The

Grand Duc

E S L   D i c t i o n a r y
a n d   T h e s a u r u s
for French-Speaking Students

Éditions Grand Duc
Groupe Éducalivres inc.
955, rue Bergar, Laval (Québec) H7L 4Z6
Téléphone: 514 334-8466 • Télécopie: 514 334-8387
InfoService: 1 800 567-3671

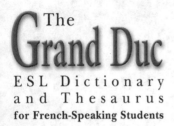

The
Grand Duc
ESL Dictionary
and Thesaurus
for French-Speaking Students

© 2001, Éditions Grand Duc, a division of Groupe Éducalivres inc.
955, rue Bergar, Laval (Québec) H7L 4Z6
Telephone: 514 334-8466 – Fax: 514 334-8387 – www.grandduc.com
All rights reserved

We acknowledge the financial support of the Government of Canada through the Canada Book Fund (CBF) for our publishing activities.

Developed by permission of **Harcourt Canada Ltd.**

 It is illegal to reproduce this publication, in full or in part, in any form or by any means (electronic, mechanical, photographic, recording, magnetic, or other) without permission from the publisher. By respecting this request, you will encourage the authors in the pursuit of their careers.

PRODUCT CODE 3041
ISBN 978-0-03-928569-2

Legal Deposit – 3rd Quarter
Bibliothèque nationale du Québec, 2001
National Library of Canada, 2001

Printed in Canada
0 L 1

Acknowledgements

ESL DICTIONARY & FRENCH LEXICON
Pedagogical designer and linguistic advisor
Thierry Pascal Karsenti

Linguistic advisor
Robert A. Papen

Coordinating editor, French-language equivalents
Suzanne Bélanger

Editorial contributors, French-language equivalents
Nadine Boccalini
Laurent Boudreault
Marc Brichau
Laila Cherrat
Johanne Delcourt
Lise Flageole
Sandra Lefebvre   (Dictionary & French Lexicon)
Catherine Léger   (Dictionary & French Lexicon)
Jacinthe Lesage   (Dictionary & French Lexicon)
Marie-Ève Morin
Huguette Paspaliaris
Olivier Pelletier
Sonia Picard
Jessica Saada
Suzie Vranderick

GRAMMAR TOOLKIT
Pedagogical designer and editor
Thierry Pascal Karsenti

Contributing editor
Peter J. Smith

THESAURUS
Pedagogical designer
Thierry Pascal Karsenti
Editorial contributors
Pamela Boyd
Krista Dalby
Clara Gabriel
Cindy Garayt
Janine Hopkinson
Olivier Pelletier
Jessica Saada

Table of Contents

▨ THESAURUS

The Grand Duc ESL Dictionary and Thesaurus Sections

 ESL DICTIONARY

- Commonly-used vocabulary
- Up to four French equivalents for every definition of each English word
- Definitions, examples or quotes from Canadian and foreign authors for main entries
- Complementary notes on the use and origin of words
- Words in the same family
- Synonyms, phrases and expressions
- References to illustrations and the Thesaurus
- **Writing Tips** and **Word Builder** entries to assist students as they write

FRENCH LEXICON

- French words, phrases, expressions and their English equivalents
- Numerous strategies to make finding words easier

GRAMMAR
TOOLKIT

- Complete English grammar
- Sample narrative and descriptive outlines
- Various strategies and methods

THESAURUS

- Banks of words classified by topics students write about most often
- French equivalents for thesaurus entries
- Topics: characters, description of characters, time, places, living world, nature, arts and culture, food, events and celebrations, travel and transportation, health, sports and recreation, and communications.

INTRODUCTION

Preface

The Grand Duc ESL Dictionary and Thesaurus is the only work of its kind. It is an English school dictionary, which includes French equivalents for every definition of each English word, a French Lexicon which can be used to look up meanings via French entries, a Grammar Toolkit including an English grammar and several methodological and reference tools, and a thesaurus containing numerous banks of words arranged according to topics that students write about most often.

The Grand Duc ESL Dictionary and Thesaurus is not just another dictionary. Its originality is the result of a desire on the part of its designers to eliminate the shortcomings of traditional English/French – French/English dictionaries, particularly with respect to their use in writing situations. *The Grand Duc ESL Dictionary and Thesaurus* responds to the needs expressed by many parents and teachers for a dictionary, to be used at school and at home, intended specifically for students learning English as a second language, and that includes definitions and examples adapted to their needs; for the reference tools required to correct and revise written texts; and for a writing tool, namely a thesaurus, that students can use to prepare and enrich their writing.

This is where all other dictionaries fail, that is, when the student is actually writing. In fact, it is generally acknowledged that students quickly learn the meaning of new words from the context, both while reading and while communicating orally. In case of doubt, they can always check the meaning of an unfamiliar word in the dictionary. However, it is also recognized that when students are actually writing, they forget even familiar words and the vocabulary they use falls below their level of general knowledge of the language. This is why the thesaurus is a perfect complement to the dictionary. Regardless of whether the student wishes to describe a character, place, time, event, etc., the thesaurus will help him/her make the necessary association between ideas and words, stimulate and feed his/her imagination and enrich his/her vocabulary as he/she prepares and polishes a piece of writing.

The Grand Duc ESL Dictionary and Thesaurus has other unique features. Most importantly, it includes a reference system which guides the students to the appropriate pages and helps them find the words listed in the thesaurus or the dictionary section at a glance. We sincerely hope that the students will use this new dictionary constantly as they read and write, and that it will become a faithful companion to them as they learn English as a second language.

⧉ ESL Dictionary Section

The purpose of this section of *The Grand Duc ESL Dictionary and Thesaurus*, which includes the largest number of articles and pages, is to define a vast array of words in current English usage. At the same time, it links one or more French equivalents to each of the different meanings given. It includes more than 20,000 entries to which can be added secondary entries touching upon differences such as phraseology, the use of the word in other parts of speech and words from the same family. Main entries are printed in bold type and their syllables are separated by periods, to make them easily identifiable. The French equivalents within each of the definitions are also set in bold type, and any words in the main entry that also appear in the Thesaurus section are printed in reversed type (white on a black background).

Word choice

Word choice is based mainly on how frequently words are used, and their importance within the school context. Nevertheless, we have not limited ourselves to the mere definition of a basic school vocabulary for ESL students; this vocabulary has been enriched by an extensive lexicon so that students may seek out, find and then understand words they may encounter more rarely. Consequently, certain technical and other more specialized terms have been included.

Content and organization of entries

Each entry offers a range of pertinent information that will be helpful to students.

Firstly, pronunciation in phonetic English is indicated in brackets, accented at two levels; syllables in upper case indicate the main accent while syllables in small upper case indicate the secondary accent. These are followed by the plural of nouns and the various verb forms (past tense, present and/or past participle). Parts of speech are always listed after that, as the case may be. Lastly, at the beginning of each separate definition of the word in question, a French-language equivalent is shown.

Each entry is followed by one or more French-language equivalents, and a definition of its most common and up-to-date meanings, with the exception of terms that are considered too technical. In this dictionary, we prefer to use the term of "equivalent" rather than "translation" since a word is usually more difficult to translate out of context (e.g. a text, a complete thought). Sometimes these French-language equivalents can't amount to only one word; then an expression or a phrase that best suits the meaning is provided. What makes *The Grand Duc ESL Dictionary and Thesaurus* a useful school dictionary for ESL students is the fact that the vast majority of definitions are accompanied by an example putting the defined word into context or illustrating its common usage. In addition a symbol (a black triangle) identifies any homographs belonging to a part of speech other than that of the main entry. Another symbol (a black square) identifies any words of the same family in the entry.

Entries may also be accompanied by synonyms. Some entries include specific remarks (NOTE) concerning pronunciation, usage, or even derivation so that other words of the same family may be formed, if and when necessary.

Cross-references

Four types of cross-references are used in the entries of *The Grand Duc ESL Dictionary and Thesaurus*: cross-references to thematic plates if a word appears in one of them, cross-references to the Writing Tips, cross-references to the Word Builders and cross-references to a particular page in the Thesaurus if the word is listed there as a main entry.

Illustrations

The dictionary section has been enriched with hundreds of illustrations and many colour plates covering major topics related to the fields of science, history, geography and physical activity, as well as certain areas of life experience. Most of the illustrations and thematic plates contain both English words and French-language equivalents set in smaller type. In some cases, the English word will not be listed as a main entry in the dictionary section; if this is the case, the French-language equivalent is still included to clarify the meaning.

Writing Tips

Writing Tips appear throughout this dictionary. Some give detailed descriptions of writing formats or techniques. Others offer spelling tips, or explanations of points of grammar or punctuation.

Word Builders

Other special boxes draw the student's attention to nuances of meaning, depending on the context in which a word is used, or to other words falling within the same lexical field as the main entry. These boxes are designed to help the student understand the content of the dictionary.

Symbols

▲   homograph belonging to another part of speech
🛱   cross-reference to the Thesaurus
👁   cross-reference to an illustration
▸   French-language equivalent
🖋   cross-reference to Word Builders
✐   cross-reference to Writing Tips
■   words of the same family

fr. French Lexicon Section

This section of *The Grand Duc ESL Dictionary and Theasurus* – identifiable by its yellow pages – is in some ways the mirror of the preceding section in that it lists all the French-language equivalents that appear in the ESL dictionary section. It is therefore not a French/English dictionary per se, but rather a gateway to the world of English that the student can use to find the equivalent of an idea that he or she is expressing as a thought in French.

Because many French-language equivalents are given as phrases or expressions, students will find that a number of main entries include secondary entries pointing to the English word that is closest in meaning to a particular sense. For example, under the entry "poste," the terms "bureau de poste" and "cachet de la poste" will be listed.

Grammar Toolkit

The Grammar Toolkit – identifiable by its blue pages – includes a range of reference tools, strategies and methods to help students in different writing situations.

It includes a concise yet comprehensive grammar, required for study programs in English as a second language. This section summarizes Basic Grammar Terminology (parts of speech, parts of a sentence) and rounds out the chapter on Grammar. Helpful methods for establishing verb/subject agreement, constructing complex and interrogative sentences, using possessives and comparatives and using various verb tenses are all included in this section.

The chapter on Writing includes narrative and descriptive outlines in the form of theoretical models or examples, to help students produce and analyse literary and other texts.

In the chapters on Spelling and Punctuation, students will find tools to assist them with spelling and etymology (prefixes, suffixes, final clauses) and the correct use of English punctuation.

Thesaurus

The word "thesaurus" is derived from Latin and means "treasure". It is this sense of the word that has inspired this section of *The Grand Duc ESL Dictionary and Thesaurus*, one that can be freely associated with the wealth that stems from words, and the invaluable ability that we seek in order to express nuanced ideas.

Much more than a usual thesaurus, this section is made up of highly-developed word banks related to topics that students write about most often. The themes it proposes, organization of sub-themes, and type of presentation given to the words that it contains make this volume suitable for school use. We have constantly kept in mind that students need to be able to use this reference work easily, since the ultimate goal is for them to be able to translate their ideas into words and freely organize their lexical fields, without having them imposed by the structure of the thesaurus itself. That is one reason why we have chosen to provide the French-language equivalent for each English entry so that students will find it easier to use this volume.

The thesaurus is not intended to be exhaustive; the word banks it contains are both rich and diversified, but do not cover every possible association of word and idea. Clearly, within the scope of a work intended for ESL students at the primary and secondary levels, it would have been presumptuous indeed to try to produce a complete catalogue of such associations.

In addition, we have deliberately chosen not to present lexical fields as such, but rather to use word banks to suggest different ways to associate ideas, so that students may learn to use and organize words.

Thematic organization

The thesaurus is organized according to two specific themes, which are relatively distinct. Firstly, we discuss themes required to produce of a story or description: characters (real, imaginary and fantastic); physical and psychological (and other) descriptions of characters (the body, clothing, appearance, attitudes and character, feelings and emotions, etc.); places (landscapes and countries, towns and neighbourhoods, housing); and time. We then outline a series of major topics that students frequently write about. Some of these touch on various disciplines, others on various aspects of life experience. They include the living world (animals and plants); nature (the sky, water, the seasons, weather, etc.); events, communications, consumerism, arts and culture, food, health, recreation and modes of transportation.

Presentation of themes

Each theme is accompanied by an explanatory chart illustrating any sub-themes that might be appropriate. In such cases, this chart is followed by a second chart including the sub-themes and their entries, presented in the form of satellites. Following these, in alphabetical order, are the entries included in the theme or sub-theme and their respective word banks.

Organization of entries

Entries in the thesaurus only include nouns, since they can be used to designate a being, a species, an idea or a thing in general. Each noun possesses its own word bank made up of lists of nouns, adjectives, verbs and, when necessary, expressions.

The list of nouns is composed mainly of synonyms and other nouns belonging to the same lexical field.

The list of adjectives is made up of most of the usual adjectives which qualify the entry, occasional quantitative adjectives, and numerous past participles in their adjectival form.

The list of verbs sometimes consist of two sub-lists, headed SUBJECT and OTHERS. Firstly, a list of verbs with an entry as their subject is provided: for example, *"air blows, circulates, cools, escapes, flows, stifles, stirs."* Then follows a list of verbs with the entry as a complement. The infinitive of the verb is then systematically followed by the entry that is its complement, in order to specify the correct prepositions to use with these complements. For example, " *to cut the fog, to disappear in the fog, to get lost in the fog, to go into the fog, to penetrate the fog.* "

The list of expressions offers many fixed or idiomatic expressions, which complete or in some way enrich the entry to which they refer. Some expressions may be found in both the dictionary and thesaurus sections; this apparent duplication is not super-fluous, however, since it allows students to refer to entries in either the dictionary or the thesaurus, as required. In addition, each expression is accompanied by a French translation of the intended meaning, as well as an equivalent expression in English.

Table of contents and thesaurus index

There are two lists at the beginning of the thesaurus, intended to give students access to the entries: a table of contents specifying themes, sub-themes, if any, and their entries; and an index of all entries in the thesaurus. These same words are printed in the dictionary section in reversed typeface and cross-referenced, offering students a third way to access the thesaurus.

◄ Message to the Teacher

Our publishing house has been developing ESL material for a number of years. Over that time, your comments and suggestions have led us to believe that traditional English/French dictionaries contain serious lacks, limiting the ability of ESL students to easily understand the correct usage of words in English, particularly with respect to context. This applies to both reading and writing.

Therefore, we have designed *The Grand Duc ESL Dictionary and Thesaurus* with more than 20,000 lexical entries, accompanied by definitions and examples in English that lie within your ESL students' level of skill. In addition, we have provided French-language equivalents to give students the information they need to properly understand the English context. Furthermore, by using the *French Lexicon* section, which contains all the French-language equivalents found in the dictionary, your students will be able to move easily from French to English. We would like to remind you that students should verify the contextual meaning of an English word found in the *ESL Dictionary* section, after consulting the *French Lexicon*. Students must clearly understand that simply translating a word is not enough. Indeed, by working with the dictionary appropriately, students will be able to retrieve the information most closely related to the meaning they are looking for.

Your comments have also led us to develop a new approach with respect to vocabulary, which can be found in the thesaurus section of *The Grand Duc ESL Dictionary and Thesaurus*. As the thesaurus was being developed, we consulted many teachers regarding the way in which writing situations are prepared and then introduced to students. This concept was enthusiastically received at both the consultative and experimental stages of the project.

The thesaurus is much more than a simple dictionary of synonyms. Its design will stimulate your students' imaginations, so that as they explore the vocabulary, they can choose terms and expressions that help them organize ideas and give their written work greater impact. In this way, their lexical range will be enriched and expanded. The theasurus will also help them develop effective and appropriate editing strategies. We would like to point out that *The Grand Duc ESL Dictionary and Thesaurus* complies with ESL study program standards. Thus, students will be able to add a valuable and effective tool to the resources they use to prepare for various writing situations.

Lastly, the *Grammar Toolkit* brings together a whole series of reference and methodological tools that students will find helpful. Examples of narrative and descriptive models and diagrams, a concise grammar that meets study program requirements, verb tables and many other features and alternative strategies all combine to enrich *The Grand Duc ESL Dictionary and Thesaurus*, making it an invaluable companion volume for students seeking to understand and write the English language.

⬛ To the Student

You can use *The Grand Duc ESL Dictionary and Thesaurus* to look up and find a word, even if you don't know how to spell it or its meaning isn't clear. Remember that all words are listed in alphabetical order and there may be several possible combinations of letters available to help you determine how to spell a particular word.

As you use *The Grand Duc ESL Dictionary and Thesaurus,* you will understand each of the different meanings a word may have, since clear and precise examples are provided for all definitions. The French-language equivalents, which are provided to help you clarify a particular meaning, are especially useful. In each dictionary entry, various types of information are provided. For example, pronunciation and tonic accents are indicated, as well as the word type and, in some instances, synonyms. Interesting information concerning grammar, etymology and spelling is also given.

In the *French Lexicon,* which is the yellow section of the dictionary, you can look up French words in order to find their English equivalents, as you would with a French/English dictionary. Most of the time, you will find a number of equivalent words for each French word. This is why it is important for you to verify how a word is used in the *ESL Dictionary* section, so that you can be sure you understand its specific meaning.

You will notice that many of the words in the dictionary are printed **like this**. This typographical format means that you can find these words in the thesaurus section of *The Grand Duc ESL Dictionary and Thesaurus*. They can be located using cross-references to the appropriate pages, as indicated by the symbol ⌖. Whenever you are preparing a piece of writing, feel free to consult the thesaurus. It will help you organize your thoughts and identify the key words you need. It will also suggest ideas for stories, or descriptions of people, animals, objects, places or events. You will also find that the thesaurus contains hundreds of English expressions, each accompanied by a definition and the French translation of that definition. Expressions are very important in the learning of a second language.

It is not always easy to find the right words to express or write down an idea. The purpose of the thesaurus is to help you discover them. Furthermore, the diagrams of the major themes in the thesaurus will show you the possibilities that are open to you. In addition, you will find the lists of themes and words at the beginning of the thesaurus, and their French equivalents, extremely helpful.

You can also explore the blue pages – the *Grammar Toolkit* – in the middle of the dictionary. It contains a whole series of reference tools, including stategies to make it easier to write in a straightforward or more literary manner, a concise grammar, and verb tables that are both clear and easy to consult. The table of contents of the *Grammar Toolkit* is the best way to find the information you are looking for.

Make this dictionary your constant companion whenever you are reading or writing in English. Knowing how to use a dictionary is one of the skills you must acquire during the course of your education. This wonderful reference source will open the universe of the English language to you.

⚜ Mot à l'élève

Tu peux te fier au *Grand Duc ESL Dictionary and Thesaurus* pour chercher et trouver un mot, si tu n'en connais pas le sens ou si tu hésites sur son orthographe. N'oublie pas que tous les mots sont classés par ordre alphabétique et qu'il peut exister plusieurs combinaisons de lettres possibles pour trouver l'orthographe d'un mot.

Avec le *Grand Duc ESL Dictionary and Thesaurus*, tu comprendras chacun des sens des mots puisque toutes les définitions sont accompagnées d'un exemple clair et précis, et surtout d'un ou de plusieurs équivalents de langue française qui t'aideront encore plus à en saisir le sens. Plusieurs informations te sont proposées dans un article du dictionnaire. Par exemple, la prononciation et les accents toniques, la classe de mot, parfois des synonymes; des remarques intéressantes sur la grammaire, l'origine et l'orthographe des mots.

Dans le *French Lexicon,* la section de couleur jaune du dictionnaire, tu pourras rechercher des mots de langue française pour leur trouver des équivalents de langue anglaise, un peu comme tu le ferais avec un dictionnaire français/anglais. Le plus souvent, tu trouveras de nombreux équivalents pour chaque mot français; c'est pourquoi il est toujours important que tu vérifies l'emploi du mot anglais dans la partie *ESL Dictionary*, pour t'assurer de bien comprendre le sens spécifique de ce mot.

Tu remarqueras que plusieurs mots du dictionnaire sont présentés **comme ceci**. Cette typographie spéciale te signale que tu peux trouver ces mots dans la partie *Thesaurus* du *Grand Duc ESL Dictionary* en te référant aux renvois aux pages précises, caractérisés par le symbole ☞. Lorsque tu prépares tes productions écrites, n'hésite pas à explorer le thésaurus: il te permettra d'organiser ta pensée et de trouver les mots importants pour écrire ton texte; il te donnera aussi des idées pour raconter une histoire, inventer un récit ou encore décrire une personne, un animal, un objet, un lieu ou un événement. Aussi, tu verras que le thésaurus recèle des centaines d'expressions anglaises accompagnées d'une définition et d'une traduction de cette dernière en français. Les expressions sont importantes dans l'apprentissage d'une langue seconde.

Il n'est pas toujours facile de trouver les bons mots pour exprimer et écrire une idée; le but du thésaurus est justement de t'aider à les découvrir. D'ailleurs, les schémas des thèmes du thésaurus te donneront un bon aperçu des possibilités qui s'offrent à toi. De plus, les listes de thèmes et de mots au début du thésaurus, auxquelles sont joints des équivalents de langue française, te seront d'une grande utilité.

Tu peux également explorer les pages bleues, intitulées *Grammar Toolkit*, au milieu du dictionnaire. Tu y découvriras toute une série d'outils de référence, des stratégies pour faciliter l'écriture des textes courants et littéraires, un condensé de grammaire ainsi que des tableaux de conjugaison clairs et faciles à consulter. La table des matières du *Grammar Toolkit* est certainement le meilleur outil pour trouver l'information que tu recherches.

Fais de ce dictionnaire un compagnon de tous les instants lorsque tu lis ou écris en anglais.

Savoir utiliser un dictionnaire fait partie des compétences que tu dois acquérir dans ta formation scolaire. Grâce à ce merveilleux outil, l'univers de la langue anglaise, t'appartient.

Explanatory Chart – ESL

Fisrt word on the page — across

Word Builder

> ✏ **Word Builder**
>
> *Act is a short, simple word, but it can be used in several different ways. An **act of kindness** is a nice thing to do. This noun-based meaning can also be a verb : To **act in a kind way** is to do something nice. **Caught in the act** means to be caught doing something (usually something wrong). […]*

Entry — **a·cross** [uh-KROS] PREPOSITION. **1. de l'autre côté de** ▸ from one side to the other : *Luke threw the ball across the street.* **2. de l'autre côté de, en face (de)** ▸ on the opposite side of : *Jenny lives across the canyon from Josh.* ▲ ADVERB. **de large** ▸ from one side to the other : *The river looks very wide ; do you know the distance across ?*

Part of speech

Part of speech

Phrasal verb — **come across** trouver, rencontrer ▸ find : *They came across a crocus pushing up through the snow.*

a·cros·tic [uh-KROS-tik] NOUN, acrostics. **acrostiche** ▸ a poem in which the first letters of each line form a word or pattern. Some acrostics are made with the end or middle letters of words.

Phonetic pronunciation

a·cryl·ic [uh-KRIL-ik] NOUN, acrylics. **acrylique** ▸ one of a group of artificial materials made mainly from petroleum, widely used in paints, fabrics, and other products.

Plural form

Cross-reference to the Thesaurus — **act** [akt] NOUN, acts. **1. acte, geste** ▸ something that is done : *Giving that poor man something to eat was an act of kindness.* **2. acte** ▸ the doing of something : *The photograph caught the player in the act of throwing a pass.* **3. loi** ▸ a law : *The Official Languages Act of 1969 guarantees all Canadians the right to communicate with the national government in either French or English.* **4. acte, numéro** ▸ one part of a play or show : *We were late for the play, so we missed part of the first act.* ▲ **agir** ▸ verb, acted, acting. **1. se comporter** ▸ to do something : *The police acted quickly to route traffic around the accident.* **2. jouer** ▸ to behave in a certain way : *I'm sorry I was rude, but I acted without thinking.* **3. jouer** ▸ to play a part in a show or movie : *Kate loves to act in our school plays.* **Note.** A person who acts is an **actor**. (✏ **p. 1126.**) SYN : deed, feat, work, accomplishment. ✏ **p. 7.** ✏ **p. 1026.**

French-language equivalent

Same entry, other part of speech

Past tense

Present participle

Cross-reference to the Thesaurus

Synonyms

Cross-reference to the Word Builder

ac·tion [AK-shun] NOUN, actions. **1. action** ▸ the doing of something : *"And suiting the action to the word, he began to blow his icy cold breath on poor Fox."* (Rosebud Yellow Robe) **2. action, acte** ▸ something that is done ; an act : *a generous action.* **3. effet** ▸ the way a thing works : *The action of the medicine made Sam feel better.* **4. combat** ▸ fighting in war : *Canada's military forces saw action on many*

Quote

Dictionary

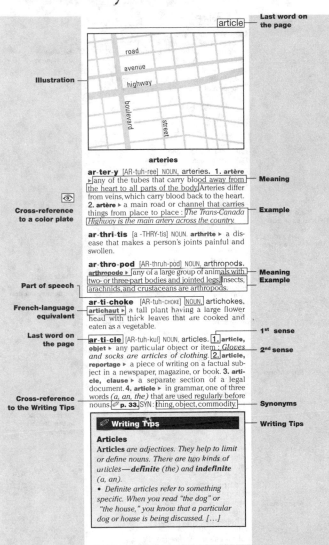

Last word on the page — article

Illustration

road
avenue
highway
boulevard
street

arteries

Cross-reference to a color plate

ar·ter·y [AR-tuh-ree] NOUN. arteries. **1.** artère ► any of the tubes that carry blood away from the heart to all parts of the body. Arteries differ from veins, which carry blood back to the heart. **2.** artère ► a main road or channel that carries things from place to place : *The Trans-Canada Highway is the main artery across the country.*

Meaning

Example

ar·thri·tis [a -THRY-tis] NOUN. arthrite ► a disease that makes a person's joints painful and swollen.

Part of speech

ar·thro·pod [AR-thruh-pod] NOUN. arthropods. arthropode ► any of a large group of animals with two- or three-part bodies and jointed legs. Insects, arachnids, and crustaceans are arthropods.

Meaning
Example

French-language equivalent

ar·ti·choke [AR-tuh-CHOKE] NOUN. artichokes. artichaut ► a tall plant having a large flower head with thick leaves that are cooked and eaten as a vegetable.

Last word on the page

ar·ti·cle [AR-tuh-kul] NOUN. articles. **1.** article, objet ► any particular object or item : *Gloves and socks are articles of clothing.* **2.** article, reportage ► a piece of writing on a factual subject in a newspaper, magazine, or book. **3.** article, clause ► a separate section of a legal document. **4.** article ► in grammar, one of three words *(a, an, the)* that are used regularly before nouns. **p. 33.** SYN. thing, object, commodity.

1ˢᵗ sense

2ⁿᵈ sense

Cross-reference to the Writing Tips

Synonyms

✏ Writing Tips

Articles

Articles *are adjectives. They help to limit or define nouns. There are two kinds of articles—**definite** (the) and **indefinite** (a, an).*

• Definite articles refer to something specific. When you read "the dog" or "the house," you know that a particular dog or house is being discussed. […]

Writing Tips

⚓ Explanatory Chart –

First word on the page — baguette – French Lexicon

baguette ► drumstick, pointer, wand
   baguettes ► chopsticks
   donner un coup de baguette ► switch ◄ **English equivalent**
bai (baie) ► bay[3]
baie[1] ► berry
   baie de Saskatoon ► saskatoon
   aller à la cueillette des baies ► berry
baie[2] ► bay[1]
   baie vitrée ► bay[5]
   fenêtre en baie ► bay[5]
baignade ► dip
   surveillant (-ante) de baignade ► lifeguard
baigner ► bathe, steep[2]
baignoire ► tub
bail (baux) ► lease
bâillement ► yawn
bailler ► yawn
bâillon ► gag
bâillonner ► gag
Main French-language entry — **bain** ► bath, dip
   Secondary entries — **maillot de bain** ► trunk
   salle de bain ► bath, bathroom
bain-marie ► boiler
baiser ► kiss
   donner un baiser ► kiss
   gros baiser retentissant ► smack
baisse ► decline, decrease, drop, reduction ◄ **[Root word] – main entry in the dictionary section**
   [reduce]
   à la baisse ► down[1]
baissé (-ée) ► down[1]
baisser ► declare, decrease, dim, dip, drop off, ebb, fade, fail, fall, hang, lower, reduce, sink, subdue, subside, turn
   se baisser ► stoop[1]
   se baisser vivement ► duck[2]
   faire baisser ► depress
bajoue ► cheek
Plural form — **bal (bals)** ► ball[2]
balai ► broom
   coup de balai ► sweep
se balader ► saunter
balance ► scale[2] ◄ **2nd main entry in the dictionary section**
balancement ► rock[2], swing
balancer ► balance, dangle, junk[1], swing
   se balancer ► roll, sway
balançoire ► swing
balayage ► sweep
balayer ► rake, scan, sweep, traverse
balcon ► balcony
   dernier balcon ► gallery
baleine ► rib, whale
Expression — **pêche à la baleine** ► whaling
balise ► beacon
   balise flottante ► buoy
ballade ► ballad
balle ► bale, ball[1], bullet, slug[1]

French Lexicon

Last word on the page —

à la balle ▶ ball[1]
balle de base-ball ▶ baseball
balle-molle ▶ softball
bonne balle ▶ fair[1]
but sur balles ▶ walk
ballet ▶ ballet
ballon ▶ ball[1], balloon

Secondary entries —
ballon de basket-ball ▶ basketball
ballon de football ▶ football
ballon de volley-ball ▶ volleyball
ballonner ▶ balloon, bulge
ballot ▶ bale, pack
ballotter ▶ buffet[2], rock[2]
balustrade ▶ railing

Feminine form —
bambin (-ine) ▶ toddler
bambou ▶ bamboo
banal (-ale, -als) ▶ everyday, ordinary
banalité ▶ cliché
banane ▶ banana
régime (bananes) ▶ bunch
banc ▶ bank[2], bench, shelf
banc de neige ▶ snowbank
banc de pénalité ▶ penalty box
banc de poissons ▶ school[2]
banc de sable ▶ shoal
banc des accusés ▶ dock[3]
bancal (-ale, -als) ▶ unstable, unsteady

Feminine and plural forms —
bandage ▶ bandage, patch, tape
1st sense — **bande[1]** ▶ band[1], band[2], chorus, clan, crowd, den, flock, gang, horde, pack, troop

1st and 2nd main entries in the dictionary section

2nd sense — **bande[2]** ▶ list[2], streak, strip[2], tape
bande de roulement ▶ tread
bande dessinée ▶ cartoon, comic
bande magnétique ▶ tape
bande publique ▶ CB
bande vidéo ▶ video, videotape

Expression — **donner de la bande** ▶ list[2]
bandeau (-eaux) ▶ bandana, blindfold
bandelette ▶ band[1]
bander ▶ bandage
bander les yeux ▶ blindfold
banderole ▶ banner, streamer
bandit ▶ bandit, gangster
bandoulière ▶ sling
banjo ▶ banjo
banlieue ▶ outskirts, suburb
de banlieue ▶ suburban [suburb]

[Root word] – main entry in the dictionary section

banni (-ie) ▶ exile
bannière ▶ banner
bannir ▶ banish, exile
banque ▶ bank[1]
banquet ▶ banquet, feast
banquette ▶ bench, booth
banquette des députés sans portefeuille ▶ backbench
Feminine form — **banquier (-ière)** ▶ banker
bantam ▶ bantam

⬩ Explanatory Chart –
Grammar Toolkit

WRITING

- Writing Formats
- The Writing Process
- Connecting Ideas
- Types of Graphs

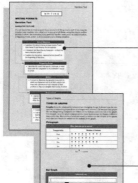

PUNCTUATION

SPELLING

— Alternative Spellings

- Prefixes
- Root Words
- Suffixes

— Abbreviations

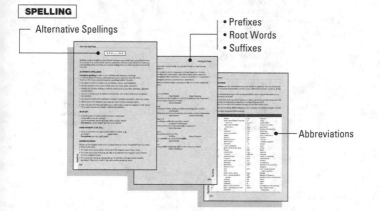

Basic Grammar terminology

Part of Speech

- Adjectives
- Adverbs
- Articles
- Conjunctions
- Interjections
- Nouns
- Prepositions
- Pronouns
- Verbs

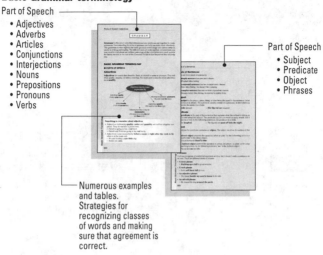

Part of Speech

- Subject
- Predicate
- Object
- Phrases

Numerous examples and tables. Strategies for recognizing classes of words and making sure that agreement is correct.

Verbs and Verb Tenses

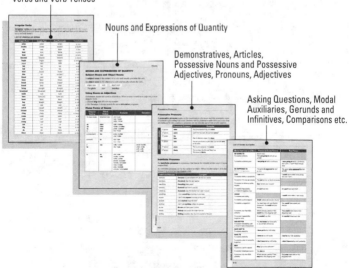

Nouns and Expressions of Quantity

Demonstratives, Articles, Possessive Nouns and Possessive Adjectives, Pronouns, Adjectives

Asking Questions, Modal Auxiliaries, Gerunds and Infinitives, Comparisons etc.

Explanatory Chart –

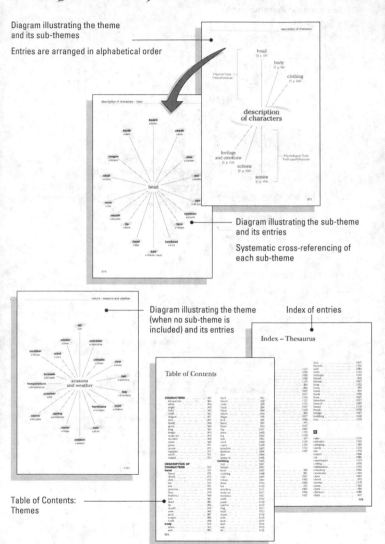

Diagram illustrating the theme and its sub-themes

Entries are arranged in alphabetical order

Diagram illustrating the sub-theme and its entries

Systematic cross-referencing of each sub-theme

Diagram illustrating the theme (when no sub-theme is included) and its entries

Index of entries

Table of Contents: Themes

Thesaurus

Entry
(These are always nouns)

List of nouns
including synonyms and other nouns belonging to the lexical field

List of adjectives

List of verbs

List of verbs
in which the word in the entry may be the object or another part of speech

List of expressions
in which the word in the entry is found

Meaning of the expression

French-language equivalent

List of verbs
in which the word in the entry may be the subject.

Expression

French translation of the expression's meaning; sometime a French-language equivalent expression

finger ▸ doigt

nouns agility, bend, bone, digit, dressing, feeling, fingernail, fingerprint, flexibility, hand, index finger, joint, little finger, pinch, plucks, pointer, ring, ring finger, splint, thimble, thumb, tip, touch.

adjectives agile, big, bulging, bumpy, chubby, clean, cold, crooked, crossed, curled, dirty, fat, fine, flexible, fractured, frozen, grabbing, grasping, hairless, hairy, hooked, injured, limber, long, missing, moving, nimble, numb, plump, probing, red, rigid, rough, short, small, stocky, swollen, tapered, tapping, wounded, wrinkled.

verbs [SUBJECT] a finger breaks, bulges, curls, grabs, grasps, hooks, moves, points, pokes, shakes, snaps, tapers, taps, touches. [OTHERS]: to injure a finger, to fracture a finger, to injure a finger, to miss a finger, to move a finger, to snap a finger, to wound a finger.

expressions ....

- *At one's fingertips:* readily available ▸ **à portée de la main.**

- *Sticky fingers:* someone with a tendency to steal ▸ **personne qui a tendance à voler.**

- *To burn one's fingers:* to be harmed ▸ **se faire blesser.**

- *To cross one's fingers:* to wish for luck, or to tell a small lie ▸ **souhaiter la chance ou dire un mensonge pieux ; croiser les doigts.**

- *To have a finger in the pie:* to be interested in something or meddle in it ▸ **s'intéresser à quelque chose ou s'en mêler.**

- *To keep one's fingers crossed:* to wish for luck ▸ **souhaiter la chance ; croiser les doigts.**

- *To lay (put) a finger on:* to barely touch what is prohibited ▸ **à peine toucher ce qui est interdit.**

- *To let slip through the fingers:* to miss an opportunity when one could have had it ▸ **laisser passer la chance ; laisser filer la chance.**

Illustrations

ESL DICTIONARY

airplane

a, A [ay] NOUN, a's, A's. **1. a, A ▸** the first letter of the English alphabet. **2. A ▸** the highest mark, grade, or level.

a [uh *or* ay] ARTICLE. **un (une), par, de ▸** a word used before a NOUN or adjective that begins with a consonant sound : *a dog; a car; a funny joke; fifty dollars a week.*

a- PREFIX. in, on, or to : *"Atop a hill" means on top of a hill.*

aard-vark [ARD-vark] NOUN, aardvarks. **fourmilier, tamanoir ▸** an animal from Africa that catches ants and termites with its long, sticky tongue.

ab- PREFIX. from ; away from : *To abduct a person means to take or carry the person away.*

ab-a-cus [AB-uh-kus] NOUN, abacuses or abaci [AB-uh-sy]. **abaque, boulier ▸** a frame with rows of beads that slide back and forth, used to do arithmetic problems. The abacus has been used for thousands of years and is considered to be an early form of the modern calculator.

a-ban-don [uh-BAN-dun] VERB, abandoned, abandoning. **abandonner, délaisser ▸** to leave behind or give up completely : *The crew had to abandon the sinking ship.* 🖉 **p. 360.**

ab-bey [AB-ee] NOUN, abbeys. **abbaye ▸** a building where nuns or monks live. **Note.** An abbess is in charge of an abbey of nuns. An abbot is in charge of an abbey of monks.

ab-bre-vi-ate [uh-BREE-vee-ATE] VERB, abbreviated, abbreviating. **1. abréger ▸** to make a word shorter by leaving out some of the letters : *Margaret abbreviates her name to Meg.* **2. raccourcir ▸** to make something shorter by cutting out a section. SYN: shorten, lessen, reduce, condense.

ab-bre-vi-a-tion [uh-BREE-vee-AY-shun] NOUN, abbreviations. **abréviation ▸** a shorter form of a word, written with some of the letters left out : *Mr. is an abbreviation for Mister.* 🖉 **p. 3.**

ab-do-men [AB-duh-mun] NOUN, abdomens. **1. abdomen ▸** the part of the body between the chest and the hips. The abdomen contains important organs of the body, such as the stomach. **2. abdomen ▸** the rear part of an insect or spider whose body has three parts. ■ **abdominal**, ADJECTIVE. ▸ abdominal (-ale, -aux).

✍ Writing Tips

Abbreviations

Abbreviations are the shortened forms of words or phrases that are formed by dropping letters from a word and often adding a period (St., Sat.).

• *Abbreviations, such as Mr., Ave., and Oct., are used most often in friendly or informal writing—for example, postcards and letters to friends and family, your diary or journal, and notes.*

• *If you want to use an abbreviation that your reader may not know, the first time the word appears in the piece of writing use the long form with the abbreviation following in brackets—United Nations (UN)—then use the abbreviation throughout the rest of the piece.*

• *Try not to use too many abbreviations at once. It makes the sentence harder to read.*

• *Abbreviations for postal addresses do not use any punctuation.*

---

ab-duct [ub-DUKT] VERB, abducted, abducting. **enlever, kidnapper ▸** to carry off a person by force or by a trick : *A group from another school abducted our school mascot.* ■ **abductor**, NOUN. ▸ **kidnappeur (-euse).** ■ **abduction**, NOUN. ▸ **enlèvement, kidnapping.** SYN: kidnap, steal, carry off, take away.

A-ben-aki [AB-uh-NAK-ee] NOUN, Abenakis. **1. Abénaquis ▸** an Aboriginal people living mostly in southern Quebec and Maine who

p. 4.

> ## ✎ Word Builder
>
> **Absolute** and **complete** can both refer to the whole amount of a thing that can be counted. **Absolute** has the idea of going to the extreme or end of something: In science, "absolute zero" is a term for the temperature that is as cold as anything can possibly get. **Complete** has the idea of bringing together all of some large thing: This book has the complete records for every player who has ever played for the Toronto Maple Leafs.

speak an Algonquian language. **2. Abénaquis ▸** the language of these people.

a-bide [uh-BIDE] VERB, abided, abiding. **1.** abide by. **obéir, suivre, accepter ▸** to accept or follow; obey : *Students must abide by the rules of the school.* **2. supporter ▸** to put up with : *I can't abide that dog's constant barking.*

a-bil-i-ty [uh-BIL-uh-tee] NOUN, abilities. **aptitude, habileté, habilité ▸** the power or skill to do something : *"Louis was greatly admired for his ability as a swimmer."* (E.B. White) SYN: talent, faculty, capacity, skill.

a-ble [AY-bul] ADJECTIVE, abler, ablest. **capable, apte ▸** having the power or skill to do something : *"[He] wished that one day he too might be able to wear the saffron robe of a monk."* (David Day)

a-board [uh-BORD] ADVERB; ADJECTIVE. **à bord ▸** in or on a ship, train, or plane : *"She swam out to the ship and climbed aboard."* (Phoebe Gilman)

a-bol-ish [uh-BOL-ish] VERB, abolished, abolishing. **abolir ▸** to put an end to; to get rid of : *The students wanted to abolish the school's dress code.* ■ **abolition,** NOUN. ▸ abolition. ■ **abolitionist,** NOUN. ▸ abolitionniste. SYN: eliminate, do away with.

Ab-o-rig-i-ne [AB-uh-RIJ-uh-nee] NOUN, Aborigines. **1. Aborigène ▸** one of a group of people who have lived in Australia for thousands of years. **2.** (sometimes aborigine) **autochtone, indigène, natif (-ive) ▸** one of a group of people who were the earliest known inhabitants of an area, such as the Inuit of northern Canada. ■ **Aboriginal,** ADJECTIVE. ▸ aborigène. ✎ p. 387.

a-bout [uh-BOWT] PREPOSITION. **1. sur, au sujet de, concernant, à propos de ▸** having something to do with : *This book is about whales.* **2. sur le point de ▸** at the point of : *They got there just as the movie was about to start.* ▲ ADVERB. **environ, à peu près ▸** nearly; almost : *The trip took them about an hour.*

a-bove [uh-BUV] PREPOSITION. **au-dessus de ▸** in a higher place than; over : *The bird flew just above the waves.* ▲ ADVERB. **en haut, plus haut ▸** in a higher place : *We heard noises from the floor above.* ▲ ADJECTIVE. **précédent (-ente), ci-dessus ▸** in an earlier part : *The above entry on this page is "about."*

a-broad [uh-BROD] ADVERB. **à l'étranger ▸** away from one's own country : *Next year she plans to go abroad to study in France.*

a-brupt [uh-BRUPT] ADJECTIVE. **soudain (-aine), brusque, abrupt (-e) ▸** sudden and not expected : *The meeting came to an abrupt end when the boss was called away to take a telephone call.* ■ **abruptly,** ADVERB. ▸ soudainement, brusquement.

ab-sence [AB-since] NOUN, absences. **absence ▸** not being present; being away : *Because of the lack of rain, there is an absence of plant life in that desert.*

ab-sent [AB-sunt] ADJECTIVE. **absent (-ente) ▸** not present; away or missing : *Maria is absent from school today because she is sick.* ■ **absently,** ADVERB. ▸ de façon absente.

ab-sent-mind-ed [AB-sunt-MINE-did] ADJECTIVE. **distrait (-aite) ▸** not paying attention to what is going on; not noticing or remembering things.

ab-so-lute [AB-suh-LUTE] ADJECTIVE. **absolu (-ue) ▸** in every way : *In the Middle Ages, monarchs had absolute power over the people they ruled.* ■ **absolutely,** ADVERB. ▸ absolument. ✎ p. 4.

ab-sorb [ub-ZORB] VERB, absorbed, absorbing. **absorber ▸** to soak up or take in : *She used a paper towel to absorb the spilled milk.*

ab-stract [AB-strakt] ADJECTIVE. **abstrait (-aite) ▸** having to do with an idea or thought, rather than with something that can be seen or sensed : *In abstract painting, ideas are expressed through the shapes and designs rather than by showing real objects.* ■ **abstractly,** ADVERB. ▸ abstraitement.

ab-surd [ub-ZERD] ADJECTIVE. **absurde ▸** not sensible; foolish : *Clowns often wear absurd-looking outfits.* ■ **absurdity,** NOUN. ▸ absurdité. ■ **absurdly,** ADVERB. ▸ absurdement.

a-bun-dant [uh-BUN-dunt] ADJECTIVE. **abondant (-ante) ▸** more than enough; plentiful : *They ate salmon, which were abundant in the lake.* ■ **abundance,** NOUN. ▸ abondance.

a-buse [uh-BYOOZ] VERB, abused, abusing. **1. maltraiter, malmener ▸** to treat in a cruel or hard way : *It is against the law to abuse a dog.* **2. abuser de ▸** to use in the wrong way : *to abuse drugs.* ▲ [uh-BYOOS] NOUN, abuses. **1. abus ▸** hard or cruel treatment : *Child abuse* *is against the law.* **2. abus** ▸ a wrong use : *an abuse of power.*

ac-a-dem-ic [AK-uh-DEM-ik] ADJECTIVE. **1. universitaire, scolaire** ▸ having to do with education : *She has a career in the academic world as a professor.* **2. académique** ▸ having to do with an idea rather than a real issue.

a-cad-e-my [uh-KAD-uh-mee] NOUN, academies. **1. académie** ▸ a school, often one for a particular field of study : *A military academy trains its students to become soldiers.* **2. académie** ▸ a group of writers, scientists, or scholars.

A-ca-di-a [uh-KAY-dee-uh] NOUN. **Acadie** ▸ the French settlements in the Maritime provinces. ■ **Acadian,** ADJECTIVE. ▸ **Acadien (-ienne).**

ac-cel-er-ate [uk-SEL-uh-RATE] VERB, accelerated, accelerating. **accélérer** ▸ to speed up; move faster : *The cheetah accelerated up to full speed.* ■ **acceleration,** NOUN. ▸ **accélération.** SYN: hasten, hurry, quicken, speed up.

ac-cel-er-a-tor [uk-SEL-uh-RATE-ur] NOUN, accelerators. **accélérateur** ▸ a pedal on the floor of a car that controls the flow of gas to the engine. A car speeds up when its accelerator is pressed down.

ac-cent [AK-sent] NOUN, accents. **1. accent** ▸ a way of speaking that is shared by the people from a particular place or region. **2. accent** ▸ stress or emphasis on a syllable or part of a word : *In the word "after," the accent is on the first syllable; in "before," it is on the second.* ▲ VERB, accented, accenting. **accentuer** ▸ to say a part of a word in a stronger way.

ac-cept [uk-SEPT] VERB, accepted, accepting. **1. accepter** ▸ to take something that is offered or given : *"She reached out to accept her gift."* (Jim McGugan) **2. admettre, accepter** ▸ to agree to, say yes to, or believe : *"It's all for the best,' he said. 'I will accept my disgrace.'"* (Robin Muller) ■ **acceptance,** NOUN. ▸ **acceptation.**

ac-cept-a-ble [uk-SEPT-uh-bul] ADJECTIVE. **acceptable, convenable** ▸ good enough to be accepted : *He always wants to get high grades; a C is just not acceptable to him.* ■ **acceptably,** ADVERB. ▸ **de façon acceptable.** SYN: adequate, agreeable, satisfactory.

ac-cess [AK-ses] NOUN, accesses. **accès** ▸ a way or means to get in to something or to have something : *The only access to the lake by car is that old dirt road.* ▲ VERB, accessed, accessing. **accéder à** ▸ to gain entry to; get in to : *In order to access that computer network, you have to know the correct password.* ■ **accessible,** ADJECTIVE. ▸ **accessible.**

ac-ces-sor-y [uk-SES-uh-ree] NOUN, accessories. **accessoire** ▸ something that is not necessary, but goes with something more important to make it more useful or attractive : *The auto*

store sells accessories for cars, such as seat covers.

ac-ci-dent [AK-suh-dunt] NOUN, accidents. **1. accident** ▸ something bad or unlucky that happens without being planned or expected : *Two cars crashing, a dish breaking, and a person falling are accidents.* **2. (par) hasard** ▸ anything that happens suddenly without being planned or expected : *I found my lost watch by accident while I was cleaning out my desk.* ⯒ p. 1143.

ac-ci-dent-al [AK-suh-DEN-tul] ADJECTIVE. **accidentel (-elle)** ▸ not planned, happening by chance : *The moving company will pay for any accidental damage to the furniture while it's being moved.* ■ **accidentally,** ADVERB. ▸ **par hasard.**

ac-com-mo-date [uh-KOM-uh-date] VERB, accommodated, accommodating. **1. loger, recevoir, contenir, accueillir** ▸ to have room for : *The hotel is very small and can accommodate only 20 guests.* **2. accommoder, obliger** ▸ to do a favour for; help out. ■ **accommodation,** NOUN. ▸ **logement, place.**

ac-com-pa-ny [uh-KUM-puh-nee] VERB, accompanied, accompanying. **1. accompagner** ▸ to go along with someone or something : *The dogs accompanied us on our walk.* **2. accompagner** ▸ to play or sing music as a background for the main part : *A guitarist accompanied the singer.* ■ **accompaniment,** NOUN. ▸ **accompagnement.** SYN: attend, escort, come or go with.

ac-com-plice [uh-KOM-plis] NOUN, accomplices. **complice** ▸ a person who helps another to commit a crime or to do something wrong.

ac-com-plish [uh-KOM-plish] VERB, accomplished, accomplishing. **accomplir, exécuter, réaliser, effectuer** ▸ to carry out or finish something : *They hoped to raise at least $200, and they accomplished that goal.* ■ **accomplishment,** NOUN. ▸ **accomplissement, réussite.** ■ **accomplished,** ADJECTIVE. ▸ **accompli (-ie), doué (-ée).**

ac-cord [uh-KORD] NOUN, accords. **1. accord, consensus** ▸ agreement; thinking or acting in the same way : *The new school will never come into being until there is some accord as to where it should be built.* **2. of one's own accord. accord, consentement** ▸ by a person's own choice. ▲ VERB, accorded, according. **s'accorder, s'entendre** ▸ to agree. ■ **accordingly,** ADVERB. ▸ **en conséquence.** SYN: agreement, treaty.

according to **d'après, selon** ▸ as stated by; on the authority of : *According to the newspaper, today's weather will be sunny and clear.*

ac-cor-di-on [uh-KOR-dee-un] NOUN, accordions. **accordéon** ▸ a musical instrument with a keyboard and buttons that is held in the hands and squeezed. ⯒ p. 539.

ac·count [uh-KOWNT] NOUN, accounts. 1. **compte** ▸a sum of money kept in a bank : *Andrew has about $50 in his savings account.* 2. **compte** ▸ a record kept by a business of how much money comes in. 3. **compte rendu, explication** ▸ a statement or record of how something happened : *There are no written accounts of how people first came to North America.* 4. on account of. **à cause de** ▸ because of : *The game was called off on account of rain.* ▲ VERB, accounted, accounting. to account for. **rendre compte de, justifier, expliquer** ▸ to explain or give á reason for : *The doctor couldn't account for her quick recovery.*

ac·count·ant [uh-KOWN-tunt] NOUN, accountants. **comptable** ▸ someone whose job is to keep track of the money spent and taken in by a person or business. **Note.** The work done by an accountant is accounting.

ac·cu·mu·late [uh-KYOOM-yuh-LATE] VERB, accumulated, accumulating. **(s') accumuler, (s') amasser, amonceler** ▸ to bring or come together in one place ; gather up :"*Over the winter snow accumulated in banks as high as two metres.*" (Robert McGhee) ■ **accumulation,** NOUN. ▸ **accumulation, amoncellement.** SYN : collect, gather, save, assemble, gain.

ac·cu·rate [AK-yur-it] ADJECTIVE. exact (-acte), précis (-ise), juste ▸ without errors or mistakes : *An accurate watch keeps the correct time.* ■ **accurately,** ADVERB. ▸ **exactement, avec précision.** ■ **accuracy,** NOUN. ▸ **exactitude, précision, justesse.** ✎ p. 503.

ac·cuse [uh-KYOOZ] VERB, accuse, accusing. **accuser** ▸ to claim that a person has done something wrong or has committed a crime : *Van accused me of eating the last cookie.* ■ **accusingly,** ADVERB. ▸ **de manière accusatrice.** ■ **accusation,** NOUN. ▸ **accusation.**

ac·cus·tomed [uh-KUS-tumd] ADJECTIVE. 1. **habituel (-elle)** ▸ according to custom or habit ; usual ; regular : *Every day, he sat in his accustomed seat in the front row.* 2. accustomed to. **(s') habituer à, (s') accoutumer à** ▸ used to : *I've lived here for years, so I'm not accustomed to moving.*

ace [ace] NOUN, aces. 1. **as** ▸ a playing card with one club, diamond, heart, or spade in the middle. The ace is usually the highest card, but in some games it can be either the highest or the lowest. 2. **as** ▸ a person who is very good at something : *Diane is an ace at computer games.*

ache [ake] NOUN, aches. **douleur** ▸ a pain, especially a dull pain that continues for a long time : *The ache in Damon's shoulder is worse when he is tired.* ▲ VERB, ached, aching. 1. **faire mal** ▸ to have an ache : *Dad's tooth ached so much he went to the dentist.* 2. **brûler de, mourir d'envie de** ▸ to want something very much : *Rista was aching for a new pair of skates.*

a·chieve [uh-CHEEV] VERB, achieved, achieving. **réaliser** ▸ to do or carry out ; successfully complete : *Let's celebrate when we achieve our goal of winning the championship.* **Note.** An achiever is a person who achieves something. SYN : accomplish, win, gain, capture.

a·chieve·ment [uh-CHEEV-munt] NOUN, achievements. **réussite, exploit** ▸ something that is achieved ; a plan or action that is carried out with courage or exceptional ability : *I think that just finishing a marathon is a great achievement.*

ac·id [AS-id] NOUN, acids. **acide** ▸ one of a large group of chemicals that unites with a base to form salt : *Acids have a sour taste, and many of them are poisonous and can burn through things.* ▲ ADJECTIVE. 1. **acide** ▸ sour or bitter in taste : *Lemons have an acid taste.* 2. **mordant (-ante)** ▸ sharp or bitter in manner : *The movie critic is known for the acid tone of his reviews.* **Note.** The quality of being acid is acidity. SYN : sour, bitter, biting, tart.

acid rain **pluies acides** ▸ rain or snow containing acid from the burning of fossil fuels such as coal and petroleum. Acid rain is harmful to plant life.

ac·knowl·edge [uk-NOWL-ij] VERB, acknowledged, acknowledging. 1. **reconnaître, avouer** ▸ to admit that something is true : *The bank acknowledged that it had made a mistake in calculating my balance.* 2. **accuser réception (de)** ▸ to make known that something has been received : *Toba acknowledged my gift with a nice thank-you note.* ■ **acknowledgement,** NOUN **reconnaître, avouer** ▸ also acknowledgment.▸ **reconnaissance, remerciement.** SYN : admit, confess, accept, declare.

a·corn [AY-korn] NOUN, acorns. **gland** ▸ the nut of an oak tree.

a·cous·tics [uh-KOO-stiks] PLURAL NOUN. 1. **acoustique** ▸ the science that studies how sounds are made and how sound carries. 2. **acoustique** ▸ the qualities of a place that make it easy or hard to hear sounds in it : *The new symphony hall has excellent acoustics.* ■ **acoustic,** ADJECTIVE. ▸ **acoustique.** Acoustic tiles on the ceiling will cut down some of the noise.

ac·quaint [uh-KWAYNT] VERB, acquainted, acquainting. **prendre connaissance de, se mettre au courant de** ▸ to get to know ; make familiar with : *Our teacher gave us time to acquaint ourselves with the equipment before we started.*

be acquainted with **connaître** ▸ have personal knowledge of someone or something : *I should improve at the game once I'm acquainted with all the rules.*

ac·quaint·ance [uh-KWAYNT-uns] NOUN, acquaintances. 1. **connaissance** ▸ a person one knows, but who is not a close friend : *Jerry is*

✎ Word Builder

*Act is a short, simple word, but it can be used in several different ways. An **act of kindness** is a nice thing to do. This noun meaning can also be a verb: To **act in a kind way** is to do something nice. **Caught in the act** means to be caught doing something (usually something wrong). An **act of the government** says that people must do things in a certain way. When people **act in a movie**, they do certain things to play the part of a character. All these different meanings of the word, as well as others, come from the idea that to act is to do something.*

---

just an acquaintance, but I'd like to get to know him better. **2. connaissance ▶** the state of being acquainted : *I have some acquaintance with cats, but I don't know anything about dogs.*

ac·quire [uh-KWIRE] VERB, acquired, acquiring. **acquérir ▶** to get as one's own; come to have : *I acquired a taste for sushi when we visited Japan last year.* **Note.** Something that is acquired is an **acquisition**: *The museum's newest acquisition is a painting by Emily Carr.* SYN: get, gain, win, receive.

ac·quit [uh-KWIT] VERB, acquitted, acquitting. **1. acquitter ▶** to declare in a court of law that a person is not guilty of a crime : *The jury acquitted him of all charges.* **2. s'acquitter de ▶** to do one's part : *The team didn't win, but each player acquitted herself well.* SYN: clear, free, release, pardon, forgive.

a·cre [AY-kur] NOUN, acres. **1. hectare ▶** a unit of measurement for land. An acre is equal to 4047 square metres. **2. acres. des kilomètres et des kilomètres de ▶** lands : *Saskatchewan has acres and acres of rich black soil.*

ac·ro·bat [AK-ruh-BAT] NOUN, acrobats. **acrobate ▶** a person who can do special tricks with the body, such as tumbling, tightrope walking, or swinging from a trapeze. ■ **acrobatic,** ADJECTIVE. **▶ acrobatique.**

ac·ro·nym [AK-ruh-nim] NOUN, acronyms. **acronyme, sigle ▶** a word made from the first letters or syllables of a series of words. Some acronyms are written as ordinary words, such as radar = <u>ra</u>dio <u>d</u>etection <u>a</u>nd <u>r</u>anging; others are sets of initials, such as NATO = North Atlantic Treaty Organization.

a·cross [uh-KROS] PREPOSITION. **1. de l'autre côté de ▶** from one side to the other : *Luke threw the ball across the street.* **2. de l'autre côté de, en face (de) ▶** on the opposite side of : *Jenny lives across the canyon from Josh.* ▲ ADVERB. **de large ▶** from one side to the other : *The river looks very wide; do you know the distance across?*

come across trouver, rencontrer ▶ find : *They came across a crocus pushing up through the snow.*

a·cros·tic [uh-KROS-tik] NOUN, acrostics. **acrostiche ▶** a poem in which the first letters of each

line form a word or pattern. Some acrostics are made with the end or middle letters of words.

a·cryl·ic [uh-KRIL-ik] NOUN, acrylics. **acrylique ▶** one of a group of artificial materials made mainly from petroleum, widely used in paints, fabrics, and other products.

act [akt] NOUN, acts. **1. acte, geste ▶** something that is done : *Giving that poor man something to eat was an act of kindness.* **2. acte ▶** the doing of something : *The photograph caught the player in the act of throwing a pass.* **3. loi ▶** a law : *The Official Languages Act of 1969 guarantees all Canadians the right to communicate with the national government in either French or English.* **4. acte, numéro ▶** one part of a play or show : *We were late for the play, so we missed part of the first act.* ▶ VERB, acted, acting. **1. agir, se comporter ▶** to do something : *The police acted quickly to route traffic around the accident.* **2. jouer ▶** to behave in a certain way : *I'm sorry I was rude, but I acted without thinking.* **3. jouer ▶** to play a part in a show or movie : *Kate loves to act in our school plays.* **Note.** A person who acts is an **actor**. (✐ p. 1126.) SYN: deed, feat, work, accomplishment. ✐ p.7. ✐ p. 1026.

ac·tion [AK-shun] NOUN, actions. **1. action ▶** the doing of something : *"And suiting the action to the word, he began to blow his icy cold breath on poor Fox."* (Rosebud Yellow Robe) **2. action, acte ▶** something that is done; an act : *a generous action.* **3. effet ▶** the way a thing works : *The action of the medicine made Sam feel better.* **4. combat ▶** fighting in war : *Canada's military forces saw action on many fronts in World War II.* **5. in action. à l'œuvre ▶** moving or at work; active : *It's exciting to watch a good athlete in action.* **6. actions. acte, geste ▶** conduct or behaviour : *It is said that actions speak louder than words.* ✐ p. 1026.

ac·ti·vate [AK-tuh-vate] VERB, activated, activating. **déclencher, mettre en marche, mettre en route ▶** to make active; put into action : *"He activated his spaceship and Whooosh! He was off."* (Tim Wynne-Jones)

ac·tive [AK-tiv] ADJECTIVE. **1. actif (-ive), en activité ▶** in action; moving or working : *an active volcano.* **2. actif (-ive) ▶** full of action; lively :

She's active in several different clubs at her school. **3. à l'actif, à la voix active ▶** in grammar, using a verb to show the subject of the sentence doing or causing the action : *In the sentence "Ted mailed the invitations to his birthday party," mailed is an active verb.* ■ **actively,** ADVERB: ▶ **activement.** *The company is actively seeking to hire more workers.*

ac·tiv·i·ty [ak-TIV-uh-tee] NOUN, activities. **1. activité ▶** something that is done or to be done : *Our main activity last week was organizing our science project.* **2. activité ▶** the state of being active; action : *Grandma still takes part in many physical activities, such as swimming, golf, and walking.* 📖 **p. 1026.**

ac·tu·al [AK-choo-ul] ADJECTIVE. **1. réel (-elle), véritable ▶** in fact; real : *What is the actual cost of the television, including tax and delivery?* ■ **actually,** ADVERB. ▶ **réellement, en fait.** *"Grama Bowman was actually her great-grandmother."* (Joseph Bruchac)

ac·u·punc·ture [AK-yoo-PUNK-chur] NOUN. **acupuncture ▶** a form of medical treatment first used in China, which eases pain and disease through the use of thin needles inserted at certain places in the body.

a·cute [uh-KYOOT] ADJECTIVE. **1. aigu (-uë), intense ▶** sharp and strong : *Carly felt an acute pain in her ankle when she slipped on the ice.* **2. fin (-ne) ▶** quick in noticing things; sharp : *Dogs have an acute sense of smell.* **3. critique ▶** very important; serious : *The drought has caused an acute shortage of food.*

acupuncture

ad [ad] NOUN, ads. **annonce, réclame ▶** short for advertisement.

ad- PREFIX. to ; toward ▶ *Advance means to move toward something. If one building adjoins another, it is next to the other building.*

A.D. [ay dee] ABBREVIATION. **après Jésus-Christ ▶** used in giving dates : *329 A.D. means 329 years*

after the birth of Christ. **Note.** A.D. is short for *Anno Domini,* a Latin phrase meaning "in the year of our Lord."

Adam's apple pomme d'Adam ▶ a bump in the front of the throat just below the chin.

a·dapt [uh-DAPT] VERB, adapted, adapting. **adapter ▶** to change in order to fit into a new situation : *The writers adapted the play for television.* **Note.** An adapter or adaptor is something that adapts one thing to another : *She needed an adapter to connect her computer to the TV set.* **Note.** Something that adapts easily is said to be adaptable.

ad·ap·ta·tion [AD-up-TAY-shun] NOUN, adaptations. **1. adaptation ▶** the act of adapting, making fit, or adjusting : *The family made a quick adaptation to their new home.* **2. adaptation ▶** something made by adapting : *The film adaptation of that novel isn't nearly as good as the book.* **3. adaptation ▶** an adjustment by which an individual or species changes to fit a change in its environment.

add [ad] VERB, added, adding. **1. additionner ▶** to put numbers together to get a total : *If you add the numbers 2 and 3, you get 5.* **2. ajouter ▶** to put a thing with something else : *Mom tasted the stew, and then added more salt.* **3. ajouter ▶** to say something more : *Sally said goodbye, adding that she hoped we'd visit again soon.* **4. ajouter à ▶** add to. **a. ajouter à ▶** put with : *He added pasta to the boiling water.* **b. ajouter à ▶** increase : *She bought a beautiful piece of art to add to her collection.*

ad·der [AD-ur] NOUN, adders. **1. vipère ▶** a small, poisonous snake of Europe : *The European viper is called an adder in Great Britain.* **2. serpent inoffensif ▶** any of several small, harmless snakes of North America.

ad·dict [AD-ikt] NOUN, addicts. **intoxiqué (-ée), toxicomane ▶** a person who is unable to control a need for something that is harmful to the body : *A drug addict finds it extremely difficult to stop using drugs.*

ad·dict·ed [uh-DIK-tud] ADJECTIVE. **dépendant (-ante) ▶** not able to do without something harmful : *Larry is addicted to cigarettes.* **Note.** The state of being addicted to something is addiction.

ad·di·tion [uh-DISH-un] NOUN, additions. **1. addition ▶** the adding of numbers together in arithmetic : *Our first arithmetic test this year was in addition.* **2. ajout ▶** the act of adding something to something else : *The addition of a little cinnamon will make the apple pie taste much better.* **3. ajout ▶** a thing that is added : *We're planning an addition to the house, which will include a bedroom and a bathroom.* **4. in addition (to). en plus (de) ▶** also : *We made baked* *beans for the picnic in addition to the potato salad.*

ad·di·tion·al [uh-DISH-uh-nul] ADJECTIVE. **additionnel (-elle), supplémentaire, de plus** ▶ that is added; extra : *Set an additional place at the table in case Kevin gets here in time for dinner.* ■ **additionally,** ADVERB. ▶ **en outre, en supplément, en plus.** *Additionally, all the winners of the weekly prize will have a chance at the grand prize.*

ad·di·tive [AD-uh-tiv] NOUN, additives. **additif** ▶ something that is added to another thing to improve it : *Additives are often added to food to preserve it.*

ad·dress [uh-DRES or AD-dres] NOUN, addresses. **1. adresse** ▶ the place where someone lives or something is located : *Clint's new address is 727 Walnut Street.* **2. adresse** ▶ the writing on a piece of mail that tells where it is to be sent : *When Nora moved, she had to change the address on all her mail.* **3. discours** ▶ a speech : *The principal gave an address at the graduation ceremony.* **4. adresse** ▶ a certain number in the memory of a computer that helps it to find a piece of information. ▲ VERB, addressed, addressing. **1. s'adresser à** ▶ to write the address on a piece of mail : *to address a letter.* **2. s'adresser à** ▶ to speak to a certain person or group : *Jane was asked to address the PTA meeting this month.*

a·dept [uh-DEPT or AD-ept] ADJECTIVE. **expert (-erte), habile, adepte** ▶ very good at something; skillful : *Pam is very adept at fixing machines.* ■ **adeptly,** ADVERB. ▶ **de façon experte.**

ad·e·quate [AD-uh-kwit] ADJECTIVE. **suffisant (-ante),** ▶ as much as is needed; enough : *Be sure that you take along an adequate supply of water on your hiking trip.* ■ **adequately,** ADVERB. ▶ **suffisamment.**

ad·he·sive [ud-HE-siv] ADJECTIVE. **adhésif (-ive), gommé (-ée)** ▶ able to stick to something; sticky : *Fasten that gauze with adhesive tape.* ▲ NOUN, adhesives. **adhésif** ▶ something that is sticky, such as tape, glue, or paste.

a·dieu [uh-DYOO] INTERJECTION. **adieu** ▶ French for goodbye.

a·di·os [AD-ee-oce or ad-ee-OCE] INTERJECTION. **adieu** ▶ Spanish for goodbye.

ad·ja·cent [uh-JAY-sunt] ADJECTIVE. **adjacent (-ente)** ▶ next to; near : *There is an orchard adjacent to the road.* 🖉 p. 391.

ad·jec·tive [AJ-ik-tiv] NOUN, adjectives. **adjectif** ▶ a word that tells something about a NOUN or PRONOUN. 🖉 p. 9.

ad·join·ing [uh-JOYN-ning] ADJECTIVE. **attenant (-ante), voisin (-ine)** ▶ being next to or near : *You can park in the lane adjoining the back of the house.*

🖉 Writing Tips

Adjectives

• Although it is the **adjective's** job to describe something or someone, try not to use too many at one time. One strong adjective is usually better than several weak ones. Try to use nouns and verbs that clearly describe what you want to say, instead of letting the adjectives do all the work. Your writing will be much more interesting. "The night was dark and stormy" could read "Strong winds blew the rain hard against the dark windows."

---

ad·journ [uh-JERN] VERB, adjourned, adjourning. **ajourner (à)** ▶ to stop until a later time : *The president adjourned the meeting until next week.*

ad·just [uh-JUST] VERB, adjusted, adjusting. **1. ajuster, régler** ▶ to change or move something to make it fit or work better : *Adjust the antenna on the TV to see if the picture comes in more clearly.* **2. (s')ajuster à** ▶ to become used to something; adapt : *He had to adjust to his new job quickly.* **Note.** Something that can be adjusted is adjustable: *an adjustable car seat.* SYN: alter, adapt, change.

ad·just·ment [uh-JUST-munt] NOUN, adjustments. **ajustement, réglage, mise au point** ▶ the act of adjusting, or something that is adjusted : *The car started when the mechanic made a small adjustment to the engine.*

ad·lib [ad-LIB] VERB, ad-libbed, ad-libbing. **improviser** ▶ to say or do something that is made up on the spot and not planned beforehand : *The comedian was quick to ad-lib responses to the shouts from the audience.* ▲ NOUN, ad-libs. **improviser** ▶ something that is said in this way : *a funny ad-lib.*

ad·min·is·ter [ud-MIN-uh-stur] VERB, administered, administering. **1. administrer, régir, gérer** ▶ to be in charge of; manage : *The Prime Minister administers the affairs of the nation.* **2. dispenser** ▶ to give out; apply : *The Red Cross administers aid and assistance to refugees.* **3. faire prêter serment (à), assermenter** ▶ to give in an official way : *The club's leader administers an oath of loyalty to all new members.* **Note.** An administrator is someone who administers.

ad·min·is·tra·tion [ad-MIN-uh-STRAY-shun] NOUN, administrations. **1. application, administration, gestion** ▶ the act of administering something : *The Supreme Court is concerned with the administration of justice.* **2. administration** ▶ the people in control of a business or group : *The Dean and her board form the administration of the college.* ■ **administrative,** ADJECTIVE. ▸ **administratif (-ive).** *The president of a large business corporation has to have administrative ability.*

ad-mi-ra-ble [AD-mur-uh-bul] ADJECTIVE. **admirable** ▸ that which should be admired; very good : *The mayor made an admirable attempt to improve the city.*

ad-mi-ral [AD-muh-rul] NOUN. admirals. **amiral (-aux)** ▸ the highest rank of officer in a navy.

ad-mi-ra-tion [AD-mu-RAY-shun] NOUN. **admiration** ▸ the act of admiring; a strong feeling of respect or pleasure : *People had great admiration for the bravery shown by the soldiers during the war.*

ad-mire [ud-MIRE] VERB. admired, admiring. **1. admirer** ▸ to think highly of; respect : *We all admire Rohan for the effort he has made to catch up after being sick so long.* **2. admirer** ▸ to think of with great pleasure : *We all admired the beautiful sunset.* ■ **admirer,** NOUN. ▸ **admirateur.**

ad-mis-sion [ud-MISH-un] NOUN. admissions. **1. prix d'entrée** ▸ the price a person must pay to enter a place : *How much is the admission to the concert?* **2. aveu (-eux)** ▸ the act of admitting something : *The police officer arrested the thief after his admission of guilt.* **3. trouver accès à, se faire admettre** ▸ the act of allowing someone to enter a place : *He applied for admission to York University.*

ad-mit [ud-MIT] VERB. admitted, admitting. **1. admettre** ▸ to agree with something in a slow or reluctant way : *I don't like what he said, but I have to admit he has a point.* **2. laisser entrer** ▸ to allow to go in : *On Tuesdays, the museum admits everyone for free.* ■ **admittance,** NOUN. ▸ **entrée.** *Admittance to the dinner is by invitation only.* SYN: grant, allow, permit, accept.

a-do-be [uh-DOH-bee] NOUN. adobes. **1. adobe** ▸ a building block made of clay mixed with straw and dried in the sun. **2. adobe** ▸ a building made of such bricks. ▲ ADJECTIVE. **d'adobe** ▸ *adobe shelters.*

ad-o-les-cent [AD-uh-LES-unt] NOUN. adolescents. **adolescent (-ente)** ▸ a person who is no longer a child but not yet an adult; a teenager : *An adolescent goes through many physical and emotional changes.* ▲ ADJECTIVE. **adolescent (-ente)** ▸ having to do with adolescents. **Note.** The time of life when a person is an adolescent is adolescence. ◪ **p. 966.**

a-dopt [uh-DOPT] VERB. adopted, adopting. **1. adopter** ▸ to take into one's family and raise as one's own : *Let's adopt that frisky puppy and take him home from the animal shelter.* **Note.** A person who adopts a child is an adoptive parent. **2. adopter** ▸ to take and use as

one's own : *Many people adopt a low-fat diet in an effort to stay fit and healthy.* **3. adopter** ▸ to accept something in a formal way : *Our school adopted a new reading program.*

a-dop-tion [uh-DOP-shun] NOUN. adoptions. **adoption** ▸ the act of adopting : *Our neighbours have four children, but they are considering the adoption of a child from Rwanda.*

a-dore [uh-DOR] VERB. adored, adoring. **adorer** ▸ to be very fond of; to love greatly : *Megan adores her grandfather.* ■ **adorable,** ADJECTIVE. ▸ **adorable.** ■ **adoration,** NOUN. ▸ **adoration.** SYN: love, cherish.

a-dorn [uh-DORN] VERB. adorned, adorning. **orner, décorer** ▸ to add something beautiful to; decorate : *She adorned her hat with flowers.* ■ **adornment,** NOUN. ▸ **ornement, décoration.**

adult [uh-DULT or AD-ult] NOUN. adults. **1. adulte** ▸ a grown-up; a person who is fully grown. **2. adulte** ▸ an animal or plant that has grown to full size and strength. ▲ ADJECTIVE. **1. adulte** ▸ fully grown; that is an adult : *Stamping one's foot and hollering is not a very adult way to act.* **2. (pour) adultes** ▸ meant for adults : *Grandpa is learning Japanese in an adult education course.* SYN: mature, full-grown. ◪ **p. 966.**

ad-vance [ud-VANCE] VERB. advanced, advancing. **1. avancer** ▸ to move forward. **2. faire avancer** ▸ to help the progress of : *The treaty between the two warring nations advanced the cause of peace.* **3. avancer** ▸ to pay money before it is due : *Dad advanced me half of my allowance so that I could buy my sister a birthday present.* ▲ NOUN. advances. **1. progrès** ▸ a forward movement. **2. avance, progression** ▸ progress or improvement : *There have been many recent advances in the field of medicine.* **3. progrès** ▸ money paid before it is due : *The author received an advance for his next book.* **4. advances. avance (s)** ▸ a first step to being friendly : *Sara ignored Robert's friendly advances.* ▲ ADJECTIVE. **à l'avance** ▸ ahead of time : *If you give us advance notice of your arrival, we'll get everything ready for you.* SYN: go ahead, continue, progress, proceed.

in advance a. à l'avant de ▸ in front : *The drum major marched in advance of the parade.* **b. d'avance, à l'avance** ▸ ahead of time : *They paid for the tickets in advance.*

ad-vanced [ud-VANST] ADJECTIVE. **1. avancé (-ée)** ▸ ahead of others of the same kind : *Egypt's civilization was one of the most advanced in ancient times.* **2. avancé (-ée)** ▸ far beyond the beginning : *Annie is taking an advanced course in mathematics at high school.* **3. un âge avancé** ▸ very old : *The cellist Pablo Casals continued performing at a very advanced age.*

ad-vance-ment [ud-VANCE-munt] NOUN. advancements. **avancement, promotion** ▸ the act of

---

📝 **Writing Tips**

Advice—Advise
Sometimes it is hard to remember which spelling is the noun and which is the verb. Think of a trick to help you remember. For example, "Advice is the noun because it has ice in it and ice is a noun."

advancing : *He took a lower-paying job because there is a greater chance for advancement with that company.*

ad·van·tage [ad-VAN-tij] NOUN, **advantages. avantage** ▸ something that is helpful or useful : *One advantage of our new home is its location.* SYN: benefit, help, assistance, upper hand.

take advantage of a. profiter de ▸ to benefit from; make good use of : *Let's take advantage of this warm weather and have a picnic.* **b. profiter de** ▸ to treat someone in an unfair way : *She took advantage of his good nature by asking him to do all her work for her.*

ad·van·ta·geous [AD-vun-TAY-jus] ADJECTIVE. **avantageux (-euse)** ▸ favourable; giving an advantage : *From our advantageous spot in the bleachers, we were able to see the whole field.* ■ **advantageously,** ADVERB. ▸ **avantageusement.**

ad·ven·ture [ud-VEN-chur] NOUN, **adventures. 1. aventure** ▸ something that involves danger and excitement; a difficult or risky experience. **2. aventure** ▸ a thrilling or unusual experience : *"I was mostly alone and made up western adventures which I acted out with my horses."* (Marilyn Halvorson) **Note.** A person who looks for and enjoys adventure is an **adventurer.** 📖 **p. 1027.**

ad·ven·tur·ous [ud-VEN-chuh-rus] ADJECTIVE. **1. aventureux (-euse), audacieux (-euse)** ▸ ready to take risks; enjoying adventures. **2. aventureux (-euse), hasardeux (-euse)** ▸ full of danger; risky. *Backpacking in the Yukon is an adventurous thing to do.* SYN: bold, dangerous, risky, daring.

ad·verb [AD-verb] NOUN, **adverbs. adverbe** ▸ a word that tells something about a verb, an adjective, or another adverb. An adverb can show "how much" *(The glass is very full);* "in which way" *(The car veered sharply);* "when" *(They arrived late);* or "where" *(Put the basket there).* **Note.** An adverbial phrase is one that is used as an adverb, such as *up and down* in the sentence *She nodded her head up and down.*

ad·ver·sar·y [AD-vurs-AIR-ee] NOUN, **adversaries. adversaire** ▸ a person or group that is against another; an enemy or opponent : *Karen is a*

worthy adversary in chess. SYN: opponent, competitor, rival, enemy.

ad·verse [AD-vers or ud-VERS] ADJECTIVE. **1. défavorable** ▸ critical or disapproving : *Her book sold well in spite of the adverse reviews.* **2. adverse, défavorable** ▸ unfavourable; not good or helpful : *The adverse weather conditions made the cycling race even more difficult.* ■ **adversely,** ADVERB. ▸ **défavorable.** SYN: unfortunate, unfavourable, opposing.

ad·ver·si·ty [ud-VER-suh-tee] NOUN, **adversities. adversité** ▸ hardship; something bad or unfavourable : *The pioneers had to overcome the adversities of harsh weather and loneliness.* SYN: misfortune, distress, trouble.

ad·ver·tise [AD-ver-TIZE] VERB, **advertised, advertising. annoncer** ▸ to announce; give public notice of : *The students put up signs to advertise their car wash.* ■ **advertiser,** NOUN. ▸ **annonceur (-euse).**

ad·ver·tise·ment [AD-ver-TIZE-munt or ad-VER-tis-munt] NOUN, **advertisements. réclame, annonce, publicité** ▸ any public statement that promotes a product, a service, or an idea. **Note.** The business of making advertisements is advertising.

ad·vice [ad-VICE] NOUN. **conseil** ▸ an opinion about what should be done : *His sister gave him advice about what courses to take in high school.* SYN: guidance, direction, suggestion. 📖 **p. 11.**

ad·vis·a·ble [ud-VIZE-uh-bul] ADJECTIVE. **conseillé (-ée)** ▸ wise; sensible : *It is advisable to study before an exam if you want to get a good mark.*

ad·vise [ud-VIZE] VERB, **advised, advising. 1. conseiller, recommander** ▸ to suggest what a person should do or say; give advice : *I advise you not to try skiing with your leg in a cast.* **2. aviser, informer (de)** ▸ to tell about something; inform : *Doctors advise bikers to wear helmets.* 📖 **p. 11. Note.** A person who advises is an **adviser** or **advisor.** SYN: counsel, guide, suggest, urge, recommend.

ad·vo·cate [AD-vuh-kate or AD-vuh-kit] VERB, **advocated, advocating. recommander (de)** ▸ to be in favour of; recommend publicly : *We advocate using the land along the river for a public park.* ▲ NOUN, **advocates. défenseur** ▸ a person who advocates something : *The speaker is an advocate for animal rights.* SYN: supporter, ally.

aer·i·al [AIR-ee-ul] NOUN, **aerials. antenne** ▸ a radio or television antenna : *The aerial on our roof helps us get a clear picture on the television screen.* ▲ ADJECTIVE. **aérien (-ienne)** ▸ in or from the air : *The plane flew over the lake to take an aerial photograph.*

aer·o·bic [uh-ROH-bik] ADJECTIVE. **aérobie** ▸ using or growing with oxygen : *Most plants are aerobic.*

aerobic exercise (also aerobics) **exercice d'aérobie ▸** exercise that strengthens the heart and lungs by increasing the efficiency of oxygen taken in by the body.

aer·o·dy·nam·ics [AIR-uh-dy-NAM-iks] NOUN. **aérodynamique ▸** the study of the forces acting on an object due to air, or other gases, moving past it : *Engineers use the principles of aerodynamics to design better airplanes.*

aer·o·naut·ics [AIR-uh-NOT-iks] NOUN. **aéronautique ▸** the science or art of designing, manufacturing, and flying aircraft.

aer·o·sol [AIR-uh-SOL] NOUN, aerosols. **aérosol ▸** a substance consisting of tiny particles of a solid or liquid held in a gas. Aerosols can be manufactured and sealed inside containers, to be released as spray or foam.

aer·o·space [AIR-oh-SPACE] NOUN. all the area above the earth; the earth's atmosphere and the space beyond it.

af·fair [uh-FAIR] NOUN, affairs. **1. affaire, événement ▸** any thing, matter, or happening : *The wedding was a formal affair.* **2.** (often affairs) **affaire (s) ▸** anything that has to be done or dealt with; a job or piece of business : *The dispute really isn't any of your affair. The magazine contains articles on current affairs.* SYN: event, happening, occasion, party, function.

af·fect¹ [uh-FEKT] VERB, affected, affecting. **1. affecter, influer sur ▸** to make a difference in : *These new glasses will affect your vision by improving it.* **2. affecter, toucher ▸** to make a person feel strongly about something : *Seeing the people begging in the street affected Zan deeply.* ✐ p. 12.

af·fect² [uh-FEKT] VERB, affected, affecting. **simuler, faire parade de ▸** to pretend to have or feel : *Ever since Nellie got back from New Orleans, she has been affecting a southern accent.* ▪ **affected**, ADJECTIVE. ▸ **affecté (-ée), maniéré (-ée).** *He stroked his moustache in an affected manner.* ✐ p. 12.

af·fec·tion [uh-FEK-shun] NOUN, affections. **affection ▸** a feeling of liking or friendship : *People often hug to show affection.* SYN: love, tenderness, fondness, attachment. ▷ p. 1017.

af·fec·tion·ate [uh-FEK-shuh-nit] ADJECTIVE. **affectueux (-euse) ▸** having or showing affection : *Grandma gives me an affectionate hug every time she sees me.* ▪ **affectionately**, ADVERB. ▸ **affectueusement.**

af·fil·i·ate [uh-FIL-ee-ATE] VERB, affiliated, affiliating. **s'affilier, se joindre à ▸** to join or connect with : *My brother will not affiliate with me at school.* ▲ NOUN [uh-FIL-ee-it], affiliates. **filiale ▸** a person or thing that is affiliated : *The TV station that my brother Jeff works for is an affiliate of the CBC.* ▪ **affiliation**, NOUN. ▸ **affiliation.**

✐ Writing Tips

Affect—Effect

*Because **affect** and **effect** sound so similar, it is important to pay close attention to the spelling of the word you want to use. In order to decide which is the right one, you have to remember what both words mean.*

- *Affect means to influence or have an impact on, or to make a show of or pretend.*

  *Tino was **affected** by the sad story.*

  *Sarah **affected** interest in the movie to please her friend.*

- *Effect is the result or consequence of an action.*

  *Adding colour to the room gave it a cosy **effect.***

af·firm·a·tive [uh-FIRM-uh-tiv] ADJECTIVE. **affirmatif (-ive) ▸** saying that something is true; saying "yes" : *The motion passed because there was a majority of affirmative votes.* ▲ NOUN, **affirmative ▸** affirmatives : *If you wish to answer in the affirmative, please nod your head.*

af·fix [uh-FIX] VERB, affixed, affixing. **apposer, attacher ▸** to fasten or attach something : *Alicia affixed the note to the front door with tape.*

af·flict [uh-FLIKT] VERB, afflicted, afflicting. **affliger ▸** to cause pain or suffering to : *Arthritis is a disease that afflicts many elderly people.* **Note.** Something that afflicts is an affliction. SYN: ail, trouble, distress.

af·flu·ent [AF-loo-unt *or* uh-FLOO-unt] ADJECTIVE. **riche ▸** having a lot of money or property; rich : *Many affluent people live in that suburb.* **Note.** The fact of being affluent is affluence.

af·ford [uh-FORD] VERB, afforded, affording. **1. avoir les moyens de, (se) permettre, pouvoir se payer ▸** to have enough money to pay for : *"He knew what the man was thinking anyway : that this job would finally afford him a new addition to the barn."* (Tim Wynne-Jones) **2. pouvoir, se permettre de ▸** to be able to do something without causing harm : *Rajib can't afford to miss a day of school, since he's been absent so often.* **3. fournir, offrir, donner ▸** to provide; give : *Seeing my old friend afforded me real pleasure.*

a·float [uh-FLOTE] ADVERB. **à flot ▸** floating in the water or the air : *They sent the toy boats afloat in the soft breeze.* ▲ ADJECTIVE. **à flot, sur l'eau ▸** on a ship : *They were afloat on a raft in the middle of the lake.*

a·fraid [uh-FRADE] ADJECTIVE. **1. effrayé (-ée) ▸** feeling scared; full of fear : *Jon isn't afraid of* *snakes, but spiders bother him.* **2. désolé (-ée)** ▶ feeling sorry or concerned about something : *Patricia was afraid she would be late for school if she missed the bus.*

af·ter [AF-tur] PREPOSITION. **1. après** ▶ later in time than : *We have soccer practice right after school.* **2. après** ▶ behind ; following : *The dog ran after the ball.* ▲ ADVERB. **après** ▶ following in time or place : *We got to the theatre after Tony.* ▲ CONJUNCTION. **après** ▶ following the time that : *There's no point in closing the door after the dog has gotten out.* **Note.** After is also combined with nouns to form such words as afterlife, aftertaste, and afterthought.

after all **après tout, finalement** ▶ in spite of ; nevertheless : *I didn't think Sean would be there, but he came after all.*

af·ter·noon [AF-tur-NOON] NOUN, afternoons. **après-midi** ▶ the time of day between noon and night.

af·ter·ward [AF-tur-wurd] ADVERB. (also afterwards) **par la suite, après** ▶ at a later time : *We had a picnic lunch, and then afterward we went for a walk.*

a·gain [uh-GEN *or* uh-GAYN] ADVERB. **encore**▶ once more ; another time : *I watched the movie again because I really liked the funny parts.*

a·gainst [uh-GENST *or* uh-GAYNST] PREPOSITION. **1. contre** ▶ in a way that is opposite to : *We play soccer against his team.* **2. contre** ▶ upon or touching : *He pressed his nose against the window, trying to see outside.*

age [ayj] NOUN, ages. **1. âge** ▶ the length of time a person, animal, or plant has been alive. **2. âge** ▶ the amount of time that a thing has existed : *What's the age of that fort?* **3.** (sometimes Age) **époque, âge** ▶ a certain period of time : *Many say that we live in the computer age.* **4. ages. une éternité, des heures** ▶ a long time : *Imagine bumping into Kamel ; I haven't seen him for ages.* ▲ VERB, aged, aging, or ageing. **vieillir, prendre de l'âge** ▶ to make or grow old : *This company ages its cheeses to improve their flavour.*

a·ged [AY-jid *or* ayjd] ADJECTIVE. **1. âgé (-ée), vieux (vieille)** ▶ of a great age ; old ; elderly : *Aaron's grandmother lives in a home for the aged.* **2.** [ayjd] **âgé de** ▶ having a certain age : *"Greta was a young widow then, with a boy aged nine."* (Thomas H. Raddall)

a·gen·cy [AY-jun-see] NOUN, agencies. **agence, bureau** ▶ a company or person that does business for others : *Hank's mother works for a real estate agency.*

a·gen·da [uh-JEN-duh] NOUN, agendas. **1. ordre du jour** ▶ a list of things to be discussed at a meeting : *Zau added that issue to the agenda for Thursday's meeting.* **2.** *Informal.* **programme, plan** ▶ any plan of things to be done :

What's on your agenda for this weekend? SYN : program, procedure.

a·gent [AY-junt] NOUN, agents. **1. agent (-ente), représentant (-ante)** ▶ a person who does business for others : *The author's business agent negotiates her book contracts with the publisher.* **2. agent (-ente)** ▶ a person who works for a government agency : *A secret agent is a spy.* **3. agent** ▶ something that produces a certain effect : *Yeast is an agent that causes dough to rise.*

ag·gra·vate [AG-ruh-VATE] VERB, aggravated, aggravating. **1.** *Informal* **exaspérer** ▶ to make someone angry by bothering the person ; irritate : *People in the audience aggravated the speaker by asking embarrassing questions.* **2. aggraver, empirer, envenimer** ▶ to make something worse : *Helen aggravated her knee injury by playing tennis.* ■ **aggravation,** NOUN. ▶ aggravation, exaspération. ✐ p. 24.

ag·gres·sion [uh-GRESH-un] NOUN, aggressions. **1. agression** ▶ an attack made without good reason : *The army's march over the border was an act of aggression.* **2. agression** ▶ behaviour or actions that are strong and forceful : *The fights among stags for leadership of the herd are forms of aggression.* **Note.** A person who commits aggression is an aggressor.

ag·gres·sive [uh-GRES-iv] ADJECTIVE. **1. agressif (-ive)** ▶ attacking without good reason ; warlike : *Our neighbour has an aggressive guard dog.* **2. énergique, dynamique** ▶ willing to compete against others ; strong and forceful : *Mary's aggressive attitude makes her a fierce opponent.* ■ **aggressively,** ADVERB. ▶ agressivement. ■ **aggressiveness,** NOUN. ▶ agressivité.

a·ghast [uh-GAST] ADJECTIVE. **atterré (-ée)** ▶ filled with surprise or horror ; shocked : *They were aghast at the damage done by the tornado.*

ag·ile [AJ-ile *or* AJ-ul] ADJECTIVE. able to move quickly and easily ; nimble : *An acrobat must be agile and strong.* **Note.** Someone who is agile has agility. SYN : nimble, quick-moving, spry.

ag·i·tate [AJ-uh-TATE] VERB, agitated, agitating. **1. agiter** ▶ to move back and forth ; shake : *The washer agitates clothes during the wash cycle.* **2. dérange, trouble** ▶ to disturb or excite : *The thought of speaking before a crowd agitates Maria.* **3. mener campagne** ▶ to try to stir up public opinion : *The speaker deliberately agitated the crowd to take action.* **Note.** A person who does this is an agitator. SYN : excite, stir, disturb, annoy, fluster, arouse.

a·go [uh-GOH] ADVERB. **il y a** ▶ in the past ; before now : *My grandma was born 70 years ago.* ▲ ADJECTIVE. **il y a longtemps** ▶ gone by ; past : *The first Ice Age occurred long, long ago.*

ag·o·nize [AG-uh-NIZE] VERB, agonized, agonizing. **1. souffrir, être au supplice** ▶ to suffer great pain. **Note.** This meaning is often used as an

ADJECTIVE: *Each step on his sprained ankle caused Ed agonizing pain.* **2. fournir de grands efforts, se vider au travail ▸** to make a great effort; struggle : *Stephanie agonized long and hard over her project.*

ag·o·ny [AG-uh-nee] NOUN. **agonies. agonie, douleur intense ▸** very great pain : *That toothache caused Ted a lot of agony.* SYN: misery, torment, anguish, torture.

a·gree [uh-GREE] VERB. **agreed, agreeing. 1. s'accorder, se mettre d'accord sur ▸** to have the same idea about something : *The boys couldn't agree on which movie to rent.* **2. accepter, consentir à, convenir de ▸** to be willing to do : *Mom agreed to let Megan stay overnight at Annie's.* **3. accorder ▸** in grammar, to go with another word in the proper way : *In a correct sentence, the verb agrees with the subject.* **4. agree with. réussir à quelqu'un ▸** be good or healthful for : *Spicy foods don't agree with my brother; they upset his stomach.* SYN: consent, accept, approve, match.

a·gree·a·ble [uh-GREE-uh-bul] ADJECTIVE. **1. consentant (-ante) ▸** willing; ready to agree : *Everyone but Lucas was agreeable to the plan.* **2. agréable ▸** nice; pleasant : *Listening to music is an agreeable way to spend a rainy afternoon.* ▪ **agreeably,** ADVERB. ▸ **agréablement, harmonieusement.** *Most of the time the children played together agreeably.*

a·gree·ment [uh-GREE-munt] NOUN. **agreements. 1. accord ▸** an understanding or arrangement between two people or groups : *The two countries made a trade agreement to buy certain products from each other.* **2. être d'accord ▸** the state of agreeing; having the same idea : *The committee was in agreement that the team's nickname should be the Wildcats.* **3. accord ▸** in grammar, the matching of two words in the proper way : *In the sentence "They were late," the verb "were" is in agreement with the subject "they."* SYN: contract, treaty, promise, accord.

ag·ri·cul·ture [AG-ruh-KUL-chur] NOUN. **agriculture ▸** the science or business of farming : *About 4 percent of Canada's workers are employed in agriculture.* ▪ **agricultural,** ADJECTIVE. ▸ **agricole.** having to do with farming.

a·ground [uh-GROWND] ADVERB. **échoué (-ée) ▸** on or onto the shore, reef, or bottom in shallow water; beached : *The boat ran aground in the low tide.*

a·head [uh-HED] ADVERB. **1. en avant de, devant ▸** in or to the front : *Just one runner crossed the finish line ahead of Su-Ann.* **2. en avance ▸** in a better or more advanced position : *The game ended with the home team three points ahead.* **3. avancer ▸** to or for the future; forward : *I set the clock 10 minutes ahead so I wouldn't be late.*

aid [ade] NOUN. **aids. 1. aide, assistance, secours ▸** help or support : *A clerk quickly came to Mom's aid when the bottom of her grocery bag split.* **2. aide ▸** something that is helpful : *A hearing aid is a device that makes sounds louder.* ▲ VERB. **aided, aiding. aider, assister ▸** to help : *It is against the law to aid a person in committing a crime.* SYN: help, assistance, support, relief.

aide [ade] NOUN. **aides. aide, assistant (-ante) ▸** a helper or assistant : *The prime minister was accompanied on the trip by several of her aides.*

AIDS [ades] NOUN. **sida ▸** a very serious disease that causes a person's body to lose the power to fight off other diseases. **Note.** AIDS is short for Acquired Immune Deficiency Syndrome. "Immune deficiency" means that a person with this condition cannot fight off infections and illnesses the way that a healthy person can.

ail [ale] VERB. **ailed, ailing. 1. tracasser, troubler ▸** to be the matter with; to cause trouble for : *We took our dog to the vet because we didn't know what ailed her.* **2. souffrir ▸** to be sick; feel ill : *Christine has been ailing for more than a week and hasn't been in school.*

ail·ment [ALE-munt] NOUN. **ailments. maladie ▸** something that ails a person; an illness, especially a minor illness : *Much to everyone's relief, Jim's ailment turned out to be just an upset stomach.* SYN: sickness, illness, disorder, complaint.

aim [ame] VERB. **aimed, aiming. 1. viser ▸** to point or direct at someone or something : *Aim the camera before you press the button.* **2. viser ▸** to have a certain goal or purpose : *The teacher aimed her talk at the students who did poorly on the test.* ▲ NOUN. **aims. 1. cible ▸** the fact of aiming : *"He took aim and shot. His arrow landed a finger's breadth from the wand."* (Sarah Hayes) **2. but, objectif ▸** goal or purpose : *His aim is to be top scorer for the season.* SYN: target, goal, mark, objective, purpose.

aim·less [AME-lis] ADJECTIVE. **sans but, sans objet ▸** lacking purpose : *She took an aimless walk in the park.* ▪ **aimlessly,** ADVERB. ▸ **sans but, sans objet.**

air [air] NOUN. **airs. 1. air ▸** what we breathe to stay alive : *Air is all around the earth and is a mixture of gases, mainly nitrogen and oxygen.* **2. air ▸** fresh air : *Open the window and get some air in here.* **3. en l'air, dans les airs ▸** the air above the earth; the sky : *Tom threw his ball in the air and caught it as it came down.* **4. air ▸** the general feeling or appearance of something : *The director has an air of importance about him.* ▲ VERB. **aired, airing. 1. aérer ▸** to place in the air or let air through : *Please open the door to air out the kitchen.* **2. exprimer ▸** to make known : *The citizens*

aired their opinions at the town meeting.
☞ **p. 1102.**

on (off) the air **diffusé (-ée), en ondes, à l'antenne** ▸ that is (or is not) being broadcast : *That program first came on the air in 1981.*

up in the air **incertain (-aine), qui n'est pas décidé** ▸ not decided; uncertain : *Plans for the rematch are still up in the air.*

air-borne [AIR-born] ADJECTIVE. **1. en vol, en l'air** ▸ in the air; flying : *The pilot said the plane would be airborne as soon as she received clearance to take off.* **2. en suspension dans l'air** ▸ carried by the air : *Some plants reproduce by means of airborne seeds.*

air-con-di-tion [AIR-CON-DISH-un] VERB, air-conditioned, air-conditioning. **climatiser** ▸ to provide a place with cooler, cleaner air. **Note.** Often used as an ADJECTIVE: *an air-conditioned car; an air-conditioning specialist.*

air conditioning **climatiseur, climatisation** ▸ a system of treating the air in a room, building, car, or other closed place. Air conditioning makes the air cooler and also drier and cleaner. **Note.** An air-conditioner is a machine used for air conditioning.

air-craft [AIR-kraft] NOUN, aircraft. **appareil, avion** ▸ anything that is made to travel through the air, such as an airplane, a helicopter, or a glider. ☞ **p. 392.**

aircraft carrier [AIR-kraft] **porte-avions** ▸ a large warship that carries airplanes. It has a long, flat deck that the planes use to land and take off.

air force (*often* Air Force) **armée de l'air** ▸ the branch of the military forces of a country that is responsible for military aircraft. **Note.** In the Canadian Forces, the function of an air force is served by Air Command.

air-line [AIR-line] NOUN, airlines. **ligne aérienne, compagnie aérienne** ▸ a company whose business is moving people and goods by aircraft. **Note.** Planes used by airlines are airliners.

air-mail [AIR-male] NOUN. **poste aérienne** ▸ (also air-mail) a system of sending mail by means of aircraft. ▲ VERB, airmailed, airmailing. to send something by airmail. **Note.** Also used as an ADJECTIVE and ADVERB: *an airmail letter; to send a package airmail.*

air-plane [AIR-plane] NOUN, airplanes. (also aeroplane) **avion** ▸ a vehicle that flies in the air . *A jet is a kind of airplane.* ☞ **p. 1152.** ☞ **p. 392.**

air-port [AIR-port] NOUN, airports. **aéroport** ▸ an area used by aircraft to take off and land. ☞ **p. 1152.**

air pressure (also atmospheric pressure) **pression de l'air** ▸ the weight of the air pressing from the top of the atmosphere on the layers of air below. You don't feel this weight because

you are supported by equal air pressure on all sides.

air-space [AIR-space] NOUN. **espace aérien** ▸ the air or sky above a country, legally agreed among nations to be part of that country's territory : *The pilot was asked to identify himself when his plane entered another country's airspace.*

air-tight [AIR-tite] ADJECTIVE. **1. hermétique** ▸ so tight that air cannot get in or out. **2. étanche** ▸ not having any weak points : *No one disagreed because Ellen had an airtight argument.*

aisle [ile] NOUN, aisles. **allée** ▸ a long, narrow passage to walk through : *The flight attendant pushed the food cart down the aisle of the plane.*

a-larm [uh-LARM] NOUN, alarms. **1. (signal d') alarme, alerte, réveil-matin** ▸ a noise that wakes people up or warns them of danger, or a device that makes such a noise : *Her alarm did not go off this morning, and she was late for work.* **2. alarme, frayeur** ▸ a sudden feeling of being afraid : *The driver was filled with alarm when he heard the loud siren behind him.* ▲ VERB, alarmed, alarming. **alarmer, effrayé (-ée)** ▸ to make afraid : *Flashbulbs alarmed the wild tiger.* **Note.** Often used as an ADJECTIVE:*The newspaper printed an alarming report about an increase in crime.* SYN: warn, frighten, agitate, disturb, excite.

alarm clock **réveil-matin** ▸ a clock that can be set to ring, buzz, or make a similar noise at a certain time, usually used to awaken a sleeping person.

al-ba-tross [AL-buh-TROS] NOUN, albatrosses. **albatros** ▸ any one of several kinds of large sea birds, found over nearly all oceans except the North Atlantic. The albatross may follow a ship for days, but is seldom seen resting.

Al-ber-to-saur-us [al-BERT-uh-SOR-us] NOUN. **albertosaure** ▸ A dinosaur similar to Tyrannosaurus rex whose remains were first found in Alberta in the 1880s.

al-bi-no [al-BY-noh] NOUN, albinos. **albinos** ▸ a person or animal that lacks colouring in the skin, eyes, and hair : *An albino is thought of as having white colouring and reddish or pink eyes.*

al-bum [AL-bum] NOUN, albums. **1. album** ▸ a long-playing record or tape. **2. album** ▸ a book with blank pages to hold stamps, photographs, autographs, or the like : *After graduation, the students signed one another's autograph albums.*

al-che-my [AL-kuh-mee] NOUN. **alchimie** ▸ an early form of chemistry practised in the Middle Ages. It was the study of how to turn ordinary metals into gold using magic and secret formulas. **Note.** A person who practised alchemy was an **alchemist**.

15

al·co·hol [AL-kuh-hol] NOUN. alcohols. **alcool** ▸ a liquid that has no colour or smell and can catch fire easily. Different kinds of alcohol are used in medicines, as fuel, and for many other products. ☞ p. 1133.

al·co·hol·ic [AL-kuh-HOL-ik] ADJECTIVE. **alcoolisé (-ée), alcoolique** ▸ containing alcohol : *Beer and wine are alcoholic drinks.* ▲ NOUN. alcoholics. **alcoolique** ▸ a person who suffers from alcoholism.

al·co·hol·ism [AL-kuh-hol-iz-um] NOUN. **alcoolisme** ▸ a disease in which a person suffers physical and mental damage from drinking too much alcohol.

ale [ale] NOUN. ales. **bière, ale** ▸ an alcoholic drink that is similar to beer, but is darker and more bitter tasting. Ale is made from malt and hops.

a·lert [uh-LERT] ADJECTIVE. **1. vigilant (-ante), attentif (-ive)** ▸ watching very carefully; ready for something to happen : *An alert motorist spotted the licence number of the stolen car.* **2. alerte, vif (-ive), éveillé (-ée)** ▸ quick to learn or understand : *a person with an alert mind.* ▲ NOUN. alerts. **alerte** ▸ a signal that warns of danger. ▲ VERB. alerted, alerting. **alerter** ▸ to make alert; warn : *Please alert me if you see anyone approach the house.* ■ **alertly,** ADVERB. ▸ **prestement.** ■ **alertness,** NOUN. ▸ **vigilance, promptitude.** SYN: watchful, attentive, vigilant, wide-awake.

al·fal·fa [al-FAL-fuh] NOUN. **luzerne** ▸ a plant with purple flowers that is related to clover. Alfalfa is grown as food for cattle and horses.

al·gae [AL-ji] PLURAL NOUN. **algues** ▸ a large group of plants that live in water. Algae do not have leaves, roots, or stems, but they do have chlorophyll. Seaweed is a type of algae.

al·ge·bra [AL-juh-bruh] NOUN. **algèbre** ▸ a form of mathematics that uses letters to stand for numbers that are not known. An algebraic expression is $4x + 3 = 9y \times 2 - 1$. **Note.** *Algebra* comes from an Arabic expression meaning "putting things together." Many English words that begin with *al-* come from Arabic; *al* is the Arabic word for "the."

Al·gon·qui·an [al-GONG-kwee-un] ADJECTIVE. **algonquien (-ienne)** ▸ the languages spoken by groups of Aboriginal peoples from Labrador to the Rockies, including Abenaki, Blackfoot, Cree, Malecite, Micmac, Ojibwa, and Ottawa. 2. (Also Algonquin) the Aboriginal people who speak these languages.

a·li·as [AY-lee-us] NOUN. aliases. **faux nom, d'emprunt** ▸ a name that a person uses other than his or her real name, especially a false name used by a criminal or secret agent to hide his or her identity : *The spy often used an alias to hide his real identity.*

al·i·bi [AL-uh-by] NOUN. alibis. **1. alibi** ▸ a claim that a suspect was somewhere else when a crime was committed and therefore could not be involved. **2. alibi, excuse** ▸ any excuse for a mistake or failure : *What is your alibi this time for getting home so late?*

a·li·en [AY-lee-un] NOUN. aliens. **1. étranger (-ère)** ▸ a person who is not a citizen of the country in which he or she is living. **2. extraterrestre** ▸ a being from another planet. ▲ ADJECTIVE. **1. étrange** ▸ very different or strange. **2. étranger à, contraire à** ▸ not natural : *Being cruel to animals is alien to my nature.*

a·li·e·nate [AY-lee-uh-NATE or ALE-yuh-NATE] VERB. alienated, alienating. **1. aliéner** ▸ to cause to become unfriendly : *Jason's unpleasant attitude has alienated most of his friends.* **2. éloigner, (se) détacher, désaffectionner** ▸ to remove or separate from a group : *The older she got, the more she alienated herself from the group.*

a·lign [uh-LINE] VERB. aligned, aligning. **1. aligner** ▸ to bring into a straight line. **2. s'aligner, se liguer** ▸ to join or co-operate with : *Canada and the U.S. are often aligned on foreign policy.* ■ **alignment,** NOUN. ▸ **alignement.** *The wheels of the car were out of alignment.*

a·like [uh-LIKE] ADJECTIVE. **semblable, pareil** ▸ like one another; similar : *Those twins look so much alike that I can't tell them apart.* ▲ ADVERB. **pareillement, de même** ▸ in the same way : *The teacher treats everyone alike.* SYN: similar, identical, resembling.

al·i·mo·ny [AL-uh-MOH-nee] NOUN. **pension alimentaire** ▸ money required by law to be paid to a former husband or wife after a divorce.

a·live [uh-LIVE] ADJECTIVE. **1. vivant (-ante)** ▸ having life; living. **2. grouillant (-ante) de, fourmillant (-ante) de** ▸ in existence; active : *The rivers in this park are alive with fish.*

all [ol] ADJECTIVE. **1. tout (-toute)** ▸ with nothing missing or left out; the whole of : *The forest fire burned all night.* **2. tous (toutes)** ▸ every one of : *After the party all the children went home.* ▲ ADVERB. **tout, complètement** ▸ completely; entirely : *Eli's clothes were all wet from the rain.* ▲ NOUN. **tout** ▸ everything one has : *She gave her all to win the race.* ▲ PRONOUN. **tout** ▸ everyone or everything : *Ten o'clock and all is well.* SYN: whole, total, entire, complete.

at all du tout, aucunement ▸ in any way : *I thought Faye would be furious, but she didn't seem at all upset.*

Al·lah [uh-LAH or AL-uh or AH-luh] NOUN. **Allah** ▸ the name of the Supreme Being or God in Islam.

al·lege [uh-LEJ] VERB. alleged, alleging. **alléguer, prétendre** ▸ to state something without presenting proof : *The police allege that he stole the money, but his case has not yet come to trial.* **Note.** Often used as an ADJECTIVE: *an* *alleged bank robber.* ■ **allegedly,** ADVERB: ▸ prétendument. *Allegedly, he was a double agent.*

al·le·giance [uh-LEE-juns] NOUN. **fidélité** ▸ being true or faithful to something : *We felt a strong allegiance to our country as we sang the national anthem.* SYN: loyalty, faithfulness, devotion.

al·le·gor·y [AL-uh-GOR-ee] NOUN, allegories. **allégorie** ▸ a story that has a hidden meaning that is different from the surface meaning.

al·ler·gic [uh-LUR-jik] ADJECTIVE. **1. allergique** ▸ having an allergy. **2.** *Informal.* **allergique, ne pas supporter** ▸ having a strong dislike : *Tan is allergic to work; he always finds something to do when it's time to do his chores.*

al·ler·gy [AL-ur-jee] NOUN, allergies. **allergie** ▸ a reaction of the body against something that is not harmful in itself and does not bother other people : *Dust, pollen, animal hair, and certain kinds of food and medicine often cause allergies.*

al·ley [AL-ee] NOUN, alleys. **ruelle** ▸ a long narrow space between buildings, especially to the side or rear of a row of buildings : *Put the garbage out in the alley behind our apartment building.*

al·li·ance [uh-LY-uns] NOUN, alliances. **alliance, association** ▸ a formal agreement to work together or combine for some purpose : *Alliances between nations are often formed by treaties.* SYN: association, union, league, affiliation.

al·lied [uh-LIDE *or* AL-ide] ADJECTIVE. **allié (-ée)** ▸ being an ally, joined or connected in some way : *The whole neighbourhood is allied against crime.*

al·li·ga·tor [AL-uh-GATE-ur] NOUN, alligators. **alligator** ▸ a large water animal with thick, tough skin : *An alligator is a reptile similar to a crocodile but with a shorter, flatter head.*

al·lit·er·a·tion [uh-LIT-uh-RAY-shun] NOUN. **allitération** ▸ in poetry and other kinds of writing, a pattern in which the same sound is repeated at the beginning of a series of words. ✐ p. 17.

al·lot [uh-LOT] VERB, allotted, allotting. **attribuer, assigner** ▸ to give as a share : *The school allotted each student 30 minutes on the computer.* ■ **allotment,** NOUN. ▸ **attribution, répartition.** SYN: allocate, assign, distribute.

al·low [uh-LOW] VERB, allowed, allowing. **1. permettre** ▸ to let a person do a certain thing; let something happen; permit : *"But allow me to ask : for whom have you prepared this royal feast?"* (Tololwa M. Mollel) **2. donner, allouer** ▸ to let have; give or provide : *The teacher allowed us more time to finish our work.* SYN: permit, let, grant, consent, authorize.

✍ **Writing Tips**

Alliteration

Alliteration is the repetition of the same sound at the beginning of words—the "s" sound of "Silly Sam"—and sometimes of sounds from the middle of a word—the "f" sound in "life's fast."

> *Silly Sam slipped silently southward.*
> *Life's fast friends forever.*

• *Writers use alliteration to catch the reader's attention in poems and advertising, or to make readers laugh.*

• *Sometimes, too much alliteration can distract the reader.*

allow for tenir compte de, prévoir ▸ to take into account; make an adjustment for : *to allow for delays because of traffic.*

al·low·ance [uh-LOW-uns] NOUN, allowances. **1. allocation, pension** ▸ a sum of money set aside for a certain purpose : *Derek gets an allowance of two dollars a week from his parents.* **2. make allowance(s) for. avoir de l'indulgence** ▸ to allow for : *We make allowances for Inez because she's younger than the other children.*

al·loy [AL-oy] NOUN, alloys. **alliage** ▸ a metal made by melting and mixing together other metals. Some alloys are stronger, harder, or lighter than the metals that combine to make them. Steel and bronze are alloys. ▲ VERB, alloyed, alloying. **allier** ▸ to make an alloy : *Copper is alloyed with zinc to make brass.*

all right 1. en bonne santé ▸ not hurt or sick. **2. satisfaisant (-ante)** ▸ good enough; satisfactory : *The book was all right, but I don't think I care to see the movie.* **3. entendu, c'est ça, ça y est** ▸ a way of saying "yes": *All right, we'll have lunch on the porch.*

all-round [OL-rownd] ADJECTIVE. (also all-around) **complet (-ète)** ▸ capable of doing many things; useful in many ways : *She's an all-round soccer player.*

al·ly [AL-i] NOUN, allies. **allié (-ée)** ▸ a person, group, or country that joins with another for some purpose : *They are allies in the fight against racism.* ▲ VERB [uh-LY *or* AL-i]. allied, allying. **s'allier à (avec)** ▸ to join with another as an ally : *Canada is allied with the U.S. on several projects.*

al·ma·nac [OL-muh-NAK] NOUN, almanacs. **almanach** ▸ a book that contains facts about different subjects, including the weather, the stars, and countries.

al·might·y [ol-MY-tee] ADJECTIVE. **tout-puissant (toute puissante)** ▶ having complete power; all-powerful. **Note.** The Almighty is a name for a Supreme Being or God.

al·mond [OM-und *or* AH-mund] NOUN, almonds. **amande** ▶ a small nut that is eaten alone or used as a flavouring for candy and other foods.

al·most [OL-most] ADVERB. **presque** ▶ very near to, but not quite : *Tasha has now saved almost $100.*

a·lo·ha [uh-LOH-hah] INTERJECTION. **bonjour, au revoir** ▶ hello or goodbye, especially in Hawaii.

a·lone [uh-LONE] ADJECTIVE. **1. seul (seule)** ▶ by oneself; not with others : *Tara offered to stay with Alan, but he wants to be alone.* **2. seul** ▶ only : *Hard work alone won't ensure success; you also need some luck.* ▲ ADVERB. **tout seul** ▶ by oneself or itself : *The bull stood alone in the pasture.*

let alone sans parler de, sans compter, encore moins ▶ not to mention : *I could hardly sit still through the first act, let alone the whole play.* ✐ p. 309.

a·long [uh-LONG] PREPOSITION. **le long de** ▶ by the length of; by or at the side of; near : *Wildflowers were growing along the fence.* ▲ ADVERB. **1. donner, transmettre** ▶ forward : *Dad passed along my baby toys to my cousin.* **2. avec** ▶ near or with someone : *Bring along a friend if you'd like.*

a·loof [uh-LOOF] ADJECTIVE. **réservé (-ée), distant (-ante)** ▶ not very friendly; removed or distant : *Mandy seems aloof, but she's really very shy.* ▲ ADVERB. (also **aloofly**) **à l'écart, à distance** ▶ at a distance : *The new boy stood aloof from his classmates.* SYN : reserved, cool, distant, unfriendly.

a·loud [uh-LOWD] ADVERB. **à voix haute (haute voix), tout haut** ▶ out loud : *"As the others took turns reading aloud, I realized with relief that I read as well as any of them, better than most."* (Jean Little)

al·pac·a [al-PAK-uh] NOUN, alpacas. **alpaga** ▶ an animal that is related to the camel and lives in the mountains of South America. The alpaca has fine, long wool that is used to make clothing.

al·pha·bet [AL-fuh-bet] NOUN, alphabets. **alphabet** ▶ the letters used to write a language, arranged in a certain order from beginning to end. In English, the order of the alphabet is A, B, C, and so on.

al·pha·bet·i·cal [AL-fuh-BET-uh-kul] ADJECTIVE. **alphabétique** ▶ arranged according to the alphabet : *In a dictionary, words appear in alphabetical order.* ■ **alphabetically,** ADVERB.

▶ **alphabétiquement.** *The students are listed alphabetically by last name.*

al·pha·bet·ize [AL-fuh-buh-TIZE] VERB, alphabetized, alphabetizing. **classer par ordre alphabétique** ▶ to arrange something in alphabetical order.

al·read·y [ol-RED-ee] ADVERB. **1. déjà** ▶ before now or before a certain time : *I've already done my homework, so I can play until dinner.* **2. déjà** ▶ so soon : *You can't be leaving already; you just got here.*

al·so [OL-soh] ADVERB. **aussi, de plus, également** ▶ as well; besides; too : *He bought a new suit, and also two shirts.* SYN : besides, too, in addition, plus, furthermore.

al·tar [OL-tur] NOUN, altars. **autel** ▶ a table or raised place used as a centre for religious services.

al·ter [OL-tur] VERB, altered, altering. **modifier, changer, transformer** ▶ to make or become different; change somewhat : *Harry's appearance had altered so much we hardly recognized him.* ■ **alteration,** NOUN. ▶ **modification.** *Our dry cleaner does minor alterations, such as shortening hems and sleeves.* SYN : adjust, change, vary, modify, revise.

al·ter·nate [OL-tur-NATE] VERB, alternated, alternating. **1. chacun son tour** ▶ to take turns; go one after another : *In the game of chess, the two players alternate in moving their pieces.* **2. alterner** ▶ to move back and forth from one to another : *The sky has alternated from sunny to cloudy this morning.* ▲ [ol-TER-nit *or* OL-tur-nit] NOUN, alternates. **remplaçant (-ante)** ▶ a person or thing that takes the place of another; a substitute : *José was chosen as an alternate on the city's all-star soccer team.* ▲ ADJECTIVE. **1. tous les deux jours, un jour sur deux** ▶ by turns; one and then another : *Mom and Mr. Tong drive us to school on alternate days.* **2. remplaçant (-ante), suppléant (-ante)** ▶ in place of another; a substitute : *Nat is the alternate bus driver on our route.* ■ **alternately,** ADVERB. ▶ **alternativement, en alternance, tour à tour.**

alternating current (AC) courant alternatif ▶ an electric current that reverses its direction at regular intervals. The electricity in homes and other buildings uses alternating current. **Note.** See also **direct current**.

al·ter·na·tive [ol-TER-nuh-tiv] NOUN, alternatives. **1. alternative** ▶ a choice from among two or more things : *Taking lunch is the alternative to buying it at school.* **2. alternative** ▶ one single choice of this kind : *If Quincy wants to make the team, he has no alternative but to practise hard.* ▲ ADJECTIVE. **alternatif (-ive)** ▶ giving a choice : *We need to choose one of the alternative plans as soon as possible.*

al-though [ol-THOH] CONJUNCTION. **bien que, quoi que ▸** in spite of ; though : *Although my room isn't large, it's comfortable and warm.*

al-ti-tude [OL-tuh-TYOOD *or* OL-tuh-TOOD] NOUN, altitudes. **altitude ▸** the height that something is above the ground or above sea level : *Mount Robson in the Canadian Rockies has an altitude of 3954 metres above sea level.*

al-to [AL-toh *or* OL-toh] NOUN, altos. **1. alto ▸** the lowest singing voice for a woman, or the highest for a man : *An alto is higher than a tenor and lower than a soprano.* **2. alto ▸** a singer or musical instrument with the same range : *an alto saxophone.*

al-to-geth-er [OL-tuh-GETH-ur] ADVERB. **1. entièrement, complètement ▸** completely ; entirely : *The restaurant seems to have closed down altogether.* **2. somme toute ▸** with all included ; counting all : *Altogether that was a great show.* **3. dans l'ensemble ▸** on the whole : *That was altogether a satisfying dinner.*

a-lu-mi-num [uh-LOO-muh-num] NOUN. **aluminium ▸** a chemical element that is a lightweight, silver-white metal. Aluminum can be easily shaped, conducts heat and electricity well, and does not rust or tarnish easily. It is used in wire, pots and pans, aircraft and car parts, and machinery. ◈ **p. 398.**

al-ways [OL-wayz *or* OL-wiz] ADVERB. **toujours ▸** all the time ; at all times : *Mom always picks me up from school at 3:30.* SYN : forever, perpetually, eternally.

am [am] VERB. **(je) suis ▸** a form of the verb to be that is used with "I" to tell about the present : *I am tired.*

AM ABBREVIATION. **AM ▸** short for amplitude modulation one of the two main kinds of signals used by radios. In AM radio the signal is sent out the same number of times per second, but the strength of the signal changes. **Note.** See also FM.

A.M., a. m. ABBREVIATION. **avant-midi, du matin ▸** a way to show that a certain time is in the morning : *A.M. means between midnight and noon.*

am-a-teur [AM-uh-chur *or* AM-uh-tur] NOUN, amateurs. **1. amateur (-trice) ▸** a person who does something for enjoyment, not for money. **2. amateur (-trice) ▸** a person who does not have skill or experience in a particular area : *This drawing shows great promise, although it is clearly the work of an amateur.* ▲ ADJECTIVE. **amateur (-trice) ▸** of or by an amateur : *a contest for amateur skaters.*

a-maze [uh-MAZE] VERB, amazed, amazing. **stupéfier ▸** to surprise greatly : *"Kileken continued to amaze the old man with his strange deeds."* (Tololwa M. Mollel) **Note.** Often used as an ADJECTIVE: *Kira demonstrated amazing skill*

on the violin. ■ **amazingly,** ADVERB. ▸ **étonnamment.** ■ **amazement,** NOUN. ▸ **stupéfaction.** SYN : surprise, astonish, astound.

am-bas-sa-dor [am-BAS-uh-dur] NOUN, ambassadors. **ambassadeur (-drice) ▸** a person who serves in a foreign country as the chief representative of her or his government in that country : *The Canadian ambassador to the U.S. works in Washington, D.C.*

am-ber [AM-bur] NOUN. **1. ambre ▸** a hard, clear yellow or brown substance that is used to make beads and jewellery. Amber is a fossil from the resin of pine trees that grew millions of years ago. **2. ambre ▸** a yellowish-brown colour.

am-bi-dex-trous [AM-buh-DEX-trus] ADJECTIVE. **ambidextre ▸** able to use both hands equally well. ■ **ambidextrously,** ADVERB. ▸ **de façon ambidextre.**

am-big-u-ous [am-BIG-yoo-us] ADJECTIVE. **ambigu (-uë) ▸** having more than one possible meaning ; not clear : *The sentence "After Ron hit Zack, he ran away" is ambiguous, because it is not clear which boy ran away.* ▲ ADVERB, ambiguously.

am-bi-tion [am-BISH-un] NOUN, ambitions. **1. ambition ▸** a strong desire to succeed or obtain something : *Suzanne has ambition and is willing to work hard to reach her goals.* **2. ambition ▸** the thing for which a person has a strong desire : *Sunil's ambition is to enter politics and become prime minister.* SYN : desire, longing, goal, aim, purpose.

am-bi-tious [am-BISH-us] ADJECTIVE. **1. ambitieux (-euse) ▸** having a strong desire to succeed or to become something : *Rosa's ambitious assistant took night courses to expand his business knowledge.* **2. ambitieux (-euse) ▸** needing effort or skill : *The students' plan to raise $300 is ambitious, but they are determined to succeed.* ■ **ambitiously,** ADVERB. ▸ **ambitieusement.**

am-biv-a-lent [am-BIV-uh-lunt] ADJECTIVE. **1. ambivalent (-ente) ▸** having conflicted feelings such as love and hate, at the same time. **2. ambivalent (-ente) ▸** uncertain, indecisive.

am-bu-lance [AM-byuh-luns] NOUN, ambulances. **ambulance ▸** a specially equipped vehicle that carries the sick or wounded : *The accident victims were rushed to the hospital in an ambulance.*

am-bush [AM-bush] NOUN, ambushes. **embuscade ▸** a surprise attack by persons who are hidden : *Our troops were on the alert for a possible ambush by the enemy.* ▲ VERB, ambushed, ambushing. **tendre une embuscade ▸** to make a surprise attack from a hidden place.

a-men [AY-MEN *or* AH-MEN] INTERJECTION. **amen ▸** a Hebrew word that means "so be it" or "let it be so." "Amen" is said at the end of a prayer, and also to show strong agreement with something another person has just said.

a·mend [uh-MEND] VERB, amended, amending. **corriger, améliorer, ajuster ▶** to change something for the better : *The company amended the plans for the new school.* ▪ **amendment,** NOUN. ▶ **modification, rectification.** SYN : adjust, improve, better, correct, reform.

a·mi·a·ble [AY-mee-uh-bul] ADJECTIVE. **aimable** ▶ easy-going ; friendly.

a·mid [uh-MID] (also amidst) PREPOSITION. **dans, parmi ▶** in the middle of ; surrounded by : *One small tree stood amid the destruction left by the tornado.*

a·mi·no acid [uh-MEE-noh] **acide aminé, aminoacide ▶** one of a group of organic compounds that are part of the structure of proteins and are essential to the workings of the human body.

a·miss [uh-MIS] ADJECTIVE. **de travers, qui ne va pas ▶** not as it should be, wrong or out of order : *I knew something was amiss when I came home and the door was open.*

am·mo·ni·a [uh-MONE-yuh *or* uh-MOE-nee-uh] NOUN, ammonias. **ammoniac ▶** a strong-smelling colourless gas that is a mixture of nitrogen and hydrogen : *Ammonia is often used for household cleaning.*

am·mu·ni·tion [AM-yuh-NISH-un] NOUN. **1. munitions ▶** bullets, shells, bombs, missiles, and other such weapons that can be fired or launched against an enemy. **2. argument ▶** facts or arguments that support a statement or point of view : *Stacey had lots of ammunition to support her side in the debate.*

am·ne·sia [am-NEE-zhah *or* am-NEE-zee-uh] NOUN. **amnésie ▶** a temporary or permanent loss of memory : *Amnesia is usually caused by an injury to the head or by a great emotional shock.*

a·moe·ba [uh-MEE-bah] NOUN, amoebas or amoebae (also ameba) **amibe ▶** a tiny, simple form of animal life that can be seen only through a microscope. Amoebas live in water and in soil and as parasites on larger animals.

a·mong [uh-MUNG] PREPOSITION. (also amongst) **1. parmi, entouré de ▶** in the middle of ; surrounded by : *He walked among the trees, admiring their beauty.* **2. parmi ▶** one of : *Carvings by Inuit artists are among my favourite sculptures.* **3. entre ▶** with a portion to each of : *Mom divided the cake equally among the three of us.* **4. entre ▶** throughout the group of : *They settled their differences among themselves.* ✐ p. 20.

a·mount [uh-MOWNT] NOUN, amounts. **1. somme, montant ▶** the total number or quantity ; the sum : *What is the amount of the lunch bill ?* **2. quantité ▶** any number or quantity :

✎ **Writing Tips**

Among—Between

As a general rule, use **among** when you are talking about more than two people or things, and **between** when you are talking about only two people or things.

Jana and Sam shared the apple **between** them.

The fruit was divided **among** all 13 students.

Andy added a small amount of pepper to his salad. ▲ VERB, amounted, amounting. **1. s'élever ▶** to add up to ; total : *The total bill amounts to over one hundred dollars.* **2. devenir ▶** to develop into ; become : *No one thought Jed would amount to anything in life, but he certainly fooled them.*

amp [amp] NOUN, amps. **ampère ▶** short for ampere. **ampères ▶** in electricity, the standard unit for measuring the strength of a current.

am·phib·i·an [am-FIB-ee-un] NOUN, amphibians. **1. amphibie ▶** one of a group of cold-blooded animals with backbones. Amphibians have moist skin without scales or fur and can live either in or out of water. Frogs and salamanders are amphibians. **2. amphibie ▶** aircraft that can take off from and land on either land or water.

amphibian

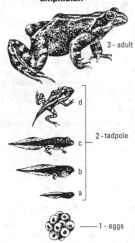

3 - adult

d

2 - tadpole

c

b

a

1 - eggs

3. véhicule amphibie ▶ a tank, a truck, or another vehicle that can travel across land or water.

am·phib·i·ous [am-FIB-ee-us] ADJECTIVE. **1.** having to do with or belonging to the amphibians : *Toads are amphibious animals.* **2.** able to operate on either land or water : *an amphibious vehicle.*

am·phi·the·a·tre [AM-fuh-THEE-uh-tur] NOUN, amphitheatres. (also amphitheater) **amphithéâtre** ▶ an oval or round building used as a theatre or sports arena : *The famous Greek tragedies of ancient times were performed in amphitheatres.*

am·ple [AM-pul] ADJECTIVE, ampler, amplest. **1. abondant (-ante), largement assez** ▶ abundant or more than enough ; plenty : *Be sure to have an ample supply of cups and napkins for the party.* **2. assez, suffisamment** ▶ enough, adequate : *The closet was not large, but there was ample room for Sherry's clothes.* **3. largement assez** ▶ large, roomy : *The garage has ample storage space.* SYN: enough, abundant, sufficient.

am·pli·fi·er [AM-pluh-FY-ur] NOUN, amplifiers. **amplificateur** ▶ a device for increasing the strength of an electronic signal : *An amplifier is part of a stereo system used to make the sound louder.*

am·pli·fy [AM-pluh-FY] VERB, amplified, amplifying. **amplifier** ▶ to make stronger : *You can amplify sound with speakers.* SYN: enlarge, increase, make louder.

am·pu·tate [AM-pyuh-TATE] VERB, amputated, amputating. **amputer** ▶ to cut off a limb of the body in a surgical operation. ∎ **amputation,** NOUN. ▶ **amputation.**

a·muse [uh-MYOOZ] VERB, amused, amusing. **1. amuser, faire rire** ▶ to cause to laugh or smile : *Tania's explanation of why she was late amused the teacher.* **2. (s') amuser, (se) divertir** ▶ to give pleasure to ; entertain : *The group amused themselves by telling ghost stories.* ∎ **amusing,** ADJECTIVE. ▶ **amusant (-ante), drôle.** *an amusing cartoon.*

a·muse·ment [uh-MYOOZ-munt] NOUN, amusements. **1. amusement, plaisir** ▶ enjoyment, pleasure : *Lou is always ready to act like a clown for the amusement of the other children.* **2. amusement, divertissement** ▶ something that amuses : *Paul's favourite summertime amusement is swimming in the lake.* SYN: fun, entertainment, pastime, pleasure.

an [un] ARTICLE. **un (une), par, de** ▶ one ; any. This is the form of the word "a" used before a noun or adjective that starts with a vowel sound : *an elephant ; an idea ; an orange ; five dollars an hour.* An is an indefinite article.

an·a·con·da [AN-uh-KON-duh] NOUN, anacondas. **anaconda** ▶ a very large, powerful snake found in South America. The anaconda is not poisonous, but it can coil around an animal and crush it to death.

an·a·gram [AN-uh-gram] NOUN, anagrams. **anagramme** ▶ a word or phrase made from switching around the letters of another word or phrase : *"Eat" is an anagram for "tea."*

a·nal·o·gy [uh-NAL-uh-jee] NOUN, analogies. **analogie** ▶ a likeness between two things that are not alike in other ways : *an analogy between the arms of a human and the tentacles of an octopus.*

an·a·lyse [AN-uh-LIZE] VERB, analysed, analysing. (also analyze) **1. analyser, décomposer** ▶ to break something down into its basic parts to find what it is made of : *We analysed the sample to see if it is truly gold.* **2. analyser, étudier** ▶ to study something carefully and in detail : *The pitcher analysed the tapes of the game to see where his form could improve.*

a·nal·y·sis [uh-NAL-uh-sis] NOUN, analyses. **1. analyse** ▶ the breaking down of something into its basic parts to find out what it is made of : *An analysis of table salt shows that it contains the elements, sodium and chlorine.* **2. analyse, étude** ▶ a careful and detailed study of something : *An analysis by the museum revealed that the painting was a fake.*

an·ar·chy [AN-ur-kee] NOUN. **1. anarchie** ▶ a condition in which people are not controlled in any way by government laws or rules. **Note.** A person who favours this kind of situation in politics is an anarchist. **2. anarchie** ▶ any state of extreme disorder. SYN: chaos, disorder, lawlessness.

a·nat·o·my [uh-NAT-uh-mee] NOUN, anatomies. **1. anatomie** ▶ the body or parts of an animal or plant : *The anatomy of a frog is like that of a toad.* **2. anatomie** ▶ a branch of science that studies the body structure of animals and plants.

an·ces·tor [AN-ses-tur] NOUN, ancestors. **ancêtre** ▶ a person in one's family line who lived long ago ; someone from whom one is descended. **Note.** All of your ancestors together make up your ancestry. ∎ **ancestral,** ADJECTIVE. ▶ **ancestral (-ale, aux)** ▶. of or inherited from ancestors : *an ancestral home.*

an·chor [ANK-ur] NOUN, anchors. **1. ancre** ▶ a heavy iron weight that is lowered into the water from a boat or ship to hold it in place. **2. attache** ▶ something that is like an anchor in giving strength or support : *The pegs acted as anchors to keep the tent firmly attached to the ground.* ▲ VERB, anchored, anchoring. **1. ancrer** ▶ to keep in place with an anchor : *We anchored the boats firmly before the storm arrived.* **2. ancrer, figer** ▶ to stay in one place, as if held by an anchor : *Instead of chasing the ball, he just stood anchored to the spot.*

an-cient [AYN-shunt] ADJECTIVE. **1. ancien (-ienne)** ▸ having to do with times long ago : *Archaeologists study the remains of ancient civilizations.* **2. très vieux** ▸ very old : *"Within, two ancient men were playing chess on a stone table."* (David Day) ▪ **the ancients,** PLURAL NOUN. ▸ **les anciens. histoire ancienne** ▸ the people who lived in ancient times, such as the early Egyptians, Greeks, and Romans. **Note.** Ancient history is the history of people from the earliest known time to the fall of the Roman Empire.

and [and] CONJUNCTION. **et, plus** ▸ a word used to connect two words, phrases, or sentences : *cats and dogs.*

an-ec-dote [AN-ik-DOTE] NOUN. **anecdotes. anec-dote** ▸ a short story that tells something funny or interesting : *Our teacher told us some anec-dotes about her trip to France last summer.*

a-ne-mi-a [uh-NEE-mee-uh] NOUN. (also anae-mia) **anémie** ▸ an unhealthy condition in which the body does not have enough red blood cells. A person with anemia feels tired and weak all the time. **Note.** Someone who suffers from ane-mia is anemic.

an-es-thet-ic [AN-us-THET-ik] NOUN. **anesthetics.** (also anaesthetic) **anesthésique** ▸ a substance that causes a loss of feeling in the body : *Before anesthetics, operations were very dangerous and painful procedures.*

an-gel [AYN-jul] NOUN. **angels. 1. ange** ▸ in some religions, a heavenly being or spirit. **2. ange** ▸ a person who is thought of as especially good and kind, like an angel : *You were an angel to help out when you were so short-handed.* ▪ **angelic,** ADJECTIVE. ▸ **angélique.** pure ; good and innocent ; like an angel. 📖 **p. 966.**

an-ger [ANG-gur] NOUN. **colère** ▸ a strong feeling of displeasure or indignation toward someone or something that opposes, hurts, or annoys one : *"He exploded with anger, like a hundred hurricanes going off at once."* (Hal Ober) ▲ VERB, **angered, angering. mettre en colère, fâcher** ▸ to make a person angry. SYN : rage, fury, ire, wrath. 📖 **p. 1017.**

an-gle [ANG-gul] NOUN. **angles. 1. angle** ▸ the area formed by two straight lines or flat surfaces that join at a given point. **2. point de vue** ▸ a point of view : *The editor asked the reporter to try a new angle on the article she was writing.* ▲ VERB, **angled, angling. obliquer, faire des angles** ▸ to move at an angle. **Note.** An acute angle is less than 90° ; a right angle is exactly 90° ; an obtuse angle is more than 90°.

An-glo-phone [ANG-gluh-FONE] NOUN, **Anglo-phones.** (also anglophone) **anglophone** ▸ a person whose first language or native language is English. Formed by combining *Anglo,* "English," with *phone,* "sound."

An-glo-Sax-on [ANG-gloh SAK-sun] NOUN, **Anglo-Saxons. 1. anglo-saxon (-onne)** ▸ a member of one of the tribes that came from what is now Germany and Scandinavia to invade England about 1500 years ago. **2. anglo-saxon** ▸ the language of these people, the earliest form of what is now the English language. Anglo-Saxon words tend to be household, personal, or basic terms : *dog, hand, moon, water.*

an-gry [ANG-gree] ADJECTIVE. **angrier, angriest. 1. en colère, fâché (-ée)** ▸ showing or feeling anger : *"But while the poor folk rejoiced, the rich grew angry."* (Sarah Hayes) **2. irrité (-ée), enflammé (-ée)** ▸ sore and painful : *That's a very angry-looking cut on your arm.* ▪ **angrily,** ADVERB. ▸ **avec colère.** SYN : mad, cross, dis-pleased.

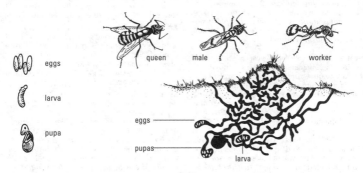

eggs

larva

pupa

queen

male

worker

eggs

pupas

larva

ants

an·guish [ANG-gwish] NOUN. **angoisse** ▶ great suffering or pain; agony. ▲ VERB, **anguished**, **anguishing. angoisser** ▶ to cause or feel great suffering or pain : *Tan anguished over the loss of his cat.*

an·i·mal [AN-uh-mul] NOUN, **animals. 1. animal (-aux)** ▶ a living being that is not a plant. Animals can move about freely and feed on plants or on other animals. They typically have a nervous system and sense organs, such as those for sight and hearing. **2. animal** ▶ any such being other than a human. **▱ p. 1084.**

an·i·mate [AN-uh-MATE] VERB, **animated**, **animating. animer** ▶ to give life to; make lively : *The jokes and games animated the party.* ▲ ADJECTIVE. **animé (-ée), vivant (-ante)** ▶ having life; living : *Tia became more animated as the others laughed at her story.* **Note.** In an animated cartoon, the drawn figures move as if they were alive.

an·i·ma·tion [AN-uh-MAY-shun] NOUN. **1. animation, vivacité, entrain** ▶ spirit; liveliness : *The chorus performed with great animation.* **2. animation** ▶ the art or work of making animated characters.

an·i·mos·i·ty [AN-uh-MOSS-uh-tee] NOUN, animosities. **animosité** ▶ active dislike : *She still has animosity toward people who teased her as a child.* SYN: ill will, hatred, hostility.

an·kle [ANG-kul] NOUN, **ankles. cheville** ▶ the joint where the foot connects to the leg : *Ellen slipped on the ice and twisted her ankle.* **▱ p. 991.**

an·nex [uh-NEKS] VERB, **annexed**, **annexing. annexer, ajouter** ▶ to add to something larger : *The growing city annexed three villages.* ▲ [AN-eks] NOUN, **annexes. annexe** ▶ a building used as an addition to another building. ■ **annexation**, NOUN. ▶ **annexion.**

an·ni·hi·late [uh-NY-uh-LATE] VERB, **annihilated**, **annihilating. annihiler, anéantir, détruire** ▶ to destroy completely, wipe out of existence : *Lava from a volcano annihilated the city of Pompeii.* **Note.** The complete destruction of something is annihilation.

an·ni·ver·sa·ry [AN-uh-VER-suh-ree] NOUN, anniversaries. **anniversaire** ▶ the return each year of a special date : *My parents celebrate their wedding anniversary on February 15.*

an·nounce [uh-NOWNCE] VERB, **announced**, **announcing. 1. annoncer** ▶ to give public notice of; make known : *The teacher announced there would be a spelling test on Friday.* **2. annoncer** ▶ to make known the arrival of a : *"Then one day it was announced that the governor of South China was coming to town."* (Paul Yee) **3. annoncer** ▶ to introduce or tell about something on radio or television. SYN: proclaim, declare, report, reveal.

an·nounce·ment [uh-NOWNCE-munt] NOUN, announcements. **annonce, avis** ▶ a public notice that makes something known : *The announcement of the resignation of the prime minister came as a shock.*

an·nounc·er [uh-NOWN-sur] NOUN, announcers. **1. présentateur (-trice)** ▶ a person on radio or television who introduces programs and performers, identifies the station, or reads the news. **2. annonceur (-euse)** ▶ a person who announces something : *The announcer at the ball game gave the names of the starting lineup.*

an·noy [uh-NOY] VERB, **annoyed**, **annoying. embêter, contrarier, importuner** ▶ to bother or disturb; make someone angry; irritate : *Jim's constant complaining annoyed his friends.* **Note.** Often used as an ADJECTIVE: *Georgia has an annoying habit of cracking her knuckles.* **Note.** A feeling of being annoyed is annoyance. SYN: irritate, bother, pester, badger, trouble. **✐ p. 24.**

an·nu·al [AN-yoo-ul] ADJECTIVE. **1. annuel (-elle)** ▶ happening or done once a year : *I have my annual physical checkup this week.* **2. annuel (-elle)** ▶ in or for one year : *The annual salary for that job is $20,000.* **3. plante annuelle** ▶ living and growing for only one year or season : *Mom's garden has a mix of annual flowers that she plants every spring.* ▲ NOUN, annuals. **annuelle** ▶ a plant or other thing that is annual. ■ **annually**, ADVERB: ▶ **annuellement.** *The company's sales meeting is held annually.*

a·non·y·mous [uh-NON-uh-mus] ADJECTIVE. **1. anonyme** ▶ from or by a person who does not want to give his or her name : *An anonymous donor made a large contribution to the Humane Society.* **2. anonyme** ▶ of unknown name; not known : *The tales of "The Arabian Nights" were written by an anonymous author.* ■ **anonymously**, ADVERB: ▶ **anonymement.** *The informant called the police anonymously to give information about the robbery.*

a·no·rak [AN-uh-RAK] NOUN, anoraks. **anorak** ▶ a parka; a waterproof jacket with a hood, originally made from fur by the Inuit.

an·o·rex·i·a [AN-uh-REK-see-yuh] NOUN. (also anorexia nervosa) **anorexie** ▶ a disease that causes a person to lose all desire to eat because of a fear of becoming overweight. **Note.** A person who has anorexia is anorexic.

an·oth·er [uh-NUTH-ur] ADJECTIVE. **1. un (une) autre, encore un (une)** ▶ one more; an additional : *I'll have another juice because I'm still thirsty.* **2. un (une) autre** ▶ different : *Try another shirt; that one is not a good colour for you.* **3. un (une) second (-onde)** ▶ of the same kind as : *Kara dreams of being another Roberta Bondar.* ▲ PRONOUN. **1. un (une) autre, encore un (une)** ▶ an additional one; one more : *He ate his*

🖉 Word Builder

Annoy, aggravate, and **pester** all mean to do something that bothers another person. *Annoy* usually means that an action goes on and on: *He annoyed her by constantly interrupting when she was speaking.* **Aggravate** has the idea of making a bad situation worse: *It was so aggravating that he drove very slowly even though he knew we were late.* **Pester** suggests something that is only a mild bother: *The boys kept pestering their mother to buy them some ice cream.*

---

ice-cream cone and then ordered another. **2. un (une) autre ▸** a different one.

an·swer [AN-sur] NOUN, answers. **1. réponse ▸** something done or said to respond to a question; a reply: *Look up the answer to your question in the encyclopedia.* **2. réponse ▸** something done in response: *I let the phone ring 10 times, but there was no answer.* ▲ VERB, answered, answering. **1. répondre à ▸** to speak or write in reply: *"There must be somewhere I can live," he called. Nobody answered."* (Nicola Morgan) **2. répondre à ▸** to act in response to something: *Mom asked Don to answer the door.* **3. répondre ▸** to agree with; conform to: *He answers to the description of the man the police are looking for.* SYN: response, reply, retort, solution.

ant [ant] NOUN, ants. **fourmi ▸** a small insect that lives in large groups called colonies. Ants live in tunnels that they make in the ground or in wood. They are related to bees and wasps. ☞ **p. 104.**

an·tag·o·nism [an-TAG-uh-niz-um] NOUN, antagonisms. **antagonisme ▸** being against something or somebody; a bad or angry feeling: *There is real antagonism between those two hockey teams.*

an·tag·o·nize [an-TAG-uh-NIZE] VERB, antagonized, antagonizing. **contrarier, éveiller l'antagonisme de ▸** to arouse anger or bad feelings: *The nasty look Joe gave me was meant to antagonize me.* **Note.** A person who antagonizes or opposes another is an antagonist. Those who act against each other are antagonistic.

Ant·arc·tic [an-TARK-tik *or* an-TAR-tik] ADJECTIVE. **antarctique ▸** at or near the South Pole, or the south polar region: *Antarctic winters drop to −100°C.* ▲ NOUN, the Antarctic. (also Antarctica) **l'Antarctique ▸** the continent surrounding the South Pole.

ant·eat·er [ANT-ee-tur] NOUN, anteaters. **fourmilier, tamanoir ▸** an animal with a very long, narrow head and a long, sticky tongue that it uses to eat ants and other insects. Anteaters have long claws that they use to dig into ant hills.

an·te·lope [AN-tuh-LOPE] NOUN, antelope or antelopes. **antilope ▸** a slender animal from Africa and southern Asia that has long horns

and runs very fast. Antelopes look like deer, but they are actually related to goats and cows.

an·ten·na [an-TEN-uh] NOUN, antennas. **1. antenne ▸** a metal rod or wire used to receive or send out radio or television signals; an aerial. **2.** *plural* antennae [an-TEN-i] **antenne ▸** one of the pair of long, thin feelers on the head of an insect or a water animal such as a crab or lobster.

an·them [AN-thum] NOUN, anthems. **hymne ▸** a song that gives praise to one's country, school, or organization: *"O Canada" is the national anthem of Canada.*

an·ther [AN-thur] NOUN, anthers. **anthère ▸** the part of the stamen of a flower that bears the pollen.

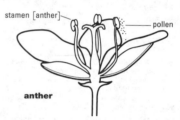

stamen [anther]

pollen

anther

an·thol·o·gy [an-THOL-uh-jee] NOUN, anthologies. **anthologie, recueil ▸** a collection in a book of poems or stories written by different authors: *an anthology of Canadian literature.*

an·thro·pol·o·gy [AN-thruh-POL-uh-jee] NOUN. **anthropologie ▸** the study of how the human race developed and of the way of life of different groups of people around the world. **Note.** An expert in anthropology is an anthropologist. ■ **anthropological,** ADJECTIVE: ▸ **anthropologique.** *an anthropological study of the native people of the Pacific Islands.*

anti- PREFIX. against; opposed to: *Someone who is antiwar is opposed to war.*

an·ti·bi·ot·ic [AN-tee-by-OT-ik] NOUN, antibiotics. **antibiotique ▸** a substance that can kill or slow the growth of germs that cause disease. In medicine, antibiotics are produced artificially from bacteria or moulds. Penicillin is an antibiotic.

an-ti-bod-y [AN-tee-BOD-ee] NOUN, antibodies. **anticorps** ▶ proteins produced by the body to weaken or destroy foreign elements such as bacteria and poisons. Antibodies can make the body able to resist certain illnesses.

an-tic-i-pate [an-TIS-uh-PATE] VERB, anticipated, anticipating. **1. prévoir, envisager, s'attendre à** ▶ to look forward to; expect : *We anticipate a large crowd for the championship game.* **2. prévoir, envisager, s'attendre à** ▶ to be aware or take care of in advance : *We don't anticipate any trouble with the car, but are prepared just in case.* **Note.** The act of anticipating is anticipation. SYN: hope for, expect, look forward to, predict.

an-ti-dote [AN-tih-DOTE] NOUN, antidotes. **1. antidote, contrepoison** ▶ something that works against the harmful effects of a poison. **2. antidote** ▶ a thing that works against something bad or harmful : *Exercise and positive thinking are antidotes for depression.*

an-ti-his-ta-mine [an-tee-HIS-tuh-MEEN *or* AN-TEE-HIS-tuh-min] NOUN, antihistamines. **antihistaminique** ▶ a drug that is used to treat colds and allergies such as hay fever and asthma.

an-tique [an-TEEK] ADJECTIVE. **antique, ancien (-ienne)** ▶ of times long ago; made or done long ago : *Sandy bought an antique chair for her collection at a garage sale.* ▲ NOUN, antiques. **antiquité** ▶ something valuable that was made long ago. SYN: ancient, very old, old-fashioned.

an-ti-sep-tic [AN-tih-SEP-tik] NOUN, antiseptics. **antiseptique** ▶ a substance that kills or stops the growth of germs that cause infections. Iodine and alcohol are commonly used antiseptics.

an-ti-so-cial [AN-tee-SOH-shul] ADJECTIVE. **1. antisocial (-ale, -aux)** ▶ behaving in a manner that goes against the social order : *Breaking the law is an antisocial act.* **2. insociable, pas sociable** ▶ avoiding other people; not friendly : *My neighbour is antisocial and never says hello to people who pass by his house.*

an-ti-tox-in [AN-tee-TOK-sin] NOUN, antitoxins. **antitoxine** ▶ a kind of antibody that protects the body against a particular disease : *Antitoxins help the body to fight diseases.*

ant-ler [ANT-lur] NOUN, antlers. **bois** ▶ one of the bony growths on the head of a deer, a moose, or an elk. Antlers usually grow in pairs. They are shed and grow back each year.

an-to-nym [AN-tuh-nim] NOUN, antonyms. **antonyme** ▶ a word that has the opposite meaning of another word : *"Go" is an antonym for "stop"; "hot" is an antonym for "cold."* 🖉 p. 25.

anx-i-e-ty [ang-ZY-uh-tee] NOUN, anxieties. **anxiété, inquiétude** ▶ an uneasy feeling of worry

---

✏ Writing Tips

Antonym

Antonyms are two words that are opposite in meaning (up/down, big/small, tall/short, sunny/cloudy).

• *Many antonyms are made by adding a prefix to the beginning of words (friendly/ unfriendly, approve/disapprove, spell/misspell).*

• *Some antonyms are made by adding a suffix at the end of words (hope/hopeless, luck/luckless).*

• *Many writers use antonyms to emphasize a point or add power to their writing. The contrast between antonyms, such as fast and slow, can add humour, intrigue, or contrast.*

The fast car slowed down.

• *You can also use antonyms in your writing to say the same thing in a different way. Instead of saying "Sam was too far away to hear me." you could write "Sam wasn't close enough to hear me."*

---

or nervousness about what might happen : *I always have feelings of anxiety when I have to speak before the class.* SYN: concern, uneasiness, worry, anguish. 📙 p. 1017.

anx-ious [ANK-shus] ADJECTIVE. **1. anxieux (-euse), inquiet (-ète), soucieux (-euse)** ▶ concerned or uneasy about what might happen; nervous; fearful : *The government has become very anxious about the situation overseas.* **2. impatient (-ente), désireux (-euse)** ▶ wanting something very much; eager : *"I went home that summer anxious to see my family and to show off my new skills."* (Christy MacKinnon) ■ **anx-iously,** ADVERB. **anxieusement, avec impatience, avec inquiétude.** in an anxious way : *She waited anxiously for the results of her medical exam.* 🖉 p. 26.

an-y [EN-ee] ADJECTIVE. **1. du tout** ▶ one of a group; one or more : *An only child doesn't have any brothers or sisters.* **2. quelque** ▶ some : *Have you read any good books lately?* **3. tous (toutes)** ▶ every : *Any person my age knows how to throw a ball.* ▲ PRONOUN. **aucun (-une)** ▶ anybody or anything : *I wanted to buy Dad a tie, but I didn't see any I liked.* ▲ ADVERB. **plus** ▶ at all : *This show can't get any worse than it already is!*

an-y-bod-y [EN-ee-BUD-ee *or* EN-ee-BOD-ee] PRONOUN. **personne** ▶ any person; anyone : *The way Ursula talks, you'd think she wasn't afraid of*

anybody. ▲ NOUN. *Informal.* **quelqu'un** ▶ an important person : *Everybody who is anybody will be at the party.*

an·y·how [EN-ee-HOW] ADVERB. **de toute manière, de toute façon, en tout cas** ▶ in any case : *Les wasn't invited to the party, but he said he had something else to do anyhow.*

an·y·more [EN-ee-MOR] (also **any more**) ADVERB. **encore, davantage** ▶ at this time; now : *The train doesn't stop in this town anymore.*

an·y·one [EN-ee-WUN] PRONOUN. **quelqu'un** ▶ any person; anybody : *Has anyone seen my keys?*

an·y·place [EN-ee-PLACE] ADVERB. **n'importe où** ▶ to, in, or at any place; anywhere : *Just put it down anyplace.*

an·y·thing [EN-ee-THING] PRONOUN. **rien** ▶ any thing : *I don't have anything to wear to the party.*

an·y·time [EN-ee-TIME] ADVERB. **quand, n'importe quand** ▶ at any time : *We can leave for the lake anytime you want.*

an·y·way [EN-ee-WAY] ADVERB. **en tout cas, de toute façon, quand même** ▶ in any case; anyhow.

an·y·where [EN-ee-WAIR] ADVERB. **n'importe où** ▶ in, at, or to any place.

a·or·ta [ay-OR-tuh] NOUN, aortas. **aorte** ▶ the main artery of the body that carries the blood from the left side of the heart to all parts of the body, except the lungs.

a·part [uh-PART] ADVERB. **1. écarté (-ée), éloigné (-ée)** ▶ away from each other in space or time : *The umpire spread her arms wide apart to show that the runner was safe.* **2. démonter** ▶ in or to pieces : *Jem took the clock apart to see if he could find what was wrong with it.*

a·part·heid [uh-PAR-tite *or* uh-PAR-tate] NOUN. **apartheid** ▶ a policy of separating people according to their race; formerly the official policy of the government of South Africa.

a·part·ment [uh-PART-munt] NOUN, apartments. **appartement, logement** ▶ a room or group of rooms to live in : *We live in an apartment on the sixth floor.* ☞ p. 1065.

ap·a·thy [AP-uh-thee] NOUN. **apathie, indifférence** ▶ a feeling of not caring; a lack of interest; indifference : *The school's apathy toward their baseball team was blamed on the team's bad play.* **Note.** A person who has this feeling is apathetic.

ape [ape] NOUN, apes. **(grand) singe (sans queue)** ▶ a large animal related to the monkey. An ape has no tail and can stand and walk on two feet. Chimpanzees, gorillas, and orangutans are kinds of apes.

a·pex [AY-peks] NOUN, apexes or apices. **sommet, point culminant** ▶ peak; the highest point : *the apex of the mountain.*

a·phid [AY-fid *or* AF-id] NOUN, aphids. **puceron** ▶ a very small insect that feeds by sucking juices from plants.

a·pi·ary [APE-ee-ER-ee] NOUN, apiaries. **rucher** ▶ a place where bees are kept.

a·piece [uh-PEES] ADVERB. **chacun (-une)** ▶ for each one; each : *These apples are fifty cents apiece.*

a·pol·o·gize [uh-POL-uh-JIZE] VERB, apologized, apologizing. **s'excuser, présenter des excuses** ▶ to say one is sorry; make an apology : *Warren apologized for interrupting Susan when she was talking.* **Note.** When someone apologizes, he or she is apologetic.

a·pol·ogy [uh-POL-uh-jee] NOUN, apologies. **excuses** ▶ words that say one is sorry for doing something wrong or for bothering or hurting someone : *Tia accepted Dan's apology for stepping on her toes.*

a·pos·tro·phe [uh-POS-truh-fee] NOUN, apostrophes. **apostrophe** ▶ a punctuation mark ['] that is used **1.** to show that one or more letters have been left out of a word : *"She's" means "she is."* **2.** to show who owns or has something : *That is my sister's book.*

ap·pall [uh-POL] VERB, appalled, appalling. (also **appal**) **épouvanter** ▶ to fill with dismay : *The mess after the party appalled the clean-up crew.*

ap·pall·ing [uh-POL-ing] ADJECTIVE. **épouvantable, effroyable** ▶ very bad; terrible; dismaying.

ap·pa·rat·us [AP-uh-RAY-tus *or* AP-uh-RAT-us] NOUN, apparatus or apparatuses. **équipement, appareil** ▶ the tools or equipment used for a certain purpose or to do a certain job : *The students set*

✐ Word Builder

Anxious has the idea of waiting for something to happen. It can mean that a person is afraid something bad might happen. **Worried** can be used instead of **anxious** for this meaning: *James is anxious (worried) about the test tomorrow because he hasn't had time to study.* **Anxious** can also mean that the person is looking forward to something good. **Eager** can be used instead of anxious for this meaning: *My parents just bought a new home computer system, and I'm anxious (eager) to get a chance to use it.*

up the apparatus to do their science experiment.

ap·par·el [uh-PAIR-ul] NOUN. **vêtement ▶** clothing; things to wear.

ap·par·ent [uh-PAIR-unt] ADJECTIVE. **1. apparent (-ente), évident (-ente) ▶** plain to see; obvious : *With each giggle, her amusement became more apparent.* **2. apparent (-ente) ▶** seeming to be true : *Lightning is the apparent cause of the fire.* SYN : obvious, clear, likely, probable.

ap·par·ent·ly [uh-PAIR-unt-lee] ADVERB. **apparemment ▶** as far as anyone can tell; seemingly : *There's no answer, so apparently no one is at home.*

ap·pa·ri·tion [AP-uh-RISH-un] NOUN, **apparitions. apparition, ▶** a strange or sudden appearance of something, especially something strange or unreal : *They were frozen with fright as the ghostly apparition seemed to float down the stairs.*

ap·peal [uh-PEEL] VERB, **appealed, appealing. 1. demander de l'aide, faire appel à ▶** to ask for help or sympathy : *We get many letters appealing for donations during the holiday season.* **2. plaire à ▶** to be attractive or interesting : *The colour of that dress appeals to me.* **Note.** Often used as an ADJECTIVE:*an appealing smile.* **3. faire appel (de), se pourvoir en appel ▶** in law, to ask that a case be tried again in a higher court : *The judge ruled that the defence counsel could not appeal the verdict.* ▲ NOUN, **appeals. 1. appel ▶** an earnest request : *The speaker made an appeal for quiet.* **2. attrait ▶** the power to attract or interest : *That TV program has maintained its appeal with the audience for many years.* **3. appel ▶** the act of appealing to a higher court.

ap·pear [uh-PEER] VERB, **appeared, appearing. 1. apparaître, paraître ▶** to be seen; come into view : *"Big spaces of bright blue appear, and by afternoon only half of the lake is covered by ice."* (Ann Blades) **2. paraître, sembler ▶** to seem to be : *"Then the ball seemed to hesitate when it got to the window of Sergeant Bouton's house. It appeared to stop and think things over before it decided to keep going."* (Roch Carrier) **3. paraître, entrer en scène ▶** to come before the public : *The marching band is appearing in the parade.* **4. comparaître, paraître ▶** to come formally into a court of law.

ap·pear·ance [uh-PEER-uns] NOUN, **appearances. 1. apparition, arrivée ▶** the act of appearing or coming into view : *The appearance of wild horses on the hill startled us.* **2. apparence, air ▶** the way a person or thing looks : *I concluded from his rumpled appearance that he'd just gotten out of bed.* **3. entrée en scène, apparition ▶** the act of coming before the public : *The tenor made his final appearance at the opera hall last month.* SYN : look, shape, form, view.

ap·pen·di·ci·tis [uh-PEN-duh-SY-tis] NOUN. **appendicite ▶** a condition in which the appendix becomes sore and swollen. **Note.** In serious cases of appendicitis, the appendix must be surgically removed in an operation called an appendectomy.

ap·pen·dix [uh-PEN-diks] NOUN, **appendixes appendice ▶** or **appendices. 1. appendice ▶** a thin, closed tube in the abdomen, attached to the large intestine. The appendix has no known useful function in the body. **2. annexe ▶** a section of writing at the end of a report or book that gives additional information.

ap·pe·tite [AP-uh-TITE] NOUN, **appetites. 1. appétit ▶** a desire to eat food : *Playing outdoors gives me a big appetite.* **2. avoir une soif de, être avide de ▶** any strong desire for something : *Diane has a great appetite for conversation and loves to talk with her friends.* **Note.** Something that pleases the appetite is appetizing. SYN : hunger, craving, longing. 📖 **p. 1133.**

ap·pe·tiz·er [ap-uh-tize-ur] NOUN, **appetizers. amuse-gueule, apéritif ▶** a small amount of food or drink served at the beginning of a meal to stimulate the appetite. Shrimp, crackers and cheese, and vegetables with dip are often served as appetizers. 📖 **p. 1133.**

ap·plause [uh-PLOD] VERB, **applauded, applauding. 1. applaudir ▶** to show approval or enjoyment by clapping the hands : *The audience stood and applauded for the orchestra to play an encore.* **2. approuver ▶** to praise or approve something : *Laura's parents applauded her decision to take a safety course.*

ap·plause [uh-PLOZ] NOUN. **applaudissements ▶** approval or enjoyment shown by the clapping of hands : *The violinist acknowledged the applause with a bow.*

ap·ple [AP-ul] NOUN, **apples. pomme ▶** a round fruit with a thin red, yellow, or green skin that grows on trees in cool climates. 👁 **p. 28.**

ap·pli·ance [uh-PLY-uns] NOUN, **appliances. appareil, électroménager ▶** any small machine or device that is used to do a particular job around the house : *Toasters, stoves, mixers, microwaves, and dishwashers are electrical appliances.* 🖉 **p. 354.**

app·li·cant [AP-luh-kunt] NOUN, **applicants. candidat (-ate) ▶** a person who applies for something, especially a job : *There were 50 applicants for the job.*

ap·pli·ca·tion [AP-luh-KAY-shun] NOUN, **applications. 1. demande, formulaire de candidature ▶** a form that must be filled out to do or get something : *Ivan filled out his application for the soccer league.* **2. application ▶** the act of applying : *It took several applications of white paint to cover that dark blue on the bedroom walls.* **3. application ▶** a program that allows a computer to perform a certain operation : *a word-processing application.*

apple trees

leaves

flowers

fruits
(apples)

pulp   stem

peel   core

seeds

apple tree

ap-ply [uh-PLY] VERB, applied, applying. **1. appliquer, mettre sur** ▶ to put on : *Dad applies shaving lotion to his face every morning.* **2. mettre en pratique** ▶ to make use of : *Try to apply what you've learned in drama class when you are on the stage.* **3. s'appliquer à, s'adresser à** ▶ to have to do with : relate to : *The rules apply to everyone in school.* **4. s'adresser, avoir recours, poser sa candidature, postuler** ▶ to make a request to get or do something : *You can apply for a learning driver's permit when you are 16.* SYN : adopt, use, employ, serve.

ap-point [uh-POYNT] VERB, appointed, appointing. **1. nommer, désigner** ▶ to name a person to some job or position; choose : *The coach appointed Sarah the captain of the lacrosse team.* **2. fixer, désigner** ▶ to set a time or place to do something : *Let's appoint a time for the next meeting.* SYN : assign, name, nominate, engage.

ap-point-ment [uh-POYNT-munt] NOUN, appointments. **1. rendez-vous** ▶ an agreement to meet someone at a certain time and place : *My doctor's appointment is at 3 :30.* **2. nomination, affectation** ▶ the selection of a person to fill a job or position.

ap-pre-ci-ate [uh-PREE-shee-ATE] VERB, appreciated, appreciating. **1. apprécier** ▶ to realize the worth or value of something : *I paused halfway up the hill to appreciate the view.* **2. être reconnaissant** ▶ to be grateful for :*Matt appreciated Ravi's help studying for the test.* **3. prendre de la valeur** ▶ to increase in value : *The value of the house appreciated over time.* SYN : enjoy, value, prize, think highly of.

ap-pre-ci-a-tion [uh-PREE-shee-AY-shun] NOUN. **1. appréciation** ▶ the act or fact of valuing something; a favourable opinion : *Shashi has a true appreciation of music.* **2. reconnaissance, gratitude** ▶ a feeling of thanks for something : *The students gave the teacher a gift in appreciation for all her help during the year.* **Note.** Showing appreciation is being appreciative.

ap-pre-hend [AP-ruh-HEND] VERB, apprehended, apprehending. **1. appréhender, arrêter** ▶ to hold or catch a person; capture : *The police apprehended the criminal at a roadblock.* **2. comprendre** ▶ to grasp mentally; understand : *We apprehended Doug's meaning even though he had a difficult time expressing himself.* **3. appréhender, craindre** ▶ to look forward to something with fear.

ap-pre-hen-sion [AP-ruh-HEN-shun] NOUN, apprehensions. **1. appréhension, crainte** ▶ a feeling of fear about what might happen; being worried or afraid : *The practice helped clear away my apprehension about the game.* **Note.** Showing apprehension is being apprehensive. **2. arrestation** ▶ the act of apprehending; an arrest or capture : *The villagers were relieved by the apprehension of the criminal.* **3. perception, compréhension** ▶ the ability to understand something.

ap-pren-tice [uh-PREN-tis] NOUN, apprentices. **1. apprenti (-ie)** ▶ a person who learns a trade or art by working under skilled supervision. **Note.** This is called an apprenticeship. **2. apprenti (-ie)** ▶ any person who is learning a skill or trade through practical experience. ▲ VERB, apprenticed, apprenticing. **placer ou mettre quelqu'un en apprentissage** ▶ to hire or place someone as an apprentice.

ap-proach [uh-PROCHE] VERB, approached, approaching. **1. (s') approcher** ▶ to come near or close to; move toward : *The judge asked the lawyers to approach the bench.* **2. approcher, aborder** ▶ to present an idea or request : *Dana approached the editor with an idea for a new feature article.* ▲ NOUN, approaches. **1. approche, venue** ▶ the act of approaching; coming near : *The cold, dark days warned of the approach of winter.* **2. voie d'accès** ▶ the way to get near a place : *The fallen treeblocked the only approach to the beach house.* **3. approche, démarche** ▶ the way in which something is done : *the best approach to solve a problem.*

Note. Someone who is easy to approach is approachable. SYN: access, entrance, path, avenue.

ap·pro·pri·ate [uh-PROH-pree-it] ADJECTIVE. **approprié (-ée), convenable** ▸ right for a situation; proper or correct : *Giggling is not an appropriate response when someone gives you a compliment.* ▪ **appropriately,** ADVERB. ▸ **convenablement.** *This is a formal affair, and everyone is expected to dress appropriately.* ▲ [uh-PROH-pre-ATE] VERB, appropriated, appropriating. **1. approprier, consacrer** ▸ to use for a special purpose : *to appropriate money to build a new public library.* **2. s'approprier, s'emparer** ▸ to take something for oneself, especially in an improper way : *The bank teller had appropriated funds and hidden them in his own account.* SYN: suitable, fitting, proper, apt, correct.

ap·pro·val [uh-PROO-vul] NOUN. **1. approbation** ▸ a good opinion ; praise : *"The robbers roared their approval."* (Sarah Hayes) **2. approbation, permission, consentement** ▸ permission or consent : *Do you have your parents' approval to go on the field trip?*

ap·prove [uh-PROOV] VERB, approved, approving. **1. approuver** ▸ to think well of ; have a good opinion : *I approve of what you are trying to do and will help as much as I can.* **2. approuver, sanctionner** ▸ to give permission or consent to something : *The school board approved the budget for the coming year.* ▪ **approvingly,** ADVERB. ▸ **avec approbation.** *Mom smiled approvingly and said I had done a good job.* SYN: accept, endorse, sanction, value.

ap·prox·i·mate [uh-PROK-suh-mit] ADJECTIVE. **approximatif (-ive)** ▸ about the same as ; close to : *Our approximate flying time is four hours, or, to be exact, four hours and six minutes.* ▪ **approximately,** ADVERB. ▸ **approximativement, à peu près, estimer** ▸ nearly or close to : *Approximately half the children in this class have brown hair.* ▲ [uh-PROK-suh-MATE] VERB, **faire une approximation** ▸ approximated, approximating. to come close to ; estimate. **Note.** An approximation is an estimate or a guess.

ap·ri·cot [AP-ruh-KOT or AY-pruh-KOT] NOUN, apricots. **abricot** ▸ a round, yellowish-orange fruit that looks like a small peach. Apricots grow on trees in warm climates.

A·pril [AY-prul] NOUN, Aprils. **avril** ▸ the fourth month of the year, between March and May. April has 30 days.

April Fools' Day (also All Fools' Day) **1ᵉʳ avril** ▸ a name for April 1, a day on which people often try to fool others with tricks and jokes.

a·pron [AY-prun] NOUN, aprons. **1. tablier** ▸ a piece of cloth or other material tied loosely around the body to protect clothing. **2. avant-**

scène ▸ the front part of an area or surface : *the apron of a stage.*

apt [apt] ADJECTIVE. **1. susceptible de, avoir tendance à** ▸ inclined to do or be ; likely : *Pay attention to what you're doing or you're apt to make mistakes.* **2. pertinent (-ente)** ▸ right for the occasion ; fitting : *Jamie's apt response to the question indicated that he had studied the material well.* **3. intelligent (-ente), habile, doué (-ée)** ▸ quick to learn : *Su May is an apt student.* SYN: likely, probable, liable, appropriate.

ap·ti·tude [AP-tuh-TYOOD or AP-tuh-TOOD] NOUN, aptitudes. **aptitude (à), disposition(s) (pour), habileté (à, pour)** ▸ a natural ability to do something ; talent : *Henri has shown an aptitude for math and wants to study physics.* **Note.** An aptitude test shows which subjects people could learn best or what kind of work they could do well. SYN: ability, talent, flair.

a·quar·i·um [uh-KWAIR-ee-um] NOUN, aquariums **aquariums** ▸ or aquaria. **1. aquarium** ▸ a glass bowl or tank containing living fish, other water animals, and water plants. **2. aquarium** ▸ a building that has a collection of fish and other water animals.

aq·uat·ic [uh-KWOT-ik or uh-KWAT-ik] ADJECTIVE. **1. aquatique** ▸ living in water : *Dolphins are aquatic mammals.* **2. nautique** ▸ taking place in or on water : *Water skiing is an aquatic sport.* **Note.** Aquatics are sports that take place in the water.

aq·ue·duct [AK-wuh-DUKT] NOUN, aqueducts. **1. aqueduc** ▸ a large pipe or channel that carries water to places at a distance. Aqueducts make it possible to build cities and grow crops in areas that were once deserts. **2. aqueduc** ▸ the structure that supports such a pipe or channel.

Ar·ab [AIR-ub] NOUN, Arabs. **Arabe** ▸ a member of a group of people who speak a language called Arabic. **arabe** ▸ These people originally lived in the area known as Arabia. ▲ ADJECTIVE. having to do with Arabs. **Note.** Arabian is another word that means the same as Arab.

Arabic numerals [AIR-uh-bik] **chiffres arabes** ▸ the signs commonly used to write numbers : 0, 1, 2, 3, 4, 5, 6, 7, 8, 9. **Note.** Arabic numerals are so called because the Europeans first learned them from the Arabs.

a·rach·nid [uh-RAK-nid] NOUN, arachnids. **arachnide** ▸ any of a group of insectlike land animals, such as a spider, scorpion, mite, or tick, having four pairs of legs. Unlike insects, arachnids do not have wings or antennae, and their bodies are divided into two main parts, not three parts.

ar·bi·trar·y [AR-buh-TRAIR-ee] ADJECTIVE. **arbitraire** ▸ not according to any rule or reasons ; based on one's feelings or wishes : *The umpire tried to be fair and not make any arbitrary decisions.* ▪ **arbitrarily,** ADVERB: ▸ **arbitrairement.**

29

She arbitrarily drew a line in the snow and dared me to step over it.

ar·bi·trate [AR-buh-TRATE] VERB, arbitrated, arbitrating. **arbitrer** ▶ to settle a dispute : *My mom's arbitrating the transit strike.* **Note.** The process of helping two sides come to an agreement is called **arbitration.** A person who does this is an **arbiter** or **arbitrator.**

arc [ark] NOUN, arcs. **1. arc** ▶ a part of a curved line, especially part of a circle : *The letter "c" is made by drawing an arc.* **2. arc** ▶ a curved line or path : *"The sun was a red arc lifting over the ridge and Grama reached out for Jamie's hand."* (Joseph Bruchac) ▲ VERB. arced, arcing. **tracer un arc** ▶ to form an arc : *The shooting star arced across the night sky.*

ar·cade [ar-KADE] NOUN, arcades. **1. arcade, galerie (marchande)** ▶ a covered passageway, usually with shops along the sides. **2. arcade** ▶ a place where people pay to play different types of games, especially electronic games. **Note.** This is also called a **video arcade.**

arch¹ [arch] NOUN, arches. **1. voûte** ▶ a curved piece of metal, wood, or other material that supports the weight of something built over an open space : *Arches often form supports for bridges.* **2. arc** ▶ anything shaped like an arch, such as a monument. **3. cambrure** ▶ the raised part of the bottom of the foot. ▲ VERB. arched, arching. **1. arquer, courber, vouter** ▶ to form into an arch ; bend or curve : *Pia arched her eyebrows in surprise.* **2. arquer, courber** ▶ to curve over an open space : *The rainbow arched across the horizon.* **Note.** A passageway or entrance covered by an arch is called an **archway.**

arch² ADJECTIVE. **1. principal, numéro un** ▶ principal ; chief : *In the Sherlock Holmes stories, Moriarty was the arch criminal.* **2. espiègle, malicieux (-euse), coquin (-ine)** ▶ playful ; mischievous : *The teacher did not appreciate Chloe's arch response to the question.*

ar·chae·ol·o·gy [AR-kee-OL-uh-jee] NOUN. (also archeology) **archéologie** ▶ the scientific study of the remains of people of ancient times. **Note.** An expert in archaeology is an **archaeologist.** Archaeologists study ancient civilizations by studying the objects the people left behind, such as buildings, artwork, tools, bones, and pottery. ■ **archaeological,** ADJECTIVE. **archéologique** ▶ having to do with archaeology or archaeologists.

ar·cha·ic [ar-KAY-ik] ADJECTIVE. **archaïque** ▶ belonging to an earlier time ; out of date : *The invention of the automobile made the use of horse-drawn carriages archaic.* **Note.** Archaic words are those that people rarely use any more, but that are still part of our language. The use of "ye" to mean "you" is archaic, but we still find it in songs and poetry.

arch·bish·op [arch-BISH-up] NOUN, archbishops. **archevêque** ▶ a bishop having the highest rank. An archbishop is the leader of all the churches in a district. **Note.** This district is called an **archdiocese.**

arch·er [AR-chur] NOUN, archers. **archer** ▶ a person who uses a bow and arrow to hunt or shoot at a target : *Robin Hood is a famous legendary archer.* **Note.** The sport or skill of shooting a bow and arrow is called **archery.**

ar·chi·pel·a·go [AR-kuh-PEL-uh-goh] NOUN, archipelagos. **archipel** ▶ a group of many islands : *The country of Malaysia is an archipelago.*

ar·chi·tect [AR-kuh-TEKT] NOUN, architects. **1. architecte** ▶ a person who designs buildings, bridges, and other structures, and then sees that the plans are carried out correctly. **2. architecte, créateur (-trice)** ▶ anyone who designs or develops something : *The coach was the architect of the winning season.*

ar·chi·tec·ture [AR-kuh-TEK-chur] NOUN. **1. architecture** ▶ the art or science of designing and planning buildings. **2. architecture** ▶ a particular style of building : *The Place Ville Marie in Montreal is an example of the modern style of architecture.* ■ **architectural,** ADJECTIVE. ▶ architectural (-ale, -aux).

Arc·tic [ARK-tik *or* AR-tik] ADJECTIVE. (sometimes arctic) **arctique** ▶ of or near the area around the North Pole : *The polar bear is an arctic animal.* ▲ NOUN. the Arctic. **l'Arctique** ▶ the area around the North Pole. **Note.** The Arctic Circle is an imaginary line around the earth at 661/3°N. No trees grow above this line.

arctic char (also Arctic char) **poisson arctique de la famille des truites** ▶ a fish of the trout family found throughout the Arctic.

are [ar] VERB. ▶ a form of the verb **to be** that is used with "you," "we," or "they" to tell about the present : *You are late. They are already gone.*

ar·e·a [AIR-ee-uh] NOUN, areas. **1. aire, superficie** ▶ a measured space or surface calculated by multiplying length by width : *Measure the area of the room so we'll know what size rug to buy.* **2. région, secteur, quartier, zone** ▶ any particular region or section : *About 24 percent of the people in Canada live in rural areas.* **3. secteur** ▶ a particular field of interest or work.

area code **code régional** ▶ a combination of three numbers used to dial long distance directly by telephone from one region to another in Canada or the world.

a·re·na [uh-REE-nuh] NOUN, arenas. **1. arène** ▶ in ancient Rome, an open space in which fights or contests were held as sport. **2. arène** ▶ a similar modern building for sports events, circuses, and shows. **3. arène, scène** ▶ any place of conflict or competition : *the arena of politics.*

ar-gue [AR-gyoo] VERB, argued, arguing. **1. se disputer** ▸ to have a disagreement; quarrel. **2. plaider, débattre** ▸ to give reasons for a point of view : *Alan argued in favour of school uniforms.* ✐ **p. 31.**

ar-gu-ment [AR-gyuh-munt] NOUN, arguments. **1. dispute, querelle** ▸ a disagreement or quarrel : *She resolved the argument by finding a solution that satisfies both sides.* **2. argument** ▸ a point of view or reason : *Fred's arguments convinced me to go camping.*

ar-id [AIR-id] ADJECTIVE. **aride** ▸ having little or no rain : *Few plants grow in the arid land of the desert.*

a-rise [uh-RIZE] VERB, arose, arisen, arising. **1. surgir, survenir** ▸ to come into being; appear : *The fog seemed to arise out of nowhere to cover the town.* **2. se lever** ▸ to stand up; get up : *As soon as the judge enters, everyone in the courtroom must arise.* **3. monter, s'élever** ▸ to move upward; rise up : *You can see the steam arising from the hot springs on cool days.*

ar-is-toc-ra-cy [AIR-uh-STOK-ruh-see] NOUN, aristocracies. **1. aristocratie** ▸ a class of people having a very high standing in society : *Princesses and dukes are part of the aristocracy.* **2. aristocratie** ▸ any group of people thought of as having great power, intelligence, or ability. **Note.** A person who belongs to the aristocracy is an aristocrat.

a-rith-me-tic [uh-RITH-muh-tik] NOUN. **calcul, arithmétique** ▸ the branch of mathematics that includes adding, subtracting, multiplying, and dividing.

ark [ark] NOUN, arks. (often Ark) **1. arche** ▸ a heavy boat : *Noah built an ark to save his family and all the animals.* **2. Arche** ▸ a chest or cupboard sacred to Judaism.

arm[1] [arm] NOUN, arms. **1. bras** ▸ the part of the body between the shoulder and the hand : *Louis throws a ball with his right arm.* **2. accoudoir** ▸ something that works or is shaped like an arm : *She rested her elbow on the arm of the chair.* ✐ **p. 991.**

arm[2] NOUN, arms. **arme** ▸ any kind of weapon, such as a gun, knife, or bomb. ▲ VERB, armed, arming. **1. armer, se munir** ▸ to supply with weapons : *The protestors, armed only with*

sticks and stones, retreated from the police. **2. s'armer, se nantir** ▸ to supply with anything that gives strength or power : *The mayor was armed with enough information to answer our questions.*

ar-ma-da [ar-MAH-duh] NOUN, armadas. **armada, flotte** ▸ a large group of warships. **Note.** The Spanish Armada was the fleet of warships from Spain that was defeated by the English in 1588.

ar-ma-dil-lo [ar-muh-DIL-oh] NOUN, armadillos. **tatou** ▸ a small insect-eating animal found in South America and southern North America. The armadillo is covered with a shell of hard, jointed plates. **Note.** *Armadillo* comes from a Spanish word meaning "little armoured thing."

ar-ma-ment [AR-muh-munt] NOUN, armaments. **1. armement, artillerie, munitions** ▸ all of a country's war forces and supplies, including its army, navy, and air force. **2. armement** ▸ the act of arming for war. **Note.** Often used with a PREFIX, as in rearmament or disarmament.

armed forces, **forces armées** ▸ the military force of a nation.

ar-mi-stice [AR-muh-stis] NOUN, armistices. **armistice** ▸ an agreement to stop fighting; a truce : *On November 11, 1918, Germany signed the armistice that officially ended World War I.*

ar-mour [AR-mur] NOUN. (also armor) **1. armure** ▸ in earlier times, a covering worn to protect the body during battle : *Knights in the Middle Ages used metal armour.* **2. carapace, blindage** ▸ any kind of hard cover that serves as protection, such as a turtle's shell or the metal plates on a tank or warship. ▪ **armoured,** ADJECTIVE. ▸ **blindé (-ée).** covered with or protected by armour : *an armoured car.*

ar-my [AR-mee] NOUN, armies. **1. armée** ▸ a large group of soldiers who are armed and trained to fight wars on land. **Note.** In the Canadian Forces, the function of an army is served by Mobile Command. **2. armée** ▸ a group of people who are organized for a common goal : *The Salvation Army works to help the poor.* **3. armée** ▸ any large group of people or animals : *An army of hungry ants invaded our kitchen.*

a-ro-ma [uh-ROH-muh] NOUN, aromas. **arôme, odeur** ▸ a pleasing smell or fragrance : *The aroma of bread baking filled the house.*

🖉 **Word Builder**

Argue, dispute, quarrel, and *debate* all mean that people do not agree about something. *Argue* refers to a situation in which two people strongly disagree with each other and become angry. *Dispute* usually means that someone does not agree with a certain idea that another person has. *Quarrel* is not as strong a word as *argue,* and it usually refers to a disagreement of people who normally are friendly. *Debate* usually refers to a formal discussion that takes place under a set of rules. The two sides disagree, but may or may not be angry about it.

Note. Something that has a fragrant or spicy aroma is **aromatic.** SYN: smell, fragrance, odour, aura, scent.

a-rose [uh-ROZE] VERB. a past form of **arise.**

a-round [uh-ROWND] PREPOSITION. **1. autour ►** in a circle about : *Columbus set out to sail around the world.* **2. autour, à l'entour ►** on all sides of : *The baby was interested in everything that went on around her.* **3. autour, aux alentours ►** along or to the side of : *Put the garbage can around the side of the house :* **4. aux environs de, à peu près ►** somewhat near : *The Schmidt farm is around 15 kilometres from here.* ▲ ADVERB. **1. en rond ►** in a circle : *Cynthia spun around and around until she couldn't stand up.* **2. de circonférence ►** in distance, about : *The tree measures five metres around.* **3. (tout) autour ►** on all sides : *The campers sat around the fire.*

a-rouse [uh-ROWZ] VERB. aroused, arousing. **1. secouer, soulever, exciter ►** to stir up; excite : *The speech aroused the crowd to action.* **2. réveiller, éveiller ►** to wake up; awaken : *The smell of coffee brewing aroused the family.* SYN: move, excite, stir, rouse.

ar-range [uh-RAYNJ] VERB. arranged, arranging. **1. arranger, disposer ►** to put into order : *Nicki arranged the flowers Kristos picked into a bouquet.* **2. s'arranger, convenir de, prévoir de ►** to plan for something; prepare : *Sam arranged to have the movers pick up the furniture on Friday.* **3. adapter, arranger ►** to change to fit; adapt or adjust : *Lida arranged the music for the song for a large orchestra.* SYN: adjust, group, sort, plan, fix, order, classify.

ar-range-ment [uh-RAYNJ-munt] NOUN. arrangements. **1. arrangement ►** the act of arranging something, or the thing that is arranged : *The flower arrangement on the table is beautiful.* **2. arrangement, adaptation ►** the act of arranging a piece of music, or a piece of music that has been arranged. **3. préparatifs ►** plans or preparations : *Arrangements for the wedding took many months.*

ar-rest [uh-REST] VERB. arrested, arresting. **1. arrêter, appréhender ►** to stop and hold someone by power of the law : *The police had enough evidence to arrest Sam.* **2. arrêter, empêcher ►** to stop something from going on; check : *The city wants to take action to arrest the decline of the downtown area.* ▲ NOUN. arrests. **arrestation ►** the act of stopping and holding someone by law : *The police were able to make an arrest in the robbery.*

ar-ri-val [uh-RY-vul] NOUN. arrivals. **1. arrivée ►** the act of arriving : *The passengers waited patiently for the arrival of the plane.* **2. nouveau venu (nouvelle venue) ►** someone or something that has arrived.

ar-rive [uh-RIVE] VERB. arrived, arriving. **1. arriver ►** to come to or reach a place : *We unpacked as soon as we arrived.* **2. arriver à, aboutir à ►** to come to or reach a goal or object : *The jury arrived at a verdict quickly.* SYN: reach, come, attain, join, gain.

ar-ro-gant [AIR-uh-gunt] ADJECTIVE. **arrogant (-ante) ►** having a feeling that one is better than other people; too proud; conceited : *an arrogant attitude.* ■ **arrogance,** NOUN. ► **arrogance.** too much pride; conceit.

ar-se-nal [AR-suh-nul] NOUN. arsenals. **arsenal (-aux) ►** a place where military equipment is made or kept.

ar-se-nic [AR-suh-nik] NOUN. **arsenic ►** a greyish-white powder that is a strong poison.

ar-son [AR-sun] NOUN. **incendie criminel ►** the crime of purposely setting fire to a building or other property. **Note.** A person who commits this crime is an arsonist.

arteries

art [art] NOUN. arts. **1. art ►** the act of doing something that has beauty or special meaning. Art is meant to bring pleasure to people. **2. art (s), beaux-arts ►** the area of art that involves creating objects to be looked at; painting, drawing, or sculpture. **3. art ►** any activity that requires special skill or talent to do well : *the art of cooking; the art of conversation.* 👁 p. 536.

ar-ter-y [AR-tuh-ree] NOUN. arteries. **1. artère ►** any of the tubes that carry blood away from the heart to all parts of the body. Arteries differ from veins, which carry blood back to the heart. 👁 p. 402. **2. artère ►** a main road or channel that carries things from place to place : *The Trans-Canada Highway is the main artery across the country.*

ar-thri-tis [a -THRY-tis] NOUN. **arthrite ►** a disease that makes a person's joints painful and swollen.

ar-thro-pod [AR-thruh-pod] NOUN. arthropods. **arthropode ►** any of a large group of animals with two- or three-part bodies and jointed legs.

Insects, arachnids, and crustaceans are arthropods.

ar-ti-choke [AR-tuh-CHOKE] NOUN, artichokes. **artichaut ▸** a tall plant having a large flower head with thick leaves that are cooked and eaten as a vegetable.

ar-ti-cle [AR-tuh-kul] NOUN, articles. **1. article, objet ▸** any particular object or item : *Gloves and socks are articles of clothing.* **2. article, reportage ▸** a piece of writing on a factual subject in a newspaper, magazine, or book. **3. article, clause ▸** a separate section of a legal document. **4. article ▸** in grammar, one of three words (*a, an, the*) that are used regularly before nouns. ✑ p. 33. SYN: thing, object, commodity, item.

ar-tic-u-late [ar-TIK-yuh-lit] ADJECTIVE. **qui s'exprime bien ▸** expressing oneself well ; speaking clearly : *Richard is a good choice for the debate team, since he is very articulate.* ▲ [ar-TIK-yuh-LATE] VERB, articulated, articulating. **articuler ▸** to speak clearly.

ar-ti-fi-cial [AR-tuh-FISH-ul] ADJECTIVE. **1. artificiel (-ielle) ▸** made by people, not by nature ; not natural. **2. artificiel (-ielle), affecté (-ée) ▸** not sincere or real ; pretended : *Tom was ill at ease and kept breaking into an odd, artificial laugh.* ∎ **artificially,** ADVERB. ▸ **artificiellement.**

artificial intelligence intelligence artificielle ▸ the things that a computer can do that are somewhat like human thinking, such as making use of previous information to solve a problem. Artificial intelligence makes it possible for a computer to play chess.

artificial respiration respiration artificielle ▸ the forcing of air into and out of the lungs of a person whose breathing has stopped.

ar-til-ler-y [ar-TIL-uh-ree] NOUN. **1. artillerie ▸** large and heavy guns used in war, such as cannons or rockets. **2. artillerie ▸** the branch of an army that uses such guns.

ar-tist [AR-tist] NOUN, artists. **1. artiste ▸** a person who is skilled in one of the arts, such as painting, music, literature, or dancing. **2. artiste ▸** a person who can do something with special skill or talent : *Rita is an artist at getting things done.* ✒ p. 1126.

ar-tis-tic [ar-TIS-tik] ADJECTIVE. **1. artiste ▸** having to do with art or artists. **2. artistique ▸** showing special skill or talent : *Marilyn has an artistic arrangement of paintings on her wall.* ∎ **artistically,** ADVERB. ▸ **artistiquement.**

as [az] ADVERB. **1. aussi ▸** to the same amount ; equally : *I am as tall as you.* **2. comme, tel (telle) que ▸** for example : *We've seen animals such as deer and rabbits in this field.* ▲ CONJUNCTION. **1. pendant que ▸** at the same time that ;

✐ Writing Tips

Articles

Articles are adjectives. They help to limit or define nouns. There are two kinds of articles – **definite** (the) and **indefinite** (a, an).

• *Definite* articles refer to something specific. When you read "the dog" or "the house," you know that a particular dog or house is being discussed.

• *Indefinite articles* refer to objects whose identity is not expected to be known. In the phrases "a dress" and "an apple," the reader does not know what dress or apple.

—Use "a" before a noun that starts with a consonant sound or a long-u sound (**a** cat, **a** watermelon, **a** uniform).

—Use "an" before a noun that starts with a vowel (**an** ant, **an** umpire, **an** orange).

while : *We talked as we cleaned the room.* **2. comme ▸** in the same way that : *Please don't argue ; just do as I say.* **3. puisque ▸** because ; since : *As there is only one apple left, you'll have to share it.* ▲ PREPOSITION. **1. en ▸** like : *He went to the party dressed as a pirate.* **2. comme, en tant que ▸** doing the work of : *a job as a production assistant.* ✑ p. 34.

as-bes-tos [ass-BES-tus or az-BES-tus] NOUN. **amiante ▸** a greyish mineral that will not burn. It can be separated into long fibres to make fireproof materials, such as clothing for firefighters. ✑ p. 397.

as-cend [uh-SEND] VERB, ascended, ascending. **1. monter, remonter ▸** to go up ; rise or climb. **2. s'élever ▸** to move upward in rank or level : *Ms. Ebata began as a salesclerk and ascended to the presidency of the company.* SYN: climb, scale, mount, go up, lift.

as-cent [uh-SENT] NOUN, ascents. **1. ascension ▸** the act of rising or climbing up : *The climbers prepared for their ascent up the mountain.* **2. ascension ▸** the act of rising to a higher rank or level. **3. montée ▸** a place that rises up.

ash[1] [ash] NOUN, ashes. **cendre ▸** the soft, light-grey powder that is left when something is burned : *The ashes from the burned logs are still hot.*

ash[2] NOUN, ashes. **frêne ▸** a kind of shade tree that has a strong, springy wood that is used for making furniture and baseball bats. ✑ p. 34.

a-shamed [uh-SHAMED] ADJECTIVE. **1. honteux (-euse) ▸** feeling shame or disgrace : *"Lin* *slipped the certificate between the pages of his music book quickly, as though he were ashamed of it."* (Barbara Novak) **2. avoir honte de** ▶ not willing to do something because of shame : *Donald was ashamed to tell us he was lost.*

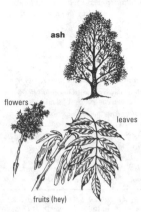

ash

flowers

leaves

fruits (hey)

a-shore [uh-SHOR] ADVERB. **à terre** ▶ on or to the shore : *As soon as the ship docked, the sailors went ashore.*

a-side [uh-SIDE] ADVERB. **1. de côté, à l'écart** ▶ on or to one side : *The actor stepped aside and addressed a few words to the audience.* **2. de côté** ▶ away or apart : *Mom sets aside ten minutes each day for meditation.*

ask [ask] VERB, asked, asking. **1. demander** ▶ to question in order to get information or permission : *Let's ask if we can go to the movies.* **2. demander, poser une question** ▶ to put a question to someone : *Cleo asked me what time it was.* **3. demander** ▶ to make a request or demand : *Travis asked me to help fix his bike.* **4. (en) demander** ▶ to try to get as a price : *The builders are asking $100,000 for this house.* **5. inviter** ▶ to invite : *We've asked a few friends to come for dinner Saturday night.* SYN: inquire, request, query, demand, require.

a-sleep [uh-SLEEP] ADJECTIVE. **1. endormi (-ie)** ▶ sleeping. **2. engourdi (-ie)** ▶ having no feeling; numb : *I sat in the same position too long, and now my foot is asleep.* ▲ ADVERB. **(tomber) endormi** ▶ to sleep : *I had just fallen asleep when my alarm clock went off.*

as-par-a-gus [uh-SPAR-uh-gus] NOUN. **asperge** ▶ a plant that is grown for food. The tender young asparagus stalks are eaten as a vegetable.

as-pect [ASS-pekt] NOUN, aspects. **1. air** ▶ appearance; look : *The house had a cheery*

✍ Writing Tips

As or Like?

• *When you speak, you can use either **as** or **like** as a conjunction or connecting word. You can say either "I make eggs **like** my father did" or "I make eggs as my father did."*

• *When you write, **as** is the preferred word to use. You would write "I make eggs **as** my father did."*

aspect with its bright curtains and fresh paint. **2. aspect** ▶ a particular way that something can be looked at or thought of : *I never thought of that aspect of the plan.*

as-pen [ASS-pun] NOUN, aspens. **tremble** ▶ any of several trees with flattened leafstalks that cause their leaves to flutter in the slightest breeze.

as-phalt [ASS-folt] NOUN. **1. asphalte** ▶ a thick, sticky, blackish-brown substance that comes from under the ground. **2. asphalte** ▶ a hard, smooth material that is used to pave roads, made from asphalt and other materials such as sand and gravel.

as-pire [uh-SPIRE] VERB, aspired, aspiring. **aspirer à, viser à** ▶ to want very much to reach a certain goal : *She aspires to be a ballet dancer and practises every day.* ■ **aspiration,** NOUN. ▶ aspiration, ambition.

as-pi-rin [ASS-prin *or* ASS-pih-rin] NOUN, aspirins. **aspirine** ▶ a drug in the form of a pill used to reduce pain and fever.

ass [ass] NOUN, asses. **1. âne** ▶ another name for a donkey. **2. imbécile, idiot (idiote), stupide** ▶ a vain, self-important, or silly person.

as-sas-si-nate [uh-SAS-uh-NATE] VERB, assassinated, assassinating. **assassiner** ▶ to murder an important or famous person, especially a political leader. **Note.** A person who does this is an **assassin.** The act of assassinating is an assassination.

as-sault [uh-SOLT] NOUN, assaults. **1. agression** ▶ in law, a threat or attempt to hurt another person. **2. assaut, attaque** ▶ any sudden and violent attack : *During the War of 1812, U.S. troops made assaults on Canadian territory.* ▲ VERB, assaulted, assaulting. **attaquer, violenter** ▶ to attack violently : *to assault a person.*

as-sem-ble [uh-SEM-bul] VERB, assembled, assembling. **1. (se) rassembler, (se) réunir** ▶ to gather or collect in one place : *The students assembled in the auditorium for the concert.* **2. assembler, monter** ▶ to fit or put together :

✐ Word Builder

Assemble, combine, collect, and ***unite*** all mean to bring different things together. ***Assemble*** has the idea of bringing together a large number of people or things in one place : *Assemble a toy.* ***Combine*** means to put together individual things to form one whole : *Combine ingredients.* ***Collect*** has the idea of gathering together various things that were separated : *Collect stamps.* ***Unite*** suggests that two or more things that had been apart, are now one unit : *Unite people.*

Dad assembled Myra's new bicycle for her birthday. ✐ p. 35, 244.

as·sem·bly [uh-SEM-blee] NOUN, assemblies. **1. assemblée, rassemblement ▸** the gathering together of a group of people : *"My first year at school ended with a special assembly."* (Christy MacKinnon) **2. montage, assemblage ▸** the act of collecting or putting together. **3.** Assembly. **assemblée ▸** a body of lawmakers, as in some provinces or foreign countries. **Note.** The one-chamber legislature in many provinces is called the Legislative Assembly. In Quebec, it is called the National Assembly.

assembly line chaîne de montage ▸ a line of workers and equipment along which a product being put together, such as a car, is passed until it is completed.

as·sess [uh-SESS] VERB, assessed, assessing. **1. évaluer ▸** to decide the worth or value of : *The minister of agriculture will fly over the flood area to assess the damage to this year's crops.* **2. exiger des frais ▸** to charge a fee or tax to : *The club assesses its members $5 a month to cover expenses.* ▪ **assessment,** NOUN. ▸ **évaluation.**

as·set [ASS-et] NOUN, assets. **1. atout, avantage ▸** something useful or valuable; an advantage : *Oil deposits are a great asset to many Middle Eastern countries.* **2.** assets. **actif, bien ▸** all the things a person or business owns that are worth money. SYN: possession, belonging, property.

as·sign [uh-SINE] VERB, assigned, assigning. **1. assigner, donner, attribuer ▸** to give out work : *The teacher did not assign any homework for the weekend.* **2. assigner, fixer ▸** to make definite; set : *The judge assigned a date for the hearing.* **3. assigner ▸** to choose or appoint to some task or duty : *Anton assigned three people to clean-up duty.* SYN: appoint, name, allot, give.

as·sign·ment [uh-SINE-munt] NOUN, assignments. **1. distribution, répartition ▸** the act of assigning : *The teacher made seating assignments on the first day of school.* **2. tâche ▸** something that is assigned : *My first assignment was to write a short paragraph about myself.*

as·sist [uh-SIST] VERB, assisted, assisting. **aider, prêter assistance ▸** to give aid or support; help : *The teacher asked Michi to assist Zoran with the lab experiment.* ▲ NOUN, assists. **passe, aide ▸** a play that helps another player to score in sports such as hockey, basketball, and soccer.

as·sis·tance [uh-SIS-tuns] NOUN. **aide, secours, assistance ▸** help; aid : *A police officer came to the assistance of the driver who was stuck in the ditch.*

as·sis·tant [uh-SIS-tunt] NOUN, assistants. **aide, assistant (-ante) ▸** any person who gives aid or support; a helper. ▲ ADJECTIVE. **adjoint (-ointe) ▸** acting to help; assisting : *Ruth has been promoted to assistant director.*

as·so·ci·ate [uh-SOH-she-ate] VERB, associated, associating. **1. associer ▸** to bring together or connect in one's mind : *Most people associate snow with winter.* **2. fréquenter ▸** to join together with a friend, fellow worker, or the like : *Jake associates with basketball players from another school.* ▲ [uh-SOH-she-it] NOUN, associates. **associé (-ée) ▸** a person who is joined with others : a friend, a fellow worker, or the like. ▲ [uh-SOH-she-it] ADJECTIVE. **associé (-ée) ▸** joined with others : *Helena is an associate professor in the biology department.* **2. adjoint (-ointe), associé (-ée) ▸** having less than full rights or privileges. SYN: partner, colleague, ally.

as·so·ci·a·tion [uh-SOH-shee-AY-shun] NOUN, associations. **1. association, société ▸** an organization of people who work together for a common purpose : *The library association will meet to discuss plans for the new building.* **2. association, fréquentation ▸** the fact of joining or being connected : *The author's association with the publishing company was long and profitable.*

as·sort·ed [uh-SOR-tid] ADJECTIVE. **assorti (-ie), varié (-ée), au choix ▸** of different kinds or varieties : *I received a box of assorted chocolates for my birthday.*

as·sort·ment [uh-SORT-munt] NOUN, assortments. **assortiment ▸** a group of assorted things : *The market has a large assortment of fall fruit this week.*

as·sume [uh-SOOM *or* uh-SYOOM] VERB, assumed, assuming. **1. supposer ▸** to believe something is true; suppose : *I assume you have a good* *excuse for coming home so late.* **2. assumer** ▸ to take on for oneself; undertake : *A newspaper publisher assumes responsibility for what is printed in the paper.* 🖉 **p. 54.**

as·sump·tion [uh-SUMP-shun *or* uh-SUM-shun] NOUN, assumptions. **supposition, hypothèse** ▸ something taken for granted : *I don't think you should act on the assumption that everyone will agree with you.*

as·sur·ance [uh-SHOOR-uns] NOUN, assurances. **1. promesse, assurance** ▸ a statement meant to make a person sure or certain ; *Tim gave me his assurance that he would be here on time.* **2. confiance** ▸ belief in one's ability ; self-confidence : *Her interest in others gave her assurance in meeting new people.* **Note.** This is also called self-assurance.

as·sure [uh-SHOOR] VERB, assured, assuring. **1. (s') assurer** ▸ to make certain or sure : *Dan tried the knob again to assure himself the door was locked.* **Note.** Often used as an ADJECTIVE: *She plays the piano with a free and assured touch.* **2. assurer** ▸ to tell in a definite way : *"I know what I'm talking about," he assured me.* ▪ **assuredly,** ADVERB. ▸ **assurément.**

as·ter [AS-tur] NOUN, asters. **aster** ▸ a star-shaped garden flower that can be white, pink, blue, or purple. **Note.** *Aster* comes from the Greek word for "star."

as·ter·isk [AS-tuh-RISK] NOUN, asterisks. **astérisque** ▸ a star-shaped mark or symbol [*]. The asterisk is used in printing or writing to tell the reader to look elsewhere on the page or on another page for more information.

as·ter·oid [AS-tuh-ROYD] NOUN, asteroids. **astéroïde** ▸ one of several thousand small, rocky planets that orbit the sun.

asth·ma [AZ-muh *or* ASS-muh] NOUN. **asthme** ▸ a disease that causes a person to have trouble breathing and to have fits of wheezing and coughing. Dust, animal hair, and certain plants can cause asthma. ▪ **asthmatic,** ADJECTIVE or NOUN. ▸ **asthmatique.**

as·ton·ish [uh-STON-ish] VERB, astonished, astonishing. **étonner, surprendre** ▸ to surprise greatly; shock or amaze : *The number of fans who had come to cheer them on astonished the team.* ▪ **astonishment,** NOUN. ▸ **étonnement, surprise.** great surprise; amazement : *We watched in astonishment as the magician vanished from sight.*

as·tound [uh-STOWND] VERB, astounded, astounding. **stupéfier, confondre** ▸ to surprise or shock greatly; amaze; astonish : *They were astounded by the news.*

as·trol·o·gy [uh-STROL-uh-gee] NOUN. **astrologie** ▸ the study of the effect that the position of the stars and planets has on events and people's lives. Some people believe astrology can be

used to predict the future. **Note.** A person who practises astrology is an astrologer.

as·tro·naut [ASS-truh-NOT] NOUN, astronauts. **astronaute** ▸ a person who is trained to travel in a spacecraft to outer space. **Note.** The word *astronaut* is only about 50 years old, but it goes back to two ancient Greek words meaning "star sailor" or "star traveller."

as·tro·nom·i·cal [ASS-truh-NOM-uh-kul] ADJECTIVE. **1. astronomique** ▸ having to do with astronomy. **2. astronomique** ▸ very large, like the numbers in astronomy : *The number of grains of sand on a beach is astronomical.*

as·tron·o·my [uh-STRON-uh-mee] NOUN. **astronomie** ▸ the scientific study of the sun, moon, stars, and other heavenly bodies. **Note.** An expert in astronomy is an astronomer.

a·sy·lum [uh-SY-lum] NOUN, asylums. **1. asile** ▸ a place that gives care and shelter to those in need. **Note.** In former times, a hospital for mentally ill people was called an insane asylum. **2. asile** ▸ protection given to people who flee their own country and enter another country.

at [at] PREPOSITION. **1. à (au)** ▸ in, on, by, or near : *at home; at school; at the front door.* **2. à (au)** ▸ in the direction of; toward : *to shoot an arrow at a target.* **3. en** ▸ in the condition of : *at war; at rest.* **4. à** ▸ in the amount of : *at 100 km per hour; at a high price.*

ate [ate] VERB. a past form of eat.

a·the·ist [AY-thee-ist] NOUN, atheists. **athée** ▸ a person who believes that there is no Supreme Being or God. ▪ **atheism,** NOUN. ▸ **athéisme.**

ath·lete [ATH-leet] NOUN, athletes. **athlète** ▸ a person who takes part in sports or games that require skill, speed, and strength.

ath·let·ic [ath-LET-ik] ADJECTIVE. **1. d'athlétisme** ▸ having to do with athletes or athletics : *an athletic club; a store that sells athletic equipment.* **2. sportif (-ive)** ▸ strong and vigorous. ▪ **athletics,** PLURAL NOUN. ▸ **athlétisme.** sports and games that require skill, speed, and strength.

At·lan·tic [ut-LAN-tik] NOUN. **l'Atlantique** ▸ the ocean between the Americas and Europe and Africa. ▲ ADJECTIVE. **atlantique** ▸ of, on, in, or near the Atlantic Ocean. **Note.** The Atlantic Provinces are Nova Scotia, New Brunswick, Prince Edward Island, and Newfoundland.

at·las [AT-lus] NOUN, atlases. **1. atlas** ▸ a book that is a collection of maps. **2. Atlas. Atlas** ▸ a god of the ancient Greeks who was thought to support the world on his shoulders.

at·mos·phere [AT-muh-SFEER] NOUN, atmospheres. **1. atmosphère** ▸ the air surrounding the earth : *Space flights go beyond the earth's atmosphere.* **2. atmosphère** ▸ the mass of air and gases that surrounds any star or planet.

3. atmosphère, ambiance ▶ the general mood or feeling of a place. ✎ **p. 37.**

at-mos-pher-ic [AT-muh-SFAIR-ik] ADJECTIVE. **atmosphérique** ▶ of or in the atmosphere : *We couldn't see the comet because of bad atmospheric conditions.*

a-tom [AT-um] NOUN, atoms. **atome** ▶ an extremely tiny unit of matter that cannot be seen with the naked eye. An atom contains even smaller parts called **protons** and **neutrons**, which appear in a core or nucleus in the centre of the atom, and **electrons**, which surround the nucleus.

a-tom-ic [uh-TOM-ik] ADJECTIVE. **1. nucléaire, atomique** ▶ of or having to do with atoms : *atomic research.* **2. atomique** ▶ using atomic energy : *an atomic submarine.*

atomic bomb **bombe atomique** ▶ a very powerful bomb whose explosion results from splitting the nuclei of atoms of a very heavy chemical element, such as uranium or plutonium. **Note.** Also called **atom bomb.**

atomic energy **énergie atomique** ▶ the energy that exists within atoms. Certain atoms can be made to release some of their energy very slowly, as in a nuclear reactor, or very quickly, as in an atomic bomb.

a-tro-cious [uh-TRO-shus] ADJECTIVE. **1. atroce, affreux (-euse)** ▶ very cruel or horrible : *The explorers suffered terribly in the atrocious cold of the Arctic.* **2. exécrable, affreux (-euse)** ▶ very bad; of poor quality : *His taste in clothes is atrocious.* **Note.** Something that is atrocious is an atrocity.

at-tach [uh-TACH] VERB, attached, attaching. **1. attacher** ▶ to fasten to or on; connect : *I attached the string to my kite with several knots.* **2. s'attacher à** ▶ to hold by feelings of love or affection. ▲ ADJECTIVE: **attaché (-ée)** ▶ *Jessie is very attached to her grandfather and was upset when he moved out of town.*

at-tach-ment [uh-TACH-munt] NOUN, attachments. **1. attachement, lien, affection** ▶ a connection through feelings of love or affection : *The attachment between Chet and his little brother is very strong.* **2. attache** ▶ a fastening together; connecting. **3. accessoire** ▶ an extra part or device that can be added to something : *The camera has a flash attachment for taking indoor photos.*

at-tack [uh-TAK] VERB, attacked, attacking. **1. attaquer, assaillir** ▶ to set upon with force; try to injure : *"At once a black cloud of hornets swept out of the sack and furiously attacked him."* (Robin Muller). **2. attaquer** ▶ to speak or write against : *The new bill before Parliament was attacked in a newspaper editorial.* **3. attaquer** ▶ to act against in a harmful way : *An outbreak of plague attacked the city.* **4. s'attaquer**

✏ **Writing Tips**

Atmosphere
The **atmosphere** *of a story, a poem, or another piece of writing is the overall feeling or mood. The atmosphere tells the reader what to expect: for example, a mystery story may have an atmosphere of suspense and uneasiness, while a funny story may have a light, silly, or cheerful atmosphere.*

à ▶ to begin to work on or deal with : *to attack a math problem.* ▲ NOUN, attacks. **1. attaque, assaut** ▶ the act of attacking. **2. attaque, crise** ▶ the sudden coming on of a disease or illness : *an attack of flu.* ■ **attacker,** NOUN. ▶ **attaquant (-ante), agresseur, assaillant (-ante).**

at-tain [uh-TANE] VERB, attained, attaining. **1. s'élever jusqu'à, réussir, parvenir à** ▶ to gain something through hard work or talent; achieve : *Jeanne Sauvé was the first woman to attain the position of governor general in Canada.* **2. atteindre, arriver à** ▶ to arrive at; reach : *The climbers attained the peak at approximately noon yesterday.* ■ **attainment,** NOUN. ▶ **obtention, réalisation.** SYN: reach, obtain, accomplish, earn.

at-tempt [uh-TEMPT] VERB, attempted, attempting. **tenter, essayer** ▶ to make an effort to do something; try : *I attempted to apologize, but he was too angry to listen.* ▲ NOUN, attempts. **1. tentative, essai** ▶ an effort or try . *Jules made four attempts before he performed the dive properly.* **2. attentat** ▶ an attack : *an attempt on a person's life.* SYN: endeavour, bid, trial, effort.

at-tend [uh-TEND] VERB, attended, attending. **1. aller à, être présent** ▶ to be present at a place or an event : *Marie attended school for four years without an absence.* **2. être attentif** ▶ to give care or thought to; pay attention to : *The teacher told me to attend to my work and stop staring out the window.* **3. être au service de** ▶ to go with as a servant or companion : *Several ladies-in-waiting attended the queen.* **Note.** A person who attends someone or something is an **attendant** or **attendee.**

at-ten-dance [uh-TEN-dunce] NOUN. **1. présence** ▶ the act of attending : *Our whole family was in attendance at my little sister's dance recital.* **2. assistance** ▶ the number of people attending an event : *The attendance at the concert was over 30 000.* **3. présences** ▶ a written record of who is present or not present : *The teacher takes attendance each morning.*

at·ten·tion [uh-TEN-shun] NOUN, attentions. **1. attention, écoute ▸** the act of listening to, watching, or fixing one's mind on a thing : *"Finally, the beautiful colour of grapes ripening in the sun caught his attention."* (Fulvio Testa) **2. garde-à-vous ▸** a military position in which soldiers stand very straight with their arms at their sides, feet together, and eyes straight ahead. SYN : care, thought, regard, consideration, notice.

at·ten·tive [uh-TEN-tiv] ADJECTIVE. **attentif (-ive) ▸** paying close attention : *an attentive listener.* ■ **attentively,** ADVERB: ▸ **attentivement.** *The children listened attentively.*

at·tic [AT-ik] NOUN, attics. **grenier ▸** a space or room directly below the roof of a house or other building, and above the other rooms.

at·ti·tude [AT-uh-TYOOD or AT-uh-TOOD] NOUN, attitudes. **1. attitude ▸** a way of thinking, acting, or feeling : *She'd make more friends if she'd change her snobbish attitude.* **2. attitude, allure, posture ▸** a position of the body that suggests some action or feeling : *He stood with his arms crossed in an attitude of defiance.*

at·tor·ney [uh-TUR-nee] NOUN, attorneys. **1. avocat (-ate) ▸** a person licensed to practise law ; a lawyer. **2. procureur (-eure), mandataire ▸** any person who is given the right to act in another person's place, especially in legal or business matters. **Note.** This is called having power of attorney.

Attorney General 1. Procureur Général ▸ the chief law officer of Canada. **2. Procureur Général ▸** the chief law officer of a province. **Note.** The plural of this word can be Attorneys General or Attorney Generals.

at·tract [uh-TRAKT] VERB, attracted, attracting. **1. attirer ▸** to draw the interest of : *"Arion's beautiful singing attracted a school of dolphins that took him to the shores of Corinth."* (Marcia Williams) **2. attirer ▸** to draw toward itself : *The light attracted the insects as if it were a magnet.*

at·trac·tion [uh-TRAK-shun] NOUN, attractions. **1. attraction, attirance ▸** the act or power of attracting. **2. attraction ▸** a thing that attracts : *I think the main attraction of the circus is the acrobats.*

at·trac·tive [uh-TRAK-tiv] ADJECTIVE. **attrayant (-ante), attirant (-ante), séduisant (-ante) ▸** having the power to attract someone or something ; pleasing to look at or think about : *It was such an attractive job offer that she couldn't pass it up.* ■ **attractively,** ADVERB. ▸ **d'une manière attrayante.** ■ **attractiveness,** NOUN ▸ **attrait.**

at·trib·ute [uh-TRIB-yoot] VERB, attributed, attributing. **1. attribuer (à) ▸** to consider as belonging or appropriate to : *The discovery of insulin is attributed to Banting and Best.*

2. attribuer (à) ▸ to consider or regard as a result of ; think of as caused by : *I attribute my good health to eating properly.* ▲ [AT-ruh-BYOOT] NOUN, attributes. **attribut, qualité ▸** a quality or characteristic of a person or thing : *Honesty is a good attribute to have.* SYN : quality, characteristic, property.

auc·tion [OK-shun] NOUN, auctions. **(vente aux) enchères, encan ▸** a public sale at which something is sold to the person who offers the highest price. ▲ VERB, auctioned, auctioning. **vendre aux enchères ▸** to sell something at an auction : *His furniture was auctioned to pay his debts.*

au·di·ence [OD-ee-uns] NOUN, audiences. **1. spectateurs, auditoire ▸** a group of people who listen to, watch, or read writings or events, such as TV programs, plays, concerts, magazines, books, or sports events : *"Our two teams applauded our friend Adeline harder than the rest of the audience."* (Roch Carrier) **2. public ▸** all the people who appreciate and support something : *There isn't a large audience for foreign films.* **3. audience ▸** a formal meeting with a person of importance or high position : *How does one get an audience with the Pope?* ✐ **p. 38.**

au·di·o [OD-ee-OH] ADJECTIVE. **1. audio ▸** having to do with sound. **2. audio ▸** having to do with sending and receiving sound by means of a TV, radio, or the like : *CD players are audio equipment.* ▲ NOUN, audios. **audio ▸** something that sends or receives sound.

au·di·tion [ah-DISH-un] NOUN, auditions. **audition ▸** a short performance to show or test the ability of a singer, an actor, a dancer, or another performer. ▲ VERB, auditioned, auditioning. **audi-**

✐ Writing Tips

Audience

Before you write anything (a story, a poem, a letter, a joke), one of the first things you should think about is your audience or who you are writing for. It could be yourself, friends, a teacher, or perhaps, a large group of people.

Once you know your audience, think about

• *Why they will be reading what you write (for enjoyment, information, and so on).*

• *What is the best way to appeal to your audience (with humour, illustrations, brief sentence, bullets)?*

• *What style of writing is best for your audience. Is a formal or informal style better?*

• *Will your audience understand the words you use? Can you use abbreviations?*

tionner ▶ to take part in an audition : *to audition for a part in a play.*

au·di·to·ri·um [OD-uh-TOR-ee-um] NOUN, auditoriums **salle** ▶ or auditoria. a large room in a school, a theatre, or another building where people can gather for a show or meeting.

Au·gust [OG-ust] NOUN, Augusts. **août** ▶ the eighth month of the year, between July and September. August has 31 days.

auk [ok] NOUN, auks. **alque, pingouin** ▶ a black-and-white sea bird found in cold northern waters. It has a heavy body, webbed feet, a short tail, and short wings.

aunt [ant *or* ont] NOUN, aunts. **1. tante** ▶ the sister of one's father or mother. **2. tante** ▶ the wife of one's uncle.

au re·voir [OH ruh-VWAR] **au revoir** ▶ a French phrase that means "until we meet again"; goodbye.

au·ro·ra bo·re·al·is [ah-ROR-uh BOR-ee-AL-is *or* BOR-ee-AY-lis] **aurore boréale** ▶ streamers of light sometimes visible in the night skies of northern regions; **Note.** Also called the northern lights.

au·then·tic [ah-THEN-tik] ADJECTIVE. **1. authentique** ▶ not false; real; genuine : *Two expert witnesses swore that the signature on the painting was authentic.* **2. authentique** ▶ being correct, reliable, or true : *Tina gave an authentic account of the accident.* SYN: valid, true, real, genuine, factual.

au·thor [OTH-ur] NOUN, authors. **auteur (-e)** ▶ a person who writes a book, an article, a poem, or another work. ☞ **p. 1126.**

au·thor·i·ty [uh-THOR-uh-tee] NOUN, authorities. **1. autorité** ▶ the power or right to act, command, or make decisions. **2. (les) autorités** ▶ a person or group that has command or certain powers : *a city's housing authority.* **3. authorities. (les) autorités** ▶ people who enforce the law : *Please report the accident to the authorities.* **4. autorité** ▶ a respected source of information : *Pierre Berton is an authority on Canadian history.*

au·thor·ize [OTH-uh-RIZE] VERB, authorized, authorizing. **1. autoriser** ▶ to give authority or power to someone : *The local police are not authorized to give traffic tickets on this highway.* **2. autoriser** ▶ to approve something officially or legally.

au·to [OT-oh] NOUN, autos. **auto** ▶ short for automobile.

auto- PREFIX. for or by itself, or for or by oneself : *An autobiography is a biography of oneself.*

au·to·bi·og·ra·phy [OT-uh-by-OG-ruh-fee] NOUN, autobiographies. **autobiographie** ▶ the story of a person's life written by that person. ▪ **autobiographical** ADJECTIVE. ▶ **autobiographique.** ✐ **p. 59.**

au·to·graph [OT-uh-GRAF] NOUN, autographs. **autographe** ▶ the signature of a person, especially a famous person, in his or her own handwriting. ▲ VERB, autographed, autographing. **écrire son autographe, signer, dédicacer** ▶ to write an autograph in or on.

au·to·mat·ic [OT-uh-MAT-ik] ADJECTIVE. **1. automatique** ▶ acting or working by itself : *an automatic garage-door opener.* **2. automatique** ▶ done without thinking : *Breathing is an automatic action.* ▲ NOUN, automatics. **automatique** ▶ any machine or device that is automatic. ▪ **automatically,** ADVERB: ▶ automatiquement. *The elevator door closes automatically.*

au·to·ma·tion [OT-uh-MAY-shun] NOUN. **automatisation** ▶ a system of working in which machines are operated by themselves or by other machines.

au·to·mo·bile [OT-uh-muh-BEEL] NOUN, automobiles. **automobile** ▶ a four-wheeled powered vehicle that is smaller than a truck or bus and that is used mainly to carry passengers rather than goods. ☜ **p. 40.** ☞ **p. 1152.**

au·top·sy [AH-top-see *or* AH-tup-see] NOUN, autopsies. **autopsie** ▶ a medical examination of a dead body to determine the cause of death.

au·tumn [OT-um] NOUN, autumns. **automne** ▶ the season of the year that comes between summer and winter; the fall.

aux·il·ia·ry [og-ZIL-yuh-ree *or* og-ZIL-ih-ree] ADJECTIVE. **auxiliaire, de secours** ▶ giving extra aid or support; helping : *The hospital has auxiliary power in case the electricity goes off.* ▲ NOUN, auxiliaries. **auxiliaire** ▶ a person or thing that is added to give aid or support.

a·vail·a·ble [uh-VALE-uh-bul] ADJECTIVE. **1. disponible** ▶ that is possible to have : *"In the days when matches were not available, starting the fire was a difficult chore."* (Lorraine O'Byrne) **2. accessible** ▶ that can be used : *The school's computers are available to all students.* ▪ **availability,** NOUN. ▶ disponibilité.

av·a·lanche [AV-uh-LANCH] NOUN, avalanches. **1. avalanche** ▶ a large, sudden fall of snow and ice down a mountain or over a cliff. **2. avalanche** ▶ something that is like an avalanche : *The tower of cards they had built so carefully came down in an avalanche.*

av·e·nue [AV-uh-NYOO *or* AV-uh-NOO] NOUN, avenues. **1. avenue** ▶ a road or street, especially a wide main road. **2. voie** ▶ a way to reach or accomplish something : *the avenue to success.*

av·er·age [AV-uh-rij *or* AV-rij] NOUN, averages. **moyenne** ▶ the number that is found by dividing the sum of several quantities by the number of the quantities : *The average of 9, 12, 15, and 20 is 14 (9 + 12 + 15 + 20 = 56; 56 ÷ 4 = 14).*

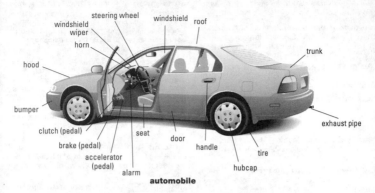

steering wheel
windshield
windshield wiper
horn
hood
bumper
clutch (pedal)
brake (pedal)
accelerator (pedal)
alarm
seat
door
handle
tire
hubcap
roof
trunk
exhaust pipe

automobile

▲ ADJECTIVE. **1. moyen (-enne)** ▶ found by figuring the average : *"The average length of the lower half of the adult thumb is 2.5 cm."* (Lorraine O'Byrne) **2. moyen (-enne)** ▶ usual or ordinary : *Lana is about average height for her age.* ▲ VERB, averaged, averaging. **1. faire la moyenne** ▶ to find the average of : *I averaged the cost of my lunches over the last three months.* **2. atteindre en moyenne** ▶ to have as an average : *The team averaged three goals a game.*

a‑vi‑a‑tion [AY-vee-AY-shun] NOUN. **aviation** ▶ the art, science, or business of building and flying airplanes or other aircraft. **Note.** A person who flies an aircraft is an aviator.

a‑void [uh-VOYD] VERB, avoided, avoiding. **éviter** ▶ to keep away from; keep clear of : *"Often they had to carry their canoe and their boxes and bundles up one side of a mountain and down the other to avoid a dangerous rapid."* (Ainslie Manson) ■ **avoidable,** ADJECTIVE. **évitable** ▶ SYN: evade, escape, dodge.

a‑wait [uh-WATE] VERB, awaited, awaiting. **attendre** ▶ to wait for : *The passengers on the platform spoke quietly as they awaited the night train.*

a‑wake [uh-WAKE] VERB, awoke **s'éveiller, se réveiller** ▶ or awaked, awaking. **1. éveiller** ▶ to wake up. **2. réveillé (-ée)** ▶ to make active; stir up : *The music awakes in him a desire to sing.* ▲ ADJECTIVE. **1. conscient (-ente) de** ▶ not asleep : *She was awake before the alarm went off.* **2. conscient (-ente)** ▶ alert to something; aware : *He is awake to the sense of danger in the air.*

a‑wak‑en [uh-WAY-kun] VERB, awakened, awakening. **éveiller, réveiller** ▶ to wake up : *As usual, I was awakened at 6 :30 by the alarm.* ■ **awakening** (☞ **p. 1027.**) NOUN. ▶ **réveil.**

a‑ward [uh-WARD] VERB, awarded, awarding. **1. décerner** ▶ to give as a prize or reward : *My neighbour awarded me $20 for finding his dog.* **2. allouer, attribuer** ▶ to grant by the decision of a court : *The jury awarded $10 000 to the injured person.* ▲ NOUN. awards. **récompense, prix, distinction** ▶ something that is awarded. ✍ **p. 183.**

a‑ware [uh-WAIR] ADJECTIVE. **conscient (-ente)** ▶ taking notice of; knowing or realizing something : *"Suddenly Sooshewan was aware of voices far away."* (Donald Gale) ■ **awareness,** NOUN. ▶ **(prise de) conscience.**

a‑way [uh-WAY] ADVERB. **1. s'éloigner** ▶ from this or that place : *Grandpa waved goodbye as we drove away.* **2. s'absenter** ▶ in another place; absent : *The neighbours went away for the weekend.* **3. faire cadeau de, donner** ▶ from or out of one's possession or use : *Mom gave away all my old clothes after I grew out of them.* **4. disparaître, s'éteindre** ▶ at or to an end; out of existence : *The smile on the Cheshire cat just faded away.* ▲ ADJECTIVE. **1. loin** ▶ at a distance : *We live far away from any stores.* **2. absent (-ente)** ▶ not present; absent : *I've been away on vacation.*

awe [ah] NOUN. **révérence, crainte** ▶ great wonder, mixed with fear or respect : *The tourists viewed the ruins in awe, struck by their size and beauty.*

awe‑some [AH-sum] ADJECTIVE. **impressionnant (-ante)** ▶ causing a feeling of awe : *an awesome sight.*

aw‑ful [AH-ful] ADJECTIVE. **1. terrible, effroyable, épouvantable** ▶ causing fear : *"You might have thought the world had come to an end. It looked so awful you kept turning your head away."* (Teddy Jam) **2. terrible, épouvantable** ▶ very bad or unpleasant : *The milk was*

40

sour and tasted awful. **3. énorme ▸** very large; great : *You have an awful lot of work to do.* **4. impressionnant (-ante) ▸** deserving respect; very impressive. SYN: horrible, terrible, shocking, frightful.

aw-ful-ly [OF-ul-ee] ADVERB. **1. terriblement, effroyablement ▸** in a terrible or unpleasant way : *He behaved awfully at the party.* **2. énor-mément ▸** very much so; extremely : *She was awfully tired and could hardly keep her eyes open.*

a-while [uh-WILE *or* uh-HWILE] ADVERB. **un moment ▸** for a short time; briefly : *Let's stop awhile and rest.*

awk-ward [OK-wurd] ADJECTIVE. **1. maladroit (-oite) ▸** without ease or grace; clumsy : *"She tried wearing gloves, but that was awkward."* (Thomas H. Raddall) **2. embarrassant (-ante) ▸** difficult or embarrassing : *Kerrie's laugh broke the awkward silence.*

aw-ning [ON-ing] NOUN, awnings. **auvent ▸** a piece of canvas, metal, plastic, or other material, used above a window or door to keep out sun or rain.

axe [aks] NOUN, axes. (also ax) **hache ▸** a tool with a sharp metal blade attached to a handle. It is used to cut wood.

ax-is [AK-sis] NOUN, axes [AK-seez]. **axe ▸** a straight line around which a body turns or seems to turn. The earth rotates on an imaginary axis.

ax-le [AK-sul] NOUN, axles. **essieu ▸** a rod or bar on which a wheel or pair of wheels turns.

aye [i] NOUN, ayes. (also ay) **oui ▸** a vote of "yes."

a-za-lea [uh-ZALE-yuh] NOUN, azaleas. **azalée ▸** a small bush with clusters of bright flowers.

butterfly

b, B [bee] NOUN, b's, B's. **1. b, B** ▸ the second letter of the English alphabet. **2. B** ▸ the second-highest mark, grade, or level.

bab·ble [BAB-ul] VERB, babbled, babbling. **1. gazouiller** ▸ to make sounds like a baby. **2. bafouiller, babiller** ▸ to talk foolishly; chatter : *"Babbling merrily, the birds landed all around him."* (Tololwa M. Mollel) **3. murmurer, gazouiller** ▸ to make a continuous, murmuring sound : *The brook babbled softly over the rocks.* ▲ NOUN, babbles. **1. bavardage** ▸ meaningless talk or sounds : *A babble of voices filled the auditorium before the concert began.* **2. babillage** ▸ foolish talk ; prattle : *Clayton's constant babble bores me.* **3. murmure** ▸ a low, murmuring sound.

ba·boon [ba-BOON] NOUN, baboons. **babouin** ▸ a large, hairy monkey with a face like a dog. Baboons live together in large groups in open areas of Africa and Southeast Asia.

ba·by [BAY-bee] NOUN, babies. **1. bébé** ▸ a young child ; an infant. **2. benjamin (-ine)** ▸ the youngest one in a family or group. ▲ VERB, babied, babying. **dorloter** ▸ to treat like a baby ; give a lot of attention to : *The doctor told Gina to baby her sprained ankle.* ▲ ADJECTIVE. **1. de bébé** ▸ for a baby : *baby toys, a baby crib.* **2. bébé** ▸ very young : *a baby animal.* ▪ **babyish**, ADJECTIVE. ▸ **enfantin.** like a baby. ⌂ p. 966.

ba·by-sit [BAY-bee-SIT] VERB, baby-sat, baby-sitting. **garder** ▸ to take care of a child or children while the parents are away from home, usually for a short period of time. **Note.** A baby-sitter is someone who baby-sits a lot.

bach·e·lor [BACH-uh-lur] NOUN, bachelors. **célibataire** ▸ a man who is not married, especially one who has never been married.

back [bak] NOUN, backs. **1. dos** ▸ the part of the human body opposite the front, from the neck to the end of the spine. **2. dos** ▸ the upper part of an animal's body. **3. dossier, arrière, au fond** ▸ the part of anything that is away from or opposite to the front : *the back of a chair ; the back of a room.* ▲ VERB, backed, backing. **1. reculer** ▸ to move backward : *Hugh carefully*

backed the car into the driveway. **2. appuyer, soutenir** ▸ to support or help : *I'm backing Yves for class president.* ▲ ADJECTIVE. **1. porte de service, à l'arrière** ▸ away from or opposite the front : *They delivered the groceries to the back door.* **2. antérieur (-eure)** ▸ not current ; past : *I looked at the back issues of the newspaper.* ▲ ADVERB. **1. s'adosser, en arrière** ▸ toward the rear : *He leaned back in the chair.* **2. retourner, de retour** ▸ to a former place or time : *Teresa forgot her book, so she went back to get it.* ⌂ p. 991.

back and forth aller-retour ▸ move one way and then the other : *She paced back and forth impatiently.*

back down retirer ses paroles, avouer ses torts ▸ give up a claim or attempt : *When challenged by his friends, Fernando backed down from his claim of seeing an alien.*

back of or in back of à l'arrière ▸ behind : *The garage is in back of the house.*

back out *Informal.* retirer sa promesse, se défiler, changer d'avis ▸ decide not to do something : *Dad said I could have a party, but he backed out at the last minute.*

back up 1. reculer, faire marche arrière ▸ move backward : *Mom said to back up the car closer to the house.* **2.** faire une copie de secours ▸ make an extra copy of work done on a computer.

back bacon bacon ▸ bacon that is cut from the back of a pig, not the sides. **Note.** Also called Canadian bacon.

back·bench [BAK-BENCH] NOUN. banquette des députés sans portefeuille ▸ the seats in a parliament or legislative assembly for members who are not in the cabinet or a leader in the opposition parties. **Note.** A person who sits here is known as a backbencher.

back·bone [BAK-BONE] NOUN, backbones. **1. colonne vertébrale, épine dorsale** ▸ the line of jointed bones down the middle of the back ; the spine or spinal column. Animals with backbones include mammals, birds, reptiles, and fish.

✎ Writing Tips

Bad—Badly

Bad is an adjective that describes or modifies a noun (a person, place, or thing). Bad can also modify linking verbs such as be, feel, smell, taste, look, sound, appear, seem, and become.

That's a bad cut on your knee.
    adjective   noun

The mildew smells really bad.
  linking verb   adjective

Badly is an adverb that modifies verbs or adjectives.

I play baseball badly.
  verb   adverb

2. pivot ▸ the most important or strongest part of something : *A good goalie is the backbone of any hockey team.* **3. avoir la force de ses convictions, courage** ▸ strength of mind ; courage : *The mayor showed a lot of backbone when she stood up to her critics.*

back-gam-mon [BAK-GAM-mun] NOUN. **jacquet** ▸ a game with two players who move pieces around a board according to the roll of the dice.

back-ground [BAK-GROWND] NOUN, backgrounds. **1. fond, arrière-plan** ▸ the part of a picture or scene behind the main object : *In this photo of Mom you can see the Rocky Mountains in the background.* **2. dans l'ombre** ▸ a position that does not get attention : *The author's husband prefers for her to get the publicity while he stays in the background.* **3. formation** ▸ the events or experiences that lead up to something : *You need a good background in math to do well in physics.* ▲ ADJECTIVE: **général (-ale)** ▸ *I did a lot of background reading on Italy before I went there.*

back-pack [BAK-PAK] NOUN, backpacks. **sac à dos** ▸ a knapsack or bag that is worn on the back. **Note.** Hiking or camping with all one's supplies in a backpack is **backpacking**.

back-ward [BAK-wurd] ADVERB. (also backwards) **1. à reculons, en arrière** ▸ toward the back. **2. à l'envers** ▸ with the back forward : *She had her cap on backward.* **3. à l'envers** ▸ opposite to the usual way : *Nyla can recite the alphabet both backward and forward.* ▲ ADJECTIVE. **1. en arrière, vers l'arrière** ▸ toward the back : *a backward movement; a backward look.* **2. arriéré (-ée), moins évolué (-ée)** ▸ behind in learning or development : *a backward area of the country.*

back-yard [BAK-YARD] NOUN, backyards. **arrière-cour** ▸ a piece of land that is in back of a house or other building.

ba-con [BAY-kun] NOUN. **bacon** ▸ a kind of smoked and salted meat that comes from a pig.

bac-te-ri-a [bak-TEER-ee-uh] PLURAL NOUN. **bactérie** ▸ **Note.** The singular form of this word is **bacterium**.

bad [bad] ADJECTIVE, worse, worst. **1. méchant, mauvais** ▸ not good ; not as is wanted or as it should be : *The bad dog ate the little girl's cookie.* **2. pourri (-ie)** ▸ rotten or spoiled : *a bad apple; bad meat.* **3. mal** ▸ sorry : *Jon felt bad about forgetting Janie's birthday.* ▪ **badly,** ADVERB. ▸ **mal.** SYN: wicked, wrong, naughty, evil, dreadful. *✐ p. 43.*

badge [baj] NOUN, badges. **1. écusson, insigne** ▸ a mark or sign that shows a person belongs to a certain group or has done a special thing : *The Boy Scout had three honour badges sewn on his sleeve.* **2. signe** ▸ a sign or symbol : *Dana says the scar he got playing soccer is a badge of honour.*

badg-er [BAJ-ur] NOUN, badgers. **blaireau (-eaux)** ▸ an animal with short legs, long, sharp claws, and heavy grey fur. Badgers feed at night and live under the ground. ▲ VERB, badgered, badgering. **harceler, tourmenter, importuner** ▸ to annoy or nag : *The players were badgered by fans wanting autographs.* SYN: tease, question, pester, bother.

bad-lands [BAD-landz] PLURAL NOUN. **badlands** ▸ an area of barren land in which ridges, gullies, and odd rock formations have been formed by wind, rain, and floods. Badlands are found in southwestern Saskatchewan, southeastern Alberta, and in semi-desert regions of the United States.

bad-min-ton [BAD-min-tun] NOUN. **badminton** ▸ a game in which racquets are used to hit a small feathered object called a **shuttlecock** or **birdie** over a high net. It is played by two or four people.

baf-fle [BAF-ul] VERB, baffled, baffling. **déconcerter** ▸ to confuse or puzzle ; bewilder : *I'm completely baffled by the directions for the VCR.* SYN: puzzle, bewilder.

bag [bag] NOUN, bags. **1. sac** ▸ a soft container that is made of paper, plastic, or cloth and is usually open at the top : *A bag is used to carry food, clothes, or other items.* **2. sac** ▸ something that can be used like a bag, such as a woman's purse or a suitcase. ▲ VERB, bagged, bagging. **1. mettre en sac, emballer** ▸ to put into a bag : *Miko bags groceries at the supermarket.* **2. empocher** ▸ to catch or capture something, as if in a bag. **3. faire des poches** ▸ to bulge like a bag : *Her jeans began to bag at the knees.*

bag·gage [BAG-ij] NOUN. **bagages** ▸ suitcases, bags, or packages that people carry on a trip ; luggage.

bag·pipe [BAG-pipe] NOUN. **bagpipes**. **corne·muse** ▸ a musical instrument where the musician blows air into a leather bag. The air in the bag then forced into several pipes to make the notes. 👁 p. 539.

bail¹ [bale] NOUN. **caution** ▸ an amount of money set by a judge and paid by a prisoner to ensure he or she will appear at the trial. ▲ VERB, bailed, bailing. **1. fournir une caution** ▸ to obtain the release of a person under arrest by paying such an amount of money : *The man bailed his son out of the city jail.* **2. tirer d'affaire** ▸ to help someone out of a difficulty : *Juan bailed me out and drove me to dance class.*

bail² VERB, bailed, bailing. **1. écoper, vider** ▸ to scoop water out of a boat : *Water seeped into the boat as fast as we could bail it out.* **2. bail out. sauter** ▸ to jump out of an airplane with a parachute.

bait [bate] NOUN, baits. **1. appât, amorce** ▸ something used to attract fish or other animals so they can be caught : *Put the bait on your hook before you cast your line into the water.* **2. appât** ▸ anything that attracts a person to do something : *Nadia used cookies as bait to get others to join her club.* ▲ VERB, baited, baiting. **1. appâter** ▸ to put bait on : *"Jodie watched with interest as the officers baited the trap."* (Marilyn Halvorson) **2. harceler, tourmenter** ▸ to tease or torment : *The crowd baited the speaker by hissing and booing at her.*

bake [bake] VERB, baked, baking. **1. (faire) cuire au four** ▸ to cook something by heating it in an oven. **Note.** A bakery is a place where baked foods are made or sold. **2. (faire) cuire au four** ▸ to dry out and make hard by heating : *The potter baked the vases in the kiln.*

bak·er [BAY-kur] NOUN, bakers. **pâtissier (-ière)** ▸ a person who bakes and sells bread, rolls, cakes, and other such foods.

bal·a·clav·a [BAL-uh-KLAV-uh] NOUN. **passe-montagne, cagoule** ▸ a knitted woollen hat that covers the head and neck except for the eyes.

bal·ance [BAL-uns] NOUN. balances. **1. équi·libre** ▸ a steady, even position of the body. **2. équilibre** ▸ a condition in which two opposing items or forces are equal, as in strength, mass, or value : *a balance of work and play.* **3. solde** ▸ a scale or object for finding the mass of things by putting them in balance with a known weight. **4. solde** ▸ the remainder of an amount due : *She paid half now and will pay the balance when the chair is delivered.* **5. maintenir en équilibre** ▸ the amount of money in a bank account : *I now have a $35 balance in my savings account.* ▲ VERB, bal-anced, balancing. **1. équilibrer** ▸ to put or keep in a steady position : *Mosi balanced her cup on her book as she walked to the TV room.* **2. balancer, régler, équilibrer** ▸ to figure the amount of money in an account : *to balance a chequebook.* ▲ ADJECTIVE: *Eat a balanced diet for better health.* **équilibré (-ée)** ▸ SYN: equalize, steady, measure.

in the balance **en suspend** ▸ undecided : *The decision regarding a new youth centre is in the balance.*

bal·co·ny [BAL-kuh-nee] NOUN, balconies. **1. balcon** ▸ a raised section that extends out from an apartment house or other building. **2. balcon** ▸ an upper floor with seats that extends out over the main floor, as in a church or theatre : *I like seats in the balcony for listening to a symphony orchestra.*

bald [bald] ADJECTIVE, balder, baldest. **1. chauve** ▸ having little or no hair on the head. **2. dépourvu (-ue), dépouillé (-ée)** ▸ without a natural covering : *There are bald spots on the lawn where the grass did not grow.* **3. simple exposition** ▸ simple or plain : *"I don't want to set down a series of bald facts in a diary like most people do."* (Anne Frank)

bale [bale] NOUN, bales. **balle, ballot** ▸ a large bundle of things wrapped together to be stored or sent somewhere : *Wheat is packed in bales to be shipped to mills.* ▲ VERB, baled, baling. **paqueter** ▸ to make into a bale : *to bale hay.* **Note.** A machine that bales something is a baler.

balk [bok] VERB, balked, balking. **1. s'arrêter, (se) dérober** ▸ to stop short and refuse to move or act : *The horse balked, and the rider went flying over its head.* **2. s'arrêter, hésiter** ▸ in baseball, a play in which the pitcher starts to pitch and then stops. ▲ NOUN, balks. **feinte, hési·tation** ▸ the act of balking : *If a pitcher commits a balk, the runners move up one base.* ■ **balky**, ADJECTIVE. ▸ **hésitant (-ante).**

ball¹ [bol] NOUN, balls. **1. balle, ballon** ▸ a round object that is used in certain games, such as basketball, baseball, tennis, and so on. **2. boule** ▸ anything having a roundish shape like this : *a snowball; a ball of yarn; a gumball.* **3. à la balle, au ballon** ▸ baseball or a similar game played with a ball : *The umpire says "Play ball" to start a baseball game.* **4. balle** ▸ in baseball, a pitch that is not a strike. ▲ VERB, balled, balling. **mettre en boule** ▸ to form the shape of a ball : *He balled up the note and threw it into the fire.*

ball² NOUN, balls. **bal (bals)** ▸ a large, formal dance : *"One day, it was announced that the Penguin Prince was giving a costume ball."* (Janet Perlman)

bal·lad [BAL-ud] NOUN, ballads. **ballade, romance** ▸ a song or poem that tells a story : *"Most of my stories about Robin Hood are* *taken from a collection of popular ballads printed in 1495."* (Sarah Hayes) ✐ **p. 45.**

✐ **Writing Tips**

Ballad

*A **ballad** is a short narrative poem that was originally created to be sung. Ballads tell a story through dialogue and action. They begin abruptly—suggesting some previous event—and often contain a refrain (a repeated verse). In music, ballads that are sung are usually slow, romantic songs about love.*

bal·let [BAL-ay *or* bal-AY] NOUN, ballets. **1. ballet** ▸ a kind of dance characterized by flowing, graceful movement: Swan Lake *is a well-known ballet.* **2. ballets** ▸ a group of dancers who perform a ballet: *Sonia is a member of the Royal Winnipeg Ballet.* **Note.** People who perform ballets are ballet dancers. Another name for a female ballet dancer is a ballerina.

bal·loon [buh-LOON] NOUN, balloons. **ballon** ▸ a bag filled with air or gas. Small rubber balloons are used as children's toys or as decorations. Larger balloons filled with helium or other gases can be attached to a basket or cabin to carry people up in the air. ▲ VERB, ballooned, ballooning. **ballonner, gonfler** ▸ to puff out or grow larger: *"All the windows were open and the lace curtains ballooned gently toward the street."* (James Joyce)

bal·lot [BAL-ut] NOUN, ballots. **1. bulletin de vote** ▸ a paper or other item used for voting. **2. bulletin de vote** ▸ the number of votes cast in an election: *We don't know who won because they haven't counted all the ballots yet.* ▲ VERB, balloted, balloting. **voter au scrutin** ▸ to vote by a ballot.

bam·boo [bam-BOO] NOUN, bamboos. **bambou (-ous)** ▸ a tall grass that grows like a tree. Bamboo has hollow, jointed stems that are used to make fishing poles, furniture, windows blinds, and other such items.

ban [ban] VERB, banned, banning. **interdire** ▸ to forbid by law or in an official way; prohibit: *Smoking is banned on all flights within Canada.* ▲ NOUN, bans. **interdiction** ▸ an official order that bans something: *High air pollution has resulted in a ban on the burning of leaves.* SYN: forbid, prohibit, block, obstruct, outlaw.

ba·nan·a [buh-NAN-uh] NOUN, bananas. **banane** ▸ a curved, finger-shaped fruit that grows in bunches and has a yellow skin when ripe. The banana plant grows in tropical areas.

band¹ [band] NOUN, bands. **1. bande, bandelette** ▸ a narrow strip of material: *Put a rubber band*

around the cards. **2. bande** ▸ a stripe or ring of colour: *Her blouse had bands of blue and green.* ▲ VERB, banded, banding. **baguer** ▸ to put a band on: *Researchers banded the birds to keep track of their migration patterns.*

band² NOUN, bands. **1. formation, groupe, orchestre** ▸ a group of people playing musical instruments: *My sister plays in the school band.* **2. bande** ▸ any group of people, animals, or objects: *"...a band of outlaws attacked the Sheriff of Nottingham, took his money and his prisoner..."* (Sarah Hayes) ▲ VERB, banded, banding. **se liguer** ▸ to form a band; unite: *The citizens banded together to protest the plan to raise their taxes.*

band·age [BAN-dij] NOUN, bandages. **bandage, pansement** ▸ a piece of cloth or tape used to cover or protect a cut or injury. ▲ VERB, bandaged, bandaging. **bander, mettre un pansement sur** ▸ to put a bandage on: *to bandage a cut.*

ban·dan·a [ban-DAN-uh] NOUN, bandanas. (also bandanna) **foulard, bandeau (-eaux)** ▸ a large handkerchief or scarf with bright colours or pattern.

ban·dit [BAN-dit] NOUN, bandits or banditti. **bandit** ▸ a robber or outlaw, especially one who is part of a gang. **Note.** From the Italian word *bandire,* which means "to band together."

bang [bang] NOUN, bangs. **détonation, claquement** ▸ a loud, sharp noise. ▲ VERB, banged, banging. **frapper** ▸ to make a loud, sharp noise: *The plumber banged on the pipe.*

bangs [bangz] NOUN, **frange** ▸ hair that is cut short and straight across the forehead.

ban·ish [BAN-ish] VERB, banished, banishing. **1. bannir, exiler** ▸ to force to leave a country: *"So Periander banished them to an ugly, barbarous land."* (Marcia Williams) **2. bannir, chasser** ▸ to send or drive away: *Uncle Andreas banished us from the living room so that he could read his book in peace.* ◾ **banishment,** NOUN. ▸ exil. SYN: exile, expel, drive away, deport.

ban·jo [BAN-joh] NOUN, banjos or banjoes. **banjo** ▸ a musical instrument that resembles a guitar, but has a longer neck and rounder body. It is played by picking the strings with the fingers. ✐ **p. 538.**

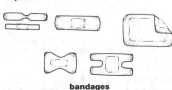

bandages

bank[1] [bank] NOUN, banks. **1. banque ▸** a place in which money is kept and other business involving money takes place : *I have a savings account in the local bank.* **Note.** This business is called banking. **2. banque ▸** a place where a large supply of something is kept : *the blood bank; the food bank.* ▲ VERB, banked, banking. **avoir un compte en banque, faire des transactions bancaires ▸** to have dealings with a bank : *We have been banking there for 10 years.* 📘 **p. 1047.**

bank[2] NOUN, banks. **1. rive, berge ▸** the land along the edge of a river or stream : *We set up camp on the banks of the river.* **2. banc, accumulation ▸** a heap or mound : *Huge banks of grey clouds rolled across the sky.* ▲ VERB, banked, banking. **1. remblayer ▸** to form into a bank : *The crane lifted the earth and banked it at the edge of the lot.* **2. surhausser, relever ▸** to slant a road so that the outer edge is higher than the inner one : *The road was banked around the curve.*

bank[3] NOUN, banks. **rangée ▸** a group of similar things together in a row : *a bank of computers; a bank of switches.*

bank-er [BANG-kur] NOUN, bankers. **1. banquier (-ière) ▸** a person whose business is banking, especially someone who manages a bank. **2. pêcheur des Grands Bancs ▸** a fisher who fishes off the Grand Banks. **3. bateau de pêche des Grands Bancs ▸** a fishing vessel that operates off the Grand Banks.

bank-rupt [BANG-krupt] ADJECTIVE. **en faillite ▸** not able to pay one's bills. ▲ VERB, bankrupted, bankrupting: *His construction company loses so much money on rainy days that it is going to bankrupt him.* **Note.** The state of being bankrupt is bankruptcy.

ban-ner [BAN-ur] NOUN, banners. **1. bannière, banderole ▸** a strip of cloth with letters or pictures on it that represent something : *Our school banner has a black bear on it.* **2. bannière, drapeau (-eaux) ▸** a flag : *Banners of all the member nations fly outside the United Nations headquarters.* ▲ ADJECTIVE, **excellent (-ente) ▸** unusually good; outstanding : *This is a banner year for apples.*

ban-nock [BAN-uk] NOUN, bannocks. **1. galette ▸** a flat, round cake made of flour, salt, and water. **2. pain plat et rond ▸** a flat cake made of oatmeal, wheat, or barley flour, usually without yeast or baking powder.

ban-quet [BANG-kwit] NOUN, banquets. **banquet ▸** a large formal dinner given to honour someone or as part of a celebration : *"For a special banquet, each restaurant in Chinatown was invited to bring its best dish."* (Paul Yee) SYN: feast, formal dinner, affair.

ban-tam [BAN-tum] NOUN, bantams. **1. coq nain, poule naine ▸** any of various breeds of small fowl. **2. coq ▸** a small but aggressive person. **3. bantam ▸** in sports, a class for players under 15 years old. ▲ ADJECTIVE: *bantam rooster, bantam hockey.*

bap-tism [BAP-tiz-um] NOUN, baptisms. **1. baptême ▸** a ceremony in which a person is sprinkled with water or immersed in water as a sign of washing away sin. Baptism is performed when someone is first admitted to a Christian church. **2. baptême ▸** any experience or ordeal that initiates or tests a person.

bap-tize [BAP-tize] VERB, baptized, baptizing. **1. baptiser ▸** to carry out a ceremony of baptism : *The priest baptized my baby brother.* **2. baptiser ▸** to give a first name to a person at baptism; christen : *The baby was baptized Maria del Carmen.*

bar [bar] NOUN, bars. **1. barre, tablette ▸** a straight piece of wood, metal, or other material that is longer than it is wide or thick : *a candy bar; a bar of soap; a bar of gold.* **2. obstacle ▸** something that blocks the way; a barrier. **3. rayure ▸** a straight band or stripe of colour. **4. bar ▸** a room with a long counter where alcoholic drinks are served. **5. barre ▸** in music, one of the straight lines drawn from top to bottom across a staff to divide it into units of time called measures. **6. mesure ▸** one of these units of rhythm; a measure : *The accent falls on the first note of each bar.* **7. barreau (-eaux) ▸** the professional body of lawyers : *She has to pass this exam before she is called to the bar.* ▲ VERB, barred, barring. **1. barrer ▸** to close or fasten with a bar : *He barred the door of the cabin.* **2. interdire, exclure ▸** to block or keep out : *For many years, the armed forces barred women.* SYN: block, obstruct, forbid, ban, exclude.

barb [barb] NOUN, barbs. **barbillon, barbelure ▸** a sharp point that sticks out backward from the object it is attached to. Fishhooks, arrows, and spears have barbs. **Note.** Something that has a barb or barbs is barbed: *Barbed wire is used to fence in cattle.*

bar-bar-i-an [bar-BAIR-ee-un] NOUN, barbarians. **1. barbare ▸** a person who is not civilized; savage. **2. barbare ▸** a person who is very crude or bad-mannered.

bar-bar-ic [bar-BAIR-ik] ADJECTIVE. **barbare, rude, primitif (-ive) ▸** uncivilized like barbarians; without culture; crude : *Ancient Rome was attacked by barbaric tribes from the north.* SYN: coarse, cruel, uncivilized, savage, brutal.

bar-be-cue [BAR-buh-kyoo] NOUN, barbecues. **1. barbecue ▸** a grill or pit for cooking food over hot coals or an open fire. **2. barbecue ▸** a meal with food cooked in this way. ▲ VERB, barbecued, barbecuing. **griller sur le barbecue ▸** to cook food over hot coals or an open fire : *to barbecue a steak.* **Note.** Barbecue comes from *barboka*, a word first used in Haiti that means "a framework of sticks."

bar-bell [BAR-bell] NOUN, barbells. **barre à disques** ▶ a metal bar to which weights are attached and used for lifting exercises.

bar-ber [BAR-bur] NOUN, barbers. **coiffeur (-euse), barbier** ▶ a person whose work is cutting hair and shaving or trimming beards. **Note.** *Barber* comes from a French word meaning "beard."

bare [bair] ADJECTIVE, barer, barest. **1. dénudé (-ée), nu (nue)** ▶ having no covering or clothing; uncovered; exposed : *"Sure enough, on a bare patch of ground I found fresh tracks."* (Janet Foster) **2. vide** ▶ empty : *The cupboards were bare of food.* ▲ VERB, bared, baring. **montrer ses dents, mettre à nu, se découvrir** ▶ to make bare; reveal or uncover : *The dog bared its teeth at the intruder.* 🖉 p. 48.

bare-ly [BAIR-lee] ADVERB. **de justesse, à peine** ▶ only just; scarcely : *More people came than we expected, and there were barely enough seats for everyone.* SYN: hardly, merely, almost.

bar-gain [BAR-gun] NOUN, bargains. **1. affaire** ▶ something for sale that is a good value at the price; a good buy : *The computer is a great bargain at that price.* **2. marché** ▶ an agreement between two people or two groups; a deal : *Duane made a bargain with his mom : if he washed her car, he could stay up late to watch the movie.* ▲ VERB, bargained, bargaining. **marchander** ▶ to try to reach an agreement to buy : *Jill likes to bargain to get the best price.*

bargain for **compter sur, s'attendre à** ▶ to be ready for; expect : *The camping trip was more than she had bargained for.*

barge [barj] NOUN, barges. **chaland, péniche** ▶ a large flat-bottomed boat : *Barges are often used to carry freight on rivers and lakes.* ▲ VERB, barged, barging. **1. se déplacer maladroitement, rentrer dans** ▶ to move clumsily, like a barge : *She barged into the chair and bruised her leg.* **2. faire brutalement irruption, rentrer dans** ▶ to push or shove rudely : *The man barged into the line and demanded immediate service.*

bar-i-tone [BAIR-uh-TONE] NOUN, baritones. **1. baryton** ▶ a male singer with a singing range lower than a tenor and higher than a bass. **2. baryton** ▶ a musical instrument that has this range. **3. baryton** ▶ a musical part written for such a voice or instrument.

bark[1] [bark] NOUN, barks. **écorce** ▶ the outer covering on the trunk and branches of a tree. 🖉 p. 253.

bark[2] NOUN, barks. **aboiement** ▶ the short, sharp sounds made by a dog or similar animal. ▲ VERB, barked, barking. **1. aboyer** ▶ to make this sound. **2. dire d'un ton brutal** ▶ to speak in a sharp, abrupt way : *The leader barked out instructions to the hikers.*

bar-ley [BAR-lee] NOUN. **orge** ▶ a plant whose grain is used for food and to make beer and whisky : *Barley is one of Canada's main products.* 👁 p. 116.

bar-mitz-vah [BAR-MITS-vuh] NOUN. **barmitsvah** ▶ a religious ceremony for a Jewish boy when he reaches the age of 13. It is a ceremony recognizing that he has become an adult and can take a full role in the Jewish religion. **Note.** A similar ceremony for a girl is called a **bas mitzvah** or **bat mitzvah**.

barn [barn] NOUN, barns. **grange, étable** ▶ a farm building used to store grain, hay, and farming equipment and to house farm animals. 👁 p. 114.

bar-na-cle [BAR-nuh-kul] NOUN, barnacles. **bernacle** ▶ a small shellfish that attaches itself to underwater objects, such as rocks or the hulls of ships.

ba-rom-e-ter [buh-ROM-uh-tur] NOUN, barometers. **1. baromètre** ▶ an instrument that measures air pressure, used to determine changes in the weather. **2. baromètre** ▶ something that gives notice of a change : *Investors often use interest rates as a barometer of how the stock market will behave.*

bar-on [BAIR-un] NOUN, barons. **1. baron (-onne)** ▶ a nobleman of the lowest rank in European countries : *"The valley was owned by a baron who lived in the castle, surrounded by his knights."* (Donald Carrick) **2. magnat** ▶ a person who has great wealth and power in a certain area : *an oil baron; a cattle baron.* **Note.** A baroness is the wife or widow of a baron, or a woman with rank equal to that of a baron.

bar-rack [BAIR-iks] NOUN, barracks. (usually barracks) **1. caserne, quartier** ▶ a large building or group of buildings in which soldiers live, as on a military base. **2. caserne** ▶ a building in which local detachments of the Royal Canadian Mounted Police live. **3. caserne** ▶ a training centre of the Royal Canadian Mounted Police.

bar-ra-cu-da [BAIR-uh-KOO-duh] NOUN, barracuda or barracudas. **barracuda** ▶ a fish with a long narrow body. Barracuda are found in warm ocean areas close to shore. Their many sharp teeth make them dangerous to other water animals.

bar-rage [buh-ROZH] NOUN, barrages. **1. tir de barrage** ▶ a rapid firing of guns, cannon, or the like. **2. déluge** ▶ any continuous series of many things of the same kind : *The prime minister was faced with a barrage of questions from the press.*

bar-rel [BAIR-ul] NOUN, barrels. **1. tonneau (-eaux), baril** ▶ a large round container with curving sides and a flat top and bottom. **2. canon** ▶ something shaped like a barrel : *the barrel of a gun.* ▲ VERB, barrelled, barrelling.

🔧 Word Builder

Barren, empty, bare, and *desolate* can all describe a place where little or nothing is growing. *Empty* is a general word: *The girls like to play in the empty lot next to their house.* *Barren* suggests a lack of life: *It was a barren desert landscape with nothing to be seen but endless sand dunes.* *Bare* indicates that something is missing: *This photo must have been taken in winter; the trees are bare.* *Desolate* gives the idea of a sad or depressing place: *The little village sits in a desolate Arctic landscape, surrounded by a blank white world of ice and snow.*

(also barreled, barreling) **foncer ▶** to travel very fast : *The sled barrelled down the steep hill.*

bar·ren [BAIR-un] ADJECTIVE. **1. stérile ▶** not able to produce much : *"There was only scrub land now, barren and drought-stricken."* (Tololwa M. Mollel) **2. stérile ▶** not able to produce new offspring : *a barren fruit tree; a barren cow.* ▲ NOUN, barrens. **lande ▶** an area of empty land; wasteland. 🖉 **p. 48.**

bar·ri·er [BAIR-ee-ur] NOUN, barriers. **1. barrage ▶** something that blocks the way or stops movement : *The police put up a barrier to keep traffic from entering the street.* **2. barrière ▶** something that blocks progress or communication : *Our disagreement has created a barrier between us.* SYN: obstacle, barricade.

bar·ter [BAR-tur] VERB, bartered, bartering. **troquer, faire du troc ▶** to trade one thing for another without using money; exchange : *Devaki bartered her old car for a new motorcycle.* ▲ NOUN. **troc, échange ▶** the act of bartering; something bartered.

base¹ [base] NOUN, bases. **1. base ▶** the lowest part of something; bottom : *We parked at the base of the hill and walked up.* **2. base, fondement ▶** the main part of something; basis. **3. but ▶** a goal or safety point in some children's games : *In hide-and-seek you have to get to base before you are caught.* **4. racine ▶** in spelling, a root word : *Cycle is the base word of bicycle.* **5. but ▶** any of the four corners of a baseball infield. **6. base ▶** a place where many ships, planes, or other military forces are kept. **7. base ▶** a number used as a standard for counting : *Our numbering system has a base of 10.* **8. base ▶** a chemical that can join with an acid to form a salt. A base will make litmus paper turn blue. ▲ VERB, based, basing. **baser, fonder ▶** to provide support or a foundation for something : *The writer based the movie on a popular children's book.*

base² ADJECTIVE, baser, basest. **1. vil (vile) ▶** low in value : *Lead is a base metal compared to gold.* **2. ignoble, indigne ▶** not honourable; low or mean : *To tell something told to you in secret is a base action.* SYN: low, mean, selfish, cowardly, inferior.

base·ball [BASE-bol] NOUN, baseballs. **1. baseball ▶** a game that is played on a field by two teams of nine players each. A player on one team tries to hit a ball with a bat and then run around the bases to score a run. The other team tries to catch the ball to get the runner out. **2. balle de base-ball ▶** the ball used in this game. **Note.** The bases form a baseball diamond.

base·ment [BASE-munt] NOUN, basements. **sous-sol ▶** the lowest floor of a building, usually partly or completely underground. 🗐 **p. 1065.**

bash·ful [BASH-ful] ADJECTIVE. **timide ▶** afraid to meet new people; timid; shy : *My little brother is very bashful and won't answer when strangers ask him questions.* ■ **bashfully,** ADVERB. ▶ **timidement.** SYN: shy, timid, uneasy, awkward.

ba·sic [BAY-sik] ADJECTIVE. **de base ▶** having to do with the simplest or most important part : *We need to know basic math before we can go on to algebra.* ■ **basics,** PLURAL NOUN. ▶ **choses essentielles.** the simplest but most important parts of something : *Reading, writing, and arithmetic are the basics of education.* SYN: first, primary, necessary, fundamental.

ba·si·cal·ly [BAY-sik-lee] ADVERB. **principalement, au fond ▶** for the most part; chiefly; mainly : *The play is basically a comedy, but there are some sad moments in it.* 🖉 **p. 49.**

ba·sin [BAY-sun] NOUN, basins. **1. cuvette, lavabo, évier ▶** a round, shallow bowl for holding liquids; a sink : *Fill the basin with water to rinse the dishes.* **2. bassin ▶** a low place in land, usually containing water. **3. bassin ▶** a sheltered area in which boats are moored. **4. bassin ▶** an area of land from which water runs down into a river.

ba·sis [BAY-sis] NOUN, bases [BAY-sees]. **base ▶** the most important part of something; foundation : *The basis of this flour is wheat.*

bask [bask] VERB, basked, basking. **1. se dorer ▶** to warm oneself pleasantly : *She basked in the warm spring air.* **2. se plaire ▶** to do well in the presence of a pleasant atmosphere or influence : *The singer basked in the praise of his teacher.*

bas·ket [BAS-kit] NOUN, baskets. **1. panier ▶** a container used to hold and carry food, clothing, and other things. **2. filet ▶** a large metal ring with a net open at the bottom that is used as the goal in basketball. **3. points ▶** a score made in

✎ Writing Tips

Basically

• The word **basically** is often used in writing when it is not really needed. For example, **basically** does not add anything useful to the meaning of this sentence:

A whale is **basically** a mammal, not a fish.

(A whale is a mammal, so **basically** is not needed to limit the statement.)

But in this sentence, **basically** is useful:

Although there are one or two boring parts, this is **basically** a good story.

(It is mainly, but not completely, a good story.)

• When you edit your writing, notice when you use **basically.** If the sentence would still have the same meaning without **basically,** take the word out.

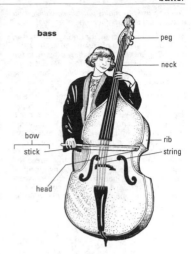

bass

peg

neck

bow

stick

rib

string

head

basketball : *Nan made six baskets in the last game.*

bas·ket·ball [BAS-kit-bol] NOUN, basketballs. **1. basket·ball ▸** a game played with a large round ball by two teams of five players each. The object of the game is to put the ball through the other team's goal, or basket. **2. ballon de basket·ball ▸** the ball used in this game. **Note.** Basketball is played on a basketball court.

bass¹ [base] NOUN, basses. **1. basse ▸** a man who has the lowest singing voice. **2. contre·basse ▸** a musical instrument that has this range. ☞ **p. 539. 3. de basse ▸** a musical part for such a voice or instrument.

bass² [bas] NOUN, bass or basses. **perche ▸** a large family of fish found all over the world. Bass live in either salt or fresh water. Common types are the striped bass and the black bass.

bas·soon [buh-SOON] NOUN, bassoons. **bas·son ▸** a long, wooden musical instrument with a low sound. ☞ **p. 539.**

bat¹ [bat] NOUN, bats. **1. bâton ▸** a long stick that is made of wood or metal, used to hit a ball in baseball or other similar games. **2. at bat. au bâton ▸** having a turn to hit in baseball or a similar game. ▲ VERB, batted, batting. **frapper la balle avec le bâton ▸** to hit a ball with a bat. SYN: hit, strike, knock.

bat² NOUN, bats. **chauve-souris ▸** a small, furry flying mammal with a body like a mouse and wings of thin skin. Bats hunt for food at night and locate prey by sending out a sound and following the echo. Most bats hang upside down while resting. ☞ **p. 110.**

batch [bach] NOUN, batches. **fournée ▸** a quantity made or used at one time : *a batch of cookies.*

bath [bath] NOUN, baths. **1. bain ▸** a washing of the body with water, usually in a tub : *Before school I take a shower instead of a bath.* **2. eau du bain ▸** the water used for this. **3. bain, salle de bain ▸** a bathroom or bathtub.

bathe [bathe] VERB, bathed, bathing. **1. se baigner ▸** to take a bath. **2. baigner ▸** to give a bath to; wash : *Mom bathes the baby in warm water.* **3. baigner ▸** to apply water or another liquid to : *She bathed the wound with cool water.* **4. baigner ▸** to seem to pour over or surround : *The sunlight bathed us in a golden glow.*

bath·room [BATH-room] NOUN, bathrooms. **salle de bain ▸** a room having a toilet, a sink, and often a bathtub or shower. ☞ **p. 1065.**

ba·ton [buh-TON] NOUN, batons. **bâton ▸** a long, thin stick used for a special purpose, as by the conductor of an orchestra or by a relay runner.

bat·tal·i·on [buh-TAL-yun] NOUN, battalions. **1. bataillon ▸** a large group of soldiers in an army, usually made up of four companies within one regiment. **2. groupe ▸** any large group organized to act together : *a battalion of volunteers.*

bat·ter¹ [BAT-ur] NOUN, batters. **frappeur (-euse) ▸** a person who takes a turn to hit the ball in baseball.

batter² NOUN, batters. **pâte ▸** a mixture of flour, eggs, and a liquid used in baking and cooking :

Batter is used to make pancakes, cakes, and biscuits and to coat other foods for cooking.

batter³ VERB, battered, battering. **maltraiter, rouer de coups ▸** to hit again and again; strike hard : *The driving rain battered against the window.* ▪ **battered,** ADJECTIVE. ▸ **délabré (-ée).** worn by hard use : *a battered old pickup truck.* SYN : beat, hit, pound.

bat·ter·y [BAT-uh-ree] NOUN, batteries. **1. batterie ▸** an electric cell or group of cells supplying current and energy : *You can't start a car if the battery is dead.* **2. voie de fait ▸** in law, the act of illegally hitting or harming somebody : *One of the men in the fight was charged with assault and battery.* **3. batterie ▸** a group of cannons or other large guns that are fired together. **4. batterie, panoplie ▸** any group of people or things that are connected or work together : *The minister of labour spoke into a battery of microphones from all the different TV channels.* 👁 p. 540.

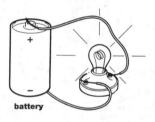

battery

bat·tle [BAT-ul] NOUN, battles. **1. bataille, combat ▸** a long, serious fight between enemies : *The opposing generals, Montcalm of France and Wolfe of Britain, were both fatally wounded in the Battle of Quebec.* **2. lutte ▸** any hard struggle or contest : *Mom never gives up on her battle to get Jo to clean her room.* ▪ VERB, battled, battling. **lutter, combattre ▸** to carry on a battle against; fight : *The swimmer had to battle against the strong current.* SYN : fight, conflict, war, combat.

bawl [bol] VERB, bawled, bawling. **1. brailler ▸** to cry loudly : *After spilling his drink, my little brother sat down and bawled.* **2. hurler, gueuler ▸** to make a loud noise : *"The cows were bawling in distress and the calves were crying back at them."* (Katherine Anne Porter) SYN : cry, weep, sob.

bawl out *Informal.* **engueuler ▸** to scold or criticize loudly : *Paul was embarrassed when his father bawled him out in front of his friends.*

bay¹ [bay] NOUN, bays. **baie ▸** a large part of a sea or lake that is partly enclosed by land : *Hudson Bay; the Bay of Fundy.*

bay² NOUN, bays. **aboiement, hurlement ▸** the long, deep barking of a dog or similar animal. ▪ VERB, bayed, baying. **aboyer, hurler ▸** to bark with a long, deep sound : *The wolf raised its head and bayed at the moon.*

at bay à distance, en échec ▸ the position of an animal or person that is being kept away : *The police held the angry crowd at bay.*

bay³ NOUN, bays. **1. bai ▸** a reddish-brown colour. **2. bai ▸** a horse that has this colour. ▪ ADJECTIVE. **bai (baie) ▸** reddish-brown.

bay⁴ NOUN, bays. **feuille odoriférante d'arbre, laurier ▸** any of several trees, such as the laurel, whose leaf (a **bay leaf**) is used to give flavour to cooking.

bay⁵ NOUN, bays. **1. enfoncement ▸** a part of a building or other structure between columns, pillars, and the like. **2. fenêtre en baie, baie vitrée ▸** a part of a wall that projects out and has a window or set of windows in it. **Note.** This is known as a **bay window. 3. silo ▸** a compartment in a barn used to store hay or grain. **4. travée, quai de chargement ▸** a compartment or platform used for a special purpose : *a loading bay.*

ba·zaar [buh-ZAR] NOUN, bazaars. **1. bazar ▸** a sale of things for a special purpose : *The church held a bazaar to raise money for building repairs.* **2. bazar ▸** a marketplace or street with shops and booths.

be [bee] is, was or were, been, being. a special kind of verb that does not show action. Be means **1. être ▸** to have reality; exist or live : *A horse that flies? Such things cannot be.* **2. être ▸** to have a certain character or quality : *Be a friend and help me out.* **3. être ▸** to occupy a certain position or condition : *I will be at school all day.* **4. avoir lieu ▸** to take place; happen : *His birthday will be next month.*

beach [beech] NOUN, beaches. **plage ▸** an area at the edge of an ocean or a lake, usually covered with sand or small rocks and sloping down to the water : *After our trip to the beach, the car was full of sand.* ▪ VERB, beached, beaching. **échouer ▸** to move or go from water onto a beach : *to beach a boat.* SYN : shore, coast, seaside.

bea·con [BEE-kun] NOUN, beacons. **phare, balise ▸** a light, fire, or radio signal used as a signal, such as a lighthouse that warns or guides ships : *"We could see the lights from a long way off, tiny beacons in a sea of snow."* (Patricia MacLachlan)

bead [beed] NOUN, beads. **1. perle ▸** a small, round piece of glass, wood, metal, or plastic. A bead has a hole through it so it can be put on a string or wire with other pieces like it. **2. perle ▸** any small, round object like this : *Beads of sweat ran down the runner's face.* ▪ VERB, beaded, beading. **couvrir de perles,**

orner de perles ▸ to decorate something with beads : *She beaded a vest.*

beak [beek] NOUN, beaks. **1. bec** ▸ the hard, horny mouth parts of a bird; bill. **2. bec** ▸ anything that projects forward in the shape of a bird's beak : *the beak of a jug.*

beak-er [BEE-kur] NOUN, beakers. **1. vase à bec** ▸ a thin glass or metal container with a small lip for pouring. Used to hold liquids or mix substances. **2. gobelet** ▸ a large drinking glass or cup with a wide mouth.

beam [beem] NOUN, beams. **1. poutre** ▸ a long, strong piece of wood or steel, used in buildings to support a floor or ceiling. **2. rayon, faisceau** ▸ a ray of light : *A beam of moonlight shone through the curtains.* ▲ VERB, beamed, beaming. **1. rayonner** ▸ to send out rays of light; shine. **2. sourire largement** ▸ to smile brightly or happily : *"The storekeeper was beaming. He was a happy man."* (E.B. White) SYN: shine, glow.

bean [been] NOUN, beans. **1. fève, haricot** ▸ a smooth, flat seed of some plants that is eaten as a vegetable, such as a lima bean or kidney bean. **2. cosse** ▸ the long pod in which bean seeds grow. Some kinds of bean pods, such as string beans, are eaten as vegetables. **3. grain, graine, fève** ▸ any other seed that looks like a bean : *Chocolate comes from cacao beans.*

bear¹ [hair] VERB, bore, borne or born, bearing. **1. supporter, soutenir, porter** ▸ to carry or support; hold up : *We didn't go skating on the pond, because the ice couldn't bear our weight.* **2. supporter** ▸ to put up with; endure : *Ravi couldn't bear to miss another soccer game.* **Note.** Something that can be borne or endured is bearable. **3. donner, porter fruit, donner naissance à** ▸ to bring forth or give birth to : *This apple tree bears delicious fruit.* **4. garder rancune** ▸ to hold in the mind : *Greta still bears a grudge against Hal after all these years.*

bear down a. pousser ▸ to press or push down. **b. foncer** ▸ to try hard : *You'd better bear down and get that job done.*

bear² NOUN, bears. **ours** ▸ a very large wild animal with thick fur, short legs, and sharp claws. **☞ p. 111.**

beard [beerd] NOUN, beards. **1. barbe** ▸ the hair that grows on a man's face. **2. barbe** ▸ something like a beard, such as the hair on a goat's chin. **☞ p. 975.**

bear-ing [BAIR-ing] NOUN, bearings. **1. port, maintien** ▸ the way a person stands, walks, and acts; manner. **2. rapport, lien** ▸ a connection in thought or meaning; relation : *"I mention this because it has some bearing on what is to follow."* (Joseph Conrad) **3. bearings. direction** ▸ a sense of where one is or is going : *"He got his bearings from his compass."* (William Steig) **4. essieu** ▸ a part of a machine that holds a moving part and allows it to move more easily. SYN: direction, way, course.

beast [beest] NOUN, beasts. **1. bête** ▸ any animal other than humans, especially a large, four-footed animal. **2. *Informal.* brute** ▸ a person who is very rude, cruel, or brutal : *Elbert is an absolute beast to his sister.* ■ **beastly,** ADJECTIVE. **1. bestial (-ale, -aux), brutal (-ale, -aux)** ▸ of or like a beast; brutal. **2. *Informal.* dégoûtant (-ante)** ▸ very unpleasant or nasty : *That was a beastly thing to say.* SYN: animal, creature, brute.

beat [beet] VERB, beat, beaten or beat, beating. **1. battre** ▸ to hit again and again; pound : *The rain was beating against the roof.* **2. battre** ▸ to get the better of; defeat : *Denise beats Nikki in Scrabble every time they play.* **3. battre** ▸ to move back and forth in a regular way : *"The bird stretched its neck and beat its wings."* (Lloyd Alexander) **4. battre** ▸ to stir rapidly; mix with force : *Beat the eggs with the shortening until the batter is fluffy.* **5. *Informal.* prendre de court** ▸ to confuse, bewilder : *It beats me how you can do those math problems so quickly.* ▲ NOUN, beats. **1. son** ▸ a blow or stroke made over and over : *We could hear the beat of the drums in the distance.* **2. battement** ▸ a single throb or pulse : *the beat of the heart.* **3. mesure, temps** ▸ a unit of time or accent in music. **4. rythme** ▸ in poetry, a stressed (strong) syllable in a word. The combination of beats creates the pattern of rhythm in a poem. **5. ronde** ▸ a regular route or round that is followed by someone in a job : *a police officer's beat.* ▲ ADJECTIVE. *Informal.* **épuisé (-ée)** ▸ very tired; exhausted : *I've got to go to bed early tonight; I'm beat.* SYN: hit, strike, knock.

beau-ti-ful [BYOO-tuh-ful] ADJECTIVE. **très beau (belle, beaux), magnifique** ▸ very pleasing to see or hear; giving pleasure to the senses or the mind : *a beautiful painting; a beautiful sunset; beautiful music.* ■ **beautifully,** ADVERB. ▸ **admirablement, à merveille.** *"She sang beautifully and would often entertain Charaxos as he ate or worked."* (Roger Lancelyn Green) **Note.** To make something beautiful is to beautify it. SYN: lovely, gorgeous.

beau-ty [BYOO-tee] NOUN, beauties. **1. beauté** ▸ the quality of being beautiful; very attractive to the eyes or other senses : *Jasper National Park is known for the beauty of its scenery.* **2. beauté** ▸ a person or thing that is beautiful : *Helen of Troy was a legendary beauty of Greek mythology.* SYN: loveliness.

bea-ver [BEE-vur] NOUN, beavers. **castor** ▸ a furry brown animal with a wide, flat tail, and webbed back feet for swimming. Beavers use their strong front teeth for gnawing down trees to build dams and nests (called lodges) in streams. The fur of the beaver was once considered very valuable and was used for coats and hats. **Note.**

beaver is the national symbol of Canada. ☞ p. 110.

be·cause [bih-KOZ *or* bih-KUZ] CONJUNCTION. **parce que ▶** for the reason that; on account of; since : *"Because she couldn't be seen, she could be squashed by koalas."* (Mem Fox) ✐ p. 52.

be·come [bih-KUM] VERB, became, become, becoming. **1. devenir ▶** to grow to be; come to be : *He became very excited when he heard the good news.* **2. bien aller à ▶** to look good on; suit :*You should wear that colour more often; it really becomes you.*

become of advenir de ▶ to happen to : *"But what has become of your beautiful piano?"* (Katherine Mansfield)

bed [bed] NOUN, beds. **1. lit ▶** a piece of furniture made for sleeping or resting on. **2. lit ▶** any place to sleep or rest : *Cinderella slept on a bed of rushes in the corner of the kitchen.* **3. carré, parterre ▶** a small area set aside for growing things : *Pansies and violets grow in the small flower bed near the back door.* **4. couche ▶** a layer at the bottom of something : *The contractors put down a bed of gravel before they set the stones of the patio.* **5. lit ▶** a layer under a body of water : *a river bed.* ▲ VERB, bedded, bedding. **se coucher, mettre au lit ▶** to put in a bed or go to bed : *The campers bedded down at 9 :00.* 🕮 p. 1065.

Bed·ou·in [BED-oh-in *or* BED-win] NOUN, Bedouin or Bedouins. **Bédouin (-ine) ▶** an Arab who is a nomadic herder in the deserts of the Middle East : *Most Bedouins are Muslims and speak Arabic.*

bed·room [BED-ROOM *or* bed-rum] NOUN, bedrooms. **chambre à coucher ▶** a room used for sleeping. 🕮 p. 1066.

bee [bee] NOUN, bees. **1. abeille ▶** an insect with four wings, a hairy body, and usually a stinger. Bees gather pollen and nectar from flowers. Some bees live together in beehives and make honey and beeswax. **Note.** A large group of bees is called a **swarm. 2. concours, compétition ▶** a gathering of people to do something together : *We have a spelling bee at school on the last Friday of the month.*

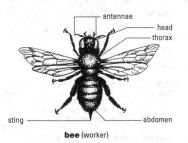

antennae
head
thorax

sting
abdomen

bee (worker)

✐ Writing Tips

Because

Because, as, and *since* are conjunctions *(words used to join other words, phrases, or clauses together), but there are small differences in the meanings of these words. You have to think about what you want to say before you choose what word to use.*

• *If you want to say "for the reason of," you can use either **because** or **since**.*

 *We didn't go hiking on Saturday **because** the trail was closed.*

 *I don't want to go to that movie, **since** I've already seen it.*

• *If you want to say "from the time of," use since.*

 *I've been waiting for you **since** lunch.*

• *If you want to say "during the time of," use as.*

 He whistled as he did the dishes.

beech [beech] NOUN. **hêtre ▶** a tree having smooth, light-grey bark and dark-green leaves. It produces a sweet-tasting nut. ☞ p. 104.

beef [beef] NOUN. **1. bœuf ▶** the meat from cattle. **2. bœuf (vache) ▶** a full-grown steer, cow, or bull that has been fattened for food. **3.** *Informal.* **plainte, objection ▶** an objection or complaint : *What's your beef with this idea?*

been [been *or* bin] VERB. a past form of be: *Megan has been very helpful today.*

beer [beer] NOUN, beers. **1. bière ▶** an alcoholic drink made from a mixture of water and a specially treated grain called **malt,** and flavoured with a fruit called **hops. 2. boisson gazeuse ▶** a soft drink made from the roots or leaves of various plants :*root beer.*

beet [beet] NOUN, beets. **betterave ▶** the thick, fleshy root of a certain kind of leafy plant. The red beet is eaten as a vegetable. Sugar is made from the white beet (also known as sugar beet).

bee·tle [BEE-tul] NOUN, beetles. **coléoptère ▶** an insect that has biting mouth parts and two hard front wings that cover its back wings when it is not flying. Common types of beetles are the ladybird or ladybug, the sweetpotato weevil, and the cucumber beetle. Some beetles cause damage to plants.

be·fore [bih-FOR] PREPOSITION. **1. avant ▶** earlier than : *The bus left just before 10:00.* **2. devant ▶** in front of : *"Startled, the old man looked down, and there before him stood a boy."* (Tololwa M.Mollel) ▲ ADVERB. **1. avant ▶** earlier : *Dinner will be ready at six, and not a moment* *before.* **2. avant, auparavant ▶** any time in the past : *I've never seen this movie before.* ▲ CONJUNCTION. **1. avant ▶** earlier than the time when : *You have to mail this in before the contest ends.* **2. avant, plutôt ▶** rather than : *I'd wait in line all night before I'd miss this concert.* SYN : earlier, prior, previously.

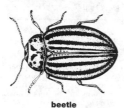

beetle

be-friend [bih-FREND] VERB. **se lier d'amitié ▶** to act as a friend to : *Wan befriended a stray dog.*

beg [beg] VERB, begged, begging. **1. mendier ▶** to ask for something as a gift because one is poor or needy : *The homeless man begged for food.* **2. supplier, prier ▶** to ask as a favour in a serious or polite way : *She begged him not to drive so fast on the icy roads.* SYN : plead, appeal.

beg-gar [BEG-ur] NOUN, beggars. **1. mendiant (-ante) ▶** a person who begs, especially one who lives by begging. **2. mendiant (-ante) ▶** a very poor person.

be-gin [bih-GIN] VERB, began, begun, beginning. **1. commencer, entamer ▶** to do the first part ; begin : *We will begin a new book today.* **2. commencer, débuter ▶** to come into being ; start to exist : *The party begins at 7:00.* SYN : start, commence.

be-gin-ner [bih-GIN-ur] NOUN, beginners. **débutant (-ante) ▶** a person who is starting to do something for the first time : *Ava dances very well for a beginner.* SYN : novice, learner, amateur.

be-gin-ning [bih-GIN-ing] NOUN, beginnings. **1. commencement ▶** a start : *When Sus and I met at summer camp, it was the begining of a long friendship.* **2. début ▶** the earliest part of something : *The beginning of the book was boring, but it got exciting later on.* SYN : start, source, root, origin.

be-go-nia [buh-GOH-nyuh] NOUN, begonias. **bégonia ▶** a plant with red, white, or pink flowers and large leaves.

be-half [bih-HAF] NOUN. **au nom de, de la part de, pour ▶** one's interest or side : *"I write again so soon because I have been making inquiries on your behalf."* (Barbara Nichol)

on behalf of or in behalf of **au nom de ▶** in the interest of : *On behalf of all the members, I'd like to welcome you to our club.* SYN : interest, good, benefit, welfare.

be-have [bih-HAYV] VERB, behaved, behaving. **1. se comporter, se conduire ▶** to act or do things in a certain way : *"Let me also explain to you how you must behave while you are a guest in the palace."* (Adèle Geras) **2. se conduire bien, se comporter bien ▶** to act properly ; do what is right : *Mom says that if we behave, we will get to stay up to watch the movie.*

be-hav-iour [bih-HAYV-yur] NOUN, behaviours. (also behavior) **comportement, conduite ▶** a way of acting ; behaving : *The scientists went to Africa to study the behaviour of elephants.* 🗋 p. 1027. SYN : conduct, action, acts.

be-hind [be-HIND] PREPOSITION. **1. derrière ▶** at or toward the back of : *He tied the apron behind his back.* **2. en retard, avoir du retard ▶** later than ; after : *Because of the storm, all the planes are behind schedule.* **3. avec ▶** in support of : *Everyone's behind the idea of a new library.* ▲ ADVERB. **1. derrière ▶** at the back ; in the rear : *The other car followed behind.* **2. prendre du retard, être en retard ▶** not on time ; slow ; late : *Glen worked hard because he didn't want to fall behind in school.*

beige [BAYZH] NOUN ; ADJECTIVE. **beige ▶** a pale-brown or greyish-tan colour : *Beige is the colour of sand.*

be-ing [BEE-ing] VERB. **verbe être ▶** the present participle of be. *Chloe is being very secretive about her plans.* ▲ NOUN. **1. existence ▶** life or existence : *Scientists aren't sure when the earth came into being.* **2. beings. être ▶** a person or animal ; a living creature : *Science-fiction stories often tell about beings from another planet.*

be-lief [bih-LEEF] NOUN, beliefs. **1. croyance, conviction ▶** something that is thought to be true or real : *It was once a common belief that the sun moved around the earth.* **2. croyance, foi ▶** the acceptance of something as true or real : *People of many religious faiths share a belief in an afterlife.* SYN : faith, conviction, confidence, trust.

be-lieve [bih-LEEV] VERB, believed, believing. **1. croire ▶** to think of as true or real : *No one believed Stan's story about seeing aliens from outer space.* **Note.** Something that can be believed is believable. **2. croire ▶** to have confidence or trust in : *I believe Tina is telling the truth.* **3. croire ▶** to think ; suppose : *I'm not sure, but I believe you are right.* **4. croire ▶** to have religious faith : *to believe in God.* ✎ p. 54.

make believe faire croire, faire semblant ▶ to pretend : *The children sipped water from the cups, making believe it was tea.*

✏ Word Builder

Believe, assume, and *suppose* all mean to think that something is probably true. *Believe* has the idea that the thought is based on facts : *From what our neighbours have said, I believe this house was built in 1952.* *Assume* indicates that a certain fact can be accepted : *We can assume this house was built after World War II, because it is not in this 1945 picture.* *Suppose* suggests that the thought is not exact : *I would suppose that this house is about 50 years old.*

bell [bel] NOUN, bells. **1. cloche** ▸ a hollow object that makes a ringing sound. A bell is shaped like an upside-down cup and is usually made of metal. **2. sonnette, timbre** ▸ anything that makes a ringing sound : *I think that must be the doorbell.* **3. cloche, pavillon** ▸ anything shaped like a bell : *the bell of a trumpet.*

bel·low [BEL-oh] VERB, bellowed, bellowing. **beugler, mugir** ▸ to make a loud, deep noise, like the sound made by a bull : *"'Quiet!' bellowed the tent leader. 'I want quiet in this tent!'"* (E.B. White) ▲ NOUN, bellows. **beuglement, mugissement** ▸ a loud, deep noise; a roar.

bel·ly [BEL-ee] NOUN, bellies. **1. ventre, bedaine** ▸ the part of the body that contains the stomach; the abdomen. **2. ventre** ▸ a lower part of something that is thought to be like this part of the body : *The airplane had to land on its belly after the wheels failed to come down.* ▲ VERB, bellied, bellying. **(s') enfler, (se) gonfler** ▸ to swell out; bulge : *The ship's sails bellied in the wind.* SYN: abdomen, stomach.

be·long [bih-LONG] VERB, belonged, belonging. **1. aller, se ranger** ▸ to have a proper place : *The sweaters belong in the top drawer.* **2. belong to. a. appartenir** ▸ to be the property of; be owned by : *All that land belongs to the Kwans.* **b. faire partie de** ▸ to be a member of : *Zafar and I belong to the same skating club.*

be·long·ings [bih-LONG-ings] PLURAL NOUN. **affaires** ▸ the things a person owns; possessions : *He carried his few belongings in the pack on his back.* SYN: possessions, property.

be·lov·ed [bih-LUV-id *or* bih-LUVD] ADJECTIVE. **bien-aimé (-ée)** ▸ dearly loved : *Our dog is beloved by the whole family.* ▲ NOUN. **bien-aimé (-ée)** ▸ a person who is dearly loved. ✏ **p. 221.**

be·low [bih-LOH] ADVERB. **1. en bas** ▸ in or at a lower place : *He called, "Watch out below!" before he jumped.* **2. en bas** ▸ to a lower floor; downstairs : *During the storm, the captain asked the passengers to go below.* ▲ ADJECTIVE. **moins, sous zéro** ▸ less than zero on a temperature scale : *It's 10 degrees below today.* ▲ PREPOSITION. **1. en bas, sous, plus bas** ▸ lower than; under : *The broom is in the closet below the stairs.* **2. au-dessous, sous** ▸ less than; lower in rank or dignity than : *On a ship, the first mate is just below the captain.*

belt [belt] NOUN, belts. **1. ceinture** ▸ a strip of leather, cloth, or other material that is worn around the waist to hold up clothing or as decoration. **2. région, zone** ▸ a place or area that is thought of as being like a belt : *Saskatchewan is part of Canada's wheat belt.* **3. courroie** ▸ a long circular band that turns two or more wheels or moves things from one place to another : *In a car, a fan belt turns a fan to cool the engine.* ▲ VERB, belted, belting. **1. ceinturer, ceindre** ▸ to put a belt on or around something. **2. frapper fort, donner une raclée** ▸ to hit hard : *The batter belted the ball out of the park.* ✏ **p. 1007.**

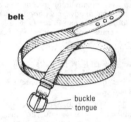

belt

buckle
tongue

be·lu·ga [buh-LOO-guh] NOUN, belugas. **1. béluga ou bélouga** ▸ a white toothed whale found from the Arctic to the Gulf of St. Lawrence. The beluga whale does not have a dorsal fin. **2. béluga ou bélouga** ▸ a large white sturgeon that is found in the Black and Caspian Seas. It is the largest inland fish in the world. ◉ **p. 110.**

bench [bench] NOUN, benches. **1. banc, banquette** ▸ a long seat for several people : *Hugh sat on the park bench and ate his lunch.* **2. établi** ▸ a strong table for working on : *a carpenter's bench.* **3. banc** ▸ the place where a judge sits in a courtroom : *The judge asked the lawyers to approach the bench.* **4. siège** ▸ the official position of a judge or judges. ▲ VERB, benched, benching. **retirer du jeu** ▸ to keep a player out of a game : *The coach benched Luna because she missed practice this week.*

bend [bend] VERB, bent, bending. **1. courber, plier, tordre** ▸ to make or become curved or crooked : *"I should bend a hairpin in the shape of a fishhook."* (E.B. White) **2. (se) pencher, (se) courber** ▸ to move part of the body lower; stoop down : *"She bent over him and wiped his face with the sleeve of her wet coat."* (Eve Bunting) ▲ NOUN, bends. **tournant, virage ▸** a curve or turn; angle : *Our house is just past the bend in the road.* SYN : curve, twist, crook.

be-neath [bih-NEETH] PREPOSITION. **1. au-dessous, sous ▸** in a lower place; below; under : *"The seal must have heard the sound beneath the water."* (James Houston) **2. au-dessous ▸** not worthy of : *Copying someone else's work is beneath you.* ▲ ADVERB. **sous, en dessous, au-dessous ▸** under; below : *"Wu walked over to the pack horses and threw back the covers to reveal the stacks of books beneath."* (David Day) SYN : below, under, underneath.

ben-e-fit [BEN-uh-fit] NOUN, benefits. **1. avantage, bienfait ▸** something that is good or helpful; an advantage : *Eating fresh fruits and vegetables can be a benefit to your health.* **2. représentation au profit de ▸** a public event or entertainment to raise money for a person or cause : *The orchestra played at a benefit for flood relief.* **3. benefits. indemnité, allocation ▸** money paid to a person by the government or an insurance company : *Clark received disability benefits when he was injured at work.* **4. indemnité, allocation ▸** something of value that a worker receives from an employer in addition to regular pay, such as paid holidays, health insurance, or a pension. **Note.** These are also called fringe benefits. ▲ VERB, benefitted, benefitting. **bénéficier, profiter ▸** (also benefited, benefiting) to be helpful to; be good for : *I think we'll all benefit from a good night's sleep.* **Note.** A thing from which one benefits is beneficial. SYN : profit, favour, advantage.

be-nev-o-lence [buh-NEV-uh-luns] NOUN, benevolences. **1. bienveillance ▸** good will; kindly feeling : *You could see the benevolence in his friendly face.* **2. bienveillance ▸** an act of kindness; something good that is done : *Her students never forgot her many benevolences.* ■ **benevolent,** ADJECTIVE: ▸ **bienveillant (-ante), disposé (-ée). ▸** *He was respected for his benevolent acts.* SYN : kindness, generosity, good will, charity.

be-nign [buh-NINE] ADJECTIVE. **1. doux (douce), bienveillant ▸** kindly; good-natured : *a benign smile.* **2. bénin (-igne) ▸** doing little or no harm : *A benign tumour is not a danger to health.*

bent [bent] VERB. ▸ a past form of bend: *I bent over to tie my shoelaces.* ▲ ADJECTIVE. **1. plié (-ée), courbé (-ée) ▸** not straight; curved or crooked : *One of the legs of the old table is badly bent.* **2. déterminé (-ée), résolu (-ue) ▸** set in one's mind; determined : *She is bent on running in the race.* SYN : twisted.

Be-o-thuk [bee-OTH-uk or bee-OT-uk] NOUN. **1. Beothuk ▸** the original inhabitants of Newfoundland, now extinct. **2. Beothuk ▸** a member of this group. **3. beothuk ▸** the language of these people.

be-queath [bee-KWEETH] VERB, bequeathed, bequeathing. **1. léguer ▸** to leave or give by will : *The duke bequeathed all his property to his first-born son.* **2. transmettre ▸** to pass on; hand down : *My parents bequeathed their love of reading to me.*

be-ret [BAIR-ay or buh-RAY] NOUN, berets. **béret ▸** a soft, round, flat cap, usually made of wool or felt.

ber-ry [BAIR-ee] NOUN, berries. **1. baie ▸** a small, juicy fruit that can be eaten, such as a strawberry or blueberry. **2. fruit ▸** any of various seeds or dried kernels : *a wheat berry; the coffee berry.* ▲ VERB, berried, berrying. **aller à la cueillette des baies ▸** to pick or gather berries : *Every summer we go berrying near the lake.* 👁 p. 251.

berth [burth] NOUN, berths. **1. couchette ▸** a space for sleeping on a train, plane, or ship : *Dana found it very hard to sleep in the narrow, hard berth on the train.* **2. poste d'amarrage ▸** a place to dock a ship.

be-side [bih-SIDE] PREPOSITION. **1. à côté de, auprès de ▸** at the side of; near : *He stopped and picked an apple from beside the road.* 👁 **p. 56. 2. hors de propos, en dehors du sujet ▸** away or apart from the main point of issue : *The price of a ticket to the concert is beside the point, since all the seats are already sold out.* **3. à côté de ▸** compared with : *My sweater looks old beside yours.*

beside oneself fou de joie, de colère, etc. ▸ very upset or excited : *"The Swan Boat passengers were beside themselves with youth and excitement."* (E.B. White)

be-sides [bih-SIDEZ] ADVERB. **en plus, sans compter, en outre ▸** in addition; also : *He owns three cars and a motorcycle besides.* ▲ PREPOSITION. **en plus ▸** in addition to : *Besides the family, two dogs live in the house.* SYN : also, too, moreover, as well. 👁 **p. 56.**

best [best] ADJECTIVE. **1. meilleur (-eure) ▸** of the highest quality; most excellent : *Zoren won first prize because he had the best science project.* **2. meilleur (-eure), préféré (-ée) ▸** most desirable, favourite : *Jess is my best friend.* ▲ ADVERB. **1. le mieux ▸** in the most excellent way : *You look best in this colour.* **2. le mieux ▸** to the highest degree; most : *Which story did you like best?* 👁 **p. 267.** ▲ NOUN. **1. le meilleur (la meilleure) ▸** a person or thing that is the most excellent. **2. faire de son mieux ▸** one's finest effort or condition : *Let's give our best in the game today.* **3. meilleurs souhaits ▸** good wishes; greeting : *Give Amy my best when you see her.* **at best au mieux ▸** under the most favourable conditions : *We have a chance to finish third at best.*

get the best of l'**emporter** ▶ defeat : *Don't let your fear get the best of you.* **make the best of** s'**arranger, s'accommoder** ▶ make do; do as well as possible with : *We've run out of the main dish, so we'll have to make the best of what's left.*

bet [bet] NOUN, bets. **1. pari** ▶ an agreement between two people or groups that the one who is wrong will give money or something of value to the one who is right. **2. pari** ▶ the amount risked in a bet : *Kevin made a bet of 25 cents that he could hit a home run.* ▲ VERB, bet or betted, betting. **1. parier** ▶ to agree to a bet : *to bet on who will win a hockey game.* **2. croire fermement** ▶ to believe strongly : *I bet it will rain tonight.* SYN : wager, gamble.

be-tray [bih-TRAY] VERB, betrayed, betraying. **1. trahir** ▶ to be unfaithful to; be false to : *He betrayed his country when he sold secret information to the enemy.* **2. trahir** ▶ to show or reveal something that one would like to hide : *"The warmth of that smile dried up the betraying tears."* (Jean Little) **Note.** The act of betraying someone or something is a betrayal.

bet-ter [BET-ur] ADJECTIVE. **1. mieux, meilleur (-eure)** ▶ of higher quality; more excellent : *This new computer is much better than our old one.* **2. aller mieux, se rétablir, se remettre** ▶ improved in health or condition : *She was sick last week, but she is better now.* **3. la plus grande partie, la majeure partie** ▶ larger : *We plan to be gone the better part of the summer.* ✐ **p. 267.** ▲ ADVERB. **1. mieux** ▶ in a more excellent way : *The car runs better after a tune-up.* **2. plus de** ▶ more : *He's been teaching math for better than 20 years.* ▲ NOUN, betters. **le meilleur (la meilleure)** ▶ the more excellent of two. ▲ VERB, bettered, bettering. s'**améliorer** ▶ to make better; improve : *Sam tried to better himself by studying hard.*

be-tween [bih-TWEEN] PREPOSITION. **1. entre** ▶ in the place or time that keeps two things apart : *February is the month between January and March.* **2. entre** ▶ having to do with; involving : *Let's have a private talk, just between you and me.* **3. entre** ▶ in relation to another : *What's the difference between a crocodile and an alligator?* ▲ ADVERB. **entre les deux** ▶ in the place or time separating : *He owns those two houses and the land between.* ✐ **p. 20, 56.**

bev-er-age [BEV-uh-rij or BEV-rij] NOUN, beverages. **boisson** ▶ a liquid for drinking; any drink : *Milk, orange juice, and coffee are popular beverages.*

be-ware [bih-WAIR] VERB. **faire attention, prendre garde (à)** ▶ to be on guard against; watch out for : *They had a big sign on their fence that said "Beware of Dog."*

be-wil-der [bih-WIL-dur] VERB, bewildered, bewildering. **désorienter, dérouter, confondre** ▶ to confuse completely; puzzle : *She was bewildered by the signs in a different language.* **Note.** The state of being bewildered is bewilderment : *He shook his head in bewilderment.* SYN : confuse, baffle, puzzle.

be-yond [bih-YOND] PREPOSITION. **1. au-delà, plus loin que** ▶ on or to the far side of : *Don't swim out to the deep water beyond the rock!* **2. plus tard que, passé** ▶ later than; past : *As a special treat, Jamie got to stay up beyond his regular bedtime.* **4. me dépasse** ▶ outside a person's knowledge or understanding : *How you could have acted that way is beyond me.* ▲ ADVERB. **au-delà** ▶ farther away : *"Lee looked out over the fields toward the swamp and the oak woods beyond."* (Judy Allen)

bi- PREFIX. two : *A bicycle has two wheels. A person who is bilingual can speak two languages.*

bi-as [BY-us] NOUN, biases. **parti pris, préjugé** ▶ a strong feeling about something without good reason; prejudice : *A referee should not show any bias for or against either team.* ▲ VERB, biased, biasing. (also biassed, biassing) to cause to have a prejudiced view.

Bi-ble [BY-bul] NOUN. **1. (Bible) Bible** ▶ the sacred book of writing of the Christian religion, consisting of the Old Testament and the New Testament. The Old Testament is also sacred to the Jewish religion. **2. bible. bible** ▶ any book that is accepted as the highest authority in a particular field : *Dr. Benjamin Spock's Baby and Child Care is known as the bible of child-raising.* **Note.** The word bible comes from the same ancient Greek word as bibliography. Both come from the name of a town that was famous for producing writing paper.

✐ **Writing Tips**

Beside—Besides

Beside and *besides* mean different things. To help you remember which word to use, think about what each word means.

• *Beside* means "next to."
  Our cars were parked beside each other.
• *Besides* means "in addition to; also."
  Besides my sister, my best friend came along too.

✐ **Writing Tips**

Between You and Me

Sometimes when people use the phrase between you and me, they aren't sure whether to use "me" or "I." The correct phrase is always between you and me.

bib·li·cal [BIB-luh-kul] ADJECTIVE. (also Biblical) **1. biblique ▸** having to do with the Bible; found in the Bible. **2. biblique ▸** according to the Bible.

bib·li·og·ra·phy [bib-lee-OG-ruh-fee] NOUN, bibliographies. **bibliographie ▸** a list of books or articles about a particular subject, or by a particular author. A bibliography often appears in a book of information or a factual report to show which sources the writer consulted for information. ✎ **p. 57.**

bick·er [BIK-ur] VERB. **se quereller, se chamailler ▸** to quarrel over something unimportant; argue in a childish or petty way.

✍ Writing Tips

Bibliography

*A **bibliography** is a list of books or articles about a certain subject or written by a particular author. Bibliographies often appear in non-fiction books or reports.*

• *When you include information from any source or directly quote from any book or article, these references should be listed in a bibliography. Some bibliographies also include other books the writer feels will be useful to the reader.*

• *Four things should be included in each entry: the author's name, the title, who published the book, and when it was published.*

The entries are listed in alphabetical order by the author's last name.

> *Lee, Dennis. Alligator Pie. Toronto: Macmillan Canada, 1974.*
>
> *Lunn, Janet, and Christopher Moore. The Story of Canada. Toronto: Key Porter Books/Lester Publishing, 1992.*

---

bi·cy·cle [BY-suh-kul] NOUN, bicycles. **bicyclette ▸** a vehicle with two large wheels, one behind the other. A bicycle has a seat, handlebars for steering, and foot pedals to turn the back wheel. ▲ VERB, bicycled, bicycling. **faire de la bicyclette ▸** to ride a bicycle. **Note.** Someone who rides a bicycle is a bicyclist or cyclist. 📖 **p. 1152.** 👁 **p. 58.**

bid [bid] VERB, bade or bid, bidden or bid, bidding. **1. dire, souhaiter ▸** to say as a greeting; tell : *They bid their parents goodbye and then set off on their camping trip.* **2. ordonner, commander ▸** to say as an order; command : *"He must be taught, and trained and bid go forth."* (William Shakespeare) **3. faire une offre ▸** to offer a certain price for something : *She bid $200 for an antique chair at the auc-*

tion. ▲ NOUN, bids. **1. soumission ▸** an offer to pay or accept a certain price : *The contract to build the new school was awarded to the company that made the lowest bid.* **2. tentative ▸** an attempt to obtain or become : *The premier made a bid for re-election.* ■ **bidder,** NOUN. ▸ **offrant.** *That land will be sold to the highest bidder.* SYN : command, order, direct.

bid·ding [BID-ing] NOUN, biddings. **1. ordre ▸** an order; command : *The sailors moved quickly to do the captain's bidding.* **2. enchère ▸** the act of making of a bid.

big [big] ADJECTIVE, bigger, biggest. **1. grand (-e) ▸** great in amount or size; large : *We want a house with a big yard so that we can have a garden.* **2. grand (grande), aîné (-ée) ▸** grown up or older : *Jeannie shares a bedroom with her big sister.* **3. important (-ante), grand (grande) ▸** important : *Our biggest game is this weekend; it will decide the championship.* SYN : large, great, huge, important.

Big·foot [BIG-foot] **Sasquatch ▸** a large, hairy creature that some people believe lives in the mountains of the Pacific Northwest. **Note.** Also known as Sasquatch.

big·horn [BIG-horn] NOUN, bighorn or bighorns. **grand mouton sauvage ▸** a large, wild sheep of the Rocky Mountains. Bighorns are known for their large, curling horns. Their hoofs are specially formed to enable them to climb steep rocks. 👁 **p. 110.**

big·ot [BIG-ut] NOUN, bigots. **sectaire ▸** a person who is intolerant and prejudiced. ■ **bigoted,** ADJECTIVE. **sectaire, sectarisme ▸** narrow-minded; prejudiced. ■ **bigotry,** NOUN. the fact of being a bigot.

bike [bike] NOUN, bikes. **vélo, bicyclette ▸** short for bicycle or motorcycle.

bi·lin·gual [by-LING-gyoo-ul or by-LING-gwal] ADJECTIVE. **bilingue ▸** able to speak two languages fluently.

bill¹ [bil] NOUN, bills. **1. facture ▸** a statement of money owed for things bought or used, or work done : *a utility bill.* **2. billet ▸** a piece of paper money : *Hans paid for the shirt with a $20 bill.* **3. projet de loi ▸** a proposed law : *A bill must go through three readings in Parliament before it becomes a law.* **4. affiche, placard ▸** a printed advertisement or public notice. ▲ VERB, billed, billing. **1. facturer ▸** to send a statement of money owed : *The phone company bills us every month.* **2. annoncer, afficher ▸** to announce or advertise by bills or posters : *The singer billed her concert at the music hall as her farewell performance.*

bill² NOUN, bills. **1. bec ▸** the horny, projecting mouth parts of a bird; a beak. **2. bec ▸** anything that looks like a bird's bill : *the bill of a cap.*

bill·board [BIL-bord] NOUN, billboards. **panneau (-eaux) d'affichage ▸** a large board used to

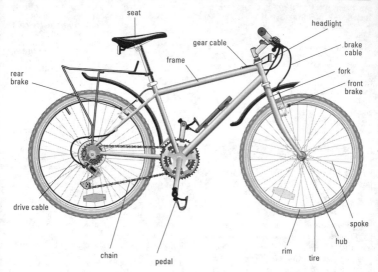

bicycle

display advertisements or announcements to the public.

bil·lion [BIL-yun] NOUN, billions. **milliard ▸** one thousand million, written as 1,000,000,000. **Note.** Someone who has a billion dollars is a billionaire.

Bill of Rights **la Charte des droits et libertés ▸** a statement of human rights and basic freedoms in a country. In Canada, the Bill of Rights was first passed by Parliament in 1960.

bil·low [BIL-oh] NOUN, billows. **lame, nuages ▸** a great wave or rising of something, such as a large mass of water, smoke, or steam. ▲ VERB, billowed, billowing. **ondoyer, se gonfler ▸** to rise or swell in a great mass : *Steam and smoke billowed from the chimneys.*

bin [bin] NOUN, bins. **coffre, bac, boîte, corbeille ▸** an enclosed box or space for storing loose items, such as flour or laundry.

bind [bynd] VERB, bound, binding. **1. attacher, lier ▸** to tie or fasten together : *She bound her hair with a red ribbon.* **2. lier, obliger, astreindre ▸** to unite or keep something together, as by love, law, or duty : *The witness was bound to tell the truth.* **3. relier ▸** to fasten in a cover : *Years ago books were bound by hand.* **Note.** A binder is a thing that binds, such as a machine that binds books or a folder used to hold loose papers together.

bi·noc·u·lars [buh-NOK-yuh-lurz] PLURAL NOUN. **jumelles ▸** a device made of two small telescopes fastened together made for use with both eyes. Binoculars make distant objects appear closer and larger.

bio- PREFIX. having to do with life : *Biochemistry is the chemistry of living things.*

bi·o·de·grad·a·ble [BY-oh-duh-GRAY-duh-bul] ADJECTIVE. **biodégradable ▸** able to break down, rot, or decay by a natural process : *This paper is biodegradable because it is made from wood, which is a natural substance.*

bi·og·ra·phy [by-OG-ruh-fee] NOUN, biographies. **biographie ▸** the written history of a person's life. ■ **biographical,** ADJECTIVE: of or having to do with a person's life. ▸ **biographique.** **Note.** Someone who writes a biography is a biographer. ✐ **p. 59.**

bi·ol·o·gy [by-OL-uh-jee] NOUN. **biologie ▸** the scientific study of plants and animals. Biology is the study of the physical makeup of living things : their development, reproduction, and relationship to their environment. It also deals with the origin and history of life on earth. **Note.** An expert in biology is a biologist.

bi·o·log·i·cal [BY-uh-LOJ-uh-kul], ADJECTIVE. **biologique ▸** having to do with or part of biology : *Botany is one of the biological sciences.*

✍ Writing Tips

Biography

*A **biography** is someone's life story told by someone else. A biography tells the major events of a person's life. Usually the person is famous, such as a politician, an athlete, an artist, an actor, or someone who has done something special in his or her life. Biographies are based on careful research. In autobiographies writers tell their own life story. You can find biographies and **autobiographies** in the non-fiction section of the library.*

bison

birch [burch] NOUN, birches. **bouleau (-eaux)** ▸ a tree with hard wood and smooth white bark that is easily peeled off in thin layers. Some Native Peoples used strips of birch bark to make canoes. 👁 **p. 254.**

bird [burd] NOUN, birds. **oiseau (-eaux)** ▸ an animal that has wings and a body covered with feathers. Birds are warm-blooded and have a backbone. They lay eggs, and most kinds can fly. 📖 **p. 1084.** 👁 **p. 108.**

birth [burth] NOUN, births. **1. naissance** ▸ the act or fact of being born; the beginning of life : *to give birth to a baby.* **2. naissance, genèse** ▸ the start or beginning of something : *the birth of a nation; the birth of the Space Age.* 📖 **p. 1143.** SYN: beginning, origin, inception, start.

birth·day [BURTH-DAY] NOUN, birthdays. **1. jour de naissance** ▸ the day on which a person is born. **2. anniversaire** ▸ the date on which this day falls in later years : *Megan's birthday is December 19.* 📖 **p. 1143.**

bis·cuit [BIS-kit] NOUN, biscuits. **biscuit** ▸ a small baked roll made from flour and baking powder, baking soda, or yeast.

bi·sect [by-SEKT or BY-sekt] VERB, bisected, bisecting. **couper en deux** ▸ to cut or divide in two equal parts : *The yellow line bisects the highway.*

bish·op [BISH-up] NOUN, bishops. **1. évêque** ▸ in a Christian church, a high-ranking member of the clergy or a minister, especially one who is in charge of a church district. **2. fou** ▸ in chess, a game piece that can move diagonally on the board.

bi·son [BY-sun] NOUN, bison. **bison** ▸ a large animal with short horns, a humped back, and a shaggy mane that is related to the ox. **Note.** The North American animal found on the western plains was mistakenly called a buffalo; it is actually a bison.

bit¹ [bit] NOUN, bits. **1. (petit) morceau** ▸ a small piece or amount : *I'll have just a bit of cake.* **2. instant** ▸ a short period of time : *I'll be ready to go in just a bit.* SYN: piece, crumb, lump.

bit² [bit] NOUN, bits. **1. mors** ▸ the metal part of a bridle that fits into a horse's mouth to control the horse's movements. **2. mèche, foret** ▸ a tool used for cutting or drilling.

bit³ VERB. a past form of bite: *I chipped my tooth when I bit into that piece of candy.*

bit⁴ NOUN, bits. **bit** ▸ the smallest unit of information that can be stored and used by a computer.

bite [bite] VERB, bit, bitten or bit, biting. **1. mordre, croquer** ▸ to cut, hold, or tear with the teeth : *to bite into an apple.* **2. mordre, piquer** ▸ to wound with fangs, a stinger, or teeth : *Does that dog bite?* **3. mordre, couper, piquer** ▸ to cause a sharp pain to; sting : *"The air bit her cheeks…with cold."* (Laura Ingalls Wilder) **4. mordre** ▸ to take or swallow bait : *Are the fish biting today?* ▲ NOUN, bites. **1. morsure** ▸ the act or fact of biting. **2. morsure, piqûre** ▸ a wound or injury that comes from biting : *a mosquito bite.* **3. bouchée** ▸ a small bit of food taken at one time; a mouthful. **4. bouchée** ▸ a light meal; snack : *Let's stop for a bite to eat.*

bit·ter [BIT-ur] ADJECTIVE. **1. amer (-ère)** ▸ having a sharp, unpleasant taste : *That medicine has a bitter taste.* **2. cinglant (-ante)** ▸ very harsh or sharp; stinging : *We felt the bitter wind on our cheeks.* **3. amer (-ère)** ▸ having angry or unhappy feelings : *He's very bitter about being fired from his job.* ▪ **bitterly,** ADVERB. ▸ **amèrement, farouchement.** *"Mr. Parnell began bitterly protesting at being abandoned."* (Lloyd Alexander) ▪ **bitterness,** NOUN. **amertume** ▸ SYN: sharp, sour, biting, pungent.

bi·zarre [buh-ZAR] ADJECTIVE. **bizarre** ▸ very odd or unusual; fantastic : *Some science-fiction stories have bizarre characters.*

black [blak] NOUN, blacks. **1. noir** ▸ a colour that is the opposite of white; the darkest colour. **2.** (also Black) **Noir (Noire)** ▸ a person with dark skin who is of African origin. ▲ ADJECTIVE, blacker, blackest. **1. noir (noire)** ▸ having the colour black : *Mark has black hair.* **2.** (also Black) **noir (noire)** ▸ of or having to do with people of African origin : *Black history; Black literature.* **3. sombre, noir (noire)** ▸ without light : *The sky was black, with no moon or stars.*

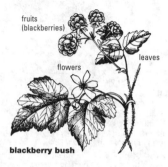

fruits
(blackberries)

leaves

flowers

blackberry bush

black-ber-ry [BLAK-BAIR-ee] NOUN, blackberries. **mûre** ▸ a small black berry that grows on a prickly bush. Blackberries are sweet-tasting and juicy, and are used for making jam and pies. 👁 **p. 251.**

black-bird [BLAK-BURD] NOUN, blackbirds. **merle** ▸ any of several birds that are so called because the male is mostly black. The male yellow-headed blackbird has a crest of yellow feathers on its head; the male redwing blackbird has a bright red marking on each wing. 👁 **p. 109.**

black-board [BLAK-BORD] NOUN, blackboards. **tableau, tableau noir** ▸ a smooth, hard surface that is used for writing or drawing with chalk, as in school classrooms. Blackboards are made of slate or other hard materials. **Note.** Such boards are now often light green or another colour rather than black, and so are also called chalk-boards.

black-fly [BLAK-FLY] NOUN, blackflies. **mouche noire** ▸ a small black or grey fly whose bite is painful.

Black-foot [BLAK-FOOT] NOUN. **1. Black foot** ▸ a confederacy of three groups of Algonquian peoples (the Blackfoot, the Blood, and the Peigan) from the western plains. **2. black foot** ▸ the people or language of these groups.

black hole 1. trou noir ▸ an object or region in outer space where the inward pull of gravity is so strong that no light or matter can escape. **2.** *Informal.* **gouffre** ▸ something that consumes a great deal of money and effort without offering any real benefit.

black-mail [BLAK-MALE] VERB, blackmailed, blackmailing. **soumettre à un chantage, faire chanter** ▸ to get money or favour from someone by threatening to tell something bad about the person : *Tim tried to blackmail Goran with information about his involvement in a robbery.* ▲ NOUN. **chantage** ▸ the crime of blackmailing someone, or the money or favour given.

black-out [BLAK-OWT] NOUN, blackouts. **1. panne de courant, panne d'électricité** ▸ the shutting down of electrical power in a certain area : *The blackout was caused by a car knocking down electrical wires.* **2. évanouissement, syncope** ▸ a loss of consciousness for a short time : *She has been having blackouts ever since the car accident.* **3. black-out** ▸ a temporary ban or shut-down : *The government imposed a news blackout during the war.* **Note.** Also used as a VERB: *The pilot almost blacked out when the plane went into a dive.*

blad-der [BLAD-ur] NOUN, bladders. **1. vessie** ▸ a small, baglike body part that holds waste liquid called **urine** before it is expelled from the body. **2. vésicule** ▸ a flexible bag that fits inside a ball or other container to hold air. ■ **blade** [blade] NOUN, blades. **1. lame** ▸ the sharp, flat cutting edge of a knife, sword, or tool. **2. pale** ▸ a thin, flat part that is like the blade of a knife : *The blades of the propeller began to whirl faster.*

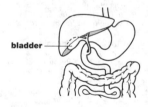

bladder

blame [blame] VERB, blamed, blaming. **1. blâmer, reprocher** ▸ to hold responsible for something wrong or bad : *The fans blamed the goalie for losing the game because he let in two easy goals.* **2. reprocher** ▸ to find fault with : *Mother blames Placido's low grades on the fact that he doesn't study enough.* ▲ NOUN. **faute, tort, reproche, responsabilité** ▸ responsibility for something wrong or bad : *Rob put the blame on his sister for breaking the window, but it was really his fault.* **Note.** Someone who does not deserve blame is blameless. SYN: accuse, charge.

bland [bland] ADJECTIVE, blander, blandest. **doux (douce), fade** ▸ not irritating; mild; soothing : *Applesauce is a bland food.*

blank [blank] ADJECTIVE, blanker, blankest. **1. blanc (blanche), vierge ▸** without printing or writing : *She pulled out a blank piece of paper and began writing.* **2. vide, sans expression ▸** vacant or empty : *Ned had a blank look on his face.* ▲ NOUN, blanks. **1. espace ▸** a space to be filled in on a form or document : *Write your name in the blank at the top of the page.* **2. formulaire ▸** a form or document having such space : *She filled out all the information requested on the entry blank.* **3. à blanc ▸** a cartridge having gunpowder, but no bullet. SYN : empty, void, vacant.

blan-ket [BLANG-kit] NOUN, blankets. **1. couverture ▸** a large covering made of soft, warm cloth, used primarily on a bed. **2. manteau, couche ▸** anything that covers things as a blanket does : *A blanket of daisies covered the field.* ▲ VERB, blanketed, blanketing. **recouvrir ▸** to cover with or as if with a blanket : *"A heavy silence blanketed the room."* (James Herriot)

blare [blair] VERB, blared, blaring. **retentir ▸** to sound loudly and harshly : *"A radio was blaring dance music."* (Arthur C. Clarke) ▲ NOUN, blares. **bruit éclatant ▸** a loud, harsh sound : *We heard the blare of sirens as the fire trucks raced by.*

blast [blast] NOUN, blasts. **1. bouffée ▸** a strong rush or gust of air : *A blast of hot air struck her when she opened the oven door.* **2. explosion ▸** an explosion : *The dynamite blast could be heard for blocks.* **3. bruit fort ▸** a loud noise : *He was awakened by the horn blast.* ▲ VERB, blasted, blasting. **faire sauter, démolir ▸** to blow apart with an explosion : *They had to blast through rock to build the road.*

blast off **décollage, décoller, être mis à feu ▸** to launch a rocket or spacecraft.

blaze[1] [blaze] NOUN, blazes. **1. flammes, brasier ▸** a bright, glowing fire or flame : *The firefighters rushed to put out the blaze.* **2. flamboiement ▸** a bright light or display : *During the spring, the fields were a blaze of colourful wildflowers.* ▲ VERB, blazed, blazing. **1. flamber ▸** to burn brightly. **2. flamboyer ▸** to shine or glow strongly : *The sun blazed overhead.* SYN : fire, flame, flare.

blaze[2] VERB, blazed, blazing. **frayer, marquer ▸** to mark a trail, as by cutting a mark in a tree. ▲ NOUN, blazes. **marque, encoche ▸** a mark to show where a trail is.

bleach [bleech] VERB, bleached, bleaching. **blanchir ▸** to make something white or light-coloured by using chemicals or exposing it to the sun : *She bleached his hair a light blond colour.* ▲ NOUN, bleaches. **eau de Javel ▸** a chemical used to make clothes or other things whiter.

bleak [bleek] ADJECTIVE, bleaker, bleakest. **1. exposé (-ée) au vent, morne, désolé (-ée)** exposed to the wind and weather; bare : *a bleak Arctic landscape.* **2. froid, glacial ▸** cold and unpleasant : *"A bleak, uneasy wind was blowing this way and that."* (Thomas H. Raddall) **3. morne, triste, lugubre ▸** depressing or gloomy : *"Our school was in a bleak building that had once been a warehouse."* (Yong Ik Kim) **d'un air morne, tristement ▸** ■ **bleakly,** ADVERB, SYN : barren, dreary, desolate.

bleed [bleed] VERB, bled, bleeding. **1. saigner ▸** to lose blood from a wound or injury : *The cut on his leg was bleeding badly.* **2. dégonfler, saigner ▸** to allow a fluid to escape : *to bleed air from a tire.* **3. avoir le cœur brisé ▸** to feel sorrow or grief : *Her heart bled for the parents of the lost child.*

blend [blend] VERB, blended, blending. **1. mélanger ▸** to mix or put together so that the parts cannot be separated : *Slowly blend the eggs with the flour.* **2. se confondre, se mêler ▸** go together well; be in harmony : *The frog blended in so well with the leaves that we could barely see it.* ▲ NOUN, blends. **1. mélange ▸** something that has been blended; a mixture : *The juice is a blend of three tropical fruits.* **2. mot composé ▸** a word that is made by joining parts of two or more words together. SYN : mix, combine, stir, join. ✐ **p. 61.**

bless [bles] VERB, blessed or blest, blessing. **1. bénir ▸** to praise or honour as holy : *to bless the Lord.* **2. bénir, faire plaisir, accorder le bonheur ▸** to bring happiness or favour to : *The child blessed us with a smile.* **3. bénir ▸** to

---

> ✐ **Writing Tips**
>
> **Blends**
>
> A **blended word** or **blend** is a word created from joining parts of two words together. When words are blended, some of the letters are left out.
>
> • For example, **brunch** is a blend of the words "breakfast" and "lunch." Brunch is a meal eaten late in the morning that combines both breakfast and lunch. **Smog** is another example—a blend of the words "smoke" and "fog."

---

make holy or sacred : *"At three o'clock in the afternoon nine priests blessed the coffin."* (Barbara Nichol)

bless-ing [BLES-ing] NOUN, blessings. **1. bénédiction ▸** a prayer or request for God's help or favour. **2. bénédiction, accord ▸** approval or honour : *Marina asked for her parents' blessing when she got married.* **3. bénédiction, chance ▸** something that brings happiness or satisfaction : *This rain is a blessing after all the dry weather we have been having lately.*

blind [blynd] ADJECTIVE, blinder, blindest. **1. aveugle** ▶ not able to see; without sight : *Raccoons are born blind.* **Note.** The condition of being blind is blindness. **2. (angle) mort, masqué (-ée), sans visibilité** ▶ hard to see; hidden or concealed : *Watch out for the blind curve in the road.* **3. aveugle (à)** ▶ not able to see or notice : *"Her stubborn pride made her blind… to the truth."* (Ann Grifalconi) ▲ VERB, blinded, blinding. **aveugler** ▶ to make blind : *The light shining in our eyes blinded us until Greg turned it off.* ▲ NOUN. **store** ▶ a window covering that shuts out light.

blind-fold [BLYND-FOLD] NOUN, blindfolds. **bandeau (-eaux)** ▶ a piece of cloth or other material tied to cover the eyes so the person can't see. ▲ VERB, blindfolded, blindfolding. **bander les yeux** ▶ to cover a person's eyes with a blindfold.

blink [blink] VERB, blinked, blinking. **1. cligner des yeux** ▶ to open and shut the eyes quickly : *"I did not dare blink. I gazed straight ahead."* (Jean Little) **2. clignoter, vaciller** ▶ to flash on and off : *The lights decorating the room blinked on and off.* ▲ NOUN, blinks. **clignotement** ▶ a quick flash of light.

bliss [blis] NOUN. **félicité, bonheur, béatitude** ▶ a feeling of perfect happiness and joy : *He was so happy that he felt the world was filled with bliss.* ■ **blissful,** ADJECTIVE. ▶ **bienheureux (-euse), heureux (-euse) heureusement, au comble du bonheur** ▶ full of bliss : *She turned to them with a blissful smile on her face.* ■ **blissfully,** ADVERB. **de façon heureuse.** *The prince and the princess lived blissfully ever after.* SYN : happiness, joy, delight, glee.

blis-ter [BLIS-tur] NOUN, blisters. **1. ampoule, cloque** ▶ a painful bump on the surface of the skin filled with a watery liquid : *A blister is usually caused by a burn or by constant rubbing.* **2. cloque, boursouflure, bulle** ▶ any small bubble or swelling of a surface : *The hot sun caused blisters to appear on the painted wall.* ▲ VERB, blistered, blistering. **provoquer des ampoules (cloques)** ▶ to form or have blisters on : *A sunburn may blister the skin.*

bliz-zard [BLIZ-urd] NOUN, blizzards. **blizzard, tempête de neige, poudrerie** ▶ a very heavy snowstorm with strong winds and cold temperatures.

block [blok] NOUN, blocks. **1. bloc** ▶ a solid piece of wood, stone, ice, or other hard material, usually having one or more flat sides : *My little brother loves to play with his set of blocks.* **2. pâté de maisons, quartier, bloc** ▶ a square area enclosed by four streets. **3. rues** ▶ the length of one side of a block : *The school is about three blocks from our house.* **4. bloc** ▶ a group of or set of things : *a block of tickets for the concert.* **5. barrage** ▶ something that is in the way; an obstacle : *The police set up a roadblock to look for the robbers.* ▲ VERB, blocked,

blocking. **1. bloquer, obstruer** ▶ to get in the way of; keep from moving : *Julie's bike blocked the driveway.* **Note.** Often used with **up** or **out**: *Something blocked up the drain, and water from the sink overflowed all over the floor.* **2. bloquer** ▶ in football and other sports, to get in the way of an opposing player so that he or she cannot move past. SYN: clog, hinder, delay, prevent, bar.

block-ade [BLOK-ADE] NOUN, blockades. **blocus** ▶ the blocking of a place by an army, a navy, or a group of people to control who or what goes in or comes out. ▲ VERB, blockaded, blockading. **barricader, barrer, bloquer** SYN : obstruction, barrier, fortification.

blond [blond] ADJECTIVE, blonder, blondest. (also **blonde**) **1. blond (blonde)** ▶ having a light-yellowish colour : *blond wood.* **2. blond (blonde)** ▶ having light-coloured hair. ▲ NOUN, blonds or blondes. **blond (blonde)** ▶ a person with light-coloured hair.

blood [blud] NOUN. **1. sang** ▶ the red liquid in the body that is pumped by the heart through the veins and arteries. Blood carries oxygen and digested food through the bloodstream to all parts of the body. **2. par le sang** ▶ family relationship; ancestry : *He is my uncle by blood.* 📖 p. 992. 👁 p. 402.

in cold blood **de sang froid** ▶ without feeling; in a cruel and deliberate way.

blood-y [BLUD-ee] ADJECTIVE, bloodier, bloodiest. **1. ensanglanté (-ée), taché (-ée) de sang** ▶ covered or stained with blood. **2. sanglant (-ante)** ▶ having much wounding or killing : *a bloody battle.*

blood pressure **tension artérielle** ▶ the amount of force that the blood has as it presses against the walls of the arteries while being pumped by the heart. Blood pressure that is too high or too low can be dangerous to one's health.

bloom [bloom] NOUN, blooms. **1. fleur** ▶ a blossom or flower. **2. floraison** ▶ the time of being in flower. **3. fleur** ▶ a time of freshness and health : *the bloom of youth.* ▲ VERB, bloomed, blooming. **1. fleurir** ▶ to bear flowers : *"Its fruit began to ripen and its flowers began to bloom with new, deeper colours."* (Hal Ober) **2. être resplendissant (-ante)** ▶ to show freshness and health. SYN: blossom, flower, glow, flourish, thrive.

blos-som [BLOS-um] NOUN, blossoms. **1. fleur** ▶ a flower or group of flowers, especially of a tree or plant that bears fruit. **2. floraison** ▶ the time of being in flower. ▲ VERB, blossomed, blossoming. **1. fleurir** ▶ to bear flowers; bloom : *The lilac bushes are full of buds ready to blossom.* **2. s'épanouir** ▶ to grow or develop : *Samantha is blossoming into quite an athlete.* SYN: develop, flower, bloom.

blot [blot] NOUN, blots. **1. tache** ▸ a stain or spot : *The ink left a blot on the paper.* **2.** something that spoils or disgraces : *The two speeding tickets are a blot on my record.* ▲ VERB, blotted, blotting. **1. tacher** ▸ to spot or stain. **2. éponger** ▸ to soak up; dry : *He blotted the spill with a paper towel.*

blot out 1. cacher, masquer ▸ to hide or cover completely : *"Suddenly a dark cloud swept across the sun, blotting it out and leaving the earth in shadow."* (E.B.White) **2. effacer, rayer, barrer** ▸ to do away with completely : *He blotted out all thoughts of the unpleasantness.*

blouse [blowz] NOUN, blouses. **blouse, chemisier** ▸ an article of women's clothing worn on the upper body. 🖝 **p. 1007.**

blow[1] [bloh] VERB, blew, blown, blowing. **1. souffler** ▸ to move with speed and force by wind or air : *"Next morning a cold wind was blowing, and storm clouds were rolling up."* (Laura Ingalls Wilder) **2. souffler sur** ▸ to send air out strongly, as with the breath : *She blew on the soup to cool it before she could eat it.* **3. faire s'envoler** ▸ to move by a current of air : *The wind blew the papers from the desk.* **4. faire** ▸ to shape or form with air : *We blew soap bubbles and watched them float away.*

blow out a. souffler, éteindre ▸ to put out or go out by blowing : *Blow out the candles on your cake.* **b. éclater** ▸ to burst suddenly : *It's lucky we weren't going very fast when the tire blew out.* **Note.** Also used as a NOUN: *We had a blowout on the highway.*

blow up a. gonfler, souffler ▸ to fill with air or gas : *Ask Uncle Jay to blow up your balloon.* **b. exploser, éclater** ▸ to damage or destroy by an explosion. **c. exagérer, faire un drame** ▸ to make something larger : *This issue has been blown up out of proportion.* **d.** *Informal.* **éclater de rage** ▸ to become very angry.

blow[2] NOUN, blows. **1. coup** ▸ a sudden hard hit with the fist or with a weapon : *The boxer took a hard blow to the chin.* **2. coup** ▸ a sudden event that causes sorrow or misfortune : *Getting that low mark on his exam was a blow to his confidence.*

blow-hole [BLOH-HOLE] NOUN, blowholes. **1. évent** ▸ a hole on the top of the head of a whale and some other animals, used for breathing. **2. trou** ▸ a hole in the ice through which whales, seals, and other sea mammals are able to breathe.

blown [blone] VERB. **souffler** ▸ a form of blow: *The wind blew blown leaves all over the yard.* ▲ ADJECTIVE. **soufflé (-ée)** ▸ formed by blowing air : *That vase is made of blown glass.*

blue [bloo] NOUN, blues. **bleu (bleus)** ▸ the colour of the sky on a clear day. ▲ ADJECTIVE, bluer, bluest. **1. bleu (bleue)** ▸ having the

colour blue. **2.** *Informal.* **bleu (bleue)** ▸ sad; unhappy. 🖉 **p. 64.**

blue-ber-ry [BLOO-BAIR-ee] NOUN, blueberries. **bleuet** ▸ a small, sweet-tasting blue berry that grows on a shrub; used in pies, jams, and pancakes. 👁 **p. 251.**

blue-bird [BLOO-BURD] NOUN, bluebirds. **oiseau bleu** ▸ a small North American songbird with bluish-coloured feathers on its back. Bluebirds are known for their sweet song and bright colours.

blue-jay [BLOO-JAY] NOUN, bluejays. **geai bleu** ▸ a bird of eastern North America with a crest on its head, and a bright blue back and wings. The bluejay is noted for its noisy, scolding cry. 👁 **p. 108.**

Blue-nose [BLOO-NOZE] **1. Bluenose** ▸ the name of a famous schooner built in Nova Scotia in 1921. The *Bluenose* was never defeated as the holder of the International Fisherman's Trophy, given to the fastest sailing vessel in the North Atlantic fishing fleets. It is shown on the back of the Canadian dime. **2. néo-écossais (-aise)** ▸ a nickname for someone or something from Nova Scotia. **Note.** Said to come from the fact that early Nova Scotian fishermen wore mittens made with blue dye that left marks on their faces.

blue-print [BLOO-PRINT] NOUN, blueprints. **1. plan** ▸ a copy of a building plan, map, or drawing showing lines against a background of another colour. For many years, blueprints had white lines on a blue background, but now the lines are often blue or black on white. **2. projet** ▸ any detailed plan or outline : *The pamphlet was a blueprint for keeping a playground safe.*

blues [blooz] PLURAL NOUN. **1. cafard** ▸ low spirits; sadness : *Casey has had the blues ever since her cat ran away.* **2. blues** ▸ a type of music that is typically slow and sad-sounding : *The blues began among people of African descent in the southern United States.*

bluff[1] [bluf] VERB, bluffed, bluffing. **bluffer** ▸ to try to fool other people by acting braver, stronger, or more sure of oneself than one actually is : *He says he'll quit the team if he can't be the first-string goalie, but he's only bluffing.* ▲ NOUN, bluffs. **bluffer** ▸ the act of bluffing : *Rosa acts as though nothing bothers her, but it's really just a bluff.* SYN: deceive, trick.

bluff[2] NOUN, bluffs. **cap, falaise** ▸ a high, steep cliff or river bank.

blun-der [BLUN-dur] VERB, blundered, blundering. **1. gaffer, faire une gaffe** ▸ to make a stupid or careless mistake : *She blundered when she locked her keys inside the car.* **2. s'avancer maladroitement** ▸ to move in a clumsy way : *He blundered through the dark room, trying to* *find a lamp.* ▲ NOUN, blunders. **gaffe** ▶ a stupid or careless mistake.

blunt [blunt] ADJECTIVE, blunter, bluntest. **1. émoussé (-ée)** ▶ having a dull edge or point; not sharp. **2. brusque, brutal (-ale), direct (directe)** ▶ speaking without worrying about the feelings of others; very plain and direct : *"He has a blunt, rough way of talking that irritates a lot of people."* (S.E. Hinton) ▲ VERB, blunted, blunting. **émousser** ▶ to make something dull or blunt. ■ **bluntly,** ADVERB: ▶ brusquement, carrément, brutalement. *I hate to put it bluntly, but you don't have a chance in this tennis game.* ■ **bluntness,** NOUN. ▶ **manque de tranchant, brusquerie.** SYN: outspoken, direct, frank, straightforward.

blur [blur] VERB, blurred, blurring. **brouiller, troubler** ▶ to make less clear or make hard to see : ▲ NOUN, blurs. **image floue** ▶ something that is not clear or is hard to see : *"All the world was a blur of white. Molly couldn't see anything around her."* (Marilynn Reynolds).

blurb [blurb] NOUN. *Informal.* **baratin publicitaire, annonce** ▶ an advertisement or announcement : *Many books have a blurb on the back cover.*

blurt [blurt] VERB, blurted, blurting. **laisser échapper, lâcher** ▶ to say something quickly and without thinking : *Without meaning to, I blurted out the secret.*

blush [blush] VERB, blushed, blushing. **rougir** ▶ to become red in the face, as from embarrassment, shame, or excitement : *Jerry blushed when we teased him about his new girlfriend.* ▲ NOUN, blushes. **rougeur** ▶ a reddening of the face.

blus-ter [BLUS-tur] VERB, blustered, blustering. **1. faire rage, souffler en rafales** ▶ of the wind, to blow in a violent and stormy way. **2. parler fort, tempêter, fulminer** ▶ to talk or act in a noisy, threatening manner. ■ **blustery,** ADJECTIVE. ▶ **venteux (-euse), en rafales.**

B.N.A. Act Acte de l'Amérique du Nord britannique ▶ short for British North America Act.

bo-a [BOH-uh] NOUN, boas. **boa** ▶ any of various large, nonpoisonous snakes that coil around and suffocate their prey. Boas include the boa constrictor, anaconda, and python.

boar [bor] NOUN, boars. **1. sanglier** ▶ a wild hog with a stiff, hairy coat and a long snout, found in Europe, Africa, and Asia. **2. verrat** ▶ a male pig.

board [bord] NOUN, boards. **1. planche, madrier** ▶ a flat, thin piece of wood, generally longer than it is wide, that is used for building. **2. planche** ▶ a flat board of hard material that is used for a special purpose : *an ironing board; a bread board; a chess board.* **3. pension** ▶ meals served for a fixed price. **Note.** Used especially in the phrase room and board. **4. conseil, comité, commission** ▶ a group of people who direct or control an organization : *a school board.* ▲ VERB, boarded, boarding. **1. boucher, clouer des planches en travers de** ▶ to cover with boards or other such material : *The broken store window had to be boarded up.* **2. prendre en pension** ▶ to get or give lodging and meals for pay. **Note.** A person who pays money for room and meals is a boarder. **3. monter à bord** ▶ to enter or get on a ship, plane, train, or the like.

boast [bohst] VERB, boasted, boasting. **1. se vanter** ▶ to talk in a very proud way about oneself; brag : *"'Come, I'll sink my teeth into him and drive him away!' the fox boasted."* (Tololwa M. Mollel) **2. être fier (fière) de posséder** ▶ to take pride in having : *Our city boasts a new convention centre.* ▲ NOUN, boasts. **objet d'orgueil** ▶ something that one brags about : *Muhammed Ali was known for his boasts about what a great boxer he was.* ■ **boastful,** ADJECTIVE. ▶ **vantard (-arde).**

boat [bote] NOUN, boats. **1. embarcation, bateau** ▶ a small, open vessel that is moved through water by means of oars, sails, or an engine. **2. bateau (-eaux), navire** ▶ a ship or vessel of any size : *Today most people cross the ocean by plane rather than by boat.* ▲ VERB, boated, boating. **faire du bateau, se promener en bateau** ▶ to use a boat : *to go boating on a lake.* 📖 p. 1153. 👁 p. 394.

bob [bob] VERB, bobbed, bobbing. **s'agiter, danser sur l'eau** ▶ to move up and down or side to side with short, jerky motions : *The little boat bobbed up and down on the waves.* ▲ NOUN, bobs. **petit coup** ▶ a short, jerky movement.

bob-cat [BOB-kat] NOUN, bobcats. **lynx** ▶ a small wild cat of North America that has a yellowish-brown coat with dark spots and a short tail.

bob-o-link [BOB-uh-link] NOUN, bobolinks. **alouette des prairies** ▶ a songbird found in North and South America, named for the sound of its call.

🖋 Word Builder

Blue and other common colour words have special meanings in addition to their colours, because of what the words suggest. Someone who feels *blue* is sad or unhappy. A person who sees *red* is very angry. A person who is *green* is new or inexperienced at something. Someone who is called *yellow* is said to be afraid or cowardly. A person who is in the *pink* is in good health.

boat

mast
lookout
sail
stern
port
bridges
hold
prow
hull
rudder
anchor
porthole   starboard

bob-sled [BOB-SLED] NOUN, bobsleds. **luge, bob ▶** a long sled having two sets of runners, a steering wheel, and brakes. The bobsled moves on a steep, curving course made of icy snow. ▲ VERB, bobsledded, bobsledding. **faire de la luge, faire du bob ▶** to ride or coast on a bobsled.

bobsled

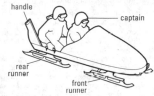

handle
captain
rear runner
front runner

bob-white [BOB-WITE] NOUN, bobwhites. **sorte de caille ▶** a North American quail whose greyish body is marked with brown and white spots.

bod-i-ly [BOD-uh-lee] ADJECTIVE or ADVERB. **à bras-le-corps, du corps, physique ▶** having to do with the body : *The woman picked up the child bodily and placed him in the chair.*

bod-y [BOD-ee] NOUN, bodies. 1. **corps ▶** all of a person or animal; the form of a living thing. 2. **cadavre ▶** a dead person or animal; a corpse. 3. **corps ▶** the main part of a person or animal, other than the head and the limbs. 4. **corps, partie principale ▶** the main part of something : *the body of an automobile ; the body of a letter.* 5. **corps ▶** a mass or group : *The student body cheered for the school hockey team.* 6. **volume, corps ▶** the quality of being full or thick : *She has beautiful hair ; it has so much body.* 📖 **p. 993.** 👁 **p. 402-405.**

bod-y-guard [BOD-ee-GARD] NOUN, bodyguards. **garde du corps ▶** someone whose job is to protect and guard another person.

bog [bog] NOUN, bogs. **marais, marécage ▶** a wet, soft area near water; a swamp or marsh.

▲ VERB, bogged, bogging. **s'embourber, s'enliser, s'enfoncer ▶** to sink or slow down, in or as if in a bog : *I can't go because I'm bogged down with work.*

boil¹ [boyl] VERB, boiled, boiling. 1. **faire bouillir, amener à ébullition ▶** to heat a liquid until bubbles form and steam rises. 2. **faire bouillir ▶** to cook food by boiling in water. **Note.** Often used as an ADJECTIVE:*boiled potatoes ; boiled beef.* 3. **bouillir ▶** to become very angry or upset : *Zan was really boiling when he heard what you said.* ▲ NOUN. **bouillir ▶** the condition of boiling : *Let the soup simmer, but don't let it come to a boil.*

boil² NOUN, boils. **furoncle ▶** a painful red swelling under the skin caused by an infection : *A boil has a hard core and is often filled with pus.*

boil-er [BOY-lur] NOUN, boilers. 1. **chaudière ▶** a large tank for holding hot water or steam, used to heat a building or to produce power for an engine. 2. **bain-marie ▶** a pan or pot in which water or another liquid is boiled, as for cooking.

bold [bold] ADJECTIVE, bolder, boldest. 1. **coura-geux (-euse), audacieux (-euse) ▶** not afraid; daring and brave : *"I feel as bold and brave and free as a cowboy again."* (Dayal Kaur Khalsa) 2. **effronté (-ée) ▶** not polite; rude : *The bold child stuck out her tongue at the teacher.* ■ **boldly,** ADVERB. ▶ **courageusement, audacieusement, effrontément. courage, effron-terie ▶** in a bold way : *"She looked Burdick boldly in the eyes."* (Lloyd Alexander) ■ **bold-ness,** NOUN. 🖉 **p. 71.**

bo-lo-gna [buh-LOH-nee] NOUN. **saucisson de Bologne ▶** a type of sausage or sandwich meat, made with seasoned beef or pork, or now sometimes with turkey or chicken. **Note.** The word *bologna* has a very unusual spelling, with the ending *gna.* This is because the word comes from Bologna, a city in Italy that is famous for this type of food.

bolt [bohlt] NOUN, bolts. 1. **éclair ▶** a single flash of lightning. 2. **verrou ▶** a sliding bar used to fasten a door. 3. **boulon ▶** a pin or rod with a head on one end and a screw thread on the other. A bolt is used with a nut to hold things in place. 4. **fuite soudaine, départ brusque ▶** a sudden, quick movement; dash. 5. **rouleau (-eaux) ▶** a large roll of cloth, wallpaper, or the like. ▲ VERB, bolted, bolting. 1. **déguerpir ▶** to make a sudden quick movement; dash : *The dog bolted for the door.* 2. **verrouiller ▶** to fasten a door with a bolt. 3. **engouffrer, engloutir ▶** to eat food too quickly without chewing : *Greta can't possibly taste her food; she bolts it down so fast.*

bomb [bom] NOUN, bombs. **bombe ▶** a container filled with material that will explode or burn, used as a weapon : *A bomb goes off when it hits something or when it is set off by a fuse or* *timer.* ▲ VERB, bombed, bombing. **bombarder** ▶ to drop or set off a bomb; attack with bombs. 👁 p. 540.

bom·bard [bom-BARD] VERB, bombarded, bombarding. **1. bombarder** ▶ to attack with bombs or heavy gunfire : *The ground troops arrived after the planes had bombarded the area.* **2. assaillir, bombarder** ▶ to attack or overwhelm, as if by bombing : *We bombarded the area with leaflets advertising the benefit concert.* ▪ **bombardment,** NOUN. ▶ **bombardement.**

bomb·er [BOM-ur] NOUN, bombers. **1. bombardier** ▶ an airplane that is specially made for dropping bombs. **2. poseur (-euse) de bombes, terroriste** ▶ a person who bombs : *The building was destroyed by a terrorist bomber.*

bond [bond] NOUN, bonds. **1. lien** ▶ something that holds or fastens things together, such as glue, rope, chains, and so on. **2. lien** ▶ something that unites people : *the bonds of friendship.* **3. obligation, bon** ▶ a note or certificate from a government or public agency promising to pay back a loan, usually with interest. ▲ VERB, bonded, bonding. **lier** ▶ to join something with a bond.

bone [bone] NOUN, bones. **os** ▶ the hard substance that forms the framework of the bodies of humans and other animals with backbones. ▲ VERB, boned, boning. **désosser** ▶ to take the bones out of : *Mom boned the fish before she served it.* 📖 p. 994.

bon·fire [BON-FIRE] NOUN, bonfires. **feu (de joie)** ▶ a large, bright fire built outdoors.

bon·net [BON-it] NOUN, bonnets. **1. bonnet** ▶ a type of hat tied under the chin and having a large, wide brim, formerly worn by women and girls : *a sun bonnet.* **2. bonnet** ▶ a similar hat worn by babies.

bo·nus [BOH-nus] NOUN, bonuses. **prime, aubaine** ▶ something extra given to a person as a reward; something more than is owed or expected.

bon·y [BOH-nee] ADJECTIVE, bonier, boniest. **1. osseux (-euse)** ▶ of or like bone : *The nose is formed of a bony material called cartilage.* **2. plein d'arêtes** ▶ having many bones : *I can't eat this fish; it's too bony.* **3. décharnée, anguleux (-euse)** ▶ having bones that stick out or that are large and noticeable.

book [book] NOUN, books. **1. livre** ▶ a set of printed pages held together inside a cover. **2. cahier** ▶ blank sheets of paper fastened together for writing on. **3. livre** ▶ one part of a very large book, such as the Bible. ▲ VERB, booked, booking. **1. réserver** ▶ to arrange ahead of time : *We booked two seats on the flight to Paris.* **2. arrêter** ▶ to record charges against someone : *The police booked him on suspicion of theft.* 📖 p. 1058. 🖎 p. 66.

✍ Writing Tips

Book Reviews

A **book review** is an article that discusses what is good or bad about a certain book and whether other people should read it. When you write a book review, include

• a short summary of the plot or subject without revealing too much, but with enough information to spark the reader's interest;

• your opinion about the book, and evidence or reasons to support this opinion;

• a recommendation as to whether your audience should read the book.

book·keep·er [BOOK-KEE-pur] NOUN, bookkeepers. **comptable** ▶ a person who keeps track of the accounts and records of a business. **Note.** The work of a bookkeeper is bookkeeping.

book·let [BOOK-lit] NOUN, booklets. **livret** ▶ a book with few pages, usually with a thin paper cover.

boom[1] [boom] NOUN, booms. **1. grondement** ▶ a loud, hollow, deep sound : *The boom of drums echoed through the valley.* **2. période d'essor, forte hausse** ▶ a time of rapid growth or activity : *There was a boom in the Yukon after gold was discovered there.* ▲ VERB, boomed, booming. **1. retentir, gronder, tonner** ▶ to make a loud noise : *The principal's voice boomed over the loudspeaker.* **2. être en plein essor** ▶ to grow or increase rapidly : *"Long lines of people were waiting to get aboard for the next ride. Business was booming."* (E.B. White) SYN : thunder, roar, rumble.

boom[2] NOUN, booms. **1. mât, perche** ▶ a long pole or beam. One kind of boom is used in a boat to keep the bottom of a sail stretched. Another kind holds a microphone for making TV shows and movies. **2. barrage flottant** ▶ a chain or line of logs used to keep other free-floating logs from floating away. **3. radeau (-eaux)** ▶ a large raft of logs being towed over water.

boom·er·ang [BOO-muh-RANG] NOUN, boomerangs. **boomerang** ▶ a flat, curved piece of wood with a bend near the middle that forms two wings. Some boomerangs can be thrown so that they circle and return to the thrower. Non-returning boomerangs were used as weapons by the Aborigines of Australia.

boost [boost] VERB, boosted, boosting. **1. soulever, remonter** ▶ to lift up or raise; push up : *"He led the sheep to the stairs, and then step by step he lugged and boosted her* *upward."* (Laura Ingalls Wilder) **2. remonter, relancer, augmenter ▸** to make bigger or grander; increase : *Winning the last game really boosted the team spirit.* ▲ NOUN, boosts. **1. poussée ▸** a push or shove upward. **2. remontant ▸** an increase or improvement : *An extra practice is a boost to our chances of winning.*

boot [boot] NOUN, boots. **botte ▸** a kind of shoe covering the foot, ankle, and lower part of the leg. Boots are usually made of leather or rubber and are stronger and heavier than ordinary shoes. ▲ VERB, booted, booting. **1. donner un coup de pied ▸** to kick : *The soccer player booted the ball.* **2. (s') amorcer, mettre en marche ▸** to start the operating system on a computer. 📘 p. 1007.

to boot en plus, de plus, par-dessus le marché ▸ besides, in addition : *If we buy the china, the store will throw in the glasses to boot.*

booth [booth] NOUN, booths. **1. stand, baraque ▸** a stand or place where things are displayed or sold : *You can get half-price tickets for plays and concerts at the booth in the mall.* **2. cabine, isoloir ▸** a small, closed space or compartment : *a telephone booth; a voting booth.* **3. banquette ▸** a partly enclosed space in a restaurant, having a table and seating for a few people.

bor·der [BOR-dur] NOUN, borders. **1. frontière ▸** a dividing line or boundary, as between two regions or provinces : *Canada and the United States have the longest undefended border in the world.* **2. bordure ▸** the edge or rim of something : *The wedding dress was made of satin with a border of lace.* ▲ VERB, bordered, bordering. **1. toucher à ▸** to be at the border of : *Alberta borders British Columbia on the east.* **2. faire le tour ▸** to put a border on : *Lilac bushes bordered the yard.* **3. border on or border upon. approcher ▸** to be near or close to : *That idea borders on brilliance.* SYN : edge, margin. 🖉 p. 69.

bore[1] [bor] VERB, bored, boring. **ennuyer ▸** to make tired or restless by being dull or uninteresting : *Watching sports like hockey, football, or baseball bores me; I'd rather go biking.* Note. The condition of being bored is **bore-dom** (📘 p. 1017). ▲ NOUN, bores. **pesonne ennuyeuse ▸** a person or thing that is dull or uninteresting : *I think he's a real bore; he's always talking about where he used to live.*

bore[2] VERB, bored, boring. **creuser, forer, percer ▸** to make a hole or tunnel; dig or drill : *The gopher bored tunnels all over our lawn.* ▲ NOUN, bores. **1. trou ▸** a hole made by boring. **2. calibre ▸** the hollow space of a pipe, cylinder, or gun. **3. calibre ▸** the diameter of a hole or tube. **4. foreuse, perceuse ▸** a drilling tool. SYN : drill, pierce, puncture.

bore[3] VERB. **porter, supporter ▸** a past form of bear; endured : *"As always, Josepha bore teasing with a smile."* (Jim McGugan)

bor·ing [BOR-ing] ADJECTIVE. **ennuyeux (-euse), ennuyant (-ante) ▸** causing boredom; dull or uninteresting : *"The grownups made friends and talked their usual boring grown-up talk."* (Jean Fritz)

born [born] VERB. **naître ▸** a past form of bear[1]: *The day you were born is your birthday.* ▲ ADJECTIVE. **né (née) ▸** by birth or natural ability : *Serge is a born athlete; he seems to be good at every sport.*

borne [born] VERB. **donner naissance ▸** a past form of bear[1]: *My grandmother has borne nine children. Let's share the load; you've borne it long enough.*

bor·ough [BUR-oh] NOUN, boroughs. **municipalité ▸** a town or township that has its own government.

bor·row [BOR-oh] VERB, borrowed, borrowing. **1. emprunter ▸** to take or get something with the understanding that it will be later returned to its owner : *You can borrow my book, if you return it to me by Friday.* **2. emprunter ▸** to take and use as one's own; adopt : *Kerry borrowed ideas from magazines when she decorated her room.*

boss [bɒs] NOUN, bosses. **patron (-onne) ▸** a person who is in charge : *You'll have to ask the boss if you can leave early.* ▲ VERB, bossed, bossing. **mener, diriger ▸** to tell someone what to do : *He started his own business because he didn't want to be bossed around by other people.* Note. A bossy person is someone who likes to tell others how to act. SYN : supervise, oversee, direct.

bot·a·ny [BOT-uh-nee] NOUN. **botanique ▸** the scientific study of plants : *Botany includes the study of plants, how and where they grow, and their effect on humans.* Note. A botanist is an expert in the field of botany. ■ **botanical,** ADJECTIVE. **botanique ▸** *A botanical garden is a place where plants are displayed and studied.*

both [bohth] ADJECTIVE. **les deux ▸** the two; one as well as the other : *Renée speaks both French and English.* ▲ PRONOUN. **tous (les) deux ▸** the two together : *Only one of the twins came to the reception, although both were invited.* ▲ CONJUNCTION or ADVERB. **à la fois ▸** together, equally : *The movie is both entertaining and educational.*

both·er [BAH-thur] VERB, bothered, bothering. **1. embêter, ennuyer, gêner, déranger ▸** to trouble or annoy : *"Big kids don't like to be bothered by little kids."* (Juanita Havill) **2. se donner la peine de, se déranger ▸** to take the trouble to do something : *Don't bother hanging up that jacket; it has to go to the cleaners.* ▲ NOUN, bothers. **ennui, inconvénient ▸** something that annoys or troubles : *If it's not too much of a bother, would you pick up a carton of milk?* **Note.** A thing or a person that causes worry is bothersome. SYN: annoy, pester, worry.

bot-tle [BOT-ul] NOUN, bottles. **bouteille ▶** a container with a narrow neck and a mouth that can be closed with a cap, usually made of glass or plastic and used to hold liquids. ▲ VERB, bottled, bottling. **embouteiller ▶** to put something in a bottle. **Note.** A company that bottles drinks is a bottler.

bot-tom [BOT-um] NOUN, bottoms. **1. fond ▶** the lowest part of something : *the bottom of a box; the bottom of a pan.* **2. fond ▶** the most deep part : *He wished from the bottom of his heart that he had never come here.* ▲ ADJECTIVE. **dernier (-ière) ▶** lowest or last : *The towels are on the bottom shelf of the linen closet.*

bot-tom-less [BOT-um-liss] ADJECTIVE. **sans fond ▶** having no bottom, or seeming to have no bottom : *a bottomless pit or lake.*

bottom line 1. solde final ▶ the last line of a business report, showing how much money has been made or lost. **2. résultat ▶** the final result or most important part of something : *Yes, we played a good game, but the bottom line is that we lost.*

bough [bow] NOUN, boughs. **branche, rameau (-eaux) ▶** a large branch of a tree : *"That night Charlie and Za cut cedar boughs, and made a bed under a big tree."* (Ann Blades)

boul-der [BOLE-dur] NOUN, boulders. **rocher ▶** a very large, rounded rock resting above or partly above the ground.

boul-e-vard [BOOL-uh-vard] NOUN, boulevards. **boulevard ▶** a wide city street or avenue, often lined with trees : *Let's stroll down the boulevard.*

bounce [bowns] VERB, bounced, bouncing. **1. rebondir, bondir ▶** to hit something and spring up or back : *"Maurice missed the shot and the ball bounced behind him."* (Juanita Havill) **2.** Informal. **être refusé pour provisions insuffisantes ▶** of a cheque to be returned by the bank without being paid ; to cause a cheque to be returned this way : *She did not have enough money in her chequing account, and her cheque bounced.* ▲ NOUN, bounces. **bond, rebond ▶** the act of bouncing ; a jump or spring : *He had a happy little bounce in his step.*

bound¹ [bownd] VERB. **attacher, lier ▶** a past form of bind: *Trevor bound the book in dark leather.* ▲ ADJECTIVE. **1. lié (-liée), attaché (-ée) ▶** fastened by bonds or as if by bonds : *He's been house-bound ever since he got sick last week.* **2. destiné (-ée) à, certain (-aine) de ▶** certain ; sure : *"If we start there and work north, we're bound to find her."* (Robert D. Ballard) **3. obligé (-ée), astreint (-einte) ▶** obliged or determined : *"Run*

if you're bound to! You'll be glad enough to come back." (Laura Ingalls Wilder)

bound² VERB, bounded, bounding. **1. bondir, sauter ▶** to leap or jump : *"They saw a deer bounding away through the underbrush."* (Vera Cleaver) **2. bondir ▶** to bounce back after striking something : *The ball hit the backboard and bounded back into the shooter's hands.* ▲ NOUN, bounds. **bond, saut ▶** a leap or jump : *In three bounds, he was across the road.*

bound³ NOUN, bounds. **limite, borne ▶** a limit marking the edge ; boundary : *The ball bounced out of bounds.* ▲ VERB, bounded, bounding. **borner, délimiter ▶** to form the boundary of : *"The river that bounded the meadow drew her like a charm."* (Philippa Pearce)

bound⁴ ADJECTIVE. **en route vers ▶** intending to go ; going : *I'm bound for the sunny south for my vacation.*

bound-a-ry [BOWN-dree] NOUN, boundaries. **limite, borne, frontière ▶** the limit or edge of something ; a dividing line : *"'You know my power will not work beyond the boundaries of our land.'"* (Robin Muller) 🖉 **p. 69.**

boun-ty [BOWN-tee] NOUN, bounties. **1. générosité ▶** generosity : *They lived simply off the bounty of the land.* **2. prime ▶** a reward for killing certain dangerous animals, or for capturing or killing an escaped criminal : *That territory has a bounty on coyotes.*

boun-ti-ful [BOWN-tuh-ful] ADJECTIVE. **abondant (-ante) ▶** generous, abundant ; plenty : *The price of oranges is down because of this year's bountiful crop.*

bou-quet [BOO-kay or BOH-kay] NOUN, bouquets. **1. bouquet ▶** a bunch of flowers, especially when tied together and given as a gift : *a bouquet of roses.* **2. bouquet ▶** a delicate smell or aroma : *the bouquet of fresh herbs.*

bout [bowt] NOUN, bouts. **1. combat ▶** a match or contest : *Max won his first five boxing bouts, but lost his sixth.* **2. accès ▶** a certain period of time, especially a period of illness : *Grandpa suffered a bout of the flu last week.* SYN: trial, struggle, battle.

bow¹ [boh] NOUN, bows. **1. arc ▶** a weapon made of a thin piece of curved wood or other material with a string (called a **bowstring**) tied from one end to another. A bow is used to shoot arrows. **2. boucle ▶** a knot with loops, as on a shoelace or on a ribbon for a gift or package. **3. archet ▶** a stick of wood with a string stretched along its length, used to play a violin or other stringed instrument.

bow² [bow] NOUN, bowed, bowing. **1. s'incliner ▶** to bend forward at the waist to show respect or politeness. **2. incliner la tête ▶** to bend the head forward : *Hajjar bowed her head in respect.* **3. se soumettre ▶** to give in ; submit : *The school bowed to the parents' wishes and* *started a new reading program.* SYN: bend, stoop, kneel.

bow³ [bow] NOUN, bows. **proue** ▸ the front part of a boat or ship. *"Jarret sleeps in his bunk in the bow."* (Alexandra Morton)

bowl¹ [bole] NOUN, bowls. **1. bol** ▸ a rounded hollow dish or container : *a soup bowl; a salad bowl; a mixing bowl.* **2. creux** ▸ any bowl-shaped part or place : *the bowl of a spoon.* **3. stade, amphithéâtre** ▸ a large, rounded stadium or amphitheatre for sporting events. **4. match de football** ▸ a football game played after the regular season between two specially invited teams : *The Super Bowl is the championship of U.S. professional football.*

bowl² VERB, bowled, bowling. **1. jouer aux quilles** ▸ to play the game of bowling. **Note.** A person who plays this game is a **bowler. 2. marquer** ▸ to get a certain score in bowling : *I bowled a 210 game last week.*

bowl over **renverser** ▸ to knock down or surprise, as if with a rolling ball : *The dog almost bowled me over when he jumped up to lick my face.*

bowl-ing [BOH-ling] NOUN. **jeu de quilles** ▸ a game played by rolling a heavy ball down a wooden lane known as a **bowling alley.** The object is to knock down five or ten pins at the end of the alley.

box¹ [boks] NOUN, boxes. **1. boîte** ▸ a container that is used to hold things. A box is shaped like a square or rectangle and has four sides, a bottom, and a top or opening. Boxes can be made of wood, cardboard, or other material. **2. boîte** ▸ the contents of a box : *Joe ate a whole box of crackers.* **3. loge** ▸ a special closed-in area like a box : *the batter's box in baseball; a box in a theatre.* ▲ VERB, boxed, boxing. **mettre en boîte, emballer** ▸ to put in a box : *Karin carefully boxed the crystal goblet for shipping.*

box² VERB, boxed, boxing. **1. boxer, faire de la boxe** ▸ to take part in the sport of boxing. **2. gifler, flanquer une claque** ▸ to hit with the hand or fist.

box³ NOUN, **buis** ▸ an ornamental shrub that stays green all winter. **Note.** Also known as box-wood.

box-er [BOKS-ur] NOUN, boxers. **1. boxeur (-euse)** ▸ a person who takes part in the sport of boxing. **2. boxer** ▸ a type of dog with a short, smooth tan or brownish coat, a sturdy build, and a short, square face. **Note.** Boxer shorts are a type of men's underwear.

box-ing [BOKS-ing] NOUN. **boxe** ▸ the sport of fighting with the fists according to certain rules. **Note.** The padded gloves worn while boxing are boxing gloves.

boy [boy] NOUN, boys. **garçon** ▸ a male child who is not yet a man or an adult.

boy-cott [BOY-kot] NOUN, boycotts. **boycottage** ▸ a plan by many people to refuse to do business or have dealings with a person or organization. People carry on a boycott to protest something or to change a policy. ▲ VERB, boycotted, boycotting. **boycotter** ▸ to take part in a boycott : *The students boycotted the snack bar because it would not serve the kinds of food they asked for.*

brace [brace] NOUN, braces. **1. prothèse** ▸ something used as a support or to hold things together : *He wore a brace on his leg to help him walk.* **2. braces. broches** ▸ a set of wires and bands used to straighten the teeth. **3. entretoise** ▸ a handle used to hold a drill or bit. **4. paire** ▸ a pair, especially a pair of animals : *a brace of pheasants.* ▲ VERB, braced, bracing. **1. soutenir** ▸ to hold or make steady : *"One hand was on his hip and the other braced his knee, as though he had a pain in his side."* (Virginia Hamilton) **2. se préparer mentalement** ▸ to prepare for something difficult or for a shock : *Brace yourself; I have some bad news to tell you.* **3. se revigorer** ▸ to fill with energy; refresh : *She braced herself with a cold shower and a glass of juice.* SYN: support, strengthen.

brace-let [BRACE-lit] NOUN, bracelets. **bracelet** ▸ a small band or chain worn as an ornament around the wrist, arm, or ankle.

brack-et [BRAK-it] NOUN, brackets. **1. parenthèse** ▸ one of a pair of symbols — for example, [ ] — that are used to enclose numbers, letters, or words. **2. support** ▸ a piece of wood or metal that is fastened to a wall to hold something up. **3. classe, groupe, tranche** ▸ a group or category into which something can be placed : *Her test scores fall into the 75 to 85 bracket.* ▲ VERB, bracketed, bracketing.

✐ Word Builder

*Boundary, border, and **margin** can all refer to the limit or edge of something. **Boundary** suggests an outer limit that may or may not be exact : This fence serves as the boundary between our yard and our neighbour's yard. **Border** has the idea of a line or limit set down by law : The Ottawa River forms part of the border between Quebec and Ontario. **Margin** has the sense of an exact outer edge : This dictionary has margins at the top and bottom of each page.*

1. mettre entre parenthèses ▶ to put numbers or words in brackets. **2. regrouper ▶** to place items together in a group.

brag [brage] VERB, bragged, bragging. **se vanter ▶** to speak highly about yourself or what you have done; praise yourself too much ▶ **Note.** A person who brags a lot is a **braggart.** SYN: boast.

braid [brade] NOUN, braids. **tresse, natte ▶** a strip made by weaving or twisting together three or more long pieces of cloth, hair, or other material : *Rita wore her hair in braids.* ▲ VERB, braided, braiding. **tresser, natter, entrelacer ▶** to make a braid.

braille [brale] NOUN. (also Braille) **braille ▶** a system of printing for visually impaired people. Braille consists of six raised dots used in many combinations to represent letters, words, and so on. People read by touching the dots with their fingertips. **Note.** Named after Louis Braille, who invented the braille alphabet and who himself was visually impaired from the age of three.

brain [brane] NOUN, brains. **1. cerveau (-eaux) ▶** the mass of nerves and tissue inside the skull. The brain is the centre of the nervous system in humans and animals. It controls our thoughts and actions. **2. brains. cerveau ▶** the mind; intelligence. **3.** *Informal.* **cerveau, génie ▶** a very smart person : *She must be a real brain to get such high marks!* ▲ VERB, brained, braining. **assommer ▶** to hit someone hard on the head.

brain

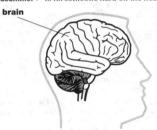

brain-storm [BRANE-storm] NOUN, brainstorms. **remue-méninges ▶** a sudden thought as to how to solve a problem or create something new. ▲ VERB. brainstormed, brainstorming. **faire un remue-méninges ▶** to think hard to try to come up with new ideas. ✐ **p. 70.**

brain-wash [BRANE-wash] VERB, brainwashed, brainwashing. **1. faire un lavage de cerveau ▶** to force someone to change his or her beliefs by putting great mental pressure on him or her. **2. faire du bourrage de crâne ▶** to persuade someone in an unfair way : *Dad says that TV commercials brainwash people into buying things.*

✐ **Writing Tips**

Brainstorming
Brainstorming is a way to come up with new ideas by writing down whatever comes to mind about a word or a subject. You can brainstorm by yourself, with a partner, or with a group. To brainstorm you need to
• *write down the subject on a piece of paper, and then list every idea suggested;*
• *accept all the suggestions offered; and*
• *build on ideas others have suggested.*

brake [brake] NOUN, brakes. **frein ▶** a part that slows or stops a moving wheel or vehicle, such as a bicycle, car, or train. ▲ VERB, braked, braking. **freiner ▶** to slow down or stop something by using a brake or brakes : *"His car almost went over the side of a hill…but he braked just in time."* (Paul Zindel)

bram-ble [BRAM-bul] NOUN, brambles. **roncier, roncière ▶** a bush or rough shrub with thorns or prickly stems, such as a blackberry bush.

bran [bran] NOUN. **son ▶** the ground-up outer shells or husks of grain. Bran from wheat, rye, or corn is used in cereal, flour, and bread.

branch [branch] NOUN, branches. **1. branche ▶** a part of a tree that grows out from the trunk. **2. succursale, branche ▶** anything that is thought of as coming out from the main part, as a branch does from a tree : *Our town has a main library downtown and several branches in other neighbourhoods.* **3. branche ▶** any part or division : *Zoology is a branch of biology.* **4. branchement ▶** a place in a computer program where there is a choice of one or more steps. ▲ VERB, branched, branching. **bifurcation ▶** to divide or separate from the main part : *That road branches off from the main highway.* 📖 **p. 1097.** ◉ **p. 253.**

branch out se diversifier ▶ to extend or add to something : *Celia is branching out and reading new authors.*

brand [brand] NOUN, brands. **1. marque ▶** a type or kind of something : *What brand of bath soap do you use?* **Note.** The name of a particular product made by a certain company is a **brand** name: *"Crest" is the brand name of a well-known toothpaste.* **2. marque ▶** a mark or sign made with a hot iron on the skin of cattle or other animals to show who owns them. ▲ VERB, branded, branding. **1. marquer ▶** to put a brand on : *The ranchers rounded up the calves and branded them.* **2. être stigmatisé, être noté comme ▶** to be marked or identified in a bad way : *to be branded a coward.* SYN: mark, tag, stamp.

brass [bras] NOUN. **cuivre, laiton** ▸ a yellow metal made of copper and zinc melted together. Brass can be made into various shapes and used to make ornaments, bowls, musical instruments, and other things.

brave [brave] ADJECTIVE, braver, bravest. **brave, courageux (-euse)** ▸ willing to face danger; showing courage; bold : *"He had always thought knights were strong, brave men who spent their time helping people."* (Donald Carrick) **Note.** The quality of being brave is bravery. ▲ VERB, braved, braving. **braver** ▸ to face danger in a brave way; take risks : *They braved the fierce storm to rescue the shipwrecked crew.* 🔖 p. 71.

brav-o [BRAHV-oh] INTERJECTION. **bravo** ▸ well done! excellent! good job!

breach [breech] NOUN, breaches. **1. brèche** ▸ a gap or opening made by a break in something : *Water came through a breach in the dam.* **2. rupture** ▸ a breaking of a law or promise. **Note.** In law, breach of contract means the failure to obey the terms of a contract. ▲ VERB, breached, breaching. **rompre, ouvrir une brèche** ▸ to make an opening in; break through.

bread [bred] NOUN, breads. **1. pain** ▸ a food made by mixing flour or meal with a liquid and baking it in an oven. **2. pain** ▸ the food needed to live : *our daily bread.* ▲ VERB, breaded, breading. **paner** ▸ to coat food with bread crumbs for cooking : *He breaded the fish before frying it.* 🔖 p. 1133.

breadth [bredth] NOUN. **largeur, ampleur** ▸ the distance from side to side of something; width.

break [brake] VERB, broke, broken, breaking. **1. casser, briser** ▸ to make something come apart in pieces; smash, crack, or split : *Jamie broke his toy when he stepped on it.* **2. se casser, se briser** ▸ to come apart; go into pieces : *That glass will break if you drop it.* **3. casser, briser** ▸ to make or become useless or damaged : *Stop fooling around with the remote or you'll break it.* **4. désobéir, rompre, enfreindre** ▸ to fail to keep or obey : *to break a promise; to break the law.* **5. briser** ▸ to do better than : *Josh broke the school record in the 10-km race.* **6. rompre** ▸ to change or become

weaker : *He's trying to break the habit of biting his nails.* ▲ NOUN, breaks. **1. brèche, rupture** ▸ a broken place : *a break in a bone; a break in a wall.* **2. pause** ▸ an opening or interruption : *to take a break from work.* **3. chance, occasion** ▸ a chance or opportunity : *a lucky break.* 🔖 p. 1076.

break down 1. tomber en panne ▸ to fail to work; stop working : *The car broke down just as we arrived.* **2. s'effondrer** ▸ to become very upset : *The witness broke down and cried when she was questioned by the lawyer.*

break in 1. (also break into) **entrer par effraction** ▸ to go in by force : *Someone broke in to the store and stole a radio.* **2. briser** ▸ to get ready for use or work : *to break in a new baseball glove.* **3. interrompre** ▸ to interrupt : *They broke into the program to give a special news report.*

break out 1. se couvrir de plaques, de boutons ▸ to have a rash or other disorder of the skin. **2. éclater** ▸ to begin suddenly : *The crowd broke out into laughter.* **3. s'évader** ▸ to escape : *to break out of jail.*

break up 1. se dissiper, se disperser ▸ to separate or scatter into parts : *The fog should break up by noon.* **2. se terminer, prendre fin** ▸ to bring or come to an end : *The party broke up early.* **3. faire rire, rire** ▸ to laugh or cause to laugh : *That comedian breaks me up.*

break-a-ble [BRAKE-uh-bul] ADJECTIVE. **cassable, fragile** ▸ that can be broken or is easily broken. SYN: fragile, delicate, weak, frail.

break-down [BRAKE-down] NOUN, breakdowns. **1. échec, insuccès** ▸ the failure to work or act properly. **2. dépression, effondrement** ▸ a failing in health, especially a mental collapse. **Note.** Also known as a **nervous breakdown**.

break-er [BRAY-kur] NOUN, breakers. **1. vague déferlante, vague brisante** ▸ a wave that breaks on shore or on a rock. **2. coupe-circuit, disjoncteur** ▸ any person or thing that breaks : *A circuit breaker stops the flow of electricity through a circuit.* 🔖 p. 72.

🖋 Word Builder

Brave, courageous, bold, and *daring* all mean that a person is willing to face danger without being afraid or running away. *Brave* is often used to refer to the dangers of war or fighting : *A brave group of Canadian soldiers landed on Juno Beach in the famous D-Day invasion.* *Courageous* can suggest that a person faces danger in a calm way : *She has been very courageous in dealing with her serious illness.* *Bold* suggests a person who is willing to take a greater risk than others : *Boxing fans are waiting to see if anyone will be bold enough to take on the champion.* *Daring* usually refers to a risk of physical danger : *It takes a daring person to ride down those rapids in a small boat.*

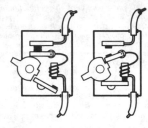

circuit **breaker**

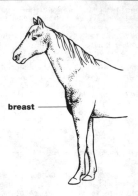

breast

break·fast [BREK-fust] NOUN, breakfasts. **petit déjeuner** ▸ the first meal of the day; the morning meal. ▲ VERB, breakfasted, breakfasting. **prendre le petit déjeuner** ▸ to eat breakfast : *He always breakfasts on fruit and toast.*

break·in [BRAKE-in] NOUN, break-ins. **effraction** ▸ the act of breaking in.

break·through [BRAKE-throo] NOUN, breakthroughs. **percée, invention révolutionnaire** ▸ a sudden finding or advance : *Doctors are hoping for a breakthrough on finding a cure for cancer.*

break·up [BRAKE-up] NOUN, break-ups. (also breakups) **1. dissolution** ▸ the fact of coming apart or separating : *the break-up of a large company into smaller units.* **2. débâcle** ▸ the breaking up of the ice layer on a lake or river in the spring. **3. débâcle** ▸ especially in northern Canada, the time when this breaking of the ice layer takes place.

break·wa·ter [BRAKE-wah-tur] NOUN, breakwaters. **brise-lames** ▸ a barrier that protects a harbour or shore from the force of waves.

breast [brest] NOUN, breasts. **1. poitrine** ▸ the front part of the body from the neck to stomach; the chest. **2. sein** ▸ a gland in women and female animals that gives milk.

breath [breth] NOUN, breaths. **1. souffle** ▸ the air taken into the lungs and forced out when breathing. **2. souffle** ▸ the ability to breathe easily : *I lost my breath climbing that steep hill.* **3. souffle** ▸ a slight breeze : *a breath of fresh air.*

breathe [breeth] VERB, breathed, breathing. **1. respirer** ▸ to take air into the lungs and force it out : *"Hush breathed deeply and began to eat."* (Mem Fox) **2. souffler** ▸ to say quietly; whisper : *Don't breathe a word to anyone; it's a secret.*

breath·tak·ing [BRETH-tay-king] ADJECTIVE. **ahurissant (-ante), palpitant (-ante), excitant (-ante)** ▸ exciting; inspiring awe : *a breathtaking view; a breathtaking performance.*

breed [breed] VERB, bred, breeding. **1. produire, engendrer** ▸ to produce or cause to produce young : *"Sled dogs are bred with wolves to maintain their wolf-like size and strength."* (Robert McGhee) **2. élever, cultiver** ▸ to raise animals or plants of a particular type : *Our neighbour breeds horses.* **3. élever, destiner** ▸ to bring up; train : *She's been bred to be well-mannered.* **4. engendrer, produire** ▸ to bring about; cause : *Good manners breed respect.* ▲ NOUN, breeds. **race** ▸ a particular type of animal or plant : *Cocker spaniels are a breed of dog.* SYN: raise, produce, develop, cultivate, bring up.

breed·ing [BREE-ding] NOUN. **1. reproduction** ▸ the act of producing young. **2. éducation** ▸ the way someone is taught to behave : *He is a person of good breeding.*

breeze [breez] NOUN, breezes. **1. vent, brise** ▸ a light, gentle wind : *The flag moved in the gentle breeze.* **2. Informal. rien** ▸ something easy to do : *That test was a breeze for him because he studied so hard.* ■ **breezy.** ADJECTIVE. ▸ **venteux (-euse).**

brew [broo] VERB, brewed, brewing. **1. brasser** ▸ to make beer, ale, or a similar drink by soaking, boiling, and fermenting malt or hops. **2. infuser** ▸ to prepare other drinks such as tea or coffee by soaking in hot water. **3. couver, prendre forme** ▸ to begin to take form; start to happen : *Look at how dark the sky is; I think a storm is brewing.* ▲ NOUN, brews. **bière, boisson** ▸ beer or another drink made by brewing.

bri·ar [BRY-ur] NOUN, briars. (also brier) **1. ronce** ▸ a bush or plant with many thorns, such as a wild rose or blackberry. **2. églantier, rosier sauvage** ▸ a hard wood often used for making pipes. **3. Pipe de Bruyère** ▸ a pipe made from such a wood.

bribe [bribe] NOUN, bribes. **pot-de-vin, paiement illicite** ▶ an offer of money or something valuable in return for doing something wrong. ▲ VERB, bribed, bribing. **corrompre, acheter, soudoyer** ▶ to give or offer a bribe : *She tried to bribe the police officer not to give her a ticket for speeding.* **Note.** The act of giving or offering a bribe is **bribery**.

brick [brik] NOUN, bricks. **1. brique** ▶ a block of clay that has been baked to make it hard. Bricks are used in making walls, fireplaces, sidewalks, and so on. **2. brique** ▶ any object shaped like a brick : *a brick of cheddar cheese.* ▲ VERB, bricked, bricking. **briqueter, murer** ▶ to cover or close up with bricks : *They bricked up the old fireplace when they remodelled the house.*

bride [bride] NOUN, brides. **future mariée, mariée** ▶ a woman who is about to be married or who has just married. **Note.** A bridesmaid is a girl or woman who serves as an attendant to the bride at a wedding. ■ **bridal** ADJECTIVE. ▶ **nuptial (-iaux).**

bride·groom [BRIDE-groom] NOUN, bridegrooms. **futur marié, marié** ▶ a man who is about to be married or has just married. **Note.** Also called a groom.

bridge [brij] NOUN, bridges. **1. pont** ▶ a structure that crosses a river, a valley, a road, or another obstacle to allow travel from one side to the other. **2. arête** ▶ the bony upper part of the nose. **3. pont** ▶ a platform above the main deck of a ship. **4. bridge** ▶ a card game played by two pairs of partners. ▲ VERB, bridged, bridging. **1. river, jeter, construire** ▶ to make a bridge over : *to bridge a river.* **2. relier, combler, surmonter** ▶ to go across or over : *The city is trying to bridge the gap between its older and younger people.* 📖 p. 1047. 👁 p. 542.

bri·dle [BRY-dul] NOUN, bridles. **bride** ▶ the part of a horse's harness that fits around its head and is used to guide and control the horse. A bridle is made of a bit, straps to hold the bit in the horse's mouth, and reins. ▲ VERB, bridled, bridling. **1. brider** ▶ to put a bridle on : *The groom bridled the horse for the rider.* **2. restreindre, maîtriser, brider, refréner** ▶ to hold back ; keep in control ; restrain : *He had to bridle his anger when the girls teased him.*

brief [breef] ADJECTIVE, briefer, briefest. **bref (brève)** ▶ short in length or time ; concise : *Ana's brief letter had only two paragraphs.* ▲ VERB, briefed, briefing. **renseigner, informer, donner des consignes** ▶ to give information or instructions : *The coach briefed the team before the game.* ▲ NOUN, briefs. **dossier** ▶ in law, the summary of facts or arguments to be used by a lawyer in preparing a court case. ■ **briefly,** ADVERB. ▶ **brique.**

bri·gade [bruh-GADE] NOUN, brigades. **1. brigade** ▶ a large unit of troops in an army. **2. brigade, corps organisé** ▶ a group of people organized for a certain purpose : *The fire brigade has only volunteer firefighters.*

bright [brite] ADJECTIVE, brighter, brightest. **1. brillant (-ante)** ▶ giving off much light ; shining with a strong light : *The full moon is very bright tonight.* **Note.** Also used as an ADVERB : *The moon was shining bright.* **2. éclatant (-ante), brillant (-ante)** ▶ strong in colour : *The door was painted bright red.* **3. brillant (-ante)** ▶ smart ; clever : *a bright girl.* ■ **brightly,** ADVERB : ▶ **brillamment.** *"He looked out at the night sky where the stars twinkled brightly in the dark."* (Nicola Morgan) ■ **brightness,** NOUN : ▶ **éclat, lustre.** *the brightness of the sun on a clear day.* SYN : brilliant, shining, gleaming.

bril·liant [BRIL-yunt] ADJECTIVE. **1. brillant (-ante)** ▶ shining brightly ; sparkling : *brilliant sunlight.* **2. brillant (-ante), excellent (-ente)** ▶ excellent ; outstanding : *"Daedalus was a brilliant craftsman who worked for the King of Athens."* (Marcia Williams) **3. brillant (-ante), très intelligent (-ente)** ▶ very intelligent : *I can't believe Clive came up with that brilliant idea.* ■ **brilliance,** NOUN : ▶ **éclat, lustre.** *The brilliance of the sun made it hard to see.*

brim [brim] NOUN, brims. **1. bord** ▶ the upper edge of a glass, cup, bowl, or similar container : *Fill the bucket almost to the brim with water.* **2. bord, rebord** ▶ the outer edge of something : *She has a hat with a wide brim to shade her face from the sun.* ▲ VERB, brimmed, brimming. **remplir** ▶ to fill to the brim ; overflow : *His eyes brimmed with tears.* SYN : edge, rim, lip.

bring [bring] VERB, brought, bringing. **1. apporter, amener, emporter, emmener** ▶ to carry or take along with one : *I'll bring my new computer game when I come over to your house.* **2. faire venir, faire monter, porter, attirer** ▶ to cause to happen : *Bring the water to a boil.* **3. amener, permettre** ▶ to cause to reach a certain condition : *Step on the brake to bring the car to a stop.* 🖋 p. 74.

bring about causer, opérer ▶ to make happen ; cause : *Computers will bring about many changes in our lives.*

bring out faire sortir, apporter ▶ to present to the public : *That studio is bringing out five new movies this month.*

bring up 1. élever, éduquer ▶ to care for or raise a child : *She's been brought up to be very polite.* **2. mentionner, suggérer, mettre sur le tapis** ▶ to mention ; suggest : *to bring up a subject for discussion.*

brink [brink] NOUN, brinks. **1. bord** ▶ the upper edge or top of a steep place : *We stood on the brink of the cliff.* **2. à la veille** ▶ the point or moment just before something is likely to happen : *the brink of disaster.* SYN : edge, verge.

brisk [brisk] ADJECTIVE, brisker, briskest. **1. vif (vive), actif (-ive)** ▶ quick and active ; lively : *We* *walked at a brisk pace.* **2. vivifiant (-ante)** ▶ cool and refreshing : *We went for a walk to enjoy the brisk spring wind.* ■ **briskly,** ADVERB. ▶ **vivement, activement.** SYN : spirited, energetic, active.

bris·tle [BRIS-ul] NOUN, bristles. **poil raide** ▶ short, stiff hair, as on a hog or other animal. Bristles are used to make brushes. ▲ VERB, bristled, bristling. **1. hérisser** ▶ to have the hairs on the back of the neck rise stiffly when excited or angry : *"The strange dog stood bristling and showing his teeth."* (Laura Ingalls Wilder) **2. se hérisser, se dresser** ▶ to stand up straight like bristles : *The boy's hair was cut so short it bristled.*

bristles

British North America Act Acte de l'Amérique du Nord britannique ▶ an act passed by the British Parliament in March 1867, which established the Dominion of Canada. **Note.** Also known as the B.N.A. Act.

brit·tle [BRIT-ul] ADJECTIVE, brittler, brittlest. **fragile** ▶ hard and easily broken ; breaking with a snap : *Gran says she has to be careful not to fall, because her bones are brittle.*

broad [brod] ADJECTIVE, broader, broadest. **1. large** ▶ large from side to side : *"She looked at Michael with a broad smile, but it quickly disappeared."* (Cynthia Rylant) **2. vaste** ▶ large in range ; not limited : *The magazine covers a broad range of subjects.* **3. grand jour, plein jour** ▶ bright and clear. **Note.** This meaning is used in the phrase broad daylight. SYN : wide, large, expansive.

broad·cast [BROD-cast] VERB, broadcast or broadcasted, broadcasting. **1. diffuser, radio-diffuser** ▶ to send out programs or information by radio or television. **2. répandre, diffuser** ▶ to make something known over a wide area : *Rumours of a test were quickly broadcast among the students.* ▲ NOUN, broadcasts. **reportage** ▶ a program sent out to the public by radio or television : *We interrupt our regular news broadcast with this special bulletin.*

bro·chure [broh-SHOOR] NOUN, brochures. **brochure, circulaire, dépliant** ▶ a small pamphlet or booklet, often with colourful pictures, that advertises a product or service or gives informa-

⌕ **Writing Tips**

Bring *or* **take**

• **Bring** *or* **Take** *Many people confuse* **bring** *and* **take**, *often using them to mean the same thing. But* **bring** *and* **take** *are opposites of each other.*

• **Bring** *means "to carry something toward the person who is speaking or writing or the person being spoken to."*
    When you are finished with my book, **bring** *it back here to me.*

• **Take** *means "to carry something away to a person or place."*
    When I am finished with this library book, I will take it back to the library.

• *Think of a trick to help you remember— for example, "Bring it to me. Take it away."*

tion about something : *We sent for brochures about all the places we want to visit on our vacation.*

broke [broke] VERB. ▶ a past form of break: *I broke the glass when I dropped it. He got a ticket because he broke the speed limit.* ▲ ADJECTIVE. *Informal.* **pauvre, sans argent** ▶ having little or no money : *I'm broke—can you loan me money for lunch?*

brok·en [BROH-kun] VERB. ▶ a past form of break: *All the glasses were broken when the shelf collapsed.* ▲ ADJECTIVE. **1. cassé (-ée), brisé (-ée)** ▶ that has or that shows a break ; in pieces : *Don't walk around barefoot; there's broken glass on the floor.* **2. brisé (-ée)** ▶ damaged or ruined by a break : *That song is about someone's broken heart.* SYN : burst, ruptured, shattered.

broker [broh-kur] NOUN. **courtier (-ière)** ▶ a person specialised in dealing on the stock exchange. *David's Father is a broker.*

bron·chi·tis [brong-KY-tus] NOUN. **bronchite** ▶ a soreness and swelling in the bronchial tubes (the tubes connecting the windpipe and lungs) causing coughs and chest pains.

bron·co [BRONG-koh] NOUN, broncos. **cheval (-aux) sauvage** ▶ a small wild or partly tamed horse of western North America.

Bron·to·sau·rus [BRON-tuh-SOR-us] NOUN, brontosauruses. **brontosaure** ▶ a huge, plant-eating dinosaur with a very small head and a long neck and tail. The Brontosaurus was up to 25 metres long and had a mass of about 30 tonnes.

bronze [bronz] NOUN. **1. bronze** ▶ a hard metal made from copper and tin, used for statues, medals, jewellery, and machine parts. **2. bronze** ▶ a reddish-brown colour like that of bronze. ▲ ADJECTIVE. **bronze** ▶ reddish-brown. ▲ VERB, bronzed, bronzing. **bronzer** ▶ to make the colour of bronze : *The artist bronzed the roof of the dollhouse he was making.*

brood [brood] NOUN, broods. **1. couvée, nichée** ▶ all the young birds that are hatched from eggs laid at the same time by one mother : *The mother hen led her brood of chicks around the farmyard.* **2.** *Informal.* **enfants** ▶ all the children in one family. ▲ VERB, brooded, brooding. **1. couver** ▶ to sit on eggs so that they will hatch. **2. songer à** ▶ to worry or think about something for a long time : *Lina is still brooding about what you said to her.*

brook [brook] NOUN, brooks. **ruisseau (-eaux)** ▶ a small stream of fresh water : *Dad and I often fish in the brook near our house.*

broom [broom] NOUN, brooms. **1. balai** ▶ a brush on a long handle, used for sweeping : *Lee used a broom to sweep out the garage.* **2. genêt** ▶ a bush with yellow flowers, small leaves, and thin branches. In early times, brooms were made from these branches. **Note.** The long handle of a broom is called a **broomstick.**

broth [BROTH] NOUN, broths. **bouillon** ▶ a thin soup made from the water used to cook meat, fish, or vegetables.

broth-er [BRUTH-ur] NOUN, brothers. **1. frère** ▶ a boy or man who has the same parents as another person. **2. frère** ▶ a male member of the same group or club. **3. frère** ▶ a male member of a religious order who is not a priest. ■ **brotherly,** ADVERB. ▶ fraternellement.

brought [brot] VERB. **apporter** ▶ a past form of bring.

brow [brow] NOUN, brows. **1. arcade sourcilière** ▶ the part of the face between the eyes and the hair ; the forehead. **2. sourcil** ▶ the eyebrow. **3. front, croupe, bord** ▶ the upper edge of a steep place : the brow of a hill. *"The soldiers rode on until they came to the brow of a high hill."* (David Day)

brown [brown] NOUN, browns. **brun, marron** ▶ a dark colour like that of chocolate or mud : *Grass will turn brown if you don't water it.* ▲ ADJECTIVE. **brun (-une), châtain (-aine)** ▶ having the colour brown. **brunir** ▶ ▲ VERB, browned, browning. **gâteau** ▶ to make or become brown : *He browned the meat before adding it to the stew.*

brown-ie [BROW-nee] NOUN, brownies. **1. gâteau au chocolat et aux noix** ▶ a small, flat chocolate cake, often made with nuts and sometimes frosted. **2. lutin** ▶ an elf in fairy tales who does kind deeds for people.

browse [browz] VERB, browsed, browsing. **1. butiner** ▶ to look through or at something in a casual way : *Zara browsed in the bookstore while waiting for her mother.* **2. brouter** ▶ to feed on grass, leaves, or twigs : *We could see the deer browsing in the meadow.*

bruise[1] [brooz] NOUN, bruises. **1. meurtrissure, contusion** ▶ an injury to the body that does not break the skin but leaves a black-and-blue mark on it. **2.** a similar injury to the outside of a fruit, vegetable, or plant. ▲ VERB, bruised, bruising. **meurtrir, contusionner** ▶ to cause a bruise on : *I bruised the pear when I dropped it.*

brush[1] [brush] NOUN, brushes. **brosse** ▶ a tool having hairs or wires attached to a handle, used for cleaning, for painting, or for arranging the hair : *Yazid likes to use a small brush when he paints.* ▲ VERB, brushed, brushing. **1. brosser** ▶ to sweep, clean, smooth, or paint with a brush : *Brush your teeth for at least one minute twice a day.* **2. effleurer, raser** ▶ to touch lightly in passing : *"I held open the door and she brushed past me without a word."* (James Herriot)

brush[2] NOUN, brushes. **1. brousse, fourré** ▶ an area where small trees, shrubs, and bushes grow together : *I think there is a rabbit hiding in the brush.* **2. broussailles** ▶ branches or twigs that are broken from trees.

bru-tal [BROOT-ul] ADJECTIVE. **brutal (-ale)** ▶ like a brute ; cruel or savage : *The treatment of the prisoners of war was brutal.* **Note.** The state of being brutal is **brutality.**

brute [broot] NOUN, brutes. **1. brute, bête** ▶ an animal, as opposed to a human ; a beast. **2. brute** ▶ a savage or cruel person. ▲ ADJECTIVE. **brute** ▶ of or like a brute ; without mind or feeling : *They were helpless against the brute force of the hurricane.*

bub-ble [BUB-ul] NOUN, bubbles. **1. bulle** ▶ a thin film of liquid shaped like a ball and filled with gas or air. Bubbles often form from soapy water and can float in the air. **2. bulle** ▶ a round space filled with air or gas inside a liquid or solid : *There are bubbles in these ice cubes.* ▲ VERB, bubbled, bubbling. **bouillonner, pétiller, dégager des bulles** ▶ to form bubbles : *The pot of stew bubbled over.*

buck [buk] NOUN, bucks. **1. daim, chevreuil** ▶ the male of deer and certain other animals, such as an antelope, rabbit, or goat. **Note.** The female of such animals is the doe. **2.** *Informal.* **billet d'un dollar** ▶ a dollar. ▲ VERB, buck, bucking. **1. sauter** ▶ to jump suddenly with the back arched and the head down : *The horse bucked and threw its rider to the ground.* **2. bouger** ▶ to move in a sudden, jerky way : *"The car bucked a few times and then roared down the street."* (Louise Fitzhugh) **3. résister** ▶ to resist or work against : *He is always bucking the system at work, and as a result he never gets promoted.*

buck-et [BUK-it] NOUN, buckets. **saut** ▶ a deep, round container with a handle, used for carrying water, dirt, sand, and other things.

buck-le [BUK-ul] NOUN, buckles. **boucle** ▸ a fastening that holds together the two ends of something, such as a belt or strap. ▲ VERB, buckled, buckling. **1. boucler** ▸ to fasten with a buckle : *We buckled our seatbelts before the plane took off.* **2. voiler** ▸ to bend or bulge : *His knees buckled when he lifted the heavy box.* SYN : fasten, clasp, hook.

buckle down travailler fort, s'atteler à un boulot ▸ to work very hard : *She buckled down and finished the job.*

bud [bud] NOUN, buds. **bourgeon** ▸ a small growth or swelling on a plant that will later develop into a leaf, flower, or branch. ▲ VERB, budded, budding. **bourgeonner** ▸ to form or put forth buds : *The trees bud in the spring.* ■ **budding,** ADJECTIVE. ▸ **qui bourgeonne.** beginning to grow or develop : *Kate is a budding swimmer.* SYN : sprout, flourish, develop. 👁 p. 249.

Bud-dhism [BOOD-iz-um] NOUN. **bouddhisme** ▸ the religion founded by Buddha and based on his teachings. Buddhism is an important religion in many countries of Asia. **Note.** A follower of Buddhism is known as a Buddhist.

bud-dy [BUD-ee] NOUN, buddies. **ami (-ie), copain (copine)** ▸ a very close friend ; pal. SYN : companion, partner, comrade, chum, pal.

budge [buj] VERB, budged, budging. **bouger, céder, reculer** ▸ to cause something to move a little : *Once Aaron has made up his mind, he just won't budge.* ✎ p. 381.

budg-et [BUJ-it] NOUN, budgets. **budget** ▸ a plan for spending money. A budget shows how much money is expected to be spent for certain things, often within a certain time such as a month or a year. ▲ VERB, budgeted, budgeting. **budgéter** ▸ to plan a budget : *Jenny should budget her time better so that she won't have to stay up so late studying.*

buff [buf] NOUN, buffs. **1. peau de buffle, cuir épais** ▸ a soft, strong leather made from the skin of a buffalo or an ox. **2. chamois** ▸ a yellowish-brown colour like this leather. **3. passionné (-ée)** ▸ a person who is very interested in some activity or subject : *Chet has turned into a real computer buff.* ▲ ADJECTIVE. **chamois** ▸ yellowish-brown. ▲ VERB, buffed, buffing. **polir** ▸ to polish or shine something with or as if with this kind of leather : *Herb buffed his shoes with his handkerchief.*

buf-fa-lo [BUF-uh-loh] NOUN, buffalo or buffaloes. **1. buffle, bison** ▸ the popular name for the bison, a large wild ox of North America, with a large, round body and long horns that curve outward. **2. bovin à cornes** ▸ any of several kinds of large wild oxen with long, curving horns, found in Asia and Africa.

buff-er [BUF-ur] NOUN, buffers. **1. amortisseur, tampon** ▸ something that comes between two things to soften a blow or shock. **2. état tampon** ▸ a person or country that serves as a barrier between others that are in conflict : *The teacher tried to act as a buffer between the two arguing students.* **3. accumulateur en tampon** ▸ a storage area in a computer that holds information that is to be printed or transferred elsewhere, so that the main memory can continue to operate.

buffalo

buf-fet[1] [buh-FAY or boo-FAY] NOUN, buffets. **1. buffet** ▸ a meal laid out on a buffet or table so that people can serve themselves. **2. buffet** ▸ a piece of furniture with a flat top that is used for serving food or for storing dishes and silverware.

buf-fet[2] [BUF-it] VERB, buffeted, buffeting. **battre, secouer, ballotter** ▸ to pound or strike again and again : *The strong winds and high waves buffeted the little sailboat.*

bug [bug] NOUN, bugs. **1. punaise** ▸ any of a large group of insects that have thick front wings and mouth parts that are used for biting and sucking. **2. insecte** ▸ any insect or animal like a true bug, such as an ant, a spider, or a beetle. **3.** *Informal.* **microbe** ▸ a germ that causes disease : *a flu bug.* **4.** *Informal.* **problème (informatique)** ▸ something wrong in the operation of a machine, especially in a computer program, that keeps it from working properly. **5.** *Informal.* **microphone clandestin** ▸ a small microphone that is hidden in a place to pick up private conversations. ▲ VERB, bugged, bugging. **1.** *Informal.* **camoufler un microphone clandestin** ▸ to hide a microphone in : *to bug a room.* **2.** *Informal.* **ennuyer** ▸ to bother or annoy someone.

bug-gy [BUG-ee] NOUN, buggies. **1. petit véhicule** ▸ a light carriage with four wheels, pulled by a single horse. **2. véhicule pour bébés** ▸ a baby carriage.

bu-gle [BYOO-gul] NOUN, bugles. **clairon** ▸ a brass musical instrument that is shaped like a trumpet. **Note.** A person who plays a bugle is a bugler.

build [bild] VERB, built, building. **1. bâtir, construire ▸** to make something by putting parts or materials together : *My sister and I like to build sand castles at the beach.* **Note.** A builder is a person who builds something, especially a person whose work is putting up buildings. **2. se développer ▸** to form little by little; develop : *My parents spent years trying to build a successful business.* ▲ NOUN, builds. **carrure, construction ▸** the way something or someone is formed : *He got his strong build by lifting weights.* SYN: construct, create, develop, manufacture.

build-ing [BIL-ding] NOUN, buildings. **1. édifice, bâtiment ▸** something that is built for use by people or to store things; a structure with walls and a roof, such as a house, store, school, or hotel. **2. construction ▸** the act or business of putting up buildings. 📖 **p. 1048.**

bulb [bulb] NOUN, bulbs. **1. bulbe ▸** a round part of certain plants, such as the onion, lily, or tulip. A bulb grows underground and produces a new growth of the plant. **2. bulbe ▸** anything that is shaped like a bulb, such as an electric light bulb.

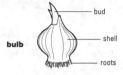

bud
shell
bulb
roots

bulge [bulj] NOUN, bulges. **bombement ▸** a part that swells out : *His wallet made a bulge in his pocket.* ▲ VERB, bulged, bulging. **bomber, ballonner ▸** to swell out : *"His pockets bulged with loose silver and balled-up notes."* (James Herriot) **Note.** Also used as an ADJECTIVE: *"Out of the flames rose a terrifying dragon, with bulging eyes and gaping jaws."* (Robin Muller)

bulk [bulk] NOUN. **1. en bloc, en quantité, en gros ▸** great size or volume : *In spite of its bulk, a tiger is very fast and graceful.* **2. la masse, le plus gros ▸** the largest part : *The bulk of Canada's population lives in urban areas.* **Note.** Something that has great bulk is bulky: *The little girl was dressed for the cold in a bulky sweater and jacket.*

bull [bul] NOUN, bulls. **1. taureau (-eaux) ▸** the full-grown male of cattle. **2. mâle ▸** the full-grown male of certain other large animals, such as an elephant, a moose, a whale, or a seal. **Note.** For those animals whose male is called a bull, the female is called a **cow.**

bull-doz-er [BUL-doh-zur] NOUN, bulldozers. **bulldozer ▸** a large tractor with a large shovel, shaped like a blade, attached to the front.

bul-let [BUL-it] NOUN, bullets. **1. balle ▸** a small piece of rounded or pointed metal that is fired

from a gun. **2. boulet ▸** the heavy dot or other graphic at the beginning of items in some lists.

bul-le-tin [BUL-uh-tun] NOUN, bulletins. **1. bulletin ▸** a brief announcement giving the latest news about something. **2. bulletin ▸** a small magazine or newspaper published regularly by a group or organization : *The church bulletin has an announcement of a picnic on Saturday.*

bulletin board 1. babillard, tableau d'affichage ▸ a board on which notices and other items are posted, as at a school, store, or other public place. **2. babillard électronique ▸** a message centre that operates by computer, so that someone can leave messages that other people can read on their own computer screens.

bul-ly [BUL-ee] NOUN, bullies. **brute ▸** a person who picks on a younger, smaller, or weaker person : *That bully always knocks down the smallest player on the other team.* ▲ VERB, bullied, bullying. **intimider, malmener, brutaliser ▸** to act like a bully; frighten someone : *"Nobody bullied us younger ones, not with Josepha standing close."* (Jim McGugan)

bum [bum] NOUN, bums. *Informal.* **1. fainéant (-ante), clochard (-arde) ▸** a person who does not work and tries to live by begging. **2. misérable ▸** a person who is thought of as bad or worthless. ▲ VERB, bummed, bumming. **1. vivre aux crochets de ▸** to take advantage of other people; beg : *He didn't have bus fare, so he tried to bum a ride.* **2. fainéanter ▸** to loaf around; do nothing : *She bummed around the country after graduating from university.*

bum-ble-bee [BUM-bul-BEE] NOUN, bumblebees. **bourdon ▸** a large yellow-and-black bee that has a thick, hairy body and makes a loud humming noise.

bump [bump] VERB, bumped, bumping. **1. cogner, frapper ▸** to move or hit against suddenly and heavily : *Brian accidentally bumped the lamp and knocked it over.* **2. avancer avec force cahots ▸** to move in an uneven, jerky, way : *The car bumped along the old dirt road.* ▲ NOUN, bumps. **1. choc, secousse ▸** a heavy knock or blow : *We felt a bump as the plane's wheels touched the runway.* **2. bosse ▸** a swelling or lump : *He has a bump on his head where the baseball hit him.* ■ **bumpy,** ADJECTIVE: **▸ cahoteux (-euse).** *a bumpy ride.*

bump-er [BUM-pur] NOUN, bumpers. **pare-chocs ▸** a heavy metal, rubber, or plastic bar or fender that is attached to the front and back of a car, truck, or bus. The bumper protects the body of the car from damage when it is hit. ▲ ADJECTIVE. **grand (grande), magnifique ▸** very large : *We had a bumper crop of wheat this year.*

bun [bun] NOUN, buns. **1. petit pain ▸** a small bread roll, often sweetened or having raisins or spices : *Dad bought tarts and sweet buns at the* *bakery.* **2. chignon ▸** a roll of hair worn on the top or back of the head.

bunch [bunch] NOUN, bunches. **groupe, régime (bananes), grappe (raisins), trousseau (-eaux) ▸** any group of things growing or placed together : *a bunch of bananas. He left a bunch of papers on the desk.* ▲ VERB, bunched, bunching. **grouper ▸** to gather in a bunch : *The sheep bunched together against the cold.*

bun·dle [BUN-dul] NOUN, bundles. **paquet ▸** a number of things tied or wrapped together : *"Harald made trip after trip to the cave, bringing Walter great bundles of reeds."* (Donald Carrick) ▲ VERB, bundled, bundling. **empaqueter ▸** to tie or wrap : *Steve bundled newspapers to be picked up for recycling.*

bun·ga·low [BUNG-guh-LOH] NOUN, bungalows. **bungalow ▸** a one-storey house or cottage.

bun·gee cord [bun-GEE] NOUN, **élastique de Bungee ▸** a stretchable cord of rubber or plastic that is often used to hold items in place.

bunk [bunk] NOUN, bunks. **lit-placard ▸** a narrow bed that is built in or set against a wall. Bunk beds are often arranged in pairs, one above the other.

bun·ny [BUN-ee] NOUN, bunnies. *Informal.* **lapin ▸** a rabbit : *the Easter Bunny.*

buoy [BOO-ee *or* boy] NOUN, buoys. **1. bouée, balise flottante ▸** a floating object that is anchored in the water. Buoys are used to show ships where they may safely go in a harbour or channel or to warn them of dangerous rocks and shallow places. **2.** (also **life buoy**) **bouée ▸** a ring made of floating material, used to keep a person afloat in the water. **buoy·ant** [BOY-ant] ADJECTIVE. **1. flottable, léger (-ère) ▸** able to float in water : *A life jacket makes you more buoyant.* **2. qui a de l'entrain ▸** cheerful : *We all smiled at Lee's buoyant mood.* **Note.** The state of being buoyant is buoyancy.

bur·den [BUR-dun] NOUN, burdens. **1. fardeau (-eaux), charge ▸** something that is carried; a load : *"He put his burden down and straightened up."* (Katherine Anne Porter) **2. poids, fardeau ▸** something that is hard to bear : *The lack of money was a burden to the family.* ▲ VERB, burdened, burdening. **charger, alourdir ▸** to put a load on : *"They were heavily burdened with blanket packs which were strapped to their shoulders."* (Jack London) ■ **burden·some,** ADJECTIVE. ▸ **onéreux (-euse).** SYN: load, weight, hardship, difficulty.

bu·reau [BYOOR-oh] NOUN, bureaus or bureaux. **1. bureau, secrétaire, commode ▸** a chest of drawers in which clothing is kept. **2. bureau ▸** an office, a department, or an agency : *Information came in to the TV station's news bureau.*

bu·reauc·ra·cy [byoo-ROK-ruh-see] NOUN, bureaucracies. **bureaucratie ▸** a system of run-

ning a government or business in which there are many different departments, and everyone does a certain job according to strict rules. A bureaucracy is often thought of as having a lot of delay and unnecessary work. **Note.** A person who works in a bureaucracy is called a bureaucrat.

buoys

bur·glar [BUR-glur] NOUN, burglars. **cambrioleur (-euse) ▸** a person who breaks into a house or building to steal something : *The police caught the burglar who stole our computer.* **Note.** This crime is known as burglary.

bur·i·al [BAIR-ee-ul] NOUN, burials. **enterrement ▸** the act of placing a dead body in a grave or tomb.

bur·ied [BAIR-eed] VERB. **enterré (-ée) ▸** a past form of bury: *Maria's shoes were buried under a pile of clothes.* ▲ ADJECTIVE. **enterré (-ée) ▸** that has been buried : *They had a map with the buried treasure marked on it.*

bur·lap [BUR-lap] NOUN. **toile d'emballage ▸** a coarse cloth woven from thick fibres of jute, hemp, or cotton. It is used mainly to make bags.

burn [burn] VERB, burned or burnt, burning. **1. brûler ▸** to be on fire or set fire to : *The logs burned in the fireplace.* **2. brûler ▸** to hurt or damage by fire or heat : *He burned the cookies when he left them in the oven too long.* **3. brûler ▸** to make or cause by fire or heat : *She accidentally burned a hole in her sweater.* **4. brûler ▸** to feel hot; give a feeling of heat to : *The baby's forehead burned with fever.* **5. brûler, consumer ▸** to use for light or heat : *Our camping stove burns kerosene.* ▲ NOUN, burns. **brûlure ▸** damage or an injury caused by fire or heat : *There are iron burns in his shirt.*

burr [bur] NOUN, burrs (also bur) **1. capsule épineuse ▸** any seed or plant part with a rough, prickly covering that causes it to stick to things. **2. capsule épineuse ▸** a plant that has burrs.

bur-row [BUR-oh] NOUN, burrows. **terrier ▸** a hole or tunnel dug in the ground by an animal to live or hide in. ▲ VERB, burrowed, burrowing. **1. fouir (la terre), se terrer, creuser ▸** to dig a hole in the ground : *The gopher burrowed holes in the lawn.* **2. fouiller ▸** to search by digging under or through : *Shanna burrowed through her dresser drawers looking for her necklace.* **3. se terrer, s'enfouir ▸** to go into something as if into a burrow : *"He burrowed down into his sleeping bag."* (James Houston)

burst [burst] VERB, burst, bursting. **1. éclater, exploser ▸** to break open suddenly : *The dam burst under the weight of too much water.* **2. regorger ▸** to be full to the point of almost breaking open : *The suitcase was bursting with clothes.* **3. éclater ▸** to come or go suddenly : *to burst into tears.* ▲ NOUN. **éclatement, explosion ▸** a sudden outbreak : *There was a burst of applause from the audience.* SYN: explode, blow up.

bur-y [BAIR-ee] VERB, buried, burying. **1. enterrer ▸** to place a dead body in a grave or tomb. **2. enterrer, enfouir ▸** to cover up with or as if with dirt : *Our dog likes to bury bones in the ground.*

bus [bus] NOUN, buses or busses. **1. autobus, bus ▸** a large motor vehicle with many rows of seats for carrying a large number of people : *Everyone in our class rides to school on the bus.* **2. conducteur (-trice) ▸** an electrical pathway that sends information from one part of a computer to another : *Data are transferred from the computer's memory to the printer by means of a bus.* ▲ VERB, bused, busing. (sometimes bussed, bussing) **aller en autobus ▸** to send or go by bus : *to bus students to school.* **Note.** The act of sending children to school by bus is busing. 📖 p. 1153.

bush [bush] NOUN, bushes. **1. buisson ▸** a low-growing plant; a shrub. A bush is smaller than a tree and has branches closer to the ground. The same plant may be called a bush or a tree, depending on its size. **2. brousse ▸** an area away from towns or cities, with a heavy growth of plants.

bush-el [BOOSH-ul] NOUN, bushels. **boisseau (-eaux) ▸** a unit of measure for dry items such as grain, fruit, and vegetables.

bush pilot **pilote de brousse ▸** a pilot who flies mainly in rough country where there are few commercial airfields, as in northern Canada.

bush-y [BOOSH-ee] ADJECTIVE, bushier, bushiest. **touffu (-ue), épais (épaisse) ▸** thick and spreading like a bush : *Squirrels have bushy tails.*

busi-ness [BIZ-nis] NOUN, businesses. **1. besogne, occupation, métier ▸** the work a person does to earn money; one's job or occupation : *Plumbing is my dad's business.* **2. affaire ▸** the making, buying, and selling of goods, or the exchange of services for money : *Business has been good at the shopping centre this year.* **3. établissement, compagnie ▸** a store, company, or factory that does business. **4. affaire, besogne ▸** an event or affair; matter : *Cleaning out the basement was a messy business.* **5. affaires ▸** one's interest or concern : *If he doesn't want to go with us, that's his business.* ▪ **businessman, businesswoman, homme (femme) d'affaires ▸** or businessperson, NOUN. SYN: work, job, occupation, employment. 📖 p. 79.

bus-tle [BUS-ul] VERB, bustled, bustling. **se remuer, s'activer ▸** to move in a busy, excited way : *The house bustled with activity before the party.* ▲ NOUN. **remue-ménage ▸** excited activity.

bus-y [BIZ-ee] ADJECTIVE, busier, busiest. **1. affairé (-ée), occupé (-ée) ▸** doing something; active : *He is busy studying for his math test.* **2. occupé (-ée) ▸** having a lot of activity : *She had a busy afternoon working at the bank.* **3. occupé (-ée) ▸** in use : *The phone has been busy all morning.* **s'occuper, s'activer ▸** to keep busy : *"Sport tried to busy himself by looking in the icebox."* (Louise Fitzhugh) ▪ **busily,** ADVERB. ▸ **de façon occupée.** SYN: occupied, engaged, active, working.

but [but] CONJUNCTION. **mais ▸** on the other hand : *I'd love to go, but I have to study.* ▲ PREPOSITION. **sauf, sans, sinon ▸** except : *She works every day but Sunday.* ▲ ADVERB. **seulement ▸** only : *He left here but a moment ago.* 📖 p. 80.

✎ Writing Tips

Business Letters
Business letters are written to request information, to make a purchase, to complain about a bad product, to ask for employment, and to take care of other business concerns. Business letters are a type of formal letter and have certain visual features.

- *Your address followed by the date goes in the upper-right corner.*
- *Two spaces down on the left are the title (Mr., Ms., Dr.), name, and address of the person to whom you're writing.*
- *The letter starts with "Dear" and the person's title and last name.*
- *The purpose of the letter is stated in the first paragraph.*
- *The letter closes with a polite ending, such as "Sincerely," your name, and your signature.*

butch·er [BOOCH-ur] NOUN, butchers. **1. boucher (-ère)** ▶ a person whose work is cutting and selling meat. **2. boucher** ▶ a person who kills in a cruel or brutal way. ▲ VERB, butchered, butchering. **abattre, égorger, massacrer** ▶ to kill or cut up for meat : *to butcher a steer.*

butte [byoot] NOUN, buttes. **butte** ▶ a steep, flat-topped hill that rises sharply from the surrounding area.

but·ter [BUT-ur] NOUN, butters. **1. beurre** ▶ a solid yellowish fat that is separated from milk or cream by churning, often used as a spread on bread and for cooking and flavouring foods. **2. beurre (de quelque chose)** ▶ another food that spreads like butter, such as peanut butter. ▲ VERB, buttered, buttering. **beurrer** ▶ to spread with butter : *to butter toast.*

but·ter·fly [BUT-ur-FLY] NOUN, butterflies. **papillon** ▶ an insect with a thin body and four large, brightly coloured wings. There are many different kinds of butterflies. 👁 **p. 105.**

butter tart **tarte au beurre** ▶ a sweet, rich tart with a butter, brown sugar, syrup, raisin, and spice filling.

but·ton [BUT-un] NOUN, buttons. **1. bouton** ▶ a flat, round piece of plastic, metal, brass, or other material that is used to fasten clothing or to decorate it. **2. bouton, interrupteur** ▶ a knob that is pushed or turned to make something work, such as a machine, an electric light, an elevator, or a doorbell. ▲ VERB, buttoned, buttoning. **boutonner** ▶ to fasten with a button.

buy [by] VERB, bought, buying. **acheter** ▶ to pay money to get something : *to buy a car.* ▲ NOUN, buys. **achat** ▶ a bargain : *They got a good buy on that house.* SYN: purchase, bargain, invest.

buzz [buz] VERB, buzzed, buzzing. **1. bourdonner, vrombir** ▶ to make a low humming sound, as bees or flies do. **2. bourdonner** ▶ to be full of activity and talk : *The school buzzed with rumours of a new principal.* **3. harceler** ▶ to fly an airplane low over something. ▲ NOUN, buzzes. **bourdonnement, vrombissement** ▶ a low humming sound, like that of a bee.

buz·zard [BUZ-urd] NOUN, buzzards. **busard (buse)** ▶ a very large bird of prey with a sharp beak, sharp claws, and dark feathers.

buzz·word [BUZ-wurd] NOUN, buzzwords. *Informal.* **néologisme** ▶ a new and important-sounding word that is used with a special meaning in a certain business or activity : *a computer buzzword.*

by [by] PREPOSITION. **1. près de, auprès de, à côté de** ▶ near; beside : *Leave the paper by the door.* **2. par** ▶ through the work of : *a play by*

✐ Writing Tips

But

Some people think that you should not start a sentence with **but.** *However, you can start a sentence with* **but** *when you want*

• *to contradict or put restrictions on the information in the sentence before :*

Businesses argue that they are doing their part to save the environment. **But** *it is clear that they aren't doing enough.*

• *to break up a very long sentence into two shorter sentences.*

• *to give force to a short statement :*
He wanted to make the climb with his friends. **But** *he couldn't do it.*

Shakespeare. **3. en, par** ▶ through the use of : *He left town by train.* **4. pour** ▶ no later than : *I hope to finish by noon.* **5. par** ▶ in the measure or amount of : *to win by a nose; to buy pop by the case.* ▲ ADVERB. **1. passer** ▶ past : *Is that Kenisha's car going by?* **2. ici** ▶ to or at someone's place : *Stop by for a visit.*

by·e·lec·tion [BY-uh-LEK-shun] NOUN, byelections. (also by-election) **élection partielle** ▶ an election held in only one riding (a political division) because of the death or resignation of its member of Parliament or of the Legislative Assembly.

by·law [BY-LAW] NOUN, bylaws. (also by-law) **arrêté municipal** ▶ a local law; a law that is made by a city, company, or club to control its own affairs.

by·pass [BY-pas] NOUN, bypasses. (also by-pass) **1. route d'évitement** ▶ a road that passes around a city or a downtown area. **2. pontage** ▶ an operation to allow blood to pass around a damaged blood vessel : *a heart bypass.* ▲ VERB, bypassed, bypassing. **éviter, dévier, détourner** ▶ to go around : *The new highway bypasses the downtown business section.*

by·prod·uct [BY-PROD-ukt] NOUN, byproducts. (also by-product) **sous-produit** ▶ something that results from making something else : *Buttermilk is a byproduct of butter.*

byte [bite] NOUN, bytes. **octet** ▶ a group of digits, usually eight, that a computer stores as one unit in its memory.

cheese

c, C [see] NOUN, c's, C's. **1. c, c** ► the third letter of the alphabet. **2.** the third-highest mark, grade, or level.

cab [kab] NOUN, cabs. **1. taxi** ► a car with a driver who is paid to take people where they want to go; a taxi. **2. cabine** ► the enclosed part of a truck, crane, or other large vehicle, where the driver or operator sits.

cab·bage [KAB-ij] NOUN, cabbages. **chou (choux)** ► a plant having a rounded head of firm, closely folded leaves of green or red. Cabbage is eaten cooked or raw as a vegetable.

cab·in [KAB-in] NOUN, cabins. **1. cabane** ► a small, simple house made of logs or rough boards. **2. cabine** ► a private room on a passenger ship where people stay during a trip. **3. cabine** ► the main section of an airplane, where the passengers sit.

cabin

cab·i·net [KAB-uh-nit] NOUN, cabinets. **1. meuble de rangement** ► a piece of furniture that has shelves and drawers for holding things: *a kitchen cabinet for dishes and glasses; filing cabinets for papers.* **2. cabinet (ministériel)** ► (also Cabinet) a group of people chosen by the head of a government to give advice on policy. In Canada, the prime minister chooses about 30 members of Parliament to be in the cabinet.

cabinet minister **ministre** ► the head of a department of the government; a member of the cabinet.

ca·ble [KAY-bul] NOUN, cables. **1. câble** ► a strong, thick rope made of twisted wire or fibres. Cables can hold up bridges or pull heavy machines. **2. câble** ► a bundle of wires protected by a covering, used to carry electricity. Telephone and telegraph systems use cables to carry messages from one place to another. **3. message ou adresse télégraphique** ► a message sent by electric cable. **Note.** Also known as a cablegram. ▲ VERB, cabled, cabling. **câbler** ► to send a message by cable.

cable television **télévision par câble** ► a system in which television shows are sent through a cable instead of over the airwaves. People pay a fee for cable TV service in order to get better reception or to receive channels available on open airwaves.

ca·boose [kuh-BOOS] NOUN, cabooses. **1. fourgon de queue** ► the last railway car on a freight train, used by the train workers. **2. cuisine** ► a kitchen on the deck of a ship.

ca·ca·o [kuh-KAY oh] NOUN, cacaos. **cacaoyer** ► a tropical evergreen tree whose seeds are used to make cocoa and chocolate.

cacao tree

leaves

flowers

fruit

seed

cache [kash] NOUN, caches. **1. cachette, cache** ► a hiding place: *The police found the cache* *of the money stolen in the robbery.* **2. butin** ▸ the things hidden in a cache.

cack·le [KAK-ul] VERB, cackled, cackling. **1. glousser, caqueter** ▸ to make a shrill, harsh sound like that of a hen. **2. glousser** ▸ to laugh or talk in a shrill or harsh way : *They cackled at the joke.*

cac·tus [KAK-tus] NOUN, cactuses or cacti. **cactus** ▸ a plant that has a thick green trunk and branches covered with sharp needle-like spines instead of leaves. Cactuses grow in hot, dry places.

ca·det [kuh-DET] NOUN, cadets. **élève officier** ▸ a person training to be an officer in the armed forces, especially a student in a military school : *Many cadets train at the Royal Military College.*

ca·fé [ka-FAY] NOUN, cafés. **café** ▸ a small, informal restaurant or bar. **Note.** The French word for coffee.

caf·e·te·ri·a [KAF-uh-TEER-ee-uh] NOUN, cafeterias. **cafétéria, cantine** ▸ a type of restaurant where customers order food that is on display at a counter and then carry it on trays to a table to eat.

caf·feine [KAF-een] NOUN. **caféine** ▸ a bitter white substance that is found in coffee, tea, chocolate, and cola drinks. Caffeine can keep a person from feeling sleepy, but too much caffeine can cause a person to be very nervous.

cage [kayj] NOUN, cages. **cage** ▸ an enclosed place with wire or bars to keep animals or birds in, as in a zoo or circus : *Juan took his cat on the train in a cage.* **2. cage** ▸ anything shaped or used like a cage : *Deep-sea divers sometimes use cages for protection while they study sharks.* ▲ VERB, caged, caging. **mettre en cage** ▸ to put something into a cage.

cake [kake] NOUN, cakes. **1. gâteau (-eaux)** ▸ a sweet food made of flour, sugar, eggs, and flavourings : *We made a cake for Sam's birthday.* **2. galette** ▸ a thin batter that is fried or baked, such as a pancake. **3. pain** ▸ any hard mass that is like a cake : *a cake of soap.* ▲ VERB, caked, caking. **mouler, former** ▸ to form or harden into a solid mass : *Toni and Pablo caked the mud into bricks.* 🗏 p. 1134.

ca·lam·i·ty [kuh-LAM-uh-tee] NOUN, calamities. **calamité** ▸ something that causes great suffering or misery : *"It seemed a small loss to others, but to Jo it was a dreadful calamity."* (Louisa May Alcott) SYN: disaster, tragedy, misfortune, catastrophe.

cal·ci·um [KAL-see-um] NOUN. **calcium** ▸ a soft, silver-white chemical element that is found in marble, chalk, and shells, and in such foods as milk and cheese. Calcium is important in the diet because it is needed for strong teeth and bones.

cal·cu·late [KAL-kyuh-LATE] VERB, calculated, calculating. **1. calculer, compter** ▸ to get the answer to a problem by using arithmetic : *She calculated how much the three books would cost.* **2. évaluer, mesurer** ▸ to think out with common sense or reason ; estimate : *The Sioux calculated time by figuring how long it took the sun to pass over a tent pole.* **3. viser, être destiné (-ée) à** ▸ to plan or design : *The commercials on some TV shows are calculated to appeal to children.* **Note.** Often used as an ADJECTIVE: *a calculated risk.* **Note.** The act or result of calculating is calculation. SYN: figure, reckon, compute, consider, estimate.

cal·cu·la·tor [KAL-kyuh-LAY-tur] NOUN, calculators. **calculatrice** ▸ a small machine that can solve number problems automatically. Calculators have keyboards with buttons for numbers and for adding, subtracting, and other mathematical operations.

ca·lèche [kuh-LESH] NOUN. **calèche** ▸ a light, two-wheeled carriage pulled by one horse. It carries two passengers, has a seat in front for the driver, and usually has a folding top.

cal·en·dar [KAL-un-dur] NOUN, calendars. **1. calendrier** ▸ a chart showing the days, weeks, and months of the year in order : *Mom marks our appointments on the calendar in the kitchen.* **2. calendrier** ▸ a schedule or list of coming events : *A calendar of events for the community centre lists all the classes starting this fall.* 🗏 p. 1102.

calf¹ [kaf] NOUN, calves. **1. veau (veaux)** ▸ the young of cattle. **2. veau (cuir de)** ▸ leather made from the skin of a calf. **Note.** Also known as calfskin. **3. petit (de gros animaux)** ▸ the young of certain other large animals, such as seals and elephants. 👁 p. 114.

calf² NOUN, calves. **mollet** ▸ the muscular back part of the lower leg, between the knee and ankle.

call [kol] VERB, called, calling. **1. appeler, crier, s'écrier** ▸ to speak or say in a loud voice ; shout or cry : *The coach called to the players from the sidelines.* **2. appeler** ▸ to ask or command to come : *to call a dog.* **3. appeler, nommer** ▸ to refer to by a name ; give a name to : *My aunt calls me "Pumpkin."* **4. annoncer, notifier** ▸ to describe or identify as : *The umpire called the runner safe.* **5. téléphoner à** ▸ to get in touch by telephone : *I'll call you when I arrive.* **6. rendre visite (à quelqu'un), passer (chez quelqu'un)** ▸ to make a short visit. **7. arrêter, suspendre** ▸ to stop or put off : *We called the game when it became too dark to play.* ▲ NOUN, calls. **1. appel, cri** ▸ a loud cry or shout : *a call for help.* **2. cri** ▸ the sound made by a bird or an animal. **3. appel** ▸ the act of getting in touch with someone by telephone. **4. courte visite** ▸ a short visit : *He paid a call on his grandparents on his way home.* **5. besoin, demande** ▸ a

---

✍ Writing Tips

Can—May

Can and may have different meanings. In writing and formal speech, it is important to choose the right word.

* Use **can** when you mean being able to or knowing how to do something.

 Chantelle **can** *speak two languages.*

* Use **may** when you mean permission to do something or the possibility of something happening.

 You **may** *leave when you are finished.*

 It **may** *rain tonight.*

---

need or demand : *courage "above and beyond the call of duty."*

calm [kom] ADJECTIVE, calmer, calmest. **1. calme, immobile ▶** quiet and still ; not moving : *Without the wind, the flag was calm.* **2. calme, serein (-eine), paisible, tranquille ▶** not nervous or excited : *He felt calm and rested after his holiday.* ▲ NOUN. **calme, tranquillité, sérénité ▶** a time or feeling of quiet and stillness : *The "calm before the storm" is an expression for a time of quiet just before something suddenly happens.* ▲ VERB. **calmed, calming. (se) calmer, apaiser, rassurer, tranquilliser ▶** to make or to become calm : *"On hearing about the monster, the little frog calmed down somewhat and thought for a moment."* (Tololwa M. Mollei) ■ **calmly,** ADVERB. ▶ **calmement, paisiblement, sereinement, tranquillement.** SYN: quiet, still, peaceful, smooth.

cal·o·rie [KAL-uh-ree] NOUN, calories. **calorie ▶** a unit for measuring heat. **Note.** A small calorie is equal to the amount of heat needed to raise the temperature of one gram of water by one degree Celsius. A **large** calorie is equal to 1000 small calories. The **large** calorie measures the amount of heat or energy that is supplied by eating a certain food.

came [kame] VERB. **venir ▶** a past form of come.

cam·el [KAM-ul] NOUN, camels. **chameau (-eaux) ▶** a large hoofed animal with a humped back and a long neck. Camels are used in the deserts of Africa and Asia for riding and carrying loads, and they can go for several days without drinking water. **Note.** A camel with one hump is also known as a **dromedary.** A camel with two humps is called a **Bactrian** camel and is found only in Asia.

cam·er·a [KAM-ur-uh or KAM-ruh] NOUN, cameras. **1. appareil photographique ▶** a device for taking photographs or motion pictures. Light passes through a small opening called a lens, causing an image to form on film or a light-sensitive material. **2. caméra ▶** a similar device used in television to form a picture and send it out as an electronic signal for broadcasting. ☞ p. 540.

cam·ou·flage [KAM-uh-FLOJ] NOUN, camouflages. **camouflage ▶** any disguise or appearance that serves to hide something : *A polar bear has a natural camouflage because it is the same white colour as the snow and ice around it.* ▲ VERB, camouflaged, camouflaging. **camoufler, dissimuler, cacher ▶** to try to hide something by changing its colour or appearance : *The soldiers' uniforms camouflaged them in the jungle.* SYN: disguise, conceal, mask.

camp [kamp] NOUN, camps. **camp, campement ▶** an outdoor area where people live in tents or cabins for a time. ▲ VERB, camped, camping. **camper ▶** to set up or live in a camp : *We camped in the mountains last summer.* **Note.** The sport of doing this is **camping** (☞ p. 1163).

cam·paign [kam-PANE] NOUN, campaigns. **1. campagne ▶** any series of actions to gain a certain goal : *The company planned an advertising campaign to introduce its new brand of soap.* **2. campagne (électorale) ▶** the activities that a political candidate carries on to try to win office. ▲ VERB, campaigned, campaigning. **faire campagne ▶** to take part in a campaign : *to campaign for student council.* ■ **campaigner,** NOUN. ▶ **militant (-ante).**

camp·er [KAM-pur] NOUN, campers. **1. campeur (-euse) ▶** a person who camps. **2. caravane ▶** a car or trailer that is built for use on camping trips.

camp·fire [KAMP-fire] NOUN, campfires. **1. feu de camp ▶** a fire in a camp that is used for heat and cooking. **2. feu de camp ▶** a social gathering around a campfire.

cam·pus [KAM-pus] NOUN, campuses. **campus ▶** the land or grounds of a school, college, or university.

can¹ [kan] VERB. **pouvoir ▶** a present form of could. Can is a special verb that is often used with other verbs in these meanings : **1. pouvoir, savoir, être capable de ▶** to be able to or know how to : *The baby can walk already.* **2. pouvoir, avoir le droit de ▶** to have the right to : *With a few exceptions, any Canadian citizen who is at least 18 can vote in a national election.* ☞ p. 83.

can² NOUN, cans. **1. cannette ou canette, conserve, boîte de conserve ▶** a metal container that is filled with food or liquid and then sealed to keep out air ; a tin : *a can of apple juice.* **2. cannette ou canette ▶** the amount that is in a can : *Add four cans of water to make the lemonade.* **3. poubelle, contenant ▶** any similar container with a lid : *a garbage can.* ▲ VERB, canned, canning. **mettre en conserve ▶** to preserve food by putting it into a can : *to can tomatoes.*

Canada Day fête du Canada ▶ A holiday on July 1 that celebrates the anniversary of Confederation. **Note.** Formerly known as Dominion Day.

Canada goose bernache du Canada ▶ a large wild goose of North America. The Canada goose has a black head and neck, white throat, and brownish-grey body.

Canada jay geai du Canada ▶ a bird of the North American conifer forests, having greyish feathers and a black-capped head.

Ca·na·di·an [kuh-NAY-dee-un] NOUN, Canadians. Canadien (-ienne) ▶ a person who lives in or comes from Canada. ▲ ADJECTIVE. canadien (-ienne) ▶ having to do with Canada.

Canadian English anglais canadien ▶ the form of English spoken by English-speaking Canadians.

Canadian Forces (also Canadian Armed Forces) Forces armées canadiennes ▶ the armed forces of Canada; the combined forces of the army (Mobile Command), navy (Maritime Command) and air force (Air Command)

Canadian French français canadien ▶ the form of French spoken by French-speaking Canadians.

Ca·na·di·en [kuh-nah-DYEN] Canadien (-ienne) français (-aise) ▶ the French word for a French Canadian. **Note.** The feminine form is Canadienne.

ca·nal [kuh-NAL] NOUN, canals. canal (-aux) ▶ a waterway that is dug across land. Canals are used to make a body of water deeper so that boats can pass through, to connect two bodies of water, or to carry water to dry lands for farming. SYN: channel, ditch, duct, waterway.

ca·nar·y [kuh-NAIR-ee] NOUN, canaries. canari ▶ a small yellow singing bird that is often kept as a pet. **Note.** The canary gets its name from the Canary Islands, where it first became known.

can·cel [KAN-sul] VERB, cancelled, cancelling. (also canceled, canceling) annuler, éliminer, supprimer ▶ **1.** to take back or do away with; end or stop : *Dale cancelled his trip to Ottawa because he was sick.* **2.** oblitérer, annuler ▶ to mark a cheque or postage stamp with lines so that it can not be used again. SYN: erase, delete, withdraw, remove, abolish.

can·cel·la·tion [KAN-suh-LAY-shun] NOUN, cancellations. annulation, élimination, suppression ▶ the act of cancelling or being cancelled : *The storm caused the cancellation of the outdoor concert.*

can·cer [KAN-sur] NOUN, cancers. **1.** cancer ▶ a very harmful disease in which cells in a body grow and develop much faster than is normal and destroy healthy tissues. Many forms of cancer can cause death. **2.** cancer ▶ something very bad that spreads in a harmful way : *Some people consider war to be a cancer of humanity.* **Note.** Cancer is the name of the constellation (a group of stars) in the shape of a crab. ■ **cancerous,** ADJECTIVE. ▶ cancéreux (-euse).

can·did [KAN-did] ADJECTIVE. **1.** franc (franche), sincère, honnête ▶ open and direct in telling the truth; frank : *Mom and I had a candid talk about my schoolwork.* **2.** naturel (-elle) ▶ not posed : *a candid photograph.*

can·di·date [KAN-duh-DATE or KAN-duh-dit] NOUN, candidates. candidat (-ate) ▶ a person who seeks or is being considered for some office or honour : *Kelly, Juanita, and Simon are all candidates for class president.* **Note.** The word candidate once meant "dressed in white." Candidates in ancient Rome wore pure white robes as a symbol of honesty.

can·dle [KAN-dul] NOUN, candles. bougie, chandelle ▶ a stick of wax, or solid fat, moulded around a string or wick that is burned to give light. **Note.** A candlestick is used to hold a candle.

can·dy [KAN-dee] NOUN, candies. bonbon, friandise, sucrerie ▶ a sweet food made of sugar or syrup, often mixed with chocolate, nuts, or fruits. ▣ p. 1134.

cane [kane] NOUN, canes. **1.** canne ▶ a long, thin stick to help in walking. **2.** canne ▶ the long, slender stem of certain tall grass plants, used to make furniture. **3.** canne ▶ the plant having such stems, such as sugarcane or bamboo.

ca·nine [KAY-nine] NOUN, canines. **1.** chien (-ienne) ▶ a dog. **2.** canine ▶ a sharp, pointed tooth on either side of the front teeth. ▲ ADJECTIVE. canin (-ine) ▶ of or like a dog.

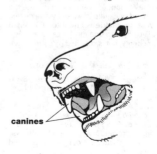

canines

can·non [KAN-un] NOUN, cannons. canon ▶ a large and heavy gun that is set on a base or mounted on wheels and shoots a heavy, round ball : *Cannons were used in wars in earlier times.* **Note.** A cannonball is the solid metal ball fired from a cannon.

ca·noe [kuh-NOO] NOUN, canoes. **canoë ▸** a light, narrow boat that is pointed at both ends and is moved by a paddle : *Connie and I paddled across the lake in a canoe.* ▲ VERB, canoed, canoeing. **faire du canoë ▸** to ride in or paddle a canoe. **☜ p. 394.**

can·ta·loupe [KANT-uh-LOPE] NOUN, cantaloupes. NOUN. **cantaloup, melon ▸** a kind of melon with sweet, orange-coloured flesh that can be eaten.

Ca·nuck [kuh-NUK] NOUN. *Informal.* **Canadien (-ienne) ▸** a Canadian.

can·tan·ker·ous [kan-TANG-kur-us] ADJECTIVE. **irritable, désagréable, de mauvaise humeur, irascible ▸** being difficult and disagreeable; ill-tempered : *Lack of sleep makes me cantankerous.*

can·teen [kan-TEEN] NOUN. **1. gourde ▸** a small container for carrying water or another drink. **2. cafétéria, cantine ▸** a place in school, camp, and so on where food is served.

can·vas [KAN-vus] NOUN, canvases. **toile ▸** a strong, coarse cloth made of cotton, flax, or hemp. Canvas is used for sails, tents, and bags, and as a covering. Artists often use oil paints on canvas.

can·yon [KAN-yun] NOUN, canyons. **canyon ▸** a deep valley with high, steep sides; a gorge.

cap [kap] NOUN, caps. **1. casquette ▸** a hat that fits closely over the head, usually without a brim but often with a visor : *a baseball cap.* **2. capsule, capuchon, bouchon ▸** something that is shaped or works like a cap : *a bottle cap.* **3. amorce ▸** a small explosive wrapped in paper, used in toy guns to make a noise like a bullet firing. ▲ VERB, capped, capping. **1. couvrir, recouvrir, capsuler, coiffer ▸** to put a cap on; cover : *Snow capped the mountains.* **2. couronner ▸** to follow with something as good or better : *She played well all game, and then to cap it off she hit a home run.*

ca·pa·ble [KAY-puh-bul] ADJECTIVE. **1. capable, apte ▸** able to do something : *"Anancy was capable of turning himself into a man."* (Faustin Charles) **2. compétent (-ente), qualifié (-ée), efficace ▸** able to do something well; efficient : *a capable worker.* SYN: able, competent, proficient.

ca·pac·i·ty [kuh-PAS-uh-tee] NOUN, capacities. **1. capacité ▸** the amount that can be held by a container or a space : *My car's gas tank has a capacity of 40 litres.* **2. capacité, aptitude, habileté ▸** mental or physical power; ability. **3. en qualité de, à titre de ▸** a position or function : *He served in the capacity of adviser to the prime minister.*

cape[1] [kape] NOUN, capes. **cape ▸** a piece of clothing worn over the shoulders like a coat, but having no sleeves.

cape[2] NOUN, capes. **cap ▸** a large piece of land that sticks out into an ocean or lake : *The boat sailed around the cape to the bay.*

cap·er [KAY-pur] VERB, capered, capering. **gambader ▸** to jump and skip about in a playful way. ▲ NOUN, capers. **gambade, cabriole ▸** a playful or silly trick or adventure : *Our holiday was filled with one caper after another.*

cap·il·lar·y [kuh-PIL-uh-ree *or* KAP-uh-LAIR-ee] NOUN, capillaries. **capillaire ▸** a blood vessel with a very slender, hairlike opening. The capillary is the smallest blood vessel in the body. They connect the smallest arteries with the smallest veins. ▲ ADJECTIVE. **capillaire ▸** like a hair; very slender.

cap·i·tal [KAP-uh-tul] NOUN, capitals. **1. majuscule ▸** the larger form of a letter of the alphabet, used at the beginning of a sentence or a proper noun such as a person's name. **2. capitale ▸** the city where the government of a province or country is located : *Ottawa is the capital of Canada.* **3. capital (-aux) ▸** money or anything that can be used to earn more money; wealth : *Some businesses can be started with only a small amount of capital.* ▲ ADJECTIVE. **1. capital (-ale, -aux), principal (-ale, -aux), primordial (-ale, -aux) ▸** most important; main : *a capital city.* **2. capital (-ale, -aux) ▸** having to do with punishment by death : *Murder is a capital offence in some states.*

cap·i·tal·ism [KAP-uh-tul-IZ-um] NOUN. **capitalisme ▸** an economic system in which people and companies rather than the government own and control the things needed to do business, such as land, factories, and goods. **Note.** A person who believes in the policy of capitalism is a capitalist.

cap·size [KAP-size *or* kap-SIZE] VERB, capsized, capsizing. **chavirer, se renverser ▸** to turn upside down; flip over. **Note.** Usually said of a boat : *From their lifeboat, the passengers watched their boat capsize.*

cap·sule [KAP-sul] NOUN, capsules. **1. capsule ▸** a very small container of medicine that can be swallowed whole. **2. capsule ▸** the part of a plant that holds and protects its seeds. **3. capsule ▸** a part of a space vehicle that separates from the rest of the vehicle in flight. ▲ ADJECTIVE. **succinct (-incte), bref (brève), court (courte) ▸** in a brief form; condensed : *The newspaper listings give a capsule description of current movies.*

cap·tain [KAP-tun] NOUN, captains. **1. capitaine ▸** the rank of an officer in the armed forces. *A captain ranks above a lieutenant and below a major.* **2. capitaine ▸** the person who is in command of a ship. **3. capitaine ▸** any person who is in command of a group; a leader : *the captain of the soccer team.* SYN: head, chief, commander.

cap·tion [KAP-shun] NOUN, captions. **légende, sous-titre ▶** the words used with a picture in a book, magazine, or newspaper to tell something about what is in the picture. ✍ p. 86.

cap·tive [KAP-tiv] NOUN, captives. **captif (-ive), prisonnier (-ière) ▶** someone who is locked up; a prisoner. ▲ ADJECTIVE. **1. captif (-ive), prisonnier (-ière), en captivité ▶** held as a prisoner; not free : *A zoo has captive animals.* **2. captif (-ive) ▶** held within bounds, as if one were a prisoner : *The passengers in the cab were a captive audience for the driver's jokes.* **Note.** The state of being held captive is captivity: *"It's against the law to hold one of these wild birds in captivity."* (E.B. White)

cap·ture [KAP-chur] VERB, captured, capturing. **1. capturer, attraper, s'emparer (de), arrêter ▶** to catch and hold a person or animal; take control of : *"This disturbed the spider, who captured the fly."* (Ruth Brown) **2. s'emparer, saisir ▶** to catch and hold, as if capturing a person : *Our team captured the trophy.* ▲ NOUN, captures. **capture, arrestation, saisie ▶** the act of capturing : *"Rewards for her capture…finally reached the sum of $40,000."* (Virginia Hamilton) SYN: catch, seize, apprehend, arrest, imprison.

car [kar] NOUN, cars. **1. voiture, auto ▶** a motor vehicle with four wheels and a motor; an automobile. **2. voiture (de tramway), wagon ▶** any similar vehicle used to carry people or things : *a railway car; a streetcar.* ✍ p. 1153.

car·at see karat.

car·a·van [KAIR-uh-van] NOUN, caravans. **1. caravane ▶** a group of traders or pilgrims travelling together, as through a desert : *The Bedouins cross the Sahara desert in a caravan.* **2. caravane ▶** any travelling group of people or vehicles : *a caravan of military trucks.* **3. caravane ▶** a large covered vehicle, usually with a living unit; a camper or van.

car·bon [KAR-bun] NOUN. **carbone ▶** a chemical element found in some amount in all living things. Coal, petroleum, and diamonds are almost pure carbon. **Note.** Carbon dioxide is a gas made up of carbon and oxygen. It is an important part of the air we breathe. **Note.** Carbon monoxide is a poisonous gas that cars and gas-burning engines produce.

car·cass [KAR-kus] NOUN, carcasses. **carcasse ▶** the dead body of an animal.

card¹ [kard] NOUN, cards. **1. carte, carton, fiche ▶** a small, stiff piece of paper or plastic with printing on it. A card usually has a rectangular shape. There are many kinds of cards, such as greeting cards, school report cards, and so on. **2. carte ▶** one of a set of 52 cards divided into four suits and marked with special symbols and

Captions
*A **caption** is a short sentence or phrase that explains or gives information about a photograph or illustration. Captions are often used in magazines, newspapers, and nonfiction books. A caption might tell who is in the photograph, describe the location, or explain an illustration.*
• When you write a caption, think about why you have included that particular photograph, illustration, or map. What information does it have that you want your readers to know? How does it connect with the story or article?

numbers, used in playing various games. **Note.** Also called playing cards. **3. cards. cartes ▶** any game played with playing cards : *I play cards with my brother when it rains.*

in the cards prévisible ▶ certain to happen : *I just knew Jill would hit that home run; it was in the cards.*

put (one's) cards on the table jouer cartes sur table ▶ be completely open about something : *I'll put my cards on the table if you will be completely honest also.*

card² NOUN, cards. **carde ▶** a wire brush or a similar machine with teeth : *A card is used to untangle wool before it is spun into yarn.* ▲ VERB, carding, carded. **carder ▶** to clean or comb with a card.

card·board [KARD-bord] NOUN, cardboards. **carton ▶** a thick, stiff kind of paper used for making boxes, cards, and so on.

car·di·nal [KAR-duh-nul or KARD-nul] NOUN, cardinals. **1. cardinal (-aux) ▶** a bright-red songbird of North America with a crest of feathers on its head. **2. pourpre, rouge vif ▶** a bright-red colour. **3. cardinal (-aux) ▶** an official in the Catholic Church having the second-highest rank, just under the Pope. ▲ ADJECTIVE. **1. capital (-ale, -aux), principal (-ale, -aux), cardinal (-ale, -aux) ▶** of first importance; primary : *The cardinal rule of good pitching is to throw strikes.* **2. pourpre, rouge vif ▶** having a bright-red colour. ✍ p. 109.

cardinal number nombre cardinal ▶ a number that shows how many : *three books; 12 houses; 365 days.* **Note.** See ordinal number.

care [kair] NOUN, cares. **1. souci, inquiétude, préoccupation, tracas ▶** a feeling of being worried or troubled; concern : *She smiled as though she hadn't a care in the world.* **2. soin, attention, vigilance ▶** close attention : *Take* *care to look both ways before you cross the street.* **3. surveillance, garde, responsabilité** ▶ a looking after; custody or keeping : *to be under a doctor's care.* ▲ VERB, cared, caring. **1. s'intéresser, se soucier, se préoccuper, s'inquiéter** ▶ to be interested in or concerned with : *"'I don't care what you eat or how you dress or where you go or what you think.'"* (Cynthia Rylant) **2. vouloir** ▶ to wish or want : *Would you care for more tea?*

ca·reer [kuh-REER] NOUN, careers. **1. carrière, profession** ▶ the work that a person does for a living : *Komiko is planning a career as a lawyer.* **2. carrière** ▶ the general course of a person's life : *Lord Stanley had an outstanding career in government, but he is best remembered for donating the Stanley Cup.* ▲ VERB, careered, careering. **aller à toute vitesse** ▶ to move or run at full speed : *The car careered down the steep road.*

care·ful [KAIR-ful] ADJECTIVE. **prudent (-ente), attentif (-ive), consciencieux (-euse), soigneux (-euse)** ▶ taking care; paying close attention. ▪ **carefully,** ADVERB: ▶ **prudemment, attentivement, consciencieusement, soigneusement.** *"Grasshopper held the boat very carefully."* (Arnold Lobel) SYN: thoughtful, cautious, watchful, prudent.

care·less [KAIR-lis] ADJECTIVE. **1. négligent (-ente), inappliqué (-ée), désordonné (-ée)** ▶ not paying close attention; not caring : *He is careless when he cooks and often ends up burning the meal.* **2. négligent (-ente), insouciant (-ante)** ▶ done without being careful; showing lack of care : *It was careless of him to leave the lights on all night.* ▪ **carelessly,** ADVERB: ▶ **négligemment, avec insouciance.** *"He turns down their invitations, dresses carelessly to visit, and arrives late for their dinners."* (Barbara Nichol) ▪ **carelessness,** NOUN. ▶ *The forest fire was caused by a camper's carelessness.*

care·tak·er [KAIR-take-ur] NOUN, caretakers. **gardien (-ienne)** ▶ a person whose work is to take care of something or some place; custodian.

car·go [KAR-goh] NOUN, cargoes or cargos. **cargaison** ▶ the goods carried by a ship, plane, or train : *The ship carried a cargo of wood.* **Note.** Cargo comes from *cargar,* a Spanish word meaning "to load."

car·i·bou [KAR-uh-boo *or* KAIR-uh-boo] NOUN, caribou or caribous. **caribou (-ous)** ▶ a type of large deer that lives in colder northern regions. Both the male and female caribou have antlers. This animal is related to the reindeer in Europe. ◉ **p. 111.**

car·ni·val [KAR-nuh-vul] NOUN, carnivals. **1. fête foraine, carnaval (-als)** ▶ a travelling amusement show with rides, games, and sideshows. **2. festival (-als), fête, célébration, foire** ▶ a time of feasting and merrymaking; a celebra-

tion; a fair or festival. **3. festivités, fête** ▶ a program of events having to do with a certain sport, institution, or the like : *a spring carnival.*

car·niv·o·rous [kar-NIV-uh-rus] ADJECTIVE. **carnivore** ▶ feeding on the flesh of other animals; meat- eating : *Lions are carnivorous animals.* **Note.** Someone or something that eats meat is a carnivore.

car·ol [KAIR-ul] NOUN, carols. **chant de Noël** ▶ a song of joy and celebration, especially a Christmas song : *"Silent Night" is a Christmas carol sung all around the world.* ▲ VERB, carolled, carolling. (also caroled, caroling) **chanter (joyeusement)** ▶ to sing songs of joy and celebration.

car·ou·sel [KAR-uh-sel] NOUN, carousels. **manège** ▶ (also **carrousels**) a merry-go-round.

carp[1] [karp] NOUN, carp or carps. **carpe** ▶ a freshwater fish, often used for food. ◉ **p. 106.**

carp[2] VERB, carped, carping. **reprocher, critiquer, blâmer** ▶ to find fault; to complain in a nagging way : *Mom is always carping at my brother about his messy room.*

car·pen·ter [KAR-pun-tur] NOUN, carpenters. **charpentier (-ière), menuisier (-ière)** ▶ a person whose work is building and fixing things made of wood, such as houses and cabinets. ▪ **carpentry,** NOUN. ▶ **charpenterie, menuiserie.**

car·pet [KAR-pit] NOUN, carpets. **1. tapis, moquette** ▶ a soft, heavy floor covering made from wool or other fibres; a rug or mat. **2. tapis** ▶ anything that covers like a carpet : *"They relaxed on a carpet of moss."* (William Steig) ▲ VERB, carpeted, carpeting. **recouvrir d'un tapis** ▶ to cover with a carpet. 🖺 **p. 1066.**

car·riage [KAIR-ij] NOUN, carriages. **1. poussette, landau** ▶ a small vehicle that is pushed by hand and used to carry a baby or doll. **2. fiacre** ▶ a four-wheeled vehicle that carries passengers and is usually pulled by a horse or horses. **3. port, maintien** ▶ the manner of holding one's head and body : *He had a proud and haughty carriage.*

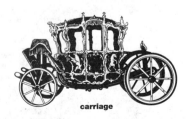

carriage

car·ri·er [KAIR-ee-ur] NOUN, carriers. **1. porteur, transporteur ▸** any person or thing that carries something : *a mail carrier; an aircraft carrier.* **2. porteur (-euse) ▸** a person or animal that does not suffer from a disease but carries the germs and can pass them on. **3. onde porteuse ▸** a radio wave that transmits speech, music, images, or other signals.

car·rot [KAIR-ut] NOUN, carrots. **carotte ▸** the long orange root of a common garden plant, eaten both cooked and raw as a vegetable.

car·ry [KAIR-ee] VERB, carried, carrying. **1. porter, apporter, transporter, emporter ▸** to hold or support something while moving it from one place to another : *He carried the dishes into the kitchen.* **2. avoir, porter (sur soi) ▸** to have with oneself or itself : *Mom carries an extra car key in her purse in case she locks her key in the car.* **3. porter ▸** to move from one place to another : *The singer's voice carried to the back of the hall.* **4. vendre ▸** to have for sale : *Does the bookstore carry tapes and CDs?* **5. porter, amener ▸** to win or capture : *Sami carried the team to victory.* 🖉 **p. 88.**

carry on 1. prendre part, diriger, mener, entretenir ▸ to take part in ; conduct : *to carry on a conversation ; to carry on business.* **2. s'énerver, être turbulent ▸** to behave or talk in a foolish or overexcited way : *If you continue to carry on in that manner, you'll have to go to your room.*

carry out exécuter, accomplir ▸ to put into action ; accomplish : *to carry out a plan.*

cart [kart] NOUN, carts. **1. charrette ▸** a strong two-wheeled vehicle used for carrying loads : *Carts are usually pulled by oxen, mules, or horses.* **2. chariot ▸** a lightweight vehicle that is pushed or pulled by hand : *Willy helped his mother load the groceries into the shopping cart.* ▲ VERB, carted, carting. **charrier ▸** to carry something in or as if in a cart : *It took all morning to cart the garbage to the dump.*

car·ti·lage [KAR-tuh-lij] NOUN. **cartilage ▸** a strong, flexible body tissue that is not as hard as bone but is able to support softer tissue, much like a bone does. The nose and the outer part of the ear are made of cartilage.

car·ton [KART-un] NOUN, cartons. **boîte ▸** a container of cardboard, paper, or plastic that comes in different shapes and sizes and can hold a variety of things : *a milk carton.*

car·toon [kar-TOON] NOUN, cartoons. **1. caricature ▸** a drawing that tells a story or shows something funny, often appearing in magazines and newspapers. **2. bandes dessinées ▸** a group of cartoons arranged in a short series in a newspaper ; a comic strip. **3. dessins animés ▸** a movie made up of a continuous series of drawings. **Note.** A person who draws a cartoon is a cartoonist.

cart·wheel [KART-weel] NOUN, cartwheels. **roue ▸** a handspring done sideways, with the weight of the body put first on the hands and then back on the legs.

carve [karve] VERB, carved, carving. **1. découper ▸** to cut or slice cooked meat into pieces : *to carve a turkey.* **2. sculpter ▸** to cut or shape something out of a solid block : *She carved a duck from a piece of wood.* **3. découper ▸** to decorate or make by cutting : *We carved a pumpkin for Halloween.* **Note.** Something that is carved is a **carving.**

case¹ [kase] NOUN, cases. **1. cas, exemple ▸** an example of something : *This is an obvious case of cheating because all his answers are the same as hers.* **2. cas, circonstances ▸** the actual facts or state of affairs : *The building was to be finished this month, but that's not the case.* **3. cas ▸** an illness or injury, or a person who is ill or injured : *a case of measles.* **4. affaire ▸** a matter that is being handled by the police or other officials, or being tried in a court of law : *a murder case.*

in case or **in case of au cas où ▸** if it should happen that ; if : *Buy some more milk, just in case we run out.*

case² NOUN, cases. **étui, boîte, caisse, coffret ▸** a box, bag, or other container used to hold and carry things : *a camera case.*

cash [kash] NOUN. **1. argent ▸** money on hand in the form of bills and coins : *I don't have enough cash to pay for the tickets.* **2. comptant ▸** money or a cheque paid at the time of buying something : *Should I pay cash, or charge it to my credit card?* ▲ VERB, cashed, cashing. **encaisser ▸** to give or get cash for : *to cash a cheque.*

cash·ew [KASH-yoo] NOUN, cashews. **noix de cajou ▸** a small, curved nut that can be eaten. It grows on an evergreen tree that is found in hot, wet climates.

🔧 **Word Builder**

*Carry is found in several expressions. For example, **carry the ball** means to take the lead or control in order to finish or accomplish something : When the lead actor got sick, Jessie carried the ball until she was better. Another expression is **carry away**, which means to excite : They got carried away with cheering at an Expos' game. **Carry the day** means to win : Our soccer team will carry the day against the champions from the northern division.*

cash·ier [KASH-eer] NOUN, cashiers. **caissier (-ière)** ▶ a person in a store, restaurant, or bank who takes in or pays out money to customers.

ca·sin·o [kuh-SEE-noh] NOUN, casinos. **casino** ▶ a room or building used for entertainment and gambling.

cas·se·role [KAS-uh-role] NOUN, casseroles. **1. cocotte** ▶ a heavy dish in which food can be baked and served. **2. ragoût en cocotte, plat en cocotte** ▶ food cooked in such a dish.

cas·sette [ka-SET] NOUN, cassettes. **cassette** ▶ a small plastic box that holds magnetic tape that is played in a tape recorder.

cast [kast] VERB, casted, casting. **1. lancer, projeter** ▶ to throw through the air : *The fisher cast a line into the water.* **2. projeter** ▶ to cause to fall on or over : *The full moon cast long shadows across the field.* **3. jeter, lancer** ▶ to direct or turn : *He cast a glance around the messy room.* **4. couler, mouler** ▶ to make or form something by pouring a liquid or soft material into a mould and letting it harden : *The artist cast a statue in bronze.* **5. donner le rôle de** ▶ to choose people to be in a play, movie, or television program : *Judy Garland was cast as Dorothy in* The Wizard of Oz. **6. voter** ▶ to record a vote : *He cast his ballot for Deva to be class president.* ▲ NOUN, casts. **1. plâtre** ▶ a stiff bandage of plaster and cloth, used for holding a broken bone or injured part of the body in place while it heals. **2. distribution** ▶ the actors in a play, movie, or television program. **3. lancer** ▶ the act of casting; a throw. **4. moulage, empreinte** ▶ something that is cast in a mould.

cast·a·way [kast-uh-way] NOUN, castaways. **naufragé (-ée)** ▶ a person lost from a shipwreck. ▲ ADJECTIVE. **jeté (-ée)** ▶ stranded or thrown away.

cas·tle [KAS-ul] NOUN, castles. **1. château (-eaux)** ▶ a very large building or group of buildings with thick walls, towers, and many rooms. Castles were built in the Middle Ages to give protection against attack. Powerful rulers lived in castles. **2. tour** ▶ one of the pieces in the game of chess. **Note.** Also known as a **rook**.

cas·u·al [KAZH-yoo-ul] ADJECTIVE. **1. fortuit (-uite), imprévu (-ue), inattendu (-ue)** ▶ happening by chance ; not expected : *a casual meeting between old friends.* **2. désinvolte, neutre** ▶ without strong feeling or concern : *"See you at noon, Jean," Mother said, her tone casual."* (Jean Little). **3. sport, décontracté (-ée)** ▶ not formal; relaxed : *After work, Jin changes into casual clothes for supper.* ■ **casually,** ADVERB. ▶ **par hasard, fortuitement, de façon décontractée.**

cat [kat] NOUN, cats. **1. chat** ▶ a small, furry animal with a long tail and sharp claws, often kept as a pet. **2. félin (-ine)** ▶ any of the larger animals that belong to the same family, such as a lion, tiger, or leopard. 🖝 **p. 1085.**

cat·a·logue [KAT-uh-LOG] NOUN, catalogues. (also catalog) **1. catalogue** ▶ a list of things in a certain order : *A library has a card catalogue — alphabetical lists of all its books by author, title, and subject.* **2. catalogue** ▶ a book or file containing such a list : *Stores mail out catalogues to show what they have for sale.* ▲ VERB, catalogued, cataloguing. **cataloguer** ▶ to list in a catalogue.

cat·a·ma·ran [KAT-uh-muh-RAN] NOUN, catamarans. **1. catamaran** ▶ a raftlike boat that has two hulls. **2. radeau (-eaux)** ▶ a raft of logs or floats lashed together, used in parts of India and South America. 🖝 **p. 394.**

cat·a·pult [KAT-uh-pult] NOUN, catapults. **1. catapulte** ▶ a large weapon that works like a slingshot. It was used long ago to throw rocks, arrows, and so on at the enemy. **2. catapulte** ▶ a machine used to launch an airplane from a ship's deck.

ca·tas·tro·phe [ka-TAS-truh-fee] NOUN, catastrophes. **catastrophe, cataclysme, désastre, fléau** ▶ a sudden and terrible disaster, such as an earthquake, a flood, or a plane crash. 🖝 **p. 1113.**

mask

glove

shin guard

knee pad

catcher

catch [kach] VERB, caught, catching. **1. attraper, saisir** ▶ to take hold of a moving object with the hands : *to catch a ball.* **2. attraper, prendre** ▶ to capture or trap : *to catch a fish.* **3. se prendre, s'accrocher** ▶ to become fastened or stuck : *She caught her sweater on a nail.* **4. surprendre** ▶ to discover by surprise : *Mom caught Steve eating candy right before dinner.* **5. attraper** ▶ to be in time for : *to catch a bus.* **6. prendre** ▶ to suddenly have or get : *The log caught fire.* **7.** *Informal.* **comprendre, saisir** ▶ to see or hear : *I'm sorry; I didn't catch your name.* ▲ NOUN, catches. **1. prise, capture** ▶ the act of catching something.

2. fermoir, loquet ▶ something that holds or fastens : *the catch on a necklace.* **3. prise ▶** something that is caught : *We fished this morning and got a great catch.* **4. jeu (jeux) de balle ▶** a game of throwing and catching a ball. **5. attrape, piège ▶** a hidden trick or difficulty : *That offer of free land can't be true ; there must be a catch.*

catch·er [KACH-ur] NOUN, catchers. **receveur (-euse) ▶** a baseball player whose position is behind home plate. ☞ **p. 89.**

catch·up or **cat·sup** see ketchup.

cat·e·go·ry [KAT-uh-GOR-ee] NOUN, categories. **catégorie, classe ▶** a group of things that are thought of as being alike in some way ; a class : *Milk, cheese, and butter are part of the category of dairy foods.* **Note.** Something that has to do with category is categorical. ▪ **categorically,** ADVERB. ▶ **catégoriquement.**

cat·er [KAY-tur] VERB, catered, catering. **1. fournir les repas ▶** to supply food, drink, and other services for a party or special event : *to cater a wedding.* **2. satisfaire, s'adresser ▶** to please someone by providing what the person needs or wants : *That hotel caters to families.*

cat·er·pil·lar [KAT-ur-PIL-ur] NOUN, caterpillars. **chenille ▶** a small, wormlike stage in the growth of moths and butterflies. A caterpillar is the larva, or first stage, in the growth of these insects. **2. tracteur à chenilles ▶** a large tractor that moves on an endless belt.

cat·fish [KAT-FISH] NOUN, catfish or catfishes. **poisson-chat ▶** a type of freshwater fish that has long feelers on the side of the head that look somewhat like a cat's whiskers. ☞ **p. 106.**

ca·the·dral [kuh-THEE-drul] NOUN, cathedrals. **1. cathédrale ▶** the official church of a bishop. Many large, impressive cathedrals were built in Europe during the Middle Ages. **2. cathédrale ▶** a large or important church.

Cath·o·lic [KATH-uh-LIK or KATH-lik] ADJECTIVE. **catholique ▶** having to do with the branch of the Christian church that is headed by the Pope. ▲ NOUN, Catholics. (also Roman Catholic) a person who is a member of the Roman Catholic Church.

cat·nap [KAT-nap] NOUN, catnaps. **somme, sieste ▶** a short, light sleep.

cat·tle [KAT-ul] NOUN. **bétail ▶** the large animals with hoofs and short horns that are commonly raised for meat, milk, and hides ; cows, bulls, and steers as a group.

caught [kot] VERB, a past form of catch.

cau·li·flow·er [KAH-lee-FLOW-ur] NOUN, cauliflowers. **chou-fleur ▶** a plant with a large round head made up of tightly packed white flowers, often eaten as a vegetable.

cause [koz] NOUN, causes. **1. cause, origine ▶** a person or thing that makes something happen : *Lightning caused the forest fire.* **2. raison, motif ▶** a reason for acting in a certain way : *His happiness caused him to smile and laugh.* **3. cause ▶** a goal or purpose that a person believes in : *We are working for the cause of peace.* ▲ VERB, caused, causing. **causer, entraîner, susciter ▶** to make something happen ; be the cause of : *"There were no more eggs to collect because the constant noise caused the chickens to stop laying."* (Donald Carrick) SYN: reason, motive, source, origin.

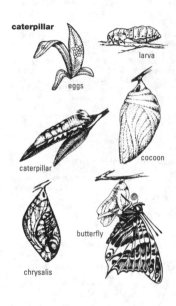

caterpillar

larva

eggs

cocoon

caterpillar

butterfly

chrysalis

cau·tion [KAH-shun] NOUN, cautions. **1. prudence, circonspection ▶** the act of being careful or watchful to avoid trouble or danger : *Motorists are warned to use caution driving on icy roads.* **2. avertissement, recommandation, conseil ▶** a warning : *We didn't listen to Lina's caution to take raincoats.* ▲ VERB, cautioned, cautioning. **avertir, mettre en garde ▶** to tell to be careful ; warn : *Dad cautioned us not to swim alone.*

cau·tious [KAH-shus] ADJECTIVE. **prudent (-ente), circonspect (-ecte) ▶** being careful ; using caution : *He was a cautious climber, and carefully checked his equipment and route before he started.* ▪ **cautiously,** ADVERB: ▶ **prudemment, avec circonspection.** *"Jodie stepped cautiously* *out onto the porch. The bear kept right on eating."* (Marilyn Halvorson)

cave [kave] NOUN, caves. **grotte, caverne** ▸ a natural hollow place in the side of a mountain or under the ground, usually with an opening to the surface. ▲ VERB, caved, caving. **s'effondrer, s'écrouler, tomber** ▸ to cave in; to fall in or down: *After the blast, the walls of the building caved in quickly.* **Note.** A cavern is a large cave, usually caused by an underground stream.

cav-i-ty [KAV-uh-tee] NOUN, cavities. 1. **carie** ▸ a hollow place in a tooth caused by decay. 2. **cavité, trou, cratère** ▸ a hollow place or hole, as in the ground. SYN: hole, pit, crater.

cay [kee *or* kay] See key².

Ca-yu-ga [kay-YOO-guh] NOUN. 1. **Cayuga** ▸ Aboriginal people of the Cayuga nation, a member of the Six Nations Iroquois Confederacy in Ontario. 2. **cayuga** ▸ the Iroquoian language of the Cayuga people.

CB ABBREVIATION. citizens band. **bande publique** ▸ a range of radio frequencies that can be used by private citizens, not the frequencies used by broadcasting stations, police departments, aircraft, and so on.

CD-Rom ABBREVIATION. **cédérom** ▸ "compact disk—read only memory." A storage device that can hold a lot of information at a low cost. CD-ROMs cannot be erased.

cease [sees] VERB, ceased, ceasing. **cesser, arrêter, finir, interrompre** ▸ to stop: *"Poor Mother! She had long since ceased to be amazed at the things Bob and I carried home."* (Todd Lee) SYN: stop, end, halt, quit, leave off, discontinue.

ce-dar [SEE-dur] NOUN, cedars. **cèdre** ▸ an evergreen tree with thick, rough bark, soft needles, reddish wood, and a pleasant smell. Clothing is often stored in closets lined with cedar wood. 👁 p. 255.

ceil-ing [SEEL-ing] NOUN, ceilings. 1. **plafond** ▸ the inside top part of a room, opposite the floor: *The crack in the wall ran from the ceiling to the floor.* 2. **plafond, limite** ▸ the upper limit; top: *The government put a ceiling on the cost of gasoline.* 3. **plafond, limite** ▸ the highest that an aircraft can fly: *That plane has a ceiling of 30000 metres.* 📖 p. 1066.

cel-e-brate [SEL-uh-BRATE] VERB, celebrated, celebrating. 1. **fêter, célébrer, commémorer** ▸ to observe a certain day or time with special activities: *Today Liza celebrates her 12th birthday.* 2. **célébrer, fêter** ▸ to have a party or enjoy oneself to honour a special occasion: *"To dance is to celebrate life. With each beat of the drum we celebrate the heartbeat of Mother Earth."* (George Littlechild) 3. **célébrer** ▸ to perform a religious ceremony: *to celebrate Mass.* 4. **célèbre** ▸ to honour or praise someone or something. Usually used as an ADJECTIVE: *He was a*

celebrated hero of the hockey team. **Note.** The act of celebrating is a **celebration** (📖 p. 1143.).

cel-eb-ri-ty [suh-LEB-ruh-TEE] NOUN, celebrities. **célébrité, personnalité** ▸ a person who is famous: *Many movie and television actors are celebrities.*

cel-er-y [SEL-uh-ree *or* SEL-ree] NOUN. **céleri** ▸ a garden plant with long, light-green stalks, eaten as a vegetable.

cell [sel] NOUN, cells. 1. **cellule, cachot** ▸ a very small, plain room, especially one in a prison, monastery, or convent. 2. **cellule** ▸ the basic unit of the body of a living thing. A cell has a centre part called the **nucleus**, which is surrounded by a fluid called **protoplasm** and enclosed in a thin wall or **membrane**. 3. **élément (de pile)** ▸ a small battery.

cel-lar [SEL-ur] NOUN, cellars. **cave, cellier** ▸ a room or rooms under a house or under the ground.

cel-lo [CHEL-oh] NOUN, cellos. **violoncelle** ▸ a musical instrument shaped like a violin, but larger and with a lower tone. A cello is held between the knees and played with a bow. 👁 p. 538.

Cel-si-us [SEL-see-us *or* SEL-shus] ADJECTIVE. **Celsius** ▸ a scale that shows how cold or hot something is. On the Celsius scale, 0 degrees is the temperature at which water freezes, and 100 degrees is the temperature at which water boils. **Note.** Also known as a centigrade scale.

Cel-tic [KEL-tik *or* SEL-tik] ADJECTIVE. **celte, celtique** ▸ having to do with a people including the Irish, Highland Scots, Welsh, and ancient Britons.

ce-ment [suh-MENT] NOUN, cements. 1. **ciment** ▸ a powdery grey mixture that is made by heating limestone and clay to a high temperature. When cement is mixed with water, the mixture dries to become very hard like stone. Cement is used in making buildings, roads, and sidewalks. 2. **colle** ▸ any soft, sticky substance that hardens to hold things together: *Rubber cement is used as a glue for household items.* ▲ VERB, cemented, cementing. **cimenter, sceller** ▸ to join together or cover with, as if with cement: *They shook hands to cement their agreement.*

cem-e-te-ry [SEM-uh-TAIR-ee] NOUN, cemeteries. **cimetière** ▸ a place where dead people are buried; a graveyard. 📖 p. 1048.

cen-sor [SEN-sur] NOUN, censors. **censeur (-eure)** ▸ a person whose job is to examine books, movies, and so on to remove parts that are thought to be harmful or improper: *a movie censor.* ▲ VERB, censored, censoring. **censurer** ▸ to act as a censor: *Tino's parents censor the TV programs he watches.* **Note.** The act or fact of censoring something is **censorship**.

cen·sus [SEN-sus] NOUN, censuses. **recensement** ▸ an official count of all the people who live in a certain country, state, or city. The national census of Canada is taken every 10 years.

cent [sent] NOUN, cents. **cent** ▸ a coin of Canada, the U.S., and other countries; the smallest coin in value. One hundred cents equals one dollar.

cent·aur [SEN-tor] NOUN, centaurs. **centaure** ▸ a creature from Greek mythology that was part man and part horse.

cen·ti·me·tre [SEN-tuh-MEE-tur] NOUN, centimetres. **centimètre** ▸ a basic measure of length in the metric system, equal to one hundredth of a metre. Symbol: cm

cen·ti·pede [SEN-tuh-peed] NOUN, centipedes. **mille-pattes** ▸ a small animal with a long, flat body, many legs, and sometimes two poisonous front fangs. **Note.** The centipede means "100 feet," but a centipede may have up to 170 legs.

cen·tral [SEN-trul] ADJECTIVE. **1. central (-ale, -aux)** ▸ in or near the middle; in between : *Central America lies between North America and South America.* **2. central (-ale, -aux), principal (-ale, -aux)** ▸ the most important; main : *Scrooge is the central character of the story* A Christmas Carol.

cen·tre [SEN-tur] NOUN, centres. (also center) **1. centre** ▸ the exact middle point of a circle, equally distant from every point on the edge. **2. milieu, centre, noyau (-jau)** ▸ the middle point or part of anything : *Kyoko put the flowers in the centre of the table.* **3. centre, cœur** ▸ the main point of activity or attention : *Ahkmed's jokes made him the centre of attention.* **4. centre** ▸ a player whose position is in the middle of the playing area in such sports as basketball, football, and hockey. ▲ VERB, centred, centring. **centrer** ▸ to put in the middle or centre : *Centre the picture on the wall.* 🖉 p. 92.

cen·tu·ry [SEN-chuh-ree] NOUN, centuries. **1. siècle** ▸ any period of 100 years : *Ten centuries ago, Native peoples were already living in North America.* **2. siècle** ▸ any of the 100-year periods before or since the beginning of the Christian era : *The year 1867 was in the 19th century.*

ce·ram·ic [suh-RAM-ik] NOUN, ceramics. **1. ceramics. céramique** ▸ the art of making things such as bricks, bowls, and pots by shaping and baking clay. **2. objet en céramique** ▸ something made from clay in this way. **Note.** Also used as an ADJECTIVE: *ceramic tiles.*

ce·re·al [SEER-ee-ul] NOUN, cereals. **1. céréale** ▸ seeds or grains that come from certain grass plants such as wheat, rice, oats, corn, and rye. **2. céréales** ▸ a breakfast food made of these seeds or grains.

ceremony [SER-uh-MON-ee] NOUN, ceremonies. **1. cérémonie** ▸ an act or series of acts carried out in a special way or by special rules : *My sister was married in a ceremony at the temple on Main Street.* **2. cérémonie** ▸ very polite behaviour based on formal rules : *The ushers at the wedding showed us to our seats with great ceremony.* **Note.** Something done according to ceremony is ceremonial or ceremonious: *The crowning of a king or queen is a ceremonial occasion.* 🖳 p. 1144.

cer·tain [SUR-tun] ADJECTIVE. **1. certain (-aine), sûr (sûre), vrai (vraie), indéniable** ▸ known to be true or right; positive; sure : *It is certain that there are 12 eggs in a dozen.* **2. certain (-aine), sûr (sûre), évident (-ente), immanquable** ▸ sure to be or happen : *With those dark clouds, it is certain to rain soon.* **3. certain (-aine), convenu (-ue), déterminé (-ée)** ▸ settled or agreed on : *To get a pilot's licence, you must have a certain number of hours of flying time.* **4. certain (-aine)** ▸ not named or stated, but known : *Certain wild animals are active only at night.* **Note.** The state or feeling of being certain is certainty. SYN: sure, positive, definite, real, established.

cer·tain·ly [SUR-tun-lee] ADVERB. **certainement, sûrement, assurément** ▸ surely or definitely; without a doubt : *She certainly studied hard for that math test.*

cer·tif·i·cate [sur-TIF-uh-kit] NOUN, certificates. **certificat, attestation** ▸ an official form or document giving information about something : *A birth certificate tells the date and place of a person's birth.*

✏ Writing Tips

Centre

Centre is one of the words that is spelled differently in Canada than it is in the United States. In Canada, we generally use the spelling **centre**. In the United States, it is spelled center.

• Other words that are different in Canada and the United States are

- Words with "re," not "er": theatre, fibre, and metric words such as litre and metre.

- Words with "our," not "or": colour, neighbour, favourite, flavour, and honour.

- Words that double the final "l" before adding "ed" or "ing": travelling and labelling.

• When you write the titles of American books, songs, movies, and organizations, or places in the United States (such as The Lincoln Center for Performing Arts), remember to use the American spelling.

cer·ti·fy [SUR-tuh-fy] VERB, certified, certifying. **1. certifier, attester, authentifier ▸** to confirm that something is true, genuine, or accurate, especially in writing. **2. certifier, attester, garantir ▸** to guarantee that something meets a certain standard : *The automobile manufacturer certified that the seatbelts were safe.*

cha·dor [chuh-DOR] NOUN, chadors. **tchador ▸** a large piece of cloth used as a cloak and veil by some Muslim women.

chain [chane] NOUN, chains. **1. chaîne ▸** a row of rings or links joined to one another. Chains are usually made of metal and are used to fasten or pull things. **2. chaîne ▸** silver or gold links made into a necklace or bracelet : *Lucy's grandmother gave her a silver chain for her birthday.* **3. chaîne, série ▸** a series of things or happenings connected to each other : *a chain of stores; a chain of events.* ▲ VERB, chained, chaining. **enchaîner ▸** to fasten or hold with a chain : *Dominic chained his bike to the fence.*

chair [chair] NOUN, chairs. **chaise ▸** a piece of furniture for one person to sit on : *A chair usually has four legs and a back, and sometimes an armrest on each side.* ▲ VERB, chaired, chairing. **présider ▸** to serve as chairperson or one in charge of a meeting. 📖 **p. 1067.**

cha·let [cha-LAY] NOUN, chalets. **1. chalet ▸** a kind of house found in the Alps, built of wood and having an overhanging roof. **2. chalet ▸** any similar house.

chalk [chok] NOUN, chalks. **1. craie ▸** a soft white rock made up mostly of tiny seashells. Chalk is used to make cement, lime, and fertilizer. **2. craie ▸** a piece of this substance used for writing or drawing. **Note.** A chalkboard is a large green or black board used for writing on with chalk.

chalk up **marquer, remporter ▸** to score or earn : *to chalk up 10 points in a game.*

chal·lenge [CHAL-unj] VERB, challenged, challenging. **1. défier, provoquer ▸** to call to a fight or contest : *Tim's team challenged us to a game.* **2. mettre en doute, contester ▸** to ask for proof that something is true or correct : *The police challenged his story of what happened to the money.* **3. représenter un défi, être exigeant (-ante) ▸** to demand effort or work : *Climbing a mountain challenged me physically and mentally.* **Note.** Often used as an ADJECTIVE: *"Now he confronted the most challenging, the deepest part of the stream."* (William Steig) ▲ NOUN, challenges. **1. défi ▸** a call to take part in a contest or fight. **2. identification ▸** a call or demand to find out who someone is. **3. défi, épreuve ▸** a job or task that calls for a lot of effort : *"Every day will bring a new challenge and adventure."* (Barbara Bondar) 🖉 **p. 468.**

cham·ber [CHAYM-bur] NOUN, chambers. **1. chambre ▸** a private room in a house, especially a bedroom. **2. chambre ▸** a large room in which lawmakers meet together, or the group itself : *The House of Commons is one of the two chambers of Parliament.* **3. cabinet ▸** also, chambers) a judge's private meeting room in a courthouse. **4. cavité ▸** any enclosed place like a chamber : *The heart has four chambers.* **Note.** Many cities have a chamber of commerce, a group that helps business in the town.

cha·me·leon [kuh-MEE-lee-un or kuh-MEEL-yun] NOUN, chameleons. **caméléon ▸** a small lizard that can change the colour of its skin. It is often thought that the chameleon changes colour to match its surroundings, but the change is a reaction to light, heat, or danger.

cham·pi·on [CHAM-pee-un] NOUN, champions. **1. champion (-onne) ▸** the winner of first place in a contest or game : *Kara is the school debating champion.* **2. champion (-onne) ▸** a person who fights for or defends other people or a cause : *Robin Hood was the champion of the poor in England.* **Note.** A championship is the position of champion, or a competition to decide a champion.

chance [chance] NOUN, chances. **1. occasion ▸** an opportunity or occasion to do something : *Today is my last chance to visit my grandparents before school starts.* **2. possibilité ▸** something that is likely to happen : *There's a slight chance that it will rain this afternoon.* **3. hasard, destin ▸** fate or luck : *"It was a matter of chance that I should have rented a house in one of the strangest communities in North America."* (F. Scott Fitzgerald) **4. risque ▸** a risk or gamble : *Don't take chances by swimming alone in rough water.* ▲ VERB, chanced, chancing. **1. se produire par hasard ▸** to happen accidentally : *Julie chanced to meet a friend from home while travelling in Europe.* **2. risquer, courir le risque de ▸** to risk : *Let's leave now; I don't want to chance being late.* **by chance 1. par hasard, fortuitement, accidentellement ▸** accidentally : *If by chance you're in the neighbourhood, please stop by.* **2. par un concours de circonstances, par hasard ▸** by some turn of events : *I met up with Jake by chance.*

chance upon or **on** **tomber sur ▸** to happen to find or meet : *I chanced upon an old cabin in the woods.* SYN: fate, luck, random, prospect.

change [chaynj] VERB, changed, changing. **1. changer, modifier, évoluer, transformer ▸** to become or make different : *"But when Michael came in the door, she always quickly changed the subject."* (Cynthia Rylant) **2. se changer, mettre ▸** to put on other clothes or coverings : *We changed into our bathing suits.* **3. faire la monnaie de ▸** to exchange money, such as dollars for coins. ▲ NOUN, changes. **1. changement, modification ▸** the act or result of changing : *They had a change of plans and drove instead*

93

of taking the bus. **2. changement, évolution ▶** something that takes the place of something else; something new or different : *There's a change in Kate's work since she spoke to her teacher.* **3. monnaie ▶** money returned when one gives a larger amount for something than what it costs : *I don't think I got the correct change for my five-dollar bill.* **4. monnaie ▶** coins, as opposed to paper money. SYN: alter, vary, replace, substitute.

change-a-ble [CHAYN-juh-bul] ADJECTIVE. **changeant (-ante), instable, variable, capricieux (-ieuse) ▶** changing often or likely to change : *changeable weather.*

chan-nel [CHAN-ul] NOUN, channels. **1. chaîne ▶** a means of carrying an electronic signal to a radio or television set through a certain range of frequencies. **2. lit, canal (-aux) ▶** the path followed by a river, or the deepest part of a river or other waterway. *"Za continues to watch the river closely, and steers the riverboat into the deepest channel."* (Ann Blades) **3. détroit ▶** a body of water joining two larger bodies : *The English Channel connects the North Sea to the Atlantic Ocean.* ▲ VERB, channelled, channelling. (also channeled, channeling) **1. canaliser, creuser un canal dans ▶** to form a channel. **2. canaliser, orienter, diriger ▶** to send as if through a channel; direct : *Mary has channelled all her energy into her studies.*

chant [chant] NOUN, chants. **chant ▶** a singing or shouting of the same words or tunes over and over again. *Chants are often used at sports events.* ▲ VERB, chanted, chanting. **scander ▶** to sing or shout a chant.

chantey (also chanty) **baraque, cabane ▶** see shanty.

Cha-nu-ka Chanuka ▶ See Hanukkah.

cha-os [KAY-os] NOUN. **chaos, confusion ▶** a state of great confusion and disorder : *The playroom was in chaos after a rainy afternoon.* **Note.** If something is in a state of chaos, it is chaotic.

chap[1] [chap] NOUN, chaps. *Informal.* **type, gars, individu ▶** a man or boy.

chap[2] VERB, chapped, chapping. **gercer, crevasser ▶** to make or become dry, rough, or cracked : *The cold wind chapped my lips.*

chap-el [CHAP-ul] NOUN, chapels. **1. chapelle ▶** a small church. **2. chapelle ▶** a small area within a larger building, used for special religious services or private prayer : *a chapel in a hospital.*

chaps [chaps] PLURAL NOUN. **jambière ▶** heavy leather pants worn over regular pants to protect legs, particularly by those who ride horses. Chaps are fastened around the waist but have no seat.

chap-ter [CHAP-tur] NOUN, chapters. **1. chapitre, section ▶** one section of a book : *I can't believe you read the last chapter of the book first.* **2. période, tranche, épisode ▶** a period of life or time that is thought of as like a chapter in a book : *The settling of Hudson Bay was an important chapter in the history of Canada.* **3. branche, division ▶** a branch of a club or other organization : *The Red Cross has chapters in many different cities.*

char-ac-ter [KAIR-ik-tur] NOUN, characters. **1. caractère, nature ▶** all the qualities and features of a thing or place that make it different from others : *The charming character of Quebec City attracts visitors from all over the world.* **2. caractère, tempérament ▶** what a person is really like, as shown by the way he or she thinks, talks, or acts. A person's character may be strong or weak, honest or dishonest, and so on. **3. caractère ▶** good personal qualities : *"Peter hasn't enough character yet, not enough willpower, too little courage and strength."* (Anne Frank) **4. personnage, rôle ▶** a person in a movie, play, book, or story. **5.** *Informal.* **numéro, personnage ▶** a person who is thought of as odd or unusual : *"Calamity Jane became known as the Heroine of Whoop-Up, because she was a rough-and-ready character."* (Linda Granfield) **6. caractère, signe ▶** a letter, number, or other mark used in printing. ✐ **p. 94.**

char-ac-ter-is-tic [KAIR-ik-tur-IS-tik] NOUN, characteristics. **caractéristique, particularité, trait, signe ▶** a special quality or feature that makes a person or thing what it is : *Megan's friendliness is her most likable characteristic.* ▲ ADJECTIVE. **typique, distinctif (-ive), particulier (-ière) ▶** being a special quality or feature of someone or something; typical : *The use of strong, bright colours is characteristic of the paintings of Vincent van Gogh.*

✐ **Writing Tips**

Characters
Characters are an important part of a story, along with the plot and the setting. When you develop characters, follow these steps :
• First focus on the main character. What is he or she like ? What are the character's strengths and weaknesses ? Likes and dislikes ? What does she or he look like ? How does the character dress ? speak ? walk ?
• Then develop the other characters in your story. What are they like ? What is their relationship with the main character ? What do they say and feel about the main character ?

characteristically, ADVERB. ▶ **typiquement, d'une façon caractéristique.**

char·ac·ter·ize [KAIR-ik-tur-ize] VERB, characterized, characterizing. **1. caractériser, marquer, déterminer** ▶ to be typical or characteristic of: *A humped back characterizes a camel.* **2. décrire, distinguer de** ▶ to tell about the character of: *Kanar's generosity characterizes him as a good-natured boy.* SYN: describe, distinguish, portray, represent.

char·coal [CHAR-kol] NOUN. **charbon de bois** ▶ a black substance that is made by heating wood in a container with very little air. Charcoal is used for drawing pictures, as a filter to make air or water pure, or for fuel, as in outdoor cooking.

charge [charj] VERB, charged, charging. **1. faire payer** ▶ to ask as a price or payment: *That store charges too much for ice cream.* **2. mettre sur le compte de** ▶ to pay later for something that is bought now: *She's not going to pay cash for the dress; she'll charge it on her credit card.* **3. inculper, dénoncer** ▶ to accuse or blame in an official way: *The police officer charged Juliet with speeding.* **4. charger, attaquer** ▶ to attack by rushing forward: *The hockey players charged the net.* **5. charger** ▶ to load with electricity: *The gas station charged our car battery.* ▲ NOUN, charges. **1. coût, frais, prix** ▶ the cost of something; price: *There is a $2 charge to enter the museum.* **2. responsable de** ▶ responsibility, care, or control. **Note.** Often used in the phrase in charge: *Juan is in charge of tidying the gym after practice.* **3. charge** ▶ the amount of electricity in a substance: *The batteries had a weak charge, so the flashlight was dim.* **4. accusation, inculpation** ▶ a formal or legal accusing or blame for something wrong: *The men were arrested on a charge of robbery.* **5. charge, attaque** ▶ a rushing attack: *"The Charge of the Light Brigade" is a poem about a famous battle.*

char·i·ot [CHAIR-ee-ut] NOUN, chariots. **char** ▶ a cart on two wheels that is pulled by horses. In ancient times, chariots were used in races, wars, and parades.

char·i·ta·ble [CHAIR-uh-tuh-bul] ADJECTIVE. **1. charitable** ▶ having to do with charity: *UNICEF is a charitable organization that helps children all over the world.* **2. généreux (-euse)** ▶ giving money or help to the poor or needy; generous. **3. bienveillant (-ante), indulgent (-ente)** ▶ kind and understanding: *Although she didn't like his painting, she made the charitable comment that he must have worked hard on it.* **charitably,** ADVERB: ▶ **charitablement.** *After Brad struck out, the coach said charitably, "You almost hit that last one."* SYN: kindly, forgiving, big-hearted, generous.

char·i·ty [CHAIR-uh-tee] NOUN, charities. **1. charité, bienfaisance** ▶ kindness and forgiveness in dealing with other people. **2. don, aumône, offrande** ▶ a gift of money or help to the poor or needy. **3. œuvre de bienfaisance, œuvre de charité** ▶ an organization or fund for helping people, such as the Red Cross.

charm [charm] NOUN, charms. **1. charme, attrait** ▶ the power to attract or please people: *The charm of the hostess soon put everyone at ease.* **2. fétiche, porte-bonheur, amulette** ▶ a magic object, saying, or action that is supposed to bring good luck or keep away evil: *Some people carry a rabbit's foot as a lucky charm.* **3. breloque** ▶ a small ornament that hangs from a bracelet or other piece of jewellery: *My grandmother has a bracelet with a charm for each one of her grandchildren.* ▲ VERB, charmed, charming. **charmer, plaire** ▶ to attract or please greatly: *Tino's letter charmed his grandparents.* **Note.** Often used as an ADJECTIVE: *Marina sent her aunt a charming thank-you note.* SYN: enchant, delight, please.

chart [chart] NOUN, charts. **1. carte, graphique, diagramme, tableau (-eaux)** ▶ information that is given in a neat or orderly way, in the form of a graph, diagram, or list of facts and figures: *Charts are used to show such information as weather, population, sales, and so on.* **2. carte marine** ▶ a map, especially a map for sailors that shows the location of coasts, reefs, shallow places, and so on. ▲ VERB, charted, charting. **1. dresser la carte de, cartographier** ▶ to make a map of: *Jacques Cartier charted the places he went in North America.* **2. afficher, indiquer, démontrer** ▶ to show or record on a chart: *The poster in the school lobby charts the progress of the food drive.*

char·ter [CHAR-tur] NOUN, charters. **1. charte** ▶ an official document that gives special rights and responsibilities to people: *Canadian banks must have a charter from the federal government.* **2. affrètement** ▶ an agreement to rent or lease a bus, an airplane, a car, or a boat for a special purpose. ▲ VERB, chartered, chartering. **affréter, louer** ▶ to rent or lease by charter: *to charter a bus.*

Charter of Rights and Freedoms Charte des droits et libertés ▶ a part of the Constitution of Canada that legally guarantees certain rights for all Canadians.

chase [chase] VERB, chased, chasing. **1. poursuivre, courir après** ▶ to go after something quickly; try to catch: *Cory chased after Kip, but he couldn't catch him.* **2. chasser** ▶ to cause to run away; drive away: *She chased the rabbit out of the garden.* ▲ NOUN, chases. **poursuite** ▶ the act of chasing or running after.

chat [chat] VERB, chatted, chatting. **bavarder, causer** ▶ to talk in a light, friendly way: *The parents sat and chatted while their children played.* ▲ NOUN, chats. **causerie, conversation,**

bavardage ▶ *The coach had a chat with our star player.* SYN: talk, gossip, converse.

cha·teau [chat-OH] NOUN, chateaux. **château (-eaux), manoir, fort** ▶ a word in French that means a castle or large house in the country.

chat·ter [CHAT-ur] VERB, chattered, chattering. **1. claquer** ▶ to make a quick, rattling sound : *Kane's teeth chattered in the cold.* **2. jacasser, bavarder** ▶ to talk quickly about unimportant things : *"All during the dance Jody had joked and laughed and chattered."* (Sylvia Plath) **Note.** A person who talks all the time is called a chatterbox. ▲ NOUN. **jacassement** ▶ a quick, rattling sound : *I think that chattering must be coming from those chipmunks.*

chauf·feur [SHOH-fur or shoh-FUR] NOUN, chauffeurs. **chauffeur (-euse), conducteur (-trice)** ▶ someone whose work is driving other people around in a car : *She hires a limousine and chauffeur whenever she is in town.*

cheap [cheep] ADJECTIVE, cheaper, cheapest. **1. bon marché, pas cher** ▶ having a low price ; not expensive : *Table salt is cheap to buy.* **2. à bas prix** ▶ charging low prices : *a cheap restaurant ; a cheap movie.* **3. de mauvaise qualité, bas de gamme** ▶ not made or done well ; of poor quality : *That cheap toy broke the first time he played with it.* **4. avare** ▶ not willing to give or spend money ; stingy : *He won't want to go to the concert ; he's too cheap to pay that much for a ticket.* ■ **cheaply,** ADVERB. ▶ **à bon marché. Note.** To lessen the value of something cheap is to cheapen it.

cheat [cheet] VERB, cheated, cheating. **1. tricher, tromper** ▶ to act in a way that is not fair ; be dishonest : *to cheat at cards by looking at the other players' hands.* **2. duper, escroquer, rouler** ▶ to take in a dishonest way : *to cheat a person out of his money.* ▲ NOUN, cheats. **tricheur (-euse), escroc** ▶ a person who cheats. **Note.** Also called a cheater. ✐ p. 96.

check [chek] NOUN, checks. **1. vérification, contrôle, inspection** ▶ a test or careful look at something to see that it is right or as it should be. **2. marque, indication** ▶ a mark [√] to show that something has been looked at or tested : *Put a check next to each correct answer.* **3. addition, note de restaurant** ▶ a piece of paper showing how much a person owes for buying food in a restaurant. **4. bulletin de consigne, bulletin de bagages** ▶ a ticket, tag, or slip of paper to show

that a thing has been left to be picked up later. **5. échec avant** ▶ something that stops or holds back : *A check in hockey is a play to keep another player from moving forward.* **6. carreaux** ▶ a shirt with red and white checks. ▲ VERB, checked, checking. **1. vérifier, examiner, inspecter, contrôler** ▶ to test or examine something to see if it is right or as it should be : *to check the oil in a car engine.* **2. pointer, cocher** ▶ to put a check mark next to something. **3. rechercher, chercher** ▶ to get information for something : *He checked the dictionary to find out what the word meant.* **4. laisser au vestiaire** ▶ to leave something to be picked up later : *She checked her coat at the door.* **5. vérifier** ▶ to stop or hold back : *to check the spread of a disease.* **6. carreler, quadriller** ▶ to mark with a pattern of squares. **Note.** Usually used as an ADJECTIVE:*a checked dress.*

check in **s'inscrire** ▶ to register as a guest : *to check in at a hotel.*

check off pointer, cocher ▶ mark as checked and found true or right : *to check off the items on a list.*

check on or check up on **se renseigner sur** ▶ find out about ; seek more information about : *The police are checking up on his alibi.*

check out régler la note ▶ to pay one's bill for being a guest and leave : *We need enough time to check out and get to the airport in time.*

in check maîtriser, contrôler ▶ controlled ; held back : *He has a hard time keeping his temper in check.*

check·ers [CHEK-urz] PLURAL NOUN. **jeu de dames** ▶ a game for two people in which each player has 12 flat, round pieces to move. **Note.** Checkers is played on a checkerboard, which has 64 squares of two different colours, often red and black.

ched·dar [CHED-ur] NOUN. **cheddar** ▶ a hard yellow or white cheese.

cheek [cheek] NOUN, cheeks. **1. joue, bajoue** ▶ the wide, fleshy part of the face between the nose and the ear : *"She had fair skin and cheeks like blushing roses."* (Roger Lancelyn Green) **2. culot, effronterie, audace** ▶ a bold, rude way of acting : *He had the cheek to push into line ahead of the others.* **Note.** A person

---

✐ **Word Builder**

Cheat, deceive, and *trick* are verbs that suggest doing something wrong deliberately. To **cheat** means to do something dishonest in order to win, or to do better without other seeing or knowing : *Although I was tempted, I didn't cheat on the test when the teacher left the room.* To **deceive** means to make someone believe something is true when it is not : *Gold-coloured flakes in the rock pyrite deceived many people into thinking they had found gold.* To **trick** is to fool someone deliberately : *My brother tricked me into thinking that his old coin was valuable.*

who acts in this way is considered **cheeky**. 📗 **p. 975.**

cheer [cheer] NOUN, cheers. **1. bonne humeur, joie ►** good feelings or good spirits; happiness : *Be of good cheer.* **2. acclamation, encouragement, ovation ►** a shout of happiness, encouragement, or praise : *"A great cheer went up from the knights."* (Donald Carrick) ▲ VERB, cheered, cheering. **1. se réjouir, s'égayer ►** to make or become happy : *We were all cheered when the rain stopped and the sun came out.* **2. encourager, soutenir, stimuler ►** to give a cheer. **Note.** A cheerleader is someone who leads cheering in cheering at a sports event. SYN: encourage, shout, yell.

cheer·ful [CHEER-ful] ADJECTIVE. **1. joyeux (-euse), enjoué (-ée) ►** full of happiness or good feelings : *"His greatest charm was this cheerful...way of making friends with people."* (Frances Hodgson Burnett) **2. réjouissant (-ante) ►** bringing cheer : *a cheerful smile.* ■ **cheerfully,** ADVERB. ► **joyeusement, gaiement.** SYN: lively, sunny, bright, happy, joyful, glad.

cheese [cheez] NOUN, cheeses. **fromage ►** a food made from milk. Cheese is made by separating solids from milk and pressing it into a solid block. 📗 **p. 1135.** 👁 **p. 117.**

chee·tah [CHEE-tuh] NOUN, cheetahs. **guépard ►** a large wild cat with spots like a leopard, found in Africa and Asia. Cheetahs can run faster than any other animal; they are able to reach a speed of 100 km per hour. **Note.** The word cheetah is from Hindi (a language of India) meaning "spotted."

chef [shef] NOUN, chefs. **chef ►** the chief cook of a restaurant.

chem·i·cal [KEM-uh-kul] NOUN, chemicals. **chimique ►** any substance that can cause other substances to change or that is the result of other substances reacting with each other. ▲ ADJECTIVE. **1. chimique ►** having to do with chemistry : *chemical engineering.* **2. chimique ►** made by or using chemicals : *a chemical reaction.*

chem·is·try [KEM-is-tree] NOUN. **1. chimie ►** the science that studies different substances to determine what they are made of, what qualities they have, and how they change when they combine or react with other substances. **Note.** A scientist who is trained in chemistry is a chemist. **2. chimie, harmonie ►** the way that a group of people or things mix or go together : *The coach of the basketball team tried to put together a lineup with the right chemistry.*

cheque [chek] NOUN, cheques. (also check) **1. chèque ►** a written order to a bank to pay a certain amount of money to the person or business named on the paper : *You can cash your cheque at that store.* **2. livret de chèques ►** a blank form on which such an order is written.

Note. A book of blank cheques is a **chequebook.**

cher·ry [CHAIR-ee] NOUN, cherries. **1. cerise ►** a small, round fruit, usually with a red skin, with a pit in the centre, which is eaten raw or in pies and other desserts : *Cherries grow in clumps on trees in cool climates.* **2. rouge cerise ►** a bright-red colour like that of a cherry. 👁 **p. 255.** ▲

chess [ches] NOUN. **échecs ►** a game for two people in which each player has 16 pieces that move in different ways according to certain rules. The object in chess is to trap the other player's main piece (the king) so that it cannot move. **Note.** The game of chess is played on a chessboard. 📗 **p. 1163.**

chest [chest] NOUN, chests. **1. poitrine ►** the upper front part of the body. The heart and lungs are inside the chest, enclosed by the ribs. **2. coffre, caisse, boîte ►** a large, strong box, used to keep things in : *a tool chest; a toy chest.* **3. commode, armoire, chiffonnier ►** a large wooden piece of furniture having several drawers, used for holding or storing clothing and other things. 📗 **p. 994.**

chest·nut [CHES-nut] NOUN, chestnuts. **1. châtaigne, marron ►** a sweet, reddish-brown nut that can be eaten. It grows inside a prickly case until it is ripe. **2. châtain ►** a reddish-brown colour like that of a chestnut.

ches·ter·field [CHES-tur-feeld] NOUN, chesterfields. **canapé, divan ►** a long sofa with padded arms and back. **Note.** Also called a couch.

chew [choo] VERB, chewed, chewing. **mâcher, chiquer, ruminer ►** to grind food or other things with the teeth : *She barely chewed her sandwich before swallowing it.* ▲ NOUN, chews. **chique ►** something that is chewed : *a chew of tobacco.* **Note.** Chewing gum is made from the gum of certain tropical trees. SYN: bite, grind, eat, nibble, gnaw.

chick [chik] NOUN, chicks. **1. poussin ►** a young chicken or other young bird. **2. poussin ►** any young bird. 👁 **p. 98.**

chick·en [CHIK-un] NOUN, chickens. **poulet ►** a type of bird that is raised for its eggs and meat; a hen or rooster. 📗 **p. 1086.** 👁 **p. 114.**

chief [cheef] NOUN, chiefs. **chef ►** the person who is the head of a group; a leader : *A fire chief is in charge of a fire department.* ▲ ADJECTIVE. **1. président (-ente), directeur (-trice) ►** being the highest in rank; most powerful : *The chief electoral officer makes sure that elections and byelections in Canada are fair.* **2. principal (-ales, -aux) ►** most important; main : *"My chief concern is the safety of the children,"* said the lifeguard. ■ **chiefly,** ADVERB. ► **surtout, principalement.** for the most part; largely; mainly : *Lemonade is chiefly water with some lemon juice and sugar.*

97

Chilcotin [CHIL-KOH-tun] NOUN. **Chilcotin** ▸ a group of Aboriginal peoples of southwestern British Columbia who speak an Athapascan language.

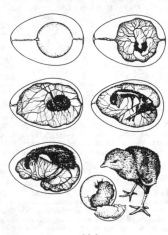

chick

child [chyld] NOUN, children. **1. enfant, gamin (-ine)** ▸ a young girl or boy. **2. enfant, fils, fille** ▸ a person's son or daughter of any age : *Mr. and Mrs. Soames have one child and three grandchildren.* **Note.** Childhood is the time in a person's life when he or she is a child. ☞ p. 967.

child·ish [CHYLD-ish] ADJECTIVE. **1. enfantin (-ine)** ▸ for or like a child : *childish games such as tag or hide-and-seek.* **2. puéril (-ile)** ▸ not suitable for an adult; not mature : *He lost his temper in a childish way when he found out the store was closed.*

chi·li [CHIL-ee] NOUN, chilies. (also **chile** or **chilli**) **1. piment rouge** ▸ the dried seed pod of a kind of red pepper, used to make a hot seasoning for food. **2. chili** ▸ a dish flavoured with chili peppers, made with meat and usually beans.

chill [chil] NOUN, chills. **1. froid, froideur** ▸ a mild but uncomfortable coldness : *"Mom passed around cinnamon buns and hot chocolate to take away the morning chill."* (Julie Lawson) **2. prendre froid, refroidissement** ▸ a feeling of being cold, often with shivering : *"His head is wet, and Virginia keeps wiping it dry so Za won't get a chill."* (Ann Blades) ▲ VERB, chilled, chilling. **se refroidir, se rafraîchir** ▸ to make or become cold. **Note.** Also used as an ADJEC-

TIVE: *"He awoke chilled and sick. There was no sun."* (Jack London)

chill·y [CHIL-ee] ADJECTIVE. **1. froid (froide), frisquet (-ette)** ▸ too cold to feel pleasant; giving a chill : *We made a fire to warm us after walking in the chilly weather.* **2. froid (froide), glacé (-ée)** ▸ not warm or friendly : *The mayor got a chilly reaction when he spoke in favour of raising taxes.*

chime [chyme] NOUN, chimes. **1. carillon** ▸ a bell or pipe tuned to a note of a musical scale. Chimes are played by being hit with small padded hammers. **2. carillonner, résonner** ▸ the ringing or piping sounds made when these bells or pipes are played. ▲ VERB, chimed, chiming. **sonner** ▸ to make a musical sound by striking or ringing bells : *The clock chimed three o'clock.*

chim·ney [CHIM-nee] NOUN, chimneys. **cheminée** ▸ a hollow, upright structure, usually of brick or stone, that carries smoke from a fireplace or furnace to the outside of a building. **Note.** One who cleans out chimneys is a chimney sweep.

chim·pan·zee [chim-pan-ZEE] NOUN, chimpanzees. **chimpanzé** ▸ a small brownish-black ape that lives in trees in Africa. Chimpanzees are among the most intelligent animals. They are one of the few creatures besides humans to make use of tools. **Note.** Informally called a chimp.

chin [chin] NOUN, chins. **menton** ▸ the bony part of the lower face, below the mouth and above the neck. The chin is the front part of the lower jaw. ▲ VERB, chin, chinning. **faire des tractions à la barre fixe** ▸ to pull oneself up to an overhead bar until the chin is higher than the bar. ☞ p. 975.

chi·na [chy-nuh] NOUN. **1. porcelaine** ▸ a fine, glasslike pottery that is made of clay or porcelain and baked twice. This pottery was first made in the country of China. **2. vaisselle, vases ou plats de (porcelaine)** ▸ dishes, vases, and other things made of china.

chi·nook [shuh-NOOK] NOUN, chinooks. **1. chinook** ▸ a warm wind that blows from the west or southwest in winter and early spring down the slopes of the Rocky Mountains into Alberta and occasionally into Saskatchewan. A chinook gets warmer as it blows down the mountain slope. **2. chinook** ▸ the largest kind of Pacific salmon.

chip [chip] NOUN, chips. **1. croustilles** ▸ a small piece that has been broken or cut off : *a potato chip; ice chips.* **2. ébréchure, brèche** ▸ the place where something has broken away : *There's a chip in that plate when I dropped it.* **3. jeton** ▸ a small disk used as a counter in some games, such as poker. **4. puce** ▸ a tiny flake of material, usually silicon, that has been specially treated to carry the circuits needed to operate a computer. ▲ VERB, chipped, chipping.

ébrécher, endommager ▸ to break or cut off a small piece of something : *They chipped the old paint off the wall before putting on the new coat.* SYN: break, crack, piece, part, small chunk. 👁 **p. 541.** ✏ **p. 99.**

chip in contribuer, collaborer, coopérer ▸ give one's share of money or help ; contribute : *We all chipped in to buy a gift for Anna.*

Chip-e-wy-an [CHIP-uh-wy-un] NOUN. **Chipe-wyan ▸** the largest group of Athapaskan-speaking Native peoples in Manitoba, Saskatchewan, and the Northwest Territories.

chip-munk [CHIP-munk] NOUN, **chipmunks. tamia ▸** a small North American animal with brown fur and a striped back. Chipmunks are related to squirrels. They can climb trees, but spend most of their time on the ground collecting seeds and nuts. 👁 **p. 111.**

chipmunk

chirp [cherp] NOUN, **chirps. gazouillis, gazouillement ▸** a quick, sharp sound made by some birds and insects. ▲ VERB, **chirped, chirping. gazouiller, bruire, murmurer ▸** to make this quick, sharp sound : *In spring, the birds begin to chirp early in the morning.*

chlo-rine [KLOR-een] NOUN. **chlore ▸** a greenish-yellow poisonous gas with a strong, unpleasant odour. Chlorine is a chemical element used to kill germs and to clean things. Compounds of chlorine are used to treat water in swimming pools. **Note.** To treat with chlorine is to chlorinate.

chlo-ro-phyll [KLOR-uh-fil] NOUN. (also chlorophyl) **chlorophylle ▸** the substance in plants that gives them their green colour. Chlorophyll uses sunlight to make food for the plant from the elements in air and water. This process is known as photosynthesis.

choc-o-late [CHOK-uh-lit] NOUN, **chocolates. 1. chocolat ▸** a food product made of ground cacao beans, used in candies and in baking. **2. chocolat ▸** candy made of chocolate or flavoured with chocolate. **3. chocolat ▸** a dark-brown colour like that of chocolate. ▲ ADJECTIVE. **1. chocolaté (-ée) ▸** made of or flavoured with chocolate. **2. basané (-ée), bronzé (-ée), tanné (-ée), brun (-une) ▸** having a dark-brown colour. ✏ **p. 1135.**

choice [choyce] NOUN, **choices. 1. choix ▸** the act of choosing ; selecting one from a group : *She had a choice of two dresses to wear to the party.* **2. choix, décision ▸** the chance or right to choose : *It's your choice which movie you go to.* **3. choix ▸** a person or thing that is chosen. ▲ ADJECTIVE, **choicer, choicest. de choix, de premier choix ▸** of high quality ; excellent : *Sam picked a choice spot to watch the ball game.*

choir [kwire] NOUN, **choirs. choeur, chorale ▸** a group that sings together, especially in a church or school.

choke [choke] VERB, **choked, choking. 1. étouffer, étrangler, suffoquer ▸** to stop or block the breathing of a person or animal : *The thick smoke choked the firefighters.* **2. suffoquer, étouffer ▸** to be unable to breathe or swallow normally : *He choked on a bone that was caught in his throat.* **3. refouler, contenir, réprimer, étouffer ▸** to hold back or stop : *Her voice choked with tears.* **4. Informal. figer, paralyser ▸** to do badly in a tense situation because of nervousness. *The tennis player choked at game point.* ▲ NOUN, **chokes. 1. suffocation ▸** the act of choking. **2. étrangleur ▸** a part of a gasoline engine that cuts down the flow of air into the engine.

cho-les-ter-ol [kuh-LES-tuh-ROL] NOUN, **cholesterols. cholestérol ▸** a fatty white substance found in food from animals. If too much cholesterol builds up in the blood vessels, it can cause health problems.

choose [chooz] VERB, **chose, chosen, choosing. 1. choisir, sélectionner ▸** to pick or select from a group : *Please choose a book from this list for your book report.* **2. décider, préférer ▸** to decide or prefer to do something : *"I can remember anything I choose to. Even the names of all my cousins.'"* (Celia Barker Lottridge) SYN: pick, select, decide on, elect.

🖉 **Word Builder**

*Chip is used in many interesting expressions. For example, **a chip off the old block** means a person is like his or her parent : Jacob looks so much like his father that everyone says he is a chip off the old block. If you say that someone has **a chip on his or her shoulder**, it means the person is ready to argue : Lana's angry expression showed that she had a chip on her shoulder. **When the chips are down** is a situation of trouble, when some action is needed : Tanya is a real friend because she's there to offer support whenever the chips are down.*

chop [chop] VERB, chopped, chopping. **1. tailader, entailler, fendre, couper** ▸ to cut by hitting with something sharp : *Tony used an axe to chop wood for the fire.* **2. hacher, couper** ▸ to cut into small pieces : *Karl chopped the vegetables for the stir-fry.* ▲ NOUN, chops. **1. coup** ▸ a quick, sharp blow : *She cut the onions with fast, even chops.* **2. côtelette** ▸ a small piece of meat with a rib in it : *lamb chops; pork chops.*

chop-py [chop-ee] ADJECTIVE. **1. saccadé (-ée), irrégulier (-ière)** ▸ short and quick, jerky : *Her running was choppy but quick.* **2. agité (-ée)** ▸ having many small, rough waves : *The lake was very choppy, making it hard to paddle the canoe.*

chop-sticks [chop-stiks] NOUN, chopsticks. **baguettes** ▸ a pair of long, thin sticks for eating solid food, used mainly in Asian countries.

chord [kord] NOUN, chords. **accord** ▸ a combination of three or more musical notes that are sounded at the same time.

chore [chor] NOUN, chores. **1. corvée, besogne** ▸ a small job around a house or farm that has to be done regularly : *Milking the cows is my chore.* **2. tâche, travail, devoir** ▸ any unpleasant or difficult task : *Sometimes homework is a chore.* SYN : task, job, work, duty, assignment.

cho-rus [KOR-us] NOUN, choruses. **1. troupe, groupe, bande** ▸ a group of singers or dancers who perform together : *Emma sings in the school chorus.* **2. refrain** ▸ a part of a song that is sung after each verse. **Note.** Also called a refrain. **3. concert** ▸ something said by many voices at the same time : *"As each howl ended, another began, until the whole night was filled with coyote song. On and on the wild chorus went."* (Janet Foster) ▲ VERB, chorused, chorusing. **chanter, dire en chœur** ▸ to sing or speak at the same time : *The children chorused "yes" when asked if they wanted ice cream.* ■ **choral,** ADJECTIVE. ▸ choral (-ale, als). something sung by a chorus : *a choral hymn.*

chose [choze] VERB. **choisir** a past form of choose.

cho-sen [CHOH-zun] VERB. **choisir** a past form of choose.

chow-der [CHOW-dur] NOUN, chowders. **soupe au poisson, soupe aux fruits de mer** ▸ a thick soup made of fish or vegetables, usually with milk and potatoes.

Christ [kryst] **1. Christ, Jésus-Christ** ▸ the saviour foretold by the ancient Hebrew prophets; the Messiah. **2. Fils de Dieu, le Messie** ▸ Jesus of Nazareth. Christ is regarded by Christians as the Son of God and the true Messiah.

Christ-mas [KRIS-mus] NOUN, Christmases. **Noël** ▸ a holiday to celebrate the birth of Jesus Christ. It falls on December 25.

chro-mo-some [KROH-muh-som] NOUN, chromosomes. **chromosome** ▸ a threadlike structure found in the nucleus of each plant and animal cell. Chromosomes are made up primarily of DNA and proteins. DNA is the coded information for the passage of characteristics from parents to offspring in every living thing.

chron-ic [KRON-ik] ADJECTIVE. **chronique** ▸ lasting a long time; coming back again and again : *Asthma and arthritis are common chronic illnesses.* ■ **chronically,** ADVERB: ▸ **chroniquement.** *to be chronically ill.*

chrys-a-lis [KRIS-uh-lis] NOUN, chrysalises or chrysalides. **chrysalide, cocon** ▸ The third stage in the life cycle of the butterfly. When the butterfly larva is mature, it sheds its skin and develops the hard-shell covering of the chrysalis.

chrys-an-the-mum [kry-SAN-thuh-mum] NOUN, chrysanthemums. **chrysanthème** ▸ a round flower with many petals. Chrysanthemums bloom in the fall and grow in many colours.

chub-by [CHUB-ee] ADJECTIVE, chubbier, chubbiest. **potelé (-ée), dodu (-ue), grassouillet (-ette)** ▸ being round and plump.

chuck-le [CHUK-ul] VERB, chuckled, chuckling. **glousser** ▸ to laugh softly and quietly : *Gary chuckled at the comics in the paper.* ▲ NOUN, chuckles. **gloussement** ▸ a soft, quiet laugh.

chum [chum] NOUN, chums. **copain (copine), ami (-ie), camarade** ▸ a close friend : *Sally and I have been chums since we were little.* ▲ VERB, chummed, chumming. **socialiser** ▸ to go about together as close friends : *They chummed around all summer.* ▲ ADJECTIVE. chummy. SYN : friend, mate, pal, buddy, companion.

chunk [chunk] NOUN, chunks. **1. gros morceau** ▸ a thick piece or lump : *He broke off a chunk of chocolate to give to his little sister.* **2.** *Informal.* **majeure partie de** ▸ a large amount : *Homework takes a big chunk of my day.* SYN : lump, mass, bulk, wad.

church [cherch] NOUN, churches. **1. église** ▸ a building for Christian religious services. **2. église, temple** ▸ public worship. **3.** (also Church) **Église** ▸ a particular branch of the Christian religion : *the United Church.*

churn [chern] NOUN, churns. **baratte** ▸ a container in which cream or milk can be shaken and stirred to make butter, often used in former times. ▲ VERB, churned, churning. **1. baratter, battre** ▸ to use a churn : *to churn butter.* **2. fouetter, battre** ▸ to move or stir with a rough motion, like that of a churn : *"His feet churned the waves as though he were running on top of the water."* (E.B. White)

chute [shoot] NOUN, chutes. **descente, chute** ▸ a steep slide or tube down which things can be moved or dropped to an opening at the other end : *a laundry chute.*

ci·ca·da [suh-KAY-duh] NOUN. cicadas or cicadae. **cigale** ▸ an insect like a large fly. Cicadas have transparent wings. The male makes a loud buzzing sound. 👁 p. 104.

ci·der [SY-dur] NOUN. ciders. **cidre** ▸ the juice that is made from apples, used as a drink and to make vinegar.

ci·gar [sih-GAR] NOUN. cigars. **cigare** ▸ a tight roll of dried tobacco leaves prepared for smoking.

cig·a·rette [SIG-uh-ret] NOUN. cigarettes. (also cigaret) **cigarette** ▸ a small roll of finely cut tobacco leaves that is wrapped tightly in paper to be smoked.

cicada

cin·e·ma [SIN-uh-muh] NOUN. cinemas. **cinéma** ▸ another name for a motion picture or motion-picture theatre. 📖 p. 1122. 👁 p. 540.

cin·na·mon [SIN-uh-mun] NOUN. **cannelle** ▸ a reddish-brown spice made from the dried inner bark of a certain tropical tree, used to flavour cookies, pies, and many other foods.

cin·quain [SING-kane or SING-kwain] NOUN. cinquains. **strophe** ▸ a poem or part of a poem that is five lines long and follows a set pattern. ✏ p. 101.

cir·ca [SUR-kah] PREPOSITION. **environ** ▸ about; used with dates and figures to show that they are not exact : *Confucius was born in China circa 550 BC.* **Note.** The ABBREVIATION for circa is ca or c.

cir·cle [SUR-kul] NOUN. circles. 1. **cercle** ▸ a line that curves around to meet itself without a break. In a circle, every part of the line is the same distance from the centre. 2. **cercle** ▸ anything that is shaped like a circle : *The square dancers all joined hands in a circle.* 3. **cercle, milieu** ▸ a group of people who share the same interests : *a circle of friends.* ▲ VERB, circled, circling. 1. **encercler, entourer** ▸ to draw or form a circle around : *Please circle the correct answer.* 2. **tourner autour** ▸ to move around in a circle : *"Fox circled the bush, trying to get at the dates."* (Jan Thornhill)

cir·cuit [SUR-kit] NOUN. circuits. 1. **circuit** ▸ a path that ends where it began; a going around : *"On his third circuit of the building, I had opened the kitchen door and Flip darted for the opening."* (Todd Lee) 2. **trajet, parcours** ▸ a route over which a person or group makes regular trips : *a judge's circuit.* 3. **circuit électrique** ▸ a path through which electric current flows : *Our air-conditioner is on its own circuit because it needs more power than our other appliances.*

cir·cu·lar [SUR-kyuh-lur] ADJECTIVE. 1. **circulaire** ▸ having a round shape; in the form of a circle : *"The corral was circular so the horses couldn't injure themselves by crowding into sharp corners."* (Linda Granfield) 2. **circulaire** ▸ moving in a circle : *The model plane flew in a circular path over the field.* ▲ NOUN, circulars. **circulaire, prospectus** ▸ a printed letter or advertisement sent out to a large number of people.

cir·cu·late [SUR-kyuh-LATE] VERB, circulated, circulating. 1. **circuler** ▸ to move around and back to a starting point; go in a circuit : *Blood circulates from the heart, around the body, and back to the heart.* 2. **faire circuler** ▸ to move about; spread : *Rumours about a movie star circulated around town.*

cir·cu·la·tion [SUR-kyuh-LAY-shun] NOUN. circulations. 1. **circulation** ▸ a going around; movement in a circuit : *They put in an attic fan to help the circulation of air through the house.* 2. **circulation, mouvement** ▸ the movement of blood through the blood vessels. **Note.** The path of blood circulation in the body is the **circulatory** system. 3. **diffusion, tirage** ▸ the number of copies of a newspaper or magazine that are sold for each issue.

✎ **Writing Tips**

Cinquain

A **cinquain** *is a five-line poem that follows a specific pattern. Each line has a purpose and is created using a set number of words or syllables.*

The number of syllables for each line :

Line 1:	two syllables
	Summer
Line 2:	four syllables
	Sunny days and
Line 3:	six syllables
	Fun in the cool water
Line 4:	eight syllables
	Playing with friends and family
Line 5:	two syllables
	Till fall

---

cir·cum·fer·ence [sur-KUM-fur-unce *or* sur-KUM-frunce] NOUN, circumferences. **1. circonférence ▸** a line that forms the outside of a circle. **2. circonférence ▸** the distance around the edge of something round : *The circumference of the earth is about 40,000 kilometres.*

circumference

cir·cum·stance [SUR-kum-stans] NOUN, circumstances. **1. circonstance, événement, situation ▸** a condition, fact, or event that happens with something else and has an effect on it : *What were the circumstances that led up to the crime?* **2. circonstance ▸** luck or chance : *She was the victim of circumstance when a tree fell on her car.* **3. circumstances. circonstance, état de chose ▸** the state or condition of something : *Under the circumstances, he has no choice but to pay the fine.*

cir·cus [SUR-kus] NOUN, circuses. **cirque ▸** a show with clowns, acrobats, trained animals, and other performers. Circuses usually travel from town to town and give their shows under a big tent.

cite [site] VERB, cited, citing. **1. citer ▸** to repeat someone else's words; quote : *Shakespeare and the Bible are cited more often than any other sources.* **2. citer, mentionner ▸** to use as an example; refer to : *Mr. Duka cited Joanne's excellent school record when he recommended her for the scholarship.* **Note.** Something that is cited is a citation: *This dictionary has many citations from famous writers.* SYN: quote, name, refer, mention, illustrate.

cit·i·zen [SIT-uh-zun] NOUN, citizens. **1. citoyen (-enne) ▸** someone who is an official member of a country, either by being born there or by choosing to live there and become a member. Citizens have certain rights, such as voting, and certain responsibilities, such as obeying the laws and paying taxes. **2. résident (-ente) ▸** anyone who lives in a town or city; a resident : *She is a citizen of Montreal.* **Note.** Citizenship is the fact of being a citizen, and the rights and responsibilities of a citizen.

cit·rus [SIT-rus] NOUN, citruses *or* citrus. **agrume, fruit ▸** any one of a family of fruit or

fruit trees that grow in warm areas, such as oranges, grapefruits, lemons, or limes.

cit·y [SIT-ee] NOUN, cities. **1. grande ville ▸** a large area where many people live and work : *Cities are larger than towns or villages.* **2. ville ▸** the people of a city : *The city made Elm a one-way street.* 🖰 **p. 1048.**

civ·ic [SIV-ik] ADJECTIVE. **1. civique ▸** having to do with a city. **2. civique ▸** having to do with a citizen or citizenship : *Voting is a civic duty.* ▪ **civics,** NOUN. **▸ instruction civique.** the study of the rights and responsibilities of citizens as a subject in school.

civ·il [SIV-ul] ADJECTIVE. **1. civil (-ile) ▸** having to do with a citizen or citizenship. **2. civil (-ile) ▸** not connected with military or church affairs : *The couple was married in a civil ceremony.* **3. civil (-ile) ▸** within a country or state : *In Canada, civil rights are protected by the Constitution.* **4. poli (-ie), courtois (-oise), aimable ▸** polite; courteous : *The least you could do is give me a civil answer.*

ci·vil·ian [sih-VIL-yun] NOUN, civilians. **civil (-ile), citoyen (-ne) ▸** a person who is not a member of the armed forces or of a police force. ▲ ADJECTIVE. **civique ▸** having to do with civilians.

civ·i·li·za·tion [SIV-uh-ly-ZAY-shun] NOUN, civilizations. **1. civilisation ▸** a stage of human society in which people have progressed in their knowledge of art, science, government, farming, trade, and so on : *the Japanese civilization.* **2. civilisation ▸** the way of life of a particular people or nation : *"At that time, in the south, the first great civilizations of Meso-America were developing."* (Robert McGhee)

civ·i·lize [SIV-uh-LIZE] VERB, civilized, civilizing. **civiliser, éduquer, évoluer ▸** to change from a primitive condition of life to a more developed one : *The ancient Romans tried to civilize the European tribes they conquered with their knowledge of government, building, and agriculture.* **Note.** Also used as an ADJECTIVE: *a civilized nation; civilized customs.*

claim [klame] VERB, claimed, claiming. **1. réclamer, demander ▸** to ask for or take as one's own : *The winner of the contest claimed his prize.* **2. affirmer, déclarer, prétendre ▸** to say that something is true; declare as fact : *Greg claims to have seen the Loch Ness Monster.* ▲ NOUN, claims. **1. revendication, réclamation, demande, requête ▸** a demand for something as one's own : *After the fire, we filed a claim with the insurance company for the damage to our house.* **2. affirmation, attestation, confirmation ▸** a statement that something is true : *We all laughed at Jenny's claim that she had seen a flying saucer.* **3. concession ▸** a thing that is claimed, especially land : *The miner found gold on his claim.*

F OOD CHAIN

omnivore
► omnivore

grain eaters
► granivores

insectivores
► insectivores

herbivore
► herbivore

carnivore
► carnivore

plants
► plantes

herbivores
► herbivores

When they die, all living beings decompose and nourish the soil.
► En mourant, tous les êtres vivants se décomposent et nourrissent le sol.

micro-organisms
► micro-organismes

mineral substances
► substances minérales

103

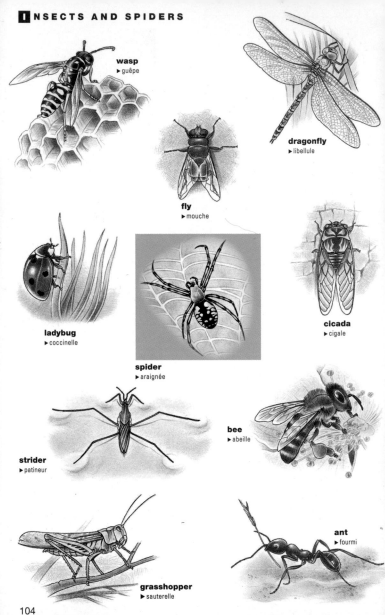

wasp
▸ guêpe

dragonfly
▸ libellule

fly
▸ mouche

ladybug
▸ coccinelle

spider
▸ araignée

cicada
▸ cigale

strider
▸ patineur

bee
▸ abeille

grasshopper
▸ sauterelle

ant
▸ fourmi

B UTTERFLIES

Canadian tiger swallowtail
▶ papillon tigré du Canada
☼

monarch butterfly
▶ grand monarque
☼

morpho menelaus
▶ morpho ménélaus
☼

American luna moth
▶ papillon-lune américain
☾

polyphemous moth
▶ polyphème d'Amérique
☾

laurel sphinx
▶ sphinx du laurier-rose
☾

cecropia moth
▶ bombyx cécropia
☾

European owl moth
▶ brahmaéide d'Hartig
☾

Legend	
☼	diurnal
☾	nocturnal

tomcod
▶ poulamon
(petit poisson des chenaux)

rainbow trout
▶ truite arc-en-ciel

lake perch; yellow perc
▶ perchaude

smallmouthed bass
▶ achigan à petite bouche

walleye
▶ doré

chain pickerel
▶ brochet maillé

carp
▶ carpe

catfish
▶ barbotte

musky
▶ maskinongé

salmon
▶ saumon

smelt
▶ éperlan

herring
▶ hareng

eel
▶ anguille

mackerel
▶ maquereau

blue shark
▶ requin bleu

sea trout
▶ truite de mer

tuna
▶ thon

cod
▶ morue

sturgeon
▶ esturgeon

107

northern gannet
▶ fou de Bassan

belted kingfisher
▶ martin-pêcheur d'Amérique

Atlantic puffin
▶ macareux moine

ring billed gull
▶ goéland à bec cerclé

mourning dove
▶ tourterelle triste

bluejay
▶ geai bleu

**ring-necked
pheasant**
▶ faisan de Colc

American kestrel
▶ crécerelle d'Amérique

loon
▶ plongeon huard

ruffed grouse
▶ gélinotte huppée

American rob
▶ merle d'Amérique

nuthatch
▶ sittelle à poitrine rousse

great horned owl
► grand-duc d'Amérique

barn swallow
► hirondelle rustique

cardinal
► cardinal rouge

snowy owl
► harfang
des neiges

**great blue
heron**
► grand héron

red-winged blackbird
► carouge à épaulettes

American goldfinch
► chardonneret jaune

**ruby-throated
humming bird**
► colibri à gorge rubis

cedar waxwing
► jaseur d'Amérique

Canada goose
► bernache du Canada

109

bat
▶ chauve-souris

bighorn
▶ mouflon

killer whale
▶ épaulard

beluga
▶ béluga

polar bear
▶ ours polaire

Arctic fox
▶ renard arctique

mountain goat
▶ chèvre de montagne

seal
▶ phoque (loup-marin)

lynx
▶ lynx

otter
▶ loutre

hare
▶ lièvre

beaver
▶ castor

groundhog
▶ marmotte

red fox
▶ renard roux

porcupine
▶ porc-epic

racoon
▶ raton laveur

squirrel
▶ écureuil

moose
▶ orignal (élan)

deer
▶ chevreuil
(cerf de Virginie)

caribou
▶ caribou (renne du Canada)

brown bear
▶ ours brun (grizzli)

elk
▶ wapiti

wolverine
▶ carcajou (glouton)

coyote
▶ coyote

skunk
▶ mouffette

wolf
▶ loup

chipmunk
▶ suisse
(tamia rayé)

muskrat
▶ rat musqué

111

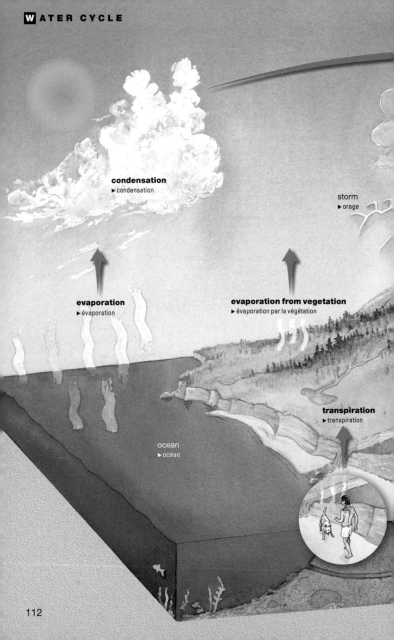

condensation
▶ condensation

storm
▶ orage

evaporation
▶ évaporation

evaporation from vegetation
▶ évaporation par la végétation

transpiration
▶ transpiration

ocean
▶ océan

clouds
► nuages

precipitation
► précipitations

ice
► glace

rain
► pluie

snow
► neige

thaw
► fonte

run-off
► ruissellement

seepage
► infiltration

evaporation
► évaporation

lake
► lac

underground run-off
► écoulement souterrain

113

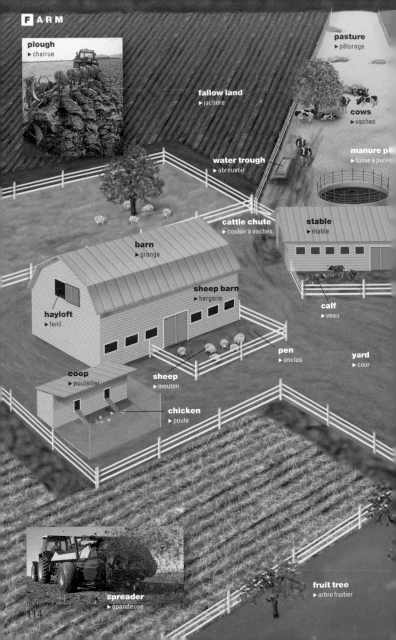

F A R M

plough
► charrue

pasture
► pâturage

fallow land
► jachère

cows
► vaches

water trough
► abreuvoir

manure pi
► fosse à purin

cattle chute
► couloir à vaches

stable
► étable

barn
► grange

sheep barn
► bergerie

calf
► veau

hayloft
► fenil

pen
► enclos

yard
► cour

coop
► poulailler

sheep
► mouton

chicken
► poule

fruit tree
► arbre fruitier

spreader
► épandeuse

114

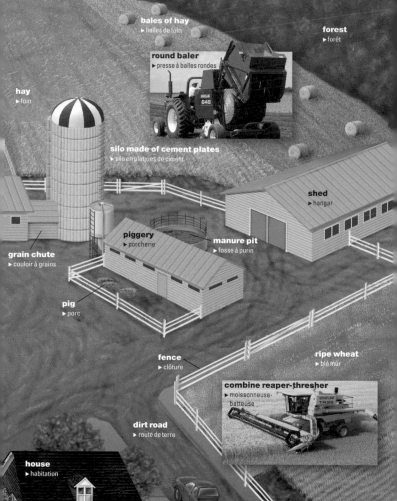

bales of hay
► balles de foin

forest
► forêt

round baler
► presse à balles rondes

hay
► foin

silo made of cement plates
► silo en plaques de ciment

shed
► hangar

piggery
► porcherie

manure pit
► fosse à purin

grain chute
► couloir à grains

pig
► porc

fence
► clôture

ripe wheat
► blé mûr

combine reaper-thresher
► moissonneuse-batteuse

dirt road
► route de terre

house
► habitation

vegetable garden
► potager

115

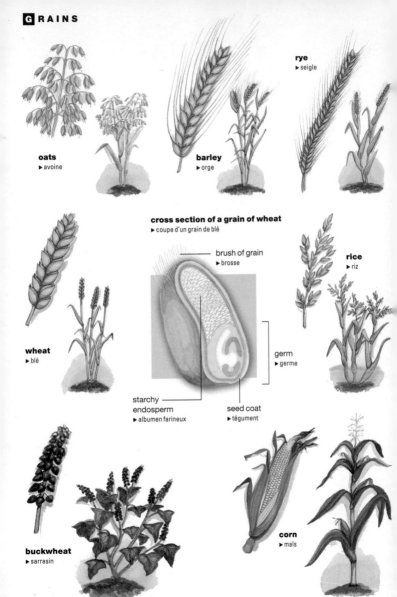

oats
▶ avoine

barley
▶ orge

rye
▶ seigle

wheat
▶ blé

cross section of a grain of wheat
▶ coupe d'un grain de blé

brush of grain
▶ brosse

germ
▶ germe

starchy endosperm
▶ albumen farineux

seed coat
▶ tégument

rice
▶ riz

buckwheat
▶ sarrasin

corn
▶ maïs

C CHEESE

cow
► vache

goat
► chèvre

sheep
► brebis

The cheeses illustrated are obtained through the coagulation of cow, goat or sheep's milk.

SOFT CHEESE

brie cheese
► brie

cheese with herbs
► roulé aux fines herbes

camembert cheese
► camembert

SEMI-FIRM CHEESE

feta cheese
► feta

Oka cheese
► Oka

goat cheese
► chèvre

blue cheese
► bleu

FIRM CHEESE

parmesan cheese
► parmesan

emmenthal cheese
► emmenthal

**cheddar cheese –
wheel and curds**
► cheddar en meule
et en grains

CANADA'S FOOD GUIDE TO HEALTHY EATING

FOR PEOPLE FOUR YEARS AND OVER

1 portion
1 slice of bread
1/2 bagel
1/2 pita bread
1/2 roll
50 to 100 g of meat
50 to 100 g of poultry
50 to 100 g of fish

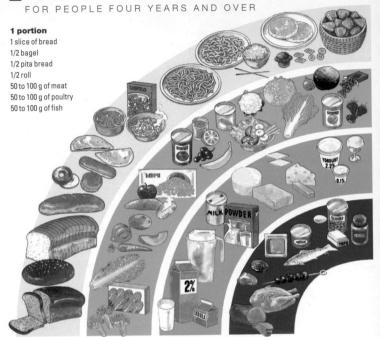

Grain products	+	Vegetables and fruits	+	Dairy products	+	Meats and meat substitutes	=	Food guide
5 TO 12 PORTIONS PER DAY		**5 TO 10** PORTIONS PER DAY		PORTIONS PER DAY children (4 to 9 years): **2 to 3** teenagers (10 to 16 years): **3 to 4** adults: **2 to 4**		**2 TO 3** PORTIONS PER DAY		Each food group is essential since each one provides a different combination of nutrients.

Grain products	Vegetables and fruits	Dairy products	Meats and meat substitutes	Food guide
proteins		proteins	proteins	proteins
		fats	fats	fats
carbohydrates	carbohydrates			carbohydrates
fibre	fibre			fibre
thiamine	thiamine		thiamine	thiamine
riboflavin		riboflavin	riboflavin	riboflavin
niacin			niacin	niacin
folacin	folacin		folacin	folacin
		vitamin B_{12}	vitamin B_{12}	vitamin B_{12}
	vitamin C			vitamin C
	vitamin A	vitamin A		vitamin A
		vitamin D		vitamin D
		calcium		calcium
iron	iron		iron	iron
zinc		zinc	zinc	zinc
magnesium		magnesium	magnesium	magnesium

Adapted from *Canada's Food Guide to Healthy Eating* with permission of the Minister of Public Works and Government Services Canada, 2001

clam [klam] NOUN, clams. **palourde** ▸ an animal that has a soft body and a double shell that is joined by a hinge. Clams are found in either salt or fresh water. Many kinds are good to eat.

clam·our [klam-ur] NOUN. (also **clamor**) **1. cla-meur, tumulte** ▸ a loud, continuous noise; shouting : *The clamour in the streets made it hard to sleep.* **2. requête, demande** ▸ a demand for something ▲ VERB, clamoured, clamouring. **vociférer, hurler** ▸ to demand noisily : *The crowd clamoured for another song.*

clamp [klamp] NOUN, clamps. **attache, crampon** ▸ a tool used for gripping or holding things together tightly. Usually, a clamp has two parts that can be tightened with a spring or screw. ▲ VERB, clamped, clamping. **1. cramponner, serrer** ▸ to hold together with a clamp : *Tom clamped the two blocks of wood until the glue was dry.* **2. clamp down. serrer la vis** ▸ to be strict : *The police clamped down on speeding cars.*

clan [klan] NOUN, clans. **1. clan, bande, tribu** ▸ a group of families who are all related to the same ancestor, especially in Scotland : *The entire Graham clan is coming to our house for dinner.* **2. association, caste, partie, classe** ▸ a group with a common interest.

clap [klap] VERB, clapped, clapping. **1. taper des mains, battre des mains** ▸ to hit together loudly : *Mia clapped her hands to get everyone's attention.* **2. applaudir** ▸ to applaud by hitting the hands together : *"As he came along the road strutting like a peacock, some animals swooned, others cheered and clapped."* (Faustin Charles) **3. donner une tape** ▸ to slap with an open hand : *He clapped me on the shoulder to celebrate our victory.* ▲ NOUN, claps. **1. claquement** ▸ a sharp, sudden noise : *a clap of thunder.* **2. tape** ▸ a friendly slap : *a clap on the shoulder.* SYN: strike, bang, applaud.

clar·i·net [klar-uh-NET] NOUN, clarinets. **clarinette** ▸ a musical instrument with a mouthpiece and a long body shaped like a tube. It is played by blowing into the mouthpiece and pressing the keys or covering the holes with the fingers. p. 539.

clash [klash] VERB, clashed, clashing. **1. entrer en contact, s'entrechoquer, résonner, se heurter** ▸ to hit or come together with a loud, hard sound. **2. entrer en conflit, s'affronter** ▸ to come into conflict; disagree strongly : *The planners clashed over where to build the park.* **3. discordance, incompatible** ▸ not to match well : *The colour of that shirt clashes with those pants.* ▲ NOUN, clashes. **1. fracas, grand bruit** ▸ a loud, hard sound. **2. conflit, désaccord, affrontement, différend** ▸ a strong disagreement; a conflict. SYN: oppose, conflict, disagree, quarrel, differ.

clasp [klasp] NOUN, clasps. **1. fermoir, agrafe** ▸ something that holds two objects or parts

together, such as a buckle or hook : *Linda asked me to fasten the clasp on her necklace.* **2. prise** ▸ a strong grip or hold : *Willy has a strong clasp for such a small boy.* ▲ VERB, clasped, clasping. **1. agrafer, attacher** ▸ to fasten with a clasp : *He clasped the watch onto his wrist.* **2. serrer, saisir, enlacer** ▸ to hold or grip strongly : *Sandy clasped her father's hand as they crossed the road.*

class [klas] NOUN, classes. **1. classe** ▸ a group of students who meet or are taught together : *The art class is visiting the museum.* **2. classe, cours** ▸ a meeting of such a group : *I have to see the teacher after class today.* **3. classe, promotion** ▸ a group of students who have graduated or will graduate in the same year : *the class of 1995.* **Note.** A person in the same class as another is a **classmate**. **Note.** School classes are held in a classroom (p. 1058). **4. classe** ▸ a division or rank based on quality : *A first-class ticket on an airplane costs more than a regular seat.* **5.** *Informal.* **classe, distinction** ▸ high quality or elegance; excellence : *Terry is a hockey player with a lot of class.* **6. classe, premier ordre, première classe** ▸ any group of people or things that are alike in some way : *Birds belong to a class of animals called "Aves."* ▲ VERB, classed, classing. **catégorie, espèce, sorte** ▸ to put in a class; classify.

clas·sic [KLAS-ik] NOUN, classics. **1. classique** ▸ a great book or work of art that has been thought of highly for a long time : *Shakespeare's plays are classics of literature.* **2. classique** ▸ anything that is thought of as outstanding in its field : *The 1937 Jaguar roadster is a classic.* **3. the classics.** (also the Classics) **classique** ▸ the literature of ancient Greece and Rome. ▲ ADJECTIVE. **1. classique** ▸ of the highest quality in literature or art : Anne of Green Gables *is a classic Canadian novel.* **2. classique** ▸ being of very high quality : *a classic movie.* **3. classique** ▸ very typical and obvious : *The accident was a classic example of careless driving.*

clas·si·cal [KLAS-uh-kul] ADJECTIVE. **1.** (also Classical) **classique, les humanités** ▸ having to do with ancient Greece and Rome, or with their literature, art, and culture : *The Parthenon, a temple in Athens, is a famous example of classical Greek architecture.* **2. classique** ▸ having to do with classical music. **Note.** Classical music is a form of music that follows certain formal rules and standards that were set down in Europe in the 1700s and early 1800s. Symphonies and operas are types of classical music.

clas·si·fy [KLAS-uh-fy] VERB, classified, classifying. **classer, répartir, diviser** ▸ to place in a class or group : *to classify mail according to city.* **Note.** Often used as an ADJECTIVE: *Classified ads are sorted according to what they are advertising.* **Note.** Classification is the act or result of classifying. SYN: organize, group, categorize, sort.

clat-ter [KLAT-ur] VERB, clattered, clattering. **entrechoquer bruyamment, faire du bruit ▸** to make a loud rattling noise : *The carts clattered over the cobblestone streets.* ▲ NOUN, clatters. **fracas, bruit, vacarme ▸** a clattering noise : *"She made a light clatter in the kitchen."* (Marjorie Kinnan Rawlings) SYN: noise, rattle, racket, din.

clause [kloz] NOUN, clauses. **1. proposition ▸** a part of a sentence that has a subject and a verb. **2. clause, disposition, condition ▸** a single part of a law, treaty, or any other written agreement : *There is a clause in her apartment lease that says pets are not allowed.*

claw [klah] NOUN, claws. **1. griffe ▸** a sharp, curved nail on the foot of an animal or a bird. **2. pince ▸** one of the grasping parts on the limb of a lobster or crab. **3. panne, marteau à panne fendue, pied de biche ▸** anything shaped like a claw, such as the part of a hammer used to pull out nails. ▲ VERB, clawed, clawing. **griffer, pincer, égratigner ▸** to scratch, tear, or dig with the claws or hands : *The searchers clawed through the dirt to get to the buried treasure.*

clay [klay] NOUN, clays. **argile ▸** a kind of soft, fine earth that can be shaped when it is wet but that hardens when it is dried or baked. Clay is used to make bricks and pottery.

clean [kleen] ADJECTIVE, cleaner, cleanest. **1. propre ▸** free from stain or dirt; not dirty : *Please change into clean clothes for dinner.* **2. honorable, honnête, franc (franche), propre ▸** free from wrong; honourable or fair : *The mayor was proud of her clean record.* **3. net (nette), franc (franche) ▸** complete; total : *She cut the branch with one clean blow.* **4. élégant (-ante) ▸** neat or, even : *an automobile with clean lines.* ▲ VERB, cleaned, cleaning. **nettoyer, récurer ▸** to remove dirt and mess from something; to make clean : *to clean a floor.* **Note.** Often used with up or out: *Please clean up your room.*

clean-er [KLEEN-ur] NOUN, cleaners. **1. nettoyeur (-euse) ▸** a person or business whose work is cleaning things : *He took his suit to the cleaners.* **2. détachant, nettoyant ▸** a machine or substance that is used to clean : *a rug cleaner.*

clear [kleer] ADJECTIVE, clearer, clearest. **1. transparent (-ente), limpide ▸** easy to see through :

The water was so clear she could see the bottom of the lake. **2. clair (claire) ▸** free from anything that darkens; bright : *The wind was just a light northern breeze and the sky was clear.* **3. clair (claire), limpide ▸** easy to see, hear, or understand : *a clear voice; clear handwriting.* ▲ VERB, cleared, clearing. **1. débarrasser, déblayer ▸** to make or become clear : *Dad cleared the dishes off the table.* **2. libérer, dégager ▸** to move away so as to make clear : *As soon as the dust cleared, we saw that we had turned onto the wrong road.* **3. dégager, désencombrer ▸** to free from something that blocks : *Mom asked us to clear our bikes from the driveway.* **4. franchir, sauter, éviter ▸** to go over or by without touching : *The horse cleared the fence with centimetres to spare.* **5. innocenter, disculper, blanchir ▸** to free from blame or guilt : *The lawyer was sure that the evidence would clear her client.* ■ **clearly,** ADVERB. ▸ **clairement.** *"Tom could always hear what went on next door as clearly as if he were there himself."* (Phillipa Pearce) 🖉 p. 120.

clear-ing [KLEER-ing] NOUN, clearings. **clairière ▸** an area of land in a forest where there are no trees and bushes.

clef [klef] NOUN, clefs. **clé, clé musicale ▸** in music, a sign at the beginning of a musical staff that shows the pitch of the notes. There are three clefs : treble clef, bass clef, and tenor or alto clef.

clench [klench] VERB, clenched, clenching. **serrer, se serrer, se crisper ▸** to hold or press together tightly : *"He clenched his jaw, trying to look like Agent 007."* (Louise Fitzhugh)

clerk [klerk] NOUN, clerks. **1. vendeur (-euse) ▸** a person who sells goods at a store : *"The storekeeper called one of his clerks to carry the brooms inside."* (Thomas H. Raddall) **2. commis, employé (-ée) de bureau ▸** a person whose work is to keep records and other papers in order in an office. ▲ VERB, clerked, clerking. **travailler comme employé (-ée) de bureau ▸** to work as a clerk : *During the summers, she clerked in a law office.*

clev-er [KLEV-ur] ADJECTIVE, cleverer, cleverest. **1. intelligent (-ente) ▸** having a quick mind; smart; bright : *The clever detective figured out who stole the jewels.* **2. ingénieux (-euse) ▸** showing skill or quick thinking : *a clever idea.* ■ **cleverly,** ADVERB. ▸ **ingénieusement.** ■ **cleverness,**

🖉 Word Builder

Clear out means to go away, often very quickly: After the game, the stadium cleared out in 15 minutes. *In the clear* means free from danger or obstacles, or free from guilt: In the football game, Damon broke through the defence and was in the clear for a pass. The expression *clear the air* means to get rid of conflicts or tensions: After their argument, they needed time to clear the air.

✍ **Writing Tips**

Climax

*The **climax** of a story is the dramatic turning point in the action—the most exciting part. The reader is in suspense up to that point, wondering if the problem will be solved.*

•   When you are developing the plot for a story, think about what the climax will be. What events will lead up to the climax to make it even more exciting?

•   Discuss two or three ideas with someone, and then develop the best one.

•   The climax is usually near the end of the story, but it's not the end. Remember to tie up all the loose ends of the story after the climax and show how the event affected the characters.

NOUN. ▸ **ingéniosité.** SYN: able, bright, smart, intelligent, skillful.

cli·ché [klee-SHAY] NOUN, clichés. **cliché, banalité** ▸ an expression or idea that has been overused : *A story about a fairy godmother helping a princess is a cliché because it has been told so often.*

click [klik] NOUN, clicks. **déclic, claquement** ▸ a short, sharp sound : *The lock clicked into place.* ▲ VERB, clicked, clicking. 1. **cliqueter** ▸ to make this sound. 2. *Informal.* **s'entendre** ▸ to fit or work together smoothly : *Suddenly everything clicked, and I understood how to solve the problem.*

cli·ent [KLY-unt] NOUN, clients. 1. **client (-ente)** ▸ a person or company that uses the services or advice of another person or company : *The lawyer defended his client in court.* 2. **clientèle** ▸ any customer of a store or business. **Note.** A group of clients is a clientele.

cliff [klif] NOUN, cliffs. **falaise** ▸ a high, steep surface of rock or earth that rises sharply above the land or water below. **Note.** A cliffhanger is a story, movie, television show, and so on that is full of suspense, especially an episode in a series in which the ending leaves the hero in a dangerous or unresolved situation.

cli·mate [KLY-mut] NOUN, climates. 1. **climat, température** ▸ the usual weather that a place has. Climate includes the temperature, rain or snow, winds, and the amount of sunshine in a region. 2. **climat** ▸ a section of the country having a certain type of weather : *The southwest coast of Canada has a mild climate.* 3. **climat, opinion** ▸ the main attitude or feeling that a certain group or place has : *the climate of public opinion.* 🗒 **p. 1102.**

cli·max [KLY-maks] NOUN, climaxes. **point culminant, apogée** ▸ the most exciting or important part of something ; the point of highest interest : *The climax of a movie usually comes just before the end.* SYN: result, end, conclusion, turning point. ✍ **p. 121.**

climb [klime] VERB, climbed, climbing. 1. **grimper, escalader, gravir** ▸ to go up something, especially by using the hands and feet : *"And the trunk was so smooth that even the monkey couldn't climb the tree."* (Celia B. Lottridge) **Note.** This meaning is also used to tell about moving down or to the side : *to climb out of bed.* 2. **monter, grimper** ▸ to move upward, as if by climbing ; rise : *The plane climbed to 20,000 metres.* ▲ NOUN, climbs. 1. **montée, côte, ascension** ▸ the act of climbing : *Their climb to the top of the hill took two hours.* 2. **montée, ascension** ▸ a place to be climbed : *That slope is a dangerous climb for beginners.*

cling [kling] VERB, clung, clinging. 1. **s'accrocher** ▸ to stick or hold tightly to something : *The little boy clung to his mother's leg when the dog came near.* 2. **s'attacher, se cramponner** ▸ to refuse to give up ; stay attached to : *She still clings to the hope that she'll become an actor.* SYN: hold, grasp, stick.

clin·ic [KLIN-ik] NOUN, clinics. 1. **clinique** ▸ a place where people can get medical help without having to stay in a hospital. 2. **clinique, maison de santé** ▸ any place where people can get help or learn certain skills : *a reading clinic.*

clip¹ [klip] VERB, clipped, clipping. 1. **couper, cisailler, tondre** ▸ to cut with scissors or shears ; trim : *to clip an article out of the newspaper.* 2. **couper** ▸ to cut something short, as if by clipping : *He clipped his sentence in the middle of a word.* ▲ NOUN, clips. **vive allure** ▸ a quick rate of moving : *The old man moved at a surprising clip.*

clip² NOUN, clips. **pince, attache, trombone** ▸ an object that holds things together : *a paper clip ; a tie clip.* ▲ VERB, clipped, clipping. **attacher, agrafer, serrer, pincer** ▸ to hold things together with a clip : *She clipped the cheque to her letter.*

clip·per [KLIP-ur] NOUN, clippers. 1. **tondeuse, coupe ongle** ▸ a tool used to cut or clip things : *fingernail clippers.* 2. (also clipper ship) **clipper** ▸ a large sailing ship of the 1800s that was built to travel at a fast speed.

clip·ping [KLIP-ing] NOUN, clippings. 1. **coupure de presse** ▸ a story, a picture, or an advertisement cut out of a newspaper or magazine. 2. **déchet** ▸ anything that is cut off or clipped from something else : *grass clippings.*

cloak [kloke] NOUN, cloaks. 1. **grande cape, manteau** ▸ a loose outer garment that covers the

121

body. **2. manteau, voile** ▸ something that covers up or hides, as a cloak covers the body : *The prisoners escaped under the cloak of darkness.* ▲ VERB, cloaked, cloaking. **dissimuler, masquer** ▸ to cover up or hide : *We cloaked the plans for Tonya's surprise party in secrecy.* SYN : hide, conceal, cover, protect, disguise.

clock [klok] NOUN, clocks. **horloge** ▸ an object that shows the time of day. A clock is meant to be left in one place rather than carried around or worn as a watch is. ▲ VERB, clock, clocking. **chronométrer** ▸ to measure time with a clock : *The police clocked the speeding car at 130 km/h.* **Note.** A digital clock shows the time directly in numbers. An analog clock has a dial with hands that point to the time. ☞ **p. 1076.**

clog [klog] VERB, clogged, clogging. **boucher, bloquer, entraver, obstruer** ▸ to stop up; block : *Traffic clogged the main street.* ▲ NOUN, clogs. **1. sabot, socque, galoche** ▸ a shoe with a thick wooden or cork bottom. **2. obstacle, entrave** ▸ something that causes clogging.

close¹ [kloze] VERB, closed, closing. **1. fermer** ▸ to cover up a space or passage ; make not open ; shut : *to close a door.* **2. fermer** ▸ to bring together the parts of : *"Miss Friel closed her book with a snap."* (Brian Moore) **3. finir, terminer** ▸ to bring or come to an end : *to close a letter with "Yours truly."* **4. fermer** ▸ to stop operating or working : *The office closed for the holiday.* **Note.** Often used with up or down : *Mr. Ross closed up the store and went home.* **Note.** Also used as an ADJECTIVE : *The mayor made a few closing remarks before ending the press conference.* ▲ NOUN, closes. **fermeture** ▸ the closing of something ; the end or finish : *"The day was drawing to a close."* (Dylan Thomas) ✐ **p. 122.**

close² [kloze] ADJECTIVE, closer, closest. **1. près de, proche** ▸ not far apart in space, time, or feeling ; near : *It's getting close to summer.* **2. clos (-ose), fermé (-ée)** ▸ without enough air or space : *This room feels close with the windows shut.* **Note.** Close quarters is a very tight or crowded space. **3. intime, personnel (-elle)** ▸ giving careful thought or attention : *Take a close look at your test paper before you turn it in.* **4. serré (-ée)** ▸ nearly even : *a close race between Danni and Jane.* ▲ ADVERB. **près de** ▸ in a close way ; near : *"I'll walk ahead and you stay close behind me."* (James Hous-

ton) ■ **closely**, ADVERB. ▸ de près. ■ **closeness**, NOUN. ▸ proximité. ✐ **p. 391.**

clos·et [KLOZ-it] NOUN, closets. **placard, armoire, penderie** ▸ a small room or cabinet for hanging clothes or storing things.

cloth [kloth] NOUN, cloths. **1. tissu, étoffe** ▸ a material made by weaving or knitting cotton, silk, wool, or other fibres. It is used to make clothes, blankets, curtains, and many other things. **2. nappe, toile** ▸ a piece of this material used for a special purpose : *a tablecloth ; a washcloth.*

clothes [kloze] PLURAL NOUN. **vêtements, habits** ▸ things worn to cover the body, such as shirts, pants, dresses, jackets, coats, and so on : *You'll need to wear heavy winter clothes to play in the snow.*

clothes-line [KLOZE-line] NOUN, clotheslines. **corde à linge** ▸ a rope or wire used to hang wet clothes on so they can dry. **Note.** Clothespins are small pins used to hold clothes on a clothesline.

cloth·ing [KLOH-thing] NOUN. **vêtements, habillement** ▸ things that cover the body ; clothes : *We store our winter clothing in the attic during the summer.* ☞ **p. 1008.**

cloud [klowd] NOUN, clouds. **1. nuage** ▸ a white, grey, or dark mass floating high in the sky. Clouds are made of tiny drops of water or ice hanging in the air. **Note.** A cloudburst is a sudden, heavy rainfall. **2. nuée** ▸ any mass or grouping of things like a cloud : *"Her truck kicked up a cloud of summer dust."* (Sheryl McFarlane) ▲ VERB, clouded, clouding. **1. s'ennuager, se voiler, se couvrir** ▸ to cover or become covered with clouds : *By the end of the day, the sky had clouded over.* **2. s'assombrir** ▸ to make or become darker or less clear : *Tea clouds when you add milk.* ☞ **p. 1117.** ☞ **p. 113.**

cloud·y [KLOWD-ee] ADJECTIVE, cloudier, cloudiest. **1. nuageux (-euse), couvert** ▸ covered with clouds : *a cloudy sky.* **2. trouble, flou (floue), sombre, nébuleux (-euse)** ▸ not clear : *The jar was filled with a cloudy brown liquid.* SYN : dark, unclear, overcast, gloomy, dismal.

clove [kloze] NOUN, cloves. **clou de girofle, gousse** ▸ the dried flower bud of a certain tropical evergreen tree. Cloves have a sharp smell and taste and are used as a spice in cooking.

🖉 Word Builder

Close in on means to come near to what you want to find : *The search and rescue team began to close in on the stranded hikers.* ***Close down*** means to shut down or stop completely : *The blizzard closed down the city.* ***Close call*** or ***close shave*** means that someone has had a narrow escape : *Evelyn had a close call when she fell from her mountain bike and rolled to the edge of the cliff.*

clo·ver [KLOH-vur] NOUN, clovers. **trèfle** ▸ a plant with leaves formed in three small, round parts and white, red, or yellow flower heads. Clover is used as food for cows and to make soil richer. ☞ **p. 250.**

clown [klown] NOUN, clowns. **1. clown, bouffon (-onne), guignol** ▸ a person whose job is to make people laugh by doing tricks, acting silly, and wearing funny clothes. Clowns often provide entertainment at circuses or parades. **2. clown, farceur (-euse), pitre** ▸ anyone who tells jokes or acts in a foolish way to make others laugh : *Matt behaves like a real clown at parties.* ▲ VERB, clowned, clowning. **faire le clown, faire le fou** ▸ to behave like a clown; act silly : *She was clowning around on her bicycle and ran into a fence.*

club [klub] NOUN, clubs. **1. club, cercle** ▸ a group of people who have joined together to do some special thing : *a swimming club; a chess club.* **2. gourdin, massue, matraque** ▸ a heavy stick that is used to hit something. **3. club** ▸ one of the long sticks used to hit the ball in the game of golf. **4. trèfle** ▸ a black cloverleaf design like this [♣], found on playing cards. **5. trèfles** ▸ clubs, the suit of cards that has this design. ▲ VERB, clubbed, clubbing. **butter, matraquer** ▸ to hit or beat with a club or stick.

clue [kloo] NOUN, clues. **indice, indication, piste** ▸ something that helps a person solve a problem or mystery : *A fingerprint was the clue that helped solve the case.*

clump [klump] NOUN, clumps. **1. bouquet, touffe, massif** ▸ a thick group or cluster : *a clump of dirt.* **2. bruit lourd** ▸ a heavy, clumsy sound : *We could hear the clump of her cane before she came into sight.* ▲ VERB, clumped, clumping. **1. rassembler** ▸ to form in a clump. **2. marcher lourdement** ▸ to walk with a heavy, clumsy sound : *The little boy clumped around the house wearing his father's shoes.*

clum·sy [KLUM-zee] ADJECTIVE, clumsier, clumsiest. **1. maladroit (-oite), gauche** ▸ not moving smoothly; awkward : *The clumsy puppies fell over each other as they tried to get out of the box.* **2. maladroit (-oite), gauche, sans tact** ▸ not well made, said, or done : *He gave a clumsy excuse for not having his homework finished.* ■ **clumsily,** ADVERB. ▸ **maladroitement.** ■ **clumsiness,** NOUN. ▸ **maladresse.** SYN: awkward, ungraceful, unskilled.

clung [klung] VERB. **s'accrocher, s'attacher, se cramponner** ▸ a past form of cling.

clus·ter [KLUS-tur] NOUN, clusters. **groupe, bouquet, grappe** ▸ a group of similar things growing or gathered together : *a cluster of stars.* ▲ VERB, clustered, clustering. **se rassembler, se grouper** ▸ to be in a cluster : *The students clustered at the front of the school, waiting for the doors to open.*

clutch[1] [kluch] VERB, clutched, clutching. **1. saisir, agripper, empoigner** ▸ to hold or grasp tightly : *"I tried to stretch up and clutch Josepha's elbow, but he broke free."* (Jim McGugan) **2. se cramponner à, s'agripper à, se raccrocher à** ▸ to reach for; try to grab : *The drowning man clutched at the rope.* ▲ NOUN, clutches. **1. embrayage** ▸ a part in an automobile or other machine that connects or disconnects the motor from the other working parts. **2. emprise, pouvoir** ▸ control or power : *She was in the clutches of the villain.* SYN: cling, hold, grasp, adhere, stick, grip, seize.

clutch[2] NOUN, clutches. **couvée, groupe** ▸ a number of things produced at one time : *a clutch of chickens.*

clut·ter [KLUT-ur] NOUN. **désordre** ▸ things scattered about in a disorganized way; a mess : *The clutter in the basement made it hard to find my hockey stick.* ▲ VERB, cluttered, cluttering. **mettre en désordre, emcombrer** ▸ to scatter or toss about; mess up : *Books, sports equipment, and my science project clutter my room.*

co- [koh] PREFIX. with another; together : *co-host.*

coach [kohch] NOUN, coaches. **1. entraîneur (-euse)** ▸ a person who is in charge of a team in sports such as hockey and basketball : *The baseball coach showed Darlene how to improve her swing.* **2. entraîneur (-euse), répétiteur (-trice), moniteur (-trice)** ▸ any person who teaches or trains a performer or athlete : *a singing coach.* **3. carrosse, diligence, wagon** ▸ a large, closed carriage on wheels that is pulled by horses : *Cinderella went to the ball in a coach pulled by white horses.* **4. voiture** ▸ a section of seats on a bus, train, or airplane that is less expensive than other sections. ▲ VERB, coached, coaching. **entraîner, former, diriger** ▸ to act as a coach : *His older sister coached him for the math exam.* SYN: tutor, trainer, teacher.

coal [kole] NOUN, coals. **charbon** ▸ a piece of glowing or burned wood, coal, or charcoal : *the glowing coals of the fire.*

co·a·li·tion [KOH-uh-LISH-un] NOUN, coalitions. **coalition, alliance, association** ▸ an agreement, usually a temporary one, between political parties, groups, or nations to work together for a special purpose.

coarse [korce] ADJECTIVE, coarser, coarsest. **1. rude, épais (épaisse), lourd (lourde)** ▸ not smooth or fine; rough : *In winter, horses have a coarse coat.* **2. grossier (-ière)** ▸ made up of large parts or pieces : *coarse soil; coarse salt.* **3. vulgaire, rude, grossier (-ière)** ▸ not having good manners; acting in a rough or crude way; rude. ■ **coarsely,** ADVERB. ▸ **grossièrement, impoliment.** ■ **coarseness,** NOUN. ▸ **grossièreté, rudesse.** SYN: rough, bumpy, choppy, unpolished.

coast [kohst] NOUN, coasts. **1. côte, littoral ▸** the edge of land touching the ocean; seashore : *"Grandma, Melissa and Oliver watched as they scrambled up the island's rocky coast."* (Phoebe Gilman) **2. rive, rivage ▸** an area of land near the ocean; waterfront : *They're looking for a small cottage on the coast.* ▲ VERB, coasted, coasting. **aller en roue libre ▸** to move without effort or power; slide : *They coasted down the snowy hill on their sleds.* ■ **coastal,** ADJECTIVE. **côtier (-ière), littoral (-ale, -aux) ▸** of or near a coast : *"Other times he walked in the nearby woods watched over by the jagged peaks of the coastal range."* (Sheryl McFarlane)

coast·er [KOH-stur] NOUN, coasters. **1. dessous de verre ▸** a small, flat object placed under a glass, bottle, or pitcher in order to protect the table or other surface beneath it : *Please put a coaster under your glass so that it won't mark the table.* **2. luge, traîneau (-eaux) ▸** a sled or toboggan.

coat [kote] NOUN, coats. **1. manteau, veston, veste ▸** a piece of clothing with sleeves, usually worn outdoors over other clothing. **2. pelage, fourrure, toison, robe ▸** the hair or fur of an animal : *a lamb's woolly coat.* **3. couvrir ▸** a thin layer of something that covers a surface : *a coat of paint.* ▲ VERB, coated, coating. **recouvrir de, enrober, garnir ▸** to cover with a layer of something : *Aunt Elsie coated the cake with sugar.* 📖 **p. 1009.**

coax [kohks] VERB, coaxed, coaxing. **cajoler, amadouer, câliner ▸** to try to get something in a nice or gentle way; persuade : *They coaxed the cat inside with some milk.* **persuader, convaincre ▸** SYN: persuade, convince, pressure, urge.

co·bra [KOH-bruh] NOUN, cobras. **cobra ▸** a large poisonous snake found in Africa and Asia. When excited, the cobra puffs out the skin around its neck into a hood.

cob·web [KOB-web] NOUN, cobwebs. **toile d'araignée ▸** another name for a spiderweb.

cock [kok] NOUN, cocks. **1. coq ▸** a male chicken; a rooster. **2. oiseau mâle ▸** the male of other birds used for food. ▲ VERB, cocked, cocking. **1. dresser ▸** to turn up; tilt or tip : *My dog cocked his ear at the loud noise.* **2. armer ▸** to pull back the hammer of a gun.

co·coa [KOH-koh] NOUN. **1. cacao ▸** a dark-brown powder made by crushing the dried seeds of the cacao tree. This powder gives a chocolate taste to foods. **2. cacao, chocolat chaud ▸** a hot drink made by mixing cocoa with sugar and milk or water.

co·co·nut [KOH-kuh-NUT] NOUN, coconuts. **noix de coco ▸** the nut of a large round fruit that comes from the coconut palm tree. It has a thick, hard shell with sweet white meat and a milky liquid inside.

co·coon [kuh-KOON] NOUN, cocoons. **cocon ▸** a silky covering that is spun by an insect to protect it while it is in an inactive stage of life called a pupa. A caterpillar lives in a cocoon while it is developing into a moth or butterfly.

cod [kod] NOUN, cod or cods. **morue ▸** a fish found in northern areas of the Atlantic Ocean. Cod is caught for food. 👁 **p. 107.**

code [kode] NOUN, codes. **1. code ▸** a set of words, signs, or symbols used to send messages. Codes are often used to keep messages short or secret. **2. code, chiffre ▸** in a computer, a method of presenting information and instructions in a form that can be understood by the computer. **3. code ▸** a system of laws arranged in an orderly way : *The building code says that the swimming pool must have a fence around it.* **4. code ▸** any set of rules or principles for doing things : *a code of honour.* ▲ VERB, coded, coding. **coder ▸** to put into code : *to code a message.*

coconut tree

fruit (coconut)

cof·fee [KOF-ee] NOUN, coffees. **1. café ▸** a dark-brown hot drink made of the crushed and roasted seeds of the coffee plant, which grows in warm, moist climates. **2. café ▸** the seeds or beans of this plant. **Note.** The word coffee comes from Arabia. The Arabs were the first people to raise coffee plants. 📖 **p. 1135.**

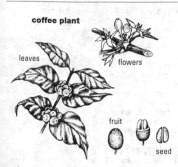

coffee plant

leaves

flowers

fruit

seed

cof-fin [KOF-in] NOUN, coffins. **cercueil ▶** a box or case in which the body of a dead person is placed to be buried.

coil [koyl] NOUN, coils. **rouleau (-eaux) ▶** anything made by winding something around in a circle many times; a connected series of circles : *a coil of rope; a coil of wire.* ▲ VERB, coiled, coiling. **enrouler ▶** to wind in a coil : *Andrew coiled up the hose.*

coin [koyn] NOUN, coins. **pièce ▶** a flat, round piece of metal used as money : *The coins in my pocket add up to $1.23.* ▲ VERB, coined, coining. **1. frapper de la monnaie ▶** to make coins from metal. **2. inventer ▶** to make up; invent : *to coin a phrase.*

co-in-ci-dence [koh-IN-suh-duns] NOUN, coincidences. **coïncidence ▶** two things happening that seem to be connected, but actually happen together by accident; chance : *It is a coincidence that we both have the same middle name.*

cold [kold] ADJECTIVE, colder, coldest. **1. froid (froide) ▶** having a low temperature; not hot : *The water was too cold to go swimming.* **2. froid (froide) ▶** not feeling warm; chilly : *She was cold, so she put on a sweater.* **3. froid (froide), sans cordialité ▶** not friendly or kind : *He gave me a cold look when I stepped on his foot.* ▲ NOUN, colds. **1. froid ▶** a lack of heat : *Some plants die if left out in the cold.* **2. rhume ▶** a common illness that causes sneezing, a runny nose, and coughing. ■ **coldly,** ADVERB: *"They looked at her coldly, as if they were finding fault with her."* (D.H. Lawrence) **froideur ▶** ■ **coldness,** NOUN. **▶ froideur.**

cold-blood-ed [kold-BLUD-ud] ADJECTIVE. **1. à sang froid ▶** having blood that changes temperature as the nearby air or water becomes colder or warmer. Fish, frogs, turtles, and snakes are cold-blooded animals. **2. sans pitié ▶** having no feelings or emotions; cruel : *a cold-blooded murderer.*

col-lab-o-rate [kuh-LAB-uh-RATE] VERB, collaborated, collaborating. **1. collaborer, participer ▶** to work together; work with others : *The three of us collaborated on our project.* **2. collaborer ▶** to help or work with an enemy against one's own country. **Note.** The act of collaborating is called **collaboration.**

col-lage [kuh-LAZH] NOUN, collages. **collage ▶** a picture that is made by gluing pieces of material such as paper, cloth, and yarn to a surface.

col-lapse [kuh-LAPS] VERB, collapsed, collapsing. **1. s'écrouler ▶** to fall down or fall in : *"One after another, the tents collapsed on the sleeping knights."* (Donald Carrick) **2. s'effondrer ▶** to lose strength; break down : *She collapsed in exhaustion on the sofa.* **3. s'écrouler, s'effondrer ▶** to fail completely or suddenly : *"His whole life would be ruined, all his plans for the future would collapse."* (E.B. White) ▲ NOUN, collapses. **écroulement, effondrement, affaissement ▶** the act or fact of collapsing : *the collapse of an old building.* **Note.** Something that can be folded together is collapsible: *a collapsible beach chair.*

col-lar [KOL-ur] NOUN, collars. **1. col, collet, encolure ▶** the band or strip around the neck of a coat, shirt, or dress : *"At once he seized Wu by the collar and pulled him up over the saddle in front of him."* (David Day) **2. collier ▶** a band or chain worn around the neck of an animal, such as a dog or cat : *a flea collar.* **3. bague ▶** anything that is like a collar, such as a ring that holds a rod or pipe in place. ▲ VERB, collared, collaring. **1. mettre un col, un collet ou une encolure ▶** to put a collar on. **2. intercepter, empoigner ▶** to catch as if by the collar : *The storekeeper collared the thief as she was sneaking out the door with a radio.*

col-league [KOL-eeg] NOUN, colleagues. **collègue, confrère, consœur ▶** someone who is in the same business or with the same company as another; a fellow worker : *While the doctor was on vacation, one of his colleagues treated his patients for him.* SYN: co-worker, associate, friend, partner, ally.

col-lect [kuh-LEKT] VERB, collected, collecting. **1. se rassembler ▶** to bring together in a group; gather together; assemble : *"There were no more eggs to collect because the constant noise caused the chickens to stop laying."* (Donald Carrick) **2. collectionner ▶** to gather for a hobby, study, or display : *Rosa collects stamps from all over the world.* **3. percevoir, recouvrer ▶** to get as payment : *Nick collected money from the people on his paper route.* **Note.** Someone or something that collects is a collector: *a coin collector.* **Note.** To be collected **maître de soi ▶** means to be calm and relaxed. SYN: bring together, gather, assemble, store up. ✍ p. 35, 244.

col·lec·tion [kuh-LEK-shun] NOUN, collections.
1. ramassage ▸ the act of gathering together or collecting : *Garbage collection happens once a week in our neighbourhood.* **2. accumulation, amas** ▸ something collected : *a collection of dust on some old books.* **3. collection** ▸ a group of things gathered for a hobby, study, or display : *"The photograph is one of a collection by a famous photographer."* (S.E. Hinton) 📑 p. 1163.

col·lege [KOL-ij] NOUN, colleges. **1. collège, université** ▸ an institution of higher education that offers training or education and gives degrees or diplomas upon completion of the course of study : *community college.* **2. collège** ▸ a special school within an entire university for instruction in one particular area : *a teachers' college.* **3. Informal. collège** ▸ university : *My sister will be going to college next fall.*

col·lide [kuh-LIDE] VERB, collided, colliding.
entrer en collision ▸ to strike or bump together in a rough or violent way ; crash : *The cars collided with a bang.* SYN : conflict, clash, band, hit, smash.

col·lie [KOL-ee] NOUN, collies. **colley** ▸ a large dog with a long, thin face and long, thick hair. The collie is a popular breed that was first used by Scottish farmers to guard sheep.

col·li·sion [kuh-LIZH-un] NOUN, collisions.
1. collision ▸ the act of hitting together ; a crash : *The automobile accident was a head-on collision.* **2. conflit, affrontement** ▸ a clash ; conflict : *a collision of opinions.*

co·lon[1] [KOH-lun] NOUN, colons. **deux-points** ▸ a punctuation mark [:] that is used to call attention to a certain group of words that follow the colon : *We are visiting many countries : Jordan, Israel, and Egypt.*

co·lon[2] NOUN, colons. **côlon** ▸ the lower part of the large intestine.

colo·nel [KER-nul] NOUN, colonels. **colonel (-elle)** ▸ an officer's rank in the armed forces, ranking above lieutenant-colonel.

co·lo·ni·al [kuh-LOH-nee-ul] ADJECTIVE. **1. colonial (-iale, -iaux)** ▸ having to do with a colony or colonies : *colonial government.* **2. colon** ▸ of the time when a nation was a colony : *colonial furniture.* ▲ NOUN, colonials. **Note.** A person who lives in a colony. **Note.** The policy of ruling other areas as colonies is colonialism.

col·o·ny [KOL-uh-nee] NOUN, colonies. **1. colonie** ▸ a group of people who leave their own country to settle in another area that is under the control of that country : *In 1608, Samuel de Champlain founded a colony in New France.* **Note.** To set up or live in a colony is to colonize. Someone who colonizes is a colonist. **2. colonie** ▸ an area of land ruled by a distant country : *Quebec was originally a French colony.* **3. colonie** ▸ a group of people who live near each other and are alike in some way : *The "Left Bank" section of Paris was a well-known artists' colony in the 1920s.* **4. colonie** ▸ a group of animals or plants of the same kind living together.

col·our [KUL-ur] NOUN, colours. (also color)
1. couleur ▸ the effects of light rays on different wavelengths : *The colour red has the longest rays, and violet has the shortest rays.* **2. couleur** ▸ Red, blue, or yellow, or any combination of these colours (green, orange, purple, and so on). **Note.** Red, blue, and yellow are called primary colours. **3. peinture, teinture** ▸ something used to produce colour, such as paint, stain, or dye. **4. couleurs** ▸ a lively or interesting quality : *The books of Charles Dickens captured the colour of life in 19th-century London.* **5. colours. drapeau (-eaux), couleurs** ▸ the flag of a certain country or military unit : *The troop hoisted its colours.* ▲ VERB, coloured, colouring. **1. colorer, colorier** ▸ to give colour; add colour : *The little child coloured the walls with a crayon.* **2. rougir** ▸ to blush ; to become flushed : *"Her face coloured scarlet as the words came out."* (Brian Moore) ▲ ADJECTIVE, colourful. coloré (-ée) ▸ 📑 p. 1009. 🖉 p. 126.

col·our·less [KUL-ur-lis] ADJECTIVE. **1. incolore** ▸ having no colour ; without colour : *He looked sadly at the dark, colourless landscape around him.* **2. terne, ennuyeux (-euse), morne** ▸ not bright or vivid ; not interesting : *The speaker had a colourless manner and soon lost the attention of her audience.* SYN : dull, uninteresting, flat, dreary.

colt [kolt] NOUN, colts. **poulain** ▸ a young horse, especially a male under four or five years old.

col·umn [KOL-um] NOUN, columns. **1. colonne, pilier, poteau (-eaux)** ▸ a tall, slender post or pillar, usually made of wood or stone, that stands upright to support a roof or other part of a building. In modern buildings, columns are often used for decoration rather than as an actual sup-

---

✎ **Word Builder**

*The expression **to lose colour** means to become pale : As she described the accident, Carol lost colour. If you **show your true colours**, you are showing yourself as you really are : Donald showed his true colours by helping out during the flood. **To pass with flying colours** means to have great success : He studied hard for the math test and passed with flying colours.*

port. **2. colonne** ▶ anything long and slender like a column : *a column of smoke.* **3. colonne** ▶ a narrow vertical section of words or figures : *Add the figures in the first column.* **4. chronique** ▶ a regular article or feature in a newspaper or magazine, usually written by the same person. **Note.** A person who writes a column is called a **columnist.**

com-a [KOH-muh] NOUN, comas. **coma** ▶ a state of deep unconsciousness from which a person cannot be woken up, caused by injury or illness.

comb [kome] NOUN, combs. **1. peigne** ▶ a plastic or metal object with teeth, used to arrange or style the hair. **2. crête** ▶ a thick, fleshy, red piece of skin on top of the head of a rooster or similar bird. ▲ VERB, combed, combing. **1. peigner** ▶ to arrange or style the hair using a comb : *I comb my hair after I wash my face.* **2. passer au peigne fin** ▶ to search for something very carefully : *The police combed the area for clues.*

com-bat [KOM-bat] NOUN, combats. **combat, bataille, affrontement** ▶ a battle or war between two military forces : *Medals are given to soldiers who are wounded in combat.* ▲ [kum-BAT], VERB, combated, combating. (also combatted, combatting) **combattre** ▶ to fight or struggle against : *Dr. Jonas Salk found a medicine to combat the spread of the disease polio.*

com-bi-na-tion [KOM-buh-NAY-shun] NOUN, combinations. **1. combinaison, assemblage** ▶ something that is formed by combining things : *A mule is a combination of a horse and a donkey.* **2. combinaison** ▶ the act of combining : *The combination of red and blue makes purple.* **3. combinaison** ▶ a series of numbers or letters used to open a lock.

com-bine [kum-BINE] VERB, combined, combining. **combiner, disposer, organiser, joindre** ▶ to put together; join or unite; mix : *She combined flour, butter, and water to make a pie crust.* **Note.** Often used as an ADJECTIVE: *The combined effort of all the players led the team to victory.* ▲ [KOM-bine] NOUN, combines. **moissonneuse-batteuse** ▶ a machine used to harvest wheat. ✐ **p. 35.**

come [kum] VERB, came, come, coming. **1. venir** ▶ to go or move toward a place : *Our dog always comes when he's called.* **2. arriver** ▶ to reach a certain place; arrive : *Come home before dark.* **3. atteindre** ▶ to reach a certain point or condition : *Heat the soup until it comes to a boil.* **4. venir** ▶ to be from a certain place : *Janet comes from Alberta.* **5. être disponible** ▶ to be available; exist : *This shirt comes in different colours.* SYN: arrive, happen, occur, draw near, advance.

com-e-dy [KOM-uh-dee] NOUN, comedies. **comédie** ▶ a play, movie, or television program that is funny and that has a happy ending. **Note.** A situation comedy is a TV comedy show that uses the same characters in a series of programs. A person whose work is entertaining others by telling jokes or doing funny things is a **comedian** or **comic.** ☞ **p. 1122.**

com-et [KOM-it] NOUN, comets. **comète** ▶ a star-like object that travels in a long path around the sun and has a bright head and a long, streaming tail. It is thought to be made of ice, frozen gases, and dust.

com-fort [KUM-furt] NOUN, comforts. **1. confort** ▶ a feeling of being free from worry, pain, or annoyances, and of having one's needs satisfied. **2. réconfort** ▶ a person or thing who gives this feeling : *The motel's ad said, "We provide all the comforts of home."* ▲ VERB, comforted, comforting. **réconforter, consoler** ▶ to give comfort to someone who is upset or in pain or difficulty : *Sergio comforted his little sister, who had fallen and hurt her knee.* SYN: console, ease, cheer, calm, soothe.

com-fort-a-ble [KUM-fur-tuh-bul] ADJECTIVE. **1. confortable** ▶ giving comfort : *comfortable clothes ; a comfortable bed.* **2. à l'aise** ▶ feeling comfort; at ease : *"You feel mighty free and easy and comfortable on a raft."* (Mark Twain) ▪ **comfortably,** ADVERB. ▶ **confortablement.**

com-ic [KOM-ik] NOUN, comics. **1. comique, drôle, amusant (-ante)** ▶ a person who tells funny stories or jokes that make people laugh ; a comedian. **2. bande dessinée** ▶ a comic strip or comic book. ▲ ADJECTIVE. **comique, drôle, amusant (-ante)** ▶ funny or amusing : *Amelia Bedelia is a comic character who always gets her words mixed up.* **Note.** Another form of this word is comical. ✐ **p. 127.**

com-ma [KOM-uh] NOUN, commas. **virgule** ▶ a mark of punctuation [,] that is used **1.** to separate parts of a sentence : *Wood floats, but iron doesn't.* **2.** to set off items in a series : *It was a cold, dark, dreary day.* **3.** to separate parts of a name, a date, or an address : *April 1, 1939 ; Halifax, Nova Scotia.*

✐ Writing Tips

Comic Strip

Comic strips are stories, riddles, or jokes told in a series of drawings called frames or panels. You can read comic strips such as Peanuts or Superman in newspapers, magazines, books, and comic books. Some jokes are told in only a single frame, such as Family Circus and Marmaduke.

• *When writing your own comic strip, you could use funny or unusual events that have happened to you or that you've heard about as story ideas.*

com·mand [kuh-MAND] VERB, commanded, commanding. **1. ordonner ▶** to give orders to; order; direct : *"She slammed supper on the table and commanded everybody to eat and be quick about it."* (Vera Cleaver) **2. commander ▶** to have power or authority over : *General Isaac Brock commanded the British troops in Upper Canada during the War of 1812.* **3. imposer ▶** to receive or demand as one's due : *"Pa's example commanded our respect and moulded us."* (Christy MacKinnon) ▲ NOUN, commands. **1. ordre, commandement ▶** an order or direction : *"The monks of Wu's monastery had no choice but to obey the command."* (David Day) **2. à la tête de ▶** the power to give orders : *to be in command of a ship.* **3. commandement ▶** the power or ability to make use of something : *a command of the English language.* **4. commande ▶** an instruction to a computer to perform a certain operation; keyboard commands : *Do you know the command for putting this list in alphabetical order?* ✐ **p. 128.**

com·mand·er [kuh-MAN-dur] NOUN, commanders. **1. commandant (-ante) ▶** a leader; a person in command. **2. commandant (-ante) ▶** an officer in charge of an army or part of an army. **3. commandant (-ante), lieutenant-colonel ▶** in the Marine Command, a naval officer equal to the rank of lieutenant-colonel.

com·mence [kuh-MENS] VERB, commenced, commencing. **commencer, amorcer, démarrer ▶** to begin : *The ceremony will commence at 8:00.* SYN : begin, start, take off.

com·ment [KOM-unt] NOUN, comments. **commentaire, remarque, observation ▶** a remark, a statement, or an opinion about someone or something : *She made the comment quietly so that no one else could hear it.* ▲ VERB, commented, commenting. **commenter, faire une remarque ▶** to make a comment : *The reporter was asked to comment on her story in the paper.* **Note.** A person whose work is to comment on the news on television or radio is a commentator. SYN : remark, note, observe, mention.

com·merce [KOM-urs] NOUN. **commerce ▶** the buying and selling of goods, especially on a large scale between different places or countries.

com·mer·cial [kuh-MUR-shul] NOUN, commercials. **publicité, annonce publicitaire ▶** an advertisement on television or radio : *A good commercial can increase the sales of the product it advertises.* ▲ ADJECTIVE. **commercial (-iale, -iaux) ▶** having to do with business : *A commercial airliner carries passengers and goods to make money, as compared to a private plane or a military aircraft.* ■ **commercially,** ADVERB. **▶ commercialement.**

✐ Writing Tips

Command Sentences

A **command sentence** gives an order or makes a request. This kind of sentence usually ends with a period, but when it's a strong command, you can use an exclamation mark.

> Close the door.
> Please be careful crossing the street.
> Wait! Stop!

com·mis·sion [kuh-MISH-un] NOUN, commissions. **1. commission ▶** a group of people given the power or authority to do a certain job : *a Human Rights Commission .* **2. brevet ▶** a position of power or authority, especially a rank in the armed forces : *My sister has received her commission as a lieutenant in the army.* **3. commission ▶** a payment of money to a person for carrying out or arranging the sale of something : *There is a commission of 5 % on the selling price of a house.* **4. perpétration ▶** the act of doing something : *the commission of a crime.* **5. out of commission. hors service ▶** out of active use or service : *Many battleships were taken out of commission after World War II.* ▲ VERB, commissioned, commissioning. **1. passer une commande, mandater, confier ▶** to give power or authority to : *We commissioned an artist to do a painting of our family.* **2. armer ▶** to put into active service : *to commission a warship.*

com·mit [kuh-MIT] VERB, committed, committing. **1. commettre, faire ▶** to do or perform something wrong or bad : *to commit an error in baseball.* **2. faire interner ▶** to be put in the care or charge of : *The court committed him to a hospital for treatment.* **3. s'engager à ▶** to promise or assign to something : *During the election, the mayor committed to making the streets safer.*

com·mit·ment [kuh-MIT-munt] NOUN, commitments. **obligation ▶** the fact of being committed to something : *Megan couldn't go on the trip; she had too many other commitments.*

com·mit·tee [kuh-MIT-ee] NOUN, committees. **comité ▶** a group of people who work together for a common purpose : *The decorations committee will hang balloons in the gym.*

com·mod·i·ty [kuh-MOD-ut-tee] NOUN, commodities. **marchandise, produit, article ▶** anything that can be bought or sold, especially raw materials produced by farming or mining : *Corn and lumber are commodities.* SYN : product, article, ware, item.

com·mon [KOM-un] ADJECTIVE, commoner, commonest. **1. commun (-une) ▶** appearing or happening often; usual or familiar : *Dogs are a common pet.* **2. courant (-ante) ▸** widespread; general : *Owning a computer is becoming more common.* **3. public (-ique), général ▸** having to do with people in general; public : *The federal government is charged with acting for the common good.* **4. commun (-une) ▸** shared by two or more people or groups : *Winning the final game was the team's common goal.* **5. commun (-une), ordinaire ▸** of no special rank or quality; average; ordinary : *common people; common table salt.* ▲ NOUN, commons. **1. terrain communal ▸** an area of public land owned or used by all the people of a city or town. **2. in common. en commun ▸** equally with another or others : *The only thing we have in common is our love of hockey.* ■ **commonly,** ADVERB: **▸ communément.** *It was once commonly believed that the earth was flat.* SYN: usual, ordinary, average, normal, everyday. ✐ **p. 129.**

Commons 1. la Chambre des Communes ▸ the House of Commons. **2. Chambre ▸** the members of the House of Commons.

com·mon·wealth [KOM-un-WELTH] NOUN, commonwealths. **1. État (I') ▸** all the people who live in a nation or state. **2. confédération ▸** a nation or state that is governed by the people. **3. Commonwealth ▸** a group of nations, persons, or the like, united by some common bond or interest. **Note.** The Commonwealth of Nations (also known as the Commonwealth) is an association of countries that were once under British law and government.

com·mo·tion [kuh-MOH-shun] NOUN, commotions. **tumulte, agitation, trouble ▸** a loud, noisy disturbance : *We were so excited about the game that the principal came over to see what all the commotion was about.* SYN: excitement, disturbance, fuss, action.

com·mu·ni·cate [kuh-MYOO-nuh-KATE] VERB, communicated, communicating. **communiquer, informer ▸** to share or exchange information, feelings, or thoughts; speak or write to someone : *My sister lives in Egypt, so we communicate by e-mail.* **Note.** Something that can be communicated is communicable. SYN: inform, tell, report, disclose.

com·mu·ni·ca·tion [kuh-MYOO-nuh-KAY-shun] NOUN, communications. **1. communication ▸** the act of communicating : *A coach should*

have good communication with the players on her team. **2. message, information, renseignement ▸** what is communicated; the information or ideas given. **3. communications. système de communication, liaison ▸** a system that is used to communicate, such as TV, radio, or telephone.

com·mun·ism [KOM-yuh-NIZ-um] NOUN. **1. communisme ▸** an economic system in which all property, goods, and services belong to the government rather than to individual people or private companies. Under communism, all people share equally in what is produced. **2.** (also Communism) **communisme ▸** a policy of government that is based on this system. **Note.** Someone who believes in communism is a communist or Communist.

com·mun·i·ty [kuh-MYOO-nuh-tee] NOUN, communities. **1. communauté ▸** a group of people who live in the same area, such as a neighbourhood or town. **2. communauté, collectivité ▸** the area or town itself : *Everyone works together to keep this community safe.* **3. communauté, congrégation, association ▸** any group of people joined by common interest : *A nun is a member of a religious community.* SYN: society, people, colony, district, town.

com·mute [kuh-MYOOT] VERB, commuted, commuting. **faire la navette ▸** to travel regularly to and from one's place of work, especially a long distance.

com·pact [KOM pakt or kum-PAKT] ADJECTIVE. **1. compact (-acte), dense, serré (-ée), tassé (-ée) ▸** packed together tightly : *The newspapers are tied in a compact pile.* **2. compact (-acte) ▸** taking up a small amount of space or room : *a compact stereo system.* ▲ [kahm-PAKT] VERB, compacted, compacting. **compacter, condenser ▸** to pack together tightly. **Note.** A compactor (also compacter) is a machine that compacts garbage into a tight bundle. ▲ [KAHM-pakt] NOUN, compacts. **1. poudrier ▸** a small case that is used to hold face powder. **2. compacte ▸** a car that is smaller than a regular sized model. **Note.** The smallest car models are called subcompacts.

compact disk NOUN, compact disks. (also compact disc) **disque compact ▸** a small, round, flat plastic device that stores information such as music, pictures, or computer programs. **Note.** A CD-ROM (compact disk—read only

---

🖉 **Word Builder**

Common, ordinary, and **familiar** are synonyms that describe something that is not special or unusual. **Common** describes something that does not stand out or is shared by many others : *A common belief is shared by many people.* **Ordinary** suggests something that is average and can be a negative comment : *That is a rather ordinary house.* **Familiar** describes something that is known and recognizable : *I felt like I had seen that movie before; the plot was familiar.*

memory) is a compact disk that cannot be recorded over.

com·pan·ion [kum-PAN-yun] NOUN, companions. **1. compagnon (compagne)** ▸ a person who spends time with another; a friend : *"'I think he needs a companion,' she said."* (Cynthia Rylant) **2. époux (épouse)** ▸ anything that matches or goes with another of the same kind : *The companion to that sock is under your bed.* **3. compagnon (compagne), partenaire** ▸ any person who goes along with another : *a travelling companion.* **Note.** The friendship between companions is known as **companionship.** SYN : friend, partner, buddy, pal, mate, match.

com·pa·ny [KUM-puh-nee] NOUN, companies. **1. compagnie, firme, société** ▸ a group of people who join together to do business; a firm or business : *The Hudson's Bay Company is the oldest company in Canada.* **2. compagnie, troupe** ▸ any group of people joined together for some purpose : *Sam has been with that theatre company for three years.* **3. de la visite** ▸ someone who visits; a guest or guests : *We're having company for dinner on Friday night.* **4. fréquentation, invité (-ée)** ▸ a group of friends; companions. **5. compagnie** ▸ companionship : *"He began to realize that his tiny desert friends came to his garden not for company, but for water."* (Richard E. Albert) **6. compagnie** ▸ a unit of soldiers in the army, under the command of a captain.

com·par·a·tive [kum-PAIR-uh-tiv] ADJECTIVE. **1. comparatif (-ive)** ▸ making a comparison : *Bob made a comparative study of the two bikes before buying one.* **2. relatif (-ive)** ▸ according to a comparison; compared to others : *Summer holidays give us a sense of comparative freedom.* ▲ NOUN, comparatives. **comparatif (-ive)** ▸ in grammar, the form of an adjective or adverb that gives the idea of comparison : *"Higher," "longer," and "more famous"* are comparatives.

com·pare [kum-PAIR] VERB, compared, comparing. **1. comparer, évaluer** ▸ to find out or show how one thing is different from or like something else : *Compare your answers with the answer key in the back of the book.* **2. comparer à, rapprocher** ▸ to say that a thing is like something else : *He compared the sound of thunder to the banging of drums.* **3. se comparer** ▸ to be similar in quality to : *I like frozen corn, but it really doesn't compare with fresh corn.* **Note.** Things that are similar and able to be compared are **comparable.**

com·par·i·son [kum-PAIR-uh-sun] NOUN, comparisons. **1. comparaison** ▸ the act of comparing : *This book gives a comparison of ancient and modern farming methods.* **2. comparaison** ▸ a likeness; similarity : *Chocolate and peppermint are both flavours of ice cream, but there's no comparison in their popularity.*

3. comparatif ▸ in grammar, the change in an adjective or adverb to show a difference in amount or quality.

com·part·ment [kum-PART-munt] NOUN, compartments. **compartiment, case, division** ▸ a separate division or part; a section : *The refrigerator has different compartments for butter, cheese, meat, and vegetables.* **Note.** A car's glove compartment holds small items such as gloves, maps, and so on.

com·pass [KUM-pus] NOUN, compasses. **1. boussole** ▸ an instrument that shows direction by means of a magnetic needle that always points toward the magnetic North Pole. **2. compas** ▸ an instrument with two legs joined at the top, used to draw circles or to measure distance.

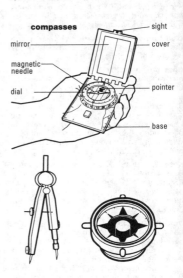

compasses

sight
mirror
cover
magnetic needle
dial
pointer
base

com·pass·ion [kum-PASH-un] NOUN. **compassion, commisération, pitié** ▸ the quality of feeling deeply sorry for others who are suffering, and wanting to help them. **Note.** A person who feels this way is **compassionate.** SYN : mercy, sympathy, pity, forgiveness.

com·pel [kum-PEL] VERB, compelled, compelling. **contraindre, forcer, obliger** ▸ to make someone do something under force.

com·pen·sate [KOM-pun-SATE] VERB, compensated, compensating. **1. compenser, racheter, réparer** ▸ to make up for something that is lacking : *Petra had to study extra hard to compensate for missing a week of classes.*

2. dédommager, payer, indemniser ▸ to pay : *My parents took me out to dinner to compensate me for all the work I did in the yard.* ■ **compensation,** NOUN. ▸ **compensation, dédommagement.** *Glasses are a compensation for weak eyesight.*

com-pete [kum-PEET] VERB, competed, competing. **rivaliser, disputer** ▸ to take part in a contest or game ; try to win : *He hopes to compete in the Olympics one day.* **Note.** Someone who competes is a competitor.

com-pe-tent [KOM-puh-tunt] ADJECTIVE. **compétent (-ente), efficace, capable, qualifié (-ée)** ▸ able to do what is needed : *She is a competent worker.* **Note.** The state of being competent is competence. SYN : able, efficient, adequate, capable, skilled.

com-pe-ti-tion [KOM-puh-TISH-un] NOUN, competitions. **1. compétition, rivalité, concurrence** ▸ the act of competing ; trying to win a contest or game : *Katie plays tennis because she loves competition.* **2. compétition, concours** ▸ a contest or game : *a spelling competition.* 🗐 **p. 1144.**

com-pet-i-tive [kum-PET-uh-tiv] ADJECTIVE. **1. compétitif (-ive)** ▸ liking to win or compete : *She's a competitive athlete.* **2. compétitif (-ive), concurrentiel (-ielle)** ▸ having to do with or using competition : *The airline industry is a highly competitive business.* ■ **competitiveness,** NOUN. ▸ **compétitivité.**

com-pile [kum-PILE] VERB, compiled, compiling. **composer, compiler, réunir** ▸ to bring together in an orderly way : *The students compiled their stories into a book.*

com-plain [kum-PLANE] VERB, complained, complaining. **1. se plaindre** ▸ to say that something is wrong or unfair ; be unhappy or annoyed : *Nora complained that her dinner was cold.* **2. se plaindre, réclamer, protester, bougonner** ▸ to make a formal report or statement that something is wrong : *to complain to the police.* SYN : grumble, find fault, protest.

com-plaint [kum-PLAYNT] NOUN, complaints. **1. plainte** ▸ the act of complaining ; an expression of unhappiness ; finding fault : *There were some complaints about the cold weather.* **2. récrimination, reproche** ▸ the cause of complaining : *The teacher's only complaint about Duane is that sometimes he talks too much in class.* **3. plainte, réclamation, protestation** ▸ a formal statement or report of complaining ; a charge :*He filed a complaint with the athletics association.*

com-ple-ment [KOM-pluh-munt] NOUN, complements. **complément** ▸ something that makes a thing whole or complete : *The sauce was a good complement for the meat.* ▲ [KOM-pluh-ment] VERB, complemented, complementing. **compléter, parfaire, terminer** ▸ to make whole or complete :*Her shoes and purse complement her dress.* **Note.** Something that complements is complementary.

com-plete [kum-PLEET] ADJECTIVE. **1. complet (-ète)** ▸ not missing anything ; whole ; having all the parts : *We have a complete set of Jean Little's books.* **2. complété (-ée), terminé (-ée), achevé (-ée)** ▸ ended ; finished : *You can watch the show when your homework is complete.* **3. entier (-ière), complet (-ète)** ▸ total ; full : *"Many times he has travelled this river at night in complete darkness."* (Ann Blades) ▲ VERB, completed, completing. **1. terminer, compléter, finir, achever** ▸ to add what is missing ; make whole : *Tasha completed the puzzle by putting in the last piece.* **2. compléter, achever, parfaire** ▸ to bring to an end ; finish : *My sister has just completed her training as a doctor.* ■ **completely,** ADVERB. ▸ **complètement.** SYN : whole, entire, total, perfect. 🖉 **p. 4.**

com-ple-tion [kum-PLEE-shun] NOUN, completions. **1. achèvement** ▸ the act of completing something : *The completion of the new bridge is scheduled for next year.* **2. achèvement, fin** ▸ a completed condition : *An architect designs a building and also sees the project through to completion.*

com-plex [kum-PLEKS *or* KOM-pleks] ADJECTIVE. **1. complexe** ▸ hard to explain or understand ; complicated : *Compared to a typewriter, a computer is very complex.* **2. complexe** ▸ made up of many parts : *Canada has a complex system of highways.* ▲ [KAHM-pleks] NOUN, complexes. **1. ensemble** ▸ something that is made up of many parts : *More than 5000 people live in that housing complex.* **2. complexe** ▸ a continuing feeling of worry or concern about some fault or problem : *I don't know why she has such a complex about her playing ; she's really very good at volleyball.* **Note.** The state of being complex is complexity: *The complexity of the instructions makes them difficult to follow.* SYN : complicated, involved, confused, mixed.

com-plex-ion [kum-PLEK-shun] NOUN, complexions. **1. teint** ▸ the natural colour and appearance of the skin, especially the face : *a pale complexion.* **2. nature** ▸ the general appearance or nature of something : *The complexion of the neighbourhood changed after the old buildings were torn down.*

com-pli-cate [KOM-pluh-KATE] VERB, complicated, complicating. **1. compliquer, obscurcir, embrouiller** ▸ to make harder to do or understand : *Don't complicate your report by adding those charts of statistics.* **2. compliquer, embrouiller** ▸ to make worse or more severe : *High blood pressure complicated her illness.* **Note.** Something that complicates is a complication. Something that is hard to do or understand is complicated: *a complicated design ; complicated instructions.*

com·pli·ment [KOM-pluh-munt or KOM-pluh-ment] VERB, complimented, complimenting. **complimenter, féliciter ▸** to say something good to or about someone; give praise to a person: *Mio complimented Laura on the poem she wrote.* ▲ NOUN, compliments. **1. compliment, louange ▸** something nice said to or about a person: *"But when compliments and tips were sent to the chef, they never reached Maylin."* (Paul Yee) **2. compliments. hommages, vœux, félicitations ▸** greetings; good wishes: *Give Naveen my compliments when you see him.* SYN: flatter, praise, congratulate, please.

com·pli·men·ta·ry [KOM-pluh-MEN-tur-ee] ADJECTIVE. **1. flatteur (-euse), louangeur (-euse) ▸** being or showing a compliment: *The teacher's remarks about Mary's work were all complimentary.* **2. gracieux, à titre gracieux ▸** given away free: *We got complimentary samples of a new drink.*

com·ply [kum-PLY] VERB, complied, complying. **se soumettre à, se conformer à, obéir à ▸** to act in agreement with something, such as a rule or request: *If you ride a bike, you must comply with the traffic laws.* **Note.** The act of complying is **compliance.** SYN: obey, conform, agree, submit.

com·po·nent [kum-POH-nunt] NOUN, components. **pièce, élément, composante ▸** one of the separate units that make up a system, machine, or program: *A stereo system has several different components, such as loudspeakers, a tape player, and a tuner.*

com·pose [kum-POZE] VERB, composed, composing. **1. composer, constituer ▸** to make up something; put together: *Oxygen and other gases compose air.* **2. composer, créer, produire ▸** to write or create: *to compose poetry.* **Note.** A composer composes something, especially music: *Mozart was the composer of* The Magic Flute.

compose oneself reprendre son calme ▸ to make oneself calm or relaxed: *She was nervous before the speech, but she composed herself and got through it easily.*

com·po·si·tion [KOM-puh-ZISH-un] NOUN, compositions. **1. composition ▸** the act of composing: *the composition of a poem.* **2. composition, agencement, arrangement ▸** something that is composed: *a composition for the piano.* **3. composition ▸** the parts of something that make up the whole: *the mineral composition of a rock.* **4. rédaction ▸** a piece of writing done as a school assignment.

com·post [KOM-post] NOUN. **compost ▸** a mixture made from decaying vegetable matter, manure, and so on, used to fertilize soil. **Note.** Leftover food, garden clippings, and so on can be put into a **composter** to make compost.

com·pound [KOM-pownd] ADJECTIVE. **composé (-ée), combiné (-ée) ▸** made up of two or more parts: *a compound leaf.* ▲ NOUN, compounds. **1. composé ▸** in chemistry, a substance formed by combining two or more elements: *Water is a compound of hydrogen and oxygen.* **2. composé ▸** anything that is a combination of parts. **3. composé ▸** a compound word. ▲ [KOM-pownd or kum-POWND] VERB, compounded, compounding. **1. combiner ▸** to mix together; combine. **2. empirer, s'aggraver, augmenter ▸** to make worse: *Her complaining compounded the problem.* 🔗 p. 132.

compound sentence phrase complexe ▸ a sentence having two or more parts that could each be separate sentences on their own. "Bees have six legs, but spiders have eight legs" is a compound sentence.

compound word mot composé ▸ a word made up of two or more parts that are words in themselves, such as *high school, high-class,* or *highway.*

com·pre·hend [KOM-pree-HEND] VERB, comprehended, comprehending. **comprendre, réaliser ▸** to understand; to grasp with the mind. **Note.** The act of understanding is **comprehension.** SYN: understand, realize, know, grasp.

com·pre·hen·sive [KOM-pree-HEN-siv] ADJECTIVE. **1. complet (-ète), vaste ▸** including everything,

---

📝 Writing Tips

Compound Word

*A **compound word** is a word made of two or more words (nighttime, ice hockey, sister-in-law). Some compounds are written as one word, some as two words, and others with a hyphen. It is not easy to know how a compound word should be written. The spelling of most compound words developed over the years and did not follow a rule. There are, however, a few general rules you can follow:*

• *Use a hyphen with compound numbers from 21 to 99.*

   *I am **twenty-four** years old.*

• *Hyphenate a compound word that is used as an adjective when it comes before the noun it describes.*

   *The novel I'm reading is a **well-written** book.*

• *Many compound words are in the dictionary, so check in a dictionary for the spelling.*

or nearly everything : *The final exam is a comprehensive test of everything we've studied in the course.* **2. large, vaste, étendu (-ue) ▸** able to understand many things : *a comprehensive mind.* SYN : wide, extensive, all-embracing, inclusive.

com-press [kom-PRES] VERB, compressed, compressing. **comprimer, condenser, refouler ▸** to force into a smaller space; press or squeeze together : *He compressed his clothes so that they would fit into his suitcase.* **Note.** Often used as an ADJECTIVE:*compressed air.* ▲ [KOM-pres] NOUN, compresses. **compresse ▸** a soft cloth or pad put on a part of the body to treat a wound or injury.

com-pro-mise [KOM-pruh-MIZE] NOUN, compromises. **compromis, transaction ▸** the settling of a disagreement by each side giving up something : *Tara wanted to eat out, but Sandy wanted to fix dinner at home; their compromise was to have a pizza delivered to the house.* ▲ VERB, compromised, compromising. **transiger, risquer, compromettre ▸** to reach a compromise. SYN : concede, meet halfway, settle, yield.

com-pul-so-ry [kum-PUL-suh-ree] ADJECTIVE. **obligatoire, nécessaire, requis (-ise) ▸** required by law or force : *If you want to drive a car, a licence is compulsory.* SYN : required, necessary.

com-pute [kum-PYOOT] VERB, computed, computing. **calculer, estimer, compter ▸** to find out by using mathematics; calculate : *Zara computed the cost of buying the dress and the sweater.* SYN : calculate, count, reckon, figure, estimate.

com-put-er [kum-PYOO-tur] NOUN, computers. hardware (the machine itself) **ordinateur ▸** and software (programs that tell the machine what to do). ☞ **p. 1168.** 👁 **p. 541.**

com-rade [KOM-rad] NOUN, comrades. **camarade, ami (-ie), copain (copine) ▸** a close companion or friend. SYN : friend, buddy, pal, companion, chum.

con-cave [kon-KAVE or KON-kave] ADJECTIVE. **concave ▸** having a shape that curves inward; the opposite of convex: *The shape of a bowl is concave.*

concave

con-ceal [kun-SEEL] VERB, concealed, concealing. **cacher, dissimuler, masquer, voiler ▸** to keep secret or out of sight; hide secretly : *Kiko*

concealed the birthday present behind the curtains. ■ **concealment,** NOUN. ▸ **dissimulation. Note.** Also used as an ADJECTIVE:*They hid in a concealed room.* SYN : hide, cover, mask, disguise, camouflage.

con-cede [kun-SEED] VERB, conceded, conceding. **1. reconnaître que, admettre ▸** to admit that something is true, usually against one's will : *After I won the race, Peter conceded that I am faster than he is.* **2. concéder, accorder ▸** to accept a loss, to give up : *Tina was so far behind that she conceded the game.* SYN : admit, allow, grant, confess.

con-ceit-ed [kun-SEE-tud] ADJECTIVE. **vaniteux (-euse), prétentieux (-euse), vantard (-arde) ▸** having too high an opinion of oneself; too proud : *He's very conceited and always talks about himself.* SYN : vain, boastful, proud, cocky.

con-ceive [kun-SEEV] VERB, conceived, conceiving. **concevoir, former, inventer, imaginer ▸** to form in the mind; think of; imagine : *It's hard to conceive of the size of the universe.* **Note.** Something that can be conceived is conceivable: *It's conceivable that our team will win.*

con-cen-trate [KON-sun-TRATE] VERB, concentrated, concentrating. **1. se concentrer ▸** to focus the mind on something; pay close attention : *We had to concentrate to finish before class ended.* **2. concentrer, grouper, réunir ▸** to gather or collect in one place : *Senora concentrated the tulips in a patch by the fence.* **3. concentrer ▸** to make a mixture stronger or thicker, especially by reducing the amount of water. **Note.** Often used as an ADJECTIVE: *concentrated orange juice.* ▲ NOUN, concentrates. **concentré ▸** a mixture that is concentrated : *This juice is made from concentrate.* SYN : think, focus, pay attention.

con-cen-tra-tion [KON-sun-TRAY-shun] NOUN. **1. concentration, application, attention, réflexion ▸** close attention : *"He ate with great concentration, as though he were doing a math problem with his teeth."* (Louise Fitzhugh) **2.** (plural, concentrations) **agglomération, regroupement, amoncellement ▸** a large gathering together; something concentrated : *The largest concentration of garbage was in the picnic area.*

con-cept [KON-sept] NOUN, concepts. **concept, idée, pensée, opinion ▸** a general idea or thought : *The teacher explained the concept of fractions by cutting up an apple.* SYN : thought, idea, notion, opinion.

con-cern [kun-SURN] VERB, concerned, concerning. **1. concerner, intéresser, toucher ▸** to be about; have to do with : *This report concerns your behaviour at school.* **2. intéresser, concerner ▸** to be of interest or importance to; affect : *Pollution concerns us all.* **3. s'inquiéter de ▸** to make troubled or anxious; worry : *Don't* *concern yourself with dinner; I'll make it.* ▲ NOUN, concerns. **1. responsabilité, tâche, charge** ▸ something that is of importance or interest : *My main concern is that we finish the job on time.* **2. inquiétude, angoisse, anxiété** ▸ something that causes trouble; a worry : *His health is a concern.* **3. entreprise** ▸ a company or business : *Tim's father is a lawyer who represents international concerns.*

con·cerned [kun-SURND] ADJECTIVE. **inquiet (-iète), soucieux (-ieuse)** ▸ troubled or anxious; worried : *My mother is concerned about our playing football in such bad conditions.*

as far as one is concerned en ce qui me concerne ▸ in one's opinion : *As far as I'm concerned, this conversation is over.*

con·cert [KON-surt] NOUN, concerts. **concert** ▸ a public performance of music, especially one with a number of musicians or singers; recital.

con·ces·sion [kun-SESH-un] NOUN, concessions. **1. concession** ▸ the act of conceding, or what is conceded : *As a concession to their age, younger runners are given a head start.* **2. franchise** ▸ a right to do something granted by the government or another authority : *a concession to sell food at the arena.* **3. lot** ▸ primarily in Ontario and Quebec, a subdivision of land within a township. **4. route rurale** ▸ a rural road running between concessions.

conch [konch *or* konk] NOUN, conchs *or* conches. **conque** ▸ a tropical sea animal having a large, one-piece shell with a spiral shape. The shell is often brightly coloured.

con·cise [kon-SISE] ADJECTIVE. **concis (-ise), abrégé (-ée)** ▸ expressing a lot of thought or meaning in a few words : *a concise short story.* SYN: brief, short.

con·clude [kun-KLOOD] VERB, concluded, concluding. **1. conclure, terminer, achever, finir** ▸ to end something : *The musical concluded with an exciting finale.* **2. déduire, conclure, inférer** ▸ to form an opinion; come to believe : *After studying the crimes, the police concluded that they were committed by the same person.* ■ **conclusive,** ADJECTIVE. ▸ **concluant (-ante), définitif (-ive).** SYN: close, end, finish.

con·clu·sion [kun-KLOO-zhun] NOUN, conclusions. **1. conclusion, fin, terme** ▸ the end or final part of something : *The conclusion of the movie will be shown after the next commercial.* **2. déduction, conclusion** ▸ something decided by thinking; a judgment or decision : *Your lack of effort leads me to the conclusion that you are lazy.* **Note.** To jump to conclusions means to make a judgment too quickly, without enough information.

con·crete [KON-kreet *or* kon-KREET] NOUN. **béton** ▸ a mixture of cement, sand, gravel, and water that becomes very hard when dry. Concrete is used for sidewalks and as a building or road material. ▲ ADJECTIVE. **1. de béton** ▸ made of concrete : *a concrete brick.* **2. réel (-elle), concret (-ète), palpable** ▸ having to do with things that can be seen or felt, as opposed to something sensed with the mind : *A book, a pencil, and a desk are concrete objects.* SYN: real, solid, substantial, tangible.

concrete poem NOUN. **poème imagé** ▸ a poem that uses words to make a visual image of the topic of the poem.

con·demn [kun-DEM] VERB, condemned, condemning. **1. accabler, censurer, critiquer, désapprouver** ▸ to strongly disapprove of someone or something : *Many parents condemn the amount of violence on TV.* **2. condamner** ▸ to state the punishment of a guilty person : *The judge condemned the convicted man to five years in prison.* **3. déclarer inhabitable, condamner** ▸ to say officially that something is not safe or fit for use : *That building has been condemned because of fire damage.*

con·dense [kun-DENS] VERB, condensed, condensing. **1. condenser, concentrer** ▸ to change from a gas or vapour to a liquid : *The hot air condensed on the cold windows.* **2. condenser, compacter** ▸ to make thick or more compressed. **3. abréger, resserrer, résumer** ▸ to make shorter by taking out some parts : *That magazine prints condensed versions of popular books.* **Note.** Often used as an ADJECTIVE: *condensed milk.* **Note.** The act of condensing is condensation: *Dew is a condensation of water vapour from the air.*

con·di·tion [kun-DISH-un] NOUN, conditions. **1. condition** ▸ the way someone or something is : *Dan keeps his car in good condition.* **2. état de santé, condition physique** ▸ a state of health or physical fitness : *"Stuart touched his toes ten times every morning to keep himself in good condition."* (E.B. White) **3. condition** ▸ a requirement necessary for something else to happen : *I'll take the job on the condition that I do not have to work on Saturdays.* **4. conditions. condition, position, situation** ▸ a state of affairs; circumstances : *The coal miners went on strike to improve their working conditions.* ▲ VERB, conditioned, conditioning. **conditionner** ▸ to make or become used to something : *She's doing a lot of running to condition herself for the marathon.* SYN: situation, state, case, form.

con·do·min·i·um [KON-duh-min-ee-um] NOUN, condominiums. **1. condominium, copropriété** ▸ an apartment building in which each of the apartments is individually owned, rather than the whole building having one owner. **2. appartement en copropriété** ▸ an apartment in such a building.

con·dor [KON-door] NOUN, condors. **condor** ▸ a very large bird with a bare head and neck. A condor is a kind of vulture found in the mountains of California and South America.

con·duct [KON-dukt] NOUN, conducts. **conduite, comportement ▶** the way someone acts or behaves : *According to Narain's teacher, his conduct in class is very good.* ▲ [kuhn-DUKT] VERB, conducted, conducting. **1. se conduire, se comporter ▶** to act in a certain way; behave. **2. conduire, mener, diriger ▶** to carry on or carry out : *to conduct a survey.* **3. conduire, mener ▶** to be in charge of; lead : *to conduct an orchestra.* **4. conduire, être conducteur (-trice) ▶** to be a path for; carry : *Aluminum conducts heat very well.* SYN: guide, lead, direct, control, manage.

con·duc·tor [kun-DUK-tur] NOUN, conductors. **1. chef d'orchestre ▶** a person who directs an orchestra or other musical group. **2. receveur, chef de train ▶** a person in charge of passengers on a train, bus, or streetcar. The conductor often has the job of collecting fares. **3. conducteur (-trice) ▶** something that conducts : *Rubber is not a good conductor of electricity.*

cone [kone] NOUN, cones. **1. cône ▶** a figure that has a round, flat base and is pointed at the other end. **2. cône, cornet ▶** anything shaped like a cone : *an ice-cream cone.* **3. cône, pomme ▶** the fruit of a pine or other evergreen tree, made up of hard, overlapping scales. It holds the seeds of the tree.

con·fed·er·a·cy [kun-FED-ur-uh-see or kun-FED-ruh-see] NOUN, confederacies. **confédération ▶** a group of countries, states, or people joined together : *Five Native groups united to form the original Iroquois confederacy.*

con·fed·er·a·tion [kun-FED-ur-AY-shun] NOUN, confederations. **1. confédération ▶** the act of forming an alliance or union, or the name of the alliance itself. **2. Confederation. fédération ▶** the name given to the union of Ontario, Quebec, Nova Scotia, and New Brunswick in 1867. **3. the Confederation. fédération ▶** the 10 provinces and the territories of Canada.

con·fer [kun-FUR] VERB, conferred, conferring. **1. conférer, s'entretenir ▶** to meet and talk things over; have a discussion : *Sandy conferred with her peer editor about the second draft of her story.* **2. attribuer, décerner ▶** to give an award or honour. SYN: consult, discuss, talk over.

con·fer·ence [KON-fur-uns or KON-fruns] NOUN, conferences. **1. conférence, congrès, assemblée, colloque ▶** a meeting to discuss something : *Teachers from across Alberta attended the reading conference.* **2. conférence ▶** a group of teams or organizations : *a football conference.* **Note.** A meeting at which news reporters can ask someone questions is a press conference.

con·fess [kun-FES] VERB, confessed, confessing. **1. avouer, confesser ▶** to say that one has done something that is wrong or against the law : *He confessed that he had stolen the money.* **2. avouer, reconnaître ▶** to make known : *What did you say? I must confess I wasn't listening.* **3. confesser ▶** to tell one's sins to a priest. **Note.** The confessing of something is called confession. SYN: admit, acknowledge, own up.

con·fi·dence [KON-fuh-duns] NOUN, confidences. **1. confiance, assurance ▶** a firm faith in oneself and belief in one's abilities : *"Dressed like a mighty warrior, Morgana set out full of confidence."* (Robin Muller) **2. confiance ▶** faith or trust in someone or something else : *I have a lot of confidence that what he says is true.* **3. confidence ▶** trust that a secret will be kept by someone : *I'm telling you this in strict confidence.*

con·fi·dent [KON-fuh-dunt] ADJECTIVE. **assuré (-ée), sûr (sûre), persuadé (-ée) ▶** having confidence; believing strongly : *Darlene is confident that she will win the race.* ■ **confidently,** ADVERB. ▶ **avec confiance, avec assurance, avec optimisme.** *"I looked confidently at Pop, waiting for the explanation."* (S.E. Hinton) SYN: certain, assured, positive, secure, positive.

con·fi·den·tial [KON-fuh-DEN-shul] ADJECTIVE. **confidentiel (-ielle) ▶** told or written as a secret : *He spoke in a confidential tone as he told her the secret.* ■ **confidentially,** ADVERB. ▶ **confidentiellement, en confidence.**

con·fine [kun-FINE] VERB, confined, confining. **limiter, restreindre ▶** to hold or keep within limits : *The speakers were asked to confine their remarks to five minutes.* ▲ [KON-fyn] NOUN, confines. **limite, borne ▶** a limit; boundary. Usually used in the PLURAL: *She was not allowed to leave the confines of the yard.* **Note.** The state of being confined is confinement: *A prisoner kept apart from other prisoners is in solitary confinement.*

con·firm [kun-FURM] VERB, confirmed, confirming. **1. confirmer, corroborer ▶** to show or prove something to be true or correct : *The singer confirmed the rumours that she is getting married.* **2. confirmer, fortifier ▶** to agree to or approve

---

✍ Writing Tips

Conflict

The conflict of a story is the problem that needs to be resolved. The conflict is very important to the events in a story and adds most of the interest.

• *When you are developing your story, think about what conflicts there could be. How will they affect the characters? What will happen as a result of the conflict?*

conflict

officially : *The mayor confirmed the budget cuts.*
3. confirmer, consolider, entériner, ratifier ▶ to
make sure of an appointment or arrangement :
The dentist's office called to confirm my appoint-ment on Monday. **4. confirmer ▶** to admit a per-son to a church or synagogue as a full member.
Note. The act of confirming is confirmation.
■ confirmed, ADJECTIVE. **▶ enduci (-ie).** not
likely to change : *He won't ever marry; he's a
confirmed bachelor.*

con-flict [KON-flikt] NOUN, conflicts. **1. conflit,
combat, dispute ▶** a long fight or struggle ; a
war : *a conflict between two countries.* **2. dis-corde, incompatible, opposition ▶** a clash of
opinions or ideas ; strong disagreement. **Note.** A
conflict of interest is a situation in which a per-son has two opposing interests in the same mat-ter. **3. conflit ▶** a situation with opposing needs
or conditions : *She can't come to the meeting
because there's a conflict in her schedule.*
▲ [kun-FLIKT] VERB, conflicted, conflicting. **miner,
être en opposition, être en désaccord ▶** to be in
conflict ; disagree : *He can work after school if it
doesn't conflict with his studies.* SYN: fight, bat-tle, contest, struggle. ✍ **p. 135, 463.**

con-front [kun-FRUNT] VERB, confronted, con-fronting. **1. confronter, affronter ▶** to meet face
to face, especially in a bold or challenging way :
He went up to her and confronted her directly.
2. confronter ▶ to bring face to face with : *The
police confronted the robbery suspect with the
stolen goods.* **Note.** The act of confronting is
confrontation. SYN: face, oppose, meet squarely,
encounter.

con-fuse [kun-FYOOZ] VERB, confused, confus-ing. **1. confondre, embrouiller ▶** to make uncer-tain or disordered ; mix up : *He was confused by
the instructions and had to ask for help.*
2. confondre ▶ to mistake one person or thing
for another : *People often confuse the words
"minor" and "miner."* **Note.** Often used as an
ADJECTIVE:*Krista stopped her explanation when
she saw that everyone looked confused.*

con-fu-sion [kun-FYOO-zhun] NOUN, confusions.
1. confusion, trouble, désordre ▶ a confused
condition or situation ; disorder : *There was a
lot of confusion in the streets when the traffic
lights went out.* **2. confusion ▶** the mistaking of
one person or thing for another : *The fact that
Tim and his twin brother look so much alike
leads to a lot of confusion.*

con-grat-u-late [kun-GRACH-yoo-LATE] VERB, con-gratulated, congratulating. **féliciter, compli-menter ▶** to give praise or good wishes to
someone for his or her success or good fortune :
Pedro congratulated the winner of the race.
Note. The act of expressing good wishes or
praise is congratulation or congratulations: *We
offered him congratulations on the birth of his
daughter.* SYN: wish well, compliment, praise.

con-gre-gate [KONG-gruh-gate] VERB, con-gregated, congregating. **rassembler, réunir,
assembler ▶** gather together in a crowd ; assem-ble : *People congregated at the park to hear the
free concert.* **Note.** A congregation is a group
of people gathered together for a purpose, espe-cially a religious service.

con-i-fer [KON-uh-fur] NOUN, conifers. **coni-fère ▶** a tree or shrub with evergreen needles.
Conifers bear their seeds in cones. **■ conifer-ous,** ADJECTIVE. **▶ conifère.** 👁 **p. 255.**

con-junc-tion [kun-JUNK-shun] NOUN, conjunc-tions. **1. conjonction ▶** in grammar, a word that
is used to join words, phrases, and sentences.
And, but, and *if* are common conjunctions.
2. conjonction, connexion, jonction, union ▶ a
joining together ; combination : *The school
board worked in conjunction with parents to
build a new playground.*

con-nect [kuh-NEKT] VERB, connected, connect-ing. **1. joindre, relier, rattacher ▶** to join or fas-ten together : *A cable connects the keyboard to
the computer.* **2. associer ▶** to think of one
thing with another ; associate : *I connect snow
with winter.* **3. relier, rattacher ▶** to join with
another or others ; have a relation to : *Those
characters are connected to the characters in
this book.* **Note.** Often used as an ADJECTIVE:*We
had to get a connecting flight in Montreal on
our way to Halifax.* SYN: join, unite, combine,
link, attach.

con-nec-tion [kuh-NEK-shun] NOUN, connec-tions. **1. connexion, liaison ▶** the act of con-necting ; the joining of things : *The proper
connection of the wires for this stereo system
is explained in the instruction book.*
2. connexion, contact ▶ the fact of being con-nected : *I couldn't tell who was on the phone
because the connection was so bad.* **3. corre-spondance ▶** a connecting of two planes, trains,
or other means of transportation : *We have an
hour to make our connection in Yellowknife.*

con-quer [KONG-kur] VERB, conquered, con-quering. **1. joindre, relier, rattacher ▶** to join or fas-ten together : *A cable connects the keyboard to
the computer.* **1. vaincre, battre, conquérir, subju-guer ▶** to get the better of in war or conflict ;
defeat by force : *Cortés sailed from Spain
to Mexico to conquer the Aztec Empire.*
2. conquérir, surmonter, vaincre ▶ to overcome
or gain control of : *She's conquered her fear of
flying and now enjoys travelling by plane.*
Note. A person who conquers is a conqueror.
SYN: overpower, defeat, crush, win, triumph.

con-quest [KON-kwest] NOUN, conquests.
1. conquête, appropriation ▶ the act of con-quering : *the conquest of an enemy in war.*
2. conquête ▶ something that is conquered :
The winning army enjoyed their conquest.

con-science [KON-shuns] NOUN, consciences.
conscience ▶ a sense of what is right and wrong

that makes one feel sorry or guilty for having done something bad : *No one had seen him cheat, but his conscience bothered him and he later confessed what he had done.*

con·scious [KON-shus] ADJECTIVE. **1. conscient (-iente)** ▶ able to see and feel; awake. **2. conscient (-iente)** ▶ able to realize some fact or feeling; aware : *He was very conscious of the fact that he was not doing well in math.* **3. conscient (-iente), intentionnel (-elle)** ▶ done on purpose; intentional. ■ **consciously,** ADVERB. ▶ **consciemment, intentionnellement, sciemment.** in a conscious way; on purpose : *She's consciously trying to be nicer to her friends.* SYN : alive, awake, alert.

con·scious·ness [KON-shus-nis] NOUN. **1. connaissance** ▶ the condition of being conscious or awake : *The diver lost consciousness when his head hit the diving board.* **2. conscience** ▶ a person's conscious thoughts and feelings; awareness : *"Our whole past experience is continually in our consciousness."* (Charles Peirce)

con·sen·sus [kun-SEN-sus] NOUN. **consensus** ▶ general agreement; the shared opinion of all or most of the people consulted.

con·sent [kun-SENT] VERB, consented, consenting. **consentir** ▶ to give permission, agree to : *The city consented to close off the street for the festival.* ▲ NOUN, consents. **consentement, accord, approbation** ▶ permission; agreement : *You need your parents' consent to go on the class trip.* SYN : permit, agree, assent, approve of, comply.

con·se·quence [KON-suh-kwens] NOUN, consequences. **1. conséquence, suite** ▶ the result or outcome of some action or happening : *As a consequence of the accident, Lee is still limping.* **2. conséquence, importance** ▶ importance : *Which runner wins the race is of no consequence to me.* SYN : effect, result, outcome.

con·se·quent·ly [KON-suh-kwent-lee] ADVERB. **donc, par conséquent, en conséquence** ▶ as a result; therefore : *Yoon slept in and was consequently late for school.* SYN : therefore, as a result, accordingly, hence.

con·ser·va·tion [KON-sur-VAY-shun] NOUN. **1. conservation, maintien** ▶ the act of conserving : *Driving at a steady speed helps in the conservation of fuel.* **2. conservation, préservation, protection, sauvegarde** ▶ the protection and careful use of natural resources such as forests, lakes and rivers, minerals, and wild animals. **Note.** Someone who supports the conservation of the environment is a conservationist.

con·serv·a·tive [kun-SUR-vuh-tiv] ADJECTIVE. **1. conservateur (-trice), traditionnel (-elle)** ▶ wanting to keep things as they have been; against change. In politics, people who are conservative generally believe that the government

should hold to the values of the past and take a limited role in human affairs. **2. conservateur (-trice)** ▶ not taking chances; cautious or careful : *That football coach uses a conservative approach and never tries tricky plays.* **3. conservateur (-trice), traditionnel (-elle), modeste** ▶ following a modest style : *He dresses in a conservative way and wears only dark suits.* ▲ NOUN, conservatives. **conservateur (-trice)** ▶ a person who is conservative. ■ **conservatively,** ADVERB. ▶ **de manière conservatrice.**

Conservative Party Le Parti conservateur ▶ In Canada, the Progressive Conservative Party.

con·serve [kon-SERVE] VERB, conserved, conserving. **conserver, préserver** ▶ to protect from loss; keep from harm : *The World Wildlife Fund works to conserve endangered species.*

con·sid·er [kun-SID-ur] VERB, considered, considering. **1. considérer, examiner, réfléchir à** ▶ to think about carefully : *to consider the effects of one's actions.* **2. considérer, tenir pour** ▶ to think of as; believe to be : *to consider skiing a dangerous sport.* **3. considérer, peser** ▶ to take into account; allow for : *to consider the price before deciding to buy something.* **4. considérer, estimer, respecter** ▶ to be thoughtful of; respect : *to consider the feelings of others.* **Note.** Also used as an ADJECTIVE:*a doctor's considered opinion.* SYN : think, study, ponder, reflect, deliberate.

con·sid·er·a·ble [kun-SID-ur-uh-bul] ADJECTIVE. **considérable, important (-ante), éminent (-ente), remarquable** ▶ worth noticing or considering; rather large : *A considerable number of people wrote letters to the station about that TV show.* ■ **considerably,** ADVERB. ▶ **considérablement.** *Theo's behaviour has improved considerably this term.*

con·sid·er·ate [kun-SID-ur-it] ADJECTIVE. **prévenant (-ante)** ▶ thoughtful of the feelings of others : *It was considerate of Jamie to take flowers to his grandmother.* ■ **considerately,** ADVERB. ▶ **avec prévenance, avec égards.** SYN : thoughtful, kind, sympathetic, unselfish.

con·sid·er·a·tion [kun-SID-uh-RAY-shun] NOUN. **1. considération, estime, égard** ▶ thoughtfulness for the feelings of other people : *He played his music quietly out of consideration for his neighbours.* **2. considération, réflexion** ▶ careful thought : *After much consideration, they decided to sell their house and buy a larger one.* **3.** (plural considerations) **préoccupation, considération** ▶ something to be thought of or taken into account : *Reliability is the most important consideration for Meryn when buying a new car.*

con·sist [kun-SIST] VERB, consisted, consisting. **consister en, se composer de** ▶ to be made up of : *The floor hockey season consists of 10 games for each team.*

con·sis·tent [kun-SIS-tunt] ADJECTIVE. **1. conséquent (-ente), logique, cohérent (-ente)** ▸ acting
or thinking in the same way : *That shortstop is a
consistent fielder who rarely makes an error.*
**2. conséquent (-ente), compatible, en accord,
conforme** ▸ in agreement : *The accused man
claimed that he was at his job the day of the
crime, but his story wasn't consistent with his
company's work records.* ■ **consistently**,
ADVERB: ▸ **immanquablement, régulièrement,
sans exception.** *Annie consistently does well
on her science tests.*

con·so·nant [KON-suh-nunt] NOUN, consonants.
1. consonne ▸ a sound in speech that is made
when the flow of air through the mouth is
blocked by the lips, teeth, or tongue. **2. consonne** ▸ a letter of the alphabet that stands for
such a sound ; any letter that is not a vowel.

con·spic·u·ous [kun-SPIK-yoo-us] ADJECTIVE.
voyant (-ante), notable, remarquable ▸ easily
seen or noticed ; attracting attention : *Lew is
conspicuous in the class picture because he is
so much taller than the other students.*

con·spir·a·cy [kun-SPEER-uh-see] NOUN, con-
spiracies. **conspiration, complot, conjuration** ▸ secret planning with others to do
something wrong·or against the law : *a conspiracy to overthrow the government.* **Note.** Someone who takes part in a conspiracy is a
conspirator.

con·spire [kun-SPIRE] VERB, conspired, conspir-
ing. **conspirer, comploter** ▸ to plan together,
usually to do something wrong ; plot.

con·stant [KON-stunt] ADJECTIVE. **1. constant
(-ante), continu (-ue),** ▸ not changing ; staying
the same : *The airplane maintained a constant
speed.* **2. constant (-ante), permanent (-ente),
durable, persistant (-ante)** ▸ going on all the
time ; not stopping : *Three days of constant rain
turned the field to mud.* **3. constant (-ante),
invariable, soutenu (-ue)** ▸ happening over and
over ; continuous : *Our TV set gets constant use.*
■ **constantly**, ADVERB. ▸ **constamment, continuellement, sans cesse.** SYN : regular, continual,
perpetual, steady.

con·stel·la·tion [KON-stuh-LAY-shun] NOUN, constellations. **constellation** ▸ a group of stars that
form a pattern in the sky. Constellations were
named long ago for things they were thought to
look like, such as the Big Dipper or Great Bear.

con·stit·u·en·cy [kun-STICH-yoo-un-see] NOUN,
constituencies. **1. circonscription** ▸ in Canada,
an area that has its own representative in a
provincial or federal government. **Note.** Also
called a riding. **2. électeur (-trice)** ▸ the voters
in such an area.

con·sti·tu·tion [KON-stuh-TOO-shun] NOUN, constitutions. **1. constitution** ▸ the basic laws and
principles used to govern a nation or state.
2. constitution ▸ the Constitution. In Canada,

the Constitution Act, 1982 includes the Charter
of Rights and Freedoms. **3. constitution,
structure, disposition** ▸ the general condition
of a person's body : *"He wanted his sons
to…have strong constitutions."* (F. Scott Fitzgerald)

con·sti·tu·tion·al [KON-stuh-TOO-shun-ul *or* KON-
stuh-TYOO-shun-ul] ADJECTIVE. **1. constitutionnel
(-elle)** ▸ allowed by a country's constitution :
*Laws against freedom of speech are not consti-
tutional.* **2. constitutionnel (-elle), parlementaire** ▸ having to do with a constitution : *a
constitutional amendment; a country with a
constitutional government.* ▲ NOUN, constitu-
tionals. **faire une petite promenade, faire un
petit tour** ▸ a walk taken for exercise.

con·strict [kun-STRIKT] VERB, constricted,
constricting. **resserrer, serrer** ▸ to make or
become smaller or narrower.

con·struct [kun-STRUKT] VERB, constructed,
constructing. **construire, bâtir** ▸ to make by
putting parts together or combining things ;
build : *They constructed a clubhouse from leftover wood.*

con·struc·tion [kun-STRUK-shun] NOUN, cons-
tructions. **1. construction, édification, assemblage, érection** ▸ the act of building
something : *Construction of the new bridge was
delayed because of the rain.* **2. construction** ▸ the business or work of building houses,
apartments, offices, and so on : *Hank has a summer job in construction.*

con·struc·tive [kun-STRUK-tiv] ADJECTIVE. **constructif (-ive)** ▸ helping to make better ; having a
useful purpose : *Tau's constructive comments
improved my story.* SYN : helpful, useful, worthwhile.

con·sult [kun-SULT] VERB, consulted, consulting. **consulter** ▸ to ask for advice or information : *to consult a doctor.* **Note.** The act of
consulting is a consultation. SYN : talk over, ask
advice of, confer, discuss.

con·sult·ant [kun-SUL-tunt] NOUN, consulttants.
**consultant (-ante), conseiller (-ère), spécia-
liste** ▸ a person who gives expert or professional advice.

con·sume [kun-SOOM] VERB, consumed, consuming. **1. consommer, brûler, employer** ▸
to use up : *A car engine consumes fuel.*
2. consumer, dévorer ▸ to destroy : *The fire
consumed most of the forest.* **3. consommer,
absorber, bouffer** ▸ to eat or drink, especially a
large amount : *At halftime, the quarterback
consumed several litres of water.* **4. consumer,
user, épuiser** ▸ to take up all the attention or
energy of : *Work consumes most of her time
lately.* **Note.** Something that is meant to be used
up is consumable.

con·sum·er [kun-SOO-mur] NOUN, consumers. **consommateur (-trice), abonné (-ée)** ▸ anyone who buys and uses things.

con·tact [KON-takt] NOUN, contacts. **1. contact, toucher** ▸ the act of touching; touching together : *We felt a jolt as the plane's wheels came into contact with the runway.* **2. contact, rapport, relation** ▸ a relation or connection : *"We would have to find some other way of making contact with these wild creatures."* (Janet Foster) **3. contact, connaissance, relation** ▸ a person one knows who can be of help or influence : *That reporter has a lot of good contacts in the city government.* ▲ VERB, contacted, contacting. **contacter, rencontrer, joindre** ▸ to get in touch with; make a connection with : *I'll contact you as soon as I have any information.*

con·ta·gious [kun-TAY-jus] ADJECTIVE. **1. contagieux (-ieuse), transmissible** ▸ easily spread from person to person by some kind of contact : *Chicken pox is a contagious disease.* **2. contagieux (-ieuse), communicatif (-ive)** ▸ causing the same feeling or action in others : *His fear was contagious, and soon all the others were feeling afraid.*

con·tain [kun-TANE] VERB, contained, containing. **1. contenir, renfermer** ▸ to be able to hold; have inside : *This can contains flour.* **2. contenir, inclure** ▸ to have as a part; include : *Ice cream contains sugar.* **3. se contenir, se retenir** ▸ to keep to oneself; hold back; control : *"Harald, who could not contain himself, jumped for joy."* (Donald Carrick) 🖉 **p. 139.**

con·tain·er [kun-TAY-nur] NOUN, containers. **récipient, contenant** ▸ anything used to hold or contain something, such as a box, can, bottle, or jar.

con·tem·plate [KON-tum-PLATE] VERB, contemplated, contemplating. **1. contempler** ▸ to look at in a thoughtful way : *to contemplate a painting in a museum.* **2. contempler, envisager, considérer, songer** ▸ to think about carefully : *This was not the future she had contemplated.*

con·tem·po·ra·ry [kun-TEM-puh-RAIR-ee] ADJECTIVE. **1. contemporain (-aine)** ▸ belonging to the same time : *Shakespeare and Galileo are contemporary figures in history; both were born in 1564.* **2. contemporain (-aine), moderne, actuel (-elle), présent (-ente)** ▸ current; modern : *Dennis Lee is a well-known contemporary*

Canadian poet. ▲ NOUN, contemporaries. **contemporain (-aine)** ▸ a person living at the same time as another.

con·tempt [kun-TEMPT] NOUN. **1. mépris, dédain, dégoût** ▸ a feeling that someone or something is mean or worthless. **2. (also contempt of court) outrage au Tribunal** ▸ in a court of law, the crime of failing to obey or show respect for a judge or for proper courtroom procedure. **Note.** Someone or something worthy of contempt is contemptible.

con·tend [kun-TEND] VERB, contended, contending. **1. combattre, lutter** ▸ to fight or struggle : *Early settlers had to contend with harsh winters and illness.* **2. se disputer, se battre** ▸ to take part in a contest; compete : *Thirty-two teams are contending for the basketball championship.* **3. soutenir, prétendre** ▸ to argue in favour of; claim : *Many experts contend that running is good for your health.* **Note.** A person who contends is a contender.

con·tent[1] [KON-tent] NOUN, contents. **1. contenu** ▸ what something holds; what is contained : *Julie had to empty the contents of her schoolbag to find her pen.* **2. contenu, contenance** ▸ something that is written or said : *the contents of a letter.* **Note.** The table of contents of a book is a list of what the book contains.

con·tent[2] [kun-TENT] ADJECTIVE. **content (-ente), satisfait (-aite)** ▸ happy with what one has; satisfied : *"Charlie knows how lucky he is, and he feels content."* (Ann Blades) **Note.** Also called contentment. ▲ VERB, contented, contenting. **contenter, satisfaire, accommoder** ▸ to make content; satisfy : *We contented ourselves with cookies and milk.*

con·test [KON-test] NOUN, contests. **concours, combat, compétition** ▸ a game, a race, or another event to be won; a struggle or competition : *a dance contest.* **Note.** Someone who takes part in a contest is a contestant. ▲ [kuhn-TEST] VERB, contested, contesting. **1. disputer, défendre, lutter** ▸ to fight or struggle over; compete for : *Three runners contested for the title of fastest runner in school.* **2. contester, discuter** ▸ to question or challenge : *The losing team contested the final goal.* SYN: fight, dispute, question, challenge.

con·text [KON-text] NOUN, contexts. **contexte, situation** ▸ the other words or sentences that

---

📎 **Word Builder**

Contain, include, and *involve* are synonyms that refer to things that are made of two or more parts. *Contain* usually refers to parts of a larger object : *The bowl contains many kinds of fruit. Include* refers to the things that make up a whole : *The car's price includes the tires, radio, and heater. Involve* refers to some but not necessarily all the parts that make something up : *Repairing the car involves fixing the brakes, lights, and signals.*

surround a particular word or sentence and are important to understanding it correctly : *The actor complained that his remarks in the newspaper were taken out of context and did not show his true feelings.*

con·ti·nent [KON-tuh-nunt] NOUN, continents. **1. continent** ▶ one of the seven large land areas of the earth. The continents are Africa, Asia, North America, South America, Europe, Australia, and Antarctica. Europe and Asia are actually part of the same land area (Eurasia), but are thought of as separate continents because they have had a different history and culture. **2. the Continent.** the continent of Europe, apart from Great Britain. ☞ **p. 1039.**

con·ti·nen·tal [KON-tuh-NEN-tul] ADJECTIVE. **1. continental (-ale, -aux)** ▶ having to do with a continent : *Hawaii is not part of the continental United States.* **2. (often Continental) continental (-ale, -aux)** ▶ having to do with the continent of Europe : *continental food.*

con·tin·u·al [kun-TIN-yoo-ul] ADJECTIVE. **continuel (-elle)** ▶ happening again and again ; frequent : *continual telephone calls.* ▪ **continually,** ADVERB. **continuellement, sans cesse** ▶ *"The animal blinked continually in the sunshine."* (Jack London)

con·tin·ue [kun-TIN-yoo] VERB, continued, continuing. **1. continuer, poursuivre** ▶ to go on without stopping ; keep happening : *The rain continued for two days.* **2. continuer, reprendre** ▶ to start again after stopping : *The game will continue in 15 minutes.* **3. continuer, rester, perpétuer, maintenir** ▶ to stay in the same place or situation ; remain : *Mrs. Leung plans to continue working until she's 65.* **Note.** The continuing of something is a continuation.

con·tin·u·ous [kun-TIN-yoo-us] ADJECTIVE. **continu (-ue), permanent (-ente)** ▶ going on without a stop : *the continuous movement of ocean waves.* ▪ **continuously,** ADVERB. **continuellement, sans interruption, sans arrêt.**

con·tract [KON-trakt] NOUN, contracts. **contrat** ▶ an agreement, usually written, that has the force of law. It states that two or more people or groups agree to do or not do certain things. ▲ [kuhn-TRAKT or KON-trakt] VERB, contracted, contracting. **1. contracter, raidir, tendre, resserrer** ▶ to make or become shorter or smaller ; draw together : *The pupils of the eyes contract when the light becomes brighter.* **2. engager** ▶ to make an agreement by contract : *My parents contracted a company to paint our house.* **3. contracter, attraper, prendre** ▶ to get something that is bad or not wanted, such as an illness : *He contracted a terrible cold.* **Note.** A person or company that agrees to do work for a certain price, especially building work, is a contractor.

con·trac·tion [kun-TRAK-shun] NOUN, contractions. **1. contraction** ▶ a word formed by putting together two words with a certain letter or letters left out : *"They're" is a contraction of "they are."* **2. contraction, crispation** ▶ the act of contracting : *The contraction of the heart pushes the blood to the arteries.*

con·tra·dict [KON-truh-DIKT] VERB, contradicted, contradicting. **contredire** ▶ to say the opposite of ; say to be false or untrue : *The mud on Jerry's shoes contradicted his claim that he hadn't been outside.* **Note.** Something that contradicts is a contradiction. SYN: oppose, deny, dispute.

con·trar·y [KON-trair-ee] ADJECTIVE. **1. contraire, opposé (-ée), en opposition** ▶ completely different ; opposite or opposed : *Kyla and I have contrary tastes in music ; she likes rock, and I like jazz.* **2.** [*also* kuhn-TRAIR-ee] liking to argue or oppose ; stubborn : *Yoes is very contrary ; he always does the opposite of what he's told.* ▲ NOUN, contraries. **contraire** ▶ something that is opposite : *I think you're wrong ; I believe the contrary.*

on (to) the contrary au contraire, contrairement à ▶ exactly the opposite ; the opposite is true.

con·trast [kun-TRAST or KON-trast] VERB, contrasted, contrasting. **1. contraster, trancher** ▶ to compare two things in order to show a difference between them : *Dad contrasted my neat room to Joel's messy room.* **2. contraster, ressortir** ▶ to show differences when compared : *The deep, cool shade contrasted with the blinding glare of the noon sun.* ▲ [KON-trast] NOUN, contrasts. **1. contraste, opposition** ▶ the comparing of things to show a difference : *Business at the store has been good this month, in contrast with last month.* **2. contraste, écart, dissemblance, disparité** ▶ a person or thing that shows such a difference : *There is a great contrast between the lives of the rich and the poor in that country.* SYN: compare, liken, measure.

con·trib·ute [kun-TRIB-yoot] VERB, contributed, contributing. **1. contribuer, cotiser** ▶ to give money or help : *I always contribute to the food bank.* **2. contribuer** ▶ to supply writing to a newspaper or magazine. **Note.** A person who contributes is a contributor.

contribute to contribuer à ▶ to help to bring about : *All the players contributed to the team's success this season.*

con·tri·bu·tion [KON-truh-BYOO-shun] NOUN, contributions. **contribution, participation** ▶ the act of contributing, or something that is contributed : *"I agree with Kate," said Marcia, making her first contribution to the discussion.*

con·trol [kun-TROLE] VERB, controlled, controlling. **1. contrôler, dominer** ▶ to have power over; rule; command : *My brother always wants to control what we watch on TV.* **2. contrôler, régler, ajuster** ▸ to direct the course of; regulate : *This dial controls the heat in the building.* **3. contrôler, contenir, maîtriser** ▸ to hold back; keep down : *"I was struggling to control the tears that were threatening to well up and spill over."* (Jean Little) ▲ NOUN, **controls. 1. contrôle** ▸ the act or fact of controlling : *I lost control of the car and hit a bush.* **2. maîtrise, contenu (-ue), contrôle** ▸ a holding back; check : *She remained calm and in complete control of herself.* **3. controls. contrôle, commande** ▸ the instruments used to run a machine : *the controls of an airplane.*

con·tro·ver·sy [KON-truh-vur-see] NOUN, controversies. **controverse, différend** ▸ an argument or a dispute; strong disagreement : *There's a big controversy about the new development downtown.* ■ **controversial,** ADJECTIVE. ▸ **discutable, discuté (-ée), controversé (-ée).** causing a lot of argument or disagreement : *Violence in movies and on TV is a controversial issue.* SYN: dispute, argument, quarrel.

con·ven·ience [kun-VEEN-yuns] NOUN, conveniences. **1. commodité, agrément, avantage** ▸ the quality of being convenient; ease and comfort : *The hotel provides transportation to the airport for the convenience of its guests.* **2. commodité** ▸ a thing that saves time or effort : *Most people expect such conveniences as hot running water and indoor plumbing in a new home.*

con·ven·ient [kun-VEEN-yunt] ADJECTIVE. **1. commode, convenable, aisé (-ée)** ▸ suited to one's needs or purposes; right for the situation : *We can meet at whatever time is convenient for you.* **2. commode, fonctionnel (-elle)** ▸ easy to reach or get to; handy : *Their house is convenient to schools and transportation.* ■ **conveniently,** ADVERB. ▸ **opportunément, convenablement.**

con·ven·tion [kun-VEN-shun] NOUN, conventions. **1. convention** ▸ a formal meeting for a special purpose : *A political party holds a convention to select a new leader.* **2. convention, usage, convenance** ▸ an accepted way of acting; a custom : *Tipping is the convention in North America.*

con·ven·tion·al [kun-VEN-shun-ul] ADJECTIVE. **1. conventionnel (-elle), classique** ▸ following the accepted practice; customary : *Shaking hands when meeting someone is the conventional thing to do in Canada.* **2. conventionnel (-elle), conformiste** ▸ of the usual or ordinary type; commonplace : *He has conventional taste in food and doesn't try new dishes.* SYN: usual, traditional, accepted, established.

con·ver·sa·tion [KON-vur-SAY-shun] NOUN, conversations. **conversation, entretien** ▸ a talk between two or more people; talking : *The con-* versation about baseball stopped when the teacher came in.

con·vert [kun-VURT] VERB, converted, converting. **1. convertir, transformer, changer** ▸ to change from one thing to another : *"I planned how to convert our garage into a stable."* (Dayal Kaur Khalsa) **2. convertir, transformer, changer** ▸ to change one's religion or beliefs. ▲ [KON-vurt] NOUN, **converts. converti (-ie)** ▸ a person who has been persuaded to accept a new religion or belief : *She is a recent convert to Islam.* **Note.** The act of converting is **conversion.**

con·vex [kon-VEKS or KON-veks] ADJECTIVE. **convexe** ▸ curved or rounded outward; the opposite of concave : *Contact lenses are curved to fit the convex shape of the eye.*

con·vey [kun-VAY] VERB, conveyed, conveying. **1. transporter, amener** ▸ to move or carry something to another place : *This cable conveys power to the computer.* **2. communiquer, transmettre** ▸ to communicate some thought or feeling; make known : *He could convey a lot of meaning with a nod of his head.*

con·vict [kun-VIKT] VERB, convicted, convicting. **déclarer coupable, reconnaître coupable** ▸ to find by a court of law that someone is guilty of a crime : *The court convicted her of driving through a red light.* ▲ [KON-vikt] NOUN, **convicts. prisonnier (-ière), détenu (-ue)** ▸ someone who has been convicted of a crime and is in prison serving a sentence.

convex

con·vic·tion [kun-VIK-shun] NOUN, convictions. **1. condamnation, sentence, jugement** ▸ the act of proving that a person is guilty of a crime : *John's conviction for speeding stays on his driving record for three years.* **2. conviction, croyance** ▸ a strong belief about something : *Because of his religious convictions, he won't work on Saturday.*

con·vince [kun-VINS] VERB, convinced, convincing. **convaincre, persuader** ▸ to make someone believe something; persuade : *Asa tried to convince me that Santa Claus isn't real.* **Note.** Also used as an ADJECTIVE:*Saeed told a convincing version of what he saw.* SYN: persuade, make certain, assure, promise.

cook [kuk] VERB, cooked, cooking. **cuisiner, préparer, cuire** ▸ to make food ready to eat by heating it : *Ned cooked the meat in the oven.*

▲ NOUN, cooks. **cuisinier (-ière)** ▸ a person who gets food ready to eat : *The cook in our school cafeteria prepares lunch every day.* **Note.** The verb is also used to form other nouns, such as cooking, cookbook, and cookout.

cook

stove

cook-ie [KUK-ee] NOUN, cookies. **biscuit** ▸ a small, sweet food, usually flat and round : *Do you like chocolate-chip cookies with nuts?*

cool [kool] ADJECTIVE, cooler, coolest. **1. frais, fraîcheur, frisquet (-ette)** ▸ lacking warmth; a little cold : *Keep butter in a cool place so that it won't melt.* **2. calme, décontracté (-ée), à l'aise** ▸ not excited; calm : *Some passengers were nervous during the storm, but the flight crew remained cool.* **3. frais (fraîche), froid (froide)** ▸ not friendly or interested : *Kara gave a cool smile to her brother.* ▲ NOUN. **fraîcheur, froid** ▸ something that lacks warmth; a cool place or thing : *The cool of the early morning always refreshed her.* ▲ VERB, cooled, cooling. **refroidir, rafraîchir** ▸ to make something cool : *The fan cooled the hot room.* ▲ ADVERB. (also coolly) **froidement** ▸ ■ **coolness,** NOUN. ▸ **froideur, sang-froid, impassibilité, flegme.** **Note.** Something that keeps food or drinks cool is a **cooler.** SYN: chilly, fresh.

coop koop] NOUN, coops. **poulailler** ▸ a cage for keeping chickens or small animals. ▲ VERB, cooped, cooping. (usually used with up) **claquemurer, cloîtrer, enfermer** ▸ to keep in a small space, as if in a coop : *The dog needs a walk; he's been cooped up all day.* 👁 **p. 114.**

co-op-er-ate [koh-OP-uh-RATE] VERB, co-operated, co-operating. (also cooperate) **coopérer, collaborer** ▸ to act with another or others to do something; work together : *We all had to co-operate to organize the school fair.* **Note.** The act or process of co-operating is **co-operation.** SYN: work together, collaborate, help, contribute.

co-op-er-a-tive [koh-OP-ur-uh-tiv *or* koh-OP-im-tiv] ADJECTIVE. **coopératif (-ive), coopérant (-ante)** ▸ willing to work with or help others : *That author is always co-operative when younger writers ask her questions.* ▲ NOUN, co-operatives. **coopérative, en copropriété** ▸ something owned and operated by the people who use it : *a housing co-operative.* **Note.** Often shortened to co-op.

co-or-di-nate [koh-OR-duh-NATE] VERB, co-ordinated, co-ordinating. (also coordinate) **coordonner, combiner, agencer** ▸ to cause different things to work together well : *The brain co-ordinates the movements of the body.* **Note.** Often used as an ADJECTIVE: *A ballet dancer must be co-ordinated.* ■ **co-ordination,** NOUN. ▸ **coordination.** *A baby learning to walk doesn't have good co-ordination.* SYN: arrange, organize, harmonize.

cop [kop] NOUN, cops. Informal. **agent de police, gardien de la paix, policier (-ère), gendarme** ▸ a police officer.

cope [kope] VERB, coped, coping. **se débrouiller, s'en tirer, s'occuper de, faire face à** ▸ to handle a difficult situation with success : *"We are having enough trouble today without having to cope with your foolishness."* (E.B. White) SYN: struggle, put up, face.

cop-per [KOP-ur] NOUN, coppers. **1. cuivre** ▸ a reddish-brown metal that is used to make pennies and other coins, electrical wire, and other products. Copper is a chemical element. It is a good conductor of heat and electricity. **2. cuivré (-ée), roux (rousse)** ▸ a reddish-brown colour like that of copper. 👁 **p. 397.**

cop-y [KOP-ee] NOUN, copies. **1. copie, reproduction** ▸ something that is made to look or be just like something else; an imitation : *This dress is*

ℳ **Word Builder**

Cook most often means to prepare food, but the verb is also found in many common phrases.
Cook up can mean to invent or make something up, such as a story: Gillian missed the soccer
practice so she cooked up a story about her stepfather's car breaking down. Cook (someone's)
goose often means to cause trouble: He cooked his goose by taking Jammu's bike without
permission. What's cooking? asks the question, "What's going on?"

a copy of one by a famous European designer.
2. exemplaire ▸ one of a number of newspapers, magazines, books, tapes, and so on printed or made at the same time : *The library has three copies of that book.* ▲ VERB, copied, copying.
1. copier ▸ to make a copy of something; duplicate : *to copy a poem out of a book.* **2. copier, imiter** ▸ to be like; imitate : *Some people copy the way a popular singer or movie star dresses.* **Note.** A copier (or photocopier) is a machine that makes copies of letters and other papers. SYN : imitate, duplicate, repeat, reproduce.

cop·y·right [KOP-ee-RITE] NOUN, copyrights. **copyright, droits d'auteurs** ▸ the right by law to be the only one to publish, produce, or sell a certain artistic work, such as a book, movie, or piece of music.

cor·al [KOR-ul] NOUN. **1. corail (-aux)** ▸ a rocklike material made up of the skeletons of tiny sea animals that live in warm waters. **Note.** A coral reef is a large formation of coral in shallow water. **2. corail (-aux)** ▸ the animal that produces this material. **3. corail** ▸ a pinkish-red colour like that of coral.

cord [kord] NOUN, cords. **1. corde** ▸ a kind of heavy string that is thicker and stronger than ordinary string. **2. cordon électrique, fil électrique** ▸ a covered wire used to connect an electric lamp or appliance to a power outlet. **3. colonne vertébrale** ▸ a part of the body that is thought of as like a cord : *the spinal cord.* **4. cordée** ▸ a unit of measure for a pile of cut firewood. A cord is 1.2 m x 2.4 m x 1.2 m.

cor·dial [KOR-jul] ADJECTIVE. **cordial (-iale, -iaux), chaleureux (-euse)** ▸ warm and friendly : *Dr. Kim always gives a cordial greeting to her patients.* ■ **cordially,** ADVERB: ▸ **cordialement.** *She gave us a wave and smiled cordially.* SYN : sincere, warm, hearty, friendly, hospitable.

core [kor] NOUN, cores. **1. trognon, cœur** ▸ the hard central part of an apple, pear, or similar fruit. The core contains the seeds of the fruit. **2. noyau (-aux), cœur** ▸ the central or most important part of something : *the core of the earth.* ▲ VERB, cored, coring. **enlever, ôter, retirer, extraire** ▸ to take or cut out the core of something : *to core an apple.*

cork [kork] NOUN, corks. **1. liège** ▸ the thick outer bark of a certain type of oak tree. Cork is very light and floats easily. It is used to make floor coverings, bulletin boards, and other things. **2. liège, bouchon de liège** ▸ something made from cork, especially a bottle stopper. ▲ VERB, corked, corking. **mettre un bouchon de liège** ▸ to push a piece of cork into a bottle as a stopper : *to cork a bottle.*

corn[1] [korn] NOUN. **maïs** ▸ a tall green plant that has large ears or cobs covered with rows of yellow or white kernels or seeds. Corn is eaten as a vegetable and is used as feed for animals. It is

also used to make many other food products, such as corn oil, cornstarch, corn bread, cornflakes, and so on. ☞ **p. 116.**

corn[2] NOUN, corns. **cor, callosité, durillon, oignon** ▸ a painful area where the skin has become hard and thick, especially on the toe.

cor·ner [KOR-nur] NOUN, corners. **1. coin, angle** ▸ the point where two lines, walls, or other surfaces come together : *the corner of a room.* **2. coin, tournant, virage** ▸ the place where two streets come together. **3. recoin** ▸ a secret, private, or faraway place : *The zoo houses animals from all corners of the earth.* **4. coincé (-ée)** ▸ a difficult or embarrassing position : *He got himself into a tight corner by charging a lot of things he couldn't afford.* ▲ VERB, cornered, cornering. **coincer, bloquer, immobiliser** ▸ to force someone into a corner; put someone in an awkward position : *Tory cornered her brother and got him to agree to take her to the movies.*

corn·y [KOR-nee] ADJECTIVE, cornier, corniest. *informal.* **à l'eau de rose** ▸ very old-fashioned, simple, or sentimental : *The movie had a corny plot about a grumpy old man who becomes friendly when he finds a puppy.*

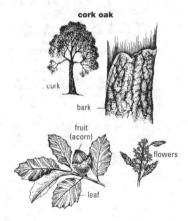

cork oak

curk

bark

fruit (acorn)

flowers

leaf

cor·po·ra·tion [KOR-puh-RAY-shun] NOUN, corporations. **corporation, conseil, société** ▸ a business; a group of people having the legal power to act as one person. ■ **corporate,** ADJECTIVE. **corporatif (-ive), constitué en corporation** ▸ having to do with corporations : *the corporate income tax.*

corps [kor] NOUN, corps. **1. corps** ▸ a military group that is trained for a special purpose : *the Medical Corps.* **2. corps** ▸ any group of people working together : *The mayor made some remarks to the press corps.*

corpse [korps] NOUN, corpses. **cadavre, corps** ▸ the body of a dead person.

cor·ral [kuh-RAL] NOUN, corrals. **corral, enclos** ▸ a fenced area or pen for keeping horses, cattle, or other animals. ▲ VERB, corralled, corralling. **1. enfermer dans un corral** ▸ to drive into or keep in a corral. **2. réunir** ▸ to hem in; surround.

cor·rect [kuh-REKT] ADJECTIVE. **1. correct (-ecte), exact (-acte), juste** ▸ having no mistakes; right : *the correct spelling of a word.* **2. correct (-ecte), convenable, d'usage, bienséant (-ante)** ▸ following certain rules or standards; proper : *Wearing shorts is not the correct way to dress for a wedding.* ▲ VERB, corrected, correcting. **1. corriger, rectifier** ▸ to mark or point out the mistakes in something : *to correct a test.* **2. corriger** ▸ to change to make right or proper : *to correct a child for acting rude.* ■ **correctly,** ADVERB: ▸ **correctement, convenablement, décemment.** *She answered all the questions correctly.* ■ **correctness,** NOUN. ▸ **exactitude, justesse. Note.** A correction is the act of changing something to make it right. SYN: true, right, exact, faultless, proper, accurate.

cor·re·spond [KOR-uh-SPOND] VERB, corresponded, corresponding. **1. correspondre, s'accorder** ▸ to agree with something; match : *The number of places at the table corresponds to the number of guests coming to the party.* **2. correspondre, équivaloir, égaler** ▸ to be similar to; be like : *The French phrase "au revoir" corresponds to "goodbye."* **3. correspondre, s'écrire** ▸ to write or exchange letters : *I correspond with pen pals from three different countries.*

cor·re·spon·dent [KOR-uh-SPOND-unt] NOUN, correspondents. **1. correspondant (-ante)** ▸ a person who corresponds with another by letter : *Mom and one of her high-school friends have been correspondents for years.* **2. correspondant (-ante), envoyé (-ée), reporter, représentant (-ante)** ▸ a person who sends in a news report to a newspaper, TV station, and so on, especially from a distant place : *Many newspapers have correspondents in countries all over the world.*

cor·ri·dor [KOR-uh-dor] NOUN, corridors. **couloir, corridor** ▸ a long, narrow hallway or passage in a building, usually with doors opening from it : *We are not allowed to run or shout in the school corridors.*

cor·rode [kuh-RODE] VERB, corroded, corroding. **corroder, attaquer, ronger** ▸ to wear away little by little over time :*Rust corrodes metal.* SYN: eat away, rot, rust.

cor·rupt [kuh-RUPT] ADJECTIVE. **corrompu (-ue), dépravé (-ée), vénal (-ale, -aux)** ▸ having poor morals : *The corrupt politician accepted a bribe to change his vote.* ▲ VERB, corrupted, corrupting. **corrompre, dépraver, pervertir** ▸ to cause someone to be dishonest; make corrupt. **Note.** The state of being corrupt is corruption. SYN: dishonest, crooked, wicked, rotten. ✎ **p. 451.**

cost [kost] NOUN, costs. **1. coût, frais, prix** ▸ the price of something; the amount paid : *What was the cost of that coat ?* **2. coût, dépens** ▸ the loss of something; a sacrifice : *The transcontinental railway was built at the cost of many workers' lives.* ▲ VERB, cost, costing. **1. coûter, valoir** ▸ to have as a price : *That book cost $19.95.* **2. coûter** ▸ to cause the loss of something : *The outfielder's error cost our team the game.*

cost·ly [KOST-lee] ADJECTIVE, costlier, costliest. **1. dispendieux (-euse), coûteux (-euse)** ▸ costing a lot; expensive : *Clothes are getting costlier all the time.* **2. coûteux (-euse)** ▸ causing a great loss : *It was a costly victory because our quarterback was injured.* SYN: valuable, expensive, rich, high-priced.

cos·tume [KOS-tyoom] NOUN, costumes. **1. costume, déguisement** ▸ clothes worn to dress up as someone or something else : *He wore a pirate costume for Halloween.* **2. costume, accoutrement, habillement** ▸ the style of clothing worn by the people of a certain place or time, or for a certain purpose : *a riding costume; the costume of a samurai warrior.* **Note.** Costume jewellery is made from inexpensive materials, not precious stones.

co·sy [KOH-zee] ADJECTIVE, cosier, cosiest. **douillet (-ette), confortable** ▸ also **cozy**) warm and soft :*a cosy chair.* SYN: comfortable, snug, homey, relaxing.

cot·tage [KOT-ij] NOUN, cottages. **cottage, villa, petite maison de campagne** ▸ a small house, especially one used for vacation : *We went to a cottage on a lake this summer.* ⌂ **p. 1067.**

cot·ton [KOT-un] NOUN. **coton** ▸ a plant that produces seeds covered with fluffy white fibres that are processed to make cloth and thread. The fibres and the cloth are also called cotton. **Note.** Often used as an ADJECTIVE:*a cotton dress.* **Note.** The word *cotton* comes from the Arabs, who introduced this plant to Europe in the Middle Ages.

couch [kowch] NOUN, couches. **1. canapé, divan, sofa, causeuse** ▸ a large piece of furniture for sleep or rest : *I sat on the couch to watch TV.* **2. coussin, tapis** ▸ any place for sleep or rest : *The lion arose from its grassy couch.* **Note.** Also called a **sofa** or a **chesterfield.** ▲ VERB, couched, couching. **1. formuler, exprimer** ▸ to put in words; express : *My father couched his question very carefully.* **2. se tapir, coucher, cacher** ▸ lie hidden, ready to attack : *They were couched down in the bush, hiding from the other team.*

cou·gar [KOO-gur] NOUN, cougars. **couguar, puma ▸** a large wild cat of North America, more often known as a **mountain lion.** The cougar is usually sand-coloured with short, black ears and a long, black-tipped tail. It usually hunts at night.

cough [kof] VERB, coughed, coughing. **tousser ▸** to force air from the lungs with a sudden effort and loud noise : *With this cold, Gwen was coughing all night.* ▲ NOUN, coughs. **1. toux ▸** the sudden, loud sound made when a person is coughing. **2. toux ▸** an illness that causes a person to cough often.

could [kood] VERB. **pouvoir, être capable ▸** a past form of **can** : *"It was very hard to get a ball past Louis—he could return almost any shot."* (E.B. White) **Note.** Could is also used in place of **can** or **may** to make a statement or question less strong or more polite : *Could you please put this away for me?*

coun·cil [KOWN-sul] NOUN. **1. conseil, assemblée ▸** a group of people who meet to discuss a problem or make a decision : *a student council.* **2. conseiller (-ère), assemblée, comité ▸** an elected group of people who make laws : *a town council.* SYN: assembly, group, committee, meeting.

coun·cil·lor [KOWN-suh-lur] NOUN, councillors. (also councilor) **1. conseiller (-ère) ▸** a member of a council. **2. conseiller (-ère) municipal ▸** an elected member of the council of a town, city, or the like.

coun·sel [KOWN-sul] NOUN. **1. conseil, recommandation, suggestion, guidance ▸** ideas or opinions about what to do; advice; guidance : *The prime minister often asks his or her cabinet for counsel.* **2. avocat (-ate) ▸** a person who gives legal advice; a lawyer or group of lawyers : *Anyone accused of a crime has a right to counsel.* ▲ VERB, counselled, counselling. (also counseled, counseling) **conseiller, proposer, suggérer, recommander ▸** to give advice or guidance to : *Mr. Yap counselled his son not to drop out of school.* SYN: advise, instruct, suggest, guide, recommend.

coun·sel·lor [KOWN-suh-lur] NOUN, counsellors. (also counselor) **1. conseiller (-ère), guide ▸** a person who advises or guides : *Meg's counsellor helped her decide which courses to take.* **2. avocat (-ate) ▸** a lawyer : *the counsellor for the defence.* **3. moniteur (-trice) ▸** a person who is in charge of activities at a children's camp : *We planned a party for the counsellors the night before we left camp.*

count¹ [kownt] VERB, counted, counting. **1. compter, additionner, calculer ▸** to find the amount or number of something; add up : *Let's count how much money we have saved.* **2. compter, dénombrer, énumérer ▸** to name or write numbers in order : *to count to 50.* **3. compter, inclure ▸** to include when adding up or thinking about something : *We need to*

count the parents in the number going to the museum. **4. compter ▸** to be taken into account : *You have to take off from behind this line, or your jump won't count.* ▲ NOUN, counts. **1. compte ▸** the act of counting. **2. compte, décompte ▸** a number that is obtained by counting; a total; sum : *At the count of three, start running.* **3. chef d'accusation ▸** a charge against a person in a court of law : *He is accused of five counts of burglary.* SYN: add, total, calculate.

count on compter sur ▸ to expect or depend on : *I was counting on using the money I've saved to buy that sweater.*

count² NOUN, counts. **comte ▸** a nobleman of high rank in some European countries.

coun·ter¹ [KOWN-tur] NOUN, counters. **1. comptoir ▸** a long, flat surface where customers in restaurants, banks, or stores are served, or where things are displayed. Kitchens and bathrooms also have counters that are used to work on or to hold things. **2. compteur ▸** an object used for counting or keeping score, as in a game : *Throw the dice; then move your counter that number of squares.*

coun·ter² ADVERB or ADJECTIVE. **à l'encontre de, à l'opposé de, contrairement à ▸** opposed to something : in the opposite : *Mia played baseball after school, counter to her parents' instructions to come right home.* ▲ VERB, countered, countering. **aller à l'encontre de, s'opposer à, contrecarrer, contre-attaquer ▸** to oppose something; act in the opposite way : *The boxer countered his opponent's punch.* **Note.** Often used in compounds to give the idea of opposing or going against something, as in counterattack, counterclockwise, counterspy.

count·ess [KOWN-tis] NOUN, countesses. **comtesse ▸** a woman of high rank in some European countries. A countess has the same rank as a count or an earl, or is the wife or widow of a count or an earl.

count·less [KOWNT-lis] ADJECTIVE. **innombrable, infini (-ie) ▸** a great many; too many to count : *There are countless stars in the sky.*

coun·try [KUN-tree] NOUN, countries. **1. pays ▸** an area of land that is under the same government; a nation. A country has certain set borders, and the people who live there are not under any government higher than that of the country itself : *Canada, France, and Chile are countries.* **2. région ▸** any area of land of a certain type : *Much of Ontario is good farming country.* **3. campagne ▸** an area of land away from cities and towns; a rural area : *She works in Montreal, but spends her weekends in the country.* ▲ ADJECTIVE. **campagnard (-arde) ▸** having to do with areas away from the city : *an old country inn.* **Note.** The countryside is a rural area outside a city. 📖 **p. 1039.**

coun-ty [KOWN-tee] NOUN, counties. **comté**
▶ one of the sections into which certain countries, states, and provinces are divided for purposes of government.

cou-ple [KUP-ul] NOUN, couples. **1. couple,
paire** ▶ two things that are the same or that go
together; a pair : *Joel and I have a couple of
tickets for the ball game.* **2. couple** ▶ two people who are thought of together because they
are màrried, engaged, partners in a dance or
game, and so on : *Mom and Dad went out to
dinner with two other couples.* ▲ VERB, coupled,
coupling. **coupler, joindre, assembler, pairer**
▶ to put together; join : *The rail workers coupled the freight cars to the engine.* SYN: join,
unite, team, link, connect.

cou-plet [KUP-let] NOUN, couplets. **distique**
▶ two lines of a poem that go together, and usually rhyme. ✐ p. 146.

cou-pon [KOO-pon *or* KYOO-pon] NOUN, coupons.
coupon, bon ▶ a printed piece of paper that can
be traded for money or merchandise or used to
get a cheaper price on a product : *Mom saves
coupons to use when she goes shopping.*

cour-age [KUR-ij] NOUN, courage, bravoure,
audace ▶ the quality of being able to face danger or pain without giving in to being afraid :
*"Did you know that an Arabian horse is the
only breed with the courage to face a lion?"*
(Walter Farley) SYN: bravery, nerve, boldness, valour, pluck.

cou-ra-geous [kuh-RAY-jus] NOUN. **courageux
(-euse), brave, audacieux (-euse)** ▶ brave or
having courage : *a courageous act.* ✐ p. 71.

cou-reur de bois [koo-RUR duh BWAH] NOUN,
coureurs de bois. **coureur des bois** ▶ formerly,
a French or Métis fur trader or woodsman in the
North or Northwest.

cou-ri-er [KUR-ee-ur] NOUN, couriers. **courrier,
messager (-ère)** ▶ a person whose job is to
carry messages: messenger.

course [korce] NOUN, courses. **1. cours** ▶ a moving from one point to another; movement
through space or time : *Passengers can watch a
movie during the course of the flight.* **2. cours,
route, parcours** ▶ a certain direction in which

something moves or goes : *The ship's course
was due west.* **3. cours** ▶ a way of acting or of
doing something : *I think the only sensible
course is to turn back.* **4. terrain** ▶ an open
area used for games or races : *a golf course.*
5. cours ▶ a series of classes in a particular subject : *an English course; a driver's education
course.* **6. plat, repas** ▶ one part of a meal :
They had soup before the main course.
SYN: direction, path, way, track, line.

of course **bien sûr, naturellement, bien
entendu, évidemment** ▶ without a doubt; certainly : *You will, of course, bring your glove to
the game.* **Note.** Often used as an answer in
conversation : *"May I borrow your geography
book?" "Of course."*

court [kort] NOUN, courts. **1. cour, tribunal
(-aux)** ▶ an official meeting at which a judge
holds trials and settles legal matters : *a traffic
court.* **2. palais de justice** ▶ the place where
such a meeting is held. **Note.** Also called a
courtroom or courthouse. **3. juge** ▶ a judge or
judges. **4. terrain, court** ▶ a space set up for a
certain game or sport : *a tennis court.* **5. Cour**
▶ the home of a king, queen, or other royal
ruler : *Hampton Court was the palace of Henry
VIII of England.* **6. honorer** ▶ respect or honour : *to pay court to someone.* ▲ VERB, courted,
courting. **1. courtiser, flatter, solliciter** ▶ to pay
attention to in order to get a favour from : *The
politician courted voters with promises of a
tax cut.* **2. courtiser, séduire** ▶ to spend time
with or pay attention to a person one hopes to
marry : *Grandpa courted Grandma 40 years
ago.* **3. s'exposer à, aller au devant de** ▶ to act
so as to get or bring on something, especially
something bad : *They're courting disaster by
building their house on the cliff.*

cour-te-ous [KUR-tee-us] ADJECTIVE. **courtois (-oise), poli (-ie)** ▶ polite and considerate
toward other people : *The children were always
courteous to their friends' parents.* ■ **courteously,** ADVERB. ▶ **courtoisement, poliment.** *The
taxi driver courteously opened the door and
helped us in.* ■ **courteousness,** NOUN. ▶ **courtoisie, politesse, civilité.** SYN: polite, civil, gracious, respectful.

cour-te-sy [KUR-tuh-see] NOUN, courtesies. **courtoisie, politesse, civilité** ▶ polite and considerate behaviour or manners; being courteous.

cous-in [KUZ-un] NOUN, cousins. **1. cousin
(-ine)** ▶ the son or daughter of one's aunt or
uncle : *My cousin Lars is Uncle Sven's son.*
2. cousin (-ine), descendant (-ante) ▶ any relative that has the same great-grandparents or
other ancestor.

cove [kove] NOUN, coves. **crique, anse** ▶ a small
bay or inlet that is sheltered by land.

cov-er [KUV-ur] VERB, covered, covering. **1. couvrir, cacher, protéger** ▶ to place upon or over or
on : *Grandma covered the baby with a blanket.*

✐ **Writing Tips**

Couplet

*A **couplet** is a two-line poem or two lines
from a poem that follow a specific pattern.
The words at the end of each line rhyme,
and the two lines together form a complete
thought.*

*Rain, rain, go away
Come again another day*

2. couvrir, recouvrir ▶ to spread over the surface of; lie over or on : *The whole field was covered with yellow daisies.* **3. couvrir, parcourir ▶** to travel or go over : *We covered 40 kilometres by bike today.* **4. couvrir, englober, traiter ▶** to deal with; include : *This social studies course covers Canadian history up to 1867.* **5. couvrir, parcourir ▶** to watch over or guard : *The police are setting up roadblocks that will cover all routes out of town.* **6. couvrir, faire compte rendu ▶** to have as one's work or interest : *Several reporters are here to cover the soccer match.* ▲ NOUN, **covers. 1. housse ▶** something that covers : *to put a cover on a chair.* **2. couverture ▶** the outside of a book, magazine, record album, or the like. **3.** (also **covers) couverture, dessus-de-lit ▶** a blanket or spread used to cover a bed. **4. abri ▶** something that protects or hides : *The soldiers took cover behind a tree.*

cover up dissimuler, cacher, recouvrir ▶ to hide or conceal : *They covered up the trap with leaves so that the animals wouldn't see it.* **Note.** Also used as a NOUN: *The story began with a cover-up of a robbery.*

cov·er·age [KUV-rij] NOUN. **1. reportage, couverture ▶** the amount of space or time given to a news event in the media. **2. couverture, garantie ▶** the amount and extent of something covered by insurance : *She has $10,000 coverage for damage to her car in an accident.*

cov·er·ing [KUV-ur-ing] NOUN, **coverings. couverture, protection, enveloppe ▶** anything that covers, protects, or hides : *A rug is a floor covering.*

co·vert [KOH vurt] ADJECTIVE. **voilé (-ée), caché (-ée), secret (-ète) ▶** hidden or secret; not in the open : *The spy was working on a covert mission, so no one knew exactly what he was doing.*

cow [kow] NOUN, **cows. 1. vache ▶** the full-grown female of cattle. **2. femelle ▶** the full-grown female of certain other large animals, such as the moose, whale, or elephant. **Note.** For those animals whose female is called a cow, the male is called a bull and the young a calf. ⌐ **p. 1087.** ◉ **p. 114.**

cow·ard [KOW-urd] NOUN, **cowards. lâche, poltron (-onne), ▲** a person who is not brave or courageous; someone who shows fear in a shameful way or who is easily frightened : *"I hung my head, just the way cowards do in books."* (Jean Fitzhugh)

cow·ard·ly [KOW-urd-lee] ADJECTIVE. **lâche, dégonflé (-ée) ▶** not brave or courageous; showing fear in a shameful way : *In* The Wizard of Oz, *the Cowardly Lion was even afraid of the little dog Toto and cried whenever he was scared.* **Note.** The state of being cowardly is cowardice.

cow·er [KOW-ur] VERB, **cowered, cowering. se recroqueviller ▶** to move away in fear of something : *"A wild glare from me was enough to make the dogs cower back in their chairs."* (James Herriot)

cow·hand [KOW-hand] NOUN, **cowhands. cow·boy ▶** a person who takes care of cattle on a ranch, usually on horseback. **Note.** Formerly cowboy or cowgirl.

Cow·i·chan [KOW-ih-chun] NOUN. **1. cowichan ▶** the Salish people of Vancouver Island. **2. cowichan ▶** (also **Cowichan sweater**) a heavy sweater made of unbleached wool and having a knitted design on the front and back, especially such a sweater knitted by the Cowichan people.

coy [koy] ADJECTIVE. **qui fait le ou la timide ▶** shy or bashful or pretending to be so : *Sandi thought Tim was shy, but he was just being coy.* SYN: shy, bashful, modest, timid.

coy·o·te [KY-ote *or* ky-OH-tee] NOUN, **coyotes** or **coyote. coyote ▶** A North American animal that is related to the wolf. Coyotes are native to the West but are now also found elsewhere. Most live and hunt alone. ◉ **p. 111.**

cozy See cosy.

crab [krab] NOUN, **crabs. 1. crabe ▶** a water animal that has a wide, flat body covered by a hard shell. Crabs have four pairs of legs and a pair of front claws. Many kinds of crabs are used as food. **2.** *Informal.* **grincheux (-euse), hargneux (-euse) ▶** someone who is cross and bad-tempered; a grouch. ■ **crabby,** ADJECTIVE. **▶ grognon (-onne), grincheux (-euse), revêche.**

crab apple NOUN, **crab apples.** (also **crabapple) pomme sauvage ▶** a small sour apple that is used to make jelly.

crack [krak] VERB, **cracked, cracking. 1. craquer, crevasser, fêler ▶** to break without completely apart; split : *The glass cracked when I dropped it into the sink.* **2. claquement ▶** to make a sudden, sharp noise : *a crack of thunder.* **3. fêler, craquer ▶** to hit with a sharp, hard blow : *I cracked my head on the cupboard door.* **4. résoudre ▶** to solve or break into : *The secret agent cracked the enemy's code.* **5. muer, se casser ▶** to change quality or pitch of a voice : *His voice cracked as he read the sad letter.* ▲ NOUN, **cracks. 1. fente, fissure, craquelure, crevasse ▶** a narrow break or split in something that is still in one piece : *This teacup has a crack in it.* **2. fente ▶** a narrow space or opening : *Light came through a crack in the door.* **3. claquement ▶** a sudden, sharp noise : *the crack of a whip.* **4. claquer ▶** a sharp, hard blow. SYN: break, split, open, slit, splinter.

crack down mesures de répressions contre ▶ to become more strict with rules or laws : *The police are cracking down on speeders by* *giving out more tickets.* **Note.** Also used as a NOUN: *a crackdown on the sale of illegal drugs.*

crack·er [krak-ur] NOUN, crackers. **craquelin, biscuit ▸** a thin, crisp piece of food, made in the same way as bread.

crack·le [krak-ul] VERB, crackled, crackling. **crépiter, grésiller ▸** to make a quick, sharp snapping sound.

cra·dle [KRAY-dul] NOUN, cradles. **1. berceau (-eaux) ▸** a small bed for a newborn baby, usually on rockers. **2. berceau (-eaux) ▸** the place where something starts : *Ancient Greece is considered the cradle of Western Civilization.* ▲ VERB, cradled, cradling. **bercer ▸** to hold as if in a cradle : *She cradled the puppy in her arms.* SYN: support, hold, carry.

craft [kraft] NOUN, crafts. **1. art, métier ▸** a special skill in doing or making something with the hands. Sewing, woodworking, and pottery are crafts. **Note.** A person who does this kind of work is an **artisan** or **craftsperson.** **2.** (plural, craft) **embarcation, barque ▸** a boat, a ship, or an aircraft : *A storm warning was sent to all small craft at sea.* **3. astuce, ruse ▸** skill in fooling or tricking others; cunning. SYN: skill, trade, art, handicraft. ☞ **p. 1163.**

cram [kram] VERB, crammed, cramming. **1. fourrer, entasser ▸** to force something into a tight place : *He crammed his clothes for the weekend into his suitcase.* **2. bachoter, préparer un examen ▸** to study hard for a test at the last minute : *Suzie crammed all day for tomorrow's exam.*

cramp [kramp] NOUN, cramps. **1. crampe ▸** a sudden, sharp pain that comes from the tightening of a muscle : *Basim got a cramp in his leg while swimming.* **2.** (usually cramps) **crampe, maux de ventre ▸** a sharp pain in the stomach or abdomen. ▲ VERB, cramped, cramping. **1. importuner, gêner ▸** to have or cause to have a cramp. **2. entasser, serrer ▸** to crowd into a tight space.

cran·ber·ry [KRAN-bair-ee] NOUN, cranberries. **canneberge ▸** a sour, shiny red berry that grows in wet places. Cranberries are used to make sauce, juice, and jelly. **Note.** The word *cranberry* is thought to be related to *crane,* because these birds live in the same swampy areas as the plant.

crane [krane] NOUN, cranes. **1. grue ▸** a tall waterbird with a long neck and very long, thin legs. **2. grue ▸** a large machine with a long movable arm. It is used to move heavy weights, as in the building of a road or tall building. ▲ VERB, craned, craning. **étirer le cou ▸** to stretch out the neck as a crane does : *The people in the back of the crowd craned their necks to see the famous movie star.*

crank [krank] NOUN, cranks. **1. manivelle ▸** a handle or rod that is turned to make a machine work : *I got tired turning the crank on the ice-*

cream maker. **2. excentrique ▸** a person who is very odd or who has very strange ideas : *Mom says that Mr. Harris is a crank, but I think he's just shy.* **3. grincheux (-euse), revêche ▸** a person who is often angry or irritated. ▲ VERB, cranked, cranking. **remonter ▸** to use or turn a crank : *My grandfather has an old car you have to crank to start.*

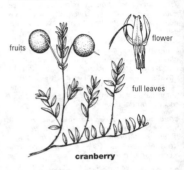

cranberry

crank·y [KRANK-ee] ADJECTIVE, crankier, crankiest. **grincheux (-euse), revêche ▸** often angry or irritated : *Chris is always cranky when she is tired.* SYN: cross, crabby, irritable.

crash [krash] VERB, crashed, crashing. **1. percuter, s'écraser, fracasser ▸** to go against something suddenly in a hard, noisy way : *The lamp crashed on the floor when the cat knocked it over.* **2. tomber en panne ▸** of a computer, to completely stop working, as from a loss of electrical power : *Always back up your work on a disk in case your computer crashes.* **3. s'effondrer ▸** to fail or collapse suddenly : *When the stock market crashes, many people lose their money.* ▲ NOUN, crashes. **1. collision, accident ▸** the act of crashing : *a car crash.* **2. fracas ▸** the noise made by this : *I heard the crash when the tree fell on the garage.* **3. faillite ▸** a sudden failure or collapse, as of a business. ▲ ADJECTIVE. **intensif (-ive) ▸** showing a very great effort over a short time : *Mary is taking a crash course in Spanish before she goes to Mexico.* SYN: strike, shatter, break, smash, clash.

crate [krate] NOUN, crates. **caisse, cageot ▸** a large box made of strips of wood : *The fruit was packed in crates to be shipped to market.*

cra·ter [KRAY-tur] NOUN, craters. **cratère ▸** a large hole in the ground, shaped like a bowl : *There are many craters on the surface of the moon.*

crave [krave] VERB, craved, craving. **avoir un besoin maladif ▸** to long for very much; desire : *I always crave ice cream.*

crawl [krol] VERB, crawled, crawling. **1. se traîner, ramper ▸** to move on the hands and knees, as a baby does before it learns to walk. **2. ramper ▸** to move in a way that is like the crawling of a baby : *"...plants that creep and crawl in the green grass forests."* (Margaret Wise Brown) **3. grouiller ▸** to be completely covered or filled with something : *The rotting wood was crawling with ants.* ▲ NOUN, crawls. **1. allure très lente, au pas ▸** the act of crawling ; a slow way of moving. **2. crawl ▸** a type of swimming stroke in which the swimmer lies face down in the water and moves the arms overhead.

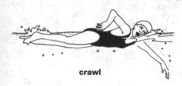

crawl

cray-on [KRAY-on] NOUN, crayons. **crayon ▸** a short stick of coloured wax or chalk, used for drawing.

cra-zy [KRAY-zee] ADJECTIVE, crazier, craziest. **1. fou (folle), cinglé (-ée), dingue ▸** not having a healthy mind ; insane. **2. idiot (idiote), fou (folle) ▸** not sensible ; foolish ; silly : *Playing in the snow in a bathing suit is a crazy thing to do.* **3.** *Informal.* **fou (folle) de, épris (-ise) ▸** very excited or enthusiastic : *She's crazy about horses and goes riding whenever she can.* **Note.** Something that is very popular for a short time is a craze.

creak [kreek] VERB, creaked, creaking. **grincer, craquer ▸** to make a sharp, squeaking sound : *"The wind...made the trees creak as the branches scratched against each other."* (Walter Farley) ▲ NOUN, creaks: *The old gate swung open with a creak.* ■ **creaky,** ADJECTIVE, creakier, creakiest: *a creaky floor.* ▸ **grincement, craquement.**

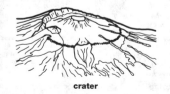

crater

cream [kreem] NOUN, creams. **1. crème ▸** the thick, yellowish part of milk that has fat in it. It rises to the top when whole milk is left standing. Cream can be separated from the milk for making butter or for use in other foods. **Note.** Something that is like cream or that has a lot of cream in it is creamy. **2. crème ▸** something that is smooth and thick like cream : *shaving cream.* **3. crème ▸** the colour of cream ; a pale-yellow shade of white. **4. la crème de ▸** the best part of something, as cream is thought to be the best part of milk : *The cream of professional basketball players will be playing in the all-star game.*

crease [krees] NOUN, creases. **pli, faux pli ▸** a line or mark made by fold or pressing something : *a crease in a pair of pants.* ▲ VERB, creased, creasing. **froisser, fripper, chiffonner, plisser ▸** to put a crease in something : *I creased my dress when I sat down, so I had to iron it again.*

cre-ate [kree-ATE] VERB, created, creating. **créer ▸** to cause something new to come into being : *The artist created a statue for the entrance to the zoo.* **Note.** Someone who creates is called a creator. ✐ **p. 464.**

cre-a-tion [kree-AY-shun] NOUN, creations. **1. création ▸** the creating of something : *"That was the wonderful thing about true creation. You made something nobody else on earth could make but you."* (Langston Hughes) **2. création ▸** something that has been created : *The beautiful ivory and soapstone sculptures are the creations of Inuit artists.* **3.** (the) Creation. **création ▸** the creating of the universe by God.

cre-a-tive [kree-AY-tiv] ADJECTIVE. **1. créatif (-ive) ▸** able to create things ; good at making new things or having new ideas : *My creative friend Beverly always comes up with ideas for new games.* **2. créatif (-ive), novateur (-trice) ▸** having or showing creativity : *Heather did a very creative science project in which she made a radio.*

crea-ture [KREE-chur] NOUN, creatures. **1. créature, bête, animal ▸** an animal of any kind : *The elephant is the largest creature I've ever seen.* **2. créature, personne ▸** any human being : *"What marvelous creatures we are!"* (Clarence Day) **3. créature, extraterrestre ▸** a strange or frightening being : *We saw a movie about creatures from outer space.*

cred-it [KRED-it] NOUN, credits. **1. crédit, honneur, mérite ▸** praise or honour for doing something good : *Erin gets the credit for our team song because she wrote it herself.* **2. à crédit ▸** a way of buying something and paying for it at a later date : *The Changs bought a TV on credit.* **3. crédit ▸** an amount of money in a person's favour in a business account : *Claire returned the sweater, and the store gave her a $20 credit.* **4. croire, accréditer, avoir confiance ▸** belief or faith in something ; trust : *I find* *it hard to credit their outlandish story.* **5. crédit ▶** a unit of work in school that counts toward graduation : *Lian is taking six credits this term.* ▲ VERB, credited, crediting. **créditer ▶** to get or give credit for something.

Cree [kree] NOUN. **1. cree ou Cri ▶** the largest group of Algonquian-speaking Aboriginals in Canada. **2. cri ▶** the language of the Cree people.

creek [kreek] NOUN, creeks. **1. crique, anse ▶** a small fresh-water stream. **2. ruisseau (-eaux) ▶** a small body of water that flows into a larger river. **Note.** The pronunciation "crick," still heard in some places, comes from the fact that the word used to be spelled *crick* or *crike*.

creep [kreep] VERB, crept, creeping. **1. ramper ▶** to move slowly and quietly; crawl : *The hunter crept silently through the woods.* **2. ramper, grimper ▶** to move or spread slowly : *The ivy crept up the garden wall.* **3. donner la chair de poule ▶** to feel as if things are crawling over one's skin : *The monster movie was so scary that it made my flesh creep.* ▲ NOUN, creeps. the creeps. *Informal.* **chose qui fait peur ▶** a feeling of being frightened or very uncomfortable : *That person is very odd; he gives me the creeps.* **■ creepy,** ADJECTIVE. **qui fait frissonner, terrifiant (-ante).**

cres·cent [KRES-unt] NOUN, crescents. **1. croissant de lune ▶** the shape of the moon when only a thin curved part of it is seen. **2. croissant ▶** something that has this shape.

crest [krest] NOUN, crests. **1. crête ▶** a group of feathers that sticks up on top of a bird's head. **2. sommet ▶** the highest part of something, such as a hill or wave : *The choppy waves were topped by white crests.*

cre·vasse [kruh-VAS] NOUN, crevasses. **crevasse ▶** a deep crack in the ice of a glacier.

crev·ice [KREV-is] NOUN, crevices. **fissure, fente ▶** a narrow opening or crack : *The mountain climber looked for crevices in the rock that she could use as a toehold as she climbed upward.*

crew [kroo] NOUN, crews. **1. équipage ▶** all the people who work on board a ship or aircraft : *That plane has a crew of 14.* **2. équipe ▶** a group of people working together on a certain job : *a road crew.*

crib [krib] NOUN, cribs. **1. berceau, lit d'enfant ▶** a small bed for a baby. A crib has high sides with bars to keep the baby from falling out. **2. mangeoire ▶** a small farm building that holds grain or corn. **3. mangeoire, crèche ▶** a box or trough that horses or cattle eat from.

crick·et[1] [KRIK-it] NOUN, crickets. **grillon ▶** a black or brown insect with long legs that looks like a small grasshopper. The male makes a chirping sound by rubbing its front wings together.

cricket

crick·et[2] NOUN. **cricket ▶** an outdoor game something like baseball, played with a ball by two teams of 11 players each.

crime [krime] NOUN, crimes. **1. crime, infraction, délit ▶** something that is against the law, especially something serious for which a person can be punished : *Murder, kidnapping, and robbery are crimes.* **2. crime, péché ▶** something thought of as cruel or very bad : *It's a crime to throw away all that food when so many people are hungry.* **☞ p. 1144.**

crim·i·nal [KRIM-uh-nul] NOUN, criminals. **criminel (-elle) ▶** a person who has committed a crime. ▲ ADJECTIVE. **1. criminel (-elle) ▶** having to do with crime : *A criminal lawyer defends people who are accused of crimes.* **2. criminel (-elle) ▶** being a crime : *Stealing a car is a criminal act.* **3. criminel (-elle) ▶** like a crime; very bad or cruel : *That is a criminal waste of food.* SYN: illegal, wrong, guilty, wicked, unlawful.

crim·son [KRIM-zun] NOUN, crimsons. **cramoisi ▶** a deep red colour. ▲ ADJECTIVE. **cramoisi (-ie) ▶** having this colour : *a crimson dress.*

cringe [krinj] VERB, cringed, cringing. **reculer ▶** to draw back or tremble with fear : *The dog cringed at the sound of thunder.*

crip·ple [KRIP-ul] NOUN, cripples. **estropié (-ée), boiteux (-euse) ▶** an older term for a person or an animal that is lame or unable to move a part of the body in a normal way. **Note.** Today it is considered rude to use *cripple* as a noun to refer to a person. ▲ VERB, crippled, crippling. **1. handicaper ▶** to make a person lame or crippled : *Until a vaccine was found, polio crippled many people.* **2. gravement endommager ▶** to make helpless or useless; cause major damage to : *The rainstorm crippled the city, knocking down telephone poles, electrical wires, and trees.*

cri·sis [KRY-sus] NOUN, crises [KRY-sees]. **crise ▶** an important point at which great change will take place; a time of danger or great difficulty : *The flooding of the river was a crisis in Quebec last spring.*

crisp [krisp] ADJECTIVE, crisper, crispest. **1. craquant (-ante), raide ▶** hard and dry, but easily broken into pieces : *crisp leaves.* **2. croquant (-ante) ▶** fresh and firm; not wilted : *crisp vegetables such as raw carrots.* **3. vif (vive),**

piquant (-ante) ▸ cool and refreshing; brisk : *a crisp October day.* **4. vif (vive), précis (-ise), tranchant (-ante)** ▸ short and exact; showing no doubt : *a paper written in crisp, clear sentences.* ▲ VERB, crisped, crisping. **raide** ▸ to make or become crisp. ■ **crisply,** ADVERB. ▸ **d'un ton tranchant, d'un ton acerbe.** ■ **crispness,** NOUN. ▸ **qualité croustillante, dureté, netteté.**

crit·ic [KRIT-ik] NOUN, critics. **1. critique** ▸ a person whose work is to judge what is good or bad about a book, play, painting, or other artistic work. **2. critique, censeur (-eure), détracteur (-trice)** ▸ a person who finds fault with someone or something : *Ms. Ginsberg has been an out-spoken critic of the prime minister's programs.*

crit·i·cal [KRIT-uh-kul] ADJECTIVE. **1. critique, sévère** ▸ looking for faults; likely to disapprove : *Her brother is a critical person who points out every little mistake she makes.* **2. critique** ▸ a well-thought-out judgment : *The editor's critical comments improved the story.* **3. critique, commentateur (-trice)** ▸ having to do with a critic or critics : *The book was a critical success, meaning that most critics thought it was good.* **4. critique, dangereux (-euse), difficile, grave** ▸ having to do with a crisis; very serious or dangerous : *The lost campers had a critical shortage of food.* ■ **critically,** ADVERB. **d'un œil critique, de façon critique** ▸ in a critical way : *The boss looked critically at Judy when she walked in two hours late.* **Note.** Hospitals use the term *critical* for patients who are in danger of dying.

crit·i·cize [KRIT-uh-size] VERB, criticized, criticizing. **1. critiquer, désapprouver** ▸ to find fault with something; disapprove. **2. critiquer, censurer, examiner, dénigrer** ▸ to judge what is good or bad about something; act as a critic. ■ **criticism,** NOUN, criticisms. ▸ **critiquer, analyser, juger. 1. critiquer, faire la critique de** ▸ the act of finding fault. **2. critique** ▸ the act of saying what is good or bad about something, such as a book or movie.

croak [kroke] NOUN, croaks. **croassement** ▸ a deep, harsh sound, such as that made by a frog. ▲ VERB, croaked, croaking. **croasser** ▸ to make this sound.

cro·chet [KROH-shay] VERB, crocheted, crocheting. **crochet** ▸ to make cloth by connecting loops of thread or yarn with a hooked needle : *My grandmother crocheted this tablecloth many years ago.*

croc·o·dile [KROK-uh-DILE] NOUN, crocodiles. **crocodile** ▸ a large animal with short legs, a long tail, thick scaly skin, and a long narrow head. it is a reptile that lives in rivers and swamps in warm areas of the United States, Africa, and Asia. Crocodiles are related to alligators, but they are faster and have a shorter snout.

crook [krook] NOUN, crooks. **1. escroc, filou, arnaqueur (-euse)** ▸ a person who is not honest ; a criminal. **2. coude** ▸ a bent or curved part : *Sara held the cat in the crook of her arm.* ▲ VERB, crooked, crooking. **courber, recourber, plier** ▸ to curve or hook.

crook·ed [KROOK-id] ADJECTIVE. **1. courbé (-ée), crochu (-ue), tordu (-ue), tortueux (-euse)** ▸ not straight; bent or twisted : *They followed a crooked path through the woods.* **2. malhonnête** ▸ not honest : *My father thinks that that sales scheme is crooked.*

crop [krop] NOUN, crops. **1.** (also **crops**) **produit, récolte** ▸ a plant grown to be used as food or to make something : *Wheat is an important crop in Canada.* **2. récolte, cueillette, moisson** ▸ the amount of a certain plant grown and harvested at one time : *this year's lettuce crop.* **3. récolte** ▸ a group of people or things that appear at the same time, as a crop does : *The Jays have a whole crop of new players this spring.* **4. jabot** ▸ a pouch in the neck of a bird, near the bottom of its throat, where food is partly digested. **5. cravache, manche** ▸ a short whip with a loop at the end, used in horseback riding. ▲ VERB, cropped, cropping. **couper** ▸ to trim; cut off the top or side of : *to crop a photograph.* SYN: produce, growth, yield, harvest.

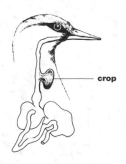

crop

cro·quet [KROH-kay] NOUN. **croquet** ▸ an outdoor game played by hitting wooden balls through a series of wire hoops known as wickets. The player hits the ball with a wooden stick known as a mallet.

cross [kros] NOUN, crosses. **1. croix** ▸ an object or mark formed by a stick or bar with another bar across it in the shape of a "t" or an "x". **2. the cross. croix** ▸ the symbol of the Christian religion, representing the cross on which Jesus died. **3. croisement, mélange** ▸ a mixing of different kinds of animals or plants : *A mule is a cross between a horse and a donkey.* ▲ VERB, crossed, crossing. **1. traverser** ▸ to go from one side of something to the other : *"Try as he might, poor Cowherd couldn't cross the river."* (Julie Lawson) **2. barrer, rayer ▸** to draw a line through : *Melissa crossed out the words that were spelled incorrectly.* **3. croiser ▸** to put or place one thing across another : *Pia crosses her arms when she gets angry.* **4. contrarier, fâcher ▸** to disagree with or oppose : *They didn't like the boss's idea, but no one was about to cross him.* ▲ ADJECTIVE, crosser, crossest. **1. croisement, carrefour ▸** placed or going across : *A crossroad is one that crosses another road.* **2. de mauvaise humeur, en colère, fâché (-ée), boudeur (-euse) ▸** angry or grouchy. **Note.** Combines with many words to form compounds : crosswalk, crosscheck, cross section, crossword. ✐ **p. 152.**

cross·ing [KROS-ing] NOUN, crossings. **traversée, croisement ▸** a place where something crosses or is crossed : *A street sign saying "School Crossing" means that children cross at that place on their way to and from school.*

crotch [kroch] NOUN, crotches. **fourche, entrejambe ▸** the place where the body or a pair of pants divides into two legs.

crouch [krowch] VERB, crouched, crouching. **s'accroupir, se tapir ▸** to stoop down or bend low ; squat : *The cat crouched, preparing to leap onto the windowsill.* ▲ NOUN, crouches. **accroupissement ▸** a position of crouching : *A catcher in baseball gets into a crouch as he or she waits for the pitch.*

crow[1] [kroh] NOUN, crows. **corneille, corbeau (-eaux) ▸** a large, shiny black bird that makes a harsh noise that sounds like "caw". Crows have long been considered pests by farmers, but studies show that they eat thousands of harmful insects each year.

crow[2] VERB, crowed, crowing. **1. chant du coq, cocorico ▸** to make a loud cry, as a rooster does : *The rooster crowed as soon as the sun started to rise.* **2. cri de triomphe, chanter victoire ▸** to speak in a happy or proud way : *"I'm good," she crowed. "I'm better than you."* (Nancy Willard)

crow·bar [KROH-bar] NOUN, crowbars. **levier, pied-de-biche ▸** a heavy steel or iron bar bent slightly at one end, used to lift or pry heavy things.

crowd [krowd] NOUN, crowds. **1. foule, masse ▸** a large number of people gathered together in one place : *There was a crowd of over 50,000 people at the game.* **2. bande, clique ▸** a group of people : *He got into trouble by hanging around with a bad crowd.* ▲ VERB, crowded, crowding. **entasser, bousculer, serrer ▸** to put or force too many people or things into too small a space : *The students crowded into the gym for an announcement.* ✐ **p. 275, 321.**

✐ Writing Tips

Crossword Puzzle

A crossword puzzle is a word puzzle that is solved by answering clues and then fitting the correct words into the crossword grid. (The grid is the pattern the empty squares make.) The letters of the word or words that answer the clue are written in a set number of squares.

• *Crossword puzzles can be on a specific theme or subject, or be about general knowledge. They also have different types of clues, such as questions, fill-in-the-blanks, synonyms or antonyms, or words or phrases that give clues to the answer.*

crown [krown] NOUN, crowns. **1. couronne ▸** a special covering or ornament for the head, worn by a king, queen, or another ruler as a sign of power. Crowns are often made of gold and have jewels set in them. **2. monarchie, règne ▸** the rank or power of a king or queen. **3. couronne de roses ou d'épines ▸** a wreath of flowers worn on the head as a sign of winning some honour. **4. couronne ▸** an honour or championship : *the heavyweight boxing crown.* **5. sommet ▸** the highest point of something : *The top of the head is called the crown.* ▲ VERB, crowned, crowning. **1. couronnement ▸** to give royal power to a ruler by placing a crown on his or her head. **2. couronner ▸** to cover the top of : *Snow crowned the peak of the mountain.*

Crown corporation Société d'état ▸ a company or agency owned by the Canadian or a provincial government : *Air Canada and the CBC are Crown corporations.*

Crown land Terre de la couronne ▸ public land ; land that is owned by the government.

cru·cial [KROO-shul] ADJECTIVE. **critique, crucial (-iale, -iaux), décisif (-ive) ▸** being a very important test or issue ; of deciding importance : *This exam is crucial for your final mark.*

crude [krood] ADJECTIVE, cruder, crudest. **1. brut (brute), non raffiné (-ée) ▸** in a natural or raw state : *Crude oil is treated with chemicals before it is used in cars.* **2. rudimentaire, qui manque de fini ▸** not done or made with skill ; rough : *The crude map showed a row of wavy lines for the ocean.* **3. grossier (-ière) ▸** without taste or good manners ; not polite : *I can't believe that his parents put up with his crude behaviour.* SYN : raw, harsh, unfinished, rough, coarse.

cru·el [KROO-ul] ADJECTIVE, crueller, cruellest. (also crueler, cruelest) **1. cruel (-elle), brutal**

(-ale, -aux), méchant (-ante), sadique ▸ willing to give pain and suffering to others; not kind; brutal : *That was a cruel practical joke.* 2. cruel (-elle), atroce, douloureux (-euse), affligeant (-ante) ▸ causing pain and suffering : *"A cruel blast of wind swept out of the north, driving chilling swirls of icy fog around them."* (James Houston) ▪ **cruelly,** ADVERB. ▸ cruellement. ▪ **cruelty,** NOUN, cruelties. ▸ cruauté. SYN : mean, unkind, heartless, brutal, ruthless.

cruise [krooz] VERB, cruised, cruising. 1. croiser ▸ to go by ship from place to place, especially for enjoyment. 2. vitesse de croisière ▸ to move or ride in a slow easy way : *The teens cruised down Main Street in Anton's new car.* ▲ NOUN, cruises. croisière ▸ a trip by ship taken for enjoyment. Note. The cruising speed of a plane, ship, or car is the speed at which it makes the best use of fuel.

cruis-er [KROOZ-ur] NOUN, cruisers. 1. yacht ▸ a motorboat with a cabin for living on board. 2. auto-patrouille ▸ a police car used for patrolling an area. 3. croiseur ▸ a large warship that is faster than a battleship but has fewer guns.

crumb [krum] NOUN, crumbs. 1. miette ▸ tiny pieces of dried food, especially a baked food such as bread, cake, crackers, or cookies : *The birds ate all the crumbs.* 2. miette, fragment ▸ a very small bit or amount : *Starting with just a few crumbs of evidence, the detective was able to figure out who the killer was.*

crum-ble [KRUM-bul] VERB, crumbled, crumbling. 1. émietter ▸ to break into small bits : *He crumbled the dry bread to feed to the birds.* 2. s'effondrer, s'écrouler ▸ to fall into pieces. Note. Often used as an ADJECTIVE: *Only crumbling ruins of buildings are left in the ancient city.* SYN : crush, wrinkle, break, fall apart.

crunch [krunch] VERB, crunched, crunching. faire craquer ▸ to move with or make a noisy, crackling sound : *The snow crunched beneath her boots as she walked.* ▲ NOUN, crunches. craquement, crissement ▸ the act or sound of crunching.

cru-sade [KROO-sade] NOUN, crusades. 1. croisade ▸ a strong movement or fight for something good or against something bad : *a crusade for human rights; a crusade against hunger.* 2. Crusade. croisade ▸ one of a series of wars fought from the 11th to 13th centuries by the Christians of western Europe to try to recapture the Holy Land (where Jesus had lived) from the Muslims. ▲ VERB, crusaded, crusading. militer, partir en croisade ▸ to take part in a crusade : *Martin Luther King crusaded for civil rights.* Note. Someone who crusades is a crusader. SYN : cause, movement, campaign.

crush [krush] VERB, crushed, crushing. 1. écraser, broyer, presser ▸ to press or squeeze something hard enough to break or harm it : *He can crush a pop can with one hand.* 2. tasser, entasser ▸ to crowd or press tightly : *"They were all crushed in the doorway as the whole school seemed to arrive at once."* (Louise Fitzhugh) ▲ NOUN, crushes. 1. foule, cohue ▸ the act of crushing, or the state of being crushed : *There was a crush of people around the exit from the subway station.* 2. avoir un béguin ▸ a strong and often foolish liking for a person : *My brother Kareem has a crush on my best friend.* SYN : pound, demolish, subdue, press, squeeze.

crust [krust] NOUN, crusts. 1. croûte ▸ the hard, crisp outer part of bread, rolls, or pies : *My dad always makes the crust for a pie, and I make the filling.* 2. croûte ▸ any hard outer covering or layer : *The earth's crust is up to 35 km thick.* ▪ **crusty,** ADJECTIVE. ▸ croustillant (-ante).

crus-ta-cean [krus-TAY-shun] NOUN, crustaceans. crustacé ▸ any of a large group of animals that have a hard shell and a jointed body and live mostly in water. Crustaceans include lobsters, crabs, shrimp, crayfish, and barnacles. Many crustaceans, such as crabs, are eaten as food.

crutch [kruch] NOUN, crutches. 1. soutien, support, béquille ▸ a support used to help a lame person walk. 2. béquille ▸ anything that gives help or support to something that is weak : *A calculator can be a crutch that prevents math students from working out problems on their own.*

cry [kry] VERB, cried, crying. 1. pleurer ▸ to shed tears; weep. 2. crier ▸ to call out loudly : *"Watch out for that rock!" she cried.* ▲ NOUN, cries. 1. cri ▸ a loud call or shout. 2. aboiement ▸ the special sound that an animal makes : *"Nights were filled with the lonely cry of the loon."* (Holling C. Holling) SYN : sob, weep, wail, bawl.

cryp-tic [KRIP-tik] ADJECTIVE. secret (-ète), énigmatique ▸ having a hidden meaning; difficult to understand : *a cryptic code.*

crys-tal [KRIS-tul] NOUN, crystals. 1. cristal (-aux) ▸ a solid object with flat surfaces that form a regular patter : *crystals of salt or sugar.* 2. cristal (-aux) ▸ a clear mineral that has no colour and can be seen through. Crystal looks like pure ice, and is a form of quartz. 3. cristal (-aux) ▸ a very fine, clear glass used to make vases, plates, bowls, and other things. ◉ p. 397.

cub [kub] NOUN, cubs. 1. petit de ▸ the young of certain animals, such as the bear, wolf, lion, or tiger. 2. jeune ▸ a person who is young and inexperienced : *Ernest Hemingway was a cub reporter for a newspaper.*

cube [kyoob] NOUN, cubes. 1. cube ▸ a solid figure with six flat, square sides that are equal in size. 2. cube ▸ something shaped like a cube : *sugar cubes.* 3. racine cubique ▸ the result of multiplying a number by itself twice : *The cube of 3 is 27, because $3 \times 3 \times 3 = 27$.* ▲ VERB, cubed, cubing. **1. couper en cubes, couper en dés ▸** to cut or form something into cubes : *to cube potatoes.* **2. mettre au carré ▸** to multiply a number by itself two times : *The number 2 cubed is equal to 2 x 2 x 2, or 8.*

cu‑bic [KYOO-bik] ADJECTIVE. **1. cubique ▸** having the shape of a cube : *Most of these toy blocks are cubic.* **2. volume, mesure ▸** having length, width, and thickness.

cuck‑oo [KOO-koo] NOUN, cuckoos. **coucou ▸** a brown bird with a long tail whose call sounds like its name. The European cuckoo lays its eggs in other birds' nests instead of hatching them itself.

cu‑cum‑ber [KYOO-kum-bur] NOUN, cucumbers. **concombre ▸** a long green vegetable with a tough skin. It is often used in salads and to make pickles.

cud [kud] NOUN, cuds. **nourriture qui a été ruminée ▸** the partly chewed food that cows, sheep, and certain other animals bring back into the mouth from the stomach to be chewed again for easier digestion.

cud‑dle [KUD-dul] VERB, cuddled, cuddling. **serrer amoureusement, câliner, caresser, embrasser ▸** hold closely in one's arms or lap; hug : *Sharon cuddled the new puppies in her arms.*

cue[1] [kyoo] NOUN, cues. **1. signal ▸** in a play or movie, a certain speech, movement, or other signal used to tell an actor to begin to do something : *When she opens the letter, that's your cue to walk onto the stage.* **2. signal, suggestion, indice ▸** any hint or suggestion as to what to do : *For a lot of people, a TV commercial is a cue to change the channel.* ▲ VERB, cued, cueing, or cuing. **donner le signal ▸** to give a person a cue : *I'll cue you when it's time for you to go on stage.*

cue[2] NOUN, cues. **queue de billard ▸** a long, thin stick used to hit a ball in the game of pool or billiards.

cuff[1] [kuf] NOUN, cuffs. **poignet, manchette, revers ▸** a band or fold of cloth at the bottom of a shirt sleeve or pants leg.

off the cuff à l'improviste, au pied levé ▸ without any preparation : *That candidate often makes mistakes when he speaks off the cuff.*

cuff[2] VERB, cuffed, cuffing. **gifler ▸** to strike with the open hand; slap. ▲ NOUN, cuffs. **gifle ▸** a blow from the open hand.

cui‑sine [kwih-ZEEN] NOUN, cuisines. **gastronomie, cuisine ▸** a style or type of cooking : *French cuisine.*

cul‑prit [KUL-prit] NOUN, culprits. **coupable ▸** someone who is guilty of a crime or of doing something wrong.

cult [kult] NOUN, cults. **1. culte ▸** a way of worshipping. **2. culte, idole ▸** an admiration or belief that lots of people share : *the cult of comic books.* ▲ ADJECTIVE: **de culte ▸** *a cult film.*

cul‑ti‑vate [KUL-tuh-VATE] VERB, cultivated, cultivating. **1. cultiver ▸** to prepare the ground for growing crops; plant and care for crops : *Ishmael cultivated his garden by turning over the soil and adding fertilizer.* **2. cultiver, développer ▸** to improve or develop something through effort, as if raising a crop of plants : *Annabelle tried hard to cultivate a friendship with Greta.* ▲ NOUN, cultivation. **agriculture, culture ▸** the act of cultivating land.

cul‑ture [KUL-chur] NOUN, cultures. **1. culture ▸** all the beliefs, habits, and customs that are common to a certain group of people at a certain time in history. Culture is made up of such things as the way people live, the work they do and the things they use for work, and the values and beliefs they share. **2. culture ▸** the qualities found in a human society that is highly developed, such as art, science, and education : *The Renaissance was a time when culture was at a high point in western Europe.* **3. culture ▸** good taste, good manners, and an appreciation for learning and the arts : *a person of great culture.* **Note.** A person of great culture is said to be **cultured. 4. culture ▸** the growing of bacteria or viruses for scientific study.

cun‑ning [KUN-ing] ADJECTIVE. **astucieux (-euse), malin (-igne) ▸** clever at fooling others : *The thieves had a cunning plan for robbing the store.* ▲ NOUN. **finesse, astuce, ruse, adresse ▸** cleverness at fooling others. ■ **cunningly,** ADVERB. **▸ astucieusement, finement, avec ruse.**

cup [kup] NOUN, cups. **1. tasse, coupe ▸** a small open container, usually with a handle, used mainly to hold coffee, tea, soup, and other hot drinks. **2. tasse ▸** a unit of measure used in cooking. One cup equals about 227 mL. ▲ VERB, cupped, cupping. **mettre en forme de coupe ▸** to make into the shape of a cup : *Thomas cupped his hands together to get a drink of water from the stream.*

cup‑board [KUB-urd] NOUN, cupboards. **placard ▸** a cabinet or closet with shelves, used for storing dishes, food, and other items.

curb [kurb] NOUN, curbs. **1. trottoir, bord ▸** the raised concrete edge of a street : *Mom pulled the car up close to the curb to load the luggage.* **2. mettre un frein à ▸** something that holds back or restrains : *The mayor wants to put a curb on the city's spending.* ▲ VERB, curbed, curbing. **réduire, restreindre ▸** to hold back or control something : *Many people believe that drinking grapefruit juice curbs your appetite and helps you lose weight.* SYN : check, stop, hold, control, restrain.

cure [kyoor] VERB, cured, curing. **1. guérir ▸** to bring or come back to health, especially by the use of medical treatment : *The doctor cured the child of the illness.* **2. se déshabituer, éliminer,**

remédier à, guérir ▶ to get rid of something that is thought to be like a sickness : *I've finally cured myself of the habit of biting my nails.* **3. traiter** ▶ to preserve or treat something by drying, smoking, or salting : *Simon cured the meat and fish by drying them in the sun.* ▲ NOUN, cures. **remède, guérison** ▶ something that cures : *At this time there is no cure for the common cold.* 📖 **p. 1159.**

cur·few [KUR-fyoo] NOUN, curfews. **1. couvre-feu** ▶ a rule or law saying that people have to be off the streets by a fixed time of night. **2. couvre-feu** ▶ any rule that something must end by a certain time of night : *The players have a 10:00 curfew the night before a game.*

cu·ri·ous [KYOOR-ee-us] ADJECTIVE. **1. curieux (-euse)** ▶ very interested in finding out about things and people : *"How was it down there?" asked Mr. Little, who was always curious to know about places he had never been to."* (E.B. White) **2. curieux (-euse)** ▶ wanting to know about things that are not one's proper concern ; nosy. **3. curieux (-euse), bizarre, singulier (-ière)** ▶ very strange, rare, or unusual : *a curious light shining in the distance.* ■ **curiously,** ADVERB. **curieusement, singulièrement** ▶ in a curious way : *Curiously, my mother and father were born on the same date.* SYN: inquisitive, searching.

cu·ri·os·i·ty [KYOOR-ee-OS-uh-tee] NOUN, curiosities. **1. curiosité** ▶ a strong interest in finding out about different things and people : *"He had the curiosity to open the door and listen, and look after them."* (Charles Dickens) **2. curiosité, rareté** ▶ something that is very strange, rare, or unusual : *The Spruce Goose was the largest plane ever built, but it flew only once and is now just a curiosity.*

curl [kurl] VERB, curled, curling. **1. boucler, friser** ▶ to form into coils or rings : *to curl one's hair.* **2. s'enrouler** ▶ (also curl up) to move or be in a curved shape : *The exhausted little girl curled up on her father's lap and went to sleep.* **3. s'enrouler, se pelotonner** ▶ to play the game of curling. ▲ NOUN, curls. **jouer au curling** ▶ anything that forms a curl. ■ **curly,** ADJECTIVE, curlier, curliest: *curly hair.* ▶ **bouclé (-ée), frisé (-ée). Note.** A curler is also a person who plays the game of curling.

cur·ling [kur-ling] NOUN. **curling** ▶ a game played on ice with two teams (known as rinks) of four players each. Players take turns sliding heavy stones from one end of the ice to the other.

cur·ren·cy [KUR-un-see] NOUN, currencies. **monnaie, argent, devise** ▶ the form of money that a country uses : *Canadian currency is based on the dollar.*

cur·rent [KUR-unt] ADJECTIVE. **courant (-ante), en cours, actuel (-elle)** ▶ belonging to the present time : *Current events are the things that are*

going on now. ▲ NOUN, currents. **1. courant (-ante)** ▶ a flow of moving gas or liquid ; a stream : *The twigs floated downstream with the current of the river.* **2. courant** ▶ a flow of electricity through a wire or other object : *A thicker wire carries more current.* **3. courant (-ante), tendance** ▶ a general trend : *The current of public opinion seems to support the prime minister's decision.* ■ **currently,** ADVERB. **actuellement, en ce moment** ▶ at this time ; now : *There are currently about 50,000 people living in our town.* 🖉 **p. 156.**

cur·ric·u·lum [kuh-RIK-yuh-lum] NOUN, curriculums or curricula. **programme** ▶ all the subjects that are offered in a school as a course of study.

cur·ry [KUR-ee] NOUN, curries. **1. curry** ▶ (also curry powder) a mixture of cumin, ginger, coriander, and other spices, used for cooking. **2. curry, cari** ▶ a dish or sauce made with curry.

curse [kurs] NOUN, curses. **1. malédiction** ▶ a wish that evil or harm will happen to someone, often made by calling on God or a spirit : *In old fairy tales, a wicked witch sometimes put a curse on people to make them sleep for a long time.* **2. malédiction, fléau (-eaux), malheur, calamité** ▶ trouble or evil that happens to someone, as if from a curse : *War is a curse of humankind.* **3. juron** ▶ a word or words used in swearing ; language that is considered very rude to use. ▲ VERB, cursed, cursing. **1. maudire** ▶ to call for a curse on someone or something. **2. jurer, saorer** ▶ to use bad language ; swear. **3. être affligé de** ▶ to cause or be caused harm by a curse : *She is cursed with a bad back that aches all the time.*

cur·sor [KUR-sur] NOUN, cursors. **curseur** ▶ a marker on a computer screen that shows where the user is working. A cursor often blinks, and may be a small line, a spot of light, an arrow, or another shape.

cur·tain [KUR-tun] NOUN, curtains. **1. rideau (-eaux)** ▶ a large piece of fabric hung across a room or over a window. **2. rideau (-eaux)** ▶ a large hanging cloth or screen that separates the stage of a theatre from the audience. **3. rideau (-eaux), voile** ▶ anything that covers or hides something as a curtain does : *A thick curtain of fog hung over the valley.* ▲ VERB, curtained, curtaining. **garnir de rideaux** ▶ to provide with a curtain : *In a hospital room, each bed usually can be curtained off from the rest of the room.*

curve [kurv] NOUN, curves. **1. courbe** ▶ a line that bends smoothly in one direction : *the curve of a rainbow.* **2. courbe, tournant, virage** ▶ anything that is shaped like a curve ; a round or bending part : *a curve in the road.* **3.** (also curveball) **balle courbe ou balle recourbée** ▶ a pitch in baseball that moves to the side, from right to left if the pitcher is right-handed. ▲ VERB, curved, curving. **se courber, s'infléchir** ▶ to move in or have the shape of a curve.

cush·ion [KUSH-un] NOUN, cushions. **1. coussin** ▸ a pillow filled with a soft material and used for sitting, lying, or resting. **2. coussin** ▸ something that is like a cushion : *A hovercraft is a vehicle that travels over water on a cushion of air.* ▲ VERB, cushioned, cushioning. **1. rembourrer, mettre un coussin** ▸ to supply with a cushion. **2. amortir, atténuer** ▸ to soften or reduce a shock, as a cushion would : *The soft snow cushioned the skier's fall.*

cus·tard [KUS-turd] NOUN, custards. **crème anglaise, crème renversée, crème pâtissière** ▸ a sweet dessert made of milk, eggs, and sugar.

cus·to·dy [KUS-tuh-dee] NOUN, custodies. **garde** ▸ the condition of being under the care of something or someone in authority : *The police held the suspected bank robbers in custody until they could go before a judge.*

cus·tom [KUS-tum] NOUN, customs. **1. coutume, usage, habitude** ▸ the way things are normally done by people in general; a usual way of acting that goes on over the years : *It is a custom in many countries for families to take a vacation during the summer.* **2. coutume, habitude** ▸ one person's usual way of acting; a habit : *"It was his custom after dinner to take a walk."* (James Thurber) **3. customs. douane** ▸ a tax paid on goods brought into a country from somewhere else, or the office that inspects these goods and collects the tax. ▲ ADJECTIVE. **sur mesure, sur commande** ▸ made in a special way for one person : *custom clothes.* SYN: tradition, habit, practice, way, manner.

cus·tom·ar·y [KUS-tuh-MAIR-ee] ADJECTIVE. **habituel (-elle), coutumier (-ière), ordinaire** ▸ what is commonly or usually done; based on custom : *It is customary to give presents on someone's birthday.* ■ **customarily,** ADVERB: ▸ **habituellement, ordinairement.** *That door is customarily kept locked.*

cus·tom·er [KUS-tuh-mur] NOUN, customers. **client (-te)** ▸ someone who buys something or uses some service, especially a person who buys something at a store.

cut [kut] VERB, cut, cutting. **1. couper, découper** ▸ to make an opening in something using a sharp tool or edge : *to cut a cake.* **2. couper, blesser, affecter** ▸ to have or get an injury from something sharp : *She cut her finger* on the broken glass. **3. couper, croiser, traverser** ▸ to move or go as if by cutting : *He cut across the field on his way home.* **4. couper, tailler** ▸ to make something shorter or smaller, by or as if by cutting : *to cut one's hair.* ▲ NOUN, cuts. **1. coupure** ▸ something that is cut or that comes from cutting : *Marshall has a cut on his foot.* **2. coupure, réduction, diminution** ▸ the act of taking away or making smaller : *a salary cut; a cut in taxes* SYN: clip, snip, trim, contract, shorten.

cute [kyoot] ADJECTIVE, cuter, cutest. **mignon (-onne)** ▸ pretty and charming; pleasing to the eye or mind : *The baby looks cute in her fuzzy pink jacket.* **Note.** Cute is usually used for something that is attractive in a light or delicate way SYN: pretty, attractive, charming.

cut·ler·y [KUT-lur-ee] NOUN. **1. coutellerie** ▸ tools for cutting such as knives and scissors. **2. couverts** ▸ tools for preparing and eating food, such as a fork, knife, and spoon.

cut·ting [KUT-ing] NOUN, cuttings. **1. coupure** ▸ a piece cut off something : *Janie used cuttings from the newspaper in her science report.* **2. bouture** ▸ a stem or twig cut from a plant and able to grow roots and develop a new plant. ▲ ADJECTIVE. **1. coupant (-ante), tranchant (-ante)** ▸ sharp and able to cut : *the cutting edge of a knife.* **2. blessant (-ante), cinglant (-ante), incisif (-ive)** ▸ hurting another's feelings; insulting : *a cutting remark.*

cy·cle [SY-kul] NOUN, cycles. **1. cycle** ▸ something that happens regularly in the same order over and over again : *The four seasons of the year are a cycle.* **2. cycle** ▸ a series of acts making one complete operation : *A washing-machine cycle includes soaking, washing, rinsing, and spinning.* **3. cycle** ▸ a short word for bicycle, motorcycle, tricycle, and so on. ▲ VERB, cycled, cycling. **cyclisme** ▸ to ride a bicycle, motorcycle, and so on. **Note.** A person who rides a cycle is a cyclist.

cy·clone [SY-klone] NOUN, cyclones. **cyclone** ▸ a storm in which winds move rapidly in a circle around a centre of low air pressure, which also moves.

cyl·in·der [SIL-un-dur] NOUN, cylinders. **1. cylindre** ▸ a hollow shape like that of a pipe or tube. **2. cylindre** ▸ something having this shape.

📝 Word Builder

Current, present, and ***popular*** are synonyms that describe what is new or what now exists. ***Current*** emphasizes recent things that are happening or popular: *Floor hockey is the current fad during school lunch hours.* ***Present*** describes what is happening right now, but it may not be happening in the near future: *With our present team, we should make it to the finals.* ***Popular*** describes something that is seen or done a lot at a specific time or place: *Overalls are the popular outfit at school this fall.*

■ **cylindrical,** ADJECTIVE: ▶ **cylindrique.** *Tennis balls come in cylindrical cans.*

cym·bal [SIM-bul] NOUN, cymbals. **cymbale** ▶ a musical instrument that is a round metal plate. A cymbal is hit with another cymbal or a drumstick. 👁 **p. 538.**

cyst [sist] NOUN, cysts. **kyste** ▶ an abnormal saclike growth filled with liquid or hard material. Both humans and animals can develop cysts.

D d

dinosaur

d, D [dee] d's, D's. **1. d, D** ▶ the fourth letter of the English alphabet. **2. D** ▶ the fourth-highest mark, grade, or level.

dab [dab] VERB, dabbed, dabbing. **tamponner** ▶ to touch in a light or gentle way : *He dabbed at the spot on his shirt.*

dad [dad] NOUN, dads. (also daddy) *Informal.* **papa, père** ▶ father.

daf-fo-dil [DAF-uh-dil] NOUN, daffodils. **jonquille** ▶ a plant that has long, thin leaves and yellow or white flowers. Daffodils grow from bulbs and bloom in the spring.

dag-ger [DAG-ur] NOUN, daggers. **poignard, dague** ▶ a small knife with a short, pointed blade.

dai-ly [DAY-lee] ADJECTIVE. **quotidien (-ienne)** ▶ done, happening, or appearing every day : *Grandpa reads the daily paper every morning.* ▲ ADVERB. **quotidiennement** ▶ day after day ; every day : *Please water the plants daily while we're away.* ▲ NOUN, dailies. **quotidien** ▶ a newspaper that is printed every day.

dain-ty [DANE-tee] ADJECTIVE, daintier, daintiest. **menu (-ue), délicat (-ate)** ▶ pretty or graceful in a light, delicate way : *The ballet dancer took small, dainty steps.* ■ **daintily,** ADVERB. ▶ **délicatement.** "*She was peeling a fig daintily with a knife.*" (Pearl Buck) SYN: delicate, small, refined, pretty.

dair-y [DAIR-ee] NOUN, dairies. **1. laiterie** ▶ a place where milk and cream are made into butter and cheese. **2. crémerie** ▶ a place where milk products are sold. **3. ferme laitière** ▶ a farm where cows are kept to produce milk.

dai-sy [DAY-zee] NOUN, daisies. **marguerite, pâquerette** ▶ a plant that has a flower of white, pink, or yellow petals around a yellow centre. 👁 **p. 250.**

Da-ko-ta [duh-KOH-tuh] NOUN. **1. Dakota** ▶ the Aboriginal people living on the southern plains of Western Canada and in the northwestern United States. **2. dakota** ▶ the language of the Dakota people.

dam [dam] NOUN, dams. **barrage, digue** ▶ a wall built across a river or creek to hold back the flow of water. ▲ VERB, dammed, damming. (usually used with up) **1. endiguer** ▶ to build a dam across ; hold back by a dam : *Sometimes, beavers dam a stream to build a place to live.* **2. retenir, faire obstacle** ▶ to block or hold back : *The leaves dammed up the drain.* 👁 **p. 400.**

dam-age [DAM-ij] NOUN, damages. **dommage** ▶ harm or injury that makes something less valuable or useful : *The river flooded, causing a great deal of damage to the city.* ▲ VERB, damaged, damaging. **endommager** ▶ to harm or injure ; hurt : *The accident damaged the front of the car.* SYN: ruin, spoil, harm, hurt, injure, sabotage.

damp [damp] ADJECTIVE, damper, dampest. **humide** ▶ a little wet ; moist : "*Sure enough, on a bare patch of ground I found fresh tracks. They showed up clearly on the damp earth.*" (Janet Foster) ▲ NOUN. **humidité, moiteur** ▶ a slight wetness ; moisture : *The grass was damp with dew.* ▲ VERB, damped, damping. **étouffer, couvrir** ▶ to check ; restrain : *to damp a fire.* ■ **dampness,** NOUN. ▶ **humidité, moiteur.** SYN: moist, humid, drizzly, drippy, wet.

damp-en [DAM-pun] VERB, dampened, dampening. **1. humecter** ▶ to make or become damp : *She dampened the cloth to wipe off the table.* **2. décourager** ▶ to make less happy or pleasant : "*He's never out to dampen your spirits or hurt you.*" (Alice Walker)

dance [dans] VERB, danced, dancing. **1. danser** ▶ to move the body in time to music or in a certain pattern of steps : *Everyone began to dance as soon as the music started.* **2. danser** ▶ to move in a quick, lively way : *The wildflowers were dancing in the spring breeze.* ▲ NOUN, dances. **1. danse** ▶ a certain set of steps or movements in time to music : *The waltz is a famous dance that began in Europe in the 1700s.* **2. danse, soirée dansante** ▶ a party where people dance : *The school dance is on*

Friday night. **Note.** A person who dances is a **dancer** (p. 1126.). p. 1122.

dan·de·li·on [DAN-duh-LY-un *or* DAN-dee-LY-un] NOUN, dandelions. **pissenlit ▸** a plant with a bright-yellow flower and long leaves with ragged edges. Dandelion leaves are sometimes eaten in salads. **Note.** The word *dandelion* comes from *dent de lion* (French for "tooth of the lion"). The leaves were thought to look like teeth.

dan·ger [DANE-jur] NOUN, dangers. **1. danger ▸** a possibility that something bad or harmful will happen : *Signs warned of danger ahead.* **2. danger ▸** something that can cause harm : *The school nurse showed a film on the dangers of smoking.* ■ **dangerous,** ADJECTIVE. ▸ **dangereux (-euse)** likely to cause harm; risky. SYN: risk, hazard, peril, threat. p. 1145.

dan·gle [DANG-gul] VERB, dangled, dangling. **balancer, suspendre ▸** to hang or swing loosely : *She dangled her hook over the side of the boat.*

dare [dair] VERB, dared, daring. **1. défier ▸** to challenge a person to do something difficult or dangerous : *Simon dared me to stand on my hands.* **2. affronter, braver ▸** to be brave enough to do something : *Amelia Earhart dared to fly across the Atlantic Ocean alone.* **3. oser ▸** to be bold or rude enough to do something : *How dare you speak to me in this tone of voice?* **Note.** Often used with another VERB: *"I did not dare blink. I gazed straight ahead."* (Jean Little) ▲ NOUN, dares. **défi ▸** a challenge. SYN: brave, challenge, venture, risk.

dar·ing [DAIR-ing] ADJECTIVE. **courageux (-euse), audacieux (-euse), hardi (-ie) ▸** willing to take chances; having courage : *Only a daring person would cross the ocean in a sailboat.* ▲ NOUN. **audace, courage, bravoure, hardiesse ▸** courage : *The skier was famous for her daring.* ✎ p. 71.

dark [dark] ADJECTIVE, darker, darkest. **1. noir (noire), sombre, obscur (-ure) ▸** having little or no light : *a dark night; a dark room.* **2. foncé (-ée), sombre ▸** not light in colour; almost black : *dark hair; a dark suit of clothes.* **3. triste ▸** sad or gloomy : *"He has a dark future—he hates everything."* (F Scott Fitzgerald) ▲ NOUN. **1. nuit ▸** night; night-time : *Yuri's mother told him to be home before dark.* **2. obscurité, noir ▸** a lack of light; darkness : *Children are sometimes afraid of the dark.* ■ **darkness,** NOUN. ▸ **noirceur.**

in the dark dans le noir ▸ without knowing; not aware : *Rashid was in the dark about his surprise party.*

dark·en [DAR-kun] VERB, darkened, darkening. **obscurcir, assombrir ▸** to make or become dark : *"Buzzards darkened the sky, waiting for cattle to die of thirst."* (Tololwa M. Mollel)

dar·ling [DAR-ling] NOUN, darlings. **chéri (-ie), bien-aimé (-ée) ▸** a person who is loved very much. ▲ ADJECTIVE. **1. bien-aimé (-ée) ▸** very much loved : *The birthday card said "To my darling daughter."* **2. ravissant (-ante), adorable ▸** cute or charming : *What a darling hat that is!*

dart [dart] NOUN, darts. **1. fléchette ▸** a thin, pointed weapon that looks like a small arrow. **2. jeu de fléchettes ▸** an indoor game in which darts are thrown at a board or other target on a wall. ▲ VERB, darted, darting. **se précipiter, s'élancer, foncer ▸** to make a quick, sudden movement : *"That was the signal for Harald to dart from tent to tent, pulling up tent pegs."* (Donald Carrick) SYN: dash, rush, scurry, run, hurry.

dash [dash] VERB, dashed, dashing. **1. se précipiter, filer ▸** to move quickly; rush : *The people at the park dashed for cover when the rain started.* **2. jeter ou lancer violemment ▸** to move or throw with great force; smash : *Sam's fall dashed his hopes of making the team.* ▲ NOUN, dashes. **1. sprint ▸** a short, fast race : *"She begged her body to move faster, but could never beat anyone in the fifty-metre dash."* (Gary Soto) **2. ruée ▸** any sudden, quick movement : *He made a dash for the open door.* **3. un peu, petite quantité, soupçon ▸** a small amount : *Luan put a dash of pepper into the soup.* **4. tiret ▸** a punctuation mark like this [—]. A dash is used to show that part of a word has been left out (May 5th, 19—) or to show a break in a sentence : *"Undoubtedly it was colder than fifty below—how much colder he did not know."* (Jack London) SYN: run, charge, hurry, hasten, sprint, sprint.

dash off partir précipitamment, partir en vitesse, finir en vitesse ▸ to do or finish something very quickly : *"He dashed off the list of calls each morning with such speed…"* (James Herriot)

da·ta [DAT-uh *or* DAY-tuh] NOUN. **1. donnée (données), information (informations) ▸** things that are known; facts or figures; information : *A census provides a large amount of data about the citizens of a country.* **2. donnée (données) ▸** any information contained in a computer. **Note.** The singular of data can be **data** or **datum.**

data base (also **database**) **base de données ▸** a large collection of information stored in a computer.

date¹ [date] NOUN, dates. **1. date ▸** the time when something happens or will happen, shown by the day, month, or year : *Please be sure to write the date on your letter.* **2. rendez-vous ▸** an appointment to meet someone or be somewhere : *They made a date to go to the movies on Saturday night.* **3. rendez-vous ▸** someone with whom one has a date : *Do you* *have a date for the dance ?* ▲ VERB, dated, dating. **1. dater** ► to mark with a date : *I dated the letter in the upper-right corner.* **2. donner une date, assigner une date** ► to assign a date to; show the age of : *The celebration of Mother's Day dates from the early 1900s.* **3. sortir avec** ► to have a series of dates with someone : *Luke and Tyra are dating.* ✐ p. 160.

✐ Writing Tips

Dates

Dates *are written out in many ways. Which style you choose depends on where the date is written.*

- *Use numbers (1, 2, 3, and so on) for most dates.*

   I was born on March 8th, 1980.

- *Avoid starting a sentence with a date, but if it is necessary, spell out the words.*

   Nineteen eighty-four *was a good year.*

- *Dates used within reports, articles, stories, invitations, and so on use a comma between the day of the week and the month, and the day of the month and the year.*

   Saturday, September 22, 1990

   December 26, 1997

- *Dates used in journals, letters, diaries, notes, and so on don't need commas.*

   October 1998

   10 April 2000

---

date[2] NOUN, dates. **datte** ► the sweet, brownish fruit of the date palm tree. Dates have been an important food in the Middle East for thousands of years. ✐ p. 160.

daugh-ter [DOT-ur] NOUN, daughters. **fille** ► a person's female child : *My cousin Marlene is my Aunt Sue's daughter.*

dawn [don] NOUN, dawns. **1. aube, aurore** ► the time when the sun rises; the first light of day : *We were so excited about going on a trip that we were up before dawn.* **2. commencement, début, aube, naissance** ► the beginning of something : *The launching of Sputnik in 1957 was the dawn of the Space Age.* ▲ VERB, dawned, dawning. **1. se lever, poindre** ► to begin to be day; grow light : *"When the next day dawned, the black and white army did not go into battle."* (David Day) **2. apparaître, naître, faire jour** ► to begin to be clear to the mind : *Finally, the answer dawned on me.* SYN: beginning, start, origin.

day [day] NOUN, days. **1. journée, jour** ► the time when the sun is out; the time that is not night :

The shortest day of the year is in December. **2. jour** ► one period of 24 hours; the time from one midnight to the next : *April has 30 days.* **3. jour** ► a special day : *New Year's Day.* **4. journée, jour** ► the part of the day spent working : *She works seven hours a day, five days a week.* **5. époque, temps** ► a time in history; age : *In Shakespeare's day, many people believed in ghosts.* ☞ p. 1076.

day-light [DAY-lite] NOUN, **1. lumière du jour, grand jour** ► the light of day; light from the sun : *The room looked cosier in the daylight.* **2. lever du jour, aube** ► the dawn; daybreak.

daze [daze] VERB, dazed, dazing. **étourdir, stupéfier, hébéter, abasourdir** ► to confuse or stun; to be unable to think clearly, as from a blow on the head : *He was dazed from falling off his bike.* ▲ NOUN, dazes. **confusion, stupéfaction, étourdissement, ahurissement** ► a confused or stunned condition : *After she heard the news, she walked around in a daze.*

dazz-le [daz-ul] VERB, dazzled, dazzling. **éblouir, aveugler** ► to make blind, confuse, or overpower with too much light. **Note.** Often used as an ADJECTIVE: *the dazzling lights of the city.*

de- PREFIX. **1.** the opposite of : *defrost.* **2.** down : *depress.* **3.** away; off : *deport.*

dead [ded] ADJECTIVE, deader, deadest. **1. mort (morte), décédé (-ée), défunt (-unte)** ► not alive; no longer having life : *The flowers are dead because I forgot to water them.* **2. inanimé (-ée)** ► never having had life : *Rocks are dead objects.* **3. sans tonalité, manque de vie, mort (morte)** ► without feeling, activity, or energy : *We couldn't call home because the phone was dead.* **4. mort (morte), plat (-plate)** ► complete or absolute, like death : *dead silence.* ■ **the dead,** PLURAL NOUN. **1. mort (morte), défunt (-unte)** ► people who are no longer living. **2. au cœur** ► the darkest, coldest, or most quiet part : *the dead of night.* ▲ ADVERB. **1. absolument, très** ► completely : *to be dead wrong about something.* **2. droit** ► directly; straight : *The sailors saw an island dead ahead.* SYN: lifeless, deceased, gone, extinct.

dead-en [DED-un] VERB, deadened, deadening. **amortir, assourdir, étouffer** ► to make dull or weak : *This restaurant needs carpeting or ceiling tiles to deaden the noise.*

dead end 1. impasse, cul-de-sac ► a street or passageway that has no way out at the other end. **2. impasse** ► a situation or course of action that does not lead to something further. **Note.** Also used as an ADJECTIVE: *She'll never get anywhere in her career if she doesn't get out of that dead-end job.*

dead-line [DED-line] NOUN, deadlines. **date limite, heure limite** ► a set time by which something must be done or finished : *Friday is the deadline for turning in our book reports.*

dead·ly [DED-lee] ADJECTIVE, deadlier, deadliest. **1. mortel (-elle)**, fatal **(-ale, -als)**, meurtrier **(-ière)** ► causing or able to cause death; fatal : *Some snakes have a deadly bite.* **2. mortel (-elle)**, fatal **(-ale) (-ale)** ► extremely; very earnestly : *He was deadly serious about flying to Mars.* SYN: fatal, harmful, destructive, poisonous.

deaf [def] ADJECTIVE, deafer, deafest. **1. sourd (sourde)** ► not able to hear or to hear well. **2. sourd (sourde), insensible** ► not willing to listen or pay attention : *The premier was deaf to the people's protests.* **Note.** The condition of being deaf is deafness.

deaf·en [DEF-un] VERB, deafened, deafening. **rendre sourd, casser les oreilles, assourdir** ► to make someone deaf : *The loud blast deafened us for a short time.* **Note.** Often used as an ADJECTIVE: *a deafening roar.*

deal [deel] VERB, dealt, dealing. **1. traiter de, parler de** ► to have to do with; be about : *That book deals with Pierre Trudeau's years as prime minister.* **2. agir, se comporter** ► to act or behave toward others in a certain way : *Mrs. Kim deals fairly with all of her students.* **3. faire le commerce** ► to buy and sell things; do business : *My aunt's store deals in antique furniture.* **4. distribuer, répartir, partager** ► to give out or distribute : *It's Harry's turn to deal the cards.* ▲ VERB, deals. **1. affaire, coup, marché** ► a bargain or agreement : *Sam made a deal to buy a car.* **2. beaucoup** ► a good deal or a great deal. a large amount; a lot : *"After a great deal of work, the three of them cleared their fields and planted crops."* (Donald Carrick) SYN: give out, allot, grant, distribute, hand out.

deal·er [DEE-lur] NOUN, dealers. **1. commerçant (-ante), marchand (-ande), fournisseur (-euse)** ► a person who buys and sells things to make a living : *an automobile dealer.* **2. donneur** ► a person who gives out the cards in a card game.

dear [deer] ADJECTIVE, dearer, dearest. **1. cher (-ère)** ► much loved; beloved : *My sister is very dear to me.* **2. cher (-ère)** ► highly regarded : *"Dear Sir" or "Dear Madam"* is a polite way to begin a letter. ▲ NOUN, dears. **cher (-ère), chéri (-ie), amour** ► a person who is loved. ▲ INTERJECTION. **mon Dieu, vraiment, pas possible, oh là là!** ► an expression of surprise or trouble : *Oh dear! I have left my wallet at home!* ► **dearly**, ADVERB. **tendrement, vraiment** ► very much; greatly : *She dearly wants to play goalie.*

dearth [durth] NOUN. **pénurie, disette, rareté** ► a lack of; shortage; scarcity.

death [deth] NOUN, deaths. **1. mort, décès** ► the end of life in people, animals, or plants. **2. anéantissement, effondrement** ► the destroying of something; like death : *Competition from CDs*

brought about the death of record albums. ■ **deathly**, ADVERB: ► **mortellement.** *deathly ill.* ☞ p. 1145.

de·bate [dih-BATE] NOUN, debates. **1. débat, discussion, délibération** ► a discussion or argument about the reasons for and against something : *The school board had a debate about closing Oak Hill School.* **2. débat** ► a contest in which two sides formally argue for and against a question. ▲ VERB, debated, debating. **1. discuter, débattre** ► to argue or discuss some issue : *The Commons debated changing the tax system.* **2. se demander** ► to think about; consider : *Wan is debating learning how to swim.* ■ **debater**, NOUN. ► **argumentateur (-trice), maître.** ☞ p. 31.

de·bris [dih-BREE] NOUN. **débris, fragment** ► scattered pieces or remains from something that has been broken or destroyed : *There was a lot of debris in the streets after that last windstorm.* ☞ p. 325.

debt [det] NOUN, debts. **1. dette** ► money that is owed by one person or business to another. **2. dette** ► anything that is owed to one person from another : *I am $5 in debt.* **3. dette** ► the state of owing money. **Note.** Usually used in the phrases in debt and out of debt. **Note.** Someone who owes a debt is a debtor. SYN: obligation, amount due, dues, money owing.

de·bug [dih-BUG *or* dee-BUG] VERB, debugged, debugging. **mettre au point, déboguer** ► to take out problems or errors from a computer program : *Jacqui's job is to debug the new program and to make sure it works.*

dec·ade [DEK-ade] NOUN, decades. **décennie** ► a period of 10 years.

de·cay [dih-KAY] NOUN. **1. pourrissement, carie, décomposition** ► the slow rotting of animal or plant matter : *I brush after each meal to avoid tooth decay.* **2. déclin, décadence** ► a gradual decline into a poor or weak condition : *The Roman Empire went through a long period of decay.* ▲ VERB, decayed, decaying. **pourrir, se gâter, se carier** ► to become rotten; suffer from decay. SYN: rot, spoil, decompose, disintegrate.

de·ceased [dih-SEEST] ADJECTIVE. **décédé (-ée), mort (morte), défunt (-unte)** ► no longer living; a person who has died recently : *The relatives of the deceased woman gathered at her funeral.* ■ **the deceased**, NOUN. ► **mort (morte), défunt (-unte).**

de·ceit [dih-SEET] NOUN, deceits. **tromperie, tricherie, mensonge, supercherie** ► something that deceives; a dishonest action : *The spy believed his deceit was necessary to win the war.* **Note.** A person or thing that uses deceit is deceitful: *a deceitful person; a deceitful comment.*

161

de·ceive [dih-SEEV] VERB, deceived, deceiving. **tromper, abuser, décevoir, duper** ▶ to make someone believe something that is not true : *Desert mirages deceive people into thinking that they see water that isn't there.* SYN: cheat, trick, lie, mislead, betray, hoax, fool. 🖉 **p. 96.**

De·cem·ber [dih-SEM-bur] NOUN, Decembers. **décembre** ▶ the 12th and last month of the year, coming after November. December has 31 days.

de·cent [DEE-sunt] ADJECTIVE. **1. décent (-ente), respectable, convenable** ▶ accepted by people as being in good taste ; proper and respectable : *It's not decent to make fun of someone's misfortune.* **2. acceptable, convenable** ▶ fairly good ; satisfying : *He's been looking for weeks, but he still can't find a decent after-school job.* ■ **decently,** ADVERB. ▶ **décemment, convenablement. Note.** The quality of being decent is decency.

de·cep·tive [dih-SEP-tiv] ADJECTIVE. **1. trompeur (-euse), menteur (-euse)** ▶ likely to deceive ; not honest : *The deceptive advertisement said that the motel was on the ocean when it was actually two kilometres inland.* **2. trompeur (-euse), illusoire** ▶ giving a false idea or impression ; misleading : *That house is deceptive; it looks small from the outside, but it has lots of room inside.* ■ **deceptively,** ADVERB. ▶ **trompeusement, faussement.** ■ **deceptiveness,** NOUN. ▶ **caractère trompeur. Note.** The act of deceiving, or something that deceives, is deception.

dec·i·bel [DES-uh-BUL] NOUN, decibels. **décibel** ▶ a unit for measuring how loud a sound is. Most people talk at about 50 decibels.

de·cide [dih-SIDE] VERB, decided, deciding. **1. se décider** ▶ to make up one's mind : *"The next morning, Za and Charlie decide to go inland for a few days."* (Ann Blades) **2. juger, trancher, régler** ▶ to judge or settle a question or argument : *The jury decided in favour of the accused man.* SYN: settle, determine, resolve, conclude, rule.

de·cid·ed [dih-SY-did] ADJECTIVE. **certain (-aine), évident (-ente), indiscutable, flagrant (-ante)** ▶ definite or certain ; sure : *Leo's height gave him a decided advantage in basketball.* ■ **decidedly,** ADVERB. ▶ **incontestablement, certainement, assurément, résolument.**

de·cid·u·ous [dih-SID-yoo-us] ADJECTIVE. **à feuilles caduques** ▶ shedding its leaves every year : *a deciduous tree.* deciduous tree

dec·i·mal [DES-uh-mul] ADJECTIVE. **décimal (-ale, -aux)** ▶ based on the number 10 : *The metric system is a decimal system of measurement.* ▲ NOUN, decimals. **décimale** ▶ a number having a decimal point. **Note.** The period in a decimal fraction, such as 0.5 or 0.75, is called a decimal point.

de·ci·pher [dih-SY-fur] VERB, deciphered, deciphering. **déchiffrer, décoder, résoudre, démê-** ler ▶ to figure out ; find the meaning of something that is not clear : *to decipher a code.* SYN: figure out, solve, explain.

de·ci·sion [dih-SIZH-un] NOUN, decisions. **1. décision, résolution** ▶ the act or result of making up one's mind ; a definite conclusion : *The whole family approved of Julie's decision to go to law school.* **2. décision, assurance, détermination** ▶ a firm or determined way of thinking. **3. décision, jugement, sentence** ▶ a judgment : *The referee's decision was final.*

de·ci·sive [dih-SY-siv] ADJECTIVE. **1. décisif (-ive), déterminant (-ante), concluant (-ante)** ▶ deciding something completely ; giving a clear result : *Our team won the game with a decisive score.* **2. décidé (-ée), déterminé (-ée), catégorique** ▶ showing decision ; firm or determined : *a decisive person; a decisive answer.* ■ **decisively,** ADVERB. ▶ **sans hésiter, ton décidé, ton catégorique, avec décision.** ■ **decisiveness,** NOUN. ▶ **caractère décisif, air décidé, ton catégorique.**

deck [dek] NOUN, decks. **1. pont** ▶ one of the floors on a ship or boat that divides it into different levels. **2. terrasse, pont** ▶ a platform that is like the deck of a ship or boat : *That house has a deck at the back.* **3. jeu de cartes** ▶ a set of playing cards. ▲ VERB, decked, decking. **décorer, orner, parer** ▶ to decorate or dress ; adorn : *He was decked out in a new suit.*

de·clare [dih-KLAIR] VERB, declared, declaring. **1. déclarer, proclamer** ▶ to announce or make something known in a formal way : *The mayor declared the new school open.* **2. déclarer, proclamer** ▶ to state in a definite way ; say strongly : *Spiro declared that the rent increase was unfair and that he did not intend to pay it.* ■ **declaration,** NOUN. **déclaration** ▶ the announcing or making known of something ; a formal statement. SYN: state, announce, pronounce, proclaim, say.

de·cline [dih-KLINE] VERB, declined, declining. **1. refuser, décliner** ▶ to refuse in a polite way to do or accept something : *Cynthia declined the invitation because she was baby-sitting.* **2. diminuer, décliner** ▶ to become less or grow weaker ; decrease : *The number of people who travel by ship declined after the airplane was developed.* **3. descendre, s'incliner** ▶ to move or slope downward : *As the road declined, the bike picked up speed.* ▲ NOUN, declines. **déclin, baisse** ▶ a slow weakening or lessening : *a decline in interest.*

de·code [dih-KODE or dee-KODE] VERB, decoded, decoding. **décoder, déchiffrer, traduire** ▶ to change secret writing into ordinary words : *We decoded the secret message.*

de·com·pose [DEE-kum-POZE] VERB, decomposed, decomposing. **décomposer, pourrir** ▶ to decay or rot : *The oranges we left outside decomposed after several weeks.* **Note.** The process of decomposing is **decomposition**. SYN: decay, rot, crumble, disintegrate.

dec·o·rate [DEK-uh-RATE] VERB, decorated, decorating. **1. décorer, orner, parer ▸** to make more beautiful, especially for an occasion : *We decorated the room with balloons and ribbons.* **2. décorer, orner, parer, peindre ▸** to add paint, wallpaper, or new furnishings to a room. **Note.** Someone whose work is decorating rooms is a **decorator**. **3. décorer ▸** to give a medal, badge, or ribbon to : *The police officer was decorated for her bravery.* SYN: adorn, trim, fix up, make beautiful.

dec·o·ra·tion [DEK-uh-RAY-shun] NOUN, decorations. **1. décoration, ornementation ▸** the act of decorating something. **2. décoration, ornement ▸** something that decorates; an ornament. **3. médaille, ruban, décoration ▸** a medal, badge, or ribbon.

de·coy [DEE-koy] NOUN, decoys. **1. appelant ▸** a model of a bird that is used by hunters to attract real birds to within shooting distance or into a trap. **2. complice, compère ▸** someone who leads another person into danger or into a trap : *The police officer dressed as an old lady to act as a decoy and catch the muggers.* ▲ [dih-KOY] VERB, decoyed, decoying. **attirer, leurrer ▸** to act as or use a decoy; lure into danger.

de·crease [dih-KREES] VERB, decreased, decreasing. **diminuer, baisser, décroître ▸** to make or become less : *Many people want the government to decrease spending on military weapons.* ▲ [DEE-krees or dih-KREES] NOUN, decreases. **1. diminution, baisse, décroissance ▸** a lessening or decline of something : *After the team dropped into last place, there was a decrease in attendance.* **2. diminution ▸** the amount by which something becomes less. SYN: reduce, diminish, lower, weaken, shorten.

ded·i·cate [DED-uh-KATE] VERB, dedicated, dedicating. **1. consacrer, réserver, employer ▸** to set apart for or direct to a special purpose or cause : *Mother Teresa of India has dedicated her life to working with the poor.* **Note.** Often used as an ADJECTIVE: *He is a dedicated scientist who puts all his energy into his work.* **2. dédier ▸** to address a book or other work to a person as a sign of respect or affection : *Herman Melville dedicated his novel* Moby Dick *to the famous author Nathaniel Hawthorne.*

ded·i·ca·tion [DED-uh-KAY-shun] NOUN. **1. dévouement, acharnement ▸** the state or attitude of being dedicated : *She'd get better grades if she had more dedication to her studies.* **2.** (plural dedications) **dédicace ▸** the act or fact of dedicating : *a dedication at the front of a book.*

de·duce [dih-DUCE] VERB, deduced, deducing. **déduire, conclure, inférer ▸** to reach a conclusion by reasoning : *Shannon deduced the answer to the mystery.*

de·duct [dih-DUKT] VERB, deducted, deducting. **soustraire, déduire, retrancher ▸** to take away one amount from another; subtract : *The store will deduct an additional 20 percent on every sale item.* SYN: subtract, remove, withdraw, take away.

de·duc·tion [dih-DUK-shun] NOUN, deductions. **1. déduction, soustraction ▸** the act of taking away : *That store offers a deduction of 5 percent for payment in cash.* **2. déduction, conclusion ▸** a thing that is deducted. **Note.** A tax **deduction** is something a taxpayer is allowed to subtract from the tax owed. If an expense can be deducted, especially from taxes, it is **deductible**. **3. (arriver à une) déduction, (tirer une) conclusion ▸** the act of reaching a conclusion.

deed [deed] NOUN, deeds. **1. action, acte, activité ▸** something done; an act or action : *"Kileken continued to amaze the old man with his strange deeds."* (Tololwa M. Mollel) **2. contrat, acte ▸** a written legal agreement stating who owns a house or piece of property SYN: feat, act, stunt, action, performance.

deep [deep] ADJECTIVE, deeper, deepest. **1. profond (-onde), épais (épaisse) ▸** going far down from the top or the surface : *The Atlantic Ocean is 8534 metres deep just north of Puerto Rico.* **2. profond (-onde) ▸** the front to the back : *Their yard is 25 m wide and 40 m deep.* **3. grave, profond (-onde) ▸** having a low pitch : *The actor has a very deep voice.* **4. absorbé (-ée), plongé (-ée) ▸** in an extreme state or condition, as if deep under water : *Sue didn't hear me because she was deep in thought.* ▲ ADVERB. (also deeply) **profondément ▸** in a way that is deep; far in, down, or back : *"The dark eyes looked deep into Winston's own."* (George Orwell) *There was something deeply wrong about the situation.*

deer [deer] NOUN, deer. **cerf (biche) ▸** a fast-running wild animal that has hoofs and chews its cud. Male deer (and some female deer) shed their antlers every year. There are many different kinds of deer in Canada, including white-tail deer, mule deer, moose, elk, and caribou. ✆ p. 111, 164.

de·face [dih-FACE] VERB, defaced, defacing. **dégrader, abîmer, détériorer, défigurer ▸** to damage the appearance of : *Someone defaced the library book by writing in it.* SYN: mar, blemish, deform, injure.

de·feat [dih-FEET] VERB, defeated, defeating. **gagner, battre, vaincre ▸** to win a victory over; beat in a battle or contest : *We defeated the other team by two goals.* ▲ NOUN, defeats. **défaite, échec, insuccès ▸** a loss in a contest or battle : *"The old man in the black robe scowled and pushed his king over to signal his defeat and the end of the game."* (David Day) SYN: win, overcome, triumph, conquer.

de·fect [dih-FEKT *or* DEE-fekt] NOUN, defects. **défaut, défectuosité, imperfection ▸** something that takes away from the quality of a thing; a fault or weakness : *The Tylers are very upset with their new car because it has so many minor defects.* **Note.** Something that has a defect or defects is defective: *The engine lost power because of a defective part.* ▲ [dih-FEKT] VERB, defected, defecting. **faire défection ▸** to leave one's country or group in order to join another : *Sean defected from his team to play with ours.* **Note.** A person who defects is a defector. SYN : fault, flaw, weakness, imperfection, failing.

deer

doe

fawn

de·fence [dih-FENS] NOUN, defences. (also defense) **1. défense, protection ▸** the act of defending : *The mayor spoke in defence of her plan to raise taxes.* **2. défenseur, protecteur (-trice) ▸** a person or thing that defends or protects : *Canada has a strong defence in its armed forces.* **3. avocat (-ate), défenseur ▸** a lawyer or lawyers who defend an accused person. **4.** [also DEE-fens] **défenseur ▸** in sports such as hockey and basketball, a player or players who try to stop the other team from scoring. **Note.** Someone or something that has no defence is defenceless.

de·fend [dih-FEND] VERB, defended, defending. **1. défendre ▸** to guard against attack or danger; protect : *The players rushed to defend their net.* **2. justifier, prendre le parti de ▸** to act, speak, or write in favour of someone or something under attack : *The president of the company defended the decision to close down two factories.* **3. défendre ▸** to serve as a lawyer for a person who is accused of a crime. **Note.** A person who defends someone or something is a defender. SYN : protect, shield, support, guard, safeguard.

de·fen·dant [dih-FEN-dunt] NOUN, defendants. **1. accusé (-ée), prévenu (-ue) ▸** a person sued in a court of law. **2. inculpé (-ée), accusé (-ée) ▸** a person in a court of law who has been charged with a crime; the accused : *The defendant asked if she could make a statement.*

de·fen·sive [dih-FENS-siv] ADJECTIVE. **1. défensif (-ive) ▸** protecting or guarding against attack : *Castles are often surrounded by moats as a defensive measure.* **2. défensif (-ive) ▸** having to do with defence in sports : *A defensive player in football.* **3. défensive ▸** expecting to be attacked or criticized : *He is very defensive about his work.* ■ **defensively,** ADVERB. **▸ défensivement, sur la défensive.** *He stood defensively, as if he had been threatened by someone.*

de·fer[1] [dih-FUR] verb, deferred, deferring. **reporter, remettre, différer ▸** to put off until later; delay; postpone : *We deferred our picnic until a sunny day.*

de·fer[2] VERB, deferred, deferring. **déférer, s'en remettre à ▸** to give in to the judgment or opinion of another person : *They deferred to their teacher's decision.* SYN : yield, submit, bow to, respect, acknowledge.

de·fi·ant [dih-FY-unt] ADJECTIVE. **provocant (-ante) ▸** refusing to obey or show respect; the act of defying. ■ **defiantly,** ADVERB. **▸ avec provocation.** ■ **defiance,** NOUN. **▸ provocation, défi, incitation.**

de·fi·cien·cy [dih-FISH-un-see] NOUN, deficiencies. **1. insuffisance, manque, carence ▸** a lack of something that is needed or important : *a vitamin deficiency.* **2. déficit ▸** the amount by which something is lacking; shortage : *When the bank teller checked her cash drawer, she found a deficiency of $1000.* ■ **deficient,** ADJECTIVE. **▸ insuffisant (-ante), manquant (-ante).** SYN : lacking, missing, incomplete, wanting.

def·i·cit [DEF-uh-sit] NOUN, deficits. **déficit ▸** the amount of money that is lacking : *There is a deficit in my monthly budget because I spend more than I earn.*

de·fine [dih-FINE] VERB, defined, defining. **1. définir ▸** to give the meaning of a word or group of words : *This dictionary defines the word "deity" as "a god or goddess".* **2. préciser, définir ▸** to describe or tell in detail; make clear : *The teacher asked us to define our role in the project.* **3. délimiter, définir ▸** to set the limits or boundary of : *The fence defines where our yard ends.* 🖉 **p. 212.**

def·i·nite [DEF-uh-nit] ADJECTIVE. **certain (-aine), sûr (-sûre) ▸** beyond doubt; certain; clear : *Is it definite that Mr. Edwards won't be teaching here next year?* ■ **definitely,** ADVERB. **▸ certainement, sans aucun doute.** *"No, Grandpa, I definitely wasn't a raven."* (Marilyn Halvorson)

164

def·i·ni·tion [DEF-uh-NISH-un] NOUN, definitions. **définition ▶** an explanation of the meaning of a word or group of words : *On this page, the word "degree" has five definitions.*

de·frost [dih-FROST] VERB, defrosted, defrosting. **dégivrer, décongeler ▶** to remove ice or frost; thaw out : *Our refrigerator defrosts automatically.* **Note.** A defroster is a device that melts or removes ice, as on a car windshield.

defroster

deft [deft] ADJECTIVE. **habile, adroit (-oite), preste ▶** quick and skillful; clever; adept : *The magician's deft movements made it easy for him to hide a coin.* **■ deftly,** ADVERB. **▶ habilement, adroitement, prestement.**

de·fy [dih-FY] VERB, defied, defying. **défier, braver ▶** to challenge boldly; resist : *"Now they wanted to know all about the young man before them, who dared to defy their leader."* (Sarah Hayes) SYN: resist, challenge, brave, mock, oppose.

de·gree [dih-GREE] NOUN, degrees. **1. degré, échelon ▶** a step or stage in a process or series : *He has reached the second degree.* **2. degré ▶** the amount or extent of something : *Burns on the skin are measured by degree.* **3. degré ▶** a unit for measuring temperature : *It's 20 degrees and sunny today.* **4. degré ▶** a unit for measuring an angle or an arc of a circle : *A square has four 90-degree angles.* **5. diplôme, baccalauréat, maîtrise, doctorat ▶** an official title given for completing a certain course of study : *My sister Talia received her engineering degree.* **Note.** The symbol for degree is [°]: *Water freezes at 0°C.*

degree

de·i·ty [DEE-uh-tee *or* DAY-uh-tee] NOUN, deities. **dieu (dieux), divinité, déité ▶** a god or goddess : *All of the planets but Earth are named after deities of the ancient world.*

de·lay [dih-LAY] VERB, delayed, delaying. **1. retarder, différer ▶** to put off until a later time; postpone : *The opening of the new shopping centre has been delayed until summer.*

2. retarder ▶ to cause to be late : *Our bus was delayed by the snowstorm.* **▲** NOUN, delays. **délai, retard ▶** a delaying or being delayed : *There will be a delay of 30 minutes before takeoff.* SYN: hold up, postpone, detain, put off, hesitate.

del·e·gate [DEL-uh-git] NOUN, delegates. **délégué (-ée), mandataire, représentant (ante) ▶** a person chosen to act or speak for another : *Each member nation of the United Nations sends delegates to the meetings.* **▲** [DEL-uh-GATE] VERB, delegated, delegating. **1. déléguer, mandater ▶** to appoint someone as a delegate. **2. déléguer ▶** to give authority or duties to another : *A good manager delegates responsibility to her employees.* SYN: assign, authorize, appoint, charge.

del·e·ga·tion [DEL-uh-GAY-shun] NOUN, delegations. **1. délégation ▶** the act of delegating or being delegated : *the delegation of authority.* **2. délégation ▶** a group of chosen representatives : *Our club sent a delegation of members to the national convention.*

de·lete [dih-LEET] VERB, deleted, deleting. **effacer, supprimer ▶** to cross out or remove something written or printed : *He deleted several paragraphs from his story because they slowed down the plot.* **Note.** Something that is deleted, or the act of deleting, is a deletion.

de·lib·er·ate [dih-LIB-ur-it] ADJECTIVE. **1. intentionnel (-elle), voulu (-ue), délibéré (-ée) ▶** done or said on purpose : *I'm sorry I forgot to sent you a birthday card; it wasn't deliberate.* **2. mesuré (-ée), posé (-ée) ▶** slow and careful; not hurried : *"Belle lowered her head and slowed to a deliberate plodding walk."* (Marilynn Reynolds) **▲** [dih-LIB-uh-RATE] VERB, deliberated, deliberating. **considérer, examiner, réfléchir (sur) ▶** to think carefully; consider : *They deliberated for days before they decided to buy the house.* **■ deliberately,** ADVERB. **▶ délibérément, volontairement, exprès.** in a deliberate way. SYN: consider, think over, study, ponder, reflect.

del·i·cate [DEL-uh-kit] ADJECTIVE. **1. délicat (-ate), fin (fine), raffiné (-ée) ▶** very finely made or shaped : *a delicate piece of lace.* **2. délicat (-ate), léger (-ère) ▶** light and pleasing : *the delicate scent of lilacs.* **3. délicat (-ate), frêle ▶** easily hurt or damaged : *"Carrie had always been delicate; she could not stand such cold much longer."* (Laura Ingalls Wilder) **4. délicat (-ate), complexe ▶** very sensitive : *a delicate situation.* **■ delicately,** ADVERB. **▶ délicatement.** *He walked delicately through the mess in his room.*

de·li·cious [dih-LISH-us] ADJECTIVE. **délicieux (-ieuse) ▶** very pleasing to the taste or smell : *a delicious cake.* **■ deliciously,** ADVERB. **▶ délicieusement. ■ deliciousness,** NOUN. **▶ délice.** SYN: tasty, pleasing, appetizing, savoury.

de·light [dih-LITE] NOUN, delights. **grand plaisir, joie** ▶ great pleasure or happiness; joy : *"When we scratched his back and stomach he would wriggle all over with delight."* (Todd Lee) ▲ VERB, delighted, delighting. **1. enchanter, réjouir** ▶ to give great pleasure or joy : *The baby-sitter delighted the children with funny stories and jokes.* **2. prendre plaisir, se délecter** ▶ to have or take great pleasure : *He delights in reading a good mystery.* 🖉 **p. 447.**

de·light·ful [dih-LITE-ful] ADJECTIVE. **réjouissant (-ante), charmant (-ante), délicieux (-ieuse)** ▶ very pleasing; giving joy : *"He found nothing more delightful than reading and being surrounded by books."* (David Day) ■ **delightfully,** ADVERB : ▶ **délicieusement.** *The weather is delightfully warm today.* SYN : charming, pleasing, appealing, pleasant.

de·liv·er [dih-LIV-ur] VERB, delivered, delivering. **1. livrer, remettre, distribuer** ▶ to carry and give out; hand over; distribute : *The mail carrier delivered a postcard to my house.* **2. prononcer** ▶ to speak or utter; say : *Sarah delivered her speech with great enthusiasm.* **3. porter, assener** ▶ to send to a target : *to deliver a blow in boxing.* **4. mettre au monde, accoucher, faire accoucher** ▶ to give birth to a baby, or help a woman to give birth. **5. délivrer, sauver** ▶ to set free or rescue from something : *They were delivered from slavery.*

de·liv·er·y [dih-LIV-uh-ree] NOUN, deliveries. **1. livraison** ▶ the act of carrying or handing over something to a place or person : *The milk truck made a delivery to the school cafeteria.* **2. débit, élocution** ▶ a way of speaking or singing : *The actor's delivery was so clear that people could hear him even in the back row.* **3. accouchement** ▶ the act of giving birth.

del·ta [DEL-tuh] NOUN, deltas. **delta** ▶ a mass of sand, mud, and earth at the mouth of a river. A delta is shaped like a fan or triangle : *The Fraser River has a large delta.*

de·mand [dih-MAND] VERB, demanded, demanding. **1. exiger, réclamer** ▶ to ask for something in a strong, forceful way; insist : *The losing candidate demanded a recount of the votes.* **2. exiger, demander** ▶ to need; require : *Opera singing demands a good, strong voice.* ▲ NOUN, demands. **1. exigence, revendication, demande** ▶ a strong request; the act of demanding : *Management refused to give in to the demands of the employees.* **2. demande** ▶ something that is demanded : *There's always a demand for people willing to play goalie.* **Note.** Also used as an ADJECTIVE: *Being police chief of a large city is a very demanding job.* SYN : inquire, want to know, request, insist, order.

dem·i- [DEM-ee] PREFIX. half : *A demigod is a god that is partly human.*

de·moc·ra·cy [dih-MOK-ruh-see] NOUN, democracies. **1. démocratie** ▶ a government that is elected and run by the people who live under it. In a direct democracy, the voters themselves make the laws, as was the case in ancient Greece. More common today is an indirect democracy, in which the voters elect representatives who make the laws, as is the case in Canada. **2. démocratie** ▶ a country in which the government is a democracy. ■ **democrat,** NOUN, democrats. ▶ **démocrate** ▶ a person who favours democracy.

dem·o·cra·tic [DEM-uh-KRAT-ik] ADJECTIVE. **1. démocratique** ▶ having to do with or favouring democracy : *Great Britain, Canada, and Japan have democratic systems of government.* **2. démocratique** ▶ favouring equal rights or treatment for all people : *The owner of that company is a democratic person who treats all workers fairly.*

de·mol·ish [duh-MOL-ish] VERB, demolished, demolishing. **démolir, détruire** ▶ to destroy completely; tear down; wreck : *They demolished the old house so that they could put up a new house on the same land.*

de·mon [DEE-mun] NOUN, demons. **1. démon, diable** ▶ a bad or evil spirit; a devil. **2. démon, diable** ▶ a person who is very cruel or wicked. **3. démon, diable** ▶ a person who has a lot of energy or determination : *Grandpa has his hands full trying to take care of Jennie—she's a little demon.* SYN : evil spirit, devil, imp.

dem·on·strate [DEM-un-STRATE] VERB, demonstrated, demonstrating. **1. démontrer, prouver, faire une démonstration** ▶ to show clearly or explain : *"Then they made her demonstrate how she had chopped the fish and carved the vegetables and blended the spices."* (Paul Yee) **2. manifester** ▶ to take part in a public display to protest or to make demands for something : *Many people demonstrated outside the jail, urging that prisoners be given better treatment.* **Note.** A person who demonstrates is a demonstrator.

dem·on·stra·tion [DEM-un-STRAY-shun] NOUN, demonstrations. **1. démonstration** ▶ the act of demonstrating; something that shows clearly or explains : *The salesperson gave us a demonstration of how the computer worked.* **2. manifestation** ▶ a public show or parade to protest or to demand something : *A demonstration was held in front of the power company to protest the cost of electricity.* 📘 **p. 1146.**

den [den] NOUN, dens. **1. tanière, antre** ▶ a wild animal's home or resting place : *a lion's den.* **2. bureau, cabinet de travail** ▶ a small room in a house where a person can read, study, or watch television. **3. groupe, bande, meute** ▶ a group of Cub Scouts. **4. repaire** ▶ something thought of as like a den, such as a hiding place for criminals.

Den-e [DEN-ay or DEN-ee] PLURAL NOUN. **Dene** ▸ the Athapaskan-speaking people of the Northwest Territories.

de-ni-al [dih-NY-ul] NOUN, denials. **démenti, dénégation** ▸ the act of denying; saying that something is not true.

den-im [DEN-um] NOUN, denim or denims. **1. jean** ▸ a sturdy cotton cloth used for work or sports clothes. **2. jean** ▸ pants or overalls made from denim.

de-nom-i-na-tor [dih-NOM-uh-NAY-tur] NOUN, denominators. **dénominateur** ▸ the number below the line in a fraction, showing the number of equal parts the whole is divided into : *In the fraction $3/4$, 4 is the denominator and 3 is the numerator.*

de-nounce [dih-NOWNCE] VERB, denounced, denouncing. **dénoncer** ▸ to speak openly against; show strong disapproval of; condemn : *The school paper denounced the school's lack of a recycling program.*

dense [dence] ADJECTIVE, denser, densest. **dense** ▸ closely packed together; thick; *The fog was so dense that we could see only a few feet in front of us.* ■ **densely,** ADVERB. ▸ **dense-ment.** ▸ *The island was densely covered with tall palm trees.*

den-si-ty [DEN-suh-tee] NOUN, densities. **1. densité** ▸ the state of being dense or close together. **2. densité** ▸ the amount of something within a unit or area : *Japan has a higher population density than Canada does.*

dent [dent] NOUN, dents. **bosse, bosselure, entaille** ▸ a place where the surface of something has been pushed in by a hard blow : *There is a dent in the roof of the car from when a branch fell on it.* ▲ VERB, dented, denting. **bosseler, cabosser, entailler** ▸ to make a dent in : *to dent the fender of a car.*

den-tal [DEN-tul] ADJECTIVE. **1. dentaire** ▸ having to do with the teeth : *Brushing your teeth regularly promotes dental health.* **2. dentaire** ▸ having to do with a dentist : *Dental school usually lasts three years.*

den-tist [DEN-tist] NOUN, dentists. **dentiste** ▸ a person who is professionally trained to take care of people's teeth. **Note.** A dentist's profession is dentistry. ☞ **p. 1159.**

de-ny [dih-NY] VERB, denied, denying. **1. nier, refuser d'admettre** ▸ to say that something is not true : *Even though the police found the TV in his house, he denied that he had stolen it.* **2. refuser, priver (de)** ▸ to refuse to give or allow : *I could not deny her the favour she asked.* SYN : refuse, dispute, contradict, reject, denounce.

de-part [dih-PART] VERB, departed, departing. **1. partir, s'en aller** ▸ to go away; leave : *"In the morning before they departed, the explorer*

painted a message on a rock." (Ainslie Manson) **2. s'écarter de, déroger à** ▸ to change from the usual way : *They departed from their morning routine to have breakfast with Daniel.*

de-part-ment [dih-PART-munt] NOUN, departments. **département, service, rayon, section** ▸ a special part or division of something : *the clothing department of a store.* ■ **departmental,** ADJECTIVE. **départemental (-ale), du département** ▸ having to do with a department : *a departmental meeting.*

de-par-ture [dih-PAR-chur] NOUN, departures. **1. départ** ▸ the going away of someone or something : *The arrival or departure of any ship was a big event in the harbour town.* **2. exception, dérogation, entorse** ▸ a change from the usual way : *Camping was a real departure for Mom; she usually stays in hotels.*

de-pend [dih-PEND] VERB, depended, depending. **1. dépendre, relever de** ▸ to rely on for help or support : *"All the animals on the island depended on the plants and the other animals for their food and well-being."* (Celia Godkin) **2. dépendre, résulter** ▸ to be controlled or determined by : *Whether or not Alec can watch that show depends on how much homework he does.* ■ **dependence,** NOUN. **dépendance** ▸ the fact or condition of depending on someone or something. SYN : rely on, trust in, confide.

de-pend-a-ble [dih-PEN-duh-bul] ADJECTIVE. **sûr (sûre), fiable, sur qui on peut compter** ▸ able to be depended on; reliable or trustworthy : *Dad doesn't want a fancy car—just a dependable one that will get him to work.*

de-pend-ant [dih-PEN-dunt] NOUN, dependants. (sometimes dependent) **personne à charge** ▸ a person who relies on another for help or support : *Children are dependants of their parents.*

de-pend-ent [dih-PEN-dunt] ADJECTIVE. **1. dépendant (-ante), tributaire** ▸ relying on the help of someone or something : *The Red Cross is dependent on contributions for the money it needs.* **2. dépendant (-ante), tributaire** ▸ controlled or determined by : *Whether or not we hold the party outdoors is dependent on the weather.* ▲ NOUN. **dépendant (-ante), personne à charge** ▸ See dependant.

de-pict [dih-PIKT] VERB, depicted, depicting. **dépeindre, décrire** ▸ to show in pictures or in words : *That picture depicts a sunset in the country.* ✐ **p. 168.**

de-plete [dih-PLEET] VERB, depleted, depleting. **diminuer, réduire, épuiser, démunir** ▸ to reduce or lessen the quantity, value, or effectiveness of something : *There is concern that we have depleted the world's oil reserves.* ■ **depletion,** NOUN. **diminution, réduction, épuisement** ▸ the act or condition of depleting.

de-port [dih-PORT] VERB, deported, deporting. **expulser** ▸ to order a person to leave a country that

🔑 Word Builder

Depict, describe, and ***portray*** *are verbs that refer to the way something is presented. Depict is often used when talking about an artistic scene or picture : The artist depicted the landscape with all its autumn colours.* ***Describe*** *means to give details to create a clear picture in the mind of the viewer or listener : Luigi vividly described the countryside around Bear Lake.* ***Portray*** *means to capture the likeness of a person : The actor playing John A. Macdonald portrayed the prime minister very well.*

is not his own : *Sam was deported from Canada because he did not have the right papers.*

de·pos·it [dih-POZ-it] VERB, deposited, depositing. **1. déposer, confier ▸** to put money or valuable things in a bank or safe place. **2. déposer, placer, mettre ▸** to put or set down : *He deposited the package on the front steps.* **3. laisser un acompte, faire un dépôt ▸** to pay money as a promise to do something or to pay more later : *We deposited the first month's rent when we signed the lease for the apartment.* ▲ NOUN, deposits. **1. dépôt ▸** something put in a bank or safe place : *a deposit of $100 in a savings account.* **2. acompte, dépôt ▸** money paid as a promise to do something or to pay more later. **3. gisement, dépôt ▸** a mass of material that has built up through the action of nature : *There are large gold deposits in South Africa.* **Note.** A person who makes a deposit is a depositor.

de·pot [DEE-poh] NOUN, depots. **1. dépôt, garage ▸** a railway or bus station. **2. dépôt, entrepôt ▸** a place for storing things, especially military supplies.

de·press [dih-PRES] VERB, depressed, depressing. **1. déprimer, décourager ▸** to make sad or gloomy : *It depressed her to stay home alone while all her friends were at the dance.* **Note.** Often used as an ADJECTIVE : *The steady rain made the whole weekend depressing.* **2. appuyer sur, abaisser ▸** to press down : *To open the door, depress the lever.* **3. faire baisser, faire diminuer ▸** to cause to sink to a lower level : *Bad weather has depressed car sales this month.*

de·pres·sion [dih-PRESH-un] NOUN, depressions. **1. découragement, dépression ▸** sadness or low spirits ; a gloomy feeling : *He sank into a deep depression after he lost his job.* **2. creux, dépression ▸** a low or sunken place in the surface of something : *Water collected in the depression in the schoolyard.* **3. dépression, marasme, récession ▸** a time when business is very bad and a great many people are out of work.

de·prive [dih-PRIVE] VERB, deprived, depriving. (usually used with of) **priver, enlever, déposséder ▸** to keep from having or doing ; take away : *As a punishment, Tina's mother deprived her of her favourite TV show.*

depth [depth] NOUN, depths. **1. profondeur ▸** how deep something is ; the distance from top to bottom or from front to back : *The depth of the lake is 10 km.* **2. (also depths) au plus profond, au cœur ▸** the deepest or most central part of something : *the depths of a mine.* **3. (also depths) fond, au plus profond, au cœur, au milieu ▸** the part that is thought of as most extreme or severe : *the depths of winter.* **4. instruction, culture, science, érudition ▸** deep learning, thinking, or feeling : *The professor is a person of great depth.* SYN: deepness, measure, extent.

in depth en profondeur ▸ in a thorough way ; in detail : *to study a problem in depth.*

dep·u·ty [DEP-yuh-tee] NOUN, deputies. **adjoint (-ointe), remplaçant (-ante), suppléant (-ante) ▸** a person appointed to work for or take the place of another : *The mayor is assisted by deputy mayors.* SYN: substitute, alternative, agent, delegate.

de·rive [dih-RIVE] VERB, derived, deriving. **1. dériver de, provenir de ▸** to get from a certain source : *Cocoa is derived from cacao seeds.* **2. tirer de, trouver ▸** to get or receive : *She derived a lot of satisfaction from helping her little brother with his art project.* SYN: get, obtain, acquire, gain, secure.

der·rick [DAIR-ik] NOUN, derricks. **1. mât de charge ▸** a large machine for lifting and moving heavy things. **2. tour de forage ▸** a tower or frame over an oil well that supports machinery for drilling.

de·scend [dih-SEND] VERB, descended, descending. **1. descendre ▸** to move from a higher to a lower place : *The rain descended without warning.* **2. descendre, être issu ▸** to come down from an earlier source : *Queen Elizabeth is descended from Queen Victoria.* **Note.** A person or animal that is descended from certain ancestors is a descendant : *Modern racehorses are descendants of Arabian horses that were brought to England about 300 years ago.* **3. s'abattre, se jeter, tomber sur ▸** to move in a sudden attack : *A swarm of grasshoppers descended on the crops.* SYN: decline, fall, drop, plunge, go down, slide.

de·scent [dih-SENT] NOUN, descents. **1. descente ▸** a moving from a higher to a lower place : *The plane landed 20 minutes after beginning its descent.* **2. descendance, lignée** ▶ family origin; ancestry : *Leif Eriksson was a Greenlander of Icelandic descent.* **3. pente, côte** ▶ a downward slope : *The ski trail makes a sharp descent just past this turn.* **4. descente, irruption** ▶ a sudden attack.

de·scribe [dih-SKRIBE] VERB, described, describing. **décrire, dépeindre** ▶ to give a picture of a thing in words; write or tell about something : *Describe your lost dog so that I'll recognize him if I see him.* Note. Something that describes is **descriptive**: *"Beautiful" is a descriptive word.* ✐ **p. 168.**

de·scrip·tion [dih-SKRIP-shun] NOUN, descriptions. **1. description, portrait, signalement** ▶ the telling of how a person or thing looked, felt, or acted, or how an event took place; an account of something. **2. sorte, espèce, genre** ▶ kind; variety : *The pond was a home for wildlife of every description—birds, fish, frogs, snakes, and even raccoons and skunks.*

des·ert[1] [DEZ-urt] NOUN, deserts. **désert** ▶ a very dry area of land. A desert is usually sandy and has little plant life. ▲ ADJECTIVE. **1. désertique** ▶ having to do with a desert : *Cactus is a desert plant.* **2. désert (-erte), désolé (-ée)** ▶ having no people : *a deserted island.* ✐ **p. 1040.** ◉ **p. 247.**

desert

de·sert[2] [dih-ZURT] VERB, deserted, deserting. **1. déserter, abandonner** ▶ to go away or leave; abandon : *Wild animals deserted the area as more people settled there.* Note. Usually used as an adjective:*We hurried through the deserted streets.* **2. déserter, faire défection** ▶ to go away from a place where one should stay : *The soldier who was on duty deserted his post.* Note. The fact or crime of leaving in this way is

desertion, and a person who does this is a deserter. **3. déserter, abandonner** ▶ to leave when needed or called for : *When I heard the news, words deserted me and I could say nothing.* ✐ **p. 360.**

de·serve [dih-ZURV] VERB, deserved, deserving. **mériter, être digne de** ▶ have the right to : *After working so hard all year, she deserves a vacation.* Note. Someone who deserves something is **deserving**: *The scholarship will be awarded to a deserving student.* SYN: earn, merit, be worthy of, rate.

de·sign [dih-ZINE] NOUN, designs. **1. plan, dessin, croquis, modèle** ▶ a plan or drawing that shows how something will look or will be made. A design can show a building, a car or other machine, a piece of clothing or furniture, or a page of a book. **2. motif, dessin** ▶ a certain pattern or arrangement of lines, colours, or shapes : *Persian rugs have very beautiful designs.* **3. dessein, intention** ▶ an idea or purpose in the mind : *Was the fire started by accident or design?* **4. designs. complot, conspiration, intrigue, machination** ▶ sly or evil plans to get or take something : *The king worried that his brother had designs on the throne.* ▲ VERB, designed, designing. **1. concevoir, dessiner, faire le plan de** ▶ to make a plan or drawing to show how something will be made : *to design the package for a new brand of cereal.* **2. concevoir, penser** ▶ to plan or make for a certain purpose : *This dictionary is designed for use by students.* ■ **designer,** NOUN. ▶ **créateur (-trice), dessinateur (-trice), décorateur (-trice).**

des·ig·nate [DEZ-ig-NATE] VERB, designated, designating. **1. désigner, indiquer** ▶ to mark or point out; show : *The signs with the arrow designate the trail.* **2. désigner** ▶ to call by a special name or title : *Each week, four students are designated Student Crossing Guards.* **3. désigner, choisir, élire** ▶ to choose; name : *The fastest runner was designated the anchor on the relay team*

de·sire [dih-ZIRE] VERB, desired, desiring. **désirer, vouloir, souhaiter, convoiter** ▶ to wish or long for; want to have : *"If you do exactly as I say, I assure you that all will be as you desire."* (Dan Yashinsky) Note. Something worth desiring is **desirable**: *You don't have to know how to type for that job, but it's certainly desirable.* ▲ NOUN, desires. **envie, goût, désir, convoitise** ▶ a strong wish or longing to have something : *After his long illness, Jack had no desire to eat.* ■ **desirably,** ADVERB. ▶ **de préférence.** SYN: wish, want, long for, yearn, crave, fancy. ✐ **p. 1018.**

desk [desk] NOUN, desks. **bureau (-eaux), pupitre** ▶ a piece of furniture with a flat top, used for writing or reading. Most desks have drawers or space for papers and other things. ✐ **p. 1067.**

des·o·late [DES-uh-lit] ADJECTIVE. **1. désolé (-ée), désert (-erte)** ► without people; deserted : *"For days and days they travelled, trudging barefoot across desolate wasteland, climbing rocky hills."* (Bob Barton) **2. désolé (-ée), éploré (-ée)** ► very unhappy : *She was desolate without her family around her.* ■ **desolation,** NOUN. ► **désolation, abattement, détresse.** ✎ **p. 48.**

de·spair [dih-SPARE] NOUN. **1. désespoir** ► a feeling of having completely lost hope : *I was so far behind the others that I almost gave up in despair.* **2. désespoir, désolation** ► something that causes this feeling : *Cory is the despair of her teacher because she's always talking in class.* ▲ VERB, despaired, despairing. **désespérer, perdre espoir** ► to lose hope; give up : *"I have often despaired, but something always happens to start me hoping again."* (C.S.Lewis)

des·per·ate [DES-pur-it] ADJECTIVE. **1. désespéré (-ée)** ► being reckless or wild because all hope is gone; feeling despair : *The desperate criminal claimed that he was innocent.* **2. désespéré (-ée)** ► causing despair; very bad or dangerous : *The skin diver was in a desperate situation when he came face to face with a shark.* ■ **desperately,** ADVERB. ► **désespérément.** *Upset as she was, she fought desperately for control.* **Note.** The feeling of being desperate is desperation: *The pilot looked in desperation for a safe place to land.* SYN: frantic, wild, reckless, hopeless.

de·spise [dih-SPIZE] VERB, despised, despising. **mépriser** ► to feel great dislike for; scorn : *They despised him for how he treated others.* **Note.** Something that deserves to be despised is despicable. SYN: hate, scorn, detest, loathe.

de·spite [dih-SPITE] PREPOSITION. **malgré, en dépit de** ► in spite of : *Rosa went to school today despite her bad cold.*

des·sert [dih-ZURT] NOUN, desserts. **dessert** ► a sweet or tasty food served at the end of a meal, such as fruit, ice cream, pie, or cake. ✎ **p. 1135.**

des·ti·na·tion [DES-tuh-NAY-shun] NOUN, destinations. **destination** ► a place where someone or something is going or is sent : *The sign on the bus said that its destination was Market Street.* SYN: end, goal, objective.

des·ti·ny [DES-tuh-nee] NOUN, destinies. **1. destin, destinée** ► what happens to a person or thing; one's fortune or fate in life : *Rachel believed that it was her destiny to become an astronaut.* **2. destin, destinée** ► the power that is thought to control what happens; fate. **Note.** Often used as an ADJECTIVE: *destined for success.*

de·stroy [dih-STROY] VERB, destroyed, destroying. **1. détruire, ravager, dévaster** ► to wreck or ruin completely; put an end to : *The city of Pompeii was destroyed by a volcano.* **2. exterminer, détruire** ► to put to death a badly injured or sick animal : *The rabid fox had to be destroyed.* SYN: spoil, ruin, wreck, devastate, demolish.

de·struc·tion [dih-STRUK-shun] NOUN. **destruction** ► the act of destroying or being destroyed : *The tornado left destruction in its path—cars were smashed, houses were knocked down, and trees were blown across the road.*

de·struc·tive [dih-STRUK-tiv] ADJECTIVE. **1. destructeur (-trice)** ► causing great damage or ruin : *a destructive fire.* **2. destructeur (-trice)** ► wanting or tending to destroy or tear down : *The destructive boy broke all the windows of the bus.*

de·tail [DEE-TALE] NOUN, details. **1. détail, renseignement** ► small or less important point or fact : *My sister gave us all the details of the baseball game, from the first pitch to the last out.* **2. (also details) détail** ► the act or fact of dealing with things one at a time : *Making a dress involves a lot of details.* **3. détachement** ► a small group of people who have a special duty : *The sergeant ordered a detail to clear the path.* ▲ [dih-TALE] VERB, detailed, detailing. **1. détailler, énumérer** ► to describe or tell fully. **2. affecter, désigner** ► to appoint or choose for a special task : *The boss detailed Ms. Edwards to collect the money for the picnic.*

de·tach [dee-TACH] VERB, detached, detaching. **détacher, séparer** ► to unfasten and separate; disconnect : *Cory detached the wheels from the toy car.*

de·tect [dih-TEKT] VERB, detected, detecting. **détecter, déceler, découvrir** ► to find out about : *A smoke alarm detects the presence of smoke in the air.* **Note.** The act of detecting is detection: *The spy escaped detection by wearing a disguise.* **Note.** Something that detects is a detector: *Airlines use a metal detector to prevent people from bringing a gun on a plane.*

de·tec·tive [dih-TEK-tiv] NOUN, detectives. **1. policier (-ière), détective, enquêteur (-euse)** ► a police officer whose work is to find out information that can be used to solve a crime. **2. (also private detective or private investigator) détective** ► a private citizen whose work is to solve crimes or to find out information about people. ▲ ADJECTIVE. **policier (-ière)** ► having to do with detectives. SYN: scout, sleuth, investigator.

de·ten·tion [dih-TEN-shun] NOUN. **1. détention, retenue** ► a keeping in custody; confinement : *The student was given a detention for misbehaving in class.* **2. détention, retenue** ► a holding back; a delay : *The accident resulted in a two-hour detention for the railway passengers.*

de·ter [dih-TUR] VERB, deterred, deterring. **dissuader, empêcher** ► to stop from doing; prevent; discourage : *I put up a fence to deter people from walking on my flowers.*

📝 **Writing Tips**

Device vs. Devise

Device and **devise** are often confused because they look so similar.

- **Device** is a noun meaning "a machine or mechanical invention" or "a scheme or trick."

    I have a **device** for chopping vegetables.

    His tears were just a **device** to get what he wanted.

- **Devise** is a verb meaning "to think out or invent."

    I **devised** a plan to solve the problem.

---

de·ter·gent [dih-TUR-junt] NOUN, detergents. **détersif, détergent ▸** a cleaning powder or liquid used like soap.

de·ter·min·a·tion [dih-TUR-muh-NAY-shun] NOUN. **1. détermination, résolution ▸** great firmness in carrying something out; a strong purpose: *Helen Keller's great determination led her to become a famous writer and speaker even though she was both blind and deaf.* **2.** (plural, determinations) **détermination, résolution ▸** a deciding or settling of something.

de·ter·mine [dih-TUR-min] VERB, determined, determining. **1. déterminer, décider, persuader ▸** to decide or settle definitely: *He was determined to make the team.* **2. déterminer, causer, déclencher, occasionner ▸** to be the reason for a certain result; have a direct effect on: *The ratings for a TV show determine whether it is kept on the air.* **3. déterminer, établir, préciser ▸** to find out: *He used a compass to determine where he was.*

de·ter·mined [dih-TUR-mind] ADJECTIVE. **déterminé (-ée) ▸** having one's mind made up firmly; showing a strong will: *The determined look on her face showed how much she wanted to win.* SYN: firm, sure, convinced, resolved, serious.

de·tour [DEE-toor] NOUN, detours. **détour, déviation ▸** a route that is different from or less direct than the regular way: *Because the main highway was flooded, we had to make a detour on an old road.* ▲ VERB, detoured, detouring. **détourner, dévier ▸** make or use a detour: *We had to detour around the accident.*

dev·as·tate [DEV-uh-STATE] VERB, devastated, devastating. **dévaster, ravager, détruire ▸** to destroy completely; ruin: *The farmer's crops were devastated by the unexpected dust storm.* SYN: destroy, ruin, wreck.

de·vel·op [dih-VEL-up] VERB, developed, developing. **1. développer, former ▸** to grow or cause to grow; bring or come into being: *Oak trees develop from acorns.* **2. développer ▸** in photography, to use chemicals on exposed film or plates in order to bring out a picture. **Note.** Someone or something that develops is a **developer**, such as a person or company that builds real estate developments.

de·vel·op·ment [dih-VEL-up-munt] NOUN, developments. **1. développement, formation ▸** the act or process of developing: *The development of the new day-care centre will begin this week.* **2. fait nouveau, rebondissement ▸** an event or happening: *The news program talked about the latest developments in education.* **3. développement ▸** a group of houses or other buildings built by the same builder.

de·vice [dih-VICE] NOUN, devices. **1. appareil, engin, mécanisme ▸** anything that is built or made by people to be used for a certain purpose. Any tool or machine is a device. **2. formule, truc, moyen ▸** a plan or scheme; trick: *A mother bird will fly quickly out of her nest as a device to draw attention away from the baby birds in the nest.* SYN: machine, took, trick, instrument, implement. ✍ **p. 171.**

dev·il [DEV-ul] NOUN, devils. **1.** (often Devil) **diable, démon ▸** the main spirit of evil. **2. diable, démon ▸** a person who is thought to be evil and cruel, like a devil. **3. diable, démon ▸** a person who is full of mischief.

de·vise [dih-VISE] VERB, devised, devising. **trainer, imaginer, inventer ▸** to plan or scheme; think out: *Taylor devised a plan to earn money to buy a bike.* ✍ **p. 171.**

de·vote [dih-VOTE] VERB, devoted, devoting. **consacrer, se dévouer ▸** to give attention, time, or help to: *Kristina plans to devote her life to community service.* **Note.** Often used as an ADJECTIVE: *The dog has been a devoted companion to my uncle for many years.*

de·vo·tion [dih-VOH-shun] NOUN, devotions. **1. dévouement, attachement ▸** the fact of being devoted. **2. devotions. dévotion, prière ▸** prayers or other religious acts. SYN: affection, dedication, love, loyalty, fondness.

dew [doo] NOUN. **rosée ▸** small drops of water that form from the night air and collect on the ground or other surface. 📖 **p. 1102.**

di·a·be·tes [DY-uh-BEE-tis or DY-uh-BEE-teez] NOUN. **diabète ▸** a serious disease in which there is too much sugar in the blood. This happens when the body does not produce enough insulin. **Note.** A person who has diabetes is a diabetic.

di·ag·nose [DY-ug-NOCE] VERB, diagnosed, diagnosing. **diagnostiquer, identifier ▸** to find out the cause of something by examination; make a diagnosis. SYN: interpret, deduce, analyse, gather.

di·ag·no·sis [DY-ug-NOH-sis] NOUN, diagnoses. **1. diagnostic ▸** a finding based on a careful study of a person by a doctor to determine whether the person has a certain disease or unhealthy condition. **2. diagnostic** ▸ any finding based on careful study aimed at learning why a certain problem exists : *The mechanic's diagnosis is that the car needs a new fuel pump.*

di-a-gram [DY-uh-GRAM] NOUN, diagrams. **diagramme, schéma** ▸ a drawing, plan, or sketch that shows or explains how something works, how it is made, or how it is arranged : *The model plane came with step-by-step diagrams for putting it together.*

di-al [DY-ul] NOUN, dials. **cadran** ▸ the front or face of an instrument that uses numbers, letters, or other marks to show how much there is of something. Some clocks, radios, TV sets, and so on have dials. ▲ VERB, dialled, dialling. (also dialed, dialing) **composer, faire** ▸ to use a dial : *In an emergency, dial 911.*

di-a-lect [DY-uh-LEKT] NOUN, dialects. **dialecte** ▸ a form of a language that is spoken in a certain area or by a certain group of people : *Newfoundlanders speak a unique dialect of English.*

di-a-logue [DY-uh-LOG] NOUN, dialogues. (sometimes dialog) **1. dialogue** ▸ the words spoken between two or more people ; a conversation. **2. dialogue** ▸ the words spoken by the characters in a book or play. 📖 **p. 1168.** ✎ **p. 172.**

di-am-e-ter [dy-AM-uh-tur] NOUN, diameters. **1. diamètre** ▸ a straight line that goes through the centre of a circle or another round object, from one side to the other. **2. diamètre** ▸ the length of such a line ; the width of something that is round : *The old fir tree was at least two metres in diameter.*

di-a-mond [DY-uh-mund or DY-mund] NOUN, diamonds. **1. diamant** ▸ a valuable mineral that is usually colourless. Diamonds are a crystal form of carbon and are the hardest natural substance. They are cut and polished for use as precious jewels, and are also used for tools to cut and grind things and for phonograph needles. **2. diamant** ▸ a figure shaped like this [♦]. **3. carreau (-eaux)** ▸ a playing card with one or more red figures having this shape. **4. carreau (-eaux)** ▸ the suit of cards that has this design. **5. losange** ▸ the section of a baseball field that has this same shape. **6. losange** ▸ anything else with a diamond shape : *A diamond-back rattlesnake is named for the shape of the markings on its skin.*

di-a-per [DY-pur or DY-uh-pur] NOUN, diapers. **couche** ▸ a soft piece of folded cloth or a pad of other absorbent material worn as underpants by a baby.

di-a-ry [DY-uh-ree] NOUN, diaries. **1. journal, agenda** ▸ a daily written record of a person's thoughts, feelings, and experiences. **2. journal intime** ▸ a book for keeping one's thoughts,

✏ **Writing Tips**

Dialogue is what we call the words of a conversation when they are written down. When characters in a story or play, for example, talk to each other, it is dialogue. Writers use dialogue to show what the characters are like, what they are thinking and feeling, and what they plan to do. Dialogue can add interest to a story. When you write dialogue :

• *Make it sound like the conversation you hear around you every day.*

• *Use words and phrases that suit the character that is speaking.*

• *Read your dialogue out loud. Does it sound natural ? Does it sound like someone talking ?*

• *Put the dialogue in quotation marks.* "When does the game start ?" Jason asked.

• *Every time a new character speaks, begin a new paragraph.*

"I've never been to the Calgary Stampede," Paula told her friend Karin.

"Well, you can come with us this year," replied Karin.

feelings, and experiences. **Note.** A person who writes a diary is a diarist. SYN : journal, account, chronicle, record book.

dice [dice] NOUN. the PLURAL of die². **1. dé** ▸ small cubes of plastic, wood, or other hard material that are marked on each side with from one to six dots. Dice are used in playing certain games of chance. **2.** *Informal.* **dé** ▸ a single one of these cubes : *Throw a dice to see who goes first in the game.* ▲ VERB, diced, dicing. **couper en dés, couper en cubes** ▸ to cut or chop food into small cube-shaped pieces : *to dice onions.* 📖 **p. 1163.**

dic-tate [DIK-TATE] VERB, dictated, dictating. **1. dicter** ▸ to say or read something out loud to be recorded or written down by another person : *People in business sometimes dictate their letters to a secretary.* **2. ordonner, dicter, imposer** ▸ to give orders or show one's authority : *The rainy weather dictated that we play inside.* ▲ NOUN, dictates. **ordre(s)** ▸ a command or rule that must be obeyed : *She followed the dictates of her conscience and returned the wallet she found to its owner.* SYN : order, demand, direct, tell, charge, rule.

dic-ta-tor [DIK-tay-tur] NOUN, dictators. **1. dicta-teur ▸** a ruler who has complete control over a country and its people. **Note.** Dictator is usually used for modern political leaders such as Adolf Hitler and Joseph Stalin, rather than for kings or emperors who had great power in ancient times. **Note.** A country ruled by a dictator is a dictatorship. **2. dictateur ▸** a person whose authority is accepted in a certain field : *Some famous designers are dictators of fashion.* **Note.** Someone who acts like a dictator is dictatorial: *"It was impossible to dispute the dictatorial commands of my uncle."* (Jules Verne)

dic-tion [DIK-shun] NOUN. **1. style, langage ▸** the manner of expressing ideas in words; the choice of words in speaking or writing : *The choice between "We finished the project" and "We finalized the project" is a matter of diction.* **2. diction, prononciation, élocution ▸** clear and proper pronunciation in speaking and singing : *He's easy to understand because he speaks with perfect diction.*

dic-tion-ar-y [DIK-shun-AIR-ee] NOUN, dictionaries. **1. dictionnaire ▸** a book that lists words of a language in alphabetical order and gives information about them. Dictionaries tell such things as how to spell and pronounce words, what they mean, how they are used, and where they come from. **2. dictionnaire ▸** a book of this kind that lists words of one language and gives their meaning in another : *a French–English dictionary.* **3. dictionnaire, lexique ▸** a book that gives information about words related to a certain subject : *a law dictionary; a sports dictionary.*

did [did] VERB. **faire ▸** a past form of do.

die[1] [dy] VERB, died, dying. **1. mourir, décéder ▸** to stop living; become dead. **2. disparaître, mourir ▸** to lose power or energy, as if dying : *"At noon on Tuesday the blizzard ended. Then the wind died down."* (Laura Ingalls Wilder) **3. mourir d'envie de ▸** to want very much; wish : *I'm dying to find out whether I was accepted at the university.*

die[2] NOUN, dice. **dé ▸** one of a pair of dice.

die[3] NOUN, dies. **matrice, étampe ▸** a metal device used to stamp, mark, or shape things. Dies cut the threads on nuts and bolts and stamp the design on coins.

di-et [DY-ut] NOUN, diets. **1. alimentation ▸** the food and drink eaten by a person or animal : *In many countries, rice is the main part of the daily diet.* **2. régime, diète ▸** a special selection of food and drink that a person chooses because of health reasons or to gain or lose weight : *Sheila is on a low-salt diet because she has high blood pressure.* ▲ VERB, dieted, dieting. **suivre un régime, se mettre au régime ▸** to eat according to a certain diet : *Rod dieted to stay in his weight class for wrestling.*

dif-fer [DIF-ur] VERB, differed, differing. **1. différer, se distinguer de ▸** to be different : *My answer differs from yours.* **2. ne pas être d'accord, ne pas s'entendre ▸** to have another opinion; disagree. SYN : disagree, contrast, clash, vary.

dif-fer-ence [DIF-ur-uns or DIF-runs] NOUN, differences. **1. différence ▸** the fact of being unlike someone or something else; being different : *Can you taste the difference between butter and margarine?* **2. différence, écart ▸** the way or amount of being different : *The difference between the two jars of jam is the amount of sugar they have.* **3. différence ▸** the amount left after one quantity is subtracted from another : *The difference between 30 and 20 is 10.* **4. divergence, désaccord ▸** a disagreement : *The company and its employees held a meeting to settle their differences over the new rules.*

dif-fer-ent [DIF-runt] ADJECTIVE. **1. différent (-ente) ▸** not like someone or something else; not alike : *My sister and I have different-colour eyes : hers are blue and mine are brown.* **2. différent (-ente) ▸** not the same as each other; separate : *"Cougar," "mountain lion," and "puma" are three different names for the same animal.* **3. différent (-ente), autre ▸** not like most others : *Ali has very different taste in clothes and never dresses like her classmates.* ■ **differently,** ADVERB. ▸ **différemment.** *The twins wear their hair differently so that people can tell them apart.* SYN : unlike, distinct, varied, assorted, diverse.

dif-fi-cult [DIF-uh-kult] ADJECTIVE. **1. difficile, dur (dure), ardu (-ue) ▸** hard to do, make, or understand : *It's difficult to make a campfire with damp wood.* **2. difficile, peu commode ▸** hard to get along with or please : *He's a difficult child who never does what his parents ask.* SYN : hard, tough, complicated, troublesome.

dif-fi-cul-ty [DIF-uh-kul-tee] NOUN, difficulties. **1. difficulté ▸** the fact of being difficult . *At first, Andrew had difficulty walking with the crutches.* **2. difficulté, obstacle, accroc, problème ▸** something that is difficult : *She is having difficulties doing her work with a broken arm.*

dif-fuse [dih-FYOOZ] VERB, diffused, diffusing. **(se) diffuser, (se) répandre ▸** to spread about or scatter widely : *They put a shade on the lamp to diffuse the glaring light.*

dig [dig] VERB, dug, digging. **1. creuser, bêcher ▸** to break up, turn over, or remove the earth. **2. creuser ▸** to make or get by digging : *to dig a hole; to dig for clams.* **3. enfoncer, donner un coup de coude, donner un coup d'épaule ▸** to push or poke, as if digging a hole : *to dig your elbow into someone's ribs.* **4. fouiller ▸** to get or search for something with difficulty, as if one were digging in the earth : *Megan went to the library and dug up some*

interesting facts for her history report.
SYN: excavate, scoop, gouge, tunnel.

di·gest [dy-JEST *or* dih-JEST] VERB, digested, digesting. **1. digérer ▸** to break down or change food in the mouth, stomach, and intestines to simpler forms that can be taken in and used by the body. **2. digérer ▸** to think something over for a time to gain a better understanding : *There was too much information in the article to digest in one reading.* **Note.** The process of digesting is **digestion.** ▲ [DY-jest] NOUN, digests. **résumé, sommaire, abrégé ▸** a shortened version of a long book or article. SYN: absorb, understand, comprehend, grasp.

di·ges·tive [dy-JES-tiv *or* dih-JES-tiv] ADJECTIVE. **digestif (-ive) ▸** relating to or helping in digestion. The **digestive system** is the group of organs that digest food and eliminate waste from the body.

dig·it [DIJ-it] NOUN, digits. **1. doigt, orteil ▸** a finger or toe. **2. chiffre ▸** a numeral, especially one of the numbers from 0 to 9.

dig·i·tal [DIJ-uh-tul] ADJECTIVE. **numérique, digital (-ale) ▸** using numbers to store, send, receive, or display information : *CDs hold music in digital form.*

dig·ni·ty [DIG-nuh-tee] NOUN, dignities. **1. dignité ▸** a quality of being worthy and honourable that commands the respect of other people : *He is an honest, hard-working man of dignity.* **2. titre, dignité ▸** pride in one's character or position : *She dresses formally to suit the dignity of her position as president.* **3. dignité ▸** a calm, serious, and formal manner : *She managed to keep her dignity even after spilling soup on herself.* **Note.** Having or showing dignity is to be **dignified.**

dike [dike] NOUN, dikes. (sometimes dyke) **barrage, digue ▸** a wall, dam, or other structure built to prevent flooding from a sea, river, or other body of water.

dike

di·lap·i·dat·ed [duh-LAP-uh-DAY-tud] ADJECTIVE. **délabré (-ée) ▸** partly fallen down or broken from lack of care : *a dilapidated old house.* SYN: neglected, ruined, battered, run-down.

di·late [dy-LATE *or* DY-LATE] VERB, dilated, dilating. **(se) dilater ▸** to make or become larger or wider : *The pupil of the eye dilates as the light gets dimmer.* SYN: expand, enlarge, widen, broaden.

di·lute [dih-LOOT] VERB, diluted, diluting. **1. diluer ▸** to make thinner or weaker by adding a liquid : *The directions said to dilute the soup mix with water.* **2. diluer, délayer, édulcorer ▸** to weaken by adding or mixing in something : *Her speech had some good points, but the effect was diluted by all the statistics.* SYN: weaken, thin out, reduce.

dim [dim] ADJECTIVE, dimmer, dimmest. **1. faible, pâle ▸** having or giving little light; not bright : *"Greta noticed that the light was growing dim. The afternoon had gone."* (Thomas H. Raddall) **2. vague, indistinct ▸** not clear or distinct; vague : *"There was no moon, and the cedar boughs were dim shadows against a gray sky."* (Mary Norton) **3. faible ▸** not seeing, hearing, or understanding well : *Old Shep's eyesight had grown dim over the years.* ▲ VERB, dimmed, dimming. **baisser, décliner, (s') estomper ▸** to make or grow dim : *The stars dimmed as dawn approached.* SYN: faint, weak, pale, vague, cloudy, obscure.

dime [dime] NOUN, dimes. **pièce de 10 cents, monnaie (10 cents) ▸** a coin of Canada and the U.S., worth 10 cents.

di·men·sion [dih-MEN-shun] NOUN, dimensions. **dimension, étendue ▸** the measurement of the length, width, or height of something. ■ **dimensional,** ADJECTIVE: **à deux dimensions, à trois dimensions.** *A cube is a three-dimensional figure.* 🖉 p. 548.

dim·ple [DIM-pul] NOUN, dimples. **fossette ▸** a small hollow place, especially in a cheek or chin.

din [din] NOUN, dins. **vacarme, tapage, chahut ▸** a loud, annoying noise that goes on for some time : *the din of traffic.* SYN: noise, racket, clamour, uproar.

dine [dine] VERB, dined, dining. **dîner ▸** to eat dinner : *They like to dine out at least once a week.*

din·er [DY-nur] NOUN, diners. **1. petit restaurant ▸** a small restaurant shaped like a dining car. **2.** (also **dining car**) **wagon-restaurant ▸** a railway car where meals are served. **3. dîneur (-euse) ▸** a person who is eating a meal, especially dinner.

din·ghy [DING-ee] NOUN, dinghies. **canot ▸** a small rowboat, especially one used to go ashore from a larger boat.

din·gy [DIN-jee] ADJECTIVE, dingier, dingiest. **terne, défraîchi (-ie), sombre, lugubre ▸** dark and dirty in appearance; not bright; dull : *The* *white kitchen curtains had turned a dingy grey from dirt and smoke.* SYN: dull, dark, dirty, grimy, faded, dim, grey.

din·ner [DIN-ur] NOUN, dinners. **1. dîner, souper** ▶ the main meal of the day, usually eaten in the evening. When the main meal is eaten in the middle of the day, it is sometimes called dinner rather than lunch, and the evening meal is then called **supper. 2. dîner** ▶ a formal meal in honour of some person or event.

di·no·saur [DY-nuh-SOR] NOUN, dinosaurs. **dinosaure** ▶ one of a group of creatures that lived on earth millions of years ago. The largest were bigger than any other land animal that has ever lived. 📖 p. 1087.

dip [dip] VERB, dipped, dipping. **1. plonger, tremper** ▶ to put into or under water or another liquid for a short time : *Megan dipped her hand into the lake to find out how cold the water was.* **2. plonger, puiser** ▶ to reach inside a thing to take something out : *Wills dipped into the bag and took out a handful of popcorn.* **3. saluer** ▶ to lower and then quickly raise again a flag to salute : *The winning sailboat dipped its flag to salute the judges as it crossed the finish line.* **4. baisser, descendre** ▶ to drop or go down : *The sun dipped out of sight behind a cloud.* ▲ NOUN, dips. **1. baignade, bain rapide** ▶ the act of dipping one's body in the water; a quick swim. **2. bain** ▶ a liquid into which something is dipped : *Sheep dip is used to kill insects and disease on the animals' skin.* **3. fondue, trempette** ▶ a soft food mixture into which other foods can be dipped : *onion dip.* **4. déclinaison, pente raide** ▶ a sinking or drop : *Be careful of that dip in the road up ahead.*

di·plo·ma [dih-PLOH-muh] NOUN, diplomas. **diplôme** ▶ a printed piece of paper given by a school, college, or university to show that a student has graduated and has completed a certain course of study.

di·plo·mat [DIP-luh-MAT] NOUN, diplomats. **1. diplomate** ▶ a person whose job is to represent his or her country in dealings with other countries around the world. **2. diplomate** ▶ any person who is good at dealing with other people. **Note.** The art or work of being a diplomat is diplomacy. SYN: ambassador, envoy, tactful person.

di·plo·ma·tic [DIP-luh-MAT-ik] ADJECTIVE. **1. diplomatique** ▶ having to do with diplomats or their work : *The ambassador is on a diplomatic mission overseas.* **2. diplomatique, plein (pleine) de tact** ▶ showing skill in dealing with people's feelings : *Nan gave a diplomatic answer to avoid hurting Cody's feelings.* ■ **diplomatically,** ADVERB. ▶ **diplomatiquement, avec diplomatie.**

dip·per [DIP-ur] NOUN, dippers. **1. louche** ▶ a cup with a long handle that is used to lift water or other liquids. **2. Grande Ourse, Petite**

Ourse ▶ either of two groups of stars in the northern sky shaped somewhat like a dipper. The larger group is the Big Dipper, and the smaller is the Little Dipper.

di·rect [dih-REKT] VERB, directed, directing. **1. diriger, gérer, administrer** ▶ to be in charge of an activity; manage or control : *Ms. Olsen directs the daily operations of the bank.* **2. ordonner, charger** ▶ to order or command : *The teacher directed her students to line up.* **3. orienter, donner la direction de, diriger** ▶ to tell or show someone the way : *Could you direct me to the nearest telephone?* **4. orienter, diriger** ▶ to send to a particular place; point or aim : *The child directed his gaze to the moving car.* ▲ ADJECTIVE. **1. direct (-ecte)** ▶ going from one point to another in a line or by the shortest route : *a direct flight to Halifax.* **2. franc (franche)** ▶ following the truth; honest : *A witness in court gave direct answers.* **3. exact (exacte)** ▶ in an exact way; exact : *a direct order.* SYN: aim, conduct, head, control, manage.

direct current (DC) **courant continu** ▶ an electric current that flows in only one direction at a constant rate. Batteries use direct current, and ordinary household electricity uses alternating current.

di·rec·tion [dih-REK-shun] NOUN, directions. **1. direction, administration** ▶ the act or fact of directing; management or control : *The orchestra has been under the direction of the same conductor for 10 years.* **2. ordre** ▶ something that is directed; an order or command : *He pulled his car to the side of the road at the police officer's direction.* **3. directions. directive, ordre, procédure** ▶ information or instructions on how to get to a place or do a certain thing : *The man gave us directions to the station.* **4. direction** ▶ the line along which something moves or the way it faces : *"She could not catch a pop-up or figure out in which direction to kick the soccer ball."* (Gary Soto)

di·rect·ly [dih-REKT-lee] ADVERB. **1. directement** ▶ in a direct line or way; straight : *"Go directly to your room!"* **2. immédiatement** ▶ at once; immediately : *He should be here directly.* **3. exactement** ▶ exactly or absolutely : *Her opinions about politics are directly opposite to mine.*

di·rec·tor [dih-REK-tur] NOUN, directors. **1. directeur (-trice)** ▶ any person who directs something : *the director of a summer camp.* **2. réalisateur (-trice), metteur (-eure) en scène** ▶ a person who directs the performance of a play, movie, or television show. **3. directeur (-trice)** ▶ a person who controls the affairs of a business as a member of its board of directors.

di·rec·to·ry [dih-REK-tree] NOUN, directories. **annuaire, répertoire** ▶ a book or sign containing a list of names, addresses, and other facts. A telephone book is a directory.

triceratops

pteranodon

tyrannosaurus

raptor

stegosaurus

brontosaurus

dirt [durt] NOUN. **1. saleté, crasse** ▸ dust, mud, or other such material that makes a thing unclean. **2. terre** ▸ loose earth or soil, as in a garden.

dirt-y [DUR-tee] ADJECTIVE, dirtier, dirtiest. **1. sale, malpropre, crasseux (-euse)** ▸ not clean; soiled by dust, mud, grease, or the like : *Karl washed his dirty hands before eating*. **2. méchant (-ante)** ▸ nasty or mean; not nice : *Why did you give me such a dirty look when I said that?* SYN : filthy, grimy, soiled, grubby, messy, untidy.

dis- [dis] PREFIX. **1.** not; the opposite of : *dishonest; disagree*. **2.** undo; reverse a process : *disassemble; dismount*. 🖉 p. 177.

dis-a-ble [dis-AY-bul] VERB, disabled, disabling. **mettre hors d'action, rendre infirme** ▸ to take away the normal ability to do something; cripple : *The disease arthritis disables many people*. **Note.** Often used as an ADJECTIVE : *Koi couldn't fix the disabled radio*. **Note.** The fact of being disabled, or something that disables, is a disability.

dis-ad-van-tage [DIS-ud-VAN-tij] NOUN, disadvantages. **1. désavantage, inconvénient** ▸ something that makes it harder to do something or succeed : *It is a disadvantage to be short if you want to be a basketball player*. **2. désavantage, inconvénient** ▸ an unfavourable condition or situation : *Noise is a disadvantage of living near the airport*. SYN : handicap, liability, inconvenience.

dis-a-gree [DIS-uh-GREE] VERB, disagreed, disagreeing. **1. être en désaccord, ne pas être du même avis** ▸ to fail to agree; differ in opinion : *The town wants to close the school, but many of the parents disagree*. **2. différer, ne pas concorder** ▸ to be unlike each other; be different . *The answer I got for that problem disagrees with the one in the book*. **3. être nuisible à, ne pas convenir à** ▸ to have a bad or unpleasant effect on; be harmful : *Mom never eats mushrooms; they disagree with her*. **Note.** The act of disagreeing is a disagreement: *They had a serious disagreement and aren't speaking to each other*. 🖉 p. 468.

dis-a-gree-a-ble [DIS-uh-GREE-uh-bul] ADJECTIVE. **1. désagréable, déplaisant (-ante)** ▸ likely to disagree; hard to get along with : *He was a most disagreeable person, and no one enjoyed his company*. **2. désagréable, déplaisant (-ante)** ▸ bad or unpleasant : *Cleaning out the basement was a dirty, disagreeable job*. ▪ **disagreeably,** ADVERB. ▸ **désagréablement, d'une façon désagréable.**

dis-ap-pear [DIS-uh-PEER] VERB, disappeared, disappearing. **1. disparaître, s'effacer** ▸ to go out of view; move out of sight; vanish : *Whenever dogs come around, our cats disappear*. **2. disparaître, s'éteindre** ▸ to pass away or go out of existence; end completely : *Dinosaurs disappeared millions of years ago*. **Note.** The act or fact of disappearing is disappearance : *The police deal with the disappearance of people*. SYN : vanish, go away, fade out.

dis-ap-point [DIS-uh-POYNT] VERB, disappointed, disappointing. **décevoir, désappointer** ▸ to fail to live up to one's hopes, wishes, or desires : *Failing to make the debating team really disappointed me*. **Note.** Often used as an ADJECTIVE: *That game was a very disappointing loss for our team*. SYN : dissatisfy, let down, displease.

dis-ap-point-ment [DIS-uh-POYNT-munt] NOUN, disappointments. **1. déception, désappointement** ▸ the act or feeling of being disappointed. **2. contrariété, déception** ▸ something or someone that disappoints : *I usually like that actor's movies, but his latest was a real disappointment*.

dis-as-ter [dih-ZAS-tur] NOUN, disasters. **désastre, catastrophe, sinistre** ▸ any event that causes great suffering or loss, such as a flood, fire, train wreck, or plane crash. ▪ **disastrous,** ADJECTIVE. ▸ **désastreux (-euse), catastrophique. désastreusement** ▸ something that causes a disaster : *a disastrous hurricane*. ▪ **disastrously,** ADVERB ▸ **désastrousement** ▸ SYN : catastrophe, misfortune, accident, calamity.

disc [disk] NOUN, discs. **disque** ▸ a disk.

dis-card [dis-KARD] VERB, discarded, discarding. **1. se débarrasser de, jeter** ▸ to throw away or give up something : *She went through her desk and discarded some old school papers*. **2. se défausser de, écarter** ▸ in card games, to put down a card that one does not want or need in one's hand. ▲ [DIS-kard] NOUN, discards. **défausse, écart, déchet** ▸ the act of discarding, or something that is discarded. SYN : throw away, reject, get rid of, dispose of.

dis-charge [dis-CHARJ] VERB, discharged, discharging. **1. renvoyer, libérer** ▸ to release or let go; dismiss : *She was discharged from the hospital*. **2. décharger, débarquer** ▸ to unload or remove cargo or passengers. **3. décharger, décocher** ▸ to fire or shoot : *to discharge a rifle*. **4. s'écouler, se déverser** ▸ to give off or let out water or other liquid or gas; flow : *The St. Lawrence River discharges into the Gulf of St.*

🖉 **Word Builder**   o

*Dis- is a prefix. Adding **dis-** to a word will change the word to mean the opposite, as in discontinue, disagree, disallow, discomfort, and displease. **Dis-** can also mean "remove," as in disconnect, disarm, disband, discolour, disorganize and disprove.*

Lawrence. ▲ [DIS-charj] NOUN, discharges. **1. renvoi, libération** ▸ a release from work or service; a dismissal : *Damon received an honourable discharge from the army.* **2. acquittement** ▸ the act of discharging : *the discharge of a debt.* **3. déversement, écoulement** ▸ a liquid or gas that is released. SYN : release, unload, dismiss, expel, dump.

dis·ci·pline [DIS-uh-plin] NOUN, disciplines. **1. discipline** ▸ strict training given to improve the body, mind, or character : *Becoming an Olympic athlete takes years of discipline.* **2. discipline** ▸ an attitude of obedience and self-control that results from such training : *Discipline is an important quality in an athlete.* **3. discipline** ▸ punishment given to train or correct. **4. discipline, matière scolaire** ▸ an area of knowledge or education : *Mathematics and physics are related disciplines.*

dis·close [dis-KLOZE] VERB, disclosed, disclosing. **1. divulguer, dévoiler, révéler** ▸ to bring into view; uncover : *The ruins of the ancient city of Pompeii were accidentally disclosed by some people digging a well.* **2. divulguer, dévoiler, révéler** ▸ to reveal something that had been secret or hidden : *The mayor disclosed the cost of the new school.* SYN : uncover, reveal, expose, show, open.

dis·com·fort [dis-KUM-furt] NOUN, discomforts. **1. inconfort** ▸ the fact of not being comfortable; a lack of comfort : *Keith felt some discomfort after his tonsils were removed.* **2. malaise, gêne** ▸ a feeling of embarrassment or confusion : *Norma's discomfort increased when everyone started to laugh.* **3. inconvénient, inconfort** ▸ something that causes discomfort : *Life in the desert has many discomforts.*

dis·count [DIS-kownt] NOUN, discounts. **escompte, remise, rabais** ▸ an amount subtracted from the regular price of something : *This store sells swimsuits at a 50% discount.* ▲ VERB, discounted, discounting. **1. faire une remise, réduire** ▸ to sell at a discount : *to discount clothing.* **2.** [dis-KOWNT] **ignorer, rabattre, écarter** ▸ to ignore part of an account; disregard : *You have to discount most of what Jack tells you because he exaggerates so much.* SYN : reduce, subtract, remove.

dis·cour·age [dis-KOOR-ij] VERB, discouraged, discouraging. **1. décourager, abattre** ▸ to cause to lose courage or hope : *The heavy rains discouraged the workers fighting the flood.* **2. décourager, déconseiller, dissuader** ▸ to try to prevent from doing something : *His parents discouraged him from playing football because they were afraid he'd get hurt.* **Note.** Often used as an ADJECTIVE: *It's discouraging not to see an improvement right away.* SYN : deter, prevent, hinder, disapprove, keep from.

dis·cov·er [dis-KUV-ur] VERB, discovered, discovering. **1. découvrir, trouver** ▸ to find out something that people did not know about before : *In 1837, Mary Ann Mantel discovered the first dinosaur bones.* **2. apercevoir, se rendre compte** ▸ to find out; learn : *I was halfway to school when I discovered I'd left my lunch at home.* **Note.** The act of discovering, or the thing discovered, is a **discovery.** SYN : reveal, see, notice, find, expose, detect.

dis·creet [dis-KREET] ADJECTIVE. **discret (-ète)** ▸ very careful about what one says or does; showing good judgment : *Nancy was discreet in not revealing her friend's secret.* **Note.** The fact of being discreet is discretion. ■ **discreetly,** ADVERB. ▸ **discrètement.** SYN : careful, prudent, cautious, thoughtful.

dis·crim·i·nate [dis-KRIM-uh-NATE] VERB, discriminated, discriminating. **1. faire de la discrimination, discriminer** ▸ to treat certain people unfairly or differently from others : *The law should not discriminate against anyone because of race, religion, or gender.* **2. distinguer, discriminer** ▸ to notice a difference between; distinguish : *He is colour-blind and can't discriminate between red and green.* SYN : separate, segregate, distinguish, set apart.

dis·crim·i·na·tion [dis-KRIM-uh-NAY-shun] NOUN, discriminations. **1. discrimination** ▸ the act or policy of treating people unfairly because of their race, religion, nationality, gender, or age. **2. distinction** ▸ the ability to make or see differences; good judgment : *Her parents think she should show more discrimination in her choice of friends.*

dis·cuss [dis-KUS] VERB, discussing. **discuter, examiner** ▸ to talk over or write about a subject : *We discussed our plans for the class trip.* **Note.** The act of discussing is discussion: *Mom and Dad had a lively discussion about next week's election.* SYN : debate, talk over, reason, consider, confer.

dis·ease [dih-ZEEZ] NOUN, diseases. **maladie, mal** ▸ condition that prevents the body or a body part from working in its normal way; a sickness or illness. A disease is a condition caused by an infection or growth, rather than by an accident or wound. People, animals, and plants can all suffer from diseases. **Note.** Something that has a disease is **diseased**: *They cut off a diseased branch from the old elm tree.* 📖 p. 1159.

dis·grace [dis-GRACE] NOUN, disgraces. **1. déshonneur, honte, disgrâce** ▸ a loss of honour or respect; shame : *Sean hung his head in disgrace when he was caught teasing his little brother.* **2. déshonneur, honte** ▸ something that causes such a lack of honour or respect : *Mom says my room is a disgrace.* **Note.** Someone or something that causes or deserves disgrace is **disgraceful.** ▲ VERB, disgraced, disgracing.

déshonorer, couvrir de honte ▶ to bring disgrace to : *He disgraced his family when he was sent to prison.* ■ **disgracefully,** ADVERB. ▶ **honteusement, scandaleusement.**

dis-guise [dis-GUYZ] VERB, disguised, disguising. **1. déguiser, costumer** ▶ to change or hide the way one looks : *The spy was disguised as a scientist so that she could take photos of the secret project.* **2. déguiser, camoufler, dissimuler** ▶ to hide or conceal :*He tried to disguise his fear of the dog by acting friendly.* ▲ NOUN, disguises. **déguisement** ▶ something that changes or hides the way one really looks : *"Then I'll cut my hair short like a man's,' cried Little Kay, 'and go to the Sultan's court in disguise!"* (Robin Muller) SYN : hide, cover, conceal, camouflage, mask.

dis-gust [dis-GUST] NOUN. **aversion, répugnance** ▶ a strong feeling of dislike caused by something very bad or unpleasant : *The smell of the rotten meat filled her with disgust.* ▲ VERB, disgusted, disgusting. **dégoûter, écœurer** ▶ to cause a feeling of disgust. **Note.** Often used as an ADJECTIVE: *She gave him a disgusted look when he ate his third piece of cake.* SYN : offend, repel, sicken, revolt.

dish [dish] NOUN, dishes. **1. plat, récipient, vaisselle** ▶ a plate or shallow bowl used to hold or serve food. **2. mets** ▶ a certain type of food : *Pizza is her favourite dish.* **3. antenne parabolique** ▶ a television antenna in the shape of a large dish, used to receive signals from a satellite. ▲ VERB, dished, dishing. **servir, verser dans un plat** ▶ to put or serve in a dish : *Dad had dinner all ready to be dished up.* 👉 p. 1068.

dis-in-te-grate [dis-IN-tuh-GRATE] VERB, disintegrated, disintegrating. **désintégrer, désagréger** ▶ to break up or separate into many small pieces : *The soft rock disintegrated when I hit it with the hammer.* **Note.** The fact of disintegrating is disintegration.

dis-in-ter-est-ed [dis-IN-tur-ES-tid *or* dis-IN-tris-tid] ADJECTIVE. **1. désintéressé (-ée), impartial (-ale, aux), objectif (-ive)** ▶ not having a selfish or personal interest; not prejudiced; fair : *A judge should take a disinterested view of the cases that come before the court.* **2.** *Informal.* **désintéressé (-ée), indifférent (-ente)** ▶ not having any interest at all; uninterested.

disk [disk] NOUN, disks. (also **disc**) **1. disque** ▶ a thin, round, flat object, such as a coin or phonograph record. **2. disquette** ▶ a metal or plastic plate with a magnetic surface, used in a computer to store information. 👉 p. 541.

disk drive NOUN, disk drives. (also **disc drive**) **lecteur de disques** ▶ a computer device that reads and records information on a disk. A disk drive spins the disk very fast to locate the information needed.

dis-like [dis-LIKE] VERB, disliked, disliking. **ne pas aimer** ▶ to not like; disapprove of, or object to : *She dislikes cooking and prefers to eat out.* ▲ NOUN, dislikes. **aversion, antipathie** ▶ a feeling of not liking someone or something.

dis-mal [DIZ-mul] ADJECTIVE. **lugubre, sombre, morne** ▶ causing gloom or sadness : *"The farther they went the more dismal and lonely the country became."* (L. Frank Baum) ■ **dismally,** ADVERB: ▶ **lugubrement.** *The rainy day dragged on dismally.* SYN : depressing, bleak, gloomy, miserable.

dis-may [dis-MAY] NOUN. **consternation, désarroi** ▶ a strong, sudden feeling of alarm or great disappointment : *To the student's dismay, the teacher announced a quiz.* ▲ VERB, dismayed, dismaying. **consterner** ▶ to feel dismay : *They were dismayed to see the brush fire racing toward their house.*

dis-miss [dis-MIS] VERB, dismissed, dismissing. **1. laisser partir, renvoyer** ▶ to tell or allow to go : *The teacher dismissed the class at 3:00 p.m.* **2. renvoyer, congédier, licencier** ▶ to remove a person from a job or position; fire : *The company dismissed an employee for stealing.* **Note.** The fact of dismissing or being dismissed is a dismissal. SYN : discharge, expel, send away.

dis-o-bey [DIS-uh-BAY] VERB, disobeyed, disobeying. **désobéir** ▶ to refuse or fail to obey : *Jan disobeyed her parents when she stayed out past 10:30 p.m.*

dis-or-der [dis-OR-dur] NOUN, disorders. **1. désordre** ▶ lack of order; confusion : *The camp counsellors allowed no disorder in the cabins.* **2. trouble** ▶ an unhealthy or harmful condition : *a stomach disorder.* ▲ VERB, disordered, disordering. **déranger, désorganiser** ▶ to throw into confusion. **Note.** Usually used as an ADJECTIVE: *Alana's CDs were disordered after her party.*

dis-play [dis-PLAY] VERB, displayed, displaying. **exposer, montrer, exhiber** ▶ to show for others to see; put in view : *She displayed her trophies on her bookshelf.* ▲ NOUN, displays. **1. exposition, étalage** ▶ the act or fact of displaying :*The Stanley Cup is on display at the Hockey Hall of Fame.* **2. écran de visualisation** ▶ the part of a computer that shows the information that is being worked on. For most computers, the display looks like a TV screen. SYN : exhibit, illustrate, present, demonstrate.

dis-pos-al [dis-POH-zul] NOUN. **1. mise au rebut, évacuation, enlèvement** ▶ the act of getting rid of something; removal. **2. disposition, arrangement** ▶ the power to use or control something : *The president for that company has a car at her disposal.*

dis-pose [dis-POZE] VERB, disposed, disposing. **1. se défaire de, se débarrasser de** ▶ to get rid of; throw away : *He disposed of the garbage at the dump.* **2. résoudre, statuer ▸** to deal with or settle : *Let's dispose of this problem before we start another discussion.* **Note.** Something that is disposable is meant to be thrown away after use instead of being used again.

dis·po·si·tion [DIS-puh-ZISH-un] NOUN, **dispositions. tempérament, caractère ▸** a person's usual way of acting, thinking, or feeling : *The baby has a happy, playful disposition.*

dis·pute [dis-PYOOT] VERB, **disputed, disputing. 1. se disputer ▸** to argue or fight about something; struggle against : *The two countries disputed a strip of land on their border.* **2. contester, mettre en doute ▸** to question the truth of something; deny : *The government disputed the millionaire's claim that he owed no income tax.* **▲** NOUN, **disputes. dispute, discussion, litige ▸** an argument or struggle. *✎ p. 31.*

dis·rupt [dis-RUPT] VERB, **disrupted, disrupting. perturber, déranger, interrompre ▸** to put out of order; break up or upset : *The woman disrupted the trial by shouting at the witness.* **■ disruption,** NOUN. **▸ perturbation, dérangement, interruption.**

dis·sat·is·fied [dis-SAT-is-FIDE] ADJECTIVE. **mécontent (-ente) ▸** not satisfied; not pleased about something : *We were dissatisfied with our new computer because it was so hard to learn to use.* **Note.** The feeling of being dissatisfied is dissatisfaction.

dis·solve [dih-ZOLV] VERB, **dissolved, dissolving. 1. dissoudre, faire fondre ▸** to mix a solid or gas into a liquid until it disappears : *The sugar dissolved when I stirred it into my tea.* **2. dissoudre ▸** to break up; end : *to dissolve a partnership.*

dis·tance [DIS-tuns] NOUN, **distances. 1. distance ▸** the amount of space between two things, places, or points : *"Everyone looked confused, so Ms. Krensky helped Kevin explain the relative distances between the earth and the sun."* (Tim Wynne-Jones) **2. au loin ▸** a place or point far away : *"In the distance they could see the walls and rooftops of a large town."* (Bob Barton) **3. distance, froideur, indifférence ▸** a feeling or attitude of being unfriendly.

dis·tant [DIS-tunt] ADJECTIVE. **1. éloigné (-ée), lointain (-aine) ▸** far away in space or time; not near : *We could hear the distant sound of the train whistle.* **2. distant (-ante), éloigné (-ée) ▸** separated by a certain amount : *The nearest shopping centre is about 5 km distant from our house.* **3. distant (-ante), froid (froide) ▸** not friendly : *No matter how hard he tried to please her, she remained cool and distant.*

dis·tinct [dis-TINKT] ADJECTIVE. **1. distinct (-incte), différent (-ente) ▸** different from others; not the same; separate : *Frogs and toads are similar but distinct animals.* **2. distinct (-incte), clair (claire), visible ▸** easy to sense or understand; clear; definite. **■ distinctly,** ADVERB. **▸ distinctivement, clairement.** *She pronounced each syllable clearly and distinctly, so everyone would understand what she was saying.* SYN : different, dissimilar, diverse, separate.

dis·tinc·tion [dis-TINK-shun] NOUN, **distinctions. 1. distinction ▸** the act or fact of making or noticing a difference. **2. distinction, différence ▸** a feature or characteristic that makes one thing different from another : *The shape of the jaw is one distinction between an alligator and a crocodile.* **3. distinction, décoration, mention, prix ▸** honour or excellence : *The Nobel Prize is given for great distinction in literature, science, and other fields.*

dis·tinc·tive [dis-TINK-tiv] ADJECTIVE. **distinctif (-ive), caractéristique ▸** showing a difference from others; special; characteristic : *She has a distinctive laugh.*

dis·tin·guish [dis-TING-gwish] VERB, **distinguished, distinguishing. 1. distinguer, discerner, percevoir ▸** to know the difference between; tell apart : *"Before moving Sluggo from his bowl, Aunt Esther marked his shell with some red fingernail polish so she could distinguish him from the rest."* (Cynthia Rylant) **2. distinguer, caractériser ▸** to cause a difference; make distinct : *The ability to laugh distinguishes humans from other animals.* **3. distinguer ▸** to bring honour or recognition to oneself. **Note.** Often used as an ADJECTIVE: *The convention will be attended by distinguished scientists from around the world.* SYN : tell apart, note, discriminate.

dis·tort [dis-TORT] VERB, **distorted, distorting. 1. déformer, altérer ▸** to twist or bend something out of its normal or true form : *Amusement parks have trick mirrors that distort the way people look.* **2. dénaturer, déformer ▸** to change from its true meaning : *The news article distorted the prime minister's remarks.* **Note.** Something that is distorted is a distortion: *Our TV set has a lot of distortion in the picture.* SYN : twist, contort, misrepresent, falsify.

dis·tract [dis-TRAKT] VERB, **distracted, distracting. distraire, déranger ▸** to take someone's attention away from what he or she is thinking or doing; divert : *Juan distracted Sewa with his video game.* **Note.** Also used as an ADJECTIVE: *Katy gave me a distracted smile but kept watching TV.* **Note.** Something that distracts is a distraction: *"Dad was right there with the net, and this time there were no distractions."* (Julie Lawson)

dis·tress [dis-TRES] NOUN, **distresses. 1. détresse, chagrin, affliction, misère ▸** a feeling of great pain or sorrow; misery; grief : *The mother quickly responded to the baby's cry of distress.*

2. péril, détresse ▸ danger, trouble, or great need : *The Coast Guard rescued the ship that was in distress.* ▲ VERB, distressed, distressing. **affliger, peiner ▸** to cause distress to a person. SYN: trouble, hurt, torment, agonize, bother, upset.

dis-trib-ute [dis-TRIB-yoot] VERB, distributed, distributing. **1. distribuer, partager, répartir ▸** to give something out in shares; deal out : *Frazer distributed pieces of his birthday cake to his classmates.* **2. étaler, répartir ▸** to spread out; scatter : *She distributed the grass seed evenly over the lawn.* **Note.** The act or fact of distributing is distribution. SYN: scatter, spread, allot, deal, give out, share.

dis-trict [DIS-trikt] NOUN, districts. **1. région, district, quartier ▸** an area of a country, province, state, or city that is officially marked for a special purpose : *a school district.* **2. quartier, région ▸** any general area with a special use or character : *Toronto has many shopping districts.* SYN: region, area, zone, neighbourhood, section.

dis-turb [dis-TURB] VERB, disturbed, disturbing. **1. troubler, inquiéter ▸** to make uneasy, upset, or nervous : *"Esther usually did not intrude in Michael's room, and seeing her there disturbed him."* (Cynthia Rylant) **2. déranger, interrompre, troubler ▸** to break in on; interrupt; bother : *"The early morning bell that woke all the other monks in the monastery at dawn did not in the least disturb Wu's slumber."* (David Day) **Note.** The act or fact of disturbing is a disturbance: *The loud noise made by jet planes create a disturbance as they land and take off.* SYN: trouble, concern, irritate, annoy, bother.

ditch [dich] NOUN, ditches. **fossé, rigole ▸** a long, narrow hole dug along the ground. Ditches are used to drain off or carry water.

Di-va-li [duh-WOL-ee *or* duh-VOL-ee] NOUN. (also Diwali or Dipavali) An important Hindu festival that celebrates the beginning of the new year. The festival has different meaning to Hindus in different parts of India and the world. **Note.** Also known as the **Festival of Light.**

dive [dive] VERB, dived *or* dove, dived, diving. **1. plonger ▸** to jump or go head first into water. **2. plonger, piquer du nez ▸** to move downward through the air quickly and at a steep angle : *The plane dived toward the airport.* **3. précipiter ▸** to go, move, or drop suddenly : *"The rabbit dived into a hole beneath a pile of rocks."* (Jim Kjelgaard) ▲ NOUN, dives. **1. plongeon ▸** a head-first jump into water : *Petra made a beautiful swan dive from the high board.* **2. plongeon ▸** a quick, steep movement downward.

div-er [DY-vur] NOUN, divers. **1. plongeur (-euse) ▸** any person who dives into water. **2. plongeur (-euse), scaphandrier ▸** a person who works or explores under the water. **3. plongeur ▸** a bird that dives into water for its food : *The loon is a diver.*

di-verse [dih-VURCE *or* DY-vurce] ADJECTIVE. **divers (-erse), différent (-ente) ▸** not the same : *The people in Canada come from many diverse backgrounds.* SYN: different, unlike, distinct, various, several.

di-ver-si-ty [dih-VUR-suh-tee] NOUN, diversities. **diversité, variété ▸** the state of being unlike; difference; variety : *The radio show explored a diversity of opinions.*

di-ver-sion [dih-VUR-zhun] NOUN, diversions. **1. déviation, détournement ▸** a change or turning aside from a planned direction. **2. diversion ▸** something that draws away attention : *Toby created a diversion while we decorated Clara's desk.* **3. divertissement, distraction ▸** something that relaxes or amuses : *Dancing is my favourite diversion.*

di-vert [dih-VURT] VERB, diverted, diverting. **1. détourner, dérouter ▸** to change the direction in which something moves : *The sign diverted us to another road.* **2. détourner ▸** to draw attention to another direction : *Kobi diverted my attention from the game.* **3. divertir, distraire, amuser ▸** to entertain; amuse : *He made funny faces to divert the crying baby.*

diver

di-vide [dih-VIDE] VERB, divided, dividing. **1. diviser, sectionner, séparer ▸** to separate into parts, pieces, or groups; split : *The teacher divided the class into small groups for the science project.* **2. diviser, partager, répartir ▸** to separate into parts and give some to each; share : *The three winners divided the prize money.* **3. diviser ▸** to show how many times one number is contained in another : *300 divided by 10 is 30.* **Note.** Something that is capable of being evenly divided is divisible: *The number 10 is divisible by the numbers 10, 5, 2, and 1.* **4. diviser ▸** to separate into opposing sides : *The idea of putting on a play divided the* *class.* ▲ NOUN, divides. **ligne de division, ligne de partage ▶** a high area of land that separates two river systems flowing in different directions.

div·i·dend [DIV-uh-dend] NOUN, dividends.
1. dividende ▶ a number that is to be divided by another number : *When you divide 8 by 4, the dividend is 8.* **2. dividende, ristourne ▶** money that is earned by a company as a profit and then divided among the people who own shares of the company.

di·vi·sion [dih-VIZH-un] NOUN, divisions. **1. division, séparation ▶** the act of dividing : *the division of a large farm into smaller plots for houses.* **2. division, classe, section ▶** one of the parts into which something is divided : *the western division of a league.* **3. séparation, division, cloison ▶** something that divides or separates. **4. division ▶** in arithmetic, the process of dividing one number by another. **Note.** A number by which another is to be divided is a divisor: *When you divide 8 by 4, the divisor is 4.* **5. division ▶** a large unit of an army.

di·vorce [dih-VORCE] NOUN, divorces. **divorce ▶** the official ending of a marriage by a court of law. ▲ VERB, divorced, divorcing. **1. divorcer ▶** to end a marriage by law. **2. séparer ▶** to separate from : *The company president tried to divorce himself from the day-to-day details of the business.*

di·vulge [dih-VULJ] VERB, divulged, divulging. **divulguer, révéler ▶** to make known ; make public : *My mother won't divulge her recipe for carrot cake.* SYN: tell, reveal, publicize, let out, make known.

diz·zy [DIZ-ee] ADJECTIVE, dizzier, dizziest. **étourdi (-ie), pris (prise) de vertige, d'étourdissement ▶** having or causing a light-headed feeling of spinning around and being about to fall. **Note.** The feeling of being dizzy is dizziness. SYN: spinning, unsteady, confused.

DNA ABBREVIATION. short for deoxyribonucleic acid. **ADN ▶** a chemical substance found in the cells of all living things. DNA carries the characteristics of an animal or plant from the parent to its offspring. DNA determines the way in which a child resembles its parents.

do [doo] VERB, did, done, doing. **1. faire ▶** to cause a certain action to happen; carry out; perform : *to do a job; to do business with someone.* **2. faire, finir, terminer ▶** to finish a certain task; complete : *She has to do her homework before she can watch TV.* **3. faire, accomplir, rendre ▶** to act in a certain way : *to do your best. This car can do 140 km/hr.* **4. faire ▶** to bring about a certain result : *A few days off will do him good.* **5. faire, s'occuper de ▶** to deal with a certain thing : *to do one's hair; to do the dishes.* **6. faire, convenir, aller ▶** to be satisfactory : *That box will do for a picnic table.* **Note.** Do is also used with other verbs as a

HELPING VERB: **1. ▶** to ask a question : *Do you know the Kwans ? Where do they live ?* **2. ▶** with the word "not": *Wolves do not like to live near people.* **3. ▶** to stand for another verb that was just used : *No one else in my family likes fish, but I do.* **4. ▶** to make something that is said stronger : *I do hope you'll be able to go with us.* SYN: perform, accomplish, achieve, act, produce.

dock¹ [dok] NOUN, docks. **bassin, dock ▶** a place at which boats or ships tie up. Docks have platforms for loading and unloading cargo and passengers. ▲ VERB, docked, docking. **1. mettre à quai ▶** to bring a boat or ship into a dock. **2. arrimer, amarrer ▶** to join two spacecraft together in space.

dock² VERB, docked, docking. **1. retenir, supprimer ▶** to take some away; make less : *The boss docked Jeffrey's pay last week because he missed three days of work.* **2. écourter, couper ▶** to cut off the end of an animal's tail or ears.

dock³ NOUN. **banc des accusés ▶** the place where the accused person stands in a court of law.

doc·tor [DOK-tur] NOUN, doctors. **1. docteur, médecin ▶** a person who has been specially trained and is licensed by law to treat sickness or injury and preserve health. A surgeon and a dentist are two types of doctors. **2. docteur ▶** a person who has the highest degree that a university gives : *A Doctor of Philosophy.* 🕮 **p. 1159.**

doc·u·ment [DOK-yuh-munt] NOUN, documents. **1. document ▶** a written or printed statement that gives official proof or information about something. A birth certificate and a driver's licence are documents. **2. document, dossier, fichier ▶** a file of the work done within a computer program or application. ▲ VERB, documented, documenting. **documenter ▶** to prove something by a document or documents : *The man documented his claim that the old house belonged to him.*

doc·u·men·ta·ry [DOK-yuh-MEN-tuh-ree *or* DOK-yuh-MEN-tree *or* dok-yoo-MEN-tuh-ree] NOUN, documentaries. **documentaire ▶** a movie or television program that gives factual information about a real-life subject.

dodge [doj] VERB, dodged, dodging. **1. esquiver, échapper à ▶** to keep away from something by moving quickly : *"Little Kay dodged between the monster's huge legs."* (Robin Muller) **2. éluder, esquiver ▶** to get away from something in a tricky way; cleverly avoid : *The witness dodged the lawyer's questions by claiming that she couldn't remember.* ▲ NOUN, dodges. **1. esquiver, échapper à ▶** a quick move to avoid something; an act of dodging. **2. truc, combine ▶** a trick used to fool or cheat someone : *The man tried to use a tax dodge so that*

🖋 Word Builder

Donate, award, and *grant* are verbs that mean to hand something over freely to someone else. *Donate* is often used when giving a gift to a needy person or charity: *They donated canned goods to the food bank.* *Award* often means that a person has earned what was given: *He was awarded the most improved student ribbon because of his hard work.* *Grant* is used when someone gives something out of generosity, fairness, or kindness: *Juanita granted a favour to her best friend.*

---

he wouldn't have to pay sales tax. SYN: avoid, sidestep, duck, evade.

doe [doh] NOUN, **does** or **doe. biche, lapine, hase ▶** the female of deer and certain other animals such as antelope, rabbit, and goat. **Note.** The male of such animals is the **buck.**

does [duz] **faire ▶** a present form of the verb **do.**

dog [dog] NOUN, **dogs. chien (-ienne) ▶** a four-legged animal that barks and is closely related to the wolf. There are many breeds of dogs that differ from each other in size and appearance. ▲ VERB, **dogged, dogging. suivre de près ▶** to follow closely, as a dog follows a trail: *to dog a person's footsteps.* 📖 **p. 1088.**

dog-sled [DOG-SLED] NOUN, **dogsleds. traîneau à chiens ▶** a sled pulled by dogs.

do-ings [DOO-ings] PLURAL NOUN. **actions, gestes ▶** things that are done; actions: *We were amazed at the odd doings going on next door.*

dole [dole] NOUN, **doles. 1. allocation, indemnité ▶** a small amount of food, goods, money, or the like given out in charity. **2. goutte, petite portion ▶** a small portion. **3. indemnité de chômage ▶** relief money given to unemployed people by their government. ▲ VERB, **doled, doling. donner au compte-gouttes ▶** to give out in small quantities: *Janine doled out the pieces of candy until there was none left.* SYN: give, hand out, allot, grant, deal out.

doll [dol] NOUN, **dolls. poupée ▶** a toy that looks like a baby, a child, or a grown person.

dol-lar [DOL-ur] NOUN, **dollars. dollar ▶** the basic unit of money used in Canada and the United States. One dollar is equal to 100 cents. **Note.** Canada's dollar coin is informally called a **loonie** (also **loony**).

dol-phin [DOL-fin] NOUN, **dolphins. dauphin ▶** a water animal that is related to the whale, but is smaller. It has a long snout like a bird's beak and two flippers. Dolphins are mammals rather than fish. Dolphins are very intelligent and can be trained to do many things.

do-main [doe-MANE] NOUN, **domains. domaine, propriété ▶** all the land under the control of one ruler, government, or owner.

dome [dome] NOUN, **domes. 1. dôme ▶** a large round roof that looks like an upside-down bowl. Domes are built on a round base or a base with

many sides: *The Alberta legislature has a beautiful dome.* **2. dôme ▶** anything shaped like a dome: *He tapped the small dome of the egg to crack the shell.*

do-mes-tic [duh-MES-tik] ADJECTIVE. **1. domestique ▶** having to do with a home, household, or family: *Cooking, washing, and cleaning are domestic chores.* **2. domestique ▶** not wild; tame: *Common domestic animals include dogs, cats, cows, and horses.* **3. intérieur (-eure), national (-ale, -aux) ▶** of one's own country; not foreign: *Domestic strawberries are tastier than imported ones.*

dom-i-nant [DOM-uh-nunt] ADJECTIVE. **dominant (-ante) ▶** having the greatest power or influence; most important: *Blue is the dominant colour in that room.*

dom-i-nate [DOM-uh-NATE] VERB, **dominated, dominating. dominer ▶** to rule or control by power, size, or importance: *Rome dominated much of the civilized world for many years.* **Note.** The dominating of something is called domination: *For many years, Egypt was under the domination of other countries.* SYN: control, rule, command, lead.

dome

do-min-ion [duh-MIN-yun] NOUN, **dominions. 1. domination, autorité ▶** rule or control: *The queen has dominion over all her subjects.* **2. territoire, possession ▶** land under the control of a ruler or government: *a king's dominion.* **3. Dominion. confédération ▶** a word used for some self-governing countries in the Commonwealth of Nations: *The Dominion of Canada was established on July 1, 1867.* **4.** (often Dominion) in Canada: **a. fédéralisme ▶** under the control or authority of the federal government. **b. fédéral, fédération, nation ▶** relating to the country as a whole; national.

Dominion Day **fête du Canada, fête de la Confédération ▶** formerly the name of Canada's

183

national holiday, July 1. The name was officially changed to Canada Day in October 1982.

dom·i·no [DOM-uh-NOH] NOUN, dominoes. domino ▶ one of a set of small black tiles or pieces of wood marked with dots, used for playing the game of dominoes.

do·nate [DOH-NATE] VERB, donated, donating. donner, faire don de ▶ to give as a gift; present : *to donate money to a charity.* **Note.** The act of donating, or something that is donated, is a donation. **Note.** Any person who donates or provides something is a donor: *a blood donor; the donor of a painting.* 🖉 p. 183.

done [dun] VERB. faire ▶ a past form of do.

don·key [DONG-kee] NOUN, donkeys. âne, baudet ▶ An animal related to the horse, but smaller and having longer ears. Donkeys are often used to pull or carry loads.

doo·dle [DOO-dul] VERB, doodled, doodling. griffonner ▶ to make drawings or other marks while thinking of something else. ▲ NOUN, doodles.

doom [doom] NOUN, dooms. destin, sort, ruine ▶ a terrible fate; ruin or death : *The warden led the condemned prisoner to his doom.* ▲ VERB, doomed, dooming. 1. condamner, destiner ▶ to subject to a terrible fate : *The court's decision doomed the spy to spend the rest of his life in prison.* 2. condamner, destiner ▶ to make bad luck, failure, or destruction certain : *Poor organization doomed that business from the very beginning.* SYN: condemn, convict, sentence.

door [dor] NOUN, doors. 1. porte, portière ▶ a movable part that is used to open or close the entrance to something, such as a room, building, cabinet, or car. 2. porte ▶ a doorway. 📖 p. 1068.

door·bell [DOR-BEL] NOUN, doorbells. sonnette ▶ a buzzer or bell outside a door that is used to signal that someone is there.

door·knob [DOR-NOB] NOUN, doorknobs. poignée, bouton de porte ▶ a round handle on a door that allows one to open the door.

door·step [DOR-STEP] NOUN, doorsteps. seuil, pas ▶ a step or flight of steps leading up to the outside door of a building.

door·way [DOR-WAY] NOUN, doorways. 1. porte, embrasure ▶ an opening in a wall that leads in and out of a room or building and is closed by a door. 2. porte, chemin ▶ a way of getting to some place or goal : *the doorway to success.*

dor·mant [DOR-munt] ADJECTIVE. en veilleuse, en sommeil, au repos ▶ not active for a period of time : *Many bulbs, such as tulips and daffodils, lie dormant over the winter and send up shoots in the spring.* SYN: sleeping, inactive.

dor·mi·to·ry [DOR-muh-TOR-ee] NOUN, dormitories. dortoir ▶ a building with many bedrooms : *My sister lives in a university dormitory.*

Dor·set [DOR-sit] NOUN. Dorset ▶ an Aboriginal culture in northeastern Canada and northern Greenland, lasting from around 500 BC to 1500 AD.

dor·y[1] [DOR-ee] NOUN, dories. doris ▶ a flat-bottomed rowboat, often used by ocean fishers.

dor·y[2] NOUN, dories. dorée, saint-pierre ▶ an edible sea fish.

DOS [dos] ABBREVIATION. short for disk operating system. environnement DOS, système d'exploitation DOS ▶ A specialized computer program that provides an easy-to-use link between the user and a computer's disk drive.

dose [doce] NOUN, doses. dose ▶ a certain amount of a medicine to be taken at one time.

dot [dot] NOUN, dots. point ▶ a small, round spot or mark like this : [.]. ▲ VERB, dotted, dotting. 1. mettre un point ▶ to mark with a dot or dots : *Be sure to dot your i's and cross your t's.* 2. parsemer ▶ to be scattered here and there : *Flowers dotted the field.* SYN: speck, spot, fleck.

dou·ble [DUB-ul] ADJECTIVE. 1. double ▶ twice as many or twice as much : *He got double pay for working on Sunday.* 2. double, pour deux ▶ made for two people or made up of two similar parts : *double doors; a double bed.* 3. double ▶ having two different sides or qualities : *The word* blue *has a double meaning :* "feeling sad" *and the colour.* ▲ ADVERB. 1. deux fois, en double ▶ two together; in pairs : *Dad claimed that his new glasses made him see double.* 2. en double ▶ twice as much : *I've made double in case lots of people come.* ▲ NOUN, doubles. 1. double ▶ a number or amount that is twice as much. 2. sosie, double ▶ a person or thing like another : *The movie star's double does all the dangerous stunts.* 3. double ▶ in baseball, a hit that allows the batter to get to second base. 4. doubles. double ▶ in tennis, a game where there are two players on each team. ▲ VERB, doubled, doubling. 1. doubler ▶ to make or become twice as many or twice as much : *Brian doubled the recipe.* 2. plier en deux, replier ▶ to fold or bend as if to make double : "*He was almost doubled over from trying to catch his breath.*" (S.E. Hinton) SYN: duplicate, copy, twice as much, twin.

doubt [dowt] VERB, doubted, doubting. douter ▶ to have a feeling of distrust or uncertainty about someone or something; question : "*But as Wu told his uncle, he could see that something made the High Priest doubt his every word.*" (David Day) ▲ NOUN, doubts. 1. doute, crainte, soupçon, appréhension ▶ a feeling of not believing or trusting : "*I had no doubt that my teacher and I would like each other.*" (Jean Little) 2. doute, incertitude ▶ a state of being uncertain or undecided : *With only half of the votes counted, the results of the election are still in doubt.* **Note.** Something that is uncertain or in doubt is doubtful: *He looked doubtful,*

184

Word Builder

*Doubt is part of many common phrases. **Beyond doubt** means surely, certainly or definitely: There were many witnesses who saw him do it; he is guilty beyond a doubt. **No doubt** can also mean surely or certainly, but it can also mean possibly. The possibility that someone did or will do something is not definite: No doubt he will return his library books on time. If something is in **doubt**, it is not certain: Only a few of the votes are counted, so the outcome is in doubt.*

and we wondered if we should take his advice.
■ **doubtfully,** ADVERB. ▶ **avec doute.** SYN: mistrust, suspect, question, challenge. 🖉 **p. 185.**

doubt-less [DOWT-lis] ADVERB. **sans aucun doute, sûrement, certainement** ▶ without doubt; certainly : *The train will doubtless be late.*

dough [doh] NOUN, doughs. **pâte** ▶ a soft, thick mixture of flour, liquid, and other ingredients, used to make such foods as bread, cookies, pies, and other baked goods.

dough-nut [DOH-nut] NOUN, doughnuts. (also donut) **beigne, beignet** ▶ a small cake of sweetened dough cooked in fat. Doughnuts are often shaped like rings with holes in the middle.

Douk-ho-bor [DOO-kuh-bor] NOUN, Doukhobors. (also Dukhobor) **Doukhobor** ▶ a member of a Christian sect that originated in Russia. Several thousand Doukhobors settled in western Canada about 100 years ago.

dove[1] [duv] NOUN, doves. **colombe** ▶ a small bird that looks like a pigeon. Doves have a thick body and make a cooing sound. Doves are often used as a symbol of peace. 👁 **p. 108.**

dove[2] [dove] VERB. **plonger** ▶ a past form of dive.

down[1] [down] ADVERB. **1. plus loin, en bas** ▶ to or at a place that is farther away : *The Perez family lives down the street from us.* **2. à la baisse, vers le bas, en bas** ▶ to or in a lower position or condition : *The price of computers has gone down since they first came down.* **3. vers le bas, en bas** ▶ to a condition that is weaker, quieter, less active, or the like : *The car slowed down.* **4. de descendance, descendant** ▶ from an earlier to a later time : *a story that comes down from my grandfather.* ▲ ADJECTIVE. **1. vers le bas, baissé (-ée)** ▶ going downward; directed down : *a down escalator.* **2. à la baisse, vers le bas, en bas** ▶ in a lowered position or state : *The stock market is down this week.* **3. se sentir mal** ▶ feeling ill or sad : *Hans is down with a bad cold.* **4. en panne, arrêté (-ée)** ▶ not working; out of order : *The computers at school are down today.* ▲ PREPOSITION. **de haut en bas** ▶ moving down along, through, or into : *Katie slid down the slide.* ▲ VERB, downed, downing. **vider** ▶ to go or bring down; make go down : *He was so thirsty, he downed three glasses of lemonade.* ▲ NOUN, downs. **essai** ▶ in football, any of the three chances that the team has to move forward at least 10 yards.

down[2] NOUN. **duvet** ▶ the fine, soft feathers that baby birds have before they grow adult feathers. **Note.** Something soft and fluffy like down is downy.

down-stairs [DOWN-stairz] NOUN. **rez-de-chaussée, étage inférieur** ▶ the lower floor or floors of a building : *That noise is coming from downstairs.* ▲ ADJECTIVE or ADVERB. **en bas, à l'étage inférieur, en dessous** ▶ down the stairs; on or to a lower floor : *Ivan tripped and fell downstairs.*

down-town [DOWN-town] NOUN. **centre-ville** ▶ the main section, often the business section, of a town or city : *City Hall is downtown.* ▲ ADVERB or ADJECTIVE. **en ville, au centre-ville** ▶ in the main part or business centre of a town or city : *My mother is driving downtown for a meeting.*

down-ward [DOWN-wurd] ADVERB. (also downwards) **vers le bas, de haut en bas, en bas** ▶ from a higher to a lower position; down.

doze [doze] VERB, dozed, dozing. **sommeiller** ▶ to sleep lightly; nap : *I was dozing off when the phone rang.*

doz-en [DUZ-un] NOUN, dozens. **douzaine** ▶ a group or set of 12 things.

Dr. ABBREVIATION. **1. docteur** ▶ a title used before a doctor's name : *Dr. A.G. Richards.* **2. promenade, avenue, rue** ▶ short for Drive: *3714 Crescent Dr., Vancouver.* **Note.** Sometimes spelled without a period (Dr).

drab [drab] ADJECTIVE. **terne, fade** ▶ not bright or interesting; dreary; dull : *The paint on this house is so old that it has become drab.*

draft [draft] NOUN, drafts. (also draught) **1. courant d'air** ▶ a current of air indoors : *"The floor and the walls were so solid that not the smallest cold draft came in."* (Laura Ingalls Wilder) **2. indicateur de tirage** ▶ something that controls the flow of air, as in a furnace. **3. brouillon, ébauche, croquis, essai** ▶ a sketch, plan, or rough copy of something to be made or written : *"The first draft is always handwritten on a clipboard and a miscellaneous collection of paper."* (Marilyn Halvorson) **4. recrutement, sélection, mobilisation, conscription** ▶ the process of selecting someone to serve for a special purpose : *During the Vietnam War, many Americans came to Canada to avoid the draft.* **5. à la pression** ▶ a drink, such as beer, that is drawn from a barrel or other large container, rather than stored in a bottle or can. ▲ VERB, drafted, drafting. **1. faire le brouillon, rédiger, dresser, esquisser ▸** to make a draft : *The architect drafted the plans for the new office building.* **2. recruter, sélectionner ▸** to select someone for a special purpose : *Each year, professional football teams draft the top university players.* ▲ ADJECTIVE. **1. de trait ▸** used for pulling heavy loads : *Horses and oxen are draft animals.* **2. prêt à être tiré ▸** ready to be drawn from a container : *draft beer.* ✐ **p. 186.**

drag [drag] VERB, dragged, dragging. **1. tirer, traîner ▸** to pull slowly and with great effort; haul : *"Each morning he would have to be shaken and dragged from his bed."* (David Day) **2. traîner, s'éterniser ▸** to go very slowly : *The meeting dragged on until almost midnight.* **3. traîner ▸** to trail along the ground : *She dragged her sled behind her.* **4. draguer ▸** to search the bottom of a body of water with a net or hook : *The police dragged the lake for the missing car.* SYN : pull, tug, haul, tow, lug.

drag-on [DRAG-un] NOUN, dragons. **dragon ▸** in old stories and legends, a beast that breathes out smoke and fire. It is often shown as a huge winged lizard with large claws. 🗋 **p. 967.**

drag-on-fly [DRAG-un-FLY] NOUN, dragonflies. **libellule, demoiselle ▸** a large insect with a long, thin body and four narrow wings. Dragonflies live near fresh water and eat other insects. 👁 **p. 104.**

dragonfly

drain [drane] VERB, drained, draining. **1. drainer, vider, assécher, égoutter ▸** to draw off or flow off slowly : *"All the blood had been drained out of my face till my tan looked like a layer of brown paint over white."* (S.E. Hinton) **2. vider, s'écouler ▸** to make empty or dry by letting liquid flow off : *drain the sink.* **3. épuiser ▸** to use up; exhaust : *The close race drained the runners of all their energy.* ▲ NOUN, drains. **1. tuyau d'écoulement ▸** a pipe or other opening that draws off liquids : *The drain in the kitchen sink is blocked.* **2. épuisement, perte ▸** a thing that uses up or exhausts something : *Car headlights are a drain on a car's battery.* SYN : empty, draw off, use, spend, exhaust.

drake [drake] NOUN, drakes. **canard ▸** a male duck.

dra-ma [DRAH-muh] NOUN, dramas. **1. pièce de théâtre ▸** a story written to be acted out by actors on a stage; a play. **2. théâtre ▸** the art of writing or presenting plays : *Shakespeare is the leading figure of English drama.* **3. drame ▸** an event in real life that is like a drama : *The TV reporter described the drama of the spacecraft blasting off for Mars.* **Note.** A person who writes plays is a **dramatist.**

dra-mat-ic [druh-MAT-ik] ADJECTIVE. **1. dramatique ▸** having to do with drama. **2. dramatique ▸** like a drama; full of excitement or feeling : *"Esther was so dramatic—leaning into the tank, her bangle bracelets clanking, earrings swinging, red pumps clicking on the linoleum—that she attracted the attention of everyone in the store."* (Cynthia Rylant) ▪ **dramatically,** ADVERB. ▸ **dramatiquement.**

✎ **Writing Tips**

Drafts

*A **draft** is an unfinished piece of writing. Most writers produce several drafts before they have a final version. How many drafts should be written? That's up to the writer, but it should be as many as are needed to make the writing well-written and clear.*

Some types of writing, such as shopping lists, telephone messages, and diary entries, don't need drafts, but a story, report, or speech will need two, three, or more drafts that involve revising and editing.

• *The first draft involves putting ideas down on paper or on the computer in a very rough form.*

• *Most people do a second draft and, depending on the changes needed, a third draft may be necessary. Second and third drafts involve revising the content, and making sure that the information is correct and that the writing is organized clearly and logically.*

• *The next stage is the editing stage—checking for correct grammar, spelling, and punctuation.*

• *The final draft is a clean copy of the work.*

dram·a·tize [DRAM-uh-tyz] VERB, dramatized, dramatizing. **1. dramatiser, adapter pour la scène, rendre dramatique** ▸ to write or present something as a drama : *The life of Helen Keller was dramatized in the play* The Miracle Worker. **2. dramatiser, rendre dramatique** ▸ to present something in a dramatic way : *Our teacher dramatizes the events of history to make them more interesting.* SYN: stage, produce, present, feature, put on.

drank [drank] VERB. a past form of drink.

drape [drape] VERB, draped, draping. **draper, recouvrir** ▸ to hang a cover loosely over something : *He draped his jacket over the back of the chair.* ▪ **drapes,** NOUN. **rideau (-eaux), draperie, tenture** ▸ cloth that hangs in long, loose folds in front of a window. **Note.** Also called drapery or curtains.

dras·tic [DRAS-tik] ADJECTIVE. **énergique, sévère, draconien (-ienne)** ▸ very strong or serious : *The flood required drastic measures to save the community.*

draught See draft.

draw [drah] VERB, drew, drawn, drawing. **1. dessiner, tracer** ▸ to make a picture with a pen, a pencil, or another writing tool : *Mika likes to draw pictures of jet planes.* **2. tirer, remorquer, traîner** ▸ to pull, drag, or haul : *Six horses drew the wagon.* **3. attirer** ▸ to bring or come close; attract : *The fiddle player soon drew a crowd on the street.* **4. tirer, puiser, préparer** ▸ to pull out or up; remove : *to draw a pail of water from a well; to draw a number in a contest.* **5. retirer, toucher** ▸ to get; receive : *I drew $10 from the bank.* **6. inspirer** ▸ to pull in air : *to draw a deep breath.* ▲ NOUN, draws. **1. partie nulle, match nul** ▸ a game or contest that ends in a tie. **2. tirage au sort** ▸ the act of drawing, especially in a contest. **3. dégainer, braquer une arme** ▸ the act of taking a pistol and aiming it. SYN: attract, lure, interest. 🖋 **p. 187.**

draw·er [dror] NOUN, drawers. **tiroir** ▸ a box-shaped container that slides in and out of a piece of furniture, such as a desk, cabinet, or chest. It is open at the top so that things can be placed inside. ▪ **drawers,** NOUN. **caleçon, culotte, pantalon** ▸ a form of underwear that fits around the waist, having long or short legs.

draw·ing [DRAH-ing] NOUN, drawings. **1. dessin, ébauche, croquis** ▸ a picture or design made by putting lines on a surface with a pencil, pen, or the like. **2. tirage** ▸ the selection of a winning ticket in a raffle or lottery. 🖋 **p. 1122.**

drawn [drawn] VERB. **dessiner** ▸ a past form of draw.

dread [dred] VERB, dreaded, dreading. **redouter, craindre, appréhender** ▸ to have a great fear; be very afraid : *"I used to dread physical education classes, especially gymnastics."* (Paul Yee) ▲ NOUN. **peur, frayeur, terreur, effroi** ▸ a feeling of great fear about something in the future : *Andrea was half sick with dread about her music exam.* ▲ ADJECTIVE. (also dreaded) **terrible, effrayant (-ante)** ▸ causing great fear : *a dread disease; a dreaded exam.*

dread·ful [DRED-ful] ADJECTIVE. **1. affreux (-euse), détestable, atroce** ▸ causing fear; terrible : *The noise of the thunder was dreadful.* **2. affreux (-euse), détestable, atroce** ▸ of poor quality; bad; awful : *I think that new TV show is absolutely dreadful.* ▪ **dreadfully,** ADVERB: ▸ **terriblement, affreusement, horriblement.** *They were dreadfully frightened by the terrible noises.* SYN: terrible, awful, horrible, serious, ghastly.

dream [dreem] NOUN, dreams. **1. rêve** ▸ pictures and thoughts that come to the mind during sleep : *"And when their voices faded away it was as quiet as a dream."* (Jane Yolen) **2. rêverie, rêvasserie** ▸ something imagined while awake; a daydream. **3. rêve, ambition** ▸ something that one hopes for and imagines coming true : *Ahmed's dream is to become an astronaut.* ▲ VERB, dreamt rêver ▸ or dreamed, dreaming. **1. rêver, rêvasser** ▸ to have a dream or daydream. **2. rêver, désirer** ▸ to think of as possible; imagine : *She dreams of becoming an artist.* ▪ **dreamer,** NOUN. ▸ **rêveur (-euse).**

drear·y [DREER-ee] ADJECTIVE. drearier, dreariest. **morne, monotone, ennuyeux (-euse)** ▸ very sad; dull; depressing : *a cold, wet, dreary day; a dreary movie.*

drench [drench] VERB, drenched, drenching. **tremper, mouiller** ▸ to make completely wet : *The rain completely drenched Casey before he could reach the porch.* SYN: soak, wet, flood, douse, saturate.

🖋 Word Builder

Draw out means to carry on or stretch out too long: *At four hours, the movie was drawn out too long.* It also means to cause someone to talk freely and openly: *Since Alysa is shy, we try to draw her out in conversation.* **Draw the line** means to set a limit, especially about behaviour : *She doesn't know where to draw the line with her rude remarks.* And if you **draw a blank**, it means you are unable to remember : *I drew a blank when the tourists asked me for directions to the library.*

dress [dres] NOUN, dresses. **1. robe** ▸ a type of clothing worn by women or girls that is a top and a skirt in one piece. **2. tenue, habillement** ▸ a particular style of clothing : *Evening dress is a style worn to a formal party.* ▲ VERB, dressed, dressing. **1. (s') habiller, (se) vêtir** ▸ to put clothes on; to wear clothes : *I dressed quickly, pulling on my boots as I ran out the door.* **2. panser, mettre un pansement** ▸ to prepare or take care of something in a special way, as if putting on clothing : *The nurse dressed my infected foot.* 🖝 **p. 1010.**

dress up s'endimancher, bien s'habiller ▸ to wear formal or fancy clothes.

dres-ser[1] [DRES-ur] NOUN, dressers. **armoire, commode, chiffonnier** ▸ a large piece of furniture, having drawers and used for storing clothes.

dresser[2] NOUN, dressers. **1. personne qui s'habille (généralement bien)** ▸ a person who dresses, especially someone who dresses in a certain way : *a fancy dresser.* **2. habilleur (-euse)** ▸ a person whose work is to help another person with dressing : *She works as a dresser for a famous TV star.* 🖝 **p. 1068.**

dres-sing [DRES-ing] NOUN, dressings. **1. habillement** ▸ the act of getting dressed; putting on clothes. **2. pansement** ▸ a bandage put on a cut or other wound. **3. sauce, vinaigrette, assaisonnement** ▸ a type of sauce used on salads and other foods. **4. farce** ▸ a mixture of bread crumbs and seasoning; also called stuffing.

drew [droo] VERB. a past form of draw.

drib-ble [DRIB-ul] VERB, dribbled, dribbling. **1. couler lentement, tomber goutte à goutte** ▸ to flow and trickle in drops : *The milk dribbled from the overturned glass onto the table.* **2. dribbler** ▸ in basketball or soccer, to move the ball along by short bounces or kicks : *"Ossie dribbled his ball down the path."* (Juanita Havill) ▲ NOUN, dribbles. **1. goutte, filet** ▸ a small amount of liquid; a series of drops : *"Meanwhile, Fox noisily lapped up every last dribble of porridge with his long pink tongue."* (Jan Thornhill) **2. dribble** ▸ the act of dribbling the ball in basketball or soccer. **Note.** A person who dribbles is a dribbler. SYN: drip, trickle, leak.

dried [dride] VERB. a past form of dry.

drift [drift] VERB, drifted, drifting. **1. dériver, dévier** ▸ to be moved or carried along by wind or water currents : *"While the cubs were poking around, the raft began to drift slowly out into the lake."* (Celia Godkin) **2. s'amonceler, s'entasser** ▸ to pile up or gather in heaps because of the wind or the water : *The snow drifted across the road.* **3. se laisser aller, flâner, être nonchalant (-ante)** ▸ to move without any purpose or goal : *We had spent a few days in Montreal and then drifted up to Quebec for the weekend.* ▲ NOUN, drifts. **1. amoncellement, tas,**

entassement ▸ loose material that is piled by wind or moving water : *The drifts of snow were so high that we couldn't see over them.* **2. force, poussée, intensité** ▸ the direction of movement of water or wind. **3. but, idée, intention** ▸ the general idea or meaning of something : *Would you repeat that—I didn't get your drift.* SYN : wander, roam, float, cruise, glide, ramble.

drift-wood [DRIFT-wood] NOUN. **bois flotté** ▸ old pieces of wood floating on water or washed up on shore.

drill [dril] NOUN, drills. **1. perceuse, vilebrequin, foreuse** ▸ a tool used to cut round holes in wood and other hard materials. **2. exercice, entraînement, manœuvre** ▸ teaching or training by doing something over and over : *Fire drills show people how to leave a burning building safely.* **3. semoir** ▸ a machine that plants seeds in rows : *The drill makes a small furrow, drops the seed, and covers the furrow.* ▲ VERB, drilled, drilling. **1. percer, forer, fraiser** ▸ to cut a hole with a drill : *The dentist drilled my tooth.* **2. s'exercer à répétition, pratiquer à répétition** ▸ to teach or train by repeating over and over : *Julio and I drill each other on our multiplication tables.*

drink [drink] VERB, drank, drunk or drank, drinking. **1. boire** ▸ to swallow water or any other liquid : *He drank two glasses of orange juice for breakfast.* **2. boire, s'enivrer, se soûler** ▸ to drink alcohol. **3. boire, absorber** ▸ to soak in or soak up : *The dry grass drank up the water from the sprinkler.* ▲ NOUN, drinks. **1. boisson** ▸ any liquid that one can drink. **2. boisson, alcool** ▸ an alcoholic drink. 🖝 **p. 1136.**

drink in absorber, boire ▸ to take in through the senses or the mind : *She drank in the beauty of the sunset.*

drip [drip] VERB, dripped, dripping. **dégoutter, dégouliner** ▸ to fall in drops : *The tennis player wiped off the sweat that was dripping into his eyes.* ▲ NOUN, drips. **1. goutte** ▸ liquid drops that fall or drip from something : *I watched the drip of water as it slid down the windowpane.* **2. bruit de l'eau qui tombe** ▸ the sound made by something dripping : *The steady drip of the faucet kept me awake half the night.*

drive [drive] VERB, drove, driven, driving. **1. conduire, piloter** ▸ to control or direct the movement of a car or other vehicle. **2. conduire, emmener** ▸ to go or travel in a car or other vehicle : *Melissa drives me to soccer practice every week.* **3. conduire, actionner, commander, diriger** ▸ to move or cause to move : *to drive a nail into a board; to drive a herd of cattle.* **4. rendre, réduire, conduire** ▸ to force to act in a certain way : *Stop making that noise! You're driving me crazy!* ▲ NOUN, drives. **1. tour, trajet, promenade** ▸ a ride in a car or another vehicle : *It's a beautiful day for a drive in* *the country.* **2. allée, avenue ▸** a street or driveway : *Lakeshore Drive.* **3. campagne de financement ▸** a strong, organized effort to do something : *We're having a drive to raise money for the club.* **4. coup droit ▸** a long hit in golf, baseball, and other games. SYN : steer, operate, run, conduct.

driv-er [DRY-vur] NOUN, drivers. **1. conducteur (-trice), automobiliste, chauffeur ▸** a person who drives a car or other vehicle : *Our bus driver expects us to stay in our seats until the bus stops.* **2. bois, driver ▸** a golf club with a wooden head, used to hit long shots.

drive-way [DRIVE-way] NOUN, driveways. **entrée, chemin d'entrée ▸** a private road that is between a house or building and the street.

driz-zle [DRIZ-ul] VERB, drizzled, drizzling. **bruiner ▸** to rain lightly in small drops. ▲ NOUN. **bruine, crachin ▸** a fine rain or mist. ■ **drizzly,** ADVERB. ▸ **de bruine, de crachin.**

drom-e-dar-y [DROM-uh-DAIR-ee] NOUN, dromedaries. **dromadaire ▸** a type of camel that has one hump, found in Arabia and North Africa.

drone [drone] VERB, droned, droning. **1. bourdonner, ronronner, vrombir ▸** to make a low humming sound that goes on and on : *The noise of construction droned outside the window.* **2. parler d'une voix monotone ▸** to speak in a tone of voice that is boring or monotonous : *The speaker droned on for what seemed like hours.* ▲ NOUN, drones. **1. bourdonnement, ronronnement, vrombissement ▸** a low, continuous humming noise. **2. faux bourdon ▸** a male bee that has no sting and does not gather honey. **3. fainéant (-ante) ▸** a person who lives off the work of others.

droop [droop] VERB, drooped, drooping. **affaisser, tomber, abaisser, pencher ▸** to sink or hang down : *"Harriet looked at her own Saturn. Her rings were drooping despite all the tape."* (Tim Wynne-Jones) SYN : hand, dangle, drag, sink, sag.

drop [drop] VERB, dropped, dropping. **1. laisser tomber, lâcher ▸** to fall or let fall; lower : *She accidentally dropped her wallet on the sidewalk.* **2. déposer, débarquer ▸** to deliver to a certain place or person : *I'll drop you a letter when I have time.* **3. passer ▸** to make a short, casual visit : *Let's drop over to Tal's house and see what she's doing.* **4. laisser tomber, abandonner, renoncer ▸** to stop or be stopped from continuing an activity : *Karen dropped ballet lessons because she was falling behind in her studies.* **5. laisser tomber, omettre ▸** to leave out; omit : *For verbs that end in "e," such as "bike," you drop the "e" before adding "ing."* ▲ NOUN, drops. **1. goutte ▸** a tiny amount of a liquid with a rounded shape like a ball : *Drops of rain rolled off the roof.* **2. pastille ▸** candy or medicine with a rounded shape like a ball : *cough drops; lemon drops.* **3. dégringolade, chute, baisse ▸** the act of dropping or falling, or

the fall itself. **4. dénivellation ▸** the distance between two levels, one higher and one lower : *There's a big drop from the top of the cliff to the river below.* **5. place, endroit ▸** a place where something may be left or dropped for someone else : *a mail drop.*

drop off 1. déposer, laisser ▸ to deliver to a place : *Drop off this package at the post office.* **2. diminuer, baisser ▸** to become less; weaken : *Sales of that computer have really dropped off lately.* **3. s'endormir ▸** to fall asleep : *After the baby dropped off, Dad put him in the crib.*

drop out décrocher (de), laisser tomber, abandonner, renoncer ▸ to stop attending to or taking part in something : *to drop out of school.* **Note.** Often used as a NOUN: *The city is setting up a special program for high-school dropouts.*

drought [drowt] NOUN, droughts. **sécheresse ▸** a long period of time when there is no rain : *The crops were very small because of the long summer drought.*

drove[1] [drove] VERB. **conduire ▸** a past form of drive.

drove[2] NOUN, droves. **1. troupeau ▸** a bunch of animals moving together, especially cattle or other farm animals. **2. foule ▸** a crowd of people : *People turned out in droves to watch the parade.*

drown [drown] VERB, drowned, drowning. **1. (se) noyer ▸** to die because water or other liquid fills the lungs so that one cannot breathe : *Lifeguards patrol the beaches to be sure that no one is drowning.* **2.** (usually used with out) **couvrir, noyer, étouffer ▸** to cover up one sound with a louder sound : *The sound of the wind and the crashing waves drowned out all other sounds.*

drow-sy [DROW-zee] ADJECTIVE, drowsier, drowsiest. **somnolent (-ente) ▸** not fully awake; sleepy : *"Little by little, peace filled me. In drowsy content I listened as she went on."* (Jean Little) ■ **drowsily,** ADVERB: ▸ **avec un air endormi.** *His head nodded drowsily, and slowly his eyes closed.*

drug [drug] NOUN, drugs. **1. remède, médicament ▸** a medical substance used to treat or cure disease or pain in the body; a medicine : *Aspirin and penicillin are common drugs.* **2. drogue, stupéfiant ▸** a substance that has a strong effect on the mind or body and that can become habit-forming : *Nicotine is an addictive drug.* ▲ VERB, drugged, drugging. **droguer ▸** to give a drug to a person : *In spy movies, people are often drugged to get them to tell secrets.* **Note.** A druggist is a person who is licensed to sell drugs. Another name for a druggist is a pharmacist. **Note.** A store in which drugs are sold is a **drugstore** (☞ **p. 1049**) or pharmacy.

drum [drum] NOUN, drums. **1. tambour, tambourin ▸** a musical instrument made of a hollow frame shaped like a bowl or circle with a tight cover. The cover is struck with the hands or with sticks to make a sound. **2. bidon, tonnelet ▸** any container shaped like a drum : *Gasoline is sometimes stored in drums.* ▲ VERB, **drummed, drumming. 1. battre le tambour, tambouriner ▸** to beat on or play a drum. **2. pianoter, tambouriner ▸** to make repeated sounds like drum beats : *Dad drummed his fingers on the table.* **3. enfoncer, fourrer ▸** to force with steady or repeated efforts : *We finally drummed it into our dog's head not to chase cars.* **Note.** A person who plays drums is a drummer. SYN : beat, tap, pound, strike. ◉ **p. 537.**

drum-stick [DRUM-stik] NOUN, **drumsticks. 1. baguette ▸** the wooden stick used to beat a drum. **2. pilon ▸** the lower part of the leg from a cooked bird such as a chicken or turkey.

drunk [drunk] VERB. **boire ▸** a past form of drink: *The other guests had drunk all the lemonade by the time we got there.* ▲ ADJECTIVE, **drunker, drunkest. soûl (soûle), ivre ▸** not in proper control of one's thoughts or actions because of drinking too much alcohol.

dry [dry] ADJECTIVE, **drier, driest. 1. sec (sèche) ▸** having very little or no water : *The desert is a hot, dry place.* **2. assoiffé (-ée) ▸** needing a drink; thirsty. **3. plat, ennuyeux (-euse), insipide ▸** boring; dull : *Zoe thought the history book was very dry.* ▲ VERB, **dried, drying. essuyer, sécher, éponger ▸** to make or become dry : *to dry the dishes ; to dry one's hair.* SYN : waterless, arid, thirsty.

dry cell **pile sèche ▸** an electric cell whose current is produced by a chemical paste that cannot spill; a dry battery.

du-al [DOO-ul] ADJECTIVE. **double, à deux ▸** made up of or having two matching or similar parts; double : *Some airplanes have dual controls for the pilot and co-pilot.*

duch-ess [DUCH-is] NOUN, **duchesses. duchesse ▸** a noble title or rank that is just below a princess.

duck[1] [duk] NOUN, **ducks. 1. canard ▸** a waterbird with webbed feet and a broad bill. Ducks have waterproof feathers. **2. cane ▸** the female of this bird. The male bird is called a drake. **Note.** A young or baby duck is a duckling.

duck[2] VERB, **ducked, ducking. 1. se baisser vivement ▸** to lower the head quickly; bend down : *Jordan ducked his head as he entered the room.* **2. plonger la tête dans l'eau ▸** to push under water for a short time : *We were splashing and ducking each other in the pool.* **3. esquiver ▸** to avoid or dodge : *The movie star ducked the reporters who wanted to interview her.*

duct [dukt] NOUN, **ducts. 1. conduite, canalisation ▸** a tube or pipe that holds moving air or liquid : *They hope to be able to use the heating ducts for the new air-conditioning system.* **2. canal, conduit ▸** a tube in the body for carrying bodily liquids : *Tears flow from tear ducts in the upper eyelids.*

due [doo] ADJECTIVE. **1. dû (due) ▸** owed to someone as a debt or right : *Don't worry, you'll get every cent that is due you.* **2. qu'on doit, qui convient ▸** proper or suitable : *"In due time I quieted down."* (Anne Frank) **3. attendu (-ue), prévu (-ue) ▸** expected, promised, or required : *The bus is due to stop here soon, so let's keep waiting.* ▲ NOUN, **dues. 1. dû ▸** something that is deserved ; something due : *to give a person his due.* **2. dues. cotisation, contribution, quote-part ▸** money that is paid by members to belong to a club or organization. ▲ ADVERB. **tout droit ▸** straight ; directly : *The reception hall is due south of the church.* ◉ **p. 190.**

due to **dû à, attribuable à ▸** because of : *The rain is due to a bad storm west of here.*

du-el [DOO-ul] NOUN, **duels. 1. duel ▸** a fight between two people to settle a quarrel or point of honour. **2. duel, bataille ▸** any fight or struggle between two opposing sides : *a duel in baseball between the batter and the pitcher.* ▲ VERB, **duelled, duelling.** (also **dueled, dueling**) **se battre en duel ▸** to fight or take part in a duel.

du-et [doo-ET] NOUN, **duets. duo ▸** a piece of music that is written for two instruments or two voices.

dug [dug] VERB. **creuser ▸** a past form of dig.

dug-out [DUG-owt] NOUN, **dugouts. 1. abri ▸** a small shelter next to a baseball field where the players sit when they are not batting or playing in the field. **2. pirogue ▸** a canoe or boat made from a hollowed-out log.

duke [dook] NOUN, **dukes. duc (duchesse) ▸** a noble title or rank that is just below a prince.

dull [dul] ADJECTIVE, **duller, dullest. 1. émoussé (-ée) ▸** not sharp or pointed ; blunt : *I can't cut the cardboard with these dull scissors.* **2. terne, sans éclat ▸** not clear or sharp to the senses : *a dull colour.* **3. lent (lente), borné (-ée), obtus (-use) ▸** slow to learn or understand ; not alert.

✎ Writing Tips

Due to vs. Due

Due to is a phrase that means "because of," "owing to," or "caused by."

- *Due to generally follows the verb "to be."*

  The delay was **due to** an accident.

- Due on its own is an adjective.

  My library books are **due**.

4. ennuyeux (-euse), insignifiant (-ante), terne, banal (-als) ▸ not exciting; boring : *Blair found life in the country rather dull after her visit to Toronto.* ▲ VERB, dulled, dulling. **atténuer, amortir, assourdir, émousser** ▸ to make or become dull : *We put special tile on the ceiling to dull the noise.*

dumb [dum] ADJECTIVE. dumber, dumbest. **1. muet (muette), sidéré (-ée), abasourdi (-ie)** ▸ not able to speak : *Everyone was struck dumb by the destruction caused by the flood.* **2.** *Informal.* **stupide, bête, idiot (idiote), imbécile** ▸ stupid ; foolish : *Running barefoot was really a dumb thing to do.*

dum·my [DUM-ee] NOUN, dummies. **1. mannequin** ▸ a copy of a human figure, used as a substitute for a person : *The dressmaker used a dummy of the actor to make her costume.* **2. maquette** ▸ anything made to look like something else and be used in its place : *When a book is being made, the publisher uses a dummy of the pages to show what they will look like.* SYN : imitation, copy, model, fake.

dump [dump] VERB, dumped, dumping. **jeter, déposer, larguer** ▸ to get rid of; unload in a pile : *Carrie dumped her laundry in a pile.* ▲ NOUN, dumps. **dépotoir** ▸ a place to throw out trash and garbage : *a city dump.* 👁 p. 261.

dune [doon] NOUN, dunes. **dune** ▸ a ridge of sand that is piled and shaped by the wind : *Many people think deserts are nothing but endless sand dunes.*

dun·geon [DUN-jun] NOUN, dungeons. **cachot** ▸ a dark underground prison or cell.

dupe [dup] VERB, duped, duping. **tromper, abuser, décevoir, duper** ▸ to deceive or trick : *Tony was duped into thinking that his coin was real.* SYN : trick, fool, hoax, deceive, betray.

du·pli·cate [DOO-pluh-kit] NOUN, duplicates. **duplicata, double, copie exacte** ▸ something that is an exact copy or just like something else : *Luke wants a duplicate of that picture.* ▲ ADJECTIVE **double, duplicata** ▸ exactly like something else : *a duplicate set of keys to the car.* ▲ [DOO-pluh-KATE] VERB, duplicated, duplicating. **1. photocopier, faire un double, reproduire** ▸ to make an exact copy : *Photocopiers are used to duplicate letters.* **2. répéter, faire un doublé** ▸ to do or make again; repeat : *Can last season's hockey champs duplicate their winning season?* SYN : copy, double, replica, reproduction.

dur·a·ble [DUR-uh-bul] ADJECTIVE. **durable, solide, résistant (-ante)** ▸ able to last a long time : *That lawn mover is very durable—I've had it for over 20 years.* SYN : enduring, endless, strong, sturdy, solid.

dur·ing [DUR-ing] PREPOSITION. **pendant, durant** ▸ throughout or at some point in the course of : *The phone rang six times during dinner.*

dusk [dusk] NOUN. **crépuscule** ▸ the time of evening just before dark : *We danced from dusk to dawn.* SYN : sunset, sundown, nightfall, evening.

dust [dust] NOUN. **poussière** ▸ fine, dry particles of dirt : *A cloud of dust surrounded the car as it raced down the dirt road.* ▲ VERB, dusted, dusting. **1. épousseter, essuyer** ▸ to wipe or brush dust off some surface : *She dusts the furniture every week.* **2. saupoudrer** ▸ to sprinkle or powder something : *The baker dusted the rolls with powdered sugar.* **Note.** Something covered with dust, or appearing this way, is **dusty**.

du·ty [DOO-tee] NOUN, duties. **1. devoir, obligation** ▸ something that a person has to do, or should do because it is right, proper, or the law : *It is a citizen's duty to vote in elections.* **2. fonction, responsabilité** ▸ a certain task or type of work that is called for by a particular job : *Your duties include keeping the play area clean.* **3. frais de douane, taxe, impôt, droit** ▸ a tax paid to the government for goods brought into a country. SYN : responsibility, task, job, chore, obligation.

dwarf [dworf] NOUN, dwarfs or dwarves. **1. nain (naine), nabot (nabote)** ▸ a full-grown person, animal, or plant that is much smaller than usual size. **2. nain (naine), nabot (nabote)** ▸ in fairy tales, a very small person who has magic powers. ▲ VERB, dwarfed, dwarfing. **rapetisser, écraser** ▸ to cause to appear small : *The tall redwoods dwarfed all the other trees in the forest.*

dwell [dwel] VERB, dwelt or dwelled, dwelling. **habiter, demeurer, résider** ▸ to live in or make one's home : *"Far away in the land of eternal snow and ice dwelt North Wind."* (Rosebud Yellow Robe) **Note.** A dweller is a person who lives somewhere : *city dweller.*

dwell on **s'étendre, insister, appuyer** ▸ to think, write, or speak about at length : *The professor was known to dwell on his favourite subject for hours at a time.* SYN : live, reside, occupy, inhabit.

dwell·ing [DWEL-ing] NOUN, dwellings. **maison, résidence, habitation** ▸ the place where someone lives; one's home : *"The houses of the Munchkins were odd-looking dwellings, for each was round with a big dome for a roof."* (L. Frank Baum)

dye [dy] NOUN, dyes. **teinture, colorant** ▸ a substance used to change the colour of things such as food, hair, and cloth. ▲ VERB, dyed, dyeing. **teindre, colorer** ▸ to add colour to or change the colour of something : *Cindy dyed an old white blouse bright red.* SYN : colour, stain, tint.

dy·ing [DY-ing] VERB. **mourir** ▸ a present form of die¹.

dy·nam·ic [dy-NAM-ik] ADJECTIVE. **1. dynamique, énergique** ▸ having to do with energy or force in motion. **2.** **dynamique, énergique, actif (-ive), entreprenant (-ante)** ▶ having great energy and enthusiasm : *The dynamic performer got a huge round of applause*. SYN: energetic, forceful, strong, lively, animated.

dy·na·mite [DY-nuh-MITE] NOUN. **dynamite** ▶ a very powerful explosive, often used in blasting rocks. Dynamite is made from nitroglycerine.

▲ VERB, dynamited, dynamiting. **dynamiter, faire sauter** ▶ to blow up with dynamite : *The workers dynamited the hillside to build a new road.*

dy·nas·ty [DY-nus-tee] NOUN, dynasties. (sometimes Dynasty) **dynastie** ▶ a series of leaders or rulers who are from the same family : China was ruled by the Ching Dynasty from 1644 to 1912.

Earth

e, E [ee] NOUN. e's, E's. **e, E** ▶ the fifth letter of the English alphabet.

each [eech] ADJECTIVE. **chaque** ▶ one of two or more people or things : *"Marion travelled to each town along the Nashua."* (Lynne Cherry) ▲ PRONOUN. **chacun (-une)** ▶ every one : *Each of the students will read one page.* ▲ ADVERB. **chacun (-une)** ▶ for or to every one : *Those books cost 90 cents each.*

ea-ger [EE-gur] ADJECTIVE. **désireux (-euse), avide, impatient (-ente), pressé (-ée)** ▶ wanting to do or have something very much : *Andrew is always eager to help in the kitchen.* ■ **eagerly,** ADVERB. ▶ **avidement, impatiemment, passionnément, ardemment.** *"When the teacher gave me my reader, I opened it eagerly."* (Jean Little) ✎ **p. 26.**

ea-gle [EE-gul] NOUN. eagles. **aigle** ▶ a large bird with a long hooked beak, strong claws, and broad wings. Eagles have keen eyesight and feed on small animals.

ear[1] [eer] NOUN. ears. **1. oreille** ▶ the part of the body that is used to hear. The human ear is divided into three parts : the outer ear, middle ear, and inner ear. **2. oreille, audition, ouïe** ▶ the ability to use the sense of hearing : *Karl has a good ear for music.* 📖 **p. 976.** ✎ **p. 194.**

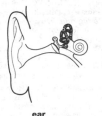

ear

ear[2] NOUN. ears. **épi** ▶ the part of corn, wheat, and other cereal plants on which the seeds grow.

earl [url] NOUN. earls. **comte** ▶ a title of noble rank in Great Britain, ranking above a viscount and below a marquis.

ear-ly [UR-lee] ADJECTIVE. earlier, earliest. **1. tôt** ▶ near the beginning : *These flowers are at their best early in the summer.* **2. tôt, à l'avance, prématuré (-ée), précoce** ▶ before the usual time : *Today, Charlie got up early to go fishing.* **3. premier (-ière), primitif (-ive), ancien (-ienne)** ▶ of a time long ago ; ancient : *Sanda's family moved to Canada in the early days of the country.* ▲ ADVERB. **1. tôt** ▶ near the beginning : *"Calves come early in the spring."* (Gary Paulsen) **2. tôt, à l'avance** ▶ before the usual time : *The train arrived early.*

ear-muffs [EER mufs] NOUN. **cache-oreilles** ▶ a pair of coverings for ears to keep them warm.

earn [urn] VERB. earned, earning. **1. gagner** ▶ to get paid for working : *Brian earns $25 a week mowing lawns.* **2. mériter** ▶ to get something one deserves : *Ali worked hard to earn a good mark on her report.* SYN: make, deserve, merit, get, gain, obtain, rate.

ear-nest [UR-nist] ADJECTIVE. **sérieux (-euse), consciencieux (-euse), sincère, ardent (-ente)** ▶ strong in one's purpose ; serious and sincere : *He made an earnest attempt to control his temper.* ■ **earnestly,** ADVERB. ▶ **sérieusement, consciencieusement, sincèrement, ardemment.** *Jon trained earnestly for the race*

in earnest *seriously : She spoke in earnest.*

earn-ings [UR-ningz] PLURAL NOUN. **1. salaire, gains** ▶ money made from working ; payment. **2. profit, bénéfice** ▶ the amount of money that a company makes after all its expenses are paid ; profit.

ear-phone [EER-fone] NOUN. earphones. **écouteur** ▶ a device worn on the ears to listen to a radio, tape player, telephone, or the like.

ear-ring [EER-ring] NOUN. earrings. **boucle d'oreille** ▶ a piece of jewellery worn on the ear.

earth [urth] NOUN. **1.** (also Earth) **Terre, monde** ▶ the planet we live on. Earth is the fifth-largest planet in the solar system and is the third

🖋 Word Builder

*When a person is **all ears,** he or she is listening very closely: Nila was all ears as she listened to her father's story. However, **in one ear and out the other** means the opposite—the person is not listening closely at all: My mother's instructions went in one ear and out the other. **Up to the ears** means a person is deeply involved in his or her work or problems: He is up to his ears in homework and can't go out. **By ear** can mean to do something without a plan, or that a person can play an instrument without reading music: Lee can't read music, he plays piano by ear.*

planet from the sun. **2. terre, sol** ▶ the surface of the earth, as opposed to the oceans or sky; soil or dirt; ground : *Helen raked the loose earth around the plants in her garden.* 📖 p. 1113. 👁 p. 391.

down to earth pratique, réaliste ▶ practical; realistic.

earth-quake [URTH-KWAKE] NOUN, earthquakes. **tremblement de terre, séisme** ▶ a very strong shaking or rolling of the ground occurring when rock or other material moves suddenly under the ground. 📖 p. 1113.

earth-worm [URTH-WURM] NOUN, earthworms. **ver de terre** ▶ a common worm that lives in the soil. Earthworms have long, tube-like bodies that they stretch out or bunch up in order to move in the ground.

ear-wig [EER-wig] NOUN, earwigs. **perce-oreille** ▶ an insect with antennae, a long, slender body, and a pair of strong pincers.

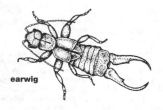

earwig

ease [eez] NOUN. **1. tranquillité, bien-être, à l'aise** ▶ freedom from worry, trouble, or pain; comfort : *Mr. Rallis looks forward to a life of ease when he retires next year.* **2. aisance, facilité** ▶ freedom from difficulty or great effort : *"He ran with such ease that his strides seemed to be a single flowing movement."* (Walter Farley) ▲ VERB, eased, easing. **1. soulager, calmer, atténuer, tranquilliser** ▶ to make free from worry, trouble, or pain; make easier : *Sally took some medicine to ease the soreness in her throat.* **2. bouger doucement, délicatement** ▶ to move slowly and carefully : *Adam eased his way through the crowd.* SYN: soothe, relieve, lessen, relax, reduce.

eas-el [EE-zul] NOUN, easels. **chevalet** ▶ a stand or rack for holding pictures or signs : *The artist often uses an easel while painting.*

eas-i-ly [EE-zuh-lee] ADVERB. **1. facilement, aisément** ▶ without trying hard; with no difficulty : *"He squatted with one knee on the ground, entranced by the sight of his daughter easily beating her brother."* (Gary Soto) **2. facilement, sans aucun doute, de loin** ▶ without doubt or question : *This was easily the best movie I've seen all summer.* **3. calmement, tranquillement** ▶ without pain or trouble : *The patient rested easily.*

east [eest] NOUN. **1. est, orient, levant** ▶ the direction that the sun comes from when it rises in the morning. **2. (usually East) est** ▶ any place or region in that direction. **3. the East. a. est** ▶ the eastern part of Canada or the United States. For western Canadians, the East includes the provinces from Ontario eastward; for Ontarians, it means the Atlantic Provinces. **b. orient** ▶ the countries to the east of Europe; the Orient. ▲ ADJECTIVE. **1. est** ▶ toward the east : *the east side of the street.* **2. est, oriental (-ale, -aux)** ▶ coming from the east : *an east wind.* ▲ ADVERB. **est** ▶ toward the east : *The plane flew due east.*

East-er [EES-tur] NOUN, Easters. **Pâques** ▶ a Christian holiday to celebrate Christ's rising from the dead, held on the Sunday after the first full moon of spring, between March 21 and April 26.

east-ern [EES-turn] ADJECTIVE. **1. est, oriental (-ale, -aux)** ▶ coming from the east : *Eastern winds bring rain.* **2. est** ▶ toward the east : *He lives at the eastern end of the valley.* **3. est, oriental (-ale, -aux)** ▶ of or in the eastern part of Canada : *Halifax is an eastern port.* **4. oriental (-ale, -aux)** ▶ having to do with Asia or the nearby islands; Asian. **Note.** An Easterner is a person born or living in the east.

east-ward [EEST-wurd] ADVERB. (also eastwards) **à l'est** ▶ to or toward the east : *Continue eastward until you come to a gate.* ▲ ADJECTIVE. *The farm is on the eastward side of the road.*

eas-y [EE-zee] ADJECTIVE, easier, easiest. **1. facile** ▶ needing only a little work or effort; not hard to do : *an easy job.* **2. aisé (-ée), facile, tranquille** ▶ comfortable; restful; relaxed : *She* had an easy way of speaking. **3. accommodant (-ante)** ▸ not hard to please : *"Christoph, I will admit that Mr. Beethoven does not seem to be an easy guest."* (Barbara Nichol) **4. facile, simple** ▸ free from pain, worry, or trouble : *I think math is an easier subject than art.* **5. modéré (-ée)** ▸ not rushed : *an easy pace.* SYN: not hard, simple, effortless, uncomplicated.

eat [eet] VERB, ate, eaten, eating. **1. manger** ▸ to chew and swallow food : *to eat an apple.* **2. déjeuner, dîner, prendre** ▸ to have a meal : *to eat lunch.* **3. saper, éroder, ronger** ▸ to wear away or destroy as if by eating : *Rust is eating away at the paint on my car.* **Note.** Someone who eats is an **eater**: *Mom says all her children are fussy eaters.* SYN: dine, chew, swallow, consume.

eaves [eevz] PLURAL NOUN. **avant-toit** ▸ the lower part of a roof that hangs out over the side of a building. **Note.** An eavestrough is a gutter placed under the eaves to catch the rain water.

eaves-drop [EEVZ-drop] VERB, eavesdropped, eavesdropping. **écouter de façon indiscrète** ▸ to listen to other people talking without their knowing it : *Moira eavesdropped on her sisters' private conversation.*

ebb [eb] NOUN, ebbs. **reflux** ▸ the flowing of the ocean tide away from shore. ▲ VERB, ebbed, ebbing. **1. refluer, descendre** ▸ of the tide, to flow out. **2. décliner, baisser** ▸ to grow less; weaken or decline : *The runner's energy ebbed 20 km into the race.* SYN: lessen, recede, subside, withdraw, diminish.

eb-on-y [EB-uh-nee] NOUN. **ébène** ▸ a hard, heavy wood that comes from trees grown in Africa and Asia. Ebony is used to make the black keys of a piano and for other woodwork.

ec-cen-tric [ik-SEN-trik] ADJECTIVE. **excentrique, original (-ale, -aux), bizarre** ▸ not in the normal or usual way; odd; peculiar : *Emily's neighbours think that she is eccentric because she has so many cats.*

ech-o [EK-oh] NOUN, echoes. **écho** ▸ a sound that is heard again because it bounces off a surface and comes back : *When I sing in the shower, the echo makes my voice sound better.* ▲ VERB, echoed, echoing. **1. répercuter, renvoyer** ▸ to send back the sound of something; make an echo : *"Their merriment increased until it rang and echoed through the trees."* (Tololwa M. Mollel) **2. répéter** ▸ to repeat what has already been said : *The second speaker just echoed what the first speaker had said.*

e-clipse [ee-KLIPS] NOUN, eclipses. **éclipse** ▸ a darkening or hiding of the sun, the moon, or a planet. A solar eclipse occurs when the moon passes between the sun and the earth, partly or completely hiding the sun. A lunar eclipse occurs when the earth passes between the sun and the moon, causing the earth's shadow to partly or completely darken the moon. ▲ VERB, eclipsed, eclipsing. **1. éclipser** ▸ to cause or form an eclipse. **2. éclipser, surpasser** ▸ to make something else seem less important; overshadow : *Rob's steady playing was eclipsed by Jean's winning goal.* SYN: hide, conceal, cover, screen, shadow.

e-col-o-gy [ih-KOL-uh-jee *or* ee-KOL-uh-jee] NOUN. **1. écologie** ▸ the scientific study of how plants and animals relate to each other and to their environment. **2. écologie** ▸ a situation in which there is a balanced relationship between living things and their environment : *Dead trees left to rot are part of the ecology of a wilderness.* ■ **ecological,** ADJECTIVE. ▸ **écologique.** *a lake's ecological balance.*

ec-o-nom-i-cal [EK-uh-NOM-uh-kul *or* EE-kuh-NOM-uh-kul] ADJECTIVE. **économique** ▸ using or operating with little waste; saving money or resources : *Mom says it's more economical to buy in bulk.* ■ **economically,** ADVERB: ▸ **économiquement.** *His car must run economically because he drives a long way to work.*

ec-o-nom-ics [EK-uh-NOM-iks *or* EE-kuh-NOM-iks] NOUN. **économie** ▸ the study of the making, selling, and using of goods and services. Economics includes the study of such matters as money, income, business, and taxes. ■ **economic,** ADJECTIVE. **économique** ▸ having to do with economics : *The prime minister proposed a new economic program that would lower taxes.* **Note.** An economist is an expert in economics.

e-con-o-my [ih-KON-uh-mee *or* EE-KON-uh-mee] NOUN, economies. **1. économie** ▸ the way that the money and goods of a country are developed and used by its people : *The country's economy is strong.* **2. économie** ▸ the careful use of money, goods, or other resources : *Mai practises many small economies to keep within her budget.*

e-co-sys-tem [EE-koh-SIS-tum *or* EK-oh-SIS-tum] NOUN, ecosystems. **écosystème** ▸ all the living plants and animals in one area or habitat, as well as their interactions.

ec-sta-sy [EK-stuh-see] NOUN, ecstasies. **extase** ▸ a very great happiness or delight : *Slowly, wonderingly, a grin of ecstasy began to stretch itself across Paul's face.* SYN: joy, happiness, delight, glee, rapture.

edge [ej] NOUN, edges. **1. bord, bordure, rive, lisière,** ▸ the line or place where something ends : *an edge of a table; the edge of the forest.* **2. tranchant, fil** ▸ the cutting side of a blade or tool. ▲ VERB, edged, edging. **1. border** ▸ to give an edge to; border : *The designer edged the dress with lace.* **2. se glisser, se faufiler** ▸ to move carefully or little by little : *Tim edged away from the cliff.* SYN: border, boundary, margin, fringe, brink.

ed·i·ble [ED-uh-bul] ADJECTIVE. **comestible** ▸ safe or fit to eat : *Some wild mushrooms are edible, and some are poisonous.*

ed·it [ED-it] VERB, edited, editing. **1. corriger, vérifier** ▸ to check, correct, and improve writing : *Elise edited her story before giving it to her teacher.* **2. éditer, diriger la publication de** ▸ to check, correct, and otherwise prepare writing to be published : *Books are edited before they are published.* **3. monter** ▸ to prepare a film, tape recording, or the like by arranging and cutting the available materials.

e·di·tion [ih-DISH-un] NOUN, editions. **1. édition** ▸ the form in which a book is printed : *Many novels are available in both hardcover and paperback editions.* **2. tirage** ▸ one of many copies of a book, newspaper, or magazine published at one time : *The first edition of a famous book is often worth a lot of money.*

ed·i·tor [ED-ih-tur] NOUN, editors. **1. éditeur (-trice)** ▸ a person who edits written material. **2. rédacteur (-trice) en chef, directeur (-trice)** ▸ the person in charge of a newspaper, magazine, reference book, or other large publication, or one of its departments : *a sports editor; a features editor.* **3. réalisateur (-trice)** ▸ a person who edits a film or tape recording. **Note.** The work that is done by an editor is **editing**.

ed·i·to·ri·al [ED-ih-TOR-ee-ul] NOUN, editorials. **éditorial (-aux)** ▸ an article in a newspaper or magazine, or a speech on television or radio, that gives an opinion on a topic rather than just the facts. ▲ ADJECTIVE. **1. éditorial (-aux)** ▸ having to do with an editorial : *editorial pages.* **2. rédactionnel (-elle)** ▸ having to do with an editor or with editing : *to make editorial changes in a paper.* ✐ p. 196.

ed·u·cate [EJ-yuh-KATE] VERB, educated, educating. **instruire, former, éduquer** ▸ to teach or train a person's mind or character in a certain way : *Both her parents were educated at the University of Alberta.* **Note.** A person whose work is educating people is an **educator**. SYN: teach, instruct, train, guide, show, lead.

ed·u·ca·tion [EJ-yuh-KAY-shun] NOUN. **1. éducation** ▸ the development of the mind and character through study, training, and experience; the gaining of knowledge about the world in general or about some particular subject. **2. éducation, instruction, études, formation** ▸ a certain type of knowledge and training : *To get that job, you have to have at least a high-school education.* **3. éducation, pédagogie, enseignement** ▸ the study of teaching and the methods and problems of teaching and learning. 🖭 p. 1058.

ed·u·ca·tion·al [EJ-yuh-KAY-shun-ul] ADJECTIVE. **1. pédagogique** ▸ having to do with education : *Many parents and teachers belong to an educational association.* **2. éducatif (-ive), instructif (-ive)** ▸ giving information or knowledge : *an educational television series.*

✐ Writing Tips

Editorial

An *editorial* is a piece of writing that gives the writer's opinion. Editorials appear in newspapers, magazines, and on radio or TV. If you write an editorial,

- state your opinion clearly at the beginning
- give some background information on the topic
- support your opinion with facts
- give reasons for the position you have taken on the issue
- restate your opinion at the end, using new wording if possible.

You could also read some editorials in newspapers and magazines to see how they work.

eel [eel] NOUN, eels. **anguille** ▸ a long, thin fish that looks like a snake and has smooth, slimy skin. 👁 p. 107.

ee·rie [EER-ee] ADJECTIVE, eerier, eeriest. **sinistre, inquiétant (-ante)** ▸ strange and scary; frightening : *Tania was scared by the eerie shadows cast by the moon.* ■ **eerily,** ADVERB. **sinistrement** ▸ *Although it was the middle of the day, the streets were eerily quiet and empty.*

SYN: strange, spooky, peculiar, weird, scary.

ef·fect [ih-FEKT] NOUN, effects. **1. effet, conséquence, résultat** ▸ something that happens because of something else; result : *The effects of that medicine last for about five hours.* ✐ p. 12. **2. effet** ▸ the power to change or influence something : *The new library hours go into effect tomorrow.* **3. effects. biens** ▸ belongings; property : *Students keep their personal effects in lockers.* **4. in effect. a. prendre effet, entrer en vigueur** ▸ in operation; active. **b. effet** ▸ in actual fact; really : *Mary is only a club member, but in effect she runs the whole thing.* ▲ VERB, effected, effecting. **effectuer, apporter, opérer, réaliser** ▸ to make happen; cause : *The new teacher has effected many changes in the way the classroom is run.* SYN: cause, bring about, achieve, produce.

ef·fec·tive [ih-FEK-tiv] ADJECTIVE. **1. efficace** ▸ able to change or influence something : *The coach's game plan was really effective—we won the game!* **2. prendre effet, entrer en vigueur** ▸ in force; in effect : *The new dress code becomes effective next term.* ■ **effectively,** ADVERB. ▸ **efficacement.** *That stain remover worked effectively on the spot on my dress.* ■ **effectiveness,** NOUN. ▸ efficacité.

ef·fi·cient [ih-FISH-unt] ADJECTIVE. **efficace** ▸ getting results without wasting time or effort : *Our new air-conditioner is much more efficient at keeping the house cool than the old fan was.* ■ **efficiently,** ADVERB: ▸ **efficacement.** *He has kept up with his schoolwork more efficiently since he got a computer.* **Note.** The state of being efficient is efficiency: *New cars are rated on fuel efficiency.* SYN: effective, skillful, competent, businesslike.

ef·fort [EF-urt] NOUN. **efforts. 1. effort** ▸ the use of energy to do something ; hard work : *With some effort, they lifted the heavy box onto the table.* **2. effort** ▸ a try or attempt : *"But the emperor, despite the governor's best efforts, was never able to taste that most delicious New World dish."* (Paul Yee) ■ **effortless,** ADJECTIVE. **facile, aisé (-ée)** ▸ with little or no effort : *That player makes tennis look effortless.* ■ **effortlessly,** ADVERB: ▸ **facilement, aisément.** *He runs so effortlessly.* 📖 p. 1028.

egg[1] [eg] NOUN. **eggs. 1. œuf** ▸ a round or oval object produced by a female bird, fish, insect, or reptile, from which the young hatches. **2. ovule** ▸ a special cell that is produced in the body of a woman or a female animal.

egg[2] VERB, **egged, egging. inciter, pousser** ▸ to encourage to do something, especially something one should not do or does not want to do : *While the two boys argued, several others egged them on to fight.* SYN: urge, provoke, put up to.

egg·plant [EG-plant] NOUN. **eggplants. aubergine** ▸ a vegetable that is shaped like a large egg, having a shiny purple skin.

e·go [EE-goh] NOUN. **egos. 1. ego, moi** ▸ a feeling in the mind that makes a person aware that he or she is different from others ; the self. **2. ego** ▸ a feeling of being better than others ; a very high opinion of oneself : *He's the star of the team, but the other players don't like him because of his big ego.*

e·gret [EE-gret] NOUN. **egrets. aigrette** ▸ a tall bird with a long neck, a pointed bill, and low white feathers. Egrets are a type of heron.

eight [ate] NOUN, ADJECTIVE. **eights. huit** ▸ the number that is one more than seven ; 8. ■ **eighth,** ADJECTIVE, NOUN. ▸ **huitième.**

eight·een [AY-teen] NOUN, ADJECTIVE. **dix-huit** ▸ the number that is eight more than ten ; 18. ■ **eighteenth,** ADJECTIVE, NOUN. ▸ **dix-huitième.**

eight·y [AY-tee] NOUN, ADJECTIVE. **quatre-vingts** ▸ the number that is equal to eight times ten ; 80. ■ **eightieth,** ADJECTIVE, NOUN. ▸ **quatre-vingtième.**

ei·ther [EE-thur or EYE-thur] ADJECTIVE. **n'importe lequel (laquelle)** ▸ one or the other of two : *We can take either road.* ▲ PRONOUN. **n'importe lequel (laquelle)** ▸ one or the other of two things : *There are two new movies in town, but I*

haven't seen either of them. ▲ CONJUNCTION. **ou** ▸ (used with or) *We can have either potatoes or rice with the chicken.* ▲ ADVERB. **soit** ▸ also ; besides : *Greg didn't go to the party, and his sister didn't go either.*

e·ject [ee-JEKT] VERB, **ejected, ejecting. éjecter, expulser** ▸ to throw or push out : *Evan ejected the tape from the VCR before turning the machine off.* SYN: remove, expel, drive out.

e·lab·o·rate [ih-LAB-ur-it or ih-LAB-rit] ADJECTIVE. **minutieux (-euse), complexe, détaillé (-ée), compliqué (-ée)** ▸ worked out or developed with great care and detail : *Elaborate plans were made for the Queen's visit to Canada.* ▲ [ih-LAB-ur-rate] VERB, **elaborated, elaborating. élaborer** ▸ to work out with great care ; add details : *Mr. Levi sent out a memo to elaborate on what he had said at the meeting.* ■ **elaborately,** ADVERB. ▸ **minutieusement, soigneusement.** SYN: expand, detail, work out, develop.

e·lapse [ih-LAPS] VERB, **elapsed, elapsing. s'écouler, passer** ▸ to pass or go by : *Hours elapsed as Trent read his new book.* SYN: run out, expire, pass, slip away.

e·las·tic [ih-LAS-tik] ADJECTIVE. **élastique** ▸ able to be stretched or squeezed and then return to its original shape : *Rubber is an elastic material.* ▲ NOUN, **elastics. élastique** ▸ something that is elastic, such as a rubber band. SYN: flexible, stretchy, springy, pliable.

el·bow [EL-boh] NOUN, **elbows. 1. coude** ▸ the joint that connects the upper and lower arm. **2. coude** ▸ something with the shape of a bent elbow, such as a piece of pipe. ▲ VERB, **elbowed, elbowing. se frayer un chemin avec les coudes, avancer en jouant des coudes, donner un coup de coude** ▸ to put or shove using the elbows : *The man elbowed his way through the crowd to get to the front.* 📖 p. 994.

eld·er [EL-dur] ADJECTIVE. **aîné (-ée)** ▸ being older than another person, especially a brother or sister : *Margaret is named after her father's elder sister.* ▲ NOUN, **elders. 1. aîné (-ée)** ▸ a person who is older : *It is polite to speak respectfully to one's elders.* **Note.** Someone who is the oldest of a number of people is the eldest. **2.** (often Elder) **aîné (-ée)** ▸ an older, influential person of a family, tribe, or community : *"One of my friends and teachers was a native elder named Swift Eagle."* (Joseph Bruchac) **3.** the elder. **aîné (-ée), père** ▸ the older of two people with the same name : *The famous painting* The Harvesters *is by Pieter Brueghel the Elder.* **Note.** A person who is very old is said to be elderly. We often speak of older people as a group as the elderly. 📖 p. 198.

e·lect [ih-LEKT] VERB, **elected, electing. 1. élire** ▸ to choose by voting : *Members of City Council are elected every two years.* **Note.** The act or fact of electing someone is an election. **2. choisir, opter** ▸ to choose or decide on a

✐ **Writing Tips**

Elder and Eldest

Elder and **eldest** are used to compare the ages of people, animals, or things.

• *Elder* is used when comparing two things

  I have two brothers Tom and Jake.

  Tom is the elder of the two.

• *Eldest* is used when more than two things are being compared.

  Rover is the eldest of my four dogs.

certain course of action : *We elected to play cards.* SYN : choose, pick, select, vote for.

e-lec-tion [ih-LEK-shun] NOUN. **élection ▶** the action of electing, of voting. *Rosa will vote in her first electon tomorrow.*

e-lec-tric [ih-LEK-trik] ADJECTIVE. 1. **électrique ▶** having to do with electricity; produced or worked by electricity : *an electric motor; an electric guitar.* 2. **électrique ▶** caused by or containing electricity : *an electric shock.* 3. **électrique ▶** very exciting : *an electric performance.*

e-lec-tric-i-ty [ih-lek-TRIS-uh-tee] NOUN. 1. **électricité ▶** a form of energy that is produced by a current of electrons flowing quickly through a wire or other object. Electricity is used to produce light and heat, provide power to motors, run TVs and radios, and so on. 2. **électricité, courant ▶** electric current : *They shut off the electricity when they closed their cottage for the winter.* **Note.** Anything having to do with electricity is **electrical**: *Modern homes have many electrical appliances.* **Note.** An electrician is a person whose work is installing, fixing, or operating electrical wiring and equipment.

e-lec-tron [ih-LEK-tron] NOUN. electrons. **électron ▶** a very tiny bit of matter that is too small to be seen. Electrons make up the part of an atom that surrounds the **nucleus**.

electronic mail NOUN. **courrier électronique, courriel ▶** a way of sending messages electronically, by means of computers. Using a special program, a message or file can be sent through telephone wires from one computer to another computer. **Note.** Also known as **e-mail**.

e-lec-tron-ics [ih-lek-TRON-iks] NOUN. 1. **électronique ▶** the scientific study of how electrons act and move. The field of electronics includes telephones, radios, TVs, tape players, computers, and so on. 2. **électronique ▶** the area of business and industry that deals with electronic products such as computers and TV sets. **Note.** Something having to do with electrons or electronics is **electronic**: *Electronic music uses sounds that are produced or changed by means of electricity.* ■ **electronically,** ADVERB. ▶ **électroniquement.**

el-e-gant [EL-uh-gunt] ADJECTIVE. **élégant (-ante), distingué (-ée), chic ▶** of a very rich and fine quality ; having beauty and style : *Shiva wore an elegant dress to the party.* **Note.** The state of being elegant is **elegance.** SYN : tasteful, polished, cultured, refined.

el-e-ment [EL-uh-munt] NOUN. elements. 1. **élément ▶** any one of the more than 100 materials from which all other things are made. An element has atoms of only one kind and cannot be broken down into any simpler substances. Carbon, oxygen, and hydrogen are common elements in nature. 2. **élément ▶** one of the basic parts of something : *Interesting characters and exciting action are elements of a good story.* 3. **élément ▶** the most natural place or setting : *Fish can live only in their own element, which is water.* 4. **the elements. éléments ▶** the forces of nature, such as wind, rain, and snow.

el-e-men-ta-ry [EL-uh-MEN-tuh-ree] ADJECTIVE. **élémentaire ▶** dealing with the basic or simplest part : *elementary science; an elementary course in math.* **Note.** An elementary school is a school of six, seven, or eight grades for children six and over. SYN : basic, primary, fundamental, beginning.

el-e-phant [EL-uh-funt] NOUN. elephants. **éléphant ▶** the largest of all land animals. Elephants have a grey body, a long trunk, big, floppy ears, and two tusks of ivory. There are two types of elephants : the **Asian elephant** and the **African elephant.** ☞ **p. 1089.**

el-e-vate [EL-uh-VATE] VERB. elevated, elevating. **hausser, élever ▶** to raise or lift to a higher level : *Elevate your sprained ankle so that the swelling will go down.*

el-e-va-tion [EL-uh-VAY-shun] NOUN. elevations. 1. **élévation, altitude, hauteur ▶** the height above sea level of a certain place : *La Paz, Bolivia, has the highest elevation of any capital city in the world.* 2. **élévation, altitude, hauteur, éminence ▶** a raised place : *Martin got dizzy in the high elevations of the Rocky Mountains.* 3. **élévation ▶** a lifting or raising up of something.

el-e-va-tor [EL-uh-VAY-tuhr] NOUN. elevators. **ascenseur, élévateur, monte-charge ▶** an enclosed car or cage that carries people and things up and down. Elevators operate by using cables and a motor to make them go from one floor to another. **Note.** A grain elevator is a building for storing grain.

e-lev-en [ih-LEV-un] NOUN, ADJECTIVE. elevens. 1. **onze ▶** the number that is one more than 10; 11. 2. **le onze, équipe ▶** a team of 11 football or cricket players. ■ **eleventh,** ADJECTIVE, NOUN. ▶ **onzième.**

elf [elf] NOUN, elves. **elfe, lutin, farfadet** ▸ in stories, a tiny being with magic powers. Elves are usually full of mischief and play tricks on people. SYN : fairy, imp, brownie, mischief-maker.

el·i·gi·ble [EL-uh-juh-bul] ADJECTIVE. **admissible** ▸ having what is required to be or do something; officially qualified : *Students must maintain good grades to be eligible to play on a school team.* **Note.** The state of being eligible is eligibility.

e·lim·i·nate [ih-LIM-uh-NATE] VERB, eliminated, eliminating. **éliminer, supprimer, exclure, écarter** ▸ to leave out or get rid of : *Many people work to eliminate pollution.* **Note.** The act of eliminating is elimination: *City Hall wants the elimination of smoking in restaurants.* SYN : get rid of, abolish, remove, discard, reject.

e·lite [ih-LEET] NOUN. (also élite) **1. élite** ▸ the best or most skilled of a particular group. **2. élite** ▸ a small and privileged group. ▲ ADJECTIVE: an elite group.

elk [elk] NOUN, elks or elk. **1. élan, original** ▸ a large deer of North America, the male of which has very large antlers. **Note.** Also known as a wapiti [WOP-ih-tee]. **2. élan** ▸ the large red deer of Europe. 👁 **p. 111.**

el·lip·sis [ih-LIP-siz] NOUN, ellipses. **ellipse** ▸ in writing or printing, punctuation marks [...] that show something has been left out. Also called ellipsis points. SEE WRITER'S TOOL KIT, PAGE 948.

elm [elm] NOUN, elms. **orme** ▸ a tall shade tree with broad leaves and arching branches. Its strong, hard wood is used for building crates and boxes. **Note.** Most North American elm trees have died from a fungus called Dutch elm disease. 👁 **p. 254.**

el·o·quent [EL-uh-kwunt] ADJECTIVE. **éloquent (-ente)** ▸ having the ability to speak and use words well : *Her eloquent speech inspired people to donate to the hospital.* SYN : well-spoken, expressive, meaningful.

else [els] ADJECTIVE. **1. autre** ▸ other or different : *Who else besides Kelly wants to study Brazil?* **2. autre, d'autre, de plus** ▸ in addition : *Do you expect anyone else?* ▲ ADVERB. **1. autrement, ailleurs** ▸ in a different manner, time, or place : *Manero's is closed today—is there anywhere else good to eat in town?* **2. autrement** ▸ otherwise : *We'd better leave now or else we'll be late.*

else·where [ELS-wair] ADVERB. **ailleurs, autre part** ▸ somewhere else; in another place : *The field is flooded, so our game will have to be played elsewhere.*

e·lude [ih-lood] VERB, eluded, eluding. **éluder, échapper, éviter, esquiver** ▸ to avoid being caught or found : *The football player eluded the other team to get a touchdown.* SYN : avoid, escape, evade, miss, dodge.

em·bark [im-BARK] VERB, embarked, embarking. **1. s'embarquer, se lancer, s'engager, commencer** ▸ to start out; set out : *After university she embarked on a career in banking.* **2. embarquer** ▸ to go onto a ship or an airplane.

em·bar·rass [im-BAIR-us] VERB, embarrassed, embarrassing. **embarrasser, gêner, déconcerter** ▸ to make someone feel uneasy, nervous, or ashamed : *"People came up to congratulate Lupe, and she felt a little embarrassed."* (Gary Soto) **Note.** Often used as an ADJECTIVE: *It was an embarrassing moment for Laura when she spelled her last name wrong on her report.* **Note.** Embarrassment is the feeling of being embarrassed. SYN : rattle, fluster, humiliate, shame, confuse.

em·bas·sy [EM-buh-see] NOUN, embassies. **ambassade** ▸ the official home and place of work of an ambassador and his or her staff in another country : *the Canadian embassy in China.*

em·brace [im-BRASE] VERB, embraced, embracing. **1. embrasser, étreindre, enlacer** ▸ to hold or take in one's arms as a sign of love or affection; hug : *"Aunt Esther, who had not embraced anyone in years, gently put her arm about his shoulder."* (Cynthia Rylant) **2. embrasser, inclure, comprendre, englober** ▸ to include; contain : *She embraced his ideas when she planned her garden.* ▲ NOUN, embraces. **étreinte, enlacement** ▸ the act of embracing someone : *The family reunion began with a whirl of embraces and loud greetings.* SYN : grasp, hug, hold, clutch, clasp, squeeze.

em·broi·der [im-BROY-dur] VERB, embroidered, embroidering. **1. broder** ▸ to stitch designs with thread onto a piece of cloth. **Note.** These designs are called embroidery. **2. broder, exagérer, enjoliver** ▸ to add extra details to the facts : *My Uncle Leo embroiders his stories about his childhood.*

em·er·ald [EM-rald] NOUN, emeralds. **1. émeraude** ▸ a valuable bright-green stone or gem : *Emeralds are used in fine jewellery.* **2. émeraude** ▸ the green colour of this stone. ▲ ADJECTIVE. **émeraude** ▸ having this colour : *Ireland is called "The Emerald Isle" because of its many green fields.*

e·merge [ih-MURJ] VERB, emerged, emerging. **1. émerger, apparaître, surgir, sortir** ▸ to come out or up; appear : *Mom emerged from the basement when I called for her.* **2. émerger, se faire jour, apparaître, surgir** ▸ to become known; develop : *The facts emerged as David told his story.*

e·mer·gen·cy [ih-MUR-jun-see] NOUN, emergencies. **urgence** ▸ a serious, sudden, and unexpected happening that needs quick action : *Call 911 in case of an emergency.* ▲ ADJECTIVE. **d'urgence, de secours** ▸ having to do with or

used for an emergency : *an emergency exit.*
SYN : crisis, distress, dilemma, crucial point.

em·i·grate [EM-uh-grate] VERB, emigrated, emigrating. **émigrer ▶** to leave one's own country to live in another : *She emigrated from Chile to Canada.* **Note.** Someone who emigrates is an emigrant. *p. 200.*

e·mo·tion [ih-MOH-shun] NOUN, emotions. **émotion, sentiment ▶** a strong feeling of any kind : *"When it was filled and ready, Alejandro waited with mixed emotions."* (Richard E. Albert) *p. 1018.*

e·mo·tion·al [ih-MOH-shun-ul] ADJECTIVE. **1. émotionnel (-elle), sentimental (-ale, -aux) ▶** having to do with a person's feelings : *The wedding was an emotional time for the bride's parents, who cried and laughed.* **2. émotionnel (-elle), sentimental (-ale, -aux), émotif (-ive) ▶** easily excited or moved by feelings : *Some people are very emotional and show their feelings easily.* **3. émotionnel (-elle), sentimental (-ale, -aux) ▶** showing or causing strong feeling : *The man gave an emotional talk about his visit to a refugee camp.* **■ emotionally,** ADVERB. **▶ sentimentalement.**

em·pha·sis [EM-fuh-sis] NOUN, emphases. [EM-fuh-sees] **1. accent ▶** special importance or attention given to something : *In revising a first draft, emphasis should be put on the ideas and content.* **2. accent ▶** extra force or meaning given to a certain word or part of a word. **Note.** To stress or give emphasis to something is to emphasize it : *Many people enjoy basketball because it emphasizes skill over power and strength.* SYN : stress, importance, accent, insistence.

em·pire [EM-pire] NOUN, empires. (often Empire) **1. empire ▶** a group of countries under one ruler or government : *the Roman Empire; the British Empire.* **2. empire ▶** any large area or activity that is ruled over by one person : *The Thomson family controls a vast communications empire.* **Note.** An emperor or empress rules over an empire.

em·ploy [im-PLOY] VERB, employed, employing. **1. employer ▶** to pay someone to work; hire : *The store plans to employ more people for the holiday season.* **2. employer, utiliser ▶** to make use of; use : *Hailey employed great skill to build the model plane.* ▲ NOUN. **à l'emploi de ▶** the fact of being employed : *Julia spent 20 years in the employ of the government.* **Note.** Someone who is paid to work for someone else is an employee : *That company has over 2000 employees.* **Note.** A person or company that pays others to do work is an employer. SYN : hire, use, engage, contract, occupy.

emp·ty [EMP-tee] ADJECTIVE, emptier, emptiest. **1. vide, vacant (-ante) ▶** having nothing inside : *"It was nine o'clock and the hall was empty."* (Jean Little) **2. vide, creux (-euse), dénué (-ée)**

✏ Writing Tips

Emigrate or Immigrate

Although **emigrate** *and* **immigrate** *both refer to the act of moving from one country to another, they have different meanings.*

• *A trick to help you remember: You* emigrate from *and* immigrate to.

• **Emigrate** *refers to the leaving of a country to live permanently in another. She emigrated from Barbados and now lives in Canada.*

• **Immigrate** *refers to coming to a new place to live. My grandmother immigrated to Canada after World War II.*

de ▶ having no force or value : *The opposing sides shouted empty threats at each other.* ▲ VERB, emptied, emptying. **1. vider, décharger, vidanger, déverser ▶** to make or become empty : *Keegan emptied the can of soup into the pot.* **2. vider, déverser, écouler, vidanger ▶** to flow out; pour out : *Many other rivers empty into the St. Lawrence.* **Note.** The fact of being empty is emptiness. *p. 48.*

en·a·ble [in-AY-bul] VERB, enabled, enabling. **permettre, habiliter ▶** to make able to do something; give the ability to : *Specially designed shoes enable people to perform more effectively in work, dance, and sports.*

en·act [in-AKT] VERB, enacted, enacting. **1. promulguer, décréter, ordonner, arrêter ▶** to make into law : *The government enacted a law against poverty.* **2. représenter, jouer ▶** play the part of; act : *to enact the lead part in the school play.*

e·nam·el [ih-NAM-ul] NOUN, enamels. **1. émail ▶** a smooth, hard, glossy coating used to protect or decorate metal or clay objects, such as pots and pans. **2. vernis ▶** a glossy paint that dries to a hard finish. **3. émail ▶** the hard outer layer of a tooth. ▲ VERB, enamelled, enamelling. (also enameled, enameling) **vernir, émailler ▶** to cover or coat with enamel.

en·chant [in-CHANT] VERB, enchanted, enchanting. **1. enchanter, ensorceler, charmer ▶** to use magic; put under a spell : *The fairy queen enchanted the princess.* **2. enchanter, ravir, charmer ▶** delight; charm : *Adam's singing enchanted everyone who heard him.* SYN : charm, please, thrill, delight.

en·close [in-KLOZE] VERB, enclosed, enclosing. **1. clôturer, entourer, ceindre, enclore ▶** to surround and shut in : *A chain fence encloses our backyard.* **2. joindre, inclure ▶** to include something else in an envelope or package : *Megan* *enclosed a picture of herself inside the letter.* SYN: surround, fence, contain, include, encircle.

en-core [ON-kor] NOUN, encores. **1. bis ▶** a call made by an audience for a performer to continue after the end of a performance. **2. bis ▶** the performance done after the audience has called for an encore.

en-count-er [in-KOWN-tur] VERB, encountered, encountering. **rencontrer ▶** to come upon; meet : *Horst encountered his neighbour at the supermarket.* ▲ NOUN, encounters. **rencontre ▶** a meeting, especially one that is unexpected or difficult : *Kevin has had several encounters with dogs while delivering newspapers, but he's never been bitten.*

en-cour-age [in-KUR-ij] VERB, encouraged, encouraging. **1. encourager ▶** to give confidence or hope : *"He knew his daughter thought she was no good at sports and he wanted to encourage her."* (Gary Soto) **Note.** Often used as an ADJECTIVE: *The patient shows encouraging signs of making a full recovery.* **Note.** Something that encourages someone, or the act of encouraging, is encouragement. **2. encourager, favoriser, inciter ▶** to help bring about or make happen : *Our school encourages recycling in the cafeteria.* ■ **encouragingly,** ADVERB, **▶ encourageant (-ante).** *The coach spoke encouragingly to Terry before she went up to bat.* ✐ p. 201.

en-cy-clo-pe-di-a [in-SY-kluh-PEE-dee-uh] NOUN, encyclopedias. (also encyclopaedia) **encyclopédie ▶** a book or set of books giving information about many things. An encyclopedia has articles explaining facts about a great number of subjects or about many different areas of one large subject.

end [end] NOUN, ends. **1. fin, limite, extrémité, bout ▶** the part where something stops; the last part : *The movie was boring, so we left before the end.* **2. fin, aboutissement, issue, achèvement ▶** the moment in time where something no longer goes on or exists : *"This was the end of the old and the start of the new."* (Eve Bunting) **3. fin, but, dessein ▶** a final purpose or goal : *The end of all our hard work was a new park.* ▲ VERB, ended, ending. **finir, terminer, conclure, achever ▶** to bring to an end; stop : *The movie ends at 9 :45.* **Note.** The ending is the end of something, especially of a

book, movie, or play : *That author is known for her surprise endings.* SYN: finish, stop, complete, close, conclude.

en-dan-ger [in-DANE-jur] VERB, endangered, endangering. **mettre en danger, compromettre, exposer, être en voie d'extinction ▶** to cause someone or something to be in danger : *She endangered herself to rescue the baby from the burning house.* **Note.** Endangered species are kinds of animals or plants that exist in such small numbers that they are likely to die out completely unless they are protected. SYN: risk, hazard, jeopardize.

en-deav-our [en-DEV-ur] VERB, endeavoured, endeavouring. (also endeavor) **s'efforcer, s'évertuer ▶** to try hard; make an effort : *She endeavoured to finish her project before bedtime.* SYN: try, attempt, struggle, labour, work, strive.

end-less [END-lis] ADJECTIVE. **1. interminable, infini (-ie), sans fin, sans borne ▶** without end; going on and on forever : *A circle is an endless figure.* **2. interminable, incessant (-ante), intarissable, inépuisable ▶** seeming to be without end : *"Eddie couldn't have imagined a time when there would not be endless forest everywhere."* (Tim Wynne-Jones) ■ **endlessly,** ADVERB. **▶ interminablement, continuellement.** SYN: continuous, constant, nonstop, infinite.

en-dorse [in-DORCE] VERB, endorsed, endorsing. **1. endosser, appuyer, approuver, adhérer ▶** to talk or act in favour of someone or something; support publicly : *The principal endorsed our peacekeeping plan.* **2. endosser ▶** to write one's name on the back of a cheque : *You will have to endorse this cheque before the bank will cash it.* ■ **endorsement,** NOUN. **▶ endossement, aval, appui, approbation.**

en-dure [in-DYOOR] VERB, endured, enduring. **1. endurer, supporter, tolérer ▶** to put up with; hold out under : *"To more easily endure the lonely hours, Alejandro planted a garden."* (Richard E. Albert) **2. durer, rester ▶** to continue or last : *The plays of Shakespeare have endured for almost 400 years.* **Note.** Also used as an ADJECTIVE: *an enduring tradition.* **Note.** The power or ability to endure is endurance. SYN: last, continue, persist, remain, stay.

🔑 **Word Builder** ♦

Encourage, support, and *inspire* are verbs that mean to give help, hope or comfort. *Encourage* is the most general of these words. It means to offer hope, confidence, or actively give help: *It is nice when famous writers encourage young writers.* **Support** suggests the thing that is supported might fail without the assistance provided: *Without the parents' support, the choir wouldn't survive.* If someone **inspires** you, it means he or she gives you confidence: *The coach's speech inspired the team to win.*

en-e-my [EN-uh-mee] NOUN, enemies. **1. ennemi (-ie)** ▸ a person who tries to hurt or wishes harm to another; someone who is strongly against another person. **2. ennemi (-ie)** ▸ a country at war with another country. **3. ennemi (-ie)** ▸ anything that is dangerous or harmful : *An elephant has no enemies in nature, except for humans.* SYN: opponent, opposition.

en-er-gy [EN-ur-jee] NOUN, energies. **1. énergie** ▸ the power needed to cause things to move or do other kinds of work. The sun, wind, gasoline, and electricity are all sources of energy. **2. énergie, vigueur** ▸ the strength or will to do something : *Exercising regularly takes a lot of energy.* **3.** (usually energies) **énergie, vigueur** ▸ the power to work; effort : *Rick is devoting all his energies to finishing his history report.* **Note.** Someone who is full of energy is said to be energetic: *Donal was tired yesterday, but he felt more energetic after a good night's sleep.* 🖉 **p. 456.**

en-force [in-FORS] VERB, enforced, enforcing. **appliquer, faire respecter** ▸ to make sure that a law or rule is obeyed : *The rule against running in the halls is strictly enforced.* ■ **enforcement,** NOUN: ▸ **mise en application, mise en vigueur.** *Kereem is interested in a career in law enforcement.* SYN: compel, force, make, oblige, drive.

en-gage [in-GAYJ] VERB, engaged, engaging. **1. get engaged. se fiancer** ▸ to promise or agree to marry a person : *Gary and Heather got engaged to each other.* **2. engager, embaucher** ▸ to hire someone for a job; employ : *The captain bought a ship and engaged a crew to sail in search of treasure.* **3. s'engager** ▸ to take part in something; participate : *The Commons engaged in a debate over health care.* **Note.** Often used as an ADJECTIVE:*The engaged couple was planning a June wedding.*

en-gage-ment [in-GAYJ-munt] NOUN, engagements. **1. fiançailles** ▸ a promise to be married; the time of being engaged : *Charles and Martha held a party to announce their engagement.* **2. engagement, rendez-vous** ▸ a meeting or appointment : *Mrs. Bishop's secretary reminded her that she had a dinner engagement that evening.* **3. engagement** ▸ the fact of being hired for work : *That singer has a two-week engagement at our club.*

en-gine [EN-jin] NOUN, engines. **1. moteur** ▸ a machine that uses energy to make something move or run; a motor. An engine may get its power from gasoline, oil, electricity, steam, or other sources of energy. **2. locomotive** ▸ a railway car with a motor that makes it able to pull other cars; a locomotive. 🖉 **p. 354.**

en-gi-neer [EN-juh-NEER] NOUN, engineers. **1. ingénieur** ▸ a person who is trained in engineering; someone who plans and builds such things as engines and other machines, and

bridges, roads, or buildings. **2. mécanicien (-ienne)** ▸ a person whose work is running a railway engine. **3. technicien (-ienne)** ▸ a person who runs or takes care of machinery or technical equipment. ▲ VERB, engineered, engineering. **1. concevoir** ▸ to plan, build, or manage as an engineer : *That company is engineering the bridge to P.E.I.* **2. gérer, diriger** ▸ to manage or carry out : *Mr. Sulu engineered a big deal that allowed his company to buy out another firm.*

Eng-lish [ING-glish] NOUN. **1. anglais** ▸ the language that was first spoken in England and that is now spoken in countries that are now or were once ruled by Great Britain, such as Australia, Canada, and the United States. **2. the English.** a. **Anglais (-aise)** ▸ the people of England. b. **Canadien-anglais** ▸ English-speaking Canadians. ▲ ADJECTIVE. **anglais (-aise)** ▸ having to do with England or the English language.

en-grave [in-GRAVE] VERB, engraved, engraving. **1. graver** ▸ to carve letters or designs into a surface : *Cory engraved the vase with flowers.* **2. graver** ▸ to cut designs into a hard surface to be used for printing, or to print something using such a surface : *Printers engraved the invitations to my sister's wedding.* **3. graver, empreindre** ▸ to impress deeply on the mind, as if by engraving : *The scene from the movie engraved itself on Matt's mind.* **Note.** Something that is engraved is an engraving.

e-nig-ma [ih-NIG-muh] NOUN, enigmas. **énigme** ▸ a puzzle; riddle; mystery.

en-joy [in-JOY] VERB, enjoyed, enjoying. **1. aimer, apprécier, goûter, prendre plaisir** ▸ to get joy or pleasure from; like to do : *On weekends, Dad enjoys watching golf on TV.* **2. jouir de** ▸ to have the use or benefit of : *to enjoy good health.* ■ **enjoyment,** NOUN. ▸ **plaisir.** **Note.** Something that is enjoyed is said to be enjoyable. SYN: like, appreciate, delight in, savour, relish.

enjoy oneself **s'amuser, prendre du bon temps** ▸ to have a good time : *I hope you enjoyed yourself at the party.*

en-large [in-LARJ] VERB, enlarged, enlarging. **agrandir, étendre** ▸ to make or become bigger : *Microscopes enlarge objects that are too small to be seen by the eye alone.* ■ **enlargement,** NOUN: ▸ **agrandissement.** *Janet ordered an enlargement of her family's picture.*

en-list [in-LIST] VERB, enlisted, enlisting. **1. s'engager, s'enrôler** ▸ to choose to join the armed forces. **2. s'assurer le concours de** ▸ to get the support of : *Luis spoke at the schools to enlist volunteers for the recycling campaign.* ■ **enlistment,** NOUN: ▸ **engagement, enrôlement.** *Jana is just finishing a four-year enlistment in the navy.*

e-nor-mous [ih-NOR-mus] ADJECTIVE. **énorme, immense, colossal (-ale, -aux)** ▸ extremely large; much bigger than usual : *"Then, at the bridge that marked the border of his land, [the magician] transformed himself into an enormous lion."* (Robin Muller) ▪ **enormously,** ADVERB: ▸ **énormément, extrêmement.** *He admired the artist enormously.* SYN : large, huge, vast, great, immense, giant.

e‧nough [ih-NUF] ADJECTIVE. **suffisant (-ante), suffisamment** ▸ not too much and not too little; just the right amount : *"She did one more set and decided that was enough push-ups for the first day."* (Gary Soto) ▲ NOUN. **assez** ▸ *an adequate amount : We've heard from everyone, and I think enough has been said on the subject.* — ADVERB : **suffisamment** ▸ I've eaten enough. SYN : sufficient, ample, adequate, satisfactory.

en‧quire [en-KWYR] VERB, enquired, enquiring. **s'enquérir, se renseigner, s'informer, demander** ▸ to inquire; to ask questions.

en‧rich [in-RICH] VERB, enriched, enriching. **1. enrichir** ▸ to make rich or richer : **2. enrichir** ▸ to make better; improve : *The farmer added compost to the soil to enrich it.* ▪ **enrichment,** NOUN. ▸ **enrichissement.** SYN : improve, better.

en‧roll [in-ROLE] VERB, enrolled, enrolling. **enrôler, inscrire, embaucher** ▸ also **enrol, enroled, enroling)** to take in a new member, or become a new member : *Dad took my little brother to school to enroll him in kindergarten.*

en‧sure [in-SHOOR] VERB, ensured, ensuring. **assurer, garantir** ▸ to make sure or certain : *She made extra sandwiches to ensure that everyone would have enough to eat.*

en‧ter [EN-tur] VERB, entered, entering. **1. entrer** ▸ to come or go into : *to enter a room or a building.* **2. entrer, commencer à** ▸ to begin; start : *Next month that store will enter its 10th year of business.* **3. entrer, s'inscrire** ▸ to sign up or register for; enroll in : *Marcia entered high school last fall.* **4. entrer, inscrire, noter, introduire** ▸ to put down an item or a figure in a book : *The teller entered my deposit in my bankbook.* ▲ NOUN. **entrée** ▸ a command that is given to a computer to record a certain item of information.

en‧ter‧prise [EN-tur-PRIZE] NOUN, enterprises. **1. entreprise** ▸ a project or undertaking, especially something that is important, complicated, or difficult. **2. entreprise** ▸ the carrying on of business activity : *Companies that are not owned by the government are considered to be part of private enterprise.*

en‧ter‧tain [EN-tur-TANE] VERB, entertained, entertaining. **1. amuser, divertir, distraire** ▸ to keep interested and amused : *Aunt Indira entertained us with stories of her trip.* **Note.** Also an ADJECTIVE: *We saw a very entertaining show on television last night.* **Note.** A person who entertains others is an **entertainer.**

2. recevoir ▸ to have a guest or guests : *Her parents often entertain on weekends.* **3. considérer, méditer, nourrir** ▸ to have in mind; consider : *He's entertaining the idea of a bicycle tour of Ireland next year.* SYN : amuse, delight, interest, fascinate, charm.

en‧ter‧tain‧ment [EN-tur-TANE-munt] NOUN, entertainments. **1. divertissement, amusement, distraction** ▸ the act of entertaining; keeping people amused or interested. **2. spectacle, attraction** ▸ something that is amusing or entertaining : *Playing on their new computer is entertainment for the whole family.*

en‧thu‧si‧asm [in-THOO-zee-AZ-um] NOUN, enthusiasms. **enthousiasme** ▸ a strong feeling of excitement and interest; a great liking : *Everyone knows about Jenny's enthusiasm for baseball.* ▪ **enthusiastic,** ADJECTIVE. ▸ **enthousiaste.**

en‧tire [en-TIRE] ADJECTIVE. **entier (-ière), tout (toute, tous, toutes)** ▸ with nothing left out; complete; whole : *We spent the entire afternoon planting the garden.* SYN : whole, full, complete, total.

en‧trance¹ [EN-truns] NOUN, entrances. **1. entrée, portail (-ails), vestibule** ▸ a door or passage through which one enters a place : *"Harald knew that once the dogs got near the entrance to the cave, all would be lost."* (Donald Carrick) **2. entrée** ▸ the act of entering : *He was stopped by the sound of someone's entrance through the back door.* **3. admission** ▸ the permission or right to go in; admission : *Barry was denied entrance to the restaurant because he was not wearing shoes.*

en‧trance² [en-TRANS] VERB, entranced, entrancing. **ravir, transporter, enivrer** ▸ to fill with wonder and delight; charm : *We were entranced by the fireworks.*

en‧try [EN-tree] NOUN, entries. **1. entrée** ▸ a place where you can enter; an entrance : *The entry to the road was blocked by a car.* **2. entrée** ▸ the act of entering . *The actress made a dramatic entry onto the stage.* **3. entrée, inscription** ▸ someone or something entered in a race or contest. **4. entrée, inscription** ▸ a written item in a record or book. **5. entrée** ▸ a word that is recorded in a dictionary.

en‧vel‧ope [EN-vuh-LOPE] NOUN, envelopes. **enveloppe** ▸ a thin, flat paper covering used to hold a letter or other piece of writing, especially for mailing.

en‧vi‧ron‧ment [in-VY-run-munt] NOUN, environments. **1. environnement, milieu** ▸ the natural conditions that make up the area in which a plant, animal, or person lives, such as air, water, and land : *Lizards are often found in a desert environment.* **2. environnement, milieu** ▸ all the conditions that surround or go with a certain person or thing : *Students become better readers in school if reading is important in their home environment.* ■ **environmental,** ADJECTIVE. ▶ **environnemental (-ale, -aux), écologique.** *Environmental studies show that pollution from cars harms plants and animals.* SYN: surroundings, neighbourhood, setting.

en·vy [EN-vee] NOUN. **1. envie, jalousie** ▶ a feeling of wanting what someone else has; jealousy : *When he saw his friend's new baseball glove, he was filled with envy.* **2. envie** ▶ a person or thing causing this feeling : *The new sports car is the envy of the neighbourhood.* ▲ VERB, envied, envying. **envier** ▶ to feel envy about something; be jealous : *He envies his sister because she's better at sports than he is.* 🖉 p. 204.

ep·ic [EP-ik] NOUN, epics. **1. épopée** ▶ a long poem telling about real or imaginary heroes and their adventures. **2. épopée** ▶ any long story with lots of action, characters, and details : *The movie* Gone With the Wind *is an epic of the U.S. Civil War.* ▲ ADJECTIVE. **1. épique** ▶ having to do with or like an epic : *Homer's* Odyssey *is an epic poem.* **2. épique, héroïque, homérique** ▶ impressive or heroic : *Alone in a tiny plane, Amelia Earhart made an epic flight across the Atlantic.*

ep·i·dem·ic [EP-uh-DEM-ik] NOUN, epidemics. **1. épidémie** ▶ the rapid spread of a disease to many people at the same time : *More than 20 million people died in a flu epidemic in 1918.* **2. épidémie** ▶ the rapid spread or increase of something that is thought of as like a disease : *There's been an epidemic of robberies in town lately.* ■ **epidemic,** ADJECTIVE. **épidémique** ▶ widespread; affecting many people : *Poverty is epidemic in some developing countries.*

ep·i·sode [EP-uh-SODE] NOUN, episodes. **épisode** ▶ one of a series of events in a story or in real life : *The last episode of that TV show was great.* SYN: event, occasion, happening, incident, affair.

e·qual [EE-kwal] ADJECTIVE. **1. égal (-ale,-aux)** ▶ having the same amount, size, or volume as something else : *One metre equals one hundred centimetres.* **2. égal (-ale, -aux)** ▶ affecting everyone in the same way : *Mom is fair, so she makes sure that all our dessert portions are equal.* **3. être à la hauteur** ▶ having enough ability or strength to do something : *After train-ing for a year, Sierra felt that she was equal to running a marathon.* ▲ VERB, equalled, equalling. (also equaled, equaling) to be equal to something else : *Five plus five equals ten.* ▲ NOUN, equals. **égaler** ▶ someone or something that is the equal of another. ■ **equally,** ADVERB. ▶ **aussi, autant, également.**

e·qual·i·ty [ih-KWAL-uh-tee] NOUN. **égalité** ▶ the state of being equal, especially in economic, social, or political rights : *Minorities have worked hard to gain equality in Canada.*

e·qua·tion [ih-KWAY-zhun] NOUN, equations. **équation** ▶ a mathematical statement showing that two things are equal, such as $3 \times 6 = 18$.

e·qua·tor [ih-KWAY-tur] NOUN, equators. **équateur** ▶ the imaginary line around the middle of the earth halfway between the North and South Poles. ■ **equatorial,** ADJECTIVE. **équatorial (-ale, -aux)** ▶ having to do with or near the equator : *Ecuador and Kenya are equatorial countries.* **Note.** *Equator* is related to the word *equal* because the equator divides the earth into two equal parts.

e·qui·nox [EE-kwuh-noks *or* EK-wuh-knoks] NOUN, equinoxes. **équinoxe** ▶ one of the two times a year when the sun is directly over the equator, and day and night are equal in length. The spring equinox is around March 21, and the fall equinox is around September 23.

e·quip [ih-KWIP] VERB, equipped, equipping. **équiper, installer, aménager, outiller** ▶ to provide what is needed; supply : *The dealer equipped this car with power steering and power brakes.*

e·quip·ment [ih-KWIP-munt] NOUN. **1. équipement, matériel** ▶ the things that are provided for a particular purpose or job : *Camping equipment includes tents and sleeping bags.* **2. équipement** ▶ the act of providing such things : *The equipment of a hockey team takes a lot of money.*

e·quiv·a·lent [ih-KWIV-uh-lunt] ADJECTIVE. **équivalent (-ente)** ▶ being the same or about the same; equal : *A temperature of 32 degrees Fahrenheit is equivalent to 0 degrees Celsius.* ▲ NOUN. **équivalent, équivalence** ▶ something that is the same or equal : *The winner of the contest gets $10,000, or the equivalent in merchandise.*

🖉 **Word Builder**

Envy and *jealousy* both mean to be resentful of another person or what that person possesses. *Envy* is the desire for the possessions or qualities of another person: *I envy his ability to pitch a great curve ball.* A *jealous* person resents what another person has, but may also fear losing his or her position or affection: *She's jealous that the coach is giving more playing time to the new player.*

e·ra [IR-uh *or* ER-uh] NOUN, eras. **ère, époque** ▶ a certain period of history or time that is thought of as a unit or marked by important events : *"The era of the cowboy lasted only about 20 years, from about 1866 to 1886."* (Linda Granfield) SYN : period, age, generation.

e·rase [ih-RASE] VERB, erased, erasing. **1. effacer, gommer** ▶ to remove by rubbing or wiping off : *Dave erased the mistake on his paper.* **2. effacer** ▶ to remove completely, as if by rubbing out : *Rosa accidentally erased two songs from her brother's tape.* Note. An eraser is something that is used to remove or rub out unwanted marks, especially on a written page.

e·rect [ih-REKT] ADJECTIVE. **droit (droite)** ▶ straight up ; not bent : *Derek walks with an erect posture.* ▲ VERB, erected, erecting. **1. ériger, construire, bâtir, élever** ▶ to build or put up : *This school was erected in 1924.* **2. élever, dresser, monter** ▶ to put into an upright position : *to erect a tent.*

e·rode [ih-RODE] VERB, eroded, eroding. **éroder, ronger, corroder** ▶ to wear or wash away slowly : *The Colorado River eroded the area known as the Grand Canyon.* ■ **erosion,** NOUN. **érosion, corrosion, effritement** ▶ the process of eroding. Note. Also used as an ADJECTIVE: *Dust from the eroding soil was blown around by the wind.* SYN : break up, disintegrate, wear away, corrode.

er·rand [FR-und] NOUN, errands. **commission, course** ▶ a short trip for the purpose of doing something, such as going to a store or to the bank. To run an errand **faire une course** ▶ to make such a trip.

er·rat·ic [uh-RAT-ik] ADJECTIVE. **irrégulier (-ière), fantasque, capricieux (-ieuse), changeant (-ante)** ▶ irregular ; not steady ; uncertain. ■ **erratically,** ADVERB: ▶ **irrégulièrement, capricieusement.** *The flat tire made the car drive erratically.*

er·ror [AIR-ur] NOUN, errors. **1. erreur, faute** ▶ something that is incorrect ; a mistake : *Chad made three errors while typing the page.* **2. erreur** ▶ in baseball, a wrong play made by a fielder that allows a runner or batter to be safe when he or she should have been out.

e·rupt [ih-RUPT] VERB, erupted, erupting. **1. entrer en éruption, exploser, éclater** ▶ to break or burst out violently : *The volcano erupted suddenly.* **2. éclater, exploser, apparaître, sortir** ▶ to develop or appear suddenly : *"The parish hall erupted in an avalanche of applause."* (Roch Carrier) ■ **eruption,** NOUN, eruptions. ▶ **éruption.**

es·ca·la·tor [ES-kuh-LAY-tur] NOUN, escalators. **escalier roulant, escalier mécanique** ▶ a moving stairway that carries people from one floor to another, such as in a store or an airport.

es·cape [es-KAPE] VERB, escaped, escaping. **1. échapper, évader, fuir, s'enfuir** ▶ to get away or get free ; break loose : *"He threw his own sword down and ran away, glad to escape with his life."* (Dan Yashinsky) **2. échapper, se soustraire** ▶ to avoid something harmful or dangerous : *"It was good to escape the smoke and fire and walk down the concession trail out to the road."* (Phoebe Gilman) **3. échapper, passer inaperçu (-ue)** ▶ to fail to be remembered, noticed, or understood : *"Learn to observe and understand everything that goes on around you. Try to know more. Let nothing escape your notice."* (Bob Barton) ▲ NOUN, escapes. **1. évasion, fuite** ▶ the act or fact of escaping : *The outlaw became famous for his daring escapes from prison.* **2. évasion** ▶ something that takes one's mind away from worries, problems, or cares : *Reading a book is a good escape.* SYN : get away, flee, evade, avoid, make off, elude.

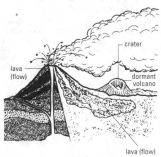

lava (flow)
lava (flow)
crater
dormant volcano

eruption

es·cort [ES-kort] NOUN, escorts. **1. escorte, cortège, suite** ▶ someone or something that goes along with another for protection or as an honour : *a police escort.* **2. escorte, cavalier (-ière)** ▶ a person who accompanies a man or woman to a dance or party : *David is my escort for the dinner.* ▲ VERB, escorted, escorting. **escorter, accompagner** ▶ to act as an escort ; to take someone somewhere or to someone : *"When she arrived at the palace, Little Kay was escorted to the Sultan."* (Robin Muller) SYN : accompany, guide, usher, attend, lead.

es·pe·cial·ly [es-PESH-uh-lee] ADVERB. **1. spécialement, particulièrement** ▶ more than usual ; in a special way : *It has been especially cold this month.* **2. spécialement, particulièrement** ▶ in a way more than others ; particularly : *"As they walked along, there was one set of tracks that Grama Bowman especially loved to see."* (Joseph Bruchac) SYN : particularly, mainly, mostly, primarily.

205

es·say [ES-ay] NOUN. essays. **essai, dissertation, rédaction, composition ▸** a short piece of writing about a true subject, especially one that tells the writer's point of view.

es·sen·tial [uh-SEN-shul] ADJECTIVE. **essentiel (-elle), indispensable, capital (-aux), fondamental (-ale, -aux) ▸** of the greatest importance; necessary; basic : *Studying is essential to getting good grades.* ▲ NOUN, essentials. **essentiel (-elle), indispensable ▸** something that is necessary or basic. ■ **essentially,** ADVERB: ▸ **essentiellement, principalement, fondamentalement.** *Chinese writing has stayed essentially the same for the last 2000 years.*

es·tab·lish [uh-STAB-lish] VERB, established, establishing. **1. établir, constituer, fonder, créer ▸** to create or begin; set up : *to establish a city.* **2. établir, prouver, démontrer ▸** to prove to be true or correct : *The facts establish that the suspect was at home at the time of the crime.* **Note.** Something that is established, especially a place of business, is an establishment.

es·tate [uh-STATE] NOUN, estates. **1. domaine, propriété, terre ▸** a large piece of land, usually with a large, impressive home on it : *"The serfs lived in huts provided for them on the lord's estate, each with its own plot of land."* (Aliki) **2. biens, fortune, succession ▸** everything that a person owns, especially the money and property that is left to others at the time of death : *When Paul's father died, he left an estate worth more than a million dollars.*

es·teem [uh-STEEM] VERB, esteemed, esteeming. **avoir de l'estime pour, apprécier, considérer ▸** to think highly of; respect : *Students, teachers, and parents all esteem our principal.* SYN: respect, regard, value, honour, appreciate.

es·ti·mate [ES-tuh-mit] NOUN, estimates. **estimation, évaluation ▸** a judgment of the amount or quality of something; a general but careful guess : *The garage gave us an estimate of what it would cost to fix the brakes on the car.* ▲ [ES-tuh-MATE] VERB, estimated, estimating. **estimer, évaluer, juger ▸** to form a general opinion; make an estimate : *Axel estimated that there were 1,000 beans in the jar.* ■ **estimation,** NOUN. **estimation, jugement, opinion, avis ▸** opinion, judgment. SYN: judge, calculate, figure, compute, gauge.

e·ter·nal [ih-TUR-nul] ADJECTIVE. **1. éternel (-elle), continuel (-elle), perpétuel (-elle) ▸** continuing forever : *"Far away in the land of eternal snow and ice dwelt North Wind."* (Rosebud Yellow-Robe) **2. éternel (-elle), continuel (-elle), perpétuel (-elle), sempiternel (-elle) ▸** seeming to continue or last forever : *An eternal complaint of teenagers is that their parents don't understand them.* ■ **eternally,** ADVERB. ▸ **éternellement, continuellement, perpétuellement, sempiternellement.**

e·ter·ni·ty [ih-TUR-nih-tee] NOUN, eternities. **1. éternité ▸** time that goes on forever; time without end. **2. éternité ▸** seeming to continue forever : *We waited an eternity until the bus arrived.*

eth·ics [ETH-iks] PLURAL NOUN. **1. éthique, morale ▸** the study of what is good and bad, and of right and wrong ways of acting. **2. éthique ▸** a set of rules or standards for a certain person or group : *According to medical ethics, doctors should not tell others about the problems of patients they are treating.* ■ **ethical,** ADJECTIVE: **éthique, moral (-ale, aux) ▸** following correct standards of ethics; proper or right.

eth·nic [ETH-nik] ADJECTIVE. **ethnique ▸** having to do with people who share the same characteristics, language, culture, homeland, and so on : *Italians, Jamaicans, and Chinese people are three of the ethnic groups in Canada.*

et·i·quette [ET-uh-kut] NOUN. **étiquette, convenance, protocole ▸** the rules of correct social behaviour.

Eur·a·sia [yoo-RAY-zhuh] NOUN. **Eurasie ▸** Europe and Asia, thought of as a single continent because they are the same land mass.

Eu·rope [YOOR-up] NOUN. **Europe ▸** the sixth-largest continent; the land east of the Atlantic Ocean and west of the Ural Mountains and the Black Sea. ■ **European,** ADJECTIVE. ▸ **européen (-enne).**

e·vade [EE-vade] VERB, evaded, evading. **éviter, esquiver, éluder, se dérober ▸** to escape or avoid through clever planning : *The criminal evaded the police with a brilliant disguise.*

e·vac·u·ate [ih-VAK-yoo-ATE] VERB, evacuated, evacuating. **évacuer ▸** to leave or go away, or to cause to do this : *Police evacuated people from the flooded area by helicopter.* SYN: leave, withdraw, remove, depart, quit.

e·val·u·ate [ih-VAL-yoo-ATE] VERB, evaluated, evaluating. **évaluer ▸** to judge or figure the value or condition of something : *to evaluate an essay or a piece of furniture.* ■ **evaluation,** NOUN. ▸ **évaluation.**

e·vap·o·rate [ih-VAP-uh-RATE] VERB, evaporated, evaporating. **1. évaporer ▸** to change from a liquid into a gas or vapour : *Water begins to evaporate at 100°C.* **2. évaporer, volatiliser, envoler, évanouir ▸** to fade away; disappear : *Our hopes of winning began to evaporate as we got closer to the end of the game.* ■ **evaporation,** NOUN. ▸ **évaporation.** SYN: vanish, disappear, fade away, dissolve.

eve [eve] NOUN, eves. **veille ▸** the evening or day before a certain day or holiday : *Lina still hadn't finished packing on the eve of her trip to Australia.*

e·ven [EE-vun] ADJECTIVE. **1. plat (plate), uni (unie) ▸** completely flat and smooth; level.

2. régulier (-ière), égal (-ale, -aux) ▸ not changing; steady : *to drive at an even speed.* **3. égal (-ale, -aux)** ▸ at the same height : *The corn was even with the top of the fence.* **4. égal (-ale, -aux)** ▸ being the same or equal : *The score was even at 3 to 3.* **5. pair (paire)** ▸ exact : *An even number is one that can be divided exactly by 2, with nothing left over, such as 4, 10, 36, and so on.* ▲ ADVERB. **1. même, jusqu'à, encore** ▸ still; yet; to a greater degree : *It's even more crowded here today than it was yesterday.* **2. même** ▸ surprising as it may seem : *We all enjoyed the rock concert, even Grandpa.* ▲ VERB. evened, evening. **égaliser, aplanir, niveler** ▸ to make or become even; make equal : *to even the score in a game.* ■ **evenly,** ADVERB. ▸ **également, régulièrement.** *Have you applied the paint evenly on the wall?* 📖 **p. 207.**

e·ven·ing [EEV-ning] NOUN. evenings. **soir, soirée** ▸ the time between late afternoon and night; the late part of the day. ▲ ADJECTIVE. **du soir** ▸ having to do with the evening : *Supper is an evening meal.* SYN: nightfall, sunset, sundown, dusk. 📖 **p. 1078.**

e·vent [ih-VENT] NOUN. events. **1. événement ou évènement** ▸ something that happens, especially an important happening : *Having a baby is an important event.* **2. événement, épreuve** ▸ a contest in a sports program or series : *Donovan Bailey won the 100-metre event at the 1996 Olympics.* SYN: happening, occurrence, incident, episode. 📖 **p. 1146.**

in any event en tout cas, de toute façon ▸ in any case; no matter what : *In any event, I'll meet you here in an hour.*

in the event of en cas de, au cas où ▸ if something happens; in case of : *In the event of a tie, the prize money will be divided between the two winners.*

e·ven·tu·al [ih-VEN-choo-ul] ADJECTIVE. **éventuel (-elle), possible, potentiel (-elle)** ▸ happening at some later time or at the end; final : *Our eventual win came after many losses.* ■ **eventually,** ADVERB. **éventuellement, finalement, en fin de compte, à la fin** ▸ at the end; finally : *"Eventually he headed west and became a cowboy, winning roping and shooting competitions in rodeos."* (Linda Granfield)

ev·er [EV-ur] ADVERB. **1. jamais, déjà** ▸ at any time : *Have you ever been to Vancouver?* **2. toujours, sans cesse** ▸ always : *People in* *fairy tales live happily ever after.* **3. jamais** ▸ in any way; by chance : *Where did you ever find that hat?*

ev·er·green [EV-ur-GREEN] ADJECTIVE. **conifère, à feuilles persistantes** ▸ having leaves or needles that stay green all year long. ▲ NOUN. evergreens. **conifère, à feuilles persistantes** ▸ a tree, shrub, or plant whose leaves or needles stay green all year round. Pines and firs are evergreens.

eve·ry [EV-ree] ADJECTIVE. **1. chaque, tout (toute, tous, toutes)** ▸ all of the ones in a group; each : *I brush my teeth every night before I go to bed.* **2. tout (toute, tous, toutes)** ▸ all that is possible : *"Sometimes he would surprise the butterflies and send them fluttering in every direction."* (Gerald McDermott)

every other chaque, à tous (toutes) les ▸ skipping one each time : *Penny visits her grandmother every other week.*

eve·ry·bod·y [EV-ree-BUD-ee or EV-ree-BOD-ee] PRONOUN. **tout le monde, chacun (-une)** ▸ every person; everyone : *Everybody in the family came to Robin's recital.*

eve·ry·day [EV-ree-DAY] ADJECTIVE. **quotidien (-ienne), banal (-ale, als), ordinaire, commun (-une)** ▸ ordinary; usual : *Jeff wasn't even excited—you'd think meeting a movie star was an everyday event.*

eve·ry·one [EV-ree-WUN] PRONOUN. **tout le monde, chacun (-une)** ▸ every person : *Shayna invited everyone in her class to her birthday party.*

eve·ry·thing [EV-ree-THING] PRONOUN. **1. tout** ▸ all things : *We packed everything we own in boxes right before we moved.* **2. tout** ▸ all that matters or is important : *Mom said she was sure we would be able to handle everything while she was gone.*

eve·ry·where [EV-ree-WAIR] ADVERB. **partout** ▸ in all places : *Julio's dog follows him everywhere.*

ev·i·dence [EV-uh-duns] NOUN. **1. évidence, preuve, signe** ▸ anything that shows or makes the truth clear; proof : *Fossils are evidence that many animals lived thousands of years ago.* **2. évidence, preuve** ▸ facts, information, or proof accepted in court : *The lawyer presented a video as evidence of his client's innocence.* SYN: fact, proof, grounds, data, clue, indication.

ev·i·dent [EV-uh-dunt] ADJECTIVE. **évident (-ente), manifeste** ▸ easy to see or understand; obvious :

📝 **Word Builder**

Even is used in some expressions to show balance or fairness. ***Break even*** means that gains or profits and losses are equal. The phrase is often heard in business situations: *After years of losing money in their sporting goods business, they finally managed to break even.* Similarly, the phrase ***get even*** is often used to mean get revenge: *I will get even with you for dumping the books out of my desk!*

It was evident from the way Nina clamped her mouth shut that she was not going to answer the question. ■ **evidently,** ADVERB. **évidemment, manifestement ▸** as it seems; clearly. SYN: clear, plain, apparent, obvious, clear-cut.

e·vil [EE-vul] ADJECTIVE. **1. mauvais (-aise), malveillant (-ante), malfaisant (-ante) ▸** against what is right or good; very bad; wicked : *an evil person; an evil crime.* **2. mauvais (-aise), néfaste, funeste ▸** causing harm : *an evil habit.* ▲ NOUN, evils. **1. mal (-aux) ▸** something bad; wickedness : *The Pied Piper was hired to rid the town from the evil caused by the rats.* **2. mal (-aux), funeste ▸** something that is evil : *an evil thought.* SYN: bad, wrong, wicked, sinful, harmful.

ev·o·lu·tion [EV-uh-LOO-shun] NOUN. **1. évolution ▸** the scientific theory that all living plants and animals came from fewer and simpler forms of life, and that these forms changed over millions of years into the many different forms that exist on the earth today. **2. évolution ▸** any slow, gradual change or development : *The Magna Carta was an important event in the evolution of British democracy.*

e·volve [ih-VOLV] VERB, evolved, evolving. **évoluer, se développer ▸** to slowly grow, develop, or change : *The space shuttle evolved from a simple rocket that was designed years ago.* SYN: develop, grow, advance, progress, unfold.

ex- PREFIX. **1.** out of : *external.* **2.** without; not including : *excluding.*

ex·act [eg-ZAKT] ADJECTIVE. **exact (-acte), juste, précis (-ise) ▸** without anything wrong; having no mistakes; correct; precise : *Markets have scales that show the exact weight of food.* ■ **exactly,** ADVERB. ▸ **exactement, précisément.** SYN: precise, correct, accurate, definite, detailed.

ex·ag·ger·ate [ig-ZAJ-uh-RATE] VERB, exaggerated, exaggerating. **exagérer, amplifier ▸** to make something seem more than it really is : *My grandpa exaggerates stories about his life.* **Note.** Something that is exaggerated is an exaggeration. SYN: stretch, overdo, magnify, expand, enlarge. 🖉 **p. 208.**

ex·am·i·na·tion [eg-ZAM-uh-NAY-shun] NOUN, examinations. **1. examen, inspection ▸** the act of examining; a careful study : *"He made an anxious examination of the paper, turning it in all directions."* (Edgar Allan Poe) **2. examen, épreuve ▸** a test. **Note.** A short word for examination is exam.

ex·am·ine [eg-ZAM-in] VERB, examined, examining. **1. examiner, inspecter ▸** to look at closely and carefully; inspect; check : *I examined the cut on my dog's paw.* **2. examiner, interroger ▸** to question closely : *Lawyers examined the witness in court.*

🖉 Writing Tips

Exaggeration

Exaggeration *is stretching the truth. Many writers use exaggeration to add humour to their writing. You will find* **exaggeration** *in tall tales, limericks, satire, and funny stories. Sometimes* **exaggeration** *is used to make something seem worse than it really is to make a point or draw attention to the problem in a gentle way.*

3. examiner ▸ to test the knowledge of : *The test examined us on our knowledge of biology.* SYN: inspect, check, study, analyse, test, question.

ex·am·ple [eg-ZAM-pul] NOUN, examples. **1. exemple ▸** something that shows what other things of the same kind are like; a usual or typical member of a group : *Cactus and sagebrush are examples of plants that grow in the desert.* **2. exemple, modèle ▸** a person or thing that is imitated; a model : *Your cheerfulness and goodness set an example for us all.* **3. exemple, cas ▸** a problem : *The teacher wrote the math example on the board so that she could explain it.* SYN: sample, model, illustration, instance.

Ex·cal·i·bur [eks-KAL-uh-bur] NOUN. **Excalibur ▸** the sword used by King Arthur in Arthurian legends.

ex·ca·vate [EKS-kuh-vate] VERB, excavating. **1. excaver, creuser ▸** to take out or make by digging; dig out : *The workers excavated dirt from the yard to create a swimming pool.* **2. excaver, creuser, dégager, déterrer ▸** to uncover by digging : *Archaeologists excavated an ancient village.* SYN: dig, scoop, unearth, pull up, mine.

ex·ceed [ek-SEED] VERB, exceeded, exceeding. **excéder, dépasser, outrepasser ▸** to be more than; go beyond : *The temperature in the desert often exceeds 40°C.* ■ **exceedingly,** ADVERB. **extrêmement, infiniment ▸** very; unusually : *Could you call back? I'm exceedingly busy at the moment.* SYN: go beyond, surpass, better, excel, beat, top.

ex·cel [ek-SEL] VERB, excelled, excelling. **exceller, briller ▸** to do better or be better than others : *My friend Krista excels in math.* SYN: be superior, exceed, do better.

ex·cel·lent [EK-suh-lunt] ADJECTIVE. **excellent (-ente), parfait (-aite), admirable ▸** of very high quality; very, very good; outstanding : *Swimming is an excellent form of exercise.* ■ **excellently,** ADVERB. ▸ **excellemment, parfaitement, admirablement.**

ex·cept [ek-SEPT] PREPOSITION. **excepté, sauf, hormis** ▸ not including; leaving out; other than : *He exercised every day except Sunday.* ▲ CONJUNCTION. **mais, à moins que, cependant** ▸ only; but : *I would like to go with you, except I have homework to do.* SYN: excluding, omitting, aside from, besides.

ex·cep·tion [ek-SEP-shun] NOUN, exceptions. 1. **exception** ▸ the fact of being left out : *I am the exception in my family—I'm the only one with brown eyes.* 2. **exception** ▸ a person or thing that is left out or different : *All of Ian Fleming's books are about James Bond, with the exception of one book for children.*

ex·cep·tion·al [ek-SEP-shun-ul] ADJECTIVE. **exceptionnel (-elle)** ▸ out of the ordinary; very unusual, especially in a good way : *All your photos are good, but the one of the sunset is exceptional.* ■ **exceptionally,** ADVERB. ▸ **exceptionnellement.** *This is an exceptionally good book I'm reading.* SYN: outstanding, extraordinary, remarkable.

ex·cerpt [ek-SURPT] NOUN, excerpts. **extrait, passage, morceau (-eaux)** ▸ a passage, selection, or quotation from a longer piece of writing. ▲ VERB, excerpted, excerpting. **extraire, citer** ▸ to take out selected passages; quote from : *Max excerpted magazine articles in his report.*

ex·cess [ek-SES] NOUN, excesses. 1. **excès, excédent** ▸ an amount that is too much or that is more than usual : *We made so much jam we gave our excess to the neighbours.* 2. **excès, excédent** ▸ the amount by which one thing is more than another. ▲ [EK-ses] ADJECTIVE. **excessif -ive), excédentaire** ▸ more than is needed or is usual; extra : *Before cooking the meat, Mom trimmed off the excess fat.* **Note.** More than is needed or wanted is excessive: *We try not to use an excessive amount of salt on our food.* ■ **excessively,** ADVERB. ▸ **excessivement.** *She is excessively concerned about her appearance and is always looking in the mirror.* SYN: leftover, additional, extra, surplus, remaining.

in excess of **plus de** ▸ more than : *The Kodiak bear can weigh in excess of 600 kilograms.*

ex·change [eks-CHAYNJ] VERB, exchanged, exchanging. **échanger** ▸ to take or give one thing for another; trade : *The sweater was too large, so the store exchanged it for a smaller size.* ▲ NOUN, exchanges. 1. **échange** ▸ the giving or taking of one thing for another : *Luis considered getting a book for a cap a fair exchange.* 2. **change, bourse** ▸ a place where things are exchanged or traded : *a stock exchange.* SYN: change, swap, trade, switch, substitute.

ex·cite [ek-SITE] VERB, excited, exciting. **exciter, passionner** ▸ to cause to have strong and lively feelings; stir up : *Mom doesn't let us play with the baby at bedtime because we'll excite him and he won't sleep.* ■ **excited,** ADJECTIVE: **excité (-ée), agité (-ée)** ▸ having strong and lively feelings : *Jody was excited about visiting her cousins.* ■ **excitedly,** ADVERB. ▸ **avec agitation.** SYN: stir up, provoke, move, affect.

ex·cite·ment [ek-SITE-munt] NOUN. 1. **excitation, agitation, fièvre, exaltation** ▸ the condition of being excited : *"The man's eyes shone with excitement."* (Tololwa M. Mollel) 2. (plural, excitements) **excitation** ▸ something that excites : *The excitements of the fair kept us busy all afternoon.*

ex·claim [eks-CLAME] VERB, exclaimed, exclaiming. **s'exclamer, s'écrier** ▸ to speak or cry out suddenly in surprise or with strong feeling : *"Then, suddenly, he heard Cowley exclaim, 'Wo ho! What's this, then?'"* (Tim Wynne-Jones)

exclamation mark (also exclamation point) **point d'exclamation** ▸ a punctuation mark [!] used to show emphasis or emotion.

ex·clude [eks-KLOOD] VERB, excluded, excluding. 1. **exclure, écarter, éliminer, rejeter** ▸ to keep from entering; shut out : *Mara and her friends exluded Alexa from their game.* **Note.** The act or fact of excluding is exclusion. 2. **exclure, soustraire** ▸ to not include : *This bus holds 60 people; that excludes the driver.*

ex·clu·sive [eks-KLOO-siv] ADJECTIVE. 1. **exclusif (-ive)** ▸ not shared with others : *"Eddie could see something pass between them, something secret and exclusive."* (Tim Wynne-Jones) 2. **exclusif (-ive), huppé (-ée), fermé (-ée), choisi (-ie)** ▸ letting in only a few people and keeping out others : *an exclusive club.* ■ **exclusively,** ADVERB. ▸ **exclusivement.**

ex·cuse [ek-SKYOOZ] VERB, excused, excusing. 1. **excuser, pardonner** ▸ to forgive; pardon : *Please excuse me for stepping on your foot.* 2. **excuser, exempter, dispenser** ▸ to let off from doing something or being in a place : *Danny asked to be excused from the table.* ▲ [ek-SKYOOS] NOUN, excuses. **excuse** ▸ something that excuses; a reason that explains something : *Ryan's excuse for missing practice was a dentist's appointment.* SYN: alibi, reason, defence, plea.

ex·e·cute [EK-suh-kyoot] VERB, executed, executing. 1. **exécuter, s'acquitter, accomplir, réaliser** ▸ to carry out; perform; do : *An Olympic diver must be able to execute several standard dives.* 2. **exécuter, s'acquitter, accomplir, réaliser** ▸ to put into effect; enforce : *Mom assigns the chores, and we execute them.* 3. **exécuter** ▸ to put someone to death, especially according to law for a crime that the person has committed.

ex·e·cu·tion [EK-suh-KYOO-shun] NOUN, executions. 1. **exécution, réalisation, accomplissement** ▸ the act of executing; carrying out or putting into effect : *the execution of the captain's orders by the crew.* **2. exécution** ▶ the executing of a person, especially by legal order. **Note.** A person who carries out the execution of a criminal is an executioner.

ex·e·cu·tive [eg-ZEK-yuh-tiv] NOUN, **executives. cadre, supérieur (-ieure)** ▶ any person who manages or helps to manage a business or organization. ▲ ADJECTIVE. **exécutif (-ive)** ▶ having to do with managing a business or organization : *The chief executive officer is the head of a company.*

ex·empt [eg-ZEMPT] VERB, **exempted, exempting. exempter, dispenser** ▶ to free from a duty or obligation; excuse; release : *High marks exempt students from writing this exam.* **Note.** The fact of exempting is exemption: *to get an exemption from jury duty.*

ex·er·cise [EK-sur-size] NOUN, **exercises. 1. exercice** ▶ activity of the body that is meant to promote good health or to train or develop the body : *Running, swimming, and playing tennis are popular forms of exercise.* **2. exercice** ▶ a question or problem that gives practice : *There are exercises at the end of each chapter in our math text.* **3. exercice** ▶ the use of a certain power or ability : *the exercise of one's imagination.* **4. exercices. cérémonie** ▶ a ceremony or program : *graduation exercises.* ▲ VERB, **exercised, exercising. 1. faire de l'exercice** ▶ to do a form of exercise. **2. exercer** ▶ to make use of; put into practice : *to exercise the right to vote.* SYN : practise, train, prepare, condition, drill.

ex·haust [eg-ZOST] VERB, **exhausted, exhausting. 1. épuiser** ▶ to use up completely : *Your constant complaining has exhausted my patience.* **2. épuiser, exténuer** ▶ to make very tired : *The long day at the beach exhausted the children.* **Note.** Usually used as an ADJECTIVE: *Cleaning out the garage is exhausting.* ▲ NOUN, **exhausts. 1. échappement** ▶ the gases or smoke released from an engine. **2.** (also **exhaust pipes**) **tuyau (-aux) d'échappement** ▶ the pipe in an automobile that carries these gases away.

ex·hib·it [eg-ZIB-it] VERB, **exhibited, exhibiting. 1. exhiber, exposer, étaler, présenter** ▶ to show a sign of; reveal : *to exhibit fear.* **2. exhiber, exposer, étaler, présenter** ▶ to put on display; show in public : *Pablo Picasso first exhibited his painting when he was only 20.* ▲ NOUN, **exhibits. objet exposé, pièce à conviction** ▶ something that is exhibited; a display. SYN : show, display, demonstrate, present, expose.

ex·hi·bi·tion [EK-suh-BISH-un] NOUN, **exhibitions. 1. exhibition, présentation, démonstration** ▶ the act of exhibiting or displaying : *Many tennis fans dislike that player because of his exhibitions of bad temper.* **2. exhibition, exposition, présentation, démonstration** ▶ a public display; a show : *an exhibition of furniture from*

Lower Canada. **Note.** In sports, an exhibition game is one that does not count as part of the regular season. 🖙 **p. 1146.**

ex·ile [EG-zile *or* EG-sile] NOUN, **exiles. 1. exil** ▶ the state of being forced to leave one's country : *Juan Perón lived in exile in Spain after he was overthrown as president of Argentina.* **2. exilé (-ée), expatrié (-ée), expulsé (-ée), banni (-nie)** ▶ a person who has been forced to leave his country : *Many Cuban exiles now live in other parts of the world.* ▲ VERB, **exiled, exiling. exiler, bannir, expatrier** ▶ to send a person into exile; banish : *After the revolution, the new government exiled many people.* SYN : banish, expel, deport, ban, exclude, cast out.

ex·ist [eg-ZIST] VERB, **existed, existing. 1. exister** ▶ to be real : *There are many stories about Robin Hood, but it is not known whether he really existed.* **2. exister, être** ▶ to be here; be present : *"Between slave and Pharaoh there existed a large gulf that had never been crossed."* (Roger Lancelyn Green) **3. exister, vivre, subsister** ▶ to continue to live; have life : *"His life would be lonely until he too, died, ceased to exist."* (James Joyce) **Note.** The fact of existing is existence: *Many people believe in the existence of ghosts.*

ex·it [EG-zit *or* EG-sit] NOUN, **exits. 1. sortie** ▶ a way out : *We left the theatre by the side exit.* **2. sortie** ▶ the act of leaving : *Linda made a quick exit from the party when she realized how late it was.* ▲ VERB, **exited, exiting. sortir** ▶ to make an exit; go out; leave : *The passengers exited from the plane.* SYN : depart, go out, leave.

ex·ot·ic [eg-ZOT-ik] ADJECTIVE. **exotique** ▶ from another part of the world; foreign; strange : *exotic birds such as the peacock or ostrich.*

ex·pand [ek-SPAND] VERB, **expanded, expanding. élargir, dilater, accroître, augmenter** ▶ to make or become larger : *A balloon expands when you blow air into it.* **Note.** The expanding of something is expansion: *Heat causes the expansion of metal.* SYN : stretch, spread, enlarge, increase, grow.

ex·pect [ek-SPEKT] VERB, **expected, expecting. 1. escompter, attendre, prévoir, s'attendre à** ▶ to look forward to; think something will probably come or happen : *Mom expects that it will be sunny tomorrow.* **2. exiger, attendre** ▶ to think of as right or proper; require : *Our teacher expects us to do our homework.* **3.** *Informal.* **penser, croire, supposer** ▶ suppose; think; believe : *I expect you're surprised to hear that.* **Note.** The act or fact of expecting is expectation. SYN : look for, think, suppose, hope, anticipate.

ex·pe·di·tion [EK-spuh-DISH-un] NOUN, **expeditions. expédition** ▶ a long trip or journey made for a special reason : *Many explorers made* *expeditions to Canada hoping to find a faster route to China.*

exotic (fruits)

ex·pel [ek-SPEKT] VERB, expelled, expelling. **1. expulser, exclure, renvoyer ▸** to force someone to leave a group or place for some wrongdoing : *Dad expelled our dog from the house for chewing the rug.* **2. expulser, évacuer, éliminer ▸** to force out from the body : *A whale expels air though a hole in the top of its head.* SYN : remove, get rid of, eject, send away.

ex·pense [ek-SPENS] NOUN, expenses. **1. dépense, frais ▸** the amount of money something costs; the price or charge for something : *"When the King announced he would visit, the lord was shaken. The expense of the preparations could cost him his fortune."* (Aliki) **2. dépense, charge ▸** a cause or reason for spending money : *Adding a new bedroom to the house was a big expense.* **3. aux dépens de ▸** a loss or sacrifice : *Maxine works long hours, but not at the expense of her health.* **Note.** Something that costs a lot of money is expensive: *"She told me that expensive toys like that were meant only for the children of kings and maharajas."* (Dayal Kaur Khalsa) ✍ **p. 650.**

ex·pe·ri·ence [ek-SPEER-ee-uns] NOUN, experiences. **1. expérience, aventure ▸** something that happens to a person; an event in one's life : *"She had always earned honours because of her brains, but winning in sports was a new experience."* (Gary Soto) **2. expérience, pratique ▸** knowledge or skill that is gained by doing something : *He has 12 years of experience as a teacher.* ▲ VERB, experienced, experiencing. **connaître, essuyer, subir ▸** to go through; have happen to : *to experience pain. Our train experienced several delays because of the snowstorm.*

ex·per·i·ment [ek-SPER-uh-munt] NOUN, experiments. **1. expérience ▸** a careful study under controlled conditions to discover or prove some fact or law of science : *We did an experiment in class to show what happens to plants if they don't get any sunlight.* **2. expérience, essai ▸** any test or trial to find something out : *We tested the strength of different materials for our science experiment.* ▲ VERB, experimented, experimenting. **expérimenter ▸** to find out by testing; perform an experiment : *The coach experimented with several different lineups before deciding on the best one.* **Note.** Something that has to do with an experiment is experimental. ■ **experimentally,** ADVERB. ▸ **expérimentalement.**

ex·pert [EK-spurt] NOUN, experts. **expert (-erte), spécialiste, connaisseur (-euse) ▸** a person who has great skill or knowledge about a certain subject; authority : *a computer expert.* ▲ ADJECTIVE. **expert (-erte) ▸** knowing a lot or having a lot of skill; being an expert : *an expert photographer.*

ex·plain [ek-SPLANE] VERB, explained, explaining. **1. expliquer, élucider, éclaircir ▸** to make something clear or easy to understand : *"Let me also explain to you how you must behave while you are a guest in the palace."* (Adèle Geras) **Note.** Something that explains is explanatory. **2. expliquer, justifier ▸** to give the reason or reasons for; justify : *"'You don't understand,' Melissa explained. 'We don't have to get away from them.'"* (Phoebe Gilman) **3. expliquer ▸** to tell the importance of; interpret : *I tried to explain my dream.* ✍ **p. 212.**

ex·pla·na·tion [EK-spluh-NAY-shun] NOUN, explanations. **1. explication, éclaircissement ▸** the explaining of something; clearing up a difficulty or mistake : *the explanation of a math problem.* **2. explication, justification ▸** something that explains; a reason : *The police have no explanation for how the money disappeared.*

ex·plode [ek-SPLODF] VERB, exploded, exploding. **1. exploser, éclater, détoner, sauter ▸** to burst suddenly with a loud noise; blow up : *The balloon exploded when Karl pricked it with a pin.* **2. exploser, éclater ▸** to burst forth suddenly and noisily : *The audience exploded with laughter.*

ex·ploit [eks-PLOYT] VERB, exploited, exploiting. **1. exploiter ▸** to make use of something : *Mines are exploited for their minerals.* **2. exploiter ▸** to use unfairly; help oneself in a selfish way : *The manager exploited the singer's trust to make more money.*

ex·plore [ek-SPLOR] VERB, explored, exploring. **1. explorer ▸** to travel to an unknown or little-known place to learn more about it : *At different times in history, people have explored western North America, central Africa, the bottom of the ocean, and the surface of the moon.*

211

🔧 Word Builder

Explain, define, and ***illustrate*** are verbs that mean to make the meaning of something clear.
Explain is the most general of these words. It can be applied to ideas, things people say, actions or operations, such as in mathematics: *The teacher gave us a clear explanation of long division.*
Define means to set limits or boundaries in an explanation: *Shayla defined what she meant by "good food" when she gave a list of desserts.* ***Illustrate*** means to show the meaning of something: *Akmet illustrated his arguments with several examples.*

Note. A person who explores something is an explorer. The act of exploring is **exploration.** **2. explorer** ▸ to go through a place that is not familiar: *Helen likes to explore the woods behind her house.* **3. explorer, sonder, examiner** ▸ to look into closely; examine: *The government is exploring ways to improve the tax system.*

ex·plo·sion [ek-SPLOH-zhun] NOUN, explosions. **1. explosion, éclatement** ▸ the blowing up of something suddenly and noisily; the act of exploding: *the explosion of a firecracker.* **2. explosion, éclatement** ▸ a sudden and sharp increase or outbreak: *a population explosion.*

ex·port [ek-SPORT *or* EK-sport] VERB, exported, exporting. **exporter** ▸ to send goods to other countries for trade or sale: *Canada exports wood to many parts of the world.* ▲ [EKS-port] NOUN, exports. **1. exportation** ▸ something that is sold or traded to another country: *Wheat is a major export of Canada.* **2. exportation** ▸ the act or process of exporting.

ex·pose [ek-SPOZE] VERB, exposed, exposing. **1. exposer, découvrir, dénuder** ▸ to leave without protection; uncover; make visible: *Jacob's fair skin was exposed to the hot sun.* **2. exposer, révéler, dévoiler, démasquer** ▸ to make something known; reveal: *The newspaper exposed the mayor's lies.* **3. exposer** ▸ to make or become subject to; allow to have an effect: *Perry exposed our whole class to chicken pox.* **4. exposer** ▸ to allow light to reach a photographic film or plate. SYN: uncover, show, display, reveal, disclose.

ex·press [ek-SPRES] VERB, expressed, expressing. **1. exprimer, émettre, formuler** ▸ to tell in words; state: *The film critic expressed her opinion of the movie in a review.* **2. exprimer, manifester, présenter** ▸ to show a thought or feeling in some way other than by words: *Clapping your hands is a way to express praise for someone.* ▲ ADJECTIVE. **1. explicite, formel (-elle)** ▸ clear and definite, certain: *Mrs. Ghandi gave money to the city with the express wish that it be used for a park.* **2. express** ▸ meant for fast travel: *An express train or bus makes only a few stops.* ▲ NOUN, expresses. **express** ▸ an express train, bus, mail service, or the like. ■ **expressly,** ADVERB. **expressément** ▸ clearly; definitely: *Dr. Marsh offered to help her, but she said that she had come expressly to see*

explosion

Dr. Chan. **Note.** Also used as an ADVERB: *to send a package express.* SYN: say, declare, state, describe, convey, show.

ex·pres·sion [ek-SPRESH-un] NOUN, expressions. **1. expression** ▸ the putting of thoughts or feelings into words or actions: *He sent us a gift as an expression of thanks for our help.* **2. expression** ▸ a look on the face that shows a certain thought or feeling: *Her expression told us how happy she was.* **3. expression, locution** ▸ a common word, phrase, or saying: *"Dead as a doornail" is a common expression.* **Note.** Something that is full of expression is expressive: *She has expressive eyes.*

ex·quis·ite [ek-SKWIZ-it *or* EKS-skwiz-it] ADJECTIVE. **exquis (-ise), raffiné (-ée), délicat (-ate)** ▸ having a special delicate beauty or charm; finely made or done: *Sam made a sweater with an exquisite design.* ■ **exquisitely,** ADVERB. ▸ **exquisément, avec finesse.**

ex·tend [ek-STEND] VERB, extended, extending. **1. élargir, étendre, agrandir, augmenter** ▸ to make longer; lengthen: *There are plans to extend the old highway to join the new one.* **2. tendre, étendre** ▸ to reach or stretch out: *A small point of land extended out into the lake.* **3. apporter, offrir, présenter, consentir** ▸ to give or offer: *to extend help; to extend a welcome.* SYN: stretch, reach out, enlarge, broaden, expand.

ex·ten·sion [ek-STEN-shun] NOUN, extensions. **1. extension, prolongation, agrandissement, rallonge** ▸ a stretching out; addition: *We built an extension onto our garage in order to park our trailer.* **2. extension, appareil supplémentaire, poste** ▸ an extra telephone connected to the main line.

ex·ten·sive [ek-STEN-iv] ADJECTIVE. **étendu (-ue), vaste, considérable, important (-ante)** ▶ covering a large area or having a large size; great : *The continent of Australia has an extensive desert in its centre.* ■ **extensively,** ADVERB. ▶ **largement, considérablement, abondamment.**

ex·tent [ek-STENT] NOUN, extents. **étendue, superficie, ampleur, importance** ▶ the length or amount to which something extends; size : *The mayor flew over the buildings that had exploded to judge the extent of the damage.*

ex·te·ri·or [ek-STEER-ee-ur] ADJECTIVE. **extérieur** ▶ outer or outside : *Exterior paints are used on the outside walls of a house.* ▲ NOUN, exteriors. **1. extérieur** ▶ an outer part or surface : *the exterior of a car.* **2. extérieur, dehors** ▶ an outward appearance or manner : *Underneath his rough exterior, he is very kind.*

ex·ter·nal [ek-STUR-nul] ADJECTIVE. **extérieur (-eure), externe** ▶ on or of the outside : *A medicine for external use is meant to be put on the skin but not swallowed.* ■ **externally,** ADVERB. ▶ **extérieurement.**

ex·tinct [ek-STINKT] ADJECTIVE. **1. disparu (-ue)** ▶ no longer existing; having died out : *Because the Beothuk are an extinct people, no one knows exactly how Beothuk words were pronounced.* **2. éteint (-einte)** ▶ not active or in use : *an extinct volcano.* **Note.** The state of being extinct is extinction: *The buffalo was once threatened with extinction because so many were killed during the late 1860s.*

ex·tin·guish [ek-STING-gwish] VERB, extinguished, extinguishing. **éteindre** ▶ to put out : *We extinguished the campfire before going to bed.*

ex·tra[1] [EKS-truh] ADJECTIVE. **supplémentaire, de plus, en sus** ▶ more than what is usual or needed; additional : *We made extra sandwiches in case more people showed up.* ▲ NOUN, extras. **1. supplément, à-côté** ▶ something added to what is usual or needed · *Our new car has a lot of extras, such as a CD player and air conditioning.* **2. supplément** ▶ a special edition of a newspaper that reports something very important. **3. figurant (-ante)** ▶ an actor appearing as part of a crowd in a film or play. ▲ ADVERB. **particulièrement, plus que d'ordinaire** ▶ more than usual : *Mother put two blankets on my bed because it was an extra cold night.*

ex·tra-[2] PREFIX. outside; besides; beyond : *extraordinary.*

ex·tract [ek-STRAKT] VERB, extracted, extracting. **1. extraire, arracher, tirer** ▶ to take or pull out, usually with some effort : *The dentist extracted Kyle's tooth.* **2. extraire** ▶ to get out by pressing, heating, or some other process : *He extracted juice from several limes.*

ex·tra·or·di·nar·y [ek-STROR-duh-NAIR-ee *or* EK-struh-OR-duh-nair-ee] ADJECTIVE. **extraordinaire, remarquable, exceptionnel (-elle)** ▶ very unusual; remarkable; exceptional : *Marco tells me that you have a rather extraordinary dog that performs all sorts of tricks.*

ex·trav·a·gant [ek-STRAV-uh-gunt] ADJECTIVE. **1. dépensier (-ière), prodigue, gaspilleur (-euse), dispendieux (-ieuse)** ▶ spending money in a careless or wasteful way : *After winning a lottery, David gave his friends extravagant gifts.* **2. extravagant (-ante), exagéré (-ée), outré (-ée), exorbitant (-ante)** ▶ going beyond what is reasonable; too extreme : *Denise didn't buy the dress because the price was too extravagant.* SYN : extreme, excessive, overdone, luxurious.

ex·treme [ek-STREEM] ADJECTIVE. **1. extrême, intense, rigoureux (-euse), très sévère** ▶ far beyond what is usual; very great or severe : *Antarctica is a region of extreme cold.* **2. extrême, dernier (-ière)** ▶ very far; farthest : *The bedrooms were at the extreme back of the house.* **3. extrême, extrémiste, exagéré (-ée), poussé (-ée)** ▶ very far from what is ordinary or typical : *That dress is extreme.* ▲ NOUN, extremes. **1. extrême** ▶ something that is extreme : *Burning hot and freezing cold are two extremes of temperature.* **2. extrémité** ▶ the greatest or highest degree : *to do something in the extreme.* ■ **extremely,** ADVERB. **extrêmement** ▶ *a joke that is extremely funny.*

go to extremes pousser les choses à l'extrême ▶ to do something in an extreme way; do more than is sensible or right.

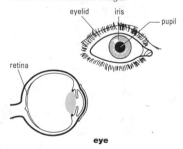

eye

eye [eye] NOUN, eyes. **1. œil (yeux)** ▶ the part of the body with which people and animals see. **2. yeux, iris** ▶ the coloured part of the eye; the iris : *Jill has blue eyes.* **3. regard** ▶ a look or gaze : *His eye fell upon a letter that had been left on the table.* **4. œil, trou, centre** ▶ something thought of as like an eye in some way, such as the hole of a needle that the thread goes through or the centre of a storm. **5. œil** ▶ an ability to see, recognize, or appreciate things : *a batter with a good eye in baseball.* ▲ VERB,

213

eyed, eyeing or eying. **regarder, observer, reluquer, toiser ▶** to watch carefully or closely : *Cory eyed the dessert.* ⎙ **p. 976.**

catch one's eye attirer l'attention de quelqu'un ▶ to attract one's attention : *The bright colour caught his eye.*

keep an eye on garder un œil sur, ne pas perdre de vue ▶ to watch carefully; look after : *Mother asked John to keep an eye on his little brother when they went to the park.*

eye·brow [EYE-BROW] NOUN, eyebrows. **sourcil ▶** the hair that grows along the bony part of the face above each eye. ⎙ **p. 978.**

eye·lid [EYE-WIT-nis] NOUN, eyelids. **paupière ▶** the fold of skin that can open and close over the eye.

eye·wit·ness [EYE-LID] NOUN, eyewitnesses. **témoin oculaire ▶** someone who has seen something happen : *Dad was an eyewitness to the car accident.*

flower

f, F [ef] NOUN, f's, F's. **1. f, F** ▸ the sixth letter of the English alphabet. **2. F** ▸ a grade, mark, or level.

fa·ble [FAY-bul] NOUN, fables. **fable, légende** ▸ a story made up to teach a lesson. Fables are usually about animals that act and talk like people. *✐ p. 215.*

fab·ric [FAB-rik] NOUN, fabrics. **tissu, étoffe** ▸ cloth; material made by weaving or knitting threads. Fabric is made from natural fibres such as cotton, wool, or silk, or from human-made fibres such as polyester. SYN: cloth, material, textile.

fab·u·lous [FAB-yuh-lus] ADJECTIVE. **1. fabuleux (-euse)** ▸ like a fable or story; beyond belief; amazing: *They must have paid a fabulous amount of money for such a beautiful house.* **2.** *Informal.* **formidable, sensationnel (-elle)** ▸ very good; outstanding; excellent: *Have you seen that movie yet? It's fabulous.* SYN: amazing, wonderful, incredible.

face [face] NOUN, faces. **1. face, visage, figure** ▸ the front part of the head, where the eyes, nose, and mouth are. **2. mine, tête, physionomie** ▸ a look or expression, especially one that shows anger or dislike: *She made a face when she tasted the sour pickle.* **3. face, côté** ▸ the front or upper part of something: *the face of a mountain; the face of a playing card.* **4. face** ▸ personal pride; self-respect. Note. Usually used in the expressions save face or lose face. ▲ VERB, faced, facing. **1. faire face** ▸ to turn the face toward: *Chloe faced the audience to give her speech.* **2. faire face** ▸ to have the front toward: *Dad backed into the garage so that the car faced forward.* **3. faire face** ▸ to meet with directly; deal with: *She smiled and prepared to face the world.* *☞ p. 979.*

face-off NOUN, face-offs. **remise en jeu, mise en jeu, confrontation** ▸ the act of putting the puck or ball into play: *a face-off at centre ice.*

fa·cial [FAY-shul] ADJECTIVE. **facial (-ale, -als, -aux)** ▸ having to do with the face: *The mime uses his facial expressions to show emotion.*

✐ **Writing Tips**

Fables are short stories told to teach a lesson or moral. In fables, animal characters act like people, often warning the reader about bad habits or what will happen if they do something wrong. The moral is often stated clearly at the end.

The most famous fable writer is Aesop, who lived in Greece around 600 BC. Well-known fables by Aesop include "The Tortoise and the Hare", "The Lion and the Mouse", and "The Ant and the Grasshopper".

Many other cultures also have their own fables. A collection of stories from India contains the "Fables of Bidpai" and the "Jataka Tales." These stories, written around 200 BC, are a lot like fables and teach others how to make wise choices in life. The "Jataka Tales" are stories of Buddha's former lives as different animals. Each tale is told to teach a moral.

▲ NOUN, facials. **soin du visage** ▸ a treatment aimed at improving the appearance of the face.

fa·cil·i·ty [fuh-SIL-uh-tee] NOUN, facilities. **1. facilité** ▸ ease or skill in doing something: *The magician had amazing facility with a deck of cards and was able to do many tricks.* **2.** (often facilities) **installation, équipement** ▸ something that makes things easier or that serves a certain purpose: *The school has excellent library facilities for research.*

fact [fakt] NOUN, facts. **1. fait** ▸ something that is known to be true or real; something that exists or that has happened: *It's a fact that the earth moves around the sun.* **2. fait** ▸ any information presented as true or real: *I hear Mr. Gagnon is retiring. Is that a fact?* Note. Something that has to do with facts or is based on

215

facts is **factual**. SYN: truth, detail, evidence, data, reality, certainty.

fac·tor [FAK-tur] NOUN, factors. **1. facteur ▶** something that helps to bring about or cause something else; one part of a situation : *Wind was a factor in the kayak race.* **2. facteur ▶** any of the numbers or expressions that produce a given number when multiplied together : *The numbers 3 and 5 are factors of 15.* ▲ VERB, factored, factoring. **factoriser, mettre en facteur ▶** to separate into factors. SYN: cause, element, part, basis, ingredient.

fac·to·ry [FAK-tuh-ree] NOUN, factories. **usine, fabrique ▶** a building or group of buildings where goods are made to be sold, especially one where large quantities of a product are made by machines.

fac·ul·ty [FAK-ul-tee] NOUN, faculties. **1. faculté ▶** all of the teachers at a school, college, or university. **2. faculté ▶** a special skill or talent for doing something : *Fatima has an excellent faculty for numbers and mathematics.* **3. faculté ▶** a natural power of the mind or senses : *the faculty of sight.* SYN: talent, gift, power, ability, capacity.

fade [fade] VERB, faded, fading. **1. se décolorer, perdre son éclat, passer ▶** to lose colour or brightness : *His bright-red shirt had faded to a dull pink.* **2. baisser, décliner, s'affaiblir, diminuer ▶** to disappear slowly; grow dim or faint : *"And when their voices faded away it was as quiet as a dream."* (Jane Yolen) SYN: dim, pale, weaken, fail, grow faint, decline.

fail [fale] VERB, failed, failing. **1. échouer ▶** to get less than a satisfactory score or mark; not pass : *to fail a test.* **2. négliger, omettre, manquer ▶** to not do what is intended; not succeed : *He failed to get to school on time.* **3. faire défaut, manquer, tomber en panne ▶** to not act or work as is expected : *The plane's engine failed, and the pilot had to make an emergency landing.* **4. faiblir, baisser ▶** to lose strength; become weak. **Note.** Often used as an ADJECTIVE: *our dog's failing eyesight.*

fail·ure [FALE-yur] NOUN, failures. **1. échec ▶** the act or fact of failing : *Gary was upset by his failure to win the election for class president.* **2. arrêt, panne ▶** a condition of not working or acting properly : *heart failure; an electrical power failure.* **3. échec, raté (-ée) ▶** a person or thing that fails : *The author's first novel was a failure, but her second became a best-seller.*

faint [faynt] ADJECTIVE, fainter, faintest. **1. faible, léger (-ère) ▶** not clearly seen, heard, or smelled; weak or dim : *Skye heard a faint noise in the kitchen.* **2. faible ▶** feeling weak and dizzy. ▲ NOUN, faints. **évanouissement, défaillance ▶** a condition in which a person appears to suddenly fall asleep for a short time and does not know what is happening. Great pain, a loss of

blood, or a shock to the mind can cause someone to fall into a faint : *"There stood an ogre so huge and so hideous that the Sultan's brave knights fainted at the sight of him."* (Robin Muller) ▲ VERB, fainted, fainting. **s'évanouir ▶** to fall into a faint. ▪ **faintly**, ADVERB. **▶ faiblement, légèrement, vaguement.** SYN: swoon, black out, pass out, keel over.

fair[1] [fare] ADJECTIVE, fairer, fairest. **1. juste, équitable, honnête ▶** not choosing or favouring one side over another; honest : *"That's not fair, Jamaica thought. Maurice is shorter than I am and he's allowed to play!"* (Juanita Havill) **2. fair-play, loyal (-ale, -aux), correct (-ecte) ▶** following the rules in a proper way : *fair play.* **3. bonne balle ▶** in baseball, not foul. **4. passable, assez bon (bonne) ▶** not too good and not too bad; average : *Beth did a fair job of washing the car—she left a few dirty spots.* **5. blond (-onde), clair (claire) ▶** of the skin, light in colouring : *"She had fair skin and cheeks like blushing roses."* (Roger Lancelyn Green) **6. beau (belle, beaux), propice, favorable ▶** of weather, clear and sunny. **7. beau (belle, beaux) ▶** pleasing to look at; beautiful : *The mayor greeted the guests by saying, "Welcome to our fair city."* ▲ ADVERB. **loyalement, franc jeu, honnêtement ▶** in a fair way; fairly : *One of the contestants cheated, but the rest played fair.* ▪ **fairness**, NOUN. **▶ justice, honnêteté, équité, impartialité.** SYN: honest, just, impartial, right, equal.

fair[2] NOUN, fairs. **1. foire ▶** a large public event where farm products and farm animals are shown and offered for sale : *"I'll braid her tail and enter her in the fair. She'll win first prize for sure."* (Marilynn Reynolds) **2. foire ▶** a large showing of goods, products, or objects : *Each year our town has a fall fair.* **3. foire ▶** any display or show of items of a certain kind : *I am working on a big project for the school science fair.* 🖉 p. 1147.

fair·ly [FAIR-lee] ADVERB. **1. honnêtement, loyalement, impartialement, équitablement ▶** in an honest or fair way : *Han quit his job because he felt he wasn't being treated fairly.* **2. assez, moyennement ▶** for the most part; somewhat; rather : *I should be finished with my homework fairly soon.*

fair·y [FAIR-ee] NOUN, fairies. **fée ▶** a small make-believe person who has magical powers. 🖉 p. 217. 🖉 p. 967.

faith [fayth] NOUN, faiths. **1. foi, confiance ▶** a strong belief in something; confidence; trust : *We're going to take the new car on the trip— Dad doesn't have much faith in the old car.* **2. foi ▶** a thought or belief that is not based on facts or proof : *I have faith that whoever found my wallet will return it to me.* **3. foi, religion ▶** a particular way or system of believing; a religion : *the Muslim faith.*

✏ Writing Tips

Fairy Tales

Fairy tales are stories full of magical and fantastic events. The characters are often extraordinary—for example, fairy godmothers, giants, wizards, leprechauns, elves, fairies, kings, queens, princesses, and princes. These characters often go out on quests or try to rescue someone. Fairy tales teach simple lessons such as that a kindness is always repaid.

When writing your own fairy tales, keep these points in mind:

- *the characters are either good or bad*
- *good wins over bad*
- *magical objects and powers are important to the story*
- *many fairy tales start with the phrase "Once upon a time" and end with "and they lived happily ever after."*

---

faith·ful [FAYTH-ful] ADJECTIVE. **1. fidèle ▸** having faith or trust; loyal; devoted : *He thought of his dog as a faithful companion.* **2. fidèle, exact (-acte), conforme ▸** keeping to the facts; true; accurate : *Only one of the witnesses could give a faithful account of the accident.* ■ **faithfully,** ADVERB. **▸ fidèlement, loyalement.** *The cook had served them faithfully for many years.* ■ **faithfulness,** NOUN. **▸ fidélité, loyauté.**

fake [fake] NOUN, fakes. **imposteur (-eure), faux (fausse) ▸** a person or thing that is not what it should be or seems to be : *The map turned out to be a fake, and there was no treasure.* ▲ VERB, faked, faking. **1. faire semblant ▸** to act so as to fool or deceive; pretend : *The quarterback faked a pass and then ran around the end.* **2. falsifier, contrefaire, truquer ▸** to make something seem real in order to fool : *Sasha forgot her lines and had to fake them.* **Note.** Often used as an ADJECTIVE: *fake money; fake fur.* SYN: imitation, fraudulent, artificial.

fal·con [FOL-kun *or* FAL-kun] NOUN, falcons. **faucon ▸** a bird related to a hawk. Falcons have long wings, a hooked bill, and strong claws. They fly very fast and can be trained to hunt other birds and animals.

fall [fol] VERB, fell, fallen, falling. **1. tomber ▸** to move or go down from a higher place : *A cold rain was falling.* **2. tomber, s'écrouler, s'effondrer ▸** to go down suddenly from a standing or sitting position : *Lynn tripped and fell to her knees.* **3. tomber, baisser ▸** to become lower in amount or position : *The temperature fell over 10 degrees yesterday.* **4. tomber ▸** to

take place on a certain date : *My birthday will fall on a Sunday this year.* **5. tomber ▸** to pass into a certain state or condition : *to fall asleep; to fall in love.* ▲ NOUN, falls. **1. automne ▸** the season of the year between summer and winter. **Note.** Also called autumn. **2. chute ▸** the act or fact of falling : *a fall from a tree.* **3. falls. chute, cascade ▸** a place on a river where the water drops sharply; a waterfall : *Niagara Falls.* SYN: drop, plunge, sink, descend, tumble, spill. 📖 **p. 1102.**

fall·en [FOL-un] ADJECTIVE. **1. tombé (-ée) ▸** having dropped; come down : *We raked the fallen leaves into piles.* **2. tombé (-ée) ▸** captured or overthrown : *The army marched into the fallen city.* **3. mort (morte), tombé (-ée) ▸** killed, especially in battle : *The soldiers observed a moment of silence in tribute to their fallen comrades.*

false [fols] ADJECTIVE, falser, falsest. **1. faux (fausse) ▸** not true, right, or correct; wrong : *Three of the answers Paula had marked true were actually false.* **2. faux (fausse) ▸** not real; artificial : *false teeth; false eyelashes.* **3. faux (fausse), mensonger (-ère), frauduleux (-euse) ▸** meant to fool or deceive; not honest or actual : *The criminal used a false name.* ■ **falsely,** ADVERB: **▸ faussement, à tort.** *The man was falsely accused of the crime.* **Note.** A falsehood is a lie. SYN: untrue, wrong, incorrect, fake, phony.

fal·ter [FOL-tur] VERB. faltered, faltering. **vaciller, chanceler, hésiter, faiblir ▸** to become unsteady; not go straight; hesitate; stumble. **Note.** Often used as an ADJECTIVE: *He nervously read his speech in a faltering voice.*

fame [fame] NOUN. **célébrité, gloire, renommée ▸** the fact of being famous; being well-known; reputation; popularity : *"From that day on Maylin was renowned in Chinatown as a great cook and a wise person. Her fame even reached as far as China."* (Paul Yee)

fa·mil·iar [fuh-MIL-yur] ADJECTIVE. **1. familier (-ière), habituel (-elle) ▸** often seen or heard; well-known; common : *Children playing in the park are a familiar sight.* **2. habitué (-ée) à, bien connu (-ue), familier (-ière), habitué (-elle) ▸** knowing something well : *Annika was familiar with that computer game.* **Note.** The state of being familiar is familiarity. 🖋 **p. 129.**

fam·i·ly [FAM-uh-lee] NOUN, families. **1. famille ▸** a parent or parents and their children : *Tickets to the fair are $2 each, or $7 for a whole family.* **2. famille, enfant ▸** the children of a mother and father : *They've been married two years and plan to start a family soon.* **3. famille, parenté ▸** a group of people related to each other; relatives : *We have to get extra tables and chairs when our whole family has dinner at Grandma's house.* **4. famille ▸** a large group of related things : *Lions and tigers are* *members of the cat family.* ▲ ADJECTIVE. **familial (-ale, -aux)** ▶ involving or belonging to the family : *a family outing.* SYN : relatives, kin, clan, folks, household. ☞ **p. 968.**

fam·ine [FAM-in] NOUN, famines. **famine** ▶ a very serious lack of food in a certain place. Famines can happen if the main food that people rely on is destroyed or does not grow.

fa·mous [FAY-mus] ADJECTIVE. **célèbre, bien connu (-ue), renommé (-ée)** ▶ known to many people ; very well-known ; noted ; famed : *Lake Louise is famous for its beautiful scenery.*

fan¹ [fan] NOUN, fans. 1. **ventilateur** ▶ a machine that uses an electric motor to turn several blades very quickly to make air move. 2. **éventail (-ails)** ▶ a piece of stiff, flat paper or other material in the shape of a half-circle, held in the hand and moved to make a cool breeze. ▲ VERB, fanned, fanning. 1. **éventer** ▶ to move air with or as if with a fan : *The passengers on the hot bus fanned themselves with their newspapers.* 2. **déployer** ▶ to spread out like an open fan : *The searchers fanned out through the woods to look for the lost child.*

fan

fan² NOUN, fans. **admirateur (-trice), enthousiaste, passionné (-ée), fan** ▶ somebody who follows or admires a certain activity, group, or person ; supporter : *a country music fan ; a soccer fan.*

fa·na·tic [fuh-NAT-ik] NOUN, fanatics. **fanatique** ▶ a person who is much too serious or enthusiastic about something ; someone who goes too far : *She's a film fanatic ; she goes to every movie that comes to town.* ▲ ADJECTIVE. **fanatique** ▶ being a fanatic ; much too serious or enthusiastic : *My brother is a fanatic follower of the Toronto Maple Leafs.*

fan·cy [FAN-see] ADJECTIVE, fancier, fanciest. **fantaisiste, de luxe** ▶ not plain or simple ; very decorated or elegant : *a fancy dress ; a fancy car.* ▲ VERB, fancied, fancying. 1. **s'imaginer, se figurer, se croire, penser** ▶ to picture in the mind ; imagine : *Can you fancy yourself wearing that hat?* 2. **aimer, avoir envie de** ▶ to like very much ; be fond of : *I rather fancy that flowered scarf.* ▲ NOUN, fancies. 1. **fantaisie, imagination** ▶ the power to picture something in the mind ; imagination. 2. **fantaisie, caprice** ▶ an odd or unusual idea or wish : *He had a sudden fancy for a peanut-butter-and-pickle sandwich.*

3. **goût, envie, se prendre d'affection pour** ▶ a liking for someone or something ; fondness.

fan·tas·tic [fan-TAS-tik] ADJECTIVE. 1. **fantastique, bizarre** ▶ seeming to come from fantasy rather than reality ; very strange ; odd : *The firelight cast fantastic shapes on the walls of the darkened room.* 2. **fantastique, invraisemblable, inouï (-ïe)** ▶ hard to accept as real ; amazing : *Space travel was a fantastic idea when my grandparents were young.* 3. **fantastique, fabuleux (-euse)** ▶ very good ; outstanding : *That chocolate cake was fantastic!* ■ **fantastically,** ADVERB. ▶ **fantastiquement, extraordinairement, fabuleusement.**

fan·ta·sy [FAN-tuh-see] NOUN, fantasies. 1. **fantaisie, imagination, fantasme** ▶ something that is made up or pictured in the mind ; something imaginary : *José has a fantasy about winning a medal at the Olympics.* 2. **fantaisie** ▶ a story, movie, or the like that deals with an imaginary world : *Tolkien's* The Hobbit *is a fantasy novel.* ✐ **p. 218.**

far [far] ADVERB, farther, farthest. (also further, furthest) 1. **loin** ▶ at or to a great distance ; not near in space or time : *to live far from town ; to study far into the night.* 2. **loin** ▶ at or to a certain point in space or time. **Note.** Usually used in the phrase **as (so) far as:** *I'll ride along with*

✐ Writing Tips

Fantasy

In **fantasy** fiction, the writer creates characters, places, and situations that aren't part of the real world. Characters include extraordinary beings such as dragons and other strange creatures. Animals or toys act like people, and human beings often have unusual powers.

Many fantasies are set in different worlds and in different times—either the past or the future. There are no scientific explanations for what happens in these worlds. Other fantasies are set in no particular time—for example, The Wonderful Wizard of Oz and Alice's Adventures in Wonderland.

Fantasies often have an underlying theme such as the idea that love overcomes hate or that getting your wish may not always make you happy.

Popular examples of fantasy include The Lion, the Witch, and the Wardrobe, The Lord of the Rings, The Hobbit, and Charlotte's Web.

you as far as the corner. **3. de loin, beaucoup, bien ▸** very much : *She's by far the fastest runner in the class.* ▲ ADJECTIVE, farther, farthest. (also further, furthest) **1. lointain (-aine), éloigné (-ée) ▸** at a distance ; not near : *a far country.* **2. plus éloigné (-ée) ▸** more distant ; farther away : *"It was there, in the far north of Australia, that they found a Vegemite sandwich."* (Mem Fox)

fare [fair] NOUN, fares. **1. prix du billet ▸** the money a person pays to travel by public transportation, as on a bus, a train, an airplane, or a ship. **2. passager (-ère), voyageur (-euse), client (-ente) ▸** a person who pays for a ticket to ride ; a passenger : *The cab driver complained because he'd had only one fare all morning.* **3. nourriture, chère ▸** food ; a meal : *We have simple fare when we go camping.* ▲ VERB, fared, faring. **réussir, aller ▸** to get along ; do : *I wondered how James was faring in his first week at camp.*

fare-well [FAIR-WEL] INTERJECTION, farewells. **adieu (-eux) ▸** good-bye and best wishes : *"'Farewell,' she shouted. 'Look for me this time next year.'"* (Robin Muller)

far-fetched [far-fecht] ADJECTIVE. **forcé (-ée), tiré (-ée) par les cheveux, bizarre ▸** unlikely, hard to believe : *I don't believe her story about meeting the movie star ; it seems far-fetched.*

farm [farm] NOUN, farms. **ferme, exploitation agricole ▸** an area of land where plants and animals are raised for food, especially a place where this is done as a business. ▲ VERB, farmed, farming. **cultiver ▸** to own or work on a farm. **Note.** A farmer is any person who lives or works on a farm. 📖 p. 1089. 👁 p. 114

far-sighted [FAR-SY-tid] ADJECTIVE. **1. hypermétrope, presbyte ▸** able to see things that are far away more clearly than things that are close up. **2. prévoyant (-ante), clairvoyant (-ante) ▸** with thought for the future.

far-ther [FAR-thur] ADVERB ; ADJECTIVE. **plus loin ▸** more distant ; more far : *We walked farther than we planned.*

far-thest [FAR-thist] ADVERB ; ADJECTIVE. **le (la) plus éloigné (-ée), le (la) plus lointain (-aine) ▸** the most distant.

fas-ci-nate [FAS-uh-NATE] VERB, fascinated, fascinating. **fasciner, captiver ▸** to attract and interest very much ; charm : *The baby was fascinated by the new toy.* ▪ **fascination,** NOUN : **▸ fascination, attrait.** *He has a fascination with trains and spends hours watching them.* SYN : attract, interest, charm, intrigue, enchant.

fash-ion [FASH-un] NOUN, fashions. **1. mode ▸** a style of clothing, especially a new or current style of women's clothing. **2. vogue, dernier cri ▸** the newest style or custom in the way someone dresses, talks, or acts : *That dress is the latest fashion, but I don't like it.* **3. façon,

manière ▸ the particular way something is done : *Don't set the table in such a careless fashion.* ▲ VERB, fashioned, fashioning. **façonner, fabriquer, confectionner ▸** to give shape or form to ; make : *"In no time she had fashioned a dish of delectable flavours and aromas, which she named Roses Sing on New Snow."* (Paul Yee) **Note.** Something that is popular is fashionable. SYN : style, mode, vogue, custom, manner, way.

fast[1] [fast] ADJECTIVE, faster, fastest. **1. rapide, vite ▸** moving or acting with speed ; going quickly ; rapid ; swift : *a fast runner ; a fast worker.* **2. avancé (-ée), en avance ▸** of a watch or clock, ahead of the correct time. **3. sûr (sûre), solide ▸** loyal ; faithful : *Sam and Adam are fast friends.* ▲ ADVERB. **1. vite, rapidement ▸** in a fast way ; quickly ; rapidly : *to swim fast ; to learn something fast.* **2. ferme, solidement ▸** tightly or firmly : *The trunk was strapped fast to the roof of the car.* SYN : quick, swift, speedy, rapid, hasty, sudden.

fast[2] VERB, fasted, fasting. **jeûner ▸** to choose to eat little or no food for reasons of health or because of one's religious or political beliefs : *During the month of Ramadan, Muslims fast during daylight hours.* ▲ NOUN, fasts. **jeûne ▸** a day or time of eating little or no food.

fas-ten [FAS-un] VERB, fastened, fastening. **1. attacher, lier ▸** to close up, attach, or connect ; make fast : *She fastened her kite to the string before letting it go.* **2. fermer solidement ▸** to fix firmly ; direct : *He fastened his eyes on the storm clouds in the distance.* SYN : tie, attach, secure, clasp, connect, bind.

fast food NOUN, fast foods. **restauration rapide ▸** food that can be prepared and served quickly, such as hamburgers and french fries.

fat [fat] NOUN, fats. **graisse, gras ▸** a soft white or yellow substance found in the body of a person or an animal, and in the seeds, nuts, and fruits of plants. Fat is an important source of energy for the human body. Too much fat in the body, however, is harmful to health. ▲ ADJECTIVE, fatter, fattest. **1. gros (grosse), gras (grasse) ▸** having a lot of fat or too much fat. **2. gros (grosse) ▸** having much in it ; full : *The movie star signed a fat new contract.*

fa-tal [FATE-ul] ADJECTIVE. **1. fatal (-ale, -als), mortel (-elle) ▸** causing death : *a fatal fire.* **2. fatal (-ale, -als), fatidique, néfaste, pernicieux (-ieuse) ▸** very bad ; causing harm or ruin : *a fatal mistake.* ▪ **fatally,** ADVERB : **▸ mortellement.** *to be fatally wounded in a car accident.* **Note.** A fatality is a death that occurs violently or by a sudden accident. SYN : deadly, killing, mortal, destructive.

fate [fate] NOUN, fates. **1. destin, destinée, fatalité, sort ▸** a power beyond human control that is thought to decide the way things happen in the world : *He decided that fate was not with* *him when everything went wrong that morning.* **2. destin, sort** ▸ something that happens to a person as if by fate; one's fortune or destiny : *"And so they set out not knowing exactly where their fate would lead them."* (Bob Barton) **3. destin, sort, avenir, lot** ▸ the end or final result of something; outcome : *City Hall will decide the fate of the park tomorrow.* SYN : fortune, destiny, lot, doom.

fa‑ther [FAH‑thur] NOUN, fathers. **1. père** ▸ the male parent of a child. **2. père, créateur, fondateur, inventeur** ▸ a man or thing thought of as like a father, because of beginning something or causing it to develop : *the Fathers of Confederation.* **3.** the Father or Our Father. **Dieu le Père** ▸ a name for God in the Christian religion. **4.** Father. **père** ▸ a title for a Catholic priest. ▲ VERB, fathered, fathering. **engendrer, procréer** ▸ to be or act as a father to : *to father a child.* ■ **fatherly,** ADJECTIVE. ▸ **paternel (-elle).** *fatherly advice.*

Fathers of Confederation les Pères de la Confédération ▸ the representatives from the original provinces of Canada who met to create the Dominion of Canada.

fath‑om [FATH‑um] NOUN, fathoms. **brasse** ▸ a unit of measurement equal to 1.83 metres, used to measure the depth of water or the length of ships.

fa‑tigue [fuh‑TEEG] NOUN. **fatigue** ▸ a feeling of being very tired from a long period of work or mental strain. ▲ VERB, fatigued, fatiguing. **fatiguer** ▸ to cause a person to be fatigued; wear out; exhaust. 📖 p. 1018.

fau‑cet [FAH‑sit] NOUN, faucets. **robinet** ▸ a device that controls the flow of water from a pipe; tap.

fault [folt] NOUN, faults. **1. défaut** ▸ something in a person's character or way of acting that is not as it should be; a personal weakness : *Fay's biggest fault is that she talks too much.* **2. défaut, anomalie, erreur** ▸ a mistake or weak point in the way something works or is made; a flaw : *a fault in an electrical wiring system.* **3. faute** ▸ the responsibility for something that is wrong : *My father apologized to my teacher and told her that it was his fault I was late for school.* **4. faille** ▸ a crack or break in the earth that causes the mass of rock on one side to move against the mass on the other side. Earthquakes are likely to take place along a fault. ▲ VERB, faulted, faulting. **blâmer, prendre en défaut** ▸ to find fault with someone; blame : *She was just trying to help. You can't fault her for that.* ■ **faulty,** ADJECTIVE, faultier, faultiest: *a car with faulty brakes.* ▸ **défectueux (-euse).** SYN : flaw, defect, weakness, shortcoming, error.

at fault responsable, en tort, en faute, fautif **(‑ive)** ▸ in the wrong; deserving blame : *Which of the two drivers was at fault in the accident?*

fau‑na [FAH‑nuh] NOUN, faunas or faunae. **faune** ▸ all the animals of a region or time : *the fauna of the Arctic.*

fa‑vour [FAY‑vur] NOUN, favours. (also favor) **1. faveur, service, grâce** ▸ a kind act that helps someone : *Would you do me a favour and drop this in the mailbox?* **2. faveur, approbation** ▸ being liked, accepted or approved. **3. faveur, cadeau (-eaux)** ▸ a small gift given at a party. ▲ VERB, favoured, favouring. **1. avoir l'amabilité de, avoir la bonté de** ▸ to do a favour for : *I hope you will favour me with a quick reply to my question.* **2. favoriser, appuyer, préférer** ▸ to think of with favour; support or approve : *Janet favours soccer over baseball.* **3. favoriser, prendre soin de** ▸ to treat in a special or careful way : *It looks as though Joe is still favouring the leg he hurt playing lacrosse.* SYN : kindness, good deed, courtesy, service.

fa‑vour‑a‑ble [FAY‑vuh‑ruh‑bul] ADJECTIVE. (also favorable) **1. favorable** ▸ showing favour; approving or liking : *That new play has received favour‑able reviews.* **2. propice** ▸ in one's favour; promising; en‑couraging : *Old sailing ships had to wait for favourable winds and tides before they left the harbour.* ■ **favourably,** ADVERB. ▸ **favorablement.** *The townspeople looked favourably on the plans for a new library.*

fa‑vour‑ite [FAY‑vuh‑rit] ADJECTIVE. (also favorite) **favori (‑ite), préféré (‑ée)** ▸ thought of with the most favour; best-liked : *"Great-grandfather played fox-and-geese in the meadow, and hide-and-seek in the barn, but his favourite game was marbles."* (Patricia MacLachlan) ▲ NOUN, favourites. **1. favori (‑ite), préféré (‑ée)** ▸ someone or something that is liked best or favoured over others : *"My favourites were the Tom Mack spoons—the lures that flashed silver in the sun."* (Tololwa M. Mollel) **2. favori (‑ite)** ▸ someone who is expected to win a game or contest : *Our school's hockey team is the favourite to win the city tournament this year.* **Note.** The practice of showing favour to a person in an unfair way is favouritism. 🖉 p. 221.

fawn [fon] NOUN, fawns. **faon** ▸ a young deer less than one year old.

fear [feer] NOUN, fears. **peur, crainte** ▸ a bad feeling that danger, pain, or something unknown is near : *"All three horses reared back in fear and panic."* (David Day) ▲ VERB, feared, fearing. **1. avoir peur de, craindre, redouter** ▸ to be scared of; be afraid of : *to fear snakes.* **2. avoir peur de, craindre, redouter** ▸ to be worried or anxious about what will happen : *He feared that he was lost.* ■ **fearful,** ADJECTIVE. ▸ **effrayant (‑ante), affreux (‑euse), épouvantable.** SYN : fright, dread, terror, horror, alarm. 📖 p. 1019.

fear‑less [feer‑lis] ADJECTIVE. **sans peur, intrépide, courageux (‑euse)** ▸ having or showing no fear; very brave; daring; bold.

🖉 Word Builder

Favourite, preferred, *and* ***beloved*** *are adjectives that indicate a strong affection for something or someone.* ***Favourite*** *means the person or thing is liked more than anyone or anything else: Misook's favourite ice cream is strawberry.* ***Preferred*** *means that someone would choose one thing over another. It is not as strong an affection as favourite: Carol prefers chocolate over vanilla.* ***Beloved*** *means a person has an extremely strong affection for someone or something: Takia took his beloved catcher's mitt everywhere he went.*

feast [feest] NOUN, feasts. **1. festin, banquet** ▸ a large or special meal with a lot of food : *"And above all, provisions had to be gathered for the great feast."* (Aliki) **2. fête** ▸ a religious holiday or celebration; a festival. ▲ VERB, feasted, feasting. **festoyer, se régaler, se délecter, se repaître** ▸ to have a feast; eat very well.

feat [feet] NOUN, feats. **prouesse, exploit, réussite, triomphe** ▸ an act or deed that shows great skill, strength, or daring :*Shooting the puck into the net from that angle was a great feat.* SYN : deed, act, exploit, stunt, achievement.

feath-er [FETH-ur] NOUN, feathers. **plume, penne** ▸ a light growth that covers and protects a bird's skin. Feathers keep birds warm and help them to fly.

fea-ture [FEE-chur] NOUN, features. **1. particularité, caractéristique** ▸ a quality or important part that stands out; something that gets attention or is especially noticed : *One nice feature of that house is the backyard.* **2. trait, particularité, caractéristique** ▸ a single part of the face or body : *His best feature is his beautiful brown eyes.* **3. long métrage, grand film** ▸ the main film of a motion-picture program; a full-length movie. **4. chronique** ▸ a special story in a newspaper or magazine. ▲ VERB, featured, featuring. **mettre en vedette, faire figurer** ▸ to have as a feature; give importance to : *The magazine will feature photos of the marathon.* ▲ ADJECTIVE. **de fond** ▸ of a special story in a newspaper or magazine · *Andrea is writing a feature story for our local newspaper.* SYN : characteristic, trait, mark, part.

Feb-ru-ar-y [FEB-roo-AIR-ee *or* FEB-yoo-AIR-ee] NOUN. Februarys. **février** ▸ the second month of the year. February has 28 days, except for every fourth year (leap year), when it has 29.

fed-er-al [FED-uh-rul] ADJECTIVE. **1. fédéral (-ale, -aux)** ▸ having to do with a nation that is formed by the coming together or agreement of many provinces, states, and the like : *Canada has a federal government.* **2. fédéral (-ale, -aux)** ▸ having to do with the central government of Canada : *Mail delivery is a federal responsibility.*

fee [fee] NOUN, fees. **honoraires, cachet, frais, prix** ▸ money asked or paid for a service or right; a charge : *There is a $4 fee to enter the race.* SYN : toll, due, fare, charge.

fee-ble [FEE-bul] ADJECTIVE, feebler, feeblest. **faible, frêle** ▸ not strong; weak; frail : *The lamp gave only a feeble light.*

feed [feed] VERB, fed, feeding. **1. nourrir, alimenter, ravitailler, donner à manger** ▸ to give food to : *Joan fed an apple to the horse.* **2. se nourrir, manger, s'alimenter** ▸ to take food into the body; eat : *The dog was feeding on the left-overs.* **3. alimenter** ▸ to provide or supply with some material : *to feed information into a computer.* ▲ NOUN, feeds. **nourriture, fourrage, pâture** ▸ food for animals, especially farm animals : *chicken feed.*

feed-back [FEED-bak] NOUN. **1. rétroaction, feed-back** ▸ a process by which a machine gets back information about how it is working and then adjusts itself according to this information. **2. réaction** ▸ information about how a process or plan is working : *The principal wants parents to give feedback on their ideas.*

feel [feel] VERB, felt, feeling. **1. palper, tâter** ▸ to find out about by touching : *Eddie felt his way carefully through the dark room.* **2. sentir, ressentir** ▸ to be aware of by touch : *Laura liked feeling the hot sand under her feet.* **3. se sentir** ▸ to have a sense of in the mind; be aware of : *to feel sick; to feel glad.* **4. avoir l'impression, considérer, estimer** ▸ to think or believe : *I'm going to vote for Keesha because I feel that she is the best person for the job.* ▲ NOUN. **toucher, sensation** ▸ the way something seems to the touch : *Velvet has a smooth, soft feel.* SYN : touch, finger, handle, grope, probe.

feel-ing [FEE-ling] NOUN, feelings. **1. sensation** ▸ the ability to feel by touching; the sense of touch. **2. sentiment, sensation** ▸ a certain sense that the body or mind feels : *a feeling of pain; a feeling of anger.* **3. feelings. sentiment, émotion, sensibilité** ▸ the sensitive part of a person's nature; one's pride : *She hurt my feelings when she made fun of me.* **4. impression, sentiment, opinion** ▸ a way of thinking; an opinion or belief : *What's your feeling about the plans for the dance?* SYN : sensation, awareness, impression. 📖 p. 1019.

feet [feet] NOUN. **pieds** ▸ the plural of foot.

fe-line [FEE-line] ADJECTIVE. **1. félin (-ine)** ▸ of a cat or of the cat family. **2. félin (-ine)** ▸ like a cat.

fell¹ [fel] a past form of fall: *He tripped and fell on his knees.*

fell² VERB, felled, felling. **1. abattre, assommer** ▶ to hit and knock down: *The knight felled his enemy.* **2. abattre** ▶ to cut down: *The wind felled many trees by the lake.*

fel-low [FEL-oh] NOUN, fellows. **1. homme, garçon, individu** ▶ any man or boy: *That fellow looks just like my brother.* **2. camarade, compagnon, pair, semblable** ▶ a person who is like another; a companion or equal. **Note.** Also used as an ADJECTIVE: *"One of her fellow slaves there had been a man called Aesop."* (Roger Lancelyn Green)

felt¹ [felt] a past form of feel.

felt² NOUN. **feutre** ▶ a heavy cloth made by rolling and pressing wool, fur, or other material together. Slippers and hats are often made of felt.

fe-male [FEE-male] NOUN, females. **1. femme, fille** ▶ a woman or girl. **2. femelle** ▶ an animal that can give birth to young or lay eggs. ▲ ADJECTIVE. **1. féminin (-ine)** ▶ having to do with women or girls: *Nursing was once thought of as a female career.* **2. femelle** ▶ of or relating to an animal that is a female: *A female pig is called a sow.*

fem-i-nine [FEM-uh-nin] ADJECTIVE. **1. féminin (-ine)** ▶ of or having to do with women or girls. **2. de femme, féminin (-ine)** ▶ typical of or suitable for women.

fence [fence] NOUN, fences. **clôture, barrière, palissade** ▶ a railing or wall that serves to mark off or protect a certain area of land. A fence is put up to keep people and animals in or out. ▲ VERB, fenced, fencing. **1. clôturer, entourer d'une clôture** ▶ to put a fence around a certain area of land; enclose. **Note.** Usually used with in or off: *We fenced in the yard to keep the dog from running away.* **2. faire de l'escrime** ▶ to fight with swords. **Note.** Fencing is the sport or art of fighting with swords. ☞ **p. 115.**

fern [furn] NOUN, ferns. **fougère** ▶ a plant that has many large, green, feathery leaves. Ferns do not have flowers or true seeds, but produce new plants by means of tiny spores. Ferns of many types grow throughout the world, usually in wet places. ☞ **p. 250.**

fe-ro-cious [fuh-ROH-shus] ADJECTIVE. **féroce** ▶ very strong and violent; fierce: *A tiger is a ferocious animal.* ■ **ferociously,** ADVERB. ▶ **férocement, avec férocité.** SYN: fierce, untamed, brutal, cruel, wild, ruthless.

fer-ret [FAIR-it] NOUN, ferrets. **furet** ▶ a small animal that looks like and is related to the weasel.

fer-ry [FAIR-ee] NOUN, ferries. **traversier, bac, ferry** ▶ a boat that goes back and forth to carry people, cars, and goods across a river or another narrow body of water. ▲ VERB, ferried, ferrying. **faire passer, transporter, emmener, conduire** ▶ to transport by a ferry or other vehicle: *The cars were ferried across the strait.* ☞ **p. 395.**

fer-tile [FUR-tul *or* FUR-tile] ADJECTIVE. **1. fertile** ▶ good for plants to grow in; able to produce crops and plants easily: *fertile soil.* **2. fécond (-onde)** ▶ able to produce eggs, seeds, pollen, or offspring. **3. fertile, fécond (-onde)** ▶ able to produce many thoughts or ideas: *a fertile imagination.* **Note.** The state of being fertile is fertility.

ferret

fer-ti-lize [FUR-tul-ize] VERB, fertilized, fertilizing. **1. fertiliser** ▶ to use a substance to make the soil richer and to help plants grow: *to fertilize a lawn or garden.* **Note.** A substance used to fertilize is a fertilizer. **2. féconder** ▶ to place pollen or sperm into a plant or female animal to develop a seed: *Bees fertilize flowers by carrying pollen from one plant to the next.* **Note.** The process of fertilizing something is fertilization.

fes-ti-val [FES-tuh-vul] NOUN, festivals. **1. fête** ▶ a day or time of celebrating: *a harvest festival.* **2. festival (-als)** ▶ a series of entertainments or cultural events of the same kind over several days: *a film festival.*

fetch [fech] VERB, fetched, fetching. **1. aller chercher, amener, apporter** ▶ to go after and bring back: *If I throw a stick, my dog will fetch it.* **2. rapporter** ▶ to be sold for: *These old coins should fetch quite a bit of money.*

feud [fyood] NOUN, feuds. **vendetta, querelle** ▶ a long and bitter fight or quarrel. ▲ VERB, feuded, feuding. **se quereller, se disputer** ▶ to take part in a feud or quarrel: *My grandfather has been feuding with his neighbour for years.*

fe-ver [FEE-vur] NOUN, fevers. **1. fièvre** ▶ a body temperature that is higher than the usual or nor-

✎ Writing Tips

Fewer vs Less

*Do not confuse **fewer** and **less**. These words should not be used to mean the same thing.*

- *Use **fewer** when referring to a number of people or things that can be counted.*
  *There were **fewer** cars on the road on the weekend.*
- *Use **less** when referring to a single amount and things that can be measured.*
  *The company made **less** profit this year than the year before.*

Note: *Use **fewer** with plural nouns and less with singular nouns.*

mal level, which is 37°C for most people. A fever is not a sickness, but is a common sign that a person is sick. **2. fièvre** ▸ a disease that causes a high fever, such as yellow fever or scarlet fever. **3. fièvre** ▸ a state of being very excited or upset : *We waited for the guests in a fever of anticipation.* 🕮 **p. 1159.**

few [fyoo] ADJECTIVE, fewer, fewest. **peu** ▸ not many : *Don't give up now; there are just a few more steps to the top.* ▲ NOUN; PRONOUN. **quelques, peu, certains (-aines)** ▸ a small number; not many : *A lot of people entered the 50-km bike race, but only a few finished the course.* SYN: not many, very little, rare, scarce. ✐ **p. 223.**

fi‑bre [FY-bur] NOUN, fibres. (also fiber) **fibre** ▸ a long, thin, threadlike piece of material : *Wool, silk, and cotton fibres are used to make cloth.*

fic‑tion [FIK-shun] NOUN. **1. fiction, roman** ▸ a form of writing in which the writer makes up the characters and the things that happen. Novels and short stories are kinds of fiction : *"Creating fiction for me is a matter of combining bits and pieces from many different sources into a unified and interesting story."* (Kevin Major) **2.** (plural, fictions) **fiction, création de l'imagination** ▸ anything that is made up or imagined : *I don't believe that story about his uncle's being a rock star; I think it's pure fiction.* ▪ **fictional,** ADJECTIVE: ▸ **fictif (-ive).** *Cinderella is a fictional character.* ✐ **p. 223.**

fid‑dle [FID-ul] NOUN, fiddles. **violon** ▸ a popular name for the violin, especially when it is used to play country or folk music. ▲ VERB, fiddled, fiddling. **1. jouer du violon** ▸ to play a fiddle. **Note.** A person who plays the fiddle is a fiddler. **2. tripoter, jouer nerveusement avec** ▸ to play restlessly : *She fiddled with the buttons on her sweater.*

fid‑dle‑head [FID-ul-HED] NOUN, fiddleheads. **crosse de fougère** ▸ the top curl of a some ferns eaten as a delicacy, especially in New Brunswick and Nova Scotia.

fidg‑et [FIJ-it] VERB, fidgeted, fidgeting. **remuer, gigoter, donner des signes d'impatience** ▸ to move in a restless or nervous way : *"I stood there fidgeting on the sidewalk, zipping the zipper of my jacket up and down."* (S.E. Hinton) SYN: wriggle, squirm, twitch, fuss, twist, jerk.

field [feeld] NOUN, fields. **1. champ** ▸ any piece of land that has few or no trees; open land; pasture. **2. champ** ▸ a piece of land that is used for growing crops : *a corn field.* **3. terrain** ▸ any area of land used for a certain purpose : *a football field.* **4. domaine, sphère** ▸ an area of activity or interest : *John Polanyi won a Nobel Prize in the field of chemistry.* ▲ VERB, fielded, fielding. **attraper** ▸ in baseball, to catch a batted ball. 🕮 **p. 1040.**

fierce [feers] ADJECTIVE, fiercer, fiercest. **1. féroce, violent (-ente), furieux (-euse)** ▸ wild or cruel; violent : *I was frightened by the fierce guard dog who bared his teeth at the gate.* **2. ardent (-ente), violent (-ente), virulent (-ente)** ▸ very strong or eager : *a fierce determination to win. They could not stay out of doors for long in the fierce cold.* ▪ **fiercely,** ADVERB: ▸ **férocement, violemment.** *"When he was aroused, he roared fiercely."* (Rosebud Yellow Robe) SYN: raging, violent, wild, ferocious, brutal.

fiery [FY-ree or FY-ur-ee] ADJECTIVE, fierier, fieriest. **1. ardent (-ente), brûlant (-ante), rougeoyant (-ante), embrasé (-ée)** ▸ containing fire; burning : *"The sleeping dragons snore a puff of smoke and steam and fiery stuff."* (Diane Dawber) **2. rougeoyant (-ante), étincelant (-ante), brillant (-ante)** ▸ glowing like a fire; very hot : *He wore*

✎ Writing Tips

Fiction

Fiction refers mainly to narratives— stories or novels that have been made up. These stories involve invented characters, settings, plots, and events. Some fiction is based on real events or people, but some features may be changed or combined with made-up characters or events. There are many different types of fiction—adventure, mystery, historical fiction, realistic fiction, science fiction, and fantasy.

Writing fiction gives writers the opportunity to use their storehouses of knowledge and their imaginations to create interesting stories and novels that entertain as well as inform the reader.

a fiery red scarf around his neck. **3. fougueux (-euse), ardent (-ente)** ▸ full of feeling; spirited : *The speaker aroused her audience with a fiery speech.* **4. fougueux (-euse), ardent (-ente)** ▸ easily excited : *Luke has a fiery temper, but he's quick to cool off.*

fif·teen [FIF-teen] NOUN, fifteens. **quinze** ▸ the number that is one more than fourteen; 15. ■ **fifteenth,** ADJECTIVE; NOUN. ▸ quinzième.

fifth [fifth] NOUN, fifths. **cinquième** ▸ the number-five item in a series; 5th. ▲ ADJECTIVE.

fif·ty [FIF-tee] NOUN, fifties. **cinquante** ▸ five times ten; 50. ■ **fiftieth,** ADJECTIVE; NOUN. ▸ cinquantième.

fig [fig] NOUN, figs. **figue** ▸ a sweet, pear-shaped fruit with many seeds that grows in warm climates. Figs are usually eaten as a dried fruit, but can also be eaten fresh off the tree.

fight [fite] NOUN, fights. **1. combat, bataille** ▸ an occasion when people try to hurt each other with weapons or fists; a battle or struggle. **2. dispute** ▸ a quarrel or argument : *Greg and his sister had a fight about who was supposed to clean up the kitchen.* **3. lutte, bataille** ▸ any contest or struggle : *the fight for equal rights.* **4. combat** ▸ a boxing match. ▲ VERB, fought, fighting. **1. se battre** ▸ to use fists or weapons against : *"He learned how to fight with knives, how to wrestle, and how to tell a good story."* (Sarah Hayes) **2. se disputer** ▸ to argue or quarrel : *Lori often fights with her brother about which TV show to watch.* **3. lutter** ▸ to take part in a contest or struggle : *They fought their way through the snow.*

fight·er [FITE-ur] NOUN, fighters. **1. combattant (-ante), lutteur (-euse)** ▸ any person who fights : *He was a fighter against injustice for his entire life.* **2. boxeur (-euse), pugiliste** ▸ a person who fights in the sport of boxing; a boxer. **3. chasseur, avion de chasse** ▸ a fast warplane with a crew of one or two.

fig·ure [FIG-yur *or* FIG-ur] NOUN, figures. **1. chiffre** ▸ a symbol that stands for a number : *1, 2, 7, 13, 57, and so on are figures.* **2. chiffre, chiffre d'affaires** ▸ an amount shown in numbers : *The company published its sales figures for last year.* **3. forme, ligne, figure** ▸ the shape or outline of something; form : *The skaters traced circular figures on the ice.* **4. silhouette, forme, ligne** ▸ the shape or form of a person's body : *Ed watches what he eats so that he'll keep his trim figure.* **5. figure, personnage** ▸ a person, especially a well-known or important person : *"He [Robin Hood] is a figure from legend, not history."* (Sarah Hayes) ▲ VERB, figured, figuring. **1. calculer** ▸ to use numbers to find an answer. **2. compter** ▸ to be important or stand out : *The book's design figured in the teacher's decision to use it in his class.* **3. penser, s'imaginer** ▸ to think or believe : *I figure we'll be there by tonight if we drive all day.*

✏ Writing Tips

Figure of Speech

A *figure of speech* is an expression that uses words in a way that is different from their ordinary meaning. A figure of speech means more than what the words say. For example, this line from Shakespeare, "Her lips are like a red, red rose," doesn't just compare a woman's lips to a rose, but suggests that the lips are soft, delicate, and beautiful like a red rose.

Figures of speech include similes, metaphors, irony, and personification.

• A simile is a comparison between two different things using like or as.

  She is as strong as an ox.

• A metaphor is a direct comparison of one thing to another. In metaphors, one thing is said to be the other.

  Her hair is spun gold.

• Personification is a figure of speech in which nonhuman things are described with human qualities.

  The stream whispered gently in the autumn breeze.

• Irony is a mocking way of using words so that they suggest a meaning that is the opposite of their usual meaning. Both the speaker and the listener are aware of the contrast. For example, saying "What a great day for a picnic" is irony if the weather is rainy.

---

figure out arriver à comprendre, résoudre ▸ to find an answer or explanation : *"She could not catch a pop-up or figure out in which direction to kick the soccer ball."* (Gary Soto)

fig·ure·head [FIG-yur-hed *or* FIG-ur-HED] NOUN, figureheads. **1. homme de paille** ▸ someone who holds a high position but does not have real power. **2. figure de proue** ▸ a carved figure on the bow of a ship for decoration.

figure of speech figure de rhétorique, façon de parler ▸ an expression that uses words in a different way from their ordinary meaning : *Carl Sandburg's "The fog comes on little cat feet" is a figure of speech.* ✏ **p. 224.**

file¹ [file] NOUN, files. **1. fichier, dossier, classeur, chemise** ▸ a folder, cabinet, or other container to hold papers, letters, cards, and so on. **2. dossier** ▸ a set of papers arranged in some order : *The doctor kept a file of all her patients' records.* **3. file** ▸ a line of people, animals, or things behind one another : *The path was narrow, so we had to walk in single file.* ► in a computer, a collection of data or programs stored under the same name. ▲ VERB, filed, filing. 1. **ranger, classer** ► to put away or store in a file : *to file a letter.* 2. **déposer, faire enregistrer** ► to send in to or put on an official record : *They filed a claim with the insurance company for the damage to their car.* 3. **marcher en file** ► to move in a line or file : *During the fire drill, we filed quietly out of the building.*

file² NOUN, files. **lime** ► a metal tool used to grind, smooth, and polish hard objects. A file has small, rough ridges in its surface that evenly cut away small amounts of material. ▲ VERB, filed, filing. **limer** ► to use or cut with a file : *Molly filed down the sharp edge on the door.*

fill [fil] VERB, filled, filling. 1. **remplir** ► to put as much into something as it will hold : *to fill the gas tank of a car.* 2. **remplir** ► to take up all the space in an area : *The crowd had filled the stadium by the start of the game.* 3. **boucher, plomber** ► to close or stop up by putting something in : *The dentist filled the cavity in Jan's tooth.* 4. **remplir, exécuter, livrer** ► to supply what is needed or asked for : *The butcher filled Ms. Ack's meat order.* 5. **remplir, compléter** ► to write information on a paper or form : *Joanna filled out an application form for a new library card.* ▲ NOUN. 1. **état d'être rassasié (-ée)** ► an amount that fills or satisfies : *to eat one's fill.* 2. **remblai** ► something used to fill an area of ground, such as dirt or gravel. **Note.** Anything used to fill something is a filling : *a pie filling.* SYN : load, cram, pack, stuff, put in, pour in.

fil-let [fih-LAY *or* FIL-ay] NOUN, fillets. **filet** ► a slice of fish or meat with no bones and very little fat.

film [film] NOUN, films. 1. **pellicule** ► a narrow strip of plastic or other material that is used with a camera to take photographs. The film is covered with a chemical substance that changes when it is exposed to light. 2. **film** ► a movie. 3. **couche, pellicule** ► a thin layer or coating over something : *There was a film of dust on the top of the dresser.* ▲ VERB, filmed, filming. **filmer** ► to take photographs on film ; make a movie : *Mr. Yeager filmed his daughter's soccer game.*

fil-ter [FIL-tur] NOUN, filters. 1. **filtre** ► a device through which a liquid or gas is passed in order to clean out substances that are unwanted. 2. **filtre** ► any material used for this purpose, such as paper, cloth, charcoal, or sand. ▲ VERB, filtered, filtering. **filtre, purifier, épurer** ► to pass a liquid or gas through a filter : *to filter water for drinking.* SYN : strain, screen, sift, purify, refine, separate.

filth-y [FIL-thee] ADJECTIVE, filthier, filthiest. **sale, crasseux (-euse), dégoûtant (-ante), répugnant**

(-ante) ► covered with dirt : *Dave's clothes were filthy after he played football in the rain.*

fin [fin] NOUN, fins. 1. **nageoire, aileron** ► one of the thin, flat parts of a fish's body. Fish use fins to swim and keep their balance in the water. Fins are also found on water animals such as dolphins and whales. 2. **palme** ► a flat rubber shoe shaped like a fin, used by swimmers for greater speed in the water. 3. **aileron, empennage** ► any object that looks like a fin, as on an airplane.

fi-nal [FINE-ul] ADJECTIVE. 1. **dernier (-ière), final (-ale, -aux)** ► coming at the end of something ; being the end ; last : *"Twenty-three complaints, young man. And this one just the final straw."* (Eve Bunting) 2. **final (-ale, -aux), définitif (-ive), décisif (-ive)** ► having or allowing no further discussion or change : *In this contest, the decision of the judges will be final.* ■ NOUN, finals. 1. (often finals) **examen** ► the last test or examination of a course in school or college. 2. (usually finals) **final (-ale, -aux)** ► the last or deciding game in a match or series. SYN : ending, last, closing, deciding.

fi-nal-ly [FY-nuh-lee] ADVERB. **finalement, enfin** ► at the end ; at last : *"When evening came and Henry finally had to crawl into bed, he could hardly wait to finish the castle."* (Cynthia Rylant)

fi-nance [FY-nans *or* fuh-NANS] NOUN, finances. 1. **finance** ► the control or management of money for a government, business, or person ; matters dealing with money. 2. finances. **finances** ► the amount of money owned by a person or group. ▲ VERB, financed, financing. **financer, commanditer** ► to provide money for someone or something : *Public schools are financed by property taxes.* ■ **financial,** ADJECTIVE. ► **financier (-ière)** ► having to do with finance ; dealing with money : *Newspaper reports on the stock market appear in the financial section.* ■ **financially,** ADVERB. ► **financièrement:** *a person who is doing well financially.* SYN : support, aid, sponsor, back, stake.

finch [finch] NOUN, finches. **fringillidé, pinson** ► songbirds with short, strong beaks. Canaries and sparrows are finches.

find [find] VERB, found, finding. 1. **trouver** ► to happen or come upon by accident : *to find a dollar on the sidewalk.* 2. **trouver, retrouver** ► to look for and locate ; get something that is hidden or lost : *They found their lost puppy a few blocks away.* 3. **trouver** ► to get or obtain by effort : *to find a job.* 4. **trouver, découvrir** ► to learn or discover something that was not known : *to find the answer to a problem.* 5. **trouver, rencontrer** ► to meet with a certain thing or condition : *Kangaroos are found in Australia.* ■ NOUN, finds. **trouvaille** ► something that is found, especially something valuable :

That old painting is a real find. SYN: locate, discover, uncover, detect, come upon.

fine[1] [fine] ADJECTIVE, finer, finest. **1. fin (fine), raffiné (-ée), délicat (-ate)** ▶ of high quality; very good or excellent : *a fine meal; fine weather for a picnic.* **2. fin (fine)** ▶ very small or thin : *The sand on the beach was fine and white.* ▲ ADVERB. **1.** (also **finely**) **finement, fin, menu (-ue)** ▶ so as to be very thin or small : *Chop the vegetables finely for the stew.* **2. juste** ▶ in an exact way : *to fine-tune a piano.* **3.** *Informal.* **bien** ▶ very well : *Madison's feeling fine and has gone back to school.*

fine[2] NOUN, fines. **amende, contravention** ▶ an amount of money that is paid as a penalty for breaking a law or rule : *The library charges a fine for books that are not returned on time.* ▲ VERB, fined, fining. **condamner à une amende, donner une contravention** ▶ to punish by charging a fine : *The police officer fined me for not wearing my seatbelt.*

fin·ger [FING-gur] NOUN, fingers. **doigt** ▶ one of the five parts at the end of a hand, also referred to as four fingers and a thumb. ▲ VERB, fingered, fingering. **manier, toucher, palper** ▶ to touch something with the fingers. 👁 p. 995.

fin·ger·nail [FING-gur-NALE] NOUN, fingernails. **ongle** ▶ the thin, hard covering on the end of the finger.

fin·ish [FIN-ish] VERB, finished, finishing. **1. finir, terminer, achever** ▶ to bring or come to the end; complete : *Mom finished painting Annie's room this morning.* **2. finir, terminer** ▶ to use until gone; use up : *We finished the cookies last night, so there are none left for lunch.* **3. mettre la dernière main, mettre la touche finale** ▶ to put a final coat or surface on something : *I finished the cabinets with a dark-coloured stain.* ▲ NOUN, finishes. **1. fin, arrivée** ▶ the end of something : *the finish of a race.* **2. finition** ▶ the final coat or surface of something : *a finish on wood furniture.* SYN: complete, end, close, conclude, stop, cease.

fiord [fy-oord *or* FE-ord] NOUN, fiords. (also **fjord**) **fiord, fjord** ▶ a narrow inlet of sea between tall, steep cliffs.

fir [fur] NOUN, firs. **sapin** ▶ a tall evergreen tree that bears upright cones and is related to the pine tree. Fir trees usually grow in northern areas and are an important source of lumber. 👁 p. 255.

fire [fire] NOUN, fires. **1. feu (feux)** ▶ the flame, heat, and light caused by something burning. **2. feu, incendie** ▶ burning that causes damage or harm : *a forest fire.* **3. feu, fougue, ardeur** ▶ a very strong feeling, like being on fire : *Her words were filled with fire.* **4. feu** ▶ the shooting of a firearm : *gunfire; cannon fire.* ▲ VERB, fired, firing. **1. renvoyer; licencier** ▶ to dismiss from a job : *Mr. Huang had to fire a worker*

today. **2. mettre le feu à, incendier** ▶ to cause something to burn : *to fire up a furnace.* **3. enflammer, échauffer, exciter** ▶ to arouse strong feelings : *to fire a person's imagination.* **4. tirer, décharger** ▶ to shoot a gun. 👁 p. 1113.

fire·fight·er [FIRE-FY-tur] NOUN, firefighters. **pompier (-ière)** ▶ a person whose job is to put out dangerous fires.

fire·fly [FIRE-FLY] NOUN, fireflies. **luciole** ▶ a small kind of beetle that gives off short flashes of light from the rear of its body when it flies in the dark.

firefly

fire·place [FIRE-PLACE] NOUN, fireplaces. **foyer, cheminée** ▶ a structure built to contain a fire for heating or cooking. Fireplaces are made of a fireproof material, such as brick, and have a chimney to carry away the smoke.

fire·works [FIRE-wurks] PLURAL NOUN. **feu d'artifice** ▶ firecrackers, rockets, and other explosives that make loud noises and fill the sky with brightly coloured lights.

firm[1] [furm] ADJECTIVE, firmer, firmest. **1. ferme** ▶ not giving way to pressure; hard; solid : *firm ground; a firm mattress.* **2. ferme, solide, constant (-ante)** ▶ not easily moved; strong or steady : *She took a firm hold on the weed and pulled.* **3. ferme** ▶ not likely to change; staying the same : *We received a firm offer for our house.* ▲ ADVERB. (also **firmly**) **fermement, avec fermeté** ▶ not moving or changing : *The door held firm against the wind. Pack the dirt down firmly around the plant.* ■ **firmness,** NOUN. ▶ **fermeté, solidité, résolution, détermination.** SYN: steady, sturdy, solid, secure, unyielding.

firm[2] NOUN, firms. **firme, compagnie** ▶ a business or company, especially one formed by two or more partners : *a law firm.*

first [furst] ADJECTIVE. **premier (-ière)** ▶ being number one; before all others; 1st : *January is the first month of the year.* ▲ ADVERB. **1. premièrement, d'abord, au préalable** ▶ before anyone or anything else : *If you want to watch TV, you'll have to clean your room first.* **2. d'abord, pour la première fois** ▶ for the first time : *I first met him when he was a small child.* ▲ NOUN, firsts. **1. premier (-ière)** ▶ someone or something that is first : *Ben was the first in his class to have his bar mitzvah.* **2. début, commencement** ▶ the beginning : *They have been friends* *from the first.* SYN: leading, main, principal, primary, chief. ✐ **p. 227.**

fish [fish] NOUN, fish or fishes. **poisson** ▶ any of a large group of animals that live in the water. Fish have a long backbone and breathe by means of gills. Almost all fish have fins to aid in swimming and balancing, and small plates on their skin called scales. ▲ VERB, fished, fishing. **1. pêcher** ▶ to catch fish or try to catch fish for food or as a sport. **Note.** This work or sport is known as fishing. **2. sortir, extirper, tirer** ▶ to draw or pull out as if by fishing : *Josie fished a quarter out of her pocket.* **3. chercher, tirer** ▶ to try to get something in an indirect or roundabout way : *I think he is just fishing for a compliment.* 📖 **p. 1090.** 👁 **p. 106.**

fish-er [FISH-ur] NOUN, fishers. **pêcheur (-euse)** ▶ a person who fishes, either for a living or for sport. **Note.** A person who fishes for sport is also called an angler.

fist [fist] NOUN, fists. **poing** ▶ a hand that is closed, with the fingers tightly folded into the palm.

fit¹ [fit] VERB, fit or fitted, fitting. **1. ajuster, adapter** ▶ to be or cause to be the right size and shape : *My mother fit my dress for the party.* **2. convenir** ▶ to be suitable or right for : *"It was a feast fit for a king."* (Aliki) ▲ ADJECTIVE, fitter, fittest. **1. convenable, correct (-ecte)** ▶ having what is needed for a purpose; suitable; right : *Some TV programs are not fit for young people.* **2. en bonne santé, en pleine forme, en état** ▶ in good physical condition; healthy : *"We can only admit racers who are strong and fit,' said another judge."* (David M. Schwartz)

✐ Writing Tips

First Person

*The **first person** is I, me, we, us—the one who is speaking. A first-person story or novel is one in which the writer speaks as "I." This means that the writer is also a character in the story, and that the story is told from his or her point of view.*

Sometimes the "I" is used but doesn't refer to the writer in an obvious way. For example, Black Beauty is written in the first person, but the main character is a horse.

*First person is often used in fiction writing, but third-person writing is more popular. In third-person writing, the story is not told from one specific character's point of view. The **third person** is shown with the pronouns "he," "she," "it," "they," "him," "her," and "them."*

▲ NOUN, fits. **taille, ajustement** ▶ the way something fits : *That dress is a perfect fit for you.* SYN: suitable, proper, right, appropriate.

fit² NOUN, fits. **accès, attaque, mouvement, quinte** ▶ a sudden attack or show of strong feeling : *a coughing fit. Tony's going to have a fit when he sees that big scratch on his car door.*

five [five] NOUN, fives. **cinq** ▶ one more than four; 5. ▪ **fifth,** ADJECTIVE; NOUN. ▶ **cinquième.**

fix [fiks] VERB, fixed, fixing. **1. réparer** ▶ to make whole; mend; repair : *to fix a broken chair.* **2. arranger, préparer, (se) passer un coup de peigne** ▶ to prepare or arrange in a certain way : *to fix your hair.* **3. fixer, attacher** ▶ to make firm or secure; fasten : *I fixed the handle onto the box.* **4. fixer, diriger** ▶ to direct or hold steadily : *"He fixed his eyes on Solomon's glittering walls and his mind on the feast that was waiting for him."* (Adèle Geras) **5. fixer, arrêter, décider, établir** ▶ to arrange or settle : *to fix a date for a doctor's appointment.* ▲ NOUN, fixes. **ennui, pétrin, embêtement** ▶ a difficult or unpleasant situation : *We'll be in a real fix if we get a flat tire, because we don't have a spare.*

fjord See fiord.

flag [flag] NOUN, flags. **1. drapeau (-eaux)** ▶ a piece of cloth having designs, symbols, and colours on it, used to represent a country, state, or other organization. **2. drapeau (-eaux)** ▶ a small piece of coloured cloth, used for giving signals : *In auto racing, a yellow flag tells drivers to slow down.* ▲ VERB, flagged, flagging. **faire signe de s'arrêter, héler** ▶ to stop or signal something with or as if with a flag. **Note.** Usually used with down : *Travis tried to flag down a taxi, but the driver didn't see him and drove right by.* 📖 **p. 1040.**

flair [flair] NOUN, flairs. **flair** ▶ a natural talent : *She has a flair for writing.*

flake [flake] NOUN, flakes. **flocon, écaille** ▶ a small, thin, flat piece of something, such as snow, dried paint, soap, breakfast cereal, and so on. ▲ VERB, flaked, flaking. **(s') écailler, effriter, peler** ▶ to come off in flakes; peel : *Paint was flaking off the garage door.*

flame [flame] NOUN, flames. **1. flamme** ▶ the glowing gas that rises up from a fire, usually seen as an orange or yellow band of light. **2. (also flames) flamme** ▶ a state of blazing fire : *The building was in flames when the firefighters arrived.* ▲ VERB, flamed, flaming. **1. flamber, brûler** ▶ to burn or blaze with flames. **2. s'embraser, prendre feu** ▶ to show red or glow, as if burning : *Gord flamed with anger.* **Note.** Also used as an ADJECTIVE: *The sun hooked its claws into the soil and a flaming sky burned up the grass and dried up the spring."* (Tololwa M. Mollel)

fla-min-go [flah-MING-goh] NOUN, flamingos or flamingoes. **flamant** ▶ a waterbird that lives in warm areas. Flamingos have pink or red feathers, a very long neck, and long thin legs.

flan-nel [FLAN-ul] ADJECTIVE. **flanelle** ▸ something made from a soft, warm woolen cloth : *flannel sheets.*

flap [flap] NOUN, flapped, flapping. **1. battement, coup** ▸ of a bird, to move the wings up and down. **2. battement, coup, claquement** ▸ to wave loosely and noisily, like the beating of a bird's wings : *The laundry drying on the line flapped in the wind.* ▲ NOUN, flaps. **rabat** ▸ something that is attached so that it can move freely : *a tent flap; a flap on an envelope.*

flare [flair] VERB, flared, flaring. **1. s'enflammer, briller** ▸ to burn suddenly and with a bright glow : *The fire flared when Dad added some dry leaves.* **2. évaser, élargir** ▸ to spread out or open up : *This skirt is designed to flare from the hips.* **3. flare up. s'embraser, se mettre en colère, s'emporter** ▸ to show sudden anger or strong feeling. ▲ NOUN, flares. **1. fusée éclairante** ▸ an emergency device that gives off a bright light. **2. flamme, flamboiement, éclat** ▸ a bright light that lasts for a short time.

flash [flash] NOUN, flashes. **1. éclat** ▸ a sudden burst of light or flame. **2. éclair, clin d'œil, tout d'un coup** ▸ a very short time ; an instant : *Quick as a flash, she grabbed the baby before he could fall.* **3. éclair, clin d'œil, tout d'un coup** ▸ a sudden feeling or thought : *Luckily, the answer came to her in a flash.* ▲ VERB, flashed, flashing. **1. étinceler, briller** ▸ to give off or show a sudden, brief light. **2. comme un éclair** ▸ to move quickly or suddenly : *The skier flashed by us on her way down the hill.* **3. projeter** ▸ to show for a moment : *A message flashed across the TV screen.* ▲ ADJECTIVE. **soudain (-aine), subit (-ite)** ▸ happening suddenly : *a flash flood; a flash fire.*

flash-light [FLASH-LITE] NOUN, flashlights. **lampe de poche, lampe électrique** ▸ a small battery-powered electric light that is usually held in the hand.

flask [flask] NOUN, flasks. **flasque, bouteille, fiole** ▸ a small bottle with a narrow neck or opening, especially one used to hold liquids.

flat[1] [flat] ADJECTIVE, flatter, flattest. **1. plat (plate)** ▸ having a surface that goes straight across ; smooth and even ; level : *The top of a table is flat.* **2. à plat** ▸ lying stretched or spread out : *He was flat on his back on the sofa.* **3. fixe** ▸ not changing ; fixed : *The garage charges a flat rate of $15 for an oil change.* **4. plat (plate), insipide, monotone, terne** ▸ dull ; not exciting : *The movie seemed a little flat and I was bored.* **5. bémol** ▸ in music, a. **faux (fausse), trop bas (basse), en-dessous du ton** ▸ half a step or half a note lower than the natural pitch : *B flat.* b. **trop bas (basse), en-dessous du ton** ▸ lower than the true or proper pitch : *Her voice sounded flat in that song.* **6. à plat, dégonflé** ▸ of a tire, not having enough air. ▲ NOUN, flats. **1. plat** ▸ a flat surface or part : *He pounded on the desk with the flat of his hand.* **2. bémol** ▸ a musical symbol b ▸ for playing a note that is half a step or half a note below the natural pitch. ▲ ADVERB. **1. dans une position horizontale, à plat** ▸ in a flat manner or position : *to lie flat on the floor.* **2. exactement, précisément** ▸ exactly : *I made it home in three minutes flat.* ■ **flatly,** ADVERB. ■ **nettement, carrément, de façon monotone.** ■ **flatness,** NOUN. ▸ **monotonie, égalité, manque de relief.**

flat[2] NOUN, flats. **appartement** ▸ a group of rooms on one floor ; an apartment.

flat-ter [FLAT-ur] VERB, flattered, flattering. **1. flatter** ▸ to try to please a person by giving praise that is false or exaggerated. **2. flatter** ▸ to please or make happy : *My desire to become a jeweller like my father flattered him.* **3. flatter** ▸ to make something seem more attractive than it really is : *Grandpa says that this photograph flatters him because it makes him seem much younger.*

fla-vour [FLAY-vur] NOUN, flavours. (also flavor) **1. saveur, goût, parfum** ▸ a certain quality that a food has that is sensed by the tongue and mouth ; a particular taste : *Chocolate is my favourite flavour of ice cream.* **Note.** Flavouring is something that is added to give flavour to food or drinks. **2. atmosphère** ▸ a special quality that a thing has that makes it different from others : *The room was decorated with model ships, paintings of the ocean, and other objects that gave it the flavour of the sea.* ▲ VERB, flavoured, flavouring. **assaisonner, relever, parfumer** ▸ to add something to give taste or flavour : *She flavoured the pasta with herbs.*

flaw [flah] NOUN, flaws. **1. défaut, imperfection** ▸ a crack, scratch, or other mark that takes away from the value of something. **2. défaut, faille, imperfection** ▸ a small fault or problem : *There's only one flaw in that plan—how did the thief get inside the vault?* SYN : defect, imperfection, crack, fault.

flea [flee] NOUN, fleas. **puce** ▸ a small, wingless insect that lives by sucking blood from animals and people. Fleas can carry diseases, which they pass on by biting through the skin.

flee [flee] VERB, fled, fleeing. **fuir, s'enfuir, se sauver** ▸ to run or get away : *"The fox fled with the hare close behind him."* (Tololwa M. Mollel)

fleet[1] [fleet] NOUN, fleets. **1. flotte** ▸ a group of naval warships under one command. **2. flotte** ▸ any group of ships or vehicles : *a fleet of buses.*

fleet[2] ADJECTIVE, fleeter, fleetest. **rapide, au pied léger** ▸ moving very fast ; swift : *The jaguar is a fleet animal.* ■ **fleetly,** ADVERB. ▸ **rapidement.**

flesh [flesh] NOUN. **1. chair ▸** the part of the body that covers the bones; muscles and other tissues. **2. chair ▸** the meat of an animal used as food. **3. chair, pulpe ▸** the part of fruits and vegetables that can be eaten.

flew [floo] VERB. **voler ▸** a past form of fly.

flex [fleks] VERB, flexed, flexing. **fléchir, faire jouer, ployer ▸** to bend and move a muscle or a certain part of the body : *He flexes his arm to show how big his muscle is.*

flex·i·ble [FLEK-suh-bul] ADJECTIVE. **1. flexible, souple ▸** able to bend easily without breaking : *That toy is made of flexible plastic.* **2. flexible, souple, ▸** able to change to meet different needs or conditions : *The hours for that job are flexible, as long as you work 40 hours a week.* SYN: pliable, limber, bendable, supple.

flight¹ [flite] NOUN, flights. **1. vol ▸** the use of wings to move through the air : *"The two birds flapped their huge wings and took flight."* (Jan Thornhill) **2. vol ▸** a movement through the air by some type of aircraft : *the flight of a balloon or rocket.* **3. vol ▸** a scheduled trip by airplane : *Flight 155 goes from Vancouver to Ottawa.* **4. élan, envolée ▸** something that goes above or beyond the usual limits : *a flight of fancy; flights of the imagination.* **5. escalier ▸** the steps leading from one floor of a building to another.

flight² NOUN, flights. **fuite ▸** the act of running or breaking away to be free; an escape.

flim·sy [FLIM-zee] ADJECTIVE, flimsier, flimsiest. **pauvre, piètre, mince ▸** light and weak; likely to break or give way : *His excuse for being late was very flimsy.*

flinch [flinch] VERB, flinched, flinching. **broncher, tressaillir, reculer, sourciller ▸** to suddenly back away in fear or pain : *The boy flinched when the dog jumped up on him.* SYN: cringe, draw back, shrink back, recoil.

fling [fling] VERB, flung, flinging. **lancer, jeter ▸** to throw or move something with great force : *"My arm is so strong that I can fling a stone over the sun."* (Robin Muller) ▲ NOUN, flings. **1. lancer ▸** the act of flinging; a sudden throw. **2. essai ▸** a short time for doing something that one enjoys : *After a brief fling as an actor, she realized she was better suited to being a director.* SYN: throw, toss, hurl, pitch, chuck.

flint [flint] NOUN, flints. **silex, pierre à briquet ▸** a hard rock that makes a spark of fire when it is scratched against iron or steel. Flint is a type of quartz and was used to start fires before matches were invented.

flip [flip] VERB, flipped, flipping. **1. retourner, faire sauter ▸** to turn over in the air : *to flip a pancake; to flip a coin.* **2. feuilleter, ouvrir d'une chiquenaude, tourner d'une pichenette ▸** to toss or move with a quick motion of the hand : *to flip through the pages of a book.*

▲ NOUN, flips. **1. chiquenaude, pichenette, petit coup ▸** a sudden move or toss in the air : *A flip of the coin will decide which side kicks off.* **2. saut périlleux ▸** a somersault made from a standing position.

float [flote] VERB, floated, floating. **1. flotter, planer ▸** to be held up by the surface of a liquid or by the air : *The paddle was floating on the water beside the canoe.* **2. flotter, planer, descendre un courant ▸** to move on a current of air or water : *In the old days, lumberjacks floated logs down this river to the mill.* ▲ NOUN, floats. **1. flotteur, bouchon ▸** something that floats on the water, such as a cork on a fishing line. **2. char ▸** a stage or platform on wheels that carries an exhibit in a parade.

flock [flok] NOUN, flocks. **1. troupeau (-eaux), volée, bande ▸** a number of animals of the same kind that live or move together : *a flock of sheep; a flock of geese.* **2. foule, troupeau (-eaux) ▸** a large group of people : *A flock of teenagers waited in line to buy tickets for the concert.* **3. ouailles ▸** a group of people who follow a certain minister or other religious leader. ▲ VERB, flocked, flocking. **aller ou venir en masse ou en foule, affluer, (s') attrouper ▸** to move together in a group or crowd : *Everyone flocked to the beach during the heat wave.* SYN: herd, group, crowd, throng, bunch, pack.

flood [flud] NOUN, floods. **1. inondation, crue ▸** a large flow of water over dry land, especially one that causes loss or damage. **2. inondation, torrent, déluge ▸** any large outpouring like a flood : *The writer received a flood of angry letters in response to his article.* ▲ VERB, flooded, flooding. **1. inonder, submerger ▸** to cover over with water : *The river flooded its banks and covered the fields.* **2. inonder ▸** to fill or pour into in large amounts or numbers : *"On Thursday, March 29, 1827, the people of Vienna flooded into the streets."* (Barbara Nichol) **3. noyer ▸** to supply too much fuel to an engine, so that it does not work properly. SYN: overflow, drench, deluge, overfill.

floor [flor] NOUN, floors. **1. sol, plancher ▸** the bottom surface of a room that a person walks or stands on. **2. fond ▸** the bottom surface of anything : *the ocean floor; the floor of a canyon.* **3. étage ▸** one level or storey of a building : *Miss Wright's office is on the 10th floor.* ▲ VERB, floored, flooring. **1. faire le plancher, faire le sol ▸** to build a floor in a house or building. **2. terrasser, envoyer au tapis ▸** to knock down to the floor : *The boxer floored his opponent with a quick jab to the chin.* **3.** *Informal.* **réduire au silence ▸** to confuse or surprise : *The last question on the test really floored me.* 📖 p. 1069.

flop [flop] VERB, flopped, flopping. **1. agiter, remuer, gigoter, faire des sauts ▸** to move or jump about in an awkward way : *The fish*

229

flopped wildly as the fisher lifted it out of the water. **2. s'affaler, s'effondrer ▸** to fall or drop in a loose, relaxed way : *"Then she flopped down on the couch beside Michael."* (Cynthia Rylant) **3.** *Informal.* **rater, faire fiasco ▸** to fail completely ; not be successful : *The play flopped after opening night.* ▲ NOUN, flops. **1. floc ▸** a flopping movement or noise. **2.** *Informal.* **fiasco, échec ▸** a complete failure : *The new musical was a flop and ran for only a week.* SYN: fall, sink, droop, slump, sap, go down.

floppy disk **disquette, disque souple ▸** a thin, flexible piece of plastic that stores computer data or information. The disk fits into a computer so that the computer can read or use the information. Sometimes shortened to floppy. **Note.** Also called a diskette.

floun·der[1] [FLOWN-dur] VERB, floundered, floundering. **patauger, bredouiller, baragouiner ▸** to struggle or stumble ; move in a clumsy way : *The actor floundered when he couldn't remember his lines.* SYN: struggle, have trouble, stumble.

flounder[2] NOUN, flounder or flounders. **flet, raie ▸** a small saltwater flatfish that is often eaten as food.

flour [flowr] NOUN, flours. **farine ▸** a fine powder made by grinding and sifting cereal grains, especially wheat. Flour is used to make bread, cake, cookies, pasta, and other foods.

flour·ish [FLUR-ish] VERB, flourished, flourishing. **1. fleurir, être en plein essor ▸** to grow or develop well : *The garden flourished after a summer of attention.* **2. prospérer ▸** to be at its most active or successful point : *The Aztec civilization flourished 500 years ago.* **3. brandir ▸** to wave about in a bold or showy way : *"This photo proves that my client is innocent!"* the lawyer shouted, flourishing it in front of the jury. ▲ NOUN, flourishes. **1. panache, moulinet ▸** a bold or showy display of something : *He bowed to her with an exaggerated flourish.* **2. fioriture, ornement ▸** a fancy addition or decoration, especially in a person's handwriting.

flow [floh] VERB, flowed, flowing. **1. couler ▸** to move along in a steady stream : *The river flows south.* **2. circuler ▸** to move in a steady, smooth way : *Traffic is flowing smoothly across the bridge.* **3. flotter, ondoyer ▸** to move or hang in a loose, graceful way. **Note.** Often used as an ADJECTIVE: *flowing hair; flowing handwriting.* ▲ NOUN, flows. **circulation, courant, flux, écoulement ▸** the act of flowing : *the flow of air from a fan; the flow of electricity through a wire.* SYN: pour, run, gush, pass, stream, glide, move.

flow·er [FLOW-ur] NOUN, flowers. **1. fleur ▸** the part of a plant that blooms and produces seeds or fruit ; a blossom. Many flowers are beautifully coloured and are used as decoration. **2. fleur ▸** a plant with flowers, especially a small plant grown for the beauty of its flowers. **3. fleur ▸** the finest part or best time of something : *the flower*

of youth. ▲ VERB, flowered, flowering. **1. fleurir ▸** to produce or have flowers; blossom : *Tulips flower in the spring.* **2. fleurir ▸** to come to full growth. 📗 p. 1097. 👁 p. 249.

flu [floo] NOUN. **grippe ▸** short for influenza.

fluff [fluf] NOUN, fluffs. **peluche, duvet ▸** light, soft material, like a cotton ball or the fur of a kitten. ▲ VERB, fluffed, fluffing. **faire bouffer, ébouriffer ▸** to make into a light, soft mass : *She dusted the room and fluffed up the cushions on the sofa.* ■ **fluffy,** ADJECTIVE. **▸ léger (-ère), aéré (-ée), mousseux (-euse), duveteux (-euse) ▸** *Mom made light, fluffy pancakes for breakfast.*

flu·id [FLOO-id] NOUN, fluids. **fluide, liquide ▸** a substance that is able to flow or move freely; a liquid or gas. A fluid takes on the shape of the container that holds it : *Water is a fluid.* ▲ ADJECTIVE. **1. fluide, liquide ▸** capable of flowing; not solid or rigid : *Some cheese becomes fluid when it is heated.* **2. fluide, coulant (-ante) ▸** having a relaxed, flowing appearance or style : *the fluid movements of a great ballet dancer.*

fluo·res·cent [fluh-RES-unt] ADJECTIVE. **fluorescent (-ente) ▸** able to give out light when acted on by certain forms of energy, such as X-rays or ultraviolet rays. A fluorescent lamp uses a narrow tube that sends out a white light when electricity passes through the fluorescent materials in the tube.

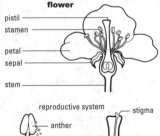

flower

pistil
stamen

petal
sepal

stem

reproductive system — stigma

anther

pollen

stamen

fluor·ide [FLOOR-ide] NOUN, fluorides. **fluorure ▸** a chemical that is added to drinking water and toothpaste to reduce tooth decay. **Note.** The process of adding fluoride to drinking water is fluoridation.

flus·ter [FLUS-ter] VERB, flustered, flustering. **énerver, agiter, troubler ▸** to make nervous or confused : *The crowd flustered the goalie and she missed an easy save.* SYN: confuse, bother, excite, agitate.

flute [floot] NOUN, flutes. **flûte ▸** a musical instrument made up of a long metal or wood pipe with several holes are covered by the fingers or by metal parts called keys. The flute is played by blowing across a hole near one end and by using one's fingers to open and close the holes. 👁 **p. 539.**

flut·ter [FLUT-ur] VERB, fluttered, fluttering. **1. voleter, voltiger ▸** to flap the wings to move in a rapid and uneven way : *The butterfly fluttered from flower to flower.* **2. voleter, flotter, s'agiter ▸** to move with a quick, uneven motion : *The drapes fluttered in the window.* **3. aller et venir dans une grande agitation, papillonner, virevolter ▸** to go about in a restless or nervous way : *Kelly fluttered about the room, tidying up before her guests arrived.* ▲ NOUN, flutters. **1. battement, palpitation ▸** a quick, uneven movement. **2. agitation, émoi, trouble ▸** a state of nervous excitement. SYN: wave, flap, tremble, move.

fly[1] [fly] VERB, flew, flown, flying. **1. voler ▸** to move through the air by means of wings, or by the force of wind. **2. voler, voyager en avion ▸** to move or travel through the air in an aircraft : *to fly to Montreal.* **3. voler, planer, filer ▸** to move or float in the air : *"The ball is flying slowly over my head as I run slowly under it."* (Arnold Adoff) **4. filer ▸** to move or pass quickly : *Is it Friday already? The week has really flown by.* **5. voler ▸** in baseball, to hit a ball high into the air. **Note.** The past form of this meaning is usually flied : *The batter flied out to left field to end the inning.* ▲ NOUN, flies. **1. braguette ▸** a flap or opening in pants or other clothing. **2.** (also fly ball) **chandelle ▸** a baseball hit high into the air. SYN: soar, float, wing, hover, flutter, sail, glide. 🖋 **p. 231.**

fly[2] NOUN, flies. **1. mouche ▸** a type of flying insect having a single pair of wings. The most common fly is the housefly, but mosquitoes and gnats are also flies. **2. mouche ▸** any of various other flying insects, such as the butterfly or dragonfly. **3. mouche ▸** a fish hook decorated with small feathers and other ornaments to look like a fly or other insect. 👁 **p. 104.**

fly·er [FLY-ur] NOUN, flyers. (also flier) **1. se dit de ce qui peut voler ▸** anything that flies, such as a bird or an insect. **2. aviateur (-trice) ▸** a person who flies in an airplane. **3. prospectus ▸** a piece of paper with an advertisement or announcement printed on it.

FM ABBREVIATION. **M.F. (modulation de fréquences) ▸** short for frequency modulation, one of the two main kinds of signals used by radio. In FM radio, the frequency of the radio wave is made higher or lower to match the sound being broadcast. **Note.** See also AM.

foam [fome] NOUN, foams. **mousse, écume ▸** a mass of tiny bubbles. Foam can be found on the top of a soft drink or inside the mouth of an animal that is sick or very hot. Some fire extinguishers contain a special foam for putting out fires. ▲ VERB, foamed, foaming. **mousser, écumer ▸** to form into foam; bubble : *The bubbles foamed up, almost overflowing the sink.*

fo·cus [FOH-kus] NOUN, focuses or foci. **1. foyer ▸** the point in the distance at which several rays of light meet after going through a glass lens or being reflected in a mirror. **2. au point, réglé (-ée) ▸** a position in which something must be placed in order to be seen or understood clearly : *The TV is out of focus, and the picture looks really fuzzy.* **3. centre ▸** a centre of activity or interest : *Tomorrow's football game was the focus of attention at school today.* ▲ VERB, focussed, focussing. (also focused, focusing) **1. mettre au point, ajuster, régler ▸** to adjust a lens or the eyes to get a sharper image or picture : *"Then she settled herself in a comfortable spot and focussed the camera on the bird feeder."* (Marilyn Halvorson) **2. concentrer ▸** to direct or fix attention on : *It was too dark to see, so he tried to focus all his other senses.*

fog [fog] NOUN, fogs. **1. brouillard, brume ▸** a misty cloud of small water drops that collects close to the ground or over a body of water. Fog can appear when winds blow warm, moist air over a cooler surface. **2. brouillard, confusion ▸** in a confused state of mind : *I'm sorry I didn't hear what you said—I've been in a fog all morning.* ▲ VERB, fogged, fogging. **embrouiller, embuer ▸** to cover with a fog; produce a fog : *She slowed the car because the windshield had fogged up.* ▪ **foggy**, ADJECTIVE, foggier, foggiest. **▸ brumeux (-euse), couvert (-erte) de buée.** 🗂 **p. 1103.**

🖋 **Word Builder**

Fly can be found in many familiar expressions. *Fly off the handle* means to get very excited or angry: *He used to fly off the handle any time someone criticized his work.* **To fly in the face of** means to disobey or defy: *Alison would fly in the face of her curfew and stay out past 9 p.m.* *Let fly* means to throw, release, or shoot something: *Roger Clemens let fly with a curve ball.*

foil[1] [foyl] VERB, foiled, foiling. **déjouer, contre-carrer ▸** to prevent a person from carrying out a plan, or a plan from being carried out; stop from succeeding : *The guards foiled the prisoners' attempt to escape.* SYN: frustrate, spoil, ruin, thwart.

foil[2] NOUN, foils. **feuille de métal, papier d'aluminium ▸** metal that has been flattened into a very thin, paperlike sheet : *Aluminum foil is used to wrap food.*

fold [fold] VERB, folded, folding. **1. plier, replier ▸** to bend something over itself one or more times : *to fold clean clothes.* **Note.** Often used as an ADJECTIVE: *a folding chair or table.* **2. croiser, envelopper, entourer, étreindre ▸** to draw close to the body : *Khalid folded his arms across his chest.* **3. fermer, disparaître ▸** to fail or close : *That business will have to fold if sales don't pick up soon.* ▲ NOUN, folds. **pli, plissement ▸** a part that is folded, or a mark made by folding.

folk [foke] NOUN. **folk** or **folks. 1. gens ▸** people of a certain type or group : *city folk; young folk.* **2. parents, famille, (les) miens ▸** a person's parents or other relatives : *Wendy brought her boyfriend home to meet her folks.* **3. les gens ▸** people in general : *"Still, it was nice being big enough in Beaver that folks could send you mail care of The Town, and you were known."* (Cynthia Rylant) **Note.** Folk is often used in compounds with other nouns and refers to the ordinary people of an area and to the way of life that they have passed down from one generation to another : *folk art; folk music. "Feed a cold and starve a fever" is a saying in folk medicine.* SYN: clan, relatives, kin, people, the public.

folklore NOUN. **folklore ▸** the stories, songs, and beliefs handed down by a people over the years. ✐ p. 232.

folk tale NOUN. (also **folk-tale** or **folktale**) **conte populaire, conte folklorique ▸** a story that has been told for many years and that has been passed down over time by word of mouth. ✐ p. 233.

fol·low [FOL-oh] VERB, followed, following. **1. suivre ▸** to come or go after : *I followed Marcel to the store so that I wouldn't get lost.* **2. suivre, longer ▸** to move or continue along a certain course : *Follow this road until you come to the main highway.* **3. suivre ▸** to act according to; obey : *To make a cake, follow the instructions.* **4. suivre ▸** to watch or observe closely : *He is a great admirer of that opera singer and has followed her career for years.* **5. suivre, comprendre ▸** to understand clearly : *Can you explain that? I don't follow you.* SYN: go after, pursue, tail, chase, track.

fol·ly [FOL-ee] NOUN, follies. **folie, sottise ▸** a complete lack of good judgment; being foolish :

✐ Writing Tips

Folklore

Folklore includes the beliefs, traditions, superstitions, and customs of a people that have been handed down from parents to their children.

Folklore can be songs, stories, myths, legends, folk tales, and proverbs. These forms can be wonderful examples of good literature and have inspired many people. The stories reappear again and again as new writers base their own stories on the different tales they have read or heard. You too can use a legend or folk tale you've read and write a new story using the same plot, with new characters or a different setting.

It was sheer folly for her to buy those expensive shoes.

fond [fond] ADJECTIVE, fonder, fondest. **1.** (used with of) **affectueux (-euse), tendre, aimer beaucoup, avoir de l'affection pour ▸** having a warm or loving feeling toward : *"In a short time he became quite fond of her and treated her like a daughter."* (Roger Lancelyn Green) **2. affectueux (-euse), tendre, cher, (chère), bon (bonne) ▸** cherished : *She has fond memories of the summers she spent at the lake.* ■ **fondly,** ADVERB. ▸ **affectueusement, tendrement.** ■ **fondness,** NOUN. ▸ **affection, tendresse, prédilection, penchant.** SYN: loving, liking, affectionate, adoring, tender.

font[1] [font] NOUN, fonts. **1. fonts baptismaux ▸** a basin that holds water for baptism. **2. fontaine, jet d'eau ▸** a fountain. **3. source ▸** a source : *That teacher is a font of knowledge.*

font[2] NOUN, fonts. **police de caractères ▸** a set of type in which letters, numbers, and so on are formed in the same style : *What fonts do you have on your computer?*

food [food] NOUN, foods. **1. nourriture ▸** something that people eat, especially something solid, as opposed to liquid. **2. aliment ▸** any substance that living things take in to keep them alive, give them strength and energy, and help them grow. ☞ p. 1136. ◉ p. 118.

fool [fool] NOUN, fools. **1. imbécile, idiot (idiote), sot (sotte), abruti (-ie) ▸** a person who does not have good judgment or good sense ; a silly or stupid person. **2. bouffon, fou ▸** in former times, a person at the court of a king who was supposed to amuse people by doing silly things; a jester. ▲ VERB, fooled, fooling. **1. berner, duper, tromper ▸** to act dishonestly toward; trick; deceive :

Folk Tales

Folk tales are traditional stories that were told hundreds of years ago and that were been passed down from generation to generation by word of mouth. Folk tales help to form and pass down the customs, beliefs, and traditions of a people. Folk tales

• *have a wide variety of characters— animals, royalty, ordinary people*

• *have a theme that is based on the beliefs and values of a people*

• *have simple plots that are based on quests, on a task to perform, or on characters who play tricks on each other.*

"You can't fool me with that one. That's the old plum trick!" (Robin Muller) **2. plaisanter ▸** to speak in a joking way; pretend : *We're not really moving away—I was only fooling when I said so.* **3. faire des bêtises, faire l'imbécile, faire l'idiot (idiote) ▸** to act in a playful or silly way : *John fooled around in class and got in trouble.* SYN : trick, deceive, bluff, mislead.

fool·ish [FOO-lish] ADJECTIVE. **1. idiot (idiote), bête, insensé ▸** showing a lack of good judgment or good sense; acting like a fool : *"It took some talking to convince Grandma that she had not been taking foolish risks."* (Marilyn Halvorson) **2. avoir l'air idiot (idiote) ▸** like a fool : *She felt foolish when she realized that she'd poured orange juice instead of milk on her cereal.*

foot [foot] NOUN, feet. **1. pied, patte ▸** the body part attached to the end of the leg, used for standing or moving. **2. pied, bout, bas ▸** something thought of as like a foot, because it is located at the end or lower part : *He pushed the blanket to the foot of the bed.* **3. pied ▸** a unit of length equal to 12 inches or about 30 cm. 📖 p. 996.

foot·ball [FOOT-bol] NOUN. **1. football américain ▸** a game played on a large field by two teams of 12 players each. (American football has 11 players.) The team that has the ball tries to carry or kick it over the other team's goal line. **2.** (plural footballs) **ballon de football ▸** the ball used in this game. **3. football, soccer ▸** in countries other than Canada and the U.S., the game of soccer.

foot·print [FOOT-print] NOUN, footprints. **empreinte de pied ▸** an outline or impression made by a person's foot or shoe : *"Our feet crunched over the crisp snow and little grey footprints followed us."* (Jane Yolen)

foot·step [FOOT-step] NOUN, footsteps. **1. pas ▸** a forward movement made by placing one foot ahead of the other. **2. pas ▸** the sound made by taking a step : *"It sounded like soft footsteps creeping down the hall."* (Marilyn Halvorson)

follow in someone's footsteps suivre les traces de quelqu'un ▸ to follow or imitate the example of another person.

for [for] PREPOSITION. **1. pour, pendant, sur ▸** to the distance, time, or amount stated : *to walk for 3 km; a book that sells for two dollars.* **2. pour, à l'intention de, à destination de, dans la direction de ▸** directed to the person or thing stated : *a movie for children; to leave for school.* **3. pour ▸** in order to serve the purpose stated : *to use an old box for a table.* **4. pour ▸** to benefit the person or thing stated : *to vote for Laura as team captain.* **5. pour, en raison de ▸** because of the reason stated : *to jump for joy.* **6. pour ▸** considering the thing stated : *Today's very cold for May.* **7. pour, comme, à la place ▸** in place of the thing stated : *What's the French word for "bread"?* ▲ CONJUNCTION. **car ▸** since; because : *We had to turn back, for the road was not passable.*

for·bid [fur-BID] VERB, forbade, forbidden, forbidding. **défendre, interdire, empêcher ▸** to order not to do; rule against; prohibit : *"Though we were forbidden to use sign language in the classroom, we always signed to each other out of school."* (Christy MacKinnon). **Note.** Often used as an ADJECTIVE:*A part of Beijing, China, is known as the Forbidden City because at one time Westerners were not allowed to go there.* SYN : prevent, prohibit, bar, ban, deter, disallow.

force [fors] NOUN, forces. **1. force, violence ▸** the ability to cause something to move or to happen; power; energy : *The force of the wind broke a branch of a tree.* **2. force ▸** in science, anything that changes the size or shape of an object, or makes it move or stop moving : *The force of gravity causes things to fall to the ground.* **3. force, violence ▸** the use of physical power on a person or thing : *The police officer had to use force to open the car door.* **4. force ▸** a power that influences the mind or thoughts : *Do you really like that cereal, or do you just eat it by force of habit?* **5. effectif ▸** a group of people organized for some purpose : *Farmers often rely on a short-term labour force to get the harvest in.* **6. forces. forces ▸** an army or other military unit : *Canadian armed forces were on peacekeeping duty in Cyprus.* ▲ VERB, forced, forcing. **1. force ▸** to use force against some object : *The door had swollen in the damp weather, and they had to force it open.* **2. forcer, contraindre, obliger ▸** to make a person do something : *The speaker was boring, and Manuel had to force himself to stay awake.* SYN : make, compel, pressure, oblige, motivate. ✏️ p. 456.

fore·cast [FOR-kast] VERB, forecast or forecasted, forecasting. **prévoir** ► to tell what is likely to happen : *The news announcer forecast rain for Friday.* ▲ NOUN, forecasts. **prévision, pronostic** ► prediction; prophecy.

fore·head [FOR-hed] NOUN, foreheads. **front** ► the upper part of the face, between the eyes and the hair. 📙 **p. 980.**

for·eign [FOR-un] ADJECTIVE. 1. **étranger (-ère), extérieur (-ieure)** ► away from one's own country : *A passport gives a person permission for foreign travel.* **Note.** A foreigner is a person who is in a country other than his or her own. 2. **à l'extérieur, à l'étranger** ► relating to another country : *I dream about travelling to foreign countries.* 3. **étranger (-ère)** ► not belonging naturally : *a foreign object in the eye.* SYN: external, alien, unknown, exotic, unfamiliar.

fore·shad·ow [for-SHAD-oh] VERB, foreshadowed, foreshadowing. **présager, annoncer, laisser prévoir** ► to be a warning of; give a sign of beforehand : *Dark clouds often foreshadow a thunderstorm.* ■ **foreshadowing,** NOUN. ► **présage.** 📎 **p. 234.**

for·est [FOR-ist] NOUN, forests. **forêt** ► a large area of land having many trees and other plants; woods. 📙 **p. 1041.** 👁 **p. 247.**

for·ev·er [for-EV-ur] ADVERB. 1. **toujours** ► without ever ending; for all time : *If we had walked off the path, we could have gotten lost forever.* 2. **sans cesse, continuellement, à tout bout de champ** ► again and again; many times or all the time; always : *I wish Jason would bring his own pen to school—he's forever borrowing mine.*

fore·word [FOR-wurd] NOUN. forewords. **avant-propos, avis au lecteur (-trice), avertissement** ► a section at the front of a book that tells the reader something about the book.

for·get [fur-GET] VERB, forgot, forgotten or forgot, forgetting. 1. **oublier** ► to not be able to call to mind something that was once known; not remember : *"The snow piled up so high that by New Year's Day I even began to forget what was under it."* (Teddy Jam) 2. **oublier, laisser**

> ✍ **Writing Tips**
>
> **Foreshadowing**
>
> *Foreshadowing is a writing technique used in stories to make the plot more interesting. The reader is given a hint of what is to come later in the story. A small event in the story, for example, may foreshadow a twist in the main plot. The atmosphere or mood of the story can be an element of foreshadowing. A dark, stormy atmosphere can foreshadow danger.*

---

tomber ► to fail to remember to do, bring, or get something : *Carol forgot to write her name on her paper.* **Note.** Someone who has a poor memory or is likely to forget things is forgetful. SYN: not remember, overlook, ignore, neglect.

for·give [fur-GIV] VERB, forgave, forgiven, forgiving. 1. **pardonner** ► to stop feeling angry toward and no longer want to blame or punish : *I hope you'll forgive me for getting here so late.* 2. **faire grâce** ► to take away the obligation to pay back a debt : *to forgive a loan.* **Note.** The act of forgiving or being willing to forgive is forgiveness. SYN: pardon, excuse, overlook.

fork [fork] NOUN, forks. 1. **fourchette** ► a small kitchen tool having two or more points attached to a handle, used to pick up and hold food. 2. **fourche** ► a large farm tool with a similar shape : *a pitchfork.* 3. **embranchement** ► a point where something divides into two or more parts : *a fork in the road.* ▲ VERB, forked, forking. 1. **manger à coups de fourchette** ► to use a fork. 2. **bifurquer** ► to divide into branches : *The road forks at the bottom of the hill.*

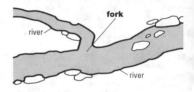

form [form] NOUN, forms. 1. **forme** ► the outward appearance that something has; the shape or outline of a thing : *Some road signs are in the form of a triangle.* 2. **forme, genre, espèce** ► an example of something; a kind or type : *Letters, poetry, and stories are forms of writing.* 3. **forme** ► a manner or style of doing something : *Top gymnasts practise daily to improve their form.* 4. **formulaire, formule, feuille, fiche** ► a piece of paper having blanks to be filled in with information. 5. **forme** ► the pronunciation or spelling of a word that changes because of the way it is used : *"Forgave" and "forgiven" are forms of the verb "forgive."* ▲ VERB, formed, forming. 1. **former, construire** ► to be or cause to be in a certain form : *"She scooped sand from the mound to form a wall."* (Juanita Havill) 2. **prendre forme, se former** ► to take on a form; come to be : *"Ice began to form in the water around the island, and along the mainland coast."* (Celia Godkin) 3. **former, composer** ► to bring into being; cause to be : *to form a club.* 4. **former** ► to be the form or nature of; be : *Ice forms much of the Antarctic.* 5. **former, composer** ► to change the form of a word in a certain way : *Most nouns in English*

form the plural by adding "s" or "es."
SYN: style, way, shape, manner, method, way.

for·mal [FOR-mul] ADJECTIVE. **1. formel (-elle), officiel (-elle), dans les règles, en bonne et due forme** ▸ following strict customs or rules : *Laura received a formal invitation to her cousin's wedding.* **2. de cérémonie, de soirée, soigné (-ée)** ▸ suitable for wearing to an important ceremony or event : *a formal dress.* **3. formaliste, cérémonieux (-euse), compassé (-ée), guindé (-ée)** ▸ very proper and polite; not relaxed : *The boss is very formal around the office and never calls people by their first names, even if he's known them for a long time.* ▪ **formally,** ADVERB. ▸ officiellement, cérémonieusement. ▪ **formality,** NOUN. ▸ formalité.

for·mat [FOR-mat] NOUN. **1. format, présentation** ▸ the size, shape, and style of a book or magazine. **2. format** ▸ a form or genre of writing. **3. présentation** ▸ any system or arrangement for doing something; a plan.

for·ma·tion [for-MAY-shun] NOUN, formations. **1. formation, élaboration** ▸ the act of forming something : *the formation of a person's character.* **2. formation** ▸ something that is formed, especially in nature : *a cloud formation; a rock formation.* **3. formation** ▸ the particular way that something is formed : *a football team that uses the "I" formation.*

for·mer [FOR-mur] ADJECTIVE. **1. ancien (-ienne), précédent (-ente)** ▸ during the past; at an earlier time : *Pierre Trudeau is a former prime minister of Canada.* **2. premier (-ière)** ▸ the first of two things that were just named or mentioned : *Wes asked Julie if she'd like to go to a movie or skating. She chose the former.* ▪ **formerly,** ADVERB. ▸ autrefois, anciennement, jadis. *I was formerly employed at the factory.* SYN: earlier, previous, prior, first, past.

for·mu·la [FOR-myuh-luh] NOUN, formulas or formulae. **1. formule** ▸ a set of symbols and figures used in mathematics to express some rule : *The formula for the area of a rectangle is "area = length x width."* **2. formule** ▸ all the things that make up a medicine, fuel, or other substance: H_2O is the formula for water. **3. formule** ▸ a certain set of methods that will lead to some result : *a formula for success.* **4. lait maternisé** ▸ a special milklike liquid for a baby to drink.

fort [fort] NOUN, forts. **1. fort** ▸ a strong building for defence against an enemy attack. **2. fort** ▸ an area where a large number of soldiers and weapons are regularly located. **3. comptoir** ▸ a trading post : *In the early days of the Hudson's Bay Company, trading posts were known as forts.* ▪ **fortress,** NOUN, fortresses. forteresse, place forte ▸ a well-protected fort.

forth [forth] ADVERB. **1. en avant** ▸ forward in direction or time : *"The stick goes back and forth and back and forth and tells musicians*

how fast they should play." (Barbara Nichol) **2. de façon à se montrer** ▸ out into sight or view : *The sun came forth from behind the clouds.* **3. de façon à s'éloigner** ▸ away : *He was told to go forth from the town and never to return.*

for·tu·nate [FOR-chuh-nit] ADJECTIVE. **heureux (-euse), chanceux (-euse),** ▸ having or bringing a good result; lucky : *"I was fortunate to have a wonderful teacher, Mr. Fearon."* (Christy MacKinnon) ▪ **fortunately,** ADVERB. ▸ heureusement, par bonheur. *Lucy left her book on the bus, but fortunately the driver found it and returned it to her.*

for·tune [FOR-chun] NOUN, fortunes. **1. fortune** ▸ a large amount of money or property; great wealth. **2. fortune, chance** ▸ something that will happen in the future; fate : *"I say we try to seek our fortune here."* (Bob Barton) **3. fortune, chance, hasard** ▸ chance; luck; fate : *to have good fortune.*

for·ty [FOR-tee] NOUN, forties. **quarante** ▸ the number that is equal to four times ten; 40. ▪ **fortieth,** ADJECTIVE; NOUN. ▸ quarantième.

for·um [FOR-um] NOUN, forums or fora. **1. forum** ▸ the public square or marketplace in ancient Rome. **2. tribune** ▸ a gathering for discussing questions of public interest.

for·ward [FOR-wurd] ADVERB. **à l'avant** ▸ (also forwards) at or toward the front : *Face forward, and don't look behind you.* ▲ ADJECTIVE. **1. en avant** ▸ at or near the front : *The pilot sits in the forward part of the plane.* **2. de manière effrontée, insolente** ▸ acting in too bold a way; rude : *It was a bit forward of him to ask for more when he had not finished eating what he was given.* ▲ VERB, forwarded, forwarding. **1. faire suivre** ▸ to send mail on to a new address : *When we moved, we forwarded our mail to our new apartment.* **2. favoriser, faire avancer** ▸ to help or advance : *to forward the cause of world peace.* ▲ NOUN, forwards. **avant** ▸ a player whose position is at the front in certain games, such as basketball, soccer, and hockey.

fos·sil [FOS-ul] NOUN, fossils. **fossile** ▸ the hardened remains of an animal or plant that lived thousands of years ago. Fossils are preserved in rock, earth, ice, or other substances.

fos·ter [FOS-tur] ADJECTIVE. **adoptif (-ive), nourricier (-ière)** ▸ having to do with the care of children by people who are not their parents by birth or by adoption : *foster care; a foster child or parent.* ▲ VERB, fostered, fostering. **élever** ▸ to help grow or develop : *My parents fostered my interest in music.* SYN: care for, support, mind, tend, feed, cultivate.

fought [fot] VERB. **se battre** ▸ a past form of fight.

foul [fowl] ADJECTIVE. **1. infect (-ecte), nauséabond (-onde), immonde ▸** having a very unpleasant smell or taste; disgusting; rotten : *the foul odour of burning rubber.* **2. gros (grosse), sale ▸** of weather, rainy and stormy : *a foul day.* **3. terrible ▸** very bad; wicked; *foul crimes.* **4. ordurier (-ière), grossier (-ière) ▸** not polite or decent : *foul language.* **▲** NOUN, fouls. **1. faute, coup défendu, coup interdit, coup irrégulier ▸** in sports and games, a move or play that is against the rules : *The soccer player committed a foul by tripping another player.* **2.** (also foul ball) **fausse balle ▸** in baseball, a ball hit outside the foul lines. **Note.** A foul line is either of the two lines in baseball that run from home plate through first or third base to the end of the outfield. A ball must be hit inside the lines to allow the batter to reach first. **▲** VERB, fouled, fouling. **1. polluer, infecter ▸** to make something foul : *Garbage fouled the river.* **2. emmêler, entortiller, embrouiller ▸** to make or become tangled : *Morgan fouled the kite string in some branches.* **3. commettre une faute ▸** to break a rule in a game or sport; commit a foul. SYN: dirty, smelly, nasty, stinky, filthy, polluted.

found[1] VERB. **trouver ▸** a past form of find.

found[2] [fownd] VERB, founded, founding. **fonder, créer, établir, constituer ▸** to bring into being; start; establish : *Samuel de Champlain founded the city of Quebec in 1608.* **Note.** A person who founds or establishes something is a founder.

foun·da·tion [fown-DAY-shun] NOUN, foundations. **1. fondations ▸** the lowest part of a house or other building, which supports the rest of the building. **2. fondement, base ▸** the basis that supports something such as a belief : *His argument has no foundation in facts.* **3. fondation, création, établissement ▸** the act of founding or establishing something. **4. fondation ▸** an organization that is set up to provide money for certain worthy causes. SYN: support, base, groundwork, foot.

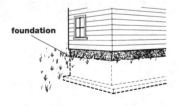

foundation

foun·tain [FOWNT-un] NOUN, fountains. **1. fontaine, jet d'eau ▸** a device that creates a small stream of water for drinking. **2. fontaine, jet d'eau ▸** a stream of water that is made to shoot up in the air or to flow out of specially designed statues and pools. **3. fontaine, source ▸** a natural stream of water rising up from the earth.

4. source ▸ a source : *That book is a fountain of information on China.*

four [for] NOUN, fours. **quatre ▸** the number that is one more than three; 4. **■ fourth,** ADJECTIVE; NOUN. **▸ quatrième.**

four·teen [FOR-teen] NOUN, fourteens. **quatorze ▸** the number that is four more than ten; 14. **■ fourteenth,** ADJECTIVE; NOUN. **▸ quatorzième.**

fowl [fowl] NOUN, fowls. **1. volaille, oiseau (-eaux), volatile ▸** any of various large birds that are raised for food, such as chickens, geese, turkeys, or ducks; poultry. **2. oiseau (-eaux), volaille, gibier à plumes ▸** any bird, especially a wild bird hunted for food.

fox [foks] NOUN, foxes. **renard ▸** a wild animal that has a pointed nose and ears, a bushy tail, and thick fur. It is related to the wolf. The red fox is found in wooded areas in most parts of North America. **▲** VERB, foxed, foxing. **tromper, berner, mystifier ▸** to trick in a sly way : *Tim foxed Toby out of his tickets to the ball game.* **👁 p. 110.**

frac·tion [FRAK-shun] NOUN, fractions. **1. fraction ▸** a number that is one or more of the equal parts of a whole or a group. A fraction is shown as two numbers with a line between them, indicating that the first number is divided by the second : 1/2, 3/16, and 8/9. **2. fraction, partie ▸** a very small part of a whole : *a fraction of a second.* SYN: part, bit, portion, segment, section.

frag·ile [FRAJ-il *or* FRAJ-ile] ADJECTIVE. **fragile, délicat (-ate) ▸** easy to break or destroy; delicate; frail : *Please pack the china carefully — it's very fragile.*

frag·ment [FRAG-munt] NOUN, fragments. **1. fragment, morceau (-eaux) ▸** a small piece broken off from an object : *a fragment of a broken plate.* **2. fragment, bribes ▸** a small or incomplete part : *He could remember only a fragment of the melody, but he kept humming it over and over.* SYN: scrap, fraction, section, portion, part, bit.

fra·grance [FRAY-gruns] NOUN, fragrances. **fragrance, parfum, senteur ▸** a pleasant smell, as of flowers or perfume : *The valley was filled with the sweet fragrance of the blossoming spring flowers.* **■ fragrant,** ADJECTIVE. **▸ parfumé (-ée), odorant (-ante).** SYN: scent, aroma, perfume, odour.

frame [frame] NOUN, frames. **1. charpente, châssis, cadre, encadrement ▸** a group of connecting parts that give support or shape to something : *Kate painted the frame of her bicycle black.* **2. cadre, encadrement ▸** a hard border or case into which something is placed : *a picture frame.* **3. charpente, ossature, corps ▸** the form of a person's body; *a woman with a small frame.* **▲** VERB, framed, framing. **1. encadrer ▸** to put a frame around : *to frame a painting or a photograph.* **2. encadrer ▸** to set within a background or border : *Sandy stood back to frame the shot of her dog with the doorway.* **3. faire porter une accusation contre quelqu'un, monter une accusation ▶** to make an innocent person seem guilty by means of tricks or false proof : *a plot to frame an innocent person.*

frame of mind **humeur, disposition d'esprit, état d'esprit ▶** the state of a person's thoughts or feelings; mood.

frame-work [FRAME-wurk] NOUN, frameworks. **structure, cadre, charpente, encadrement ▶** the basic structure around which a thing is built.

Fran-co-phone [FRANG-kuh-fone] ADJECTIVE. (also francophone) **francophone ▶** a person whose first language is French.

frank [frank] ADJECTIVE. franker, frankest. **franc (-anche), direct (-ecte), ouvert (-erte) ▶** honest and open in expressing what one thinks and feels; sincere : *I'm going to be frank with you; you aren't ready to compete in the tennis tournament.* ■ **frankly,** ADVERB. ▶ **franchement, sincèrement.** ■ **frankness,** NOUN. ▶ **franchise.** SYN: open, sincere, blunt, outspoken, candid.

fran-tic [FRAN-tik] ADJECTIVE. **frénétique, effréné (-ée), hors de soi, fou (folle) ▶** not in control of one's feelings; very excited with fear, worry, anger, or pain : *"Hare was frantic with worry."* (Jan Thornhill) ■ **frantically,** ADVERB. ▶ **frénétiquement, avec frénésie, comme un fou (une folle).** *"They were separated from us earlier today and I have been searching frantically for them."* (Bob Barton) SYN: crazy, wild, excited, hysterical.

fraud [frod] NOUN, frauds. **1. fraude, imposture, tromperie, escroquerie ▶** a dishonest act or trick, especially one that cheats someone : *The store owner was arrested for fraud because he sold cheap machine-made blankets as handwoven blankets.* **2. imposteur (-eure), fraudeur (-euse) ▶** a person or thing that is not what is claimed; a fake. **Note.** Someone or something that is a fraud is fraudulent.

freck-le [FREK-ul] NOUN, freckles. **tache de rousseur, tache de son ▶** a small brown spot on the skin, usually caused by being exposed to sunlight. ▲ VERB, freckled, freckling. ■ **freckly** or freckled, ADJECTIVE. ▶ **couvert (-erte) de taches de rousseur.**

free [free] ADJECTIVE. freer, freest. **1. gratuit (-uite) ▶** not costing anything; with no cost : *The telephone company gives away free telephone books.* **2. libre ▶** not under the control or power of another : *a free country.* **3. libre ▶** not held or kept in; not confined : *"I tried to stretch up and clutch Josepha's elbow, but he broke free."* (Jim McGugan) **4. libre, sans ▶** not troubled or bothered; clear : *free of worry.* **5. libre ▶** not busy or in use : *I have two free afternoons this week.* ▲ ADVERB. **gratuitement, gratis ▶** at no cost : *Children under six are admitted to the museum free.* ▲ VERB, freed, freeing. **libérer, affranchir ▶** to make or set free : *"He told them about William Wilberforce and Harriet Tubman helping to free the slaves."* (Jean Little) ■ **freely,** ADVERB: ▶ **librement, sans contrainte, franchement.** *to speak freely about a problem.* 🖉 p. 237.

free-dom [FREE-dum] NOUN, freedoms. **1. liberté ▶** the state of being free; liberty : *When the jury found him innocent, the accused man was given his freedom.* **2. liberté, indépendance ▶** the right to be free; being able to act, think, speak, and write as one wishes : *"A fifteen-year-old boy does need a little freedom."* (Eve Bunting) **3. libéré (-ée) ▶** the condition of being free of a burden or worry.

freeze [freez] VERB, froze, frozen, freezing. **1. geler ▶** to change from a liquid to a solid by cold. **2. geler ▶** to become covered or filled with ice : *The pipes had frozen while we were away during the winter.* **3. geler ▶** to make or become very cold : *The cold wind froze my hands as I walked to the store.* **4. (se) figer ▶** to stop moving suddenly, as if turning to ice : *Deer often freeze in their tracks when they hear a noise.* **5. geler, bloquer ▶** to set or fix at a certain amount : *The premier wants to freeze rents at the present level.* ▲ NOUN, freezes. **1. gel ▶** a period of very cold weather : *A January freeze destroyed the orange crop.* **2. gel ▶** the act of freezing : *The company ordered a freeze on pay raises.*

freez-er [FREE-zur] NOUN, freezers. **1. congélateur ▶** a separate part of a refrigerator that has a temperature below freezing, used to make ice, freeze food, and store frozen foods. **2. congélateur ▶** a special refrigerator used for this same purpose.

🖉 Word Builder

Make free with means to use something as if you own it: *My brother made free with my bike when I was away.* If you get something *for free,* you do not have to pay for it: *I got this book for free at the fair.* A *free-for-all* is a fight, an argument, or a competition without order that anyone present can participate in: *The debate turned into a free-for-all.* A *free lunch* or *free ride* is something gotten without work or payment: *Sally got a free ride on the project because Vithya did all the work.*

freight [frate] NOUN. **1. transport ▸** the act or business of moving goods by land, air, or water : *We sent the package by air freight.* **2. cargaison ▸** the goods carried in this way, as in a plane, ship or truck : *Railway trains are often used to move freight.* **Note.** A freighter is a ship used for carrying freight. SYN: load, cargo, shipment, goods. ☞ **p. 395.**

French Canadian 1. Canadien (-ienne) français (-aise) ▸ one of the French-speaking people of Canada. **2. français ▸** the language of these Canadians. ■ **French-Canadian,** ADJECTIVE. **canadien (-ienne) français (-aise) ▸** having to do with French Canadians or their language.

french fry NOUN, french fries. (often French fry) **pomme de terre frite, frite ▸** potatoes cut in thin strips and fried in fat until brown and crisp.

fre·quen·cy [FREE-kwun-see] NOUN, frequencies. **1. fréquence ▸** the fact of being frequent; happening again and again : *It rains frequently in Prince Rupert.* **2. fréquence ▸** the number of times that something happens or appears : *The letter in English that has the highest frequency is "e."* **3. fréquence ▸** the number of times per second that something such as sound or light vibrates.

fre·quent [FREE-kwunt] ADJECTIVE. **fréquent (-ente), nombreux (-euse), courant (-ante) ▸** happening again and again ; taking place often : *People living along the Gulf of Mexico must expect frequent rainstorms.* ▲ [free-KWENT] VERB, frequented, frequenting. **fréquenter ▸** to be in a certain place often : *to frequent a restaurant; to frequent a museum.* ■ **frequently,** ADVERB. **▸ fréquemment, souvent.** SYN: common, regular, many, habitual.

fresh [fresh] ADJECTIVE, fresher, freshest. **1. frais (fraîche) ▸** something just gathered, caught, or produced : *fresh fruit; fresh fish.* **2. frais (fraîche) ▸** just made or done : *fresh bread; fresh animal tracks in the snow.* **3. nouveau (-elle, -eaux) ▸** another; different : *Dan decided to move to Australia to get a fresh start in life.* **4. frais (fraîche) ▸** not stale; cool or refreshing : *a fresh breeze.* **5. doux (douce) ▸** of water, not part of the ocean; not salty. **6. impertinent (-ente) ▸** not polite; rude : *The boy gave a fresh answer when he was asked to be quiet.* ■ **freshly,** ADVERB: ▸ **fraîchement.** *The breeze blew freshly after the spring rain.* ■ **freshness,** NOUN. ▸ fraîcheur.

fresh·wa·ter [FRESH-WAH-tur] ADJECTIVE. (also fresh-water) **d'eau douce ▸** Having to do with or living in water that is not salty.

fret [fret] VERB, fretted, fretting. **s'agiter, se tourmenter, se tracasser ▸** to make or become worried or upset, especially over something small or unimportant.

fric·tion [FRIK-shun] NOUN. **1. friction ▸** the rubbing of one object against another. **2. friction, frottement ▸** a force that slows down or stops the movement of two objects that touch each other : *A stone will slide on ice more easily than dirt because the ice has less friction.* **3.** (plural, frictions) **friction, désaccord ▸** the effect of opposing forces or ideas; conflict; disagreement : *There's a lot of friction between my sister and me.*

Fri·day [FRY-day] NOUN, Fridays. **vendredi ▸** the day after Thursday and before Saturday.

fried [fride] VERB. **frire ▸** a past form of fry. **Note.** Often used as an ADJECTIVE:*fried fish ; fried potatoes.*

friend [frend] NOUN, friends. **1. ami (amie), camarade ▸** a person whom one knows well and likes; someone with whom a person likes to spend time. **2. ami (amie), bienfaiteur (-trice) ▸** a person who helps or supports someone or something : *He is a friend of the opera and gave a lot of money for the new opera house.* SYN: mate, pal, buddy, chum, companion, ally. ☞ **p. 1058.**

friend·ly [FREND-lee] ADJECTIVE, friendlier, friendliest. **1. amical (-ale, -aux) ▸** like a friend; warm and kind : *a friendly smile.* **2. amical (-ale, -aux) ▸** without anger or fighting; on good terms : *"We are friendly with all our neighbours."* SYN: kind, helpful, agreeable, neighbourly.

friend·ship [FREND-ship] NOUN, friendships. **amitié ▸** the feeling between friends; the relationship of being friends. ☞ **p. 1020.**

fright [frite] NOUN, frights. **1. effroi, peur ▸** a sudden feeling of deep fear or alarm. **2. épouvantail, horreur ▸** something that looks shocking, ugly, or ridiculous : *The outfit he wore on Halloween made him look a fright.* SYN: fear, alarm, terror, dread, dismay, panic.

fright·en [FRITE-un] VERB, frightened, frightening. **1. effrayer, faire peur à ▸** to make or become suddenly afraid or alarmed : *That scream frightened me so much that my heart is still beating fast.* **Note.** Often used as an ADJECTIVE: ▸ *"I couldn't hear my mother's frightened call as the frisky horse leaped over me."* (Christy MacKinnon) **2. effrayé (-ée), effarouché (-ée) ▸** to drive away by scaring : *The dog barked at the birds and frightened them away.* ■ **frightful,** ADJECTIVE. ▸ **effrayant (-ante), effroyable, épouvantable.** ✐ **p. 239.**

fringe [frinj] NOUN, fringes. **1. frange ▸** an edge of hanging threads or cord used as a decoration on curtains, bedspreads, clothing, and so on. **2. bord, bordure, lisière ▸** the part away from the middle; the edge : *He hung on the fringe of the crowd, never quite joining in on the celebration.* ▲ VERB, fringed, fringing. **franger ▸** to

🖋 **Word Builder**

Frighten, scare, and *terrify* are all verbs that mean to fill with fear. *Frighten* often means to be afraid of physical harm, but it can also be fears from your emotions (feelings) or imagination: *Riding elevators always frightens Megan.* *Scare* is similar in meaning to frighten, but it can also suggest that what frightens you happens suddenly: *When the elevator stopped between floors, it really scared Megan.* *Terrify* is the strongest of the three words and it suggests a very extreme fear: *When the elevator started to drop suddenly, Megan was terrified.*

make a fringe for : *Long, dark lashes fringed his eyes.*

frisk·y [FRIS-kee] ADJECTIVE. **fringant (-ante), vif (vive), sémillant (-ante)** ▸ lively; playful : *Our new puppy is always frisky.*

friv·o·lous [FRIV-uh-lus] ADJECTIVE. **frivole, léger (-ère), superficiel (-ielle)** ▸ not serious or important; silly : *a frivolous conversation.* SYN: silly, light, unimportant, trivial, shallow.

frog [frog] NOUN, frogs. **grenouille** ▸ a small animal with webbed feet, smooth skin, no tail, and strong back legs that it uses for jumping. Frogs are good swimmers and usually live in or near water.

from [frum] PREPOSITION. **1. de, du, des** ▸ used to show a starting place or time : *I believe he comes from Vancouver.* **2. de, du, des** ▸ used to show a starting point or position : *She took a dollar from her pocket.* **3. de, du, des** ▸ used to show the source or cause : *Bread is made from flour.* **4. de, du, des** ▸ used to show a difference : *Some people have trouble telling red from green.*

front [frunt] NOUN, fronts. **1. avant, devant, couverture, façade** ▸ a part that is forward or near the beginning; the opposite side from the back : *She wrote her name on the front of her notebook.* **2. bord, front** ▸ the land at the edge of a street or body of water : *They have a home on the lakefront.* **3. front** ▸ in a war, a place where the fighting is going on. **4. contenance** ▸ an outward appearance that is different from what is real : *He was very nervous, but he tried to keep up a brave front.* **5. front** ▸ in weather, the division between two masses of air that have different temperatures : *a cold front.* ▲ ADJECTIVE. **de devant, (en) avant, frontal (-ale, -aux)** ▸ facing or near the front; in front : *the front door of a house.* ▲ VERB, fronted, fronting. **donner sur, faire face** ▸ to look out on; face : *Her house fronts the stream.*

fron·tier [frun-TEER] NOUN, frontiers. **1. frontière** ▸ the last edge of a settled area before the part that is not built up or developed begins : *the Western frontier of the 1800s.* **2. frontière** ▸ the border area between two countries. **3. frontière** ▸ any place or area of knowledge that has not yet been fully explored or developed : *the frontiers of space.*

frost [frost] NOUN, frosts. **1. givre** ▸ a covering of thin ice that forms when cold temperatures freeze the water vapour in the air. **2. gel, gelée** ▸ weather cold enough to cause freezing. ▲ VERB, frosted, frosting. **1. geler** ▸ to cover with frost : *The windshield frosted up as they sat in the car talking.* **2. glacer** ▸ to cover a cake or pastry with frosting or icing. ■ **frosty,** ADJECTIVE. ▸ **glacial (-ale, -als), froid (froide).** *We could see our breath in the frosty air.*

frown [frown] VERB, frowned, frowning. **froncer les sourcils, se renfrogner** ▸ to draw the eyebrows together so that lines appear in the forehead. People frown when they are upset or angry, when they are thinking hard, when the light is very bright, and so on : *"'I have never seen a dog frown,' I said."* (Patricia MacLachlan) ▲ NOUN, frowns. **froncement** ▸ the act of frowning : *"Esther seemed perfectly comfortable, although she looked over at him with a frown on her face."* (Cynthia Rylant)

frown on **désapprouver** ▸ to be against, disapprove : *She frowns on going barefoot outdoors, even on hot summer days.* SYN: scowl, pout, glare, look sullen or displeased.

fro·zen [FROH-zun] VERB. **geler** ▸ a past form of freeze: *The pond had frozen over night.*

fruit [froot] NOUN, fruits. **1. fruit** ▸ a sweet, juicy plant part that is good to eat, often served as a snack or for dessert. Apples, oranges, strawberries, bananas, grapes, and peaches are popular fruits. **2. fruit** ▸ the part of any flowering plant that contains the seeds. **3. fruit** ▸ a product; result : *The new playground was the fruit of many people's efforts.* 📖 **p. 1097.**

frus·trate [FRUS-trate] VERB, frustrated, frustrating. **1. contrecarrer, faire échouer, déjouer** ▸ to prevent or block from reaching a goal : *The firefighters fought the brush fire all day, but the hot, dry winds frustrated their efforts to put it out.* **2. frustrer, décevoir** ▸ to have a feeling of being discouraged, irritated, or helpless : *Trying to fix the air-conditioner really frustrated Dad.* **Note.** Also used as an ADJECTIVE: *He was a frustrated athlete who never made the big leagues.* SYN: foil, spoil, ruin, defeat, thwart.

frus·tra·tion [frus-TRAY-shun] NOUN, frustrations. **1. frustration** ▸ the feeling of being frustrated : *Pam gave up in frustration after trying three* *times to open the jar.* **2. frustration ▶** something that causes this : *the frustrations of city driving.*

fry [fry] VERB, fried, frying. **frire ▶** to cook food in a pan, usually with hot oil or fat : *John was frying bacon and eggs over the fire.* ▲ NOUN, fries. **friture ▶** a meal of fried food : *They marked the end of summer with a fish fry on the beach.*

fudge [fuj] NOUN. **fudge, fondant ▶** a soft candy, usually made of chocolate, sugar, milk, and butter, and sometimes containing nuts.

fu-el [fyool] NOUN. fuels. **combustible, carburant ▶** anything that is burned to provide heat or energy, such as wood, coal, or oil.

full [ful] ADJECTIVE, fuller, fullest. **1. plein (pleine), rempli (-ie), comble, complet (-ète) ▶** holding as much or as many as possible : *a full stomach. The hotel is full, so we'll have to stay somewhere else.* **2. complet (-ète) ▶** with nothing missing; complete : *a full deck of cards; a full day's work.* **3. plein (pleine), rempli (-ie) ▶** having a large amount : *During the summer, the town is full of tourists.* **4. tout (toute) ▶** to the greatest amount or degree : *to go at full speed.* **5. plein (pleine), rond (ronde), joufflu (-ue), charnu (-ue) ▶** of the body, having a rounded shape : *a full face.* **6. large, ample ▶** of clothes, wide or loose-fitting : *a full skirt.* ▲ ADVERB. **1. plein (pleine) ▶** completely; entirely : *He filled the bag full of apples.* **2. droit (droite) ▶** straight on; directly : *to look a person full in the face.* ▪ **fully,** ADVERB. **▶ complètement, entièrement, au maximum, à plein.** *to answer someone's questions fully.* ▪ **fullness,** NOUN. ▶ **abondance.** SYN : complete, whole, entire, stuffed, packed.

fum-ble [FUM-bul] VERB, fumbled, fumbling. **1. tâtonner, fouiller ▶** to feel around in a clumsy way : *She fumbled about in the dark.* **2. manier gauchement, manier maladroitement, répondre avec maladresse ▶** to handle something awkwardly : *The announcer fumbled the player's name.* **3. échapper, mal attraper ▶** to lose hold of; drop : *He fumbled the ball.*

fun [fun] NOUN. **1. plaisir, amusement ▶** a time of playing, enjoying oneself, or being amused; a good time : *We always have fun at the beach.* **2. amusement ▶** someone or something that causes enjoyment or amusement : *The fun we had playing baseball was incredible.*

make fun of se moquer de quelqu'un, rire de quelqu'un, ▶ to laugh at in a cruel or unkind way; tease.

func-tion [FUNK-shun] NOUN, functions. **1. fonction, charge ▶** the proper activity or use of a person or thing; role; purpose : *The function of the chairperson is to be in charge of the meeting.* **2. cérémonie publique, réception, réunion ▶** a formal social event or ceremony : *The awards banquet is an annual function at our school.* ▲ VERB, functioned, functioning. **faire**

fonction de, servir de, fonctionner, marcher ▶ to have or perform a function; work or act : *A cowboy's hat also functioned as a pillow or water bucket.*

fund [fund] NOUN. funds. **1. fonds ▶** money set aside or raised for a special purpose : *My parents have set up a special account they call my university fund.* **2. funds. fonds ▶** money that is available for use : *to raise funds for a charity.* **3. fond ▶** a supply of something that is ready for use : *A dictionary is a fund of information about words.* ▲ VERB, funded, funding. **financer, doter en capital ▶** to provide funds for : *Large corporations fund many sporting competitions.*

fun-da-men-tal [FUN-duh-MENT-ul] ADJECTIVE. **fondamental (-ale, -aux), de base, essentiel (-elle) ▶** forming a necessary or very important part; basic, essential : *The law of gravity is a fundamental principle of science.* ▲ NOUN, fundamentals. **fondamental (-als, -aux), essentiel (-elle) ▶** a basic principle or part : *Blocking and tackling are fundamentals of football.* ▪ **fundamentally,** ADVERB. ▶ **fondamentalement, essentiellement.** SYN : essential, basic, primary, underlying.

fu-ner-al [FYOO-nur-ul] NOUN. funerals. **funérailles, enterrement, obsèques ▶** a religious service or special ceremony held for a dead person, especially at the time the person is buried.

fun-gus [FUNG-gus] NOUN, fungi or funguses. **champignon ▶** one of a very large group of plants that have no flowers or leaves or green colouring matter. Mushrooms and mould are fungi.

fun-nel [FUN-ul] NOUN, funnels. **1. entonnoir ▶** a utensil with a wide cone or cup at one end that narrows to a thin tube at the other. A funnel is used to avoid spilling while pouring a liquid into a container with a small opening. **2. cheminée ▶** the smokestack of a steamship or steam engine.

fun-ny [FUN-ee] ADJECTIVE, funnier, funniest. **1. drôle, amusant (-ante), comique ▶** causing laughter; amusing : *a funny story; a funny joke.* **2. drôle, curieux (-euse), bizarre ▶** unusual in a strange way; odd; peculiar : *The rocking of the boat made me feel funny.*

fur [fur] NOUN, furs. **1. poil, pelage, fourrure ▶** the thick, soft hair that covers the skin of many types of animals. Tigers, bears, and rabbits have fur. **2. fourrure ▶** a coat made from animal fur. ▪ **furry,** ADJECTIVE, furrier, furriest. ▶ **poilu (-ue), à poil.**

fur-i-ous [FYOOR-ee-us] ADJECTIVE. **1. furieux (-euse) ▶** filled with or showing great anger; in a rage : *Mr. Meta was furious when the baseball went through his window.* **2. déchaîné (-ée), acharné (-ée), fou (folle) ▶** violent or extreme; very strong or fierce : *The racing cars roared around the track at a furious* *pace.* ■ **furiously,** ADVERB. ▶ **furieusement.** SYN: angry, mad, raging, violent, upset, enraged.

fur·nace [FUR-nis] NOUN, furnaces. **fournaise, chaudière, chaufferie** ▶ an enclosed chamber where fuel is burned to produce heat to warm houses and other buildings.

fur·nish [FUR-nish] VERB, furnished, furnishing. **1. meubler** ▶ to supply or decorate with furniture : *She furnished her apartment with old furniture from her family.* **Note.** Often used as an ADJECTIVE: *A furnished apartment is rented with furniture in it.* **2. fournir, donner, pourvoir, munir** ▶ to supply what is needed; provide : *That power plant furnishes the entire city.* SYN: supply, equip, provide, give, outfit.

fur·ni·ture [FUR-nih-chur] NOUN. **meubles, mobilier, ameublement** ▶ movable items, such as tables, chairs, and beds, that are used to sit or lie down on, keep things in, work at, and so on.
📖 **p. 1069.**

fur·ther [FUR-thur] ADJECTIVE. **additionnel (-elle), supplémentaire, nouveau (-elle, -eaux)** ▶ additional; more : *I'd like to take that empty box, if you have no further use for it.* ▲ ADVERB. **1. davantage, plus** ▶ to a greater degree or amount : *The principal is going to look into the matter further.* **2. plus loin** ▶ at a more distant point; farther. ▲ VERB, furthered, furthering. **servir, avancer, favoriser** ▶ to help the progress of; support or advance : *to further the cause of world peace.*

fur·ther·more [FUR-thur-mor] ADVERB. **en outre, de plus, qui plus est, par ailleurs** ▶ in addition to; besides, also : *That road is much too narrow; furthermore, it's not well lighted.*

fu·ry [FYOOR-ee] NOUN, furies. **fureur, furie, violence, acharnement** ▶ the state of being furious; great anger : *the fury of a hurricane.* SYN: rage, frenzy, wrath, ferocity.

fuse [fyooz] NOUN, fuses. **1. amorce, détonateur** ▶ a piece of cord or other easily burned material that is used to set off a bomb or other explosive. **2. fusible, plomb** ▶ a safety device consisting of a strip of metal that melts and breaks an electric circuit when the current becomes too strong. New buildings use a circuit breaker for this purpose rather than fuses. ▲ VERB, fused, fusing. **1. fondre, mettre en fusion,** to melt or soften by heating : *The heat of the fire fused the plastic toy into a shapeless lump.* **2. fusionner, unifier, amalgamer** ▶ to unite by or as if by melting. SYN: join, blend, melt, unite, combine, weld.

fuss [fus] NOUN, fusses. **1. tapage pour peu, agitation pour peu** ▶ great attention to small or unimportant things : *"He couldn't understand why everyone made such a fuss about playing the piano."* (Barbara Novak) **2. faire grand cas de, être aux petits soins** ▶ a great show of interest or affection : *Grandma always makes a big fuss about how big we've grown.* ▲ VERB, fussed, fussing. **faire un tas d'histoire** ▶ to make a fuss : *Jessie did fuss when she had to go to the doctor to get a shot.* **Note.** A person who fusses or is hard to please is fussy: *My dog is a fussy eater.* SYN: worry, bother, fret.

fu·tile [FYOO-tul or FYOO-tile] ADJECTIVE. **futile, vain (vaine)** ▶ having no effect; not successful : *I spent the afternoon in a futile search for my book.* ■ **futilely,** ADVERB. ▶ **futilement.** ■ **futility,** NOUN. ▶ **futilité.**

fu·ture [FYOO-chur] NOUN, futures. **1. avenir** ▶ the time that is yet to come : *They're planning a sequel to that movie in the near future.* **2. avenir** ▶ a chance of success : *"We are very hopeful and the future looks promising."* (Marilyn Halvorson) **3. futur** ▶ in grammar, a verb that shows action in the time to come. ▲ ADJECTIVE. **futur (-ure)** ▶ happening in the future : *If it gets too dark, we'll finish the game at some future date.* 📖 **p. 1078.**

fuzz·y [FUZ-ee] ADJECTIVE. fuzzier, fuzziest. **1. crépu (-ue), crêpelé (-ée), moutonné (-ée)** ▶ like or covered with loose fibres or hair : *a fuzzy caterpillar.* **2. flou (floue), confus (-use)** ▶ not clear; blurred; hazy : *We can't get that station very well; the picture is always fuzzy.*

galley

g, G [jee] NOUN, g's, G's. **g, G** ▶ the seventh letter of the English alphabet.

gadg·et [GAJ-it] NOUN, gadgets. **gadget, machin, truc** ▶ a name for any small tool or machine : *Dad is always buying the latest gadgets for the kitchen, such as an electric knife sharpener and a juice maker.* SYN : device, tool, utensil.

gag [gag] NOUN, gags. **1. bâillon** ▶ something such as a scarf put in or across the mouth to stop a person from talking or crying out. **2. farce, blague, plaisanterie** ▶ a joke : *The comedian told a gag about a three-legged horse that ran in triangles.* ▲ VERB, gagged, gagging. **1. bâillonner, museler** ▶ to stop someone from talking or crying out by using a gag. **2. étouffer, suffoquer, avoir un haut-le-cœur** ▶ to not be able to swallow ; choke : *She gagged on a piece of popcorn.* SYN : choke, muffle, silence, restrain, strangle.

gain [gane] VERB, gained, gaining. **1. gagner, obtenir, acquérir** ▶ to come to have ; get or win, especially by some effort : *to gain control of oneself.* **2. prendre** ▶ to get as an increase or addition : *The baby gained a lot of weight last month.* ▲ NOUN, gains. **1. profit, bénéfice, gain** ▶ something that is gained. **2. (also gains) profit, bénéfice, augmentation, gain** ▶ an increase in value ; profit : *If a house sells for more than it cost to buy, there is a gain on the sale.*

gain on rattraper ▶ to catch up to ; get closer : *The red car was gaining on the others in the race.*

gait [gate] NOUN, gaits. **démarche** ▶ a way of stepping, walking, or running : *A horse's fastest gait is a gallop.*

gal·ax·y [GAL-uk-see] NOUN, galaxies. **galaxie** ▶ a group of many millions of stars. There are millions of different galaxies in the universe. The earth, sun, and other planets in our solar system are part of the Milky Way galaxy.

gale [gale] NOUN, gales. **1. rafale, grand vent, bourrasque** ▶ in weather reports, a wind that blows with a speed of 50–90 km/hr. **2. rafale, coup de vent, grand vent, bourrasque** ▶ any

very strong wind : *They could hear the roar of the gale and the smashing of waves against the boat.* **3. éclat** ▶ a sudden noise that is like a strong wind : *gales of laughter.* SYN : wind, windstorm, squall, cyclone, tempest.

gall bladder NOUN. **vésicule biliaire** ▶ a small organ in the body near the liver. It holds a liquid known as gall or bile that helps to digest food.

gal·ler·y [GAL-uh-ree] NOUN, galleries. **1. galerie d'art, musée** ▶ a room or building where works of art are shown or sold. **2. dernier balcon, poulailler** ▶ the highest balcony of a theatre, church, or other such building.

gal·ley [GAL-ee] NOUN, galleys. **1. galère** ▶ a long, low ship with sails and oars, used in early times. **2. aire de travail** ▶ the kitchen on a ship or an airplane.

galley

gal·lon [GAL-un] NOUN, gallons. **gallon** ▶ a unit of measure for liquids. An imperial gallon equals 4.55 litres.

gal·lop [GAL-up] NOUN, gallops. **galop** ▶ the fastest way of running for a horse or other four-footed animal. During a gallop, all four feet come off the ground at once. ▲ VERB, galloped, galloping. **galoper** ▶ to move or ride at a gallop.

gam·ble [GAM-bul] VERB, gambled, gambling. **1. jouer, miser, spéculer, risquer** ▶ to try to win money on the outcome of some game or other event whose result cannot be known ahead of time. **Note.** This is known as **gambling.** **Note.** A person who gambles is a **gambler.** **2. compter sur, miser sur** ▶ to take a chance on any future event that is uncertain : *Kate didn't* *study the lesson and gambled that the teacher wouldn't call on her.* SYN: risk, bet, speculate, try one's luck.

game [game] NOUN, games. **1. jeu ▶** something that is done to have fun or as a way of playing : *a game of tag.* **2. partie, match ▶** a way of playing in which there are certain rules and one side tries to win; a sport or contest : *a baseball game; a card game.* **3. gibier ▶** wild animals, birds, or fish hunted or caught for sport or food. ▲ ADJECTIVE, **gamer, gamest. 1. courageux (-euse), brave, décidé (-ée), déterminé (-ée) ▶** full of spirit and courage; brave : *a game boxer.* **2. prêt (prête), consentant (-ante) ▶** ready; willing : *Who's game for a swim?* SYN: sport, match, contest, fun, amusement. ⌷ **p. 1164.**

gan·der [GAN-dur] NOUN, ganders. **jars ▶** a full-grown male goose.

gang [gang] NOUN, gangs. **1. bande, gang, clan, troupe ▶** a number of people who act together to do something that is against the law; a group of criminals : *Jesse James led a gang of train robbers in the 1870s.* **2. bande, gang, clan ▶** a group of young people from one area who form a group under a certain name. Gang members often commit minor crimes and fight with other gangs. **3. équipe ▶** any group of people who work or act together : *A road gang repaired the holes in the highway.* ▲ VERB, ganged, ganging. (usually used with **up**) **faire équipe contre, se mobiliser contre ▶** to act against as a group : *Tim and Jeff often gang up on their little sister.* SYN: band, crowd, pack, group, mob, bunch.

gang·ster [GANG-stur] NOUN, gangsters. **bandit, gangster, malfaiteur (-euse), voleur (-euse) ▶** a member of a gang of criminals; mobster : *Al Capone was a famous gangster.*

gap [gap] NOUN, gaps. **1. brèche, trouée, vide, ouverture ▶** an open space; an opening or break : *a gap in a fence; a gap between a person's front teeth.* **2. trouée, brèche ▶** an opening or pass between mountains. **3. trou, vide, lacune ▶** a blank or empty space : *gaps in a person's memory.* **4. écart ▶** a big difference in character, ideas, or opinions : *a generation gap.* SYN: opening, break, pass, crevice, hole, space.

ga·rage [guh-RAZH *or* guh-RAJ *or* guh-ROZH *or* guh-ROJ] NOUN, garages. **1. garage ▶** a building or part of a building used for parking a car. **2. garage ▶** a place or business for repairing cars. **Note.** A garage sale is a sale of personal belongings such as old furniture, toys, and clothes, often held in or in front of a garage. ⌷ **p. 1069.**

gar·bage [GAR-bij] NOUN. **1. ordure, déchet, détritus ▶** waste food and other unwanted things that are thrown away from a kitchen. **2. rebut, déchet ▶** any worthless material. SYN: waste, trash, rubbish, litter, refuse, debris.

gar·den [GARD-un] NOUN, gardens. **jardin, potager ▶** a small area of land where vegetables or flowers are grown. ▲ VERB, gardened, gardening. **jardiner ▶** to work in a garden. **Note.** A person who takes care of a lawn or garden is a gardener. ⌷ **p. 1050.**

gar·gle [GAR-gul] VERB, gargled, gargling. **se gargariser ▶** to rinse the inside of the mouth and throat with liquid : *The doctor said I should gargle with warm salt water to help my sore throat.*

gar·goyle [GAR-goyl] NOUN, gargoyles. **gargouille ▶** an ugly or scary stone figure, part human and part animal. Many churches and buildings from the Middle Ages had gargoyles on the edge of their roofs.

gar·lic [GAR-lik] NOUN. **ail (ails) ▶** a plant that looks like a small onion. The bulb of a garlic plant has a very strong smell and taste and is used for flavour in cooking. **Note.** Garlic is a member of the lily family.

gar·ment [GAR-munt] NOUN, garments. **vêtement ▶** any piece of clothing.

gar·nish [GAR-nish] NOUN, garnishes. **garniture ▶** something put on or around food to make it look more attractive. Radishes, parsley, and lemon slices are often used as garnishes. ▲ VERB, garnished, garnishing. **garnir, orner, décorer ▶** to decorate foods with a garnish. SYN: decorate, trim, dress up, adorn, embellish.

garter snake **couleuvre ▶** a brown or green snake with yellow stripes. Garter snakes live in North America and are harmless to humans.

gas [gas] NOUN, gases *or* gasses. **1. gaz ▶** one of the three basic forms of matter, along with a liquid and a solid. A gas does not have a shape and does not occupy a fixed space. Air itself is a gas, and it is made up of other gases such as hydrogen and oxygen. **2. gaz ▶** a gas or mixture of gases burned for cooking or heating. **3. essence ▶** short for gasoline. **Note.** Something in the form of a gas is gaseous.

gas·o·line [GAS-uh-LEEN] NOUN. **essence ▶** a liquid fuel that burns easily, made from petroleum. Gasoline is used to run cars, trucks, airplanes, boats, lawn mowers, and many other vehicles.

gasp [gasp] VERB, gasped, gasping. **haleter, suffoquer, chercher sa respiration ▶** to breathe in air suddenly or with difficulty : *They gasped in fright at the sight of a shadow moving outside.* SYN: pant, puff, choke, gulp.

gate [gate] NOUN, gates. **porte, portillon ▶** a part of a fence that opens and closes like a door.

gath·er [GATH-ur] VERB, gathered, gathering. **1. rassembler, réunir, grouper ▶** to bring or come together : *The whole family gathered together for my grandmother's birthday.* **2. ramasser, cueillir, recueillir ▶** to pick up or collect : *"And above all,*

243

🖋 Word Builder

Gather, collect, and **assemble** all mean to bring things together in a group. **Gather** means to bring things that have been scattered over an area into one place: *They gathered lilies from the side of the road.* **Collect** often means there is some judgment in the selection process: *Gregor collects stamps from Asian countries.* **Assemble** is used when people are brought together for a purpose: *The students assembled in the gym for the awards ceremony.*

provisions had to be gathered for the great feast." (Aliki) **3. déduire, conclure ▶** to put together in the mind : *Since you're packing a bag, I gather that you're going on a trip.* **4. froncer, plisser ▶** to bring together in folds : *The dress was gathered at the waist* 🖉 **p. 244.**

gath·er·ing [GATH-uh-ring] NOUN, **gatherings. rassemblement, réunion, assemblée ▶** the act or fact of bringing or coming together : *We played games at the family gathering.*

gave VERB. **donner ▶** a past form of give.

gauge [gayj] NOUN, **gauges.** (also **gage**) **1. jauge, indicateur ▶** an instrument for measuring the amount or size of something. Different types of gauges measure temperature, air or water pressure, and the level of water or other liquids. **2. calibre, jauge, écartement ▶** a standard measure for certain manufactured objects. There are gauges for the thickness of a wire and for the distance between two railway tracks. ▲ VERB, **gauged, gauging. 1. mesurer, jauger, calibrer ▶** to measure something by means of a gauge. **2. jauger, mesurer, évaluer ▶** to judge or estimate something, as if by using a gauge : *to gauge a person's character; to gauge how long it will take to get somewhere.*

gaze [gaze] VERB, **gazed, gazing. fixer, regarder, contempler ▶** to look at something steadily for a long time, without looking away ; stare : *We gazed at the stars in the sky.* SYN: stare, watch, observe, look, peer.

gear [geer] NOUN, **gears. 1. engrenage ▶** a wheel having teeth that fit into the teeth of another wheel. Gears are used to allow motion to be passed from one part of a machine to another, so as to control speed, power, or direction. **2. engrenage ▶** an arrangement of such wheels. **3. train ▶** a group of connected parts in a machine that have a certain purpose : *the landing gear of an airplane.* **4. équipement, matériel, attirail ▶** the equipment needed for a certain activity : *mountain-climbing gear.* ▲ VERB, **geared, gearing. adapter, préparer ▶** to fit to a certain purpose ; make suitable : *That computer program is geared to business rather than home use.*

geese [gees] NOUN. **oies ▶** the plural of goose.

gem [jem] NOUN, **gems. 1. pierre précieuse, gemme ▶** a valuable stone that has been cut and polished ; a jewel : *Diamonds and emeralds*

are gems. **2. bijou (-oux), perle, merveille ▶** a person or thing that is very special or valuable, like a gem : *The boss says that her new assistant is a real gem.*

gene [jeen] NOUN, **genes. chromosomes. gène ▶** Genes determine what colour a person's eyes and hair will be and influence other qualities such as height and weight.

gen·er·al [JEN-ur-ul] NOUN, **generals. 1. général (-aux) ▶** an officer of the highest rank in either the Moblie Command or the Air Command of the armed forces. ▲ ADJECTIVE. **1. général (-ale, -aux) ▶** having to do with everyone or with the whole ; not limited : *That beach is open only to people who live in this town, and not to the general public.* **2. général (-ale, -aux) ▶** not giving details ; not specific or exact : *I'm not a mechanic, but I've got a general idea how a car engine works.*

in general en général ▶ as a rule ; usually ; generally : *In general, mammals live on land.* SYN: common, widespread, broad, usual, normal.

gen·er·al·ize [JEN-ruh-lɪz or JEN-uh-ruh-lʌz] VERB, **generalized, generalizing. 1. généraliser ▶** to form a general rule or conclusion. **2. généraliser ▶** to state an idea that is too broad or too general : *Just because you've had trouble with your car, don't generalize and say that all cars of that model are badly made.* **Note.** The act of generalizing is a generalization.

gear

gen·er·al·ly [JEN-uh-ruh-lee or JEN-ruh-lee] ADVERB. **1. généralement, habituellement, en général, ordinairement ▶** as a rule ; in most cases ; usually : *I generally have a sandwich or a salad for lunch.* **2. généralement, habituellement, en général, ordinairement ▶** among most people ; widely ; commonly : *It's not generally known that the mayor's husband was once a reporter.*

gen·er·ate [JEN-uh-RATE] VERB, generated, gee-rating. **produire, générer, provoquer, engendrer ▸** to cause to be; bring about; produce : *That article in the school paper generated a lot of discussion.* SYN: bring about, make, produce, create.

gen·er·a·tion [JEN-uh-RAY-shun] NOUN, generations. **1. génération, postérité ▸** one step in the line of descent in a family : *Three generations of our family live together :me, my mom, and my grandfather.* **2. génération ▸** a group of people born in the same period of time : *my grandparents' generation.* **3. génération ▸** a period of about 30 years, or roughly the time from the birth of one generation of a family to the next. **4. production ▸** the act of generating : *The force of a waterfall can be used for the generation of electric power.*

gen·er·a·tor [JEN-uh-RAY-tur] NOUN, generators. **génératrice, groupe électrogène ▸** a machine that produces electricity from other forms of energy, such as by burning fuel.

✎ Writing Tips

Geographical Names

Geographical names include the names of continents, countries, islands, mountains, provinces, territories, cities, towns, and streets. These words should be capitalized. For example :

continents	*Africa*
countries	*Canada*
islands	*the West Indies*
mountains	*the Rocky Mountains*
territories	*the Northwest Territories*
provinces	*Newfoundland*
regions	*Wentworth Region*
cities	*Saskatoon*
towns	*Woodbridge*
streets	*Queen Street*

• Words such as city, island, river, street, and park are capitalized only when they are part of a name.

Quebec City
I took a trip to the big city.

• Words such as north, south, east, and west are not capitalized when they indicate direction.

capitals	*no capitals*
the wild West	*north of Toronto*
down East	*a south wind*
a Northerner	*northern Quebec*

---

gen·er·ous [JEN-uh-rus] ADJECTIVE. **1. généreux (-euse), charitable, prodigue ▸** willing and happy to give to others; not selfish : *He is a kind and generous person, always willing to help others.* **2. généreux (-euse), copieux (-ieuse), abondant (-ante) ▸** large in amount : *Lou took a generous helping of the birthday cake.* **■ generously,** ADVERB. **▸ généreusement. ■ generosity,** NOUN. **▸ générosité, bonté, charité, altruisme.** SYN: kind, big-hearted, charitable, liberal.

gen·ius [JEEN-yus] NOUN, geniuses. **1. génie ▸** a person with an outstanding intelligence; someone who is able to produce great thoughts or lasting works of art or science. **2. génie, talent, don ▸** the mental ability that such a person has : *Shakespeare's plays and Einstein's scientific theories are works of genius.* **3. génie ▸** any person who is thought of as very intelligent or as highly skilled at some mental activity : *a genius at writing advertising copy.*

gen·re [ZHON-ruh] NOUN, genres. **genre ▸** style, kind, or sort, especially in works of literature, art, and so on : *The novel is a literary genre.*

gen·tle [JENT-ul] ADJECTIVE. **1. doux (douce), aimable, gentil (-ille) ▸** not hard, rough, or wild : *a gentle horse that is easy to ride; to give a person a gentle tap on the arm.* **2. doux (douce), léger (-ère) ▸** not having great force; soft, low, or mild : *"And if you feel a gentle ruin on your face, you'll know that Weaving Maid is crying for joy."* (Julie Lawson) **■ gently,** ADVERB. **doucement, gentiment ▸** in a gentle way. SYN: soft, tender, bland, moderate, mild.

gen·tle·man [JENT-ul-mun] NOUN, gentlemen. **1. gentilhomme ▸** in former times, a man born into a good family and having a high social position : *He has such fine clothes and such good manners; he must be a gentleman.* **2. gentilhomme ▸** a man who is honourable and treats others well. **3. monsieur (messieurs) ▸** a polite way to refer to any man : *"Ladies and gentlemen—may I have your attention, please."*

gen·u·ine [JEN-yoo-in] ADJECTIVE. **1. véritable, authentique, réel (-elle) ▸** not false; real : *a genuine diamond.* **2. sincère, franc (franche), honnête ▸** not pretended; honest; sincere : *April made a genuine effort to help me.* **■ genuinely,** ADVERB **▸ vraiment, sincèrement, franchement, véritablement.** *From his warm welcome, I knew he was genuinely glad to see me.* SYN: real, true, honest, pure, authentic, sincere.

ge·og·ra·phy [jee-OG-ruh-fee] NOUN. **géographie ▸** the study of the natural features of the earth, such as mountains, deserts, and bodies of water; natural events such as plant and animal life and climate; and human features of the earth, such as the cities and countries people live in and the resources and products they use. **■ geographic** or **geographical,** ADJECTIVE.

▶ **géographique.** Note. An expert in geography is a geographer. ✏ p. 245.

ge·ol·o·gy [jee-OL-uh-jee] NOUN. **géologie** ▶ the scientific study of the rocks, soil, and other minerals that make up the earth's crust. Geology also includes the study of how these materials were formed, how they are arranged, and how they have changed throughout the history of the earth. ■ **geologic** or geological, ADJECTIVE. ▶ **géologique.** Note. An expert in geology is a geologist.

ge·om·et·ry [jee-OM-uh-tree] NOUN. **géométrie** ▶ the branch of mathematics that is concerned with the study of points, lines, angles, shapes, and solid figures. Geometry is used to determine the shape and size of an object or the distance between two points. ■ **geometric** or geometrical, ADJECTIVE. ▶ **géométrique.**

ger·bil [JUR-bul] NOUN, gerbils. **gerbille** ▶ a small furry animal like a mouse, with a long tail and long hind legs. Gerbils are often kept as pets.

germ [jurm] NOUN, germs. 1. **germe** ▶ any one of many types of tiny plants or animals that can be seen only through a microscope and that can cause disease. 2. **germe** ▶ the earliest form of a living thing, especially the part of a seed, nut, or bud that can sprout into a new plant : *wheat germ.* 3. **embryon, germe** ▶ the earliest form or beginning of something : *the germ of an idea.* ✏ p. 116, 249.

ges·ture [JES-chur] NOUN, gestures. 1. **geste, signe** ▶ a movement of the hand, head, or body to show what a person feels or thinks : *Waving one's hand is a gesture that can mean hello or goodbye.* 2. **geste, signe** ▶ some action that is done to show a certain feeling : *a gesture of friendship.* ▲ VERB, gestured, gesturing. **faire un geste, gesticuler** ▶ to make a gesture. 📖 p. 1028.

get [get] VERB, got, got or gotten, getting. 1. **avoir, obtenir, recevoir** ▶ to come to have for oneself : *to get a job; to get a birthday present.* 2. **avoir, obtenir, recevoir** ▶ to cause to be or to happen : *to get a haircut; to get ready for bed.* 3. **devenir, se faire** ▶ to be or become : *to get sick; to get mad about something.* 4. **aller, se rendre, arriver** ▶ to move or go to a place : *to get home late.* 5. **comprendre, saisir** ▶ to understand : *to get a story; to get the point of a story.* 6. **falloir, devoir** ▶ to have to or need to : *I've got to be home by ten.* ✏ p. 246. SYN: obtain, gain, earn, acquire, receive, bring.

gey·ser [GY-zur] NOUN, geysers. 1. **geyser** ▶ a spring that shoots hot water and steam into the air from time to time. 2. **geyser** ▶ anything that rises into the air like a geyser : *"A little geyser of dirt spouted out on either side."* (Jim Kjelgaard)

ghast·ly [GAST-lee] ADJECTIVE, ghastlier, ghastliest. **horrible, effrayant (-ante), affreux (-euse),**

Get/got/gotten

• *Get* is a common verb with many meanings—to obtain, to become, to understand, to reach, to catch, to persuade. It is also used in many popular expressions, such as get going, get lost, get ahead.

• *Got* and *gotten* are past-tense forms of *get*. When referring to something that has been obtained, either form is correct; *gotten* is more common in North America.

   Karac had gotten us tickets to the circus.

   Karac had got us tickets to the circus.

For simple possession, *got* is always used :

   I got $10 for baby-sitting last night.

• When revising your work, check how often you use these words. Think about replacing some of them with another verb that says what you mean more clearly. For example :

   I've **gotten** them to change their minds.

can be changed to

   I've **persuaded** them to change their minds.

épouvantable ▶ causing great fear; horrible; terrible; shocking : *That was a ghastly accident.*

ghost [gohst] NOUN, ghosts. 1. **fantôme, revenant, spectre** ▶ the spirit of a dead person as it supposedly appears to living people, usually thought of as a pale or shadowy form like a human figure. 2. **fantôme, revenant, spectre** ▶ something very dim or faint, like a ghost : *The woman was covered in mist and looked like a ghost.* 3. **écrivain fantôme, écrivain anonyme** ▶ short for ghostwriter, a person who writes a book for someone else without taking credit as the author. ■ **ghostly,** ADJECTIVE, ghostlier, ghostliest. **fantomatique, spectral (-ale, -aux)** ▶ like a ghost : *A ghostly shape moved past the window of the deserted house.* 📖 p. 968.

gi·ant [JY-unt] NOUN, giants. 1. **géant (-ante)** ▶ a creature that is much larger than an ordinary person. Giants often appear in Greek myths and in folk tales like "Jack and the Beanstalk." 2. **géant (-ante), colosse** ▶ a person who is much taller and heavier than usual : *Wilt Chamberlain was a giant among pro basketball players at roughly 2.2 metres and nearly 135 kilos.* 3. **géant (géante)** ▶ any person or thing having great power or influence : *That company is a giant in the computer industry.* ▲ ADJECTIVE.

prairie (Canada) ▽
► prairie (Canada)

savanna (Kenya) △
► savane (Kenya)

mixed forest (Canada) △
► forêt mixte (Canada)

tundra (Canada) ▽
► toundra (Canada)

tropical forest (Australia) △
► forêt tropicale (Australie)

boreal forest (Canada) △
► taïga (Canada)

steppe (Mongolia) △
► steppe (Mongolie)

desert (Morocco) ▷
► désert (Maroc)

P OLLINATION

by insects
▶ par les insectes

by humans
▶ par les humains

by the water
▶ par l'eau

by the wind
▶ par le vent

by animals
▶ par les animaux

248

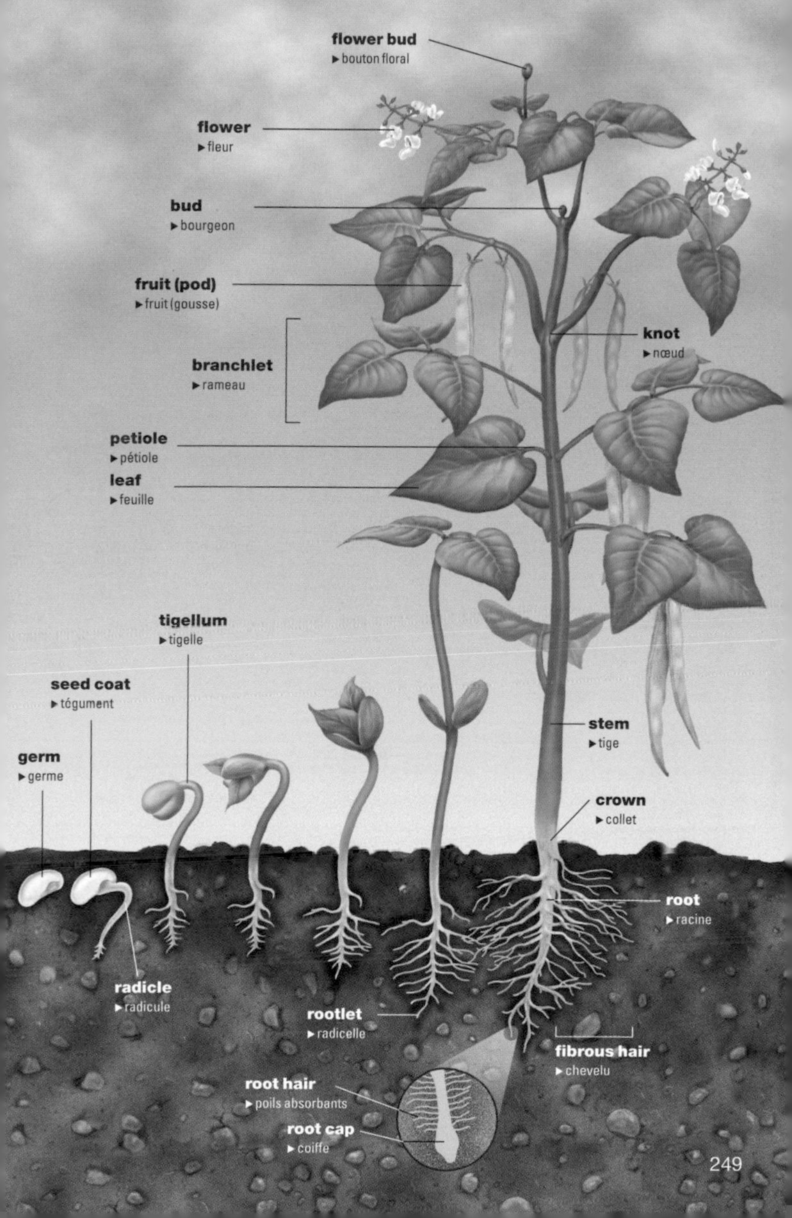

flower bud
▶ bouton floral

flower
▶ fleur

bud
▶ bourgeon

fruit (pod)
▶ fruit (gousse)

knot
▶ nœud

branchlet
▶ rameau

petiole
▶ pétiole

leaf
▶ feuille

tigellum
▶ tigelle

seed coat
▶ tógument

stem
▶ tige

germ
▶ germe

crown
▶ collet

root
▶ racine

radicle
▶ radicule

rootlet
▶ radicelle

fibrous hair
▶ chevelu

root hair
▶ poils absorbants

root cap
▶ coiffe

249

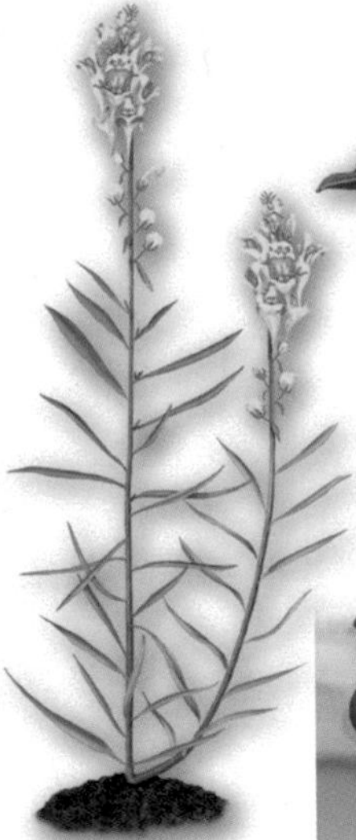

purple trillium
▶ trille rouge

daisy
▶ marguerite

water lily
▶ nénuphar

toadflax
▶ linaire vulgaire

red clover
▶ trèfle rouge

kelp; seaweed
▶ laminaire

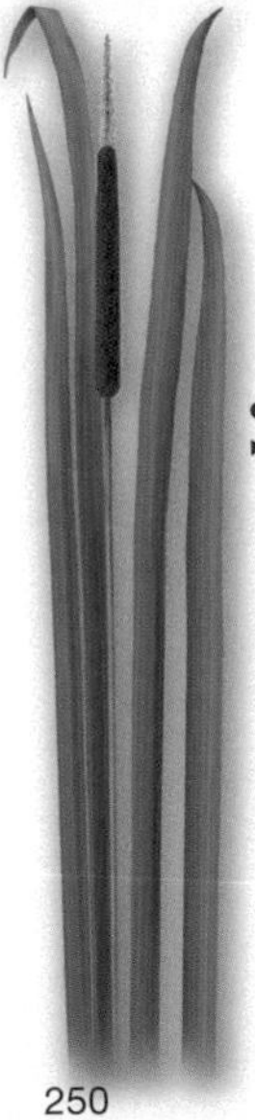

cattail
▶ quenouille

fern
▶ fougère

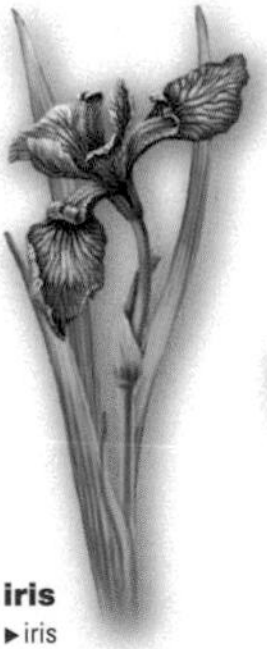

iris
▶ iris

yellow buttercup
▶ bouton d'or

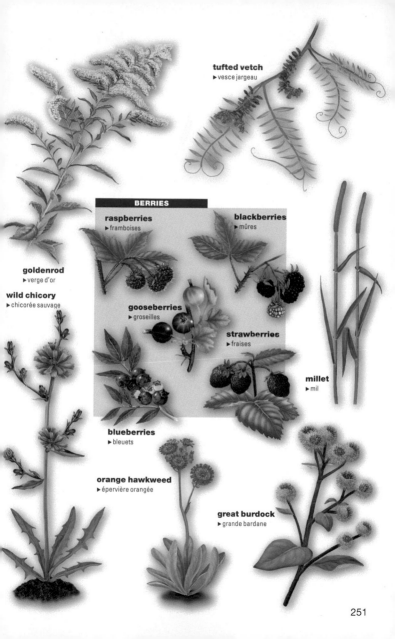

tufted vetch
▶ vesce jargeau

BERRIES

raspberries
▶ framboises

blackberries
▶ mûres

goldenrod
▶ verge d'or

wild chicory
▶ chicorée sauvage

gooseberries
▶ groseilles

strawberries
▶ fraises

millet
▶ mil

blueberries
▶ bleuets

orange hawkweed
▶ épervière orangée

great burdock
▶ grande bardane

251

MUSHROOMS

hedgehogs △
▶ hydnes (hydne ombiliqué)

gilled △
▶ à lames (pleurote en huître)

morels △
▶ morilles (morille conique)

clavaria ▽
▶ clavaires (clavaire de Zollinger)

chanterelle ▽
▶ chanterelles (chanterelle commune)

cross section of a gilled mushroom
▶ coupe d'un champignon à lames

cap
▶ chapeau

gills
▶ lames

partial veil
▶ voile partiel (anneau)

stipe
▶ pied

universal veil
▶ voile général (volve)

gilled △
▶ à lames (lactaire indigo)

puffballs ▽
▶ vesses-de-loup (vesse-de-loup perlée)

boletes △
▶ bolets (bolet comestible)

gilled shaggy mane △
▶ à lames (coprin chevelu)

polypores ▽
▶ polypores (polypore écailleux)

All of the musrooms illustrated are found in Quebec and are edible

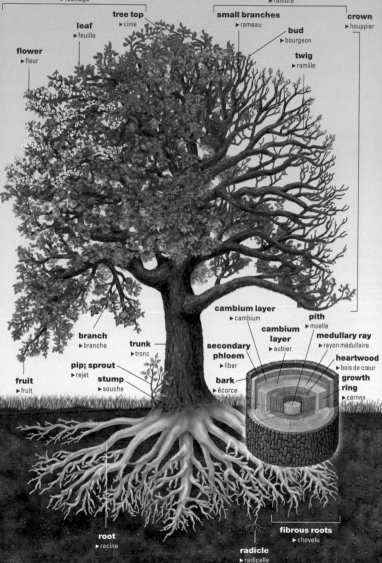

S STRUCTURE OF A TREE

foliage
▶feuillage

boughs
▶ramure

tree top
▶cime

small branches
▶rameau

crown
▶houppier

leaf
▶feuille

bud
▶bourgeon

flower
▶fleur

twig
▶ramille

cambium layer
▶cambium

pith
▶moelle

cambium layer
▶aubier

medullary ray
▶rayon médullaire

branch
▶branche

trunk
▶tronc

secondary phloem
▶liber

heartwood
▶bois de cœur

pip; sprout
▶rejet

bark
▶écorce

growth ring
▶cernes

fruit
▶fruit

stump
▶souche

fibrous roots
▶chevelu

root
▶racine

radicle
▶radicelle

253

H ARDWOOD TREES

maple ▷
▸érable

weeping willow ▷
▸saule pleureur

◁ **American elm**
▸orme d'Amérique

◁ **Lombardy poplar**
▸peuplier de Lombardie

linden ▷
▸tilleul

black walnut ▷
▸noyer noir

◁ **white birch**
▸bouleau à papier

◁ **red oak** ▸chêne rouge

C ONIFEROUS TREES

◁ **spruce**
▶ épinette

larch ▷
▶ mélèze

◁ **balsam fir**
▶ sapin baumier

black pine ▷
▶ pin noir

◁ **northern white cedar**
▶ thuya de l'Est (cèdre)

F RUIT TREES

bird cherry tree
▶ cerisier à grappes

crabapple
▶ pommetier

plum tree
▶ prunier

255

MAKING PAPER

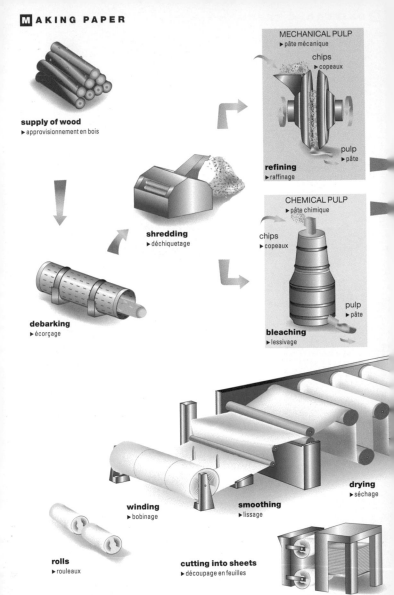

supply of wood
▶ approvisionnement en bois

debarking
▶ écorçage

shredding
▶ déchiquetage

MECHANICAL PULP
▶ pâte mécanique

chips
▶ copeaux

pulp
▶ pâte

refining
▶ raffinage

CHEMICAL PULP
▶ pâte chimique

chips
▶ copeaux

pulp
▶ pâte

bleaching
▶ lessivage

drying
▶ séchage

winding
▶ bobinage

smoothing
▶ lissage

rolls
▶ rouleaux

cutting into sheets
▶ découpage en feuilles

chips
▶ copeaux

bleaching ▷
▶ blanchiment

bleaching
▶ blanchiment

cleaning
▶ épuration de la pâte

mixing
▶ mélange

recovery of used paper
▶ récupération de vieux papiers

headbox
▶ caisse d'arrivée

pressing
▶ pressage

shaping table
▶ table de formation

fourdrinier machine ▽
▶ machine à papier à table plate

reams of paper
▶ rames de papier

257

R ECYCLING

cardboard
▶ papier, carton

glass, tires
▶ verre, pneus

plastic
▶ plastique

refillable bottle
▶ bouteille réutilisable

textile
▶ textile

glass and tires used to manufacture paving materials
▶ verre et pneus entrent dans la fabrication du revêtement routier

sorting centre
▶ centre de tri

recycling bin and container
▶ bac et cabanon de récupération

recycling truck
▶ benne à recyclage

258

biodegradable material
▶ matières biodégradables

compost
▶ compost

metal, dangerous materials
▶ métal, matières dangereuses

materials that cannot be recycled
▶ matières non récupérables

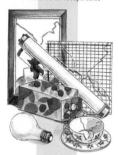

landfill
▶ décharge contrôlée

Legend

recyclable

recycled

recycling bin for biodegradable materials
▶ bac de récupération des matières biodégradables

Deposit Centres

• for metal
• for dangerous materials such as oils, paints and batteries

garbage truck
▶ benne à ordures

259

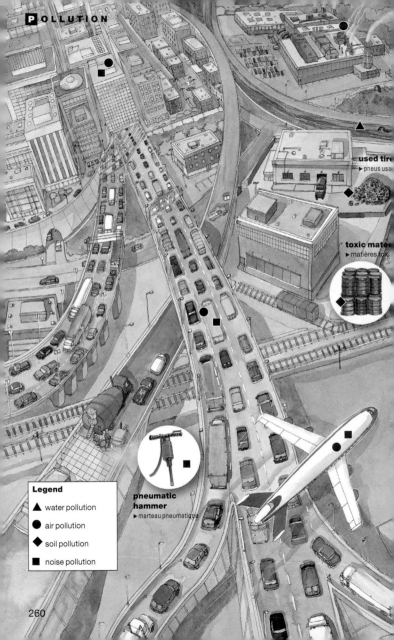

P OLLUTION

used tire
► pneus usa

toxic mate
► matières toxi

pneumatic
hammer
► marteau pneumatique

Legend

▲ water pollution

● air pollution

◆ soil pollution

■ noise pollution

manure pit
▸ fosse à purin

pesticides
▸ pesticides

septic tank
▸ fosse septique

chemical fertilizer spreader
▸ épandeur d'engrais chimique

nuclear waste
▸ déchets nucléaires

dump
▸ dépotoir

261

MAPLE SYRUP PRODUCTION

old-fashioned process for collecting and processing sap
▶ procédé révolu pour la cueillette et la transformation

traditional sugarhouse ▽
▶ cabane à sucre traditionnelle

temperature for manufacturing maple products ▽
▶ température de fabrication des produits de l'é

°C

125	granulated sugar
120	very hard sugar
	hard sugar
115	maple taffy or soft sugar ●
110	maple taffy on snow
105	maple butter ●
	temperature for cooking syrup
100	temperature at which water boils

traditional method for collecting sap: bucket and spout
▶ méthode de cueillette traditionnelle : seau et chalumeau

Modern sap collection method: conduit system ▽
▶ méthode de cueillette moderne : le réseau de tubulures

modern sugarhouse △
▶ cabane à sucre moderne

262

géant (géante) ▶ being a giant; very large : *"The trees stood still as giant statues."* (Jane Yolen)

gift [gift] NOUN, gifts. **1. cadeau (-eaux), présent, don** ▶ something that is given : *a birthday gift.* **2. don, talent, avantage naturel** ▶ a special talent that a person has : *Rick has a gift for languages and learns to speak them easily.* ■ **gifted,** ADJECTIVE. **doué (-ée), talentueux (-euse)** ▶ having a special talent : *Paula is a gifted pianist.* SYN: present, donation, offering, favour.

gi-gan-tic [jy-GAN-tik] ADJECTIVE. **gigantesque, géant (géante), monumental (-ale, -aux)** ▶ like a giant; very large; huge : *"The old man continued to grow a huge garden, an enormous garden, a gigantic garden."* (Sheryl McFarlane) SYN: huge, immense, massive, great, enormous.

gig-gle [GIG-ul] VERB, giggled, giggling. **pouffer, éclater de rire** ▶ to laugh in an excited or silly way, especially in a high voice. ▲ NOUN, giggles. **rire étouffé, gloussement** ▶ such a laugh.

gill [gil] NOUN, gills. **ouïes** ▶ the body part that fish and many other water animals use for breathing. Gills take in oxygen from the water.

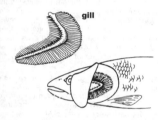

gill

gim-mick [GIM-ik] NOUN, gimmicks. *Informal.* **truc, trouvaille, combine, astuce** ▶ a clever way to attract attention : *The company is looking for a gimmick to help sell a new movie.*

gin-ger [JIN-jur] NOUN, gingers. **gingembre** ▶ a spice with a strong, sharp taste, used in food and medicine. Ginger comes from the root of a tropical plant. **Note.** Gingerbread is a cookie or cake flavoured with ginger.

gi-raffe [juh-RAF] NOUN, giraffes. **girafe** ▶ a large African mammal with long legs, a very long neck, and a light-coloured coat with brown patches. Giraffes are the tallest living animals and can grow up to 5.5 metres or more.

girl [gurl] NOUN, girls. **fille, petite fille, jeune fille** ▶ a female child who is not yet a woman or an adult.

give [giv] VERB, gave, given, giving. **1. donner, offrir** ▶ to take something that one has and pass it to another person as a present : *I gave Lois a book for her birthday.* **2. donner, payer, offrir** ▶ to hand over or let have : *I'll give you*

two dollars for that picture. **3. donner, rendre, rapporter** ▶ to provide or supply : *a cow that gives a lot of milk.* **4. donner, occasionner, accorder** ▶ to cause to have or to happen : *The car's been giving us trouble lately.* **5. faire, donner, présenter, pousser** ▶ to perform or put on : *to give a speech; to give a party.* **6. céder, se dérober, s'effondrer, casser** ▶ to move or bend under pressure : *The door gave slightly as he leaned against it.* ■ **given,** ADJECTIVE: ▶ **donné (-ée), déterminé (-ée).** *You must finish the test in the given time.* SYN: present, donate, offer, award, supply, grant. ✐ **p. 264.**

gla-cier [GLAY-shur] NOUN, glaciers. **glacier** ▶ a huge mass of ice that moves very slowly down a mountain or over land. A glacier is formed over a long period of time from snow that has not melted. At one time, glaciers covered much of North America and Europe. ■ **glacial,** ADJECTIVE. **1. glaciaire** ▶ of or like a glacier : *Glacial deposits of clay and sand can form hills or ridges.* **2. glacial (-ale, -als)** ▶ very cold; icy : *Her attitude was glacial; she did not speak or look at him.*

glad [glad] ADJECTIVE, gladder, gladdest. **content (-ente), heureux (-euse), joyeux (-euse)** ▶ feeling good about something; pleased, happy : *Jen was glad to be home again.* ■ **gladly,** ADVERB: ▶ **avec joie, avec plaisir, volontiers.** *I'll gladly give you a hand with the yardwork.* ■ **gladness,** NOUN. ▶ **joie, contentement.** SYN: happy, delighted, merry, joyful, cheerful.

giraffes

baby giraffe

glam-our [GLAM-ur] NOUN. (also glamor) **séduction, fascination, prestige, éclat** ▶ a power of charm and beauty that can attract people : *The Eiffel Tower and sidewalk cafés add to the glamour of Paris.* ■ **glamorous,** ADJECTIVE: **séduisant (-ante), fascinant (-ante), prestigieux**

🖋 Word Builder

*The verb **give** is found in many phrases, such as **give and take**, which means to exchange evenly or fairly: A true compromise requires give and take. To **give in** can mean to stop fighting and admit defeat: Stella gave in to her friends' pleas and went to the movie. Or, **to give up** can mean to hand over, surrender, or stop doing: I won't give up until I finish the race.*

(-euse), éclatant (-ante) ▸ having glamour : *Old movies often featured glamorous stars such as Audrey Hepburn.*

glance [glance] VERB, glanced, glancing. **1.** jeter un coup d'œil, lancer un regard ▸ to look at something quickly : *They glanced at me but not long enough for a good look.* **2.** ricocher, dévier ▸ to hit something at a slant and fly off to one side : *The rock glanced off the side of the tree.* ▲ NOUN, glances. regard, coup d'œil ▸ a quick look. SYN : look, glimpse, skim, peer, peek.

gland [gland] NOUN, glands. gland ▸ one of the organs that make one or more special substances that are used or released by the body. Glands produce such things as tears or sweat, juices that help the body digest food, and cells that help it fight disease germs. The liver, kidneys, and stomach are important glands.

glare [glair] NOUN, glares. **1.** éclat aveuglant, lumière éblouissante, éblouissement ▸ a strong, harsh light : *He was blinded by the glare of the sun on the snow.* **2.** regard furieux ▸ an angry look or stare : *"Little Kay stood before him with his fists on his hips and her face scrunched into a most ferocious glare."* (Robin Muller) ▲ VERB, glared, glaring. **1.** éblouir, aveugler, briller ▸ to shine with a strong, harsh light : *The metal door glared in the sunlight.* **2.** lancer un regard furieux ▸ to give an angry look or stare : *The two furious boys glared at each other.* SYN : shine, dazzle, glitter, glow, flash, beam.

glass [glas] NOUN, glasses. **1.** verre ▸ **2.** verre, vitre ▸ a container of glass or plastic that is used for drinking, or the contents of such a container : *Toba drank two glasses of orange juice at breakfast.* **3.** verre ▸ something made of glass, such as a mirror or telescope. **4.** glasses. (also eyeglasses) verre ▸ a pair of lenses made of glass or plastic, used to help people see better.

glaze [glaze] NOUN, glazes. **1.** vernis, lustre ▸ a thin, shiny coating over something : *The sidewalk was covered with a glaze of ice.* **2.** vernis, enduit vitrifié ▸ the material used to glaze. ▲ VERB, glazed, glazing. **1.** glacer, vernir, lustrer ▸ to put a thin coating on : *to glaze doughnuts.* **2.** vitrer ▸ to put glass in or on : *to glaze windows.* **3.** vitreux (-euse), éteint (-einte) ▸ of the eyes, to become glassy. ■ **glazed,** ADJECTIVE: vitré (-ée), glacé (-ée), verni (-ie), lustré (-ée) ▸ a glazed expression. SYN : polish, gloss, lustre, wax, coat, cover.

gleam [gleem] NOUN, gleams. lueur, rayon, reflet ▸ a bright flash or beam of light : *There was a brief gleam from the flashlight, and then the battery went dead.* ▲ VERB, gleamed, gleaming. briller, luire, reluire ▸ to shine brightly : *A light gleamed in the distance.* ■ **gleaming,** ADJECTIVE. ▸ luisant (-ante). *The cat had sharp, gleaming white teeth.* SYN : shine, glow, sparkle, beam, glitter, twinkle.

glee [glee] NOUN. réjouissance, jubilation ▸ great happiness or joy; delight : *The children laughed with glee at the clown.* ■ **gleeful,** ADJECTIVE. ▸ joyeux (-euse), réjouissant (-ante), jubilant (-ante). ■ **gleefully,** ADVERB. ▸ joyeusement.

glide [glide] VERB, glided, gliding. **1.** glisser, entrer/sortir avec grâce, entrer/sortir avec douceur ▸ to move smoothly and easily, with little effort : *The dancers glided gracefully around the floor.* **2.** planer ▸ of an aircraft, to travel through the air without using a motor or other form of power. **Note.** An aircraft that does this is called a glider. NOUN, glides. glissement, vol plané ▸ the act or fact of gliding. SYN : coast, slide, cruise, sail, move easily. ◉ **p. 392.**

glimpse [glimps] NOUN, glimpses. aperçu, voir un instant ▸ a short, quick look at something : *A crowd of people waited to catch a glimpse of the actor.* ▲ VERB, glimpsed, glimpsing. apercevoir, entrevoir ▸ to get a quick view; see for a moment : *He glimpsed someone waving as the car raced by.*

glis·ten [GLIS-un] VERB, glistened, glistening. briller, miroiter, scintiller, chatoyer ▸ to shine with a soft, reflected light; sparkle : *The sunlight glistened on the still water.*

glit·ter [GLIT-ur] VERB, glittered, glittering. briller, étinceler, scintiller, rutiler ▸ to shine with bright flashes; sparkle brightly : *Her bracelet was studded with stones that glittered in the sun.* ▲ NOUN. **1.** scintillement, éclat ▸ something that glitters or seems to glitter : *There was a glitter of tears in his eyes.* **2.** prestige, éclat ▸ an attractive or showy quality; glamour : *the glitter of Hollywood.* ■ **glittery or glittering,** ADJECTIVE. ▸ brillant (-ante), étincelant (-ante), scintillant (-ante). *glittering eyes.* SYN : sparkle, twinkle, glisten, shine, gleam.

globe [globe] NOUN, globes. **1.** globe, sphère, boule ▸ any object or shape that is round like a ball; sphere. **2.** terre, globe ▸ the earth : *an ocean liner that circles the globe.* **3.** globe terrestre ▸ a round model of the earth or the sky.

■ **global,** ADJECTIVE. global (-ale, -aux), entier (-ière), total (-ale, -aux) ▸ concerning the entire world : *Hunger is a global problem.* ■ **globally,** ADVERB. ▸ **globalement.**

gloom [gloom] NOUN. **1. obscurité, ténèbres, noirceur** ▸ dim light; darkness : *"Suddenly, out of the gloom, the Boat Deck of the ship came into view."* (Robert D. Ballard) **2. tristesse, mélancolie** ▸ low spirits; sadness : sorrow. ■ **gloomy,** ADJECTIVE, gloomier, gloomiest. **1. obscur (-ure), sombre, ténébreux (-euse)** ▸ partly or completely dark; dim : *It was a dark, gloomy night.* **2. triste, mélancolique, sombre** ▸ causing or full of sorrow or low spirits; sad : *After his friends left, he sat alone in gloomy silence.*

glo·ri·ous [GLOR-ee-us] ADJECTIVE. **1. glorieux (-euse), honorable** ▸ having or deserving great praise or glory : *a glorious accomplishment.* **2. magnifique, splendide** ▸ very beautiful or splendid; magnificent; grand : *The band members marched proudly in their glorious new uniforms.* ■ **gloriously,** ADVERB. ▸ **glorieusement.** SYN : wonderful, marvellous, splendid, superb.

glo·ry [GLOR-ee] NOUN, glories. **1. gloire, célébrité, popularité, prestige** ▸ great honour or praise that comes to a person for some success; great fame : *Abner Doubleday got the glory for inventing baseball, although it turned out later that he had had nothing to do with it.* **2. gloire, splendeur** ▸ great beauty or splendour : *They were stunned by the glory and size of the palace.* **3. gloire** ▸ a person or thing that brings great honour or pride : *Although she is very smart, her true glory is her good nature.* SYN : honour, fame, praise.

glos·sa·ry [GLOS-uh-ree] NOUN, glossaries. **glossaire, lexique** ▸ a list of difficult or special words with their meanings. A glossary appears at the end of a book or article to explain words used in the text. 📖 p. 265.

glos·sy [GLOS-ee] ADJECTIVE, glossier, glossiest. **brillant (-ante), luisant (-ante), lustré (-ée)** ▸ smooth and shiny : *The glossy yellow paint matched the satin that covered the chairs.*

glove [gluv] NOUN, gloves. **gant** ▸ a covering for the hand, especially one with a separate part for each finger : *winter gloves; a baseball glove.*

glow [gloh] NOUN, glows. **1. lueur, rougeoiement, éclat** ▸ a soft, steady light or shine : *the glow of candles; the glow of hot coals in a fireplace.* **2. éclat** ▸ a warm, bright colour of the skin. **3. rayonnement** ▸ a warm or happy feeling : *Jordy felt a warm glow when he hit the ball.* ▲ VERB, glowed, glowing. **1. luire, rougeoyer, s'embraser, rayonner** ▸ to give off a soft, steady light : *The light glowed in the darkness.* **2. être florissant (-ante) de santé** ▸ to have a shining, healthy colour : *Her cheeks glowed pink.*

3. rayonner, flamboyer ▸ to have or show a warm feeling : *As Sara received her diploma, her family glowed with pride.* SYN : shine, gleam, glint, twinkle, flame, glare.

glue [gloo] NOUN, glues. **colle, glu** ▸ any sticky substance used to hold or join things together. ▲ VERB, glued, gluing. **1. coller** ▸ to stick things together with glue : *He glued the broken pieces of the vase back together.* **2. coller** ▸ to fasten or hold tight, or to be so fastened, as if with glue : *Erica's eyes were glued to the TV set as she watched her favourite program.* SYN : fasten, bind, paste, stick together, cement.

gnat [nat] NOUN, gnats. **moucheron** ▸ a tiny biting insect having two wings. There are many kinds of gnats found in all parts of the world.

gnaw [nah] VERB, gnawed, gnawing. **1. ronger** ▸ to bite at and chew so as to wear away : *"The deer were so hungry they gnawed bark from the trees."* (Celia Godkin) **2. ronger, dévorer, miner** ▸ to cause pain or worry, as if by chewing : *Fear gnawed at his confidence.*

gnome [nome] NOUN, gnomes. **lutin, gnome, esprit** ▸ in old stories, a dwarf or other tiny creature who lives under the ground and guards treasures. **Note.** Gnome comes from an old word meaning "wise," because gnomes were thought to have a special knowledge of the earth.

gnu [noo or nyoo] NOUN, gnus or gnu. **gnou (gnous)** ▸ a large African antelope with curved horns, a tail like a horse, and a head and humped shoulders like a buffalo. **Note.** Also called a wildebeest.

go [goh] VERB, went, gone, going. **1. aller, se rendre** ▸ to move from one place to another; move along : *to go to Halifax.* **2. aller, faire** ▸ to take part in or do : *to go shopping.* **3. aller,**

🖊 **Writing Tips**

Glossary

A glossary is a list of special, technical, or difficult words found in a back section of a book or article. The words are listed alphabetically with definitions or comments.

- *A glossary is a good way to explain terms you have used that your readers might not know. Instead of interrupting your writing with a definition, you can include it in a glossary.*

- *A glossary entry may look like this :*
  fable: *a story meant to teach a lesson. Fables often focus on human weaknesses but use talking animals as characters instead of humans.*

mener ▶ to reach or extend : *Does this road go to town?* **4. devenir, se faire** ▶ to be in a state of ; become : *to go to sleep.* **5. aller, se mettre, se ranger** ▶ to have a place ; belong : *Those books go on the shelf.* **6. aller** ▶ to turn out ; happen : *How are things going with you?* **7. aller** ▶ to be suited ; fit : *That purple tie does not go with the orange shirt.*

goal [gole] NOUN, goals. **1. but, objectif** ▶ something that a person wants and tries for ; an aim or purpose : *Ruth worked hard to reach her goal of running 10 km.* **2. but** ▶ in games such as football, soccer, basketball, or hockey, a space that players get the ball or puck into or through in order to score. **3. but** ▶ a point earned by reaching the goal in such a game. **Note.** Goalkeeper, goaltender, and goalie are terms for the person who defends a goal in a sport. SYN : objective, aim, ambition, destination, end.

goat [gote] NOUN, goats. **chèvre** ▶ an animal with short horns and rough hair. Goats are related to sheep and are raised for their milk, meat, and hair. Wild goats usually live in mountain areas. **Note.** A goatherd is someone who looks after goats. **Note.** A scapegoat is a person who is blamed for something, often unfairly. ☞ p. 110.

gob·ble[1] [GOB-ul] VERB, gobbled, gobbling. **avaler gloutonnement, engloutir, engouffrer** ▶ to eat in a very fast, noisy way ; eat quickly and greedily : *They gobbled the food as though they hadn't eaten in weeks.*

gobble[2] NOUN, gobbles. **glouglou** ▶ a harsh sound like that made by a male turkey. ▲ VERB, gobbled, gobbling. **glouglouter** ▶ to make this sound.

god [god] NOUN, gods. (also God) **dieu, divinité, idole** ▶ a being who is believed to live forever and have powers far beyond those of ordinary people. In many ancient civilizations, people believed in many different gods and told stories about them.

god·dess [GOD-is] NOUN, goddesses. **déesse, divinité** ▶ a female god : *The ancient Romans worshipped Venus as the goddess of love.*

god·moth·er [GOD-MUTH-ur] NOUN, godmothers. **marraine** ▶ a woman who takes vows for a child being baptized. **Note.** A godfather is a man who takes vows for a child being baptized. **Note.** A godparent is a godmother or godfather. **Note.** A godchild is a child for whom a godparent takes vows at baptism.

gold [gohld] NOUN. **1. or** ▶ a soft, heavy, very valuable yellow metal used to make jewellery and coins. **2. d'or, en or, or** ▶ something thought of as very valuable or special, like gold : *a person with a heart of gold.* **3.** (plural, golds) **d'or, en or, or** ▶ a bright-yellow colour like gold. ☞ p. 397.

gold·en [GOHLD-un] ADJECTIVE. **1. d'or, en or** ▶ made of or containing gold. **2. doré (-ée), d'or** ▶ having the colour or shine of gold ; deep, bright yellow. **3. magnifique, rêvée (-ée), splendide** ▶ very good or excellent ; very valuable : *a golden opportunity.* **4. d'or, en or** ▶ having to do with the 50th year in a series : *His grandparents celebrated their golden wedding anniversary this year.*

gold·fish [GOHLD-FISH] NOUN, goldfish or goldfishes. **poisson rouge** ▶ a small freshwater fish that usually has an orange-gold colour, often kept in home aquariums or ponds.

golf [golf] NOUN. **golf** ▶ an outdoor game in which a player hits a small, hard ball with special clubs. The object of the game is to use as few strokes as possible to hit the ball into a series of holes called a golf course. ▲ VERB, golfed, golfing. **jouer au golf** ▶ to play the game of golf. ■ **golfer,** NOUN. **golfeur (-euse).**

good [good] ADJECTIVE. **1. bon (bonne), beau (belle, beaux)** ▶ having the right qualities ; above average ; not poor or bad : *good weather ; to have a good time.* **2. bon (bonne), charitable, généreux (-euse)** ▶ honest and kind ; not evil : *a good deed ; a person with a good character.* **3. bon (bonne)** ▶ as it should be ; all right : *good health ; a good appetite.* **4. bon (bonne), compétent (-ente)** ▶ useful or helpful for a certain purpose : *good advice ; a good exercise for keeping in shape.* **5. bon (bonne)** ▶ proper and correct : *good manners.* **6. bon (bonne), valide, sûr (sûre)** ▶ in use or effect : *This train ticket is good for one month.* **7. bon (bonne), au moins, grand (grande)** ▶ at least the amount stated : *We waited a good half an hour for him to arrive.* ✐ p. 267. ▲ NOUN. **bien, bonheur, intérêt** ▶ something that is good : *A vacation would really do her a lot of good.* SYN : excellent, fine, nice, first-rate, wonderful. ✐ p. 268.

goodbye [good-BY] INTERJECTION ; NOUN, goodbyes. (also good-bye or good-by) **au revoir, adieu (-eux)** ▶ what someone says to another person when one or the other is leaving.

good·ness [GOOD-nis] NOUN. **1. bonté, bienveillance, générosité** ▶ the quality of being good. **2. bonté, bienveillance, générosité** ▶ the quality of having a good character ; caring for others ; kindness : *He did that purely from the goodness of his heart.*

goods [goodz] PLURAL NOUN. **1. marchandise, article** ▶ anything made to be bought and sold ; merchandise : *The artists spread out their goods on tables set up in tents at the fair.* **2. bien, avoir, richesse** ▶ the things that belong to someone ; belongings : *"They attacked the people and stole their goods."* (Leonard Everett Fisher)

goose [goos] NOUN, geese. **oie** ▶ a web-footed waterbird that looks like a duck but is larger and has a longer neck. Some kinds of geese, such as

Writing Tips

Good vs well

*Some people are not sure how to use **good** and **well**.*

- **Good** *is an adjective, so it always describes a noun.*
  *She is a **good** singer.*
- **Well** *is an adjective and an adverb.*
  *– As an adverb, **well** means "with skill" or "satisfactorily" and is used to describe verbs.*
  *He played the guitar **well**.*
  *She writes **well**.*
  *– As an adjective, **well** is used with the verb "feel" to mean "healthy" or "satisfactory in appearance or condition."*
  *Do you **feel** well?*
  *Paul looks **well** in his new coat.*
- *Feel well and feel good mean different things. Feel well means "to feel healthy." Feel good means to "feel happy or pleased."*

the Canada goose, are wild; others, such as the large white variety that is raised for meat, are tame. 👁 **p. 109.**

goose

go-pher [GOH-fur] NOUN, gophers. **spermophile ▸** a small, furry North American animal that lives in long tunnels that it burrows under the ground. Gophers have long teeth and large claws that are used for digging, and large cheek pouches to carry food.

gorge [gorj] NOUN, gorges. **gorge ▸** a deep, narrow valley that has steep and rocky walls on either side, usually formed by a river that runs through it. ▲ VERB, gorged, gorging. **se bourrer, se gorger, se rassasier ▸** to eat a very large amount of food; stuff oneself with food: *He gorged himself at the picnic, eating three helpings of everything.* SYN: valley, ravine, gully.

gor-geous [GOR-jus] ADJECTIVE. **somptueux (-euse), splendide, magnifique, sensationnel (-elle) ▸** beautiful to look at : *a gorgeous sunset; a gorgeous movie star.* SYN: beautiful, stunning, brilliant, dazzling.

go-ril-la [guh-RIL-uh] NOUN, gorillas. **gorille ▸** a very large, strong ape. Gorillas have a broad, heavy chest and shoulders, long arms, and short legs. They live in the rain forests of central Africa and feed on fruits and vegetables.

gos-ling [GOZ-ling] NOUN, goslings. **oison ▸** a young goose.

gos-sip [GOS-ip] NOUN, gossips. **1. commérage, potin, cancan, bavardage ▸** talk or news about the personal lives of other people that is often not kind or true : *Some newspapers print gossip about TV stars and other famous people.* **2. commère, bavard (-arde), cancanier (-ière) ▸** a person who likes to spread gossip. ▲ VERB, gossiped, gossiping. **commérer, potiner, cancaner, bavarder ▸** to repeat stories and rumours about other people; spread gossip.

got [got] VERB. **recevoir, avoir, chercher ▸** a past form of get: *I got two letters in the mail yesterday. That's not the style of dress I've got in mind for you.* 👁 **p. 246.**

got-ten [GOT-un] VERB. **recevoir, avoir, chercher ▸** a past form of get: *He has never gotten over his fear of the dark.* 👁 **p. 246.**

gourd [gord *or* goord] NOUN. gourds. **potiron ▸** a rounded fruit with a hard outer shell. Gourds grow on vines and are related to pumpkins and squash.

gour-met [gor-MAY *or* goor-MAY] NOUN, gourmets. **gourmet, gastronome ▸** a person who has a great appreciation for fine food and drink and

Writing Tips

Good/better/best

Good, better, and best are adjectives used to describe or compare nouns.

- **Good** *describes one thing: I am a **good** hockey player.*
- **Better** *compares two things: My sister is a **better** hockey player than I am.*
- **Best** *compares three or more things: My sister is the **best** hockey player in our family.*

*Good is unusual because it is irregular. Most adjectives keep the same root or base word and add **er** and **est** (long, longer, longest).*

knows a lot about them. ▲ ADJECTIVE. **de gourmet, gastronomique** ▸ having to do with or suited for a gourmet : *gourmet meals; a gourmet cook.*

gov·ern [GUV-urn] VERB, governed, governing. **1. gouverner, administrer, conduire** ▸ to be in charge of a country, province, state, city, or other body; rule : *Canada is governed by the prime minister and Parliament.* **2. gérer, administrer, diriger** ▸ to be in charge of something; control or manage : *She tried hard to govern her temper.* **3. déterminer, régir** ▸ to decide or influence the nature of something; determine : *The movements of the moon govern the flow of ocean tides.* SYN : rule, control, regulate, command, determine.

gov·ern·ment [GUV-urn-munt] NOUN, governments. **1. gouvernement, administration, autorité** ▸ a system of controlling a country, province, state, city, or other body and managing its affairs : *Canada combines a federal form of government with a cabinet system.* **2. gouvernement, gestion, administration, direction** ▸ the act of ruling; governing. **3. gouvernement, cabinet, ministère** ▸ the group of people who manage or govern a certain place. SYN : authority, rule, regime, administration.

gov·er·nor [GUV-ur-nur] NOUN, governors. **1. gouverneur (-eure)** ▸ a person appointed to manage a colony or territory on behalf of a ruling country. **2. administrateur (-trice)** ▸ an official who is in charge of an organization : *a board of governors.* **3. gouverneur (-eure)** ▸ an elected official who is the head of a state government in the United States.

Governor General NOUN, Governors General. (sometimes governor general) **gouverneur (-eure) général** ▸ in Canada and other Commonwealth countries, the representative of the king or queen appointed on the advice of the prime minister.

gown [gown] NOUN, gowns. **1. robe** ▸ a dress, especially a long, formal dress worn for special occasions : *a wedding gown; a ball gown.* **2. toge** ▸ a long, loose robe worn for an important event, as by a judge in a courtroom or by a student at graduation. **3. robe** ▸ a long, loose robe or similar garment : *a dressing gown; a nightgown.*

grab [grab] VERB, grabbed, grabbing. **1. saisir, agripper, empoigner** ▸ to take hold of suddenly by the hand : *"When we could hear the rumble of the train, Grandma would grab my hand."* (Paulette Bourgeois) **2. se saisir de, prendre, mettre la main sur, s'accaparer** ▸ to take something in a sudden or hasty way : *to grab a bite to eat.* ▲ NOUN, grabs. **mouvement rapide, geste vif** ▸ the act of grabbing : *She made a grab at the ball as it flew past.* SYN : snatch, seize, grasp, clutch, catch, grip.

grace [grace] NOUN, graces. **1. grâce, aisance, charme, chic** ▸ a way of moving that is smooth and easy and beautiful to see : *Champion figure skater Kurt Browning is known for his grace on the ice.* **2. charme, chic, distinction, grâce** ▸ a highly pleasing or agreeable quality; charm : *Their home is decorated with grace and style.* **3. grâce, délicatesse** ▸ kindness or politeness : *He stepped on my foot and didn't even have the grace to apologize.* **4. grâce, répit** ▸ a period of extra time that is allowed for something : *The video's due back at noon, but the store allows a one-hour grace period before charging for an extra day.* **5. bénédicité, action de grâces** ▸ a short prayer of thanks given before a meal. ▲ VERB, graced, gracing. **1. embellir, orner** ▸ to add grace to : *Freshly cut flowers graced the dining table.* **2. honorer** ▸ to be blessed with : *He was graced with a good mind.* ■ **graceful,** ADJECTIVE : **gracieux (-ieuse), élégant (-ante).** *The dancer has very graceful movements.* ■ **gracefully,** ADVERB. ▸ **gracieusement, avec élégance, avec grâce, élégamment.**

gra·cious [GRAY-shus] ADJECTIVE. **gracieux (-ieuse), aimable, élégant (-ante)** ▸ showing kindness and courtesy; well-mannered. ■ **graciously,** ADVERB. ▸ **gracieusement, aimablement.**

grade [grade] NOUN, grades. **1. classe** ▸ one year or level of school. **2. note** ▸ a letter or number showing how well a student has done; a mark : *Sheila got a grade of "B" on her book report.* **3. calibre, catégorie, qualité** ▸ one level on a scale of value : *"Choice" and "Prime" are grades of beef.* **4. rampe** ▸ the amount of slope on a road, hill, or railway track : *a hill with a steep grade.* ▲ VERB, graded, grading. **1. noter** ▸ to give a grade or mark to : *The teacher's assistant graded the test papers.*

✏ Word Builder

Good *is used when speaking of someone's or something's positive qualities.* ***Make good*** *means to prosper or succeed: Everyone knew she would make good and go to university.* ***For good*** *means permanently or forever: When they sold the farm, my family left the country for good.* ***As good as*** *means just about or practically: Farid was as good as can be until his sister started teasing him.* ***Good and*** *means thoroughly or very: I'll leave when I am good and ready.*

2. classer, calibrer ▶ to place according to level or quality : *to grade eggs by their size.*
3. niveler ▶ to change the amount of slope in an area of ground : *The bulldozer graded the hillside so that a house could be built there.*

grad·u·al [GRAJ-yoo-ul] ADJECTIVE. **graduel (-elle), progressif (-ive) ▶** happening little by little; changing or moving slowly : *There was a gradual drop in the temperature, and we started to feel chilly.* ■ **gradually,** ADVERB. ▶ **graduellement, progressivement.**

grad·u·ate [GRAJ-yoo-ATE] VERB, graduated, graduating. **1. obtenir un diplôme ▶** to complete a full course of study and be given a certificate or paper showing this : *My cousin just graduated from law school.* **2. graduer ▶** to mark off something in equal amounts for measuring : *This measuring cup is graduated in millilitres.* **3. changer graduellement, passer graduellement ▶** to advance to some higher level or status : *My little sister has graduated from her crib to a bed.* ▲ [GRAJ-yoo-it] NOUN, graduates. **diplômé (-ée) ▶** a person who has graduated from a school, college, or university : *To get that job you must be a high-school graduate.*

grad·u·a·tion [GRAJ-yoo-AY-shun] NOUN, graduations. **1. collation des grades, remise des diplômes ▶** a ceremony that honours people who have graduated : *The students wore caps and gowns for their graduation.* **2. obtenir un diplôme ▶** the act or fact of graduating : *Jackie needs to pass two more courses for graduation.* 📖 **p. 1059.**

graf·fi·ti [gruh-FEE-tee] PLURAL NOUN. **graffiti ▶** words or drawings scribbled or painted without permission in a public place, as on a wall, sidewalk, rock, and so on.

grain [grane] NOUN, grains. **1. grain ▶** the seed of wheat, corn, rice, and other such food plants. **2. grain ▶** a tiny, hard piece of something : *a grain of salt; a grain of sand.* **3. grain ▶** the lines or marks that run through wood, stone, meat, and other substances : *It's easier to saw this wood if you cut along the grain.* **4. poussière, brin, grain ▶** the smallest possible amount; a tiny bit : *I don't think there's a grain of truth in his story.* 👁 **p. 115, 116.**

gram [gram] NOUN, grams. **gramme ▶** a way of measuring weight. The gram is the basic unit used for small weight measurements in the metric system. There are 1 000 grams in a kilogram. Symbol : **g**

gram·mar [GRAM-ur] NOUN. **1. grammaire ▶** the way in which words are used in a language. When a person has a thought to express, grammar determines how the person should form this thought into a sentence that will sound natural and correct to others. **2. grammaire ▶** the way words are used in acceptable or standard speech or writing : *It's not correct grammar to say "they was here."* **Note.** Anything that has to

do with grammar or that follows the rules of grammar is said to be grammatical. ✎ **p. 269.**

grand [grand] ADJECTIVE, grander, grandest. **1. grand (grande), magnifique, splendide ▶** very large and impressive; magnificent; splendid : *"The king of the Skylanders welcomed the guests with a grand festival."* (Tololwa M. Mollel) **2. impressionnant (-ante), important (-ante), considérable ▶** greatest in size or importance; main : *the Grand Canal in Venice, Italy.* **Note.** This meaning is often used to form compound nouns : *a grand piano; a grand slam.*

✍ Writing Tips

Grammar

Grammar is the study of how words are used to make sentences so that the meaning is clear. In writing and formal speech the rules for making sentences are stricter than for casual conversation. To be good speakers and writers, we need a basic knowledge of these rules of grammar. Here are a few of the rules:

• *There are eight parts of speech that can make up a sentence: noun, pronoun, verb, adjective, adverb, preposition, conjunction, and interjection.*

• *Nouns and pronouns (the names of people, places, and things) should agree with the verbs used. If the noun is singular (it refers to one only) place, or thing), the verb should also be singular. If the noun is plural, the verb should be plural.*

My <u>mother</u> **was** late for work.
The <u>three boys</u> **were** late for school.

• *Verbs have tenses, which tell when the action in the sentence happened—in the past, present, or future.*

I <u>drove</u> yesterday. (past tense)
I <u>am driving</u> to work. (present tense)
I <u>will drive</u> tomorrow. (future tense)

• *Adjectives modify (describe) nouns or pronouns.*

a <u>black</u> cat   a <u>strong</u> person

• *Adverbs modify verbs, adjectives, or another adverb.*

The dog barked <u>loudly</u>.
Sue ran <u>incredibly</u> fast.
He walked <u>very</u> carefully.
The room was **<u>beautifully</u>** painted.

3. résultat final (-ale, -aux), somme globale (global, -aux) ▸ taking in everything; complete : *She won $3000 on the quiz show today and $5000 yesterday, for a grand total of $8000.* **4. magnifique, sensationnel (-elle), formidable** ▸ very good; excellent : *He thought the horse was the grandest animal in the world.* SYN : great, large, big, magnificent, stately.

Grand Banks (also **Grand Bank**) **Grands bancs** ▸ a shallow region covering about 360 000 square kilometres off the southeast coast of Newfoundland. The Grand Banks area is one of the world's best fishing grounds.

grand-child [GRAND-CHILD] NOUN, grandchildren. **petits-enfants (petit-enfant)** ▸ the child of one's son or daughter; a granddaughter or grandson.

grand-daugh-ter [GRAND-DOT-ur] NOUN, granddaughters. **petite-fille** ▸ the daughter of one's son or daughter.

grand-fa-ther [GRAND-FAH-thur] NOUN, grandfathers. **grand-père** ▸ the father of one's mother or father.

grand-moth-er [GRAND-MUTH-ur] NOUN, grandmothers. **grand-mère** ▸ the mother of one's mother or father.

grand-par-ent [GRAND-PAIR-unt] NOUN, grandparents. **(grands-parents)** ▸ the parent of one's mother or father; a grandmother or grandfather.

grand-son [GRAND-SUN] NOUN, grandsons. **petit-fils** ▸ the son of one's son or daughter.

gran-ite [GRAN-it] NOUN. **granit** ▸ a hard, heavy type of rock that is often used in buildings and monuments. ☞ **p. 397.**

gra-no-la [gruh-NOH-luh] NOUN. **granule, grain, muesli** ▸ a dry breakfast or snack food made of rolled oats, wheat germ, brown sugar or honey, and sometimes dried fruit and nuts.

grant [grant] VERB, granted, granting. **1. accorder, allouer, exaucer, octroyer** ▸ to give or allow what one asks : *"I will fight you. Before I do so, grant me two hours to complete a certain errand."* (Dan Yashinsky) **2. admettre, accorder, concéder** ▸ to admit to be true; agree : *I'll grant you that he has the best voice in the cast, but he's not a very good actor.* ▲ NOUN, grants. **1. concession, octroi, subvention** ▸ something that is granted. **2. subvention, bourse** ▸ money that is provided for education or the arts : *The doctor received a $30 000 grant to study cancer.* **Note.** A land grant is property given by the government to a person, as for farming. ✏ **p. 183.**

take for granted prendre pour acquis ▸ to be aware of without questioning or thinking about : *We just take everything Mom does for granted, never thinking about how much time and effort it all takes.*

grape [grape] NOUN, grapes. **raisin** ▸ a small, juicy, round fruit that grows in bunches on vines.

Grapes are usually green or purple and have a smooth, thin skin. They are eaten raw and are also used to make juice, wine, raisins, and jam.

grape-fruit [GRAPE-FROOT] NOUN, grapefruit or grapefruits. **pamplemousse** ▸ a round fruit with a pale-yellow skin and white, yellow, or pink pulp. Grapefruit are like oranges, but are larger and sourer in taste.

leaves

fruit (grapefruit)

grapefruit tree

grape-vine [GRAPE-VINE] NOUN, grapevines. **1. vigne** ▸ a vine that grapes grow on. **2. téléphone arabe** ▸ a secret or informal way of passing news or rumours from person to person : *I heard through the grapevine at school that Nina is moving away.*

graph [graf] NOUN, graphs. **graphique** ▸ a drawing that shows how certain numbers or facts relate to each other. Graphs use a set of lines, bars, or pictures to show many different types of information. SYN : diagram, chart, outline, drawing. ✏ **p. 271.**

grasp [grasp] VERB, grasped, grasping. **1. saisir, prendre, empoigner** ▸ to take hold of firmly with the hands : *Don't grasp the pencil so tightly or you will get a cramp in your hand.* **2. saisir, comprendre** ▸ to take hold of with the mind; understand : *I finally grasped the teacher's explanation about how to solve the math problem.* ▲ NOUN, grasps. **1. poigne, prise, étreinte** ▸ a firm hold or grip. **2. compréhension** ▸ the fact of grasping with the mind; understanding : *He just started the course and*

doesn't have a good grasp of the subject yet.
SYN: seize, catch, clasp, grip, hold, clutch.

grass [gras] NOUN, grasses. **1. pelouse, gazon, herbe ▸** any of the various types of grass plants that are used to cover lawns, playgrounds, and sports fields, or grown in fields as feed for farm animals. Common grasses include rye, bluegrass, and Bermuda grass. **2. graminée ▸** one of a family of green plants that have long, thin leaves and grow throughout the world. Members of this family include sugarcane, bamboo, reeds, and cereal grasses such as wheat, rice, and corn. **▪ grassy,** ADJECTIVE, grassier, grassiest. **▸ herbeux (-euse).**

grass-hop-per [GRAS-hop-ur] NOUN, grasshoppers. **sauterelle ▸** an insect that has wings and long, powerful legs that it uses for jumping. ☞ p. 104.

grate [grate] VERB, grated, grating. **1. râper ▸** to grind or shred into small pieces by rubbing against a rough surface : *He grated carrots for his salad.* **Note.** A grater is a device used to shred food. **2. grincer, crisser ▸** to make a hard grinding noise by rubbing or scraping : *The bottom of the car grated on the sidewalk.* **3. grincer, écorcher, crisser ▸** to be unpleasant or irritating : *That noise really grates on my nerves.*

grate-ful [GRATE-ful] ADJECTIVE. **reconnaissant (-ante) ▸** feeling or showing appreciation for some favour or something good that has happened : *"Jodie was grateful that the bear had gone in the opposite direction from the one they had taken."* (Marilyn Halvorson) **Note.** A feeling of being grateful is gratitude: *He accepted his award with gratitude and pride.* **▪ gratefully,** ADVERB. **▸ avec reconnaissance, avec gratitude.** *He smiled gratefully as the police car pulled over to help him.* SYN: thankful, appreciative, obliged, indebted.

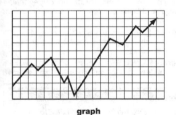

graph

grave[1] [grave] NOUN, graves. **1. tombe, sépulture ▸** a hole dug in the ground to bury a dead body. **2. tombe, sépulture ▸** any place of death or burial : *It is sometimes said that a ship that sinks has gone to a watery grave.* **Note.** A graveyard is a place where dead people are buried. It is also called a cemetery.

> ### ✍ Writing Tips
>
> #### Graphs
>
> A **graph** is a chart or drawing that shows information in a visual form. There are different types of graphs : bar graphs, line graphs, pie charts or circle graphs, and pictographs.
>
> • A bar graph shows quantities as bars of different lengths.
>
> • In a line graph, points are plotted on a chart, and then connected.
>
> • A pie chart or circle graph shows parts of a whole as larger or smaller pieces of a pie or circle. Numbers on a pie chart are usually shown in percentages—for example, 10% or 90%. The total of the percentages on a pie chart should equal 100%. • A pictograph compares using pictures that represent objects.

grave[2] ADJECTIVE, graver, gravest. **1. sérieux (-ieuse), important (-ante) ▸** of great importance ; very serious : *Being prime minister of Canada is a grave responsibility.* **2. grave, sérieux (-ieuse), inquiétant (-ante), alarmant (-ante) ▸** very dangerous or threatening ; causing great concern : *The patient is in grave condition.* **3. grave, sérieux (-ieuse), solennel (-elle), digne ▸** very serious in manner ; solemn : *From the grave look on her face, I knew the news could not be good.* **▪ gravely,** ADVERB. **▸ gravement, sérieusement, solennellement.**

grav-el [GRAV-ul] NOUN. **gravier, gravillon ▸** a loose mixture of pebbles and small pieces of rock, often used for making driveways and roads.

grav-i-ty [GRAV-uh-tee] NOUN. **1. gravité ▸** the force that pulls things toward the centre of the earth. Gravity causes things to have weight and to fall to earth when they are dropped. **2. gravité, sérieux, danger ▸** the state of being grave ; seriousness ; importance : *This is treason, an affair of the deepest gravity.*

gray. See grey.

gra-vy [GRAY-vee] NOUN, gravies. **sauce, sauce au jus de viande ▸** the juices that drip from meat while it is cooking, or a sauce made from these juices.

graze[1] [graze] VERB, grazed, grazing. **brouter, paître ▸** of a cow, sheep, or other such animal, to feed on growing grass : *Huge herds of buffalo used to graze on the North American prairies.*

graze[2] VERB, grazed, grazing. **frôler, effleurer, raser ▸** to touch or scrape lightly : *The tall grass* *grazed his bare legs as he ran through the field.* SYN : scrape, rub, skim, glance, brush.

grease [grees] NOUN. **1. graisse ▸** soft, melted animal fat : *We poured the bacon grease into a can.* **2. graisse, lubrifiant ▸** any thick, oily substance : *She put grease on the bicycle chain to help it turn more easily.* ▲ VERB, greased, greasing. **graisser, lubrifier ▸** to rub or put grease on : *I greased the frying pan so that the meat wouldn't stick to it.* ■ **greasy,** ADJECTIVE, greasier, greasiest. **1. gras (grasse), graisseux (-euse), huileux (-euse) ▸** covered or soiled with grease. **2. gras (grasse), graisseux (-euse), huileux (-euse) ▸** containing grease or fat; oily : *greasy food.*

great [grate] ADJECTIVE, greater, greatest. **1. grand (grande), illustre, célèbre ▸** much better than is usual; of very high quality; excellent : *Emily Carr and Tom Thomson are thought of as great Canadian artists.* **2. grand (grande), étendu (-ue), vaste ▸** very large or important : *the Great Wall of China.* **3. grand (grande), merveilleux (-euse), magnifique, sensationnel (-elle) ▸** much more than usual : *great happiness. It came as a great surprise to me.* **4. grand (grande), excellent (-ente), merveilleux (-euse) ▸** very good; first-rate : *a great vacation; a restaurant that serves great hamburgers.* **5. petit-enfant, arrière-petit-enfant ▸** of a relative, belonging to the next-earlier or next-later generation : *They have six grandchildren and five great-grandchildren.* ■ **greatly,** ADVERB. **beaucoup, énormément, fort, bien ▸** very much; highly. 🖉 **p. 272.**

greed [greed] NOUN. **avidité, cupidité, gloutonnerie, voracité ▸** a selfish desire to get more than one's fair share of something; a great wish for money, power, and so on : *One folk tale tells of a king who had so much greed that he wanted everything he owned turned into gold.*

greed-y [GREED-ee] ADJECTIVE, greedier, greediest. **1. avide, cupide, rapace ▸** showing greed; wanting very much to have more than one needs or more than one's share. **2. glouton (-onne), vorace, goulu (-ue) ▸** wanting to eat or drink a very large amount. ■ **greedily,** ADVERB. **▸ avidement, voracement, gloutonnement, cupidement.** *The dog lapped greedily at his water bowl.*

green [green] NOUN, greens. **1. vert, pelouse, gazon ▸** the colour of growing grass and leaves. **place ▸ 2. vert, place ▸** an area of ground that is covered with grass : *Our town has a village green in the centre.* **3. vert, verdure, légumes verts ▸** on a golf course, the area of smooth, short grass around the hole. **4. greens.** green leaves and stems of plants that are used for food. ▲ ADJECTIVE, greener, greenest. **1. vert (verte) ▸** having the colour green. **2. verdoyant (-ante), herbeux (-euse) ▸** covered with growing plants, grass, or leaves : *Green hills surrounded the peaceful valley.* **3. vert (verte), pas mûr (mûre) ▸** not full-grown; not ripe : *green apples.* **4. jeune, inexpérimenté (-ée) ▸** without training; not experienced : *He's a good young player, but he's too green to be in the major leagues.* 🖉 **p. 64.**

green-house [GREEN-hows] NOUN, greenhouses. **serre ▸** a glass or plastic building with a controlled temperature, used for growing plants all year round.

greet [GREET] VERB, greeted, greeting. **1. accueillir, saluer ▸** to welcome or speak to a person in a friendly or polite way : *She greeted her grandmother with a big hug.* **2. accueillir, saluer ▸** to respond to; meet or receive : *The students greet the news of a field trip with cheers.* SYN : address, hail, talk to, welcome, meet.

greet-ing [GREET-ing] NOUN, greetings. **1. salutation, accueil ▸** the act or words of a person who greets someone; a welcome : *We were welcomed with greetings from the whole family.* **2. greetings. souhait, vœu (vœux) ▸** a friendly message that someone sends : *holiday greetings.*

grew VERB. **croître ▸** a past form of grow.

grey [gray] NOUN, greys (also gray) **1. gris ▸** a colour that is a mixture of black and white : *Clouds are usually grey right before it rains.* **2. gris ▸** not cheerful or bright : *a grey winter day.* ▲ ADJECTIVE. **gris (grise) ▸** having the colour grey.

grief [greef] NOUN. **peine, chagrin, douleur ▸** a great feeling of sadness or sorrow, as at the death of a loved one.

grieve [greev] VERB, grieved, grieving. **avoir de la peine, avoir du chagrin, se désoler,**

🖉 Word Builder

Great, outstanding, and *superb* are all adjectives that can describe a person noted for or distinguished by his or her accomplishments. *Great* can refer to people who have wealth or influence, or who have achieved something: *Glenn Gould was a great pianist. Outstanding* has the idea that a person's excellence sets him or her apart from others: *Nobel-prize winner John Polanyi is an outstanding scientist in Canada and around the world. Superb* is the strongest word. It suggests the highest degree of excellence: *Karen Kain's ballet career has been superb.*

s'affliger ▶ to feel grief; be very sad : *The entire country grieved over the death of the young king.*

grill [gril] NOUN, grills. **gril ▶** a framework of metal bars to hold food for cooking over an open fire : *We broiled steaks on the grill.* ▲ VERB, grilled, grilling. **1. griller ▶** to cook food on a grill. **2. cuisiner, faire subir un interrogatoire ▶** to question severely for a long time : *The police grilled the suspect for hours before she finally admitted she'd been lying.*

grim [grim] ADJECTIVE, grimmer, grimmest. **1. menaçant (-ante), effrayant (-ante), sinistre ▶** causing fear; horrible or frightening : *Jack London's "To Build a Fire" is a grim tale of a man freezing to death.* **2. impitoyable, implacable, inflexible ▶** very stern or harsh; forbidding : *The boy stood in grim silence, refusing to answer the angry man.* **■ grimly,** ADVERB. **▶ avec acharnement, inexorablement, inflexiblement.** SYN: fierce, terrible, stern, severe, hard, harsh.

grin [grin] VERB, grinned, grinning. **large sourire ▶** to smile in a very happy way; have a wide smile : *Wai was so happy that he grinned as he walked home.* ▲ NOUN, grins. **large sourire ▶** a wide, happy smile.

grind [grynd] VERB, ground, grinding. **1. moudre, écraser, broyer ▶** to crush or chop into small pieces or fine powder : *to grind coffee; to grind beef for hamburger.* **2. aiguiser, affiler, affûter ▶** to make something smooth or sharp by rubbing it against something rough : *to grind a knife to sharpen it.* **3. grincer, crisser, crier ▶** to rub together harshly and noisily : *People who are nervous sometimes grind their teeth when they sleep.* **Note.** Something that grinds is a grinder.

grip [grip] NOUN, grips. **1. poigne, prise, étreinte ▶** a tight, strong hold; a firm grasp : *"In that split second, I lost my grip. The rod leaped out of my hands."* (Julie Lawson). **2. maîtrise ▶** a full hold; control : *Keep calm, now; get a grip on yourself.* **3. poignée ▶** a place to take hold of; a handle : *the grip on a golf club or tennis racquet.* ▲ VERB, gripped, gripping. **empoigner, serrer, saisir ▶** to hold something in a tight, strong way : *She gripped his wrist so tightly that it began to ache.* **Note.** Also used as an ADJECTIVE: *a gripping story.* SYN: hold, grasp, clasp, clutch, seize.

grizzly bear (also grizzly) **grizzli ▶** very large, fierce bear of western North America. Grizzly bears have long claws and brown or black fur tipped with grey.

groan [grone] NOUN, groans. **plainte, gémissement, lamentation ▶** a deep, sad sound that people make when they are in pain, unhappy, or upset. ▲ VERB, groaned, groaning. **se plaindre, gémir, geindre ▶** to give a deep, sad sound; make a groan. *"The animals didn't even groan.*

They were too tired and too hungry." (Celia Barker Lottridge) SYN: moan, cry, sob, wail, whimper, whine.

gro·cer·y [GROCE-uh-ree] NOUN, groceries. **1. supermarché, épicerie ▶** a store that sells food and household supplies. A grocery store is smaller than a supermarket and is usually not part of a larger chain of stores. **Note.** A person who owns or runs a grocery is a grocer. **2. groceries. articles d'épicerie ▶** food and household supplies.

groom [groom] NOUN, grooms. **1. palefrenier (-ière) ▶** a person whose work is taking care of horses. **2. marié ▶** short for bridegroom. ▲ VERB, groomed, grooming. **1. panser, faire la toilette ▶** to take care of a horse by washing, brushing, and feeding it. **2. soigner, coiffer ▶** to make neat and clean in appearance. **Note.** Usually used as an ADJECTIVE:*a person who is well-groomed.* **3. préparer, former, façonner ▶** to prepare someone for a certain job or responsibility : *The coach is grooming Kirby to be the goalie.*

grope [grope] VERB, groped, groping. **1. tâtonner, aller à l'aveuglette ▶** to feel about with the hands because one cannot see clearly : *Wesley groped in the dark for the light switch.* **2. tâtonner, hésiter ▶** to search in one's mind, as if feeling for something :*She groped for the answer.*

gross [groce] ADJECTIVE, grosser, grossest. **1. brut (brute) ▶** with nothing taken out; total :*A person's gross income is the total amount that is earned before any taxes are paid.* **2. évident (-ente), flagrant (-ante), indéniable ▶** obviously wrong or bad : *a gross error.* **3. effronté (-ée), impoli (-ie), impertinent (-ente), grossier (-ière) ▶** not polite or proper; disgusting; vulgar : *a gross remark; a gross habit.* ▲ NOUN. **1.** (plural, grosses) **montant brut ▶** the total amount. **2.** (plural, gross) **grosse ▶** a group of 12 dozen or 144, used as a way of measuring goods in business.

ground¹ [grownd] NOUN, grounds. **1. terre, sol, terrain ▶** the solid part of the earth's surface; the earth; land : *A pass in football must be caught before it touches the ground.* **2. grounds. cour, terrain ▶** the land around a house or school. **3.** (also grounds) **cour ▶** an area of land that is used for a certain purpose : *picnic grounds; a camp ground.* **4.** (also grounds) **raison, motif, cause ▶** a cause for thinking or doing something; a reason : *The police believe that they have grounds for charging him with the crime.* **5. grounds. grains de café, marc ▶** small pieces of coffee that settle at the bottom of a cup or pot. ▲ VERB, grounded, grounding. **1. empêcher de voler, retenir au sol, interdire de voler ▶** to force to stay on the ground or come down to the ground : *An ice storm grounded the plane.* **2. s'échouer, s'ensabler ▶** to cause to hit the bottom of a river or other body of water.

273

ground

3. brancher à la prise de terre ▶ to connect an electric wire with the ground so that its circuit will be safely completed. **4. roulant** ▶ in baseball, to hit a ball so that it bounces or rolls along the ground. ✐ **p. 274.**

ground² VERB. **moudre** ▶a past form of grind: *Millers ground grains of wheat to make flour.*

ground-hog [GROWND-hog] NOUN, groundhogs. **marmotte** ▶ an animal with a plump body and a bushy tail. **Note.** Also called a **woodchuck.** ☞ p. 110.

group [groop] NOUN, groups. **1. groupe** ▶ a number of persons or things together : *A group of people waited outside for the store to open.* **2. groupe** ▶ a number of persons or things that belong together or are thought of together : *All the children in Karen's reading group are using the same book.* ▲ VERB, grouped, grouping. **grouper, réunir** ▶ to form into or belong to a group : *The children group the blocks according to colour.* ✐ **p. 275.**

grove [grove] NOUN, groves. **bosquet, bouquet, massif** ▶ a group of trees standing together : *"The blue jay had followed us from the maple grove."* (Teddy Jam)

grow [groh] VERB, grew, grown, growing. **1. grandir, pousser, croître** ▶ of a growing thing, to become bigger in size : *My brother grew 10 cm this year.* **2. pousser, croître** ▶ to live and be able to develop : *Lemon trees grow in warm areas.* **3. faire pousser** ▶ to cause or allow to grow : *to grow tomatoes; to grow a beard.* **4. augmenter, grandir** ▶ to become larger; increase : *The town grew rapidly after the gold boom.* **5. devenir** ▶ to become tired of something. SYN: increase, get bigger, expand, develop. **grow up devenir adulte** ▶ to become an adult.

growl [growl] VERB, growled, growling. **1. gronder, grogner** ▶ to make a deep, low, rumbling sound in the throat, as a dog does when it is angry or as a sign of warning. **2. grogner, ronchonner** ▶ to speak in a tone of voice like this. ▲ NOUN, growls. **grondement, grognement, ronchonnement** ▶ a growling sound. SYN: snarl, bark, roar, grumble, complain.

grown-up [GRONE-up] NOUN, grown-ups. **adulte, grande personne** ▶ a person who is fully grown; an adult.

growth [growth] NOUN. **1. croissance, développement** ▶ the process of growing : *the growth of a child; the growth of a plant.* **2. développement, expansion** ▶ something that has grown : *There was a thick growth of weeds along the fence.*

grudge [gruj] NOUN, grudges. **rancune, rancœur** ▶ a feeling of anger, dislike, or ill will against a person that is held for a long time : *They don't talk to each other; they have an old grudge about a coat that wasn't returned.*

grunt [grunt] NOUN, grunts. **grognement** ▶ a short, deep, harsh sound. ▲ VERB, grunted, grunting. **grogner** ▶ to make a short, deep, harsh sound : *They could hear him grunt as he lifted the heavy trunk.*

guar-an-tee [GAIR-un-TEE] NOUN, guarantees. (sometimes guaranty) **1. garantie** ▶ a promise to fix or replace something or to give back the money paid for it if something goes wrong with it during a certain period of time : *We have a three-year guarantee on our new refrigerator.* **2. garantie** ▶ a way of being certain that something will happen or will be done : *The Charter of Rights is a guarantee of certain basic freedoms.* ▲ VERB, guaranteed, guaranteeing. **1. garantir, assurer** ▶ to give a guarantee for : *The manufacturers guarantee this car for the first 50,000 km of driving.* **2. garantir, certifier** ▶ to make sure or certain : *We guarantee satisfaction to all our customers.*

guard [gard] VERB, guarded, guarding. **1. garder, surveiller** ▶ to watch over; protect from harm; keep safe : *The dogs guarded the door.* **2. garder, détenir, séquestrer** ▶ to watch over to keep from escaping or keep under control : *Several police officers guarded the prisoner on her way to court.* **3. garder, surveiller** ▶ in sports, to stay close to a player from the other team to try to prevent him or her from scoring. ▲ NOUN, guards. **1. garde** ▶ a police officer, soldier, or other person who watches over or protects someone or something. **2. protection** ▶ anything that protects or provides safety : *Soccer players wear shin guards in case another player kicks them.* **3. défenseur,**

✐ **Word Builder**

Ground *means a solid part of the earth's surface. When people **break new ground,** they do something for the very first time, or they do something in an original way: The scientist's discovery breaks new ground in cancer research. When someone **gains ground,** he or she is going forward, usually catching up on someone else: The sprinter is gaining ground on her opponent. On the other hand, someone who **loses ground** is falling behind: Every day he misses school, he loses ground in his studies.*

✐ **Writing Tips**

Guides

*Written **guides** offer information on a place or topic.*

• *Guides come in different forms. A guide could be a one-page fact sheet about a new product, a museum brochure, or even a book about a country.*

• *Guides present information in different ways—text, pictures, maps, diagrams, photographs, and charts.*

• *Guides tell where something takes place, explain why something happens, describe what something does, or show how something works.*

• *When you write a guide, remember to:*
  – collect and read a variety of guides
  – include an introduction explaining what the guide is about
  – use headings to organize the information
  – use diagrams, charts, photographs, and illustrations where needed.

arrière ▸ in sports, a player whose job is to prevent scoring. SYN: defend, protect, shield, watch, care for.

guard·i·an [GAR-dee-un] NOUN, guardians. **1. tuteur (-trice) ▸** a person chosen by law to take care of someone who is young or who is not able to take care of himself or herself : *The boy's aunt and uncle were appointed by the court to be his guardians after his parents died in an accident.* **2. gardien (-ienne), protecteur (-trice) ▸** something that guards or protects : *My older sister is my guardian.*

guer·ril·la [guh-RIL-uh] NOUN, guerrillas. (sometimes querilla) **guérillero ▸** a member of a small group of soldiers who make quick surprise attacks in enemy territory.

guess [ges] VERB, guessed, guessing. **1. deviner, supposer ▸** to have an idea about something without being sure that it is right;

decide when one does not know exactly : *She felt that she knew him well enough to guess what his answer would be.* **2. deviner, évaluer ▸** to judge by guessing : *to guess a person's name.* **3. croire, penser, avoir l'impression ▸** to believe or suppose : *"Harriet guessed that he had made the black box with its glittery smears of stars."* (Tim Wynne-Jones) ▲ NOUN, guesses. **supposition, conjecture, hypothèse ▸** an opinion formed without having enough information to be sure; the act of guessing. SYN: suppose, imagine, think, speculate, assume.

guest [gest] NOUN, guests. **1. invité (-ée) ▸** someone who is at another person's home for a meal or a visit : *We have four guests coming over for dinner tonight.* **2. client (-ente), invité (-ée) ▸** someone who stays at a hotel or motel.

guide [gíde] NOUN, guides. **1. guide ▸** a person who leads a group of explorers, travellers, campers, or other such people through an area that they are not familiar with. **2. (also tour guide) guide ▸** a person whose work is leading visitors through a museum, famous building, amusement park, or the like. **3. guide, indication ▸** anything that shows the way or shows how something should be done : *"Let your conscience be your guide" is a well-known old saying.* **4. guide, manuel ▸** a book that shows how to do something or gives facts about something : *Carol bought a guide to flowers in Canada.* ▲ VERB, guided, guiding. **1. guider, conduire, piloter ▸** to serve as a guide : *I guided the visitors around the museum.* **2. guider, conduire, piloter ▸** to lead in a certain way : *The usher used a small flashlight to guide people to their seats.* SYN: leader, conductor, escort, usher, pilot. ✐ **p. 275.**

guilt [gilt] NOUN, guilts. **1. culpabilité ▸** the fact of having done wrong or broken the law : *The evidence convinced the jury of the woman's guilt.* **2. culpabilité ▸** a feeling of having done something wrong; shame : *He felt a lot of guilt because he hadn't done his homework.*

guilt·y [GIL-tee] ADJECTIVE, guiltier, guiltiest. **1. coupable ▸** having been convicted of a crime in a court of law : *to be found guilty of theft.* **2. coupable, responsable, fautif (-ive) ▸** having done something wrong; deserving blame or punishment : *She was guilty of eating the last piece of pie.* **3. coupable, confus (-use) ▸** feeling or showing guilt : *Todd looked guilty when*

✐ **Word Builder**

Group, crowd, *and **pack** are all nouns that refer to gatherings of people or things. **Group** can be used to describe small or large gatherings of people that come together informally: A group of students met in the lunch room. A **crowd** is a large gathering of people: A crowd gathered outside the hotel where the rock group was staying. **Pack** is often used when describing a group of animals that run and hunt together: The pack of wolves ran through the woods.*

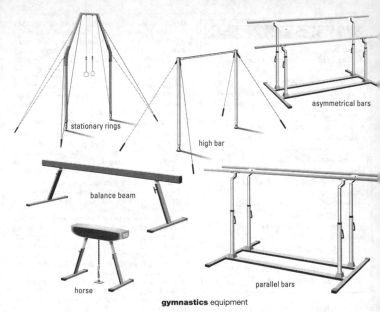

gymnastics equipment

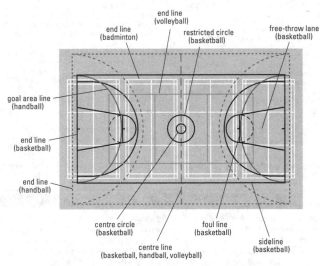

gymnasium

his mother asked what had happened to the cookies.

gui·tar [gih-TAR] NOUN, guitars. **guitare** ▶ a musical instrument with a long neck and six or more strings. Guitars are played by plucking or strumming the strings. **Note.** Electric guitars make sounds that are different from, and louder than, those made by acoustic guitars. 👁 **p. 538.**

gulf [gulf] NOUN, gulfs. **1. golfe, estuaire** ▶ an area of an ocean or sea that is partly enclosed by land. A gulf is usually larger and deeper than a bay. **2. gouffre, abîme** ▶ a great separation or difference : *The strike may last a long time, because there's a wide gulf between the two sides.*

gull [gul] NOUN, gulls. **mouette, goéland** ▶ a bird with gray and white feathers, webbed feet, and long wings. Gulls live on or near bodies of water. 👁 **p. 108.**

gul·ly [GUL-ee] NOUN, gullies. **rigole, caniveau (-eaux)** ▶ a narrow ditch or trench cut in the earth by heavy rains or running water.

gum[1] [gum] NOUN, gums. **1. gomme** ▶ a thick, sticky juice that comes from different trees and plants. Gum is used to coat the back of a stamp or the flap of an envelope. It is also used to make candies and chemicals. **2.** (also **chewing gum**) **gomme à mâcher, chewing-gum** ▶ a gum that is sweetened for chewing.

gum[2] NOUN, gums. **gencive** ▶ the firm pink flesh around the teeth.

gun [gun] NOUN, guns. **1. revolver, pistolet, fusil** ▶ a weapon that shoots bullets or shells through a metal tube. Rifles, pistols, and cannons are types of guns. **2. pistolet** ▶ any device that looks like a gun and shoots something out : *Mom used a staple gun to fasten the paper on the shelves.* ▲ VERB, gunned, gunning. **1. chasser, tuer, abattre** ▶ to shoot or hunt with a gun : *to go gunning for rabbits.* **2. faire ronfler le moteur, appuyer sur le champignon** ▶ to speed up a motor or engine suddenly : *Josette gunned past the slower cars.*

guy[1] [gy] NOUN, guys. **corde, cordage, filage, chaîne** ▶ a rope, chain, or wire used to steady or fasten something : *Guy wires are used to hold up a large tent.*

guy[2] NOUN, guys. *Informal.* **gars, garçon** ▶ any man or boy : *We'll start the game as soon as the guys arrive.*

gym [jim] NOUN, gyms. **1. gymnase** ▶ short for gymnasium. **2. classe ou cours de gymnastique** ▶ a course in physical education that is taught in a school or college.

gym·na·si·um [jim-NAY-zee-um] NOUN, gymnasiums or gymnasia. **gymnase** ▶ a room or building with equipment for physical exercise or training and for indoor sports. 🏳 **p. 1059.**

Gyp·sy [JIP-see] NOUN, Gypsies. (also **gipsy**) **Tsigane** ▶ a person belonging to a wandering group of people who are thought to have come from India hundreds of years ago. **Note.** The more correct term is Romany.

H h

helicopter

h, H [aych] NOUN. h's, H's. **h,H ▶** the eighth letter of the English alphabet.

hab·it [HAB-it] NOUN, habits. **1. habitude, manie ▶** something a person does so often or for so long that it is done without thinking. A habit is usually hard to stop or control : *"East Wind had the habit of shedding bitter tears over the least little thing."* (Rosebud Yellow Robe) **2. routine ▶** a usual way of acting or behaving; custom : *It was his habit to have an egg for breakfast.* **3. habit, tenue ▶** a special kind of clothing : *A riding habit is an outfit worn for horseback riding.* SYN: practice, custom, pattern, routine, way.

hab·i·tat [HAB-uh-tat] NOUN, habitats. **habitat ▶** the place where an animal or a plant naturally lives or grows : *A swamp is a habitat for water lilies.*

hack [hak] VERB, hacked, hacking. **1. hacher, tailler, taillader, couper ▶** to cut or chop roughly with heavy blows : *Jed hacked up the old box to use as firewood.* **2. tousser ▶** to cough with harsh, dry sounds. SYN: cut, sever, split, chop.

hack·er [HAK-ur] NOUN, hackers. **passionné (-ée), mordu (-ue) d'informatique ▶** a person who likes to experiment with computers; someone who is interested in computers as a hobby.

had [had] VERB. **avoir ▶** a past form of have.✍ **p. 283.**

had·dock [HAD-uk] NOUN, haddocks or haddock. **églefin, aiglefin ▶** an ocean fish found in the northern Atlantic, often used for food.

Hai·da [HY-da] NOUN, Haida. **1. Haida ▶** a member of the Haida, Native peoples of western British Columbia who are known for their totem poles. **2. Haida ▶** the language of the Haida people. ▲ ADJECTIVE. **haida ▶** having to do with the Haida people or language.

hai·ku [HY-koo] NOUN, haiku or haikus. **haïku ▶** a form of poetry that originated in Japan. A haiku is made up of three lines of different lengths that do not rhyme.

hail[1] [hale] NOUN, hails. **1. grêle ▶** small lumps of ice that fall from the sky during a storm. A hail-storm usually occurs during a thunderstorm. Note. A single lump of hail is a hailstone. **2. pluie ▶** a heavy shower of something, thought of as like hail falling from the sky : *a hail of bullets during a battle.* ▲ VERB, hailed, hailing. **grêler ▶** to pour down as hail : *It hails more often in spring than in other seasons.*

hail[2] VERB, hailed, hailing. **1. héler, interpeller ▶** to get someone's attention by shouting or waving : *He hailed a taxi with the wave of his hand.* **2. saluer, acclamer ▶** to give honour or approval to ; praise : *The crowd hailed Botan as the hero of the game.* SYN: greet, cheer, welcome, call, shout.

hail from être originaire de **▶** to come from a certain place : *Both my grandparents hail from Saskatoon.*

hair [hair] NOUN, hairs. **1. poil, duvet ▶** a very thin, fine growth, like a thread, on the skin of people and animals. **2. cheveux (eux), chevelure ▶** a mass or covering of such growths. Note. A haircut or hairstyle is the way a person wears the hair. 🖙 **p. 981.**

hair·y [HAIR-ee] ADJECTIVE, hairier, hairiest. **1. chevelu (-ue), poilu (-ue), velu (-ue) ▶** covered with hair ; having a lot of hair. **2. peluché (-ée) ▶** like hair : *a hairy blanket.*

half [haf] NOUN, halves. **1. demi (-ie), moitié ▶** one of two equal parts of something : *Mother divided the apple in halves and gave half to me and half to my sister.* **2. demie ▶** in certain sports, one of the two equal time periods that make up a game. ▲ ADJECTIVE. **1. demi (-ie) ▶** amounting to half ; being a half : *a half litre of milk.* **2. demi ▶** related through one parent only : *a half brother or sister.* ▲ ADVERB. **1. à demi ▶** to the amount of one half : *The gas tank is half full.* **2. à moitié ▶** partly or nearly : *Colleen was so tired that she was half asleep during dinner.*

half·way [HAF-way] ADVERB. **1. à mi-chemin, à moitié chemin ▶** half the way between two things : *I paused halfway up the hill to appreciate the view.* **2. à moitié, à peu près ▶** not fully or completely; partway : *to do a halfway decent job.* ▲ ADJECTIVE: *the halfway mark in a race.*

hal·i·but [HAL-uh-but] NOUN, halibut or halibuts. **flétan** ▸ a very large fish with a flat body, often used for food. Halibut are found in the northern Pacific and Atlantic Oceans.

hall [hol] NOUN, halls. **1.** (also hallway) **couloir, corridor** ▸ a long narrow area in a building, from which other rooms open; a way of passing through a house or building; corridor. **2. entrée, hall, vestibule** ▸ a space or room just inside the entry to a house or building : *We left our wet boots on the mat in the front hall.* **3. salle, réfectoire** ▸ a large room or building for meetings or other public gatherings : *a concert hall; a dining hall.* **4. hôtel de ville** ▸ a building containing offices of local government : *The mayor's office is in City Hall.*

Hal·low·een [HAL-oh-EEN, HAL-uh-WEEN, *or* HOL-uh-WEEN] NOUN, Halloweens. (also Hallowe'en) **Halloween** ▸ the evening of October 31. Children celebrate Halloween by dressing up in costumes, playing tricks, and collecting candy and other treats.

halt [holt] VERB, halted, halting. **(s') arrêter, faire halte** ▸ to stop for a time : *She halted her horse to gaze at the scenery below.* ▲ NOUN, halts. **halte, arrêt, pause, interruption** ▸ a stopping of something : *The jeep screeched to a halt.* SYN: spot, rest, pause, come to a standstill.

ham [ham] NOUN, hams. **1. jambon** ▸ the meat from the back leg of a pig. Ham is often salted or smoked before being eaten. **2. radioamateur** ▸ a person who sends and receives radio messages as a hobby on home equipment (a ham radio). **3.** *Informal.* **cabotin (-ine)** ▸ an actor who uses a very showy, exaggerated style to get the audience's attention.

ham·burg·er [HAM-bur-gur] NOUN, hamburgers. **1. bœuf haché** ▸ ground beef. **2. hamburger, hambourgeois** ▸ a sandwich consisting of a round, flat piece of cooked ground beef inside a bun. **Note.** Informally called a **burger**. **Note.** The word *hamburger* comes from an earlier name, Hamburg Steak, from the city of Hamburg, Germany.

ham·mer [HAM-ur] NOUN, hammers. **1. marteau (-eaux) , masse** ▸ a tool with a heavy metal head attached to a long handle, used to drive nails and shape metal. **2. marteau** ▸ something that looks like or is used like a hammer : *In a piano, the hammer hits a string to make a sound.* ▲ VERB, hammered, hammering. **1. marteler, frapper à coup de marteau** ▸ to hit with a hammer. **2. frapper, tabasser, cogner dur sur** ▸ to hit with a hard blow : *"Their stilt legs hammered the ground and their crimson robes swirled as they sang and danced and swayed."* (Tololwa M. Mollel)

ham·mock [HAM-uk] NOUN, hammocks. **hammac** ▸ a swinging cot or bed made of netting or sturdy cloth that is hung between two supports.

ham·ster [HAM-stur] NOUN, hamsters. **hamster** ▸ a small, furry animal with a plump body, a short tail, and cheek pouches. Hamsters are part of the rodent family. They are often kept as pets.

hand [hand] NOUN, hands. **1. main** ▸ the end of the arm from the wrist down, made up of the palm, four fingers, and the thumb. **2. aiguille** ▸ something thought of as like a hand : *the hands of a clock.* **3. applaudissement** ▸ a round of applause; clapping : *They gave the singer a big hand.* **4. écriture** ▸ handwriting : *He signed the letter in a shaky hand.* **5.** hands. **entre les mains de** ▸ control or possession : *The decision is now in the hands of the teacher.* **6. part, responsabilité, rôle** ▸ a part in doing something; share; role : *Everyone on the team had a hand in our winning the game.* **7. main-d'œuvre, ouvrier (-ière)** ▸ a worker : *The farmer had a hired hand who helped with the work.* **8. main** ▸ the cards a player holds in a card game, or one round in a game. ▲ VERB, handed, handing. **donner, remettre, retourner, passer** ▸ to give or pass with the hand : *"Then she wrote another request, handed him the book, and winked at me."* (Barbara Nichol) SYN: turn over, give, deliver, pass, transfer. ☞ **p. 997.**

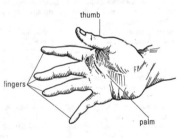

thumb

fingers

palm

hand

hand·ful [HAND-ful] NOUN, handfuls. **1. poignée** ▸ the amount a hand can hold at one time : *She took a handful of popcorn from the box.* **2. poignée, petit nombre** ▸ a small number or amount : *"At last there were only a handful of pieces left on the board and the old man commanding the white pieces smiled."* (David Day)

hand·i·cap [HAN-dee-kap] NOUN, handicaps. **1. handicap, désavantage** ▸ anything that makes it harder for a person to do something; a disadvantage : *Not having the proper education can be a handicap in trying to get a job.* **2. désavantage, handicap** ▸ a disadvantage given in a race or contest to try to make the chances of winning equal for all : *In a horse race, faster horses carry more weight as a handicap.* ▲ VERB, handicapped, handicapping. **être handicapé (-ée), être gêné (-ée)** ▶ to have or give a handicap : *When her arm had healed, Marilyn realized how much the injury had handicapped her.* **Note.** The words handicap or handicapped have been used to refer to people with physical or mental challenges, but this usage is no longer the most acceptable term.

hand·ker·chief [HANG-kur-chif *or* HANG-kur-CHEEF] NOUN, handkerchiefs. **mouchoir** ▶ a soft, square piece of cloth used to wipe the nose, eyes, or face.

han·dle [HAND-ul] NOUN, handles. **manche, bras, poignée, anse** ▶ the part of an object that is held, turned, or lifted by the hand. A car door, a pair of scissors, and a frying pan all have handles. ▲ VERB, handled, handling. **1. manipuler, toucher, tâter** ▶ to hold or touch with the hands : *He handled the china very carefully as he washed it.* **2. s'y prendre avec, (s') occuper** ▶ to deal with, control, or manage something, as if holding it in the hands : *We'll handle the decorations for the dance, if you deal with the food.* **3. manœuvrer, gouverner, conduire** ▶ to act or move in a certain way : *This car handles very well on icy roads.* **4. vendre, tenir, distribuer** ▶ in business, to sell or deal in a certain item : *That bookshop handles magazines as well as books.*

hand·some [HAND-sum] ADJECTIVE, handsomer, handsomest. **1. beau (belle)** ▶ good-looking; having a pleasing appearance : *He looked very handsome in his new suit.* **2. élégant (-ante)** ▶ good-looking in a way that is thought of as strong or dignified : *a handsome white horse.* ■ **handsomely,** ADVERB. ▶ **élégamment, généreusement.**

hand·shake [HAND-SHAKE] NOUN, handshakes. **poignée de main** ▶ the holding and shaking of another person's right hand as a greeting or to show friendship or agreement.

hand·stand [HAND-STAND] NOUN, handstands. **équilibre sur les mains** ▶ the act of supporting the body with hands while the legs and body are stretched straight in the air.

hand·writ·ing [HAND-RY-ting] NOUN, handwritings. **1. écriture, manuscrit** ▶ writing done by hand, rather than typed or printed by machine. **2. écriture, calligraphie** ▶ the style or look of a person's writing : *His handwriting is hard to read because the letters are so small.*

hand·y [HAN-dee] ADJECTIVE, handier, handiest. **1. proche** ▶ within easy reach; at hand; nearby : *Mom keeps a flashlight handy in case the electricity goes out.* **2. habile, adroit (-oite)** ▶ good at working with one's hands; skillful : *If you're handy with a needle and thread, would you sew this button on for me?* **3. pratique,**

commode, utile ▶ helpful or easy to use; convenient : *This little vacuum cleaner is a handy thing to have for cleaning out odd places.* SYN: useful, helpful, ready, near, convenient.

hang [hang] VERB, hung, hanging. **1. suspendre, accrocher, être accrocher** ▶ to fix or fasten something from above, leaving the lower part free; suspend : *We hung our coats on hooks outside the classroom.* **2. baisser, courber, replier** ▶ to bend over or bend down : *to hang one's head in shame.* **3. (hanged, hanging) pendre** ▶ to put a person to death by hanging from a rope tied around the neck. **Note.** A person who hangs criminals was formerly called a hangman. ✐ **p. 299. 4. planer** ▶ to float above; be in the air over : *The smoke hung in the air.* ▲ NOUN. **1. façon de pendre ou d'être suspendu** ▶ the way something hangs : *the hang of a jacket.* **2. Informal. habileté** ▶ the skill or ability to do something easily : *I just can't seem to get the hang of this new computer game.*

hang back rester en arrière, être réticent (-ente) ▶ to hold off; stay back : *Some of the children seemed to be hanging back.*

hang·ar [HANG-ur] NOUN, hangars. **hangar** ▶ a shed or building where airplanes are kept.

hang·er [HANG-ur] NOUN, hangers. **1. cintre** ▶ a wire, wood, or plastic frame on which clothes are hung. **2. crochet, support** ▶ anything used to hang something, such as a hook for hanging a picture.

Ha·nuk·kah [HAH-nuh-kuh] NOUN. **hanoukka** ▶ (also **Chanukah**) the Jewish celebration of the Feast of Lights, for eight days in December.

hap·pen [HAP-un] VERB, happened, happening. **1. arriver, se produire, se passer** ▶ to take place; occur : *Nothing ever happens in this town.* **2. arriver, se passer** ▶ to take place without plan or reason; occur by chance : *I don't know what caused the book to fall; it just happened.* **3. trouver par hasard** ▶ to come upon by chance or accident : *I happened upon a good book.* **4. arriver, se produire, se passer** ▶ to cause a change, especially a bad change : *What happened to the radio? It worked yesterday.* SYN: occur, take place, befall, transpire.

hap·pen·ing [HAP-uh-ning] NOUN, happenings. **événement, incident** ▶ something that happens; an incident or event.

hap·py [HAP-ee] ADJECTIVE, happier, happiest. **1. heureux (-euse), joyeux (-euse)** ▶ having or showing a good feeling; pleased; glad : *"He thought about how happy all the animals would be, and how they would thank him and be grateful to him."* (Celia Barker Lottridge) **2. heureux (-euse), chanceux (-euse)** ▶ having or showing good luck; fortunate : *By a happy accident two passengers didn't show up, and we got their seats.* **3. heureux (-euse)** ▶ pleased or willing : *"I would be most happy to have you as a companion. You are welcome to live here as long as you want."* (Tololwa M. Mollel) ■ **happily,** ADVERB. ► **heureusement.** ■ **happiness** (☞ p. 1020), NOUN. ► **bonheur, joie.** SYN: cheerful, glad, contented, delighted, joyful.

har·ass [huh-RAS *or* HAIR-us] VERB, harassed, harassing. **harceler, tracasser, tourmenter** ► to bother or annoy someone again and again : *She is always being harassed by her brother to play catch with him.* SYN: bother, badger, trouble, haunt, plague.

har·bour [HAR-bur] NOUN, harbours. **1. port** ► (also **harbor**)an area of water that is protected from the rougher waters of an ocean, a river, or a lake. A harbour provides a safe place for ships or boats to stay. **Note.** A harbourmaster (also harbour chief) is a person who controls a harbour or port and who enforces its rules. **2. refuge, havre, maison** ► a place thought of as safe or protected like a harbour; a shelter : *He found a safe harbour in the orchard, far away from the teasing of the others.* ▲ VERB, harboured, harbouring. **1. donner asile à, héberger** ► to give shelter or protection : *to harbour a prisoner of war.* **2. nourrir, entretenir, garder rancune** ► to hold or keep in the mind : *to harbour a grudge against someone.* SYN: shelter, protect, shield, defend, house.

hard [hard] ADJECTIVE, harder, hardest. **1. dur (dure), rigide** ► solid and firm to the touch; not easy to bend or push in : *The ice was as hard as a rock.* **2. difficile, dur (dure)** ► not easy to do or understand, difficult : *It was a hard climb to the top of the mountain.* **3. pénible** ► full of sorrow, pain, or trouble : *"Winter is a hard time for animals, but this winter was harder than most."* (Celia Godkin) **4. sévère, dur (dure), ferme** ► not gentle or kind : *a person with a hard heart.* **5. fort (forte)** ► having or using great force, strength, or energy : *a hard rain; a hard worker.* ▲ ADVERB. **sérieusement, fortement, durement** ► in a hard way : *"He was thinking so hard I could see his thoughts."* (Ann Cameron) SYN: firm, solid, dense, rigid, inflexible.

hard drive **disque dur** ► a hard plate made from metal or clay and coated with magnetic material, used in a computer to store a very large amount of information. **Note.** Also known as a hard disk.

hard·en [HAR-dun] VERB, hardened, hardening. **durcir, endurcir, raffermir** ► to make or become hard : *The melted candle wax hardened as it cooled.*

hard·ly [HARD-lee] ADVERB. **1. presque, à peine, tout juste** ► only just; almost not : *Shauna could hardly wait for her birthday.* **2. sûrement pas, pas précisément** ► not likely; probably not : *You could hardly expect the train to wait*

just for you. SYN: just, barely, not quite, scarcely, nearly.

hard·ship [HARD-ship] NOUN, hardships. **épreuve, souffrance** ► something hard to bear; sorrow, pain, or trouble : *Early pioneers in Canada had to put up with a lot of hardships, such as sickness and loneliness.*

hard·ware [HARD-wair] NOUN. **1. quincaillerie** ► things made of metal that are used to make and fix other items. Tools, nails, screws, and locks are kinds of hardware. **2. matériel d'informatique** ► the machine parts that make up a computer, such as a display screen, a keyboard, disks, wires, and a printer. Hardware is the "hard" or physical parts of the computer, as opposed to the programs stored inside, which are software.

har·dy [HAR-dee] ADJECTIVE, hardier, hardiest. **robuste, résistant (-ante), vigoureux (-euse)** ► strong and healthy; able to stand hardships : *The players on our football team are strong and hardy.* SYN: strong, healthy, powerful, rugged.

hare [hair] NOUN, hares. **lièvre** ► a furry animal that is very much like a rabbit, but with longer ears and longer back legs. ☞ p. 110.

harm [harm] NOUN. **1. tort, mal, dommage** ► something that causes pain, damage, or loss : *The sudden rain caused great harm to the wheat crop.* **2. mal** ► something that is wrong : *I don't see any harm in using a calculator to do my math homework.* ▲ VERB, harmed, harming. **faire du mal à, faire du tort à, léser, nuire à** ► to cause or feel harm; hurt or damage : *"'And harm innocent travellers for gold?' interrupted Robert."* (Sarah Hayes) SYN: hurt, damage, injure, ruin, wrong.

harm·ful [HARM-ful] ADJECTIVE. **nuisible, nocif (-ive)** ► causing or able to cause harm; damaging : *Eating too many sweets can be harmful to your teeth.*

harm·less [HARM-lis] ADJECTIVE. **inoffensif (-ive), innocent (-ente)** ► causing no harm or damage : *Some snakes are poisonous, but most are harmless to humans.* ■ **harmlessly,** ADVERB. ► **innocemment, sans faire de mal, gentiment.**

har·mo·ny [HAR-muh-nee] NOUN, harmonies. **1. harmonie, mélodie** ► a combination of musical notes sounded at the same time in a pleasant-sounding way. **2. harmonie** ► musical notes played or sung to go along with a melody. **3. accord, entente, harmonie** ► a state of being in agreement or at peace : *There has been harmony between Canada and the U.S. for almost 200 years.* **4. harmonie, accord** ► a pleasing or orderly arrangement of parts; things that go well together : *The two wrote together in harmony and produced many great books.*

har·ness [HAR-nis] NOUN, harnesses. **1. harnais, attelage** ► a set of leather straps and bands used to attach a horse or other work animal to a

wagon, plough, or other vehicle to be pulled.
2. sangle ▶ any set of straps used to fasten or control something : *a parachute harness.*
▲ VERB, **harnessed, harnessing. 1. harnacher, atteler ▶** to put a harness on. **2. exploiter, aménager ▶** to control and put to work : *The town wants to harness the power of the waterfall to make electricity.*

harp [harp] NOUN, harps. **harpe ▶** a stringed musical instrument shaped like a very large triangle with a curved top. A harp is played by plucking the strings with fingers. **Note.** A person who plays the harp is a harpist. ▲ VERB, harped, harping. **jouer de la harpe ▶** to play on a harp. 👁 p. 537.

harp

harpist

harp on rebattre les oreilles, revenir sur ▶ to talk about a subject too much or for too long a time : *The gym teacher kept harping on the importance of exercise for good health.*

har·poon [HAR-POON] NOUN, harpoons. **harpon, lance ▶** a spear with a rope attached to it. Harpoons are thrown by hand or shot from guns. ▲ VERB, harpooned, harpooning. **harponner ▶** to kill or catch with a harpoon.

harsh [harsh] ADJECTIVE, harsher, harshest.
1. désagréable, dur (dure), âpre, strident (-ente) ▶ painful or unpleasant to the senses; rough : *The noise from the machines is harsh and unpleasant.* **2. sévère, cruel (-elle), rigoureux (-euse), austère ▶** not kind; cruel or severe : *That seems like a harsh punishment.* ■ **harshly,** ADVERB: ▶ **durement, sévèrement.** *She felt that life had treated her harshly.* ■ **harshness,** NOUN. ▶ **dureté, rudesse, sévérité.** SYN: rough, coarse, severe, sharp, grating.

har·vest [HAR-vist] NOUN, harvests. **1. moisson, récolte ▶** the gathering or picking of a crop when it is ripe :*"Without a harvest, his family*

would have no food and could not pay the Baron for the use of his land."* (Donald Carrick) **2. récolte ▶** a crop; the food that is gathered : *The potato harvest was small this year because of the bad weather.* ▲ VERB, harvested, harvesting. **récolter, cueillir, moissonner ▶** to gather in a crop : *"I wanted to help you harvest. I wanted to be a farmer."* (Jan Andrews) **Note.** A machine that harvests crops is a harvester. SYN: crop, yield, output, product, proceeds.

has [haz] VERB. **avoir ▶** a present form of have. Has is used with the third person singular : *She, he, or it has.* 🖉 p. 283.

has·sle [HAS-ul] VERB, **avoir ▶**hassled, hassling. **ennuyer, embêter ▶** to bother or annoy : *My dad is always hassling me about my haircut.* ▲ NOUN, hassles. **problème, embêtement ▶** something that bothers; a problem or difficulty : *We took a taxi because parking is too much of a hassle.*

haste [haste] NOUN. **1. hâte, rapidité ▶** speed in getting something done; quickness : *Make haste, and get to shelter before the storm breaks.* **2. empressement ▶** too much of a hurry; careless speed : *In her haste to catch the bus, she forgot her lunch.*

has·ten [HAY-sun] VERB, hastened, hastening. **hâter, s'empresser, presser, accélérer ▶** to move or act quickly; hurry : *Ken hastened to set the table before the guests arrived.*

hast·y [HACE-tee] ADJECTIVE, hastier, hastiest. **1. précipité (-ée), pressé (-ée) ▶** done with speed; quick; speedy : *She ate a hasty breakfast before rushing off to school.* **2. irréfléchi (-ie), hâtif (-ive) ▶** done too quickly : *He made a hasty judgment without finding out all the facts.* ■ **hastily,** ADVERB: ▶ **à la hâte, précipitamment, trop vite.** *He left after hastily writing a note to say goodbye.* ■ **hastiness,** NOUN. ▶ **hâte, précipitation.**

hat [hat] NOUN, hats. **chapeau (-eaux) ▶** a covering worn on the head. Hats are usually worn outside for protection or decoration. 🗂 p. 1010.

to pass the hat faire passer le chapeau, faire la quête ▶ to collect money for something.

to keep under one's hat garder pour soi ▶ to keep a secret.

hatch¹ [hach] VERB, hatched, hatching. **1. faire éclore, incuber ▶** of a baby bird, fish, reptile, and so on, to come out of an egg : *"Once these fish were little fry that hatched from eggs in this very spot."* (Julie Lawson) **Note.** A place where eggs are hatched is called a hatchery. **2. (se) tramer, comploter, conspirer, manigancer ▶** to plan or bring forth, often in secret : *They put their heads together and hatched a scheme to make money.* SYN: plot, plan, arrange, invent, make up, scheme.

hatch² NOUN, hatches. **1. écoutille ▶** an opening or a small door in the deck of a ship, leading

✍ Writing Tips

Have/has/had

Have is an irregular verb—it does not add "d" or "ed" to the base form of the verb to make it past tense. (The tense of a verb shows the time of the action or state of being expressed by the verb.)

The verb **to have** has many forms:

- *Two present-tense forms:*

  has and **have**.

    He **has** a new car.

    I **have** a broken ankle.

- *A past-tense form,* **had.**

    I **had** cereal for breakfast yesterday.

- *A past-participle form,* **had.**

    I **have had** three operations.

Note: *When the past participle of any verb is used as the main verb in a sentence, a helping verb is needed. One of the main helping verbs is "have" or "has."*

    I **have given** away my old coat.

    (**have** is the helping verb)

    Charlie **has worked** all summer.

    (**has** is the helping verb)

to a lower level. **2. trappe ▸** any trap door or small opening like this.

hatch·et [HACH-it] NOUN. hatchets. **hachette ▸** a small axe with a short handle, used with one hand.

hate [hate] VERB. hated, hating. **haïr, détester ▸** to dislike very much; have deep, strong feelings against : *The tugboat hauled the Megan and Todd both hate snakes.* ▲ NOUN. hates. **haine ▸** a deep, strong dislike. SYN : dislike, detest, loathe, object to.

ha·tred [HAY-trid] NOUN. **haine, aversion ▸** a deep, strong feeling against a person or thing; hate.

haugh·ty [HAH too] ADJECTIVE. haughtier, haughtiest. **hautain (-aine), arrogant (-ante) ▸** having or showing too much pride; feeling that one is better than other people : *The haughty movie star wouldn't have anything to do with his old friends after he became famous.* SYN : arrogant, proud, scornful.

haul [hol] VERB. hauled, hauling. **1. tirer ▸** to pull or drag with effort : *The tugboat hauled the ship out of the harbour.* **2. traîner, transporter, remorquer ▸** to move or carry : *They hauled in dirt to make a garden.* ▲ NOUN. hauls. **1. parcours, trajet (d'un objet traîné ou remorqué) ▸** a strong pulling or dragging; the act of hauling. **2. parcours, trajet, distance ▸** a distance that something moves or goes : *Let's stop to eat now—it's a long haul to the next town.* **3. prise, butin, saisie ▸** an amount collected : *I got a big haul of presents on my birthday.* SYN : drag, draw, tug, tow.

haunt [hont] VERB. haunted, haunting. **1. hanter ▸** to visit or return to a place as a ghost, spirit, or other strange form. **2. fréquenter ▸** to visit a place often : *The kids haunted the park, looking for a game of ball.* **3. obséder, hanter, troubler ▸** to stay in the mind or come to mind often : *Memories of the accident haunted Alex.* ▲ NOUN. haunts. **lieu (lieux) fréquenté(s), repère ▸** a place that is often visited : *When we returned for our class reunion, we visited all our old haunts, like the library and the old movie theatre.* SYN : visit often, frequent, hang around.

have [hav] VERB. had, having. **1. avoir, posséder ▸** to be in possession of; own or hold : *Do you have a pencil I could borrow? I have an idea for earning some money.* **2. avoir, posséder ▸** to own or hold as a quality or feature : *A tiger has stripes on its body.* **3. avoir ▸** to go through; experience : *to have breakfast; to have a talk with someone.* **4. avoir ▸** to cause to happen or be done; bring about : *to have your hair cut. I'll have Dad pick you up at 3:00.* **5. avoir ▸** to carry on; be part of : *We're going to have a meeting on Friday.* **6. avoir ▸** to give birth to or be a parent of : *to have a baby. We have three children.* **Note.** Have is also used with other verbs : **1. ▸** to show a previous action : *We have finished our project.* **2. ▸** with to. to show need or obligation : *I have to leave now.* ✐ p. 283.

hawk¹ [hok] NOUN. hawks. **faucon ▸** a large bird of prey having a sharp, hooked beak, and powerful feet with sharp, curved claws. Hawks catch and eat small animals.

hawk² VERB. hawked, hawking. **colporter, faire du porte à porte ▸** to offer goods for sale in a public place by calling out or shouting; peddle : *Ryan hawks peanuts and popcorn at the baseball stadium.*

hay [hay] NOUN. **foin ▸** grass, clover, or other plants that have been cut and dried for use as food for horses, cattle, and other farm animals. 👁 p. 115.

haz·ard [HAZ-urd] NOUN. hazards. **danger, risque, péril ▸** something that can cause harm or injury; a risk or danger : *That pile of old newspapers is a fire hazard.* **Note.** Something that is a hazard is hazardous. ▲ VERB. hazarded, hazarding. **risquer, hasarder ▸** to take a risk : *to hazard a guess.* SYN : risk, chance, gamble, wager, dare.

haze [haze] NOUN. hazes. **brume (légère) ▸** a thin layer of smoke, mist, or dust in the air : *A haze of smoke hung over the neighbourhood long after the fire had been put out.*

ha-zel [HAY-zul] NOUN, hazels. **1. noisetier** ▶ a tree with light-brown nuts that can be eaten. **2. noisette, bistre** ▶ a light-brown or greenish-brown colour.

fruit

flowers

leaves

hazel

ha-zy [HAY-zee] ADJECTIVE, hazier, haziest. **1. brumeux (-euse), embrumé (-ée)** ▶ covered by or blurred with haze : *a hazy summer afternoon.* **2. vague, flou (floue), nébuleux (-euse)** ▶ not clear; dim; blurred : *"It's a bit hazy around the edges, but when I give it a polish it comes out bright and clear and shining."* (Julie Lawson) SYN: foggy, cloudy, misty, muddy, filmy.

he [hee] PRONOUN. **il** ▶ the boy, man, or male animal that has been mentioned : *I called Jim on the phone, but he wasn't home.* ▲ NOUN, hes. **mâle** ▶ a male : *Is your cat a he or a she?* ✐ p. 284.

head [hed] NOUN, heads. **1. tête** ▶ the top part of the body, containing the eyes, ears, mouth, nose, and brain. **2. tête, esprit** ▶ the power of the brain; the mind : *She has a good head for figures.* **3. tête** ▶ anything thought of as like a head in shape or position : *a head of lettuce; the head of a pin.* **4. tête, haut, bout** ▶ something that is at the top or front : *to stand at the head of the stairs; to march at the head of a parade.* **5. chef, maître, supérieur (-ieure)** ▶ a person who is at the top; a leader : *In Canada, the prime minister is the head of the government.*

6. (plural, head) **têtes** ▶ one of a group of cattle or other such animals : *That ranch has about 600 head of cattle.* **7. point déterminant** ▶ an important or crucial point : *to bring matters to a head.* **8.** heads. **face** ▶ the side of a coin having a face on it. ▲ VERB, headed, heading. **1. aller, se diriger** ▶ to move in a certain direction; go toward : *We're heading north for the weekend.* **2. mener, diriger, être à la tête de** ▶ to be or go at the head of; lead : *He heads a large company.* **3. faire une tête, renvoyer d'un coup de tête** ▶ in soccer, to strike the ball with the head. **Note.** A play of this kind is called a **header.** ▲ ADJECTIVE. **de tête** ▶ being the head : *the head chef in a restaurant.* **Note.** Head is used in many compound words : *headstrong, headband, headwind, head-start,*

✐ **Writing Tips**

He; he or she; they

Do your best to avoid sentences that make it necessary to choose between **he** *and* **she; his** *and* **hers;** *or* **him** *and* **her;** *or* **himself** *and* **herself.**

In the past, when a pronoun could refer to either a male or female, the masculine pronoun—he, his, or him—was chosen. This approach is not used anymore because it is sexist language.

• Another solution is to use "he or she," or "he/she." Many writers believe that this approach is clumsy and ugly.

  If a student loses a textbook, **he or she** should replace it.

• Other writers use the plural form of the pronoun.

  If a student loses a textbook, **they** should replace it.

While this approach is becoming more accepted, it is not grammatically correct because it uses a plural pronoun to refer to a singular noun. This usage is more accepted in conversation than in writing.

• Another option is to make the sentence plural if possible.

  If students lose textbooks, **they** should replace it.

• Your best option is to rewrite the sentence to get rid of he or she. This is not always easy to do.

  Students who lose textbooks should replace them.

✍ Writing Tips

Headlines

Headlines are the words printed in large type at the top of a newspaper or magazine article. They sum up the main idea of the article in just a few words. They also attempt to grab the readers' attention and spark their interest in the story. Some headlines are written in complete sentences, others are phrases.

When writing a headline,

* choose the most exciting or important part of your story or an interesting fact.

* use a clever play on words or give straight information.

* use active verbs, for example, *"Blue Jays **trample** the Braves."*

headphone, headroom, headlong, and so on. 📖 **p. 982.** 🖉 **p. 285.**

head·ache [HED-AKE] NOUN, **headaches. mal (maux) de tête, migraine ▸** a pain in the head.

head·ing [HED-ing] NOUN, **headings. 1. en-tête ▸** something written at the top of a page, such as the first part of a letter, the title of a page, chapter, or book, and so on. **2. sous-titre ▸** a title that sets apart or describes a section such as a chapter, paragraph, or topic. **3. orientation, sens ▸** the direction of a vehicle as indicated by a compass : *a heading of west.*

head·light [HED-LITE] NOUN, **headlights. phare, feu avant ▸** a bright light attached to the front of a car, bicycle, or other vehicle.

head·line [HED-LINE] NOUN, **headlines. 1. (gros) titre, manchette ▸** several words printed in large, dark type at the beginning of a newspaper article telling what the story is about. **2. (grand) titre ▸** a similar title above a magazine article or an advertisement. 🖉 **p. 285.**

head·quar·ters [HED-KWOR-turz] NOUN. **1. quartier général, état major ▸** a main location or office for the operations of an army, a police force, or another such group : *The soldiers were waiting for orders from headquarters.* **2. siège social ▸** the main office of a business or an organization.

heal [heel] VERB, **healed, healing. 1. guérir ▸** to make or become well; return to health : *"By the end of winter holidays, the eagle's wing had healed enough to take the bandages off."* (Sheryl McFarlane) **2. cicatriser, corriger, réparer ▸** to repair or make right : *The passing of time healed the bad feelings between them.* SYN: cure, mend, correct, repair, remedy.

health [helth] NOUN. **1. bonne santé ▸** a condition in which the body and mind are as they should be; being free from sickness and feeling well : *Eating the proper foods is important to good health.* **2. santé ▸** the condition of the body and mind, whether good or bad : *He wants to retire from his job because he's been in poor health for several years.* 📖 **p. 1160.**

health·y [HELTH-ee] ADJECTIVE, **healthier, healthiest. 1. sain (saine), salubre ▸** having or showing good health : *"The island animals were healthy. There was plenty of food for all."* (Celia Godkin) **2. bon pour la santé, salutaire ▸** good for one's health : *Swimming is a healthy exercise.* **3. considérable, grand (grande) ▸** large in amount : *The old sailor had a healthy respect for the power of the sea.* SYN: fit, well, sound, hearty vigorous.

heap [heep] NOUN, **heaps. 1. tas, amas ▸** a group of things thrown together; a pile : *"The sticks had fallen in a heap and begun to rot."* (Margaret Read MacDonald) **2.** *Informal.* **tas, masse ▸** a large number or amount : *to be in a heap of trouble.* ▲ VERB, **heaped, heaping. 1. entasser, empiler ▸** to pile in a heap : *He heaped his dirty clothes in a pile.* **2. accabler, couvrir de ▸** to give or provide in large amounts : *She was embarrassed by the praise that her parents heaped on her.*

hear [heer] VERB, **heard, hearing. 1. entendre ▸** to take in sound through the ear : *I could hear the whistle of the train in the distance.* **2. écouter ▸** to pay attention to; listen to : *We waited to hear all options before we made our decision.* **3. apprendre, entendre (dire), entendre (parler de) ▸** to get a message or information about; learn or find out : *I hear that there's a party at Ellen's this weekend.*

🔧 Word Builder

Head up means to be careful: *Keep your head up when hiking along the Niagara Escarpment.* When you *put your head together* with a friend, you're consulting or planning with that person: *Cora and I put our heads together to plan a surprise party.* *Talk someone's head off* means to talk endlessly: *My sister is a chatterbox. She can talk your head off.* *Go to someone's head* means that a person takes too much pride in his or her accomplishments: *He won't take supporting roles anymore. I guess all the praise has gone to his head.*

hear of savoir, entendre (parler de), connaî-tre ▶ to know of; be aware of : *I've never heard of that actor.*

hear·ing [HEER-ing] NOUN, hearings. **1. ouïe** ▶ the sense by which sounds are received by the ear. Note. A hearing aid is a device worn on the ear by people who are hearing-impaired. It makes sounds louder. **2. audition** ▶ the act of getting information. **3. audience, audition, séance** ▶ an official meeting or trial allowing someone the chance to be heard : *The judge set a date for the hearing.* 🖝 p. 1034.

heart [hart] NOUN, hearts. **1. cœur** ▶ a large, hol-low muscle that pumps blood to all parts of the body. **2. cœur** ▶ the heart is thought of as the centre of a person's feelings : *When he saw the hungry children, his heart was moved to pity.* **3. cœur, courage** ▶ energy and courage : *a hockey player with a lot of heart.* **4. cœur** ▶ the centre or main part of some-thing : *We hike many hours, deep into the heart of the forest.* **5. cœur, de cœur** ▶ a heart-shaped design like this [♥], as on a playing card or a Valentine. **6. hearts. cœur** ▶ the suit of cards that has this design. 🖝 p. 999. 👁 p. 402.

by heart par cœur ▶ by memory : *She's already learned her lines for the play by heart.*

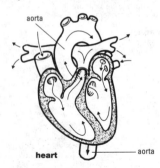

heart   — aorta

heart attack crise cardiaque ▶ a sudden fail-ure of the heart to work normally, often resulting in death or serious damage to the heart.

heart-bro-ken [HART-BROH-kun] ADJECTIVE. qui a le cœur brisé, chagriné (-ée), peiné (-ée) ▶ suf-fering great sorrow or grief.

hearth [harth] NOUN, hearths. foyer, âtre ▶ the floor of a fireplace and the area around it. A hearth is usually made of brick or stone.

heart·y [HART-ee] ADJECTIVE, heartier, heartiest. **1. cordial (-iale, -iaux), chaleureux (-euse), sincère** ▶ showing warmth and feeling; friendly : *Hank had a hearty laugh that made you want to laugh with him.* **2. vigoureux (-euse), robuste, solide** ▶ strong and healthy : *a hearty meal; a person with a hearty appetite.* ■ **heartily,** ADVERB: ▶ cordialement, de tout cœur, sincèrement, chaleureusement. *"He spoke to Sadie through the tube and laughed heartily when she answered back."* (Christy MacKinnon) ■ **heartiness,** NOUN. ▶ cordialité, sincérité, vigueur, chaleur. SYN: healthy, robust, well, sound.

heat [heet] NOUN. **1. chaleur** ▶ a form of energy that causes the temperature of something to become higher. Heat is produced by the sun, by fire, by friction, and by certain chemical reac-tions. **2. chaleur** ▶ a high temperature; the state of being hot : *She didn't like living in Arizona because of the heat.* **3. chauffage** ▶ warm air supplied to a room or building. Note. A heater is a device that provides heat, as to a building or car. Stoves, radiators, furnaces, and fireplaces are types of heaters. **4. feu de l'action** ▶ a point of strong feelings or excitement : *In the heat of the game, he forgot all about his sore leg.* ▲ VERB, heated, heating. **chauffer, réchauffer** ▶ to make warm or hot; give heat to : *to heat soup before serving it.* Note. Also used as an ADJEC-TIVE: *a heated garage; a heated argument with strong feelings.* 🖝 p. 1103.

heav·en [HEV-un] NOUN, heavens. **1.** (also Heaven) **paradis, ciel (cieux)** ▶ in religious teaching, the place where God lives and where good people go after they die, usually thought of as a place of complete happiness. **2.** (also the heavens) **ciel (cieux)** ▶ the area above the earth; the sky : *The heavens seemed to open up, and rain began to pour down.* **3. au para-dis, aux anges, au septième ciel** ▶ a state of great happiness like heaven : *She was in heaven when she won a prize for her short story.*

heav·i·ly [HEV-uh-lee] ADVERB. lourdement, forte-ment ▶ in a heavy way : *The rain was falling heavily.*

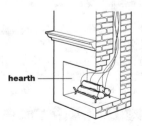

hearth

heav·y [HEV-ee] ADJECTIVE, heavier, heaviest. **1. lourd (lourde), pesant (-ante)** ▶ having a lot of weight; hard to pick up or move : *"Michael fig-ured he'd have a heart attack before he got the heavy tank into their living room."* (Cynthia Rylant) **2. lourd (lourde), gros (grosse)** ▶ having more than the usual weight for its kind : *a heavy* *sweater; heavy cardboard.* **3. lourd (lourde), gros (grosse), fort (forte)** ▸ greater than usual in size or amount : *"When the heavy rains come, the soil will be washed away and the forest will become a desert."* (Lynne Cherry) **4. pesant (-ante), lourd (lourde)** ▸ seeming to be under a great weight : *moist, heavy air; a sad and heavy heart.* ■ **heaviness,** NOUN. ■ **lourdeur, pesanteur.** SYN : weighty, fat, burdensome.

hec·tic [HEK-tik] ADJECTIVE. **trépidant (-ante), agité (-ée), mouvementé (-ée)** ▸ filled with activity; busy in a hurried or confusing way : *It was hectic trying to get to school on time after we had all slept late.* SYN : frantic, busy, exciting, moving.

hedge [hej] NOUN, **hedges.** **haie** ▸ a row of closely planted shrubs or small trees. Hedges often form a boundary or fence in a yard or garden. ▲ VERB, **hedged, hedging. 1. mettre une haie autour de, enclore** ▸ to close in or separate something with a hedge : *We hedged our backyard with shrubs.* **2. éviter de se compromettre, chercher des faux-fuyants, patiner** ▸ to avoid giving a direct answer : *The candidate for mayor hedged when the reporters asked him what he planned to do about the city's high crime rate.*

hedge

hedge·hog [HEJ-hog] NOUN, **hedgehogs. hérisson** ▸ an insect-eating animal related to the porcupine. It has a pointed snout and is covered with sharp, stiff spines. When a hedgehog is frightened, it rolls into a ball with its spines pointed out for protection.

heed [heed] VERB, **heeded, heeding. faire attention à, prendre garde, tenir compte de** ▸ to pay attention to : *He failed to heed the stop sign and kept driving.* ▲ NOUN. **souci, attention** ▸ one's attention; notice : *She paid no heed to the soft rain that was falling.* SYN : notice, observe, follow, mind, attend.

heel [heel] NOUN, **heels. 1. talon** ▸ the rounded back part of the foot below the ankle. **2. talon** ▸ the part of a shoe or sock at the heel.

3. talon ▸ anything that has the shape or position of a heel : *The heel of the hand is the lower part of the palm.* ▲ VERB, **heeled, heeling. talonner, être sur les talons de** ▸ to follow on the heels of; follow closely : *The dog trainer taught the puppy to heel at her side.*

height [hite] NOUN, **heights. 1. hauteur, taille, grandeur** ▸ the distance from the top to the bottom of something; elevation : *The height of the tower is 35 metres.* **2. grandeur, hauteur** ▸ the state of having great height; being high : *I guessed he was a basketball player because of his height.* **3.** (often **heights**) **hauteurs** ▸ a high place : *He didn't want to go up on the roof because he's afraid of heights.* **4. sommet, apogée, faîte** ▸ the highest point; peak : *August is the height of the tourist season in Europe.*

heir [ayr] NOUN, **heirs. héritier (ière)** ▸ a person who has the right to own or hold money, property, or a title after the owner dies; a person who inherits something : *She is heir to her parents' fortune.* **Note.** An heirloom is a possession handed down from one generation to another.

held [held] VERB. **tenir** ▸ a past form of hold.

hel·i·cop·ter [HEL-ih-KOP-tur] NOUN, **helicopters. hélicoptère (re)** ▸ an aircraft without wings that is lifted up by one or more large blades called rotors or propellers. Helicopters can move forward, backward, sideways, up, or down. 👁 p. 393.

he·li·um [HEE-lee-um] NOUN. **hélium** ▸ a very light gas that has no colour or smell and does not burn. It is used to fill balloons because it is lighter than air. Helium is a chemical element that is found in small amounts in the earth's atmosphere, but in large amounts in the sun and stars.

hedgehog

hell [hel] NOUN, **hells. 1.** (also Hell) **enfer** ▸ in religious teaching, the place where evil people are punished after death. **2. enfer** ▸ something that causes great suffering; a very bad place or condition.

hel·lo [heh-LOH or huh-LOH] INTERJECTION; NOUN, **hellos. allô!, salut, bonjour** ▸ a word of greeting used when meeting someone or answering the telephone.

hel·met [HEL-mit] NOUN, helmets. **casque ▸** a hard covering worn to protect the head in certain sports, in warfare, in doing dangerous work, and so on.

help [help] VERB, helped, helping. **1. aider, assister, seconder, collaborer ▸** to do part of the work; do what is needed or wanted : *"Maylin's father and brothers loved eating food, but they didn't help Maylin in the kitchen."* (Paul Yee) Note. A person who helps is a helper. **2. empêcher ▸** to keep from; avoid or prevent : *I can't help thinking that I have forgotten something.* ▲ NOUN, helps. **1. aide, secours, assistance ▸** the act of helping; aid ; assistance : *We never could have done it without her help.* **2. aide, secours ▸** a person or thing that helps. **3. domestique, employé (-ée) de maison ▸** a hired worker or workers, especially someone paid to do housework. SYN: aid, assist, lend a hand, support, collaborate.

help oneself se servir ▸ to serve oneself : *Help yourself to some of the cookies.*

help·ful [HELP-ful] ADJECTIVE. **utile, serviable ▸** giving help : *helpful advice. Ian finds it helpful to use a dictionary.* ■ **helpfully,** ADVERB. ▸ **gentiment, utilement.** ■ **helpfulness,** NOUN. ▸ **utilité, serviabilité.**

help·less [HELP-lis] ADJECTIVE. **impuissant (-ante), faible ▸** not being able to take care of oneself or to act without help : *A newborn baby is helpless.* ■ **helplessly,** ADVERB. ▸ **faiblement, en vain, sans ressource, désespérément.** ■ **helplessness,** NOUN. ▸ **impuissance, incapacité, faiblesse.**

hem [hem] NOUN, hems. **bord, ourlet ▸** the smooth edge on the bottom of a piece of clothing. A hem is made by turning the rough edge under and sewing it in place. ▲ VERB, hemmed, hemming. **faire l'ourlet de ▸** to put a hem on : *to hem a skirt.*

hem in encercler, entourer, cerner ▸ to close in ; surround : *The house stood on a small plot of ground, hemmed in by trees and bushes.*

hem·i·sphere [HEM-is-FEER] NOUN, hemispheres. **hémisphère ▸** one half of the earth. The Northern Hemisphere and the Southern Hemisphere are divided by the equator. The Western Hemisphere and the Eastern Hemisphere are not divided by an exact line in this way, but the Western Hemisphere is thought of as consisting of North and South America.

hen [hen] NOUN, hens. **1. poule ▸** an adult female chicken. **2. femelle ▸** the adult female of certain other birds, such as a turkey or pheasant.

hence [hence] ADVERB. **1. dont, par conséquent, de là, d'où ▸** as a result; for this reason : *She was named after her father, George ; hence the name Georgia.* **2. d'en ▸** from this time : *When*

he left, he promised to return a week hence. SYN: therefore, thus, consequently.

her [hur] PRONOUN. **1. elle, lui, la ▸** the pronoun she when used as an object : *Give me Eve's address so that I can send her a letter.* **2. son (sa, ses) ▸** the pronoun she when used as a possessive : *I don't know Eve's address, but I do have her phone number.* ✐ p. 284.

her·ald [HAIR-uld] NOUN, heralds. **messager (-ère), annonciateur (-trice), crieur (-euse), héraut ▸** in former times, a person who carried messages for a king and gave important news. ▲ VERB, heralded, heralding. **annoncer, proclamer ▸** to give a message or sign of : *The bright morning sun seemed to herald a beautiful day.* SYN: announce, shout, proclaim, bring news.

herb [urb or hurb] NOUN, herbs. **herbe (aromatique médicinale), fines herbes ▸** any plant whose stems, leaves, roots, or seeds are used for flavouring food or as a medicine. Common herbs include parsley, basil, mint, and sage.

herd [hurd] NOUN, herds. **1. troupeau (-eaux), harde ▸** a group of farm animals or other large animals that feed and stay together : *a herd of cattle. "One day Elephant came crashing out of the jungle, followed by his herd."* (Jan Thornhill) **2. gardien (-ienne) de troupeau (-eaux) ▸** a person who herds animals : *a goatherd.* ▲ VERB, herded, herding. **1. rassembler en troupeau (-eaux) ▸** to gather a group of animals into a herd. **2. regrouper, rassembler ▸** to form or gather into a large group : *The teachers herded the children into the building.*

here [heer] ADVERB. **1. ici ▸** in, at, or to this place : *Jason, you stand here, next to Brian. Here comes our bus now.* **2. là ▸** at the time being spoken about; now : *Here it is Thursday already.* ▲ NOUN. **d'ici ▸** this place : *Do you know how to get to the theatre from here ?*

here·af·ter [heer-AF-tur] ADVERB. **dorénavant, désormais, ci-après, ▸** in the future; after this : *Hereafter, please print your name.* ▲ NOUN. **l'audelà, dans l'autre monde ▸** the time after death.

he·red·i·tar·y [huh-RED-ih-TAIR-ee] ADJECTIVE. **1. héréditaire ▸** able to be passed on from a parent to its offspring : *Colour blindness is hereditary.* **2. hérité (-ée) ▸** passing from a parent to a child by inheritance : *"Baron" is a hereditary title in Britain.*

he·red·i·ty [huh-RED-ih-tee] NOUN, heredities. **hérédité ▸** the process by which living things pass on their characteristics from parent to child. All humans, animals, and plants do this through tiny substances called genes.

her·i·tage [HAIR-ih-tij] NOUN, heritages. **héritage, patrimoine ▸** what has been handed down from the past ; the beliefs and customs that people take from earlier generations : *Our Canadian*

✐ **Writing Tips**

Hero Tales

Hero tales come from all over the world. These stories were often based on real events or real people and were handed down from generation to generation. The stories may have changed with each telling, sometimes becoming more and more exaggerated. But they kept their main purpose: to teach the lesson that good actions are rewarded and bad actions are punished.

• *Well-known hero tales include stories about Robin Hood, Vasilisa the Wise, King Arthur and the Knights of the Round Table, and Ishikawa.*

• *The word* **hero** *usually refers to the main or central character of a story. In these stories a hero*

– has a problem to solve or an obstacle to overcome,

– may have a special characteristic such as wisdom, strength, courage, intelligence,

– acts for the good of others.

• *When developing a hero tale, you need a hero with a special skill or characteristic. You might also use exaggeration or humour to help "teach the lesson" of the tale.*

heritage has elements from English, French, and Native cultures, as well as many others.

her·mit [HUR-mit] NOUN, hermits. **ermite** ▶ a person who chooses to live alone, away from other people; recluse. In former times, people often became hermits for religious reasons.

he·ro [HEER-oh] NOUN, heroes. **1. héros (héroïne)** ▶ a person who is admired by others for great achievements or outstanding qualities. **2. héros (héroïne)** ▶ a person who shows great courage: *She is a hero for saving her little brother in the fire.* **3. héros (héroïne)** ▶ the leading character in a book, play, or movie. **Note.** Female heroes used to be called heroines. ✐ **p. 289.**

he·ro·ic [hih-ROH-ik] ADJECTIVE. **1. héroïque** ▶ having to do with a hero: *Sir Thomas Malory wrote heroic tales of King Arthur and his knights.* **2. héroïque, brave, courageux (-euse), vaillant (-ante)** ▶ showing the qualities of a hero; very brave or outstanding: *The lifeguard made a heroic rescue of the drowning man.* SYN: brave, valiant, courageous, bold.

her·on [HAIR-un] NOUN, herons. **héron** ▶ a wading bird that has very long legs, a long, slender neck, and a narrow head with a sharply pointed bill. 👁 p. 109.

hers [hurz] PRONOUN. **le sien, la sienne, les siens, les siennes** ▶ a possessive form of she: *This book is mine, and that one is hers.* ✐ **p. 284.**

her·self [hur-SELF] PRONOUN. **1. elle-même, se** ▶ her own self: *My little sister just learned to tie her shoes herself.* **2. elle-même** ▶ her usual or normal self: *Katie was up late last night, so she's not really herself today.* **3. elle-même** ▶ a stronger form of she or her, used to call attention to the person who was just mentioned: *Yvonne claimed that she, herself, answered the phone.* ✐ **p. 284.**

hes·i·tate [HEZ-uh-TATE] VERB, hesitated, hesitating. **hésiter** ▶ to stop or wait for a time; be slow in acting because one is unsure: *He hesitated a moment before knocking on the door.* ▪ **hesitation,** NOUN: **hésitation, doute.** *When Chloe was offered the new job, she accepted without hesitation.* SYN: pause, rest, falter, waver, doubt.

hex·a·gon [HEK-suh-GON] NOUN, hexagons. **hexagone** ▶ a closed figure having six sides and six angles.

hey [hay] INTERJECTION. ▶ a word used to attract someone's attention or to show a certain feeling: *Hey! That was my juice you just drank.*

hi [hy] INTERJECTION. **salut, allô!** ▶ a word used to greet people, like "hello."

hi·ber·nate [HY-bur-NATE] VERB, hibernated, hibernating. **hiberner** ▶ of an animal, to spend a long period of time in a very quiet and inactive state like sleep. Bears and some other animals hibernate during the winter, living off fat that is stored in their bodies. **Note.** This period of rest is called hibernation.

hi·bis·cus [hy-BIS-kus] NOUN, hibiscuses. **hibiscus** ▶ a flower, shrub, or small tree from tropical regions, with large, bell-shaped white, pink, red, yellow, or blue flowers.

hic·cup [HIK-up] NOUN, hiccups. (also hiccough) **1. hoquet** ▶ a sudden gasp of breath that one cannot control, producing a short, clicking sound. A hiccup is caused by a sudden tightening of the breathing muscles. **2. the hiccups. hoquet** ▶ the condition of having hiccups one after the other. ▲ VERB, hiccuped, hiccupping. **avoir le hoquet, hoqueter** ▶ to have hiccups.

hick·o·ry [HIK-ur-ee] NOUN, hickories. **noyer d'Amérique** ▶ a tall North American hardwood tree with grey bark. Hickory nuts can be eaten.

hid·den [HID-un] VERB. **caché (-ée), dissimulé (-ée)** ▶ a past form of hide: *I had hidden my diary under my sweater.* ▲ ADJECTIVE. **caché (-ée), dissimulé (-ée), secret (-ète)** ▶ put or kept out of sight; secret: *His face was hidden behind a mask.*

hide[1] [hide] VERB. hid, hidden or hid, hiding.
1. cacher, dissimuler ▶ to put or keep out of
sight : *"It makes us afraid, so we hide from the
sunlight and the noise."* (Gerald McDermott)
2. cacher, dissimuler ▶ to keep secret; conceal : *Phil tried to hide his disappointment
when his poem didn't win first prize.*
Note. Hide-and-seek is a children's game in
which some players hide and others seek (try to
find) them. SYN : conceal, cover up, disguise, camouflage.

hide[2] NOUN, hides. **peau (peaux), cuir** ▶ the skin
of an animal; pelt. Hides are used to make
leather for shoes, clothing, and other products.

hid·e·ous [HIDE-ee-us] ADJECTIVE. **laid (laide),
hideux (-euse), monstrueux (-euse), affreux
(-euse)** ▶ very ugly or frightening; horrible : *a
hideous monster.* SYN : ugly, frightful, horrible,
dreadful, ghastly.

hide·out [HIDE-out] NOUN, hideouts. **cachette** ▶ a safe place to hide : *Our treehouse is
a great hideout because no one knows where
it is.*

hi·er·o·glyph·ic [HY-roh-GLIF-iks] NOUN, hieroglyphics. **1. hiéroglyphe** ▶ a picture or symbol
that stands for a word, an idea, or a sound, such
as two wavy lines, which means "water" in many
Native languages of North America. **2. hiéroglyphe** ▶ any form of writing in which pictures
and symbols are used to present ideas : *The
Egyptians used hieroglyphics before they
developed an alphabet.*

hieroglyphics

high [hy] ADJECTIVE. higher, highest. **1. haut
(haute), élevé (-ée)** ▶ going far up above the
ground; tall : *a high building.* **2. haut
(haute)** ▶ at a point far above the ground : *a balloon that is high in the air.* **3. haut (haute)** ▶ at
the stated distance above the ground : *That
fence is two metres high.* **4. grand (grande),
élevé (-ée)** ▶ greater than is normal or usual :
high winds; high prices. **5. éminent (-ente),
important (-ante), grand (grande)** ▶ above others in rank or importance : *a high government
official.* **6. aigu (aiguë)** ▶ of music or other
sound, nearer to the top of the range of sound

that the human ear can hear. ▲ NOUN, highs.
1. sommet, haut ▶ something that is high; a
high place or point : *Today's temperature of
37°C was a new high for this date.* **2. anticyclone** ▶ a weather condition in which there
is a central area of air with higher pressure than
the areas around it. ▲ ADVERB. **en haut, en hauteur** ▶ to a high place or point : *to hit a ball
high in the air.* **Note.** High is a part of many
compound words : *highlight, high jump, high
school, highrise, high sticking,* and so on.
SYN : tall, towering, elevated.

high·land [HY-lund] NOUN, highlands. **1. région
montagneuse** ▶ a region that is higher and
hillier than the surrounding areas : *Lewa Downs
is a huge private range in the highlands of
Kenya.* **2. the Highlands. Highlands** ▶ a hilly
region in northern and western Scotland.

high·ly [HY-lee] ADVERB. **1. très, grandement,
fortement, extrêmement** ▶ to a great degree;
very much; very : *This restaurant was highly
recommended by one of our neighbours.*
2. en bien (de) ▶ in a good or favourable way :
*Nadya's teachers think very highly of her
writing ability.*

high school see secondary school.

high·way [HY-way] NOUN, highways. **autoroute**
▶ a public road that is a main route. 🔲 **p. 1050.**

hike [hike] VERB, hiked, hiking. **faire une randonnée pédestre, faire une promenade à pied**
▶ to go on a long walk, especially one that is
taken for exercise or enjoyment : *We hiked
to the lake for a swim.* ▲ NOUN, hikes. **randonnée** ▶ a long walk.

hi·lar·i·ous [hih-LAIR-ee-us] ADJECTIVE. **hilarant
(-ante), tordant (-ante), amusant (-ante), drôle**
▶ very funny; full of or causing loud laughter :
I think the Pink Panther movies are hilarious.
SYN : funny, amusing, laughable.

hill [hil] NOUN, hills. **1. colline** ▶ a raised piece of
ground that is higher than the surrounding land,
but smaller than a mountain. **2. butte** ▶ a small
heap or pile : *There's a big ant hill in our backyard.*

hill

hill·side [HIL-side] NOUN, hillsides. **flanc de
montagne** ▶ the sloping side of a hill.

him [him] PRONOUN. **lui, le ▶** the pronoun he when used as an object : *If that's Doug on the phone, ask him to call back later.* ✏ p. 284.

him-self [him-SELF] PRONOUN. **1. lui-même, se ▶** his own self : *"Papagayo came flying along just then, singing and chuckling to himself."* (Gerald McDermott) **2. lui-même ▶** his usual or normal self : *Don't be upset with Jeff for acting so rude; he's just not himself today.* **3. lui-même ▶** a stronger form of he or him, used to call attention to the person who was just mentioned : *This copy of the book was signed by the author himself.* ✏ p. 284.

hind [hynd] ADJECTIVE. **de derrière, postérieur ▶** at the back; rear. **Note.** Used to refer to animals : *"There, standing on his hind legs and helping himself to some fat, was the biggest, fattest, shiniest, blackest bear she had ever seen."* (Marilyn Halvorson)

hin-der [hin-dur] VERB, hindered, hindering. **gêner, entraver, embarrasser ▶** to get in the way of; hold back; delay; interfere with : *Strong winds hindered our efforts to put up a tent.* **Note.** Someone or something that hinders is a **hindrance.** SYN : prevent, obstruct, impede, block, hold back.

Hin-du [HIN-doo] NOUN, Hindus. **Hindou ▶** a person who believes in the religion of Hinduism. Many people in India are Hindus.

hinge [hinj] NOUN, hinges. **gond, charnière ▶** a jointed device that allows a door, gate, lid, or other swinging part to open or move.

hint [hint] NOUN, hints. **1. indice ▶** a piece of information that is meant to help someone answer a question or to do something more easily : *You still can't guess? All right, I'll give you a hint — his last name begins with "S."* **2. soupçon ▶** a very small amount of something that can barely be noticed : *"She turned at her desk. Was there the hint of a smile on her face?"* (Tim Wynne-Jones) ▲ VERB, hinted, hinting. **insinuer, laisser entendre (que) ▶** to suggest something without saying it directly; show by a hint : *"I bet you have to get up early tomorrow,"* she hinted when she wanted her guests to go home. SYN : clue, tip, suspicion, suggestion.

hip [hip] NOUN, hips. **1. hanche ▶** the bony part on either side of the human body where the legs join the body. **2. hanche ▶** in an animal, where the back legs join the body. ☐ p. 1001.

hip-po-pot-a-mus [HIP-uh-POT-uh-mus] NOUN, hippopotamuses or hippopotami. **hippopotame ▶** a very large plant-eating animal that lives in or near lakes, rivers, or ponds in central and southern Africa. It has a broad body, short legs, and thick grey or brown skin without hair. **Note.** Also called hippo for short.

hire [hire] VERB, hired, hiring. **1. engager, employer, embaucher ▶** to get someone to do work for pay; employ : *Dad hired someone to paint the house.* **2. louer, emprunter ▶** to get the use of something for a time in return for payment; rent : *to hire a cab; to hire a hall for a dance.* ▲ NOUN. **location, embauche ▶** the act or fact of hiring : *Several places at the lake have fishing boats for hire.*

his [hiz] PRONOUN. **le sien (la sienne), son (sa, ses) ▶** the pronoun he when used as a possessive : *Mike left his jacket at the park yesterday and had to borrow mine.* ✏ p. 284.

hiss [hiss] VERB, hissed, hissing. **1. siffler, chuinter ▶** to make a sharp, long "s" sound : *Air hissed out of the hole in the bicycle tire.* **2. siffler ▶** to show anger or dislike by making this sound : *In earlier times, the audience hissed when the villain of a play appeared.* ▲ NOUN. hisses. **sifflement ▶** a hissing sound.

his-tor-i-cal [his-TOR-ih-kul] ADJECTIVE. **1. historique ▶** having to do with history : *a historical museum.* **2. *Informal.* historique ▶** historic : *a historical site.*

historical fiction **récit historique ▶** writing that is set in the past and includes accurate details of life during that period. The stories can include real people, places, or events.

his-to-ry [HIS-tuh-ree] NOUN, histories. **1. histoire ▶** all the things that have happened in the time before now; all past events : *the history of Canada.* **Note.** A historian is a person who studies or writes about history. **2. histoire ▶** a story or record of certain past events : *"Histories of Japan mention ball-kicking games played thousands of years ago on special holidays."* (Kathy Stinson) **3. histoire ▶** the study of past events, especially as a subject in school. **Note.** Something that is important or famous in history is historic.

hit [hit] VERB, hit, hitting. **1. frapper, heurter ▶** to go hard against; give a blow to; strike : *The car went off the road and hit a tree.* **2. atteindre, toucher, frapper, affecter ▶** to affect in a bad way, as if with a blow : *The news that she'd failed the test hit her hard.* **3. arriver à, atteindre, ▶** to come to; reach : *Stay on this road and you'll hit the main highway in about a kilometre* **4. trouver ▶** discover, meet, or find : *They hit upon a new idea to raise money for the school.* ▲ NOUN, hits. **1. coup ▶** the act or fact of hitting. **2. succès ▶** something that is very popular; a great success : *The movie* Star Wars *was a big hit when it first came out.* Often used as an ADJECTIVE: *a hit song.* **3. coup sûr ▶** in baseball, a ball that is hit so that the batter can reach base safely. SYN : strike, blow, knock, punch, slug, bat, swat. ☐ p. 1028.

hitch [hich] VERB, hitched, hitching. **1. attacher, accrocher ▶** to fasten or tie something with a rope, strap, or the like : *Julia hitched the horse trailer to her truck.* **2. remonter ▶** to move or raise with a jerking motion : *Jimmy hitched up his football pants.* **3. faire de l'auto-stop,**

291

du pouce ▸ to hitchhike : *to hitch a ride on a truck.* ▲ NOUN, hitches. **1. attache** ▸ something that hitches; a fastening : *A trailer hitch is used to connect a trailer to a car.* **2. empêchement, anicroche, contretemps** ▸ an unexpected problem or delay : *The play went on without a hitch.* **3. accroc** ▸ a jerking motion : *He's having trouble hitting the ball because he has such a hitch in his swing.* **4. nœud** ▸ any of several types of knots used to fasten things. SYN : fasten, hook up, clasp, bind, tie.

hitch-hike [HICH-HIKE] VERB, hitchhiked, hitchhiking. **faire de l'auto-stop, faire du pouce** ▸ to travel by walking or standing at the side of a road and trying to get free rides from passing cars or trucks. **Note.** A person who does this is a hitchhiker.

hive [hive] NOUN, hives. (also beehive) **1. ruche** ▸ a box, house, or nest where bees live. **2. ruche, fourmilière** ▸ a very busy, active place; a place crowded with people : *The gym is a hive of activity after school.*

hoarse [horse] ADJECTIVE, hoarser, hoarsest. **enroué (-ée), rauque** ▸ having a harsh or rough sound : *My voice is hoarse from cheering at the game.* ■ **hoarsely,** ADVERB. ▸ **d'une voix rauque/enrouée.** *"Shut up!" Frank said hoarsely when threatened."* (Richard E. Albert) SYN : rough, grating, harsh, husky.

hoax [hohks] NOUN, hoaxes. **canular, farce, tour** ▸ a story or trick meant to fool people : *The alien invasion is a hoax.*

hob·by [HOB-ee] NOUN, hobbies. **passe-temps** ▸ something that a person does regularly for enjoyment in his or her free time. Popular hobbies include photography, stamp collecting, and building models. 🖉 p. 1164.

hock·ey [HOK-ee] NOUN. (also ice hockey) **hockey** ▸ a game played on ice by two teams of six players each. The players wear skates and use long, curved sticks to try to hit a small, hard rubber disk called a puck into the other team's goal. **Note.** Similar games played on different surfaces are *field hockey, floor hockey,* and *ball hockey.*

hoe [hoh] NOUN, hoes. **binette, houe** ▸ a garden tool with a thin, flat blade at the end of a long handle, used mainly to dig up weeds and loosen the soil around plants. ▲ VERB, hoed, hoeing. **sarcler, biner, désherber** ▸ to use a hoe : *to hoe a garden.* SYN : plow, dig, till, loosen.

hog [hog] NOUN, hogs. **1. porc, cochon** ▸ a pig raised for its meat. **2. porc** ▸ any animal of the pig family. **3.** *Informal.* **salaud** ▸ a greedy, selfish, or dirty person : *A "road hog" is a driver who stays in the middle of the road and won't let anyone by.* ▲ VERB, hogged, hogging. *Informal.* **accaparer, prendre plus que sa part de** ▸ to take more than one's share : *Jonah hogged all the cookies and didn't give us any.*

hoist [hoyst] VERB, hoisted, hoisting. **hisser, lever** ▸ to lift or raise up : *to hoist the sails.* ▲ NOUN, hoists. **1. treuil, grue** ▸ a machine or device used to lift or raise something heavy. **2. levage, poussée** ▸ the act of lifting. SYN : raise, lift, elevate, boost.

hold¹ [hold] VERB, held, holding. **1. tenir** ▸ to take and keep in one's hands : *Hold my books while I open the door.* **2. tenir, retenir** ▸ to keep in a certain place or position : *Mom told Bret to hold still while she cut his hair.* **3. contenir, renfermer** ▸ to be able to keep, contain, or support : *Our car's gas tank holds 40 litres.* **4. détenir, posséder** ▸ to control or possess : *The president of that company holds a lot of its stock.* **Note.** Something that is held or owned is a holding : *an oil company with large holdings in Alberta.* **5. tenir, diriger, mener, effectuer** ▸ to carry on; conduct : *to hold a meeting; to hold a garage sale.* ▲ NOUN, holds. **1. prise** ▸ the act or fact of holding something in the hands; a grasp or grip. **2. emprise** ▸ a controlling power or influence : *In the classroom, teachers have a hold on their students.* **3. attente** ▸ a way of interrupting a telephone call so that a person is not on the line but is not completely disconnected : *He put me on hold while he answered another call.* SYN : grasp, clutch, grip, cling to, keep, retain. 🖉 p. 293.

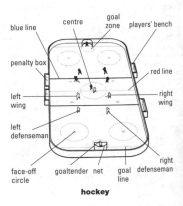

hockey

hold² NOUN, holds. **cale, soute** ▸ the area of a ship or airplane where cargo is stored. 🖉 p. 293.

hold·er [HOLE-dur] NOUN, holders. **possesseur (-euse), détenteur (-trice), titulaire** ▸ a person or thing that holds : *Who is the holder of the world record in the high jump?* **Note.** Often used in compounds to form other words : *a potholder; a knifeholder.*

✎ Writing Tips

Holidays and Holy Days

The names of holidays and holy days are always capitalized because they are proper nouns.

Holidays	*Holy days*
Thanksgiving	*Yom Kippur*
New Year's Day	*Ramadan*
Canada Day	*Easter*

hold-up [HOHLD-up] NOUN, holdups. **1. vol à main armée, hold-up** ▸ a robbery by someone who either has or pretends to have a weapon. **2. arrêt, interruption** ▸ a delay : *A strike at the factory caused a holdup of shipments.* **Note.** Also used as a VERB: *Sorry we're late; we were held up by traffic.*

hole [hole] NOUN, holes. **1. trou, cavité, brèche** ▸ an open place in something solid : *a hole in a sock.* **2. tanière, terrier** ▸ an animal's burrow or den : *a rabbit hole.* **3. Informal. trou, lacune, vide** ▸ a flaw; a weakness : *He says he had nothing to do with the surprise, but there are several holes in his story.* **4. trou** ▸ in golf, a shallow opening in the ground into which the player must hit the ball. SYN: opening, hollow, cavity, pit, gap.

hol·i·day [HOL-uh-DAY] NOUN, holidays. **1. congé, jour de congé, jour férié** ▸ a day when most people do not work and business offices are closed, usually because of the celebration of some special day or event : *Major holidays in Canada include Canada Day, Christmas, and New Year's Day.* **2. holidays. vacances** ▸ a period of rest from work or school; a vacation : *the summer holidays.* 🖰 p. 1147. ✎ p. 293.

hol·low [HOL-oh] ADJECTIVE, hollower, hollowest. **1. creux (creuse)** ▸ having a hole or empty space inside : *Owls often make their nests in hollow trees.* **2. caverneux (-euse), sourd (sourde)** ▸ suggesting a sound made in an empty place; deep and muffled : *He made a hollow whistling sound by blowing across the mouth of a bottle.* **3. faux (fausse), trompeur (-euse)** ▸ with no real meaning, truth, or worth : *She made hollow promises she never kept.*

▲ NOUN, hollows. **1. creux** ▸ an empty space; a hole : *"During the midday heat, peccaries often sleep in hollows in the ground."* (Richard E. Albert) **2. creux** ▸ a low area of land with hills around it; a small valley. ▲ VERB, hollowed, hollowing. **creuser, évider** ▸ to make an empty space : *He hollowed out the piece of wood to make a bowl.* SYN: empty, vacant, bare void, concave.

hol·ly [HOL-ee] NOUN, hollies. **houx** ▸ an evergreen plant that has bright-red berries and shiny green leaves with sharp, pointed edges. Holly is often used as a decoration at Christmas.

ho·lo·caust [HOL-uh-KOST] NOUN, holocausts. **1. holocauste** ▸ great destruction or loss of life, especially because of fire. **2. the Holocaust. Holocauste** ▸ the mass killing of European Jews by Nazi Germany during World War II.

hol·ster [HOLE-stur] NOUN, holsters. **étui de revolver** ▸ a leather case for carrying a pistol, usually worn attached to a belt or on a strap across the shoulder.

ho·ly [HOH-lee] ADJECTIVE, holier, holiest. **1. saint (sainte), sacré (-ée)** ▸ having to do with God; deserving worship; sacred : *Jerusalem is a holy city of the Christian, Jewish, and Muslim religions.* **2. pieux (-euse), saint (sainte)** ▸ very religious; like a saint : *a holy man of the Hindu religion.* SYN: scared, spiritual, religious, pure, godly. ✎ p. 293.

home [home] NOUN, homes. **1. maison, habitat, foyer, demeure** ▸ the place where a person or family lives : *She worked late and didn't get home until after seven.* **2. habitat** ▸ the place where an animal lives : *Beavers make their homes in ponds and streams.* **3. patrie, terre natale** ▸ the place where something comes from or is typically found : *Toronto is the home of the Blue Jays.* **4. résidence, maison d'hébergement, foyer, centre d'accueil** ▸ a place that cares for ill people or for people with special needs : *a nursing home.* **5.** (also home plate) **but, arrivée** ▸ the goal or point to be reached in certain games, such as hide-and-seek. **6. marbre** ▸ in baseball, the base at which the batter stands to hit and that a runner must reach to score a run. ▲ ADJECTIVE. **1. domestique, à la maison** ▸ having to do with or used in the home : *home cooking; a home computer.* **2. à domicile, qui reçoit** ▸ having to do with or being in a base or home area : *The home team*

✐ Word Builder

Hold back *means to keep back someone or something:* He tried to hold back his anger. ***Hold down*** *can mean to keep something down, but it can also mean to have or keep:* She needs to hold down a job to pay for her education. ***Hold the fort*** *means to assume responsibility while someone is away:* While my parents are away, my uncle is holding down the fort. ***Hold out*** *means to resist giving in:* They offered him a good job but he held out for more money.

bats last. ▲ ADVERB. **chez soi** ▶ to or at one's home : *to stay home for the weekend.* 📖 p. 1070.

at home a. **chez-soi** ▶ at or in one's home. b. **se sentir à l'aise, confortable** ▶ relaxed and comfortable; at ease : *She's just started driving and doesn't feel at home behind the wheel yet.*

home-land [HOME-LAND] NOUN, homelands. **patrie, terre natale** ▶ the country where a person was born.

home-less [HOME-lis] ADJECTIVE. **sans abri** ▶ without a home.

home-made [HOME-MADE or HOME-MADE] ADJECTIVE. **fait (faite) à la maison** ▶ made at home; not made in a factory or by a professional : *I like my mom's homemade cookies more than store-bought ones.*

home run (also homer) **coup de circuit** ▶ a hit in baseball that allows the batter to run around all the bases and score a run.

home-sick [HOME-sik or HOME-sik] ADJECTIVE. **qui a le mal du pays, nostalgique** ▶ sad and lonely because of being away from one's home and family. ■ **homesickness,** NOUN. ▶ **mal du pays.**

home-ward [HOME-wurd] ADVERB; ADJECTIVE. (also homewards) **vers la maison, vers la patrie** ▶ toward home : *to sail homeward; a homeward journey.*

home·work [HOME-wurk or HOME-wurk] NOUN. **1. devoir** ▶ school lessons or studying done outside of the regular class period. **2. étude, leçon** ▶ reading or study done to prepare for something : *The mayor had done her homework and had an answer ready for all the reporters' questions.* 📖 p. 1059.

hom·o·graph [HOM-uh-graf] NOUN, homographs. **homographe** ▶ a word that is spelled the same way as another word but has a different meaning : *A bat used in baseball and a bat that flies through the air.* .

hom·o·nym [HOM-uh-nim] NOUN, homonyms. **homonyme** ▶ a word that has either the same spelling or the same sound as another word. Both homographs and homophones are homonyms.

hom·o·phone [HOM-uh-FONE] NOUN, homophones. **homophone** ▶ a word that has the same sound as another word but is spelled differently : *too, two,* and *to.*

hon·est [ON-ist] ADJECTIVE. **1. honnête, droit (droite), véritable, sincère** ▶ not lying, cheating, or stealing; able to be trusted; fair and truthful : *He's an honest man and won't lie to you.* **2. honnête, sincère** ▶ showing these qualities; without lying, cheating, or stealing : *an honest answer.* ■ **honestly,** ADVERB. ▶ **honnêtement, sincèrement, franchement. Note.** The quality of being honest is honesty. SYN: true, sincere, honourable, truthful, genuine.

hon·ey [HUN-ee] NOUN, honeys. **1. miel** ▶ a sweet, thick liquid that is made by certain bees called **honeybees.** Honey comes from nectar, a thin liquid that bees gather from flowers. People eat honey or use it to sweeten things. **2. chéri (-ie), amour** ▶ a name for a person who is loved; darling; dear.

hon·ey·moon [HUN-ee-MOON] NOUN, honeymoons. **1. lune de miel, voyage de noces** ▶ a trip or vacation taken by a couple who have just been married. **2. lune de miel** ▶ a pleasant or peaceful period at the start of something : *The news reporters didn't criticize the mayor much when he first took office, but now the honeymoon is over.* ▲ VERB, honeymooned, honeymooning. **être en voyage de noces, aller en voyage de noces, partir en lune de miel** ▶ to be on or have a honeymoon : *They honeymooned at Lake Louise.*

honk [honk] NOUN, honks. **cri, coup de klaxon** ▶ a loud, harsh sound such as that made by a goose or a car horn. ▲ VERB, honked, honking. **klaxonner, pousser un cri** ▶ to make or cause to make this sound : *Ethan honked his car horn.*

hon·our [ON-ur] NOUN, honours. (also honor) **1. honneur** ▶ a sense of what is right to do; being fair and honest : *He's a man of honour who would never go back on a promise.* **2. honneur** ▶ a good name or reputation : *Kelly gave the teacher her word of honour that she had done the whole project by herself.* **3. honneur, respect, reconnaissance, gloire** ▶ a sign of great respect; a special recognition or award : *"He knew that if he succeeded, he would not only a reward and honours but would be looked upon as great and wise."* (Rosebud Yellow Robe) **4. Honour. votre/son Honneur** ▶ a title of respect for a judge, mayor, or other high official. **Note.** Used in the phrase Your (His, Her) Honour. **5. honours. honneurs, distinction, mention** ▶ a special mention or recognition given to a student for outstanding work : *to graduate with honours.* ▲ VERB, honoured, honouring. **honorer** ▶ to show great respect for; give honour to. SYN: respect, praise, regard, renown, fame, glory.

hon·our·a·ble [ON-ur-uh-bul] ADJECTIVE. (also honorable) **1. honorable** ▶ having or showing a sense of honour; doing what is right, fair, and honest : *Turning in the $100 bill you found on the bus was an honourable thing to do.* **2. honorable** ▶ deserving or bringing honour or great respect. **Note.** An honourable mention is a recognition or an award given to someone who has done very well, but not well enough to win top honours. ■ **honourably,** ADVERB. ▶ **honorablement, décemment.**

hood [hood] NOUN, hoods. **1. capuchon** ▶ a protective covering for the head and neck, usually attached to the collar of a coat or jacket.

2. capot ► a hinged metal cover over the engine of an automobile. **3. hotte ►** something that looks or acts like a hood : *Our new stove has a hood over it to draw out smoke.*

hoof [huf *or* hoof] NOUN, hoofs or hooves. **sabot ►** a hard, tough covering that protects the feet of horses, cows, deer, pigs, or similar animals ; foot. ■ **hoofed,** ADJECTIVE. ► **à sabots.**

hook [hook] NOUN, hooks. **1. crochet, agrafe ►** a bent or curved piece of metal, wood, plastic, or another strong material : *a coat hook.* **2.** (also fishhook) **hameçon ►** a curved piece of metal with a sharp point at one end, used for catching fish. **3. crochet ►** anything shaped like a hook. ▲ VERB, hooked, hooking. **1. accrocher, prendre ►** to fasten, hold, or catch, as with a hook : *After hours, he finally hooked a fish.* **2. accrocher ►** to form a hook or a hooked shape : *Mary hooked her arm through her mother's as they crossed the street.* ■ **hooked,** ADJECTIVE. ► **accroché (-ée) à, crochu (-ue).** SYN : fasten, clasp, clip, latch, snap, bind.

hook up se brancher, se raccorder ► to set up a piece of electrical equipment so that it is ready to work. **Note.** Also used as a NOUN: *a telephone hookup.*

hoop [hoop] NOUN, hoops. **1. cerceau (-eaux) ►** a band or flat ring in the form of a circle : *Metal hoops are used to hold wooden barrels together.* **2. cerceau (-eaux) ►** a circular ring used as a child's toy. Many years ago, children used to roll hoops as a street game. Plastic hula hoops were a popular toy in the 1950s. **3. panier ►** another name for the basket in basketball.

hoot [hoot] NOUN, hoots. **1. hululement ►** the sound made by an owl. **2. huée ►** a sound like this used to show anger, disbelief, or disappointment. ▲ VERB, hooted, hooting **huer, crier, siffler ►** to make this sound. SYN : yell, call, cry, jeer.

hop[1] [hop] VERB, hopped, hopping. **sautiller ►** to move with short, quick jumps : *Dave grabbed his injured foot and hopped around like a bird.* ▲ NOUN, hops. **sautillement, saut, bond ►** a short jump or movement : *The shortstop caught the ball on the first hop.* SYN : spring, jump, vault, leap, bound, bounce.

hop[2] NOUN, hops. **1. houblon ►** a climbing vine with clusters of greenish flowers that look like small pine cones. **2. hops. houblon ►** the dried ripe flower clusters of this plant, used to give flavour to beer.

hope [hope] VERB, hoped, hoping. **espérer ►** to want something and believe that it is possible ; wish and expect that something will happen : *"I hope I live long enough to hear you on the radio giving the Yankees a good licking."* (Roch Carrier) ▲ NOUN, hopes. **1. espoir, espérance ►** a strong wish for something and a belief that it will happen : *Keith has hopes of*

doing well in English this term. **2. espoir ►** a person or thing that gives hope. SYN : wish for, desire, long for, expect, yearn for.

hope-ful [HOPE-ful] ADJECTIVE. **1. plein (pleine) d'espoir ►** feeling or showing hope : *"He was hopeful, yet he couldn't forget what had happened the first time."* (Richard E. Albert) **2. encourageant (-ante) ►** giving cause for hope ; promising : *"We are very hopeful and the future looks promising."* (George Littlechild) SYN : confident, optimistic.

hope-less [HOPE-lis] ADJECTIVE. **sans espoir, désespéré (-ée), impossible ►** not having or giving any chance of success ; without hope : *He felt alone and hopeless and wanted to cry.* SYN : discouraged, desperate, useless, in vain.

hop-scotch [HOP-skoch] NOUN. **marelle ►** a child's game in which a stone or other object is thrown onto a pattern of numbered squares drawn on the ground. A player has to hop through the squares in a certain way to pick up the object.

horde [hord] NOUN, hordes. **horde, foule, troupe, bande ►** a large group ; a crowd or swarm : *a horde of ants.*

hor-i-zon [huh-RY-zun] NOUN, horizons. **1. horizon ►** the distant line where the land or sea seems to touch the sky **2. horizons, perspectives ►** the limit or range of a person's experience or knowledge : *Her four years of university have really broadened her horizons.*

hor-i-zon-tal [HOR-uh-zONT-ul] ADJECTIVE. **horizontal (-ale, -aux) ►** in line with the ground ; straight across ; level : *The walls of a room are vertical, and the floor and ceiling are horizontal.* ■ **horizontally,** ADVERB. ► **horizontalement.**

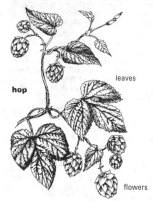

leaves

hop

flowers

hor-mone [HOR-mone] NOUN, hormones. **hormone ►** a chemical substance made in certain glands of the body and carried by blood to various body parts. Hormones control body growth and development and regulate such activities as breathing, digestion, and perspiration.

horn [horn] NOUN, horns. **1. corne** ▶ a hard, permanent growth on the head of certain animals, such as cattle, sheep, goats, or rhinoceroses. Horns usually are curved and pointed and grow in pairs. **2. klaxon, avertisseur** ▶ a device in a car, truck, or other vehicle that can make a loud noise as a warning to someone in the way. **3. cuivre** ▶ any one of musical instruments played by blowing into a narraow opening at one end of a large, curved tube. The earliest of these instruments are usually made of brass. Trumpets, trombones, and tubas are horns. ▪ **horned,** ADJECTIVE. ▶ **cornu (-ue)** ▶ having horns or something like horns : *a horned owl.* ☞ p. 539.

hor-net [HOR-nit] NOUN, hornets. **frelon, guêpe** ▶ a large type of wasp that has a painful sting.

hor-o-scope [HOR-uh-skope] NOUN, horoscopes. **horoscope** ▶ the influence of the sun and stars on a person's life according to their position at the time of birth.

hor-ri-ble [HOR-uh-bul] ADJECTIVE. **1. horrible, affreux (-euse), atroce, monstrueux (-euse)** ▶ causing horror; very frightening or shocking; terrible : *Seeing the skyscraper on fire was a horrible sight.* **2. désagréable, atroce, horrible** ▶ very bad or unpleasant; awful : *Rotten eggs have a horrible smell.* ▪ **horribly,** ADVERB. ▶ **horriblement, affreusement.** SYN : frightful, shocking, terrible, horrid, awful.

hor-rid [HOR-id] ADJECTIVE. **1. horrible, affreux (-euse), méchant (-ante)** ▶ causing great fear or shock; horrible. **2. horrible, affreux (-euse)** ▶ very bad or unpleasant.

hor-ri-fy [HOR-uh-FY] VERB, horrified, horrifying. **1. horrifier, effrayer** ▶ to cause a feeling of horror; fill with great fear or shock : *The number of robberies in the neighbourhood horrifies Mrs. Ellis.* **2. scandaliser, choquer, indigner, offusquer** ▶ to surprise in an annoying or unpleasant way : *The mess I made in the kitchen horrified my parents.*

hor-ror [HOR-ur] NOUN, horrors. **1. horreur, terreur, effroi** ▶ a feeling of great fear or shock; terror : *She screamed in horror as the huge rock plummeted toward her.* **2. horreur, aversion, répugnance** ▶ something that causes this feeling : *the horrors of war.*

horse [hors] NOUN, horses. **1. cheval (-aux)** ▶ a large, grass-eating animal that has four legs with hoofs and has a flowing mane and tail. Horses are strong and fast and are used for riding and pulling. **2. chevalet, tréteau (-eaux)** ▶ a frame with legs that is used to hold something up. **Note.** A carpenter uses a **sawhorse** to support

a board while cutting it. **3. cheval (-aux) d'arçons** ▶ in gymnastics, a padded block with legs that is used for vaulting exercises. ☞ **p. 1090.**

horse

horse-back [HORS-bak] NOUN. **à cheval** ▶ on the back of a horse : *"In the midst of all this confusion, Wu found two soldiers on horseback blocking his way."* (David Day)

horse-pow-er [HORS-pow-ur] NOUN. **cheval-vapeur, puissance en chevaux-vapeur** ▶ a unit that measures the power of an engine. One horsepower is equal to the amount of power needed to lift 550 pounds (roughly 249 kg) one foot (roughly 30.5 cm) in one second : *a boat with a 20-horsepower engine.*

horse-shoe [HORS-shoo] NOUN, horseshoes. **1. fer à cheval** ▶ a U-shaped piece of metal that is nailed to the bottom of a horse's hoof to protect it. **2. horseshoes. fer à cheval** ▶ a game in which players throw a horseshoe, or an object shaped like this, so that it will land around a post in the ground.

hose [hoze] NOUN, hoses. **1. boyau (-aux), tuyau (-aux)** ▶ a tube made of rubber, plastic, or other material used to carry liquid, as for watering a garden or moving gasoline from a pump into a car's gas tank. **2.** (also hosiery) **bas, chaussette** ▶ socks; stockings. ▲ VERB, hosed, hosing. **arroser au jet, laver au jet** ▶ to spray with a hose : *Mr. Weiss hoses down the sidewalk outside his store every morning.*

hos-pi-tal [HOS-pit-ul] NOUN, hospitals. **hôpital (-aux)** ▶ a place where doctors, nurses, and other medical workers provide care and treatment for people who are sick, injured, or in need of medical care. ☞ **p. 1160.**

host [hohst] NOUN, hosts. **1. hôte (hôtesse)** ▶ a person who invites and entertains guests : *"Crow thought Fox was an incredibly rude host, but he didn't say anything."* (Jan Thornhill)

2. animateur (-trice) ▸ a person who is the main performer on a television variety show or talk show. ▲ VERB, hosted, hosting. **animer, recevoir** ▸ to act as a host : *to host a dinner.*

hos·tage [HOS-tij] NOUN, hostages. **otage** ▸ a person who is held as a prisoner until certain demands have been met.

hos·tile [HOS-tul *or* HOS-TILE] ADJECTIVE. **1. hostile** ▸ showing anger or dislike; unfriendly : *"I did not feel the hostile glances aimed at my back."* (Jean Little) **2. ennemi (-ie)** ▸ of or belonging to an enemy : *The town was attacked by hostile troops.* SYN: unfriendly, aggressive, belligerent, nasty.

hot [hot] ADJECTIVE, hotter, hottest. **1. chaud (chaude)** ▸ having a high temperature; very warm. **2. épicé (-ée), piquant (-ante), fort (forte)** ▸ having a sharp, burning taste : *This pepper sauce is really hot.* **3. emporté (-ée)** ▸ easily excited; violent : *Watch how you deal with him, because he's got a hot temper.* **4. à la mode** ▸ very active or successful : *She's the hottest young actor around and is being offered many starring roles.* **5. aux trousses** ▸ following closely : *Nancy Drew was hot on the heels of her suspect.* **6.** Informal. **recherché (-ée) par la police** ▸ recently stolen or obtained in an illegal way : *The police stopped him because he was driving a hot car.*

ho·tel [hoh-TEL] NOUN, hotels. **hôtel** ▸ a place that rents rooms for sleeping, and usually offers meals as well.

hound [hownd] NOUN, hounds. **chien de meute, chien de chasse** ▸ a type of dog with droopy ears, a very good sense of smell, and a deep bark. Hounds were originally trained to hunt animals. Beagles, foxhounds, and dachshunds are hounds. ▲ VERB, hounded, hounding. **traquer, pourchasser, poursuivre** ▸ to follow someone in an annoying way; pester : *The reporter hounded the singer for days until she finally agreed to give him an interview.*

hour [owr] NOUN, hours. **1. heure** ▸ a unit of time equal to 60 minutes : *From 6:52 to 7:52 is one hour.* **2. heure** ▸ one of the points of time indicating such a period : *That radio station gives news on the hour and the half-hour.* **3. heure** ▸ the amount of distance that can be travelled in one hour : *It's about two hours from here to Vancouver.* **4. heure** ▸ a certain point in time : *Mom doesn't like to get calls at the dinner hour.* **5.** hours. **heures** ▸ a fixed time for doing something : *The store's hours are from 9:00 a.m. to 6:00 p.m.* 📗 **p. 1078.**

house [hows] NOUN, houses. **1. maison** ▸ a building for people to live in, separate from other buildings. **2. maisonnée, famille, ménage** ▸ the people living in a house; a household : *Lee had a bad nightmare, and his yelling woke up the whole house.* **3. maison** ▸ any building used for a certain purpose : *a doghouse; an*

apartment house. *We saw a movie at the Rye Playhouse.* **4. maison, famille** ▸ a royal family or other important family : *the House of Rothschild was once the leading banking group in Europe.* **5. Chambre** ▸ a group of people who make laws : *the House of Commons.* **6. salle, auditoire, assistance** ▸ an audience in a theatre : *There was a full house at the school play.* ▲ [howz] VERB, housed, housing. **loger, héberger** ▸ to provide a place for someone or something to live, stay, or be kept : *My collection of rocks is housed in a special case.* SYN: shelter, dwelling, home, lodge, residence. 📗 **p. 1070.** 👁 **p. 115.**

house·hold [HOWS-hohld] NOUN, households. **maisonnée, famille, ménage** ▸ all the people living together in one house. ▲ ADJECTIVE. **1. ménager (-ère)** ▸ having to do with a house : *household jobs such as cooking, cleaning, and washing dishes.* **2. familier (-ière), connu (-ue)** ▸ very well-known; common; familiar : *"Xerox" became a household word after the company's copying machine became famous.*

house·keep·er [HOWS-kee-pur] NOUN, housekeepers. **gouvernante** ▸ a person whose work is taking care of a house and doing housework.

House of Commons 1. Chambre des communes ▸ in Canada, the elected representatives who meet in Ottawa to make laws and debate questions of government. **2. Chambre des communes** ▸ the chamber in which these representatives meet.

house·work [HOWS-wurk] NOUN. **ménage, travaux ménagers** ▸ the work done in a home, such as cleaning, cooking, washing, ironing, and so on.

hous·ing [HOW-zing] NOUN. **1. logement** ▸ houses as a group; places to live : *The city is building new public housing downtown.* **2.** (plural, housings) **boîtier** ▸ a covering that protects the moving parts of a machine : *the housing on an electric drill.*

how [how] ADVERB. **1. comment** ▸ in what way or by what means : *How do you work this computer? How do you say "friend" in Spanish?* **2. comment** ▸ in what condition or state : *How is Ahmed since his operation?* **3. combien, comment** ▸ to what degree or amount : *How did you like the movie? How much does that camera cost?* ▲ CONJUNCTION. **combien, comment** ▸ the fact that; the way that : *Remember how we played until long after dark in the summer?*

how·ev·er [how-EV-ur] CONJUNCTION. **cependant, toutefois, mais** ▸ in spite of that; but still; yet : *I thought that joke was really funny; however, no one else laughed.* ▲ ADVERB. **de quelque manière que, comment** ▸ in whatever way : *You can arrange the boxes however you want.* SYN: yet, still, but, nevertheless, notwithstanding. ✎ **p. 298.**

howl [howl] VERB, howled, howling. **1. hurler** ▸ to make a long, loud crying sound : *In the distance, we could hear the wolves howling.* **2. hurler** ▸ yell ; shout : *The crowd howled with laughter.* ▲ NOUN, howls. **hurlement** ▸ a loud, wailing cry : *"I was just falling asleep, my mind already half dreaming, when I heard a thin, high-pitched howl."* (Janet Foster) SYN : cry, yell, shout, bark, bellow, yelp, wail.

hub [hub] NOUN, hubs. **1. moyeu (-eux)** ▸ the centre part of a wheel. **Note.** A hubcap is a metal cap that fits over the hub of a car's wheel. **2. centre (d'activités)** ▸ a centre of activity. SYN : centre, middle, core, nucleus.

hud·dle [HUD-ul] VERB, huddled, huddling. **se serrer les uns (unes) contre les autres, s'entasser** ▸ to crowd together in a tight group ; bunch up : *"My French partner and friend Jean-Louis Michel and I huddled over the maps and charts spread out before us."* (Robert D. Ballard)

hue [hyoo] NOUN, hues. **teinte, nuance** ▸ a colour, or a shade of a colour : *The winter sky had a greyish hue.*

hug [hug] VERB, hugged, hugging. **1. étreindre, embrasser, serrer** ▸ to put one's arms around someone or something and hold him, her, or it close. **2. longer** ▸ to stay close to : *The small sailboat hugged the coastline.* ▲ NOUN, hugs. **étreinte, enlacement** ▸ a close, tight hold : *"Henry was thrilled. He gave his parents a big hug. He gave Mudge a big hug."* (Cynthia Rylant) SYN : hold, clasp, embrace, squeeze, press.

huge [hyooj] ADJECTIVE. **immense, énorme, gigantesque** ▸ having a great size ; very large ; enormous : *"Huge horses. Huge to adults, enormous mountains to young people."* (Gary Paulsen) SYN : enormous, vast, immense, gigantic.

hull [hul] NOUN, hulls. **1. coque** ▸ the sides and bottom of a ship : *a sailboat with a wooden hull.* **2. cosse, gousse** ▸ the outer covering of a seed. A pea pod and a nutshell are hulls.

hum [hum] VERB, hummed, humming. **1. fredonner, chantonner** ▸ to make a soft, musical sound while keeping the lips together : *If you hum that tune for me, maybe I can remember the words.* **2. bourdonner, ronronner** ▸ to make a low, even buzzing sound. **3. bourdonner** ▸ to be busy and active : *The classroom was humming as students prepared for the school fair.* ▲ NOUN, hums. **bourdonnement** ▸ a soft sound like that made by a bee : *"Before he knew it, the heat and hum of the forest had lulled him to sleep."* (Lynne Cherry) SYN : drone, buzz, murmur.

hu·man [HYOO-mun] ADJECTIVE. **humain** ▸ having to do with a person or people : *The human body has 12 pairs of rib bones. Great writers such as Shakespeare and Dickens give a true picture of human nature.* ▲ NOUN, humans. (also human

being) **être humain** ▸ a person. ✐ p. 356. SYN : person, mortal, being. ◉ p. 402-405.

hu·mane [HYOO-MANE] ADJECTIVE. **humain** ▸ acting as a person should toward human beings or animals ; showing human kindness : *"So humane was she that she used nearly all of the money to maintain her home, later known as the Harriet Tubman Home, as a refuge for the needy."* (Virginia Hamilton) SYN : compassionate, kind, tender.

hu·man·i·ty [hyoo-MAN-uh-tee] NOUN. **1.** (also humankind) **humanité** ▸ the human race ; all people as a group. **2. humanité, charité, générosité, altruisme** ▸ the state of being humane ; kindness. ✐ p. 437.

hum·ble [HUM-bul] ADJECTIVE, humbler, humblest. **1. humble** ▸ not proud ; modest : *He's very humble and doesn't talk about his accomplishments.* **2. modeste** ▸ not large or important : *Some people have risen from humble beginnings to become great world leaders.* ▲ VERB, humbled, humbling. **humilier** ▸ to make humble : *The girls' soccer team humbled the boys' team, beating them easily.* ■ **humbly,** ADVERB : ▸ **humblement, modestement.** *"The*

✎ Writing Tips

However

However is used as a conjunction to show contrast or argument against what has just been said, much in the same way as "but" is used.

• At the beginning of a sentence, *however* shows contrast to the sentence before. For example,

 I have never believed in UFOs. However, what happened last night changed my mind.

• When you use *however* in the middle of a sentence, make sure it follows the idea that it is contrasting.

 I really liked the movie I saw last night ; my friend, however, was not impressed.

• *However* should always follow a period, semicolon, or comma, and it should always be followed by a comma.

• Don't overuse *however*, or it will lose its effectiveness. When you revise your work, think about how you have used *however*. Are all of the "howevers" in the right place ? Are they really necessary ? Would "but" or "yet" work better ?

✍ Writing Tips

Hung and *hanged* are both past-tense forms of the verb *hang*.

• *Hung* should be used to show that something has been fastened.

Stella hung a new picture in her bedroom.

• *Hanged* should only be used to talk about the punishment.

In the past, the British hanged people for spying.

Sultan smiled humbly." (Robin Muller) SYN: modest, meek, unpretentious, unassuming.

hu·mid [HYOO-mid] ADJECTIVE. **humide ▸** of the air, damp or moist : *a hot, humid July day.* SYN: moist, damp, wet, muggy.

hu·mid·ex [HYOO-mih-deks] NOUN. **taux d'humidité ▸** a combined measurement of temperature and humidity that shows what dry-air temperature would cause the same amount of discomfort as the temperature with the humidity : *Most people find that a humidex of 85 or more is uncomfortable.*

hu·mid·i·ty [hyoo-MID-uh-tee] NOUN. **humidité ▸** the amount of water vapour in the air : *The humidity is higher near the ocean than it is in the desert.*

hu·mil·i·ate [hyoo-MIL-ee-ATE] VERB, humiliated, humiliating. **humilier, abaisser, rabaisser ▸** to make someone feel foolish or worthless; make ashamed : *Nicky's nasty comment humiliated me.* SYN: embarrass, disgrace, shame.

hu·mil·i·ty [hyoo-MIL-uh-tee] NOUN. **humilité, modestie ▸** the quality of being humble; lack of pride : *She accepted the honour with great humility.*

hum·ming·bird [HUM-ing-BURD] NOUN, hummingbirds. **colibri, oiseau-mouche ▸** a small, brightly coloured bird with a long, narrow beak from the Americas. Hummingbirds move their wings with great speed to fly forward, backward, or sideways, or to hover in one place.

hu·mour [HYOO-mur] NOUN, humours. (also humor) **1. humeur ▸** something that is funny; something that makes people laugh. **Note.** Something that is full of humour is humorous. **2.** the way a person feels; one's mood : *to be in a good or bad humour.* ▲ VERB, humoured, humouring. **se plier, se prêter, ne pas contrarier ▸** to give in to what someone wants; go along with a person's mood or wishes : *Mom knew that Ravi's leg really wasn't badly hurt, but just to humour him she put a bandage on it anyway.*

sense of humour sens de l'humour **▸** the ability to see and enjoy something funny or to make people laugh.

hump [hump] NOUN, humps. **bosse ▸** a rounded part that sticks up : *Camels and buffalo have humps on their backs.* SYN: bump, bulge, hunch, lump.

hu·mus [HYOO-mus] NOUN. **humus, terreau (-eaux) ▸** the dark-brown part of the soil that is formed by material from dead plants. Humus is rich in substances that help plants grow.

hunch [hunch] VERB, hunched, hunching. **courber, arrondir ▸** to bend over; to form a hump : *Mason hunched over his plate as though he expected someone to steal his food.* ▲ NOUN, hunches. **pressentiment, intuition ▸** a guess made because of a strong feeling : *I had a hunch it would rain, so I brought along my umbrella.* SYN: feeling, impression, suspicion.

hun·dred [HUN-drid] NOUN, hundred or hundreds. **cent, centaine ▸** ten times ten; 100. **Note.** Also used as an ADJECTIVE. **■ hundredth,** NOUN; ADJECTIVE. **▸ centième.**

hung [hung] VERB. **pendre, accrocher, suspendre ▸** a past form of hang: *"She hung from a branch with one claw at a time till she ached."* (Mem Fox) ✐ **p. 299.**

hun·ger [HUNG-ur] NOUN. **1. faim ▸** a feeling of wanting or needing food : *She hadn't eaten in so long that she had pangs of hunger.* **2.** (plural, hungers) **faim ▸** a strong wish or need for anything. ▲ VERB, hungered, hungering. **avoir faim de, désirer, être assoiffé (-ée) de ▸** to have a strong need or wish for something : *From an early age, Adam has hungered to be an artist.* SYN: starvation, appetite, craving, desire. 📖 **p. 1137.**

hun·gry [HUNG-gree] ADJECTIVE, hungrier, hungriest. **1. affamé (-ée) ▸** needing or wanting food : *We were quite hungry after a day of working in the garden.* **2. avide ▸** having a strong need or wish for something : *She was hungry for knowledge.* **■ hungrily,** ADVERB. **▸ voracement, avidement.**

hunk [hunk] VERB, hunks. *Informal.* **bout, morceau (-eaux) ▸** a big piece or lump of something. SYN: lump, piece, mass, bulk, chunk.

hunt [hunt] VERB, hunted, hunting. **1. chasser ▸** to chase wild animals in order to catch or kill them : *"Without wolves to hunt the deer, there were now too many deer on the island for the amount of food available."* (Celia Godkin) **Note.** A person or animal that hunts, especially one that hunts wild animals, is a hunter. **2. pourchasser, chasser ▸** to chase after a person in the same way. **3. chercher ▸** to search hard for something : *to hunt for a lost pair of socks.* ▲ NOUN, hunts. **1. chasse ▸** a chase made to catch or kill : *a deer hunt.* **2. recherche ▸** a search to find something : *We had to find a red* *maple leaf for the scavenger hunt.* SYN: search, seek, look for, pursue, chase.

hur·dle [HURD-ul] NOUN, hurdles. **1. haie ▶** a fence or small frame that is to be jumped over during a race. **2.** hurdles. **course de haies ▶** a race in which runners jump over a series of such barriers. **Note.** An athlete who runs in a hurdle race is a hurdler. **3. obstacle ▶** a problem or obstacle that has to be overcome : *Once the exchange student got over the language hurdles, he did very well.* ▲ VERB, hurdled, hurdling. **sauter, franchir ▶** to leap over something. SYN: block, obstacle, hitch, catch, snag, barrier.

hurl [hurl] VERB, hurled, hurling. **lancer violemment avec force ▶** to throw something hard and fast : *"She slipped the swallow into her hand, and with a mighty pitch, hurled the bird into the sky."* (Robin Muller) SYN: throw, fling, pitch, toss, cast, heave, chuck.

Hu·ron [HYUR-un *or* HYUR-on] NOUN, Huron **Huron ▶** or Hurons. **1. Huron (-onne) ▶** a member of the Native peoples who used to live in the area between Lake Huron and Lake Ontario. The Huron lived in longhouses and farmed. **2. huron ▶** the Iroquoian language of these peoples. ▲ ADJECTIVE.

hur·ri·cane [HUR-uh-KANE] NOUN, hurricanes. **ouragan ▶** a large, powerful storm with strong, swirling winds and heavy rains. To be officially called a hurricane, a storm must have winds blowing at least 120 km per hour. 📖 **p. 1103.**

hur·ried [HUR-eed] ADJECTIVE. **pressé (-ée), précipité (-ée), fait (faite) à la hâte, bousculé (-ée) ▶** more quickly than usual; rushed; hasty : *She got up late and had time only for a hurried breakfast of toast and juice.* ▪ **hurriedly,** ADVERB. ▶ **à la hâte, précipitamment.**

hur·ry [HUR-ee] VERB, hurried, hurrying. **se hâter, se dépêcher, (se) presser ▶** to move more quickly than usual; rush : *"They piled everything into huge baskets and then hurried back."* (Paul Yee) ▲ NOUN, hurries. **hâte, empressement, précipitation ▶** the act of moving fast; the wish or need to move fast : *Zach was in such a hurry, he didn't notice that he had left his coat behind.* ✏ **p. 300.**

hurt [hurt] VERB, hurt, hurting. **1. blesser, faire du mal à ▶** to cause pain to; injure : *Gary hurt his arm when he fell off his bike.* **2. faire mal, faire**

hurdle ▶ to feel pain : *Grandpa says that his knees hurt whenever the weather is cold and damp.* **3. faire du mal, faire de la peine, blesser ▶** to cause pain to a person's feelings; make sad or upset : *"Then she thought, but I don't like my brother to say that. It hurts my feelings."* (Juanita Havill) **4. endommager, faire mal à, offenser ▶** to have a bad effect on; harm : *Failing that test will really hurt her chances of getting a good mark for the course.* ▲ NOUN, hurts. **mal (maux), blessure ▶** something that hurts; an injury. SYN: injure, harm, wound, damage, wrong. 📖 **p. 1021.**

hur·tle [hurt-ul] VERB, hurtled, hurtling. **aller à toute allure, avancer à toute vitesse ▶** to move with great speed; rush with force : *My bike hurtled off the path and into the bush.*

hus·band [HUZ-bund] NOUN, husbands. **mari, époux ▶** a man who is married.

hush [hush] VERB, hushed, hushing. **calmer, faire taire ▶** to make quiet : *to hush a crying baby.* ▲ NOUN. **silence ▶** a time of complete quiet; silence : *"As she stepped toward the tree, a hush fell over the crowd."* (Mem Fox) ▲ INTERJECTION: **chut! ▶** *"Hush!"* she said to the noisy children.

hush up étouffer ▶ to keep secret : *Whitney and Pat hushed up about Taylor's surprise party when she came into the room.*

husk [husk] NOUN, husks. **enveloppe ▶** the dry outside covering of corn or certain other fruits and vegetables. ▲ VERB, husked, husking. **décortiquer, éplucher ▶** to remove the husk from : *to husk corn.*

husk·y[1] [HUS-kee] ADJECTIVE, huskier, huskiest. **1. costaud (-aude), fort (forte) ▶** big and strong : *a husky weightlifter.* **2. enroué (-ée), rauque ▶** deep and rough-sounding : *a husky voice.*

husky[2] NOUN, huskies. (also huskie) **husky (huskies), chien de traîneau ▶** a large, strong dog with a thick, bushy coat. Huskies are used in the Far North to pull dogsleds.

hus·tle [HUS-ul] VERB, hustled, hustling. **1. se dépêcher, se presser ▶** to move or work quickly and with lots of energy : *Brad really has to hustle to deliver all the newspapers on his route each morning.* **2. Informal. arnaquer ▶** to try to make money in a clever and energetic way, espe-

---

✏ Word Builder

Hurry, urge, and *hustle* all refer to moving or doing something quickly. *Hurry* means to do things in a very rushed way: *Since Raginder is 10 minutes late, he will have to hurry to get to school on time.* *Urge* can mean to move or speed something or someone along: *Mai Ling tends to dally in the morning so her mother must urge her along.* A person who *hustles* moves quickly and displays a lot of energy: *Marci hustles after the balls in every basketball game she plays.*

cially by doing something that is not completely honest. **Note.** A person who hustles is a hustler. ▲ NOUN, hustles. **effervescence, tourbillon ▶** the act or fact of hustling : *"He was delighted to leave the palace and wander about, watching the hustle and bustle of the marketplaces."* (Dan Yashinsky) ✐ **p. 300.**

hut [hut] NOUN, huts. A small, roughly built house or other shelter; cabin; shed.

hy·a·cinth [HY-uh-sinth] NOUN, hyacinths. **jacinthe ▶** a plant with a cluster of bell-shaped flowers. Hyacinths grow from bulbs and have long leaves that grow from the base of the stem.

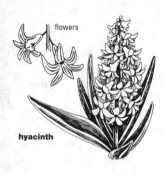

flowers

hyacinth

hy·brid [HY-brid] NOUN, hybrids. **hybride ▶** a plant or an animal that comes from parents of two different kinds. A mule is a hybrid that comes from crossing a female horse and a male donkey. Hybrids are important in developing better varieties of plants and farm animals. **Note.** Also used as an ADJECTIVE: *hybrid cattle that produce more milk.*

hy·drant [HY-drunt] NOUN, hydrants. **prise d'eau, borne d'incendie, borne-fontaine ▶** a wide, thick water pipe that stands above ground near a street. Hydrants are connected to main water pipes under the ground. They provide water for fighting fires or washing the streets.

hy·dro [HY-droh] NOUN. **1. hydro-électricité, énergie hydraulique ▶** power made from harnessing the force of water; short for hydroelectric power. **2. électricité ▶** electricity distributed by a power company. ✐ **p. 400.**

hy·dro·gen [HY-druh-jun] NOUN. **hydrogène ▶** a gas that cannot be seen, tasted, or smelled, but that burns easily. Hydrogen is the lightest of all chemical elements. It mixes with oxygen to make water, and is the most common element on earth.

hy·e·na [hy-EEN-uh] NOUN, hyenas. **hyène ▶** (also hyaena) a wild animal of Africa and Asia that looks similar to a dog. Hyenas have strong jaws, and make a cry that sounds like a person laughing.

hy·giene [HY-JEEN] NOUN. **hygiène ▶** the things that people do to keep their bodies clean and healthy. Washing the body and hair and brushing the teeth are important parts of hygiene.

hymn [him] NOUN, hymns. **hymne, cantique ▶** a song of praise or thanksgiving, usually part of a religious service.

hype [hipe] NOUN. *Informal.* **battage publicitaire ▶** exaggerated promotion or advertising : *There's a lot of hype about that new action movie.* ▲ VERB, hyped, hyping. **1. promouvoir, faire de la publicité à outrance ▶** to promote or advertise. **2. faire mousser ▶** to excite or add interest : *The company hired a basketball player to hype its new line of clothing.*

hy·per·bo·le [hy-PUR-buh-lee] **hyperbole ▶** exaggeration ; a figure of speech used for emphasis or comic effect.

hy·phen [HY-fun] NOUN, hyphens. **trait d'union ▶** a short line [-] used to join two or more words, as in "merry-go-round" or "a two-day trip." In writing, a hyphen is also used to show that a word has been divided between lines.

hyp·no·tize [HIP-nuh-TIZE] VERB, hypnotized, hypnotizing. **hypnotiser ▶** to put people in a special state of mind in which they are very relaxed, as if asleep, but are still able to move and to sense things around them. **Note.** Hypnosis is the state of mind of a person who has been hypnotized. The act or fact of hypnotizing a person is hypnotism. A hypnotist is someone who is able to do this. SYN: entrance, spellbind, mesmerize.

hyp·o·crite [HIP-uh-KRIT] NOUN, hypocrites. **hypocrite ▶** people who pretend to be what they are not ; someone who speaks of being honest, kind, and so on, but doesn't really act that way. **Note.** The fact of being a hypocrite is hypocrisy. ■ **hypocritical,** ADJECTIVE. ▶ **hypocrite.** SYN : pretender, fake.

hy·po·the·sis [hy-POTH-uh-sis] NOUN, hypotheses. **1. hypothèse ▶** an explanation of a set of facts that can be tested by further investigation : *The researcher was disappointed when her tests did not support her hypothesis.* **2. hypothèse ▶** something that is taken to be true for the sake of argument ; a theory : *The teams debated the hypothesis that all humans are created equal.*

hys·ter·i·cal [his-TAIR-ih-kul] ADJECTIVE. **1. hystérique ▶** losing control of oneself because of fear, sorrow, or other strong feeling. **2.** *Informal.* **hilarant (-ante), tordant (-ante), très drôle ▶** very funny : *That cartoon was hysterical.* SYN : uncontrollable, frantic, overexcited.

insect

i, I [eye] NOUN, i's, I's. **i, I ▶** the ninth letter of the English alphabet.

I PRONOUN. **je, moi ▶** the person who is speaking or writing : *My sister takes piano lessons, but I don't. ✎ p. 362.*

ice [ice] NOUN. **1. glace ▶** water that has been made solid by cold; frozen water. Ice forms when the temperature of water falls to 0°C. **2.** (plural **ices**) **sorbet, glace ▶** a frozen dessert made with sweetened fruit juice. **3. patinoire, glace ▶** the frozen surface for skating, hockey, or curling. ▲ VERB, **iced, icing. 1. refroidir, rafraîchir ▶** to make cold or keep cold with ice : *We iced our drinks while we swam.* **Note.** Also used as an ADJECTIVE: *iced tea.* **2. geler ▶** to become covered with ice; freeze : *This lake ices over in winter.* **3. dégagement ▶** in hockey, shooting the puck from your defensive zone past the goal line of the other team. **Note.** This is known as icing. ⌨ p. 1108. 👁 p. 113.

Ice Age période glaciaire ▶ a period of time when glaciers covered large parts of the earth's surface. The most recent Ice Age began about 1.75 million years ago and ended about 10,000 years ago.

ice-berg [ICE-burg] NOUN, icebergs. **iceberg ▶** a very large piece of ice that has broken off a glacier and is floating in the ocean. Icebergs can be dangerous to ships.

ice-break-er [ICE-brake-ur] NOUN, icebreakers. **brise-glace ▶** a large, heavy ship used to break a path through ice so that other ships can pass.

ice cream crème glacée, glace ▶ a smooth, frozen food that is served as a dessert, made of milk or cream with various sweeteners and flavourings.

ice-house [ICE-hows] NOUN, icehouses. **1. igloo, iglou ▶** a dome-shaped house made from blocks of ice or snow, especially one used by the Inuit. Icehouses are built for temporary shelter while hunting or travelling. **Note.** Some people use the word igloo, but *icehouse* is the correct term. **2. glacière ▶** a building for storing ice. **3. glacière, chambre froide ▶** a pit or building for cold storage of meat and other food.

i-ci-cle [I-suh-kul] NOUN, icicles. **glaçon ▶** a pointed, hanging piece of ice formed by water that freezes as it drips.

ic-ing [I-sing] NOUN, icings. **glaçage, glace ▶** a sweet, smooth mixture of sugar, butter, and flavouring used to cover and decorate cakes, cookies, and other baked goods. **Note.** Also called frosting.

i-cy [I-see] ADJECTIVE, icier, iciest. **1. glacé (-ée)▶** covered with ice : *an icy road.* **2. glacial (-ale, -als) ▶** very cold, like ice : *an icy wind.* **3. glacial (-ale, -als), glacé (-ée) ▶** cold and unfriendly : *Meg gave her brother an icy stare when he teased her.*

i-de-a [i-DEE-uh] NOUN, ideas. **1. idée ▶** a thought, plan, or picture that has been formed in the mind; something that exists in the mind : *"The giant shadows his father cast on the wall gave Harald an idea."* (Donald Carrick) **2. idée, opinion ▶** a certain belief or opinion : *Many people have strong ideas about how students should be taught.* **3. intention, but, dessein ▶** the purpose or point of something : *The idea of recycling is to help the environment.* SYN : thought, plan, notion, opinion, impression.

i-de-al [i-DEE-ul] NOUN, ideals. **1. idéal (ale, -aux) ▶** a person or thing that is thought of as being perfect; a perfect example : *Getting front-row seats for the concert would be ideal, but I'd settle for seats anywhere.* **2. ideals. idéal (ale, -als, -aux) ▶** standards for thinking or acting : *a person of high ideals.* ▲ ADJECTIVE. **idéal (-ale, -als, -aux), parfait (-aite) ▶** being exactly what is wanted or hoped for; the best possible : *A sunny, warm day is ideal for a picnic.* ■ **ideally,** ADVERB. ▶ **idéalement.** *Ideally, we should plant the tulip bulbs in the fall.* SYN : perfect, faultless, model, flawless.

i-den-ti-cal [i-DEN-tuh-kul] ADJECTIVE. **1. identique, pareil (-eille) ▶** being exactly alike : *"Side by side they heated two woks, and then stirred in identical ingredients."* (Paul Yee) **2. identique ▶** being the very same : *The two golfers hit long shots that landed in almost the identical spot.* ■ **identically,** ADVERB.

✍ Writing Tips

Idioms

An **idiom** is an expression that is difficult to understand from the meaning of the individual words. The words work together to create a special meaning; for example, Keep an eye on… means "to watch or take care of something or someone." It's raining cats and dogs means "it's raining heavily."

A few idioms can make your writing more interesting, but too many can ruin a piece of writing.

identiquement. SYN: same, duplicate, alike, equal, equivalent.

i·den·ti·fi·ca·tion [i-DEN-tuh-fuh-KAY-shun] NOUN, identifications. **1. identification ▸** the act of identifying; recognizing someone or something : *Alex made an identification of his jacket at the lost and found.* **2. pièce d'identité ▸** something that is used to prove which a person is : *Bank tellers ask for identification before they will cash a cheque.*

i·den·ti·fy [i-DEN-tuh-FY] VERB, identified, identifying. **identifier ▸** to know or show who a person is or what a thing is; recognize : *She identified her suitcase by the yellow tape on the handle.*

identify with a. **identifier, assimiler ▸** to think one thing is the same as another; consider the same : *People sometimes identify happiness with having a lot of money.* b. **identifier, reconnaître ▸** to feel something in common with : *"An attraction to a crab is something I cannot identify with."* (Cynthia Rylant)

i·den·ti·ty [i-DEN-tuh-tee] NOUN, identities. **identité ▸** who a person is or what a thing is : *The movie star wore a big hat and dark glasses to hide her identity from the crowd of fans.*

id·i·om [ID-ee-um] NOUN, idioms. **expression, tournure, idiome, locution ▸** a group of words whose meaning cannot be understood by putting together the regular meaning of each separate word in the group, such as "play it by ear" and "keep your nose to the grindstone." ▪ **idiomatic,** ADJECTIVE: ▸ **idiomatique.** *an idiomatic expression.* ✐ p. 303.

i·dle [IDE-ul] ADJECTIVE, idler, idlest. **1. inactif (-ive), inoccupé (-ée), désœuvré (-ée) ▸** not working or busy; doing nothing : *All the teams in the league have games today except the Lions, who are idle until Saturday.* **2. paresseux (-euse), fainéant (-ante), oisif (-ive) ▸** not willing to work; lazy : *He spent too much of his time in*

idle company. **3. inutile, vain (vaine), futile, oiseux (-euse) ▸** not producing anything useful; worthless : *Paula says that my big plans for the future are only idle talk.* ▲ VERB, idled, idling. **1. gaspiller, paresser ▸** to spend time doing nothing; waste time : *He planned to idle away his vacation doing nothing.* **2. tourner au ralenti ▸** to run a motor or machine slowly and out of gear : *The driver left the cab idling when he stopped to make a phone call.* ▪ **idly,** ADVERB. ▸ **paresseusement.** *Many of the spectators stood idly by instead of trying to help.* ▪ **idleness,** NOUN. ▸ **inaction, inactivité, inutilité.**

i·dol [IDE-ul] NOUN, idols. **1. idole ▸** an object or other image that is worshipped as a god. An idol is usually a statue or similar figure. **2. idole ▸** a person who is greatly admired or loved. **Note. ▸** To idolize someone means to admire the person very much : *Teenagers often idolize athletes or rock singers.*

if [if] CONJUNCTION. **1. si ▸** in the event that; should it happen that : *"You will leave many of us homeless if you chop down this great Kapok tree."* (Lynne Cherry) **2. si ▸** whether : *Do you know if we have school next Monday?* **3. si ▸** that : *Is it all right if I borrow your pen for a minute?*

ig·loo [IG-loo] NOUN, igloos. **igloo, iglou ▸** The Inuit word for any dwelling, not just those made of ice. **Note.** See icehouse.

ig·ne·ous [IG-nee-us] ADJECTIVE. **igné (-ée) ▸** of rocks, produced by the cooling and hardening of very hot material. For example, when lava from a volcano hardens, it forms a type of igneous rock.

ig·nite [ig-NITE] VERB, ignited, igniting. **1. mettre le feu à, enflammer ▸** to set fire to something; cause to burn. **2. prendre feu, s'enflammer ▸** to begin to burn; catch fire : *The leaves ignited quickly, and the bonfire lit up.* SYN: set on fire, burn, light.

ig·ni·tion [ig-NISH-un] NOUN, ignitions. **1. allumage, ignition ▸** the act of setting on fire or catching fire : *The ignition of gasoline starts an engine.* **2. allumage ▸** an electrical system that starts the engine of a car, a boat, or another motor vehicle.

ig·no·rance [IG-nur-uns] NOUN. **ignorance ▸** the fact or state of not knowing; a lack of knowledge : *In his ignorance, he tried to make the flashlight work without putting in the batteries.*

ig·no·rant [IG-nur-unt] ADJECTIVE. **1. ignorant (-ante), illettré (-ée) ▸** knowing nothing; having little or no knowledge or education : *People who live in the city are often ignorant about country life.* **2. ignorant (-ante) ▸** not aware of a certain thing; not knowing : *She found it hard to follow the baseball game because she was ignorant of its rules.* **3. ignorant (-ante) ▸**

showing a lack of information or knowledge : *He made the ignorant remark that horses are the fastest animals on earth.* ▪ **ignorantly**, ADVERB. ▶ **par ignorance.** SYN: uneducated, unintelligent, foolish, unaware.

ig·nore [ig-NOR] VERB, ignored, ignoring. **ne pas tenir compte de, ne pas relever, passer sous silence** ▶ to pay no attention to; not take notice of : *"Other kids his own age he just simply ignored."* (Michael Chesworth) SYN: disregard, overlook, snub, slight, scorn.

i·gua·na [ih-GWAH-nuh] NOUN, iguanas. **iguane** ▶ a large lizard with a row of spines along its back. It is found in very warm parts of the Americas.

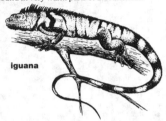

iguana

ill [il] ADJECTIVE. **1. malade, souffrant (-ante), indisposé (-ée)** ▶ having a disease; not healthy; sick : *Jan has been ill with the flu for several days now.* **2. mauvais (-aise), méchant (-ante), dur (dure), cruel (-elle)** ▶ bad or harmful; unfortunate : *The farmer's crops are suffering from the ill effects of bad weather.* ▲ ADVERB. **mal** ▶ in a harmful way; badly : *There is an old saying "Do not speak ill of the dead."* **Note.** Often used in combination with another word, such as *ill-tempered, ill-mannered,* and so on. ▲ NOUN, ills. **1. maladie, mal (maux), malaise, affection** ▶ a sickness; disease. **2. mal** ▶ something that is bad or harmful. SYN: sick, unwell, under the weather, ailing, sickly.

ill at ease **mal à l'aise, gêné (-ée), embarrassé (-ée)** ▶ not comfortable, uneasy : *Kelly is very ill at ease about giving speeches.*

il·le·gal [ih-LEE-gul] ADJECTIVE. **illégal (-ale, -aux)** ▶ not legal; against the law. ▪ **illegally**, ADVERB. ▶ **illégalement.** *He got a ticket because his car was illegally parked.*

il·leg·i·ble [ih-LEJ-uh-bul] ADJECTIVE. **illisible** ▶ hard or impossible to read : *His handwriting is illegible.*

il·lit·er·ate [ih-LIT-ur-it] ADJECTIVE. **1. illettré (-ée), analphabète** ▶ not able to read or write at all; having no education. **2. illettré (-ée), analphabète** ▶ not able to read and write well enough (for example, to read a newspaper or write out a cheque) to get along in the world. ▪ **illiteracy**, NOUN. ▶ **analphabétisme.**

ill·ness [IL-nis] NOUN, illnesses. **1. maladie, mal (maux), malaise, affection** ▶ the fact or state of being ill ; sickness ; disease : *Our teacher is away today because of illness.* **2. maladie** ▶ a certain disease : *Polio was a very dangerous illness until doctors learned how to prevent it in the 1950s.* 📖 **p. 1160.**

il·lu·mi·nate [ih-LOO-muh-NATE] VERB, illuminated, illuminating. **1. éclairer, illuminer** ▶ to light up; shine light on : *Lights at each corner illuminated the tennis court.* **2. éclairer, faire la lumière sur** ▶ explain; make clear : *Marc's explanation illuminated how the machine works.* ▪ **illumination**, NOUN. ▶ **éclairage, illumination.**

il·lu·sion [ih-LOO-zhun] NOUN, illusions. **1. illusion** ▶ something that fools the eyes, ears, or other senses : *Mirrors on a wall will give the illusion that the room is bigger.* **2. illusion, rêve, mirage** ▶ a false idea or belief : *Taylor has the illusion that she'd be happier if she were taller.* SYN: fantasy, trick, misconception.

il·lus·trate [IL-us-TRATE] VERB, illustrated, illustrating. **1. illustrer, imager** ▶ to add a picture or illustration to a book or other written work in order to explain the text, give it decoration, or make it more interesting : *Our neighbour writes books for children, and her husband illustrates them.* **Note.** A person who does this is called an illustrator. **2. donner un exemple, éclairer, illustrer** ▶ to explain something by giving an example or by comparing it to something else : *This dictionary illustrates the meanings of many words by showing how they are used by writers.* 🖉 **p. 212.**

il·lus·tra·tion [IL-us-TRAY-shun] NOUN, illustrations. **1. image, dessin, illustration** ▶ a picture, diagram, map, and so on used to explain or decorate something written. **2. illustration, à titre d'exemple** ▶ something such as a story, comparison, or example that is used to explain : *Falling leaves are a good illustration of the law of gravity.*

im- PREFIX. **not**; the opposite of : *immature.*

im·age [IM-ij] NOUN, images. **1. portrait, image** ▶ a person or thing that looks like another; likeness : *Ted is the image of his father.* **2. idée, image** ▶ a picture formed in the mind; representation : *I had an image of the crowded train station where we met.* **3. image** ▶ in writing, a word or words used to suggest a certain picture in the mind : *The poet's words brought lovely images to my mind.* **Note.** The use of words in this way by a writer is called imagery. 🖉 **p. 305.** **4. image de marque** ▶ public opinion about a person or thing; the way something is thought of by others : *The oil company hired an advertising firm to improve its image.* **5. reflet, image** ▶ a picture formed when light shines in a mirror or through a camera lens : *You have to adjust the focus to make the image clear.*

✏ **Writing Tips**

Imagery

*When writers use words to create pictures in a reader's mind it is called **imagery**. The words call on our senses—taste, smell, touch, sight, and sound—to draw a picture, strengthen a feeling, reveal characters, even create a mood or explain an idea. The following paragraph has images that make readers feel like they are right in the scene.*

The hot summer sun burned its way across the cloudless sky. The children splashed about in the pool, as playful as fish in the sea. They were surrounded by the sharp smell of chlorine and the coconut scent of suntan lotion. Their shouts of joy echoed off the concrete walls of the public pool.

i·mag·i·nar·y [ih-MAJ-uh-NAIR-ee] ADJECTIVE. **imaginaire, irréel (-elle), fictif (-ive)** ▶ existing only as a picture in the mind ; not real : *He has imaginary friends and a real horse.* SYN: unreal, make-believe, fanciful, fictitious.

i·mag·i·na·tion [ih-MAJ uh-NAY-shun] NOUN. **imaginations. 1. imagination** ▶ the ability of the mind to form images and pictures of things that are not there : *In her imagination, Lucy could see her old house.* **2. imagination, créativité** ▶ the ability of the mind to create something new or different, or to create a new or different use for something that already exists : *Science-fiction writers use their imagination to create new worlds.*

i·mag·ine [ih-MAJ-in] VERB, **imagined, imagining. 1. imaginer, concevoir, envisager** ▶ to form an idea or image in the mind ; have a mental picture of something : *"She saw her mother in the crowd and imagined her saying again, 'Koala Lou, I DO love you!'"* (Mem Fox) **2. imaginer, penser, supposer, croire** ▶ to believe to be true; suppose; guess : *"You can imagine how overwhelmed, how excited and how flattered Bavsi*

was." (Adèle Geras) **3. croire, s'imaginer, se figurer** ▶ to think or believe : *He imagines that people make fun of him because he has braces, so he tries not to smile.* **Note.** Something that can be imagined is **imaginable**: *"They will think we are boring unless we choose the fanciest new names imaginable."* (Tololwa M. Mollel) ✏ **p. 305.**

im·i·tate [IM-uh-TATE] VERB, **imitated, imitating. 1. imiter, copier,** ▶ to try to act or be like someone or something else; follow an example; copy : *A mockingbird can imitate the call of almost anyother bird.* **2. ressembler, paraître** ▶ to look like; resemble : *Artificial playing fields are coloured green to imitate grass.*

im·i·ta·tion [IM-uh-TAY-shun] NOUN. **imitations. 1. imitation, caricature, parodie** ▶ the act of imitating; copying : *My uncle does a good imitation of a rooster crowing.* **2. imitation, copie, contrefaçon** ▶ a copy of something else : *an imitation of a famous painting.* ▲ ADJECTIVE. **imité (-ée), copié (-ée)** ▶ made to look like something else; not real : *She bought an imitation diamond, because real diamonds are so expensive.*

im·ma·ture [IM-uh-CHOOR or IM-uh-TOOR] ADJECTIVE. **1. vert (verte), pas mûr (mûre)** ▶ not fully grown or developed; not ripe : *Immature tomatoes are hard and green.* **2. immature** ▶ behaving in a childish way; not acting according to one's age; foolish.

im·me·di·ate [ih-MEE-dee-it] ADJECTIVE. **1. immédiat (-ate), instantané (-ée), subit (-ite)** ▶ happening at once; without delay : *The townspeople are cut off by flood waters and need immediate help.* **2. immédiat (-ate), proche** ▶ close; near : *There are no grocery stores in the immediate neighbourhood.* ■ **immediately,** ADVERB : ▶ **immédiatement, aussitôt, instantanément.** *He left immediately after his mom called to ask him to come home.*

im·mense [ih-MENCE] ADJECTIVE. **immense, énorme, vaste** ▶ of very great size ; huge; enormous : *The immense wedding cake almost covered the table it was placed on.* ■ **immensely,** ADVERB: ▶ **extrêmement, immensément, énormément.** *Joshua admired his father immensely.* ■ **immensity,** NOUN. ▶ **immensité.**

✏ **Word Builder**

Imagine, visualize, and think are verbs meaning to create pictures, ideas, or plans in a person's mind. Imagine means to create pictures of things that go beyond facts : Imagine what the world would be like without cars. Visualize also has the idea of creating pictures in one's head. Sometimes these pictures can be drawn from real things : When he's afraid, it gives him great comfort to visualize the safety of his own room. Think is a general word but it can mean to develop ideas or plans in one's mind : I thought of the idea in the middle of the night.

im‑mi‑grant [IM-uh-grunt] NOUN, immigrants. **immigrant (-ante), immigré (-ée)** ► a person who comes into a country to live after leaving the country where he or she was born : *My parents were immigrants to Canada when they moved here from Jamaica.*

im‑mi‑grate [IM-uh-GRATE] VERB, immigrated, immigrating. **immigrer** ► to go to live in a country in which you were not born : *Many people immigrate to Canada each year.* **Note.** The process of immigrating is called immigration. ✐ p. 200.

im‑mor‑tal [ih-MORT-ul] ADJECTIVE. 1. **immortel (-elle), éternel (-elle)** ► living forever; never dying : *The ancient Greeks believed that their gods were immortal.* 2. **immortel (-elle), éternel (-elle), impérissable** ► lasting forever : *William Shakespeare's immortal plays.* **Note.** The state of being immortal is immortality.

im‑mune [ih-MYOON] ADJECTIVE. 1. **immunisé (-ée), protégé (-ée)** ► protected from a disease : *Most people are immune to chicken pox after they have had it once.* 2. **immunisé (-ée), protégé (-ée)** ► not affected by, or free from, something unpleasant : *The author claims that he is immune to criticism and never pays attention to reviews of his books.* **Note.** The fact of being immune is immunity.

im‑pact [IM-pakt] NOUN, impacts. 1. **impact, choc** ► the striking of one object against another; a collision : *The impact of the crash damaged the front of my car.* 2. **impact** ► the force or effect of something : *"Keep a journal. Write down things that have a strong impact on you."* (Marilyn Halvorson) SYN: collision, contact, crash, bump, blow.

im‑pal‑a [im-PAL-uh] NOUN, impalas. **impala** ► a small reddish or brown African antelope with curved horns. An impala can run very fast and make long, high leaps through the air.

impala

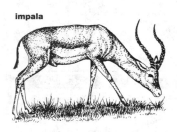

im‑par‑tial [im-PAR-shul] ADJECTIVE. **impartial (-ale, -aux), objectif (-ive), juste, équitable** ► not favouring one person or side over another; with-

out bias; fair : *A judge must be impartial.* SYN: just, unbiased, neutral, equal, unprejudiced.

im‑pa‑tient [im-PAY-shunt] ADJECTIVE. 1. **impatient (-ente)** ► not willing to put up with delay or problems; not patient : *The server took so long to come to our table that we all became impatient.* 2. **impatient (-ente),** ► anxious; eager : *Patrice was impatient for the movie to start.* ■ **impatiently,** ADVERB. ► impatiemment. ■ **impatience,** NOUN. ► impatience, énervement. *"The room surged with excitement and impatience."* (Eve Bunting) SYN: anxious, restless, eager, fretful.

im‑pe‑ri‑al [im-PEER-ee-ul] ADJECTIVE. **impérial (-ale, -aux)** ► having to do with an empire or with its ruler : *The emperor of Japan lives in an imperial palace.*

im‑per‑son‑al [im-PUR-sun-ul] ADJECTIVE. 1. **impersonnel (-elle), neutre** ► referring to any person or thing, not to any specific one : *"All for one and one for all"* is an impersonal expression. 2. **impersonnel (-elle), froid (froide), distant (-ante)** ► not affected by personal feelings : *a big impersonal company.*

im‑ple‑ment [IM-pluh-munt] NOUN, implements. **outil, instrument, appareil** ► a tool or piece of equipment that is used to do a particular job : *A shovel and a rake are common gardening implements.* ▲ [IM-pluh-ment] VERB, implemented, implementing. **exécuter, effectuer, mettre en pratique** ► to put into action; carry out : *to implement a plan.*

im‑ply [im-PLY] VERB, implied, implying. **suggérer, insinuer, laisser entendre, laisser supposer** ► to express something without saying it directly; suggest; hint : *Her expression implied that she didn't agree with me.* **Note.** Something that is implied is an implication. SYN: hint at, suggest.

im‑po‑lite [IM-puh-LITE] ADJECTIVE. **impoli (-ie), effronté (-ée), insolent (-ente), grossier (-ière)** ► not polite; having bad manners; rude; disrespectful. ■ **impolitely,** ADVERB. ► impoliment, grossièrement. ■ **impoliteness,** NOUN. ► impolitesse, insolence, impertinence.

im‑port [im-PORT] VERB, imported, importing. **importer** ► to bring in something from another country for sale or use : *Canada imports coffee from Brazil and Colombia.* ▲ [IM-port] NOUN, imports. 1. **importations** ► something that is imported. 2. **importance** ► importance : *a matter of great import.*

im‑por‑tant [im-PORT-unt] ADJECTIVE. **important (-ante), sérieux (-ieuse)** ► worth caring about or being concerned with; having value or meaning : *"Feeling that I belong to a community is important to me."* (Paul Yee) **Note.** The state or quality of being important is importance: *This book deals with the importance of eating* *proper food.* SYN: significant, meaningful, essential, valuable.

im-pose [im-POZE] VERB, imposed, imposing. **1. imposer, obliger, commander, infliger** ▶ to take unfair advantage; force oneself on someone : *I'd love to stay for dinner if you're sure I'm not imposing.* **2. imposer** ▶ to apply by force : *to impose a new tax; to impose a jail sentence.* **Note.** Something that is imposing is large and impressive : *Niagara Falls is an imposing sight.*

im-pos-si-ble [im-POS-uh-bul] ADJECTIVE. **1. impossible, irréalisable** ▶ not able to be or to happen; not possible : *It's impossible to drop a stone and have it go upward instead of falling to the ground.* **2. impossible, irréalisable** ▶ not able to be done : *"For without the ancient books, it is impossible to prove who should be the true emperor."* (David Day) **3. impossible, insupportable** ▶ hard to put up with or get along with; very unpleasant or difficult : *His sullen attitude made him impossible to talk to.* SYN: unimaginable, unthinkable, absurd.

im-pos-tor [im-POS-tur] NOUN, impostors. (sometimes imposter) **imposteur (-eure), menteur (-euse), charlatan** ▶ a person who pretends to be someone else in order to gain or to get something : *She tried to get into the party by claiming that she was the host's cousin, but she was an impostor.*

im-press [im-PRESS] VERB, impressed, impressing. **1. impressionner, frapper, étonner** ▶ to have a strong effect on the mind or feelings, especially in a good way : *Tanya's hockey skills impressed the coach.* **2. faire comprendre** ▶ to fix in the mind : *The mother impressed upon her children the importance of looking both ways before crossing a road.* **3. imprimer** ▶ to make a mark or pattern by pressing.

im-pres-sion [im-PRESH-un] NOUN, impressions. **1. impression** ▶ a strong effect produced in the mind; an idea or feeling about what something is like : *It's hard to sell a house if people get a bad impression when they first see the property.* **2. impression** ▶ an idea; understanding; notion : *I had the impression that you had already finished your homework.* **3. empreinte, trace, impression** ▶ a mark or pattern made on a surface by pressing : *The dog's paws made an impression in the mud.* **4. imitation, caricature** ▶ an imitation of the way someone speaks, acts, or looks; an impersonation.

im-pres-sive [im-PRESS-iv] ADJECTIVE. **impressionnant (-ante), frappant (-ante), saisissant (-ante), imposant (-ante)** ▶ having a powerful effect on the mind or feelings; making a strong or lasting impression : *All your debating awards are impressive—you must be very good!* ■ **impressively,** ADVERB. ▶ **de façon impressionnante.** ■ **impressiveness,** NOUN. ▶ impres-

sionnabilité. SYN: moving, stirring, exciting, thrilling, notable.

im-prop-er [im-PROP-ur] ADJECTIVE. **incorrect (-ecte), faux (fausse), inexact (-acte), impoli (-ie)** ▶ not correct; wrong : *You can't turn left here; you just made an improper turn!* SYN: incorrect, wrong, unfit, bad, unsuitable.

im-prove [im-PROOV] VERB, improved, improving. **améliorer, perfectionner, développer** ▶ to make or become better : *My piano playing improves when I practise every day.*

im-prove-ment [im-PROOV-munt] NOUN, improvements. **1. amélioration, progrès, développement** ▶ the act or fact of improving; making or becoming better : *Tim's work has shown a lot of improvement since he started studying more.* **2. amélioration** ▶ a person or thing that is better; something that adds value : *When they bought the house, they put aside extra money to pay for a new roof and other improvements.*

im-pulse [IM-puls] NOUN, impulses. **1. idée, pensée, impulsion, influence** ▶ a sudden wish to act; something decided without real thought : *My first impulse was to run away, but I decided to stay and face my angry brother.* **Note.** A person who acts according to impulse is impulsive. **2. poussée, impulsion** ▶ a sudden wave or force : *Impulses of the nervous system carry messages to the brain.* SYN: thought, idea, notion, urge, inclination.

im-pure [im-PYOOR] ADJECTIVE. **1. malpropre, sale, impur (-ure)** ▶ not pure; unclean : *After the flood, they had to boil the impure water before they could use it.* **2. mélangé (-ée), impur (-ure)** ▶ mixed with something, especially something of lower value : *She was disappointed to learn that the gold in her new ring is impure.* SYN: unclean, dirty, foul, polluted.

in [in] PREPOSITION. **1. dedans** ▶ inside : *Put your shoes in the closet.* **2. dans** ▶ into : *Get in the car.* **3. à, au (aux), en, dans** ▶ at a certain place : *She was born in Quebec City.* **4. dans, en** ▶ at a certain time : *I'll be finished in an hour.* **5. en, au, dans** ▶ to or at a certain condition : *to be in pain; to get in trouble.* **6. à, par, en, au (aux)** ▶ by a certain way or method : *to sign a letter in ink; to pay for something in cash.* ▲ ADVERB. **dedans, à l'intérieur** ▶ inside or within : *It might rain, so bring the wash in.*

in- PREFIX. not; the opposite of : *incapable.*

in-a-bil-i-ty [IN-uh-BIL-uh-tee] NOUN. **incapacité, impuissance** ▶ a lack of ability or power; not being able.

in-ad-e-quate [in-AD-uh-kwit] ADJECTIVE. **insuffisant (-ante), inadéquat (-ate), inadapté (-ée), inapproprié (-ée)** ▶ not adequate : *The space in the tent is inadequate for six sleeping people.* ■ **inadequately,** ADVERB. ■ **insuffisamment.** SYN: not enough, insufficient, unsatisfactory.

in·cen·tive [in-SEN-tiv] NOUN, incentives. **motivation, motif, prétexte, mobile** ▶ something that makes a person want to try harder or do more work : *Abdul's father offered him a bike as an incentive to work harder in school.*

inch [inch] NOUN, inches. **pouce** ▶ a unit of measure for length. Twelve inches equal one foot. An inch is equal to 2.54 centimetres. ▲ VERB, inched, inching. **bouger petit à petit** ▶ to move very slowly, a little bit at a time : *The bumper-to-bumper rush-hour traffic inched along at a snail's pace.*

in·ci·dent [IN-suh-dunt] NOUN, incidents. 1. **évènement, expérience, incident** ▶ something that happens; an event : *Marilyn keeps a journal in which she notes any important incidents that occur.* 2. **incident** ▶ a minor conflict; something that causes trouble or problems : *There are hard feelings between those two countries because of the many incidents along their border.* SYN: event, happening, occurrence, experience.

in·ci·den·tal·ly [IN-suh-DENT-uh-lee] ADVERB. **incidemment** ▶ by the way; along with something else : *I really like that particular series of books; and incidentally, I still have one that you loaned me.*

in·cline [in-KLINE] VERB, inclined, inclining. 1. **pencher, incliner, courber** ▶ to be or move at an angle; slant; slope : *My father inclined his head slightly, indicating that he was willing to listen.* 2. **avoir tendance, pencher, incliner** ▶ to be willing to; favour : *I'm inclined to agree with you about that.* 3. **pencher, incliner** ▶ to be likely to; tend : *"Moose seldom eat grass but are more inclined to browse off the tender buds of trees and bushes."* (Todd Lee) ▲ [IN-kline or in-KLINE] NOUN, inclines. **pente, inclinaison** ▶ a slanted or sloped surface : *the incline of a hill.*

in·clude [in-KLOOD] VERB, included, including. 1. **inclure, comprendre, compter** ▶ to be made up of; have as a part; contain : *This recipe includes sugar, flour, and milk.* 2. **inclure, comprendre, compter** ▶ to make someone or something part of a group : *"I say we because they always try to include me in everything they do."* (Alice Walker) ✐ **p. 139.**

in·cog·ni·to [in-KOG-nee-TOH or IN-kog-NEE-toh] ADJECTIVE; ADVERB. **incognito** ▶ with one's name, character, rank, face, and so on concealed : *The rock star travelled incognito so that she would not be recognized.*

in·co·her·ent [IN-koh-HEER-unt] ADJECTIVE. 1. **incohérent (-ente), illogique, absurde** ▶ not sticking together. 2. **incohérent (-ente), illogique, absurde** ▶ not making sense; confused : *His reason for being late was incoherent.*

in·come [IN-kum or IN-KUM] NOUN, incomes. **revenu, salaire, rente** ▶ the money that a person or business earns for work that is done, things that are sold, or property that is owned.

Note. Income tax is a tax collected on the money earned by a person or business. SYN: salary, wages, earnings, profit, gains.

in·com·plete [IN-kum-PLEET] ADJECTIVE. **incomplet (-ète), inachevé (-ée)** ▶ missing some part; unfinished; not complete : *The puzzle is incomplete; three pieces are missing.*

in·con·ven·ient [IN-kun-VEEN-yunt or in-kun-VEEN-ee-unt] ADJECTIVE. **malcommode, peu pratique, incommode, inopportun (-une)** ▶ causing trouble or bother; not convenient : *I can't make the meeting at six; that's a really inconvenient time for me.*

in·cor·po·rate [in-KOR-puh-RATE] VERB, incorporated, incorporating. 1. **incorporer, mélanger, inclure, insérer** ▶ to join something with something else; make a part of something else : *Leigh incorporated Avi's suggestions into her story.* 2. **fusionner, réunir, grouper, unifier** ▶ to form, or make into, a corporation : *As the business grew, the partners felt that it would be more profitable to incorporate.*

in·cor·rect [in-kuh-REKT] ADJECTIVE. **incorrect (-ecte), faux (fausse), inexact (-acte), erroné (-ée)** ▶ not correct or proper; wrong; containing errors : *an incorrect answer.* ■ **incorrectly,** ADVERB. ▶ **incorrectement, inexactement.**

in·crease [in-KREES] VERB, increased, increasing. **augmenter, hausser, monter, accroître** ▶ to make or become larger in size, number, or amount : *The car's speed increased as we went downhill.* ▲ [IN-krees] NOUN, increases. 1. **augmentation, hausse** ▶ the amount by which something is made larger : *The workers are asking for a 10% increase in pay.* 2. **augmentation, accroissement** ▶ the act of increasing; growth : *The census will tell us how large the population increase has been in the past 10 years.* ■ **increasingly,** ADVERB. **de plus en plus** ▶ more and more : *It's becoming increasingly difficult to find an affordable house.* SYN: enlarge, expand, add to, extend, raise, grow.

in·cred·i·ble [in-KRED-uh-bul] ADJECTIVE. **incroyable, étonnant (-ante), surprenant (-ante), renversant (-ante)** ▶ hard to believe or imagine; amazing : *The new ride at the amusement park is incredible!*

in·cu·ba·tor [IN-kyuh-BAY-tur] NOUN, incubators. 1. **incubateur, couveuse** ▶ a heated container used in hospitals for newborn babies who are born too early or who have serious health problems. 2. **incubateur, couveuse** ▶ a heated container used for hatching eggs artificially.

in·de·ci·sive [IN-dih-SY-siv] ADJECTIVE. 1. **indécis (-ise), hésitant (-ante)** ▶ not settling or deciding a matter. 2. **indécis (-ise), hésitant (-ante), irrésolu (-ue)** ▶ having a habit of not making decisions or hesitating : *She is indecisive about what to eat in a restaurant.*

✏️ **Writing Tips**

Index

*An **index** can help you as you conduct research. For example, if you are writing a report on acid rain and you've found a book that covers many environmental issues, look up "acid rain" in the index at the back of the book. The entry for acid rain will give you all the pages on which acid rain is discussed.*

in-deed [in-DEED] ADVERB. **en effet, vraiment** ► in truth; really : *"As the weeks passed the Sultan saw that Little Kay could indeed ride, joust, and swing a scimitar as well as any of the others."* (Robin Muller) SYN: in fact, certainly, of course, absolutely.

incubator

in-def-i-nite [in-DEF-uh-nit] ADJECTIVE. **imprécis (-ise), indéterminé (-ée), vague, indéfini (-ie)** ► not clear or exact; not definite; vague : *The movie will play at some indefinite date in the future.* ■ **indefinitely,** ADVERB. ► **indéfiniment.** *Let's get this settled now so that it won't drag on indefinitely.*

in-dent [in-DENT] VERB, indented, indenting. **mettre en retrait, renfoncer** ► to start a line of a written work farther to the right than other lines : *I like to indent the first line of each paragraph.* ▲ [IN-dent] NOUN, indents. **alinéa, retrait, renfoncement.**

in-de-pen-dent [IN-dih-PEN-dunt] ADJECTIVE. **1. indépendant (-ante), autonome** ► not connected with others; separate : *He's leaving his job with the TV network to set up an independent film company.* **2. indépendant (-ante), autonome** ► thinking or acting for oneself; not depending on others : *My great-grandmother is very independent and still lives alone in her own house.* **3. indépendant** ► not under the control of another country; not ruled by others; free. *Canada and the U.S. are independent nations.* **Note.** The fact of being independent is independence. 📖 **p. 309.**

in-dex [IN-deks] NOUN, indexes or indices. **1. index, répertoire, table alphabétique** ► an alphabetical list at the end of a book that shows the page or pages where information on a particular subject can be found. **2. indice, signe** ► something that shows a certain value or quality : *The number of people using the park is an index of how popular it is.* 📖 **p. 309.**

In-di-an [IN-dee-un] ADJECTIVE. **1. indien (-ienne)** ► having to do with the country of India or with the people, languages, and cultures found there. **2. indien (-ienne), amérindien (-ienne)** ► having to do with the original inhabitants of the Americas, their language or culture. **Note.** When the first European explorers arrived in the Americas, they thought they had reached India and called the people they met "Indians. 📖 **p. 387.**

in-di-cate [IN-duh-KATE] VERB, indicated, indicating. **1. indiquer, montrer** ► to point out; show : *"He got a pointer and indicated the faraway island that the Chinese called Taiwan, where I had lived for the first six years of my life."* (Jean Little) **2. indiquer, dénoter, révéler** ► to be a sign of; reveal or suggest : *His smile indicated how happy he was.* ■ **indicator,** NOUN. ► **indication, signe, indice.** SYN: show, demonstrate, display, suggest, imply.

in-dif-fer-ent [in-DIF-ur-unt] ADJECTIVE. **indifférent (-ente), froid (froide), neutre, insensible** ► not caring one way or the other how something happens or turns out; having or showing no interest : *Kate and Jeff were excited about the soccer game, but I was indifferent.* ■ **indifference,** NOUN. **indifférence, insensibilité, froideur** ► a lack of concern or interest. SYN: neutral, impersonal, unconcerned, unbiased.

🔧 **Word Builder**

Independent, alone, and ***self-reliant*** *all mean someone or something is not connected with a group. An **independent** person thinks for himself or herself and is not influenced by others : René is independent and prefers to work on his own. **Alone** means to be set apart from others : Taylor raised the flag alone. **Self-reliant** means to be able to do things on one's own : Ritta showed that she is self-reliant by surviving alone in the woods for two days.*

in·di·ges·tion [IN-duh-JES-chun] NOUN. **indigestion** ▸ difficulty digesting food and the pain or uncomfortable feeling this causes.

in·dig·nant [in-DIG-nunt] ADJECTIVE. **indigné (-ée)** ▸ surprised and angry about something that is thought to be unfair : *Patrice was indignant that others were cheating at the game.* ■ **indignantly,** ADVERB. ▸ **avec indignation.** ■ **indignation,** NOUN. ▸ **indignation.** *Chris couldn't contain his indignation over the cruel remark.*

in·di·rect [IN-duh-REKT] ADJECTIVE. **1. indirect (-ecte), détourné (-ée)** ▸ not in a straight path or line; not direct. **2. indirect (-ecte), détourné (-ée)** ▸ not directly mentioned or connected : *His offer to think over her request was an indirect way of saying no.* ■ **indirectly,** ADVERB. ▸ **indirectement.**

in·di·vid·u·al [IN-duh-VIJ-yoo-ul] ADJECTIVE. **1. individuel (-elle), particulier (-ière)** ▸ single; separate from others; particular : *individual students; individual questions.* **2. individuel (-elle)** ▸ by or meant for only one : *The cereal package had 12 small boxes, each containing an individual serving.* ▲ NOUN., **individuals. 1. individu, personne** ▸ a single person or thing. **2. individualité** ▸ a distinct person : *Oprah always does her own thing; she's a real individual.* ■ **individually,** ADVERB.: ▸ **individuellement.** *The teacher met with each student individually to discuss the stories.* **Note.** A quality that makes someone or something different from others is individuality. 🖉 **p. 432.**

in·door [IN-DOR] ADJECTIVE. **intérieur** ▸ of or taking place inside a house or other building : *Bowling is an indoor sport.* ■ **indoors,** ADVERB. ▸ **à l'intérieur, à la maison, à l'abri.** *We played indoors because it was raining.*

in·dus·tri·al [in-DUS-tree-ul] ADJECTIVE. **1. industriel (-ielle)** ▸ having to do with or made by industry. **2. (also industrialized) industriel (-ielle)** ▸ having highly developed industry : *Japan and Germany are industrial countries.*

in·dus·tri·ous [in-DUS-tree-us] ADJECTIVE. **travailleur (-euse), appliqué (-ée), studieux (-ieuse)** ▸ working hard; diligent; busy : *Leslie is very industrious and has already finished her science project.* ■ **industriously,** ADVERB. ▸ **avec application, industrieusement.**

in·dus·try [IN-dus-tree] NOUN, **industries. 1. industrie** ▸ the producing and selling of goods; the work of factories and manufacturing plants. Industry takes natural materials and uses machines to change them into products to be sold. **2. industrie** ▸ a particular type of manufacturing, trade, or business : *the television industry; the fishing industry.* **3. industrie** ▸ manufacturing and business activity in general : *The mayor was praised for bringing new industry to our city.* **4. application, zèle, assiduité** ▸ hard work; steady effort : *It took a lot of indus-*try and self-discipline for her to become the success she is today.*

in·ept [in-EPT] ADJECTIVE. **inapte, gauche, malhabile** ▸ awkward, clumsy, or out of place : *With some practice, you won't be so inept in the kitchen.*

in·ev·i·ta·ble [in-EV-uh-tuh-bul] ADJECTIVE. **inévitable, immanquable, fatal, inéluctable** ▸ that which cannot be avoided; sure to happen; happening very often : *Be ready for the inevitable delay because of rush-hour traffic.* ■ **inevitably,** ADVERB. ▸ **inévitablement, immanquablement, fatalement.** SYN: unavoidable, inescapable, sure, certain.

in·ex·pen·sive [IN-ik-SPEN-siv] ADJECTIVE. **bon marché, pas cher (chère), peu coûteux (-euse)** ▸ not costing much; cheap; low-priced : *Tia bought an inexpensive poster to decorate her room.*

in·fa·mous [IN-fuh-mus] ADJECTIVE. **infâme, détestable** ▸ having a bad reputation : *Al Capone was an infamous criminal.*

in·fant [IN-funt] NOUN, **infants. petit enfant, bébé, enfant en bas âge** ▸ a very young child or baby. **Note.** Infancy is the time of being an infant.

in·fect [in-FEKT] VERB, **infected, infecting. 1. infecter, contaminer, transmettre** ▸ to cause disease by allowing germs to enter the body : *His cut became sore when it got infected.* **2. communiquer, infecter, contaminer** ▸ to spread easily from one person to another : *The excitement of the festival infected the whole school.* **Note.** Something that can infect is infectious: *The common cold is an infectious disease.*

in·fec·tion [in-FEK-shun] NOUN, **infections. 1. infection, contamination, contagion** ▸ the fact of being infected : *A bacterial infection usually takes seven days to show itself.* **2. infection, contamination** ▸ a disease caused by germs infecting the body, especially a painful swelling where germs have entered an open cut or sore.

in·fer [in-FUR] VERB, **inferred, inferring. déduire, conclure, inférer** ▸ to know or learn something by judging the facts or by noticing something, rather than by being told directly : *He inferred how worried I was by the frown on my face.* SYN: presume, suppose, conclude, gather, reason.

in·fer·i·or [in-FEER-ee-ur] ADJECTIVE. **inférieur (-eure), moindre** ▸ lower in quality, value, or rank; not as good or as high : *Kelly is so good in math that she makes the rest of the class feel inferior.* **Note.** The state of being inferior is inferiority. An inferiority complex is a strong and disturbing feeling that one is not as important or as good at things as other people are.

in·fi·nite [IN-fuh-nit] ADJECTIVE. **1. infini (-ie), illimité (-ée), sans borne** ▸ having no limits or boundaries; endless : *I gazed across the infinite expanse of the sea.* **Note.** The state of being infinite is infinity. **2. infini (-ie), illimité (-ée), sans borne** ▸ very great; as much as is possible : *It takes infinite patience to be a good teacher.* ■ **infinitely,** ADVERB. ▸ **Infiniment, énormément, immensément.** SYN: unlimited, endless, eternal, countless.

in·flame [in-FLAME] VERB, inflamed, inflaming. **1. enflammer, irriter** ▸ to have or cause an inflammation : *An infection inflamed Tony's throat.* **2. enflammer, attiser, allumer** ▸ to make angry or greatly excited : *The speaker inflamed the crowd with her passionate speech.*

in·flam·ma·tion [in-fluh-MAY-shun] NOUN, inflammations. **inflammation** ▸ a condition where part of the body becomes swollen, hot, and painful.

in·flate [in-FLATE] VERB, inflated, inflating. **1. gonfler** ▸ to expand or swell by filling with air or another gas : *You inflate a balloon by blowing into it.* **Note.** Something that can be inflated is inflatable. **2. faire monter, hausser, gonfler, dilater** ▸ to increase or enlarge beyond what it should be. **Note.** Usually used as an ADJECTIVE: *inflated ego.* SYN: swell, enlarge, expand, puff out, blow up.

in·fla·tion [in-FLAY-shun] NOUN. **1. inflation** ▸ a situation in which the prices of important goods and services rise, and the same amount of money will purchase less than it did before. **2. gonflement** ▸ the act of expanding something by filling it with air or another gas.

in·flu·ence [IN-floo-uns] NOUN. influences. **1. influence, emprise, autorité** ▸ the power to cause a change or to have an effect : *The pull of the moon's gravity has an influence on the tides.* **2. influence, prestige** ▸ the power to affect a person's mind or actions without using force : *My sister used her influence to get me a summer job.* **3. influence, emprise** ▸ a person or thing with this power : *Shayne's physics teacher had a great influence on his choice of career.* ▲ VERB, influenced, influencing. **influencer, entraîner** ▸ to have an influence on : *The friendly neighbourhood influenced our decision to move here.* **Note.** Someone who has or uses influence is influential. SYN: power, control, authority, force, pressure.

in·flu·en·za [IN-floo-EN-zuh] NOUN. **influenza, grippe** ▸ a disease like a very bad cold, but more dangerous; more often called flu. Its symptoms include a fever, a cough, and muscle aches.

in·form [in-FORM] VERB, informed, informing. **1. informer, avertir, aviser, renseigner** ▸ to give information to a person; tell : *The message informed Devi that her dentist appointment had been cancelled.* **2. dénoncer, informer contre quelqu'un** ▸ to tell something that is secret or that will harm a person : *The case was solved when one of the thieves informed on*

the rest of the gang. **Note.** A person who informs against another is an informer. SYN: tell, notify, report, communicate, advise.

in·for·mal [in-FOR-mul] ADJECTIVE. **1. simple, sans façon, familier (-ière)** ▸ not formal; casual; relaxed : *Dad plays basketball in an informal league where there are no uniforms and they don't really keep score.* **2. familier (-ière)** ▸ of language, used in everyday conversation and friendly writing, but not appropriate for more serious or formal situations. ■ **informally,** ADVERB. ▸ **sans cérémonie, officieusement, de façon informelle.**

in·for·ma·tion [IN-fur-MAY-shun] NOUN. **1. information, renseignement** ▸ facts; knowledge; news : *A dictionary is a book of information about words.* **2. information, renseignement** ▸ a service provided to answer customers' questions and give other facts : *I got Joanna's new telephone number by calling Information.* **Note.** Something that gives information is informative. SYN: news, data, evidence, material, knowledge.

in·gre·di·ent [in-GREE-dee-unt] NOUN, ingredients. **ingrédient** ▸ any one of the parts in a mixture : *Flour is the main ingredient in bread.*

in·hab·it [in-HAB-it] VERB, inhabited, inhabiting. **habiter, vivre, résider** ▸ to live in or on : *Animals that inhabit the desert have become used to living without much water.* **Note.** An inhabitant is a person or an animal that inhabits a place for a length of time : *My brother-in-law is an inhabitant of Newfoundland.* SYN: live, dwell, occupy, reside, stay, room.

in·hale [in-HALE] VERB, inhaled, inhaling. **inhaler, respirer, avaler** ▸ to breathe into the lungs : *Firefighters wear masks so that they won't inhale dangerous smoke.*

in·her·it [in-HAIR-it] VERB, inherited, inheriting. **1. hériter** ▸ to get money, property, or personal possessions from someone who has died : *"He figured he'd die and Aunt Esther would inherit twenty-one crabs and funeral expenses."* (Cynthia Rylant) **2. hériter, acquérir** ▸ to get a quality or characteristic from one's parent or ancestors : *Analise inherited her father's brown eyes and dark hair.* **Note.** Something that is inherited is an inheritance.

in·i·tial [ih-NISH-ul] NOUN, initials. **1. initiale** ▸ the first letter of a word or name. **2. initials. initiale** ▸ the first letter or letters of someone's full name, used instead of a signature : *My dad's initials are D. W. F.* ▲ ADJECTIVE. **initial (-iale, -iaux), premier (-ière)** ▸ coming or belonging at the beginning; first; earliest : *The initial sound of the word "capital" is [kap].* ▲ VERB, initialled, initialling. (also initialed, initialing) **parapher, signer** ▸ to mark or sign one's initials : *The teacher initialled the report to show that she had read it.* ■ **initially,** ADVERB. ▸ **au commencement, au début, initialement.**

in·i·ti·ate [ih-NISH-ee-ATE] VERB, initiated, initiating. **1. entreprendre, lancer, initier ▸** to be the first one to do something; set up; start : *The music teacher initiated a new concert program at the school.* **2. initier ▸** to admit someone to a group or club by some special ceremony : *The French club initiated new members by asking them to recite a poem in French.* ▪ **initiation,** NOUN. ▸ **initiation.**

in·i·ti·a·tive [ih-NISH-ee-uh-tiv *or* ih-NISH-uh-tiv] NOUN. **1. initiative, décision ▸** the ability to begin or carry out a plan or action : *Max had so much initiative that he began his own business while still in high school.* **2.** (*plural,* initiatives) the first step in doing something; the lead : *On her own initiative, Ali had invited Julio to join them.*

in·ject [in-JEKT] VERB, injected, injecting. **1. injecter ▸** to force a liquid through the skin with a needle : *The dentist injected medicine into her gums to make her mouth numb.* **2. communiquer, insuffler, inspirer ▸** to throw in or put in : *Carrie injected some humour into her speech.*

in·jure [IN-jur] VERB, injured, injuring. **blesser, faire du mal ▸** to cause pain or harm to; damage; hurt : *Klara injured her arm when she fell off her horse.* SYN : hurt, harm, damage, wound, spoil.

in·ju·ry [IN-jur-ee] NOUN, injuries. **blessure, lésion ▸** harm; damage; a wound or hurt : *The doctor checked Cliff's injury to make sure it wasn't serious.*

in·jus·tice [in-JUS-tice] NOUN, injustices. **injustice ▸** a lack of justice; something that is not fair or right : *We all did Nori an injustice when we didn't believe that she would finish the race.*

ink [ink] NOUN, inks. **1. encre ▸** a coloured liquid that is used for writing, drawing, or printing. **2. encre ▸** a dark liquid that squid and octopuses release for protection. ▲ VERB, inked, inking. **encrer ▸** to put ink on : *The police officer inked the suspect's fingers in order to take his fingerprints.* ▪ **inky,** ADJECTIVE. ▸ **encré (-ée).** 🖉 p. 363.

ink·ling [INK-ling] NOUN, inklings. ▸ a slight suggestion or hint : *I didn't have an inkling that they were planning a surprise party for me!* SYN : hint, suspicion, idea, impression.

in·land [IN-land] ADJECTIVE. **intérieur (-eure) ▸** away from the coast : *Manitoba is an inland province.* ▲ ADVERB. **à l'intérieur ▸** in or toward the inner part : *The hurricane along the coast is expected to move inland.*

in·law [IN-LAH] NOUN, in-laws. **belle-famille ▸** a relative by marriage instead of by birth. In-laws include mother-in-law, brother-in-law, and daughter-in-law.

in·let [IN-LET *or* IN-lit] NOUN, inlets. **crique, anse ▸** a narrow strip of water leading from a larger body of water into the land.

in·line skates [IN-LINE] NOUN. **patins à roues alignées ▸** roller skates with the wheels in one row, one behind the other.

inn [in] NOUN, inns. **1. auberge, hôtel ▸** in former times, a small hotel by the roadside providing rooms and meals for travellers. **2. hôtel, cabaret ▸** a hotel or tavern.

in·ner [IN-ur] ADJECTIVE. **1. intérieur (-eure), en dedans, interne ▸** located farther in; inside : *The doctor sees her patients in an inner room.* **2. intime, secret (-ète), profond (-onde) ▸** private; secret : *People often keep a diary to record their inner feelings.*

in·ning [IN-ing] NOUN, innings. **manche ▸** in baseball, one of the playing periods in which each team has a chance to bat until it has made three outs.

in·no·cent [IN-uh-sunt] ADJECTIVE. **1. innocent (-ente), non coupable ▸** free from doing wrong or guilt : *He claimed that he was innocent, insisting that he was out of the country when the crime was committed.* **2. innocent (-ente), sans malice, candide ▸** causing or meaning no harm : *Don't be upset by what she said — it was an innocent remark.* **3. innocent (-ente), naïf (naïve), candide ▸** not aware of evil or sin; simple and trusting. **Note.** The state or quality of being innocent is innocence. ▪ **innocently,** ADVERB. ▸ **innocemment.**

in·no·va·tion [IN-uh-VAY-shun] NOUN, innovations. **innovation, changement ▸** a new idea or way of doing something : *The telephone was a major innovation in the way people communicated.* ▪ **innovative,** ADJECTIVE. ▸ **innovant (-ante).**

In·nu [IN-oo] NOUN. **1. Innu (-ue), Montagnais (-aise) ▸** a member of the Algonquian people living in northern and eastern Québec and in Labrador, who used to be known as Montagnais-Kapaski. **2. innu (-ue), montagnais (-aise) ▸** the Algonquian language of Innu people.

in·put [IN-POOT] NOUN. **1. donnée ▸** data or information entered into a computer. **2. commentaire, avis ▸** any comments or advice added : *We asked several people for input on our plan.* ▲ VERB, inputted *or* input, inputting. **entrer les données ▸** to enter information into a computer.

in·quire [in-KWIRE] VERB, inquired, inquiring. **demander, s'informer de, s'enquérir ▸** to get information by asking questions : *He inquired at the post office to see if they'd found the missing package.* **Note.** An inquiry is the act or fact of asking questions. SYN : ask, question, interrogate, pry, interview.

in·quis·i·tive [in-KWIZ-uh-tiv] ADJECTIVE. **curieux (-ieuse), indiscret (-ète) ▸** curious; asking many questions : *Darren was very inquisitive about my plans to start a new club.* SYN : curious, questioning, nosy, snooping.

in-sane [in-SANE] ADJECTIVE. **1. fou (folle), déséquilibré (-ée), insensé (-ée), dément (-ente)** ▸ having a serious mental illness. **2. insensé (-ée), absurde, ridicule** ▸ without sense; very foolish; wild : *He has some insane scheme to attach a sail to the back of the car as a way of saving gasoline.* ■ **insanely,** ADVERB. ▸ **comme un fou.**

in-sect [IN-sekt] NOUN, insects. **insecte** ▸ a small animal with six legs, no backbone, and a body divided into three main parts. Most insects have wings. Beetles, ants, moths, flies, mosquitoes, cockroaches, bees, and grasshoppers are among the hundreds of thousands of kinds of insects. 🖪 p. 1091. 👁 p. 104.

in-sert [in-SERT] VERB, inserted, inserting. **insérer, ajouter, annexer, incorporer** ▸ to put, set, or place in : *Rashid inserted the key into the lock and opened the door.* ▲ [IN-sert] NOUN, inserts. **encart, insertion, pièce insérée** ▸ something put on or set in : *The weekend paper has many advertising inserts.*

in-side [IN-side *or* in-SIDE] NOUN, insides. **dedans, intérieur** ▸ the part that is in; the inner part : *The inside of the box is blue.* ▲ ADJECTIVE. **1. intérieur (-ieure), interne** ▸ being in, on, or toward the inside : *an inside pocket of a jacket.* **2. interne, intérieur (-ieure)** ▸ from the inside of some group : *We think the robbery was an inside job, because whoever did it knew where the jewellery was kept.* ▲ ADVERB: on, at, or to the inside of a place or thing; within : *We walked inside the house.* ▲ PREPOSITION. **dedans, au-dedans, à l'intérieur** ▸ within : *The keys are on the table just inside the door.* 🖉 p. 313.

in-sig-ni-fi-cant [IN-sig-NIF-uh-kunt] ADJECTIVE. **insignifiant (-ante), négligeable, sans importance** ▸ small in size, number, or value; not important; meaningless : *The difference between the two is insignificant.*

in-sist [in-SIST] VERB, insisted, insisting. **insister, réclamer** ▸ to stand up strongly for one's idea or position; say in a firm way : *"I insist on going. I would rather risk my life than see you in disgrace."* (Robin Muller) SYN: demand, assert, request, urge, press, stress.

in-spect [in-SPEKT] VERB, inspected, inspecting. **inspecter, scruter** ▸ to look at closely and carefully; examine : *The doctor inspected Carly's sprained ankle.* **Note.** The act of inspecting is inspection. **Note.** Someone who inspects is an inspector.

in-spi-ra-tion [IN-spuh-RAY-shun] NOUN, inspirations. **1. inspiration** ▸ a force that stirs the mind or feelings : *Martin Luther King's speeches gave inspiration to civil-rights workers in the 1960s.* **2. inspiration** ▸ a person or thing that inspires : *Mount Fuji has been an inspiration for many Japanese artists.*

in-spire [in-SPIRE] VERB, inspired, inspiring. **1. inspirer, stimuler** ▸ to cause strong feelings or a wish to do something important : *The beautiful sunset inspired me to write a poem.* **2. inspirer, stimuler, enthousiasmer** ▸ to cause an action, feeling, or thought : *Inez's hard work and efforts inspired her whole team to do better.* 🖉 p. 201.

in-stall [in-STOL] VERB, installed, installing. (sometimes instal) **1. poser, installer** ▸ to put a mechanical device in place and set it up for use : *to install an air-conditioner.* **2. installer** ▸ to place a person in a position or an office by means of some ceremony : *to install a judge on the Supreme Court.* ■ **installation,** NOUN: ▸ **installation.** *If you buy that stove, there's a charge for installation.*

in-stance [IN-stunce] NOUN, instances. **exemple, cas** ▸ a situation in which a general point is true; an example : *Coyotes don't usually live near people, but in some instances they are found in major cities.*

for instance **par exemple** ▸ as an example; such as : *Picasso was an artist in many fields — for instance, painting, sculpture, and pottery.*

in-stant [IN-stunt] NOUN, instants. **1. instant, moment** ▸ a very short period of time; a moment : *She stopped talking for an instant when a dog ran in front of her.* **2. instant, moment** ▸ a certain moment or point in time : *"The name-calling began the instant I left the shelter of the playground."* (Jean Little) ▲ ADJECTIVE. **1. immédiat (-ate), instantané (-ée)** ▸ without delay; immediate : *The clown was an instant hit with the children.* **2. instantané (-ée), préparation rapide** ▸ of foods, needing very little time or effort to prepare : *instant cake mix.* ■ **Instantly,** ADVERB. ▸ **instantanément, aussitôt.**

🖉 **Word Builder**

Inside of means within or in a period of time less than : *Donovan Bailey runs the 100 metres inside of 10 seconds.* The expression *on the inside* means that a person enjoys a position of influence or confidence : *She is **on the inside** with the organizers of the field hockey tournament.* **Inside out** means that the inside of something is now on the outside : *He pulled his pockets inside out.* **From the inside out** means to know something completely : *Patrice knows engines from the inside out.*

in·stead [in-STED] ADVERB. **au lieu de, plutôt ▸** in place of someone or something : *He usually walks to work, but today he took the bus instead.* SYN : in place of, rather than, in lieu of.

instead of au lieu de, plutôt que ▸ rather than ; in place of : *Do you want juice instead of milk?*

in·stinct [IN-stinkt] NOUN, instincts. **1. instinct ▸** an inner force that causes an animal to act in a certain way. Instinct is something an animal is born with, rather than something it learns or decides to do : *Spiders spin webs and birds build nests by instinct.* **2.** (also instincts) **instinct ▸** a natural feeling or ability : *Everyone urged her to try the easier shot, but her instincts told her to try the harder one.* ▪ **instinctive** or instinctual, ADJECTIVE. **▸ instinctif (-ive).** 📖 p. 1021.

in·sti·tute [IN-stuh-TOOT] NOUN, institutes. **institut ▸** a school, organization, or society set up for a special purpose : *Terry is going to study at the Art Institute.* ▲ VERB, instituted, instituting. **instituer, établir, fonder ▸** to set up or establish ; start : *The school instituted a series of tests to identify students who are gifted.*

in·sti·tu·tion [IN-stuh-TOO-shun] NOUN, institutions. **1. institution ▸** an organization set up for some public purpose, such as a hospital, school, or library. **2. institution ▸** an established custom or practice : *Marriage is an institution in many societies.*

in·struct [in-STRUKT] VERB, instructed, instructing. **1. enseigner, instruire, éduquer, former ▸** to give skill or knowledge to ; teach : *The teacher instructed us in the correct way to use the computer.* **2. avertir, aviser, informer, renseigner ▸** to give an order or direction : *The police instructed motorists to drive with care because of the icy roads.* SYN : teach, guide, show, tell, advise, train, direct.

in·struc·tion [in-STRUK-shun] NOUN, instructions. **1. instruction, enseignement, éducation ▸** the act or fact of teaching. **2. instructions.** **a. instructions, directives, explications ▸** the steps or processes involved in doing something ; directions : *Don't start the test until you've read all the instructions.* **b. instructions, consignes, directives ▸** orders : *Our instructions are to meet at the park at noon.* **Note.** Something that gives instruction is instructive. ✎ p. 314.

in·struc·tor [in-STRUK-tur] NOUN, instructors. **professeur (-eure), maître, moniteur (-trice) ▸** a person who instructs ; a teacher : *Olisa worked as a swimming instructor last summer.*

in·stru·ment [IN-struh-munt] NOUN, instruments. **1. instrument ▸** an object that makes musical sounds, such as a piano, violin, trumpet, or drum. **2. instrument, outil, appareil ▸** a device used to do a certain kind of work ; a tool : *A scalpel is an instrument used by a doctor for an operation.* **3. instrument ▸** a device that records or mea-

✐ Writing Tips

Instructions

Instructions tell people what to do or how to do it.

• When you write instructions for others to follow, remember :

– include every step in the procedure,

– explain any words or processes your audience might not recognize,

– put your steps in the correct order, and

– include diagrams or photographs if necessary.

• Ask someone to review your instructions. Can he or she follow all the steps ? Are any steps missing ? Are the steps in the correct order ? Is there anything that needs to be explained ?

sures information : *The astronauts checked their instruments when they prepared to take off.* 📖 **p. 1130.** 👁 **p. 538.**

in·su·late [IN-suh-LATE] VERB, insulated, insulating. **1. isoler ▸** to cover, fill, or surround something with a special material in order to slow or stop the flow of heat, sound, or electricity : *We insulated the attic to keep heat from escaping in winter.* ▪ **insulation,** NOUN. **1. isolant ▸** any material that insulates something. **2. isolation ▸** the act or fact of insulating.

in·sult [in-SULT] VERB, insulted, insulting. **insulter, injurier, outrager ▸** to say something bad about a person, or treat the person in a rude way ; show a lack of respect ; offend : *Dave insulted Lara by ignoring her at the party.* ▲ [IN-sult] NOUN, insults. **insulte, injure, affront, outrage ▸** something said or done to hurt a person's feelings.

in·sur·ance [in-SHOOR-uns] NOUN. **1. assurance ▸** a way of protecting against loss by such things as fire, accident, or death. **2. assurance, police, couverture, garantie ▸** a contract in which a company promises to pay a certain sum of money in the event of loss of an insured item or person. To get insurance, a person agrees to pay a regular amount of money in return. **3. prime ▸** the money a person pays to get insurance. **4. assurance, protection ▸** anything that is thought of as a protection against loss or damage : *We were winning 1–0 late in the game, but we wanted to get another goal as insurance.*

in·sure [in-SHOOR] VERB, insured, insuring. **1. assurer ▸** to get or have insurance for something : *People often insure their lives, homes, cars, or valuable property such as jewellery and diamonds.* **2. assurer, garantir, certifier**

314

▶ to make certain; ensure : *Jillian checked the door to insure that it was locked.* SYN : protect, defend, shelter, cover, safeguard.

in·tact [in-TAKT] ADJECTIVE. **intact (-acte), entier (-ière), indemne** ▶ having all parts; whole : *The glass vase survived the fall intact, much to everyone's surprise.* SYN : whole, complete, unharmed, untouched.

in·take [IN-take] NOUN, intakes. **1. ouverture, prise** ▶ an opening where a fluid enters into a container or pipe. **2. consommation** ▶ the act of taking in : *Eating requires the intake of food.* **3. consommation** ▶ the amount or thing that is taken in : *We need an accurate measurement of the daily intake of water through that pipe.*

in·te·grate [IN-tuh-GRATE] VERB, integrated, integrating. **intégrer, incorporer, inclure** ▶ to bring parts together into a whole : *The committee integrated the ideas of the members to develop a plan for the school fair.*

in·teg·ri·ty [in-TEG-ruh-tee] NOUN. **1. honnêteté, intégrité** ▶ honesty; honour : *She is a person of integrity, and you can be sure she'll do as she promises.* **2. intégrité, entier** ▶ wholeness; the condition of being undivided : *The treaty guaranteed the country's integrity.* SYN : honesty, sincerity, honour, respectability.

in·tel·lec·tu·al [IN-tuh-LEK-choo-ul] ADJECTIVE. **intellectuel (-elle),** ▶ having to do with the mind or intellect : *She's well over 80, but her intellectual powers are as strong as ever.* ▲ NOUN, intellectuals. **intellectuel (-elle)** ▶ an intelligent and well-educated person who has an interest in the arts and other activities of the mind. ■ **intellectually,** ADVERB. ▶ **intellectuellement.**

in·tel·li·gence [in-TEL-uh-junce] NOUN. **1. intelligence, raison** ▶ the ability to learn new things, understand ideas, remember facts, and solve problems; mental ability. **2. information, renseignement** ▶ information about the activities and plans of another country or business : *Most nations have an agency that obtains intelligence about other nations.* **Note.** To be intelligent is to have or show intelligence : *Masika is an intelligent student who does well in school.* ■ **intelligently,** ADVERB ▶ **intelligemment.**

in·tend [in-TEND] VERB, intended, intending. **1. avoir l'intention, vouloir, se proposer, projeter** ▶ to have in mind as a plan or purpose; mean to : *"I intend to put your words to the test. We shall see if you are telling the truth."* (Bob Barton) **2. destiner, réserver, attribuer** ▶ to mean for a certain person or use : *The gift was intended for both boys, not just for Hugh.*

in·tense [in-TENCE] ADJECTIVE. **1. intense, excessif (-ive), extrême, violent (-ente)** ▶ very great or strong; extreme : *"Flip's devotion to his human companions was intense."* (Todd Lee) **2. intense, démesuré (-ée), excessif (-ive)** ▶ full of strong feelings; very emotional : *intense joy.*

■ **intensely,** ADVERB : ▶ **intensément.** *He wasn't sure why, but he disliked her intensely.* ■ **intensity,** NOUN. ▶ **intensité, violence.** SYN : strong, forceful, severe, considerable.

in·tent[1] [in-TENT] ADJECTIVE. **1. absorbé (-ée), attentif (-ive), résolu (-ue)** ▶ determined; directed toward a certain plan or purpose : *Neper ignored the noise around him, intent on finishing his work.* **2. absorbé (-ée), attentif (-ive)** ▶ having or showing deep feeling; intense : *The students watched the teacher with intent expressions.* ■ **intently,** ADVERB. ▶ **avec une vive attention.**

in·tent[2] NOUN, intents. **intention, but, dessein** ▶ meaning; significance : *What was the intent of that comment?*

in·ten·tion [in-TEN-shun] NOUN, intentions. **intention, idée, dessein** ▶ something that a person plans or intends to do; a purpose or aim : *"I went to Memorial University in St. John's and studied pre-med for three years with the intention of becoming a doctor."* (Kevin Major) ■ **intentional,** ADJECTIVE. ▶ **intentionnel (-elle), voulu (-ue), volontaire, délibéré (-ée).** SYN : intent, object, plan, purpose, motive, idea.

in·ter- [IN-tur] PREFIX. **1.** together; with one another. **2.** between : *interschool game; interface.*

in·ter·est [IN-tur-ist] NOUN, interests. **1. intérêt** ▶ a feeling of wanting to put one's attention on something and know more about it : *The book captured my interest from the first page.* **2. intérêt** ▶ something that causes this feeling : *Collecting stamps is one of my interests.* **Note.** Something or someone that causes or creates interest is interesting. **3.** (also interests) **intérêt, profit, avantage** ▶ something that helps a person; an advantage or benefit. **4. intérêts** ▶ money paid for the use of someone else's money. A bank pays interest to a person who leaves money in the bank for saving, and charges interest to a person who borrows money. ▲ VERB, interested, interesting. **intéresser** ▶ to catch or hold the attention; cause to have an interest : *Trevor tried to interest us in a game of hockey.*

in·ter·est·ing [IN-tuh-RES-ting *or* IN-trus-ting] ADJECTIVE. **intéressant (-ante), passionnant (-ante), captivant (-ante)** ▶ causing or creating interest : *That was an interesting article about the finding of the* Titanic. ■ **interestingly,** ADVERB. ▶ **de façon intéressante.** SYN : fascinating, intriguing, provoking, entertaining, gripping, captivating, appealing.

in·ter·fere [in-tur-FEER] VERB, interfered, interfering. **1. contrecarrer, contrarier, entraver** ▶ to get in the way; interrupt or block : *The rain interfered with our day at the beach.* **2. s'immiscer, s'ingérer** ▶ to get involved with the affairs of others without being asked; meddle :

315

When Cal and his friends argue, you shouldn't interfere.

in·te·ri·or [in-TEER-ee-ur] NOUN, interiors. **1. intérieur** ▸ the inside or inner part : *"The large rooms of the interior included a great hall and private rooms for the lord and his family."* (Gillian Clements) **2. intérieur** ▸ a region away from the coast or border; an inland area : *Brazil has several large cities near the ocean, but not many people live in the interior.* ▲ ADJECTIVE. **intérieur (-eure)** ▸ of or having to do with the inner part : *an interior wall.* **Note.** An interior decorator designs and decorates the interior of a room or building. SYN: inside, inner, middle, heart, core.

in·ter·ject·ion [in-tur-JEK-shun] NOUN, interjections. **interjection** ▸ a word or phrase that shows a sudden or strong feeling. *"Ouch!" "Help!"* and *"Hey!"* are interjections.

in·ter·me·di·ate [in-tur-MEE-dee-it] ADJECTIVE. **intermédiaire** ▸ in the middle; in between : *The intermediate ice-skating class is for people who already know how to skate, but aren't ready to start advanced figure skating yet.*

in·ter·nal [in-TER-nul] ADJECTIVE. **1. interne** ▸ in or having to do with the inside of the body : *Max suffered internal injuries from the car accident.* **2. intérieur (-eure)** ▸ having to do with matters within a country, company, or organization : *The prime minister is more experienced in internal affairs than in foreign affairs.* ▪ **internally**, ADVERB. ▸ **intérieurement**.

in·ter·na·tion·al [in-tur-NASH-un-ul] ADJECTIVE. **international (-ale, -aux)** ▸ having to do with two or more nations; between nations : *international trade; international waters.* ▪ **internationally**, ADVERB. ▸ **internationalement**.

In·ter·net [IN-tur-net] NOUN. **Internet** ▸ a system of connected computer networks, used for e-mail, access to information stored in computers, on-line discussions, and other features. **Note.** *Internet* is short for inter-network. Also called the Net ☞ **p. 541.**

in·ter·pret [in-TUR-prit] VERB, interpreted, interpreting. **1. traduire, interpréter** ▸ to take something that has just been said in one language and repeat it in another. **Note.** A person who does this is an interpreter. **2. comprendre, expliquer, interpréter** ▸ to understand or explain the meaning of something : *He interpreted her silence to mean that she was angry with him.* **3. interpréter, exécuter** ▸ to perform or depict in a certain way; bring out the meaning : *to interpret a piece of music.* ▪ **interpretation**, NOUN. ▸ **interprétation**. *The actor Kenneth Branagh is known for his interpretation of Shakespeare's* Hamlet. SYN: explain, clarify, define, translate, analyze.

in·ter·rupt [in-tuh-RUPT] VERB, interrupted, interrupting. **1. interrompre, couper, déranger** ▸ to break in upon : *Mother was annoyed when Juanita interrupted her while she was talking on the telephone.* **2. interrompre, couper** ▸ to stop something : *A fire alarm interrupted the awards ceremony.* **Note.** The act or fact of interrupting is an interruption. SYN: break in, stop, hinder, intrude, interfere.

in·ter·val [IN-tur-vul] NOUN, intervals. **intervalle, période** ▸ a period of time or space between; break or pause : *We've had a lot of rain, with only a few intervals of sunny weather, this spring.*

in·ter·view [IN-tur-vyoo] NOUN, interviews. **1. entrevue, interview, entretien** ▸ a meeting or conversation in which one person asks another person questions in order to get information : *Brooke has an interview with a police officer for the school paper.* **2. interview** ▸ a printed or broadcast report of such a meeting. **3. entrevue, interview** ▸ a meeting at which a person is asked questions to determine whether he or she is qualified for a job or position : *The store is holding interviews for new salesclerks.* ▲ VERB, interviewed, interviewing. **interviewer** ▸ to have an interview with : *The reporter interviewed the author about her new book.* ▪ **interviewer**, NOUN. ▸ **interviewer**. SYN: question, examine, quiz.

in·tes·tine [in-TES-tun] NOUN, intestines. **intestin** ▸ a long, twisting tube in the body that runs downward from the stomach. It is important in digesting food. The intestine is made up of the small intestine and the large intestine. ☞ **p. 403.**

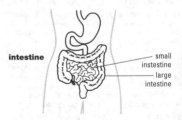

intestine — small instestine / large instestine

in·ti·mate [IN-tuh-mit] ADJECTIVE. **intime, proche** ▸ known very well; close and well-acquainted : *intimate friends.* ▪ **intimacy**, NOUN. ▸ **intimité**.

in·to [IN-too] PREPOSITION. **1. dans, dedans** ▸ to the inside of : *Put the carrots into the stew.* **2. dans** ▸ so as to hit against : *He backed the car right into a tree.* **3. en** ▸ to the form or condition of : *At 0°C, water turns into ice.* **4.** *Informal.* **par, avec** ▸ very interested in or involved with : *Zoë is really into country music now.*

in·tol·er·ant [in-TOL-ur-unt] ADJECTIVE. **intolérant (-ante), intransigeant (-ante)** ▸ unwilling to let others think or do as they choose; unwilling to accept differences in opinions or beliefs.

in·trigue [in-TREEG] VERB, intrigued, intriguing. **intriguer** ▸ to make curious or interested : *The parcel that came in the mail intrigued us all until Mom came home to open it.* ■ **intriguing**, ADJECTIVE. ▸ **intrigant (-ante)**.

in·tro·duce [in-truh-DOOS] VERB, introduced, introducing. 1. **présenter** ▸ to present someone for the first time; to make known or acquainted with : *I introduced my teacher to my parents.* 2. **introduire, présenter** ▸ to bring into use or notice, especially for the first time : *In 1964, Ford introduced the popular Mustang automobile.* 3. **présenter, aborder** ▸ to begin; start : *A short quotation introduces each chapter.*

in·tro·duc·tion [in-truh-DUK-shun] NOUN, introductions. 1. **introduction** ▸ the act of introducing : *Spanish explorers were responsible for the introduction of horses into the Americas.* 2. **présentation** ▸ the act of introducing people to each other. 3. **introduction** ▸ something that serves to introduce : *This course is an introduction to computer programming.* 4. **introduction, préface, avant-propos** ▸ a part at the beginning of a book, a play, or the like that tells something about it.

in·trude [in-TROOD] VERB, intruded, intruding. **(s') imposer** ▸ to come in without being invited or wanted. **Note.** Someone who intrudes in an intruder. SYN: interfere, trespass, meddle, cut in, invade.

In·u·it [IN-yoo-it *or* IN-oo-it] NOUN. 1. **Inuit (-te)** ▸ the aboriginal peoples from Arctic areas of North America and Greenland. 2. **Inuktitut (-c)** ▸ any of the languages of the Inuit peoples. ▲ ADJECTIVE. **inuit (-te)** ▸ having to do with the Inuit people. **Note.** Inuk is the word for one Inuit.

in·vade [in-VADE] VERB, invaded, invading. 1. **envahir, prendre** ▸ to enter with force; attack : *"Because the Persians were threatening to invade Egypt, Amasis welcomed many Greeks into his country."* (Roger Lancelyn Green) 2. **envahir, couvrir, remplir, infester** ▸ to enter in great numbers : *Thousands upon thousands of grasshoppers invaded the fields and ate the crops.* 3. **violer, enfreindre, transgresser** ▸ to enter where one is not wanted : *My little sister always invades my privacy.* **Note.** The act or fact of invading is invasion. SYN: intrude, trespass, raid, attack.

in·vent [in-VENT] VERB, invented, inventing. 1. **inventer, créer, découvrir** ▸ to make or think of for the first time; create something new : *We invented a new way to compost leaves for our science project.* **Note.** A person who invents something is an inventor. 2. **inventer, forger** ▸ to make up; think up : *Every time Rashid is*

late, he invents some wild excuse. SYN: discover, create, conceive, devise, contrive.

in·ven·tion [in-VEN-shun] NOUN, inventions. 1. **invention** ▸ the act or fact of inventing : *Alexander Graham Bell is known for the invention of the telephone.* 2. **invention, découverte** ▸ something invented : *The computer has become one of the most important inventions of modern times.* 3. **invention, imagination, inspiration** ▸ the power to invent things. **Note.** A person with this ability is inventive: *Charles Dickens was an inventive author who created many well-known characters.* 👁 p. 540.

in·ven·to·ry [IN-vun-TOR-ee] NOUN, inventories. 1. **inventaire** ▸ a detailed list of items on hand and their value : *The publishing company's inventory shows how many books are in the warehouse and what they are worth.* 2. **inventaire** ▸ all of the articles listed; stock : *The store holds a sale every August to reduce its inventory of bathing suits.*

in·vest [in-VEST] VERB, invested, investing. 1. **investir, placer** ▸ to put money in something in order to make more money : *People invest in real estate because they expect the price of land to go up.* 2. **investir** ▸ to spend time or energy in order to get some benefit : *She's invested years in ballet lessons, hoping to dance on the stage someday.*

in·ves·ti·gate [in-VES-tuh-GATE] VERB, investigated, investigating. **enquêter, étudier, examiner, scruter** ▸ to look into carefully in search of information; try to learn the facts about : *The students investigated the volume of six different containers.* **Note.** The act of investigating is investigation. ■ **investigator,** NOUN. ▸ **enquêteur (-euse), investigateur (-trice).** SYN: inquire, search, examine, inspect, explore.

in·vest·ment [in-VEST-munt] NOUN, investments. 1. **investissement, placement** ▸ the fact of investing; using money to earn a future profit : *Bank savings accounts are a common form of investment.* 2. **investissement, placement** ▸ something in which money is invested.

in·vin·ci·ble [in-VIN-suh-bul] ADJECTIVE. **invincible** ▸ impossible to overcome; unbeatable : *Everyone said that that team was invincible, but we beat them.*

in·vis·i·ble [in-VIZ-uh-bul] ADJECTIVE. **invisible** ▸ not able to be seen; not visible; hidden : *"Because she couldn't be seen, she was safe from snakes, which is why Grandma Poss had made her invisible in the first place."* (Mem Fox)

in·vite [in-VITE] VERB, invited, inviting. 1. **inviter, convier** ▸ to ask someone to come somewhere or do something : *Rigel invited the whole class to his birthday party.* **Note.** An invitation is the act or fact of inviting. 2. **inviter** ▸ to be the cause of; bring on : *Her unpleasant attitude invites dislike from others.* ■ **inviting,** ADJECTIVE. ■ **invitant (-ante), tentant (-ante), attirant (-ante).** *After the long race, a cool drink sounded very inviting.*

in-volve [in-VOLV] VERB, involved, involving. **1. impliquer, comporter, entraîner** ▸ to have as a necessary part; include : *Doing well in school involves hard work and effort.* **2. impliquer, mêler, entraîner** ▸ to bring into a difficult or damaging situation : *His friends involved him in a dangerous prank.* ■ **involved** or involving, ADJECTIVE. **compliqué (-ée), complexe** ▸ taking up all one's attention, or having all one's attention taken up ; being absorbed or absorbing : *Her job is extremely involving.* **Note.** The fact of being involved is involvement. ✐ **p. 139.**

in-ward [IN-wurd] ADVERB. (also inwards) toward the inside or centre : *The door to the kitchen opens inward.* ▲ ADJECTIVE. **vers l'intérieur, en dedans de** ▸ toward or on the inside. ■ **inwardly,** ADVERB. ▸ **intérieurement, à l'intérieur, au-dedans.**

i-o-dine [I-uh-DINE] NOUN. **1. iode** ▸ a chemical element that is used in medicine and in photography. **2. teinture d'iode** ▸ a liquid medicine that contains iodine, used to treat cuts and prevent infections.

IQ [I KYOO] ABBREVIATION. **quotient intellectuel (QI)** ▸ short for Intelligence Quotient, a way of determining intelligence by comparing scores from a standard test. An IQ of 100 represents the average score.

i-ris [I-ris] NOUN, irises or irides. **1. iris** ▸ the coloured part of the eye around the pupil. It controls the amount of light that enters the eye. **2. iris** ▸ a plant that has long leaves and large flowers of different colours. ◉ **p. 250.**

i-ron [I-run] NOUN, irons. **1. fer** ▸ a hard, greyish metal that is a chemical element. Iron is needed in the body by all plants, animals, and people to live and grow. **Note.** Iron ore is used to make steel for tools and machines. **2. fer** ▸ a household appliance used to press wrinkles out of clothes. **3. fer** ▸ something that is made from iron, such as a golf club. ▲ ADJECTIVE. **1. en fer** ▸ made of iron. **2. en fer, de fer** ▸ strong and hard, as if made of iron : *He has an iron will and never gives up once he starts.* ▲ VERB, ironed, ironing. **repasser, donner un coup de fer** ▸ to press or smooth with a heated iron : *to iron a shirt.*

i-ron-y [I-run-ee] NOUN, ironies. **1. ironie, moquerie, raillerie, sarcasme** ▸ the art of using words to express the opposite of what is really intended. **2. ironie** ▸ something that is the opposite of what is naturally expected or what would usually happen. **Note.** Something that shows or

is full of irony is ironic or ironical. ■ **ironically,** ADVERB. ▸ **ironiquement.** ✐ **p. 319.**

Ir-o-quois [IR-uh-KWAH] NOUN. **1. Iroquois** ▸ The Aboriginal peoples originally living in Ontario, Quebec, and New York State that speak an Iroguoian language. The Mohawk, Oneida, Onondaga, Cayuga, Seneca, and Tuscaroran peoples make up the Six Nations Iroquois Confederacy. Other Iroguoian groups include the Huron and Cherokee people. **2. iroquois (-oise), iroquoien (-ienne)** ▸ the language of these peoples. ■ **Iroquoian,** ADJECTIVE. ▸ **iroquois.**

ir-reg-u-lar [ih-REG-yuh-lur] ADJECTIVE. **1. irrégulier (-ière)** ▸ not usual or normal : *an irregular heartbeat.* **2. irrégulier (-ière), asymétrique** ▸ not even or smooth ; rough : *I cut myself on the irregular edge of that glass.* **3. irrégulier** ▸ in grammar, not following the normal pattern : *The verb "make" is irregular, because the past form is "made" rather than "maked."* ■ **irregularly,** ADVERB. ▸ **irrégulièrement, de façon irrégulière.**

iris

ir-ri-gate [IR-uh-GATE] VERB, irrigated, irrigating. **irriguer** ▸ to supply land or crops with water from another place, through a system of canals or pipes. **Note.** The process of irrigating or a system for doing this is irrigation.

ir-ri-tate [IR-uh-TATE] VERB, irritated, irritating. **1. agacer, énerver, irriter, contrarier** ▸ to make angry or impatient ; annoy ; bother : *Traffic jams irritate Dad when he's in a hurry.* **2. irriter** ▸ to make sore or sensitive : *Cutting raw onions often irritates a person's eyes.* SYN: stir up, bother, madden, annoy, anger.

ir-ri-ta-tion [IR-uh-TAY-shun] NOUN, irritations. **irritation** ▸ the fact of being irritated, or something that does this : *That's a very strong soap that can cause a skin irritation.*

✍ **Writing Tips**

Irony

Irony is a literary technique that occurs when a writer or speaker makes a statement that is the opposite of (or different from) what he or she really means. The writer or speaker gives clues to the intended meaning by the context of the statement or tone of voice so that the audience will understand what is really meant—for example, "Nice weather, isn't it?" the cabbie asked as the hurricane tore the door from her cab. Irony is used to draw attention to an issue indirectly or to treat it with humour.

Over time, irony has also come to mean something that is the opposite to what is normally expected: Many people consider the sinking of the Titanic ironic, because the builders claimed that the ship was unsinkable.

When you write stories, try not to use ironic statements or situations too often. If you use irony only once in a while, it will have a greater effect.

---

is [iz] VERB. **être** ▶ a form of the verb to be used with "he," "she," or "it" to tell about the present : *Toronto is the largest city in Canada. Rina is tall.*

Is·lam [iss-LOM *or* IZ-lam] NOUN. **Islam** ▶ a name of the religion that was founded by the prophet Muhammad ; the Muslim religion. ■ **Islamic**, ADJECTIVE. ■ **islamique**.

is·land [I-lund] NOUN. **islands**. **1. île** ▶ a piece of land that is completely surrounded by water. **Note.** All land on earth is actually surrounded by water, but *island* usually refers to a land area smaller than a **continent. 2. îlot, refuge** ▶ something thought of as like an island : *A traffic island is a place in the middle of a street where people can stand while crossing the street.* 📖 **p. 1041.**

isle [ïle] NOUN. **isles. île** ▶ another word for an island, especially a small island. **Note.** Usually used in poetry and other literary writing.

i·so·late [I-suh-LATE] VERB. **isolated, isolating. isoler** ▶ to set or keep apart from others ; separate : *Doctors isolated me when I got chicken pox, so that others would not catch the disease from me.* **Note.** Often used as an ADJECTIVE : *The weather report says to expect isolated showers today.* **Note.** The state of being isolated or the act of isolating is isolation.

is·sue [ISH-yoo] NOUN. **issues. 1. question, sujet, point, problème** ▶ a subject that is being talked about or considered ; a matter to be dealt with : *The environment is an issue in this election.* **2. numéro** ▶ a copy of a newspaper or magazine. **3. émission** ▶ something that is sent or given out : *There was a special issue of postage stamps in honour of the Olympic Games.* ▲ VERB. **issued, issuing. donner, distribuer, émettre** ▶ to send or give out : *Mom issued orders for us to clean up the kitchen.* SYN : topic, problem, subject, theme, cause, point.

it [it] PRONOUN. **1. le, la, il, elle** ▶ the thing or animal that has been mentioned ; that one : *You can have this book —I've finished reading it.* **2. ce, ça, ceci, cela** ▶ a condition that is mentioned : *It looks like rain.* **3. il, ce, ça, ceci, cela** ▶ a subject that is not mentioned : *How did you like it in Vancouver?*

itch [ich] NOUN. **itches. 1. démangeaison** ▶ an irritating or slightly painful feeling in the skin that makes one want to scratch. **2. démangeaison** ▶ a restless, uneasy feeling or desire : *Wendy has an itch to go to Morocco.* ▲ VERB. **itched, itching. 1. démanger** ▶ to feel or cause to feel an itch. **2. démanger** ▶ to have a strong restless desire to do something : *While everyone talked, Dougall itched to eat the cake.* ■ **itchy**, ADVERB. ▶ **qui démange**.

i·tem [I-tum] NOUN. **items. 1. objet, chose, article** ▶ a single thing ; one of something : *I made a list of the items to pack for the trip.* **2. article** ▶ a piece of news : *I read an item in the paper saying that Miya's sister got a new job.* **Note.** To make a list of items is to itemize.

i·tin·er·ary [ih-TIN-ur-ER-ee *or* i-TIN-ur-air ee] NOUN, itineraries. **itinéraire** ▶ a plan or route for a trip.

its [its] PRONOUN. **son (sa, ses)** ▶ the pronoun it when used as a possessive ; belonging to it : *That silly dog is chasing its own tail.*

it·self [it-SELF] PRONOUN. **lui-même (elle-même)** ▶ its own self : *This oven turns itself on and off automatically with a timer.*

i·vo·ry [I-vuh-ree] NOUN, ivories. **1. ivoire** ▶ a hard white substance that forms a very long pointed tooth called a tusk in elephants and certain other animals. **Note.** The sale of new ivory is now banned by many countries in an effort to protect the animals that are killed for their tusks. **2. ivoire** ▶ a creamy white colour like that of ivory.

i·vy [I-vee] NOUN, ivies. **1. lierre** ▶ a vine that has shiny leaves and that grows by climbing up walls or along the ground. **2. lierre** ▶ a plant that is like ivy, such as poison ivy.

Jupiter

j, J [jay] NOUN. j's, J's. **j, J** ▸ the 10th letter of the English alphabet.

jack [jak] NOUN. jacks. **1. cric** ▸ a tool or machine used for lifting heavy objects, such as a car, a short distance off the ground. **2. valet** ▸ a playing card with a picture of a young man dressed as a court page. A jack ranks between a ten and a queen. **3. jacks. osselets** ▸ a game using small pebbles or six-pointed metal pieces that players pick up quickly while bouncing a small ball. **4. prise (à fiche)** ▸ an electrical device to receive a plug. ▲ VERB, jacked, jacking. **soulever avec un cric** ▸ to lift something with a jack : *Meli jacked up the car to change the flat tire.*

jack-al [JAK-ul] NOUN. jackals. **chacal** ▸ a wild animal that is related to the dog. Jackals live on the plains of Africa and Asia. They are pack animals that hunt at night, feeding on small animals and the remains of larger animals left by other predators.

jack-et [JAK-it] NOUN. jackets. **1. veste, veston** ▸ a short coat for the upper body, ending at the waist or hips. **2. couverture, pelure** ▸ an outer covering that is thought of as like a jacket, such as the skin of a potato or the paper wrapping that protects the cover of a book.

jack-knife [JAK-nife] NOUN. jack-knives. (also jackknife) **1. couteau (-eaux) de poche, canif** ▸ a large, strong pocketknife with blades that fold into the knife handle. **2. carpé (-ée), de carpe** ▸ a dive in which the diver bends forward while in the air to touch the toes and then straightens out. ▲ VERB, jack-knifed, jack-knifing. **mise en travers** ▸ to bend or fold like a jackknife : *Traffic on the highway stopped after a tractor-trailer jack-knifed and turned over.*

jack-o'-lan-tern [JAK-uh-LAN-tern] NOUN. jack-o'-lanterns. **feu follet** ▸ a pumpkin that has been hollowed out and carved with holes to look like a face, used for decoration at Halloween. A candle or light is often placed inside to show the carved face.

jade [jade] NOUN. **jade** ▸ a hard, green stone used in jewellery and carvings.

jag-ged [JAG-id] ADJECTIVE. **irrégulier (-ière), dentelé (-ée), déchiqueté (-ée)** ▸ cut or shaped in a rough, uneven way, often with sharp points : *jagged glass.* SYN : ragged, pointed, notched.

jag-uar [JAG-war or JAG-yoo-ar] NOUN. jaguars. **jaguar** ▸ a large, wild animal of the cat family having yellowish-brown fur with black spots. Jaguars are found in Mexico and in Central and South America.

jail [jale] NOUN. jails. **1. prison** ▸ a building where people who have been arrested and are waiting for trial, or who have been found guilty of a minor crime, are locked up. **2. prison** ▸ any place where prisoners are kept; a prison. ▲ VERB, jailed, jailing. **emprisonner, incarcérer, mettre en prison** ▸ to put someone into jail.

jam¹ [jam] VERB, jammed, jamming. **1. enfoncer, tasser, entasser, fourrer en forçant** ▸ to push or squeeze into a tight space : *Max jammed his hands into his pocket.* **2. serrer, comprimer, écraser, coincer** ▸ to hurt by squeezing or crushing : *Dina jammed her finger in a drawer.* **3. freiner brutalement** ▸ to push, place, or shove hard : *to jam on the brakes.* **4. coincer** ▸ to wedge or get stuck tight : *Jam the window open with a stick.* **5. brouiller** ▸ in radio, to send out signals that interfere with a broadcast. ▲ NOUN, jams. **1. masse, foule, embouteillage, encombrement** ▸ a group of people or things that are crowded tightly together : *a traffic jam.* **2. pétrin** ▸ a difficult situation : *We'll be in a jam if the car breaks down; it's 30 kilometres to the next town.* 🖉 p. 321.

jam² NOUN. jams. **confiture** ▸ a sweet, thick food made by boiling fruit with sugar : *strawberry jam.* 🖝 p. 1137.

jan-i-tor [JAN-ih-tur] NOUN. janitors. **concierge** ▸ a person whose job is to clean and make repairs to a building; caretaker. 🖝 p. 1059.

Jan-u-ar-y [JAN-yoo-air-ee or JAN-yuh-wur-ee] NOUN. Januarys. **janvier** ▸ the first month of the year, before February. January has 31 days.

jar¹ [jar] NOUN. jars. **pot, bocal, jarre** ▸ a glass or clay container with a wide mouth used to hold food. Foods such as peanut butter, jelly, and pickles come in jars.

jar² VERB, jarred, jarring. **1.** vibrer, trembler ▸ to cause to shake violently; rattle : *The passing of the subway train jarred the windows.* **2.** irriter, agacer ▸ to have an upsetting effect on ears, nerves, or feelings; disturb or shock : *The loud siren jarred him from a deep sleep.* **3.** grincer, crisser, rendre un son discordant ▸ to make a harsh, grating sound. ▲ NOUN, jars. secousse, choc ▸ the act or fact of jarring; a shaking or shock. SYN: jolt, shake, bump, vibrate.

jar·gon [JAR-gun] NOUN. **1.** jargon, baragouin, charabia ▸ writing that is hard to understand because it is full of long or unfamiliar words. **2.** jargon, baragouin, charabia ▸ the special words used in a particular profession or activity : *The engineer's report was full of jargon.*

jav·e·lin [JAV-uh-lin] NOUN. javelin. javelot ▸ a long, thin, lightweight spear. Athletes compete to see how far they can throw a javelin in a track-and-field event.

jaw [jah] NOUN, jaws. **1.** mâchoire ▸ the upper and lower bony parts of the mouth that hold the teeth. The upper jaw is fixed, while the lower jaw is movable. **2.** mâchoire ▸ the parts of a tool or machine that hold or grip something : *the jaws of a trap.*

jay [jay] NOUN, jays. geai ▸ any of a group of brightly coloured, noisy birds of the crow family. The best-known type in North America is the blue jay.

jay·walk [JAY-wok] VERB, jaywalked, jaywalking. marcher dans la rue en contravenant à la sécurité routière ▸ to cross the street without paying attention to the traffic laws. Crossing when a "Don't walk" sign is displayed is an example of jaywalking.

jazz [jaz] NOUN. jazz ▸ a type of music developed by Black musicians in the southern United States. Jazz has a strong and lively rhythm, with musicians often making up their own notes and changing rhythms as they play. ■ **jazzy**, ADJECTIVE. ▸ criard (-arde), tapageur (-euse), qui a du chic.

jeal·ous [JEL-us] ADJECTIVE. **1.** jaloux (-ouse) ▸ worried or fearful that someone is taking the love or affection a person has or wants : *The boy was jealous of his new baby sister.* **2.** jaloux (-ouse) ▸ unhappy with another person because of something he or she has or can do; envious. **3.** vigilant (-ante) ▸ watchful; guarding

something : *The dog kept a jealous watch over her pups.* ■ **jealously,** ADVERB. ▸ jalousement. ■ **jealousy** (☞ p. 1021), NOUN, jealousies. jalousie ▸ the condition of being jealous. ✎ p. 204.

jeans [jeenz] NOUN. jean ▸ pants made of a heavy cotton cloth. **Note.** Also called blue jeans because for many years, these pants were always dark blue.

jel·ly [JEL-ee] NOUN, jellies. gelée ▸ a clear, firm food usually made by boiling fruit juice with sugar. Jelly is served with other foods, such as bread or meat, or used as a filling for pastries.

jel·ly·fish [JEL-ee-FISH] NOUN, jellyfish or jelly-fishes. méduse ▸ a sea animal shaped like an umbrella and having a soft body that looks like jelly. A jellyfish has many long, trailing parts, called tentacles, that can cause a painful sting.

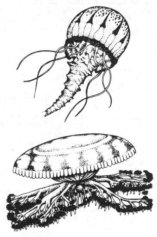

jellyfishes

jerk [jurk] NOUN, jerks. secousse, saccade, à-coup ▸ a quick, sharp pull or twist : *"She urged the horse on with a jerk of the reins."* (Thomas H. Raddall) ▲ VERB, jerked, jerking.

✎ **Word Builder**

*The verb **jam** means to press, hold, or squeeze something into a tight space : The kayak was jammed between two rocks. To **crowd** suggests a number of things are placed in a limited space and those things are very close together : After the ceremony, we crowded into the lobby for a party. To **load** can mean to add a quantity of material to a limited space : Mustafa loaded his plate with mashed potatoes.*

tirer brusquement, secouer, donner une secousse ▶ to move with a quick, sudden motion : *"Grandma would grab my hand. If there were people around I'd jerk it back, embarrassed."* (Paulette Bourgeois) **Note.** Something that has a jerking motion is said to be **jerky. SYN :** pull suddenly, jolt, yank, tug, twist.

jer·sey [JUR-zee] NOUN, jerseys. **1. jersey** ▶ a type of soft, stretchy cloth knitted from cotton, wool, or other material. **2. chandail** ▶ a pullover shirt or sweater made from this material, often used as part of a sports uniform : *a football jersey.*

jet [jet] NOUN, jets. **1. jet, giclée** ▶ a powerful stream of gas, liquid, or vapour that is forced through a small opening by great pressure : *The fireboat sent jets of water high into the air.* **2. jet, avion à réaction** ▶ an aircraft powered by a jet engine. ▲ VERB, jetted, jetting. **gicler, jaillir** ▶ to shoot out in a stream ; spurt : *Water from a broken lawn sprinkler jetted high in the air.* **Note.** Jet lag is a feeling of being tired and slightly sick after a long airplane flight through several time zones.

jet·ty [JET-ee] NOUN, jetties. **jetée, digue** ▶ a wall of rocks, concrete, or other material built out into the ocean or another body of water ; wharf. A jetty is used to break the force of waves or to control the flow of water.

jew·el [JOO-ul] NOUN, jewels. **1. joyau (-aux), pierres précieuses** ▶ a diamond, a ruby, an emerald, or another such precious stone ; a gem : *The treasure chest was full of jewels and gold.* **2. bijou (-oux), trésor, perle** ▶ a person or thing that is very valuable or precious : *The city of Cairo in Egypt is sometimes called "the jewel of the Nile."*

jew·el·ler·y [JOO-ul-ree *or* JOO-ler-ee] NOUN. (also jewelry) **bijoux, joyaux** ▶ ornaments such as rings, necklaces, earrings, and pins usually made of a precious metal such as gold or silver, often set with gems. **Note.** A person who makes, sells, or repairs jewellery and watches is a jeweller. **p. 1011.**

jig [jig] NOUN, jigs. **gigue** ▶ a lively dance, or the music for this dance.

jig·gle [JIG-ul] VERB, jiggled, jiggling. **secouer légèrement** ▶ to move back and forth with a small quick motion ; shake : *Carmen jiggled the keys in her hand.*

jigsaw puzzle puzzle, casse-tête ▶ a puzzle with small cardboard or wooden pieces cut into different shapes that are fitted together to form a picture. **Note.** A jigsaw is a special saw for cutting wavy or curving lines.

jin·gle [JING-ul] VERB, jingled, jingling. **faire tinter, faire sonner** ▶ to make a gentle ringing or tinkling sound : *The coins jingled in my pocket.* ▲ NOUN, jingles. **1. tintement, cliquetis** ▶ a tinkling or clinking sound, as of small metal objects

hitting against each other. **2. sonal ou ritournelle publicitaire** ▶ a short verse or tune that is easy to remember and often used in radio and television advertisements.

job [job] NOUN, jobs. **1. emploi, travail, poste, boulot** ▶ any form of work done for pay : *Julie has an after-school job at the supermarket.* **2. travail, besogne, tâche** ▶ anything that must be worked at or done : *It's my job to wash the dishes.* **SYN :** work, task, business, chore, duty, position.

jock·ey [JOK-ee] NOUN, jockeys. **jockey, femme jockey** ▶ a person who is paid to ride a horse in a horse race.

jog¹ [jog] VERB, jogged, jogging. **1. faire du jogging, faire du footing** ▶ to run slowly, for exercise : *"She jogged and puffed and lifted weights and panted."* (Mem Fox) **2. pousser** ▶ give a little push or nudge : *Jog Rashid to see if he is awake.* ▲ NOUN, jogs. **jogging** ▶ a slow, steady run : *He takes a jog around the lake each morning.* **Note.** A person who jogs is called a jogger.

jog someone's memory rafraîchir la mémoire de quelqu'un ▶ to help someone remember something.

jog² NOUN, jogs. **irrégularité, changement de direction abrupt** ▶ a part that is uneven or changes direction suddenly : *There's a jog in the path where it goes around the tree.* ▲ VERB, jogged, jogging. **changer de direction de façon abrupte** ▶ to make a jog : *The road jogs to the left in front of the store.*

join [joyn] VERB, joined, joining. **1. joindre, unir, relier** ▶ to bring or come together ; connect : *Everyone joined hands.* **2. rejoindre, retrouver** ▶ to meet : *Paul joined me at the game.* **3. adhérer à, devenir membre de, s'inscrire à** ▶ to become a member or part of : *Everyone is invited to join the theatre group.* **p. 323.**

joint [joynt] NOUN, joints. **1. articulation** ▶ a place where two or more bones fit together, usually in such a way that they can move. Wrists, elbows, knees, and ankles are joints. **2. joint, jointure, articulation** ▶ the place where two or more things are fixed together : *The plumber tightened the joint between the pipes so that water won't leak out.* ▲ ADJECTIVE. **commun (-une), conjugué (-ée), réuni (-ie)** ▶ shared by two or more people or groups : *"The expedition I had waited so long for was a joint French–American undertaking."* (Robert D. Ballard) ■ **jointly,** ADVERB. ▶ conjointement, en commun.

joke [joke] NOUN, jokes. **1. plaisanterie, blague, farce** ▶ something said to make people laugh : *Many comedians tell jokes.* **2. tour, farce** ▶ something that is done to be funny : *Peter filled the sugar bowl with salt as a joke, but Dad didn't laugh when he put some in his*

✍ Writing Tips

Joke

Jokes come in many forms : knock-knock jokes, puns, one-liners, question-and-answer jokes, plays on words, or stories.

• Here are some things to think about when you're writing jokes :

– Read lots of joke books. What jokes were the funniest?

– Think about jokes you've heard. What made them funny? How did the teller build anticipation or set up the joke? How was the punch line delivered? The punch line is what makes others laugh.

– In many jokes, the punch line uses a play on words, including words that sound alike, or words that have more than one meaning.

coffee. ✎ **p. 323.** ▲ VERB, joked, joking. **plaisanter, blaguer** ▶ to tell or make jokes : *Ramiro joked about his awful day and made everyone laugh.* **Note.** A person who tells jokes or likes to play tricks on others is a **joker**.

jol·ly [JOL-ee] ADJECTIVE, jollier, jolliest. **enjoué (-ée), jovial (-iale, -iaux)** ▶ full of fun ; very cheerful ; merry ; joyful.

jolt [johlt] VERB, jolted, jolting. **cahoter, tressauter** ▶ to move suddenly or shake roughly : *I jolted along the path on my bicycle.* ▲ NOUN, jolts. **1. cahot, secousse, à coup** ▶ a sudden rough movement ; a bump or jerk : *With a little jolt, the plane climbed into the air.* **2. choc** ▶ a sudden shock or surprise : *With a jolt, Oba realized that he was lost.* SYN : jerk, jar, shake, startle, shock.

jot [jot] VERB, jotted, jotting. **noter, prendre note de** ▶ to write a short, quick note : *Ivan jotted down his ideas.* ▲ NOUN, jots. **brin, iota** ▶ a little bit ; a very small amount : *Taylor put a jot of jam on her toast.* SYN : write, note, record, mark down.

jour·nal [JUR-nul] NOUN, journals. **1. journal (-aux)** ▶ a daily record of events ; a diary. **2. journal (-aux), revue** ▶ a newspaper or magazine. ✎ **p. 324.**

jour·nal·ism [JUR-nuh-liz-um] NOUN. **journalisme** ▶ the work of gathering and presenting the news, as by a newspaper or magazine, or by a radio or TV station. **Note.** A person whose work is journalism is a journalist.

jour·ney [JUR-nee] NOUN, journeys. **voyage, trajet, parcours** ▶ a trip from one place to another, especially a long trip : *"When the shuttle blasts free of the gantry, the Discovery astronauts begin their skyward journey."* (Barbara Bondar) ▲ VERB, journeyed, journeying. **voyager** ▶ to take a long trip ; travel. ✎ **p. 628.**

joy [joy] NOUN, joys. **1. joie** ▶ a feeling of being very happy or pleased ; delight : *Maria jumped for joy when she won the race.* **2. joie** ▶ a thing that brings happiness : *"At first Icarus stayed close behind his father, but soon he was overwhelmed with the joy of flying."* (Marcia Williams)

joy·ful [JOY-ful] ADJECTIVE. **joyeux (-euse)** ▶ feeling, showing, or causing joy : *The crowd's joyful cheers made José very happy.* ■ **joyfully,** ADVERB: ▶ **joyeusement.** *The man smiled joyfully as his son came into view.* SYN : glad, happy, cheerful, merry, gleeful.

joy·ous [JOY-us] ADJECTIVE. **joyeux (-euse)** ▶ filled with joy ; glad : *It was a joyous day when my grandfather came from Italy to visit.* ■ **joyously,** ADVERB. ▶ **joyeusement.** ■ **joyousness,** NOUN. ▶ **joie.**

judge [juj] NOUN, judges. **1. juge** ▶ a public official with the power to hear and decide cases in a court of law. **2. juge** ▶ someone who decides the winner of a contest : *The winner in such sports as diving and gymnastics is decided by judges.* **3. juge** ▶ a person who gives an opinion about the value or quality of something : *someone who is a good judge of writing.* ▲ VERB, judged, judging. **1. juger, rendre un jugement** ▶ to hear cases and make decisions in a court of law. **2. juger** ▶ to decide on the winner of a contest or settle an argument. **3. juger** ▶ to make a decision or form an opinion : *She judged the answer to be no.* **4. juger, estimer** ▶ to guess or estimate : *to judge a distance.*

judg·ment [JUJ-munt] NOUN, judgments. (also judgement) **1. jugement** ▶ an official decision given by a judge or a jury in a court of law : *The judgment of the court was that the man should be sentenced to six months in prison.* **2. jugement, discernement** ▶ the ability to decide

✍ Word Builder

Join means to bring things or people together. *Join up* is a phrase that means to sign up or enlist, especially for the armed forces : *Tricia joined up with the Canadian Armed Forces.* *Join hands* can mean to hold hands or to work together : *If we all join hands, we can clean up the yard quickly.* *Join in* means to participate : *Everyone joined in to fix up the playground.*

something : *She shows good judgment in choosing her friends.* **3. jugement, opinion, avis ▸** an opinion reached after thinking carefully about something.

jug [jug] NOUN, jugs. **pichet, cruche, carafe ▸** a round container with a small handle and a narrow neck, used for holding liquids.

jug·gle [JUG-ul] VERB, juggled, juggling. **1. jongler ▸** to keep two or more objects in motion in the air at the same time by tossing and catching them as they fall : *The clown juggled five apples while riding a unicycle.* **Note.** A person who can juggle is a juggler. **2. jongler ▸** to deal with several problems or tasks at the same time : *Cassie juggles school and a part-time job.*

juice [joos] NOUN, juices. **1. jus ▸** the liquid from fruit, vegetables, or meat. **2. suc ▸** a natural fluid in the body : *Digestive juices act to digest food.* 📖 **p. 1137.**

juic·y [JOOS-ee] ADJECTIVE, juicier, juiciest. **juteux (-euse) ▸** full of juice : *fresh, juicy peaches.*

Ju·ly [JOO-ly] NOUN, Julys. **juillet ▸** the seventh month of the year, between June and August. July has 31 days.

jump [jump] VERB, jumped, jumping. **1. sauter, bondir ▸** to spring up from the ground into the air; leap; bound. **2. sauter ▸** to go over something by leaping : *The horse jumped the fence.* **3. sursauter, tressauter ▸** to move suddenly or quickly : *Vic jumped out of his seat when I touched his arm.* **4. monter en flèche, faire un bond ▸** to rise quickly in value or amount : *The price of that baseball card has jumped to $10 since the player retired.* ▲ NOUN, jumps. **1. saut, bond ▸** the act of jumping; a leap or spring. **2. obstacle ▸** something to be jumped over : *In this race, runners go over a water jump.* **3. sursaut ▸** a sudden movement : *Gary gave a jump when the phone rang.* SYN: spring, leap, vault, hurdle, hop, bound. 📖 **p. 1029.** 📖 **p. 324.**

jump·er[1] [JUM-pur] NOUN, jumpers. **sauteur (-euse) ▸** a person or thing that jumps.

jumper[2] NOUN, jumpers. **robe chasuble ▸** a dress with no sleeves or collar. Jumpers are usually worn over sweaters or blouses.

junc·tion [JUNK-shun] NOUN, junctions. **1. jonction, carrefour ▸** a place where things join or

cross : *The city is located at the junction of the two rivers.* **2. jonction ▸** the act of joining. SYN: union, meeting, joining, connection.

June [joon] NOUN, Junes. **juin ▸** the sixth month of the year, between May and July. June has 30 days.

jun·gle [JUNG-gul] NOUN, jungles. **jungle ▸** an area of tropical land that is covered with thick masses of trees, vines, and bushes.

jun·ior [JOON-yur] ADJECTIVE. **1. junior, fils ▸** the younger : *A son who is given the same name as his father is called "junior."* **2. subalterne ▸** having a lower rank or position : *In the army, a second lieutenant is a junior officer.* ▲ NOUN, juniors. **cadet (-ette) ▸** a person who is younger or has a lower rank than another.

junk[1] [junk] NOUN. **bric-à-brac, vieilleries, ferraille ▸** old, worn-out things that have no use or value; things to be thrown away; trash : *We've got to clear out all the junk that's lying around the garage.* ▲ VERB, junked, junking. **balancer ▸** to get rid of as useless or worthless; throw out : *to junk a broken-down old car.* 📖 **p. 325.**

junk[2] NOUN, junks. **jonque ▸** a flat-bottomed Chinese or Japanese boat with square sails.

junk food NOUN. *Informal.* **aliments sans valeur nutritive, cochonneries ▸** popular foods that

---

✒ **Writing Tips**

Journals

A journal is a personal written record that someone keeps from day to day. In journals, writers can record their ideas, feelings, experiences, observations, what they've done or plan to do, conversations they've had, or questions they have. To start your own journal, all you need is a blank notebook and a pen. Write anything you want within it, and try to write something each day. Remember to begin each entry with the date.

✒ **Word Builder**

Get a jump on means to hold an advantage over someone : She decided to get a jump on her family and do her chores before the others were awake. **Jump the gun** *means to start something too soon : He jumped the gun and answered before I finished asking the question. When you* **jump on** *someone, you are criticizing or blaming him or her : Stella really jumped on me for telling her secret.* **Jump at** *means to accept something eagerly and quickly : I jumped at the opportunity to take a trip to Prince George.*

Junk, debris, and *litter* refer to things that have been discarded or are left behind. *Junk can mean worthless items or ones that are no longer used: They keep their broken toys and other junk in a basement room. Debris is often used to describe piles or scattered things, such as the remaining pieces after a crash: After the plane crashed, debris was everywhere. Litter has the sense of carelessly discarded garbage such as waste paper: After lunch there's always litter in the schoolyard.*

Word Builder

Junk, debris, and *litter* refer to things that have been discarded or are left behind. *Junk can mean worthless items or ones that are no longer used: They keep their broken toys and other junk in a basement room. Debris is often used to describe piles or scattered things, such as the remaining pieces after a crash: After the plane crashed, debris was everywhere. Litter has the sense of carelessly discarded garbage such as waste paper: After lunch there's always litter in the schoolyard.*

have little or no nutritional value. Candy, cookies, potato chips, and other snacks are thought of as junk food.

Ju·pi·ter [JOO-puh-tur] NOUN. **1. Jupiter** ▶ the largest planet in the solar system. Jupiter is the fifth-closest planet to the sun. **2. Jupiter** ▶ in the religion of the ancient Romans, the ruler of the gods. **Note.** Also called Jove. 👁 **p. 391.**

ju·ry [JOOR-ee] NOUN, juries. **jury (jurés)** ▶ in a court of law, a group of people officially chosen to listen to the evidence at a trial and to decide on a verdict. **Note.** A person who serves on a jury is a juror.

just [just] ADVERB. **1. juste** ▶ only or merely : *The ball didn't break the window; it just bounced off it.* **2. juste, exactement, justement, précisément** ▶ neither more nor less; exactly : *I am just 160 cm tall.* **3. juste, de justesse** ▶ not by much; barely : *I just made the team.* **4. venir de faire** ▶ a very short while ago; very recently : *I'm sorry—Amy just left.* **5. juste** ▶ very close; immediately : *The store is just around the corner.* ▲ ADJECTIVE. **1. juste, équitable** ▶ as it should be; honest and right; fair : *We believe in just treatment for everyone.* **2. juste, mérité (-ée)** ▶ deserved; earned : *just rewards.*

jus·tice [JUS-tis] NOUN, justices. **1. justice, équité** ▶ honest and fair treatment according to

honour or law : *Justice is everyone's right.* **2. justice** ▶ the condition of being proper or correct : *How could we lose when we played better than they did—there's no justice to it!* **3. juge** ▶ a judge. **Note.** A justice of the peace is a public official with powers that are more limited than those of a judge. **do justice to a. rendre justice à** ▶ treat fairly. **b. montrer la juste valeur de** ▶ see the good points of. **c. faire honneur** ▶ show appreciation for : *Brooke's compliments did justice to the wonderful dinner Seth had cooked.*

jus·ti·fy [JUS-tuh-fy] VERB, justified, justifying. **1. justifier, légitimer** ▶ to show that something is fair and reasonable : *She justified her opinion by presenting supporting facts.* **2. justifier** ▶ to give a good reason for something. ■ **justification,** NOUN: ▶ **justification.** *Jean had justification in yelling—he had stubbed his toe.*

ju·ve·nile [JOO-vuh-nile *or* JOO-vuh-nul] ADJECTIVE. **1. juvénile, pour enfants** ▶ for or about children or young people : *Alice's Adventures in Wonderland is one of the world's best-known juvenile books.* **2. juvénile, puéril (-rile)** ▶ youthful; childish; immature. ▲ NOUN, juveniles. **jeune, adolescent (-ente)** ▶ a young person or animal.

K k

koalas

k, K [kay] NOUN, k's, K's. **k, K** ▶ the 11th letter of the English alphabet.

ka·lei·do·scope [kuh-LY-duh-SKOPE] NOUN, kaleidoscopes. **kaléidoscope** ▶ a tube containing bits of coloured glass at one end and a small hole at the other end. When someone looks through the hole and turns the tube, two mirrors inside show the changing patterns of the moving glass.

kan·ga·roo [KANG-guh-ROO] NOUN, kangaroos or kangaroo. **kangourou** ▶ an animal that lives in Australia. It has small front legs and very strong back legs that it uses for jumping. The female kangaroo carries her young in a pouch on the front of her body.

kar·at [KAIR-ut] NOUN, karats. (also carat) **carat** ▶ a unit of measure that shows the amount of gold in a certain metal mixture. Pure gold is 24 karats, but most gold jewellery is between 10 and 18 karats.

ka·ra·te [kuh-RAH-tee] NOUN. **karaté** ▶ a Japanese style of self-defence fighting in which the hands, elbows, feet, and knees are used instead of weapons.

— kimono

— belt

karate

kay·ak [KY-AK] NOUN, kayaks. **kayak** ▶ a lightweight canoe for one person that is moved by one long paddle with a blade at both ends. **Note.** Kayaks were developed by the Inuit.

kayak

keel [keel] NOUN, keels. **1. quille** ▶ a wooden or steel piece that runs along the bottom of a ship or boat. The keel is the main support of the ship, and the frame or hull is attached to it. **2. quille** ▶ a fin-shaped piece attached to the bottom of a sailboat that hangs down into the water to balance the boat. ▲ VERB, keeled, keeling. (used with over) **1. chavirer** ▶ to turn upside down; capsize : *Our boat keeled over in the big waves.* **2. tourner de l'œil** ▶ to fall over suddenly : *When I heard I'd won the prize, I nearly keeled over.*

keen [keen] ADJECTIVE, keener, keenest. **1. tranchant (-ante), aiguisé (-ée), affilé (-ée)** ▶ sharp enough to cut : *a knife with a keen edge.* **2. vif (vive), aigu (aiguë), fin (fine), pénétrant (-ante)** ▶ able to think or understand well; bright. **3. fin (fine), pénétrant (-ante), perçant (-ante)** ▶ sharp or quick in the use of the mind or senses : *Dogs have keen ears.* ■ **keenly,** ADVERB: ▶ **vivement, profondément.** *We were keenly aware of the falling temperature.* ■ **keenness,** NOUN: ▶ **ardeur, enthousiasme.** *Her keenness for chemistry was well-known.*

keep [keep] VERB, kept, keeping. **1. garder, conserver, avoir** ▶ to have for a long time or to own : *You may keep it forever.* **2. garder, mettre en réserve** ▶ to hold or guard and not give away. **3. tenir, garder** ▶ to stay the same or continue : *Indira kept quiet as she watched the squirrel.* **4. garder, ranger, mettre en lieu sûr** ▶ to put or hold in a safe place : *to keep a* car in a garage. **5. garder, empêcher, retenir** ▶ to hold back or stop something from happening : *The noise kept her from sleeping.* **6. garder, avoir, élever** ▶ to take care of or protect : *to keep a pet.* **7. garder, tenir** ▶ to manage, organize, or maintain : *I like to keep my room clean.* **8. tenir, respecter, rester fidèle à** ▶ to carry out or follow as expected : *to keep a promise.* **9. tenir** ▶ to make a regular record : *to keep a diary.* **10. garder, conserver** ▶ to stay fresh or in good condition : *Milk keeps better in the fridge.* ▲ NOUN. **1. de quoi vivre, entretien** ▶ a place to live and food to eat : *People who work hard earn their keep.* **2. donjon** ▶ the safest place in a castle. SYN: reserve, maintain, have, hold, save, protect. 🖉 p. 454.

keep·er [KEEP-ur] NOUN, keepers. **gardien (-ienne), surveillant (-ante)** ▶ a person who takes care of or is in charge of something : *The keeper fed the animals in the zoo.* **Note.** Often combined with other words, as in *shopkeeper, gatekeeper,* or *goalkeeper.*

kelp [kelp] NOUN. **varech** ▶ the large brown varieties of seaweed. Some kinds of kelp are used to make fertilizer and iodine.

ken·nel [KEN-ul] NOUN, kennels. **1. niche** ▶ a doghouse. **2. chenil** ▶ a place where dogs are raised or trained, or where owners may leave their dogs to be cared for. **Note.** *Kennel* comes from the Latin word *canis,* meaning "dog."

kept [kept] VERB. a past form of **keep.**

ker·chief [KUR-chif] NOUN, kerchiefs. **1. fichu, fanchon** ▶ a piece of cloth worn over the head or around the neck. **2. mouchoir, foulard** ▶ a handkerchief.

ker·nel [KURN-ul] NOUN, kernels. **1. grain** ▶ a grain or seed of wheat or corn or other cereal. **2. amande** ▶ the soft part inside the shell of a nut, fruit, or seed. **3. noyau (-aux)** ▶ the central or most important part of something : *the kernel of an argument.*

ker·o·sene [KAIR-uh-SEEN] NOUN. **kérosène, pétrole** ▶ a thick, light-coloured oil made from petroleum. Kerosene is used as fuel in some lamps and stoves.

ketch·up [KECH-up] NOUN. (also **catchup** or **catsup**) **ketchup** ▶ a thick red sauce made from tomatoes, onions, spices, sugar, and salt. Ketchup is used to add flavour to foods. **Note.** The word *ketchup* comes from Chinese.

ket·tle [KET-ul] NOUN, kettles. **1. marmite** ▶ a metal pot, usually with a lid, used for boiling liquids or cooking foods. **2. bouilloire** ▶ a metal container with a small opening, used for heating water, as for tea.

key¹ [kee] NOUN, keys. **1. clé** ▶ a small piece of metal with a special shape that fits into a lock to open or close it. **2. clé, remontoir** ▶ anything shaped or used like a key : *Some old clocks are wound with keys.* **3. clé** ▶ something that

solves or explains a puzzle or problem : *This math book has an answer key in the back.* **4. clé** ▶ the most important element or part : *Most people believe that hard work is the key to success.* **5. touche** ▶ one of a set of parts that is pressed down to play a musical instrument or use a machine : *computer keys; the black keys on a piano.* **6. ton** ▶ in music, a set of notes that are all related to each other, based on one note (the keynote) : *a song written in the key of G.* ▲ ADJECTIVE. **clé** ▶ very important; major : *Several key employees make most of the decisions for the company.*

key in faire la saisie de ▶ to input information into a computer using a keyboard.

keyed up surexcité (-ée), tendu (-ue) ▶ excited or nervous; tense.

key² NOUN, keys. (sometimes **cay**) **caye** ▶ a low island or reef : *You can visit the keys off the coast of southern Florida.*

key·board [KEE-bord] NOUN, keyboards. **clavier** ▶ a set of keys in rows on a piano, typewriter, computer, and so on : *Our band uses an electronic keyboard instead of a piano.* ▲ VERB, keyboarded, keyboarding. **faire la saisie de** ▶ to use a computer keyboard. ▪ **keyboarder,** NOUN. ▶ **opérateur (-trice), pupitre, claviériste.** **Note.** Also called an **inputter.**

key·board·ist [KEE-bor-dist] NOUN, keyboardists. **joueur (-euse) d'un instrument à clavier** ▶ a person who plays a musical instrument that has a keyboard, such as a piano.

khak·i [KAK-ee *or* KAR-kee] NOUN, khakis. **1. kaki** ▶ a dull yellowish-brown or tan colour. **2. kaki** ▶ a heavy cotton cloth of this colour, often used to make uniforms. **3. khakis. kaki** ▶ a uniform made of this cloth.

kick [kik] VERB, kicked, kicking. **1. donner un coup de pied, lancer un coup de pied** ▶ to hit or strike with the foot : *He kicked the wall in frustration.* **2. battre des pieds** ▶ to strike out with the foot or feet : *The swimmer kicked harder as she neared the finish line.* **3. botter** ▶ to move or force by kicking : *to kick a field goal in football.* ▲ NOUN, kicks. **1. coup de pied** ▶ a hit or blow with the foot. **2.** *Informal.* **être émoustillé (-ée), être excité (-ée)** ▶ a feeling of excitement or pleasure : *Grandpa got a big kick out of the present Abdul gave him.* **3.** *Informal.* **se tourner à plein dans** ▶ a strong new interest or concern : *Fatima has been on a money-saving kick lately.* 🖉 p. 328.

kick·off [KIK-off] NOUN, kickoffs. **1. coup d'envoi** ▶ a kick in football or soccer that puts the ball into play at the beginning of the game or after a touchdown or goal. **2.** *Informal.* **coup d'envoi** ▶ the start of any activity : *the kickoff of a festival.*

kid [kid] NOUN, kids. **1. chevreau (-eaux), chevrette** ▶ a young goat. **2. de chevreau (-eaux)**

✎ Word Builder

Kick is found in many familiar expressions. To *kick around* can mean to treat a person badly or to move from place to place without any real purpose: *On Saturday, we kicked around the park.* The expression *kick off* is used in football. It means to put the ball in play, usually to start each half. To *kick off* can also mean the start of something: *The parade kicked off the spring festival.* If people *kick up their heels,* they are having a good time.

▶ soft leather made from the skin of young goat: *kid gloves.* **3.** *Informal.* **gamin (-ine), gosse, jeune** ▶ a child or young person. ▲ ADJEC-TIVE. *Informal.* **petit (-ite)** ▶ younger: *I had to baby-sit my kid brother and couldn't go to the movies.* ▲ VERB, kidded, kidding. **raconter des blagues, faire marcher quelqu'un** ▶ to make fun of or joke with someone: *Mom likes to kid Tomas about how much time he spends combing his hair.*

kid-nap [KID-nap] VERB, kidnapped, kidnapping. (also kidnaped, kidnaping) **kidnapper, enle-ver** ▶ to take away and hold someone by force. **Note.** A person who does this is a kidnapper.

kid-ney [KID-nee] NOUN, kidneys. **1. rein** ▶ one of a pair of body organs that removes waste from the bloodstream. **2. rognon** ▶ the kidney or kid-neys of an animal cooked for food.

kill [kil] VERB, killed, killing. **1. tuer, assas-siner** ▶ to end the life of or cause the death of. **2. tuer, détruire** ▶ to put an end to; destroy; ruin: *Failing that test killed my chances of get-ting an "A" in the course.* **3. tuer** ▶ to use up free time: *We killed an hour wandering through the mall.* **4.** *Informal.* **tuer** ▶ to cause great pain; hurt badly: *This toothache is killing me.* ▲ NOUN, kills. **mise à mort** ▶ the act of killing, or an animal that is killed. SYN: murder, slaughter, execute, end, finish.

kill-er [KIL-ur] NOUN, killers. **tueur (-euse), assas-sin, meurtrier (-ière)** ▶ a person or thing that kills, especially one who kills another person.

kiln [kiln] NOUN, kilns. **four** ▶ an oven or furnace for burning, baking, or drying things at a very high temperature. Kilns are used to make bricks, pottery, and charcoal.

kil-o-gram [KIL-uh-GRAM] NOUN, kilograms. **kilo-gramme** ▶ a unit of weight or mass in the metric system. A kilogram is equal to 1000 grams. Sym-bol: kg

kil-om-e-tre [KIL-uh-MEE-tur *or* kih-LOM-uh-tur] NOUN, kilometres. **kilomètre** ▶ a unit of length in the metric system. A kilometre is equal to 1000 metres. Symbol: km

kilt [kilt] NOUN, kilts. **kilt** ▶ a pleated plaid skirt that reaches to the knees. Kilts are a traditional form of clothing worn by men in Scotland.

ki-mo-no [kih-MOH-noe *or* kih-MOH-nuh] NOUN, kimonos. **1. kimono** ▶ a long, loose robe or gown that has wide sleeves and is tied with a wide sash called an **obi. kimono** ▶ In Japan, kimonos are a traditional form of clothing for both men and women. **2. kimono** ▶ a loose dressing gown or housecoat.

kin [kin] NOUN. **parents, famille** ▶ a person's fam-ily; relatives: *Your parents, brothers, and sisters are your next of kin.* ■ **kinship,** NOUN. ▶ **parenté.** SYN: family, relatives, relations, folks.

kind[1] [kynd] ADJECTIVE, kinder, kindest. **1. gentil (-ille), bon (bonne), aimable** ▶ wanting to help others and make them happy; friendly; caring: *It is kind of you to help me.* **2. gentil (-ille), bon (bonne), aimable** ▶ showing or coming from a feeling of caring; warm and generous: *kind words; a kind act.* **Note.** The quality of being kind, or a kind act, is kindness: *Treat animals with kindness.* SYN: thoughtful, friendly, consid-erate, gentle.

kind[2] NOUN, kinds. **sorte, genre, espèce** ▶ a group of things that are alike in some way; a type: *I like all kinds of food.*

kind of *Informal.* **assez** ▶ more or less; rather; somewhat: *It was kind of dark, so we stopped the game.*

one of a kind unique ▶ unique. *My dad says the coin I found is one of a kind and worth a lot of money.* SYN: sort, type, variety, class.

kin-der-gar-ten [KIN-dur-GART-un] NOUN, kinder-gartens. **1. maternelle** ▶ a class in school that comes before grade one. **2. jardin d'enfants** ▶ a school for younger children; a nursery school.

kin-dle [KIND-ul] VERB, kindled, kindling. **1. allumer** ▶ to set on fire; start something burn-ing: *She kindled a fire to warm up the room.* **Note.** The small pieces of material used to start a fire, such as twigs, leaves, paper, or thin branches, are called kindling. **2. enflammer** ▶ to catch fire: *The dry wood kindled quickly.* **3. allumer, enflammer** ▶ to stir up or excite; arouse: *The trip to the museum kindled Lina's interest in dinosaurs.*

kind-ly [KYND-lee] ADJECTIVE, kindlier, kindliest. **bienveillant (-ante), plein (pleine) de bonté, gentil (-ille)** ▶ warm and friendly; kind: ▲ ADVERB. **1. avec bonté, avec gentillesse** ▶ in a kind way: *The vet treated the sick dog kindly.* **2. avec bonté, avec obligeance** ▶ as a favour: *Sid kindly helped me change my tire.*

king [king] NOUN, kings. **1. roi ▸** a man who is the ruler of a country, and whose power has been passed down from the previous ruler. **2. roi ▸** a person or thing that is very important or powerful : *The lion is sometimes called the king of beasts.* **3. roi ▸** a playing card with a picture of a king on it. A king ranks between a queen and an ace. **4. roi, dame ▸** the most important piece in the game of chess or checkers. ■ **kingly,** ADJECTIVE. **royal (-ale, -aux), de roi ▸** of or like a king : *kingly robes.* 🖙 **p. 968.**

king·dom [KING-dum] NOUN, kingdoms. **1. royaume ▸** a country or territory that is ruled by a king or queen. **2. royaume ▸** a place or area where one is in control : *My home is my kingdom.* **3. règne ▸** one of the three main groups into which the natural world is divided. They are the animal kingdom, the plant kingdom, and the mineral kingdom. 🖙 **p. 1041.**

kink [kink] NOUN, kinks. **1. noeud, entortillement, pli ▸** a short, tight curl or twist in hair, wire, rope, and so on : *Karlene has kinks in her hair.* **2. crampe ▸** a pain or stiffness in a muscle; a cramp. **3. petit problème ▸** a small problem in the working of something : *There are still a few kinks to be worked out in our plan.* ▲ VERB, kinked, kinking. **se nouer, s'entortiller ▸** to curl or twist sharply; form a kink.

kiss [kis] VERB, kissed, kissing. **1. embrasser, donner un baiser ▸** to touch with the lips as a sign of love, affection, or greeting. **2. effleurer ▸** to touch gently : *The wind kissed the flowers.* ▲ NOUN, kisses. **1. baiser ▸** a touch with the lips as a sign of love, affection, or greeting. **2. baiser ▸** a gentle touch.

kit [kit] NOUN, kits. **1. kit ▸** a set of parts to be put together to make something : *a model-airplane kit.* **2. trousse ▸** a special set of tools, equipment, or information : *a first-aid kit; a visitor's kit.* **3. équipement, matériel, attirail ▸** the uniform and equipment for an activity : *a camping kit.*

kit·chen [KICH-un] NOUN, kitchens. **cuisine ▸** a room where food is cooked. **Note.** A kitchenette is a small kitchen. 🖙 **p. 1071.**

kite [kite] NOUN, kites. **1. cerf-volant ▸** a light frame covered with paper, plastic, or cloth that is flown in the air at the end of a long string. **2. milan ▸** a hawk with long, pointed wings, a forked tail, and a hooked bill.

kit·ten [KIT-un] NOUN, kittens. **chaton, petit (-ite) chat (-atte) ▸** a young cat.

knack [nack] NOUN. **avoir le talent, tour de main ▸** a special talent or skill; the ability to do something easily : *Elaine has a knack for science.* SYN : skill, talent, ability, art, know-how.

knap·sack [NAP-sack] NOUN, knapsacks. **sac à dos, havresac ▸** a canvas or leather bag used to carry clothes, camping equipment, books, and so on. It is strapped over the shoulders and carried on the back.

knead [need] VERB, kneaded, kneading. **1. pétrir, travailler ▸** to mix dough or clay by pressing or working it with the hands : *to knead bread.* **2. masser ▸** to press and rub with the hands; massage : *Molly kneaded the kinks out of my neck muscles.*

knee [nee] NOUN, knees. **1. genou (-oux) ▸** the joint of the leg between the thigh and the lower leg, or the area around this joint. **2. genou (-oux) ▸** clothing that covers this leg joint : *the shredded knees of her jeans.* **Note.** The kneecap is the flat, movable bone in front of the knee. Its medical name is patella. 🖙 **p. 1002.**

kneel [neel] VERB, knelt or kneeled, kneeling. **s'agenouiller, se mettre à genoux ▸** to go down or stay on bent knee or knees : *She knelt to look under the bed.*

knew [noo] VERB. a past form of know.

knife [nife] NOUN, knives. **couteau (-eaux), canif ▸** a tool made of a sharp blade attached to a handle, used for cutting. ▲ VERB, knifed, knifing. **1. donner un coup de couteau ▸** to cut or stab with a knife. **2. fendre ▸** to move quickly through, as if by cutting : *The speedboat knifed through the water.* 🖉 **p. 330.**

knight [nite] NOUN, knights. **1. chevalier ▸** in the Middle Ages, an armed warrior who fought on horseback and served a king or other ruler. Knights pledged to follow a code of honour. **2. chevalier ▸** in modern times, a person raised to the honorary rank of knight for great achievements or service to his or her country. A man who has been honoured in this way uses the title "Sir" before his name, a woman uses the title "Dame." **3. cavalier ▸** a piece in the game of chess, usually shaped like a horse's head. ▲ VERB, knighted, knighting. **faire chevalier ▸** to raise to the rank of knight : *King George V knighted Frederick Banting for his part in the discovery of insulin.* ■ **knightly,** ADJECTIVE; ADVERB. ● **chevaleresque.** 🖙 **p. 969.**

knit [nit] VERB, knitted or knit, knitting. **1. tricoter ▸** to make cloth or clothing by looping yarn or thread together with knitting needles or with a machine : *Aunt Joan knitted Avi a sweater.* **2. se souder ▸** to grow together : *Kerry's broken wrist knitted well as it healed.* 🖉 **p. 330.**

knob [nob] NOUN, knobs. **1. bouton ▸** a round handle for opening a door or drawer. **2. bouton ▸** a round handle on things like radios, televisions, and so on. **3. nœud, protubérance, bosse ▸** a round lump, such as a lump on the trunk of a tree.

knock [nok] VERB, knocked, knocking. **1. frapper ▸** to strike with a hard blow or shove; hit : *"How dare you push me and knock me around!"* (Dan Yashinsky) **2. frapper, cogner ▸** to hit and make a noise; bang : *to knock on a door.* **3. défoncer, démolir ▸** to hit and cause to

329

Silent K

*The words knight, knife, knit, knot, and knuckle have a **silent k**. The **k** sound at the beginning of each word isn't pronounced. These words are pronounced in the same way as they would be if they began with **n**. In earlier times, the **k** was pronounced.*

fall or move : *They knocked down the wall.* ▲ NOUN, knocks. **1. coup, choc, heurt ▸** a sharp, hard blow : *We were startled by a loud knock on the window.* **2. cognement ▸** a pounding or clanking noise in a car engine : *Engine knock may be caused by using the wrong gasoline.*

knock out 1. assommer ▸ to hit so hard as to make unconscious : *The boxer knocked out his opponent in the first round.* **2.** *Informal.* **mettre à plat ▸** to make a very great effort : *He knocked himself out to get his project in on time.* **Note.** Also used as a NOUN: *to win a fight by a knockout.* SYN : bang, hit, strike, jab, tap, rap, beat.

knoll [nole] NOUN, knolls. **monticule, tertre ▸** a small, rounded hill.

knot [not] NOUN, knots. **1. nœud ▸** a fastening made by tying together pieces of string, rope, or thread. **2. nœud ▸** a tight tangle of hair. **3. petit groupe ▸** a small group; a cluster : *A knot of people were standing near the statue.* **4. nœud**

▸ a hard, dark, roundish spot in a wooden board. A knot is a place where a branch grew out from the trunk of a tree. **5. nœud ▸** a hard mass or lump : *a knot in a muscle.* **6. nœud ▸** a measure of speed for ships, boats, and aircraft. A knot is equal to one nautical mile, or 1852 metres, per hour. ▲ VERB, knotted, knotting. **nouer, faire un nœud ▸** to tie in or with a knot.

know [noe] VERB, knew, known, knowing. **1. savoir ▸** to have information in the mind; be certain of the truth or facts about : *I know she lives on Queen Street.* **2. connaître ▸** to be familiar with; to be acquainted with : *We've known each other since we were kids.* **3. savoir ▸** to have learned; be experienced or skilled in : *My sister already knows how to drive a car.* **4. connaître, reconnaître ▸** to tell apart from others; identify or recognize : *Do you know the new teacher?*

in the know *Informal.* **être au courant, être au parfum ▸** to have inside information.

know-how *Informal.* **savoir-faire ▸** the knowledge needed to do things.

know-it-all un (une) je-sais-tout ▸ someone who thinks that he or she knows everything.

knowl·edge [NOL-ij] NOUN. **1. savoir, connaissance, science ▸** what a person knows; information : *Elders share their knowledge with others.* **2. connaissance ▸** what is generally known; learning : *scientific knowledge.* **3. connaissance ▸** the fact of knowing; understanding or awareness : *I had no knowledge of*

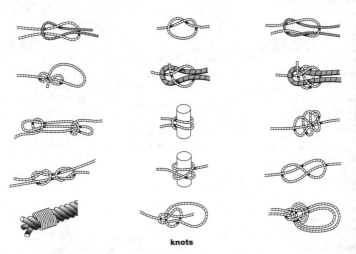

knots

your success! **Note.** A person who has a great deal of knowledge is knowledgeable.

known [nohn] VERB. a past form of know. ▲ ADJECTIVE. **connu (-ue), reconnu (-ue)** ▸ generally recognized or accepted : *a known fact.*

knuck‧le [NUK-ul] NOUN, knuckles. **articulation, jointure du doigt** ▸ a joint of a finger, especially the joint between a finger and the rest of the hand.

koalas

ko‧a‧la [koh-AH-luh] NOUN, koalas. (also koala bear) **koala** ▸ a furry, chubby animal of Australia that looks like a small bear. It carries its young in a pouch and is actually distantly related to the kangaroo. Koalas live in trees and feed on the leaves of a certain type of eucalyptus tree.

Koo‧ten‧ay [KOO-ten-ay] NOUN, Kootenay or Kootenays. (also Kutenai) **1. kootenay** ▸ a member of the Aboriginal peoples living in southeastern British Columbia and the northeastern United States. **2. kootenay** ▸ the language of the Kootenay people.

Ko‧ran [kor-RAN *or* kuh-RON] NOUN. (also Qur'an) **Coran** ▸ the sacred book of Islam, believed by Muslims to have been revealed to Muhammad by the archangel Gabriel.

ko‧sher [KOH-shur] ADJECTIVE. **kascher** ▸ of food, prepared according to the traditional rules of the Jewish religion.

Krish‧na [KRISH-nuh] NOUN. **Krishna, Krisna** ▸ The human form of the Hindu god Vishnu, usually pictured as a young man playing a flute.

kung fu [KOONG foo] NOUN. **kung fu** ▸ an ancient Chinese art of fighting similar to karate.

Kwan‧za [KWON-zuh] NOUN, Kwanzas. **kwanza** ▸ An African-heritage cultural festival celebrated from December 26 to January 1.

ladybug

I, L [el] NOUN, I's, L's. **i, L** ▶ the 12th letter of the English alphabet.

la-bel [LAY-bul] NOUN, labels. **1. étiquette** ▶ a piece of cloth or paper attached to something to tell what it is or give other information about it : *an address label on a package; a label on a jacket.* **2. marque, étiquette, label** ▶ a word or phrase used to describe or name something : *In this dictionary, words are given part-of-speech labels.* ▲ VERB, labelled, labelling. (also labeled, labeling) **1. étiqueter** ▶ to put a label on : *The movers labelled each box as they packed it.* **2. nommer** ▶ to describe or name something with a label; name or call : *The child labelled every object she saw.*

lab-o-ra-to-ry [LAB-ruh-TOR-ee *or* luh-BOR-uh-tur-ee] NOUN, laboratories. **laboratoire** ▶ a room or building with special equipment for scientific research or experiments. **Note.** The short form for laboratory is lab.

la-bour [LAY-bur] NOUN, labours. (also labor) **1. travail, labeur** ▶ hard work, especially physical work : *It took years of labour to build the bridge.* **2. travailleur (-euse), main-d'œuvre, ouvrier (-ière)** ▶ working people as a group, especially people who work with their hands : *A work force can be divided into two groups—labour and management.* **Note.** A labour union is an organization that protects and promotes the interests of workers. ▲ VERB, laboured, labouring. **1. travailler, peiner** ▶ to work hard; toil : *The editors often laboured far into the night.* **2. peiner** ▶ to move slowly and with difficulty : *"She closed her eyes and hung on fiercely as the old horse laboured through the storm."* (Marilyn Reynolds) ■ **laborious,** ADJECTIVE. ▶ **laborieux (-euse), pénible, fatigant (-ante).** needing much labour or effort. **Note.** A labourer is a person who does work, especially physical work. SYN: work, task, toil, employment, industry.

Labour Day **Fête du travail** ▶ a holiday to honour working people. It is celebrated on the first Monday in September.

lab-y-rinth [LAB-uh-rinth *or* LAB-rinth] NOUN, labyrinths. **1. labyrinthe, dédale** ▶ a place through which it is hard to find one's way; a maze : *The streets of her new neighbourhood seemed like a labyrinth to Roberta.* **2. laby-rinthe** ▶ in Greek mythology, the maze built by Daedalus for King Minos of Crete, where a beast called the Minotaur was kept. **3. labyrinthe** ▶ the inner ear.

lace [lace] NOUN, laces. **1. lacet** ▶ a cord or string used to pull or hold together : *a shoelace.* **2. dentelle** ▶ a fabric that is woven of fine threads in a loose, open pattern : *lace on a wedding dress.* ▲ VERB, laced, lacing. **1. lacer** ▶ to fasten with a lace or laces : *to lace up a pair of shoes.* **2. faire de la dentelure** ▶ to mark with a loose, woven pattern like lace : *Hundreds of tiny hairline cracks laced the old table.* ■ **lacy,** ADJECTIVE. ▶ **de dentelle.**

lack [lak] VERB, lacked, lacking. **manquer de** ▶ to be without; be in need of : *We lack two ingredients for making this cake.* ▲ NOUN. **manque** ▶ the state of being without something; need : *"I've got dark rings under my eyes from lack of sleep."* (Anne Frank) SYN: want, need, require, fall short.

lac-quer [LAK-ur] NOUN, lacquers. **laque** ▶ a substance used to give something a protective, shiny coat, as on the surface of wood. ▲ VERB, lacquered, lacquering. **laquer** ▶ to coat with lacquer. SYN: varnish, polish.

la-crosse [luh-KROS] NOUN. **crosse** ▶ a game played on a field with two teams of 10 players. A long stick with a net at one end that is used to throw or catch a small, hard ball. Points are scored by throwing the ball into a goal. **Note.** A lacrosse stick is the stick used in lacrosse.

lad [lad] NOUN, lads. **garçon, jeune homme** ▶ a boy or young man.

lad-der [LAD-ur] NOUN, ladders. **1. échelle** ▶ a device used for climbing up or down. It has two long side rails with rungs between them to step on. **2. échelon, palier, niveau (-eaux)** ▶ a way of moving up or making progress : *Studying at* *university can be the first step on the ladder to success.*

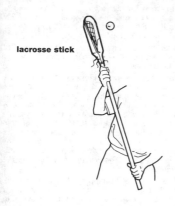

lacrosse stick

la·dle [LAY-dul] NOUN, ladles. **louche** ▸ a bowl-shaped spoon with a long handle, used to scoop out liquids. ▲ VERB, ladled, ladling. **servir à la louche** ▸ to spoon out or dip : *Sharlene ladled soup into my bowl.*

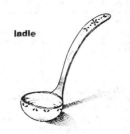

ladle

la·dy [LAY-dee] NOUN, ladies. 1. **dame, femme** ▸ a woman who has a high social position. 2. Lady. **Lady** ▸ in the United Kingdom and its colonies, a title for a woman of noble rank. 3. **dame** ▸ a woman or girl with very polite manners and habits. 4. **femme** ▸ any woman : *We received a note from the lady across the street.*

la·dy·bug [LAY-dee-BUG] NOUN, ladybugs. **coccinelle** ▸ a small, round beetle that is red or orange with black spots on its back. Ladybugs eat several kinds of insects that are harmful to plants. **Note.** Also called a ladybird. ☞ p. 104.

lag [lag] VERB, lagged, lagging. **traîner derrière** ▸ to fall behind : *Kerry lagged behind her friends on a trip to the museum.* ▲ NOUN, lags.

décalage, délai ▸ a delay or following after. SYN : linger, straggle, delay.

la·goon [luh-GOON] NOUN, lagoons. **lagon, lagune** ▸ a shallow area of water that is partly cut off from a larger body of water by a narrow strip of land or by a coral reef.

laid [lade] VERB **poser, placer, mettre** ▸ a past form of lay¹: *Olivia laid the cloth on the table. We had laid carpet in the bedrooms before we moved into the house.*

lain [lane] a past form of lie¹ **s'allonger, se trouver sur** ▸: *The towel had lain on the floor most of the day.*

lair [lair] NOUN, lairs. **tanière, repère** ▸ the den or place where a wild animal lives, especially a bear, a wolf, or another large animal.

lake [lake] NOUN, lakes. **lac** ▸ a body of fresh or salt water that is completely surrounded by land : *"You must use this ferry boat to get across the lake."* (Arnold Lobel) ☞ **p. 1108.** ☞ p. 113.

lamb [lam] NOUN, lambs. 1. **agneau (-eaux)** ▸ a young sheep. 2. **agneau** ▸ the meat of a young sheep. 3. **agneau (-eaux), ange** ▸ an innocent, gentle person.

lame [lame] ADJECTIVE, lamer, lamest. 1. **boiteux (-euse), estropié (-ée), éclopé (-ée)** ▸ not able to walk well because of being hurt or disabled ; limping. 2. **courbaturé (-ée)** ▸ sore, stiff, or painful : *a lame back; a lame shoulder.* 3. **piètre, boiteux (-euse)** ▸ not satisfactory ; weak : *a lame excuse for not doing something.* ▲ VERB, lamed, laming. **estropier** ▸ to make lame.

la·ment [luh-MENT] VERB, lamented, lamenting. 1. **se lamenter sur, pleurer, se plaindre** ▸ to express deep sorrow or grief. 2. **regretter** ▸ regret : *She lamented her actions.* ▲ NOUN, laments. 1. **lamentation** ▸ an expression of grief. 2. **complainte, lamentation** ▸ a song or poem that expresses grief. SYN : mourn, grieve, bemoan, bewail.

lamp [lamp] NOUN, lamps. **lampe** ▸ a device that gives off light. Most lamps use electric bulbs. Some lamps burn kerosene, gas, or oil to give light. ☞ p. 1071.

lance [lance] NOUN, lances. 1. **lance** ▸ a long spear that is made of wood and has a sharp metal tip. Knights in the Middle Ages used lances as weapons. 2. **bistouri** ▸ a tool that looks like this weapon. Doctors use small lances for operating. ▲ VERB, lanced, lancing. **percer, inciser** ▸ to cut open with a sharp knife or instrument.

land [land] NOUN, lands. 1. **terre** ▸ the part of the earth's surface not covered by water. 2. **terrain, terre(s)** ▸ property ; real estate : *Mrs. Raymond bought some land near the new highway.* 3. **terre, sol** ▸ soil or ground of a particular type : *farmland.* 4. **pays, terre** ▸ a country or region and its people : *the land of Oz.* ▲ VERB,

landed, landing. 1. débarquer, atterrir ▸ to arrive or bring to shore : *Cabot landed in Newfoundland in 1497.* **2. (faire) atterrir ▸** to bring or come down to the ground from the air : *The plane landed on time.* **3. amener à terre ▸** to bring a fish out of the water. ⬙ p. 1042. SYN: earth, ground, soil, sod, shore, terrain.

land-ing [LAND-ing] NOUN, landings. **1. atterrissage, débarquement ▸** the act of coming to land from the water or the air : *an airplane landing.* **2. débarcadère ▸** a place where passengers land or where cargo is unloaded. **3. palier ▸** a wide, flat area at the top or bottom of a set of stairs.

land-lord [LAND-LORD] NOUN, landlords. **propriétaire ▸** a person who owns apartments, houses, or rooms that are rented to other people.

land-mark [LAND-MARK] NOUN, landmarks. **1. repère, borne ▸** a familiar or easily seen object that is used as a guide. **2. événement marquant ▸** an event or discovery that is important in history : *Gutenberg's invention of the printing press is a landmark event in communications.*

land-scape [LAND-SKAPE] NOUN, landscapes. **1. paysage ▸** a view of a large area of land. **2. paysage ▸** a painting or photograph showing a view of such an area, especially one of rivers, lakes, woods, and so on. **3. paysage ▸** the landforms of a region. ▲ VERB, landscaped, landscaping. **aménager en parc, faire l'aménagement paysager ▸** to make an area more beautiful by planting trees, flowers, and other plants according to a plan. ⬙ p. 1043.

land-slide [LAND-SLIDE] NOUN, landslides. **1. éboulement, affaissement, glissement ▸** a sliding or falling of rock and soil down the side of a mountain. **2. vague ▸** a large number of votes that cause a candidate or political party to win.

lane [lane] NOUN, lanes. **1. chemin, ruelle, petite route, passage ▸** a narrow, often winding path or road, especially between hedges or fences. **2. voie ▸** a division of a road for a single line of traffic going in one direction. **3. voie, couloir ▸** any narrow path or way : *In a race, the runners must stay in their own lanes.* **4. piste de jeu ▸** in bowling, the long strip of floor down which the ball is rolled. SYN: path, road, alley, pass, aisle.

lan-guage [LANG-gwij] NOUN, languages. **1. langue, langage ▸** spoken or written words; human speech. People use language to communicate thoughts and feelings. **2. langue ▸** the particular system of words or gestures used in a country or by a large group of people : *the French language; sign language.* **3. langage, langue ▸** the words used in a subject or activity : *the language of science.* **Note.** A way of expressing thoughts and feelings without using words is called body language. SYN: speech, words, talk, tongue. ⬙ p. 1168.

lan-tern [LAN-turn] NOUN, lanterns. **lanterne ▸** a covering or container for holding a light, usually with a handle and glass sides or openings through which the light can shine.

lap[1] [lap] NOUN, laps. **genoux ▸** the front part of the body from the waist to the knees of a person who is sitting.

lap[2] VERB, lapped, lapping. **1. chevaucher, recouvrir ▸** to place something so that it lies partly over something else; overlap. **2. enrouler ▸** to wind or wrap around : *She lapped herself in a blanket.* **3. doubler ▸** to get ahead in a race by one full lap. ▲ NOUN, laps. **1. tour (de piste) ▸** the entire length of something, or the entire distance around : *They ran three laps around the track.* **2. étape ▸** a stage of a journey or process : *The last lap of the hike was the hardest.*

lap[3] VERB, lapped, lapping. **1. laper ▸** to drink by licking up with the tongue : *The cat lapped up every last drop of cream.* **2. clapoter ▸** to splash or move against gently : *The waves lapped against the boat.*

lap-top [LAP-top] NOUN, laptops. **microordinateur portable ▸** a small, lightweight portable computer. Laptops usually have a flat screen and a battery power source.

lard [lard] NOUN. **saindoux ▸** a greasy white substance made from the fat of pigs. Lard is used in cooking.

large [larj] ADJECTIVE, larger, largest. **grand (grande), gros (grosse) ▸** more than the usual size, amount, or number; big : *Toronto is a large city.* SYN: big, great, huge, vast, immense, massive.

at large 1. libre, en liberté ▸ on the loose; escaped; free : *Three wolves are at large somewhere in the city.* **2. en général ▸** as a whole : *This magazine is sent only to doctors and is not sold to the public at large.*

large-ly [LARJ-lee] ADVERB. **majoritairement ▸** to a great amount or extent; mostly; mainly : *The central part of Australia is largely desert.*

lar-i-at [LAIR-ee-ut]. **lasso ▸** See lasso.

lark[1] [lark] NOUN, larks. **alouette ▸** a small, grey-brown bird that sings while flying. The skylark is common in Europe; the horned lark is found in North America.

lark[2] NOUN, larks. **farce, blague, plaisanterie ▸** something done for fun or amusement : *Tomas had a lark at the party.* SYN: fun, joke, prank, trick, adventure, fling.

lar-va [LAR-vuh] NOUN, larvas or larvae [LAR-vy *or* LAR-vee]. **1. larve ▸** an early stage of an insect's life cycle, when it has just been hatched and looks like a worm. A caterpillar is the larva of a butterfly or moth. **2. larve ▸** an early stage of development of a fish or water animal that looks different from its adult form. A tadpole is the larva of a frog or toad.

lar·ynx [LAIR-inks] NOUN, larynxes. **larynx ▶** the upper part of the throat, between the tongue and the windpipe. A person's voice is produced in the larynx by means of the vocal cords. **Note.** Laryngitis is a painful swelling of the larynx, often causing a faint, hoarse voice.

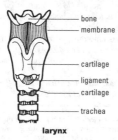

bone
membrane
cartilage
ligament
cartilage
trachea

larynx

la·ser [LAY-zur] NOUN, lasers. **laser ▶** a device that produces a very narrow and very powerful beam of light that travels in a single direction. Laser beams can melt or cut metal and are also used to send long-distance telephone, radio, and TV signals, to perform surgical operations, and to print information from a computer. **Note.** The word *laser* started out as an acronym for *light amplification by stimulated emission of radiation.* ☞ **p. 541.**

lash¹ [lash] NOUN, lashes. **1. a. fouet, lanière, cravache ▶** a whip. **b. coup de fouet ▶** a stroke or blow given with a whip. **2. cil ▶** a hair growing from the edge of the eyelid; an eyelash. ▲ VERB, lashed, lashing. **1. fouetter, flageller ▶** to strike with or as if with a whip: *The driving rain and sleet lashed his face.* **2. fouetter, cingler ▶** to move or strike suddenly: *The dragon lashed at the knight with its tail.*

lash² [lash] VERB, lashed, lashing. **attacher ▶** to tie with a cord or rope: *We lash branches together to make a frame.*

lass [las] NOUN, lasses. **fille, jeune fille ▶** a girl or young woman.

las·so [la-SOO *or* LAS-oh] NOUN, lassos *or* lassoes. **lasso ▶** a long rope with a loop at one end that can be tightened, used for catching cattle and horses: *The rider twirled her lasso and roped the calf.* **Note.** Also called a lariat. ▲ VERB, lassoed, lassoing. **prendre au lasso ▶** to rope with a lasso: *to lasso a steer.*

last¹ [last] ADJECTIVE. **1. dernier (-ière) ▶** coming after all others; at the end: *We missed the last bus home.* **2. dernier (-ière), récent (-ente) ▶** most recent: *I saw a great movie on television last night.* **3. dernier (-ière) ▶** not likely: *Rina was the last person I expected to meet at the art gallery.* ▲ ADVERB. **1. en dernier ▶** at the end: *The letter "z" comes last in the alphabet.* **2. à la fin ▶** most recently: *Where did you last see your keys?* ▲ NOUN. **1. le (la) dernier (-ière) ▶** after all others: *Ewan was the last in line at the movies.* **2. le (la) fin ▶** the end: *We haven't heard the last of this problem.* SYN: final, end, cling, ultimate, latest, concluding.

at last enfin, finalement ▶ after a long time; finally.

the last straw une chose de trop, la goutte qui fait déborder le vase ▶ causes an outburst: *When the company cancelled her vacation time, it was the last straw*

last² VERB, lasted, lasting. **1. durer, se maintenir ▶** to go for a time; continue; not end: *The storm lasted all day.* **2. durer ▶** to remain in use or in good condition: *That cedar fence should last for several years.* SYN: stay, remain, endure, persist.

last³ NOUN, lasts. **forme à chaussure ▶** a block or form shaped like a person's foot, used in making or repairing shoes.

stick to (one's) **last s'occuper de ses affaires ▶** pay attention to one's own work; mind one's own business.

latch [lach] NOUN, latches. **loquet ▶** a lock or catch used to fasten a window, door, or gate. It usually has a bar of metal or wood that fits into a notch. ▲ VERB, latched, latching. **verrouiller ▶** to fasten a door or gate with a latch.

late [late] ADJECTIVE, later, latest. **1. en retard, retardé (-ée) ▶** coming after the expected or usual time: *We had a late lunch.* **2. tard, vers la fin de ▶** occurring near the end of some period of time: *Cars were first used in the late 1800s.* **3. récent (-ente) ▶** not long past; recent: *Donna always wears the latest style in clothing.* **4. le (la) regretté (-ée), défunt (-unte), feu (feue) ▶** dead: *She keeps a picture of her late husband on the table.* ▲ ADVERB. **1. en retard ▶** after the proper or expected time: *Karin arrived late.* **2. tard ▶** toward the end of a certain time: *Our maple tree loses its leaves late in the fall.* SYN: slow, delayed, tardy, behind schedule.

late·ly [LATE-lee] ADVERB. **récemment, dernièrement ▶** not long ago; recently: *Have you seen any good movies lately?*

lat·er·al [LAT-er-ul] ADJECTIVE. **latéral (-ale, -aux) ▶** coming from, going to, or having to do with the side: *a lateral pass in football.* ■ **laterally,** ADVERB. **▶** latéralement.

lathe [layth] NOUN, lathes. **tour ▶** a machine used for holding and spinning a piece of wood or metal while a cutting tool shapes it.

lath·er [LATH-ur] NOUN, lathers. **1. mousse ▶** a thick white foam made by rapidly mixing soap and water. **2. écume ▶** a foam caused by heavy sweating, especially on a horse. ▲ VERB, lathered, lathering. **savonner, mousser ▸** to make or cover with a lather.

Lat-in [LAT-un] NOUN. 1. **latin ▸** the language that was spoken in ancient Rome and the Roman Empire. 2. (plural, Latins) **Latin (-ine) ▸** a person who speaks one of the languages that come from Latin, such as Italian, French, Spanish, or Portuguese. 3. (plural, Latins) **Latino-Américain (-aine) ▸** a person born in or coming from Latin America. **Note.** Also called a Latin-American or a Latino. ▲ ADJECTIVE. 1. **latin (-ine) ▸** having to do with the Latin language. 2. (also Latin-American or Latino) **latino-américain (-aine) ▸** having to do with Latin America.

lat-i-tude [LAT-ih-TOOD] NOUN, latitudes. 1. **latitude ▸** the distance north or south of the equator. Latitude is measured in degrees; each degree represents about 111 kilometres. On a map, latitude is shown by lines that run east and west, parallel to the equator. 2. **latitude, liberté ▸** freedom of action or expression : *Our teacher gives us a lot of latitude in choosing report topics.* **Note.** See also longitude. ✎ **p. 336.**

lat-ter [LAT-ur] ADJECTIVE. 1. **deuxième, dernier (-ière) ▸** the second of two things just named or mentioned. 2. **deuxième, dernier (-ière) ▸** nearer the end; later : *The student council will meet in the latter part of the month.*

laugh [laf] VERB, laughed, laughing. **rire, rigoler ▸** to make the sounds and movements of the face that show one is happy or finds something funny. ▲ NOUN, laughs. **rire ▸** the act or sound of laughing. **Note.** The act or sound of laughing is also called laughter. ▪ **laughable,** ADJECTIVE. ▸ **risible, ridicule, comique.** amusing; ridiculous; causing laughter. SYN: chuckle, giggle, howl, roar, guffaw.

no laughing matter pas de quoi rire ▸ something that is serious.

launch¹ [lonch] VERB, launched, launching. 1. **lancer, mettre à l'eau ▸** to put a boat or ship into the water. 2. **lancer ▸** to send an aircraft, a spacecraft, or another vehicle into the air. 3. **se lancer ▸** to start out on something, as if setting out in a ship : *With a deep breath, Anita launched into her speech.* ▲ NOUN, launches. **lancement ▸** the act of launching : *Karly watched the launch of the space shuttle on TV.* **Note.** A launching pad or launch pad is a platform or structure from which rockets and missiles are launched into the air.

launch² NOUN, launches. **chaloupe, bateau (-eaux) de plaisance ▸** an open motorboat, especially one used for short pleasure trips.

laun-dry [LON-dree] NOUN. 1. (plural, laundries) **buanderie, blanchisserie ▸** a place or business where clothes and other fabrics are washed.

✎ p. 336.

✐ Writing Tips

Latitude and Longitude
Latitude and *longitude* are imaginary lines that circle the earth. Latitude lines run from the North Pole to the South Pole. Longitude lines run east and west around the world, parallel to the equator. You can see latitude and longitude lines marked in atlases, on maps, and on globes.

These lines are used by people such as geographers and navigators for directions or to show the location of a place in the world.

Ottawa is located at a latitude of 45°25'N and a longitude of 75°42'E.

---

2. **lessive ▸** clothes that have just been washed or that need to be washed. **Note.** To wash or to wash and iron clothes is to launder them.

lau-rel [LOR-ul] NOUN, laurels. 1. **laurier ▸** an evergreen shrub that has stiff, fragrant leaves. In ancient times, laurel wreaths were given to people as a sign of victory in a battle or contest. 2. **laurels. lauriers ▸** honour or fame.

rest on (one's) **laurels dormir sur ses lauriers ▸** to be satisfied with what one has already done.

la-va [LA-vuh or LAH-vuh] NOUN. 1. **lave ▸** the red-hot melted rock that flows out of a volcano when it erupts. 2. **lave ▸** the hardened rock that forms from the cooling of this melted rock.

lav-en-der [LAV-un-dur] NOUN, lavenders. 1. **lavande ▸** a small plant related to mint. It has light-purple flowers and a strong, sweet smell. 2. **lavande ▸** a light purple colour.

law [lah] NOUN, laws. 1. **loi ▸** a rule made and enforced by the government of a country, state, province, or city, to be followed by the people who live there : *It is a law that you must have a licence to drive.* **Note.** A person who helps to make the laws of a country is a lawmaker. 2. **loi, législation ▸** a system or set of these rules : *provincial law; federal law.* 3. **droit ▸** the study of such a set of rules; the profession of a lawyer or a judge. 4. **loi, principe ▸** a statement in science or mathematics about something that happens under certain conditions : *the law of gravity.* 5. **loi ▸** any similar statement about what is expected to happen in a certain situation : *"Murphy's Law" says that "anything that can go wrong will."* SYN: rule, regulation, act, decree, proclamation.

law-ful [LAH-FUL] ADJECTIVE. **légal (-ale, -aux), légitime ▸** allowed or recognized by law; legal. ▪ **lawfully,** ADVERB. ▸ **légalement, légitimement.**

✐ Writing Tips

Lay vs. Lie

The verbs **lay** *and* **lie** *are often confusing for writers. The verb "to lay" means "to put or place," and "to lie" means "to rest or recline."*

Dad asked Sandy to lay his tools on the workbench.

Mom said we could lie in her bed.

Adding to the confusion is the fact that **lay** *is both a present form of "to lay" and a past form of "to lie."*

I always lay my clothes on my bed before I get dressed.

Last night, I lay down on the couch after dinner.

law·less [LAH-lis] ADJECTIVE. **sans loi** ▸ not ruled or controlled by laws : *the lawless gold-rush towns in the Yukon.*

lawn [lon] NOUN, lawns. **pelouse** ▸ an area around a house or building that is planted with grass.

lawn mower [MOH-ur] **tondeuse à gazon** ▸ a machine with revolving blades used to cut grass.

law·suit [LAH-SOOT] NOUN, lawsuits. **procès, action judiciaire** ▸ a case in a court of law that asks the court to decide a claim or question between two sides : *The lawsuit claimed that the author had copied parts of his best-selling novel from someone else's book.*

law·yer [LAH-yur or LOY-yur] NOUN, lawyers. **avocat (-ate)** ▸ a person who is trained and licensed to give people advice about the law and to represent them in court.

lay¹ [lay] VERB, laid, laying. **1. poser, placer, mettre** ▸ to place or set : *Just lay the package on that table.* **2. poser** ▸ to put down and attach in place : *to lay tiles for a kitchen floor.* **3. pondre** ▸ to produce an egg or eggs. SYN: put, place, set, rest, deposit. ✐ p. 337.

lay off licencier, congédier ▸ to dismiss from a job : *The company had to lay off 60 workers because business was slow.* **Note.** Also used as a NOUN: *Our town has really suffered from all the layoffs this spring.*

lay² VERB. **s'allonger, être couché (-ée), se trouver sur** ▸ a past form of lie¹: *The over-turned car lay on its left side.*

lay·er [LAY-ur] NOUN, layers. **1. couche** ▸ a single thickness or level of something : *A layer cake has two or more layers with filling between them.* **2. poseur (-euse)** ▸ a person or thing that lays : *a bricklayer.*

la·zy [LAY-zee] ADJECTIVE, lazier, laziest. **1. paresseux (-euse), fainéant (-ante)** ▸ not liking to work or be active; unwilling to do things : *The lazy dog slept all day.* **2. indolent (-ente)** ▸ causing a lazy feeling : *a lazy summer day.* **3. nonchalant (-ante)** ▸ slow-moving : *a lazy stream.* ■ **lazily,** ADVERB. ▸ **paresseusement, nonchalamment.** ■ **laziness,** NOUN. ▸ **paresse, nonchalance, indolence, fainéantise.** the condition of being lazy. SYN: inactive, lax, slothful.

lead¹ [leed] VERB, led, leading. **1. mener, conduire, guider** ▸ to show the way; go along before or with : *Jordan led the way through the forest.* **2. mener** ▸ to be first, or to be ahead of others : *Our team leads the other teams in wins.* **3. conduire, mener** ▸ to go in a certain direction; be a way or road to : *The steps lead to the basement.* **4. diriger, conduire** ▸ to be in charge of; direct or control : *A conductor leads an orchestra.* ▲ NOUN, leads. **1. avance** ▸ the fact of being ahead, or the amount that one is ahead : *The Expos have a three-game lead.* **2. tête** ▸ the position of guiding or giving direction : *in the lead.* **3. rôle principal (-aux), premier rôle** ▸ the main or most important part in a play, film, or other performance : *She played the lead in* Harriet the Spy. **4. chapeau (-eaux), attaque, introduction, article d'appel** ▸ the opening paragraph in a newspaper article. **5. piste** ▸ a clue : *He followed many leads to help solve the mystery.* SYN: guide, steer, escort, head, direct, command.

lead² [led] NOUN, leads. **1. plomb** ▸ a soft, heavy grey metal that is easily bent or shaped. Lead is a chemical element and one of the oldest known metals. **2. mine de plomb** ▸ the thin strip in the middle of a pencil that makes marks; now, it is made of graphite, a mineral that looks like lead.

lead·er [LEE-dur] NOUN, leaders. **chef, dirigeant (-ante), meneur (-euse), leader** ▸ someone or something that leads, or who is well able to lead : *a natural leader.* **Note.** The fact or quality of being a leader is leadership. SYN: chief, head, director, conductor, captain.

leaf [leef] NOUN, leaves. **1. feuille** ▸ one of the thin, flat green parts growing from a stem or branch on trees, bushes, flowers, grass, and other plants. **2. feuille, page** ▸ a sheet of paper, usually from a book or magazine; a page : *You can take pages out of a loose-leaf notebook.* **3. feuille** ▸ a very thin sheet of metal, especially gold. **4. rallonge** ▸ an extra piece that is inserted into or folded out from a table to make it larger. ▲ VERB, leafed, leafing. **1. feuiller** ▸ of a plant, to produce or grow leaves. **2. feuilleter** ▸ to quickly glance at and turn pages : *to leaf through a magazine.* ■ **leafy,** ADJECTIVE, leafier, leafiest. ▸ **feuillu (-ue).** covered with or having many leaves : *leafy vegetables.* ✐ p. 1097. ☞ p. 249, 253.

leaf-let [LEEF-lit] NOUN, leaflets. **prospectus, tract, brochure, dépliant ▸** a small booklet or sheet of paper : *I received a leaflet about the new exhibit at the art gallery.*

league[1] [leeg] NOUN, leagues. **1. ligue ▸** a group of sports teams that play against each other : *a bowling league; a hockey league.* **2. ligue, société, association ▸** a group of people, organizations, or countries working together for a common purpose : *The League of Nations was an earlier form of the United Nations.* SYN : union, association, group, alliance, federation.

in league liguer, être en coalition, s'unir contre ▸ united : *They are in league against us.*

league[2] NOUN, leagues. **lieue ▸** an old measure of distance equal to about 5 kilometres.

leak [leek] NOUN, leaks. **1. fuite, infiltration ▸** a crack or hole that allows something to pass through by accident. **Note.** Something that is leakproof will not leak. **2. fuite ▸** information that was supposed to be secret, but that somehow becomes known : *There was a leak, and information got to the press.* ▲ VERB, leaked, leaking. **fuir, avoir une fuite ▸** to cause or have a leak; to pass through a hole or gap : *The boat leaks.* **2. divulguer, (s') ébruiter ▸** make or become known by accident or by a deliberate break in secrecy : *The information leaked out.* ▪ **leaky,** ADJECTIVE. ▸ **fuyant (-ante), percé (-ée).** having a leak or leaks : *a leaky faucet.*

lean[1] [leen] VERB, leaned or leant, leaning. **1. pencher, incliner ▸** to go at an angle; not be straight up and down. **2. (s') appuyer ▸** to rest against someone or something : *Erika leaned back in her chair.* **3. compter sur ▸** to count on for support; rely or depend : *to lean on a friend during a difficult time.* **4. favoriser, avoir un penchant pour, préférer ▸** to have a tendency toward; favour : *Kai's taste leans toward mystery stories.* ▲ NOUN. **inclinaison, penchant ▸** the act or fact of leaning : *The tree has a lean to the right.* SYN : bend, slant, slope, incline, tilt.

lean[2] ADJECTIVE, leaner, leanest. **1. maigre ▸** having very little fat : *a tall, lean basketball player.* **2. maigre, mauvais (-aise), rare ▸** not producing or having enough; scarce : *a lean harvest.* SYN : thin, spare, slight, slim, slender, scant.

leap [leep] VERB, leaped or leapt, leaping. **1. bondir, sauter ▸** to make a jump or spring, especially a high, sudden jump : *Some fish leap right out of the water.* **2. se précipiter ▸** to make a sudden or eager move like this : *Aaron leaped to help the crying child.* **3.** to happen or appear suddenly : *A new idea leaped to mind.* ▲ NOUN, leaps. **saut, bond, jet ▸** the act of leaping. SYN : jump, spring, vault, hop, hurdle, plunge, dive.

learn [lurn] VERB, learned or learnt, learning. **1. apprendre ▸** to come to know something that one did not know before, or be able to do something that one could not do before : *to learn to read.* **2. apprendre ▸** to fix in the mind; memorize : *The actor has to learn his lines for the play.* **3. apprendre ▸** to come to know or realize; find out : *At the ticket office, we learned that the tickets were sold out.* ▪ **learned** [LUR-nid], ADJECTIVE. ▸ **savant (-ante), éduqué (-ée).** having or showing much education or knowledge : *a learned scholar.* ▪ **learner,** NOUN. ▸ **apprenant (-ante), débutant (-ante), apprenti (-ie), élève.**

learn-ing [LUR-ning] NOUN. **apprentissage ▸** the act or process of gaining knowledge, or the knowledge and skill that comes from this : *Colleges and universities are called institutions of higher learning.* **Note.** A learning disability is a term used to describe one of various kinds of problems that can cause a person to have difficulty learning things.

learnt [lernt] VERB. **apprendre ▸** a past form of learn.

lease [lees] NOUN, leases. **bail (baux) ▸** a written agreement stating how long a property will be rented and how much money will be paid for it : *I just signed the lease for my apartment.* ▲ VERB, leased, leasing. **louer ▸** to rent by means of a lease : *Many people lease cars rather than buy them.* SYN : rent, hire, let, charter.

least [leest] ADJECTIVE. **plus petit (-ite) ▸** the smallest : *A penny is worth the least amount of any Canadian coin.* ▲ ADVERB. **moins ▸** to the smallest amount or degree : *I liked that book least of all.* ▲ NOUN. **le (la) moins, le (la) dernier (-ière) ▸** the smallest in size or importance : *The job of cleaning my room is the least of my worries.* SYN : slightest, tiniest, fewest, smallest, minimum.

at least a. au moins ▸ not less than : *She tries to get at least eight hours' sleep a night.* **b. au moins, du moins ▸** in any case; at any rate : *We lost, but at least it was a close game.*

leath-er [LETH-ur] NOUN, leathers. **cuir ▸** a material made from the skin of an animal. Leather is used to make shoes, belts, gloves, purses, jackets, and many other things. Most leather comes from cattle, though other animals are also used. ▪ **leathery,** ADJECTIVE. ▸ **tanné (-ée).**

leave[1] [leev] VERB, left, leaving. **1. quitter, partir ▸** to go away from : *Our train leaves in 10 minutes.* **2. quitter ▸** to withdraw from; quit : *to leave the country.* **3. laisser ▸** to cause to be or stay in a certain place : *to leave food on your plate.* **4. laisser ▸** to cause to be or stay in the same condition : *I left the door open.* **5. laisser ▸** to give to someone else to do or use : *He left the talking to me.* SYN : go away, depart, exit, retreat, quit, abandon.

✎ Writing Tips

Legends

A **legend** *is a tale that tells of the deeds and adventures of a heroic figure, such as Cleopatra, Robin Hood, Joan of Arc, or King Arthur.*

• *Often a legend is based on a real figure, and his or her deeds and adventures are exaggerated. As the tale is told from one generation to another, this hero will become "larger than life." Over time, the exaggerated figure takes over, and the real figure disappears.*

• *If you're writing a legend, remember to include realistic details as well as exaggerating the heroic deeds and adventures.*

leave² NOUN, leaves. **1. autorisation, permission** ▸ official permission to be absent from work, school, or other duty : *My cousin is home on a month's leave from the armed forces.* **2. autorisation, permission** ▸ permission to do something.

leaves [leevs] NOUN. **1. feuilles** ▸ the plural of leaf. **2. permissions** ▸ the plural of leave².

lec·ture [LEK-chur] NOUN, lectures. **1. conférence, cours** ▸ a prepared speech or talk given to an audience, especially as part of a course of study. **2. sermon, réprimande** ▸ a serious talk that warns or scolds someone : *Jonah got a lecture about leaving his clothes on the floor.* ▲ VERB, lectured, lecturing. **donner un cours, prononcer une conférence** ▸ to give a lecture. ■ **lecturer,** NOUN. ▸ **conférencier (-ière), professeur (-eure).** SYN: speech, address, talk, discourse, sermon.

led [led] VERB. **diriger, guider** ▸ a past form of lead¹.

ledge [lej] NOUN, ledges. **1. rebord, corniche** ▸ a narrow shelf that sticks out from a wall : *a window ledge.* **2. corniche, crête** ▸ a flat, narrow place like this on the side of a cliff or mountain. SYN: shelf, ridge, edge, rim.

ledg·er [LEJ-ur] NOUN, ledgers. **grand livre** ▸ a book used by a business to keep track of its money.

leech [leech] NOUN, leeches. **sangsue** ▸ a worm that lives in water and damp soil and sucks the blood of other animals for food.

leek [leek] NOUN, leeks. **poireau (-eaux)** ▸ a vegetable related to the onion that has long, thick green leaves and a narrow white bulb.

left¹ [left] NOUN, lefts. **1. gauche** ▸ the opposite of right; the left direction or side. **2. gauche** ▸ a political belief or party supporting social equality and liberal policies. Often somewhat radical. ▲ ADJECTIVE. **gauche** ▸ on or for the left side : *a left shoe.* ▲ ADVERB. **à gauche** ▸ to the left : *to turn left.*

left² VERB. **laisser, quitter** ▸ a past form of leave¹.

left·o·ver [LEFT-oh-vur] NOUN, leftovers. **reste, surplus** ▸ something that remains or is left, such as food after a meal. ▲ ADJECTIVE: *leftover meat.*

leg [leg] NOUN, legs. **1. jambe, patte** ▸ one of the parts of the body that supports a person or animal while standing or walking. **2. jambe** ▸ the part of a piece of clothing that covers the leg. **3. pied** ▸ something that is shaped or used like a leg : *the leg of a table.* **4. étape, relais** ▸ one part or stage of a trip or activity : *Bobbie ran the first leg of the relay race.* 📄 p. 1002.

not having a leg to stand on être sans excuse, être sans argument valable ▸ not having any reason, excuse, or defence.

shake a leg a. **se dépêcher** ▸ hurry up. b. **danser** ▸ dance.

leg·a·cy [LEG-uh-see] NOUN, legacies. **1. legs, héritage** ▸ money or other property left to someone in the will of a person who has died. **2. héritage, hérédité** ▸ something that has been handed down from someone from the past : *His love of jokes is a legacy from his grandmother.*

le·gal [LEE-gul] ADJECTIVE. **1. légal (-ale, -aux)** ▸ having to do with the law : *You ask a lawyer for legal advice.* **2. légal (-ale, -aux), autorisé (-ée), permis (-ise)** ▸ according to law; allowed by law : *a legal parking space.* SYN: lawful, authorized, rightful, permitted.

leg·end [LEJ-und] NOUN, legends. **1. légende** ▸ a story passed down by people over many years, usually based in some way on facts. Legends often tell about real or make-believe heroes such as Laura Secord or Robin Hood : *"No one knows exactly when Robin Hood lived. He is a figure from legend, not history."* (Sarah Hayes) **2. légende** ▸ words that explain a picture or map; caption : *Use the legend to help you read that map.* ✎ p. 339.

leg·end·ar·y [LEJ-un-DAIR-ee] ADJECTIVE. **légendaire** ▸ having to do with legends : *the legendary knights of King Arthur's Round Table.*

leg·i·ble [LEJ-uh-bul] ADJECTIVE. **lisible, net (nette)** ▸ that can be read; easy to read : *legible handwriting; legible type.*

le·gion [LEE-jun] NOUN, legions. **1. légion** ▸ a large military unit of the ancient Roman army, made up of several thousand soldiers. **2. légion** ▸ any great military force. **3. légion, multitude** ▸ a very large number : *The singer*

legislate

has legions of fans. **4.** the Legion. **Légion**
▶ short for the Royal Canadian Legion.

leg·is·late [LEJ-iss-LATE] VERB, legislated, legis-
lating. **légiférer, promulguer une loi** ▶ to make or
pass a law or laws. **Note.** The act or fact of doing
this is legislation: *Parliament is considering legislation to create a new national park.*

leg·is·la·tive [LEJ-iss-LAY-tiv *or* LEG-iss-luh-tiv]
ADJECTIVE. **1. législatif (-ive)** ▶ having the power
to create and pass laws : *Parliament is the
legislative branch of the federal government.*
2. législatif (-ive) ▶ having to do with the making of laws. **Note.** The Legislative Assembly is
the group of representatives elected to the legislature in the provinces and the Yukon Territory.

leg·is·la·tor [LEJ-iss-LAY-tur] NOUN, legislators.
législateur (-trice) ▶ a person who makes laws;
someone who belongs to a group that makes
laws.

leg·is·la·ture [LEJ-iss-LAY-chur *or* LEJ-iss-luh-chur]
NOUN, legislatures. **corps législatif** ▶ a group of
people elected to create and pass laws for a
country, province, or state. Each Canadian
province has a legislature.

le·git·i·mate [luh-JIT-uh-mit] ADJECTIVE. **1. légitime** ▶ according to the law; legal : *The court
ruled that she had a legitimate claim to the
property.* **2. légitime, admissible, justifié (-ée)**
▶ according to what is right or allowed : *She
had a legitimate reason for missing school
today.* ■ **legitimately,** ADVERB. ▶ **légitimement,
équitablement.** SYN : lawful, rightful, allowed,
valid, just.

lei·sure [LEE-zhur *or* LEZH-ur] NOUN. **loisir** ▶ a condition or time of not having to work; free time to
do as one wishes : *When I have time for leisure,
I enjoy fishing.* — adjective: *leisure hours.*
■ **leisurely,** ADJECTIVE. ▶ **de loisir.** *They strolled
around the park at a leisurely pace.*
🖾 p. 1165.

lem·on [LEM-un] NOUN, lemons. **1. citron** ▶ a
juicy yellow fruit that has a sour taste. Lemons
grow on trees in warm climates and are related
to grapefruits, oranges, and limes. **Note.** Lemonade is a drink made of lemon juice, sugar, and
water. **2. (jaune) citron** ▶ a bright yellow colour
like that of a lemon. **3.** *Informal.* **citron** ▶ a car
or other machine that is badly made or has
many things wrong with it.

lend [lend] VERB, lent, lending. **1. prêter** ▶ to let
someone have or use something for a while :
Uncle Dave lent us his car. **2. prêter** ▶ to give
someone money that must be paid back by a
stated time, usually with interest; to make a
loan : *The bank will lend us the money.*
3. donner ▶ to give or add; provide : *The fireworks over the lake will lend excitement to
that concert.* ■ **lender,** NOUN. ▶ **prêteur (-euse).**
someone who lends.

**lend a hand donner un coup de main, prêter
assistance, prêter main-forte, aider** ▶ help : *If
everyone lends a hand, we'll have this tent up
in no time.*

length [length] NOUN, lengths. **1. longueur**
▶ how long a thing is from one end to the other
end : *The length of the boat is 16 metres.*
2. durée ▶ the amount of time from beginning
to end; the time something lasts : *The movie
was more than two hours in length.* **3. longueur** ▶ a piece of something that is long : *a
length of rope.* **4. longueur** ▶ the fact or condition of being long : *I read the book quickly, in
spite of its length.* ■ **lengthy,** ADJECTIVE. ▶ **trop
long (longue), interminable.** long; too long.
SYN : span, measure, reach, stretch, distance.

length·en [LENGTH-un] VERB, lengthened,
lengthening. **allonger, rallonger, prolonger** ▶ to
make or become longer : *The tailor lengthened
Goran's pants. The days lengthened as spring
arrived.*

lens [lenz] NOUN, lenses. **1. lentille, verre** ▶ a
piece of glass or other material that is curved to
make light rays move apart or come together. A
lens can make objects look larger, clearer, or
closer. Lenses are used in cameras, eyeglasses,
telescopes and so on. **2. cristallin** ▶ the clear,
colourless part of the eye that focuses light rays
onto the retina.

lent [lent] VERB. **prêter** ▶ a past form of lend:
*Crystal lent her book to Juan. He had lent his
book to Pat.*

leop·ard [LEP-urd] NOUN, leopards. **léopard** ▶ a
large wild cat that lives in Africa and Asia. Most
leopards have a yellowish coat with black spots,
but a few (called **panthers**) are all black.

le·o·tard [LEE-uh-TARD] NOUN, leotards. **1. maillot, léotard** ▶ a thin one-piece garment that
stretches to fit tightly over the body from the
shoulders to the hips, worn for dancing or exercising. **2. collant** ▶ tights.

less [les] ADJECTIVE. **moins (de), plus petit (-ite)
que** ▶ not as great an amount; not as much :
*He's been trying to use less salt and butter on
food.* ▲ ADVERB. **moins** ▶ a smaller amount : *She
eats less.* ▲ PREPOSITION. **moins** ▶ minus; without :
Five less three equals two. ▲ NOUN. **moins** ▶ a
smaller amount or part : *I want more, not less.*
SYN : fewer, smaller, reduced. ✐ p. 223.

less·en [LES-un] VERB, lessened, lessening.
diminuer, réduire, atténuer ▶ to make or
become less.

less·er [LES-ur] ADJECTIVE. **moindre** ▶ smaller in
size or amount.

les·son [LES-un] NOUN, lessons. **1. cours, leçon**
▶ something to be learned in school; an activity
that is assigned or taught : *a math lesson.*
2. cours, leçon ▶ any form of study or instruction for the purpose of learning something or
gaining a skill : *swimming lessons.* **3. leçon**

▸ an experience or event in life that gives knowledge or understanding : *Jeff's accident taught him a lesson; he drives more carefully now.*

let [let] VERB, let, letting. **1. permettre, faire en sorte que** ▸ to cause to happen. **2. laisser** ▸ to allow or permit : *Our teacher let us choose our own stories.* **3. permettre, autoriser** ▸ to allow to pass, go, or come : *to let a dog in; to let air out of a balloon.* SYN: allow, permit, authorize, enable, grant. 📖 **p. 341.**

let-ter [LET-ur] NOUN, letters. **1. lettre** ▸ a mark or symbol that stands for a speech sound and is used to spell words; one part of the alphabet. **2. lettre** ▸ a written message : *I received a letter from my cousin.* ▲ VERB, lettered, lettering. **faire du lettrage, marquer avec des lettres, graver des lettres** ▸ to mark with letters : *Kobi lettered "Stay Out" in red on her door.*

let-tuce [LET-us] NOUN, lettuces. **laitue** ▸ a plant with large green leaves. Several different kinds of lettuce are eaten in salads and in sandwiches.

lev-ee [LEV-ee] NOUN, levees. **levée, digue** ▸ a wall built up along a river bank to keep the water from overflowing during a flood.

lev-el [LEV-ul] ADJECTIVE. **1. plat (plate), ras (rase)** ▸ having a flat surface : *to build a house on level ground.* **2. égal (-ale, -aux)** ▸ at the same height or position · *The water rose until it was level with the dock.* **3. assuré (-ée), égal (-ale, -aux)** ▸ steady; even : *to speak in a level tone of voice.* ▲ NOUN, levels. **1. niveau (-eaux)** ▸ something that is level, such as the top of a hill or one floor of a building. **2. niveau (-eaux), hauteur** ▸ the height of something : *The water is at its highest level in weeks.* **3. niveau (-eaux)** ▸ the position of someone or something in a rank or scale; a grade : *He plays piano at a professional level.* ▲ VERB, levelled, levelling. (also leveled, leveling) **1. niveler, aplanir, égaliser** ▸ to make level : *They levelled the ground to make a soccer field.* **2. raser** ▸ to knock down to the ground; tear down : *The wrecking crew levelled the old building.* **3.** *Informal.* **parler franchement** ▸ to be honest : *I'm going to level with you.*

lev-er [LEEV-ur or LEV-ur] NOUN, levers. **1. levier** ▸ a rod or bar used to lift things or to pry things open. To lift something, a lever rests on a fixed object called a fulcrum, and is pushed down on one end to raise the weight at the other end.

2. levier, manette ▸ a rod or bar that is moved to control or operate a machine : *a gearshift lever or a parking-brake lever in a car.*

lev-y [LEV-ee] VERB, levied, levying. **prélever, percevoir** ▸ to order to be paid : *to levy a tax; to levy a fine.*

li-a-bil-i-ty [LY-uh-BIL-uh-tee] NOUN, liabilities. **1. responsabilité** ▸ the fact of being held responsible for some wrong or crime. **2. liabilities. dettes** ▸ all the money that a person or business owes; debts. **3. désavantage, handicap** ▸ something that hinders or holds back; a disadvantage : *The car's lack of power is a real liability on these hilly roads.*

li-a-ble [LY-uh-bul] ADJECTIVE. **1. tenu (-ue)** ▸ responsible by law; legally bound to pay : *If you break something in a store, you are liable for it.* **2. susceptible, sujet (-ette) à, exposé (-ée)** ▸ likely : *You're liable to get sick after getting so cold and wet.*

li-ar [LY-ur] NOUN, liars. **menteur (-euse)** ▸ a person who says things that are not true.

lib-er-al [LIB-ur-ul] ADJECTIVE. **1. libéral (-ale, -aux), large** ▸ not exact or strict : *A liberal translation of the French phrase "c'est la vie" is "that's the way it goes."* **2. généreux (-euse)** ▸ generous : *Mr. Stein is a liberal supporter of the museum.* **3. tolérant (-ante), libéral (-ale, -aux)** ▸ free from narrow ideas; broad-minded : *She is a liberal thinker.* **4. libéral (-ale, -aux)** ▸ wanting to change something to improve it; in favour of change. **Note.** In politics, people who are liberal believe that the government should create laws and programs that solve social problems. ▲ NOUN, liberals. **1. libéral (-ale, -aux)** ▸ a person who is liberal, especially in politics. **2.** Liberal. **Libéral (-aux)** ▸ a member of the Liberal Party. ■ **liberally,** ADVERB. ▸ **libéralement, généreusement, largement.**

Liberal Party le Parti Libéral ▸ one of the major political parties in Canada.

lib-er-ate [LIB-uh-RATE] VERB, liberated, liberating. **libérer, dégager** ▸ to set free; release : *to liberate slaves.* ■ **liberator,** NOUN. ▸ **libérateur (-trice).** Something or someone who sets others free. **Note.** The act of liberating or the fact of being liberated is liberation.

lib-er-ty [LIB-ur-tee] NOUN, liberties. **1. liberté** ▸ freedom to act, speak, and think as one wishes : *People have the right to liberty of*

📝 **Word Builder**

Let down means to lower, but it can also mean to disappoint : *I let down my parents when I didn't come home on time.* **Let on** often means to allow to be known : *He didn't let on that he knew Surjit had won the essay contest.* **Let up** means to pause or stop : *The runner let up near the finish line and another runner passed her.* **Let loose** can mean to free or not to hold back : *Inez let loose all her opinions on why Prince Edward Island is the prettiest province in Canada.*

speech and action. **2.** (also independence) **indépendance, liberté ▸** freedom from the control or rules of others : *Iceland gained its liberty from Denmark in 1944.*

li·brar·i·an [ly-BRAIR-ee-un] NOUN, librarians. **bibliothécaire ▸** someone who is in charge of a library, or someone trained to work in a library.

li·brar·y [LY-brair-ee] NOUN, libraries. **1. bibliothèque ▸** a room or building where a large collection of books is kept for public or general use. Public libraries also have magazines, newspapers, CDs, records, films, videotapes, computerized databases, and so on. **2. bibliothèque ▸** a collection of books in a person's home. **3. collection ▸** any large collection of films, photos, records, or the like. ⌨ **p. 1050.**

li·cence [LY-sunce] NOUN, licences. (sometimes license) **1. autorisation, licence ▸** legal permission to do or own something : *People need a licence to drive a car, get married, or operate a business.* **2. permis ▸** the card, paper, or other document that gives proof of this permission. **3. licence, débauche, libertinage ▸** freedom that is taken too far; too much freedom.

li·cense [LY-sunce] VERB, licensed, licensing. **autoriser, donner une licence ▸** to give a licence to a person; to give someone permission : *The province licenses people who want to drive a car or truck.*

lick [lik] VERB, licked, licking. **1. lécher ▸** to pass the tongue over. **2. effleurer ▸** to pass over like a tongue : *The flames from the bonfire licked the wood.* **3.** *Informal.* **battre, donner une raclée ▸** to defeat : *I licked my older brother at chess.* ▲ NOUN, licks. **1. coup de langue ▸** a movement of the tongue over something : *The dog gave its paw a lick.* **2.** (also **salt lick**) **pain de sel ▸** a natural salt deposit that animals can lick. **3.** *Informal.* **brin, peu ▸** a small amount : *Get Jared to help you—he hasn't done a lick of work all day.*

lid [lid] NOUN, lids. **1. couvercle ▸** a movable cover for a container; a top : *the lid of a jar; the lid of a box.* **2. paupière ▸** the covering of skin over the eye; an eyelid.

lie¹ [ly] VERB, lay, lain, lying. **1. s'allonger ▸** to put one's body in a flat position on a surface : *to lie in bed.* **2. être couché (-ée), être étendu (-ue), se trouver ▸** to be or rest on a surface : *A spoon lay on the rug under the table.* **3. se trouver ▸** to be in a certain place or condition : *The small airport lies in the middle of farming country.* **4. se trouver, résider dans ▸** to be found; to be or exist : *The answer lies in research.* ✐ **p. 337.**

lie² NOUN, lies. **mensonge ▸** something that a person says, knowing that it is not true. ▲ VERB, lied, lying. **mentir ▸** to tell a lie. SYN: untruth, falsehood, invention.

lieu·ten·ant [lef-TEN-unt *or* loo-TEN-unt] NOUN, lieutenants. **1. lieutenant (-ante) ▸** a military or police officer ranking below a captain. **2. adjoint (-ointe) ▸** someone who acts on behalf of a higher authority; a deputy : *The president of the company sent her trusted lieutenant to check on the problems.* **Note.** A lieutenant-governor is the Queen's representative in each province. The position is held for five years.

life [life] NOUN, lives. **1. vie ▸** the condition of being alive. People, plants, and animals have life. Rocks and machines do not. Something that has life can develop young like itself and can grow. **2. vie ▸** the time between birth and death; one's lifetime. *My grandmother has had a long life.* **3. vie ▸** a living person : *Penicillin has saved many lives.* **4. vie ▸** living things as a group : *animal life; vegetable life.* **5. vie, durée ▸** the time during which something is in use or in effect : *the life of a car.* **6. vitalité, animation ▸** energy; spirit : *Noel is always the life of the party.* **7. vie ▸** a particular way of living : *an adventurous life; city life.* **8. vie, existence ▸** human existence in general : *Life is a precious gift.* ⌨ **p. 1078.**

as large as life a. grandeur nature ▸ as big as the living person or thing. **b. en personne, en chair et en os ▸** in person.

true to life réaliste, véritable ▸ as in real life.

life·boat [LIFE-bote] NOUN, lifeboats. **canot de sauvetage ▸** an open boat used for saving lives at sea. Lifeboats are carried on large boats or ships.

life·guard [LIFE-gard] NOUN, lifeguards. **surveillant (-ante) de baignade, sauveteur (-eure) ▸** a person who works at a pool or beach to rescue swimmers or protect them from danger.

life·like [LIFE-like] ADJECTIVE. **1. réaliste, vivant (-ante) ▸** looking as if alive : *a lifelike picture.* **2. ressemblant (-ante) ▸** copying real life.

life·time [LIFE-time] NOUN, lifetimes. **vie, (le) temps d'une vie ▸** the period of time a person or animal lives or a thing lasts; the time of being alive.

lift [lift] VERB, lifted, lifting. **1. soulever, lever ▸** to raise into the air; take to a high position; pick up : *She lifted the suitcase and put it in the overhead rack.* **2. se lever, se dissiper ▸** to rise and go; go away : *After the morning fog lifts, we'll have a beautiful day.* **3. (s') élever ▸** to go up; be raised to a higher level : *Their spirits lifted when they heard the good news.* ▲ NOUN, lifts. **1. haussement ▸** the act of lifting. **2. trajet dans la voiture de quelqu'un ▸** a ride in a car or other vehicle : *Can you give me a lift to the post office?* **3. stimulant ▸** a happy feeling; a rise in spirits : *Grandma says that my visits give her a real lift.* **4. ascenseur, monte-charge, élévateur, remonte-pente ▸** a machine or device for lifting : *a ski lift.* SYN: raise, elevate, pick up, hoist, boost.

lift-off [LIFT-off] NOUN, liftoffs. **décoller** ▶ the launching or takeoff of a rocket or spacecraft.

lig-a-ment [LIG-uh-munt] NOUN, ligaments. **ligament** ▶ a band of strong tissues that connects bones or holds organs of the body in place.

light¹ [lite] NOUN, lights. **1. lumière** ▶ the form of energy given off by the sun, an electric bulb, and so on that makes it possible for us to see. **2. lumière** ▶ anything that gives off any of these forms of energy, especially an electric lamp : *Turn off the light when you come in.* **3. feu (feux)** ▶ something used to set fire to something else : *We need a light to get the bonfire going.* **4. lumière** ▶ a way of seeing or regarding something : *to shed light on a problem.* ▲ VERB, lit or lighted, lighting. **1. allumer** ▶ to burn or cause to burn : *Mother lit the candles on the birthday cake.* **2. éclairer** ▶ to make bright; give brightness to : *One bulb will light the whole room well enough.* **3. illuminer** ▶ to make or become lively or bright : *A smile lit up her face.* ▲ ADJECTIVE, lighter, lightest. **1. clair (claire)** ▶ not dark; bright : *It gets light at about 6:30 a.m. this time of year.* **2. clair (claire)** ▶ pale in colour : *Her hair is light — almost blonde.*

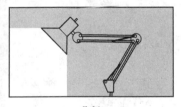

light

light² ADJECTIVE, lighter, lightest. **1. léger (-ère)** ▶ having little weight; not heavy : *Feathers and sponges are light.* **2. léger (-ère)** ▶ having less than the usual weight for its kind : *a light truck.* **3. léger (-ère), petit (-ite)** ▶ small in amount or degree : *a light meal; a light snowfall.* **4. léger (-ère), délicat (-ate)** ▶ moving easily; graceful : *The gymnast was light on her feet.* **5. léger (-ère), frivole, insouciant (-ante)** ▶ not serious; meant to entertain : *Spy stories are light reading.* **6.** (sometimes lite, especially in product names) **léger (-ère)** ▶ low in fat or calories : *light popcorn.* **7. facile** ▶ easy to do or endure : *light work.* ▲ ADVERB. **légèrement** ▶ in a light way : *Mark always travels light, carrying everything in one small bag.* ▪ **lightly**, ADVERB: ▶ **légèrement, délicatement.** *The dancer moved lightly on his feet.*

light³ VERB, lighted or lit, lighting. **se poser, atterrir** ▶ to come down from flight : *Pigeons often light on our window sills.*

light-en¹ [LITE-un] VERB, lightened, lightening. **éclairer, éclaircir** ▶ to make or become lighter or less dark; brighten : *I added white to lighten the colour of the paint.*

lighten² VERB, lightened, lightening. **1. alléger** ▶ to make less heavy; make lighter : *Charlie removed some books to lighten his knapsack.* **2. faciliter, simplifier** ▶ to make less difficult to do or hard to bear : *Tim lightened my load.* **3. dérider, réjouir, égayer** ▶ to make or become more cheerful.

light-er [LY-tur] NOUN, lighters. **briquet** ▶ a device that produces a small flame : *a barbecue lighter.*

light-house [LITE-hows] NOUN, lighthouses. **phare** ▶ a tower with a powerful light at the top built near dangerous places along the coast to warn and guide ships at night and during storms and fog.

light-ning [LITE-ning] NOUN. **éclair, foudre** ▶ a sudden flash of light in the sky caused by a powerful charge of electricity between clouds, or between clouds and the ground. This electric charge also produces the sound of thunder. 📖 **p. 1117.**

lightning rod **paratonnerre** ▶ a metal rod attached to the top of a building to protect it against damage from lightning by conducting the electric charge harmlessly into the ground.

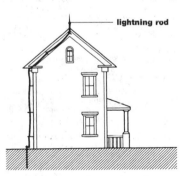

lightning rod

lik-a-ble [LIKE-uh-bul] ADJECTIVE. (also likeable) **agréable, sympathique** ▶ easy to like; having a pleasing personality : *a likable person.*

like¹ [like] VERB, liked, liking. **1. aimer** ▶ to feel good toward something or someone; be fond of; enjoy : *to like reading.* **2. vouloir** ▶ to want; wish : *Would you like some cake?* ▪ **likes,**

NOUN. ▸ **préférences, goûts** the things a person enjoys or prefers : *What are your likes and dislikes ?* SYN : care for, prefer, be fond of, enjoy.

like[2] PREPOSITION. **1. comme, semblable, pareil (-eille) à, tel (telle) que** ▸ being the same as something else; similar; alike : *This bike is just like that one.* **2. comme** ▸ what one expects of; typical of : *It's just like Larry to forget his homework.* **3. comme, tel (telle)** ▸ much the same as; in the same way as : *She swims like a fish.* *✐ p. 34.* **4. comme, tel (telle) que, par exemple** ▸ for example; such as : *Many people watch sports like hockey and basketball.* **5. pour** ▸ in the mood for : *Do you feel like eating out tonight?* ▲ ADJECTIVE. **semblable, pareil (-eille)** ▸ exactly or nearly the same. ▲ NOUN. **semblable, similitude** ▸ a person or thing like another; an equal.

and the like et cetera ▸ and others of the same kind; and so on : *peas, beans, corn, and the like.*

like-ly [LIKE-lee] ADJECTIVE. likelier, likeliest. **1. probable, vraisemblable** ▸ more or less certain to happen; probable : *Dark clouds in the sky mean that it's likely to rain.* **2. vraisemblable** ▸ believable; reliable : *His story just doesn't sound likely.* **3. convenable, propice,** ▸ right for the time or purpose; fitting : *a likely spot for a picnic.* ▲ ADVERB. **probablement, vraisemblablement, possible** ▸ probably : *We'll likely get homework.* **Note.** Likelihood is the fact of being likely. SYN : liable, probable, possible.

like-wise [LIKE-wize] ADVERB. **pareillement, aussi, de même** ▸ in the same way; also : *The coach spread his arms wide and told the players to do likewise.* SYN : also, too, as well, similarly, moreover.

li-lac [LY-luk *or* LY-lok] NOUN, lilacs. **1. lilas** ▸ a bush with clusters of tiny, sweet-smelling purple, pink, or white flowers. **2. lilas** ▸ a pale pinkish-purple colour.

lil-y [LIL-ee] NOUN, lilies. **1. lys** ▸ a plant with large, bell-shaped, brightly coloured flowers and narrow leaves. The lily grows from a bulb. The **prairie** lily is the provincial flower of Saskatchewan. The white **garden** lily is the provincial flower of Quebec. **2. nénuphar** ▸ any other plant with flowers like a lily's, such as the water lily. *👁 p. 250.*

lima bean [LY-muh] NOUN, lima beans. **haricot/fève de lima** ▸ a flat, pale green bean that is eaten as a vegetable.

limb [lim] NOUN, limbs. **1. (grosse) branche** ▸ a large branch growing out from the trunk of a tree. **2. membre** ▸ a leg, an arm, a wing, or a flipper.

out on a limb être sur la corde raide ▸ in or into a dangerous or exposed position : *Ariel was left out on a limb when her car broke down.*

limb-er [LIM-bur] ADJECTIVE. **souple, flexible, agile** ▸ able to move or bend easily; flexible. ▲ VERB, limbered, limbering. (used with up) **s'échauffer, assouplir** ▸ to make or become limber : *The gymnast limbered up before performing his routine.* SYN : flexible, pliable, elastic, bendable.

lime[1] [lime] NOUN, limes. **1. lime, citron vert** ▸ a juicy, light-green fruit that grows on a tree in warm climates. Limes are related to lemons and oranges, and they have a sour taste. **2. vert lime** ▸ a bright green colour.

lime[2] NOUN. **chaux** ▸ a white powder made by burning limestone, a kind of rock. It is used to make cement, glass, and fertilizer. **Note.** Limelight is a white light produced when lime is heated. In the past, theatres used limelights to light the stage. Today, limelight means the centre of public attention : *My sister Diane enjoys being in the limelight.*

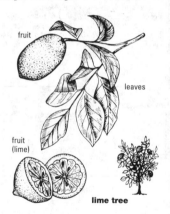

fruit

leaves

fruit (lime)

lime tree

lim-er-ick [LIM-uh-rik *or* LIM-rik] NOUN, limericks. **limerick, poème burlesque et grivois** ▸ a funny poem having five lines. The first and second lines rhyme with the last line. The third and fourth lines are shorter and rhyme with each other. *✐ p. 345.*

lim-it [LIM-it] NOUN, limits. **1. limite** ▸ the farthest edge or point that one can go to; the point where something stops : *Mom said that four laps around the track was her limit.* **2.** (also **limits**) **limite, frontière** ▸ the edge or boundary of a certain area : *the Calgary city limits.* **3. limite** ▸ the greatest amount or number that is officially allowed : *The speed limit near a school is 40 km/h.* ▲ VERB, limited, limiting. **limiter, restreindre** ▸ to set a limit; restrict : *The rules limit each speaker to five minutes.*

✐ Writing Tips

Limericks

Limericks are nonsense poems that tell a joke or a funny story. They can be written about a person, an animal, or anything else that sparks the writer's imagination. Limericks have a special pattern of rhyme and rhythm. Read this limerick aloud :

> There once was a bear of Kamloops   a
> Who put purple bugs in her soups.   a
> She knocked down trees,   b
> And she angered bees,   b
> That wild, hungry bear of Kamloops.   a

Notice the rhyming scheme of aabba, and that the last word of the first line is repeated in the last line. This is the pattern of classic limericks; in modern limericks, the last line is often used to deliver the conclusion or a surprising twist.

Note. Something that limits is a limitation. SYN : boundary, end, tip, border, edge.

lim‑ou‑sine [LIM-uh-zeen] NOUN, limousines. **limousine ▸** a very large and expensive automobile that usually has a glass panel between the front and back seats. Limousines are driven by a paid driver while the passengers sit in back. **Note.** Limo is a short form for this word.

limp¹ [limp] VERB, limped, limping. **boiter, claudiquer ▸** to walk in an uneven way, with less weight on one leg, usually because of pain or injury. ▲ NOUN, limps. **boitement, claudication ▸** a limping walk or movement : *to have a limp.*

limp² ADJECTIVE, limper, limpest. **mou (molle), faible, flasque ▸** not stiff or firm; drooping : *Her limp hair could not hold a curl.* ■ **limply,** ADVERB. ▸ **mollement, faiblement.** *They shook hands limply.*

line¹ [line] NOUN, lines. **1. ligne ▸** a long, thin mark : *Notebook paper has lines to write on.* **2. ligne, corde ▸** a long, thin piece of string, rope, or the like : *a fishing line; a clothesline.* **3. ligne ▸** a border or edge marked by or as if by a line : *Donovan was the first runner to cross the finish line.* **4. ride ▸** a wrinkle or mark on the skin : *Grandpa has a lot of laugh lines around his eyes.* **5. ligne, rang, rangée, fil ▸** a row of people or things side by side or one behind the other : *People stood in line for hours to get tickets to the concert.* **6. ligne ▸** a row of words on a page : *A sonnet is a poem*

with 14 lines. **7.** lines. **texte ▸** the words spoken by an actor. **8. ligne ▸** a system of transportation : *a bus line; an airline.* **9. ligne, gamme de produits ▸** a type or brand of goods for sale : *a line of clothes.* **10. métier, branche, domaine ▸** a person's job or business : *What line of work is she in?* ▲ VERB, lined, lining. **1. ligner ▸** to mark with lines : *to line a tennis court.* **2. (s') aligner ▸** to form into a line; place or arrange in line : *People lined both sides of the hall waiting to see Mrs. Kwan.* **Note.** Often used with up: *Line up here to get the tickets.* The NOUN form for this meaning is line-up: *a long lineup at the checkout counter.*

line² VERB, lined, lining. **1. doubler ▸** to cover the inside of : *to line gloves with fur.* **2. recouvrir, garnir, tapisser ▸** to be used as a lining or covering : *Posters line my bedroom wall.*

lin‑en [LIN-un] NOUN, linens. **1. lin ▸** a strong cloth made from the stalks of a plant called flax. **2.** (often linens) **linge ▸** household articles such as tablecloths, sheets, towels, and napkins, made of linen or a similar fabric.

lin‑ger [LING-gur] VERB, lingered, lingering. **s'attarder, traîner ▸** to stay on longer than usual; move or go away slowly : *A damp chill lingered in the autumn air.* ■ **lingeringly,** ADVERB. ▸ **à retardement.** SYN : stay, lag, delay, wait, remain.

lin‑ing [LY-ning] NOUN, linings. **doublure, revêtement intérieur ▸** a layer of material that covers the inside surface of something : *the lining of a coat.*

link [link] NOUN, links. **1. chaînon, maillon, maille ▸** a ring or loop that is part of a chain. **2. intermédiaire, lien, liaison ▸** anything that joins things as if by a chain : *This old photo album is a link to my past.* ▲ VERB, linked, linking. **relier ▸** to join or connect.

li‑on [LY-un] NOUN, lions. **lion ▸** a large, powerful animal of the cat family that lives in Africa or India. Lions have a smooth, light-brown coat and a long tail. A male lion has a darker shaggy mane around the neck, head, and shoulders. 📖 **p. 1091.**

li‑on‑ess [LY-uh-nes] NOUN, lionesses. **lionne ▸** a female lion.

lip [lip] NOUN, lips. **1. lèvre, babine ▸** one of the two movable folds of flesh that form the opening to the mouth. **2. bord, rebord ▸** the edge or rim of a container or opening : *the lip of a glass.* 📖 **p. 984.**

li‑quid [LIK-wid] NOUN, liquids. **liquide ▸** a form of matter that is not a gas or a solid. A liquid flows easily, and it can take on the shape of its container. Unlike a gas, the liquid may not fill its container. A liquid becomes a gas if heated to a certain point, or a solid if cooled to a certain point. Water is a liquid. ▲ ADJECTIVE. **liquide ▸** in the form of a liquid : *liquid soap.*

liq-uor [LIK-ur] NOUN, liquors. **spiritueux, alcool**
▸ an alcoholic drink such as gin, vodka, or
scotch.

list[1] [list] NOUN, lists. **liste** ▸ a series of names,
numbers, or other things written one after the
other : *Dad makes a shopping list when he
goes to the store.* ▲ VERB, listed, listing. **enregistrer, inscrire sur une liste, lister** ▸ to make
a list of; enter in a list : *I list my chores in my
calendar.*

list[2] NOUN, lists. **bande, gîte** ▸ an inclination or
tilt to one side. ▲ VERB, listed, listing **prendre de
la gîte, donner de la bande** ▸: *The ship listed
badly to the left after it became stuck on a
sand bar.*

lis-ten [LIS-un] VERB, listened, listening. **écouter** ▸ to try to hear; to pay attention in order to
hear : *to listen to music; to listen to what someone is saying.* ▪ **listener,** NOUN, listeners.
▸ **auditeur (-trice).** *That radio station has
many loyal listeners.*

lit[1] [lit] VERB. **allumer** ▸ a past form of light[1]: *The
new lamp lit up the room. We had lit the bon-
fire by the time it started to rain.*

lit[2] VERB. **allumer** ▸ a past form of light[3]: *The
bird lit on the branch.*

lit-er-al [LIT-ur-ul] ADJECTIVE. **littéral (-ale, -aux)**
▸ following the exact wording or meaning;
word for word : *a literal translation.* ✐ **p. 346.**

lit-er-al-ly [LIT-ur-uh-lee] ADVERB. 1. **littéralement** ▸ using words according to their exact
or strict meaning : *When I said, "Go jump in a
lake," I didn't mean it literally.* 2. **réellement,
exactement** ▸ really; actually : *There are literally hundreds of coins in the fountain.*
SYN : actually, really, exactly, word for word.

lit-er-a-ture [LIT-ur-uh-chur *or* LIT-ruh-chur] NOUN.
1. **littérature** ▸ Well-written poetry, fiction, and
other works showing imagination, powerful
ideas, beauty, or great style in a way that has lasting value. **Note.** Someone or something having
to do with literature is literary: *a literary critic.*
2. **littérature, documentation** ▸ all of the published information on a particular subject :
the literature of science. 3. **prospectus, brochure** ▸ a leaflet, booklet, or other printed material to advertise or promote something : *Thierry
asked for literature on the new computer.*

li-tre [LEE-tur] NOUN, litres. (also liter) **litre** ▸ the
basic metric unit for measuring volume or
capacity. One litre of water weighs one kilogram
(1000 grams). The litre is used to measure
liquids like juices and sauces. Symbol : L

lit-ter [LIT-ur] NOUN, litters. 1. **ordure, détritus**
▸ bits of paper and other waste material lying
around; rubbish. 2. **portée** ▸ a number of young
animals born at one time to the same mother :
Lions usually have two or three cubs in a litter.
3. **civière** ▸ a stretcher for carrying sick or

wounded people. ▲ VERB, littered, littering. **couvrir de, mettre en désordre** ▸ to scatter things
around to make a mess : *They littered the room
with paper and leftover food.* ✐ **p. 325.**

lit-tle [LIT-ul] ADJECTIVE, littler, littlest. 1. **petit
(-ite)** ▸ small in size or amount; not big : *That's
a little puppy. How old is she ?* 2. **petit
(-ite)** ▸ small in importance : *He has to clear up
a few little problems at the office.* ▲ ADVERB.
peu ▸ not much; slightly : *to feel a little tired or
a little sick.* ▲ NOUN. **(le) peu** ▸ a small amount :
Let me have a little of that bread. 2. **(un)
peu** ▸ a short time or distance : *a little past
3:00.* SYN : small, tiny, miniature, slight, puny.

live[1] [liv] VERB, lived, living. 1. **vivre** ▸ to be
alive ; have life : *We live in the 20th century.*
2. **vivre de** ▸ to keep up life ; feed or support
oneself : *A hawk lives on rabbits, mice, and
other small animals.* 3. **vivre, habiter, demeurer** ▸ to make one's home : *My friend Chanda
lives across the street.* 4. **vivre** ▸ to spend one's
life or time in a certain way : *to live well; to live
alone.*

live[2] [live] ADJECTIVE. 1. **vivant (-ante)** ▸ having
life; not dead : *a live rattlesnake.* 2. **ardent
(-ente)** ▸ burning or glowing : *The campers
poured water over the live coals to put them
out.* 3. **chargé (-ée) d'électricité, sous tension** ▸ carrying electricity : *After the storm, a
live wire was dangling over the street.*
Note. The expression **a live wire** also refers to
an energetic or a lively person. 4. **en direct** ▸ of
a TV program, shown while actually taking
place, rather than being taped or filmed for later
showing.

✐ **Writing Tips**

Literal and Figurative Language

• *Sometimes writers describe people,
places, and things exactly as they are,
in plain, simple language that does not
exaggerate or compare one thing to
another. This is called* literal language.

*The speckled, white horse pulled the red
wagon through the dusty village streets.*

• *At other times, writers want to describe
people, places, and things in a more
dramatic or exaggerated way. To do this,
they use writing devices such as*
**exaggeration, metaphors, similes,
personification,** *and* **hyperbole.**
This is called figurative language.

*Ellen was as brave as a lion; her strength
was the strength of 20 charging bulls,
and she had the wisdom of an owl.*

live-li-hood [LIVE-lee-HOOD] NOUN, livelihoods. **gagne pain** ▶ the way a person earns a living.

live-ly [LIVE-lee] ADJECTIVE, livelier, liveliest. **vivant (-ante), actif (-ive), animé (-ée), plein (pleine) d'entrain** ▶ full of life or energy : *a person with a lively imagination.* ▲ ADVERB. **avec entrain** ▶ in a lively way : *to step lively.* SYN : spirited, exciting, active, energetic, vigorous.

liv-er [LIV-ur] NOUN, livers. **1. foie** ▶ a large organ in the body. As blood passes through it, the liver absorbs fats, stores vitamins, and cleans the blood. **2. foie** ▶ the liver of an animal used as food, such as a calf or chicken liver. 👁 p. 403.

live-stock [LIVE-STOK] NOUN. **bétail, cheptel** ▶ animals raised on a farm or ranch for profit : *Cows, horses, pigs, and sheep are livestock.*

liv-ing [LIV-ing] NOUN, livings. **1. vie, vivant** ▶ the fact or condition of being alive : *She was filled with the joy of living.* **2. vie** ▶ a way of supporting oneself or earning the means to live : *He earns his living by giving music lessons.* **3. vie** ▶ a certain way of life : *suburban living.* ▲ VERB. a present form of live[1]. ▲ ADJECTIVE. **1. vivant (-ante)** ▶ having life; alive : *living plants and animals.* **2. de vie, d'existence** ▶ having to do with life or a certain way of life : *clean living conditions.* **3. vivant (-ante)** ▶ still in use; active : *English is a living language.*

liz-ard [LIZ-urd] NOUN, lizards. **lézard** ▶ a reptile that usually has a scaly body, four legs, and a long tail. Lizards are usually found in warm climates.

lla-ma [LAH-muh] NOUN, llamas. **lama** ▶ a South American animal that is related to the camel but is smaller and has no hump. Llamas are raised for their thick, soft wool.

load [lode] NOUN, loads. **1. charge, chargement** ▶ something that is lifted or carried : *Alan has a load of lumber on his truck.* **2. fardeau (-eaux)** ▶ something that bothers a person; a burden or worry : *I found my wallet—that really takes a load off my mind.* **3. Informal. tas** ▶ any large amount of something : *I've still got loads of homework to do.* ▲ VERB, loaded, loading. **1. charger** ▶ to put a load in or on something : *"And it takes another day just to load the donkeys with water."* (Tololwa M. Mollel) **2. charger, remplir** ▶ to put materials into a machine : *to load a dishwasher.* 👁 p. 321.

loaf[1] [lofe] NOUN, loaves. **1. pain, miche de pain** ▶ bread shaped and baked in one large piece. **2. pain** ▶ anything shaped like a loaf of bread : *a meat loaf.*

loaf[2] VERB, loafed, loafing. **paresser, traîner** ▶ to do nothing; rest or relax in a lazy way : *They loafed around all day doing nothing.* **Note.** A person who loafs is a **loafer.** SYN : lounge, lie around, idle.

loan [lone] NOUN, loans. **1. prêt** ▶ money that is given for a time and paid back later, usually with

interest : *I got a bank loan to buy a new car.* **2. emprunt** ▶ anything that is borrowed. **3. prêt** ▶ the act of lending : *I asked my sister for the loan of her bike.* ▲ VERB, loaned, loaning. **prêter** ▶ to give something as a loan; lend : *I loaned him money for lunch.*

lob-by [LOB-ee] NOUN, lobbies. **1. hall, vestibule** ▶ a waiting room or hall at the entrance to a hotel, a theatre, an apartment, or another building. **2. lobby, groupe de pression** ▶ a person or organized group that works to try to change the way lawmakers vote or act : *The anti-smoking lobby supported a ban on smoking in all public places.* **Note.** A person who does this is a lobbyist. ▲ VERB, lobbied, lobbying. **faire pression sur** ▶ to act to change the way lawmakers vote or act : *The townspeople lobbied to have a new community centre built.*

lob-ster [LOB-stur] NOUN, lobsters. **homard** ▶ a sea animal with a hard outer shell and no backbone. Lobsters have five pairs of legs, with large claws on the front pair. They are often eaten as food.

lo-cal [LOH-kul] ADJECTIVE. **1. local (-ale, -aux)** ▶ having to do with one place, especially the town or neighbourhood one lives in : *Most children go to their local school, the one closest to where they live.* **Note.** A local area, such as a neighbourhood or town, is a locality or a locale. ▲ NOUN, locals. **habitants du coin** ▶ a person from the area. ■ **locally,** ADVERB. ▶ localement.

lo-cate [LOH-KATE *or* loh-KATE] VERB, located, locating. **1. localiser, situer** ▶ to be or exist in a certain place : *That store is located on the other side of the mall.* **2. (s') installer, implanter** ▶ to put in a certain place : *They've decided to locate their new store in the north end of Winnipeg.* **3. repérer, localiser** ▶ to find the position of; search out : *Once you locate the fish, you will have to catch them.*

lo-ca-tion [loh-KAY-shun] NOUN, locations. **1. emplacement** ▶ a place where something is located : *My grandparents know a perfect location for our camp-site.* **2. repérage, localisation** ▶ the act of locating. SYN : place, position, area, spot, territory, district.

on location sur le site, sur place, en extérieur ▶ at a place outside the studio where a movie or TV show is normally filmed : *That movie was shot on location in the Rockies.*

lock[1] [lok] NOUN, locks. **1. serrure** ▶ a small device used to keep a door, window, drawer, or other object closed until it is opened by a key or by some other means. **2. écluse** ▶ a part of a canal or waterway closed off with gates. The water level can be changed by letting water in or out to raise or lower boats and ships. ▲ VERB, locked, locking. **1. verrouiller, fermer à clé** ▶ to fasten with a lock : *Don't forget to lock the door.* **2. mettre sous clé, mettre sous les verrous,**

enfermer ▶ to shut away or hold in place : *We locked the money into the safe.* **3. (se) bloquer** ▶ to join or hold firmly in place, as if with a lock : *The ice locked our ship in place.* SYN : fasten, close, latch, seal, clasp.

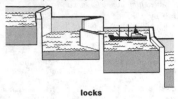

locks

lock² NOUN, locks. **1. mèche** ▶ a piece of hair from the head. **2. locks. cheveux, cheve-lure** ▶ the hair of the head : *a young child with curly locks.*

lock·er [LOK-ur] NOUN, lockers. **casier** ▶ a small closet or cabinet that can be locked, used for storing personal belongings in a public place. 📖 **p. 1059.**

lock·et [LOK-ut] NOUN, lockets. **médaillon** ▶ a small metal case with a picture, a lock of hair, or something else that one wants to keep, usually worn on a chain around the neck.

lock·smith [LOK-smith] NOUN, locksmiths. **serrurier (-ère)** ▶ a person who makes, installs, or fixes locks.

lo·co·mo·tive [LOH-kuh-MOH-tiv] NOUN, loco-motives. **locomotive** ▶ a railway car with an engine, used for pulling or pushing other cars. 👁 **p. 540.**

lo·cust [LOH-kust] NOUN, locusts. **1. sauterelle** ▶ a type of grasshopper that sometimes travels in huge swarms eating all the plants in their path. They can cause great damage to farm crops. **2. caroubier** ▶ a tree with small, feathery leaves and sweet-smelling white flowers.

lodge [loj] NOUN, lodges. **1. pavillon, camp** ▶ a house or cottage, especially one used for a spe-cial purpose : *a fishing lodge.* **2. section** ▶ a branch of a larger organization or club : *My uncle belongs to a local lodge of the Lions Club.* **3. hutte, terrier** ▶ the den or home of an animal : *a beaver lodge.* ▲ VERB, lodged, lodg-ing. **1. loger, habiter, rester** ▶ to live in a place for a time : *We lodged in a cabin near the water.* **2. héberger** ▶ to provide a place to stay : *Our friends lodged us at their place overnight.* **3. (se) loger** ▶ to be stuck or caught in some-thing : *The kite lodged in the tree between two branches.* **4. porter plainte, formuler, présen-ter** ▶ to place a formal charge or complaint : *The tenants lodged a complaint about their landlord.*

lodg·ing [LOJ-ing] NOUN, lodgings. **1. loge-ment** ▶ a place to sleep or live in for a while :

They found temporary lodging in a small motel. **2. lodgings. chambre, pension, appare-ment, logement** ▶ a rented room or rooms in someone else's home. **Note.** A person who lives in another person's home and pays rent is a lodger.

loft [loft] NOUN, lofts. **1. grenier** ▶ an open space or room under the roof of a building; an attic. **2. grenier** ▶ any large, open space on the upper floor of a building used as a work or storage area. **3. grenier** ▶ an open area under the roof of a barn, used for storing hay.

log [log] NOUN, logs. **1. bûche, rondin** ▶ a large, rough piece of wood cut from a tree, with the bark still on it. **2. journal de bord, carnet** ▶ a daily record of a ship's voyage. (also logbook) **3. registre, carnet, journal (-aux)** ▶ any similar record of events : *The truckdriver's log showed how long the trip took.* ▲ VERB, logged, logging. **1. bûcher, tronçonner** ▶ to chop down trees and cut them into pieces. **Note.** A person who does this work is a logger. **2. inscrire, noter, consigner** ▶ to make a record of something in a log : *Our boss logs the hours we work.*

log·ic [LOJ-ik] NOUN. **1. logique** ▶ an exact form of reasoning that uses accurate information and thought to reach a conclusion. **2. logique** ▶ cor-rect thinking of any kind : *Marcel used logic to solve the problem.*

log·i·cal [LOJ-uh-kul] ADJECTIVE. **1. logique** ▶ according to the rules of logic : *logical thought.* **2. logique** ▶ showing correct thinking; reason-able; sensible : *It is logical to expect a ball to fall when you drop it.* ■ **logically,** ADVERB. ▶ **logiquement.** SYN : sensible, reasonable, sound, rational.

lone [lone] ADJECTIVE. **1. seul (seule), solitaire** ▶ not with another; alone : *There was a lone pine tree in the middle of the field.* **Note.** A loner is someone who likes to live or be alone.

lone·ly [LONE-lee] ADJECTIVE, lonelier, loneliest. **1. seul (seule), solitaire** ▶ unhappy about being alone; missing other people : *a lonely person.* **2. délaisé (-ée), isolé (-ée) esseulé (-ée)** ▶ causing a person to have this feeling : *A train whistle is a very lonely sound.* **3. isolé (-ée), déserté (-ée)** ▶ not visited by people; deserted : *a lonely prairie road.* ■ **loneliness,** NOUN. ▶ **solitude, isolement.** the fact of being lonely : *Loneliness can make the first day of school very difficult.* SYN : friendless, lonesome, alone, isolated, solitary.

lone·some [LONE-sum] ADJECTIVE. **1. solitaire, seul (seule)** ▶ unhappy about being alone; lonely : *Chuck was lonesome at summer camp.* **2. solitaire, seul (seule)** ▶ making one feel lonely : *He read and slept, trying to fill the lone-some hours.*

long¹ [long] ADJECTIVE, longer, longest. **1. long (longue)** ▶ being a great distance from one end to the other; not short : *a long tunnel.* **2. long (longue)** ▶ lasting a great amount of time; a great duration : *a long wait in line.* **3. long (longue) de** ▶ having an exact length or time : *a race that is 5 km long; a play that was three hours long.* **4. long (longue)** ▶ of vowel sounds, spoken like the name of the letter itself. The *a* in the word *late* is long. ▲ ADVERB. **1. long, longtemps** ▶ for a great amount of time : *It won't be long now.* **2. durant, pendant, tout au long de** ▶ for or during a certain time; throughout : *all night long.*

long[2] VERB, longed, longing. **avoir très envie de** ▶ to want very much; have a great desire for : *"Claire longed to be brave."* (Jean Little)

long·ing [LONG-ing] NOUN, longings. **envie, désir** ▶ a feeling of wanting something very much; a strong desire : *"Each day his longing to know the boy's secret sharpened until he thought of nothing else."* (Tololwa M. Mollel) ▲ ADJECTIVE. **plein (pleine) d'envie** ▶ showing a deep wish or a strong desire : *The hungry man cast a longing glance at the food.* ■ **longingly,** ADVERB: ▶ **avec envie.** *Cody looked longingly at the new computer games.*

lon·gi·tude [LON-juh-TOOD *or* LON-guh-TOOD] NOUN, longitudes. **longitude** ▶ A way of measuring distance on the earth's surface. Longitude is expressed in degrees east or west of the meridian line at Greenwich, England. On a map, longitude is shown by lines running north and south between the North and South Poles. 🖉 **p. 336**.

look [look] VERB, looked, looking. **1. regarder** ▶ to use the eyes to see : *to look out the window; to look at a picture.* **2. chercher** ▶ to search : *They looked for the ball.* **3. sembler, paraître** ▶ to appear to be; seem : *It looks new. You look tired.* **4. donner sur** ▶ to face in a certain direction : *Our window looks out over the park.* ▲ NOUN, looks. **1. coup d'œil** ▶ the act of looking : *Take a look at this picture.* **2. air, aspect, regard** ▶ a way of looking; an appearance or expression : *She had a worried look on her face.* **3. looks. apparence** ▶ personal appearance; what one looks like : *That movie star is famous for his good looks.* SYN: see, observe, view, gaze, peek, glance, stare. 🖉 **p. 349**.

look·out [LOOK-out] NOUN, lookouts. **1. vigie, guetteur (-euse), veilleur (-euse)** ▶ a person

whose job it is to watch carefully for something : *The ship's lookout spotted land.* **2. recherche, quête** ▶ a careful watching for something : *to be on the lookout for a good book.* **3. poste de guet** ▶ a place from which to see a long way : *From the lookout, they could see clear across the lake.*

lookout

loom[1] [loom] NOUN, looms. **métier à tisser** ▶ a machine or frame for weaving thread into cloth.

loom[2] VERB, loomed, looming. **1. apparaître indistinctement** ▶ to rise up into view as a large shape : *Clouds loomed overhead as we finished our picnic.* **2. apparaître indistinctement** ▶ to come into the mind as large or threatening : *The fear of being late loomed in her mind.* SYN: appear, come into sight, show up, emerge.

loon [loon] NOUN, loons. **huard** ▶ a water bird with short legs, webbed feet, and a back with small whitish spots. Loons are good swimmers and divers and use their pointed bills to catch fish. Their cry sounds like a wild laugh. 👁 **p. 108**.

loop [loop] NOUN, loops. **1. boucle** ▶ the rounded part of a string or rope folded over itself.

🖉 **Word Builder**

Look after means to take care of something or someone : *I can't go to the concert because I have to look after my baby brother.* ***Look alive*** has the idea or hurrying or responding quickly : *The coach told us to look alive on the field.* If you ***look down on*** someone, you feel superior to that person : *Jennifer looks down on anyone who can't do as many chin-ups as her.* On the other hand, someone you ***look up to*** is a person you admire : *Keeok looked up to the tennis player Arthur Ashe.*

2. boucle ▸ anything that has or makes a loop : *The path makes a loop around the pond.* ▲ VERB. looped, looping. **faire une boucle, enrouler** ▸ to make or form a loop : *He looped the rope around the pony's neck.*

loose [loos] ADJECTIVE. looser, loosest. **1. défait (-aite), détaché (-ée)** ▸ not fastened or attached tightly : *a loose shoelace.* **2. libre, détaché (-ée)** ▸ not tied or fastened at all; free : *Maggie has a loose tooth.* **3. ample** ▸ not fitting tightly : *a loose dress.* **4. détacher, délier, en vrac** ▸ not tied, bound, or packed together : *Damon put loose pieces of paper into his binder.* **5. vague, peu exact (-acte)** ▸ not strict or exact : *I made a loose count of the fans at the game.* ▲ ADVERB. **librement, de façon décontractée, relâchée** ▸ in a loose way : *A set of keys hung loose at his belt.* ■ **loosely,** ADVERB. ▸ **de manière lâche, sans serrer.** ■ **looseness,** NOUN. ▸ **relâchement, desserrement.**

loos-en [LOO-sun] VERB, loosened, loosening. **(se) défaire, (se) desserrer, (se) délier, (se) relâcher** ▸ to make or become loose : *When Dad gets home, he loosens his tie.*

lop-sid-ed [LOP-SY-did] ADJECTIVE. **de travers, asymétrique, disproportionné (-ée)** ▸ leaning too far to one side ; larger or heavier on one side than the other : *After the big branch fell, the tree looked lopsided.*

lord [lord] NOUN. lords. **1. seigneur** ▸ in the Middle Ages, a man who held a high rank in a kingdom. A lord ruled over the other people in the area. **2. seigneur, maître** ▸ a person who holds great power or rules over others. **3. Lord. Lord** ▸ in the United Kingdom and some of its colonies, a title for a man of noble rank. **4. Lord (also the Lord) Seigneur** ▸ a title for God. ▲ VERB, lorded, lording. (used with it over) **agir comme un seigneur, snober** ▸ to act in a proud or bossy way toward others : *Gina lorded it over us after she scored perfect on the test.* ■ **lordly,** ADJECTIVE. ▸ **snob.**

lose [looz] VERB, lost, losing. **1. perdre, égarer** ▸ to not have something anymore; forget or not know where something is : *to lose a pen.* **2. perdre, égarer** ▸ to fail to keep or have : *Try not to lose the book I gave you.* **3. perdre** ▸ to fail to win : *to lose a game.* **4. perdre** ▸ to have taken away : *to lose a mark.* **5. perdre** ▸ to have less of : *to lose money.* **6. perdre** ▸ to fail to see, understand, or hear; miss : *I lost the point of the argument.* **7. se perdre** ▸ to be completely taken up with : *I lost myself in the book.*

loss [los] NOUN, losses. **1. perte** ▸ the fact of losing something : *This year our soccer team had only six losses.* **2. perte** ▸ something that is lost : *I am upset about the loss of my favourite hat.* **3. perte** ▸ in business, the amount of money owed when a company earns less money than it spends.

lost [lost] VERB. **perdre** ▸ a past form of lose : *Pierre lost his new gloves.* ▲ ADJECTIVE. **1. perdu (-ue)** ▸ missing or unable to be found : *a lost dog.* **2. perdu (-ue)** ▸ not won : *a lost game.* **3. perdu (-ue), gaspillé (-ée)** ▸ wasted ; not used : *a lost chance.* **4. perdu (-ue)** ▸ puzzled; uncertain : *Amanda felt lost in the city.* SYN : missing, vanished, misplaced.

lot [lot] NOUN, lots. **1. beaucoup de** ▸ a large number or amount : *There are many people here, making a lot of noise.* **2. lot, terrain** ▸ a piece of land : *a parking lot; an empty lot.* **3. lot** ▸ a number of persons or things as a group : *This book is the best of the lot.* **4. tirage au sort** ▸ a piece of paper, straw, wood, or the like, used to decide something by chance : *People sometimes draw lots to decide who will do something.* **5. lot** ▸ one's fate or fortune : *It's their lot in life to work for a living.* ▲ ADVERB. **beaucoup** ▸ very much : *Our new school is a lot bigger than our old one.* SYN : many, bunch, group, cluster, clump, batch.

lo-tion [LOH-shun] NOUN. lotions. **lotion** ▸ a smooth liquid mixture used on the skin to soften, protect, or heal it : *hand lotion; suntan lotion.*

lot-ter-y [LOT-uh-ree] NOUN, lotteries. **loterie** ▸ a contest where the winners are chosen by drawing lots. Many provinces hold lotteries to raise money for the government.

loud [lowd] ADJECTIVE, louder, loudest. **1. bruyant (-ante), fort (forte)** ▸ having a great or strong sound; noisy : *Turn the TV down; it's too loud.* **2.** *Informal.* **criard (-arde), voyant (-ante)** ▸ having colours too bright to be pleasing; not in good taste : *a loud shirt with green, purple, and orange designs.* ▲ ADVERB. **fort, haut** ▸ in a loud way : *The bell rang, loud and clear.* ■ **loudly,** ADVERB. ▸ **bruyamment, fort, haut.** ■ **loudness,** NOUN. ▸ **sonorité, force, bruit.** SYN : noisy, riotous, deafening, thunderous.

loud-speak-er [LOWD-SPEE-kur] NOUN, loudspeakers. **1. haut-parleur (haut-parleurs), enceinte** ▸ a device for making sounds louder. Loudspeakers are used to make announcements in public places.

lounge [lownj] VERB, lounged, lounging. **se prélasser, flâner** ▸ to stand or sit in a comfortable, relaxed way : *It was so hot that we lounged on the porch all afternoon.* ▲ NOUN, lounges. **salon** ▸ a room where a person can relax : *the ship's lounge.*

love [luv] NOUN, loves. **1. amour** ▸ a very deep, strong feeling of caring for another person : *family love; romantic love.* **2. amour** ▸ a great liking for something : *a love of music.* **3. amour** ▸ a person for whom one feels love : *You are my love.* ▲ VERB, loved, loving. **1. aimer** ▸ to have a very deep, strong feeling of caring for someone. **2. adorer** ▸ to like very much : *Jerry*

loves chocolate ice cream. ■ **loving,** ADJECTIVE.
▶ **aimant (-ante), affectueux (-euse).** SYN: affection, tenderness, devotion, respect. 📖 p. 1021.

love·ly [LUV-lee] ADJECTIVE, lovelier, loveliest.
1. beau (belle), ravissant (-ante) ▶ very pleasing to look at; beautiful : *a lovely bouquet of spring flowers.* **2. charmant (-ante)** ▶ very nice or pleasant; delightful : *I had a lovely time at your party.* ■ **loveliness,** NOUN. ▶ **beauté, charme.** SYN: pretty, beautiful, delightful, charming.

lov·er [LUV-ur] NOUN, lovers. **1. amant (-ante), amoureux (-euse)** ▶ someone who loves another person : *Romeo and Juliet are a famous pair of young lovers.* **2. amateur (-trice)** ▶ a person who loves a certain thing : *a music lover.*

low [loh] ADJECTIVE, lower, lowest. **1. bas (basse)** ▶ close to the ground or surface; not high or tall : *Strawberries grow on a low plant.* **2. bas (basse)** ▶ below the usual or general level : *It hasn't rained lately, so the lake is low.* **3. bas (basse), peu élevé (-ée)** ▶ below the normal amount : *The discount store has very low prices.* **4. bas (basse)** ▶ of little value or quality; bad; poor : *Kyan got a low mark on the test.* **5. bas (basse), grave** ▶ deep in pitch; not high : *A bass singer can hit very low notes.* **6. déprimé (-ée)** ▶ sad or unhappy : *Denise has been in low spirits since her best friend moved away.* **7. peu élevé (-ée), bas niveau** ▶ almost gone; used up : *low in supplies.* ▲ ADVERB, lower, lowest. **au plus bas** ▶ at or to a low place or level : *The plane flew low over the treetops.* ▲ NOUN, lows. **bas** ▶ something that is low : *The temperature had a new low last night.* ■ **lowly,** ADJECTIVE. ▶ **modeste, humble, inférieur (-eure).** having a low rank or position.

low·er [LOH-ur] ADJECTIVE. **inférieur (-eure)** ▶ the comparative form of low: *a lower floor of a building; students in the lower grades.* ▲ VERB, lowered, lowering. **baisser** ▶ to bring or move down : *Please lower your voice — you're talking too loud.*

lower oneself s'abaisser ▶ to act in a wrong or unworthy way : *I won't lower myself by replying to that insult.*

low·er case minuscule ▶ see small letter.

loy·al [LOY-ul] ADJECTIVE. **loyal (-ale, -aux), fidèle, dévoué (-ée)** ▶ true to a person, country, or idea; faithful : *I am loyal to my friends and always support them.* **Note.** The fact or condition of being loyal is loyalty: *Loyalty must be given : it can't be bought.* ■ **loyally,** ADVERB. ▶ **loyalement, fidèlement.** SYN: faithful, true, constant, reliable, devoted.

loy·al·ist [LOY-uh-list] NOUN, loyalists. **1. loyaliste** ▶ a person who supports an existing government, king, queen, or other ruler, especially in times of rebellion. **2. Loyalist (also United Empire Loyalist) Loyaliste** ▶ a colonist who remained loyal to Great Britain during the American Revolution. Many Loyalists left the United States to live in Canada.

luck [luk] NOUN. **1. chance, hasard** ▶ the way some things happen by accident, without being controlled or planned; fate : *The winner of a lottery is decided by luck.* **2. chance** ▶ success; good fortune : *I wish you good luck.* SYN: chance, fate, lot, destiny, good fortune.

luck·i·ly [LUK-uh-lee] ADVERB. **heureusement, par chance** ▶ in a lucky way; by good luck; fortunately : *Luckily, it didn't rain, so we had the party outside.*

luck·y [LUK-ee] ADJECTIVE, luckier, luckiest. **1. chanceux (-euse)** ▶ having or showing good luck : *You'll be lucky to win even one game against that team.* **2. chanceux (-euse)** ▶ thought of as bringing good luck : *Kayla held her lucky penny all through her speech.*

lug [lug] VERB, lugged, lugging. **traîner, tirer** ▶ to pull or carry with great effort; drag : *He lugged his suitcase onto the bus.*

lug·gage [LUG-ij] NOUN. **bagage** ▶ the suitcases and bags that a traveller takes along on a trip; baggage.

luke·warm [LUKE warm] ADJECTIVE. **1. tiède** ▶ slightly warm; neither hot nor cold. **2. tiède** ▶ showing little interest or enthusiasm : *a lukewarm greeting.*

lull [lul] VERB, lulled, lulling. **1. calmer** ▶ to make or become calm; quiet down . *Her reassuring words lulled my fears.* **2. endormir, bercer** ▶ to cause to sleep or rest : *The song lulled the baby to sleep.*

lul·la·by [LUL-uh-by] NOUN, lullabies. **berceuse** ▶ a soft song intended to lull a baby to sleep : "Rock-a-Bye Baby" *is a well-known lullaby.*

lum·ber¹ [LUM-bur] NOUN. **bois de charpente, bois de construction** ▶ boards and planks cut from logs.

lum·ber² VERB, lumbered, lumbering. **marcher pesamment** ▶ to move in a noisy, clumsy way : *The bear lumbered along through the forest.*

lu·mi·nous [LOO-muh-nus] ADJECTIVE. **lumineux (-euse), brillant (-ante), fluorescent (-ente)** ▶ giving off light; glowing; shining : *a luminous sign.* SYN: radiant, clear, bright, brilliant, shining.

lump [lump] NOUN, lumps. **1. morceau (-eaux), grumeau (-eaux)** ▶ a small, solid piece of something having no special shape : *a lump of clay.* **2. bosse** ▶ a swelling or bump : *Brett had a lump on his head where the baseball had hit him.* ▲ VERB, lumped, lumping. **1. mettre en tas** ▶ to form into a lump or lumps. **2. mettre dans la même sac** ▶ to put together in one group : *Let's lump everyone into one group.* ■ **lumpy,** ADJECTIVE. ▶ **grumeleux (-euse), bosselé (-ée).**

lu-nar [LOO-nur] ADJECTIVE. **lunaire** ▶ having to do with the moon : *In a lunar eclipse, the moon passes through the earth's shadow.*

lu-na-tic [LOO-nuh-tik] NOUN, lunatics. **1. fou (folle), cinglé (-ée)** ▶ someone who is mentally ill. **2. fou (folle)** ▶ someone who acts in a wild and foolish way. ▲ ADJECTIVE. **1. aliéné (-ée), dément (-ente), fou (folle)** ▶ insane. **2. fou (folle), insensé (-ée), bête** ▶ very foolish.

lunch [lunch] NOUN, lunches. **lunch, dîner** ▶ a meal eaten in the middle of the day, between breakfast and dinner (or supper). ▲ VERB, lunched, lunching. **luncher, dîner** ▶ to eat lunch : *We lunched at the new restaurant.* 📖 **p. 1060.**

lunch-eon [LUN-chun] NOUN, luncheons. **lunch, repas (du midi), dîner** ▶ lunch, especially a formal or special lunch.

lung [lung] NOUN, lungs. **poumon** ▶ one of a pair of large organs in the chest used for breathing. The lungs take in oxygen from the air and give out carbon dioxide into the air. 👁 **p. 403.**

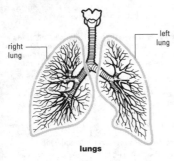

right lung · left lung

lungs

lunge [lunj] NOUN, lunges. **coup, mouvement brusque** ▶ a sudden movement or rush forward : *The outfielder made a lunge for the ball.* ▲ VERB, lunged, lunging. **se jeter** ▶ to make a sudden movement forward : *Mark lunged to catch the falling cup.* SYN: attack, push, thrust, plunge.

lure [loor] NOUN, lures. **1. attrait** ▶ something that strongly attracts or tempts a person : *The lure of the beautiful spring day made it hard for her to work.* **2. leurre, appât** ▶ an artificial bait used to catch fish. ▲ VERB, lured, luring. **attirer, séduire, charmer** ▶ to attract strongly; tempt : *"We always took pity on the horses, however, and lured Flip away with a lump of sugar."* (Todd Lee) SYN : attract, seduce, coax, tempt, trick, trap.

lush [lush] ADJECTIVE, lusher, lushest. **luxuriant (-ante), abondant (-ante)** ▶ thick, rich, and healthy : *The trees in the forest were lush and green.*

lux-u-ry [LUK-shur-ee or LUG-zhur-ee] NOUN, luxuries. **1. luxe** ▶ something that gives pleasure but is not necessary, especially something expensive : *A silk shirt is a luxury.* **2. luxe** ▶ a very rich, splendid, or costly way of living : *"But he never again lived in such luxury and plenty as he had among the Lakota people."* (Rosebud Yellow Robe) SYN : extravagance, frills, splendour, elegance.

ly-ing[1] [LY-ing] **s'allonger, être couché (-ée), se trouver sur** ▶ a present form of lie[1]: *The dog is lying in the shade.*

ly-ing[2] [LY-ing] **mentir** ▶ a present form of lie[2]: *The police think that he's lying about where he was that night.*

lynx [links] NOUN, lynx or lynxes. **lynx** ▶ a wild animal of the cat family, with long legs, a short tail, and fur in bunches around its ears. 👁 **p. 110.**

ly-ric [LIR-ik] NOUN, lyrics. **1. lyrics. paroles** ▶ the words to a song. **2. poème lyrique** ▶ a short poem that tells a poet's personal feelings.

mushroom

m, M [em] NOUN, m's, M's. **m, M** ▸ the 13th letter of the English alphabet.

ma'am [mam] NOUN, ma'ams. **madame** ▸ the contraction for madam.

mac-a-ro-ni [mak-uh-ROH-nee] NOUN. **macaroni** ▸ a type of noodle that is shaped like a small, short tube. Macaroni is cooked in boiling water before being eaten.

ma-caw [muh-kaw] NOUN, macaws. **ara** ▸ a large, brightly coloured parrot with a long tail, found in Central and South America.

ma-chine [muh-SHEEN] NOUN, machines. **1. machine, appareil** ▸ any device that uses energy and motion to do work. Most machines combine moving and fixed parts. Automobiles, dishwashers, printing presses, and computers are all types of machines. **2.** (also **simple machine**) **machine** ▸ a basic device that makes it easier to do physical work, such as a lever, pulley, wedge, screw, or wheel, or an inclined plane. ✐ **p. 354.**

ma-chin-er-y [muh-SHEEN-uh-ree] NOUN. **1. machinerie** ▸ machines as a group : *They worked quickly to fix the machinery.* **2. mécanisme** ▸ the working parts of a machine or machines : *The elevator isn't working because something got caught in the machinery.* **Note.** A person who works with machinery is a **machinist**.

mad [mad] ADJECTIVE, madder, maddest. **1. furieux (-euse), en colère** ▸ feeling or showing anger; angry. **2. fou (folle, fous, folles), dément (-ente), cinglé (-ée)** ▸ not in one's right mind; insane. **3. insensé (-ée)** ▸ not sensible; very foolish : *Swimming in the lake in the dark was a mad thing to do.* **4. effréné (-ée)** ▸ wild and confused : *The children made a mad scramble across the lawn as the scavenger hunt began.* **5. enragé (-ée)** ▸ of an animal (especially a dog), having a dangerous disease called rabies that causes the animal to run about wildly and attack people. ■ **madly**, ADVERB. ▸ follement. ■ **madness**, NOUN. ▸ folie. SYN : angry, furious, irate.

ma-dam [MAD-um] NOUN, madams. (often Madam) **madame** ▸ a polite way of speaking to a woman : *"Madam, your table is ready now,"* the waiter told her.

made [made] VERB. a past form of make.

mag-a-zine [mag-uh-ZEEN or MAG-uh-zeen] NOUN, magazines. **1. magazine, revue** ▸ a printed collection of writing, often with pictures, that is published at regular times, usually weekly or monthly. **2. magasin** ▸ a room for storing explosives or ammunition. **Note.** Magazine comes from an Arabic word meaning "to store."

ma-gic [MAJ-ik] NOUN. **1. magie, sorcellerie** ▸ a special power that allows a person to control what happens or to do things that would otherwise be impossible : *"But the best magic of all…was the magic that made Hush invisible."* (Mem Fox) **2. magie** ▸ the performing of certain tricks that seem impossible, such as pulling a rabbit out of an empty hat. **3. magie, enchantement** ▸ a powerful effect that seems to work by magic : *Music calmed the crying baby like magic.* ▲ ADJECTIVE. **magique** ▸ having to do with the power of magic : *"Way off in the distance a small planet twinkled like a magic blue marble."* (Nicola Morgan) **Note.** Something of magic or done by magic is magical: *Cinderella's fairy godmother used her magical powers to turn a pumpkin into a beautiful cariage.* ■ **magically**, ADVERB. ▸ magiquement. SYN : spell, charm, sorcery, witchcraft, wizardry.

ma·gi·cian [muh-JISH-un] NOUN, magicians. **1. magicien (-ienne), illusionniste** ▸ a person who performs magic tricks to entertain people : *The magician Harry Houdini was famous for his amazing escapes.* **2. fée, sorcier (-ière)** ▸ a person who supposedly has magical powers. ✐ **p. 969.**

mag-net [MAG-nit] NOUN, magnets. **1. aimant** ▸ a piece of metal, rock, or other material that has the power to attract iron and steel toward it. **2. aimant** ▸ anything that strongly attracts people to it : *The new video game acted like a magnet, drawing all the players to it.*

mag-net-ic [mag-NET-ik] ADJECTIVE. **1. magnétique** ▸ having the properties of a magnet : *Compass needles are magnetic and show direction*

🔧 Word Builder

*Machine, engine, and appliance are all devices that apply energy to do work for people. A **machine** is a device in which power is given at one point and work is done at another such as levers and earth diggers. An **engine** is a machine such as a car engine that changes heat, electrical, waterpower, or other types of energy into mechanical power. An **appliance** is thought of as an electrically powered device used to do household work such as a washing machine or toaster.*

by pointing to the north. **2. magnétique** ▶ having a great power to attract, as if by a magnet. **Note.** Magnetic north is the point on the earth that compass needles point to. It is south of the North Pole.

mag·ni·fi·cent [mag-NIF-uh-sunt] ADJECTIVE. **magnifique, splendide, superbe** ▶ very grand, beautiful, or outstanding : *"The Tong monastery possessed the most magnificent library in all of China."* (David Day) ▪ **magnificence,** NOUN. ▶ **magnificence, splendeur, richesse.** SYN : splendid, noble, grand, glorious, brilliant.

mag·ni·fy [MAG-nuh-fy] VERB, magnified, magnifying. **1. grossir** ▶ to make something look larger than it actually is : *A microscope magnifies almost invisible objects so that people can see them.* **2. exagérer** ▶ to make something seem greater or more important than it really is; exaggerate : *Rod sometimes magnifies a small problem until he can think of nothing else.* **Note.** A magnifying glass is a lens or combination of lenses that makes objects look larger than they are.

mag·ni·tude [MAG-nuh-TOOD] NOUN. **ampleur, importance** ▶ of great size, importance, effect, or extent : *The magnitude of the problem weighed them down like a stone.*

ma·hog·a·ny [muh-HOG-uh-nee] NOUN. **1. acajou** ▶ an evergreen tree that grows in tropical climates. Its strong reddish-brown wood is of very high quality and is often used to make furniture and musical instruments. **2. acajou** ▶ a dark, reddish-brown colour like this wood. **Note.** Also used as an ADJECTIVE : *a mahogany table.*

maid [made] NOUN, maids. **1. domestique** ▶ a woman servant, especially one who does washing and cleaning. **2. jeune fille** ▶ an old word for an unmarried girl or young woman ; a maiden.

maid·en [MADE-un] NOUN, maidens. **jeune fille** ▶ an old word for a girl or young woman who is not married : *"South Wind was a beautiful maiden."* (Rosebud Yellow Robe) ▲ ADJECTIVE. **premier (-ière), inaugural (-ale, -aux)** ▶ first; earliest : *The ocean liner* Titanic *sank on its maiden voyage.*

mail[1] [male] NOUN, mails. **1. courrier** ▶ letters, packages, postcards, and the like sent from one place to another through the post office. **Note.** Often the mail: *I got the mail early today.*

2. poste ▶ the public system by which mail is sent and delivered : *She sent out the invitations by mail.* ▲ VERB, mailed, mailing. **poster, envoyer par la poste** ▶ to send by mail. **Note.** A mailbox is a public box from which mail is collected or a private box to which mail is delivered.

mail[2] **mailles** ▶ in the Middle Ages, a type of armour made of small metal plates or rings linked together, used to protect the body during battle.

main [mane] ADJECTIVE. **principal (-ale, -aux)** ▶ first in size or importance : *the main street of a town.* **Note.** Main is part of several compound words—for example, *mainsail, mainstream,* and *mainstay.* ▲ NOUN, mains. **canalisation ou conduite maîtresse** ▶ a large pipe that carries water, gas, electricity, or the like to or from a central location. SYN : major, leading, primary, central, principal.

main·frame [MANE-frame] NOUN, mainframes. **ordinateur central** ▶ a very powerful computer that is able to process huge amounts of information. One mainframe can handle information for many different terminals that are connected to it.

main·land [MANE-LAND or MANE-lund] NOUN, mainlands. **continent** ▶ the main land mass of an area or a continent, apart from outlying islands : *There is a small island just off the mainland.*

main·ly [MANE-lee] ADVERB. **principalement** ▶ for the most part; chiefly : *His bookcase holds mainly mysteries, which he reads over and over.*

main·tain [mane-TANE] VERB, maintained, maintaining. **1. maintenir, garder, conserver** ▶ to continue or carry on in the same way : *"Even today, sled dogs are bred with wolves to maintain their wolf-like size and strength."* (Robert McGhee) **2. entretenir** ▶ to keep in good condition; take care of : *The house is in good shape because the owners maintained it carefully.* **3. soutenir** ▶ to say strongly; declare; insist : *"Do you know, though, to his dying day he maintained that he didn't know which lake he'd caught it in."* (Ted Stone) **Note.** Maintenance is the act or fact of maintaining something : *People are responsible for the maintenance of their pets.* SYN : keep, provide for, support, preserve.

maize [maze] NOUN. **maïs** ▸ the corn plant or its ears or kernels.

ma·jes·tic [muh-JES-tik] ADJECTIVE. **majestueux (-euse)** ▸ having or showing majesty, very grand or dignified : *The parade was a majestic sight as it wound its way through town.* ■ **majestically,** ADVERB. ▸ **majestueusement.** SYN: grand, magnificent, splendid, noble.

ma·jes·ty [MAJ-is-tee] NOUN. majesties. **1.** Majesty. **Sa (Votre) Majesté** ▸ the title used with Her, His, or Your when speaking to or about a king or queen. **2. majesté** ▸ a very grand and impressive quality : *"As he rose quickly into the air, the sun gradually regained its sparkle and majesty."* (Tololwa M. Mollel)

ma·jor [MAY-jur] ADJECTIVE. **1. majeur (-eure)** ▸ great in size or importance : *The major meeting place was the town square.* **2. principal (-ale, -aux)** ▸ greater than another or others; main : *The major idea of her speech was that peace is worth the effort.* ▲ NOUN. majors. **1. major** ▸ a rank in the armed forces, above a captain and below a lieutenant-colonel. **2. majeure** ▸ a student's main subject at university : *Eileen's major is physics.* SYN: superior, senior, important.

ma·jor·i·ty [muh-JOR-uh-tee] NOUN. majorities. **1. majorité** ▸ the greater of two numbers; more than half : *The majority of Canadians live in or near large cities.* **2. majorité** ▸ the difference between a larger and a smaller number : *The last bill passed with a majority of 12—55 votes for and 43 against.*

make [make] VERB. made, making. **1. faire, fabriquer, construire** ▸ to bring something into being, especially by putting parts or materials together : *"The old man set to making a bed for the boy to sleep on."* (Tololwa M. Mollel) **2. faire** ▸ to cause something to happen; bring about : *to make a telephone call.* **3. rendre** ▸ to cause someone or something to be in a certain condition : *I don't eat mushrooms because they make me sick.* **4. faire, obliger, forcer** ▸ to force someone to act in a certain way : *They put speed bumps in the parking lot to make people slow down.* **5.** *Informal.* **attraper** ▸ to catch : *to make a 6:30 train.* **6. gagner** ▸ to gain or earn : *I make $2.50 an hour baby-sitting.* ▲ NOUN. makes. **marque** ▸ the way in which something is made; a brand or style : *What make is your new TV set?* SYN: build, construct, create, manufacture. ✐ **p. 355.**

make up a. inventer, fabriquer ▸ to invent : *to make up a story.* **b. se réconcilier** ▸ to become friends again after a quarrel.

make over reprendre, convertir ▸ to make different; change.

make-be·lieve [MAKE-bih-LEEV] NOUN. **fiction, imaginaire** ▸ imagination; pretence : *the world of make-believe.* ▲ ADJECTIVE. **fictif (-ive), imaginaire** ▸ a make-believe pet.

mak·er [MAY-kur] NOUN. makers. **fabricant (-ante)** ▸ a person or thing that makes something : *The maker of this furniture is famous.* **Note.** Often used in combination with other words : *a dressmaker; a watchmaker.*

make-up [MAKE-up] NOUN. make-ups. (also makeup) **1. constitution** ▸ the particular way that something is formed or arranged : *The make-up of the team provided a strong defence, but a weak offence.* **2. maquillage** ▸ powders, creams, lipstick, and other cosmetics put on the face to change one's appearance. Actors often wear make-up to appear much older, to look frightening or silly, and so on. ✐ **p. 1011.**

ma·lar·i·a [muh-LAIR-ee-uh] NOUN. **paludisme, malaria** ▸ a disease that causes a high fever, sweating, and severe chills. Malaria is carried from one person to another by the female of certain types of mosquitoes, which transmit the disease when they bite someone.

male [male] ADJECTIVE. **1. mâle** ▸ having to do with the sex that can father young : *A male elephant is called a bull.* **2. masculin (-ine), mâle** ▸ having to do with men or boys : *a male choir; male students.* ▲ NOUN. males. **mâle** ▸ a male person or animal.

mal·ice [MAL-iss] NOUN. **méchanceté** ▸ a wish to hurt someone or to see him or her suffer : *He showed no malice toward the person who had won the contest.* ■ **malicious,** ADJECTIVE. ▸ **méchant (-ante),** wishing to hurt others; spiteful. ■ **maliciously,** ADVERB. ▸ **avec méchanceté.**

mall [mol] NOUN. malls. **1. rue piétonnière, mail** ▸ a public walkway that is closed to auto traffic. **2. centre commercial** ▸ a shopping

---

✐ **Word Builder**

*Make is found in the expression **make do**, which means to get along with whatever is available : I'll make do with these shoes. **Make up** means to resolve a quarrel and become friends again after a disagreement : Sheila and Miko made up after an argument over who won the race. If a person **makes good**, it means he or she have become successful. **Make good** can also mean that a person is able to deliver on a commitment : Cherry will make good on her promise to take out the garbage.*

centre, especially one that is enclosed and has a central walkway with shops on either side.

mal·lard [MAL-urd] NOUN, mallards. **colvert ▶** a common wild duck found in many parts of the world. The female has a brownish body, with blue bands on the wings, and the male has a green head, a white band around the neck, a reddish-brown chest, and a grey back.

mallard

mam·mal [MAM-ul] NOUN, mammals. **mammifère ▶** a member of the large group of animals that are warm-blooded, have a backbone, and usually have fur or hair on their bodies. Female mammals produce milk for their young. Almost all mammals are born alive, rather than hatched from eggs. Mammals include humans, dogs, cattle, mice, and whales. 📙 **p. 1092.** 👁 **p. 110.**

mam·moth [MAM-uth] NOUN, mammoths. **mammouth ▶** a type of elephant that lived in ancient times. The last ones died out about 10,000 years ago. ▲ ADJECTIVE. **géant (-ante) ▶** very large; huge: *Brazil's national soccer team plays in a mammoth stadium that holds 200,000 people.* SYN: giant, huge, gigantic, colossal.

mammoth

✎ Writing Tips

Man/Woman/People

*In earlier times, the words **man** and **men** were used to refer to all humans.*

"All men are created equal."

"No man is an island."

*Nowadays, expressions like these are avoided because they are considered offensive to women. If you want to write a statement that refers to all of the human race, use the word **people, humanity,** or **humankind.***

man [man] NOUN, men. **1. homme ▶** a full-grown male person; a male who is no longer a boy. **2. hommes ▶** adult men as a group. **Note.** At one time this word was used to refer to all humans, male or female: *All men were created equal.* ▲ VERB, manned, manning. **pourvoir en personnel ▶** an older word meaning "to supply with people for work": *Most of the village manned the crumbling dam, piling up sandbags.* **Note.** Now considered sexist language. To avoid it, rewrite the sentence: *Most of the village worked at the crumbling dam.* SYN: male, fellow, guy, gentleman, sir. ✐ **p. 356.**

man·age [MAN-ij] VERB, managed, managing. **1. gérer, diriger ▶** to be in charge of something; control; direct: *to manage a store.* **Note.** A person who manages something is a manager: *the manager of a movie theatre.* **2. réussir, parvenir à ▶** to be able to deal with a situation, especially a difficult one; get along: *We managed to put the fire out.* SYN: direct, deal with, govern, control, administer.

man·age·ment [MAN-ij-munt] NOUN. **1. gestion, administration ▶** the act of managing something: *Careful management of her money allowed her to take a trip each year.* **2.** (plural, managements) **direction, cadres ▶** the people who manage a business or company. SYN: direction, administration, government.

man·do·lin [MAN-duh-LIN *or* MAN-duh-LIN] NOUN, mandolins. **mandoline ▶** a small musical instrument somewhat like a guitar. A mandolin has a pear-shaped body and four to six pairs of strings.

mane [mane] NOUN, manes. **crinière ▶** a growth of long, thick hair on the neck and shoulders of some animals, such as horses and male lions.

man·i·a [MAY-nee-uh] NOUN. **1. manie ▶** a mental illness that can cause a person to become very excited or violent. **2.** (plural manias) **manie ▶** a very strong liking for something: *Mom has a mania for crossword puzzles and does one every morning.*

ma·ni·ac [MAY-nee-ak] NOUN, maniacs. **maniaque** ▸ a person who behaves wildly or violently : *He drives like a maniac.*

man·kind [MAN-kynd or MAN-KYND] NOUN. **humanité, le genre humain** ▸ an old word for human beings as a group ; the human race ; humanity ; humankind.

man·ner [MAN-ur] NOUN. **1. manière, façon** ▸ the way in which something happens or is done : *She packed the glasses in a very careful manner.* **2. comportement, attitude** ▸ a certain way of acting or behaving : *He has a gentle and kind manner.* **3. manners. manières** ▸ a way of behaving that is considered polite or proper : *It is a sign of bad manners to interrupt someone who is speaking.* **4. sorte, genre** ▸ a kind or type : *"Here…fences, chairs, and every manner of basket."* (Donald Carrick) ▪ **mannerly,** ADJECTIVE: having or showing good manners ; polite. ▸ **poli (-ie), bien élevé (-ée).** **Note.** To be mannerless is to have bad manners. SYN: fashion, form, kind, sort, type, way, style.

ma·noeu·vre [muh-NOO-vur] NOUN, manoeuvres. (also maneuver) **1. manœuvre, intrigue, manège** ▸ a clever plan or action, usually one meant to fool or trick someone : *Good basketball players learn many manoeuvres with the ball.* **2. manœuvre** ▸ a planned movement of military troops or ships : *The surprise attack on the enemy was a brilliant manoeuvre.* **3. manoeuvres. manœuvres** ▸ such movements carried out as a training exercise : *The fleet is on manoeuvres in the Indian Ocean this month.* ▲ VERB, manoeuvred, manoeuvring. **1. manœuvrer pour faire entrer, faire sortir, faire passer** ▸ to move or guide something : *The passengers manoeuvred their luggage through the narrow door.* **2. manœuvrer** ▸ to plan cleverly ; scheme : *Alberto manoeuvred to get a seat next to Kristen.*

man·sion [MAN-shun] NOUN, mansions. **manoir, hôtel particulier** ▸ a very large, expensive house with many rooms.

man·tel [MAN-tul] NOUN, mantels. **manteau de cheminée, dessus de cheminée** ▸ a shelf, beam, or arch located above a fireplace. **Note.** Also called a mantelpiece.

man·tle [MAN-tul] NOUN, mantles. **1. cape, mante** ▸ a loose cape ; a sleeveless cloak. **2. manteau** ▸ anything that covers like a mantle : *In the morning, a fresh mantle of snow lay on the ground.* **3. manteau** ▸ the part of the earth beneath the crust and above the outer core. ▲ VERB, mantled, mantling. **couvrir, recouvrir** ▸ to cover with a mantle.

man·u·al [MAN-yoo-ul] ADJECTIVE. **1. manuel (-elle)** ▸ having to do with the hands ; involving the use of the hands : *Cutting down trees, washing windows, and painting a house are forms of manual labour.* **2. manuel (-elle)** ▸ not operating automatically : *A manual typewriter does*

not run on electricity. ▲ NOUN, manuals. **manuel** ▸ a book of instructions on how to do something ; a handbook or guidebook : *A new car comes with an owner's manual showing how the car works.* **Note.** Manual comes from *manus,* the Latin word for "hand."

man·u·fac·ture [MAN-yuh-FAK-chur] VERB, manufactured, manufacturing. **1. fabriquer** ▸ to make a product in large amounts by hand or by machine : *to manufacture trucks ; to manufacture clothing.* **2. fabriquer, inventer** ▸ to invent or make up : *They manufactured an excuse for being late.* ▲ NOUN, manufactures. **fabrication** ▸ the act of manufacturing, or something that is manufactured. ▪ **manufacturer,** NOUN. ▸ **fabricant (-ante).** *Many auto manufacturers use robots to build cars.* SYN: make, build, construct, produce.

ma·nure [muh-NOOR or muh-NYOOR] NOUN. **fumier** ▸ waste products of animals, such as cattle or chickens, used as a fertilizer to enrich the soil.

man·u·script [MAN-yuh-skript] NOUN, manuscripts. **1. manuscrit** ▸ in early times, a book or paper written by hand. **2. manuscrit** ▸ in modern times, an unpublished copy of a book, an article, or another piece of writing.

man·y [MEN-ee] ADJECTIVE. **beaucoup, un grand nombre** ▸ being a large number ; great in number : *"He won so many prizes that it took twelve porters to carry them to the ship."* (Marcia Williams) ▲ NOUN; PRONOUN. **beaucoup** ▸ a large number : *Many of us went to the movies. A lot of people enter contests, but not many win.* SYN: several, numerous, various, plenty.

map [map] NOUN, maps. **carte** ▸ a drawing or chart showing a place and its important features, such as oceans, rivers, mountains, countries, cities, roads, and so on. ▲ VERB, mapped, mapping. **dresser la carte de** ▸ to make a map of ; show on a map : *Amerigo Vespucci mapped the coastline of South America in the early 1500s.*

map out tracer ▸ to plan something in careful detail, as if making a map : *Our committee has mapped out plans for a spring festival.*

ma·ple [MAY-pul] NOUN, maples. **érable** ▸ a tall tree that grows widely in the northern half of the world. Maple wood is strong and hard and is used to make furniture. **Note.** The best-known North American maple tree is the sugar maple, whose sap is used to make maple syrup and maple sugar. **Note.** The maple leaf is a Canadian symbol and appears on the Canadian flag. The flag itself is often called the Maple Leaf. 👁 p. 254, 262, 358.

mar [mar] VERB, marred, marring. **1. gâcher, gâter** ▸ to damage or spoil the appearance of : *The table is marred by several deep scratches.* **2. gâcher** ▸ to spoil the quality of ; damage : *The team's victory was marred by an injury to the* *goalie.* SYN: mark, spoil, damage, blemish, deface.

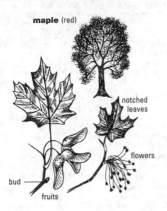

maple (red)

notched leaves

flowers

bud

fruits

mar-a-thon [MAIR-uh-THON] NOUN, marathons. **1. marathon ▸** a foot race of 42.195 kilometres, run over roads and open ground rather than around a track. **Note.** The marathon race gets its name from the Battle of Marathon in 490 B.C., in which the Greeks defeated the Persians. A long-distance runner carried news of the victory to the city of Athens. **2. marathon ▸** any very long race or competition : *In a dance marathon, people try to dance for days.*

mar-ble [MAR-bul] NOUN. **1. marbre ▸** a very hard, smooth stone that is used in buildings, floors, and statues. Marble is usually white or streaked with different colours. **2. marbles. billes ▸** a children's game played with small balls that were once made of marble, but now are glass. Players take turns shooting their marbles to knock other players' marbles out of a ring. **3.** (plural, marbles) **bille ▸** a small ball of marble or glass used in this game.

march [march] VERB, marched, marching. **1. marcher ▸** to walk with regular, even steps, as is done by members of a band, people in a parade, soldiers, and so on. **2. marcher au pas ▸** to walk in a steady determined way. **3. s'écouler ▸** to move or advance in a steady way : *Time marches on.* ▲ NOUN, marches. **1. marche ▸** the act of marching, or the distance marched : *The campers faced a march of 10 kilometres.* **2. marche ▸** a piece of music with a strong, steady beat, used for marching : *A dignified march is often played at school graduation ceremonies.*

March [march] NOUN, Marches. **mars ▸** the third month of the year, between February and April. March has 31 days.

mare [mair] NOUN, mares. **jument ▸** the female of a horse or related animal, such as a donkey or zebra.

mar-ga-rine [MAR-juh-rin] NOUN, margarines. **margarine ▸** a soft, smooth food that is used in place of butter. Margarine is made from vegetable oil and colouring or flavouring.

mar-gin [MAR-jin] NOUN, margins. **1. bord ▸** the edge of something and the area next to it ; border. **2. marge ▸** the blank space between the edges of a page and the printed or written part. **3. marge ▸** an extra part or amount in addition to what is needed : *Candy won the race by a wide margin.* 🖉 p. 69.

mar-i-gold [MAIR-uh-GOLD] NOUN, marigolds. **souci ▸** a garden plant that has orange, yellow, or red flowers.

ma-rine [muh-REEN] ADJECTIVE. **1. marin (-ine) ▸** having to do with the ocean : *Marine mammals include whales and dolphins.* **2. marin (-ine) ▸** having to do with ships and boats : *He bought paint for his sailboat at the marine supply store.* ▲ NOUN, marines. **marines ▸** a soldier once serving only at sea, but now serving on land and in the air. Canada does not have marines.

mar-i-time [MAIR-ih-TIME] ADJECTIVE. **1. maritime ▸** on or near the sea : *Dartmouth and Halifax are maritime cities.* **2. maritime ▸** living near the sea. **3.** Maritime. **Maritimes ▸** of or having to do with the Maritime Provinces.

Maritime Provinces (also the Maritimes) **Provinces maritimes ▸** three provinces on the Atlantic coast of Canada : New Brunswick, Nova Scotia, and Prince Edward Island. **Note.** When Newfoundland is included, use the term Atlantic Provinces.

mark [mark] NOUN, marks. **1. marque ▸** anything on an object that shows where something has touched the surface, leaving a spot, a line, a chip, and so on : *The baby left finger marks on the wall.* **2. signe ▸** a line, sign, or symbol written or printed to show something : *The teacher put a check mark next to each right answer.* **3. note, point ▸** a letter or number used in school to show the level a student has earned ; a grade : *Dana got the highest mark on the math test.* **4. signet, repère ▸** something used to show a certain position or place : *a bookmark.* **5. cible, but ▸** a goal or target that is aimed at : *Robin Hood always hit the mark with his arrows.* ▲ VERB, marked, marking. **1. marquer ▸** to make a mark : *"Before moving Sluggo from his bowl, Aunt Esther marked his shell with some red fingernail polish so she could distinguish him from the rest."* (Cynthia Rylant) **2. noter ▸** to give a school mark to ; grade : *to mark a test paper.* **3. indiquer, signaler ▸** to be a mark or feature of ; show or indicate : *The falling leaves marked the coming of winter.* 🖉 **p. 359.**

✒ Word Builder

Mark down means to write or note something down. Often you might see the term used in a store where *mark down* means to offer at a lower price. On the other hand, *mark up* can mean to increase the price or to spoil by making marks on something: *The dogs marked up the window with their muddy paws. Mark time* can mean to pass time or go through the motions of doing things without accomplishing anything: *While waiting for the bus, we marked time by playing tag.*

mar·ket [MAR-kit] NOUN, markets. **1. marché ▸** a store or other place where goods are sold : *We bought steak at the market.* **2. marché ▸** a public place for buying and selling goods or services. **3. marché ▸** buyers of a certain type : *That science-fiction movie was intended for the teenage market.* **4. marché, demande, clientèle ▸** a demand for something that is for sale : *There is still a large market for TV sets and VCRs.* ▲ VERB, marketed, marketing. **1. vendre, mettre en marché ▸** to sell or offer to sell : *Italian shoe companies often market their products in other countries.* **Note.** Marketing is the process by which companies try to find buyers for their products or services. Advertising and selling are major parts of marketing. **2. faire le marché, faire les courses ▸** to go shopping for food and supplies : *Most people market on weekends.* SYN : shop, store, fair, bazaar.

mar·ket·place [MAR-kit-PLACE] NOUN, marketplaces. **1. marché, place du marché ▸** a place in which a market is held. **2. marché ▸** the world of business. **3. marché ▸** an exchange of works, opinions, and ideas.

ma·roon[1] [muh-ROON] VERB, marooned, marooning. **1. abandonner ▸** to put people on shore in a deserted or isolated place and leave them there : *In olden times, a ship's captain could maroon sailors on a deserted island as punishment.* **2. abandonner ▸** to leave someone alone or helpless; strand : *Tyler was marooned at the cabin all weekend without a car or a boat.* ✒ **p. 360.**

maroon[2] NOUN, maroons. **bordeaux ▸** a dark brownish-red colour.

mar·riage [MAIR-ij] NOUN, marriages. **1. mariage ▸** the fact of being married : *My grandparents have had a long and happy marriage.* **2. mariage ▸** the act or ceremony of marrying; a wedding : *The marriage will take place next week.*

mar·ry [MAIR-ee] VERB, married, marrying. **1. marier ▸** to legally join a man and a woman as husband and wife : *Judges, priests, and ministers have the power to marry couples.* **2. se marier, épouser ▸** to take someone for one's husband or wife : *"That's Cowherd. He married Weaving Maid, who weaves the clouds in their sunset colours."* (Julie Lawson) SYN : matrimony, wedlock, union, match.

Mars [marz] NOUN. **1. Mars ▸** the seventh-largest planet in the solar system. Mars has two moons and is the fourth-closet planet to the sun. **2. Mars ▸** in the religion of the ancient Romans, the god of war. 👁 **p. 391.**

marsh [marsh] NOUN, marshes. **marécage, marais ▸** an area of soft, low land that is partly or completely covered by water. ■ **marshy,** ADJECTIVE. **1. marécageux (-euse) ▸** soft and wet like a marsh. **2. marécageux (-euse) ▸** having many marshes.

marsh·mal·low [MARSH-mal-oh *or* MARSH-mel-oh] NOUN, marshmallows. **guimauve ▸** a soft white candy covered with powdered sugar.

mar·vel [MAR-vul] NOUN, marvels. **merveille ▸** someone or something that is very surprising, outstanding, or unusual : *She is a marvel at organizing people to get things done.* ▲ VERB, marvelled, marvelling. (also marveled, marveling) **s'émerveiller ▸** to be filled with wonder, amazement, or astonishment : *"Leif marvelled at the stories—and at how Bjarni could pass by such tempting new lands without bothering to go ashore."* (Charnan Simon)

mar·vel·lous [MAR-vuh-lus] ADJECTIVE. (also marvelous) **1. merveilleux (-euse), magnifique ▸** causing wonder or great admiration; astonishing; amazing : *a marvellous sunset.* **2. splendide, formidable ▸** very good; excellent; splendid : *a marvellous day.* ■ **marvellously,** ADVERB. **▸ merveilleusement.** SYN : wonderful, fabulous, amazing, remarkable.

mas·cot [MAS-kot] NOUN, mascots. **mascotte ▸** an animal, person, or thing that is supposed to bring good luck : *My sister's club has an eagle for a mascot.*

mas·cu·line [MAS-kyuh-lin] ADJECTIVE. **1. masculin (-ine) ▸** of or belonging to men or boys. **2. masculin (-ine) ▸** typical or suited for men.

mash [mash] VERB, mashed, mashing. **écraser, broyer ▸** to beat or crush something into a soft mass : *Dad asked me to mash the potatoes for dinner.* ▲ NOUN, mashes. **pâtée, purée ▸** a soft mixture of grain and warm water that is used for feeding horses and other animals.

mask [mask] NOUN, masks. **1. masque ▸** a covering worn to protect or hide the face : *Firefighters wear masks when they enter a smoke-filled building.* **2. masque ▸** anything that hides or

✏ Word Builder

Maroon, abandon, and *desert* all mean to leave a person behind. *Maroon* means to intentionally leave a person behind on a deserted island or a coastal area: *The sailor was marooned on a deserted island.* *Abandon* can mean to give someone or something up that a person was interested in or felt responsible for: *We abandoned our sinking rowboat.* The meaning of *desert* is very similar to abandon, but it also suggests that leaving someone behind was the wrong thing to do: *She felt bad that she deserted her friend in a time of need.*

covers something like a mask : *"The moon made his face into a silver mask."* (Jane Yolen) ▲ VERB, masked, masking. **1. masquer ▶** to cover the face with a mask : **2. masquer, cacher, dissimuler ▶** to hide or cover up : *The new paint masked the cracks in the wall.* SYN: hide, disguise, veil.

mass [mas] NOUN. **1. amas, masse ▶** a body of matter that has no particular shape; a pile or lump : *The heavy rains left a mass of mud at the bottom of the driveway.* **2. masse, multitude ▶** a large quantity or amount : *A mass of wildflowers covered the hillside.* **3. the masses. masses ▶** ordinary or average people as a group; the common people. **4. masse ▶** the amount of matter in an object or body. Mass causes a thing to have a certain weight from the pull of gravity. ▲ VERB, massed, massing. **(se) masser, (se) réunir ▶** to gather or form into a mass. ▲ ADJECTIVE. **1. massif (-ive), collectif (-ive), grand (grande) ▶** of or including many people : *Farmers of this region held a mass protest this week.* **2. de masse ▶** on a large-scale : *Mass media are large-scale communication systems with a wide audience, such as television, radio, magazines, newspapers, and the Internet.* **Note.** Mass production is the use of machinery to make many items of the product, such as a car.

Mass [mas] NOUN, Masses. (sometimes mass) **messe ▶** the main religious service in the Catholic Church and some other Christian churches.

mas·sa·cre [MAS-uh-kur] NOUN, massacres. **massacre, extermination, tuerie ▶** a cruel and needless killing of many people or animals; slaughter. ▲ VERB, massacred, massacring. **massacrer, exterminer ▶** to kill in this way.

mas·sive [MAS-iv] ADJECTIVE. **massif (-ive), énorme, imposant (-ante) ▶** having great size or mass; strong and heavy; huge : *The Tyrannosaurus rex was one of the most massive animals on earth.* SYN: big, large, imposing, huge.

mast [mast] NOUN, masts. **mât ▶** a long pole that rises straight up from the deck of a ship, used to hold up the sails.

mas·ter [MAS-tur] NOUN, masters. **1. maître (-esse) ▶** a person who has power or control over others : *The dog ran over as soon as its master called.* **2. maître (-esse) ▶** a person who has great skill or is a great expert at something : *She is a master of the Japanese tea ceremony and always performs it beautifully.* **3. Master. monsieur ▶** an old word used instead of "Mister," to address a boy. **4. capitaine ▶** the captain of a merchant ship. ▲ ADJECTIVE. **1. maître (-esse) ▶** very skilled at working or doing things with the hands : *a master carpenter; a master printer.* **2. maître (-esse), original (-ale, -aux), principal (-ale, -aux) ▶** most important; main : *A master copy of a song is the original recording from which CDs and tapes are recorded.* **3. général (-ale, -aux) ▶** being in control of a system or operation : *a master switch.* ▲ VERB, mastered, mastering. **1. maîtriser, surmonter ▶** to become the master of; bring under control : *She mastered her fear of speaking in public and gave a speech to the entire school.* **2. apprendre, posséder ▶** to become an expert in; become skillful at : *Dana has mastered in-line skating and now skates every day.* **Note.** The act or fact of mastering something is mastery.

mas·ter·piece [MAS-tur-PEES] NOUN, masterpieces. **chef-d'œuvre ▶** an outstanding work or accomplishment, especially in the arts.

mat [mat] NOUN, mats. **1. tapis ▶** a small piece of material used as a floor covering : *Our neighbours have a welcome mat outside their front door.* **2. napperon ▶** a small piece of material put under a dish, lamp, or other object to protect a surface or act as a decoration : *He set the table with place mats and matching napkins.* **3. tapis ▶** a thick pad used on the floor of a gymnasium or other sports area to protect someone who falls or jumps. **4. enchevêtrement, fouillis ▶** a thick or tangled mass : *a mat of hair.* ▲ VERB, matted, matting. **emmêler ▶** to become tangled in a thick mass.

match¹ [mach] NOUN, matches. **allumette ▶** a small stick of wood or cardboard coated on one end with chemicals that will catch fire when the match is rubbed against a rough surface. **Note.** *Matchbook, matchbox,* and *matchstick* are compounds associated with this meaning of *match*.

match² NOUN, matches. **1. équivalent (-ente), égal (-ale, -aux) ▶** a person or thing that is equal to or very much like another : *That jacket is a match for one I have at home.* **2. assorti (-ie)** ▶ someone or something that goes well with another : *That blue sweater would be a good match for your grey pants.* **3. match, partie** ▶ a game or contest : *a chess match; a soccer match.* ▲ VERB, matched, matching. **1. aller bien avec, assortir, appareiller** ▶ to be similar or go well together : **2. égaler** ▶ to be the same as : *In the card game "Go Fish," you collect cards that match.* **3. être à la hauteur, rivaliser** ▶ to compete with as an equal : *She worked hard to match her tennis partner's skill.*

mate [mate] NOUN, mates. **1. double** ▶ one of a pair : *I'm looking for the mate to this sock.* **2. mari, femme** ▶ a husband or wife. **3. mâle, femelle** ▶ the male or female of a pair of animals or birds : *A female lion does much more hunting than her mate does.* **4. second (-onde)** ▶ an officer on a merchant ship : *The first mate ranks just below the ship's master or captain.* ▲ VERB, mated, mating. **(s') accoupler** ▶ of animals, to join together for breeding : *Canada geese mate for life.*

ma-te-ri-al [muh-TEER-ee-ul] NOUN, materials. **1. matériau (-aux)** ▶ what something is made of or used for : *Wood and brick are common building materials.* **2. tissu, étoffe** ▶ fabric for clothing : *The material was a blend of cotton and linen.* ▲ ADJECTIVE. **1. matériel (-elle)** ▶ made of matter; physical : *We live in the material world, not the world of imagination.* **2. matériel (-elle)** ▶ having to do with the body or the physical world : *material needs such as food and clothing.* ■ **materially,** ADVERB. ▶ **matériellement.**

ma-te-ri-al-ize [muh-TEER-ee-ul-IZE] VERB, materialized, materializing. **1. se matérialiser** ▶ to take on a physical form. **2. se réaliser** ▶ to become real : *Their ideas for the house materialized after years of work.*

math [math] NOUN. **math(s)** ▶ short for mathematics.

math-e-mat-ics [MATH-uh-MAT-iks] NOUN. **mathématique(s)** ▶ the study of numbers, quantities, and the way these things are measured and relate to one another. Arithmetic, algebra, and geometry are branches of mathematics. **Note.** An expert in mathematics is called a mathematician.

mat-i-née [MAT-uh-NAY] NOUN, matinées. (also matinee) **concert en matinée, spectacle en matinée** ▶ a play or other performance in the afternoon.

mat-ter [MAT-ur] NOUN, matters. **1. matière** ▶ anything that has weight and takes up space. All things are made up of matter. Matter can be a solid, liquid, or gas. **2. sujet, question** ▶ anything to be dealt with or thought about ; a subject that is given attention : *Mom knows a lot* *about financial matters.* **3. problème** ▶ trouble ; a problem : *Let's deal with the matter quickly.* **Note.** Used in the phrase the matter: *What's the matter with Judy? She hasn't said a word all morning.* ▲ VERB, mattered, mattering. **importer, compter** ▶ to be important ; make a difference : *All that matters is whether or not I make the team.* SYN: object, thing, material, substance.

no matter a. peu importe ▶ it is not important. **b. peu importe comment** ▶ regardless of : *No matter how often Yasmin hikes in the Rockies, she is always filled with awe and wonder.*

mat-tress [MAT-rus] NOUN, mattresses. **matelas** ▶ a thick pad used for sleeping on. A mattress usually fits within the frame of the bed.

ma-ture [muh-CHOOR or muh-TOOR] ADJECTIVE. **1. mûr (mûre)** ▶ fully grown or developed : *Mature oak trees can be over 30 metres high.* **2. adulte** ▶ having to do with or suitable for an adult : *This movie is recommended for mature audiences only.* ▲ VERB, matured, maturing. **mûrir** ▶ to become full-grown ; become an adult. ■ **maturity,** NOUN. ▶ **maturité.**

max-i-mum [MAKS-suh-mum] NOUN, maximums or maxima. **maximum** ▶ the greatest or highest number or point : *The gas tank of our car holds a maximum of 40 litres.* ▲ ADJECTIVE. **maximal (-ale, -aux)** ▶ greatest or highest possible : *The maximum speed limit on that road is 60 km/hr.*

may [may] VERB. **May pouvoir** ▶ is a special verb that is used with other verbs in these meanings : **1. se pouvoir** ▶ it is more or less likely : *I may have left my jacket at school.* **2. permettre, avoir la permission** ▶ it is allowed : *Swimmers may use any part of the south beach.* **3. espérer, souhaiter** ▶ it is hoped that : *May fortune be good to you.* 🖝 p. 83.

May [may] NOUN, Mays. **mai** ▶ the fifth month of the year, between April and June. May has 31 days. **Note.** May Day is a spring festival held on May 1.

may-be [MAY-be] **peut-être** ▶ possibly ; perhaps : *Maybe next month I'll win the lottery.*

May-day [MAY-DAY] NOUN, Maydays. (also mayday) **S.O.S.** ▶ an international distress signal used in emergencies by ships and aircraft.

may-on-naise [MAY-uh-NAZE or MAY-uh-NAZE] NOUN. **mayonnaise** ▶ a thick dressing for salads, sandwiches, and other foods. Mayonnaise is made of egg yolks, oil, vinegar or lemon juice, and seasonings, beaten together until thick.

may-or [MAY-ur] NOUN, mayors. **maire (mairesse)** ▶ a person who is the head of a city or town government.

maze [maze] NOUN, mazes. **1. labyrinthe, dédale** ▶ a complicated series of paths through which it is hard to find one's way : *"He had to find his way through a maze of streets with*

Writing Tips

May and Might
May and *might* can both be used to express desire or doubt. They are different forms of the same verb, and most of the time you will be able to tell what form you should use by the other verbs in the sentence.
• Use *may* when there is a good chance something will happen, and *might* when the chances are not as good.
  We *may* get a puppy on Sunday. We might get a cat as well.
• *May* and *might* express the possibility that something will happen, so avoid using them with "possibly," "perhaps," or "maybe."
  For example,
  We *may* eat at the new diner. Not we *may possibly* eat at the new diner.

high walls." (Hal Ober) 2. **labyrinthe, dédale** ▶ any complicated situation like a maze : *He finds the tax system very confusing and says that it's a maze of rules and forms.*

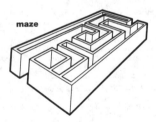

maze

me [mee] PRONOUN. **m', me, moi** ▶ the pronoun *I* when used as an object : *Call me tomorrow. Daryl lent this tape to me.* 🖉 **p. 362.**

mead·ow [MED-oh] NOUN, meadows. **pré, prairie** ▶ a large area of grassy land, especially one where farm animals feed or where hay is grown.

meal[1] [meel] NOUN, meals. **repas** ▶ the food served or eaten at one time : *a meal of soup and salad.* 🗁 **p. 1137.**

meal[2] NOUN, meals. **farine** ▶ corn or other grain that has been ground up into a coarse powder.

mean[1] [meen] VERB, meant, meaning. 1. **vouloir dire, signifier** ▶ to have the sense of; be defined as : *What does that word mean?* 2. **avoir l'intention, vouloir** ▶ to want to do or say; to intend : *When I'm older, I mean to travel the*

world 3. **annoncer** ▶ to be a sign of : *A solid yellow line in the road means cars aren't supposed to cross it.* 4. **entraîner** ▶ to have a certain effect : *"Having such an important pig was going to mean plenty of extra work."* (E.B. White) SYN : signify, intend, convey, stand for.

mean[2] ADJECTIVE, meaner, meanest. 1. **mesquin (-ine), méchant (-ante), méprisable** ▶ not kind or good; nasty; cruel : *"And he was the meanest, most penny-pinching scoundrel who ever drew breath."* (Adèle Geras) 2. **méchant (-ante), terrible** ▶ hard to handle or deal with; tough : *That's a mean storm coming in; we should get home before it hits.* 3. **misérable** ▶ low in rank or quality; poor : *He lived in a mean shack on the edge of the field.* Note. This last meaning is used mostly in older writing. 🖉 **p. 363.**

mean[3] NOUN, means. 1. **milieu** ▶ something that is halfway between two extremes; an average; a middle point, condition, or action : *The mean between 2 and 10 is 6.* 2. means. **moyen** ▶ the way that something is done or can be done : *She searched the toolbox for some means of fixing the broken hinge.* 3. means. **moyens** ▶ money or property; wealth : *She was a woman of independent means.* ▲ ADJECTIVE. **moyen (-enne)** ▶ being in a mean or middle position; average.

mean·ing [MEE-ning] NOUN, meanings. **sens, signification** ▶ the way a thing is meant; what is

Writing Tips

Me, Myself, and I
The words *me*, *myself*, and *I* all have different roles to play.
• *I* is the subject of a verb.
  I am going to town today.
  Gillian and *I* will be at the meeting.
  No one can dance as well as *I* can.
• *Me* is the object of a verb or preposition.
  Rico lent *me* his jacket.
  They asked *Rudy and me* to pick up the dog.
  The plate of spaghetti landed *on me*.
• *Myself* should be used to refer to the subject of the sentence.
  I hurt *myself* playing soccer.
  I asked *myself* if a second piece of cake was really necessary.
• *Myself* can also be used for emphasis, but don't overuse *myself* in this way, or it will lose its impact.
  I *myself* will make sure that the project is completed.

intended : *I became excited when I realized the full meaning of the note.* ■ **meaningful,** ADJECTIVE. ▶ **significatif (-ive).** having a serious meaning; important. ■ **meaningless,** ADJECTIVE. dénué (-ée) de sens, sans signification ▶ having no meaning. SYN: purpose, intent, sense, point, aim.

meant [ment] VERB. a past form of mean: *Your support has meant a lot to me.*

mean-time [MEEN-TIME] NOUN. in the meantime. **en attendant, pendant ce temps** ▶ in the time between : *Mom said that dinner would be ready in a hour, and in the meantime we could help clean the garage.*

mean-while [MEEN-WILE *or* MEEN-WHILE] ADVERB. **1. en attendant, pendant ce temps** ▶ in the time between; in the meantime : *"His arms would not hold up the air and he plunged toward the sea. Meanwhile, Daedalus had lost sight of his son."* (Marcia Williams) **2. entre temps, aussi** ▶ at the same time : *I'll clear the table; meanwhile, you start washing the dishes.*

mea-sles [MEE-zulz] NOUN. **1. rougeole** ▶ a disease that is caused by a virus and that can spread easily from one person to another. It causes red spots on the skin, a fever, coughing, and other symptoms of a bad cold. **2. rubéole** ▶ any similar disease, such as German measles.

meas-ure [MEZH-ur] VERB, measured, measuring. **1. mesurer** ▶ to find out how big something is, what it weighs, how much of it there is, and so on : *Common instruments for measuring include a ruler, a scale, and a thermometer.* **2. mesurer, délimiter** ▶ to mark off by length, weight, distance, and so on : *Measure out a litre of gas for the lawn mower.* ▲ NOUN, measures. **1. mesure** ▶ the amount or size of something found by measuring : *The measure of the table is 2 metres by 3 metres.* **2. mesure** ▶ something used to measure, such as a tape measure. **3. mesure, évaluation** ▶ a way of judging something; a standard : *Grades in school are not necessarily a true measure of intelligence.* **4. mesure** ▶ an action done to make something happen : *Speed bumps were put in the parking lot as a safety measure.* **5. mesure** ▶ a bar of music. **Note.** Often used as an ADJECTIVE: *a measured beat; a measuring cup.*

1 kilogram (kg)	=	1000 grams (g)
1 kilometre (km)	=	1000 metres (m)
1 metre (m)	=	1000 millimetres (mm)
1 metre (m)	=	100 centimetres (cm)
1 metre (m)	=	10 decimetres (dm)
1 decimetre (dm)	=	10 centimetres (cm)
1 centimetre (cm)	=	10 millimetres (mm)
1 litre (l)	=	1000 millilitres (ml)
1 litre (l)	=	100 centilitres (cl)
1 litre (l)	=	10 decilitres (dl)
1 decilitre (dl)	=	10 centilitres (cl)
1 centilitre (cl)	=	10 millilitres (ml)

measures

meas-ure-ment [MEZH-ur-munt] NOUN, measurements. **1. mesure, mesurage** ▶ the act of measuring; a way of finding the size or amount of a thing : *We used a metre-stick for the measurement of the bathroom.* **2. mesures, mensurations** ▶ the size or amount found by measuring : *His measurements were taken by the tailor.*

meat [meet] NOUN, meats. **1. viande** ▶ the flesh of an animal that is eaten for food. Beef and pork are kinds of meat. **2. chair** ▶ the part of anything that can be eaten : *the meat of a walnut.* **3. substance** ▶ the main part of something : *Newspaper reporters get the meat of their story into the first few sentences.* ■ **meaty,** ADJECTIVE. ▶ **de viande, étoffé (-ée), substantiel (-elle).** ⌂ **p. 1138.**

me-chan-ic [muh-KAN-ik] NOUN, mechanics. **mécanicien (-ienne)** ▶ a person who is skilled at fixing or working with machines : *an auto mechanic.*

me-chan-i-cal [muh-KAN-ih-kul] ADJECTIVE. **1. mécanique** ▶ using or having to do with machines or tools : *mechanical drawing; mechanical engineering.* **2. mécanique** ▶ acting like a machine; without any feeling or expression. ■ **mechanically,** ADVERB. ▶ **mécaniquement.**

✎ Word Builder

Mean, unkind, and *vicious* describe unattractive characteristics of people or animals. *Mean* is used when someone lacks feelings and is hurtful or unfair: *He was very mean to throw dirt lumps at the animal.* *Unkind* means a person is not friendly or considerate: *She was unkind not to open the door for the woman carrying all those packages.* *Vicious* is the strongest of the words. It can mean a person or creature is very wicked, violent, or destructive: *The vicious dog attacked the delivery person.*

me·chan·ics [muh-KAN-iks] NOUN. **1. mécanique ►** the branch of science that deals with motion, and with the effect of force on bodies in motion or at rest : *Knowledge of mechanics is needed when designing an aircraft or building a bridge.* **2. mécanisme, processus ►** the way in which some action is carried out : *A famous baseball pitcher wrote a book on the mechanics of pitching.*

mech·a·nism [MEK-uh-niz-um] NOUN, mechanisms. **1. mécanisme ►** the working parts of a machine : *the mechanism of a watch.* **2. appareil, mécanisme ►** the arrangement of the parts of a large or complicated system : *the mechanism of the federal government.*

med·al [MED-ul] NOUN, medals. **médaille ►** a small, flat piece of metal usually shaped like a coin, with a design or writing on it. Medals are often given as awards for bravery or for some outstanding achievement : *Winners at the Olympic Games receive gold medals.* **Note.** A medallion is a large, round medal, or an ornament shaped like this.

med·dle [MED-ul] VERB, meddled, meddling. **se mêler, intervenir, s'ingérer ►** to interfere in other people's business in a rude or unwanted way. ■ **meddler,** NOUN. **► touche-à-tout.** ■ **meddlesome,** ADJECTIVE. **► qui se mêle de tout, importun.** SYN: interfere, butt in, tamper with, intervene.

me·di·a [MEE-dee-uh] PLURAL NOUN. **1. média ►** a plural form of medium. **2.** (also, **the media**) **médias ►** the means of public communication, such as newspapers, television, and radio. *◇ p. 364.*

med·i·cal [MED-uh-kul] ADJECTIVE. **médical (-ale, -aux) ►** having to do with the study and use of medicine : *a medical school; a problem needing medical attention.*

med·i·cine [MED-uh-sun] NOUN, medicines. **1. médicament ►** a drug or other substance that is used to treat, prevent, or cure disease or to relieve pain or injuries. **Note.** Something used this way is said to be medicinal. **2. médecine ►** the science of treating and understanding disease. Medicine deals with methods or efforts aimed at keeping people alive, free of pain, and in good health.

me·di·e·val [MUH-dee-EE-vul or mid-EE-vul] ADJECTIVE. (also mediaeval) **médiéval (-ale, -aux) ►** having to do with the Middle Ages : *After studying the Middle Ages, we are going to hold a medieval feast.*

me·dicine man sorcier **►** or

me·dicine woman sorcière **►** see shaman.

me·di·um [MEE-dee-um] NOUN, mediums or media. **1. milieu ►** something that is in the middle between two extremes. **2. milieu ►** the conditions in which something lives or acts : *Sandy soil is the proper medium for growing straw-*

berry plants. **3. véhicule, moyen (d'expression) ►** a means of communication or expression : *Poetry is the medium he uses to express his feelings.* **Note.** For definitions 2 and 3 the plural is usually media. ▲ ADJECTIVE. **moyen (-enne) ►** having a middle position; in the middle : *She likes her steak medium, not well-done or rare.*

meek [meek] ADJECTIVE. **doux (douce), humble ►** gentle, humble, mild. ■ **meekly,** ADVERB. **► doucement, humblement.**

meet [meet] VERB, met, meeting. **1. rencontrer, tomber sur, faire face à ►** to come face to face with; to come upon : **2. rencontrer, faire la connaissance de ►** to be introduced to : *Dad, I'd like you to meet my teacher, Mr. Randoja.* **3. rencontrer, donner rendez-vous ►** to keep an appointment with : *I'll meet you at 8 :00.* **4. croiser ►** to come together with; join : *The yard has a row of bushes that meets the back fence.* ▲ NOUN, meets. **compétition ►** a gathering for competition : *a track meet.*

meet with a. **rencontrer, avoir, faire face à ►** to experience : *to meet with bad weather.* b. **rencontrer, parler avec ►** to talk with.

meet·ing [MEE-ting] NOUN, meetings. **1. réunion ►** a gathering of a group of people, especially one that is arranged for a certain purpose : *The students held a meeting to discuss the yearbook.* **2. rencontre ►** the act of coming together : *I had a chance meeting with my sister on the subway.* SYN: assembly, get-together, gathering.

meg·a·byte [MEG-uh-bite] NOUN, megabytes. **1. méga-octet ►** a unit of measure for storage capacity on a computer. One megabyte (MB) equals 1048576 bytes. **2. méga-octet ►** one million bytes. **Note.** Mega- is a PREFIX meaning "very large."

mel·an·chol·y [MEL-un-kol-ee] ADJECTIVE. **1. mélancolique, triste ►** feeling sad or depressed low in spirits; gloomy : *"'Only it is so very lonely here,' Alice said in a melancholy voice."* (Lewis Carroll) **2. mélancolique ►** caus-

✐ Writing Tips

Media

Media—*the methods of mass communication such as radio, newspapers, television, and the Internet*—*is a plural noun. The verb that follows this noun should be in the plural:*

*All the media **have** stories about the explosion.*

*Most of the media **are** governed by federal laws.*

ing this feeling. ▲ NOUN. **mélancolie** ▶ low spirits; sadness : *His melancholy made him forget that he had ever been happy.* SYN: sad, gloomy, unhappy, sorrowful, dejected.

mel·low [MEL-oh] ADJECTIVE, mellower, mellowest. **1. doux (douce), moelleux (-euse), riche** ▶ soft, full, and rich : *a mellow voice.* **2. mûri (-ie), assagi (-ie), adouci (-ie)** ▶ made wise and gentle by age and experience : *Our supervisor used to be quick-tempered, but she's very mellow now.* ▲ VERB, mellowed, mellowing. **mûrir** ▶ to make or become mellow.

mel·o·dra·mat·ic [MEL-uh-druh-MAT-ik] ADJECTIVE. **mélodramatique** ▶ sensational and exaggerated : *She's so melodramatic—she makes every little problem into a tragedy.* ■ **melodramatically,** ADVERB. ▶ **d'un air ou d'une façon mélodramatique.**

mel·o·dy [MEL-uh-dee] NOUN, melodies. **1. mélodie** ▶ a series of musical notes that make up a tune : *I know the melody, but I can't remember the words of the song.* **2. mélodie** ▶ the main part of a piece of music. ■ **melodic,** ADJECTIVE. ▶ **mélodique.** 📖 p. 1130.

mel·on [MEL-un] NOUN, melons. **melon** ▶ a large fruit that grows on a vine. Melons have a sweet, juicy pulp that can be eaten. Cantaloupes and watermelons are well-known types of melons.

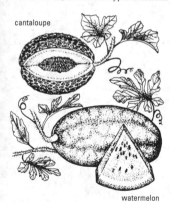

cantaloupe

watermelon

melons

melt [melt] VERB, melted, melting. **1. fondre** ▶ to change from a solid into a liquid by heating : *The ice cream melted in the hot sun.* **2. fondre, se dissoudre** ▶ to turn to liquid; dissolve : *The sugar melted in the cup of tea.* **3. fondre, disparaître, se dissiper** ▶ to disappear; fade : *The fog melted away as the sun came out.* **4. attendrir, émouvoir** ▶ to become gentle or tender; soften : *His kindness melted my heart.* SYN: dissolve, thaw, soften.

mem·ber [MEM-bur] NOUN, members. **membre** ▶ a person, animal, or thing that belongs to a certain group : *Lions, tigers, and leopards are members of the cat family.* **Note.** The fact of being a member is membership.

mem·brane [MEM-BRANE] NOUN, membranes. **membrane** ▶ a thin layer of skin or tissue that lines parts of the body.

me·men·to [muh-MEN-toh] NOUN, mementos or mementoes. **souvenir** ▶ something that serves as a reminder of an event or time in the past; souvenir.

mem·o [MEM-oh] NOUN, memos. **1. note de service** ▶ an informal note, letter, or report. **2. note** ▶ any brief note or letter written to remind a person of something. **Note.** The full form of this word is memorandum.

me·mo·ri·al [muh-MOR-ee-ul] NOUN, memorials. **monument, à la mémoire de** ▶ something that serves to honour the memory of an important person or event : *They built a statue as a memorial to Terry Fox.*

mem·o·rize [MEM-uh-RIZE] VERB, memorized, memorizing. **mémoriser** ▶ to learn by heart; commit to memory : *Actors memorize their lines.*

mem·or·y [MEM-uh-ree *or* MEM-ree] NOUN, memories. **1. mémoire** ▶ the ability to remember things : *My aunt has a great memory and never forgets people's names.* **2. souvenir** ▶ someone or something that is remembered : *We shared our memories of past camping trips.* **3. mémoire** ▶ all that can be remembered : *She searched her memory for the name of the hockey player.* **4. mémoire** ▶ the place in a computer that stores the information put into it, or the amount of information it can store : *four megabytes of memory.*

in memory of à la mémoire de ▶ as a help in remembering : *Remembrance Day is a holiday in memory of those who died fighting for our country.*

memory chip NOUN. **puce de mémoire** ▶ a device that stores information in the form of electrical charges.

men [men] NOUN. **hommes** ▶ the plural of man.

men·ace [MEN-is] NOUN, menaces. **menace** ▶ something that can cause harm; a threat; danger : *He was frightened by the menace of the storm.* ▲ VERB, menaced, menacing. **menacer** ▶ to put in danger; threaten. **Note.** Usually used as an ADJECTIVE:*The actor used a menacing voice to frighten the audience.* ■ **menacingly,** ADVERB. ▶ **d'un air ou d'un ton menaçant.** *The bear growled menacingly.*

mend [mend] VERB, mended, mending. **1. réparer, repriser** ▶ to put back in good condition; repair; fix. **2. aller mieux, s'améliorer** ▶ to get better; heal or improve : *Her sprained ankle has mended, and now she's running again.* ▲ NOUN, mends. **reprise** ▶ a place that has been mended.

men·tal [MEN-tul] ADJECTIVE. **1. mental (-ale, -aux)** ▶ having to do with the mind : *a mental test; mental health.* **2. mental (-ale, -aux)** ▶ having to do with people suffering from a disease of the mind : *mental illness.* ■ **mentally,** ADVERB. ▶ mentalement.

men·tion [MEN-shun] VERB, mentioned, mentioning. **mentionner, parler de, faire mention de** ▶ to speak or write about; refer to : *Don't mention it to Kira.* ▲ NOUN, mentions. **mention** ▶ the fact of mentioning; a statement or reference : *There was no mention of the accident in today's paper.* SYN: speak of, name, remark, refer to, tell. *✐ p. 366.*

men·u [MEN-yoo] NOUN, menus. **1. menu** ▶ a list of the food and drinks that are available in a restaurant or other eating place, along with their prices. **2. menu** ▶ in a computer, a list on the screen showing the different things that a program can do.

mer·chan·dise [MUR-chun-DICE or MUR-chun-DIZE] NOUN. **marchandise** ▶ things that are bought and sold; goods : *That store sells books, magazines, newspapers, and other such merchandise.* ▲ VERB, merchandised, merchandising. **commercialiser, mettre en marché** ▶ to sell products.

mer·chant [MUR-chunt] NOUN, merchants. **1. marchand (-ande)** ▶ a person in the business of buying and selling goods for a profit. **2. commerçant (-ante)** ▶ a person who owns or is in charge of a store; a storekeeper. ▲ ADJECTIVE. **marchand (-ande)** ▶ having to do with business or trade : *a merchant ship.*

mer·cu·ry [MUR-kyuh-ree] NOUN. **mercure** ▶ a heavy, silver-white metal that is a chemical element. Mercury is a liquid at normal temperatures. It is used in thermometers and batteries. *✐ p. 391.*

Mer·cu·ry [MUR-kyuh-ree] NOUN. **1. Mercure** ▶ the smallest planet in the solar system. Mercury is the closest planet to the sun. **2. Mercure** ▶ in the religion of the ancient Romans, the god who served as a messenger for other gods. *✐ p. 391.*

mer·cy [MUR-see] NOUN, mercies. **1. pitié, indulgence** ▶ kind or gentle treatment, especially not giving punishment that is deserved or expected. **2. chance, reconnaissance** ▶ something one is thankful for; a blessing : *It's a mercy that someone saw the smoke and called for help.* ■ **merciful,** ADJECTIVE. ▶ **miséricordieux (-euse), clément (-ente).** with mercy; showing or feeling mercy. ■ **merciless,** ADJECTIVE. ▶ **impitoyable, sans pitié.** SYN: compassion, clemency, sympathy, pity.

mere [meer] ADJECTIVE, merest. **simple, pur (pure), seul (seule)** ▶ nothing more or less than; only; simple : *There was a mere scratch on his leg, but he acted as if it had been broken.*

mere·ly [MEER-lee] ADVERB. **simplement, purement, seulement** ▶ not more than; only : *I'm not trying to interfere; I merely want to help you.*

merge [murj] VERB, merged, merging. **se rencontrer, se joindre, se fondre** ▶ to come together; join : *The streams merged.*

mer·it [MAIR-it] NOUN, merits. **1. mérite, valeur** ▶ the fact of having value or worth; having a good quality : *The teacher thought that Jana's essay had merit.* **2. (often merits) mérite** ▶ the actual facts or qualities of something. ▲ VERB, merited, meriting. **mériter** ▶ to be worthy of something; deserve : *I think Lin's performance merits a round of applause.* SYN: deserve, be worthy of, qualify for.

mer·ry [MAIR-ee] ADJECTIVE, merrier, merriest. **joyeux (-euse)** ▶ full of fun and good cheer; very happy. ■ **merrily,** ADVERB: ▶ joyeusement. *"Babbling merrily, the birds landed all around him."* (Tololwa M. Mollel) SYN: jolly, happy, glad, festive, merry, jovial.

mer·ry-go-round [MAIR-ee-goh-ROWND] NOUN, merry-go-rounds. **manège** ▶ a round revolving platform with seats in the shape of horses and other animals on which people ride. **Note.** Also called a **carousel** or **carrousel.**

mess [mes] NOUN, messes. **1. désordre, gâchis, fouillis** ▶ an area that is dirty and unpleasant, with useless or unwanted things lying around : *"The whittling made such a mess in her clean kitchen that she took part of the barn for a workshop."* (Thomas H. Raddall) **2. pétrin, gâchis, mauvais pas** ▶ a situation that is

---

✐ Word Builder

Mention, name, and ***tell*** are all verbs that refer to communicating with others through speaking or writing. ***Mention*** means to refer to in a very casual fashion : *I think he mentioned that Meredith would be coming.* ***Name*** means to mention, but to do so by specifying names. *She can name all the prime ministers of Canada.* ***Tell*** can mean to make something known or reveal something : *Gia would not tell who she saw talking to Clayton.*

Metaphor

*A **metaphor** is an expression that describes a person, place, or thing by comparing it to something else.*

• *In a **metaphor** a word or phrase that usually means one thing is used to describe another. For example, in the following sentence Alise is compared to a live electrical wire, meaning she's fun and exciting.*

> *Invite Alise to the party; she's a real live wire.*

• *A **metaphor** is different from a simile because **similes** use the words "like," "as," or "than" in the comparison.*

Note: *A mixed metaphor is the term used when two or more metaphors are used together in the same expression to describe one subject.*

> *Riding the rapids was a roller-coaster ride without a parachute.*

Mixed metaphors should be avoided because they tend to complicate a sentence.

unpleasant, confusing, or hard to deal with : *"Oh, what would your mother think, Michael, if she could see this mess we've gotten ourselves into!"* (Cynthia Rylant) **3.** (also **mess hall**) **mess, cantine** ▶ in the armed forces, a place for a large group of people to eat : *The soldiers all gathered in the mess.* ▲ VERB, messed, messing. (often **mess up**) **gâcher, mettre en désordre** ▶ to make a mess : *Don't mess the place up before Mom and Dad come home.* ■ **messy,** ADJECTIVE. ▶ **sale, désordonné (-ée).** ■ **messily,** ADVERB. ▶ **salement, mal.** SYN: disorder, clutter, confusion, muddle.

mess about or **mess around** **perdre son temps** ▶ to busy oneself without accomplishing anything.

mes·sage [MES-ij] NOUN, messages. **1.** **message** ▶ information passed on from one person to another or others : *I left a message on Tina's voice mail.* **2.** **message** ▶ a lesson, moral, or other point contained in a story :*"Crime doesn't pay" is the message of that movie.*

mes·sen·ger [MES-un-jur] NOUN, messengers. **messager (-ère)** ▶ a person who carries messages, packages, and so on from one place to another.

met [met] VERB. a past form of meet: *I met my parents for lunch. I had met Jason earlier.*

met·al [MET-ul] NOUN, metals. **métal (-aux)** ▶ any of a large group of substances such as iron, gold, lead, aluminum, and copper. Alloys are made by combining one metal with another. Most metals conduct heat and electricity well, and can be melted down, hammered into a thin sheet, or drawn out into a wire. ■ **metallic,** ADJECTIVE. ▶ **métal (-aux). métallique** ▶ made of, containing, or like metal : *metallic paints.*

met·a·phor [MET-uh-FOR] NOUN, metaphors. **métaphore, image** ▶ a way of describing something by suggesting that it is like another thing. Writers often use metaphors to describe a person, place, or thing : *"His icy heart melted,"* she said, using a metaphor. ■ **metaphorical,** ADJECTIVE. ▶ **métaphorique.** ■ **metaphorically,** ADVERB. ▶ **métaphoriquement.** ✐ **p. 367.**

me·te·or [MEE-tee-ur] NOUN, meteors. **météore** ▶ a piece of metallic or rocky matter from space that glows and burns as it enters the earth's atmosphere at high speed, often resembling a streak of light. **Note.** Meteors are sometimes called **falling stars** or **shooting stars**. ■ **meteoric,** ADJECTIVE. ▶ **fulgurant (-ante).** flashing like a meteor; brilliant; swift : *The rock group had a meteoric rise to fame.*

me·te·or·ite [MEE-tee-uh-RITE] NOUN, meteorites. **météorite** ▶ a meteor that has fallen to earth without being totally burned up.

me·ter [MEE-tur] NOUN, meters. **compteur** ▶ a device or machine used to measure or record the amount of something : *An electric meter measures how much electricity is used.* **Note.** Also used in such combinations as *thermometer* and *speedometer*.

meth·od [METH-ud] NOUN, methods. **méthode** ▶ a way of doing something : *This book claims to present a new method for learning a language.*

Mé·tis [MAY-tee, may-TEE, or may-TEES] NOUN, Métis. **Métis (-isse)** ▶ the descendants of French, Scottish, or English fathers and Cree or Ojibway mothers who form a distinct cultural group.

me·tre¹ [MEE-tur] NOUN, metres. (also **meter**) **mètre** ▶ the basic unit of length or distance in the metric system. There are 100 centimetres in a metre. Symbol: m

me·tre² NOUN, metres. **1.** **mètre** ▶ the regular arrangement of words in a line, according to which words are accented (spoken strongly) and which words are not. The metre of a poem is determined by which syllable in a group of two or three gets the accent. **2.** **mesure** ▶ in music, a similar pattern of rhythm, based on the number of strong and weak beats in a bar.

met·ric [MET-rik] ADJECTIVE. **1.** **métrique** ▶ having to do with the metric system : *a metric ruler.* **2.** (also **metrical**) **métrique** ▶ having to do with metre in poetry or music.

metric system **système métrique** ▶ a system of measurement that is based on units of 10. In the metric system, the *metre* is the basic way to measure length, the *gram* is the basic way to measure weight or mass, and the *litre* is the basic way to measure capacity (how much something holds). Many countries use an expanded version of the metric system called Système international d'unités or SI, but the U.S. still uses a system based on feet, miles.

me·tro·pol·i·tan [MET-ruh-POL-uh-tun] ADJECTIVE. **métropolitain (-aine)** ▶ having to do with a large city : *a metropolitan transit system*. **Note.** A metropolitan area is made up of a central city and its nearby smaller towns and suburbs.

mice [mice] NOUN. **souris** ▶ the plural of mouse.

Mic·mac [mik-mak] NOUN. Micmac or Micmacs. (also Mi'kmaq) **1. Micmac** ▶ a member of the Aboriginal peoples living in the Maritimes and in the Gaspé region of Quebec. **2. micmac** ▶ the Algonquian language of the Micmac people.

mi·cro·com·put·er [MY-kroh-kum-PYOO-tur] NOUN, microcomputers. (also micro) **microordinateur** ▶ a small computer that has all its functions stored in the same unit and is designed to be used by one person at a time. **Note.** Often called a personal computer or PC.

mi·cro·film [MY-kruh-FILM] NOUN. **microfilm** ▶ film on which images have been reduced to a very small size. Microfilm is viewed with a projector that enlarges the image : *One month of the* Globe and Mail *newspaper can be stored on two rolls of microfilm.*

mi·cro·or·gan·ism [MY-kroh-OR-gun-iz-um] NOUN, microorganisms. **microorganisme** ▶ a very tiny living thing that can be seen only with a microscope. Bacteria and viruses are microorganisms. **Note.** The study of such organisms is called microbiology.

mi·cro·phone [MY-kruh-FONE] NOUN, microphones. **microphone** ▶ an instrument used to make sound louder, to broadcast radio and TV shows, and to record sound for movies, CDs, and other recordings. Microphones change sound waves into electrical signals. **Note.** Often called a mike.

mi·cro·pro·ces·sor [MY-kroh-PROH-ses-ur] NOUN, microprocessors. **microprocesseur** ▶ a single chip that contains everything a computer needs to process information.

mi·cro·scope [MY-kruh-SKOPE] NOUN, microscopes. **microscope** ▶ a device that is used to look at something that is too small to see with the eye alone. A microscope uses a combination of lenses to make the object look much larger. Microscopes are often used in science to study bacteria, body cells, and so on. ■ **microscopic,** ADJECTIVE. ▶ **microscopique.**

mi·cro·wave [MY-kruh-WAVE] NOUN, microwaves. **micro-onde** ▶ an electromagnetic wave that has a very short length, used in radar and to send long-distance television signals. 2. *Informal.* **micro-ondes** ▶ a microwave oven.

microwave oven **four à micro-ondes** ▶ an oven that uses microwaves to cook foods much more quickly than a gas or electric oven.

mid [mid] ADJECTIVE. **mi-, au milieu de** ▶ at or in the middle. **Note.** Usually used as a PREFIX in other words : *a man in his mid-thirties; mid-day.*

mid·dle [MID-ul] ADJECTIVE. **du milieu, central (-ale, -aux)** ▶ at or near the centre; away from the sides, the front and back, or the beginning and end : *On our plane trip, I sat in the middle seat between Mom and Dad.* ▲ NOUN, middles. **milieu, centre** ▶ something that is in this place or position : *The phone always seems to ring when we're right in the middle of eating dinner.*

Middle Ages **Moyen Âge** ▶ the period in European history between ancient times and the beginning of modern times. The Middle Ages is usually considered to have started in the year 476 A.D., when the Western Roman Empire fell, and to have ended in about 1500, when life in Europe began to change greatly.

mid·night [MID-NITE] NOUN. **minuit** ▶ 12:00 at night; the middle of the night.

midst [midst] NOUN. **milieu** ▶ the middle : *The farming areas of the country are in the midst of a long dry spell.*

mid·way [MID-way or MID-WAY] ADJECTIVE; ADVERB. **à mi-chemin** ▶ halfway; in the middle : *My grandparents' house is midway between ours and my uncle's.* ▲ [MID-way] NOUN, midways. **fête foraine** ▶ an amusement park at a fair, circus, or carnival, usually including rides and games.

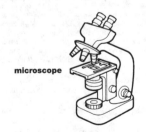

microscope

might[1] [mite] VERB. a past form of may. 🖝 p. 362.

might[2] NOUN. **force, puissance** ▶ great strength or power : *She pushed with all her might and the rock moved.*

might·y [MY-tee] ADJECTIVE, mightier, mightiest. **puissant (-ante)** ▶ showing great strength or

MICROCOMPUTERS

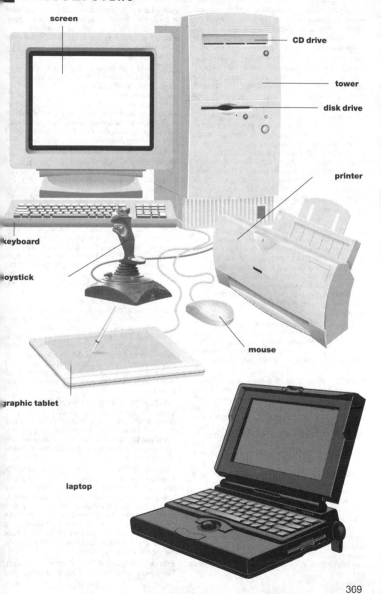

screen

CD drive

tower

disk drive

printer

keyboard

joystick

mouse

graphic tablet

laptop

369

power; very strong. ■ **mighty,** ADVERB. ▶ rudement, extrêmement. very; extremely : *He'll be mighty upset if he doesn't get to go with us.* ■ **mightily,** ADVERB. ▶ vigoureusement, puissamment. SYN : great, strong, powerful, forceful.

mi-grant [MY-grunt] NOUN, migrants. **migrateur (-trice) , nomade, itinérant (-ante)** ▶ an animal, person, or plant that migrates : *Canada geese are migrants that fly south for the winter months.* ▲ ADJECTIVE: *Migrant workers are often hired to pick fruit, vegetables, or other crops.*

mi-grate [MY-GRATE] VERB, migrated, migrating. **1. migrer** ▶ to move from one place to another with the seasons : *Whales in the northern Pacific migrate thousands of kilometres south every winter.* **2. émigrer** ▶ to move from one place to live in another : *Many North American pioneers migrated west in search of good farmland.* **Note.** Migration is the act or fact of migrating : *Caribou form herds of up to 100 000 animals during their migrations.* ✐ **p. 628.**

mike NOUN, mikes. **micro** ▶ short for microphone.

mild [mild] ADJECTIVE, milder, mildest. **1. doux (douce), tempéré (-ée), clément (-ente)** ▶ not having great force; not rough or harsh : *"Winter was mild that year, with little snow."* (Celia Godkin) **2. doux (douce)** ▶ calm and gentle : *In movies, this actor plays a mild-mannered character.* **3. doux (douce), léger (-ère)** ▶ not strong in taste or smell; not sharp, sour, or bitter : *a mild Cheddar cheese.* ■ **mildly,** ADVERB. ▶ légèrement.

mil-dew [MIL-DOO] NOUN. **moisissure, rouille, mildiou** ▶ a fungus that forms on plants, leather, paper, cloth, and other things in damp weather. ▲ VERB, mildewed, mildewing. **moisir, rouiller, frapper de mildiou** ▶ to become coated with mildew.

mile [mile] NOUN, miles. **1. mille** ▶ a way of measuring distance. A mile is equal to about 1.6 kilometres. **2. nautical mile. mille nautique** ▶ a way of measuring distance for sea or air travel, equal to about 1852 metres. **Note.** A milestone was a marker by a road used in ancient times to show distances. Milestone has come to mean an important event in history or in one's life : *The publishing of her first book was a milestone in her writing career.*

mile-age [MY-lij] NOUN. **1. distance, millage (= kilométrage)** ▶ the number of miles that have been travelled or that are to be travelled : *What's the mileage from Montreal to Quebec City?* **2. consommation de carburant au mille (= au kilomètre)** ▶ the number of miles that a vehicle can travel on a certain amount of fuel : *Diesel engines can usually get better mileage than ordinary gas engines can.* **3.** *Informal.* **maximum** ▶ an amount or period of use : *Uncle Carl has really gotten a lot of mileage out of that old joke.*

mil-i-ta-ry [MIL-uh-TAIR-ee] ADJECTIVE. **militaire** ▶ having to do with soldiers, the armed forces, or war : *Officers in the armed forces are often trained at a military academy.* ▲ NOUN. the military. **armée, militaires** ▶ the armed forces of a country.

milk [milk] NOUN, milks. **1. lait** ▶ a white liquid made in the bodies of female mammals to feed their babies. Cow's milk is often drunk by people. **2. lait** ▶ the white juice of some fruits or plants : *coconut milk.* ▲ VERB, milked, milking. **traire** ▶ to draw milk from an animal. ■ **milky,** ADJECTIVE: ▶ au lait, lacté (-ée), laiteux (-euse). *"Waiting for him there in his favourite bowl was steaming hot, milky tea."* (Tololwa M. Mollel) ✐ **p. 1138.**

Milky Way 1. Voie lactée ▶ a white path of light that can be seen across the night sky. The Milky Way is made up of billions of stars. **2. Milky Way galaxy. Voie lactée** ▶ a galaxy that includes the stars seen as the Milky Way. Earth and the other planets orbiting the sun are part of this galaxy.

mill [mil] NOUN, mills. **1. moulin** ▶ a large machine that grinds wheat or other grain into flour or meal. **2. moulin** ▶ any similar machine that crushes or grinds food : *a pepper mill.* **3. moulin, minoterie** ▶ a building containing machines that grind grain. **Note.** A person who owns or operates a mill is a miller. **4. usine, fabrique** ▶ a building where large machines make a certain product : *a paper mill; a steel mill.* ▲ VERB, milled, milling. **1. moudre** ▶ to grind or make something with a mill. **2. tourner sur place, tourner en rond, grouiller autour de** ▶ to move around in a circle or moving mass with no special direction : *"Dumbfounded, the knights milled about the camp gathering their wits and their horses."* (Donald Carrick) **Note.** Also used in compound words, such as *millpond, millstone, millstream, roue d'un moulin* ▶ and *mill wheel.*

mil-lion [MIL-yun] NOUN, millions. **million** ▶ one thousand times one thousand; 1 000 000. **Note.** A millionaire is a person who has a million dollars or more in money or property. ■ **millionth,** NOUN; ADJECTIVE. ▶ **millionième.** *a millionth of a second. The millionth customer received a free turkey.*

mim-ic [MIM-ik] VERB, mimicked, mimicking. **1. imiter** ▶ to copy someone or something; imitate : *Tim mimics other children to tease them.* **2. imiter** ▶ to resemble closely in appearance : *The viceroy butterfly mimics the monarch butterfly because birds don't like to eat the monarch.* ▲ NOUN, mimics. **imitateur (-trice)** ▶ a person or animal that mimics. **Note.** The act or fact of mimicking something else is mimicry. SYN : mime, imitate, ape, parrot.

mince [mince] VERB, minced, mincing. **1. hacher** ▶ to cut or chop meat or other food into very small pieces : *We minced onions and mushrooms and added them to the sauce.* **2. mâcher (ses mots), parler du bout des lèvres ▸** to choose words very carefully; keep from saying something directly : *The principal did not mince matters but spoke to us openly.* SYN : *dice, cube, shred.*

mince-meat [MINCE-MEET] NOUN. **hachis de fruits secs ▸** a sweet filling for pie. Mincemeat is made of spices, raisins, finely cut fruits, and sometimes meat.

mind [mynd] NOUN. minds. **1. esprit, intelligence ▸** the part of a person that can think; the part that learns, knows, remembers, and decides things. **2. esprit, intelligence ▸** the ability of the brain to think and feel; intelligence. **3. raison ▸** a normal state of the mind : *We speak of people losing their minds.* **4. esprit, attention ▸** the use of the mind; one's thoughts or attention : *He almost had an accident because he didn't keep his mind on his driving.* **5. idée, avis ▸** one's opinion or point of view : *I've changed my mind; I'll have the lasagna, not the steak.* ▲ VERB, minded, minding. **1. garder, surveiller, prendre soin ▸** to take care of; watch over : *to mind a baby.* **2. s'opposer à ▸** to not like something; be against; object to : *Do you mind if we stay home tonight?* **3. prêter attention à, s'occuper de ▸** to pay attention; be concerned about. **Note.** This meaning is used in special phrases such as mind your manners, mind your own business, ne faites pas attention ▸ and never mind. ∎ **mindful,** VERB, ADJECTIVE. ▸ **attentif (-ive), soucieux (-euse) ▸** SYN : brain, intelligence, intellect. ✐ **p. 371.**

mine[1] [mine] PRONOUN. **le mien (la mienne, les miens) ▸** the pronoun I when used as a possessive after a verb; belonging to me; the one that belongs to me : *That coat is mine, not yours.*

mine[2] NOUN, mines. **1. mine ▸** a place where people dig into the earth to take out useful or valuable substances, such as coal, iron, copper, silver, gold, uranium, and so on. **2. mine, source ▸** a person or thing that is a source of something useful or valuable : *She's a mine of information about the park.* **3. mine ▸** a bomb or other explosive charge that is hidden under the ground or the water. A mine is set to explode when something touches it. ▲ VERB, mined,

mining. **1. extraire ▸** to take something useful or valuable out of the ground : *Today, most of the world's diamonds are mined in South Africa.* **Note.** This work is called mining. **Note.** A person who works in a mine is a miner. **2. miner, semer des mines ▸** to hide bombs under the ground or under water : *The harbour had been mined to keep enemy ships from entering.*

min-er-al [MIN-ur-ul] NOUN, minerals. **1. minéral (-aux) ▸** a solid substance that is found in nature, but that is not alive and is not plant or animal matter. Rocks are made up of different minerals. Lead, iron, gold, and quartz are minerals. **2. minerai, combustible fossile ▸** any natural substance that is mined from the earth because it is useful or valuable, such as oil, copper, and gold. **3. minéral (-aux) ▸** any of certain chemical elements that are important to the nutrition of people, animals, and plants : *People need the mineral calcium in order to have healthy bones and teeth.* ✐ **p. 397.**

min-gle [MING-gul] VERB, mingled, mingling. **1. mêler, mélanger ▸** to mix with another thing; combine : *When he saw the mouse, Joe's reaction was fear mingled with disgust.* **2. se mêler ▸** to mix with other people; be part of a group : *Delia was friendly and tried to mingle with the other guests.*

min-i-a-ture [MIN-ee-uh-chur *or* MIN-uh-chur] NOUN, miniatures. **1. miniature ▸** something that is a smaller copy of something else. **2. miniature ▸** a very small painting. Artists used to paint miniatures of people to be worn inside a locket or other piece of jewellery. ▲ ADJECTIVE. **miniature ▸** very small; tiny : *a miniature poodle.* **Note.** Miniature golf is played in an area much smaller than a regular golf course. ∎ **miniaturize,** VERB, miniaturized, miniaturizing. ▸ **miniaturiser.** to make small.

min-i-mum [MIN-uh-mum] NOUN, minimums or mimima. **minimum ▸** the smallest amount; the least possible : *You have to get a minimum of 30 correct answers in order to pass the test.* ▲ ADJECTIVE. **minimal (-ale, -aux) ▸** being the lowest or smallest amount : *a minimum speed.* SYN : least, smallest, lowest.

min-is-ter [MIN-ih-stur] NOUN, ministers. **1. pasteur ▸** in some churches, a person who is in charge of the religious services. **2. ministre ▸** a

---

🖋 Word Builder

Mind is the part of the body that allows a person to think. Bear in mind means to remember or keep in one's attention : Bear in mind that dinner is at six o'clock. To be of one mind means to agree : They are of one mind on which movie to see. A person who has a mind of his or her own is very independent : Gitta has a mind of her own when it comes to what she wears. If you make up your mind, you have decided something : He made up his mind to make the basketball team.

cabinet member who is the head of a large department of the government : *the prime minister; the minister of finance.* ▲ VERB, ministered, ministering. **donner des soins à ▶** to take care of; give help to : *Dr. Crusher ministered to the wounded alien's needs.*

min·is·try [MIN-is-tree] NOUN, ministries. **1. ministère ▶** the office or work of a minister. **2. ministère ▶** a government department headed by a cabinet minister : *In Canada, the armed forces are governed by the Ministry of Defence.*

mink [mink] NOUN, minks. **1. vison ▶** a small animal related to the weasel. In the wild, minks live in wooded areas near water. **2. vison ▶** the fur of this animal, often used to make or trim clothing.

min·now [MIN-oh] NOUN, minnows or minnow. **vairon, fretin ▶** any one of a group of small freshwater fish. Many types of minnows are found in North America and other parts of the world.

mi·nor [MY-nur] ADJECTIVE. **secondaire, mineur (-eure) ▶** not of great size or importance; smaller; lesser, unimportant : *a minor injury; a minor mistake.* ▲ NOUN, minors. **mineur (-eure) ▶** a person who is not considered an adult by law for certain things, such as voting. In different provinces, minors are persons under 18, 19, or 21 years old.

mi·nor·i·ty [muh-NOR-uh-tee *or* my-NOR-uh-tee] NOUN, minorities. **1. minorité ▶** the smaller of two unequal numbers; less than half : *The survey showed that only a minority of those asked liked the new cereal — two out of every 10 people.* **2. minorité ▶** a group of people who are of a different race, nationality, or religion than a larger group living in the same area : *the Francophone minority in Canada.* **Note.** Often used as an adjective :*a minority group.*

mint[1] [mint] NOUN, mints. **1. menthe ▶** a plant used for flavouring such foods as jelly, ice cream, gum, and tea. **2. bonbon à la menthe ▶** a candy flavoured with mint.

mint[2] NOUN, mints. **1. hôtel de la Monnaie ▶** a place where the national government makes the coins and paper money used in the country. **2.** *Informal.* **fortune ▶** a large amount of money : *That's a beautiful watch—it must have cost a mint.* ▲ VERB, minted, minting. **frapper une monnaie ▶** to make money in a mint : *to mint quarters.*

mint condition neuf (neuve) ▶ as good as new : *The used car we bought was in mint condition.*

mi·nus [MY-nus] PREPOSITION. **1. moins ▶** made less by; less : *Eight minus two is six.* **2.** *Informal.* **sans, en moins ▶** without : *Jerry finished the race minus his left shoe.* ▲ ADJECTIVE. **1. moins ▶** less than or lower than : *In that course, a grade of 80 to 82 percent is a B minus.* **2. moins, négatif (-ive) ▶** less than zero : *The temperature fell to minus 10 degrees last*

night. ▲ NOUN, minuses. (also minus sign) a sign [–] showing that something is to be subtracted.

min·ute[1] [MIN-it] NOUN, minutes. **1. minute ▶** a way of measuring time. One minute is equal to 60 seconds, and 60 minutes make one hour. **2. minute, instant, moment ▶** a very small amount of time; a moment : *I knew she was your sister the minute I saw her.* **3. minutes. compte rendu, procès-verbal ▶** an official written record of what was said or done at a meeting.

up-to-the-minute récent (-ente), mis (mise) à jour ▶ up-to-date : *The information on the Web site was up-to-the-minute.*

mi·nute[2] [my-NOOT] ADJECTIVE. **1. minuscule, infime ▶** very, very small; tiny : *They found some minute specks of gold dust in the shallow river water.* **2. minutieux (-euse), détaillé (-ée) ▶** made up of many fine points; very detailed; careful or exact : *The drawings of Leonardo da Vinci are famous for their minute detail.* ■ **minutely,** ADVERB. ▶ **minutieusement.**

mir·a·cle [MEER-uh-kul] NOUN, miracles. **1. miracle ▶** an amazing event that goes beyond the laws of nature. Many religions tell of miracles performed by a holy leader. **2. miracle ▶** any event that is very amazing, lucky, or surprising : *If I get an A in this course, it will be a miracle.* SYN: marvel, surprise, wonder.

mi·rac·u·lous [muh-RAK-yuh-lus] ADJECTIVE. **1. miraculeux (-euse), merveilleux (-euse), prodigieux (-euse) ▶** highly amazing; wonderful; marvellous : *Getting that job is miraculous good luck.* **2. miraculeux (-euse) ▶** like a miracle : *a miraculous recovery from an illness.* ■ **miraculously,** ADVERB. ▶ **miraculeusement.**

mi·rage [mih-ROZH] NOUN, mirages. **1. mirage ▶** a sight that seems to appear but is not really there. Mirages are common in hot countries, especially in the desert, where travellers often imagine that they see a lake where no lake exists. **2. mirage, illusion ▶** something that is not what it seems or that cannot come true; an illusion. SYN: optical illusion, delusion, hallucination.

mir·ror [MEER-ur] NOUN, mirrors. **1. miroir, glace ▶** a smooth, shiny surface that reflects the image of whatever is in front of it. Most mirrors are made of glass with a thin coating of silver, aluminum, or other metal on the back. **2. miroir, reflet ▶** anything thought of as being like a mirror in the sense of showing or reflecting something in an exact way : *Newspapers are a mirror of what happens in our world.* ▲ VERB, mirrored, mirroring. **refléter, réfléchir ▶** to reflect with or as if with a mirror : *The gleaming brass of the hearth mirrored the crackling fire.*

mis- PREFIX. bad, wrong : *mischief; mistake; misspell.* ✐ **p. 373.**

mis-chief [MIS-chif] NOUN. **1. sottise, mauvais tour, espièglerie ▸** an act that is not truly bad, but that causes some harm or damage : *The puppies made mischief in the kitchen, knocking over cans and boxes of foods.* **2. malice, tort, dommage ▸** a feeling of wanting to tease or cause harm : *You could almost see the mischief in his eyes.* SYN : trick, prank, joke, lark, caper.

mis-chie-vous [MIS-chih-*vus* or mis-CHEE-vee-us] ADJECTIVE. **1. espiègle, farceur (-euse), malicieux (-euse) ▸** full of or caused by mischief : *a mischievous child.* **2. espiègle, malicieux (-euse) ▸** suggesting mischief : *a mischievous wink.*

mi-ser [MY-zur] NOUN. misers. **avare ▸** a person who loves money for its own sake. A miser may live like a poor person in order to avoid spending money. ■ **miserly,** ADJECTIVE. ▸ avare, pingre.

mis-er-a-ble [MIZ-ur-uh-bul] ADJECTIVE. **1. malheureux (-euse), triste ▸** very unhappy : *Keith felt miserable because he was too sick to go on the class trip.* **2. misérable ▸** of very poor quality; very bad : *a miserable hut; miserable conditions.* **3. maussade, détestable ▸** causing trouble or unhappiness : *a miserable, wet spring; a miserable cold.* ■ **miserably,** ADVERB. ▸ misérablement.

mis-er-y [MIZ-ur-ee] NOUN. miseries. **douleur, détresse ▸** a feeling of great pain or suffering; great unhappiness : *a poor, homeless person who lives in misery.* SYN : sorrow, grief, suffering, agony, woe.

mis-fit [MIS-fit] NOUN. misfits. **inadapté (-ée) ▸** a person who does not seem to fit in to a place or group.

mis-for-tune [mis-FOR-chun] NOUN. misfortunes. **1. malchance ▸** a lack of good fortune; bad luck : *They had the great misfortune of losing all their savings.* **2. malheur ▸** an unlucky or unfortunate event : *Getting stranded in a snowstorm was a great misfortune for Cassie.* SYN : disaster, tragedy, hardship, mishap, trouble.

mis-giv-ing [mis-GIV-ing] NOUN. misgivings. **crainte, doute, appréhension ▸** an idea that things might turn out wrong; feelings of doubt or worry : *Angelo had misgivings about driving long distances by himself.* SYN : apprehension, doubt, hesitation, mistrust.

mis-guid-ed [mis-GY-did] ADJECTIVE. **malavisé (-ée) ▸** led in the wrong way; led into wrong actions or ideas.

mis-hap [MIS-hap] NOUN. mishaps. **mésaventure, contretemps ▸** an unlucky accident, especially one that is not serious : *Patrice had a mishap and spilled juice all over herself.*

mis-judge [MIS-JUJ] VERB. misjudged, misjudging. **sous-estimer, mal évaluer ▸** to judge in a way that is wrong or incorrect : *I misjudged how much material I would need to make the dress.*

miss¹ [mis] VERB. missed, missing. **1. manquer, rater ▸** to fail to connect in some way; not hit, catch, or get something : *to swing at and miss a pitch in baseball; to miss the train.* **2. manquer, rater ▸** to not do what is expected or intended; fail to do : *to miss a question on a test; to miss three days of school.* **3. ne pas voir, ne pas entendre, ne pas comprendre ▸** to fail to see, hear, or understand : *They missed the point of the story.* **4. éviter ▸** to get away from; avoid : *Mom likes to leave early so that she'll miss the rush-hour traffic.* **5. regretter, remarquer l'absence ▸** to notice that something or someone is lost or absent : *I missed you.* ▲ NOUN. misses. **manque ▸** the fact of missing, or something that misses.

miss² NOUN. misses. **1. mademoiselle (mesdemoiselles) ▸** Miss. a title sometimes used for a girl or for a woman who is not married. **2. jeune fille ▸** any young woman or girl. Note. Many women now prefer the title Ms. **3. mademoiselle (mesdemoiselles) ▸** a way of addressing a woman or girl whose name is not known : *Excuse me, miss; do you know if Dr. Orta's office is in this building?*

mis-sile [MIS-ul] NOUN. missiles. **missile ▸** any object that is thrown or shot through the air, especially a weapon such as an arrow, a bullet, a rocket, or a guided missile; a projectile.

mis-sing [MIS-ing] ADJECTIVE. **1. disparu (-ue), perdu (-ue), égaré (-ée) ▸** not present or found; lost : *They found the missing cat hiding in the barn.* **2. manquant (-ante) ▸** lacking : *What is missing from this soup?* **3. absent (-ente) ▸** absent : *Who was missing from class yesterday?* SYN : lost, mislaid, misplaced, absent, gone, away.

mis-sion [MISH-un] NOUN. missions. **1. mission ▸** sending a person or group to perform a special job : *The search pilot's mission is to*

🖋 Word Builder

***Mis-** is a prefix. Adding mis- to a word can change the word to mean something negative as in mischief, misbehave, misinformation, and misadventure. **Mis-** also has the sense of something going badly, unfavourably, or wrongly as in words such as misunderstand, misconduct, miscalculation, mispronounce, misjudge, misdeed, mislead, misshapen, mistrust, and misspell.*

locate the shipwrecked passengers. **2. mission ▶** a church or other place where missionaries do their work : *A mission was set up in South America by the Anglican Church.* **Note.** A missionary is a person who is sent by a church to teach the people of a foreign country about, and help spread, the religion of that church. **3. mission ▶** a purpose or task in life that one feels chosen for or required to do : *"The eagle flew purposefully, as if on a mission for the gods."* (Roger Lancelyn Green) SYN : errand, task, assignment, purpose.

mis·spell [mis-SPEL] VERB, misspelled, misspelling. **mal épeler, mal orthographier ▶** to spell a word incorrectly : *Many people misspell the word "misspell," giving it only one "s."*

mist [mist] NOUN, mists. **1. brume ▶** a cloud of very fine drops of water in the air; a light fog. **2. voile ▶** anything that makes things dim or cloudy like a mist : *His eyes clouded with a mist of tears.* ▲ VERB, misted, misting. **1. s'embuer ▶** to become covered with a mist : *The car windows misted over in the damp spring night.* **2. bruiner ▶** to rain in fine drops; come down as mist. **■ misty,** ADJECTIVE, mistier, mistiest. **1. embué (-ée) ▶** clouded or covered with mist. **2. flou (floue), nébuleux (-euse) ▶** unclear; vague.

mis·take [MIS-STAKE] NOUN, mistakes. **erreur, faute ▶** something that is not correct; something done, said, or thought in the wrong way : *I want to read my story one more time to check for spelling mistakes.* ▲ VERB, mistook, mistaken, mistaking. **se tromper ▶** to make a mistake; understand something in the wrong way. SYN : error, slip, blunder, fault, inaccuracy.

mis·tak·en [mis-STAY-kun] ADJECTIVE. **erroné (-ée), faux (fausse) ▶** being a mistake; not correct; wrong : *Some people are frightened of king snakes because of a mistaken belief that they are poisonous.* **■ mistakenly,** ADVERB. **▶ par erreur, par mégarde.**

mis·ter [MIS-tur] NOUN, misters. **1.** Mister. **Monsieur ▶** a title used before a man's name. In writing, it is usually abbreviated as Mr. **2. monsieur ▶** a way of speaking to a man whose name is not known : *Hey, mister, you left your car's headlights on.*

mis·tle·toe [MIS-ul-toh] VERB. **gui ▶** a plant with small, light-green leaves and white berries. Mistletoe grows as a parasite on the branches of trees. It is often used as a Christmas decoration.

mis·tress [MIS-tris] NOUN, mistresses. **maîtresse ▶** a girl or woman who has power or control over others : *The horse ran over to the fence when it saw its mistress standing there.*

mis·un·der·stand [MIS-un-dur-STAND] VERB, misunderstood, misunderstanding. **mal comprendre, mal interpréter ▶** to understand incorrectly; not understand : *We misunderstood her directions and got off at the wrong stop.*

mis·un·der·stand·ing [MIS-un-dur-STAND-ing] NOUN, misunderstandings. **1. erreur, méprise ▶** a failure to understand; lack of understanding. **2. malentendu ▶** a minor argument or quarrel; a disagreement.

mitt [mit] NOUN, mitts. **1. gant de base-ball ▶** a baseball glove that is worn on one hand to catch the ball : *a catcher's mitt.* **2. mitaine, moufle ▶** short for mitten.

mit·ten [MIT-un] NOUN, mittens. **mitaine, moufle ▶** a covering used to keep the hands warm. A mitten is like a glove but covers the four fingers together, with only the thumb having a separate part.

mix [miks] VERB, mixed, mixing. **1. mélanger, mêler, malaxer ▶** to put different things together as one or in one group. **2. se mêler ▶** to join with other people at a party or other social gathering : *Kasey is very shy and finds it hard to mix with others.* **3.** (usually used with up) **mêler, mélanger ▶** to put together in a confusing way : *I dropped my essay, and the pages got mixed up.* **Note.** Also used as a NOUN: *We almost boarded the wrong plane because there was a mix-up at the gate.* ▲ NOUN, mixes. **1. préparation ▶** a food that is sold partly prepared, with some ingredients already mixed : *a cake mix.* **2. mélange, amalgame ▶** any group of different things : *an unusual mix of guests at dinner.* **Note.** A mixture is something that is made up of different things : *Her expression was a mixture of surprise and anger.* SYN : combine, blend, mingle, merge, unite.

mixed [mikst] ADJECTIVE. **1. mélangé (-ée), mêlé (-ée) ▶** made up of more than one kind : *a can of mixed nuts.* **2. mixte ▶** made up of both males and females : *a mixed softball team.* SYN : assorted, various, varied.

moan [mone] NOUN, moans. **gémissement, plainte ▶** a long, low sound, especially one that expresses pain or suffering. ▲ VERB, moaned, moaning. **1. gémir ▶** to give a moan or sound like this : *The wind moaned through the trees.* **2. se plaindre, maugréer, geindre ▶** to speak with moans; complain :*"I don't want to go," he moaned.*

moat [mote] NOUN, moats. **fossé ▶** a deep, wide ditch that is usually filled with water. In the Middle Ages, moats were dug around castles or towns for protection against enemies.

mob [mob] NOUN, mobs. **foule ▶** a large, excited group of people who are likely to cause harm or break the law : *A mob of people waited outside the theatre to see the actors.* ▲ ADJECTIVE. *Mob violence broke out during the protest march.* ▲ VERB, mobbed, mobbing. **désordonné (-ée) ▶** to form a large, excited crowd : *Thousands of screaming fans mobbed the airport to greet the* *winning team.* SYN: crowd, mass, swarm, jam.

mo-bile [MOH-bul *or* MOH-bile] ADJECTIVE. **1. mobile, transportable** ▸ able to move or be moved easily : *In spite of her broken leg, she was very mobile.* **2. expressif (-ive), changeant (-ante)** ▸ easily changed; quick to change from one position to another : *a mobile mind. The actor's mobile face changed expression quickly.* **Note.** A mobile home is another name for a large trailer that can be moved from place to place. ▲ [MOH-bile *or* MOH-beel] NOUN, **mobiles.** **mobile** ▸ a type of sculpture in which parts hang from wires or strings, so that they can move in the air. SYN: movable, portable.

moc-ca-sin [MOK-uh-sun] NOUN, **moccasins.** **mocassin** ▸ a soft leather shoe with a soft sole and no heel, first made and worn by the Aboriginal peoples of North America.

mock [mok] VERB, **mocked, mocking. se moquer de, ridiculiser,** ▸ to laugh at or make fun of someone, especially by copying the person's speech or actions. ▲ ADJECTIVE. **faux (fausse), simili-** ▸ being an imitation; make-believe; fake : *a mock diamond.* ■ **mockery,** NOUN. ▸ **moquerie.** SYN: tease, laugh at, imitate, jeer at, mimic.

mode [mode] NOUN, **modes. 1. manière, mode** ▸ a way of doing something; manner; means : *The letter was in a very flowery style, much different from her regular mode of writing.* **2. mode** ▸ a style of dressing; fashion. SYN: style, manner, way, fashion, form, custom.

mod-el [MOD-ul] NOUN, **models. 1. maquette, modèle (réduit)** ▸ something made as a copy or an example of something else, especially in a smaller form than the original : *Nat collects models of ships and planes.* **2. modèle** ▸ a certain style or type of some product that is manufactured : *The 1964 Ford Mustang was a very popular model of car.* **3. modèle** ▸ a person or thing that is a good example of what something should be like : *Diane is a model of good cheer.* **4. mannequin** ▸ a person whose job is to wear new clothes, jewellry, cosmetics, and so on to show them for sale, as in an advertisement or a fashion show. **5. modèle** ▸ a person who poses for an artist or photographer. ▲ VERB, **modelled, modelling.** (also modeled, modeling) **1. modeler** ▸ to make or design a model : *Val modelled a dinosaur out of clay.* **2. être mannequin, présenter les modèles de** ▸ to work as a model : *to model clothes.* **3. dessiner d'après le modèle de** ▸ to use something as an example : *Architects have modelled many modern buildings after buildings of ancient Greece.* ▲ ADJECTIVE. **1. modèle, témoin** ▸ being a model or copy : *A builder of homes often provides a model home for buyers to visit.* **2. modèle** ▸ serving as a good example; being a model for others : *a model citizen.*

mo-dem [MOH-dum] NOUN, **modems. modem** ▸ a device that allows a computer to communicate with other computers, usually over telephone lines. A modem allows information and instructions to be passed between computers.

mod-er-ate [MOD-ur-it] ADJECTIVE. **modéré (-ée), tempéré (-ée)** ▸ neither too great nor too little; not extreme : *The city of Victoria has a moderate climate—not too hot in the summer or too cold in the winter.* **Note.** The act or fact of being moderate is moderation. ▲ NOUN, **moderates. modéré (-ée)** ▸ a person who had moderate ideas or opinions, especially in politics. ▲ [MOD-uh-RATE] VERB, **moderated, moderating. (se) modérer** ▸ to make or become less extreme. ■ **moderately,** ADVERB. ▸ **modérément.** *clothing that is moderately priced.* SYN: reasonable, medium, middle-of-the-road.

mod-ern [MOD-urn] ADJECTIVE. **1. moderne** ▸ having to do with the present time or with the recent past : *VCRs, personal computers, and microwave ovens are modern inventions.* **2. moderne** ▸ up to date; not old-fashioned : *modern furniture; a modern hairstyle.* ▲ NOUN, **moderns. moderniste** ▸ a person who is modern or who has modern ideas. **Note.** To make something more modern is to modernize it : *The house was built in 1920, but the kitchen was modernized last year.* SYN: up to date, current, new, recent, present.

mod-est [MOD-ist] ADJECTIVE. **1. modeste, réservé (-ée), effacé (-ée)** ▸ not thinking too highly of oneself; not talking about what one is good at or calling attention to things one has done. **2. modeste, humble** ▸ not grand, impressive, or fancy; plain and simple : *It's a modest little house, not a mansion.* **3. réservé (-ée), pudique** ▸ decent and proper in a quiet way, as in one's dress or actions. ■ **modesty,** NOUN. ▸ **pudeur.** the condition or quality of being modest. ■ **modestly,** ADVERB. ▸ **modestement.** *Although he spoke modestly, it was clear that he was an expert in the field.* SYN: humble, unassuming, reserved, quiet.

mod-i-fy [MOD-uh-fy] VERB, **modified, modifying. 1. modifier, changer** ▸ to make different in some way; change somewhat : *The plans for the campout have been modified because of the rain.* **2. modifier** ▸ in grammar, to limit the meaning of another word or describe what it means : *In Rudyard Kipling's line "The great gray-green, greasy Limpopo River," all of the other words modify "Limpopo River."* SYN: change, alter, revise, convert, transform.

mod-ule [MOJ-ool *or* MOD-yool] NOUN, **modules. 1. module** ▸ a separate unit of a spacecraft, used for a special job or jobs : *a landing module.* **2. module** ▸ in a computer, any device that is a separate unit and that can be added to the computer system. A printer, a disk drive, and a mouse are types of modules.

Mo·hawk [MOH-hok] NOUN, Mohawk or Mohawks. **1. Mohawk** ▸ a member of the Aboriginal peoples who originally lived in northeastern New York State but now live mostly in southern Ontario and Quebec. The Mohawk are members of the Six Nation Iroquois Confederacy. **2. mohawk** ▸ the Iroquoian language of the Mohawk people.

moist [moyst] ADJECTIVE, moister, moistest. **humide, moite** ▸ slightly wet; damp : *moist air.* ■ **moisten,** VERB, moistened, moistening. ▸ **(s')** **humecter, (se) mouiller légèrement.** to make moist : *"She bathed his forehead with snow and moistened his lips."* (Donald Gale)

mois·ture [MOYS-chur] NOUN. **humidité** ▸ a small amount of wetness; water or other liquid that forms in small drops on a surface.

mold See mould.

mole¹ [mole] NOUN, moles. **grain de beauté** ▸ a small raised spot on the skin, usually brown or black.

mole² NOUN, moles. **taupe** ▸ a small animal that lives in underground burrows. Moles have tiny eyes that are covered by fur, powerful front feet for digging, and soft, greyish fur. **Note.** A molehill is a small mound of earth made by moles as they dig.

make a mountain out of a molehill faire une montagne d'un rien ▸ to exaggerate the importance of something that is unimportant.

mol·e·cule [MOL-uh-kYOOL] NOUN, molecules. **molécule** ▸ the smallest particle into which a substance can be divided and still keep the same qualities as the original substance. A molecule is made up of two or more atoms. A molecule of water has two atoms of hydrogen and one of oxygen. ■ **molecular,** ADJECTIVE. ▸ **moléculaire.**

mol·lusc [MOL-usk] NOUN, molluscs. (also mollusk) **mollusque** ▸ one of a large group of animals having a soft body and no backbone. Most molluscs (such as clams, oysters, and octopuses) live in the ocean. Other kinds (such as snails and slugs) live on land or in fresh water.

mol·ten [MOLE-tun] ADJECTIVE. **fondu (-ue)** ▸ made into a liquid or melted by great heat : *Volcanoes often spill molten rock called lava.*

mom [mom] NOUN, moms. (also mommy) *Informal.* **maman** ▸ a mother : *Children often call*

their mothers "Mom" or "Mommy." My mom is a doctor.

mo·ment [MOH-munt] NOUN, moments. **1. instant, moment** ▸ a very short period of time; an instant : *Please wait for just a moment.* **2. instant, moment** ▸ a certain point in time : *The moment he left the building, the rain started.* ■ **momentary,** ADJECTIVE. ▸ **momentané (-ée).** ■ **momentarily,** ADVERB. ▸ **momentanément.** SYN: instant, flash, second. 🖉 **p. 376.**

mo·men·tum [moh-MEN-tum] NOUN, momentums or momenta. **1. vitesse acquise** ▸ the amount of force that a moving object has as a result of its combined weight and speed : *An object will gain momentum as it rolls down a hill.* **2. dynamisme** ▸ any force that grows or advances : *Her campaign to become class president gained momentum as the election got closer.*

mon·arch [MON-ark] NOUN, monarchs. **1. monarque** ▸ a ruler who is not elected to power, but takes over at the death of a parent or other relative and then rules for life. Kings, queens, and emperors are monarchs. **2. monarque** ▸ a North American butterfly with orange-and-black wings.

mon·arch·y [MON-ur-kee] NOUN, monarchies. **1. monarchie** ▸ a form of government headed by a monarch. **2. monarchie** ▸ a country ruled by a monarch, such as Saudi Arabia. Countries such as Spain, Denmark, and Great Britain are called limited or constitutional monarchies because a person has the title king or queen but little actual power.

mon·as·ter·y [MON-es-TAIR-ee] NOUN, monasteries. **monastère** ▸ a building or buildings where a group of monks live according to certain religious rules.

Mon·day [MUN-day] NOUN, Mondays. **lundi** ▸ the day after Sunday and before Tuesday.

mon·ey [MUN-ee] NOUN, moneys or monies. **1. argent** ▸ objects that are in the form of coins or paper bills and that have an accepted value, for use in buying and selling things or in paying for work done. **2. monnaie** ▸ any system of using objects in this way. At different times in history, gold, stones, shells, beads, and many other things have been used as money. **3. fonds, argent** ▸ a large amount of money; wealth : *She's in the*

🖉 Word Builder

Moment usually refers to a very short period of time, but it can also refer to longer periods : The War of 1812 was an important moment in our history. Second is a unit of time : Sixty seconds make up a minute. Often it can be used just to mean a short period of time : Can I put you on hold for a second ? An instant often means an extremely short, almost noticeable, amount of time : In an instant, the birthday cake was gone.

money since she won the lottery. SYN: cash, funds, currency, coin, legal tender.

mon-grel [MONG-rul] NOUN, mongrels. **bâtard (-arde), hybride ▸** a dog or other animal that is a mixture of different breeds. **Note.** Such a dog is often called a mutt.

mon-i-tor [MON-uh-tur] NOUN, monitors. **1. moniteur (-trice), chef de classe ▸** a student who is given a special duty in school, such as helping teachers take attendance or keeping order in the hall. **2. moniteur (-trice) ▸** someone or something used to keep watch or give warning of trouble : *The monitors in the space shuttle showed that everything was working well.* **3. moniteur ▸** a television set or speaker used in a broadcasting studio to check what is being broadcast. **4. moniteur, écran, téléviseur ▸** the screen or television set that displays information from a computer, VCR, or the like. ▲ VERB, monitored, monitoring. **surveiller, contrôler ▸** to watch over or check on something : *The principal is monitoring the new class schedule.*

monk [munk] NOUN, monks. **moine ▸** a man who has become a member of a religious group called an order and lives a life of prayer, obeying rules set by that order, such as not being married or owning property.

mon-key [MUNG-kee] NOUN, monkeys. **singe ▸** one of a family of animals that have long arms and legs, hands with thumbs, and a long tail. Monkeys usually live in trees, are very good climbers, and are among the most intelligent animals. ▲ VERB, monkeyed, monkeying. *Informal.* **faire l'imbécile ▸** to play around with something in a foolish way. ☞ **p. 1092.**

mo-no-gram [MON-uh-GRAM] NOUN, monograms. **monogramme ▸** a person's initials written together in a fancy way. Monograms are used on towels, clothing, stationery, and such other items.

mo-no-logue [MON-uh-LOG] NOUN, monologues. (sometimes monolog) **1. monologue ▸** a play or part of a play during which one actor speaks alone : *"To be or not to be" is the beginning of a famous monologue in Shakespeare's* Hamlet. **2. monologue ▸** a series of jokes or stories told by one person : *The talk-show host starts her show with a monologue.* **3. monologue ▸** any long speech given by one person, without allowing others to speak.

mo-nop-o-ly [muh-NOP-uh-lee] NOUN, monopolies. **1. monopole ▸** complete control over selling or making a certain product or service : *The telephone company used to have a monopoly in supplying long-distance service.* **2. monopole ▸** a company or other organization that has this complete control. If a company has a monopoly on something, someone who wants to buy it has no choice but to buy from that company. **3. monopole ▸** complete control over any situation, as if by a monopoly : *Sarah won't*

listen to anyone else; she thinks that she has a monopoly on all good ideas

mo-not-o-nous [muh-NOT-uh-nus] ADJECTIVE. **1. monotone, uniforme ▸** continuing without change at the same level : *The monotonous beat of the drums sounded throughout the night.* **2. monotone ▸** tiring or boring because of a lack of change; dull : *Megan finds riding the train really monotonous, so she takes a book along to read.* **Note.** This feeling or quality is called **monotony.** SYN: boring, bland, dull, uninteresting, tedious.

mon-soon [mon-SOON] NOUN, monsoons. **1. mousson ▸** a strong, steady wind that blows in southern Asia and the Indian Ocean. The winds blow in opposite directions in summer and winter, bringing either heavy rains or dry weather. **2. mousson (d'été) ▸** in India or southern Asia, the season of heavy rain, or a heavy rainstorm during this season.

[MON-stur] NOUN, monsters. **1. monstre ▸** a huge imaginary creature that has a strange and frightening appearance. Old folk tales often tell of dragons, sea serpents, and other such monsters. **2. monstre ▸** a person who is very cruel or evil. **3. monstre ▸** any person or thing that is very large : *a monster of a storm.* ☞ **p. 969.**

mon-strous [MON-strus] ADJECTIVE. **1. monstrueux (-euse), abominable ▸** not natural or normal, especially in an ugly or frightening way. **2. monstrueux (-euse), abominable ▸** very wrong or evil : *Prisoners in Nazi concentration camps were treated with monstrous cruelty.* **3. colossal (-ale) monstrueux (-euse) ▸** very large; huge : *"…a muffled roar of energy, as though some monstrous, gigantic, machine were spinning its wheels at breakneck speed."* (Roald Dahl) ▪ **monstrously,** ADVERB. ▸ monstrueusement.

Mon-ta-gnais [MON-tuh-NYAY or mon-tuh-NYEE] NOUN, Montagnais. **Montagnais ▸** a member of the Aboriginal peoples living in eastern and northern Quebec and Labrador. See Innu.

month [munth] NOUN, months. **mois ▸** one of the 12 parts into which a year is divided. ☞ **p. 1079.**

month-ly [MUNTH-lee] ADJECTIVE. **1. mensuel (-elle) ▸** done or happening once a month : *This is a monthly magazine—there are 12 issues a year.* **2. mensuel (-elle) ▸** of or for a month : *Monthly sales of video games for December were way up this year.* ▲ ADVERB. **mensuellement ▸** once a month; every month. ▲ NOUN, monthlies. **mensuel ▸** a magazine published once a month.

mon-u-ment [MON-yuh-munt] NOUN, monuments. **1. monument ▸** a statue, building, or other object that is built to honour and preserve the memory of some important person or event. **2. témoignage ▸** anything that keeps alive the memory of a person or an event : *His book was a monument to his sister.* **Note.** Something that is very large or important is **monumental.**

mood [mood] NOUN, moods. **humeur, dispositions** ▸ a person's feelings ; a person's state of mind : *to be in a good mood.* **Note.** A person who changes moods quickly, or who is often in a bad mood, is **moody.** SYN : feeling, frame of mind, temper, disposition. *p. 378.*

moon [moon] NOUN, moons. **1. lune** ▸ a heavenly body that revolves around the earth about once every 29.5 days. The light that appears to shine from the moon is actually light reflected from the sun. The moon has a rocky surface of craters and mountains with no water or atmosphere. **2. lune** ▸ a similar body that revolves around another planet : *Titan is one of the 23 moons of Saturn.* ▲ VERB, mooned, mooning. **flâner** ▸ to spend time in a lazy or wasteful way : *Claude has spent most of his vacation mooning about the house.* p. 1117.

moon-light [MOON-lite] NOUN. **clair de lune** ▸ the light of the moon. ▲ ADJECTIVE. **au clair de lune** ▸ of or happening by the light of the moon : *We took a moonlight cruise around the lake.* ▲ VERB, moonlighted, moonlighting. **travailler au noir, faire du travail au noir** ▸ to work at a second job besides one's full-time job, especially at night : *He works for the bank and moonlights as a cab driver.*

moor¹ [moor] VERB, moored, mooring. **amarrer** ▸ to fasten or tie a boat in place : *Several sailboats were moored in the harbour.*

moor² NOUN, moors. **lande** ▸ a large area of open, empty land with few trees on it. There are moors in parts of Scotland and England.

moose

moose [mooce] NOUN, moose. **original** ▸ a large animal of the deer family. A moose has a heavy body with large humped shoulders, long legs, and a large head. The male has wide, flat antlers.

Moose are found in North America and in northern parts of Europe and Asia. **Note.** In Europe it's called an elk. **élan** ▸ In North America, elk and moose are different animals. p. 111.

mop [mop] NOUN, mops. **vadrouille** ▸ a household tool with a long handle that ends in either a sponge or a thick bundle of soft string used for cleaning floors. ▲ VERB, mopped, mopping. **1. essuyer, éponger** ▸ to use a mop. **2. (s') éponger** ▸ to use a cloth or other material to soak up moisture : *He mopped his brow with a handkerchief.*

mope [mope] VERB, moped, moping. **broyer du noir, se morfondre** ▸ to move slowly, in a dull, sad way : *Jean moped around the house because he couldn't go out to play.*

mor·al [MOR-ul] ADJECTIVE. **1. moral (-ale, -aux)** ▸ having to do with what is right and wrong : *Justin found $5 and had to make a moral decision about whether to return or keep it.* **2. moral (-ale, -aux)** ▸ honest or good : *The store owner is a moral person who would never cheat a customer.* **3. moral (-ale, -aux)** ▸ having to do with the mind or spirit rather than with action : *Dad went with Joanie to see the principal, just to give her moral support.* ▲ NOUN, morals. **1. morals. moralité** ▸ a person's beliefs or actions in matters of right and wrong.

✐ Writing Tips

Mood

*All pieces of writing, particularly stories and poems, have a certain **mood**—a feeling that they give the reader. The mood may be dark and serious, or light and comic. The mood may change throughout the piece of writing as events unfold. **Mood** is also called **atmosphere.***

• *When you begin to write a story, you establish a mood.*

It was a bright, sunny day. People were walking their dogs and kites were flying.

This beginning raises certain expectations in the reader. As a writer, you can meet these expectations by continuing with a cheerful story. Or you can turn these expectations upside down by introducing new elements that disrupt this mood.

As I watched, the sky was suddenly filled with smoke, and in the distance I could hear shouting.

• *Remember that writers have the power to make their readers feel. Good writers use this power carefully.*

2. morale, moralité ▸ a lesson about right and wrong : *Some fables have a moral stated at the end.* ■ **morally,** ADVERB. ▸ **moralement.**

mor-ale [muh-RAL] NOUN. **moral ▸** the state of mind of a person or group; how people feel about their situation in life or about what will happen to them in the future : *Morale in the office was low after many people were let go.*

mo-ral-i-ty [muh-RAL-uh-tee] NOUN. moralities. **1. moralité ▸** the right or wrong of something. **2. morale ▸** right conduct; acting in the proper way. **3. mœurs ▸** a set of moral standards : *middle-class morality.*

more [mor] ADJECTIVE. **1. plus de ▸** greater in number or amount : *The mail carrier says that there seems to be more mail to deliver on Monday than on any other day.* **2. d'autres, encore (de) ▸** additional; extra : *You'd better bring more money, in case we decide to eat out.* ▲ NOUN. **plus ▸** a larger or extra amount. ▲ ADVERB. **1. plus, davantage ▸** to a great number or amount : *Large colour TVs cost more than small ones.* **2. encore ▸** in addition; again : *I'll try to call her once more.*

more-o-ver [mor-OH-vur] ADVERB. **d'ailleurs, de plus, en outre ▸** not only that; besides; also : *I don't want to go to the party; moreover, I don't have anything to wear.*

morn-ing [MOR-ning] NOUN, mornings. **matin, matinée ▸** the early part of the day, from the time the sun rises up until noon. ▲ ADJECTIVE. **matinal (-ale, -aux), du matin ▸** of or during the early part of the day : *a morning walk.* 📖 **p. 1079.**

morph [morf] VERB, morphed, morphing. **1. transformer par morphing ▸** to use a computer to change one digital image into another so that the first image transforms seamlessly into the second. **2. transformer ▸** of an image, to change in this way.

Morse code [mors] **morse ▸** either of two systems of short and long signals, or dots and dashes, that represent letters in the alphabet. Morse code was once the most common way of sending long-distance messages. **Note.** It was named after its inventor, Samuel F.B. Morse.

mor-sel [MOR-sul] NOUN. morsels. **bouchée, petit bout ▸** a small bit or piece of something.

mor-tal [MOR-tul] ADJECTIVE. **1. mortel (-elle) ▸** sure to die sometime : *All living things are mortal.* **Note.** The fact of being mortal is mortality. **2. mortel (-elle), fatal (-ale, -als) ▸** causing death or able to cause death : *mortal combat.* **3. mortel (-elle) ▸** very serious or intense : *mortal terror.* ■ **mortally,** ADVERB. ▸ **mortellement.** *to be mortally wounded.*

mort-gage [MOR-gij] NOUN. mortgages. **hypothèque ▸** an agreement by which someone borrows money to buy a house or other property, or borrows against the value of real estate that is already owned. If the borrower does not pay back the loan, the lender can take ownership of the property. ▲ VERB. mortgaged, mortgaging. **hypothéquer ▸** to place a mortgage on property.

mo-sa-ic [moh-ZAY-ik] NOUN. mosaics. **1. mosaïque ▸** a picture or design made of small pieces of coloured tile, glass, stone, or other material fastened together : *Mosaics are used on walls and floors.* **2. mosaïque ▸** something made up of different parts or elements : *Canada is often called a cultural mosaic because of its many different cultures.*

Mos-lem musulman (-ane) ▸ See Muslim.

mosque [mosk] NOUN. mosques. **mosquée ▸** a Muslim temple or place of worship. The Great Mosque in Mecca, Saudia Arabia, is considered to be the centre of the Muslim religion.

mos-qui-to [musk-HEE-toh] NOUN. mosquitoes **maringouin, moustique ▸** or mosquitos.

moss [mos] NOUN. mosses. **mousse ▸** a type of small green plant that has no flowers and that grows together in clumps to form a soft, dense mat. Moss grows in damp, shady places on the surface of rocks, at the base of trees, or along the ground. ■ **mossy,** ADJECTIVE, mossier, mossiest. ▸ **mousseux (-euse).**

most [mohst] ADJECTIVE. **1. le plus ▸** the greatest in number or amount : *Toronto has the most people of any Canadian city.* **2. la plupart, la majorité ▸** to a great extent or amount; nearly all : *"Like most Greeks, Periander, King of Corinth, was a music lover."* (Marcia Williams) ▲ ADVERB. **le plus ▸** to the greatest amount : *It was the most beautiful day of the summer.* ▲ NOUN. **le plus, au plus, le maximum, au maximum ▸** the greatest number or amount : *We'll be gone about two hours, three at the most.* ■ **mostly,** ADVERB. ▸ **principalement, surtout.** for the most part; largely; mainly.

moth [moth] NOUN. moths. **papillon de nuit, mite ▸** any of a very large group of insect found throughout the world. Moths are like butterflies, but are less brightly coloured, have smaller wings and larger bodies, and are active mainly at night. Some kinds of moths damage trees, plants, and clothing. moths.

moth-er [MUTH-ur] NOUN. mothers. **1. mère, maman ▸** the female parent of a child. **2. mère ▸** a woman or thing thought of as like a mother : *We saw a mother goose with her babies.* **Note.** Mother Nature is the world of animals, plants, and so on. ▲ VERB, mothered, mothering. **materner, servir de mère à ▸** to be or act as a mother to. ■ **motherly,** ADJECTIVE. ▸ **maternel (-elle).**

Mother's Day fête des Mères ▸ a holiday in honour of mothers, celebrated on the second Sunday in May.

mo-tion [MOH-shun] NOUN. motions. **1. mouvement ▸** the fact of moving; not staying

still; movement : *the motion of the waves.*
2. motion. **geste ▸** one single or particular way
of moving : *he made a slight motion towards
him.* **3. proposition, motion ▸** in a meeting, a
plan or suggestion that is put forward for a vote
or decision : *Erin proposed a motion to end
the meeting.* ▲ VERB, motioned, motioning. **faire
signe, inviter ▸** to make a motion; move the
hand or body as a signal to do something : *Kiko
stopped at a house and motioned us to follow
him.* ■ **motionless,** ADJECTIVE. **▸ immobile,
sans bouger.** SYN : movement, action, direction.

motion picture **film, long métrage ▸** See
movie.

mo·ti·vate [MOH-tuh-VATE] VERB, motivated,
motivating. **motiver, stimuler, pousser, inciter
▸** to give someone a motive or reason to
do something. ■ **motivation,** NOUN. **▸ motivation.** something that causes a person to act.
SYN : inspire, drive, impel, encourage, sway.

mo·tive [MOH-tiv] NOUN, motives. **1. motif, raison ▸** the reason that a person does something :
*A desire to escape persecution was one motive
for the first settlers to come to Canada.*
2. mobile ▸ the reason that a person commits a
crime. SYN : reason, cause, purpose, impulse,
incentive.

mo·tor [MOH-tur] NOUN, motors. **moteur ▸** a
machine that changes power into motion.
Motors are used to make other machines work,
such as washing machines, vacuum cleaners,
electric fans, and so on. ▲ ADJECTIVE. **1. motorisé
(-ée), à moteur ▸** run by a motor. **2. automobile ▸** having to do with cars or other motor
vehicles : Motor Trend *magazine reports on the
auto industry.* **3. moteur (-trice) ▸** having to do
with motion, especially the motion of the body :
*Very young children usually don't have enough
motor control to catch a baseball or ride
a bicycle.* **Note.** Compound words formed
with motor include *motorboat,* **motorcycle**
(📖 **p. 1154**), *motorbike,* and *motor home.*

mot·to [MOT-oh] NOUN, mottoes or mottos.
devise ▸ a short phrase or sentence that sums
up what a person or group believes in or stands
for; guiding idea or principle; slogan : *"'An
apple a day keeps the doctor away' has
always been my motto," said the 100-year-old
woman.*

mould¹ [mold] NOUN, moulds. (also mold ▲ VERB,
moulded, moulding. **1. mouler, modeler, façonner ▸** to form something with or as if with a
mould. **2. former, façonner ▸** to give something
a certain form or character, as if with a mould :
*"Pa's example commanded our respect and
moulded us."* (Christy MacKinnon)

mould² NOUN, moulds. (also mold) **moisissure
▸** a type of fungus. Mould can be seen as a soft,
fuzzy growth, often bluish or greenish in colour,
that grows on such foods as bread, cheese and
fruits. ▲ VERB, moulded, moulding. **moisir ▸** to
develop or become covered with mould.

mould·y [MOLE-dee] ADJECTIVE, mouldier, moul-
diest. (also moldy, moldier, moldiest) **1. moisi
(-ie) ▸** covered with mould : *The cheese is
mouldy.* **2. nauséabond (-onde) ▸** having a stale,
damp smell : *The garage is always mouldy.*

mound [mownd] NOUN, mounds. **1. monticule,
butte ▸** a hill or heap of dirt, stones, or other
material : *"About 2000 years ago, on the hills of
central Ontario, large mounds were built as
burial structures."* (Robert McGhee) **2. monticule ▸** in baseball, the raised ground in the centre of the infield from which the pitcher throws
the ball to the batter. **3. tas, montagne ▸** a large
pile or heap : *Sira says that she can't go to the
movie because she has a mound of laundry to
do.*

mount [mownt] VERB, mounted, mounting.
1. monter ▸ to go or climb up something : *They
slowly mounted the winding staircase.* **2. monter, enfourcher ▸** to get up on : *Sue mounted
the horse.* **3. fixer, installer ▸** to set firmly in
place; fix : *They mounted photographs on the
walls of the gallery.* **4. monter, s'élever ▸** to go
up in amount or level; rise; increase : *"As we
settled in to the new ship, tension began
to mount."* (Robert D. Ballard) ▲ NOUN, mounts.
1. monture ▸ a horse or other animal for riding.
2. cadre, support ▸ a frame or support for
mounting something, such as a painting.
3. mont ▸ a short word for mountain, often used
in names : *Mount Everest.*

moun·tain [MOWN-tun] NOUN, mountains.
1. montagne ▸ a large mass of land that rises
high above the land around it. The difference
between a mountain and a high hill is not exact,
but a mountain is usually thought of as being
more than 600 metres above its surroundings.
Note. A group or series of mountains is called a
mountain range. **2. montagne, tas ▸** a large
pile or amount of something; a heap : *Ken dug
into the mountain of mashed potatoes heaped
on his plate.* ▲ ADJECTIVE. **montagnard (-arde),
des montagnes ▸** having to do with a mountain
or mountains : *mountain people; mountain air.*
📖 **p. 1043.**

moun·tain·ous [MOWN-tun-us] ADJECTIVE.
1. montagneux (-euse) ▸ having many mountains. **2. gigantesque, énorme ▸** like a mountain; very high or large : *Sunset Beach in Hawaii
is famous for its mountainous waves.*

Moun·tie [MOWN-tee] NOUN, Mounties. (also
mountie) *Informal.* **membre de la Gendarmerie
royale du Canada ▸** a member of the Royal
Canadian Mounted Police.

mourn [morn] VERB, mourned, mourning.
pleurer ▸ to be very sad over the loss of someone or something; feel great sorrow. **Note.** A
mourner is a person who is mourning a loss.

mournful, ADJECTIVE. ▶ **triste, mélancolique, affligé (-ée).** feeling great sorrow; very sad : *He felt a mournful sinking of his heart when he thought of leaving his home.* ■ **mournfully,** ADVERB. ▶ **tristement, mélancoliquement.** SYN : grieve, regret, lament, feel sorrow.

mourn·ing [MOR-ning] NOUN. **1. deuil** ▶ the act or fact of showing great sadness over a death or loss. **2. deuil, vêtements de deuil** ▶ black clothing worn to show sorrow over someone's death.

mouse [mowce] NOUN, mice. **1. souris** ▶ a small furry animal with a pointed nose, large, sharp front teeth, and a long tail. There are many kinds of mice found in different parts of the world. **2. souris** ▶ a small device used to give instructions to a computer without the use of the keyboard, thought to be shaped somewhat like a mouse.

mous·tache [MUS-tash or muh-STASH] NOUN, moustaches. (also mustache) **moustache** ▶ hair that is grown on a man's upper lip.

mouth [mowth] NOUN, mouths. **1. bouche, gueule** ▶ the opening in the face of a person or animal through which food and drink are taken into the body, and from which sounds come. **2. embouchure, entrée, ouverture, goulot** ▶ an opening that is like a mouth : *the mouth of a river.* ▲ VERB, mouthed, mouthing. **articuler, former des mots avec les lèvres** ▶ to move the mouth in a certain way : *She mouthed each word slowly to be sure she was being understood.* **Note.** A mouthful is the amount the mouth can hold or take in at one time. 🗐 p. 985. 🔊 p. 403.

mouth-to-mouth [MOWTH-tuh-MOWTH] ADJECTIVE. **bouche-à-bouche** ▶ of or having to do with a method of artificial resuscitation in which the rescuer places his or her mouth tightly over the mouth of a person who has stopped breathing and forces air into the person's lungs.

mouth·wash [MOWTH-wash or MOWTH-wosh] NOUN, mouthwashes. **rince-bouche, gargarisme** ▶ a liquid, usually flavoured, used for rinsing out the mouth and freshening the breath.

mouth·wa·ter·ing [MOWTH-wah-tur-ing] ADJECTIVE. **appétissant (-ante), alléchant (-ante)** ▶ very appealing to the taste.

move [moov] VERB, moved, moving. **1. bouger, déplacer** ▶ to change the place where something is; go or cause to go from one place to another. **2. déménager** ▶ to change the place where one lives. **3. agir** ▶ to begin to take action; act : *After the owner's son took over the business, he moved quickly to hire a number of new people.* **4. proposer** ▶ to make a formal suggestion at a meeting; make a motion : *I move that we have a vote on the issue.* **5. causer** ▶ to cause a person to act or feel in a certain way : *The play moved him to tears.* ▲ NOUN, moves. **1. mouvement** ▶ the act of moving : *The phone rang, but no one made a move to answer it.* **2. coup, tour** ▶ the act of moving a piece in a game, or a turn that allows a player to do this : *In chess, the player with the white pieces has the first move.* 🖉 p. 381.

St. Lawrence River

Atlantic Ocean

mouth

get a move on **se dépêcher, se hâter** ▶ hurry up; make haste : *Get a move on—we're going to be late.*

move in **emménager** ▶ move oneself and one's belongings into a new place to live or work.

move·ment [MOOV-munt] NOUN, movements. **1. mouvement** ▶ the act of moving : *"She saw no movement when she scanned the ice."* (Donald Gale) **2. mouvement** ▶ the moving parts of a machine : *the movement of a watch.* **3. mouvement** ▶ the efforts or actions of a group of people : *Those who belong to the peace movement oppose war.* **4. mouvement** ▶ one part of a larger piece of music, such as a symphony.

🖉 **Word Builder**

Move, shift, and *budge* are all verbs that mean to transport something from one place to another. It can refer to transporting something a short or much longer distance. Move can also mean to change the place where someone lives : *They moved from Brandon to Winnipeg. **Shift** often implies a slight move : He had to shift seats when a person with a large hat sat down in front of him. **Budge** means to move something slightly, often with great effort : After a lot of pushing, they were finally able to budge the refrigerator away from the wall.*

mov-ie [MOOV-ee] NOUN, movies. **1. film ▸** a story or other work of entertainment or education, presented in the form of a motion picture; also called a film. **2. movies. cinéma ▸** the showing of a movie, or a theatre where movies are shown : *to go to the movies.* ☞ **p. 1123.**

mov-ing [MOOV-ing] ADJECTIVE. **1. mobile ▸** that which moves or is able to move : *the moving parts of a machine.* **2. émouvant (-ante) ▸** having a strong effect on the feelings : *The class president gave a moving speech at graduation.*

mow [moh] VERB, mowed, mowing. **tondre, faucher ▸** to cut grass or other growing plants in a lawn or field. ■ **mower,** NOUN. ▸ **faucheur (-euse), tondeuse.**

Mr. [MIS-tur] ABBREVIATION. (sometimes Mr) **M. ▸** a title used before a man's name.

Mrs. [MIS-iz] ABBREVIATION. (sometimes Mrs) **Mme ▸** a title sometimes used before a married woman's name. **Note.** Many women now prefer the title Ms.

Ms. [miz] ABBREVIATION. (also Ms) **Mme ▸** a title used before a woman's name when it is not known, or does not matter, whether she is married or single. Many women prefer to be addressed this way, while others prefer Miss or Mrs.

much [much] ADJECTIVE, more, most. **beaucoup (de) ▸** being a large amount; great in amount : *With much noise and fuss, the party started.* ADVERB. **combien ▸** being a certain amount : *How much does it cost to get into the zoo?* ▲ NOUN: *Much of what happened has been forgotten.* SYN: a lot, loads, plentiful, abundant, substantial.

mud [mud] NOUN. **boue ▸** dirt that is wet, soft, and sticky. ■ **muddy,** ADJECTIVE, muddier, muddiest. ▸ **boueux (-euse).**

mud-dle [MUD-ul] VERB, muddled, muddling. **embrouiller, brouiller ▸** to mix up; confuse : *Janine muddled her explanation of the experiment.* SYN: mix up, confuse, rattle, bungle, bewilder.

muff [muf] NOUN, muffs. **manchon ▸** a soft, thick roll of fur open at each end for warming the hands. In the past, women carried a muff in cold weather.

muf-fin [MUF-in] NOUN, muffins. **muffin ▸** a small piece of bread like a little cake, baked in a small container and often eaten hot.

muf-fle [MUF-ul] VERB, muffled, muffling. **assourdir, étouffer ▸** to make a sound softer or weaker : *She tried to muffle the sound of her laughter.* ■ **muffler,** NOUN. **1. silencieux ▸** a device used to soften the noise of an automobile engine. **2. cache-col ▸** a long scarf worn around the neck. SYN: silence, drown, deaden, squelch.

mug [mug] NOUN, mugs. **chope, gobelet ▸** a large, heavy drinking cup that has a flat bottom,

straight sides, and a handle. ▲ VERB, mugged, mugging. **agresser ▸** to suddenly attack someone in order to rob the person, especially on the street. **Note.** Someone who robs in this way is a mugger.

mug-gy [MUG-ee] ADJECTIVE, muggier, muggiest. **chaud (chaude) et humide ▸** warm and damp; humid : *This summer is one of the muggiest we have ever had.*

muk-luk [MUK-luk] NOUN, mukluks. **mukluk ▸** a traditional Inuit boot made of soft hide.

mule [myool] NOUN, mules. **mulet, mule ▸** an animal that is produced by mating a female horse and has a male donkey. A mule looks like a horse, but has the long ears and tail of a donkey. Mules are used as work animals. ■ **mulish,** ADJECTIVE. ▸ **buté (-ée), têtu (-ue).** stubborn; like a mule.

mul-ti-cul-tur-al [MUL-tee-KUL-chur-ul] ADJECTIVE. **multiculturel (-elle) ▸** of or having many distinct cultures existing side by side in the same place : *Canada is a multicultural country.*

mul-ti-ple [MUL-tuh-pul] ADJECTIVE. **multiple ▸** being more than one; many : *Multiple copies of a letter can be made quickly with a photocopier.* ▲ NOUN, multiples. **multiple ▸** a number that is the result of multiplying one number by another.

mul-ti-pli-ca-tion [mul-tuh-pluh-KAY-shun] NOUN. **multiplication ▸** in mathematics, a short way of adding a number to itself a certain number of times. The multiplication of 16 x 4 is the same as $16 + 16 + 16 + 16 = 64$.

mul-ti-ply [MUL-tuh-ply] VERB, multiplied, multiplying. **1. multiplier ▸** in mathematics, to perform the operation of multiplication. **2. (se) multiplier ▸** to become greater in number, especially very quickly or by a large amount : *When there are no larger animals to hunt them, rabbits multiply rapidly.* SYN: increase, make more, extend, reproduce.

mul-ti-tude [MUL-tuh-TOOD] NOUN, multitudes. **multitude, foule ▸** a very large number of people or things. SYN: mass, crowd, throng, flock, swarm.

mum-ble [MUM-bul] VERB, mumbled, mumbling. **murmurer, marmotter, marmonner ▸** to speak in a soft way with the mouth partly closed, so that one cannot be easily understood. SYN: whisper, murmur, mutter.

mumps [mumps] NOUN. **oreillons ▸** a contagious disease that causes a painful swelling in the lower cheeks and around the jaw, making it difficult to chew or swallow.

mu-ni-ci-pal [myoo-NIS-uh-pul] ADJECTIVE. **municipal (-ale, -aux) ▸** having to do with a city or its government : *a municipal court; municipal parks.*

mu-ral [MYOOR-ul] NOUN, murals. **peinture murale ▸** a large painting or design on a wall.

mur-der [MUR-dur] NOUN, murders. **meurtre, assassinat, homicide** ▸ the killing of one person by another. ▲ VERB, murdered, murdering. **assassiner** ▸ to commit the crime of murder. Note. A person who does this is a murderer. ■ **murderous**, ADJECTIVE. ▸ **meurtrier (-ière)**. ■ **murderously**, ADVERB. ▸ **d'une façon meurtrière**.

mur-ky [MUR-kee] ADJECTIVE, murkier, murkiest. **sombre, trouble** ▸ very dark or cloudy : the murky water of a lake.

mur-mur [MUR-mur] NOUN, murmurs. **murmure, bourdonnement** ▸ a soft, low sound that goes on and on : We could hear the murmur of the ocean far below. ▲ VERB, murmured, murmuring. **murmurer** ▸ to make this sound : She murmured the words under her breath.

mus-cle [MUS-ul] NOUN, muscles. 1. **muscle** ▸ a particular body part made up of this tissue : The biceps and triceps are arm muscles. 2. **muscle** ▸ strength of the muscles; physical strength : We'll need some extra muscle on moving day. 👁 p. 402.

mus-cu-lar [MUS-kyuh-lur] ADJECTIVE. 1. **musclé (-ée)** ▸ having well-developed muscles; strong : Pat was a tall, well-built athlete with muscular arms and legs. 2. **musculaire** ▸ having to do with the muscles : muscular aches and pains.

muse [myooz] VERB, mused, musing. **songer, méditer** ▸ to think in a dreamy way; think : to muse on the meaning of life.

Muse [myooz] NOUN. 1. **Muse** ▸ in Greek mythology, one of the nine goddesses of the fine arts and sciences. 2. **muse** ▸ a spirit that inspires a poet or composer.

mu-se-um [myoo-ZEE-um] NOUN, museums. **musée** ▸ a building or room used for keeping and displaying works of art, or things of value and interest from other fields, such as history, science, technology, or animal and plant life. 👁 p. 1051.

mush-room [MUSH-room] NOUN, mushrooms. **champignon** ▸ a type of plant that has a stalk with a cap on top shaped like a cup or umbrella. A mushroom is a kind of fungus. Many kinds of mushrooms can be eaten; others are poisonous and are called toadstools. ▲ VERB, mushroomed, mushrooming. **pousser comme un champignon, se multiplier** ▸ to suddenly appear or grow, in the way that mushrooms spring from the ground : What started out as a small party has mushroomed into a huge celebration. 👁 p. 252.

mu-sic [MYOO-zik] NOUN. 1. **musique** ▸ the art of making sounds that are beautiful or pleasing to the ear, and of putting these sounds together in a pattern that expresses feelings or ideas. 2. **musique** ▸ a particular way of arranging these sounds; a musical composition : Healey Willan wrote music for choirs. Note. A **musi-**

cian (👁 **p. 1127**) is a person who plays or sings music. 3. **musique, partition** ▸ the notes of a musical composition set down on paper : Many early jazz musicians could not read music and created their own versions of songs. 4. **musique** ▸ a sweet or pleasing sound like music : the music of the breeze in the trees. 👁 p. 1130.

mu-si-cal [MYOO-zuh-kul] ADJECTIVE. 1. **musical (-ale, -aux)** ▸ having to do with music. 2. **musical (-ale, -aux), harmonieux (-euse)** ▸ having a pleasant sound like music : the musical sound of the stream. ▲ NOUN, musicals. **comédie musicale** ▸ a stage show or movie that includes songs and dancing as well as ordinary spoken words. Well-known musicals include The Sound of Music and My Fair Lady.

mus-keg [MUS-keg] NOUN, muskegs. 1. **muskeg** ▸ a swamp or marsh. 2. **tourbière** ▸ an area of bog made of decaying plant life : Northern Alberta contains large areas of muskeg.

musk-rat [MUSK-rat] NOUN, muskrats. **rat musqué** ▸ a small rodent with dark brown fur that lives in wet, swampy areas of North America. 👁 p. 111.

Mus-lim [MOZ-lim or MOOS-lim] NOUN, Muslims. (also **Moslem**) a member of the religion of Islam. ▲ ADJECTIVE. **musulman (-ane)** ▸ of or having to do with this religion : a Muslim temple. **musulman (-ane)** ▸

mus-sel [MUS-ul] NOUN, mussels. **moule** ▸ a type of water animal that can be eaten. Mussels have a two-part shell with a bluish black colour. They are related to clams.

must [must] VERB. Must is a special verb used with other verbs to show 1. **devoir** ▸ that something is absolutely certain : A person must have food and water to live. 2. **devoir** ▸ that something is likely : Who's that at the door? It must be Brian. 3. **devoir** ▸ that something is needed or required : "He is far to the north by the sea. Someone must go to him." (Donald Gale) Note. This meaning is also used as a NOUN: You've got to hand in your paper by Friday; it's an absolute must.

mus-tache See moustache.

mus-tard [MUS-turd] NOUN, mustards. 1. **moutarde** ▸ a yellow or brownish-yellow paste or powder with a sharp taste, used to give flavour to meats and other foods. 2. **moutarde** ▸ the plant from which this seasoning is made.

mutt **bâtard (-arde), hybride** ▸ See mongrel.

mut-ter [MUT-ur] VERB, muttered, muttering. **marmotter, murmurer, marmonner** ▸ to speak in a low tone that cannot be clearly understood. SYN: growl, mumble, grumble, complain.

mu-tu-al [MYOO-choo-ul] ADJECTIVE. **mutuel (-elle)** ▸ shared or felt by two or more people or

383

✐ **Writing Tips**

Mystery

*A **mystery** story involves suspense, and the development and solving of some crime or other puzzle. When you're writing mysteries, provide enough clues so that the reader can try to solve the mystery. Some of your clues could be false clues or "red herrings"—information designed to lead the reader away from the correct solution.*

groups : *Rashid and Julia have a mutual love of science fiction.*

my [my] PRONOUN. **mon (ma, mes)** ▶ belonging to me : *I think that's my book, not yours.*

my-self [my-SELF] PRONOUN. **1. me, moi, moi-même** ▶ my own self : *I painted this picture myself.* **2. moi-même** ▶ my usual self : *I'm not feeling myself today.* **3. moi-même** ▶ a stronger form of I or me: *I, myself, paid the bill.* **Note.** Note that *myself* has to follow "I" or "me" in a sentence. It is not used alone. ✐ **p. 362.**

mys-te-ri-ous [mis-TEER-ee-us] ADJECTIVE. **mystérieux (-euse)** ▶ full of mystery ; hard to explain or understand : *a mysterious event.* ■ **mysteriously,** ADVERB: ▶ **mystérieusement.** *"Many a starving peasant had his grain sack mysteriously filled, and hungry families found food waiting on their doorsteps."* (Sarah Hayes)

mys-ter-y [MIS-tur-ee] NOUN, **mysteries. 1. mystère** ▶ something that cannot be explained or understood by normal means ; something that is hidden or unknown. **2. drame policier, mystère** ▶ a book, movie, TV show, or other story in which there is a crime or other unexplained problem that has to be solved. SYN : riddle, puzzle, secret. ✐ **p. 384.**

✐ **Writing Tips**

Myth

*A **myth** is a traditional folkloric story that can involve humans, animals, other beings—supernatural creatures such as the Minotaur, Anansi—gods, and so on. The origins of these stories are unknown, but every culture has some myths that supposedly explain nature and natural events, such as the sun's rising, the pattern on a turtle's shell, or the tides. Other myths are tales of heroes and their adventures or about relationship between the gods and humans.*

• If you want to try writing a myth, read lots of different myths. Remember that a myth's ending isn't always happy, and that there isn't always a lesson learned.

myth [mith] NOUN, **myths. 1. mythe** ▶ a story from very early times that tries to explain why things happen as they do, such as the weather, the changing of seasons, or the creation of the world, animals, and human beings. **Note.** Mythology is a collection of myths and legends, or myths as a group. **2. mythe** ▶ a story or idea that is not true : *It's a myth that the koala is a kind of bear; koalas are actually distantly related to kangaroos.* ✐ **p. 384.**

myth-i-cal [MITH-uh-kul] ADJECTIVE. **mythique** ▶ having to do with myths and legends : *a mythical character.* ■ **mythically,** ADVERB. ▶ **de façon mythique.**

nest

n, N [en] NOUN, n's, N's. **n, N** ► the 14th letter of the English alphabet.

nail [nale] NOUN, nails. **1. clou (clous)** ► a long, thin piece of metal with a pointed end and a flat, circular top. Nails are hammered into pieces of wood or other material to hold them together. **2. ongle** ► the flat, hard layer protecting the top end of a person's finger or toe. ▲ VERB, nailed, nailing. **clouer** ► to fasten something together with nails. 🖝 **p. 1002.**

hit the nail on the head *Informal.* **tomber juste, mettre le doigt dessus** ► to guess or understand correctly; do or say something just right : *You hit the nail on the head, Naveen — that's exactly what happened.*

na·ive [ny-EVE] ADJECTIVE. (also **naïve**). **naïf (naïve)** ► not having experience or knowledge; believing or accepting things without question. ■ **naively,** ADVERB. ► **naïvement.**

na·ked [NAY-kid] ADJECTIVE. **1. nu (nue)** ► not wearing clothing; bare. **2. dénudé (-ée), dépouillé (-ée)** ► without the usual or natural covering : *In winter, the maple tree's naked branches wave in the wind.* **3. pur (pure), nu (nue)** ► nothing to hide or disguise; plain : *the naked truth.* SYN : nude, exposed, bare, uncovered, undressed.

naked eye à l'œil nu ► the eye alone; not helped by any glass, telescope, or microscope : *Germs can't be seen with the naked eye.*

name [name] NOUN, names. **1. nom** ► the word or words by which someone or something is known : *His brother's name is Ben.* **2. réputa-**
tion, renom ► the fact of having one's name be well-known ; fame : *Barbra Streisand has made a name for herself as a singer, an actor, and a director.* ▲ VERB, named, naming. **1. nommer, appeler** ► to give a name to someone or something : *We named our new kitten "Fluffy."* **2. nommer, citer** ► to mention by name; identify : *Can you name all the provinces in Canada?* **3. désigner, nommer** ► to choose for some position or honour : *The hockey team has just named a new captain.* **4. fixer** ► to settle on; decide : *I'd like to buy that painting—just name your price.* **Note.** A namesake is a person named for another : *Stan is Uncle Stanley's namesake.* 🖝 **p. 969.** 🖋 **p. 366, 385.**

name·ly [NAME-lee] ADVERB. **c'est-à-dire, à savoir** ► that is to say : *There are only two students from our class left in the spelling bee— namely, Zoe and Dustin.*

nap [nap] NOUN, naps. **sieste, (petit) somme** ► a short sleep, especially during the day. ▲ VERB, napped, napping. **faire une sieste, sommeiller** ► to sleep for a short time; take a nap.

nap·kin [NAP-kin] NOUN, napkins. **serviette de table** ► a small piece of cloth or paper used at meals to keep food and drink off clothes and to wipe the hands and mouth. **Note.** Also called a serviette.

nar·cis·sus [nar-SIS-is] NOUN, narcissuses, narcissus, or narcissi. **narcisse** ► a type of spring plant that grows from a bulb, having white or yellow flowers with a cup-shaped part in the centre.

🖋 **Word Builder**

Name often means the word or words by which a person is known. *Call names* means to insult someone: *The bully called us names.* If you know someone *by name,* you know the person only because you have heard about him or her: *I've never met my second cousin, but I know her by name.* *In the name of* can mean by the authority of someone or for the sake of: *We held a concert in the name of charity.* *To one's name* means all that belongs to a person: *He only has 17 cents to his name.*

nar·rate [NAIR-ATE *or* nuh-RATE] VERB, narrated, narrating. **1. raconter, relater ▶** to serve as the narrator of a movie, play, and so on. **2. raconter ▶** to tell a story, especially in a book. **Note.** A narrative is a story or tale. SYN: tell, recount, describe, recite, relate.

nar·ra·tor [NAIR-ATE-ur *or* nuh-RAY-tur] NOUN, narrators. **1. narrateur (-trice) ▶** a person who speaks along with the action of a film, play, TV show, or the like, to tell the audience what is going on or to give background information. **Note.** The words spoken or written by a narrator, or the act of narrating, are narration. **2. narrateur (-trice) ▶** anyone who tells or writes a story.

nar·row [NARE-oh] ADJECTIVE, narrower, narrowest. **1. étroit (-oite) ▶** having a slender width; not broad or wide : *"She wiped away her tears and began to climb a narrow gully which cut into the cliff."* (Donald Gale) **2. restreint (-einte), étroit (-oite), limité (-ée) ▶** small in amount or extent; limited : *Tonya has a narrow circle of friends.* **Note.** Someone who is narrow-minded has very strict opinions and does not like to change his or her way of thinking. **3. réussi (-ie) de justesse ▶** almost not enough; close to failing : *"Charlotte felt greatly relieved to see him go. It had been a narrow escape."* (E.B. White) ▲ VERB, narrowed, narrowing. restreindre, limiter, rétrécir ▶ to make or become narrow : *They still haven't decided which car to buy, but they've narrowed it down to two choices.* ▲ NOUN, narrows. **étranglement, passage étroit ▶** a thin or narrow part in a body of water. ■ **narrowly,** ADVERB: ▶ **de justesse.** *The tree branch that fell narrowly missed the garage.*

nas·ty [NAS-tee] ADJECTIVE, nastier, nastiest. **1. déplaisant (-ante), méchant (-e) ▶** acting in a rude or angry way; mean; cruel. **2. vilain (-aine) ▶** very serious or harmful : *a nasty cut; a nasty cough.* ■ **nastiness,** NOUN. ▶ **méchanceté.**

na·tion [NAY-shun] NOUN, nations. **1. nation ▶** a place that has certain borders, its own form of government, and is not part of any larger area of government; a country. **2. peuple ▶** the people of a nation. **3. nation ▶** a large and organized tribe : *The Cree Nation is the largest nation of Native peoples in Canada.* **4. the nation. pays ▶** the country : *Rain is predicted for all parts of the nation this weekend.* SYN: country, community, tribe, society, land.

na·tion·al [NASH-uh-nul *or* NASH-nul] ADJECTIVE. **national (-ale, -aux) ▶** having to do with or belonging to a nation : *The prime minister is chosen in a national election.* ▲ NOUN, nationals. **ressortissant (-ante) ▶** a citizen of a certain nation : *a Swiss national.* ■ **nationally,** ADVERB. ▶ **au niveau national.**

na·tion·al·ism [NASH-uh-nuh-LIZ-um *or* NASH-nul-IZ-um] NOUN. **1. nationalisme, patriotisme ▶** a deep feeling of loyalty to one's own country. **Note.** A person who has this attitude is nationalistic. **2. nationalisme ▶** a feeling of belonging to a certain nation and of wanting that nation to rule itself independently : *After World War II, nationalism led many African countries to demand self-government.* **Note.** A person who supports nationalism is a nationalist. **3. nationalisme ▶** the desire of a people to preserve its own language, religion, and traditions.

na·tion·al·i·ty [NASH-uh-NAL-uh-tee *or* nash-NAL-uh-tee] NOUN, nationalities. **1. nationalité, citoyenneté ▶** the fact of being a citizen of a certain country. **2. nationalité ▶** a group of people having the same homeland, language, and culture.

na·tive [NAY-tiv] NOUN, natives. **1. natif (-ive) de, originaire de ▶** a person who was born or grew up in a certain place : *John now lives in Newfoundland, but he is a native of Ontario.* **2. indigène, autochtone ▶** an animal, plant, or group of people that has lived in a place from the earliest times. ▲ ADJECTIVE. **1. de souche ▶** having to do with the place where a person was born or grew up : *Both of Elaine's parents are native Quebeckers.* **2. originaire de, naturel (-elle) ▶** living or growing somewhere from the earliest times : *Potatoes are now grown all over Europe, but they are native to South America.* **3. natal (-e, -als) ▶** having to do with a person's birth. SYN: natural, original. ✐ **p. 387.**

Native people NOUN. **autochtone ▶** any of the Aboriginal inhabitants of the continent of North America, or their descendants : *Many Native people live in Canada.* ✐ **p. 387.**

nat·u·ral [NACH-uh-rul] ADJECTIVE. **1. naturel (-elle) ▶** made by or found in nature; not caused or produced by people; not artificial. **2. naturel (-elle) ▶** having to do with nature, as opposed to people : *Gravity is a natural law.* **3. naturel (-elle), normal (-ale, -aux) ▶** happening normally in nature or in life; usual; ordinary : *The lion is the natural enemy of the antelope.* **4. naturel (-elle), inné (-ée) ▶** present from birth; not needing to be taught : *Henri has a natural talent for music.* **5. naturel (-elle), simple ▶** not pretended or artificial : *The actor gave a very natural performance.* ▲ NOUN, naturals. **doué (-ée) ▶** a person who has a natural talent or ability : *That player is a natural as a hitter.*

nat·u·ral·ly [NACH-uh-ruh-lee] ADVERB. **1. naturellement, de nature ▶** by nature; without anything artificial : *Darcy's hair is naturally blonde.* **2. simplement, avec naturel ▶** in a normal, natural way : *"Leif came by his love of adventure naturally!"* (Charnan Simon) **3. naturellement, bien sûr ▶** as would be expected; of course : *Naturally, we went to the wedding.*

✍ Writing Tips

Native Peoples

• *In the early 1500s, when European explorers were searching for a quicker route to India, they landed in North America. They mistakenly thought it was India, so they called the people they met there Indians. Even once the mistake was discovered, Europeans continued to call these people Indians or American Indians.*

• *Although most people shy away from using the word Indian, many Native peoples themselves use and accept this word. Rather than use Indian, you could use Native peoples, first peoples, Aboriginal peoples, or First Nations. (First Nations, however, refers only to status Indians [people who are officially registered as Indians with the Canadian government], not non-status Indians, Métis, the Inuit.) It is best to use the specific name of the group you are referring to—for instance, Métis, Mohawk, Haida, Cree, and so on.*

• *Also, for many years the Native peoples of the Far North were referred to as Eskimos, but their name for themselves, and the preferred term, is the Inuit.*

---

natural resources ressources naturelles ▶ things supplied by nature that are important for human life such as water, minerals, and plants.

na·ture [NAY-chur] NOUN, natures. **1.** (also Nature) **nature** ▶ the universe and everything in it, such as animals, plants, mountains, oceans, and the weather; anything that is not made by people. **2. nature** ▶ the world of wildlife and the outdoors. **3. nature, tempérament, caractère, naturel** ▶ the basic qualities or characteristics of someone or something; personality : *Cassia has a restless and adventurous nature.* **4. sorte, nature, espèce** ▶ type; kind : *She enjoys camping, hiking, and activities of that nature.*

naugh·ty [NAW-tee] ADJECTIVE, naughtier, naughtiest. **vilain (-aine)** ▶ not obedient : *The naughty puppy chewed up the newspaper.* SYN : mischievous, bad, misbehaving.

na·val [NAY-vul] ADJECTIVE. **naval (-ale, -als)** ▶ having to do with the navy or with warships : *Ariza is training to be a naval officer.*

na·vel [NAY-vul] NOUN, navels. **nombril** ▶ a small round mark on the abdomen of people and

other mammals that is made when the cord connecting a newborn baby to its mother is cut. **Note.** A similar mark on one kind of orange has led to the name navel orange.

nav·i·gate [NAV-uh-GATE] VERB, navigated, navigating. **1. naviguer, piloter, diriger** ▶ to control or steer a ship or aircraft. **Note.** A navigator is someone who plans and directs the course of a ship or airplane. **2. naviguer** ▶ to travel on or over a certain body of water : *Samuel de Champlain, with the help of Native guides, was one of the first Europeans to navigate the St. Lawrence River.* SYN : steer, pilot, guide, cruise, sail.

nav·i·ga·tion [NAV-uh-GAY-shun] NOUN. **1. navigation** ▶ the science of determining where a ship or aircraft is, how far it has travelled, and what direction it is going in. **2. navigation, pilotage, conduite** ▶ the act of navigating : *A bad storm made navigation of the plane difficult.*

na·vy [NAY-vee] NOUN, navies. **1.** (also Navy) **marine** ▶ the part of a country's armed forces that has to do with war on the seas. **Note.** In the Canadian Forces, the function of a navy is served by Maritime Command. **2.** (also navy blue) **bleu marine** ▶ a very dark blue colour like that of some naval uniforms.

near [neer] ADVERB, nearer, nearest. **près, à proximité** ▶ at a short distance or time away; not far; close. ▲ ADJECTIVE. **1. proche, voisin (-ine)** ▶ close by; not far away : near neighbours. **2. évité (-ée) de près, évité (-ée) de justesse** ▶ done or missed by a small amount or margin; close : *a near accident,* **3. proche, intime** ▶ close in feeling or relationship : *"My teacher is so near to me that I scarcely think of myself apart from her."* (Helen Keller) ▲ PREPOSITION. **près de** ▶ close to; by : *There's a well near the cottage.* ▲ VERB, neared, nearing. **(s') approcher** ▶ to come close or closer to; approach : *The ship neared land.* ■ **nearness,** NOUN. ▶ **proximité, intimité.** the state or condition of being near. SYN : close, closely, nearly, nearby, at hand.

near·by [NEER-by] ADJECTIVE. **proche, avoisinant (-ante)** ▶ not far away; close : *Avi attends a nearby school.* [NEER-BY] ADVERB.

near·ly [NEER-lee] ADVERB. **presque, à peu près** ▶ almost but not quite; close; practically : *I was nearly hit by the speeding car.*

near·sight·ed [NEER-SITE-id] ADJECTIVE. **1. myope** ▶ unable to see objects that are far away as clearly as objects that are close by. **2. myope** ▶ without thought for the future. SYN : almost, close to, just about, approximately.

neat [neet] ADJECTIVE, neater, neatest. **1. propre, soigné (-ée), net (nette)** ▶ being clean and in good order; arranged as it should be; tidy : *a neat room.* **2. habile, adroit (-oite), ingénieux (-ieuse)** ▶ done in a skillful or clever way :

That's a neat trick. **3.** *Informal.* **beau (belle), bon (bonne)** ▶ very good; fine : *He had the neatest smile.* ■ **neatly,** ADVERB. ▶ **soigneusement.** ■ **neatness,** NOUN. ▶ netteté, propreté, habileté, adresse.

nec·es·sar·i·ly [NES-uh-SAIR-uh-lee] ADVERB. nécessairement, forcément ▶ in a way that must be or that cannot be avoided : *The fact that the car is old doesn't necessarily mean it's not in good condition.*

nec·es·sar·y [NES-uh-SAIR-ee] ADJECTIVE. **1.** nécessaire, essentiel (-elle) ▶ impossible to do without; needed ; required : *I don't have the necessary information to finish my science report.* **2.** inévitable, nécessaire ▶ that cannot be avoided ; that must be ; certain : *Tiredness is a necessary result of not getting enough sleep.* **Note.** A necessary evil is something bad a person must put up with to get something good : *Working hard in the spring is necessary if you want a nice garden in the summer.* SYN : required, essential, compulsory, needed.

ne·ces·si·ty [nuh-SES-uh-tee] NOUN. necessities. **1.** nécessité ▶ something needed or required : *"Necessity is the mother of invention" means that people invent things because they need them.* **2.** nécessité, besoin ▶ the fact of being necessary.

neck [nek] NOUN, necks. **1.** cou ▶ the part of the body that connects the head to the shoulders. **2.** col, encolure ▶ the part of clothing that fits around the neck : *He wears shirts with a size 16 neck.* **3.** col, goulot ▶ something thought to be like a neck, as by being long and narrow : *the neck of a bottle.* ⌖ p. 1003.

neck and neck à égalité ▶ being equal or even in a race or contest : *The horses were neck and neck as they crossed the finish line.*

neck·lace [NEK-lis] NOUN, necklaces. **collier** ▶ jewellery that is worn around the neck as an ornament, such as a chain of gold or silver, or a string of beads or pearls. ⌖ p. 1011.

nec·tar [NEK-tur] NOUN, nectars. **1.** nectar ▶ a sweet liquid found in the centre of some flowers, collected by bees to make honey. **2.** nectar ▶ in ancient Greek and Roman myths, the drink of the gods.

need [need] NOUN, needs. **1.** besoin ▶ the lack of something that is useful, important, or wanted : *Jodie's paper had a lot of careless mistakes and showed a need for more time and effort.* **2.** (usually needs) besoins ▶ something that is useful, important, or wanted : *the needs of a newborn baby.* **3.** besoin ▶ something that must be done; an obligation : *There is a need for settling this strike.* **4.** besoin, indigence, dénuement, gêne ▶ the condition of being without something important; being poor or in difficulty. ▲ VERB, needed, needing. **1.** avoir besoin de ▶ to want and be without; having a need for :

We need milk. **2.** devoir ▶ to be obligated; have to : *Carlo needs to leave for a doctor's appointment.* ■ **needy,** ADJECTIVE. ▶ nécessiteux (-euse), indigent (-ente). SYN : require, want, lack.

nee·dle [NEED-ul] NOUN, needles. **1.** aiguille ▶ a small, thin tool used for sewing, usually made of metal. One end has a sharp point, and the other end has a hole through which thread is passed and fastened. **2.** aiguille à tricoter ▶ a long, slender rod used in knitting to hold and form the stitches. **3.** aiguille ▶ a thin, pointed, needle-shaped leaf found on certain trees, such as the pine, spruce, or fir. **4.** aiguille ▶ a hollow tube with a sharp, thin point that is used to inject medicine or another liquid into the body. **5.** aiguille ▶ any of various other things that are long, thin, and pointed like a needle : *the needle of a compass.* ▲ VERB, needled, needling. **agacer, piquer** ▶ to bother or annoy a person; tease.

need·less [NEED-lis] ADJECTIVE. **inutile** ▶ not needed or necessary : *Rosi went to a lot of needless trouble to find that book when Ari had a copy all along.* ■ **needlessly,** ADVERB. ▶ inutilement.

neg·a·tive [NEG-uh-tiv] ADJECTIVE. **1.** négatif (-ive) ▶ saying or meaning "no"; showing that something is not true, not to be done, and so on. **2.** négatif (-ive) ▶ not helpful or friendly; not positive : *Steven has had a negative attitude about Toronto ever since he got lost in the downtown traffic.* **3.** négatif (-ive) ▶ of a number, being less than zero. **4.** négatif (-ive) ▶ showing that a certain disease or harmful condition is not present : *Christos was afraid he'd broken his finger, but luckily the X-rays were negative.* ▲ NOUN, negatives. **1.** négation ▶ a word or phrase that says "no" or that denies or refuses : *"Not" and "no" are negatives.* **2.** négatif ▶ in photography, an image on a piece of film that is developed into a print.

neg·lect [nih-GLEKT] VERB, neglected, neglecting. **1.** négliger, délaisser ▶ to not give the proper attention or care to : *Annie was busy reading and neglected her homework.* **Note.** Often used as an ADJECTIVE:*neglected chores.* **2.** négliger, oublier, manquer à ▶ to fail to do; leave undone : *Pat neglected to tell Jenny that he had made the team.* ▲ NOUN. négligence, manque de soins ▶ the fact or condition of being neglected : *It's a sad case of neglect.* SYN : miss, skip, omit, ignore, be careless.

ne·go·ti·ate [nih-GOH-she-ATE] VERB, negotiated, negotiating. **1.** négocier ▶ to talk over a problem or an issue in order to reach an agreement or to make arrangements : *The two countries were negotiating a peace treaty to end the war.* **2.** franchir, traverser ▶ to go safely on or over : *The horse negotiated the last jump and headed for the finish line.* ■ **negotiation,** NOUN. ▶ négociation. the act or fact of negotiating : *Ms. Gaynor has just begun negotiations to sell her business.* SYN: talk over, settle, mediate, discuss, arrange.

neigh-bour [NAY-bur] NOUN, neighbours. (also neighbor) **1. voisin (-ine)** ▸ a person who lives next door or nearby : *We went over to meet our new neighbours.* **2. voisin (-ine)** ▸ a person or thing located next to another : *Sami is my neighbour in English class.* ■ **neighbouring,** ADJECTIVE. ▸ **voisin (-ine), avoisinant (-ante),** close by; near : *We invited the people from the neighbouring village to our festival.* ■ **neigh-bourly,** ADJECTIVE **amical (-ale, -aux), obligeant (-ante)** ▸ like a good neighbour; friendly.

neigh·bour·hood [NAY-bur-HOOD] NOUN, neighbourhoods. **1. quartier** ▸ one particular area that is within a larger city or town and that has certain characteristics of its own : *We go down-town when we want to see a movie, because there's no theatre in our neighbourhood.* **2. voisinage, environs, alentours** ▸ all the people who live in a certain area : *Stop making so much noise!You'll wake up the whole neighbourhood!* ▲ ADJECTIVE:*to play ball in the neighbourhood park.* 🕮 p. 1051.

nei·ther [NEE-thur *or* NY-thur] ADJECTIVE. **ni l'un (l'une) ni l'autre, aucun (-une) des deux** ▸ not one nor the other : *Neither book was very well-written.* ▲ PRONOUN. **ni l'un (l'une) ni l'autre, aucun (-une) des deux** ▸ not the one or the other : *Would you like pie or cake? Neither; I'm going to skip dessert.* ▲ CONJUNCTION. **ni ... ni** ▸ not either; not in either case (used with nor to present two negative alternatives) : *We have neither the time nor the money to take a vacation this year.*

ne·on [NEE-on] NOUN. **néon** ▸ a chemical element that's a gas with no colour or smell. It is used in tubes to light up signs and lamps because it glows when electricity is applied to it.

neph·ew [NEF-yoo] NOUN, nephews. **1. neveu (-eux)** ▸ the son of a person's brother or sister. **2. neveu (-eux)** ▸ the son of a person's brother-in-law or sister-in-law.

Nep·tune [NEP-TOON] NOUN. **1. Neptune** ▸ the fourth-largest planet in the solar system, and the eighth-closest planet to the sun. **2. Neptune** ▸ in the religion of the ancient Romans, the god of the sea. 👁 **p. 391.**

nerve [nurv] NOUN, nerves. **1. nerf** ▸ a fibre or bundle of fibres connecting the brain and spinal cord to other parts of the body, such as the eyes, ears, muscles, and organs. Nerves carry messages to and from the brain that make the body work. **2. courage** ▸ strength of the mind or will; courage : *"When the children and their parents had looked at the face of the monster, they had lost their nerve."* **3. toupet, culot** ▸ the fact of being rude or impolite : *You have a lot of nerve walking right by me like that.* **4. nerves. ner-**

vosité ▸ a feeling of being upset or nervous; nervousness.

ner·vous [NUR-vus] ADJECTIVE. **1. nerveux (-euse), tendu (-ue), inquiet (-iète)** ▸ quick to become upset or excited; not relaxed; tense : *Lin was nervous about giving a speech to the whole school.* **2. nerveux (-euse), agité (-ée)** ▸ showing this feeling : *a nervous person.* **3. nerveux (-euse)** ▸ having to do with the nerves or the mind : *Polio and epilepsy are nervous disorders.* ■ **nervously,** ADVERB. ▸ **nerveusement.** *Trent laughed nervously.* ■ **nervousness,** NOUN. ▸ **nervosité, agitation, crainte.** SYN: tense, upset, restless, flustered, agitated.

nervous system système nerveux ▸ the sys-tem in the body made up of the brain, spinal cord, and nerves.

nest [nest] NOUN, nests. **1. nid** ▸ a place built by a bird from grass, mud, twigs, or other materials, and used for laying its eggs and raising its young. **2. nid** ▸ a similar place used by other animals, such as fish, turtles, or snakes. **3. nid** ▸ any shel-ter or comfortable home. ▲ VERB, nested, nest-ing. **nicher, faire son nid** ▸ to make or live in a nest. **Note.** A nest egg is money saved for the future.

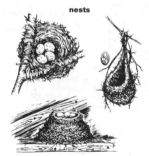

nests

nes·tle [NES-ul] VERB, nestled, nestling. **se blot-tir, se pelotonner** ▸ to settle down or lie in a comfortable place : *Kyle nestled in a chair to read his book.*

net[1] [net] NOUN, **nets. 1. filet** ▸ a fabric made of thread, cord, or rope woven or knotted together, leaving evenly spaced openings. Nets are used to catch, stop, or hold things : *a fishing net.* **2. filet** ▸ a net used as a goal or dividing line in such games as tennis, volleyball, hockey, or soccer. ▲ VERB, **netted, netting. prendre au filet, ramasser dans ses filets** ▸ to catch in a net : *Leah netted a beautiful rainbow trout on her last fishing trip.*

net[2] ADJECTIVE. **1. net (nette)** ▸ what is left after all charges, costs, and allowances have been made : *The net weight of a truckload of furniture is the weight of the furniture and does not include the weight of the truck.* **2. net (nette)** ▸ after everything has been taken into account; final : *The new magazine was tested in six different cities, but the net result was that people weren't very interested in it.* ▲ VERB, netted, netting. **rapporter, produire** ▸ to receive as a profit : *They netted $20 000 on the sale of their house.*

net-work [NET-wurk] NOUN, **networks. 1. réseau** ▸ a system or pattern of crossing lines, wires, routes, or the like :"*She went about establishing a network of Underground stations from the South all the way into Canada.*" (Virginia Hamilton) **2. réseau** ▸ a group of radio or TV stations that are joined together so that they can use the same broadcasts. **3. réseau** ▸ a system of computers connected to one another so that they can share and exchange information. ▲ VERB, networked, networking. **établir un réseau, faire partie d'un réseau** ▸ to co-operate with a group of others to do or get something, especially to advance in business.

neu-tral [NOO-trul] ADJECTIVE. **1. neutre** ▸ not taking sides in a contest, argument, or war : *Sweden was neutral in World War II and did not side with either the Allies or the Axis countries.* **Note.** The fact of being neutral is neutrality. **2. neutre** ▸ having little or no colour, or a colour that blends easily with others : *Grey, tan, and cream are neutral colours.* **3. neutre** ▸ in chemistry, neither an acid nor a base : *a neutral solution.* ▲ NOUN. **au point mort** ▸ a position of gears in an automobile in which no power is sent from the engine to the wheels. **Note.** To make something neutral is to neutralize it. SYN: detached, unprejudiced, independent.

neu-tron [NOO-tron] NOUN, **neutrons. neutron** ▸ in an atom, a tiny particle that has neither a positive nor a negative charge of electricity. Neutrons and protons together make up almost all the mass of the nucleus of the atom. Neutrons are found in all atoms except hydrogen.

nev-er [NEV-ur] ADVERB. **jamais** ▸ not at any time; not ever : *"In time he regarded Kileken as the son he'd never had."* (Tololwa M. Mollel)

nev-er-the-less [NEV-ur-thuh-LES] ADVERB. **malgré tout, cependant, pourtant** ▸ in any case; in

spite of that; anyway : *I'm afraid I won't be able to go; nevertheless, thanks for asking me.* SYN: however, notwithstanding, although, but.

new [nyoo or noo] ADJECTIVE, **newer, newest. 1. nouveau (-elle, -eaux), neuf (neuve)** ▸ made or done just now or a short time ago; not in being for long; not old : *At the end of the winter, trees grow new leaves.* **2. nouveau (-elle, -eaux)** ▸ just seen, found, or learned about; not known before : *In 1930, scientists discovered a new planet and named it Pluto.* **3. nouveau (-elle, -eaux), débutant (-ante)** ▸ being in a place or condition for only a short time : *Cynthia has just started her new job.* **4. nouveau (-elle, -eaux)** ▸ taking the place of what was there before : *a new edition of a book.* **5. nouveau (-elle, -eaux)** ▸ beginning again : *a new moon; the start of a new day.*

New Democratic Party Nouveau parti démocratique ▸ one of the major political parties in Canada.

new-ly [NYOO-lee or NOO-lee] ADVERB. **récemment, nouvellement** ▸ not long ago; recently, lately. **Note.** Used in combination with an ADJECTIVE: *newly cut hair.* **Note.** A newlywed is a person who has been recently married.

news [nooz] NOUN. **1. nouvelles, informations, actualités** ▸ a newspaper, television, or radio report about something important that has recently happened or become known. **2. nouvelles** ▸ any report about something that has recently happened : *Grandma sends us a letter every week with the latest news about the family.*

news-cast [NOOZ-kast] NOUN, **newscasts. bulletin d'informations, informations, nouvelles** ▸ a radio or television program on which news events are reported. **Note.** A person who presents the news on such a show is a newscaster.

news-let-ter [NOOZ-let-ur] NOUN, **newsletters. bulletin** ▸ a written or printed letter presenting news in an informal way.

news-pa-per [NOOZ-pay-pur] NOUN, **newspapers. journal (-aux)** ▸ a paper that is printed and sold each day or each week and that reports the news to the public. Newspapers also contain other writing besides news stories, such as editorials and columns, as well as advertisements.

news-print [NOOZ-print] NOUN. **papier journal** ▸ a cheap, coarse paper made from wood pulp. Newspapers are usually printed on this kind of paper.

newt [noot] NOUN, **newts. triton** ▸ a small, brightly coloured animal with smooth skin, short legs, and a long tail. It lives part of the time in water and part on land, and looks like a lizard.

New Year's Day NOUN. **jour de l'An, Nouvel An** ▸ the first day of the year; January 1.

Pluto
▶ Pluton
5,900 million km

Sun
▶ Soleil

Mercury
▶ Mercure
58 million km

Neptune
▶ Neptune
4,490 million km

Venus
▶ Vénus
108 million km

Uranus
▶ Uranus
2,869 million km

Earth
▶ Terre
150 million km

Mars
▶ Mars
228 million km

Saturn
▶ Saturne
1,427 million km

Jupiter
▶ Jupiter
778 million km

	ORBIT AROUND THE SUN	ROTATION	NUMBER OF KNOWN SATELLITES
Mercury	87.969 d	58.646 d	0
Venus	224 d 18 h 49 m	243.1 d	0
Earth	365.256 d	23 h 56 m 45 s	1
Mars	1 yr 321 d	24 h 37 m 39 s	2
Jupiter	11 yrs 314 d	9 h 50 m	16
Saturn	29 yrs 167 d	10 h 02 m	18
Uranus	84 yrs 7.4 d	17 h 02 m	20
Neptune	164 yrs 280 d	17 h 07 m	8
Pluto	248 yrs	6 d 9 h 17 m	1

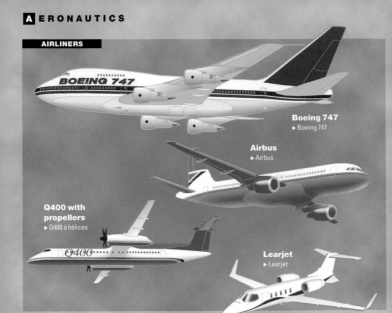

Boeing 747
▶ Boeing 747

Airbus
▶ Airbus

Q400 with propellers
▶ Q400 à hélices

Learjet
▶ Learjet

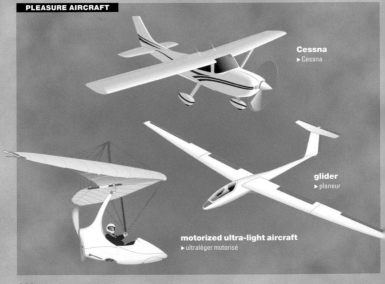

Cessna
▶ Cessna

glider
▶ planeur

motorized ultra-light aircraft
▶ ultraléger motorisé

MILITARY AIRCRAFT

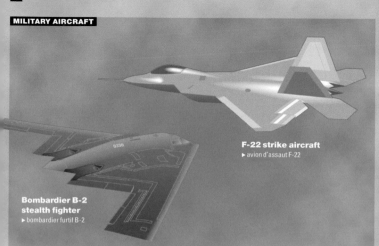

F-22 strike aircraft
▶ avion d'assaut F-22

Bombardier B-2 stealth fighter
▶ bombardier furtif B-2

UTILITARIAN AIRCRAFT

helicopter
▶ hélicoptère

tiltrotor aircraft - Osprey V-22
▶ avion à rotors basculants V-22 Osprey

CL 415 water bomber
▶ avion citerne CL 415

B OATS

yacht
▶yacht

sailboat
▶voilier

catamaran
▶catamaran

rubber canoe
▶canot de caoutchouc

cruise ship
▶paquebot de croisière

tugboat
▶ remorqueur

trawler
▶ chalutier

hydrofoil
▶ hydroptère

container freighter ▽
▶ cargo porte-conteneurs

ferry △
▶ traversier

395

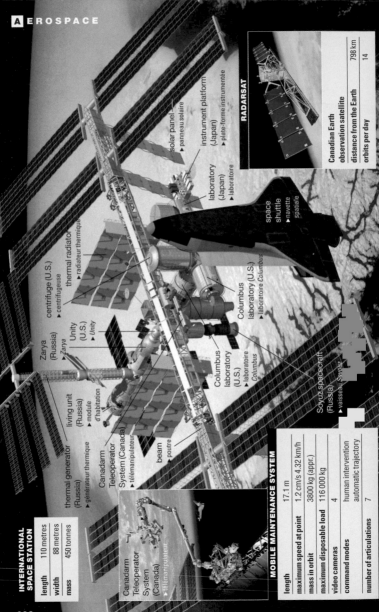

RADARSAT

Canadian Earth	
observation satellite	
distance from the Earth	798 km
orbits per day	14

solar panel
▲ panneau solaire

instrument platform (Japan)
▲ plate-forme instrumentée

laboratory (Japan)
▲ laboratoire

space shuttle
▲ navette spatiale

thermal radiator
▲ radiateur thermique

centrifuge (U.S.)
▲ centrifugeuse

Columbus laboratory (U.S.)
▲ laboratoire Columbus

Unity (U.S.)
▲ Unity

Columbus laboratory (U.S.)
▲ laboratoire Columbus

Zarya (Russia)
▲ Zarya

Soyuz spacecraft (Russia)
▲ vaisseau Soyouz

living unit (Russia)
▲ module d'habitation

thermal generator (Russia)
▲ générateur thermique

Canadarm Teleoperator System (Canada)
▲ télémanipulateur

beam
▲ poutre

INTERNATIONAL SPACE STATION

length	110 metres
width	88 metres
mass	450 tonnes

Canadarm Teleoperator System (Canada)
▲ télémanipulateur

MOBILE MAINTENANCE SYSTEM

length	17.1 m
maximum speed at point	1.2 cm/s 4.32 km/h
mass in orbit	3800 kg (appr.)
maximum disposable load	116 000 kg
video cameras	4
command modes	human intervention automatic trajectory
number of articulations	7

M INERALS

quartz ▷
▶ quartz

synthetic ▷
bismuth
crystal
▶ cristal
synthétique
de bismuth

pyrite ▽
▶ pyrite

gold ▷
▶ or

garnet ▽
▶ grenat

asbestos △
▶ amiante

amethyst △
▶ améthyste

salt rock △
▶ halite (sel de table)

gypsum flower ▽
▶ rose des sables

copper △
▶ cuivre

granite △
▶ granit

gypsum △
▶ gypse

agglomerate ▷
▶ conglomérat

397

BAUXITE
► bauxite

bauxite mine
► mine de bauxite

rolling
► laminage

can
► conserve

CRUSHER
► broyeur

crystalization of aluminum hydrate
► cristallisation de l'alumine hydratée

alloying of metals
► alliage de métaux

dissolution of alumina contained in the bauxite
► dissolution de l'alumine de la bauxite

removal of red mud residue
► retrait des résidus de boue rouge

INCINERATION FURNACE
► four de calcination

drying of hydrate and transformation into fine, white powder (alumina)
► séchage de l'hydrate et transformation en fine poudre blanche (alumine)

siphoning
► siphonnage

aluminum deposit
► dépôt d'aluminium

ELECTROLYTIC CELL
► cuve d'électrolyse

separation of metal from aluminum using an electric current
► séparation par courant électrique du métal de l'alumine

HOLDING FUR
► four d'atten

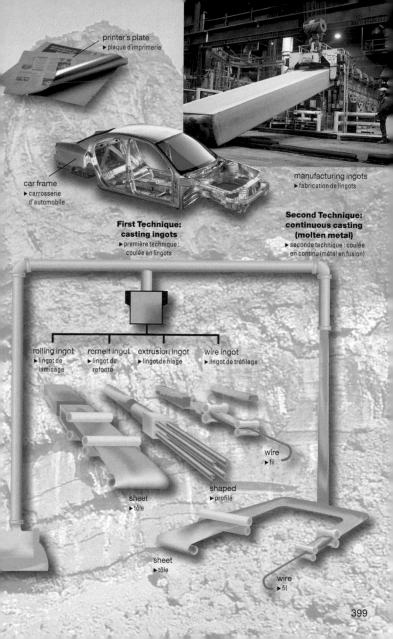

printer's plate
▶ plaque d'imprimerie

manufacturing ingots
▶ fabrication de lingots

car frame
▶ carrosserie
d'automobile

**First Technique:
casting ingots**
▶ première technique :
coulée en lingots

**Second Technique:
continuous casting
(molten metal)**
▶ seconde technique : coulée
en continu (métal en fusion)

rolling ingot
▶ lingot de
laminage

remelt ingot
▶ lingot de
refonte

extrusion ingot
▶ lingot de filage

wire ingot
▶ lingot de tréfilage

wire
▶ fil

sheet
▶ tôle

shaped
▶ profilé

sheet
▶ tôle

wire
▶ fil

399

HYDROELECTRICITY

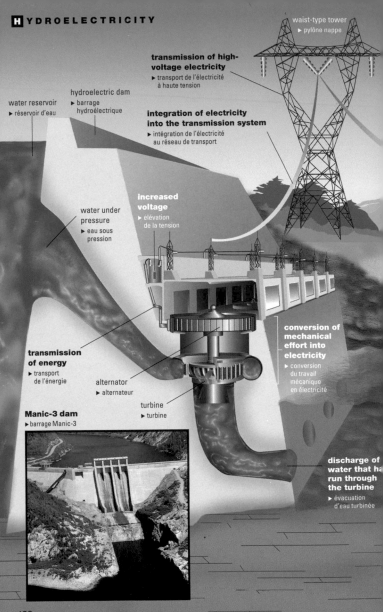

waist-type tower
▶ pylône nappe

transmission of high-voltage electricity
▶ transport de l'électricité à haute tension

integration of electricity into the transmission system
▶ intégration de l'électricité au réseau de transport

water reservoir
▶ réservoir d'eau

hydroelectric dam
▶ barrage hydroélectrique

increased voltage
▶ élévation de la tension

water under pressure
▶ eau sous pression

conversion of mechanical effort into electricity
▶ conversion du travail mécanique en électricité

transmission of energy
▶ transport de l'énergie

alternator
▶ alternateur

turbine
▶ turbine

Manic-3 dam
▶ barrage Manic-3

discharge of water that ha run through the turbine
▶ évacuation d'eau turbinée

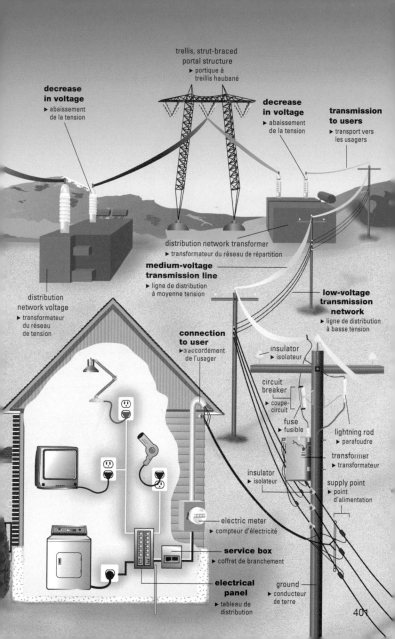

trellis, strut-braced
portal structure
► portique à
treillis haubané

**decrease
in voltage**
► abaissement
de la tension

**decrease
in voltage**
► abaissement
de la tension

**transmission
to users**
► transport vers
les usagers

distribution network transformer
► transformateur du réseau de répartition

**medium-voltage
transmission line**
► ligne de distribution
à moyenne tension

distribution
network voltage
► transformateur
du réseau
de tension

**low-voltage
transmission
network**
► ligne de distribution
à basse tension

**connection
to user**
► raccordement
de l'usager

insulator
► isolateur

circuit
breaker
► coupe-
circuit

fuse
► fusible

lightning rod
► parafoudre

transformer
► transformateur

insulator
► isolateur

supply point
► point
d'alimentation

electric meter
► compteur d'électricité

service box
► coffret de branchement

**electrical
panel**
► tableau de
distribution

ground
► conducteur
de terre

401

CIRCULATORY SYSTEM

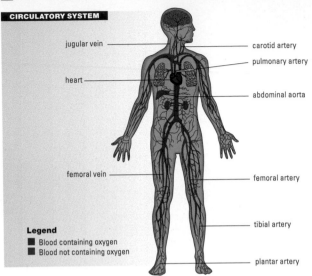

jugular vein

carotid artery

pulmonary artery

heart

abdominal aorta

femoral vein

femoral artery

tibial artery

Legend
- ■ Blood containing oxygen
- ■ Blood not containing oxygen

plantar artery

MUSCULAR SYSTEM

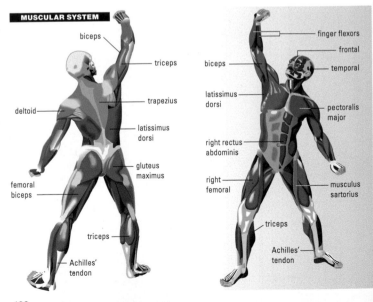

biceps

triceps

trapezius

deltoid

latissimus dorsi

gluteus maximus

femoral biceps

triceps

Achilles' tendon

finger flexors

frontal

biceps

temporal

latissimus dorsi

pectoralis major

right rectus abdominis

right femoral

musculus sartorius

triceps

Achilles' tendon

RESPIRATORY SYSTEM
ORGANS

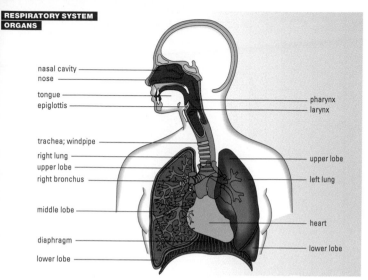

nasal cavity
nose
tongue
epiglottis
trachea; windpipe
right lung
upper lobe
right bronchus
middle lobe
diaphragm
lower lobe

pharynx
larynx
upper lobe
left lung
heart
lower lobe

DIGESTIVE SYSTEM
ORGANS AND GLANDS

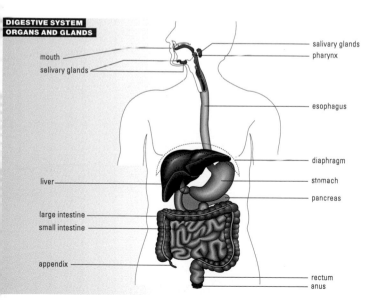

mouth
salivary glands
liver
large intestine
small intestine
appendix

salivary glands
pharynx
esophagus
diaphragm
stomach
pancreas
rectum
anus

FEMALE REPRODUCTIVE SYSTEM

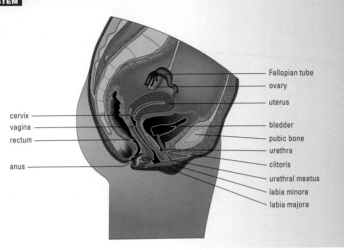

Fallopian tube
ovary
uterus
cervix
vagina
bladder
rectum
pubic bone
urethra
anus
clitoris
urethral meatus
labia minora
labia majora

MALE REPRODUCTIVE SYSTEM

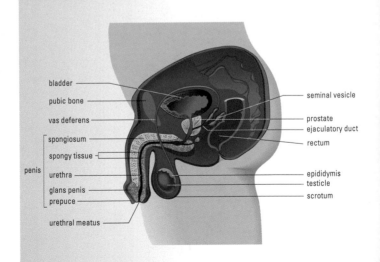

bladder
pubic bone
vas deferens
spongiosum
spongy tissue
penis
urethra
glans penis
prepuce
urethral meatus
seminal vesicle
prostate
ejaculatory duct
rectum
epididymis
testicle
scrotum

H UMAN BODY (HUMAN REPRODUCTION)

A FERTILIZATION

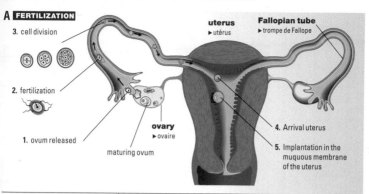

3. cell division

2. fertilization

1. ovum released

maturing ovum

ovary
► ovaire

uterus
► utérus

Fallopian tube
► trompe de Fallope

4. Arrival uterus

5. Implantation in the muquous membrane of the uterus

B GROWTH OF THE EMBRYO

head

tail

3 weeks (approximately 3 mm) approximately 0.2 g

beginnings of:
eye
arm
leg

4 weeks (approximately 4 mm, the size of an apple seed) approximately 0.4 g

12 weeks
(approximately 10 cm)
15 g approximately, the weight of a chicken egg

C GROWTH OF FETUS

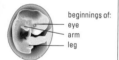

ear

umbilical cord

8 weeks
(between 2.5 and 3.5 cm, the size of a strawberry)
and approximately 1 to 2 g

20 weeks
(approximately 22 cm)
approximately 30 g

D BIRTH

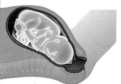

At **40 weeks,**
the baby measures approximately 50 cm and weighs approximately 3.5 kg. He/she is ready to be born.

Dilation of cervix
The uterus contracts and the cervix dilates to allow the baby to pass through.

Birth
Each contraction of the uterus and each push causes the baby to slide outwards until he/she is completely expelled.

405

crossing for people with disabilities
▶ passage de personnes handicapées

crossing for children near a playground
▶ passage d'enfants près d'un terrain de jeux

school bus stop warning
▶ signal avancé d'arrêt d'autobus scolaire

pedestrian access prohibited
▶ accès interdit aux piétons

school zone
▶ début de zone scolaire

stop at intersection
▶ arrêt à l'intersection

seat belt required
▶ obligation de porter la ceinture de sécurité

no entrance
▶ accès interdit

bicycle access prohibited
▶ accès interdit aux bicyclettes

bicycle crossing
▶ passage de bicyclettes

arena
▶ aréna

indoor public pool
▶ piscine publique intérieure

outdoor public pool
▶ piscine publique extérieure

library
▶ bibliothèque

community centre
▶ centre communautaire

telephone
▶ téléphone

one-way
▶ sens unique

bicycle path
▶ piste cyclable

button for pedestrians or cyclists
▶ bouton-poussoir pour piétons ou cyclistes

municipal park
▶ parc municipal

electrical hazard
▶ danger électrique

inflammable
▶ inflammable

explosive
▶ explosif

poison
▶ poison

corrosive
▶ corrosif

next [nekst] ADJECTIVE. **prochain (-aine), suivant (-ante)** ► just after this one or after the one before : *the next day*. **Note.** Also used as an ADVERB or a PREPOSITION: *"Next, it will be Mother Owl's turn to hunt."* (Tejima) ℘ **p. 407.**

next door **la maison voisine, la maison d'à côté, à côté** ►in or at the nearest house, building, or room : *Tomas has just moved next door to his best friend.* **Note.** Also used as an ADJECTIVE: *a next-door neighbour.*

next of kin **le (la) plus proche parent (-ente)** ► a person's nearest blood relative or relatives.

nib-ble [NIB-ul] VERB, nibbled, nibbling. **grignoter, mordiller** ► to take quick, small bites : *"I nibbled on carrot sticks while I made my dinner."*

nice [nice] ADJECTIVE, nicer, nicest. **beau (belle), gentil (-ille), agréable, aimable** ► pleasing or good in some way, as by being kind, friendly, well-done, well-made, and so on : *It is a nice day for a picnic.* ■ **nicely,** ADVERB. ► **bien, gentiment, agréablement, aimablement.** SYN: friendly, agreeable, pleasing, pleasant, good.

niche [nich *or* neesh] NOUN, niches. **1. niche** ► a sunken or hollowed-out place in a wall, used to hold something for decoration, such as a small vase. **2. voie** ► a place or activity for which a person is well-suited : *Mia has yet to find her niche in the world.*

nick [nik] NOUN, nicks. **1. coupure, entaille, encoche** ► a small cut or chip on the edge or surface of something. *"They have found flakes of flint and nicks on animal bones suggesting they had been killed with flint knives."* (Robert McGhee) ▲ VERB, nicked, nicking. **entailler, faire une entaille** ► to make a nick.

in the nick of time **juste à temps** ► at the last moment; just in time.

nick-el [NIK-ul] NOUN, nickels. **1. nickel** ► a strong, hard, silver-coloured metal that is often combined with other metals. **2. pièce de cinq cents** ► a coin containing nickel; a five-cent piece.

nick-name [NIK-NAME] NOUN, nicknames. **surnom, diminutif, sobriquet** ► a name used in place of a person's real name. A nickname can be a short form of the person's name, such as

Joey or Joe for *Joseph*. It can also be a description of the person, such as *Red* for someone with red hair. ▲ VERB, nicknamed, nicknaming. **surnommer** ► to give a nickname to a person.

nic-o-tine [NIK-uh-TEEN] NOUN. **nicotine** ► a poison that is found in small amounts in the leaves, roots, and seeds of tobacco plants. Nicotine is one of the harmful substances in cigarettes. It is used as an insect poison and in some medicines.

niece [nees] NOUN, nieces. **1. nièce** ► the daughter of a person's brother or sister. **2. nièce** ► the daughter of a person's brother-in-law or sister-in-law.

night [nite] NOUN, nights. **nuit** ► the time when it is dark; the time between sunset and sunrise. ▲ ADJECTIVE. **de nuit, nocturne** ► of or relating to the night. ℘ **p. 1080.**

night-gown [NITE-GOWN] NOUN, nightgowns. **chemise de nuit** ► a loose, dresslike garment worn to bed.

night-in-gale [NITE-in-GAYL] NOUN, nightingales. **rossignol** ► a small, reddish-brown bird with a grey or white underside. The males are known for their beautiful songs and often sing at night.

night-ly [NITE-lee] ADJECTIVE; ADVERB. **de soir, de nuit, nocturne** ► happening or done every night : *a nightly newscast. Riley takes a walk nightly.*

night-mare [NITE-MAIR] NOUN, nightmares. **1. cauchemar** ► a dream that is frightening or disturbing; a bad dream : *Last night I had a nightmare that I was falling out of my apartment window.* **2. cauchemar** ► a frightening or horrible experience that is thought of as being like a bad dream : *We ran out of gas on the bridge at rush hour—what a nightmare!*

nim-ble [NIM-bul] ADJECTIVE, nimbler, nimblest. **agile, alerte, vif (vive), preste** ► moving in a light, graceful way; agile : *"The bass players say their instruments aren't nimble enough for Mr. Beethoven's quick notes."* (Barbara Nichol) ■ **nimbly,** ADVERB: ► **agilement, légèrement, prestement.** *to run nimbly across a floor that is covered with toys.*

nine [nine] NOUN, nines. **neuf** ► one more than eight; 9. ■ **ninth,** ADJECTIVE; NOUN. ► **neuvième.**

✎ Word Builder

Next, closest, and adjacent all refer to the order or relationship between two things. Next can mean when something follows right after something else: Chandra was the next person in the bank lineup. It can also mean the first time after something happens: Visit us the next time you're in town. Closest means the nearest in terms of space, time, or a relationship: Savona is the closest town to Kamloops. Adjacent can mean that two things are close together, or that they share a common boundary: Sam and Emily lived in adjacent apartments.

nine-teen [nine-TEEN] NOUN, nineteens. **dix-neuf** ▸ one more than eighteen; 19. ■ **nine-teenth**, ADJECTIVE; NOUN. **dix-neuvième**.

nine-ty [NINE-tee] NOUN, nineties. **quatre-vingt-dix** ▸ nine times ten; 90. ■ **ninetieth**, ADJECTIVE; NOUN. ▸ **quatre-vingt-dixième**.

ni-tro-gen [NY-truh-jun] NOUN. **azote** ▸ a gas that has no colour, smell, or taste. It makes up about 70% of the air and is found in all living things. Nitrogen is a chemical element.

no [noh] ADVERB. **1. non** ▸ the opposite of "yes"; a word used to mean that something can't be, won't be, shouldn't be, and so on. **2. pas, non** ▸ not any; not at all : *Your reports must be ready no later than Friday.* ▲ NOUN, nos. **non** ▸ a negative response.

no-holds-barred 1. sans règle, sans restriction ▸ without rules or restrictions : *a no-holds-barred game.* **2. complet (-ète)** ▸ complete : *a no-holds-barred effort.*

Nobel Prize **prix Nobel** ▸ an international award given each year for important work in the fields of physics, chemistry, medicine, literature, and advancing the cause of peace. Prizes have been awarded since 1901, and a prize in economic science was added in 1969 : *Lester B. Pearson won the Nobel Peace Prize in 1957 for helping to settle the Suez Canal crisis.*

no-ble [NOH-bul] ADJECTIVE, nobler, noblest. **1. noble** ▸ having a high rank or title in society. **2. noble, grand (grande)** ▸ having great value or character; distinguished; outstanding : *He was very noble, and gave up his trip to help his parents.* **3. majestueux (-euse), remarquable, imposant (-ante)** ▸ very grand or impressive in appearance; splendid : *The Grand Canyon is a noble sight.* ▲ NOUN, nobles. **noble** ▸ a person of high rank or title. **Note.** People who are born into or who are given a high rank or title in society belong to the nobility. **Note.** Such a person is also called a nobleman or noblewoman. ■ **nobly**, ADVERB. ▸ **noblement**.

no-bod-y [NOH-BUD-ee or NOH-BOD-ee] PRONOUN. **personne, nul (nulle), aucun** ▸ no person; not anybody; no one : *Nobody likes hearing bad news.* ▲ NOUN, nobodies. **moins que rien, nullité** ▸ a person of no importance : *He hoped she wouldn't think he was a nobody, hanging around doing nothing.*

noc-tur-nal [nok-TUR-nul] ADJECTIVE. **nocturne** ▸ having to do with or happening at night : *Nocturnal animals such as the owl sleep during the day.*

nod [nod] VERB, nodded, nodding. **1. hocher la tête, incliner la tête** ▸ to move the head up and down. **2. faire oui, faire un signe de tête affirmatif, consentir d'un signe de tête** ▸ to do this as a sign to show that one agrees, is saying "yes," and so on : *"The animals nodded, for this was true."* (Celia Barker Lottridge) ▲ NOUN, nods.

signe de tête affirmatif, signe d'assentiment ▸ a nodding motion : *a nod of her head.* SYN : bow, bob, tip, bend, signal.

noise [noyz] NOUN, noises. **1. bruit** ▸ a sound that is loud, unpleasant, or unwanted : *Our neighbour's house alarm made a loud noise.* **2. bruit, son** ▸ any sound : *"A loud chewing noise awakened us one night."* (Janet Foster) ■ **noisy**, ADJECTIVE. ▸ **bruyant (-ante).** full of noise. ■ **noisily**, ADVERB. ▸ **bruyamment:** *Karly shut the door noisily.* ■ **noiseless**, ADJECTIVE. **silencieux (-ieuse)** ▸ making little or no sound : *a noiseless engine.*

no-mad [NOH-MAD] NOUN, nomads. **1. nomade** ▸ a member of a tribe or group that often moves from place to place, rather than staying in one permanent home : *Bedouins are nomads who live in and travel across the Sahara desert.* **Note.** A group that does this is nomadic. **2. nomade** ▸ any person who wanders about from place to place.

nom-i-nate [NOM-uh-NATE] VERB, nominated, nominating. **1. proposer, présenter** ▸ to choose someone to run for office : *Jenny nominated Beth for president of their club.* **2. nommer, désigner** ▸ to name to a high office or position. SYN : propose, name, recommend, appoint.

nom-i-na-tion [NOM-uh-NAY-shun] NOUN, nominations. **nomination** ▸ the act or fact of nominating. **Note.** A person who is nominated is a nominee.

non- [non] PREFIX. not : *nonsense; non-stop.*

none [nun] PRONOUN. **aucun (-une)** ▸ not one; not any : *She tried several keys in the lock, but none fit.* ▲ ADVERB. **pas tellement** ▸ not at all : *The tomatoes from the vegetable garden were none too good this year.*

none-the-less [NUN-the-LES] ADVERB. **néanmoins** ▸ nevertheless; however.

non-sense [NON-sence or NON-sunce] NOUN. **absurdités, sottises, idioties, inepties** ▸ talk or actions that do not make sense; things that have a foolish meaning or no meaning at all.

noo-dle [NOOD-ul] NOUN, noodles. **nouille** ▸ a mixture of flour, water, and egg rolled and cut into strips. Noodles come in different sizes and shapes and are used in soups, stews, and other meals. **Note.** Noodle comes from the German word for this food.

noon [noon] NOUN. **midi** ▸ 12:00 in the daytime; the middle part of the day.

no one (sometimes no-one) **personne** ▸ not one person; nobody : *I rang the doorbell, but no one answered.*

Noot-ka [NOOT-kuh] NOUN. **1. Nootka** ▸ a member of the Aboriginal peoples living mainly on Vancouver Island. **2. nootka, nutka** ▸ the Wakashan language of the Nootka.

nor [nor] CONJUNCTION. **ni ▸** and not : *Something that is lukewarm is neither hot nor cold.*

nor-mal [NOR-mul] ADJECTIVE. **1. normal (-ale, -aux) ▸** as it should be; healthy and natural. **2. ordinaire ▸** as it usually is; like most others; typical : *It was just a normal Saturday; we did chores and watched* Star Trek. ■ **normally,** ADVERB. ▸ **normalement:** *I really enjoyed* The Sound of Music, *even though I don't normally like musicals.* SYN: regular, typical, natural, ordinary, usual.

north [north] NOUN. **1. nord ▸** the direction that is on your right when you face the sun at sunset; the opposite of south. **2.** (usually **North**) **Nord ▸** any place or region in that direction. **3. the North. Nord ▸** in Canada, the northern parts of the provinces from Quebec westward and the territories lying north of these provinces. ▲ ADJECTIVE. **1. nord ▸** toward the north : *the north side of the street.* **2. du nord, nordique ▸** coming from the north : *a north wind.* ▲ ADVERB. **vers le nord, au nord ▸** toward the north : *to travel north.*

north-east [NORTH-EEST] NOUN. **1. nord-est ▸** the direction that is halfway between north and east : *The wind is coming from the northeast.* **2. Nord-Est ▸** a place or region lying to or located in the northeast : *That city is in the northeast.* ▲ ADJECTIVE. **au nord-est, du nord-est, vers le nord-est ▸** of, at, in, toward, or from the northeast : *a northeast wind.* ▲ ADVERB: *They travelled northeast.*

north-ern [NOR-thurn] ADJECTIVE. **1. nord, septentrional (-ale, -aux) ▸** of, in, or toward the north : *the northern border.* **2. du nord, septentrional (-ale, -aux), nordique ▸** coming from the north : *a cold northern air mass.* **3.** (often **Northern**) **nordique ▸** of, in, or having to do with the North. **Note.** A Northerner is a person born or living in the north.

northern lights aurore boréale ▸ bands of bright light and colour in the northern sky at night, especially in the Arctic regions. **Note.** Also called the aurora borealis, northern lights

North Pole pôle Nord ▸ the northernmost part of the earth, near the middle of the Arctic Ocean.

North Star étoile polaire ▸ a bright star in the northern sky, almost directly above the North Pole. **Note.** Also called Polaris.

north-ward [NORTH-wurd] ADVERB. (also **northwards**) **vers le nord ▸** to or toward the north : *Sheila turned the car northward.* ▲ ADJECTIVE. **nordique ▸** moving to or toward the north : *They began their northward hike.*

north-west [NORTH-WEST] NOUN. **1. nord-ouest ▸** the direction that is halfway between north and west : *That storm is coming from the northwest.* **2. Nord-Ouest ▸** a place or region lying to or located in the northwest. ▲ ADJECTIVE. **au nord-ouest, du nord-ouest, vers le nord-ouest ▸** of, at, in, toward, or from the northwest : *a northwest wind.* ▲ ADVERB. **vers le nord-ouest ▸** toward the northwest : *They walked northwest.*

nose [noze] NOUN. noses. **1. nez ▸** the part of the face that is used for breathing and smelling. **2. odorat ▸** the sense of smell : *a dog with a good nose.* **3. flair ▸** an ability to sense or search out things : *a reporter with a nose for news.* **4. nez ▸** something that sticks out in front the way a nose does : *the nose of an airplane.* ▲ VERB. nosed, nosing. **1. renifler, flairer ▸** to use the nose : *The dog nosed out the steak bones in the trash.* **2. fouiller, fureter, fouiner ▸** to search for something in a prying or annoying way; snoop : *She nosed around for the presents that her parents had hidden.* 📖 p. 986. 👁 **p. 403.**

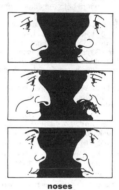

noses

on the nose exactement, pile, dans le mille ▸ exactly : *She guessed my height right on the nose.*

by a nose par une petite différence, par une faible marge ▸ a very small difference : *Channah won the race by a nose.*

nos-tal-gi-a [nos-TAL-juh *or* nos-TAL-jee-uh] NOUN. **1. nostalgie, mal du pays ▸** homesickness. **2. nostalgie ▸** a longing for something in the past; longing for the return of some former condition or circumstance : *Karin thought with nostalgia of her high-school days.* ▲ ADJECTIVE. nostalgic. **nostalgique ▸** having to do with nostalgia.

nos-tril [NOS-tril] NOUN. nostrils. **narine ▸** one of the two outer openings of the nose. The nostrils are the passageways through which air is pulled into the body by the lungs and through which air is expelled.

nos·y [NOZ-ee] ADJECTIVE, nosier, nosiest. (also nosey) **curieux (-ieuse), fureteur (-euse)** ▸ curious about things that are not one's business : *It's nosy to listen to other people's phone calls.*

not [not] ADVERB. **ne ... pas** ▸ in no way : *A whale is not a fish; it's a mammal.*

no·ta·ble [NOH-tuh-bul] ADJECTIVE. **notable, éminent (-ente), remarquable** ▸ worth being noticed; important; outstanding. ▲ NOUN, notables. **notable** ▸ a person who is important : *The opening of the new bridge will be attended by the mayor, the city councillors, and various other notables.* ■ **notably**, ADVERB. ▸ **notamment, notablement.** SYN : important, memorable, special, famous.

note [note] NOUN, notes. **1. mot, note** ▸ a short letter or message : *Axel left his mother a note to say that he'd gone to his friend's house.* **2. note** ▸ a few words or sentences that a person writes down to help explain some larger thought or idea. **3. annotation** ▸ a short comment or item of information in a book to explain something or to refer to another place in the book. **4. note** ▸ notice or attention : *Take note of what she says.* **5. touche, accent, note** ▸ a little bit; a hint or suggestion : *There was a note of sadness in her voice.* **6. note** ▸ one musical sound, or the sign representing this sound. A written note shows how long a certain sound is to be held and how high or low it is. ▲ VERB, noted, noting. **1. noter, inscrire, écrire** ▸ to write down; to make a short record of : *Elaine noted what had happened in her diary.* **2. remarquer, constater** ▸ to pay attention to; notice : *I noted his new hat.* ☞ p. 1130.

compare notes confronter des vues ▸ exchange ideas or opinions : *Shameil and Pat compared notes on the movie.*

make a note of prendre note de ▸ write down as something to be remembered : *Chris made a note of Tan's request.*

note-book [NOTE-book] NOUN, notebooks. **carnet, calepin, bloc-notes** ▸ a book with blank pages for taking notes or for writing or drawing.

not·ed [NOH-tid] ADJECTIVE. **célèbre, illustre, réputé (-ée)** ▸ well-known, famous : *a noted singer; a noted author.*

noth·ing [NUTH-ing] NOUN. **1. rien** ▸ not having anything or things; not anything. **2. zéro** ▸ zero : *The Blue Jays won by a score of one to nothing.* **3. rien, vétille** ▸ something that is not at all important : *Don't worry about this cut; it's nothing but a scratch.* ▲ ADVERB. **aucunement** ▸ not in any way; not at all.

no·tice [NOH-tis] NOUN, notices. **1. avis, annonce** ▸ a short written message that announces something : *There was a notice on the bulletin board that someone had lost a wallet.* **2. avertissement** ▸ a warning or action that shows something is about to happen : *The guard stood*

close to the door, ready to slam it shut at a moment's notice. **3. préavis** ▸ a formal statement ahead of time that someone will be moving, leaving a job, or the like. **4. attention** ▸ the fact of knowing about or being aware of something; attention : *Let nothing escape your notice.* ▲ VERB, noticed, noticing. **remarquer, noter** ▸ to pay attention to; see or sense : *"At first the cubs didn't notice anything wrong."* (Celia Godkin) **Note.** Something that can be noticed is noticeable.

no·ti·fy [NOH-tuh-fy] VERB, notified, notifying. **signaler, aviser, avertir, notifier** ▸ to make some information known to a person; announce something : *The letter notified her that she had been accepted into acting school.* ■ **notification**, NOUN. ▸ **avis, annonce, notification.** SYN : announce, inform, tell, advise, report.

no·tion [NOH-shun] NOUN, notions. **1. idée, notion** ▸ a vague or general idea about something : *"It happened so suddenly, Thomas had the notion that time had stopped."* (Virginia Hamilton) **2. idée** ▸ a sudden or odd desire to do something : *After reading about the Yukon, Pilar got a notion to go there.* **3. (notions) articles de mercerie** ▸ small items that are used in sewing, such as needles, thread, pins, and ribbons : *Diane bought notions at the fabric store.* SYN : idea, understanding, belief, thought, view.

no·to·ri·ous [noh-TOR-ee-us] ADJECTIVE. **notoire, tristement célèbre** ▸ well-known, especially for something bad or unpleasant; infamous : *Kay is notorious for exaggerating when she tells a story.* **Note.** The fact of being notorious is notoriety. ■ **notoriously**, ADVERB. ▸ **notoirement.**

noun [NOWN] NOUN, nouns. **nom** ▸ a word that names a person, place, thing, or idea. A NOUN can act as the SUBJECT of a verb (The *dog* just got out), the OBJECT of a verb (I forgot to close the *door*), or the OBJECT of a PREPOSITION (He ran across the *street*).

nour·ish [NUR-ish] VERB, nourished, nourishing. **nourrir, alimenter** ▸ to provide food and other things to plants and animals so that they can live and grow. **Note.** Sometimes used as an ADJECTIVE: *Fruit is a nourishing snack.* ■ **nourishment**, NOUN. ▸ **nourriture, aliments.**

no·va [NOH-vuh] NOUN, novas or novae. **nova** ▸ a star that explodes and sends huge masses of matter into space. It becomes tremendously bright for a time and then fades to its former lower level of brightness.

nov·el¹ [NOV-ul] NOUN, novels. **roman** ▸ a written story that is long enough to fill a book. A novel tells a story made up by the author, rather than presenting actual facts. **Note.** A novelist is a person who writes novels.

nov·el² ADJECTIVE. **nouveau (-elle, -eaux)** ▸ not known before; new and unusual : *Toni has a* *novel way to ride a bike.* SYN: different, unusual, new, original, unique.

nov·el·ty [NOV-ul-tee] NOUN, novelties. **1. nouveauté, étrangeté ►** something that is novel; a new and unusual thing : *José enjoyed the novelty of going to his first opera.* **2. nouveauté ►** the fact or condition of being new or different : *Wes played with his new toy all the time, but the novelty soon wore off and he lost interest.* **3. novelties. articles de fantaisie ►** small items for sale, such as toys and games : *Tourists like to buy novelties like cheap jewellery and key chains.*

No·vem·ber [noh-VEM-bur] NOUN, Novembers. **novembre ►** the 11th month of the year between October and December. November has 30 days.

no·vice [NOV-us] NOUN, novices. **1. novice ►** a person who is new to a job or activity; a beginner : *She is a novice at hockey.* **2. novice ►** a monk or a nun who has entered a religious order but has not yet taken final vows.

now [now] ADVERB. **1. maintenant, en ce moment, actuellement ►** at this time; at the present : *Pat was born in Regina, but now lives in Winnipeg.* **2. maintenant ►** at once; right away : *We'd better leave now or we'll miss the bus.* ▲ CONJUNCTION. **maintenant que ►** considering that; since : *Now that it's stopped raining, we can finish the game.* ▲ NOUN. **maintenant, en ce moment ►** the present time : *He should have been here by now.*

now·a·days [NOW-uh-DAZE] ADVERB. **aujourd'hui, actuellement, de nos jours ►** these days; now : *Nowadays most people own a TV set.*

no·where [NOH-WAIR] ADVERB. **nulle part ►** at, to, or in no place : *One moment the dog was in the yard, and the next he was nowhere to be seen.*

noz·zle [NOZ-ul] NOUN, nozzles. **ajutage, bec, gicleur ►** a small opening or spout at the end of a hose or pipe : *the nozzle of a garden hose.*

nu·cle·ar [NOO-klee-ur] ADJECTIVE. **1. nucléaire ►** having to do with a nucleus : *nuclear particles.* **2. nucléaire ►** using power from the nucleus of an atom : *There is a nuclear-powered submarine in the harbour.* **3. nucléaire ►** having to do with nuclear weapons : *nuclear war.*

nuclear energy énergie nucléaire ► power or energy that can be released from the nucleus of an atom.

nu·cle·us [NOO-klee-us] NOUN, nuclei or nucleuses. **1. noyau (-aux), nucléus ►** the tiny roundish centre of an animal or plant cell that controls the cell's growth and other important activities. **2. noyau (-aux) ►** the central part of an atom. The nucleus contains protons and neutrons, and has a positive charge of electricity. **3. noyau (-aux), fond ►** the central or most important part of something.

nude [nood] ADJECTIVE. **nu (nue) ►** naked; unclothed.

nudge [nuj] VERB, nudged, nudging. **pousser du coude, pousser légèrement ►** to push or move something slightly, In a gentle way : *"Three Names would nudge him with his cool wet nose."* (Patricia MacLachlan) ▲ NOUN, nudges. **coup de coude ►** a gentle push. SYN: push, prod, shove, poke, prompt.

nui·sance [NYOO-sunce or NOO-sunce] NOUN, nuisances. **fléau, plaie, peste ►** something or someone that annoys or causes trouble; a bother : *"The long, full skirts worn by women were yet another nuisance of the times."* (Linda Granfield)

numb [num] ADJECTIVE. **engourdi (-ie) ►** having lost feeling or movement : *My fingers were numb from the cold.* ▲ VERB, numbed, numbing. **engourdir ►** to lose or cause to lose the ability to feel or move in a normal way : *The dentist numbed Irene's gums before filling the cavity.*

num·ber [NUM-bur] NOUN, numbers. **1. nombre ►** how many there are of something; the amount of things in a group : *"They showed up clearly on the damp earth, and from the number of paw prints I knew there had been two coyotes, maybe even three."* (Janet Foster) **2. nombre, chiffre ►** a sign or word that tells how many, such as four, 10, 16th, 80th, and so on. **3. numéro ►** a certain number that is given or assigned to someone : *Do you know Jill's telephone number?* **4. un grand nombre ►** a large but not exact amount : *A number of people have told her how nice her new car looks.* ▲ VERB, numbered, numbering. **1. numéroter ►** to give a number or numbers to : *The city numbered the houses on our block 100 to 150.* **2. compter, comprendre ►** to amount to; include : *The population of our town numbers around 85,000.* **3. compter ►** to limit the number of : *The arrival of CDs numbered the days of vinyl records.* SYN: amount, quantity, sum, whole, volume.

nu·mer·al [NYOO-muh-rul or NOO-muh-rul] NOUN, numerals. **chiffre ►** a sign or symbol that represents a certain number or quantity : *X is the Roman numeral for 10.*

nu·mer·a·tor [NYOO-muh-RAY-tur or NOO-muh-RAY-tur] NOUN, numerators. **numérateur ►** in a fraction, the number above the line : *In the fraction [$\frac{1}{4}$], 1 is the numerator and 4 is the denominator.*

nu·mer·ous [NYOO-muh-rus or NOO-muh-rus] ADJECTIVE. **nombreux (-euse), abondant (-ante) ►** being or made up of a large number; very many : *We have made numerous changes to our garden over the years.* SYN: many, several, various, considerable.

nun [nun] NOUN, nuns. **religieuse, sœur ►** a woman who belongs to a religious order through which she dedicates her life to serving

411

God. Nuns do not marry and usually live together as part of a group. They do such work as teaching, caring for the sick, and helping the poor. **Note.** Nuns sometimes live in **nunneries** or **convents.**

nurse [nurs] NOUN, **nurses. infirmier (-ière) ▸** a person who is specially trained to take care of sick people and carry on other medical duties. Nurses work in hospitals or in private homes, and also in nursing homes, where elderly or ill people are cared for. ▲ VERB, **nursed, nursing. 1. soigner ▸** to act as a nurse ; care for the sick : *to nurse someone back to health.* **2. soigner, entretenir, faire durer ▸** to treat something in a careful and gentle way : *He sat for a while, nursing his coffee.* **3. allaiter, nourrir ▸** to feed a baby its mother's milk.

nurs·er·y [NUR-suh-ree] NOUN, **nurseries. 1. chambre d'enfant, pouponnière ▸** a room or place for babies or young children. **2. pépinière ▸** a place where plants are grown and sold.

nursery rhyme comptine ▸ a short song or poem for children, such as "Humpty Dumpty."

nursery school centre de la petite enfance, garderie, école maternelle ▸ a school for young children who are not old enough to go to kindergarten.

nut [nut] NOUN, **nuts. 1. noix, fruit à écale ▸** the dry fruit of certain plants, made up of a hard outer shell with a seed inside. Walnuts, almonds, and cashews are nuts. **2. écrou ▸** a small piece of metal with a hole in the centre, through which a bolt is turned or screwed.

nut·meg [NUT-meg] NOUN, **nutmegs. 1. muscadier ▸** an evergreen tree with spicy seeds found in the East Indies. **2. nutmeg. muscade ▸** a sweet-smelling spice made from grinding the hard seeds of this tree.

nu·tri·ent [NYOO-tree-unt *or* NOO-tree-unt] NOUN, **nutrients. élément nutritif, substance nutritive, nutriment ▸** the special elements found in food that people, animals, and plants need to live and grow, such as proteins and vitamins.

nu·tri·tion [nyoo-TRISH-un *or* noo-TRISH-un] NOUN. **1. alimentation, nutrition ▸** the fact of taking in food ; nourishment : *Good nutrition is very important to health.* **2. nutrition ▸** the process by which food is taken in and used by living things. **Note.** Food that is healthful and gives nourishment is **nutritious.**

ny·lon [NY-LON] NOUN. **nylon ▸** a strong artificial material that is used for many purposes, such as to make clothing, rope, or brushes, and for machine parts.

nymph [nimf] NOUN, **nymphs. 1. nymphe ▸** in stories of the ancient Greeks and Romans, one of a group of beautiful goddesses who lived in woods, trees, water, and so on. **2. nymphe ▸** a young insect that has not yet developed into its adult state.

ocelot

o, O [oh] NOUN, o's, O's. **o, O ▸** the 15th letter of the English alphabet.

oak [oke] NOUN, oaks. **chêne ▸** a tree with large, notched leaves and nuts that are called acorns. An oak tree has strong, hard wood that is used in building furniture. ▪ **oaken,** ADJECTIVE. ▸ **en chêne, de chêne. ◎ p. 254.**

oak

notched leaves

flowers

fruits (acorns)

oar [or] NOUN, oars. **rame, aviron ▸** a long pole with a flat blade at one end, used for rowing a boat.

o-a-sis [oh-AY-sis] NOUN, oases [oh-AY-seez]. **1. oasis ▸** an area in the middle of a desert where trees and other plants can grow because there is water. **2. oasis, havre ▸** any place or thing that is thought of as giving comfort or relief.

oath [ohth] NOUN, oaths. **1. serment, promesse ▸** a strict promise by a person to tell the truth, obey the law, act in a proper way, or the like : *The witness took an oath to tell the truth.* **2. juron ▸** a word or phrase used to express anger or other strong feelings; a swear word or a curse. SYN: promise, vow, pledge, commitment.

under oath sous serment ▸ bound by an oath : *Darlene told her story under oath.*

oat-meal [OTE-meel] NOUN. **1. flocons d'avoine▸** ground or rolled oats; oats made into meal. **2. gruau ▸** porridge or hot cereal made by boiling such oats.

oats [otes] NOUN. **1. avoine ▸** grain that is related to wheat, used in breakfast cereals and as food for horses and other animals. **2. oat. avoine▸** the tall grass plant that produces this grain. **◎ p. 116.**

o-be-di-ent [oh-BEE-dee-unt] ADJECTIVE. **obéissant (-ante), docile ▸** willing to obey; doing what one is told or is supposed to do : *the obedient dog stopped on command.* ▲ NOUN, obedience. **obéissance, docilité ▸** the fact of being obedient. ▪ **obediently,** ADVERB ▸ **docilement.** *The children lined up obediently when the bell rang.* SYN: well-behaved, dutiful, orderly, quiet.

o-bey [oh-BAY] VERB, obeyed, obeying. **1. obéir à, écouter, se soumettre ▸** to do as one is told or asked to do. **2. observer, obéir à, se conformer à, obtempérer ▸** to follow a rule or a law. SYN: submit to, agree with, heed, mind, listen to.

ob-ject [OB-jikt *or* OB-jekt] NOUN, objects. **1. objet, chose ▸** a real thing that can be seen and touched; a thing; an article. **2. objet ▸** a person or thing that draws attention or that causes certain feelings : *The gift-wrapped box was an object of much interest to the children.* **3. but, objectif ▸** something aimed at or worked toward; a purpose or goal : *The object of chess is to capture the other player's pieces.* **4.** in grammar, **a. complément direct ou indirect ▸** a word that receives the action of a verb. In the sentence *She rode her bike, bike* is the object of the verb *rode.* **b. complément ▸** a word that follows a preposition. In the phrase "on the wall," *wall* is the object of the preposition "on." ▲ [ob-JEKT] VERB, objected, objecting. **1. s'opposer, désapprouver ▸** to be against; dislike; oppose : *Kira objects to animal testing.* **2. objecter que, faire valoir que, prétexter ▸** to 413 give a reason against : *Rocco objected that the weather was too warm for skating.*

ob·jec·tion [ub-JEK-shun *or* ob-JEK-shun] NOUN, objections. **objection, opposition ▸** the fact of objecting, or a reason for this : *The mayor had no objection to publicity.* ■ **objectionable,** ADJECTIVE. **▸ contestable, attaquable, désobligeant (-ante).**

ob·jec·tive [ub-JEK-tiv *or* ob-JEK-tiv] ADJECTIVE. **1. objectif (-ive), impartial (-ale, -aux) ▸** dealing with facts, rather than with opinions or personal feelings : *The reporter always wrote objective articles that didn't favour any side.* **2. objectif (-ive) ▸** real; existing outside the mind as an actual object : *Some objective evidence was needed to solve the case.* ▲ NOUN, objectives. **objectif, but ▸** the goal or purpose of something : *When Tia joined the band, her objective was to play a solo.* ■ **objectively,** ADVERB. **▸ objectivement.** SYN: unbiased, impartial, unprejudiced. ✐ **p. 414.**

ob·li·gate [OB-luh-GATE] VERB, obligated, obligating. **obliger, contraindre, forcer ▸** to make someone do something because of a contract, promise, or feeling of duty, or because it is required by law : *Edward was obligated to pay the parking ticket.*

ob·li·ga·tion [OB-luh-GAY-shun] NOUN, obligations. **1. obligation, devoir ▸** the fact of being obligated, or something that obligates; a duty. **2. obligation, engagement ▸** money or something else that is owed; a debt : *I took care of my sister's obligations.* SYN: duty, responsibility, debt, liability, task.

o·blige [uh-BLYJE] VERB, obliged, obliging. **1. obliger, forcer, contraindre ▸** to make someone feel that something should be done; force to happen : *Before Jovita could watch TV, she was obliged to finish her homework.* **2. être reconnaissant (-ante), savoir gré ▸** to make a person thankful for something done or given : *I'd be obliged if you'd turn the music down.* **3. faire une faveur, rendre service ▸** to do someone a favour : *I can oblige you with a free ticket to the show.*

o·bliv·i·on [uh-BLIV-ee-un] NOUN. **oubli ▸** the state of being completely forgotten : *Many famous writers have passed into oblivion.* **Note.** A person who is oblivious to something does not notice it : *Luan was oblivious to what was happening around her.*

ob·long [OB-LONG] ADJECTIVE. **oblong (-ongue), rectangulaire ▸** having a shape that is longer than it is wide. ▲ NOUN, oblongs.

ob·nox·ious [ub-NOK-shus] ADJECTIVE. **odieux (-ieuse), détestable, exécrable ▸** very rude or unpleasant; nasty : *His obnoxious behaviour turned off everyone he met.* SYN: offensive, unpleasant, disgusting.

414

Objective/Subjective Writing

• *As a writer you can write in two ways :* **objectively** *or* **subjectively**. *If you write objectively you state facts, without giving opinion. As the writer, you remain separate from the action or characters; you do not seem to judge them. If you write subjectively, you colour the facts with feelings or personal opinions.*

• *When you write reports or articles it is important to remain objective—to state the facts, rather than your opinions or theories.*

• *When you write an editorial or essay, you are subjective but you support your opinions with facts.*

• *When you write fiction, you can be subjective or objective. The advantage of being subjective is that readers know exactly how they should feel about a character or an event. However, sometimes it's good to let readers form their own opinions, to give them just the facts, and allow them to draw their own conclusions.*

---

o·boe [OH-boe] NOUN. **hautbois ▸** a musical instrument of the woodwind family, made of a long tube that has a double reed for the mouthpiece. ☜ **p. 539.**

ob·scene [ob-SEEN *or* ub-seen] ADJECTIVE. **obscène, indécent (-ente), immoral (-ale, -aux) ▸** going against accepted standards of what is decent or moral : *TV shows don't allow performers to make obscene comments on air.*

ob·scure [ub-SKYOOR] ADJECTIVE. **1. obscur (-ure), confus (-use) ▸** not easy to understand; not clear : *The author Gertrude Stein is known for obscure statements such as "There is no there there."* **2. obscur (-ure) ▸** not likely to be noticed; not well-known : *They had dinner in an obscure little restaurant in their neighbourhood.* **3. indistinct (-incte), imprécis (-ise) ▸** not easily seen or heard; not distinct : *an obscure shape in the distance.* ▲ VERB, obscured, obscuring. **obscurcir, cacher ▸** to make obscure; hide from view : *Heavy fog obscured the view of the mountain.* ■ **obscurity,** NOUN. **obscurité, noirceur ▸** the fact of being obscure. SYN: unclear, vague, dim, faint, shadowy, hazy.

ob·ser·va·tion [OB-zur-VAY-shun] NOUN, observations. **1. observation ▸** the act of watching or noticing : *It is necessary to wear special glasses or other eye protection for the observation of a solar eclipse.* **2. surveillance ▸** the fact of being seen or observed : *We used the back door to avoid observation.* **3. observation** ▶ the act of observing something in a scientific way and noting what is seen. **4. observation, remarque** ▶ a comment or remark : *The speaker started by making a few observations about how crowded the meeting hall was.*

ob·serve [ub-ZURV] VERB, observed, observing. **1. observer, remarquer** ▶ to see and notice; pay attention to : *A neighbour observed two men running from the building just before the fire broke out.* **2. surveiller, épier** ▶ to watch carefully for a special purpose : *On a stakeout, the detective observed the building across the street.* **3. célébrer, fêter** ▶ to follow or obey a certain custom or rule : *Canada Day is observed on the first day of July.* **4. faire remarquer, faire observer** ▶ to make a comment or remark : *Joachim observed that the day was almost over.* Note. Someone who is observant is quick or careful to observe. SYN: watch, notice, see, study, perceive.

ob·sta·cle [OB-stuh-kul] NOUN, obstacles. **obstacle, barrière** ▶ something that blocks or stands in the way : *The runner Wilma Rudolph overcame obstacles, such as polio, to win three Olympic gold medals.* SYN: barrier, hurdle, hitch, snag, catch.

ob·sti·nate [OB-stih-nit] ADJECTIVE. **obstiné (-ée), entêté (-ée)** ▶ not wanting to change or co operate; stubborn; determined : *Molly and Wendy are both obstinate, and neither will ever admit that the other is right.*

ob·tain [ub-TANE *or* ob-TANE] VERB, obtained, obtaining. **obtenir, se procurer** ▶ to get or gain, especially through some effort : *During the camping trip, we obtained most of our food from hunting and fishing.* Note. Something that can be obtained is obtainable.

ob·vi·ous [OB-vee-us] ADJECTIVE. **évident (-ente), certain (-aine), clair (claire)** ▶ very easy to see or understand; plain; clear : *It was obvious from their yawning that the children were bored.* ■ **obviously,** ADVERB. ▶ **évidemment, certainement.** SYN: plain, clear, visible, conspicuous, evident.

oc·ca·sion [uh-KAY-zhun *or* oh-KAY-zhun] NOUN, occasions. **1. occasion** ▶ the time when a certain event takes place; a particular time : *On another occasion, we'll visit Niagara Falls.* **2. occasion** ▶ a time that is favourable; a chance; an opportunity : *She never missed an occasion for going to the library.* **3. événement, ou évènement** ▶ a special event : *Our family always makes birthdays into festive occasions with a special meal, cake, and presents.* **4. raison, motif** ▶ a cause or reason : *You have no occasion to behave so badly.*

oc·ca·sion·al [uh-KAY-zhun-ul *or* oh-KAY-zhun-ul] ADJECTIVE. **occasionnel (-elle), de temps en temps** ▶ happening only once in a while; not

regular or frequent : *Winter is always a quiet time, with only an occasional visitor now and then.* ■ **occasionally,** ADVERB. ▶ **occasionnellement, à l'occasion.**

oc·cu·pant [OK-yuh-punt] NOUN, occupants. **occupant (-ante)** ▶ a person who occupies a place : *That apartment has no occupants right now.*

oc·cu·pa·tion [OK-yuh-PAY-shun] NOUN, occupations. **1. occupation, profession, métier, emploi** ▶ the kind of work a person regularly does to earn money; one's profession : *Teaching is a rewarding occupation.* **2. occupation** ▶ the act or fact of occupying; possession : *The occupation of a building by a business.* SYN: job, work, profession, trade, calling. 📖 p. 1029.

oc·cu·py [OK-yuh-py] VERB, occupied, occupying. **1. occuper** ▶ to take up the space of; fill : *The airplane's washroom was already occupied.* **2. s'occuper, passer le temps** ▶ to take up one's time or attention : *He usually takes a book to occupy him on long trips.* **3. occuper** ▶ to take and keep possession of a place : *During World War II, Germany occupied France.* **4. habiter** ▶ to live in : *occupy a house.* **5. occuper** ▶ to have or hold : *She occupied the position of company president.*

oc·cur [uh-KUR *or* oh-KUR] VERB, occurred, occurring. **1. se produire, arriver** ▶ to take place; happen : *"They wanted to know what had occurred on their land, and how their ancestors had lived."* (Donalda Badone) **2. se trouver, se rencontrer** ▶ to be found; appear; exist : *"E" is the letter that occurs most often in English words.* **3. venir à l'esprit** ▶ to suggest itself; come to mind : *"It occurred to him that hockey season would soon be over."* (Barbara Novak) ■ **occurrence,** NOUN. **événement, circonstance** ▶ SYN: happen, take place, come about, transpire.

o·cean [OH-shun] NOUN, oceans. **1. océan** ▶ the large body of salt water that covers about three fourths of the earth's surface. **2. océan** ▶ any one of the four main parts into which this water is divided; the Atlantic, Pacific, Indian, or Arctic Ocean. ■ **oceanic,** ADJECTIVE. ▶ **océanique.** 📖 p. 1108. 👁 p. 112.

o·cean·og·ra·phy [OH-shun-OG-ruh-fee] NOUN. **océanographie** ▶ the science or study of the ocean and its animals and plants. Note. A person who studies oceanography is an oceanographer.

oc·e·lot [OS-uh-late *or* OH-suh-lot] NOUN, ocelots. **ocelot** ▶ a medium-sized wild cat that has a yellowish coat with a pattern of black spots and stripes. Ocelots are found in the southwestern United States, in Mexico, and in parts of South America. 👁 p. 416.

o'clock [uh-KLOK *or* oh-KLOK] ADVERB. **heure(s)** ▸ of or by the clock, used in stating an exact hour of the day : *Classes start at nine o'clock.*

oc·ta·gon [OK-tuh-GON *or* OK-tuh-gun] NOUN, octagons. **octogone** ▸ a closed geometric figure that has eight angles and eight sides. ■ **octagonal,** ADJECTIVE. ▸ **octogonal (-ale, -aux).**

ocelot

Oc·to·ber [ok-TOH-bur] NOUN. **octobre** ▸ the 10th month of the year, between September and November. October has 31 days.

oc·to·pus [OK-tuh-pus] NOUN, octopuses *or* octopi. **pieuvre, poulpe** ▸ a saltwater animal having a soft body with no backbone and eight long arms called tentacles. The tentacles have rows of small suction pads underneath that help the octopus grip rocks and food.

odd [od] ADJECTIVE, odder, oddest. **1. bizarre, étrange, curieux (-ieuse)** ▸ not as it should be or is expected to be; not normal; strange; unusual. **2. impair (-aire)** ▸ of numbers, not able to be divided exactly by 2; not even. **3. occasionnel (-elle)** ▸ happening from time to time; occasional : *Trish does odd jobs in her spare time.* **4. dépareillé (-ée)** ▸ not part of a matched pair or set : *an odd sock.* ■ **oddly,** ADVERB. ▸ **bizarrement, étrangement, curieusement.** ■ **oddness,** NOUN. ▸ **bizarrerie, étrangeté.** SYN: curious, unusual, peculiar, irregular, weird.

odds [odz] PLURAL NOUN. **1. probabilités, chances** ▸ numbers used to show the chance that a certain thing is true or will happen : *If you flip a coin, the odds are 50–50 that it will turn up heads.* **2. avantage** ▸ difference favouring one side over another : *Ravi overcame great odds to win the race.*

at odds **en désaccord** ▸ disagreeing or quarrelling : *Jamie and Alexa were at odds about which game to play.*

odds and ends **restes** ▸ items left over; odd pieces or scraps.

416

ode [ode] NOUN, odes. **ode** ▸ a lyric poem full of noble feeling, usually addressed to a particular person or thing : *an ode to Shakespeare.* ✐ p. 416.

odometer [oh-DOM-it-ur] **compteur (kilométrique), odomètre** ▸ an instrument or device that shows how far a vehicle has travelled. **Note.** Usually part of the speedometer.

o·dour [OH-dur] NOUN, odours. (also odor) **odeur, senteur, arôme** ▸ a scent or smell : *They put a fan over the stove to carry off smoke and kitchen odours.*

of [uv *or* ov] PREPOSITION. **1. de** ▸ belonging to : *the pages of a book.* **2. de** ▸ having or containing : *a glass of water.* **3. de** ▸ named as ; that is : *the city of Calgary.* **4. de** ▸ having to do with : *the chief of police ; to be afraid of dogs.* **5. de, en** ▸ made with or from : *a house of wood.* **6. de** ▸ away from : *2 km north of town.*

off [of] ADVERB. **1. s'éloigner** ▸ away from or free from : *The bird flew off into the night.* **2. éteint (-einte), fermé (-ée)** ▸ not active or working : *Turn the radio off.* **3. en moins** ▸ less than usual : *Everything in the store is selling for 20% off.* **4. enlevé (-ée)** ▸ no longer on ; not attached : *Take off your coat.* ▲ ADJECTIVE: **1. annulé (-ée)** ▸ cancelled : *The game is off because of the rain.* **2. enlevé (-ée)** ▸ not on : *His mittens are off.* **3. éteint (-einte)** ▸ not in use or operation : *The television was off.* ▲ PREPOSITION. **1.** ▸ relieved from : *Sue gets off work at 4:30 p.m.* **2.** ▸ so as to be removed or away from : *Pablo took the book off the shelf.* ✐ p. 417.

off and on **de temps à autre** ▸ at some times and not at others : *Tran plays hockey off and on throughout the year.*

of·fence [uh-FENS] NOUN, offences. (also offense) **1. délit, infraction** ▸ the breaking of a rule or law; a crime : *The judge gave him a small fine because it was his first offence.* **2. offense, affront** ▸ the fact of offending someone, or something that causes offence.

✐ Writing Tips

Ode

An ode is a type of poem that can take various forms. However, it is usually a long lyrical or musical poem that has a serious subject—such as life, death, or victory. The poet often relates personal feelings or deep, reflective thoughts.

The original ode form comes from Greece, where odes were performed to music with singers and dancers, and used to celebrate special events.

✎ **Word Builder**

Off-the-wall and **offbeat** mean the same thing—unusual or different: *Trey's shirt is really off-the-wall. Andrea has an offbeat sense of humour that always makes me laugh.* **Off-the-cuff** and **offhand** also have similar meanings. If you do something **off-the-cuff**, it is not planned or prepared. If you say something **offhand**, it is said without thinking or preparation: *Aline made an off-the-cuff remark that got her into a lot of trouble. I didn't realize that Ranat took my offhand remark so seriously.*

3. [AH-fens] in sports such as football or basketball, the team or players who have the ball and are trying to score.

of·fend [uh-FEND] VERB, offended, offending. **offenser, offusquer, choquer** ▸ to cause someone to feel upset or angry; hurt a person's feelings; insult : *I was hurt and offended when I didn't hear from you on my birthday.* **2. déranger, déplaire** ▸ be unpleasant to; displease; hurt : *Loud music offends my ears.*

of·fen·sive [uh-FEN-siv] ADJECTIVE. **1. offensant (-ante), choquant (-ante), blessant (-ante), vexant (-ante)** ▸ causing someone to be offended : *That loud-mouthed bully is very offensive.* **2.** [OF-en-siv] **offensif (-ive)** ▸ having to do with offence in sports. ▲ NOUN, offensives. **offensif (-ive)** ▸ an attack or position of attack : *The team went on the offensive and scored a goal.*

of·fer [OF-ur] VERB, offered, offering. **1. offrir, proposer** ▸ to present something that may or may not be taken : *He offered us dessert.* **2. offrir de, proposer de** ▸ to be willing to do something : *"Michael's parents had died and only Esther could take him in—or, only she had offered to."* (Cynthia Rylant) **3. offrir, proposer** ▸ to put forward as a suggestion or an attempt : *The dealer offered us $2000 for our old car.* **4. émettre, soulever** ▸ give or show : *My mom offered no protest when I asked for a raise in my allowance.* ▲ NOUN, offers. **proposition** ▸ the act of offering, or something that is offered. SYN: present, suggest, propose, submit, give.

of·fer·ing [OF-ur-ing *or* OF-ring] NOUN, offerings. **don, offrande** ▸ something given; a contribution : *They gave an offering of $10 dollars to the church.*

off·hand [OF-HAND] ADJECTIVE. **spontané (-ée), impulsif (-ive)** ▸ on the spur of the moment without thought or planning : *an offhand answer.* ▲ ADVERB. **de but en blanc** ▸ without previous thought or preparation : *The mechanic couldn't tell offhand how much the repairs would cost.*

of·fice [OF-is] NOUN, offices. **1. bureau (-eaux), cabinet, étude** ▸ a building or other place where the work of a business is carried on : *a dentist's office.* **2. fonction, charge** ▸ an impor-

tant position, especially in government : *the office of prime minister.* ☞ **p. 1051.**

of·fi·cer [OF-uh-sur] NOUN, officers. **1. officier** ▸ a person who has a high rank in the armed forces, such as a general or captain. **2. agent** ▸ a member of the police force. **3. membre de la direction, dirigeant (-ante)** ▸ a person who holds an important position : *Contracts can be signed only by someone who is an officer of this company.*

of·fi·cial [uh-FISH-ul] NOUN, officials. **1. fonctionnaire** ▸ a person who holds an office or position of authority, especially in government : *City officials have approved the plans to build a new park near us.* **2. officiel (-elle)** ▸ in sports, a person who decides when a rule has been broken and what the penalty should be, such as a referee or umpire. ▲ ADJECTIVE. **1. officiel (-elle)** ▸ having to do with a position of authority : *a mayor's official duties.* **2. officiel (-elle)** ▸ having been decided or determined by officials. ▪ **officially,** ADVERB: ▸ **officiellement.** *The president of the student council officially takes office at the beginning of the fall term.*

off·key [OF-KEE] ADJECTIVE. **1. faux (fausse)** ▸ in music, not in the correct musical key. **2. déplacé (-ée), inapproprié (-ée)** ▸ improper, not timed well : *off-key remarks.*

off·line [OF-LINE] ADJECTIVE. **non connecté (-ée), hors ligne, autonome** ▸ not connected to a computer or computer network : *The printers are often off-line.*

off·set [OF-SET *or* OF-set] VERB, offset, offsetting. **compenser** ▸ to make up for; balance : *The company got a lot of sales from its new store in the shopping mall to offset the loss of business downtown.*

off·shore [OF-shore] ADJECTIVE; ADVERB. **en mer, au large, côtier (-ière)** ▸ away from the shore : *an offshore breeze; offshore drilling for oil.*

off·spring [OF-spring] NOUN, offspring *or* offsprings. **progéniture** ▸ the young of a person, animal, or plant.

off the record [awf the REK-urd] ADJECTIVE; ADVERB. **1. officieux (-ieuse), confidentiel (-ielle)** ▸ not for publication or release of news : *The mayor made her comments off the record.* **2. hors procès-verbal** ▸ not to be written in the minutes of a meeting.

417

oft·en [OF-un *or* OF-tun] ADVERB. **souvent** ▸ happening again and again; frequently : *The restaurant is right near her office, and she eats there often.* ■ **oftentimes,** ADVERB. ▸ **souvent.** SYN: regularly, many times, repeatedly.

o·gre [oh-gur] NOUN, ogres. **ogre** ▸ a monster or giant from folklore that is cruel or terrifying.

oh [oh] INTERJECTION. **oh, ah** ▸ a word used to show a certain feeling, such as surprise, happiness, or fear : *"Oh, no—not again!"*

oil [oyl] NOUN, oils. 1. **pétrole** ▸ a thick, dark liquid that is found in the earth and that is used to make gasoline and other fuels. **Note.** Also called petroleum. 2. **huile** ▸ any of various other thick, greasy substances that are usually in a liquid form, will float on water, and will burn easily. Oils may be mineral, vegetable, or animal, and are used for cooking, for fuel, or to make machines run more smoothly. 3. **huile** ▸ a paint made by mixing colouring material with an oil, or a painting using such paints : *That oil by Van Gogh sold for $1.4 million.* ▲ VERB, oiled, oiling. **huiler, graisser, lubrifier** ▸ to put oil on something : *Oil your new baseball glove so that it'll be softer and more flexible.* ■ **oily,** ADJECTIVE. ▸ **huileux (-euse), graisseux (-euse), gras (grasse).**

oint·ment [OYNT-munt] NOUN, ointments. **onguent, pommade** ▸ an oily cream rubbed into the skin to soften it or to cure a skin disorder : *The doctor gave me an ointment for my poison-ivy rash.*

O·jib·wa [oh-JIB-way] NOUN. (also Ojibway) 1. **Ojibway** ▸ an Aboriginal people living around Lake Superior and westward. The Ojibwa traditionally occupied an area stretching from the Ottawa Valley to the prairies. 2. **ojibway** ▸ an Algonquian language spoken by the Ojibwa.

OK [OH-KAY] ADVERB; ADJECTIVE; INTERJECTION. (also O.K., Okay, or okay) all right; fine : *If you want to use my book, it's OK with me.* ▲ VERB, OK'd, OK'ing. **d'accord, très bien** ▸ to approve; say "yes" to : *My parents OK'd our fishing trip.* **être d'accord, approuver.**

O·ka·nag·an [oh-kuh-NOG-un] NOUN. 1. **Okanagan** ▸ the Aboriginal people living in south central British Columbia. 2. **okanagan** ▸ the Salish language of the Okanagan people.

old [old] ADJECTIVE. 1. **vieux (vieille), âgé (-ée)** ▸ having lived for a long time; not young. 2. **vieux (vieille)** ▸ having existed or been in use for a long time : *an old car.* 3. **âgé (-ée) de** ▸ having a certain age : *The Kentucky Derby is a race for three-year-old horses. My goddaughter is 11 years old.* SYN: ancient, antique, used, out of date, mature.

old-fash·ioned [OLD-FASH-und] ADJECTIVE. 1. **démodé (-ée)** ▸ having to do with past times; out of date : *old-fashioned clothes.* 2. **tradi-**

tionnel (-elle) ▸ favouring old ways and ideas : *an old-fashioned family.*

ol·ive [OL-iv] NOUN, olives. 1. **olive** ▸ a small oval fruit that is yellowish-green or black in colour and has a hard pit in the centre. Olives come from a small evergreen tree that is grown in hot, dry areas. 2. **vert olive, olive** ▸ a dull greenish-brown color. **Note.** An olive branch is a symbol of peace.

O·lym·pic Games [OH-lim-pik] NOUN. 1. (also the Olympics) **Jeux olympiques** ▸ an international sports competition held once every four years, each time in a different country. Athletes from all over the world take part in these events, which are divided into the Summer Olympics and the Winter Olympics. 2. **Jeux olympiques** ▸ a contest in sports, poetry, and music held every four years at Olympia in ancient Greece. It was the model for the modern Olympics.

om·e·lette [OM-uh-lit *or* OM-lit] NOUN, omelettes. **omelette** ▸ a food made from a mixture of eggs beaten with milk or water, and then cooked and folded over. Often a filling, such as cheese or meat, is added.

o·men [OH-mun] NOUN, omens. **présage, augure** ▸ anything that is thought of as a sign of good or bad luck in the future : *A black cat crossing your path is said to be a bad omen, but finding a four-leaf clover is believed to be a good omen.*

om·i·nous [OM-uh-nus] ADJECTIVE. **de mauvais augure, menaçant (-ante)** ▸ being a bad omen; seeming to tell of something bad to come; threatening : *The heavy, dark clouds overhead had an ominous look.*

o·mit [OH-mit] VERB, omitted, omitting. **omettre, oublier** ▸ to leave out; not include or do : *Tell me everything; don't omit a single detail.* ■ **omission,** NOUN. ▸ **omission, oubli.** SYN: exclude, overlook, neglect, skip, miss.

on [on] PREPOSITION. 1. **sur** ▸ held up by something or attached to it : *to hang a picture on a wall.* 2. **près de, au bord de, sur** ▸ located at or near : *a house on the beach.* 3. **sur, en** ▸ having to do with the thing or condition stated : *a book on Africa; a dress that is on sale.* ▲ ADVERB. 1. **sur** ▸ so as to be touching or covering : *Heather put her raincoat on.* 2. **allumé (-ée), en marche** ▸ so as to be in use or operation : *Turn the TV on.* **Note.** Also used as an ADJECTIVE: *All the lights were on when we got home.* ✐ p. 419.

once [wuns] ADVERB. 1. **une fois** ▸ one time : *That magazine comes out once a month.* 2. **autrefois, jadis** ▸ at a certain time in the past, but no longer : *They lived in that house once.* ▲ CONJUNCTION. **quand, une fois que** ▸ as soon as; whenever : *That will be a beautiful building*

✍ Writing Tips

On, onto, on to

When you're confused about whether to use **on**, **onto** *or* **on to**, *remember,*

- **on** *means "on top of,"*
- **onto** *means "to a position on."*
- *You use* **on to** *only when the word* **on** *is an adverb, closely connected to the verb, and the word* **to** *is a preposition that forms part of the phrase following the verb.*
- *You can see how these meanings differ in the following sentences :*

  She's walking **on** *the boat. (Meaning "she's taking a stroll on a boat.")*

  She's walking **onto** *the boat. (Meaning "she's boarding the boat.")*

  She's walking **on to** *the bow of the boat. (Meaning "she is continuing to walk, heading toward the bow.")*

✍ Writing Tips

Onomatopoeia

- *Onomatopoeia is a word used to describe the effect of such words as buzz, click, bang, hiss, and screech. When these words are spoken out loud they sound like the sounds they are supposed to represent.*
- *Onomatopoeia is a device that writers, especially poets, often use to make their writing more effective by creating sharper images for the reader.*
- *Which of the following sentences does the best job of letting you hear the machine at work ?*

  The cranks and cogs whirred and clicked in time with the ticking clock.

  The cranks and cogs turned just as the hands of the clock did.

once it is finished. ▲ NOUN. **(juste) pour une fois** ▸ one single time : *I'll help just this once.*

once in a while de temps en temps, de temps à autre ▸ now and then.

at once a. immédiatement, tout de suite, sur-le-champ ▸ immediately. b. **en même temps, à la fois** ▸ at the same time.

one [wun] NOUN, ones. 1. **un** ▸ the number that is larger than zero and less than two ; 1. 2. **un (une)** ▸ a single person or thing. ▲ ADJECTIVE. **un (une)** ▸ being a single person or thing : *one table and four chairs.* ▲ PRONOUN. 1. **un (une)** ▸ a particular person or thing : *One of the glasses is cracked.* 2. **on** ▸ any person ; anyone : *That wasn't much of a meal, but one can hardly expect great food at those prices.*

O-nei-da [oh-NY-dah] NOUN, Oneida or Oneidas. 1. **Oneida** ▸ an Aboriginal people who originally lived only in central New York State but who now also live in Ontario and in Wisconsin. The Oneida are members of the Six Nations Iroquois Confederacy. 2. **oneida** ▸ the Iroquoian language of the Oneida.

on-ion [UN-yun] NOUN, onions. **oignon** ▸ a vegetable that is used in cooking, having a sharp taste and a strong smell. Onions grow as bulbs below the surface of the ground, just above the plant's roots.

on-line [ON-LINE] ADJECTIVE. (often online) of computers, a. **en ligne, en direct, connecté (-ée)** ▸ being connected directly with a central computer and ready to operate. b. **branché (-ée)** ▸ being connected to the Internet.

on-ly [OHN-lee] ADJECTIVE. 1. **seul (seule), unique** ▸ without any others of the same kind or type ; alone : *An only child doesn't have any brothers or sisters.* 2. **seul (seule)** ▸ finest ; best : *It's the only perfume for me.* ▲ ADVERB. 1. **seul (seule), rien que** ▸ without anyone or anything else : *Only 10 people showed up for the movie.* 2. **seulement, à peine** ▸ merely ; just : *It's only 2:00.* ▲ CONJUNCTION. **mais** ▸ but, except that : *I'd go to the library, only I'm too tired.* SYN: just, barely, solely, hardly, merely, simply.

on-o-mat-o-poe-ia [ON-uh-MAT-uh-poe uh] ADJECTIVE. 1. **onomatopée** ▸ the forming of a word by imitating the sound associated with the action or thing named — for example, the *buzz* of a bee. 2. **onomatopée** ▸ the use of such words in poetry. ✍ **p. 419.**

On-on-da-ga [ON-un-DOG-uh *or* ON-un-DAG-uh] NOUN. 1. **Onondaga** ▸ an Aboriginal people that live in parts of southeast Ontario and west-central New York State. The Onondaga are members of the Six Nations Iroquois Confederacy. 2. **onondaga** ▸ the Iroquoian language of the Onondaga.

on-to [ON-too] PREPOSITION. **sur** ▸ to a position on or upon : *The skater stepped onto the ice.* ✍ **p. 419.**

on-ward [ON-wurd] ADVERB ; ADJECTIVE. (also onwards) **depuis, à partir de** ▸ in or to a forward direction or position : *From that day onward, they were friends.*

o-paque [OH-pake] ADJECTIVE. **opaque** ▸ not allowing light to pass through ; not transparent ; cloudy-looking : *opaque paper.*

o·pen [OH-pun] ADJECTIVE. **1. ouvert (-erte)** ▸ allowing things to pass through; not shut : *an open window.* **2. ouvert (-erte)** ▸ not covered, sealed, fastened, and so on : *an open can of pop.* **3. à la campagne, en plein champ** ▸ having a clear space; not closed in : *open country.* **4. ouvert (-erte)** ▸ ready for business; doing business : *That store is open from 9:00 to 5:00.* ▲ VERB, opened, opening. **1. ouvrir** ▸ to make or become open. **2. commencer par, débuter** ▸ to begin; start : *The movie opens with a view of mountain scenery.* ▲ NOUN. the open. **en plein champ** ▸ *Deer usually live in the woods but can also be seen in the open.* ∎ **openness,** NOUN. ▸ ouverture, franchise. ∎ **openly,** ADVERB. ▸ ouvertement ▸ so as to be seen or noticed : *The students were staring openly at the new boy.* SYN: unlocked, exposed, uncovered. ✐ **p. 420.**

o·pen·ing [OH-pun-ing] NOUN, openings. **1. ouverture, brèche** ▸ an open space; a hole; a gap. **2. poste vacant** ▸ a job or position that is available or not yet filled : *There are several openings for salespeople.* **3. première** ▸ the beginning of something : *the opening of a new play.*

op·er·a [OP-uh-ruh *or* OP-ruh] NOUN, operas. **opéra** ▸ a musical play in which all or most of the characters' lines are sung rather than spoken. **Note.** Something that has to do with opera is operatic.

op·er·ate [OP-uh-RATE] VERB, operated, operating. **1. fonctionner** ▸ to run or work in a certain way : *These machines can operate without people around to run them.* **2. exploiter, gérer** ▸ to be in control of the way something runs or functions : *She operates a restaurant on Main St.* **3. opérer** ▸ to perform surgery or a medical procedure : *Dr. Thuc operated on Laura's knee.*

op·er·a·tion [OP-uh-RAY-shun] NOUN, operations. **1. fonctionnement** ▸ the act or fact of working or running something : *This booklet explains the operation of the computer.* **2. opération** ▸ treating by surgery to take out a diseased part or correct some harmful condition. **3. opération** ▸ an organized activity for a certain purpose : *a rescue operation.* **4. opération** ▸ a mathematical process such as addition or multiplication.

op·er·a·tor [OP-uh-RAY-tur *or* OP-ur-ay-tur] NOUN, operators. **1. téléphoniste, standardiste** ▸ a person who works for a telephone company giving information and assistance to customers. **2. opérateur (-trice)** ▸ any person who operates a machine, computer, switchboard, and so on.

o·pin·ion [uh-PIN-yun *or* oh-PIN-yun] NOUN, opinions. **1. opinion, avis** ▸ information that is based on what a person believes, rather than on what can be shown to be true or real : *It's a fact that Toronto has more people than any other Canadian city; it's an opinion that Toronto has fewer good restaurants than Montreal does.* **2. opinion** ▸ a particular idea or judgment formed in this way; what a person thinks about something : *He has a high opinion of her singing ability.* **3. avis** ▸ the judgment of an expert, formed after careful thought : *Dr. Vadin advised her to get a second opinion.* SYN: view, conviction, theory, belief, judgment.

o·pos·sum [uh-POS-um] NOUN, opossums *or* opossum. (also possum) **opossum** ▸ a small, four-legged animal that lives in trees and carries its young in a special pouch. When it becomes very frightened, it sometimes lies completely still and appears to be dead.

op·po·nent [uh-POH-nunt] NOUN, opponents. **adversaire, concurrent (-ente), rival (-ale, -aux)** ▸ a person or group on the opposite side in a contest or struggle; someone who is against another : *Marie finished the race seconds before her opponent did.* SYN: rival, foe, competitor, enemy, antagonist.

op·por·tu·ni·ty [OP-ur-TOO-nuh-tee] NOUN, opportunities. **occasion** ▸ a favourable time or situation; a good chance : *He is waiting for an opportunity to talk to his boss about his new idea.* SYN: chance, occasion, time, opening.

op·pose [uh-POZE] VERB, opposed, opposing. **s'opposer à, faire opposition à** ▸ to be against; act or go against; resist : *The residents opposed the building of a hydro plant in their neighbourhood.* SYN: resist, fight, dispute, conflict with.

op·po·site [OP-uh-zit] NOUN, opposites. **contraire** ▸ something that is completely different from another thing : *The opposite of "fast" is "slow."* ▲ ADJECTIVE. **1. opposé (-ée)** ▸ completely different : *the opposite direction.* **2. en face de** ▸

🖉 **Word Builder**

Open up *can mean to open up a way for development: The discovery will open up mining in the North. Or,* ***open up*** *can mean to talk freely: She is shy in large groups and it takes some time before she opens up. If a person* ***opens their eyes*** *to something, they are becoming aware of the truth a situation: Terry opened his eyes to the fact he would not pass the test if he doesn't study. If something is* ***open and shut,*** *it is straight forward or not complicated: The police had an open-and-shut case against the thief caught in the act.*

across from; facing : *The Yakovs live opposite us on the other side of the street.*

op-po-si-tion [OP-uh-ZISH-un] NOUN. **1. opposition, désaccord ▶** the act or fact of opposing; being against : *The mayor announced her opposition to the new tax plan.* **2. opposition, désapprobation ▶** something that is an opposing obstacle : *The plan met with strong opposition from my father.* **3.** (often the Opposition) **opposition ▶** a political party opposed to the party in power in government.

op-ti-cal [OP-tik-ul] ADJECTIVE. **(d') optique ▶** of or having to do with sight : *An optical illusion occurs when a person seems to see something that is not there.*

op-ti-mis-tic [OP-tuh-MIS-tik] ADJECTIVE. **optimiste ▶** expecting things to turn out well; looking at the good side of a situation rather than the bad side : *Even when he was very sick, Mats remained optimistic and spoke of what he would do when he got better.* **Note.** This kind of hopeful, cheerful attitude is known as optimism, and a person who has it is called an optimist. SYN: positive, hopeful, happy, cheerful.

op-tion [OP-shun] NOUN, options. **1. option, choix ▶** the right or freedom to choose. **2. option ▶** choice; what is chosen : *Air conditioning and cassette players are popular options in a car.* ■ **optional,** ADJECTIVE. ▶ **facultatif (-ive), en option, optionnel (-elle).**

op-tom-e-trist [OP-tum-uh-trist] NOUN, optometrists. **optométriste ▶** a person trained and licensed to examine people's eyes and to prescribe eyeglasses or contact lenses to correct their eyesight.

or [ore] CONJUNCTION. **1. ou ▶** the word *or* is used to show a choice in the following ways : a. one of a group of things : *Do you want water, milk, or juice?* b. the second of only two things, with the word "either" or "whether" coming before the first : *I want either a mystery or an adventure story to read.* **2. sinon, autrement ▶** otherwise : *Close the door or the dog will get out.*

o-ral [OR-ul] ADJECTIVE. **1. oral (-ale, -aux), verbal (-ale, -aux) ▶** spoken rather than written : *I have to give an oral report to the class.* **2. buccal (-ale, -aux) ▶** having to do with the mouth : *A dentist who operates on someone's teeth or jaw is an oral surgeon.* ■ **orally,** ADVERB. ▶ **oralement, verbalement.**

or-ange [OR-inj] NOUN, oranges. **1. orange ▶** a round fruit with a thick reddish-yellow skin and sweet, juicy pulp. Oranges are citrus fruits related to lemons, limes, and grapefruits. **2. orangé, orange ▶** the colour that is like this fruit.

o-rang-u-tan [oh-RANG-uh-tan *or* uh-RANG-uh-tan] NOUN, orangutans. (also orangoutang) **orangoutang ▶** a large ape that lives in trees on some islands of southern Asia. Orangutans have long arms, short legs, and shaggy reddish-brown hair.

Note. The word *orangutan* means "man of the woods" in Malaysian.

or-bit [OR-bit] NOUN, orbits. **1. orbite ▶** the path of a heavenly body as it moves in a circle around another body in space : *The moon is in an orbit around the earth.* **2. orbite ▶** the path of a satellite or spacecraft around the earth. ▲ VERB, orbited, orbiting. **graviter autour de, être en orbite autour de ▶** to move in an orbit around the earth or another body in space.

or-chard [OR-churd] NOUN, orchards. **1. verger ▶** an area of land where fruit trees are grown. **2. arbres fruitiers ▶** the trees in this area.

or-ches-tra [OR-kus-truh] NOUN, orchestras. **1. orchestre ▶** a group of musicians who play various instruments under the direction of a leader called a conductor. **2. instruments d'orchestre ▶** the musical instruments that are played by such a group. **3. fosse d'orchestre, fauteuil d'orchestre ▶** the place just in front of and below the stage where the musicians sit to play in a theatre, or the seats near this area.

orchestrate, VERB, orchestrated, orchestrating. **orchestrer ▶** to compose and arrange music for performance by an orchestra.

or-deal [or-DEEL *or* OR-deel] NOUN, ordeals. **épreuve, supplice ▶** a very difficult or painful test or experience : *It's an ordeal taking my cat to the vet.*

or-der [OR-dur] NOUN, orders. **1. ordre ▶** a certain way in which things are placed in relation to each other : *Words in a dictionary are listed in alphabetical order.* **2. ordre, consigne ▶** a command or direction given to a person to do something or act in a certain way. **3. ordre ▶** a situation in which things are arranged or done in the proper way : *to put a room in order.* **4. commande ▶** a serving of food in a restaurant. **5. commande ▶** a request to buy, sell, or supply goods in business : *The computer company just got a large order from the government.* ▲ VERB, ordered, ordering. **1. ordonner, commander ▶** to tell someone to do something; give a command. **2. commander ▶** to ask for; request : *Mom called the restaurant and ordered a pizza.* SYN: command, direct. ✐ **p. 422.**

in order a. **en ordre ▶** in its proper place : *All the rooms are in order.* b. **en bon état ▶** working properly : *The car is in order now.*

in order to afin de, pour ▶ for the purpose of : *She studied in order to get good grades.*

or-der-ly [OR-dur-lee] ADJECTIVE. **1. ordonné (-ée) ▶** placed in a neat way; in order; tidy : *She kept her clothes arranged in very orderly rows in her closet.* **2. discipliné (-ée), docile ▶** not causing trouble or making noise : *An orderly crowd stood outside the store waiting for it to open.* ▲ NOUN, orderlies. **préposé (-ée) aux soins ▶** a

---

Word Builder

In short order means quickly: *The mechanic told Mom he would fix the car in short order.* When something is *made to order*, it is made to fit a particular person: *Henri's new suit was made to order.* The expression *out of order* has several different meanings. It can mean in the wrong position: *The pages are be out of order.* The phrase also means not working properly: *A stamp machine is out of order.* *Out of order* may mean not according to the rules: *During our discussion, Tarissa often spoke out of order.*

---

worker whose job is to keep things in order, as in a hospital.

ordinal number [OR-duh-nul] **nombre ordinal** ▶ a number that shows where (what order) something comes in a series. The sentence *Jenny and Nicole were fourth and fifth in line at the water fountain* contains two ordinal numbers: *fourth* and *fifth*. **Note.** See cardinal number.

or·di·nar·i·ly [OR-duh-NARE-uh-lee] ADVERB. **ordinairement, habituellement, normalement** ▶ in most cases; normally; usually: *Ordinarily he orders fries with his burger.*

or·di·nar·y [OR-duh-NARE-ee] ADJECTIVE. **ordinaire, banal (-ale, -als), commun (-une)** ▶ being as it usually is or is expected to be; normal; common: *It is an ordinary house.* ✐ **p. 129.**

ore [ore] NOUN. **ores. minerai** ▶ any rock or mineral that contains a certain amount of a valuable metal, such as iron.

or·gan [OR-gun] NOUN. **organs. 1. orgue(s)** ▶ a musical instrument played by pressing keys or pedals to blow air through pipes of varying sizes to produce different notes. **Note.** A person who plays this instrument is called an **organist.** **2. organe** ▶ a part of an animal or plant that does a particular job. The heart, eyes, lungs, and stomach are organs in the human body. 📖 **p. 1003.** 👁 **p. 403.**

or·gan·ic [or-GAN-ik] ADJECTIVE. **1. organique** ▶ having to do with one or more of the organs of the body. **2. organique** ▶ having to do with living things, as opposed to artificial products: *Cover the plant's roots with organic materials such as wood chips, dead leaves, or grass.* **3. biologique** ▶ of food, grown without artificial fertilizers or pest controls: *organic vegetables.*

or·gan·ism [OR-guh-NIZ-um or OR-gan-izm] NOUN. **organisms. organisme** ▶ any living animal or plant.

or·gan·i·za·tion [OR-guh-nuh-ZAY-shun or or-guh-ny-ZAY-shun] NOUN. **organizations. 1. organisation, organisme, association** ▶ a group of people who are joined together for some purpose: *a parent–teacher organization at a school.* **2. organisation** ▶ the act or fact of organizing; putting things together according to a system.

or·gan·ize [OR-gun-IZE] VERB. **organized, organizing. 1. organiser, agencer, structurer** ▶ to arrange or place things according to some plan or system. **2. organiser** ▶ to bring people together into a group: *They organized a search party to find the missing camper.* SYN: arrange, categorize, sort, group.

o·ri·ent [OR-ee-ent] VERB. **oriented, orienting. 1. (s') orienter** ▶ to place or locate in a certain position; a direction: *Jeremy looked at his compass to orient himself before setting out across the fields.* **2. (se) familiariser** ▶ to make or become familiar with a new situation. ▪ **orientation,** NOUN: ▶ **accueil.** *New students go through orientation at the beginning of the school year.*

or·i·gin [OR-uh-jin] NOUN. **origins. origine, source** ▶ the point from which something comes; the cause, beginning, or source.

o·rig·i·nal [uh-RIJ-uh-nul] ADJECTIVE. **1. original (-ale, -aux), innovateur (-trice)** ▶ not in being before; not copied; completely new: *an original idea.* **2. premier (-ière), d'origine** ▶ having to do with the origin or beginning; earliest; first: *The original Bluenose was built in 1921.* **Note.** The fact of being original is originality: *Sandy's science project showed a lot of originality.* ▲ NOUN, originals. **original (-aux)** ▶ something that is not a copy or imitation.

o·rig·i·nal·ly [uh-RIJ-uh-nul-ee] ADVERB. **à l'origine, au départ, originalement** ▶ at first; from the start.

o·rig·i·nate [uh-RIJ-uh-NATE] VERB. **originated, originating. 1. donner naissance à, prendre naissance** ▶ to bring into being; create; invent: **2. provenir** ▶ to start; begin: *She got on the plane in Ottawa, but the flight originated in Toronto.*

or·na·ment [OR-nuh-munt] NOUN. **ornaments. décoration, ornement** ▶ something that is added to give beauty; something pretty; a decoration. ▲ VERB, ornamented, ornamenting. **décorer, orner** ▶ to decorate with ornaments; add beauty to. ▪ **ornamental,** ADJECTIVE: ▶ **ornemental (-ale, -aux), décoratif (-ive).** *decorative ornamental flowers.*

or·phan [OR-fun] NOUN. **orphans. orphelin** ▶ a child whose parents are dead. **Note.** An orphanage is a home that takes care of a number of orphans.

or-tho-dox [OR-thuh-doks] ADJECTIVE. **1. traditionnel (-elle), orthodoxe** ▸ following the usual or accepted way; typical; customary : *The orthodox method of setting a table is to put the forks on the left and the knives and spoons on the right of the plate.* **2. orthodoxe** ▸ having or following generally accepted beliefs, especially in religion. SYN: usual, traditional, customary, accepted.

os-mo-sis [oz-MOE-sis *or* os-MOE-sis] NOUN. **osmose** ▸ the movement of fluid through a membrane until it becomes mixed with fluid on the other side of that membrane. Osmosis allows fluid to move through cell walls in the human body.

os-trich [OS-trich] NOUN, ostriches. **autruche** ▸ a very large African bird that has long legs and a long neck. An ostrich cannot fly, but it can run very fast. Ostriches are the largest of all living birds.

oth-er [UTH-ur] ADJECTIVE, others. **1. autre** ▸ being the one remaining of two or more; extra : *Pia's gone, but the other girls are here.* **2. autre** ▸ not the same as was already mentioned; not this one or ones; another; alternative : *Call again some other day.* **3. autre** ▸ additional; extra : *I have no other hats.* ▲ PRONOUN. **autre** ▸ another person or thing : *Rashid got there at 5:00, but the others didn't arrive until 6:00.* 🖉 **p. 423.**

every other tous les deuxièmes ▸ every second one : *His column appears in the paper every other morning.*

oth-er-wise [UTH-ur-wize] ADVERB. **1. mais, néanmoins** ▸ other than that; in a different way or a different condition : *"They watched as, scarred but otherwise unharmed, the iceberg sailed on."* (Eve Bunting) **2. sinon, autrement** ▸ or else : *We'd better get to work; otherwise, we'll never finish.*

ot-ter [OT-ur] NOUN, otters or otter. **loutre** ▸ a small animal that is related to the weasel, with a long, slender body, webbed feet, and thick brown fur. Otters live in or near the water. 👁 **p. 110.**

ouch [owch] INTERJECTION. **aïe!** ▸ a word used to express sudden pain.

ought [ot] ▲ VERB. **devoir** ▸ used with other verbs to show **1.** that something is right or should be done : *I ought to finish my homework.* **2.** that something can be expected to happen : *They ought to be here any minute now.* SYN: should, must, need to, have to.

ounce [owns] NOUN, ounces. **1. once** ▸ a unit for measuring weight in the imperial system equal to about 28 grams. **2. once** ▸ a unit of measure for liquids, equal to about 28 millilitres. **3. once, gramme** ▸ a little bit : *I didn't have an ounce of strength left after the soccer game was over.*

our [owr] PRONOUN. **notre (nos)** ▸ the pronoun we when used as a possessive; belonging to us : *My brother and I took our dog to the park.*

ours [owrz] PRONOUN. **le nôtre (la nôtre, les nôtres)** ▸ the pronoun we when used as a possessive after a verb; the one or ones that belong to us or have to do with us : *Both cars are the same make, but ours is newer.*

our-selves [owr-SELVZ] PRONOUN. **1. nous** ▸ our own selves : *We scared ourselves by telling ghost stories.* **2. nous-mêmes** ▸ our usual or normal selves : *His column appears in the paper.* **3. nous-mêmes** ▸ a stronger form of we or us used : *We painted the room ourselves.*

out [owt] ADVERB. **1. hors** ▸ away from the inside : *The water rushed out of the hole.* **2. en dehors de, sortir** ▸ away from the usual place : *The doctor has stepped out for a minute.* **3. éteindre** ▸ so as to be at an end : *to put out a fire.* **4. apparaître** ▸ so as to be seen or known : *The sun came out from behind a cloud.* **5. distribuer** ▸ so as to be available for use : *to give out free tickets.* ▲ ADJECTIVE. **1. hors de question** ▸ not a choice; not possible : *Going to the beach this weekend is out unless I can get all my homework done.* **2. démodé (-ée)** ▸ not in style; no longer popular : *Wide collars are out this year.* **3. retiré (-ée)** ▸ in baseball, no longer at bat and not safely on base.

out-come [OWT-kum] NOUN, outcomes. **résultat, issue, conclusion** ▸ the way something turns out; the end or result : *We waited to hear the outcome of the vote.* SYN: end, result, conclusion, consequence.

out-door [OWT-dor] ADJECTIVE. **de plein air** ▸ done or used in the open, rather than in a house or building : *Fishing and hiking are outdoor sports.* ◼ **outdoors,** ADVERB. **en plein air,**

🔧 **Word Builder**

Other can mean *left over*, *extra*, or *not the same as*. Many expressions have *other* in them. *Every other* means on alternate or every second time : *She goes to the skating rink every other day.* *The other day* means recent or not long ago : *I saw Preman just the other day and now you tell me he's moved to Sydney.* *None other than* means no one else but : *None other than the president presented the award.*

---

dehors ▸ in or into the open air : *playing outdoors.*

out·er [OW-tur] ADJECTIVE. **extérieur (-ieure)** ▸ on the outside; exterior; farther out.

outer space 1. **espace** ▸ space immediately beyond the air around the earth. 2. **espace** ▸ space between the planets and between the stars.

out·fit [OWT-FIT] NOUN, outfits. 1. **tenue** ▸ the clothing or equipment needed for some work or activity : *an outfit for camping; an exercise outfit.* 2. **brigade** ▸ a group of people who work together, especially in the military : *My dad and Mrs. Lewis were in the same outfit in the armed forces.* ▲ VERB, outfitted, outfitting. **équiper** ▸ to provide the necessary clothing or equipment for some work or activity. ⬧ p. 1012.

out·go·ing [OWT-GO-ing] ADJECTIVE. 1. **sortant (-ante), en partance** ▸ going out; departing; leaving. 2. **sociable, aimable** ▸ friendly and talkative.

out·let [OWT-LET *or* OWT-let] NOUN, outlets. 1. **déversoir** ▸ a place for something to get out; an opening or exit : *the outlet of a lake.* 2. **exutoire** ▸ a way of expressing or releasing something : *Playing basketball is a good outlet for excess energy.* 3. **prise de courant** ▸ a place in a wall where an electric device can be plugged in.

out·line [OUT-LINE] NOUN, outlines. 1. **contour, profil, silhouette** ▸ a line that marks the outer edge or boundary of something and shows its shape : *The outline of Italy looks like a boot.* 2. **esquisse** ▸ a drawing that shows only the outer edge of something. 3. **aperçu, grandes lignes** ▸ a short list or plan that gives the main points of a longer report, speech, article, or the like : *"For my writing, I do outlines, as detailed as possible, whether for fiction or non-fiction."* (Paul Yee) ▲ VERB, outlined, outlining. 1. **donner un aperçu, exposer les grandes lignes** ▸ to make or give an outline : *At the meeting, the boss will outline his plan to open a new office.* 2. **esquisser** ▸ to show something in outline. ⬧ p. 424.

out·look [OWT-LOOK] NOUN, outlooks. 1. **vue** ▸ what can be seen from a place; a view. 2. **point de vue** ▸ a way of thinking or feeling about things : *She's a happy person and has a cheerful outlook on life.* 3. **perspectives** ▸ what is likely to happen in the future; prospect. SYN : view, attitude, position.

out·put [OUT-PUT] NOUN. 1. **production** ▸ the amount of something made or done : *The auto factory has an output of 1000 cars a day.* 2. **rendement** ▸ the act of putting forth something : *the output of energy from a generator.* 3. **données de sortie** ▸ any information that comes out of a computer and can be understood by the user. SYN : production, proceeds, crop, harvest, yield.

✍ Writing Tips

Outlines

• *Whenever you write a report or story, develop an **outline** first. An outline uses one or two words to describe each section of a report or the plotline of a story. Each subsection can also be described with a few words.*

• *Outlines can help you organize and sequence your ideas. The following outline shows how a short story is going to be organized.*

Spaceship to Venus
1. Boarding the Ship
    A.   Saying goodbye to friends
    B.   Settling in
    C.   Getting ready for takeoff
2. Taking Off!
3. In Space
    A.   Zero gravity
    B.   Space food
    C.   Space games
4. Landing on Venus

out·rage [OWT-RAJE] NOUN, outrages. 1. **outrage** ▸ an action that is very cruel or wrong and that causes great harm : *The mindless destruction of the environment is an outrage.* 2. **indignation** ▸ angry feelings caused by an injury or insult : *Newspapers all over the world expressed outrage over the hijacking of the plane.* ▲ VERB, outraged, outraging. **outrager, insulter** ▸ to make very angry; offend greatly; insult.

out·ra·geous [owt-RAY-jus] ADJECTIVE. 1. **atroce, monstrueux (-euse), effroyable** ▸ very cruel or wrong : *an outrageous crime.* 2. **scandaleux (-euse)** ▸ very bad or insulting; shocking : *You want $50 for that hat? That's outrageous!* ▪ **outrageously,** ADVERB. ▸ outrageusement.

out·right [OWT-RITE] ADJECTIVE. 1. **complet (-ète), total (-ale, -aux)** ▸ completely; totally : *an outright lie.* ▲ ADVERB. 2. **complètement, entièrement** ▸ completely; entirely : *I now own my car outright; I've finished paying for it.* 2. **franchement, carrément, sincèrement** ▸ directly; honestly : *She told me about the problem outright.*

out·side [OUT-SIDE] NOUN, outsides. **extérieur (-eure)** ▸ the opposite of inside; the outer side, surface, or part : *Meg put a big "Keep Out!" sign on the outside of her bedroom door.* ▲ ADVERB. **dehors, à l'extérieur** ▸ on or to the outside; outdoors : *Let's go outside and have a game of catch.* ▲ PREPOSITION. **de** ▸ to the outer side of :

She lives about 15 km outside Vancouver. ▲ ADJECTIVE. **1. extérieur (-eure)** ▶ on, to, or from the outside : *the outside walls of a house.* **2. très faible** ▶ very small; not likely; slight : *We've got only an outside chance of winning the game.* **Note.** A person who does not belong to a certain group is an **outsider.**

out·skirts [OWT-SKURTS] PLURAL NOUN. **périphérie, banlieue** ▶ the edge or outer area of a town or other place : *This bus runs all the way to the outskirts of the city.*

out·stand·ing [owt-STAN-ding] ADJECTIVE. **1. exceptionnel (-elle), remarquable, extraordinaire** ▶ better than others; standing out from the rest : *Larry won an award as the outstanding student in his class.* **2. impayé (-ée)** ▶ not paid or settled : *There is still $2,000 outstanding on the loan she took out to buy that car.* ■ **outstandingly,** ADVERB. ▶ remarquablement, exceptionnellement. 🖉 p. 272.

out·ward [OWT-wurd] ADJECTIVE. **1. vers l'extérieur** ▶ toward the outside : *an outward movement.* **2. extérieur (-eure), apparent (-ente)** ▶ that is seen; outer : *He gave an outward appearance of being calm, even though he was nervous inside.* ▲ ADVERB. (also **outwards**) toward the outside : *Fire exit doors in a public place always open outward.* ■ **outwardly,** ADVERB. ▶ vers l'extérieur, extérieurement, en apparence.

o·val [OH-vul] ADJECTIVE. **ovale** ▶ shaped like an egg : *Auto races sometimes take place on an oval track.* ▲ NOUN. **ovals. ovale** ▶ something that has an oval shape.

ov·en [UV-un] NOUN. **ovens. 1. four** ▶ a kitchen appliance with an enclosed space that can be heated in order to cook food inside it. **2. four** ▶ any similar device used to heat or dry things : *a pottery oven.*

o·ver [OH-vur] PREPOSITION. **1. au-dessus** ▶ higher than and not touching; above : *Hang the picture over the fireplace.* **2. par-dessus** ▶ from one side to the other of : *That bridge goes over the widest part of the river.* **3. par-dessus** ▶ on or across the surface of; covering : *She put on a jacket over her sweater.* **4. plus de** ▶ higher in amount or position; more than : *Don't spend over $10 on the birthday present.* **5. pendant** ▶ during the time of : *He's visiting his family over summer vacation.* **6. à propos de** ▶ about; concerning : *You really shouldn't be so upset over such a little thing.* ▲ ADVERB. **1. faire tomber** ▶ down from an upright position : *The dog knocked the lamp over.* **2. chez, rendre visite** ▶ to another place or person : *Jerry came over to see me today.* **3. encore** ▶ another time; again : *She listened to her favourite song over and over.* ▲ ADJECTIVE. **fini (-ie)** ▶ at an end; finished : *We left as soon as the movie was over.*

o·ver·alls [OH-vur-OLZ] PLURAL NOUN. **salopette** ▶ sturdy, loose-fitting work trousers with a top piece that covers the chest, held up by straps that go over the shoulders.

o·ver·board [OH-vur-BORD] ADVERB. **par-dessus bord** ▶ over the side of a ship or boat into the water : *A passenger fell overboard, but the crew rescued him.*

go overboard aller trop loin, s'emballer ▶ to go too far; become too intense or excited about something.

o·ver·coat [OH-vur-KOTE] NOUN. **overcoats. pardessus, paletot** ▶ a long, heavy coat worn over other clothes for warmth.

o·ver·come [OH-vur-KUM] VERB, **overcame, overcome, overcoming. 1. surmonter, vaincre, triompher** ▶ to get the better of; defeat. **2. affaiblir, accabler** ▶ to make helpless or weak : *The firefighter was overcome by smoke from the fire.* SYN: upset, overpower, defeat, conquer.

o·ver·due [OH-vur-DO] ADJECTIVE. **en retard** ▶ delayed past the usual or proper time; not done or paid at the time due : *The fine for overdue library books is 10 cents a day for each book.*

o·ver·flow [OH-vur-FLO] VERB, **overflowed, overflowing. 1. déborder** ▶ to flow over the top or beyond the usual limits; flood : *Before the Aswan Dam was built, the Nile River overflowed its banks almost every year.* **2. déborder** ▶ to spill or spread over; be very full or too full : *The bookshelves in the den were overflowing with books.* ▲ NOUN. **overflows. débordement** ▶ something that flows over.

o·ver·head [OH-vur-HED] ADVERB; ADJECTIVE. **au-dessus de la tête** ▶ above the head : *"He sees an eagle circling high overhead."* (Ann Blades) ▲ NOUN. **overhead. frais généraux** ▶ the general costs of running a business, such as rent, taxes, repairs, heat, and electricity.

o·ver·joyed [OH-vur-JOYD] ADJECTIVE. **enchanté (-ée), ravi (-ie)** ▶ filled with joy; delighted.

o·ver·load [OH-vur-LODE] VERB, **overloaded, overloading. surcharger** ▶ to put too much of a load on : *to overload a moving truck with furniture.* ▲ NOUN. **overloads.** *Too many electrical appliances working at once can put an overload on a power system.*

o·ver·look [OH-vur-LOOK] VERB, **overlooked, overlooking. 1. omettre, oublier, négliger** ▶ to fail to see or notice; miss : *The detective Sherlock Holmes was known for finding important clues that others had overlooked.* **2. passer sur, fermer les yeux** ▶ to choose not to see or pay attention to; ignore; excuse : *Klaus overlooked Mike's nasty remark because he was usually very polite.* **3. donner sur, avoir vue sur** ▶ to have a view of from a higher place : *Your room overlooks the water.*

o·ver·night [OH-vur-NITE] ADVERB; ADJECTIVE.
1. pendant la nuit ▸ during or through the
night : *Kani is staying overnight at her friend
Katie's house.* **2. du jour au lendemain ▸** very
quickly; suddenly : *I didn't learn to play guitar
overnight; it took years of practice.*

o·ver·seas [OH-vur-SEEZ] ADVERB. **outre-mer
▸** across the sea; abroad : *He's going to join
CUSO and hopes to serve somewhere overseas.* ▲ ADJECTIVE. **outre-mer ▸** of, to, or from
countries across the sea : *an overseas flight.*

o·ver·shoe [OH-vur-SHOO] NOUN, **overshoes.
couvre-chaussures ▸** a waterproof shoe or boot
that is worn over another shoe to keep the foot
dry : *"They saw the worn overshoes, the home-
knit woollen cap, the hands twisting anxiously
inside the grey mittens."* (Thomas H. Raddall)

o·ver·sight [OH-vur-SITE] NOUN. **oubli,
omission, inattention ▸** a careless mistake that
is not made on purpose.

o·ver·take [OH-vur-TAKE] VERB, **overtook, over-
taken, overtaking. 1. dépasser ▸** to catch up
with : *The bus quickly overtook and passed the
car.* **2. surprendre ▸** to come upon suddenly :
*A snowstorm overtook her as she was driving
home.*

o·ver·time [OH-vur-TIME] NOUN, **overtimes.
1. heures supplémentaires ▸** extra time worked
beyond regular working hours, or the pay for this
time. **Note.** Also used as an ADJECTIVE or ADVERB:
overtime pay; to work three hours overtime.
2. prolongation ▸ in sports, an extra amount of
playing time to decide the winner of a game that
has ended in a tie.

o·ver·whelm [OH-vur-WELM] VERB, **overwhelmed, overwhelming. accabler, submerger,
écraser ▸** to overcome completely; overpower;
crush : *"At first Icarus stayed close behind his
father, but soon he was overwhelmed with the
joy of flying."* (Marcia Williams)

owe [oh] VERB, **owed, owing. 1. devoir ▸** to have
to pay; be required to pay : *I owe Nancy $5 that
I borrowed from her.* **2. devoir ▸** to have or feel
the need to give or do : *He owes me an apology
for wrecking my bike.*

owing to en raison de, à cause de ▸ because
of : *Ruth missed her flight owing to the traffic
on the way to the airport.*

owl [owl] NOUN, **owls. hibou (-oux) ▸** a bird with a
large round head, large eyes, and a short hooked
bill. Owls hunt at night for mice, frogs, snakes,
and insects. The **great horned owl** and the
snowy owl are two common North American
owls. ■ **owlish**, ADJECTIVE. ▸ **comme un hibou,
qui a l'air d'un hibou.** ☞ **p. 109.**

own [own] ADJECTIVE. **propre ▸** of or belonging to
oneself or itself : *Roger fixed his own breakfast.*
▲ VERB, **owned, owning. 1. posséder ▸**
▸ to have as belonging to one; possess : *to own
a car; to own a house.* **Note.** A person who

owns something is an **owner.** The condition of
owning something is **ownership. 2. avouer,
confesser ▸** to admit; confess : *I owned up to
my mistake.* ✐ **p. 454.**

ox [oks] NOUN, **oxen. bœuf ▸** the full-grown male
of cattle. Oxen are used as work animals or
eaten for beef.

ox·y·gen [OK-suh-jin] NOUN. **oxygène ▸** a gas that
has no colour, taste, or smell. Oxygen is the most
common chemical. Water is mostly oxygen, and
the air is about one-fifth oxygen. Plants, animals,
and people all need oxygen to live.

oys·ter [OYS-tur] NOUN, **oysters. huître ▸** a sea animal that has a soft body inside a rough shell
with two hinged parts. Oysters are found in
warm shallow water along coasts. Many kinds of
oysters are eaten as food; some form pearls
inside their shells.

owl

snowy owl

owls

pigeon

p, P [pee] NOUN, p's, P's. **p, P ▶** the 16th letter of the English alphabet.

pace [pace] NOUN, paces. **1. pas ▶** one step taken in walking or running, or the length of such a step : *The ledge is six paces from the door.* **2. allure, vitesse ▶** the speed with which some activity is done; tempo : *a quick pace.* ▲ VERB, paced, pacing. **1. arpenter, faire les cent pas ▶** to walk back and forth again and again. **2. mesurer au pas ▶** to measure the length of something with paces : *Ashwin and I paced off the boundaries for the game.*

pack [pak] NOUN, packs. **1. a. paquet, ballot ▶** a number of things that are wrapped or tied together to be carried. **b. sac, sac à dos ▶** a sturdy bag that can be strapped on : *a backpack; a fanny pack.* **2. paquet, bande ▶** a group of things of the same type that go together : *a pack of playing cards; a wolf pack.* ▲ VERB, packed, packing. **1. emballer, mettre, empaqueter ▶** to put something in a box, suitcase, or other container : *to pack for a trip.* **2. remplir, entasser ▶** to fill something up : *The stadium was packed with fans.* 🖉 **p. 275, 427.**

pack-age [PAK-ij] NOUN, packages. **1. paquet, colis ▶** something wrapped, tied, or sealed inside a box, bag, or other container. **Note.** These containers are referred to as packaging. **2. forfait, ensemble, globalité ▶** a number of things grouped together and thought of as one : *Our vacation package includes airfare, hotel, and all meals.* ▲ VERB, packaged, packaging. **emballer, empaqueter ▶** to wrap or make into a package : *When we bought the camera, film was packaged with it.* **Note.** Often used as an ADJECTIVE: *a package deal.*

pact [pact] NOUN, pacts. **pacte ▶** an agreement between people or countries; a contract; treaty: *Jenny and Patrice made a pact not to tease each other.*

pad [pad] NOUN, pads. **1. bloc-note, bloc ▶** a number of sheets of paper glued or stuck together along one end, used for writing. **2.** (also padding) **coussinet, coussin ▶** a thick, soft piece of material used to make furniture or clothing more comfortable. **3. protecteur rembourré ▶** a similar material used to protect something : *Football and hockey players wear shoulder pads.* **4. coussinet ▶** the under part of an animal's paw, which is thick and soft like a cushion. ▲ VERB, padded, padding. **1. rembourrer, capitonner ▶** to cover or line something with a pad or cushion : *The workers padded the walls of the elevator before they loaded the furniture on to it.* **2. marcher à pas feutrés ▶** to walk with soft, quiet steps.

pad-dle [PAD-ul] NOUN, paddles. **1. pagaie ▶** a long-handled pole with a wide blade at one end used to move and steer a canoe or other small boat. **2. raquette ▶** a small, flat board with a handle, used to hit the ball in table tennis and other games. ▲ VERB, paddled, paddling. **1. pagayer ▶** to move a canoe or boat with paddles. **2. barboter, patauger ▶** to move the hands and feet with short strokes when swimming.

pad-lock [PAD-lok] NOUN, padlocks. **cadenas ▶** a removable lock that has a curved bar that twists open when unlocked. ▲ VERB, padlocked, padlocking. **cadenasser ▶** to lock something with such a lock.

🖉 **Word Builder**

*You might often hear people using expressions containing the word **pack**. **Send packing** means to send away very quickly: Cory was sent packing to her room after throwing a tantrum. **Pack it in** means to stop work or an activity: After several knee operations, the tennis player decided to pack it in and retire. **Pack off** can mean to send away: The children were packed off to bed after watching their favourite show.*

page[1] [paje] NOUN, pages. **page** ▸ one side of a sheet of paper in a book, newspaper, magazine, and so on.

page[2] NOUN, pages. **1. page** ▸ in the Middle Ages, a youth who was in training to become a knight and who acted as a knight's servant. **2. page** ▸ a messenger in the House of Commons, the Senate, or a legislative assembly. ▲ VERB, paged, paging. **1. faire appeler** ▸ to try to find someone in a public place by having his or her name called out. **2. appeler** ▸ to call a person by means of a device called a **pager** or a beeper.

paid [pade] VERB. a past form of **pay**.

pail [pale] NOUN, pails. **seau (seaux)** ▸ a round, open container with a flat bottom and a curved handle; a bucket.

pain [pane] NOUN, pains. **1. douleur** ▸ a bad feeling that a person does not like having and that shows that something is wrong. A headache, a cut on the arm, or an upset stomach can cause pain. **2. peine** ▸ an emotional feeling rather than a physical feeling; sadness : *the pain of having a family member die.* **3. pains. peine** ▸ great care or effort (usually used with the verb take) : *She took pains to make sure that every word of her report was correct.* **4.** *Informal.* **casse-pieds, emmerdant (-ante), ennuyant (-ante)** ▸ a person or thing that is annoying; a nuisance : *Inez is being a real pain today and keeps trying to ruin our game.* ▲ VERB, pained, paining. **faire souffrir, peiner, attrister** ▸ to cause or feel pain. SYN : ache, sore, hurt, suffering, agony. 📖 p. 1022.

pain-ful [PANE-ful] ADJECTIVE. **1. douloureux (-euse)** ▸ causing pain : *a painful injury.* **2. pénible** ▸ causing worry or concern. ■ **painfully**, ADVERB. ▸ **douloureusement.**

paint [paynt] NOUN, paints. **peinture** ▸ a mixture of colouring matter and water, oil, or other liquid. Paint is put on walls and other surfaces to colour, decorate, or protect them. ▲ VERB, painted, painting. **1. peindre** ▸ to cover something with paint. **2. peindre** ▸ to make a picture or a design with paint. **3. dépeindre, décrire** ▸ to tell about something so as to create a picture in the mind : *Laila painted a glowing picture of her new job.*

paint-er [PANE-tur] NOUN, painters. **1. peintre** ▸ a person whose work is painting things, such as walls, buildings, and so on. **2. artiste peintre** ▸ a person who paints pictures; an artist. **3. amarre** ▸ a rope attached to the front of a boat, used for tying it to a dock or another object. 📖 p. 1127.

paint-ing [PANE-ting] NOUN, paintings. **1. tableau (-eaux), peinture** ▸ a picture made with paints. **2. peinture** ▸ the art of painting pictures : *She's studying the history of Canadian painting.* 📖 p. 1123. 👁 p. 536.

pair [pare] NOUN, pairs. **1. paire** ▸ a set of two things that are together or are supposed to be together : *a pair of shoes.* **2. paire** ▸ one thing made up of two similar parts : *a pair of scissors; a pair of pants.* **3. paire, couple** ▸ two people or animals that go or work together : *The farmer used a pair of oxen to plough the field.* ▲ VERB, paired, pairing. **appareiller, faire la paire** ▸ to make or form a pair. SYN : set, two, twins, mates.

pal [pal] NOUN, pals. *Informal.* **copain (copine)** ▸ a good friend.

pal-ace [PAL-is] NOUN, palaces. **1. palais, château (-eaux)** ▸ a very large, grand building that is an official home of a king, queen, or other ruler. **2. palais, palace** ▸ any very large and impressive house or building that resembles a royal palace. **Note.** Something that is like a palace is called palatial.

pale [pale] ADJECTIVE, paler, palest. **1. pâle, blême** ▸ without the usual amount of colour in the face : *Her face grew pale when she heard about the accident.* **2. pâle, clair (claire)** ▸ of a light shade; not bright; faint : *a pale blue.* ▲ VERB, paled, paling. **pâlir, blêmir** ▸ to turn pale.

pal-ette [PAL-et] NOUN, palettes. **palette** ▸ a thin board used by artists to mix paints. A palette usually has an oval shape, with a hole for the thumb.

palm[1] [pom] NOUN, palms. **paume** ▸ the inside of the hand between the wrist and the fingers. ▲ VERB, palmed, palming. **escamoter, subtiliser** ▸ to hold or hide something in the hand.

palm[2] NOUN, palms. **palmier** ▸ a tree, shrub, or vine that has a long trunk with no branches, and a cluster of broad leaves at the top shaped like huge feathers or fans. Palm trees grow in warm climates, especially in the tropics.

pam-per [PAM-pur] VERB, pampered, pampering. **1. dorloter** ▸ to treat someone in too kind a way; give too much attention to : *She likes to pamper her pets.* **Note.** Also used as an ADJECTIVE: *a pampered child.* **2. gâter, choyer** ▸ to treat someone kindly. SYN : indulge, cater to, spoil, favour.

pam-phlet [PAM-flit] NOUN, pamphlets. **brochure, dépliant, opuscule** ▸ a very short book with a paper cover; a booklet : *The power company sent us a pamphlet describing ways to use less electricity.* ✎ p. 429.

pan [pan] NOUN, pans. **1. casserole, poêle** ▸ a shallow, open container, usually made of metal and having a handle, used for cooking foods. **2. batée** ▸ any shallow metal container like this, such as one used to sift gold ore from earth or gravel. ▲ VERB, panned, panning. **1. laver à la batée** ▸ to separate gold from earth or gravel by washing it in a pan. **2. éreinter, démolir** ▸ to criticize strongly : *I thought the new play was good, but the critics really panned it.*

✐ Writing Tips

Pamphlets

*Pamphlets (sometimes called **brochures** or **booklets**) are written to persuade readers either to buy a product or service, or to care about an issue or an idea. Organizations such as travel agencies and environmental groups might use pamphlets. Pamphlets use persuasive writing, photographs, and/or illustrations to win their readers' support. Headings help to organize ideas and grab the readers' attention. Often pamphlets include an address, telephone number, Internet address, or order form so that readers can get more information or order the service or product.*

pan·cake [PAN-kake] NOUN, pancakes. **crêpe** ▶ a thin, flat cake made by frying a mixture called batter, usually made of milk, eggs, and flour. ☞ **p. 1139.**

pan·da [PAN-duh] NOUN, pandas. 1. (also giant panda) **panda, panda géant** ▶ a large animal that looks like a bear. Pandas have shaggy coats with black-and-white markings and live in bamboo forests in southern China and Tibet. 2. (also lesser panda) **panda, petit panda** ▶ a small reddish-brown animal that looks like a raccoon. It lives in the mountains of southern Asia.

pane [pane] NOUN, panes. **carreau (-eaux)** ▶ a single sheet of glass that is set into a door or window frame.

pan·el [PAN-ul] NOUN, panels. 1. **panneau (-eaux), caisson** ▶ a section of a wall or door that is different from the rest of the surface : *a wooden door with glass panels.* 2. **tableau (-eaux) de bord, panneau (-eaux)** ▶ a board with dials and controls for operating something : *an instrument panel in an airplane.* 3. **table ronde, comité, jury** ▶ a group of people who meet to talk about or judge something : *a panel of experts.* **Note.** Members of such a panel are panelists. ▲ VERB, **panelled, panelling.** (also paneled, paneling) **recouvrir de panneaux, lambrisser** ▶ to decorate or fit with panels : *They panelled the walls of their family room with pine.* **Note.** A group of panels joined together is called **panelling.**

pan·ic [PAN-ik] NOUN, panics. **panique** ▶ a sudden feeling of great fear that makes a person or an animal want to get away quickly : *The fire caused panic.* ▲ VERB, **panicked, panicking. paniquer, affoler** ▶ to feel or cause panic : *The rabbit panicked when it heard the thunder of*

hooves. ■ **panicky,** ADJECTIVE. ▶ **sujet (-ette) à la panique.** SYN : alarm, terror, fear, fright, scare, dread.

pant [pant] VERB, panted, panting. **haleter** ▶ to breathe very hard and fast in short, sharp breaths : *"There, at the foot of the bed, lay Miss Dog, panting."* (Marilyn Halvorson)

pan·ther [PAN-thur] NOUN, panthers or panther. **panthère** ▶ a large, wild cat or leopard, especially one with a black coat.

pants [pants] PLURAL NOUN. **pantalon** ▶ clothing for the lower half of the body from the waist to the ankles, divided to cover each leg separately; trousers; slacks. ☞ **p. 1012.**

pa·per [PAY-pur] NOUN, papers. 1. **papier** ▶ a material used for writing on and for printing books, magazines, and newspapers. Paper is usually made from wood, or from rags or grasses. It is also used in making napkins, tissues, bags, packages, cartons, and so on. 2. **feuille de papier** ▶ a single piece or sheet of this material : *Clara wrote her name on her test paper.* 3. **papier, document** ▶ a piece of paper with information on it : *Mom bought a car, and the dealer is drawing up the papers now.* 4. **devoir écrit, épreuve** ▶ a written report or other such assignment in school. ▲ VERB, **papered, papering. tapisser** ▶ to cover with, or as if with, wallpaper : *to paper a room. We papered the neighbourhood with posters about our garage sale.* ☞ **p. 256.**

par·a·chute [PARE-uh-shoot] NOUN, parachutes. **parachute** ▶ a large piece of fabric shaped like an umbrella, which unfolds in midair to slow the fall of a person or object. ▲ VERB, **parachuted, parachuting. descendre en parachute, sauter en parachute** ▶ to come down by parachute.

pa·rade [PAH-rade] NOUN, parades. 1. **parade, cortège** ▶ a public march in honour of a person or a special event. In a parade, marching bands, vehicles, and floats pass before crowds of spectators. 2. **défilé** ▶ any procession of a large group of people : *There has been a parade of people in and out of my office all day.* ▲ VERB, **paraded, parading.** 1. **parader** ▶ to march in a parade. 2. **exhiber, parader** ▶ to display in a proud way; show off : *"He loved parading himself in a new suit every day, walking erect and proud, holding his head high in the air."* (Faustin Charles)

par·a·dise [PARE-uh-dice] NOUN. 1. **paradis** ▶ another name for heaven. 2. **paradis** ▶ a place or condition of perfect beauty or happiness : *a tropical paradise.*

par·a·graph [PARE-uh-graf] NOUN, paragraphs. **paragraphe** ▶ one part of a piece of writing starting on a new line, usually set in, or indented, from the other lines. The sentences in a paragraph all relate to one topic or idea. ✐ **p. 430.**

par·a·keet [PARE-uh-keet] NOUN, parakeets. **perruche** ▸ a small parrot with brightly coloured feathers and a long tail.

par·al·lel [PARE-uh-lel] ADJECTIVE; ADVERB. **parallèle, parallèlement** ▸ f two lines or paths, going in the same direction and always staying the same distance apart, without meeting or crossing : *Railway tracks have two parallel rails.* ▲ NOUN, parallels. **1. parallèle** ▸ a parallel line or surface. **2. parallèle, analogie** ▸ a situation in which two things are closely connected : *This article draws a parallel between lowering the speed limit and the drop in highway accidents.* ▲ VERB, paralleled, paralleling. **1. être parallèle** ▸ to lie in a parallel direction : *The road parallels the river.* **2. être analogue à** ▸ to have a close connection.

equator

parallels

par·a·lyse [PARE-uh-lize] VERB, paralysed, paralysing (also paralyze) **1. paralyser** ▸ to take away the power to feel or move a part of the body : *A fall from a horse paralysed actor Christopher Reeve from the neck down.* **Note.** The condition of being paralysed is called paralysis. **2. paralyser** ▸ to make unable to act or function ; make helpless : *A blizzard paralysed the city for several hours.*

par·a·site [PARE-uh-site] NOUN, parasites. **1. parasite** ▸ a plant or animal that lives on or in a larger plant or animal. A parasite takes its food from the animal or plant and is often harmful to it. Fleas, ticks, and tapeworms are parasites. **2. parasite** ▸ a person who lives off another, without doing anything useful.

par·cel [PAR-sul] NOUN, parcels. **1. colis, paquet** ▸ something that is wrapped up ; a package. **Note.** The sending of such packages through the mail is called parcel post. **2. parcelle** ▸ a section or piece of land. ▲ VERB, parcelled, parcelling. (also parceled, parceling) (used with out) to divide or give out in parts : *The teacher parcelled out our assignments for the open house.*

par·don [PAR-dun] VERB, pardoned, pardoning. **1. pardonner** ▸ to forgive. **2. gracier, amnis-**

✍ Writing Tips

Paragraphs

*A **paragraph** is a group of sentences about one topic or idea. The first sentence in a paragraph often tells readers what the rest of the paragraph will be about. The following sentences in the paragraph provide more detail. The closing sentence sums up the idea of the whole paragraph. Remember that by dividing your text into paragraphs, you help your readers to follow your ideas and to pick out key points.*

When you are reading, notice how the authors have divided their writing into paragraphs.

tier ▸ to free someone without punishment for a crime or offence. ▲ NOUN, pardons. **pardon** ▸ the act of pardoning.

Pardon me or **I beg your pardon. demander pardon, pardon, excusez-moi** ▸ to ask another to excuse one : *I beg your pardon for being late.*

par·ent [PARE-unt] NOUN, parents. **1. parents, père, mère** ▸ a mother or father. **Note.** Parenthood is the fact of being a parent. **2. parent** ▸ an animal or plant that produces another of its own kind.

pa·ren·the·sis [puh-REN-thuh-sis] NOUN, parentheses [puh-REN-thuh-seez]. **parenthèse** ▸ one of a pair of curved lines like these ( ) used to set apart a word or phrase within a sentence : *The length of the race is 5 000 metres (about 3 miles).* **Note.** Sometimes called round brackets.

park [park] NOUN, parks. **1. parc** ▸ a piece of public land set apart for people to use for rest and enjoyment. **2. parc** ▸ a large area of land that is left in its natural form for public use : *Canada has many large national parks.* ▲ VERB, parked, parking. **stationner** ▸ to leave a car or other vehicle for a time. **Note.** Can be used as an ADJECTIVE: *a parking lot; a parking garage.* ▪ **parking,** NOUN. **stationnement** ▸ the act of parking a car, or the place for parking.

par·ka [PAR-kuh] NOUN, parkas. **parka, anorak** ▸ a heavy fur or cloth jacket with a hood.

par·lia·ment [PAR-luh-munt] NOUN, parliaments. **1. parlement** ▸ a group of people who have been given the power to make the laws of a country. **2. Parliament. Parlement** ▸ in Canada, the House of Commons and the Senate make up Parliament.

par·lour [PAR-lur] NOUN, parlours. (also parlor) **1. salon** ▸ a room used for entertaining guests. Houses built in recent times do not have a separate parlour. **2. salon** ▸ a room or building used for a certain type of business : *a beauty parlour; an ice-cream parlour.*

par·o·dy [PARE-uh-dee] NOUN, parodies. **1. parodie ▸** a funny imitation of a serious piece of writing. A parody follows the form of the original but changes its meaning to nonsense. **2. parodie ▸** any piece of work that makes fun of another. 🖉 p. 431.

par·rot [PARE-ut] NOUN, parrots. **perroquet ▸** a large bird with brightly coloured feathers, a short, hooked beak, and a long tail. Some parrots can be taught to copy human speech and other sounds. ▲ VERB, parroted, parroting. **répéter comme un perroquet ▸** to copy another person's words or actions exactly.

part [part] NOUN, parts. **1. partie ▸** something that belongs to a thing, but is not all of the thing : *That part of the movie was unbelievable.* **2. partie, pièce ▸** one of the pieces that are put together to make up a whole thing : *Headlights and spark plugs are parts of a car.* **3. rôle ▸** the role of an actor in a play or movie. **4. raie ▸** a line that is made in the hair, with some hair being combed to one side and the rest to the other. ▲ VERB, parted, parting. **1. séparer, diviser ▸** to come between; break up; separate : *The teacher parted the arguing children.* **2. se séparer ▸** to leave one another; go different ways; separate : *The two men shook hands as they parted.* ▲ ADVERB. **partiellement, en partie ▸** in part; not completely. *A mule is part horse and part donkey.*

take part prendre part, participer, collaborer ▸ to do something along with others : *Sara takes part in a soccer league at school.*

par·tial [PAR-shul] ADJECTIVE. **1. partiel (-ielle) ▸** not all; only a part; not complete : *The photo was not big enough to show more than a partial view of the building.* **2. partial (-iale, -iaux), injuste ▸** favouring one side over another; prejudiced : *A judge should not be partial.* **3. friand (-ande) de ▸** especially fond of or attracted to : *to be partial to ice cream.* ■ **partially,** ADVERB. **▸ partiellement, en partie, avec partialité, partialement.**

par·tic·i·pate [par-TIS-uh-pate] VERB, participated, participating. **participer ▸** to join with others in doing something; take part : *Everyone in the class is participating in the food drive.* **Note.** The act or fact of participating in something is participation. **Note.** Someone who participates is a participant. SYN: take part in, co-operate, enter into, join in.

par·ti·ci·ple [par-tuh-sip-ul] NOUN, participles. **participe ▸** in grammar, either of two verb forms used with other verbs to form certain tenses. The present participle of the verb is usually formed with the ending -ing. The past participle is usually formed with the ending -ed: *I like flying. I have never skated.*

🖉 Writing Tips

Parody

In a **parody**, a writer exaggerates and imitates the work of another author. A parody is used to entertain readers and to criticize the other author—perhaps for being too wordy, too sentimental, or too serious. Parodies work only if the readers know the original work that is being parodied. Parodies can imitate the words, structure, point of view, narrative voice, style, tone, plot, characterization, setting, or ideas of another author. For example, most of the songs written and recorded by Weird Al Yankovic are parodies of other songs.

If you wished to parody the opening lines of A Tale of Two Cities by Charles Dickens —It was the best of times, it was the worst of times…. —you could start a story about a clown with She was the best of mimes; she was the worst of mimes.

par·ti·cle [PAR-ti-kul] NOUN, particles. **particule ▸** a tiny piece or bit : *particles of dust; sand particles.*

par·tic·u·lar [pur-TIK-yuh-lur] ADJECTIVE. **1. particulier (-ière) ▸** apart from others; being a certain one : *That particular book is on sale.* **2. particulier (-ière) ▸** not the same as others; special; unusual : *He wanted that one particular hockey card more than any others.* **3. méticuleux (-euse), pointilleux (-euse) ▸** paying close attention to details : *My uncle is very particular about food.* ▲ NOUN, particulars. **détail ▸** a single or separate fact or detail. ■ **particularly,** ADVERB. **particulièrement ▸** especially : *She acted the part of Juliet particularly well.* SYN: specific, distinct, special, different, exact. 🖉 p. 432.

part·ly [PART-lee] ADVERB. **partiellement, en partie ▸** in part; not completely : *The clothes are partly dry.*

part·ner [PART-nur] NOUN, partners. **1. partenaire, collègue ▸** a person who works with another person on a project. **2. associé (-ée) ▸** in business, someone who joins with another person or persons to run a company and who shares in the profits or losses of that company. **Note.** A partnership is the fact of being a partner, or a business that is run by partners. **3. partenaire ▸** one of two people who play together on the same side in a game : *Doubles is a form of tennis in which each player has a partner.*

🔧 Word Builder

Particular, special, and *individual* are adjectives that describe something or someone that is different from others. When something is *particular,* it is a specific person group, thing, or category: *I have a particular person in mind for the job.* **Special** refers to something or someone different because of a positive or unusual quality: *This ring is special because my grandmother gave it to me.* **Individual** suggests only one thing or person, separate from others: *There are 30 individual desks in that classroom.*

part of speech catégorie grammaticale
▶ one of the basic classes into which words are grouped according to how they are used. The parts of speech in English are noun, pronoun, verb, adjective, adverb, preposition, conjunction, and interjection.

par·ty [PAR-tee] NOUN, parties. **1.** fête, partie, soirée, réception ▶ a gathering of a group of people to have a good time or to mark some special occasion. **2.** parti ▶ a group of people who act or work together in politics to win an election: *the Liberal Party; Conservative Party.* **3.** équipe, groupe ▶ any group of people who act together: *A search party was organized to find the boys who were lost in the woods.* SYN: gathering, celebration, festivity, affair. ☞ p. 1147, 1165.

pass [pas] VERB, passed, passing. **1.** passer, dépasser ▶ to move beyond; go past: *"Early the next day, the other cyclists passed Gustaf."* (David M. Schwartz) **2.** passer ▶ to go from one place or condition to another; move: *"Time passed. Spring grew into summer on the island, and summer into fall."* (Celia Godkin) **3.** réussir ▶ to complete a test or problem in an acceptable way: *To get a driver's licence, she had to pass a written exam and a road test.* **4.** adopter, voter ▶ to vote in favour of; approve: *The council passed a law.* **5.** passer, donner ▶ to hand or throw from one person to another: *Pass me the butter.* **6.** passer ▶ to use up or spend time: *He got there early and passed the time reading a book.* ▲ NOUN, passes. **1.** passe ▶ in sports, the act of throwing the ball from one player to another. **2.** laissez-passer ▶ a ticket or piece of paper that allows a person to do something or go past a certain point. **3.** passage ▶ an opening or gap to go through: *a mountain pass.* **4.** billet gratuit ▶ a free ticket: *The store is giving away passes to the amusement park.* 🖉 p. 433.

pas·sage [PAS-ij] NOUN, passages. **1.** passage, couloir, corridor ▶ a way of passing from one point to another: *an underground passage.* **2.** traversée, passage, voyage ▶ a journey: *a passage by boat.* **3.** passage, changement ▶ the fact of passing: *the passage of time.* **4.** passage ▶ a small part of a written work or piece of music, presented by itself: *"Lin recognized a passage from the Minute Waltz, some-*

thing he'd never wanted to learn."* (Barbara Novak) **Note.** A passageway is a way along which a person or thing can pass: *"After he delivered the baskets, he wandered through the passageways, exploring the wondrous stone chambers."* (Donald Carrick)

pas·sen·ger [PAS-un-jur] NOUN, passengers. passager (-ère) ▶ a person who gets a ride in a bus, a train, an airplane, or another such vehicle.

pass·ing [PAS-ing] NOUN, passings. passage ▶ the act of going or going past. ▲ ADJECTIVE. **1.** qui passe, en passant ▶ moving by; going by: *He waved at me from the window of the passing train.* **2.** passager (-ère), de passage, éphémère ▶ lasting only a short time; brief: *Angie had a passing interest in golf last year.*

in passing en passant ▶ while dealing with something else; incidentally: *In his speech the mayor mentioned in passing that his son had just gotten married.*

pas·sion [PASH-un] NOUN, passions. **1.** passion ▶ a very strong feeling or emotion: *Love, hate, and anger are passions.* **2.** passion ▶ a very strong liking: *She has a passion for art and goes to the gallery almost every weekend.* ■ **passionate,** ADJECTIVE. ▶ passionné (-ée), fervent (-ente), ardent (-ente). ☞ p. 1023.

pas·sive [PAS-iv] ▲ ADJECTIVE. **1.** passif (-ive) ▶ not acting or responding, especially at a time when one should act or is expected to act: *He is too passive and lets everyone take advantage of him.* **2.** (also passive voice) passif (-ive) ▶ in grammar, a verb form showing that something happens to the subject, rather than that the subject causes something to happen. In the sentence *Judy was stung by a bee,* **passive-ment, au passif** ▶ the verb is passive. That sentence in the active voice is *The bee stung Judy.* ■ **passively,** ADVERB. ▶ passivement.

Pass·o·ver [PAS-oh-ver] NOUN. Pâques ▶ a Jewish holiday that celebrates the escape of Jews from slavery in Egypt in ancient times. Passover comes in the spring and lasts for eight days.

pass·port [PAS-port] NOUN, passports. passeport ▶ an official paper given to a person by the government of a country. It identifies the person as a citizen of the country and gives permission to travel to other countries.

pass-word [PAS-wurd] NOUN, passwords. **mot de passe** ▸ a secret word or phrase that a person has to know in order to pass a guard, get into a special place, and so on.

past [past] NOUN. **1. passé** ▸ the time that has come before now; what has already happened : *In the past, people did most of their work by hand rather than with machines.* **2. passé** ▸ short for past tense. ▲ ADJECTIVE. **1. passé (-ée)** ▸ in the time gone by; before now : *We haven't had any rain for the past two months.* **2. passé (-ée), ancien (-ienne)** ▸ of an earlier time; former : *Can you name all the past prime ministers?* ▲ ADVERB. **au-delà, par-delà, plus loin que** ▸ going by; beyond. ▲ PREPOSITION. **devant, au-delà** ▸ beyond in place or amount : *Xavier streaked past the others to win the race.* 📖 **p. 1080.**

pas-ta [PAS-tuh] NOUN. **pâte alimentaire** ▸ a food made by mixing flour and water into a paste or dough. Spaghetti, macaroni, and noodles are types of pasta. 📖 **p. 1139.**

paste [paste] NOUN, pastes. **1. colle** ▸ a soft mixture that is used to stick paper and other things together, often made of flour and water. **2. pâte** ▸ anything that is soft and sticky like this : *toothpaste.* ▲ VERB, pasted, pasting. **coller** ▸ to stick or fasten with paste : *The children pasted down pictures for their project.*

pas-tel [pas-TEL] NOUN. **1. pastel** ▸ a soft chalk used like a crayon for drawing pictures, or a picture made with these chalks. **2. pastel** ▸ a soft, pale shade of colour : *She painted her walls pastel blue.*

pas-try [pay-STREE] NOUN, pastries. **1. pâtisserie** ▸ sweet, baked foods such as pies. **2. pâte** ▸ the dough that is used to make the crusts of such foods.

past tense **passé** ▸ in grammar, a verb form showing that something happened or existed in the past.

pas-ture [PAS-chur] NOUN, pastures. **pâture, pâturage, herbage** ▸ a field or piece of land covered with plants that are eaten by farm animals such as cows, horses, and sheep; grassland; meadow. 📖 **p. 114.**

pat [pat] VERB, patted, patting. **flatter, caresser, tapoter** ▸ to touch or strike softly with an open hand; pet; tap : *to pat a dog.* ▲ NOUN, pats. **1. petite tape** ▸ a gentle stroke or tap. **2. noix** ▸ a small, flat piece of butter.

pat on the back **féliciter, complimenter** ▸ praise; compliment : *Dan's father gave him a pat on the back for writing a wonderful story.*

patch [pach] NOUN, patches. **1. pièce** ▸ a small piece of material used to cover a hole or rip in something : *a patch for jeans.* **2. bandage** ▸ a piece of cloth or bandage put over a wound or injury for protection : *an eye patch.* **3. pan, tache** ▸ a small area that is different from what is around it : *a patch of moonlight.* ▲ VERB, patched, patching. **rapiécer, recoudre, réparer** ▸ to put a patch on; mend.

patch up **se raccommoder, rafistoler** ▸ to make right; settle : *to patch up a quarrel between two old friends.*

path [path] NOUN, paths. **1. sentier, chemin** ▸ a way or trail on which people or animals walk : *We strolled along the path.* **2. route** ▸ a line along which something or someone moves; a route : *He almost stepped into the path of an oncoming car.* SYN: trail, track, route, way, road, lane, pass.

pa-tience [PAY-shuns] NOUN. **patience** ▸ the condition or quality of being patient : *She had great patience with her baby sister.* SYN: tolerance, calmness, persistance, endurance. ✏ **p. 434.**

pa-tient [PAY-shunt] ADJECTIVE. **patient (-iente)** ▸ able to deal with delays and problems without immediately getting upset; willing to wait for something. ■ **patiently,** ADVERB: ▸ **patiemment.** *They waited patiently.* ▲ NOUN, patients. **patient (-iente)** ▸ a person who is staying in a hospital or is being treated by a doctor.

pat-i-o [PAT-ee-oh] NOUN, patios. **1. patio** ▸ an outdoor space near a house that is usually paved with stone or tile and is used for cooking, eating, or relaxing. **2. patio** ▸ an inner yard or court that is open to the sky. Houses in Spain and Mexico are often built around patios.

pa-tri-ot [PAY-tree-ut] NOUN, patriots. **patriote** ▸ one who loves and supports his or her country. **Note.** This quality is patriotism. ■ **patriotic,** ADJECTIVE. ▸ **patriotique, patriote.**

pa-trol [puh-TROLE] VERB, patrolled, patrolling. **patrouiller** ▸ to go through or around an area to

---

✏ Word Builder

Pass is a simple word, but it can be found in many expressions. *Pass away* means to come to an end or die: *Ismail was sad when his stepmother passed away after a long illness.* When a person *passes out,* he or she has fainted or lost consciousness: *George passed out in the extreme heat. Pass for* means to be accepted as or believed to be: *The identical twins could pass for each other. Pass the buck* means to pass responsibility to someone else: *She tried to pass the buck to Liam when it was her turn to baby-sit.*

guard it and make sure there is no trouble. ▲ NOUN, patrols. 1. **patrouille** ▸ the act of patrolling an area. **Note.** A police car that does this is a patrol car. 2. **patrouille** ▸ a person or group that does this. SYN: watch, guard, police, protect.

pat·tern [PAT-urn] NOUN, patterns. 1. **motif** ▸ the way in which colours, shapes, or lines are arranged; a design. 2. **patron, modèle** ▸ a guide or model that is to be followed in making something : *a dress pattern.* 3. **schème, routine, mode** ▸ a set of actions or conditions that continue or are repeated : *a learning pattern.* ▲ VERB, patterned, patterning. **modeler** ▸ to make according to a pattern; follow a model. 🖙 p. 1012.

pause [poz] VERB, paused, pausing. **s'interrompre, faire une pause** ▸ to stop for a short time and then continue; stop in the middle of something. ▲ NOUN, pauses. **pause, arrêt** ▸ the act of pausing : *There was a pause in the music.*

pave [pave] VERB, paved, paving. **paver** ▸ to cover a street, walk, or other such place with a hard, level surface : *pave the driveway.*

pave the way préparer le terrain ▸ to go before something and prepare the way; make it easier for something to happen.

pave·ment [PAVE-munt] NOUN, pavements. **pavé** ▸ a paved surface, such as a street, sidewalk, or parking lot.

pa·vil·ion [puh-VIL-yun] NOUN, pavilions. 1. **pavillon** ▸ an open building with a roof and a raised wooden floor, used in a park or at a fair. 2. **chapiteau (-eaux)** ▸ a large, fancy tent used for shows or parties.

paw [pah] NOUN, paws. **patte** ▸ the foot of an animal that has claws or nails, such as a cat or dog. ▲ VERB, pawed, pawing. 1. **donner un (des) coup(s) de patte à** ▸ to touch or strike with a paw or foot. 2. **tripoter** ▸ to handle something in a rough or awkward way.

pay [pay] VERB, paid, paying. 1. **payer** ▸ to give money to someone in return for something or for work done : *to pay $10 for a shirt.* 2. **payer** ▸ to give money that is owed or due : *to pay rent.* 3. **payer** ▸ to be worth doing or having : *It pays to read as much as you can.* 4. **payer** ▸ to

have to put up with or suffer : *If I eat another piece of cake, I'll pay for it later with a stomachache.* 5. **faire, présenter, donner** ▸ to give, do, say, or make : *to pay attention in class; to pay a visit to a friend.* ▲ NOUN. **paie, salaire** ▸ money that is given for work or goods : *I got a raise in my pay.*

pay·ment [PAY-munt] NOUN, payments. 1. **paiement** ▸ the act of paying. 2. **paiement, versement** ▸ the amount that is paid : *The payments on his car loan are $165 a month.*

pea [pee] NOUN, peas. **pois, petit pois** ▸ a small, round green seed that is eaten as a vegetable. Peas grow inside long green pods on a low-growing garden plant.

peace [pees] NOUN. 1. **paix** ▸ the state of being free from fighting or war. 2. **paix** ▸ a time when things are quiet and calm; freedom from trouble or disorder : *Karin enjoyed the peace and quiet.*

peace·ful [PEES-ful] ADJECTIVE. 1. **paisible, calme, tranquille** ▸ in a state of peace; free from fighting or trouble; calm. 2. **pacifique** ▸ not wanting to fight; not warlike. ■ **peacefully,** ADVERB. ▸ **paisiblement, tranquillement.** "*Then she lay down and slept peacefully in the little shelter.*" (Donald Gale) SYN: calm, quiet, still, tranquil, untroubled.

peach [peech] NOUN, peaches. 1. **pêche** ▸ a sweet, round, juicy fruit that has a smooth, fuzzy skin and a hard pit inside. Peach trees are found in most areas of the world that have a mild climate. 2. **pêche** ▸ a yellowish-pink colour like the skin of a peach.

peak [peek] NOUN, peaks. 1. **pic, sommet, cime** ▸ the pointed top of a mountain or hill. 2. **pic** ▸ a mountain, especially one that stands alone. 3. **pointe, sommet, extrémité** ▸ any pointed top or end : *the peak of a roof.* 4. **apogée** ▸ the highest point : "*By now the storm had reached its peak.*" (Robert D. Ballard) SYN: top, crest, summit, tip, hilltop, crown.

peal [peel] NOUN, peals. 1. **sonnerie, carillon** ▸ the loud ringing of a set of bells. 2. **éclat** ▸ any long, loud sound like this : *a peal of laughter.*

pea·nut [PEE-nut] NOUN, peanuts. **cacahuète, arachide** ▸ a plant seed that grows in pods that ripen underground. Peanuts look and taste like

---

🖉 **Word Builder**

A person with ***patience*** *has calmness, self-control, and is able to live with any delays that might come up: Tina's patience with us wasn't shattered by our fighting and delay tactics. Someone with* ***tolerance*** *can be open-minded and doesn't make judgments quickly or show disapproval: Byron showed great tolerance in putting up with his little sister's endless questioning.* ***Persistence*** *means to keep trying and not to give up: The mountain climbers demonstrated great persistence in finally reaching the mountain peak.*

nuts. They are eaten whole or ground to make peanut butter, and peanut oil is used in cooking.

pear [pare] NOUN, pears. **poire** ▸ a sweet, juicy fruit with a smooth yellowish skin. Pear trees are found in mild climates throughout the world.

pearl [purl] NOUN, pearls. **1. perle** ▸ a small round gem that is formed inside the shell of some oysters. Most pearls have a soft white or cream-coloured shine. **2. perle** ▸ something that looks like or has the colour of a pearl. ■ **pearly,** ADJECTIVE. ▸ **perlé (-ée).**

peas-ant [PEZ-unt] NOUN, peasants. **paysan (-anne)** ▸ one of a group of people who live and work on small farms.

peb-ble [PEB-ul] NOUN, pebbles. **caillou (-oux), galet** ▸ a small stone that is smooth and round.

peck [pek] VERB, pecked, pecking. **picorer, picoter** ▸ to strike or poke at something, as a bird does with its beak. ▲ NOUN, pecks. **1. coup de bec** ▸ a short stroke made by pecking. **2. bise, bécot** ▸ a light, quick kiss : *a peck on the cheek.*

pe-cul-iar [pih-KYOOL-yur] ADJECTIVE. **1. bizarre, curieux (-ieuse), original (-ale, -aux)** ▸ not as it usually is; odd or strange : *Jonah had a peculiar laugh.* **2. propre à, particulier (-ière)** ▸ belonging to a particular person, group, place, or thing : *Bengal tigers are peculiar to Asia.*

ped-al [PED-ul] NOUN, pedals. **pédale** ▸ a lever that is worked or operated by the foot to control machinery. A bicycle is moved by pushing down on the pedals. Pedals are used to control the brakes or gas in a car. ▲ VERB, pedalled, pedalling. (also pedaled, pedaling) **pédaler** ▸ to work or use the pedals of something : *to pedal a bicycle.*

ped-es-tri-an [puh-DES-tree-un] NOUN. **piéton (-onne)** ▸ a person who travels on foot : *Drivers should be careful of pedestrians.*

peek [peek] VERB, peeked, peeking. **jeter un coup d'œil furtif** ▸ to look quickly or secretly : *to peek at a present.* ▲ NOUN, peeks. **coup d'œil, regard furtif** ▸ a quick or secret look. SYN: look slyly, peep, peer, glance, glimpse.

peel [peel] NOUN, peels. **pelure, écorce** ▸ the skin or outer covering of some fruits or vegetables : *a lemon peel.* ▲ VERB, peeled, peeling. **1. peler, éplucher** ▸ to remove the skin or outer covering from : *to peel potatoes.* **2. enlever, détacher, décoller** ▸ to remove something in this way; strip off : *Sharon peeled the address label from the magazine.* **3. peler, (s') écailler** ▸ to come off in pieces or thin strips : *Skin was peeling off her shoulders where she was sunburned.*

peep[1] [peep] VERB, peeped, peeping. **1. jeter un coup d'œil furtif** ▸ to look quickly or secretly; peek. **2. émerger partiellement** ▸ to come partly into view; begin to be seen : *The moon was just peeping over the horizon.* ▲ NOUN, peeps. **coup d'œil** ▸ a quick or secret look; a peek.

peep[2] NOUN, peeps. **pépiement, piaulment** ▸ any short, high sound like that made by a young bird or chicken; chirp. ▲ VERB, peeped, peeping. **pépier, piauler** ▸ to make such a sound.

peer[1] [peer] VERB, peered, peering. **scruter** ▸ to look closely at something to see it clearly : *"I had to lean forward and peer over my toes just to see the next step."* (Paulette Bourgeois)

peer[2] NOUN, peers. **1. pair** ▸ a person who has the same rank or quality as another; an equal : *Babe Ruth had no peers among the baseball players of his time.* **2. pair, noble** ▸ a person who has a noble title, such as a duke. ■ **peer-less,** ADJECTIVE. **sans pareil, sans égal, hors pair** ▸ having no peer or equal; very outstanding.

peer group **pairs** ▸ people of about the same age, social status, and so on within a community.

peg [peg] NOUN, pegs. **cheville, piquet** ▸ a thick pin of wood or metal used to fasten things together, hang things on, plug holes, and so on. ▲ VERB, pegged, pegging. **accrocher, cheviller, fixer** ▸ to fasten or hold with pegs : *The campers pegged the tent to hold it in place.*

pelt[1] [pelt] VERB, pelted, pelting. **1. lancer, bombarder, cribler** ▸ to throw things at. **2. frapper ou heurter violemment** ▸ to hit or beat against something heavily : *The rain pelted the roof.* **3. aller à toute vitesse, foncer** ▸ to hurry or rush : *The runner pelted past us.*

pelt[2] NOUN, pelts. **peau (peaux), fourrure** ▸ the skin of an animal with the fur or hair still on it.

pen[1] [pen] NOUN, pens. **stylo** ▸ a tool used for writing or drawing with ink : *a ballpoint pen.*

pen[2] NOUN, pens. **1. enclos** ▸ a small, fenced area for keeping cows, chickens, pigs, or other farm animals. **2. parc** ▸ any small enclosed area : *a baby's playpen.* ▲ VERB, penned, penning. **parquer, enfermer** ▸ to keep in or as if in a pen. ☜ p. 114.

pen-al-ty [PEN-ul-tee] NOUN, penalties. **1. pénalité, peine** ▸ a punishment for breaking a rule or law. **2. pénalité** ▸ in sports or contests, a disadvantage that is placed on a team or player for breaking a rule.

penalty box **banc de pénalité** ▸ a special bench in hockey or lacrosse where players serve penalties.

pen-cil [PEN-sul] NOUN, pencils. **crayon** ▸ a thin, pointed tool that is used for writing and drawing. Pencils are usually made of a stick of black or coloured material inside a wooden covering. ▲ VERB, pencilled, pencilling. (also penciled, penciling) **écrire à l'aide d'un crayon, dessiner au crayon** ▸ to write, draw, or mark with a pencil : *Mom pencilled in the time of my piano lesson on the calendar.*

pen·e·trate [PEN-uh-trate] VERB, penetrated, penetrating. **1. pénétrer ▸** to go into or pass through : *The light from the flashlight penetrated the darkness.* **2. pénétrer, découvrir ▸** to study and understand : *to penetrate the mysteries of the brain.*

pen·guin [PENG-gwin] NOUN, penguins. **manchot ▸** a black-and-white sea bird with narrow wings that are like flippers. Penguins cannot fly, but they use their wings for swimming. They live in large colonies in the Antarctic and in other cold areas of the Southern Hemisphere.

pen·i·cil·lin [PEN-uh-SIL-in] NOUN. **pénicilline ▸** a powerful medicine used to kill bacteria that cause diseases and infections. Penicillin is an antibiotic made from plant mould.

pen·in·su·la [puh-NIN-suh-luh *or* puh-NINSE-yuh-luh] NOUN, peninsulas. **péninsule, presqu'île ▸** a piece of land that is almost completely surrounded by water and is still connected to a larger body of land : *Nova Scotia is a large peninsula.*

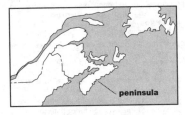

peninsula

pen·man·ship [PEN-mun-ship] NOUN. **calligraphie ▸** the act or art of writing by hand ; handwriting.

pen·ny [PEN-ee] NOUN, pennies. **1. sous, cent ▸** a Canadian or U.S. coin worth one cent, or 1/100 of a dollar. **2. pièce de un cent ▸** a British coin worth 1/100 of a pound.

pen·sion [PEN-shun] NOUN, pensions. **pension, rente ▸** a sum of money paid regularly by a company or by the government to someone who used to work but has now retired. **Note.** A person who receives a pension is a pensioner. SYN: allowance, aid, assistance, help, subsidy.

pen·ta·gon [PEN-tuh-gone] NOUN, pentagons. **pentagone ▸** a closed geometric figure with five sides and five angles.

peo·ple [PEE-pul] NOUN, people. **1. personne ▸** men, women, and children ; persons as a group : *That stadium holds 100,000 people.* **2.** (plural, peoples) **peuple, population, nation ▸** all of the persons of a certain nation : *the Canadian people.* **3. gens ▸** the members of a certain group, place, or class ; persons who

have something in common : *city people.* **4. personne, gens ▸** persons in general ; the average person : *People need to eat.* ▲ VERB, peopled, peopling. **peupler ▸** to fill with people ; populate : *The west was peopled largely by Europeans.* ✎ p. 437. ✐ p. 356.

pep [pep] NOUN. **entrain, fougue ▸** the fact of being lively and having a lot of energy : *The puppy was full of pep as it ran around the yard.* ▲ VERB, pepped, pepping. **revigorer, ragaillardir ▸** to fill with energy : *A quick run on a cold morning always peps me up.* ▪ **peppy,** ADJECTIVE. **plein (pleine) d'entrain ▸** full of energy. SYN: energy, spirit, vigour, life, vitality.

pep·per [PEP-ur] NOUN, peppers. **1. poivre ▸** a seasoning with a sharp, spicy taste. Pepper plants have small berries called peppercorns that are dried and then ground into a powder. **2. poivron ▸** any of several garden plants with large, hollow fruits that are green, red, or yellow. Peppers are eaten as a vegetable or are used to flavour other foods. ▲ VERB, peppered, peppering. **1. poivrer ▸** to season with pepper. **2. pimenter, parsemer ▸** to hit or shower with small things : *Janet's conversation was peppered with references to her new home.*

per [per] PREPOSITION. **1. par ▸** for each : *The school has one computer per classroom.* **2.** *Informal.* **selon ▸** according to : *He prepared his report per the teacher's instructions.*

per·ceive [pur-SEEV] VERB, perceived, perceiving. **1. percevoir ▸** to become aware of through the senses ; see, hear, taste, smell, or feel : *He perceived someone standing just at the outer edge of his vision.* **Note.** The act or fact of perceiving something is perception. **2. (s') apercevoir ▸** to sense with the mind ; understand ; realize : *She perceived that he was upset and changed the subject.* **Note.** A person who is perceptive is quick to sense and understand things.

per·cent [pur-SENT] NOUN. (also per cent) **1. pour cent ▸** a certain number of parts in each hundred : *Ten percent of one hundred is ten.* **Note.** A percentile is a point on a scale of 100 that shows how many within a group are at or below that point. **2. pour cent ▸** for each hundred : *Ninety percent of the students passed.* Symbol : %

per·cent·age [pur-SEN-tij] NOUN, percentages. **1. pourcentage ▸** a part of the whole stated in hundreds ; percent : *The percentage of unemployed has dropped slightly this month.* **2. proportion, pourcentage ▸** a part of some larger whole ; ratio : *Mr. Roggi says that if I help him sell the Christmas trees, there'll be a percentage in it for me.*

perch[1] [purch] NOUN, perches. **1. perchoir ▸** a bar or branch on which a bird can rest. **2. perchoir ▸** any resting place, especially a high one : *The climbers looked down toward the valley*

Word Builder

People, *society*, and *humanity* all describe groups of individuals. *People* can describe any group of more than one person: *There were two people in the store.* Or, it can be a very large group: *There were thousands of people at the concert.* *Society* often describes a large group of people who share characteristics such as culture, interests, or relationships: *Our school is a good representative of Canadian society.* *Humanity* describes the entire group of all human beings on earth: *Environmental problems affect all of humanity.*

from their perch on the side of the mountain. ▲ VERB, perched, perching. **1. se percher** ▸ of a bird, to sit or rest. **2. (se) percher, (se) jucher** ▸ to place or sit : *The teacher was perched on a stool in front of the chalkboard.*

perch[2] NOUN, perch or perches. **perche, perchaude** ▸ a freshwater fish found in North America and Europe. The yellow perch is popular game for fishing and for food. 👁 p. 106.

per-fect [PUR-fikt] ADJECTIVE. **1. parfait (-aite)** ▸ that which cannot be made better; having no faults or mistakes; exactly as it should be : *A grade of 100% on a test is a perfect score.* **2. parfait (-aite) idéal (-ale, -aux)** ▸ just as a person wishes or needs it to be; ideal; excellent : *"The morning is perfect for spotting whale blows."* (Alexandra Morton) **3.** *Informal.* **parfait (-aite)** ▸ total; complete : *perfect strangers.* ▲ [pur-FEKT] VERB, perfected, perfecting. **perfectionner, parfaire** ▸ to make perfect; remove errors or faults from. SYN: faultless, flawless, correct, ideal, accurate.

perfect tense in grammar, a verb tense formed with *have* or *had* and another verb. It is used to show that an action began in the past, such as *Jack had already left when we got there*, or *We have lived here for six years*.

per-fec-tion [pur-FEK-shun] NOUN. **1. perfection** ▸ the state of being perfect. **2. perfectionnement** ▸ the act or process of making something perfect : *Polio became a much less dangerous disease after the perfection of a medicine to combat it.* **Note.** A person who seeks or expects perfection is a perfectionist.

per-fect-ly [PUR-fikt-lee] ADVERB. **1. parfaitement** ▸ in a perfect way. **2. complètement** ▸ very much; totally; completely : *perfectly still.*

per-form [pur-FORM] VERB, performed, performing. **1. exécuter, effectuer** ▸ to do or carry out an action; do : *He practised the dive over and over until he could perform it without fault.* **2. jouer, exécuter, représenter** ▸ to do something before an audience, such as singing or acting. **Note.** A person who performs is a performer. SYN: act, do, accomplish, carry out, achieve.

per-for-mance [pur-FOR-muns] NOUN, performances. **1. représentation** ▸ a play, musical program, or other such entertainment that is pre-

sented before an audience. **2. performance, exécution** ▸ the act of performing or doing something : *His performance at school improved once he asked for extra help.*

per-fume [PUR-fyoom] NOUN, perfumes. **1. parfum** ▸ a specially prepared liquid that has a pleasant smell, worn by a person on the body or clothing. **2. parfum, fragrance** ▸ a sweet, pleasant smell; fragrance : *I love the perfume of the flowers.* ▲ [pur-FYOOM] VERB, perfumed, perfuming. **parfumer, embaumer** ▸ to fill with a sweet, fragrant odour : *The smell of jasmine perfumed the night air.*

per-haps [pur-HAPS] ADVERB. **peut-être** ▸ it is possible; maybe : *Perhaps Meeta will call today.* SYN: maybe, possibly, probably, conceivably.

per-il [PARE-ul] NOUN, perils. **péril, danger** ▸ a serious chance of harm or loss; danger : *Tornadoes put people in peril.* ■ **perilous,** ADJECTIVE: ▸ **périlleux (-euse), dangereux (-euse).** *"After a long and perilous journey, Bjarni and his men had brought their ship safely to shore."* (Charnan Simon) ■ **perilously,** ADVERB. ▸ **dangereusement, périlleusement.**

pe-ri-od [PEER-ee-ud] NOUN, periods. **1. point** ▸ a punctuation mark [.] used in writing to show the end of a sentence. It is also used at the end of abbreviations or after numbers in a list. SEE WRITER'S TOOL KIT, PAGE 623. **2. période, ère, époque** ▸ a certain part of a school day : *the lunch period.* **3.** (often Period) a certain time in history; era : *Many dinosaurs are from the Cretaceous period.* **4. période** ▸ any amount or portion of time : *We're having a period of cold weather.* 📖 p. 1080.

pe-ri-od-ic [PEER-ee-OD-ik] ADJECTIVE. **périodique** ▸ happening over and over again, especially at regular times : *This car should have periodic oil changes, every 15,000 km or so.* ■ **periodically,** ADVERB. ▸ **périodiquement.**

per-ish [PARE-ish] VERB, perished, perishing. **1. périr** ▸ to be destroyed; die : *"One thing was certain, she was freezing there in the bitter wind and snow. So was the little horse. They must move or perish."* (Thomas H. Raddall) **2. pourrir, se détériorer** ▸ spoil; decay : *Fruit perishes quickly in the heat.*

perk [purk] VERB, perked, perking. (usually with up) **1. dresser ▶** to pick up or lift quickly : *The cat perked up her ears at the sound of the front door opening.* **2. se ragaillardir, se requinquer, s'animer ▶** to become more lively or cheerful : *Nicola perked up at the suggestion of going to see a movie.* **■ perky,** ADJECTIVE. **éveillé (-ée), gai (gaie), vif (vive), plein (pleine) d'entrain, joyeux (-euse) ▶** lively; cheerful; energetic : *a perky personality.*

per-ma-nent [PUR-muh-nunt] ADJECTIVE. **permanent (-ente) ▶** lasting or meant to last for a long time without change; not temporary : *She gave up her temporary job for a permanent position.* **Note.** The fact of being permanent is permanence. **■ permanently,** ADVERB. **▶ de façon permanente.** **▲ NOUN, permanents. permanente ▶** a chemical treatment for the hair that produces a long-lasting curl. SYN: enduring, lasting, durable, endless.

per-mis-sion [pur-MISH-un] NOUN. **permission ▶** the act of permitting; allowing a person to do something : *He had permission to leave early.*

per-mit [pur-MIT] VERB, permitted, permitting. **1. permettre, autoriser ▶** to agree that a person may do something; let; allow : *She was permitted to go skiing.* **2. permettre (de) ▶** to make possible; allow to happen : *The picnic will be held Saturday, if the weather permits.* **▲ [PUR-mit]** NOUN, permits. **permis, laissez-passer, autorisation écrite ▶** a written statement from some authority allowing or giving permission to do something : *You need a permit to fish in this lake.* SYN: allow, authorize, let, grant, consent.

per-pen-dic-u-lar [PUR-pun-DIK-yoo-lur] ADJECTIVE. **1. perpendiculaire ▶** straight up and down. **2. perpendiculaire ▶** at a right angle to a straight line.

per-pet-u-al [pur-PECH-yoo-ul] ADJECTIVE. **1. perpétuel (-elle), éternel (-elle) ▶** going on for ever; never stopping; forever. **2. perpétuel (-elle), continuel (-elle), sans fin ▶** happening over and over without stopping.

per-sist [pur-SIST] VERB, persisted, persisting. **1. persister, s'obstiner ▶** to continue doing something in spite of difficulty; refuse to give up : *Liam persisted until he solved the mystery.* **2. persister, continuer ▶** to go on and on; continue : *Shayla's cough persisted through the winter.* **■ persistent,** ADJECTIVE. **▶ persistant (-ante), tenace. ■ persistence,** NOUN. **▶ persistance, ténacité, obstination.** SYN: keep on, persevere, continue, hold on. ✏ **p. 434.**

per-son [PUR-sun] NOUN, persons. **1. personne, individu ▶** a human being; a man, woman, or child. **2. personne ▶** in language, a word showing who or what the subject is. The first person (*I* or *we*) tells who is speaking. The second person (*you*) tells who is spoken to. The third person (*he, she, it,* or *they*) tells who is spoken about. **in person en personne ▶** physically there; present : *He had to appear in person to pay the traffic fine.*

per-son-al [PUR-sun-ul] ADJECTIVE. **1. personnel (-elle) ▶** having to do with only one person rather than with people in general; private : *a personal opinion.* **2. personnel (-elle) ▶** about or against a person : *Instead of sticking to the issues, the candidate made a lot of personal remarks about his opponent.* **3. en personne ▶** done in person : *a personal appearance by a famous singer.* **4. personnel (-elle) ▶** having to do with the body : *Soap, toothpaste, and deodorant are personal-care products.* **■ personally,** ADVERB. **▶ personnellement.**

personal computer (PC) ordinateur personnel **▶** a small computer meant to be used on its own by one person.

per-son-al-i-ty [PUR-suh-NAL-ih-tee] NOUN, personalities. **1. personnalité ▶** the way a person acts; all the habits, feelings, and other such qualities that show what someone is like : *He's well-liked by his classmates because he has a friendly personality.* **2. personnalité ▶** personal qualities that are pleasing to others : *I really like Jana; she has a lot of personality.* **3. personnalité célèbre ▶** a person who is well-known : *I'm sure that woman is a well-known television personality, but I can't think of her name.*

per-son-al-ly [PUR-sun-ul-ee or PURSE-nul-ee] ADVERB. **1. personnellement ▶** by oneself rather than through someone else; in person; directly : *I'll personally drop off the rent cheque on my way to work.* **2. personnellement, pour ma part ▶** as far as oneself is concerned; speaking for oneself : *A lot of my friends watch that TV show, but personally I think it's silly.* **3. personnellement ▶** in a personal way : *I wouldn't let her remarks bother you—I don't think she meant them personally.*

per-son-i-fi-ca-tion [PUR-son-uh-fih-KAY-shun] NOUN. **personnification, incarnation ▶** a figure of speech in which things and abstract ideas are given human qualities—for example, the "cruel sun." ✏ **p. 439.**

per-son-nel [PUR-suh-nul] NOUN. **personnel ▶** all the people who work in a company or organization : *With the holiday season coming, the store will be hiring additional sales personnel.*

per-spec-tive [pur-SPEK-tiv] NOUN, perspectives. **1. perspective ▶** in art, a way of painting or drawing a picture so that things in the background seem to be farther away and harder to see, as they would be in a real-life view of the same scene. **2. perspective ▶** a certain way of thinking about or judging something; a point of view : *Try to see the problem from the other person's perspective.* ✏ **p. 440.**

per-suade [pur-SWADE] VERB, persuaded, persuading. **persuader, convaincre ▶** to make a person or group of people do or believe something; win over; convince : *Pia persuaded her parents to start recycling.* **Note.** The act or fact of persuading is **persuasion.** SYN: convince, coax, influence, win over.

pest [pest] NOUN, pests. **1. animal, insecte nuisible ou plante ▸** an animal, insect, or plant that destroys crops or causes other damage : *Mice and ants are common household pests.* **Note.** A chemical used to kill pests is a pesticide. **2. peste ▸** a very annoying person; a nuisance. ▲ VERB, pested, pesting. **tourmenter, importuner ▸** to keep bothering or annoying. 🖉 p. 24. .

pet [pet] NOUN, pets. **1. animal domestique, animal familier, animal de compagnie ▸** a dog, cat, bird, fish, or other tame animal that is kept by people as a companion. **2. chouchou (-oute) ▸** a person who is treated with special kindness; a favourite. ▲ ADJECTIVE. **1. domestique ▸** kept or treated as a pet : *my pet goldfish.* **2. favori (-ite) ▸** favourite; liked better than others. ▲ VERB, petted, petting. **câliner, caresser ▸** to pat or touch in a kind and gentle way : *She petted the puppy on the head.* 📖 p. 1093.

pet·al [PET-ul] NOUN, petals. **pétale ▸** one of the parts of a flower that give it a special shape and bright colour.

pe·ti·tion [puh-TISH-un] NOUN, petitions. **pétition, requête ▸** a formal request directed to someone in authority, asking that some action take place : *The people in our neighbourhood signed a petition to the city council asking that a traffic light be put on the corner.* ▲ VERB, petitioned, petitioning. **pétitionner, adresser une pétition ▸** to submit such a request. SYN: request, demand, appeal, plea.

pet·ri·fy [PFT-ruh-fy] VERB, petrified, petrifying. **1. pétrifier ▸** to become hard like stone over a very long period of time by replacing plant and animal cells with minerals. **2. pétrifier, paralyser ▸** to make or become unable to move, as if turned to stone : *Fear of the dark petrified him.* **Note.** Can be used as an ADJECTIVE: *petrified wood; the Petrified Forest.*

pe·tro·le·um [puh-TROH-lee-um] NOUN. **pétrole ▸** a thick, oily liquid that can burn easily and is usually found underground. Petroleum is believed to have formed from plant or animal remains that were buried under rock for millions of years. It is used for making fuels such as gasoline, natural gas, kerosene, heating oil, and for many other industrial products.

Pe·tun [pe-TUN] NOUN. **Pétun ▸** an Aboriginal people who were part of the Huron Nation. They originally lived in central and southern Ontario, but now live in Oklahoma, where they are known as the Wyandot.

phan·tom [FAN-tum] NOUN, phantoms. **fantôme, spectre ▸** an image that appears to be real, but does not actually exist.

phar·aoh [FARE-oh *or* FAR-oh] NOUN, pharaohs. (often Pharaoh) **pharaon ▸** the title of the rulers of ancient Egypt. 👁 p. 440.

phase [faze] NOUN, phases. **1. phase ▸** one of the changing stages of development for a person or thing : *Being a caterpillar is a phase in the life of a butterfly.* **2. phase ▸** any of the forms in which the moon or the planets appear.

pheas·ant [FEZ-unt] NOUN, pheasant or pheasants. **faisan (-ane) ▸** a long-tailed bird with brightly coloured feathers, often hunted for sport. 👁 p. 108.

phe·nom·e·non [fuh-NOM-uh-non] NOUN, phenomena. **1. phénomène ▸** any fact or event in nature that can be observed or studied, especially one that is unusual or interesting : *A tornado is a natural phenomenon.* **2.** (plural, phenomenons) **phénomène ▸** someone or something that is very unusual or remarkable : *Her amazing musical ability made her something of a phenomenon in the town.* ■ **phenomenal,** ADJECTIVE. **phénoménal (-ale, -aux), prodigieux (-ieuse) ▸** extraordinary; amazing.

phi·los·o·pher [fih-LOS-uh-fur] NOUN, philosophers. **1. philosophe ▸** a person who has a great knowledge of philosophy or has studied questions of philosophy. **2. philosophe ▸** any person who thinks deeply or makes judgments about the nature of life : *The cab driver who drove us home last night was quite a philosopher.*

phi·los·o·phy [fih-LOS-uh-fee] NOUN, philosophies. **1. philosophie ▸** the study of the nature and meaning of life. Philosophy deals with such questions as how to think and learn, what is true or real, what is right and wrong, and how to judge art and beauty. **2. philosophie ▸** any system of ideas based on this kind of study. **3. philosophie ▸** any set of beliefs that determines how a person acts; a guide to living : *Work hard and play hard—that's his philosophy.* ■ **philosophical** (also philosophic),

---

🖋 **Writing Tips**

Personification

*Writers use **personification** to make their writing more poetic or to add sharper images. In personification, ideas or things are given human qualities.*

> *The stream whispered to the trees and it wound through the woods. (The stream is given the human ability to whisper.)*
> *The North Wind's icy breath chilled us. (The North Wind is given the human ability to breathe.)*

✐ Writing Tips

Perspective/Point of View

Point of view or *perspective* refers to the way writers choose to present the events of a story. Every piece of writing is written from a perspective or point of view—it could be from the point of view of the main character, that of another character, or that of an impartial reporter. Different perspectives change the way a story is told. Little Red Riding Hood would be a different story if it were told from the Wolf's point of view rather than from that of either Little Red Riding Hood or an unknown narrator.

A writer who uses the **observer's point a of view** doesn't look into anyone's mind. The reader must judge the characters by the way they act and what they say. Most nonfiction is written from this point of view.

Writers use the **personal point of view** to present the story from the perspective of one character in the story. The writing directly tells the readers what that character sees, hears, and thinks.

With the **single point of view**, writers are not writing as a character in the story, but as if they can see into the mind of one character. Writers use this point of view when the key to the story is understanding that character's perspective.

With the **general point of view**, writers write as if they can see into the mind of more than one character, allowing the reader to know what several or all of the characters are thinking and feeling.

Before you write fiction, think carefully about the events of the story from the perspective of each of the characters. This will help you understand everyone's actions. You may then choose to tell the story from just one perspective, but it's important to have an understanding of all the characters.

ADJECTIVE. **philosophique, philosophe** ▶ having a calm attitude in the face of problems.

phone [fone] NOUN, phones. **téléphone** ▶ short for telephone. ▲ VERB, phoned, phoning. **téléphoner** ▶ to call someone on the telephone.

pho·net·ics [foh-NET-iks] NOUN. **phonétique** ▶ the study of the sounds people make when they speak and of how these sounds are produced. ■ **phonetic,** ADJECTIVE. **phonétique** ▶ having to do with the sounds of speech.

pho·nics [FON-iks] NOUN. **phonique** ▶ a way of teaching people to read by showing how the letters used in writing stand for certian speech sounds.

pharaoh

phos·pho·rus [FOS-fur-us] NOUN. **phosphore** ▶ a chemical element that is found in several different forms. The basic form is a waxy yellowish substance that is very poisonous and glows in the dark. Another form of phosphorus is needed by plants and animals in order to grow.

pho·to [FOH-toh] NOUN, photos. **photo, photographie** ▶ short for photograph.

pho·to·cop·y [FOH-toh-KOP-ee] NOUN, photocopies. **photocopie** ▶ an exact copy of something written or printed on a page, made by a special photographic process. ▲ VERB, photocopied, photocopying. **photocopier** ▶ to make a photocopy. ■ **photocopier,** NOUN. **photocopieur, photocopieuse** ▶ a machine that makes photocopies.

pho·to·graph [FOH-tuh-graf] NOUN, photographs. ▲ VERB, photographed, photographing. **photo, photographie** ▶ to make a photograph of something. ■ **photographic,** ADJECTIVE. ▶ **photographier, prendre en photo. Note.** Photography is the art or work of taking photographs. **Note.** A photographer is a person who takes photographs, especially someone who does this as a job.

pho·to·syn·the·sis [FOH-toh-SIN-thuh-sis] NOUN. **photosynthèse** ▶ the process by which green plants make food from water and carbon dioxide. A substance called chlorophyll allows plants to change the energy of sunlight into food.

phrase [fraze] NOUN, phrases. **1. syntagme, locution** ▶ a group of words that go together to express an idea, but that do not form a complete sentence : *"The red car"* is a phrase; *"The red car raced past us"* is a sentence. **2. expres-**

sion ▸ a short, simple, or forceful expression : *The phrase "the real McCoy" is said to refer to an invention by Elijah McCoy.* ▲ VERB, phrased, phrasing. **exprimer** ▸ to say or write something in a particular way : *He tried to think of a way to phrase his request so that Dad would be sure to grant it.*

phys·i·cal [FIZ-i-kul] ADJECTIVE. **1. physique** ▸ having to do with the body : *physical exercise.* **2. physique, concret (-ète)** ▸ having to do with solid, material things that can be seen, as opposed to thoughts or feelings; concrete : *Trees, rocks, and clouds are all physical objects.* ▪ **physically,** ADVERB. ▸ **physiquement.** Note. The physical sciences are those that deal with earth, matter, and the universe, such as physics, chemistry, and geology.

phy·si·cian [fih-ZISH-un] NOUN, physicians. **médecin** ▸ a person who is trained and licensed to practise medicine ; a doctor.

phys·ics [FIZ-iks] NOUN. **physique** ▸ the science that studies matter and energy, such as motion, heat, light, sound, electricity, and magnetism. Physics includes the study of atoms and nuclear energy. Note. A person who is an expert in physics is a physicist.

pi·an·o [pee-AN-oh] NOUN, pianos. **piano** ▸ a large musical instrument with a keyboard. A musical sound is made by pressing a key, which causes a felt-covered hammer to strike a certain metal string. Note. A person who plays the piano is a pianist. ☞ p. 538.

pick[1] [pik] VERB, picked, picking. **1. choisir, sélectionner** ▸ to take just one from a group ; choose; select : *Pick a card from the deck and I'll tell you what it is.* **2. cueillir** ▸ to take up with the hands ; gather : *She picked fresh flowers for the table.* **3. picoter** ▸ to dig at with something pointed : *Don't pick at your food.* **4. pincer** ▸ to play a guitar or other such instrument with the fingers ; pluck. ▲ NOUN, picks. **1. choix, sélection** ▸ something that is chosen from a group ; a choice : *Take your pick of any kind of fruit you want.* **2. plectre, médiator** ▸ a small piece of plastic or other hard material used to play a guitar, banjo, or other such instrument.

pick a fight chercher la bagarre, chercher la querelle ▸ to start a fight or argument.

pick on taquiner, s'en prendre à ▸ to bother or make fun of ; tease. ✎ p. 442.

pick[2] NOUN, picks. **1. (pickaxe or pickax) pioche** ▸ a tool consisting of a curved metal bar sharpened at each end and attached to a long wooden handle. A pick is used to break up hard ground, rocks, paved surfaces, and so on. **2. pic** ▸ any tool with a sharp point used to break up or poke at something : *an ice pick; a toothpick.*

pick·et [PIK-it] NOUN, pickets. **1. piquet** ▸ a pointed stake or post driven into the ground. Note. A group of these can be used to make up a picket fence. **2. gréviste** ▸ a person who stands or marches back and forth outside a building to protest something. Pickets may be seen carrying signs outside a business where there is a strike going on, or in front of public buildings as a political protest. ▲ VERB, picketed, picketing. **faire le piquet de grève** ▸ to stand or march as a picket : *People picketed in front of that company to protest the way it harms the environment.*

pick·le [PIK-ul] NOUN, pickles. **cornichons** ▸ any food, especially a cucumber, that has been preserved and flavoured by keeping it in a mixture of salt water or vinegar. ▲ VERB, pickled, pickling. **mariner, saumurer** ▸ to preserve food in this way. ▪ **pickled,** ADJECTIVE: ▸ **mariné (-ée).** *pickled beets.*

picket fence

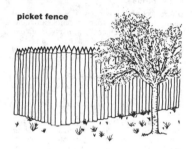

pick·up [PIK-up] NOUN, pickups. **1. ramassage, collecte** ▸ the act of picking up something : *There is no trash pickup today because of the holiday.* **2. accélération** ▸ a quick increase in speed : *A diesel engine doesn't have as much pickup as a regular gas engine.* **3. (also pickup truck) camionnette** ▸ a small truck with an open back for carrying light loads.

pic·nic [PIK-nik] NOUN, picnics. **pique-nique** ▸ a meal eaten outdoors. ▲ VERB, picnicked, picnicking. **pique-niquer** ▸ to go on a picnic. ☞ p. 1165.

pic·ture [PIK-chur] NOUN, pictures. **1. peinture, image, dessin** ▸ a likeness of a person or thing; a drawing, painting, photograph, or the like. **2. image** ▸ what is seen on a television or movie screen : *The picture is always fuzzy on this set.* **3. film** ▸ a movie : *In 1939, Gone With the Wind won the Academy Award for Best Picture.* **4. image, tableau (-eaux), description** ▸ a clear description given in words ; image : *That author gives a great picture of life in the Klondike.* ▲ VERB, pictured, picturing. **1. présenter** ▸ to

441

🖉 Word Builder

Pick on *often means to annoy, bother, or tease: We pick on Todd because he is so good natured and knows how to take it.* ***Pick off*** *is sometimes used in baseball to describe when a runner is caught off base: Ari picked off a runner at first base. It can also mean to shoot one at a time.* ***Pick and choose*** *means to select with great care: I pick and choose movies carefully because I don't like to be disappointed.* ***Pick to pieces*** *means to criticize very strongly: During a peer evaluation, Eduard picked my science project to pieces.*

make a picture of. **2. (s') imaginer, se représenter ▸** to form an image in the mind; imagine: *Stephen did not look at all as I had pictured him.* **3. dépeindre, décrire ▸** to give a picture of in words; describe.

pie [py] NOUN, pies. **tarte, tourte ▸** a food made up of a pastry crust and a filling of fruit, vegetables, or meat, usually baked in a shallow round pan. 📖 p. 1139.

piece [peece] NOUN, pieces. **1. morceau (-eaux), bout ▸** a part that has been cut, broken, or otherwise taken off a larger thing: *a piece of cake.* **2. parcelle, morceau (-eaux), bout ▸** a portion; a limited part of some larger group: *a piece of land.* **3. pièce, article ▸** one part of a set: *She plays the drums in a six-piece band.* **4. pièce, morceau (-eaux), article ▸** a single work in painting, music, writing, and so on: *a piece of art.* **5. exemple ▸** an example of something: *Elaine's term paper was a fine piece of work.* ▲ VERB, pieced, piecing. **joindre, assembler, rassembler ▸** to join pieces together: *Yvon tried to piece together the broken coffee cup with glue.* SYN: part, bit, portion, section, segment, share.

pier [peer] NOUN, piers. **1. jetée ▸** a structure built out from the shore over the water and used as a dock or a walkway. **2. pilier, colonne ▸** a large post or pillar used to support a bridge.

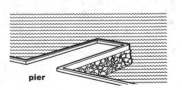

pier

pierce [peers] VERB, pierced, piercing. **1. percer, transpercer ▸** to go into or through: *A shaft of sunlight pierced the gloom.* **2. percer ▸** to make a hole in: *The nail pierced the tire on my bike.* **Note.** Can be used as an ADJECTIVE: *A piercing shout broke the quiet of the night.*

pig [pig] NOUN, pigs. **porc, cochon ▸** a four-legged animal with a fat body, short legs, a broad nose, and a short, curly tail. Pigs are raised on farms to provide meats such as pork, ham, and bacon, and for many other products such as lard and leather. **Note.** Also called a **hog** or **swine.** 📖 p. 1093. 👁 p. 115.

pi·geon [PIJ-un] NOUN, pigeons. **pigeon ▸** a common bird with short legs, a small head, and a plump body. Pigeons and doves are actually the same type of bird, and the pigeon that is often seen in large cities is also called a **rock dove.**

pigeon

pike [pike] NOUN, pike or pikes. **brochet ▸** one of a family of long, thin freshwater fish with a large mouth and many sharp teeth. Pike are popular for game fishing and for food.

pile¹ [pile] NOUN, piles. **1. pile, tas, amas ▸** many things lying on top of each other; a heap: *a wood pile.* **2.** Informal. **paquet ▸** a large amount: *She made piles of money with her invention.* ▲ VERB, piled, piling. **1. empiler ▸** to stack or heap so as to form a pile: *Pile the books on the table.* **2. empiler, entasser ▸** to crowd together as if in a pile: *The hockey fans piled into the arena.* SYN: heap, mound, stack, mass, quantity, batch.

pile² NOUN, piles. **pieu (-eux), pilotis ▸** a heavy beam of concrete, wood, or steel used to help hold up a bridge, pier, or building. **Note.** Also called a **piling.**

pile³ NOUN, piles. **poil ▸** the soft, thick fibres on the surface of a carpet or on materials such as velvet.

piles

pil·grim [PIL-grim] NOUN, pilgrims. **1. pèlerin (-ine)** ▸ a person who travels to a holy place. **Note.** A journey of this kind is called a **pilgrimage. 2. Pilgrim fathers. Père pèlerin** ▸ one of the group of English settlers who travelled to Plymouth, Massachusetts, in 1620 to seek religious freedom.

pill [pil] NOUN, pills. **1. pilule** ▸ medicine in the form of a small ball or tablet that is swallowed whole. **2.** Informal. **fatigant (-ante)** ▸ something or someone unpleasant : *Judy always nags her friends; she's such a pill.*

pil·lar [PIL-ur] NOUN, pillars. **1. pilier** ▸ an upright column that is used as a support in a building or that stands by itself as a monument. **2. pilier** ▸ a person who is thought of as an important source of strength or support : *She is a pillar of her community.*

pil·low [PIL-oh] NOUN, pillows. **oreiller** ▸ a bag or case filled with feathers or other soft material, used as a support for the head while lying down. **Note.** A pillowcase is a cloth cover for a pillow.

pi·lot [PY-lut] NOUN, pilots. **1. pilote** ▸ a person who flies an aircraft. **2. pilote** ▸ a person who steers and controls a ship. **3. pilote** ▸ a person who is specially trained to guide ships into and out of a harbour or through dangerous waters. ▲ VERB, piloted, piloting. **piloter** ▸ to act as a pilot; steer or guide.

pin [pin] NOUN, pins. **1. épingle** ▸ a short length of metal with a point at one end and a flat or rounded head at the other. A pin is used to fasten pieces of cloth or paper together. **2. épingle** ▸ any similar thing used to hold or fasten : *a clothespin.* **3. broche** ▸ an ornament with a clasp for attaching it to clothing. **4. quille** ▸ in the game of bowling, one of the 5 or the 10 bottle-shaped wooden pieces to be knocked down by the ball. ▲ VERB, pinned, pinning. **1. épingler** ▸ to fasten or join together with a pin : *He wore a flower pinned to his jacket.* **2. immobiliser, fixer, clouer** ▸ to hold in

one place : *The wrestler won the match by pinning her opponent.*

on pins and needles être sur des charbons ardents ▸ worried or anxious.

pinch [pinch] VERB, pinched, pinching. **1. pincer** ▸ to squeeze between the thumb and finger, or between hard surfaces : *He pinched his finger in the door.* **2. tirer, serrer** ▸ to make tight or wrinkled : *His face was pinched with cold.* ▲ NOUN, pinches. **1. pincement** ▸ the act of squeezing hard on a person's skin. **2. pincée** ▸ a very small amount of something, such as can be held between the thumb and finger : *He added a pinch of salt to the soup.* **3. au besoin** ▸ a time of sudden difficulty or trouble; an emergency : *Don't throw away that old flashlight—we can always use it in a pinch if the lights go out.* SYN: squeeze, press, nip.

pine¹ [pine] NOUN, pines. **1.** (also pine tree) **pin** ▸ any one of a large group of evergreen trees that bear cones and have long, very thin leaves called needles. **2. pin** ▸ the wood of a pine tree, used in building. 👁 p. 255.

pine² VERB, pined, pining. **se languir** ▸ to become weak or sick from sadness or from wanting something too much : *Dianne is pining for ice cream.*

pine·ap·ple [PINE-ap-ul] NOUN, pineapples. **ananas** ▸ a large, juicy tropical fruit that looks somewhat like a large pine cone. Pineapples have a tough brownish skin and stiff, pointed leaves on top.

pink [pink] NOUN, pinks. **1. rose** ▸ a pale red colour. **2. œillet** ▸ a garden plant bearing pink, red, or white flowers with a sweet smell. 🖉 p. 64.

pint [pint] NOUN, pints. **pinte** ▸ a unit of measure in the imperial system. A pint is equal to 0.57 litres.

pi·o·neer [py-uh-NEER] NOUN, pioneers. **1. pionnier (-ière)** ▸ one of the first people to live in a new land, preparing the way for others. **2. pionnier (-ière), précurseur (-eure)** ▸ a person who does something first and leads the way for others. ▲ VERB, pioneered, pioneering. **ouvrir, être à l'avant garde, défricher** ▸ to act as a pioneer : *That company pioneered the sale of small, inexpensive computers.* SYN: settler, leader, colonist, forerunner.

pipe [pipe] NOUN, pipes. **1. tuyau (-aux)** ▸ a long, hollow tube used to carry water, steam, oil, and other liquids or gases from one place to another. **2. pipe** ▸ a tube with a small bowl at one end, used to hold tobacco for smoking. **3. pipeau (-eaux), chalumeau (-eaux)** ▸ the long, tube-shaped part of certain musical instruments, such as the organ. **4. pipes. cornemuse** ▸ short for bagpipes. ▲ VERB, piped, piping. **1. canaliser, transporter par tuyau** ▸ to carry by a pipe or pipes : *Oil is piped south from Alaska.*

2. jouer ▸ to play music or give a signal on a pipe or pipes : *to pipe a tune on the bagpipes.* **3. parler d'une voix flûtée ▸** to speak up in a shrill voice : *"I'm bored," piped a small voice from the third row.*

pi·rate [PY-rit] NOUN, pirates. **1. pirate, flibustier, corsaire ▸** a person who attacks and robs a ship at sea. **2. pirate, voleur (-euse) ▸** any person who takes and uses the work or property of others in a way that is against the law. **Note.** The crime of being a pirate is piracy. ▪ **pirate or pirated,** ADJECTIVE. ▸ **pirate, piraté (-ée):** *to rent a movie and make a pirate copy.* ▲ VERB, pirated, pirating. **pirater, contrefaire, voler ▸** to make one or more copies of a copyrighted work such as a movie, CD, or computer program, and sell or use them illegally. ☞ p. 971.

pis·til [PIS-tul] NOUN, pistils. **pistil ▸** the part of a flower where the seeds grow.

pis·tol [PIS-tul] NOUN, pistols. **pistolet ▸** a small gun that is held and fired in one hand. **Note.** Also called a handgun.

pis·ton [PIS-tun] NOUN, pistons. **piston ▸** in a machine, a solid part that fits inside a hollow cylinder and moves back and forth by the force of liquid or steam.

pit¹ [pit] NOUN, pits. **1. fosse, trou ▸** a hole in the ground, especially one made by digging something out : *a sand pit.* **2. alvéole ▸** a small hole or hollow in the surface of anything : *The surface of a golf ball is covered in pits.* ▲ VERB, pitted, pitting. **1. trouer, piquer ▸** to make pits in something. **2. se mesurer, opposer ▸** to match one person or group against another : *The chess player was pitted against the former champion.*

pit² NOUN, pits. **noyau (-aux) ▸** the seed in the middle of certain fruits, such as peaches or cherries.

pitch¹ [pich] VERB, pitched, pitching. **1. lancer ▸** in baseball, to throw the ball to the batter. **2. lancer, jeter ▸** to throw or toss anything in this way : *They're out back pitching horseshoes.* **3. tanguer ▸** to fall roughly forward, or go roughly up and down : *"For ten hours the wind howled across our rolling deck as the Knorr pitched and heaved in the rough sea."* (Robert D. Ballard) **4. dresser, monter ▸** to set up : *pitch a tent.* **5. donner le ton ▸** to set at a certain level of sound : *The speaker's voice was pitched so low that the audience had a difficult time hearing him.* ▲ NOUN, pitches. **1. lancer ▸** a throw by the pitcher in baseball. **2. hauteur, ton, registre ▸** the level of a certain sound, in the sense of how high or low it is : *A singer who can sing each note exactly at the right level is said to have perfect pitch.*

pitch in s'y mettre, s'atteler au travail ▸ work or begin to work hard : *If everyone pitches in, we'll get done much quicker.*

pitch² NOUN. **bitume ▸** a black, gummy substance made from tar, used to pave streets or to make things waterproof. ▲ ADJECTIVE. **noir absolu, noir complet ▸** very dark or black, like pitch : *The room was pitch black with the lights out.*

pitch·er¹ [PICH-ur] NOUN, pitchers. **cruche, pichet ▸** a container with a handle on the side and a lip for pouring liquids; a jug.

pitch·er² NOUN, pitchers. **lanceur (-euse) ▸** in baseball, the player who throws the ball to the batter.

pitcher plant sarracénie ▸ a plant with leaves shaped like pitchers. The leaves contain a liquid in which insects are trapped. Pitcher plants are found in the bogs of northern and eastern Canada.

pit·i·ful [PIT-ih-ful] ADJECTIVE. **1. pitoyable, lamentable ▸** causing a feeling of pity. **2.** *Informal* **pitoyable, lamentable ▸** badly done; poor : *Our team lost 14–0? That's really pitiful.* SYN: sad, sorry, wretched, miserable.

pi·ty [PIT-ee] NOUN, pities. **1. pitié, compassion ▸** a feeling of sorrow for the unhappiness or suffering of another : *"One by one, they took pity on the pathetic creature before them."* (Tololwa M. Mollel) **2. dommage ▸** a cause for sorrow or regret : *It would be a pity to miss the game.* ▲ VERB, pitied, pitying. **avoir pitié de, plaindre ▸** to feel pity for another or others : *She pitied the dog, who was left alone all day.* SYN: mercy, compassion, sympathy, grief.

piz·za [PEET-suh] NOUN, pizzas. (also pizza pie) **pizza ▸** an Italian dish that is made up of a thin baked crust covered with tomato sauce, cheese, and seasonings, and that can also be topped with sausages, mushrooms, onions, and so on.

place [place] NOUN, places. **1. endroit, lieu (lieux) ▸** a certain part of space; any point in space thought of by itself : *That's a good place to fish.* **2. endroit, lieu (lieux) ▸** a house, city, or other such location on the earth : *Quebec City is an interesting place to visit.* **3. lieu (lieux) ▸** a room, building, or other area used for a certain purpose : *This office is my place of business.* **4. place ▸** any position in time, space, rank, and so on : *He finished the race in first place.* **5. rue ▸** a name for a short street : *My friend Anton lives at 37 Berec Place.* ▲ VERB, placed, placing. **1. placer, mettre ▸** to put something in a certain place or position. **2. se rappeler, remettre ▸** to identify something by connecting it with proper facts, location, and so on : *She looks familiar to me, but I just can't place her at the moment.* **3. se classer ▸** to finish in a certain place in a competition : *Anna placed third in the science fair.* **Note.** The act or fact of placing is placement. SYN: region, spot, location, site. ✏ p. 445.

pla·gia·rize [PLAY-juh-rize] VERB, plagiarized, plagiarizing. **plagier, copier ▸** to copy the writ

plagiarism

ing or words of another and to present it as one's own. **Note.** The fact of doing this is called **plagiarism.**

plague [playg] NOUN, plagues. **1. peste** ▶ a deadly disease with a high fever and chills, spreading rapidly from one person to another. **Note.** A serious plague was bubonic plague, also known as **Black Plague** or **Black Death.** Bubonic plague is caused by a certain type of bacteria carried by fleas. In the Middle Ages, this disease swept through Europe and Asia killing millions of people. **2. plaie, fléau (fléaux), invasion** ▶ anything that causes trouble or suffering : *Farmers fear a plague of locusts.* ▲ VERB, plagued, plaguing. **harceler, tourmenter** ▶ to trouble or distress; cause to suffer; annoy : *Jared has been plagued with allergies all summer.*

plaid [plad] NOUN, plaids. **1. tartan, tissu écossais** ▶ a pattern of squares formed by checks and stripes of different colours that cross each other. **2. tartan, tissu écossais** ▶ any fabric having this pattern. **3. plaid** ▶ a long cloth worn over the shoulder by Scottish Highlanders.

plain [plane] ADJECTIVE, plainer, plainest. **1. clair (claire), évident (-ente)** ▶ easy to see, hear, or understand : *I found the pen right away—it was in plain sight, on the table.* **2. simple** ▶ not fancy or elegant; without decoration : *Male cardinals have bright-red crests, but female and young cardinals are a plain brown.* **3. quelconque** ▶ not good-looking. **4. franc (franche)** ▶ very direct in expressing thoughts and feelings; frank : *I like that candidate; she's a plain talker.* **5. nature** ▶ with nothing else added; by itself : *I'll have a plain hamburger, with no ketchup or mustard.* ▲ NOUN, plains. **plaine** ▶ a large area of land that is flat or nearly flat. **plainly,** ADVERB. ▶ **simplement, clairement, nettement.** SYN : simple, clear, obvious, distinct, unadorned.

plan [plan] NOUN, plans. **1. projet, plan** ▶ a way or idea worked out ahead of time for what to do or how to do it : *Serge made a plan for completing his class project on time.* **2. plan** ▶ a drawing or diagram showing how to make something or how something is arranged : *the plans for a new house.* ▲ VERB, planned, planning. **projeter, organiser, planifier** ▶ to think about or work out how to do something; make a plan : *She plan-*

plane[1] [plane] NOUN, planes. **1. plan** ▶ a smooth surface : *Plane geometry deals only with flat surfaces, rather than solid objects.* **2. avion** ▶ short for **airplane** (p. 1152).

plane[2] [plane] NOUN, planes. **rabot** ▶ a hand tool with a wide, sharp blade that is used to smooth away the rough parts of a wood surface. ▲ VERB, planed, planing. **raboter, aplanir, planer** ▶ to make smooth or level using a plane on something : *to plane a table top.*

plan·et [PLAN-it] NOUN, planets. **planète** ▶ one of the large round bodies that move in an orbit around the sun. The nine planets in our solar system are Mercury, Venus, Earth, Mars, Jupiter, Saturn, Uranus, Neptune, and Pluto. p. 1117. p. 391.

plank [plank] NOUN, planks. **planche, madrier** ▶ a long, heavy, flat piece of wood that has been sawed : *The floor is made of pine planks.*

plank·ton [PLANK-tun] NOUN. **plancton** ▶ the mass of very tiny plants and animals that float with the current on an ocean or lake. Many sea animals live by eating plankton.

plant [plant] NOUN, plants. **1. végétal (-ale, -aux)** ▶ a living thing that is not an animal, cannot move about by itself, and can make its own food through photosynthesis. **2. plante** ▶ a vegetable, flower, or other small form of plant life with a soft stem, as opposed to a larger tree or shrub. **3. usine** ▶ a building where something is made or manufactured; a factory : *Books are produced in a printing plant.* ▲ VERB, planted, planting. **1. planter** ▶ to set a plant or seed into the ground so that it can grow. **2. planter** ▶ to set very firmly in place : *Henry planted his feet firmly and refused to move.* p. 1098. p. 249.

plant·er [PLAN-tur] NOUN, planters. **1. pot, jardinière** ▶ a container in which house plants are grown. **2. planteur (-euse)** ▶ a person or machine that plants.

plaque [plak] NOUN. **1.** (plural, plaques) **plaque** ▶ a flat piece of board or metal that has writing or designs on it. Plaques are often placed at historic spots to give information, or are given

---

✏ Word Builder

Place is often a particular area. To **go places** means to be successful or advance toward a goal: *She has good money sense and will go places in business.* **In place of** means instead of: *The coach put Anita in goal instead of Bryan.* **Out of place** can mean something is inappropriate or badly timed: *His remark about Raginder's money troubles was way out of place.* To **take place** is to happen or occur: *The awards ceremony will take place on Friday afternoon.*

as an award for something. **2. plaque ▸** a thin film left by food on the surface of teeth. Plaque contains bacteria that can cause cavities.

plas-ma [PLAZ-muh] NOUN. **plasma ▸** the clear, almost colourless liquid part of the blood, in which red blood cells and white blood cells are suspended. Plasma is what makes the blood able to flow through the body.

plas-ter [PLAS-tur] NOUN. **plâtre ▸** a pasty mixture of lime, sand, and water that becomes hard as it dries. Plaster is used to coat walls and ceilings. ▲ VERB, plastered, plastering. **1. plâtrer ▸** to cover a wall or ceiling with plaster. **2. coller, plaquer ▸** to cover closely, as if with plaster : *Joanna surfaced from her dive with her hair plastered to her head.*

plas-tic [PLAS-tik] NOUN, plastics. **plastique ▸** an artificial material that is soft and can be shaped when it is hot. When it cools, it becomes very hard. Many common items are made partly or completely of plastic. ▲ ADJECTIVE. **1. plastique, en plastique ▸** made of plastic : *a plastic cup.* **2. malléable ▸** able to be moulded or shaped : *Wax is a plastic material.*

plate [plate] NOUN, plates. **1. assiette ▸** a round, nearly flat dish from which food is eaten. **2. assiette ▸** the food on such a plate : *I ordered a fruit plate for lunch.* **3. plaque ▸** a thin, flat, smooth piece of metal or other such material : *Battleships and tanks are protected by steel plates.* **4. plaque ▸** a thin piece of metal that is stamped, printed, or engraved : *a car's licence plate.* ▲ VERB, plated, plating. **1. plaquer ▸** to cover with a thin layer of metal, such as gold or silver. **2. métalliser, blinder ▸** to cover with metal plates, as for armour.

pla-teau [pla-TOH] NOUN, plateaus or plateaux. **1. plateau (-eaux) ▸** a large, flat area of land that is higher than the land around it. **2. plateau (-eaux) ▸** a length of time in which progress stops for a while : *After improving all fall, the basketball team seems to have hit a plateau.*

plat-form [PLAT-form] NOUN, platforms. **1. plateforme, quai ▸** a floor or flat surface that is raised off the ground : *The passengers stood on the platform, waiting for the train.* **2. plate-forme ou plateforme, programme ▸** a statement of beliefs and policies : *A political party has a platform that explains its position on the issues.*

plat-i-num [PLAT-uh-num] NOUN. **platine ▸** a valuable metal that looks like silver. It is used to make jewellery and in tools and machinery.

plat-ter [PLAT-ur] NOUN, platters. **plat ▸** a large plate for serving food, usually having an oval shape : *a turkey platter.*

plat-y-pus [PLAT-uh-pus] NOUN, platypuses or platypi. **ornithorynque ▸** a water animal of Australia that has a bill like a duck, webbed feet, a broad, flat tail, and dark-brown fur. Platypuses are among the few mammals that lay eggs.

play [play] VERB, played, playing. **1. jouer ▸** to do something for fun; pass the time in an enjoyable way : *"Why don't you laugh and play all day as I do?"* (Gerald McDermott). **2. jouer ▸** to take part in a sport or game : *to play baseball.* **3. jouer ▸** to act out a part on the stage, in a movie, and so on. **4. jouer ▸** to make music or sound : *to play the piano; to play a CD.* **5. jouer ▸** to act in a certain way : *to play a trick on someone; to play fair.* ▪ **playful,** ADJECTIVE. ▸ **enjoué (-ée), espiègle.**

play-er [PLAY-ur] NOUN, players. **1. joueur (-euse) ▸** a person who plays a game or a musical instrument : *a basketball player; a piano player.* **2. lecteur ▸** a machine that reproduces something that was recorded before : *a cassette player.* **3. acteur (-trice) ▸** an actor or actress.

play-ground [PLAY-grownd] NOUN, playgrounds. **terrain de jeu, cour de récréation, parc ▸** an outdoor area where children can play, usually having swings, slides, and other such equipment.

play-mate [PLAY-mate] NOUN, playmates. **camarade ▸** someone who plays with another person; a friend.

pla-za [PLAZ-uh or PLAH-zuh] NOUN, plazas. **1. centre commercial ▸** a shopping centre. **2. place ▸** an open square or other public area in a city.

plea [plee] NOUN, pleas. **1. appel ▸** a serious request for something; an appeal : *The mayor made a plea to all citizens to save water during the long dry spell.* **2. défense ▸** in law, the answer that an accused person gives in court to the charges made against him or her : *a plea of not guilty.*

plead [pleed] VERB, pleaded or pled, pleading. **1. supplier, implorer ▸** to make a serious request; ask for something with deep feeling : *to plead for help.* **2. plaider ▸** to respond to a charge in court : *The accused thief pleaded guilty.* SYN: beg, implore, coax, pray.

pleas-ant [PLEZ-unt] ADJECTIVE. **1. agréable ▸** giving pleasure; enjoyable : *The wind was warm, the stars shone in the night sky, and the ride home was very pleasant.* **2. agréable, aimable, affable ▸** having nice manners or behaviour; friendly : *Tim's kindergarten teacher is a very pleasant person.* ▪ **pleasantly,** ADVERB. ▸ **agréablement.** SYN: agreeable, likable, enjoyable, charming.

please [pleez] VERB, pleased, pleasing. **1. plaire à, faire plaisir à ▸** to cause someone to feel good; give pleasure to : *The song pleased the audience.* **2. plaire, agir à sa guise, s'il vous plaît ▸** to like or wish to do; prefer; choose : *as you please.* **Note.** Also used to ask a person politely to do something : *Please pass me the salt.* ▪ **pleasing,** ADJECTIVE. **agréable ▸** giving pleasure; pleasant; enjoyable : *a pleasing smile; a pleasing combination of colours.* 🖋 p. 447.

plea·sure [PLEZH-ur] NOUN, pleasures. **1. plaisir** ▶ a feeling of being happy; enjoyment; liking something : *It has been a pleasure meeting you.* **2. plaisir** ▶ fun or enjoyment, as opposed to work : *They played games all day, just for the pleasure of it.* **Note.** Often used as an ADJECTIVE: *The harbour was filled with sailboats, speedboats, and other pleasure craft.* ▪ **pleasurable,** ADJECTIVE. ▶ **agréable.** SYN : joy, delight, thrill, satisfaction. 🗐 p. 1023.

pleat [pleet] NOUN, pleats. **pli** ▶ a flat fold made in cloth by folding it over on itself and then sewing or pressing it in place. ▪ **pleated,** ADJECTIVE. **plissé (-ée)** ▶ having pleats : *a pleated skirt.*

pled [pled] VERB. a past form of plead.

pledge [plej] NOUN, pledges. **1. promesse, parole** ▶ a serious promise or agreement that is meant to be kept : *The organizers of the fundraising drive signed a pledge to give the money to charity.* **2. gage** ▶ something given as a guarantee or token of something : *He left his bike as a pledge to return quickly.* ▲ VERB, pledged, pledging. **promettre, s'engager** ▶ to make a pledge; promise.

plen·ty [PLEN-tee] NOUN. **abondance** ▶ as much as or more than is needed; a full supply : *There is plenty of food for everyone.* ▪ **plentiful,** ADJECTIVE. ▶ **abondant (-ante), copieux (-ieuse).** more than enough; abundant. SYN : enough, ample, sufficient, abundant.

pli·ers [PLY-urs] PLURAL NOUN. **pince(s)** ▶ a tool that looks like a pair of scissors, with two handles and two short grips that close tightly together. Pliers are used for holding, bending, or cutting things.

plot [plot] NOUN, plots. **1. conspiration, complot** ▶ a secret plan to do something, especially something wrong : *Two thieves formed a plot to steal the gold.* **2. terrain** ▶ a small area or piece of ground : *They had a plot of land for a garden.* **3. intrigue, action** ▶ the main story or action in a book, play, movie, or the like. ▲ VERB, plotted, plotting. **1. comploter, conspirer** ▶ to make a secret plan or plot. **2. tracer** ▶ to make a map, diagram, or chart of : *The weather service plotted the path of the approaching storm.* SYN : scheme, plan, intrigue, conspiracy. 🖋 p. 448.

plough [plow] NOUN, ploughs. (also plow) **1. charrue** ▶ a large, heavy farm tool used for breaking up and turning the soil to prepare it for planting. **2. charrue, chasse-neige** ▶ something that works the way a plough does, especially a snowplough. ▲ VERB, ploughed, ploughing. (also plowed, plowing) **1. passer la charrue** ▶ to use a plough to work the soil or to move snow. **2. avancer péniblement** ▶ to move along with a strong effort : *The ships ploughed steadily through the rough sea.*

plough

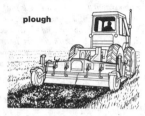

pluck [pluk] VERB, plucked, plucking. **1. arracher, cueillir** ▶ to pull or pick something off or out : *She plucked the apples from the tree.* **2. plumer** ▶ to pull the feathers off a chicken or other such bird to prepare it for cooking. **3. tirer** ▶ to grasp at; pull at : *The child plucked at her father's coat.* ▲ NOUN, plucks. **1. extirpation, arrachement** ▶ the act of plucking at something; a pull or tug. **2. courage** ▶ courage; bravery **Note.** A plucky person is one who shows a lot of courage.

plug [plug] NOUN, plugs. **1. bouchon** ▶ a piece of rubber, metal, or other material used to fill or cover a hole : *the plug for the sink.* **2. prise, fiche** ▶ a device attached to the end of an electric wire or cord, used to make an electrical connection. It has points sticking out that fit into holes in a socket. ▲ VERB, plugged, plugging. **1. boucher, obturer** ▶ to fill or stop up. **2. brancher** ▶ to put the plug of an electrical device into an outlet. **3. persévérer, bûcher, piocher** ▶ to work slowly but steadily : *to plug away at an assignment.* SYN : block, clog, stop, jam, obstruct, stuff.

plum [plum] NOUN, plums. **1. prune** ▶ a small, round, juicy fruit that grows on a small tree. Plums usually have a smooth purple or red skin.

🖋 Word Builder

Please, delight, and **satisfy** *refer to the positive way a person responds to something.*
If something **pleases** *you, it makes you happy: It pleases me to watch the waves at the beach.*
Delight *indicates strong feelings of pleasure: It is a real delight to watch you skate.*
When you are **satisfied,** *your needs and wishes have been met: I was satisfied by the dinner and went to bed happy.*

✐ Writing Tips

Plot

The **plot** of a story is the series of events in the story, the line of action. The plot of a story often centres on a problem or conflict. The plot of *Charlotte's Web*, which is built around the problem of Wilbur's survival, can be described in the following way:

> When Wilbur the pig is born, he is the runt of the litter. But as he grows bigger, he is in danger of being sold for his meat. His life is saved by Charlotte, a spider, and the other farm animals he has come to know. Charlotte cleverly saves him by writing messages in her web.

A plot develops with **rising action,** a term used to describe how conflict builds or is introduced as the story progresses. **Climax** is a term used to describe the most exciting point of the story. The **falling action** comes after the climax; things happen quickly, and loose ends are beginning to be cleared up. The **resolution** of the story comes at the end; it ties up all the loose ends and gives the reader a satisfactory conclusion or resolution to the problem or conflict.

2. prune ▶ a dark reddish-purple colour. 👁 p. 255.

plumb·er [PLUM-ur] NOUN, plumbers. **plombier (-ière) ▶** a person whose work is putting in and repairing water pipes and fixtures.

plumb·ing [PLUM-ing] NOUN. **plomberie, tuyauterie ▶** the system of pipes and fixtures that brings water to a building and carries waste away.

plum·met [PLUM-it] VERB, plummeted, plummeting. **tomber à pic, plonger, chuter ▶** to drop or fall suddenly.

plump [plump] ADJECTIVE, plumper, plumpest. **grassouillet (-ette), dodu (-ue) ▶** having a full or round figure; fat in a healthy way : *We had a nice plump chicken for dinner.*

plunge [plunj] VERB, plunged, plunging. **1. plonger, enfoncer ▶** to go or move quickly and with force : *He plunged his hand into the icy cold water.* **2. plonger ▶** to make a sudden and complete change : *There was a crack of lightning, and the room was plunged into darkness.* **3. se jeter, se lancer ▶** to begin something in a hurried or hasty way : *Mom plunged into another of her long stories about the "good old*

days." ▲ NOUN, plunges. **plongeon ▶** the act of plunging; a quick jump or movement : *She took a plunge in the lake.*

plu·ral [PLOOR-ul] NOUN, plurals. **pluriel ▶** the form of a word used to show more than one : *The plural of "door" is "doors."* ▲ ADJECTIVE. **pluriel (-ielle) ▶** more than one. ✐ p. 448.

plus [plus] PREPOSITION. **1. plus ▶** added to : *Four plus four is eight.* **2.** *Informal.* **plus ▶** along with; increased by : *It takes skill plus practice to win a competition.* ▲ ADJECTIVE. **1. supérieur (-ieure), plus ▶** more than or higher than : *A grade of 85 is a B, and 89 is a B plus.* **2. positif (-ive) ▶** greater than zero. ▲ NOUN, pluses or plusses. **1.** (also plus sign) **plus ▶** a sign [+] showing that something is to be added. **2. plus, avantage, atout ▶** a good point or feature; an advantage : *It was a plus that the new hockey coach had a large van.*

Plu·to [ploo-toh] NOUN. **1. Pluton ▶** the smallest planet in the solar system. Pluto is the farthest planet from the sun. **2. Pluton ▶** in the religion of the ancient Romans, the god of the dead. 👁 p. 391.

P.M., p.m. ABBREVIATION. **1. après-midi ▶** a way to show that a certain time is in the afternoon or evening : *Karla's hockey game is at 7 p.m.* **Note.** P.M. means from noon until midnight; A.M. means between midnight and noon. **2. Premier ministre ▶** prime minister : *Canada's P.M. lives at 24 Sussex Dr.*

pneu·mo·nia [nyoo-MONE-yuh or noo-MONE-yuh] NOUN. **pneumonie ▶** a serious disease of the lungs, usually caused by bacteria or viruses. People with pneumonia may get a sore throat, a high fever, chest pains, and a dry cough.

pock·et [POK-it] NOUN, pockets. **1. poche ▶** a small bag sewn inside clothing, used to hold items such as money, keys, pens or pencils, and so on. **2. poche, compartiment ▶** any small compartment like this found in a car, suitcase, purse, and so on. **3. poche ▶** a small area that is different from what is around it : *The divers found an air pocket inside the sunken ship.* ▲ ADJECTIVE. **de poche ▶** small enough to fit inside a pocket, or meant for carrying in a pocket : *a pocket camera.* ▲ VERB, pocketed, pocketing. **empocher, mettre dans sa poche ▶** to put something in a pocket : *Kyle pocketed the change from the $20 bill.*

✐ Writing Tips

Plurals

The most common way to form **plural** words in English is to add **s** to the end of words—one **chicken** becomes two **chickens,** and one **egg** becomes two **eggs.**

pod [pod] NOUN, pods. **cosse** ▸ on a plant, the shell or case in which seeds grow. When it is ripe, a pod splits open and releases its seeds : *Peas grow inside pods.* 👁 **p. 249.**

po-em [POH-um] NOUN, poems. **poème** ▸ a form of writing that expresses ideas or feelings through the sound and rhythm of words, as well as through their meaning. The words and lines of a poem are usually arranged to create a pattern of rhythm and sound, sometimes including rhymes. **Note.** Someone who writes poems is a **poet. Note.** Something that has to do with a poem or is like a poem is **poetic.**

po-et-ry [POH-uh-tree] NOUN. **1. poésie** ▸ the art or process of writing poems. **2. poésie** ▸ poems as a part of literature : *Canadian poetry includes the works of Dennis Lee, Margaret Atwood, and many others.* **3. poésie** ▸ something very beautiful, like a poem : *The ballet dancing of Karen Kain has been called pure poetry.*

point [poynt] NOUN, points. **1. pointe** ▸ a sharp, thin end : *the point of a pencil or knife.* **2. pointe** ▸ a narrow piece of land that sticks out into the water. **3. point** ▸ any particular area or spot of land : *The South Pole is the point on earth that is farthest south.* **4. point** ▸ a dot or period. **5. point** ▸ a certain time, position, or condition : *The boiling point of water is 100°C.* **6. propos** ▸ the main idea of an article or report : *The point of her article was that we need more volunteers.* **7. point, qualité, défaut** ▸ a fact or characteristic : *Spelling is one of his weak points* **8. point** ▸ one unit of scoring in a game : *A touchdown counts for six points.* ▲ VERB, pointed, pointing. **pointer, montrer du doigt** ▸ to show the way or indicate something. SYN : aim, goal, purpose, objective, intention. 🖉 **p. 449.**

point-er [POYN-tur] NOUN, pointers. **1. baguette** ▸ something used to point to things : *Teachers sometimes use a pointer to call attention to something on the board.* **2. pointeur, pointer** ▸ a hunting dog that is trained to stand very still and point in the direction toward the position of game. **3. tuyau (-aux), conseil** ▸ a helpful piece of advice ; tip : *Thanks for that pointer about pitching a baseball.*

point-less [POYNT-les] ADJECTIVE. **futile, inutile, vain (vaine)** ▸ without purpose or meaning ; having no point : *a pointless argument.*

point of view **point de vue** ▸ the way a person looks at or judges things ; viewpoint ; perspective. 🖉 **p. 440.**

poise [poyz] VERB, poised, poising. **équilibrer, tenir en équilibre** ▸ to balance or hold steady in one place : *"And with its wings poised for flight, the eagle called out its anger."* (Sheryl McFarlane) ▲ NOUN. **1. assurance** ▸ the quality of being calm and in control of oneself. **2. équilibre** ▸ the act of holding steady ; balance. ■ **poised,** ADJECTIVE. **posé (-ée)** ▸ confident ; composed : *Sandy remained poised during the questions after her presentation.*

poi-son [POY-zun] NOUN, poisons. **poison** ▸ a substance that can kill or seriously harm a person, animal, or plant. Common poisons include arsenic, and lead. Poison is contained in the bite of many snakes and insects, and also in some plants. ▲ VERB, poisoned, poisoning. **1. empoisonner, intoxiquer** ▸ to cause injury or death with a poison. **2. empoisonner** ▸ to add poison to. **3. corrompre, pervertir** ▸ to have a very bad influence : *Lies poison the mind.* ■ **poisonous,** ADJECTIVE. ▸ **vénéneux (-euse), venimeux (-euse), toxique.** 📖 **p. 1161.** 🖉 **p. 451.**

poison ivy **herbe à puce, sumac vénéneux** ▸ a North American plant that has shiny leaves made up of three leaflets. The oil of this plant can cause a severe, itchy rash when it is touched. **Note.** Another form of the plant is called **poison oak.**

poke [poke] VERB, poked, poking. **1. piquer** ▸ to push against with a pointed object ; give a sharp blow : *He poked the needle through the cloth.* **2. sortir, dépasser** ▸ to thrust or stick out : *The turtle poked its head out of its shell.* **3. avancer lentement** ▸ to move or act very slowly : *The old truck poked along in the right lane.* ▲ NOUN, pokes. **coup, poussée** ▸ a sharp, quick blow.

po-ker¹ [POH-kur] NOUN, pokers. **tisonnier** ▸ a pointed metal rod used to stir up or tend a fire.

poker² NOUN. **poker** ▸ a card game in which players bet that their cards have a higher value than those in the other players' hands. The winning player gets what everyone else has bet.

po-lar [POH-lur] ADJECTIVE. **polaire** ▸ having to do with the North or South Pole : *a polar expedition.*

🖉 **Word Builder**

*At the point of can mean very near to: When we visited Indira, she was at the point of making dinner. **Beside the point** means having little or nothing to do with a subject: Jeremy's story about brown bears was beside the point in our discussion of Arctic creatures. On the other hand, **to the point** means very direct, concise, and relevant: Su Ling's ideas about walruses were really to the point. Make **a point of** can mean to make a special effort to do something: Diane makes a point of swimming every day.*

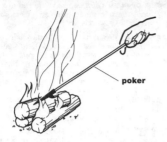

poker

polar bear OURS (OURSE) **polaire ▶** a large bear with heavy white fur. Polar bears live in the Far North.

pole[1] [pole] NOUN, poles. **perche, poteau (-eaux), mât, canne ▶** a long, slender rod or post of wood, metal, or other material : *a fishing pole ; a telephone pole ; a flagpole.*

pole[2] NOUN, poles. **1. pôle ▶** the north or south end of the earth's axis. **2. pôle ▶** either of the two ends of a magnet, where the opposite magnetic forces are the strongest.

pol·ice [puh-LESE] PLURAL NOUN. **police ▶** a group of people who work for the government to keep order and enforce the law. **Note.** A member of a police force is called a police officer. ▲ VERB, policed, policing. **maintenir l'ordre dans ▶** to control or keep order : *The downtown streets were heavily policed during the Queen's visit.*

pol·i·cy[1] [POL-uh-see] NOUN, policies. **politique ▶** a plan that guides the way something is done ; a set of rules or ideas for action ; procedure : *That restaurant has a no-smoking policy.*

policy[2] NOUN, policies. **police ▶** a written agreement or contract between an insurance company and a person whose life or property is insured.

po·li·o [POH-lee-oh] NOUN. **Note.** Other names for this disease are poliomyelitis and infantile paralysis. **polio, poliomyélite ▶**

pol·ish [PAH-lish] VERB, polished, polishing. **1. polir, cirer ▶** to make something shiny and smooth by rubbing it with a cloth or other material : *to polish a floor.* **2. polir, lisser ▶** to make smooth or neat ; work on to take out problems and rough spots : *Tyler spent hours polishing his essay before he handed it in.* ▲ NOUN, polishes. **1. poli ▶** a smooth, shiny surface. **2. vernis, crème, cire, ▶** something used to produce such a surface : *nail polish ; silver polish.*

po·lite [puh-LITE] ADJECTIVE, politer, politest. **poli (-ie) ▶** having or showing good manners ; acting toward other people in a nice and proper way : *"He wished South Wind a polite good-bye."*

(Rosebud Yellow Robe) ■ **politely,** ADVERB. ▶ **poliment.** ■ **politeness,** NOUN. ▶ **politesse.** SYN : well-mannered, proper, civil, courteous.

po·lit·i·cal [puh-LIT-uh-kul] ADJECTIVE. **politique ▶** having to do with politics ; concerning the activities of government : *Lester B. Pearson's political career began in 1928.* ■ **politically,** ADVERB. ▶ **politiquement.**

pol·i·ti·cian [POL-uh-tish-un] NOUN, politicians. **1. homme (femme) politique ▶** a person who is elected to public office or is running for office, such as a mayor, member of Parliament, premier, or prime minister. **2. politicien (-ienne) ▶** any person who works for a political party or is involved in politics.

pol·i·tics [POL-uh-tiks] NOUN. **1.** (used with a singular VERB) **politique ▶** the science or practice of holding public office or taking part in government. **2.** (used with a plural VERB) **conviction ▶** a person's attitudes or beliefs about government : *My mom's politics are very conservative.*

poll [pol] NOUN, polls. **1. sondage ▶** a survey of a group of people to find out what they think about a subject : *We took a poll to decide whether or not to change the name of our school mascot.* **2. suffrage, scrutin, vote ▶** the process of casting and counting votes in an election. **3. polls. bureau de vote, bureau de scrutin ▶** the place where people vote : *The polls were open for 12 hours on election day.* ▲ VERB, polled, polling. **1. sonder ▶** to get information by using a poll : *Auto makers often poll car buyers to find out what kinds of safety features they prefer.* **2. obtenir des votes ▶** to receive a certain number of votes in an election : *The mayor polled the majority of the votes.* SYN: survey, vote, questionnaire.

pol·len [POL-un] NOUN. **pollen ▶** in flowers, the fine yellow powder made by the male part of the plant. These male cells join with the female cells of the same plant or a related one to produce seeds. **Note.** This process is known as pollination. ☞ p. 248.

pol·lute [puh-LOOT] VERB, polluted, polluting. **polluer ▶** to put something into the air, water, or ground that makes it dirty or harmful to living things : *That factory is polluting the lake with its toxic waste.* ■ **polluted,** ADJECTIVE. ▶ **pollué (-ée).** *a polluted lake ; polluted air.* ✎ p. 451.

pol·lu·tion [puh-LOO-shun] NOUN. **1. pollution ▶** the condition of being polluted : *Air pollution is a serious problem in big cities.* **2. pollution ▶** things that pollute : *The pollution in our province's lakes is killing the fish.* **Note.** Something that pollutes is a pollutant : *Car exhaust is a pollutant.* ☞ p. 1161. ☞ p. 260.

po·lo [POH-loh] NOUN. **1. polo ▶** a game played on a large grassy field by two teams of riders on horseback. The players use long-handled mallets to try to knock a wooden ball into a goal. **2. water-polo** ▶ short for water polo.

polo

pol·y·es·ter [POL-ee-ES-tur] NOUN. **polyester** ▶ an artificial fibre made from chemicals, often used for making clothes.

pol·y·gon [POL-ee-gon] NOUN, polygons. **polygone** ▶ any geometric figure having three or more straight sides. Squares are polygons.

pome-gran·ate [POM-GRAN-it or POM-uh-GRAN-it] NOUN, pomegranates. **grenade** ▶ a round red fruit with a thick skin and many small seeds contained in a juicy pulp.

pon·cho [PON-choh] NOUN, ponchos. **poncho** ▶ a loose type of clothing made of a large piece of material with a hole in the middle for the head to go through. Ponchos are worn over other clothes to keep a person warm or dry.

pond [pond] NOUN, ponds. **1. étang, mare, bassin** ▶ a small, shallow body of fresh water that is completely surrounded by land. Ponds may be formed by nature or dug by people, as on a farm. **2. étang** ▶ a lake. ☞ p. 1108.

pon·der [PON-dur] VERB, pondered, pondering. **considérer, peser, réfléchir (à, sur), méditer (sur)** ▶ to think about something very seriously : *Aidan pondered the information he planned to include in his report.* **Note.** Something that is heavy or serious is ponderous: *a dull and ponderous speech.*

po·ny [POH-nee] NOUN, ponies. **poney** ▶ a very small, gentle horse.

poo·dle [POO-dul] NOUN, poodles. **caniche** ▶ a type of dog with thick, curly hair.

pool[1] [pool] NOUN, pools. **1.** (also swimming pool) **piscine** ▶ a large tank of water for swimming and diving, set either into the ground or above it. **2. mare** ▶ a body of still water.

3. flaque ▶ a small amount of any liquid : a puddle : *There was a pool of water next to the broken fish tank.*

pool[2] NOUN, pools. **1. billard (américain)** ▶ a game played with a stick (called a cue) and 16 balls on a large table that has six holes called pockets. **2. coopération, collaboration, partage, covoiturage** ▶ an arrangement by which a group of people share work or effort : *Carmen rides to work in a car pool with three other people.* ▲ VERB, pooled, pooling. **mettre en commun** ▶ To put things together for common use ; share : *The children pooled their allowances to buy a new puppy.*

poor [poor] ADJECTIVE, poor, poorest. **1. pauvre, dans le besoin** ▶ not having enough money to pay for things that are needed, such as food, clothing, or shelter. **2. mauvais (-aise), médiocre** ▶ not as good or as much as is expected or needed ; bad : *poor health ; a poor grade on a test.* **3. pauvre, malheureux (-euse)** ▶ worth feeling sorry for ; deserving pity or care : *The poor rabbit was shivering from cold and fear.* ■ **poorly,** ADVERB. ▶ **pauvrement, médiocrement.** *The band performed poorly when they didn't practise.*

pop[1] [pop] VERB, popped, popping. **1. éclater, faire pan** ▶ to make or cause to make a sudden, short sound : *The balloon popped when it broke.* **2. apparaître, (se) déplacer brusquement, fourrer** ▶ to go or place quickly up, down, in, or out ; move in a sudden way : *He popped it into his mouth.* ▲ NOUN, pops. **1. pan** ▶ a short, sharp sound. **2. soda** ▶ short for soda pop. **3. papa** ▶ short for father. ✐ p. 453.

pop[2] *Informal.* **populaire** ▶ short for popular: *pop music.*

pop-corn [POP-corn] NOUN. **maïs éclaté, pop-corn** ▶ a type of corn with kernels that pop open and become white and puffy when they are heated.

pope [pope] NOUN, popes. (usually Pope) **pape (papesse)** ▶ the head of the Roman Catholic Church.

pop-lar [POP-lar] NOUN, poplars. **peuplier** ▶ a tall, thin tree that grows quickly and has oval or heart-shaped leaves. Poplar trees have light, soft wood. ☞ p. 254.

pop·u·lar [POP-yuh-ler] ADJECTIVE. **1. populaire** ▶ liked or enjoyed by many people : *a popular*

✐ **Word Builder**

Pollute can mean to add to air, water, or land something that is harmful to health or life : If the factory pollutes the stream, the fish will die. Corrupt means to introduce something new or harmful into something that was once very pure : A virus corrupted the hard drive on my computer. Poison is to add a harmful substance that is very dangerous and could cause death : Alonzo tried to poison the weeds with a spray.

451

song. **2. populaire, très apprécié (-ée)** ► having many friends; well-liked : *a popular person.* **3. populaire** ► having to do with people in general; of or by the people : *The members of the House of Commons in Canada are elected by popular vote.* **4. de notoriété publique** ► accepted by many people; widespread; common : *It is a popular belief that 13 is an unlucky number.* ■ **popularly,** ADVERB. ► **populairement, communément.** ✐ p. 156.

leaves

flowers

poplar

pop·u·lar·i·ty [POP-yuh-LAR-uh-tee] NOUN. **popularité** ► the condition of being popular; being liked by most people.

pop·u·late [POP-yuh-late] VERB, populated, populating. **1. peupler, habiter** ► to live in a certain place; inhabit : *Pigeons and squirrels populate the parks of most cities.* **2. peupler** ► to move into an area; settle : *Many Eastern Europeans populated the Canadian West.*

pop·u·la·tion [POP-yuh-LAY-shun] NOUN. populations. **1. population** ► the total number of people who live in a place : *The population of Canada in 1996 was nearly 30 million people.* **2. population** ► a particular group of people or animals : *The deer population in this area has doubled.*

por·ce·lain [POR-suh-lin *or* POR-slin] NOUN. **1. porcelaine** ► a hard white ceramic material that is so thin that light can be seen through it. Porcelain is used to make cups, dishes, and vases. **2. porcelaine** ► an object made from this material. ▲ ADJECTIVE. **délicat (-ate)** ► looking like porcelain : *a baby with porcelain skin.*

porch [porch] NOUN. porches. **porche, véranda** ► a platform at the entrance to a house or other building, usually covered by a roof but open at the sides.

por·cu·pine [POR-kyuh-PINE] NOUN. porcupines. **porc-épic** ► an animal that is covered with long, sharp quills, which it uses to protect itself. ☜ p. 110.

pore[1] [por] NOUN. pores. **pore** ► a very small opening that allows liquid or air to go through : *Sweat passes through the pores in our skin.* **Note.** Something that is porous has many pores or holes.

pore[2] VERB, pored, poring. (used with **over**) **être absorbé dans, étudier de près** ► to look at and study very carefully; examine : *"Michael and I pored over the treasures in his rusty old tackle box."* (Julie Lawson)

pork [pork] NOUN. **porc** ► the meat of a pig or hog used for food.

por·poise [POR-pus] NOUN. porpoises or porpoise. **marsouin** ► a warm-blooded sea mammal that is like a small whale, with a round head and a blunt snout. Porpoises are smaller than dolphins.

por·ridge [POR-ij] NOUN. **porridge, bouillie de flocons d'avoine** ► a soft breakfast food made by boiling oatmeal or other cereal in water or milk until it thickens.

port [port] NOUN. ports. **1. port** ► a place where boats and ships can dock or anchor; a harbour. **2. port** ► a city that has a harbour where ships can load and unload cargo and passengers : *Halifax is an important port in Nova Scotia.* **3. bâbord, gauche** ► the left side of a boat, a ship, or an aircraft when facing the front.

port·a·ble [POR-tuh-bul] ADJECTIVE. easy to move from one place to another; able to be carried; movable : *a portable typewriter.* ▲ ADJECTIVE. **portatif (-ive), portable** ► a temporary building on the grounds of a school, used as an extra classroom.

port·age [POR-taj] NOUN. portages. **1. portage** ► carrying boats, canoes, supplies, and so on overland from one stretch of water to another. **2. portage** ► a place where such a carrying takes place. ▲ VERB, portaged, portaging. **faire un portage** ► to carry a canoe, boat, supplies, and so on from one stretch of water to another.

por·ter [POR-tur] NOUN. porters. **1. porteur (-euse), bagagiste** ► a person who is hired to carry luggage or packages, as in a hotel or at a railway station. *"He won so many prizes that it took twelve porters to carry them to the ship."* (Marcia Williams) **2. employé (-ée) des wagons-**

✏️ Word Builder

*The expression **pop off** has different meanings depending on the situation. **Pop off** can mean to fall asleep: Grandpa often pops off halfway through the news. It can also mean to leave very quickly: They frequently just pop off to the lake for the weekend. As well, **pop off** can mean to die suddenly: The actor popped off during the filming of the movie. And **pop off** can mean to speak thoughtlessly, often showing anger: She would pop off whenever she was teased.*

---

lits ▶ a person who assists passengers on a train.

port·fo·li·o [port-FOH-lee-oH] NOUN, portfolios. **1. porte-documents** ▶ a folder or case for holding loose papers and other materials. **2. portfolio** ▶ a sample of one's work : *The students' portfolios contained their best work.*

port·hole [PORT-hole] NOUN, portholes. **hublot** ▶ a small, round window in the side of a ship or boat to let in air and light.

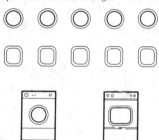

portholes

por·tion [POR-shun] NOUN, portions. **1. partie** ▶ a part of some larger thing or amount; a share : *They give a portion of their allowance to charity.* **2. portion** ▶ a serving of food : *Have a portion of pie.* ▲ VERB, portioned, portioning. **répartir** ▶ to divide or give out something in portions. SYN: part, share, piece, fraction.

por·trait [POR-trit *or* POR-trate] NOUN, portraits. **1. portrait** ▶ a painting or photograph of someone : *The Mona Lisa is a famous portrait.* **2. portrait** ▶ a realistic description of something in words.

por·tray [por-TRAY] VERB, portrayed, portraying. **1. représenter** ▶ to show in a picture : *The paintings of Allen Sapp portray Native life on the reserve.* **2. dépeindre** ▶ to create a picture of something in words; describe : *The article portrayed the ambassador as a kind and competent woman.* **3. jouer (le rôle de)** ▶ to act out a part in a play, film, or the like. **Note.** The act or fact of portraying something is a portrayal. **représentation, portrait** ▶ 📖 p. 168.

pose [pose] NOUN, poses. **pose** ▶ a way of standing or sitting; posture. ▲ VERB, posed, posing. **1. poser** ▶ to hold or place in position : *The campers posed next to the tent for a group picture.* **2. pose as. se faire passer pour** ▶ to pretend to be : *The spy posed as a businessman.* **3. poser, présenter** ▶ to put forward or present : *to pose a question.*

po·si·tion [puh-ZISH-un] NOUN, positions. **1. place** ▶ the place where a person or thing is : *The clowns took up a position at the head of the parade. Her position on the softball team is third base.* **2. position** ▶ the way someone or something is placed : *a sitting position; a standing position.* **3. situation** ▶ a particular situation or condition : *Being caught lying is an embarrassing position to be in.* **4. position, opinion** ▶ a certain way of thinking; point of view : *I don't agree with your position on that issue.* ▲ VERB, positioned, positioning. **(se) placer, (se) mettre en place, (se) poster** ▶ to position : *The choir director positioned the altos behind the sopranos.* SYN: location, place, spot, site.

pos·i·tive [POZ-uh-tiv] ADJECTIVE. **1. certain (-aine), formel (-elle)** ▶ with no doubt; absolutely sure; certain : *I am positive that this is the answer.* **2. affirmatif (-ive)** ▶ that agrees with or approves of something : *"Yes" is a positive answer to a question.* **3. positif (-ive), constructif (-ive)** ▶ meant to make things better; helpful or useful : *The teacher's positive comments on Sean's story encouraged him to continue writing.* **4. positif (-ive)** ▶ of a number, being larger than zero. **5. positif (-ive)** ▶ having one of two possible electrical charges : *A radio battery has a negative charge at one end and a positive charge at the other end.* **6. positif (-ive)** ▶ of a medical test, showing that a disease or condition is present. ▲ NOUN, positives. **1. épreuve positive, positif** ▶ an image on film that shows the light and dark areas as they actually appear, rather than reversed as in a negative. **2. nombre positif** ▶ a number greater than zero. ■ **positively,** ADVERB. **1. de façon positive, affirmativement, formellement** ▶ in a positive way. **2.** *Informal.* **positivement, assurément** ▶ actually; indeed : *It is so cold today that I am positively freezing.* SYN: definite, sure, certain, absolute.

pos·sess [puh-ZES] VERB, possessed, possessing. **1. posséder, avoir, être en possession**

453

de ▶ to have or keep for oneself; own : *This story tells of three men who each want to possess a golden statue.* 2. **posséder, obséder** ▶ to feel a very strong influence that takes over one's mind or will : *Cory was possessed by a dream of competing in the Olympics.* SYN: own, have, keep, hold, control. 🖉 **p. 454.**

pos·ses·sion [puh-ZESH-un] NOUN, possessions. 1. **fait d'entrer en possession de, fait de s'emparer de** ▶ the fact of possessing something : *The school won possession of the hockey trophy for one year.* 2. **possession** ▶ something owned; a belonging : *The family packed all their possessions for the move.*

pos·ses·sive [puh-ZES-iv] ADJECTIVE. 1. **possessif (-ive)** ▶ in grammar, showing that something belongs to a person or thing. 2. **possessif (-ive), jaloux (-ouse) de** ▶ wanting very much to own or completely control something : *My brother is very possessive about his toys and never lets me play with any of them.* ▲ NOUN, possessives. **possessif** ▶ a word that shows possession.

pos·si·ble [POS-uh-bul] ADJECTIVE. 1. **possible** ▶ that can be done; that can happen : *It is possible to get straight A's.* 2. **possible** ▶ that could be used, considered, or done : *Each student was given a list of four possible topics to write about.* ▲ NOUN, possibilities. 1. **possibilité, éventualité** ▶ the fact of being possible : *There is still a possibility that we can win.* 2. **possibilité** ▶ something that is possible : *What are the possibilities?*

pos·si·bly [POS-uh-blee] ADVERB. 1. **possiblement, probablement** ▶ according to what is possible : *You can't possibly be in two places at once.* 2. **peut-être (bien), possiblement** ▶ it is possible that; perhaps : *My neighbour is 80, or possibly 90, years old.*

possum opossum ▶ SEE opossum.

post[1] [pohst] NOUN, posts. **poteau (-eaux)** ▶ a piece of wood, metal, or other material that is placed upright in the ground to support something. ▲ VERB, posted, posting. **afficher** ▶ to put up a notice.

post[2] NOUN, posts. 1. **poste** ▶ a system for carrying letters, packages, and so on from one place to another; the mail. 2. **poste, courrier** ▶ a single delivery of mail : *Has today's post come yet?* ▲ VERB, posted, posting. 1. **poster, mettre à la**

poste ▶ to mail a letter or package. 2. keep (someone) posted. **tenir au courant** ▶ to let someone know the latest news. ■ **postal,** ADJECTIVE. **postal (-ale, aux)** ▶ having to do with mail or post offices : *Remember to put your postal code on your letters and cards.*

post[3] NOUN, posts. 1. **poste** ▶ the place where a soldier, guard, or police officer is supposed to stay when on duty. 2. **poste, affectation** ▶ a place where soldiers are stationed. 3. **poste** ▶ a job or position. 4. **comptoir** ▶ short for trading post.

post- PREFIX. after : *postdate; postscript.*

post·age [POHS-tuj] NOUN. **tarif(s) postal (-aux), tarif(s) d'affranchissement, frais de port** ▶ the amount of money charged by the post office for sending something by mail. ▲ ADJECTIVE: *postage stamp.*

post·card [POHST-kard] NOUN, postcards. **carte postale** ▶ a small card used for sending short notes through the mail. Postcards usually have a picture on one side and space for the address and message on the other side.

postal code **code postal** ▶ a code designed to speed up the processing of mail sorted by machines. In Canada, the postal code is a mix of numbers and letters : *M4W 1S3.*

post·er [POH-stur] NOUN, posters. **affiche** ▶ a large printed sign, often with an illustration or photograph, used for advertising or as a decoration. 🖉 **p. 1168.**

pos·ter·i·ty [pos-TAYR-uh-tee] NOUN. **postérité** ▶ the generations of the future; descendants : *She thought of her writing as a gift to posterity.*

post·mark [POHST-mark] NOUN, postmarks. **cachet de la poste, oblitération** ▶ an official mark placed on mail to cancel the stamp and show the date and place of mailing. ▲ VERB, postmarked, postmarking. **tamponner, oblitérer** ▶ to stamp mail with a postmark.

post office 1. **bureau de poste** ▶ an official government office that accepts, sorts, and delivers mail and sells postage stamps. 2. (often Post Office) **Société canadienne des postes** ▶ the Crown corporation that is in charge of mail. **Note.** Officially called the Canada Post Corporation. 🖉 **p. 1052.**

post·pone [pohst-PONE] VERB, postponed, postponing. **remettre (à plus tard), ajourner** ▶ to

---

🖉 Word Builder

Possess, own, and *keep* can all refer to the relationship between a person and what belongs to him or her. Possess is often used when talking about someone's belongings: I **possess** six cat's-eye marbles. **Own** can be used in place of possess, but it suggests an object that legally belongs to a person: My parents used to rent an apartment: now, they **own** a house. **Keep** suggests that something is in a person's possession, and that it can be held for a long or short time: I'll keep your bike while you're away.

put off until some later time : *They postponed the picnic because of rain.* SYN : delay, hold over, put off, defer, stall.

pos-ture [POS-chur] NOUN, postures. **pos-ture ▶** the way a person holds or carries the body when standing, sitting, or walking. ▲ VERB, postured, posturing. **poser, prendre des attitudes ▶** to take a posture ; pose : *The dancer postured before the mirror.*

pot [pot] NOUN, pots. **1. théière, pot, marmite, casserole ▶** a deep, usually round container used for holding food and liquids in cooking : *a teapot ; a pot of soup.* **2. pot ▶** a container for a growing plant : *a flower pot.* ▲ VERB, potted, potting. **mettre en pot ▶** to put something into a pot : *We should pot these young plants before they get much bigger.* SYN : bowl, pan, basin, vessel.

po-ta-to [puh-TAY-toh] NOUN, potatoes. **pomme de terre, patate ▶** a round or oval-shaped vegetable that grows under the ground as part of a leafy plant. Potatoes are white inside and have a brown or reddish skin.

po-tent [POH-tent] ADJECTIVE. **puissant (-ante) ▶** having great strength or force ; very powerful : *a potent tropical storm ; a potent cure.*

po-ten-tial [puh-TEN-chul] ADJECTIVE. **potentiel (-elle), éventuel (-elle), en puissance ▶** able to happen ; possible but not yet true or real : *Several potential buyers took the new car out for a test drive.* ▲ NOUN. **potentiel ▶** a quality that is able to develop : *Teresa is a student who has great potential for success.*

po-tion [POH-shun] NOUN, potions. **potion, philtre ▶** a drink that acts as a medicine.

pot-latch [POT-lach] NOUN, potlatches. **pot-latch ▶** a gift-giving ceremony among some of the Aboriginal peoples of the west coast of North America.

pot-pour-ri [POH-puh-REE] NOUN, potpourris. **1. pot(s)-pourri(s), fleurs séchées ▶** a fragrant mixture of dried flower petals and spices. **2. pot(s)-pourri(s) ▶** any miscellaneous collection, especially of musical or literary pieces.

pot-ter-y [POT-ur-ee] NOUN. **1. poterie ▶** pots, dishes, vases, and other such things shaped from clay and hardened by heat. **2. poterie ▶** the art or business of making such things. **Note.** A person who makes pottery is a **potter.**

pouch [powch] NOUN, pouches. **1. petit sac ▶** a soft container that is open at the top ; a bag or sack. **2. poche ▶** a part of an animal that is like a bag : *a kangaroo's pouch.*

poul-try [POLE-tree] NOUN, poultry. **volaille ▶** chickens, turkeys, ducks, geese, and other birds that are raised for their meat or eggs. **p. 1139.**

pounce [powns] VERB, pounced, pouncing. **bondir sur ▶** to jump down on something sud-denly to grab or stop it : *The cat pounced on the mouse.* ▲ NOUN. **bond ▶** a sudden jump or grab : *With a pounce, the cat was on the chair.*

pound[1] [pownd] NOUN, pounds. **1. livre ▶** a unit for measuring weight equal to 16 ounces (about 454 grams). **2. livre sterling, monnaie ▶** a unit of money in various countries, including Great Britain, where it is also called a **pound sterling.** Written with the symbol [£]: *Twenty pounds is $20.*

pound[2] VERB, pounded, pounding. **1. taper, frapper à grands coups, marteler ▶** to hit some-thing hard over and over : *The baby pounded on the board with her toy hammer.* **2. concasser, piler, broyer, pulvériser ▶** to beat something down into a powder or pulp by hitting it with a heavy object. **3. battre fort ▶** to beat hard ; throb : *My heart pounded.* ▲ NOUN, poundings. **martèlement ▶** the act of hitting hard. ▲ ADJEC-TIVE ▶ **d'un pas lourd** *"As I fled, each pounding step jarred my whole body."* (Jean Little) SYN : strike, bat, hammer, knock, bang, thump.

pound[3] NOUN, pounds. **fourrière ▶** an enclosed place for keeping stray dogs and other animals until their owners claim them or new owners can be found.

pour [por] VERB, poured, pouring. **1. verser, servir ▶** to cause a liquid to flow in a steady stream : *She poured a glass of juice.* **2. se déverser, affluer ▶** to move in a steady way : *The ants came pouring out of their hole in a huge mass.* **3. pleuvoir à verse, pleuvoir à tor-rents ▶** to rain hard. **4. pour out. raconter d'un seul jet, (s') épancher, se répandre en flots de paroles ▶** to tell about something freely ; talk openly : *The lost camper poured out her story of hunger and fear.*

pout [powt] VERB, pouted, pouting. **faire la moue ▶** to push out the lips with a frown to show that one is angry or upset : *The little boy pouted when his mother insisted that he go to bed on time.* ▲ NOUN : *The little girl walked away with a pout on her face.* SYN : frown, scowl, sulk, mope, fret.

pov-er-ty [POV-ur-tee] NOUN. **1. pauvreté ▶** the fact of being poor ; being without money for things that are necessary to life. **2. pauvreté ▶** any lack of something needed : *The poverty of the soil made farming difficult.*

pow-der [POW-dur] NOUN, powders. **1. poudre, poussière ▶** a fine dust made by grinding or crushing something solid : *Stone dust covered everything in the quarry.* **2. poudre ▶** some-thing made or used as a powder : *baking powder ; face powder.* ▲ VERB, powdered, pow-dering. **saupoudrer, poudrer ▶** to cover or sprin-kle something with powder : *The model wanted to powder his face before the photo shoot.*

pow-er [POW-ur] NOUN, powers. **1. pouvoir, faculté ▶** the fact of being able to do some-thing : *the power to fly ; the power to decide.*

2. puissance ▸ a force or strength; energy : *The runner has lots of power in her legs.* **3. électricité, courant électrique ▸** electricity : *The thunderstorm knocked power out all over the city.* **4. pouvoir, influence ▸** the ability to control or influence others : *In the 1970s, Prime Minister Pierre Trudeau had great power over Canadian politics.* **5. puissance ▸** in mathematics, the number of times that a number is multiplied by itself to get a result : *8 to the second power is 64 (8 times 8).* ▲ VERB, powered, powering. **(faire) marcher, (faire) fonctionner, actionner, propulser ▸** to provide with power : *Electricity powers this lawn mover.* ▲ ADJECTIVE. **qui marche à, qui fonctionne à ▸** powered by a motor : *a power boat.* ■ **powerful,** ADJECTIVE. **puissant (-ante) ▸** having great power : *The actor had a powerful voice.* 🖋 **p. 456.**

pow·er·less [POW-ur-les] ADJECTIVE. **impuissant (-ante) ▸** without power; not able to do something.

prac·ti·cal [PRAK-tuh-kul] ADJECTIVE. **1. pratique ▸** having to do with what is real and actual, rather than with theories or ideas : *practical advice.* **2. pratique ▸** suited for actual use; useful : *Please wear practical shoes for the hike.* **3. qui a le sens pratique, plein (pleine) de bon sens ▸** showing good sense; reasonable : *"What are you going to use for money?" asked his practical wife."* (E.B. White) SYN: workable, useful, sensible, useful, effective.

prac·ti·cal·ly [PRAK-tik-lee] ADVERB. **1. presque, pratiquement ▸** very close to, but not quite; nearly : *He read practically the whole book in one night.* **2. en pratique, d'une manière pragmatique ▸** in a practical or useful way.

prac·tice [PRAK-tis] NOUN. practices. **1. habitude ▸** the experience that comes from doing something over and over to develop and improve it : *Practice makes perfect.* **2. (mise en) pratique ▸** actual use or action; performance : *They put what they learned into practice.* **3. entraînement, exercice ▸** a time set aside for exercise or drill in some activity : *She had hockey practice every Saturday.*

prac·tise [PRAK-tis] VERB, practised, practising. (also practice) **1. s'entraîner (à), s'exercer (à), répéter ▸** to do something again and again so as to become better at it : *She practises the*

piano every day. **2. (s') exercer (à) ▸** to do regularly or make a habit of it : *to practise self-control.* **3. exercer, pratiquer ▸** to work at a profession : *My sister practises law.* SYN: train, rehearse, exercise, drill, repeat.

prai·rie [PRAYR-ee] NOUN, prairies. **1. prairie, plaine ▸** a large, open area of flat or gently rolling land with very few trees. **2. the Prairies. les Prairies ▸** the prairie lands in central Canada. 🗂 **p. 1043.** 👁 **p. 247.**

Prairie Provinces (sometimes the Prairies) **les Prairies ▸** Alberta, Saskatchewan and Manitoba.

praise [prayz] NOUN, praises. **éloge, louange ▸** the act of saying that someone likes or thinks highly of a person or thing; words showing something is good : *The delicious dessert earned the praise of all the guests at the dinner party.* ▲ VERB, praised, praising. **1. louer, faire l'éloge (de) ▸** to give praise to someone; speak favourably about. **2. louer, glorifier ▸** to worship or give honour to a god or gods.

prance [prans] VERB, pranced, prancing. **1. caracoler ▸** of a horse, to step or spring forward with high, lively steps. **2. marcher allègrement, se pavaner ▸** to move or walk in a proud, happy way : *When she won the race, Julie pranced happily around the playing field.*

prank [prank] NOUN, pranks. **farce, tour ▸** a joke or trick. **Note.** Someone who plays a prank is a prankster. SYN: mischief, trick, joke, whim, antic, caper.

pray [pray] verb, prayed, praying. **prier ▸** to give a prayer; address words or thoughts to a god or gods.

pray·er [prayr] NOUN, prayers. **1. prière ▸** thoughts or words directed to a god or gods. **2.** *Informal.* **chance ▸** a hope or chance : *In all this rain, we haven't a prayer of staying dry.* 🗂 **p. 1029.**

pre- PREFIX. before; earlier than; prior to : *prehistoric; prearrange; prepay.*

preach [preech] VERB, preached, preaching. **prêcher ▸** to speak in public about religion : *preach a sermon.* **Note.** A person who preaches is a preacher.

pre·car·i·ous [prih-CARE-ee-us] ADJECTIVE. **précaire ▸** not safe or secure; dangerous : *The kit-*

✐ Word Builder

Power, strength, force, and *energy* all describe the ability or capacity to make an effort for a reason or purpose. *Power* is a general term to describe the ability to do something: *The car has enough power to go 200 km/hr.* Force is the use of power: *The force of the wind knocked down branches.* Strength is the ability to exert force: *She had to use all her strength to move the old trunk.* Energy usually applies to the use of stored-up power: *Alcino had enough energy to ride his bike home after running in a long-distance race.*

ten had a precarious hold on the tree branch. ■ **precariously,** ADVERB. ▶ **précairement.**

pre·cau·tion [prih-KAH-shun] NOUN, precautions. **précaution** ▶ something done ahead of time to avoid danger or harm.

pre·cede [pree-SEED] VERB, preceded, preceding. **précéder** ▶ to come before; go ahead of : *A calm, quiet period often precedes a rainstorm.* **Note.** Often used as an ADJECTIVE: *Don't fill out Section B until you've completed the preceding section.*

pre·ce·dent [PRES-sih-dent] NOUN, precedents. **précédent** ▶ something used as an example or guide for future decisions : *If I let you stay up late, it will set a precedent for your brothers and sisters.*

pre·cious [PRESH-us] ADJECTIVE. **1. précieux (-ieuse)** ▶ worth much; very rare or expensive; very valuable : *A diamond is a precious stone, and gold is a precious metal.* **2. précieux (-ieuse), chéri (-ie), adoré (-ée)** ▶ greatly loved; dear. ■ **preciousness,** NOUN. ■ **valeur.** ✐ p. 650.

prec·i·pice [PRES-uh-pis] NOUN, precipices. **1. précipice** ▶ a very steep, high wall of rock or earth; a cliff. **2. catastrophe, désastre, précipice** ▶ a dangerous situation.

pre·cip·i·tate [prih-SIP-uh-tate] VERB, precipitated, precipitating. **1. précipiter, hâter** ▶ to cause something to happen suddenly : *The damage from the earthquake precipitated our move from our house.* **2. condenser** ▶ to change from vapour to water and fall to earth as rain, snow, and so on.

pre·cip·i·ta·tion [prih-SIP-uh-TAY-shun] NOUN. **précipitation** ▶ any form of water that falls from the sky, including rain, snow, hail, or sleet. ✐ p. 113.

pre·cise [prih-SISE] ADJECTIVE. **précis (-ise)** ▶ having the proper order or details; strictly as it should be; exact : *Pilots must follow precise instructions when landing planes.* ■ **precisely,** ADVERB. **précisément, exactement** ▶ in a precise or accurate way; exactly : *The movie starts at precisely 7 :15.* SYN: exact, definite, accurate, correct, careful.

pre·ci·sion [prih-SIZH-un] NOUN. **précision, exactitude, minutie** ▶ the quality of being precise or exact : *It takes precision to be good at math.*

pre·co·cious [prih-KOH-shus] ADJECTIVE. **précoce** ▶ of a child, learning and doing things at a much earlier age than other children; advanced : *The precocious five-year-old could already read fluently.*

pred·a·tor [PRED-uh-tur] NOUN, predators. **prédateur (-trice), animal de proie** ▶ an animal that lives by hunting other animals for food : *Lions and hyenas are predators.* ■ **predatory,** ADJECTIVE. ▶ **prédateur (-trice), de proie.**

pred·e·ces·sor [PRED-uh-ses-ur *or* PREE-duh-ses-ur] NOUN, predecessors. **prédécesseur (-eure)** ▶ someone or something that comes before; a person or thing that precedes : *The current government blames the country's problems on its predecessors.*

pre·dic·a·ment [prih-DIK-uh-munt] NOUN, predicaments. **situation difficile, situation fâcheuse** ▶ a difficult or embarrassing problem : *When he spilled gravy on his shirt right before his speech, Joseph found himself in an embarrassing predicament.* SYN: mess, situation, complication, difficulty.

pred·i·cate [PRED-ih-kit] NOUN, predicates. **prédicat** ▶ in grammar, one of the two basic parts that make up a sentence. The subject tells what the sentence is about. The predicate tells what the subject is or does.

pre·dict [prih-DIKT] VERB, predicted, predicting. **prédire** ▶ to know or tell about something before it happens : *It's hard to predict the weather.* ■ **predictable,** ADJECTIVE: that can be predicted. ▶ **prévisible. Note.** A prediction is the act of predicting something, or the thing predicted.

pre·face [PREF-is] NOUN, prefaces. **préface** ▶ a short introduction at the beginning of a book or speech that tells something about the main part : *In the preface, the author thanks the people who helped him finish the book.* ✐ p. 458.

pre·fer [prih-FUR] VERB, preferred, preferring. **préférer** ▶ to like one person or thing better than another; choose one over another : *Many people prefer chocolate rather than vanilla ice cream.* ■ **preferable** [PREF-ur-uh-bul *or* PREF-ruh-bul] ADJECTIVE. ▶ **préférable, de préférence** ▶ to be preferred : *The thank-you note may be typed, but a handwritten note is preferable.* ■ **preferably,** ADVERB. ▶ **préférablement.** *They wanted a small cottage, preferably with a view of the lake.* ✐ p. 221.

pref·er·ence [PREF-uh-runs *or* PREF-runs] NOUN, preferences. **préférence** ▶ the fact of preferring one thing to another : *We can spend our vacation in Vancouver or Victoria—what's your preference?*

pre·fix [PREE-fiks] NOUN, prefixes. **préfixe** ▶ a group of letters put before a word to change the meaning. *Un-* and *non-* are prefixes meaning "not," as in <u>un</u>known and <u>non</u>fiction.

preg·nant [PREG-nunt] ADJECTIVE. **enceinte** ▶ of a female human or animal, having young growing inside the body before birth. **Note.** The fact of being pregnant is pregnancy.

pre·his·tor·ic [PREE-his-TOR-ik] ADJECTIVE. **préhistorique** ▶ having to do with the time before written records were kept, which was about 6000 years ago.

pre·ju·dice [PREJ-uh-dis] NOUN, prejudices. **1. préjugé** ▶ a strong feeling against another person because of the race, religion, or group to which he or she belongs. **2. préjugé, idée préconçue ▶** any opinion formed without knowing the facts. ▲ VERB, prejudiced, prejudicing. **prévenir (contre, en faveur de) ▶** to cause a person to have prejudice : *The food poisoning she experienced prejudiced her against eating seafood.* SYN: bias, unfairness, intolerance.

pre·ma·ture [pree-muh-CHUR *or* PREM-uh-CHUR] ADJECTIVE. **prématuré (-ée), avant terme ▶** before the usual or normal time; too early : *A premature baby is one that is born a month or more earlier than it should be.* **■ prematurely,** ADVERB. **▶ prématurément.** SYN: early, advanced, too soon, hasty.

pre·mier [PREE-mir *or* PREE-myir *or* prih-MIR] NOUN, premiers. **1. Premier ministre ▶** in Canada, the head of a provincial government. **2. chef du gouvernement ▶** in some countries, the person who is the chief officer of the government. The premier of some countries such as China is like the prime minister in Canada. ▲ ADJECTIVE. **premier (-ière) ▶** highest or most important; first in rank or quality : *William Shakespeare was the premier playwright of his day.*

pre·miere [prih-MEER *or* pre-MYER] NOUN, premieres. (also première) **première ▶** the first public performance of a new play, movie, or other such work. ▲ VERB, premiered, premiering. **donner la première de ▶** to give a first public performance or showing of : *A wonderful new play premiered last night.*

prem·ise [PREM-is] NOUN, premises. **1. prémisse, principe ▶** a statement that is the basis of an argument or conclusion : *The peace movement is based on the premise that war is evil.* **2. premises. locaux, lieux ▶** a piece of land and the buildings on it : *This restaurant does not allow smoking on its premises.*

pre·mi·um [PREE-mee-um] NOUN, premiums. **1. prime ▶** something extra given as a prize or reward, or to persuade a person to do something : *Magazines sometimes offer free gifts as a premium to anyone who buys a subscription.* **2. prime ▶** the amount paid at one time for an insurance policy. ▲ ADJECTIVE. **de marque, de qualité supérieure ▶** of higher value or quality : *You pay more for premium ice cream.*

put (place) a premium on donner la primauté à ▶ to value something highly : *My parents put a premium on high grades and quality work.*

prep·a·ra·tion [PREP-uh-RAY-shun] NOUN, preparations. **1. préparatif ▶** the fact of preparing, or something done to prepare : *The town was busy with preparations for the summer festival.* **2. préparation ▶** something prepared for a purpose, such as food or medicine. SYN: plans, arrangements, groundwork.

pre·pare [prih-PARE] VERB, prepared, preparing. **1. (se) préparer ▶** to get ready for something :

🖉 **Writing Tips**

Preface

An opening section in a book may be called a **preface,** *a* **prologue,** *an* **introduction,** *or a* **foreword.** *A preface often comes before the first chapter or section of a nonfiction text. It may include background information about the subject, explain how the writer gathered information or what the purpose of the book is, or acknowledge the contributions of others. It is usually not necessary to read the preface in order to understand the rest of the book.*

"They have been training together for three years to prepare for this brief shuttle mission." (Barbara Bondar) **2. préparer ▶** to make something by putting things together : *to prepare a video presentation.* SYN: arrange, get ready, fix, plan, equip.

prep·o·si·tion [PREP-uh-ZISH-un] NOUN, prepositions. **préposition ▶** in grammar, a word relating a NOUN or PRONOUN to another word. In the sentence *The dog ran to the mailbox,* the word *to* is a preposition. It shows the relationship of the NOUN *mailbox* to the rest of the sentence.

pre·pos·ter·ous [pruh-POS-tur-us *or* prih-POS-trus] ADJECTIVE. **absurde, ridicule, grotesque ▶** not making sense; very silly or foolish; ridiculous. **■ preposterously,** ADVERB. **▶ absurdement, ridiculement, grotesquement.**

pre·scribe [prih-SKRIBE] VERB, prescribed, prescribing. **1. prescrire ▶** to order a treatment or medicine for a patient : *The doctor prescribed penicillin and bed rest for Karin's bronchitis.* **Note.** A written order from a doctor for a certain medicine or treatment is a prescription. **2. prescrire ▶** to set as a rule to be followed; order : *Laws prescribe what we may and may not do.* SYN: order, recommend, suggest, advise, assign.

pres·ence [PREZ-uns] NOUN. **1. présence ▶** the condition of being in a certain place; being present : *His presence was noted by the teacher.* **2. présence, prestance, allure ▶** the way that a person appears or acts : *The famous actor had such a commanding presence that everyone turned to look at her.*

pre·sent[1] [PREZ-unt] ADJECTIVE. **1. présent (-ente) ▶** being in a certain place at a certain time : *All the students were present in class.* **2. actuel (-elle) ▶** going on now; at this time; current : *Present-day computers are much different from computers of 20 years ago.* ▲ NOUN. **1. présent ▶** the current time; now : *My grandmother tells me to live in the present, not in*

the past. **2. présent** ▸ short for **present** tense.
📖 **p. 156.**

pres·ent² [PREZ-unt] NOUN, presents. **cadeau (-eaux)** ▸ something that is given to a person by another as a sign of love, friendship, gratitude, and so on. ▲ [prih-ZENT] VERB, presented, presenting. **1. offrir** ▸ to give something as a present : *I presented my grandma with a bouquet of flowers.* **2. présenter** ▸ to bring before the public or a group; show or display : *The author presented his new book at a press conference.* **3. présenter** ▸ to bring forward; cause to be : *You must present a reason for your decision.* **4. présenter (à)** ▸ to introduce a person, especially in a formal way : *May I present my niece, Megan Pratt?* **Note.** Something that is fit to be seen or presented is presentable.

pres·en·ta·tion [PREZ-un-TAY-shun] NOUN, presentations. **présentation, exposé, représentation** ▸ the act of presenting, or something that is presented.

pres·ent·ly [PREZ-unt-lee] ADVERB. **1. actuellement, en ce moment** ▸ at the present time; now : *Mitchell is presently studying to be a mechanic.* **2. bientôt** ▸ in or after a little while; soon : *I can't help you right now, but I will presently.*

present tense **présent** ▸ in grammar, a verb form showing that something happens or exists at the present time.

pres·er·va·tion [PREZ-ur-VAY-shun] NOUN. **protection, sauvegarde, préservation, conservation** ▸ the act of preserving; protection : *The preservation of endangered species is an important concern of environmentalists.* SYN: safekeeping, saving, conservation.

pre·serv·a·tive [prih-ZUR-vuh-tiv] NOUN, preservatives. **agent de conservation** ▸ anything that is used to preserve something : *Sugar, vinegar, or salt can be used as a preservative in jams and pickles.*

pre·serve [prih-ZERV] VERB, preserved, preserving. **1. préserver, protéger** ▸ to keep from harm; keep safe; protect. **2. conserver** ▸ to keep in the same state; keep up; maintain : *Museums preserve many interesting objects from the past.* **3. conserver** ▸ to prepare food so that it will not rot or spoil : *Smoking fish can help to preserve it.* ▲ NOUN, preserves. **1. réserve** ▸ an area of forest or other wild land where wild animals are protected. **2. preserves. confiture** ▸ fruit that has been cooked with sugar. SYN: protect, keep, guard, shelter, save, conserve.

pre·side [prih-ZIDE] VERB, presided, presiding. **présider** ▸ to be in charge; control or direct : *Nelson presided over the meeting.* SYN: direct, lead, govern, administer, officiate.

pres·i·dent [PREZ-uh-dunt] NOUN, presidents. **1. président (-ente)** ▸ the chief officer of a company, club, society, or other such organization :

As president of the company, Ms. Atwood oversees all major decisions. **2. président (-ente)** ▸ the highest-ranking officer in some countries, such as the United States or France. ▪ **presidential,** ADJECTIVE. ▸ **présidentiel (-elle).** *a presidential election.* **Note.** The position of president or the period of time that one person holds that position is called the presidency.

press [pres] VERB, pressed, pressing. **1. (s') appuyer sur, (se) presser (contre)** ▸ to push against something in a firm, steady way. **2. repasser** ▸ to make clothing smooth, as with an iron. **3. se frayer un chemin** ▸ to move or go with force : *They pressed forward through the crowd so that they could see what everyone was looking at.* **4. presser** ▸ to ask for something in a strong way : *The little boy pressed him until they gave him a cookie.* ▲ NOUN, presses. **1. pressoir** ▸ a machine used to press things : *A wine press crushes grapes to make wine.* **2.** (also printing press) **presse** ▸ a machine that prints newspapers, magazines, or books. **3.** (usually the press) **presse** ▸ newspapers, magazines, radio, and TV, or the people who report for them : *The press waited outside city hall to interview the mayor.* **Note.** Also called the media or the mass media. **4. pression** ▸ the fact of pressing : *The press of the crowd pushed her forward.* SYN: force, squeeze, crush, push, tighten, smooth.

pres·sure [PRESH-ur] NOUN, pressures. **1. pression** ▸ the force that is caused by one thing pushing against another : *She applied pressure to the brake.* **2. pression** ▸ a strong force or influence to do something : *peer pressure.* ▲ VERB, pressured, pressuring. **forcer à, contraindre à** ▸ to put pressure on; force or influence strongly : *Tim's brother pressured him into eating the last cookie.*

pres·tige [pres-TEEZH or pres-TEEJ] NOUN. **prestige** ▸ respect or high position that comes from some outstanding accomplishment. **Note.** Something or someone that has prestige is prestigious.

pre·sume [prih-ZOOM or prih-ZYOOM] VERB, presumed, presuming. **1. présumer, supposer** ▸ to accept something as true without full proof; suppose; assume : *I presume that you know how to read.* **2. se permettre de** ▸ to do something without having the right or permission. **Note.** Someone who presumes in this way is presumptuous. ▪ **presumably,** ADVERB. ▸ **vraisemblablement.** SYN: suppose, believe, assume, guess, think, infer.

pre·tend [prih-TEND] VERB, pretended, pretending. **1. faire semblant (de, que), feindre** ▸ to act as if something is true or real when it is not : *He pretended to be asleep.* **2. faire semblant, prétendre** ▸ to imagine that something is true as a game; make believe : *I used to pretend to be a magician.* **Note.** Something that is pretended is a pretence (also pretense) : *She made a pre-*

tence of reading while looking around the room. SYN: fake, make believe, bluff, act, mimic.

pret-ty [PRIT-ee] ADJECTIVE, prettier, prettiest. **1. joli (-ie)** ▶ pleasing to the eyes; nice to look at; attractive. **2. joli (-ie)** ▶ pleasing to the senses in any way : *a pretty melody.* ▲ ADVERB. **assez, plutôt** ▶ somewhat; rather; quite : *I was pretty happy about winning the race.* SYN: lovely, beautiful, handsome, good-looking.

pret-zel [PRET-sul] NOUN, pretzels. **bretzel** ▶ a thin roll of dough that is shaped like a knot or a stick and baked until crisp. Pretzels are usually coated with salt.

pre-vent [prih-VENT] VERB, prevented, preventing. **1. prévenir, empêcher (de)** ▶ to keep something from happening : *Brushing and flossing regularly prevents cavities and gum disease.* **2. empêcher** ▶ to keep someone from doing something; hold back or stop : *"A bad attack of flu has prevented me from writing to you until today."* (Anne Frank) **Note.** Something that serves or intends to prevent is **preventive** (sometimes **preventative**) : *preventive medicine.* SYN: stop, hinder, block, keep from, obstruct.

pre-ven-tion [prih-VEN-shun] NOUN. **prévention** ▶ the act or fact of preventing something : *fire prevention.*

pre-view [PREE-vyoo] NOUN, previews. **1. avant-première** ▶ an advance showing of a movie, show, or play before its regular opening. **2. aperçu** ▶ any advance showing or example : *The museum workers got a preview of the new exhibit.* ▲ VERB, previewed, previewing. **voir en avant-première, prévisionner** ▶ view before.

pre-vi-ous [PREE-vee-us] ADJECTIVE. **précédent (-ente), antérieur (-ieure), préalable** ▶ coming or made before something else; earlier : *Have you seen any of her previous movies?* ■ **previously,** ADVERB. ▶ **précédemment, avant, auparavant, par le passé.** SYN: earlier, prior, former.

prey [pray] NOUN. **1. proie** ▶ an animal that is hunted and killed by another animal for food. **2. proie, victime** ▶ a person who is hurt or taken advantage of by another; a victim. ▲ VERB, preyed, preying. (used with on) **1. faire sa proie de** ▶ to hunt animals for food : *Tyrannosaurus rex preyed on smaller, plant-eating dinosaurs.* **2. faire sa victime de, s'attaquer à** ▶ to harm or take advantage of. **3. ronger, miner, travailler** ▶ to bother or irritate : *The thought preyed on his mind.*

price [prise] NOUN, prices. **1. prix** ▶ the amount of money paid or asked for something being sold. **2. prix** ▶ what a person has to give up or do to get something else : *The price of success is hard work and less play.* **Note.** Something that is very valuable is **priceless** : *a priceless jewel.* ▲ VERB, priced, pricing. **1. se vendre (à)** ▶ to set a certain price for something : *The bicycle was priced $50 higher than Max could*

afford. **2.** *Informal.* **s'informer du prix de** ▶ to find out the price of something : *Shea priced many shoes before he found a pair he could afford.* SYN: cost, value, expense, amount, worth, charge.

prick [prik] VERB, pricked, pricking. **piquer, percer** ▶ to make a tiny hole with a sharp, pointed object : *He pricked his finger on a needle while sewing.* ▲ NOUN. **piqûre** ▶ a sharp point or the feeling of being touched by a sharp point. ■ **prickly,** ADJECTIVE. ▶ **épineux (-euse), hérissé (-ée), armé (-ée) de piquants** ▶ having small sharp points or thorns : *a prickly rose bush.*

pride [pride] NOUN. **1. fierté, amour-propre** ▶ a proper sense of one's worth and ability; self-respect : *She had great pride in his abilities.* **2. fierté** ▶ a person or thing that is highly thought of : *Their new twins are their pride and joy.* **3. orgueil** ▶ too high an opinion of oneself; a feeling that one is better than other people : *"Tortoise…swelled up with pride even though he knew it hadn't been his plan at all."* (Jan Thornhill) ■ **proud,** ADJECTIVE. ▶ **fier (fière).** *Amy is proud of her brother.* ▲ VERB, prided, priding. **pride oneself on. être fier (fière) de** ▶ to take pride in; think highly of : *Mario prides himself on being a peacemaker in class.*

priest [preest] NOUN, priests. **1. prêtre** ▶ a person specially trained to lead religious ceremonies : *a Buddhist priest; a Catholic priest.* **2. prêtre, ecclésiastique** ▶ a member of the clergy in the Roman Catholic Church and in certain other Christian churches.

pri-ma-ry [PRY-mer-ee *or* PRY-muh-ree] ADJECTIVE. **1. premier (-ière), principal (-ale, -aux), primordial (-iale, -aux), fondamental (-ale, -aux)** ▶ first in importance : *Her primary reason for staying late was to get help with a math problem.* **2. premier (-ière)** ▶ first in order or time : *In Québec, grades one through six are called the primary grades.* SYN: first, important, chief, principal, leading.

primary colour (also primary color) **couleur primaire, couleur fondamentale** ▶ one of the three basic colours — red, yellow, and blue — that can combine with each other to make all the other colours.

pri-mate [PRY-mate] NOUN, primates. **primate** ▶ one of the group of mammals made up of human beings, apes, and monkeys.

prime [prime] ADJECTIVE. **1. principal (-ale, -aux), fondamental (-ale, -aux), primordial (-ale, -aux)** ▶ first in importance or value; primary : *His prime purpose is to pass the exam.* **2. de premier choix, de première qualité** ▶ of the best quality : *prime beef; prime tickets.* ▲ VERB, primed, priming. **préparer** ▶ to get someone or something ready; prepare : *An opening act primes* *the audience for the show to follow.* ▲ NOUN. **fleur de l'âge, apogée** ▸ the best or highest condition : *She is in the prime of her life.*

prime minister **Premier ministre** ▸ the head of the government in Canada, Great Britain, and some other countries.

prime number **nombre premier** ▸ a number (such as 3, 7, and 19) that cannot be divided evenly except by itself and by 1.

prim·er [PRIM-ur] NOUN, primers. **1. livre élémentaire, premier livre** ▸ a reading book for beginning readers. **2. manuel d'introduction** ▸ any textbook or instruction book for those beginning to learn about a subject. **3. apprêt** ▸ paint or other such material used to prepare a surface for painting.

prim·i·tive [PRIM-uh-tiv] ADJECTIVE. **1. primitif (-ive)** ▸ having to do with the earliest times or stages of something, especially the development of living things on earth. **2. primitif (-ive)** ▸ not advanced; simple and crude : *He made a primitive hut out of branches and palm leaves.*

prince [prins] NOUN, princes. **1. prince** ▸ the son of a king or queen. **2. prince consort** ▸ the husband of a ruling queen. **3. prince régnant** ▸ a male ruler of a small country or territory.

prin·cess [PRIN-sis or PRIN-ses] NOUN, princesses. **1. princesse** ▸ the daughter of a king or queen. **2. princesse** ▸ the wife of a prince. **3. princesse** ▸ a woman having the same rank as a prince.

prin·ci·pal [PRIN-suh-pul] NOUN, principals. **1. directeur (-trice)** ▸ the person who is in charge of a school. **2. premier rôle** ▸ a person who has a leading or important position : *The principals in a play are the actors with the most lines.* ▲ ADJECTIVE. **principal (-ale, -aux)** ▸ first in importance; main : *The principal problem with the new shopping centre is that it doesn't have enough parking.* SYN : main, important, leading, head, primary. ✏ **p. 462.** 📖 **p. 1060.**

prin·ci·ple [PRIN-suh-pul] NOUN, principles. **1. principe** ▸ any important belief or truth that serves as a guide to thoughts or action : *It is against my principles to steal or cheat.* **2. principe** ▸ a law of nature or science that explains how things act : *"The Italian physicist Galileo discovered the principle of the pendulum while watching a hanging lamp swing back and forth."* (A.G. Smith) SYN : belief, truth, standard, rule, law. ✏ **p. 462.**

print [print] VERB, printed, printing. **1. écrire en majuscules** ▸ to write words with separate letters. **2. imprimer** ▸ to put words or images on paper using a machine : *to print a newspaper, book, or magazine or other publication.* **3. publier** ▸ to include writing in a newspaper or magazine; publish : *an advertisement printed in a newspaper.* ▲ NOUN, prints. **1. trace,**

empreinte ▸ a mark made by pressing on or into something : *The child's fingers left prints on the window.* **Note.** Usually used in compounds : *a footprint; a fingerprint.* **2. caractères** ▸ letters made by printing. **3. épreuve** ▸ a copy of a photograph. **4. gravure** ▸ a painting or other picture reproduced by printing. **5. imprimé** ▸ fabric or clothing with a design pressed or marked on it : *a shirt with a floral print.*

print·er [PRIN-tur] NOUN, printers. **1. imprimeur (-euse), imprimerie** ▸ a person or business that prints books, magazines, or other such material. **2. imprimante** ▸ a machine used to print information from the computer.

printing press **presse typographique** ▸ a machine that prints letters, words, or pictures on paper.

print·out [PRINT-out] NOUN, printouts. **sortie sur imprimante** ▸ the printed material that comes out of a computer printer.

pri·or [PRY-ur] ADJECTIVE. **préalable, précédent (-ente)** ▸ coming before; earlier : *I can't go with you; I have a prior commitment.* **Note.** Also used in the phrase **prior to:** *Mr. Havill taught grade three prior to teaching grade four.*

prism [PRIZ-um] NOUN, prisms. **prisme** ▸ a solid glass object that breaks rays of light into the individual colours of the rainbow.

pris·on [PRIZ-un] NOUN, prisons. **prison** ▸ a building in which convicted criminals are forced to stay for a certain time.

pris·on·er [PRIZ-uh-nur or PRIZ-nur] NOUN, prisoners. **1. prisonnier (-ière), détenu (-ue)** ▸ a person who is forced to stay in a prison. **2. prisonnier (-ière), captif (-ive)** ▸ anyone who is held by force; a captive.

pri·vate [PRY-vit] ADJECTIVE. **1. personnel (-elle), confidentiel (-ielle)** ▸ not meant to be shared with or known by others; personal : *Rick wrote all of his private thoughts and feelings in his diary.* **Note.** The fact of being away from the notice or attention of others is called privacy. **2. privé (-ée)** ▸ not for people in general; not public : *a private boarding school; a private road.* ▲ NOUN, privates. **simple soldat, soldat de deuxième classe** ▸ a soldier having the lowest rank. SYN : confidential, personal, intimate, secret.

priv·i·lege [PRIV-lij] NOUN, privileges. **privilège, prérogative** ▸ a special right or permission given to a person or group of people. **Note.** Someone who is privileged has special advantages in life.

prize [prize] NOUN, prizes. **prix, lot** ▸ something won in a game or contest; award. ▲ ADJECTIVE: *The prize money was locked in the vault.* ▲ VERB, prized, prizing. **du prix** ▸ to value highly : *My neighbour prizes his award-winning roses.*

pro [proh] NOUN. pros. **1. professionnel (-elle)** ▸ short for professional: *a tennis pro.* **2. pour, en faveur de, partisan (-ane) de** ▸ in favour of : *Zoran made a list of all the pros of staying on the team.*

prob·a·bil·i·ty [PROB-uh-BIL-uh-tee] NOUN. probabilities. **1. probabilité** ▸ the fact of being likely to happen ; likelihood : *When there is an east wind, the probability of rain increases.* **2. probabilité, chance** ▸ something likely to happen : *Since he missed the bus, there is a strong probability that he'll be late.*

prob·a·ble [PROB-uh-bul] ADJECTIVE. **probable** ▸ fairly certain to happen or be true : *It is more probable that we will have snow in November than in September.* ■ **probably,** ADVERB. **probablement** ▸ almost certain or definite ; likely : *Look at those clouds ; I think it will probably rain this afternoon.* SYN : likely, possible, reasonable, presumable.

pro·ba·tion [proh-BAY-shun] NOUN. probations. **essai, mise à l'épreuve, sursis, probation** ▸ a set period of time for testing a person's ability, qualification, or behaviour : *After a three-week probation, Carmela was given the job permanently.*

probe [probe] NOUN. probes. **1. enquête, investigation** ▸ a careful study of something : *to conduct a probe into the causes of poverty.* **2. sonde** ▸ a device or tool used to explore or test something : *NASA launched a space probe that will gather rock samples from Venus.* ▲ VERB, probed, probing. **examiner avec une sonde, chercher à localiser, faire des recherches, sonder** ▸ to carry out a careful search or investigation : *The doctor probed Kirk's abdomen for signs of an infected appendix.* SYN : examine, investigate, search, explore.

prob·lem [PROB-lum] NOUN. problems. **1. problème** ▸ something that causes difficulty or trouble : *It's always a problem choosing a gift for my father.* **2. problème** ▸ a question for which an answer is needed : *Our teacher assigned the math problems on page 129 as homework.* SYN : difficulty, obstacle, puzzle, riddle, question. 🖉 p. 463.

pro·ce·dure [pruh-SEE-jur] NOUN. procedures. **procédure** ▸ the proper or correct way to do something, especially a set of steps to be done in order. SYN : method, process, plans.

pro·ceed [pruh-SEED *or* proh-SEED] VERB. proceeded, proceeding. **1. continuer, avancer** ▸ to go on or move forward ; continue : *The conductor proceeded with the rehearsal, even though half of the musicians had left.* **2. entreprendre (de)** ▸ to carry on an activity : *He boiled the water and proceeded to make the coffee.* ▲ NOUN, proceeds. **produit** ▸ the amount of money gained from a sale or other business activity : *The proceeds from the fundraiser will be given to the shelter for homeless people.*

proc·ess [pruh-SES *or* proh-SES] NOUN. processes. **1. processus, être en train de** ▸ a series of actions done in a certain way to make or do something : *I'm in the process of making a cake.* **2. processus** ▸ a series of events in nature that happen in a certain way : *The process by which green plants make food is called "photosynthesis."* ▲ VERB, processed, processing. **traiter** ▸ to prepare or do something using a series of steps : *Computers process information.* SYN : method, procedure, course, mode, way.

pro·ces·sion [pruh-SESH-un] NOUN. processions. **1. cortège, défilé** ▸ the act of moving forward in an even, orderly way : *"Clouds drifted across the sky in an endless procession."* (E.B. White) **2. cortège, procession** ▸ a group of people moving in this way : *a wedding procession.*

pro·ces·sor [PROH-ses-ur *or* PRAH-ses-ur] NOUN. processors. **traiteur (-euse), processeur, robot culinaire** ▸ a person or thing that processes something : *a word processor ; a food processor.*

pro·claim [pruh-KLAYM] VERB. proclaimed, proclaiming. **proclamer, déclarer** ▸ to make known or announce to the public : *Our class declared Friday a "garbage-free" day.* **Note.** A proclamation is an official public announcement. SYN : declare, announce, advertise, inform.

pro·cras·ti·nate [proh-KRAS-tih-NATE] VERB. procrastinated, procrastinating. **remettre à plus tard, temporiser, tergiverser, atermoyer** ▸ to put off something that should be done ; delay without good reason : *Sydney procrastinated all*

📝 **Writing Tips**

Principle/Principal

*Many people get confused about when to use the words **principle** (a noun that means a basic idea, belief, or rule) and **principal** (an adjective that can sometimes be used as a noun—the principal of a school).*

Here are some tips to help you remember which word to use :

*Principle spelled with an **e** is a noun, like words used to describe a belief, idea, or rule.*

*Principal with an **a** is an adjective, like major or main. Or the principal of a school is spelled with an a because the principal is your pal.*

---

week and had to write her essay the night before it was due. **Note.** Procrastination is the act of procrastinating.

prod [prod] VERB, prodded, prodding. **1. pousser du doigt, pousser du pied ▸** to push or jab with something pointed. **2. pousser à, inciter à ▸** to urge or press a person to do something. ▲ NOUN, prods. **petit coup de doigt ▸** the act of prodding, or a thing used for this. SYN: spur, drive, jab, urge, drive.

prod-i-gy [PROD-uh-jee] NOUN, prodigies. **prodige, génie, surdoué (-ée) ▸** a child or young person who is very brilliant or who has some amazing talent : *The child prodigy graduated from high school at age 15 and from university at 18.*

pro-duce [pruh-DOOS *or* pruh-DYOOS] VERB, produced, producing. **1. produire, fabriquer ▸** to make or build something; manufacture : *Each year, Japan produces thousands of automobiles.* **2. donner ▸** to bring forth from something grown or from animals : *Sunflowers produce seeds. Hens produce eggs.* **3. produire, sortir (de), exhiber ▸** to bring forth into view; show : *Gary produced the keys from his pocket.* **4. mettre en scène, produire, réaliser ▸** to bring a play, movie, TV show, or the like before the public. ▲ [PROH-doos *or* PRAH-doos] NOUN. **produits alimentaires, produits agricoles ▸** fresh vegetables or fruit grown for selling. ✎ p. 464.

pro-duc-er [pruh-DOO-sur *or* pruh-DYOO-sur] NOUN, producers. **1. producteur (-trice) ▸** a person or thing that produces something : *Switzerland is known as a producer of fine clocks and watches.* **2. producteur (-trice) ▸** a person in charge of producing a play, movie, and so on.

pro-duct [PROD-ukt] NOUN, products. **1. produit ▸** a thing that is made or manufactured; something produced : *Corn, wheat, and oats are all farm products.* **2. produit ▸** in mathematics, the number you get when you multiply two or more numbers together : *The product of 7 times 2 is 14.* **3. produit, résultat, fruit ▸** anything that comes from thought or action; a result : *This artwork is the product of a creative mind.*

pro-duc-tion [pruh-DUK-shun] NOUN, productions. **1. production ▸** the act of producing something : *The invention of the assembly line greatly sped up automobile production.* **2. mise en scène, réalisation ▸** something that is produced : *a school production of Shakespeare's play* Hamlet.

pro-duc-tive [pruh-DUK-tiv] ADJECTIVE. **1. productif (-ive), fécond (-onde), prolifique ▸** able to produce things, especially in large amounts : *She's a productive writer, publishing a book every year.* **2. fertile, fructueux (-euse) ▸** able to produce a useful result : *On a productive evening, I get all my homework done.*

✏ Writing Tips

Problem or Conflict

*Whenever writers develop a story, they usually have a **conflict**—a **problem** that involves the main characters and is resolved by the end of the story. The conflict usually causes change or growth in the characters. A conflict could be a disagreement between people, a disaster or crisis, or friction between groups. Other features of a story are the **setting** (the place where the problem occurs) and the **characters** (the people who are affected by the problem).*

Note. The ability to produce things is productivity.

pro-fes-sion [pruh-FESH-un] NOUN, professions. **1. profession, métier ▸** a type of work that calls for special education and training, such as the law, medicine, or teaching. **2. corps de métier ▸** the group of persons doing such work : *the teaching profession.*

pro-fes-sion-al [pruh-FESH-uh-nul *or* pruh-FESH-nul] NOUN, professionals. **1. professionnel (-elle) ▸** a person who is paid to do something that others do for enjoyment or as a hobby : *She played tennis as a professional.* **2. professionnel (-elle), exercer une profession libérale ▸** a person who works in a profession, such as a lawyer, doctor, dentist, and so forth. ▲ ADJECTIVE. **1. professionnel (-elle) ▸** doing something for pay that others do without pay : *a professional pianist; a professional clown.* **2. professionnel (-elle) ▸** having to do with a profession, or acting in a way that is seen as being the way a professional should act : *Shayla has such a professional attitude.* **3. excellent (-ente) ▸** done in a skillful way, as if by a professional : *You did a professional job of building the deck.* ■ **professionally,** ADVERB. ▸ **professionnellement, de manière professionnelle, en professionnel (-elle).**

pro-fes-sor [pruh-FES-ur] **professeur (-eure) ▸** a teacher of the highest rank at a college or university.

pro-file [PROH-file] NOUN, profiles. **1. profil ▸** the view of something as seen from the side, especially the human face. **2. profil ▸** a short description of a person or thing : *The school newspaper published a profile of the new history teacher.*

pro-fit [PROF-it] NOUN, profits. **profit, bénéfice ▸** the money that a business has left over after all its costs have been paid. ▲ VERB, profited, profiting. **1. faire un bénéfice** ▸ to make a profit; gain money. **2. tirer profit de** ▸ to gain or benefit from something : *to profit from a challenging experience.* SYN : gain, earnings, proceeds, returns, benefits.

pro·fit·a·ble [PROF-ih-tuh-bul] ADJECTIVE. **1. rentable, lucratif (-ive), payant (-ante)** ▸ making or giving a profit : **2. fructueux (-euse), payant (-ante), profitable** ▸ giving a gain or benefit : *Lisa had a profitable study session and got an "A" on the test.* ■ **profitably,** ADVERB. ▸ à profit, avec profit, utilement.

pro·found [pruh-FOWND] ADJECTIVE. **1. profond (-onde)** ▸ having or showing a deep knowledge or understanding : *a profound book.* **2. profond (-onde)** ▸ very strongly felt; very great : *profound joy; profound apologies.* ■ **profoundly,** ADVERB. ▸ profondément.

pro·gram [PROH-gram] NOUN, programs. (also programme) **1. programme, émission** ▸ a show on television or radio : *a news program.* **2. programmation, programme** ▸ a list of the order of events in a show, concert, or meeting, along with the people performing or involved : *a program for a piano recital.* **3. programme** ▸ the performance itself : *David will be playing the violin in the school's winter program.* **4. programme** ▸ a plan for doing something : *a town improvement program.* **5. programme** ▸ a set of instructions telling a computer how to carry out a job. ▲ VERB, programmed, programming. **1. programmer** ▸ to enter instructions into a computer or another machine so that it can perform a function. **2. prévoir à son programme** ▸ to include in a program : *He programmed an evening of entertainment for his friends.* **Note.** A person who develops programs for use in computers is called *programmer.* The act of doing this is called *programming.*

pro·gress [PROH-gres or PROG-res] NOUN. **1. progression** ▸ the act of moving forward toward a goal : *They made rapid progress on their journey to the Arctic Circle.* **2. progrès, amélioration** ▸ a gradual change or improvement : *The patient's progress was slow, but she was feeling better.* **3. in progress. en cours** ▸ happening at the time; going on. ▲ [pruh-GRES] VERB, progressed, progressing. **progresser** ▸ to move forward or toward a goal; advance : *Now that the roof is on, the construction of the*

house will progress more quickly. **Note.** The act of progressing is progression. SYN : advance, proceed, go ahead, move, develop.

pro·gres·sive [pruh-GRES-iv] ADJECTIVE. **1. progressif (-ive), par étapes, par degrés** ▸ moving forward step by step : *a progressive school system.* **2. progressiste** ▸ working for improvement or change in politics and social issues. ▲ NOUN, progressives. **progressiste** ▸ a person who favours change or reform.

Progressive Conservative Party (sometimes Conservative Party or Conservatives) **Parti progressiste-conservateur (du Canada)** ▸ one of the major political parties in Canada.

pro·hi·bit [proh-HIB-it] VERB, prohibited, prohibiting. **interdire, défendre** ▸ to officially forbid by law or other authority : *The law prohibits fishing in the spring.* SYN : forbid, deny, ban, prevent, bar.

pro·ject [PROJ-ekt or PROH-jekt] NOUN, projects. **1. projet, plan** ▸ a plan to carry out an important task : *My project for the summer is to learn to swim.* **2. étude, dossier** ▸ a special assignment done by students as part of their studies : *a class project on the solar system.* **3. cité, lotissement, ensemble** ▸ a group of houses or apartment buildings built and operated as a unit; a housing project. ▲ [pruh-JEKT] VERB, projected, projecting. **1. saillir, surplomber** ▸ to reach forward; stick out : *The huge rock projects at least 10 metres out of the water.* **2. projeter** ▸ to cause something to be seen or heard over a distance : *to project a voice; to project a movie on a screen.* **3. prévoir (par extrapolation)** ▸ to think forward about how something will turn out; make a prediction : *We project a snowfall of one to three centimetres overnight.* **4. projeter** ▸ to throw something forward. **Note.** Any object, such as a stone, that is thrown or hurled through the air is a projectile. SYN : plan, scheme, plot, undertaking, venture.

pro·jec·tion [pruh-JEK-shun] NOUN, projections. **1. saillie** ▸ a part that projects : *The climber was able to grasp several projections on the side of the cliff as he made his way to the top.* **2. projection** ▸ the act or fact of projecting : *Most television sets use rear projection, which means that the picture comes from behind the*

Word Builder

Produce, **make,** and **create** are all verbs that mean to bring into being something that did not exist before. **Produce** can refer to turning out works : *The author will produce a new play sometime this year.* **Make** is the most general of the three words and is used to describe any type of production : *They make soap at the factory.* **Create** most often suggests something is brought into being as the result of a person's talent, control, or determination. *The author creates a vivid picture of the landscape around Kelowna.*

screen instead of from in front of it, as is usual in a movie theatre.

pro-jec-tor [pruh-JEK-ter] NOUN, projectors. **projecteur ▸** a machine that shows a picture on a screen by means of a beam of light and special lenses.

pro-long [pruh-LONG] VERB, prolonged, prolonging. **prolonger ▸** to make something longer; extend : *Don't prolong your speech with useless information.* SYN: increase, stretch, lengthen, continue.

pro-logue [proh-LOG] NOUN, prologues. (sometimes prolog) **1. prologue ▸** a speech or poem addressed to the audience by one of the actors at the beginning of a play. **2. prologue ▸** an introduction to a novel, poem, or other literary work.

prom-i-nent [PROM-uh-nunt] ADJECTIVE. **1. célèbre, important (-ante), en vue ▸** important and well-known : *The dinner party was attended by the Governor General and many other prominent Canadians.* **2. bien en vue ▸** easy to see; obvious : *Alexa took a prominent position at the head of the line.* **3. proéminent (-ente) ▸** standing or sticking out : *A fly has prominent, bulging eyes.*

prom-ise [PROM-is] NOUN, promises. **1. promesse, serment ▸** a statement guaranteeing a person will or will not do something. **2. promesse, espérance ▸** a sign of something that might happen in the future : *Her work shows the promise of great things to come.* ▲ VERB, promised, promising. **1. promettre, assurer ▸** to give a promise : *"You'll fly again. I promise," he whispered to the injured bird."* (Sheryl McFarlane) **2. promettre, annoncer ▸** to give a reason to expect something to happen : *The clear sky and gentle wind promised a day of good sailing.* SYN: vow, pledge, agreement, word, guarantee.

pro-mote [pruh-MOTE] VERB, promoted, promoting. **1. promouvoir ▸** to move a person up in rank or grade. **2. promouvoir, favoriser, encourager ▸** to help the growth or development of something : *a program designed to promote peace.* **3. promouvoir ▸** to try to sell or advance a product or idea : *Terry Fox ran across Canada in 1980 to promote cancer research.*

pro-mo-tion [pruh-MOH-shun] NOUN, promotions. **1. promotion, avancement ▸** the act or fact of promoting : *She got a promotion to vice-president in charge of sales.* **2. promotion, lancement, publicité ▸** an activity designed to help the selling of something : *the promotion of a new breakfast cereal.*

prompt [prompt] ADJECTIVE. **1. ponctuel (-elle), à l'heure ▸** at the expected time; not late : *Dinner will be served at 6:30. Please be prompt.* **2. rapide, prompt (prompte) ▸** done without delay; quick : *The emergency fire department*

made a prompt response to the call for help. ▲ VERB, prompted, prompting. **1. pousser, inciter, entraîner ▸** to cause someone to act : *Seeing Marlin prompted me to ask him about his plans for Saturday.* **2. souffler (une réplique) ▸** to remind speakers of something they are supposed to say : *He prompted the actor who couldn't remember his lines.* ■ **promptly,** ADVERB. ▸ **promptement, ponctuellement.** ■ **promptness,** NOUN. ▸ **promptitude, empressement, ponctualité.** SYN: ready, punctual, quick, swift, immediate.

prone [prone] ADJECTIVE. **1. enclin (-ine), sujet (-ette) à, prédisposé (-ée) ▸** likely to act or be a certain way : *to be accident-prone; to be prone to forget names.* **2. couché (-ée) sur le ventre, prostré (-ée) ▸** lying flat with the front or face downward.

prong [prong] NOUN, prongs. **1. dent ▸** one of the sharp points of a fork or other such tool. **2. pointe ▸** any sharp pointed end like this.

pro-noun [PROH-nown] NOUN, pronouns. **pronom ▸** in grammar, a word used in place of a NOUN to refer to a person, place, or thing. In the sentence *She lent me her book,* the words *She, me,* and *her* are pronouns.

pro-nounce [pruh-NOWNCE] VERB, pronounced, pronouncing. **1. prononcer ▸** to speak the sound of a word or letter : *How do you pronounce the word "hippopotamus"?* **2. déclarer, prononcer ▸** to state something in an official or serious way : *The minister said, "I now pronounce you husband and wife."* SYN: state, announce, express, speak, say.

pro-nounced [pruh-NOWNST] ADJECTIVE. **fort (forte), prononcé (-ée), marqué (-ée) ▸** easy to notice, obvious, distinct : *He spoke with a pronounced Danish accent.*

pro-nun-ci-a-tion [pruh-nun-see-AY-shun] NOUN, pronunciations. **prononciation ▸** the act of pronouncing a word or letter, or the way that it is pronounced.

proof [proof] NOUN, proofs. **1. preuve ▸** papers, facts, or any other way to show beyond a doubt that something is true; evidence. **2. preuve ▸** in science or mathematics, the process of checking to make sure that a certain statement is true. **3. épreuve ▸** a copy of a photograph or a piece of writing, to be checked over for mistakes and problems before final printing. ▲ ADJECTIVE. **à l'épreuve de ▸** able to protect against something that is harmful or unwanted : *a waterproof raincoat; a soundproof room.*

proof-read [PROOF-reed] VERB, proofread, proofreading. **corriger les épreuves de ▸** to read over a piece of writing in order to find and correct any mistakes in it. **Note.** A person who does this work is called a proofreader. *⊘* **p. 466.**

prop [prop] VERB, propped, propping. **1. caler, maintenir ouvert (-te) ▸** to hold something up by placing a support under or against it : *The farmer propped open the trap door with a pitchfork.* **2. adosser à ▶** to place in a leaning or resting position : *He propped the cookbook up in front of him.* ▲ NOUN, props. **1. support, perche, étai ▶** a support used to keep something from falling. **2. accessoire ▶** an object used as part of a scene in a play or movie, not including the costumes or scenery. SYN: support, brace, hold up.

prop-a-gan-da [PROP-uh-GAN-duh] NOUN. **1. propagande ▶** a method of trying to make people think or believe something. Propaganda usually gives only one side of an issue, and often slants the truth or even tells lies. **2. propagande ▶** information in this form.

pro-pel [pruh-PEL] VERB, propelled, propelling. **propulser, faire avancer ▶** to make something move forward or keep it moving : *She used a paddle to propel the canoe through the water.* SYN : push, move, drive, force, thrust.

pro-pel-ler [pruh-PEL-ur] NOUN, propellers. (also propellor) **hélice ▶** a device that has blades sticking out from a shaft that turns very quickly. The blades produce a force that is used to move an aircraft through the air or a boat through the water.

pro-per [PROP-ur] ADJECTIVE. **1. adéquat (-ate), indiqué (-ée), approprié (-ée) ▶** suited to a certain use or purpose; fitting; correct : *She needed the proper tools to fix the sink.* **2. même, proprement dit (dite) ▶** in the strict sense of the word; actual : *The marathon will be held right in Vancouver proper, not out in the suburbs.* ▪ **properly,** ADVERB. ▶ **correctement, convenablement.** ✎ p. 503.

proper noun (sometimes proper name) **nom propre ▶** a noun that names one particular person, place, or thing and begins with a capital letter : *Clayton Brown; St. John's; Pacific Ocean.*

prop-er-ty [PROP-ur-tee] NOUN, properties. **1. propriété, biens ▶** anything that is owned by a person. **2. propriété, terres, biens immobiliers ▶** a specific area of land : *We are going to build a cabin on our property in the mountains.* **3. propriété, vertu ▶** a quality or fact belonging specifically to something : *It is a property of water to freeze at zero degrees Celsius.* SYN : belongings, possessions, land, wealth.

proph-e-cy [PROF-uh-see] NOUN, prophecies. **1. prophétie ▶** the act of telling or warning about something that is supposed to happen in the future. **2. prophétie ▶** something that is said in this way : *George Orwell made many accurate prophecies concerning the future in his book 1984.*

pro-por-tion [pruh-POR-shun] NOUN, proportions. **1. (à la) mesure (de) ▶** the amount or size of something when compared to something else : *Your success will be in proportion to the*

effort you make. **2.** (often proportions) **proportion ▶** the size or extent of something : *The house was of large proportions.* **3. (en) proportion de, proportionné (-ée) à ▶** a proper or balanced relationship between the parts of a thing : *The dog's short legs were not in proportion to its long body.* **4. pourcentage, part, partie ▶** a part or share : *A large proportion of the earth is covered in water.* SYN : ratio, percentage, measure, portion, share.

pro-po-sal [pruh-POH-zul] NOUN, proposals. **1. proposition, suggestion ▶** the act or fact of proposing ; suggesting : *The principal is studying our proposal to start an after-school art class.* **3. demande en mariage, offre de mariage ▶** an offer of marriage.

pro-pose [pruh-POZE] VERB, proposed, proposing. **1. proposer, suggérer ▶** to suggest something for others to consider : *I propose that Leslie head the group.* **2. se proposer de, compter faire ▶** to plan to do something : *She proposes to leave in two days.* **3. demander en mariage ▶** to make an offer of marriage. SYN : suggest, offer, put forward, submit.

⌖ Writing Tips

Proofreading

Proofreading is one of the basic steps in the writing process. When proofreading, an editor looks for spelling and grammar mistakes. The best time to proofread is before you write your final draft. There is no point in checking a paragraph for punctuation if you're not sure that you will keep that paragraph in the final draft.

Professional proofreaders use different methods to look for errors. Some read the paper aloud and say the punctuation marks and capital letters: "We (capital **W**) stopped at Ben's (capital **B**, apostrophe **s**) house. (period)" This makes you more conscious of missing items. Others read through several times, looking for a different kind of mistake each time. Some proofreaders read the pages out of order, so that they can concentrate on proofreading without being distracted by the content of the writing. Other proofreaders read the text backwards, starting at the last word. This is good for locating spelling mistakes because one is not distracted by trying to understand the text.

prop·o·si·tion [PROP-uh-ZISH-un] NOUN, propositions. **1. proposition, offre** ▸ something that is proposed; a plan : *The owner made a proposal to buy the hotel next door to his building.* **2. proposition** ▸ a statement put forward for argument or discussion : *Ashwin and Shauna are going to debate the proposition that students should wear uniforms.*

prose [prose] NOUN. **prose** ▸ the usual form of spoken or written language; speech or writing that is not poetry.

pros·pect [PROS-pekt] NOUN, prospects. **1. perspective** ▸ something expected or looked forward to; a strong hope or possibility : *The prospect of a trip to the Rocky Mountains thrilled us.* **2. client (-ente) potentiel (-ielle), candidat (-ate) éventuel (-elle)** ▸ a person who is a possible candidate or customer : *She sold two cars this morning and has another prospect coming in at 3:00 p.m.* **3. perspective, vue** ▸ a view looking out over an area : *There is a grand prospect from the top of the mountain.* ▲ VERB, prospected, prospecting. **prospecter** ▸ to search for valuable minerals : *Thousands of people flocked into the Yukon after 1896 to prospect for gold.* **Note.** A prospector is a person who searches an area for gold, oil, uranium, or other valuable minerals. SYN: hope, chance, expectation, likelihood.

pro·spec·tive [pruh-SPEK-tiv] ADJECTIVE. **éventuel (-elle), possible** ▸ likely to be; very possible : *a prospective buyer.*

pros·per [PROS-per] VERB, prospered, prospering. **prospérer** ▸ to do very well; be successful : *Her business prospered when she added some new clients.*

pros·per·i·ty [pros-PAIR-uh-tee] NOUN. **prospérité** ▸ the condition of doing very well or being successful : *The new business brought prosperity to the town.*

pros·per·ous [PROS-per-us] ADJECTIVE. **prospère** ▸ having wealth or good fortune; successful : *Mr. Rashad is a prosperous owner of four restaurants.*

pro·tag·o·nist [proh-TAG-uh-nist] NOUN. **1. protagoniste** ▸ the main character in a play, story, or novel. **2. protagoniste** ▸ a person who takes a leading part.

pro·tect [pruh-TEKT] VERB, protected, protecting. **protéger** ▸ to keep or guard against harm or danger : *Quills protect a porcupine from danger.* SYN: shield, guard, shelter, defend, keep.

pro·tec·tion [pruh-TEK-shun] NOUN, protections. **1. protection** ▸ the fact of keeping someone or something from harm : *The security guard was hired for the politician's protection.* **2. protection** ▸ something or someone that prevents damage or harm : *The fox used the dense underbrush as protection from the hunters.*

pro·tec·tive [proh-TEK-tiv] ADJECTIVE. **protecteur (-trice), de protection** ▸ helping to protect : *a protective covering.*

pro·tein [PROH-teen] NOUN, proteins. **protéine** ▸ a substance found in all living animals and plant cells. Proteins are necessary to life. Foods such as eggs, milk, meat, beans, and cheese are good sources of protein.

pro·test [PROH-test] NOUN, protests. **protestation, contestation** ▸ something said or done to show that a person disagrees with some policy, action, or decision : *The students made a formal protest to their teacher after he doubled their homework.* ▲ [proh-TEST] VERB, protested, protesting. **protester, objecter** ▸ to make a protest; object : *"But Mom, I don't have time to do the dishes!" she protested.* 🖉 **p. 468.**

Prot·es·tant [PROT-is-tunt] NOUN, Protestants. **protestant (-ante)** ▸ a person of the Christian religion who does not belong to a Catholic or an Orthodox church. **Note.** Protestant churches include the Anglican, the Baptist, the Lutheran, the Presbyterian, the United, and many other churches.

pro·ton [PROH-ton] NOUN, protons. **proton** ▸ a basic particle of an atom found in the nucleus, or centre part, of the atom. A proton has a positive electrical charge.

pro·to·zo·an [PROH-tuh ZOII-un] NOUN, protozoans or protozoa. (sometimes protozoon) **protozoaire** ▸ one of a group of tiny animals that have only one cell and can be seen only under a microscope.

pro·trude [proh-TROOD] VERB, protruded, protruding. **dépasser (de)** ▸ to stick out : *The rabbit's ears protruded from the top of its head.*

proud [prowd] ADJECTIVE, prouder, proudest. **1. fier (fière)** ▸ being pleased with something you have made or done, or something that relates to you; satisfaction : *She was proud of herself for doing well in math.* **2. qui suscite de la fierté** ▸ causing or able to cause this feeling : *The day my brother graduated from university was a proud moment for my parents.* **3. orgueilleux (-euse), hautain (-aine), vaniteux (-euse)** ▸ thinking too highly of oneself; conceited : *That boy is very vain and proud.* ■ **proudly,** ADVERB. ▸ **fièrement.**

prove [proov] VERB, proved or proven, proving. **1. prouver, démontrer** ▸ to show that something is true or as it is said to be : *"You have proven yourself both brave and clever, and I appoint you Captain of my Royal Company of Knights."* (Robin Muller) **2. s'avérer, se révéler, se trouver être** ▸ to turn out to be : *What we thought were ancient arrowheads proved to be modern imitations.* SYN: confirm, show, demonstrate, establish.

prov·erb [PROV-urb] NOUN, proverbs. **proverbe** ▸ a short, well-known saying that contains a truth or makes a point : *"Haste makes waste"* and *"Don't count your chickens before they hatch"* are proverbs. ✎ p. 468.

pro·vide [pruh-VIDE] VERB, provided, providing. **1. fournir** ▸ to give what is needed or wanted; supply : *Trees provide wood for building and fuel.* **2. pourvoir, subvenir aux besoins de** ▸ to take care of; support : *Parents provide for their children.* **3. prévoir** ▸ to make plans; prepare for something : *Have you provided for an alternative day in case it rains ?* ■ **provided** or providing, CONJUNCTION. **pourvu que, à condition que, à condition de, sous réserve que** ▸ on the condition that; if : *Mary will go with us, providing we can give her a ride home.* SYN: arrange, supply, equip, produce, give.

prov·ince [PROV-ins] NOUN, provinces. **1. province** ▸ one of 10 divisions of Canada. **2. province, région, état** ▸ similar territories in other countries. ■ **provincial,** ADJECTIVE. **provincial (-iale, -iaux)** ▸ of or related to a province : *Halifax is the seat of the provincial government in Nova Scotia.* 📖 p. 1044.

pro·vi·sion [pruh-VIZH-un] NOUN, provisions. **1. fourniture, approvisionnement** ▸ the act or fact of providing. **2. provisions. provision(s)** ▸ a supply of food : *"And above all, provisions had to be gathered for the great feast."* (Aliki) ■ **provisional,** ADJECTIVE. **provisoire** ▸ for the time being; temporary : *The new business partners drew up a provisional agreement to be used until a legal contract was signed.*

pro·voke [pruh-VOKE] VERB, provoked, provoking. **1. provoquer, faire naître, susciter** ▸ to cause to happen; bring about : *The principal's speech provoked discussion among the students.* **2. provoquer, pousser, inciter** ▸ to excite or stir up : *People who see bears in the wild should be careful not to provoke them to attack.* **Note.** Something that provokes is a provocation. SYN: enrage, anger, infuriate, annoy, irritate, vex.

prow [prow] NOUN, prows. **proue** ▸ the front part of a boat or ship; the bow.

prowl [prowl] VERB, prowled, prowling. **1. rôder** ▸ of an animal, to move slowly or quietly while looking for something to eat : *"Once he saw a wolf prowling a little too close to the sleeping men."* (Ainslie Manson) **2. arpenter,**

✏ **Writing Tips**

Proverb

A proverb is a short expression that states a general truth—for example, A stitch in time saves nine, A bird in the hand is worth two in the bush, or The early bird catches the worm.

You can add spice to your writing by using proverbs with slight alterations :
A fish in the tank is worth two on the floor or *The early bird catches the worm, but then has to eat it.*

faire les cent pas ▸ to move in a quiet, restless way : *He prowled around the room, waiting for the phone to ring.* ▲ NOUN, prowls. **fait de rôder** ▸ the act of prowling : *a stray dog on the prowl.* SYN: roam, wander, sneak.

pru·dent [PROO-dunt] ADJECTIVE. **prudent (-ente), circonspect (-ecte)** ▸ looking ahead to possible risks or problems; showing care and good judgment : *A prudent shopper compares prices and quality before buying.* SYN: cautious, careful, wise, sensible.

prune¹ [proon] NOUN, prunes. **pruneau (-eaux)** ▸ a plum that is dried for eating.

prune² VERB, pruned, pruning. **tailler, élaguer, émonder** ▸ to cut off some parts from a plant to help it grow or to make it look better : *Roses are pruned so that they will produce better flowers.*

pry¹ [pry] VERB, pried, prying. **ouvrir en employant la force, forcer** ▸ to move or raise by force : *I pried the lid off with a crowbar.*

pry² VERB, pried, prying. **fouiner, fureter** ▸ to be too curious or to ask personal questions about something that is not one's business : *My nosy neighbour always watches everyone and pries into their business.*

psy·chi·a·trist [sy-KY-uh-trist *or* suh-KY-uh-trist] NOUN, psychiatrists. **psychiatre** ▸ a doctor who is specially trained to treat people who are mentally ill or have serious mental problems.

✏ **Word Builder**

Protest, disagree, and *challenge* can all refer to a lack of agreement between two or more persons' ideas. *Protest* means that someone strongly and openly opposes an idea : *The class protested the proposed clear-cutting of the trees.* When people *disagree,* they most often voice their dispute over facts or ideas : *They disagree over the best way to solve the problem.* If a person *challenges* something, he or she raises objections or calls into question another person's position : *I challenged the politician on the new pollution law.*

Note. The medical treatment of mental illness is psychiatry.

psy-cho-lo-gi-cal [sy-kuh-LOJ-ih-kul] ADJECTIVE. **1. psychologique ▶** having to do with psychology. **2. psychologique, psychique ▶** having to do with the mind : *His great fear of going out in public is a psychological problem.*

psy-chol-o-gy [sy-KOL-uh-jee] NOUN. **psychologie ▶** the study of the human mind. Psychology studies how people think, why they act as they do, and how we can learn to change our behaviour if we want to. **Note.** A person who is specially trained to practise psychology is a psychologist.

pu-ber-ty [PYOO-bur-tee] NOUN. **puberté ▶** the age or time at which a person's body becomes physically mature and able to produce children.

pub-lic [PUB-lik] ADJECTIVE. **1. public (-ique) ▶** having to do with people as a group ; of people in general : *Public opinion is divided on the issue of limiting violence on television.* **2. public (-ique), commun (-une), communautaire ▶** meant for or serving everyone ; not private : *a public school.* **3. public (-ique), national (-ale, -aux), social (-ale, -aux) ▶** working or acting for the people : *Members of Parliament are public officials.* **4. public (-ique) ▶** done or presented in front of people : *a public performance.* ▲ NOUN. **public, population ▶** people in general : *The media informed the public of the election results.* ■ **publicly,** ADVERB. ▶ **publiquement.**

in public en public ▶ not secretly or privately ; publicly, openly : *The meeting will be held in public so that anyone may attend.*

pub-li-ca-tion [pub-luh-KAY-shun] NOUN. **publications. 1. publication ▶** something that is published ; a book, newspaper, magazine, or other printed material. **2. publication, parution ▶** the act or fact of publishing : *The publication date for the new novel is set for June 1.*

pub-lic-i-ty [pub-LIS-uh-tee] NOUN. **1. publicité ▶** public notice ; information that is given out so that the public will know more about something. Newspaper stories, radio announcements, and posters are types of publicity. **2. publicité ▶** the process of getting public notice. 🖰 **p. 1169.**

pub-lish [PUB-lish] VERB, published, publishing. **1. publier, éditer, faire paraître ▶** to produce a book, newspaper, magazine, or other such printed item and offer it to the public. **Note.** A person or company that publishes is a publisher, and their work or business is called publishing. **2. publier, faire connaître ▶** to make known or announce. 🖉 **p. 470.**

puck [puk] NOUN, pucks. **rondelle, disque, palet ▶** a hard rubber disk used in hockey.

puck-er [PUK-ur] VERB, puckered, puckering. **(se) plisser ▶** to come together in small folds or wrinkles : *Anton puckered his lips and whistled.*

pud-ding [POOD-ing] NOUN, puddings. **pouding ▶** a sweet, creamy dessert made with milk, eggs, and flavourings such as chocolate or vanilla.

pud-dle [PUD-ul] NOUN, puddles. **flaque ▶** a small pool of water or some other liquid on a surface : *a mud puddle.*

puff [puf] NOUN, puffs. **1. bouffée, souffle ▶** a short, sudden blast of air, wind, smoke, and so on : *Grandpa puffed on his pipe.* **2. objet d'aspect cotonneux, pâte feuilletée, houppe, houppette ▶** anything soft, light, and fluffy : *a cream-filled puff pastry ; a powder puff.* ▲ VERB, puffed, puffing. **1. haleter, souffler ▶** to give off a short blast of air or sound. **2. gonfler ▶** to fill or swell : *"His red cheeks were puffed out with breath."* (David M. Schwartz) ■ **puffy,** ADJECTIVE : ▶ **moelleux (-euse).** *a puffy feather pillow.*

puf-fin [PUF-un] NOUN, puffins. **macareux ▶** a black-and-white sea bird with a plump body, a short, thick neck, and a large, brightly coloured bill. Puffins live in large groups on northern seacoasts. 👁 **p. 108.**

puffin

pull [pul] VERB, pulled, pulling. **1. tirer, traîner ▶** to take something and move it toward or along with oneself : *The little boy walked down the street, pulling his toy wagon behind him.* **2. arracher, extirper ▶** to draw something up or out in this way : *to pull weeds.* **3. entrer dans ▶** to go or move to a certain place : *to pull into a parking space.* **4. se déchirer, se froisser, se claquer ▶** to hurt or strain, especially by stretching too hard : *to pull a muscle.* **5. démolir, abattre ▶** to tear or rip : *to pull down a wall.* ▲ NOUN, pulls. **1. attraction ▶** the act or fact of pulling : *the pull of the ocean tide.* **2.** *Informal.* **influence ▶** a special kind of influence or advantage : *My mother used her pull to get me a summer job at her office.* SYN: haul, tow, drag, tug, yank. 🖉 **p. 470.**

pul-ley [PUL-ee] NOUN, pulleys. **poulie ▶** a wheel with a groove around its edge and a rope or

✏️ **Writing Tips**

Publishing

The basic meaning of publish is "to make public." You can publish poetry, stories, instructions, letters, and much more in books, newspapers, magazines, pamphlets, and brochures. Making something available on the Internet is a new way to publish. Not everything published is done by professional writers or publishers. You can take one of your stories or articles through the writing process and publish it yourself.

chain that moves through the groove. A pulley is used to lift or lower heavy things.

pulp [pulp] NOUN, pulps. **1. pulpe, chair ▸** the soft, juicy part of a fruit or vegetable. **2. pulpe, pâte ▸** any wet, soft mass of material like this : *Wood pulp is used to make paper products.*

pulse [puls] NOUN, pulses. **1. pouls ▸** in the body, the steady beating of the arteries caused by the rush of blood after each pump of the heart. By feeling the pulse in your wrist, you can count the rate at which your heart is beating. **2. battement rythmique ▸** any steady or regular beat like this : *the pulse of flashing lights; the pulse of a drum machine.*

pu-ma [PYOO-muh *or* POO-muh] NOUN, pumas. **puma ▸** a large wild cat found in North and South America. **Note.** Often called a mountain lion or a cougar.

pump [pump] NOUN, pumps. **pompe ▸** a machine that forces liquid or a gas into or out of something : *a water pump; a gas pump.* ▲ VERB, pumped, pumping. **1. pomper ▸** to move a liquid or gas from one place to another using a pump : *We pump our water from the well.* **2. gonfler, remplir de ▸** to blow air or other gas into : *to pump up a flat tire.* **3. marcher en cadence, lever et abaisser régulièrement ▸** to move hard up and down, as if pumping water from a well : *She pumped her legs as she ran up the hill.* **4.** *Informal.* **essayer de soutirer, cuisiner, tirer les vers du nez ▸** to try to get

information by careful questioning : *The reporter pumped the actor for information about his latest movie.*

pump-kin [PUMP-kin] NOUN, pumpkins. **citrouille ▸** a large, round yellow-orange fruit with a hard outer shell and many seeds, used for making pies.

pun [pun] NOUN, puns. **calembour, jeu de mots ▸** a funny play on words, using words that have the same sound or spelling but have different meanings. The following pun plays on the meaning of *due* and *dew* : *Rain falls, but it goes up again in dew time.* 📖 p. 471.

punch¹ [punch] VERB, punched, punching. **1. donner un coup de poing ▸** to hit hard with the fist. **2. taper sur, enfoncer ▸** to push or poke something : *to punch computer keys; to punch an elevator button.* ▲ NOUN, punches. **coup de poing ▸** a blow with the fist. SYN: pound, beat, hammer, strike, hit.

punch² NOUN, punches. **perforateur, poinçonneuse, étampe, poinçon ▸** a tool for making holes or for pressing a design into something. ▲ VERB, punched, punching. **perforer, poinçonner, estamper ▸** to make a hole or design with a punch.

punch³ NOUN, punches. **punch ▸** a sweet drink made by mixing different fruit juices, soda, and so on.

punch line chute, conclusion ▸ the final line or sentence of a joke, necessary for understanding the joke.

punc-tu-al [PUNK-choo-ul] ADJECTIVE. **ponctuel (-elle), à l'heure ▸** at the proper or expected time : *Brent is so punctual that he has never been late for school.* ■ **punctually,** ADVERB. ▸ **exactement, à l'heure pile.** *We will start punctually at 12:00 noon.*

punc-tu-ate [PUNK-choo-ATE] VERB, punctuated, punctuating. **1. ponctuer ▸** to mark writing with periods, commas, and other symbols so as to make the meaning clear. **2. marquer, souligner ▸** to give emphasis to : *He punctuated the end of the reading by slamming the book shut.* **3. interrompre ▸** to interrupt : *Applause punctuated her speech.*

punc-tu-a-tion [PUNK-choo-AY-shun] NOUN. **ponctuation ▸** the use of periods, commas, and other

✏️ **Word Builder**

Pull apart *means to separate into pieces by pulling or to criticize very severely: She was a tough editor and pulled apart my entire essay. To* ***pull for*** *is to offer one's support: He always pulls for the Edmonton Oilers during the play-offs.* ***Pull off*** *means to do something successfully or perform in the face of difficulties: We pulled off the surprise party without a hitch.* ***Pull one's weight*** *means to do one's share of the work: Although Shawna is much younger, she pulls her weight around the house.*

✏ **Writing Tips**

Pun

Puns are usually thought of as silly, and people will groan at a pun as often as they laugh. Puns involve a play on words, twisting them around; for example— what do you call a monkey who jokes? A chimpunzee. If you use puns in your writing, be careful not to overuse them. A few puns go a long way.

symbols to make the meaning of written material clear. **Note.** A punctuation mark is used to do this.

punc‑ture [PUNK-chur] VERB, punctured, puncturing. **crever ▸** to make a hole in something with a sharp object : *A nail in the street had punctured the front tire of our car.* ▲ NOUN, punctures. **crevaison, piqûre, ponction ▸** a hole made by a sharp object.

pun‑gent [PUN-junt] ADJECTIVE. **âcre, piquant (-ante) ▸** having a strong, sharp taste or smell : *The pungent smell of burning leaves filled the air.*

pun‑ish [PUN-ish] VERB, punished, punishing. **1. punir ▸** to make a person suffer for doing something wrong : *They were punished for breaking the window.* **2. malmener ▸** to treat harshly or roughly. **Note.** Often used as an ADJECTIVE: *A punishing wind ripped shingles off the roof of the house.* SYN: discipline, correct.

pun‑ish‑ment [PUN-ish-munt] NOUN, punishments. **1. punition, châtiment ▸** the act or fact of punishing. **2. punition, sanction ▸** the way in which someone is punished : *Her punishment for speeding was a $20 fine.* **3. Informal. mauvais traitement ▸** rough treatment : *Toys should be built to take a lot of punishment.*

pu‑ny [PYOO-nee] ADJECTIVE, punier, puniest. **chétif (-ive), malingre, frêle ▸** small or weak : *The runt of the litter was a puny little puppy.*

pup [pup] NOUN, pups. **chiot, jeune animal ▸** a young dog; a puppy. **Note.** The young of certain other animals, such as sharks or seals, are sometimes called pups.

pu‑pa [PYOO-puh] NOUN, pupas or pupae. **chrysalide, pupe ▸** an insect in a resting stage before it becomes an adult. A caterpillar is a pupa when it is in its cocoon.

pu‑pil[1] [PYOO-pul] NOUN, pupils. **élève ▸** a person who is in a school; a student.

pupil[2] NOUN, pupils. **pupille ▸** the opening in the centre of the eye. The pupil, which looks like a black dot, gets smaller in bright light and larger in darkness.

pup‑pet [PUP-it] NOUN, puppets. **1. marion‑nette ▸** a small figure of a person or animal that is used as a toy or to act out a puppet show. Some puppets fit over the hand and are moved by the fingers; others have strings that are pulled from above. **Note.** A person who works the puppets in a puppet show is a puppeteer. **2. pantin ▸** a person or group that is completely controlled by someone else.

puppets

pup‑py [PUP-ee] NOUN, puppies. **chiot ▸** a young dog.

pur‑chase [PUR-chus] VERB, purchased, purchasing. **acheter ▸** to get something by paying money; buy : *to purchase a new computer.* ▲ NOUN, purchases. **1. achat ▸** a thing that is purchased; something bought : *All purchases are paid for at the checkout counter.* **2. achat ▸** the act of purchasing : *the purchase of a new coat.* SYN: buy, get, bargain for, acquire, shop.

pure [pyoor] ADJECTIVE, purer, purest. **1. pur (pure) ▸** free from dirt, germs, or harmful substances; perfectly clean : *pure water from a clean mountain spring.* **Note.** The condition of being pure is purity. **2. pur (pure) ▸** not mixed with anything else : *a coin made of pure gold.* **3. pur (pure) ▸** free from evil or faults : *A person who has not done anything wrong has a pure conscience.* **4. pur (pure), simple ▸** nothing other than : *No skill is involved in winning the lottery—it's pure luck.* ■ **purely,** ADVERB. **▸ purement.** SYN: clean, spotless, unpolluted.

pu‑ri‑fy [PYOOR-uh-fy] VERB, purified, purifying. **purifier, épurer ▸** to make pure or clean : *The hikers used a special filter to purify the water from the stream so that it would be safe to drink.* **Note.** The process of doing this is purification. SYN: clean, filter, refine, cleanse.

pu·ri·tan [PYOOR-uh-tun] NOUN, puritans. **1. puritain (-aine), personne austère ▸** a person who follows very strict rules for living and does not approve of certain freedoms and pleasures. **2. Puritan. puritain (-aine), rigoriste ▸** a member of a group in the 1500s and 1600s who wanted to "purify" the Church of England by making church services simpler and by living strictly according to the teachings of the Bible.

pur·ple [PUR-pul] NOUN, purples. **pourpre, violet ▸** the colour made by mixing red and blue together.

pur·pose [PUR-pus] NOUN, purposes. **but, objet, utilité ▸** the reason why something is made or done; a plan or goal; use : *The purpose of a dictionary is to give information about words.* ▪ **purposely,** ADVERB. **à dessein, exprès, délibérément ▸** for a reason; on purpose. SYN: aim, goal, target, intent, ambition, design. ✍ **p. 472.**

on purpose intentional; not by accident : *My little sister spilled her juice on purpose, just to get some attention.*

purr [pur] NOUN, purrs. **ronronnement, ronron ▸** a soft, low rumbling sound like that made by a cat. ▲ VERB, purred, purring. **ronronner, faire ronron, roucouler ▸** to make this sound : *"His voice was almost purring with pleasure now, like a well-tuned engine."* (Betsy Byars)

purse [purs] NOUN, purses. **1. sac à main ▸** a bag used by women for carrying money, keys, a comb or brush, and other small personal items. **Note.** Also called a handbag or pocketbook. **2. porte-monnaie ▸** a small bag or pouch used to hold money : *a coin purse.* **3. prix, récompense ▸** a sum of money given as a prize or gift : *A purse of $10,000 will be given to the winner of the horse race.* ▲ VERB, pursed, pursing. **pincer (les lèvres), faire la moue ▸** to pull or draw together; wrinkle; pucker : *The manager pursed her lips in thought as she considered the problem.*

pur·sue [pur-SOO] VERB, pursued, pursuing. **1. poursuivre, pourchasser ▸** to follow in order to catch up to or capture : *The cat pursued the mouse until he caught it.* **2. poursuivre ▸** to carry or keep on with something : *to pursue a dream.* SYN: follow, chase, track, trail, go after, hunt.

pur·suit [pur-SOOT] NOUN, pursuits. **1. poursuite ▸** the act of pursuing; chasing or following something : *in pursuit of a criminal.* **2. poursuite, recherche ▸** the act of making a continued effort to reach some goal : *the pursuit of happiness.* **3. occupation, travail, activité, passe-temps ▸** a particular activity : *Many people enjoy the relaxing pursuit of fishing.*

push [poosh] VERB, pushed, pushing. **1. pousser ▸** to press against something in order to move it; shove : *to push open a door.* **2. se frayer un chemin ▸** to press or move forward :

The dog sled pushed ahead through the snow. **3. appuyer sur, enfoncer ▸** to press with the finger : *"But when Alistair pushed the button to take the judges through time, nothing happened."* (Marilyn Sadler) **4. pousser à, obliger ▸** to try to make a person do something by urging or by force : *The teacher pushed Maya to do her best.* **5. faire la réclame pour ▸** to try to sell or promote something : *a TV commercial that pushes a new kind of toy.* ▲ NOUN, pushes. **poussée ▸** the act or fact of pushing. ▪ **pushy,** ADJECTIVE. *Informal.* **arriviste, qui se met trop en avant ▸** too anxious to get ahead or to be noticed; very forward. SYN: press, nudge, prod, force, drive, shove.

push-up [POOSH-up] NOUN, push-ups. **exercice de traction ▸** an exercise done by lying face down, then raising and lowering the body by straightening and bending the arms.

pussy willow **saule blanc ▸** a small willow tree with silky grey flower clusters that look like a cat's fur and that appear in the spring.

put [poot] VERB, put, putting. **1. mettre ▸** to cause to be in a certain place : *Put this letter in the mailbox.* **2. mettre ▸** to cause to be in a certain condition : *"Arion's music always put Periander in a good mood."* (Marcia Williams) **3. dire, exprimer ▸** to say something in a certain way : *When you tell her that she didn't make the team, put it to her gently.* SYN: place, set, lay, position, arrange, deposit.

✒ **Writing Tips**

Purpose

You might say "The purpose of this letter is to thank Uncle Jack for the present he sent me, or "The purpose of my English report is to get extra credit in the course." Teachers of writing, however, would say that these are **motives** *or* **goals** *for writing. A writer's purpose, on the other hand, is the effect that he or she hopes to have on the reader. If you write a science report, your purpose is to inform. You wouldn't include jokes, slang, made-up words, and so on. But suppose you are writing a note to cheer up a sick friend. Now your purpose is to entertain; jokes, puns, and slang will all suit your purpose. Sometimes your purpose is to persuade, as in a letter to the editor. Here you would be serious, as in a science paper. But now you need to give opinions as well as facts, so your approach will be different.*

put aside mettre de côté ▸ to save for future use.

put down 1. écrire, inscrire, noter ▸ to write. **2.** *Informal.* critiquer, dénigrer ▸ to find fault with.

put in passer du temps, investir du temps, consacrer du temps ▸ to spend time doing something.

put off retarder, repousser, différer ▸ to not do something; delay.

put on 1. mettre, passer, enfiler ▸ to dress oneself. **2.** organiser ▸ to present a show on stage.

put up 1. construire, ériger ▸ build or erect. **2.** offrir ▸ to offer something, such as money. **3.** loger, héberger ▸ to give lodging or food to.

put up with tolérer, supporter ▸ to endure or bear with patience.

put-ter [PUT-ur] VERB, puttered, puttering. bricoler ▸ to keep busy without doing anything important; work at small, minor tasks : *My father likes to putter around the house, doing odd jobs.*

put-ty [PUT-ee] NOUN, putties. mastic ▸ a soft mixture that starts out moist like clay when put on and then dries and slowly hardens. It is used to fill cracks and to hold panes of glass in place.

puz-zle [PUZ-ul] NOUN, puzzles. **1.** casse-tête, rébus, mots croisés, puzzle ▸ a game in which a person tries to solve a problem as a test of mental skill, such as a jigsaw puzzle or crossword puzzle. **2.** énigme, mystère ▸ a question or problem that is hard to understand; a mystery : *It's a puzzle to me how he knew where to find me.* ▲ VERB, puzzled, puzzling. tenter de résoudre, tenter de comprendre, rendre perplexe, laisser perplexe ▸ think hard; be perplexed : *"The old man was still puzzled, but he decided not to ask any more questions."* (Tololwa M. Mollel) SYN: mystery, problem, question, confusion. ✐ **p. 152.**

py-ja-mas [puh-JAM-uz *or* puh-JAH-muz] NOUN. (also pajamas) **pyjama** ▸ a set of clothes worn for sleeping, usually made up of a shirt and trousers or shorts.

pyr-a-mid [PEER-uh-mid] NOUN, pyramids. **1.** pyramide ▸ a solid shape or object with a flat base and three or more triangles that slope upward to meet in a point at the top. **2.** the Pyramids. pyramide ▸ the huge stone structures with four triangle-shaped sides that were built thousands of years ago in Egypt.

py-thon [PY-thon *or* PY-thun] NOUN, pythons. python ▸ a very large snake that is not poisonous, but that coils around its prey and crushes it to death. Pythons are found in Africa, Asia, and Australia.

quartz

q, Q [kyoo] NOUN, q's, Q's. **q, Q ▸** the 17th letter of the English alphabet.

quack [kwak] NOUN, quacks. **coin-coin ▸** the sound that a duck makes. ▲ VERB, quacked, quacking. **faire coin-coin ▸** to make such a sound.

quad-ri-lat-er-al [KWOD-ruh-LAT-uh-rul] NOUN, quadrilaterals. **quadrilatère ▸** a flat geometric figure with four sides and four angles. Squares, rectangles, and trapezoids are quadrilaterals.

quad-ru-ped [KWOD-ruh-ped] NOUN, quadrupeds. **quadrupède ▸** an animal that has four feet. Cats, dogs, bears, and the like are quadrupeds.

quad-ru-plet [kwod-ROO-plit or KWOD-ruh-plit] NOUN, quadruplets. **1. quadruplés ▸** one of four children born of the same mother in a single birth. **2. quadruplé ▸** one of a group of four.

quail [kwale] NOUN, quail or quails. **caille ▸** a small bird with a plump body, a short tail, and brownish feathers. It is often hunted as game.

quaint [kwaynt] ADJECTIVE, quainter, quaintest. **curieux (-ieuse), surprenant (-ante), singulier (-ière) ▸** interesting or attractive in an odd and old-fashioned way : *I had a quaint little doll-house with handmade furniture when I was young.* SYN: odd, curious, unusual, old-fashioned.

quake [kwake] VERB, quaked, quaking. **trembler, vaciller ▸** to shake or tremble : *"Maylin's father and brothers quaked with fear and fell to their knees."* (Paul Yee) ▲ NOUN, quakes. **1. tremblement ▸** the act of trembling or shaking. **2. tremblement de terre, séisme ▸** a short word for earthquake. SYN: tremble, shake, shudder, shiver, vibrate.

qual-i-fi-ca-tion [KWOL-uh-fuh-KAY-shun] NOUN, qualifications. **1. compétence(s), qualification, aptitude ▸** something that makes a person or thing suited for a job or task : *Being able to use computers is a qualification for many jobs today.* **2. restriction, réserve ▸** something that limits or restricts : *Michi supported the plan wholeheartedly and without qualification.*

qual-i-fy [KWOL-uh-fy] VERB, qualified, qualifying. **1. (se) qualifier ▸** to cause to be fit or suited for something; make able to do or have : *The winner of today's contest will qualify for the national championship in Ottawa next month.* **2. mettre des conditions, nuancer ▸** to change so as to limit or restrict : *Our teacher promised us no homework for the holiday, but qualified that by saying "no homework for those who finish all their work."* SYN: change, modify, alter, moderate.

qual-i-ty [KWOL-uh-tee] NOUN, qualities. **1. qualité ▸** something that makes a person or thing what it is; the nature or character of something : *Marie has many wonderful qualities—she is friendly, confident, happy, and intelligent.* **2. qualité ▸** the amount of worth or value that something has : *the quality of a good education.* SYN: characteristic, trait, property, feature.

quan-ti-ty [KWON-tuh-tee] NOUN, quantities. **1. quantité ▸** something that can be counted or measured; a number or amount : *Shiva measured the quantity of flour she needed to make bread.* **2. quantité, nombre ▸** a large number or amount : *We packed a large quantity of water for our trip across the desert.*

quar-an-tine [KWOR-un-teen] NOUN, quarantines. **quarantaine ▸** a period of time during which someone or something that may carry a dangerous disease is kept away from people, so that the disease will not spread. ▲ VERB, quarantined, quarantining. **mettre en quarantaine ▸** to put a person or thing in quarantine : *After the dog bit the postal carrier, it was quarantined while it was tested for rabies.* SYN: separate, isolate, confine, seclude.

quar-rel [KWOR-ul] NOUN, quarrels. **querelle, dispute, désaccord ▸** an angry fight or disagreement with words; an argument. ▲ VERB, quarrelled, quarrelling. (also quarreled, quarreling) **1. se quereller, se disputer, se mailler ▸** to have a quarrel; argue : *My mom was tired of hearing us quarrel so she sent us to our rooms.* **2. critiquer, désapprouver ▸** to

474

find fault; disagree : *I can't quarrel with my coaches' methods because I have improved so quickly.* 🖊 **p. 31.**

quar-ry[1] [KWOR-ee] NOUN, quarries. **carrière ▸** a place where stone is cut or blasted out of the ground to be used for building. ▲ VERB, quarried, quarrying. **extraire ▸** to cut and remove stone from a quarry.

quarry[2] NOUN, quarries. **proie ▸** an animal that is being hunted; prey : *A wolf's quarry is the old, sick, or injured caribou in a herd.*

quart [kwort] NOUN, quarts. **pinte ▸** a unit of measure for liquids in the imperial system, equal to about 1.14 litres.

quar-ter [KWOR-tur] NOUN, quarters. **1. quart ▸** one of four equal parts; one fourth : *Seven students is a quarter of our class of 28.* **2. quart d'heure ▸** a time of 15 minutes, equal to one fourth of an hour : *6:45 is a quarter to seven.* **3. pièce de vingt-cinq cents, monnaie ▸** a coin of Canada and the United States that is worth 25 cents, or one fourth of a dollar. **4. trimestre ▸** one fourth of a year; three months : *Profits increased in the last quarter.* **5. quart ▸** one of four equal time periods of play in football, basketball, and certain other games. **6. quartier ▸** a certain section or neighbourhood of a city : *the French quarter of town.* **7. quarters. logement, gîte ▸** a place to live or stay : *The hotel was very elegant; we couldn't have asked for better quarters.* ▲ VERB, quartered, quartering. **1. diviser en quatre ▸** to divide into four equal parts : *to quarter an apple.* **2. cantonner ▸** to give a place to live or stay : *to quarter an army official at a military base.*

quar-ter-back [KWOR-tur-BAK] NOUN, quarterbacks. **quart, quart arrière ▸** in football, the player who takes the ball from the centre to start the play and either hands it off to another player or passes it or runs with it.

quar-ter-ly [KWOR-ter-lee] ADJECTIVE; ADVERB. **trimestriel (-ielle) ▸** happening or done once every quarter of the year : *A quarterly magazine comes out four times a year.*

quar-tet [kwor-TET] NOUN, quartets. (sometimes quartette) **1. quatuor ▸** a musical composition written for four voices or instruments. **2. quatuor ▸** a group of four singers or musicians performing together : *A barbershop quartet has four male singers who each take a different harmonizing part.* **3. quatuor ▸** any group of four persons or things. **Note.** *Quartette* refers to a group of four performers.

quartz [kworts] NOUN. **quartz ▸** a very hard that is one of the most common minerals founds on earth. It is colourless in its pure form but often appears coloured when it is mixed with other minerals. Quartz crystals are used in watches and clocks and in transmitters for radio and TV sets.

qua-sar [KWAY-zar] NOUN, quasars. **quasar ▸** a starlike object that sends out powerful radio waves and very bright light. Quasars are at very great distances from the earth, and it is not certain what their exact properties are. 👁 **p. 397.**

qua-ver [KWAY-vur] VERB, quavered, quavering. **chevroter, trembloter ▸** to shake or tremble : *"A white-throated sparrow whistled its quavering three-note song."* (Tim Wynne-Jones)

quay [kee] NOUN, quays. **quai ▸** a landing place for boats, often built of stone, used for the loading and unloading of ships.

quea-sy [KWEE-zee] ADJECTIVE, queasier, queasiest. **qui donne mal au cœur, qui met mal à l'aise ▸** a feeling of nausea or unease : *Rollercoasters make some people feel queasy.*

queen [kween] NOUN, queens. **1. reine ▸** a woman who rules a country as the head of a royal family. **2. reine ▸** the wife or widow of a king. **3. reine ▸** a woman or girl thought of as ruling like a queen, or as important as a real queen : *The Red Cross nurses were known as the "queens of the battlefield" during World War II.* **4. reine ▸** a female bee, ant, or other insect that is larger than the others of its kind and is usually the only one that lays eggs. **5. reine ▸** a playing card with a picture of a queen on it. A queen ranks between a jack and a king. **6. reine ▸** a powerful piece in the game of chess. 📖 **p. 971.**

queer [kweer] ADJECTIVE, queerer, queerest. **bizarre, étrange ▸** not what is expected or normal; strange; odd : *My chair made a queer noise when I stood up.*

quench [kwench] VERB, quenched, quenching. **1. éteindre ▸** to put out a fire or light : *The firefighters quenched the fire with water.* **2. étancher, satisfaire ▸** to put an end to; satisfy : *to quench your thirst with lemonade.*

que-ry [KWEER-ee] NOUN, queries. **question, requête ▸** a question : *The external-affairs minister fielded many queries from the media about Canada's trade policies.* ▲ VERB, queried, querying. **demander, poser une question ▸** to ask a question.

quest [kwest] NOUN, quests. **quête, recherche ▸** the act of looking for something valuable or important; a search : *The character Don Quixote went on a quest to right the world's wrongs.* ▲ VERB, quested, questing. **être en quête de, rechercher ▸** to go in search of something; go on a quest.

ques-tion [KWES-chun] NOUN, questions. **1. question ▸** something that is said or written to get an answer, to find something out, or to test what a person knows. **2. question, problème ▸** a matter to be thought about, discussed, or settled; an issue or problem : *How to raise money for our library is the question we are discussing at this meeting.* **3. incertitude, doute ▸** the fact of being uncertain or in doubt : *Whether or not we were finished was open to question, but we decided to stop anyway.* **4. out of the question. hors de question ▸** not to be considered.▲ VERB, questioned, questioning. **1. questionner, interroger ▸** to ask a question or questions. **2. contester, mettre en doute ▸** to have or show doubts about : *My teacher questioned my story about how my homework was lost.* ■ **questioningly,** ADVERB. ▸ **d'un air interrogateur.** *"She looked back at him questioningly, as if to say, 'Where are you taking me?'"* (Isaac Bashevis Singer) **Note.** Something that is questionable is uncertain or open to question : *His leg is sore, so it is questionable whether he will play in Saturday's game.* SYN: ask, inquire, demand, quiz, interrogate, query. *✐* **p. 476.**

question mark point d'interrogation ▸ a punctuation mark [?] that goes at the end of a sentence to show that a question is being asked.

ques·tion·naire [KWES-chun-air] NOUN, questionnaires. **questionnaire ▸** a written or printed list of questions that is used to get information : *When Ann went to a new doctor, she filled out a long questionnaire about her medical history.*

queue [kyoo] NOUN, queues. **queue, file d'attente ▸** a line of waiting people, cars, or the like : *There was a long queue for the water fountain.* ▲ VERB, queued, queuing. (often used with up) to form a line or to wait in a line : *We queued up for the new movie.*

quib·ble [KWIB-ul] VERB, quibbled, quibbling. **chicaner, disputer ▸** to argue about a very small point in order to avoid dealing with the main point or problem : *Don't quibble over a few cents in tax when you're getting a $200 discount.*

quick [kwik] ADJECTIVE, quicker, quickest. **1. rapide, vite, prompt (prompte) ▸** moving or acting with speed; fast : *"The bass players say their instruments aren't nimble enough for Mr. Beethoven's quick notes."* (Barbara Nichol) **2. rapide, furtif (-ive) ▸** done or happening in a short time; brief : *Kyle took a quick glance at his notes before beginning his speech.* **3. vif (vive), rapide, prompt (prompte) ▸** able to understand and learn easily : *a person with a quick mind.* ▲ ADVERB. **vite, rapidement, promptement ▸** in a quick way; fast : *Quick, run and get help.* ▲ NOUN, quicks. **1. chair à vif ▸** the tender, sensitive skin under the fingernails. **2. vif, point sensible ▸** the tender, sensitive part of one's feelings. ■ **quickly,** ADVERB. ▸ **rapidement, promptement.** ■ **quickness,** NOUN. ▸ **rapidité, vitesse, promptitude.** SYN: fast, rapid, swift, hasty, speedy.

quick·sand [KWIK-sand] NOUN, quicksands. **sables mouvants ▸** a soft, wet mixture of sand and water that will not hold up a heavy object. A person who steps in quicksand will sink down into it.

✐ Writing Tips

Questions

There are two kinds of questions.

• **Yes/no questions** *ask for a yes or a no answer.*

"Is that your brother?"
"Do you need help?"

• **Information questions** *ask for information, rather than just a yes or a no. Information questions are formed using the five W's : who, what, when, where, and why (also how).*

"Who was that on the phone?"
"Why did Josée leave early?"

• *A* **direct question** *always has a question mark at the end, rather than a period.*

Jashir asked, "Why was the talent show called off?"

• *An* **indirect question** *uses a period. Jashir asked me why the talent show was called off.*

---

qui·et [KWY-ut] ADJECTIVE, quieter, quietest **1. tranquille, silencieux (-ieuse), paisible ▸** with little or no noise; silent. **2. faible, léger (-ère ▸** not loud : *The injured man let out a quie moan.* **3. tranquille, silencieux (-ieuse), calme ▸** without movement or activity; calm; peaceful : *"Alejandro paused, keeping very quiet a the squirrel approached the garden."* (Richard E. Albert) **4. discret (-ète) ▸** not standing out o making a show; modest : *She faded into the crowd in her quiet navy-blue dress.* ▲ NOUN **tranquillité, silence, calme ▸** a lack of noise silence : *the quiet of evening.* ▲ VERB, quieted quieting. **(se) calmer, apaiser, tranquilliser ▸** tc make or become quiet : *The father quietee the crying baby with a bottle of warm milk* ■ **quietly,** ADVERB. ▸ **tranquillement, calme ment, paisiblement.** SYN: silent, noiseless hushed, soundless, calm.

quill [kwil] NOUN, quills. **1. penne ▸** a bird': feather, especially one from a wing or tail **2. plume d'oie ▸** a pen made from such a feather. Quill pens were used from ancient times up to the late 1800s. **3. piquant ▸** one of the sharp spines of a porcupine or other such ani mal.

quilt [kwilt] NOUN, quilts. **courtepointe ▸** a cove. for a bed, made of two pieces of cloth stuffec with soft material and held together by stitching across the surface. ▲ VERB, quilted, quilting **1. matelasser, ouater et piquer ▸** to make a

✐ **Writing Tips**

Direct and Indirect Quotations

When you quote someone directly in your writing, use quotation marks. The following is a **direct quotation:**

"My ideas come from my community. Chinese people have lived in Canada since before Confederation," Paul Yee said of his writing.

However, you can also summarize what someone has said in an **indirect quotation:**

Paul Yee talked about how his ideas came from the Chinese people who have lived in Canada since Confederation.

quilt. **2. ouatiner ▸** to stitch together with padding. **Note.** A piece of clothing that is quilted is made in this same way: *a quilted vest.*

quin·tet [kwin-TET] NOUN, quintets. (sometimes quintette) **1. quintette ▸** a musical piece written for five voices or instruments. **2. quintette ▸** a group of five singers or five musicians performing together.

quin·tu·plet [kwin-TUP-lit *or* KWIN-tuh-plit] NOUN, quintuplets. **1. quintuplés ▸** one of five children born of the same mother in a single birth. **2. quintuplé ▸** one of a group of five. **Note.** Often shortened to quint.

quip [kwip] NOUN, quips. **trait d'esprit, boutade, plaisanterie ▸** a clever, often teasing or funny remark. ▲ VERB, quipped, quipping. **lancer avec esprit ▸** to make such a remark: *"Someone forgot to order a set of legs for that snake,"* he quipped.

quirk [kwirk] NOUN, quirks. **bizarrerie, quolibet, excentricité ▸** a strange or peculiar way of acting: *Our lawn mower has many quirks, like suddenly stopping for no reason.* ■ **quirky,** ADJECTIVE. ▸ **bizarrement, étrangement.**

quit [kwit] VERB, quit *or* quitted, quitting. **1. arrêter, cesser, abandonner ▸** to stop doing something, especially something that is not wanted: *I quit going to bed late every night so that I can get up early for swimming practice.* **2. quitter, laisser ▸** to leave a job or position. **Note.** A quitter is a person who gives up too easily in the face of problems or difficulty. SYN: end, stop, leave, abandon, depart.

quite [kwite] ADVERB. **1. tout à fait, complètement ▸** completely; entirely: *"She was surprised to notice her hands were not quite steady as she took the camera on the table."* (Marilyn Halvorson) **2. plutôt ▸** more than usual; very; rather. **3. quite a. un assez grand nombre de ▸** very much; more than usual: *A few years ago, quite a few people had never even seen a computer.*

quiv·er[1] [KWIV-ur] VERB, quivered, quivering. **frémir, frissonner ▸** to shake slightly; tremble: *"Instantly, the water quivered and rippled, making the moon's reflection burst into hundreds of shimmering pieces."* (Jan Thornhill) **Note.** Also used as a NOUN: *A quiver of excitement ran down her spine as she stepped up to the starting block for the race.*

quiver[2] NOUN, quivers. **carquois ▸** a case for holding arrows.

quiz [kwiz] NOUN, quizzes. **quiz, petit test ▸** a short test: *We had a quiz in our math class today.* ▲ VERB, quizzed, quizzing. **interroger ▸** to question: *Cara quizzed the reporter about his training.*

quo·ta [KWOH-tuh] NOUN, quotas. **1. part ▸** one part or share of a total amount: *We had to pick our quota of berries if we wanted some pie.* **2. quota ▸** the amount or percentage of a certain type of thing or people that is allowed: *Fishing quotas were set to prevent overfishing.*

quo·ta·tion [kwoh-TAY-shun] NOUN, quotations. **citation ▸** something that is quoted; the exact words of another person: *Denise used a quotation from the fire chief in her report.* **Note.** Also called a quote. ✐ **p. 477.**

quotation mark guillemets ▸ one of a pair of punctuation marks [" "] used to show the beginning or ending of a quotation or to set off the title of a newspaper or magazine article, story, poem, and so on.

quote [kwote] VERB, quoted, quoting. **1. citer ▸** to repeat the exact words of another person: *to quote the poetry of Dennis Lee.* **2. établir un prix ▸** to name the price or cost of something. ▲ NOUN, quotes. **1. citation ▸** the act of quoting another's words; a quotation. **2. proposition (de prix) ▸** a price that is quoted: *Jim got two quotes on the cost of having his car repaired.*

quo·tient [KWOH-shunt] NOUN, quotients. **quotient ▸** a number obtained by dividing one number by another: *In the equation $6 \div 2 = 3$, the quotient is 3.*

Qur·'an see Koran.

rice

r, R [ar] NOUN, r's, R's. **r, R ▶** the18th letter of the English alphabet.

rab·bi [RAB-i] NOUN, rabbis. **rabbin ▶** in the Jewish religion, a trained religious teacher who is usually the leader of a congregation.

rab·bit [RAB-it] NOUN, rabbits. **lapin (-ine) ▶** a small animal that has soft fur, large front teeth, long ears, and a short tail. Rabbits are found in most parts of the world.

ra·bies [RAY-beez] NOUN. **rage ▶** a very serious disease that can cause death in warm-blooded animals, such as humans, dogs, and squirrels. Rabies is caused by a virus, usually passed on by the bite of an animal that already has the disease. **Note.** An animal that is affected with this disease is **rabid**.

rac·coon [ruh-KOON] NOUN, raccoons. **raton laveur ▶** a North American animal with a plump body, a sharp, pointed nose, a bushy tail, and dark markings around the eyes. Raccoons are active at night and can eat almost any kind of food.

race[1] [race] NOUN, races. **1. course ▶** a contest to decide who or what is fastest : *a relay race; a bicycle race.* **2. course, concours ▶** any contest like a race : *"When we arrived it was a race to see who could strip off his clothes first."* (Todd Lee) ▲ VERB, raced, racing. **1. courir, faire la course ▶** to take part in a contest of speed. **2. se précipiter, courir, filer à toute allure ▶** to run fast, as if in a race : *After lunch she raced back to school to play baseball.* **3. faire à toute vitesse, se dépêcher, se hâter à faire ▶** to do something very fast : *Kelly raced through her homework so that she'd have more time to play.*

race[2] NOUN, races. **1. race ▶** a large group of people who share some physical features, such as the colour of the skin and the shape of the body and face. **2. race ▶** a group of people who share a common history or cultural traditions. ■ **racial**, ADJECTIVE. **racial (-iale, -iaux) ▶** having to do with a person's race : *racial characteristics.* **Note.** A person who opposes another or others because of race is a **racist**. Such an attitude is called **racism**.

rack [rak] NOUN, racks. **1. support ▶** a frame or stand for hanging or storing things : *a coat rack; a towel rack.* **2. ramure, bois de cervidés ▶** a pair or set of antlers. ▲ VERB, racked, racking. **torturer, tourmenter, assaillir, tenailler ▶** to suffer greatly : *She was racked with guilt over breaking her mother's favourite lamp.*

rack one's brains **se creuser la tête, se creuser la cervelle ▶** to think as hard as one can.

rack·et [RAK-it] NOUN, rackets. **1. tapage, vacarme ▶** a loud, unpleasant noise : *We made such a racket that Jon couldn't hear the phone ring.* **2.** *Informal.* **fraude, trafic, escroquerie, racket ▶** a way to get money that is not honest or fair. **Note.** A racketeer is a criminal who carries on illegal business.

rac·quet [RAK-it] NOUN, racquets. (also racket) **raquette ▶** a round or oval fame having tightly laced strings in a crisscross pattern, and a handle at the end. It is used in such games as tennis, badminton, and squash.

ra·dar [RAY-dar] NOUN. **Note.** The word *radar* **radar ▶** started out as an acronym for *radio detecting and ranging.*

ra·di·ant [RAY-dee-unt] ADJECTIVE. **1. radieux (-ieuse) ▶** giving off bright light; shining or glowing : *a radiant sunrise.* **2. radieux (-ieuse), rayonnant (-ante) ▶** glowing with happiness or joy : *Megan was radiant with excitement as she received her award.* **3. radiant (-iante) ▶** sent out in waves or made up of waves : *Heat and radio waves are forms of radiant energy.* **Note.** The quality of being radiant is **radiance**.

ra·di·ate [RAY-dee-ATE] VERB, radiated, radiating. **1. rayonner ▶** to give off heat or light as rays : *Heat radiated from the campfire.* **2. rayonner ▶** to move or spread out from a central point : *Spokes of a wheel radiate out from the centre of the wheel.*

ra·di·a·tion [RAY-dee-AY-shun] NOUN. **1. irradiation, rayonnement, radiation ▶** light or other energy that radiates through the air. The sun's rays are a form of radiation. **2. radiation ▶** cer-

478

tain rays given off by a radioactive material. Radiation can be very dangerous.

ra·di·a·tor [RAY-dee-AY-ter] NOUN, radiators. **1. radiateur** ▸ a heating device made up of a series of pipes or tubes through which hot water or steam passes. **2. radiateur** ▸ a device for cooling an engine or a machine, such as a car engine.

radiator

rad·i·cal [RAD-ih-kul] ADJECTIVE. **1. radical (-ale, -aux)** ▸ having to do with the source or most important part : *He had radical surgery to remove a tumour from his stomach.* **2. radical (-ale, -aux)** ▸ being in favour of or working toward extreme changes, especially in politics : *The radical politician wants to abolish sales tax.* ▲ NOUN, radicals. **radical (-ale, -aux)** ▸ a person who has extreme opinions in politics. ■ **radically,** ADVERB: ▸ **radicalement, fondamentalement, complètement :** *There is something radically wrong with the car; the engine is making an awful clanking noise.*

ra·di·o [RAY-dee-oh] NOUN, radios. **1. radio** ▸ a way of sending and receiving sounds through the air by means of electrical waves. **2. radio** ▸ a device that receives sounds that are sent out this way. ▲ VERB, radioed, radioing. **envoyer un message radio, communiquer par radio** ▸ to send a message by radio : *The pilot radioed the control tower for help landing in the foggy weather.* 📖 p. 1169. 👁 p. 540.

ra·di·o·ac·tiv·i·ty [RAY-dee-oh-ak-TIV-ih-tee] NOUN. **radioactivité** ▸ the energy that is given off when the nucleus of an atom breaks apart or decays. This usually causes the atom to give off particles in the form of invisible waves or rays called radiation. Some elements, such as uranium and radium, have natural radioactivity. Scientists cause radioactivity in other elements for use as a source of energy or for nuclear weapons. ■ **radioactive,** ADJECTIVE. **radioactif (-ive)** ▸ caused by, having, or showing radioactivity.

rad·ish [RAD-ish] NOUN, radishes. **radis** ▸ a garden vegetable with a root that is usually eaten raw. The radish has a crisp white inside with a sharp taste and a thin red or white skin.

ra·di·us [RAY-dee-us] NOUN, radii [RAY-dee-i] or radiuses. **1. rayon** ▸ any line going straight from the centre to the outside edge of a circle or sphere : *The straight side of a piece of pie is a radius.* **2. rayon** ▸ a circular area that is measured by the length of its radius : *There are four schools within a two-kilometre radius of our house.*

raf·fle [RAF-ul] NOUN, raffles. **tombola** ▸ a game of chance in which people buy tickets in hopes of winning a prize. ▲ VERB, raffled, raffling. (often used with off) **mettre en tombola** ▸ to offer a prize in a raffle : *Our school raffled off a car to raise money for computers.*

raft [raft] NOUN, rafts. **radeau (-eaux)** ▸ a floating platform of logs, boards, or other materials bound together.

rag [rag] NOUN, rags. **1. lambeau (-eaux), chiffon, loque** ▸ a small piece of old cloth, usually one that is worn out or torn. **2. rags. guenilles, haillons** ▸ old, worn-out clothing.

rage [raje] NOUN, rages. **1. rage, furie, fureur** ▸ a feeling of very strong, wild anger that one cannot control ; fury : *"If anyone came near his property, he flew into a terrible rage."* (Roch Carrier) **2. vogue, mode, fureur, engouement** ▸ something that is very popular at a certain time ; a fad or fashion : *During the 1950s, the hula hoop was the rage on every playground.* ▲ VERB, raged, raging. **1. rager, éprouver de la colère, être furieux (-ieuse)** ▸ to feel or show great anger. **2. faire rage, se déchaîner, être en furie** ▸ to act or move in a strong, violent way : *The storm raged through the night, leaving drifts of snow everywhere.* SYN: fury, passion.

rag·ged [RAG-id] ADJECTIVE. **1. en lambeaux, en loques** ▸ worn or torn into rags : *My little brother's teddy bear is old and ragged, but he doesn't want a new one.* **2. irrégulier (-ière), inégal (-ale, -aux)** ▸ rough or uneven ; not smooth : *"The eagle's wing was torn, a bone had snapped, and its breathing came in ragged gasps."* (Sheryl McFarlane)

rag·weed [RAG-WEED] NOUN, ragweeds. **herbe à poux** ▸ a plant found in North America that produces a lot of pollen, which causes allergies.

raid [rade] NOUN, raids. **raid, incursion, descente, rafle** ▸ a sudden surprise attack or invasion. ▲ VERB, raided, raiding. **1. attaquer, faire une incursion, faire une descente** ▸ to make a raid : *"In the north, fierce Mongol horsemen raided Chinese villages."* (Leonard Everett Fisher) **2. dévaliser, rafler** ▸ to enter and take what is there : *We raided the kitchen for cookies.* ■ **raider,** NOUN. ▸ **attaquant (-ante), agresseur, braqueur.**

rail [rale] NOUN, rails. **1. garde-fou, rail, traverse, main courante** ▸ a long, narrow piece of wood, metal, or other material used as a guard or support. Wooden rails are often held up by posts as part of a fence. Steel rails are placed in pairs on the ground to form a track for railway cars. **2. chemin de fer, voie ferrée, rail ▸** a railway : *The shipment was sent east by rail.*

rail·ing [RAY-ling] NOUN, railings. **balustrade ▸** a fence made of a rail or rails, especially one used to keep people from falling : *a railing on a stairway.*

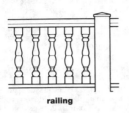

railing

rail·road [RALE-RODE] NOUN, railroads. **chemin de fer, voie ferrée, rail ▸** another word for railway. ▲ VERB, railroaded, railroading. *Informal.* **forcer quelqu'un à faire quelque chose ▸** to push to get something done quickly without concern for fairness : *My boss railroads his ideas through without asking anyone else's opinion.*

rail·way [RALE-way] NOUN, railways. (also railroad) **1. voie ferrée, chemin de fer ▸** a path or track made of two metal rails on which a train runs. **2. système ferroviaire ▸** a system of transportation in which people and goods are moved along such tracks, including the trains, tracks, and stations, and the workers who operate the system.

rain [rane] NOUN, rains. **1. pluie ▸** drops of water that fall to the earth from the sky. **2. pluie ▸** the falling of such drops : *a heavy summer rain.* **3. pluie ▸** a heavy, fast fall of anything like rain : *a rain of angry words.* ▲ VERB, rained, raining. **1. pleuvoir ▸** to fall as rain : *It rained all day.* **2. pleuvoir ▸** to fall in the way rain does : *The wind caused the leaves to rain down onto our heads.* 📖 p. 1118. 👁 p. 113.

rain·bow [RANE-BOH] NOUN, rainbows. **arc-en-ciel ▸** a band of coloured light shaped like an arc, sometimes seen in the sky after or during a rain shower. It is caused by sunlight reflecting through tiny drops of water in the sky.

rain·coat [RANE-COTE] NOUN, raincoats. **imperméable, manteau (-eaux) de pluie ▸** a coat made from waterproof material, used to keep a person dry when it rains.

rain·fall [RANE-FOL] NOUN, rainfalls. **1. chute de pluie ▸** the falling of rain : *A heavy rainfall caused the mudslide.* **2. pluviosité, taux de précipitations ▸** the amount of water that falls as rain, snow, sleet, or hail in a given area in a certain period of time.

rain forest forêt tropicale (humide) ▸ a dense forest in an area that has a high rainfall throughout the year.

rain·y [RANE-ee] ADJECTIVE, rainier, rainiest. **pluvieux (-ieuse) ▸** having a lot of rain : *a rainy day.*

raise [raze] VERB, raised, raising. **1. lever, soulever ▸** to move to a higher place or position : *She raised her hand to show that she knew the answer.* **2. hausser, élever, augmenter ▸** to move to a higher condition or amount : *to raise your voice; to raise a worker's salary.* **3. réunir, rassembler, collecter ▸** to bring together; collect : *A bake sale was held to raise money for schoolyard equipment.* **4. élever, cultiver, faire pousser ▸** to bring up and take care of : *to raise goats or orchids.* **Note.** When referring to bringing up children, **rear** is the correct word to use in formal writing. **5. soulever ▸** to ask or talk about : *to raise a question or an issue.* ▲ NOUN, raises. **1. augmentation de salaire ▸** an increase in the rate of pay given to a worker. **2. augmentation ▸** any increase in amount or value.

rai·sin [RAY-zin] NOUN, raisins. **raisin sec ▸** a sweet dried grape that is eaten as a snack or used in cooking.

rake [rake] NOUN, rakes. **râteau (-eaux) ▸** a garden tool having a long handle with a row of teeth or prongs attached at one end. Rakes are used to smooth dirt or to gather loose leaves, grass, and so on. ▲ VERB, raked, raking. **1. ratisser, râteler ▸** to gather or smooth with a rake : *Wan raked up all the leaves and twigs in the yard.* **2. balayer, parcourir ▸** to sweep or go over something with a movement like a rake : *"Thorns raked his arms, but he did not feel the sting."* (Betsy Byars) **3. ratisser, fouiller avec soin ▸** to search carefully : *She raked through the papers on her desk to find her notes.*

ral·ly [RAL-ee] VERB, rallied, rallying. **1. rassembler, rallier, regrouper ▸** to bring back together; bring back to order : *Renate rallied the spectators to cheer louder.* **2. reprendre des forces, aller mieux ▸** to get back strength and health; recover : *The patient rallied and was out of the hospital in a week.* ▲ NOUN, rallies. **1. rassemblement, ralliement ▸** the act of rallying. **2. rassemblement ▸** a gathering of many people to show support for a person or cause : *a victory rally; a protest rally.*

ram [ram] NOUN, rams. **bélier ▸** a male sheep. ▲ VERB, rammed, ramming. **1. emboutir, percuter, heurter violemment ▸** to strike with great force; hit against : *"Ouch!" he yelled as he rammed into the corner of the table.* **2. enfoncer, tasser, entasser ▸** to force to press into place : *She rammed her clothes into her bag.* SYN: jam, thrust, force.

RAM [ram] ABBREVIATION. **RAM ▸** short for random-access memory, the part of a computer or similar device that can locate information at random rather than in a certain set order.

Ram·a·dan [RAM-uh-DON *or* ROM-uh-DON] NOUN. *ramadan* ▶ the ninth month of the Muslim year, when no food or drink can be taken during daylight.

Ram·a [ROM-uh] NOUN. **Rama** ▶ a human form of the Hindu god Vishnu. Rama is known for his goodness and justice toward people.

ram·ble [RAM-bul] VERB, rambled, rambling. **1. se promener au hasard, errer** ▶ to go about without trying to get to any special place; wander. **2. serpenter, sinuer, aller çà et là, divaguer** ▶ to grow or move in an irregular way : *The ivy rambled over the wall and fence.* **3. radoter, parler pour ne rien dire, divaguer** ▶ to talk or write without any order or purpose : *"Grandma rambled on with her comments, going through the pictures so slowly...." (Marilyn Halvorson)* **Note.** Also used as an ADJECTIVE: *a rambling old building; a rambling speech.* SYN : roam, wander.

ramp [ramp] NOUN. ramps. **rampe, voie d'accès** ▶ a section of a surface, such as a floor, that slopes to connect a lower area with a higher one : *Marg rolled her wheelchair up the ramp to the door.*

ram·page [ramp] NOUN, rampages. **déchaînement, emportement** ▶ a fit of violent or reckless behaviour.

ran [ran] VERB. a past form of run.

ranch [ranch] NOUN, ranches. **1. ranch** ▶ a large farm on which herds of cattle, sheep, or horses are raised. **2. ranch, ferme** ▶ any farm that is used to raise one particular animal or crop : *a turkey ranch.* **Note.** A person who owns or works on a ranch is a rancher.

ran·dom [RAN-dum] ADJECTIVE. **soumis (-ise) au hasard, à l'aveuglette, aléatoire** ▶ without any pattern, plan, or purpose; by chance : *The winner was chosen at random from the many entries.*

rang [rang] VERB. a past form of ring.

range [raynj] NOUN, ranges. **1. écart, échelle, étendue, éventail (-ails)** ▶ the distance between certain limits or amounts : *The choir accepts members in the age range of 8 to 12 years.* **2. rayon d'action, portée, autonomie** ▶ the longest distance something can work or travel : *This aircraft has a range of about 4,000 kilometres.* **3. champ de tir, stand de tir, polygone de tir** ▶ a place to practise or test shooting a gun or other weapon : *a rifle range.* **4. prairie, pâturage** ▶ a large open area of land on which farm animals can be kept and fed. **5. chaîne** ▶ a row or series of mountains : *The Rockies, a chain of mountain ranges, extend from Canada into the United States.* **6. fourneau (-eaux) de cuisine** ▶ a stove for cooking : *a gas*

range. ▲ VERB, ranged, ranging. **1. s'étendre, varier** ▶ to go or extend between certain limits : *The library's collection ranges from picture books to encyclopedias.* **2. parcourir** ▶ to move through or over : *The cattle ranged over the grassland.*

ran·ger [RANE-jur] NOUN, rangers. **1.** (also forest ranger *or* park ranger) **garde forestier, gardien (-ienne) de parc national** ▶ a person whose job is to look after and look after a forest or natural area. **2.** Ranger. **guide aînée** ▶ a senior Girl Guide 15 years or older.

rank[1] [rank] NOUN, ranks. **1. grade, rang** ▶ a certain level within a group; a position or grade : *Captain, sergeant, and general are different ranks in the armed forces.* **2. rangée, rang** ▶ a row or line of people or things, placed side by side : *Ranks of seats filled the gym for the play.* **3. ranks.** (also rank and file) **hommes de troupe, simples soldats** ▶ the people in the armed forces who are not officers; the ordinary members of any group, as opposed to its leaders. ▲ VERB, ranked, ranking. **se classer, avoir un certain classement** ▶ to have a certain rank : *Pierre ranked second in his graduating class.* SYN : class, level, position, status.

rank[2] ADJECTIVE. **1. fétide, nauséabond (-onde), rance** ▶ having a strong, very unpleasant taste or smell. **2. pur (pure), parfait (-aite), criant (-ante), flagrant (-ante)** ▶ a complete or extreme example of a bad quality; total : *Her rude behaviour showed rank ingratitude to her friends.*

ran·sack [RAN-sak] VERB, ransacked, ransacking. **fouiller à fond, fouiller en mettant tout sens dessus dessous** ▶ to search in a rough way : *Tina ransacked her room looking for her lost wallet.*

ran·som [RAN-sum] NOUN, ransoms. **1. rançon** ▶ money paid to set free a person who is being held as a prisoner : *The kidnappers demanded a million-dollar ransom to return the businessman.* **2. rançon, rançonnement** ▶ the fact of holding someone captive in this way. ▲ VERB, ransomed, ransoming. **libérer contre une rançon, rançonner** ▶ to set a prisoner free by paying the ransom.

rap[1] [rap] VERB, rapped, rapping. **frapper bruyamment, donner un coup sec** ▶ to knock or tap sharply. ▲ NOUN, raps. **petit coup sec, tape** ▶ a quick, sharp blow or knock; tap : *Shashi heard a rap on the window and went out to see what had made the noise.*

rap[2] NOUN, raps. **rap** ▶ a form of music in which the lyrics are spoken or chanted to a rhythm.

rap·id [RAP-id] ADJECTIVE. **rapide** ▶ moving or done with great speed; very quick; fast : *the rapid movement of a hummingbird's wings.* ■ **rapidly,** ADVERB. ▶ **rapidement.** *He ran rapidly toward the finish line.* ■ **rapidity,** NOUN. ▶ **rapidité.**

rap·ids [RAP-idz] NOUN. **rapides** ▶ a part of a river or stream where the water flows very fast.

rare¹ [rair] ADJECTIVE. rarer, rarest. **1. rare** ▶ not often seen or found; not happening often; unusual : *Snow is rare in the summer.* **2. rare** ▶ very valuable or special because of not being common : *That book is very rare; only 100 copies were printed.* **Note.** Something that is rare is a rarity. ▪ **rarely**, ADVERB: ▶ **rarement.** *A roadrunner is a bird that rarely flies.*

rare² ADJECTIVE. **peu cuit (cuite), saignant (-ante)** ▶ of meat, lightly cooked : *a rare steak.*

ras·cal [RAS-kul] NOUN. rascals. **polisson (-onne), fripon (-onne), espiègle, coquin (-ine)** ▶ someone who does bad things that are not really harmful; a person who is naughty or full of mischief.

rash¹ [rash] NOUN. rashes. **rougeur, éruption, urticaire, tache rouge** ▶ a condition in which small red spots or patches break out on the skin, causing pain or itching. Poison ivy, measles, and allergies can cause a rash.

rash² ADJECTIVE. **imprudent (-ente), irréfléchi (-ie)** ▶ in too much of a hurry; reckless or careless : *Kerry made a rash promise to sing in the talent show.* SYN : careless, hasty.

rasp·ber·ry [RAZ-bair-ee] NOUN. raspberries. **framboise** ▶ a sweet berry that grows on a prickly plant. Raspberries are usually red or black. ☜ **p. 251.**

raspberry bush

leaf

flower

fruits (raspberries)

rat [rat] NOUN. rats. **1. rat (rate)** ▶ an animal that looks like a mouse, but is larger. Rats have a long nose, round ears, and a long, thin tail. They can spread disease and germs, kill small animals, and damage food supplies. **2.** *Informal.* **salaud (salope), dégueulasse, ordure** ▶ a person who is considered mean, sneaky, or destructive.

rate [rate] NOUN. rates. **1. taux, vitesse, rythme** ▶ an amount or number that is measured against something else : *The space shuttle travels at a rate of 8 km per second.* **2. taux** ▶ a price or charge for something, especially a service : *The mechanic's rate is $15 an hour.* ▲ VERB, rated, rating. **évaluer, classer** ▶ to place at a certain level : *Michael was rated the top student in his class this year.*

rath·er [RATH-er] ADVERB. **1. plutôt** ▶ more willing to do one thing than another : *I would rather walk than drive.* **2. plutôt, quelque peu** ▶ to a certain amount or extent; somewhat : *"He had a kind voice and rather dark, deep eyes."* (Margaret Read MacDonald) **3. plutôt** ▶ in the opposite or a different way; instead : *We took a side road rather than the main highway.* **4. plutôt, plus exactement** ▶ more correctly or more exactly : *The nearest town is 100 km away — or rather, almost 100.*

rat·i·fy [RAT-ih-fy] VERB, ratified, ratifying. **ratifier** ▶ to accept and approve in an official way : *Parliament must ratify any treaties made with foreign countries.* ▪ **ratification**, NOUN. ▶ **ratification.**

rat·ing [RAY-ting] NOUN. ratings. **1. indice d'écoute, audimat, médiamat** ▶ a rank given to a TV show, radio program, song, and so on to show how many people watch, listen to, or buy it : *The Channel 8 News has the highest ratings for a news broadcast.* **2. classement** ▶ any grade or rank that shows relative value; position : *Our school has an excellent academic rating.*

ra·ti·o [RAY-shoh *or* RAY-shee-oh] NOUN. ratios. **rapport** ▶ a comparison of the number or size of two different things. A ratio is the number of times the second thing can be divided into the first : *If there are 8 apples and 2 oranges, the ratio of apples to oranges is 4 to 1, or 4:1.*

ra·tion [RASH-un *or* RAY-shun] NOUN. rations. **ration** ▶ a fixed amount or share of food allowed for one person or animal : *We carry our own rations of water when we hike.* ▲ VERB, rationed, rationing. **rationner** ▶ to limit food or other important supplies to a fixed amount : *The government rationed gasoline, meat, butter, and other items during the two world wars.*

ra·tion·al [RASH-un-ul] ADJECTIVE. **1. rationnel (-elle), logique** ▶ having a sound mind; able to think clearly : *Most problems can be solved with rational thought.* **2. rationnel (-elle), raisonnable** ▶ based on sound thinking; reasonable : *There must be a rational explanation for this broken window; it couldn't have just broken by itself.*

rat·tle [RAT-ul] VERB, rattled, rattling. **1. crépiter, cliqueter** ▶ to make a series of short, sharp sounds : *The wind rattled the windows all night.* **2. rattle off. débiter à toute allure** ▶ to talk or say something quickly : *She loves that movie and can rattle off all its funniest lines.* **3. déconcerter, ébranler** ▶ to make nervous or upset : *The pitcher was so rattled by the* *noise that he walked four batters in a row.* ▲ NOUN, rattles. **1. cliquetis, crépitement ▸** a short, sharp sound. **2. hochet, crécelle ▸** something that makes this sound : *a baby's toy rattle.*

rat-tle-snake [RAT-ul-SNAKE] NOUN, rattlesnakes. **serpent à sonnette, crotale ▸** a poisonous snake with several horny rings at the end of its tail that rattle when shaken.

rave [rave] VERB, raved, raving. **1. divaguer, déraisonner ▸** to talk in a very excited or wild way; say things that do not make sense. **2. s'extasier, parler avec enthousiasme, louanger, faire l'éloge ▸** to give something great praise or approval : *The critics all raved about that new book.* ▲ NOUN, raves. **éloge, louange, dithyrambe ▸** very great praise or approval. **Note.** Also used as an ADJECTIVE: *a rave review for a new movie.*

ra-ven [RAY-vun] NOUN, ravens. **corbeau (-eaux) ▸** a large black bird that is related to and looks very much like a crow, but is larger. Ravens have a harsh cry. ▲ ADJECTIVE. **noir (noire) comme un corbeau, noir (noire) comme l'ébène ▸** shiny black : *raven hair.*

ra-vine [ruh-VEEN] NOUN, ravines. **ravin ▸** a deep, narrow valley, usually formed when running water wears down a space between two hills over a long period of time.

raw [rah] ADJECTIVE, rawer, rawest. **1. cru (crue) ▸** not cooked : *Raw carrots are much crunchier than cooked ones.* **2. brut (brute) ▸** in a natural condition; not processed : *raw wool.* **3. inexpérimenté (-ée), non aguerri (-ie) ▸** not trained or experienced : *New members of the armed forces are called raw recruits.* **4. à vif ▸** having the skin rubbed off : *Melissa scraped her knee raw on the pavement.* **5. glacial (-iale, ials) ▸** of weather, damp and cold.

raw material matière première ▸ a substance that is still in its natural state and has not been refined, manufactured, or processed. Coal, wood, and cotton are important raw materials.

ray[1] [ray] NOUN, rays. **1. rayon ▸** a narrow beam or line of light : *"In the evenings, he looked out over the water shimmering with the last rays of light."* (Sheryl McFarlane) **2. rayon ▸** any similar line or stream of some other form of energy : *X-rays are used to photograph bones inside the body.* **3. rayon ▸** one of a group of lines going out from a centre. **4. rayon, lueur ▸** a very small amount : *a ray of hope.*

ray[2] NOUN, rays. **raie ▸** any one of a large group of saltwater fish that are related to sharks. A ray has a wide, flat body, broad fins, and a long tail.

ray-on [RAY-on] NOUN. **rayonne ▸** an artificial material made from the cellulose fibre of wood or cotton.

ra-zor [RAY-zur] NOUN, razors. **rasoir ▸** a small tool with a thin, sharp blade that is used for shaving hair from the face or body.

re- PREFIX. **1.** again : *redo; retest.* **2.** back : *recall; return.*

reach [reech] VERB, reached, reaching. **1. tendre le bras, essayer de prendre, tendre le bras pour prendre ▸** to put out the hand to try to hold or touch something : *He reached up to pick an apple from the tree.* **2. atteindre ▸** to stretch out as far as; extend to : *"But the tree was so tall and the branches so high that even the giraffe couldn't reach the fruit."* (Celia Barker Lottridge) **3. arriver, parvenir, atteindre ▸** to come to a certain place or condition; arrive at : *to reach a decision. At this speed we will reach Montreal by noon.* **4. joindre, rejoindre ▸** to get in touch with someone; communicate : *I tried all day, but I could not reach John on the phone.* ▲ NOUN, reaches. **1. portée, atteinte ▸** the act of reaching, or the distance that can be covered by doing so : *She always keeps a dictionary within reach when she writes.* **2. allonge ▸** the distance that a person can extend his or her arms. **3. étendue ▸** a long stretch or extent : *"His footsteps echoed through the vast silent reaches of the house."* (Esther Forbes)

re-act [ree-AKT] VERB, reacted, reacting. **1. réagir ▸** to act because something else happened or was done; respond : *Most people react to being tickled by laughing, screaming, or pulling away.* **2. réagir ▸** to have a chemical reaction; to change.

re-ac-tion [ree-AK-shun] NOUN, reactions. **1. réaction ▸** the fact of reacting; a response : *What was Mom's reaction when you asked her whether we could go to the beach?* **2. réaction ▸** a condition in nature that occurs as a direct result of something else : *For every action, there is an equal and opposite reaction.* **3. réaction ▸** in chemistry, a process by which substances are changed into new substances : *A reaction between iron and water creates rust.*

read [reed] VERB, read [red], reading. **1. lire ▸** to look at something that is written or printed and understand its meaning. **2. lire ▸** to say aloud printed or written words : *Randy read them a story.* **3. lire ▸** to learn about something by reading : *Kristen read about how to grow peas in* The Old Farmer's Almanac. **4. lire, discerner ▸** to get the meaning of; understand : *"I watched his face to see if I could read his reactions."* (Irene Hunt) **5. lire, interpréter ▸** to get information from observation; interpret : *He read the sky to determine the weather for the day.* **6. indiquer ▸** of an instrument, to give or show information : *The thermometer read 17 degrees.* **7. lire ▸** of a computer, to locate information on a disk or other storage device. **Note.** Something that can be read is readable.

read-er [REE-dur] NOUN. **1. lecteur (-trice) ▸** a person who reads : *Jeff is a very fast reader.*

2. livre de lecture ▸ a book used by students for learning and practising the skill of reading.

read·i·ly [RED-uh-lee] ADVERB. **volontiers, de bon gré, facilement, aisément** ▸ in a willing way; without difficulty; easily : *After losing badly, the team readily agreed to an extra practice.*

read·ing [REE-ding] NOUN, **readings**. **1. lecture** ▸ the fact of reading : *a reading of a poem.* **2. lecture** ▸ something to be read : *This novel makes for suspenseful reading.* **Note.** Also used as an ADJECTIVE:*reading glasses.*

read-out [REED-out] NOUN. **sortie papier** ▸ information from a computer in a printed form that can be read by the user.

read·y [RED-ee] ADJECTIVE, **readier, readiest. 1. prêt (prête)** ▸ in a condition to be used; prepared : *Dinner is ready.* **2. prêt (prête), sur le point de** ▸ likely or about to happen : *Elijah was ready to sing when he won the contest.* **3. à portée de la main, à sa disposition** ▸ able to be put into use quickly; available : *We have a ready supply of food in case of a snowstorm.* ▲ VERB, **readied, readying. préparer** ▸ to make ready; prepare. SYN: available, equipped.

re·al [reel] ADJECTIVE. **1. vrai (vraie), réel (-elle), véritable** ▸ not imagined or made-up; true : *Samuel Clemens was the real name of the author Mark Twain.* **2. vrai (vraie), authentique** ▸ not artificial; genuine : *She's a real astronaut, not an actor who pretends to be one.* ▲ ADVERB. *Informal.* **très, vraiment** ▸ very. **Note.** The fact of being real is reality. SYN: authentic, true. ✍ **p. 484.**

real estate NOUN. **biens immobiliers** ▸ land and the buildings, plants, water, and so on that are on or in the land.

re·al·ism [REE-uh-LIZ-um] NOUN. **réalisme** ▸ the fact of seeing or showing things as they really are; being realistic. **Note.** A realist is someone who sees or presents things as they really are.

re·al·is·tic [REE-uh-LIS-tik] ADJECTIVE. **1. réaliste** ▸ looking or seeming to be real; like real life : *The museum has realistic dinosaurs on display.* **2. réaliste** ▸ dealing with real life; seeing things as they really are : *I hope to win, but I am realistic enough to know that I don't have much chance.* ■ **realistically,** ADVERB. ▸ **de façon réaliste, avec réalisme.**

re·al·ize [REE-uh-LIZE] VERB, **realized, realizing. 1. se rendre compte, s'apercevoir, comprendre** ▸ to notice or be aware of; know about; understand : *When she got to school, she realized that she had left her book at home.* **2. réaliser** ▸ to make or become real : *I realized my goal of saving $50.* **Note.** The act or fact of realizing is realization. SYN: comprehend, understand.

re·al·ly [REEL-ee] ADVERB. **1. en fait, en réalité** ▸ in fact; actually : *He really didn't want to go, but he went anyway.* **2. vraiment, réellement** ▸ very much; truly : *a really difficult test.* SYN: indeed, truly, especially. ✍ **p. 484.**

✐ Writing Tips
Real/Really
Many people misuse *real* and use it as an adverb—she drove real fast. The word that should be used in this sentence is *really*. Some words have the same form for both the adjective and the adverb (He's a fast runner. He ran fast). Don't use real as an adverb, only use really, the -ly adverb form of the adjective.

realm [relm] NOUN, **realms**. **1. royaume** ▸ a kingdom. **2. domaine** ▸ an area of interest, knowledge, influence, or activity : *the realm of science.*

reap [reep] VERB, **reaped, reaping. 1. moissonner, faucher** ▸ to cut down and gather wheat or similar crops. **2. récolter** ▸ to get as a reward : *Your kindness will reap rewards.*

rear[1] [reer] NOUN. **arrière, derrière** ▸ the part that is away from or opposite to the front; the back. ▲ ADJECTIVE. **arrière, de derrière** ▸ at or in the back : *He left by the rear door.*

rear[2] VERB, **reared, rearing. 1. élever** ▸ to take care of a child while he or she is growing up; raise : *Jenny was reared by her grandparents.* **Note.** Sometimes used to refer to animals or plants, though **raise** is more common in this sense. **2. se cabrer** ▸ of an animal, to rise up on the hind legs : *"The deer in the centre reared and started in sudden fright."* (Farley Mowat) **3. dresser, se dresser** ▸ to rise or lift up : *The cliffs reared almost straight up from the beach.*

rea·son [REE-zun] NOUN, **reasons**. **1. raison** ▸ a fact or cause that explains why something happens as it does : *The reason the grass is so green is all the rain this spring.* **2. raison** ▸ the act or fact of thinking in a clear, sensible way : *She solved the problem with reason.* ▲ VERB, **reasoned, reasoning. 1. raisonner** ▸ to give reasons in an effort to change someone's mind : *I tried to reason with my dad about letting me go to the dance.* **2. raisonner** ▸ to think clearly.

rea·son·a·ble [REE-zuh-nuh-bul or REEZ-nuh-bul] ADJECTIVE. **1. raisonnable** ▸ acting with good reason; sensible; fair : *My teacher is reasonable about the amount of homework she gives us, never giving us too much.* **2. raisonnable** ▸ not too much or too great : *This jacket is on sale for a reasonable price.* ■ **reasonably,** ADVERB. ▸ **assez, relativement, raisonnablement.** *I'm not positive, but I am reasonably sure your keys are on the table.*

rea·son·ing [REE-zun-ing] NOUN. **1. raisonnement** ▸ the process of using reason and facts to make a judgment; using the mind carefully and well : *A scientist uses reasoning to form a hypothesis.* **2. raisonnement** ▸ the reason or reasons for something.

re·as·sure [REE-uh-SHOOR] VERB, reassured, reassuring. **rassurer** ▸ to give confidence or courage to someone who is worried, afraid, or in doubt : *The mother reassured her child that she would not leave him alone.* ■ **reassurance,** NOUN. ▸ réconfort, assurance, garantie.

re·bate [REE-bate] NOUN, rebates. **rabais** ▸ a part of the money paid for something, returned as a discount or refund : *The company offers a $1 rebate if you send in two proof-of-purchase seals.* ▲ VERB, rebated, rebating. **accorder un rabais, consentir un rabais, faire un rabais** ▸ to give a rebate.

reb·el [REB-ul] NOUN, rebels. **1. rebelle** ▸ a person who fights against and will not obey a government or ruler : *The rebels protested a new tax on food.* **2. rebelle** ▸ any person who goes against authority : *Robi is a rebel and never does what she is told to do.* ▲ [rih-BEL] VERB, rebelled, rebelling. **1. se révolter, se rebeller** ▸ to fight against one's government or ruler. **2. se révolter, se rebeller** ▸ to go against authority or control.

re·bel·lion [rih-BEL-yun] NOUN, rebellions. **1. rébellion, révolte** ▸ an armed revolt against the government : *In the Rebellion of 1837, armed settlers beat back British troops near Montreal.* **2. rébellion, révolte** ▸ the fact of rebelling against any authority or control : *The labourers were in rebellion over the cut in wages.* ■ **rebellious,** ADJECTIVE. ▸ rebelle.

re·bound [ree-BOWND] VERB, rebounded, rebounding. **1. rebondir** ▸ to bounce back after hitting something : *The puck rebounded off the boards.* **2. se rétablir, guérir** ▸ to recover : *She rebounded after a long illness.* ▲ [rih-bownd] NOUN. ▸ rebond, rebondissement.

re·call [rih-KOL] VERB, recalled, recalling. **1. appeler, se rappeler, se souvenir** ▸ to bring back to memory; remember : *Michelle recalls the way her grandfather used to bounce her on his knee.* **2. rappeler, retirer de la vente** ▸ to call or order back; withdraw : *The car maker recalled all of its vans because of a problem with the brakes.* ▲ [REE-kol] NOUN. **rappel, remémoration** ▸ the fact of calling back : *People with total recall can remember every detail of what they have seen, read, or heard.*

re·cede [rih-SEED] VERB, receded, receding. **s'éloigner, s'estomper** ▸ to go or move away : *The water receded as the tide went out.* **Note.** Often used as an ADJECTIVE : *A person who is going bald has a receding hairline.*

re·ceipt [rih-SEET] NOUN, receipts. **1. reçu** ▸ a written statement that something such as money, mail, or merchandise has been received : *Sarah checked her receipt from the grocery store to see how much the grapes had cost.* **2.** receipts. **recettes** ▸ the amount of money received : *Yesterday, the store collected almost $5000 in receipts.* **3.** (also reception) **réception** ▸ the act or fact of receiving.

re·ceive [rih-SEEV] VERB, received, receiving. **1. recevoir** ▸ to get or take on what is given; accept : *I received a letter from home.* **2. recevoir, accueillir** ▸ to greet or welcome in a formal way : *Marina received her guests as they arrived at the party.* SYN: acquire, obtain, accommodate.

re·ceiv·er [rih-SEE-ver] NOUN, receivers. **1. récepteur, combiné** ▸ the part of a telephone that is held up to the ear for hearing and speaking. **2. récepteur** ▸ a device that can receive a radio or TV signal and convert it to sound or sound and pictures. **3.** (also recipient) **récipiendaire** ▸ a person who receives : *the receiver of this award.*

receiver

re·cent [REE-sunt] ADJECTIVE. **récent (-ente)** ▸ happening, done, or made just before the present; not old : *A recent news story discussed the discovery of a new star.* ■ **recently,** ADVERB. ▸ récemment, dernièrement. *I recently learned to dance.* SYN: fresh, new, current.

re·cep·ta·cle [rih-SEP-tuh-kul] NOUN, receptacles. **réceptacle, récipient** ▸ a container used to hold something : *a garbage receptacle.*

re·cep·tion [rih-SEP-shun] NOUN, receptions. **1. réception** ▸ the act or fact of receiving : *He acknowledged the reception of the package with his signature.* **2. réception** ▸ a party or social gathering to welcome guests : *The school held a reception to welcome new students.* **3. réception** ▸ the quality of signals received by a radio or a television set. **Note.** A receptionist is someone whose job is answering telephones, giving information, and greeting visitors.

re·cep·tive [rih-SEP-tiv] ADJECTIVE. **réceptif (-ive)** ▸ ready to receive; open to ideas or sugges-

485

tions : *A child with a receptive mind is eager to learn.*

rec·ess [REE-sess *or* rih-SESS] NOUN, recesses. **1. récréation, pause ▸** a time when work or other activity stops : *Our school has recess in the morning and the afternoon.* **2.** (often **recesses**) **recoin ▸** a part in a wall or other structure that is set back from the rest : *Ashley hid the present in the dark recess of the closet.* ▲ VERB, recessed, recessing. **suspendre ▸** to stop an activity for a short time. ⏰ **p. 1060.**

re·ces·sion [rih-SESH-un] NOUN, recessions. **récession ▸** a period of time when business conditions are bad. In a recession, sales and production fall, and there are fewer people working.

rec·i·pe [RES-uh-pee] NOUN, recipes. **1. recette ▸** a set of directions for preparing something to eat or drink. **2. recette, secret ▸** any method or set of steps for reaching a goal : *a recipe for losing weight.*

re·cite [rih-SITE] VERB, recited, reciting. **1. réciter ▸** to repeat something from memory : *We recite a passage from literature each week to improve our memories.* **2. énumérer, faire le récit ▸** to tell about in detail : *Benito recited the events of his day.* ◾ **recital,** NOUN. ▸ **récitation, récit, récital (-als).** SYN : quote, repeat.

reck·less [RECK-lis] ADJECTIVE. **imprudent (-ente), insouciant (-ante), irresponsable ▸** not thinking about or using care with something ; careless : *A reckless driver didn't stop at the lights.* ◾ **recklessly,** ADVERB. ▸ **imprudemment.** ◾ **recklessness,** NOUN. ▸ **imprudence, insouciance.** SYN : rash, wild.

reck·on [REK-un] VERB, reckoned, reckoning. **1. calculer, compter ▸** to find the value or amount of ; count ; calculate : *The committee reckoned that the new playground would cost $5,000.* **2.** *Informal.* **penser, supposer ▸** to think or guess ; suppose : *I reckon it's time for us to leave.*

re·cline [rih-KLINE] VERB, reclined, reclining. **s'allonger, s'étendre, s'incliner ▸** to lie down or lean back. **Note.** A recliner is a stuffed chair that adjusts so that a person can lie back.

re·cluse [rih-KLOOS *or* REK-loos] NOUN, recluses. **reclus (-use), solitaire ▸** a person who lives apart from the rest of the world. **Note.** Also called a hermit. ◾ **reclusive,** ADJECTIVE. ▸ **reclus (-use).**

rec·og·ni·tion [REK-ug-NISH-un] NOUN. **reconnaissance, identification ▸** the fact of recognizing or being recognized ; being known : *When she saw the dog, a look of recognition came over her face.*

rec·og·nize [REK-ug-NIZE] VERB, recognized, recognizing. **1. reconnaître ▸** to know who a person is, because of something that was known before : *Although I hadn't met Brad, I recognized him from your description.* **2. recon-**

naître ▸ to know something for what it is ; identify : *I recognized the song from the first few notes.* **3. reconnaître ▸** to accept or acknowledge that a person or thing has a certain standing or value : *Wayne Gretzky is recognized as one of the greatest hockey players of all time.*

re·coil [rih-KOYL] VERB, recoiled, recoiling. **reculer ▸** to draw back suddenly ; move back : *Martin recoiled when he saw a snake on the path.*

rec·om·mend [REK-uh-MEND] VERB, recommended, recommending. **1. recommander ▸** to speak in favour of someone or something : *Ms. Ng recommended me to her neighbours as a good baby-sitter.* **2. recommander ▸** to suggest or advise something as being a good idea : *The waiter recommended the salmon ; he said that it was the best thing on the menu.* **Note.** The act or fact of recommending is a recommendation.

re·con·cile [REK-un-SILE] VERB, reconciled, reconciling. **1. réconcilier ▸** to become friends again : *Steven and Alexi reconciled after their fight.* **2. régler ▸** to settle : *to reconcile an argument.* **3. réconcilier, faire accepter, résigner ▸** to make accept : *Time has reconciled us to the loss of our dog.*

re·cord [REK-urd] NOUN, records. **1. rapport ▸** a written statement of facts, events, or other such information : *Marie keeps a record of each day in her diary.* **2. dossier ▸** a history of facts about someone or something : *His school record shows that he is a fine, well-behaved student.* **3. record ▸** a performance or action that is the best of its kind : *The women's rowing team set a record in the 5000-metre race.* **4. disque ▸** a plastic disk on which music or other sounds can be stored to be played back on a record player. ▲ [rih-KORD] VERB, recorded, recording. **1. enregistrer, noter, consigner ▸** to set down facts in writing. **2. enregistrer ▸** to keep track of or display : *A barometer records air pressure.* **3. enregistrer ▸** to put sounds and/or images on tape, on disk, or on another device. ✎ **p. 487.**

re·cord·er [rih-KOR-der] NOUN, recorders. **1. enregistreur (-euse), magnétophone, magnétoscope ▸** a machine that records something, such as a tape recorder. **2. archiviste, greffier (-ière) ▸** a person who keeps records. **3. flûte à bec ▸** a musical instrument that is blown through like a whistle or flute, having a wooden body and finger holes to change the pitch of the sound. 👁 **p. 539.**

re·cov·er [rih-KUV-ur] VERB, recovered, recovering. **1. récupérer ▸** to get back something that was lost or stolen : *Hana recovered her ring from the bottom of the lake.* **2. se rattraper ▸** to make up for ; regain : *He recovered from his slow start and finished the test in time.* **3. récupérer, se rétablir ▸** to get back to a

> ✏️ **Word Builder**
>
> A **record** is an account or set of facts usually set down in writing. To **break the record** means to do better than all people who have competed or performed in that event before: *Donovan Bailey broke the record for the 100-metre race at the Olympics.* **Off the record** means something is not written down, quoted, or published: *The fire chief made his comments about the fire off the record.* When things are **on the record,** they are written down or made public: *In her speech, the mayor went on the record as a supporter of the new law.*

normal state or condition: *It took Sean three weeks to recover from a cold.* **Note.** The act of recovering or returning to normal is recovery.

rec·re·a·tion [REK-ree-AY-shun] NOUN. recreations. **détente, récréation ▸** something that is done for fun or relaxation; amusement; play: *Caitlin likes to read for recreation.* ■ **recreational,** ADJECTIVE. ▸ **pour les loisirs, de loisirs.**

re·cruit [rih-KROOT] NOUN. recruits. 1. **recrue ▸** a person who has recently joined the armed forces. 2. **recrue ▸** any new member or newcomer: *The French Club is small and needs some new recruits.* ▲ VERB. recruited, recruiting. **recruter ▸** to get people to join: *The group wants to recruit new volunteers.* **Note.** Someone who finds recruits is a recruiter.

rec·tan·gle [REK-TANG-gul] NOUN. rectangles. **rectangle ▸** a flat geometric shape with four sides and four right angles. A rectangle's opposite sides are parallel and equal in length. ■ **rectangular,** ADJECTIVE. ▸ **rectangulaire.**

re·cur [rih-KUR] VERB. recurred, recurring. **se reproduire, réapparaître, se représenter, se répéter ▸** to come or happen again: *Josh's dream that he is lost in the woods recurred last night.*

re·cy·cle [ree-SY-kul] VERB. recycled, recycling. **recycler ▸** to prepare or treat something so that it can be used again, instead of being thrown away: *Newspapers, glass bottles, and cans are recycled.* 👁 **p. 258.**

red [red] NOUN. reds. **rouge ▸** a bright colour that is the colour of blood. ▲ ADJECTIVE. ▸ **rouge, roux (rousse).** **Note.** To make or become red is to redden. Something that is somewhat red is reddish. 🖊 **p. 64.**

re·deem [rih-DEEM] VERB. redeemed, redeeming. 1. **échanger ▸** to exchange or turn in for a prize: *We redeemed a coupon for $2 off when we ordered a pizza.* 2. **racheter, compenser ▸** to make up for; balance: *The wonderful food redeemed the restaurant's poor service.* 3. **racheter ▸** to buy back or recover.

re·duce [rih-DOOS] VERB. reduced, reducing. 1. **réduire, diminuer, baisser ▸** to make less or smaller in size or amount; decrease: *The price of that bicycle was just reduced by $50.* 2. **réduire ▸** to cause or bring to a specific condition: *Tim's teasing reduced Nicky to tears.*

3. reduce to. **réduire ▸** to bring to a lower state or condition: *Maria was once a chef, but she has been reduced to cooking for a fast-food place.* ■ **reduction,** NOUN. ▸ **réduction, diminution, baisse.**

re·dun·dant [rih-DUN-dunt] ADJECTIVE. **redondant (-ante) ▸** extra; not needed: *It is redundant to say "Every day, I take a daily walk," because "every day" and "daily" mean the same thing.*

red·wood [RED-wood] NOUN. redwoods. **séquoia, wellingtonia ▸** a very large evergreen tree that grows along the Pacific coast of North America. **Note.** Also called a sequoia.

reed [reed] NOUN. reeds. 1. **roseau (-eaux) ▸** a tall, slender grass plant with long, narrow leaves and hollow stems. Reeds grow in swamps and marshes. 2. **anche ▸** a thin piece of wood or plastic that is used in the mouthpiece of some musical instruments. When air is blown over it, the reed vibrates and makes a sound. 3. **instrument à anche ▸** a musical instrument that uses a reed, such as a clarinet, a saxophone, or an oboe.

reef [reef] NOUN. reefs. **récif, écueil ▸** a chain or ridge of coral, rocks, or sand, often rising to the surface of the ocean.

reel¹ [reel] NOUN. reels. **bobine, moulinet, rouleau (-eaux) ▸** a roller or spool on which something is wound. Fishing line, tape, rope, film, or string can be wound on a reel. ▲ VERB. reeled, reeling. 1. **ramener, remonter, bobiner, embobiner ▸** to wind on a reel or pull in by winding a reel: *to reel in a fish.* 2. reel off. **débiter ▸** to say in a quick, easy way; rattle off: *Carla reeled off the names of all the students in her class.*

reel² VERB. reeled, reeling. 1. **chanceler, tituber, vaciller ▸** to be thrown off balance; sway or rock; feel as if one is turning: *Mr. Davis reeled when the ball hit him.* 2. **tourner, tourbillonner, tournoyer ▸** to turn around and around; whirl: *Her mind reeled as she remembered everything she had done this summer.*

reel³ NOUN. reels. **reel ▸** a lively folk dance.

re·fer [rih-FUR] VERB. referred, referring. 1. **se référer, consulter, recourir ▸** to direct attention to; speak or write about: *During his speech, Alan referred frequently to his notes.* 2. **diriger, envoyer ▸** to send or direct a person somewhere for help or information : *The librarian referred me to the encyclopedia for information on Louis Riel.*

ref-er-ee [REF-uh-REE] NOUN, referees. **arbitre** ▶ in sports such as hockey, soccer, and boxing, an official who makes sure that the rules are obeyed. The referee can call a foul or penalty if a rule is broken. ▲ VERB, refereed, refereeing. **arbitrer, servir d'arbitre** ▶ to act as a referee : *to referee a hockey game.*

ref-er-ence [REF-ur-runs *or* REF-runs] NOUN, references. **1. référence** ▶ the fact of referring to something : *During dinner, Alec didn't make any reference to the fight he'd had with his brother.* **Note.** Often used in the phrase in reference to: *Sandra wrote a letter to the company in reference to its excess packaging.* **2. référence, renvoi** ▶ a note in a book, an essay, or a speech that refers to another source of information : *This essay has two references to an excellent book on whales.* **Note.** Sometimes called a *citation.* **3. ouvrage de référence** ▶ a standard source of useful information, such as a dictionary, an encyclopedia, an almanac, and so on. **4. référence** ▶ a statement about how suitable someone is for a certain job or position, or the person who can give such a statement : *When I applied for a job, the store's owner asked me for two references.* ▲ ADJECTIVE. **de référence** ▶ used for reference or information : *a reference book.*

re-fine [rih-FINE] VERB, refined, refining. **1. raffiner** ▶ to make pure or free from other materials : *Sugar-cane is refined to make granulated sugar.* **2. raffiner, améliorer, soigner** ▶ to make more polished or elegant; improve : *Before you eat with me, you'll have to refine your table manners.* ■ **refinement,** NOUN. ▶ **raffinage, affinage, perfectionnement.**

re-fin-er-y [rih-FY-nuh-ree] NOUN, refineries. **raffinerie** ▶ a place where a product is refined, especially one where crude oil is made into gasoline and other products.

re-flect [rih-FLEKT] VERB, reflected, reflecting. **1. refléter, réfléchir** ▶ to turn or throw something back, such as light or heat : *The sun reflected off the water.* **Note.** Something that reflects is called a reflector. **2. refléter** ▶ to show as a result : *The faces of the children reflected their excitement.* **3.** reflect on. **a. réfléchir** ▶ to think carefully and seriously about : *The class quietly reflected on the poem.* **b. se répercuter** ▶ to bring about a certain result or feeling : *A good showing at the debating tournament reflects well on the school.*

re-flec-tion [rih-FLEK-shun] NOUN, reflections. **1. reflet** ▶ an image that is reflected by a surface, such as a mirror or still water. **2. réflexion** ▶ careful and serious thinking : *After serious reflection, Ryan decided to stay home and do his homework.* **3. reflet** ▶ something

that expresses or shows something else ; a result : *The improvement in Elsa's marks this year is a reflection of her hard work.*

re-flex [REE-fleks] NOUN, reflexes. **1.** (also reflex action) **réflexe** ▶ an automatic action that takes place when certain nerves are touched. Jerking your lower leg when your knee is tapped with a mallet and closing your eyes when you sneeze are reflex actions. **2.** reflexes. **réflexes** ▶ the ability of the body to react quickly to an action or event. **3. réflexe** ▶ something done automatically, as if by reflex.

re-form [rih-FORM] VERB, reformed, reforming. **réformer** ▶ to make a change for the better; correct something that is wrong : *Maka is trying to reform her eating habits with a healthier diet.* ▲ NOUN, reforms. **réforme** ▶ a change for the better. **Note.** A person who works for or favours reform is a *reformer.*

re-frain[1] [rih-FRANE] VERB, refrained, refraining. **se retenir, s'abstenir** ▶ to hold back from ; avoid : *Please refrain from talking during the show.*

refrain[2] NOUN, refrains. **refrain** ▶ a phrase repeated regularly in a song or poem ; a chorus.

re-fresh [rih-FRESH] VERB, refreshed, refreshing. **1. rafraîchir** ▶ to make fresh again ; renew or relax : *After a long walk, he refreshed himself with a glass of cold water.* **2.** refresh (one's) memory. **rafraîchir la mémoire, se rafraîchir la mémoire** ▶ to help a person remember ; remind. SYN : renew, restore.

re-fresh-ment [rih-FRESH-munt] NOUN, refreshments. **1.** refreshments. **rafraîchissements-** ▶ food or drink : *After the play, we had cookies and punch for refreshments.* **2. rafraîchissement, délassement** ▶ the fact of refreshing : *On a hot day, nothing provides as much refreshment as a swim.*

re-frig-er-ate [rih-FRIJ-uh-RATE] VERB, refrigerated, refrigerating. **réfrigérer** ▶ to keep something at a low temperature ; make or keep cool or cold : *Refrigerate meat to keep it from spoiling.* **Note.** The process of doing this is called refrigeration.

re-frig-er-a-tor [rih-FRIJ-uh-RAY-tur] NOUN, refrigerators. **réfrigérateur** ▶ a storage device used to keep things cold, especially a kitchen appliance.

re-fuge [REF-yooj] NOUN, refuges. **1. refuge** ▶ protection from trouble or danger; a safe place or condition : *The wet cat found refuge from the rain under a porch.* **2. réserve** ▶ a place that gives such protection : *a refuge for endangered birds.*

ref-u-gee [REF-yoo-JEE *or* REF-yoo-JEE] NOUN, refugees. **réfugié (-ée)** ▶ a person who flees from a place to find safety and protection somewhere else : *The school gave shelter to refugees from the flood.* **Note.** See also sanctuary.

✍ Writing Tips

Regardless

Regardless is a very useful word that means "not considering; not taking into account."

In our youth soccer league every player has to play at least half the game, *regardless* of what the score is.

But this useful word has a very unpopular cousin—irregardless. There is no such word in English. Why then do people make the mistake of using it? They probably share of similar word pairs —*relevant* means "to the point", and *irrelevant*, adding ir-, means "off the point". But *regardless* already carries the sense of "not" and doesn't need *ir*-So remember, *regardless* of what you hear sportscasters saying, *irregardless* is not a word.

re·fund [rih-FUND] VERB, refunded, refunding. **rembourser ▸** to give or pay back : *I returned the scratched CD to the store, and they refunded the money I paid for it.* ▲ [REE-FUND] NOUN, refunds. **remboursement ▸** the return of money that was paid.

re·fus·al [rih-FYOO-zul] NOUN, refusals. **refus ▸** the act of refusing .*Jason's refusal to get out of bed this morning made him late for school.*

re·fuse¹ [rih-FYOOZ] VERB, refused, refusing. **1. refuser ▸** to decide not to do or allow something : *He refused to eat his peas.* **2. refuser ▸** to say no; turn down : *She refused dessert because she was already full.* SYN: decline, deny, forbid, reject.

ref·use² [REF-yooce] NOUN. **détritus, débris, ordures, déchets ▸** anything worthless that is thrown away; garbage or trash.

re·gain [rih-GANE] VERB, regained, regaining. **récupérer, se rétablir ▸** to get back again; recover : *to regain health after a long illness.*

re·gal [REE-gul] ADJECTIVE. **royal (-ale, -aux) ▸** royal; having to do with a king or queen.

re·gard [rih-GARD] VERB, regarded, regarding. **1. considérer ▸** to think of in a certain way; consider to be : *"In time he regarded Kileken as the son he'd never had."* (Tololwa M. Mollel) **2. observer ▸** to look at closely; observe : *The cat and the dog regarded each other cautiously.* **3. tenir en grande estime, respecter, estimer ▸** to respect; pay attention to : *My father has earned the respect of his peers.* ▲ NOUN, regards. **1. considération, égard ▸**

thought or consideration : *That man rescued us with no regard for his own safety.* **2. regard ▸** a look or gaze. **3. regards. meilleurs souvenirs, meilleurs vœux ▸** best wishes : *When you see Mrs. Sorensen, give her my regards.*

regardless [rih-GARD-less] ADJECTIVE; ADVERB. **indifférent (-ente), insouciant (-ante), indépendamment, quand même ▸** with no thought or regard for; in spite of : *I will finish this book tonight, regardless of how late it is.* ✍ p. 489.

re·gard·ing [rih-GARD-ing] PREPOSITION. **pour, en ce qui concerne, quant à ▸** having to do with; about : *There is a meeting tonight regarding the new library.*

re·gime [rih-ZHEEM or ra-ZHEEM] NOUN, regimes. (also régime) **régime, règne ▸** a system or way of government, or a time when a certain ruler or government is in power : *The regime of Queen Victoria lasted from 1837 until 1901.*

reg·i·ment [REJ-uh-munt] NOUN, regiments. **régiment ▸** a large military unit, usually led by a colonel. ▲ VERB, regimented, regimenting. **imposer une discipline trop stricte ▸** to act or think in a strict, unchanging way, as if part of a military unit. ▪ **regimented** or regimental, ADJECTIVE: **▸ régimentaire, enrégimenté.** *Camp is so regimented that there is never any time to play.*

re·gion [REE-jun] NOUN, regions. **région ▸** any large area of land : *Gorillas are found in the forested regions of Africa.* ▪ **regional**, ADJECTIVE. **régional (-ale, -aux) ▸** having to do with or happening in a certain large area : *Our team won the regional soccer tournament.* 📘 p. 1044. SYN: territory, district.

reg·is·ter [REJ-us-tur] VERB, registered, registering. **1. inscrire, enregistrer ▸** to enter something on an official list or record : *You can register for night classes in the main office.* **2. indiquer, marquer ▸** to show on a scale or meter : *The temperature today registered 20°C.* **3. exprimer, refléter ▸** to show or express : *Miguel's face registered surprise when I told him that I had won the lead in the play.* ▲ NOUN, registers. **1. inscription, liste ▸** an official list or record. **2.** (also cash register) a machine that records the money that comes in from sales in a store, a restaurant, or another business.

reg·is·tra·tion [REJ-us-TRAY-shun] NOUN, registrations. **inscription, enregistrement ▸** the act of registering : *Kindergarten registration is being held at the elementary school today.*

re·gret [rih-GRET] VERB, regretted, regretting. **regretter ▸** to feel sorry or disappointed about something : *Robert regretted missing Sheena's party.* ▲ NOUN, regrets. **regret ▸** a feeling of being sorry.

reg·u·lar [REG-yuh-lur] ADJECTIVE. **1. régulier (-ière), normal (-ale, -aux), habituel (-elle) ▸** being what is usual or expected; normal;

489

standard : *Class starts at our regular time tomorrow, but it will end early.* **2. régulier (-ière)** ▶ happening over and over at the same time or in the same way; steady : *I heard the sound of his deep, regular breathing.* **3. régulier (-ière), assidu (-ue), fidèle** ▶ according to habit, custom, or usual behaviour : *My uncle is a regular visitor at our house.* **4. régulier (-ière)** ▶ even; balanced; orderly : *The design on the fabric followed a regular pattern.* ▲ NOUN, regulars. **habitué (-ée)** ▶ a person who is part of a regular group : *We had all our regular and two new players last night.* ■ **regularly,** ADVERB. ▶ **régulièrement.** SYN : customary, typical, habitual.

reg·u·late [REG-yuh-LATE] VERB, regulated, regulating. **1. régir, régler** ▶ to control or direct something according to a system or set of rules : *Laws regulate how people drive their cars.* **2. régler, ajuster** ▶ to adjust a machine or device so that it works in a certain way : *The thermometer regulates the temperature of the room.*

reg·u·la·tion [REG-yuh-LAY-shun] NOUN, regulations. **1. réglementation, ajustement** ▶ the act of regulating. **2. règlement, règle** ▶ something that regulates, such as a law, a rule, or an order : *This school's attendance regulations are strict.* ▲ ADJECTIVE. **réglementaire** ▶ according to the rules : *a regulation uniform.*

re·hearse [rih-HURS] VERB, rehearsed, rehearsing. **répéter** ▶ to practise or train for a play, concert, speech, or similar event before performing : *The choir rehearsed their songs for months before the concert.* ■ **rehearsal,** NOUN, rehearsals. **répétition** ▶ a practice session before the actual performance.

reign [rane] NOUN, reigns. **1. règne** ▶ the period of time when a king or queen rules : *the reign of King Hussein.* **2. règne** ▶ a period of time when someone has great power or influence over others : *The Beatles enjoyed a long reign at the top of pop music in the 1960s.* ▲ VERB, reigned, reigning. **1. régner** ▶ to hold power as a ruler. **2. régner** ▶ to have great influence or power; rule : *When the war was over, peace reigned over the land once more.*

re·im·burse [REE-im-BURS] VERB, reimbursed, reimbursing. **rembourser** ▶ to pay back; repay : *My dad reimbursed me for the book I bought for him.*

rein [rane] NOUN, reins. **1. rêne, bride** ▶ a long, narrow strap used to control and guide a horse. **2. rêne, bride** ▶ any way of controlling or guiding something : *Emily is trying to keep a tight rein on her spending.*

rein·deer [RANE-deer] NOUN, reindeer. **renne** ▶ a large deer found in cold northern areas of Europe, Asia, and North America. Reindeer are sometimes used as work animals and for food.

Note. Wild reindeer of North America are called caribou.

re·in·force [REE-in-FORCE] VERB, reinforced, reinforcing. **renforcer** ▶ to make something stronger by adding parts, making repairs, and so on : *We reinforced the sagging wall by propping it up with wooden beams.* ■ **reinforcement,** NOUN. ▶ **renfort, renforcement.** *We need reinforcements to win the contest.*

re·ject [rih-JEKT] VERB, rejected, rejecting. **1. rejeter** ▶ to refuse to use or accept : *Mr. Green rejected our offer of help and fixed the tire himself.* **2. mettre au rebut, jeter au rebut** ▶ to throw away or put aside; discard : *Monika rejected several bags of clothes that didn't fit anymore.* ▲ [REE-jekt] NOUN, rejects. **rejet, rebut** ▶ something that is rejected. ■ **rejection,** NOUN. **1. rejet, refus** ▶ the act of rejecting. **2. rejet, refus** ▶ the thing that is rejected.

re·joice [rih-JOYS] VERB, rejoiced, rejoicing. **se réjouir** ▶ to show or feel great joy; be very happy : *The school rejoiced when their team won the science fair.*

re·lapse [REE-laps] NOUN, relapses. **rechute, récidive** ▶ the fact of falling back into a weaker or poorer condition. ▲ [rih-LAPS] VERB, relapsed, relapsing. **rechuter, récidiver** ▶ to fall back or return to an earlier condition : *After keeping her room neat for a month, Julie relapsed into her usual sloppiness.*

re·late [rih-LATE] VERB, related, relating. **1. relater, raconter** ▶ to tell the story of; give an account : *The hiker related everything she had seen on the mountain.* **2. rapprocher, relier, établir un lien** ▶ to make or show a connection between two things. **3. entretenir des bons rapports, avoir le sens des contacts, se lier facilement** ▶ to understand and get along with other people; be connected with others : *Mr. Wong is a good teacher; he relates well to children.* ■ **related,** ADJECTIVE. **1. parent (-ente), apparenté (-ée)** ▶ belonging to the same family : *Rio and I are related because our mothers are sisters.* **2. apparenté (-ée), connexe, analogue** ▶ having something in common; connected : *We are studying crabs, lobsters, and related sea animals.* SYN : communicate, describe, report.

re·la·tion [rih-LAY-shun] NOUN, relations. **1. rapport** ▶ a connection between two or more things : *A kangaroo has huge hind legs in relation to the rest of its body.* **2. relation, rapport** ▶ the fact of understanding and getting along with one another : *Canada and the United States have had friendly relations for most of their history.* **3. relation, récit** ▶ the act of telling about something. **4. parent (-ente)** ▶ a person who belongs to the same family; a relative.

re·la·tion·ship [rih-LAY-shun-SHIP] NOUN, relationships. 1. **rapport, lien, relation** ▶ the fact of being related or connected to another person. 2. **rapport, lien, relation** ▶ a connection between ideas or things : *There is a strong relationship between studying and good marks.*

re·la·tive [REL-uh-tiv] NOUN, relatives. **parent (-ente)** ▶ a person who belongs to the same family. ▲ ADJECTIVE. 1. **lié (liée), relié (-ée), pertinent (-ente)** ▶ having a connection; being related : *Is that idea really relative to this discussion?* 2. **relatif (-ive)** ▶ in comparison to; depending on something else for its meaning or importance : *When I say that he's a slow skater, I mean that he's slow relative to the others on the team.* ■ **relatively,** ADVERB. ▶ relativement.

re·lax [rih-LAKS] VERB, relaxed, relaxing. 1. **relâcher, desserrer** ▶ to make loose or less tight : *At the bottom of the hill, Toba relaxed her tight grip on the bike's brakes.* 2. **se détendre, se relaxer, se reposer** ▶ to take it easy without work or worry; rest : *My parents took a vacation to relax in the sun.* 3. **assouplir, modérer** ▶ to be less strict or severe : *After Kim showed that he was responsible, his mother relaxed the rules a little.* ■ **relaxation,** NOUN. ▶ **relaxation, détente.** *Jane finds relaxation working in the garden.*

re·lay [REE-LAY] NOUN, relays. 1. **relais** ▶ a fresh supply of something to help or relieve another : *They made the cross-country trip in two weeks by using relays of fresh horses.* 2. (also relay race) **course de relais** ▶ a race between teams in which each team member races a certain distance before being relieved by another member, who continues the race. ▲ [rih-LAY *or* ree-LAY] VERB, relayed, relaying. **relayer, transmettre, faire passer de main en main** ▶ to pass along : *Paco asked Jun to relay a message to his father that he would be late.*

relay race

re·lease [rih-LEES] VERB, released, releasing. 1. **libérer, relâcher** ▶ to set free or let go : *Renée released the horses into the field.* 2. **sortir,** paraître, mettre en vente ▶ to provide to the public for use or sale : *The movie* Star Wars *was released in 1977.* ▲ NOUN, releases. 1. **communiqué, nouveauté** ▶ the fact of releasing. 2. **libération, relâchement, parution, mise en vente** ▶ a letter or document granting freedom from something : *Mark's parents signed a release form allowing him to go on the field trip.* 3. **communiqué, nouveauté** ▶ something that is released to the public : *The actor issued a press release about his new movie.* SYN: deliver, liberate, detach.

re·lent [rih-LENT] VERB, relented, relenting. **s'adoucir** ▶ to become less strict or demanding; to be more compassionate : *After making me paint the fence as a punishment, Mom relented and took me out for ice cream.*

re·lent·less [rih-LENT-lis] ADJECTIVE. **incessant (-ante), continu (-ue)** ▶ going on and on in a strict or harsh way; not stopping or letting up : *The relentless noise of the rain kept me awake.* ■ **relentlessly,** ADVERB. ▶ **avec acharnement, sans cesse, continuellement.** *My brother questioned us relentlessly about dinosaurs.*

rel·e·vant [REL-uh-vunt] ADJECTIVE. **pertinent (-ente), relié (-ée), lié (liée)** ▶ having to do with the subject or question being considered; related or connected : *That story is certainly interesting, but is it relevant to this discussion?*

re·li·a·ble [rih-LY-uh-bul] ADJECTIVE. **digne de confiance, fiable** ▶ that can be trusted or relied on; dependable : *She is a reliable baby-sitter and has worked for me many times.* ■ **reliably,** ADVERB. ▶ **de manière fiable.** SYN: trustworthy, responsible.

rel·ic [REL-ik] NOUN, relics. **vestige, relique** ▶ something from the ancient past that has survived to the present time : *The pyramids of Egypt are extraordinary relics of the past.*

re·lief¹ [rih-LEEF] NOUN, reliefs. 1. **soulagement** ▶ something that brings freedom from pain, suffering, or sorrow; a form of comfort or help : *"As the others took turns reading aloud, I realized with relief that I read as well as any of them, better than most."* (Jean Little) 2. **secours, aide** ▶ help such as food, shelter, or medical care that is given to those in need. 3. **relève** ▶ release from a job or duty : *At midnight, the nurse's relief arrived to take over his duties.*

relief² NOUN, reliefs. 1. **relief** ▶ a figure or design that is raised or carved to stand out from a flat background. 2. relief map. **carte en relief** ▶ a map that shows the height or depth of land and water areas.

re·lieve [rih-LEEV] VERB, relieved, relieving. 1. **soulager** ▶ to make free from pain, suffering, or sorrow; give relief : *Some medicines help to relieve pain.* 2. **soulager, diminuer, apaiser** ▶

491

to make free from worry or tension; relax : *The walk relieved his tension from the day at work.* **3. relayer, prendre la relève ▸** to take over or free someone from a duty or job : *The firefighters were relieved by a second crew from a neighbouring town.* SYN: ease, lessen, aid.

re·li·gion [rih-LIJ-un] NOUN, religions. **1. religion ▸** a system of belief in something that cannot be known through the senses and that goes beyond human powers; belief in a god or gods. A religion usually teaches certain beliefs and values and that people should show their faith by special acts and ceremonies. **2. religion, culte ▸** a particular branch or form of this belief : *the Jewish religion; the Islamic religion.* **3. religion, confession ▸** anything that is very strongly believed in or seriously practised : *Hockey is a religion to many Canadians.* 📖 p. 1148.

re·li·gious [rih-LIJ-us] ADJECTIVE. **1. religieux (-ieuse) ▸** having to do with religion : *Christmas is a religious holiday.* **2. religieux (-ieuse) ▸** following the practices of a religion very closely : *The rabbi is a very religious man who spends most of his time studying the Torah.*

re·lin·quish [re-LING-kwish] VERB, relinquished, relinquishing. **abandonner, renoncer ▸** to give up or put aside : *"We know that no one seized power with the intention of relinquishing it."* (George Orwell)

rel·ish [REL-ish] NOUN, relishes. **1. relish ▸** a mixture of chopped vegetables, spices, and other things, used to add flavour to foods such as hot dogs, or eaten as a side dish. **2. délectation ▸** enjoyment; pleasure : *She ate the candy with great relish.* ▲ VERB, relished, relishing. **se délecter, savourer ▸** to think of with pleasure; enjoy : *He relished the thought of hiking in the woods.*

re·luc·tant [rih-LUK-tunt] ADJECTIVE. **réticent (-ente) ▸** not wanting to do something; slow or unwilling to act or decide : *The cold and wind made me reluctant to go skating.* ▸ **reluctantly,** ADVERB. ▸ **à contrecœur, avec réticence.** Note. The fact of being reluctant is reluctance. SYN: hesitant.

re·ly [rih-LY] VERB, relied, relying. **compter, dépendre, se fier ▸** to have trust or confidence in; depend on : *"Since I could no longer see what was happening I had to rely upon my other senses."* (Farley Mowat)

re·main [rih-MANE] VERB, remained, remaining. **1. rester, demeurer ▸** to stay in the same place; not move or go away : *Teri remained in goal despite having let two shots in.* **2. rester, demeurer ▸** to go on doing; keep on; continue : *Owen remained happy at school.* **3. rester, demeurer ▸** to still be in the same condition after other things have changed : *The dining room is the only part of the original house that*

remains. ▪ **remains,** PLURAL NOUN. **1. restes ▸** what is left after things change or move on. **2. restes ▸** a dead body.

re·main·der [rih-MANE-dur] NOUN, remainders. **1. reste, restant ▸** a part left over or remaining : *We had a piece of cake each and put the remainder back in the fridge.* **2. reste ▸** the number left when one number is subtracted from another : *The remainder of 10 minus 6 is 4.* **3. reste ▸** the number left over when another number cannot be divided evenly : *When 17 is divided by 4, the remainder is 1.*

re·mark [rih-MARK] NOUN, remarks. **remarque ▸** something that is said; a short statement or opinion : *The doctor made a few opening remarks about the operation and then answered questions from the press.* ▲ VERB, remarked, remarking. **faire une remarque, remarquer, observer, constater ▸** to say in a few words; mention : *My mother remarked that it looked as if I hadn't washed my hands in days.* SYN: comment, mention, observe.

re·mark·a·ble [rih-MAR-kuh-bul] ADJECTIVE. **remarquable ▸** very much out of the ordinary; worth being noted or spoken about; unusual : *That painting is remarkable; I've never seen another one like it.* ▸ **remarkably,** ADVERB. ▸ **extrêmement, remarquablement.** SYN: exceptional, uncommon.

re·me·di·al [rih-MEE-dee-ul] ADJECTIVE. **curatif (-ive), correctif (-ive), de rattrapage, de soutien ▸** meant to improve or cure a problem : *A remedial-reading class helps people to read better.*

rem·e·dy [REM-uh-dee] NOUN, remedies. **1. remède ▸** something that cures pain or illness : *Gran says that a good night's sleep is the best remedy for an illness.* **2. remède ▸** something that corrects a problem : *Rachel finds that the best remedy for stage fright is to be well-prepared.* ▲ VERB, remedied, remedying. **remédier ▸** to provide a remedy for; cure.

re·mem·ber [rih-MEM-bur] VERB, remembered, remembering. **1. se souvenir, se rappeler ▸** to bring or call back to the mind; think of again : *Cathy remembers the day her brother was born, even though she was only four at the time.* Note. Something that is remembered is a remembrance. **2. se souvenir, se rappeler ▸** to keep carefully in the memory : *Remember to talk quietly in a hospital so that you don't disturb the patients.* Note. Remembrance Day is held every November 11 to honour the people who have served in Canada's armed forces since World War I. SYN: recall, recollect.

re·mind [rih-MYND] VERB, reminded, reminding. **1. rappeler, faire penser ▸** to cause a person to remember : *Remind me to bring a raincoat on the hike.* Note. Something that helps a person to remember is a reminder. **2. rappeler ▸** to cause a person to think of someone or something else : *Rachel reminds me of my sister.*

re-morse [rih-MORCE] NOUN. **remords ▸** a feeling of guilt or sorrow : *Danni was filled with remorse after hitting her sister with the ball.*

re-mote [rih-MOTE] ADJECTIVE, remoter, remotest. **1. éloigné (-ée), lointain (-aine) ▸** far away in place or time ; distant : *I grew up in a remote village, far from any other town.* **2. isolé (-ée), à l'écart, retiré (-ée) ▸** out of the way ; secluded : *He drove his car off the highway and onto a remote dirt road that cut through the woods.* **3. mince, vague, faible ▸** slight or small : *There is a remote chance that I won't be able to go out on Friday.* ■ **remotely,** ADVERB. ▸ **absolument, tant soit peu, d'une manière distante, à distance.** ■ **remoteness,** NOUN. ▸ **éloignement, isolement, attitude distante, attitude réservée.** SYN : isolated, solitary.

remote control 1. télécommande ▸ the control of a machine or device from a distance by using radio waves, electricity, or a similar method. TV sets and model planes can be controlled this way. **2. télécommande ▸** the device used to control a machine in this way. Note. Often shortened to remote.

re-mov-al [rih-MOO-vul] NOUN, removals. **enlèvement ▸** the act of taking away : *Volunteers are needed for the removal of garbage from the wildlife refuge.*

re-move [rih-MOOV] VERB, removed, removing. **1. enlever, ôter ▸** to move away from one place to another ; take off or take out : *"Esther removed the last pan from the dishwasher and hung it above the oven."* (Cynthia Rylant) **2. dissiper, supprimer, éliminer ▸** to get rid of : *This plan should remove any doubts you have.* SYN : eliminate, erase, withdraw.

ren-dez-vous [RON-day-voo] NOUN, rendezvous. **1. rendez-vous ▸** a plan to meet at a certain time and place : *The hikers have a rendezvous at the park every Sunday.* **2. rendez-vous, lieu de rencontre ▸** the meeting place. ▲ VERB, rendezvoused, rendezvousing. **se retrouver, se rencontrer, se réunir ▸** to meet at a set place : *We plan to rendezvous at the park at noon*

re-new [rih-NOO] VERB, renewed, renewing. **1. renouer ▸** to make new or as if new again ; restore : *Sasha and Will renewed their friendship after bumping into each other on a bus.* **2. renouveler, recommencer ▸** to begin again : *I renewed my efforts to convince Dad to let me go to the party.* **3. renouveler ▸** to extend the time or term of something : *Daniel renewed his library books for two more weeks.* ■ **renewal,** NOUN. ▸ **réabonnement, renouvellement.** *the renewal of a magazine subscription.*

ren-o-vate [REN-uh-vATE] VERB, renovated, renovating. **rénover, remettre à neuf, restaurer ▸** to restore ; repair ; make new or like new : *The Hans*

renovated their house by replacing the roof, windows, plumbing, and wires.

rent [rent] NOUN, rents. **prix de location, loyer ▸** money paid for the use of something that someone else owns. ▲ VERB, rented, renting. **1. louer ▸** to have or give the right to use something in exchange for payment : *We rented a video to watch on our TV tonight.* **2. se louer ▸** to be available for rent : *An apartment rents for about $800 a month in that building.*

rent-al [REN-tul] NOUN, rentals. **location ▸** something that is rented, or the amount of rent received or paid.

re-pair [rih-PAIR] VERB, repaired, repairing. **1. réparer, arranger ▸** to put something that is broken or not working back in the proper condition ; fix ; mend : *to repair a flat tire.* **2. réparer, corriger ▸** to make up for some damage or harm : *to repair a wrong.* ▲ NOUN, repairs. **1. réparation ▸** the act of repairing : *The repair will take two days.* **2. état ▸** the general condition of something : *They keep their home in beautiful repair.* ■ **repairable** or reparable, ADJECTIVE. **réparable ▸** able to be repaired.

re-pay [rih-PAY] VERB, repaid, repaying. **rembourser, remettre, rendre ▸** to pay something back : *to repay a bank loan ; to repay a good deed with kindness.*

re-peat [rih-PEET] VERB, repeated, repeating. **répéter, se répéter ▸** to say, do, or happen again : *"Maylin's father waddled forward and repeated the lie he had told so often before."* (Paul Yee) ▲ [REE-peet or rih-PEET] NOUN, repeats. **répétition ▸** the act of repeating ; something that is repeated. ■ **repeatedly,** ADVERB. ▸ **à plusieurs reprises, sans cesse, de façon répétée.**

re-per-cus-sion [REE-pur-KUSH-un] NOUN, repercussions. **1. répercussion ▸** a reaction or consequence : *Ani didn't think about the repercussions of staying up late to watch a movie.* **2. répercussion ▸** a bouncing or recoiling back from a surface : *The repercussion of your call echoed through the valley.*

re-pel [rih-PEL] VERB, repelled, repelling. **1. repousser ▸** to drive back or force away : *The defence repelled the other team's attack.* **2. repousser, éloigner ▸** to hold off ; keep out : *My raincoat repels water.* **3. répugner, dégoûter, inspirer de la répulsion ▸** to cause a strong feeling of dislike or disgust : *She was repelled by his dirty clothes and rude manner.* Note. Something that repels is repellent : *mosquito repellent.*

rep-e-ti-tion [rep-uh-TISH-un] NOUN, repetitions. **répétition ▸** the act of repeating or something that is repeated : *The repetition of the poem many times helped me to memorize it.* Note. Something that repeats over and over is repetitious: *the repetitious ringing of a telephone.* ✍ **p. 494.**

re·place [rih-PLACE] VERB, replaced, replacing. **1. remplacer ▸** to take the place of : *After Hui gave up three easy goals, the coach replaced him with another goalie.* **2. replacer, remettre à sa place ▸** to put back into place : *Please replace the books on the shelf when you are finished.* **3. remplacer ▸** to get or give something in the place of : *He bought a new umbrella to replace his old one.*

re·place·ment [rih-PLACE-munt] NOUN, replacements. **1. remplacement ▸** the act of replacing or being replaced : *If your watch stops working, you might need a battery replacement.* **2. remplaçant (-ante), produit de remplacemen, pièce de rechange ▸** a person or thing that takes the place of another : *I've lost a part for this toy; I'll have to order a replacement.*

rep·li·ca [REP-luh-kuh] NOUN, replicas. **réplique, copie ▸** a copy that is very close to the original : *I thought it was an original painting, but it was just a replica.*

re·ply [rih-PLY] VERB, replied, replying. **répondre ▸** to respond; give an answer : *José replied "yes" when I asked if he wanted ice cream.* ▲ NOUN, replies. **réponse ▸** the act of replying; an answer or response : *Marta sent a letter to Ted three months ago and still hasn't received a reply.*

re·port [rih-PORT] NOUN, reports. **1. rapport, compte rendu, reportage ▸** an account or statement telling the facts about something; a description in writing or speech : *There was a report about the flood on the news.* **2. rapport, compte rendu ▸** a school assignment that requires giving information about a certain thing : *a book report; an oral report.* **3. détonation ▸** a loud noise like an explosion or a shot : *The booming report of cannon fire.* ▲ VERB, reported, reporting. **1. rapporter, rendre compte, faire le compte rendu, présenter ▸** to tell about; give an account of : *Jayanti reported on our science experiment.* **2. se présenter ▸** to present oneself : *Anton reports for work at 7:00.* SYN: description, essay, narrative.

report card bulletin scolaire ▸ a written account sent from a school to parents or guardians, giving information on a student's work, behaviour, and so on.

re·port·er [rih-POR-tur] NOUN, reporters. **reporter, journaliste ▸** a person whose work is to gather and report the news for a newspaper, magazine, TV or radio station, and so on.

rep·re·sent [REP-rih-ZENT] VERB, represented, representing. **1. représenter ▸** to stand for or be a symbol of : *Each letter in the alphabet represents a sound.* **2. représenter ▸** to speak or act for officially : *A lawyer can represent you in court.* **3. représenter, constituer ▸** to be an

---

✏ **Writing Tips**

Repetition

Repetition occurs needlessly in expressions like "a tall giant" or "an expensive mansion." By definition, a giant is tall and a mansion is expensive. You don't say "new innovation," because an innovation by definition is new. "Past history" is also needlessly repetitive : history is the past. There is a tendency in English nowadays to say "plan for the future." But of course you can't plan for anything else ; it's too late to plan for the past or the present. Expressions like this are also called **redundant.**

However, there are times when repetition does serve a purpose. Repeating a certain phrase is an effective way to give rhythm to your sentences, or to emphasize or clarify a point.

example of : *This detailed report represents a lot of hard work.* ■ **representation,** NOUN. ▸ **représentation.** *Jared built a scale-model representation of the real airplane.*

rep·re·sen·ta·tive [REP-rih-ZEN-tuh-tiv] NOUN, representatives. **représentant (-ante), porte-parole ▸** a person chosen to speak or act for others : *A representative from the World Wildlife Fund spoke to our class about endangered animals.* ▲ ADJECTIVE. **1. représentatif (-ive) ▸** being an example of a group or type; typical : *The lion is a representative of the cat family.* **2. représentatif (-ive) ▸** having its members elected : *Canada has representative government.*

re·pro·duce [REE-proh-DOOS] VERB, reproduced, reproducing. **1. reproduire ▸** to make a copy; produce again : *I tried to reproduce the cake we had had at the restaurant, but I didn't have the recipe.* **2. se reproduire ▸** to produce offspring : *Seeds and spores are two ways that plants reproduce.* ■ **reproduction,** NOUN. ▸ **reproduction.**

rep·tile [REP-TILE] NOUN, reptiles. **reptile ▸** one of a large group of cold-blooded animals that have backbones and dry, scaly skin made up of scales or plates. Most reptiles lay eggs. Snakes, lizards, alligators, and turtles are types of reptiles. ✍ **p. 1094.**

re·pub·lic [rih-PUB-lik] NOUN, republics. **1. république ▸** a form of government in which the citizens are governed by representatives whom they elect to manage the government. The head of a republic is usually a president. **2. république** ▸ a country that has this form of government. **Note.** Something or someone that has to do with a republic is a **republican**.

rep·u·ta·tion [REP-yuh-TAY-shun] NOUN, reputations. **réputation** ▸ a general opinion of someone or something that is held by the public; what others think a person or thing is like : *Pierre Trudeau had a reputation of being both glamorous and tough.*

re·quest [rih-KWEST] VERB, requested, requesting. **demander, demander poliment, prier** ▸ to ask for something; ask in a polite way : *Oretta called the travel agency to request some information on discount airfares.* ▲ NOUN, requests. **1. demande, requête** ▸ the act of requesting. **2. demande, requête** ▸ something asked for : *Isiah is a vegetarian, so when he flies he always makes a request for a special meal.*

re·quire [rih-KWIRE] VERB, required, requiring. **1. requérir, demander, exiger** ▸ to have need of; need or demand : *"Flying in a shuttle requires years of training and hard work."* (Barbara Bondar) **2. requérir, exiger, obliger** ▸ to order or command someone to do something : *Wearing shin guards during games is required by our soccer league.* **Note.** Also used as an ADJECTIVE: *a course that is required for graduation.*

re·quire·ment [ri-KWIRE-munt] NOUN, requirements. **exigence, nécessité, condition requise** ▸ something that is required : *Computer skills are a requirement for that job.*

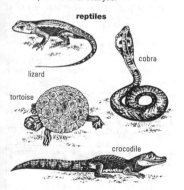

reptiles

cobra
lizard
tortoise
crocodile

res·cue [RES-kyoo] VERB, rescued, rescuing. **sauver, secourir** ▸ to save or free from danger : *The firefighter rescued a child from the burning building.* ▲ NOUN, rescues. **sauvetage, secours** ▸ the fact of rescuing someone or something. ■ **rescuer,** NOUN. ▸ **sauveteur (-euse).**

re·search [REE-surch or rih-SURCH] NOUN. **recherche** ▸ the careful study or testing of something to learn new facts : *The scientist announced the results of his research into new cancer treatments.* ▲ VERB, researched, researching. **faire une recherche** ▸ to do research on : *Kelly is at the library researching information on Egypt for her report.* **Note.** Someone who conducts research is a researcher.

re·sem·ble [rih-ZEM-bul] VERB, resembled, resembling. **ressembler** ▸ to look like or be like in some ways; be similar to : *Maria resembles her sister, except that Maria is taller and has darker hair.* **Note.** The fact of resembling someone or something is a **resemblance**.

re·sent [rih-ZENT] VERB, resented, resenting. **être contrarié (-ée), être indigné (-ée), éprouver de l'amertume** ▸ to feel angry or annoyed toward; be bitter about : *Karem resented having to clean the kitchen while his sister played outside.* ■ **resentful,** ADJECTIVE. ▸ **rempli (-ie) de ressentiment, qui éprouve du ressentiment.** ■ **resentment,** NOUN. ▸ **ressentiment.**

res·er·va·tion [rez-ur-VAY-shun] NOUN, reservations. **1. réservation** ▸ an arrangement to reserve something for someone : *a dinner reservation at a restaurant.* **2. réserve** ▸ an uncertain feeling; doubt : *My parents had several reservations about the idea of my taking a bus trip to Ottawa with my friends.* **3. réserve** ▸ land that is set aside by the government for a particular purpose or use. **Note.** In Canada, usually called a reserve.

re·serve [rih-ZURV] VERB, reserved, reserving. **1. réserver** ▸ to set aside : *to reserve tickets to a play.* **2. réserver** ▸ to save or hold for some special purpose : *He is very busy at work, but he always reserves time for his family.* **3. réserver, conserver, garder** ▸ to keep for oneself : *I will reserve my opinion on that issue until I know more.* ▲ NOUN, reserves. **1. réserve** ▸ something set aside for future use : *The climber called on a reserve of energy to make it to the top.* **2. réserve** ▸ the quality of holding back one's thoughts or feelings : *Not many people have been able to see through Jenny's reserve to discover her sense of humour.* **3. reserves. réserves** ▸ a part of the armed forces who are not on actual duty but who keep ready to serve if needed. **4. réserve** ▸ public land set aside for a particular use : *a wildlife reserve.* **Note.** Sometimes called a preserve or a reservation. SYN : hoard, conserve.

res·er·voir [REZ-ur-vwar or REZ-ur-vwor] NOUN, reservoirs. **réservoir** ▸ a place where water or another substance is stored for later use : *a reservoir that supplies water for a region.*

re·side [rih-ZIDE] VERB, resided, residing. **résider, habiter** ▸ to have one's home at a certain place : *I reside at 1620 Danbury Lane.*

res-i-dence [REZ-uh-dunce] NOUN, residences.
1. résidence ▸ the place where a person lives; one's home : *"Owl lived at the Chestnuts, an old-world residence of great charm."* (A.A. Milne) **2. résidence, domicile** ▸ the fact of living in a certain place : *"His hunger was gnawing at him, just as though a large rat had taken up residence in his stomach."* (Adèle Geras) **3. résidence** ▸ a building where people live.

res-i-dent [REZ-uh-dunt] NOUN, residents. **résidant (-ante)** ▸ someone who lives in a certain place : *The seniors' home has a cafeteria for its residents.*

res-i-den-tial [REZ-uh-DEN-shul] ADJECTIVE. **résidentiel (-ielle)** ▸ used as or suitable for residences : *A residential area has homes, not offices or businesses.*

re-sign [rih-ZINE] VERB, resigned, resigning. **1. démissionner** ▸ to give up a job, position, or office; quit : *Lester Pearson resigned from the office of prime minister of Canada in 1968.* **2. resign oneself. se résigner** ▸ to accept problems or difficulties patiently, without complaining : *We've missed the 11:00 train, so resign yourselves to waiting for the 11:30 train.* **Note.** A person who is willing to accept suffering in this way is resigned.

res-ig-na-tion [REZ-ig-NAY-shun] NOUN, resignations. **1. démission** ▸ the fact of resigning : *Ms. Bell is moving to Ottawa, so she will hand in her resignation at work today.* **2. résignation** ▸ the fact of accepting problems or difficulties patiently.

res-il-ient [rih-ZIL-yunt] ADJECTIVE. **1. résistant (-ante), élastique, souple** ▸ able to bounce back into original form : *After I had an accident, I got a resilient bumper for my car.* **2. résistant (-ante), qui a du ressort, tenace, robuste** ▸ able to recover quickly from illness or misfortune.

res-in [REZ-un] NOUN, resins. **résine** ▸ a sticky substance that flows from pine, balsam, and other trees. Resin is used in medicine, in varnishes, and in plastics.

re-sist [rih-ZIST] VERB, resisted, resisting. **1. résister** ▸ to fight or go against; oppose : *The townspeople resisted the invading army.* **2. résister** ▸ to keep from giving in to; not accept : *I could not resist the temptation to jump into the cool pool of water.* **3. résister** ▸ to withstand the effects of : *The castle's thick stone walls resisted both fire and the battering ram.* **Note.** Someone or something that resists is resistant: *My new coat is water-resistant.* SYN: defy.

re-sist-ance [ri-ZIS-tuns] NOUN. **1. résistance, opposition, objection** ▸ the act or fact of resisting : *There was no resistance to the plan to use our basement for our club meetings.* **2. résistance** ▸ the ability or power to resist : *Because she was so tired, her resistance was low and*

she caught the flu. **3. résistance** ▸ a force that goes against or prevents a motion : *The sleek canoe met with little resistance as it moved through the still water.* **4. résistance** ▸ the power with which something resists an electric current that is passing through it.

res-o-lu-tion [rez-uh-LOO-shun] NOUN, resolutions. **1. résolution** ▸ the act of firmly deciding or promising to do something : *Amanda made a New Year's resolution to practise the piano more.* **2. résolution** ▸ something that has been officially decided : *The United Nations passed a resolution to support peacekeeping efforts in the Middle East.* **3. résolution, entente** ▸ the fact of settling or solving something, such as a problem or a quarrel : *The neighbours finally reached a resolution in the dispute over their property line.* **4. résolution, définition** ▸ the sharpness or clearness of an image, such as a picture on a video screen. ✐ p. 496.

re-solve [rih-ZOLV] VERB, resolved, resolving. **1. résoudre, décider, se résoudre, se décider** ▸ to make up one's mind; make a firm decision; determine : *Kyoko resolved to do better in school.* **2. résoudre, régler** ▸ to find an answer to a problem or difficulty; settle : *Our teacher told us to find a non-violent way to resolve our differences of opinion.* **3. résoudre, statuer** ▸ to decide by a vote : *Parliament resolved to pass the new law.*

re-sort [rih-ZORT] NOUN, resorts. **1. lieu de séjour, lieu de vacances, lieu de villégiature** ▸ a place where people often go for a vacation or to relax : *Banff is a popular resort in the Rockies.* **2. recours** ▸ someone or something used or appealed to for help : *If we miss our ride to school, as a last resort we can walk.* ▲ VERB, resorted, resorting. **avoir recours, recourir** ▸ to turn to something as a way of solving a problem : *Mrs. Cook had to resort to bribing her dog with a bone to get it to come out from under the house.*

re-sound [rih-ZOWND] VERB, resounded, resounding. **1. résonner, retentir** ▸ to be filled with sound : *The stadium resounded with the cheers of the fans.* **2. résonner, retentir** ▸ to make a long, loud sound. **Note.** Often used as an ADJEC-

---

✎ Writing Tips

Resolution

*The **resolution** of a story occurs when all of the loose ends are tied up, and everyone, including the reader, has been satisfactorily taken care of. The resolution may involve a happy ending, but doesn't always.*

TIVE:*"In my hurry, I let it go down with a resounding bang."* (Jean Little)

re·source [rih-ZORCE or REE-zorce] NOUN, resources. **1. ressource** ► someone or something to turn to for help; a source of aid or support : *We had no money, so our only resources were time and hard work.* **2.** (also **resources**) **ressource** ► a source of wealth : *Oil, water, and minerals are important natural resources.* **Note.** A person who is good at making use of available resources is **resourceful.**

re·spect [rih-SPEKT] NOUN, respects. **1. respect** ► a good opinion of the worth or value of something or someone; high regard; admiration : *I would like your advice about this because I have a lot of respect for your opinion.* **2. respect** ► a polite attitude toward or consideration for someone who is older, of higher rank, and so on : *My parents taught me to show respect to my teachers.* **3. égard** ► a certain point or detail to be considered : *House cats and panthers are similar to each other in some respects.* **4.** respects, **hommages** ► a polite expression of greeting. ▲ VERB, respected, respecting. **respecter** ► to think highly of someone or something. SYN: admiration, esteem, regard, honour.

re·spect·a·ble [rih-SPEK-tuh-bul] ADJECTIVE. **1. respectable** ► worth being respected; having a good reputation : *In earlier times, a respectable woman did not travel by herself.* **2. respectable** ► fairly good or large : *He inherited a respectable sum of money from his great-uncle.* ■ **respectably,** ADVERB. ► **convenablement, honorablement.** Note. The fact of being respectable is **respectability.**

re·spect·ful [rih-SPEKT-ful] ADJECTIVE. **respectueux (-euse)** ► having or showing respect; polite : *"It doesn't seem respectful for a boy to call a senior citizen just Bob."* (E.L. Konigsburg) ■ **respectfully,** ADVERB. ► **respectueusement.** *The young boy bowed respectfully to the king as he backed out of the room.*

re·spec·tive [rih-SPEK-tiv] ADJECTIVE. **respectif (-ive)** ► belonging to each; individual; separate; *After recess, the students returned to their respective classrooms.* ■ **respectively,** ADVERB. **respectivement** ► in the order given : *Jane, Emily, and Sarah are 15, 12, and 6 years old, respectively.*

res·pi·ra·tion [RES-puh-RAY-shun] NOUN. **respiration** ► the process of breating. During respiration, oxygen is taken in from the air (or water), and carbon dioxide is given off as a waste product. In humans and other land animals, respiration occurs in the lungs : in fish, it occurs through the gills. In plants, gases flow freely into and out of cells.

res·pi·ra·tor·y [RES-pruh-TOR-ee] ADJECTIVE. **respiratoire** ► having to do with breathing or the organs involved in breathing : *Lung cancer is a*

respiratory disease. **Note.** A machine or device used to help a person breathe is called a **respirator.**

respiration

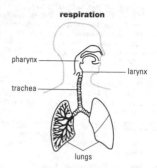

pharynx — larynx

trachea

lungs

re·spond [rih-SPOND] VERB, responded, responding. **1. répondre** ► to give an answer; reply : *"If I could just give the right call, they might think I was another coyote and respond."* (Janet Foster) **2. réagir, répondre** ► to act in return; react : *My Aunt Lorraine is responding well to treatments and hopes to be cured.*

re·sponse [rih-SPONCE] NOUN, responses. **réponse, réaction** ► something said or done as an answer : *Goose bumps are the body's response to cold.*

re·spon·si·bil·i·ty [rih-SPON-suh-BIL-ih-tee] NOUN, responsibilities. **1. responsabilité** ► the fact of being responsible : *Regular homework helps students develop responsibility for their own work.* **2. responsabilité** ► something that a person is responsible for : *It is Aziz's responsibility to walk the dog.*

re·spon·si·ble [rih-SPON-suh-bul] ADJECTIVE. **1. responsable, chargé (-ée)** ► having a job, duty, or assignment : *"The astronauts responsible for operating the shuttle and keeping the crew safe are called the orbiter crew."* (Barbara Bondar) **2. responsable** ► being the cause of : *Since you left the gate open, you are responsible for the dog's getting out.* **3. fiable, digne de confiance** ► able to be trusted or relied on; dependable : *Rista is a good class president because she is very responsible and makes sure things get done.* ■ **responsibly,** ADVERB. ► **de façon responsable, avec sérieux.**

rest[1] [rest] NOUN, rests. **1. repos** ► a time of sleep, relaxing, or not being active : *I had a long rest this afternoon.* **2. arrêt, état immobile** ► a state of not moving; a stop : *The driver brought the bus to a rest at the bus stop.* **3. support, appui** ► something used as a support : *Seats on a plane have an armrest on each side.*

4. soupir ▸ in music, a period of silence between tones in a measure, or a symbol that shows this. ▲ VERB, rested, resting. **1. reposer, se reposer** ▸ to stop work or activity; relax or allow to relax : *Rest your voice so that you won't be hoarse for the choir's performance tomorrow.* **2. se reposer, dormir** ▸ to lie down or sleep. **3. reposer, poser, appuyer** ▸ to be placed on or against; sit or lie on : *Rest the shovel against the fence.*   SYN: leisure, relaxation, recess, pause.

rest² NOUN. **reste, restant** ▸ what is left over; the remainder : *"Crickets fiddled and owls hooooted, but the rest of the world was quiet."* (Mary Bahr)

res·tau·rant [RES-tuh-RONT or RES-tuh-runt] NOUN, restaurants. **restaurant** ▸ a business where meals are prepared and served to customers. 🖙 **p. 1053.**

rest·less [REST-lis] ADJECTIVE. **1. agité (-ée)** ▸ not able to relax and be comfortable; continually moving in a nervous or impatient way : *"They were restless after the long winter they had spent inside the castle."* (Donald Carrick) **2. agité (-ée)** ▸ causing or having such a feeling : *The mother spent a restless night listening to the baby's coughing.* ■ **restlessly**, ADVERB. ▸ **avec agitation, nerveusement.** *He walked restlessly back and forth, waiting for his train to arrive.* ■ **restlessness**, NOUN. ▸ agitation, nervosité.

re·store [rih-STOR] VERB, restored, restoring. **1. restaurer** ▸ to bring something back to an earlier and better condition : *Sections of the Great Wall of China have collapsed, but the government is working to restore them.* **2. rétablir** ▸ to bring back into being or into use : *My faith in people was restored when a passerby stopped to help me change my flat tire.* **Note.** Something that has been restored is a restoration.   SYN: repair, revive.

re·strain [rih-STRANE] VERB, restrained, restraining. **1. retenir, maîtriser** ▸ to hold in or hold back : *Yousef restrained the horse by pulling hard on the reins.* **2. empêcher** ▸ to keep someone from acting in a certain way : *The press secretary restrained the reporters from asking the prime minister any more questions.* **Note.** Often used as an ADJECTIVE: *The judge lectured the outspoken lawyer in restrained tones, trying to keep calm despite his anger.*

re·straint [rih-STRAYNT] NOUN, restraints. **1. empêchement, limitation, contrainte** ▸ the fact of being restrained, or something that is used to do this : *The dog pulled against the firm restraint of the rope, which was tied to a post.* **2. retenue** ▸ the fact of restraining one's actions or feelings : *Rajan showed great restraint in not laughing out loud when Matt tripped over the rope.*

re·strict [rih-STRIKT] VERB, restricted, restricting. **restreindre, limiter, confiner** ▸ to keep within certain limits; confine : *The city restricts swimming to the south beach, where there are no rocks.*

re·stric·tion [rih-STRIK-shun] NOUN, restrictions. **1. restriction** ▸ the act or fact of restraining : *George's restriction for his poor grades was to do his homework after school instead of going to a friend's house.* **2. restriction, limitation** ▸ anything that restricts, especially a law or rule : *There is a restriction against bicycling on sidewalks.*

re·sult [rih-ZULT] NOUN, results. **1. résultat** ▸ something that happens because of something else ; outcome : *The results of the race were posted on the notice board.* **2. (bons) résultats** ▸ something good that happens in this way : *This plant fertilizer promises noticeable results in five days.* ▲ VERB, resulted, resulting. **1. résulter, découler** ▸ to be a result of : *His citizenship award resulted from months of good behaviour.* **2. résulter, causer** ▸ to have as a result : *Reckless driving often results in an accident.* SYN: outcome, consequence, effect.

re·sume [rih-ZOOM] VERB, resumed, resuming. **1. reprendre, recommencer** ▸ to go on again after a break or interruption : *Grandpa resumed his walk after stopping to talk to a neighbour.* **2. reprendre** ▸ to take or occupy again : *After intermission, we resumed our seats and watched the second half of the play.*

rés·u·mé [REZ-uh-MAY] NOUN, résumés. (sometimes resumé or resume) **curriculum vitæ** ▸ a report that a person prepares when applying for a new job, listing past jobs, educational background, skills, and so on.

re·tail [REE-tale] NOUN. **détail, vente au détail** ▸ the selling of goods directly to the general public, rather than selling to a dealer or distributor who then sells to the public. **Note.** A person who does this is a retailer. ▲ ADJECTIVE. **de détail, au détail** ▸ having to do with the selling of products at retail : *the retail price; a retail store.*

re·tain [rih-TANE] VERB, retained, retaining. **1. conserver, garder, maintenir** ▸ to keep or hold on to : *Celeste retained her lead in the race and finished in first place.* **2. retenir** ▸ to keep in a certain position or condition : *The metal pan had retained enough heat to burn his hand when he touched it.* **Note.** The fact of retaining something is retention.

re·tal·i·ate [rih-TAL-ee-ATE] VERB, retaliated, retaliating. **se venger, riposter, user de représailles** ▸ to take action against or harm, in response to harm done : *The wolf will retaliate if you hurt it.* ■ **retaliation**, NOUN. ▸ représailles, vengeance.

ret·i·na [RET-uh-nuh] NOUN, retinas or retinae. **rétine ▸** the lining on the back of the eyeball, containing nerve cells that are sensitive to light. The retina sends images to the brain through a special pathway called the optic nerve.

re·tire [rih-TIRE] VERB, retired, retiring. **1. prendre sa retraite ▸** to leave a job, business, or other work for good because of having reached a certain age, which is now usually 65 or 70. **2. se retirer ▸** to give up one's work permanently; end a career : *Pelé, the famous soccer player, has now retired from active play.* **3. aller se coucher, se retirer ▸** to go away to one's room or to a quiet place, as to sleep, relax, and so on : *After the long trip across the dusty desert, the travellers wanted only to bathe and then retire early.*

re·tire·ment [rih-TIRE-munt] NOUN. **retraite ▸** the act of retiring, or the fact of being retired, from work, or the time when this takes place.

re·tir·ing [rih-TY-ring] ADJECTIVE. **réservé (-ée) ▸** wanting to avoid attention or notice; shy; reserved : *Helen, who has a retiring nature, doesn't like giving oral reports in class.*

re·tort [rih-TORT] VERB, retorted, retorting. **répliquer, rétorquer, riposter ▸** to answer or reply to what is said, especially in a quick or angry way : *When Yves asked her why she had been absent from school, Alanna retorted that it was none of his business.* **Note.** Also used as a NOUN: *a stinging retort.* **réplique, riposte ▸**

re·treat [rih-TREET] VERB, retreated, retreating. **se retirer, reculer ▸** to pull or move back; withdraw : *We like to watch the water retreat from shore.* ▲ NOUN, retreats. **1. retraite ▸** the act of retreating : *The victorious citizens cheered the retreat of the army.* **2. lieu de retraite ▸** a place to get away to rest and relax : *I have a retreat in the woods where I go to be alone and think.*

re·trieve [rih-TREEV] VERB, retrieved, retrieving. **1. récupérer ▸** to get back; recover : *In early games of basketball, players had to retrieve the ball from the net.* **2. rapporter ▸** in hunting, to find and bring back dead or wounded game. **■ retrieval,** NOUN. **▸ récupération.**

re·trie·ver [rih-TREE-vur] NOUN, retrievers. **retriever ▸** a type of hunting dog that is trained to find and bring back dead or wounded game. The Labrador retriever and golden retriever are two popular breeds of this type.

re·turn [rih-TURN] VERB, returned, returning. **1. retourner ▸** to come or go back : *Bees return to their hives by the most direct route.* **2. retourner ▸** to take, bring, or send back : *The sweater I bought is too small, so I am going to return it to the store.* ▲ NOUN, returns. **1. retour ▸** the act of returning : *The baby-sitter looked forward to the parents' return.* **2. déclaration ▸** an official record or statement : *a tax*

return. **3. returns. profits, bénéfices ▸** money made from a business; profits. **4. rendu, article rendu ▸** a giving back; exchange : *During the first week after Christmas, this store doesn't accept returns.* ▲ ADJECTIVE. **de retour, aller-retour ▸** for or in return : *a return airline ticket.*

re·un·ion [ree-YOON-yun] NOUN, reunions. **réunion ▸** a coming together of friends, family, or other groups of people who have not seen each other in some time.

re·veal [rih-VEEL] VERB, revealed, revealing. **1. révéler ▸** to make known something that was hidden or unknown : *to reveal a secret.* **2. révéler, laisser voir ▸** to show or display something; allow to be seen : *"Mr. Magic grinned, revealing two neat rows of very small teeth."* (Steven Kroll) SYN : bare, expose, disclose, divulge.

re·venge [rih-VENJ] NOUN. **revanche, vengeance ▸** damage or injury done to another person to pay back the harm done by that person : *Sybil hid Alec's notebook in revenge for the time Alec had lost her assignment.*

rev·e·nue [REV-uh-noo] NOUN, revenues. **1. revenu, bénéfices ▸** income; the money a business makes. **2. revenu ▸** the money taken in by the government from taxes, fees, and so on.

rev·er·ence [REV-uh-runce] NOUN. **révérence ▸** a feeling of great respect and honour, mixed with love : *She felt great reverence as she entered the old cathedral and gazed at the beautiful paintings.* **■ reverent,** ADJECTIVE. **▸ révérencieux (-ieuse), avec révérence ▸** feeling or showing reverence : *The priest's reverent attitude showed in the way he knelt at the altar.* **■ reverently,** ADVERB. **▸ avec déférence.** *"He shared P.J.'s feeling about John Wayne, and he always spoke reverently about him."* (Jill Klevin)

re·verse [rih-VERCE] NOUN, reverses. **1. contraire, inverse ▸** something that is the opposite of something else : *No matter what I want to do, my little brother always wants to do the reverse.* **2. marche arrière ▸** the gear position on a machine that causes the machine to move backward : *Jean put the car in reverse and backed out of the driveway.* **3. revers, verso, endos, envers ▸** the back or rear part : *Moesha drew the pattern on the reverse of the fabric.* **4. revers ▸** a change of luck for the worse; a setback. ▲ ADJECTIVE. **à l'envers ▸** : turned backward; opposite : *Molly's sweater is reversed; she's wearing it back to front.* ▲ VERB, reversed, reversing. **1. renverser, inverser, reculer ▸** to go backward or in the opposite way : *Our teacher reverses the order of roll call, starting with "Z" and ending with "A."* **2. renverser, se renverser ▸** to change to the opposite position. SYN : contrary, opposite.

re·view [rih-VYOO] VERB, reviewed, reviewing. **1. repasser, réviser ▸** to look over or study again : *Lynn spent time before class reviewing her notes for the test.* **2. faire la critique d'une œuvre, critiquer ▸** to give an opinion as to the quality of a book, play, movie, and so on ; act as a critic. **Note.** A person who does this is a reviewer. **3. passer en revue, inspecter ▸** to inspect in a formal or official way : *The admiral reviewed the crew before the ship went to sea.* ▲ NOUN, reviews. **1. révision ▸** the act or fact of studying something again : *Our teacher gave a review of the books we had read earlier in the year.* **2. critique, compte rendu ▸** a report on a book, movie, or other work of art, giving its good and bad points. **3. revue, inspection ▸** an official inspection : *Troops marched past the general for an official review.*

re-vise [rih-VIZE] VERB, revised, revising. **1. réviser, corriger ▸** to check over a piece of writing before it is put in final form, in order to correct mistakes, add or take out material as needed, and make other improvements. **2. réviser, mettre à jour ▸** to make changes in a finished book to correct errors, bring it up to date, and so on : *Encyclopedias need to be revised every few years to include new information and technology.* **3. réviser, modifier ▸** to change something to meet new conditions : *Catherine revised her ideas about the value of car insurance after she had an accident.* **Note.** Something that has been revised is a revision.

re-vive [rih-VIVE] VERB, revived, reviving. **1. ranimer, réanimer ▸** to bring back to life or activity ; make healthy or conscious again : *The man who fainted in the restaurant was revived by the ambulance crew.* **2. relancer, raviver, faire revivre, faire renaître ▸** to bring back into use or action : *It is important to revive the old traditions before they are all forgotten.* **Note.** Something that is revived is a revival : *TV movies are often revivals of movies shown some years ago in theatres.*

re-voke [rih-VOKE] VERB, revoked, revoking. **révoquer ▸** to officially take away or cancel : *If you misbehave, permission to work here will be revoked.*

re-volt [rih-VOLT] NOUN, revolts. **révolte ▸** the act of rising up or fighting against a government or leader ; a rebellion : *In 1837, Toronto's William Lyon Mackenzie led a revolt against the privileged in Upper Canada.* ▲ VERB, revolted, revolting. **1. se révolter, se rebeller ▸** to stage a revolt ; rebel. **2. révolter ▸** to cause a feeling of sickness or disgust. **Note.** Usually used as an ADJECTIVE: *the revolting smell of old garbage.*

rev-o-lu-tion [REV-uh-LOO-shun] NOUN, revolutions. **1. révolution ▸** the overthrow of one government in order to set up a new one : *In the French Revolution, the monarchy was overthrown and a republic was formed.* **2. révolution ▸** a great or complete change : *The invention of the radio caused a revolution in*

the entertainment industry. **3. révolution ▸** a complete movement in a circle around a certain point : *One revolution of the earth on its axis takes about 24 hours.*

rev-o-lu-tion-ar-y [REV-uh-LOO-shuh-NAIR-ee] ADJECTIVE. **1. révolutionnaire ▸** of or having to do with revolution : *a revolutionary war.* **2. révolutionnaire ▸** leading to or causing a great change : *Computers have created a revolutionary way of doing business.*

re-volve [rih-VOLV] VERB, revolved, revolving. **1. tourner ▸** to move in a circle around an object : *The earth revolves around the sun.* **2. tourner ▸** to turn or spin around a centre point : *a toy top revolves on a small point.* **3. tourner ▸** to centre on ; have as a main point : *All night her thoughts revolved around whether to sell her house.*

re-volv-er [rih-VOL-vur] NOUN, revolvers. **revolver ▸** a handgun that holds several bullets in a chamber that revolves each time the gun is shot.

re-ward [rih-WORD] NOUN, rewards. **1. récompense ▸** something given or gained in return for some work or service : *The rewards of being a doctor include the satisfaction of knowing that you have made many lives better.* **2. récompense ▸** an offer of money made so that a missing person or thing can be found, lost or stolen property can be recovered, and so on : *We're offering a reward to anyone who finds our dog.* ▲ VERB, rewarded, rewarding. **récompenser ▸** to give a reward : *After comforting the little girl who had fallen down, I was rewarded with a hug.* **Note.** Also used as an ADJECTIVE: *She had a rewarding experience helping out at the shelter.*

re-write [ree-RITE] VERB, rewrote, rewritten, rewriting. **récrire ▸** to write something again ; greatly revise a piece of writing.

rhet-o-ric [RET-ur-ik] NOUN. **1. rhétorique ▸** the art or talent of using language well, especially in public speaking or in formal writing. **2. rhétorique ▸** a false or exaggerated use of language : *There were no facts in his report, it was all rhetoric.*

rheu-ma-tism [ROO-muh-TIZ-um] NOUN. **rhumatisme ▸** a disease that causes a painful swelling and stiffening of the muscles or joints.

rhi-noc-er-os [ry-NOSS-ur-us] NOUN, rhinoceroses or rhinoceros. **rhinocéros ▸** a very large powerful animal that has thick, loose skin and either one or two horns rising from its nose. Different types of rhinoceroses live in Africa, India and Southeast Asia.

rho-do-den-dron [ROH-duh-DEN-drun] NOUN, rhododendrons. **rhododendron ▸** a shrub with large, shiny evergreen leaves and clusters of large, colourful flowers shaped like bells.

rhyme [rime] NOUN, rhymes. **rime, vers ▸** a word or line that has the same ending sound as another : *The words "side," "cried," and "guide" are rhymes.* ▲ VERB, rhymed, rhyming. **rimer** ▸ to sound alike or cause to sound alike.

rhythm [RITH-um] NOUN, rhythms. **1. rythme** ▸ a regular repeating of sounds or movements in a certain pattern. Poetry, music, and dancing have rhythm. **2. rythme** ▸ a similar repeating pattern in the way something happens : *"The rhythm of the rails" is a term for the sound that a moving train makes.* **Note.** Something that has rhythm is rhythmic or rhythmical. 🖙 **p. 1131.**

rib [rib] NOUN, ribs. **1. côte** ▸ one of the long bones that are attached to the backbone and that curve around to the front of the body. The ribs enclose and protect the chest. **2. baleine, côte, membrure** ▸ a curved part that gives support like a rib : *The curved metal bars that hold out the fabric of an umbrella are called ribs.*

rib·bon [RIB-un] NOUN, ribbons. **1. ruban** ▸ a long, narrow strip of cloth, paper, or other material used for decoration or to tie something : *ribbons tied in hair; a ribbon on a present.* **2. ruban** ▸ something that looks like a ribbon : *A ribbon of light shone through the curtains.* **3. ruban** ▸ a special ribbon given as a prize or award : *Amelia won a ribbon in the science fair for her project on magnetism.*

rice [rice] NOUN, rice. **riz** ▸ a grain that is grown in warm, wet climates in many parts of the world. Rice is the main part of people's diet in China, India, and other Asian countries. 🖙 **p. 116.**

rich [rich] ADJECTIVE, richer, richest. **1. riche** ▸ having a lot of money, property, or valuable things. **2. riche** ▸ having a great supply of something; having a lot : *The forests of northern Canada are rich in animal life.* **3. riche** ▸ of food, containing a lot of sugar, cream, eggs, and so on : *a rich chocolate-mousse dessert.* **4. riche** ▸ having a lot of a certain good quality : *"The cabin glowed inside from the rich colour of the logs."* (Janet Foster) ■ **richly**,

ADVERB. ▸ **richement.** SYN : abundant, wealthy, affluent, prosperous.

rich·es [RICH-iz] PLURAL NOUN. **richesse** ▸ things that make a person rich, such as money or property ; wealth.

Rich·ter scale [RIK-tur] **échelle de Richter** ▸ a scale ranging from 1 to 10 that is used to measure the strength of earthquakes. An earthquake measuring 1.5 is considered mild, and one measuring 8.5 would cause very great damage. **Note.** The scale is named for Charles Richter, the scientist who developed it.

rice

ric·o·chet [RIK-uh-SHAY *or* rik uh-SHAY] NOUN, ricochets. **ricochet** ▸ the act of bouncing back off a surface at an angle. ▲ VERB, ricocheted, ricocheting. **ricocher** ▸ to skip or glance off a surface in this way: *The ball ricocheted off the table and hit the chair.*

rid [rid] VERB, rid or ridded, ridding. **se défaire de, se débarrasser de** ▸ to become free of; do away with : *Our cat got rid of the mice in our house.*

rid·den [RID-un] VERB. a past form of ride.

rid·dle[1] [RID-ul] NOUN, riddles. **1. énigme, devinette** ▸ a tricky or difficult question to be answered by guessing. **2. énigme, mystère** ▸ anything that is hard to understand ; a mystery : *What I do with my time is a riddle my parents can't figure out.*

riddle[2] VERB, riddled, riddling. **cribler** ▸ to put a lot of holes through something : *"It was late ; the July night was bright and riddled with stars."* (Roch Carrier)

ride [ride] VERB, rode, ridden, riding. **1. aller, monter, se déplacer** ▸ to sit on or in something and cause it to move : *to ride a bicycle.* **2. pren-**

rhododendron
sweet azalea

501

dre, faire un tour ▶ to travel in or on something : *to ride an elevator.* **3. voguer, planer, se laisser porter par le vent** ▶ to float or move over a surface : *The eagle rode the air current in a steady glide.* ▲ NOUN, rides. **1. tour, promenade** ▶ the act of riding : *Can I go for a ride on your pony?* **2. tour de manège, tour de montagnes russes** ▶ something ridden on or in for fun, as at an amusement park : *That roller coaster is the scariest ride I have ever been on.* ■ **rider,** NOUN. ▶ **cavalier (-ière), cycliste, motocycliste.**

ridge [rij] NOUN, ridges. **1. crête, chaîne** ▶ a long, narrow hill or range of hills. **2. faîte, crête** ▶ any long, thin part at the top of something : *The dog's hair bristled along the ridge of its back.*

rid·i·cule [RID-uh-KYOOL] VERB, ridiculed, ridiculing. **ridiculiser** ▶ to make fun of a person or thing; laugh at in an unkind way : *When he first played soccer, the other players ridiculed him because he didn't know not to use his hands.* ▲ NOUN. **raillerie, moquerie, risée** ▶ words or actions that make fun of someone.

ri·dic·u·lous [rih-DIK-yuh-lus] ADJECTIVE. **ridicule** ▶ deserving to be laughed at; very foolish or silly : *The bulldog looked ridiculous in the pink coat.* ■ **ridiculously,** ADVERB. ▶ **ridiculement.**

ri·fle [RY-ful] NOUN, rifles. **fusil** ▶ a gun that has a long barrel. A rifle is usually shot from the shoulder.

rifle

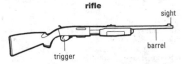

rig [rig] VERB, rigged, rigging. **1. gréer** ▶ to equip a boat with the necessary ropes, sails, masts, and so on. **2. garnir, approvisionner, munir** ▶ to supply or equip something as needed : *The backpack was rigged out with all he would need for his hike.* ▲ NOUN, rigs. **1. gréement** ▶ an arrangement of sails on a ship. **2. plate-forme** ▶ equipment or machinery made for a certain purpose : *an oil-drilling rig.*

right [rite] ADJECTIVE, righter, rightest. **1. droit (droite)** ▶ on the side opposite the left; on the right side : *my right hand.* **2. exact (-acte), juste, correct (-ecte)** ▶ without a mistake; correct : *She got all the questions right on the math test.* **3. bon (bonne), approprié (-ée)** ▶ being fair, good, and just : *The right thing to do would be to return the stolen candy.* ▲ NOUN, rights. **1. droite** ▶ the opposite of left; the right direction or side : *To your right is the CN Tower.* **2. droit** ▶ something that is fair and proper for a

person to do or have : *For many years, women have been seeking equal rights in the workplace.* **3. droite** ▶ a political belief or party that supports conservative policies. ▲ ADVERB. **1. à droite** ▶ to the right : *Turn right at the stoplight.* **2. bien** ▶ in the correct way : *Ever since I added that new program, my computer hasn't worked right.* **3. exactement, juste** ▶ in an exact way or place : *Where are my keys? I know I put them right here.* ▲ VERB, righted, righting. **réparer, rectifier, corriger** ▶ to make right : *Melanie, who is always involved in good causes, tries to right any wrongs she comes across.* ■ **rightly,** ADVERB. ▶ **bien, avec raison, à juste titre.** ✐ p. 503.

right angle angle droit ▶ an angle measuring 90 degrees. A square is made up of four right angles. **Note.** A right triangle is a triangle with one angle that measures 90 degrees.

right·eous [RY-chus] ADJECTIVE. **droit (droite), honnête** ▶ acting in a way that is right or moral. ■ **righteously,** ADVERB. ▶ **vertueusement.** ■ **righteousness,** NOUN. ▶ **droiture, vertu.**

rig·id [RIJ-id] ADJECTIVE. **1. rigide, raide** ▶ hard to bend or move; not flexible; stiff : *This piece of cardboard is rigid, and I can't bend it easily.* **2. rigide, strict (-icte)** ▶ not likely to change; fixed; strict : *a person with rigid ideas.* ■ **rigidly,** ADVERB. ▶ **rigoureusement, rigidement, avec raideur.**

rim [rim] NOUN, rims. **1. bord** ▶ the outer edge or border of something, especially something curved or round : *the rim of a basketball hoop.* **2. jante** ▶ the outside part of a car or bicycle wheel, the part to which a tire is fitted. ▲ VERB, rimmed, rimming. **1. border, cercler** ▶ to form or put a rim around. **2. encercler, entourer, border, ourler** ▶ to go around the rim of : *Tears rimmed my eyes.*

rind [rynd] NOUN, rinds. **peau (peaux), écorce, pleure, croûte** ▶ a hard, thick outer covering on some fruits and other foods : *lemon rind; cheese rind.*

ring[1] [ring] NOUN, rings. **1. cercle, rond** ▶ a circle that is open in the centre : *In this game, every one forms a ring around the person who is "It."* **2. anneau (-eaux), bague** ▶ a circular band worn as jewellery or used to hold or fasten something : *an engagement ring; a key ring.* **3. piste, ring** ▶ an enclosed area used for sports, shows, and so on : *a boxing ring; a circus ring.* ▲ VERB, ringed, ringing. **entourer, encercler, ceinturer** ▶ to form a circle or ring around : *The city is ringed by the suburbs.* ✐ p. 1013.

ring[2] VERB, rang, rung, ringing. **1. sonner, retentir** ▶ to make a sound like a bell. **2. sonner, téléphoner** ▶ to call someone with a bell, buzzer, or telephone. **3. bourdonner** ▶ of the ears, to seem to be filled with a steady buzzing or humming

---

✎ Word Builder

Right, accurate, and **proper** suggest that a person meets a standard of behaviour or action. **Right** is very similar in meaning to correct, but suggests there is a goodness to the person's action: *Jamie followed the right course of action when he returned the money.* **Accurate** suggests that something matches the facts: *Maraya gave an accurate description of the accident.* **Proper** refers to something that is appropriate in a certain situation: *It is proper to say thank you when someone holds the door for you.*

---

sound. ▲ NOUN, rings. **1. sonnerie** ▸ a sound like that of a bell. **2. coup de téléphone, coup de fil** ▸ a telephone call : *If you need a baby-sitter, just give me a ring and I'll be right over!*

rink [rink] NOUN, rinks. **patinoire** ▸ an enclosed area with a smooth surface that is used for skating, hockey, or curling.

rinse [rince] VERB, rinsed, rinsing. **1. rincer** ▸ to wash with clear water to remove soap or other matter : *Jim scrubbed all the dirt off the car, and then rinsed it with the hose.* **2. rincer** ▸ to wash lightly with water : *The dentist gave me a cup of water to rinse my mouth.* ▲ NOUN, rinses. **1. rinçage** ▸ the act of rinsing. **2. rinçage** ▸ a liquid solution that temporarily changes the colour of a person's hair.

ri·ot [RY-ut] NOUN, riots. **1. émeute** ▸ a violent, noisy disturbance caused by a group of people. **Note.** A person who takes part in a riot is a rioter. **2. débauche, profusion** ▸ a bright or colourful display : *The garden was a riot of blooming flowers.* **3.** *Informal.* **partie de plaisir** ▸ something that is very funny or enjoyable : *We had so much fun spending the day at the water park — it was a real riot.* ▲ VERB, rioted, rioting. **participer à une émeute, être turbulent (-ente)** ▸ to take part in a riot; act in a violent and noisy way. ■ **riotous,** ADJECTIVE. ▸ **très animé (-ée), déchaîné (-ée), dissipé (-ée), amusant (-ante).** SYN: protest, revolt.

rip [rip] VERB, ripped, ripping. **déchirer** ▸ to split or cut open in a rough way; tear apart : *He ripped the bag of chips open.* ▲ NOUN, rips. **déchirure** ▸ a ripped place; a tear : *There's a rip in my jeans.* ✎ **p. 570.**

ripe [ripe] ADJECTIVE, riper, ripest. **1. mûr (mûre)** ▸ of fruits and vegetables, fully grown and ready to be eaten : *Ripe peaches are soft, not hard.* **2. mûr (mûre)** ▸ fully developed or prepared; ready : *The farmers, angry over a new tax, were ripe for rebellion.*

rip·en [RY-pun] VERB, ripened, ripening. **mûrir** ▸ to become ripe : *The fruit on the top of that tree gets more sun so it ripens faster.*

rip·ple [RIP-ul] NOUN, ripples. **1. onde, ride, ondulation** ▸ a tiny wave on the surface of water : *A stone thrown into the water makes rings of ripples.* **2. clapotis, murmure, cascade** ▸ anything thought of as being like the movement or shape of small waves on the shore : *ripples of laughter.* ▲ VERB, rippled, rippling. **onduler** ▸ to form ripples : *The sand in the desert rippled like waves on the ocean.*

rise [rize] VERB, rose, risen, rising. **1. lever, se lever** ▸ to move from a lower to a higher place : *The sun rises in the east.* **2. se lever** ▸ to stand up from a sitting, kneeling, or lying position : *to rise from bed.* **3. monter, accroître, augmenter, hausser** ▸ to increase in size, number, amount, or value : *During the summer, temperatures rise steadily.* ▲ NOUN, rises. **1. augmentation, hausse** ▸ the act or fact of rising; an increase : *a rise in the price of gasoline.* **2. côte, pente** ▸ a gentle slope : *She walked up the rise behind her house.*

risk [risk] NOUN, risks. **risque** ▸ a chance of loss, harm, or injury; danger : *No one would take the risk of swimming in shark-infested water.* ▲ VERB, risked, risking. **1. risquer** ▸ to take a chance of loss or harm; face danger : *The fire-fighter risked her life to save the child.* **2. risquer, courir le risque** ▸ to take the risk of : *"Not one knight wanted to stay on and risk seeing the giant again."* (Donald Carrick)

risk·y [RISK-ee] ADJECTIVE, riskier, riskiest. **risqué (-ée), dangereux (-euse)** ▸ involving a risk; dangerous : *Skydiving is a risky sport.*

rit·u·al [RICH-oo-ul] NOUN, rituals. **1. rite, rituel** ▸ an action or set of actions that is always done in the same way, especially as part of a religious ceremony : *the ritual of baptism; a wedding ritual.* **Note.** Also called a rite. **2. rite, coutume** ▸ any action that is often repeated in the same way : *Making pancakes on Sunday morning is a ritual at our house.*

ri·val [RY-vul] NOUN, rivals. **rival (-ale, -aux), adversaire, compétiteur (-trice)** ▸ a person who tries to do better at something than another; a competitor : *The fox and the crow are often rivals in Aesop's fables.* **Note.** The fact of competing with a rival is rivalry. ▲ VERB, rivalled, rivalling. (also rivaled, rivaling) **rivaliser** ▸ to be a rival for; be as good as : *The beauty of her singing rivalled the song of a nightingale.* **Note.** Often used as an ADJECTIVE: *Two rival hockey teams are meeting in the championship game tomorrow night.*

riv·er [RIV-ur] NOUN, rivers. **1. rivière, fleuve ▸** a large, natural stream of moving water that empties into a lake, an ocean, or another large body of water. **2. rivière ▸** an abundant flow of something that moves like a river : *"A river of nervous sweat ran down his palms."* (Gary Soto) 📖 **p. 1109.**

road [rode] NOUN, roads. **1. route, chemin ▸** a smooth path or way that has been specially prepared for travel by cars, trucks, and so on. **2. chemin ▸** a path or way that leads to some goal : *Good marks can start you on the road to success.* 📖 **p. 1053.**

roam [rome] VERB, roamed, roaming. **parcourir, errer, vagabonder ▸** to travel around with no goal or purpose ; wander : *The cattle roamed the valley, looking for something to eat.*

roar [ror] VERB, roared, roaring. **1. rugir, hurler, gronder ▸** to make a very loud, deep noise : *"The wind god roared as if there were no end to his voice."* (Hal Ober) **2. s'éclater de rire, s'esclaffer, rire à gorge déployée ▸** to laugh loudly : *The audience roared when the clown fell over.* ▲ NOUN, roars. **rugissement, hurlement, grondement ▸** a very loud, deep sound : *the roar of a lion.*

roast [rohst] VERB, roasted, roasting. **1. griller, rôtir, faire rôtir, faire griller ▸** to cook food in an oven, over a fire, or on hot coals : *to roast a hot dog over a campfire.* **2. griller, rôtir, faire rôtir, faire griller ▸** to dry and brown by heating : *Most nuts are roasted before they are packaged.* **3. rôtir ▸** to make or be very hot : *Let's go swimming — I'm roasting in this heat!*

rob [rob] VERB, robbed, robbing. **1. voler ▸** to take someone else's money or property in a way that is against the law : *"They sailed their pirate ship around the world, robbing and plundering everywhere."* (Phoebe Gilman) **2. dérober, voler ▸** to keep a person from getting something in an unfair way : *The other team cheated and won the game, robbing us of the city championship.*

rob·ber·y [ROB-uh-ree] NOUN, robberies. **vol ▸** the unlawful act of taking money or property that belongs to someone else.

robe [robe] NOUN, robes. **1. robe de chambre, peignoir, tunique ▸** a loose piece of clothing worn as a covering or for warmth : *a bathrobe.* **2. robe, toge ▸** a long, flowing piece of clothing worn for ceremonies or to show rank or office : *a graduation robe ; a judge's robes.*

rob·in [ROB-in] NOUN, robins. **1. rouge-gorge américain, merle américain ▸** a common North American songbird with a brown or black upper body and, in the male, a reddish-orange breast. **2. rouge-gorge européen, rouge-gorge familier ▸** a similar but smaller European bird. 👁 **p. 108.**

ro·bot [ROH-bot] NOUN, robots. **robot ▸** a machine that is designed to perform certain tasks that a human being can do. Robots are often shown in movies as looking somewhat like a human. **Note.** Karel Capek made up this word for a play in 1921.

rock[1] [rok] NOUN, rocks. **1. roche ▸** a large mass of solid material forming part of the crust of the earth. Rock is usually made up of a combination of several different materials. Sandstone, granite, and quartz are types of rocks. **2. roche, pierre ▸** a small, separate piece of this material ; a stone. **3. rocher ▸** a large mass of rock : *The waves broke on the rocks at the base of the cliff.* **4. dur (dure), coriace, indépendant (-ante) ▸** someone or something thought of as like a rock, because of being very strong or dependable. ■ **rocky,** ADJECTIVE. **rocheux (-euse), rocailleux (-euse) ▸** covered with many rocks. 📖 **p. 1114.** 👁 **p. 397.**

rock[2] VERB, rocked, rocking. **1. bercer ▸** to move back and forth or from side to side : *I rocked the baby to sleep.* **2. secouer, ébranler, ballotter ▸** to cause to shake or sway in a sudden way : *An earthquake rocked the house.* ▲ NOUN, rocks. **1. bercement, balancement, ébranlement ▸** a rocking movement. **2. rock ▸** short for Rock and Roll, a popular form of music. ■ **rocky,** ADJECTIVE. **instable, branlant (-ante), chancelant (-ante), fragile ▸** not firm or steady.

rock·er [ROK-ur] NOUN, rockers. **1.** (also rocking chair) **berceuse, chaise berçante ▸** a chair mounted on rockers or springs that allow it to rock back and forth. **2. bascule ▸** a curving piece of metal or wood on which an object, such as a cradle or a rocking chair, rocks.

rock·et [ROK-it] NOUN, rockets. **1. fusée, roquette ▸** a device that is moved at great speed by the force of burning gases being released from the rear. Very large and powerful rockets are used to launch spacecraft into space and to power guided missile in warfare. **2. vaisseau (-eaux) spatial (-iaux), missile, roquette ▸** a space vehicle or missile that is powered by such an engine. **3. fusée ▸** a type of firework that is shot through the air by gunpowder or another explosive. ▲ VERB, rocketed, rocketing. **monter en flèche, passer en trombe ▸** to rise up or travel very fast : *The flames of the burning forest fire rocketed into the air.* 📖 **p. 1154.**

rod [rod] NOUN, rods. **1. canne, tige, tringle ▸** a thin, straight bar of metal, wood, plastic, or other such hard material : *a fishing rod ; a curtain rod.* **2. perche ▸** a unit of length once used for measuring land. It is equal to about five metres.

rode [rode] VERB. a past form of ride.

ro·dent [RODE-unt] NOUN, rodents. **rongeur ▸** one of a large family of animals with large, sharp front teeth used for gnawing. There are nearly 2000 different kinds of rodents, including mice, rats, squirrels, beavers, gophers, and porcupines.

ro-de-o [ROH-dee-oh *or* roh-DAY-oh] NOUN, rodeos. **rodéo ▸** a contest to test skills used by people who handle cattle, such as roping calves, riding bulls, and wrestling steers.

role [role] NOUN, roles. 1. **rôle ▸** a character or part in a play, movie, or the like. 2. **rôle ▸** a part or position taken by a person in some activity : *A teacher's role is to help students learn.* **Note.** A role model is someone whom another person follows or imitates.

roll [role] VERB, rolled, rolling. 1. **rouler ▸** to move by turning over many times : *to roll a ball along the ground.* 2. **rouler, enrouler, retrousser ▸** to turn something around on itself or on something else : *"The governor nodded, rolled up his sleeves, and donned an apron."* (Paul Yee) 3. **onduler, se balancer, osciller ▸** to move up, down, or from side to side : *"For ten hours the wind howled across our rolling deck as the Knorr pitched and heaved in the rough sea."* (Robert D. Ballard) 4. **rouler, aller bon train ▸** to move or pass by in a smooth, steady way : *The construction of the school is rolling right along, and it should be finished next month.* ▲ NOUN, rolls. 1. **rouleau (-eaux) ▸** anything that is rolled up in the shape of a tube or cylinder : *a roll of pennies; a roll of foil.* 2. **petit pain, pâtisserie ▸** a small, round piece of baked bread dough : *dinner rolls; cinnamon rolls.* 3. **liste ▸** a list of names : *The teacher called the roll to see who was absent.* 4. **roulement ▸** a deep, loud rumble : *a drum roll.*

roll-er [ROH-lur] NOUN, rollers. 1. **rouleau (-eaux), enrouleur ▸** a rod or cylinder on which something is rolled up : *a roller for a window blind; hair rollers.* 2. **rouleau (-eaux) ▸** something that turns around and around and that is used to smooth, flatten, or spread things : *a paint roller.* 3. **roulette ▸** a small wheel or set of wheels attached to something so it can be moved : *a chair on rollers.*

roller coaster **montagnes russes ▸** an amusement-park ride in which a set of open cars travels very fast on tracks that form steep hills and sharp turns.

roller skate **patin à roulettes ▸** a shoe or boot that fastens to a plate with four wheels attached to the bottom. It is worn for skating on sidewalks or other hard, flat surfaces. ▲ VERB, roller-skated, roller-skating. **faire du patin à roulettes ▸** to move along on roller skates.

ROM [rom] ABBREVIATION. **mémoire morte ▸** short for Read-Only Memory, the part of a computer's memory, or a computer CD, that can be read that cannot be erased or changed.

Roman Catholic Church **Église catholique romaine ▸** a Christian church that is headed by

the Pope. **Note.** A member of this church is called a Roman Catholic or Catholic.

Roman numeral **chiffre romain ▸** a numeral in a numbering system used by the ancient Romans, in which letters are used instead of numbers. In this system, $I = 1, V = 5, X = 10, L = 50, C = 100, D = 500,$ and $M = 1000.$ Either capital letters or small letters may be used.

ro-mance [roh-MANCE *or* ROH-mance] NOUN, romances. 1. **idylle ▸** a love affair : *Shakespeare made the romance of Romeo and Juliet famous by writing a play about it.* 2. **roman ▸** a story or poem about adventure, love, or great deeds, especially one that is set in a distant place or time : *The novel Ivanhoe is a romance.* 3. **charme, poésie ▸** a quality of love, mystery, or adventure : *The romance of the stage makes a live play very appealing to me.*

ro-man-tic [roh-MAN-tik] ADJECTIVE. 1. **romantique ▸** having to do with or showing romance : *Sending me a dozen red roses was such a romantic thing to do!* 2. **romantique ▸** having ideas or feelings suitable for a romance; not practical or realistic : *In the 1800s, many people had a romantic view of the West and were unprepared for harsh conditions.* ■ **romantically,** ADVERB. ▸ **de façon romantique, amoureusement.**

romp [romp] VERB, romped, romping. **jouer bruyamment, s'ébattre ▸** to run and play in a lively, noisy way : *The children and puppies romped together on the front lawn.* ▲ NOUN, romps. **ébats ▸** a time of carefree and lively play : *a romp in the snow.*

roof [roof] NOUN, roofs. 1. **toit ▸** the outer, top part covering a building. 2. **toit, voûte ▸** something that covers like a roof : *the roof of your mouth; a car roof.* ▲ VERB, roofed, roofing. **couvrir d'un toit ▸** to cover a building with a roof. ■ **roofer,** NOUN. ▸ **couvreur (-euse).**

rook[1] [rook] NOUN, rooks. **freux ▸** a large black European bird that is like a crow. Rooks live in large groups and build their nests together.

rook[2] NOUN, rooks. **tour ▸** a piece used in the game of chess. A rook can move in a straight line parallel to the sides of the board. **Note.** Also called a castle.

rook-ie [ROOK-ee] NOUN, rookies. **bleu (bleue, bleus), novice, débutant (-ante) ▸** any person without much experience; a beginner, such as an athlete in his or her first season with a professional team.

room [room] NOUN, rooms. 1. **place, espace ▸** a space or area for a certain purpose : *The elevator has room for 15 people.* 2. **salle, pièce, chambre ▸** an area in a house or building that is enclosed by walls : *a* **dining room** (☞ p. 1067); *a bathroom.* 3. **place, trou, espace inoccupé, temps libre ▸** a chance or occasion to do something : *The doctor doesn't* *have any room in her schedule to see me today.* ▲ VERB, roomed, rooming. **1. partager une chambre, partager un appartement, être en colocation ▸** to live with another person as a roommate : *Dana and I roomed together at camp.* **Note.** A roommate is a person who shares a room or an apartment with someone else. **2. vivre en chambre, vivre en appartement, être en colocation ▸** to live in a rented room or a set of rooms. 🗐 p. 1072. SYN : area, space, range.

room·y [ROO-mee] ADJECTIVE, roomier, roomiest. **spacieux (-euse) ▸** having plenty of room; large : *a roomy tent that sleeps four comfortably.* SYN : spacious, sizeable, large.

roost [roost] NOUN, roosts. **perchoir, juchoir ▸** a place where a bird sleeps or rests. ▲ VERB, roosted, roosting. **se percher, se jucher ▸** to rest or sleep on a roost.

roost·er [ROO-stur] NOUN, roosters. **coq ▸** a male chicken.

root beer **racinette ▸** a soft drink that was originally flavoured with the roots of plants such as sassafras and sarsaparilla.

root[1] [root] NOUN, roots. **1. racine ▸** the part of a plant that grows down into the ground. Roots hold the plant in place and draw water and minerals from the earth. **2. racine ▸** something like a root in the way it is formed or attached : *the roots of a tooth.* **3. racine, origine ▸** the part from which something grows or starts; the source or cause : *the root of the problem.* **4. racine ▸** the main part of a word to which other parts may be added : *"Real" is the root of "unrealistic."* **5. racine ▸** a number that when multiplied by itself a given number of times produces a certain quantity : *6 is the square root of 36 (6 times 6).* **6. roots. racines ▸** the feeling of belonging to a certain place : *I live in Vancouver, but my roots are in Saskatchewan.* ▲ VERB, rooted, rooting. **1. s'enraciner, prendre racine ▸** of a plant, to develop roots; grow. **2. clouer sur place, prendre racine ▸** to keep from moving; fix in one place : *He saw the truck coming, but he was.rooted by fear to his spot in the road.* 👁 p. 249, 253. 🖉 p. 506.

root[2] VERB, rooted, rooting. **1. fouiller avec le groin ▸** to dig in the soil with the nose, as a pig does. **2. fouiller ▸** to look for something in a similar way; rummage : *Kevin rooted through the garbage can, frantically looking for the homework he had accidentally thrown away.*

root[3] VERB, rooted, rooting. **encourager, applaudir, supporter ▸** to cheer for or be in favour of one side in a game or contest : *I grew up in Toronto and have always rooted for the Maple Leafs.* ■ **rooter,** NOUN. ▸ supporteur (-trice).

rope [rope] NOUN, ropes. **1. corde ▸** a thick, strong cord or line made by twisting together strands of materials such as plant fibres, nylon,

or wire. **2. collier, torsade ▸** a number of things twisted or strung together : *a rope of pearls.* ▲ VERB, roped, roping. **1. corder, attacher à l'aide d'une corde ▸** to tie or fasten something with a rope : *She roped the logs together.* **2. prendre au lasso, capturer au lasso ▸** to catch with a lasso : *to rope a calf.* **3. rope off. délimiter à l'aide d'une corde, entourer d'une corde ▸** to enclose an area with a rope.

rose[1] [roze] NOUN, roses. **1. rosier ▸** any one of a large group of plants that grow as a bush, vine, or small tree and have beautiful, sweet-smelling flowers and thorny stems. **2. rose ▸** the flower of such a plant. Roses have several layers of large, colourful petals, usually red, pink, yellow, or white. **3. rose ▸** a pinkish-red colour.

rose[2] VERB. a past form of rise.

Rosh Hashanah [rosh huh-SHAH-nuh] (also Rosh Hashana, Rosh ha-Shana, Roch ha-Shana ▸** the Jewish New Year, celebrated in September or early October.

ros·y [ROH-zee] ADJECTIVE, rosier, rosiest. **1. rosé (-ée), rose ▸** having a pinkish-red colour : *the rosy glow of a sunset.* **2. optimiste, rose ▸** full of cheer; bright and hopeful : *a rosy view of life.*

rot [rot] VERB, rotted, rotting. **pourrir ▸** to become rotten or spoiled; decay : *The apple rotted in the sun.* ▲ NOUN. **1. pourriture ▸** the process of rotting; a state of decay **2. pourriture ▸** any one of several plant diseases in which the plant decays, caused by bacteria or fungi.

ro·ta·ry [ROH-tur-ee] ADJECTIVE. **rotatif (-ive) ▸** turning around a centre, or having parts that turn in a circle : *a rotary blade on a lawn mower.*

✐ Writing Tips

Root Words

*The root of a word is the part from which other words develop. For instance, kind is the root word for unkind and for kindness. Notice that you can add to the beginning or end of a root word. If you add to the beginning of a root word, you will be adding prefixes like un-, re-, co-, pre-, non-, anti-, and so on. Suffixes are added to the end of root words; -ness, -er, -or, -ly, and -able are all suffixes. Sometimes when you figure out what the root of a word is, you can figure out how to spell it—**dishonourable**, for instance, has a prefix and a suffix. But the root word is a very familiar word—**honour**.*

ro‑tate [ROH‑TATE] VERB, rotated, rotating.
1. tourner, pivoter ▸ to turn or cause to turn in
a circle on a centre point called an axis : *It takes
about 24 hours for the earth to rotate once.*
**2. faire en rotation, faire tour à tour, faire à tour
de rôle, faire en alternant ▸** to take turns in a
fixed order : *Sunil, Georgia, and I will rotate
turns as president.*

ro‑ta‑tion [roh‑TAY‑shun] NOUN, rotations. **rota‑
tion, tour ▸** the fact of rotating around a centre
point : *the rotation of a wheel.*

rot‑ten [ROT‑un] ADJECTIVE, rottener, rottenest.
1. pourri (‑ie) ▸ of food, not fit to eat because
of being spoiled or decayed : *a rotten egg.*
2. pourri (‑ie) ▸ worn out and likely to give way ;
weak : *The bridge had to be closed after it was
found that its support timbers were rotten.*
3. *Informal.* **minable, pitoyable ▸** very bad or
poor : *I have a fever and chills — I just feel
rotten.*

rouge [roozh] NOUN, rouges. **rouge à joues, fard à
joues ▸** a pink or red makeup that is used to
add colour to the cheeks. **Note.** Often called
blusher or blush.

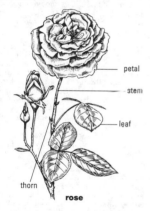

petal

stem

leaf

thorn

rose

rough [ruf] ADJECTIVE, rougher, roughest. **1. rude,
rêche, rugueux (‑euse) ▸** having a surface that is
bumpy, scratchy, or jagged ; not smooth or even.
2. rude, brutal (‑ale, ‑aux) ▸ having or showing
force or violence : *Tim gave the wagon a rough
push and tipped it over.* **3. ébauché (‑ée),
inachevé (‑ée) ▸** not in a final or complete state ;
unfinished : *I need to rewrite my rough draft of
the essay.* **4. approximatif (‑ive) ▸** not exact or
detailed : *The mechanic gave us a rough esti‑
mate for how much it would cost to fix our car.*
5. rude, difficile ▸ hard to deal with or get
through ; difficult or unpleasant : *Mom had a
rough week, working overtime every day.*

▲ VERB, roughed, roughing. **1. malmener, bruta‑
liser, traiter avec rudesse ▸** to treat in a mean
or violent way. **2. ébaucher, esquisser ▸** to
make or plan in an unfinished way : *The
architect roughed in the basic shape of the
building.* **■ roughly,** ADVERB. **1. rudement,
brutalement ▸** in a rough way : *They play too
rough.* **2. environ, approximativement, à peu
près ▸** about ; approximately : *She owes me
roughly $100, give or take a few cents.*
■ roughness, NOUN. **▸ rudesse, brutalité,
caractère rudimentaire.** SYN : coarse, harsh, tur‑
bulent, rugged.

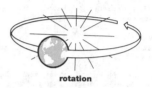

rotation

round [rownd] ADJECTIVE. **1. rond (ronde) ▸**
shaped like a ball or a globe : *The moon is
round.* **2. rond (ronde), arrondi (‑ie) ▸** shaped
like a circle or curve : *a round corner.* ▲ NOUN,
rounds. **1. rond, cercle ▸** something shaped
like a ball or cylinder. **2. ronde, tournée ▸** a reg‑
ular movement or route around a certain area :
*The security guard made rounds through the
museum each hour.* **3. partie ▸** a complete
game or contest, or a section of one : *a round of
golf ; a round of cards.* **4. salve, série, suite ▸** a
series or set of things that happen :
a round of cheers from an audience. ▲ VERB,
rounded, rounding. **1. arrondir ▸** to make or
become round : *She rounded the mud with her
hands.* **2. tourner, contourner ▸** to pass around
something ; go to the other side : *Gord rounded
the corner on his bicycle.* **3. arrondir ▸** of a
number, to make it more simple or less exact by
changing it : *You can round the number 978
to 980.* ▲ ADVERB ; PREPOSITION. **autour, autour
de ▸** around : *We spent the day walking round
the city.*

round‑a‑bout [ROWND‑uh‑BOWT] ADJECTIVE. **dé‑
tourné (‑ée), indirect (‑ecte) ▸** in a way that is
not straight or direct : *Katrina took a round‑
about way to school, detouring through the
woods and the candy store.*

round trip aller et retour ▸ a trip that includes
going to a place and then returning to the start‑
ing point. **Note.** Also used as an ADJECTIVE : *The
round‑trip airfare between here and Halifax is
$400.*

round‑up [ROWND‑up] NOUN, roundups. **1. ras‑
semblement, rodéo ▸** a gathering together of
farm animals such as cows, horses, or sheep, so
that they can be counted, moved to another

place, and so on. **2. rassemblement, rafle ▸** any similar gathering of people or things : *a roundup of suspects in a crime case.* SYN : rodéo.

rouse [rowz] VERB, roused, rousing. **1. réveiller, éveiller ▸** to disturb someone from sleep or rest : *My dad was roused from his afternoon nap by an urgent phone call.* **2. agiter, exciter ▸** to cause to move or become active; stir up : *The barking dogs roused three ducks from the reeds.* **Note.** Also used as an ADJECTIVE: **entraînant (-ante) ▸** *a rousing piece of music.*

rout [rowt] NOUN, routs. **déroute, défaite ▸** a complete defeat : *The game turned into a complete rout, with a final score of 10–3.* ▲ VERB, routed, routing. **vaincre, battre, mettre en déroute ▸** to defeat completely : *The soldiers routed the enemy, driving them far behind the battle line.*

route [root *or* rowt] NOUN, routes. **1. route, trajet, chemin, itinéraire ▸** a way to get from one place to another; a road, course, or path : *This road is the fastest route to the border.* **2. parcours, itinéraire ▸** a regular series of stops for a vehicle, delivery person, and so on : *a newspaper route; a bus route.* ▲ VERB, routed, routing. **acheminer, expédier ▸** to send or be sent by a certain way : *to route a package.*

rou-tine [roo-TEEN] NOUN, routines. **1. routine ▸** a regular or usual way of doing something; something that is repeated time after time : *My after-school routine includes eating a snack, doing my homework, and playing outside.* **2. numéro ▸** an act or part of an act performed for a show : *The circus has a very funny clown routine.* ▲ ADJECTIVE. **routinier (-ière), systématique ▸** according to a routine; regular or repeated : *At first driving a car was exciting, but now it is just routine.* ▪ **routinely,** ADVERB. ▸ **systématiquement, de façon routinière.** SYN : habit, method.

row[1] [roh] NOUN, rows. **1. rang, rangée ▸** a line of people or things : *a row of seats in a theatre; a row of corn in a field.* **2. suite, file ▸** a series of things, one right after the other, with no breaks in between : *Nunzio has been so sick that he has missed school five days in a row.*

row[2] [roh] VERB, rowed, rowing. **ramer ▸** to use oars to move a boat : *We rowed across the lake.* SYN : paddle.

row[3] [row] NOUN, rows. **dispute, querelle, engueulade ▸** a noisy quarrel or fight : *The two candidates got into a row about taxes.*

row-boat [ROH-bote] NOUN, rowboats. **canot à rames ▸** a small boat that is moved by the use of oars.

row-dy [ROW-dee] ADJECTIVE, rowdier, rowdiest. **chahuteur (-euse), bruyant (-ante) ▸** acting in a way that is noisy, rough, or rude; disorderly : *A few rowdy students in class disturb the rest of us.*

roy-al [ROY-ul] ADJECTIVE. **1. royal (-ale, -aux) ▸** having to do with a king or queen : *the royal family.* **2. royal (-ale, -aux) ▸** serving or belonging to a king or queen : *the royal crown; royal command.* **3. royal (-ale, -aux) ▸** suited for a king or queen : *On Parents' Day at our school, visiting parents are given a royal welcome.* ▪ **royally,** ADVERB. ▸ **royalement, complètement.**

roy-al-ty [ROY-ul-tee] NOUN, royalties. **1. famille royale, membre de la famille royale ▸** a royal person such as a king, queen, prince, or princess. **2. royauté ▸** the position, rank, or powers of such a person. **3. droits d'auteur ▸** a share of the money earned from the sale or performance of a work such as a book, a play, or a piece of music, paid to the author or composer of the work.

rub [rub] VERB, rubbed, rubbing. **1. frotter ▸** to press down on a surface while moving back and forth over it. **2. frotter, frictionner ▸** to put on spread over a surface : *Martin rubbed lotion into his chapped hands.* **3. frotter ▸** to move one thing over another, or two things against each other : *The boat was rubbing against the dock.* **4. frotter, astiquer ▸** to clean, polish, or smooth something by applying pressure to it. SYN : massage, buff, shine.

rub-ber [RUB-ur] NOUN, rubbers. **1. caoutchouc ▸** a strong substance that keeps out water and that can be easily stretched. Natural rubber is made from the milky sap of certain tropical plants, such as the rubber tree. Artificial rubber can be made using coal, oil, and chemicals. **2. rubbers. caoutchoucs ▸** waterproof over shoes made from this substance, used for wearing in the rain. **Note.** Also called **boots or galoshes.** ▪ **rubbery,** ADJECTIVE. **caoutchouteux (-euse) ▸** like rubber in some way, as by being floppy or stretchy : *I had to sit down because my legs felt rubbery from climbing up the mountain.*

rub-bish [RUB-ish] NOUN. **1. détritus, ordures, déchets ▸** things that are not wanted and are thrown away; useless or waste material; trash. **2. bêtise, idiotie, sottise ▸** foolish talk; nonsense.

rub-ble [RUB-ul] NOUN. **décombres ▸** broken pieces of stone, brick, and other solid material, such as the ruins of buildings that have been demolished.

ru-by [ROO-bee] NOUN, rubies. **1. rubis ▸** a precious stone with a clear red colour. **2. rubis ▸** deep-red colour.

rud-der [RUD-ur] NOUN, rudders. **1. gouvernail (-ails) ▸** a wide, flat movable part attached to the back of a boat or ship, used for steering. **2. gouvernail (-ails) ▸** a similar part attached to the tail of an aircraft.

rud·dy [RUD-ee] ADJECTIVE, ruddier, ruddiest. **rose** ▸ having a rich, healthy reddish colour of the skin.

rude [rood] ADJECTIVE, ruder, rudest. **1. rude, impoli (-ie), grossir (-ière)** ▸ showing or having bad manners; not polite : *"Lin would have liked to know exactly how tall Sister Noella was but he was afraid it would be rude to ask."* (Barbara Novak) **2. rudimentaire** ▸ made or done with little skill; crude or rough : *a rude hut built out of branches and palm leaves.* ■ **rudely,** ADVERB. ▸ **rudement, impoliment, brutalement, grossièrement.** ■ **rudeness,** NOUN. ▸ **impolitesse, grossièreté.** SYN: impolite, inconsiderate, tactless.

ruf·fle [RUF-ul] NOUN, ruffles. **jabot, fraise, manchette** ▸ a strip of cloth, ribbon, or lace that has folds or waves at one edge, used for trimming. ▲ VERB, ruffled, ruffling. **1. ébouriffer, agiter, déranger, froisser** ▸ to disturb something that was smooth or calm : *"Grandpa grinned and ruffled her hair with his big hand as he went by."* (Marilyn Halvorson) **2. froisser, contrarier, irriter** ▸ to make someone annoyed or upset : *Pam was tired and easily ruffled by her pesky younger brother.*

rug [rug] NOUN, rugs. **tapis, carpette** ▸ a piece of thick, heavy fabric that is used to cover a floor.

rug·by [RUG-bee] NOUN. **rugby** ▸ a form of football played by teams of 13 or 15 players, in which bouncing and kicking the ball are permitted but not passing it forward or taking time out from play.

rug·ged [RUG-id] ADJECTIVE. **1. accidenté (-ée), sauvage** ▸ having a rough or broken surface or outline : *Some parts of Honduras are so rugged that they are still unexplored.* **2. solide** ▸ able to stand up to hard treatment; strong and sturdy : *a rugged four-wheel-drive vehicle.* **3. difficile, escarpé (-ée), d'accès difficile** ▸ hard to do or get through; severe; harsh : *a rugged path through the valley.*

rudder

ruin [ROO-in] NOUN, ruins. **1. ruine** ▸ the fact of being completely destroyed; very great damage : *The earthquake left the city in ruins.* **2. ruine** ▸ something that causes such a destruction or collapse. **3. ruines** ▸ what is left of something that has been destroyed; remains : *The Coliseum in Rome is one of many famous ruins in Italy.* ▲ VERB, ruined, ruining. **1. ruiner** ▸ to bring or cause destruction or collapse : *Last summer's drought brought about the ruin of many farmers.* **2. ruiner, gâcher** ▸ to spoil or harm : *The cold temperatures ruined my plans for a winter party.*

rule [rool] NOUN, rules. **1. règlement, règle** ▸ a statement telling what is allowed or not allowed : *In basketball, it is a rule that you cannot run carrying the ball.* **2. règle** ▸ the regular or usual way that something is done : *As a rule, I like to be in bed by 10:00.* **3. autorité, domination** ▸ the fact of being in control or governing : *Senegal was under the rule of France.* **4. ligne droite** ▸ a straight line. ▲ VERB, ruled, ruling. **1. gouverner, diriger, dominer** ▸ to have control over or govern : **2. décider, déclarer** ▸ to make a rule, or a decision about a rule : *The umpire ruled the player out.* SYN: regulation, policy, decree.

rul·er [ROO-lur] NOUN, rulers. **1. chef, chef d'État, dirigeant (-ante)** ▸ a person who rules others, especially as the head of a country. **2. règle** ▸ a strip of wood, plastic, or other material, used to measure and draw straight lines.

rum·ble [RUM-bul] VERB, rumbled, rumbling. **gronder, gargouiller** ▸ to made a deep, heavy, rolling sound : *Loud thunder rumbled across the darkened sky.* ▲ NOUN, rumbles. **grondement, gargouillement** ▸ a deep, heavy rolling sound : *a rumble in my stomach.*

rum·mage [RUM-ij] VERB, rummaged, rummaging. **fouiller, farfouiller** ▸ to search through something by moving things aside : *"She hopped out of bed and rummaged through the closet until she found a can full of her brother's marbles."* (Gary Soto)

rummage sale **vente de bric-à-brac, vente d'objets usagés** ▸ a sale of used clothes, furniture, and other household items.

ru·mour [ROO-mur] NOUN, rumours. (also rumor) **1. rumeur, bruit** ▸ a story or report that is passed from person to person and believed to be true without any proof : *"No one was sure where the rumour had started, but it was a strong one, and most people believed it."* (Judy Allen) **2. rumeur, bruit** ▸ what people are saying in general; the general opinion : *Rumour has it that the prime minister will be vacationing here next week.* ▲ VERB, rumoured, rumouring. **faire courir des rumeurs** ▸ to spread or tell rumours : *It is rumoured that school is closing early.* SYN: hearsay, gossip.

rump [rump] NOUN, rumps. **1. croupe** ▶ the part of an animal's body where the legs meet the back. **2. culotte** ▶ a cut or piece of meat from this part.

rum-ple [RUM-pul] VERB, rumpled, rumpling. **froisser, ébouriffer** ▶ to mess something by handling it roughly; wrinkle or crumple : *Sally rumpled her new dress while playing in the yard.*

run [run] VERB, ran, run, running. **1. courir** ▶ to go by moving the legs more quickly than one does when walking. **2. se présenter, être candidat (-ate), participer** ▶ to take part in a race or contest : *Brian is running for president.* **3. passer, assurer le service** ▶ to travel regularly : *This ferry runs between Victoria and Vancouver.* **4. aller, passer** ▶ to make a small trip or trips to do routine things; do errands : *I'm going to run to the store for some fruit.* **5. parcourir, vagabonder, laisser aller** ▶ to let something move or operate freely; roam : *Randy let the hose run in the dry part of the garden.* **6. rencontrer, tomber** ▶ to pass into or let into a place or condition : *I ran into a problem when I tried to program the computer.* **7. se dérouler, se passer, se transmettre entre générations** ▶ to happen or to be in effect : *The semester runs for 16 weeks. Big feet run in her family.* **8. diriger, gérer, administrer** ▶ to be in charge of : *to run a day-care center.* **9. déteindre, couler, fuir, courir** ▶ to spread or leak out : *That red towel ran in the wash and stained my white T-shirt pink.* **10. courir, faire** ▶ to experience something bad : *to run a high temperature; to run a risk.* **11. faire marcher, faire fonctionner** ▶ to operate a program on a computer. ▲ NOUN, runs. **1. course** ▶ the act of running : *I go for a run every morning.* **2. tour, tournée** ▶ a trip : *The mail carrier made daily delivery runs.* **3. jouissance** ▶ the freedom to move around or to use something : *Mother told our guests that they could have the run of the house.* **4. série de représentations, durée** ▶ a period of time when something continues to happen : *The play had a two-year run before it ended.* **5. maille** ▶ a part of a knitted cloth where the stitches have broken and come undone : *Melanie got a run in her sweater after she snagged it on a twig.* **6. point** ▶ a score earned in baseball after a player has gone around the bases and returned to touch home plate without being put out. 📖 **p. 1030.** SYN: race, sprint, compete. 🖉 **p. 510.**

run-a-way [RUN-uh-WAY] NOUN, runaways. **fugitif (-ive), fugueur (-euse), fuyard (-arde)** ▶ a person, animal, or thing that runs away or runs out of control. ▲ ADJECTIVE. **fou (folle, fous, folles), hors de contrôle** ▶ running away or moving without any control : *a runaway truck.*

run-down [RUN-DOWN] ADJECTIVE. **1. à plat, fatigué (-ée), affaibli (-ie), épuisé (-ée)** ▶ having bad health; sick or tired : *I am likely to get ill when I am run-down.* **2. délabré (-ée)** ▶ needing to be fixed, falling apart : *a run-down apartment that needs paint and new carpet.*

rung[1] [rung] VERB. a past form of ring.

rung[2] NOUN, rungs. **1. barreau (-eaux), échelon** ▶ a bar or rod that forms a step on a ladder. **2. barreau (-eaux)** ▶ a piece between the legs or within the framework of a chair that gives strength or support.

run-ner [RUN-ur] NOUN, runners. **1. coureur (-euse)** ▶ a person or animal that runs. **2. lame** ▶ the part on which an ice skate, sled, iceboat, and so on moves along the ice or snow. **3. chemin** ▶ a narrow strip of carpeting in a hallway or on a stairway. **4. stolon** ▶ a thin stem of a plant that crawls along the ground and roots in another place to make a new plant. **5. coureur** ▶ a player in baseball who is on base or trying to reach base.

run-ner-up [RUN-ur-UP] NOUN, runners-up. **personne en deuxième position, équipe en deuxième position** ▶ a person or team that finishes in second place in a race or contest.

runt [runt] NOUN, runts. *Informal.* **avorton** ▶ an animal that is much smaller than normal.

run-way [RUN-way] NOUN, runways. **piste d'envol, piste d'atterrissage** ▶ a long, narrow roadway where an airplane can take off and land.

ru-ral [ROOR-ul] ADJECTIVE. **rural (-ale, -aux)** ▶ having to do with or being in the country; away from cities or towns : *My dad doesn't like cities, so we have always lived in rural areas.*

rush[1] [rush] VERB, rushed, rushing. **1. se précipiter, se dépêcher** ▶ to hurry or move quickly : *I rushed home to take the dog for a walk.* **2. faire à la hâte, faire à toute vitesse** ▶ to do something in too much of a hurry : *Jason rushed through the test and missed six questions.* ▲ NOUN, rushes. **1. précipitation, hâte, empressement** ▶ the act or fact of rushing; quick or

---

✏️ **Word Builder**

Run means to move your legs in rapid steps so you travel faster than when you walk. ***Run into*** means to meet someone by chance : *I ran into my cousin Cyril at the park.* ***Run away with*** can mean to do much better than others : *The Raptors outscored the Pistons by 20 points in the third quarter and ran away with the game.* ***Run in the family*** means that something can be found in most family members of many generations : *Long legs run in the Sese family.*

hurried movements: *I am always in a rush to get to school in the morning.* **2. ruée ▶** the fact of many people rushing to do something: *a gold rush.* SYN: gush, hasten, surge.

rush² NOUN, rushes. **jonc ▶** a grasslike plant that grows in very wet places. Most rushes have thin, hollow stems and bunches of little green or brown flowers. The stems are used to weave mats, baskets, and chair seats.

rush hour heure de pointe, heure d'affluence ▶ a time of day when many people are travelling either to or from work.

rust [rust] NOUN, rusts. **1. rouille ▶** a reddish-brown or orange coating that forms on iron when it is exposed to moisture or air for a long time. **2. rouille ▶** a plant disease that marks leaves and stems with reddish-brown or orange spots or streaks. **3. rouille ▶** a reddish-brown colour. ▲ VERB, rusted, rusting. **rouiller ▶** to become covered with rust. ■ **rusty,** ADJECTIVE. **1. rouillé (-ée) ▶** covered with rust: *a rusty nail.* **2. rouillé (-ée) ▶** having the look or colour of rust. **3. rouillé (-ée) ▶** not as good as it should be, because of not being used or practised: *My tennis game is rusty.*

rus·tle [RUSS-ul] VERB, rustled, rustling. **1. bruire, froisser ▶** to make a soft crackling or fluttering sound: *papers rustling during a test.*

2. faire bruire ▶ to lift or move something so that it makes a sound like this: *"Above him, the wind rustled the remaining dead leaves of the oak tree."* (Betsy Byars) **3. voler du bétail ▶** to steal cattle. **Note.** A person who does this is a rustler. ▲ NOUN, rustles. ■ **bruissement, froissement ▶** a soft, whispering sound: *The audience made a rustle as they shifted in their seats.*

rut [rut] NOUN, ruts. **1. ornière ▶** a deep wheel track or groove made in the ground from repeated use. **2. routine, ornière ▶** a way of living or doing things that is the same day after day; a boring routine: *All I do is homework and baby-sitting—I'm in a real rut!* ▲ VERB, rutted, rutting. **sillonner, tracer des ornières ▶** to make ruts in something.

ruth·less [ROOTH-lis] ADJECTIVE. **impitoyable, sans pitié ▶** having or showing no pity or kindness; harsh and cruel. ■ **ruthlessly,** ADVERB. **▶ impitoyablement, sans pitié.** ■ **ruthlessness,** NOUN. **▶ caractère impitoyable, cruel (-elle).**

rye [ry] NOUN, ryes. **seigle ▶** a grass plant with thin stems. Its grain is used to make flour, and food for animals, and an alcoholic drink. Rye bread is made from this flour 👁 **p. 116.**

saw

s, S [es] NOUN, s's, S's. **1. s, S** ▶ the 19th letter of the English alphabet. **2.** a mark meaning satisfactory work. **3.** a suffix, or ending, used to make a word plural, as in *ships*. **4.** shaped like the letter *S*.

Sab·bath [SAB-uth] NOUN, Sabbaths. **sabbat** ▶ the day of the week that is set aside for worship and rest. The Sabbath is Sunday for most Christians and Friday evening to Saturday evening for Jews.

sa·ble [SAY-bul] NOUN, sables. **zibeline, martre** ▶ a small animal of Europe and Asia that is similar to the mink.

sab·o·tage [SAB-uh-TAZH] NOUN. **sabotage** ▶ any damage done in order to harm the owner, such as destroying machines, tools, factories, or roads. ▲ VERB, sabotaged, sabotaging. **saboter** ▶ to damage or destroy by sabotage : *The secret agent sabotaged the phone lines so no one could call for help.*

sa·bre [SAY-bur] NOUN, sabres. (also **saber**) **sabre** ▶ a long sword with a curved blade. Once a weapon, today it is used mainly in the sport of fencing.

sabre-toothed tiger [SAY-bur-TOOTHT] **tigre à dents de sabre** ▶ a large cat with two long curved upper teeth. It lived about 12,000 years ago but is now extinct.

sac [sak] NOUN, sacs. **sac, vessie** ▶ a baglike part of a plant or animal that usually holds liquid such as poison.

sack[1] [sak] NOUN, sacks. **1. sac** ▶ a large bag made of strong, rough material : *a sack of potatoes.* **2. sac** ▶ any bag. ▲ VERB, sacked, sacking. **ensacher, mettre dans un sac** ▶ to put in a sack.

sack[2] VERB, sacked, sacking. **1. saccager, piller** ▶ to capture and rob a place; loot : *Invaders sacked the city.* **2. plaquage du quart-arrière** ▶ in North American football, to tackle the quarterback behind the line while he or she is trying to pass the ball. ▲ NOUN, sacks. **mise à sac** ▶ the act of sacking.

sa·cred [SAY-krid] ADJECTIVE. **1. sacré (-ée)** ▶ belonging to a god; holy : *The Koran is the sacred book of Islam.* **2. sacré (-ée)** ▶ worthy of special respect or honour : *a sacred promise.*

sac·ri·fice [SAK-ruh-FICE] NOUN, sacrifices. **1. sacrifice** ▶ the act of offering something to a god as a form of worship. **2. sacrifice** ▶ the giving up of something one values for the sake of someone or something else : *Luc thought it was a small sacrifice to give one of his kidneys to his sister.* **3. jeu sacrifice** ▶ a play in baseball in which the batter is put out but another runner advances. ▲ VERB, sacrificed, sacrificing. **1. sacrifier** ▶ to make a religious sacrifice. **2. sacrifier** ▶ to give up something for the sake of someone or something else : *The soldier sacrificed his life for his country.* **3. sacrifier** ▶ to lose value : *The student sacrificed her honour by cheating on the test.*

sad [sad] ADJECTIVE, sadder, saddest. **1. triste** ▶ not happy; feeling sorrow : *Asa was sad to be away from home.* **2. triste** ▶ causing or showing this feeling : *sad news.* ■ **sadly,** ADVERB. ▶ **tristement, mélancoliquement.** ■ **sadness** (☞ p. 1023), NOUN. ▶ **tristesse.** SYN: unhappy, depressed, miserable, blue.

sad·den [SAD-un] VERB, saddened, saddening. **(s') attrister** ▶ to make sad : *The bad news saddened us all.*

sad·dle [SAD-ul] NOUN, saddles. **selle** ▶ a seat for a rider on the back of a horse or other animal. ▲ VERB, saddled, saddling. **1. seller** ▶ to put a saddle on : *to saddle a horse.* **2. imposer, alourdir** ▶ to put a load on; burden : *Mom is saddled with a big tax bill this year.*

sa·fa·ri [suh-FAR-ee] NOUN, safaris. **safari** ▶ a trip through wild country to hunt or photograph animals, especially in eastern or central Africa.

safe [safe] ADJECTIVE, safer, safest. **1. sans danger, sûr (sûre)** ▶ free from danger or harm : *It's not safe to drive fast on a mountain road.* **2. sans danger** ▶ not able or likely to cause harm : *Dad keeps the knives in a safe place.* **3. sûr (sûre)** ▶ without the risk of being wrong or failing : *It is safe to say that the house will be built by summer.* **4. sauf (sauve)** ▶ in baseball, reaching base without being put out. ▲ NOUN,

512

safes. coffre-fort ▸ a strong box with a lock, used to keep valuable things from being lost or stolen. ■ **safely,** ADVERB. ▸ **sans risque, sans danger.**

safe-ty [SAFE-tee] NOUN. **sécurité ▸** the fact of being safe; freedom from harm or danger : *"See-ing Alejandro, the skunk darted to safety."* (Richard E. Albert)

safety pin épingle de sûreté ▸ a U-shaped pin with a special guard at one end to cover the sharp point.

sag [sag] VERB, sagged, sagging. **(s')affaisser, pendre ▸** to bend or droop down loosely : *"When they reached the top at last, they sagged against the sled exhausted."* (James Houston) ▲ NOUN, sags. **pendant (-ante) ▸** the act of sagging, or a part that sags. SYN: droop, slacken, slump, hang, sink.

sa-ga [SAG-uh *or* SOG-uh] NOUN, sagas. **1. saga ▸** an ancient storytelling of the deeds of heroes of Norway and Iceland. **2. saga ▸** any long story of adventure with many episodes : *We enjoyed Grandma's saga of sailing around the world.*

sage¹ [saje] NOUN, sages. **sage ▸** a person thought to be very wise. ▲ ADJECTIVE. **sage ▸** having wisdom; wise : *sage advice.* ■ **sagely,** ADVERB. ▸ **sagement.**

sage² [saje] NOUN. **sauge ▸** a strong-smelling leaf that is used in cooking or as a medicine.

sage-brush [SAJE-brush] NOUN. **armoise ▸** a bushy shrub that grows in dry areas of western North America.

said [sed] VERB. a past form of say.

sail [sale] NOUN, sails. **1. voile ▸** a piece of heavy cloth attached to a boat or ship. It collects the force of the wind to move the boat move forward in the water. **2. voyage en bateau à voile ▸** a trip on a boat or ship using sails. ▲ VERB, sailed, sailing. **1. piloter, barrer ▸** to guide or control a boat with a sail. **Note.** The sport of doing this is sailing. **2. naviguer ▸** to move or travel by ship : *The cruise ship will sail at noon tomorrow.* **3. filer, glisser ▸** to move or glide smoothly, as if sailing on a boat : *The skater sailed across the frozen pond.*

sail-boat [SALE-bote] NOUN, sailboats. **voilier ▸** a boat fitted with sails and powered by wind. 👁 **p. 394.**

sail-or [SAY-lur] NOUN, sailors. **marin ▸** a person who helps guide or control a boat or ship, especially someone who does this as a job : *The sailors got their boat ready to leave.*

saint [saynt] NOUN, saints. **1.** (also Saint) **saint (sainte) ▸** a very holy person. In some religions, a saint is believed to have special powers, such as the ability to perform miracles. **Note.** The fact of being a saint is sainthood. **2. saint (sainte) ▸** a person thought of as having qualities like a saint, such as being very good, kind, or patient.

■ **saintly,** ADJECTIVE. ▸ **plein (pleine) de bonté, digne d'un saint (d'une sainte).**

Saint Ber-nard [BUR-nard *or* bur-NARD] **saint-bernard ▸** a very large, powerful dog with thick brown-and-white hair. **Note.** These dogs were first bred by monks at the monastery of St. Bernard, in the Swiss Alps, and were used to find people lost in the snow.

sake [sake] NOUN, sakes. **1. intérêt, égard, amour ▸** benefit or good : *Don't stay for my sake.* **2. raison, but ▸** reason or purpose : *For the sake of saving money, let's go together.*

sal-ad [SAL-ud] NOUN, salads. **salade ▸** a dish of vegetables, fruits, meat, or fish served cold, usually with dressing. 👁 **p. 1139.**

sal-a-man-der [SAL-uh-man-dur] NOUN, salamanders. **salamandre ▸** a small animal that looks like a lizard, but is related to frogs and toads. A salamander is an amphibian that lives in or near damp places.

salamander

sal-a-ry [SAL-uh-ree] NOUN, salaries. **salaire, traitement ▸** a fixed amount of money paid for work done. A salary is paid at regular times, such as by the week or month, rather than by the hour or the job.

sale [sale] NOUN, sales. **1. vente ▸** an exchange of goods for money; the selling of something. **2. solde ▸** the selling of goods or property at lower than usual prices : *The store has a sale on turkeys this week.*

sales-per-son [SALES-pur-sun] NOUN, salespeople *or* salespersons. **vendeur (-euse) ▸** a person who sells things or services. **Note.** Also called a salesclerk or sales representative.

sales tax taxe sur les ventes ▸ money that is collected as tax on the price of the goods sold.

Sa-lish [SAY-lish] NOUN. **1. Salish ▸** an Aboriginal people in British Columbia and the northwestern United States. There are several groups : the Coastal Salish, the Interior Salish, and the Straits Salish. **2. salish ▸** the languages of the Salish people. ▲ ADJECTIVE. ▸ **salish.**

513

sa·li·va [SUH-LY-vuh] NOUN. **salive ▸** a clear, taste-less fluid given off into the mouth by special glands, to moisten food and help digestion.

salm·on [SAM-un] NOUN, salmon or salmons. **1. saumon ▸** a large, silver-coloured fish that is hatched in fresh water but lives in the ocean as an adult. Salmon return to the fresh water where they were born to lay their eggs. The meat of salmon is widely used as food. **2. saumon ▸** an orange colour like that of the flesh of a salmon. 👁 p. 107.

sal·mon·ber·ry [SAM-un-BAIR-ee] NOUN, salmon-berries. **1. ronce remarquable ▸** a large bush of the Pacific coast with red flowers and pink, edible fruit. **2. fruit de la ronce remarquable ▸** the fruit of this bush, which resembles a raspberry.

sa·loon [suh-LOON] NOUN, saloons. **1. bar ▸** a place where alcoholic drinks are served; a bar. **2. salon ▸** a large room for public use, such as on steamships. Note. *Saloon* is a more old-fash-ioned word than *bar*.

salt [salt] NOUN, salts. **1.** (also **table salt**) **sel ▸** a white crystal mined from the earth or taken from sea water. Its chemical name is **sodium chloride**. Salt is used to season and preserve foods and is important in the diet of people and animals. **2. sel ▸** a chemical compound. **3. sel ▸** any of various substances that look like salt : *bath salts.* ▲ VERB, salted, salting. **1. saler ▸** to season or preserve food with salt : *to salt pork.* **2. salt away. mettre de côté, épargner ▸** to save for use at a later time. *Each week, Darius salted away money for a trip.* ■ **salty,** ADJECTIVE. **▸ salé (-ée).** ■ **saline,** ADJECTIVE. **salin (-ine) ▸** having or containing salt : *saline solution.* 📖 p. 1140.

salt·wa·ter [SALT-WAH-tur] (also **salt-water**) ADJECTIVE. **de mer ▸** having to do with or living in the ocean, rather than in the fresh water of lakes, rivers, and so on : *Sharks are saltwater fish.*

sal·u·ta·tion [SAL-yoo-TAY-shun] NOUN, saluta-tions. **salutation (s) ▸** an act or expression of greeting, especially the greeting used in writing a letter. 🖎 p. 514.

sa·lute [suh-LOOT] VERB, saluted, saluting. **1. saluer ▸** to show respect or honour in a for-mal way, especially by touching the open right hand to the forehead : *A soldier salutes a senior officer.* **2. saluer ▸** to greet with friendly words or actions : *Rachel saluted the new teacher with a smile.* ▲ NOUN, salutes. **salut, salve ▸** the act or fact of saluting.

sal·vage [SAL-vij] VERB, salvaged, salvaging. **1. sauver ▸** to save something from being lost or damaged : *Divers salvaged treasure from the sunken ship.* **2. sauvegarder ▸** to save from being thrown away or destroyed : *He salvaged an old chair from the garbage.* ▲ NOUN. **sauve-tage ▸** the act or fact of salvaging something. SYN: save, rescue, recover.

sal·va·tion [sal-VAY-shun] NOUN. **salut ▸** the fact of being saved from danger, destruction, or loss.

salve [salv or sav] NOUN, salves. **onguent ▸** a creamy substance used in healing or soothing a sore or burn on the skin; an ointment.

same [same] ADJECTIVE. **1. même ▸** being the one and only; not another : *Terek's family has owned the same house for 20 years.* **2. iden-tique, pareil (-eille) , même ▸** being exactly like another; identical : *My friends and I all listen to the same radio station.* ▲ PRONOUN:*She ordered the fish, and I had the same.* ■ **sameness,** NOUN. **▸ de même, répétitivité ▸** the fact of being the same, especially if boring or repetitive.

sam·ple [SAM-pul] NOUN, samples. **échan-tillon ▸** a small piece or amount that shows what something is like : *He tried the free sam-ples of the cookies.* Note. Also used as an ADJEC-TIVE:*a sample copy of the newspaper.* ▲ VERB, sampled, sampling. **prendre un échantillon, essayer ▸** to take a sample of; test a part or piece : *Vijay sampled six flavours of ice cream before ordering.* SYN: example, model, illustra-tion, specimen.

sanc·tion [SANK-shun] VERB, sanctioned, sanc-tioning. **approuver, sanctionner ▸** to approve of something in an official way : *The prime minis-ter would not sanction a deal with terrorists.* ▲ NOUN, sanctions. **1. approbation, sanction ▸** the fact of approving something officially. **2. sanctions. sanction ▸** an agreement by two or more countries to act against another coun-try. SYN: permit, allow, authorize, approve.

sanc·tu·ar·y [SANK-choo-AIR-ee] NOUN, sanc-tuaries. **1. sanctuaire ▸** a holy or sacred place. **2. refuge ▸** a refuge; safety or protection : *The refugee asked Canada for sanctuary.* **3. ré-serve ▸** a natural area where wild animals are protected : *a bird sanctuary.*

✐ Writing Tips

Salutation

*A salutation is a greeting such as "Hello"
or "Good Evening." In letters, the salutation
comes just before the body of the
letter.*

• *A salutation begins with a capital letter:
"Dear Karin" or "Friends."*

• *In business letters and other formal
letters, the salutation is punctuated by a
colon: "Dear Ms. Medieros:" or "Dear Sir
or Madam:". For friendly letters you can
use a comma: "Dear Grandma," or "Hello
Tomas,".*

sand [sand] NOUN, sands. **sable ▸** loose, tiny grains of crushed or worn rock, often found in the desert or at the seashore. Sand is used to make products such as glass, cement, bricks, and sandpaper. ▲ VERB, sanded, sanding. **1. sabler ▸** to smooth or polish with sandpaper : *The carpenter sanded the desk before painting it.* **2. sabler ▸** to sprinkle or spread over with sand : *The icy roads were sanded to keep cars from skidding.*

san-dal [SAN-dul] NOUN, sandals. **sandale ▸** an open shoe made up of a sole that is attached to the foot by straps or ties.

sand-bar [SAND-bar] NOUN, sandbars. **barre de sable ▸** a shallow place in a body of water, where sand has built up to form a ridge.

sand-pa-per [SAND-pay-pur] NOUN, sandpapers. **papier de verre ▸** heavy paper that is coated with sand or other rough material, used to smooth surfaces. ▲ VERB, sandpapered, sandpapering: *Jana sandpapered the old paint off the table.*

sand-pi-per [SAND-py-pur] NOUN, sandpipers. **bécasseau ▸** a small bird with a long, pointed bill, long legs, and brown or grey speckled feathers. Sandpipers live near the shore.

sand-wich [SAND-wich (es)] NOUN, sandwiches. **sandwich (s) ▸** slices of bread with a filling between them, such as meat, cheese, or peanut butter and jam. ▲ VERB, sandwiched, sandwiching. **serrer entre, coincer entre ▸** to squeeze or fit tightly between two things : *I sandwiched myself between Dean and José to watch the game.*

sand-y [SAN-dee] ADJECTIVE, sandier, sandiest. **1. sablonneux (-euse) ▸** like or covered with sand : *a sandy beach.* **2. blond roux ▸** light tan or reddish-blond colour : *sandy hair.*

sane [sane] ADJECTIVE, saner, sanest. **1. sain (saine) d'esprit ▸** having a mind that is healthy or normal; not crazy. **2. sensé (-ée) ▸** showing good sense : *a sane approach to exercise.* **Note.** The fact of having a healthy mind or behaviour is sanity.

sang [sang] VERB. a past form of sing.

san-i-tar-y [SAN-ih-TAIR-ee] ADJECTIVE. **sanitaire ▸** mostly clean and free of germs : *The drinking glasses were covered with a sanitary wrapper.* SYN: antiseptic, germ-free, sterile, clean.

san-i-ta-tion [san-ih-TAY-shun] NOUN. **système sanitaire, hygiène publique ▸** the protection of the public health by doing such things as collecting garbage, providing safe drinking water, and building sewer systems.

sank [sank] VERB. ▸ a past form of sink.

San-ta Claus [SAN-tuh KLOZ] **le Père Noël, Saint-Nicolas ▸** a man who represents the spirit of Christmas and who leaves presents for children on Christmas Eve.

sap[1] [sap] NOUN, saps. **sève ▸** the liquid that flows through plants, carrying food and other materials : *Sap from maple trees makes maple syrup.*

sap[2] VERB, sapped, sapping. **saper ▸** to weaken by draining away; cause to lose power or energy. SYN: weaken, drain, deplete.

sap-phire [SAF-ire] NOUN, sapphires. **1. (de) saphir ▸** a clear blue gemstone. **2. saphir ▸** a blue colour.

sar-cas-tic [sar-CAS-tik] ADJECTIVE. **sarcastique ▸** using sharp, hurtful remarks, tone of voice, or expressions to insult or make fun of someone. ■ **sarcastically**, ADVERB. ▸ **sarcastiquement.** *"I hope you had a nice nap," she said sarcastically after cleaning the kitchen with no help.* ■ **sarcasm**, NOUN. ▸ **sarcasme.** SYN: biting, bitter, cutting, sneering, sharp.

sar-dine [sar-DEEN] NOUN, sardines or sardine. **sardine ▸** a small herring or similar fish eaten as food, often packed tightly in oil in small, flat cans. **Note.** The expression like sardines is used when things are crowded very tightly, like sardines in a tin : *Fans packed the gym like sardines.*

sa-ri [SAR-ee] NOUN, saris. **sari ▸** a length of cotton or silk material wrapped around the body, as in the traditional outer clothing of Hindu women.

sash[1] [sash] NOUN, sashes. **écharpe, ceinture (d'étoffe) ▸** a length of cloth or ribbon worn around the waist or over a shoulder.

sash[2] NOUN, sashes. **châssis ▸** a frame into which the glass of a window or door is fitted.

sas-ka-toon [SAS-kuh-TOON] NOUN. saskatoons. **1. amélanchier de Saskatoon ▸** a small bush or tree that has large, sweet fruit. **2. baie de Saskatoon ▸** the fruit of this tree. **Note.** This name comes from the Cree word for "fruit from the tree of many branches."

Sas-quatch [SAS-kwotch] NOUN. **Sasquatch ▸** a large, hairy, humanlike creature thought to live in the mountains of the Pacific Northwest. **Note.** Also known as Bigfoot.

sat [sat] VERB. a past form of sit.

sat-el-lite [SAT-ih-lite] NOUN, satellites. **1. satellite ▸** a natural body that revolves around a planet or another larger body in space : *The moon is a satellite of the earth.* **2. satellite ▸** an artificial body put into orbit from earth to collect information, transmit radio and TV signals, and so on. **3. satellite ▸** a country or organization that is controlled by another : *Cuba was once a satellite of the Soviet Union.* 👁 p. 391, 540.

sat-in [SAT-un] NOUN. **satin ▸** a smooth, shiny fabric made of silk or other material. **Note.** Also used as an ADJECTIVE: *satin pyjamas.*

sat·ire [SAT-ire] NOUN. satires. **satire** ▸ a written work that uses humour to show the foolishness or evil of a well-known custom or idea : *This play is a satire on the government's social policy.* **Note.** A person who writes or creates a satire is a satirist.

sat·is·fac·tion [SAT-is-FAK-shun] NOUN. **satisfaction** ▸ the state of being satisfied, or something that causes this : *I feel satisfaction after reading a good book.* SYN: pleasure, comfort, enjoyment.

sat·is·fac·tory [SAT-iss-FAK-tur-ee] ADJECTIVE. 1. **satisfaisant (-ante)** ▸ giving satisfaction : *Mika had a satisfactory excuse for her behaviour.* 2. **satisfaisant** ▸ good enough but not outstanding; adequate : *Rico's mark in math is only satisfactory.* ▪ **satisfactorily,** ADVERB. ▸ de manière satisfaisante.

sat·is·fy [SAT-iss-fy] VERB. satisfied, satisfying. 1. **satisfaire** ▸ to get what is wanted to fill a need or a desire; to be pleased : *Nori worked hard to satisfy her track coach.* 2. **satisfaire** ▸ to free from doubt; convince : *I had to look twice to satisfy myself that my wallet was in my bag.* SYN: please, content, fulfill, gratify. 🖋 **p. 447.**

sat·u·rate [SACH-uh-RATE] VERB. saturated, saturating. **saturer** ▸ to make as wet as possible; soak :*"He squirmed over the wet moss, saturating his clothes and chilling his body."* (Jack London) ▪ **saturation,** NOUN. ▸ saturation.

Sat·ur·day [SAT-ur-DAY] NOUN. Saturdays. **samedi** ▸ the day after Friday and before Sunday.

Sat·urn [SAT-urn] NOUN. 1. **Saturne** ▸ the second-largest planet in the solar system, and the sixth-closest to the sun. Saturn is surrounded by large rings made up of particles of ice and water. 2. **Saturne** ▸ in the religion of the ancient Romans, the god of agriculture. 👁 **p. 391.**

sauce [soss] NOUN. sauces. **sauce** ▸ a liquid mixture used to add flavour to foods, usually poured or spooned on top of the food when it is served. **Note.** Sauce comes from the Latin *sal,* meaning "salt." *Sausage, salami,* and *salad* also come from *sal.* 🏳 **p. 1140.**

sau·cer [SAH-sur] NOUN. saucers. **soucoupe** ▸ a small shallow dish used to hold a cup.

saun·ter [SON-tur] VERB. sauntered, sauntering. **se balader, se promener** ▸ to walk at a slow, easy pace. SYN: ramble, stroll, wander.

sau·sage [SOS-ij] NOUN. sausages. **saucisse** ▸ chopped meat that is mixed with spices and then stuffed into a thin covering and shaped like a tube. **Note.** Salami is a kind of sausage made of pork or beef.

sav·age [SAV-ij] ADJECTIVE. 1. **féroce, violent (-ente)** ▸ acting in a violent way; cruel or fierce : *The savage storm blew the tree down.* 2. **sauvage** ▸ not tamed; wild : *a savage animal, such as the tiger.* ▲ NOUN, savages. 1. **primitif** ▸ an uncivilized person. 2. **sauvage** ▸ a cruel, violent person. ▪ **savagely,** ADVERB. ▸ **sauvagement.** ▪ **savagery,** NOUN. ▸ sauvagerie.

save [save] VERB. saved, saving. 1. **sauver** ▸ to make free from harm or danger; make safe : *The dog saved the child from drowning.* 2. **économiser** ▸ to put away for later use : *saving for a vacation.* 3. **épargner** ▸ to keep from wasting or losing something : *A dishwasher saves me time.* ▲ NOUN, saves. **arrêter un but** ▸ a play in hockey or soccer in which the goalie prevents a goal from being scored. ▲ PREPOSITION. **sauf, à l'exception de** ▸ except for; but : *The whole family was there save my oldest sister.*

sav·ings [SAVE-ings] PLURAL NOUN. **épargnes, économies** ▸ money that is saved : *to keep savings in a bank.*

sav·iour [SAVE-yur] NOUN. saviours. (also savior) 1. **sauveur** ▸ a person who saves another or others from harm. 2. **Saviour. Sauveur** ▸ a name for Jesus Christ.

sa·vour [SAY-vur] VERB. (also savor) savoured, savouring. **savourer** ▸ to enjoy in an intense way; take great pleasure in : *Trina savoured the last days of summer.* ▪ **savoury,** ADJECTIVE. ▸ **succulent (-ente), savoureux (-euse), appétissant (-ante).** *Dinner was a savoury stew.*

saw[1] [sah] VERB. a past form of see. 🖋 **p. 516.**

saw[2] NOUN. saws. **scie** ▸ a tool having a thin, flat blade with V-shaped teeth on one edge, used for cutting wood and other hard materials. ▲ VERB. sawed, sawed or sawn, sawing. **scier** ▸ to cut with a saw.

saw·dust [SAH-DUST] NOUN. **sciure, brin de scie** ▸ fine grains or dust that come from wood that has been sawed.

🖋 Writing Tips

Saw/Seen

*The difference between the two words **seen** and **saw** may seem obvious, but many people confuse them. **Seen** and **saw** are both past forms of **see**, but they are not interchangeable.*

- *Saw is the form of the past tense that can be used on its own.*

  I know he was at the baseball tryouts.
  I saw him there myself.

- *Seen must be used with a form of be or have.*

  She's a Jay's fan; she'd never be seen in an Expo cap.

saw-mill [SAH-MILL] NOUN, sawmills. **scierie** ▶ a place where logs are sawed into lumber.

sax-o-phone [SAKS-uh-FONE] NOUN, saxophones. **saxophone** ▶ a musical instrument that has a curved metal body shaped something like the letter "J." Notes are played by blowing through a mouthpiece and pressing keys. ◉ **p. 539.**

say [say] VERB, said, saying. **1. dire** ▶ to speak words out loud : *to say "goodbye."* **2. dire** ▶ to make known in words; express : *He says he left the key in the car.* **3. dire** ▶ to guess or assume : *Let's say the others aren't coming.* ▲ NOUN, says. **avoir droit au chapitre** ▶ a chance to speak : *The other candidate got her say at the next meeting.* SYN : speak, tell, declare, utter, state.

say-ing [SAY-ing] NOUN, sayings. **expression, dicton, proverbe** ▶ a well-known phrase or expression containing some statement of common sense or wisdom, such as "A stitch in time saves nine."

go without saying **il va sans dire** ▶ something completely understood; obvious : *It goes without saying that our team is best.*

scab [skab] NOUN, scabs. **croûte, gale** ▶ a crust that forms over a cut or scrape on the skin to protect it as it heals.

scaf-fold [SKAF-old *or* SKAF-uld] NOUN, scaffolds. **échafaud** ▶ a platform used to support people working in a high place, such as a building.

scale[1] [skale] NOUN, scales. **1. écaille** ▶ one of the thin, hard plates that cover the body of animals, such as fish, lizards, and snakes. **2. écaillure, écaille** ▶ any plate-like piece that comes off a surface : *The paint peeled off in scales.* ▲ VERB, scaled, scaling. **écailler** ▶ to remove scales from : *We scaled the fish before cooking it.*

scale[2] [skale] NOUN, scales. **balance** ▶ a device used to find the mass of something. A scale works by balancing an object against an object whose mass is known or against the force of a spring.

scale[3] [skale] NOUN, scales. **1. graduation** ▶ a series of marks or numbers evenly spaced out a line used for measuring, as on a thermometer or a ruler. **2. échelle** ▶ a series of steps or stages; a range : *the pay scale for a job.* **3. échelle** ▶ an exact way of comparing the size of a plan, model, or map of something with the original : *The scale for this map is one centimetre equals one kilometre.* **4. gamme** ▶ in music, a series of notes that go up higher or lower in pitch in equal steps. A scale is usually made up of eight notes that form an octave. ▲ VERB, scaled, scaling. **1. escalader** ▶ to climb up : *He tried to scale the rock, but it was too slippery.* **2. reproduire à l'échelle** ▶ to make larger or smaller according to a certain measurement : *to scale down a sewing pattern for a smaller person.*

sca-lene [SKAY-leen] ADJECTIVE. **scalène** ▶ in geometry, having three unequal sides : *a scalene triangle.*

scal-lion [SKAL-yun] NOUN, scallions. **échalote** ▶ a mild-flavoured onion that is long and narrow, with a small white bulb and a green top.

scal-lop [SKAL-up *or* SKOL-up] NOUN, scallops. **1. coquille Saint-Jacques, pétoncle** ▶ a shellfish with a soft body in a double fan-shaped shell with grooves that form wavy edges. The body of the scallop is used for food. **2. festonné (-ée), ondoyant (-ante), ondulé (-ée), ondulatoire** ▶ a wavy shape, like the edge of a scallop : *The skirt has scallops around the hem.* ▲ VERB, scalloped, scalloping. **festonner, ondoyer, onduler** ▶ to make a wavy edge. **Note.** Also used as an adjective : *She made scalloped potatoes by alternating sliced potatoes with onion and cheese.*

scalp [skalp] NOUN, scalps. **cuir chevelu** ▶ the skin covering the area at the top of the head.

scam-per [SKAM-pur] VERB, scampered, scampering. **gambader, trottiner** ▶ to run or hop quickly; scurry : *The chipmunk scampered into the bushes.*

scan [skan] VERB, scanned, scanning. **1. parcourir, feuilleter** ▶ to read over quickly : *to scan the dictionary for a word.* **2. scruter, examiner** ▶ to look at carefully; examine closely : *Orma scanned the crowd for her brother.* **3. balayer** ▶ to use a special machine to check for certain information : *Airline passengers are scanned by metal detectors.* **Note.** A machine that does this is a scanner. ▲ NOUN, scans. **lecture au scanner, examen au scanner** ▶ the act or fact of scanning : *A brain scan shows if a brain has an injury or disease.* SYN : examine, inspect, look at, study, review.

scan-dal [SKAN-dul] NOUN, scandals. **scandale** ▶ something that shocks people and makes them feel that a serious wrong has happened; a disgrace : *Cuts to hospital funding are a scandal.* **Note.** Something that causes a scandal is **scandalous**. SYN : disgrace, humiliation, shame, offence.

scant [skant] ADJECTIVE. **insuffisant (-ante), peu abondant (-ante)** ▶ not quite enough or just barely enough : *Gasoline was in scant supply during World War II.* ■ **scanty,** ADJECTIVE. ▶ **minuscule, insuffisant (-ante).** *The scanty supply of wood barely kept us warm.*

scar [skar] NOUN, scars. **1. cicatrice** ▶ a mark that is left when skin has healed from a cut or other injury. **2. cicatrice** ▶ any such mark or sign of damage : *The buildings showed the scars of a fire.* ▲ VERB, scarred, scarring. **marquer d'une cicatrice** ▶ to form or cause a scar.

scarce [skairce] ADJECTIVE, scarcer, scarcest. **rare** ▶ difficult to find; hard to get; rare : *Gold is* *expensive because it is scarce.* ■ **scarcity,** NOUN. ▶ **rareté.**

scarce-ly [SKAIRCE-lee] ADVERB. **1. à peine, très peu** ▶ almost not; barely : *The kitten scarcely made a sound.* **2. sûrement pas** ▶ definitely not; hardly : *You can scarcely expect the little girl to walk home alone.*

scare [skair] VERB, scared, scaring. **faire peur, épeurer, effrayer** ▶ to cause fear; make afraid; frighten : *He was scared by a siren in the middle of the night.* ▲ NOUN, scares. **peur** ▶ something that causes fear : *The growling dogs gave the children a scare.* ✐ p. 239.

scare-crow [SKAIR-crow] NOUN, scarecrows. **épouvantail** ▶ a straw figure dressed up like a person to scare birds away from a field or garden.

scarf [skarf] NOUN, scarves or scarfs. **foulard, écharpe** ▶ a piece of cloth worn on the head or around the neck or shoulders. ☞ p. 1013.

scar-let [SKAR-lit] NOUN, scarlets. **écarlate** ▶ a bright red colour. ▲ ADJECTIVE: *a scarlet dress.*

scar-y [SKAIR-ee] ADJECTIVE, scarier, scariest. **terrifiant (-ante), effrayant (-ante)** ▶ causing fear or panic; frightening : *a scary movie about creatures from another planet.*

scat-ter [SKAT-tur] VERB, scattered, scattering. **éparpiller, (se) disperser** ▶ to go or cause to go in different directions; separate : *The wind scattered leaves over the yard.*

scav-en-ger [SKAV-un-jur] NOUN, scavengers. **1. charognard** ▶ an animal, such as a coyote or vulture, that feeds on the remains of dead animals. **2. fouilleur (-euse) d'ordures** ▶ a person who looks through garbage for useful objects that have been thrown away. ▲ VERB, scavenged, scavenging: *The children scavenged the garage for old wood to build their clubhouse.*

scene [seen] NOUN, scenes. **1. scène** ▶ the place where something happens : *the scene of a crime.* **2. scène** ▶ one part of a play or movie : *Remember the scene in Jurassic Park where the dinosaur sneezes?* **3. tableau (-eaux)** ▶ the view of a certain place or area : *The artist painted sunset scenes of the ocean.* **4. scène** ▶ a public show of anger or strong feelings : *The boy made a scene when his mother wouldn't buy the toy.*

sce-ne-ry [SEE-nuh-ree or SEEN-ree] NOUN. **1. paysage** ▶ the general way a place looks, especially an outdoor scene : *Banff National Park is famous for its beautiful scenery.* **2. décor** ▶ in a play or movie, the painted walls and decorations that give an idea of the place where the action is happening.

scent [sent] NOUN, scents. **1. senteur, odeur** ▶ the smell of something : *the scent of a wood fire.* **2. odorat** ▶ an animal's sense of smell. **3. parfum** ▶ a pleasant smell; perfume. ▲ VERB,

scented, scenting. **1. flairer, sentir** ▶ to know or sense by scent; smell. **2. parfumer** ▶ to fill with a certain smell : *Apple blossoms scented the air.* SYN: smell, odour, aroma.

sched-ule [SKEJ-yool or SHEJ-yool] NOUN, schedules. **1. horaire, plan** ▶ a record or list of events according to the times they happen : *Check the schedule to find out when the train leaves.* **2. à l'heure, à temps** ▶ the normal or expected time for something to happen : *The new store opened on schedule.* ▲ VERB, scheduled, scheduling. **planifier** ▶ to place or be on a schedule : *I scheduled my vacation for the summer.*

scheme [skeem] NOUN, schemes. **1. plan, projet** ▶ a plan of doing something; an idea : *Lara has a scheme to build a time machine.* **2. combine, astuce, complot** ▶ a secret plan to do something wrong or bad : *a scheme to steal computers.* **3. arrangement, classification** ▶ an arrangement of things in an orderly or pleasing way : *a colour scheme.* ▲ VERB, schemed, scheming. **conspirer, comploter** ▶ to make up a scheme; to plot. ■ **schemer,** NOUN. ▶ **intrigant (-ante).** SYN: plan, plot, intrigue, design.

schol-ar [SKOL-ur] NOUN, scholars. **1. érudit (-ite), savant (-ante)** ▶ a person who has great knowledge from study. **2. étudiant (-ante)** ▶ an old word for student. ■ **scholarly,** ADJECTIVE. ▶ **érudit (-ite), savant (-ante), instruit (-uite).**

schol-ar-ship [SKOL-ur-ship] NOUN. **1. bourse** (plural, scholarships) money given to a student to help pay the cost of studies. **2. érudition** ▶ the practice of gaining knowledge or learning.

scho-las-tic [shuh-LAS-tik] ADJECTIVE. **scolaire** ▶ having to do with students or with school : *She is proud of her scholastic record.*

school[1] [skool] NOUN, schools. **1. école** ▶ a place that holds regular classes for learning and teaching. **2. école** ▶ the period of time that a person spends in such a place : *Meet me after school.* **3. école** ▶ the students, teachers, and staff of a school. **Note.** This word is often used to form compounds such as schoolteacher, schoolbook, schoolmate, schoolwork. ▲ VERB, schooled, schooling. **enseigner, entraîner** ▶ to train or teach : *Naveen schooled his dog to obey commands.* ☞ p. 1061.

school[2] NOUN, schools. **banc de poissons** ▶ a large group of fish or other water animals of the same kind swimming together : *We saw a school of bass in the bay.*

schoon-er [SKOO-nur] NOUN, schooners. **goélette** ▶ a ship that has the masts and sails arranged so that the sails stretch along the length of the ship, rather than across from side to side.

sci-ence [SY-uns] NOUN, sciences. **1. science** ▶ a body of knowledge that results from the study of things in nature and in the universe, along with the forces that affect these things. **2.** science ▸ a particular area of science, such as biology, chemistry, or physics. **3.** science ▸ something thought of as like a science : *The great baseball player Ted Williams wrote a book called* The Science of Hitting.

sci·en·tif·ic [SY-un-TIF-ik] ADJECTIVE. **1.** scientifique ▸ having to do with science : *scientific equipment.* **2.** scientifique ▸ showing or using the methods or rules of science : *a scientific approach.* ▪ **scientifically,** ADVERB. ▸ scientifiquement.

sci·en·tist [SY-un-tist] NOUN, scientists. scientifique ▸ a person who works in an area of science or who knows a great deal about science.

scis·sors [SIZ-urz] PLURAL NOUN. ciseaux ▸ a tool for cutting that is made up of two sharp blades that close against each other : *That pair of scissors is sharp, but our new scissors are even sharper.*

scold [skold] VERB, scolded, scolding. gronder, réprimander, reprocher ▸ to blame someone with angry words; find fault with : *He scolded his son for running into the street.* SYN: lecture, talk to, blame, reprimand, chide.

scoop [skoop] NOUN, scoops. cuiller, pelle ▸ a tool shaped like a bowl with a handle, used for shovelling or dipping. ▲ VERB, scooped, scooping. ramasser, pelleter ▸ to take something with or as if with a scoop : *Cora scooped ice cream into the bowls.*

scope [skope] NOUN. limites, ampleur ▸ the area covered by an idea or action : *The scope of Matt's knowledge of insects is wide.* SYN: extent, degree, range, reach.

scorch [skorch] VERB, scorched, scorching. brûler légèrement ▸ to burn just slightly on the surface : *The iron was too hot, and it scorched Gino's shirt.* ▪ **scorching,** ADJECTIVE. brûlant (-ante) ▸ very hot : *the scorching sun.* ▲ NOUN, scorches. a slight burn; a surface burn.

score [skor] NOUN, scores. **1.** score, marque ▸ a group of numbers or points used to show how one person or thing compares with others in a game, contest, or test : *Our team won the game by a score of 3 to 1.* **2.** partition ▸ written music that shows the parts for the musicians. **3.** des comptes à régler ▸ a wrong or injury that must be taken care of : *They had a score to settle with the other team.* **4.** (plural) vingtaine ▸ an older word for a group of 20 : *Four score means four 20s, or 80.* **5.** scores. masse, foule ▸ a large number; a crowd : *On opening night, scores of people stood in line for the movie.* ▲ VERB, scored, scoring. **1.** marquer ▸ to have or record a certain score : *Katie scored perfect on her math exam.* **2.** graver, incruster ▸ to cut lines or make scratch marks on something : *Mom scores the roast so that the spices soak in.*

know the score comprendre, connaître la situation ▸ to understand what is happening : *After the argument, he knew the score when the others ignored him.*

scorn [skorn] NOUN. mépris ▸ a feeling that someone or something is very bad or of very low quality; a complete lack of respect : *She felt our scorn after she was caught cheating.* ▲ VERB, scorned, scorning. mépriser, dédaigner ▸ to treat with scorn; look down on. ▪ **scornful,** ADJECTIVE. ▸ méprisant (-ante). ▪ **scornfully,** ADVERB. ▸ avec mépris.

scor·pi·on [SKOR-pee-un] NOUN, sorpions. scorpions ▸ a small animal related to the spider. Scorpions live a long tail with a poisonous stinger, a jointed body, and gripping claws attached to the head. They live mainly in hot, dry areas, such as Mexico and the southwestern U.S., but can also be found in Alberta and British Columbia.

scour¹ [skowr] VERB, scoured, scouring. récurer ▸ to polish or clean by scrubbing : *Dad scoured the dirty frying pan with steel wool.*

scour² VERB, scoured, scouring. fouiller ▸ to search thoroughly : *We scoured the woods for our dog.*

scout [skowt] NOUN, scouts. **1.** éclaireur (-euse) ▸ a military person sent out to get information, such as the location of the enemy. **2.** dénicheur (-euse) de talents ▸ a person who seeks out new information in sports or entertainment, such as finding talented new people or players or the strategy of opposing teams : *The actor heard that a scout from Hollywood was in the audience.* **3.** scout ▸ a member of the Scouts, a program for young people aged 11–14. ▲ VERB, scouted, scouting. aller en reconnaissance ▸ to act as a scout : *Baseball teams often send someone to scout the team they will be playing next.*

scowl [skowl] NOUN, scowls. air renfrogné, air de mauvaise humeur ▸ an angry expression; a deep frown. ▲ VERB, scowled, scowling. froncer les sourcils ▸ to make an angry expression : *The baby cried when her brother scowled at her.*

scram·ble [SKRAM-bul] VERB, scrambled, scrambling. **1.** grimper à quatre pattes ▸ to move quickly by climbing or crawling : *The mouse scrambled under the cupboard.* **2.** (se) bousculer ▸ to struggle to get something first : *The children scrambled to the doors.* **3.** brouiller, brasser, mélanger ▸ to mix or stir things together : *Bill scrambled up the cards during the magic trick.* **4.** brouiller ▸ to cook eggs by stirring them together in a frying pan, blending the yolks and whites. ▲ NOUN. ruée, bousculade ▸ the act or fact of scrambling : *There was a scramble for the last cookie.* SYN: hurry, scurry, rush.

scrap [skrap] NOUN, scraps. **1. bout, morceau (-eaux) ▸** a small piece or amount; a bit : *a scrap of paper.* **2. ferraille ▸** something that is thrown away but may be used by someone else; a used item : *The metal in my old car can be sold for scrap.* **3. scraps. restes, restants ▸** bits of left-over food from a meal : *to feed a dog scraps.* **4.** *Informal.* **querelle, bagarre, ▸** a fight or quarrel. ▲ VERB, scrapped, scrapping. **1. mettre au rebut, jeter au rancart ▸** to break up for use as scrap : *The old airplanes were scrapped.* **2. mettre aux oubliettes, laisser tomber ▸** give up something as useless or unwanted : *Let's scrap that idea and start over.* SYN: bit, piece, portion, fragment, morsel.

scrap-book [SKRAP-book] NOUN, scrapbooks. **album (de coupures, etc.) ▸** a book with blank pages to which newspaper clippings, photos, and other items can be attached.

scrape [skrape] VERB, scraped, scraping. **1. érafler ▸** to damage or remove the surface of something by rubbing or scratching it : *I scraped my knee when I fell.* **2. racler, gratter ▸** to make a harsh, unpleasant sound by rubbing or dragging something over a surface : *chalk scraping on a chalkboard.* **3. frotter, gratter ▸** to clean or smooth a surface by rubbing it against something : *Scrape the mud off your shoes before coming inside.* **4. rassembler, réunir ▸** to gather or collect something with difficulty : *Jonah scraped together the money to buy a bike.* ▲ NOUN, scrapes. **1. grattement, éraflure, égratignure ▸** the act of scraping, or the damage caused by this. **2.** *Informal.* **pétrin ▸** a bad situation; a problem : *Pilar's quick thinking got us out of a scrape.* **Note.** A scraper is a tool that scrapes off paint or smooths a surface.

scratch [skrach] VERB, scratched, scratching. **1. égratigner ▸** to cut, dig, or scrape a shallow mark with a sharp object : *The cat scratched Larissa's arm with its claws.* **2. (se) gratter ▸** to rub or scrape the skin when it itches : *Don't scratch a mosquito bite; it might get worse.* **3. gratter, érafler ▸** to make a sound when rubbing or scraping something : *A branch scratched against the car.* **4. retirer ▸** to remove or cancel : *Horst was scratched from the race when he pulled a muscle.* ▲ NOUN, scratches. **grattement, éraflure ▸** a mark or sound made by scratching. ■ **scratchy,** ADJECTIVE. ▸ rugueux (-euse).

from scratch **partir de zéro, de rien ▸** from nothing; starting at the beginning : *My grandmother makes cake from scratch, not from a mix.*

scrawl [skrol] VERB, scrawled, scrawling. **griffonner ▸** to write in a messy or hurried way : *Tony quickly scrawled a message.* ▲ NOUN, scrawls. **gribouillage ▸** messy writing or drawing.

scraw-ny [SKRAH-nee] ADJECTIVE, scrawnier, scrawniest. **très maigre ▸** very thin; bony; skinny.

scream [skreem] VERB, screamed, screaming. **pousser un cri, crier, hurler ▸** to cry out with a sudden, loud, and high-pitched sound, usually in fright or in pain. ▲ NOUN, screams. **cri perçant ▸** a sudden, loud sound or cry. SYN: yell, cry, shout, shriek.

screech [skreech] VERB, screeched, screeching. **crisser, pousser des cris perçants ▸** to make a loud, high, shrill sound : *car brakes screeching to a stop.* ▲ NOUN, screeches: *the screech of monkeys in a jungle.*

screen [skreen] NOUN, screens. **1. moustiquaire ▸** a frame holding wire netting, placed in a window or door to allow air in but keep insects out. **2. grillage, grille, écran de cheminée ▸** a similar pattern of wire used to cover or protect something : *Close the screen on the fireplace to keep sparks from flying out.* **3. paravent ▸** a curtain, wall, or frame used to separate or hide part of a room : *He closed the screen for privacy in the voting booth.* **4. écran ▸** anything that acts like a screen to cover or hide something : *A thick screen of fog hid the houses.* **5. écran ▸** a flat surface that reflects light, used to show movies or slides. **6. écran ▸** the surface on which images from a movie, television, or computer appear. ▲ VERB, screened, screening. **1. cacher, abriter ▸** to protect, hide, or shade with a screen : *We screened our porch.* **2. filtrer ▸** to go through carefully to separate, as if sifting through a wire screen : *The secretary screens phone calls for the president of the company.*

screw [skrew] NOUN, screws. **vis ▸** a type of nail with a ridge that winds around its length. It is twisted into things to hold them together. **Note.** A screw is usually turned by a tool called a screwdriver. ▲ VERB, screwed, screwing. **1. visser ▸** to join materials together with a screw. **2. visser ▸** to tighten something with a twist or turn : *Ella screwed the lid onto the jar.*

scrib-ble [SKRIB-ul] VERB, scribbled, scribbling. **griffonner, gribouiller, barbouiller ▸** to draw or write in a quick, sloppy way. ▲ NOUN, scribbles: *Jim put scribbles on his book.*

scribe [skribe] NOUN, scribes. **scribe ▸** in earlier times, a person who wrote or copied books and other writing by hand.

scrim-mage [SKRIM-ij] NOUN, scrimmages. **1. mêlée, cohue ▸** a rough fight or struggle. **2. mêlée ▸** in sports, a practice game. **Note.** The line of scrimmage in football is the imaginary line that separates the two teams as they line up before a play.

script [skript] NOUN, scripts. **1. écriture script ▸** a type of handwriting in which the letters are connected, not separated as in printing.

2. scénario, texte ▶ the written lines of a play, movie, television show, or other such spoken performance.

Scrip-ture [SKRIP-chur] NOUN, Scriptures. **1.** (also [the] Scriptures) **Écriture sainte ▶** the Bible or a passage from the Bible. **2.** scripture. **écriture(s) ▶** a holy book of a religion.

scroll [skrole] NOUN, scrolls. **parchemin, rouleau (-eaux) ▶** a written piece of paper or parchment that is rolled up. ▲ VERB, scrolled, scrolling. **défiler ▶** in a computer, using the controls to view different areas of a document.

scrub¹ [skrub] VERB, scrubbed, scrubbing. **frotter (à la brosse), récurer ▶** to rub hard or roughly, as in cleaning or drying something : *Hans had to scrub the pan to get the burned food off.* ▲ NOUN. **récurage ▶** the act of scrubbing : *to give the floor a good scrub.*

scrub² NOUN. **broussailles ▶** low-growing trees or shrubs.

scruff [skruf] NOUN, scruffs. **peau (du cou) ▶** the back part of the neck, or the loose skin that covers it : *The dog picked her newborn puppy up by the scruff.*

scru-pu-lous [SKROO-pyuh-lus] ADJECTIVE. **scrupuleux (-euse) ▶** following what is right or what should be done ; taking care ; honest : *Clara was scrupulous in following the directions.* **■ scrupulously,** ADVERB. **▶ scrupuleusement.** SYN: strict, careful, precise, exacting, fussy.

scu-ba [SKOO-buh] NOUN. **scuba ▶** the special air tanks worn by swimmers for breathing under water. **Note.** The sport of doing this is scuba diving. **Note.** The word *scuba* started out as an acronym for *self-contained underwater breathing apparatus.*

souff [skuf] VERB, scuffed, scuffing. **érafler, rayer ▶** to scrape or scratch a surface : *Stavros scuffed his new shoes playing soccer.*

scuf-fle [SKUF-ul] NOUN, scuffles. **chamaillerie, bagarre, querelle, dispute ▶** a sudden, confused fight or struggle, usually not long or serious : *There was a scuffle when the candy in the dish fell to the ground.* ▲ VERB, scuffled, scuffling. **(se) chamailler ▶** to fight or struggle in this way.

sculp-tor [SKULP-tur] NOUN, sculptors. **sculpteur (-eure) ▶** an artist who makes sculptures. 📖 **p. 1127.**

sculp-ture [SKULP-chur] NOUN, sculptures. **1. sculpture ▶** the art of making figures or designs out of stone, wood, metal, or other such materials. Sculpture is made by carving, moulding, or changing the shape of a material into artwork. **2. sculpture ▶** artwork made in this way. ▲ VERB, sculptured, sculpturing. **sculpter ▶** to make figures or designs out of materials ; to shape : *Moosa sculpted the clay into a horse.* 📖 **p. 1123.**

scum [skum] NOUN. **écume ▶** a thin layer of material that rises to, or forms on, the surface of a liquid : *In the summer, scum forms around the edge of a pond.*

scur-ry [SKUR-ee] VERB, scurried, scurrying. **se précipiter, détaler ▶** to move or run quickly ; hurry : *Their father's call made them scurry down to breakfast.*

scur-vy [SKUR-vee] NOUN. **scorbut ▶** a disease caused by not having enough vitamin C which causes swollen and bleeding gums and weakness. In former times, sailors on long sea voyages sometimes died from scurvy because they didn't have fruits and vegetables to eat.

scut-tle [SKUT-ul] VERB, scuttled, scuttling. **courir précipitamment ▶** to move with quick, short motions : *"A large grey rat scuttled around the corner of the house."* (Madeleine L'Engle)

sea [see] NOUN, seas. **1.** (also the sea) **mer ▶** a large body of salt water ; an ocean. **2. mer ▶** the name of certain parts of this area of water : *the Caribbean Sea.* **3. mer ▶** the waves or heavy swell of the ocean : *The fishing boat travelled in rough seas.* **4. mer ▶** a great number ; a huge amount : *a sea of faces.* **Note.** Used to form many compounds such as **seafood** (📖 p. 1140), seashore, seagull, sea water, and sea port. 📖 **p. 1109.**

sea a-nem-o-ne [uh-NEM-uh-nee] **actinie, anémone de mer ▶** a sea animal with a flexible body shaped like a tube and a mouth that is surrounded by many highly coloured, flowerlike tentacles.

sea horse hippocampe ▶ a type of fish with a head that looks something like a horse's head, and a curved tail with which it hangs on to ocean plants.

sea horses

sea level niveau de la mer ▶ a measurement of the surface of the sea that is taken halfway between high tide and low tide. **Note.** All measurements of the height of features of the earth are figured from sea level : *Death Valley has the lowest point below sea level in North America*

sea lion otarie ▶ a large seal that lives in the Pacific Ocean.

seal[1] [seel] NOUN, seals. phoque ▶ a large animal with flippers and sleek, shiny fur, found in cold ocean waters. Seals are mammals; they live mainly in the water and rest on land. ☜ **p. 110.**

seal[2] NOUN, seals. 1. sceau (-eaux) ▶ a design on a mould or stamp that is pressed into ink, wax, paper, or other material : *The queen put her seal on the treaty to show that it was official.* 2. sceau ▶ any similar design or mark of authority : *Each province or territory has an official seal.* 3. sceau ▶ something that keeps things tightly closed : *If the seal on a package of medicine is broken, don't buy that package.* ▲ VERB, sealed, sealing. 1. sceller ▶ to close or fasten tightly : *The plumber sealed the water pipe so that it would not leak.* 2. cacheter ▶ to put an official seal or stamp on.

seam [seem] NOUN, seams. 1. couture ▶ the line that is made when two pieces of cloth or other material are sewn together. 2. joint ▶ any line like this where two things or parts come together, as in the hull of a ship. 3. veine ▶ a line or layer of mineral in the earth : *a seam of coal.* ▲ VERB, seamed, seaming. faire une couture, coudre ▶ to join together in a seam; make a seam.

sea-plane [SEE-plane] NOUN, seaplanes. hydravion ▶ a plane that can take off from, or land on, the water.

search [surch] VERB, searched, searching. chercher, fouiller, rechercher ▶ to look carefully to find something; go over closely : *I searched my room for my shoe.* ▲ NOUN, searches. recherche ▶ the act or fact of searching. ■ **searcher**, NOUN, searchers. ▶ chercheur (-euse). SYN: look for, seek, hunt, rummage.

search-light [SURCH-LITE] NOUN, searchlights. projecteur ▶ a very large light that gives off a powerful beam, and that may be moved to shine in different directions to search or signal.

sea-sick [SEE-sik] ADJECTIVE. qui a le mal de mer ▶ ill and dizzy from the rocking motion of a ship at sea.

sea-son [SEE-zun] NOUN, seasons. 1. saison ▶ one of the four parts of the year; spring, summer, fall, or winter. 2. temps, saison ▶ a period of time thought of as a separate part of the year : *the holiday season.* ▲ VERB, seasoned, seasoning. assaisonner ▶ to add spices or flavouring to food : *Indira seasoned the rice with curry.* ■ **seasoning**, NOUN, seasonings. assaisonnement ▶ something that

adds flavour, such as salt, pepper, or garlic. ⏏ p. 1104.

sea-son-al [SEE-zun-ul] ADJECTIVE. saisonnier (-ière) ▶ having to do with the seasons of the year; a special season : *the seasonal migration of monarch butterflies.*

seat [seet] NOUN, seats. 1. siège ▶ a place to sit on, such as a chair or bench. 2. derrière, fond ▶ the part of the body that a person sits on, or the clothing that covers that part. 3. siège ▶ a position as a member of a group or organization : *My sister has a seat on the board of directors.* 4. haut lieu, siège ▶ a special place that is the centre of something : *Brasilia is the seat of government in Brazil.* ▲ VERB, seated, seating. 1. (faire) asseoir, asseoir, s'asseoir ▶ to be taken to, or placed on, a seat. 2. avoir une capacité, accueillir ▶ to have seats for : *The school auditorium seats 300 people.*

seat-belt [SEET-BELT] NOUN, seatbelts. ceinture de sécurité ▶ a strap or set of straps holding a person in place in the seat of a car, airplane, or other moving vehicle, to help prevent injury in the case of an accident or sudden stop. **Note.** Also called a safety belt.

sea-way [SEE-way] NOUN, seaways. route maritime, voie maritime ▶ a path for travelling over the sea; an inland water route that is connected to the ocean and where large ships may travel : *the Saint Lawrence Seaway.*

sea-weed [SEE-weed] NOUN, seaweeds. algue marine ▶ a general name for many kinds of plants that grow in the ocean. ☜ p. 250.

se-cede [suh-SEED] VERB, seceded, seceding. faire sécession, se séparer ▶ to withdraw officially from an organization : *In 1992, it looked as if Quebec would secede from Canada.* ■ **secession**, NOUN. sécession, séparation ▶ the act of seceding.

se-clude [sih-KLOO] VERB, secluded, secluding. 1. isoler, (se) retirer ▶ to keep apart from others; isolate : *When Terry had chicken pox, he was secluded from others.* 2. dissimuler, masquer ▶ to hide from view; screen. **Note.** Sometimes used as an adjective : *We found a secluded spot in the forest for our picnic.*

sec-ond[1] [SEK-und] ADJECTIVE. 1. deuxième, second (-onde) ▶ next after the first : *second place in a contest.* 2. deuxième, second (-onde) ▶ below the first or the best : *Mario was on the second team in football.* ▲ ADVERB. deuxième, en second ▶ coming after the first; next : *Lily will run second.* ▲ NOUN, seconds. 1. deuxième, second (-onde) ▶ a person or thing that is next. 2. second, assistant ▶ a person who helps or supports another. 3. seconds. deuxième assiettée ▶ an extra helping of food : *Would you like seconds?* ▲ VERB, seconded, seconding. appuyer ▶ in a meeting, to support a motion or nomination so that it can be voted on : *to second a motion.* ■ **secondly**, ADVERB. ▶ **deuxièmement.**

second² NOUN, seconds. **1. seconde** ▶ a small unit of time. Sixty seconds equal one minute. **2. seconde** ▶ any short period of time : *I'll be there in a second.* 🖉 p. 376. 🗂 p. 1081.

sec·ond·ar·y [SEK-un-DAIR-ee] ADJECTIVE. **1. secondaire** ▶ coming after the first; next in order, place, or time. **2. secondaire** ▶ not as important as the first or main thing : *Your excuses are secondary to the fact that you are late.*

secondary school école secondaire ▶ the school that students attend after elementary school and junior high school, and before college or university. **Note.** Also called **high school.**

sec·ond-hand [SEK-und-HAND] ADJECTIVE. **usagé (-ée), d'occasion** ▶ having been used before; owned first by another : *This secondhand shop sells old clothes.*

se·cre·cy [SEE-krih-see] NOUN. **secret** ▶ the fact of being secret or of keeping a secret : *The surprise party was organized in complete secrecy.* **Note.** A person who tries to keep things secret is **secretive.**

se·cret [SEE-krit] NOUN, secrets. **1. secret** ▶ information that is kept hidden and that is known only by one person or by a few. **2. secret** ▶ a hidden reason or cause : *The secret to her success is hard work.* ▲ ADJECTIVE. **secret (-ète)** ▶ known to only one person or a few; kept from most people : *I keep my diary in a secret place.* ■ **secretly**, ADVERB. ▶ **secrètement, en secret, dans le secret.** SYN: mystery, confidence.

sec·re·tar·y [SEK-ruh-TAIR-ee] NOUN, secretaries. **1. secrétaire** ▶ a person in business whose job is to assist another person by doing such work as typing letters, answering the telephone, keeping records. **Note.** Someone who does this job is also known as an **administrative assistant. 2. secrétaire** ▶ a person in a club or other organization who keeps the records of the group. **3. secrétaire** ▶ a piece of furniture with a surface to write on and drawers and shelves for papers and books. **Note.** The word *secretary* is related to the word *secret.* In early times, a secretary was a king's officer who dealt with secret papers and records. 🗂 p. 1061.

se·crete [suh-KREET] VERB, secreted, secreting. **sécréter** ▶ of an animal or plant, to give off a liquid from some part of the body : *to secrete tears.* ■ **secretion**, NOUN. ▶ **sécrétion.** SYN: produce, give off, discharge.

sect [sekt] NOUN, sects. **secte** ▶ a smaller group within a larger religion, with special customs or beliefs.

sec·tion [SEK-shun] NOUN, sections. **1. section** ▶ one part of a whole thing : *a section of a pie.* **2. section, partie** ▶ a part of something that is written : *Turn to the last section in your book.* ▲ VERB, sectioned, sectioning. **trancher, sectionner, diviser** ▶ to cut or separate into parts; divide : *She sectioned an orange.* ■ **sectional**, ADJECTIVE; NOUN. ▶ **démontable.**

sec·tor [SEK-tor] NOUN, sectors. **secteur** ▶ a section or area : *the business sector.*

sec·u·lar [SEK-yuh-lur] ADJECTIVE. **profane, laïque** ▶ having to do with matters of the earth and humankind, rather than with a god or gods and religion.

se·cure [sih-KYOOR] ADJECTIVE. **1. sûr (sûre), assuré (-ée)** ▶ safe or protected against danger or loss : *Many castles had high walls and moats to make them secure against attack.* **2. solide, ferme, sûr (sûre)** ▶ not likely to give way; firmly fastened; steady : *"Those roots held onto the only secure thing down there, the rocks."* (Teddy Jam) **3. en sécurité, sécurisant (-ante)** ▶ free from fear or worry : *Eleni feels secure when she is home.* ▲ VERB, secured, securing. **1. protéger (de), sécuriser** ▶ to make secure : *He secured the door with a padlock.* **2. assurer** ▶ to get, especially through some effort : *Your last goal secured the win.* SYN: safe, protected, sure, sound.

se·cu·ri·ty [sih-KYOOR-ih-tee] NOUN, securities. **1. sécurité, sûreté** ▶ the fact of being secure; protection against danger or loss : *For security, she always keeps some extra money in her pocket.* **2. sécurité** ▶ the fact of protecting against violence, crime, and so on : *There will be tight security when the Queen visits.* **Note.** Often used in compounds : *a security guard.* **3. caution, garantie** ▶ property that is offered to get a loan. **4. securities. investissement** ▶ stocks, bonds, or other investments.

se·dan [suh-DAN] NOUN, sedans. **berline** ▶ a car with two or four doors, a front seat and a back seat, a permanent roof, and a trunk.

sed·i·ment [SED-ih-munt] NOUN, sediments. **sédiment, dépôt** ▶ small pieces of matter that settle at the bottom of a liquid : *Sediment of dead leaves and sand lay at the bottom of the swimming pool.*

see [see] VERB, saw, seen, seeing. **1. voir** ▶ to sense with the eyes; look at : *I saw her walk past my house.* **2. voir** ▶ to be able to use this sense : *Preman sees much better with new glasses.* **3. voir, saisir, comprendre** ▶ to sense with the mind; understand; to know : *I see what you mean.* **4. voir** ▶ to find out : *See how you like this new CD.* **5. voir** ▶ to visit or meet : *I saw the doctor today.* **6. se voir, se fréquenter** ▶ to date or have a romance : *Darijan and Abel are seeing each other.* **7. s'assurer, s'occuper (de)** ▶ to make sure : *Please see that it doesn't happen again.* SYN: observe, notice, watch, look, view.

seed [seed] NOUN, seeds or seed. **1. germe** ▶ the part of a plant that can grow into a new plant. **2. graine** ▶ something thought of as being like a seed, because it is the source or beginning point : *a seed of doubt.* ▲ VERB, **seeded, seeding.** **1. semer, ensemencer** ▸ to plant land with seeds; sow : *Abou seeded his yard for a lawn.* **2. égrener** ▸ to remove seeds from : *Peel and seed six oranges for the salad.*

seek [seek] VERB, **sought, seeking.** **1. chercher, rechercher** ▸ to try to find; search for : *"It was hot enough now to make us seek the shade."* (Evelyn Waugh) **2. chercher à, tâcher de** ▸ to try to get or have : *"I must not tell you and you must never seek to know."* (Tololwa M. Mollel) **3. rechercher, demander** ▸ to ask for : *I seek your advice.* ■ **seeker,** NOUN. ▸ **chercheur (-euse).** *Newton was a seeker of scientific knowledge.* SYN : hunt, search, look for, scour.

seem [seem] VERB, **seemed, seeming.** **1. paraître, apparaître** ▸ to appear to be; look like : *Grandma seems younger than her age because she is so active.* **2. sembler** ▸ to appear to be true; appear to exist : *You seem to have trouble understanding me.* **3. sembler** ▸ to appear to oneself : *I seem to have forgotten my manners.* ■ **seemingly,** ADVERB. **apparemment** ▸ as far as one can tell; as it seems : *She was seemingly unhappy at the party.*

seen [seen] VERB. a past form of see. ✐ **p. 516.**

seep [seep] VERB, **seeped, seeping. suinter, filtrer** ▸ to spread or flow slowly : *Water seeped in through a crack in the lid.*

see-saw [SEE-saw] NOUN, **seesaws. 1. bascule** ▸ play equipment for children, made of a long board balanced in the middle so that when one end goes up, the other goes down. **2. basculement** ▸ a movement back and forth like that of a seesaw. ▲ VERB, **seesawed, seesawing. basculer** ▸ to move up and down, on or as if on, a seesaw : *The score seesawed during the game.*

seethe [seethe] VERB, **seethed, seething. 1. être en effervescence** ▸ to foam and bubble. **2. bouillir de colère** ▸ to be very excited or angry : *My mother is seething about the stain on the rug.*

seg-ment [SEG-munt] NOUN, **segments. segment** ▸ one of the parts into which a whole is or can be divided; a division or section : *segments of a grapefruit.*

seg-re-gate [SEG-ruh-GATE] VERB, **segregated, segregating. séparer** ▸ to set apart from others : *Balraj was segregated so others wouldn't get sick.* **Note.** Often used as an ADJECTIVE: *In a segregated school system, students of different religions go to separate schools.* ■ **segregation,** NOUN. **ségrégation** ▸ the act or fact of separating; isolation : *South Africa used to have a policy of racial segregation.* ✐ **p. 526.**

seis-mo-graph [SIZE-muh-GRAF] NOUN, **seismographs. sismographe** ▸ an instrument that

records when and where an earthquake occurs, how long it lasts, and how strong it is.

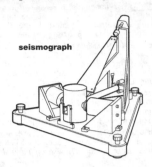

seismograph

seize [seez] VERB, **seized, seizing. 1. saisir** ▸ to take hold of suddenly; grab : *He seized Jin's bag of marbles.* **2. saisir** ▸ to take by force or authority; capture : *"We don't want our belongings to be seized by the Germans."* (Anne Frank) SYN : grip, grasp, clutch, grab, snatch.

sei-zure [SEE-zyur] NOUN, **seizures. 1. saisie** ▸ the act of seizing : *The Coast Guard ordered the seizure of the boat for illegal fishing.* **2. crise, attaque** ▸ a sudden loss of control of the body : *Epilepsy is a disease of the brain that causes seizures.*

sel-dom [SEL-dum] ADVERB. **rarement** ▸ not often; rarely : *"The pond Sam had discovered... was seldom visited by any human being."* (E.B. White)

se-lect [suh-LEKT] VERB, **selected, selecting. sélectionner** ▸ to pick out from a group; choose : *The teacher selected me to show the new student around school.* ▲ ADJECTIVE. **1. choisi (-ie), sélectionné (-ée)** ▸ picked or chosen specially : *a select display of the artist's work.* **2. sélect (-ecte), sélectif (-ive)** ▸ careful in choosing; exclusive : *The select soccer team is made up of the best players in the league.* SYN : choose, pick, designate, single out.

se-lec-tion [suh-LEK-shun] NOUN, **selections. 1. sélection (de choix)** ▸ the act or fact of selecting something; choice : *Mark your selection on the form.* **2. sélection** ▸ a person or thing that is or may be chosen : *a selection of desserts.*

self [self] NOUN, **selves. 1. la personne** ▸ one's own person apart from all others. **2. soi-même** ▸ one's normal self : *After a long illness, Vithya is her old self again.*

self- PREFIX. of, for, or by oneself or itself : *A self-cleaning oven is one that can clean itself.* **Note.** Among the common *self*- compounds are self-confident, self-control, self-defence, self-respect, self-service, and self-sufficient. ☞ p. 309.

self·ish [SEL-fish] ADJECTIVE. **égoïste** ▸ caring too much about one's own needs; acting to help oneself without regard for others : *That selfish man went right up to the front of the line without waiting his turn.* ■ **selfishly,** ADVERB. ▸ **égoïstement.** ■ **selfishness,** NOUN. ▸ **égoïsme.**

sell [sel] VERB, sold, selling. **1. vendre** ▸ to give an item to someone else in return for money : *Tak is selling his bicycle for $25.* **2. vendre** ▸ to offer a certain item in this way : *a store that sells books.* **3.** *Informal.* **être emballé (-ée)** ▸ to agree to or approve of : *He was sold on the idea of going to Fiji instead of Hawaii.*

sell out trahir, laisser tomber ▸ to act in a disloyal way.

sell·er [SEL-ur] NOUN, sellers. **1. vendeur (-euse), marchand (-ande)** ▸ a person who sells something : *The seller is asking $2000 for that car.* **2. best-seller** ▸ a product that sells in a certain way : *That book is a best-seller.*

selves [selvz] NOUN. **êtres, individus** ▸ the plural of self.

se·mes·ter [SUH-mes-tur] NOUN, semesters. **semestre** ▸ one of the two terms into which a school year is divided. **Note.** A school year can also be divided into three terms called trimesters.

semi- PREFIX. **1.** partly; not completely : *a semi-desert area.* **2.** twice : *a semi-annual event.*

sem·i·cir·cle [SEM-ee-SUR-kul] NOUN, semicircles. **demi-cercle** ▸ half a circle.

sem·i·co·lon [SEM-ee-KOH-lun] NOUN, semicolons. **point-virgule** ▸ a mark of punctuation [;] that shows a greater break in thought than a comma does, but less of a break than a period does.

sem·i·con·duc·tor [SEM-ee-kun-DUK-tur] NOUN, semiconductors. **semi-conducteur** ▸ a material, such as silicon, that conducts electricity better when it is heated. Semiconductors are widely used in TV sets, radios, and computers.

sem·i·fi·nal [SEM-ee-FY-nul] NOUN, semifinals. **demi-finale** ▸ a game or round that comes just before the final one, and must be won to participate in the final. ■ **semifinalist,** NOUN. ▸ **demi-finaliste.**

sem·i·nar [SEM-uh-NAR] NOUN, seminars. **séminaire** ▸ a meeting for exchanging and discussing special information : *a seminar on new technology.*

sem·i·nar·y [SEM-uh-NAIR-ee] NOUN, seminaries. **séminaire, colloque** ▸ a school that trains students to be priests, ministers, or rabbis.

sen·ate [SEN-ut] NOUN, senates. (usually Senate) **sénat** ▸ the upper and smaller branch of a parliament or any similar lawmaking or govern-

ing body : *The Canadian Senate has representatives from every province and territory.*

sen·a·tor [SEN-uh-tur] NOUN, senators. **sénateur (-trice)** ▸ a member of a senate. ■ **senatorial,** ADJECTIVE. ▸ **sénatorial.**

Sen·e·ca [SEN-uh-kuh] NOUN, Seneca **Sénèques** or Senecas. **1. Sénèque** ▸ a member of the Aboriginal group originally living in western New York State and now in Ontario. The Seneca are part of the Six Nations Iroquois Confederacy. **2. sénèque** ▸ the Iroquoian language of these people.

send [send] VERB, sent, sending. **1. envoyer** ▸ to cause a thing to move from one place to another : *to send a letter.* **2. envoyer** ▸ to cause a person to go : *She was sent to camp.* **3. précipiter** ▸ to cause a certain feeling or condition : *Playing with the puppy sent Jim into gales of laughter.* ■ **sender,** NOUN. ▸ **expéditeur (-trice).**

sen·ior [SEEN-yur] ADJECTIVE. **1. père** ▸ the older of two people with the same name : *John Brown Senior and his son, John Junior.* **2. supérieur (-ieure)** ▸ having higher rank or longer service : *Captain Lewis was the senior officer on duty.* **Note.** The fact of having this rank is seniority. ▲ NOUN, seniors. **1. aîné** ▸ a person who is older than another : *Sue has an older sister who is her senior by five years.* **2. personne âgée, de l'âge d'or** ▸ short for senior citizen.

senior citizen personne âgée, de l'âge d'or ▸ an older person, especially one who is retired from work.

sen·sa·tion [sen-SAY-shun] NOUN, sensations. **1. sensation** ▸ the use of the senses; the ability to see, hear, touch, taste, or smell. **2. sensation** ▸ something known by one of the senses; a feeling : *In space, there was no sensation of motion.* **3. sensation** ▸ great excitement or interest : *The new pop star is creating a sensation everywhere she goes.*

sen·sa·tion·al [sen-SAY-shuh-nul] ADJECTIVE. **1. sensationnel (-elle)** ▸ creating great excitement or interest : *Tia made a sensational play to catch the ball.* **2. à sensation** ▸ trying to arouse great excitement or interest : *Sensational headlines helped sell the newspaper.* SYN: exciting, stimulating, thrilling, marvellous.

sense [sence] NOUN, senses. **1. sens** ▸ any of the powers by which a living being can be aware of itself and of what goes on around it; the ability to see, hear, feel, smell, or taste things. **2. sentiment** ▸ a feeling in the mind : *a sense of pride.* **3. sens** ▸ the ability to use the physical senses or the mind to make judgments : *She has a good sense of direction.* **Note.** Often used in expressions, such as a sense of humour or common sense. **4. bon sens** ▸ the proper use of the mind; good judgment : *There's no sense planting flowers now—the frost will kill them.*

5. sens ▶ meaning : *When I say that the show is funny, I mean in the sense of "strange."* **6. senses. raison, conscience, bon sens ▶** a clear state of mind; the ability to think or reason : *He came to his senses and didn't buy the car.* ▲ VERB, sensed, sensing. **sentir, connaître par intuition ▶** to understand something without being told directly; have a certain feeling : *My dentist sensed that I was uncomfortable, and was careful.* ■ **sensory,** ADJECTIVE. **sensoriel (-elle) ▶** having to do with the senses. 📖 **p. 1034.**

sense-less [SENCE-lis] ADJECTIVE. **1. sans connaissance ▶** not having the use of the senses; unconscious. **2. insensé (-ée) ▶** not showing proper use of the mind; foolish. ■ **senselessly,** ADVERB. ▶ **stupidement.** ■ **senselessness,** NOUN. ▶ **manque de bon sens.**

sen-si-ble [SEN-suh-bul] ADJECTIVE. **sensé (-ée) ▶** having or showing good sense; reasonable : *She is sensible enough to come home when it gets dark.* ■ **sensibly,** ADVERB. ▶ **raisonnablement.** SYN : intelligent, reasonable, wise, sane.

sen-si-tive [SEN-sih-tiv] ADJECTIVE. **1. sensible ▶** quick to show the effect of some physical force; sensing or responding quickly : *My eyes were sensitive to the sunlight after being in the dark basement.* **2. sensible ▶** easily hurt or upset; having delicate feelings : *Miro is sensitive to any mention of the accident.* **3. sensible ▶** having deep feelings : *The minister was very sensitive to the poor family's problems.* ■ **sensitivity,** NOUN. ▶ **sensibilité.** ■ **sensitively,** ADVERB. ▶ **avec sensibilité.**

sent [sent] VERB. a past form of send.

sen-tence [SEN-tuns] NOUN, sentences. **1. phrase ▶** a group of words expressing a complete thought. A sentence has both a subject (a noun or pronoun) and a verb. **2. sentence ▶** punishment given to a person who is found guilty by a court of law. ▲ VERB, sentenced, sentencing. **condamner (à) ▶** to set the punishment of : *The accused was sentenced to 90 days in jail.*

sen-ti-ment [SEN-tuh-munt] NOUN, sentiments. **1. sentiment ▶** a thought mixed with feeling or emotion : *Fatima cared for that sick puppy out of sentiment.* **2. sentiment ▶** tender feelings. **3.** (usually sentiments) **sentiment ▶** an attitude or point of view; an opinion.

sen-ti-men-tal [SEN-tih-men-tul] ADJECTIVE. **1. sentimental (-ale, -aux) ▶** having or showing tender, sensitive feelings : *Jim becomes sentimental when he sings that old song.* **2. sentimental (-ale, -aux) ▶** having or showing too much sentiment; too emotional : *This sentimental plot is about an orphan girl and a grouchy old man who adopts her.* ■ **sentimentally,** ADVERB. ▶ **sentimentalement.** SYN : warm, loving, affectionate, tender.

sen-try [SEN-tree] NOUN, sentries. **sentinelle ▶** a soldier or other person who is stationed at a place to keep watch. **Note.** Also called a sentinel.

se-pal [SEE-pul] NOUN, sepals. **sépale ▶** one of the parts that make up the outer covering of a flower. Sepals are usually green, but in some flowers they have the same colour as the petals. **Note.** The outermost layer of sepals is called the calyx.

sep-a-rate [SEP-uh-RATE] VERB, separated, separating. **1. séparer ▶** to keep apart; be between; divide : *Fences separate the yards in our neighbourhood.* **2. séparer ▶** to break into parts; set or place apart : *Separate paper products from the rest of the garbage for recycling.* **3. se séparer ▶** of a married couple, to make an agreement to live apart while still remaining legally married. ▲ [SEP-uh-rit or SEP-rit] ADJECTIVE. **1. séparé (de) ▶** apart from another or others; not joined : *Those are separate pieces; they don't go together.* **2. distinct (-incte), séparé (-ée) ▶** different; distinct : *Those are separate questions.* ■ **separately,** ADVERB. ▶ **séparément.** SYN : divide, part, segregate, sort, keep apart. 🖋 **p. 526.**

sep-a-ra-tion [SEP-uh-RAY-shun] NOUN, separations. **1. séparation ▶** the act or fact of separating. **2. séparation ▶** something that separates.

Sep-tem-ber [sep-TEM-bur] NOUN, Septembers. **septembre ▶** the ninth month of the year, between August and October. September has 30 days.

se-quel [SEE-kwil] NOUN, sequels. **1. suite ▶** a complete story that continues from where an earlier story ended : *The movie* Return of the Jedi *was a sequel to* Star Wars. **2. séquelle ▶** something that follows because of something else; a result.

🖋 **Word Builder**

Separate, sort, and *segregate* all mean to break down a group into smaller parts. *Separate* can mean to take apart things that have been closely joined together : *The recipe said to separate the egg whites from the yolks. Sort* can mean to group things according to common elements or characteristics : *I sorted the fruit by colour. Segregate* means to isolate something from a main group : *The teacher segregated the students working on their projects from the rest of the class.*

se-quence [SEE-kwince] NOUN, sequences. **1. succession** ▶ the fact of one thing coming after another in a certain order : *Customers are served in sequence, depending on who came first.* **2. séquence** ▶ a series of connected things : *The sequence of photos showed how the city had grown over the last 100 years.*

se-quoi-a [sih-KWOY-uh] NOUN, sequoias. **séquoia** ▶ a very large evergreen tree that bears cones and has a reddish-brown bark and pointed leaves. **Note.** Also called a redwood.

se-rene [suh-REEN] ADJECTIVE. **serein (-eine)** ▶ calm and quiet; peaceful : *A walk along the beach at sunset gave her a serene feeling.* **Note.** The fact of being serene is serenity. ■ **serenely,** ADVERB. ▶ sereinement.

serf [surf] NOUN, serfs. **serf** ▶ in Europe in earlier times, a poor farm worker who was forced by law to work on a certain piece of land and pay rent to its owner.

ser-geant [SAR-junt] NOUN, sergeants. **1. sergent (-ente)** ▶ in Canada, an officer in the military ranking above master corporal but below warrant officer. **2. sergent (-ente)** ▶ a police officer ranking above detective or constable but below inspector or staff sergeant.

se-ri-al [SEER-ee-ul] NOUN, serials. **série, feuilleton** ▶ a long story that is broken up into smaller parts that are published or broadcast one at a time. ▲ ADJECTIVE. **de série, en série** ▶ arranged in a series.

serial number numéro de série ▶ a number given to a member of a large group to identify one from the others, as with soldiers, cars, or appliances.

se-ries [SEER-eez] NOUN, series. **1. série** ▶ a number of things of the same kind that come one after another : *There has been a series of accidents at that intersection.* **2. série, feuilleton** ▶ a number of books, movies, and the like that deal with the same subject, or are otherwise related to each other : *a TV series.*

se-ri-ous [SEER-ee-us] ADJECTIVE. **1. sérieux (-ieuse)** ▶ not joking or acting in fun; not fooling : *Are you serious ? I thought the test was tomorrow.* **2. sérieux (-ieuse)** ▶ having a quiet, thoughtful manner; solemn; grave. **3. sérieux (-ieuse)** ▶ important, difficult, or dangerous : *a serious illness.* ■ **seriously,** ADVERB. ▶ sérieusement. ■ **seriousness,** NOUN. ▶ sérieux.

ser-mon [SUR-mun] NOUN, sermons. **1. sermon** ▶ a talk on religious or moral behaviour as part of a church service. **2.** *Informal.* **sermon** ▶ any long, serious talk about how someone should behave.

ser-pent [SUR-pent] NOUN, serpents. **serpent** ▶ a snake, especially a large snake.

se-rum [SEER-um] NOUN, serums or sera. **1. sérum** ▶ a liquid that is used to cure or treat a disease. It is made from the blood of an animal that is immune to the disease. **2. sérum** ▶ the thin, clear liquid that separates from blood as a blood clot forms.

ser-vant [SUR-vunt] NOUN, servants. **domestique, serviteur, servant (-ante)** ▶ a person whose job is to work for another person, doing jobs such as cooking, cleaning, or gardening. **Note.** People who work for the government are often called public servants or civil servants.

serve [surv] VERB, served, serving. **1. servir** ▶ to place food on the table for eating : *to serve breakfast.* **2. servir** ▶ to be of use or help to : *to serve a customer.* **3. servir, être membre de** ▶ to carry out a certain job, duty, or obligation : *to serve in the military.* **4. délivrer, signifier, notifier une assignation** ▶ to present in an official or legal way : *She was served with a summons to appear in court.* **5. service** ▶ in tennis and similar games, to hit the ball to begin play. ▲ NOUN, serves. **servir** ▶ the act of putting the ball in play in a game such as tennis or volleyball.

ser-vice [SUR-viss] NOUN, services. **1. service** ▶ the act or fact of helping others : *The doctor was honoured for her many years of service to the village.* **2. services. service** ▶ professional help or advice : *You need the services of a lawyer.* **3. service** ▶ the act of waiting on or helping customers : *This restaurant is known for its fine food and excellent service.* **4. service** ▶ a system of providing things to the public : *bus service.* **5. office** ▶ a religious ceremony : *a funeral service.* **6. service militaire** ▶ the armed forces : *Grandfather was in the service during the war.* **7. service de table** ▶ a set of dishes for a meal. ▲ VERB, serviced, servicing. **révision, entretien** ▶ to put or keep in good condition : *The new car should be serviced every 15,000 kilometres.* ▲ ADJECTIVE. **(de) service** ▶ having to do with or giving service : *a service award.*

service station station-service ▶ a place where cars and trucks can get gas, oil, and so on, or be maintained and repaired. **Note.** Also called a gas station.

ser-vi-ette [SUR-vee-ET] NOUN, serviettes. **serviette de table** ▶ a cloth or paper napkin used during meals to protect clothing and wipe hands and face.

serv-ing [SUR-ving] NOUN, servings. **assiettée, portion** ▶ a portion of food for one person : *a serving of potatoes.*

ses-sion [SESH-un] NOUN, sessions. **1. session, séance** ▶ a formal meeting of a council, club, or organization : *Court is now in session.* **2. séance** ▶ a series of such meetings, or the time when they take place : *a session of Parliament.* **3. séance** ▶ any meeting at a fixed time : *The rock group has a recording session this week.*

set [set] VERB, set, setting. **1. poser, mettre ▶** to put something in a certain place : *Set the ham on the table.* **2. libérer, rendre en liberté ▶** to put in a certain condition : *to set a prisoner free.* **3. mettre le couvert ▶** to put in the proper condition : *to set the table for dinner.* **4. mettre ▶** to fix at a certain point or level : *Set your alarm for 6:30 a.m.* **5. se mettre en route ▶** to begin a trip or journey : *The pioneers set out for Alberta.* **6. se coucher ▶** to go out of sight below the horizon : *The sun set.* **7. durcir ▶** to make or become solid : *Let the glue set overnight.* ▲ ADJECTIVE. **1. avoir ses habitudes, être coincé dans ses habitudes ▶** fixed or decided : *The man was "set in his ways," and did not like things to change.* **2. prêt (prête) ▶** ready ; prepared : *Are you all set for your trip?* ▲ NOUN, sets. **1. ensemble, collection ▶** a group of things or people that belong together : *a set of encyclopedias.* **2. décor ▶** the scenery for a play, film, or television program. **3. téléviseur ▶** a device for receiving television signals. **4. set ▶** one part of a tennis match.

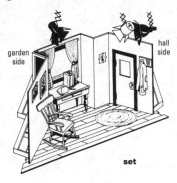

set

set-back [SET-bak] NOUN, setbacks. **contre-temps, retard ▶** a lack of progress or success ; a reverse or defeat : *The mayor had a setback when the tax plan failed.*

set-ter [SET-ur] NOUN, setters. **1. setter ▶** a large hunting dog with a long coat, that points its nose and stands still when it senses prey. **2. sertisseur (-euse), compositeur (-trice) ▶** a person or thing that sets : *a typesetter.*

set-ting [SET-ing] NOUN, settings. **1. mise, création ▶** the act of a person or thing that sets. **2. monture ▶** a thing in which something else is set : *a diamond ring in a gold setting.* **3. cadre ▶** the place and time of the action in a book, play, or other such work.

set-tle [SET-ul] VERB, settled, settling. **1. décider, régler ▶** to agree or decide some issue or problem : *to settle an argument.* **2. s'établir**
▶ to make a home ; live in a certain place : *Australia was settled by people from Britain in the 1800s.* **3. (s') installer ▶** to come to rest on something : *The birds settled on the ledge.* **4. (s') enfoncer, (s') affaisser ▶** to sink slowly or gradually down : *The ship settled into the mud.* **5. calmer ▶** to make or become calm or less active : *to settle one's nerves.*

set-tle-ment [SET-ul-munt] NOUN, settlements. **1. établissement, colonisation ▶** the act or fact of settling. **2. colonie ▶** a small village or community.

set-tler [SET-lur] NOUN, settlers. **colon ▶** a person who goes to live in a new area or country : *British and French settlers came to Canada.*

sev-en [SEV-un] NOUN, sevens ; ADJECTIVE. **sept ▶** one more than six ; 7. **■ seventh,** ADJECTIVE ; NOUN. ▶ **septième.**

sev-en-teen [SEV-un-teen *or* SEV-un-TEEN] NOUN, seventeens ; ADJECTIVE. **dix-sept ▶** one more than sixteen ; 17. **■ seventeenth,** ADJECTIVE ; NOUN. ▶ **dix-septième.**

sev-en-ty [SEV-un-tee] NOUN, seventies ; ADJECTIVE. **soixante-dix ▶** seven times ten ; 70. **■ seventieth,** ADJECTIVE ; NOUN. ▶ **soixante-dixième.**

sev-er [SEV-ur] VERB, severed, severing. **trancher, couper ▶** to cut or break off, especially in a sharp, sudden way : *Lightning severed a branch off the old tree.*

sev-er-al [SEV-ur-al *or* SEV-rul] ADJECTIVE ; NOUN. **plusieurs, quelques ▶** more than two, but not many : *Soo Nor borrowed several books from the library.* SYN : many, various, numerous.

se-vere [suh-VEER] ADJECTIVE, severer, severest. **1. sévère ▶** not kind and gentle ; strict ; harsh : *The troublemakers were subject to severe discipline.* **2. grave ▶** hard to bear or deal with ; causing great pain, discomfort, or damage : *a severe toothache.* **■ severely,** ADVERB. ▶ **sévèrement.** Note. The state of being severe is severity.

sew [soh] VERB, sewed, sewed or sewn, sewing. **coudre ▶** to make or mend clothes with a needle and thread : *Mom sewed the torn seam in the jacket.* Note. The art or work of doing this is **sewing** (☞ p. 1166).

sew up (se) garantir ▶ to make certain of getting or having : *His excellent play sewed up a spot on the team.*

sew-age [SOO-ij] NOUN. **eau d'égout, eaux usées ▶** waste matter from homes, factories, and other buildings. Sewage is carried off in sewers or drains.

sewed [sohd] VERB. a past form of **sew.**

sew-er[1] [SOO-ur] NOUN, sewers. **égout ▶** a pipe or channel located underground and used to carry away waste matter and dirty water.

sew·er² [SOH-ur] NOUN. sewers. **couturier (-ière), couseur (-euse)** ▸ a person who sews.

sewing machine machine à coudre ▸ a mechanical device that sews, usually having an electric motor to run it.

sewn [sohn] VERB. a past form of sew.

sex [seks] NOUN. sexes. **1. sexe** ▸ one of the two groups, male or female, that humans, animals, and some plants are divided into. **2. sexe** ▸ the fact or condition of being male or female : *Public washrooms are usually divided by sex.* **3. rapport sexuel** ▸ the manner in which humans and animals reproduce young. ▪ **sexual,** ADJECTIVE. **sexuel (-elle)** ▸ having to do with sex : *Bright-coloured feathers are a sexual trait found in many male birds.*

sex·ism [seks-izm] NOUN. **sexisme** ▸ prejudice against a person or persons because of his, her, or their sex. ▪ **sexist,** ADJECTIVE: ▸ **sexiste.** *a sexist comment.* ✐ **p. 529.**

shab·by [SHAB-ee] ADJECTIVE, shabbier, shabbiest. **usé (-ée), miteux (-euse)** ▸ showing too much wear; faded and ragged : *I put on my shabbiest clothes to clean the garage.* ▪ **shabbily,** ADVERB. ▸ **pauvrement, mesquinement.**

shack [shak] NOUN, shacks. **1. baraque, hutte, cabane** ▸ a small, roughly built house or cabin. **2. cabane, cabanon, remise** ▸ a hut or shed.

shack·le [SHAK-ul] NOUN, shackles. **carcan, fers** ▸ a band or chain used to hold a prisoner, work animal, and so on in one place. ▲ VERB, shackled, shackling. **mettre les fers à** ▸ to hold or confine with, or as if with shackles : *shackled by responsibility.* SYN: handcuff, bind, tie, chain.

shad [shad] NOUN, shad or shads. **alose** ▸ a small fish related to the herring. Shad live in the Atlantic Ocean and swim to freshwater streams to lay their eggs. Both the shad itself and its eggs are valued as food.

shade [shade] NOUN, shades. **1. ombre** ▸ an area that is darker and cooler because sunlight is blocked off. **2. pare-soleil, abat-jour, store** ▸ something that blocks off light : *a lamp shade.* **3. ton, nuance** ▸ the distinct nature of a colour that makes it different from another similar one : *My room is a pale shade of blue.* **4. légèrement** ▸ a small amount or difference; a little bit : *The water is still a shade too cold to swim.* ▲ VERB, shaded, shading. **1. ombrager** ▸ to keep direct light or heat away from something : *The baby-sitter shaded the baby from the sun.* **2. ombrer** ▸ to make or have different degrees of light and dark : *The artist shaded the parts of the drawing that were in shadow.*

shad·ow [SHAD-oh] NOUN, shadows. **1. ombre, ombrage** ▸ a dark area caused by something blocking the sunlight. **2. ombre, marqueur** ▸ a person or thing that follows another very closely : *In soccer, a shadow is a player assigned to cover the other team's star player on the field.* **3. ombre (de)** ▸ a small amount; a bit. **Note.** Usually used in the phrase (beyond) a shadow of a doubt. ▲ VERB, shadowed, shadowing. **1. ombrager** ▸ cover with a shadow; make a shadow on : *"The room, shadowed well with awnings, was dark and cool."* (F. Scott Fitzgerald) **2. faire suivre, prendre en filature** ▸ to follow very closely : *The police shadowed the suspected thief.* ▪ **shadowy,** ADJECTIVE. **sombre** ▸ covered with, or as if with, shadows : *A shadowy figure led us to a secret passage.*

shad·y [SHAY-dee] ADJECTIVE, shadier, shadiest. **1. ombragé (-ée)** ▸ giving shade, or in the shade : *a shady tree.* **2.** *Informal.* **louche** ▸ not strictly honest or legal; doubtful : *He approached me with a shady deal on a watch.*

✐ Writing Tips

Sexist Language
Sexist language is any language that treats males and females differently, or favours one sex over the other. Today, most writers work to avoid sexist language in their writing. They do this by using words like **actor** (*rather than actress*), **police officer** (*rather than policeman or police woman*), and **humans** or **humankind** (*rather than mankind or man*).

Sometimes people use sexist language without realizing it. For example, a news report is sexist if it describes women by their looks or marital status, while describing men by what they do. If a story talks about a "farmer and his wife," it is sexist. If both people share the chores and responsibilities of farm life, they both should be referred to as farmers. To be fair, you must describe or speak about men and women in the same way. Also, be sure that you look at both sexes as equal and equally capable.

Traditionally, it was acceptable to use just **he** when the person being discussed could be male or female. This is sexist, however, because it doesn't include women. To avoid sexist language, use **he or she** or **she/he** or rewrite the sentence to use **they**.

shaft [shaft] NOUN, shafts. **1. manche ▸** the long, narrow part of an arrow or spear that is attached to the head. **2. hampe, manche ▸** a similar part of a golf club, hockey stick, axe, hammer, and so on. **3. arbre (de moteur) ▸** a bar in a machine that supports moving parts or sends motion to other parts of the machinery : *the driveshaft of a car.* **4. éclair ▸** a ray or beam of light : *shafts of sunlight.* **5. cage, puits ▸** a long, narrow opening that goes up and down : *an elevator shaft; a mine shaft.*

shag·gy [SHAG-ee] ADJECTIVE, shaggier, shaggiest. **hirsute ▸** having hair, fur, wool, and so on, that is long, rough, and thick : *the shaggy sheepdog.*

shake [shake] VERB, shook, shaken, shaking. **1. brasser, agiter, secouer ▸** to move up and down or from side to side in quick, quick movements : *The instructions read "Shake well before using."* **2. trembler ▸** to make a series of small, quick body movements because of illness, cold, fear, excitement, and so on; tremble : *The thunder made us shake with fear.* **3. ébranler ▸** to upset, weaken, or disturb : *The athlete's confidence was shaken by a few bad plays.* **4. secouer ▸** to get rid of; get away from : *She shook off the negative feelings about the plane trip.* ▲ NOUN, shakes. **1. secousse ▸** the act of shaking : *a handshake.* **2. lait fouetté ▸** a drink made by mixing several things together using a shaking motion : *a milk shake.* SYN: tremble, shiver, vibrate, shudder, quake.

shak·y [SHAKE-ee] ADJECTIVE, shakier, shakiest. **branlant (-ante), tremblant (-ante) ▸** that shakes or is likely to shake; not steady : *a shaky old ladder.* ■ **shakily,** ADVERB. ▸ **en tremblant.**

shale [shale] NOUN. **schiste argileux ▸** a rock formed from hardened clay, with thin layers that split easily.

shall [shal] VERB. used with other verbs to show the future : *We shall go to a movie tomorrow.*

shal·low [SHAL-loh] ADJECTIVE, shallower, shallowest. **1. peu profond ▸** not far from top to bottom; not deep : *the shallow end of the pool.* **2. superficiel (-ielle) ▸** not deep in thought or feeling : *He's a shallow person who only wants friends for the things they will give him.* ■ **shallowness,** NOUN. ▸ **manque de profondeur.**

sham [sham] NOUN, shams. **imposture, imitation ▸** something that is not true or real; imitation. ▲ ADJECTIVE. ▲ VERB, shammed, shamming. **faux (fausse) ▸** to pretend. SYN: hoax, fraud, fake, pretence, cheat.

sha·man [SHAH-mun or SHAY-mun] NOUN, shamans. **chaman ▸** in some religions, a priest or priestess who is believed to be able to influence the spirits. Note. Also known as a **medicine man** or **medicine woman**, especially among the Native peoples of North America.

sham·bles [SHAM-bulz] NOUN. **fouillis, désordre ▸** a mess or a scene of confusion : *Pia's room is a shambles.*

shame [shame] NOUN. **1. honte ▸** a painful feeling that comes from doing something wrong or being connected with something bad : *She felt shame for lying to her friend.* **2. dommage ▸** something that should not be; something unfortunate or unwanted : *It is a shame that we lost the game.* ▲ VERB, shamed, shaming. **faire honte à ▸** to cause to feel shame : *We shamed him for cheating.* ■ **shameless,** ADJECTIVE. ▸ **éhonté (-ée).** ■ **shamelessly,** ADVERB. ▸ **effrontément.** *She shamelessly cancelled her date with one boy to be with another.*

sham·poo [SHAM-POO] VERB, shampooed, shampooing. **(se) faire un shampooing, (se) laver la tête ▸** to wash the hair. ▲ NOUN, shampoos. **shampooing ▸** a special soap used for washing the hair. Note. The word *shampoo* comes from Hindi.

sham·rock [SHAM-rok] NOUN, shamrocks. **trèfle ▸** a small plant related to clover, having leaves with three leaflets.

shant·y[1] [SHAN-tee] NOUN, shanties. **baraque ▸** a small, roughly built shelter or cabin; a shack.

shanty[2] NOUN, shantys or shanties. (also chantey or chanty) **chanson de marin ▸** a song sung by sailors : *a sea shanty.*

shape [shape] NOUN, shapes. **1. forme ▸** the outer form or outline of something : *a pie shape.* **2. état ▸** the physical condition of a person or thing, whether good or bad : *The ship was not in shape for the voyage.* **3. en forme ▸** good physical condition : *Conor runs to keep in shape.* ▲ VERB, shaped, shaping. **façonner ▸** to give a certain shape to : *The baker shaped the cookies to look like animals.*

share [shair] NOUN, shares. **1. part ▸** the part of a larger thing that belongs to one particular person : *Everyone did his or her fair share of the work.* **2. action ▸** one of the equal parts of ownership of a company : *shares in a company.* ▲ VERB, shared, sharing. **1. partager ▸** to use or take part in with others : *Althina and her sister share a bedroom.* **2. partager ▸** to divide into parts and give to others as well as to yourself : *I'll share my lunch with you.* SYN: part, portion, quota, lot.

shark [shark] NOUN, sharks. **requin ▸** a saltwater fish that lives in warm seas and has rough grayish skin and rows of sharp teeth. Sharks attack other fish and the larger ones can be dangerous to people. ☞ p. 107.

sharp [sharp] ADJECTIVE, sharper, sharpest. **1. pointu (-ue) ▸** having an edge or point that will cut easily : *a sharp point on a pencil.* **2. aiguisé (-ée) ▸** having a point or edge; not rounded : *the sharp peaks of the Rocky Moun-*

tains. **3. net (nette)** ▶ quick and exact in a way that is thought to be like the cutting of a knife : *Our new computer screen is much sharper than the old one.* **4. violent (-ente), perçant (-ante)** ▶ affecting the senses in a quick, cutting way : *a sharp pain.* **5. brusque** ▶ having a sudden change in size, direction, amount, and so on : *a sharp turn.* ▲ ADVERB. **pile** ▶ exactly ; promptly : *Meet me here at 3:00 sharp.* ▲ NOUN, sharps. **dièse** ▶ in music, a tone or note that is half a note above its natural tone, or the symbol [#] that indicates this. ▪ **sharply,** ADVERB: "*Miss Crail looked up sharply from her card index, as if she had heard a rude word.* ▶ **brusquement.** " (John Le Carré) ▪ **sharpness,** NOUN. ▶ netteté.

sharp-en [SHAR-pen] VERB, sharpened, sharpening. **aiguiser** ▶ to make or become sharp or sharper : *to sharpen a knife.*

shat-ter [SHAT-ur] VERB, shattered, shattering. **1. fracasser** ▶ to break into pieces in a sudden, violent way : *The force of the wind shattered windows.* **2. anéantir, détraquer** ▶ to have a very bad effect on ; to distress : *News of a death in the family shattered Anwar.*

shave [shave] VERB, shaved, shaved **raser** ▶ or shaven, shaving. **1. (se) raser** ▶ to cut hair from the body with a razor or sharp blade. **2. raboter, planer** ▶ to cut off thin strips or pieces : *With a knife, Lars shaved off some kindling to start a fire.* ▲ NOUN, shaves. **1. rasage** ▶ the fact of shaving. **2. close shave. frôlement** ▶ a close call ; a narrow escape.

shawl [shol] NOUN, shawls. **châle** ▶ a piece of soft, heavy cloth that is worn over the shoulders or head, especially by women. ☞ **p. 1013.**

she [shee] PRONOUN. **elle** ▶ the girl, woman, or female animal that has been mentioned ; that female one : *Sarita sat down after she finished her speech.* ▲ NOUN, shes. **femelle** ▶ a female. ✍ **p. 284.**

shear [sheer] VERB, sheared, sheared or shorn, shearing. **tondre** ▶ to cut or clip something with a sharp tool : *Sheep are shorn to remove their wool.* ▲ NOUN, shears. (usually **shears**) **cisailles** ▶ a cutting tool similar to scissors, but larger and heavier : *The garden sheurs do a fine job of cutting the hedge.*

shed[1] [shed] NOUN, sheds. **hangar, remise** ▶ a small building or hut used for storing things : *a tool shed.* ☞ **p. 115, 117.**

shed[2] VERB, shed, shedding. **1. perdre** ▶ of an animal or plant, to cast off or lose an outer covering : *Many trees shed their leaves in fall.* **2. se dépouiller, perdre, enlever** ▶ to throw off some covering or burden in this way : *The hikers shed their heavy backpacks and went swimming.* **3. répandre, verser** ▶ to let flow or cause to flow : "*If you have tears, prepare to shed them now.*" (William Shakespeare)

4. jeter de la lumière, éclairer ▶ to send out ; give off : *The winter sun doesn't seem to shed any warmth.*

sheep [sheep] NOUN, sheep. **mouton** ▶ a farm animal that is raised for its wool, meat, and milk. Other kinds of sheep live wild in mountain areas of Asia, southern Europe, and western North America. ☞ **p. 114.**

sheer [sheer] ADJECTIVE, sheerer, sheerest. **1. fin (fine), transparent (-ente)** ▶ very thin and light so that it can be seen through : *a sheer fabric for a wedding veil.* **2. abrupt (-upte)** ▶ straight up or down ; very steep : "*The tide had risen and the sea lapped the bottom of the sheer cliff.*" (Donald Gale) **3. pur (pure), véritable** ▶ complete ; total : *sheer exhaustion.*

sheet [sheet] NOUN, sheets. **1. drap** ▶ one of a pair of large pieces of cloth used as a bed covering : a *bedsheet.* **2. feuille** ▶ any thin, wide piece of material : *a sheet of paper ; sheets of plywood.* **3. plaque, feuille, tôle** ▶ a broad, thin surface thought of as lying flat like a bedsheet : *A sheet of ice covered the lake.*

sheik [shake *or* sheek] NOUN, sheiks. (also **sheikh**) **cheik, scheik** ▶ an Arab leader or ruler.

shelf [shelf] NOUN, shelves. **1. étagère** ▶ a thin, flat piece of wood, metal, glass, or other such material that is attached to a wall or frame and used to hold things, such as books. **2. plate-forme, banc** ▶ anything that is like a shelf : *The Continental Shelf is a flat, shallow region of the Atlantic Ocean.*

shell [shel] NOUN, shells. **1. coquille, coche, enveloppe** ▶ a hard outer covering that protects the body of certain animals, such as turtles, clams, and snails. **2. carapace, coquille, coquillage** ▶ a similar covering of an egg, nut, seed, and so on. **3. carcasse** ▶ any outer covering or protection : *The builders had constructed only the shell of the house when the rain came.* **4. obus, cartouche** ▶ a metal case holding a bullet or explosive charge for a gun, or the bullet or charge itself. ▲ VERB, shelled, shelling. **1. écosser, écaler** ▶ to remove the shell from something : *to shell peas.* **2. bombarder** ▶ to attack with shells, cannons, or guns : *Bombers shelled the city of London during World War II.*

shel-lac [shuh-LAK] NOUN, shellacs. **gomme-laque** ▶ a thick liquid that dries to form a shiny protective covering for furniture, floors, and so on. ▲ VERB, shellacked, shellacking. **traiter à la gomme-laque** ▶ to cover or coat a surface with shellac.

shell-fish [SHEL-FISH] NOUN, shellfish or shell-fishes. **coquillages, crustacés, fruits de mer** ▶ any animal that lives in the water and has a shell to protect its body. Clams, oysters, crabs, and shrimp are shellfish.

shel-ter [SHEL-tur] NOUN, shelters. **1. abri** ▶ something that protects from the weather or from danger : *We ran into the house for shelter from the wind.* **2. foyer, refuge** ▸ a place for homeless people to stay for a time : *a Red Cross shelter.* ▲ VERB, sheltered, sheltering. **mettre à l'abri de** ▸ to give shelter to ; protect : *The trees sheltered us from the rain.* ■ **sheltered**, ADJECTIVE. **à l'abri, à couvert** ▸ away from harm or difficulty : *"The cove was partly sheltered from the wind."* (Scott O'Dell) SYN : protection, harbour, refuge, cover.

shelve [shelv] VERB, shelved, shelving. **1. mettre sur les rayons** ▸ to put on a shelf : *The librarian shelved several books.* **2. ajourner** ▸ to put aside to be considered later : *Let's shelve the plans for a new pool until next year.*

shelves [shelvz] NOUN. **étagères, tablettes** ▸ the plural of shelf.

shep-herd [SHEP-urd] NOUN, shepherds. **berger (-ère)** ▸ a person whose work is taking care of or herding sheep in the field. **Note.** At one time, the word *shepherdess* was used for a woman who did this job ; *shepherd* now means either a man or woman. ▲ VERB, shepherded, shepherding. **1. garder, guider** ▸ to watch over or herd sheep. **2. guider, conduire, piloter** ▸ to guide or watch over something, as shepherds do with their herds : *The guide shepherded the tour group through the museum.*

sher-bet [SHUR-bit] NOUN, sherbets. **sorbet** ▸ a frozen dessert like ice cream, made mostly of fruit juice, water, and sugar.

sher-iff [SHAIR-if] NOUN, sheriffs. **1. shérif** ▸ in Canada, a law officer whose job is to carry out court orders. **2. chef de la police, shérif** ▸ the chief law officer of a county.

shied [shide] VERB. a past form of shy.

shield [sheeld] NOUN, shields. **1. bouclier** ▸ a heavy piece of armour that was carried on one arm by knights in the Middle Ages, to protect against blows or weapons during a battle. **2. bouclier** ▸ an object that protects in this way : *A shield covers the blade on the electric saw.* **3. écusson** ▸ something shaped like a knight's shield, such as a police badge. ▲ VERB, shielded, shielding. **protéger** ▸ to protect from harm or danger : *Father shielded us from the wind.*

shift [shift] VERB, shifted, shifting. **1. déplacer, changer, bouger** ▸ to move or change from one to another : *Now, please shift your attention to the front.* **2. changer de vitesse** ▸ to change the gears in a car. ▲ NOUN, shifts. **1. changement, glissement** ▸ the act or fact of shifting : *There's been a shift in opinion on that issue.* **2. levier** ▸ a part used for shifting : *the gearshift of an automobile.* **3. poste, équipe** ▸ a certain group of workers, or the period of time that they work together : *Mom is tired after working the night shift this week.* ✐ **p. 381.**

shil-ling [SHIL-ing] NOUN, shillings. **shilling** ▸ a coin once used in Britain, equal to 1/20 of a pound sterling.

shim-mer [SHIM-ur] VERB, shimmered, shimmering. **miroiter** ▸ to shine with a faint, waving light : *Moonlight shimmered over the ocean.* SYN : glisten, twinkle, shine.

shin [shin] NOUN, shins. **devant du tibia** ▸ the front part of the leg from the knee to the ankle. ▲ VERB, shinned, shinning. **grimper** ▸ to climb up something using both arms and legs to hold on.

shine [shine] VERB, shone or shined, shining. **1. briller** ▸ to give off a light ; be bright ; glow : *The sun shone all day.* **2. polir, briller** ▸ to make bright ; polish : *to shine shoes.* **3. briller** ▸ to be outstanding : *Elizabeth really shines at math.* ▲ NOUN. **brillant** ▸ a bright reflection or light : *a beautiful shine on a waxed floor.*

shin-gle [SHING-gul] NOUN, shingles. **bardeau, aisseau** ▸ a thin piece of wood or other material that is used to cover a roof or wall in overlapping rows. Shingles protect against rain and weather. ▲ VERB, shingled, shingling. **couvrir de bardeaux** ▸ cover with shingles.

shin-y [SHY-nee] ADJECTIVE, shinier, shiniest. **brillant (-ante)** ▸ bright and shining : *a shiny new penny.*

ship [ship] NOUN, ships. **1. navire** ▸ a large seagoing boat. **2. vaisseau (-eaux)** ▸ an airplane or a spacecraft. ▲ VERB, shipped, shipping. **1. expédier (par bateau)** ▸ to send something by ship. **2. expédier, envoyer** ▸ to send by land or air : *to ship a package.* **3. ship out. mettre les voiles** ▸ to go on a ship as a crew member : *Krendra is shipping out today.* ◉ **p. 394.**

ship-ment [SHIP-munt] NOUN, shipments. **cargaison** ▸ the act of shipping, or something that is shipped : *a shipment of toys.*

ship-ping [SHIP-ing] NOUN. **1. expédition, envoi** ▸ the act or business of sending goods by water, land, or air. **2. navires** ▸ ships as a group : *The seaway is open to shipping.*

ship-wreck [SHIP-rek] NOUN, shipwrecks. **naufrage** ▸ the sinking or destruction of a ship at sea, or such a ship itself. ▲ VERB, shipwrecked, shipwrecking. **faire naufrage** ▸ to cause to suffer a shipwreck.

shirt [shurt] NOUN, shirts. **chemise, chemisier** ▸ a piece of clothing worn on the upper body, usually having sleeves and a collar. ☞ **p. 1013.**

shiv-er [SHIV-ur] VERB, shivered, shivering. **frissonner** ▸ to shake from cold or fear ; tremble : *I shivered as I got out of bed to shut the window.* ▲ NOUN, shivers. **frisson** ▸ the act of shivering or trembling.

shoal [shohl] NOUN, shoals. **haut-fond, banc de sable** ▸ a shallow place in a lake, river, or ocean.

shock[1] [shok] VERB, shocked, shocking. **1. choquer** ▶ to disturb or upset the mind and feelings : *His rude attitude shocked us.* **2. produire, recevoir une décharge** ▶ to cause an electric shock. ▲ NOUN, shocks. **1. choc** ▶ a sudden, very strong blow to the mind and feeling that comes from some bad or unexpected event : *Mr. Lang was fired, instead of being promoted — what a shock!* **2. choc** ▶ a dangerous condition of the body caused by the blood's sudden failure to circulate properly. Shock can be brought on by an injury, heavy bleeding, a great fright, or emotional distress. **3. choc électrique** ▶ a feeling of pain caused by electricity passing through the body. **4. secousse** ▶ a strong and sudden blow, jolt, or crash : *The earthquake caused violent shocks along the surface of the earth.* SYN : startle, frighten, appall, jolt, alarm, surprise.

shock[2] NOUN, shocks. **1.** (also stook) **botte, gerbe** ▶ a bundle of grain stalks, such as corn or wheat, set on end in a field to dry. **2. tignasse** ▶ a thick mass of hair.

shock·ing [SHOK-ing] ADJECTIVE. **bouleversant (-ante)** ▶ causing a shock; very wrong or bad : *Her nasty behaviour was shocking.* ■ **shockingly**, adverb. ▶ **affreusement**. ✎ **p. 609.**

shod·dy [SHOD-dee] ADJECTIVE, shoddier, shoddiest. **de camelote, minable** ▶ poorly made, or of poor quality; inferior.

shoe [shoo] NOUN, shoes. **1. soulier, chaussure** ▶ an outer covering worn on the foot. **2. fer à cheval** ▶ something like a shoe, such as a horseshoe. ▲ VERB, shod or shoed or shodden, shoeing. **chausser, ferrer** ▶ to put a shoe or shoes on : *to shoe a horse.* ✎ **p. 1014.**

shone [shon *or* shone] VERB. a past form of shine.

shook [shook] VERB. a past form of shake.

shoot [shoot] VERB, shot, shooting. **1. tirer** ▶ to fire a gun or other such weapon. **2. tirer** ▶ to hit with a bullet, arrow, or the like : *The hunters shot two elk.* **3. tourner** ▶ to photograph or film something : *They shot a movie in Halifax.* **4. (s') élancer, se projeter** ▶ to move or grow quickly, as if sent from a gun : *Water shot out of the hose when the tap was turned on.* ▲ NOUN, shoots. **pousse** ▶ a new growth that comes out from a plant.

shop [shop] NOUN, shops. **1. magasin, boutique** ▶ a small store where goods are sold : *a candy shop.* **2. atelier** ▶ a public place where a certain kind of work is done : *a TV repair shop.* ▲ VERB, shopped, shopping. **1. magasiner** ▶ to visit stores or shops to look for and buy goods. **2. shop around. comparer les prix** ▶ to compare prices in various stores before making a purchase.

shop·lift·er [SHOP-LIF-tur] NOUN, shoplifters. **voleur (-euse) à l'étalage** ▶ a person who steals goods from a store while pretending to be a customer.

shopping centre **centre commercial** ▶ a separate group of stores, restaurants, and other businesses in one area with a common parking area **Note.** Also called a **shopping mall** or **shopping plaza** (often shortened to **mall** or **plaza**). ✎ **p. 1054.**

shore [shor] NOUN, shores. **1. côte, bord, rivage** ▶ the area of land along an ocean, a lake, or a river. **2. terre** ▶ dry land : *The sailors ate on shore when the ship docked.* SYN : coast, waterfront, beach, bank. ✎ **p. 1109.**

shorn [shorn] VERB. a past form of shear.

short [short] ADJECTIVE, shorter, shortest. **1. court (courte)** ▶ not far from one end to the other; not long or tall : *short hair.* **2. petit (petite), court (courte)** ▶ not long in distance or time : *a short walk.* **3. à court de** ▶ not having enough; lacking : *I am short on cash and can't go to the movie.* **4. brève** ▶ of a vowel, having a sound that is said quickly and with little force. The *i* in the word *hit* is short, but the *i* in *mine* is long. ▲ ADVERB. **1. net (nette)** ▶ suddenly : *The car stopped short to avoid the dog.* **2. ne pas atteindre** ▶ not quite as far as; on the near side of : *The arrow fell short of the target.* ▲ NOUN, shorts. **1. court métrage** ▶ something that is short, such as a movie lasting a few minutes. **2. short, culotte courte** ▶ pants that end around the knees. **3. caleçon** ▶ men's underpants. ✎ **p. 533.**

short·age [SHOR-tij] NOUN, shortages. **manque, pénurie** ▶ the fact of having less than is needed; too small an amount : *We were careful of the water we used during the water shortage.* SYN : lack, want, need, deficiency.

short circuit **court-circuit** ▶ an electric circuit that allows too much current to flow through it. A short circuit may blow a fuse or start a fire.

✎ **Word Builder**

Short appears in the expression *short end of the stick,* which means the worst side of an unequal deal : *Dwayne thinks he got the short end of the stick, since he had to wash the dishes and all I did was set the table.* The phrase *make short work of* means to deal with quickly : *She made short work of the chocolate cake at Marcella's birthday party.* *Cut short* means to end suddenly : *My mother cut short our card game and sent us to bed.*

short-com-ing [SHORT-kum-ing] NOUN, short-comings. **défaut, imperfection ▸** a failure to reach the level needed; a fault or weakness : *She soon realized the shortcomings of the cheap telephone.*

short cut raccourci ▸ a quicker or shorter way to go somewhere or do something.

short-en [SHORT-un] VERB, shortened, shortening. **raccourcir, abréger ▸** to make or become short : *to shorten a pair of pants that are too long.*

short-en-ing [SHORT-ning] NOUN. **matière grasse ▸** any kind of fat that is used in baking or cooking, such as butter, lard, or vegetable oil.

short-hand [SHORT-hand] NOUN. **sténo, sténographie ▸** a method of writing that uses symbols or letters to take the place of longer words. It is used by some reporters and secretaries to write down quickly what someone else is saying.

short-ly [SHORT-lee] ADVERB. **bientôt, prochainement ▸** in a short time; soon : *Lee is at the store and will be back shortly.*

short-stop [SHORT-stop] NOUN, shortstops. **arrêt-court, inter ▸** in baseball, the position between second and third base, or a player who plays there.

short story nouvelle ▸ a work of fiction that is shorter than a novel.

shot[1] [shot] NOUN, shots. **1. coup de feu ▸** the act of firing a gun, cannon, or other such weapon. **2. tireur (-euse) ▸** a person who shoots a gun or other weapon : *Claire is a good shot.* **3. plomb, grenaille de plomb ▸** a ball of lead or steel that is fired from a shotgun or cannon. **4. tir ▸** the launching of a rocket or missile toward a target : *a moon shot.* **5. piqûre ▸** an injection of medicine given with a needle : *a flu shot.* **6. tir ▸** in games such as basketball, hockey, or soccer, an effort to score a goal. **7. prise de vue, photo ▸** a photograph or view with a camera : *The photographer took a good shot of the race.* **8. poids ▸** the heavy metal ball used in the shot put.

shot[2] VERB. a past form of **shoot.**

shot-gun [SHOT-gun] NOUN, shotguns. **fusil de chasse ▸** a gun that is fired from the shoulder like a rifle.

shot put lancer de poids ▸ an event in track and field in which people compete to see how far they can throw a heavy metal ball. ■ **shot-putter,** NOUN. ▸ **lanceur (-euse).**

should [shood] VERB. used with other verbs to show **1.** a duty or obligation : *You should drive slowly on the icy road.* **2.** a condition that would lead to something else : *You should come to the movie, if you've done your work.* **3.** what is expected or likely : *My cold should be better soon.*

shoul-der [SHOLE-dur] NOUN, shoulders. **1. épaule ▸** the part on either side of the body between the neck and arm. **2. accotement ▸** an edge or border alongside a road or highway. ▲ VERB, shouldered, shouldering. **1. se frayer un chemin à coup d'épaules ▸** to push with the shoulders : *He shouldered his way through the crowd.* **2. endosser ▸** to place a load on, or as if on, the shoulders : *to shoulder the blame for something.* 📘 **p. 1003.**

shout [showt] VERB, shouted, shouting. **crier ▸** to cry out loudly; yell : *Daria shouted to Anton to pass the ball.* ▲ NOUN, shouts. **cri ▸** a loud cry; a yell. SYN: yell, shriek, holler, bellow, scream.

shove [shuv] VERB, shoved, shoving. **pousser, enfoncer ▸** to push or press roughly, especially in a rude way : *"I shoved my way off the bleachers and ran to the locker room."* (S.E. Hinton) ▲ NOUN, shoves. **poussée ▸** a rough push. SYN: push, jostle, ram, bump, nudge.

shov-el [SHUV-ul] NOUN, shovels. **pelle ▸** a tool with a handle and a broad scoop, used for digging and moving dirt, snow, and other loose matter. ▲ VERB, shovelled, shovelling. (also shoveled, shoveling) **1. pelleter ▸** to dig up and move with a shovel. **2. enfourner, pelleter ▸** to move or throw in large amounts, as with a shovel : *We shovelled down lunch in a hurry.*

show [shoh] VERB, showed, shown or showed, showing. **1. montrer ▸** to allow to be seen; bring into view : *Maheed showed us the story he had written.* **2. se voir ▸** to be in sight; be able to be seen : *The sun showed through the clouds.* **3. exposer ▸** to make known; reveal : *This cave painting shows a deer hunt.* **4. montrer ▸** to tell the proper way or course; guide or direct : *I showed Robin how to use the computer.* ▲ NOUN, shows. **1. démonstration ▸** the act or fact of showing : *A show of hands decided the vote.* **2. exposition ▸** something that is seen or presented to the public; an exhibition or display : *a dog show.* **3. spectacle ▸** a play, movie, television or radio program, or other such entertainment. **4. semblant, mine de ▸** a display that is intended to attract attention or to give a false impression : *Laurie put on a show of courage.* ■ **showy,** ADJECTIVE. **voyant ▸** putting on a show; attracting attention. 📘 **p. 1148.**

show-er [SHOW-ur] NOUN, showers. **1. averse ▸** a short rainfall. **2. douche ▸** a bath in which water sprays down on a person from an overhead fixture with small holes in it. **3. douche ▸** this fixture itself, or an enclosed space containing it. **4. pluie, déluge de ▸** a fall of many small things like a rain shower : *a shower of sparks from a fire.* **5. réception, fête ▸** a party at which gifts are given to celebrate an event such as a wedding or the birth of a baby. ▲ VERB, showered, showering. **1. verser, pleuvoir ▸** to fall or cause to fall in a shower

THE SEVEN WONDERS OF THE ANCIENT WORLD

Pharos of Alexandria
▶ le phare d'Alexandrie

Hanging gardens of Babylon
▶ les jardins suspendus de Babylone

Temple of Artemis at Ephesus
▶ le temple d'Artémis à Éphèse

Mausoleum at Halicarnassus
▶ tombeau de Mausole Halicarnasse

Pyramids of Egypt
▶ les pyramides d'Égypte

Colossus at Rhodes
▶ le colosse de Rhodes

Statue of Zeus at Olympia
▶ la statue de Zeus à Olympie

535

Alfred PELLAN,
Mascarade, 1942

Collection, Montreal Museum of Contemporary Art

Paul-Émile BORDUAS,
Les carquois fleuris, 1947

Anne KAHANE,
Runners, 1952
Private collection

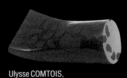

Jean DALLAIRE,
Peintre maudit !, 1954

Lavalin collection. Montreal Museum of Contemporary Art

Jean-Paul MOUSSEAU,
Sans titre, 1956

Ulysse COMTOIS,
Foot Prints, 1964

Collection, Montreal Museum
of Contemporary Art

Pierre AYOT,
Et boule de gomme, 1972

Collection, Montreal Museum of Contemporary Art

Marcel BARBEAU,
Rétine virevoltante, 1966

1953
Commercial computer by IBM
(U.S.)

1954
Nuclear power plant
(Russia)

1957
Artificial satellite
Sputnik 1 (Russia)

1959
• **Snowmobile**
  by Joseph Armand Bombardier
  (Canada)

• **Electronic chip**
  by Bob Noyce
  (U.S.)

printed circuit ▶

1960
Laser by Theodore Maiman
(U.S.)

1961
**Inhabited space
capsule,** *Vostok 1*
(Russia)

1962
• **Roboticized assembly line** by
  Unimation (U.S.)
• **Skateboard**
  by Mickey Munoz
  and Phil Edwards
  (U.S.)

◀ 1973 model with
polyurethane
wheels

1965
Snowboard
by Sherman Poppen

◀ 1977 model
by Jake Burton Carpenter
(U.S.)

1970
IBM diskette
(U.S.)

1971
Space station
Saliut 1 (Russia)

1972
Video game
by Ralph Baer
(U.S.)

1973
Genetic manipulation
by Stanley Cohen and Herbert Boyer
(U.S.)

1974
Chip card
by Roland Moreno
(France)

1978
Microcomputer
by Steve Jobs and Steve Wozniak
(U.S.)

◀ Apple

1979
Sony **Walkman**
(Japan)

1980
In-line skates
by the Olsen brothers
(U.S.)

1981
• *Columbia*
  **space
  shuttle**
  (U.S.)

• "**Canadarm**" used during the second
  flight of the *Columbia*

1982
Discman
by Sony (Japan)
and Philips
(Netherlands)

1985
CD-ROM by Sony (Japan) and Philips
(Netherlands)

1986
International space station
Mir
(Russia)

1989
Nintendo **Game
Boy** (Japan)

1991
Marketing of first
virtual reality game
in London
(Great Britain)

1994
Public access to the **Internet**

1996
DVD-video by Sony (Japan) and
Philips (Netherlands)

B RIDGES

GIRDER BRIDGE

cantilever bridge △
(Quebec City Bridge)
► cantilever

◁ **box girder bridge**
(Confederation Bridge,
Prince Edward Island)
► à poutres-caissons

SUSPENSION BRIDGE

cable-stayed bridge △
(Papineau Bridge, Montreal)
► à haubans

MOVABLE BRIDGE

cable-supported bridge △
(Pierre-Laporte Bridge, Quebec City
► à câbles

ARCH BRIDGE

(Laviolette Bridge, Trois-Rivières) ▽
► en arc

single-leaf bascule bridge △
(lock located at Sainte-Catherine)
► pont basculant à simple volée

542

The wind showered the ground with leaves from the tree. **2. prendre une douche ▸** to bathe in a shower. **3. inonder de ▸** to give in large amounts; give generously : *The parents showered their son with praise at his graduation.*

shown [shohn] VERB. a past form of show.

shrank [shrank] VERB. a past form of shrink.

shred [shred] NOUN, shreds. **1. lambeau (-eaux) ▸** a narrow strip or small piece that has been torn or cut off : *He used shreds of newspaper to pack the dishes.* **2. morceau (-eaux), moindre preuve ▸** a small amount; a bit : *There wasn't a shred of evidence.* ▲ VERB, shredded or shred, shredding. **déchiqueter ▸** to cut or tear into shreds. **Note.** A machine that shreds paper is a shredder.

shrew [shroo] NOUN, shrews. **musaraigne ▸** a very small animal somewhat like a mouse, having a long nose, short ears, and brownish fur.

shrewd [shrood] ADJECTIVE, shrewder, shrewdest. **astucieux (-euse) ▸** clever and sharp, especially in acting for one's own benefit : *The shrewd politician kept his opponents off guard.* ■ **shrewdly,** ADVERB. ■ **astucieusement.** ■ **shrewdness,** NOUN. ▸ **astuce.** SYN: clever, smart, cunning, crafty, knowing.

shriek [shreek] NOUN, shrieks. **cri perçant ▸** a loud, piercing sound or cry. ▲ VERB, shrieked, shrieking. **hurler, pousser un cri ▸** to make such a sound : *The children shrieked when they saw a mouse.*

shrill [shril] ADJECTIVE, shriller, shrillest. **criard (-arde) ▸** having a high, piercing sound : *a shrill whistle.*

shrimp [shrimp] NOUN, shrimp or shrimps. **crevette ▸** a small shellfish with a long tail that is related to the lobster. Shrimp are highly valued as food.

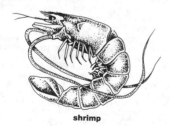

shrimp

shrine [shrine] NOUN, shrines. **1. lieu saint, châsse, reliquaire ▸** a holy place, such as the tomb of a saint, an altar in a church, or a box holding a holy object : *The shrine at Ste-Anne-de-Beaupré attracts visitors from around the world.* **2. lieu saint ▸** a place or object that is

respected or highly valued because of its history or memories : *The old Montreal Forum was often called "the shrine of hockey."*

shrink [shrink] VERB, shrank or shrunk, shrunk or shrunken, shrinking. **1. faire rétrécir ▸** to make or become smaller in size : *She shrank her jeans in hot water.* **2. reculer devant ▸** to draw back; move away from : *People shrank away from the snarling dog.*

shriv-el [SHRIV-ul] VERB, shrivelled, shrivelling. (also shriveled, shriveling) **(se) flétrir ▸** to dry up; shrink : *The plants shrivelled in the dry weather.*

shroud [shrowd] NOUN, shrouds. **1. linceul ▸** a cloth used to cover a dead body for burying. **2. voile ▸** something that covers or hides. ▲ VERB, shrouded, shrouding. **envelopper ▸** to cover with, or as if with, a shroud : *A fog shrouded the beach with an eerie mist.*

shrub [shrub] NOUN, shrubs. **arbuste ▸** a woody plant that is smaller than a tree, and that usually has several stems rather than a single trunk. **Note.** A grouping of shrubs is shrubbery.

shrug [shrug] VERB, shrugged, shrugging. **hausser les épaules ▸** to raise the shoulders slightly to show doubt, dislike, or lack of interest. ▲ NOUN, shrugs. **haussement d'épaules ▸** the act of raising the shoulders in this way.

shrunk [shrunk] VERB. a past form of shrink.

shrunken [shrunk-un] VERB. a past form of shrink.

shud-der [SHUD-ul] VERB, shuddered, shuddering. **frissonner, frémir ▸** to shake or tremble : *The hikers shuddered to think of their narrow escape.* ▲ NOUN, shudders. **frisson, frémissement ▸** the act of shuddering : *Shudders came from the car engine, but it wouldn't start.*

shuf-fle [SHUF-ul] VERB, shuffled, shuffling. **1. traînement de pieds ▸** to walk by dragging the feet along the ground. **2. mêler, mélanger, battre ▸** to mix playing cards to change their order before dealing them out. **3. brasser ▸** to move things from one place to another : *Josh shuffled the papers on his desk trying to look busy.*

shun [shun] VERB, shunned, shunning. **éviter ▸** to avoid on purpose; stay away from : *Frank shuns greasy foods and sweets.*

shut [shut] VERB, shut, shutting. **1. fermer ▸** to move something so that it blocks an entrance or opening; close : *Shut the screen door; you're letting mosquitoes into the house.* **2. fermer ▸** to bring together the parts of : *Shut the book and go to sleep.* **3. couper, arrêter, fermer ▸** to stop the operation or activity of (used with an ADVERB) : *to shut off a radio.* **4. bloquer ▸** to stop the passage or movement of; block : *Dark drapes shut out the daylight.*

shut out blanchissage ▶ in sports, to stop the other team from scoring. **Note.** Also used as a NOUN:*to pitch a shutout.*

shut-ter [SHUT-ur] NOUN, shutters. **1. volet** ▶ a movable cover for a window or door, used to shut out light, and so on. **2. obturateur** ▶ a movable cover over a camera lens that lets in light for a very short time when a picture is taken. ▲ VERB, shuttered, shuttering. **fermer les volets** ▶ to close with, or as if with, shutters.

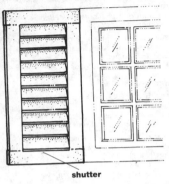

shutter

shut-tle [SHUT-ul] NOUN, shuttles. **1. navette** ▶ a train, a bus, or an airplane that makes short trips between two places : *Someday the space shuttle will take people to the moon and back.* **2. navette** ▶ in the weaving of cloth, a device that carries the thread back and forth across the piece that is being woven. ▲ VERB, shuttled, shuttling. **véhiculer** ▶ to move back and forth between two places. ✪ p. 396.

shy [shy] ADJECTIVE, shyer, shyest. (also shier, shiest) **1. timide** ▶ not comfortable in public or in a group of people; bashful : *Anwar is too shy to talk much.* **2. sauvage, farouche** ▶ of an animal, easily frightened; timid. **3.** *Informal.* **manquer de** ▶ short of; lacking : *I am two cents shy of a dollar.* ▲ VERB, shied, shying. **1. se cabrer (devant)** ▶ to move back suddenly because of fear : *The horse shied at the sight of the rattlesnake.* **2. éviter** ▶ to stay away from, out of doubt or dislike : *Kate shied away from the large horse.* ■ **shyly,** ADVERB. ▶ **timidement.** ■ **shyness,** NOUN. ▶ timidité.

sick [sik] ADJECTIVE. **1. malade** ▶ not in good health; having a disease; ill. **Note.** A person who is often sick is sickly. **2. qui a mal au cœur** ▶ having an upset stomach; feeling nausea. **3. écœuré (-ée) par, qui en a assez de** ▶ feeling strong dislike or unhappiness : *I'm sick of tuna sandwiches.* ■ **sickness,** NOUN. ▶ maladie.

side [side] NOUN, sides. **1. côté** ▶ a surface or part of something, other than the front, top, bottom, or back : *The van has doors on both sides.* **2. côté** ▶ an outside line or surface : *A triangle has three sides.* **3. côté** ▶ one of the two similar surfaces of a flat object : *Write on both sides of the paper.* **4. partie, côté** ▶ a point or place away from the centre of something : *the west side of the city.* **5. aspect, point de vue, côté** ▶ one of two opposing groups or points of view : *Which side are you cheering for?* **6. côté** ▶ a certain quality that a person or thing has : *He has a funny side, too.* ▲ ADJECTIVE. **1. de côté** ▶ at or near one side : *a side view.* **2. secondaire** ▶ less important; secondary : *Don't worry about that right now; it's a side issue.* ▲ VERB, sided, siding. side with. **prendre parti** ▶ to take sides; support : *We sided with Taylor in the argument.*

sideburns [SIDE-burnz] PLURAL NOUN. **favoris** ▶ the hair that grows along the side of a man's face, next to the ears.

side effect effet, réaction secondaire ▶ a secondary effect of a drug, chemical, or other medicine, besides the intended effect : *The medicine had the side effect of making me sleepy.*

side-walk [SIDE-wok] NOUN, sidewalks. **trottoir** ▶ a path or place alongside a street where people can walk. It is usually paved.

side-ways [SIDE-wayz] ADVERB; ADJECTIVE. (also sidewise) **1. de côté** ▶ to or toward one side : *to move sideways instead of forward.* **2. latéralement** ▶ with one side forward : *to walk sideways through a narrow passageway.*

siege [seej] NOUN, sieges. **siège** ▶ the surrounding of a fort, city, or position for a long time by an army trying to capture it. Supplies are cut off from those who are under siege, in an effort to force them to surrender.

sieve [siv] NOUN, sieves. **tamis, crible** ▶ a utensil that has many small holes in the bottom, used to separate solids from liquid or smaller pieces from larger ones.

sift [sift] VERB, sifted, sifting. **1. tamiser, passer au tamis, cribler** ▶ to separate larger pieces from smaller ones by shaking through a sieve, net, or the like : *They sifted the soil to remove pieces of wood and stones.* **2. tomber doucement, couler** ▶ to fall in a light, loose way, as if through a sieve : *Snow was sifting down from the branches above.* **3. examiner minutieusement** ▶ to examine the individual items of a group, as if putting them through a sieve : *She sifted through the box to find an old picture.*

sigh [sy] VERB, sighed, sighing. **1. soupirer** ▶ to let out a long, deep breathing sound to show that one is sad, tired, relieved, and so on. **2. soupirer** ▶ to make this sound : *Antonio sighed with exhaustion.* ▲ NOUN, sighs. **soupir** ▶ the act or sound of sighing.

sight [site] NOUN, sights. **1.** (also eyesight) vue ▸ the ability to see. **2. vision, aperçu** ▸ the act or fact of seeing. **3. (en) vue** ▸ the range or distance that one can see : *The mother put the candy out of the child's sight.* **4. attraction touristique** ▸ something that is worth seeing : *Ivan visited the famous sights of Spain.* **Note.** A sightseer is someone who visits places of interest. **5. qui est dans un drôle d'état** ▸ something that looks strange or unpleasant : *My hair was a sight after the rainstorm.* **6.** (usually sights) **mire** ▸ a device on a gun or other such object that helps in seeing and taking aim. ▲ VERB, sighted, sighting. **1. apercevoir** ▸ to sense with the eyes ; observe : *The sailors cheered when they sighted land.* **2. viser** ▸ to look at a target through a sight. 📖 **p. 1034.**

sign [sine] NOUN, signs. **1. panneau (-eaux), enseigne** ▸ a board or other such object that has words or numbers on it to give information : *The sign on the building had the company's name and address.* **2. signe** ▸ a mark or object used to stand for something else, a symbol : *The plus sign means addition.* **3. signe** ▸ a thing that shows or suggests some fact or quality : *Lisette showed no sign of being tired.* **4. signe** ▸ a movement of the hand or body that carries some meaning ; a signal : *"He held up one hand as a sign, although Ben's father could clearly hear."* (Virginia Hamilton) ▲ VERB, signed, signing. **1. signer** ▸ to write one's name on : *to sign a cheque.* **2. signer, parler dans le langage des signes** ▸ to use sign language. ▪ **signer,** NOUN. **signataire** ▸ a person who signs something.

sig·nal [SIG-nul] NOUN, signals. **1. signal** ▸ an action, sound, or object that is meant to give a warning or message : *A flashing yellow light is a signal of danger ahead.* **2. signal** ▸ a sign or action that causes something to happen : *The flag went down as a signal to start the race.* ▲ VERB, signalled, signalling. (also signaled, signaling) **signaler** ▸ to give a signal : *Mom signalled to Dad with a nod that she was ready to go home.*

sig·na·ture [SIG-nuh-chur] NOUN, signatures. **1. signature** ▸ a person's name written in his or her own handwriting. **2. armature** ▸ a sign at the beginning of a section of music to show the key and metre.

sig·nif·i·cance [sig-NIF-ih-kuns] NOUN. **importance** ▸ the fact of being significant ; importance or meaning.

sig·nif·i·cant [sig-NIF-ih-kunt] ADJECTIVE. **significatif (-ive)** ▸ having special meaning ; important : *a significant game.* ▪ **significantly,** ADVERB. ▸ **d'une manière significative, considérablement.**

sig·ni·fy [SIG-nih-FY] VERB, signified, signifying. **signifier** ▸ to be a sign of ; show : *A bell signifies that class is over.*

sign language langage des signes, langage signé ▸ a way of communicating by using hand and body movements to represent words and ideas : *Aboriginal tribes on the Great Plains used sign language to communicate with each other.*

si·lence [SY-luns] NOUN, silences. **silence** ▸ a lack of sound ; complete quiet : *"They sit in silence, waiting for the sound of the plane."* (Ann Blades) ▲ VERB, silenced, silencing. **faire taire, réduire au silence** ▸ to make silent ; keep quiet : *The storyteller silenced the audience with his tale.*

si·lent [SY-lunt] ADJECTIVE. **1. silencieux (-ieuse)** ▸ having or making no sound ; quiet ; still : *"The big bird gave an angry hiss, rose and flew away on silent wings."* (James Houston) **2. silencieux (-ieuse)** ▸ not spoken out loud : *a silent vote.* ▪ **silently,** ADVERB. ▸ **silencieusement.**

sil·hou·ette [SIL-oo-ET] NOUN, silhouettes. **1. silhouette** ▸ a picture or drawing showing only the outline of the object filled in with a single colour. **2. silhouette** ▸ a dark outline of something against a lighter background : *A silhouette of tree branches seemed like spiderwebs over the moon.* ▲ VERB, silhouetted, silhouetting. **silhouetter, projeter en silhouette** ▸ to show a silhouette : *"The lion looked huge, silhouetted on the rise of bank in the gray morning light."* (Ernest Hemingway)

sil·i·con [SIL-uh-kon] NOUN. **silicone** ▸ a non-metallic element that exists as a brown powder or dark grey crystals and is the second most common element in the earth's crust. Silicon is widely used in making computers and other electronic devices. **Note.** A compound of silicon and oxygen, silicone is used in oils, plastics, and so on.

silk [silk] NOUN, silks. **1. soie** ▸ the soft, shiny thread that a silkworm produces, or the cloth made from this thread. Silk is noted for its great strength and for its deep, rich colours when dyed. **2. de soie, en soie** ▸ anything like silk, such as the strands on an ear of corn. ▪ **silken** or **silky,** ADJECTIVE: ▸ **soyeux (-euse), doux (douce).** *She combed the horse's silky mane.*

silk·worm [SILK-wurm] NOUN, silkworms. **ver à soie** ▸ a caterpillar that spins silk to make its cocoon.

sill [sil] NOUN, sills. **rebord, seuil** ▸ the piece of wood or stone across the bottom of a door or window.

sil·ly [SIL-lee] ADJECTIVE, sillier, silliest. **bête, stupide, idiot (idiote)** ▸ not serious or intelligent ; not showing good sense ; foolish : *We giggled* *and made silly remarks to each other during the movie.* ■ **silliness,** NOUN. ▶ **bêtise, idiotie.**

si-lo [SY-loh] NOUN, silos. **1. silo** ▶ a tall, round building used to store food for farm animals. **2. silo** ▶ a deep hole in the ground used to store and launch guided missiles. 👁 **p. 115.**

silt [silt] NOUN. **vase** ▶ very fine pieces of sand, clay, or other such matter that are carried along by flowing water and then settle at the bottom.

sil-ver [SIL-vur] NOUN. **1. argent** ▶ a shiny white soft metal that is a chemical element. Silver is easily shaped to make such objects as coins, jewellery, or spoons, knives, and forks. **Note.** A person who makes or repairs silver is a silver-smith. **2. monnaie d'argent** ▶ coins that are made of silver. **3. argenterie** ▶ short for silverware. **4. gris argenté, argenté** ▶ a greyish-white colour like silver. ▲ ADJECTIVE. **argenté** ▶ made of, coated with, or having the colour of silver. ▲ VERB, silvered, silvering. **étamer, argenter** ▶ to coat with silver. ■ **silvery,** ADJECTIVE: ▶ **argenté (-ée).** *the silvery moonlight.*

sil-ver-ware [SIL-vur-WAIR] NOUN. **argenterie** ▶ knives, forks, spoons, and the like, sometimes made of silver or containing silver.

sim-i-lar [SIM-uh-lur] ADJECTIVE. **semblable** ▶ not exactly the same but very much alike; of the same kind : *Many animals are a similar colour to their surroundings.* ■ **similarly,** ADVERB. ▶ **de la même façon.**

sim-i-lar-i-ty [SIM-uh-LAIR-ih-tee] NOUN, similarities. **similitude** ▶ the fact of being similar; a likeness or resemblance. SYN : alikeness, sameness, closeness.

sim-i-le [SIM-uh-lee] NOUN. **comparaison** ▶ a phrase or expression in which one thing is compared to another to suggest they are alike. 🖉 **p. 546.**

sim-mer [SIM-ur] VERB, simmered, simmering. **1. (faire) mijoter** ▶ to cook below or just below the boiling point : *The stew simmered for 15 minutes.* **2. bouillonner** ▶ to be just below the point of breaking out : *Jan's temper was simmering as he picked up the broken jar.*

sim-ple [SIM-pul] ADJECTIVE, simpler, simplest. **1. simple** ▶ easy to understand or do; not difficult : *a simple math problem.* **2. simple** ▶ without ornament or decoration; not fancy; plain : *He has simple tastes in clothes.* **3. simple** ▶ of the basic or ordinary kind; not complicated : *"I see." is a simple sentence.* **4. niais (-aise), naïf (naïve)** ▶ not intelligent; stupid or foolish : *a simple remark.* **Note.** The fact of being simple is simplicity.

sim-pli-fy [SIM-pluh-FY] VERB, simplified, simplifying. **simplifier** ▶ to make easier or plainer; make simpler : *The teacher simplified the problem to be sure that we all would understand it.*

🖉 **Writing Tips**

Simile

*A **simile** is a writing technique that compares one thing with another, using like, as, or than to connect the two things. Similes are useful writing tools to help describe something unfamiliar by comparing it with something familiar.*

> *Our flight to Kamloops was as bumpy as a roller-coaster ride.*

When you write similes, use comparisons that your reader will recognize. It's no use saying "Alfie was as smart (tall, kind, hungry) as Kelly," unless the reader already knows how smart (tall, kind, hungry) Kelly is.

---

sim-ply [SIM-pul] ADVERB. **1. avec simplicité** ▶ in a simple way : *to dress simply.* **2. simplement** ▶ only; just : *I'm simply asking you to do part of the housework, not to clean the whole house.* **3. tout simplement** ▶ really; absolutely : *Tanya simply yearns to learn how to ride a horse.*

sim-u-late [SIM-yuh-LATE] VERB, simulated, simulating. **simuler** ▶ to give a show or appearance of; imitate : *The space centre simulates weightlessness to prepare the astronauts.* ■ **simulation,** NOUN. ▶ **simulation.**

si-mul-ta-ne-ous [SY-mul-TAY-nee-us] ADJECTIVE. **simultané (-ée)** ▶ existing or happening at the same time : *"The beginning of civilization and the appearance of temples are simultaneous in history."* (H.G. Wells) ■ **simultaneously,** ADVERB. ▶ **simultanément.**

sin [sin] NOUN, sins. **1. péché** ▶ the act of breaking a moral or religious law : *Murder is a sin.* **2. péché, mal** ▶ any action that is thought of as very wrong or bad : *It's a sin the way that dog is chained up.* ▲ VERB, sinned, sinning. **pécher** ▶ to break a moral or religious law. **Note.** A person who sins is a sinner. ■ **sinful,** ADJECTIVE. ▶ **coupable, honteux (-euse).** SYN : offence, vice, crime, wrongdoing.

since [since] ADVERB. **1. depuis** ▶ from then until now : *I saw her last summer, but I haven't seen her since.* **2. depuis** ▶ at some time between then and now : *Amar arrived this morning : he has since painted the kitchen.* ▲ PREPOSITION. **depuis** ▶ from then until now : *She has lived in British Columbia since 1981.* ▲ CONJUNCTION. **1. depuis (que)** ▶ after the time when : *He's been looking for work since he was laid off.* **2. puisque** ▶ because : *Since we had to go to the store, dinner will be late.* 🖉 **p. 52.**

sin·cere [sin-SEER] ADJECTIVE, sincerer, sincerest. **sincère** ▶ telling or showing the truth; honest and real; not false : *a sincere apology.* ■ **sincerely,** ADVERB: ▶ **sincèrement.** *Even though she didn't win, Jennifer was sincerely happy that she completed the race.* ■ **sincerity,** NOUN. ▶ **sincérité.** SYN: genuine, true, real, honest, trustworthy.

sing [sing] VERB, sang or sung, sung, singing. **1. chanter** ▶ to make sounds or words with musical tones; produce music with the voice. **2. chantonner, fredonner** ▶ to make a whistling, ringing, or humming sound that is like a song. **3. chanter** ▶ to tell of or praise something in a song or poem : *"Come near me, while I sing the ancient ways."* (William Butler Yeats)

sing·er [SING-ur] NOUN, singers. **chanteur (-euse)** ▶ a person or bird that sings. ▶ **p. 1128.**

sin·gle [SING-gul] ADJECTIVE. **1. seul (seule), unique** ▶ only one; one : *Liza has only a single shoe.* **Note.** A line in which people stand one behind the other is called single file. **2. pour une personne** ▶ meant to be used by one person only : *a single serving.* **3. célibataire** ▶ not married : *Joaquim is single, but wants to marry after law school.* ▲ NOUN, singles. **1. simple** ▶ a hit in baseball that allows the runner to reach first base safely. **2. célibataire** ▶ a person who is not married. ▲ VERB, singled, singling. **1. single out. isoler, choisir** ▶ to pick or choose from a group : *She singled out the black puppy as the one she wanted.* **2. frapper un simple** ▶ to hit a single in baseball. ■ **single-handed,** ADJECTIVE. **tout seul (toute seule)** ▶ without anyone's help or support. ▶ **p. 643.**

sin·gu·lar [SING-gyuh-lur] ADJECTIVE. **1. singulier (-ière)** ▶ showing only one person or thing : *"Mouse" is a singular noun; "mice" is plural.* **2. singulier (-ière), bizarre** ▶ out of the ordinary; unusual : *The sighting of the comet was a singular event that excited scientists around the world.* ▲ NOUN, singulars. **singulier (-ière)** ▶ the form of a word showing only one person or thing.

sin·is·ter [SIN-uh-stur] ADJECTIVE. **sinistre** ▶ evil or suggesting evil; threatening : *That character in the film had a strange, sinister appearance.*

sink [sink] VERB, sank or sunk, sunk, sinking. **1. couler** ▶ to go down below water or another such surface : *After hitting a rock, our rowboat sank into the lake.* **2. baisser** ▶ to become less or weaker : *Noise in the classroom sank to a whisper when the teacher entered.* **3. creuser** ▶ to dig or drill into the earth : *The diggers had sunk several holes into the ground looking for water.* **4. sombrer, s'endormir** ▶ to pass or fall gradually into a certain condition : *to sink into sleep.* ▲ NOUN, sinks. **évier** ▶ a basin of metal, porcelain, or the like, that is used for washing. Sinks have faucets that supply water, and a drain for emptying.

si·nus [SY-nus] NOUN, sinuses. **sinus** ▶ one of the openings or air-filled spaces in the bones of the skull that connect to the nostrils. **Note.** Sinus trouble or sinusitis occurs when these openings become swollen and cause painful pressure.

Sioux [soo] NOUN, Sioux. **1. Sioux** ▶ an Aboriginal people living on the American Plains; also known as Dakota. **2. sioux** ▶ the language of these people. ■ **Siouan,** ADJECTIVE. **sioux.**

sip [sip] VERB, sipped, sipping. **boire à petites gorgées** ▶ to drink in small amounts; take a little drink. ▲ NOUN, sips. **petite gorgée** ▶ a little drink : *a sip of tea.*

si·phon [SY-fun] NOUN, siphons. **siphon** ▶ a bent tube or pipe that has the shape of an upsidedown ∩. Siphons are used to transfer liquid from one container to another by means of air pressure. ▲ VERB, siphoned, siphoning. **siphonner** ▶ to transfer liquid with a siphon : *Brynne siphoned some gas from her car to Aaron's car.*

sir [sur] NOUN, sirs. **1. monsieur** ▶ a title or form of address used in place of a man's name : *Sir, do you know when the next bus arrives?* **2. Sir. sir** ▶ a title used for a man who has been knighted : *Sir Francis Drake was a famous British explorer.*

si·ren [SY-run] NOUN, sirens. **sirène** ▶ a device that makes a loud, shrill noise as a signal or warning, as on an ambulance, police car, or fire truck.

sis·ter [SIS-tur] NOUN, sisters. **1. sœur** ▶ a girl or woman who has the same parents as another person. **2. sœur** ▶ a female member of a group or club. **3. sœur** ▶ a female member of a religious order; a nun.

sit [sit] VERB, sat, sitting. **1. (s') asseoir, être assis (-ise)** ▶ to be in the position in which the body is supported by the lower back and bottom, with little weight on the feet. **2. asseoir** ▶ to cause someone to be in this position : *The child was so agitated, the teacher had to sit him on his chair.* **3. être posé (-ée)** ▶ to occupy a certain place or position, as if sitting : *The house sits high on the mountain.* **4. siéger** ▶ to be a member of an official group : *Ms. Patel sits on the recycling committee.*

site [site] NOUN, sites. **emplacement** ▶ the position or location of something : *The province put up a historical marker at the site of the Rebellion of 1837.* SYN: place, location, position, spot, situation.

sit·u·at·ed [SICH-ooh-ATE-id] ADJECTIVE. **situé (-ée)** ▶ in a certain place or position : *I was situated directly across from Thuy at dinner.*

sit·u·a·tion [SICH-yooh-AY-shun] NOUN, situations. **situation** ▶ any set of conditions that can apply at a given time; a state of affairs : *The situation in the Middle East is getting more serious.*

six [siks] NOUN, sixes; ADJECTIVE. **six** ▸ one more than five; 6. ■ **sixth**, ADJECTIVE; NOUN. ▸ sixième.

six-teen [SIKS-TEEN] NOUN, sixteens; ADJECTIVE. seize ▸ one more than fifteen; 16. ■ **sixteenth**, ADJECTIVE; NOUN. ▸ seizième.

six-ty [SIKS-tee] NOUN, sixties; ADJECTIVE. soixante ▸ six times ten; 60. ■ **sixtieth**, ADJECTIVE; NOUN. ▸ soixantième.

size [size] NOUN, sizes. 1. **grandeur, taille** ▸ the amount of space that a thing takes up; the height, width, or length that something has : *My dog is the same size as yours.* 2. **nombre, montant** ▸ a number or amount : *The size of my income is hardly enough to pay the bills.* 3. **taille, grosseur, pointure** ▸ a number that shows how large clothing, shoes, and other such goods are : *Dennis wears size 10 shoes.* ▲ VERB, sized, sizing. 1. **être d'une taille** ▸ to have a certain size or number. 2. size up. **jauger, juger** ▸ to form a judgment or opinion about : *The teams sized each other up.* ■ **sizeable**, ADJECTIVE. (also sizable) **considérable** ▸ fairly large : *We raised a sizeable amount.* 🖉 p. 548.

siz-zle [SIZ-ul] VERB, sizzled, sizzling. **grésiller** ▸ to make a hissing or crackling sound : *The campfire sizzled.* ▲ NOUN, sizzles. **grésillement** ▸ a hissing or crackling sound : *the sizzle of bacon frying.*

skate[1] [skate] NOUN. skates. 1. (also ice skate) **patin** ▸ a shoe or boot with a metal blade attached to the bottom, used for gliding over ice. 2. (also roller skate or in-line skate) **patin à roues alignées** ▸ a shoe or boot with small wheels mounted on the bottom, used for moving over hard surfaces, such as streets and sidewalks. ▲ VERB, skated, skating. **patiner** ▸ to move on skates. 📖 p. 1154.

skate[2] NOUN, skates or skate. **raie** ▸ a flat fish that has two wide fins on the side of its body and a long, slender tail.

skate-board [SKATE-bord] NOUN, skateboards. **planche à roulettes, rouli-roulant** ▸ a low, flat board that has wheels mounted on the bottom, used for riding. The rider usually balances in a standing position. 👁 p. 541.

skel-e-ton [SKEL-uh-tun] NOUN, skeletons. 1. **squelette** ▸ the complete set of bones that supports the body of a human or animal.

2. **charpente** ▸ a framework thought of as being like this : *The skeleton of the house was all that remained after the fire.* 📖 p. 1004. 👁 p. 549.

skep-ti-cal [SKEP-tih-kul] ADJECTIVE. (also sceptical) **sceptique** ▸ having or showing doubt; not believing : *Mom was skeptical when a free trip was offered for buying a stove.* **Note.** A person who is skeptical is a skeptic.

sketch [skech] NOUN, sketches. 1. **croquis, esquisse** ▸ a quick, rough drawing : *The artist drew cartoon sketches of people for $5 each.* 2. **sketch, saynète** ▸ a short piece of writing : Stephen Leacock's *Sunshine Sketches of a Little Town* are funny stories about life in a small town. ▲ VERB, sketched, sketching. 1. **faire des croquis, esquisses** ▸ to make a sketch. 2. **ébaucher, esquisser** ▸ to present or outline in a rough way, with few details : *We sketched out plans for the party.* **Note.** Something that is sketchy is quickly or roughly done, without enough detail.

ski [skee] NOUN, skis. **ski** ▸ one of a pair of long, narrow runners made of wood, metal, or other material, worn to glide over snow or water. Snow skis are worn with special boots attached to the runner. Water skis have a rubber or plastic shoe into which the foot slides. ▲ VERB, skied, skiing. **skier** ▸ to move on skis : *My little brother skied the beginners' slope.* **Note.** The sport of doing this is skiing.

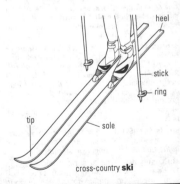

cross-country **ski**

📎 **Word Builder**

Size, dimension, and volume refer to the measure of something. *Size* is the most general of the three words. It can refer to something being large or small in quantity, space, or degree: *Quebec ranks as Canada's largest province in terms of size. Dimension* can refer to the width, height, or length of an object: *The dimensions of the closet were five metres by four metres. Volume* is the amount of cubic space an object takes up or is needed to fill a container: *The volume of our pool is measured in litres.*

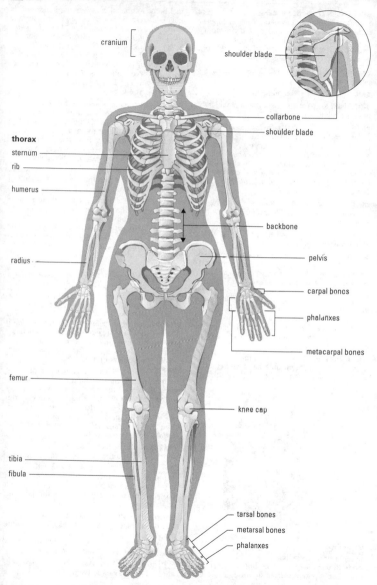

cranium

shoulder blade

collarbone

shoulder blade

thorax

sternum

rib

humerus

radius

backbone

pelvis

carpal bones

phalanxes

metacarpal bones

femur

knee cap

tibia

fibula

tarsal bones

metarsal bones

phalanxes

skid [skid] NOUN, skids. 1. **dérapage** ▶ the act of slipping or sliding sideways on a wet or slippery surface : *The car went into a skid on the icy road.* 2. **palette** ▶ a plank or frame to carry heavy objects. ▲ VERB, skidded, skidding. **déraper** ▶ to slip or slide sideways.

ski-er [SKEE-ur] NOUN, skiers. **skieur (-euse)** ▶ a person who uses skis.

skies [skize] NOUN. ▶ the plural of sky.

skiff [skif] NOUN, skiffs. **esquif** ▶ a small, light boat, especially a rowboat.

skill [skil] NOUN, skills. **adresse, habileté** ▶ an ability to do something well that comes from practice, training, or experience : *The carpenter's skill could be seen in the beautiful furniture.* ■ **skillful,** ADJECTIVE. ▶ **habile, adroit (-oite).** (also skilful) *The seagull opened the clam with one quick, skillful motion.* ■ **skillfully,** ADVERB. ▶ **habilement.**

skilled [skild] ADJECTIVE. **habile à** ▶ having or showing special skill : *Electricians are skilled workers.*

skil-let [SKIL-it] NOUN, skillets. **poêle (à frire)** ▶ a shallow frying pan with a handle.

skim [skim] VERB, skimmed, skimming. 1. **feuilleter** ▶ to read or examine quickly; scan : *Mari skimmed over her notes just before the test.* 2. **écrémer, dégraisser, écumer** ▶ to remove floating matter from the surface of a liquid : *The cleaner skimmed dirt off the bottom of the pool.* Note. A tool or machine that does this is a skimmer. 3. **glisser** ▶ to glide or move swiftly over a surface : *"In the far distance a helicopter skimmed down between the roofs."* (George Orwell)

skim milk **lait écrémé** ▶ milk that has had the cream removed. Skim milk has fewer calories and less fat than whole milk.

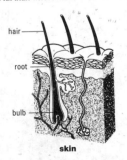

hair

root

bulb

skin

skin [skin] NOUN, skins. 1. **peau (peaux)** ▶ the outer layer of tissue that covers and protects the body. 2. **peau (peaux)** ▶ the outer covering or hide that is removed from an animal. Some animal skins are treated and used to make leather. Some animal skins are treated and used to make leather. Some animal skins are treated and used to make leather. ▶ any surface or outer layer that is like skin : *Peel the skins off the potatoes.* ▲ VERB, skinned, skinning. 1. **(s') écorcher** ▶ to injure by scraping or removing the skin from : *Gwen skinned her knees while skateboarding.* 2. **écorcher, dépouiller** ▶ to cut off the skin of an animal : *Bjorn skinned the chicken to make the meal less fatty.* 🖰 **p. 1004.**

skin diving **plongée sous-marine** ▶ an underwater swimming activity in which the diver stays under for long periods of time using a mask, flippers, and a snorkel. ■ **skin-dive,** VERB, skin-dived or skin-dove, skin-dived, skin-diving. ▶ **faire de la plongée sous-marine.** Note. A person who does this sport is a skin diver.

skin-ny [SKIN-nee] ADJECTIVE, skinnier, skinniest. **(très) maigre** ▶ very thin, especially in an unhealthy or unattractive way.

skip [skip] VERB, skipped, skipping. 1. **sautiller** ▶ to move with a springing step, hopping from one foot to another. 2. **sauter** ▶ to jump lightly over : *to skip rope.* 3. **sauter** ▶ to pass over; leave out : *to skip a meal.* 4. **faire ricocher** ▶ to bounce across a surface : *We skipped stones across the lake.* ▲ NOUN, skips. **bond** ▶ a light, springing step.

skip-per [SKIP-ur] NOUN, skippers. **capitaine** ▶ a nickname for the captain of a ship.

skir-mish [SKUR-mish] NOUN, skirmishes. **escarmouche, échauffourée** ▶ a quick fight or contest involving two small groups : *The skirmish was between the army and the rebels hiding in the hills.* ▲ VERB, skirmished, skirmishing. **se livrer à une guerre d'escarmouches** ▶ to fight in a battle or contest in this way. SYN : clash, scuffle, encounter, conflict.

skirt [skurt] NOUN, skirts. 1. **jupe** ▶ a piece of women's clothing that hangs down from the waist. 2. **jupe** ▶ the part of a dress or other longer piece of clothing that hangs down from the waist. ▲ VERB, skirted, skirting. **contourner** ▶ to go around the edge of something rather than through it; avoid : *The editorial skirted the serious issues.* 🖰 **p. 1014.**

skit [skit] NOUN, skits. **numéro comique** ▶ a short, quick performance or play, usually funny.

skull [skul] NOUN, skulls. **crâne** ▶ the bony framework that forms the head of humans and other animals that have a backbone. The skull protects the brain and supports the jaw and other bones of the face. 🖰 **p. 987.**

skunk [skunk] NOUN, skunks. **mouffette** ▶ a North American animal with black fur, a white stripe down its back, and a long, bushy tail. Skunks spray a bad-smelling liquid when they are frightened or attacked. 👁 **p. 111.**

sky [sky] NOUN, skies. **ciel** ▶ the upper space or atmosphere above the earth : *Blue skies mean* *good weather.* ■ **skyward,** ADVERB. **vers le ciel** ▶ toward the sky. 🖙 **p. 1118.**

sky-div-ing [SKY-DY-ving] NOUN. **parachutisme en chute libre** ▶ a type of parachute jumping in which the jumper falls through the air for a long distance before opening the parachute.

sky-light [SKY-LITE] NOUN, skylights. **lucarne** ▶ a window in a ceiling or roof that lets in outside light.

sky-line [SKY-LINE] NOUN, skylines. **1. ligne d'horizon** ▶ the line along which the sky and the earth seem to come together; the horizon. **2. silhouette** ▶ the outline of buildings, trees, or mountains against the sky : *a city skyline.*

sky-rock-et [SKY-ROK-ut] VERB, skyrocketed, skyrocketing. **monter en flèche** ▶ to rise, succeed, or become famous very quickly, like a skyrocket moving across the sky : *The Beatles skyrocketed to fame during the 1960s.* ▲ NOUN, skyrockets. **fusée** ▶ a firework that goes off high in the sky and showers coloured sparks and lights.

sky-scra-per [SKY-SCRAY-pur] NOUN, skyscrapers. **gratte-ciel** ▶ a very tall building, thought of as so high it touches (scrapes) the sky. 🖙 **p. 1054.**

slab [slab] NOUN, slabs. **plaque, dalle** ▶ a thick, flat piece of something . *a slab of concrete.*

slack [slak] ADJECTIVE, slacker, slackest. **1. mou (molle)** ▶ not tight or firm; loose : *As the line went slack, Tal realized she'd lost the fish.* **2. stagnant (-ante), faible** ▶ not lively; slow : *Business at the store has been slack since the holidays ended.* ▲ NOUN. **mou** ▶ the part of something that hangs loose : *Take up the slack in that rope.*

slack-en [SLAK-un] VERB, slackened, slackening. **relâcher, détendre, ralentir** ▶ to make or become slack; let up ; *The storm slackened and we went outside.*

slacks [slaks] PLURAL NOUN. **pantalon** ▶ trousers or pants, especially when worn as casual wear.

slain [slane] VERB. a past form of slay.

sla-lom [SLAL-um] NOUN. **1. slalom** ▶ in skiing, a zigzag course downhill in which the skier goes in between posts. **2. slalom** ▶ in water skiing, using one ski.

slam [slam] VERB, slammed, slamming. **1. claquer** ▶ to shut with force, causing a loud sound : *She slammed the door.* **2. freiner à fond, se fracasser contre** ▶ to move or throw with force and a loud noise : *Quang slammed on the brakes when a dog ran into the street.* ▲ NOUN, slams. **claquement** ▶ a noisy closing or striking done with great force.

slan-der [SLAN-dur] NOUN, slanders. **calomnie, médisance, diffamation** ▶ a false spoken statement that is made to damage another person's reputation : *The mayor sued the radio station for slander when it stated that he took money*

illegally. ▲ VERB, slandered, slandering. **calomnier, diffamer** ▶ to talk in a false and harmful way about someone. ■ **slanderous,** ADJECTIVE. ▶ **diffamatoire, calomnieux (-ieuse).** SYN : smear, libel, slur, discredit.

slang [slang] NOUN. **argot** ▶ a type of language that is more relaxed than standard language. Slang uses new or made-up words and expressions that are humorous, exaggerated, impolite, and so on.

slant [slant] VERB, slanted, slanting. **1. incliner, pencher** ▶ to move or lie at an angle, rather than straight across or up and down. **2. interpréter dans une perspective, favoriser** ▶ to present facts or ideas so that they favour one side or point of view : *The reporter slanted the facts to make the article more interesting.* ▲ NOUN, slants. **biais, pente** ▶ a slanting line or direction : *to write on a slant.*

slap [slap] VERB, slapped, slapping. **gifler, claquer** ▶ to strike quickly and sharply with the open hand or something flat · *Hallip slapped at the fly with a newspaper.* ▲ NOUN, slaps. **gifle, tape, taloche, claque** ▶ a sharp, quick blow.

slap-shot [SLAP-SHOT] NOUN, slapshots. **lancer-frappé** ▶ in hockey, a fast shot made with a quick stroke.

slash [slash] VERB, slashing. **1. tail-lader** ▶ to cut with a sweeping stroke of a knife or other sharp object : *A thief slashed the seats in our car.* **2. casser, réduire** ▶ to reduce sharply : *to slash prices.* ▲ NOUN, slashes. **cingler** ▶ the act or fact of slashing. **2. barre oblique** ▶ a punctuation mark (/) that shows choice. SYN : slit, cut, chop, carve.

slat [slat] NOUN, slats. **lame, lamelle** ▶ a thin, narrow strip of wood, metal, or other such material : *The fence was missing a few slats of board.*

slate [slate] NOUN. **1. ardoise** ▶ a bluish-grey rock that splits easily into smooth, thin layers. Slate is used to make blackboards, roofs, and garden tiles. **2. (plural slates) ardoise** ▶ a small board used to write on with chalk.

slaugh-ter [SLOT-ur] VERB, slaughtered, slaughtering. **1. abattre** ▶ to kill a farm animal for food : *to slaughter a hog.* **Note.** A building where this is done is a slaughterhouse. **2. massacre** ▶ to kill many people in a cruel and brutal way. **3.** *Informal.* **massacrer** ▶ to defeat very badly : *The first-place team slaughtered us.* ▲ NOUN, slaughters. **massacre** ▶ the act of slaughtering.

slave [slave] NOUN, slaves. **1. esclave** ▶ a person who is legally owned by another person and who can be sold like a piece of property : *In ancient Greece and Rome, prisoners captured in war were often kept as slaves.* **2. esclave** ▶ a person who is completely controlled by some harmful habit or need : *a slave to junk food.* **3.** *Informal.* **esclave** ▶ a person who works long and hard for little pay. ▲ VERB, **slaved**, **slaving**. **trimer ▶** to work like a slave; work long and hard : *The settlers slaved under hot, dusty conditions to make the dry land into a farm.*

slav·er·y [SLAVE-uh-ree *or* SLAVE-ree] NOUN. **1. esclave ▶** the practice of owning another person as a slave : *Slavery ended in the U.S. after the Civil War.* **2. esclavage ▶** the condition of being a slave : *His ancestors had been sold into slavery.*

Slavey [SLAY-vee] NOUN, Slavey *or* Slaveys. **Atha-paskan, Esclave ▶** is from the Cree, who often enslaved them. **2. athapaskan ▶** the Athapaskan language of these people.

slay [slay] VERB, slew, slain, slaying. **tuer ▶** to kill in a violent way; put to death : *to slay a dragon.*

sled [sled] NOUN, sleds. **traîneau (-eaux), luge ▶** a wooden vehicle, mounted on metal runners, used to carry people and goods over the snow. ▲ VERB, **sledded**, **sledding**. **aller en traîneau, faire de la luge ▶** to ride or travel by sled.

sledge-ham·mer [SLEJ-HAM-mur] NOUN, sledge-hammers. **marteau (-eaux) de forgeron ▶** a large, heavy hammer with a long handle, usually held with both hands, used to drive large posts into the ground or break up heavy surfaces such as concrete and rocks.

sleek [sleek] ADJECTIVE, sleeker, sleekest. **1. lis-se, luisant (-ante) ▶** soft and shiny; smooth. **2. lisse, brillant (-ante) ▶** having a neat, trim, smooth, or stylish appearance : *a sleek car.*

sleep [sleep] NOUN. **sommeil ▶** a natural state of rest for humans and animals that occurs at regular times from day to day. Sleep is a time for the mind and body to regain strength and energy. ▲ VERB, slept, sleeping. **dormir ▶** to be or fall into this state. SYN: slumber, dose, nap, rest, snooze. 🖙 p. 1030.

sleeping bag **sac de couchage ▶** a thickly padded, warm bag in which a person may sleep outdoors.

sleep·less [SLEEP-lis] ADJECTIVE. **sans som-meil ▶** going without sleep; not sleeping : *Tika was sleepless the night before the big test.* ■ **sleeplessness,** NOUN. ▶ insomnie.

sleep·y [SLEE-pee] ADJECTIVE, sleepier, sleepiest. **1. somnolent (-ente) ▶** needing seep; drowsy. **2. endormi (-ie), somnolent (-ente) ▶** as if asleep; not active; quiet : *a sleepy town.*

sleet [sleet] NOUN. **verglas ▶** frozen or partly frozen rain : *The sleet caused slippery roads.* ▲ VERB, sleeted, sleeting. **faire du verglas ▶** to come down as sleet.

sleeve [sleev] NOUN, sleeves. **manche ▶** the part of clothing that covers all or part of the arm.

sleigh [slay] NOUN, sleighs. **traîneau (-eaux), luge ▶** a vehicle or carriage on runners, used to travel over snow and ice. A sleigh is usually pulled by a horse.

slen·der [SLEN-dur] ADJECTIVE, slenderer, slen-derest. **1. mince, svelte ▶** not big around; thin, especially in a graceful and attractive way : *The slender skater seemed to float over the ice.* **2. mince ▶** small in size or amount; not as large as it could be : *to win by a slender margin.* SYN: thin, narrow, slight, slim.

slept [slept] VERB. a past form of sleep.

slew [sloo] VERB. a past form of slay.

slice [slice] NOUN, slices. **tranche ▶** a thin, flat piece cut from something larger : *a slice of bread.* ▲ VERB, sliced, slicing. **1. couper en tranches, rondelles ▶** to cut into a thin, flat piece or pieces : *to slice potatoes.* **2. cou-per ▶** to cut or move like a knife : *The boat sliced through the water.*

slick [slik] ADJECTIVE, slicker, slickest. **1. glissant (-ante), lisse ▶** having a smooth or slippery sur-face : *The winding roads were slick with rain.* **2. rusé (-ée) ▶** clever or skillful; smooth : *a slick TV commercial.* ▲ NOUN, slicks. **endroit glisant ▶** a smooth or slippery place. **Note.** A place where spilled oil is floating in the water is called an oil slick. ▲ VERB, slicked, slicking. **lisser ▶** to make slick.

slide [slide] VERB, slid, sliding. **1. glisser ▶** to move smoothly and quickly across a surface : *She slid and slid across the mud.* **2. (se) glisser ▶** to shift or move suddenly : *"I slid into the seat, my head down, my cheeks flaming."* (Jean Little) ▲ NOUN, slides. **1. glissade, glisse-ment ▶** the act of sliding : *The runner made a hard slide into second base.* **2. glissoire, tobog-gan ▶** a piece of playground equipment with a smooth, slanting surface to slide down. **3. glisser ▶** the fall or slipping of a mass of earth, rocks, or snow down a hill. **4. diaposi-tive ▶** a small piece of photographic film viewed on a projector. 🖙 p. 1166.

slight [slite] ADJECTIVE. **1. léger (légère) ▶** not much; small in amount or importance : *a slight cough.* **2. petit (petite) ▶** small in size; thin. ▲ VERB, slighted, slighting. **traiter sans considé-ration ▶** to treat as unimportant; not pay atten-tion to; insult : *Becky slighted Nydia when she didn't invite her to the party.* ■ **slightly,** ADVERB. ▶ un peu, quelque peu.

slim [slim] ADJECTIVE, slimmer, slimmest. **1. svel-te, mince ▶** slender; thin : *She looked slimmer after dieting.* **2. faible ▶** small; in amount; slight : *He has a slim chance of passing if he doesn't study.* ▲ VERB, slimmed, slimming: *to slim down by exercising.*

slime [slime] NOUN. **vase ▶** thick, slippery mud or a similar substance. ■ **slimy,** ADJECTIVE. ▶ visqueux (-euse).

sling [sling] NOUN, slings. **1. fronde ▶** a hand-held device for throwing stones or other small objects : *David used a sling to throw rocks over the barn.* **2. écharpe, bandoulière** ▶ a piece of cloth that is folded in a triangle and tied around the neck, to support an arm or shoulder while it is recovering from an injury. ▲ VERB, slung, slinging. **1. jeter** ▶ to hurl a stone or other small object. **2. jeter par derrière l'épaule** ▶ to hang or throw loosely : *She slung her jacket over her shoulder.*

sling·shot [SLING-shot] NOUN, slingshots. **fronde** ▶ a Y-shaped piece of wood or metal that has an elastic band fastened to the ends of the prongs, used for shooting rocks or other small objects.

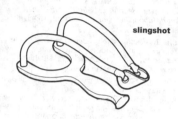

slingshot

slink [slink] VERB, slunk or slinked, slinking. **aller furtivement, partir en catimini, s'éclipser** ▶ to move in a quiet, sneaking way, as if ashamed, trying to hide, and so on : *Sandi slunk to her room so her sister would not hear her.*

slip[1] [slip] VERB, slipped, slipping. **1. glisser, faire une chute** ▶ to slide or move suddenly, so as to lose control : *to slip on ice.* **2. sortir (sans être vu)** ▶ to move quietly, quickly, or smoothly : *Chloe slipped through the guests at the party.* **3. enfiler** ▶ to put on or take off clothing quickly : *Slip on your coat.* **4. faire une gaffe** ▶ to make a mistake : *I slipped up and left the package at the wrong address.* **5. oublier, (s') échapper** ▶ to fail to notice or remember : *It slipped my mind.* **6. glissement, chute** ▶ to become worse; decline : *Sales have slipped recently.* ▲ NOUN, slips. **1. gaffe, faux pas** ▶ the act of slipping. **2. jupon** ▶ a lightweight piece of cloth, worn under a skirt or dress. **3. lapsus** ▶ an error; mistake : *a slip of the tongue.*

slip[2] NOUN, slips. **1. bout, bon, fiche** ▶ a small piece of paper, usually printed : *For information, fill out the slip.* **2. bouture** ▶ a small twig cut from a plant to start a new plant.

slip·per [SLIP-ur] NOUN, slippers. **pantoufle, chausson** ▶ a lightweight, low-cut shoe or sandal : *ballet slippers.*

slip·per·y [SLIP-ur-ee or SLIP-ree] ADJECTIVE, slipperier, slipperiest. **1. glissant (-ante)** ▶ likely to slip or cause slipping : *The wet floor was slippery.* **2. retors (-orse)** ▶ not to be trusted; sly;

tricky : *The slippery thief took the jewels right under the guard's nose.*

slit [slit] NOUN, slits. **fente, déchirure** ▶ a long, narrow opening or cut : *Kiet peeked through a slit in the curtains.* ▲ VERB, slit, slitting. **fendre, couper** ▶ to make a slit or cut in something : *to slit open an envelope.* SYN: cut, split, tear.

slith·er [SLITH-ur] VERB, slithered, slithering. **glisser, ramper** ▶ to move with a slipping, twisting motion : *The snake slithered along the sand.*

sliv·er [SLIV-ur] NOUN, slivers. **petite tranche, éclat** ▶ a small, thin piece of something that has been broken off to a sharp point; a splinter : *slivers of glass.*

slo·gan [SLOH-gun] NOUN, slogans. **slogan** ▶ a phrase or saying that expresses the goals or beliefs of a group. Slogans are often used to draw attention to something in politics or advertising : *Mayor Murray's slogan for the election was "No need to worry with Murray."* SYN: motto, saying, phrase, expression.

sloop [sloop] NOUN, sloops. **sloop** ▶ a small sailboat with one mast.

slop [slop] VERB, slopped, slopping. **1. déverser, répandre** ▶ to spill or splash a liquid in a careless manner. **2. donner de la pâtée** ▶ to give leftover food or wet garbage to farm animals, especially to pigs.

slope [slope] VERB, sloped, sloping. **pencher, être en pente** ▶ to lie or move at an angle; not be straight across; slant : *The stream sloped down the hill to the river below.* ▲ NOUN, slopes. **pente** ▶ land or any other surface that is not flat or level : *a ski slope.*

slop·py [SLOP-ee] ADJECTIVE, sloppier, sloppiest. **1. mouillé (-ée)** ▶ very wet; wet and dirty : *His clothes were sloppy with mud.* **2. négligé (-ée), négligent (-ente), bâclé (-ée)** ▶ not neatly done or made; careless; messy : *sloppy handwriting.*

slot [slot] NOUN, slots. **1. fente** ▶ a straight and narrow opening in something; a groove : *Pay phones and vending machines have slots for coins.* **2. créneau (-eaux)** ▶ a place or position : *I had the fourth slot in the race.*

sloth [sloth] NOUN, sloths. **1. paresseux (-euse)** ▶ a slow-moving animal of South America. It uses its legs and long, curved claws to hang upside down from trees and can even sleep in this position. **2. paresseux (-euse)** ▶ someone who is lazy or not willing to work. ☞ **p. 554.**

slouch [slowch] VERB, slouched, slouching. **être avachi (-ie), avoir une démarche molasse** ▶ to sit, stand, or walk in a loose, drooping position. ▲ NOUN, slouches. **démarche molasse, allure avachie** ▶ a drooping of the head and shoulders.

slow [sloh] ADJECTIVE, slower, slowest. **1. lent (lente)** ▶ not fast or quick; moving without

553

much speed : *slow traffic.* **2. lent (lente)** ▶ taking longer than usual; taking a long time : *a slow game.* **3. en retard** ▶ of a watch or clock, behind the correct time. ▲ ADVERB. (also slowly) **lentement** ▶ in a slow manner : *This clock runs slow. Drive slowly when you pass the school.* ▲ VERB, slowed, slowing. **ralentir** ▶ to make or become slow : *Denzel slowed his bicycle to cross the street.* ■ **slowness**, NOUN. ▶ **lenteur.**

sloth

slug[1] [slug] NOUN, slugs. **1. limace** ▶ a slow-moving animal related to and resembling a snail, but usually without a shell. Some slugs live in moist places such as gardens, and others live in the ocean. **2. balle** ▶ a piece of lead or other metal that is fired from a gun. **3. fausse pièce** ▶ a coin-shaped piece of metal used illegally in place of a coin in a vending machine.

slug[2] *Informal.* VERB, slugged, slugging. **assommer, frapper** ▶ to hit hard, as with the fist or a weapon. ▲ NOUN, slugs. **coup violent** ▶ a hard hit or punch. ■ **slugger**, NOUN. ▶ **frappeur (-euse).**

slug-gish [SLUG-ish] ADJECTIVE. **mou (molle), lent (lente)** ▶ slow to move or act : *The car was sluggish on the cold morning.* ■ **sluggishly**, ADVERB. ▶ **mollement.** ■ **sluggishness**, NOUN. ▶ **mollesse.**

slum [slum] NOUN, slums. **taudis, bidonville** ▶ a poor section of a city where buildings are in bad condition and people live crowded together.

slum-ber [SLUM-bur] VERB, slumbered, slumbering. **1. dormir (paisiblement)** ▶ to sleep or doze. **2. sommeiller** ▶ to be quiet or inactive, as if sleeping. ▲ NOUN. **sommeil** ▶ a sleep or rest.

slump [slump] VERB, slumped, slumping. **1. s'effondrer, s'affaisser** ▶ to sink or fall heavily; slouch : *I was so tired I slumped against the wall.* **2. s'effondrer** ▶ to go down in strength or quality; decline : *The player's batting average*

slumped recently and is down to .200. ▲ NOUN, slumps. **effondrement, chute, crise** ▶ the act or fact of slumping : *Business has been in a bit of a slump.*

slung [slung] VERB. a past form of sling.

slunk [slunk] VERB. a past form of slink.

slur[1] [slur] VERB, slurred, slurring. **mal articuler** ▶ to pronounce words in an unclear way, running together certain sounds : *After her visit to the dentist, she slurred her speech until the medicine wore off.*

slur[2] VERB, slurred, slurring. **insulter** ▶ to say bad things about; criticize in an unfair way. ▲ NOUN, slurs. **insulte** ▶ an insulting remark or comment : *Seanna was hurt by the slur Edgar made about her story.* SYN: insult, slight, libel, slander.

slush [slush] NOUN. **neige fondante, neige fondue** ▶ partly melted snow; watery snow. ■ **slushy**, ADJECTIVE, slushier, slushiest. ▶ **couvert (-erte) de neige fondue.**

sly [sly] ADJECTIVE, slyer, slyest. (also slier, sliest) **1. sournois (-oise)** ▶ able to fool or trick; cunning; shrewd : *The sly fox escaped from the hunters.* **2. malin (-ine)** ▶ full of mischief; playful in a clever way : *a sly grin.* **3. on the sly. à la dérobée, en cachette** ▶ in a sly way; secretly. ■ **slyly**, ADVERB. ▶ **avec ruse, sournoisement.** SYN: cunning, tricky, crafty, sneaky.

smack [smak] VERB, smacked, smacking. **1. claquer la langue** ▶ to make a sharp sound by closing and opening the lips quickly. **2. claquer** ▶ to strike or bump sharply making a loud noise : *The door smacked shut in the wind.* ▲ NOUN, smacks. **1. claquement** ▶ a noisy or sharp blow against a surface; a slap. **2. gros baiser retentissant, grosse bise** ▶ a loud kiss. ▲ ADVERB. **en plein** ▶ straight into; directly : *I walked smack into the light pole.*

small [smol] ADJECTIVE, smaller, smallest. **1. petit (petite)** ▶ not large in size or number; little : *Small amounts of rain each year made this place a desert.* **2. petit (petite)** ▶ not important or serious : *a small problem.* **3. petit (-ite)** ▶ of a business, having limited property or activity : *small businesses such as a candy store or a barber.* **4. mesquin (-ine)** ▶ mean or bitter in a petty way : *That was a small remark you made about Eli's old clothes.* SYN: little, slight, puny, insignificant, tiny.

small letter minuscule ▶ a letter that is not a capital; a lower-case letter : *"I" is a capital letter, and "i" is a small letter.*

small-pox [SMOL-poks] NOUN. **variole** ▶ a very serious, contagious disease marked by chills, fever, and headaches, and by small blisters that can leave deep, permanent scars on the skin.

smart [smart] ADJECTIVE, smarter, smartest. **1. habile, intelligent (-ente), vif (vive)** ▶ having a good mind; quick to learn and understand; intelligent; bright. **2. à l'esprit vif, qui a des idées, dégourdi (-ie)** ▸ making good judgments, clever : *Chapa is a smart shopper and always finds bargains.* **3. vif (vive), rapide** ▸ quick and lively; brisk : *"Look smart!" the officer called out to the soldiers.* **4. élégant (-ante)** ▸ in style; fashionable : *Colin has a smart outfit on today.* ▲ VERB, **smarted, smarting. 1. irriter** ▸ to cause or feel a sharp, stinging pain : *My sunburn really smarts; don't touch my back!* **2. être piqué (-ée) au vif** ▸ to feel distress or hurt feelings : *Lana is still smarting over the scolding her father gave her.* ■ **smartly,** ADVERB. ▸ **rapidement, élégamment.** *A jackrabbit ran smartly from bush to bush, alert for coyotes.*

smash [smash] VERB, **smashed, smashing. 1. casser, briser** ▸ to break into many pieces with great force : *The captain smashed a bottle of champagne against the bow of the new ship.* **2. s'écraser contre** ▸ to strike or hit with a hard blow : *Waves smashed against the rocks.* ▲ NOUN, **smashes. fracassement, collision** ▸ the act of something breaking in a violent way. SYN: shatter, break, crush, destroy, ruin.

smear [smeer] VERB, **smeared, smearing. 1. barbouiller, salir, étaler** ▸ to spread or stain using a sticky, dirty, or greasy substance : *to smear wax on a floor.* **2. brouiller** ▸ to be or cause to be blurred or messy : *The rain smeared the writing on the envelope.* **3. porter atteinte à (la réputation), diffamer, calomnier, salir** ▸ to harm or spoil someone's reputation. ▲ NOUN, **smears. 1. salissure** ▸ a spot or stain caused by smearing : *an oily smear on wallpaper.* **2. calomnie** ▸ a false charge or criticism : *The editorial accused the politician of using smear tactics.* SYN: stain, mark, soil, tarnish, spot.

smell [smel] VERB, **smelled or smelt, smelling. 1. sentir** ▸ to recognize or discover an odour by using the nose. **2. sentir** ▸ to have or give off an unpleasant odour : *The harbour smelled of dead fish.* ▲ NOUN, **smells. 1. odorat** ▸ the sense used to recognize odours. **2. odeur** ▸ a particular odour or scent : *The smell of freshly baked bread filled the shop.* 📖 **p. 1035.**

smelt[1] [smelt] NOUN, **smelts or smelt. éperlan** ▸ a small, silvery fish related to trout. Smelts live in the cool waters of the Northern Hemisphere and are used for food. 👁 **p. 107.**

smelt[2] VERB, **smelted, smelting. fondre, extraire par fusion** ▸ to melt ores to separate the metal from them : *Iron ore must be smelted before it can be made into steel.*

smelt[3] VERB. a past form of smell.

smile [smile] NOUN, **smiles. sourire** ▸ an expression of the face in which the corners of the mouth turn upward, to show a feeling of being happy, amused or friendly. ▲ VERB, **smiled, smiling. sourire** ▸ to have or show a smile : *Tika smiled hello.* 📖 **p. 1024.**

smock [smok] NOUN, **smocks. sarrau** ▸ a loosely fitting garment like a coat or shirt, worn over regular clothing to keep it from getting dirty.

smog [smog] NOUN. **smog** ▸ polluted air that is a mixture of smoke and fog. Smog is caused by the exhaust from cars and factories in larger cities.

smoke [smoke] NOUN, **smokes. fumée** ▸ a substance that is given off by something burning. Smoke is a combination of gases and tiny pieces of soot and ash. ▲ VERB, **smoked, smoking. 1. fumer** ▸ to give off smoke : *The forest was still smoking a day after the fire was put out.* **2. fumer** ▸ to take in and blow out smoke from a cigarette, cigar, or pipe. **3. fumer** ▸ to preserve meat or fish by using smoke from certain kinds of wood : *smoked salmon.* **Note.** A smokehouse is a place where foods are prepared and treated with smoke to preserve them.

smok-er [SMOKE-ur] NOUN, **smokers. fumeur (-euse)** ▸ a person who smokes cigarettes or other forms of tobacco.

smoke-stack [SMOKE-stak] NOUN, **smokestacks. cheminée** ▸ a tall chimney that sends smoke into the air, as in a factory or on an ocean liner.

smok-y [SMOKE-ee] ADJECTIVE, **smokier, smokiest. 1. enfumé (-ée)** ▸ giving off a lot of smoke, or filled with smoke : *a smoky room.* **2. fumé (-ée)** ▸ having the colour or taste of smoke : *smoky glass.*

smooth [smooth] ADJECTIVE, **smoother, smoothest. 1. lisse** ▸ having a surface that is not rough or uneven : *The lake was smooth because there was no wind.* **2. confortable** ▸ free from bumps or jolts; gentle : *a smooth ride.* **3. sans anicroches** ▸ free from trouble or problems : *Our planning made the vacation smooth and carefree.* **4. doux (douce)** ▸ not harsh or bitter to the taste : *a smooth cheese.* ▲ VERB, **smoothed, smoothing. 1. lisser, égaliser, aplatir** ▸ to level or make even; flatten : *to smooth wrinkles out of material.* **2. faire oublier, aplanir les difficultés** ▸ to make easy or easier; take away troubles or problems. ■ **smoothly,** ADVERB. ▸ **en douceur.** ■ **smoothness,** NOUN. ▸ **égalité, douceur.**

smoth-er [SMUTH-ur] VERB, **smothered, smothering. 1. étouffer, suffoquer** ▸ to keep from getting enough air, suffocate : *Young children could smother themselves with plastic bags.* **2. étouffer** ▸ to cause a fire to go out by covering it : *Put a lid on the pan to smother a grease fire.* **3. couvrir** ▸ to cover thickly with something : *The houses in the desert were smothered by the sandstorm.* **4. étouffer, retenir** ▸ to hide; conceal : *We smothered our giggles when the teacher came into the classroom.*

smoul-der [SMOLE-dur] verb, **smouldered, smouldering. (also smolder) 1. couver, brûler lentement** ▸ to burn or smoke with little or no flame. **2. se consumer de colère, de passion** ▸

to show strong feelings that are just below the surface : *His eyes smouldered with anger at the insult.*

smudge [smuj] VERB, smudged, smudging. **salir, maculer ▶** to make dirty by smearing; mark. *Her shoes smudged dirt on the carpet.* ▲ NOUN, smudges. **tache, traînée ▶** a dirty mark or stain made by smearing.

smug [smug] ADJECTIVE, smugger, smuggest. **suffisant (-ante), satisfait (-aite) de soi-même ▶** pleased with oneself to the point of annoying others; showing great self-satisfaction: *"I'm the best dancer," she said in a smug voice.* ■ **smugly,** ADVERB. ▶ **d'un air suffisant.** SYN: vain, conceited, self-satisfied, arrogant.

smug-gle [SMUG-ul] VERB, smuggled, smuggling. **1. faire de la contrebande ▶** to take goods into a country in a secret and illegal way : *to smuggle exotic animals.* **2. faire entrer (sortir) clandestinement ▶** to carry or take secretly : *He smuggled candy into the theatre.* ■ **smuggler,** NOUN. ▶ **contrebandier (-ière).**

snack [snak] NOUN, snacks. **casse-croûte ▶** a small amount of food or drink taken between regular meals; a light meal.

snag [snag] NOUN, snags. **1. accroc ▶** a sharp or rough place on which things can be caught or torn, such as a branch or stump of a tree that is under water. **2. obstacle ▶** a hidden or unexpected problem that blocks progress : *Their plans for a picnic hit a snag when it began to rain.* ▲ VERB, snagged, snagging. **faire un accroc à, accrocher ▶** to catch on a snag : *to snag stockings.*

snail [snale] NOUN, snails. **escargot ▶** a small, slow-moving animal that has a soft body protected by a coiled shell. There are thousands of kinds of snails throughout the world, both on land and in water.

snake [snake] NOUN, snakes. **serpent ▶** a reptile that has a long, slender body with no limbs, lidless eyes, and a covering of dry scales. A snake can swallow an animal larger than itself because its jaws can stretch very wide. Some kinds of snakes have a poisonous bite. ▲ VERB, snaked, snaking. **serpenter ▶** to move in a twisting or winding pattern, as a snake moves along the ground : *The river snakes through the valley.* 📖 p. 1094.

snap [snap] VERB, snapped, snapping. **1. claquer ▶** to make a sharp, quick sound : *to snap your fingers.* **2. claquer, casser net ▶** to break suddenly : *The branch snapped in two.* **3. rafler, saisir ▶** to grab at or take quickly and eagerly : *Shoppers snapped up everything on sale.* **4. se mettre au garde-à-vous ▶** to act or go with a quick, exact movement : *"The sentry snapped to attention as the great man appeared."* (C.S. Forester) **5. photographier, prendre en photo ▶** to take a photograph : *I'll snap your picture as you finish the race.* ▲ NOUN, snaps. **1. bruit sec, claquement ▶** the act or sound of snapping. **2. bouton-pression ▶** a fastener that makes a clicking sound when opened or closed. **3. courte période de temps froid, coup de froid ▶** a short period of very cold weather. **4. Informal. chose aisée, jeu d'enfant ▶** something that is easy to do : *Making instant pudding is a snap.* ▲ ADJECTIVE. **subit (-ite) ▶** made suddenly, without careful thought : *I carefully studied the problem, rather than make a snap decision.*

snap-dra-gon [SNAP-DRAG-un] NOUN, snapdragons. **gueule de loup ▶** a yellow, white, red, or pink flower that grows in clusters on a long stalk.

snap-shot [SNAP-SHOT] NOUN, snapshots. **instantané ▶** a quick or informal photograph.

snare [snair] NOUN, snares. **piège ▶** a trap for catching small animals. ▲ VERB, snared, snaring. **prendre au piège ▶** to catch with, or as if with, a snare : *to snare a fish.*

snarl[1] [snarl] VERB, snarled, snarling. **1. grogner, gronder (en montrant les dents) ▶** of a dog or similar animal, to growl while showing the teeth. **2. grogner, gronder ▶** to speak in an angry or bad-tempered way : *"Get out of my yard,"* snarled my neighbour. ▲ NOUN, snarls. **grondement, grognement ▶** an angry growl.

snarl[2] NOUN, snarls. **1. enchevêtrement ▶** a mass of knots, twists, and so on; a tangled mess : *Her hair was full of snarls from the wind.* **2. embouteillage ▶** a tangled, confused situation or condition. ▲ VERB, snarled, snarling. **emmêler, enchevêtrer ▶** to put into a snarl; make tangled or confused : *The accident snarled traffic on the highway.*

snatch [snach] VERB, snatched, snatching. **s'emparer brusquement de ▶** to grab suddenly : *A dog snatched the food from my hand.* ▲ NOUN, snatches. **1. saisir ▶** the act of grabbing or snatching. **2.** (usually snatches) **fragment ▶** a short period or amount; a little bit : *I caught snatches of that new song on the radio.* SYN: take, seize, grab, clutch, grasp.

sneak [sneek] VERB, sneaked or snuck, sneaking. **se faufiler furtivement ▶** to move or act in a quiet, secret way, so as not to be seen or noticed : *He tried to sneak into his sister's room.* ▲ NOUN, sneaks. **cachottier (-ière), hypocrite, rapporteur (-euse) ▶** a person who is dishonest or who does things in a cunning, secret way. ■ **sneaky,** ADJECTIVE. ▶ **sournois (-oise).**

sneer [sneer] VERB, sneered, sneering. **ricaner, se moquer, lancer des sarcasmes ▶** to say or act with disrespect, dislike, and anger. ▲ NOUN, sneers. **sourire de mépris, ricanement ▶** an expression that sneers, often like a twisted smile. SYN: mock, jeer, cut down, ridicule, scorn.

sneeze [sneez] VERB, sneezed, sneezing. **éternuer ▶** to force air out through the nose and mouth in a sudden, violent way that cannot be stopped or controlled. ▲ NOUN, sneezes. **éternuement** ▸ the act of sneezing.

snick-er [SNIK-ur] NOUN, snickers. **ricanement** ▸ a sly or cruel laugh that shows scorn, dislike, or disrespect. ▲ VERB, snickered, snickering. **ricaner** ▸ to laugh in this way : *The other team snickered as Todd missed the ball.*

sniff [snif] VERB, sniffed, sniffing. **1. renifler** ▸ to breathe in through the nose in short, quick breaths. **2. flairer** ▸ to smell by sniffing : *The dog sniffed my clothes.* ▲ NOUN, sniffs. **reniflement** ▸ the act or sound of air being drawn quickly through the nose.

snif-fle [SNIF-ul] VERB, sniffled, sniffling. **renifler, pleurnicher** ▸ to breathe loudly by sniffing through the nose, as when crying or when sick with a cold. ▲ NOUN, sniffles. **1. reniflement** ▸ the act or sound of sniffling. **2. sniffles. petit rhume** ▸ a slight cold in the nose and head.

snip [snip] VERB, snipped, snipping. **couper** ▸ to cut with scissors in short, quick strokes : *The barber snipped the hair around his ears.* ▲ NOUN, snips. **petit coup de ciseaux, petit bout** ▸ the act of snipping, or a piece that is snipped off.

snip-er [SNIPE-ur] NOUN, snipers. **tireur (-euse) embusqué (-ée)** ▸ a person who uses a gun from a hidden place.

snob [snob] NOUN, snobs. **1. snob** ▸ someone who thinks he or she is better than others because of wealth or position. **2. snob** ▸ a person who claims great knowledge or taste in some area, and who looks down on the taste of others.

snoop [snoop] NOUN, snoops. **fouine, fouineur (-euse)** ▸ a person who looks secretly into other people's private affairs : *Tima called her brother a snoop for reading her diary.* ▲ VERB, snooped, snooping. **mettre son nez dans** ▸ to pry or sneak in this way.

snooze [snooz] VERB, snoozed, snoozing. *Informal.* **sommeiller, faire un petit somme** ▸ to sleep or nap; doze off. ▲ NOUN, snoozes. **petit somme** ▸ a quick nap or sleep : *an afternoon snooze.*

snore [snor] VERB, snored, snoring. **ronfler** ▸ to make loud, rough breathing sounds while sleeping. ▲ NOUN, snores. **ronflement** ▸ such a noise.

snor-kel [SNOR-kul] NOUN, snorkels. **tuba** ▸ a short tube through which a person can breathe while swimming just under the surface of the water.

snort [snort] VERB, snorted, snorting. **grogner, renâcler** ▸ to blow air through the nose with great force and noise. ▲ NOUN, snorts, **ébrouement, grognement** ▸ a loud, forceful noise made through the nose, as by a horse.

snout [snowt] NOUN, snouts. **museau (-eaux), groin** ▸ in certain animals such as dogs, pigs, or crocodiles, the long front part of the head that extends outward.

snow [snoh] NOUN, snows. **1. neige** ▸ the white crystals or flakes of frozen water vapour that fall from the sky. **2. chute de neige** ▸ a snowfall: *There are heavy snows in the mountains.* ▲ VERB, snowed, snowing. **1. neiger** ▸ to fall as snow. **2. être bloqué (-ée) par la neige** ▸ to cover, block, or shut in with snow, or as if with snow : *A blizzard snowed us in.* **3. neiger** ▸ to fall like snow : *Ash from the fire snowed on the city.* 📖 p. 1104. 👁 p. 113.

snow-ball [SNOH-bol] NOUN, snowballs. **boule de neige** ▸ a small mass of snow that is packed together to resemble a ball. ▲ VERB, snowballed, snowballing. **faire boule de neige** ▸ to grow bigger very quickly : *Her lies snowballed and Una soon found herself in trouble.*

snow-bank [SNOH-bank] NOUN, snowbanks. **banc de neige** ▸ a large mass of snow piled up against something. **Note.** Also called a snow-drift.

snow-board [SNOH-bord] NOUN, snowboards. **planche à neige** ▸ a flat board that can be attached to boots, used to go down a snow-covered hill. ▲ VERB, snowboarded, snowboarding. **faire de la planche à neige** ▸ to go down a hill on a snowboard. 👁 p. 541.

snow-fall [SNOH-fol] NOUN, snowfalls. **chute de neige** ▸ the amount of snow that falls in a certain amount of time or at a particular place.

snow-flake [SNOH-flake] NOUN, snowflakes. **flocon de neige** ▸ a single flake or crystal of snow.

snow man [SNOH-man] NOUN, snowmen. **bonhomme de neige** ▸ snow shaped into a figure similar to a person.

snow-mo-bile [SNOH-moh-beel] NOUN, snowmobiles. **motoneige** ▸ a small open motor vehicle that travels over snow on ski-like runners. 👁 p. 541.

snowmobile

snow-plough [SNOH-plow] NOUN, snowploughs. (also snowplow) **chasse-neige** ▸ a truck with a wide, blade on the front, used to push snow off a road or other surface. ▲ VERB, snowploughed, snowploughing. **déneiger** ▸ to remove snow with a snowplough.

snow-shoe [SNOH-shoo] NOUN, snowshoes. **raquette** ▸ one of a pair of flat frames woven with strips of leather or other material. Snow-

557

shoes are attached to boots and are used to walk on deep snow.

snow·y [SNOH-ee] ADJECTIVE, snowier, snowiest. **1. neigeux (-euse)** ▶ covered with or having snow : *a snowy field.* **2. (blanc) comme neige** ▶ like snow : *a snowy beard.*

snuck [snuk] VERB. a past form of sneak.

snug [snug] ADJECTIVE, snugger, snuggest. **1. confortable** ▶ warm and secure; comfortable; cozy : *I was snug in bed.* **2. serré (-ée)** ▶ tight or close-fitting : *These shoes are too snug and I got a blister.* ■ **snugly,** ADVERB. ▶ bien, à l'aise.

snug·gle [SNUG-ul] VERB, snuggled, snuggling. **se blottir (contre)** ▶ to move up against; cuddle : *The little boy snuggled with his stuffed bear.*

so [soh] ADVERB. **1. tellement** ▶ to a certain extent or degree : *How can you be so sad about the race when you came in second?* **2. cela** ▶ in a way stated or suggested : *We have to clean our room; Mom said so.* **3. de même** ▶ in the same way; likewise; also : *Lydia likes chocolate, and so does Kumar.* **4. tellement** ▶ very much; extremely : *There was so much laundry and so little detergent.* **en effet** ▶ most certainly; indeed : *You did so take my cookie!* ▲ ADJECTIVE. **ainsi** ▶ true : *He thinks we are bad sports, but that's just not so.* ▲ CONJUNCTION. **donc** ▶ with the result or purpose that : *She stayed up too late, so she's tired this morning.* **Note.** Often used with that : *I stayed home so that I could finish my project.* ▲ INTERJECTION: ▶ alors, donc. *So, you are the thief!*

soak [sohk] VERB, soaked, soaking. **1. faire tremper** ▶ to let sit in water or other liquid : *Soak your shirt in cold water and the juice stain may come out.* **2. tremper** ▶ to make very wet; wet completely : *The rain soaked the children.* **3. absorber** ▶ to take or draw in; absorb : *Shayla soaked up the warmth of the sun.* SYN: wet, drench, saturate, steep.

soap [sope] NOUN, soaps. **savon** ▶ a common cleaning substance usually made from fat and lye. Soap comes in the forms of bars, liquids, powders, or flakes. VERB, soaped, soaping. **savonner** ▶ to rub or cover with soap. ■ **soapy,** ADJECTIVE. ▶ savonneux (-euse).

soar [sor] VERB, soared, soaring. **1. monter en flèche, prendre son essor, s'élever** ▶ to fly very high and seemingly without effort : *Eagles soared on the air currents looking for prey below.* **2. s'élever, augmenter de façon vertigineuse** ▶ to rise or greatly increase; go very high : *Temperatures will soar into the 30s today.*

sob [sob] VERB, sobbed, sobbing. **sangloter** ▶ to cry with short, quick catches of breath; cry hard. ▲ NOUN, sobs. **sanglot** ▶ the act of crying in this way : *Sobs of grief could be heard during the memorial service.* SYN: cry, weep, wail, howl.

so·ber [SOH-bur] ADJECTIVE, soberer, soberest. **1. sobre** ▶ not drinking alcohol; not drunk. **2. grave, posé (-ée)** ▶ very serious; solemn; grave : *The sober look of the judge made everyone nervous.* ▲ VERB, sobered, sobering. **dégriser** ▶ to make sober : *A stern look sobered the giggling children.* ■ **soberly,** ADVERB. ▶ avec modération.

so·called [SOH-KAHLD] ADJECTIVE. **soi-disant, prétendu (-ue)** ▶ called such, but not actually so : *The so-called hero who reported the fire had actually started it.*

soc·cer [SOKE-ur] NOUN. **soccer, football** ▶ a game played on a large field by two teams of 11 players each who try to get a ball into a goal by kicking it or moving it with the body except for hands and arms. **Note.** Many countries call this game football.

so·cia·ble [SOH-shuh-bul] ADJECTIVE. **sociable** ▶ liking to be with other people; friendly : *Thuy was not feeling sociable; so, he stayed in his room.*

so·cial [SOH-shul] ADJECTIVE. **1. social (-ale, -aux)** ▶ having to do with society; having to do with people in groups or people in general : *Great social changes came during the 1960s.* **2. social (-ale, -aux)** ▶ of animals, living together in groups, as humans do : *Bees and ants are social insects.* **3. social (ale, -aux)** ▶ having to do with friends or friendly relations : *If my grades don't improve, I'll have to cut back on my social life.* **4. social (ale, -aux)** ▶ having to do with people who are rich, famous, fashionable, and so on : *The party was the social event of the year.* ▲ NOUN, socials. **soirée, réunion** ▶ a friendly gathering; a party : *a church social.* ■ **socially,** ADVERB. ▶ en société, socialement.

Social Credit Party Le Parti du Crédit Social ▶ a political party founded in the 1930s in Alberta.

so·cial·ism [SOH-shul-iz-um] NOUN. (also Socialism) **socialisme** ▶ an economic and political system in which factories, land, businesses, and other means of producing goods are owned by the government rather than by individuals.

so·cial·ist [SOH-shul-ist] NOUN, socialists. (also Socialist) **socialiste** ▶ a person who believes in or practises socialism.

social science 1. sciences humaines ▶ the study of human relationships and the way society works. History, government, economics, geography, sociology, and anthropology are social sciences. **2.** (usually **social studies**) **sciences humaines** ▶ the study of history, geography, and other social sciences as a subject in school.

social work travail social ▶ a profession that brings assistance to people in need, in areas such as health care, mental health, and family and child welfare. **Note.** A person trained to do this work is a **social worker.**

so·ci·e·ty [suh SY-ih-tee] NOUN, **societies.** **1. société** ▸ all human beings; people living and working together as a large group : *Medical research benefits society.* **2. société** ▸ a certain group of people : *Canadian society.* **3. société, association** ▸ a group of people who share a common interest or purpose : *the Cancer Society.* 🖉 p. 437.

sock¹ [sok] NOUN, **socks. chaussettes** ▸ a knitted or woven covering for the foot and lower leg.

sock² VERB, **socked, socking.** *Informal.* **flanquer un coup** ▸ to hit or punch.

sock·et [SOK-it] NOUN, **sockets. douille, prise de courant** ▸ an opening or hollow place forming a holder for something : *Screw the bulb into the light socket.*

sod [sod] NOUN. **1. tourbe** ▸ the surface of ground including grass and its roots. **2. motte de gazon** ▸ a piece or layer of ground held together by grass and roots and not tightly secured to the earth : *On the prairies, people made houses using sod for walls.* ▲ VERB, **sodded, sodding. poser de la tourbe** ▸ to cover or plant with sod.

so·da [SOH-duh] NOUN, **sodas. 1. bicarbonate de soude** ▸ a white powder made with sodium, used in soap, in making glass, and in cooking and medicine. **2.** (sometimes **soda pop**) **soda** ▸ a drink made with carbonated water and sweet flavouring, and sometimes ice cream; a soft drink.

so·di·um [SOH-dee-um] NOUN. **sodium** ▸ a soft, waxy, silvery element. Sodium occurs in nature only in combination with other substances. Table salt and soft drinks contain sodium.

so·fa [SOH-fuh] NOUN, **sofas. sofa, canapé** ▸ a long, padded seat or couch with a back and arms. **Note.** Also called a **couch** or a **chesterfield.** 🖉 p. 1072.

sofa

soft [soft] ADJECTIVE, **softer, softest. 1. doux (douce)** ▸ easily giving way to the touch : *soft pillows.* **2. soyeux (-euse)** ▸ not rough or coarse; smooth and light to the touch : *Cats have soft fur.* **3. doux (douce)** ▸ not too strong or extreme; gentle; mild : *They kept the music*

soft; we could talk at the party. **4. faible** ▸ not in good physical condition; lacking strength; weak. *The dogs became soft and lazy from lack of exercise.* **5. tendre** ▸ affected by the emotions; gentle and kind : *Carlo's soft heart makes him take home all the stray dogs he sees.* ■ **softly,** ADVERB. ▸ **doucement, faiblement.** ■ **softness,** NOUN. ▸ **douceur.**

soft·ball [SOFT-bol] NOUN, **softballs. 1. balle molle** ▸ a game like baseball but played with lighter bats and a larger, softer ball that is pitched underhand. **2. balle (molle)** ▸ the ball used in this game.

soft drink (**boisson gazeuse**) ▸ a sweet, carbonated drink made without alcohol.

soft·en [SOF-un] VERB, **softened, softening. ramollir, adoucir, atténuer** ▸ to make or become softer : *I heated the butter to soften it.*

soft·ware [SOFT-wair] NOUN. **logiciel** ▸ the programs that make a computer operate; the information and instructions for a computer. **Note.** Hardware is machinery such as a keyboard, a display screen, or a printer.

sog·gy [SOG-ee] ADJECTIVE, **soggier, soggiest. trempé (-ée), détrempé (-ée)** ▸ soaked with water; wet and heavy : *After the storm, the soggy trail made hiking difficult.* SYN: damp, soaked, wet, saturated.

soil [soyl] NOUN, **soils. 1. sol, terre** ▸ the loose surface part of the earth in which plants grow; dirt; earth : *Farmers like dark, rich soil for vegetables.* **2. terre** ▸ country; land. ▲ VERB, **soiled, soiling. salir** ▸ to make or become dirty, stain : *Don't soil your new outfit.* 🖉 p. 1114.

so·lar [SOH-lur] ADJECTIVE. **solaire** ▸ having to do with the sun : *Solar energy uses the heat from the sun.*

solar system système solaire ▸ the sun and all the things that orbit around it, including planets, comets, and other natural objects in outer space.

sold [sohld] VERB. a past form of sell.

sol·der [SOD-ur] NOUN. **soudure** ▸ a metal that is melted and used to join two metal surfaces. A mixture of lead and tin is a common solder. ▲ VERB, **soldered, soldering. souder** ▸ to bind or mend with a solder.

sol·dier [SOLE-jur] NOUN, **soldiers. soldat** ▸ a person who serves in the army, especially one who is not an officer. **Note.** The term *soldier* goes back to *solidus,* a gold coin that was used to pay soldiers in the ancient Roman army.

sole [sole] NOUN, **soles. semelle** ▸ the bottom part of the foot, or of a shoe, slipper, or boot. ▲ VERB, **soled, soling. ressemeler** ▸ to put a sole on a shoe or boot; repair a sole : *Mike soled his boots again because the old soles were worn through.*

sole[2] ADJECTIVE. **1. seul (seule), unique** ▸ being the only one; single; alone : *Selma is our sole daughter.* **2. exclusif (-ive)** ▸ limited to one person or group; exclusive : *Our school has sole use of that area.* ■ **solely,** ADVERB. ▸ **seulement.**

sole[3] NOUN, sole or soles. **sole** ▸ a flatfish related to the flounder, usually found near shore in warmer seas. The sole is a popular food fish.

sol-emn [SOL-um] ADJECTIVE. **grave, solennel (-elle)** ▸ very serious; grave : *The solemn look on Mom's face told us something had happened.* ■ **solemnly,** ADVERB. ▸ **solennellement.** *The witness solemnly swears to tell the truth.* SYN: sombre, sad, serious, grave.

sol-id [SOL-id] ADJECTIVE. **solide** ▸ having a definite shape and some amount of firmness; not a liquid or gas : *Ice is the solid form of water.* **2. massif (-ive)** ▸ made entirely of one material : *a solid gold bracelet.* **3. solide** ▸ in firm agreement; united : *The countries had a solid agreement.* **4. d'affilée, continu (-ue)** ▸ without breaks; entire : *We danced for two solid hours.* ▲ NOUN, solids. **solide** ▸ a substance that has shape and firmness and is not a liquid or gas. Wood, rocks, and metal are examples of solids. ■ **solidly,** ADVERB. ▸ **solidement, unanimement.** *Most countries solidly back the peace plan.* **Note.** The fact of being solid is solidity. SYN: firm, sound, stable, sturdy, strong, hard.

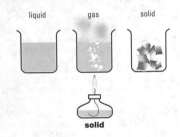

liquid · gas · solid

solid

sol-i-taire [SOL-ih-TAIR] NOUN, solitaires. **1. patience, solitaire, réussite** ▸ a card game for one player. **2. solitaire** ▸ a single diamond or other gem set alone in a ring.

sol-i-tar-y [SOL-ih-TAIR-ee] ADJECTIVE. **1. solitaire** ▸ being the only one; alone or single : *"The mole's a solitary soul who minds his own affairs."* (Jack Prelutsky) **2. solitaire** ▸ by itself; isolated; lonely. **Note.** The fact of being alone is solitude. ✎ p. 643.

so-lo [SOH-loh] NOUN, solos. **solo** ▸ music played or sung by a single person : *a violin solo.* **Note.** A person who performs a solo is a soloist.

▲ ADJECTIVE; ADVERB. **en solitaire** ▸ done or performed by a single person : *a solo flight.*

sol-stice [SOL-stis *or* SOLE-stis] NOUN, solstices. **solstice** ▸ the two times of the year when the sun is farthest away from the earth's equator. In the Northern Hemisphere, June 21 or 22 is the summer solstice (the longest day of the year), and December 21 or 22 is the winter solstice (the shortest day).

sol-u-ble [SOL-yuh-bul] ADJECTIVE. **1. soluble** ▸ able to be dissolved in liquid : *The dry soup mix is soluble in water.* **2. soluble** ▸ able to be solved : *The detective was convinced that the case was soluble.*

so-lu-tion [suh-LOO-shun] NOUN, solutions. **1. solution** ▸ an answer to a problem; an explanation : *The solutions to the crossword puzzles are in the back of the book.* **2. solution** ▸ a mixture of a substance dissolved in a liquid. **Note.** A substance in which another can be dissolved is called a solvent.

solve [solv] VERB, solved, solving. **résoudre, élucider** ▸ to find an answer or solution for; explain : *Anup always uses wisdom to solve problems, never violence.* SYN: answer, work out, clear up, explain.

som-bre [SOM-bur] ADJECTIVE. (also **somber**) **sombre** ▸ dark, gloomy, and depressing : *The forest was a sombre and scary place to be alone at night.* SYN: dismal, murky, shadowy, dreary, bleak.

some [sum] ADJECTIVE. **1. quelques, un peu** ▸ a number or quantity that is not known : *Do you want some cheese on your sandwich?* **2. quelconque** ▸ being a thing that is referred to, but not named or known : *James said he'd call back some other time.* ▲ PRONOUN.: **certains** ▸ *Almost all the guests are here, but some are coming late.*

some-bod-y [SOM-bud-ee *or* SUM-bud-ee, *or* SUM-bod-ee] PRONOUN. **quelqu'un** ▸ a person; some person who is not known or not identified : *Somebody left a present on my desk.*

some-day [SUM-day] ADVERB. **un jour** ▸ at some time in the future : *Tanis wants to fly a plane someday.*

some-how [SUM-how] ADVERB. **d'une manière ou d'une autre** ▸ in a way that is not known or stated; in one way or another : *Somehow, the skunk got into our house.*

some-one [SUM-wun] PRONOUN. **quelqu'un** ▸ some unknown or unnamed person; somebody.

som-er-sault [SUM-ur-salt] NOUN, somersaults. **culbute, saut périlleux** ▸ the act of rolling the body in a complete circle by bringing the feet up and over the head. ▲ VERB, somersaulted, somersaulting. **faire la culbute, faire un saut périlleux** ▸ to do a somersault.

some-thing [SUM-THING] PRONOUN. **quelque chose ▸** an unknown or unnamed thing : *Something is wrong with the car—it's making a funny noise.* ▲ ADVERB. **quelque peu ▸** to some degree ; somewhat : *A zebra looks something like a horse.*

some-time [SUM-TIME] ADVERB. **un jour ou l'autre ▸** at an indefinite time ; at one time or another : *Let's go to a ball game sometime.*

some-times [SUM-TIMEZ] ADVERB. **parfois ▸** now and then ; at times : *Sometimes it's very hot in Calgary.*

some-what [SUM-WUT] ADVERB. **quelque peu ▸** to some amount ; rather : *Jorge is somewhat disappointed with his new computer.*

some-where [SUM-WAIR] ADVERB. **1. quelque part ▸** in or to an unknown or unnamed place : *Your hockey stick is somewhere in the garage.* **2. à peu près, dans les environs de ▸** at an unknown or unnamed point ; about : *The poet Chaucer was born somewhere around 1340.*

get somewhere avancer ▸ to make progress ; have some success.

son [sun] NOUN. **sons. fils ▸** a person's male child : *My son Peter made dinner for the whole family.*

so-nar [SOH-NAR] NOUN. **sonars. sonar ▸** an instrument that uses reflected sound waves for navigation and to determine the location of objects under water, such as fish or icebergs. **Note.** The word *sonar* started out as an acronym for sound navigation and ranging.

so-na-ta [suh NAI-tuh] NOUN. **sonatas. sonate ▸** a musical composition written for one or two instruments and having three or four distinct sections.

song [song] NOUN. **songs. 1. chanson, chant ▸** a musical piece performed by the voice ; music that is sung. **2. chant, ramage, gazouillis ▸** music-like sounds made by a bird, or something able to produce such sounds. 🖐 **p. 1131.**

song-bird [SONG-BURD] NOUN. **songbirds. oiseau chanteur ▸** any bird that sings or has a musical call.

son-ic [SON-ik] ADJECTIVE. **sonique ▸** having to do with, or caused by, sound waves. **Note.** A sonic boom is an explosive sound that occurs when aircraft travel at speeds faster than sound (1,225 km/h).

son-net [SON-it] NOUN. **sonnets. sonnet ▸** a 14-line poem that has 10 syllables in each line, and set rhythm and rhyme patterns.

soon [soon] ADVERB. **1. bientôt ▸** in the near future ; before long : *Dad will be home from work soon.* **2. tôt ▸** ahead of time ; early : *I took the cake out of the oven too soon.* **3. rapidement ▸** quickly ; fast : *Rena soon tired of the new game.* **4. just as soon or sooner. plutôt, mieux ▸** by choice : *I'd just as soon read a book than watch TV.* SYN : shortly, presently, promptly, quickly.

soot [soot] NOUN. **suie ▸** a clinging, greasy, black powder formed when fuel such as wood or coal is burned. Soot gives smoke a greyish or black colour and makes the insides of chimneys and fireplaces dirty. ■ **sooty,** ADJECTIVE. ▸ **couvert (-erte) de suie, noir (noire) de suie.**

soothe [sooth] VERB. **soothed, soothing. 1. apaiser, calmer, tranquilliser ▸** to calm down or quiet ; comfort : *The farmer soothed the frightened horse.* **2. apaiser, calmer ▸** to ease pain ; relieve : *This heating pad will soothe sore muscles.* ■ **soothing,** ADJECTIVE. ▸ **calmant (-ante), apaisant (-ante).** ■ **soothingly,** ADVERB. ▸ **d'une manière calmante.** SYN : calm, comfort, quiet, settle, pacify.

so-phis-ti-cat-ed [suh-FIS-tih-KAY-tid] ADJECTIVE. **1. élégant (-ante), raffiné (-ée) ▸** having or showing much knowledge of the world ; very cultured : *Spy novels are often set in sophisticated cities like New York and Paris.* **2. sophistiqué (-ée) ▸** drawing on high levels of knowledge ; complex ; complicated : *That software program is so sophisticated that it can do many tasks at once.* **Note.** The fact of being sophisticated is sophistication.

so-pran-o [suh-PRAN-oh] NOUN. **sopranos. 1. soprano ▸** the highest singing voice for women and boys, or a person who has such a voice. **2. soprano ▸** a singer or musical instrument with such a range : *My sister is a soprano.* **Note.** Often used as an ADJECTIVE : *a soprano saxophone.*

sor-cer-er [SOR-sur-ur] NOUN. **sorcerers. sorcier (-ière) ▸** a person who practises magic. **Note.** Sorcery is the use of magic or witchcraft.

sore [sor] ADJECTIVE. **sorer, sorest. 1. douloureux (-euse), irrité (-ée), endolori (-ie) ▸** causing pain ; aching : *Karen has sore arms from working out.* **2. sensible ▸** causing hurt feelings : *Vacation is a sore subject with him, because he wanted to go to camp.* **3.** *Informal.* **fâché (-ée), vexé (-ée) ▸** mad ; angry. ▲ NOUN. **sores. plaie ▸** an injured or painful place on the body. SYN : painful, aching, tender, throbbing.

sor-rel¹ [SOR-ul] NOUN. **sorrels. oseille ▸** a plant with long clusters of small green flowers and sour-tasting leaves that are used in salads and sauces.

sor-rel² ADJECTIVE. **roux, brun rouge ▸** a reddish-brown colour. **Note.** The name comes from the colour of the seeds of the sorrel plant. ▲ NOUN. **sorrels. alezan ▸** a horse of this colour.

sor-row [SOR-oh] NOUN. **sorrows. chagrin, tristesse ▸** a feeling of pain or unhappiness over a loss or bad event ; sadness : *"Gone was the trust they had shared. In its place was only sorrow."* (Tololwa M. Mollel) ▲ VERB. **sorrowed, sorrowing. éprouver du chagrin, de la tristesse ▸** to feel sorrow; be sad. ■ **sorrowful,** ADJECTIVE. ▶ chagriné (-ée), attristé (-ée). ■ **sorrowfully,** ADVERB. ▶ avec chagrin, tristement. SYN: sadness, grief, regret, heartache, anguish.

sor-ry [SORE-ee] ADJECTIVE, sorrier, sorriest. **1. désolé (-ée)** ▶ feeling or causing sorrow; sad : *We are sorry to hear that Petra is ill.* **2. désolé (-ée)** ▶ feeling regret or shame over something one has done : *I'm sorry I fought with you.* **3. triste, lamentable, piteux (-euse)** ▶ not very good; poor : *a sorry excuse.*

sort [sort] NOUN, sorts. **sorte** ▶ a group of similar things; a type or kind : *What sort of food do you like to eat?* ▲ VERB, sorted, sorting. **trier (selon), assortir** ▶ to place by kind or group; arrange : *Sort the dirty laundry by colour.* ▲ ADVERB. **sort of.** *Informal.* **plutôt, un peu** ▶ a little; somewhat : *My jeans are sort of dirty.* 🖉 p. 526.

SOS ▶ an international distress signal used to call for help : *The sinking ship sent an urgent SOS.*

sought [sot] VERB, a past form of seek.

soul [sole] NOUN, souls. **1. âme** ▶ the part of a person that is not the physical body; the spiritual force within a person that controls thoughts and feelings : *Many people believe a person's soul lives on after death.* **2. personne, âme** ▶ a person : *"Indeed, with never a soul to talk to, the days dragged even more heavily than before."* (George Orwell)

sound[1] [sownd] NOUN, sounds. **1. son, bruit** ▶ something that can be heard; something that is sensed by the ear. **2. son** ▶ one of the distinct noises making up human speech : *"City" begins with an "s" sound.* ▲ VERB, sounded, sounding. **1. sonner, résonner** ▶ to make or cause something to make a noise : *The howl of coyotes sounded over the hills.* **2. sembler** ▶ to make an impression; seem to be : *Mehta sounded lonely; I think we should go visit her.* **3. se prononcer** ▶ to pronounce or be pronounced : *"Sole" and "soul" sound alike.*

sound[2] ADJECTIVE, sounder, soundest. **1. sain (saine)** ▶ free from illness, damage, or fault : *having a sound mind and body.* **2. solide** ▶ strong and safe; secure; solid : *a sound foundation for a house.* **3. judicieux (-euse)** ▶ wise or sensible : *sound advice.* ▲ ADVERB. **profondément** ▶ thoroughly; completely : *Walk quietly; the baby is sound asleep.* ■ **soundly,** ADVERB. ▶ judicieusement. *The voters soundly rejected the proposed new law.* ■ **soundness,** NOUN. ▶ solidité.

sound[3] VERB, sounded, sounding. **sonder** ▶ to measure the depth of a body of water by letting down a weighted rope or string until it touches bottom.

sound out **sonder** ▶ to try to discover the thoughts, feelings, or views of a person : *Dad sounded Mom out on the idea of buying a new house.*

sound[4] NOUN, sounds. **détroit, bras de mer** ▶ a long, wide body of water that either connects two larger bodies or separates an island from the mainland.

sound-proof [SOWND-proof] ADJECTIVE. **insonorisé (-ée)** ▶ not allowing sound to pass in or out : *This apartment is so soundproof that we don't hear our neighbours.* ▲ VERB, soundproofed, soundproofing. **insonoriser** ▶ to make a room or building soundproof.

soup [soop] NOUN, soups. **soupe, potage** ▶ a liquid food made by cooking meat, fish, or vegetables in milk, water, or another liquid, often with solid pieces of food. 🖉 p. 1140.

sour [sowr] ADJECTIVE, sourer, sourest. **1. sur (sure), acide, aigre** ▶ having a sharp or biting taste : *Lemons are sour.* **2. sur (sure), suret (-ette), acidulé (-ée), aigre** ▶ spoiled or decayed : *sour milk.* **3. revêche, aigre** ▶ not happy or pleasant; having or showing bad feelings : *Take that sour expression off your face.* ▲ VERB, soured, souring. **surir, (s') aigrir** ▶ to make or become sour : *The milk soured in my glass overnight.*

source [sorce] NOUN, sources. **source** ▶ the place or thing that something comes from; the origin : *The source of the Alberta River is in Montana.*

sour cream **crème sure** ▶ a smooth, thick cream made sour with acids and used as an ingredient in soups, salads, and other dishes, or as a topping.

sour-dough [SOWR-doh] NOUN. **1. pain au levain** ▶ a type of bread mix that has active yeast, of which a small amount is saved and used to make the next batch. **2. vétéran (des placers d'Alaska)** ▶ a pioneer or prospector in northwestern Canada or Alaska.

south [sowth] NOUN. **1. sud** ▶ the direction that is on your left as you face the sun at sunset; the opposite of north. **2.** (also South) **Sud** ▶ a region or place located in this direction. **3.** (also the South) **du sud** ▶ the southeastern U.S. ▲ ADJECTIVE; ADVERB. **du sud, méridional (-ale, -aux)** ▶ from, toward, or at the south : *a south wind; to head south.*

south-east [SOUTH-EAST] NOUN. **Sud-Est** ▶ the direction that is halfway between south and east. ▲ ADJECTIVE; ADVERB. **du sud-est** ▶ of, at, in, toward, or from the southeast. ■ **southeastern,** ADJECTIVE. ▶ du sud-est.

south-ern [SUTH-urn] ADJECTIVE. **1. méridional (-ale, -aux), sud, austral (-ale, -als)** ▶ in, toward, or of the south. **2.** (also Southern) **méridional (-ale, -aux), du sud, austral (-ale, -als)** ▶ in or having to do with the South : *a southern accent.*

south·ern·er [SUTH-urn-ur] NOUN, southerners. (also Southerner) **méridional (-ale, -aux)** ▸ a person born or living in the south part of a country or region.

south·ward [SOWTH-wurd] ADJECTIVE; ADVERB. (also southwards) **vers le sud** ▸ toward or at the south.

south·west [SOWTH-WEST] NOUN. **Sud-Ouest** ▸ the direction that is halfway between south and west. ▲ ADJECTIVE; ADVERB. **vers le sud-ouest** ▸ toward or at the southwest. ■ **south·western**, ADJECTIVE. ▸ **du sud-ouest**.

sou·ve·nir [SOO-vuh-EER or SOO-vuh-NEER] NOUN, souvenirs. **souvenir** ▸ something kept as a reminder of a person, place, or event : *I have a jar of sand as a souvenir of Prince Edward Island.*

sov·er·eign [SOV-rin or SOV-ur-in] NOUN, sovereigns. **souverain (-aine)** ▸ the highest ruler, a king, queen ; monarch. ▲ ADJECTIVE. **1. souverain (-aine)** ▸ having control or authority ; ruling : *a sovereign command.* **2. souverain (-aine)** ▸ ruling itself ; self-governing : *India, once under British control, became a sovereign state in 1947.*

sow[1] [soh] VERB, sowed, sown or sowed, sowing. **semer** ▸ to plant or scatter seeds in order to grow plants : *to sow a wheat field.*

sow[2] [sow] NOUN, sows. **truie** ▸ an adult female pig.

soy·bean [SOY-been] NOUN, soybeans **graine de soja** ▸ a protein-rich bean used in making flour and oil and eaten as an additive in many foods. Soybeans grow in pods on leafy green bushes.

space [space] NOUN, spaces. **1. espace** ▸ the area beyond the earth's air that has no known end or limits ; the outer area where the sun, moon, planets, and stars are. **Note.** Also called outer space. **2. espace** ▸ the empty area of air that surrounds objects on the earth : *Mona didn't hear me — she just stared off into space.* **3. place** ▸ an open distance or empty area between two things : *Leave space on the page for a picture.* **4. place, espace** ▸ a place or area to be filled in some way : *a parking space.* **5. espace, intervalle** ▸ a period of time : *He's made several trips over the space of a month.* ▲ VERB, spaced, spacing. **espacer** ▸ to leave space between ; keep apart ; separate : *Let's space the chairs out around the room.* ☞ p. 396.

space·craft [SPACE-kraft] NOUN, spacecraft. **engin spatial** ▸ any vehicle used for travelling outside the earth's atmosphere. **Note.** Also called a spaceship.

space shuttle **navette spatiale** ▸ a vehicle that is launched into space by a rocket, used to carry people and supplies between earth and space. It can return to earth, land on an airstrip, and be used over again.

space suit **combinaison spatiale** ▸ a special airtight suit that astronauts wear. It protects them from radiation and heat and provides oxygen.

spa·cious [SPAY-shus] ADJECTIVE. **spacieux (-ieuse)** ▸ having a lot of space ; large and open ; roomy : *The house had spacious rooms and acres of land.*

spade[1] [spade] NOUN, spades. **bêche, pelle** ▸ a digging tool with a long handle attached to a flat, metal blade, which is pushed into the ground with the foot.

spade[2] NOUN, spades. **1. pique** ▸ a playing card marked with one or more black figures like this [♠]. **2. spades. les piques** ▸ the suit of cards that has this design.

spa·ghet·ti [spuh-GET-ee] NOUN. **spaghetti** ▸ very thin, long, stringlike noodles that are cooked by boiling. Spaghetti is made of flour and water.

span [span] NOUN, spans. **1. travée, distance, portée** ▸ the distance or section between two objects or supports : *Each span of the bridge is 100 metres.* **2. espace, durée** ▸ a time period : *The average life span of a person is about 75 years.* ▲ VERB, spanned, spanning. **franchir, enjamber, traverser** ▸ to reach or stretch across or over : *The bridge spans a wide river.*

span·iel [SPAN-yul] NOUN, spaniels. **épagneul** ▸ a small or medium-sized dog that has long, wavy, silky hair and droopy ears.

spank [spank] VERB, spanked, spanking. **donner un coup ou donner une claque sur les fesses, donner une fessée** ▸ to hit the rump with a flat object or the open hand in order to punish : *I spanked the puppy for biting me.*

spare [spare] VERB, spared, sparing. **1. épargner, ménager** ▸ to keep from being hurt or punished ; not harm or destroy : *I chased away the cat to spare the life of the bird.* **2. se passer de, donner** ▸ to give up as not needed ; allow : *I can spare you only 10 minutes before I have to go.* ▲ ADJECTIVE. **1. disponible, en trop** ▸ more than is needed ; extra : *In her spare time, she goes sailing.* **2. maigre, frugal (-ale)** ▸ not generous ; lean : *The spare breakfast didn't satisfy my hunger.* ▲ NOUN, spares. **1. rechange, remplacement** ▸ something extra or available as a replacement : *I have lost my house key but there's a spare in the garage.* **2.** (also spare tire) **pneu de rechange, pneu de secours** ▸ a tire that is carried in a car to replace one that goes flat. **3. abat** ▸ in bowling, the knocking down of all 10 pins with two balls.

spark [spark] NOUN, sparks. **1. étincelle** ▸ a tiny burning piece : *Sparks from the fire jumped out onto the rug.* **2. étincelle** ▸ a small flash of light made when electricity jumps across open space. Spark plugs use sparks to explode the fuel mixture in an automobile engine. **3. étincelle** ▸ a small but important part :

A spark of an idea came into the scientist's mind. ▲ VERB, sparked, sparking. **1. produire une étincelle** ▸ to produce or throw off sparks. **2. provoquer, déclencher** ▸ to set off or cause to begin : *That gossip sparked a lot of bad feelings around town.*

spar·kle [SPAR-kul] VERB, sparkled, sparkling. **1. produire des étincelles** ▸ to give off small flashes of bright light : *Waves on the pond sparkled in the sunlight.* **2. étinceler, briller** ▸ to be lively : *a sparkling conversation.* **3. pétiller** ▸ to give off bubbles of gas : *Champagne is a sparkling wine.* ▲ NOUN, sparkles. **scintillement, étincellement** ▸ a spark or glitter ; a flash. SYN : twinkle, glimmer, glint, gleam, shine, glitter.

spar·row [SPAIR-oh] NOUN, sparrows. **moineau (-eaux)** ▸ any of various kinds of small brownish or greyish songbirds commonly found in North America, such as the house sparrow.

sparse [sparce] ADJECTIVE, sparser, sparsest. **clairsemé (-ée)** ▸ scattered here and there ; small in number or amount : *There is a sparse amount of land available downtown.* ▪ **sparsely,** ADVERB. ▸ peu, d'une façon clairsemée.

spasm [SPAZ-um] NOUN, spasms. **1. spasme** ▸ a sudden and violent movement that cannot be controlled : *She had spasms of coughing all night long.* **2. accès, éclatement** ▸ a sudden burst or outbreak : *spasms of laughter.*

spat[1] [spat] NOUN, spats. **prise de bec, petite dispute** ▸ a small or unimportant quarrel ; a fight.

spat[2] VERB. a past form of spit.

spat·ter [SPAT-ur] VERB spattered, spattering. **éclabousser, asperger** ▸ to splash or scatter in drops or pieces : *Mud spattered her clothing as the car sped off.*

spat·u·la [SPACH-uh-luh] NOUN, spatulas. **spatule, abaisse-langue** ▸ a tool with a long handle and a flat, wide blade, used to slide under foods in order to turn them over or spread thick substances such as icing or plaster.

spawn [spon] NOUN. **œuf** ▸ the eggs of water animals such as fish and frogs. ▲ VERB, spawned, spawning. **1. frayer, pondre** ▸ to lay eggs or produce offspring : *Salmon travel many miles upstream in order to spawn in fresh water.* **2. engendrer, faire naître** ▸ to create a new idea or product ; produce : *The book spawned a TV series.*

speak [speek] VERB, spoke, spoken. **1. parler** ▸ to use words ; talk : *The baby spoke his first word today.* **2. parler de, mentionner** ▸ to mention in talking : *Maria spoke to Donato about the book.* **3. parler** ▸ to be able to use a certain language : *to speak Hindi.* **4. parler, prendre la parole** ▸ to give a speech.

speak·er [SPEEK-ur] NOUN, speakers. **1. celui (celle) qui parle, interlocuteur, orateur (-trice), conférencier (-ière)** ▸ a person who speaks, especially someone who gives a speech. **2. (often Speaker) président (-ente)** ▸ the head officer of an assembly or lawmaking body : *the Speaker of the House of Commons.* **3. (also loudspeaker) haut-parleur, enceinte** ▸ a device or instrument that changes electrical signals into sounds : *Timo bought speakers for his stereo.*

spear [speer] NOUN, spears. **1. lance** ▸ a weapon with a long, thin shaft and a sharp pointed head. **2. pointe** ▸ the long, thin stalk of plants : *asparagus spears.* ▲ VERB, speared, spearing. **piquer, transpercer** ▸ to catch with, or as if with, a spear : *Jasinder speared a piece of meat with a fork.*

spear·mint [SPEER-mint] NOUN. **menthe verte** ▸ a pleasant-smelling plant whose leaves are shaped like the head of a spear. Spearmint is used to give flavour to foods and to chewing gum.

spe·cial [SPESH-ul] ADJECTIVE. **1. exceptionnel (-elle), particulier (-ière), spécial (-ale, -aux)** ▸ different from others ; unusual, especially in a good way : *The clearing by the lake was her special place.* **2. spécial (-ale, -aux), réservé (-ée)** ▸ meant for a certain use or situation ; particular : *That rare book is kept in a special case.* ▲ NOUN, PLURAL, specials. **1. spécialité** ▸ something that is special : *In addition to their regular food, the restaurant offers a special every day.* **2. émission spéciale** ▸ a television show that is not part of a regular series. ▪ **specially,** ADVERB : ▸ spécialement. *Those pants were specially made for him.* 🖋 p. 432.

spe·cial·ist [SPES-uh-list] NOUN, specialists. **1. spécialiste** ▸ a doctor who deals with a particular area of medicine : *a heart specialist.* **2. spécialiste** ▸ anyone who concentrates on one limited area of a larger activity : *The football team has 22 offensive players, 21 defensive, and two kicking specialists.*

spe·cial·ize [SPESH-uh-LIZE] VERB, specialized, specializing. **se spécialiser** ▸ to study or work in one specific area of a larger field : *She sings all kinds of songs, but she specializes in folk songs.* **Note.** The act or fact of specializing is specialization.

spe·cial·ty [SPESH-ul-tee] NOUN, specialties. **1. spécialité, caractère spécial** ▸ a special product, attraction, or feature ; something outstanding or unusual : *The restaurant's specialty is shellfish.* **2. spécialité** ▸ what a person specializes in ; a special area of training or knowledge.

spe·cies [SPEE-seez *or* SPEE-sheez] NOUN, species. **espèce** ▸ a group of plants or animals with common features that set them apart from others : *Coyotes and wolves are different species of the dog family.*

spe·cif·ic [spih-SIF-ik] ADJECTIVE. **particulier (-ière), précis (-ise), clair (claire)** ▸ clearly stated; naming a certain one or ones; definite : *Let me be specific; I want the white cake on the left.* ▲ NOUN. **specifics. détail** ▸ something that is exact and definite : *Teresa couldn't give any specifics about the accident.* ■ **specifically,** ADVERB. ▸ **explicitement, précisément, particulièrement.** SYN: definite, precise, particular, special, exact.

spec·i·fi·ca·tion [SPESS-uh-fih-kaY-shun] NOUN, specifications. **précision, spécification** ▸ something specified; an exact or detailed statement : *Here are specifications for the wood for the table.*

spec·i·fy [SPESS-uh-FY] VERB, specified, specifying. **préciser** ▸ to ask for or explain in a clear and precise way; say exactly : *Did you specify a time for the furniture delivery?*

spec·i·men [SPESS-uh-mun] NOUN, specimens. **spécimen, échantillon, prélèvement** ▸ one person, animal, or thing that can represent and give information about the whole group : *Kai collected 20 different insect specimens.* SYN: sample, representative, example, type.

speck [spek] NOUN, specks. **grain, petite tache, poussière** ▸ a small piece, spot, or mark : *a speck of dust.* ■ **speckled,** ADJECTIVE. ▸ **tacheté (-ée), moucheté (-ée).** *A speckled trout has small reddish spots on the sides of its body.*

spec·ta·cle [SPEK-tuh-kul] NOUN, spectacles. 1. **spectacle** ▸ a very unusual or impressive sight : *The circus was an exciting spectacle of colour and acts.* 2. **(se donner en) spectacle** ▸ a silly or embarrassing sight : *I'm not going to sing—I'll make a spectacle of myself.* 3. spectacles. **lunettes** ▸ a pair of eyeglasses to correct poor vision.

spec·tac·u·lar [spek-TAK-yuh-lur] ADJECTIVE. **spectaculaire, impressionnant** ▸ sure to be noticed and remembered; very unusual or impressive : *The house had spectacular views of the ocean and the city.*

spec·ta·tor [SPEK-tay-tur] NOUN, spectators. **spectateur (-trice)** ▸ a person who watches a game or other scheduled event : *The spectators cheered the players.*

spec·trum [SPEK-trum] NOUN, spectrums or spectra. 1. **spectre (lumineux)** ▸ the bands of colour that are separated and displayed together in a rainbow when sunlight passes through raindrops. The colours of the spectrum are red, orange, yellow, green, blue, indigo, and violet. 2. **gamme, éventail** ▸ a wide range; a variety : *The debaters presented a broad spectrum of opinions on the issue.*

spec·u·late [SPEK-yuh-LATE] VERB, speculated, speculating. 1. **s'interroger, spéculer** ▸ to think about something without having all the facts or evidence; guess : *We can only speculate on*

how the dinosaurs died out. 2. **spéculer** ▸ to take risks in business that may pay off in a good profit : *to speculate on a new invention.* ■ **speculation,** NOUN. ▸ **spéculation, conjecture, supposition.** ■ **speculator,** NOUN. ▸ **spéculateur (-trice).**

sped [sped] VERB. a past form of speed.

speech [speech] NOUN, speeches. 1. **parole, articulation, langage** ▸ the act of speaking; the use of spoken words to express thoughts and feelings. 2. **discours, allocution, sermon** ▸ something that is spoken, especially a formal talk given by one person to a group : *The premier gave a speech to the students.* 3. **articulation, prononciation, accent** ▸ the way a person or group speaks : *We guessed she was from Australia by her speech.*

speech·less [SPEECH-less] ADJECTIVE. **interloqué (-ée), muet (muette)** ▸ unable to speak for a moment because of a shock or great surprise : *Our neighbour was speechless when he won a million dollars in the lottery.*

speed [speed] NOUN, speeds. 1. **rapidité, vitesse** ▸ fast movement or action; quickness : *The greyhound is known for its speed.* 2. **vitesse** ▸ any given rate of movement, whether fast or slow : *Cars passing a school must reduce their speed.* ▲ VERB, sped or speeded, speeding. 1. **aller à toute vitesse, aller à toute allure** ▸ to go at a fast rate; move quickly : *She sped out the door, racing after her dog.* 2. **conduire trop vite, excéder la vitesse limite** ▸ to drive a car, truck, or other such vehicle faster than the law allows (the speed limit).

speed·om·e·ter [spih-DOM-ih-tur] NOUN, speedometers. **compteur de vitesse, indicateur de vitesse** ▸ an instrument or device that shows how fast a car, truck, or bicycle is moving. Many speedometers also contain an odometer, which shows how far the vehicle has travelled.

speed·y [SPEED-ee] ADJECTIVE, speedier, speediest. **rapide** ▸ going or able to go at a fast rate; swift : *Josh is a speedy runner.* ■ **speedily,** ADVERB. ▸ **rapidement.** SYN: fast, rapid, swift, hasty, quick.

spell¹ [spel] VERB, spelled or spelt, spelling. 1. **épeler, orthographier, écrire** ▸ to say or write the letters of a word in a certain order. 2. **épeler, orthographier** ▸ to say or write letters in the correct order : *He doesn't spell well, but he has good ideas for stories.* 3. **signifier, représenter** ▸ to show or indicate; mean : *It spelled trouble for the game when dark clouds appeared overhead.*

spell out expliquer clairement ▸ to explain in a clear, simple way.

spell² NOUN, spells. 1. **sort, sortilège** ▸ a magic power to control a person's actions : *The fairy cast a spell over the villagers to put them to sleep.* 2. **formule magique, incantation** ▸ the words or action used to put a magic spell on someone. **3. charme ▶** a power of great charm or attraction, like magic : *Pat fell under the spell of Cape Breton's rugged coast.* **Note.** A person who is controlled by a spell is spellbound: *Clara was spellbound by the ballet.*

spell[3] NOUN, spells. **1. moment, instant ▶** a short, indefinite period of time : *Let's stop and rest for a spell.* **2. période ▶** a period of a certain action or condition : *a cold spell.*

spell-er [SPEL-ur] NOUN, spellers. **1. personne sachant épeler ▶** a person who spells words : *I am one of the best spellers in the class.* **2. livre d'orthographe ▶** a book that teaches spelling.

spell-ing [SPEL-ing] NOUN, spellings. **1. orthographe ▶** the act of putting letters together to form words, or a school subject that teaches this. **2. orthographe ▶** the correct written form of a word : *Some words have different spellings, such as "theatre" and "theater."* **Note.** A spelling bee is a contest to see who can spell the most words correctly.

spelt [spelt] VERB. a past form of spell.

spend [spend] VERB, spent, spending. **1. dépenser ▶** to give money in return for something; pay out : *The girls each spent $5 for the movie.* **2. consacrer, employer, passer ▶** to use time for : *Muhamud spends hours reading.* **3. épuiser, dépenser ▶** to use up; wear out : *Don't spend all your energy playing ball.* ■ **spender,** NOUN. ▶ **dépensier (-ière).** *She is a big spender, so look for a good tip.*

spent [spent] VERB. épuisé (-ée) ▶ a past form of spend. ▲ ADJECTIVE: *We were completely spent after the race.*

sperm [spurm] NOUN, sperms. **sperme ▶** a cell produced by a male animal that can fertilize the egg of a female animal in order to produce new life.

sperm whale **cachalot ▶** a large, toothed whale of warm seas that has a huge, flat head.

spew [spyoo] VERB, spewed, spewing. **jaillir, fuser ▶** to pour out; move in a strong, quick flow : *Fire spewed from the upstairs windows.*

sphere [sfeer] NOUN, spheres. **1. sphère ▶** a solid figure that has a round shape, or an object shaped like this. The earth and the moon are spheres. **2. sphère, domaine ▶** a certain area of interest or activity : *Eastern Europe was once under the Soviet Union's sphere of influence.* ■ **spherical,** ADJECTIVE. **sphérique ▶** having the shape of a sphere.

sphinx [sfinks] NOUN, sphinxes or sphinges. **sphinx ▶** an ancient Egyptian figure having the head of a man and the body of a lion.

spice [spice] NOUN, spices. **épice ▶** the seeds, leaves, or other parts of a plant that are used to flavour foods. Pepper, ginger, cinnamon, and sage are spices. ▲ VERB, spiced, spicing. **épicer ▶** to

use spices to flavour foods. ■ **spicy,** ADJECTIVE. ▶ **piquant (-ante), épicé (-ée).** 📖 **p. 1141.**

spi·der [SPY-dur] NOUN, spiders. **araignée ▶** one of a large group of animals that have thin, jointed legs and can spin webs. Spiders differ from insects in that they have eight legs and a body with two parts, and don't have wings. Spiders live mainly on insects that they trap in their webs. 📖 **p. 1095.** 👁 **p. 104.**

spied [spide] VERB. a past form of spy.

spike[1] [spike] NOUN, spikes. **1. pointe ▶** a large, pointed, thin piece of metal shaped like a nail. Spikes are used for holding things in place, such as the rails and wooden ties on a railway track. **2. crampon ▶** a sharp, pointed object or projection : *Golfers often wear shoes with spikes on the bottom.* ▲ VERB, spiked, spiking. **empaler ▶** to pierce or stab with a spike.

spike[2] NOUN, spikes. **1. épi ▶** an ear of a grain plant such as corn or wheat. **2. épi ▶** a long cluster of flowers on a single stem.

spill [spil] VERB, spilled or spilt, spilling. **1. renverser, répandre ▶** to let something flow, fall, or run out by accident : *Jordan spilled his milk on the table.* **2. tomber ▶** to flow or fall : *Michi's long hair spilled over her shoulders.* SYN. overflow, run over, cascade, flood.

spin [spin] VERB, spun, spinning. **1. tourner ▶** to turn quickly around in circles : *The wheel spun on the ice.* **2. tourner ▶** to feel dizzy from, or as if from, turning quickly around : *The excitement made my head spin.* **3. filer ▶** to twist and draw out wool, cotton, or other fibres to make thread. **4. tisser ▶** of a spider, silkworm, or other such animal, to make a web or cocoon by giving off and stretching a special threadlike substance from its body. ▲ NOUN, spins. **1. tournoiement, vrille ▶** the act of spinning : *The skater made several graceful spins.* **2. tour ▶** a short ride or trip for pleasure : *Would you like to take a spin in my boat?* ■ **spinner,** NOUN. ▶ **fileur (-euse), essoreur (-euse).** SYN. turn, rotate, revolve, circle, twirl, wheel.

spin·ach [SPIN-ich] NOUN. **épinard ▶** a dark green vegetable leaf that is eaten raw in salads or cooked.

spi·nal cord [SPY-nul] **moelle épinière ▶** the thick band of nerve tissue running through the centre of the spine. It carries messages between the brain and the rest of the body.

spine [spine] NOUN, spines. **1. épine dorsale, colonne vertébrale ▶** the bones down the centre of the back that support the body and protect the nerves of the spinal cord; also called the backbone or spinal column. **2. dos ▶** the strip on the narrow edge of a book that joins the front cover to the back. The spine usually shows the title and the author. **3. épine ▶** a needlelike part that grows on some plants, such as cactus, and on some animals, such as a porcupine. ■ **spiny,**

ADJECTIVE. **épineux (-euse)** ▸ of an animal or plant, having spines.

spinning wheel **rouet** ▸ a device used to spin thread by hand before spinning machines were invented.

spi·ral [SPY-rul] NOUN, spirals. **spirale** ▸ a curve that keeps winding in layers above or below itself; a coil. Screws and mattress springs take the shape of a spiral. ▲ VERB, spiralled, spiralling. (also spiraled, spiraling) **tourner en spirale** ▸ to move in a spiral.

spire [spire] NOUN, spires. **flèche** ▸ the narrow, pointed top of a building such as a cathedral.

spir·it [SPEER-it] NOUN, spirits. **1. esprit, âme** ▸ the part of a person's being that exists apart from the body; the soul. **2. esprit** ▸ a dead person thought of as continuing to exist apart from the body : *The mine is said to hold the spirits of workers who died there.* **3. esprit** ▸ a force that gives life and energy : *Her lovely spirit shows when she smiles.* **4.** (often spirits) **humeur, moral** ▸ a state of mind; attitude : *Stuart is in high spirits and is ready for fun.* **5. spirits. spiritueux** ▸ a distilled alcoholic beverage. ▲ VERB, spirited, spiriting. **faire sortir discrètement** ▸ to move or take something away secretly : *Someone spirited away the school mascot.*

spir·it·ed [SPEER-ih-tid] ADJECTIVE. **1. fougueux (-euse), animé (-ée), plein (pleine) de verve** ▸ full of spirit; lively, energetic, and so on : *The music was spirited and everyone clapped in time.* **2. d'humeur, d'esprit** ▸ having a certain feeling or spirit : *That hateful, mean-spirited person is no longer my friend.*

spir·it·u·al [SPEER-ih-choo-ul] ADJECTIVE. **spirituel (-elle)** ▸ having to do with the spirit, the mind, religion, and so on, rather than the body or the physical world. ▲ NOUN, spirituals. **spirituel (-elle)** ▸ a religious song developed by black people of the southern United States in the 1800s. ■ **spiritually,** ADVERB. ▸ **spirituellement.** SYN : religious, sacred, holy, divine.

spit[1] [spit] VERB, spat or spit, spitting. **cracher** ▸ to push or force saliva or other matter out of the mouth : *The cat hissed and spat at the dog.* ▲ NOUN, spits. **crachat, salive** ▸ the watery fluid in the mouth; saliva.

spit[2] NOUN, spits. **1. broche** ▸ a thin rod on which meat is roasted, as in a fireplace or barbecue. **2. pointe de terre, langue de terre** ▸ a narrow point of land that juts into a body of water.

spite [spite] NOUN. **1. in spite of. en dépit de, malgré** ▸ even though there are opposing facts or conditions; despite : *In spite of the cold, I was thirsty.* **2. rancune** ▸ a feeling of wanting to hurt or annoy another person : *He just rooted for the other team out of spite.* ▲ VERB, spited, spiting. **vexer, contrarier** ▸ to show spite; act to hurt or annoy someone. ■ **spiteful,** ADJECTIVE.

▸ **rancunier (-ière).** ■ **spitefully,** ADVERB. ▸ **par rancune.**

splash [splash] VERB, splashed, splashing. **éclabousser, faire des éclaboussures** ▸ to cause water or other liquids to scatter or fly about : *Mud splashed against the windows of the car.* ▲ NOUN, splashes. **1. éclaboussement** ▸ the sound or feel of something hitting water : *to dive into the water with a splash.* **2. éclaboussure** ▸ a spot or patch of colour made by splashing : *The painting has splashes of bright colour against a grey background.* **3. sensation** ▸ something that creates excitement : *The new band is causing a big splash in our town.*

splat·ter [SPLAT-ur] NOUN, splatters. **éclaboussure** ▸ a splash or spatter : *The sauce splattered all over my clothes.* ▲ VERB, splattered, splattering.

spleen [spleen] NOUN. **rate** ▸ an organ in the body near the stomach that filters and stores blood.

splen·did [SPLEN-did] ADJECTIVE. **1. splendide** ▸ very beautiful or impressive to look at; brilliant or magnificent : *a splendid sunset.* **2. magnifique** ▸ very good; excellent. ■ **splendidly,** ADVERB. ▸ **splendidement.** SYN : gorgeous, superb, excellent, glorious.

splint [splint] NOUN, splints. **éclisse** ▸ a straight piece of wood or other material that is used to hold a broken bone in place.

splin·ter [SPLIN-tur] NOUN, splinters. **écharde** ▸ a thin, sharp piece broken off from wood or other such material : *I got a splinter in my hand when I picked up an old board.* ▲ VERB, splintered, splintering. **se fendre en éclats** ▸ to break into splinters.

split [split] VERB, split, splitting. **1. (se) fendre** ▸ to break or divide along a length : *Split that wood into smaller pieces and it will fit into the fireplace.* **2. diviser** ▸ to divide or go into parts : *The plan split the community.* **3. partager** ▸ to divide into even parts; share : *The neighbours split the cost of the fence.* ▲ NOUN, splits. **1. fente, fissure, déchirure** ▸ the act or fact of splitting. **2. division** ▸ a parting or division within a group : *There is a split in opinion.* **3. grand écart** ▸ an exercise in which the legs are opened straight out over the floor. ✐ p. 570.

spoil [spoil] VERB, spoiled or spoilt, spoiling. **1. gâcher** ▸ to hurt or ruin in some way : *A little rain won't spoil our fun.* **2. gâter** ▸ to become decayed or rotten : *The fruit spoiled in the sun.* **3. gâter** ▸ to allow a person, especially a child, to become selfish or self-satisfied because of easy treatment : *Eileen tried not to spoil the puppy.* ▲ NOUN, spoils. **bénéfices, butin** ▸ property that is taken by force, as by the

SUMMER SPORTS

hiking

baseball

football

skateboarding

horseback riding

soccer

wind surfing

swimming

roller-skating

operating personal watercraft

cycling

568

WINTER SPORTS

mountain climbing

downhill skiing

snowmobiling

surf boarding

luge

snowshoeing

tobogganing

cross-country skiing

hockey

skating

569

winning side in a battle. SYN: harm, injure, hurt, damage, ruin, mar.

spoke[1] [spoke] VERB. a past form of **speak**. **Note**. A spokesperson speaks formally for another person, or for a group or organization.

spoke[2] NOUN. spokes. **rayon ▸** a thin rod or bar that connects the rim of a wheel to the hub, as on a bicycle tire.

spo·ken [SPOKE-un] VERB. a past form of **speak**. ▲ ADJECTIVE. **1. parlé ▸** expressed in speech; oral : *Letters are symbols that represent the sounds of spoken language.* **2. à la voix ▸** speaking in a certain way : *a shy, soft-spoken person.*

sponge [spunj] NOUN. sponges. **1. éponge ▸** a water animal that lives attached to rocks or other solid objects. A sponge skeleton is light and strong and full of holes. Household sponges are made from these animals. **2. éponge ▸** an artificial cleaning pad that looks somewhat like a true sponge and is used in the same way. ▲ VERB, sponged, sponging. **éponger ▸** to clean or wipe off with a sponge. ■ **spongy**, ADVERB. **▸ spongieux (-ieuse).**

spon·sor [SPON-sur] NOUN. sponsors. **1. commanditaire ▸** a company, business, or other group that pays for all or part of a television or radio show, in order to advertise on the program. **2. commanditaire ▸** any person or group that pays to support some event or activity. **3. parrain, marraine ▸** a person who is responsible for or supports something : *Our member of Parliament is the sponsor of a new human-rights bill.* ▲ VERB, sponsored, sponsoring. **commanditer, être le garant de, répondre de, se porter caution pour ▸** to act as a sponsor.

spon·ta·ne·ous [spon-TAY-nee-us] ADJECTIVE. **spontané (-ée) ▸** happening by itself; not planned or forced : *There was spontaneous applause when the clown appeared.* ■ **spontaneously**, ADVERB. **▸ spontanément.** SYN: instinctive, impulsive, natural, automatic.

spool [spool] NOUN. spools. **bobine ▸** a rounded piece or cylinder of wood or plastic, used to hold thread, wire, or tape.

spoon [spoon] NOUN. spoons. **cuiller ▸** a kitchen tool with a handle connected to a little bowl, used in eating, serving, or preparing foods. ▲ VERB, spooned, spooning. **prendre à la cuiller,**

verser à la cuiller ▸ to use a spoon. ■ **spoonful,** NOUN. **▸ cuillerée.**

spore [spor] NOUN. spores. **spore ▸** a tiny cell that can grow into a plant or animal. Ferns, mould, and fungi grow from spores.

sport [sport] NOUN, sports. **1. sport ▸** a game or other activity in which people actively use the body, play according to certain fixed rules, and compete to win : *Baseball and soccer are widely played sports.* **2. sport ▸** any physical activity carried on for enjoyment or recreation, such as swimming, biking, or mountain climbing. **3. beau joueur (belle joueuse), mauvais perdant (mauvaise perdante) ▸** a person judged as to how fairly she or he plays a game and reacts to winning or losing : *a good sport.* ▲ VERB, sported, sporting. **arborer ▸** to wear or display in public; show off : *Dominic sported a new jacket.* ⌐ p. 1166. ◉ p. 568, 569.

sports car voiture de sport ▸ a small, low car seating one or two people, designed for high speed and quick turns.

spot [spot] NOUN. spots. **1. tache ▸** a mark or stain left on clothes, furniture, and so on, by pieces of dirt, food, oil, paint, or other things. **2. pois ▸** a small part or area that looks different from what is around it : *A dalmatian is a white dog with black spots.* **3. endroit, lieu (lieux) ▸** a particular place : *The café is a popular spot with artists.* **1. tacher, souiller ▸** to mark or stain with spots : *Paint spotted my shirt.* **2. repérer ▸** to catch sight of; see : *I spotted Haroon in the crowd.*

spot·less [SPOT-lis] ADJECTIVE. **immaculé (-ée) ▸** not having any marks, stains, flaws; completely clean : *a spotless window.* ■ **spotlessly**, ADVERB. **▸ impeccable, d'une propreté impeccable.**

spot·light [SPOT-lite] NOUN. spotlights. **1. projecteur ▸** a bright light that is focussed on a performer on stage. **2. vedette, centre de la scène ▸** a position of public notice : *The mayor's husband doesn't enjoy the spotlight of public life.*

spouse [spows or spowz] NOUN. spouses. **conjoint (-ointe), époux (épouse) ▸** a wife or husband.

spout [spowt] VERB, spouted, spouting. **1. jaillir, rejaillir, gicler ▸** to force out water or liquid in a

---

🖉 Word Builder

Split, *rip*, and *tear* all suggest pulling or breaking something apart by using force. When someone **splits** something, he or she usually breaks or cuts it into two pieces : *She split all the wood in the pile for kindling.* *Rip* often means to cut a part of something from a whole : *I ripped my pants on a nail.* *Tear* means to pull apart pieces of material, such as paper or cloth, often leaving rough edges on the resulting pieces : *Nico didn't have any scissors so he tore the paper into strips.*

powerful stream; spray or spurt : *A whale spouts water from the hole in its back.* **2. débiter, déclamer** ▸ to pour forth a stream of words : *He was spouting nonsense, so we ignored him.* ▲ NOUN. **spouts. bec, goulot** ▸ a small opening, tube, or lip from which liquid is poured or flows out : *the spout of a teapot.*

sprain [sprane] VERB. sprained, spraining. **se fouler, se faire une entorse à** ▸ to hurt a joint of the body by twisting or straining it : *Sybil sprained her ankle during the game*

sprang [sprang] VERB. a past form of spring.

sprawl [sprol] VERB. sprawled, sprawling. **1. s'étaler, s'affaler** ▸ to sit or stretch out in a loose, awkward way : *Cory sprawled on the couch to watch TV.* **2. s'étendre de tous les côtés** ▸ to spread out or over an area in an uncontrolled way : *The city sprawls for 20 miles.* ▲ NOUN. sprawls. **position affalée** ▸ a sprawling position, or something that sprawls.

spray [spray] NOUN. sprays. **1. (nuage de) gouttelettes** ▸ drops of water or other liquid flying through the air : *The hose sent out sprays of water onto the flowers.* **2. fixatif à cheveux, laque** ▸ a stream of very tiny drops forced out from a can or container : *hair spray keeps hair in place* ▲ VERB. sprayed, spraying. **1. arroser, vaporiser** ▸ to fall or cause to fall in a spray : *to spray paint.* **2. pulvériser** ▸ to apply spray to : *Farmers spray to protect their crops against disease and insects.* ■ **sprayer,** NOUN. ▸ vaporisateur, pulvérisateur.

spread [spred] VERB. spread, spreading. **1. déployer** ▸ to open wide or stretch open : *The hawk spread its wings and flew away.* **2. étaler, étendre** ▸ to put on or cover a surface : *to spread butter on bread.* **3. étaler, déployer** ▸ to reach out or extend over an area : *The grasslands spread out before us.* ▲ NOUN. spreads. **1. étendue** ▸ the amount or extent that something can stretch out or open : *the spread of my fingers.* **2. couvre-lit** ▸ the covering or top cover of a bed. **3. tartinade, produit (à tartiner)** ▸ a soft food that can be spread on a piece of bread or cracker : *a cheese spread.* SYN : stretch out, extend, sprawl, scatter.

spree [spree] NOUN. sprees. **fête** ▸ a short burst of activity : *They went on a shopping spree today.*

spring [spring] VERB. sprang **sauter, bondir** ▸ or sprung, sprung, springing. **1. sauter, bondir** ▸ to move quickly up or out; jump; leap : *A gazelle can spring high into the air.* **2. s'ouvrir d'un coup, se fermer d'un coup** ▸ to open or close quickly and with force : *The door sprang open and startled me.* **3. surgir, apparaître soudain** ▸ to come into being or appear quickly : *Weeds are springing up in the garden.* **4. prendre par surprise, faire une surprise** ▸ to make happen suddenly : *to spring a surprise on*

someone. ▲ NOUN. springs. **1. printemps** ▸ the season of the year between winter and summer. **2. source** ▸ a place where water comes out in a stream from under the ground. **3. ressort** ▸ a metal or plastic spiral that can be pulled or bent but that always returns to its first shape or position. **4. bond** ▸ the act of springing; a jump or leap. ■ **springy,** ADJECTIVE. ▸ **élastique, souple,** ☞ p. 1104.

spring-board [SPRING-bord] NOUN. springboards. **1. tremplin** ▸ a board used to spring high into the air. Divers use springboards to dive into the water. **2. tremplin** ▸ something that gets things moving quickly; a starting point : *The right law school is a springboard to success.*

sprin-kle [SPRING-kul] VERB. sprinkled, sprinkling. **1. saupoudrer, arroser légèrement** ▸ to scatter or spread around in tiny pieces or small drops : *He sprinkled chocolate on the cake.* **2. pleuvoir légèrement** ▸ to rain lightly or gently. ■ **sprinkler,** NOUN. **arroseur, gicleur** ▸ a device used to spray or sprinkle water over lawns and gardens SYN : spray, splatter, splash, spot.

sprint [sprint] NOUN. sprints. **sprint** ▸ a short, fast race in which the runners run at top speed for the entire race. The 100-metre dash is a sprint. ▲ VERB. sprinted, sprinting. **sprinter** ▸ to run a sprint.

sprout [sprowt] VERB. sprouted, sprouting. **1. bourgeonner, pousser, germer** ▸ of a seed or plant, to start to grow. **2. bourgeonner, pousser** ▸ to come forth or out like a growing plant : *The catfish has whiskers sprouting from the sides of its face.* **3. pousser, surgir, naître** ▸ to arise or develop : *Cabins sprouted up along the beach.* ▲ NOUN. sprouts. **pousse** ▸ a new growth on a plant.

needles

fruits (cones)

spruce

spruce [sprooce] NOUN. spruces. **épicéa, épinette** ▸ an evergreen tree with short, needle-shaped leaves, light strong wood, and cones that carry seeds. Spruces grow in colder temperatures. ▲ VERB. spruced, sprucing. **se faire beau (belle), donner de l'éclat à** ▸ to make neat and attractive : *We spruced up our house with a coat of paint.* ☜ p. 255.

sprung [sprung] VERB. a past form of spring.

spry [spry] ADJECTIVE, spryer, spryest. (also sprier, spriest) **vif (vive)** ▶ active; lively : *Regular exercise keeps my grandmother spry.* ■ **spryly,** ADVERB. ▶ **vivement.** ■ **spryness,** NOUN. ▶ **vivacité.**

spun [spun] VERB. a past form of spin.

spur [spur] NOUN, spurs. **éperon** ▶ a sharply pointed device on the heel of a rider's boot to get a horse to move faster. ▲ VERB, spurred, spurring. **1. éperonner** ▶ to use spurs on a horse. **2. pousser à agir** ▶ to get someone to move faster or do better : *Clayton spurred me to finish the race.*

spurn [spurn] VERB, spurned, spurning. **rejeter avec mépris, repousser avec mépris** ▶ to turn away from; reject : *She spurned all offers of help.*

spurt [spurt] VERB, spurted, spurting. **jaillir, gicler** ▶ to pour or flow out in a strong stream; gush; spout : *The drink spurted out of the bottle.* ▲ NOUN, spurts. **1. jaillissement, giclée, jet** ▶ a bursting out of water or some other liquid. **2. par à-coups** ▶ a short action or feeling that lasts only a short time : *He cleaned his room in spurts.*

sput-ter [SPUT-tur] VERB, sputtered, sputtering. **1. crépiter, grésiller** ▶ to make spitting, hissing, or popping noises : *"We had a great wood-fire crackling and sputtering on the hearth."* (Arthur Conan Doyle) **2. bredouiller** ▶ to speak in a rushed or confused way : *The nervous girl sputtered her lines and ran off stage.*

spy [spy] NOUN, spies. **espion (-ionne)** ▶ a person who secretly watches others and gathers information about them. ▲ VERB, spied, spying. **1.** (used with on) **espionner** ▶ to watch others secretly; act as a spy : *I spied on my sister's party.* **2. apercevoir** ▶ to catch sight of; spot or see : *Marc spied Julie talking to Hussein.*

squab-ble [SKWOB-ul] NOUN, squabbles. **chamaillerie** ▶ a minor fight or argument. ▲ VERB, squabbled, squabbling: *The children squabbled over a toy.*

squad [skwod] NOUN, squads. **1. escouade** ▶ the smallest unit in an army, made up of about 12 soldiers. **2. équipe, groupe, brigade** ▶ any small group that acts or works together : *a football squad.* **Note.** A police patrol car is sometimes called a **squad car.**

squad-ron [SKWOD-run] NOUN, squadrons. **escadron** ▶ a unit of airplanes, warships, or other such forces that operate together.

squall[1] [skwol] NOUN, squalls. **bourrasque** ▶ a sudden and harsh wind storm, often with rain, or snow.

squall[2] NOUN, squalls. **cri rauque, cri discordant, braillement** ▶ a harsh cry or scream. ▲ VERB, squalled, squalling. **crier, brailler** ▶ to make loud cries or screams.

Squam-ish [SKWOM-ish] NOUN. **1. Squawmish, Squamish** ▶ an Aboriginal group living on the southwest coast of British Columbia related to the Interior Salish tribes. **2. squawmish, squamish** ▶ the Salish language of these people.

squan-der [SKWON-dur] VERB, squandered, squandering. **dilapider** ▶ to spend money in a foolish or careless way; waste money : *Jamie squandered his whole month's allowance in the first week.*

square [skwair] NOUN, squares. **1. carré** ▶ a flat figure that has four equal sides and angles, or an object or design with this shape : *a checkerboard with red and black squares.* **2. place, carré** ▶ a four-sided open area that is surrounded by streets or buildings. **3. carré** ▶ in mathematics, the number that results when any number is multiplied by itself : *The square of 4 is 16.* ▲ ADJECTIVE, squarer, squarest. **1. carré (-ée)** ▶ having four equal sides and angles : *a square box.* **2. à angle (s) droit (s)** ▶ making a right angle : *Most boxes have square corners.* **3. carré** ▶ a unit of area having the same width and length : *An area that is 10 metres by 15 metres is 150 square metres.* **4. honnête** ▶ honest; fair : *This store gives its customers a square deal.* ▲ VERB, squared, squaring. **1. rendre carré** ▶ to make square : *He squared his shoulders and marched to his parents' room.* **2. élever au carré** ▶ to multiply a number by itself. ■ **squarely,** ADVERB. **carrément** ▶ exactly or firmly : *She looked him squarely in the face and said, "No!"*

square dance **danse carrée** ▶ a type of folk dance that is done by four or more couples who form a square at the beginning of the dance.

square root **racine carrée** ▶ a number that, when multiplied by itself (squared), produces a certain other number : *The square root of 25 is 5.*

squash[1] [skwosh] VERB, squashed, squashing. **1. aplatir, écraser** ▶ to press or force down into a flat mass; crush : *He accidentally stepped on the toy and squashed it.* **2. écraser** ▶ to put down or stop something : *The army squashed the rebels.* ▲ NOUN. **squash** ▶ a game played with a racquet and a rubber ball in a walled court. SYN: crush, press, smash, mash.

squash[2] NOUN, squash or squashes. **courge** ▶ an orange, yellow, or green vegetable that grows on a vine along the ground and is related to the pumpkin.

squat [skwot] VERB, squatted or squat, squatting. **1. s'accroupir, s'asseoir sur les talons** ▶ to sit on the lower part of the legs while the knees are drawn close to the body : *Craig* squatted beside Quang. **2. occuper un terrain illégalement, squatter** ▸ to live on land without owning it or having a legal right to it. **3. squatter** ▸ to live or settle on public land in order to become its owner. ▲ ADJECTIVE. **courtaud (-aude), trapu (-ue)** ▸ having a low, broad shape : *A badger is a small, squat animal.*

squawk [skwok] VERB, squawked, squawking. **1. pousser des cris rauques** ▸ to make a loud, shrill cry : *The radio squawked when I turned it on.* **2.** *Informal.* **rouspéter, râler** ▸ to complain noisily. ▲ NOUN, squawks: *"The jay gave a loud squawk that sounded like he was scolding right back at her."* (Marilyn Halvorson)

squeak [skweek] VERB, squeaked, squeaking. **couiner, grincer, crisser, pousser des petits cris** ▸ to make a short, sharp, high sound or cry. ▲ NOUN, squeaks: **couinement, grincement, glapissement** ▸ *the squeak of a rusty hinge on a gate.* ■ **squeaky,** ADJECTIVE. **grinçant (-ante).**

squeal [skweel] VERB, squealed, squealing. **pousser des cris perçants, grincer** ▸ to make a loud shrill cry or sound : *Their boots squealed on the waxed floor.* ▲ NOUN, squeals: *the squeal of tires.*

squeeze [skweez] VERB, squeezed, squeezing. **1. presser** ▸ to push together the sides or parts of; press hard : *to squeeze a toothpaste tube.* **2. s'introduire, presser** ▸ to force by pressing; force into a tight space : *The people squeezed into the bus.* ▲ NOUN, squeezes. **étreinte, embrassade** ▸ *the act of squeezing.*

squid [skwid] NOUN, squid or squids. **calmar** ▸ a sea animal that is like an octopus, with a long tube-shaped body and 10 arms. Some squid are very small, but the giant squid can be over 15 metres long.

squash

squint [skwint] VERB, squinted, squinting. **1. plisser les yeux** ▸ to look with the eyes slightly open : *to squint in the sun.* **2. donner un coup d'œil** ▸ to give a quick look out of the corner of the eye. ▲ NOUN, squints. **coup d'œil, loucherie** ▸ the act of squinting.

squire [skwire] NOUN, squires. **1. écuyer** ▸ in the Middle Ages, a young man who acted as a servant to a knight while training to become a

knight himself. **2. châtelain (-aine)** ▸ in England, a landowner or other wealthy man in a village or country area.

squirm [skwurm] VERB, squirmed, squirming. **1. se tortiller** ▸ to twist or turn the body; wriggle : *The cat squirmed from my arms and ran up a tree.* **2. être mal à l'aise, se tordre** ▸ to act or feel nervous or uneasy : *The witness squirmed while telling a lie in court.*

squir-rel [SKWUR-ul] NOUN, squirrels. **écureuil** ▸ a small, furry animal with a long bushy tail and grey, reddish, or dark-brown fur. Squirrels live in trees and feed mostly on nuts. ☜ p. 110.

squirt [skwurt] VERB, squirted, squirting. **1. faire gicler** ▸ to force out liquid through a narrow opening in a thin stream : *I squirted oil on the squeaking hinge.* **2. mouiller, arroser** ▸ to wet by squirting : *Ali squirted us with the hose.* ▲ NOUN, squirts. **jet, giclée** ▸ the act of squirting. SYN: spew, spout, spurt, spray, gush, jet.

stab [stab] VERB, stabbed, stabbing. **1. poignarder** ▸ to cut or wound with a knife or other pointed weapon. **2. donner des coups de** ▸ to strike with, or as if with, a pointed object : *Pain stabbed her leg.* ▲ NOUN, stabs. **1. coup de couteau** ▸ a wound or blow made with a pointed weapon. **2. élancement** ▸ a sharp, brief feeling of pain. **3. essayer de faire, tenter** ▸ an attempt; try : *I'll take a stab at answering that question.*

sta-ble[1] [STAY-bul] NOUN, stables. **1. écurie** ▸ a building where horses, cattle, or other such animals are kept and fed. **2. écurie** ▸ a group of racehorses belonging to a particular owner. ▲ VERB, stabled, stabling. **mettre dans une écurie** ▸ to keep an animal in a stable. ☜ p. 114.

sta-ble[2] ADJECTIVE, stabler, stablest. **stable** ▸ not easily moved, changed, or shaken; firm; steady : *That bridge was built to remain stable during an earth-quake.* **Note.** The fact of being stable is stability.

stack [stak] NOUN, stacks. **1. pile, tas** ▸ a pile of things on top of one another : *a stack of pancakes.* **2. meule** ▸ a large pile of straw or hay that is shaped like a cone or mound. **3. cheminée** ▸ short for smokestack. **4. stacks. rayons** ▸ the area in a library where the books are kept on shelves. ▲ VERB, stacked, stacking. **empiler** ▸ to put in a stack; pile up : *He stacked the newspapers.*

sta-di-um [STAY-dee-um] NOUN, stadiums or stadia. **stade** ▸ a large structure that has many rows of seats built around an open field or playing area. Stadiums are used for sports events, concerts, rallies, and so on.

staff [staf] NOUN, staffs. **1. bâton, hampe, mât** ▸ a stick, rod, or pole : *A flagpole is also called a flagstaff.* **2. personnel** ▸ a group of people who work under a manager or boss : *The* *hospital staff works hard.* **3. portée ▸** a set of five lines and four spaces on which music is written. **▲ VERB, staffed, staffing. pourvoir en personnel ▸** to provide with employees : *The information desk is staffed with volunteers.*

stag [stag] NOUN, stags. **cerf ▸** a full-grown male deer ; a buck.

stage [staje] NOUN, stages. **1. scène ▸** the raised platform in a theatre on which actors and other entertainers perform. **2.** (also **the stage**) **théâtre ▸** the art or work of the theatre : *The actor works on the stage.* **3. stade, phase ▸** a step, period, or point in a process of development : *The baby was in a teething stage.* **4. diligence ▸** short for stagecoach. **▲ VERB, staged, staging. 1. mettre en scène, monter, porter à la scène ▸** to put on in a theatre ; present : *to stage one of Shakespeare's plays.* **2. monter, organiser ▸** to put before the public ; carry out : *The union staged a strike.* **3. monter ▸** to act in an artificial way ; put on a false performance : *The police staged a raid for the news cameras.*

stage-coach [STAJE-KOHCH] NOUN, stage-coaches. **diligence ▸** a large coach drawn by horses. Stagecoaches were used to carry passengers and mail.

stag-ger [STAG-ur] VERB, staggered, staggering. **1. tituber ▸** to move or walk in a weak, unsteady way, as if about to fall : *The movers staggered under the weight of the piano.* **2. stupéfier ▸** to act strongly and suddenly on the mind or feelings ; shock ; stun : *The flood damage staggered the townspeople.* **3. échelonner ▸** to schedule so as to begin at different times : *Mom staggered her work hours so that she can be at my game on Tuesdays.* **▲ NOUN, staggers. allure chancelante ▸** a weak, unsteady motion or walk. SYN : sway, reel, totter, waver.

stag-nant [STAG-nunt] ADJECTIVE. **1. stagnant (-ante) ▸** of water or air, being still, especially becoming foul or polluted : *A leak had caused a pool of stagnant water under the sink.* **2. stagnant (-ante) ▸** not active ; dull ; lifeless.

stain [stane] VERB, stained, staining. **1. tache ▸** to mark with an unwanted area of colour that is hard to get out ; soil ; spot : *Juice stained my shirt.* **2. teindre ▸** to colour with a dye or tint : *We stained the dresser a dark brown.* **3. souiller, ternir, tacher ▸** to mark by a wrong or dishonour ; disgrace : *A speeding ticket will stain your driving record.* **▲ NOUN, stains. 1. tache ▸** a place that is stained ; a mark or spot : *Tory had grass stains on her jeans.* **2. tache ▸** a mark of disgrace or dishonour.

stainless steel acier inoxydable ▸ a form of steel that does not rust or stain easily, often used for household products such as knives, forks, pots, and so on.

stair [stair] NOUN, stairs. **1. stairs. escalier ▸** a series of steps, used to go from one floor or level

to another. **2. marche ▸** one of these steps : *The cat was curled up on a stair.*

stair-case [STAIR-kace] NOUN, staircases. (also stairway) **escalier ▸** a flight of stairs.

stake [stake] NOUN, stakes. **1. pieu (pieux) ▸** a stick or post pointed at one end for driving into the ground : *The plants were tied to stakes as they grew taller.* **2. enjeu ▸** something offered as a bet in a game, race, or contest. **3. part, intérêts ▸** an interest or share in a business, investment, or other such activity. **4. at stake. en jeu ▸** in danger of being lost : *We played well with the championship at stake.* **▲ VERB, staked, staking. 1. soutenir à l'aide de pieux ▸** to fasten or support with a stake. **2. miser ▸** to gamble or risk ; bet : *He staked his reputation on the results of the race.* **3. jalonner ▸** to mark off an area with, or as if with, stakes : *to stake a claim.*

sta-lac-tite [stuh-LAK-TITE] NOUN, stalactites. **stalactite ▸** a formation that looks like an icicle and hangs from the ceiling of a cave. A stalactite is formed over a long period of time when water containing minerals drips down from the roof of a cave.

stalactites

stalagmites

sta-lag-mite [stuh-LAG-MITE] NOUN, stalagmites. **stalagmite ▸** a formation that is built up from moisture dripping down onto the floor of a cave.

stale [stale] ADJECTIVE, staler, stalest. **1. rassis (-ie), vicié (-ée), qui n'est plus frais ▸** of air, water, or certain foods, not having the proper taste or quality ; not fresh : *I used the stale pieces of bread to make a bread pudding.* **2. qui a perdu tout enthousiasme ▸** having lost its energy or interest ; worn out ; dull : *The politician made the same stale speech every year.*

stalk¹ [stok] NOUN, stalks. **1. tige ▸** the main stem of a plant : *a bean stalk ; a corn stalk.* **2. tige ▸** any long plant part that supports leaves or flowers.

stalk[2] VERB, stalked, stalking. **1. chasser à l'affût, traquer ▶** to hunt or follow in a careful, quiet way, so as not to be seen or heard : *The lion stalked the zebra from a distance.* **2. suivre furtivement ▶** to follow after something in a dangerous way, as if hunting prey. **3. marcher d'un air digne, avec raideur ▶** to walk in a stiff or proud manner : *"Eddie stood… watching a blue heron stalk the shore with her improbable long legs."* (Tim Wynne-Jones)

stall [stol] NOUN, stalls. **1. stalle ▶** a place in a stable for one animal. **2. kiosque, stand ▶** a small booth or counter where goods are sold : *food stalls at a fair.* ▲ VERB, stalled, stalling. **1. mettre à l'étable ▶** to put an animal in a stall. **2. caler ▶** to stop or bring to a stop : *The car stalled on the highway.* **3. retarder ▶** to put off action; slow down; delay : *I'll stall Jim until you get home.*

stal-lion [STAL-yun] NOUN, stallions. **étalon ▶** a male horse.

sta-men [STAY-mun] NOUN, stamens. **étamine ▶** the part of a flower that produces pollen. The stamen is made up of a thin stalk with a pollen-bearing tip called the **anther**.

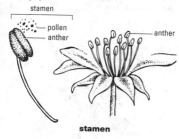

stamen

pollen
anther
anther

stamen

stam-i-na [STAM-ih nuh] NOUN. **endurance ▶** the strength to keep going; endurance : *Runners need great stamina to complete a marathon race.*

stam-mer [STAM-ur] VERB, stammered, stammering. **bégayer ▶** to repeat the same sound; stutter. ▲ NOUN, stammers: *a nervous stammer.* SYN: stutter, falter, stumble.

stamp [stamp] NOUN, stamps. **1.** (also postage stamp) **timbre, timbre-poste ▶** a small piece of paper with a design on the front and a sticky substance on the back. Stamps are put on letters and packages to show that a mailing charge has been paid. **2. estampille ▶** a mark or message : *They put a stamp on my hand so that I could go on all the rides.* **3. estampe, tampon ▶** a tool for making a design or letters : *The clerk used a stamp to mark "Paid" on our bill.*

▲ VERB, stamped, stamping. **1. timbrer, affranchir ▶** to put a stamp on : *The librarian stamped the due date on the book.* **2. taper du pied ▶** to bring down the foot heavily and with force : *"She stamped her foot and said, 'Shoot!'"* (Gary Soto) **3. stamp out. écraser, éteindre ▶** to get rid of; do away with : *The new mayor promises to stamp out illegal drugs in our city.* ✍ p. 540.

stam-pede [stam-PEED] NOUN, stampedes. **1. ruée ▶** a sudden, wild rush of a frightened herd of animals. **2. panique, ruée ▶** a sudden, wild rush of many people : *A stampede of fans met the team in the parking lot.* **3. rodéo ▶** a rodeo and fair : *the Calgary Stampede.* ▲ VERB, stampeded, stampeding. **1. semer la panique, se ruer, se précipiter ▶** to be a part of or cause a stampede : *The cattle stampeded at the loud noise.* **2. ne pas laisser le temps de la réflexion ▶** to force to act in a careless or thoughtless way : *The salesperson tried to stampede us into buying a car today.*

stand [stand] VERB, stood, standing. **1. se lever, se mettre debout ▶** to be on one's feet : *Carla stood up.* **2. être debout ▶** to be in an upright position : *Only a few trees stood after the fire.* **3. se trouver ▶** to be in a certain place or condition : *My desk stands next to the window.* **4. avoir une position ▶** to have a certain opinion or attitude : *Dad sure knows where he stands on rudeness.* **5. supporter, endurer ▶** to put up with; bear : *I can't stand the sight of blood!* **6. se mettre au garde-à-vous ▶** to carry out a certain duty or action : *to stand guard.* ▲ NOUN, stands. **1. position ▶** the act of standing, or a place where something stands : *a stand of trees.* **2. position ▶** an attitude or opinion : *Her stand on rent control was reasonable.* **3. combat ▶** a stop for battle or resistance : *Louis Riel made a last stand at the Battle of Batoche.* **4. support ▶** a rack or other structure for placing things : *an umbrella stand.* **5. étalage ▶** a booth, stall, or counter for selling things : *a fruit stand.*

stand-ard [STAND-urd] NOUN, standards. **1.** (usually standards) **niveau (-eaux) ▶** a certain level of quality or value : *That school has high academic standards.* **2. critère, norme ▶** anything that is accepted as an example or used as a model : *safety standards for cars.* **3. étendard, drapeau (-eaux) ▶** a flag or banner used as a symbol. ▲ ADJECTIVE. **1. modèle standard ▶** used as a model or guide : *Computer disks come in standard sizes.* **2. norme, normal (-ale, -aux) ▶** generally accepted; usual; typical : *It is standard practice to tip the server in most restaurants.* **3. standard, étalon, référence ▶** used as a guide or authority : *standard English.* SYN: criterion, level, ideal, principle, rule.

standard of living **niveau de vie ▶** the level at which a country, group, or person lives, based on how well basic needs and wants are satisfied.

standard time heure normale, temps légal, fuseau horaire ► the accepted measure of time in a certain region. *British Columbia follows Pacific Standard Time.*

stand·ing [STAND-ing] NOUN, standings. rang, position ► a certain rank or position : *the standings for the teams in a league.* ▲ ADJECTIVE. 1. debout ► that stands ; in an upright or fixed position : *The runners began the race from a standing start.* 2. permanent (-ente) ► not moving or changing : *Pierre has a standing invitation to come and visit his cousins.*

stand·point [STAND-poynt] NOUN, standpoints. point de vue ► a way of thinking about or judging things ; a point of view : *From my standpoint, polluting is a crime.*

stand·still [STAND-stil] NOUN. arrêt, immobilisation ► a complete stop : *The storm brought the town to a standstill.* SYN : stop, halt, pause.

stank [stank] a past form of stink.

stan·za [STAN-zuh] NOUN, stanzas. strophe ► a group of lines that form one part of a poem or song.

sta·ple¹ [STAY-pul] NOUN, staples. 1. agrafe ► a similar piece of thin metal that is used to hold papers and other thin materials together. 2. crampon ► a U-shaped piece of metal with pointed ends. Staples are driven into a surface to hold a hook, pin, or bolt in place. ▲ VERB, stapled, stapling. agrafer ► to hold together or fasten with a staple. ■ **stapler,** NOUN. ► agrafeuse.

stapler

staple² NOUN, staples. 1. aliment de base ► a product or food that is used widely and often, such as salt, sugar, meat, or flour. 2. culture de base ► a major product or crop grown in a certain region.

star [star] NOUN, stars. 1. étoile ► a celestial body that looks like a steady, bright point in the sky at night. 2. étoile ► a figure in the shape that a star appears to have in the sky : *a gold star on an excellent paper.* 3. étoile, vedette ► a person who is an outstanding performer in some field : *a baseball star; a rock star.* 4. étoile, vedette ► an actor who plays a leading part in a movie, play, or television show. ▲ VERB, starred, starring. 1. marquer d'un astérisque ► to mark with a star : *Mike starred the chores on his list that he had done.* 2. être la vedette ► to play a leading role : *to star in a play.* ▲ ADJECTIVE. vedette ► outstanding; excellent : *The star athlete is on several teams.* 🗐 **p. 1118.**

star·board [STAR-burd] NOUN. tribord ► the right side of a boat, a ship, or an aircraft when facing forward. ▲ ADJECTIVE. à tribord ► on the right side : *the starboard engine.*

starch [starch] NOUN, starches. 1. fécule, amidon ► a white powdery food substance that has no taste or smell and is found in most green plants. Starch is an important element in the diet. Foods such as potatoes, corn, and rice contain starch. 2. amidon ► a form of this substance that is used to stiffen clothes or cloth. ▲ VERB, starched, starching. empeser, amidonner ► to make stiff by using starch. ■ **starchy,** ADJECTIVE. ► féculent. of food, containing a high amount of starch : *Noodles are starchy foods.* ■ **starched,** ADJECTIVE. empesé (-ée), amidonné (-ée) ► of cloth, having been stiffened with starch : *a starched shirt.*

stare [stair] VERB, stared, staring. regarder fixement ► to look long or hard with the eyes wide open : *The people stared at the barking dog.* ▲ NOUN, stares. regard fixe ► a long, direct look. SYN : gaze, look, peer, glare.

star·fish [STAR-fish] NOUN, starfish or starfishes. étoile de mer ► a sea animal with five arms and a body shaped like a star.

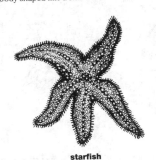

starfish

Star of David étoile de David ► a six-pointed star that is the symbol of the Jewish religion and of the country of Israel.

stark [stark] ADJECTIVE. 1. absolu, pur (pure) ► in every way; absolute; complete. Note. Usually used with negative words : *stark terror.* 2. austère ► bare and plain in appearance; harsh; bleak : *The picture showed a stark view of the frozen fields.* ▲ ADVERB. complètement ► absolutely; completely : *stark raving mad.* ■ **starkly,** ADVERB. ► complètement. SYN : simple, completely, downright, entirely.

star·ling [STAR-ling] NOUN, starlings. étourneau (-eaux) ► a bird with a plump body, pointed wings, a short tail, and glossy dark-green or purple feathers. Starlings live in large flocks and are found in great numbers in North America.

starling

star·ry [STAR-ee] ADJECTIVE, starrier, starriest. **1. étoilé (-ée)** ▶ full of stars; lighted by stars : *a clear, starry summer night.* **2. étincelant (-ante)** ▶ shining like stars; bright : *We could see the starry lights of the city.*

starry-eyed idéaliste, ingénu (-ue) ▶ too hopeful or optimistic; dreamy.

start [start] VERB, started, starting. **1. partir, démarrer, commencer** ▶ to go into action; get moving; set out : *Let's get started, or we'll be late for school.* **2. commencer** ▶ to come into operation or being : *My vacation starts May 1st.* **3. commencer, mettre en marche** ▶ to cause to be in motion or in being : *to start a fire.* **4. sursauter** ▶ to move suddenly, from surprise or fear. ▲ NOUN, starts. **1. début, départ** ▶ the act of starting : *Let's get an early start to beat the traffic.* **2. sursaut** ▶ a sudden movement : *With a start, he opened his eyes in alarm.* SYN : begin, commence, set out, launch, initiate.

star·tle [STAR-tul] VERB, startled, startling. **faire sursauter** ▶ to come upon without warning; frighten or excite suddenly : *The loud noise startled me.* SYN : frighten, alarm, surprise, shock, scare,

star·va·tion [STAR-VAY-shun] NOUN. **inanition** ▶ the fact of starving; death or suffering from lack of food.

starve [starve] VERB, starved, starving. **1. mourir de faim** ▶ to suffer or die from lack of food. **2. mourir de faim, être affamé** ▶ to be very hungry : *I am starving; I haven't eaten since breakfast.* **3. être privé (-ée) de** ▶ to suffer from the lack of something; need or want greatly. **Note.** Usually used as an ADJECTIVE: *she was starved for attention.*

state [state] NOUN, states. **1. État** ▶ a group of people living together under one government; a nation : *Many African states became independent in the 1950s and 1960s.* **2. état** ▶ a unit of government within a country : *Alaska became a U.S. state in 1959.* **3. l'État** ▶ the power or activity of government : *In some countries, the state provides medical care.* **4. état** ▶ a certain condition of a person or thing : *a state of happiness.* **5. état** ▶ one of the three conditions (solid, liquid, or gas) in which all matter exists. ▲ VERB, stated, stating. **déclarer** ▶ to tell in speech or writing; express : *Devadas carefully stated the instructions.* SYN : say, tell, inform, report, express, declare.

state-of-the-art [STATE-uv-thee-ART] ADJECTIVE. **dernier cri** ▶ of the best or most advanced quality that is currently available : *This CD-ROM has state-of-the-art graphics.*

state·ly [STATE-lee] ADJECTIVE, statelier, stateliest. **majestueux (-euse)** ▶ grand and dignified in appearance or manner; elegant; majestic : *a stately building.*

state·ment [STATE-munt] NOUN, statements. **1. déclaration** ▶ something that is stated; an idea expressed in speech or writing : *What do you mean by that statement?* **2. déclaration** ▶ a formal comment on something that has happened : *The prime minister issued a statement condemning the terrorists.* **3. relevé** ▶ a written summary or report of money owed, paid out, received, and so on : *a bank statement.* SYN : account, report, declaration, notice.

stat·ic [STAT-ik] NOUN. **électricité statique, parasites** ▶ electrical charges in the air that interfere with television or radio broadcast signals. ▲ ADJECTIVE. **1. statique** ▶ not moving; staying in one place or condition. **2. parasites** ▶ having to do with radio or television interference . *During the storm, there was only static on the radio.* **Note.** Static electricity does not flow in a current.

sta·tion [STAY-shun] NOUN, stations. **1. gare** ▶ a stopping place along the route of a train, bus, or the like : *I'll meet you at the train station.* **2. poste** ▶ a company or location for sending out broadcast signals : *Janet keeps her radio tuned to a pop station.* **3. poste, caserne** ▶ a building or place that is used for a particular purpose : *gas station,* **fire station, police station** (⌐ p. 1049, 1052). **4. position** ▶ a person's place or rank in society. ▲ VERB, stationed, stationing. **(se) poster** ▶ to assign to a certain position : *The Armed Forces stationed my aunt in England.* ⌐ p. 1169.

sta·tion·a·ry [STAY-shuh-NAIR-ee] ADJECTIVE. **1. stationnaire** ▶ not moving or changing; remaining still : *Hold your arms stationary in that position for five seconds.* **2. immobile** ▶ not able to be moved; fixed : *Don't try to move that bookcase — it's stationary.*

sta·tion·er·y [STAY-shuh-NAIR-ee] NOUN. **1. papeterie** ▶ writing paper and envelopes. **2. articles de bureau** ▶ materials used for writing, such as pens and pencils.

577

station wagon (voiture) familiale ▸ a car with a rear door that can be used for loading and unloading, and a rear seat or seats that can be folded down.

sta·tis·tics [stuh-TIS-tiks] PLURAL NOUN. **1. statistiques** ▸ facts and figures that are collected to give information about a particular subject. **2. statistic. statistique** ▸ a single number in a set of statistics : *For my report, I need the statistic for the number of non-smokers in our country.*

stat·ue [STACH-oo] NOUN. statues. **statue** ▸ a likeness of a person or animal that is made out of stone, clay, metal, or other solid material. Statues are carved, moulded, or cast into shape.

sta·ture [STACH-ur] NOUN. **1. stature** ▸ the height of the body : *She has an average stature for a girl her age, about 155 cm.* **2. envergure** ▸ a level of achievement or development : *Many writers of great stature, such as Tolstoy and Chekhov, were Russian.*

sta·tus [STAY-tus *or* STAT-us] NOUN. **1. statut, état** ▸ the condition or rank of a person or thing ; state : *The team will give the status of the pitcher's arm before the game.* **2. standing, statut** ▸ a person's rank or standing in society : *They're very status-minded and are always seen at cultural events.*

stat·ute [STACH-oot] NOUN. statutes. **loi** ▸ a law written down and put into effect by a legislature. **Note.** Something that is statutory is fixed or controlled by this kind of law.

staunch [stonch] ADJECTIVE. stauncher, staunchest. **sûr (sure), ardent (-ente), loyal (-ale, -aux)** ▸ strong and solid ; firm : *Our teacher is a staunch believer in homework.* ■ **staunchly,** ADVERB. ▸ **loyalement.** *Inez staunchly defends her rights.* SYN : loyal, steadfast, devoted, firm, reliable.

stay [stay] VERB. stayed, staying. **1. rester** ▸ to continue to be in one place ; not move on or leave ; remain : *Riley stayed after school because she was rude to the teacher.* **2. rester, veiller** ▸ to go on in the same manner or condition ; continue : *to stay up late.* **3. rester** ▸ to live in or visit for a time : *to stay overnight at a friend's house.* ▲ NOUN. stays. **1. séjour** ▸ a short period of visiting or living in a place. **2. ajournement** ▸ a delay or putting off of an official action, especially of a criminal sentence : *a stay of execution.* SYN : remain, wait, continue.

stead·fast [STED-fast] ADJECTIVE. **inébranlable** ▸ not moving or changing ; constant ; fixed : *Darrin is steadfast in his devotion to his dog.* ■ **steadfastly,** ADVERB. ▸ **inébranlablement.**

stead·y [STED-ee] ADJECTIVE. steadier, steadiest. **1. ferme, stable** ▸ firm in position ; not likely to move, shake, or shift : *Hold the chair steady while I stand on it to change the light bulb.* **2. régulier (-ière), continu (-ue)** ▸ moving at an even rate ; not changing : *a steady downpour of rain.* **3. régulier (-ière)** ▸ that can be relied on ; regular or dependable : *a steady job.* **4. calme** ▸ not easily upset or excited ; calm : *Test pilot Chuck Yeager was known for his steady nerves.* ▲ VERB, steadied, steadying. **raffermir, affermir** ▸ to make or become steady : *He steadied himself for the difficult test.* ■ **steadily,** ADVERB. ▸ **régulièrement.** *to work steadily all day.* ■ **steadiness,** NOUN. ▸ **régularité, stabilité.** SYN : constant, fixed, regular, continuous, reliable.

steak [stake] NOUN. steaks. **bifteck, tranche, darne** ▸ a slice of meat or fish for broiling or frying.

steal [steel] VERB, stole, stolen, stealing. **1. voler** ▸ to take property that belongs to another in a way that is against the law : *to steal a car.* **2. voler** ▸ to take or get in a dishonest way : *They stole the idea for the movie from another author.* **3. aller furtivement, se faufiler** ▸ to act or move in a sly, secret way : *The children stole into the neighbour's yard to find their ball.* **4. conquérir le cœur de** ▸ to get or win by charm : *His kindness stole her heart.* **5. voler** ▸ in baseball, to run suddenly to the next base, without being advanced by a hit. SYN : rob, take, burglarize, plunder.

stealth [stelth] NOUN. **(à la) dérobée** ▸ the fact of moving in a quiet, secret way : *The cat moved with stealth to pounce on the bird.* ■ **stealthy,** ADJECTIVE. ▸ **furtif (-ive).** ■ **stealthily,** ADVERB. ▸ **furtivement.**

steam [steem] NOUN. **1. vapeur** ▸ water that has changed into the form of gas or vapour by being heated to a boil. Steam is used for heating, cooking, and a source of energy. **2. vapeur** ▸ the power produced by steam under pressure : *In the 1800s trains were powered by steam.* **3.** *Informal.* **vapeur** ▸ a driving force or power : *Katie finished the race under her own steam.* ▲ VERB, steamed, steaming. **1. fumer** ▸ to give off steam : *The kettle steamed.* **2. cuire à la vapeur, étuver** ▸ to cook, soften, or work on with steam : *to steam vegetables.* **3. avancer (à la vapeur)** ▸ to move by, or as if by, steam : *A ship steamed into port.* **4.** *Informal.* **bouillonner, fulminer** ▸ to be very angry : *I was steaming about the trick.* ■ **steamy,** ADJECTIVE. ▸ **plein (pleine) de vapeur, couvert (-erte) de buée, humide.** 📖 p. 1109.

steam·boat [STEEM-boht] NOUN. steamboats. **bateau (-eaux) à vapeur** ▸ a boat moved by steam.

steam engine machine à vapeur, locomotive à la vapeur ▸ an engine that is powered by the force of steam.

steam·er [STEEM-ur] NOUN. steamers. **1. paquebot, bateau (-eaux) à vapeur** ▸ a steamboat or steamship. **2. cuit-vapeur, marmite à étuver** ▸

a special container in which food is steamed : *a rice steamer.* **3. palourde ▶** a clam with a soft shell, usually cooked by steaming.

steam-roll-er [STEEM-ROLE-ur] NOUN, steam-rollers. **rouleau compresseur ▶** a vehicle on heavy rollers that is used for crushing and smoothing road surfaces.

steam-ship [STEEM-SHIP] NOUN, steamships. **bateau (-eaux) à vapeur, paquebot ▶** a steam-powered ship that travels on the sea.

steed [steed] NOUN, steeds. **coursier ▶** a horse, especially a lively or high-spirited one. **Note.** Used mostly in older stories : *a knight and his steed.*

steel [steel] NOUN. **acier ▶** a hard, strong metal that is made of iron mixed with carbon. Steel is used to make machines, automobiles, tools, the framework for large buildings, and many other things. ▲ VERB, steeled, steeling. **s'armer de courage ▶** to make oneself strong like steel : *He steeled himself to face his parents about his marks.* ■ **steely,** ADJECTIVE. ▶ **d'acier.**

steel wool laine d'acier, paille de fer, tampon métallique ▶ a pad made of fine threads of steel, used for cleaning and polishing.

steep[1] [steep] ADJECTIVE, steeper, steepest. **1. escarpé (-ée), raide ▶** having a sharp slope; rising at a sharp angle : *a steep climb.* **2. excessif (-ive) ▶** very high; too high : *The price of this computer is a bit steep.*

steep[2] VERB, steeped, steeping. **1. faire tremper ▶** to soak in liquid : *Yang steeped the teabag for several minutes.* **2. baigner ▶** to be full of, involve deeply : *Moonlight steeped the room in silvery light.*

stee-ple [STEE-pul] NOUN, steeples. **clocher, flèche ▶** a high tower that rises from the roof of a church or other building and narrows to a point at the top.

steer[1] [steer] VERB, steered, steering. **1. diriger ▶** to guide the course of a car, boat, or other such vehicle. **2. être guidé (-ée), être dirigé (-ée) ▶** to follow a certain cause; be guided : *Abe was steered to religion by a priest.* SYN: direct, guide, manage, control, lead, pilot.

steer[2] NOUN, steers. **bouvillon boeuf ▶** a male animal of the cattle family that is raised for beef, rather than to produce young.

steg-o-sau-rus [STEG-uh-SOR-us] NOUN, stegosauruses. (also stegosaur) **stégosaure ▶** a large dinosaur that had a spiked tail and two rows of bony plates standing upright on its back.

stem[1] [stem] NOUN, stems. **1. tige ▶** the main part of a plant above the ground, from which leaves and flowers grow. **2. tige ▶** a stalk supporting a leaf, flower, or fruit. **3. pied ▶** something that is like the stem of a plant : *the stem of a wine glass.* ✎ p. 249.

stem[2] VERB, stemmed, stemming. **1. arrêter, contenir ▶** to stop the flow or movement of; check : *to stem the flow of water.* **2. stem from. provenir de ▶** to come from : *Many Canadian place names stem from Aboriginal words.*

sten-cil [STEN-sil] NOUN, stencils. **stencil, pochoir ▶** a thin sheet of metal, paper, or other material that has letters or designs cut through it. When it is laid on a surface and ink or colour is spread on it, these designs are made on the surface. ▲ VERB, stencilled, stencilling. (also stenciled, stenciling) **marquer au pochoir ▶** to mark with a stencil.

step [step] NOUN, steps. **1. pas ▶** a movement made by lifting the foot and putting it down again in a new position : *Our baby took his first step today.* **2. pas ▶** a short distance : *Their cabin is just a few steps from the lake.* **3. marche ▶** a place to put the foot on to go up or come down, such as a stair or a rung of a ladder. **4. pas, empreinte ▶** a sound or mark made by walking; a footstep or footprint. **5. mesure, pas ▶** an action or actions to reach a goal : *Let's take steps to save money.* **6. cran ▶** a grade or rank : *That scooter is barely a step above a bicycle!* ▲ VERB, stepped, stepping. **1. marcher ▶** to move by taking a step. **2. marcher sur ▶** to put or press the foot down : *She stepped on glass and cut her foot.*

step-fath-er [STEP-FAH-thur] NOUN, stepfathers. **beau-père ▶** a man who has married someone's mother after the person's father has died or been divorced from the mother. **Note.** A stepfather has one or more stepsons or stepdaughters.

step-lad-der [STEP-LAD-dur] NOUN, stepladders. **escabeau (-eaux) ▶** a ladder that stands by itself on four legs and has flat steps instead of rungs.

stems

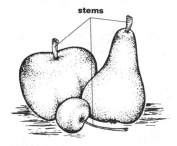

step-moth-er [STEP-MUTH-ur] NOUN, stepmothers. **belle-mère ▶** a woman who has married someone's father after the person's mother has died or been divorced from the father. **Note.** A stepmother has one or more stepsons or stepdaughters.

steppe [step] NOUN, steppes. **steppe ▶** a dry, flat area with low grass and few trees, especially the large region of this type that is found in southeastern Europe and parts of Asia. ☞ **p. 247.**

ster·e·o [STAIR-ee-oh] NOUN, stereos. **(chaîne) stéréo ▶** a radio, CD, or tape player that produces realistic sound by using two or more speakers

ster·e·o·type [STAIR-ee-oh-TYPE] NOUN, stereotypes. **stéréotype ▶** an oversimplified image of a group that makes all of them seem the same : *It's a stereotype to think owls are wise.* ▲ VERB, stereotyped, stereotyping. ✐ **p. 580.**

ster·ile [STAIR-ul *or* STAIR-ILE] ADJECTIVE. **1. stérile ▶** free from harmful germs and dirt : *Doctors use sterile instruments for operations.* **2. stérile ▶** not able to produce young; not fertile. **3. stérile ▶** without life or energy; empty; barren : *The street seemed sterile and deserted.*

ster·i·lize [STAIR-uh-LIZE] VERB, sterilized, sterilizing. **1. stériliser ▶** to make free from germs or dirt : *While camping, Zis sterilizes the water by boiling it.* **2. stériliser ▶** to make unable to produce young. SYN: disinfect, decontaminate, clean.

ster·ling [STUR-ling] NOUN. **1.** (also sterling silver) **argent fin, de bon aloi ▶** a valuable metal that is made of a mixture of 92.5 % pure silver with 7.5 % copper. **2. livre sterling ▶** the British system of money. ▲ ADJECTIVE. **1. (fait) d'argent fin ▶** made of sterling silver. **2. excellent (-ente) ▶** very fine or valuable, like sterling silver : *a sterling reputation.*

stern[1] [sturn] ADJECTIVE, sterner, sternest. **sévère ▶** very strict and serious; not giving in easily : *I saw the stern face of the principal.* ■ **sternly,** ADVERB. ▶ **sévèrement.**

stern[2] NOUN, sterns. **poupe ▶** the rear part of a boat or ship.

steth·o·scope [STETH-uh-SKOPE] NOUN, stethoscopes. **stéthoscope ▶** an instrument used by doctors and nurses to listen to sounds made by the heart, lungs, and other parts of the body.

stew [stoo] NOUN, stews. **ragoût ▶** a dish made of a mixture of meat or fish with various vegetables, cooked slowly for a time in a liquid : *vegetable stew.* ▲ VERB, stewed, stewing. **mijoter ▶** to cook slowly in a liquid : *to stew a chicken.*

stew·ard [STOO-urd] NOUN, stewards. **1. hôte (hôtesse), steward ▶** a person in charge of food and other services on a ship, airplane, or train, or at a club or hotel. **2. intendant (-ante) ▶** a person in charge of the household of a ruler or wealthy person.

stick [stik] NOUN, sticks. **1. bâton, brindille ▶** a long, thin piece of wood : *We used sticks to start our campfire.* **Note.** Often used in compounds, such as drumstick, matchstick. **2. bâton,**

✎ Writing Tips

Stereotyping

A **stereotype** is an idea or opinion that is fixed and unchanging. In writing, stereotype refers to types of characters who always have the same qualities regardless of the story in which they appear. (These are also known as **stock characters.**) Their characters do not change throughout the story, despite events happening that would naturally change them.

One type of stereotyping is the gender stereotype, often seen in commercials and TV comedies. The males and females take on traditional roles—the men have positions of power and play active roles, and the women have passive roles and little power.

Other types of stereotyping may involve a character's race, religion, or profession. For instance, the mad scientist is a common stereotype in bad science fiction. The most important thing to remember about this kind of stereotyping is that it doesn't represent people or reality accurately.

When you write, avoid stereotyping your characters, since stereotypes don't really show how complex people are. Use your imagination to create characters who are realistic, interesting, and three-dimensional.

---

morceau (-eaux) ▶ something shaped like a stick : *a stick of gum.* ▲ VERB, stuck, sticking. **1. piquer, enfoncer ▶** to push in with a pointed object : *I stuck a fork into the cake to see if it was done.* **2. coller ▶** to keep fixed in a certain spot; fasten or hold fast : *Stick the pieces together with glue.* **3. se coincer ▶** to keep from moving or making progress; bring to a stop : *The windows stick in damp weather.* **4. attendre, rester ▶** to stay in one place or condition; keep on : *Stick around after soccer practice for some extra help.*

stick·er [STIK-ur] NOUN, stickers. **1. autocollant ▶** a label or other printed paper that has glue or gum on the back. **2. objet pointu ▶** something that sticks, such as a sharp or rough part of a plant.

stick·y [STIK-ee] ADJECTIVE, stickier, stickiest. **1. collant (-ante), gluant (-ante) ▶** likely to stick, or covered with something that makes things

stick : *Her hands were sticky with pie dough.*
2. moite ▸ hot and humid : *The weather has been hot and sticky this summer.*

stiff [stif] ADJECTIVE, stiffer, stiffest. **1. raide, rigide, dur (dure) ▸** not easily bent; not flexible; rigid : *My leather gloves are still very stiff.* **2. raide, guindé (-ée) ▸** not easy or natural in manner; very formal : *a stiff manner of speaking.* **3. fort (forte) ▸** more extreme or severe than usual; hard to accept or deal with : *a stiff wind.* ▲ ADVERB: *Informal.* **complètement ▸** completely; extremely : *I was scared stiff on that ride.* ■ **stiffly,** ADVERB. ▸ avec raideur. ■ **stiffness,** NOUN. ▸ raideur.

stiff-en [STIF-un] VERB, stiffened, stiffening. **(se) raidir ▸** to make or become stiff : *My hands stiffened in the cold.*

sti-fle [STY-ful] VERB, stifled, stifling. **1. réprimer ▸** to hold back a sound from the mouth or throat : *Jill stifled a yawn.* **2. réprimer ▸** to hold back; keep in : *"And I don't know how long I shall be able to stifle my rage."* (Anne Frank) **3. étouffer ▸** to become or cause to become short of breath : *The desert air stifled me.* SYN : smother, stop, suppress, choke, suffocate.

stig-ma [STIG-muh] NOUN, stigmas. **1. honte ▸** a mark or sign of disgrace or dishonour. **2. stigmate ▸** the part of a flower that receives the pollen.

still [stil] ADJECTIVE, stiller, stillest. **1. immobile, tranquille ▸** not moving; without motion : *"He was never quite still, there was always a tapping foot somewhere, the impatient opening and closing of a hand."* (F Scott Fitzgerald) **2. tranquille ▸** without sound; quiet; silent : *On a still day you can hear the hum of bees.* ▲ VERB, stilled, stilling. **tranquilliser, apaiser ▸** to make or become quiet. ▲ NOUN, stills. **tranquillité, calme ▸** the fact of being quiet : *the still of the early morning.* ▲ ADVERB. **1. immobile ▸** not moving; without motion : *The ship was still in the harbour.* **2. encore ▸** now the same as before; even now : *Are you and Casey still friends?* ■ **stillness,** NOUN. ▸ tranquillité. *Thunder broke the stillness of the night.* SYN : quiet, motionless, calm, tranquil, peaceful.

stilt [stilt] NOUN, stilts. **échasse ▸** one of a long pair of slender poles with a small support for the foot that makes it possible to walk with the feet high above the ground.

stim-u-late [STIM-yuh-LATE] VERB, stimulated, stimulating. **stimuler ▸** to stir or rouse to action; excite : *The movie stimulated us to become pilots.* **Note.** Something that can stimulate the activity of the body is a stimulant: *Coffee and tea contain the stimulant caffeine.* ■ **stimulation,** NOUN. ▸ stimulation.

stim-u-lus [STIM-yuh-lus] NOUN, stimuli [STIM-yuh-LY]. **stimulus, encouragement ▸** something that stimulates; something producing a reaction : *A talk with my teacher was the stimulus I needed to work harder.*

sting [sting] VERB, stung, stinging. **1. piquer ▸** to pierce or wound with a small, sharp point, as a bee or wasp does. **2. piquer ▸** to cause or suffer a quick, sharp pain : *The scrape on her knee stung for a few seconds.* ▲ NOUN, stings. **1. piqûre ▸** a wound made by an insect or animal stinger : *The bee sting raised a bump on Lee's arm.* **2. piquant, dard ▸** the sharp part of an insect or animal that is used for stinging; also called a stinger.

sting-ray [STING-RAY] NOUN, stingrays. **pastenague ▸** a large, flat ocean fish that has a long whip-like tail with poisonous, stinging spines that can inflict a painful wound.

sting-y [STIN-jee] ADJECTIVE, stingier, stingiest. **avare, chiche ▸** not willing to give or share something, especially money; not generous : *In the story* A Christmas Carol, *Scrooge is a stingy and mean man.*

stink [stink] NOUN, stinks. **puanteur ▸** a strong, bad smell. ▲ VERB, stank or stunk, stunk, stinking. **puer ▸** to have a strong, unpleasant smell.

stilts

stir [stur] VERB, stirred, stirring. **1. brasser, remuer, tourner ▸** to mix something by moving it in a circular motion with a spoon or similar tool : *Keep stirring the sauce so that it doesn't burn.* **2. remuer, faire bouger ▸** to move or cause to move : *Wind stirred the lake water into choppy waves.* **3. remuer, émouvoir, éveiller, agiter ▸** to cause a certain thought or action; bring about : *to stir up trouble.* ▲ NOUN, stirs. **1. action de remuer ▸** the act of stirring. **2. agitation ▸** excitement or interest : *There was quite a stir when the rock group visited town.* SYN : mix, blend, combine, scramble, jumble.

stir·rup [STEER-up *or* STUR-up] NOUN, stirrups. **étrier ▸** a loop or ring that hangs from a saddle and supports the rider's foot, usually made of leather or metal.

stitch [stich] NOUN, stitches. **1. point, maille ▸** in sewing, a single, complete movement of a thread and needle through a piece of cloth. **2. point, maille ▸** any similar movement used in knitting, crocheting, or embroidering. **3. point ▸** a loop created by such a movement. **4. suturer ▸** the act of closing up a cut with a threadlike material to help it heal properly. **Note.** The medical term for this is suture. **5. point de côté ▸** a sharp pain in the side. ▲ VERB, stitched, stitching. **coudre, piquer, suturer ▸** to make a stitch or stitches.

in stitches (rire) aux larmes, se tordre de rire ▸ laughing very hard.

stock [stok] NOUN, stocks. **1. stock ▸** a supply of things stored for future use or sale : *The store has that popular CD in stock again.* **2.** (also **livestock**) **bétail ▸** animals raised or kept on a farm or ranch, such as cows, sheep, and pigs. **3. bouillon ▸** broth made from the liquid in which fish, meat, or poultry has been cooked : *chicken stock.* **4. titre, action ▸** shares of ownership in a business : *to buy stock in a company.* ▲ VERB, stocked, stocking. **avoir en stock, s'approvisionner en vivres, stocker ▸** to keep on hand; keep a supply : *We stocked up on chips and drinks for the party.* ▲ ADJECTIVE. **1. en stock ▸** on hand; in supply : *This bracelet is not a stock item; it was a special order.* **2. courant (-ante) ▸** in common use : *a stock character.*

stock-brok·er [STOK-broke-ur] NOUN, stockbrokers. **courtier (en valeurs mobilières) ▸** a person who buys and sells shares of stock for others, in return for a fee.

stock·ing [STOK-ing] NOUN, stockings. **bas ▸** a close-fitting covering for the leg.

stock market (also **stock exchange**) **marché financier, Bourse ▸** a place where stocks and bonds are bought and sold.

stocks [stoks] PLURAL NOUN. **pilori ▸** a wooden frame made for a prisoner to sit or stand in, with holes for the feet and sometimes for the head and hands. In earlier times, people were punished for minor crimes by being put in the stocks.

stock·y [STOK-ee] ADJECTIVE, stockier, stockiest. **trapu (-ue) ▸** having a short, heavy shape or build : *a stocky wrestler.*

stock·yard [STOK-yard] NOUN, stockyards. **parc à bestiaux ▸** a place where livestock is kept in pens before being shipped to market or to be slaughtered.

stole [stole] VERB. a past form of steal.

sto·len [STOLE-in] VERB. a past form of steal.

stom·ach [STUM-ik] NOUN, stomachs. **1. esto-mac ▸** the baglike part of the body that holds food and begins digesting it. **2. ventre ▸** the area of the body between the middle of the chest and the hips. ▲ VERB, stomached, stomaching. **supporter, endurer ▸** to put up with something or someone; bear : *I can't stomach that show.* ⌐ p. 1005. ☉ p. 403.

stomp [stomp] VERB, stomped, stomping. **frapper du pied ▸** to walk or step heavily and with force : *We stomped loudly around the gym.*

stone [stone] NOUN, stones. **1. pierre ▸** the hard mineral substance that makes up rocks. **2. pierre, caillou (-oux) ▸** a piece of this material that is larger than a pebble but smaller than a boulder. **3.** (also called **precious stone**) **pierre ▸** a gem or jewel. **4. noyau (-aux) ▸** the hard pit or seed of certain fruits, such as cherries and peaches. ⌐ p. 1114.

Stone Age l'âge de (la) pierre ▸ an early period of human history when tools and weapons were made of stone rather than metal.

stood [stood] VERB. a past form of stand.

stook [stook *or* stuke] NOUN, stooks. **choc ▸** another word for shock². ▲ VERB, stooked, stooking. **mettre en moyettes ▸** to arrange grain or hay into stooks.

stool [stool] NOUN, stools. **tabouret ▸** a seat without arms or a back.

stoop¹ [stoop] VERB, stooped, stooping. **1. se baisser, se pencher ▸** to bend the body forward and down : *to stoop over to tie a shoe.* **2. marcher voûté, avoir le dos rond ▸** to stand or walk with the shoulders pushed forward. **3. s'abaisser ▸** to lower oneself to do something one should not do : *We didn't think he'd stoop to cheating.* ▲ NOUN. **dos rond ▸** a bending forward of the head and shoulders : *to walk with a stoop.*

stoop² NOUN, stoops. **porche, terrasse, véranda ▸** a small platform or porch with stairs leading up to the entrance of a house or other building.

stop [stop] VERB, stopped, stopping. **1. (s') arrê-ter ▸** to keep from moving or going on : *to stop for a red light.* **2. empêcher ▸** to keep from doing something : *Paul stopped his brother from running into the street.* **3. s'arrêter ▸** to come to an end : *After the rain stopped, we continued our game.* **4. bloquer ▸** to close up or block : *Clay stopped up the sink.* ▲ NOUN, stops. **1. arrêt, halte ▸** the act of stopping or being stopped : *The driver made a quick stop to avoid hitting the skunk.* **2. arrêt ▸** a place or location where a stop is made : *Clyde missed his bus stop because he fell asleep.* **3. taquet, butoir ▸** something used to stop or block : *a doorstop.* **4. clé ▸** the part on a musical instrument that controls the tone and pitch. SYN: end, halt, cease, quit, suspend, discontinue.

stop-per [STOP-ur] NOUN, stoppers. **bouchon** ▸ something used to stop up or close the opening of a bottle, jar, or other container.

stop-watch [STOP-WOCH] NOUN, stopwatches. **chronomètre** ▸ a special watch that can be stopped to give the exact length of time that something takes.

stopwatch

stor-age [STOR-ij] NOUN. **1. emmagasinage, entreposage** ▸ the act or fact of storing something : *We put our winter clothes in storage.* **2. mise en mémoire** ▸ the fact or process of saving information in a computer.

store [stor] NOUN, stores. **1. magasin** ▸ a place where things are sold to the public : *a grocery store.* **2. provisions** ▸ a supply of things that are intended for future use : *Some animals gather a store of food for the winter.* ▲ VERB, stored, storing. **1. entreposer** ▸ to put away and keep for future use : *We stored our skis in the attic until next year.* **2. mettre en mémoire** ▸ to put information into a computer memory or onto a computer device such as a tape, CD-ROM, or floppy disk. ▷ **p. 1054.**

store-house [STOR-HOWCE] NOUN, storehouses. **1. entrepôt** ▸ a building or other place where things are stored for future use. **2. mine de renseignements** ▸ a large supply or source : *A farmer's almanac is a storehouse of useful information.*

stor-ey [STOR-ee] NOUN, storeys. (also story) **étage** ▸ one floor of a building that has different levels : *a 20-storey building.*

stork [stork] NOUN, storks. **cigogne** ▸ a long-legged bird with a long neck and bill.

storm [storm] NOUN, storms. **1. orage, tempête** ▸ a change in the weather that brings strong wind along with rain, snow, hail, or sleet. **2. torrent** ▸ a sudden and strong outburst of noise or feeling : *a storm of boos from the crowd.* ▲ VERB, stormed, storming. **1. pleuvoir, neiger, souffler** ▸ to rain, snow, or blow strongly. **2. aller furieusement** ▸ to rush or attack violently and quickly : *Darla teased her until she stormed out of the room.* ▷ **p. 1104 , 1119.** ◉ **p. 112.**

by storm d'assaut ▸ with a sudden and powerful attack : *to take a castle by storm.*

storm-y [STOR-mee] ADJECTIVE, stormier, stormiest. **1. orageux (-euse)** ▸ having to do with a storm or storms : *stormy weather.* **2. violent (-ente), orageux (-euse)** ▸ like a storm; noisy, violent, angry, and so on : *The friends had a stormy relationship with many arguments.*

sto-ry [STOR-ee] NOUN, stories. **1. histoire** ▸ words telling about something that has happened : *Did you read the magazine story about Mother Teresa?* **2. histoire, conte** ▸ an account or tale that is made up : *the story of Cinderella.* **3. histoire** ▸ a lie : *My uncle likes to tell stories about his adventures during the war.* **4. étage** ▸ a storey. SYN : tale, yarn, account, narrative, anecdote.

stout [stowt] ADJECTIVE, stouter, stoutest. **1. corpulent (-ente), gros (grosse), robuste** ▸ large and heavy; fat : *a stout cabinet.* **2. intrépide** ▸ having courage; brave : *In old stories, the hero is often a "stout fellow."* **3. solide** ▸ strong and solid : *stout walls.*

stove [stove] NOUN, stoves. **cuisinière, poêle** ▸ a kitchen appliance that is used for cooking food. **Note.** A stovepipe is a large metal pipe used to carry smoke away from a stove.

portable **stove**

stow [stoh] VERB, stowed, stowing. **1. ranger** ▸ to put or pack away : *We stowed supplies for our hike in the packs.* **2. stow away. être un ou une passager (-ère) clandestin (-ine)** ▸ to be a stowaway.

stow-a-way [STOH-uh-WAY] NOUN, stowaways. **passager (-ère) clandestin (-ine)** ▸ a person who hides on a ship or plane to avoid paying for a ticket.

strad-dle [STRAD-dul] VERB, straddles, straddling. **enfourcher, se mettre à califourchon** ▸ to have one leg or part on either side of something : *to straddle a horse.*

strag·gle [STRAG-gul] VERB, straggled, straggling. **1. traîner en arrière ▸** to go off from the main group or main path ; wander ; stray : *The little ones straggled behind the bigger children.* **2. marcher sans ordre ▸** to move in an uneven or crooked way : *We straggled up the hill.* ▪ **straggler,** NOUN. ▸ **traînard (-arde).** *A few stragglers were left after the game.* SYN: wander, ramble, roam, drift away.

straight [strate] ADJECTIVE, straighter, straightest. **1. droit ▸** not curved or crooked ; following one direction : *Notebook paper is marked with straight lines.* **2. droit (droite) ▸** in the proper order or arrangement : **3. franc (franche) ▸** honest and direct. **4. sérieux (-ieuse) ▸** not joking ; serious : *We tried to keep straight faces as she opened the gag gift.* ▲ ADVERB. **1. (tout) droit ▸** in a straight manner or way : *to stand up straight.* **2. directement ▸** without delay : *Come straight home after school.*

straight·en [STRAY-tun] VERB, straightened, straightening. **devenir droit, redresser ▸** to make or become straight : *She straightened the picture.*

straight·for·ward [strate-FOR-wurd] ADJECTIVE. **franc (franche) ▸** acting or speaking in a direct way ; honest.

strain¹ [strane] VERB, strained, straining. **1. faire un grand effort ▸** to make a great effort ; try hard : *Clara looked back, straining for a last look at the lake.* **2. tendre ▸** to draw or pull tight ; pull with force : *The dog strained at the rope and growled at the cat.* **3. se froisser ▸** to weaken or damage by stretching or putting too much pressure on : *to strain a muscle.* **4. passer, filtrer ▸** to pour or press something through a strainer. ▲ NOUN, strains. **fatigue, épuisement ▸** the fact or condition of being strained : *The strain on his face was evident as Father told us about the accident.*

strain² NOUN, strains. **1. race ▸** a breed or type of animal : *The cat is from an ancient Egyptian strain.* **2. lignée ▸** a family line ; ancestry. **3. accords, accents ▸** a piece of music ; a melody or tune : *Strains of Debussy's "Clair de Lune" could be heard through the open window.*

strain·er [STRANE-ur] NOUN, strainers. **passoire ▸** a device for separating liquids from solids, with small holes to stop the solids as the liquid flows through.

strait [strate] NOUN, straits. **1. détroit ▸** a narrow channel between two larger bodies of water : *Davis Strait connects Baffin Bay with the Atlantic Ocean.* **2. straits. ennuis ▸** a difficult situation ; a problem or trouble : *to be in tough straits.*

strand¹ [strand] VERB, stranded, stranding. **abandonner ▸** to leave behind or in a helpless position : *We were stranded when our car broke down.*

strand² NOUN, strands. **1. brin, toron, fibre ▸** one of the threads or wires that is twisted together to form a rope or cable. **2. mèche ▸** a hair or thread.

strange [straynj] ADJECTIVE, stranger, strangest. **1. étrange ▸** not known before ; not familiar : *I would rather not spend the night in a strange place.* **2. étrange ▸** not normal or ordinary ; odd ; unusual : *Is this clock supposed to make this strange buzzing noise?* ▪ **strangely,** ADVERB. ▸ **bizarrement, de façon étrange.** ▪ **strangeness,** NOUN. ▸ **bizarrerie, étrangeté.** SYN : unusual, peculiar, unfamiliar, odd, curious.

strang·er [STRANE-jur] NOUN, strangers. **1. étranger (-ère) ▸** a person who is not known or is not familiar : *"We'd never seen this stranger before."* (Roch Carrier) **2. étranger (-ère) ▸** a person from another place : *They were strangers in the town.*

stran·gle [STRANG-ul] VERB, strangled, strangling. **1. étrangler ▸** to kill by squeezing the throat to cut off the breath. **2. étouffer, étrangler ▸** to be or feel unable to breathe ; choke. ▪ **strangulation,** NOUN. ▸ **strangulation.**

strap [strap] NOUN, straps. **courroie, sangle, lanière ▸** a long, narrow strip of leather, cloth, or some other material used to tie or hold something : *The strap on Val's shoe broke and she had to change shoes.* ▲ VERB, strapped, strapping. **attacher avec une courroie, sangler ▸** to fasten or hold with a strap.

shoulder **strap**

strat·e·gy [STRAT-uh-jee] NOUN, strategies. **1. stratégie ▸** the technique of planning and directing troops and other forces during a war. **Note.** Strategy deals with planning before a battle ; tactics involves decisions made in or at the battle itself. **2. stratégie ▸** a careful plan for reaching a goal : *What's the best strategy to use to get my sister to help with the dishes?* ▪ **strategic,** ADJECTIVE. **stratégique ▸** having to do with strategy or important to strategy.

straw [strah] NOUN, straws. **1. paille ▸** a narrow tube of paper or plastic, used for sucking up liquids into the mouth. **2. paille ▸** the thin, dried stalks of grains or grasses after they have been harvested and the seeds have been removed. Straw is also used as animal bedding in barns and to make objects such as a straw hat and a straw broom.

straw-ber-ry [STRAH-BAIR-ee] NOUN, strawberries. **fraise ▸** a small, red berry with a sweet taste, growing on a plant that grows low to the ground. **◉ p. 251.**

stray [stray] VERB, strayed, straying. **s'écarter ▸** to move off from a group or from the proper place; wander away: *The speech strayed from the main issue.* ▲ ADJECTIVE. **1. errant (-ante), perdu (-ue) ▸** wandering or lost: *stray cats.* **2. épars (-arse) ▸** scattered about: *There were only a few stray plants growing along the desert road.* ▲ NOUN, strays. **animal (-aux) égaré(s), perdu (s), errant (s) ▸** a lost or homeless animal. SYN: drift, wander, roam, straggle.

streak [streek] NOUN, streaks. **1. bande, traînée ▸** a long, thin mark that is usually a different colour than the surrounding area: *streaks of dirt on a window.* **2. suite, série ▸** a continuing pattern or series of events: *a 10-game winning streak.* **3. tendance à ▸** a small amount or trace of something: *a mean streak.* ▲ VERB, streaked, streaking. **1. sillonner de ▸** to mark with streaks: *Tears streaked the face of the child.* **2. passer comme un éclair ▸** to move very fast: *A shooting star streaked across the sky.*

stream [streem] NOUN, streams. **1. ruisseau (-eaux) ▸** a small body of running water: *The stream feeds into a pond beyond the barn.* **2. flot continu ▸** a steady flow or movement of something: *a stream of people.* ▲ VERB, streamed, streaming. **1. sortir à flots, couler à flots ▸** to flow steadily: *Light streamed into the street from the all-night store.* **2. flotter au vent ▸** to wave or float in the air, as a flag does. **⬒ p. 1110.**

stream-er [STREE-mur] NOUN, streamers. **banderole ▸** a long, ribbonlike flag or banner.

stream-line [STREEM-LINE] VERB, streamlined, streamlining. **1. rendre aérodynamique ▸** to design and build something in the shape that offers the least resistance for moving through air or water. *The company streamlined their new car to get better gas mileage.* **2. rationaliser ▸** to make something more efficient or able to work better: *Let's streamline the way we check in students for the meeting.*

street [street] NOUN, streets. **rue ▸** a public road in a city or town. A street has houses or other buildings on one or both sides. **⬒ p. 1055.**

street-car [STREET-KAR] NOUN, streetcars. **tramway ▸** a vehicle that runs on rails in the streets and carries passengers.

strength [strenkth] NOUN, strengths. **force ▸** the quality of being strong; power or force: *"The sun's rays appeared to lose their strength little by little."* (Jules Verne) **✐ p. 456.**

strength-en [STRENK-thun] VERB, strengthened, strengthening. **renforcer ▸** to make or grow stronger: *The prime minister felt that the country should strengthen its stand on human rights.*

stren-u-ous [STREN-yoo-us] ADJECTIVE. **1. fatigant (-ante), acharné (-ée) ▸** with great effort: *It is a strenuous climb up that steep hill.* **2. énergique ▸** very active: *There is strenuous opposition to new development.* **■ strenuously,** ADVERB: **▸ vigoureusement.** *Laura works strenuously in her garden.*

stress [stres] NOUN, stresses. **1. tension ▸** the force with which one body acts on another, as by pulling or pressing down: *We tested the metal to see how much stress it can take.* **2. stress ▸** pressure or strain on the mind and feelings: *A new job or an illness in the family can cause stress.* **3. accent ▸** a special meaning, emphasis, or importance: *Our team put stress on a strong conclusion for the debate.* **4. accent ▸** a stronger tone of voice used to emphasize a certain sound, word, or phrase: Note. In the word *firefighter,* "fire" has primary stress, "fight" has secondary stress, and "er" has no stress. ▲ VERB, stressed, stressing. **1. accentuer ▸** to give special meaning or importance to: *The mayor stressed the need for a new community centre.* **2. accentuer ▸** to pronounce a word or syllable of a word with greater emphasis: *We stress the first syllable in the word "streamline."*

stretch [strech] VERB, stretched, stretching. **1. (s') étirer ▸** to draw out to become larger or wider: *to stretch a rubber band.* **2. (s') étirer, (s') étendre ▸** to spread or reach out to full length: *Minga was stretched out in front of the TV.* **3. s'étendre ▸** to move or lie over an area; extend: *The prairies stretch across three of Canada's provinces.* ▲ NOUN, stretches. **1. étirement ▸** the act of stretching: *The catcher made a long stretch to catch the ball.* **2. étendue ▸** a straight or level area: *Great stretches of wheat fields lay before us.* **3. longtemps, période ▸** an unbroken period of time or activity: *He reads for hours at a stretch.*

stretch-er [STRECH-ur] NOUN, stretchers. **brancard ▸** a frame or simple bed on which a sick or injured person can be carried.

strew [stroo] VERB, strewed, strewed or strewn, strewing. **éparpiller ▸** to spread around by throwing or scattering: *He strewed his clothes around the room.*

strick-en [STRIK-un] VERB. a past form of strike. ▲ ADJECTIVE. **atteint (-einte), frappé (-ée) ▸** affected by sickness or trouble: *Her face was drawn and stricken with fear.*

strict [strikt] ADJECTIVE, stricter, strictest. **1. strict (-icte), sévère** ▶ following or enforcing a rule in an exact, careful manner : *I have strict orders to be home by dark.* **2. strict (-icte)** ▶ closely enforced; exact : *I call her a sister, but in the strictest sense she is my stepsister.* **3. strict (-icte)** ▶ absolute or complete : *His real identity was a strict secret.* ■ **strictly,** ADVERB. ▶ **strictement, sévèrement.** ■ **strictness,** NOUN. ▶ **rigueur.**

stride [stride] VERB, strode, stridden, striding. **marcher à grands pas** ▶ to walk with long steps : *The man strode down the road in a hurry to get home.* ■ **strides,** PLURAL NOUN. **1. grands pas** ▶ a long step : *One of his strides equalled three of my steps.* **2. grands progrès** ▶ the fact of advancing; progress or improvement : *Great strides have been taken to improve working conditions.*

strike [strike] VERB, struck, struck or stricken, striking. **1. frapper** ▶ to contact with force; hit : *The player struck the ball so hard it went out of the park.* **2. frapper, venir (à l'esprit)** ▶ to come to the mind quickly or with force : *The idea struck me in the middle of the night.* **3. impressionner** ▶ to affect the mind or feelings in a certain way : *The stark beauty of the Northwest Territories struck him.* **4. sonner** ▶ to show the time by sound : *The clock struck 3:00.* **5. découvrir, allumer** ▶ to set on fire by scratching : *to strike a match.* **6. trouver** ▶ to discover suddenly : *to strike gold.* **7. faire grève** ▶ of workers, to stop work as a protest until certain demands are met, such as higher pay. ▲ NOUN, strikes. **1. grève** ▶ the stopping of work as a method of forcing an employer to agree to certain demands. **2. découverte** ▶ a sudden discovery : *an oil strike.* **3. prise** ▶ in baseball, a pitch that the batter either swings at and misses or hits into foul territory. **Note.** A pitch is also called a **strike** if the batter does not swing, but the ball passes over home plate in an area called the **strike zone.** *✐* **p. 586.**

strike•out [stry-owt] **1. retirer** ▶ to make an out in baseball by getting three strikes. **2.** *Informal.* **échouer** ▶ to fail completely : *He asked for a raise but struck out.* **3. commencer, prendre une direction** ▶ to begin to move or go; set out : *She struck out for the next village on*

foot. **Note.** Also used as a NOUN: *That pitcher has set a record for strikeouts.*

strik•ing [STRY-king] ADJECTIVE. **1. frappant (-ante)** ▶ making a strong impression, as by being attractive or unusual : *a striking picture.* **2. en grève** ▶ on strike : *striking employees.* ■ **strikingly,** ADVERB. ▶ **remarquablement.**

string [string] NOUN, strings. **1. ficelle** ▶ a thin cord made of twisted fibres or wire. **2. fil** ▶ something that is like this in appearance or use : *a string of lights.* **3. collier, rang, suite** ▶ a series of persons, things, or events : *a string of good luck.* **4. strings. cordes** ▶ musical instruments that have strings and are usually played with a bow, such as the violin or cello. ▲ VERB, strung, stringing. **1. enfiler, tendre** ▶ to put on a string or provide with strings : *to string beads for a necklace.* **2. enchaîner** ▶ to arrange in a row or series : *"I never heard so many old, played out jokes strung together in my life."* (Mark Twain) ■ **stringy,** ADJECTIVE. ▶ **fibreux (-euse), filandreux (-euse). ☜ p. 538.**

string bean haricot vert ▶ a long, green bean that is cooked and eaten along with the pod.

strip¹ [strip] VERB, stripped, stripping. **1. (se) déshabiller** ▶ to take off clothing; undress : *Strip off those dirty clothes and get into the bathtub.* **2. enlever** ▶ to remove the covering or outer layer of something : *She stripped the wrapping paper off the present.*

strip² NOUN, strips. **bande** ▶ a long, narrow piece of some material : *a strip of paper or cloth.*

stripe [stripe] NOUN, stripes. **rayure** ▶ a narrow, even band of colour : *A candy cane has a red stripe on it.* ▲ VERB, striped, striping. **rayer** ▶ to mark with a stripe or stripes. **Note.** Often used as an ADJECTIVE: *a striped shirt.*

strive [strive] VERB, strove or strived, striven or strived, striving. **s'efforcer de** ▶ to make a great effort to get or do something; try hard : *The author strives to create realistic characters.* SYN: struggle, endeavour, attempt, try, labour.

strode [strode] VERB. a past form of stride.

stroke¹ [stroke] NOUN, strokes. **1. coup** ▶ the act of hitting or striking something : *the stroke of an axe.* **2. coup** ▶ the act of hitting the ball in a game : *a backhand stroke in tennis.* **3. coup**

🔧 Word Builder

*The expression **on strike** means to participate in a work stoppage : The workers rejected the contract offer and went on strike. **Strike it rich** can mean to find a rich pocket or vein of ore, but it can also mean to have sudden financial success or good fortune : They struck it rich in a lottery. **Strike out** is a baseball phrase that means to fail to hit a fair ball in three attempts but it is also used to mean to not succeed : He struck out trying to convince his dad that he needs a new bike.*

▸ a single motion that is repeated, as in swimming or in rowing a boat. **4. attaque** ▸ the sudden breaking or blocking of a blood vessel in the brain.

stroke² [strohk] VERB, stroked, stroking. **caresser** ▸ to rub or pat gently : *Our dog likes to be stroked on her belly.*

stroll [strole] VERB, strolled, strolling. **se promener, flâner** ▸ to walk around in a slow and relaxed way : *"Grandpa finally came strolling in."* (Marilyn Halvorson) ▲ NOUN, strolls. **promenade** ▸ a slow, relaxed walk : *They went for a stroll in the park to watch the children play.*

strol-ler [STROLE-lur] NOUN, strollers. **poussette** ▸ a baby carriage in which a child can sit upright.

strong [strong] ADJECTIVE, stronger, strongest. **1. fort** ▸ having much power or energy to lift or move things : *Naveen got stronger by lifting weights.* **2. fort** ▸ having much more than the usual power or force : *a strong wind.* **3. solide** ▸ able to stand up to strain or pressure; not easily damaged : *Denim is a strong fabric.* **4. solide, sérieux (-euse)** ▸ not easily moved or changed; firm : *a strong belief.* ■ **strongly,** ADVERB. ▸ **fortement.** *"The oysters had to be torn from the rocks to which they were so strongly attached."* (Jules Verne) SYN: powerful, forceful, mighty, sturdy.

strove [strove] VERB. a past form of strive.

struck [struk] VERB. a past form of strike.

struc-ture [STRUK-chur] NOUN, structures. **1. construction** ▸ something that is built; a house or other building. **2. structure** ▸ the way in which the parts of something are organized into a whole : *We are studying the structure of plants.* ▲ VERB, structured, structuring. **structurer** ▸ to organize in a certain way : *She structured her report in three parts.*

strug-gle [STRUG-ul] VERB, struggled, struggling. **1. se battre (contre)** ▸ to make a great effort; try hard to get or do something : *"I was struggling to control the tears that were threatening to well up and spill over."* (Jean Little) **2. se débattre** ▸ to fight or do battle. ▲ NOUN, struggles. **lutte** ▸ the fact of struggling. SYN: attempt, try, endeavour, strive, battle.

strum [strum] VERB, strummed, strumming. **racler, gratter** ▸ to stroke the strings of a musical instrument in an easy or relaxed way : *to strum a guitar.*

strung [strung] VERB. a past form of string.

stub [stub] NOUN, stubs. **bout** ▸ the short part that remains when something is torn off or worn down : *The usher at the theatre door tore our tickets in half and gave us the stubs.* ▲ VERB, stubbed, stubbing. **se cogner** ▸ to bump one's

toe or foot against something. ■ **stubby,** ADJECTIVE. ▸ **courtaud (-aude).**

stub-ble [STUB-ul] NOUN. **1. chaume** ▸ the short stalks of grain left standing in the ground after a crop is harvested. **2. barbe rêche, barbe de plusieurs jours** ▸ a short, rough growth of hair, especially on a man's face.

stub-born [STUB-urn] ADJECTIVE. **1. têtu (-ue), obstiné (-ée), entêté (-ée)** ▸ not giving in easily; not willing to change or to go along with others : *Joseph was very stubborn and kept doing it the way he always had.* **2. rebelle** ▸ hard to change or deal with : *a stubborn stain.* ■ **stubbornly,** ADVERB. ▸ **obstinément.** ■ **stubbornness,** NOUN. ▸ **entêtement.** SYN: willful, obstinate, headstrong, rigid.

stuck [stuk] VERB. a past form of stick.

stud [stud] NOUN, studs. **1. clou (décoratif), bouton, crampon** ▸ a small, round nail or other such object sticking out from a surface : *Snow tires have metal studs that grip slippery roads.* **2. poteau montant, poteau intermédiaire** ▸ one of the vertical posts in a wall to which boards and other materials are nailed or fastened. ▲ VERB, studded, studding. **parsemer** ▸ to cover with, or as if with, studs : *Diamonds studded the expensive pin.*

stu-dent [STOO-dunt] NOUN, students. **1. étudiant (-ante), élève** ▸ a person who goes to school. **2. étudiant (-ante), élève** ▸ anyone who studies something : *The painter was a student of nature.* 📖 p. 1061.

stu-di-o [STOO-dee-oh] NOUN, studios. **1. studio** ▸ a place where an artist works. **2. studio** ▸ a place where movies are filmed or where radio and television programs are made.

stud-y [STUD-ee] VERB, studied, studying. **1. étudier** ▸ to try to learn, know, or understand something by reading and thinking about it : *to study for a test.* **2. examiner** ▸ to examine or look at something very closely : *"I studied how to be a cowboy, watching every movie my cowboy heroes made."* (Dayal Kaur Khalsa) ▲ NOUN, studies. **1. étude** ▸ the act of studying : *It took years of study for her to be a concert pianist.* **2. étude** ▸ a subject that is studied : *He's been neglecting his studies, and his marks show it.* **3. bureau (-eaux)** ▸ a room used for studying. ■ **studious,** ADJECTIVE. **studieux (-ieuse)** ▸ serious about one's studies; likely to spend time studying.

stuff [stuf] NOUN. **1. choses, affaires, trucs** ▸ things in a group; a mass or collection of things : *Is that your stuff on the floor?* **2. matière, substance, chose** ▸ useless or unwanted things : *There was brown stuff at the bottom of the jar.* **3.** *Informal.* **chose** ▸ something that is known about or mentioned, but not definitely named : *Dad bought some stuff to make the grass grow.* ▲ VERB, stuffed, stuffing.

1. bourrer ▸ to pack full of; fill up : *She stuffed her bag with clothes.* **2. farcir** ▸ to put stuffing in food. **3. empailler** ▸ to fill the skin of a dead animal to make it look natural : *Hunters sometimes stuff the animals they kill.*

stuff·ing [STUF-ing] NOUN, stuffings. **1. rembourrage** ▸ material that is used to fill or pack something : *The stuffing is coming out of that old chair.* **2. farce** ▸ a seasoned mixture of food put inside some other kind of food : *The turkey stuffing is made from corn bread, celery, and onions.*

stuff·y [STUF-ee] ADJECTIVE, stuffier, stuffiest. **1. mal aéré (-ée)** ▸ without enough fresh air : *I need fresh air after working in that stuffy room.* **2. collet monté, snob** ▸ too serious and formal; dull ; boring : *That teacher is rather stuffy.*

stum·ble [STUM-bul] VERB, stumbled, stumbling. **1. trébucher** ▸ to trip or lose one's balance; fall or almost fall. **2. hésiter, avancer en trébuchant** ▸ to speak or act in a clumsy, hesitating way : *The new teacher stumbled over our names on the first day.* **3. tomber sur par hasard** ▸ to discover accidentally or come upon by accident : *Keegan stumbled upon an old box under the bush.* SYN: trip, blunder, falter, totter.

stump [stump] NOUN, stumps. **1. souche** ▸ the lower part of a tree trunk left in the ground after the tree has been cut down. **2. moignon, chicot,** ▸ the part of something that is left after most of it has been used or worn down. ▲ VERB, stumped, stumping. ▸ to confuse or puzzle someone : *The last question stumped me.* ☞ p. 253.

stun [stun] VERB, stunned, stunning. **1. assommer** ▸ to make unconscious for a short time; daze. **2. abasourdir** ▸ to make unable to act; shock or surprise greatly : *The mistake stunned the crowd.* ■ **stunning**, ADJECTIVE. superbe ▸ very attractive or stylish : *a stunning gown.*

stung [stung] VERB. a past form of sting.

stunk [stunk] VERB. a past form of stink.

stunt[1] [stunt] NOUN, stunts. **acrobatie** ▸ a difficult and daring act of skill : *The pilots did some amazing stunts with their airplanes.* **Note.** A stunt person does the dangerous actions during the filming of a movie.

stunt[2] VERB, stunted, stunting. **rabougrir, retarder, ralentir** ▸ to stop or slow the growth of something : *"There are no trees on the island except the small ones stunted by the winds."* (Scott O'Dell)

stu·pid [STOO-pid or STYOO-pid] ADJECTIVE. **stupide** ▸ not having intelligence or common sense; not smart. ■ **stupidly,** ADVERB. ▸ **stupidement.** ■ **stupidity,** NOUN. ▸ stupidité, bêtise.

stur·dy [STUR-dee] ADJECTIVE, sturdier, sturdiest. **robuste, vigoureux (-euse)** ▸ able to bear up to strain and hard use; strong : *They lived in a sturdy brick house.* ■ **sturdily,** ADVERB. ▸ **avec robustesse, vigoureusement.** ■ **sturdiness,** NOUN. ▸ **robustesse, solidité.** SYN: strong, rugged, well-built, sound.

stur·geon [STUR-jun] NOUN, sturgeon or sturgeons. **esturgeon** ▸ a large food fish that has a long, narrow body with bony scales. It is found in northern waters. Sturgeon eggs are the source of caviar. ☞ p. 107.

stut·ter [STUT-ur] VERB, stuttered, stuttering. **bégayer** ▸ to speak in a jerky, uneven way, often repeating sounds. ▲ NOUN. **bégaiement** ▸ the act of stuttering.

style [stile] NOUN, styles. **1. style** ▸ a way of writing that makes one writer different from another; a particular way of writing. **2. style** ▸ the particular qualities of a work of art that make it distinct : *a film in the style of Alfred Hitchcock.* **3. style** ▸ any particular design, fashion, or way of doing things : *hairstyles; an affluent lifestyle.* **4. mode** ▸ the way of dressing and acting that is currently accepted; fashion : *A black dress like that never goes out of style.* ■ **stylish,** ADJECTIVE. **élégant (-ante), à la mode** ▸ showing the latest style; fashionable.

sub- a PREFIX meaning "below" or "less than": *subzero; substandard.*

sub·due [sub-DOO] VERB, subdued, subduing. **1. soumettre, subjuguer** ▸ to bring under control; conquer or defeat : *It took several zoo workers to subdue the injured tiger.* **2. baisser** ▸ to make less in force or strength; soften : *They talked in subdued voices in the library.*

sub·ject [SUB-jikt] NOUN, subjects. **1. sujet** ▸ something that is thought about, talked about, or written about; topic : *When we started gossiping, Dylan told us to change the subject.* **2. sujet** ▸ the word or words in a sentence that tell what the sentence is about. A complete sentence must have a subject, and a verb to show what the subject is or does. **3. matière** ▸ a course of study in school : *My favourite subject is math.* **4. sujet** ▸ a person or thing who is under the control of a ruler such as a king. **5. sujet** ▸ a person or thing that is used in an experiment : *The subject of my experiment is wind power.* ▲ ADJECTIVE. **1. assujetti (-ie)** ▸ under the control or influence of another : *India was a subject colony ruled by the British for over 100 years.* **2. subject to. a. sujet (-ette) à** ▸ likely to have or be affected by : *She's subject to colds.* **b. sous réserve de** ▸ depending on : *The plan is subject to her approval.* ▲ [sub-JEKT] VERB, subjected, subjecting. **1. assujettir** ▸ to rule or control : *The teacher subjected the class with a stern look.* **2. soumettre** ▸ to cause a person to experience something, especially something negative or unpleasant : *The doctors subjected me to many tests in the hospital.*

sub·ma·rine [SUB-muh-reen *or* sub-muh-REEN] NOUN, submarines. **sous-marin ▶** any ship that can travel under water. ▲ ADJECTIVE. **sous-marin ▶** under water.

sub·merge [sub-MURJ] VERB, submerged, submerging. **1. immerger ▶** to put or go below water or down into another liquid : *I submerged the toy in the bathwater.* **2. plonger, submerger ▶** to keep below the surface; cover or hide : *She submerged her sadness behind a cheerful face.*

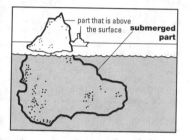

part that is above the surface **submerged part**

sub·mit [sub-MIT] VERB, submitted, submitting. **1. se soumettre ▶** to give in to some power or authority; yield : *The city quickly submitted to the attacking army.* **Note.** The fact of submitting is submission, and a person or animal who submits easily is submissive. **2. soumettre ▶** to present or bring forward; offer : *You must submit your reports by Friday.* SYN : yield, surrender, comply, bow, cave in.

sub·or·di·nate [sub-OR-duh-nit] ADJECTIVE. **subordonné (-ée) ▶** lower in rank or less important. **Note.** In a sentence, a subordinate clause is not as important as the main clause, as in "When the phone rang (*subordinate*), we were eating dinner (*main*)." ▲ NOUN, subordinates. **subordonné (-ée) ▶** a person who is lower in rank or importance : *The general ordered his subordinates to meet.* ▲ [sub-OR-duh-NATE] VERB, subordinated, subordinating. **subordonner ▶** to treat as less important.

sub·scribe [sub-SKRIBE] VERB, subscribed, subscribing. **1. souscrire, s'abonner ▶** to pay for a magazine, newspaper, or other item that comes in the mail or to one's house at certain regular times : *We subscribe to a local newspaper.* **2. souscrire ▶** to agree with : *Dad subscribes to the idea that we should earn our spending money.* **3. s'abonner ▶** to join a discussion group on the Internet. **■ subscriber,** NOUN. **▶ abonné (-ée).**

sub·scrip·tion [sub-SKRIP-shun] NOUN, subscriptions. **abonnement ▶** an agreement to pay for and receive a certain number of newspapers, magazines, theatre tickets, and so on : *Our subscription to the magazine has expired.*

sub·se·quent [SUB-si-kwint] ADJECTIVE. **suivant (-ante), ultérieur (-ieure) ▶** happening as a result; coming after : *The characters reappear in subsequent books in the series.* **■ subsequently,** ADVERB. **▶ plus tard, par la suite.** SYN : next, succeeding, following, later.

sub·side [sub-SIDE] VERB, subsided, subsiding. **1. s'affaisser, baisser ▶** to go down or fall back to a lower level : *The fever subsided, and my temperature returned to normal.* **2. s'apaiser, se calmer ▶** to become less; ease up; decrease : *Her anger subsided and she was happy again.* SYN : fall, drop, decrease, diminish, lessen, sink.

sub·stance [SUB-stunce] NOUN, substances. **1. substance ▶** the material that something is made of; matter : *Ice, steam, and water are all forms of the same substance.* **2. substance ▶** the main idea or part; essence : *The substance of the speech was world peace.*

sub·stan·tial [sub-STAN-shul] ADJECTIVE. **1. important (-ante) ▶** of a large or important amount : *There was substantial evidence that the dog ate the cheese.* **2. solide ▶** strong and solid : *That substantial desk is too heavy to be easily moved.* **3. de substance ▶** having to do with the physical world; real. **■ substantially,** ADVERB. **▶ considérablement.** *It costs substantially more to fly first class.*

sub·sti·tute [SUB-stih-TOOT] VERB, substituted, substituting. **1. substituer, remplacer ▶** to put or use in place of another : *to substitute margarine for butter.* **2. remplacer ▶** to take the place of someone else : *Vahid substituted for Rod on first base.* ▲ NOUN, substitutes. **remplaçant (-ante), suppléant (-ante) ▶** a person or thing that takes the place of another : *We had a substitute today because our teacher was sick.* **■ substitution,** NOUN. **▶ remplacement, substitution.** SYN : change, replace, switch, exchange.

sub·tle [SUT-ul] ADJECTIVE, subtler, subtlest. **subtil (-ile) ▶** hard to see, notice, or understand; not obvious : *The difference between the two pictures was so subtle that I didn't notice it.* **■ subtly,** ADVERB: **▶ subtilement.** *The suspense in the movie develops very subtly and is resolved in a surprising way.*

sub·tract [sub-TRAKT] VERB, subtracted, subtracting. **soustraire ▶** to take one number away from another : *When you subtract 2 from 8, you have 6.* SYN : take away, deduct, remove,

sub·trac·tion [sub-TRAK-shun] NOUN, subtractions. **soustraction ▶** the subtracting of one number from another to find the difference.

sub·urb [SUB-urb] NOUN, suburbs. **banlieue** ▸ a town or area that is outside of but near a larger city : *Commuters from the suburbs travel into Montreal to work.* ■ **suburban,** ADJECTIVE. ▸ **de banlieue.**

sub·way [SUB-way] NOUN, subways. **1. métro** ▸ an underground railway that is powered by electricity. Subways serve the people of major cities such as Toronto, Montreal, London, and New York. **2. passage souterrain** ▸ a passage under a street; an underpass.

suc·ceed [suk-SEED] VERB, succeeded, succeeding. **1. réussir** ▸ to do something very well, or to have something turn out well : *The kicker missed on the first try but succeeded on the second.* **2. succéder à** ▸ to come or be next : *Vasa succeeds me as club president.* SYN: prosper, thrive, flourish, achieve success.

suc·cess [suk-SES] NOUN, successes. **1. succès** ▸ the fact of succeeding; a good result : *She had great success with the new cookie recipe.* **2. succès** ▸ something that succeeds : *Drew's success in school makes his parents very proud.*

suc·cess·ful [suk-SES-ful] ADJECTIVE. **réussi (-ie), couronné (-ée) de succès** ▸ having or gaining a good result; resulting in success : *The bake sale was a success; we raised lots of money for the library.* ■ **successfully,** ADVERB. ▸ **avec succès.**

suc·ces·sion [suk-SESH-un] NOUN, successions. **1. suite** ▸ a series of people or things coming one after another : *Fireworks exploded in quick succession.* **2. suite** ▸ the following of one person by another to fill an office or position : *A succession of students have led the group over the years.* ■ **successive,** ADJECTIVE. **successif (-ive)** ▸ following one after the other; in succession : *We've had severe winters for three successive years.* ■ **successively,** ADVERB. ▸ **successivement.**

such [such] ADJECTIVE. **1. tel (telle), pareil (-eille), semblable** ▸ of this kind; of the same kind : *I'm not used to such excitement.* **2. tel (telle)** ▸ of the kind just mentioned, or about to be mentioned : *Nagi enjoys such water sports as swimming, sailing, and fishing.* **3. tel, tellement, si** ▸ so much so : *It was such a cold day that I wore two scarves.* **4. such as tel (telle) que** ▸ for example : *There are many stories about mysterious creatures such as Sasquatch or the Loch Ness Monster.* ▲ PRONOUN. **et autres de la sorte** ▸ someone or something of that kind : *The soup is full of tomatoes, carrots, peas, celery, and such.*

suck [suk] VERB, sucked, sucking. **1. téter, boire** ▸ to draw up into the mouth : *Darlene sucked on a milk shake with a straw.* **2. sucer** ▸ to hold or keep in the mouth and lick : *to suck on candy.* **3. aspirer, absorber** ▸ to draw in : *The vacuum cleaner sucked up the dirt.*

suc·tion [SUK-shun] NOUN, suctions. **succion** ▸ the force of drawing or pulling a solid, liquid, or gas that is caused by lowering the air pressure on its surface. Vacuum cleaners use suction to lift dirt, and pumps use it to draw water.

sud·den [SUD-un] ADJECTIVE. **1. soudain** ▸ happening quickly and with little or no warning; not expected : *a sudden flash of light.* **2. all of a sudden. soudain** ▸ in a sudden way; suddenly : *"Daddy's lamp blew a fuse, and all of a sudden we were sitting in darkness."* (Anne Frank) ■ **suddenly,** ADVERB. ▸ **soudainement.** *"I'm going to be a clown," he blurted suddenly.* ■ **suddenness,** NOUN.: **soudaineté.** *The marriage happened with a suddenness that surprised us all.* SYN: unexpected, hasty, impulsive, abrupt.

suds [sudz] PLURAL NOUN. **eau savonneuse** ▸ the foam and bubbles found on top of and in soapy water.

sue [soo] VERB, sued, suing. **poursuivre en justice** ▸ to begin a court case against someone; take a complaint before a judge or jury : *He sued the city because a large hole in his street had wrecked his car.*

suede [swade] NOUN. **suède** ▸ very soft, somewhat fuzzy leather. Suede is used to make clothes, purses, shoes, and other items.

su·et [SOO-it] NOUN. **graisse (de rognon)** ▸ the hard fat from the bodies of cattle and sheep. Suet is used in cooking.

suf·fer [SUF-ur] VERB, suffered, suffering. **1. souffrir** ▸ to feel pain or sadness : *She was suffering from an aching tooth.* **2. subir** ▸ to experience something bad or unpleasant : *The car suffered only a little damage in the accident.* **3. souffrir** ▸ to bear or endure : *I won't suffer their teasing any longer.*

suf·fer·ing [SUF-ur-ing or SUF-ring] NOUN, sufferings. **souffrance** ▸ a feeling of pain or sadness : *the horror and suffering of war.*

suf·fi·cient [suh-FISH-unt] ADJECTIVE. **assez, suffisant (-ante)** ▸ just as much as is needed or wanted; enough : *He had sufficient money to buy the book.* ■ **sufficiently,** ADVERB. ▸ **suffisamment.** *When you feel you are sufficiently prepared, begin your presentation.* SYN: enough, ample, abundant, adequate.

suf·fix [SUF-iks] NOUN, suffixes. **suffixe** ▸ a word ending that changes or adds to the meaning of the root word. *Paint*er, *paint*ed, and *paint*ing are formed by adding suffixes to the word *paint.*

suf·fo·cate [SUF-uh-kate] VERB, suffocated, suffocating. **1. suffoquer, étouffer** ▸ to die or cause to die from lack of air. **2. étouffer** ▸ to keep from breathing well. **3. suffoquer** ▸ to have or give a closed-in feeling, as if from lack of breath : *She was suffocating in the small town and decided to move.* ■ **suffocation,** NOUN. ▸ **étouffement.**

suf·frage [SUF-rij] NOUN. **droit de vote** ▸ the right to vote: *Nellie McClung fought for women's suffrage in Canada.*

sug·ar [SHOOG-ur] NOUN, sugars. **sucre** ▸ a white or brown sweet substance that usually comes in crystal or powder form, used to sweeten foods. Sugar is made from sugarcane or sugar beets. ▲ VERB, sugared, sugaring. **1. sucrer** ▸ to coat or mix food with sugar in order to sweeten it. **2. faire du sirop d'érable** ▸ to make maple syrup. 📗 **p. 1141.** 👁 **p. 262.**

sug·ar·cane [SHOOG-ur-KANE] NOUN. **canne à sucre** ▸ a tall grass with thick stalks that are pressed for their juices, which are dried into sugar. Sugarcane grows best in hot climates.

sug·gest [suj-EST or sug-JEST] VERB, suggested, suggesting. **1. suggérer** ▸ to put forward an idea; say or write something: *The students asked classmates to suggest names for their mascot.* **2. insinuer, venir à l'esprit** ▸ to bring to mind; cause to think of: *Her yawning suggested that she was tired.* SYN: imply, hint, offer, intimate, insinuate.

sug·ges·tion [suj-ES-chun or sug-JES-chun] NOUN, suggestions. **1. suggestion** ▸ the act of suggesting, or something that is suggested: *Mom asked us for some suggestions for dinner.* **2. trace, soupçon** ▸ something that is indirectly brought to mind; a hint or trace: *There was a suggestion of fear in his eyes.* SYN: proposal, idea, tip, recommendation.

su·i·cide [SOO-ih-SIDE] NOUN, suicides. **1. suicide** ▸ the act of killing oneself in a way that is planned and deliberate. **2. suicidé (-ée)** ▸ a person who does this.

commit suicide se suicider ▸ to kill oneself.

suit [soot] NOUN, suits. **1. costume, tailleur** ▸ a set of clothes designed to be worn together. Suits usually have trousers or a skirt and a matching jacket. **2. (also lawsuit) procès** ▸ a legal question that is brought before a judge or jury: *The woman's suit stated that the newspaper had suggested that she was involved in the robbery.* **3. couleur** ▸ any of the four sets of playing cards in a deck. ▲ VERB, suited, suiting. **1. convenir (à)** ▸ to be right for or meet the needs of: *The test reveals what jobs the students are suited to.* **2. aller bien (à)** ▸ to be becoming to; flatter: *The green dress suited her.* **3. convenir** ▸ to please or satisfy: *Come over whenever it suits you.* 📗 **p. 1015.**

suit·a·ble [SOOT-uh-bul] ADJECTIVE. **convenable, approprié (-ée)** ▸ right or correct for the purpose; proper: *The word "ain't" is not suitable for use in a school report.* ■ **suitably,** ADVERB. ▸ **convenablement.** SYN: correct, proper, apt, fitting, satisfactory.

suit·case [SOOT-KACE] NOUN, suitcases. **valise** ▸ a flat, boxlike container for carrying clothes and other items while travelling.

suite [sweet] NOUN, suites. **1. suite** ▸ a group of connected rooms in a hotel or motel: *Our family stayed in a suite in the hotel.* **2. ensemble** ▸ a matching set of furniture: *a bedroom suite.*

sulk [sulk] VERB, sulkier, sulkiest. **bouder** ▸ to be quiet while in a bad mood; refuse to talk: *Eva sulked when her sister went to a party.* ■ **sulky,** ADJECTIVE. ▸ **boudeur.** ■ **sulkily,** ADVERB. ▸ **en boudant.** *Joe sulkily kicked at his shoes because he didn't like them.*

sul·len [SUL-un] ADJECTIVE. **1. renfrogné (-ée)** ▸ quiet and unhappy because of anger, dislike, and so on. **2. maussade** ▸ dark and unpleasant; gloomy: *The sullen sky cast a gloom over the party.* ■ **sullenly,** ADVERB. ▸ **d'un air renfrogné.** *Mary sullenly did the dishes as a punishment.* SYN: gloomy, glum, dismal, moody, sulky.

sul·phur [SUL-fur] (also sulfur) NOUN. **soufre** ▸ a chemical element that appears in nature as a yellowish substance. Sulphur is found in underground deposits. It is used to make gunpowder, matches, insecticides, and other products. ■ **sulphuric,** ADJECTIVE. **sulfurique** ▸ containing sulphur.

sul·tan [SUL-tun] NOUN, sultans. **sultan** ▸ a title of a ruler in Muslim countries, especially in former times.

sul·try [SUL-tree] ADJECTIVE, sultrier, sultriest. **étouffant (-ante)** ▸ very hot, humid, and uncomfortable: *The air was thick and sultry before the summer storm.*

sum [sum] NOUN, sums. **1. somme** ▸ a number that comes from adding two or more numbers together: *The sum of 6 plus 2 plus 4 is 12.* **2. somme (d'argent)** ▸ an amount of money: *He paid a huge sum of money for the house.* **3. somme totale** ▸ the full amount; the total: *The sum of our efforts was a new playground.* ▲ VERB, summed, summing, sum up. **résumer** ▸ to go over the main points; summarize: *The speaker summed up her points and then asked for questions.*

su·mac [SOO-MAK] NOUN, sumacs. (also sumach) **sumac** ▸ a small tree or shrub that has clusters of small flowers that turn into berries. Some kinds of sumacs have leaves that can cause a rash when touched.

sum·ma·rize [SUM-uh-RIZE] VERB, summarized, summarizing. **résumer** ▸ to tell the main points briefly; make a summary: *Can you summarize the plot of the book in a few sentences?*

sum·ma·ry [SUM-uh-ree] NOUN, summaries. **résumé** ▸ a short statement or brief account of the main points: *Farouk wrote up a summary of the meeting.* ▲ ADJECTIVE. **1. résumé** ▸ having

a brief account of the main points.
2. résumé ▶ done quickly and without delay.
■ **summarily,** ADVERB. ▶ **sommairement.** *The principal dealt with her bad behaviour summarily.*

sum·mer [SUM-ur] NOUN, summers. **été** ▶ the season of the year between spring and fall. ▲ VERB, summered, summering. **passer l'été** ▶ to spend the summer in a certain place : *They live in Victoria but summer in the mountains.* ▲ ADJECTIVE. **(d') été** ▶ suitable for the summer season : *a light summer suit.* 📘 **p. 1105.**

sum·mit [SUM-it] NOUN, summits. **1. sommet** ▶ the highest point of a mountain or hill. **2. sommet** ▶ the highest point or level ; the top : *The summit of his sports career was winning an Olympic medal.* **3. au sommet** ▶ meetings or talks that are held by the highest government officials : *The prime minister held a summit meeting with the Russian president.*

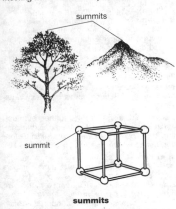

summits

summit

summits

sum·mon [SUM-un] VERB, summoned, summoning. **1. convoquer** ▶ to call or send for someone, especially in an official or urgent way : *The principal summoned me to her office.* **2. (usually, summon up) faire appel à** ▶ to gather together or call up ; arouse : *He summoned up the courage to face the bully.*

sum·mons [SUM-unz] NOUN, summonses. **citation, assignation** ▶ an official order or notice to appear somewhere or do something, especially to appear in court.

sun [sun] NOUN, suns. **1. soleil** ▶ the star around which the earth and the other planets revolve. **2. soleil** ▶ a similar star in another solar system. **3. lumière du soleil** ▶ the light and heat that comes from the sun ; sunshine. ▲ VERB, sunned, sunning. **prendre un bain de soleil,**

faire le lézard ▶ to put in the sunlight ; be out in the sun : *He sunned himself in the yard.* 📘 **p. 1119.** 👁 **p. 391.**

sun·bathe [SUN-bayth] VERB, sunbathed, sunbathing. **prendre un bain de soleil, se faire bronzer** ▶ to lie in the sun ; spend time in the sun.

sun·burn [SUN-burn] NOUN, sunburns. **coup de soleil** ▶ a redness or burn on the skin caused by staying in the sun too long. A bad sunburn can cause serious damage to the skin and can cause sickness. ▲ VERB, sunburned or sunburnt, sunburning. **brûler** ▶ to be affected by sunburn. **Note.** Also used as an ADJECTIVE: *a sunburned nose.*

sun·dae [SUN-day] NOUN, sundaes. **coupe glacée** ▶ a serving of ice cream with syrup, fruits, whipped cream, or nuts on it.

Sun·day [SUN-day *or* SUN-dee] NOUN, Sundays. **dimanche** ▶ the day after Saturday and before Monday.

sun·dial [SUN-dile] NOUN, sundials. **cadran solaire** ▶ a device that shows time by the movement of the sun. It has a round dial or plate marked with the hours and a pointer that casts a shadow from the sun onto the dial.

sun·flow·er [SUN-flow-ur] NOUN, sunflowers. **tournesol** ▶ a large flower that has bright-yellow petals around a brownish centre and that grows on a very tall stalk. It is thought to look like the sun. The seeds that grow in the centre of the flower are pressed into an oil or baked and eaten as food.

sung [sung] VERB. a past form of sing.

sun·glass·es [SUN-glas-iz] PLURAL NOUN. **lunettes de soleil** ▶ eyeglasses with specially coloured or shaded lense to protect the eyes from the sun's glare.

sunk [sunk] VERB. a past form of sink.

sunk·en [SUNK-un] ADJECTIVE. **1. englouti (-ie)** ▶ having gone to the bottom of water : *sunken treasure.* **2. encastré (-ée)** ▶ lower than other areas : *a sunken living room.*

sun·light [SUN-lite] NOUN. **lumière du soleil** ▶ the light of the sun. ■ **sunlit,** ADJECTIVE. ▶ **éclairé (-ée), ensoleillé (-ée).** *a sunlit room.*

sun·ny [SUN-ee] ADJECTIVE, sunnier, sunniest. **1. ensoleillé (-ée)** ▶ full of sunlight or warmth from the sun. **2. radieux (-euse), rayonnant (-ante), joyeux (-euse)** ▶ bright and happy ; cheerful : *Semareh has a sunny attitude and is always pleasant.*

sun·rise [SUN-rize] NOUN, sunrises. (also sunup) **lever du soleil** ▶ the time of day when the sun appears to rise in the sky ; early morning, when the sun is first seen.

sun·set [SUN-set] NOUN, sunsets. (also sundown) **coucher de soleil** ▶ the time of day when the sun appears to go down; evening, when the sun goes out of sight.

sun·shine [SUN-SHINE] NOUN. **lumière du soleil** ▸ the light from the sun.

sun·spot [SUN-SPOT] NOUN, sunspots. **tache solaire** ▸ a darker area on the surface of the sun, where the temperature is relatively cooler than in the surrounding areas. Scientists believe that sunspot activity may affect weather on earth.

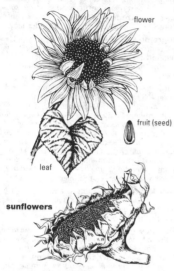

flower

fruit (seed)

leaf

sunflowers

sun·stroke [SUN-STROKE] NOUN, sunstrokes. **insolation** ▸ illness caused by being exposed to too much heat from the sun. A person with sunstroke has a high body temperature and feels dizzy and very weak. In some cases, the victim may become unconscious or even die.

su·per [SOO-pur] ADJECTIVE. *Informal.* **super** ▸ very good; outstanding; excellent.

su·per- PREFIX. over; above : _superhuman_; _superglue_.

su·perb [suh-PERB *or* soo-PERB] ADJECTIVE. **superbe, magnifique, excellent (-ente)** ▸ excellent or outstanding; very fine : *"We are having a superb spring after our long, lingering winter."* (Anne Frank) ∎ **superbly,** ADVERB. ▸ **superbement.** ✎ **p. 272.**

su·per·fi·cial [soo-pur-FISH-ul] ADJECTIVE. **superficiel (-ielle)** ▸ on the surface; not deep or serious : *The accident caused only superficial wounds, such as small bruises and cuts.* ∎ **superficially,** ADVERB. ▸ **superficialité.**

su·per·in·ten·dent [soo-pur-in-TEN-dunt *or* soop-rin-TEN-dunt] NOUN, superintendents. **1. directeur (-trice)** ▸ a person who is in charge of or manages something : *a superintendent of schools.* **2. concierge** ▸ someone who is responsible for the repair or cleaning of an apartment building or office building.

su·pe·ri·or [suh-PEER-ee-ur] ADJECTIVE. **1. supérieur (-ieure)** ▸ better, higher, or greater than others of its kind; exceptional : *The leather is of a superior grade.* **2. supérieur (-ieure)** ▸ having higher rank or office : *The soldiers followed their superior officer without question.* **3. hautain (-aine)** ▸ thinking oneself better than others; too proud : *He thinks he is superior because he got perfect on the test.* ▲ NOUN, superiors. **1. supérieur (-ieure)** ▸ a person who is higher in rank or office. **2. supérieur (-ieure)** ▸ the head of a religious community : *Mother Superior.*

su·pe·ri·or·i·ty [suh-PEER-ee-OR-ih-tee] NOUN. **supériorité** ▸ the fact of being superior : *The boxer soon showed his superiority over the challenger.*

su·per·la·tive [suh-PUR-lih-tiv *or* soo-PUR-lih-tiv] NOUN, superlatives. **superlatif** ▸ in grammar, the form of an adverb or adjective that describes the highest, the best, or the most of something : *The superlative of "fast" is "fastest."* ▲ ADJECTIVE. **1. superlatif (-ive)** ▸ above all others; supreme : *The diamond is of superlative quality.* **2. superlatif (-ive)** ▸ describing the highest, the best, or the most.

su·per·mar·ket [SOO-pur-MAR-kit] NOUN, supermarkets. **supermarché** ▸ a large food store where customers serve themselves and then pay as they leave. Supermarkets also sell many nonfood items, such as cleaning and health-care products. ✎ **p. 1055.**

su·per·nat·u·ral [soo-pur-NACH-uh-rul] ADJECTIVE. **surnaturel (-elle)** ▸ outside of the natural world; not part of normal human powers or understanding : *The book was about supernatural beings such as aliens, ghosts, and monsters.* ▲ NOUN. the supernatural. **surnaturel (-elle)** ▸ the world of supernatural beings, especially that of ghosts, spirits, and magic.

su·per·sti·tion [soo-pur-STISH-un] NOUN, superstitions. **superstition** ▸ a belief that events can be affected by ordinary actions that are not important in themselves. Well-known superstitions say that bad luck can be brought on by breaking a mirror or that bad luck can be kept away by carrying a rabbit's foot. ∎ **superstitious,** ADJECTIVE. **superstitieux (-ieuse)** ▸ caused by or likely to believe in superstitions : *Petra is superstitious and won't walk under a ladder.*

su·per·vise [SOO-pur-VIZE] VERB, supervised, supervising. **surveiller** ▸ to watch over, direct, or manage : *A more experienced worker super-*

vised the new clerks. **Note.** The act or fact of supervising is supervision: *My little sister is not allowed to play outside without supervision.*

su·per·vi·sor [SOO-pur-vy-zur] NOUN, supervisors. **superviseur (-euse)** ▸ a person who supervises; someone who is in charge : *Ab is the supervisor of 15 workers.* ■ **supervisory,** ADJECTIVE. ▸ de surveillance.

sup·per [SUP-ur] NOUN, suppers. **souper** ▸ the last meal of the day, especially a lighter meal when the main meal is eaten at midday. **Note.** Also called dinner.

sup·ple [SUP-ul] ADJECTIVE, suppler, supplest. **souple** ▸ able to bend easily; flexible : *The gymnast's body is so supple that she bends backward effortlessly.*

sup·ple·ment [SUP-luh-munt] NOUN, supplements. 1. **supplément** ▸ something added to a thing to make it better : *I take vitamin supplements daily.* 2. **supplément** ▸ a part added to a book, magazine, or newspaper to give further information or to concentrate on a special subject. ▲ VERB, supplemented, supplementing. **ajouter un supplément** ▸ to add to something; add as a supplement. ■ **supplementary,** ADJECTIVE. ▸ supplémentaire. *He earns a supplementary income by writing children's books.*

sup·ply [suh-PLY] VERB, supplied, supplying. **fournir, approvisionner** ▸ to give what is needed; provide : *The bakery supplies bread to many local stores.* ▲ NOUN, supplies. 1. **fourniture, approvisionnement** ▸ an amount of things ready for use : *Japan depends on foreign countries for its oil supply.* 2. supplies. **vivres, provisions** ▸ food and other such necessary items : *We had enough supplies for a three-day hike.*

sup·port [suh-PORT] VERB, supported, supporting. 1. **soutenir** ▸ to hold the weight of something; keep from falling or collapsing; hold up : *Four legs support the table.* 2. **subvenir aux besoins de** ▸ to take care of the needs of; provide for : *The Kwons support their grandparents, who live with them.* 3. **appuyer** ▸ to help or back; favour : *The school supports the recycling program.* 4. **soutenir, corroborer** ▸ to help to prove true or correct : *The research supports the scientist's theory.* ▲ NOUN, supports. 1. **appui, soutien** ▸ the act of supporting : *Grandpa walks using a cane for support.* 2. **support** ▸ something that supports : *the supports of a bridge.* ■ **supporter,** NOUN. ▸ partisan (-ane). 🖉 **p. 201.**

sup·pose [suh-POZE] VERB, supposed, supposing. 1. **imaginer, supposer** ▸ to imagine or think to be possible; believe : *I suppose that there could be life on Mars.* 2. **supposer** ▸ to assume : *Suppose Jim's not there. What will we do?* 3. **être sensé (-ée)** ▸ to expect or require something : *Kalida is supposed to be home by now.* ■ **supposedly,** ADVERB. **supposément** ▸ as is believed; as it appears : *She is suppos-*

edly an excellent chess player, but I've never seen her play the game. SYN: believe, guess, think, imagine, consider. 🖉 **p. 54.**

sup·press [suh-PRESS] VERB, suppressed, suppressing. **réprimer, refouler** ▸ to hold back or keep down : *Hsui suppressed his excitement.* ■ **suppression,** NOUN. ▸ répression.

su·preme [suh-PREEM] ADJECTIVE. 1. **suprême** ▸ highest or greatest in authority : *a supreme commander.* 2. **suprême** ▸ greatest in importance; highest or most extreme : *a supreme sacrifice.* ■ **supremely,** ADVERB. ▸ suprêmement. **Note.** The fact of being supreme is supremacy.

Supreme Court 1. **Cour suprême** ▸ the highest court in Canada, which acts as the final authority for any disputed court case. It consists of nine judges. 2. **Cour suprême** ▸ a similar court in some provinces and countries.

sure [shoor] ADJECTIVE, surer, surest. 1. **sûr (sure)** ▸ having no doubt about something; certain : *I'm sure I saw him—I should know my own brother!* 2. **sûr (sûre), assuré (-ée)** ▸ certain to be or happen : *Gail is the sure winner of any race she enters.* 3. **sûr (sûre), assuré (-ée)** ▸ firm and steady : *He had a sure grip on me when we crossed the bridge.* ▲ ADVERB. *Informal.* **vraiment** ▸ certainly : *She is quiet today; something must be wrong.* ■ **surely,** ADVERB. ▸ sûrement, tout de même.

surf [surf] NOUN. **vagues déferlantes** ▸ the rise and swelling of ocean waves that break on the shore. ▲ VERB, surfed, surfing. **faire du surf** ▸ to take part in the sport of surfing.

sur·face [SUR-fus] NOUN, surfaces. 1. **surface** ▸ the outside of a solid object or the upper level of a liquid : *Tree bark is a rough surface.* 2. **apparence** ▸ the outer appearance of something : *Laurie is quiet on the surface, but underneath she's very funny.* ▲ ADJECTIVE. **de surface** ▸ having to do with a surface. ▲ VERB, surfaced, surfacing. **faire surface** ▸ to come to or emerge on the surface : *The whales surfaced near our boat.*

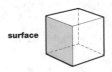

surface

surf·board [SURF-bord] NOUN, surfboards. **planche de surf** ▸ a long, flat board, usually made of a strong, light plastic covered with fibreglass, a material that helps it float. It is used to ride a wave of water to shore.

surf·ing [SUR-fing] NOUN. **surf** ▸ the sport of riding waves to shore, usually on surfboards. ▲ VERB, surfed, surfing. **faire du surf** ▸ to ride on waves

> ### ✑ Writing Tips
>
> **Suspense**
>
> *Any time you're reading a book and anxiously asking yourself, "What's going to happen next?" you are feeling **suspense**. When the reader feels concerned and uncertain about what will happen to the characters and what will happen, the writer has successfully created suspense. Most mystery, adventure, spy, and action stories use suspense, but sometimes even realistic and humorous stories have suspense.*

of water. **Note.** A person who does this is a surfer.

surge [surj] VERB, surged, surging. **déferler ▸** to move forward or swell up, like a powerful wave : *The water surged wildly through the channel.* ▲ NOUN, surges. **mouvement ▸** the act of surging; a rushing movement : *Jonas felt a surge of energy as he neared the finish line.*

sur·geon [SUR-jun] NOUN, surgeons. **chirurgien (-ienne) ▸** a medical doctor who has special skill and training in performing surgery.

sur·ger·y [SUR-juh-ree] NOUN, surgeries. **1. chirurgie ▸** the branch of medicine that deals with treating disease and injury by cutting into the body to remove, repair, or replace affected parts. **2. (en) chirurgie ▸** a place where a medical operation is performed : *There were several patients in surgery that morning.* ■ **surgical,** ADJECTIVE. **de chirurgie, chirurgical (-ale, -aux) ▸** having to do with surgery : *surgical instruments.*

sur·ly [SUR-lee] ADJECTIVE, surlier, surliest. **bourru (-ue) ▸** rude and unfriendly : *Mother scolded him for his surly remarks.*

sur·name [SUR-name] NOUN, surnames. **nom de famille ▸** a last name or family name : *The surname of Carmen Lopez is "Lopez."*

sur·pass [sur-PAS] VERB, surpassed, surpassing. **surpasser ▸** to do more than; be better or greater : *This book surpasses all her other books.* SYN: excel, exceed, go beyond.

sur·plus [SUR-plus *or* SUR-plus] NOUN, surpluses. **surplus ▸** an amount greater than what is needed : *a surplus of candies after Halloween.* ▲ ADJECTIVE. **en surplus ▸** greater than is needed; leftover. SYN: extra, excess, leftover, remaining, spare.

sur·prise [suh-PRIZE *or* sur-PRIZE] ▲ NOUN, surprises. **1. surprise ▸** the fact of coming suddenly without warning : *Troy took me by surprise.* **2. surprise ▸** a feeling of wonder or amazement caused by something unexpected :

I was surprised by everyone's kindness. **3. surprise ▸** something that gives this feeling; something unexpected : *Don't tell Billy about the new computer; it's a surprise.* ▲ VERB, surprised, surprising. **1. surprendre ▸** to cause to feel surprise : *The ending of the movie surprised me.* **2. surprendre ▸** to come upon suddenly without warning. ■ **surprisingly,** ADVERB. **▸ étonnamment.** *The food was surprisingly good.*

sur·ren·der [suh-REN-dur] VERB, surrendered, surrendering. **1. se rendre ▸** to give up in a fight or battle; accept defeat : *The rebels surrendered after the battle.* **2. abandonner ▸** to give in; yield : *The mayor surrendered to pressure and supported the bylaw.* **3. renoncer à ▸** to give up a claim or right to : *He had to surrender his driver's licence for speeding.* ▲ NOUN, surrenders. **reddition ▸** the act of surrendering : *They raised a white flag as a sign of surrender.*

sur·round [suh-ROWND] VERB, surrounded, surrounding. **entourer ▸** to make a circle around; close in on all sides : *A forest surrounded the house.*

sur·round·ings [suh-ROWN-dingz] PLURAL NOUN. **environs ▸** the things or conditions that are around a person, animal, or thing; the environment : *Many animals blend into their surroundings.*

sur·vey [sur-VAY] VERB, surveyed, surveying. **1. inspecter ▸** to study or examine in detail; look over : *Lydia surveyed herself in the mirror.* **2. arpenter ▸** to measure the size, shape, or boundaries of a piece of land : *They surveyed the area for a road.* ▲ [SUR-vay] NOUN, surveys. **1. examen ▸** a careful, detailed examination : *Officials made a survey of the damage.* **2. étude, sondage ▸** a gathering of detailed information about some topic or issue, as by asking questions : *Ranjit took a survey to find out what his classmates read.* **3. étude ▸** a view or description of a broad subject : *a survey of world history.* **4. relevé ▸** the act of surveying land, or the report of a survey.

sur·vey·or [sur-VAY-ur] NOUN, surveyors. **arpenteur (-euse), géomètre ▸** a person whose work is surveying land.

sur·viv·al [sur-VY-vul] NOUN. **survie ▸** the fact of surviving. **Note.** Survival of the fittest or natural selection is the process in nature by which animals that are better able to live under certain conditions survive, and weaker ones die out.

sur·vive [sur-VIVE] VERB, survived, surviving. **1. survivre ▸** to live or continue to live : *The American camel did not survive the last Ice Age in North America.* **2. survivre ▸** to continue to exist; remain : *Only a few buildings survived the fire.* ■ **survivor,** NOUN. **survivant (-ante) ▸** a person or thing that survives.

sus·cep·ti·ble [suh-SEP-tih-bul] ADJECTIVE. **sensible, susceptible** ▸ easily influenced or affected : *Charley is very susceptible to colds.*

sus·pect [suh-SPEKT] VERB, suspected, suspecting. **1. soupçonner** ▸ to think that someone is guilty without having proof : *We suspect that the clerk is stealing money from the store.* **2. soupçonner** ▸ to believe that something is true or possible; suppose : *Dad suspected that I wanted to borrow the car when he saw me washing it.* **3. soupçonner** ▸ to be aware of; realize or sense : *I didn't suspect a thing.* ▲ [SUS-pekt] NOUN, suspects. **suspect (-ecte)** ▸ someone who is suspected. ▲ ADJECTIVE. **suspect (-ecte)** ▸ that can be doubted or mistrusted; uncertain : *A treatment to improve memory is highly suspect.*

sus·pend [suh-SPEND] VERB, suspended, suspending. **1. suspendre** ▸ to hang down from above; be attached from above : *Large, glittering lamps were suspended from the ceiling.* **2. suspendre** ▸ to hang as if floating : *The bird was suspended on the wind.* **3. suspendre** ▸ to stop for a certain period of time : *The carpenters suspended work for the holidays.* **4. suspendre** ▸ to take away a privilege or rank : *The players were suspended for poor behaviour.* ■ **suspension,** NOUN, suspensions. ▸ suspension.

sus·pend·ers [suh-SPEND-urz] PLURAL NOUN. **bretelles** ▸ a pair of straps worn over the shoulders to hold up a pair of pants or a skirt.

sus·pense [suh-SPENCE] NOUN. **suspense** ▸ the condition of not knowing what will happen next; being uncertain : *Everyone was in suspense until the last two minutes of the movie.* ✐ p. 595.

suspension bridge pont suspendu ▸ a bridge suspended from cables that are stretched between two towers.

sus·pi·cion [suh-SPISH-un] NOUN, suspicions. **1. soupçon** ▸ a feeling that something is wrong or bad; the doubting or distrusting of someone : *Our suspicions about him were wrong; he really cares about the environment.* **2. soupçon** ▸ the condition of being suspected of a crime or wrongdoing.

sus·pi·cious [suh-SPISH-us] ADJECTIVE. **1. suspect (-ecte)** ▸ causing or arousing suspicion : *We saw a suspicious character hanging around the store before the robbery.* **2. méfiant (-ante)** ▸ showing or expressing suspicion : *She gave me a suspicious look when I said that the dog ate my homework.* ■ **suspiciously,** ADVERB. ▸ **avec méfiance, d'une manière suspecte.** SYN: doubtful, questionable, wary, suspecting.

sus·tain [suh-STANE] verb, sustained, sustaining. **1. supporter, soutenir** ▸ to keep going in a certain way for an extended time; continue : *to sustain a friendship.* **2. supporter, soutenir** ▸ to provide what is needed to keep on : *People need three meals a day to sustain good health.* **3. éprouver, subir** ▸ to suffer or undergo : *He sustained many injuries in the car accident.* ■ **sustenance,** NOUN. **subsistance** ▸ something that provides life or strength.

swal·low[1] [SWOL-oh] VERB, swallowed, swallowing. **1. avaler, déglutir** ▸ to cause food to pass from the mouth down into the stomach : eat or drink. *Chanka swallowed the berry.* **2. avaler, engloutir** ▸ to take in or cover, as if by swallowing : *Edgar was swallowed by the crowd in the street.* **3. ravaler, retenir** ▸ to hold back some feeling : *I swallowed my pride and asked for help.* **4.** *Informal.* **avaler** ▸ to accept or believe without question : *I swallowed the whole story.* ▲ NOUN, swallows. **avalement, gorgée, bouchée** ▸ the act of swallowing.

swal·low[2] NOUN, swallows. **hirondelle** ▸ a small bird that has a forked tail and long wings. Swallows catch insects in the air and fly gracefully. ✐ p. 109.

swam [swam] VERB. a past form of swim.

swamp [swomp] NOUN, swamps. **marécage, marais** ▸ an area of wet, muddy land with a growth of trees and shrubs. ▲ VERB, swamped, swamping. **1. inonder, emplir** ▸ to fill with water or become soaked : *A large wave swamped the rowboat.* **2. déborder** ▸ to cover or load with a large amount : *My parents swamped me with chores on Saturday.* ■ **swampy,** ADJECTIVE. ▸ **marécageux (-euse).**

swan [swon] NOUN, swans. **cygne** ▸ a large bird that has a long, graceful neck, webbed feet, and usually, white feathers. Swans are related to ducks and geese but are larger.

swap [swop] *Informal.* VERB, swapped, swapping. **échanger** ▸ to trade or exchange one item for another : *Joelle and I swapped seats so I could sit next to the window.* ▲ NOUN, swaps. **échange, troc** ▸ a trade or exchange.

swarm [sworm] NOUN, swarms. **1. essaim** ▸ a large colony of bees that leave a hive with a queen bee to start a new colony somewhere else. **2. essaim, troupe** ▸ a large group or gathering : *A swarm of reporters were waiting for the prime minister.* ▲ VERB, swarmed, swarming. **1. essaimer** ▸ of bees, to fly off in a group to start a new colony. **2. aller en masse, fourmiller** ▸ to move or gather in a large group : *"The guests swarmed into the Great Hall at half past ten in the morning."* (Aliki)

swat [swot] VERB, swatted, swatting. **écraser (avec une tapette)** ▸ to hit or smack quickly or sharply : *to swat a fly.* ▲ NOUN, swats. **coup de tapette** ▸ a sharp slap; a smack.

sway [sway] VERB, swayed, swaying. **1. se balancer** ▸ to swing slowly back and forth or from side to side : *Branches swayed in the* *breeze.* **2. influencer ▶** to change the thinking or opinion of; influence : *The jury was swayed by the woman's story.* ▲ NOUN, sways. **1. oscillation ▶** the act of swaying. **2. domination ▶** control or influence : *The country was under the sway of a dictator.* SYN : swing, reel, rock, roll, pitch.

swear [swair] VERB, swore, sworn, swearing. **1. jurer ▶** to make a formal or serious promise to do something : *You must swear to tell the truth in court.* **2. jurer ▶** to say in a very definite way : *"If I listened very carefully I'd swear I could hear something like a low growl."* (Paulette Bourgeois) **3. sacrer, jurer ▶** to use bad language; curse.

sweat [swet] NOUN. **1. sueur, transpiration ▶** salty liquid given off through the skin; perspiration. **2. sueur ▶** moisture that collects in drops on a surface. ▲ VERB, sweated or sweat, sweating. **1. suer, transpirer ▶** to give off sweat; perspire. **2. suer, transpirer ▶** to gather drops of moisture : *The glass of ice water sweated in the sun.* ■ **sweaty,** ADJECTIVE. ▶ **en sueur, de sueur.**

sweat-er [SWET-ur] NOUN, sweaters. **chandail, tricot, pull-over ▶** a piece of clothing that is knitted from wool or other fibres and worn on the upper part of the body. A sweater is often worn for warmth.

sweep [sweep] VERB, swept, sweeping. **1. balayer ▶** to clean with a broom, brush, or the like : *to sweep the kitchen floor.* **2. balayer ▶** to carry or move, as with a broom : *We were swept along in the crowd.* **3. balayer ▶** to pass over or through in a quick, steady motion : *Searchlights swept back and forth in the dark.* ▲ NOUN, sweeps. **1. balayage, coup de balai ▶** a sweeping motion : *The dog cleared off the coffee table with a sweep of its tail.* **2. étendue ▶** an open area : *a sweep of parkland in the middle of the city.*

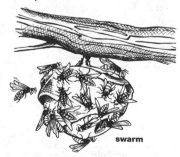

swarm

sweep-ing [SWEE-ping] ADJECTIVE. **radical (-ale, -aux), vaste, large ▶** passing over a broad area : *The new government made sweeping changes to the educational system.*

sweet [sweet] ADJECTIVE, sweeter, sweetest. **1. sucré (-ée), frais (fraîche) ▶** having a pleasing taste, like that of sugar or honey : *the sweet taste of ripe fruit.* **2. doux (douce) ▶** pleasing to smell, hear, and so on : *sweet words.* **3. gentil (-ille) ▶** pleasant or kind; nice : *It was sweet of you to wait for me.* **4. doux (douce) ▶** not salty or sour : *Sweet butter does not have salt added to it.* ▲ NOUN, sweets. **sucreries, friandises ▶** something that is sweet, such as candy. ■ **sweetly,** ADVERB. ▶ **agréablement.** ■ **sweetness,** NOUN. ▶ **douceur, gentillesse.**

sweet-en [SWEET-un] VERB, sweetened, sweetening. **sucrer ▶** to make sweet or sweeter : *to sweeten tea by adding sugar.* ■ **sweetener,** NOUN. ▶ **édulcorant.**

sweet-heart [SWEET-hart] NOUN, sweethearts. **amoureux (-euse) ▶** a person who is loved by another.

sweet pea **pois de senteur ▶** a climbing vine that has sweet-smelling red, white, pink, or purple flowers.

sweet potato **patate douce ▶** the sweet, thick root of a tropical plant that is cooked and eaten as a vegetable.

swell [swel] VERB, swelled, swelled or swollen, swelling. **1. enfler, gonfler ▶** to grow or increase in size : *Her broken finger swelled to twice its normal size.* **2. grossir ▶** to rise above the ordinary level; fill up : *The river had swelled from all the rain.* ▲ NOUN, swells. **1. houle ▶** a rolling wave on an ocean or lake. **2. enflure ▶** the act of swelling : *There was a swell of pride when the school won the championship.* ▲ ADJECTIVE. *Informal.* **épatant (-ante) ▶** excellent or good; fine : *a swell party.* SYN : grow bigger, increase, expand, inflate.

swell-ing [SWEL-ing] NOUN, swellings. **enflure ▶** an enlarged or swollen part : *Put ice on your sprained ankle to keep down the swelling.*

swept [swept] VERB. a past form of sweep.

swerve [swurv] VERB, swerved, swerving. **dévier (de), faire un écart ▶** to turn or move to the side quickly : *The driver swerved to avoid hitting the stalled car.* SYN : dodge, sidestep, turn, veer, shift.

swift¹ [swift] ADJECTIVE, swifter, swiftest. **1. rapide ▶** moving or able to move with speed; fast : **2. rapide ▶** happening quickly : *I received a swift reply to my letter of complaint.* ■ **swiftly,** ADVERB. ▶ **rapidement.** *The boat moved swiftly down the river.* ■ **swiftness,** NOUN. ▶ **rapidité.**

swift² NOUN, swifts. **martinet ▶** a bird similar to a swallow. It has narrow wings and flies very fast.

swim [swim] VERB, swam, swum, swimming. **1. nager ▶** to move through the water by using the arms and legs, or the fins, tail, and so on. **2. traverser à la nage ▶** to cross by swimming :

597

to swim the English Channel. **3. nager ▸** to be in or covered by a liquid : *The ice-cream sundae was swimming in chocolate syrup.* **4. tourner ▸** to have a dizzy feeling; be lightheaded : *All the excitement made my head swim.* ▲ NOUN, **swims. nage ▸** the act of swimming, or the distance covered : *Let's swim across the lake.* **Note.** A **swimming pool** is a special indoor or outdoor pool for swimming.

swim-mer [SWIM-ur] NOUN, **swimmers. nageur (-euse) ▸** a person or animal that swims.

swin-dle [SWIN-dul] VERB, swindled, swindling. **escrouer ▸** to take someone's money or property in a dishonest way : *He swindled people by selling fake diamonds.* ▲ NOUN, **swindles. escroquerie ▸** the act of swindling. ■ **swindler,** NOUN. **▸ escroc.** SYN : cheat, con, defraud, trick.

swine [swine] NOUN, **swine. pourceau (-eaux) ▸** a pig or hog.

swing [swing] VERB, swung, swinging. **1. (se) balancer ▸** to move back and forth with a steady motion : *The children swung from a rope.* **2. (essayer de) frapper ▸** to move with a curving or sweeping motion : *to swing at a pitch in baseball.* ▲ NOUN, **swings. 1. balancement, oscillation ▸** the act of swinging. **2. balançoire ▸** a seat that hangs by a rope or chain, in which a person can swing back and forth. *We have a swing in our backyard.* **3. courant, mouvement ▸** activity; movement : *It took me a while to get into the swing of things.*

in full swing à son plein ▸ at the highest point of activity : *The party was in full swing when I arrived.*

swirl [swurl] VERB, swirled, swirling. **faire tourbillonner ▸** to go around and around in a circular, twisting motion : *The dust swirled on the desert road like a small tornado.* ▲ NOUN, **swirls. tourbillon ▸** a twisting motion or shape : *All we could see were the swirls of her large, colourful skirt as she danced.*

swish [swish] VERB, swished, swishing. **faire siffler, faire bruire ▸** to make a soft, brushing sound; rustle : *The horse swished its tail to brush flies from its hindquarters.* ▲ NOUN, **swishes. bruissement ▸** a soft, rustling sound : *the swish of skis through the snow.*

switch [swich] NOUN, **switches. 1. changement ▸** a change or shift from one thing to another, especially a change that is not expected : *The coach made a switch; Rena will play for Davis, who is injured.* **2. interrupteur, commutateur ▸** a device for breaking an electrical circuit : *a light switch.* **3. canne, fouet, cravache ▸** a long, thin rod or stick, especially one used for whipping. **4. voie de raccordement, aiguille ▸** a device for changing a train from one track to another. ▲ VERB, switched, switching. **1. échanger, changer ▸** to change : *They switched sweaters.* **2. allumer, éteindre**

▸ to turn on or off using an electrical switch : *He switched on the radio to get the news.* **3. donner un coup de baguette ▸** to strike with a rod or switch : *The jockey switched the horse to make it run faster.* **4. aiguiller ▸** to change a train from one track to another. SYN : change, exchange, substitute, replace, swap.

switch-board [SWICH-bord] NOUN, switch-boards. **tableau de distribution ▸** a control panel with plugs or switches to connect and disconnect electrical circuits.

swiv-el [SWIV-ul] NOUN, swivels. **pivot ▸** a device linking two parts so that one or both can turn freely. *Office chairs often turn on a swivel.* ▲ VERB, swivelled, swivelling. (also swiveled, swiveling) **faire pivoter ▸** to turn or twist freely, as if on a swivel.

swol-len [SWOH-lun] VERB. a past form of swell. ▲ ADJECTIVE. **enflé (-ée); gonflé (-ée) ▸** made larger by swelling : *Her broken finger was bruised and swollen.*

swoop [swoop] VERB, swooped, swooping. **fondre, piquer sur ▸** to move or go down suddenly and quickly, with a sweeping motion : *"Father Owl swoops down to rest upon a drifting log."* (Tejima) ▲ NOUN, **swoops. 1. descente en piqué ▸** the act of swooping. **2. un fell swoop. un seul coup ▸** one quick motion or action : *We gave a party to meet all our new neighbours in one fell swoop.*

sword [sord] NOUN, swords. **épée ▸** a weapon used especially in former times, having a long, sharp blade set into a handle or hilt.

sword-fish [SORD-fish] NOUN, swordfish or swordfishes. **espadon ▸** a large saltwater fish with a long upper jawbone shaped in a point like a sword. It is a popular food and game fish.

swore [swor] VERB. a past form of swear.

sworn [sworn] VERB. a past form of swear.

swum [swum] VERB. a past form of swim.

swung [swung] VERB. a past form of swing.

syc-a-more [SIK-uh-MOR] NOUN, sycamores. **sycomore ▸** a North American tree with broad leaves and smooth bark that peels off in thin layers.

syl-la-ble [SIL-uh-bul] NOUN, syllables. **syllabe ▸** a single sound in speech that forms a word or part of a word : *The word "go" has one syllable; "going" has two syllables.*

sym-bol [SIM-bul] NOUN, symbols. **symbole ▸** something chosen to stand for something else : *The maple leaf is a national symbol for Canada.* ■ **symbolic,** ADJECTIVE. **symbolique ▸** being or using a symbol ■ **symbolically,** ADVERB. ▸ **symboliquement.** ◉ p. 406.

sym-bol-ize [SIM-buh-lize] VERB, symbolized, symbolizing. **symboliser ▸** to be a symbol;

stand for something; represent : *In that poem, the bird symbolized freedom.*

sym·me·try [SIM-ih-tree] NOUN, symmetries. **1. symétrie** ▸ an exact match of the shape or form on both sides of a body or object. **2. symétrie** ▸ a pleasing, balanced form resulting from such an arrangement. — **symmetrical,** ADJECTIVE:*Two symmetrical rows of trees lined the driveway.*

sym·pa·thet·ic [SIM-puh-THET-ik] ADJECTIVE. **1. compréhensif (-ive), compatissant (-ante)** ▸ showing kindness or sympathy : *Everyone was very sympathetic when Purun broke his leg.* **2. en sympathie** ▸ in favour of; supporting : *Several politicians are sympathetic to our cause.* ▪ **sympathetically,** ADVERB. ▸ sympathiquement.

sym·pa·thize [SIM-puh-thize] VERB, sympathized, sympathizing. **sympathiser** ▸ to have or show sympathy : *Margot could sympathize with the skater who fell, because she skated in competitions too.*

sym·pa·thy [SIM-puh-thee] NOUN, sympathies. **1. sympathie** ▸ a feeling of sharing the troubles of others in an understanding way : *The volunteers have great sympathy for the people they help.* **2. sympathie** ▸ support in thought or feelings; agreement : *The children were trying to get the neighbourhood's sympathy for their request for a new playground.* SYN: understanding, empathy, pity, compassion.

sym·pho·ny [SIM-fuh-nee] NOUN, symphonies. **1. symphonie** ▸ a long musical piece written for an orchestra. **2. orchestre symphonique** ▸ a large orchestra that plays symphonies or other such musical pieces. It usually has string, percussion, and wind instruments.

symp·tom [SIM-tum *or* SIMP-tum] NOUN, symptoms. **1. symptôme** ▸ a change from the normal condition of the body, showing that a disease or illness is present : *A sore throat and fever can be symptoms of a virus.* **2. symptôme** ▸ a sign or indication of something bad : *High unemployment is a symptom of a bad economy.*

syn·a·gogue [SIN-uh-GOG] NOUN, synagogues. **synagogue** ▸ a place or building used for worship and instruction in the Jewish religion.

syn·o·nym [SIN-uh-NYM] NOUN, synonyms. **synonyme** ▸ a word that has the same or almost the same meaning as another word : *"Courage" and "bravery" are synonyms.*

syn·on·y·mous [sih-NON-uh-mus] ADJECTIVE. **1. synonyme (de)** ▸ having the same or a similar meaning : *"fast" is synonymous with "quick."* **2. synonyme (de)** ▸ very closely connected : *The song "Auld Lang Syne" has become synonymous with New Year's Eve.*

syn·tax [SIN-taks] NOUN. **syntaxe** ▸ the way in which words are put together to form sentences : *"I the tree climbed" is not the proper syntax, because the verb "climbed" is in the wrong place.*

syn·thet·ic [sin-THET-ik] ADJECTIVE. **synthétique** ▸ made artificially with chemicals; not found in nature : *Many types of clothing are now made from synthetic fabrics.*

syr·up [SUR-up *or* SEER-up] NOUN, syrups. **sirop** ▸ a thick, sweet liquid made by boiling sugar and water, or sometimes by boiling tree sap or fruit juice. ◉ **p. 262.**

sys·tem [SIS-tim] NOUN, systems. **1. système** ▸ a group of things that are related and form a whole : *the solar system.* **2. système** ▸ a set of beliefs, laws, or principles : *a democratic system of government.* **3. méthode, système** ▸ an orderly method of doing something : *What version of that operating system is your computer using?* ▪ **systematic,** ADJECTIVE. **systématique** ▸ following a system : *Kara keeps her school notebook arranged in a very systematic way.* ▪ **systematically,** ADVERB. ▸ systématiquement. SYN: method, scheme, plan, design, arrangement.

Système international d'unités an expanded form of the metric system of measurement that is now used in most countries. **Note.** Often used shortened to SI: *Use SI symbols in your report.*

trumpet

t, T [tee] NOUN, t's, T's. **t, T** ▶ the 20th letter of the English alphabet.

tab [tab] NOUN, tabs. **étiquette, attache, languette, patte** ▶ a small flap or tag that is attached or stuck to some object : *A zipper has a tab that is used to open and close it.* 2. *Informal.* **note, addition** ▶ a bill or cheque : *Put it on my tab.*

ta·ble [TAY-bul] NOUN, tables. 1. **table** ▶ a piece of furniture with a flat top, supported by one or more legs. 2. **table, tablée** ▶ the food served at a table, or the people who sit at a table to eat : *Hamish sets a fine table with the best food and company.* 3. **plateau (-eaux)** ▶ a flat surface of land; plateau. 4. **table, tableau (-eaux)** ▶ a short list or chart of facts or information. **Note.** The **table of contents** is a list of information in a book or magazine. ⌖ p. 1072.

ta·ble·spoon [TAY-bul-SPOON] NOUN, tablespoons. 1. **cuiller à soupe, cuiller de service** ▶ a large spoon. 2. **cuillerée à soupe** ▶ a unit of measure in cooking, equal to about 15 mL or three teaspoons.

tab·let [TAB-lit] NOUN, tablets. 1. **tablette, plaque** ▶ a thin, flat slab of wood or stone that is used to write or draw on : *People in ancient times used tablets before paper was invented.* 2. **bloc de papier à lettres** ▶ a number of sheets of paper held together at one edge. 3. **cachet, comprimé, pastille** ▶ a small, flat piece of medicine or candy : *vitamin C tablets.*

table tennis ping-pong, **tennis de table** ▶ a game that is similar to tennis, played on a table with paddles and a small plastic ball. **Note.** This game is also called ping-pong.

ta·boo [tuh-BOO *or* ta-BOO] NOUN, taboos. **tabou, interdit** ▶ a strong social or religious rule against doing certain things : *Some cultures have strict taboos against wearing shoes inside a home.*

tack [tak] NOUN, tacks. 1. **punaise, petit clou** ▶ a small, sharp-pointed nail with a wide, flat head. 2. **bord, bordée** ▶ a change in the direction of a sailing ship. 3. **tactique, méthode** ▶ a course of action : *No one believed my excuse, so I tried a different tack and told the truth.* ▲ VERB, tacked, tacking. 1. **fixer avec une punaise, clouer** ▶ to fasten with a tack or tacks : *Cara tacked the posters up on the bulletin board.* 2. **louvoyer, tirer une bordée** ▶ of a sailing ship, to change direction : *To sail a boat into the wind, you must tack back and forth.*

tack on rajouter ▶ to add something extra at the end : *Delivery charges are tacked on to the bill.*

tack·le [TAK-ul] NOUN, tackles. 1. **équipement, matériel** ▶ the equipment used for a certain activity or sport, especially the rod, reel, line, hooks, and so on used for fishing. 2. **appareil de levage** ▶ a system of ropes and pulleys used for raising and lowering things, such as the sails of a ship. 3. **bloqueur (-euse)** ▶ in football, a player whose position is between the guard and the end on offence, or in the middle of the line on defence. 4. **tacle** ▶ in football or soccer, the act of stopping a player who is moving with the ball. ▲ VERB, tackled, tackling. 1. **plaquer (au sol)** ▶ to grab and force to the ground : *A guard tackled the bank robber.* 2. **aborder, s'attaquer à** ▶ to deal with or take on : *I have so much homework—there's just no way I could tackle another project.* ■ **tackler,** NOUN. ▶ **plaqueur (-euse).**

tack·y [TAK-ee] ADJECTIVE. tackier, tackiest. 1. **collant (-ante), adhésif (-ive)** ▶ sticky, adhesive : *A piece of tape is tacky.* 2. *Informal.* **de mauvais goût, moche** ▶ of poor quality or cheap; shabby : *Unfortunately, there were only tacky souvenirs.*

tact [takt] NOUN. **tact, doigté, délicatesse** ▶ the ability to say and do the right thing so as not to hurt someone's feelings; dealing with people in a careful and sensitive way. **Note.** A person who has this ability is tactful: *My friends tried to be tactful when they told me my clothes didn't match.* ■ **tactfully,** ADVERB. ▶ **avec tact.**

tac·tic [TAK-tik] NOUN, tactics. 1. tactics. **tactique** ▶ the art or science of arranging and moving troops and other military forces in battle. 2. (also tactics) **plan, stratégie, tactique** ▶ any plan or method of action to reach a goal : *The lawyer used delaying tactics to keep the case from coming to trial.* ■ **tactical,** ADJECTIVE. ▶ **tactique.** *a tactical error.*

tad·pole [TAD-pole] NOUN, tadpoles. **têtard** ▶ a very young frog or toad in the stage of development when it lives in the water and has gills, a tail, and no legs.

taf·fy [TAF-ee] NOUN, taffies. **(bonbon au) caramel, tire d'érable** ▶ a chewy candy made with molasses, brown sugar, or maple syrup.

tag¹ [tag] NOUN, tags. **étiquette, marque, plaque d'identité** ▶ a piece of paper, plastic, or other material that is attached to, or hanging loosely from, something. It is used to label, identify, or give information : *an identification tag on a dog's collar.* ▲ VERB, tagged, tagging. **1. étiqueter, marquer** ▶ to label with or as if with a tag. **2. suivre, coller aux talons** ▶ to follow closely : *My brother likes to tag along wherever I go.* SYN : label, mark.

tag² NOUN, tags. **1. jeu du chat** ▶ a game in which a player who is "it" chases the others until he or she touches one of them. The person who is touched then becomes "it" and must chase the others. **2. toucher (action de)** ▶ in baseball, the act of putting out a runner by touching him or her with the ball or with the hand holding the ball. ▲ VERB, tagged, tagging. **toucher** ▶ to touch or tap with the hand : *Mei tagged the runner at first base.*

Tahl·tan [TOL-tan] NOUN, Tahltan or Tahltans. **1. Tahltan, Athapascan** ▶ the Aboriginal people living in northwest British Columbia. **2. tahltan, athapascan** ▶ the Athapaskan language of these people.

tai·ga [TY-guh] NOUN. **taïga** ▶ the dense, damp pine forests of northern Canada and Siberia, just south of the tundra.

tail [tale] NOUN, tails. **1. queue** ▶ the movable part of an animal's body that sticks out from the rear, usually having a long, thin shape. **2. pan, basque** ▶ anything thought of as trailing behind or out like this : *the tail of a shirt.* **3. fin, bout** ▶ the end, rear, or last part of something : *the tail end of the show.* **4. tails. pile** ▶ one of the two sides of a coin, opposite the head. **5. tails. queue de pie** ▶ a man's formal evening wear. ▲ VERB, tailed, tailing. **filer, suivre de près** ▶ to follow closely and watch : *We tailed the dog to the park.* ▲ ADJECTIVE. **arrière, postérieur (-ieure)** ▶ of or at the tail.

tail·or [TALE-ur] NOUN, tailors. **tailleur, couturier (-ière)** ▶ a person who makes, alters, or repairs clothing, especially men's suits and coats. ▲ VERB, tailored, tailoring. **1. faire sur mesure, ajuster** ▶ to work on clothing as a tailor does : *She tailored the suit to fit me.* **2. adapter** ▶ to make or adjust in a special way :

The company offers several plans that it tailors to the needs of each client.

take [take] VERB, took, taken, taking. **1. prendre** ▶ to get hold of; get possession of : *Max took the puppy in his arms and petted it gently.* **2. apporter, emporter, amener, emmener** ▶ to go along with, or cause to go : *Take this map with you so you don't get lost.* **3. prendre** ▶ to deal with or experience in some way; get, use, have, and so on : *to take piano lessons; to take notes in class.* **4. demander, nécessiter** ▶ to need or require : *This wonderful dinner must have taken a lot of work.* **5. prendre (pour)** ▶ to accept as true; assume : *"Do you take me for a fool?" he bellowed.* (Paul Yee) ▲ NOUN, takes. **prise de vue(s)** ▶ a portion or scene of a movie, TV program, or recording that is photographed or recorded without interruption. SYN : get, seize, obtain, grasp, snatch, grab. ✍ p. 74.

take·off [TAKE-off] NOUN, takeoffs. **1. décollage** ▶ the act of an aircraft rising up in flight from the ground. **Note.** Also used as a VERB: *The plane will take off in 20 minutes.* **2. imitation, pastiche** ▶ a copy or imitation of something, meant to amuse people : *That new movie is a takeoff of one of Shakespeare's plays.*

take·over [TAYK-oh-vur] NOUN, takeovers. **prise de contrôle, rachat** ▶ in business, the act of taking control or ownership of a company by buying up a certain amount of the company's stock.

tale [tale] NOUN, tales. **1. conte, histoire, récit** ▶ an imaginary story : *The tales of Peter Rabbit have delighted children for years.* **2. conte populaire** ▶ short for folk tale. **3. récit** ▶ an account of real events : *She told us the sad tale of how the house had burned down.* **4. histoire, fable** ▶ a false story; a lie. SYN : story, yarn, account, narrative, anecdote.

tal·ent [TAL-unt] NOUN, talents. **1. talent, don** ▶ a special ability that is natural or inborn : *It takes talent and work to be an opera singer.* **2. future vedette** ▶ a person who has this special ability : *Scouts from professional teams will watch high-school games, looking for new talent.* ■ **talented,** ADJECTIVE. ▶ **talentueux (-euse), doué (-ée).** *a talented writer.* SYN : ability, aptitude, flair, gift, skill.

talk [tok] VERB, talked, talking. **1. parler** ▶ to express words or ideas by using speech; speak : *Please do not talk during the test.* **2. discuter, parler de** ▶ to speak about a certain subject; discuss : *Can you talk to her about driving us to the store?* **3. convaincre, persuader** ▶ to bring about or influence by speech : *Eric talked his dad into taking him to the game.* ▲ NOUN, talks. **1. discussion, conversation** ▶ the act of talking : *I had a talk with Jenny about baseball.* **2. bavardage** ▶ a short or informal speech. **Note.** A person who likes to talk a lot is talkative. SYN : speak, communicate, converse, discuss.

talk·er [TOK-ur] NOUN, talkers. **causeur (-euse)** ▸ a person who talks, usually one who talks fast or well : *Ravi told stories for two hours ; he's really a talker.*

tall [tol] ADJECTIVE, taller, tallest. **1. grand (grande), haut (haute)** ▸ higher than average ; not short : *She is very tall.* **2. mesurer** ▸ having a certain height : *Sean is 176 cm tall.* **Note.** A tall tale is one that is exaggerated and hard to believe. ✐ p. 602.

tal·ly [TAL-ee] NOUN, tallies. **compte** ▸ a count or record of votes, points, and so on ; a score : *The final tally showed that our class collected the most books.* ▲ VERB, tallied, tallying. **pointer, tenir le compte** ▸ to make or keep a tally : *The cashier tallied the cost of all my groceries.*

tal·on [TAL-un] NOUN, talons. **serre** ▸ the claw of a bird or animal, especially an eagle, hawk, owl, or other such bird of prey.

tam·bou·rine [TAM-buh-REEN] NOUN, tambourines. **tambourin, tambour de basque** ▸ a small drum with loose metal disks attached to the rim. The tambourine is played by shaking or striking it with the hand. ✇ p. 538.

tame [tame] ADJECTIVE, tamer, tamest. **1. apprivoisé (-ée)** ▸ of an animal, taken from the wild and trained to live or work with humans. **2. docile, pas farouche** ▸ not afraid of people ; not wild or dangerous : *The deer was so tame that it ate out of my hand.* **3. insipide, monotone, terne** ▸ not lively or exciting ; dull : *This TV show is too tame.* ▲ VERB, tamed, taming. **dresser, apprivoiser, dompter, mater** ▸ to make or become tame : *to tame a horse.* SYN : domesticated, subdued, gentle, obedient.

tam·per [TAM-pur] VERB, tampered, tampering. tamper with. **toucher à, altérer, essayer d'ouvrir** ▸ to deal with in a harmful or careless way ; meddle : *Look at this envelope — someone's been tampering with my mail!*

tan [tan] VERB, tanned, tanning. **1. tanner** ▸ to make animal skins into leather by soaking them in a special liquid. **Note.** This process is called tanning. **2. bronzer, brunir, hâler** ▸ of a person, to have the skin become darker because of being out in the sun. ▲ NOUN, tans. **1. fauve** ▸ a yellowish-brown colour like that of leather that has been tanned. **2. hâle, bronzage** ▸ a darker colour of the skin caused by the sun. ▲ ADJECTIVE. **ocre, marron clair** ▸ yellowish-brown.

tan·ger·ine [tan-juh-REEN] NOUN, tangerines. **1. mandarine** ▸ a small, juicy fruit that is related to the orange. It has a skin that peels away easily. **2. orange soutenu** ▸ a reddish-orange colour like the colour of this fruit. ▲ ADJECTIVE. **orange soutenu** ▸ reddish-orange.

tan·gi·ble [TAN-juh-bul] ADJECTIVE. **1. tangible, palpable** ▸ able to be sensed by touch ; having a physical existence : *A table is tangible, but an idea is not.* **2. tangible, concret (-ète), réel (-elle)** ▸ not imaginary ; certain ; real : *The broken window was tangible evidence that someone had broken into the house.* ■ **tangibly,** ADVERB. ▸ **tangiblement, manifestement.** SYN : real, actual, concrete, touchable, physical.

tan·gle [TANG-ul] VERB, tangled, tangling. **1. (s') emmêler, (s') enchevêtrer** ▸ to twist or mix together in a confused mass : *The wind tangled my hair.* **2. tangle with. se colleter avec, avoir une prise de bec avec** ▸ to have a fight or dispute with. ▲ NOUN, tangles: *The wool for my sweater was in tangles.*

tank [tank] NOUN, tanks. **1. réservoir, cuve, citerne** ▸ a large container for holding liquid or gas : *a car's gas tank.* **2. tank, char d'assaut, char de combat** ▸ a large, heavy vehicle used in warfare, covered with thick metal plates and carrying a cannon and machine guns. A tank runs on two continuous metal belts rather than on wheels.

tank·er [TANK-ur] NOUN, tankers. **pétrolier, camion-citerne, avion-ravitailleur** ▸ a ship, truck, or airplane that is built to carry large amounts of oil or other liquids.

tan·ta·lize [TAN-tuh-LIZE] VERB, tantalized, tantalizing. **tourmenter** ▸ to tease or disturb a person by keeping something that she or he wants just out of reach : *Troy tantalized me by talking*

✐ Writing Tips

Tall Tale

*A **tall tale** is a type of folk tale that uses exaggeration. Tall tales often tell of someone's heroic deeds, but they can also be humorous.*

• *Heroic tall tales are stories about heroes, such as Paul Bunyan and John Henry, who are characters that are bigger than life or who accomplish the impossible. If you are writing a heroic tall tale, you could create your own superhero — a hero able to do impossible things — and put this character into situations that call for action.*

• *If you are writing a humorous tall tale, your characters can be ordinary people involved in extraordinary and amusing events. You could write about a student who does impossible things on the way to school one day, or about the impossible events that take place during a family camping trip. Use your imagination and think of impossible situations in which to place your ordinary character.*

---

about going to the movie when he knew I had to stay home.

tan-trum [TAN-trum] NOUN, tantrums. **crise de colère** ▸ an outburst of temper; a fit of anger : *I had a tantrum when my sister borrowed a dress without asking.*

tap[1] [tap] VERB, tapped, tapping. **frapper légèrement, tapoter** ▸ to touch or strike lightly : *We tapped our feet to the music.* ▲ NOUN, taps. **petit coup** ▸ a light or gentle blow :*A tap on the door told her Soo Nor had arrived.* SYN : pat, beat, rap.

tap[2] [tap] NOUN, taps. **1. robinet, manette** ▸ a device for turning water or other liquid on or off; a faucet. **2. bonde** ▸ a plug or cork that closes a hole in a barrel. ▲ VERB, tapped, tapping. **1. percer, inciser, saigner** ▸ to make a hole in something to draw liquid out : *People tap maple trees to draw the sap for syrup.* **2. mettre sur écoute, placer sur table d'écoute** ▸ to cut in on a telephone line and secretly listen to another person's conversation. **3. exploiter, utiliser** ▸ to draw upon; employ; use : *Ang tapped into the Internet to find information on Africa.*

tape [tape] NOUN, tapes. **1. ruban adhésif** ▸ a long, narrow strip of paper, plastic, or other material, having a sticky substance on one side and used for wrapping, fastening, or sealing things. **2. ruban, bande, bandage** ▸ any long, narrow band of cloth, steel, paper, and so on. **3. bande magnétique, cassette, cassette vidéo** ▸ a long narrow piece of specially treated plastic for recording sounds, or sounds and pictures : *videotape.* ▲ VERB, taped, taping. **1. attacher avec du ruban** ▸ to fasten with tape. **2. enregistrer (sur bande)** ▸ to record sounds or images on tape :*Dad videotaped the play so we could see ourselves performing.*

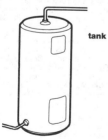

tank

ta-per [TAPE-ur] VERB, tapered, tapering. **1. (s') effiler, fuseler, tailler en pointe** ▸ to make or become gradually smaller at one end : *A spear tapers to a sharp point.* **2. s'estomper, s'effilocher** ▸ to slowly become less and less; slowly decrease : *By morning the storm had begun to taper off.*

tape recorder **magnétophone** ▸ a machine that records sounds on specially treated plastic tape so that they can be played back later.

tap-es-try [TAP-iss-tree] NOUN, tapestries. **tapisserie** ▸ a heavy fabric with designs or pictures woven into it. Tapestries are hung on walls or laid over furniture as decoration.

taps [taps] NOUN. **sonnerie aux morts** ▸ a bugle call that is played at night as a signal to put out all lights for the night.

tar [tar] NOUN. **goudron, bitume, asphalte** ▸ a thick, black, sticky substance that is made from wood or coal. It is used to pave roads and to waterproof roofs, and in making many industrial products. ▲ VERB, tarred, tarring. **goudronner, bitumer, asphalter** ▸ to cover or coat with tar : *to tar a roof.*

ta-ran-tu-la [tuh-RAN-chuh-luh] NOUN, tarantulas. **tarentule** ▸ a large, hairy spider whose bite is painful but generally not dangerous. Tarantulas are found mainly in tropical parts of the world.

tar-dy [TAR-dee] ADJECTIVE, tardier, tardiest. **tardif (-ive), lent (lente), en retard** ▸ coming or happening late; behind time : *Lunch is at noon; don't be tardy.* ▪ **tardiness,** NOUN. ▸ **lenteur, manque d'empressement, manque de ponctualité.**

tar-get [TAR-git] NOUN, targets. **1. cible** ▸ a mark or object that is aimed or fired at : *The arrow hit the target.* **2. cible, victime** ▸ a person or thing that is attacked or made fun of : *a target of criticism.* ▲ VERB, targeted, targeting. **s'adresser à, destiner à, viser, cibler** ▸ to set as a goal or target : *Some advertisers target their ads at children.*

tar-iff [TAIR-if] NOUN, tariffs. **tarif douanier** ▸ a tax or duty that a government puts on goods coming into a country : *The merchant paid a tariff on the imported clothing made in Indonesia.*

tar-nish [TAR-nish] VERB, tarnished, tarnishing. **1. ternir** ▸ to dull the shine or colour of : *Rain tarnished the metal finish.* **2. ternir, souiller** ▸ to lose purity or quality : *Rumours tarnished my reputation.* ▲ NOUN. **ternissure** ▸ a thin, dull coating; a loss of brightness or colour.

tar-pau-lin [TAR-puh-lin *or* tar-POL-in] NOUN, tarpaulins. **toile goudronnée, bâche (goudronnée)** ▸ a piece of waterproof canvas or other material that is used as a protective covering for objects exposed to the weather. **Note.** A tarpaulin is often called a **tarp.**

tart[1] [tart] ADJECTIVE, tarter, tartest. **1. âpre, sur (sure)** ▸ having a sharp or sour taste; not sweet. **2. acerbe, âpre** ▸ sharp or harsh in tone or meaning :*I was angry and gave a tart reply to his question.* ▪ **tartness,** NOUN. ▸ **acerbité, aigreur, acidité.** SYN : sour, sharp, bitter, pungent, acidic.

tart[2] NOUN, tarts. **tarte, tartelette** ▶ a pastry shell filled with fruit, jam, or custard.

tar-tan [TAR-tun] NOUN, tartans. **tartan** ▶ a plaid pattern or design, first made in Scotland. Scottish clans or families have their own tartan.

tar-tar [TAR-tur] NOUN. **tartre** ▶ a yellowish substance that forms on the teeth. Tartar will form into a hard crust if it is not removed.

task [task] NOUN, tasks. **tâche** ▶ a piece of work to be done; a job or duty : *Feeding the dog is my task.* SYN: assignment, chore, duty, job.

tas-sel [TAS-ul] NOUN, tassels. **pompon, gland** ▶ a hanging bunch of threads or cords that are fastened together at one end.

taste [tayst] NOUN, tastes. **1. (sens du) goût** ▶ the sense felt in the mouth when food or drink is taken in : *Sweet, sour, salty, and bitter are the four basic tastes.* **2. goût** ▶ a particular sensation felt in the mouth; a flavour : *the taste of the sea.* **3. un petit peu de, une pincée de, une goutte de** ▶ a small amount of food or drink; a bit. **4. aperçu, échantillon, avant-goût** ▶ a small amount or brief experience : *Paula got a taste of being a cowhand when she spent a week at a ranch.* **5. goût** ▶ the ability to judge things and to appreciate what has beauty, style, quality, and so on : *Duleta has wonderful taste in clothes and always looks stylish.* ▲ VERB, tasted, tasting. **avoir un goût de** ▶ to get the flavour of; have a certain flavour : *This milk tastes sour.* ■ **taster,** NOUN. ▶ **dégustateur (-trice).** ☞ p. 1035.

taste-ful [TAYST-ful] ADJECTIVE. **de bon goût** ▶ having or showing good taste. ■ **tastefully,** ADVERB. ▶ **avec goût.**

taste-less [TAYST-lis] ADJECTIVE. **1. insipide, fade** ▶ having little or no flavour : *The soup was watery and tasteless.* **2. de mauvais goût** ▶ having or showing bad taste : *a tasteless comment.* ■ **tastelessly,** ADVERB. ▶ **sans goût, avec mauvais goût.**

tast-y [TAYST-ee] ADJECTIVE, tastier, tastiest. **savoureux (-euse), délicieux (-ieuse), succulent (-ente)** ▶ pleasing to the sense of taste; having a good flavour : *a tasty treat.*

tat-tered [TAT-urd] ADJECTIVE. **en loques, en lambeaux, déguenillé (-ée)** ▶ torn or hanging in shreds; ragged : *The coat was old and tattered.*

tat-tle [TAT-ul] VERB, tattled, tattling. **cafarder, moucharder** ▶ to tell someone what another person has done wrong : *Sandy tattled on her brother when he teased her.* ■ **tattler** or tattle-tale, NOUN. ▶ **rapporteur (-euse), mouchard (-arde).** SYN : report, gossip, repeat.

tat-too [ta-TOO] VERB, tattooed, tattooing. **tatouer** ▶ to mark the skin with permanent pictures or designs by pricking it with special needles that are dipped in coloured ink. ▲ NOUN,

tattoos. **tatouage** ▶ a picture or design on the skin that is made in this way.

taught [tot] VERB. a past form of teach.

taunt [tont] VERB, taunted, taunting. **railler, se moquer de, accabler de sarcasmes** ▶ to make fun of; insult with bitter remarks : *The other children taunted the little boy when he cried.* ▲ NOUN, taunts. **raillerie, moquerie, sarcasme** ▶ an insulting or cruel remark. SYN : ridicule, mock, jeer.

taut [tot] ADJECTIVE, tauter, tautest. **1. (bien) tendu (-ue)** ▶ stretched or drawn tight : *When the fish took the bait, the fish line snapped taut.* **2. tendu (-ue)** ▶ tense; strained : *Ab's nerves were taut as he waited to perform.*

tav-ern [TAV-urn] NOUN, taverns. **1. taverne** ▶ a place where alcoholic drinks are sold and drunk; a bar. **2. auberge** ▶ in former times, a place where travellers could stay overnight; an inn.

tax [taks] NOUN, taxes. **taxe, impôts, contributions** ▶ money that people must pay to the government to pay for public services such as hospitals, school, and roads. ▲ VERB, taxed, taxing. **1. taxer, imposer** ▶ to put a tax on : *The Canadian government taxes goods that are imported from other countries.* **Note.** Income or goods that can be taxed are taxable. **2. mettre à l'épreuve, éprouver** ▶ to make a heavy demand on; tire out or strain : *Amelia taxed her memory, trying to recall where she had left her book.* ■ **taxpayer,** NOUN. **contribuable** ▶ someone who pays taxes.

tax-a-tion [tak-SAY-shun] NOUN. **imposition** ▶ the act or system of collecting taxes.

tax-i [TAK-see] NOUN, taxis. **taxi** ▶ a car that can be hired to take a person somewhere. **Note.** Also called a taxicab or cab. ▲ VERB, taxied, taxiing. **rouler au sol** ▶ of an airplane, to move slowly over the ground before taking off or after landing.

tea [tee] NOUN, teas. **1. thé** ▶ a drink that is made by pouring boiling water over the leaves of a certain Asian plant. **2. thé** ▶ the dried leaves of this plant, or the plant itself. **3. infusion, tisane** ▶ a similar drink made from another plant : *herb tea.* **4. thé, goûter** ▶ a light meal in the late afternoon at which tea is served.

teach [teech] VERB, taught, teaching. **1. enseigner, apprendre (à)** ▶ to cause a person to know something; give knowledge : *to teach someone to speak French.* **2. apprendre à, montrer** ▶ to show or explain how to perform some physical action or skill : *Teach me to ride a bike.* **3. apprendre** ▶ to show by example : *Sam's determination taught me an important lesson about achieving goals.* **4. enseigner** ▶ to give lessons as one's job; work as a teacher in school. SYN : instruct, educate, inform, tutor, show, guide.

teach·er [TEE-chur] NOUN, teachers. **enseignant (-ante), professeur (-eure), instituteur (-trice)** ▸ a person whose job is teaching in a school or giving lessons. 🅟 p. 1062.

teach·ing [TEE-ching] NOUN, teachings. 1. **enseignement** ▸ the profession or work of a teacher. 2. **enseignements, leçon** ▸ what is taught : *the teachings of the prophet Muhammad.*

teak [teek] NOUN. **teck** ▸ a strong, hard wood that comes from a tree of southeast Asia, used in furniture, floors, and shipbuilding.

team [teem] NOUN, teams. 1. **équipe** ▸ in sports, a group of people who play together against other groups of the same kind : *There are 11 players on a soccer team.* **Note.** A player on the same team as another is a teammate. 2. **équipe** ▸ a group of people who work or act together : *A team of firefighters put out the blaze.* 3. **attelage** ▸ two or more horses or other animals joined or harnessed together to do work : *A team of horses pulled the wagon.* ▲ VERB, teamed, teaming. **team up. faire équipe, collaborer, s'associer avec, s'allier à** ▸ to work or join together as a team : *Students teamed up on their projects.*

team·ster [TEEM-stur] NOUN, teamsters. 1. **conducteur (-trice) d'attelage** ▸ a person who drives a team of animals. 2. **routier (-ière), camionneur (-euse)** ▸ a person whose work is driving a truck.

team·work [TEEM-wurk] NOUN. **collaboration, travail d'équipe** ▸ the smooth working together of members of a team or group to reach the same goal.

tea·pot [TEE-pot] NOUN, teapots. **théière** ▸ a pot with a handle and spout, used to brew and serve tea.

tear¹ [tair] VERB, tore, torn, tearing. 1. **déchirer, arracher** ▸ to pull apart in a rough, sudden way; split into pieces; rip : *Van tore the wrapping off his present.* 2. **aller à toute allure, foncer** ▸ to move quickly or with great force : *The excited puppy tore around the lawn.* 3. **tirailler, déchirer** ▸ to divide between two sides; force or draw apart : *Sally was torn between going to the movies or visiting her aunt.* ▲ NOUN, tears. **déchirure, accroc** ▸ a torn part or place. 🖉 p. 570.

tear² [teer] NOUN, tears. 1. **larme** ▸ a drop of clear, salty liquid that comes from the eye **Note.** Also called a teardrop. It is produced by glands called tear ducts. 2. **tears. (en) larmes, (en) pleurs** ▸ the fact of crying from pain or sadness : *to burst into tears.* 🅟 p. 1024.

tease [teez] VERB, teased, teasing. 1. **taquiner** ▸ to annoy or bother someone in a playful way; make fun of : *Albert teased me about my hair.* 2. **coiffer à rebrousse-poil** ▸ to comb the hair backward to make it stand out and look fuller. ▲ NOUN, teases. **taquin (-ine)** ▸ a person

who teases someone. SYN: harass, mock, badger, annoy, bother, taunt.

tea·spoon [TEE-spoon] NOUN, teaspoons. 1. **petite cuiller, cuiller à café, à thé** ▸ a small spoon. 2. **cuillerée à café, à thé** ▸ a unit of measure used in cooking, equal to 5 mL or one-third of a tablespoon.

tech·ni·cal [TEK-nih-kul] ADJECTIVE. 1. **technique** ▸ having to do with the use of science to deal with practical problems : *Engineering is a technical field of study.* 2. **technique** ▸ having to do with one special field or profession : *Medicine uses many technical words.* 3. **précis (-ise), exact (-acte)** ▸ according to strict and exact rules or judgment : *To be technical, that animal is a bison, not a buffalo.* ■ **technically,** ADVERB. ▸ **techniquement, sur le plan technique.**

tech·ni·cian [tek-NISH-un] NOUN, technicians. **technicien (-ienne)** ▸ a person who has skill in some technical field ; a person skilled in the use of certain instruments or machinery.

tech·nique [tek-NEEK] NOUN, techniques. **technique** ▸ a particular way of doing something or dealing with a problem ; a method or plan of action : *Morphing is an animation technique done on computers.*

tech·nol·o·gy [tek-NOL-uh-jee] NOUN, technologies. **technologie** ▸ the use of tools, machines, inventions, and scientific principles to do work and solve problems. ■ **technological,** ADJECTIVE. **technologique** ▸ having to do with technology : *Technological innovations include the computer and the airplane.*

te·di·ous [TEE-dee-us] ADJECTIVE. **ennuyeux (-euse), fastidieux (-ieuse)** ▸ long and tiring ; very boring : *Weeding the garden is a slow and tedious job.* ■ **tediously,** ADVERB. ▸ **de façon ennuyeuse, fastidieusement.**

tee [tee] NOUN, tees. **tee** ▸ a small peg on which a golf ball may be placed for the first stroke in playing a hole. ▲ VERB, teed, teeing. **tee off. placer sur le tee, partir du tee** ▸ to hit the ball off a tee to start playing a hole.

teem [teem] VERB, teemed, teeming. **grouiller (de)** ▸ to be filled with ; have in large numbers : *The street was teeming with people celebrating the new year.*

teen·ag·er [TEE-nay-jur] NOUN, teenagers. **adolescent (-ente)** ▸ a person who is between the ages of 13 and 19. ■ **teenage** or teenaged, ADJECTIVE. ▸ **adolescent (-ente), pour adolescents (-entes).** *Skateboarding is primarily a teenage sport.*

teens [teenz] PLURAL NOUN. **adolescence** ▸ the years of a person's life from the age of 13 to 19.

tee·pee [TEE-pee] NOUN, teepees. (also tepee or tipi) **wigwam, tipi** ▸ a cone-shaped tent originally made of animal skins or tree bark, used by some native North Americans as a dwelling, especially among the Plains tribes.

tee-ter [TEE-tur] VERB, teetered, teetering. **chanceler, vaciller ▸** to stand or move in an unsteady way : *Tim teetered before regaining his balance.*

teeth [teeth] **dents ▸** the plural of tooth. **Note.** The fact or time of a baby growing teeth is called teething.

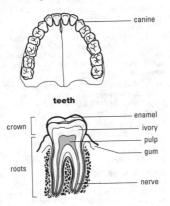

teeth

tel-e-cast [TEL-uh-KAST] NOUN, telecasts. **émission de télévision ▸** a program broadcast by television.

tel-e-com-mu-ni-ca-tions [TEL-uh-kuh-myoo-nuh-KAY-shunz] PLURAL NOUN. **télécommunications ▸** the process of sending messages or broadcasts by telephone, radio, television, computer, and so on.

tel-e-gram [TEL-uh-GRAM] NOUN, telegrams. **télégramme ▸** a message that is sent by telegraph.

tel-e-graph [TEL-uh-GRAF] NOUN, telegraphs. **télégraphe ▸** a method of sending and receiving messages over a long distance with electronic signals carried by wires or cables. ▲ VERB, telegraphed, telegraphing. **télégraphier ▸** to send a message by telegraph. **☞ p. 540.**

tel-e-phone [TEL-uh-FONE] NOUN, telephones. **téléphone ▸** an instrument used to send and receive sounds or speech over a distance. The sound is sent over wires or through the air. ▲ VERB, telephoned, telephoning. **téléphoner ▸** to call or talk by telephone. **☞ p. 1169. ☞ p. 540.**

tel-e-scope [TEL-uh-SKOPE] NOUN, telescopes. **télescope ▸** an instrument that makes distant objects seem much closer and larger. It uses a system of lenses or mirrors inside a long tube.

Telescopes are used to study the stars and planets.

tel-e-vise [TEL-uh-VIZE] VERB, televised, televising. **téléviser ▸** to send by television : *The Olympic games are televised throughout the world.*

tel-e-vi-sion [TEL-uh-VIZH-un] NOUN, televisions. **1. télévision ▸** a system of sending pictures and sounds through the air by means of electronic signals, so that they can be seen and heard in other places. **2.** (also television set) **poste de télévision, téléviseur ▸** a device used to receive such signals. **3. programme télévisé ▸** programs broadcast in this way : *I can watch television when my homework is done.* **☞ p. 1170. ☞ p. 540.**

tell [tel] VERB, told, telling. **1. dire, raconter ▸** to make known by words; say or write : *You must not tell this secret to anyone!* **2. indiquer ▸** to make known by some sign or indication : *A thermometer tells how hot or cold it is.* **3. reconnaître, voir, distinguer ▸** to know or sense; recognize : *I could tell he was upset by the look in his eyes.* **4. ordonner ▸** to order; command : *I told my dog to sit.* **✎ p. 366.**

tell-er [TEL-ur] NOUN, tellers. **1. guichetier (-ière), caissier (-ière), préposé (-ée) ▸** a person who works in a bank and takes in, pays out, and counts money. **2. conteur (-euse) ▸** a person who tells : *a storyteller.*

telescope

tem-per [TEM-pur] NOUN, tempers. **1. tempérament, caractère, disposition ▸** a particular state of the mind or feelings : *Our baby never cries and has a very sweet temper.* **2. (de) mauvaise humeur, (en) colère ▸** an angry mood or state of mind : *Sarita's in a temper because Brad ate her lunch.* **3. (perdre son) calme ▸** control of the emotions : *lose your temper.* **4. trempe ▸** the degree of hardness of a metal or other substance. ▲ VERB, tempered, tempering. **1. tempérer ▸** to make less harsh; ease or soften : *Mom tempered my disappointment by buying me a book.* **2. tremper ▸** to make metal harder or more flexible. SYN: disposition, character, nature, tendency.

tem-per-a-ment [TEM-pruh-munt] NOUN, temperaments. **tempérament, naturel ▸** the normal state of the mind and feelings; a person's nature : *Ani and I have different temperaments —she is outgoing and I am quiet.*

tem·per·a·men·tal [TEM-pruh-MEN-tul] ADJECTIVE. **1. capricieux (-ieuse), fantasque, d'humeur instable ▸** easily upset or made angry : *The king is very temperamental and will lock up anyone who offends him.* **2. d'un naturel, du tempérament ▸** having to do with temperament; caused by one's nature. ■ **temperamentally,** ADVERB. ▸ **par nature.**

tem·per·ate [TEM-puh-rit *or* TEM-prit] ADJECTIVE. **1. tempéré (-ée) ▸** not too hot nor too cold; not extreme : *Ireland has a temperate climate — not too hot or too cold.* **2. modéré (-ée), mesuré (-ée) ▸** having or showing self-control.

tem·per·a·ture [TEM-puh-ruh-chur *or* TEM-pruh-chur] NOUN, temperatures. **1. température ▸** the level of heat or cold in a place or object, as measured by a thermometer : *Water turns to ice at a temperature of 0° Celsius.* **2. température ▸** the level of heat of the human body : *Normal body temperature is about 37° Celsius.* **3. fièvre ▸** a body temperature that is higher than normal; a fever : *When Jin had the flu, he ran a high temperature.* 🗒 **p. 1105.**

tem·pest [TEM-pist] NOUN, tempests. **tempête ▸** a very strong wind or storm.

tem·ple¹ [TEM-pul] NOUN, temples. **temple ▸** a building used for the worship of a god or gods :

Pyramids in Central and South America are ancient Mayan and Aztec temples. **Note.** A Jewish synagogue is often called a temple.

tem·ple² NOUN, temples. **tempe ▸** the flat area on either side of the forehead, in front of the ear.

tem·po [TEM-poh] NOUN, tempos. **1. tempo ▸** the speed at which music is played. **2. rythme ▸** the rate of speed of an activity : *During the summer the tempo of my job slows down.*

tem·po·rar·y [TEM-puh-RAIR-ee] ADJECTIVE. **provisoire, temporaire ▸** lasting only for a short time; not permanent : *Jenny has a temporary cast on her arm.* ■ **temporarily,** ADVERB. ▸ **provisoirement, temporairement.** *Because of the power outage, the grocery store is temporarily closed.*

tempt [tempt] VERB, tempted, tempting. **1. tenter ▸** to lead to do something unwise or wrong : *Seeing a copy of the test on the teacher's desk tempted him to look at the answers.* **2. tenter, persuader ▸** to appeal strongly to; attract : *Could I tempt you with a cookie?* SYN: lure, seduce, invite.

temp·ta·tion [temp-TAY-shun] NOUN, temptations. **tentation ▸** the fact of being tempted, or something that tempts : *It is always a temptation to stay up late to watch a good movie.*

ten [ten] NOUN, tens; ADJECTIVE. **dix ▸** one more than nine; 10. ■ **tenth,** ADJECTIVE; NOUN. ▸ **dixième.**

telephone equipment

te·na·cious [tuh-NAY-shus] ADJECTIVE. **tenace, obstiné (-ée), entêté (-ée) ▸** holding or grasping tight; not letting go or giving in : *The starfish had a tenacious grip on the rocks and was not swept away.* **Note.** The fact of being tenacious is tenacity. ■ **tenaciously,** ADVERB. ▸ **avec ténacité, obstinément.**

ten·ant [TEN-unt] NOUN, tenants. **locataire ▸** a person who pays rent for the use of property owned by another person : *New tenants just moved into the apartment down the hallway from ours.*

tend¹ [tend] VERB, tended, tending. **avoir tendance à ▸** to move or develop in a certain way; be likely :*"When things fall in deep water, they tend to be scattered by ocean currents."* (Robert D.Ballard)

tend² VERB, tended, tending. **s'occuper de, garder ▸** to take care of; look after :*"Most mornings found Alejandro tending the garden, watching it grow."* (Richard E.Albert)

ten·den·cy [TEN-dun-see] NOUN, tendencies. **tendance ▸** the way that something tends to be or go; a leaning : *Mark's tendency to be late drives me crazy.*

ten·der¹ [TEN-dur] ADJECTIVE, tenderer, tenderest. **1. tendre ▸** of food, not tough; easily chewed : *The meat was boiled until it was tender.* **2. sensible, douloureux (-euse) ▸** painful or sore; very sensitive : *She has a tender spot on her forehead where she bumped it.* **3. délicat (-ate), fragile ▸** not strong; delicate. **4. tendre, doux (douce) ▸** showing love or kindness : *a tender embrace.* ■ **tenderly,** ADVERB. ▸ **tendrement.** ■ **tenderness,** NOUN. ▸ **tendresse, délicatesse, sensibilité, tendreté.**

tender² VERB, tendered, tendered. **faire une soumission, soumissionner ▸** to offer or present, especially in a formal way : *Trey tendered an offer to buy the house.*

tender³ **préposé (-ée) ▸** a person who tends or takes care of something : *A bartender serves drinks in a bar.*

ten·don [TEN-dun] NOUN, tendons. **tendon ▸** a cord or band of tough tissue that connects muscles to bones. ☞ **p. 402.**

ten·nis [TEN-is] NOUN. **tennis ▸** a game played by two or four persons. The players use racquets to hit a ball back and forth over a net stretched across a level playing surface called a court.

ten·or [TEN-ur] NOUN, tenors. **1. ténor ▸** usually the highest adult male singing voice, or a singer who has this voice. **2. ténor ▸** an instrument having this range. ▲ ADJECTIVE: *tenor saxophone.*

tense¹ [tence] ADJECTIVE, tenser, tensest. **1. tendu (-ue) ▸** stretched or pulled out tightly; strained : *Alec's muscles were tense as he waited for the race to start.* **2. tendu (-ue), crispé (-ée) ▸** causing or showing strain, excite-ment, or worry : *The class was tense as they waited for the results of the exam.* ▲ VERB, tensed, tensing. **(se) tendre, (se) crisper ▸** to make or become tense. ■ **tensely,** ADVERB. ▸ **d'une manière tendue.** SYN: strained, tight, taut, stretched.

tense² NOUN, tenses. **temps ▸** the form of a verb that shows the time of the action or state of being : *The past tense of the verb "bring" is "brought."*

ten·sion [TEN-shun] NOUN, tensions. **1. tension ▸** the fact or condition of being strained or stretched out : *The tension on a bow must be tight to shoot an arrow far.* **2. tension, nervosité ▸** mental strain or worry; nervousness : *Julian was filled with tension about his speech.* **3. animosité ▸** an unfriendly or hostile feeling.

tent [tent] NOUN, tents. **tente ▸** an outdoor shelter that can be put up and taken down, consisting of a fabric supported by poles and ropes.

ten·ta·cle [TEN-tuh-kul] NOUN, tentacles. **1. tentacule ▸** a long, flexible part attached to the body of certain saltwater animals, used for holding things and for moving about. An octopus has eight tentacles, and a squid has ten. **2. tentacule ▸** a thread-like growth extending from an animal.

ten·ta·tive [TEN-tuh-tiv] ADJECTIVE. **provisoire ▸** done or made as a trial; uncertain; not confirmed : *She had made tentative plans to go to the beach, if it didn't rain.* ■ **tentatively,** ADVERB. ▸ **provisoirement, à titre d'essai, expérimentalement.**

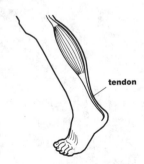

tendon

ten·ure [TEN-yur] NOUN. **exercice, mandat ▸** the act or right of holding some office or position : *The mayor is elected for a two-year tenure.*

term [turm] NOUN, terms. **1. terme ▸** a word or phrase having a certain meaning : *Many medical terms come from Latin, such as "osteo" and "cardio."* **Note.** The special terms used in a certain field are terminology. **2. durée, période, terme ▸** a certain period of time : *The usual*

✎ **Word Builder**

Terrible, unfortunate, and *shocking* all describe undesirable things, events, or people. *Terrible* means that something has happened to cause great fear or alarm: On the way home from our cottage, we saw a terrible car accident. *Unfortunate* is a much milder word and suggests it is regrettable or unlucky that something has happened: It was unfortunate that he did not hand in his science project on time. *Shocking* describes something that surprises because it goes against what is expected or acceptable: Aileen dyed her hair a shocking green.

---

term for a member of the House of Commons in Canada is five years. **3. terms. conditions, termes ▸** the conditions or requirements of an agreement : *The terms of the rental agreement say that no pets are allowed in the apartment.* **4. terms. rapports, termes ▸** a relationship between people : *to be on good terms with someone.* ▲ VERB, **termed, terming. appeler, qualifier, nommer ▸** to call or name something : *The critic termed the play a great success.*

ter·mi·nal [TUR-muh-nul] NOUN, terminals. **1. terminus, aérogare ▸** a station at either end of a route of travel for a train, bus, plane, and so on. **2. terminal (-ale, -aux) ▸** a single keyboard and screen for a computer. **3. borne ▸** any of the points in an electrical circuit where connections can be made. ▲ ADJECTIVE. **1. dernier (-ière), final (-ale, -aux) ▸** at the end; coming last : *Pierre has made 23 of the 24 payments due on his loan; the terminal payment is due next week.* **2. incurable, en phase terminale ▸** relating to an illness that will end in death.

ter·mi·nate [TUR-muh-NATE] VERB, terminated, terminating. **(se) finir, arriver à terme, mettre fin, résilier ▸** to bring to an end; stop; finish : *My contract terminates at the end of this year.* ■ **termination,** NOUN. ▸ **conclusion, résiliation, terminaison.**

ter·mite [TUR-mite] NOUN, termites. **termite ▸** a small insect that eats and destroys wood. Termites live in very large groups and can cause severe damage to wooden buildings and furniture.

ter·race [TAIR-is] NOUN, terraces. **1. terrasse ▸** a flat area made on the side of a hill or slope to provide a level surface for growing crops. **2. terrasse ▸** a paved area next to a house; a patio. **3. terrasse ▸** a small porch or balcony. ■ **terraced,** ADJECTIVE. ▸ **en terrasses, attenant (-ante).**

ter·rain [tuh-RANE] NOUN. **terrain ▸** an area of land, especially its physical features : *Few people live in the rugged terrain of the Yukon.*

ter·rar·i·um [tuh-RAIR-ee-um] NOUN, terrariums or terraria. **terrarium ▸** an enclosed glass container for keeping live plants and small animals.

ter·ri·ble [TAIR-uh-bul] ADJECTIVE. **1. terrible, effroyable, atroce, horrible ▸** causing great

fear or suffering; dreadful; horrible : *a terrible airplane crash.* **2. épouvantable, abominable ▸** very damaging; very extreme : *A terrible wind blew down a tree.* **3. Informal. très désagréable ▸** very bad or unpleasant : *It would be terrible to run out of gas and miss the game!* 🖉 p. 609.

ter·ri·bly [TAIR-uh-blee] ADVERB. **1. gravement, terriblement, atrocement ▸** in a terrible way; very badly : *to be terribly injured in an accident.* **2. Informal. très ▸** very : *They were terribly tired and just wanted to go to bed.*

ter·ri·er [TAIR-ee-ur] NOUN, terriers. **terrier ▸** a breed of small, active dogs, originally used to hunt rats and other small animals that burrow in the ground.

ter·rif·ic [tuh-RIF-ik] ADJECTIVE. **1. terrifiant (-ante), épouvantable ▸** causing great fear or suffering; terrible : *"The plants began to dry up in the sun's terrific heat."* (Lois Lenski) **2. Informal. excellent (-ente), formidable, sensationnel (-elle) ▸** very good; excellent : *a terrific book.* ■ **terrifically,** ADVERB. ▸ **formidablement, terriblement, incroyablement.**

ter·ri·fy [TAIR-uh-fy] VERB, terrified, terrifying. **terrifier, rendre fou de terreur ▸** to frighten greatly; fill with terror : *The howling of the wolves terrified the children.* **Note.** Often used as an ADJECTIVE: *The bookcase fell over with a terrifying crash.* 🖉 p. 239.

ter·ri·to·ri·al [TAIR-uh-TOR-ee-ul] ADJECTIVE. **territorial (-ale, -aux) ▸** having to do with a territory or territories.

ter·ri·to·ry [TAIR-uh-TOR-ee] NOUN, territories. **1. territoire ▸** an area of land; a region : *Wolves mark the territory where they live and hunt.* **2. territoire ▸** the land and waters that make up a state or nation. **3. Territoire ▸** an area that is part of Canada but is not a province, with some self-government : *Yukon Territory.*

ter·ror [TAIR-ur] NOUN, terrors. **1. terreur, épouvante ▸** very great fear : *"With the first clap of thunder Flip began to race around the house bleating with terror."* (Todd Lee) **2. terreur ▸** a person or thing causing great fear. SYN: apprehension, dread, panic, fear, alarm.

ter·ror·ism [TAIR-uh-RIZ-um] NOUN. **terrorisme ▸** the use or threat of violence to gain a political goal. **Note.** A person who uses acts of terrorism is a terrorist.

ter·ror·ize [TAIR-uh-rize] VERB, terrorized, terrorizing. **terroriser** ▶ to make very frightened; terrify.

test [test] NOUN, tests. **1. examen, épreuve, interrogation, test** ▶ a series of questions or problems to find out what someone knows or can do : *I need to study for a math test.* **2. analyse, examen** ▶ any way to study or examine something to find out its nature or quality : *a blood test.* ▲ VERB, tested, testing. **essayer, mettre à l'épreuve** ▶ to give a test to; examine; question : *The company is testing a new flavour of ice cream to see if people like it.* ⌐ p. 1062. SYN: examination, quiz, trial.

tes·ti·fy [TES-tuh-FY] VERB, testified, testifying. **1. témoigner** ▶ to make a formal statement giving proof or evidence about something : *My uncle, who saw the car accident, will have to testify at the trial.* **2. attester** ▶ to show as proof; indicate : *Her beautiful painting testified to years of training and work.*

tes·ti·mo·ny [TES-tuh-MOH-nee] NOUN, testimonies. **1. témoignage** ▶ the fact of testifying; a formal statement made in a court of law. **2. preuve** ▶ evidence or proof : *Their beautiful garden is a testimony to their hard work and determination.*

test tube **éprouvette** ▶ a small glass tube closed at one end, used in laboratory tests.

tet·a·nus [TET-uh-nus] NOUN. **tétanos** ▶ a serious disease caused by bacteria. Tetanus causes the muscles to stiffen, especially the muscles of the jaw. **Note.** It is commonly called lockjaw.

teth·er [TETH-ur] NOUN, tethers. **longe** ▶ a rope or chain used to tie an animal to limit how far it can wander. ▲ VERB, tethered, tethering. **attacher (à)** ▶ to tie an animal in this way.

text [tekst] NOUN, texts. **1. texte** ▶ a book used for studying; a textbook. **2. texte** ▶ the words that form the main part of a book, as opposed to the introduction, pictures, index, and so on. **3. texte** ▶ the actual wording of something : *If you missed the Mayor's speech, you can read the full text in the paper.*

text·book [TEKST-book] NOUN, textbooks. **manuel scolaire, livre scolaire** ▶ a book that provides facts, lessons, and so on for a class or course of study. ⌐ p. 1063.

tex·tile [TEKS-tul *or* TEKS-TILE] NOUN, textiles. **textile** ▶ fabric or cloth made by weaving or knitting fibres, such as cotton, wool, linen, or silk.

tex·ture [TEKS-chur] NOUN, textures. **texture, grain** ▶ the way a surface feels to the touch; the roughness or smoothness of some object or fabric : *Velvet has a very soft texture.*

than [than] CONJUNCTION. **1. que** ▶ a word used to introduce the second part of a comparison : *A*

cheetah is a faster runner than a lion is. **2. que** ▶ a word used to show a preference : *I'd rather drive a truck than a car.*

thank [thank] VERB, thanked, thanking. **remercier** ▶ to say that one is pleased or grateful : *Thank you for the lovely gift you gave me for my birthday.*

thank·ful [THANK-ful] ADJECTIVE. **reconnaissant (-ante)** ▶ feeling or showing thanks; grateful. ■ **thankfully,** ADVERB. ▶ **avec gratitude, avec reconnaissance.** ■ **thankfulness,** NOUN. ▶ **reconnaissance, gratitude.**

thanks [thanks] INTERJECTION. **merci** ▶ a word showing that one is pleased or grateful : *Thanks, I'd love a ride to school.* ▲ PLURAL NOUN. **remerciements** *Marta expressed her thanks to her friends for their help.*

Thanks·giv·ing [THANKS-GIV-ing] NOUN, Thanksgivings. **1. Action de grâce(s)** ▶ a holiday celebrated by feasting and giving thanks. In Canada, Thanksgiving is celebrated on the second Monday in October. **2. thanksgiving. rendre grâces (fait de)** ▶ the act or fact of giving thanks.

that [that] PRONOUN; those. **1. ce (cet, cette), cela** ▶ being the one seen, named, or known : *That was your last chance to tell me the truth.* **2.** ADJECTIVE, PRONOUN. **ce (cet, cette), celui (celle), celui-là (celle-là)** ▶ being the one at a greater distance : *This puppy is too wild; let me see that one over there.* ▲ ADVERB. **si, aussi** ▶ to a certain amount or degree : *I don't want to go to bed yet; I'm tired, but not that tired.* ▲ CONJUNCTION. **que** ▶ used to begin another part of a sentence that gives a result or reason : *They were so late that they missed half the movie.*

thaw [thah] VERB, thawed, thawing. **1. (faire) fondre, dégeler, décongeler** ▶ to change a solid to a liquid by raising the temperature; melt : *Please take the roast out of the freezer so it can thaw out.* **2. se détendre, s'améliorer, se**

✎ Writing Tips

Theme

In fictional writing the term **theme** *refers to the underlying idea of a story. For instance, the theme in The Lion, the Witch and the Wardrobe is that having faith in goodness gives one the power to triumph over evil. The theme of a story is like its* **message.** *Most writers do not decide on a theme and then write a story. The theme develops as their stories do. Observant readers can find out a lot about a writer's own beliefs by looking at the themes of their writing.*

réchauffer ▶ to become warmer or more friendly : *Relations between Canada and China have recently begun to thaw.* ▲ NOUN, thaws. **1. dégel, décongélation ▶** the fact of thawing. **2. dégel, fonte ▶** a period when the weather is warm enough for ice and snow to thaw : *The spring thaw led to some minor flooding.* 👁 p. 113.

the [thuh *or* thee] ARTICLE. **1. le, la, les ▶** used to point out or name a certain person or thing : *The roses were red, and the daisies were white.* **2. le fameux (la fameuse), le meilleur (la meilleure) ▶** being the only one or a special one : *This is the day I've been waiting for—my birthday!* ▲ ADVERB. ▶ to that degree; by that amount : *The sooner you clean your room, the sooner you'll get to play.*

the-a-tre [THEE-uh-tur] NOUN, theatres. (also theater) **1. théâtre, salle de cinéma ▶** a building or place where plays or motion pictures are presented. **2. théâtre ▶** the art or work of presenting plays : *She loves acting and wants to have a career in the theatre.* **3. théâtre ▶** an area where action takes place : *During the war, many battles took place in the Pacific theatre.* 📖 p. 1123.

the-at-ri-cal [thee-AT-rih-kul] ADJECTIVE. **1. théâtral (-ale, aux) ▶** having to do with the theatre. **2. théâtral (-ale, aux), dramatique ▶** like a play or drama; showy and dramatic : *He carried on in a theatrical manner, but he wasn't badly hurt.*

theft [theft] NOUN, thefts. **vol ▶** the crime of stealing : *The theft left her with no money for groceries* SYN: robbery, burglary, thievery.

their [thair] ADJECTIVE. **leur, leurs ▶** belonging to them : *Their car is the same make and model as ours.*

theirs [thairz] PRONOUN. **le leur, la leur, les leurs ▶** something belonging to them : *That's not our dog—it's theirs.*

them [them] PRONOUN. **les, eux, elles, leur ▶** a form of they: *Don't worry your parents—tell them when you go out.*

theme [theem] NOUN, themes. **1. thème, sujet ▶** the main subject or idea : *A theme in many of Shakespeare's plays is the corrupting influence of power.* **Note.** Something that has to do with a theme is thematic. **2. thème ▶** the main melody of a song. **3.** (also theme song) **thème, musique de film, indicatif ▶** the main melody associated with a movie, a radio or television show, or particular entertainer. SYN: subject, topic, problem, issue, point. 👁 p. 610.

them-selves [thum-SELVZ] PRONOUN. **eux-mêmes, elles-mêmes, se, tout seuls, toutes seules ▶** their own selves : *The two boys ate the whole cake all by themselves.*

then [then] ADVERB. **1. alors, en ce temps-là, à cette époque-là ▶** at that time : *I don't know how you could remember that—you were only three years old then.* **2. ensuite, puis ▶** next after that : *First, mix the sugar and butter; then, mix in the eggs.* **3. dans ce cas, donc, alors ▶** in that case : *If you study now, then you will be ready for the test.* ▲ NOUN. à ce moment-là ▶** that time : *Check with me tomorrow; I should know by then.*

the-ol-o-gy [thee-OL-uh-jee] NOUN, theologies. **théologie ▶** the study of God and religion. **■ theological,** ADJECTIVE. ▶ théologique.

the-o-ret-i-cal [THEE-uh-RET-ih-kul] ADJECTIVE. **théorique ▶** having to do with or existing in theory, rather than reality : *It is a theoretical possibility that there could be life on Mars, although nothing has been proved.* **■ theoretically,** ADVERB. ▶ théoriquement.

the-o-rize [THEE-uh-RIZE] VERB, theorized, theorizing. **élaborer une théorie, émettre une hypothèse ▶** to form or express a theory.

the-o-ry [THEE-uh-ree] NOUN, theories. **1. théorie ▶** a set of facts or ideas generally accepted as an explanation of some event or condition in nature : *The theory of relativity proposes that nothing in the universe travels faster than light.* **2. théorie ▶** the rules and principles of an art or science, rather than the actual practice of it : *In chemistry we study the scientific theory before we do lab work.* **3. hypothèse ▶** an idea or opinion that is presented without real proof : *My theory is that the butler did it.* SYN: explanation, idea, hypothesis, opinion.

ther-a-py [THAIR-uh-pee] NOUN, therapies. **thérapie ▶** the treatment of an illness of the mind or body, especially in a way that does not involve drugs or operations : *Soothing music is good therapy for the soul.* **Note.** A person who is trained to give a certain kind of therapy is a therapist.

there [thair] ADVERB. **là ▶** in, at, or to that place : *Your book is over there on the table.* ▲ PRONOUN. **il (y a) ▶** used to introduce a sentence in which the subject comes after the VERB:*There are 60 seconds in a minute.* ▲ INTERJECTION. **voilà ▶** used to express strong feelings : *There! It's all fixed.*

there-fore [THAIR-FOR] ADVERB. **par conséquent, donc ▶** for that reason : *I cooked dinner; therefore, you can wash up.*

ther-mal [THUR-mul] ADJECTIVE. **thermique ▶** having to do with heat : *This jacket has excellent thermal insulation and will be perfect for cold weather.*

ther-mom-e-ter [thur-MOM-uh-tur] NOUN, thermometers. **thermomètre ▶** an instrument for measuring temperature. It usually consists of a glass tube containing mercury or another liquid, with a scale marked off in degrees on the side of the tube. The mercury rises or falls according to how hot or cold the temperature is.

ther·mos [THUR-mus] NOUN, thermoses. **1. thermos, bouteille isolante** ▶ an insulated container used to keep liquids either hot or cold. **2. Thermos** ▶ a trademark name for a brand of such containers.

ther·mo·stat [THUR-muh-STAT] NOUN, thermostats. **thermostat** ▶ a device that automatically controls the temperature of something: *The temperature inside a house can be raised by turning up the thermostat that is connected to the furnace.*

the·sau·rus [thih-SOR-us] NOUN, thesauruses or thesauri. **thésaurus, dictionnaire (analogique)** ▶ a reference book that contains groups of words that share a similar meaning. Writers use it to find a synonym that will replace a word, or to choose the most suitable word from a group.

these [theez] ADJECTIVE; PRONOUN. **ces, ceux (celles), ceux-ci (celles-ci)** ▶ the plural form of this: *These cookies are mine, and those are yours.*

the·sis [THEE-siss] NOUN, theses. **1. thèse** ▶ a statement or position that is to be proved or defended. **2. thèse** ▶ a formal report or essay written by a university student.

they [thay] PRONOUN. **1. ils, elles** ▶ those persons or things previously named: *Andreas and Sally entered the contest, and they both won awards.* **2. on** ▶ people in general: *They say the movie is really funny.* ✐ p. 284.

thick [thik] ADJECTIVE, thicker, thickest. **1. épais (épaisse)** ▶ with a large distance between its opposite sides or surfaces; not thin: *The thick walls of very old buildings helped keep out the heat.* **2. d'épaisseur** ▶ having a certain size when measured between opposite sides: *The walls surrounding the castle are two metres thick.* **3. épais (épaisse), consistant (-ante)** ▶ of a liquid, not flowing easily; not watery: *a thick, meaty soup.* **4. dense, touffu (-ue), fourni (-ie)** ▶ with many parts or objects close together; tightly packed: *The forest was thick with trees and brush.* ▲ ADVERB. (also thickly) **en une couche épaisse, en tranches épaisses** ▶ so as to be thick; thickly: *I sliced the bread thick.* ▲ NOUN. **au cœur** ▶ the most active or dangerous part or place: *That reporter is always in the thick of a good story.* ■ **thickness,** NOUN. ▶ épaisseur. SYN: broad, massive, bulky, wide.

thick·en [THIK-un] VERB, thickened, thickening. **(s') épaissir, grossir** ▶ to make or become thicker: *Flour and cornstarch are used to thicken soups.*

thick·et [thik-it] NOUN, thickets. **fourré** ▶ a group of bushes or small trees growing close together.

thief [theef] NOUN, thieves. **voleur (-euse)** ▶ a person who steals. SYN: robber, burglar, crook.

✐ **Writing Tips**

Thing

Thing is a useful word because it can refer to almost any object, idea, or action.

> *I'm not sure what controls the sprinklers;*
> *I think it's that green **thing.***

*Because the word **thing** fits so many different situations, writers sometimes overuse it. Don't use **thing** if you are referring to something specific that you know the name of.*

> *Instead of writing She picked up some things for her bike,*
> *you could write She picked up some new tires and a bicycle pump.*

*In the first sentence below, **thing** is misused. The second sentence shows how to get rid of the unnecessary thing.*

> *Instead of writing The thing is, he really doesn't want to go to the party,*
> *you could write He really doesn't want to go to the party.*

thigh [thy] NOUN, thighs. **1. cuisse** ▶ the upper part of the leg, between the knee and the hip. **2. cuisse** ▶ the same part on the back leg of an animal.

thim·ble [THIM-bul] NOUN, thimbles. **dé à coudre** ▶ a small cover that is worn when sewing, to protect the tip of the finger that pushes the needle.

thin [thin] ADJECTIVE, thinner, thinnest. **1. mince** ▶ with a small distance between its opposite sides or surfaces; not thick: *The letter was written on thin, crackly paper.* **2. mince, maigre** ▶ not having a heavy body; not fat: *The stray cat was thin and hungry.* **3. clair (claire), liquide** ▶ of a liquid, flowing easily; watery. **4. clairsemé (-ée)** ▶ few and far apart; not closely packed: *My grandfather has very thin hair, especially on top of his head.* **5. faible, grêle, fluet (-ette)** ▶ lacking strength; weak: *"I was just falling asleep…when I heard a thin, high-pitched howl."* (Janet Foster) ▲ ADVERB. (also thinly) **en fines tranches** ▶ so as to be thin; thinly: *He asked the butcher to slice the meat very thin.* ▲ VERB, thinned, thinning. **(se) disperser, (s')éclaircir** ▶ to make or become thin: *The farmer thinned the seedlings to make room for the remaining ones to grow.* ■ **thinness,** NOUN. ▶ minceur, finesse, légèreté, maigreur. SYN: slender, slim, slight, lean.

thing [thing] NOUN, things. **1. chose, objet** ▶ an item that can be known to the senses but is not alive; a physical object: *He treats that stuffed* *dog as if it were real, not just a thing.* **2. chose, truc, machin ▶** an object that is not known or named : *What is that green thing crawling on your arm?* **3. chose ▶** any idea or subject that is talked about or thought about : *The best thing about summer vacation is no homework.* **4. créature ▶** a person or animal thought of in a certain way : *That dog is a friendly thing.* **5. things. a. affaires, choses ▶** personal belongings : *Get your things; it's time to leave.* **b. choses, ça ▶** the state of affairs; general conditions : *Things have gone well since last summer.* **6. truc, objet de prédilection ▶** an activity or interest that appeals to or suits a person : *Rachel plays the piano, flute, and guitar—music is just her thing.* 🖋 **p. 305.** 🖋 **p. 612.**

think [thingk] VERB, thought, thinking. **1. penser, réfléchir ▶** to use the mind to form an idea or opinion; have a thought : *I will answer the question, if you give me a minute to think about it.* **2. penser à, réfléchir à ▶** to have a certain idea : *Iqbal has to think of a way to fix his bicycle.* **3. penser, croire ▶** to have an opinion; suppose : *Jan thinks we'll go to the cottage this weekend.* ■ **thinker,** NOUN: ▶ **penseur (-euse)**. *Aristotle was a great thinker.* 🖋 **p. 305.**

third [thurd] NOUN, thirds. **tiers ▶** one of three equal parts ▲ ADJECTIVE. **troisième ▶** next after the second.

thirst [thurst] NOUN. **1. soif ▶** a feeling of desire or need for something to drink. **2. soif (de) ▶** any strong desire for something : *a thirst for knowledge.* 📖 **p. 1141.**

thirst-y [THUR-stee] ADJECTIVE, thirstier, thirstiest. **1. assoiffé (-ée) ▶** feeling thirst; having the desire or need to drink something. **2. desséché (-ée) ▶** lacking water or moisture; very dry : *the thirsty desert soil.*

thir-teen [thur-TEEN *or* THURT-TEEN] NOUN, thirteens; ADJECTIVE. **treize ▶** one more than twelve; 13. ■ **thirteenth,** ADJECTIVE; NOUN. ▶ **treizième.**

this [this] ADJECTIVE; PRONOUN, these. **1. ce, cet (cette), ça, ceci ▶** being the one seen, named, or known : *This is my favourite class.* **2. ce (cet, cette), celui (celle), celui-ci (celle-ci) ▶** being the closer one of two things : *This is my book, and that one over there is yours.* ▲ ADVERB. **si, aussi ▶** to the amount or extent mentioned; so : *I expected the test to be hard, but not this hard.*

this-tle [THIS-ul] NOUN, thistles. **chardon ▶** a prickly, wild plant with spiny leaves and purple, red, or yellow flowers, often growing as a weed in fields and pastures.

tho-rax [THOR-acks] NOUN, thoraxes. **1. thorax ▶** the part of the body between the neck and the abdomen; the chest. **2. thorax ▶** the part of an insect's body between the head and abdomen.

thorn [thorn] NOUN, thorns. **1. épine, aiguille, piquant ▶** a sharp point on a branch or stem of a plant : *Roses have thorns.* **2. arbre ou buisson épineux ▶** a tree or shrub that has thorns.

thorn-y [THORN-ee] ADJECTIVE, thornier, thorniest. **1. épineux (-euse) ▶** full of thorns; prickly : *a thorny bush.* **2. épineux (-euse) ▶** causing trouble; difficult : *a thorny problem.*

thor-ough [THUR-oh] ADJECTIVE. **approfondi (-ie), minutieux (-ieuse), consciencieux (-ieuse) ▶** careful and complete; leaving nothing out : *I go to my doctor for a thorough exam each year.* ■ **thoroughly,** ADVERB. ▶ **à fond, minutieusement.** *I cleaned my room thoroughly before my cousin came to visit.* SYN: full, complete, detailed, intensive, accurate.

thor-ough-bred [THUR-uh-BRED] NOUN, thoroughbreds. **1. animal de race ▶** a pet or farm animal that is of a pure breed. **2.** (also Thoroughbred) **pur-sang ▶** a special type of racing or jumping horse originally bred in England. ▲ ADJECTIVE. **de pure race ▶** of a pure or unmixed breed.

those [thoze] ADJECTIVE; PRONOUN. **ces, ceux (celles), ceux-là (celles-là) ▶** the plural of that: *These socks are mine, but those over there are yours.*

thistle

though [thoh] CONJUNCTION. **1. bien que, quoique, malgré (que) ▶** even if; although : *"But though he was curious, he asked no questions."* (Tololwa M. Mollel) **2. as though. comme si ▶** as if : *"Lin slipped the certificate between the pages of his music book quickly, as though he were ashamed of it."* (Barbara Novak) ▲ ADVERB. **pourtant, cependant ▶** however; nevertheless : *The book was difficult to read; I did enjoy it, though.*

thought [thot] VERB. a past form of think. ▲ NOUN, thoughts. **1. pensée, perspective ▶** the act or fact of thinking : *The thought of visiting her grandparents made her smile.* **2.** the result of thinking; ideas, feelings, or opinions : *We don't need to go—it was just a thought.* SYN : concept, view, notion, opinion, belief, idea.

thought·ful [THOT-ful] ADJECTIVE. **prévenant (-ante), attentionné (-ée), plein d'égards, gentil (-ille)** ▸ showing the proper thought; having care and concern for other people : *It was so thoughtful of Barry to bring me some soup when I was ill.* ▪ **thoughtfully,** ADVERB. ▸ **avec prévenance, gentiment.** ▪ **thoughtfulness,** NOUN. ▸ **prévenance, considération.**

thought·less [THOT-lis] ADJECTIVE. **étourdi (-ie), irréfléchi (-ie), inconsidéré (-ée)** ▸ showing a lack of thought; not thinking; careless or rude. ▪ **thoughtlessly,** ADVERB. ▸ **étourdiment, à la légère, négligemment.** ▪ **thoughtlessness,** NOUN. ▸ **étourderie, légèreté, manque de prévenance ou d'égards.**

thou·sand [THOW-zund] NOUN, thousands; ADJECTIVE. **mille** ▸ ten times one hundred; 1000. ▪ **thousandth,** ADJECTIVE; NOUN. ▸ **millième.**

thrash [thrash] VERB, thrashed, thrashing. **1. donner une (bonne) correction, rosser, rouer de coups, battre à plate (s) couture (s)** ▸ to beat hard : *"If I were big, I'd thrash all the knights and send them running," said Harald."* (Donald Carrick) **2. se débattre** ▸ to move wildly; toss about : *A trout was thrashing about in the river.*

thread [thred] NOUN, threads. **1. fil** ▸ a very thin string or cord used in sewing and weaving cloth. **2. fil** ▸ anything thin and long like a thread : *My father has threads of grey throughout his brown hair.* **3. pas, filetage** ▸ a narrow, winding ridge around a screw, nut, or bolt : *The thread of a screw helps hold it in place.* **4. fil (conducteur)** ▸ the main idea that connects different parts of a story, argument, and so on : *That movie was so complicated that it was hard to follow the thread of the plot.* ▲ VERB, threaded, threading. **1. enfiler** ▸ to put a piece of thread through : *to thread a needle.* **2. se faufiler** ▸ to move in a winding, twisting way : *The lion silently threaded its way through the trees.*

thread·bare [THRED-bair] ADJECTIVE. **usé (-ée), râpé (-ée), élimé (-ée)** ▸ worn out so much that pieces of thread show; shabby : *an old threadbare quilt on the bed.*

threat [thret] NOUN, threats. **1. menace** ▸ a warning or plan of hurting or punishing someone : *The threat of no dessert stopped my giggles.* **2. menace** ▸ a person or thing that can be dangerous or harmful : *The strong winds are a threat to several houses.* **3. signe** ▸ a sign that something might be dangerous or harmful : *The day was beautiful with no threat of rain.* SYN : menace, peril, hazard.

threat·en [THRET-un] VERB, threatened, threatening. **1. menacer, proférer des menaces** ▸ to say that something will be done to hurt or punish; to make a threat against : *Greg threatened to leave if I didn't play his way.* **2. menacer de** ▸ to be the cause of danger or harm : *"I was struggling to control the tears that were threatening to well up and spill over."* (Jean Little) **3. menacer de, risquer** ▸ to be a sign of something dangerous : *The branch swung wildly in the storm and threatened to break right off.* SYN : warn, caution, advise, alert.

three [three] NOUN, threes; ADJECTIVE. **trois** ▸ one more than two; 3. **Note.** A three-dimensional object has the dimensions of height, width, and depth.

thresh [thresh] VERB, threshed, threshing. **battre** ▸ to separate seeds or grain from plants by beating or striking. **Note.** A thresher is a farm machine that does this.

thresh·old [THRESH-HOLD] NOUN, thresholds. **1. seuil, pas (de la porte)** ▸ a piece of wood or stone at the base of a doorway. **2. seuil, sur le point de** ▸ a point of beginning or entering : *She was on the threshold of making a new discovery.*

threw [throo] VERB. a past form of throw.

thrift·y [THRIF-tee] ADJECTIVE, thriftier, thriftiest. **économe** ▸ careful in the use of money; likely to save; not wasteful : *A thrifty shopper uses coupons and watches for sales.* ▪ **thrift,** NOUN. ▸ **économie.**

thrill [thril] NOUN, thrills. **frisson, émotion** ▸ a strong sudden feeling of excitement or joy : *Meeting an astronaut was a big thrill for Antoine.* ▲ VERB, thrilled, thrilling. **exciter, réjouir, transporter** ▸ to give a thrill to; fill with excitement or joy : *Winning the award thrilled me!* ▲ ADJECTIVE: *a thrilling boat ride.*

thrill·er [THRIL-ur] NOUN, thrillers. **roman, pièce, film à suspense** ▸ a person or thing that thrills, especially a story or movie that is full of suspense and excitement.

thrive [thrive] VERB, thrived or throve, thrived or thriven, thriving. **se développer (bien), prospérer** ▸ to do well; be successful : *The calf thrived on its mother's rich milk.* ▲ ADJECTIVE:*a thriving business.* SYN : flourish, prosper, grow, develop.

throat [throte] NOUN, throats. **1. gorge** ▸ the front part of the neck. **2. gorge** ▸ the passage from the mouth to the stomach or lungs.

throb [throb] VERB, throbbed, throbbing. **élancer, battre, palpiter, vibrer** ▸ to beat strongly or quickly; pound : *Eva's head throbbed.* ▲ NOUN, throbs. **élancement, pulsation, battement, vibration** ▸ a quick or strong beat.

throne [throne] NOUN, thrones. **1. trône** ▸ a special chair that a king or queen sits in for ceremonies or important decisions. **2. trône** ▸ the power or authority of a king or queen : *Queen*

Elizabeth ascended to the throne of England in 1952.

throng [throng] NOUN, throngs. **foule, cohue** ▸ a large group of people; a crowd : *Throngs of people crowded into the theatre for the premiere of the new movie.*

throt-tle [THROT-ul] NOUN, throttles. **accélérateur, arrivée de gaz, papillon des gaz** ▸ a valve that controls the flow of fuel to an engine. ▲ VERB, throttled, throttling. **1. mettre au ralenti** ▸ to slow an engine by closing this valve. **2. étrangler** ▸ to stop the breath by closing off the throat; choke.

through [throo] PREPOSITION. **1. dans, à travers** ▸ from one side or part to the other : *We walked through the park.* **2. tout le long (de), pendant, durant (tout)** ▸ from beginning to end : *Laura talked all the way through the play, so I couldn't follow what was going on.* **3. par l'entremise de, par l'intermédiaire de** ▸ because of or by means of : *I ordered the dress through this store.* ▲ ADVERB. **1. à travers, de part en part** ▸ from one side or end to the other : *The phone lines are down and no one can get through.* **2. complètement, entièrement** ▸ completely : *After 20 minutes in the rain, Marianne was wet right through.* ▲ ADJECTIVE. **1. fini (-ie), terminé (-ée)** ▸ finished; done : *Are you through with the computer?* **2. direct (-ecte)** ▸ going from one point to another in a direct way : *This isn't a through street; it's a dead end.*

through-out [throo-OWT] PREPOSITION. **partout dans, dans tout** ▸ in every part of; from beginning to end : *"It was a spot well known throughout the New World for its fine food."* (Paul Yee)

throw [throh] VERB, threw, thrown, throwing. **1. lancer** ▸ to send something through the air with force, by a sudden movement of the arm and hand : *to throw a snowball.* **2. jeter, projeter, rejeter** ▸ to move suddenly and with force : *When the alarm rang, Zack threw off his covers and jumped out of bed.* **3. lancer, jeter** ▸ to cause to go through the air : *Penelope threw an angry look at the driver who honked at her.* **4. se lancer, se jeter** ▸ to go suddenly or with force into a certain condition : *Hoping to get a scholarship, she threw herself into her schoolwork.* ▲ NOUN, throws. **(action de) lancer** ▸ the act of throwing : *The throw to the catcher was way off.*

throw away or **throw out** **jeter, se débarrasser de** ▸ to get rid of something that is not wanted : *I try not to throw away anything that can be reused or recycled.* SYN : hurl, toss, cast, fling, pitch, chuck.

thrown [throne] VERB. a past form of **throw**.

thrush [thrush] NOUN, thrushes. **grive** ▸ one of a group of birds noted for their beautiful song. The **wood thrush** and **hermit thrush** are common in North America.

thrust [thrust] VERB, thrust, thrusting. **enfoncer, plonger, fourrer** ▸ to push with force; shove : *She thrust her hands into her pockets to keep them warm.* ▲ NOUN, thrusts. **poussée, coup** ▸ a sudden strong push or shove : *With a violent thrust, the robber pushed her to the ground.*

thud [thud] NOUN, thuds. **bruit sourd, son mat** ▸ a dull sound; a thump. ▲ VERB, thudded, thudding. **émettre un bruit sourd, battre sourdement** ▸ to move or hit with a dull sound : *My heart was thudding as I reached the top of the hill.*

thumb [thum] NOUN, thumbs. **pouce** ▸ the short, thick finger on a hand, nearest to the wrist. ▲ VERB, thumbed, thumbing. **feuilleter** ▸ to turn and look through the pages of : *She thumbed through a magazine.*

thumb-tack [THUM-tak] NOUN, thumbtacks. **punaise** ▸ a tack with a flat, round head that can be pressed into place with the thumb.

thump [thump] NOUN, thumps. **bruit lourd et sourd** ▸ a dull, heavy sound; a thud : *"One flock passed so low over our camp that I could hear the thump, thump of their wings beating the air."* (Janet Foster) ▲ VERB, thumped, thumping. **marteler** ▸ to beat or hit with a dull, heavy sound : *My dog thumps his tail on the ground every time he sees me.*

thun-der [THUN-dur] NOUN, thunders. **1. tonnerre** ▸ the loud rumbling or crashing sound that follows lightning. Thunder is caused by the sudden heating and expanding of air. **2. tonnerre, tempête** ▸ any very loud noise like thunder : *the thunder of applause.* ▲ VERB, thundered, thundering. **tonner, produire un bruit retentissant** ▸ to make thunder or any noise like thunder : *The old tree thundered as it hit the ground.* ■ **thunderous**, ADJECTIVE. ▸ **tonitruant (-ante), fracassant (-ante).** 🔲 p. 1119.

thun-der-bolt [THUN-dur-BOLT] NOUN, thunderbolts. **coup de foudre, coup de tonnerre** ▸ a flash of lightning together with a clap of thunder.

thun-der-head [THUN-dur-HED] NOUN, thunderheads. **tête de cumulonimbus** ▸ a rounded mass of dark cloud that often appears before a thunderstorm. **Note.** Thunderheads usually develop into **thunderclouds**—clouds that produce thunder and lightning.

thun-der-storm [THUN-dur-STORM] NOUN, thunderstorms. **orage** ▸ a storm having thunder and lightning.

Thurs-day [THURZ-DAY or THURZ-dee] NOUN, Thursdays. **jeudi** ▸ the day after Wednesday and before Friday.

thus [thus] ADVERB. **1. ainsi, de cette façon, comme ceci** ▸ in this manner; in this way; so : *My father stood angrily, and thus told me I was grounded.* **2. ainsi, donc, par conséquent** ▸ because of this; therefore : *The detec-*

tive figured out who took the statue and thus solved the mystery.

thwart [thwort] VERB, thwarted, thwarting. **contrecarrer, contrarier** ▶ to keep from doing or succeeding; oppose and defeat : *The storm thwarted our plans of a picnic.* SYN: frustrate, foil, oppose, defeat, obstruct.

thyme [time] NOUN, thymes. **thym** ▶ a small plant with sweet-smelling leaves belonging to the mint family. Thyme leaves are used to flavour foods.

thy-roid [THY-royd] NOUN, thyroids. **thyroïde** ▶ a large gland in the neck that controls the body's rate of growth and the rate at which it burns up food for energy.

tick¹ [tik] NOUN, ticks. **tic-tac** ▶ a light, clicking sound such as is made by a clock or watch. ▲ VERB, ticked, ticking. **1. tictaquer, faire tic-tac** ▶ to make this sound. **2. passer, s'écouler** ▶ of time, to pass away : *Time ticked by slowly as she waited for the bus.* **3. cocher** ▶ to mark with a check, dot, or slash : *He ticked off each item on his grocery list as he put it in the cart.*

tick² NOUN, ticks. **tique** ▶ a tiny animal with eight legs, related to the spider. A tick attaches itself to the skin of animals or people to suck their blood. In this way it can spread serious diseases.

tick-et [TIK-it] NOUN, tickets. **1. billet** ▶ a piece of paper or a card that gives a person certain services or rights. You pay money for a ticket to get into a movie or show, to get onto a plane or train, and so on. **2. étiquette** ▶ a tag that shows something, such as the price or size of clothing. **3. contravention** ▶ a notice for someone to pay a fine or go to court for breaking a traffic law : *A person who drives too fast may get a speeding ticket.* ▲ VERB, ticketed, ticketing. **1. étiqueter** ▶ to put a card or tag on. **2. émettre une contravention, donner une contravention** ▶ to give a notice for someone to pay a fine or go to court.

tick-le [TIK-ul] VERB, tickled, tickling. **1. chatouiller** ▶ to touch the body lightly, causing a tingling feeling : *When I tickled the baby, he started to laugh.* **2.** *Informal.* **faire plaisir, amuser** ▶ to be delighted or pleased : *Our mother was really tickled when we gave her flowers.* ▲ NOUN, tickles. **chatouillement** ▶ a tingling feeling.

tick-lish [TIK-lish] ADJECTIVE. **1. chatouilleux (-euse)** ▶ sensitive to tickling : *Evan, who is very ticklish, starts to giggle before you even touch him.* **2. délicat (-ate)** ▶ needing careful handling; difficult; delicate : *Telling my boss that she made a mistake was a ticklish situation.*

tidal wave **raz-de-marée** ▶ a huge, powerful ocean wave caused by an underwater earthquake or by a heavy storm at sea. Tidal waves can be as high as a tall building and can cause great damage. **Note.** These waves are also called by their Japanese name, tsunami [soo-NAH-mee].

tid-bit [TID-bit] NOUN, tidbits. **1. friandise, bon morceau** ▶ a small but good piece of food. **2. nouvelle croustillante** ▶ an interesting bit of information or news.

tide [tide] NOUN, tides. **1. marée** ▶ the regular rise and fall in the level of the ocean or other large bodies of water. Tides are caused by the pull of gravity from the moon or sun, and they change from high to low and back to high about every 12 hours. **2. courant, cours, marche** ▶ anything that is thought to rise and fall like the tide : *a tide of events.* ▲ VERB, tided, tiding. **tide over. dépanner** ▶ to give help through a difficult period : *We had a snack to tide us over till dinner.*

tid-ings [TY-dingz] PLURAL NOUN. **nouvelles** ▶ information; news : *Glenna brought tidings from her family.*

ti-dy [TY-dee] ADJECTIVE, tidier, tidiest. **1. ordonné (-ée), soigné (-ée), bien rangé (-ée)** ▶ clean and in good order; neat : *Her tidy bedroom looks as though no one lives in it.* **2. coquet (-ette)** ▶ fairly large : *The antique dresser sold for a tidy sum of money.* ▲ VERB, tidied, tidying. **ranger** ▶ to make neat : *Keeok scurried about, dusting and tidying the room.* ■ **tidily,** ADVERB. ▶ **soigneusement, avec soin.** ■ **tidiness,** NOUN. ▶ **ordre, propreté.** SYN: orderly, neat, trim, well-kept.

tie [ty] VERB, tied, tying. **1. lacer, attacher** ▶ to fasten with string or rope : *to tie your shoelaces.* **2. être à égalité, être ex æquo** ▶ to equal the score in a game or contest : *The game was tied at 5–5.* **3. relier, attribuer** ▶ to join together; connect : *Scientists tie the poor weather to the volcano eruption.* **4. tie down or tie up. limiter, être pris (prise), être retenu (-ue)** ▶ to keep from moving or acting; limit; restrict : *Mom called to say she was tied up at work and wouldn't be home for dinner.* **Note.** Also used as a noun : *a traffic tie-up.* ▲ NOUN, ties. **1. lien, entrave** ▶ something that fastens or holds something together, such as a string or rope. **2. cravate** ▶ a strip of cloth worn around the neck; a necktie. **3. match nul, égalité (de points)** ▶ an equal score in a game or contest. **4. liens, attaches** ▶ something that joins or connects : *That business has strong ties to the community.* **5. traverse** ▶ a piece of wood or metal that holds together and strengthens other parts : *Railway tracks have metal rails with wooden ties going across them.* SYN: fasten, bind, strap, attach. 📙 p. 1015.

tier [teer] NOUN, tiers. **gradin, étage** ▶ a number of rows or layers arranged one above the other : *A wedding cake often has several tiers.*

ti-ger [TY-gur] NOUN, tigers. **tigre (tigresse)** ▶ a large, powerful wild cat with orange-brown fur and black stripes. Tigers are found in Asia and are among the largest members of the cat family.

tight [tite] ADJECTIVE, tighter, tightest. **1. serré (-ée), ferme, solide, fort (forte)** ▸ closely fastened, held, or tied; fixed firmly in place : *My little brother had a tight grip on my hand.* **2. juste, étroit (-oite)** ▸ fitting close to the body : *a tight skirt.* **3. étanche, hermétique** ▸ made so nothing can pass through. **Note.** Also used in combination : airtight, watertight. **4. serré (-ée), à l'étroit** ▸ having little room or space; close or confined : *The room was so full, it was a tight squeeze.* **5. avare** ▸ not generous; stingy : *a miser is tight with his money.* ▲ ADVERB. **solidement, bien** ▸ so as to be tight; firmly; securely : *Hold on tight!* ◼ **tightly,** ADVERB. ▸ **étroitesse, rigueur, sévérité, avarice.** ◼ **tightness,** NOUN. ▸ **étroitesse.** SYN : taut, tense, firm, secure, close.

tight-en [TITE-un] VERB, tightened, tightening. **resserrer, tendre, ajuster** ▸ to make or become tight : *I tightened the bolts on my bike wheel so it wouldn't be so wobbly.*

✎ Writing Tips

Time

• *There are several ways to write out* **time** *in your writing.*

  A bank was robbed at **three thirty in the afternoon.**

  The car chase started at **3:55 p.m.**

  The bank robber was caught at **four o'clock.**

  Police officers wrote their report at **18:00.**

Remember, once you use a style, continue using it in that piece of writing. If you are using figures (12:06, 1:59), don't suddenly switch to using written numbers with "o'clock."

• *When you refer to a specific time, it helps readers if you also tell them the time of day (six in the evening, four in the morning, and so on) or use "a.m." and "p.m." ("a.m." refers to the hours between 12 midnight and 12 noon; "p.m." refers to the hours between 12 noon and 12 midnight). The 24-hour clock (I woke up at 06:00; We ate dinner at 18:00) has the advantage of making the time of day quite clear. When you use the 24-hour clock, you don't need to use "o'clock," "a.m." or "p.m." or refer to the time of day.*

---

tights [tites] PLURAL NOUN. **collant(s)** ▸ a close-fitting garment that stretches to fit the legs and lower part of the body.

tile [tile] NOUN, tiles. **tuile, carreau** ▸ a thin slab or piece of baked clay or other material. Tiles are usually square and are placed side by side to cover walls, floors, countertops, and so on. ▲ VERB, tiled, tiling. **couvrir de tuiles, carreler** ▸ to cover with tiles : *to tile a shower wall.*

till[1] [til] PREPOSITION; CONJUNCTION. **jusqu'à** ▸ up to the time of; until : *I waited till my brother was in bed before I wrapped his present.*

till[2] VERB, tilled, tilling. **labourer, cultiver** ▸ to prepare and use farm land for growing crops : *Farmers till the soil by turning it over with a hoe or plough.* ◼ **tiller,** NOUN. ▸ **laboureur, cultivateur (-trice).**

till[3] NOUN, tills. **caisse enregistreuse, tiroircaisse** ▸ a small drawer for holding money, such as one under a counter in a store.

till-er [TIL-ur] NOUN, tillers. **barre** ▸ a handle or bar used to turn a rudder to steer a boat.

tilt [tilt] VERB, tilted, tilting. **pencher, incliner** ▸ to raise one end or side higher than the other; slant or tip : *"She unhooked one of the buckets and tilted it so that Jamie could drink."* (Joseph Bruchac) ▲ NOUN, tilts. **1. inclinaison** ▸ a slanting position. **2. full tilt. à toute vitesse, à fond de train** ▸ full speed or force : *She ran down the hill at full tilt.* SYN : incline, lean, slope, slant, tip.

tim-ber [TIM-bur] NOUN, timbers. **1. bois de construction, bois d'oeuvre** ▸ wood for building houses, boats, and other such items. **2. poutre, madrier** ▸ a long, large piece of wood for building. **3. arbres, bois, taillis, terre boisée** ▸ a group of trees, or an area where trees grow; a forest. **Note.** A timberline is the line on a mountain above which trees do not grow.

tim-bre [TIM-bur or TAM-bur] NOUN. **timbre** ▸ the quality of a sound that makes it distinct from other sounds : *His soft voice has a different timbre when he is angry.*

time [time] NOUN, times. **1. fuseau horaire** ▸ a quality that goes on and on without end, separating things that happened before from those that will happen. Time is measured in hours, days, years, and so on. The moving of a clock's hands or the passing of time. **fuseau horaire 2. temps** ▸ a way of measuring this quality : *Vancouver is on Pacific Standard Time.* **Note.** This is also known as a time zone. **3. heure** ▸ a certain point or moment in the past, present, or future : *What time does the show start?* **4. moment, époque** ▸ a certain period of history : *in the time of the Vikings.* **5. époque, ère, temps** ▸ an occasion or period having a particular purpose : *It is time to clean up!* **6. fois** ▸ one of a number of occasions on which something happens : *That's the third time I've been late this term.*

▲ VERB, timed, timing. **1. règler** ▶ to set to a certain time : *The house lights are timed to come on at 8:00.* **2. fixer** ▶ to measure the time of : *The sprinter in the 100-metre race was timed at 10.3 seconds.* ⌀ p. 617.

time·less [TIME-lis] ADJECTIVE. **intemporel (-elle)** ▶ not affected or limited by time : *the timeless appeal of fables.*

tim·er [TIME-ur] NOUN, timers. **chronométreur (-euse), chronomètre, minuterie** ▶ a person or thing that keeps track of time : *a kitchen timer.*

times [times] PREPOSITION. **fois** ▶ multiplied by : *Three times four is 12.*

time·ta·ble [TIME-TAY-bul] NOUN, timetables. **1. horaire** ▶ a list of the times when trains, buses, or the like arrive or leave. **2. emploi du temps, calendrier** ▶ a schedule or plan : *What's your timetable to get this project done by April?*

tim·id [TIM-id] ADJECTIVE. **craintif (-ive), timoré (-ée), timide** ▶ not brave or bold; easily frightened; shy : *The mouse was too timid to come out when a cat was near.* ■ **timidly,** ADVERB. ▶ **craintivement, timidement.** ■ **timidity,** NOUN. ▶ **timidité, caractère timoré, caractère craintif.** SYN: meek, fearful, bashful, retiring, shy, afraid.

tin [tin] NOUN, tins. **1. étain, fer-blanc** ▶ a soft, silver-white metal that is a chemical element. Tin is useful because it protects things from rust, and it is often used to coat other metals. **2. boîte** ▶ something made out of tin : *a tin of cookies.* ▲ ADJECTIVE. **de fer-blanc, d'étain** ▶ made out of tin, or coated with tin : *a tin can.*

tin·der [TIN-dur] NOUN. **petit bois** ▶ any dry material that burns easily and is used to start a fire. Wood shavings, dry pine cones, and paper are tinder.

tine [tine] NOUN, tines. **dent** ▶ a sharp or projecting part : *the tines of a fork.*

tin·foil [TIN-FOYL] NOUN. **papier d'aluminium** ▶ a very thin sheet of tin, aluminum, or other metal used for wrapping.

tinge [tinj] NOUN, tinges. **un soupçon de, très peu** ▶ a slight amount; a trace : *There is a tinge of ginger in these cookies, but you can barely taste it.* ▲ VERB, tinged, tingeing or tinging. **1. teinter** ▶ to give a slight amount of colour to : *Light from the sunset tinged the horizon.* **2. nuancer, teinter** ▶ to show a slight amount of some quality. *Fear tinged my excitement of acting in a school play.*

tin·gle [TING-ul] VERB, tingled, tingling. **picoter, piquer, fourmiller** ▶ to have a slight prickly, stinging feeling : *My foot is asleep, and it is tingling.* ▲ NOUN, tingles. **picotement, fourmillement, sensation cuisante** ▶ a tingling feeling. ■

tin·ker [TINK-ur] VERB, tinkered, tinkering. **bricoler** ▶ to fix or work with something in an unskilled or casual way : *Tora likes to tinker with old cars to get them running.* ▲ NOUN, tinkers. **romanichel (-elle), rétameur (-euse)** ▶ in former times, a person who travelled around mending pots, pans, and other such household items.

tin·kle [TINK-ul] VERB, tinkled, tinkling. **tinter, tintinnabuler** ▶ to make a light, clear ringing sound like the sound of tiny bells : *The bells tinkled in the wind.* ▲ NOUN, tinkles. **tintement** ▶ a light, clear ringing sound.

tint [tint] NOUN, tints. **teinte, nuance** ▶ a shade of a colour, especially a pale or delicate colour : *The paint had a blue tint.* ▲ VERB, tinted, tinting. **teindre** ▶ to give a tint to.

ti·ny [TY-nee] ADJECTIVE. tinier, tiniest. **minuscule** ▶ very, very small : *a tiny speck of dust.* SYN: small, minute, little, slight, puny.

tip[1] [tip] NOUN, tips. **1. extrémité** ▶ the end or farthest point of anything : *the southern tip of Africa.* **2. bout, pointe** ▶ a small piece on the end of something : *the tip of a pen.*

tip[2] VERB, tipped, tipping. **1. faire basculer, renverser** ▶ to knock over; overturn or upset : *"My father jumped up so fast he tipped over his lemonade cup."* (Ann Cameron) **2. soulever un bord, relever une extrémité** ▶ to raise one end or side; tilt or slant : *The cowhand tipped his hat as a greeting.*

tip[3] NOUN. **1. pourboire** ▶ a small amount of money given for service, beyond the normal amount due : *Ilanko gave the waiter an excellent tip.* **2. conseil, renseignement** ▶ a helpful hint; useful information : *a safety tip.* ▲ VERB, tipped, tipping. **1. donner un pourboire** ▶ to give a small amount of money for a service : *We tipped the person who delivered our pizza.* **2. tip off. avertir, prévenir** ▶ to give someone private or secret information : *A noise tipped off the spy that he had been discovered.* ■ **tipper,**

✍ Writing Tips

To/Too

*The words **too** and **to** are often misused.*

• *Too is used whenever you mean "more"*
  or "a greater amount."
    *There were **too** many rotten jokes.*

• *To is used to indicate direction, action,*
  comparison, or purpose.
    *She went **to** the movies.*
    *He went **to** school.*

Tip: One way to remember when to use too is to remember that too has too many o's.

NOUN. ▶ **personne qui donne le pourboire, (camion à) benne (basculante).**

tip-toe [TIP-TOH] VERB, tiptoed, tiptoeing. **marcher sur la pointe des pieds** ▶ to walk on the tip of one's toes : *Lily tiptoed out of the room where her brother slept.*

tire¹ [tire] VERB, tired, tiring. **(se) fatiguer** ▶ to make or become tired : *I wonder if the mail carrier ever tires of doing the same thing every day.* ▲ ADJECTIVE:*Mowing the lawn is a hot and tiring job.* SYN: exhaust, wear out, fatigue, weary.

tire² NOUN, tires. **pneu** ▶ a covering for a wheel of a car, truck, bicycle, or other such vehicle. Tires are usually made of rubber. Most tires have air in them, but some are solid rubber.

tired [tired] ADJECTIVE. **fatigué (-ée)** ▶ feeling or showing a lack of energy in the mind or body ; wanting to rest or sleep : *She was too tired even to eat dinner.* 2. **las (lasse)** ▶ no longer interested ; bored or annoyed : *"A long time ago there was no moon. The people got tired of going around at night in the dark."* (Joseph Bruchac) ▪ **tiredness,** NOUN. ▶ **fatigue, lassitude.** Something that is tiresome is boring or annoying : *The tiresome noise of the engine annoyed us all.*

tire-less [TIRE-lis] ADJECTIVE. **infatigable, inlassable** ▶ never tiring ; going on and on : *a tireless worker.* ▪ **tirelessly,** ADVERB: ▶ **infatigablement, inlassablement.** *George-Étienne Cartier worked tirelessly to bring Quebec into Confederation in the 1800s.*

tis-sue [TISH oo] NOUN, tissues. 1. **mouchoir en papier** ▶ a soft, thin paper used as a handkerchief. 2. **tissu** ▶ a group of cells in a plant or animal that are alike in what they do : *Connective tissue forms the ligaments and tendons in animals.* **Note.** Tissue paper is a soft, thin paper used for wrapping or packing things.

ti-tle [TITE-ul] NOUN, titles. 1. **titre** ▶ the name of a book, song, movie, painting, or other such work. 2. **titre** ▶ a word or name used with a person's name to show a rank or position, such as "Ms.," "Doctor," or "Her Majesty." 3. **titre** ▶ a championship : *Our school captured the regional lacrosse title after a close match with a rival school.* 4. **titre** ▶ the legal right a person has to own property, or a document that shows this right. ▲ VERB, titled, titling. **intituler, appeler** ▶ to give a name or title to : *Mozart titled one of his operas "The Magic Flute."*

to [too] PREPOSITION. 1. **à, vers, en, chez** ▶ in the direction of ; toward : *The family drove to Manitoba for their vacation.* 2. **à** ▶ as far as the point or condition of : *The season is changing from winter to spring.* 3. **(jusqu') à** ▶ through and including : *The market is open from 6:00 a.m. to 10:00 p.m.* 4. **à** ▶ compared with : *We lost the game, 1–4.* 5. **pour** ▶ for the purpose of ; for : *She went to get the key.* **Note.** To is also

used : 1. **à** ▶ to introduce an indirect object : *Give this book to Vasa.* 2. **pour, envers** ▶ to show a relation to a noun or adjective : *You were always so kind to him.* 3. to indicate the infinitive : *I didn't know whether to go or to stay.* ✐ p. 618.

toad [tode] NOUN, toads. **crapaud** ▶ an animal that is very much like a frog but has shorter legs, a thicker body, and dry, bumpy skin. A toad hatches and develops in water but spends most of its adult life on land.

toad-stool [TODE-STOOL] NOUN, toadstools. **champignon vénéneux** ▶ a name for a mushroom with an umbrella-shaped top, especially one that is poisonous.

toast¹ [tohst] NOUN. **rôtie, pain grillé, toast** ▶ a crisp slice of bread that has been browned on both sides by heat. ▲ VERB, toasted, toasting. **(faire) griller** ▶ to brown by heating : *Alison likes to toast marshmallows over a camp fire.*

toast² NOUN, toasts. **toast** ▶ a short speech made before drinking in honour of someone : *The president made a toast to Aunt Duleta for her years of hard work.* ▲ VERB, toasted, toasting. **porter un toast** ▶ to drink in honour of someone : *Everyone toasted the bride and groom at the wedding reception.*

toast-er [TOHST-ur] NOUN, toasters. **grille-pain** ▶ an electric device for making bread into toast.

to-bac-co [tuh-BAK-oh] NOUN. 1. **(pied de) tabac** ▶ a tall plant with pink and white flowers and broad, sticky leaves. 2. **(feuilles de) tabac** ▶ the dried leaves of this plant are used for smoking, as in cigarettes, and chewing.

to-bog-gan [tuh-BOG-un] NOUN, toboggans. **traîne sauvage, toboggan, luge** ▶ a long, flat wooden sled used for sliding down hills. The front of a toboggan is curled up. ▲ VERB, tobogganed, tobogganing. **faire du toboggan, faire de la luge** ▶ to ride on a toboggan.

to-day [tuh-DAY] NOUN. **aujourd'hui** ▶ the present day or time : *Today is my birthday.* ▲ ADVERB. 1. **aujourd'hui** ▶ on or during the present day : *Is it going to rain today?* 2. **aujourd'hui, de nos jours** ▶ at the present time ; nowadays : *Today, people change jobs more often than they used to.*

tod-dler [TOD-lur] NOUN, toddlers. **bambin (-ine), enfant en bas âge** ▶ a small child who is just learning to walk. **Note.** Someone who walks in small and uncertain steps is said to toddle.

toe [toh] NOUN, toes. 1. **orteil** ▶ one of the five parts at the end of the foot. 2. **bout** ▶ the part of a sock, shoe, or boot that covers the toes.

to-geth-er [tuh-GETH-ur] ADVERB. 1. **ensemble** ▶ with one another : *"They spent the rest of the evening sitting quietly together out under the stars."* (Tololwa M. Mollel) 2. **ensemble** ▶

mixed or in contact with : *Mix the ingredients together.* **3. unanimement** ▶ in agreement : *The council voted together to defeat the proposal.*

toil [toyl] NOUN, toils. **labeur, dur travail** ▶ long, hard work : *The pyramids were built by the toil of thousands of workers.* ▲ VERB, toiled, toiling. **travailler dur, peiner** ▶ to work hard and long : *We toiled for hours in the fields.*

toi·let [TOY-lit] NOUN, toilets. **toilettes** ▶ a bowl that is filled with water and has a seat attached to it. It is found in a bathroom and is used to carry away body wastes.

to·ken [TOH-kun] NOUN, tokens. **1. gage, marque, signe** ▶ something that stands for another thing that is larger or greater; a sign or symbol : *My mother smiled at me as a token of support.* **2. jeton** ▶ a piece of metal or plastic that looks like a coin and is used in place of money. A token is sometimes used to pay for a ride on a bus, train, or subway. ▲ ADJECTIVE. **symbolique** ▶ done only to meet a requirement; slight or insignificant : *It seems you have only made a token effort to clean your room.*

told [tohld] VERB. a past form of tell.

tol·er·a·ble [TOL-ur-uh-bul] ADJECTIVE. **tolérable, supportable, acceptable, passable** ▶ that can be tolerated; acceptable. ■ **tolerably,** ADVERB. ▶ **passablement**.

tol·er·ance [TOL-ur-uns] NOUN. **1. tolérance** ▶ an attitude of allowing others to have ideas and beliefs that are different from one's own, and of accepting people who are from a different background. **2. tolérance** ▶ the ability or quality of being able to resist or endure something : *A person with low tolerance for stress usually doesn't deal well with pressure.* ✐ **p. 434.**

tol·er·ant [TOL-ur-unt] ADJECTIVE. **tolérant (-ante), indulgent (-ente)** ▶ showing tolerance : *Mara is tolerant of my brother's tricks, but I usually get mad.* ■ **tolerantly,** ADVERB. ▶ **d'une manière tolérante, avec indulgence.** SYN: forgiving, lenient, indulgent.

tol·er·ate [TOL-ur-RATE] VERB, tolerated, tolerating. **1. tolérer, accepter** ▶ to allow something that one does not agree with to be done : *Members of Parliament fiercely debate the issues, but they must tolerate laws once they are passed.* **2. tolérer, supporter** ▶ to be willing to accept or put up with : *Our teacher will not tolerate any talking during tests.* SYN: let, allow, permit, bear, endure, stand.

toll[1] [tole] NOUN, tolls. **1. péage** ▶ a fee that is paid for the right to do something, such as to travel on a road or bridge. **2. bilan, nombre de victimes** ▶ any serious loss or damage : *the death toll in the plane crash.*

toll[2] VERB, tolled, tolling. **sonner** ▶ of a bell, to ring in a slow, regular way. ▲ NOUN, tolls. **son de cloche** ▶ the slow, regular ringing of a bell.

✐ Writing Tips

Tone

Tone reflects a writer's attitude toward a subject. The tone may be angry, happy, critical, serious, humorous, and so on. A writer's tone can usually be sensed from reading just a paragraph or two, and will affect how the reader feels about the subject. For example, a letter to a friend will be friendly and chatty, while a letter of complaint will be formal, and maybe a little angry.

When you're writing, make sure your tone is what you want it to be. Read your writing aloud, or ask someone else to read it, to find out what tone others think the writing has.

---

tom·a·hawk [TOM-uh-HOK] NOUN, tomahawks. **tomahawk, hache de guerre** ▶ a small, light axe used as a tool and weapon by some Aboriginal peoples.

tomahawk

to·ma·to [tuh-MAY-toh *or* tuh-MAH-toh] NOUN, tomatoes. **tomate** ▶ a juicy fruit that grows on a vine and is red when ripe. Tomatoes are eaten raw or cooked.

tomb [toom] NOUN, tombs. **tombe, tombeau (-eaux)** ▶ a place where a dead body is buried, especially a large decorated building in which the body is placed. **Note.** A tombstone marks a grave and usually has the name and the dates of birth and death of the dead person.

to·mor·row [tuh-MOR-oh] NOUN. **1. demain** ▶ the day after today. **2. demain, futur, avenir** ▶ the future : *The show discussed how robots will be used in the world of tomorrow.* ▲ ADVERB. **demain** ▶ on the day after today.

ton [tun] NOUN. **tonne** ▶ a measure of weight used in the United States and formerly in Canada, equal to 2000 pounds (about 907 kg).

tone [tone] NOUN, tones. **1. sonorité, timbre**
▶ the nature of a sound in terms of its pitch,
loudness, length, and so on : *The deep, mellow
tones of a cello.* **2. tonalité** ▶ the difference in
higher or lower pitch between two musical
notes on a scale. **3. ton** ▶ the quality of the
voice that shows some feeling or meaning :
*Ralph's tone sharpened as he questioned me
about his missing jacket.* **4. ton** ▶ a quality of a
colour that makes it distinct : *The tone of that
colour is much deeper than this colour.*
5. ton ▶ the style or character of something : *It
was obvious from the tone of the meeting that
the deal had fallen through.* ✐ p. 620.

tongs [tongz] PLURAL NOUN. **pinces** ▶ a tool used
to hold or pick up something. Tongs have two
long arms joined to form a handle at one end :
*She used a pair of tongs to lift the meat off the
barbecue.*

tongue [tung] NOUN, tongues. **1. langue** ▶ the
movable, muscular piece of flesh in the mouth
that is used in the tasting, chewing, and swallowing of food. When a person speaks, the tongue helps form certain sounds in words.
2. langue ▶ the tongue of an animal used for
food : *ox tongue.* **3. langue** ▶ a language : *German is my mother tongue but I also speak
French and English.* **4. langue, capacité de
parler** ▶ the ability to speak : *When I had nothing to say, Tim teased, " Have you lost your
tongue?"* **Note.** When this happens, the person
is said to be tongue-tied. **5. languette** ▶ the
narrow, flat piece of leather located under the
laces or buckle of a shoe. **6. langue** ▶ something
shaped like a tongue : *Tongues of flame licked
the side of the house.* ✐ p. 988. 👁 p. 403.

ton·ic [TON-ik] NOUN, tonics. **tonique, fortifiant** ▶ something that is meant to bring a person strength or health, such as a medicine.

to·night [tuh-NITE] NOUN. **ce soir, cette
nuit** ▶ the night of the present day. ▲ ADVERB. **ce
soir, cette nuit** ▶ on or during this night : *We
are going to the symphony tonight.*

tonne [tun] NOUN, tonnes. **tonne** ▶ a unit of measure for weight, equal to 1000 kg. **Note.** Formerly
spelled ton.

ton·sil [TON-sul] NOUN, tonsils. **amygdale**
▶ either of two small, oval pieces of flesh

located on the inside back part of the throat.
Note. Tonsillitis is an infection of the tonsils.

too [too] ADVERB. **1. aussi, également** ▶ also ;
besides : *Ella came too.* **2. trop, excessivement** ▶ more than enough ; more than it
should be : *Farhid has grown so much this year
that his clothes are too small.* **3. trop, extrêmement** ▶ very ; very much : *Thank you for all
your help ; you are too kind.* ✐ p. 618.

took [took] VERB. a past form of take.

tool [tool] NOUN, tools. **1. outil, instrument** ▶ an
instrument or device used for doing work, especially one that is held in the hand. Hammers,
saws, and screwdrivers are types of tools. **2. outil,
instrument** ▶ a person or thing that is used for a
certain purpose : *Computers are excellent
research tools.* ▲ VERB, tooled, tooling. **travailler** ▶ to use a tool on something : *The
leather on this boot was tooled by hand.*

toot [toot] NOUN, toots. **coup de klaxon, coup de
sifflet, note** ▶ a short, loud blast of sound.
▲ VERB, tooted, tooting. **donner un coup de
klaxon, donner un coup de sifflet, klaxonner** ▶ to make or cause such a sound : *The driver tooted the horn.*

tooth [tooth] NOUN, tooth. **1. dent** ▶ one of a set
of hard, bony parts in the mouth used for biting
and chewing. Teeth are set in the gums and supported by the jaws. Animals also use their teeth
to protect themselves and to kill prey.
2. dent ▶ something that looks or works like a
tooth : *the teeth of a saw.* ✐ p. 988.

tooth-brush [TOOTH-brush] NOUN, toothbrushes.
brosse à dents ▶ a small brush with a long handle, used to clean the teeth.

tooth-paste [TOOTH-payst] NOUN, toothpastes.
dentifrice ▶ a paste used in cleaning the teeth.

tooth-pick [TOOTH-pik] NOUN, toothpicks. **cure-
dent** ▶ a small, thin piece of wood, plastic, or
other material, used to remove food from
between the teeth.

top¹ [top] NOUN, tops. **1. sommet, cime, haut,
crête** ▶ the highest part or point of something :
We ran up to the top of the hill. **Note.** Also
used in combinations such as mountaintop,
hilltop, and rooftop. **2. (en) tête** ▶ the highest
level or degree : *Our team is at the top of the*

🔧 **Word Builder**

Top is a very short word that is found in many common expressions. ***Blow one's top*** means a
person has lost his or her temper and become very excited : *Dad blew his top when he found out
that I hadn't cleaned my room.* A ***top dog*** is the most important person in an organization :
As president, Leah is the top dog in the science club. When someone does something ***off the top***
of their head, he or she does it without any practice or rehearsing : *Mrs. Singh asked us to do
a short speech off the top of our heads.*

league. **3. bouchon, capsule, couvercle, capuchon ▸** something that goes on the higher or upper part : *Please put the top back on the jar.* ▲ ADJECTIVE. **dernier (-ière), supérieur (-ieure), du haut ▸** of or at the top; highest : *Mom keeps dishes that she doesn't use often in the top cupboard.* ▲ VERB, **topped, topping. 1. napper, recouvrir ▸** to cover or put a top on : *Top the potatoes with butter.* **Note.** Something put on food in this way is a **topping. 2. dépasser, faire mieux ▸** to be at or reach the top : *I can do a hundred sit-ups. Can you top that?* 🖉 **p. 621.**

top[2] NOUN, tops. **toupie ▸** a toy, usually cone-shaped, that can be made to spin very fast on a point.

to-paz [TOH-PAZ] NOUN. **topaze ▸** a mineral, usually yellow or brown, that is valued as a gemstone.

top-ic [TOP-ik] NOUN, topics. **sujet, thème ▸** something that is dealt with in speech or writing; the subject of a paper, book, discussion, and so on : *The topic of my speech on Canadian unity.* SYN: subject, theme, issue, point, question.

to-pog-ra-phy [tuh-POG-ruh-fee] NOUN, topographies. **1. topographie ▸** the surface features of an area of land, such as mountains, valleys, rivers, lakes, and so on. **2. topographie ▸** the science of showing these features on a map. ▪ **topographical,** ADJECTIVE. ▸ **topographique.**

top-ple [TOP-ul] VERB, toppled, toppling. **(faire) renverser, basculer, tomber, perdre l'équilibre ▸** to push or fall over : *"The steps had rotted from the dampness in the air and one good shove could have toppled the railing."* (Paulette Bourgeois)

top-soil [TOP-SOYL] NOUN. **terre, couche arable ▸** a rich surface layer of soil that has most of the materials needed by plants to grow.

Tor-ah [TOR-ah] NOUN. (also torah) **1. Torah, Thora, Tora ▸** the first five books of the Jewish bible. **2. Torah, Thora, Tora ▸** the sacred writings and laws of the Jewish religion.

torch [torch] NOUN, torches. **1. flambeau, lampe de poche ▸** a bright flame or light that is carried to light the way. **Note.** In Britain a flashlight is called a **torch. 2. torche, chalumeau (-eaux) ▸** a device that produces a very hot flame, such as a blowtorch.

tore [tor] VERB. a past form of tear.

tor-ment [tor-MENT] VERB, tormented, tormenting. **tourmenter, torturer ▸** to cause great pain or suffering : *"Do your twin sisters still torment you with their terrible shouts?"* (Barbara Nichol) ▲ [TOR-MENT] NOUN, torments. **tourment, supplice ▸** great pain or suffering. SYN: pain, torture, agonize, plague, persecute.

torn [torn] VERB. a past form of tear.

tor-na-do [tor-NAY-doh] NOUN, tornadoes or tornados. **tornade ▸** a very strong wind storm that

creates a dark, funnel-shaped cloud. This cloud twists around and around with great speed and force as it moves in a narrow path. Objects in the path of the tornado are often damaged by the force of the wind. **Note.** Also called a **twister.** 🖼 **p. 1105.**

tor-pe-do [tor-PEE-doh] NOUN, torpedoes. **torpille ▸** a weapon used to sink ships, made up of a long, tube-shaped metal shell that is filled with explosives. Torpedoes are fired from submarines, ships, or planes and then travel under the water to the target. ▲ VERB, torpedoed, torpedoing. **torpiller ▸** to hit an object with a torpedo.

tor-rent [TOR-unt] NOUN, torrents. **1. torrent ▸** a heavy, fast-moving stream of water or other liquid : *"The storm grew worse as Wu came to cross a creek that had flooded into a raging torrent."* (David Day) **2. torrent ▸** any strong, steady stream : *"Her tears streamed down in torrents."* (Rosebud Yellow Robe) ▪ **torrential,** ADJECTIVE. ▸ **torrentiel (-ielle).**

tor-so [TOR-soh] NOUN, torsos. **torse, buste ▸** the upper part of the human body; the trunk.

tor-toise [TOR-tus] NOUN, tortoise or tortoises. **tortue ▸** a turtle, especially one that lives only on land.

tor-ture [TOR-chur] VERB, tortured, torturing. **1. torturer, mettre au supplice ▸** to cause a person great pain or suffering, as a punishment or to force the person to do something. **2. tourmenter, torturer ▸** to cause suffering to ; torment : *He tortures his little brother by jumping out and scaring him.* ▲ NOUN. **torture, tourment, supplice ▸** great pain or suffering.

toss [toss] VERB, tossed, tossing. **1. lancer, jeter ▸** to make a quick or short throw : *The catcher tossed the ball to the pitcher.* **Note.** In a tossed salad, the ingredients are tossed or stirred to mix them together. **2. rejeter en arrière, secouer ▸** to throw or move about quickly : *The horse tossed its mane.* ▲ NOUN, tosses. **lancer, coup (de pile ou face) ▸** a quick or short throw : *A coin toss decides which team goes first.*

toss-up **égalité (de chances) ▸** an even chance : *It's a toss-up whether Kevin or Jayanti will win the school election.* SYN: throw, fling, chuck, pitch, hurl.

to-tal [TOH-tul] ADJECTIVE. **total (-ale, -aux), absolu (-ue), global (-ale, -aux), complet (-ète) ▸** making up the whole; complete : *When the power went out, we were in total darkness.* ▲ NOUN, totals. **total (-aux), somme ▸** the complete amount : *The cost of the new bike, including tax, comes to a total of $146.50.* ▲ VERB, totalled, totalling. (also totaled, totaling) **1. totaliser, additionner, s'élever à ▸** amount to ; come to as a total : *The cashier totalled our bill.* **2.** Informal. **démolir, détruire complètement ▸** to destroy completely : *The car was* *totalled in the accident.* SYN: entire, comprehensive, absolute.

to‑tal‑i‑tar‑i‑an [toh‑TAL‑uh‑TAIR‑ee‑un] ADJECTIVE. **totalitaire** ▶ having to do with a country in which the central government has complete power and greatly controls the lives of the citizens.

to‑tal‑ly [TOH‑tuh‑lee] ADVERB. **totalement, entièrement, complètement** ▶ completely; entirely : *The bridge was totally destroyed by the flood; nothing was left standing.*

tote [tote] VERB, toted, toting. *Informal.* **porter, trimballer** ▶ to carry around or on one's person : *We toted the picnic basket from the car to the top of the hill.* **Note.** A tote bag is used to carry small personal items.

to‑tem [TOH‑tum] NOUN, totems. **totem** ▶ in the beliefs of certain cultures, an animal, plant, or other natural object that is taken as the symbol for a family or tribe. **Note.** A totem pole is a pole with carved and painted images of totems created by some Aboriginal tribes of the Pacific coast.

totem

tot‑ter [TOT‑ur] VERB, tottered, tottering. **chanceler, vaciller, tituber** ▶ to move in a shaky or unsteady way : *"Several times he stumbled, and finally he tottered, crumpled up, and fell."* (Jack London) ▪ **tottery,** ADJECTIVE. ▶ chancelant (‑ante).

tou‑can [TOO‑kan] NOUN, toucans. **toucan** ▶ a brightly coloured tropical bird with a large curving beak and a heavy body.

touch [tuch] VERB, touched, touching. **1. toucher** ▶ to put a hand, finger, or other part of the body against : *The lake was so deep that he could not touch the bottom.* **2. se toucher, être contigu (‑uës)** ▶ to put one thing against another so that there is no space between : *The*

pictures were hung closely together, but not touching. **3. toucher, émouvoir** ▶ to affect the feelings : *Marla was touched by a neighbour's offer of help during her illness.* **4. toucher, affecter** ▶ to relate or refer to : *Brent is hoping the scandal won't touch him, since he wasn't involved.* **5. touch up. retoucher** ▶ to make small changes or improvements : *We touched up a few places where the paint had chipped.* ▲ NOUN, touches. **1.** **toucher** ▶ the sense by which objects are felt and known by the hands and other body parts. **2. (au) toucher** ▶ a particular feeling sensed in this way : *Velvet has a silky, smooth touch.* **3. toucher (action, fait de)** ▶ the act or fact of touching. **4. un soupçon (de)** ▶ a small amount : *I like a touch of lemon in my tea.* **5. (en) contact (avec)** ▶ communication between people : *My mother and her sister keep in touch by letter.* SYN: feel, finger, handle, contact. ☞ p. 1036.

touch‑down [TUCH‑down] NOUN, touchdowns. **1. touché** ▶ a score in football that is worth six points, made by carrying or catching the ball beyond the other team's goal line. **2. atterrissage, amerrissage, alunissage** ▶ the landing or moment of landing of a spacecraft or other aircraft.

touch‑y [TUCH‑ee] ADJECTIVE, touchier, touchiest. **susceptible** ▶ easily insulted or very sensitive.

tough [tuf] ADJECTIVE, tougher, toughest. **1. dur (dure), solide, robuste** ▶ not easily damaged by breaking, cutting, or tearing; strong : *The tough meat was very difficult to cut.* **2. endurant (‑ante), coriace, endurci (‑ie)** ▶ able to put up with hardship and difficulty : *Pioneers had to be tough to survive.* **3. dur (dure)** ▶ likely to fight; mean and rough : *Kalya always acts tough so that we'll be afraid of her.* **4. dur (dure), difficile** ▶ hard to do; difficult : *The play dealt with tough issues like racism and poverty.* ▪ **toughness,** NOUN. ▶ dureté, solidité, robustesse, endurance. SYN: hardy, durable, rugged, sturdy, strong.

tough‑en [TUF un] VERB, toughened, toughening. **(se) renforcer, (se) durcir, (s') endurcir, (s') aguerrir** ▶ to make or become tough : *The lacrosse team needs to toughen up for the big match.*

tou‑pee [too‑PAY] NOUN, toupees. **postiche** ▶ a small wig, worn to cover a bald spot on the head.

tour [toor] NOUN, tours. **1. voyage organisé** ▶ a trip where many places are visited for a short period of time : *We saw 10 cities on our tour of Europe.* **2. excursion, visite** ▶ a short trip around or through a place to see it : *Our science class went on a tour of the botanical gardens.* **3. période (de service), durée (d'une mission)** ▶ a period of time for fulfilling a required task or service : *a tour of duty peacekeeping in Haiti.* ▲ VERB, toured, touring. **voyager, visiter, être en**

tournée ▸ to travel in or through a place; make a tour : *Our band is touring schools in Ontario.*

tour-ist [TOOR-ist] NOUN, tourists. **touriste** ▸ a person who travels to visit a place for pleasure. **Note.** The fact of doing this is **tourism.**

tour-na-ment [TUR-nuh-munt or TOOR-nuh-munt] NOUN, tournaments. **tournoi** ▸ a series of contests involving two or more persons or teams : *a volleyball tournament.*

tour-ni-quet [TUR-nuh-kit or TUR-nuh-KIT or TOOR-nuh-kit] NOUN, tourniquets. **tourniquet, garrot** ▸ a bandage or cloth used to stop the flow of blood from a serious cut or wound. Bleeding can be stopped by wrapping the cloth around the wound and twisting it tight with a short stick.

tow [toh] VERB, towed, towing. **remorquer** ▸ to pull or drag something behind : *After the accident, the car had to be towed to a body shop for repairs.* ▲ NOUN, tows. **remorquage** ▸ the act of towing.

to-ward [tuh-WORD] PREPOSITION. (also towards) **1. vers** ▸ in the direction of : *The children ran toward the puppy.* **2. pour, en vue de** ▸ in regards to; concerning : *I am saving toward a new bike.*

tow-el [towl] NOUN, towels. **serviette, torchon** ▸ a piece of cloth or paper that is used for drying or wiping something. ▲ VERB, towelled, towelling. (also toweled, toweling) **essuyer avec une serviette** ▸ to wipe or dry with a towel : *Dad towelled Henri dry as he stepped out of the bath.*

tow-er [TOW-ur] NOUN, towers. **tour** ▸ a very tall building or the narrow top part of a tall building : *a bell tower.* ▲ VERB, towered, towering. **se dresser de manière imposante, dominer** ▸ to rise or extend high into the air : *My brother towers over the rest of us.*

tow-er-ing [TOW-ur-ing] ADJECTIVE. **1. imposant (-ante), énorme** ▸ very tall : *A towering cloud appeared on the southern horizon.* **2. imposant (-ante), dominant (-ante)** ▸ very great; outstanding : *Albert Einstein is a towering figure in science.*

town [town] NOUN, towns. **1. (petite) ville** ▸ an area with a group of houses and other buildings in which people live and work. **Note.** The word town is used for a place that is smaller than a city but larger than a village. **2. ville** ▸ the people of a town : *The whole town came to the fair.* **3. en ville, au centre-ville** ▸ the downtown area of a city, or the city itself : *Let's drive into town and see a movie.* **4. ville, municipalité** ▸ a unit of local government; more often called a **township. Note.** The town hall is a meeting place in which the official business of a community takes place.

town-ship [TOWN-ship] NOUN, townships. **1. canton** ▸ an area of local government within a county. A township may be rural areas or have

towns and cities within it. **2. canton** ▸ in the Prairie Provinces, an area of land of about 93 square kilometres.

tox-ic [TOK-sik] ADJECTIVE. **toxique** ▸ having to do with or being a poison : *toxic fumes.* **Note.** Toxic waste is the poisonous remains of some industrial chemicals.

tox-in [TOK-sin] NOUN, toxins. **toxine** ▸ any of various poisons produced by certain bacteria and viruses and causing diseases.

toy [toy] NOUN, toys. **1. jouet** ▸ something that is made to amuse or entertain; an object that can be played with. **2. miniature, petit chien (chienne) d'appartement** ▸ a dog that is much smaller than one of the regular breed : *a toy poodle.* ▲ VERB, toyed, toying. **toy with. 1. jouer avec, s'amuser avec, tripoter** ▸ to play with; to amuse oneself with : *We toyed with our papers and books as we waited for class to begin.* **2. caresser l'idée** ▸ to think of in a light or casual way : *I am toying with the idea of becoming a nurse.* 📖 **p. 1166.**

trace [trace] NOUN, traces. **1. trace** ▸ a small amount left behind showing that something was there at one time : *Scientists measure for traces of radioactivity in dinosaur bones.* **2. ombre** ▸ any small amount or quantity : *"The boy grinned at the audience, shook his head, and loped off the stage without a trace of embarrassment."* (Barbara Novak) ▲ VERB, traced, tracing. **1. suivre la piste de, retrouver, dépister** ▸ to follow the route, trail, or course of someone or something : *We traced the route of the settlers.* **2. décalquer** ▸ to copy something by following the lines as seen through a piece of paper. **Note.** Tracing paper is special thin paper used to do this.

tra-che-a [TRAY-kee-uh] NOUN, tracheas. **trachée** ▸ the tube in the body that runs between the throat and the lungs; the windpipe.

track [trak] NOUN, tracks. **1. empreinte, trace** ▸ a mark or footprint left by a person, an animal, or an object when moving over the ground : *deer tracks in dirt.* **2. piste** ▸ a race course : *Olympic relay races are run on a track in a stadium.* **3. voie ferrée, rails** ▸ a set of rails that a train runs on. **4. chenille** ▸ the continuous metal belts that tanks and tractors move on. ▲ VERB, tracked, tracking. **1. suivre la piste de, dépister** ▸ to follow the marks or prints left by a person, animal, or thing. **2. retrouver** ▸ to follow the course or path of : *My grandmother is trying to track down her ancestors for a family history.* **3. laisser des traces, laisser des empreintes** ▸ to make tracks on something : *The children tracked mud on the floor.*

keep (lose) track of garder (perdre) contact, garder (perdre) la notion du temps ▸ to keep (fail to keep) informed about or in communication with : *We had so much fun that we lost* *track of the time.* SYN: sign, mark, trace, clue, evidence.

track and field athlétisme ▸ a group of sporting events that involve running, jumping, and throwing. **Note.** A track meet is a scheduled meeting of athletes to compete in such events.

tract [trakt] NOUN, tracts. **1. étendue, lotissement** ▸ a large area of land : *My family owns a tract of land by the lake.* **2. appareil, système** ▸ a system of parts or organs in the body that work together : *the digestive tract.*

trac·tion [TRAK-shun] NOUN. **traction, adhérence** ▸ the power to grip the surface of the road or ground and not slip while in motion ; traction : *Deep grooves in tires give them better traction on the road.*

trac·tor [TRAK-tur] NOUN, tractors. **tracteur** ▸ a work vehicle with large tires or continuous metal tracks. Tractors are used to pull farm machinery, move other heavy objects, and so on.

trachea

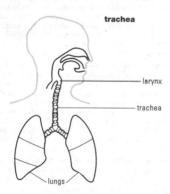

— larynx

— trachea

— lungs

trade [trade] NOUN, trades. **1. commerce** ▸ the act or business of buying and selling goods : *Canada carries on trade with other nations, such as the United States and Japan.* **Note.** A policy of free trade means that the government does not limit or tax goods coming into the country. **2. métier** ▸ a particular type of business : *the construction trade.* **3. échange** ▸ the exchange of one thing for another. ▲ VERB, traded, trading. **1. échanger** ▸ to give one thing for another ; exchange : *Professional sports teams often trade players.* **2. trade in. faire reprendre** ▸ to give something as part of the payment when buying a new item of the same kind : *Let's trade in our old truck and get a new one.* **3. faire le commerce** ▸ to buy and sell goods ; carry on trade. SYN: barter, exchange, swap, deal, switch.

trade-mark [TRADE-mark] NOUN, trademarks. **1. marque déposée, marque de commerce** ▸ a picture, word, or symbol put onto an item so that it can be easily recognized as the product of a certain maker : *The panda is a trademark of the World Wildlife Fund.* **2. marque distinctive** ▸ any distinctive feature that identifies a person or thing : *Prime Minister Trudeau's trademark was a flower in his lapel.*

trad·er [TRAY-dur] NOUN, traders. **1. commerçant (-ante), marchand (-ande), négociant (-ante)** ▸ a person who takes part in trade : *a fur trader.* **2. navire marchand** ▸ a ship that is used to carry on trade. **Note.** A trade route is a sea or land route used to travel from one place to another for trade, especially in former times.

trading post comptoir (commercial) ▸ a store in a frontier region where people can sell or exchange things for food and other supplies.

tra·di·tion [truh-DISH-un] NOUN, traditions. **tradition, coutume** ▸ a custom or belief that is passed from one generation to another : *A popular Canadian tradition is setting off fireworks on Canada Day.*

tra·di·tion·al [truh-DISH-un-ul] ADJECTIVE. **traditionnel (-elle)** ▸ according to or following tradition ; passed down over time : *Irene wore a traditional Greek costume for the parade.* ∎ **traditionally**, ADVERB. ▸ **traditionnellement.**

traf·fic [TRAF-ik] NOUN. **1. circulation, trafic** ▸ the moving of cars, trucks, ships, planes, or other vehicles along a certain route : *I avoid driving in downtown traffic by taking the bus.* **2. trafic** ▸ the business of buying and selling goods, especially illegal goods : *the drug traffic.* ▲ VERB, trafficked, trafficking. **faire le trafic de, trafiquer** ▸ to buy, sell, or deal in goods ; especially stolen or illegal goods : *It's illegal to traffic in endangered animals.*

trag·e·dy [TRAJ-uh-dee] NOUN, tragedies. **1. tragédie, drame, malheur** ▸ a very sad or unfortunate event ; something that brings great unhappiness : *The death of the two children in*

✏ Writing Tips

Tragedy

*In literature, a **tragedy** is a play or story with a main character (a tragic hero) who has a character flaw that will lead to downfall and general disaster. Tragedies usually end with most of the characters being killed or dying. In older tragedies, the tragic heroes were often royal figures — kings, princes, and so on. Modern tragedies usually involve ordinary characters.*

a house fire was a terrible tragedy. **2. tragédie ▶** a serious play in which the main character, an important or heroic person, meets death or ruin through fate or because of some fault in his or her nature. **3. tragédie ▶** any story that has a sad ending. ✎ **p. 625.**

trag·ic [TRAJ-ik] ADJECTIVE. **tragique ▶** causing great suffering or sorrow; very sad : *the tragic Halifax explosion.* **2. tragique ▶** having to do with a dramatic tragedy : *Shakespeare's characters Romeo and Juliet are tragic figures.* ■ **tragically,** ADVERB. ▶ tragiquement.

trail [trale] NOUN, trails. **1. sentier ▶** a path for moving through an area that is not settled or built up, such as a forest, desert, or mountain region : *a hiking trail.* **2. piste, empreintes, traces ▶** a mark, scent, or set of tracks made by an animal or person : *The guide followed the lion's trail into the mountains.* **3. traînée ▶** something that marks a trail or follows along behind : *Hansel and Gretel left a trail of bread crumbs to help them find their way home.* ▲ VERB, trailed, trailing. **1. suivre ▶** to follow the tracks or path of : *We trailed behind our dog as she ran down the street.* **2. se faire mener (de), se faire distancer (par) ▶** to be behind in a race or game : *Our team trailed by two goals at half time.* **3. pousser le long de ▶** to grow along or over a surface : *The ivy trailed up the side of the house.* **4. trail off. s'estomper ▶** to become weaker and fade away : *The sound of the band slowly trailed off as they marched off the stage.*

trail·er [TRAY-lur] NOUN, trailers. **1. caravane ▶** an enclosed room or house on wheels that can be pulled behind a car. When parked, the trailer can be used as a home or office. **2. remorque ▶** a platform or box on wheels that is pulled behind a truck to move or carry something.

train [trane] NOUN, trains. **1. train ▶** a line of connected railway cars being pulled by an engine. **2. caravane ▶** a group of vehicles, pack animals, or people travelling together : *Wagon trains crossed the frontier and headed across the wilderness.* **3. fil ▶** a connected series of ideas or events : *a train of thought.* **4. traîne ▶** the part of a formal dress or gown that trails on the ground behind the wearer : *the train of a wedding gown.* ▲ VERB, trained, training. **1. former, dresser, recevoir une formation ▶** to show or teach how to act in a certain way or carry out a particular task : *We trained our dog to walk on his hind legs.* **Note.** A person who is being trained is called a trainee. **2. se préparer, s'entraîner ▶** to get ready for some test or activity by repeated practice : *The speed skater trains for the Olympics six days a week.* **3. faire grimper, faire pousser le long de ▶** to make something grow or go a certain way : *Ariella trained the vines to grow along the fence.* ▲ ADJECTIVE: *a trained bird that can talk.* ✑ **p. 1155.**

train·er [TRAY-nur], NOUN, trainers. **1. entraîneur (-euse) ▶** someone who helps an athlete get into condition and prepare for a sporting event. A trainer also treats minor injuries during a game or practice. **2. dresseur (-euse), dompteur (-euse) ▶** someone who teaches animals to perform, as in a circus.

train·ing [TRAY-ning] NOUN. **1. formation ▶** education or instruction in how to do something : *Dr. Piers had years of special training before she became a surgeon.* **2. entraînement, préparation ▶** a program for good physical condition : *You should be in training for many months before you run a marathon.*

trait [trate] NOUN, traits. **trait (de caractère), caractéristique ▶** a special feature or quality that sets one person or thing apart from others; a characteristic : *Mikeala never loses her temper; that's a trait I greatly admire.* SYN: attribute.

trai·tor [TRAY-tur] NOUN, traitors. **1. traître (-esse), criminel (-elle) d'État ▶** a person who betrays his or her own country and helps its enemies. **Note.** A person who acts in this way is traitorous. **2. traître (-esse) ▶** anyone who betrays a cause or duty : *Colin promised to take me to the movie, but he took Jana instead—what a traitor!*

tramp [tramp] VERB, tramped, tramping. **1. marcher d'un pas lourd ▶** to step or walk heavily. **2. se déplacer à pied, faire une randonnée ▶** to travel by foot; walk or hike : *We tramped through the snow to Derek's house.* ▲ NOUN, tramps. **1. vagabond (-onde), itinérant (-ante) ▶** a person who has no home or job and wanders from place to place. **2. pas lourd, bruit de pas ▶** a heavy step, or the sound made by this.

tram·ple [TRAM-pul] VERB, trampled, trampling. **piétiner ▶** to walk heavily on, so as to crush or damage : *A herd of stampeding buffaloes trampled a path through the grass.*

tram·po·line [TRAM-puh-LEEN] NOUN, trampolines. **trampoline ▶** a piece of strong netting or cloth that is attached by springs to a large metal frame. People bounce up and down and perform tumbling exercises on a trampoline.

trance [trance] NOUN, trances. **1. transe, état de transe ▶** a condition of the mind in which a person is only partly conscious and seems to be asleep : *In a trance, the sleepwalker went out the door.* **2. absorption ▶** a state of mind in which a person is completely absorbed by something and not aware of what is happening : *Alana sat in a trance staring at the waves.*

tran·quil [TRANK-wil] ADJECTIVE. **tranquille, paisible ▶** free from trouble or worry; calm; peaceful : *There wasn't a ripple on the tranquil lake.* ■ **tranquillity,** NOUN. (also tranquility) ▶ tranquillité, calme. ▪ **tranquilly,** ADVERB. ▶ tranquillement, calmement, paisiblement

tran·quill·iz·er [TRANK-wuh-IZE-ur] NOUN, tranquillizers. (also tranquilizer) **tranquillisant** ▶ a drug used to calm the nerves or make a person less upset.

trans·con·ti·nen·tal [TRANS-kon-tuh-NEN- tul] ADJECTIVE. **transcontinental (-ale, -aux)** ▶ going from one side of a continent to the other : *a transcontinental flight.*

trans·scribe [tran-SKRIBE] VERB, transcribed, transcribing. **transcrire** ▶ to make a written copy of something. **Note.** Such a copy is a transcription.

trans·fer [TRANS-fur or TRANZ-fur or trans-FUR] VERB, transferred, transferring. **1. transférer** ▶ to change or move from one place to another : *Vijay transferred a file from the hard drive to a disk.* **2. muter, transférer** ▶ to move a person officially from one job, position, or location to another : *The company transferred its headquarters from Brandon to Winnipeg.* ▲ NOUN, [TRANS-fur or TRANZ-fur] transfers. **1. transfert, mutation** ▶ the act or fact of transferring ; a move from one place to another : *Computers speed up the transfer of information.* **2. correspondance** ▶ a ticket or pass that allows a person to change from one bus, train, or plane to another without paying again.

trans·fix [trans-FIKS] VERB, transfixed, transfixing. **pétrifier, clouer au sol** ▶ to make unable to move, as from shock or surprise : *I was transfixed by the beautiful sunset.*

trampoline

trans·form [trans-FORM] VERB, transformed, transforming. **transformer** ▶ to change greatly in form or appearance : *Makeup transforms me into a clown.* **Note.** The fact of transforming is a

transformation. SYN : change, convert, alter, modify.

trans·fu·sion [trans-FYOO-zhun] NOUN, transfusions. **transfusion** ▶ the transfer of blood from one person to another by medical means, usually given because the patient has been in an accident or had an operation.

tran·sis·tor [tran-ZIS-tur] NOUN, transistors. **transistor** ▶ a small, electronic device that is used to control the flow of electricity in computers, radios, televisions, and so on.

tran·sit [TRAN-zit] NOUN. **transit, transport** ▶ the act of carrying or moving something : *A city's bus system is often called mass transit.*

tran·si·tion [tran-ZISH-un] NOUN, transitions. **transition** ▶ the fact of changing from one place or form to another : *Karl managed the transition of moving to a new city very well.*

trans·late [tranz-LAYT or TRANZ-layt] VERB, translated, translating. **1. traduire** ▶ to change something spoken or written into another language : *The novels of Marie-Claire Blais have been translated from French into many other languages.* **2. se traduire (par), signifier** ▶ to explain or say in other words : *She took a "little nap," which translates into a five-hour sleep.* **Note.** A person who translates words from one language to another is a translator.

trans·la·tion [trans-LAY-shun or tranz-LAY-shun] NOUN, translations. **traduction** ▶ the changing of something spoken or written into another language : *The announcement was given in English, followed by a French translation.*

trans·lu·cent [trans-LOO-sunt or tranz-LOO-sunt] ADJECTIVE. **translucide** ▶ allowing some light to pass through, but not allowing what is on the other side to be seen clearly : *translucent curtains.*

trans·mis·sion [tranz-MISH-un] NOUN, transmissions. **1. transmission** ▶ the act of transmitting ; sending or passing something from one place to another : *Some wild rodents can be dangerous because of their role in the transmission of rabies.* **2. transmission, émission, diffusion** ▶ the broadcasting or sending out of radio and television signals. **3. boîte de vitesses** ▶ the series of gears that transfer power from the engine to the wheels of a car, truck, or other such vehicle.

trans·mit [tranz-MIT] VERB, transmitted, transmitting. **1. transmettre** ▶ to send or pass on from one person or place to another : *The secret agent transmitted the documents to the president.* **2. émettre, diffuser** ▶ to send out radio or television signals. SYN : send, pass along, forward, transfer.

trans·mit·ter [tranz-MIT-ur] NOUN, transmitters. **transmetteur, émetteur** ▶ an electronic device for sending out radio and television signals.

trans-par-ent [tranz-PAIR-unt] ADJECTIVE. **1. transparent (-ente)** ► able to be seen through clearly : *Most windows are transparent.* Note. The fact of being transparent is transparency. **2. transparent (-ente), évident (-ente)** ► easily understood or detected ; not able to hide or conceal : *Anwar's excuse was so transparent that I knew it was a lie.* ■ **transparently,** ADVERB. ► **clairement, de manière transparente.**

trans-plant [tranz-PLANT] VERB, transplanted, transplanting. **1. transplanter** ► to dig up and move a plant from one place to another : *We transplanted the flowers from the containers into the garden.* **2. transplanter** ► to move from one place to another : *My mom transplanted the family to Regina when she got a new job.* **3. transplanter, greffer** ► to transfer an organ or body part from one person to another by a surgical operation : *The doctor transplanted a new heart into the baby.* ▲ NOUN: *a kidney transplant.*

trans-port [tranz-PORT] VERB, transported, transporting. **transporter** ► to bring or carry someone or something from one place to another : *The truck transported apples from the Okanagan Valley to Edmonton.* ▲ [TRANZ-port] NOUN, transports. **1. transport** ► the act or fact of transporting : *My only means of transport is my bicycle.* **2. transport** ► a ship, truck, or airplane used to carry soldiers or military supplies.

trans-por-ta-tion [TRANZ-pur-TAY-shun] NOUN. **transport** ► the fact of moving people or things from one place to another : *Cars, trains, planes, and horses are all forms of transportation.* ⌂ p. 1155.

trap [trap] NOUN, traps. **1. piège** ► a device used to catch and hold a wild animal : *a mousetrap.* **2. piège** ► a trick used to catch someone by surprise : *The police set a trap to catch the thief.* ▲ VERB, trapped, trapping. **piéger, prendre au piège** ► to catch in a trap.

trap door trappe ► a small door that is set in a ceiling, floor, or roof and that is slid or lifted to open.

tra-peze [truh-PEEZ] NOUN, trapezes. **trapèze** ► a strong, short bar hung between two ropes. Acrobats swing on the trapeze in circus acts.

trap-e-zoid [TRAP-uh-zoyd] NOUN, trapezoids. **trapèze** ► a flat, geometric figure having four sides, with only two sides being parallel to each other.

trap-per [TRAP-ur] NOUN, trappers. **trappeur (-euse)** ► a person who uses traps, especially someone who catches wild animals for their fur.

trash [trash] NOUN. **ordures** ► things that are of no use and are to be thrown away ; garbage ; rubbish.

trau-ma [TROM-uh] NOUN, traumas. **traumatisme** ► a serious physical injury or mental shock : *A concussion is usually caused by severe trauma to the head.* ■ **traumatic,** ADJECTIVE. **traumatisant (-ante), traumatique** ► being or causing a great injury or shock.

trav-el [TRAV-ul] VERB, travelled, travelling. (also traveled, traveling) **1. voyager** ► to go from one place to another for business or pleasure : *I travelled to India to see my grandparents.* **2. se déplacer, parcourir, faire le tour** ► to pass or move from one point to another : *The news about the fire travelled quickly around school.* ■ **traveller,** NOUN. ► **voyageur (-euse).** ⌂ p. 1155. ✎ p. 628.

trapezes

trapeze acrobat

trav-erse [TRAV-urce *or* truh-VURCE] VERB, traversed, traversing. **traverser, balayer** ► to pass or go over or through : *to traverse a ski slope.*

trawl [trol] NOUN, trawls. **chalut** ► a long fishing line with many hooks, or a net that is dragged

---

✐ **Word Builder**

Travel, migrate, and ***journey*** all describe the movement of people or animals from one place to another. ***Travel*** often means to take a trip to a place where a person does not live : *They travelled to Quebec City to visit all the historical sites.* ***Migrate*** suggests the movement of a large group of animals : *Each year Canada geese migrate south for winter.* ***Journey*** often means to travel by land over a great distance and for a long time : *Rick Hansen was successful in his journey around the world.*

slowly along an ocean or lake bottom to catch fish. ▲ VERB, trawled, trawling. **pêcher au chalut** ▶ to fish with a trawl. **Note.** A boat used to fish in this way is a trawler. ☞ **p. 395.**

tray [tray] NOUN, trays. **plateau (-eaux)** ▶ a flat, shallow dish with a small rim, used for carrying or displaying things : *I carried my lunch on a tray.*

treach·er·ous [TRECH-ur-us] ADJECTIVE. **1. traître (-resse), déloyal (-ale, -aux), perfide** ▶ not to be trusted or relied on ; disloyal : *The treacherous double agent was feeding false information to both sides.* **dangereux (-euse), traître (-resse)** ▶ The fact of being treacherous is treachery. **2. traître (-esse), perfide, dangereux (-euse)** ▶ not as safe as it appears to be ; dangerous : *Tides can be treacherous to swimmers.* ■ **treacherously,** ADVERB. ▶ **traîtreusement, dangereusement.**

tread [tred] VERB, trod, trodden or trod, treading. **marcher sur** ▶ to walk on, along, or over something, especially in a rough way : *Carol trod carefully through the flower garden to get her ball.* ▲ NOUN, treads. **1. pas, bruit de pas** ▶ the act or sound of walking. **2. bande de roulement, semelle** ▶ the grooved surface of a tire or the bottom of the shoe. **3. giron** ▶ the top surface of a step on a staircase.

trea·son [TREE-zun] NOUN. **trahison** ▶ the crime of betraying one's country by aiding its enemies. Acts of treason can include fighting against one's own country in wartime, or giving away a country's military secrets.

treas·ure [TREZH ur] NOUN, treasures. **1. trésor** ▶ wealth such as gold, silver, jewels, and so on, stored away or kept hidden : *treasures of King Tut's tomb.* **2. trésor** ▶ anything that is very precious or valuable : *"Michael and I pored over the treasures in his rusty old tackle box."* (Julie Lawson) ▲ VERB, treasured, treasuring. **tenir à, attacher une grande valeur à, garder précieusement** ▶ to value highly ; prize : *Nila treasures the ring her parents gave her.*

treas·ur·er [TREZH-ur-ur] NOUN, treasurers. **trésorier (-ière)** ▶ the person who is responsible for taking care of the money that belongs to a business, club, government, or other organization.

treas·ur·y [TREZH-ur-ee] NOUN, treasuries. **1. trésorerie** ▶ the money belonging to a business, government, or other organization. **2. Treasury. le Trésor, ministère des Finances** ▶ a government department that is in charge of manufacturing, collecting, and managing the country's money.

treat [treet] VERB, treated, treating. **1. traiter** ▶ to act or deal with in a particular way : *"In a short time he became quite fond of her and treated her like a daughter."* (Roger Lancelyn Green) **2. traiter, soigner** ▶ to give medical care or treatment : *Doctors treat many people every day.* **3. offrir, payer** ▶ to pay for the food or entertainment of another person : *Let me treat you to an ice-cream cone.* **4. traiter** ▶ to expose to a chemical or physical process to improve or change : *Dad treated the new deck with a preservative.* ▲ NOUN, treats. **plaisir, gâterie** ▶ anything that is a special or unexpected pleasure : *"Eagles, gulls, and crows lined the trees, waiting for a chance to pluck a tasty treat from the shallow waters."* (Sheryl McFarlane) SYN: handle, attend, manage, behave toward.

treat·ment [TREET-munt] NOUN, treatments. **traitement, soin, accueil** ▶ the fact or way of treating a person or thing : *I'll be back to this hotel—the treatment is wonderful!*

treat·y [TREE-tee] NOUN, treaties. **traité** ▶ a formal agreement made between two or more groups or countries : *The Treaty of Versailles in 1919 officially ended World War I.*

tree [tree] NOUN, trees. **arbre** ▶ a tall, woody plant that has a main stem or trunk from which branches and leaves or needles grow. ☞ **p. 1098.** ☞ **p. 114, 253-255.**

trek [trek] NOUN, treks. **randonnée, expédition** ▶ a long, difficult journey : *Many pioneers made the long trek across the continent.* ▲ VERB, trekked, trekking. **faire du trekking, faire de la randonnée** ▶ to make a long, difficult journey : *The nomads trekked across the Sahara desert on their camels.*

trel·lis [TREL-is] NOUN, trellises. **treillis** ▶ a framework of wood or other material for plants to grow on.

trem·ble [TREM-bul] VERB, trembled, trembling. **1. trembler, frémir, frissonner** ▶ to shake or shiver without control : *The thunder made me tremble.* **2. trembler, secouer** ▶ to move quickly back and forth or shake : *The whole earth seemed to tremble when the volcano erupted.*

tre·men·dous [tuh-MEN-dus] ADJECTIVE. **énorme, prodigieux (-ieuse)** ▶ very large, strong, or great : *The fireworks lit the sky with a tremendous shower of coloured lights.* ■ **tremendously,** ADVERB. ▶ **énormément, prodigieusement.**

tre·mor [TREM-ur] NOUN, tremors. **tremblement, secousse** ▶ a shaking or vibrating movement : *an earthquake tremor.*

trench [trench] NOUN, trenches. **1. tranchée** ▶ a long, narrow ditch : *Workers dug a trench to hold the pipes for the new house.* **2. tranchée** ▶ a long ditch with earth piled high on one side, dug by soldiers for protection from enemy fire. **3. fosse** ▶ a long, narrow depression in the ocean floor.

trend [trend] NOUN, trends. **tendance** ▶ a particular direction or course that is being followed, as by a group of people : *Unfortunately, the trend*

in movies seems to be toward more violence.
SYN : tendency, direction, fad, fashion.

trend-y [TREN-dee] ADJECTIVE. *Informal.* trendier, trendiest. **à la mode ▸** keeping up with or influenced by the latest styles : *a trendy hairstyle.*

tres-pass [TRES-pus *or* TRES-pas] VERB, trespassed, trespassing. **s'introduire sans permission, violer la propriété ▸** to break the law by entering or passing through someone else's property without permission. **Note.** A person who commits the crime of trespassing is a trespasser. ▲ NOUN, trespasses. **1. violation de propriété, atteinte (aux droits de) ▸** in law, the act of trespassing. **2. offense, péché ▸** an older word for a sin or a wrong act.

tres-tle [TRES-ul] NOUN, trestles. **tréteau (-eaux) ▸** the framework that supports a bridge or other structure.

tri- PREFIX. three : *tricycle; triangle.*

tri-al [TRY-ul] NOUN, trials. **1. procès, jugement ▸** the process of hearing and judging evidence in a court of law, to determine if a person is guilty of a crime, if someone should pay damages to another, and so on. **2. épreuve, souci ▸** something that causes suffering or is difficult to deal with : *The cast on my right arm made writing a trial.* **3. essai ▸** any test or study to determine the value or quality of a thing : *a trial of a new engine.*

tri-an-gle [TRY-ang-gul] NOUN, triangles. **1. triangle ▸** a figure having three sides and three angles, like this : ▲. **2. triangle ▸** a musical instrument made from a bent metal bar in the shape of a triangle. A triangle is struck with a small stick to make a bell-like sound. ◉ **p. 538.**

tri-an-gu-lar [try-ANG-gyuh-lur] ADJECTIVE. **triangulaire ▸** being or having to do with a triangle.

tri-bal [TRY-bul] ADJECTIVE. **tribal (-ale, aux) ▸** having to do with tribes or a specific tribe : *tribal customs and beliefs.*

tribe [tribe] NOUN, tribes. **tribu ▸** a group of peole who live in the same area and have certain things in common, such as the same language, customs, and religious beliefs.

trib-u-tar-y [TRIB-yuh-TAIR-ee] NOUN, tributaries. **affluent ▸** a river or stream that flows into and joins a larger river.

trib-ute [TRIB-yoot] NOUN, tributes. **1. hommage ▸** an act done to show respect or to honour someone : *The award paid tribute to all the work Lucien had done for others.* **2. tribut ▸** a forced payment : *For many years, countries in the Middle East had to pay taxes as tribute to the Roman Empire.*

trick [trik] VERB, tricked, tricking. **tromper, attraper, tricher ▸** to deceive someone with a trick ; fool or cheat : *Del tricked her parents into thinking she was asleep.* ▲ NOUN, tricks. **1. ruse, supercherie ▸** something done to fool or cheat

a person : *Hiding my homework is a nasty trick.* **2. tour ▸** an act that shows cleverness or skill ; a stunt : *My dog can do many tricks, including walking on his hind legs.* **Note.** The use of tricks to fool or cheat someone is trickery. SYN : deceive, trick, fool, hoax, dupe, betray. 🖉 **p. 96.**

trick-le [TRIK-ul] VERB, trickled, trickling. **1. couler doucement, dégouliner ▸** to flow or fall in drops or in a thin, slow, stream : *"A tear or two trickled down his cheek."* (Lewis Carroll) **2. arriver (s'éloigner) peu à peu ▸** to move slowly, a little at a time : *One by one, the runners trickled across the finish line.* ▲ NOUN, trickles. **filet ▸** a slow, thin stream : *A tiny trickle of water seeped out of the rock.*

trick-y [TRIK-ee] ADJECTIVE. trickier, trickiest. **1. rusé (-ée), sournois (-oise), espiègle ▸** using tricks to fool or deceive ; cunning ; sly : *a tricky plan.* **2. difficile ▸** requiring careful handling or skill : *Steering a boat through the narrow, rocky channel can be very tricky.*

tri-cy-cle [TRY-sik-ul] NOUN, tricycles. **tricycle ▸** a vehicle that has three wheels and is usually moved by pedals. Tricycles are easier for young children to learn to ride than bicycles.

tried [tride] VERB. a past form of try.

tri-fle [TRY-ful] NOUN, trifles. **1. bagatelle ▸** something of little value or importance ; a small amount : *One rainy day on our trip is a trifle when all the other days were sunny.* **2. diplomate ▸** a dessert made of cake, custard, and jam. ▲ VERB, trifled, trifling. **se jouer de, traiter à la légère ▸** to play with or treat something in a careless or joking way : *Don't trifle with me ; I'm serious !*

trig-ger [TRIG-ur] NOUN, triggers. **détente, gâchette ▸** a small lever pressed or pulled by the finger to fire a gun. ▲ VERB, triggered, triggering. **déclencher, provoquer ▸** to cause or start something : *to trigger a chain reaction.*

trig-o-nom-e-try [TRIG-uh-NOM-uh-tree] NOUN. **trigonométrie ▸** a branch of mathematics that deals with the relations of the sides and angles of triangles.

tril-lion [TRIL-yun] NOUN, trillions. **billion ▸** a thousand billion ; 1 000 000 000 000.

tril-o-gy [TRIL-uh-jee] NOUN, trilogies. **trilogie ▸** a group of three novels, plays, or other works, each complete in itself but related to the others.

trim [trim] VERB, trimmed, trimming. **1. tailler ▸** to make something neat by cutting or chopping : *to trim the branches off a bush.* **2. décorer, orner ▸** to decorate : *to trim a tree with lights.* ▲ NOUN. **1. forme ▸** the state of being in good physical shape or condition. **2.** (*plural,* trims) **coupe d'entretien, finitions, garniture ▸** something used to decorate or finish. ▲ ADJECTIVE, trimmer, trimmest. **net (nette), soigné (-ée),**

en forme ▸ in good condition or shape; neat : *Lucia runs to stay fit and trim.*

trim-ming [TRIM-ing] NOUN, trimmings. **1. décoration, garniture** ▸ something used as a decoration or ornament. **2.** (plural, trims) trimmings. **garniture, accompagnement** ▸ things that usually go along with something else : *a steak dinner with all the trimmings.* **3. chutes** ▸ cuttings from something that has been trimmed : *trimmings from a rose bush.*

trin-ket [TRINK-it] NOUN, trinkets. **bibelot, babiole, colifichet** ▸ a small ornament, toy, or piece of inexpensive jewellery.

tri-o [TREE-oh] NOUN, trios. **trio** ▸ a group of three, especially three musicians or singers who perform together.

trip [trip] NOUN, trips. **voyage, excursion** ▸ the act of travelling from one place to another, as in a car, train, bus, plane, and so on : *The Kon-Tiki made the trip across the Pacific in 101 days.* ▲ VERB, tripped, tripping. **1. trébucher** ▸ to catch the foot and lose one's balance; fall or almost fall : *I tripped over the rug and fell with a thud.* **2. marcher d'un pas léger** ▸ to walk with quick, light steps. ☞ **p. 1149.**

trip up induire en erreur ▸ to cause to make a mistake : *The last question tripped me up.* SYN : journey, voyage, trek, tour, expedition.

tripe [tripe] NOUN. **1. tripes** ▸ the walls of the stomach of cattle used as food. **2.** *Informal.* **bêtises, inepties** ▸ something bad or useless : *She thought her story was quite good, but now she thinks it is tripe.*

tri-ple [TRIP-ul] ADJECTIVE. **1. triple** ▸ having three parts : *a triple-scoop ice-cream cone.* **2. triple** ▸ three times as much or as many : *The last question is worth triple the points of the other questions.* ▲ NOUN, triples. **triple, coup à trois buts** ▸ a series or combination of three, especially a hit in baseball by which the batter reaches third base. ▲ VERB, tripled, tripling. **tripler** ▸ to make or become three times as much : *Sales have tripled since the beginning of summer.*

trip-let [TRIP-lit] NOUN, triplets. **1. triplés (-ées)** ▸ one of three children born to the same mother at the same time. **2. tercet** ▸ any group of three, such as three lines of poetry.

tri-pod [TRY-pod] NOUN, tripods. **trépied** ▸ a three-legged support or stand used for holding a camera or telescope steady.

tri-umph [TRY-umf] VERB, triumphed, triumphing. **triompher (de)** ▸ to win or gain victory : *Because of his determination, runner Terry Fox triumphed over the limitations of only having one leg.* ▲ NOUN, triumphs. **triomphe, victoire** ▸ a great victory : *The winning team ran off the field cheering in triumph.*

tri-um-phant [try-UM-funt] ADJECTIVE. **triomphal (-ale, -aux), triomphant (-ante), victorieux (-leuse)** ▸ showing or being a triumph : *the triumphant team.* ■ **triumphantly,** ADVERB. ▸ **triomphalement.**

triv-i-al [TRIV-ee-ul] ADJECTIVE. **insignifiant (-ante), frivole** ▸ not important; minor; insignificant : *Shashi always focuses on trivial details, such as how many spaces to indent a paragraph.* ■ **trivia,** PLURAL NOUN. **1. broutilles, bagatelles, futilités** ▸ things that are not important. **2. jeu-questionnaire** ▸ a quiz or game of short factual questions about details of history, the arts, and so on.

trod [trod] VERB. a past form of tread.

trod-den [TROD-un] VERB. a past form of tread.

troll[1] [trole] VERB, trolled, trolling. **pêcher à la cuiller** ▸ to fish by moving a line and hook, as from a slow-moving boat.

troll[2] NOUN, trolls. **troll** ▸ in folk tales, a dwarf or giant that lives underground, under a bridge, or in a cave or hill.

trol-ley [TROL-ee] NOUN, trolleys. **1. caténaire** ▸ a small wheel that moves along an overhead electrical wire to run a streetcar, train, or bus. **2.** (also trolley car) **tramway** ▸ an electric streetcar that gets its power from a trolley.

trom-bone [trom-BONE *or* TROM-bone] NOUN, trombones. **trombone** ▸ a brass musical instrument made up of two long U-shaped tubes that are connected. The sound is changed by moving a sliding piece back and forth. ☞ **p. 539.**

troop [troop] NOUN, troops. **1. groupe, bande** ▸ a group or gathering of people doing something together : *A troop of children played ball in the park.* **2. troupes. escadron, troupes** ▸ a group of soldiers; a military unit, such as a unit of cavalry. ▲ VERB, trooped, trooping. **aller en groupe, (s') attrouper** ▸ to march or walk in a group : *The students trooped from the gym back to their classroom.* ■ **trooper,** NOUN. **agent (-ente) de la police d'État, soldat (de cavalerie)** ▸ a mounted police officer.

tro-phy [TROH-fee] NOUN, trophies. **trophée** ▸ a small statue, cup, or other object awarded to someone for winning a contest or sports event.

trop-i-cal [TROP-ih-kul] ADJECTIVE. **tropical (-ale, aux)** ▸ having to do with or found in the tropics : *Parrots live mainly in tropical rain forests.* ☞ **p. 247.**

trop-ics [TROP-iks] PLURAL NOUN. **tropiques** ▸ the region of the earth that lies on or near the equator. The sun is closest to the equator, so areas in the tropics have hot or warm weather almost all the time.

trot [trot] NOUN, trots. **trot** ▸ a movement of a four-legged animal, between a walk and a run. When a horse moves at a trot, it lifts one front foot and the opposite rear foot off the ground at the same time. ▲ VERB, trotted, trotting. **1. trotter, faire trotter ▶** of an animal or a rider, to move or go at a trot. **2. aller au trot, marcher d'un pas pressé ▶** to move more quickly than walking : *We trotted around the park.*

trou‑ble [TRUB‑ul] NOUN, troubles. **1. problème, difficulté, ennui ▶** something that causes danger, suffering, worry, and so on ; a problem or difficulty : "*Someone has given him another piano, and there was a lot of trouble getting it up the stairs.*" (Barbara Nichol) **2. peine ▶** extra effort or work : *Please don't go to a lot of trouble ; sandwiches are fine.* **3. maladie ▶** an illness or ailment : *heart trouble.* ▲ VERB, troubled, troubling. **1. préoccuper, troubler, agiter ▶** to cause someone to be worried, anxious, upset, and so on ; disturb ; distress : *Thoughts of her unfinished essay troubled Marina.* **2. déranger ▶** to cause someone to do extra work : *Can I trouble you to carry this box for me?* **3. faire souffrir ▶** to cause pain or illness : *Matt's injured knee keeps troubling him.* 🖉 p. 639.

trou‑ble‑some [TRUB‑ul‑sum] ADJECTIVE. **pénible, gênant (‑ante), incommodant (‑ante) ▶** causing trouble ; difficult or annoying : *There are some troublesome weeds that I can't get rid of.*

trough [trof] NOUN, troughs. **1. auge ▶** a long, narrow box or container used for feeding or watering farm animals. **2. dépression ▶** any long, narrow, hollow place like this. 👁 p. 114.

troupe [troop] NOUN, troupes. **troupe ▶** a group of actors or other performers.

trou‑sers [TROW‑zurz] PLURAL NOUN. **pantalon ▶** a piece of clothing with two legs that covers the body from the waist to the ankles ; pants ; slacks.

trout [trowt] NOUN, trout or trouts. **truite ▶** any of several kinds of fish that live in cool, clear, fresh water, such as the brook trout, lake trout, or brown trout. Trout are often eaten as food and are a very popular game fish. 👁 p. 106‑107.

trout

tru‑ant [TROO‑unt] ADJECTIVE. **absentéiste, qui fait l'école buissonnière ▶** of a student, absent from school without permission. ▲ NOUN, truants. **1. élève absent (‑ente) sans autorisation ▶** a student who is absent from school without

permission. **2. vagabond (‑onde) ; élève absentéiste ▶** a person who fails to do his work or duty. **Note.** The act or fact of being a truant is truancy.

truce [trooce] NOUN, truces. **trêve ▶** a time when fighting is stopped ; a break in a battle or war : *The warring sides declared a truce.* SYN : pause, rest, break, peace.

truck [truk] NOUN, trucks. **1. camion ▶** a motor vehicle that is larger, heavier, and more strongly built than a car, and that is used mainly for carrying goods. **Note.** There are many types of trucks, from light pickup trucks that carry loads of one or two tonnes, to huge tractor‑trailer trucks carrying 40 tonnes or more. **2.** (also hand truck) **diable ▶** a low frame or vehicle having wheels at one end and a handle at the other, used for moving heavy objects by hand, such as a refrigerator or heavy boxes. ▲ VERB, trucked, trucking. **(faire) transporter par camion, camionner ▶** to drive a truck or carry something on a truck : *The farmers trucked their crops to local markets.* **Note.** A person whose work is driving a truck is a trucker. 📖 p. 1156.

trudge [truj] VERB, trudged, trudging. **marcher péniblement, se traîner ▶** to walk in a slow, tired way : *We trudged up the hill carrying our skis.* ▲ NOUN, trudges : *It's a long trudge home through the woods.*

true [troo] ADJECTIVE, truer, truest. **1. vrai (vraie), exact (‑acte), véridique ▶** agreeing with the facts ; not false or made up : *The story about the explosion is true ; I saw it too.* **2. véritable, authentique ▶** actually being what it is called ; genuine ; authentic : *a true astronaut.* **3. fidèle à ▶** faithful and loyal : *She was true to her promise and was home before dinner.* ▲ ADVERB. **vraiment, véritablement ▶** in a true way ; truly.

come true se réaliser ▶ to happen just as was dreamed, hoped, expected, and so on. SYN : certain, correct, actual, accurate, authentic.

tru‑ly [TROO‑lee] ADVERB. **1. vraiment, franchement, réellement ▶** in a true way ; sincerely : *Tell me if you truly like this painting.* **2. effectivement, bien ▶** in fact ; indeed : *This sweater is truly mine.*

trum‑pet [TRUM‑pit] NOUN, trumpets. **1. trompette ▶** a brass musical instrument, made up of a long tube that is curved into a loop and has a wide opening at one end. It is played by blowing into a mouthpiece at the other end and pressing down on valves on top of the tube. **2. cornet, barrissement ▶** something that is shaped like a trumpet or that makes such a sound. ▲ VERB, trumpeted, trumpeting. **trompeter ▶** to blow a trumpet or make a sound like that of a trumpet : *The winning team trumpeted their victory with loud shouts from the bus.* 👁 p. 539.

trunk [trunk] NOUN, trunks. **1. tronc ▶** the thick main stem of a tree, from which the branches and roots grow. **2. tronc ▶** the part of the human body from which the head, arms, and legs extend. **3. coffre, malle ▶** a large, strong box used to store clothes and belongings, or carry them for travel. **4. coffre ▶** an enclosed area in a car, usually at the rear, for carrying or storing things. **5. trompe ▶** the long, flexible nose part of an elephant, used for drawing in air, food, and water, or for grasping objects. **6. trunks. short, maillot de bain ▶** shorts worn by swimmers, boxers, and so on : *swimming trunks.* 👁 **p. 253.**

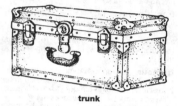

trunk

trust [trust] VERB, trusted, trusting. **1. avoir confiance (en) ▶** to believe that someone is honest, fair, reliable, and so on; have confidence in : *Jerry knew Eva was a good driver, so he trusted her with his car.* **2. faire confiance, se fier à ▶** to believe in the strength or soundness of something; depend on : *I trust the bridge to hold us all.* **3. être certain (-aine), être sûr (sûre), espérer ▶** to feel sure of; expect : *I trust you all know what to do in case of a fire.* **Note.** Often used as an adjective : *a trusted friend.* ▲ NOUN. **1. confiance ▶** the act or fact of trusting. **Note.** A person, animal, or thing who deserves trust is trustworthy. **2.** (*plural*, **trusts**) **(en) fiducie ▶** property or money held and managed by one person or group for the benefit of another. **Note.** A trust fund is money or property held in this way. **3. trust ▶** an agreement by which a group of different businesses or companies combine to control how much of a product is available and how much it costs. Trusts of this type are often illegal because they eliminate competition and drive up prices. SYN: believe, rely on, credit, put hope in.

trus-tee [trus-TEE] NOUN, trustees. **1. fiduciaire, curateur (-trice), fidéicommissaire ▶** a person who has the legal authority to manage the property of another. **2. administrateur (-trice), syndic ▶** one of a group of people who manage the affairs of a school district, church, or other such organization.

truth [trooth] NOUN, truths. **1. vérité ▶** something that agrees with the facts; something that is true : *A witness in court must swear to tell the truth.* **2. vérité ▶** the fact or quality of being true : *"The*

truth of the matter was that he was already extremely hungry." (Adèle Geras)

truth-ful [TROOTH-ful] ADJECTIVE. **franc (franche), sincère, véridique ▶** telling the truth, or likely to tell the truth; honest : *The article takes an honest, truthful look at life in the city.* ∎ **truthfully,** ADVERB. **▶ franchement, sincèrement.** ∎ **truthfulness,** NOUN. **▶ véracité.**

try [try] VERB, tried, trying. **1. essayer, tenter, tâcher ▶** to work toward doing something; make an effort : *She is trying to get better grades this year and is studying hard.* **2. essayer ▶** to use something in order to test its quality or effect : *Let's try arranging the furniture.* **3. mettre à l'épreuve, éprouver ▶** to strain a person's nerves, patience, energy, and so on : *Baby-sitting four children tried my patience.* **Note.** Also used as an adjective : *a trying experience.* **4. juger ▶** to examine a case in a court of law; put a person on trial. **5. try on. essayer ▶** to put on clothing to see how it looks or fits. ▲ NOUN, tries. **essai, tentative ▶** an attempt to do something; an effort : *In volleyball, you get three tries to get the ball over the net.* SYN: attempt, tackle, undertake, endeavour, test.

try-out [TRY-owt] NOUN, tryouts. **mise à essai ▶** a test to see how well a person can do something : *tryouts for the basketball team.* **Note.** Also used as a VERB : *Do you want to try out for the school play?*

T-shirt [TEE SHURT] NOUN, T-shirts. **tee-shirt, gaminet ▶** a light shirt with short sleeves, worn under other clothes or as an outer shirt.

Tsim-shi-an [TSIM-shuh-un *or* TSIM-shan *or* TSIM-shun] NOUN, Tsimshian or Tsimshians. **1. Tsimshian ▶** an Aboriginal people living on the western coast of British Columbia. **2. tsimshian ▶** the group of languages spoken by these people.

tub [tub] NOUN, tubs. **1. baignoire ▶** a large, open container for taking a bath; a bathtub. **2. contenant ▶** a small, round container used to keep or serve butter or other such foods.

tu-ba [TOO-buh] NOUN, tubas. **tuba ▶** a very large brass musical instrument with a deep tone. 👁 **p. 539.**

tube [toob] NOUN, tubes. **1. tube, tuyau (-aux) à ▶** a hollow piece of rubber, plastic, glass, or metal that is shaped like a long pipe. **2. tube ▶** any long, tubelike part or organ of the body : *bronchial tubes.* **3. tube ▶** a container that is long and narrow and must be squeezed to get its contents out : *a tube of toothpaste.* **4. métro ▶** an underground or underwater tunnel through which a train or subway runs.

tu-ber-cu-lo-sis [tuh-BUR-kyuh-LOH-sis] NOUN. **tuberculose ▶** a serious disease that affects the lungs or other parts of the body. **Note.** Also called **TB** or (formerly) **consumption.** It is caused by bacteria that can be passed from one person to another. Modern drugs can now prevent and treat this disease, but it is still a threat in some places.

tuck [tuk] VERB, tucked, tucking. **1. rentrer ▸** to fold or push the ends or edges of something into place : *Frieda stopped to tuck her scarf more securely into her coat.* **2. border ▸** to wrap or cover a person snugly in bed : *Ben read his sister a story and then tucked her into bed.* **3. ranger ▸** to hide or put into a safe or covered space : *She tucked the money into her wallet.* ▲ NOUN, tucks. **rempli ▸** a fold of cloth that is sewn into a piece of clothing as a decoration or to make it fit better.

Tues·day [TOOZ-day *or* TOOZ-dee] NOUN, Tuesdays. **mardi ▸** the day after Monday and before Wednesday.

tuft [tuft] NOUN, tufts. **touffe ▸** a bunch of feathers, hair, grass, threads, or other material growing or fastened together at one end and loose at the other.

tug [tug] VERB, tugged, tugging. **tirer (sur) ▸** to give a hard pull on something : *The little girl tugged on her mother's sleeve.* ▲ NOUN, tugs. **1. (petit) coup, traction ▸** a give a hard pull : *to tug at a door that is stuck.* **2. remorqueur ▸** a tugboat. SYN: tow, pull, jerk, yank, haul.

tug·boat [TUG-bote] NOUN, tugboats. **remorqueur ▸** a small but powerful boat that pushes or pulls larger boats or ships, or barges loaded with cargo. **Note.** This boat is also called a tug or a towboat. ☞ p. 395.

tugboat

tu·i·tion [too-ISH-un] NOUN. **frais de scolarité ▸** the money that is paid for a student's instruction at a university or private school.

tu·lip [TOO-lip] NOUN, tulips. **tulipe ▸** a cup-shaped flower with thick petals. Each flower grows at the end of a long stem that comes out of the ground from a bulb. A tulip may be one of many bright colours, such as red, yellow, or pink.

tum·ble [TUM-bul] VERB, tumbled, tumbling. **1. faire une chute, tomber, culbuter, dégringoler ▸** to lose one's balance and fall or roll over in an awkward way : *"Sometimes in winter when the trails were rough, she would slip and tumble off the horse's back into the snow."*

(Marilynn Reynolds) **2. se bousculer ▸** to move or go in a confused or disorganized way : *He spoke so fast that his words tumbled over one another.* **3. faire des culbutes, faire des cabrioles ▸** to do gymnastic or acrobatic exercises, such as flips or somersaults. ▲ NOUN, tumbles. **chute ▸** a fall : *The skater took a tumble on the ice.* SYN: fall, topple, descend, plunge.

tum·bler [TUM-blur] NOUN, tumblers. **1. acrobate, tambour rotatif ▸** a person or thing that tumbles. **2. gorge (de serrure) ▸** a part inside a lock that holds the bolt until it is lifted by a key. **3. verre (droit), gobelet ▸** a drinking glass that has no handle or stem.

tum·ble·weed [TUM-bul-WEED] NOUN, tumbleweeds or tumbleweed. **amarante ▸** any of several plants growing in dry areas. The branches of a tumbleweed break off from their roots and are rolled along by the wind, scattering seeds as they go.

tu·mour [TOO-mur] NOUN, tumours. (also tumor) **tumeur ▸** a swelling or abnormal growth in the body. **Note.** A benign tumour [buh-nine] is generally not harmful and usually does not spread to other parts of the body. A malignant tumour [muh-LIG-nunt] is dangerous and can spread elsewhere in the body, destroying other tissue.

tu·mult [TOO-mult] NOUN. **tumulte, vacarme ▸** a loud noise or disturbance; confusion and excitement : *He was awakened during the night by the thunderous tumult of the storm.* ■ **tumultuous,** ADJECTIVE. ▸ **tumultueux (-euse).** *A tumultuous yell went up from the crowd as the winning goal was scored.*

tu·na [TOO-nuh] NOUN, tuna or tunas. **thon ▸** any of several kinds of large ocean fish found in warm seas throughout the world. Tuna are caught in large numbers for use as food. ☞ p. 107.

tun·dra [TUN-druh] NOUN, tundras. **toundra ▸** a large, flat area with no trees, found in arctic regions. **Note.** Below the surface of the ground, tundra has a layer of soil that is always frozen. This soil layer is called permafrost. ☞ p. 247.

tune [toon] NOUN, tunes. **air ▸** the series of notes that make up a melody or piece of music : *What's the tune to that song?* ▲ VERB, tuned, tuning. **1. accorder ▸** to put into tune; fix the pitch of : *to tune a piano.* **2. (also tune up) mettre au point, régler ▸** to put into better working order; adjust the parts of : *A mechanic tuned up the engine.* **Note.** Also used as a NOUN: *Cars need a regular tuneup.* **3. régler, mettre au point ▸** to adjust a radio or television set so as to get a clearer sound or picture, or bring in a certain station.

in (out) of tune a. **accordé (-ée), désaccordé (-ée), juste, faux (fausse) ▸** at (not at) the correct musical pitch or key. b. **en accord, en désaccord ▸** in agreement or sympathy.

tun-er [TOO-nur] NOUN, tuners. **1. syntonisateur, syntoniseur ▸** the part of a radio or television set that receives signals and changes them to sound or pictures. **2. accordeur (-euse) ▸** a person who tunes a musical instrument to the proper pitch : *a piano tuner.*

tu-nic [TOO-nik] NOUN, tunics. **1. tunique ▸** a piece of clothing reaching from the shoulders to the knees, somewhat like a long shirt. Tunics were worn by both men and women in ancient Greece and Rome. **2. tunique ▸** a modern item of clothing that looks something like this, such as a short, close-fitting jacket worn as part of a military uniform.

tuning fork diapason ▸ a U-shaped metal object that always sounds the same tone when struck, used as a guide in tuning a musical instrument.

tun-nel [TUN-ul] NOUN, tunnels. **tunnel, galerie ▸** a long, narrow passageway under the ground or the water : *Prairie dogs dig a network of underground tunnels.* ▲ VERB, tunnelled, tunnelling. (also tunneled, tunneling) **creuser un tunnel, percer une galerie ▸** to dig through or under something to make a tunnel or something shaped like a tunnel : *"There were spring storms, and sometimes tornadoes with thin dark clouds tunnelling down from the sky."* (Patricia MacLachlan)

tuque [tuke] NOUN, tuques. (also toque) **tuque ▸** a knitted hat or cap.

tur-ban [TUR-bun] NOUN, turbans. **turban ▸** a covering for the head made of a long scarf that is wound around and around, worn especially by Muslim and Sikh men.

tur-bine [TUR-bine] NOUN, turbines. **turbine ▸** a machine with blades that are turned by the force of moving air, steam, water, and so on. Turbines are used to power electric generators, water pumps, jet engines, and other devices. 👁 **p. 400.**

tur-bu-lent [TUR-byuh-lunt] ADJECTIVE. **agité (-ée), turbulent (-ente) ▸** causing or full of disorder, violence, or confusion : *World War II was a turbulent period in history.* **Note.** The state of being turbulent is turbulence : *The pilot blamed the bumpy flight on air turbulence.*

turf [turf] NOUN. **1. tourbe ▸** the top layer of soil from which grasses and small plants grow. **2.** (also **the turf**) **piste de course hippique, turf ▸** a grass course over which horses race, or the sport of horse racing itself. **3.** *Informal.* **turf, piste ▸** an area controlled by a certain person or group : *My brother considers the basement his turf.*

tur-key [TUR-kee] NOUN, turkeys. **dindon, dinde ▸** a large reddish-brown bird with a spreading tail, a long neck, and a head with no feathers. The turkey is a North American bird that is found in the wild and also raised for food.

tur-moil [TUR-moyl] NOUN. **agitation, trouble, émoi ▸** great disorder or confusion : *"As they rode, Wu saw the countryside in turmoil. Soldiers were everywhere, farms and homes were burning."* (David Day)

turn [turn] VERB, turned, turning. **1. tourner ▸** to move in a circle or part of a circle : *Bicycle wheels turn when you pedal.* **2. (se) tourner ▸** to move or go to a different direction or position : *When you get to the corner, turn right.* **3. augmenter, baisser ▸** to move or set a dial or other such control : *Please turn up the volume.* **4. devenir, (se) changer en ▸** to change the condition or form of : *When the sun sets, day turns into night.* **5. changer d'avis ▸** to change one's attitude or feelings : *At first I didn't like him, but his kindness turned me around.* **6. turn on (off). mettre en marche, allumer, éteindre ▸** to cause a machine or device to operate (stop operating). ▲ NOUN, turns. **1. tournant ▸** the act of turning : *A bicyclist should use hand signals when making a turn.* **2. (bonne) action ▸** an act or deed. **Note.** Usually used in the phrase **a good turn**. **3. tour ▸** a person's proper chance or time in a certain order : *After John takes a few more shots at the basket, it will be Riya's turn.* **Note.** Often used in the phrase **to take turns**.

turn out a. se rassembler ▸ to gather for a meeting or event. **Note.** Also used as a NOUN : *a big voter turnout.* **b. s'avérer, se révéler ▸** to end up; prove to be : *This game turned out to be fun.*

tur-nip [TUR-nip] NOUN, turnips. **navet ▸** a white or yellow rounded root that is cooked and eaten as a vegetable. A turnip plant has large, soft leaves and clusters of bright yellow flowers.

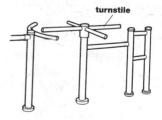

turnstile

turn-stile [TURN-stile] NOUN, turnstiles. **tourniquet ▸** a gate with horizontal bars that move around as people pass through one at a time, used at the entrance to a subway, stadium, or other public areas.

tur-pen-tine [TUR-pun-tine] NOUN. **térébenthine ▸** a strong-smelling, oily liquid that is made from the sap of certain pine trees.

635

Turpentine is used mainly to thin paints or to remove paint stains.

tur·quoise [TUR-koyz] NOUN, turquoises. **1. turquoise** ▶ a bright-blue to greenish-blue mineral that is valued as a gemstone. **2.** ▶ the colour of this stone. ▲ ADJECTIVE. **turquoise** ▶ having a turquoise colour; greenish-blue.

tur·ret [TUR-it] NOUN, turrets. **1. tourelle** ▶ a small tower that is built onto a house or other building. Castles of the Middle Ages often had turrets from which soldiers could fire down on the enemy. **2. tourelle** ▶ a structure on a military ship, tank, or aircraft that has cannons or guns mounted inside it.

tur·tle [TUR-tul] NOUN, turtles. **tortue de mer** ▶ one of a group of reptiles that have a low, flat body covered by a hard upper shell. A turtle can pull its head and limbs inside its shell for protection. **Note.** Turtles that live on land are usually called **tortoises.**

tur·tle·neck [TUR-tul-nek] NOUN, turtlenecks. **col roulé** ▶ a sweater or shirt that has a high, turned-down collar that fits closely around the neck.

Tus·ca·ror·a [tus-kuh-ROR-uh] NOUN, Tuscarora or Tuscaroras. **1. Tuscarora** ▶ an Aboriginal people who originally lived in North Carolina but now live in Ontario and New York. **2. tuscarora** ▶ The Iroquoian language of these people.

tusk [tusk] NOUN, tusks. **défense** ▶ a very long, thick, pointed tooth that grows out from the sides of some animals' mouths. Elephants, wild boars, and walruses have tusks.

tu·tor [TOO-tur or TYOO-tur] NOUN, tutors. **précepteur (-trice)** ▶ a teacher or helper who gives special lessons to a particular student or students outside of regular class time. ▲ VERB, tutored, tutoring. **donner des cours particuliers à** ▶ to act as a tutor : *Our math teacher says that she will tutor students who are having problems.*

tux·e·do [tuk-SEE-doh] NOUN, tuxedos or tuxedoes. **smoking** ▶ a man's dress jacket, usually all black, that is worn for serious formal occasions.

tweed [tweed] NOUN, tweed. **tweed** ▶ a rough cloth made of wool and woven with two or more colours of yarn.

twelve [twelv] NOUN, twelves; ADJECTIVE. **douze** ▶ one more than eleven; 12. ■ **twelfth,** ADJECTIVE; NOUN. ▶ **douzième.**

twen·ty [TWEN-tee] NOUN, twenties; ADJECTIVE. **vingt** ▶ two times ten; 20. ■ **twentieth,** ADJECTIVE; NOUN. ▶ **vingtième.**

twice [twice] ADVERB. **deux fois** ▶ two times : *You shouldn't make the same mistake twice!*

twig [twig] NOUN, twigs. **brindille** ▶ a very small branch growing from a tree or other woody plant. 👁 p. 253.

twi·light [TWY-lite] NOUN. **1. aube naissante** (morning), **crépuscule** (evening) ▶ a time just after sunset or just before sunrise when the sun's light is very soft and the sky appears somewhat grey. **2. déclin, crépuscule** ▶ a time when a period of success or glory begins to fade away, or of advancing age : *the twilight of a career.*

twin [twin] NOUN, twins. **1. jumeau (-elle, -eaux)** ▶ one of two children born to the same mother at the same time. **Note.** Identical twins **exacte réplique, copie conforme** ▶ are always the same sex and look very much alike. Fraternal twins may or may not be the same sex and don't always look alike. **2. jumeau (-elle, -eaux)** ▶ one of two things that are exactly alike. ▲ ADJECTIVE: *a twin brother.*

twine [twine] NOUN, twines. **ficelle** ▶ a strong cord or string made of two or more strands twisted together. ▲ VERB, twined, twining. **(s') enrouler, serpenter** ▶ to twist or wind : *"They began to grow tall and thin and to twine together like a rope."* (Hal Ober)

twinge [twinj] NOUN, twinges. **1. élancement** ▶ a sudden, sharp pain : *Daria felt a twinge of pain when she put weight on her swollen ankle.* ▲ VERB, twinged, twinging. **ressentir un élancement (de douleur)** ▶ to feel a twinge.

twin·kle [TWINK-ul] VERB, twinkled, twinkling. **scintiller** ▶ to shine or sparkle with short, quick flashes of light : *The stars twinkled in the dark night sky.* ▲ NOUN, twinkles. **scintillement** ▶ a flash or flicker of light. SYN: flicker, glimmer, glitter, sparkle.

twirl [twurl] VERB, twirled, twirling. **(faire) tournoyer, tortiller** ▶ to cause to turn quickly; spin : *Henry twirled me around the dance floor.* ■ **twirler,** NOUN. ▶ **majorette.**

twist [twist] VERB, twisted, twisting. **1. (s') entortiller, (s') enrouler** ▶ to turn around something; wind around : *George twisted the rope around the tree trunk and tied a knot.* **Note.** A tornado is called a **twister** because of the way it spins around as it moves. **2. zigzaguer, serpenter** ▶ to move in a curving or winding course : *The bumpy road twisted and turned as it climbed steadily up the mountain.* **3. tordre, tirebouchonner** ▶ to move out of shape; change from its normal shape or position : *"The girl beside Lin had taken off her mittens and was twisting them into tight blue balls."* (Barbara Novak) **4. (se) tordre, se fouler** ▶ to hurt a part of the body by turning it out of its normal position : *to twist one's ankle.* **5. déformer** ▶ to change the meaning or : *to twist someone's words to mean something else.* ▲ NOUN, twists. **1. tortillon, torsion, tour, tournant** ▶ something having a curled or bending shape. **2. tournure, coup de théâtre** ▶ an unexpected change or development : *Our trip took an unforeseen twist when our suitcases were lost.*

twitch [twich] VERB, twitched, twitching. **avoir un tic, se convulser, avoir un mouvement convulsif ▶** to move or pull with a sudden tug or jerk : *His lips twitched as he tried not to smile.* ▲ NOUN, twitches. **tic, coup sec, saccade▶** a sharp, sudden movement.

two [too] NOUN, twos; ADJECTIVE. **deux ▶** one more than one ; 2.

ty-coon [ty-KOON] NOUN, tycoons. **magnat ▶** a wealthy and powerful business leader.

ty-ing [TY-ing] VERB. a present form of tie.

type [tipe] NOUN, types. **1. type, sorte, genre ▶** a group or class of things that are alike in some way and different from others ; a kind : *My blood type is O positive.* **2. caractère ▶** a piece of film, metal, wood, and so on, with a letter, number, or design on it, for use in printing : *This sentence is in italic type.* **Note.** A particular style or design of type is called a typeface. ▲ VERB, typed, typing. **1. dactylographier ▶** to write using a typewriter : *I type my reports myself.* **2. classifier, catégoriser, cantonner ▶** to find out what group a person or thing belongs to ; consider to be of a certain type. SYN : kind, class, group, sort, category, variety.

type-wri-ter [TIPE-ry-tur] NOUN, typewriters. **machine à écrire ▶** a machine that prints letters on paper. It has a set of keys that are pressed down to cause type letters to mark the paper. **Note.** Something that is printed on a typewriter is typewritten. ☞ **p. 540.**

ty-phoid fever [TY-foyd] **fièvre typhoïde ▶** a serious disease caused by bacteria in food, milk,

or water. Typhoid fever shows up as spots on the skin, fever, great physical weakness, and disorders of the stomach and intestines.

ty-phoon [ty-FOON] NOUN, typhoons. **typhon ▶** a violent windstorm that begins over tropical waters in the western Pacific Ocean and the China Sea.

typ-i-cal [TIP-uh-kul] ADJECTIVE. **typique, caractéristique ▶** having qualities or characteristics that are common to a certain group : *My typical breakfast includes juice and cereal.* ■ **typically,** ADVERB. ▶ typiquement, de manière caractéristique.

ty-ran-no-saur-us [tih-RAN-uh-SOR-us] NOUN, tyrannosauruses. **tyrannosaure ▶** a huge, meat-eating dinosaur that lived in North America about 100 million years ago. The tyrannosaurus had a large head, small front legs, and powerful hind legs that it walked on. **Note.** This animal is also called tyrannosaurus rex or tyrannosaur.

tyr-an-ny [TEER-uh-nee] NOUN. **1. tyrannie ▶** a government in which one ruler has total power and control of all people and laws. **2. tyrannie ▶** total or absolute power that is used cruelly and unfairly. ■ **tyrannical,** ADJECTIVE. ▶ **tyrannique.** *a tyrannical king.*

ty-rant [TY-runt] NOUN, tyrants. **1. tyran, despote, dictateur (-trice) ▶** a ruler who has absolute power over others and uses it in a cruel and unfair way. **2. tyran ▶** any person who uses power cruelly or unfairly : *The boss was a tyrant who would fire someone for the smallest mistake.*

uranus

u, U [yoo] NOUN. u's, U's. **u, U** ▶ the 21st letter of the English alphabet.

ud·der [UD-ur] NOUN. udders. **pis** ▶ a baglike part of a female cow or goat in which milk is produced.

ug·ly [UG-lee] ADJECTIVE, uglier, ugliest. **1. laid (laide), hideux (-euse), horrible, affreux (-euse)** ▶ not pleasing to look at; not pretty or attractive : *an ugly monster; an ugly scar.* **2. menaçant (-ante), inquiétant (-ante), dangereux (-euse)** ▶ not pleasant; dangerous or disagreeable : *An ugly storm brought the sailboats into shore.* ■ **ugliness,** NOUN. ▶ laideur .

u·ku·le·le [yoo-kuh-LAY-lee] NOUN. ukeleles. **ukulélé** ▶ a small musical instrument shaped like a guitar and having four strings.

ul·cer [UL-sur] NOUN. ulcers. **ulcère** ▶ an open sore that can be on the outside or inside of the body, and may be very painful.

ul·ti·mate [UL-tuh-mit] ADJECTIVE. **1. ultime, dernier (-ière), final (-ale, -aux)** ▶ coming at the end; last or final : *She is a nurse, but her ultimate goal is to become a pilot.* **2. suprême** ▶ greatest or extreme : *My ultimate challenge is to sail around the world alone.* ■ **ultimately,** ADVERB. ultimement ▶ in the end; at last; finally : *Mom ultimately makes the decision about whether or not we get a dog.*

ultra- PREFIX. to go beyond the ordinary; excessive : *ultramodern; an ultralight plane.*

ul·tra·vi·o·let [UL-truh-VY-uh-lit] ADJECTIVE. **ultraviolet (-ette)** ▶ of light rays, lying just beyond the violet end of the spectrum and thus not visible. The sun is the main source of ultraviolet rays.

u·lu [OO-LOO] NOUN. ulu ▶ a traditional knife used by the Inuit, having a crescent blade and handle made of wood, ivory, or bone.

um·brel·la [UM-BREL-uh] NOUN. umbrellas. **parapluie, parasol** ▶ a circular piece of cloth or plastic stretched on a frame that can be folded up when not in use. It is held over the head by a handle or pole and used to give protection from the rain or sun.

um·iak [OO-mee-AK] NOUN. (also **oomiak**) **umiak** ▶ a flat-bottomed boat made of skins stretched over a wood frame, traditionally used by the Inuit for carrying goods and families.

um·pire [UM-PIRE] NOUN. umpires. **arbitre** ▶ in baseball and other sports, a person who rules on plays. ▲ VERB, umpired, umpiring. **arbitrer** ▶ to act as an umpire : *Dad was asked to umpire the softball game at the picnic.* **Note.** The short form of this word is ump.

un- PREFIX. **1.** not : *unhappy; untrue.* **2.** reverse to an action : *unscrew; untie.*

un·able [un-AY-bul] ADJECTIVE. **incapable, inapte** ▶ not able : *Areetha was so tired that she was unable to stay up to watch the whole movie.* SYN : incapable, unfit, unqualified.

un·ac·cep·ta·ble [UN-ak-SEP-tuh-bul] ADJECTIVE. **inacceptable, inadmissible** ▶ that will not or should not be accepted : *Jeans are unacceptable at this job.*

u·nan·i·mous [yoo-NAN-uh-mus] ADJECTIVE. **unanime** ▶ showing total agreement : *It was unanimous; we all voted to see the adventure movie.* ■ **unanimously,** ADVERB. ▶ à l'unanimité, unanimement.

un·a·ware [un-uh-WAIR] ADJECTIVE; ADVERB. **ignorant (-ante) de, inconscient (-ente) de** ▶ not knowing; not aware : *As he stared out the window, he was unaware that the teacher was calling on him.* **Note.** The ADVERB form of this word is usually written unawares.

un·bear·a·ble [UN-BAIR-uh-bul] ADJECTIVE. **insupportable, intolérable, intenable, insoutenable** ▶ not bearable; too harsh or extreme to bear : *unbearable sorrow; unbearable pain.*

un·be·liev·a·ble [UN-bee-LEE-vuh-bul] ADJECTIVE. **1. incroyable, invraisemblable, extraordinaire** ▶ that cannot be believed : *The teacher thought her story was unbelievable and called her parents.* **2. incroyable, étonnant (-ante), inconcevable** ▶ very hard to believe; very surprising or shocking : *Ewen's rude behaviour at dinner was unbelievable!* SYN : incredible, doubtful, questionable.

un·bro·ken [UN-BROKE-in] ADJECTIVE. **1. intact (-acte)** ▸ not broken : *The seal on the bottle of medicine was unbroken.* **2. ininterrompu (-ue)** ▸ not interrupted; continuous : *They saw unbroken desert for miles around them.*

un·can·ny [UN-KAN-ee] ADJECTIVE. **mystérieux (-euse), inexplicable** ▸ seeming to be beyond normal powers; not natural or usual; mysterious : *It was uncanny how Marina knew when I was in trouble.*

un·cer·tain [UN-SUR-tin] ADJECTIVE. **incertain (-aine), hésitant (-ante)** ▸ not certain; doubtful; unsure : *Tan was uncertain of the answer and decided not to raise his hand.* ▪ **uncertainly,** ADVERB. ▸ *d'une manière incertaine, avec hésitation.* ▪ **uncertainty,** NOUN. ▸ *incertitude, hésitation, doute.*

un·changed [UN-CHAYNJD] ADJECTIVE. **inchangé (-ée), pareil (-eille), identique** ▸ not changed or changing : *The patient's condition is unchanged since yesterday.*

un·cle [UNK-ul] NOUN, uncles. **1. oncle** ▸ the brother of one's father or mother. **2. oncle** ▸ the husband of one's aunt.

un·clear [un-KLEER] ADJECTIVE. unclearer, unclearest. **obscur (-ure), confus (-use), ambigu (-uë)** ▸ not easy to understand; not clear : *He didn't explain, and it's unclear what he wants.*

un·com·fort·a·ble [UN-KUM-fur-tuh-bul *or* UN-KUMF-tur-bul] ADJECTIVE. **mal à l'aise, inconfortable** ▸ not comfortable : *"No one had ever seen Sergeant Bouton smile. I felt uncomfortable."* (Roch Carrier) ▪ **uncomfortably,** ADVERB. ▸ *inconfortablement.* ✎ p. 639.

un·com·mon [UN-KOM-un] ADJECTIVE. **rare, peu commun (-une), inhabituel (-elle)** ▸ not common; unusual or different : *Laura's uncommon sense of humour leads to lots of practical jokes.* ▪ **uncommonly,** ADVERB: ▸ *exceptionnellement.* *" He was uncommonly tired and nervous."* (Ivan Southall) SYN : rare, unusual, novel, extraordinary.

un·con·di·tion·al [UN-kun-DISH-un-ul] ADJECTIVE. **inconditionnel (-elle)** ▸ not having any terms; not restricted; without exceptions : *An unconditional surrender means that the defeated side must do whatever is asked of it.*

un·con·scious [UN-KON-shus] ADJECTIVE. **1. inconscient (-ente), sans connaissance** ▸ not fully awake; not conscious : *He was unconscious after hitting his head in a car accident.* **2. inconscient (-ente) de, ignorant (-ante) de** ▸ not knowing; not aware : *Unconscious of her beauty, Su Mei never acted as though she was different.* ▪ **unconsciously,** ADVERB. ▸ *inconsciemment.*

un·con·sti·tu·tion·al [UN-kon-stih-TOO-shun-ul] ADJECTIVE. **inconstitutionnel (-elle)** ▸ not in keeping with or not following the constitution of a country : *Some laws in Canada have been declared unconstitutional by the Supreme Court.*

un·con·ven·tion·al [UN-kun-VEN-shun-ul] ADJECTIVE. **original (-ale, -aux), non conformiste** ▸ out of the ordinary; not following the usual customs of society : *His unconventional style of clothing made him stand out in a crowd.*

un·couth [un-KOOTH] ADJECTIVE. **grossier (-ière), impoli (-ie)** ▸ not showing good manners; not polite; crude : *The uncouth boys grabbed at the food on the table.*

un·cov·er [UN-KUV-ur] VERB, uncovered, uncovering. **1. découvrir** ▸ to take off a cover or top : *When they uncovered the furniture, they saw how beautiful it was.* **2. découvrir, mettre au jour, révéler** ▸ to discover and make known; reveal : *The spy uncovered a secret plan.*

un·daunt·ed [UN-DON-tid] ADJECTIVE. **intrépide, hardi (-ie), audacieux (-euse)** ▸ not frightened or discouraged : *The captain remained undaunted and headed into the storm.* SYN. fearless, courageous, bold, daring, confident.

un·de·cid·ed [UN-dih-SY-did] ADJECTIVE. **1. indécis (-ise), incertain (-aine)** ▸ not having made up one's mind : *Esmé is undecided about attending Jeff's party.* **2. non résolu (-ue), non réglé (-ée)** ▸ not yet settled : *an undecided issue.*

un·der [UN-dur] PREPOSITION. **1. sous, au-dessous de** ▸ lower than or down from; below; beneath : *They sat under a tree for shade.* **2. de moins de, au-dessous de** ▸ less than a certain amount or level : *Children must be under 12 years old to get the discount.* **3. sous, en** ▸ controlled or affected by in some way : *under the care of a doctor; under repair.* **4. sous** ▸ in a certain

---

✎ **Word Builder**

Uncomfortable, **troubled,** and **distressed** all describe when a person is not feeling pleasure or contentment. *Uncomfortable* can suggest a person does not have peace of mind or physical contentment: *He was quite uncomfortable sitting on the lumpy couch.* **Troubled** suggests a person is bothered or upset: *Angela's mother was troubled by all the break-ins in the neighbourhood.* **Distressed** is the strongest of the three words. It suggests a person is extremely upset: *Mustafa's father was distressed by the news of fighting in his homeland.*

group or category : *I found information about the goalie under the subject "Hockey."* ▲ ADVERB. **au-dessous de** ► in or to a lower place; below : *The boy could not swim and was in danger of going under.* ▲ ADJECTIVE. **au-dessous de** ► lower in position or amount.

un·der·brush [UN-dur-BRUSH] NOUN. **sous-bois** ► low plants, bushes, and shrubs growing among larger trees in a woods or forest. **Note.** Also called undergrowth.

un·der·cov·er [UN-dur-KUV-ur] ADJECTIVE; ADVERB. **en civil, secret (-ète)** ► in a secret or hidden way : *An undercover police officer dresses in regular clothes rather than in a uniform.*

un·der·de·vel·oped [UN-dur-DIH-VEL-upt] ADJECTIVE. **sous-développé (-ée)** ► not completely or properly developed : *Poor children are often underdeveloped from an improper diet and little exercise.*

un·der·dog [UN-dur-DOG] NOUN, underdogs. **1. négligé (-ée)** ► a person or team who is expected to lose a game or contest : *Sewa likes to root for the underdog in a game.* **2. opprimé (-ée)** ► a person or group treated in an unfair way by those in power.

un·der·foot [UN-dur-FUT] ADVERB. **1. sous les pieds** ► under the feet : *The floor underfoot was not secure, and we were in danger of falling through.* **2. dans les jambes** ► in the way, as if under one's feet : *Their three little dogs were always getting underfoot.*

un·der·go [UN-dur-GOH] VERB. underwent, undergone, undergoing. **subir** ► to go through or experience something, especially something difficult or unpleasant : *He underwent surgery to fix his broken leg.* SYN: experience, endure, go through, suffer.

un·der·grad·u·ate [UN-dur-GRAJ-oo-it] NOUN, undergraduates. **étudiant (-ante) de premier cycle (universitaire)** ► a student in university who has not yet received an academic degree.

un·der·ground [UN-dur-GROWND] ADJECTIVE. **1. souterrain (-aine)** ► below the ground : *The new shopping mall has underground parking.* **2. clandestin (-ine), secret (-ète)** ► secret or hidden : *The Underground Railway brought many Blacks to Canada.* ▲ NOUN, undergrounds. **1. souterrain, tunnel** ► an area below the ground. **2. mouvement clandestin, résistance** ► a group that works in secret to oppose the government in power : *In World War II, members of the underground carried out secret attacks against the Germans.* ▲ [UN-dur-GROWND] ADVERB. **1. sous (la) terre** ► below the ground. *"The fire had been smouldering underground all winter beneath the snow."* (Teddy Jam) **2. secrètement, clandestinement** ► secretly.

un·der·hand [UN-dur-HAND] ADJECTIVE; ADVERB. (also underhanded) **1. par en dessous** ► with the hand below the level of the shoulder : *Throw*

underhand to your little brother because he's just learning to catch the ball. **2. sournois (-oise), hypocrite** ► in a dishonest or secret way : *an underhanded trick.*

un·der·line [UN-dur-LINE] VERB, underlined, underlining. **1. souligner** ► to draw a line under something, like this: *to underline an important word in a sentence.* **2. souligner, mettre en évidence, insister (sur), faire ressortir** ► to show to be important; emphasize : *The mayor's speech underlined the need for more safe parks for children.*

un·der·mine [UN-dur-MINE] VERB, undermined, undermining. **1. saper, miner** ► to dig out or wear away the ground under : *The constant action of the waves has undermined the supports for the bridge.* **2. ébranler, miner, saper** ► to weaken or ruin slowly : *Rumours undermined people's confidence in the government.*

un·der·neath [UN-dur-NEETH] PREPOSITION; ADVERB. **sous** ► under; below : *Kristal wore a heavy sweater underneath her jacket.*

un·der·pass [UN-dur-PASS] NOUN, underpasses. **passage inférieur** ► a road that goes under another road or a bridge.

un·der·score [UN-dur-SKOR] VERB, underscored, underscoring. **1. souligner** ► another word for underline. **2. souligner, mettre en évidence, insister (sur), faire ressortir** ► to make important; to stress : *The need for safer school buses was underscored by the recent accidents.*

un·der·side [UN-dur-SIDE] NOUN, undersides. **dessous** ► the side underneath; the bottom : *The cow was mostly black except for a white underside.*

un·der·stand [UN-dur-STAND] VERB, understood, understanding. **1. comprendre, saisir** ► to get the meaning of; be clear about : *The students understood the lesson, so the teacher went on to the next section.* **2. comprendre** ► to know a person's nature or character; be in sympathy with : *My best friend understands me very well.* **3. comprendre** ► to assume or accept as true : *If a book is a "limited edition," it's understood that only a certain number of copies will be made.* SYN: comprehend, grasp, take in, follow.

un·der·stand·ing [UN-dur-STAN-ding] NOUN, understandings. **1. compréhension, connaissance** ► the fact of knowing or getting the meaning of something : *Science often requires an understanding of mathematics.* **2. compréhension** ► something assumed; a belief or opinion : *It's my understanding that this pass can only be used by an adult.* **3. entente** ► a private agreement : *They have an understanding that they will get married after university.* ▲ ADJECTIVE. **compréhensif (-ive), tolérant (-ante)** ► able to understand the feelings of others : *Our neighbour was very understanding about the broken window.*

un·der·stood [UN-dur-STOOD] VERB. a past form of understand.

un·der·take [UN-dur-TAKE] VERB, undertook, undertaken, undertaking. **entreprendre** ▶ to agree or attempt to do something; take on oneself : *"When a man undertakes a job, he has to stick to it till he finishes it."* (Laura Ingalls Wilder) ▪ **undertaking**, NOUN, undertakings. *Writing a dictionary can be quite an undertaking.* ▶ **entreprise.** SYN : try, attempt, pursue, take up, embark on.

un·der·tak·er [UN-dur-TAY-kur] NOUN, undertakers. **entrepreneur de pompes funèbres** ▶ a person whose job is to prepare a dead person for burying and to arrange the person's funeral.

un·der·tone [UN-dur-TONE] NOUN, undertones. **1. voix basse, nuance** ▶ a low tone, as of the voice, a colour, and so on. **2. sous-entendu** ▶ a partly hidden feeling or thought.

un·der·took [UN-dur-TOOK] VERB. a past form of undertake.

un·der·tow [UN-dur-TOW] NOUN, undertows. **courant sous-marin** ▶ in the ocean, a strong current below the surface of the water that flows back out to sea or along the beach while waves break on the shore.

un·der·wa·ter [UN-dur-WAT-ur] ADJECTIVE. **sous-marin (-ine)** ▶ used, done, or lying below the surface of the water : *The "Chunnel" is an underwater tunnel across the English Channel.* ▲ ADVERB: *I like to swim underwater.* **Note.** Generally written as two words when it appears after a VERB: *At high tide, the beach is under water.*

un·der·wear [UN-dur-WAIR] NOUN. **sous-vêtement** ▶ clothing worn next to the skin under one's outer clothing, such as an undershirt or underpants. **Note.** Also called **underclothes** or **underclothing.**

un·der·went [UN-dur-WENT] VERB. a past form of undergo.

un·de·sir·a·ble [UN-dih-ZIRE-uh-bul] ADJECTIVE. **indésirable** ▶ not pleasing or wanted; disagreeable. ▲ NOUN, undesirables. **indésirable** ▶ an undesirable person.

un·did [UN-DID] VERB. a past form of undo.

un·do [UN-DOO] VERB, undid, undone, undoing. **1. défaire, détacher, dénouer** ▶ to loosen or untie something : *Tanis undid the bow on her present.* **2. annuler, détruire** ▶ to do away with something that has already been done : *His determination to finish writing the book was undone by long hours working at a regular job.* ▪ **undoing,** NOUN. **perte** ▶ a cause of ruin or failure : *I was trying to eat healthily, but the cake was my undoing.*

un·done¹ [UN-DUN] ADJECTIVE. **inachevé (-ée), pas fait (faite)** ▶ not done; not finished : *She left her cleaning undone while the hockey playoffs were on.*

undone² VERB. a past form of undo.

un·doubt·ed·ly [UN-DOW-tud-lee] ADVERB. **indubitablement, certainement, sans aucun doute** ▶ without a doubt; certainly.

un·eas·y [UN-EE-zee] ADJECTIVE. **agité (-ée), nerveux (-euse), inquiet (-ète)** ▶ not calm or relaxed; nervous; worried : *"The child was uneasy, fluttering up and down, like a bird on the point of taking flight."* (Nathaniel Hawthorne) ▪ **uneasily,** ADVERB. ▶ **avec inquiétude, nerveusement.** *Kai glanced uneasily down the street.* ▪ **uneasiness,** NOUN. ▶ **inquiétude, nervosité.**

un·em·ployed [UN-im-PLOYD] ADJECTIVE. **au chômage** ▶ without a job; out of work. **Note.** Also used as a NOUN: *The unemployed are people without a job who are actively looking for work.* ▪ **unemployment,** NOUN. **chômage** ▶ the state of being without a job.

un·e·ven [UN-EE-vin] ADJECTIVE. (sometimes unevener, unevenest) **1. inégal (-ale, -aux), raboteux (-euse), irrégulier (-ière)** ▶ not even : *The wooden floor had a bumpy, uneven surface.* **2. inégal (-ale, -aux), disproportionné (-ée)** ▶ not fair or balanced : *It was an uneven game as the other team was much better than we were.*

un·ex·pect·ed [UN-ik-SPEK-tid] ADJECTIVE. **inattendu (-ue), imprévu (-ue), imprévisible** ▶ not expected; coming or happening without notice : *I was an unexpected guest but was welcomed warmly.* ▪ **unexpectedly,** ADVERB: ▶ **de façon inattendue.** *We found California to be unexpectedly cloudy.* SYN: unforeseen, sudden, unanticipated, swift.

un·fair [UN-FAIR] ADJECTIVE. **injuste, inéquitable** ▶ not fair; not right or proper : *an unfair start.* ▪ **unfairly,** ADVERB. ▶ **injustement, d'une façon inéquitable.** *He thought that he had been treated unfairly when his idea was rejected by the group.*

un·fa·mil·iar [UN-fuh-MIL-yur] ADJECTIVE. **inconnu (-ue)** ▶ not familiar; not well-known : *My home town has changed so much that the streets look unfamiliar to me.* SYN: strange, uncommon, unusual, different.

un·fin·ished [UN-FIN-isht] ADJECTIVE. **inachevé (-ée), incomplet (-ète)** ▶ not finished : *When the writer died, she left behind an unfinished novel.*

un·fit [UN-FIT] ADJECTIVE. **inapproprié (-ée)** ▶ not fit; not suited or qualified for something : *The boss was afraid that Darrin was unfit to work on the new project.*

un·fold [UN-FOLD] VERB, unfolded, unfolding. **1. déplier** ▶ to open up or spread out : *to unfold a map.* **2. révéler, dévoiler** ▶ to come to be known; reveal : *As the story unfolds, the village is getting ready for the Queen's visit.*

un·for·get·ta·ble [UN-for-GET-uh-bul] ADJECTIVE. **inoubliable, mémorable ▸** impossible or difficult to forget; memorable : *The meeting with the Prime Minister was an unforgettable experience for the students.*

un·for·tu·nate [UN-FOR-chuh-nit] ADJECTIVE. **regrettable, malchanceux (-euse) ▸** not fortunate; unlucky : *"Its light might have the unfortunate effect of attracting some of the more dangerous inhabitants of these waters."* (Jules Verne) ■ **unfortunately,** ADVERB. ▸ **malheureusement.** 🔑 **p. 609.**

un·friend·ly [UN-FREND-lee] ADJECTIVE, unfriendlier, unfriendliest. **inamical (-ale, -aux), hostile, agressif (-ive) ▸** showing dislike or coldness towards others; not friendly.

un·gain·ly [UN-GANE-lee] ADJECTIVE. **gauche, maladroit (-oite) ▸** awkward or clumsy : *The handsome man had been tall, thin, and ungainly as a teen.*

un·grate·ful [UN-GRATE-ful] ADJECTIVE. **ingrat (-ate) ▸** not thankful or grateful : *She did not want to appear ungrateful and acted as if she liked the food.*

un·hap·py [UN-HAP-ee] ADJECTIVE, unhappier, unhappiest. **malheureux (-euse), triste ▸** not happy; sad : *The loss of his dog made Jake very unhappy.* ■ **unhappily,** ADVERB. ▸ **malheureusement.** ■ **unhappiness,** NOUN: *"His daughters sensed their father's unhappiness.* ▸ **tristesse."** (Robin Muller)

un·health·y [UN-HELTH-ee] ADJECTIVE, unhealthier, unhealthiest. **1. en mauvaise santé ▸** not in good health; sick; ill. **2. malsain (-aine), insalubre ▸** causing poor health : *His unhealthy eating habits made him dangerously overweight.*

un·heard-of [UN-HURD-uv] ADJECTIVE. **1. sans précédent ▸** not heard of before; not previously known or done. **2. étonnant (-ante), surprenant (-ante) ▸** not normally done; strange or unusual : *The women did something unheard-of as they demanded to join the men's club.*

uni- PREFIX. one : *unicolour; unicycle.*

u·ni·corn [YOO-nih-KORN] NOUN, unicorns. **licorne ▸** an imaginary animal that looks like a white horse with a single, pointed horn in the middle of its forehead. **Note.** Unicorns often appeared in art and stories of the Middle Ages.

u·ni·cy·cle [YOO-nih-SY-kul] NOUN, unicycles. **monocycle ▸** a vehicle that is like a bicycle, but with only one wheel and a seat above.

un·i·form [YOO-nuh-FORM] NOUN, uniforms. **uniforme ▸** a special sort of clothes that identifies a person who wears it as belonging to a certain group. Soldiers, police officers, and members of sports teams wear uniforms. ▲ ADJECTIVE. **uniforme, uni (unie) ▸** being the same; having the same appearance, form, rate, and so on : *The building was a uniform blue throughout.* **Note.** The fact of being uniform is uniformity. ■ **uniformly,** ADVERB. ▸ **uniformément.**

un·i·formed [YOO-nuh-FORMD] ADJECTIVE. **en uniforme ▸** wearing a uniform. *A uniformed police officer entered the courtroom with a handcuffed man.*

un·in·hab·it·ed [UN-in-HAB-ih-tid] ADJECTIVE. **inhabité (-ée), désert (-erte) ▸** not lived in; having no inhabitants : *Early European explorers thought that North America was mostly uninhabited.*

un·in·tel·li·gi·ble [UN-in-TEL-uh-juh-bul] ADJECTIVE. **inintelligible, incompréhensible ▸** not able to be understood : *The noise from the storm made the plane's radio almost unintelligible.*

un·in·ter·est·ed [un-IN-tur-es-tid or un-IN-tris-tid] ADJECTIVE. **inintéressé (-ée) ▸** not interested : *Miko gazed blankly out the window, completely uninterested in what was being said by the teacher.*

un·ion [YOON-yun] NOUN, unions. **1.** (also labour union) **syndicat ▸** a group of workers who join together to deal with the company manager and to protect the workers' needs, such as trying to gain higher pay or better working conditions. **2. union ▸** the fact of joining together as one : *the union of marriage.* **3. union ▸** a group of states or countries joined as one : *the Union of South Africa.*

u·nique [yoo-NEEK] ADJECTIVE. **1. unique ▸** being one of a kind; different from all others : *"The most important things are to know why you want to write and to figure out what you have to say that is unique."* (Paul Yee) **2.** Informal. **exceptionnel (-elle), rare, extraordinaire, exclusif (-ive) ▸** very rare or unusual. ■ **uniquely,** ADVERB. ■ **uniquement.** ■ **uniqueness,** NOUN. ▸ **caractère unique, unicité.** 🔑 **p. 643.** 🔑 **p. 643.**

u·ni·son [YOO-nuh-sin] NOUN. **in unison. unisson ▸** sounding the same notes, making the same sounds, or doing the same thing at the same time : *The whole class will recite the poem in unison.*

u·nit [YOO-nit] NOUN, units. **1. unité, élément, chapitre, section ▸** a single person, group, or thing that is part of a larger group : *We're studying Unit Ten of our history book.* **2. unité ▸** a fixed amount that is used as a standard of measurement : *Seconds, minutes, and hours are units of time.* **3. appareil ▸** a piece of equipment or furniture having a special purpose : *an air-conditioning unit.*

u·nite [yoo-NITE] VERB, united, uniting. **unir ▸** to bring or join together; make one; combine : *Three neighbourhoods united to combat the new highway.* ■ **united,** ADJECTIVE: *The United Nations Children's Fund (UNICEF) helps children around the world.* ▸ **uni (unie). Note.** The fact of being united is unity. 🔑 **p. 35.**

✒ **Writing Tips**

Unique

Unique is an absolute word that means "unlike any other." You cannot say something is "almost unique" or "somewhat unique." To do so is to misuse the word.

*Every person, every leaf, every fingerprint, and every tree is unique. So when you say something is unique, you're not really telling the reader anything new. In your writing, try to avoid the word and be more specific in your descriptions. Instead of saying, "Aunt Helena is really **unique**," you could write, "There's no one as unpredictable and as much fun as Aunt Helena."*

United Nations Nations Unies ▶ an organization that contains many nations from all over the world. The United Nations was formed after World War II to keep world peace and encourage countries to work together to solve problems. Over 180 countries belong to the United Nations.

u·ni·ver·sal [YOO-nuh-VUR sul] ADJECTIVE. **1. universel (-elle)** ▶ of, for, or shared by everyone : *Jean Little's novels touch on universal themes, such as loneliness and family problems.* **2. universel (-elle)** ▶ being or happening everywhere : *Universal time is the standard time calculated in Greenwich, England, that serves as the basis for figuring time throughout the world.* **Note.** The Universal Product Code is the series of black bars and lines appearing on food packages and other products to allow them to be automatically identified by a computer. ■ **universally,** ADVERB. ▶ **universellement.**

u·ni·verse [YOO-nuh-vurs] NOUN, **universes. univers** ▶ all of the area that exists and everything that exists within it ; the earth, planets, stars, and all other things.

u·ni·ver·si·ty [YOO-nuh-VUR-suh-tee] NOUN, **universities. université** ▶ a place of higher learning where people study special fields such as medicine, law, the arts, sciences, and business. 📖 p. 1056.

un·just [un-JUST] ADJECTIVE. **injuste, inéquitable** ▶ not fair or just. ■ **unjustly,** ADVERB. ▶ **injustement, d'une façon inéquitable.**

un·kempt [un-KEMPT] ADJECTIVE. **négligé (-ée), peu soigné (-ée)** ▶ not neat, clean, in place, and so on : *The unkempt dog was homeless and had no one to look after it.*

un·kind [un-KIND] ADJECTIVE, **unkinder, unkindest. méchant (-ante), cruel (-elle)** ▶ not kind ; cruel or mean : *It was unkind of you to mention his bad haircut.* ■ **unkindly,** ADVERB. ▶ **méchamment, cruellement.** ■ **unkindness,** NOUN. ▶ **méchanceté, cruauté.** 📖 p. 363.

un·known [un-NOHN] ADJECTIVE. **inconnu (-ue)** ▶ not known or familiar : *The owner of this coat is unknown, so I'll put it in the lost and found.* **Note.** Also used as a NOUN: *a political unknown.*

un·law·ful [un-LAH-ful] ADJECTIVE. **illégal (-ale, -aux)** ▶ against the law ; illegal.

un·less [un-LES] CONJUNCTION. **à moins que** ▶ except in the case that ; except that : *"During free-fall, or reduced gravity, the astronauts' arms float in front of them unless they make a conscious effort to hold them down."* (Barbara Bondar)

un·like [un-LIKE] PREPOSITION. **1. contrairement** ▶ different from ; not like . *Unlike other deer, male and female caribou both have antlers.* **2. contrairement** ▶ not typical of : *"Unlike other stars, it neither flickered nor twinkled."* (Tololwa M. Mollel) ▲ ADJECTIVE. **différent (-ente)** ▶ not the same ; different.

un·like·ly [un-LIKE-lee] ADJECTIVE, **unlikelier, unlikeliest. 1. improbable, douteux (-euse)** ▶ not expected or probable ; not likely : *Her ring dropped in the grass, and so it's unlikely that she'll find it.* **2. invraisemblable, impossible** ▶ not likely to happen or be true : *Achmed said that the man described an unlikely scheme for making money.*

un·lim·it·ed [un-LIM-uh-tid] ADJECTIVE. **illimité (-ée)** ▶ having no bounds or limits : *I have a pass that allows unlimited travel on the train for a month.*

un·load [un-LODE] VERB, **unloaded, unloading. décharger** ▶ to take off or remove a load from :

🔧 **Word Builder**

*Unique, single, and **solitary** can be used to describe one person or thing. **Unique** describes something that is one-of-a-kind: Graeme's lime-green suit is unique. **Single** means there is just one of something: A single CD was left on the shelf. **Solitary** can refer to a person or thing that stands alone or the only one that exists: A solitary tree stood in the middle of the field.*

The driver unloaded boxes off the truck into the store.

un·lock [UN-LOK] VERB. unlocked, unlocking. **1. déverrouiller ▸** to open the lock of : *to unlock a door.* **Note.** Often used as an ADJECTIVE: *an unlocked window.* **2. ouvrir ▸** to open something that is closed tight : *It was hard to unlock the legs of the frightened cat from around the tree branch.* **3. découvrir, résoudre ▸** to make known something that was hidden or secret; reveal : *Louis Pasteur unlocked the mystery of how diseases spread.*

un·luck·y [UN-LUK-ee] ADJECTIVE. unluckier, unluckiest. **malchanceux (-euse) ▸** bringing or causing bad luck; not lucky : *Many people think that 13 is an unlucky number.*

un·mis·tak·a·ble [UN-mis-TAKE-uh-bul] ADJECTIVE. **reconnaissable, évident (-ente) ▸** not able to be mistaken or misunderstood; clear; obvious : *I know that was Luis I heard, because his laugh is unmistakable.* ■ **unmistakably,** ADVERB. ▸ **indubitablement, sûrement, certainement.** *The rattling noise was unmistakably that of a startled rattlesnake.*

un·moved [UN-MOOVD] ADJECTIVE. **1. insensible, indifférent (-ente) ▸** not affected by feelings of pity or sympathy : *Dad was unmoved by Celia's tears and scolded her for being rude.* **2. qui n'a pas été déplacé ▸** not changed in position; not moved or disturbed.

un·nat·ur·al [UN-NACH-ur-ul] ADJECTIVE. **anormal (-ale, -aux) ▸** not natural or normal; strange : *The paintings of Picasso often feature unnatural-looking people with two eyes on one side of the face.*

un·nec·es·sar·y [UN-NESS-uh-sair-ee] ADJECTIVE. **inutile, superflu (-ue) ▸** not needed; not necessary : *The directions said not to make any unnecessary marks on the test paper.* ■ **unnecessarily,** ADVERB. ▸ **inutilement.**

un·of·fi·cial [UN-uf-FISH-ul] ADJECTIVE. **non officiel (-elle), officieux (-euse) ▸** not formal or official : *The unofficial opening of the park is this weekend.* ■ **unofficially,** ADVERB. ▸ **de façon non officielle, officieusement.**

un·or·tho·dox [UN-OR-thuh-DOKS] ADJECTIVE. **inhabituel (-elle) ▸** not usual or typical : *The basketball star has an unorthodox method of throwing the ball.*

un·paid [UN-PADE] ADJECTIVE. **1. impayé (-ée) ▸** not yet paid or settled : *an unpaid debt.* **2. sans solde ▸** without pay : *She took an unpaid leave of absence from her job.*

un·pleas·ant [UN-PLEZ-unt] ADJECTIVE. **désagréable ▸** not agreeable or pleasing; not pleasant : *The coach had the unpleasant job of telling some people that they didn't make the team.* ■ **unpleasantly,** ADVERB. ▸ **désagréablement.** *"The lane was becoming unpleasantly*

slippery, for the mist was passing into rain." (George Eliot)

un·pre·dict·a·ble [UN-prih-DIK-tuh-bul] ADJECTIVE. **imprévisible ▸** not possible to predict; not able to be known or judged in advance : *The currents are unpredictable in the ocean, so swimmers need to be careful.*

un·pre·pared [UN-prih-PAIRD] ADJECTIVE. **non préparé (-ée) ▸** not ready; not prepared : *She was unprepared and couldn't answer the teacher's question.*

un·real [UN-REEL or UN-REE-ul] ADJECTIVE. **irréel (-elle), imaginaire ▸** not true or real; imaginary. ■ **unrealistic,** ADVERB. **irréaliste ▸** not realistic or practical : *He was unrealistic about being a singing star when he had no talent.*

un·rea·son·a·ble [UN-REE-zun-uh-bul] ADJECTIVE. **déraisonnable, excessif (-ive) ▸** not reasonable; not sensible or fair : *It is unreasonable to expect a child to keep up with adults while walking.* ■ **unreasonably,** ADVERB. ▸ **de façon déraisonnable, excessivement.**

un·re·li·a·ble [UN-rih-LY-uh-bul] ADJECTIVE. **peu fiable, indigne de confiance ▸** not to be trusted or depended on; not reliable : *The new babysitter is unreliable and often arrives late for the job.*

un·rest [UN-REST] NOUN. **agitation, remous ▸** an uneasy or troubled state; lack of peace or ease : *The late 1960s was a time of great unrest because of student protests and changes in society.*

un·ru·ly [UN-ROO-lee] ADJECTIVE. unrulier, unruliest. **indiscipliné (-ée), incontrôlé (-ée) ▸** hard to control; out of order : *The hockey crowd became unruly when the referee called a penalty against the home team.*

un·scru·pu·lous [UN-SKROO-pyuh-lus] ADJECTIVE. **sans scrupules ▸** not having the proper standards or principles; not careful about right and wrong : *The unscrupulous lawyer gambled her clients' money in get-rich-quick schemes and bad investments.* SYN: sly, cheating, underhanded.

un·seem·ly [UN-SEEM-lee] ADJECTIVE. unseemlier, unseemliest. **inconvenant (-ante), déplacé (-ée), impoli (-ie) ▸** not done with good manners or proper behaviour; not polite : *It is unseemly the way you spit out the foods you don't like.*

un·set·tled [UN-SET-uld] ADJECTIVE. **1. inhabité (-ée), sauvage ▸** not lived in : *Most of the North is unsettled wilderness.* **2. non résolu (-ue), non réglé (-ée), en suspens ▸** not decided : *an unsettled land claim.* **3. instable, changeant (-ante), perturbé (-ée) ▸** not calm or peaceful. ■ **unsettling,** ADJECTIVE. **perturbateur (-trice) ▸** making uneasy or disturbed : *I found the high-wire act at the circus unsettling.*

un-skilled [UN-SKILD] ADJECTIVE. **inexpérimenté (-ée)** ▸ not having or requiring a skill or special training : *The city hired a group of unskilled workers to clean up vacant lots and unoccupied buildings.*

un-sound [UN-SOWND] ADJECTIVE. **1. fragile, instable, précaire** ▸ not strong or solid ; weak : *The bridge was built on unsound foundations, and it is sinking.* **2. douteux (-euse), mal fondé (-ée), peu sûr (sûre), contestable** ▸ not based on truth or clear thinking : *unsound ideas.*

un-speak-a-ble [UN-SPEE-kuh-bul] ADJECTIVE. **1. inexprimable, indescriptible, horrible, atroce** ▸ bad beyond description ; horrible : *the unspeakable horrors of war.* **2. indicible** ▸ not able to be said in words : *The name of god is unspeakable by the followers of certain religions.*

un-sta-ble [UN-STAY-bul] ADJECTIVE. **1. instable, branlant (-ante), bancal (-ale, -als)** ▸ not firm or steady ; shaky : *That table is too unstable to hold a heavy vase.* **2. instable, changeant (-ante), inconstant (-ante)** ▸ not having a firm control of the mind or feelings : *The girl became unstable after she suffered a terrible fright.*

un-stead-y [UN-STED-ee] ADJECTIVE. unsteadier, unsteadiest. **instable, branlant (-ante), bancal (-ale, -als)** ▸ not firm or steady ; shaky.

un-suc-cess-ful [UN-suk-SES-ful] ADJECTIVE. **sans succès, infructueux (-euse), vain (vaine)** ▸ not having a good result ; not successful. ▪ **unsuccessfully,** ADVERB. ▸ **sans succès, vainement, en vain.** *For years, she tried unsuccessfully to beat the school record in track.*

un-sure [UN-SHOOR] ADJECTIVE. **mal assuré (-ée), hésitant (-ante), peu sûr (sûre)** ▸ not sure ; doubtful : *He's just started skiing and is still very unsure of himself on the slopes.*

un-think-a-ble [UN-THINK-uh-bul] ADJECTIVE. **impensable, inconcevable, inimaginable** ▸ not to be thought of or considered ; not acceptable : *Cheating on a test is unthinkable to me.*

un-ti-dy [UN-TY-dee] ADJECTIVE. untidier, untidiest. **désordonné (-ée), en désordre** ▸ not in order ; not tidy.

un-tie [UN-TY] VERB, untied, untying. **dénouer, détacher, défaire** ▸ to unfasten a knot or something tied ; loosen or undo : *He untied the ribbon on his present.*

un-til [un-TIL] PREPOSITION ; CONJUNCTION. **jusqu'à (ce que)** ▸ up to the time of ; up to the stated time : *"I've been at it all afternoon, from two o'clock until now."* (Anne Frank)

un-to [UN-TOO] PREPOSITION. **à** ▸ an old and more formal form of the word to : *Do others as you would have others do unto you.*

un-told [UN-TOLD] ADJECTIVE. **1. jamais raconté (-ée), inédit (-ite)** ▸ not reported or told : *Her book contains several untold stories about great*

scientific discoveries. **2. incalculable, innombrable** ▸ too great to be counted : *The war brings suffering to untold numbers of people.*

un-used [UN-YOOZD] ADJECTIVE. **1. inutilisé (-ée), inemployé (-ée)** ▸ not in use ; not put to use : *He put the unused milk in the refrigerator.* **2. non habitué (-ée), inaccoutumé (-ée)** ▸ not used to ; not accustomed to : *Kathleen is unused to speaking in front of a big group and is a bit nervous about it.*

un-u-su-al [UN-YOO-zhoo-ul] ADJECTIVE. **inhabituel (-elle), exceptionnel (-elle), extraordinaire** ▸ not ordinary or common ; not usual : *Mr. Kassim must be ill ; it's very unusual for him to miss his morning walk.* ▪ **unusually,** ADVERB. ▸ **exceptionnellement, extraordinairement.** *Her fever was unusually high, so they took her to the hospital.* SYN: uncommon, out-of-the-ordinary, different.

un-veil [UN-VALE] VERB, unveiled, unveiling. **dévoiler, révéler** ▸ to remove a veil or covering from ; reveal : *"The airplane has unveiled for us the true face of the earth."* (Antoine de St. Exupéry)

un-want-ed [un-WON-tid] ADJECTIVE. **malvenu (-ue), non désiré (-ée)** ▸ not needed or wished for ; not wanted.

un-wel-come [UN-WEL-kum] ADJECTIVE. **importun (-une), déplaisant (-ante)** ▸ not well-received ; not welcome : *The storm was an unwelcome surprise during the picnic.*

un-wind [UN-WYND] VERB, unwound, unwinding. **1. se dérouler** ▸ to loosen or undo something that has been wound up : *The ball of yarn unwound as it rolled down the stairs.* **2. se détendre, se reposer, se délasser, se relaxer** ▸ to become free from tension ; relax : *Dad likes to unwind by sitting on the back porch with a cup of coffee.*

un-wise [UN-WIZE] ADJECTIVE. **imprudent (-ente), malavisé (-ée), inconsidéré (-ée), irréfléchi (-ie)** ▸ showing poor judgment ; not wise.

un-wor-thy [UN-WUR-thee] ADJECTIVE. **indigne, déshonorant (-ante), inconvenant (-ante)** ▸ not worthy ; not suitable : *Your nasty comment is unworthy of you.*

un-wound [UN-WOWND] VERB. a past form of unwind.

un-wrap [UN-RAP] VERB, unwrapped, unwrapping. **déballer** ▸ to remove the wrapping from ; open or uncover : *to unwrap a package.*

un-writ-ten [UN-RIT-tun] ADJECTIVE. **verbal (-ale, -aux), tacite** ▸ not in writing ; spoken : *We have an unwritten agreement — I clean the house and you do the yard work.* **Note.** An unwritten law or rule is something that does not have legal force but is accepted as common practice.

up [up] ADVERB. **1. vers le haut** ▸ from a lower to a higher place : *The dog jumped up onto the* couch. **2. plus haut ▶** in, at, or to a higher point or level : *Please turn up the TV; I can't hear the show.* **3. plus loin ▶** to a place that is thought of as above, farther along, or farther away : *They live up the river in Emmerson.* **4. debout, éveillé (-ée) ▶** out of bed : *Michi asked if she could stay up until Aunt Kyoko arrived.* ▲ ADJEC-TIVE. **1. levé (-ée) ▶** going to or in a higher place or position : *We want to be on the road before the sun is up.* **Note.** Often used in combination : *Upland is the higher land in an area.* **2. debout, levé (-ée) ▶** out of bed : *She was up early.* **3. au bâton ▶** in baseball, at bat : *How many times have you been up?* **4. rétabli (-ie) ▶** of a computer, working : *It took us a while to get the network up after it crashed.* ▲ PREPOSITION. **en haut ▶** from a lower to a higher place or level : *to climb up a tree.* **Note.** Often used with to: *That school goes up to grade six.* 🖋 *p. 646.*

up·com·ing [UP-KUM-ing] ADJECTIVE. **à venir, prochain (-aine), imminent (-ente) ▶** coming up; coming near : *The school band is practising for an upcoming concert.*

up·date [up-DATE] VERB, updated, updating. **mettre à jour, actualiser ▶** to bring up-to-date; make more modern or current : *When a dictionary is updated, new words are added to it.* ▲ NOUN, updates: *The report gave an update on the election results.*

up·grade [up-GRADE] VERB, upgraded, upgrading. **améliorer, perfectionner, bonifier ▶** to improve the quality or level of : *The cafeteria upgraded to become a fancy restaurant.* ▲ NOUN [UP-grade] upgrades: *The airline gave him an upgrade from regular to first-class.*

up·heav·al [up-HEE-vul] NOUN, upheavals. **bouleversement, émeute, soulèvement ▶** a time of great change or sudden disturbance : *The upheaval of revolution made the country a lawless and dangerous place.*

up·hill [UP-HIL] ADVERB; ADJECTIVE. **1. vers le haut ▶** going up a hill or toward a higher place; upward : *Water does not flow uphill.* **2. pénible, ardu (-ue), difficile ▶** filled with obstacles; difficult : *The baseball team faced an uphill battle to win the series, after losing the first three games.*

up·hold [up-HOLD] VERB, upheld, upholding. **soutenir, appuyer ▶** to support or agree with :

The Supreme Court has upheld the decision of the lower courts, and the law will stay in effect.

up·hol·ster [up-HOL-stur] VERB, upholstered, upholstering. **rembourrer ▶** to fit furniture with padding, cushions, or coverings. ▲ ADJECTIVE:*an upholstered sofa.* **Note.** The materials used to pad and cover furniture are called upholstery.

up·keep [UP-keep] NOUN. **entretien, soins, maintien ▶** the keeping of something in good condition, or the cost of doing this : *The upkeep on this old house is too expensive.*

up·lift [up-LIFT] VERB, uplifted, uplifting. **1. lever ▶** to raise or lift up : *Thousands of faces were uplifted to watch the fireworks.* **2. inspirer, encourager ▶** to raise the spirit; encourage good feeling : *The lively music uplifted the crowd, and everyone began to sing.*

up·on [uh-PON] PREPOSITION. **sur ▶** on : *Minoru put fresh flowers upon the table.*

up·per [UP-pur] ADJECTIVE. **1. supérieur (-ieure) ▶** higher in position : *The bedrooms are on the upper floor.* **2. uppercase.** (also **upper case**) **majuscule ▶** in printing, the capital or big letters : *A, B, and C are uppercase letters.*

the upper hand dessus, avantage ▶ a position of control; the advantage : *to have the upper hand in a game.*

up·right [UP-RITE] ADJECTIVE. **1. droit (droite), debout ▶** standing straight up. **2. honnête, intègre ▶** honest; trustworthy : *Jorge earned an honest living and lived an upright life.* ▲ ADVERB:*I put the shovel upright against the shed.*

up·ris·ing [UP-ry-zing] NOUN, uprisings. **soulèvement, révolte, émeute ▶** a revolt against a government or others with power; a rebellion : *José Marti began an uprising to free Cuba from Spain.*

up·roar [UP-ror] NOUN, uproars. **tumulte, vacarme, clameur ▶** a loud, confusing disturbance : *The backyard was in an uproar when a pack of dogs ran through.* SYN: confusion, clamour, tumult, chaos.

up·root [up-ROOT] VERB, uprooted, uprooting. **1. déraciner, arracher ▶** to tear or pull up by the roots : *Two huge trees were uprooted by the tornado.* **2. déraciner, arracher (de) ▶** to send or

---

🖋 Word Builder

The word **up** appears in many familiar expressions. **On the up and up** means someone is very open and honest: *The coach was on the up and up when he told Jamie he wouldn't make the team if he didn't work harder.* **Up against** means confronted with or facing: *Look at all the obstacles they are up against in raising money for the hospital.* **Up and about** means that a person is active, especially after an illness: *My grandfather was up and about two days after his surgery.*

force away; remove : *The family was uprooted after losing everything in the flood.*

up•set [up-SET] VERB. upset, upsetting. **1.** renverser, faire tomber ▶ to tip or knock over : *The wrestling children upset the lamp and broke it.* **2.** déranger, bouleverser ▶ to disturb the order of; interfere with : *Her travel plans were upset when she lost her wallet.* **3.** contrarier, agacer, énerver ▶ to make worried, nervous, or unhappy : *Your nasty remark upset me.* **4.** déranger ▶ to make slightly sick, especially in the stomach. **5.** gagner (contre toute attente) ▶ to win a game or contest that one had been expected to lose. *The challenger upset the champion.* ▲ [up-SET or US-pet] ADJECTIVE. **1.** fâché (-ée), contrarié (-ée), agacé (-ée), énervé (-ée) ▶ worried, nervous, or unhappy. **2.** dérangé (-ée) ▶ sick to one's stomach. ▲ [UP-set] NOUN. upsets. déception, désappointement, contrariété, agacement ▶ the act or fact of upsetting : *The hockey team's loss in the finals was a big upset.*

up•side down [UP-side DOWN] ADVERB. **1.** à l'envers ▶ having the top part or side turned to the bottom part of something : *The opossum can hang upside down by its tail.* **2.** à l'envers ▶ in disorder or confusion : *We turned the house upside down looking for the escaped hamster.*

up-stairs [up-STAIRZ] ADVERB; ADJECTIVE; NOUN. **1.** en haut, là-haut, à l'étage, étage ▶ up the stairs or on a higher floor : *Please go upstairs and clean your bedroom.*

up-stream [up-STREEM] ADVERB; ADJECTIVE. en amont ▶ toward the start or source of a stream; up a stream : *Salmon go upstream in fresh water to give birth to their young.*

up-to-date [UP-to-DATE] ADJECTIVE. à jour, actuel (-elle) ▶ keeping up with new or recent things; having the latest information. SYN: modern, current, contemporary, fashionable.

up-ward [UP-wurd] ADVERB; ADJECTIVE. (also upwards) vers le haut ▶ from a lower to a higher place or stage : *The fields sloped upward onto the sides of the mountains.*

u-ra-ni-um [yuh-RAY-nee-um] NOUN. uranium ▶ a heavy, silver-white metal that is used to make nuclear energy. Uranium is radioactive.

U-ra-nus [yuh-RANE-us or YUR-uh-nus] NOUN. **1.** Uranus ▶ the third-largest planet in the solar system and the seventh-closest planet to the sun. Uranus has five moons circling it. **2.** Uranus ▶ in the religion of the ancient Greeks, the god of the sky and the father of a race of giants. ◉ p. 391.

ur-ban [UR-bun] ADJECTIVE. urbain (-aine) ▶ having to do with a city or with city life : *Many urban people like to get away to the country for a vacation.*

urge [urj] VERB. urged, urging. **1.** presser, pousser ▶ to push or force on : *"Glorfindel still urged them on, and only allowed two brief*

halts during the day's march." (J.R.R.Tolkien) **2.** exhorter, inciter, persuader ▶ to try to convince or persuade; argue for : *Gandhi urged people to achieve their goals in a nonviolent way.* ▲ NOUN. urges. forte envie, besoin pressant ▶ a strong desire or wish : *"Suddenly an urge to understand everything came over the old man."* (Tololwa M.Mollel) ✐ p. 300.

ur-gent [UR-jint] ADJECTIVE. urgent (-ente), pressant (-ante) ▶ needing to be dealt with or taken care of right away; pressing; demanding : *There was the urgent sound of a siren in the middle of the night.* Note. The fact of being urgent is urgency. ■ **urgently,** ADVERB. ▶ d'urgence. *I called urgently for help.* SYN: pressing, important, critical, essential.

u-rine [YUR-in] NOUN. urine ▶ a clear yellow fluid made of body wastes. Urine is given off by the kidneys and discharged from the body.

urn [urn] NOUN. urns. **1.** urne ▶ a large vase set on a base. **2.** fontaine (à café, à thé) ▶ a large metal container that holds several gallons of coffee or tea and that is used to serve large groups of people.

us [us] PRONOUN. nous ▶ the pronoun we when used as an object : *We needed to go home, so Thuy's mom gave us a ride.*

us-age [YOO-sij] NOUN. usages. **1.** utilisation ▶ a way of using or handling something; treatment . *Your CD player will not work properly under such rough usage.* **2.** usage ▶ the way in which words are used in speaking or writing : *The word "thine," meaning "yours," is no longer in common usage.*

use [yooz] VERB. used, using. **1.** utiliser, user, employer, se servir de ▶ to put into action or service for a special purpose : *Sandy used a wooden match to light the stove.* **2.** (also use up) consommer, épuiser ▶ to finish or consume : *Maria used up all the hot water washing her car.* **3.** utiliser, se servir de, profiter de quelqu'un ▶ to take advantage of : *She is just using Eddie so that he will drive her to school.* ▲ [yoos] NOUN. uses. **1.** utilisation, emploi, usage ▶ the act or fact of being used : *Constant use of the heater keeps her room warm despite the cold.* **2.** utilité ▶ the quality of being useful or helpful : *It is no use trying to look for the dog; he has been gone for a month.* **3.** utilisation ▶ a need or purpose for which something is used : *The Internet has many uses, such as research, news updates, paying bills, or buying products.* **4.** usage ▶ the power or right to use something : *She had the use of her parents' car for the summer.* SYN: utilize, apply, employ, take advantage of.

used [yoozd] ADJECTIVE. usagé (-ée), d'occasion ▶ of a car or other such item, having been used by someone else; not new.

used to 1. **habitué (-ée), accoutumé (-ée)** ▸ having the habit of; accustomed to : *"Some of the older children are used to coming to the mission school, but the smaller children are not."* (Alice Walker) 2. **avoir l'habitude de** ▸ did at one time or did in the past : *"Father used to carry me down to the riverbank on his shoulders."* (Barbara Nichol)

use·ful [YOOS-ful] ADJECTIVE. **utile, pratique, commode, avantageux** ▸ having a good use or purpose; helpful : *I found the World Wide Web to be very useful when I was doing my science project* ■ **usefulness,** NOUN. ▸ **utilité.** SYN: helpful, practical, handy, valuable.

use·less [YOOS-lis] ADJECTIVE. **inutile, superflu (-ue)** ▸ having no use; not helpful; worthless : *A flashlight without batteries is useless.*

us·er [YOO-zur] NOUN. **utilisateur (-trice), usager** ▸ a person who uses some stated thing : *The saw blades are covered to protect the user against getting cut.*

us·er-friend·ly [yooz-ur-FREND-lee] ADJECTIVE. **convivial (-ale, -aux)** ▸ of a computer or computer program, easy to understand and operate for people who are not computer experts.

ush·er [USH-ur] NOUN, **ushers. placeur (-euse)** ▸ a person who shows people to their seats in a church, theatre, stadium, and so on. ▲ VERB, ushered, ushering. 1. **accompagner, escorter, conduire** ▸ to act as an usher; escort someone : *Dad ushered Mom into the room to surprise her with the finished shelves.* 2. usher in (out). **annoncer, marquer, signaler** ▸ to cause something to come or go; lead the way : *Warm weather ushered in an early spring season.*

u·su·al [YOO-zhoo-ul] ADJECTIVE. **habituel (-elle), courant (-ante), ordinaire** ▸ as normal or to be expected; ordinary; common : *"We were playing in our usual field among the daisies."* (Roch Carrier) **Note.** Often used in the phrase **as usual:** *"As usual, Mother was busy with the twins, so I climbed the stairs and crept along the hall to Mr. Beethoven's room."* (Barbara Nichol) SYN: normal, regular, ordinary, general, typical.

u·su·al·ly [YOO-zhu-lee *or* YOO-zhoo-uh-lee] **habituellement, normalement, couramment, ordi-** nairement ▸ in a way that is usual; normally : *"Pomegranates are usually green at this time of the year."* (Bob Barton)

u·ten·sil [yoo-TEN-sul] NOUN, utensils. **ustensile, outil** ▸ a tool or small object that is useful and has a special purpose : *Forks and spoons are kitchen utensils.*

u·til·i·ty [yoo-TIL-uh-tee] NOUN, utilities. 1. **service public** ▸ a company that sells a basic service to the public. Telephone, gas, and electric companies are utilities. 2. **utilité** ▸ the quality of being useful; usefulness : *We tested the utility of the new computer program, and it was faster than the old version.*

u·til·ize [YOO-tuh-LIZE] VERB, utilized, utilizing. **utiliser, employer, user, se servir de** ▸ to put into use; to make use of : *We surveyed to find out how people utilized the library.*

ut·most [UT-most] ADJECTIVE. **le plus grand** ▸ greatest or most possible : *He used the utmost care while bathing the baby.* **Note.** Also used as a NOUN: *The new show was the utmost in family entertainment.*

u·to·pi·a [yoo-TOW-pee-yuh] NOUN, utopias. (also Utopia) **utopie** ▸ an imaginary place offering a perfect life where complete happiness is enjoyed by all. ■ **utopian,** ADJECTIVE. ▸ **utopique. Note.** This word comes from the name of a book by Sir Thomas More, in which he describes an island called Utopia where all people are wise, healthy, and prosperous.

ut·ter[1] [UT-ur] VERB, uttered, uttering. **prononcer, exprimer, formuler** ▸ to say out loud; speak : *"But before anyone could utter a word, the palace shuddered as though hit by an earthquake."* (Robin Muller) ■ **utterance,** NOUN. ▸ **expression.** *With an utterance of disgust, my mom told us to clean up.* SYN: say, speak, express, talk, declare, tell.

ut·ter[2] ADJECTIVE. **parfait (-aite), complet (-ète), total (-ale, -aux)** ▸ complete or total; absolute : *Lydia made an utter fool of herself by yelling at Ivan for taking her usual seat in the cafeteria.* ■ **utterly,** ADVERB. ▸ **absolument, totalement, complètement.** *The sunset was utterly beautiful with colours streaking across the sky.*

violin

v, V [vee] NOUN, v's, V's. **v, V** ▶ the 22nd letter of the English alphabet.

va·can·cy [VAY-kun-see] NOUN, vacancies. **chambre libre** ▶ the fact of being vacant or empty : *A motel with a vacancy has a room for rent.*

va·cant [VAY-kunt] ADJECTIVE. **1. inoccupé (-ée), libre, disponible, vacant (-ante)** ▶ not in use; not occupied; empty : *"The story begins when a stranger appears and moves into a house that was vacant for years."* (Joan W. Blos) **2. absent (-ente), sans expression, vide** ▶ without expression or thought : *Julie was so tired that she had just a vacant expression on her face.*

va·cate [VAY-KATE] VERB, vacated, vacating. **quitter, vider** ▶ to make vacant; leave empty : *When the police arrived at the bank after the robbery, they asked everyone to vacate the building.*

va·ca·tion [vuh-KAY-shun or vay-KAY-shun] NOUN, vacations. **1. vacances** ▶ a period away from school, work, or other regular activity : *Jeremy is feeding the neighbours' dog while they are on vacation.* **2. vacances, voyage de vacances** ▶ a time spent in travel or amusement; a pleasure trip. ▲ VERB, vacationed, vacationing. **prendre des vacances** ▶ to take a vacation : *to vacation in the Bahamas.* 📖 **p. 1156.**

vac·ci·nate [VAK-suh-NATE] VERB, vaccinated, vaccinating. **vacciner** ▶ to give a vaccine in order to protect a person from disease : *The nurse has vaccinated the children against such diseases as measles, polio, and tetanus.* ▪ **vaccination,** NOUN. ▶ **vaccination.**

vac·cine [vak-SEEN or VAK-seen] NOUN, vaccines. **vaccin** ▶ a solution containing weakened or dead disease germs, injected into a person's bloodstream to help the person build up resistance against the actual disease.

vac·u·um [VAK-yoo-um or VAK-yoom] NOUN, vacuums. **1. vacuum, vide** ▶ a space that has nothing in it, not even air. **2. aspirateur** ▶ short for vacuum cleaner. **3. vide, néant** ▶ an area or condition cut off from outside events and influences : *Ilias knows nothing about current events; it's as though he lives in a vacuum.* ▲ VERB, vacuumed, vacuuming. **passer l'aspirateur, passer à l'aspirateur** ▶ to clean with a vacuum cleaner : *to vacuum the carpet.*

vacuum cleaner **aspirateur** ▶ an electrical machine that is used to suck up dirt and dust from carpets, floors, furniture, and so on.

va·grant [VAY-grunt] NOUN, vagrants. **vagabond (-onde), clochard (-arde)** ▶ a person without a settled home or regular job. **Note.** The fact of being vagrant is **vagrancy.**

vague [vayg] ADJECTIVE, vaguer, vaguest. **vague, flou (floue), imprécis (-ise)** ▶ not clear or definite : *Melissa wasn't exactly sure where Sarita lived, but she had a vague idea.* ▪ **vaguely,** ADVERB. ▶ **vaguement.** *I was in such a rush that I was only vaguely aware of the rain.* SYN: unclear, indistinct, fuzzy, faint, obscure.

vain [vane] ADJECTIVE, vainer, vainest. **1. vaniteux (-euse)** ▶ having too much pride in one's appearance or ability; conceited : *"This girl is very vain and proud. She thinks people are always admiring her!"* (Ann Grifalconi) **2. vain (vaine), inutile** ▶ not successful; useless. **Note.** Used in the phrase in vain: *Alberto tried to lift the trunk, but it was too heavy and his efforts were in vain.* ▪ **vainly,** ADVERB. ▶ **vainement, en vain, vaniteusement, avec vanité.**

val·en·tine [VAL-un-TINE] NOUN, valentines. **1.** (also Valentine) **carte de la Saint-Valentin** ▶ a card, present, or greeting given to a sweetheart, friend, or family member on Valentine's Day, February 14. **2. valentin (-ine)** ▶ a sweetheart chosen on this day. **Note.** Valentine's Day was named after Saint Valentine, a Christian saint who lived in Rome in the 3rd century A.D.

val·iant [VAL-yunt] ADJECTIVE. **vaillant (-ante), valeureux (-euse), courageux (-euse)** ▶ full of bravery or courage; heroic : *Harriet Tubman's valiant efforts rescued many slaves from cruel masters.*

val·id [VAL-id] ADJECTIVE. **1. valable** ▶ based on facts or truth; sound : *a valid argument.* **2. valable, valide** ▶ having force under the law : *a* *valid driver's licence.* SYN : sound, true, good, established, convincing.

val·ley [VAL-ee] NOUN, valleys. **vallée** ▸ an area of low land between hills or mountains, often with a river flowing through it. ☞ **p. 1045.**

val·our [VAL-ur] NOUN. (also **valor**) **courage, bravoure** ▸ great courage or bravery, especially in war.

val·u·a·ble [VAL-yoo-uh-bul *or* VAL-yuh-bul] ADJECTIVE. **1. de (grande) valeur** ▸ worth a lot of money : *Several hundred years ago, salt was as valuable as gold.* **2. précieux (-euse), très utile, très important (-ante)** ▸ very important or useful : *When Emily was almost hit by a car, she learned a valuable lesson about looking both ways before crossing the street.* ▲ NOUN, **valuables. objets de valeur** ▸ something that is worth a lot of money or is of great importance : *Mr. Barnes keeps jewellery, his stamp collection, and other valuables in his safe.* 🔑 **p. 650.**

val·ue [VAL-yoo] NOUN, values. **1. valeur** ▸ how much money, goods, or services a thing will bring in return; the worth of something when compared to other things : *The dealer said the coin has a value of $54.* **2. valeur** ▸ the quality of something that makes it important, useful, or helpful : *the value of a good friend.* **3. values. valeurs** ▸ the standards or beliefs that someone has about how to act or to conduct one's life : *Her values prevent her from cheating.* ▲ VERB, valued, valuing. **1. évaluer, estimer** ▸ to set or estimate the worth of : *This painting is valued at $10 000.* **2. apprécier, importer** ▸ to consider important or valuable; think highly of : *I really value your opinion.* SYN : price, merit, significance, worth.

valve [valv] NOUN, valves. **1. valve** ▸ a movable part that can control the flow of a liquid or gas from one part of a machine or device to another. **2. valvule** ▸ a similar part in the body that controls the flow of blood or other fluids : *The heart has four main valves.* **3. valve** ▸ one of the halves of the shell of an oyster or similar animal.

vam·pire [VAM-pire] NOUN, vampires. **1. vampire** ▸ in folk tales, a dead body that rises from its grave at night to suck the blood of sleeping people. **2.** (also **vampire bat**) **vampire** ▸ a bat in tropical countries that drinks the blood of animals. ☞ **p. 971.**

van [van] NOUN, vans. **1. camion, fourgon** ▸ a large, covered truck that is used to haul goods or animals. **2. camionnette, fourgonnette** ▸ a motor vehicle like a small truck, having seats for passengers and extra room for cargo : *A moving van is used to move furniture and household goods.*

van·dal·ism [VAN-duh-LIZ-um] NOUN. **vandalisme** ▸ the crime of destroying or damaging someone's property on purpose : *Graffiti is an act of vandalism.* **Note.** A person who does this is a vandal.

vane [vane] NOUN, vanes. **1. aile (d'un moulin à vent), pale (d'une hélice), aube (d'une roue hydraulique), hélice (d'un ventilateur)** ▸ a blade that is moved around a centrepoint by water or wind. Fans, propellers, and windmills have vanes. **2. girouette** ▸ a short form of **weather vane.**

va·nil·la [vuh-NIL-uh] NOUN. **vanille, extrait de vanille** ▸ a liquid flavouring made from the dried seed pods of a tropical plant, used in sweets such as cake and candy.

valve

van·ish [VAN-ish] VERB, vanished, vanishing. **1. disparaître** ▸ to suddenly go out of sight; become invisible; disappear : *Suddenly, my dog*

🔧 **Word Builder**

Valuable, expensive, *and* ***precious*** *all suggest that things have worth.* ***Valuable*** *can apply to the cost of something, but it can also refer to its importance or excellence: Shane made many valuable contributions to our discussion.* ***Expensive*** *usually refers to an item's high cost: Unfortunately, the bike I wanted was the most expensive.* ***Precious*** *can mean an item has great worth and that it is loved or cherished: Madeline's mother keeps her precious porcelain in a glass cabinet.*

vanished under a bush. **2. disparaître** ▶ to stop existing; come to an end : *The dodo bird vanished in the late 1600s.*

van-i-ty [VAN-uh-tee] NOUN, vanities. **vanité** ▶ the fact of being vain; too much pride in one's looks, accomplishments, or abilities.

van-quish [VANK-wish] VERB, vanquished, vanquishing. **vaincre** ▶ to conquer or defeat, as an enemy in war : *to vanquish one's fears.*

va-pour [VAY-pur] NOUN, vapours. (also vapor) **vapeur** ▶ tiny particles of a liquid or gas that can be seen or smelled floating in the air. Clouds, steam, and gasoline fumes are kinds of vapour. **Note.** A vaporizer is a device that adds moisture to the air.

var-i-a-ble [VAIR-ee-uh-bul *or* VA-ree-uh-bul] ADJECTIVE. **variable, changeant (-ante)** ▶ that varies; able or likely to change : *My sister, who is a nurse, works variable hours from week to week.* ▲ NOUN, variables. **variable** ▶ something that can change or be changed : *Math problems often contain variables such as x and y that can stand for different numbers.*

var-i-ant [VAIR-ee-unt *or* VA-ree-unt] NOUN, variants. **variante** ▶ something that varies; a different form : *The word "color" is a variant of the word "colour."* ▲ ADJECTIVE: *a variant spelling.*

var-i-a-tion [vair-ee-AY-shun *or* va-ree-AY-shun] NOUN, variations. **1. variation** ▶ the fact of varying; a change from the normal or usual way : *a jazz variation of a folk song.* **2. variation** ▶ a similar but slightly different form of something.

var-ied [VAIR-eed *or* VA-reed] ADJECTIVE. **varié (-ée)** ▶ that changes or has changed : *Canada's varied landscape often made travel difficult.*

va-ri-et-y [vuh-RY-uh-tee] NOUN, varieties. **1. variété, diversité** ▶ the fact of being different : *I do the same thing every day; I need some variety in my life.* **2. variété** ▶ things that are different; an assortment or collection : *That store sells a variety of magazines.* **3. variété, type** ▶ a particular type that is different from others : *McIntosh is a popular variety of apple.* SYN: assortment, collection, diversity.

var-i-ous [VAIR-ee-us *or* VA-ree-us] ADJECTIVE. **1. divers (-erse), plusieurs** ▶ more than one; several or many : *Various people protested the plan.* **2. divers (-erse), différent (-ente)** ▶ not like each other; different : *The dog show included contests for various types of dogs.* ■ **variously,** ADVERB. ▶ **d'une manière diverse, de plusieurs façons différentes, diversement.** SYN: assorted, miscellaneous, numerous, many.

var-nish [VAR-nish] NOUN, varnishes. **vernis** ▶ a paint-like liquid spread on wood or another surface to give it a hard, shiny coating. ▲ VERB, varnished, varnishing. **vernir** ▶ to cover with varnish : *to varnish the hull of a boat.*

var-y [VAIR-ee *or* VA-ree] VERB, varied, varying. **varier, différer, changer** ▶ to make or become different; change : *"The longhouse might vary in length, but it was usually as high as it was wide."* (Bonnie Shemie)

vase [vaze] NOUN, vases. **vase** ▶ a container used to hold flowers or as a decoration.

vast [vast] ADJECTIVE, vaster, vastest. **vaste, énorme, immense, très grand (grande)** ▶ very large; huge : *I travelled over vast stretches of sand, riding in jeeps and on horseback.* ■ **vastly,** ADVERB. **extrêmement, largement, nettement, considérablement** ▶ very much : *Our hotel was vastly different from the one in the brochure.* ■ **vastness,** NOUN. ▶ **immensité.** SYN: immense, spacious, unlimited, huge.

vault[1] [volt] NOUN, vaults. **1. chambre forte, salle des coffres, coffre-fort** ▶ a large compartment or room with strong walls and locks, used for storing valuable things and keeping them safe : *Banks keep money in a vault.* **2. voûte** ▶ an arched ceiling or roof : *There are vaults in the Parliament buildings in Ottawa.* **3. voûte** ▶ something like an arched ceiling : *The sky is sometimes called the vault of heaven.*

vault[2] [volt] VERB, vaulted, vaulting. **sauter quelque chose d'un bond** ▶ to jump or leap over something : *The horse vaulted over the fence and galloped away.* ▲ NOUN, vaults. **saut** ▶ a high leap or jump, as in the pole vault.

veal [veel] NOUN. **veau (veaux)** ▶ the meat from a calf.

veer [veer] VERB, veered, veering. **virer, tourner, changer de direction** ▶ to change direction; turn : *The driver veered to the left to avoid hitting a dog.*

veg-e-ta-ble [VEJ-uh-tuh-bul *or* VEJ-tuh-bul] NOUN, vegetables. **légume** ▶ any plant or plant part eaten for food, such as corn, peas, beans, lettuce, tomatoes, and potatoes. **Note.** Vegetables usually refer to plants eaten as part of a main meal or in a salad, rather than sweet fruits (apples, oranges, berries, and so on) eaten separately or for dessert. ▲ ADJECTIVE. **légumier (-ière), végétal (-ale, -aux), de légumes, à légumes** ▶ made from or having to do with vegetables : *vegetable soup.* ⮥ **p. 1098.**

veg-e-tar-i-an [VEJ-uh-TAIR-ee-un] NOUN, vegetarians. **végétarien (-ienne)** ▶ a person who chooses not to eat meat. ▲ ADJECTIVE: *a vegetarian meal.*

veg-e-ta-tion [VEJ-uh-TAY-shun] NOUN. **végétation** ▶ plant life : *The vegetation in tropical rain forests is thick and lush.* ◉ **p. 247.**

ve-he-ment [VEE-uh-munt] ADJECTIVE. **véhément (-ente)** ▶ marked by strong feeling or passion; intense : *a vehement protest.* ■ **vehemence,** NOUN. ▶ **véhémence.** ■ **vehemently,** ADVERB. ▶ **avec véhémence, violemment.**

ve·hi·cle [VEE-uh-kul] NOUN, vehicles. **véhi·cule** ▶ anything that is used to move or carry people or goods : *trucks, trains, and other vehicles.*

veil [vale] NOUN, veils. 1. **voile** ▶ a very thin cloth or netting that a woman wears over her head or face as a covering or decoration : *a bridal veil.* 2. **voile** ▶ something that covers or hides : *A veil of clouds hid the sun.* ▲ VERB, veiled, veiling. **voiler, couvrir d'un voile** ▶ to cover with or as if with a veil : *A thin layer of dust veiled the desk.*

vein [vane] NOUN, veins. 1. **veine** ▶ one of the blood vessels that carries blood back to the heart from all parts of the body. 2. **nervure** ▶ a tube-like structure that carries food and water in a leaf, or provides support in an insect's wing. 3. **veine** ▶ a long, narrow mineral deposit in a rock : *a rich vein of silver ore.* 4. **veine, veinure** ▶ a streak of different colour or texture in wood or marble. 5. **veine, esprit, style** ▶ a certain style or mood : *This song is not in the same vein as the band's other songs.* ☞ p. 402.

ve·loc·i·ty [vuh-LOS-uh-tee] NOUN, velocities. **vélocité, vitesse** ▶ the rate of motion of an object; speed : *The velocity of sound under water is much slower than it is through the air.*

vel·vet [VEL-vit] NOUN, velvets. **velours** ▶ a kind of fabric that has a very soft, thick, raised surface. ▲ ADJECTIVE. 1. **de velours** ▶ made with velvet. 2. (also velvety) **velouteux (-euse), velouté (-ée), de velours** ▶ very soft and smooth, like this fabric : *The ice cream was as smooth as velvet.*

vend·ing machine [VEN-ding] **distributeur automatique** ▶ a machine with a slot where money is deposited in order to get soft drinks, candy, stamps, and other such small items from the machine.

ven·dor [VEN-dur] NOUN, vendors. (also vender) 1. **marchand (-ande)** ▶ a person who sells something on the street or from door to door : *a hot-dog vendor.* 2. **marchand (-ande), vendeur (-euse)** ▶ anyone who sells something.

ve·neer [vuh-NEER] NOUN, veneers. 1. **placage, vernis** ▶ a thin sheet of fine wood glued or bonded to something of lesser material, to give it a nicer finish or a stronger structure. 2. **vernis, apparence** ▶ any outer covering or surface meant to hide some weakness or fault : *A veneer of self-confidence hid Kiet's shyness.*

venge·ance [VEN-junce] NOUN. 1. **vengeance** ▶ punishment given in return for a wrong or injury. 2. **with a vengeance. avec furie, avec rage** ▶ with great force or violent energy.

ven·i·son [VEN-uh-sun] NOUN. **venaison** ▶ the meat from a deer eaten as food.

ven·om [VEN-um] NOUN, venoms. 1. **venin** ▶ the poison that some snakes, spiders, and other animals can pass on through a bite or sting.

2. **venin** ▶ strong, bitter feelings; hatred. ■ **venomous,** ADJECTIVE. ▶ **venimeux (-euse).**

vent [vent] NOUN, vents. 1. **orifice, tuyau (-aux), conduit** ▶ an opening that allows gas or liquid to escape or enter : *a heating vent.* 2. **échappatoire, exutoire** ▶ a means of escape or release; an outlet : *After keeping his feelings to himself, Mark finally gave vent to all his frustrations.* ▲ VERB, vented, venting. **laisser s'échapper, donner libre cours, laisser libre cours** ▶ to allow to escape through or as if through a vent : *to vent smoke through a chimney.*

ven·ti·la·tion [VEN-tuh-LAY-shun] NOUN. 1. **ventilation** ▶ the movement of air through or around an area. 2. **ventilation** ▶ a way of supplying fresh air to a place.

ven·tri·lo·quist [ven-TRIL-uh-kwist] NOUN, ventriloquists. **ventriloque** ▶ someone who can talk without moving the mouth, making it sound as if a voice is coming from another source, such as from a puppet.

ven·ture [VEN-chur] VERB, ventured, venturing. 1. **risquer, se risquer, s'aventurer** ▶ to face a risk or danger; take a chance : *Edmund ventured into the dark woods.* 2. **hasarder, avancer** ▶ to say something that may be objected to; dare to say : *I will venture a guess.* ▲ NOUN, ventures. **tentative, coup d'essai, projet** ▶ the act of venturing; a course of action in which there is some risk : *a business venture.*

Ve·nus [VEE-nus] NOUN. 1. **Vénus** ▶ the second-closest planet to the sun and sixth-largest planet in the solar system. It is the brightest natural object in the sky after the sun and moon. 2. **Vénus** ▶ in the religion of the ancient Romans, the goddess of love. ☞ p. 391.

ve·ran·da [vuh-RAN-duh] NOUN, verandas. (also verandah) **véranda** ▶ a long, usually open porch that has a roof and that is attached to one or more sides of a house.

verb [vurb] NOUN, verbs. **verbe** ▶ a word that expresses an action or a state of being. The words *write, sing, run, have, are,* and *do* are verbs.

ver·bal [VUR-bul] ADJECTIVE. **verbal (-ale, -aux)** ▶ of or having to do with words : *Although she didn't sign any papers, she gave her verbal consent to the operation.*

ver·dict [VER-dikt] NOUN, verdicts. 1. **verdict** ▶ the judgment or decision made by a judge or jury in a court trial. 2. **jugement, opinion, verdict** ▶ any judgment or opinion : *Did you like the movie or not—what's your verdict?*

verge [vurj] NOUN. **au bord de, sur le point de, à la veille de, au seuil de** ▶ the point at which some action or condition is just about to take place. **Note.** Usually used in the phrase **on the verge of:** *The lost little girl was on the verge of tears.* SYN : edge, rim, brink, border.

ver·i·fy [VAIR-uh-FY] VERB, verified, verifying. **vérifier** ▸ to prove the truth of; show to be true : *Please show us your driver's licence so that we can verify who you are.* ■ **verification,** NOUN. ▸ **vérification.**

ver·sa·tile [VUR-suh-TILE *or* VUR-suh-tul] ADJECTIVE. **polyvalent (-ente), aux talents variés, à usages multiples** ▸ able to do a number of things well or be used for many purposes : *This versatile pocket knife has eight different uses.*

verse [vurce] NOUN, verses. **1. vers, poésie** ▸ words put together in a certain pattern of sounds, often with rhyme; poetry. **2. strophe, couplet** ▸ a group of lines within a poem or song; a stanza or section. **3. verset** ▸ a short, numbered section of the Bible.

ver·sion [VUR-zhun] NOUN, versions. **1. version** ▸ an account or description given from one person's point of view : *Each witness gave a different version of the crime.* **2. version, traduction** ▸ a translation, especially a translation of the Bible. **3. version** ▸ a form of a written work or other work of art : *I haven't read the play, but I have seen the movie version.*

ver·sus [VUR-sus] PREPOSITION. **contre, versus** ▸ opposed to; against : *Today's game features the Edmonton Oilers versus the Montreal Canadiens.*

ver·te·bra [VUR-tuh-bruh] NOUN, vertebrae [VUR-tuh-bray] *or* vertebras. **vertèbre** ▸ one of the bones in the backbone of animals such as humans and snakes.

ver·te·brate [VUK-tuh-BRATE] NOUN, vertebrates. **vertébré** ▸ an animal with a backbone. Mammals, fish, birds, reptiles, and amphibians are vertebrates. ▲ ADJECTIVE: *A frog is a vertebrate animal.*

ver·ti·cal [VUR-tuh-kul] ADJECTIVE. **vertical (-ale, -aux)** ▸ going straight up and down rather than across; upright : *vertical stripes running up the wall.*

ver·y [VAIR-ee] ADVERB. **1. très, beaucoup** ▸ more than usual; to a high degree; extremely : *It gets very cold on Baffin Island.* **2. vraiment, réellement** ▸ really; actually : *This book is the very best that I've read.* ▲ ADJECTIVE. **même, précis (-ise)** ▸ same; exact : *That's the very hat I'm looking for.* SYN: exceedingly, truly, exceptionally, greatly.

ves·sel [VESS-ul] NOUN, vessels. **1. vaisseau (-eaux)** ▸ a ship or large boat. **2. récipient** ▸ a large, hollow container for holding liquids, such as a pitcher or tank. **3. vaisseau (-eaux)** ▸ a long, narrow tube that carries fluids through the body of an animal or plant : *a blood vessel.*

vest [vest] NOUN, vests. **gilet** ▸ a piece of clothing without sleeves or a collar, worn over a shirt or blouse and extending to the waist. 🄿 p. 1015.

vet·er·an [VET-uh-run] NOUN, veterans. **1. vétéran, ancien combattant** ▸ a person who has served in the armed forces, especially during wartime. **2. vétéran** ▸ a person who has held a position for a long time or has a lot of experience : *After 20 years, Ms. Gilles is a veteran in the classroom.* ▲ ADJECTIVE: **d'expérience** ▸ *a veteran teacher.*

vet·er·i·nar·i·an [VET-uh-ruh-NAIR-ee-un] NOUN, veterinarians. **vétérinaire** ▸ a person trained and licensed to be a doctor for animals. **Note.** This type of medicine is known as veterinary medicine.

ve·to [VEE-TOH] NOUN, vetoes. **1. veto** ▸ the legal right or power to forbid or prevent : *In Canada, the Senate has the power of veto over most bills passed by the House of Commons.* **2. veto** ▸ a similar power held by someone in authority. ▲ VERB, vetoed, vetoing. **1. mettre son veto, opposer son veto** ▸ to stop the passage of a law with a veto. **2. mettre son veto, opposer son veto, interdire** ▸ to refuse to approve; forbid : *Mom vetoed ice-cream cones before dinner.*

vex [veks] VERB, vexed, vexing. **contrarier, fâcher, vexer** ▸ to bother or annoy; irritate. ▲ ADJECTIVE: *a vexing situation.*

vi·a [VY-uh *or* VEE-uh] PREPOSITION. **via, par, au moyen de** ▸ by way of; through : *We travelled from Victoria to Vancouver via a ferry boat.*

vi·a·ble [VY-uh-bul] ADJECTIVE. **1. viable** ▸ able to continue living and growing. **2. viable** ▸ able to succeed or function : *a viable idea for a fundraiser.*

vi·brant [VY-brunt] ADJECTIVE. **1. vibrant (-ante)** ▸ having vibrations; vibrating : *the vibrant voice of an opera singer.* **2. vivant (-ante), vif (vive), dynamique** ▸ full of energy; lively : *Erin is popular because she has such a vibrant personality and is involved in many activities.* ■ **vibrantly,** ADVERB. ▸ **de façon dynamique, vivement.**

vi·brate [VY-BRATE] VERB, vibrated, vibrating. **vibrer** ▸ to shake back and forth quickly; quiver : *Guitar strings vibrate and make sounds when plucked.*

vi·bra·tion [vy-BRAY-shun] NOUN, vibrations. **vibration** ▸ the act of vibrating; a quick moving back and forth, or up and down : *The vibrations caused by the truck made the windows rattle.*

vice[1] [vice] NOUN, vices. **vice** ▸ a bad or evil habit or form of behaviour : *Smoking is a vice.*

vice[2] NOUN. **étau** ▸ another spelling of vise.

vice-pres·i·dent **vice-président (-ente)** ▸ an official next in rank to the president of a country or an organization, who can take the president's place if needed.

vi·ce ver·sa [VY-suh VUR-suh *or* VICE-VUR-suh] ADVERB. **vice versa** ▸ in the opposite way; the other way around : *Mia said it was my fault, and vice versa.*

vi·cin·i·ty [vih-SIN-uh-tee] NOUN, vicinities. **environs, alentours ▸** the area around or near a particular place : *My coat was found in the vicinity of the school.*

vi·cious [VISH-us] ADJECTIVE. **1. haineux (-euse), méchant (-ante), acerbe ▸** having or showing hate or cruelty; evil; mean : *vicious gossip.* **2. méchant (-ante), vicieux (-euse), féroce ▸** likely or able to cause harm; dangerous; fierce : *a vicious mountain lion.* ■ **viciously,** ADVERB. ▸ **brutalement, violemment, méchamment.** ■ **viciousness,** NOUN. ▸ **méchanceté, brutalité, agressivité.** 🔎 p. 363.

vic·tim [VIK-tum] NOUN, victims. **1. victime ▸** a living thing that is killed, injured, or made to suffer : *a victim of a car accident.* **2. victime ▸** a person who is cheated, fooled, or taken advantage of by another : *Ernest was the victim of Michi's practical joke.* **Note.** A person who is fooled in this way is said to be victimized.

vic·to·ri·ous [vik-TOR-ee-us] ADJECTIVE. **victorieux (-euse) ▸** having won a fight or struggle; having gained victory : *Our swim team was victorious at the meet.* **Note.** A person who is victorious is a victor.

vic·to·ry [VIK-tur-ee] NOUN, victories. **victoire ▸** the act of winning a battle, struggle, or contest : *We had a party to celebrate our debating victory.*

vid·e·o [VID-ee-oh] ADJECTIVE. **1. vidéo ▸** having to do with what is seen on a television or computer screen. **2. vidéo ▸** having to do with television or the television industry. ▲ NOUN, videos. **1. vidéo, écran ▸** the picture on a television or a computer screen. **2. bande vidéo, cassette vidéo ▸** short for videotape. **3. clip vidéo ▸** a short film that goes with the music of a popular song.

vid·e·o·cas·sette [VID-ee-oh-kuh-SET] NOUN, videocassettes. **vidéocassette, cassette vidéo ▸** a plastic case with a roll of videotape, on which pictures may be recorded or played using a special machine. **Note.** This machine is called a videocassette recorder or VCR.

vid·e·o·disc [VID-ee-oh-DISK] NOUN, videodiscs. **vidéodisque ▸** a disk resembling a phonograph record, containing recorded pictures and sounds that can be played back on a television set. **Note.** A videodisc stores more information than a videotape and can refer to this information at random, but cannot make new recordings.

video game jeu vidéo ▸ an electronic game that is played by moving images around on a screen such as a television or computer screen. **Note.** Also called a computer game or electronic game.

vid·e·o·tape [VID-ee-oh-TAPE] NOUN, videotapes. **bande vidéo, cassette vidéo ▸** a special type of magnetic tape that records television perfor-

mances for later showing. ▲ VERB, videotaped, videotaping. **enregistrer (sur bande vidéo) ▸** to record something on videotape : *to videotape a TV show.*

view [vyoo] NOUN, views. **1. vue ▸** the act or fact of seeing something : *"Eddie watched the men ride away long after they had disappeared from view."* (Tim Wynne-Jones) **2. vue, panorama ▸** something that is seen : *The view of the valley was spectacular.* **3. vue, opinion ▸** a way of thinking; an opinion : *Karla has strong views on protecting the environment.* **4. in view of. vu, étant donné que ▸** because of; considering : *In view of your poor marks, I think you should study more.* ▲ VERB, viewed, viewing. **1. regarder, voir ▸** to look at; see : *We viewed the parade from a balcony.* **2. considérer, envisager, voir ▸** to think about; consider : *My parents view music lessons as an important part of my education.* SYN: scene, vista.

view·er [VYOO-ur] NOUN, viewers. **1. spectateur (-trice), téléspectateur (-trice) ▸** a person who watches something, especially someone who watches television. **2. viseur ▸** a device to look through to see something, as on a camera.

viewer

view·point [VYOO-POYNT] NOUN, viewpoints. **point de vue ▸** a way of thinking; a point of view.

vig·il [VIJ-ul] NOUN, vigils. **1. veille, veillée ▸** a time of staying awake at night to keep watch or guard something. **2. veille, veillée ▸** any such time of careful watching : *Hollis kept a close vigil over her dog, knowing that the puppies could be born any day.* **Note.** A person who is watchful and alert is vigilant.

vig·or·ous [VIG-ur-us] ADJECTIVE. **1. vigoureux (-euse), énergique ▸** full of energy; healthy and active : *Linda is a vigorous sportsperson, enjoying swimming, hiking, and basketball.* **2. vigoureux (-euse), robuste ▸** having force and strength : *Vitus gave his horse a vigorous rubdown after a long ride.* ■ **vigorously,** ADVERB. ▸ **vigoureusement.**

vig·our [VIG-ur] NOUN. (also vigor) **vigueur, énergie, vitalité ▸** the fact of being vigorous; healthy energy : *Mark has the vigour of a boy accustomed to eating well and spending a lot of time outdoors.*

Vi·king [VY-king] NOUN, Vikings. **Viking** ▶ one of a group of Scandinavian warriors who raided the coasts of northern Europe from the late 700s to about 1100.

vil·la [VIL-uh] NOUN, villas. **villa, maison de campagne** ▶ a large and expensive house, especially one located in the country or at the seashore.

vil·lage [VIL-ij] NOUN, villages. **village** ▶ houses and other buildings located near each other, forming a community that is smaller than a town.

vil·lain [VIL-un] NOUN, villains. **méchant (-ante)** ▶ in a story or play, an evil character who commits crimes or otherwise harms people : *A wicked witch is the villain of many fairy tales.* ▪ **villainous,** ADJECTIVE. ▶ **ignoble, infâme, abominable.** ✎ p. 655.

vine [vine] NOUN, vines. **plante grimpante** ▶ a plant with a long, thin stem that crawls along or around something, such as a tree or fence, and holds on to it for support : *Ivy and grapes grow as vines.*

vin·e·gar [VIN-uh-gur] NOUN, vinegars. **vinaigre** ▶ a sour liquid made by fermenting cider, wine, or other liquids. It is used in salad dressing, to flavour foods, and to preserve foods such as pickles.

vine·yard [VIN-yurd] NOUN, vineyards. **vignoble** ▶ an area of land where grapes are grown to make wine.

vin·tage [VIN-tij] NOUN, vintages. **cru** ▶ a season's crop of wine grapes in a certain district or place, or a wine made from such a harvest. ▲ ADJECTIVE **1. d'époque** ▶ the crop or product of a certain time : *vintage clothing from the 1920s.* **2. de grand cru, du meilleur cru, millésimé (-ée)** ▶ outstanding; excellent : *a vintage crop.*

vi·nyl [VY-nul] NOUN, vinyls. **vinyle** ▶ any of several kinds of shiny, flexible plastic used to make floor covering, raincoats, and other products.

vi·o·la [vee-OH-luh] NOUN, violas. **alto** ▶ a stringed musical instrument that is like a violin, but slightly larger and with a deeper tone. ◉ p. 538.

vi·o·late [VY-uh-LATE] VERB, violated, violating. **violer, enfreindre, transgresser** ▶ to break a rule or law; fail to obey : *John violated the law by driving through the red light.* ▪ **violator,** NOUN. ▶ **violateur (-trice), contrevenant (-ante).**

vi·o·la·tion [VY-uh-LAY-shun] NOUN, violations. **violation, infraction** ▶ the fact of violating; breaking a law or rule : *Using hands to stop the ball is a rule violation in soccer.*

vi·o·lence [VY-uh-lens] NOUN. **1. violence** ▶ the use of strong physical force to cause injury or damage : *I believe there is too much violence on television.* **2. violence** ▶ great force or strength : *The tree was uprooted by the violence of the tornado.*

✐ **Writing Tips**

Villain

*The **villain** of a story is the person who works against the **hero**, often creating problems that the hero has to solve or putting the hero in danger. Villains are usually evil, nasty, clever, sly, devious, dangerous people. They often think very highly of themselves, which means a bigger fall when they fail to conquer the heroes. When you are writing a story, remember to give your villain some motivation: Why is the villain so nasty? Why does this person want to harm the hero?*

vi·o·lent [VY-uh-lunt] ADJECTIVE. **1. violent (-ente)** ▶ with strong physical force; rough and dangerous : *The dog became violent and started biting people.* **2. violent (-ente)** ▶ caused by or showing strong, rough force : *Violent waves battered the shore.* ▪ **violently,** ADVERB. ▶ **violemment, avec violence.** SYN : fierce, vicious, turbulent, wild.

vi·o·let [VY-uh-lit] NOUN, violets. **1. violette** ▶ a small plant with flowers that are usually bluish-purple but can be yellow or white. **2. violet** ▶ a bluish-purple colour. ▲ ADJECTIVE. **violet (-ette)** ▶ having this colour.

vi·o·lin [vy-uh-LIN] NOUN, violins. **violon** ▶ a musical instrument that is played by drawing a bow across four strings. A violin is held under the chin with one arm as it is played. **Note.** A violinist is a person who plays the violin. ◉ p. 538.

vir·gin [VUR-jin] ADJECTIVE. **vierge** ▶ not yet touched, used, or marked; pure : *Virgin wilderness is territory that has not been explored or settled.*

vir·tu·al·ly [VUR-choo-ul-ee] ADVERB. **pratiquement, quasiment** ▶ almost completely; practically : *Virtually every early culture has stories about how the world began.* ▪ **virtual,** ADJECTIVE. ▶ **de fait, virtuel (-elle).**

vir·tue [VUR-choo] NOUN, virtues. **1. moralité** ▶ the right way of thinking and acting; good living; morality. **2. vertu, qualité** ▶ a certain good quality of character : *Tran tells me that my determination and willingness to work hard are my best virtues.* **3. vertu, mérite, avantage** ▶ something good; a benefit or advantage : *He made it into a good college by virtue of his academic abilities.*

vir·tu·ous [VUR-choo-us] ADJECTIVE. **vertueux (-euse), moral (-ale, -aux)** ▶ having or showing virtue; moral; pure.

vi·rus [VY-rus] NOUN, viruses. **1. virus ▶** a tiny, living thing that grows in the cells of other living things. They can cause diseases, such as the common cold or influenza. **2. virus ▶** in computers, an illegal program hidden in apparently normal software that can disrupt normal computer functioning.

vi·sa [VEE-zuh] NOUN, visas. **visa ▶** an official mark placed on a person's passport in a foreign country to show that the person has permission to enter or leave that country.

vise [vice] NOUN, vises. (also **vice**) **étau ▶** a device for holding an object in place while it is worked on.

vis·i·bil·i·ty [viz-uh-BIL-uh-tee] NOUN. **visibilité ▶** the ability to see, especially the distance at which an object can be seen: *During the snowstorm, drivers had poor visibility.*

vis·i·ble [VIZ-uh-bul] ADJECTIVE. **1. visible ▶** able to be seen: *The bowl has a visible crack in it.* **2. notable, apparent (-ente), visible ▶** able to be understood or noticed; apparent: *The candidate promised to cut taxes, but a year later there are no visible signs of tax cuts.* ■ **visibly,** ADVERB. ▶ **visiblement, manifestement.** *The children were visibly frightened by the movie.*

vi·sion [VIZH-un] NOUN, visions. **1. vision ▶** the power to see; the power of sight: *I have much better vision with my glasses.* **2. vue, champ de vision ▶** the range or distance of sight: *"Something moved at the edge of her vision and she turned her head slowly."* (Joseph Bruchac) **3. vision ▶** a thing that is seen, especially something of great beauty. **4. vision ▶** the power or ability to think of what things will be like in the future: *Egerton Ryerson's vision led to equal access to schools.* **5. vision ▶** something imaginary that is seen in the mind, as in a dream: *The scientist has visions of winning a Nobel prize.*

vis·it [VIZ-it] VERB, visited, visiting. **rendre visite, visiter ▶** to go to see a person or a place for a time: *Every Sunday I visit my grandmother.* ▲ NOUN, visits. **visite, séjour ▶** a short stay with someone or at some place: *a doctor's visit.* 🖺 **p. 1031.**

vis·i·tor [VIZ-uh-tur] NOUN, visitors. **visiteur (-euse) ▶** a person who visits; a guest: *Thousands of visitors come to the museum each year.*

vi·sor [VY-zur] NOUN, visors (also vizors) **1. visière ▶** a brim on the front of a hat to protect the eyes and face from the sun, as on a baseball cap. **2. pare-soleil ▶** a wide flap inside a car that can be turned down over part of the windshield to block the sun.

vis·ta [VIS-tuh] NOUN, vistas. **vue, perspective ▶** a view, especially one that is seen through a long, narrow opening: *A beautiful ocean vista spread out before them.*

vis·u·al [VIZH-oo-ul] ADJECTIVE. **1. visuel (-elle) ▶** having to do with the sense of sight: *The lovely table decorations were a visual feast.* **2. visuel (-elle) ▶** able to be seen; visible: *In teaching, visual aids such as pictures or maps can help students.*

vis·u·al·ize [VIZH-oo-ul-IZE] VERB, visualized, visualizing. **visualiser, se représenter, s'imaginer ▶** to form a mental picture of; see in the mind: *I can visualize what our new house will look like when it is all built.* 🖊 **p. 305.**

vi·tal [VY-tul] ADJECTIVE. **1. vital (-ale, -aux) ▶** important or necessary to life: *The heart, liver, and lungs are vital organs of the body.* **Note.** In medicine, the vital signs are basic indications of a person's health, such as pulse rate and blood pressure. **2. vital (-ale, -aux) ▶** very important or needed; essential: *It is vital that you have your passport when you leave the country.* **3. énergique, dynamique ▶** full of life and energy; lively. ■ **vitally,** ADVERB. ▶ **de façon cruciale, de façon essentielle, tellement, absolument. Note.** The fact of being vital or lively is vitality.

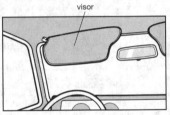

visor

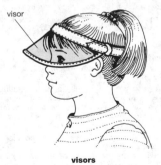

visor

visors

vi·ta·min [VY-tuh-min] NOUN, vitamins. **1. vitamine ▶** one of the natural substances that are found in small quantities in food and that are necessary to keep the body healthy and functioning properly. Vitamins are identified by letters of the alphabet, such as vitamin C. **2. vita-mine** ▸ one or more of these substances concentrated in the form of a pill or liquid, taken as an aid to health.

viv·id [VIV-id] ADJECTIVE. **1. vif (vive), éclatant (-ante)** ▸ of colour or light, bright and strong : *a vivid picture.* **2. vif (vive)** ▸ full of life and energy; lively; active : *a vivid imagination.* **3. vivant (-ante), saisissant (-ante), net (nette)** ▸ giving a clear picture to the mind; lifelike : *a vivid description.* ▪ **vividly,** ADVERB. ▸ **nettement, distinctement, de façon vivante, de façon frappante.** ▪ **vividness,** NOUN. ▸ **vivacité, éclat, netteté.**

vo·cab·u·lar·y [voh-KAB-yuh-LAIR-ee] NOUN, vocabularies. **1. vocabulaire** ▸ all the words that a person uses and understands. **2. lexique** ▸ all the words of a language. **3. jargon** ▸ the particular set of words that is used by a certain group of people : *the vocabulary of medicine.* **4. vocabulaire** ▸ a list of words and their meanings, used in studying a language.

vo·cal [VOH-kul] ADJECTIVE. **vocal (-ale, -aux)** ▸ having to do with the voice; using the voice. **Note.** Vocal cords are folds of skin in the throat. As air passes through the vocal cords, the vibration creates voice sounds.

vo·ca·tion [voh-KAY-shun] NOUN, vocations. **1. vocation, profession** ▸ the work that a person does or is suited to do; a business or trade. **2. vocation** ▸ a strong desire to enter a certain type of work, especially religious service. ▪ **vocational,** ADJECTIVE. **professionnel (-elle), technique** ▸ having to do with a job or career.

voice [voyce] NOUN, voices. **1. voix** ▸ the sound that is made through the mouth by a person in speaking or singing : *"Now the wild voices came together in a duet of yips, barks, and howls."* (Janet Foster) **2. voix** ▸ the power or ability to produce sounds : *Her voice was clear as she sang.* **3. opinion** ▸ the right to state an opinion : *In a democracy, your voice in government is guaranteed.* ▲ VERB, voiced, voicing. **exprimer, formuler** ▸ to say or express in words : *My mother voiced strong disapproval of our gossiping.* ✐ **p. 657.**

void [voyd] ADJECTIVE. **1. vide, dépourvu (-ue), dénudé (-ée)** ▸ not holding or having anything; empty or lacking : *His sleeping face was void of all expression.* **2. nul (nulle), non valide** ▸ having no power in law; not legally valid : *The contract is void because Janis had signed it without a witness.* ▲ NOUN, voids. **vide** ▸ an empty space or place.

vol·ca·no [vol-KAY-noh] NOUN, volcanoes. **1. vol-can** ▸ an opening in the earth's crust from which hot gases, lava, and ashes are thrown up. A volcano creates a cone-shaped hill or mountain. **2. volcan** ▸ the mountain or hill formed by a

┌─────────────────────────────────────┐
│ ✐ **Writing Tips** │

Voice (Passive and Active)
*In grammar, voice can be either **active** or **passive**.*

• *In the active voice, the subject does the action.*

   *Inez **opened** the store.*

• *In the passive voice, the action is done to the subject.*

   *The store **was opened** by Inez.*
When you're writing, it's best to avoid overusing the passive voice, which many experts consider weak, indirect, and wordy.
└─────────────────────────────────────┘

volcano. ▪ **volcanic,** ADJECTIVE. ▸ **volcanique.** *a volcanic eruption.* ✐ **p. 1115.**

vol·ley·ball [VOL-ee-bol] NOUN, volleyballs. **1. volley-ball** ▸ a ball game between two teams who try to keep the ball in the air and return it over the net to the other team. **2. ballon de volley-ball** ▸ the ball used in this game.

volt [vohlt] NOUN, volts. **volt** ▸ a unit used to measure the strength of electric current. A volt is the amount of force necessary to carry a certain amount of current through a certain kind of material.

vol·tage [VOLE-tij] NOUN, voltages. **voltage, tension** ▸ the force of an electric current, usually measured in volts. ✐ **p. 401.**

vol·ume [VOL-yoom *or* VOL-yum] NOUN, volumes. **1. volume** ▸ the amount of sound; loudness : *I can't hear the radio; could you turn the volume up?* **2. volume** ▸ the amount of space an object takes up, measured by multiplying its height, width, and length : *A box that is 5 cm wide by 5 cm deep by 6 cm tall has a volume of 150 cubic centimetres.* **3. volume** ▸ a number of pages bound together as a book. **4. volume** ▸ one of a set of books : *The article on "Zebras" is in the last volume of the encyclopedia.* ✐ **p. 548.**

volume

vol·un·tar·y [VOL-un-tair-ee] ADJECTIVE. **1. volontaire** ▸ done by choice or of one's own free will, not forced : *a voluntary contribution to a charity.* **2. volontaire** ▸ of an action of the body, done by thought and controlled by the mind.

vol·un·teer [VOL-un-TEER] NOUN, volunteers.
1. volontaire ▸ a person who enters military service without being drafted or forced to join.
2. bénévole ▸ a person who willingly does some job without pay : *Cindy is a volunteer at a seniors' home.* **3. volontaire** ▸ any person who agrees to take a difficult or unpleasant task. *Mom asked for a volunteer to help weed the garden.* ▲ VERB, volunteered, volunteering.
1. s'engager comme volontaire ▸ to choose to join the armed forces. **2. s'offrir pour faire quelque chose, se proposer pour faire quelque chose** ▸ to give help without being asked ; offer to do something : *My neighbour volunteered to look after my plants while I'm away.* ▲ ADJECTIVE: **pompier (-ière) bénévole** ▸ *a volunteer firefighter.*

vom·it [VOM-it] VERB, vomited, vomiting. **vomir** ▸ to become sick and throw up matter from the stomach. **Note.** Also used as a NOUN.

vote [vote] VERB, voted, voting. **1. voter** ▸ to show an opinion or choice in an election ; choose one person or course of action. People may vote by marking a ballot in secret, or by speaking or raising their hand to show their choice. **2.** *Informal.* **voter** ▸ to make a choice or decision : *Our family voted on where to go for vacation.* ▲ NOUN, votes. **1. vote** ▸ the act or fact of voting ; a choice in an election : *Kirk received 20 more votes than his opponent.* **2. vote** ▸ the right to take part in an election : *Canadian women gained the right to vote in 1918.*

vow [vow] NOUN, vows. **vœu (vœux)** ▸ a serious promise that a person is determined to keep :

marriage vows. ▲ VERB, vowed, vowing. **jurer** ▸ to make a vow : *She vowed she would never make that mistake again.*

vow·el [VOW-ul] NOUN, vowels. **voyelle** ▸ a sound in speech made by letting air pass freely through the open mouth as opposed to a consonant where the air is blocked in some way. In English, the vowels are spelled with the letters *a, e, i, o, u* and sometimes *y.* Every syllable has at least one vowel.

voy·age [VOY-ij] NOUN, voyages. **voyage (par mer), traversée** ▸ a trip or journey, especially a long trip over water. ▲ VERB, voyaged, voyaging. **voyager (par mer), traverser** ▸ to travel on a voyage. ■ **voyager,** NOUN. ▸ **passager (-ère), voyageur (-euse).**

vul·gar [VUL-gur] ADJECTIVE. **vulgaire** ▸ showing poor taste or bad manners ; crude or disgusting. **Note.** The fact of being vulgar is vulgarity.

vul·ner·a·ble [VUL-nur-uh-bul] ADJECTIVE. **vulnérable** ▸ easily able to be hurt or injured ; not strong or well-protected : *In hockey, protective equipment shields the vulnerable parts of the body.*

vul·ture [VUL-chur] NOUN, vultures. **1. vautour** ▸ a very large bird with dark feathers and a bare head and neck, related to hawks and eagles. It feeds on the decaying bodies of dead animals. **2. vautour** ▸ a cruel, greedy person who gains from the troubles of others.

whale

w, W [DUB-ul-yoo] NOUN, w's, W's. **w, W ▶** the 23rd letter of the English alphabet.

wad [wad] NOUN, wads. **1. tampon ▶** a small, soft mass : *a wad of cotton.* **2.** *Informal.* **liasse ▶** a large roll of paper money. ▲ VERB, **wadded, wadding. faire un tampon de ▶** to roll, squeeze, or crush into a wad : *Luisa wadded up the paper and threw it into the wastebasket.*

wad·dle [WAD-ul] VERB, waddled, waddling. **se dandiner ▶** to walk or move with short steps, with the body swaying from side to side, as a duck does : *A bear waddled slowly back into the woods.* ▲ NOUN, waddles. **dandinement ▶** a heavy, awkward way of walking.

wade [wade] VERB, waded, wading. **1. patauger, marcher avec difficulté ▶** to walk in or through water, mud, snow, or another such substance that covers the feet and makes movement difficult. **2. passer à travers, travailler laborieusement ▶** to move or make one's way slowly and with difficulty : *Rolf stayed late to wade through the pile of extra work.*

waf·fle[1] [WAH-ful] NOUN, waffles. **gaufre ▶** a crisp cake made of batter. Waffles are marked with little squares on them that are made as they are cooked in a special appliance, called a waffle iron.

waffle iron

waf·fle[2] VERB, waffled, waffling. **parler pour ne rien dire, parler avec ambiguïté ▶** to avoid making a decision.

wag [wag] VERB, wagged, wagging. **agiter, remuer, frétiller ▶** to move back and forth or up and down with short, quick movements : *My dog wags her tail a lot.* ▲ NOUN, wags. **remuement, frétillement ▶** the act of moving in this way.

wage [waje] NOUN, wages. **salaire, paie ▶** payment for work done : *The government sets a minimum hourly wage.* ▲ VERB, waged, waging. **faire la guerre ▶** to carry on a struggle or effort of some kind : *to wage a war.*

wag·on [WAG-un] NOUN, wagons. **1. chariot, char, voiture ▶** a large, heavy, four-wheeled vehicle that is used for carrying heavy loads. It is pulled by horses, oxen, mules, and so on. **2. train ▶** a low, small, four-wheeled vehicle like this that is pulled by hand, used as a toy. 📖 p. 1156.

wail [wale] VERB, wailed, wailing. **1. gémir, pleurer ▶** to make a long, loud cry because of sadness or pain : *"Soon they will fall on us,"* wailed the emperor's oldest son." (Leonard Everett Fisher) **2. hurler ▶** to make a long, mournful sound like this : *The ambulance siren wailed.* ▲ NOUN, wails. **pleurer ▶** a long, loud cry.

waist [waste] NOUN, waists. **1. taille ▶** the part of the human body between the ribs and the hips. **2. taille ▶** a piece of clothing that covers this area : *The pants have an elastic waist.*

wait [wate] VERB, waited, waiting. **1. attendre ▶** to stay in a place or do nothing, until someone comes or something happens : *"Waiting for him in his favourite bowl was steaming hot tea."* (Tololwa M. Mollel) **2. patienter, attendre ▶** to delay or be delayed : *Let's wait until next weekend to do the yardwork.* **3.** (usually **wait on** or **wait upon**) **servir ▶** to attend to people's needs, as in a store or restaurant. ▲ NOUN, **attente ▶** the act of waiting, or the time spent in waiting : *We had a two-hour wait in traffic before we got home.*

waive [wave] VERB, waived, waiving. **renoncer à, abandonner ▶** to agree to give up a right or claim : *The doctor waives her fee for people who can't afford to pay.* ■ **waiver,** NOUN. **renonciation, abandon ▶** the act or fact of waiving.

Wak-a-shan [wah-KASH-un *or* WOK-uh-SHON] NOUN. **wakashan** ▸ the group of languages spoken by the Nootka, the Kwakiutl, and other aboriginal groups in the Pacific Northwest.

wake[1] [wake] VERB, woke or waked, waked or woken, waking. **1. se réveiller, s'éveiller, sortir du sommeil** ▸ to stop sleeping : *Mary woke to the noise of the garbage truck.* **2. réveiller, tirer du sommeil** ▸ to cause to stop sleeping : *Don't talk so loud; you'll wake the baby.* **3. wake up. a. se réveiller** b. **se réveiller, se ranimer** ▸ to become active or aware : *He woke up when the coach said he'd be off the team if he didn't improve his marks.*

wake[2] NOUN, wakes. **veillée mortuaire** ▸ a gathering to watch over the body of a dead person before burial and to pay last respects to the one who died.

wake[3] NOUN, wakes. **1. sillage** ▸ the track left by a ship, boat, or other object moving through water. **2. sillage, trace** ▸ any similar track or path that is left by something. **3. in the wake of. marcher sur les traces de, dans le sillage de** ▸ following close behind; after.

walk [wok] VERB, walked, walking. **1. marcher** ▸ to move on foot at the normal rate. **2. se rendre, faire à pied** ▸ to move over or through something on foot : *Michelle walked to the store.* **3. promener** ▸ to cause to walk : *to walk a dog.* **4. but sur balles** ▸ in baseball, to allow a batter to go to first base by pitching four balls. ▲ NOUN, walks. **1. promenade, randonnée, excursion** ▸ the act of walking, especially for pleasure or exercise : *We went for a walk in the park.* **2. de marche, à pied de** ▸ the distance or time to be walked : *It is a five-minute walk to the bus stop.* **3. chemin, sentier** ▸ a place set apart for walking : *Rows of daffodils lined the walk.* **Note.** Often used in combinations such as sidewalk, walkway, and crosswalk. **4. but sur balles, base sur balles** ▸ in baseball, the act of allowing a batter to go to first base by pitching four balls. ☞ **p. 1031.**

walk-er [WOK-ur] NOUN, walkers. **1. piéton (-onne), marcheur (-euse), promeneur (-euse)** ▸ a person who walks : *I can't keep up; you're a fast walker.* **2. déambulateur, trotteuse** ▸ a device used to help a person in walking, as for a young child or a person who is disabled.

wall [wal] NOUN, walls. **1. mur** ▸ a solid, standing structure that divides or closes off an area. Walls form the sides of a building or room. **2. mur** ▸ something that looks or acts like a wall : *A wall of mud swept through the flooded town.* **3. paroi** ▸ the side or inner surface of something, such as a body part : *the wall of the stomach.* **4. mur** ▸ something that separates or forms a barrier : *The reporter found a wall of silence about the robbery.* ▲ VERB, walled, walling. **entourer d'un mur** ▸ to close off or protect with, or as if with, a wall : *"The three huge*

barns and the fence walled in the snug yard." (Laura Ingalls Wilder) ☞ **p. 1073.**

wal-let [WAL-it] NOUN, wallets. **portefeuille** ▸ a small, flat folding case used for holding money, cards, photographs, and so on.

wal-low [WAL-oh] VERB, wallowing. **1. se vautrer** ▸ to roll about in deep mud, water, dirt, or the like : *Pigs wallowed in mud to cool off.* **2. se complaire** ▸ to take too much pleasure in : *I wallowed in self-pity about the accident.*

wall-pa-per [WAL-PAY-pur] NOUN, wallpapers. **papier peint, tapisserie** ▸ paper that is used to cover and decorate the walls of a room. Wallpaper is printed with colours and designs. ▲ VERB, wallpapered, wallpapering. **tapisser** ▸ to put wallpaper on : *to wallpaper a room.*

wal-nut [WAL-nut] NOUN, walnuts. **1. noix** ▸ a large nut that can be eaten, having a hard, thick shell that is evenly divided into two parts. **2. noyer** ▸ the tree that this nut grows on. **3. noyer** ▸ the hard, strong wood of the walnut tree, used to make furniture. ☞ **p. 254.**

wal-rus [WOL-rus] NOUN, walrus or walruses. **morse** ▸ a large sea animal of the Arctic that looks like and is related to the seal. A walrus has a thick neck, two long tusks, and a thick, wrinkled hide.

walrus

waltz [woltz] NOUN, waltzes. **1. valse** ▸ a smooth, gliding dance for couples. **2. valse** ▸ music for this dance. ▲ VERB, waltzed, waltzing. **1. valser, danser la valse** ▸ to dance a waltz. **2. entrer avec désinvolture** ▸ to move in an easy or confident way : *Daniel waltzed into the room as if he was a star.*

wam-pum [WOM-pum] NOUN. **wampum** ▸ small shell beads strung together into necklaces, belts, or bracelets. It was once used as money by some Native peoples in eastern North America.

wand [wond] NOUN, wands. **baguette** ▸ a thin stick or rod, especially one held or waved around by a magician during a magic act : *a magic wand.*

wan-der [WON-dur] VERB, wandered, wandering. **1. flâner, errer** ▸ to go or move around with no particular place to go : *We wandered around the fair until it was time to meet the others for lunch.* **Note.** A person who wanders is a wanderer. **2. s'égarer** ▸ to lose one's way : *Our puppy wandered into the neighbour's yard.* **3. s'égarer, déconcentrer, être distrait (-aite)** ▸ to move away from a certain point or place; move about without purpose : *My attention wandered from the movie.* SYN: roam, stroll, ramble.

wane [wane] VERB, waned, waning. **1. diminuer** ▸ to lose size gradually; become smaller : *The moon is said to wane during the time after the full moon when it appears to be growing smaller in the sky.* **2. décliner, être en déclin, décroître** ▸ to lose power, strength, or importance : *Carla's energy waned at the end of the busy day.*

want [wont] VERB, wanted, wanting. **1. vouloir, désirer** ▸ to wish to do or have; have a desire for : *Ask Sybil what she wants for her birthday.* **2. avoir besoin par manque, avoir besoin faute de** ▸ to have a need for; lack : *Jashir is such a good host that we didn't want for anything.* ▲ NOUN, wants. **1. besoin** ▸ the fact of needing or lacking something : *For want of money, Asad could not buy the desk.* **2.** (usually **wants**) **besoin (s)** ▸ something that is desired or needed.

wan-ton [WON-tun] ADJECTIVE, **injustifié (-iée), gratuit (-uite)** ▸ done without any reason or purpose; reckless : *Fences were knocked down in wanton acts of destruction.* SYN: reckless, unruly, inconsiderate.

war [wor] NOUN, wars. **1. guerre** ▸ a large, continued fight between the armed forces of different countries or groups : *a civil war.* **2. guerre, lutte** ▸ a long, serious fight or struggle : *a war against a disease.* ▲ VERB, warred, warring. **faire la guerre** ▸ to take part in a war; fight. **Note.** Also used as an ADJECTIVE: *warring nations.* 📖 **p. 1149.**

ward [word] NOUN, wards. **1. salle, pavillon** ▸ a part of a hospital in which there are a number of patients of the same kind : *the children's ward.* **2. section électorale** ▸ an election district or other such local division of a city. **3. pupille** ▸ a person placed under the care or supervision of a guardian or of a court : *After my parents died, I became my uncle's ward.* ▲ VERB, warded, warding. ward off. **parer, éviter** ▸ to keep away; turn back : *Knights used shields to ward off the blows of an attacker.*

war-den [WOR-den] NOUN, wardens. **1. directeur (-trice), gardien (-ienne)** ▸ a person who is in charge of a prison. **2. gouverneur (-eure), directeur (-trice)** ▸ an official who makes sure that certain laws are obeyed.

ward-robe [WORD-robe] NOUN, wardrobes. **1. garde-robe** ▸ a person's clothes; a collection or supply of clothing : *Ashley added a new coat to her winter wardrobe.* **2. armoire, penderie, garde-robe** ▸ a large piece of furniture or a closet for hanging and keeping clothes.

ware [wair] NOUN, wares. **1. wares. marchandise, article, produit** ▸ articles for sale. **2. article de** ▸ manufactured items of a certain kind. **Note.** Used in combinations such as kitchenware, hardware, and software.

ware-house [WAIR-hows] NOUN, warehouses. **entrepôt, magasin** ▸ a building where goods are stored, especially one where items for sale are kept before being delivered to a store or to a customer.

war-fare [WOR-fair] NOUN. **guerre, lutte** ▸ fighting between armed forces; war.

war-head [WOR-hed] NOUN. **ogive** ▸ the front part of a torpedo, missile, or the like, which carries the explosive charge.

war-i-ly [WAIR-uh-lee] ADVERB. **avec prudence, avec précaution** ▸ in a wary manner; cautiously : *The chipmunk ate warily, ready to run if we came any closer.*

war-like [WOR-like] ADJECTIVE, **guerrier (-ière), belliqueux (-euse)** ▸ ready for war; favouring or threatening war.

warm [worm] ADJECTIVE, warmer, warmest. **1. chaud (chaude), assez chaud (chaude)** ▸ somewhat hot; not cold : *the warm afternoon sun.* **2. chaud (chaude), assez chaud (chaude)** ▸ giving off or holding in heat : *Come sit by the fire where it is warm.* **3. chaleureux (-euse), cordial (-iale, -iaux)** ▸ having or showing lively and friendly feeling : *a warm smile.* **4. chaud (chaude)** ▸ of a colour, suggesting heat : *Red, yellow, and orange are known as warm colours.* ▲ VERB, warmed, warming. **1. réchauffer, chauffer** ▸ to make or become warm : *Warm the buns on the barbecue.* **2. warm up. a. réchauffer** ▸ to make or become warm : *"Work hard and it will warm you up a little."* (James Houston) **b. se réchauffer** ▸ to get a person or thing to perform or operate : *It is good to let the car engine warm up for a while before driving.* **Note.** Also used as a NOUN and an ADJECTIVE: *a 10-minute warmup; a warmup suit.* ▪ **warmly,** ADVERB. ▸ **chaudement, chaleureusement, cordialement** ▸. *The villagers warmly welcomed the stranded travellers into their homes.*

warm-blood-ed [WORM-BLUD-id] ADJECTIVE. **à sang chaud** ▸ of an animal, having blood that stays at about the same temperature, even when the temperature of the surrounding air or water changes. Mammals and birds are warm-blooded.

warmth [wormth] NOUN. **chaleur** ▸ the fact of being warm : *the warmth of an electric blanket.*

warn [worn] VERB, warned, warning. **1. prévenir, avertir** ▸ to give notice of something bad that might happen : *the radio warned listeners that it might rain today.* **2. déconseiller, mettre en garde contre** ▸ to give advice about possible harm or danger : *"Be careful," she warned.* SYN: caution, advise, notify, give notice.

warn·ing [WORN-ing] NOUN, warnings. **avertisse-ment, avis ▸** a notice of harm or danger : *This toy has a warning that it is not suitable for children under three.* ▲ ADJECTIVE. **d'avertissement, d'alarme, avertisseur (-euse) ▸** that warns; serving to warn : *Jamie caught a warning glance from Mr. Sanchez.*

warp [worp] VERB, warped, warping. **1. gauchir, voiler ▸** to bend or twist out of shape : *Water has warped the wall outside the shower.* **2. fausser, pervertir, corrompre ▸** to turn from what is right : *Many parents complain that advertising warps children's ideas about clothes and toys.*

war·rant [WOR-unt] NOUN, warrants. **mandat ▸** an official written order that gives a person legal authority to do something : *A search warrant gives the police the right to search someone's home.* ▲ VERB, warranted, warranting. **justifier, légitimer ▸** to give or be a good reason for : *The rude way my sister spoke to Mom warrants punishment.*

war·ran·ty [WOR-un-tee] NOUN, warranties. **garantie ▸** a written statement from the seller of a product guaranteeing that the product is being sold as it is described, and that for a certain period of time, the seller will repair or replace the item if it fails to work as expected.

war·ri·or [WOR-ee-ur *or* WOR-yur] NOUN, warriors. **1. guerrier (-ière), soldat, militaire ▸** a person who is experienced in fighting wars or battles. **2. guerrier (-ière), combattant (-ante) ▸** any person who takes part in a difficult struggle or conflict : *She is considered a warrior in the fight for human rights.*

war·ship [WOR-SHIP] NOUN, warships. **navire de guerre, vaisseau (-eaux) de guerre ▸** a ship that is built for combat and armed with weapons.

wart [wort] NOUN, warts. **verrue ▸** a small hard lump that grows on the skin. Warts are caused by a virus.

wart·hog [WORT-HOG] NOUN, warthogs. (also wart hog) **phacochère ▸** a wild hog of Africa having long, curving tusks and large, wartlike growths sticking out from its cheeks. .

war·y [WAIR-ee] ADJECTIVE, warier, wariest. **prudent (-ente), sur ses gardes, circonspect (-ecte) ▸** looking out for danger; on guard; alert : *The deer were wary and would not come near us.* SYN : aware, wakeful, attentive.

was [wuz] VERB. a past form of be.

wash [wosh] VERB, washed, washing. **1. laver ▸** to clear away dirt or stains by using water, or water and soap : *to wash your hands.* **2. s'en aller, partir à l'eau ▸** to move or carry away by the action of water : *Heavy rains washed away the hillside.* ▲ NOUN, washes. **1. lavage ▸** the act of washing; or a place where this is done : *a car wash.* **2. lavage, lessive ▸** the amount of clothes or other items that are washed at one time. **3. clapotis ▸** a flow of water, or the sound made by this. **4. oasis ▸** an area in a desert or other dry place where water sometimes flows.

wash·er [WASH-ur] NOUN, washers. **1. laveur (-euse) ▸** a person who washes : *A window washer is coming to clean the windows.* **2. lave-linge, machine à laver ▸** another name for a washing machine. **3. rondelle, joint ▸** a flat ring used to give a tighter fit to two parts that go together. A metal washer goes between a nut and a bolt.

washing machine lave-linge, machine à laver **▸** an electric machine used for washing clothes, towels, and other such items automatically.

wasp [wosp] NOUN, wasps. **guêpe ▸** a flying insect related to bees and ants, having a powerful sting and a slender body with a narrow abdomen. Hornets and yellow jackets are types of wasps. 👁 p. 104.

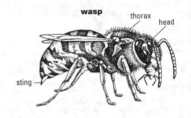

wasp

thorax

head

sting

waste [wayst] VERB, wasted, wasting. **1. gaspiller ▸** to use or spend in a careless and foolish way : *Nan doesn't like to waste anything, so she reuses all her jars.* **2. dépérir ▸** to slowly lose health, strength, or force : *to waste away to skin and bones.* ▲ NOUN. **1. perte, gaspillage, gâchis ▸** the act or fact of wasting : *a waste of time.* **2. déchet, ordure ▸** things of no use or value; worthless material to be thrown away. **3. déchet, excrément ▸** material that is not digested for use as food and that is sent out from the body. ▲ ADJECTIVE. **perdu (-ue), superflu (-ue), usé (-ée) ▸** having to do with or used for waste : *wastepaper.* ■ **wasteful,** ADVERB. **▸ de façon peu économique, de façon peu rentable, de façon excessive.**

waste·bas·ket [WAYSTE-bas-kit] NOUN, wastebaskets. **corbeille à papier ▸** a basket or other container that is used to hold paper scraps and other things to be thrown away. **Note.** Also called a wastepaper basket.

waste·land [WAYST-land] NOUN, wastelands. **1. désert ▸** an area of land where there are very few plants and animals and where few people live, such as a desert or a polar region. **2. terrain**

vague ▸ an area that is without life or spirit : *This part of town is an industrial wasteland because no one lives here.*

watch [woch] VERB, watched, watching. **1. regarder** ▸ to look carefully at some event or activity that is going on : *to watch television.* **2. observer, regarder** ▸ to look at carefully; keep one's attention on : *"The Mongols watched from distant hills."* (Leonard Everett Fisher) **3. surveiller, observer** ▸ to keep guard over; look at so as to care for or protect : *Mom sent me outside to watch my sister.* **4. surveiller, guetter, observer** ▸ to be careful or concerned about : *The shoppers watched to see how low the prices would go.* ▲ NOUN, watches. **1. montre, montre-bracelet** ▸ a small device that tells time, usually worn on the wrist or sometimes carried in a pocket. **2. guetter, faire le guet, monter la garde** ▸ one or more people ordered to stay awake and alert to guard or protect others, as on a ship at night. **3. être de quart** ▸ the period of time when someone does this : *Lieutenant Brown's watch was from midnight to 4 a.m.* **4. surveiller de près, surveiller avec vigilance** ▸ the act or fact of looking carefully; close attention. ☞ p. 1081.

watch·dog [WOCH-dog] NOUN, watchdogs. **1. chien de garde** ▸ a dog that is kept to guard a house or property and to warn of intruders. **2. gardien (-ienne)** ▸ a person or group that tries to guard against loss, crime, and so on : *Amnesty International acts as a watchdog against countries that abuse human rights.*

watch·ful [WOCH-ful] ADJECTIVE. **vigilant (-ante), attentif (-ive)** ▸ carefully watching; alert. ▪ **watchfully,** ADVERB. ▪ **attentivement.**

wa·ter [WAH-tur] NOUN, waters. **eau** ▸ the common liquid that is used for drinking and washing; the substance that falls from the sky as rain and forms the world's oceans, lakes, rivers, and so on. Water has no colour, smell, or taste in its pure form. ▲ VERB, watered, watering. **1. arroser** ▸ to supply with water : *Please water the garden.* **2. larmoyer, pleurer** ▸ to give off a fluid like water : *My eyes began to water when I smelled the onion.* **3. water down. a. couper** ▸ to make a liquid weaker by adding water. **b. atténuer, affaiblir** ▸ to make weaker or less effective : *The committee watered down the resolution so everyone would agree to it.* ☞ p. 1110. ☞ p. 112, 400.

water-bed [WAH-tur-bed] NOUN, waterbeds. **lit d'eau** ▸ a type of bed that uses a plastic bag filled with water rather than an ordinary mattress.

water buffalo arni, kérabau, buffle (des Indes) ▸ a large, powerful buffalo found chiefly in Asia and Africa, having very wide horns that curve backward.

water colour (also **water color**) **1. aquarelle** ▸ a paint that is made by mixing colour with water instead of with oil. **2.** (also **water-colour**) **aquarelle** ▸ a picture done with such paints, or the art of painting in this way.

wa·ter·cress [WAH-tur-kres] NOUN. **cresson** ▸ a type of plant that grows in water, having sharp-tasting leaves that are used in salads and sandwiches.

wa·ter·fall [WAH-tur-fol] NOUN, waterfalls. **chute d'eau, cascade** ▸ a stream of water that falls straight down from a high place, as over a cliff.

wa·ter·front [WAH-tur-frunt] NOUN, waterfronts. **1. front de mer** ▸ land that is at the edge of a body of water. **2. quai** ▸ the part of a city that is alongside a body of water, especially where there are docks.

wa·ter·logged [WAH-tur-logd] ADJECTIVE. **imprégné (-ée) d'eau, imbibé (-ée) d'eau, détrempé (-ée)** ▸ said of something that is completely soaked through with water : *The water-logged boat sank.*

wa·ter·mel·on [WAH-tur-mel-un] NOUN, watermelons. **melon d'eau, pastèque** ▸ a large melon that has sweet, juicy, red or pink flesh, many seeds, and a hard green outer skin. Watermelons grow on vines.

wa·ter·proof [WAH-tur-proof] ADJECTIVE. **imperméable** ▸ keeping water from passing through : *a waterproof raincoat.* ▲ VERB, waterproofed, waterproofing. **imperméabiliser** ▸ to make something waterproof : *Dad waterproofed our deck.*

wa·ter·shed [WAH-tur-shed] NOUN, watersheds. **1. ligne de partage des eaux** ▸ a ridge of mountains or other high land, separating river systems that flow in different directions. **2. bassin hydrographique** ▸ the total land area from which a river or lake drains its water. **3. moment critique, moment décisif (-ive), grand tournant** ▸ a crucial dividing point in the course of events : *The debate was a watershed in the mayor's defeat.*

wa·ter·ski [WAH-tur-skee] VERB, water-skied, water-skiing. **ski nautique** ▸ to glide over water on skis (water skis) while holding on to a tow rope that is attached to a power boat.

wa·ter·way [WAH-tur-way] NOUN, waterways. **voie navigable** ▸ a river, canal, or other such body of water that ships and boats travel on.

wa·ter·wheel [WAH-tur-weel] NOUN, waterwheels. **roue hydraulique** ▸ a wheel that is turned by the weight of water falling on it, used to provide power.

wa·ter·y [WAH-tur-ee] ADJECTIVE, waterier, wateriest. **trop liquide** ▸ full of water or containing too much water : *a watery soup.*

watt [wot] NOUN, watts. **watt** ▸ a unit used to measure electrical power : *a 100-watt bulb.*

wave [wave] VERB, waved, waving. **1. saluer** ▸ to move something in the air, such as the hand, as a signal or greeting : *Yat-San and I* *waved good-bye.* **2. flotter ▶** to move freely back and forth in the air : *The flag waved in the breeze.* **3. ondulation, cran ▶** to give a series of curls to the hair. **▲ NOUN, waves. 1. vague ▶** a moving ridge or high point on the surface of a body of water. **2. onde ▶** any movement like the shape of an ocean wave. Sound and heat move in waves, and radio and TV programs travel through the air as waves. **3. vague ▶** a strong feeling or condition that is thought of as moving like a wave : *"He felt a sudden wave of disgust sweep over him."* (Arthur C. Clarke) **4. signe de la main, geste ▶** the act of waving.

wave-length [WAVE-lenkth] NOUN, wavelengths. **1. longueur d'ondes ▶** the distance from a certain point on one wave to the same point on the next wave, especially from the top of one wave to the top of another. Often used in the measurement of light or sound. **2. longueur d'ondes ▶** a certain way of thinking, in relation to how another or others think : *Kate and I are on the same wavelength when it comes to music.*

wa-ver [WAY-vur] VERB, wavered, wavering. **1. vaciller ▶** to move back and forth in an unsteady way : *Joel wavered for a moment after he walked into the wall.* **2. vaciller, hésiter ▶** to be uncertain ; hesitate : *"Older people have formed their opinions about everything, and don't waver before they act."* (Anne Frank) SYN : quiver, shake, tremble.

wav-y [WAVE-ee] ADJECTIVE, wavier, waviest. **ondulé (-ée) ▶** having waves : *Some terrier dogs have wavy hair.*

wax¹ [waks] NOUN, waxes. **1. cire ▶** any of various thick, fatty substances that come from plants or animals or are made artificially. Wax melts or softens when it is heated. **2.** (also beeswax) **cire ▶** such a substance made by bees. **3. de cire ▶** any of various materials containing wax or a similar substance and used as a polish for floors and cars, to make candles, and for other items. **▲ VERB, waxed, waxing. cirer ▶** to coat or polish with wax : *She waxed her car until it shone.* **■ waxy,** ADJECTIVE. **▶ cireux (-euse).**

wax² VERB, waxed, waxing. **croître ▶** to become larger or greater : *The Moon is said to wax when it appears to grow larger and closer to being a full moon.*

way [way] NOUN, ways. **1. façon, méthode, manière, moyen ▶** the certain manner or method in which something happens or is done : *Do it this way.* **2. chemin, route ▶** a road or course going from one place to another ; a route : *The quickest way to the store is across the park.* **3. en chemin vers, sur la route de ▶** a certain direction : *Please mail this letter on your way to the library.* **4. être loin, distance ▶** a distance in space or time : *Summer's still a long way off.* **5. égard, point ▶** a point or item to be considered : *In many ways I agree with you.* **6. caprice, volonté ▶** what someone

wants ; a wish. **Note.** Used mainly in the phrase **get (have) one's way.** **▲ ADVERB. très loin ▶** far : *We are way off our course.*

we [wee] PLURAL PRONOUN. **nous ▶** the person speaking or writing, and another or others thought of as in the same group : *Sanjeet and I will help you when we get there.*

weak [week] ADJECTIVE, weaker, weakest. **1. faible ▶** not having the needed power or energy ; not strong : *"Za is too old and too weak to have the strength to get well."* (Ann Blades) **2. faible, mou (molle) ▶** lacking strength of character or will : *He is weak and just follows the others.* **■ weakly,** ADVERB. **▶ faiblement, mollement.** ✍ p. 664.

weak-en [WEEK-in] VERB, weakened, weakening. **s'affaiblir, faiblir ▶** to make or become weak.

weak-ness [WEEK-nis] NOUN, weaknesses. **1. faiblesse, fragilité, mollesse, impuissance ▶** the fact of being weak ; a lack of strength. **2. faiblesse, défaut ▶** a weak point ; a fault or flaw : *His poor start was his weakness in the race.* **3. faiblesse, goût, penchant ▶** a special liking that is hard to resist : *My weakness is for chocolate.*

wealth [welth] NOUN. **1. richesse, fortune ▶** a great amount of money, property, or valuable things ; riches. **2. en abondance, à profusion ▶** a great amount : *a wealth of decorating ideas.*

wealth-y [WEL-thee] ADJECTIVE, wealthier, wealthiest. **riche, fortuné (-ée) ▶** having wealth ; rich.

weap-on [WEP-un] NOUN, weapons. **1. arme ▶** any tool or device used in fighting or killing, such as a gun, knife, and so on : *the murder weapon.* **2. arme ▶** anything used for attack or defence : *Words are sometimes stronger weapons than force.*

wear [wair] VERB, wore, worn, wearing. **1. porter ▶** to have certain clothes on the body : *to wear a coat.* **2. avoir, afficher ▶** to have or show on the face or body : *She wore a look of disbelief as a pig walked into the yard.* **3. user ▶** to damage, weaken, or use up by rub-

---

✏ **Writing Tips**

Weak Ending

*A **weak ending** can damage a reader's opinion of the whole story. To make sure your endings are strong, think of the following questions : Is the story resolved too quickly or too easily ? Will the reader be left with unanswered questions ? Will the reader be satisfied by the ending ? Are all the loose ends tied up neatly ?*

bing or scraping, or by continued use : *My coat has worn thin*. **Note**. Usually used with a following ADVERB : *to wear out a pair of shoes*. **4. résis- ter à l'usure ▶** to hold up to such long use ; to last : *These gloves have worn well and still look good*. ▲ NOUN. **1. port ▶** the act or fact of wearing. **2. usure ▶** the damage caused by long use : *Our sofa is showing signs of wear*. **3. vête- ment, tenue, habillement, toilette ▶** things to be worn ; clothing of a certain type. **Note**. Used in combinations such as **sportswear** and **evening wear**.

wea·ry [WEER-ee] ADJECTIVE, wearier, weariest. **las (lasse), fatigué (-ée), épuisé (-ée) ▶** very tired : *"'I did my best,' sighed weary Ngwele. 'No one could have done better.'"* (Tololwa M. Mollel) ▲ VERB, wearied, wearying. **fati- guer, lasser ▶** to make or become tired. ▪ **wearily,** ADVERB. ▶ **avec lassitude, pénible- ment.** ▪ **weariness,** NOUN. ▶ **fatigue, épui- sement.** *The weariness showed in each firefighter's face.* SYN : exhausted, spent, over- worked.

wea·sel [WEE-zul] NOUN, weasels or weasel. **belette ▶** a small animal that has a long, slim body with soft, thick fur, short legs, and a long tail.

weath·er [WETH-ur] NOUN. **temps, température, climat ▶** the condition of the outside air at a certain time and place, as to whether it is cold, hot, sunny, rainy, windy, and so on. ▲ VERB, weath- ered, weathering. **1. user, abîmer ▶** to change by being exposed to the air or weather : *Years of sun and rain have weathered the fence.* **2. surmonter, réchapper à, survivre à ▶** to pass through a difficult experience safely, as if going through a storm : *to weather a problem.* 📄 p. 1105.

weather vane girouette ▶ a device that is moved by the wind and that has an arrow or pointer to show the direction in which the wind is blowing.

weave [weev] VERB, wove or weaved, woven or weaved, weaving. **1. tisser, entrelacer ▶** to pass threads or strips over and under each other to form cloth or other material : *to weave a rug.* **2. tisser ▶** of an insect, to spin a web or cocoon. **3. se faufiler ▶** to move quickly in and out ; go by twisting or turning : *I wove in and out of the crowd to race to a phone.* ▲ NOUN, weaves. **tissage ▶** a pattern or method of weaving : *Men's dress shirts are often made in a style called a basket weave.* **Note**. A person who weaves is a **weaver**.

web [web] NOUN, webs. **1. toile ▶** the pattern of fine threads that is spun by a spider to catch its prey. **Note**. Also called a **cobweb** or **spider- web. 2. tissu ▶** a piece of cloth that is being woven. **3. enchaînement ▶** something that is thought of as being like a spider's web, as by being complicated, by trapping or deceiving

someone, and so on : *Her web of lies made us believe she was a famous actor.* **4. palmure ▶** the skin between the toes of a swimming bird or animal, such as a duck, otter, or frog. **Note**. Such a bird or animal is said to be web- footed.

wed [wed] VERB, wedded, wedded or wed, wed- ding. **1. marier, épouser ▶** to take a husband or wife ; marry. **2. marier ▶** to join a couple as hus- band and wife. **3. allier ▶** to join or attach closely.

wed·ding [WED-ing] NOUN, weddings. **mariage, noce ▶** a marriage ceremony, or a celebration that goes along with a marriage. 📄 p. 1150.

wedge [wej] NOUN, wedges. **1. pointe, part ▶** anything that has the triangular shape of a wedge : *a wedge of pie.* ▲ VERB, wedged, wedg- ing. **1. enfoncer quelque chose dans une fente ▶** to split or separate with, or as if with, a wedge : *to wedge open a window.* **2. caler, enfoncer ▶** to push or crowd into a tight space : *We wedged five people into the tiny booth.*

Wed·nes·day [WED-unz-day or WENZ-day] NOUN, Wednesdays. **mercredi ▶** the day after Tuesday and before Thursday.

weed [weed] NOUN, weeds. **mauvaise herbe ▶** a wild plant that grows where it is not wanted in a garden or field, harming the growth of other plants that are wanted. Crabgrass and dande- lions are common weeds in a lawn. ▲ VERB, weeded, weeding. **1. désherber, sarcler ▶** to take the weeds out of : *to weed a garden.* **2. weed out. éliminer, trier ▶** to remove some- thing not wanted : *Chanda weeded out all her clothes that are too small.*

week [week] NOUN, weeks. **1. semaine ▶** a period of seven days in a row, especially one starting with Sunday and ending with Saturday. **2. semaine ▶** the part of a seven-day period when a person works or goes to school : *Friday is the end of the work week.*

week·day [WEEK-day] NOUN, weekdays. **jour de la semaine ▶** any day of the week except Satur- day and Sunday.

week·end [WEEK-end] NOUN, weekends. **fin de semaine, week-end ▶** the time from the end of one work or school week to the beginning of the next, usually Saturday and Sunday.

week·ly [WEEK-lee] ADJECTIVE. **1. hebdomadaire, de la semaine ▶** of or for a week : *a weekly visit.* **2. chaque semaine, hebdomadaire ▶** done or happening once a week : *a weekly TV show.* ▲ NOUN, weeklies. **hebdomadaire ▶** a newspaper or magazine published once a week. ▲ ADVERB. **hebdomadairement ▶** once a week ; every week.

weep [weep] VERB, wept, weeping. **pleurer, verser des larmes ▶** to cry ; shed tears : *Lara wept until she couldn't cry anymore.*

wee-vil [WEE-vil] NOUN. weevils. **charançon** ▸ a type of small beetle that has a long snout. Weevils do great damage to grain and cotton crops.

weigh [way] VERB, weighed, weighing. **1. peser** ▸ to find out how heavy someone or something is : *The doctor weighed the baby.* **2. peser** ▸ to have a certain weight : *This books weighs 2 kg.* **3. peser** ▸ to think about carefully ; consider : *Ishmael weighed all the choices before deciding on one.* **4.** weigh down. **faire plier, ployer, courber** ▸ to put a heavy load or weight on : *Snow weighed down the branches.*

weight [wate] NOUN, weights. **1. poids, pesanteur** ▸ how heavy a thing is : *His weight is about 30 kilograms.* **2. poids, haltère** ▸ a metal object that has a standard weight, used in the sport of weight lifting or for judging the weight of other objects on a balance scale. **3. presse-papier** ▸ a heavy metal object used to hold something down : *A paperweight keeps papers in place.* **4. poids** ▸ something that bears down on a person like a heavy load : *Darlene felt the weight of all the work she had to do.* **5. avoir du poids, avoir de l'influence** ▸ value or importance : *Your ideas have a lot of weight with the boss.* ▲ VERB, weighted, weighting. **peser** ▸ to put a load or weight on : *At practice, Sunil weights his bat to strengthen his swing.*

weight-less [WATE-lis] ADJECTIVE. **1. apesanteur** ▸ having little or no weight. **2. en état d'apesanteur** ▸ free from the pull of gravity, as objects are in a spacecraft in outer space.

weight lifting halterophilie ▸ an exercise or competition in which a person lifts an iron bar with heavy weights attached to it. **Note.** A person who does this is a weightlifter.

weight-y [WATE-ee] ADJECTIVE, weightier, weightiest. **grave, important (-ante), pesant (-ante), lourd (lourde)** ▸ having great importance ; serious : *a weighty decision.*

weird [weerd] ADJECTIVE, weirder, weirdest. **1. bizarre, étrange** ▸ strange in a way that is frightening or disturbing : *Mom had a weird feeling that something had happened to me, so she hurried home.* **2.** *Informal.* **bizarre, étrange, singulier (-ière), curieux (-ieuse)** ▸ odd or unusual : *The shirt has a weird pattern.*

wel-come [WEL-kum] VERB, welcomed, welcoming. **1. accueillir, souhaiter la bienvenue** ▸ to greet in a friendly way ; meet with warm feelings : *to welcome guests.* **2. accepter** ▸ to be glad to accept ; get with pleasure : *I welcome your ideas.* ▲ NOUN, welcomes. **bienvenue, accueil** ▸ a friendly greeting : *"Mr. Johnston came to meet us, smiling a welcome."* (Jean Little) ▲ ADJECTIVE. **1. bienvenu (-ue)** ▸ greeted or received with pleasure : *Your help was very welcome.* **2. bienvenu (-ue)** ▸ free to have or use : *You're welcome to take that book ; I'm through with it.* **3.** You're welcome. **de rien** ▸ a polite remark made in answer to a

person who has thanked you for something. ☞ **p. 1031.**

weld [weld] VERB, welded, welding. **souder** ▸ to join two pieces of metal or other material by heating the pieces until they can be pressed together. **Note.** This work is called welding, and a person who does it is a welder.

wel-fare [WEL-fair] NOUN. **1. bien, bien-être** ▸ the fact of being happy and healthy and of having what one needs to live comfortably : *The welfare of the students is a principal's most important concern.* **2. aide sociale** ▸ a government program to provide money, food, housing, medical care, or other forms of aid to those in need.

well¹ [wel] ADVERB, better, best. **1. bien** ▸ in a good, proper, or favourable way : *Casey and Lien play well together.* **2. bien** ▸ to a great extent ; very much : *Pietro didn't know the new neighbour well and he decided to pay a visit.* ▲ ADJECTIVE. **1. en santé** ▸ in good health ; healthy : *I don't think she's well ; she's missed a week of school.* **2. bien, bon** ▸ as it should be ; in good order or condition : *In olden times, a guard would call out "All's well" if there was nothing wrong.* ▲ INTERJECTION. **1.** ▸ used to show surprise : *Well! I thought you were never coming home!* **2. donc** ▸ used to begin a new remark, or to continue with one after a pause or interjection : *Well, I guess it's time to eat.* ☞ **p. 267.**

well² NOUN, wells. **1. puits** ▸ a deep hole dug in the ground to bring up water. **2. puits** ▸ a similar hole to bring up oil or gas. **3. puits** ▸ a natural spring or fountain used as a source of water. ▲ VERB, welled, welling. **monter** ▸ to rise or flow, like water filling a well : *My eyes welled with tears at the happy news.*

well-be-ing [WEL-BEE-ing] NOUN. **bien-être** ▸ the fact of being healthy and happy ; health and happiness.

well-done [WEL-DUN] ADJECTIVE. **1. bien fait** ▸ done well or properly : *The mayor congratulated the volunteers on a job well-done.* **2. bien cuit (cuite)** ▸ cooked for a long time ; thoroughly cooked : *I ordered my steak well-done, not rare.*

well-known [WEL-NOHN] ADJECTIVE. **bien connu (-ue), célèbre** ▸ generally or widely known : *It's a well-known fact that the world is round.*

well-mean-ing [WEL-MEE-ning] ADJECTIVE. **bien intentionné (-ée)** ▸ done with good intentions, though not always having the result wanted : *He's well-meaning, but he rarely finishes a project.*

went [went] VERB. a past form of go.

wept [wept] VERB. a past form of weep.

were [wur] VERB a past form of be.

were-wolf [WAIR-WULF] **loup-garou** ▶ in old stories, a person who temporarily turns into a wolf while keeping human intelligence.

west [west] NOUN. **1. ouest, au couchant** ▶ the direction that the sun goes in when it sets in the evening. **2. à l'ouest, de l'ouest** ▶ often West. any place or region in this direction. **3. the West. a. l'Ouest** ▶ the western part of North America. **b. l'Occident** ▶ the countries in Europe and America rather than those in Asia. ▲ ADJECTIVE. **1. ouest** ▶ toward the west : *the west side of the city.* **2. de l'ouest, d'ouest** ▶ coming from the west : *a west wind.* ▲ ADVERB. **à l'ouest, vers l'ouest** ▶ toward the west : *They travelled west to British Columbia.*

west-ern [WES-turn] ADJECTIVE. **1. de l'ouest** ▶ toward the west : *Red Deer is in western Canada.* **2. de l'ouest, d'ouest** ▶ coming from the west : *a west wind.* **3. de l'Ouest, occidental (-ale, -aux)** ▶ often Western. having to do with the western part of the world : *Countries in the Western world are technologically advanced.* Note. A Westerner is a person born or living in the West. ▲ NOUN, westerns. also, Western. **western** ▶ a book, movie, or TV show about life in the North American West in the 1800s.

west-ward [WEST-wurd] ADVERB; ADJECTIVE. **à l'ouest** ▶ toward the west.

wet [wet] ADJECTIVE. wetter, wettest. **1. mouillé (-ée), trempé (-ée)** ▶ covered or soaked with water or another liquid : *It was still wet outside from last night's rain.* **2. frais (fraîche)** ▶ not yet dry or hardened : *wet paint.* **3. pluvieux (-ieuse)** ▶ rainy . *This wet weather has caused a lot of traffic accidents.* ▲ VERB, wet or wetted, wetting. **mouiller** ▶ to cause to be wet : *Wet the cloth with warm water.* ■ **wetness,** NOUN. ▶ humidité.

wet-land [WET-LAND] NOUN, wetlands. (usually Wetlands) **marais, zone humide** ▶ a low-lying area that is partly covered with water and has very damp soil, such as a swamp or marsh. Wetlands are important as a home for animal and plant life.

✏️ Writing Tips

The Five W's
The five W's are the five basic question words: who, what, where, when, and why. These are the questions reporters ask when they go out to cover a story. If you have written a report, reread it to make sure you've answered these five questions. Are there any other questions that your readers might ask?

---

whack [wak] *Informal.* VERB, whacked, whacking. **fesser** ▶ to hit sharply; smack. ▲ NOUN, whacks. **grand coup, claquement** ▶ a loud or sharp blow.

whale [wale] NOUN, whales. **baleine** ▶ a very large sea animal that looks like a fish but is actually an air-breathing mammal. ☞ **p. 1095.** ☞ **p. 110.**

whal-ing [WALE-ing] NOUN. **pêche à la baleine** ▶ the work or business of hunting whales for their meat, bone, and fat called blubber. This fat produces a valuable oil that was widely used in former times. Many countries now have laws against whaling because of the threat to the whale population.

wharf [worf] NOUN, wharves or wharfs. **quai** ▶ a structure that is built along the shore for the loading and unloading of ships, often a platform set on pillars.

what [wut] PRONOUN. **1. que** ▶ which thing or things : *What are you going to do today?* **2. ce que** ▶ that or those; which : *She took what she could carry.* ▲ ADJECTIVE. **1. quel (quelle), lequel (laquelle, lesquels, lesquelles)** ▶ which or which type : *What shoes are you wearing tonight?* **2. quel (quelle)** ▶ how surprising or unusual . *What a story he told!* ▲ INTERJECTION. **quoi!** ▶ used to show surprise or annoyance : *What! You forgot to tell Mom that we'd be late!* ✍ **p. 667.**

what-ev-er [wut-EV-ur] PRONOUN. **1. tout ce que** ▶ anything that : *Jacob did whatever he could to repair his bike.* **2. quoi que** ▶ no matter what : *Whatever you do, be careful not to let the cat out* ▲ ADJECTIVE. **1. quel (quelle) que soit** ▶ any and all : *Whatever dinner is left over we'll save for tomorrow's lunch.* **2. quoi que ce soit** ▶ of any kind or type : *Steve looked at me blankly, with no expression on his face whatever.*

what-so-ev-er [wut-soh-EV-ur] PRONOUN; ADJECTIVE. **quel (quelle) que soit** ▶ of any kind; at all : *There's no reason whatsoever why you can't be on time for school.*

wheat [weet] NOUN. **blé, froment** ▶ a tall grass plant that has a thin stem and long leaves, and that is a very important source of food. The seeds (kernels) of wheat are ground up to make bread, breakfast cereal, spaghetti, noodles, and other foods. ☞ **p. 116.**

wheat germ **germe de blé** ▶ the centre or inner part of a kernel of wheat. Wheat germ has a high amount of vitamins and is often added to other foods.

wheel [weel] NOUN, wheels. **1. roue** ▶ a round frame that turns around a central point to allow a car, bicycle, or other vehicle to move or allow a machine to work. **2. rouet, roue hydraulique** ▶ a machine or other thing that uses a wheel, such as a *spinning wheel* or a *waterwheel.* **3.** (also steering wheel) **volant** ▶ the circular frame used to control the movement of a car or other such vehicle : *Mom took the wheel so that Dad could rest.* ▲ VERB, **wheeled**, **wheeling. 1. rouler, pousser** ▶ to roll or move on wheels : *Ayesha wheeled her baby in a carriage.* **2. tourner** ▶ to turn or change direction : *The car wheeled away from the accident.*

wheel·bar·row [WEEL-BAIR-oh *or* WEEL-BA-roh] NOUN, **wheelbarrows. brouette** ▶ a small vehicle with a wheel on the front, two handles in the back, and a flat container in which small loads of dirt or other materials can be carried.

wheel·chair [WEEL-CHAIR] NOUN, **wheelchairs. fauteuil roulant** ▶ a special chair mounted on wheels, used as a way of moving about by people who cannot use their legs or who are too ill to walk.

wheeze [weez] VERB, **wheezed**, **wheezing. respirer bruyamment** ▶ to breathe with difficulty or with a rough, whistling sound. ▲ NOUN, **wheezes. respiration bruyante, respiration sifflante** ▶ a wheezing sound. ■ **wheezy,** ADJECTIVE, **wheezier**, **wheesiest. ▶ poussif (-ive) asthmatique.**

when [wen] ADVERB. **1. quand, à quel (quelle)** ▶ at what time : *When do we leave for the show?* **2. quand** ▶ the time at which : *Goran knows when we have to leave.* ▲ CONJUNCTION. **1. quand, lorsque** ▶ at the time that : *I had just walked in when you called.* **2. quand, lorsque** ▶ at any time that : *When he's at the beach, he likes to jog.* **3. quand, alors que, étant donné** ▶ considering that ; since : *How can you eat that greasy pizza when you've had an upset stomach?* ▲ PRONOUN. **(depuis) quand** ▶ what or which time : *Since when have you become an expert on computers?* ✐ **p. 667.**

whence [wence] ADVERB ; CONJUNCTION. **d'où** ▶ from what place or cause : *"If you know whence you came, there is really no limit to where you can go."* (James Baldwin)

when·ev·er [wen-EV-ur] ADVERB ; CONJUNCTION. **quand, chaque fois que, toutes les fois que** ▶ at any time : *Whenever one of the students has a problem, the school counsellor helps.*

where [wair] ADVERB. **où** ▶ at or in what place : *Where did I leave my keys?* ▲ CONJUNCTION. **1. là où, à l'endroit que** ▶ in or at which place : *See that house—that's where I live.* **2. où** ▶ in that case or situation : *Bryn is getting to the point where all she does is play computer games.* ✐ **p. 667.**

where·a·bouts [WAIR-uh-BOWTS] ADVERB. **où, où donc** ▶ near or in what location or place : *Whereabouts did you last see my book?* ▲ NOUN, **whereabouts. où, lieu (lieux), endroit** ▶ the place where someone or something is : *The whereabouts of our cat is unknown.*

where·as [wair-AZ] CONJUNCTION. **alors que, tandis que** ▶ on the other hand ; while : *Mammals give birth to live animals, whereas most reptiles and birds hatch their young from eggs.*

where·by [wair-BY] ADVERB ; CONJUNCTION. **par quoi, par lequel (laquelle, lesquels, lesquelles)** ▶ by means of which ; through which : *Education is the process whereby people learn new skills.*

where·fore [WAIR-FOR] ADVERB ; CONJUNCTION. **pourquoi** ▶ for what reason ; why. **Note.** Used mainly in older writings : *"O Romeo, Romeo! wherefore art thou Romeo?"* (William Shakespeare)

where·in [WAIR-IN] ADVERB ; CONJUNCTION. **1. où, en quoi, dans quoi, dans lequel (laquelle, lesquels, lesquelles)** ▶ in what way or manner. **2. en quoi, dans quoi** ▶ in which. **Note.** Wherein and whereby are used mainly in literary or formal writing.

where·up·on [WAIR-uh-PON] CONJUNCTION. **sur quoi, après quoi, et sur ce** ▶ at which time : *Whereupon the Queen knighted the peasant boy and gave him the finest horse.*

wher·ev·er [WAIR-EV-ur] CONJUNCTION ; ADVERB. **1. où que** ▶ in or to whatever place : *The cat sleeps wherever it will get the sun.* **2. mais où donc** ▶ where : *I don't swim every day. Wherever did you get that idea?*

whet [wet] VERB, **whetted**, **whetting. 1. aiguiser, affûter** ▶ to sharpen a knife or blade, as by rubbing it against a sharpening stone. **2. stimuler** ▶ to make more keen or eager : *Prizes whetted our interest in the contest.*

wheth·er [WETH-ur] CONJUNCTION. **1. si** ▶ if it is likely that ; if : *Quang wants to know whether you have done your homework.* **2. si** ▶ if one or the other ; in either or any case : *Briana was so happy she didn't know whether to laugh or cry.*

whey [way] NOUN. **petit-lait** ▶ the clear, watery part of milk that separates when milk turns sour. Whey is used in making cheese.

which [wich] PRONOUN. **1. quel (quelle), lequel (laquelle, lesquels, lesquelles)** ▶ what one or ones : *I know you liked both my stories, but which do you think is better?* **2. celui (celle, ceux, celles)** ▶ the thing or things mentioned before : *My old school, which I mentioned before, is having a spring fair.* ▲ ADJECTIVE. **lequel (laquelle, lesquels, lesquelles)** ▶ what one or ones : *Which room is yours?*

which·ev·er [wich-EV-ur] PRONOUN ; ADJECTIVE. **celui (celle) qui, celui (celle) que** ▶ any one of a group that ; whatever one or ones : *I have three flavours of ice cream ; you can have whichever one you like best.*

whiff [wif] NOUN, **whiffs. bouffée, odeur** ▶ a light puff or breath, as of air or smoke : *I got a whiff of the bread baking and suddenly felt hungry.*

while [wile] NOUN. a while. **quelque temps, un moment, un instant ▸** a period of time, especially a short time : *Let's stop and rest for a while, then we can go on.* ▲ CONJUNCTION. **1. pendant que , durant que, alors que ▸** during the time that : *While you were sleeping, your friends came by.* **2. quoi que, bien que ▸** on the other hand ; although : *While I enjoy swimming, I'm not sure I want to go out for the team.* **3. alors que, tandis que ▸** whereas ; but : *This computer is easy to use, while the other one is more up-to-date.* ▲ VERB, whiled, whiling. while away. **passer ▸** to spend time relaxing : *We whiled away the day fishing and picnicking on the river.*

whim [wim] NOUN, whims. **caprice, fantaisie ▸** a sudden desire or wish to do something, especially something that is not serious or sensible : *On a whim, we went dancing.*

whim‑per [WIM-pur] VERB, whimpered, whimpering. **gémir ▸** to cry in a low, broken sound : *A lost puppy whimpered at our door.* ▲ NOUN, whimpers. a whimpering sound.

whim‑si‑cal [WIM-zih-kul] ADJECTIVE. **fantaisiste, étrange, curieux (-ieuse) ▸** full of humorous or lighthearted ideas : *The room was decorated in a whimsical way for the party.*

whine [wine] VERB, whined, whining. **1. gémir, geindre, pleurer, brailler ▸** to cry in a complaining way : *The baby whined all day because he was teething.* **2. se lamenter ▸** to complain in a childish way : *Karen whined about missing her favourite TV show.* ▲ NOUN, whines. **gémissement, lamentation, pleurnicheries, braillement ▸** the sound or act of whining. ■ **whiny,** ADJECTIVE. ▸ **pleurnicheur (-euse), grognon (-onne), brailleur (-euse).**

whin‑ny [WIN-ee] NOUN, whinnies. **hennissement ▸** a low, gentle sound like that made by a horse or a similar animal. ▲ VERB, whinnied, whinnying. **hennir ▸** to make this sound.

whip [wip] NOUN, whips. **1. fouet, cravache ▸** a device made up of a long cord or rope with a handle at one end. A rider in a race may hit a horse with a whip to get it to go faster. **2. whip ▸** in parliament, a member of each party whose job is to make sure the members of their party are present for voting. ▲ VERB, whipped, whipping. **1. fouetter, battre ▸** to hit with a whip, strap, or other such device. **2. fouetter ▸** to make go suddenly : *The wind whipped at the sails, moving the boat.* **3. enlever brusquement ▸** to move or pull out suddenly : *Greg whipped the ball out of my hands.* **4. battre ▸** to defeat : *Our team would like to whip the Cougars just once.* **5. fouetter ▸** to beat cream, eggs, or other food into a foam. **Note.** Cream treated this way is called whipped cream.

whip‑lash [WIP-lash] NOUN, whiplashes. **1. coup de fouet ▸** a blow from a whip. **2. syndrome**

cervical traumatique ▸ an injury to the neck caused by a sudden forward and backward movement of the head, such as can happen in a car accident.

whip‑poor‑will [WIP-ur-wil] NOUN, whippoor‑wills. **engoulevent ▸** a North American bird with brown and black feathers and an unusual whistling call that sounds like its name.

whir [wur] VERB, whirred, whirring. (also whirr) **vrombir, ronronner ▸** to move or operate with a buzzing or humming sound. ▲ NOUN, whirs. **vrombissement, ronronnement ▸** such a sound : *the whir of a blender.*

whirl [wurl] VERB, whirled, whirling. **tourbillon‑ner, tournoyer ▸** to turn or move quickly in a circle ; spin around : *Papers were whirling up in the air in the sudden burst of wind.* ▲ NOUN, whirls. **1. tourbillon ▸** a quick, turning movement : *The little boat was spun in a whirl of water.* **2. étourdissement ▸** a confused condition : *"I felt in such a whirl after hearing a lot of sad news."* (Anne Frank)

whirl‑pool [WURL-pool] NOUN, whirlpools. **tour‑billon ▸** a strong current of water that moves quickly in a circle and pulls things below the surface.

whirl‑wind [WURL-wind] NOUN, whirlwinds. **tor‑nade ▸** a small windstorm in which a mass of air spins rapidly in a circle.

whisk [wisk] VERB, whisked, whisking. **1. en‑lever brusquement ▸** to brush off lightly : *Gina whisked crumbs off her face.* **2. filer à toute allure, quitter brusquement ▸** to move or go quickly : *Dean whisked through the room, grabbed his sweater, and left.*

whisk‑er [WIS-kur] NOUN, whiskers. **1. whiskers. poil ▸** the hair growing on a man's face. **2. barbe ▸** one hair of a man's beard. **3. mous‑tache ▸** a stiff hair on the face of an animal, such as a cat.

whis‑per [WIS-pur] VERB, whispered, whisper‑ing. **chuchoter, murmurer ▸** to speak in a low or soft voice : *"Are you awake?" Juan whispered.* ▲ NOUN, whispers. **chuchotement, murmure ▸** a soft spoken sound. *The whispers stopped when a teacher came into the room.*

whis‑tle [WIS-ul] VERB, whistled, whistling. **1. siffler ▸** to make a clear, sharp, or musical sound by forcing air out through the lips or the teeth : *to whistle for a taxi.* **2. siffler ▸** to cause a similar sound : *"Down, down he hur‑tled, the wind whistling in his ears."* (Tololwa M. Mollel) ▲ NOUN, whistles. **1. sifflet ▸** a small instrument that makes a clear, musical tune when air is blown through it. **2. sifflement ▸** a whistling sound.

white [wite] NOUN, whites. **1. blanc (blanche) ▸** the lightest of all colours ; the colour of milk or snow. **2.** (also White) **blanc (blanche) ▸** a member of the race having light skin. ▲ ADJECTIVE, whiter, whitest. **1. blanc (blanche)** ▶ being the opposite of black; the lightest of colours. **2. blanc (blanche)** ▶ light in colour as compared to other things of the same kind : *white rice*. **3.** (also White) **blanc (blanche)** ▶ belonging to the race of people having light skin. ■ **whiteness,** NOUN. ▶ **blancheur.**

white-col-lar [WITE-KOL-ur] ADJECTIVE. **de bureau** ▶ having to do with jobs that are done in offices or indoors and that do not call for heavy physical activity : *Joseph left his white-collar job at the bank to work outdoors in forestry.* Note. From the white dress shirts often worn by men who are office workers.

whit-en [WITE-un] VERB, whitened, whitening. **blanchir** ▶ to make or become white or whiter.

white-out [WITE-owt] NOUN, whiteouts. **1. visibilité nulle à cause de la poudrerie** ▶ a weather condition in which blowing snow blankets and blinds the field of vision : *During the whiteout, drivers couldn't see the car ahead of them.* **2. poudrerie** ▶ a temporary blindness from being exposed to this weather.

white-wash [WITE-wash] NOUN, whitewashes. **lait, blanc de chaux** ▶ a watery white paint made from lime and chalk, often used in former times to paint wooden fences or walls. ▲ VERB, whitewashed, whitewashing. **1. blanchir à la chaux, chauler** ▶ to cover a fence or other surface with whitewash. **2. camoufler, blanchir** ▶ to cover up a crime or mistake.

whith-er [WITH-ur] ADVERB; CONJUNCTION. **où** ▶ to what or which place; where.

whit-tle [WIT-ul] VERB, whittled, whittling. **tailler au couteau** ▶ to cut away small pieces of wood with a knife, either as a pastime or to form some shape : *Lekh whittled a duck from an old piece of wood.*

whiz [wiz] VERB, whizzed, whizzing. **filer à toute allure** ▶ to make a buzzing or humming sound while moving fast : *Cars whizzed by without slowing down.* ■ **whiz,** NOUN, whizzes. ▶ **sifflement.** *Informal.* **champion** ▶ a person with a special skill : *a whiz at computers.*

who [hoo] PRONOUN. **1. qui** ▶ what or which person : *Who do you think called me last night? Miguel!* **2. qui** ▶ the person or persons mentioned before : *My Aunt Margrite, who lives in Denmark, will be coming for a visit next month.* ✐ **p. 667.**

whoa [woh] INTERJECTION. ▶ a word said to a horse or other such animal to get it to stop.

who-ev-er [hoo-EV-ur] PRONOUN. **quiconque, qui que ce soit, celui (celle) qui** ▶ any person who; whatever person : *Whoever came in last left the door wide open.*

whole [hole] ADJECTIVE. **tout (toute, tous, toutes), entier (-ière)** ▶ being all that there is or should

be; complete; entire : *We spent the whole afternoon swimming.* ▲ NOUN. **tout (toute, tous, toutes)** ▶ all the parts that make up something; the complete amount.

on the whole or **as a whole dans l'ensemble** ▶ in general : *A few people complained about the noise, but on the whole, the party was a success.* SYN : entire, complete, total, all, undivided.

whole number nombre entier ▶ a number that does not contain a fraction or decimal, such as 12 or 367, as opposed to 12.5 or 3672/3.

whole-sale [HOLE-sale] NOUN. **vente en gros** ▶ the selling of goods in large quantities, usually to store owners who then sell the goods to the public at a higher price. ▲ ADJECTIVE; ADVERB. **1. de gros, en gros** ▶ having to do with the sale of goods in quantity : *wholesale prices.* **2. en masse, en série** ▶ in too large an amount or quantity : *In the late 1800s, hunters caused the wholesale slaughter of buffalo.* ■ **wholesaler,** NOUN. ▶ **grossiste, marchand en gros.**

whole-some [HOLE-sum] ADJECTIVE. **1. sain (saine)** ▶ good for the health; healthful : *Ian eats only wholesome foods, no candy or chips.* **2. sain (saine)** ▶ good for the mind or character : *wholesome family entertainment.*

whole-wheat [HOLE-WEET] ADJECTIVE. **complet** ▶ of bread or flour, made from the entire grain of wheat.

whol-ly [HOH-lee] ADVERB. **complètement, entièrement** ▶ in a whole way; entirely; completely : *I was wholly responsible for the mistake in the report; no one else is to blame.*

whom [hoom] **qui** ▶ a form of who, used as the object of a verb or preposition : *To whom are you speaking?*

whoop [woop or hoop] NOUN, whoops. **cri** ▶ a loud cry or shout. ▲ VERB, whooped, whooping. **pousser des cris** ▶ to give a loud cry or shout : *The players whooped and cheered as they won the match.*

whooping cough toux aspirante, coqueluche, toux coquelucheuse ▶ a serious disease of the lungs, causing violent coughing fits that end with a high-pitched whooping sound.

whooping crane grue blanche ou grue d'Amérique ▶ a tall North American bird with long legs, a white body, and wings with black tips. The whooping crane is almost extinct. It was named for the loud cry it makes.

whose [hooz] PRONOUN. **à qui** ▶ a form of who or which : *Whose dirty dishes are those on the table?*

why [wy] ADVERB; CONJUNCTION. **pourquoi** ▶ for what cause or reason : *Why are you leaving so soon?* ▲ INTERJECTION. ▶ used to show surprise : *Why, I had no idea that Anton was such a fine musician!* ✐ **p. 667.**

wick [wik] NOUN, wicks. **mèche** ▸ a cord or band of twisted fibres used in an oil lamp, candle, or lighter to draw up fuel for burning.

wick·ed [WIK-id] ADJECTIVE, wickeder, wickedest. **mauvais (-aise), malfaisant (-ante), méchant (-ante), vilain (-aine)** ▸ evil or bad : *"'Right!' howled the ogre with a wicked smile."* (Robin Muller) ▪ **wickedly,** ADVERB. ▸ vilainement, malicieusement. ▪ **wickedness,** NOUN. ▸ méchanceté, cruauté.

wick·er [WIK-ur] NOUN. 1. **osier** ▸ flexible twigs or reeds that are woven together. Furniture and baskets are sometimes made of wicker. 2. **vannerie** ▸ also, wickerwork. an object made of wicker.

wide [wide] ADJECTIVE, wider, widest. 1. **grand (grande), large, immense** ▸ extending far from side to side; broad : *a wide truck.* 2. **de large** ▸ having a certain distance from one side to another side : *The river is 150 metres wide.* 3. **grand (grande), vaste, considérable** ▸ large in range or amount : *This cookbook has a wide range of dishes.* 4. **passer à coté, loin de la cible** ▸ away from the target or goal : *The throw was wide and the runner stole second.* ▲ ADVERB. 1. **large** ▸ over a large area or space. **Note.** Usually used in the expression far and wide: *Susan looked far and wide for her lost dog.* 2. **grand (grande)** ▸ to the full extent or amount : *The gate was wide open and the dog ran off.* ▪ **widely,** ADVERB. ▸ beaucoup. *My grandparents have travelled widely through India.*

wid·en [WY-dun] VERB, widened, widening. **élargir** ▸ to make or become wide or wider . *to widen a path.*

wide-spread [WIDE-SPRED] ADJECTIVE, **très répandu (-ue)** ▸ happening over or affecting a large area : *The flooding caused widespread damage in Manitoba.*

wid·ow [WID-oh] NOUN, widows. **veuve** ▸ a woman whose husband is dead and who has not married again.

wid·o·wer [WID-oh-ur] NOUN, widowers. **veuf** ▸ a man whose wife is dead and who has not married again.

width [width] NOUN, widths. **largeur** ▸ the distance from one side of an object to the other : *This box has a width of 21 centimetres.*

wield [weeld] VERB, wielded, wielding. 1. **manier** ▸ to hold or use a weapon or tool : *The surgeon wielded the scalpel skilfully.* 2. **exercer** ▸ to hold or use power or authority : *A president wields a lot of the power in a company.*

wife [wife] NOUN, wives. **femme, épouse** ▸ a woman who is married.

wig [wig] NOUN, wigs. **perruque, postiche** ▸ a covering for the head, made of artificial or real hair.

wig·gle [WIG-ul] VERB, wiggled, wiggling. **agiter, remuer** ▸ to move or twist from side to side in quick, short motions : *All six puppies wiggled through the hole in the fence and escaped.*

wig·wam [WIG-wom] NOUN, wigwams. **wigwam** ▸ a type of house or hut used by certain Native peoples, made of a frame of wooden poles covered with bark or with hides.

wild [wyld] ADJECTIVE, wilder, wildest. 1. **sauvage** ▸ not under the care or control of people; living or growing in nature : *a wild animal.* **Note.** A flower that grows in this way is a wildflower. 2. **sauvage** ▸ not lived in or settled : *wild jungles.* 3. **intense, brusque** ▸ rough or violent : *That roller coaster is a wild ride!* 4. **fou (folle)** ▸ not under proper control or discipline : *a wild party.* 5. **à tout hasard** ▸ not having the proper aim or direction : *He took a wild guess.* ▲ ADVERB. **en liberté** ▸ in a wild way; not under control : *We let the dogs run wild in the country.* ▲ NOUN, wilds. (usually the wild or the wilds) **fou (folle)** ▸ of a natural area away from people; a wilderness. ▪ **wildly,** ADVERB. ▸ région sauvage, région reculée. *to laugh wildly.* ▪ **wildness,** NOUN. ▸ de façon extravagante, frénétiquement. 👁 p. 250. ✎ p. 671.

wild·cat [WYLD-kat] NOUN, wildcats. **chat sauvage** ▸ a name for various small, wild members of the cat family, such as the bobcat or lynx. ▲ ADJECTIVE. **sauvage** ▸ in business, done in an unusual or irregular way : *A wildcat strike is one where workers go on strike without permission.*

wil·der·ness [WIL-dur-nis] NOUN, wildernesses. **jungle, région sauvage** ▸ an area that is in its natural state, with wild animals and plants and with few people living there : *Much of the Yukon is still wilderness.*

wild·fire [WYLD-FIRE] NOUN, wildfires. 1. **feu de fôret** ▸ a fire that spreads quickly. 2. like

---

📝 **Word Builder**

Wild can mean out of control. To **run wild** often means to live and grow without rules or restrictions : *The Jamesons let their six-year-old twins run wild in the playground.* **Wild and woolly** is often used to describe a place that is very rough and uncivilized : *The gold-rush town was wild and woolly after the miners got paid.* **In the wild** frequently refers to the wilderness : *Benito's uncle works downtown, but whenever he can he goes camping in the wild.*

wildfire. **comme une traînée de poudre, très rapidement ▶** in a very fast, uncontrolled way : *The news of the factory closing spread like wildfire around town.*

wild-life [WYLD-LIFE] NOUN. **faune et flore ▶** animals and plants that live naturally in a wild area.

will[1] [wil] VERB. used with other verbs to show **1.** something expected to happen in the future : *I will go with you tonight.* **2.** something that should be done : *You will clean up your room now!* **3.** something that is able to be done : *This theatre will seat 150 people.* **4.** something that is done by habit or custom : *Often, she will find herself walking to her old house.* **5.** something that a person is asked to do or agrees to do : *Will you stay for lunch ? Thank you ; I will.*

will[2] NOUN. wills. **1.** **volonté, désir ▶** the power that the mind has to make a decision and then select actions to carry it out. **Note.** Often used in the phrase **free will.** **2.** **volonté, vouloir ▶** a determination to make things happen in a certain way : *A championship team has the will to win.* **Note.** This is also called **willpower:** *My mother stopped smoking by sheer willpower.* **3.** **testament ▶** a legal document that states what a person wants done with his or her money and property after he or she dies. ▲ VERB, willed, willing. **1.** **vouloir ▶** to use the power of the mind to decide or control what goes on : *The swimmers willed themselves to be calm for the race.* **2.** **léguer ▶** to give away one's property by a will.

will-ful [WIL-ful] ADJECTIVE. (also wilful) **têtu (-ue), obstiné (-ée), entêté (-ée) ▶** determined to get one's own way, even at the expense of others ; stubborn : *a willful child.* ■ **willfully,** ADVERB. ▶ **obstinément, avec entêtement.**

will-ing [WIL-ing] ADJECTIVE, **être prêt (prête), disposé (-ée) à faire ▶** ready or wanting to do something : *Bret is always willing to help make dinner.* ■ **willingly,** ADVERB. ▶ **volontiers, de bon cœur, volontairement.** ■ **willingness,** NOUN. ▶ **bonne volonté, empressement.**

wil-low [WIL-oh] NOUN, willows. **saule ▶** a tree or bush that has long, thin branches that droop. Willows have thin, pointed leaves and clusters of tiny flowers. 👁 **p. 254.**

wilt [wilt] VERB, wilted, wilting. **1.** **dessécher, se flétrir ▶** of a plant, to lose freshness ; become limp or droopy : *Celery wilts when it gets old.* **2.** **s'affaiblir, s'alanguir, incommoder ▶** to lose strength or energy : *The runners wilted in the heat.*

win [win] VERB, won, winning. **1.** **gagner, l'emporter ▶** to be the best or first in a game or contest ; come out ahead : *to win a contest.* **2.** **gagner, remporter ▶** to gain as a reward for success in a game or contest : *to win a trophy.* **3.** **gagner ▶** to get or achieve through an effort : *The mayor won the union's support in*

her campaign for reelection. ▲ NOUN, wins. **victoire ▶** a victory or success : *Our chess team has a record of six wins and one loss.*

wince [wince] VERB, winced, wincing. **tressaillir, grimacer ▶** to draw back slightly or draw in the breath, as from pain or danger : *Tim winced as the door slammed.*

winch [winch] NOUN, winches. **treuil ▶** a device used for lifting or pulling heavy objects, made up of a large drum or pulley with a rope or chain that wraps around it. Winches can be operated by hand or by a motor.

wind[1] [wind] NOUN, winds. **1.** **vent ▶** the air that moves over the surface of the earth. **2.** **souffle ▶** the breath, or the ability to breathe : *The runners got their second wind as they reached the end of the course.* **3.** winds. **instruments à vent ▶** Wind instruments as a group. ▲ VERB, winded, winding. **essouffler ▶** to be or cause to be out of breath : *The soccer game winded all of us.* 📖 **p. 1106.** 👁 **p. 539.**

weeping willow

leaves

male flowers

female flowers

buds

leaves

pussy willow

willows

wind[2] [wynd] VERB, wound, winding. **1.** **enrouler ▶** to twist or wrap string, thread, wire, or the like around itself or around something else : *The cowhand wound the rope around the fencepost.* **2.** **remonter ▶** to turn a part on a watch or other such device to adjust it or make it work.

3. serpenter ▸ to move in a series of twists and turns : *A road wound up the mountainside.* **4. wind up. a. tirer à sa fin, terminer, finir ▸** to bring to a close : *It's time to wind up practice for the day.* **b. relais ▸** of a pitcher in baseball, to move the arms and body before throwing the ball. **c. enrouler ▸** the act of turning or twisting. **Note.** Also used as a noun and an adjective : *a pitcher's windup; a windup toy.*

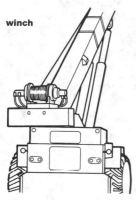

winch

wind-break-er [WIND-BRAY-kur] NOUN, wind-breakers. **coupe-vent ▸** a short, light jacket that protects against wind.

wind chill refroidissement dû au vent ▸ a way to measure how cold the air feels to the surface of the skin. The **wind-chill factor** takes into account both the actual air temperature and the force of the wind. Thus, if the temperature is -10°C and there is a strong wind, the wind-chill factor might make a person feel as cold as if it were -20°C.

wind-fall [WIND-fol] NOUN, windfalls. **chance, aubaine ▸** an unexpected, lucky event : *Winning the lottery was a lucky windfall.*

wind-ing [WINE-ding] ADJECTIVE, **sinueux (-euse), tortueux (-euse) ▸** full of bends or turns : *a winding mountain road.*

wind instrument instrument à vent ▸ any musical instrument that is played by blowing air into it, such as a bugle, trumpet, flute, or clarinet.

wind-mill [WIND-mil] NOUN, windmills. **moulin à vent ▸** a machine that uses large blades to capture the power of the wind and turn it into energy. Windmills are now used mainly to pump water.

win-dow [WIN-doh] NOUN, windows. **1. fenêtre ▸** an opening in a wall that is fitted with a frame and glass to let in light, and that usually can also be opened to let in air. **2. fenêtre ▸** a separate viewing area on a computer screen giving different information from the rest of the screen. ☞ **p. 1073.**

win-dow-pane [WIN-doh-PANE] NOUN, window-panes. **vitre, carreau (-eaux) ▸** a sheet of glass used in a window.

wind-pipe [WIND-pipe] NOUN, windpipes. **trachée ▸** the tube that connects the throat to the lungs, carrying air in and out. **Note.** The medical term is trachea. ☞ **p. 403.**

wind-shield [WIND-sheeld] NOUN, windshields. **pare-brise ▸** the clear window at the front of a car or other vehicle. **Note.** A windshield wiper is a device used to clear rain or dirt from a windshield.

wind-y [WIN-dee] ADJECTIVE, windier, windiest. **1. venteux (-euse) ▸** having much wind : *It's a great day for sailing because it is so windy.* **2.** *Informal.* **verbeux (-euse) ▸** using a lot of wasteful talk : *a windy speech.*

wine [wine] NOUN, wines. **1. vin ▸** a drink containing alcohol, made from the juice of grapes. **2. vin ▸** a similar drink made from another fruit or plant, such as apples or blackberries.

windmill

wing [wing] NOUN, wings. **1. aile ▸** one of the movable parts used by a bird, insect, or bat to move through the air. **2. aile ▸** a flat structure extending out from either side of an airplane that helps it stay in the air as it moves forward. **3. aile ▸** a smaller part that projects out from the main part of a building : *a new wing of the school.* **4. coulisse ▸** an area to the side of a stage not visible to the audience : *The dancers waited in the wings until the music began.* **5. ailier ▸** in sports such as soccer and hockey, a player whose position is near the side of the playing area. ▲ VERB, winged, winging. **1. voler ▸** to use the wings; fly : *The geese were winging their way north.* **2. blesser ▸** to wound slightly in the wing or arm : *The bear had been winged by the bullet.*

673

winged [wingd *or* WING-id] ADJECTIVE. **ailé (-ée)** ▸ having wings : *Beetles and flies are winged insects.*

wing-span [WING-span] NOUN, wingspans. **enver-gure** ▸ the distance between the tip of one extended wing and the other, used to measure the size of a bird or an aircraft. **Note.** Also called wingspread.

wink [wink] VERB, winked, winking. **cligner de l'œil** ▸ to close and open one eye quickly, usu-ally as a private message or signal to someone : *Grandpa winked at me to let me know he had hidden the coin.* ▲ NOUN, winks. **1. faire un clin d'œil** ▸ the act of winking. **2. court moment** ▸ a short period of time, especially a short sleep ; a nap : *I was so excited I didn't sleep a wink.*

win-ner [WIN-ur] NOUN, winners. **vainqueur (-euse), gagnant (-ante)** ▸ a person or thing that wins or is successful.

win-ning [WIN-ing] ADJECTIVE, **1. gagnant (-ante)** ▸ being the one that wins : *The winning team goes on to the World Series.* **2. charmant (-ante), adorable** ▸ able to win favour or attention ; charming ; attractive : *a winning smile.* ▲ NOUN, winnings. **1. gagner** ▸ the act of a person or thing that wins. **2. winnings. gain** ▸ something that is won, especially money won by gambling.

win-ter [WIN-tur] NOUN, winters. **hiver** ▸ the coldest season of the year ; the season after fall and before spring. ▲ ADJECTIVE: *winter clothing.* ▣ p. 1106.

win-ter-green [WIN-tur-green] NOUN, winter-greens. **gaulthérie** ▸ a shrub having red berries and evergreen leaves with a spicy scent. The oil from the leaves is used as a flavouring.

win-try [WIN-tree] ADJECTIVE, wintrier, wintriest. **hivernal (-ale, -aux), d'hiver** ▸ having to do with or like winter : *It's only October but it feels win-try outside.*

wipe [wipe] VERB, wiped, wiping. **1. essuyer** ▸ to clean or dry by rubbing on or with something : *"Father wiped the grease off his cheek with a hunk of fresh bread."* (Tim Wynne-Jones) **2. essuyer** ▸ to remove by rubbing lightly : *to wipe away tears with a tissue.* **3. wipe out. anéantir** ▸ to kill or destroy completely : *The beaver was almost wiped out by hunters.*

wire [wire] NOUN, wires. **1. fil** ▸ a long, thin, flexi-ble piece of metal that has a standard thickness for its entire length, often used to join or fasten things : *"He put a nice chunk of spoiled bacon in the far end and attached it to a trip wire."* (Marilyn Halvorson) **2. fil électrique** ▸ such a piece of metal used to carry electricity. **3. télé-gramme** ▸ a message sent by telegraph wire ; a telegram. ▲ VERB, wired, wiring. **1. faire l'instal-lation électrique de** ▸ to install wires for elec-tricity : *to wire a house for electricity.* **2. relier,**

attacher ▸ to fasten something with wire. **3. télégraphier** ▸ to send a telegram.

wir-ing [WIRE-ing] NOUN, wiring. **installation électrique** ▸ a system of wires used to carry electricity.

wir-y [WIRE-ee] ADJECTIVE, wirier, wiriest. **1. dru (drue)** ▸ like wire : *wiry hair.* **2. nerveux (-euse)** ▸ thin, but strong : *Dennis was a tall, wiry boy with good running ability.*

wis-dom [WIZ-dum] NOUN. **sagesse** ▸ good judg-ment as to what is true and right, gained through knowledge and experience : *We studied the wis-dom of Greek thinkers such as Aristotle and Socrates.*

wisdom tooth **dent de sagesse** ▸ one of four teeth located at the very back of each side of the upper and lower jaws. **Note.** These teeth are so called because they come in later than the other teeth, when a person is older.

wise [wize] ADJECTIVE, wiser, wisest. **1. sage, averti (-ie)** ▸ able to understand people and sit-uations and choose the right course of action ; having knowledge and intelligence : *Solomon was a wise king who was skilled in dealing with people and solving problems.* **2. sage, avisé (-ée)** ▸ showing this ability to judge and decide ; sensible : *a wise decision.* **3. Informal. fantasque** ▸ showing off one's knowledge in a rude or insulting way ; fresh. **Note.** A remark or joke of this kind is a **wisecrack.** ▪ **wisely,** ADVERB. ▸ **sagement, prudemment, judicieuse-ment.** SYN : intelligent, informed, clever, sensible.

wish [wish] VERB, wished, wishing. **1. souhaiter, vouloir** ▸ to want something that at present it is not possible to get ; have a hope for : *"I wished I was a horse wrangler or the scout for a wagon train."* (Dayal Kaur Khalsa) **2. souhaiter, désirer** ▸ to have a desire for ; want to be or to happen : *I wish you the best in your new job.* ▲ NOUN, wishes. **vœu (vœux), souhait, désir** ▸ the act of saying or thinking that one wants to get something or have something happen : *It is her wish to skate at the national finals.* ▪ **wishful,** ADJECTIVE. **avec envie de, en prenant ses désirs pour des réalités** ▸ based only on a wish. **Note.** Wishful thinking means hoping that something will happen, even though it is not likely, because that is what one wants. SYN : desire, crave, long for, yearn, hope.

wisp [wisp] NOUN, wisps. **fine mèche, brin** ▸ a small bunch or bit : *a wisp of hair ; wisps of smoke.* ▪ **wispy,** ADJECTIVE. ▸ **fin (fine), mince.**

wist-ful [WIST-ful] ADJECTIVE, **nostalgique, mélancolique, rêveur (-euse)** ▸ showing sadness because of a wish that did not come true or a memory of something lost ; longing : *"There was a wistful quality about the words which defeated me ; a hint of a wild hope."* (James Herriot) ▪ **wistfully,** ADVERB. ▸ **avec mélancolie, avec**

tristesse, avec nostalgie. ■ **wistfulness,** NOUN.
▶ nostalgie, mélancolie, regret.

wit [wit] NOUN, wits. **1. esprit, intelligence, astuce** ▶ the talent to describe things in a clever and funny way; a sense of humour. **2. esprit** ▶ a person who has this talent : *The noted Irish wit, Oscar Wilde once said, "I can resist everything except temptation."* **3. intelligence** ▶ the ability to know and understand things; intelligence. Now used mainly in combinations such as quick-witted or slow-witted. **4. wits. esprit, intelligence** ▶ the quickness of the mind. **Note.** Used in special expressions such as *"be scared out of your wits," "keep your wits about you," "live by your wits."*

witch [wich] NOUN, witches. **sorcière** ▶ a woman thought to have magic powers and to use them for evil purposes. In former times people believed that a witch could bring bad luck, illness, and so on. 📖 p. 971.

witch-craft [WICH-kraft] NOUN. **sorcellerie** ▶ the magic power of a witch.

with [withe *or* with] PREPOSITION. **1. avec** ▶ in the company of; beside or among : *Glenn sat with several friends.* **2. avec** ▶ having or showing : *Debra's shoes were covered with mud.* **3. avec** ▶ by means of : *Dad waters the yard with a hose.* **4. avec** ▶ because of or concerning : *I have a problem with my computer.*

with-draw [with-DRAH] VERB, withdrew, withdrawing. **1. retirer** ▶ to take money out of a bank account : *He withdrew his savings to buy a bike.* **2. retirer** ▶ to move away or take something away : *"A servant leaned in and withdrew one green pomegranate."* (Bob Barton) **3. se retirer** ▶ to go away in order to be alone; stay to oneself : *Martin has withdrawn from his friends lately.*

with-draw-al [with-DRAH-ul *or* with-DROL] NOUN, withdrawals. **1. retrait** ▶ the act of withdrawing, especially taking money out of a bank account. **2. sevrage** ▶ the process of breaking a drug addiction.

with-drawn [with-DRON] VERB. a past form of withdraw. ▲ ADJECTIVE. **renfermé (-ée)** ▶ wanting to be alone ; not friendly : *Mr. Carter was a withdrawn person who rarely came out of his house.*

with-er [WITH-ur] VERB, withered, withering. **se flétrir, se faner, dépérir** ▶ of a plant, to dry up from lack of moisture : *The tomato plants withered in the hot weather.*

with-hold [with-HOHLD] VERB, withheld, withholding. **retenir** ▶ to refuse to give ; hold back : *You shouldn't withhold information from the police.*

with-in [with-IN] PREPOSITION. **1. à l'intérieur de** ▶ in the limits of : *I live within the city limits.* **2. dedans, intérieur** ▶ in the inner part of : *"Go outside, laugh, and take a breath of fresh air, a*

voice cries within me." (Anne Frank) ▲ NOUN. ▶ **intérieur.** *"Enter," called a voice from within.*

with-out [with-OWT] PREPOSITION. **sans** ▶ not having or doing; lacking : *I'd like a piece of pie without whipped cream.*

with-stand [with-STAND] VERB, withstood, withstanding. **résister à** ▶ to hold out against; resist : *The dike withstood the pressure of the water from the flooding river.*

wit-ness [WIT-nis] NOUN, witnesses. **1. témoin** ▶ someone who is present and sees a crime, accident, or other such event : *Several witnesses saw the accident.* **2. témoin** ▶ a person who gives evidence in a court of law about something she or he knows or has seen. **3. témoin** ▶ a person who is present at an important event to give proof that the event took place : *a witness to a marriage ceremony.* **4.** *Informal.* **témoin** ▶ any person who is present when something takes place : *You heard Kerry say she'd take me riding—you're my witness.* ▲ VERB, witnessed, witnessing. **être témoin, assister à** ▶ to be a witness.

wit-ty [WIT-ee] ADJECTIVE, wittier, wittiest. **spirituel (-elle), plein d'esprit** ▶ having a good wit; able to make clever, amusing remarks : *She's very witty and makes us all laugh.*

wives [wives] NOUN. the plural of wife.

wiz-ard [WIZ-urd] NOUN, wizards. **1. magicien (-ienne), enchanteur (-teresse), sorcier (-ière)** ▶ a person — usually a man — thought to have magic powers. **2. génie** ▶ a person with great skill or cleverness : *Tina is a wizard with the computer.* 📖 p. 972.

wob-ble [WOB-ul] VERB, wobbled, wobbling. **trembler, osciller, branler** ▶ to move from side to side in a shaky or unsteady way : *The old ladder wobbled when I stood on it.* ▲ NOUN, wobbles. **pas chancelant (-ante), démarche chancelante** ▶ a wobbling movement. ■ **wobbly,** ADJECTIVE, ▶ **branlant (-ante), tremblant (-ante).**

woe [woh] NOUN, woes. **malheur** ▶ sorrow or suffering. **Note.** It is used mainly in older writings. When woe is used today it is usually in a lighter way : *I'm ready to hear your sad tale of woe.* ■ **woeful,** ADJECTIVE. ▶ **malheureux (-euse), très triste, cruel (cruelle).** ■ **woefully,** ADVERB. ▶ **malheureusement, tristement, cruellement.**

wok [wok] NOUN, woks. **wok** ▶ a wide, bowl-shaped pot, used especially in Asian cooking.

woke [woke] VERB. a past form of wake.

wo-ken [WOH-kin] VERB. a past form of wake.

wolf [woolf] NOUN, wolves. **loup (louve)** ▶ a large, powerful wild animal related to the dog. Wolves band together in packs to hunt larger animals. Wolves once lived over most of the northern half of the world, but hunting by humans has driven them into a few remote regions. ▲ VERB, wolfed,

675

wolfing. engloutir ▶ to eat quickly and hungrily : *Joshua wolfed down a huge plate of mashed potatoes.* 👁 p. 111.

wol·ver·ine [WOOL-vuh-REEN] NOUN, wolverines. **glouton, carcajou** ▶ an animal with a heavy, powerful body, thick fur, and a bushy tail. Wolverines feed on other animals and live mostly in northern areas. 👁 p. 111.

wolves [woolvz] NOUN. the plural of wolf.

wom·an [WOOM-un] NOUN, women. **1. femme** ▶ a full-grown female person; a female who is no longer a girl. **2. femme** ▶ adult females as a group. ✐ p. 356.

womb [woom] NOUN, wombs. **utérus, matrice** ▶ the organ in a woman's body where a baby is developed and nourished before it is born. **Note.** The medical term for the womb is the uterus.

wom·en [WIM-in] NOUN. the plural of woman.

won [wun] VERB. a past form of win.

won·der [WUN-dur] VERB, wondered, wondering. **se demander** ▶ to be curious or doubtful about; want to know : *"I wondered if anyone had heard them falling."* (Teddy Jam) ▲ NOUN, wonders. **1. merveille, prodige, miracle** ▶ something that causes surprise or amazement, and also respect : *Snowcapped mountains are only one of the many wonders of Banff National Park.* **2. émerveillement, étonnement** ▶ a feeling of surprise and admiration : *to stare at in wonder.* **3. étonnement** ▶ something that is surprising or unusual : *"No wonder, before the first recess bell had rung, I had forty enemies."* (Jean Little)

won·der·ful [WUN-dur-ful] ADJECTIVE, **1. merveilleux (-euse), étonnant (-ante), extraordinaire** ▶ causing wonder; amazing; marvellous. **2. merveilleux (-euse), magnifique, formidable, sensationnel (-elle)** ▶ very good; excellent; fine : *"Ngwele was a wonderful maker of things and was Mbeku's only friend."* (Tololwa M. Mollel) ▪ **wonderfully**, ADVERB. ▶ **admirablement, merveilleusement.** *"Mars was wonderfully clear in the telescope, but even with the naked eye she could imagine canals and raging storms."* (Tim Wynne-Jones)

wood [wood] NOUN, woods. **1. bois** ▶ the hard material that makes up the trunk and branches of a tree or shrub. Wood can be cut up into various shapes and used as building material, burned as fuel, or to make furniture. **2. bois, forêt** ▶ usually **woods**) an area having a thick growth of trees; a forest.

wood·chuck [WOOD-chuk] NOUN, woodchucks. **marmotte d'Amérique** ▶ a small animal having a thick body, short legs, and a short hairy tail. They live in burrows dug in the ground, and they sleep during the winter months. **Note.** Also known as a groundhog.

wood·ed [WOOD-ud] ADJECTIVE. **boisé (-ée)** ▶ having trees; covered with many trees : *acres of wooded land.*

wood·en [WOOD-un] ADJECTIVE. **1. de bois, en bois** ▶ made of wood : *a wooden desk.* **2. sans expression, inexpressif (-ive), impassible** ▶ like wood; stiff and lifeless : *The adults knew that the girls were lying; each had the same wooden answer.*

wood·peck·er [WOOD-pek-ur] NOUN, woodpeckers. **pic-bois** ▶ a bird with a long, pointed bill that it uses to peck holes in trees to find insects to eat. It is found in many parts of the world.

woodpecker

wood·wind [WOOD-wind] NOUN, woodwinds **bois** ▶ a musical instrument, originally made of wood, that makes a sound when air is blown trough the mouthpiece. Some woodwinds, such as the clarinet, have a reed in the mouthpiece that vibrates to make sound. Others, such as the flute, have an openeing in the mouthpiece.

wood·work [WOOD-wurk] NOUN. **menuiserie** ▶ things made of wood, especially on the inside of a house, such as around a window or door or the strip at the bottom of a wall.

wood·work·ing [WOOD-wur-king] NOUN. **ébénisterie** ▶ the art or skill of making objects out of wood, especially furniture.

wood·y [WOOD-ee] ADJECTIVE, woodier, woodiest. **1. ligneux (-euse)** ▶ made of or containing wood : *The woody part of a tree includes the trunk and branches, but not the leaves.* **2. boisé (-ée)** ▶ having many trees; wooded.

wool [wool] NOUN, wools. **1. laine** ▶ the thick, curly hair of sheep and some other animals that is used to make clothing, rugs, blankets, and other items. **2. laine** ▶ the fabric or yarn made from this hair. ▲ ADJECTIVE. **de laine** ▶ made of wool; woolen.

wool·en [WOOL-un] ADJECTIVE. (also **woollen**) **de laine, en lainage** ▶ having to do with or made of wool : *a woolen sweater.*

wool·ly [WOOL-ee] ADJECTIVE, woollier, woolliest. (also wooly) **laineux (-euse)** ▶ made of, covered with, or like wool.

word [wurd] NOUN, words. **1. mot** ▶ the smallest part of a language that can mean something when used by itself. In speaking, a word is a sound or group of sounds with a short pause before and after it. In writing, it is a letter or group of letters with a space before and a space or a punctuation mark after it. **2. mot** ▶ a certain one of these items, having its own particular sound, spelling, and meaning : *"The" is the most common word in English.* **3. mot** ▶ a short talk or remark : *If you say a word to anyone, I'll be really upset.* **4. mot** ▶ a promise : *Give me your word.* **5. parole, promesse** ▶ information ; views : *What is the word on Mike's condition ? Is he better ?* **6. words. mot, nouvelles** ▶ an argument or quarrel. ▲ VERB, worded, wording. **dire, écrire, formuler, rédiger** ▶ to say or write in words : *Sami worded his comment carefully.* ✐ **p. 506.**

word·ing [WUR-ding] NOUN. **terme, formulation** ▶ the way of expressing something in words : *The strong wording of this letter means that the company is in serious trouble.*

word processing **traitement de texte** ▶ the activity of producing written documents by means of a computer. Word processing allows the writer to change, add to, or reprint a document without retyping it. **Note.** A word processor is a machine used in word processing, or a person who uses one.

word·y [WURD-ee] ADJECTIVE, wordier, wordiest. **verbeux (-euse)** ▶ using too many words ; using

---

📝 **Writing Tips**

Wordiness

When you revise your writing, one thing to look for is wordiness — words that aren't needed, that don't add information, or that repeat something already said. Wordiness can confuse and annoy the reader.

Think about these questions as you revise your writing : Have you used large words when small ones would do ? Have you repeated yourself ? Have you used too many large words ? Are there too many clauses, adjectives, or adverbs within one sentence ? Is your writing style clear and simple ? Ask a classmate to edit your draft for wordiness.

---

more words than is necessary for the thought expressed. ■ **wordiness,** NOUN. ▶ **verbosité.**

wore [wor] VERB. a past form of **wear.**

work [wurk] NOUN, works. **1. travail** ▶ the use of the body or the mind to do something or to reach some goal : *I have too much work, so I can't go to the movies.* **2. travail, emploi** ▶ what a person does regularly to earn money ; a job : *What kind of work are you looking for ?* **3. œuvre, ouvrage** ▶ something that is made or done : *a work of art.* **4. works. mécanisme** ▶ the moving parts of a machine or instrument, such as a clock. ▲ VERB, worked, working. **1. travailler** ▶ to use the body or mind to do or get something : *I work hard at school.* **2. travailler** ▶ to do something for pay ; have a job : *Julia works as a dental assistant.* **3. faire fonctionner** ▶ to cause to act in the proper way ; operate : *The video showed us how to work the new computer.* **4. fonctionner** ▶ to act or operate in a certain way : *The new system is really working out well.* 🖙 **p. 1032.**

work·a·ble [WUR-kuh-bul] ADJECTIVE. **possible, réalisable** ▶ able to work ; that will work well : *a workable plan.*

work·er [WUR-kur] NOUN, workers. **1. travailleur (-euse), employé (-ée)** ▶ a person who works. **2. ouvrier (-ière)** ▶ a female bee, ant, or other insect that does most of the work of the hive or colony, but is unable to produce young.

work·out [WURK-out] NOUN, workouts. **séance d'entraînement** ▶ a period of using the body in an active way, as a form of exercise for health or training.

work·shop [WURK-shop] NOUN, workshops. **1. atelier** ▶ a room or building where work is done by hand or with machines. **2. atelier** ▶ a meeting of people to work on or study a special subject : *Mom's office had a workshop on their new computer software.*

world [wurld] NOUN, worlds. **1. monde, globe, terre** ▶ the planet on which human beings live ; the earth. **2. monde** ▶ a certain area or part of the earth : *the Western world.* **3. monde** ▶ an activity or way of life involving a large part of the earth or a large number of people : *the plant world.* **4. monde** ▶ all people ; everyone : *The whole world watched as the astronauts landed on the moon.* **5. monde** ▶ a large amount ; a great deal : *The Red Cross has done a world of good for people in need.*

world·ly [WURLD-lee] ADJECTIVE, worldlier, worldliest. **1. de ce monde, terrestre** ▶ of or having to do with ordinary or human existence, rather than with gods or religion. **2. attaché au bien de ce monde, qui a l'expérience du monde** ▶ knowing or caring a lot about the affairs of the world : *Emily was a worldly girl who had travelled widely.* ■ **worldliness,** NOUN. ▶ **mondanité.**

world-wide [WURLD-WIDE] ADJECTIVE; ADVERB. **mondial (-iale), universel (-elle)** ▶ all over the world : *Mickey Mouse is a cartoon character who is famous worldwide.*

World Wide Web **World Wide Web, toile Internet** ▶ a network of information stored in computer files, accessed through the Internet.

worm [wurm] NOUN, worms. **ver** ▶ a small animal with a long, thin body and no legs or backbone. ▲ VERB, wormed, worming. **1. avancer en rampant, ramper** ▶ to move by crawling or wriggling, as a worm does. **2. worm out. insinuer** ▶ to get something by a special trick or effort : *My sister wormed out of doing the dishes by pretending she was sick.*

worn [worn] VERB. a past form of wear. ▲ ADJECTIVE. **1. usé (-ée)** ▶ damaged or made thin by long, hard use : *My jacket is old and worn.* **2. las (lasse), fatigué (-ée), épuisé (-ée)** ▶ looking tired or weak : *"I saw her in front of me, clothed in rags, her face thin and worn."* (Anne Frank)

worn-out [WORN-OWT] ADJECTIVE. **1. complètement usé (-ée)** ▶ having had such long and hard wear that it is no longer useful : *worn-out shoes.* **2.** (also worn out) **épuisé (-ée), éreinté (-ée)** ▶ very tired or weak; exhausted.

wor-ry [WUR-ee] VERB, worried, worrying. **1. s'inquiéter, se faire du souci** ▶ to have a thought or feeling that something bad may happen; be uneasy or concerned : *Sharlene worried about the math test.* **2. jouer avec, secouer** ▶ of an animal, to bite at or shake something with the teeth over and over again : *a dog worrying a bone.* ▲ NOUN, worries. **1. souci, inquiétude** ▶ the act or fact of worrying; a feeling of being anxious or uncomfortable : *the worry of looking after a sick child.* **2. inquiétude, anxiété, tracas** ▶ something that causes this feeling : *Marc's big worry is that no one will come to his party.* ■ **worriedly,** ADVERB. ▶ avec inquiétude, avec anxiété. ✎ p. 26.

worse [wurs] ADJECTIVE. **pire, plus mauvais (-aise)** ▶ the COMPARATIVE form of bad. *—The snowstorm was bad yesterday, but it's even worse today.* Note. Also used as a NOUN and an ADVERB.

wors-en [WURS-un] VERB, worsened, worsening. **empirer, se détériorer, s'aggraver, se dégrader** ▶ to make or become worse : *Instead of getting better, her cough worsened.*

wor-ship [WUR-ship] VERB, worshipped, worshipping. (also worshiped, worshiping) **1. vénérer, vouer un culte à, adorer** ▶ to show love and respect to a god, as by taking part in a religious service. **2. adorer, honorer, rendre un culte à** ▶ to love and respect a person greatly, often too greatly : *Ansa worshipped her older sister and tried to be exactly like her.* ▲ NOUN. **1. adoration, culte, vénération** ▶ great love and

respect for a god, or an action showing this. **2. liturgie, cérémonial (-aux)** ▶ religious services : *Churches and synagogues are sometimes called houses of worship.*

worst [wurst] ADJECTIVE. **pire, le (la) plus mauvais (-aise)** ▶ the SUPERLATIVE form of bad or ill: *He has the worst grade in the class —he's failing.* Note. Also used as a NOUN and an ADVERB. *"The worst is surely behind us now."* (Bob Barton)

worth [wurth] PREPOSITION. **1. valoir** ▶ of the same value as : *That bike is not worth $60.* **2. valoir, s'élever à** ▶ having property or money amounting to : *His uncle is worth over a million dollars.* **3. valoir, mérite** ▶ deserving of; good enough for : *This is a movie worth seeing.* ▲ NOUN. **valeur** ▶ the value or importance of a person or thing : *They took the ring to a jeweller to get an idea of its worth.*

worth-less [WURTH-lis] ADJECTIVE. **sans valeur, bon à rien** ▶ having no worth; without value; useless : *The cheap watch broke within a day; it's worthless.*

worth-while [WURTH-WILE] ADJECTIVE. **utile, qui mérite de, qui vaut la peine** ▶ having value or importance; worth spending time or money on : *It's not worthwhile to get this television fixed; it would cost less to buy a new one.*

wor-thy [WUR-thee] ADJECTIVE, worthier, worthiest. **1. digne, louable, noble, notable** ▶ having value or importance; worthwhile : *This charity is a worthy cause.* **2. digne, mérite** ▶ having merit; deserving support : *This wonderful book is worthy of the many awards it received.*

would [wood] VERB. a past form of will. Note. Also used in a polite request or question : *Would you like to see a movie with me?*

wound¹ [woond] NOUN, wounds. **blessure** ▶ an injury to the body caused by cutting or tearing the skin and flesh. ▲ VERB, wounded, wounding. **1. blesser, mutiler** ▶ to harm the body by a cut or other injury : *A fall from a horse wounded his shoulder.* **2. blesser** ▶ to hurt someone's feelings : *Hajjar's pride was wounded when she didn't make the team.* ✎ p. 1161.

wound² [wownd] VERB. a past form of wind.

wove [wove] VERB. a past form of weave.

wo-ven [WOH-ven] VERB. a past form of weave.

wrap [rap] VERB, wrapped or wrapt, wrapping. **1. envelopper, emballer** ▶ to cover by winding or folding something around : *We wrapped the birthday presents in blue paper.* **2. enlacer** ▶ to wind or fold about something : *Mom wrapped her arms around me.* **3. wrapped up in. absorber** ▶ completely or only interested in : *Cory is always wrapped up in skating.* ▲ NOUN, wraps. **manteau, châle, écharpe** ▶ an outer garment worn for warmth, such as a coat.

wrap-per [RAP-ur] NOUN, wrappers. **papier d'emballage ▸** a covering, usually made of paper, used to wrap something : *a candy wrapper.*

wrap-ping [RAP-ing] NOUN, wrappings. **papier, papier d'emballage ▸** paper or other material used to wrap something.

wrath [rath or roth] NOUN, wraths. **colère, courroux ▸** great anger; rage : *The children felt Mr. Harlow's wrath when their ball broke his window for a second time.*

wreath [reeth] NOUN, wreaths. **couronne, gerbe ▸** a group of branches, leaves, or flowers woven together to form a ring : *A wreath was placed around the winning horse's neck.*

wreck [rek] NOUN, wrecks. **1. accident ▸** the damaging or destroying of a car, train, ship, or other vehicle, by its striking heavily against another object : *a car wreck.* **2. épave, décombre ▸** the remains of something that has been damaged in this way : *the wreck of the boat.* ▲ VERB, wrecked, wrecking. **détruire, démolir ▸** to damage badly or destroy; ruin : *An accident wrecked my car.*

wreck-age [REK-ij] NOUN. **1. épave ▸** the fact of being wrecked. **2. débris, décombre ▸** the broken parts of something that has been wrecked : *Wreckage from the plane crash was pulled from the ocean.*

wren [ren] NOUN, wrens. **roitelet ▸** a very small songbird having brown feathers with black and white markings.

wrench [rench] NOUN, wrenches. **1. clé à écrous, clef en croix, clé polygonale, clé à fourche ▸** a tool used to hold and turn nuts, bolts, or pipes, usually having two jawlike parts that can be moved together to grip the object tight. **2. entorse, déchirement ▸** a sharp twist or pull, or an injury caused by such a movement. ▲ VERB, wrenched, wrenching. **tirer violemment, arracher ▸** to give a sudden, sharp twist to : *Paula wrenched her ankle during baseball tryouts.*

wres-tle [RESS-ul] VERB, wrestled, wrestling. **1. lutter, pratiquer la lutte ▸** to take part in the sport or contest of wrestling. **2. lutter ▸** to struggle in an attempt to hold a person or throw him to the ground : *The boys wrestled each other to the ground.* **3. se débattre contre ▸** to struggle to overcome : *to wrestle with a problem.*

wres-tling [RESS-ling] NOUN. **lutte ▸** a sport in which two opponents compete to try to force each other to the ground or hold each other in certain positions, in a test of strength. **Note.** A wrestler is a person who takes part in wrestling.

wretch [rech] NOUN, wretches. **1. malheureux (-euse), misérable ▸** a very sad or unhappy person. **2. affreux (-euse), misérable ▸** a cruel person.

wretch-ed [RECH-id] ADJECTIVE. **1. déprimé (-ée), démoralisé (-ée) ▸** very unfortunate or unhappy; suffering : *"The tears made dark spots on the red of my apron and I felt very wretched."* (Anne Frank) **2. misérable, maudit (-ite) ▸** causing unhappiness or suffering : *This wretched headache won't let me concentrate on my work.* ■ **wretchedly,** ADVERB. ▸ **misérablement.** ■ **wretchedness,** NOUN. ▸ **misère, extrême pauvreté, extrême tristesse.**

wrig-gle [RIG-ul] VERB, wriggled, wriggling. **se tortiller, gigoter, se faufiler ▸** to move by twisting from side to side; squirm, as a worm or snake does : *We wriggled through a hole in the fence.*

wring [ring] VERB, wrung, wringing. **1. essorer ▸** to twist or squeeze water from : *I had wrung out my wet bathing suit and hung it up to dry.* **2. serrer, tordre ▸** to twist or squeeze : *I could see Mother worried and wringing her hands.* **3. arracher ▸** to get by force or threat : *Workers tried to wring better conditions from their employers.*

wrin-kle [RINK-ul] NOUN, wrinkles. **ride, pli ▸** a small ridge or crease on a smooth surface, such as cloth or skin : *Carol smoothed the wrinkles out of her skirt.* ▲ VERB, wrinkled, wrinkling. **rider ▸** to have wrinkles : *Skin wrinkles as it gets older.*

wrist [rist] NOUN, wrists. **poignet ▸** the joint of the body that connects the hand and the arm.

wrist-watch [RIST-woch] NOUN, wristwatches. **montre-bracelet ▸** a type of watch that is held onto the wrist by a band made of metal, leather, or cloth.

write [rite] VERB, wrote, written, writing. **1. écrire ▸** to put letters and words on paper or another such surface : *Please write your name at the top of your test paper.* **2. écrire, composer ▸** to create a book, article, or other work involving words : *to write a story.*

writ-er [RITE-ur] NOUN, writers. **1. auteur ▸** any person who writes. **2. auteur, écrivain ▸** someone who writes stories, articles, and so on as a job or for money. 📖 **p. 1128.**

writhe [rithe] VERB, writhed, writhing. **se tordre ▸** to twist and turn because of pain : *The stomach flu made Hussein writhe in discomfort.*

writ-ing [RY-ting] NOUN, writings. **1. écrit, écriture ▸** the fact of putting words on paper. **2. écriture ▸** something in the form of words on paper; something written : *Your writing is impossible to read.* **3. écriture ▸** the activity of creating a poem, story, play, article, or the like; the art of a writer : *I am taking creative writing at school.* **4. écrit, œuvre ▸** a work of literature : *the writings of Jean Little.* ✍ **p. 680.**

writ-ten [RIT-un] VERB. a past form of write. ▲ ADJECTIVE. **écrit, par écrit ▸** in the form of writing : *a written note.*

679

wrong [rong] ADJECTIVE. **1.** **incorrect (-ecte), inexact (-acte)** ▸ not agreeing with the facts; not correct : *My watch is wrong; it says 12:10 but it's really 12:30.* **2.** **mal** ▸ not according to what is good or proper : *You were wrong to lie.* **3.** **inadéquat (-ate), peu approprié (-ée), mauvais (-aise)** ▸ not suited to the purpose : *David wore the wrong clothes and felt embarrassed.* ▲ ADVERB. **incorrectement** ▸ in an incorrect or improper way : *to spell a word wrong.* ▲ NOUN, wrongs. **injustice, tort** ▸ something that is bad, incorrect, or improper : *Two wrongs don't make a right.* ▲ VERB, wronged, wronging. **traiter injustement, faire tort à** ▸ to treat in an unfair way : *The man claimed that the government had wronged him.*

wrote [rote] VERB. a past form of write.

wrung [rung] VERB. a past form of wring.

wry [ry] ADJECTIVE, wrier, wriest. **1.** **forcé (-ée), désabusé (-ée)** ▸ of a smile, remark, and so on, showing dislike or lack of feeling; forced or twisted. **2.** **désabusé (-ée), empreint (-einte) d'une ironie désabusée** ▸ humorous and slightly sarcastic. ■ **wryly,** ADVERB. ▸ **avec une ironie désabusée.**

✎ Writing Tips

Writing Strategies

*Most writers have problems getting from the first blank page to their last draft. Whenever you have trouble beginning your writing, use one of the **writing strategies** below. Some of these work better with fiction; some with non-fiction.*

• *Read a newspaper and use one headline as the basis of a story.*

• *Listen to the lyrics of a song and think about the story behind the song.*

• *Study a photograph or illustration and think about the story behind it.*

• *Read through a book of quotations until you find one that jump-starts your imagination.*

• *Arrange words connected to your subject in a list, chart, or web. Cluster together words with connections to one another.*

• *Make a chart of the five W's : Who? What? Where? When? and Why?*

• *Write an outline of some of your ideas.*

• *Talk with other people about the subject you are thinking of writing about.*

• *Review your research and think about new angles on a familiar subject.*

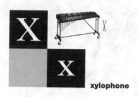

xylophone

x, X [eks] NOUN, x's, X's. **x, X ▶** the 24th letter of the English alphabet.

Xan-a-du [ZAN-uh-DOO] NOUN. **paradis, Eden ▶** a beautiful, perfect place. **Note.** The word *Xanadu* comes from the poem "Kubla Khan" by Samuel Taylor Coleridge.

Xe-rox [ZEER-OKS] NOUN, Xeroxes. **1. photo-copie ▶** a trademark name for a process of making photographic copies of written and printed material. **2. photocopie ▶** a copy made in this way. ▪ **Xeroxed, Xeroxing. photocopier ▶** to make such a copy : *to Xerox a report.* **Note.** The Xerox Corporation often points out in its advertisements that this word correctly applies only to machines made by their company, and they oppose the use of the word in a general sense, as in "That's the original, not a *xerox* copy," or "I *xeroxed* the letter at the library." Legally, the general word should be *photocopy*, not *xerox*.

X-mas [KRIS-mus *or* EKS-mus] NOUN. *Informal.* **Noël (fête de) ▶** a short word for **Christmas. Note.** *Xmas* is a very old word, going back to the 1500s. The letter "X" is an ancient symbol for Christ. In Greek, Christ's name begins with the letter "X," which is said as *ky*.

X-ray [EKS-RAY] NOUN, X-rays. (also x-ray) **1. rayon x ▶** a powerful form of energy made up of waves of very short length. It is similar to ordinary light but has the power to pass through solid objects in a way that light cannot. **2. radio-graphie ▶** a photographic film made with X-rays. X-rays are used by doctors to study the bones and the inside of the body. ▲ VERB, X-rayed, X-raying. **radiographier, faire une radio ▶** to examine or photograph by the use of X-rays : *The last time I went to the dentist, she X-rayed my teeth to see if I had any cavities.* **Note.** In science and mathematics, "X" stands for something that is not known. When the German scientist Wilhelm Roentgen discovered X-rays in 1895, at first he did not know what they were or why they acted in such an unusual way.

xy-lem [ZY-lum] NOUN. **bois ligneux ▶** the woody part of a tree, bush, or plant.

xy-lo-phone [ZY-luh-FONE] NOUN, xylophones. **xylophone ▶** a musical instrument that is made up of a series of flat wooden or metal bars of different sizes. It is played by striking the bars with small wooden mallets. **Note.** This word comes from two Greek terms, *xylo* (meaning "wood") and *phone* (meaning "sound"). ☜ **p. 538.**

yacht

y, Y [wy] NOUN, y's, Y's. **y, Y ▶** the 25th letter of the English alphabet.

yacht [yot] NOUN, yachts. **yacht, voilier, bateau (-eaux) de plaisance ▶** a large, expensive boat used for pleasure cruising or for racing. 👁 **p. 394.**

yak [yak] NOUN, yaks. **yack, yak ▶** a long-haired animal that is a type of ox and that lives in the high mountains of central Asia. It is raised for meat and milk and used to pull heavy loads.

yam [yam] NOUN, yams. **1. igname ▶** a trailing tropical vine that has a thick root that can be eaten as a vegetable. **2. patate douce ▶** a type of sweet potato.

yank [yank] VERB, yanked, yanking. **arracher, extirper ▶** to pull or jerk something suddenly : *He yanked hard on the doorknob, but he could not open the door.* ▲ NOUN, yanks. **coup, saccade ▶** a sharp, sudden pull.

Yan·kee [YANK-ee] NOUN, Yankees. **Note.** Yankee or Yank is a nickname for : **a. Yankee ▶** a person from one of the six New England states of the northeastern United States. **b. Yankee ▶** a person who fought on the side of the Union in the U.S. Civil War. **c. Yankee des États-Unis ▶** any person from the United States.

yard¹ [yard] NOUN, yards. **1. cour, préau (-aux) ▶** an area of ground around a house or other building : *Play outside in the yard.* **Note.** Often used in combinations such as barnyard, backyard, schoolyard, and so on. 📖 **p. 1074. Note.** Yard sale is another way of saying garage sale. **2. chantier ▶** an area used for a certain type of work : *a junkyard.* 👁 **p. 114.**

yard² NOUN, yards. **1. verge ▶** a way of measuring the length of something. A yard is equal to three feet, 36 inches, or about 91 cm. **2. vergue ▶** a long pole set across the mast of a ship and used to support the top edge of the sails.

yard·stick [YARD-stik] NOUN, yardsticks. **1. mesure ▶** a measuring stick that is one yard in length. **2. mesure ▶** any way of measuring or comparing something : *Scores on a standard test are one yardstick for judging a teacher's effectiveness.*

yarn [yarn] NOUN, yarns. **1. fil ▶** twisted thread or fibres used for knitting or weaving. **2. longue histoire ▶** an adventure story, especially one that is told for entertainment : *Grandpa likes to tell an old yarn about finding a gold mine.*

yawn [yon] VERB, yawned, yawning. **1. bailler ▶** to open the mouth wide and take a deep breath, as when one is tired, sleepy, or bored. **2. béant ▶** to be or stand wide open : *a yawning hole where the door used to be.* ▲ NOUN, yawns. **bâillement ▶** the act of yawning.

ye [yee] PRONOUN. **vous ▶** an old word for you, used in such writings as the Bible and Shakespeare.

yea [yay] NOUN, yeas. **oui ▶** a vote in favour of something, as opposed to "nay." ▲ ADVERB. **vieux oui ▶** an old way of saying "yes."

year [yeer] NOUN, years. **1. an, année, âge ▶** the period of 12 months or 365 days from January 1st to December 31st, during which the earth moves around the sun once. **2. année scolaire, année fiscale, etc. ▶** any period of 12 months : *Sam will be 12 years old next Saturday.* **3. année ▶** a period of time, usually less than a year, used to measure some activity : *The school year is really only 10 months long.* 📖 **p. 1081.**

year·book [YEER-book] NOUN, yearbooks. **1. annuaire ▶** a book that is published once a year with information about the previous year. **2. annuaire (d'un organisme) ▶** a book published once a year by a school with information about the students and school activities.

year·ling [YEER-ling] NOUN, yearlings. **âgé d'un an ▶** a racehorse, farm animal, or deer between one and two years of age.

year·ly [YEER-lee] ADJECTIVE. **1. chaque année, tous les ans ▶** happening or done once a year; annual : *My parents have a yearly barbecue for our neighbours.* **2. annuel ▶** lasting for one year : *a yearly income.* ▲ ADVERB.

yearn [yurn] VERB, yearned, yearning. **avoir envie de, aspirer, avoir désir de ▶** to feel a

682

strong desire to have or do something; want very much : *After spending three hours in the storm, she yearned for a blanket and a cup of hot tea.* SYN : desire, crave, wish for, long for.

yeast [yeest] NOUN, yeasts. **levure** ▶ a substance used to make bread rise and to brew beer. It is made of the tiny cells of a certain fungus plant.

yell [yel] VERB, yelled, yelling. **crier, hurler** ▶ to cry out in a loud voice; shout : *"Digging her heels into the donkey's flanks, she yelled, 'Charge!'"* (Robin Muller) ▲ NOUN, yells. **cri, hurlement** ▶ a loud cry or shout : *the yells of the excited fans.* SYN : scream, holler, bellow, roar, cry out.

yel·low [YEL-oh] NOUN, yellows. 1. **jaune** ▶ the colour of butter or ripe lemons. 2. **jaune** ▶ something having this colour. ▲ ADJECTIVE. **jaune** ▶ having the colour yellow. ▲ VERB, yellowed, yellowing. **jaunir** ▶ to make or become yellow in colour. ✐ p. 64.

yellow fever **fièvre jaune** ▶ a tropical disease that is carried by the bite of certain female mosquitoes. Yellow fever causes fever, chills, and sometimes death. It was once very common in areas of the Caribbean but is now largely under control.

yellow jacket **guêpe** ▶ a type of wasp that has bright yellow markings on its body.

Yel·low·knife [YEL-oh-nife] NOUN, Yellowknife **Yellowknife** ▶ or Yellowknifes. 1. **Yellowknife** ▶ an Aboriginal people originally living in the southeast of the Northwest Territories. The Yellowknife have not joined with the Chipewyan. 2. **yellowknife** ▶ the Athapaskan language of these people.

yelp [yelp] VERB, yelped, yelping. **japper, glapir** ▶ to give a sharp, quick cry, as a dog does when it is excited or in pain : *"Beside us Duke and Chuck raced, barking and yelping their pleasure at the outing."* (Todd Lee) ▲ NOUN, yelps. **jappement** ▶ a sharp, quick cry.

yen[1] [yen] NOUN, yen. **yen** ▶ the unit of money that is used in Japan.

yen[2] NOUN. *Informal.* **grande envie de, désir intense** ▶ a strong desire; an urge : *He has a yen for some chocolate cake.*

yes [yes] ADVERB; NOUN, yeses. **oui** ▶ it is so; it is correct; the opposite of "no."

yes·ter·day [YES-tur-DAY or YES-tur-dee] ADVERB, NOUN, yesterdays. 1. **hier** ▶ the day before today. 2. **hier** ▶ the past : *It's your turn to do the dishes; I did them yesterday.*

yet [yet] ADVERB. **encore** ▶ up to or at this time; so far : *"I had not yet met a teacher who had not liked me."* (Jean Little) ▲ CONJUNCTION. **jusqu'à présent** ▶ even so; but; nevertheless : *"He was hopeful, yet he couldn't forget what had happened the first time."* (Richard E. Albert)

yew [yoo] NOUN, yews. **bois d'if** ▶ an evergreen tree that grows in Europe and Asia. It has reddish-brown bark and flat, needle-shaped leaves.

Yid·dish [YID-ish] NOUN. **yiddish** ▶ a language that developed from German, spoken by Jews in central and eastern Europe and by Jewish immigrants in other places.

yield [yeeld] VERB, yielded, yielding. 1. **céder, se rendre** ▶ to give up; surrender : *Ann yielded to temptation and ate the last piece of pie.* 2. **céder, abandonner** ▶ to give way under force : *The shelf finally yielded to the weight of all the books.* 3. **rapporter, produire, rendre** ▶ to bring forth; produce : *That orchard yields thousands of kilos of apples each fall.* ▲ NOUN, yields **rendement, production** ▶ the amount yielded or obtained.

yo·gurt [YOH-gurt] NOUN, yogurts. (also yoghurt or yoghourt) **yogourt, yaourt** ▶ a food prepared from milk that has been thickened by the addition and action of certain bacteria.

yoke [yoke] NOUN, yokes. 1. **attelage** ▶ a wooden crosspiece that is fastened over the necks of two oxen or other animals so that they can move together to pull a plough, wagon, or other device. 2. **empiècement** ▶ a part of a shirt or dress that covers the shoulders and includes the neckline. ▲ VERB, yoked, yoking. **atteler** ▶ to join or attach with a yoke : *The farmer yoked the horses to the wagon.*

yolk [yoke] NOUN, yolks. **jaune d'œuf** ▶ the yellow part of an egg.

Yom Kippur [YOM-kih-PUR] **Yom Kippour** ▶ a Jewish holiday that falls in September or October. It is a day of not eating and of praying for forgiveness of sins. **Note.** Also called the Day of Atonement.

yon·der [YON-dur] ADVERB. **là-bas, là-haut** ▶ in that place; over there : *"We were always near the kitchen window, which faced the road and the barn, the railroad and the lake yonder."* (Christy MacKinnon) **Note.** Also used as an ADJECTIVE, mainly in older writings : *"What light through yonder window breaks?"* (William Shakespeare)

you [yoo] PRONOUN, you. 1. **tu, vous** ▶ the person or persons being spoken to : *Why didn't you tell me today is your birthday?* 2. **toi, vous** ▶ a person; anyone : *You must have your birth certificate to get a passport.* ✐ p. 684.

young [yung] ADJECTIVE, younger, youngest. **jeune, petit (petite)** ▶ having lived or existed for a short period of time, not old : *Young children enjoy having stories read to them before they can read themselves.* ▲ NOUN. 1. the young. **jeunes** ▶ young people as a group. 2. **petit, jeune, enfant** ▶ an animal's young offspring : *"Deer and moose especially are in the habit of hiding their young while they go off to feed."* (Todd Lee) SYN: youthful, juvenile, fresh, new.

✍ Writing Tips

You

It's an old saying among advertising writers that the most powerful word in an ad is **you.** *You refers to the reader. There are two situations in which writers use* **you.**

• *One situation is when the writer is speaking directly to the reader, as if having a conversation.*

My little brother is a pest. If you have a little brother, **you** *know exactly what I mean.*

• *The other situation is when the reader is placed right in the middle of a story.*

You *look around and all* **you** *can see is the fire.* **You** *see smoke and steam, and people, too. All looking at the fire.* **You're** *scared, but too ashamed to say so.*

Writers use **you** *to make an experience more real to readers. This is a good idea, but it has to be controlled. If you overuse* **you,** *the effect becomes forced or artificial.*

young-ster [YUNG-stur] NOUN, youngsters. **jeune enfant, jeune garçon ▸** a young person; a child.

your [yoor *or* yor] ADJECTIVE. **1. ton (ta, tes) votre (vos) ▸** of or belonging to you : *Hang your coat up in the closet.* **2. à ta, à votre ▸** of or relating to any person : *The art museum is the building on your left.* **3.** *Informal.* **un (une), ton (ta, tes), vos ▸** any one; a, an, or the : *My grandmother is not your average grandparent; she's travelling around Africa on foot!*

yours [yorz *or* yoorz] PRONOUN. **le tien (la tienne), les tiens, les tiennes), le vôtre (la vôtre, les vôtres) ▸** belonging or relating to you : *Someone turned in homework without a name on it. Is it yours?*

your-self [yur-SELF] PRONOUN, yourselves. **toi-même, vous-mêmes ▸** the one that you are; your own self : *I knew I couldn't fix this; you should have done it yourself.*

youth [yooth] NOUN, youths or youth. **1. jeunesse ▸** the time of being young, especially the part of life between early childhood and adulthood : *Erin spent her youth travelling all over Canada with her family.* **2. jeune, jeune homme ▸** a young person, especially a young man : *The city honoured three youths who had started a basketball league in an inner city neighbourhood.* **3. the youth. jeunes, jeunesse ▸** young people as a group. **4. jeunesse ▸** the fact of being young. SYN: adolescence, childhood, juvenile.

youth-ful [YOOTH-ful] ADJECTIVE. **jeune, juvénile ▸** having youth or the qualities of youth; being young : *"The old man's heart was full of joy. His face became brighter and his step more youthful."* (Tololwa M. Mollel) SYN: young, fresh, juvenile, childlike.

yo-yo [YOH-yoh] NOUN, yo-yos. **yo-yo ▸** a toy that is made of two disks connected at the centre by a piece which has a string wrapped around it. A yo-yo goes up and down as the string winds and unwinds around the centre piece.

Yule [yool] NOUN. (also yule or Yuletide) **les fêtes, période de Noël ▸** Christmas or the Christmas season.

zebra

z, Z [zed] NOUN, z's, Z's. **z, Z** ▸ the 26th letter of the English alphabet.

zeal [zeel] NOUN. **zèle, ardeur** ▸ great interest and enthusiasm in working for some cause or goal : *Her love of debating is partly based on her competitive zeal.* ■ **zealous** [ZEL-us], ADJECTIVE. **zélé (-ée), enthousiaste** ▸ having or showing zeal. ■ **zealously,** ADVERB. ▸ **avec zèle, avec ardeur.**

ze-bra [ZEE-bruh] NOUN, zebras or zebra. **zèbre** ▸ an African animal that looks like a horse with a black-and-white or brown-and-white striped coat.

zebra

ze-nith [ZEE-nith] NOUN, zeniths. **1. zénith** ▸ the point in the sky directly above where a person is standing. **2. zénith, apogée** ▸ the highest or most important point ; the peak : *the zenith of power.*

ze-ro [ZEE-roh] NOUN, zeros or zeroes. **1. zéro** ▸ the number that leaves any other number the same when added to it ; 0. **2. zéro** ▸ a point on a scale of measurement : *On a Celsius scale, water freezes at zero.* **3. zéro, rien, néant** ▸ nothing ; none at all : *The score was three to zero.* ▲ ADJECTIVE. **nul (nulle)** ▸ of or at zero : *During the snowstorm, there was zero visibility.*

zest [zest] NOUN. **entrain, enthousiasme** ▸ an exciting or interesting quality : *Shiu Ngoi has a*

zest for life. SYN: passion, spirit, zeal, enjoyment, enthusiasm.

zig-zag [ZIG-zag] NOUN, zigzags. **zigzag, lacet** ▸ a series of short, sharp turns or angles. ▲ VERB, zigzagged, zigzagging. **zigzaguer, faire des zigzags** ▸ to move or form a zigzag : *The skiers zigzagged back and forth down the hill.*

zinc [zink] NOUN. **zinc** ▸ a greyish-white metal that is a chemical element.

zin-ni-a [ZIN-ee-uh] NOUN, zinnias. **zinnia** ▸ a garden plant with brightly coloured flowers.

zip [zip] VERB, zipped, zipping. **1. fermer à l'aide d'une fermeture éclair** ▸ to close or fasten something with a zipper : *to zip up a jacket.* **2.** *Informal.* **passer comme une flèche, passer rapidement** ▸ to move quickly or with energy : *I'll just zip over to the store.* ■ NOUN. *Informal.* **entrain, vitalité, enthousiasme** ▸ energy, vitality : *This salsa has a lot of zip to it.*

zip-per [ZIP-ur] NOUN, zippers. **fermeture éclair, fermeture à glissière** ▸ a fastener made up of two rows of metal or plastic teeth that can be joined or separated by sliding a catch up or down. Zippers are used on clothing, suitcases, and other items. ■ **zipped,** ADJECTIVE. ▸ **fermé (-ée) à l'aide d'une fermeture éclair.**

zith-er [ZITH-ur] NOUN, zithers. **cithare** ▸ a musical instrument having 30 to 40 strings stretched across a wooden sounding box. It is played by plucking the strings.

zo-di-ac [ZOH-dee-ak] NOUN. **zodiaque** ▸ an imaginary belt in the sky along which the sun appears to travel. The zodiac is divided into 12 sections, called **signs**, each of which is named after a different group of stars, such as Taurus or Libra.

zone [zone] NOUN, zones. **1. zone, secteur** ▸ any area that has some special quality, condition, or use : *a war zone.* **2. zone climatique** ▸ any of the five regions of the earth's surface divided according to climate. **Note.** Near the North and South Poles are the two **Frigid Zones**. The area on either side of the equator, with hot temperatures, is the **Torrid Zone**. Between these are the

685

two Temperate Zones, which have a more even climate. **3. zone, secteur** ▸ a certain part of a city or town, classified by what kind of buildings are permitted there : *an industrial zone.* **Note.** The process of controlling land use in this way is called zoning. ▲ VERB, zoned, zoning. **diviser en zones, diviser en secteurs** ▸ to divide land into zones : *That area is zoned for business.* SYN : area, region, district, section, part, division.

zoo [zoo] NOUN, ZOOS. **zoo** ▸ a special park or other place where wild animals are kept to be seen by the public.

zo-ol-o-gy [zoh-OL-uh-jee] NOUN. **zoologie** ▸ the science that studies animals and animal life.

zoom [zoom] VERB, zoomed, zooming. **démarrer, traverser en trombe** ▸ to move or go suddenly and quickly : *We zoomed about the lake in a speed boat.* SYN : shoot, speed, streak.

zuc-chi-ni [zoo-KEE-nee] NOUN, zucchini or zucchinis. **courgette** ▸ a type of green-skinned squash that looks like a cucumber, eaten as a vegetable.

FRENCH LEXICON

à ► at, in, to, unto
abaisse-langue ► spatula
abaisser ► depress, droop, humiliate
    s'abaisser ► lower oneself, stoop[1]
abandon ► waive
abandonner ► abandon, desert[2], drop, drop out, maroon[1], quit, relinquish, surrender, waive, yield
abaque ► abacus
abasourdi (-ie) ► dumb
abasourdir ► daze, stun
abat ► spare
abat-jour ► shade
abattement ► desolation [desolate]
abattre ► butcher, discourage, fell[2], gun, pull, slaughter
    s'abattre ► descend
abbaye ► abbey
abdomen ► abdomen
abdominal (-ale, -aux) ► abdominal [abdomen]
abeille ► bee
abénaquis ► Abenaki
abîme ► gulf
abîmer ► deface, weather
    s'abîmer ► spoil
aboiement ► bark[2], bay[2], cry
abolir ► abolish
abolition ► abolition [abolish]
abolitionniste ► abolitionist [abolish]
abominable ► monstrous, terrible, villainous [villain]
abondamment ► extensively [extensive]
abondance ► abundance [abundant], fullness [full], plenty
    en abondance ► wealth
abondant (-ante) ► abundant, ample, bountiful, generous, lush, numerous, plentiful [plenty]
    peu abondant (-ante) ► scant
abonné (-ée) ► consumer, subscriber [subscribe]
abonnement ► subscription
s'abonner ► subscribe
d'abord ► first
aborder ► approach, introduce, tackle
Aborigène ► Aborigine
aborigène ► Aboriginal [Aborigine]
aboutir ► arrive
aboutissement ► end
aboyer ► bark[2], bay[2]
abrégé ► digest
abrégé (-ée) ► concise
abréger ► abbreviate, condense, shorten
abréviation ► abbreviation

abri ► cover, dugout, shelter
    à l'abri ► indoor, sheltered [shelter]
    mettre à l'abri de ► shelter
abricot ► apricot
abriter ► screen
abrupt (-upte) ► abrupt, sheer
abruti (-ie) ► fool
absence ► absence
    remarquer l'absence ► miss[1]
absent (-ente) ► absent, away, missing, vacant
    de façon absente ► absently [absent]
s'absenter ► away
absentéiste ► truant
absolu (-ue) ► absolute, stark, total
absolument ► absolutely [absolute], dead, remotely [remote], utterly [utter[2]], vitally [vital]
absorbé (-ée) ► deep, intent[1]
absorber ► absorb, consume, drink, drink in, soak, suck, wrapped up in [wrap]
    être absorbé dans ► pore[2]
absorption ► trance
abstrait (-aite) ► abstract
abstraitement ► abstractly
absurde ► absurd, incoherent, insane, preposterous
absurdement ► absurdly [absurd], preposterously [preposterous]
absurdité ► absurdity [absurd]
    absurdités ► nonsense
abus ► abuse
abuser ► deceive, dupe
    abuser de ► abuse
académie ► academy
académique ► academic
Acadie ► Acadia
acadien (-ienne) ► Acadian [Acadia]
acajou ► mahogany
accabler ► condemn, heap, overcome, overwhelm
    accabler de sarcasmes ► taunt
accaparer ► hog
    s'accaparer ► grab
accéder à ► access
accélérateur ► accelerator [accelerate], throttle
accélération ► acceleration [accelerate], pickup
accélérer ► accelerate, hasten
accent ► accent, emphasis, note, speech, stress
    accents ► strain[2]
accentuer ► accent, stress
acceptable ► acceptable, decent, tolerable
    de façon acceptable ► acceptably [acceptable]
acceptation ► acceptance [accept]

accepter ▸ abide, accept, agree, tolerate, welcome
    faire accepter ▸ reconcile
accès[1] ▸ access, bout, fit[2]
    d'accès difficile ▸ rugged
accès[2] ▸ spasm
    voie d'accès ▸ approach, ramp
    trouver accès à ▸ admission
accessible ▸ accessible [access], available
accessoire ▸ accessory, attachment, prop
accident ▸ accident, crash, wreck
accidenté (-ée) ▸ rugged
accidentel (-elle) ▸ accidental
accidentellement ▸ by chance [chance]
acclamation ▸ cheer
acclamer ▸ hail[2]
accommodant (-ante) ▸ easy
accommoder ▸ accommodate, content[2]
    s'accommoder ▸ make the best of
accompagnement ▸ accompaniement [accompany], trimming
accompagner ▸ accompany, escort, usher
accompli (-ie) ▸ accomplished [accomplish]
accomplir ▸ accomplish, carry out, do, execute
accomplissement ▸ accomplishment [accomplish], execution
accord ▸ accord, agreement, blessing, chord, consent, harmony
    accords ▸ strain[2]
    d'accord ▸ OK
    en accord ▸ consistent, in (out) of tune
    être d'accord ▸ agreement, OK
    ne pas être d'accord ▸ differ
    se mettre d'accord sur ▸ agree
accordé (-ée) ▸ in (out) of tune
accordéon ▸ accordion
accorder ▸ agree, concede, give, grant, tune
    s'accorder ▸ accord, agree, correspond
accordeur (-euse) ▸ tuner
accotement ▸ shoulder
accouchement ▸ delivery
accoucher ▸ deliver
accoudoir ▸ arm[1]
accoupler ▸ mate
accoutrement ▸ costume
accoutumé (-ée) ▸ used to
(s')accoutumer à ▸ accustomed to [accustomed]
accréditer ▸ credit
accroc ▸ difficulty, hitch, snag, tear[1]
    faire un accroc à ▸ snag
accroché (-ée) ▸ hooked [hook]
accrocher ▸ hang, hitch, hook, peg, snag
    s'accrocher ▸ catch, cling
accroissement ▸ increase
accroître ▸ expand, increase, rise

accroupissement ▸ crouch
s'accroupir ▸ crouch, squat
accueil ▸ greeting, orientation [orient], treatment, welcome
    centre d'accueil ▸ home
accueillir ▸ accommodate, greet, receive, seat, welcome
accumulateur en tampon ▸ buffer
accumulation ▸ accumulation [accumulate], bank[2], collection
(s')accumuler ▸ accumulate
accusation ▸ accusation, charge
    chef d'accusation ▸ count[1]
    faire porter une accusation contre quelqu'un ▸ frame
    monter une accusation ▸ frame
    de manière accusatrice ▸ accusingly [accuse]
accusé (-ée) ▸ defendant
    banc des accusés ▸ dock[3]
accuser ▸ accuse
    accuser réception (de) ▸ acknowledge
acerbe ▸ tart[1], vicious
    d'un ton acerbe ▸ crisply [crisp]
acerbité ▸ tartness [tart[1]]
acharné (-ée) ▸ furious, strenuous
acharnement ▸ dedication, fury
    avec acharnement ▸ grimly [grim], relentlessly [relentless]
achat ▸ buy, purchase
acheminer ▸ route
acheter ▸ bribe, buy, purchase
achèvement ▸ completion, end
achevé (-ée) ▸ complete
achever ▸ complete, conclude, end, finish
acide ▸ acid, sour
    acide aminé ▸ amino acid
    pluies acides ▸ acid rain
acidité ▸ tartness [tart[1]]
acidulé (-ée) ▸ sour
acier ▸ steel
    acier inoxydable ▸ stainless steel
    d'acier ▸ steely [steel]
acompte ▸ deposit
    laisser un acompte ▸ deposit
à-côté ▸ extra[1]
à-coup ▸ jerk
    par à-coup ▸ spurt
acoustique ▸ acoustic, acoustics
acquérir ▸ acquire, gain, inherit
    prendre pour acquis ▸ take for granted
acquittement ▸ discharge
acquitter ▸ acquit
    s'acquitter ▸ acquit, execute
âcre ▸ pungent
acrobate ▸ acrobat, tumbler
acrobatie ▸ stunt[1]

acrobatique ► acrobatic [acrobat]
acronyme ► acronym
acrostiche ► acrostic
acrylique ► acrylic
acte ► act, action, actions, deed
   Acte de l'Amérique du Nord britannique ► B.N.A. Act, British North America Act
acteur (-trice) ► player
actif ► asset
   à l'actif ► active
actif (-ive) ► active, brisk, dynamic, lively
   à la voie active ► active
actinie ► sea anemone
action[1] ► action, deed
   actions ► doings
   action de grâces ► grace
   Action de grâce(s) ► Thanksgiving
   action judiciaire ► lawsuit
   (bonne) action ► turn
   feu de l'action ► heat
   rayon d'action ► range
action[2] ► plot
action[3] ► share, stock
actionner ► drive, power
activement ► actively [active], briskly [brisk]
s'activer ► bustle, busy
activité ► activity, deed, pursuit
   en activité ► active
   centre (d'activités) ► hub
actualiser ► update
actualités ► news
actuel (-elle) ► contemporary, current, present[1], up-to-date
actuellement ► currently, now, nowadays, presently
acupuncture ► acupuncture
adaptation ► adaptation, arrangement
adapter ► adapt, arrange, fit[1], gear, tailor
   adapter pour la scène ► dramatize
additif ► additive
addition[1] ► addition, check
addition[2] ► tab
additionnel (-elle) ► additional, further
additionner ► add, count[1], total
adepte ► adept
adéquat (-ate) ► proper
adhérence ► traction
adhérer ► endorse
   adhérer à ► join
adhésif ► adhesive
   ruban adhésif ► tape
adhésif (-ive) ► adhesive, tacky
adieu ► adieu, adios, farewell, goodbye
adjacent (-ente) ► adjacent
adjectif ► adjective

adjoint (-ointe) ► assistant, associate, deputy, lieutenant
admettre ► accept, admit, concede, grant
   refuser d'admettre ► deny
   se faire admettre ► admission
administrateur (-trice) ► governor, trustee
administratif (-ive) ► administrative [administration]
administration ► administration, direction, government, management
administrer ► administer, direct, govern, run
admirable ► admirable, excellent
admirablement ► beautifully [beautiful], excellently [excellent], wonderfully [wonderful]
admirateur (-trice) ► admirer, fan[2]
admiration ► admiration
admirer ► admire
admissible ► eligible, legitimate
admission ► entrance[3]
ADN ► DNA
adobe ► adobe
adolescence ► teens
adolescent (-ente) ► adolescent, juvenile, teenager
adopter ► adopt, pass
adoptif (-ive) ► foster
adoption ► adoption
adorable ► adorable [adore], darling, winning
adoration ► adoration [adore], worship
adoré (-ée) ► precious
adorer ► adore, love, worship
adosser ► prop
   s'adosser ► back
adouci (-ie) ► mellow
adoucir ► soften
adresse[1] ► address
   adresse télégraphique ► cable
adresse[2] ► cunning, neatness [neat], skill
adresser ► address
   s'adresser à ► address, apply, target
   adresser une pétition ► petition
adroit (-oite) ► deft, handy, neat, skillful [skill]
adroitement ► deftly [deft]
adulte ► adult, grown-up, mature
   devenir adulte ► grow up
advenir de ► become of
adverbe ► adverb
adversaire ► adversary, opponent, rival
adverse ► adverse
adversité ► adversity
aéré (-ée) ► fluffy [fluff]
   mal aéré (-ée) ► stuffy
aérer ► air
aérien (-ienne) ► aerial
   poste aérienne ► airmail
aérobie ► aerobic

exercice d'**aérobie** ► aerobic exercise
aérodynamique ► aerodynamics
   rendre aérodynamique ► streamline
aérogare ► terminal
aéronautique ► aeronautics
aéroport ► airport
aérosol ► aerosol
affable ► pleasant
affaibli (-ie) ► run-down
affaiblir ► overcome, water
   s'affaiblir ► fade, weaken, wilt
affaire ► affair, bargain, business, case[1], deal
   affaires ► affair, belongings, business,
   stuff, things [thing]
   chiffre d'affaires ► figure
affairé (-ée) ► busy
affaissement ► collapse, landslide
affaisser ► droop
   s'affaisser ► sag, settle, slump, subside
position **affalée** ► sprawl
affamé (-ée) ► hungry
affectation ► appointment, post[3]
affecté (-ée) ► affected [affect[2]], artificial
affecter ► affect[1], cut, detail, hit, touch
affection ► affection, attachment, fondness
[fond], ill, illness
   avoir de l'affection pour ► fond
   se prendre d'affection pour ► fancy
affectueusement ► affectionately
[affectionate], fondly [fond]
affectueux (-cuse) ► affectionate, fond,
loving [love]
affermir ► steady
tableau d'**affichage** ► bulletin board
affiche ► bill[1], poster
afficher ► bill[1], chart, post[1], wear
affilé (-ée) ► keen
d'**affilée** ► solid
affiler ► grind
affiliation ► affiliation [affiliate]
s'**affilier** ► affiliate
affinage ► refinement [refine]
affirmatif (-ive) ► affirmative, positive
   signe de tête affirmatif ► nod
affirmation ► claim
affirmativement ► positive
affirmer ► claim
affliction ► distress
affligé (-ée) ► mournful [mourn]
affligeant (-ante) ► cruel
affliger ► afflict, distress
   s'affliger ► grieve
heure d'**affluence** ► rush hour
affluent ► tributary
affluer ► flock, pour
affoler ► panic
affranchir ► free, stamp

affrètement ► charter
affréter ► charter
affreusement ► dreadfully [dreadful], horribly
[horrible], shockingly [shocking]
affreux (-euse) ► atrocious, dreadful, fearful
[fear], ghastly, hideous, horrible, horrid, ugly,
wretch
affront ► insult, offence
affrontement ► clash, collision, combat
affronter ► confront, dare
   s'affronter ► clash
chasser à l'**affût** ► stalk[2]
affûter ► grind, whet
afin de ► in order to
agacé (-ée) ► upset
agacement ► upset
agacer ► irritate, jar, needle, upset
âge ► age, year
   un âge avancé ► advanced
   l'âge de (la) pierre ► Stone Age
   fleur de l'âge ► prime
   prendre de l'âge ► age
âgé (-ée) ► aged, old
   âgé (-ée) de ► old
   âgé d'un an ► yearling
   personne âgée ► senior, senior citizen
agence ► agency
agencement ► composition
agencer ► coordinate, organize
agenda ► diary
agent (-ente) ► agent, officer
   agent de conservation ►
   preservative
   agent (-ente) de police ► cop
   agent (-ente) de la police d'état ►
   trooper [troop]
agglomération ► concentration
aggravation ► aggravation [aggravate]
aggraver ► aggravate
agile ► limber, nimble
agilement ► nimbly [nimble]
agir ► act, deal, move
   agir à sa guise ► please
   pousser à agir ► spur
agitation ► commotion, excitement, flutter,
nervousness [nervous], restlessness
[restless], stir, turmoil, unrest
   avec agitation ► excitedly [excite],
   restlessly [restless]
agité (-ée) ► choppy, excited [excite], hectic,
nervous, restless, turbulent, uneasy
agiter ► flop, fluster, rouse, ruffle, shake, stir,
trouble, wag, wiggle
   s'agiter ► bob, flutter, fret
agneau (-eaux) ► lamb
agonie ► agony
agrafe ► clasp, hook, staple[1]

agrafer ► clasp, clip², staple¹
agrafeuse ► staple¹
agrandir ► enlarge, extend
agrandissement ► enlargement [enlarge], extension
(s')aggraver ► compound, worsen
agréable ► agreeable, likable, nice, pleasant, pleasing [please], pleasurable [pleasure]
agréablement ► agreeably [agreeable], nicely [nice], pleasantly [pleasant], sweetly [sweet]
agrément ► convenience
agresser ► mug
agresseur ► attacker, raider [raid]
agressif (-ive) ► aggressive, unfriendly
agression ► aggression, assault
agressivement ► aggressively [aggressive]
agressivité ► agressiveness [aggressive], viciousness [vicious]
agricole ► agricultural [agriculture]
   produits agricoles ► produce
agriculture ► agriculture, cultivation [cultivate]
agripper ► clutch¹, grab
agrume ► citrus
(s')aguerrir ► toughen
   non aguerri (-ie) ► raw
ahurissant (-ante) ► breathtaking
ahurissement ► daze
aide ► aid, aide, assist, assistance, assistant, help, relief¹
   aide sociale ► welfare
   demander de l'aide ► appeal
aider ► aid, assist, help, lend a hand
aigle ► eagle
aiglefin ► haddock
aigre ► sour
aigrette ► egret
aigreur ► tartness [tart¹]
(s')aigrir ► sour
aigu (-uë) ► acute, high, keen
aiguille ► hand, needle, switch, thorn
   aiguille à tricoter ► needle
aiguiller ► switch
aiguisé (-ée) ► keen, sharp
aiguiser ► grind, sharpen, whet
ail (ails) ► garlic
aile ► wing
   aile (d'un moulin à vent) ► vane
ailé (-ée) ► winged
aileron ► fin
ailier ► wing
ailleurs ► else, elsewhere
   d'ailleurs ► moreover
   par ailleurs ► furthermore
aimable ► amiable, civil, gentle, gracious, kind¹, nice, outgoing, pleasant

aimablement ► graciously [gracious], nicely [nice]
aimant ► magnet
aimant (-ante) ► loving [love]
aimer ► enjoy, fancy, like¹, love
aîné ► senior
aîné (-ée) ► big, elder
ainsi ► so, thus
air¹ ► air
   en l'air ► air, airborne
   dans les airs ► air
   armée de l'air ► air force
   courant d'air ► draft
   plein air ► outdoor
   pression de l'air ► air pressure
air² ► appearance, aspect, look
   air décidé ► decisiveness [decisive]
   avec un air endormi ► drowsily
   d'un air interrogateur ► questioningly [question]
   d'un air morne ► bleakly [bleak]
   air renfrogné ► scowl
   d'un air renfrogné ► sullenly [sullen]
   d'un air suffisant ► smugly [smug]
   avoir l'air idiot (idiote) ► foolish
air³ ► tune
aire ► area
   aire de travail ► galley
aisance ► ease, grace
à l'aise ► comfortable, cool, ease, snugly [snug]
   mal à l'aise ► ill at ease, uncomfortable
   qui met mal à l'aise ► queasy
   se sentir à l'aise ► at home
aisé (-ée) ► convenient, easy, effortless [effort]
aisément ► easily, effortlessly [effort], readily
aisseau ► shingle
ajournement ► stay
ajourner ► adjourn, postpone, shelve
ajout ► addition
ajouter ► add, annex, insert
   ajouter à ► add to [add]
   ajouter un supplément ► supplement
ajustement ► adjustment, fit, regulation
ajuster ► adjust, amend, control, fit¹, focus, regulate, tailor, tighten
ajutage ► nozzle
s'alanguir ► wilt
alarmant (-ante) ► grave²
alarme ► alarm
   d'alarme ► warning
alarmer ► alarm
albatros ► albatross
albertosaure ► Albertosaurus
albinos ► albino

album ► album
   album (de découpures, etc.) ► scrapbook
alchimie ► alchemy
alcool ► alcohol, drink, liquor
alcoolique ► alcoholic
alcoolisé (-ée) ► alcoholic
alcoolisme ► alcoholism
ale ► ale
aléatoire ► random
alentours ► neighbourhood, vicinity
   aux alentours ► around
alerte ► alarm, alert, nimble
alerter ► alert
algèbre ► algebra
algonquien (-ienne) ► Algonquian
algonquin (-ine) ► Algonquian
algues ► algae
   algue marine ► seaweed
alibi ► alibi
aliéné (-ée) ► lunatic
aliéner ► alienate
alignement ► alignment [align]
aligner ► align
   (s')aligner ► line[1]
aliment ► food
   aliments ► nourishment [nourish]
   aliment de base ► staple[2]
   aliments sans valeur nutritive ► junk food
produits alimentaires ► produce
alimentation ► diet, nutrition
alimenter ► feed, nourish
alinéa ► indent
Allah ► Allah
allaiter ► nurse
alléchant (-ante) ► mouth-watering
allée ► aisle, drive
(s')alléger ► lighten[2]
allégorie ► allegory
alléguer ► allege
aller ► belong, do, fare, get
   aller et retour ► round trip
aller[1] ► go, head, ride, run
   aller à ► attend
   aller à l'encontre de ► counter[2]
   aller à toute vitesse ► career, hurtle, pelt[1], speed, tear[1]
   aller au devant de ► court
   aller au trot ► trot
   aller bien (à) ► become, suit
   aller bien avec ► match[2]
   aller bon train ► roll
   aller çà et là ► ramble
   aller chercher ► fetch
   aller chez quelqu'un ► over
   aller en autobus ► bus

   aller en groupe ► troop
   aller en masse ► swarm
   aller en reconnaissance ► scout
   aller en roue libre ► coast
   aller en traîneau ► sled
   aller en voyage de noces ► honeymoon
   aller et venir dans une grande agitation ► flutter
   aller furieusement ► storm
   aller furtivement ► slink, steal
   aller mieux ► better, mend, rally
   aller ou venir en masse ► flock
   aller se coucher ► retire
   aller trop loin ► go overboard
   qui ne va pas ► amiss
   s'en aller ► depart, wash
aller-retour ► back and forth, return
allergie ► allergy
allergique ► allergic
alliage ► alloy
alliance ► alliance, coalition
allié (-ée) ► allied, ally
allier ► alloy, wed
   s'allier à (avec) ► ally, team
alligator ► alligator
allitération ► alliteration
allô ► hello, hi
allocation ► allowance, benefit, dole
allocution ► speech
allonge ► reach
allonger ► lengthen
   s'allonger ► lie[1], recline
allouer ► allow, award, grant
allumage ► ignition
allumé (-ée) ► on
allumer ► inflame, kindle, light[1], strike, switch, turn on (off) [turn]
allumette ► match[1]
allure ► attitude, pace, presence
   allure avachie ► slouch
   allure très lente ► crawl
   filer à toute allure ► race[1], whisk, whiz
almanach ► almanac
alors ► so, then
   alors que ► when, whereas, while
alose ► shad
alouette ► lark[1]
   alouette des prairies ► bobolink
alourdir ► burden, saddle
alpaca (alpaga) ► alpaca
alphabet ► alphabet
alphabétique ► alphabetical
   table alphabétique ► index
   classer par ordre alphabétique ► alphabetize
alphabétiquement ► alphabetically
alque ► auk

693

altérer ► distort, tamper
en **alternance** ► alternately
alternatif (-ive) ► alternative
alternative ► alternative
alternativement ► alternately
alterner ► alternate
   faire en alternant ► rotate
altitude ► altitude, elevation
alto ► alto, viola
altruisme ► generosity [generous], humanity
aluminium ► aluminum
   papier d'aluminium ► foil[2], tinfoil
alunissage ► touchdown
alvéole ► pit[1]
avoir l'**amabilité de** ► favour
amadouer ► coax
amalgame ► mix
amalgamer ► fuse
amande ► almond, kernel
amant (-ante) ► lover
amarante ► tumbleweed
amarre ► painter
amarrer ► dock[1], moor[1]
amas ► collection, heap, mass, pile[1]
(s')amasser ► accumulate
amateur ► amateur
amateur (-trice) ► amateur, lover
ambassade ► embassy
ambassadeur (-drice) ► ambassador
ambiance ► atmosphere
ambidextre ► ambidextrous
   de façon ambidextre ► ambidextrously [ambidextrous]
ambigu (-uë) ► ambiguous, unclear
   de façon ambiguë ► ambiguously [ambiguous]
ambitieusement ► ambitiously [ambitious]
ambitieux (-euse) ► ambitious
ambition ► ambition, aspiration [aspire], dream
ambivalent (-ente) ► ambivalent
ambre ► amber
ambulance ► ambulance
âme ► soul, spirit
amélanchier de Saskatoon ► saskatoon
amélioration ► improvement, progress, upgrade
améliorer ► amend, improve, refine, upgrade
   s'améliorer ► better, mend, thaw
amen ► amen
faire l'**aménagement paysager** ► landscape
aménager ► equip, harness
   aménager en parc ► landscape
amende ► fine[2]
   condamner à une amende ► fine[2]

amener ► bring, carry, convey, fetch, take
   amener à ébullition ► boil[1]
   amener à terre ► land
amer (-ère) ► bitter
amèrement ► bitterly [bitter]
amérindien (-ienne) ► Indian
amerrissage ► touchdown
amertume ► bitterness [bitter]
   éprouver de l'amertume ► resent
ameublement ► furniture
ami (-ie) ► buddy, chum, comrade, friend
amiante ► asbestos
amibe ► amoeba
amical (-ale, -aux) ► chummy [chum], friendly, neighbourly [neighbour]
amidon ► starch
amidonné (-ée) ► starched [starch]
amidonner ► starch
aminoacide ► amino acid
amiral (-aux) ► admiral
amitié ► friendship
   se lier d'amitié ► befriend
ammoniac ► ammonia
amnésie ► amnesia
amnistier ► pardon
amonceler ► accumulate
   s'amonceler ► drift
amoncellement ► accumulation [accumulate], concentration, drift
en **amont** ► upstream
amorce ► bait, cap, fuse
amorcer ► commence
   (s')amorcer ► boot
amortir ► cushion, deaden, dull
amortisseur ► buffer
amour[1] ► dear, honey
amour[2] ► love
amoureusement ► romantically [romantic]
   serrer amoureusement ► cuddle
amoureux (-euse) ► lover, sweetheart
amour-propre ► pride
ampère ► amp
amphibie ► amphibian
amphithéâtre ► amphitheatre, bowl[1]
ample ► full, loose
ampleur ► breadth, extent, magnitude, scope
amplificateur ► amplifier
amplifier ► amplify, exaggerate
ampoule ► blister
   provoquer des ampoules (cloques) ► blister
amputation ► amputation [amputate]
amputer ► amputate
amulette ► charm
amusant (-ante) ► amusing [amuse], comic, funny, hilarious, riotous [riot]

amuse-gueule ► appetizer
amusement ► amusement, entertainment, fun
amuser ► amuse, divert, entertain, tickle
    s'amuser ► enjoy oneself, toy
amygdale ► tonsil
an ► year
    tous les ans ► yearly
    jour de l'an ► New Year's Day
    nouvel an ► New Year's Day
anaconda ► anaconda
anagramme ► anagram
analogie ► analogy, parallel
analogue ► related [relate]
analphabète ► illiterate
analphabétisme ► illiteracy [illiterate]
analyse ► analysis, criticism [criticize], test
analyser ► analyse, criticize
ananas ► pineapple
anarchie ► anarchy
anatomie ► anatomy
ancestral (-aux) ► ancestral [ancestor]
ancêtre ► ancestor
anche ► reed
    instrument à anche ► reed
ancien (-ienne) ► ancient, antique, early, former, past
anciennement ► formerly [former]
ancre ► anchor
ancrer ► anchor
âne ► ass, donkey
anéantir ► annihilate, shatter, wipe out [wipe]
anéantissement ► death
anecdote ► anecdote
anémie ► anemia
anémone de mer ► sea anemone
anesthésique ► anesthetics
ange ► angel, lamb
    aux anges ► heaven
angélique ► angelic [angel]
anglais ► English
    anglais canadien ► Canadian English
Anglais (-aise) ► the English [english]
    Canadien-anglais (Canadienne-anglaise) ► the English [english]
angle ► angle, corner
    angle droit ► right angle
    à angle (s) droit (s) ► square
    (angle) mort ► blind
    faire des angles ► angle
anglophone ► Anglophone
anglo-saxon (-onne) ► Anglo-Saxon
angoisse ► anguish, concern
angoisser ► anguish
anguille ► eel
anguleux (-euse) ► bony
anicroche ► hitch

sans anicroches ► smooth
animal (-aux) ► animal, creature
    petit (de gros animaux) ► calf[1]
    jeune animal ► pup
    animal égaré ► stray
    animal de compagnie ► pet
    animal de proie ► predator
    animal de race ► thoroughbred
    animal domestique ► pet
    animal familier ► pet
    animal nuisible ► pest
animateur (-trice) ► host
animation ► animation, life
animé (-ée) ► animated cartoon, lively, spirited
    très animé (-ée) ► riotous [riot]
    dessins animés ► cartoon
animer ► animate, host
animosité ► animosity, tension
anneau (-eaux) ► ring[1]
année ► year
    chaque année ► yearly
    année scolaire ► year
    année fiscale ► year
annexe ► annex, appendix
annexer ► annex, insert
annexion ► annexation [annex]
annihiler ► annihilate
anniversaire ► anniversary, birthday
annonce ► ad, advertisement, announcement, blurb, notice, notification [notify]
    annonce publicitaire ► commercial
annoncer ► advertise, announce, bill[1], call, foreshadow, herald, mean[1], promise, usher in (out) [usher]
annonceur ► advertiser
annonceur (-euse) ► announcer
annonciateur (-trice) ► herald
annotation ► note
annuaire ► directory, yearbook
annuel ► yearly
annuel (-elle) ► annual
    plante annuelle ► annual
annuellement ► annually [annual], yearly
annulation ► cancellation
annulé (-ée) ► off
annuler ► cancel, undo
anomalie ► fault
anonyme ► anonymous
anonymement ► anonymously [anonymous]
anorak ► anorak, parka
anorexie ► anorexia
anormal (-ale, -aux) ► unnatural
anse ► cove, creek, handle, inlet
antagonisme ► antagonism
    éveiller l'antagonisme de ► antagonize

Antarctique ► Antarctic
antenne ► aerial, antenna
   à l'antenne ► on (off) the air [air]
   antenne parabolique ► dish
antérieur (-ieure) ► back, previous
anthère ► anther
anthologie ► anthology
anthropologie ► anthropology
anthropologique ► anthropological
antibiotique ► antibiotic
anticorps ► antibody
anticyclone ► high
antidote ► antidote
antihistaminique ► antihistamine
antilope ► antelope
antipathie ► dislike
antique ► antique
antiquité ► antique
antiseptique ► antiseptic
antisocial (-ale, -aux) ► antisocial
antitoxine ► antitoxin
antonyme ► antonym
antre ► den
anxiété ► anxiety, concern, worry
   avec anxiété ► worriedly [worry]
anxieusement ► anxiously [anxious]
anxieux (-euse) ► anxious
aorte ► aorta
août ► August
apaisant (-ante) ► soothing [soothe]
apaiser ► calm, quiet, relieve, soothe, still
   s'apaiser ► subside
apartheid ► apartheid
apathie ► apathy
apercevoir ► discover, glimpse, perceive, sight, spy
   s'apercevoir ► realize
aperçu ► glimpse, outline, preview, sight, taste
   donner un aperçu ► outline
apéritif ► appetizer
apesanteur ► weightless
   en état d'apesanteur ► weightless
aplanir ► even, level, plane^2
   aplanir les difficultés ► smooth
aplatir ► smooth
apogée ► climax, height, peak, prime, zenith
apostrophe ► apostrophe
apparaître ► appear, dawn, emerge, erupt, out, pop^1, seem
   apparaître indistinctement ► loom^2
   apparaître soudain ► spring
appareil^1 ► aircraft
appareil^2 ► apparatus, appliance, device, implement, instrument, machine, mechanism, tract, unit

appareil supplémentaire ► extension
   appareil de levage ► tackle
appareiller ► match^2, pair
appareil-photo ► camera
apparemment ► apparently, seemingly [seem]
apparence ► appearance, look, surface, veneer
   en apparence ► outwardly [outward]
apparent (-ente) ► apparent, outward, visible
apparenté (-ée) ► relate, related [relate]
apparition ► apparition, appearance
appartement ► apartment, flat^2, lodging
   appartement en copropriété ► condominium
   partager un appartement ► room
   vivre en appartement ► room
appartenir ► belong to [belong]
appât ► bait, lure
appâter ► bait
appel^1 ► appeal, call
appel^2 ► plea
   faire appel à ► appeal, summon
   faire appel (de) ► appeal
   se pourvoir en appel ► appeal
appelant ► decoy
appeler ► call, name, page^2, recall, term, title
   faire appeler ► page^2
appendice ► appendix
appendicite ► appendicitis
appétissant (-ante) ► mouth-watering, savoury [savour]
appétit ► appetite
applaudir ► applaud, clap, root^3
applaudissement ► hand
   applaudissements ► applause
application ► administration, application, concentration, industry
   avec application ► industriously [industrious]
   mise en application ► enforcement [enforce]
appliqué (-ée) ► industrious
appliquer ► apply, enforce
   s'appliquer à ► apply
   s'appliquer (au travail) ► buckle
apporter ► bring, bring out, carry, effect, extend, fetch, take
apposer ► affix
appréciation ► appreciation, criticism [criticize]
apprécier ► appreciate, enjoy, esteem, value
   très apprécié (-ée) ► popular
appréhender ► apprehend, arrest, dread
appréhension ► apprehension, doubt, misgiving

apprenant (-ante) ► learner [learn]
apprendre ► hear, learn, master, teach
apprenti (-ie) ► apprentice, learner [learn]
apprentissage ► learning
   placer ou mettre quelqu'un en apprentissage ► apprentice
apprêt ► primer
apprivoisé (-ée) ► tame
apprivoiser ► tame
approbation ► approval, consent, endorsement [endorse], favour, sanction
   avec approbation ► approvingly [approve]
approche ► approach
approcher ► approach, border on, border to [border], near
approfondi (-ie) ► thorough
appropriation ► conquest
approprié (-ée) ► appropriate, proper, right, suitable
   peu approprié (-ée) ► wrong
s'approprier ► appropriate
approuver ► applaud, approve, endorse, OK, sanction
approvisionnement ► provision, supply
approvisionner ► rig, supply
   s'approvisionner en vivres ► stock
approximatif (-ive) ► approximate, rough
faire une approximation ► approximate
approximativement ► approximately [approximate], roughly [rough]
appui ► endorsement [endorse], rest[1], support
appuyer ► back, dwell on, endorse, favour, lean[1], rest[1], second[1], support, uphold
   appuyer sur ► depress, press, push
   appuyer sur le champignon ► gun
âpre ► harsh, tart[1]
après ► after, afterward
   d'après ► according to
   après Jésus-Christ ► A.D.
   après quoi ► whereupon
   après tout ► after all
   ici après ► hereafter
après-midi ► afternoon, P.M., p.m.
apte ► able, capable
aptitude ► ability, aptitude, capacity, qualification
aquarelle ► water colour
aquarium ► aquarium
aquatique ► aquatic
aqueduc ► aqueduct
ara ► macaw
Arabe ► Arab
arabe ► Arabic, arabian
   chiffres arabes ► Arabic numerals
   téléphone arabe ► grapevine

couche ou terre arable ► topsoil
arachide ► peanut
arachnide ► arachnid
araignée ► spider
   toile d'araignée ► cobweb
arbitraire ► arbitrary
arbitrairement ► arbitrarily [arbitrary]
arbitre ► referee, umpire
   servir d'arbitre ► referee
arbitrer ► arbitrate, referee, umpire
arborer ► sport
arbre[1] ► tree
   arbre ou buisson épineux ► thorn
   arbres ► timber
   arbres fruitiers ► orchard
   à feuilles caduques ► deciduous
arbre[2] (de moteur) ► shaft
arbuste ► shrub
arc ► arc, arch[1], bow[1]
arcade ► arcade
   arcade sourcilière ► brow
arc-en-ciel ► rainbow
archaïque ► archaic
arche ► ark
archéologie ► archaeology
archéologique ► archeological [archeology]
archer ► archer
archet ► bow[1]
archevêque ► archbishop
archipel ► archipelago
architecte ► architect
architectural (-ale, -aux) ► architectural [architecture]
architecture ► architecture
archiviste ► recorder
cheval d'arçons ► horse
arctique ► Arctic
ardemment ► eagerly [eager], earnestly [earnest]
ardent (-ente) ► earnest, fierce, fiery, live[2], passionate [passion], staunch
ardeur ► fire, keenness [keen], zeal
   avec ardeur ► zealously [zeal]
ardoise ► slate
ardu (-ue) ► difficult, uphill
arène ► arena
arête ► bridge
   plein d'arêtes ► bony
argent ► cash, currency, money, silver
   argent fin ► sterling
   sans argent ► broke
   monnaie d'argent ► silver
   somme (d'argent) ► sum
argenté (-ée) ► silver, silvery [silver]
argenter ► silver

697

argenterie ► silver, silverware
argile ► clay
    schiste (argileux) ► shale
argot ► slang
argument ► ammunition, argument
    être sans argument valable ► not having a leg to stand on
argumentateur (-trice) ► debater [debate]
aride ► arid
aristocratie ► aristocracy
arithmétique ► arithmetic
armada ► armada
armature ► signature
arme ► arm[2], weapon
    braquer une arme ► draw
    vol à main armée ► holdup
armée ► army, the military [military]
    armée de l'air ► air force
armement ► armament
armer ► arm[2], cock, commission
    s'armer de courage ► steel
armistice ► armistice
armoire ► chest, closet, dresser[1], wardrobe
armoise ► sage-brush
armure ► armour
arnaquer ► hustle
arnaqueur (-euse) ► crook
arni ► water buffalo
arôme ► aroma, odour
arpenter ► pace, prowl, survey
arpenteur (-euse) ► surveyor
arquer ► arch[1]
arrachement ► pluck
arracher ► extract, pluck, pull, tear[1], uproot, wrench, wring, yank
arrangement ► arrangement, composition, disposal, scheme
arranger ► arrange, fix, repair
    s'arranger ► make the best of
arrestation ► apprehension, arrest, capture
arrêt ► failure, halt, holdup, pause, rest[1], standstill, stop
    sans arrêt ► continuously [continuous]
arrêt-court ► shortstop
arrêté municipal ► bylaw
arrêté (-ée) ► down[1]
arrêter ► apprehend, arrest, balk, book, call, capture, cease, enact, fix, halt, quit, shut, stem[2], stop
arrière ► back, guard, rear[1], tail
    à l'arrière ► back, back of
    en arrière ► back, backward
    vers l'arrière ► backward
    marche arrière ► reverse
    faire marche arrière ► back up
    rester en arrière ► hang back
    traîner en arrière ► straggle

arrière-cour ► backyard
arrière-petit-enfant ► great
arrière-plan ► background
arrimer ► dock[1]
arrivée ► appearance, arrival, finish, home
    arrivée de gaz ► throttle
arriver ► arrive, come, get, happen, occur, reach
    arriver à ► arrive, attain, hit
    arriver (s'éloigner) peu à peu ► trickle
    arriver à comprendre ► figure out
    arriver à terme ► terminate
arriviste ► pushy [push]
arrogance ► arrogance [arrogant]
arrogant (-ante) ► arrogant, haughty, lordly [lord]
arrondi (-ie) ► round
arrondir ► hunch, round
arroser ► spray, squirt, water
    arroser légèrement ► sprinkle
    arroser au jet ► hose
arroseur ► sprinkler [sprinkle]
arsenal (-aux) ► arsenal
arsenic ► arsenic
art ► art, craft
artère ► artery
arthrite ► arthritis
arthropode ► arthropod
artichaut ► artichoke
article ► article, commodity, goods, item, piece, ware
    article rendu ► return
    articles de fantaisie ► novelty
    articles de mercerie ► notion
    articles de bureau ► stationery
articulation ► joint, knuckle, speech
articuler ► articulate, mouth
    mal articuler ► slur[1]
artificiel (-ielle) ► artificial
    respiration artificielle ► artificial respiration
artificiellement ► artificially [artificial]
artillerie ► armament, artillery
artiste ► artist, artistic
    artiste peintre ► painter
artistique ► artistic
artistiquement ► artistically [artistic]
as ► ace
ascenseur ► elevator, lift
ascension ► ascent, climb
asile ► asylum
    donner asile à ► harbour
aspect ► aspect, look, side
    aspect sauvage ► wildness [wild]
asperge ► asparagus
asperger ► spatter

asphalte ► asphalt, tar
asphalter ► tar
aspirateur ► vacuum, vacuum cleaner
aspiration ► aspiration [aspire]
aspirer ► suck, yearn
   aspirer à ► aspire
aspirine ► aspirin
assagi (-ie) ► mellow
assaillant (-ante) ► attacker
assaillir ► attack, bombard, mob, rack
assaisonnement ► dressing, seasoning [season]
assaisonner ► flavour, season
assassin ► killer
assassinat ► murder
assassiner ► assassinate, kill, murder
assaut ► assault, attack
   d'assaut ► by storm
   char d'assaut ► tank
assécher ► drain
assemblage ► assembly, combination, construction
assemblée ► assembly, conference, council, gathering
assembler ► assemble, congregate, couple, piece
assener ► deliver
asseoir ► seat, sit
assermenter ► administer
assez ► ample, enough, fairly, kind of, pretty, reasonably [reasonable], sufficient
assidu (-ue) ► regular
assiduité ► industry
assiéger ► mob
assiette ► plate
assiettée ► serving
assignation ► summons
   notifier une assignation ► serve
assigner ► allot, assign
   assigner une date ► date[1]
assimiler ► identify with
assistance ► aid, assistance, attendance, help, house
   prêter assistance ► assist
assistant (-ante) ► aide, assistant, second[1]
assister ► aid, help
   assister à ► witness
association ► alliance, association, clan, coalition, community, league[1], organization, society
associé (-ée) ► associate, partner
associer ► associate, connect, team
assoiffé (-ée) ► dry, thirsty
assombrir ► darken
   s'assombrir ► cloud
assommer ► brain, fell[2], knock out [knock], slug[2], stun

assorti (-ie) ► assorted, match[2]
assortiment ► assortment
assortir ► match[2], sort
assouplir ► limber, relax
assourdir ► deaden, deafen, dull, muffle
assujetti (-ie) ► subject
assujettir ► subject
assumer ► assume
assurance ► assurance, confidence, decision, insurance, poise, reassurance [reassure]
   avec assurance ► confidently [confident]
assuré (-ée) ► confident, level, secure, sure
   mal assuré (-ée) ► unsure
assurément ► assuredly [assure], certainly, decidedly [decided], positively [positive]
assurer ► assure, ensure, guarantee, insure, promise, secure
   s'assurer ► see
   assurer le service ► run
   s'assurer le concours de ► enlist
aster ► aster
astérisque ► asterisk
   marquer d'un astérisque ► star
astéroïde ► asteroid
asthmatique ► asthmatic [asthma]
   poussif (-ive) asthmatique ► wheeze
asthme ► asthma
astiquer ► rub
astreindre ► bind
astreint (-einte) ► bound[1]
astrologie ► astrology
astronaute ► astronaut
astronomie ► astronomy
astronomique ► astronomical
astuce ► craft, cunning, gimmick, scheme, shrewdness [shrewd], wit
astucieusement ► cunningly [cunning], shrewdly [shrewd]
astucieux (-euse) ► cunning, shrewd
asymétrique ► irregular, lopsided
atelier ► shop, workshop
atermoyer ► procrastinate
athapascan ► Tahltan
athapascan ► Slavey, Tahltan
athée ► atheist
athéisme ► atheism [atheist]
athlète ► athlete
athlétisme ► athletics, track and field
   d'athlétisme ► athletic
atlantique ► Atlantic
atlas ► atlas
atmosphère ► atmosphere, flavour
atmosphérique ► atmospheric
atome ► atom
atomique ► atomic
   bombe atomique ► atomic bomb

atout ► asset, plus

âtre ► hearth

atroce ► atrocious, cruel, dreadful, horrible

atroce ► outrageous, terrible, unspeakable

atrocement ► terribly

attache ► anchor, attachment, clamp, clip[2], hitch, tab

    attaches ► tie

attaché (-ée) ► attach, bound[1]

    attaché (-ée) aux biens de ce monde ► worldly

attachement ► attachment, devotion

attacher ► affix, attach, bind, clasp, clip[2], fasten, hitch, lash[2], tether, tie, wire

    s'attacher ► cling

    attacher à l'aide d'une corde ► rope

    attacher avec du ruban ► tape

    attacher avec une courroie ► strap

    attacher beaucoup de prix à ► prize

    attacher une grande valeur à ► treasure

attaquable ► objectionable [objection]

attaquant (-ante) ► attacker, raider [raid]

attaque ► assault, attack, charge, fit[2], lead[1], offence, offensive, seisure, stroke[1]

attaquer ► assault, attack, charge, corrode, raid

    s'attaquer à ► attack, prey, tackle

atteindre ► attain, come, hit, reach

    atteindre en moyenne ► average

    ne pas atteindre ► short

atteint (-einte) ► stricken

atteinte ► reach

    atteinte (aux droits de) ► trespass

attelage ► harness, team, yoke

    conducteur (-trice) d'attelage ► teamster

atteler ► harness, yoke

    s'atteler au travail ► pitch in

    s'atteler à un boulot ► buckle down

attenant (-ante) ► adjoining, terraced [terrace]

attendre ► await, expect, stick

    s'attendre à ► anticipate, bargain for, expect

    en attendant ► meantime, meanwhile

attendrir ► move, soften, melt

attendu (-ue) ► due

attentat ► attempt

attente ► hold[1], wait

    file d'attente ► queue

attentif (-ive) ► alert, attentive, careful, intent[1], mindful [mind], watchful

attention ► attention, care, concentration, heed, mind, notice

    attirer l'attention de quelqu'un ► catch one's eye

    avec une vive attention ► intently [intent[1]]

    faire attention ► beware

attentionné (-ée) ► thoughtful

attentivement ► attentively [attentive], carefully [careful], watchfully [watchful]

atténuer ► cushion, dull, ease, lessen, soften, water

atterré (-ée) ► aghast

atterrir ► land, light[3]

atterrissage ► landing, touchdown

    piste d'atterrissage ► runway

attestation ► certificate, claim

attester ► certify, testify

attirail ► gear, kit

attirance ► attraction

attirant (-ante) ► attractive, invite

attirer ► attract, bring, decoy, draw, lure

    attirer l'attention de quelqu'un ► catch one's eye

attiser ► inflame

attitude ► attitude, manner

    attitude distante ► remoteness [remote]

    attitude réservée ► remoteness [remote]

    prendre des attitudes ► posture

attraction ► attraction, entertainment, pull

    attraction touristique ► sight

attrait ► appeal, attractiveness [attractive], charm, fascination [fascinate], lure

attrape ► catch

attraper ► capture, catch, contract, field, make, trick

    mal attraper ► fumble

attrayant (-ante) ► attractive

    d'une manière attrayante ► attractively [attractive]

attribuable à ► due to

attribuer ► allot, assign, attribute, award, confer, intend, tie

attribut ► attribute

attribution ► allotment [allot]

attristé (-ée) ► sorrowful [sorrow]

attrister ► pain

    (s')attrister ► sadden

(s')attrouper ► flock, troop

au ► voir à

aubaine ► bonus, windfall

aube[1] ► dawn, daylight

    aube naissante ► twilight

aube[2] (d'une roue hydraulique) ► vane

auberge ► inn, tavern

aubergine ► eggplant

aucun (-une) ► any, nobody, none

    aucun (-une) des deux ► neither

aucunement ► at all, nothing

audace ► cheek, courage, daring

audacieusement ▸ boldly [bold]
audacieux (-euse) ▸ adventurous, bold, courageous, daring, undaunted
au-dedans ▸ inside, inwardly [inward]
au-delà ▸ beyond, past
   l'au-delà ▸ hereafter
au-dessous ▸ below, beneath, under
au-dessus ▸ above, over
   au-dessus de la tête ▸ overhead
audience ▸ audience, hearing
audimat ▸ rating
audio ▸ audio
auditeur (-trice) ▸ listener
audition ▸ audition, ear[2], hearing
auditionner ▸ audition
auditoire ▸ audience, house
auge ▸ trough
augmentation ▸ gain, increase, raise, rise
   augmentation de salaire ▸ raise
augmenter ▸ increase, boost, compound, expand, extend, grow, raise, rise, turn
   augmenter de façon vertigineuse ▸ soar
augure ▸ omen
   de mauvais augure ▸ ominous
aujourd'hui ▸ nowadays, today
aumône ▸ charity
auparavant ▸ before, previously [previous]
auprès de ▸ beside, by
aurore ▸ dawn
   aurore boréale ▸ aurora borealis, northern lights
aussi ▸ also, as, equally [equal], likewise, meanwhile, then, this, too
aussitôt ▸ immediately [immediate], instantly [instant]
austère ▸ harsh, stark
   personne austère ▸ puritan
austral (-ale, -als) ▸ southern
autant ▸ equally [equal]
autel ▸ altar
auteur ▸ author, writer
   droits d'auteur ▸ copyright, royalty
authentifier ▸ certify
authentique ▸ authentic, genuine, real, true
auto ▸ auto, car
autobiographie ▸ autobiography
autobiographique ▸ autobiographical [autobiography]
autobus ▸ bus
autochtone ▸ Aborigine, native, Native people
autocollant ▸ sticker
autographe ▸ autograph
automatique ▸ automatic
automatiquement ▸ automatically [automatic]

automatisation ▸ automation
automne ▸ autumn, fall
automobile ▸ automobile, motor
automobiliste ▸ driver
autonome ▸ independent, off-line
autonomie ▸ range
auto-patrouille ▸ cruiser
autopsie ▸ autopsy
autorisation ▸ leave[2], licence, permit
   élève absent (-ente) sans autorisation ▸ truant
autorisé (-ée) ▸ legal
autoriser ▸ authorize, let, licence, permit
autorité ▸ authority, dominion, government, influence, rule
autoroute ▸ highway
autour ▸ around
   autour de ▸ round
   tourner autour ▸ circle
autre[1] ▸ another, different, else, other, variant
   d'autre ▸ else
   d'autres ▸ more
   autre part ▸ elsewhere
autrefois ▸ formerly [former], once
autrement ▸ else, or, otherwise
autruche ▸ ostrich
auvent ▸ awning
auxiliaire ▸ auxiliary
aval ▸ endorsement [endorse]
avalanche ▸ avalanche
avalement ▸ swallow[1]
avaler ▸ inhale, swallow[1]
   avaler gloutonnement ▸ gobble[1]
avance ▸ advance, lead[1]
   à l'avance ▸ advance, early, in advance [advance]
   d'avance ▸ in advance [advance]
   en avance ▸ ahead, fast[1]
avancé (-ée) ▸ advanced, fast[1]
   un âge avancé ▸ advanced
avancement ▸ advancement, promotion
avancer ▸ advance, ahead, forward, further, get somewhere, proceed, venture
   avancer (à la vapeur) ▸ steam
   avancer à toute vitesse ▸ hurtle
   avancer avec force cahots ▸ bump
   avancer en jouant des coudes ▸ elbow
   avancer en rampant ▸ worm
   avancer en trébuchant ▸ stumble
   avancer péniblement ▸ plough
   avancer lentement ▸ poke
   s'avancer maladroitement ▸ blunder
   faire avancer ▸ advance, propel
avant ▸ before, forward, front, previously [previous]

en avant ► ahead, forth
à l'avant de ► in advance [advance]
avantage ► advantage, asset, benefit, convenience, interest, odds, plus, the upper hand, virtue
avantage naturel ► gift
avantageusement ► advantageously [advantageous]
avantageux (-euse) ► advantageous, useful
avant-goût ► taste
avant-midi ► AM
avant-première ► preview
avant-propos ► foreword, introduction
avant-scène ► apron
avant-toit ► eaves
avare ► cheap, miser, miserly [miser], stingy, tight
avarice ► miserliness
avec ► along, behind, into, with
avenir ► fate, future, tomorrow
aventure ► adventure, experience
s'aventurer ► venture
aventureux (-euse) ► adventurous
avenue ► avenue, drive
s'avérer ► prove, turn out
averse ► shower
aversion ► disgust, dislike, hatred, horror
averti (-ie) ► wise
avertir ► caution, inform, instruct, notify, tip off [tip[3]], warn
avertissement ► caution, foreword, notice, warning
d'avertissement ► warning
avertisseur ► horn, warning
aveu (-eux) ► admission
aveugle ► blind
aveuglement ► whiteout
aveugler ► blind, dazzle, glare
à l'aveuglette ► random
aller à l'aveuglette ► grope
aviateur (-trice) ► flyer
aviation ► aviation
avide ► eager, greedy, hungry
avidement ► eagerly [eager], greedily [greedy], hungrily [hungry]
avidité ► greed
avion ► aircraft, airplane, plane[1]
par avion ► airmail
avion à réaction ► jet
avion de chasse ► fighter
avion-ravitailleur ► tanker
porte-avions ► aircraft carrier
voyager en avion ► fly[1]
aviron ► oar
avis ► announcement, estimation [estimate], input, judgement, mind, notice, notification [notify], opinion, warning

avis au lecteur (-trice) ► foreword
changer d'avis ► back out, turn
ne pas être du même avis ► disagree
avisé (-ée) ► wise
aviser ► advise, inform, instruct, notify
avocat (-ate) ► attorney, counsel, counsellor, defence, lawyer
avoine ► oats
flocons d'avoine ► oatmeal
bouillie de flocons d'avoine ► porridge
avoir ► carry, get, goods, have, keep, meet with, possess, wear
avoisinant (-ante) ► nearby, neighbour
avorton ► runt
avoué ► attorney
avouer ► acknowledge, confess, own
avouer ses torts ► back down
avril ► April
premier avril ► April Fools' Day
axe ► axis
azalée ► azalea
azote ► nitrogen

B

babillage ► babble
babillard ► bulletin board
babiller ► babble
babine ► lip
babiole ► trinket
bâbord ► port
babouin ► baboon
bac ► bin, ferry
baccalauréat ► degree
bâche (goudronnée) ► tarpaulin
bachoter ► cram
backgammon ► backgammon
bâclé (-ée) ► sloppy
bacon ► back bacon
bactérie ► bacteria
bad-lands ► badlands
badminton ► badminton
bafouiller ► babble
bagage ► luggage
bagages ► baggage
bulletin de bagages ► check
bagagiste ► porter
bagarre ► scrap, scuffle
chercher la bagarre ► pick a fight
bagatelle ► trifle
bagatelles ► trivial
bague ► collar, ring
baguer ► band[1]
baguette ► drumstick, pointer, wand
baguettes ► chopsticks
donner un coup de baguette ► switch
bai (baie) ► bay[3]

baie[1] ► berry
    baie de Saskatoon ► saskatoon
    aller à la cueillette des baies ► berry
baie[2] ► bay[1]
    baie vitrée ► bay[5]
    fenêtre en baie ► bay[5]
baignade ► dip
    surveillant (-ante) de baignade ► lifeguard
baigner ► bathe, steep[2]
baignoire ► tub
bail (baux) ► lease
bâillement ► yawn
bailler ► yawn
bâillon ► gag
bâillonner ► gag
bain ► bath, dip
    maillot de bain ► trunk
    salle de bain ► bath, bathroom
bain-marie ► boiler
baiser ► kiss
    donner un baiser ► kiss
    gros baiser retentissant ► smack
baisse ► decline, decrease, drop, reduction [reduce]
    à la baisse ► down[1]
baissé (-ée) ► down[1]
baisser ► declare, decrease, dim, dip, drop off, ebb, fade, fail, fall, hang, lower, reduce, sink, subdue, subside, turn
    se baisser ► stoop[1]
    se baisser vivement ► duck[2]
    faire baisser ► depress
bajoue ► cheek
bal (bals) ► ball[2]
balai ► broom
    coup de balai ► sweep
se balader ► saunter
balance ► scale[2]
balancement ► rock[2], swing
balancer ► balance, dangle, junk[1], swing
    se balancer ► roll, sway
balançoire ► swing
balayage ► sweep
balayer ► rake, scan, sweep, traverse
balcon ► balcony
    dernier balcon ► gallery
baleine ► rib, whale
    pêche à la baleine ► whaling
balise ► beacon
    balise flottante ► buoy
ballade ► ballad
balle ► bale, ball[1], bullet, slug[1]
    à la balle ► ball[1]
    balle de base-ball ► baseball
    balle-molle ► softball
    bonne balle ► fair[1]

    but sur balles ► walk
ballet ► ballet
ballon ► ball[1], balloon
    ballon de basket-ball ► basketball
    ballon de football ► football
    ballon de volley-ball ► volleyball
ballonner ► balloon, bulge
ballot ► bale, pack
ballotter ► buffet[2], rock[2]
balustrade ► railing
bambin (-ine) ► toddler
bambou ► bamboo
banal (-ale, -als) ► everyday, ordinary
banalité ► cliché
banane ► banana
    régime (bananes) ► bunch
banc ► bank[2], bench, shelf
    banc de neige ► snowbank
    banc de pénalité ► penalty box
    banc de poissons ► school[2]
    banc de sable ► shoal
    banc des accusés ► dock[3]
bancal (-ale, -als) ► unstable, unsteady
bandage ► bandage, patch, tape
bande[1] ► band[1], band[2], chorus, clan, crowd, den, flock, gang, horde, pack, troop
bande[2] ► list[2], streak, strip[2], tape
    bande de roulement ► tread
    bande dessinée ► cartoon, comic
    bande magnétique ► tape
    bande publique ► CB
    bande vidéo ► video, videotape
    donner de la bande ► list[2]
bandeau (-eaux) ► bandana, blindfold
bandelette ► band[1]
bander ► bandage
    bander les yeux ► blindfold
banderole ► banner, streamer
bandit ► bandit, gangster
bandoulière ► sling
banjo ► banjo
banlieue ► outskirts, suburb
    de banlieue ► suburban [suburb]
banni (-ie) ► exile
bannière ► banner
bannir ► banish, exile
banque ► bank[1]
banquet ► banquet, feast
banquette ► bench, booth
    banquette des députés sans portefeuille ► backbench
banquier (-ière) ► banker
bantam ► bantam
baptême ► baptism
baptiser ► baptize
bar ► bar, saloon
baragouin ► jargon
baragouiner ► flounder[1]

baraque ▸ booth, chantey, shack, shanty
baratin publicitaire ▸ blurb
baratte ▸ churn
baratter ▸ churn
barbare ▸ barbarian, barbaric
barbe ▸ beard, whisker
    barbe rêche, de plusieurs jours ▸ stubble
barbecue ▸ barbecue
barbelure ▸ barb
barbier ▸ barber
barbillon ▸ barb
barboter ▸ paddle
barbouillage ▸ scribble
barbouiller ▸ scribble, smear
bardeau ▸ shingle
baril ▸ barrel
bar-mitsvah ▸ bar mitzvah
baromètre ▸ barometer
baron (-onne) ▸ baron
barque ▸ craft
barracuda ▸ barracuda
barrage ▸ barrier, block, dam, dike
    barrage flottant ▸ boom[2]
    tir de barrage ▸ barrage
barre[1] ▸ stand
barre[2] ▸ bar, tiller
    barre à disques ▸ barbell
    barre oblique ▸ slash
barreau ▸ bar
barreau (-eaux) ▸ rung[2]
barrer[1] ▸ bar, blockade, blot out, cross
barrer[2] ▸ sail
barricader ▸ blockade
barrière ▸ barrier, fence, obstacle
barrissement ▸ trumpet
baryton ▸ baritone
bas[1] ▸ foot, hose, low
    de haut en bas ▸ down[1], downward
    en bas ▸ below, down[1], downstairs, downward
    plus bas ▸ below
    vers le bas ▸ down[1], downward
bas[2] ▸ stocking
bas (basse) ▸ low
    trop bas (basse) ▸ flat[1]
    voix basse ▸ undertone
basané (-ée) ▸ chocolate
bascule ▸ rocker, seesaw
basculement ▸ seesaw
basculer ▸ seesaw, topple
    faire basculer ▸ tip[2]
base ▸ base[1], basis, foundation
    de base ▸ basic, fundamental
    base de données ▸ data base
    culture de base ▸ staple[2]
base-ball ▸ baseball

gant de base-ball ▸ mitt
balle de base-ball ▸ baseball
baser ▸ base[1]
basket-ball ▸ basketball
    ballon de basket-ball ▸ basketball
basque ▸ tail
    tambour de basque ▸ tambourine
basse ▸ bass[1]
bassin ▸ basin, dock[1], pond
    bassin hydrographique ▸ watershed
basson ▸ bassoon
bataille ▸ battle, combat, duel, fight
bataillon ▸ battalion
bâtard (-arde) ▸ mongrel, mutt
bateau ▸ boat
    bateau (-eaux) à vapeur ▸ steamboat, steamer, steamship
    bateau (-eaux) de pêche des Grands Bancs ▸ banker
    bateau (-eaux) de plaisance ▸ launch[2], yacht
    voyage en bateau à voile ▸ sail
batée ▸ pan
bâtiment ▸ building
bâtir ▸ build, construct, erect
bâton ▸ bat[1], baton, staff, stick
    au bâton ▸ at bat [bat[1]], up
battage publicitaire ▸ hype
battement ▸ beat, flap, flutter, throb
    battement rythmique ▸ pulse
batterie ▸ battery
battre ▸ beat, buffet[2], churn, conquer, defeat, lick, rout, shuffle, thresh, throb, whip
    se battre ▸ contend, fight, struggle
    battre fort ▸ pound[2]
    battre sourdement ▸ thud
    battre des mains ▸ clap
    battre des pieds ▸ kick
    battre le tambour ▸ drum
    se battre en duel ▸ duel
baudet ▸ donkey
bavard (-arde) ▸ gossip
bavardage ▸ babble, chat, gossip, talk
bavarder ▸ chat, chatter, gossip
bazar ▸ bazaar
béatitude ▸ bliss
beau ▸ handsome
beau (belle, beaux) ▸ fair[1], good, lovely, neat, nice
    très beau (belle, beaux) ▸ beautiful
    se faire beau (belle, beaux) ▸ spruce
beaucoup ▸ far, good deal, great deal [deal], greatly [great], lot, many, much, very, widely [wide]
beau-père ▸ stepfather
beauté ▸ beauty, loveliness [lovely]

grain de beauté ▸ mole[1]
beaux-arts ▸ art
bébé ▸ baby, infant
    véhicule pour bébés ▸ buggy
bec ▸ beak, bill[2], nozzle, spout
    avoir une prise de bec avec ▸ tangle
    with [tangle]
    coup de bec ▸ peck
    flûte à bec ▸ recorder
    vase à bec ▸ beaker
bécasseau ▸ sandpiper
bêche ▸ spade[1]
bêcher ▸ dig
bécot ▸ peck
bedaine ▸ belly
Bédouin (-ine) ▸ Bedouin
bégaiement ▸ stutter
bégayer ▸ stammer, stutter
bégonia ▸ begonia
avoir un **béguin** ▸ crush
beige ▸ beige
beigne ▸ doughnut
beignet ▸ doughnut
belette ▸ weasel
bélier ▸ ram
belle-famille ▸ in-law
belle-mère ▸ stepmother
belliqueux (-euse) ▸ warlike
béluga ▸ beluga
bémol ▸ flat[1]
bénédicité ▸ grace
bénédiction ▸ blessing
bénéfice ▸ earnings, gain, profit
    bénéfices ▸ return, revenue, spoil
    faire un bénéfice ▸ profit
bénéficier ▸ benefit
bénévole ▸ volunteer
bénin (-ine) ▸ benign
bénir ▸ bless
benjamin (-ine) ▸ baby
(camion à) **benne (basculante)** ▸ tipper [tip[3]]
beothuk ▸ Beothuk
béquille ▸ crutch
berceau (-eaux) ▸ cradle, crib
bercement ▸ rock[2]
bercer ▸ cradle, lull, rock[2]
berceuse ▸ lullaby, rocker
béret ▸ beret
berge ▸ bank[2]
berger (-ère) ▸ shepherd
berline ▸ sedan
bernache du Canada ▸ Canada goose
bernacle ▸ barnacle
berner ▸ fool, fox
besogne ▸ business, chore, job
besoin ▸ call, necessity, need, want
    au besoin ▸ pinch

    dans le besoin ▸ poor
    besoin pressant ▸ urge
    avoir un besoin maladif ▸ crave
    subvenir aux besoins de ▸ provide,
    support
bestial (-ale, -aux) ▸ beastly [beast]
    parc à bestiaux ▸ stockyard
best-seller ▸ seller
bétail ▸ cattle, livestock
    voler du bétail ▸ rustle
bête ▸ beast, brute, creature, dumb, foolish,
lunatic, silly
bêtise ▸ rubbish, silliness [silly], stupidity
[stupid]
    bêtises ▸ tripe
béton ▸ concrete
betterave ▸ beet
beuglement ▸ bellow
beugler ▸ bellow
beurre ▸ butter
    tarte au beurre ▸ butter tart
beurrer ▸ butter
biais ▸ slant
bibelot ▸ trinket
bible ▸ Bible
bibliographie ▸ bibliography
bibliothécaire ▸ librarian
bibliothèque ▸ library
biblique ▸ biblical
bicarbonate de soude ▸ soda
biche ▸ doe
bicyclette ▸ bicycle, bike
bidon ▸ drum
bidonville ▸ slum
bien[1] ▸ asset, good, goods,
    biens ▸ effect, estate, property
    biens immobiliers ▸ property, real estate
    attaché (-ée) aux biens de ce monde ▸
    worldly
bien[2] ▸ far, fine[1], greatly [great], nicely [nice],
right, rightly [right]
    en bien (de) ▸ highly
    très bien ▸ OK
    bien fait ▸ well-done
bien[3] ▸ welfare, well[1]
bien-aimé (-ée) ▸ beloved, darling
bien entendu ▸ of course
bien-être ▸ ease, welfare, wellbeing
bienfaisance ▸ charity
bienfait ▸ benefit
bienfaiteur (-trice) ▸ friend
bienheureux (-euse) ▸ blissful [bliss]
bien que ▸ although, while
bienséant (-ante) ▸ correct
bien sûr ▸ naturally, of course
bientôt ▸ presently, shortly, soon

bienveillance ► benevolence, goodness
bienveillant (-ante) ► benevolent
[benevolence], benign, charitable, kindly
bienvenue ► welcome
bière ► ale, beer, brew
bifteck ► steak
bifurcation ► branch
bifurquer ► fork
bijou (-oux) ► gem, jewel, jewellery
bilan ► toll[1]
bilingue ► bilingual
billard (américain) ► pool[2]
   queue de billard ► cue[2]
bille ► marble
billet ► bill[1], ticket
   billet d'un dollar ► buck
   billet gratuit ► pass
   prix du billet ► fare
billion ► trillion
biner ► hoe
binette ► hoe
biodégradable ► biodegradable
biographie ► biography
biographique ► biographical [biography]
biologie ► biology
biologique ► biological, organic
bis ► encore
biscuit ► biscuit, cookie, cracker
bise ► peck
   grosse bise ► smack
bison ► bison, buffalo
bistouri ► lance
bistre ► hazel
bit ► bit[4]
bitume ► pitch[2], tar
bitumer ► tar
bizarre ► bizarre, curious, eccentric,
fantastic, far-fetched, funny, odd, peculiar,
queer, singular, strange, weird
bizarrement ► oddly [odd], quirky [quirk],
strangely [strange]
bizarrerie ► oddness [odd], quirk,
strangeness [strange]
black foot ► Blackfoot
black-out ► blackout
blague ► gag, joke, lark[2]
blaguer ► joke, kid
blaireau (-eaux) ► badger
blâmer ► blame, carp[2], fault
blanc (blanche) ► blank, white
   à blanc ► blank
   (blanc) comme neige ► snowy
   de but en blanc ► off-hand
blancheur ► whiteness [white]
blanchir ► bleach, clear, whiten, whitewash
blanchissage ► shut out
blanchisserie ► laundry

blé ► wheat
   blé d'Inde ► corn[1]
   germe de blé ► wheat germ
   de blé entier ► whole-wheat
blême ► pale
blêmir ► pale
blessant (-ante) ► cutting, offensive
blesser ► cut, hurt, injure, wing, wound[1]
blessure ► hurt, injury, wound[1]
bleu (bleue, bleus) ► blue, rookie
   bleu marine ► navy
bleuet ► blueberry
blindage ► armour
blindé (-ée) ► armoured [armour]
blinder ► plate
blizzard ► blizzard
bloc ► block, pad
   en bloc ► bulk
   bloc de papier à lettres ► tablet
bloc-note ► notebook, pad
blocus ► blockade
blond (blonde) ► blond, fair[1]
   blond roux ► sandy
bloquer ► block, blockade, clog, corner,
freeze, lock[1], shut, stop
bloqueur (-euse) ► tackle
blouse ► blouse
se blottir ► nestle, snuggle
Bluenose ► Bluenose
blues ► blues
bluffer ► bluff[1]
boa ► boa
bob ► bobsled
bobine ► reel[1], spool
bobiner ► reel[1]
bocal ► jar
bœuf ► beef, ox, steer[2]
   bœuf haché ► hamburger
boire ► drink, drink in, drunk, suck
   boire à petites gorgées ► sip
bois[1] ► driver
bois[2] ► timber, wood, woodwind
   de bois ► wooden
   petit bois ► tinder
   bois de charpente ► lumber[1]
   bois de construction ► lumber[1], timber
   bois d'if ► yew
   bois flotté ► driftwood
   bois ligneux ► xylem
   charbon de bois ► charcoal
   coureur des bois ► coureur de bois
   sous-bois ► underbrush
bois[3] ► antler
   bois de cervidés ► rack
boisé (-ée) ► wooded, woody
   terre boisée ► timber
boisseau (-eaux) ► bushel

boisson ▸ beverage, brew, drink
    boisson gazeuse ▸ beer, soft drink
boîte ▸ bin, box[1], case[2], chest, tin
    boîte (en carton) ▸ carton
    boîte de conserve ▸ can[2]
    boîte de vitesses ▸ transmission
    mettre en boîte ▸ box[1]
boitement ▸ limp[1]
boiter ▸ limp[1]
boiteux (-euse) ▸ cripple, lame
boîtier ▸ housing
bol ▸ bowl[1]
bombardement ▸ bombardment [bombard]
bombarder ▸ bomb, bombard, pelt[1], shell
bombardier ▸ bomber
bombe ▸ bomb
    bombe atomique ▸ atomic bomb
    poseur (-euse) de bombes ▸ bomber
bombement ▸ bulge
bomber ▸ bulge
bon ▸ bond, coupon, slip[2]
bon (bonne) ▸ fond, good, kind[1], neat, right, well[1]
    assez bon (bonne) ▸ fair[1]
    bon à rien ▸ worthless
    bon pour la santé ▸ healthy
bonbon ▸ candy
    bonbon à la menthe ▸ mint[1]
    (bonbon au) caramel ▸ taffy
bonbonne d'oxygène ▸ scuba
bond ▸ bound[2], hop[1], jump, leap, pounce, skip, spring
    faire un bond ▸ jump
    sauter quelque chose d'un bond ▸ vault[2]
bonde ▸ tap[2]
bondir ▸ bounce, bound[2], jump, leap, spring
    bondir sur ▸ pounce
bonheur ▸ bliss, good, happiness [happy]
    par bonheur ▸ fortunately [fortunate]
    accorder le bonheur ▸ bless
    au comble du bonheur ▸ blissfully [bliss]
    porte-bonheur ▸ charm
bonhomme de neige ▸ snowman
bonifier ▸ upgrade
bonjour ▸ aloha, hello
bonnet ▸ bonnet
bonté ▸ generosity [generous], goodness
    avec bonté ▸ kindly
    plein (pleine) de bonté ▸ kindly, saintly [saint]
    avoir la bonté de ▸ favour
boomerang ▸ boomerang
bord ▸ brim, brink, brow, curb, edge, fringe, front, hem, lip, margin, rim, shore, tack
    à bord ▸ aboard

    au bord de ▸ on, verge
    par-dessus bord ▸ overboard
    journal de bord ▸ log
    tableau (-eaux) de bord ▸ panel
    monter à bord de ▸ board
    soulever un bord ▸ tip[2]
bordeaux ▸ maroon[2]
bordée ▸ tack
    tirer une bordée ▸ tack
border ▸ edge, rim, tuck
bordure ▸ border, edge, fringe
aurore boréale ▸ aurora borealis, northern lights
borne ▸ bound[3], boundary, confine, landmark, terminal
    sans borne ▸ endless, infinite
    borne d'incendie ▸ hydrant
borné (-ée) ▸ dull
borne-fontaine ▸ hydrant
borner ▸ bound[3]
bosquet ▸ grove
bosse ▸ bump, dent, hump, knob, lump
bosselé (-ée) ▸ lumpy [lump]
bosseler ▸ dent
bosselure ▸ dent
botanique ▸ botanical [botany]
botte[1] ▸ boot
botte[2] ▸ shock[2]
botter ▸ kick
bouche ▸ mouth
bouche-à-bouche ▸ mouth-to-mouth
bouchée ▸ bite, morsel, swallow[1]
boucher (-ère) ▸ board, butcher, clog, fill, plug
bouchon ▸ cap, float, plug, stopper, top[1]
    bouchon de liège ▸ cork
boucle ▸ bow[1], buckle, loop
    boucle d'oreille ▸ earring
    faire une boucle ▸ loop
bouclé (-ée) ▸ curly [curl]
boucler ▸ buckle, curl
bouclier ▸ shield
bouddhisme ▸ Buddhism
bouder ▸ sulk
    en boudant ▸ sulkily [sulk]
boudeur (-euse) ▸ cross, sulky [sulk]
boue ▸ mud
bouée ▸ buoy
boueux (-euse) ▸ muddy [mud]
bouffée ▸ blast, puff, whiff
bouffer ▸ consume
    faire bouffer ▸ fluff
bouffon (-onne) ▸ clown, fool
bouger ▸ buck, budge, move, shift
    bouger doucement ▸ ease
    bouger petit à petit ▸ inch
    sans bouger ▸ motionless [motion]

faire bouger ► stir
bougie ► candle
bougonner ► complain
bouillie de (flocons d'avoine) ► porridge
bouillir ► boil[1]
   bouillir de colère ► seethe
   faire bouillir ► boil[1]
bouilloire ► kettle
bouillon ► broth, stock
bouillonner ► bubble, simmer, steam
boule ► ball[1], globe
   boule de neige ► snowball
   mettre en boule ► ball[1]
bouleau (-eaux) ► birch
boulet ► bullet
boulevard ► boulevard
bouleversant (-ante) ► shocking
bouleversement ► upheaval
bouleverser ► upset
boulier ► abacus
boulon ► bolt
boulot ► job
   s'atteler à un boulot ► buckle down
bouquet ► bouquet, clump, cluster, grove
bourdon ► bumblebee
   faux bourdon ► drone
bourdonnement ► buzz, drone, hum, murmur
bourdonner ► buzz, drone, hum, ring[2]
bourgeon ► bud
bourgeonner ► bud, sprout
   qui bourgeonne ► budding [bud]
bourrasque ► gale, squall[1]
bourrer ► stuff
   se bourrer ► gorge
bourru (-ue) ► surly
bourse ► exchange, grant, scholarship
   Bourse ► stock market
boursouflure ► blister
bousculade ► scramble
bousculé (-ée) ► hurried
bousculer ► crowd, scramble
   se bousculer ► tumble
boussole ► compass
bout ► end, foot, head, hunk, piece, scrap, slip[2], stub, tail, tip[1], toe
   petit bout ► morsel, snip
   à tout bout de champ ► forever
boutade ► quip
bouteille ► bottle, flask
   bouteille isolante ► thermos
boutique ► shop
bouton ► button, knob, stud
   bouton de porte ► doorknob
   se couvrir de boutons ► break out
boutonner ► button
bouton-pression ► snap

bouture ► cutting, slip[2]
bouvillon ► steer[2]
bovin à cornes ► buffalo
boxe ► boxing
boxer ► box[2], boxer
boxeur (-euse) ► boxer, fighter
boyau (-aux) ► hose
boycottage ► boycott
boycotter ► boycott
bracelet ► bracelet
braguette ► fly[1]
braille ► braille
braillement ► squall[2], whine
brailler ► bawl, squall[2], whine
brailleur (-euse) ► whiny [whine]
brancard ► stretcher
branche ► bough, branch, chapter, line[1]
   (grosse) branche ► limb
branché (-ée) ► on-line
branchement ► branch
brancher ► plug
   se brancher ► hook up
   brancher à la prise de terre ► ground[1]
brandir ► flourish
branlant (-ante) ► rocky [rock[2]], shaky, unstable, unsteady, wobbly [wobble]
branler ► wobble
braquer (une arme) ► draw
braqueur ► raider [raid]
bras ► arm[1], handle
   bras de mer ► sound[4]
   tendre le bras ► reach
brasier ► blaze[1]
à bras-le-corps ► bodily
brasse ► fathom
brasser ► brew, scramble, shake, shuffle, stir
brave ► brave, courageous, game, heroic
braver ► brave, dare, defy
bravo ► bravo
bravoure ► courage, daring, valour
brèche ► breach, break, chip, gap, hole, opening
   ouvrir une brèche ► breach
bredouiller ► flounder[1], sputter
bref (brève) ► brief, capsule
breloque ► charm
bretelles ► suspenders
bretzel ► pretzel
brève ► short
brevet ► commission
bribes ► fragment
bric-à-brac ► junk[1]
   vente de bric-à-brac ► rummage sale
bricoler ► putter, tinker
bride ► bridle, rein
brider ► bridle

bridge ► bridge
brièvement ► briefly [brief]
brigade ► brigade, outfit, squad
brillamment ► brightly [bright]
brillant ► shine
brillant (-ante) ► bright, brilliant, fiery, glittery, glittering [glitter], glossy, luminous, shiny, sleek
briller ► excel, flare, flash, glare, gleam, glisten, glitter, shine, sparkle
brin ► grain, jot, lick, strand[2], wisp
   brin de scie ► sawdust
brindille ► stick, twig
brique ► brick, brief
briquet ► lighter
   pierre à briquet ► flint
briqueter ► brick
brise ► breeze
brisé (-ée) ► broken
   qui a le cœur brisé ► heartbroken
brise-glace ► icebreaker
brise-lames ► breakwater
briser ► break, break in, smash
   se briser ► break
   vague brisante ► breaker
broche ► pin, spit[2]
   broches ► brace
brochet ► pike
brochure ► brochure, leaflet, literature, pamphlet
broder ► embroider
broncher ► flinch
bronchite ► bronchitis
brontosaure ► Brontosaurus
bronzage ► tan
bronze ► bronze
bronzé (-ée) ► chocolate
bronzer ► bronze, tan
   se faire bronzer ► sunbathe
brosse ► brush[1]
   brosse à dents ► toothbrush
brosser ► brush[1]
brouette ► wheelbarrow
brouillard ► fog
brouiller ► blur, jam[1], muddle, scramble, smear
brouillon ► draft
   faire le brouillon ► draft
broussailles ► brush[2], scrub[2]
brousse ► brush[2], bush
   pilote de brousse ► bush pilot
brouter ► browse, graze
broutilles ► trivial
broyer ► crush, grind, mash, pound[2]
   broyer du noir ► mope
bruine ► drizzle
   de bruine ► drizzly
bruiner ► drizzle, mist

bruire ► chirp, rustle
   faire bruire ► rustle, swish
bruissement ► rustle, swish
bruit ► clatter, loudness [loud], noise, rumour, sound[1]
   bruit éclatant ► blare
   bruit fort ► blast
   bruit lourd ► clump, thump
   bruit sec ► snap
   bruit sourd ► thud, thump
   grand bruit ► clash, fuss
   bruit de l'eau qui tombe ► drip
   bruit de pas ► tramp, tread
   faire du bruit ► clatter
   émettre un bruit sourd ► thud
   produire un bruit retentissant ► thunder
brûlant (-ante) ► fiery, scorching [scorch]
brûler ► burn, consume, flame, sunburn
   brûler légèrement ► scorch
   brûler lentement ► smoulder
   brûler de ► ache
brûlure ► burn
brume ► fog, mist
   brume (légère) ► haze
brumeux (-euse) ► foggy [fog], hazy
brun (-une) ► brown, chocolate
   brun rouge ► sorrel[2]
brunir ► brown, tan
brusque ► abrupt, blunt, sharp, wild
brusquement ► abruptly [abrupt], bluntly [blunt], sharply [sharp]
   quitter brusquement ► whisk
   s'emparer brusquement de ► snatch
   tirer brusquement ► jerk
brusquerie ► bluntness [blunt]
brut (brute) ► crude, gross, raw
brutal (-ale, -aux) ► beastly [beast], blunt, brutal, cruel, rough
brutalement ► bluntly [blunt], rough, rudely [rude], viciously [vicious]
brutaliser ► bully, rough
brutalité ► roughness [rough], viciousness [vicious]
brute ► beast, brute, bully
bruyamment ► loudly [loud], noisily [noise]
   respirer bruyamment ► wheeze
bruyant (-ante) ► loud, noisy [noise], rowdy
   respiration bruyante ► wheeze
buanderie ► laundry
buccal (-ale, -aux) ► oral
bûche ► log
bûcher ► log, plug
budget ► budget
budgéter ► budget
buée ► steam
   couvert (-erte) de buée ► foggy [fog], steamy [steam]

buffet ▸ buffet[1]
buffle ▸ buffalo
   buffle (des Indes) ▸ water buffalo
   peau de buffle ▸ buff
buis ▸ box[3]
buisson ▸ bush
   arbre ou buisson épineux ▸ thorn
bulbe ▸ bulb
bulldozer ▸ bulldozer
bulle ▸ blister, bubble
   dégager des bulles ▸ bubble
bulletin ▸ bulletin, newsletter
   bulletin de bagages ▸ check
   bulletin de consigne ▸ check
   bulletin de vote ▸ ballot
   bulletin d'informations ▸ newscast
   bulletin scolaire ▸ report card
bungalow ▸ bungalow
bureau (-eaux) ▸ agency, bureau, den,
desk, office, study
   de bureau ▸ white-collar
   bureau de poste ▸ post office
   bureau de scrutin ▸ poll
   bureau de vote ▸ poll
   articles de bureau ▸ stationery
   employé (-ée) de bureau ▸ clerk
bureaucratie ▸ bureaucracy
bus ▸ bus
busard (buse) ▸ buzzard
buste ▸ torso
but ▸ aim, base[1], drift, end, goal, home, idea,
intent[2], mark, object, objective, purpose, sake
   sans but ▸ aimless, aimlessly [aimless]
   but sur balles ▸ walk
   de but en blanc ▸ off-hand
   coup à trois buts ▸ triple
   arrêter un but ▸ save
buté (-ée) ▸ mulish [mule]
butin ▸ cache, haul, spoil
butiner ▸ browse
butoir ▸ stop
butte ▸ butte, hill, mound
butter ▸ club

C

ça ▸ it, that, things [thing], voir **cela**
   ça y est ▸ all right
   c'est ça ▸ all right
cabane ▸ cabin, chantey, hut, shack
cabanon ▸ shack
cabaret ▸ inn
cabine ▸ booth, cab, cabin
cabinet ▸ chamber, government, office
   cabinet (ministériel) ▸ cabinet
   cabinet de travail ▸ den
câble ▸ cable

câbler ▸ cable
cabosser ▸ dent
cabotin (-ine) ▸ ham
se cabrer ▸ rear[2]
   se cabrer (devant) ▸ shy
cabriole ▸ caper
   faire des cabrioles ▸ tumble
cacahuète ▸ peanut
cacao ▸ cocoa
cacaoyer ▸ cacao
cachalot ▸ sperm whale
cache ▸ cache
caché (-ée) ▸ covert, hidden
cache-col ▸ muffler [muffle]
cache-oreilles ▸ earmuffs
cacher ▸ blot out, camouflage, conceal,
couch, cover, cover up, hide[1], mask, obscure,
screen
   cacher derrière un rideau ▸ curtain
cachet ▸ fee, tablet
   cachet de la poste ▸ postmark
cacheter ▸ seal[2]
cachette ▸ cache, hideout
   en cachette ▸ on the sly [sly]
cachot ▸ cell, dungeon
cachottier (-ière) ▸ sneak
cactus ▸ cactus
cadavre ▸ body, corpse
cadeau (-eaux) ▸ favour, gift, present[2]
   faire cadeau de ▸ away
cadenas ▸ padlock
cadenasser ▸ padlock
cadet (-ette) ▸ junior
cadran ▸ dial
   cadran solaire ▸ sundial
cadre ▸ executive, frame, framework, mount,
setting
   cadres ▸ management
cafard ▸ blues
cafarder ▸ tattle
café ▸ café, coffee
   cuiller à café ▸ teaspoon
   cuillerée à café ▸ teaspoon
caféine ▸ caffeine
cafétéria ▸ cafeteria, canteen
cage ▸ cage, shaft
   mettre en cage ▸ cage
cageot ▸ crate
cagoule ▸ balaclava
cahier ▸ book
cahot ▸ jolt
   avancer avec force cahots ▸ bump
cahoter ▸ jolt
cahoteux (-euse) ▸ bumpy [bump]
caille ▸ quail
   sorte de caille ▸ bobwhite
caillou (-oux) ▸ pebble, stone

caisse ► case[2], chest, crate
   tiroir-caisse ► till[3]
   caisse enregistreuse ► register, till[3]
caissier (-ière) ► cashier, teller
caisson ► panel
cajoler ► coax
calamité ► calamity, curse
calcium ► calcium
calcul ► arithmetic
calculatrice ► calculator
calculer ► calculate, compute, count[1], figure, reckon
cale ► hold[2]
calèche ► calèche
caleçon ► drawer, short
calembour ► pun
calendrier ► calendar, timetable
calepin ► notebook
caler ► prop, stall, wedge
calibre ► bore[2], gauge, grade
calibrer ► gauge, grade
câliner ► coax, cuddle, pet
calligraphie ► handwriting, penmanship
callosité ► corn[2]
calmant (-ante) ► soothing [soothe]
   d'une manière calmante ► soothingly [soothe]
calmar ► squid
calme ► calm, cool, peaceful, quiet, steady, still, tranquillity [tranquil]
   (perdre son) calme ► temper
   reprendre son calme ► compose oneself
calmement ► calmly [calm], easily, quietly [quiet], tranquilly [tranquil]
calmer ► calm, ease, hush, lull, quiet, settle, soothe
   se calmer ► subside
calomnie ► slander, smear
calomnier ► slander, smear
calomnieux (-euse) ► slanderous [slander]
calorie ► calorie
camarade ► chum, comrade, fellow, friend, playmate
cambrioleur (-euse) ► burglar
cambrure ► arch[1]
caméléon ► chameleon
de camelote ► shoddy
caméra ► camera
camion ► truck, van
   (camion à) benne (basculante) ► tipper [tip[3]]
   (faire) transporter par camion ► truck
camion-citerne ► tanker
camionner ► truck
camionnette ► pickup, van

camionneur (-euse) ► teamster
camouflage ► camouflage
camoufler ► camouflage, disguise, whitewash
   camoufler un microphone clandestin ► bug
camp ► camp, lodge
campagnard (-arde) ► country
campagne ► campaign, country
   à la campagne ► open
   campagne de financement ► drive
   maison de campagne ► villa
   faire campagne ► campaign
   mener campagne ► agitate
campement ► camp
camper ► camp
campeur (-euse) ► camper
campus ► campus
canadien (-ienne) ► Canadian
   Canadien (-ienne) ► Canuck
   Société canadienne des postes ► post office
   Canadien-anglais ► the English [english]
   canadien (-ienne) français (-aise) ► French Canadian, French-Canadian
canal (-aux) ► canal, channel, duct
   creuser un canal dans ► channel
canalisation ► duct, main
canaliser ► channel, pipe
canapé ► chesterfield, couch, sofa
canard ► drake, duck[1]
canari ► canary
cancan ► gossip
cancaner ► gossip
cancanier (-ière) ► gossip
cancer ► cancer
cancéreux (-euse) ► cancerous [cancer]
candidat (-ate) ► applicant, candidate
   être candidat (-ate) ► run
   candidat (-ate) éventuel (-elle) ► prospect
candidature ► application
   poser sa candidature ► apply
candide ► innocent
cane ► duck[1]
canette ► can[2]
caniche ► poodle
canif ► jack-knife
canin (-ine) ► canine
canine ► canine
caniveau (-eaux) ► gully
canne ► cane, pole, rod, switch
   canne à sucre ► sugarcane
canneberge ► cranberry
cannelle ► cinnamon
cannette ► can[2]
canoë ► canoe

canon ► barrel, cannon
canot ► dinghy
   canot de sauvetage ► lifeboat
cantaloup ► cantaloupe
cantine ► cafeteria, canteen, mess
cantique ► hymn
canton ► township
cantonner ► quarter, type
canular ► hoax
canyon ► canyon
caoutchouc ► rubber
caoutchouteux (-euse) ► rubbery [rubber]
cap ► bluff^2, cape^2
capable ► able, capable, competent
capacité ► capacity
   capacité de parler ► tongue
   avoir une capacité ► seat
cape ► cape^1, mantle
   grande cape ► cloak
capillaire ► capillary
capitaine ► captain, master, skipper
capital (-aux) ► capital
   doter en capital ► fund
capital (-ale, -aux) ► capital, cardinal,
essential
capitale ► capital
capitalisme ► capitalism
capitonner ► pad
capot ► hood
caprice ► fancy, way, whim
capricieusement ► erratically [erratic]
capricieux (-ieuse) ► changeable, erratic,
temperamental
capsule ► cap, capsule, top^1
   capsule épineuse ► burr
capsuler ► cap
captif (-ive) ► captive, prisoner
captivant (-ante) ► interesting
captiver ► fascinate
en **captivité** ► captive
capture ► capture, catch
capturer ► capture
   capturer au lasso ► rope
capuchon ► cap, hood, top^1
caqueter ► cackle
car ► for
caracoler ► prance
caractère ► character, disposition, nature,
temper, type
   caractère craintif ► timidity [timid]
   caractère décisif ► decisiveness
   [decisive]
   caractère impitoyable ► ruthlessness
   [ruthless]
   caractère rudimentaire ► roughness
   [rough]

   caractère spécial ► specialty
   caractère timoré ► timidity [timid]
   caractère trompeur ► deceptiveness
   [deceptive]
   caractère unique ► uniqueness [unique]
caractères ► print
caractériser ► characterize, distinguish
caractéristique ► characteristic, distinctive,
feature, trait, typical
   de manière caractéristique ► typically
   [typical]
   d'une façon caractéristique ►
   characteristically [characteristic]
caramel ► taffy
carafe ► jug
carapace ► armour, shell
carat ► karat
caravane ► camper, caravan, trailer, train
carbone ► carbon
carburant ► fuel
   consommation de carburant au mille
   (= au kilomètre) ► mileage
carcajou ► wolverine
carcan ► shackle
carcasse ► carcass, shell
carde ► card^2
carder ► card^2
cardinal (-ale, -aux) ► cardinal
cardinal (-aux) ► cardinal
carence ► deficiency
caresser ► cuddle, pat, pet, stroke^2
   caresser l'idée ► toy
cargaison ► cargo, freight, shipment
cari ► curry
caribou ► caribou
caricature ► cartoon, imitation, impression
carie ► cavity, decay
se **carier** ► decay
carillon ► chime, peal
carillonner ► chime
carnaval (-als) ► carnival
carnet ► log, notebook
carnivore ► carnivorous
carotte ► carrot
caroubier ► locust
carpe ► carp^1
carpé (-ée) ► jack-knife
carpette ► rug
carquois ► quiver
carré^1 ► bed
carré^2 ► square
   danse carrée ► square dance
   élever au carré ► square
   rendre carré ► square
carré (-ée) ► square
carreau (-eaux) ► diamond, Diamonds
[diamond], pane, tile, windowpane

carreaux ▶ check
carrefour ▶ cross, junction
carreler ▶ check, tile
carrément ▶ bluntly [blunt], flatly [flat[1]], outright, squarely [square]
carrière ▶ career, quarry[1]
carrosse ▶ coach
carrure ▶ build
carte ▶ card[1], chart, map
   carte de la Saint-Valentin ▶ valentine
   carte en relief ▶ relief map [relief[2]]
   carte marine ▶ chart
   carte postale ▶ postcard
   dresser la carte de ▶ chart, map
cartilage ▶ cartilage
cartographier ▶ chart
carton ▶ card[1], cardboard, carton
cartouche ▶ shell
cas ▶ case[1], example, instance
   grand cas ▶ fuss
   au cas où ▶ in case, in the event of
   dans ce cas ▶ then
   en tout cas ▶ anyhow, anyway, in any event
   en cas de ▶ in the event of
   faire grand cas de ▶ prize
cascade ▶ fall, ripple, waterfall
case ▶ compartment
caserne ▶ barracks, station
casier ▶ locker
casino ▶ casino
casque ▶ helmet
casquette ▶ cap
cassable ▶ breakable
cassé (-ée) ▶ broken
casse-croûte ▶ snack
casse-pieds ▶ pain
casser ▶ break, give, slash, smash
   se casser ▶ break, crack
   casser les oreilles ▶ deafen
   casser net ▶ snap
casserole ▶ pan, pot
casse-tête ▶ jigsaw puzzle
cassette ▶ cassette, tape
   cassette vidéo ▶ tape, video, videocassette, videotape
caste ▶ clan
castor ▶ beaver
cataclysme ▶ catastrophe
catalogue ▶ catalogue
cataloguer ▶ catalogue
catamaran ▶ catamaran
catapulte ▶ catapult
catastrophe ▶ catastrophe, disaster, precipice
catastrophique ▶ disastrous [disaster]

catégorie ▶ category, class, grade
   catégorie grammaticale ▶ part of speech
catégorique ▶ decisive
   ton catégorique ▶ decisively [decisive], decisiveness [decisive]
catégoriquement ▶ categorically [category]
catégoriser ▶ type
cathédrale ▶ cathedral
catholique ▶ Catholic
   Église catholique romaine ▶ Roman Catholic Church
partir en catimini ▶ slink
cauchemar ▶ nightmare
cause ▶ cause, ground[1]
   à cause de ▶ on account of [account], owing to
causer[1] ▶ bring about, cause, determine, move, result
causer[2] ▶ chat
causerie ▶ chat
causeur (-euse) ▶ talker
causeuse ▶ couch
caution ▶ bail[1], security
   fournir une caution ▶ bail[1]
   se porter caution pour ▶ sponsor
cavalier ▶ knight
cavalier (-ière) ▶ escort, rider [ride]
cave ▶ cellar
caverne ▶ cave
caverneux (-euse) ▶ hollow
cavité ▶ cavity, chamber, hole
caye ▶ key[2]
cayuga ▶ Cayuga
ce ▶ it
   ce que ▶ what
ceci ▶ it, this
   comme ceci ▶ thus
ce (cet, cette) ▶ this, that
céder ▶ budge, give, yield
cédérom ▶ CD-ROM
cèdre ▶ cedar
ceindre ▶ belt, enclose
ceinture ▶ belt
   ceinture de sécurité ▶ seatbelt
   ceinture (d'étoffe) ▶ sash[1]
ceinturer ▶ belt, ring[1]
cela ▶ it, so, that
célébration ▶ carnival
célèbre ▶ celebrate, famous, great, noted, prominent, well-known
   tristement célèbre ▶ notorious
   personnalité célèbre ▶ personality
célébrer ▶ celebrate, observe
célébrité ▶ celebrity, fame, glory
céleri ▶ celery
célibataire ▶ bachelor, single

celle ► that
   celle-ci ► this
   celles-là ► those
cellier ► cellar
cellule ► cell
Celsius ► Celsius
celte ► Celtic
celtique ► Celtic
celui (celle) ► that, which
   celui (celle) que ► whichever
   celui (celle) qui ► whichever, whoever
   celui (celle) qui parle ► speaker
celui-ci (celle-ci) ► this
celui-là (celle-là) ► that
cendre ► ash[1]
censeur (-eure) ► censor, critic
censurer ► censor, condemn, criticize
cent[1] ► cent, hundred
   pour cent ► percent
cent[2] ► penny
   pièce de un cent ► penny
   pièce de cinq cents ► nickel
   pièce de dix cents ► dime
   pièce de vingt-cinq cents ► quarter
centaine ► hundred
centaure ► centaur
centième ► hundredth [hundred]
centimètre ► centimetre
central (-ale, -aux) ► central, middle
centre ► centre, eye, focus, middle
   centre commercial ► mall, plaza,
   shopping centre
   centre d'accueil ► home
   centre (d'activités) ► hub
   centre de la petite enfance ► nursery
   school
   centre de la scène ► spotlight
centrer ► centre
centre-ville ► downtown
cependant ► except, however, nevertheless,
though
céramique ► ceramic
   objet en céramique ► ceramic
cerceau (-eaux) ► hoop
cercle ► circle, club, ring[1], round
cercler ► rim
cercueil ► coffin
céréale ► cereal
cérémonial (-aux) ► worship
cérémonie ► ceremony, exercise
   cérémonie publique ► function
   de cérémonie ► formal
   sans cérémonie ► informally [informal]
cérémonieusement ► formally [formal]
cérémonieux (-euse) ► formal
cerf ► stag, deer
cerf-volant ► kite

cerise ► cherry
   rouge cerise ► cherry
cerner ► hem in
certain[1] **(-aine)** ► certain, decided, definite,
obvious, positive
   certain (-aine) de ► bound[1]
certain[2] **(-aine)** ► few, some
certainement ► certainly, decidedly
[decided], definitely [definite], doubtless,
obviously [obvious], undoubtedly,
unmistakably [unmistakable]
certificat ► certificate
certifier ► certify, guarantee, insure
cerveau (-eaux) ► brain
   faire un lavage de cerveau ► brainwash
   se creuser la cervelle ► rack one's brain
ces ► these, those
cesser ► cease, quit
   sans cesse ► constantly [constant],
   continually [continual], ever, forever,
   relentlessly [relentless], repeatedly [repeat]
c'est-à-dire ► namely
ceux (celles) ► these, those
ceux-ci (celles-ci) ► these
ceux-là (celles-là) ► those
chacal ► jackal
chacun (-une) ► apiece, each, everybody,
everyone
   chacun son tour ► alternate
chagrin ► distress, grief, sorrow
   avec chagrin ► sorrowfully [sorrow]
   avoir du chagrin ► grieve
   éprouver du chagrin ► sorrow
chagriné (-ée) ► heartbroken, sorrowful
[sorrow]
chahut ► din
chahuteur (-euse) ► rowdy
chaîne ► chain, channel, guy, range, ridge
   chaîne de montage ► assembly line
   chaîne stéréo ► stereo
chaînon ► link
chair ► flesh, meat, pulp
   chair à vif ► quick
   en chair et en os ► as large as life
chaise ► chair
   chaise berçante ► rocker
chaland ► barge
châle ► shawl, wrap
chalet ► chalet
chaleur ► heartiness [hearty], heat, warmth
chaleureusement ► heartily [hearty], warmly
[warm]
chaleureux (-euse) ► cordial, hearty, warm
chaloupe ► launch[2]
chalumeau (-eaux) ► pipe, torch
chalut ► trawl

pêcher au chalut ► trawl
(se) chamailler ► bicker, quarrel, scuffle
chamaillerie ► scuffle, squabble
chaman ► shaman
chambre ► chamber, lodging, room
  chambre à coucher ► bedroom
  chambre d'enfant ► nursery
  chambre froide ► icehouse
  chambre forte ► vault[1]
  chambre libre ► vacancy
  robe de chambre ► robe
  vivre en chambre ► room
Chambre ► Commons, house
  chambre des Communes ► House of Commons
chameau (-eaux) ► camel
chamois ► buff
champ ► field
  champ de tir ► range
  champ de vision ► vision
  à tout bout de champ ► forever
champignon ► fungus, mushroom
  champignon vénéneux ► toadstool
  appuyer sur le champignon ► gun
  pousser comme un champignon ► mushroom
champion (-ionne) ► champion, whiz
chance ► blessing, break, fortune, luck, mercy, prayer, probability, windfall
  chances ► odds
  par chance ► luckily
  égalité (de chances) ► toss up
chancelant (-ante) ► rocky [rock[2]], tottery [totter]
  pas chancelant (-ante) ► stagger, wobble
chanceler ► falter, reel[2], teeter, totter
chanceux (-euse) ► fortunate, happy, lucky
chandail ► jersey, sweater
chandelle ► candle, fly[1]
change ► exchange
changeant (-ante) ► changeable, erratic, mobile, unsettled, unstable, variable
changement ► change, innovation, passage, shift, switch
  changement de direction abrupt ► jog[2]
changer ► alter, change, convert, modify, shift, switch, turn, vary
  changer graduellement ► graduate
  se changer ► change
  changer d'avis ► back out, turn
  changer de direction ► veer
  changer de direction de façon abrupte ► jog[2]
  changer de vitesse ► shift
chanson ► song
  chanson de marin ► shanty

chant ► chant, song
  chant de Noël ► carol
  chant du coq ► crow[2]
chantage ► blackmail
chanter ► chorus, sing
  chanter (joyeusement) ► carol
  chanter victoire ► crow[2]
  faire chanter ► blackmail
chanteur (-euse) ► singer
chantier ► yard[1]
chantonner ► hum, sing
Chanuka ► Chanuka
chaos ► chaos
chapeau[1] (-eaux) ► hat
  faire passer le chapeau ► to pass the hat
chapeau[2] (-eaux) ► lead[1]
chapelle ► chapel
chapiteau (-eaux) ► pavilion
chapitre ► chapter, unit
  avoir droit au chapitre ► say
chaque ► each, every, every other
char ► chariot, float, wagon
  char d'assaut ► tank
  char de combat ► tank
charabia ► jargon
charançon ► weevil
charbon ► coal
  charbon de bois ► charcoal
  être sur des charbons ardents ► on pins and needles
chardon ► thistle
charge ► burden, charge, concern, expense, function, load, office
  mât de charge ► derrick
  personne à charge ► dependant, dependent
chargé (-ée) ► responsible
  chargé (-ée) d'électricité ► live[2]
chargement ► load
  quai de chargement ► bay[5]
charger ► burden, charge, direct, load
chariot ► cart, wagon
charitable ► charitable, generous, good
charitablement ► charitably [charitable]
charité ► charity, generousity [generous], humanity
  œuvre de charité ► charity
charlatan ► impostor
charmant (-ante) ► delightful, glamourous [glamour], lovely, winning
charme ► charm, grace, loveliness [lovely], romance, spell[2]
charmer ► charm, enchant, lure
charnière ► hinge
charnu (-ue) ► full
charognard ► scavenger
charpente ► frame, framework, skeleton

bois de charpente ▸ lumber[1]
charpenterie ▸ carpentry [carpenter]
charpentier (-ière) ▸ carpenter
charrette ▸ cart
charrier ▸ cart
charrue ▸ plough
    passer la charrue ▸ plough
charte ▸ charter
    Charte des droits et libertés ▸ Charter of Rights and Freedoms
chasse ▸ hunt
    avion de chasse ▸ fighter
    chien de chasse ▸ hound
    fusil de chasse ▸ shotgun
châsse ▸ shrine
chasse-neige ▸ plough, snowplough
chasser ▸ banish, chase, gun, hunt
    chasser à l'affût ▸ stalk[2]
chasseur ▸ fighter
châssis ▸ frame, sash[2]
robe chasuble ▸ jumper[2]
chat ▸ cat
    petit (petite) chat (-atte) ▸ kitten
    chat sauvage ▸ wildcat
    jeu du chat ▸ tag[2]
châtaigne ▸ chest-nut
châtain ▸ chestnut
châtain (-aine) ▸ brown
château (-eaux) ▸ castle, chateau, palace
châtelain (-aine) ▸ squire
châtiment ▸ punishment
chaton ▸ kitten
chatouillement ▸ tickle
chatouiller ▸ tickle
chatouilleux (-euse) ▸ ticklish
chatoyer ▸ glisten
chaud (chaude) ▸ hot, warm
    assez chaud (chaude) ▸ warm
    chaud (chaude) et humide ▸ muggy
chaudement ▸ warmly [warm]
chaudière ▸ boiler, furnace
chauffage ▸ heat
chauffer ▸ heat, warm
chaufferie ▸ furnace
chauffeur (-euse) ▸ chauffeur, driver
chauler ▸ whitewash
chaume ▸ stubble
chausser ▸ shoe
chaussette ▸ hose
    chaussettes ▸ sock[1]
chausson ▸ slipper
chaussure ▸ shoe
    couvre-chaussures ▸ overshoe
    forme à chaussure ▸ last[3]
chauve ▸ bald
chauve-souris ▸ bat[2]
chaux ▸ lime[2], whitewash

blanchir à la chaux ▸ whitewash
chavirer ▸ capsize, keel
cheddar ▸ cheddar
chef ▸ chef, chief, head, leader, ruler
    chef d'accusation ▸ count[1]
    chef de classe ▸ monitor
    chef de la police ▸ sheriff
    chef de train ▸ conductor
    chef d'État ▸ ruler
    chef d'orchestre ▸ conductor
    chef du gouvernement ▸ premier
chef-d'œuvre ▸ masterpiece
cheik ▸ sheik
chemin ▸ doorway, lane, path, road, route, runner, walk, way
    à moitié chemin ▸ halfway
    en chemin vers ▸ way
    chemin de fer ▸ rail, railroad, railway
    chemin d'entrée ▸ driveway
    se frayer un chemin ▸ press, push
    se frayer un chemin des coudes ▸ elbow
    se frayer un chemin à coup d'épaules ▸ shoulder
cheminée ▸ chimney, fireplace, funnel, smokestack
    écran de cheminée ▸ screen
    dessus de cheminée ▸ mantel
    manteau de cheminée ▸ mantel
chemise ▸ file[1], shirt
    chemise de nuit ▸ nightgown
chemisier ▸ blouse, shirt
chêne ▸ oak
    de chêne ▸ oaken [oak]
    en chêne ▸ oaken [oak]
chenil ▸ kennel
chenille ▸ caterpillar, track
    tracteur à chenilles ▸ caterpillar
cheptel ▸ livestock
chèque ▸ cheque
    livret de chèques ▸ cheque
cher[1] (-ère) ▸ dear, fond
cher[2] (-ère) ▸ expensive [expense]
    pas cher (chère) ▸ cheap, inexpensive
chercher ▸ check, fish, hunt, look, search, seek
    aller chercher ▸ fetch
    chercher la querelle ▸ pick a fight
    chercher à localiser ▸ probe
    chercher des faux-fuyants ▸ hedge
    chercher la bagarre ▸ pick a fight
    chercher sa respiration ▸ gasp
chercheur (-euse) ▸ searcher [search], seeker [seek]
chéri (-ie) ▸ darling, dear, honey, precious
chétif (-ive) ▸ puny
cheval (-aux) ▸ bronco, horse

à cheval ▶ horseback
cheval d'arçons ▶ horse
cheval sauvage ▶ bronco
fer à cheval ▶ horseshoe
chevaleresque ▶ knightly [knight]
chevalet ▶ easel, horse
chevalier ▶ knight
cheval-vapeur ▶ horsepower
puissance en chevaux-vapeur ▶
horsepower
chevaucher ▶ lap[2]
chevelu (-ue) ▶ hairy
chevelure ▶ hair, lock[2]
cheveu (-eux) ▶ hair, lock[2]
fixatif à cheveux ▶ spray
(se) laver les cheveux ▶ shampoo
cheville ▶ ankle, peg
cheviller ▶ peg
chèvre ▶ goat
chevreau (-eaux) ▶ kid
chevrette ▶ kid
chevreuil ▶ buck
chevronné (-ée) ▶ veteran
chevroter ▶ quaver
chez ▶ over, to
chez soi ▶ home
chez-soi ▶ at home
chic ▶ elegant, grace
qui a du chic ▶ jazzy [jazz]
chicaner ▶ quibble
chiche ▶ stingy
chicot ▶ stump
chien (-ienne) ▶ dog, canine
chien de chasse ▶ hound
chien de garde ▶ watchdog
chien de meute ▶ hound
chien de traîneau ▶ husky[2]
petit chien d'appartement ▶ toy
traîneau à chiens ▶ dogsled
chiffon ▶ rag
chiffonner ▶ crease
chiffonnier ▶ chest, dresser[1]
chiffre ▶ code, digit, figure, number, numeral
chiffre d'affaires ▶ figure
chiffre romain ▶ Roman numeral
chiffres arabes ▶ Arabic numerals
chignon ▶ bun
chilcotin ▶ Chilcotin
chili ▶ chili
chimie ▶ chemistry
chimique ▶ chemical
chimpanzé ▶ chimpanzee
chinook ▶ Chinook
chiot ▶ pup, puppy
chipewyan ▶ Chipewyan
chique ▶ chew
chiquenaude ▶ flip

chiquer ▶ chew
chirurgical (-ale, aux) ▶ surgical [surgery]
chirurgie ▶ surgery
de chirurgie ▶ surgical [surgery]
chirurgien (-ienne) ▶ surgeon
chlore ▶ chlorine
chlorophylle ▶ chlorophyll
choc ▶ bump, impact, jar, jolt, knock, shock[1],
stook
choc électrique ▶ shock[1]
chocolat ▶ chocolate
chocolat chaud ▶ cocoa
chocolaté (-ée) ▶ chocolate
chœur ▶ choir
dire en chœur ▶ chorus
choisi (-ie) ▶ exclusive, select
choisir ▶ choose, designate, elect, pick[1],
single out [single]
choix ▶ choice, option, pick[1]
au choix ▶ assorted
de choix ▶ choice
de premier choix ▶ choice, prime
sélection (de choix) ▶
cholestérol ▶ cholesterol
chômage ▶ unemployment [unemployed]
au chômage ▶ unemployed
indemnité de chômage ▶ dole
chope ▶ mug
choquant (-ante) ▶ offensive
choquer ▶ horrify, offend, shock[1]
choral (-ale, -als) ▶ choir, choral [chorus]
chose ▶ item, object, stuff, thing
choses ▶ stuff, things [thing]
chose aisée ▶ snap
chose de trop ▶ the last straw
chose qui fait peur ▶ creep
choses essentielles ▶ basic
état de chose ▶ circumstance
quelque chose ▶ something
pousser les choses à l'extrême ▶ go to
extremes
chou (choux) ▶ cabbage
chouchou (-oute) ▶ pet
chou-fleur ▶ cauliflower
choyer ▶ pamper
Christ ▶ Christ
chromosome ▶ chromosome
chronique ▶ chronic, feature
chroniquement ▶ chronically
chronomètre ▶ stopwatch, timer
chronométrer ▶ clock, time
chronométreur (-euse) ▶ timer
chrysalide ▶ chrysalis, pupa
chrysanthème ▶ chrysanthemum
chuchotement ▶ whisper
chuchoter ▶ whisper

chuinter ► hiss
chute ► chute, drop, fall, punch line, slip[1], slump, tumble
    chutes ► trimming
    chute d'eau ► waterfall
    chute de neige ► snow, snowfall
    chute de pluie ► rainfall
    faire une chute ► slip[1], tumble
chuter ► plummet
cible ► aim, mark, target
    loin de la cible ► wide
cibler ► target
cicatrice ► scar
    marquer d'une cicatrice ► scar
cicatriser ► heal
ci-dessus ► above
cidre ► cider
ciel ► heaven, sky
    ciels ► skies
    cieux ► heaven
cigale ► cicada
cigare ► cigar
cigarette ► cigarette
cigogne ► stork
cil ► lash[1]
cime ► peak, top[1]
ciment ► cement
cimenter ► cement
cimetière ► cemetery
cinéma ► cinema, movie
    salle de cinéma ► theatre
cinglant (-ante) ► bitter, cutting
cinglé (-ée) ► crazy, lunatic, mad
cingler ► lash, slash
cinq ► five
cinquante ► fifty
cinquantième ► fiftieth [fifty]
cinquième ► fifth, fifth [five]
cintre ► hanger
circonférence ► circumference
    de circonférence ► around
circonscription ► constituency
circonspect (-ecte) ► cautious, prudent, wary
circonspection ► caution
    avec circonspection ► cautiously [cautious]
circonstance ► circumstance, occurrence [occur]
    circonstances ► case[1]
circuit ► circuit
    circuit électrique ► circuit
    coup de circuit ► homerun
circulaire ► brochure, circular
circulation ► circulation, flow, traffic
circuler ► circulate, flow
    faire circuler ► circulate

cire ► polish, wax[1]
cirer ► polish, wax[1]
cireux (-euse) ► waxy [wax[1]]
cirque ► circus
cisailler ► clip[1]
cisailles ► shear
ciseaux ► scissors
    petit coup de ciseaux ► snip
citation[1] ► quotation, quote
citation[2] ► summons
cité ► project
citer ► cite, excerpt, name, quote
citerne ► tank
cithare ► zither
citoyen (-enne) ► citizen, civilian
citoyenneté ► nationality
citron ► lemon
    citron vert ► lime[1]
    (jaune) citron ► lemon
citrouille ► pumpkin
civière ► litter
civil (-ile) ► civil, civilian
    en civil ► undercover
civilisation ► civilization
civiliser ► civilize
civilité ► courteousness [courteous], courtesy
civique ► civic, civilian
clair (claire) ► clear, distinct, fair[1], light[1], obvious, pale, plain, specific, thin
    clair de lune ► moonlight
clairement ► clearly, distinctly [distinct], plainly [plain], transparently [transparent]
clairière ► clearing
clairon ► bugle
clairsemé (-ée) ► sparse, thin
    d'une façon clairsemée ► sparsely [sparse]
clairvoyant (-ante) ► far-sighted
clameur ► clamour, uproar
clan ► clan, gang
clandestin (-ine) ► underground
    passager (-ère) clandestin (-ine) ► stowaway
clandestinement ► smuggle, underground
clapoter ► lap[3]
clapotis ► ripple, wash
claque ► slap
    donner une claque sur les fesses ► spank
claquement ► bang, clap, click, crack, flap, slam, smack, snap, whack
claquemurer ► coop
claquer ► chatter, crack, slam, slap, snap
    se claquer ► pull
    claquer la langue ► smack
clarinette ► clarinet

classe ► bracket, category, clan, class, division, grade
    salle de classe temporaire ► portable
    chef de classe ► monitor
classement ► rating
    avoir un certain classement ► rank[1]
classer ► class, classify, file[1], grade, rate
    se classer ► place, rank[1]
    classer par ordre alphabétique ► alphabetize
classeur ► file[1]
classification ► scheme
classifier ► class, type
classique ► classic, classical, conventional
claudication ► limp[1]
claudiquer ► limp[1]
clause ► article, clause
clavier ► keyboard
    joueur (-euse) d'un instrument à clavier ► keyboardist
claviériste ► keyboarder [keyboard]
clé[1] ► clef, key[1], stop
    mettre sous clé ► lock[1]
    fermer à clé ► lock[1]
    clé musicale ► clef
    trousseau (clés) ► bunch
clé[2] ► wrench
clément (-ente) ► merciful [mercy], mild
cliché ► cliché
client (-ente) ► client, customer, fare, guest
    client (-ente) potentiel (-lelle) ► prospect
clientèle ► client, market
cligner de l'œil ► wink
    cligner des yeux ► blink
clignotement ► blink
clignoter ► blink
climat ► climate, weather
    zone climatique ► zone
climatisation ► air conditioning
climatiser ► air-condition
climatiseur ► air conditioner, air conditioning
clin d'œil ► flash
clinique ► clinic
clip vidéo ► video
clipper ► clipper
clique ► crowd
cliqueter ► click, rattle
cliquetis ► jingle, rattle
clochard (-arde) ► bum, vagrant
cloche ► bell
    son de cloche ► toll[2]
clocher ► steeple
cloison ► division
cloîtrer ► coop
cloque ► blister
    provoquer des ampoules (cloques) ► blister

clos (close) ► close[2]
clôture ► fence
clôturer ► enclose, fence
clou (clous) ► nail
    petit clou ► tack
    clou (décoratif) ► stud
    clou de girofle ► clove
clouer ► nail, pin, tack
    clouer au sol ► transfix
    clouer des planches en travers de ► board
    clouer sur place ► root[1]
clown ► clown
    faire le clown ► clown
club ► club
coalition ► coalition
    être en coalition ► in league
cobra ► cobra
coccinelle ► ladybug
coche ► shell
cocher ► check, check off, tick[1]
cochon ► hog, pig
cochonneries ► junk food
noix de coco ► coconut
cocon ► chrysalis, cocoon
cocorico ► crow[2]
cocotte ► casserole
    plat en cocotte ► casserole
code ► code
    code postal ► postal code
    code régional ► area code
coder ► code
cœur ► centre, core, heart, hearts [heart]
    au cœur ► dead, depth, thick
    de cœur ► heart
    de bon cœur ► willingly [willing]
    de tout cœur ► heartily [hearty]
    par cœur ► by heart
    avoir le cœur brisé ► bleed
    conquérir le cœur de ► steal
    dire en cœur ► chorus
    qui donne mal au cœur ► queasy
    qui a mal au cœur ► sick
    qui a le cœur brisé ► heartbroken
coffre ► bin, chest, trunk
    salle des coffres ► vault[1]
coffre-fort ► safe, vault[1]
coffret ► case[2]
cognement ► knock
cogner ► bump, knock
    se cogner ► stub
    cogner dur sur ► hammer
cohérent (-ente) ► consistent
cohue ► crush, scrimmage, throng
coiffer ► cap, groom
    coiffer à rebrousse-poil ► tease

coiffeur (-euse) ► barber
coin ► corner, wedge
coincé (-ée) ► corner
coincer ► corner, jam[1]
   se coincer ► stick
   coincer entre ► sandwich
coïncidence ► coincidence
coin-coin ► quack
   faire coin-coin ► quack
col ► collar, neck
   col roulé ► turtleneck
   mettre un col ► collar
coléoptère ► beetle
colère ► anger, wrath
   avec colère ► angrily
   de colère ► beside oneself
   en colère ► angry, cross, mad, temper
   crise de colère ► tantrum
   se mettre en colère ► flare
   bouillir de colère ► seethe
   éprouver de la colère ► rage
   mettre en colère ► angrily [anger]
colibri ► hummingbird
colifichet ► trinket
colis ► package, parcel
collaboration ► pool[2], teamwork
collaborer ► chip in, collaborate, cooperate, help, take part, team
collage ► collage
collant ► leotard
   collant(s) ► tights
collant (-ante) ► sticky, tacky
collation des grades ► graduation
colle ► cement, glue, paste
collecte ► pickup
collecter ► raise
collectif (-ive) ► mass
collection ► collection, library, set
collectionner ► collect
collectivité ► community
collège ► college
collègue ► colleague, partner
coller ► glue, paste, plaster, stick
   coller aux talons ► tag[1]
collet ► collar
   collet monté ► stuffy
se **colleter avec** ► tangle with [tangle]
colley ► collie
collier ► collar, necklace, rope, string
colline ► hill
collision ► collision, crash, smash
   entrer en collision ► collide
colloque ► conference
colloque ► seminary
colombe ► dove
colon ► colonial, settler
côlon ► colon[2]

colonel (-elle) ► colonel
colonial (-ale, -aux) ► colonial
colonie ► colony, settlement
colonisation ► settlement
colonne ► column, pier
   colonne vertébrale ► backbone, cord, spine
colorant ► dye
coloré (-ée) ► colourful [colour]
colorer ► colour, dye
colorier ► colour
colossal (-ale, -aux) ► enormous, monstrous
colosse ► giant
colporter ► hawk[2]
colvert ► mallard
coma ► coma
combat ► action, battle, bout, combat, conflict, contest, fight, stand
   char de combat ► tank
combattant (-ante) ► fighter, warrior
   ancien combattant ► veteran
combattre ► battle, combat, contend
combien ► how, much
combinaison ► combination
   combinaison spatiale ► space suit
combine ► dodge, gimmick, scheme
combiné ► receiver
combiné (-ée) ► compound
combiner ► combine, compound, coordinate
comble ► full
   au comble du bonheur ► blissfully [bliss]
combler ► bridge
combustible ► fuel
   combustible fossile ► mineral
comédie ► comedy
   comédie musicale ► musical
comestible ► edible
comète ► comet
comique ► comic, funny, laughable [laugh]
   numéro comique ► skit
comité ► board, committee, council, panel
commandant (-ante) ► commander
commande[1] ► control
commande[2] ► command, order
   passer une commande ► commission
   sur commande ► custom
commandement ► command
commander ► bid, command, drive, impose, order
commanditaire ► sponsor
commanditer ► finance, sponsor
comme ► as, for, like[2]
   comme ceci ► thus
   comme si ► though
commémorer ► celebrate
commencement ► beginning, dawn, first

au commencement ► initially [initial]
commencer ► begin, commence, embark, enter, start
   commencer (à) ► strike out
   commencer par ► open
comment ► how, however
   peu importe comment ► no matter
commentaire ► comment, input
commentateur (-trice) ► critical
commenter ► comment
commérage ► gossip
commerçant (-ante) ► dealer, merchant, trader
commerce ► commerce, trade
   marque de commerce ► trademark
   faire le commerce ► deal, trade
commercial (-ale, -aux) ► commercial
commercialement ► commercially [commercial]
commercialiser ► merchandise
commère ► gossip
commérer ► gossip
commettre ► commit
   commettre une faute ► foul
commis ► clerk
commisération ► compassion
commission ► board, commission, errand
   faire des commissions ► to run an errand
commode[1] ► bureau, chest, dresser[1]
commode[2] ► convenient, handy, useful
   peu commode ► difficult
commodité ► convenience
Commonwealth ► Commonwealth
commun (-une) ► common, everyday, joint, ordinary, public
   peu commun (-une) ► uncommon
   en commun ► in common [common], jointly [joint]
   mettre en commun ► pool[2]
Communes ► House of Commons
   chambre des Communes ► House of Commons
communautaire ► public
communauté ► community
communément ► commonly [common], popularly [popular]
communicatif (-ive) ► contagious
communication ► communication
communiqué ► release
communiquer ► communicate, convey, infect, inject
   communiquer par radio ► radio
communisme ► communism
commutateur ► switch
compact (-acte) ► compact
   disque compact ► compact disk

compacter ► compact, condense
compagnie ► business, company, firm[2]
   compagnie aérienne ► airline
   animal de compagnie ► pet
compagnon ► fellow
compagnon (compagne) ► companion
comparable ► comparable
comparaison ► comparison, simile
comparaître ► appear
comparatif ► comparison
comparatif (-ive) ► comparative
comparer ► compare
   comparer à ► compare
   se comparer ► compare
   comparer les prix ► shop around [shop]
compartiment ► compartment, pocket
compas ► compass
compassé (-ée) ► formal
compassion ► compassion, pity
compatible ► consistent
compatissant (-ante) ► sympathetic
compensation ► compensation [compensate]
compenser ► compensate, offset, redeem
compère ► decoy
compétence ► qualification
compétent (-ente) ► capable, competent, good
compétiteur (-trice) ► rival
compétitif (-ive) ► competitive
compétition ► bee, competition, contest, meet
compétitivité ► competitiveness [competitive]
compiler ► compile
complainte ► lament
se complaire ► wallow
complément ► complement, object
   complément direct ou indirect ► object
complet (-ète) ► all-round, complete, comprehensive, full, no-holds-barred, outright, total, utter[2]
complété (-ée) ► complete
complètement ► all, altogether, completely [complete], fully [full], outright, perfectly, quite, radically [radical], royally [royal], stark, starkly [stark], stiff, through, totally, utterly [utter[2]], wholly
compléter ► complement, complete, fill
complexe ► complex, delicate, elaborate, involve
complice ► accomplice, decoy
compliment ► compliment
complimenter ► compliment, congratulate, pat on the back
compliqué (-ée) ► elaborate, involve
compliquer ► complicate
complot ► conspiracy, design, plot, scheme

comploter ▸ conspire, hatch[1], plot, scheme

comportement ▸ behaviour, conduct, manner

comporter ▸ involve

    se comporter ▸ act, behave, conduct, deal

    se comporter bien ▸ behave

composante ▸ component

composé ▸ compound

composé (-ée) ▸ compound

composer ▸ compile, compose, dial, form, write

    se composer ▸ consist

compositeur (-trice) ▸ setter

composition ▸ composition, essay

compost ▸ compost

compréhensif (-ive) ▸ sympathetic, understanding

compréhension ▸ apprehension, grasp, understanding

comprendre[1] ▸ apprehend, catch, comprehend, follow, get, grasp, interpret, know the score, realize, see, understand

    ne pas comprendre ▸ miss[1]

    mal comprendre ▸ misunderstand

    faire comprendre ▸ impress

    tenter de comprendre ▸ puzzle

comprendre[2] ▸ embrace, include, number

compresse ▸ compress

rouleau **compresseur** ▸ steamroller

comprimé ▸ tablet

comprimer ▸ compress, jam[1]

compromettre ▸ compromise, endanger

    éviter de se compromettre ▸ hedge

compromis ▸ compromise

comptable ▸ accountant, bookkeeper

comptant ▸ cash

compte ▸ account, count[1], tally

    avoir un compte en banque ▸ bank[1]

    mettre sur le compte de ▸ charge

    rendre compte ▸ account, report

    se rendre compte ▸ discover, realize

    tenir le compte ▸ tally

    tenir compte de ▸ allow for [allow], heed

    des comptes à régler ▸ score

compter ▸ calculate, compute, count[1], figure, include, matter, number, reckon, rely

    compter sur ▸ bargain for, count on, gamble, lean[1]

    compter faire ▸ propose

    sans compter ▸ besides, let alone [alone]

    sur qui on peut compter ▸ dependable

compte rendu ▸ account, minute[1], report, review

    faire compte rendu ▸ cover, report

compteur ▸ counter[1], meter

compteur de vitesse ▸ speedometer

compteur (kilométrique) ▸ odometer

comptine ▸ nursery rhyme

comptoir ▸ counter[1], fort, post[3]

    comptoir (commercial) ▸ trading post

comte ▸ count[2], earl

comté ▸ county

comtesse ▸ countess

concasser ▸ pound[2]

concave ▸ concave

concéder ▸ concede, grant

concentration ▸ concentration

concentré ▸ concentrate

concentrer ▸ concentrate, condense, focus

concept ▸ concept

concernant ▸ about

concerner ▸ concern

    en ce qui concerne ▸ regarding

    en ce qui me concerne ▸ as far as one is concerned

concert ▸ chorus, concert

    concert en matinée ▸ matinée

concession ▸ claim, concession, grant

concevoir ▸ conceive, design, engineer, imagine

concierge ▸ janitor, superintendent

concis (-ise) ▸ concise

concluant (-ante) ▸ conclusive [conclude], decisive

conclure ▸ conclude, deduce, end, gather, infer

conclusion ▸ conclusion, deduction, outcome, punch line, termination [terminate]

concombre ▸ cucumber

ne pas concorder ▸ disagree

concours ▸ bee, competition, contest, race[1]

    s'assurer le concours de ▸ enlist

    par un concours de circonstances ▸ by chance [chance]

concret (-ète) ▸ concrete, physical, tangible

concurrence ▸ competition

concurrent (-ente) ▸ opponent

concurrentiel (-ielle) ▸ competitive

condamnation ▸ conviction

condamner ▸ condemn, doom

    condamner (à) ▸ sentence

    condamner à une amende ▸ fine[2]

condenser ▸ compact, compress, condense, precipitate

condition ▸ clause, condition

    conditions ▸ terms [term]

    à condition de ▸ provide

    à condition que ▸ provide

    condition physique ▸ condition

    condition requise ▸ requirement

conditionner ▸ condition

condominium ▸ condominium

condor ► condor
conducteur (-trice) ► bus, chauffeur, conductor, driver
   conducteur (-trice) d'attelage ► teamster
conduire ► conduct, drive, ferry, govern, guide, handle, lead[1], shepherd, usher
   conduire trop vite ► speed
   se conduire ► behave, conduct
   se conduire bien ► behave
conduit ► duct, vent
conduite ► behaviour, conduct, navigation
   conduite maîtresse ► main
cône ► cone
confectionner ► fashion
confédération ► commonwealth, confederacy, confederation, Dominion
   les Pères de la Confédération ► Fathers of Confederation
   fête de la Confédération ► Dominion Day
conférence ► conference, lecture
   prononcer une conférence ► lecture
conférencier (-ière) ► lecturer [lecture], speaker
conférer ► confer
confesser ► confess, own
confession ► religion
confiance ► assurance, confidence, faith, trust
   avec confiance ► confidently [confident]
   digne de confiance ► reliable, responsible
   indigne de confiance ► unreliable
   avoir confiance ► credit, trust
   faire confiance ► trust
confidence ► confidence
   en confidence ► confidentially [confidential]
confidentiel (-ielle) ► confidential, off the record, private
confidentiellement ► confidentially [confidential]
confier ► commission, deposit
confiner ► restrict
confirmation ► claim
confirmer ► confirm
confiture ► jam[2], preserve
conflit ► clash, collision, conflict
   entrer en conflit ► clash
confondre ► astound, bewilder, confuse
   se confondre ► blend
conforme ► consistent, faithful
   se conformer à ► comply, obey
conformiste ► conventional
   non conformiste ► unconventional

confort ► comfort
confortable ► at home, comfortable, cosy, cozy, smooth, snug
confortablement ► comfortably [comfortable]
confrère ► colleague
confrontation ► face-off
confronter ► confront
   confronter des vues ► compare notes
confus (-use) ► fuzzy, guilty, obscure, unclear
confusion ► chaos, confusion, daze, fog
congé ► holiday
   jour de congé ► holiday
congédier ► dismiss, lay off
congélateur ► freezer
congrégation ► community
congrès ► conference
conifère ► conifer, coniferous [conifer], evergreen
conjecture ► guess, speculation [speculate]
conjoint (-ointe) ► spouse
conjointement ► jointly [joint]
conjonction ► conjunction
conjugué (-ée) ► joint
conjuration ► conspiracy
connaissance ► acquaintance, consciousness, contact, knowledge, understanding
   sans connaissance ► senseless, unconscious
   faire la connaissance de ► meet
   prendre connaissance de ► acquaint
connaisseur (-euse) ► expert
connaître ► be acquainted with [acquaint], experience, hear of, know
   connaître la situation ► know the score
   connaître par intuition ► sense
   faire connaître ► publish
connecté (-ée) ► on-line
   non connecté (-ée) ► off-line
connexe ► related [relate]
connexion ► conjunction, connection
connu (-ue) ► household, known
   bien connu (-ue) ► familiar, famous, well-known
conque ► conch
conquérir ► conquer
conquête ► conquest
consacrer ► appropriate, dedicate, devote, spend
   consacrer du temps ► put in
consciemment ► consciously [conscious]
conscience ► conscience, consciousness, sense

(prise de) conscience ▸ awareness [aware]

consciencieusement ▸ carefully [careful], earnestly [earnest]

consciencieux (-euse) ▸ careful, earnest, thorough

conscient (-ente) ▸ awake, aware, conscious

conscription ▸ draft

conseil ▸ advice, board, caution, corporation, council, counsel, pointer, tip[3]

conseillé (-ée) ▸ advisable

conseiller (-ère) ▸ advise, counsel, consultant, council, councillor, counsellor

   conseiller (-ère) municipal ▸ councillor

consensus ▸ accord, consensus

consentant (-ante) ▸ agreeable, game

consentement ▸ accord, approval, consent

consentir ▸ consent, extend

   consentir à ▸ agree

   consentir d'un signe de tête ▸ nod

   consentir un rabais ▸ rebate

conséquence ▸ consequence, effect

   en conséquence ▸ accordingly [accord], consequently

conséquent (-ente) ▸ consistent

   par conséquent ▸ consequently, hence, therefore, thus

conservateur (-trice) ▸ conservative

   Parti progressiste-conservateur (du Canada) ▸ Progressive Conservative Party, Conservative Party

   de manière conservatrice ▸ conservatively [conservative]

conservation ▸ conservation, preservation

   agent de conservation ▸ preservative

conserve ▸ can[2]

   boîte de conserve ▸ can[2]

   mettre en conserve ▸ can[2]

conserver ▸ conserve, keep, maintain, preserve, retain

considérable ▸ considerable, extensive, grand, healthy, sizeable [size], wide

considérablement ▸ considerably [considerable], extensively [extensive], significantly [significant], substantially [substantial], vastly [vast]

considération ▸ consideration, regard, thoughtfulness [thoughtful]

   traiter sans considération ▸ slight

considérer ▸ consider, contemplate, deliberate, entertain, esteem, feel, ponder, regard, view

consigne[1] ▸ order, instruction

   donner des consignes ▸ brief

bulletin de **consigne[2]** ▸ check

consigner ▸ log, record

consistant (-ante) ▸ thick

consister ▸ consist

consœur ▸ colleague

consoler ▸ comfort

consolider ▸ confirm

consommateur (-trice) ▸ consumer

consommation ▸ intake

   consommation de carburant au mille (= au kilomètre) ▸ mileage

consommer ▸ consume, use

consonne ▸ consonant

conspiration ▸ conspiracy, design, plot

conspirer ▸ conspire, hatch[1], plot, scheme

constamment ▸ constantly [constant]

constant (-ante) ▸ constant, firm[1]

constater ▸ note, remark

constellation ▸ constellation

consternation ▸ dismay

consterner ▸ dismay

constituer ▸ compose, establish, found[2], represent

   constitué en corporation ▸ corporate [corporation]

constitution ▸ constitution, make-up

constitutionnel (-elle) ▸ constitutional

constructif (-ive) ▸ constructive, positive

construction ▸ build, building, construction, structure

   bois de construction ▸ lumber[1], timber

construire ▸ bridge, build, construct, erect, form, make, put up

consultant (-ante) ▸ consultant

consulter ▸ consult, refer

consumer ▸ burn, consume

   se consumer de colère ▸ smoulder

contact ▸ connection, contact

   (en) contact (avec) ▸ touch

   avoir le sens des contacts ▸ relate

   entrer en contact ▸ clash

   garder (perdre) contact ▸ keep (lose) track of

contacter ▸ contact

contagieux (-euse) ▸ contagious

contagion ▸ infection

contamination ▸ infection

contaminer ▸ infect

conte ▸ story, tale

   conte folklorique ▸ folk tale

   conte populaire ▸ folk tale

contempler ▸ contemplate, gaze

contemporain (-aine) ▸ contemporary

contenance ▸ content[1], front

contenant ▸ can[2], container, tub

contenir ▸ accommodate, choke, contain, control, hold[1], stem[2]

content (-ente) ▸ content[2], glad

contentement ▸ gladness [glad]

contenter ► content[2]
contenu ► content[1]
contenu (-ue) ► control
contestable ► objectionable [objection], unsound
contestation ► protest
contester ► challenge, contest, dispute, question
conteur (-euse) ► teller
contexte ► context
continent ► continent, mainland
  Continent (le) ► continent
continental (-ale, -aux) ► continental
continu (-ue) ► constant, continuous, relentless, solid, steady
continuel (-elle) ► continual, eternal, perpetual
continuellement ► constantly [constant], continually [continual], continuously [continuous], endlessly [endless], eternally [eternal], forever, relentlessly [relentless]
continuer ► continue, persist, proceed
contour ► outline
contourner ► round, skirt
contracter ► contract
contraction ► contraction
contradiction ► contradiction
contraindre ► compel, force, obligate, oblige, pressure
contrainte ► restraint
  sans contrainte ► freely [free]
contraire ► contrary, opposite, reverse
  au contraire ► on (to) the contrary
  contraire à ► alien
contrairement ► counter[2], on (to) the contrary, unlike
contrariant (-ante) ► vex
contrarié (-ée) ► upset
contrarier ► annoy, antagonize, cross, interfere, irritate, ruffle, spite, thwart, upset, vex
  ne pas contrarier ► humour
contrariété ► disappointment, upset
contraste ► contrast
contraster ► contrast
contrat ► contract, deed
contravention ► fine[2], ticket
  donner une contravention ► fine[2], ticket
contre ► against, versus
contre-attaquer ► counter[2]
faire de la **contrebande** ► smuggle
contrebandier (-ière) ► smuggler [smuggle]
contrebasse ► bass[1]
contrecarrer ► counter[2], foil[1], frustrate, interfere, thwart
à **contrecœur** ► reluctantly [reluctant]
contredire ► contradict
contrefaçon ► imitation
contrefaire ► fake, pirate

contrepoison ► antidote
contretemps ► hitch, mishap, setback
contrevenant (-ante) ► violator [violate]
contribuable ► taxpayer [tax]
contribuer ► chip in, contribute
  contribuer à ► contribute to
contribution ► contribution, due
  contributions ► tax
contrôle ► check, control
  hors de contrôle ► runaway
contrôler ► check, control, in check, monitor
controverse ► controversy
controversé (-ée) ► controversial [controversy]
contusion ► bruise
contusionner ► bruise
convaincre ► coax, convince, persuade, talk
convenable ► acceptable, appropriate, convenient, correct, decent, fit[1], likely, suitable
convenablement ► appropriately [appropriate], conveniently [convenient], correctly [correct], decently [decent], properly [proper], respectably [respectable], suitably [suitable]
convenance ► convention, etiquette
convenir ► do, fit[1], suit
  convenir de ► agree, arrange
  qui convient ► due
convention ► convention
conventionnel (-elle) ► conventional
convenu (-ue) ► certain
conversation ► chat, conversation, talk
converti (-ie) ► convert
convertir ► convert, make over
convexe ► convex
conviction ► belief, conviction, politics
  avec conviction ► deadly
  pièce à conviction ► exhibit
  avoir la force de ses convictions ► backbone
convier ► invite
convivial (-ale, -aux) ► user-friendly
convoiter ► desire
convoitise ► desire
convoquer ► summon
se **convulser** ► twitch
coopérant (-ante) ► cooperative
coopératif (-ive) ► cooperative
coopération ► pool[2]
coopérative ► cooperative
coopérer ► chip in, cooperate
coordination ► coordination [coordinate]
coordonner ► coordinate
copain (copine) ► buddy, chum, comrade, pal
copie ► copy, imitation, replica
  copie conforme ► twin

copie exacte ▸ duplicate
copié (-ée) ▸ imitation
copier ▸ copy, imitate, plagiarize
copieux (-euse) ▸ generous, plentiful [plenty]
copropriété ▸ condominium
   en copropriété ▸ cooperative
copyright ▸ copyright
coq ▸ bantam, cock, rooster
   coq nain ▸ bantam
   chant du coq ▸ crow[2]
coque ▸ hull
coqueluche ▸ whooping couch
coquet (-ette) ▸ tidy
coquillage ▸ shell
   coquillages ▸ shellfish
coquille ▸ shell
   coquille Saint-Jacques ▸ scallop
coquin (-ine) ▸ arch[2], rascal
cor ▸ corn[2]
corail (-aux) ▸ coral
Coran ▸ Koran
corbeau (-eaux) ▸ crow[1], raven
   noir (noire) comme un corbeau ▸
   raven
corbeille ▸ bin
   corbeille à papier ▸ wastebasket
cordage ▸ guy[1]
corde ▸ cord, guy[1], line[1], rope
   cordes ▸ string
   corde à linge ▸ clothes-lines
   attacher à l'aide d'une corde ▸ rope
   délimiter à l'aide d'une corde ▸ rope
   off [rope]
   être sur la corde raide ▸ out on the limb
cordée ▸ cord
corder ▸ rope
cordial (-ale, -aux) ▸ cordial, hearty, warm
cordialement ▸ cordially [cordial], heartily
[hearty], warmly [warm]
cordialité ▸ heartiness [hearty]
   sans cordialité ▸ cold
cordon électrique ▸ cord
coriace ▸ rock[1], tough
corne ▸ horn
   bovin à cornes ▸ buffalo
corneille ▸ crow[1]
cornemuse ▸ bagpipe
cornet ▸ cone, trumpet
corniche ▸ ledge
cornichon ▸ pickle
cornu (-ue) ▸ horned [horn]
corporatif (-ive) ▸ corporate [corporation]
corporation ▸ corporation
   constitué en corporation ▸ corporate
   [corporation]
corps ▸ body, corps, corpse, frame
   du corps ▸ bodily

corps de métier ▸ profession
corps législatif ▸ legislature
corps organisé ▸ brigade
garde du corps ▸ bodyguard
corpulent (-ente) ▸ stout
corral ▸ corral
   enfermer dans un corral ▸ corral
correct (-ecte) ▸ correct, fair[1], fit[1], right
correctement ▸ correctly [correct], properly
[proper]
correctif (-ive) ▸ remedial
donner une (bonne) correction ▸ thrash
correspondance ▸ connection, transfer
correspondant (-ante) ▸ correspondent
correspondre ▸ correspond
corridor ▸ corridor, hall, passage
corriger ▸ amend, correct, edit, heal, repair,
revise, right
   corriger les épreuves ▸ proofread
corroborer ▸ confirm, support
corroder ▸ corrode, erode
corrompre ▸ bribe, corrupt, poison, warp
corrompu (-ue) ▸ corrupt
corrosion ▸ erosion [erode]
corsaire ▸ pirate
cortège ▸ escort, parade, procession
corvée ▸ chore
cosse ▸ bean, hull, pod
costaud (-aude) ▸ husky[1]
costume ▸ costume, suit
costumer ▸ disguise
côte ▸ climb, coast, descent, rib, rise, shore
côté ▸ face, side
   à côté ▸ next door
   à côté de ▸ beside, by
   de côté ▸ aside, sideways
   de l'autre côté de ▸ across
   point de côté ▸ stitch
   mettre de côté ▸ put aside, salt
   passer à coté ▸ wide
   s'étendre de tous les côtés ▸ sprawl
côtelette ▸ chop
côtier (-ière) ▸ coastal [coast], offshore
cotisation ▸ due
cotiser ▸ contribute
coton ▸ cotton
cottage ▸ cottage
cou ▸ neck
   peau (du cou) ▸ scruff
   étirer le cou ▸ crane
au couchant ▸ west
couche ▸ bed, blanket, coat, diaper, film,
layer
   couche arable ▸ topsoil
   en une couche épaisse ▸ thick
coucher[1] ▸ put to bed
   se coucher ▸ go to bed, lie down

chambre à coucher ▸ bedroom
couché (-ée) sur le ventre ▸ prone
aller se coucher ▸ retire
coucher[2] **(de soleil)** ▸ sunset
couchette ▸ berth
coucou ▸ cuckoo
coude ▸ crook, elbow
   coup de coude ▸ nudge
   se frayer un chemin des coudes ▸ elbow
   donner un coup de coude ▸ dig
   pousser du coude ▸ nudge
coudre ▸ seam, sew, stitch
   machine à coudre ▸ sewing machine
couguar ▸ cougar
couinement ▸ squeak
couiner ▸ squeak
coulant (-ante) ▸ fluid
couler ▸ cast, flow, run, sift, sink
   couler doucement ▸ trickle
   couler lentement ▸ dribble
   couler à flots ▸ stream
couleur ▸ colour, suit
   couleur fondamentale ▸ primary colour
   couleur primaire ▸ primary colour
couleuvre ▸ garter snake
coulisse ▸ wing
couloir ▸ corridor, hall, lane, passage
coup ▸ blow[2], chop, deal, flap, hit, knock, lunge, move, poke, stroke[1], thrust, yank
   petit coup ▸ bob, flip, tap[1], tug
   petit coup sec ▸ rap[1]
   petit coup de doigt ▸ prod
   petit coup de ciseaux ▸ snip
   grand coup ▸ whack
   à coup ▸ jolt
   un seul coup ▸ one fell swoop [swoop]
   tout d'un coup ▸ flash
   coup à trois buts ▸ triple
   coup de circuit ▸ homerun
   coup de balai ▸ sweep
   coup de bec ▸ peck
   coup de coude ▸ nudge
   coup de couteau ▸ stab
   coup de feu ▸ shot[1]
   coup de fil ▸ ring[2]
   coup de fouet ▸ lash[1], whiplash
   coup de froid ▸ snap
   coup de klaxon ▸ honk, toot
   coup de langue ▸ lick
   coup de pied ▸ kick
   coup (de pile ou face) ▸ toss
   coup de poing ▸ punch[1]
   coup de sifflet ▸ toot
   coup de soleil ▸ sunburn
   coup de tapette ▸ swat
   coup de téléphone ▸ ring[2]

coup de théâtre ▸ twist
coup de vent ▸ gale
coup défendu ▸ foul
coup d'envoi ▸ kick off
coup d'essai ▸ venture
coup d'œil ▸ glance, look, peek, peep[1], squint
coup droit ▸ drive
coup interdit ▸ foul
coup irrégulier ▸ foul
coup sec ▸ twitch
coup sûr ▸ hit
coup violent ▸ slug[2]
donner un coup ▸ spank
donner des coups de ▸ stab
donner un (des) coup(s) de patte à ▸ paw
donner un coup de baguette ▸ switch
donner un coup de coude ▸ dig
donner un coup de couteau ▸ knife
donner un coup de fer ▸ iron
donner un coup de klaxon ▸ toot
donner un coup de main ▸ lend a hand
donner un coup de pied ▸ boot, kick
donner un coup de poing ▸ punch[1]
donner un coup de sifflet ▸ toot
donner un coup d'épaule ▸ dig
donner un coup d'œil ▸ squint
donner un coup sec ▸ rap[1]
s'ouvrir d'un coup ▸ spring
frapper à grands coups ▸ pound[2]
coupable ▸ culprit, guilty, sinful [sin]
   non coupable ▸ innocent
   déclarer coupable ▸ convict
   reconnaître coupable ▸ convict
coupant (-ante) ▸ cutting
coupe ▸ cup
   coupe glacée ▸ sundae
   coupe d'entretien ▸ trim
   mettre en forme de coupe ▸ cup
coupe-circuit ▸ breaker
coupe ongle ▸ clipper
couper ▸ bite, chop, clip[1], crop, cut, dock[2], hack, interrupt, sever, shut, slice, slit, snip, water
   couper en cube ▸ cube
   couper en cubes ▸ dice
   couper en dés ▸ cube, dice
   couper en deux ▸ bisect
   couper en tranches ▸ slice
coupe-vent ▸ windbreaker
couple ▸ couple, pair
coupler ▸ couple
couplet ▸ verse
coupon ▸ coupon
coupure ▸ cut, cutting, nick
   coupure de presse ▸ clipping

cour[1] ► court
   Cour suprême ► Supreme Court
cour[2] ► court
cour[3] ► ground[1], yard[1]
   cour de récréation ► playground
courage ► backbone, boldness [bold], courage, daring, heart, nerve, pluck, valour
courageusement ► boldly [bold]
courageux (-euse) ► bold, brave, courageous, daring, fearless, game, heroic, valiant
couramment ► usually
courant ► current, electricity, flow, swing, tide
   courant alternatif ► alternating current (AC)
   courant continu ► direct current (DC)
   courant d'air ► draft
   courant électrique ► power
   courant sous-marin ► undertow
   descendre un courant ► float
   être au courant ► in the know
   tenir au courant ► post[2]
courant (-ante) ► common, current, frequent, stock, usual
courbaturé (-ée) ► lame
courbe ► curve
   balle courbe ► curve
courbé (-ée) ► bent, crooked
courber ► arch[1], bend, crook, hang, hunch, incline, weigh down [weigh]
   se courber ► curve
coureur (-euse) ► runner
   coureur des bois ► coureur de bois
courge ► squash[2]
courgette ► zucchini
courir ► race[1], run
   courir après ► chase
   courir précipitamment ► scuttle
   courir le risque ► chance, risk
couronne ► crown, wreath
   couronne de roses ou d'épines ► crown
   Terre de la couronne ► Crown land
couronnement ► crown
couronner ► cap, crown
   couronné (-ée) de succès ► successful
courriel ► electronic mail
courrier ► courier, mail[1], post[2]
   courrier électronique ► electronic mail
courroie ► belt, strap
   attacher avec une courroie ► strap
courroux ► wrath
cours[1] ► class, course, lecture, lesson
   donner un cours ► lecture
   donner des cours particuliers à ► tutor
cours[2] ► tide
   en cours ► current, in progress [progress]

   donner libre cours ► vent
   laisser libre cours ► vent
course ► errand, race[1], run
   course de haies ► hurdle
   course de relais ► relay
   piste de course hippique ► turf
   faire les courses ► market
   faire des courses ► to run an errand
   faire la course ► race[1]
coursier ► steed
court ► court
court (courte) ► capsule, short
   à court de ► short
   prendre de court ► beat
courtaud (-aude) ► squat, stubby [stub]
court-circuit ► short circuit
courtepointe ► quilt
courtier (en valeurs mobilières) ► broker, stockbroker
courtiser ► court
court-métrage ► short
courtois (-oise) ► civil, courteous
courtoisement ► courteously [courteous]
courtoisie ► courteousness [courteous], courtesy
couseur (-euse) ► sewer
cousin (-ine) ► cousin
coussin ► couch, cushion, pad
   mettre un coussin ► cushion
coussinet ► pad
coût ► charge, cost
couteau (-eaux) ► knife
   couteau (-eaux) de poche ► jack-knife
   coup de couteau ► stab
   donner un coup de couteau ► knife
   tailler au couteau ► whittle
coutellerie ► cutlery
coûter ► cost
coûteux (-euse) ► costly
   peu coûteux (-euse) ► inexpensive
coutume ► custom, ritual, tradition
coutumier (-ière) ► customary
couture ► seam
   faire une couture ► seam
couturier (-ière) ► sewer, tailor
couvée ► brood, clutch[2]
couver ► brew, brood, smoulder
couvercle ► lid, top[1]
couvert ► cloudy
   à couvert ► sheltered [shelter]
   mettre le couvert ► set
couverts ► cutlery
couverture ► blanket, cover, coverage, covering, front, insurance, jacket
couveuse ► incubator
couvre-chaussures ► overshoe
couvre-feu ► curfew

couvre-lit ▸ spread
couvreur (-euse) ▸ roofer [roof]
couvrir ▸ cap, coat, cover, damp, drown, heap, invade, litter, mantle, smother
    se couvrir ▸ cloud
    se couvrir de plaques ▸ break out
    couvrir de bardeaux ▸ shingle
    couvrir de honte ▸ disgrace
    couvrir de perles ▸ bead
    couvrir de tuiles ▸ tile
    couvrir d'un toit ▸ roof
    couvrir d'un voile ▸ veil
covoiturage ▸ pool^2
cow-boy ▸ cowhand
cowichan ▸ Cowichan
coyote ▸ coyote
crabe ▸ crab
crachat ▸ spit^1
cracher ▸ spit^1
crachin ▸ drizzle
    de crachin ▸ drizzly
craie ▸ chalk
craindre ▸ apprehend, dread, fear
crainte ▸ apprehension, awe, doubt, fear, misgiving, nervousness [nervous]
craintif (-ive) ▸ timid
craintivement ▸ timidly [timid]
cramoisi (-ie) ▸ crimson
crampe ▸ cramp, kink
crampon ▸ clamp, stud, spike^1, staple^1
cramponner ▸ clamp
    se cramponner ▸ cling, clutch^1
cran ▸ step, wave
crâne ▸ skull
    faire du bourrage de crâne ▸ brainwash
crapaud ▸ toad
craquant (-ante) ▸ crisp
craquelin ▸ cracker
craquelure ▸ crack
craquement ▸ creak, crunch
craquer ▸ crack, creak
    qui craque ▸ creaky [creak]
    faire craquer ▸ crunch
crasse ▸ dirt
crasseux (-euse) ▸ dirty, filthy
cratère ▸ cavity, crater
cravache ▸ crop, lash^1, switch, whip
cravate ▸ tie
crawl ▸ crawl
crayon ▸ crayon, pencil
    dessiner au crayon ▸ pencil
    écrire à l'aide d'un crayon ▸ pencil
créateur (-trice) ▸ architect, designer [design], father
créatif (-ive) ▸ creative
création ▸ creation, foundation, setting
    création de l'imagination ▸ fiction

créativité ▸ imagination
créature ▸ creature, thing
crécelle ▸ rattle
crèche ▸ crib
crédit ▸ credit
créditer ▸ credit
cree ▸ Cree
créer ▸ compose, create, establish, found^2, invent
crème ▸ cream, polish
    la crème de ▸ cream
    crème anglaise ▸ custard
    crème glacée ▸ ice cream
    crème pâtissière ▸ custard
    crème renversée ▸ custard
    crème sure ▸ sour cream
crémerie ▸ dairy
créneau (-eaux) ▸ slot
crêpe ▸ pancake
crêpelé (-ée) ▸ fuzzy
crépitement ▸ rattle
crépiter ▸ crackle, rattle, sputter
crépu (-ue) ▸ fuzzy
crépuscule ▸ dusk, twilight
cresson ▸ watercress
crête ▸ comb, crest, ledge, ridge, top^1
creuser ▸ bore^2, burrow, dig, excavate, hollow, sink
    creuser un canal ▸ channel
    creuser un tunnel ▸ tunnel
    se creuser la cervelle ▸ rack one's brain
    se creuser la tête ▸ rack one's brain
creux ▸ bowl^1, depression, hollow
creux (-euse) ▸ empty, hollow
crevaison ▸ puncture
crevasse ▸ crack, crevasse
crevasser ▸ chap^2, crack
crever ▸ puncture
crevette ▸ shrimp
cri^1 ▸ call, cry, honk, shout, whoop, yell
    cri de triomphe ▸ crow^2
    cri discordant ▸ squall^2
    cri perçant ▸ scream, screech, shriek, squeal
    cri rauque ▸ squall^2, squawk
    dernier cri ▸ fashion, state-of-the-art
    pousser un cri ▸ honk, scream, shriek
    pousser des cris ▸ whoop
    pousser des petits cris ▸ squeak
cri^2 ▸ Cree
criant (-ante) ▸ rank^2
criard (-arde) ▸ jazzy [jazz], loud, shrill
crible ▸ sieve
cribler ▸ pelt^1, riddle^2, sift
cric ▸ jack
    soulever avec un cric ▸ jack

cricket ► cricket
crier ► call, cry, grind, hoot, scream, shout, squall[2], yell
crieur (-euse) ► herald
crime ► crime
criminel (-elle) ► criminal
    criminel (-elle) d'État ► traitor
crinière ► mane
crique ► cove, creek, inlet
crise ► attack, crisis, seizure, slump
    crise cardiaque ► heart attack
    crise de colère ► tantrum
crispation ► contraction
crispé (-ée) ► tense[1]
crisper ► tense[1]
    se crisper ► clench
crissement ► crunch, screech
crisser ► grate, grind, jar, screech, squeak
cristal (-aux) ► crystal
cristallin ► lens
critère ► standard
critique[1] ► acute, critical, crucial
    d'un œil critique ► critically [critical]
    de façon critique ► critically [critical]
critique[2] ► critic, criticism [criticize], review
    faire la critique ► criticize
    faire la critique d'une œuvre ► review
critiquer ► carp[2], condemn, criticize, put down, quarrel, review
croassement ► croak
croasser ► croak
crochet ► crochet, hanger, hook
    vivre aux crochets de ► bum
crochu (-ue) ► crooked, hooked [hook]
crocodile ► crocodile
croire ► believe, credit, expect, guess, imagine, think
    croire fermement ► bet
    se croire ► fancy
    faire croire ► make believe
croisade ► crusade
croisement ► cross, crossing
croiser ► cross, cruise, cut, fold, meet
croiseur ► cruiser
croisière ► cruise
    vitesse de croisière ► cruise
croissance ► growth
croissant (-ante) ► crescent
    croissant de lune ► crescent
croître ► grow, wax[2]
croix ► cross
croquant (-ante) ► crisp
croquer ► bite
croquet ► croquet
croquis ► design, draft, drawing, sketch
    faire des croquis ► sketch
crosse ► lacrosse

crosse de fougère ► fiddlehead
crotale ► rattlesnake
croupe ► brow, rump
croustillant (-ante) ► crusty [crust]
    qualité de ce qui est croustillant ► crispness [crisp]
croustilles ► chip
croûte ► crust, rind, scab
croyance ► belief, conviction
    croyances ► religion
cru ► vintage
cru (crue) ► raw
cruauté ► cruelty [cruel], unkindness [unkind], wickedness [wicked]
cruche ► jug, pitcher[1]
crucial (-ale, -aux) ► crucial
    de façon cruciale ► vitally [vital]
crue ► flood
cruel (-elle) ► cruel, harsh, ill, ruthlessness [ruthless], unkind, woeful [woe]
cruellement ► cruelly [cruel], unkindly [unkind], woefully [woe]
crustacé ► crustacean, shellfish
cube ► cube
    mettre au cube ► cube
cubique ► cubic
cueillette ► crop
    aller à la cueillette des baies ► berry
cueillir ► gather, harvest, pick[1], pluck
cuiller ► scoop, spoon
    petite cuiller ► teaspoon
    cuiller à café ► teaspoon
    cuiller à soupe ► tablespoon
    cuiller de service ► tablespoon
    pêcher à la cuiller ► troll[1]
    prendre à la cuiller ► spoon
    verser à la cuiller ► spoon
cuillerée ► spoonful [spoon]
    cuillerée à café ► teaspoon
    cuillerée à soupe ► tablespoon
cuir ► hide[2], leather
    cuir chevelu ► scalp
    cuir épais ► buff
    veau (cuir de) ► calf[1]
cuire ► cook
    cuire à la vapeur ► steam
    cuire au four ► bake
    bien cuit (cuite) ► well-done
    peu cuit (cuite) ► rare[2]
cuisine ► caboose, cuisine, kitchen
cuisiner ► cook, grill, pump
cuisinier (-ière) ► cook
cuisinière ► stove
cuisse ► thigh
cuit-vapeur ► steamer
cuivre ► brass, copper, horn

cuivré (-ée) ► copper
culbute ► somersault
  faire des culbutes ► tumble
  faire la culbute ► somersault
culbuter ► tumble
cul-de-sac ► dead end
culot ► cheek, nerve
culotte ► drawer, rump
  culotte courte ► short
culpabilité ► guilt
culte ► cult, religion, worship
  rendre un culte à ► worship
  vouer un culte à ► worship
cultivateur (-trice) ► tiller [tilt[2]]
cultiver ► breed, cultivate, farm, raise, tilt[2]
culture ► cultivation [cultivate], culture, depth
  culture de base ► staple[2]
cupide ► greedy
cupidement ► greedily [greedy]
cupidité ► greed
curateur (-trice) ► trustee
curatif (-ive) ► remedial
cure-dent ► toothpick
curieusement ► curiously [curious], oddly [odd]
curieux (-euse) ► curious, funny, inquisitive, nosy, odd, peculiar, quaint, weird, whimsical
curiosité ► curiosity
curling ► curling
  jouer au curling ► curl
curriculum vitæ ► résumé
curry ► curry
curseur ► cursor
cuve ► tank
cuvette ► basin
cycle ► cycle
cyclisme ► cycle
cycliste ► rider [ride]
cyclone ► cyclone
cygne ► swan
cylindre ► cylinder
cylindrique ► cylindrical [cylinder]
cymbale ► cymbal

D

dactylographier ► type
dague ► dagger
daim ► buck
dakota ► Dakota
dalle ► slab
dame ► king, lady
  jeu de dames ► checkers
dandinement ► waddle
se dandiner ► waddle
danger ► danger, gravity, hazard, peril
  sans danger ► safe, safely [safe]

  mettre en danger ► endanger
dangereusement ► perilously [peril], treacherously [treacherous]
dangereux (-euse) ► critical, dangerous [danger], perilous [peril], risky, treacherous, ugly
dans ► amid, in, inside, into, through
  partout dans ► throughout
danse ► dance, reel[3]
  danse carrée ► square dance
danser ► dance, shake a leg
  danser la valse ► waltz
  danser sur l'eau ► bob
  soirée dansante ► dance
dard ► sting
darne ► steak
date ► date[1]
  assigner une date ► date[1]
  date limite ► deadline
  donner une date ► date[1]
dater ► date[1]
datte ► date[2]
dauphin ► dolphin
davantage ► anymore, further, more
de ► a, an, from, of, off, outside
dé ► dice, die[2]
  couper en dés ► cube, dice
  dé à coudre ► thimble
déambulateur ► walker
débâcle ► break-up
déballer ► unwrap
débarcadère ► landing
débarquement ► landing
débarquer ► discharge, drop, land
débarrasser ► clear
  se débarrasser de ► discard, dispose, get rid of [rid], throw away, throw out
débat ► debate
débattre ► argue, debate
  se débattre ► struggle, thrash, wrestle
débauche ► licence, riot
débit ► delivery
débiter ► reel[1], spout
  débiter à toute allure ► rattle
déblayer ► clear
déboguer ► debug
débordement ► overflow
déborder ► overflow, swamp
debout ► standing, up, upright
  être debout ► stand
  se mettre debout ► stand
débris ► debris, refuse[2], wreckage
se débrouiller ► cope
début ► beginning, dawn, first, start
  au début ► initially [initial]
débutant (-ante) ► beginner, learner [learn], new, rookie

débuter ▸ begin, open
décadence ▸ decay
décalage ▸ lag
décalquer ▸ trace
décédé (-ée) ▸ dead, deceased
décéder ▸ die[1]
déceler ▸ detect
décembre ▸ December
décemment ▸ correctly [correct], decently [decent], honourably [honourable]
décennie ▸ decade
décent (-ente) ▸ decent
déception ▸ disappointment, upset
    coup d'une déception ▸ rebound
décerner ▸ award, confer
décès ▸ death
décevoir ▸ deceive, disappoint, dupe, frustrate
déchaîné (-ée) ▸ furious, riotous [riot]
se déchaîner ▸ rage
déchaînement ▸ rampage
décharger ▸ discharge, empty, fire, unload
    recevoir une décharge ▸ shock[1]
décharné (-ée) ▸ bony
déchet ▸ clipping, discard, garbage, waste
    déchets ▸ refuse[2], rubbish
déchiffrer ▸ decipher, decode
déchiqueté (-ée) ▸ jagged
déchiqueter ▸ shred
déchirement ▸ wrench
déchirer ▸ rip, tear[1]
    se déchirer ▸ pull
déchirure ▸ rip, slit, split, tear[1]
décibel ▸ decibel
décidé (-ée) ▸ decisive, game
    qui n'est pas décidé ▸ up in the air [air]
    ton décidé ▸ decisively [decisive]
décider ▸ choose, determine, fix, resolve, rule, settle
    se décider ▸ decide, resolve
décimal (-ale, -aux) ▸ decimal
décimale ▸ decimal
décisif (-ive) ▸ crucial, decisive, final
décision ▸ choice, decision, initiative
    avec décision ▸ decisively [decisive]
déclamer ▸ spout
déclaration ▸ declaration [declare], return, statement
déclarer ▸ claim, declare, proclaim, pronounce, rule, state
    déclarer coupable ▸ convict
    déclarer inhabitable ▸ condemn
déclencher ▸ activate, determine, spark, trigger
déclic ▸ click
déclin ▸ decay, decline, twilight
    être en déclin ▸ wane

déclinaison ▸ dip
décliner ▸ decline, dim, ebb, fade, wane
décocher ▸ discharge
décoder ▸ decipher, decode
décollage ▸ blast off, takeoff
décoller ▸ blast off, lift off, peel
se décolorer ▸ fade
décombre ▸ wreck, wreckage
    décombres ▸ rubble
décomposer ▸ analyse, decompose
décomposition ▸ decay
décompte ▸ count[1]
déconcentrer ▸ wander
déconcerter ▸ baffle, embarrass, rattle
décongélation ▸ thaw
décongeler ▸ defrost, thaw
déconseiller ▸ discourage, warn
décontracté (-ée) ▸ casual, cool
    de façon décontractée ▸ casually [casual], loose
décor ▸ scenery, set
décorateur (-trice) ▸ designer [design]
décoratif (-ive) ▸ ornamental [ornement]
décoration ▸ adornment [adorn], decoration, distinction, ornament, trimming
décorer ▸ adorn, deck, decorate, garnish, ornament, trim
décortiquer ▸ husk
découler ▸ result
découper ▸ carve, cut
découragement ▸ depression
décourager ▸ dampen, depress, discourage
découverte ▸ invention, strike
découvrir ▸ detect, discover, expose, find, invent, penetrate, strike, uncover, unlock
    se découvrir ▸ bare
décréter ▸ enact
décrire ▸ characterize, depict, describe, paint, picture
décrocher ▸ drop out
décroissance ▸ decrease
décroître ▸ decrease, wane
dédaigner ▸ scorn
dédain ▸ contempt
dédale ▸ labyrinth, maze
dedans ▸ in, inside, into, within
    au-dedans ▸ inside, inwardly [inward]
    en dedans ▸ inner, inward
dédicace ▸ dedication
dédicacer ▸ autograph
dédier ▸ dedicate
dédommagement ▸ compensation [compensate]
dédommager ▸ compensate
déduction ▸ conclusion, deduction
déduire ▸ conclude, deduce, deduct, gather, infer

déesse ► goddess
défaillance ► faint
défaire ► loosen, undo, untie
   se défaire de ► dispose, get rid of [rid]
défait (-aite) ► loose
défaite ► defeat, rout
défausse ► discard
défaut ► defect, fault, flaw, point, shortcoming, weakness
   faire défaut ► fail
   prendre en défaut ► fault
défavorable ► adverse
défavorablement ► adversely
faire **défection** ► defect, desert[2]
défectueux (-euse) ► fault
défectuosité ► defect
défendre ► contest, defend, forbid, prohibit
défense ► defence, ivory, plea, tusk
défenseur ► advocate, defence, guard
défensif (-ive) ► defensive
défensive ► defensive
   sur la défensive ► defensively [defensive]
défensivement ► defensively [defensive]
avec **déférence** ► reverently [reverence]
déférer ► defer[2]
déferler ► surge
défi ► challenge, dare, defiance [defiant]
   représenter un défi ► challenge
déficit ► deficiency, deficit
défier ► challenge, dare, defy
défilé ► parade, procession
défiler ► scroll
   se défiler ► back out
défigurer ► deface
définir ► define
définitif (-ive) ► conclusive [conclude], final
   en définitive ► eventually [eventual]
définition ► definition, resolution
défoncer ► knock
déformer ► distort, twist
défraîchi (-ie) ► dingy
défricher ► pioneer
défunt (-unte) ► dead, deceased, late, the dead [dead], the deceased [deceased]
dégagement ► ice
dégager ► clear, excavate, liberate
   dégager des bulles ► bubble
dégainer ► draw
dégel ► thaw
dégeler ► thaw
dégivrer ► defrost
déglutir ► swallow[1]
dégonflé (-ée) ► cowardly, flat[1]
dégonfler ► bleed
dégouliner ► drip, trickle
dégourdi (-ie) ► smart

dégoût ► contempt
dégoûtant (-antc) ► beastly [beast], filthy
dégoûter ► disgust, repel
dégoutter ► drip
dégrader ► deface
   se dégrader ► worsen
se **délasser** ► unwind
dégraisser ► skim
degré ► degree
   par degrés ► progressive
dégringolade ► drop
dégringoler ► tumble
dégriser ► sober
déguenillé (-ée) ► tattered
déguerpir ► bolt
dégueulasse ► rat
déguisement ► costume, disguise
déguiser ► disguise
dégustateur (-trice) ► taste
dehors ► exterior, outdoor, outside
   en dehors de ► out
   en dehors du sujet ► beside
déité ► deity
déjà ► already, ever
déjeuner[1] ► eat
petit **déjeuner**[2] ► breakfast
   prendre le petit déjeuner ► breakfast
déjouer ► foil[1], frustrate
délabré -(ée) ► battered [batter[3]], dilapidated, run-down
délai ► delay, lag
délaissé (-ée) ► lonely
délaisser ► abandon, neglect
délassement ► refreshment
se **délasser** ► unwind
délayer ► dilute
délectation ► relish
se **délecter** ► delight, feast, relish
délégation ► delegation
délégué (-ée) ► delegate
déléguer ► delegate
délibération ► debate
délibéré (-ée) ► deliberate, intentional [intention]
délibérément ► deliberately [deliberate], purposely [purpose]
délicat (-ate) ► dainty, delicate, exquisite, fine[1], fragile, light[2], porcelain, tender[1], ticklish
délicatement ► daintily [dainty], delicately [delicate], ease, lightly [light[2]]
délicatesse ► grace, tact, tenderness [tender[1]]
délice ► deliciousness [delicious]
délicieusement ► deliciously [delicious], delightfully [delightful]
délicieux (-euse) ► delicious, delightful, tasty

733

délier ▶ loose, loosen
délimiter ▶ bound[3], define, measure
    délimiter à l'aide d'une corde ▶ rope off [rope]
délit ▶ crime, offence
délivrer ▶ deliver, serve
déloyal (-ale, -aux) ▶ treacherous
delta ▶ delta
déluge ▶ barrage, flood, shower
demain ▶ tomorrow
demande ▶ application, call, claim, clamour, demand, market, request
    demande en mariage ▶ proposal
demander ▶ ask, claim, demand, enquire, inquire, query, request, require, seek, take
    se demander ▶ debate, wonder
    (en) demander ▶ ask
    demander de l'aide ▶ appeal
    demander en mariage ▶ propose
    demander pardon ▶ pardon me or I beg your pardon
    demander poliment ▶ request
démangeaison ▶ itch
démanger ▶ itch
    qui démange ▶ itchy [itch]
démarche ▶ approach, gait
    démarche chancelante ▶ wobble
    démarche molasse ▶ slouch
    avoir une démarche molasse ▶ slouch
démarrer ▶ commence, start, zoom
démasquer ▶ expose
démêler ▶ decipher
déménager ▶ move
dément (-ente) ▶ insane, lunatic, mad
démenti ▶ contradiction, denial
démesuré (-ée) ▶ intense
demeure ▶ home
demeurer ▶ dwell, live[1], remain
demi (-ie) ▶ half
demi-cercle ▶ semicircle
demie ▶ half
demi-finale ▶ semifinal
demi-finaliste ▶ semifinalist [semifinal]
démission ▶ resignation
démissionner ▶ resign
démocrate ▶ democrat [democracy]
démocratie ▶ democracy
démocratique ▶ democratic
    Nouveau parti démocratique ▶ New Democratic Party
démodé (-ée) ▶ old-fashioned, out
demoiselle ▶ dragonfly
démolir ▶ blast, demolish, knock, pan, pull, total, wreck
démon ▶ demon, devil
démonstration ▶ demonstration, exhibition, show

    faire une démonstration ▶ demonstrate
démontable ▶ sectional [section]
démonter ▶ apart
démontrer ▶ chart, demonstrate, establish, prove
démoralisé (-ée) ▶ wretched
démunir ▶ deplete
dénaturer ▶ distort
dene ▶ Dene
dénégation ▶ denial
déneiger ▶ snowplough
dénicheur (-euse) de talents ▶ scout
dénigrer ▶ criticize, put down
dénivellation ▶ drop
dénombrer ▶ count[1]
dénominateur ▶ denominator
dénoncer ▶ charge, denounce, inform
dénoter ▶ indicate
dénouer ▶ undo, untie
dense ▶ compact, dense, thick
densément ▶ densely [dense]
densité ▶ density
dent ▶ prong, tine, tooth
    dents ▶ teeth
    brosse à dents ▶ toothbrush
    dent de sagesse ▶ wisdom tooth
dentaire ▶ dental
dentelé (-ée) ▶ jagged
dentelle ▶ lace
    de dentelle ▶ lacy [lace]
faire de la dentelure ▶ lace
dentifrice ▶ toothpaste
dentiste ▶ dentist
dénudé (-ée) ▶ bare, naked, void
dénuder ▶ expose
dénué (-ée) de ▶ empty
dénuement ▶ need
dépanner ▶ tide
dépareillé (-ée) ▶ odd
départ ▶ departure, start
    au départ ▶ originally
    départ brusque ▶ bolt
département ▶ department
    du département ▶ departmental [department]
départemental (-ale) ▶ departmental [department]
dépasser ▶ exceed, overtake, pass, poke, protrude, top[1]
se dépêcher ▶ get a move on, hurry, hustle, race[1], rush[1], shake a leg
dépeindre ▶ depict, describe, paint, picture, portray
dépendance ▶ dependence [depend]
dépendant (-ante) ▶ addicted, dependent
dépendre ▶ depend, rely
dépens ▶ cost, expense

dépense ► expense
dépenser ► spend
dépensier (-ière) ► extravagant, spender [spend]
dépérir ► waste, wither
dépister ► trace, track
en dépit de ► despite
déplacé (-ée) ► off-key, unseemly
déplacer ► move, shift
   se déplacer ► ride, travel
   qui n'a pas été déplacé ► unmoved
   (se) déplacer brusquement ► pop[1]
   se déplacer maladroitement ► barge
   se déplacer à pied ► tramp
déplaire ► offend
déplaisant (-ante) ► disagreeable, nasty, unwelcome
dépliant ► brochure, leaflet, pamphlet
déplier ► unfold
déployer ► fan[1], spread
   rire à gorge déployée ► roar
déposer ► deposit, drop, drop off, dump, file[1]
déposséder ► deprive
dépôt ► deposit, depot, sediment
   faire un dépôt ► deposit
dépotoir ► dump
dépouillé (-ée) ► bald, naked
dépouiller ► skin
   se dépouiller ► shed[2]
dépourvu (-ue) ► bald, void
dépravé (-ée) ► corrupt
dépraver ► corrupt
dépression ► breakdown, depression, trough
déprimé (-ée) ► low, wretched
déprimer ► depress
depuis ► onwards, since
   depuis (que) ► since
déraciner ► uproot
déraisonnable ► unreasonable
   de façon déraisonnable ► unreasonably [unreasonable]
déraisonner ► rave
dérangé (-ée) ► upset
dérangement ► disruption [disrupt]
déranger ► agitate, bother, disorder, disrupt, distract, disturb, interrupt, offend, ruffle, trouble, upset
dérapage ► skid
déraper ► skid
dérider ► lighten[2]
dériver ► derive, drift
dernier (-ière) ► bottom, extreme, final, last[1], latter, least, terminal, top[1], ultimate
   en dernier ► last[1]
   le dernier ► least
dernièrement ► lately, recently [recent]
à la dérobée ► on the sly [sly], stealth

dérober ► balk, rob
   se dérober ► evade, give
dérogation ► departure
déroger ► depart
se dérouler ► run, unwind
dérouter ► rout
   mettre en déroute ► rout
dérouter ► bewilder, divert
derrière ► behind, rear[1], seat
   de derrière ► hind, rear[1]
   traîner derrière ► lag
des ► voir de
désabusé (-ée) ► wry
désaccord ► clash, difference, friction, opposition, quarrel
   en désaccord ► at odds, in (out) of tune
   être en désaccord ► conflict, disagree
désaccordé (-ée) ► in (out) of tune
désaffectionner ► alienate
désagréable ► cantankerous, disagreeable, harsh, horrible, unpleasant
   très désagréable ► terrible
   d'une façon désagréable ► disagreeably [disagreeable]
désagréablement ► disagreeably [disagreeable], unpleasantly [unpleasant]
désagréger ► disintegrate
désappointement ► disappointment, upset
désappointer ► disappoint
désapprobation ► opposition
désapprouver ► condemn, criticize, frown on, object, quarrel
désarroi ► dismay
désastre ► catastrophe, disaster, precipice
désastreusement ► disastrously [disaster]
désastreux (-euse) ► disastrous [disaster]
désavantage ► disadvantage, handicap, liability
descendance ► descent
   de descendance ► down[1]
descendant (-ante) ► cousin, down[1]
descendre ► decline, descend, dip, ebb
   descendre en parachute ► parachute
   descendre un courant ► float
descente ► chute, descent, raid
   descente en piqué ► swoop
   faire une descente ► raid
description ► description, picture
désencombrer ► clear
déséquilibré (-ée) ► insane
désert ► desert[1], wasteland
désert (-erte) ► desert[1], desolate, uninhabited
déserté (-ée) ► lonely
déserter ► desert[2]
désertique ► desert[1]
désespéré (-ée) ► desperate, hopeless
désespérément ► desperately [desperate], helplessly

désespérer ► despair
désespoir ► despair
(se) **déshabiller** ► strip[1]
désherber ► hoe, weed
se **déshabituer** ► cure
déshonneur ► disgrace
déshonorant (-ante) ► unworthy
déshonorer ► disgrace
désigner ► appoint, designate, detail, name, nominate
désillusion ► awakening [awaken]
désintégrer ► disintegrate
désintéressé (-ée) ► disinterested
désinvolte ► casual
désir ► desire, longing, will[2], wish
   désir intense ► yen[2]
   avoir désir de ► yearn
désirer ► desire, dream, hunger, want, wish
   non désiré (-ée) ► unwanted
désireux (-euse) ► anxious, eager
désobéir ► break, disobey
désobligeant (-ante) ► objectionable [objection]
désœuvré (-ée) ► idle
désolation ► desolation [desolate], despair
désolé (-ée) ► afraid, bleak, desert[1], desolate, sorry
se **désoler** ► grieve
désordonné (-ée) ► careless, messy [mess], mob, untidy
désordre ► clutter, confusion, disorder, mess, shambles
   mettre en désordre ► clutter, litter, mess
   en désordre ► untidy
désorganiser ► disorder
désorienter ► bewilder
désormais ► hereafter
désosser ► bone
despote ► tyrant
desséché (-ée) ► thirsty
dessécher ► wilt
dessein ► design, end, idea, intent[2], intention
   à dessein ► purposely [purpose]
desserrement ► looseness [loose]
desserrer ► loosen, relax
dessert ► dessert
dessin ► design, drawing, illustration, picture
   dessins animés ► cartoon
   bande dessinée ► cartoon, comic
dessinateur (-trice) ► designer [design]
dessiner ► design, draw
   dessiner au crayon ► pencil
   dessiner d'après le modèle de ► model
dessous ► underside
   au-dessous ► below, beneath, under
   en dessous ► beneath, downstairs
   par en dessous ► underhand

   dessous de verre ► coaster
dessus ► the upper hand
   au-dessus ► over
   au-dessus de la tête ► overhead
   dessus de cheminée ► mantel
dessus-de-lit ► cover
destin ► chance, destiny, doom, fate
destination ► destination
   à destination de ► for
destiné (-ée) ► bound[1]
destinée ► destiny, fate
destiner ► breed, doom, intend, target
destructeur (-trice) ► destructive
destruction ► destruction
détachant ► cleaner
détaché (-ée) ► loose
détachement ► detail
détacher ► detach, loose, peel, undo, untie
   (se) détacher ► alienate
détail[1] ► detail, particular, specific
détail[2] ► retail
   vente au détail ► retail
détaillé (-ée) ► elaborate, minute[2]
détailler ► detail
détaler ► scurry
détecter ► detect
détective ► detective
déteindre ► run
détendre ► slaken
   se détendre ► relax, thaw, unwind
détendu (-ue) ► leisurely [leisure]
détenir ► guard, hold[1], own
détente ► recreation, relaxation [relax], trigger
détenteur (-trice) ► holder
détention ► detention
détenu (-ue) ► convict, prisoner
détergent ► detergent
détériorer ► deface
   se détériorer ► perish, worsen
déterminant (-ante) ► decisive
   point déterminant ► head
détermination ► decision, determination, firmness [firm[1]]
déterminé (-ée) ► bent, certain, decisive, determined, game, given [give]
déterminer ► characterize, determine, govern
déterrer ► excavate
détersif ► detergent
détestable ► dreadful, infamous, miserable, obnoxious
détester ► hate
détonateur ► fuse
détonation ► bang, report
détoner ► explode
détour ► detour
détourné (-ée) ► indirect, roundabout

détournement ► diversion

détourner ► bypass, detour, divert, steer[1]

détracteur (-trice) ► critic

détraquer ► shatter

détrempé (-ée) ► soggy, waterlogged

détresse ► desolation [desolate], distress, misery

détritus ► garbage, litter, refuse[2], rubbish

détroit ► channel, sound[4], strait

détruire ► annihilate, demolish, destroy, devastate, kill, undo, wreck

    détruire complètement ► total

dette ► debt

    dettes ► liability

deuil ► mourning

deux ► two

    à deux ► dual

    les deux ► both

    pour deux ► double

    aucun (-une) des deux ► neither

    un jour sur deux ► alternate

    tous les deux jours ► alternate

    tous (les) deux ► both

    couper en deux ► bisect

    plier en deux ► double

deux-points ► colon[1]

deuxième ► latter, second[1]

    tous les deuxièmes ► every other

    personne en deuxième position ► runner-up

deuxièmement ► secondly [second[1]]

dévaliser ► raid

devant[1] ► ahead, before, past

devant[2] ► front

    de devant ► front

    aller au devant de ► court

    devant du tibia ► shin

dévaster ► destroy, devastate

développement ► development, growth, improvement

développer ► cultivate, develop, improve

    sous-développé (-ée) ► underdeveloped

    se développer ► build, evolve, thrive

devenir ► amount, become, get, go, grow, turn

    devenir adulte ► grow up

    devenir droit ► straighten

    devenir membre ► join

déverrouiller ► unlock

déversement ► discharge

déverser ► empty

    se déverser ► discharge, pour

déversoir ► outlet

déviation ► detour, diversion

dévier ► bypass, detour, drift, glance, swerve

deviner ► guess

devinette ► riddle[1]

devise ► currency, motto

dévoiler ► disclose, expose, unfold, unveil

devoir[1] ► get, must, need, ought, owe

    qu'on doit ► due

devoir[2] ► chore, duty, homework, obligation

    devoir écrit ► paper

dévorer ► consume, gnaw

dévotion ► devotion

dévoué (-ée) ► loyal

dévouement ► dedication, devotion

se dévouer ► devote

diabète ► diabetes

diable ► demon, devil, truck

diagnostic ► diagnosis

diagnostiquer ► diagnose

diagramme ► chart, diagram

dialecte ► dialect

dialogue ► dialogue

diamant ► diamond

diamètre ► diameter

diapason ► tuning fork

diapositive ► slide

dictateur (-trice) ► dictator, tyrant

dicter ► dictate

diction ► diction

dictionnaire ► dictionary

    dictionnaire (analogique) ► thesaurus

dicton ► saying

dièse ► sharp

diète ► diet

dieu (dieux) ► deity, god

    Dieu le Père ► Father

diffamation ► slander

diffamatoire ► slanderous [slander]

diffamer ► slander, smear

différemment ► differently [different]

différence ► difference, distinction

    par une petite différence ► by a nose

différend ► clash, controversy

différent (-ente) ► different, distinct, diverse, unlike, various

    légèrement différent (-ente) ► variant

différer ► defer[1], delay, differ, disagree, put off, vary

difficile ► critical, difficult, hard, rough, rugged, tough, tricky, uphill

    situation difficile ► predicament

difficulté ► difficulty, trouble

    aplanir les difficultés ► smooth

    marcher avec difficulté ► wade

diffusé (-ée) ► on (off) the air [air]

diffuser ► broadcast, diffuse, transmit

diffusion ► circulation, transmission

digérer ► digest

digestif (-ive) ► digestive

digne ► grave[2], worthy

    digne de confiance ► reliable, responsible

digne d'un saint (d'une sainte) ► saintly [saint]
    marcher d'un air digne ► stalk[2]
dignité ► dignity
digue ► dam, dike, jetty, levee
dilapider ► squander
dilater ► dilate, expand, inflate
diligence ► coach, stage, stagecoach
diluer ► dilute
dimanche ► Sunday
dimension ► dimension
    à deux dimensions ► dimensional [dimension]
    à trois dimensions ► dimensional [dimension]
diminuer ► decline, decrease, deplete, drop off, fade, lessen, reduce, relieve, wane
    faire diminuer ► depress
diminutif ► nickname
diminution ► cut, decrease, depletion [deplete], reduction [reduce]
dinde ► turkey
dindon ► turkey
dîner ► dine, dinner, eat, lunch, luncheon
dîneur (-euse) ► diner
dingue ► crazy
dinosaure ► dinosaur
diplomate ► diplomat, trifle
avec **diplomatie** ► diplomatically [diplomatic]
diplomatique ► diplomatic
diplomatiquement ► diplomatically [diplomatic]
diplôme ► degree, diploma
    remise des diplômes ► graduation
    obtenir un diplôme ► graduate, graduation
diplômé (-ée) ► graduate
dire ► bid, put, say, tell, word
    proprement dit (dite) ► proper
    c'est-à-dire ► namely
    dire d'un ton brutal ► bark[2]
    il va sans dire ► go without saying
direct (-ecte) ► blunt, direct, frank, through
    en direct ► live[2], on-line
directement ► directly, straight
directeur (-trice) ► chief, director, editor, principal, superintendent, warden
direction[1] ► bearing
    dans la direction de ► for
    changement de direction abrupt ► jog[2]
    changer de direction ► veer
    donner la direction de ► direct
    prendre une direction ► strike out
direction[2] ► command, direction, government, management
    membre de la direction ► officer
directive ► direction, instruction

dirigeant (-ante) ► leader, officer, ruler
diriger ► boss, carry on, channel, coach, conduct, direct, drive, engineer, fix, govern, head, hold[1], lead[1], manage, navigate, refer, rule, run, steer[1]
    diriger la publication ► edit
    se diriger ► head
    être dirigé (-ée) ► steer[1]
discernement ► judgement
discerner ► distinguish, read
discipline ► discipline
    imposer une discipline trop stricte ► regiment
discipliné (-ée) ► orderly
discordance ► clash
    rendre un son discordant ► jar
discorde ► conflict
discours ► address, speech
discret (-ète) ► discreet, quiet
discrètement ► discreetly [discreet]
discrimination ► discrimination
    faire de la discrimination ► discriminate
discriminer ► discriminate
disculper ► clear
discussion ► debate, dispute, talk
discutable ► controversial [controversy]
discuté (-ée) ► controversial [controversy]
discuter ► contest, debate, discuss, talk
disette ► dearth
disgrâce ► disgrace
disjoncteur ► breaker
disparaître ► away, die[1], disappear, fold, melt, vanish
disparité ► contrast
disparu (-ue) ► extinct, missing
dispendieux (-euse) ► costly, extravagant
dispenser ► administer, excuse, exempt
disperser ► scatter, thin
    se disperser ► break up
disponibilité ► availability [available]
disponible ► available, spare, vacant
disposé (-ée) ► benevolent, willing
disposer ► arrange, combine
disposition ► clause, constitution, disposal, temper
    disposition d'esprit ► frame of mind
    disposition(s) ► aptitude, mood
    à sa disposition ► ready
disproportionné (-ée) ► lopsided, uneven
dispute ► argument, conflict, dispute, fight, quarrel, row[3], scuffle, word
    petite dispute ► spat[1]
disputer ► compete, contest, quibble
    se disputer ► argue, contend, dispute, feud, fight, quarrel
disque ► disc, disk, puck, record
    disque compact ► compact disk

disque dur ► hard drive
disque souple ► floppy disk
barre à disques ► barbell
disquette ► disk, floppy disk
dissemblance ► contrast
dissertation ► essay
dissimulation ► concealment [conceal]
dissimulé (-ée) ► hidden
dissimuler ► camouflage, cloak, conceal, cover up, disguise, hide[1], mask, seclude
dissipé (-ée) ► riotous [riot]
dissiper ► remove
se dissiper ► break up, lift, melt
dissolution ► break-up
dissoudre ► dissolve
se dissoudre ► melt
dissuader ► deter, discourage
distance ► distance, haul, mileage, span, way
à distance ► aloof, aloofly, at bay, remotely [remote]
se faire distancer (par) ► trail
distant (-ante) ► aloof, distant, impersonal
d'une manière distante ► remotely [remote]
distinct (-incte) ► distinct, separate
distinctement ► vividly [vivid]
distinctif (-ive) ► characteristic, distinctive
distinction ► award, class, discrimination, distinction, grace, Honour [honour]
distinctivement ► distinctly [distinct]
distingué (-ée) ► elegant
distinguer ► discriminate, distinguish, tell
distinguer de ► characterize
distique ► couplet
distraction ► diversion, entertainment
distraire ► distract, divert, entertain
distrait (-aite) ► absent-minded
distraitement ► absently [absent]
distribuer ► deal, deliver, distribute, handle, issue, out
distributeur automatique ► vending machine
distribution ► assignment, cast
tableau de distribution ► switchboard
district ► district
dithyrambe ► rave
divaguer ► ramble, rave
Divali ► Divali
divan ► chesterfield, couch
divergence ► difference
divers (-erse) ► diverse, various
d'une manière diverse ► variously [various]
diversement ► variously [various]
se diversifier ► branch out
diversion ► diversion

diversité ► diversity, variety
divertir ► amuse, divert, entertain
divertissement ► amusement, diversion, entertainment
dividende ► dividend
divinité ► deity, god, goddess
diviser ► classify, divide, part, section, split
diviser en quatre ► quarter
diviser en secteurs ► zoning
diviser en zones ► zoning
division ► chapter, compartment, division, split
ligne de division ► divide
divorce ► divorce
divorcer ► divorce
divulguer ► disclose, divulge, leak
dix ► ten
dix-huit ► eighteen
dix-huitième ► eighteenth [eighteen]
dixième ► tenth [ten]
dix-neuf ► nineteen
dix-neuvième ► nineteenth [nineteen]
dix-sept ► seventeen
dix-septième ► seventeenth [seventeen]
docile ► obedient, orderly, tame
docilement ► obediently [obedient]
docilité ► obedience [obedient]
dock ► dock[1]
docteur ► doctor, Dr.
doctorat ► degree
document ► document, paper
porte-documents ► portfolio
documentaire ► documentary
documentation ► literature
documenter ► document
se documenter ► background
dodu (-ue) ► chubby, plump
doigt ► digit, finger
jointure du doigt ► knuckle
mettre le doigt dessus ► hit the nail on the head
montrer du doigt ► point
petit coup de doigt ► prod
pousser du doigt ► prod
doigté ► tact
dollar ► dollar
billet d'un dollar ► buck
domaine ► domain, estate, field, line[1], realm, sphere
dôme ► dome
domestique ► domestic, help, home, maid, pet, servant
animal domestique ► pet
domicile ► residence
à domicile ► home
dominant (-ante) ► dominant, towering
domination ► dominion, rule, sway

739

dominer ► control, dominate, rule, tower
domino ► domino
dommage ► damage, harm, mischief, pity, shame
dompter ► tame
dompteur (-euse) ► trainer
don ► charity, genius, gift, offering, talent
   faire don ► donate
donc ► consequently, so, then, therefore, thus, well[1]
donjon ► keep
donné (-ée) ► given [give]
donnée ► input
   données ► data
   données de sortie ► output
   base de données ► data base
   entrer les données ► input
donner ► afford, allow, along, assign, away, bear[1], donate, furnish, give, hand, issue, lend, pass, pay, produce, spare
   donner sur ► front, look, overlook
   donner au compte-gouttes ► dole
donneur ► dealer
dont ► hence
doré ► dory[2]
doré (-ée) ► golden
se dorer ► bask
dorénavant ► hereafter
doris ► dory[1]
dorloter ► baby, pamper
dormir ► rest[1], sleep
   dormir (paisiblement) ► slumber
   dormir sur ses lauriers ► rest on
Dorset ► Dorset
dortoir ► dormitory
dos ► back, spine
   dos rond ► stoop[1]
   sac à dos ► backpack, knapsack
   avoir le dos rond ► stoop[1]
dose ► dose
dossier ► back, brief, document, file[1], project, record
doter en capital ► fund
douane ► custom
   frais de douane ► duty
   tarif douanier ► tarif
double ► double, dual, duplicate, mate
   en double ► double
   faire un double ► duplicate
   faire un doublé ► duplicate
doubler ► double, lap[2], line[2]
doublure ► lining
doucement ► gently [gentle], meekly [meek], softly [soft]
douceur ► smoothness [smooth], softness [soft], sweetness [sweet]
   en douceur ► smoothly [smooth]

entrer/sortir avec douceur ► glide
douche ► shower
   prendre une douche ► shower
doué (-ée) ► accomplished [accomplish], apt, gifted [gift], natural, talented [talent]
douille ► socket
douillet (-ette) ► cosy, cozy
Doukhobor ► Doukhobor
douleur ► ache, grief, misery, pain
   douleur intense ► agony
   ressentir un élancement (de douleur) ► twinge
douloureusement ► painfully [painful]
douloureux (-euse) ► cruel, painful, sore, tender[1]
doute ► doubt, hesitation, misgiving, question, uncertainty [uncertain]
   avec doute ► doubtfully [doubt]
   mettre en doute ► challenge, dispute, question
   sans aucun doute ► definitely [definite], doubtless, easily, undoubtedly
douter ► doubt
douteux (-euse) ► unlikely, unsound
doux (douce) ► benign, bland, fresh, gentle, meek, mellow, mild, silken [silk], smooth, soft, sweet, tender[1]
douzaine ► dozen
douze ► twelve
douzième ► twelfth [twelve]
draconien (-ienne) ► drastic
dragon ► dragon
draguer ► drag
drainer ► drain
dramatique ► dramatic, theatrical
   rendre dramatique ► dramatize
dramatiquement ► dramatically
dramatiser ► dramatize
drame ► drama, tragedy
   drame policier ► mystery
   faire un drame ► blow up
drap ► sheet
drapeau (-eaux) ► banner, colour, flag, standard
draper ► drape
draperie ► drape
dresser ► cock, draft, erect, perk, pitch[1], rear[2], tame, train
   se dresser ► bristle, rear[2]
   se dresser de manière imposante ► tower
dresseur (-euse) ► trainer
dribble ► dribble
dribbler ► dribble
drogue ► drug
droguer ► drug
droit[1] ► law

droit[2] ► duty, right
   droits d'auteur ► copyright, royalty
   droit de vote ► suffrage
   atteinte (aux droits de) ► trespass
   avoir droit au chapitre ► say
   avoir le droit de ► can[1]
   Charte des droits et libertés ► Charter of Rights and Freedoms
droit[3] ► dead, upright
   tout droit ► due, straight
droit (droite) ► erect, full, honest, right, righteous, straight, upright
droite ► right
   à angle (s) droit (s) ► square
droiture ► righteousness [righteous]
drôle ► amusing [amuse], comic, funny, hilarious
   très drôle ► hysterical
dromadaire ► dromedary
dru (drue) ► wiry
du ► from
dû (due) ► due
   dû à ► due to
duc ► duke
duchesse ► duchess
duel ► duel
   se battre en duel ► duel
dune ► dune
duo ► duet
duper ► cheat, deceive, dupe, fool
duplicata ► duplicate
dur (dure) ► difficult, hard, harsh, ill, rock[1], stiff, tough
   disque dur ► hard drive
durable ► constant, durable
durant ► during, long[1]
   durant (tout) ► through
   durant que ► while
durcir ► harden, set
   (se) durcir ► toughen
durée ► length, life, run, span, term
   durée (d'une mission) ► tour
durement ► hard, harshly [harsh]
durer ► endure, last[2]
   faire durer ► nurse
dureté ► crispness [crisp], harshness [harsh], toughness [tough]
durillon ► corn[2]
duvet ► down[2], fluff, hair
duveteux (-euse) ► fluffy [fluff]
dynamique ► aggressive, dynamic, vibrant, vital
   de façon dynamique ► vibrantly [vibrant]
dynamisme ► momentum
dynamite ► dynamite
dynamiter ► dynamite
dynastie ► dynasty

E

eau ► water
   sur l'eau ► afloat
   sous l'eau ► underwater
   eau de Javel ► bleach
   eau d'égout ► sewage
   eau du bain ► bath
   eau savonneuse ► suds
   eaux usées ► sewage
   chute d'eau ► waterfall
   lit d'eau ► waterbed
   melon d'eau ► watermelon
   prise d'eau ► hydrant
   à l'eau de rose ► corny
   bruit de l'eau qui tombe ► drip
   d'eau douce ► freshwater
   danser sur l'eau ► bob
   mettre à l'eau ► launch[1]
   partir à l'eau ► wash
   plonger la tête dans l'eau ► duck[2]
ébats ► romp
s'ébattre ► romp
ébauche ► draft, drawing
ébauché (-ée) ► rough
ébaucher ► rough, sketch
ébène ► ebony
   noir (noire) comme l'ébène ► raven
ébénisterie ► woodworking
éblouir ► dazzle, glare
éblouissement ► glare
éboulement ► landslide
ébouriffer ► fluff, ruffle, rumple
ébranlement ► rock[2]
ébranler ► rattle, rock[2], shake, undermine
ébrécher ► chip
ébréchure ► chip
ébrouement ► snort
(s')ébruiter ► leak
écaille ► flake, scale[1]
écailler ► flake, peel, scale[1]
écaillure ► scale[1]
écaler ► shell
écarlate ► scarlet
écart ► contrast, difference, discard, gap, range
   à l'écart ► aloof, aloofly, aside, remote
   grand écart ► split
   faire un écart ► swerve
écarté (-ée) ► apart
écartement ► gauge
écarter ► discard, discount, eliminate, exclude
   s'écarter ► depart, stray
ecclésiastique ► priest

échafaud ► scaffold
échalote ► scallion
échange ► barter, exchange, swap, trade
échanger ► exchange, redeem, swap, switch, trade
échantillon ► sample, specimen, taste
   prendre un échantillon ► sample
échappatoire ► vent
échappement ► exhaust
   tuyau (-aux) d'échappement ► exhaust pipes
échapper ► dodge, elude, escape, fumble, slip[1]
   laisser échapper ► blurt
   laisser s'échapper ► vent
écharde ► splinter
écharpe ► sash[1], scarf, sling, wrap
échasse ► stilt
échauffer ► fire
   s'échauffer ► limber
échauffourée ► skirmish
échec ► breakdown, defeat, failure, flop
   échecs ► chess
   échec avant ► check
   en échec ► at bay
   coup d'un échec ► rebound
échelle ► ladder, range, scale[3]
   échelle de Richter ► Richter scale
   reproduire à l'échelle ► scale[3]
échelon ► degree, ladder, rung[2]
échelonner ► stagger
écho ► echo
échoué (-ée) ► aground
échouer ► beach, fail, strike out
   s'échouer ► ground[1]
   faire échouer ► frustrate
éclaboussement ► splash
éclabousser ► spatter, splash, splatter
éclaboussure ► splash, splatter
   faire des éclaboussures ► splash
éclair ► bolt, flash, lightning, shaft
   comme un éclair ► flash
   passer comme un éclair ► streak
éclairage ► illumination [illuminate]
éclaircir ► explain, lighten[1], thin
éclaircissement ► explanation
éclairé (-ée) ► sunlit [sunlight]
éclairer ► illuminate, illustrate, light[1], lighten[1], shed[2]
éclaireur (-euse) ► scout
éclat ► brightness [bright], brilliance [brilliant], flare, flash, gale, glamour, glitter, glow, peal, sliver, vividness [vivid]
   éclat aveuglant ► glare
   sans éclat ► dull
   donner de l'éclat à ► spruce

   perdre son éclat ► fade
   se fendre en éclats ► splinter
éclatant (-ante) ► bright, glamorous [glamour], vivid
éclatement ► burst, explosion, spasm
éclater ► blow out, blow up, break out, burst, erupt, explode, pop[1]
   éclater de rage ► blow up
   s'éclater de rire ► giggle, roar
éclipse ► eclipse
éclipser ► eclipse
   s'éclipser ► slink
éclisse ► splint
éclopé (-ée) ► lame
faire éclore ► hatch[1]
écluse ► lock[1]
écœurer ► disgust
   écœuré (-ée) par ► sick
école ► school[1]
   école maternelle ► nursery school
   école secondaire ► secondary school
   qui fait l'école buissonnière ► truant
écologie ► ecology
écologique ► ecological [ecology], environmental [environment]
économe ► thrifty
économie ► economics, economy, thrift [thrifty]
   économies ► savings
économique ► economic [economics], economical
   de façon peu économique ► wasteful [waste]
économiquement ► economically [economical]
économiser ► save
écoper ► bail[2]
écorce ► bark[1], peel, rind
écorcher ► grate, skin
écosser ► shell
écosystème ► ecosystem
écoulement ► discharge, flow
   tuyau d'écoulement ► drain
écouler ► empty
   s'écouler ► discharge, drain, elapse, march, tick[1]
écourter ► dock[2]
écoute ► attention
   indice d'écoute ► rating
   mettre sur écoute ► tap[2]
écouter ► hear, listen, obey
   écouter de façon indiscrète ► eavesdrop
écouteur ► earphone
écoutille ► hatch[2]
écran ► monitor, screen, video
   écran de visualisation ► display

écraser ► crush, dwarf, grind, jam[1], mash, overwhelm, squash[1], stamp
   écraser (avec une tapette) ► swat
écrémer ► skim
s'écrier ► call, exclaim
écrire ► note, put down, spell[1], word, write
   écrire à l'aide d'un crayon ► pencil
   écrire en majuscules ► print
   écrire son autographe ► autograph
   machine à écrire ► typewriter
   mal écrire ► misspell
écrit ► writing, written
écriture ► hand, handwriting
   écriture(s) ► Scripture
   Écriture sainte ► Scripture
   écriture script ► script
écrivain ► writer
   écrivain anonyme ► ghost
   écrivain fantôme ► ghost
écrou ► nut
écroulement ► collapse
s'écrouler ► cave, collapse, crumble, fall
écueil ► reef
écume ► foam, lather, scum
écumer ► foam, skim
écureuil ► squirrel
écurie ► stable[1]
   mettre dans une écurie ► stable[1]
écusson ► badge, shield
écuyer ► squire
Eden ► Xanadu
édification ► construction
édifice ► building
éditer ► edit, publish
éditeur (-trice) ► editor
édition ► edition
éditorial (-aux) ► editorial
éducatif (-ive) ► educational
éducation ► breeding, education, instruction
édulcorant ► sweetener [sweeten]
édulcorer ► dilute
éduqué (-ée) ► learned [learn]
éduquer ► bring up, civilize, educate, instruct
effacé (-ée) ► modest
effacer ► blot out, delete, erase
effarouché (-ée) ► frighten
effectif ► force
effectivement ► truly
effectuer ► accomplish, effect, hold[1], implement, perform
effervescence ► hustle
   être en effervescence ► seethe
effet ► action, effect, in effect [effect], side effect
   en effet ► indeed, so
   prendre effet ► effective, in effect [effect]

efficace ► capable, competent, effective, efficient
efficacement ► effectively [effective], efficiently [efficient]
efficacité ► effectiveness [effective]
(s')effiler ► taper
s'effilocher ► taper
effleurer ► brush[1], graze, kiss, lick
effondrement ► breakdown, collapse, death, slump
s'effondrer ► break down, cave, collapse, crash, crumble, fall, flop, give, slump
effort ► effort
   faire un grand effort ► strain[1]
   fournir de grands efforts ► agonize
s'efforcer ► endeavour, strive
   entrer par effraction ► break in
effraction ► break-in
effrayant (-ante) ► dread, dreaded, fearful [fear], frightful [frighten], ghastly, grim, scary
effrayé (-ée) ► alarm, afraid, frightful [frighten]
effrayer ► frighten, horrify, scare
effréné (-ée) ► frantic, mad
effritement ► erosion [erode]
effriter ► flake
effroi ► dread, fright, horror
effronté (-ée) ► bold, gross, impolite
   de manière effrontée ► forward
effrontément ► boldly [bold], shamelessly [shame]
effronterie ► boldness [bold], cheek
effroyable ► appalling, awful, frightful [frighten], outrageous, terrible
effroyablement ► awfully
égal (-ale, -aux) ► equal, even, level, match[2]
   sans égal ► peerless [peer[2]]
également ► also, equally, evenly [even], too
égaler ► correspond, equal, match[2]
égaliser ► even, level, smooth
égalité ► equality, flatness [flat[1]], smoothness [smooth]
   à égalité ► neck and neck
   égalité (de chances) ► toss up
   égalité (de points) ► tie
   être à égalité ► tie
égard ► consideration, regard, respect, sake, way
   avec égards ► considerately [considerate]
   plein d'égards ► thoughtful
   manque de prévenance ou d'égards ► thoughtlessness [thoughtless]
égaré (-ée) ► missing
égarer ► lose
   s'égarer ► wander
égayer ► lighten[2]

s'égayer ▸ cheer
églantier ▸ briar
églefin ▸ haddock
église ▸ church
   Église ▸ Church
   Église catholique romaine ▸ Roman
Catholic Church
ego ▸ ego
égoïsme ▸ selfishness [selfish]
égoïste ▸ selfish
égoïstement ▸ selfishly [selfish]
égorger ▸ butcher
égout ▸ sewer
   eau d'égout ▸ sewage
égoutter ▸ drain
égratigner ▸ claw, scratch
égratignure ▸ égratignure
égrener ▸ seed
éhonté (-ée) ▸ shameless [shame]
éjecter ▸ eject
élaboration ▸ formation
élaborer ▸ elaborate
   élaborer une théorie ▸ theorize
élaguer ▸ prune^2
élan ▸ elk, flight^1, moose
élancement ▸ stab, throb, twinge
   ressentir un élancement (de douleur)
   ▸ twinge
élancer ▸ throb, shoot
   s'élancer ▸ dart
élargir ▸ expand, extend, flare, widen
élastique ▸ elastic, resilient, springy [spring]
   élastique de Bungee ▸ bungee cord
électeur (-trice) ▸ constituency
élection ▸ election
   élection partielle ▸ by-election
   section électorale ▸ ward
électricité ▸ electricity, hydro, power
   électricité statique ▸ static
   chargé (-ée) d'électricité ▸ live^2
   panne d'électricité ▸ blackout
électrique ▸ electric
électroménager ▸ appliance
électron ▸ electron
électronique ▸ electronic [electronics]
électroniquement ▸ electronically
[electronics]
élégamment ▸ gracefully [grace],
handsomely [handsome], smartly [smart]
   avec élégance ▸ gracefully [grace]
élégant (-ante) ▸ clean, elegant, graceful
[grace], gracious, handsome, smart,
sophisticated, stylish [style]
élément ▸ component, element, unit
   éléments ▸ the elements [element]
   élément (de pile) ▸ cell
   élément nutritif ▸ nutrient

élémentaire ▸ elementary
éléphant ▸ elephant
élévateur ▸ elevator, lift
élévation ▸ elevation
élève ▸ learner [learn], pupil^1, student
   élève absentéiste ▸ truant
   élève officier ▸ cadet
élevé (-ée) ▸ high
   peu élevé (-ée) ▸ low
   bien élevé (-ée) ▸ mannerly [manner]
élever ▸ breed, bring up, elevate, erect,
foster, keep, lift, raise, rear^2
   s'élever jusqu'à ▸ attain
   s'élever ▸ amount, arise, ascend, soar,
total, worth
   élever au carré ▸ square
elfe ▸ elf
élimé (-ée) ▸ threadbare
élimination ▸ cancellation
éliminer ▸ cancel, cure, eliminate, exclude,
expel, remove, weed
élire ▸ designate, elect
élite ▸ elite
elle ▸ her, it, she
   elles ▸ them, they
   elle-même ▸ herself
   elles-mêmes ▸ themselves
ellipse ▸ ellipsis
élocution ▸ delivery, diction
éloge ▸ praise, rave
   faire l'éloge ▸ praise, rave
éloigné (-ée) ▸ apart, away, distant, far, off,
remote
   plus éloigné (-ée) ▸ far
   le (la) plus éloigné (-ée) ▸ farthest
éloignement ▸ remoteness [remote]
éloigner ▸ alienate, repel
   s'éloigner ▸ recede
   s'éloigner de façon à ▸ forth
   arriver (s'éloigner) peu à peu ▸ trickle
éloquent (-ente) ▸ eloquent
élucider ▸ explain, solve
éluder ▸ dodge, elude, evade
émail ▸ enamel
émailler ▸ enamel
emballer ▸ bag, box^1, pack, package, wrap
   s'emballer ▸ go overboard
embarcation ▸ boat, craft
embarquer ▸ embark
   s'embarquer ▸ embark
embarrassant (-ante) ▸ awkward
embarrassé (-ée) ▸ ill at ease
embarrasser ▸ embarrass, hinder
embauche ▸ hire
embaucher ▸ engage, enroll, hire
embaumer ▸ perfume
embellir ▸ grace

embêtement ► fix, hassle
embêter ► annoy, bother, hassle
embobiner ► reel[1]
embouchure ► mouth
embouteillage ► jam[1], snarl[2]
embouteiller ► bottle
emboutir ► ram
s'embourber ► bog
embranchement ► fork
embrassade ► squeeze
embrasé (-ée) ► fiery
embrasser ► cuddle, embrace, hug, kiss
   s'embraser ► flame, flare, glow
embrasure ► doorway
embrayage ► clutch[1]
embrouiller ► complicate, confuse, fog, foul, muddle
embrumé (-ée) ► hazy
embryon ► germ
embué (-ée) ► misty [mist]
embuer ► fog
   s'embuer ► mist
embuscade ► ambush
   tendre une embuscade ► ambush
emcombrer ► clutter
émeraude ► emerald
émerger ► emerge
   émerger partiellement ► peep[1]
émerveillement ► wonder
s'émerveiller ► marvel
émetteur ► transmitter
émettre ► express, issue, offer, transmit
   émettre un bruit sourd ► thud
   émettre une contravention ► ticket
   émettre une hypothèse ► theorize
émeute ► riot, upheaval, uprising
   participer à une émeute ► riot
émietter ► crumble
émigrer ► emigrate
éminence ► elevation
éminent (-ente) ► considerable, high, notable
émission ► issue, program, transmission
   émission de télévision ► telecast
   émission spéciale ► special
emmagasinage ► storage
emmêler ► foul, mat, snarl[2], tangle
emménager ► move in
emmener ► bring, drive, ferry, take
emmerdant (-ante) ► pain
émoi ► flutter, turmoil
émonder ► prune[2]
émotif (-ive) ► emotional
émotion ► emotion, feeling, thrill
émotionnel (-elle) ► emotional
émoussé (-ée) ► blunt, dull
émousser ► blunt, dull

émouvant (-ante) ► moving
émouvoir ► melt, stir, touch
empailler ► stuff
empaler ► spike[1]
empaqueter ► bundle, pack, package
s'emparer ► appropriate, capture
   s'emparer brusquement de ► snatch
empêchement ► hitch, restraint
empêcher ► arrest, deter, forbid, help, keep, prevent, restrain, stop
   empêcher de voler ► ground[1]
empennage ► fin
empesé (-ée) ► starched [starch]
empeser ► starch
empiècement ► yoke
empiler ► heap, pile[1], stack
empire ► empire
empirer ► aggravate, compound, worsen
emplacement ► location, site
emplir ► swamp
emploi ► employ, job, occupation, use, work
   emploi du temps ► timetable
employé (-ée) ► worker
   employé (-ée) de bureau ► clerk
   employé (-ée) de maison ► help
   employé (-ée) des wagons-lits ► porter
employer ► consume, dedicate, employ, hire, spend, use, utilize
empocher ► bag, pocket
empoigner ► clutch[1], collar, grab, grasp, grip
empoisonner ► poison
emporté (-ée) ► hot
emportement ► rampage
emporter ► bring, carry, take
   s'emporter ► flare
   l'emporter ► get the best of, win
empreindre ► engrave
empreinte ► cast, impression, print, step, track
   empreintes ► trail
   empreinte de pied ► footprint
   laisser des empreintes ► track
empressement ► haste, hurry, promptness [prompt], rush[1], willingness [willing]
   manque d'empressement ► tardiness [tardy]
s'empresser ► hasten
emprise ► clutch[1], hold[1], influence
emprisonner ► jail
emprunt ► loan
   nom d'emprunt ► alias
emprunter ► borrow, hire
en ► as, at, by, in, into, of, on, to, under
   d'en ► hence
encadrement ► frame, framework
encadrer ► frame
encaisser ► cash

encan ▸ auction
encart ▸ insert
encastré (-ée) ▸ sunken
enceinte ▸ loudspeaker, pregnant
encercler ▸ circle, hem in, rim, ring[1]
enchaînement ▸ web
enchaîner ▸ chain, string
enchanté (-ée) ▸ overjoyed
enchantement ▸ magic
enchanter ▸ delight, enchant
enchanteur (-teresse) ▸ wizard
enchère ▸ bidding
   vendre aux enchères ▸ auction
   (vente aux) enchères ▸ auction
enchevêtrement ▸ mat, snarl[2]
enchevêtrer ▸ snarl[2], tangle
enclin (-ine) ▸ prone
enclore ▸ enclose, hedge
enclos ▸ corral, pen[2]
encoche ▸ blaze[2], nick
encolure ▸ collar, neck
encombrement ▸ jam[1]
à l'encontre de ▸ counter[2]
encore ▸ again, anymore, even, more, over, still, yet
   encore moins ▸ let alone [alone]
   encore un (une) ▸ another
encourageant (-ante) ▸ encouragingly [encourage], hopeful
encouragement ▸ cheer, stimulus
encourager ▸ cheer, encourage, promote, root[3], uplift
encre ▸ ink
encré (-ée) ▸ inky [ink]
encrer ▸ ink
encyclopédie ▸ encyclopedia
endiguer ▸ dam
s'endimancher ▸ dress up
endolori (-ie) ▸ sore
endommager ▸ chip, damage, hurt
endormi (-ie) ▸ asleep, sleepy
endormir ▸ lull
   s'endormir ▸ asleep, drop off, sink
endos ▸ reverse
endossement ▸ endorsement [endorse]
endosser ▸ endorse, shoulder
endroit ▸ drop, place, spot, whereabouts
   à l'endroit que ▸ where
enduit vitrifié ▸ glaze
endurance ▸ stamina, toughness [tough]
endurant (-ante) ▸ tough
endurci (-ie) ▸ confirmed [confirm], tough
endurcir ▸ harden, toughen
endurer ▸ endure, stand, stomach
énergie ▸ energy, vigour
   énergie atomique ▸ atomic energy

   énergie hydraulique ▸ hydro
   énergie nucléaire ▸ nuclear energy
énergique ▸ aggressive, drastic, dynamic, strenuous, vigorous, vital
énervé (-ée) ▸ excited [excite], upset
énervement ▸ impatience [impatient]
énerver ▸ fluster, irritate, upset
   s'énerver ▸ carry on
enfant ▸ child, family, young
   enfants ▸ brood
   enfant en bas âge ▸ infant, toddler
   jeune enfant ▸ youngster
   petit-enfant ▸ grandchild, great
   arrière-petit-enfant ▸ great
   centre de la petite enfance ▸ nursery school
   chambre d'enfant ▸ nursery
   jardin d'enfants ▸ kindergarten
   jeu d'enfant ▸ snap
   lit d'enfant ▸ crib
enfantin (-ine) ▸ babyish [baby], childish
enfer ▸ hell
enfermer ▸ coop, lock[1], pen[2]
   enfermer dans un corral ▸ corral
enfiler ▸ put on, slip[1], string, thread
enfin ▸ at last, finally
enflammé (-ée) ▸ angry
enflammer ▸ fire, ignite, inflame, kindle
   s'enflammer ▸ flare, ignite
enflé (-ée) ▸ swollen
enfler ▸ belly, swell
enflure ▸ swell, swelling
enfoncement ▸ bay[5]
enfoncer ▸ dig, drum, jam[1], plunge, punch[1], push, ram, settle, shove, stick, thrust, wedge
   s'enfoncer ▸ bog
enfouir ▸ bury
   s'enfouir ▸ burrow
enfourcher ▸ mount, straddle
enfourner ▸ shovel
enfreindre ▸ break, invade, violate
s'enfuir ▸ escape, flee
engagement ▸ engagement, enlistment [enlist], obligation
engager ▸ contract, engage, hire
   s'engager ▸ commit, embark, engage, enlist, pledge
   s'engager comme volontaire ▸ volunteer
engendrer ▸ breed, father, generate, spawn
engin ▸ device
   engin spatial ▸ spacecraft
englober ▸ cover, embrace
englouti (-ie) ▸ sunken
engloutir ▸ bolt, gobble[1], swallow[1], wolf
engouement ▸ rage
engouffrer ▸ bolt, gobble[1]

engoulevent ► whippoorwill
engourdi (-ie) ► asleep, numb
engourdir ► numb
engrenage ► gear
engueulade ► row[3]
engueuler ► bawl out
énigmatique ► cryptic
énigme ► enigma, puzzle, riddle[1]
enivrer ► entrance[2]
　　s'enivrer ► drink
enjamber ► span
enjeu ► stake
enjoliver ► embroider
enjoué (-ée) ► cheerful, jolly, playful [play]
enlacement ► embrace, hug
enlacer ► clasp, embrace, wrap
enlevé (-ée) ► off
enlèvement ► abduction [abduct], disposal, removal
enlever ► abduct, core, deprive, kidnap, off, peel, remove, shed[2], strip[1]
　　enlever brusquement ► whip, whisk
s'enliser ► bog
ennemi (-ie) ► enemy, hostile
ennui ► bother, fix, trouble
　　ennuis ► straits [strait]
s'ennuager ► cloud
ennuyant (-ante) ► boring, pain
ennuyer ► bore[1], bother, bug, hassle
ennuyeux (-euse) ► boring, colourless, dreary, dry, dull, tedious
　　de façon ennuyeuse ► tediously [tedious]
　　personne ennuyeuse ► bore[1]
énorme ► awful, enormous, huge, immense, massive, mountainous, towering, tremendous, vast
énormément ► awfully, enormously [enormous], greatly [great], immensely [immense], infinitely [infinite], tremendously [tremendous]
s'enquérir ► enquire, inquire
enquête ► probe
enquêter ► investigate
enquêteur (-euse) ► detective, investigator [investigate]
s'enraciner ► root[1]
enragé (-ée) ► mad
enrégimenté (-ée) ► regimented [regiment]
enregistrement ► registration
enregistrer ► list[1], record, register, store
　　enregistrer (sur bande vidéo) ► videotape
　　enregistrer (sur bande) ► tape
　　faire enregistrer ► file[1]
enregistreur (-euse) ► recorder
enrichir ► enrich
enrichissement ► enrichment [enrich]

enrober ► coat
enrôlement ► enlistment [enlist]
enrôler ► enroll
　　s'enrôler ► enlist
enroué (-ée) ► hoarse, husky[1]
enrouler ► coil, lap[2], loop, roll, twine, twist, wind up [wind[2]]
　　s'enrouler ► curl
enrouleur ► roller
à l'entour ► around
s'ensabler ► ground[1]
s'entrechoquer ► clash
　　entrechoquer bruyamment ► clatter
par l'entremise de ► through
ensacher ► sack[1]
ensanglanté (-ée) ► bloody
enseignant (-ante) ► teacher
enseigne ► sign
enseignement ► education, instruction, teaching
enseigner ► instruct, school[1], teach
ensemble ► complex, package, set, suite, together
　　dans l'ensemble ► altogether, on the whole or as a whole
ensemencer ► seed
ensoleillé (-ée) ► sunlit [sunlight], sunny
ensorceler ► enchant
ensuite ► then
entaille ► dent, nick
　　faire une entaille ► nick
entailler ► chop, dent, nick
entamer ► begin
entassement ► drift
entasser ► cram, cramp, crowd, crush, heap, jam[1], pack, pile[1], squash[1], wedge
　　s'entasser ► drift, huddle
entendre ► hear
　　entendre (dire) ► hear
　　entendre (parler de) ► hear, hear of
　　laisser entendre ► imply
　　laisser entendre (que) ► hint
　　ne pas entendre ► miss[1]
　　ne pas s'entendre ► differ
entendu ► all right
　　sous-entendu ► undertone
　　bien entendu ► of course
entente ► harmony, resolution, understanding
entériner ► confirm
enterré (-ée) ► buried
enterrement ► burial, funeral
enterrer ► bury
en-tête ► heading
entêté (-ée) ► obstinate, stubborn, tenacious, willful

entêtement ► stubbornness [stubborn]
   avec entêtement ► willfully [willful]
enthousiasme ► enthusiasm, keenness [keen], zest, zip
   qui a perdu tout enthousiasme ► stale
   parler avec enthousiasme ► rave
enthousiasmer ► inspire
enthousiaste ► enthusiastic [enthusiasm], fan[2], zealous [zeal]
entier (-ière) ► complete, entire, global [globe], intact
   tout (toute, tous, toutes) entier (-ière) ► whole
   nombre entier ► whole number
entièrement ► altogether, fully [full], outright, through, totally, wholly
entièreté ► integrity
entonnoir ► funnel
entorse ► departure, wrench
   se faire une entorse à ► sprain
entortillement ► kink
entortiller ► foul, kink, twist
entouré de ► among
entourer ► circle, enclose, fold, hem in, rim, ring[1], surround
   entourer d'une clôture ► fence
   entourer d'une corde ► rope off [rope]
   entourer d'un mur ► wall
entrain ► animation, pep, zest, zip
   avec entrain ► lively
   qui a de l'entrain ► buoyant
   plein (pleine) d'entrain ► lively, peppy [pep], perky [perk]
entraînant (-ante) ► rouse
entraînement ► drill, practice, training
   séance d'entraînement ► workout
entraîner ► cause, coach, influence, involve, mean[1], prompt, school[1]
   s'entraîner ► practise, train
entraîneur (-euse) ► coach, trainer
entrave ► clog, tie
entraver ► clog, hinder, interfere
entre ► among, between
   entre les deux ► between
   entre les mains ► hand
entre temps ► meanwhile
entrechoquer bruyamment ► clatter
entrée ► admittance [admit], driveway, enter, entrance[1], entrance[2], entry, hall, mouth
   entrée en scène ► appearance
   chemin d'entrée ► driveway
   prix d'entrée ► admission
entre-jambe ► crotch
entrelacer ► braid, weave
entreposage ► storage
entreposer ► store
entrepôt ► depot, storehouse, warehouse

entreprenant (-ante) ► dynamic
entreprendre ► initiate, proceed, undertake
entreprise ► concern, enterprise, undertaking [undertake]
entrer ► enter
   entrer dans ► pull
   faire entrer ► smuggle
   laisser entrer ► admit
   entrer avec désinvolture ► waltz
   entrer en collision ► collide
   entrer en conflit ► clash
   entrer en contact ► clash
   entrer en éruption ► erupt
   entrer en scène ► appear
   entrer en vigueur ► effective, in effect [effect]
   entrer les données ► input
   entrer par effraction ► break in
   entrer/sortir avec douceur ► glide
   entrer/sortir avec grâce ► glide
entretenir ► carry on, harbour, maintain, nurse
   s'entretenir ► confer
   entretenir des bons rapports ► relate
entretien ► conversation, interview, keep, service, upkeep
   coupe d'entretien ► trim
entretoise ► brace
entrevoir ► glimpse
entrevue ► interview
énumérer ► count[1], detail, recite
envahir ► invade
enveloppe ► covering, envelope, husk, shell
envelopper ► fold, shroud, wrap
envenimer ► aggravate
envergure ► stature, wingspan
envers ► reverse, to
   à l'envers ► backward, reverse, upside down
envie ► desire, envy, fancy, longing
   forte envie ► urge
   grande envie de ► yen[2]
   plein (pleine) d'envie ► longing
   avec envie ► longingly [longing], wishful [wish]
   avoir très envie de ► long[2]
   avoir envie de ► fancy, yearn
   mourir d'envie de ► ache, die[1]
envier ► envy
environ ► about, circa, roughly [rough]
   environs ► neighbourhood, surroundings, vicinity
environnement ► environment
   environnement DOS ► DOS
environnemental (-ale, -aux) ► environmental [environment]

envisager ► anticipate, contemplate, imagine, view
envoi ► shipping
    coup d'envoi ► kick off
envolée ► flight[1]
envoler ► evaporate
    faire s'envoler ► blow[1]
    piste d'envol ► runway
envoyé (-ée) ► correspondent
envoyer ► refer, send, ship
    envoyer au tapis ► floor
    envoyer un message radio ► radio
    envoyer par la poste ► mail[1]
épagneul ► spaniel
épais (épaisse) ► bushy, coarse, deep, thick
épaisseur ► thickness [thick]
    d'épaisseur ► thick
(s')épaissir ► thicken
s'épanouir ► blossom
épargner ► salt, save, spare
épargnes ► savings
éparpiller ► scatter, strew
épars (-arse) ► stray
épatant (-ante) ► swell
épaule ► shoulder
    donner un coup d'épaule ► dig
    hausser les épaules ► shrug
    se frayer un chemin à coup d'épaules ► shoulder
épave ► wrock, wreckage
épée ► sword
épeler ► spell[1]
    personne sachant épeler ► speller
éperlan ► smelt[1]
éperon ► spur
éperonner ► spur
épeurer ► scare
éphémère ► passing
épi ► ear[2], spike[2]
épice ► spice
épicé (-ée) ► hot, spicy [spice]
épicéa ► spruce
épicer ► spice
épicerie ► grocery
épidémie ► epidemic
épidémique ► epidemic
épier ► observe
épinard ► spinach
épine ► spine, thorn
    épine dorsale ► backbone, spine
    couronne de roses ou d'épines ► crown
épinette ► spruce
épineux (-euse) ► prickly [prick], spiny [spine], thorny
épingle ► pin

    épingle de sûreté ► safety pin
épingler ► pin
épique ► epic
épisode ► chapter, episode
éploré (-ée) ► desolate
éplucher ► husk, peel
éponge ► sponge
éponger ► blot, dry, mop, sponge
épopée ► epic
époque ► age, day, era, period, time
    d'époque ► vintage
    à cette époque-là ► then
époux (épouse) ► companion, spouse
    époux ► husband
    épouse ► wife
épouser ► marry, wed
épousseter ► dust
épouvantable ► appalling, awful, fearful [fear], frightful [frighten], ghastly, terrible, terrific
épouvantail ► fright, scarecrow
épouvante ► terror
épouvanter ► appall
épreuve ► challenge, event, examination, hardship, ordeal, paper, print, proof, test, trial
    épreuve positive ► positive
    à l'épreuve de ► proof
    mise à l'épreuve ► probation
    corriger les épreuves de ► proofread
    mettre à l'épreuve ► tax, test, try
épris (-ise) ► crazy
éprouver ► sustain, tax, try
    qui éprouve du ressentiment ► resentful [resent]
    éprouver de la colère ► rage
    éprouver de l'amertume ► resent
    éprouver du chagrin ► sorrow
éprouvette ► test tube
épuisé (-ée) ► beat, run-down, spent, weary, worn, worn-out
épuisement ► drain, depletion [deplete], fatigue, strain[1], weariness [weary]
épuiser ► consume, deplete, drain, exhaust, spend, use
épurer ► filter, purify
équateur ► equator
équation ► equation
équatorial (-ale, -aux) ► equatorial [equator]
équilibre ► balance, poise
    équilibre sur les mains ► handstand
    maintenir en équilibre ► balance
    perdre l'équilibre ► topple
    tenir en équilibre ► poise
équilibré (-ée) ► balance
équilibrer ► balance, poise
équinoxe ► equinox
équipage ► crew

équipe ► crew, eleven, gang, party, shift, squad, team

    équipe en deuxième position ► runner-up

    faire équipe ► gang, team

équipement ► apparatus, equipment, facility, gear, kit, tackle

équiper ► equip, outfit

équitable ► fair[1], impartial, just

équitablement ► fairly, legitimately [legitimate]

équité ► fairness [fair[1]], justice

équivalence ► equivalent

équivalent ► equivalent

équivalent (-ente) ► equivalent, match[2]

équivaloir ► correspond

érable ► maple

    tire d'érable ► taffy

érafler ► scrape, scratch, scuff

éraflure ► scrape, scratch

ère ► era, period, time

érection ► construction

éreinté (-ée) ► worn-out

éreinter ► pan

ériger ► erect, put up

ermite ► hermit

éroder ► eat, erode

érosion ► erosion [erode]

errant (-ante) ► stray

errer ► ramble, roam, wander

erreur ► error, fault, mistake, misunderstanding

    par erreur ► mistakenly [mistaken]

    induire en erreur ► trip up

erroné (-ée) ► incorrect, mistaken

érudit (-ite) ► scholar, scholarly [scholar]

érudition ► depth, scholarship

éruption ► eruption [erupt], rash[1]

    entrer en éruption ► erupt

escabeau ► stepladder

escadron ► squadron, troop

escalader ► climb, scale[3]

escalier ► flight[1], stair, staircase

    escalier mécanique ► escalator

    escalier roulant ► escalator

escamoter ► palm[1]

escargot ► snail

escarmouche ► skirmish

escarpé (-ée) ► rugged, steep[1]

s'esclaffer ► roar

esclavage ► slavery

esclave[1] ► slave

esclave[2] ► Slavey

escompte ► discount

escompter ► expect

escorte ► escort

escorter ► escort, usher

escouade ► squad

faire de l'escrime ► fence

escroc ► cheater, crook, swindler [swindle]

escroquer ► cheat, swindle

escroquerie ► fraud, racket, swindle

espace ► blank, outer space, room, space, span

    espace aérien ► airspace

    espace inoccupé ► room

espacer ► space

espadon ► swordfish

espèce ► class, description, form, kind[2], nature, species

espérance ► hope, promise

espérer ► hope, may, trust

espiègle ► arch[2], mischievous, playful [play], rascal, tricky

espièglerie ► mischief

espion (-ionne) ► spy

espionner ► spy

espoir ► hope

    plein (pleine) d'espoir ► hopeful

    sans espoir ► hopeless

    perdre espoir ► despair

esprit ► gnome, head, mind, spirit, vein, wit

    à l'esprit vif ► smart

    d'esprit ► spirited

    disposition d'esprit ► frame of mind

    état d'esprit ► frame of mind

    sain (saine) d'esprit ► sane

    trait d'esprit ► quip

    lancer avec esprit ► quip

    venir à l'esprit ► occur, suggest, strike

esquif ► skiff

esquisse ► outline, sketch

esquisser ► draft, outline, rough, sketch

esquiver ► dodge, duck[2], elude, evade

essai ► attempt, down[1], draft, essay, experiment, fling, probation, trial, try

    à titre d'essai ► tentatively [tentative]

    coup d'essai ► venture

    mise à l'essai ► tryout

essaim ► swarm

essaimer ► swarm

essayer ► attempt, endeavour, sample, test, try, try on [try]

essence ► gas, gasoline

essentiel (-elle) ► essential, fundamental, necessary

    de façon essentielle ► vitally [vital]

essentiellement ► essentially, fundamentally [fundamental]

esseulé (-ée) ► lonely

essieu ► axle, bearing

essorer ► wring

essoreuse (-euse) ► spinner [spin]

essouffler ► wind[1]

essuyer ► dry, dust, experience, mop, wipe
   essuyer avec une serviette ► towel
est ► east, the East [east], eastern
   à l'est ► eastward
   vers le nord-est ► northeast
estampe ► stamp
estamper ► punch[2]
estampille ► stamp
estimation ► estimate, estimation [estimate]
estime ► consideration
   avoir de l'estime pour ► esteem
   tenir en grande estime ► regard
estimer ► approximate, compute, consider, estimate, feel, judge, regard, value
   sous-estimer ► misjudge
estomac ► stomach
estomaquer ► stump
(s')estomper ► dim, recede, taper, trail off [trail]
estropié (-ée) ► cripple, lame
estropier ► lame
estuaire ► gulf
esturgeon ► sturgeon
et ► and
   et sur ce ► whereupon
et cetera (etc.) ► and the like, beside oneself
étable ► barn
   mettre à l'étable ► stall
établi ► bench
établir ► determine, establish, fix, found[2], institute
   s'établir ► settle
   établir un lien ► relate
   établir un prix ► quote
   établir un réseau ► network
établissement ► business, foundation, settlement
étage ► floor, storey, storey [story], tier, upstairs
   étage inférieur ► downstairs
   à l'étage ► upstairs
   à l'étage inférieur ► downstairs
étagère ► shelf
étai ► prop
étain ► tin
   d'étain ► tin
étalage ► display, stand
   voleur (-euse) à l'étalage ► shoplifter
étaler ► distribute, exhibit, smear, spread
   s'étaler ► sprawl
étalon ► stallion, standard
étamer ► silver
étamine ► stamen
étampe ► die[3], punch[2]
étanche ► airtight, tight
étancher ► quench
étang ► pond

étant donné ► when
   étant donné que ► view
étape ► lap[2], leg
   par étapes ► progressive
état[1] ► condition, repair, shape, state, status
   état de chose ► circumstance
   état de transe ► trance
   état d'esprit ► frame of mind
   état immobile ► rest[1]
   état major ► headquarters
   état tampon ► buffer
   en état ► fit[1]
   en bon état ► in order
   en état d'apesanteur ► weightless
état[2] ► province, state
   chef d'État ► ruler
   criminel (-elle) d'État ► traitor
   État (l') ► commonwealth
étau ► vice[2], vise
été ► summer
   passer l'été ► summer
éteindre ► blow out, extinguish, quench, stamp, switch, turn on (off) [turn]
   s'éteindre ► away, disappear
éteint (-einte) ► extinct, glaze, off
étendard ► standard
étendre ► enlarge, extend, spread, stretch
   s'étendre ► dwell on, range, recline, stretch
   s'étendre de tous les côtés ► sprawl
étendu (-ue) ► comprehensive, extensive, great
étendue ► dimension, extent, range, reach, spread, stretch, sweep, tract
éternel (-elle) ► eternal, immortal, perpetual
éternellement ► eternally [eternal]
s'éterniser ► drag
éternité ► eternity
   une éternité ► ages [age]
éternuement ► sneeze
éternuer ► sneeze
éthique ► ethical [ethics]
ethnique ► ethnic
étincelant (-ante) ► fiery, glittery, glittering [glitter], starry
étinceler ► flash, glitter, sparkle
étincelle ► spark
   produire une étincelle ► spark
   produire des étincelles ► sparkle
étincellement ► sparkle
étiqueter ► label, tag[1], ticket
étiquette ► etiquette, label, tab, tag[1], ticket
étirement ► stretch
étirer ► stretch
   étirer le cou ► crane
étoffe ► cloth, fabric, material
   ceinture (d'étoffe) ► sash[1]

étoffé (-ée) ► meaty [meat]
étoile ► star
  étoile de David ► Star of David
  étoile de mer ► starfish
  étoile polaire ► North Star
étoilé (-ée) ► starry
étonnamment ► amazingly [amaze], surprisingly [surprise]
étonnant (-ante) ► incredible, unbelievable, unheard-of, wonderful
étonnement ► astonishment [astonish], wonder
étonner ► astonish, impress
étouffant (-ante) ► sultry
étouffement ► suffocation [suffocate]
étouffer ► choke, damp, deaden, drown, gag, hush up, muffle, smother, stifle, suffocate
  rire étouffé ► giggle
étourderie ► thoughtlessness [thoughtless]
étourdi (-ie) ► dizzy, thoughtless
étourdiment ► thoughtlessly [thoughtless]
étourdir ► daze
étourdissement ► daze, whirl
  d'étourdissement ► dizzy
étourneau ► starling
étrange ► alien, odd, queer, strange, weird, whimsical
  de façon étrange ► strangely [strange]
étrangement ► oddly [odd], quirky [quirk]
  à l'étranger ► abroad, foreign
étranger (-ère) ► alien, foreign, stranger
étrangeté ► novelty, oddness [odd], strangeness [strange]
étranglement ► narrow
étrangler ► choke, strangle, throttle
étrangleur ► choke
être ► be, being, exist
  c'est ça ► all right
  ça y est ► all right
êtres ► selves
étreindre ► embrace, fold, hug
étreinte ► embrace, grasp, grip, hug, squeeze
étrier ► stirrup
étroit (-oite) ► narrow, tight
  à l'étroit ► tight
  passage étroit ► narrow
étroitesse ► tightness [tight]
étude ► analysis, homework, office, project, study, survey
  études ► education
étudiant (-ante) ► scholar, student
  étudiant (-ante) du premier cycle (universitaire) ► undergraduate
étudier ► analyse, investigate, study
  étudier de près ► pore²
étui ► case²

étui de revolver ► holster
étuver ► steam
Eurasie ► Eurasia
Europe ► Europe
européen (-enne) ► European [Europe]
eux ► them
  eux-mêmes ► themselves
évacuation ► disposal
évacuer ► evacuate, expel
évader ► escape
  s'évader ► break out
évaluation ► assessment [assess], estimate, evaluation [evaluate], measure
évaluer ► assess, calculate, compare, estimate, evaluate, gauge, guess, rate, value
  mal évaluer ► misjudge
évanouir ► evaporate
  s'évanouir ► faint
évanouissement ► blackout, faint
évaporation ► evaporation [evaporate]
évaporer ► evaporate
évaser ► flare
évasion ► escape
éveillé (-ée) ► alert, perky [perk], up
éveiller ► arouse, awake, awaken, stir
  s'éveiller ► awake, wake¹
  éveiller l'antagonisme de ► antagonize
événement ► affair, circumstance, event, happening, incident, occasion, occurrence [occur]
  événement marquant ► landmark
évent ► blowhole
éventail¹ (-ails) ► fan¹
éventail² (-ails) ► range, spectrum
éventer ► fan¹
éventualité ► possible
éventuel (-elle) ► eventual, potential, prospective
éventuellement ► eventually [eventual]
évêque ► bishop
s'évertuer ► endeavour
évidemment ► evidently [evident], obviously [obvious], of course
évidence ► evidence
  mettre en évidence ► underline, underscore
évident (-ente) ► apparent, certain, decided, evident, gross, obvious, plain, transparent, unmistakable
évider ► hollow
évier ► basin, sink
évitable ► avoidable [avoid]
éviter ► avoid, bypass, clear, elude, evade, miss¹, shun, shy, ward
  éviter de se compromettre ► hedge
  évité (-ée) de justesse ► near
  évité (-ée) de près ► near

route d'évitement ► bypass
évoluer ► change, civilize, evolve
évolution ► change, evolution
exact (-acte) ► accurate, correct, direct, exact, faithful, right, technical, true
   peu exact (-acte) ► loose
   exacte réplique ► twin
exactement ► accurately [accurate], directly, exactly [exact], flat[1], just, literally, on the nose, precisely [precise], punctually [punctual], right
   plus exactement ► rather
exactitude ► accuracy [accurate], correctness [correct], precision
exagéré (-ée) ► extravagant, extreme
exagérer ► blow up, exaggerate, magnify
exaltation ► excitement
examen ► examination, final, survey, test
   examen au scanneur ► scan
   préparer un examen ► cram
examiner ► check, consider, criticize, deliberate, discuss, examine, explore, investigate, scan, study
   examiner minutieusement ► sift
   examiner avec une sonde ► probe
exaspération ► aggravation [aggravate]
exaspérer ► aggravate
exaucer ► grant
Excalibur ► Excalibur
excaver ► excavate
excédent ► excess
excédentaire ► excessive [excess]
excéder ► exceed
   excéder la vitesse limite ► speed
excellemment ► excellently [excellent]
excellent (-ente) ► banner, brilliant, excellent, great, professional, sterling, superb, terrific
exceller ► excel
excentricité ► quirk
excentrique ► crank, eccentric
excepté ► except
exception ► departure, exception
   sans exception ► consistently [consistent]
   à l'exception de ► save
exceptionnel (-elle) ► exceptional, extraordinary, outstanding, special, unique, unusual
exceptionnellement ► exceptionally [exceptional], outstandingly [outstanding], uncommonly [uncommon], unusually [unusual]
excès ► excess
excessif (-ive) ► excessive [excess], intense, steep[1], unreasonable
   de façon excessive ► wasteful [waste]
excessivement ► excessively [excess], too, unreasonably [unreasonable]

excitant (-ante) ► breathtaking, thrill
excitation ► excitement
excité (-ée) ► excited [excite]
exciter ► arouse, excite, fire, thrill
point d'exclamation ► exclamation mark
s'exclamer ► exclaim
exclure ► bar, eliminate, exclude, expel
exclusif (-ive) ► exclusive, sole[2], unique
exclusivement ► exclusively [exclusive]
excrément ► waste
excursion ► tour, trip, walk
excuse ► alibi, excuse
   excuses ► apology
   être sans excuse ► not having a leg to stand on
excuser ► excuse
   s'excuser ► apologize
   excusez-moi ► pardon me or I beg your pardon
exécrable ► atrocious, obnoxious
exécuter ► accomplish, carry out, execute, fill, implement, interpret, perform
exécutif (-ive) ► executive
exécution ► execution, performance
exemplaire ► copy
exemple ► case[1], example, instance, piece
   à titre d'exemple ► illustration
   par exemple ► for instance, like[2]
   donner un exemple ► illustrate
exempter ► excuse, exempt
exercer ► exercise, practise, wield
   s'exercer à répétition ► drill
exercice ► drill, exercise, practice, tenure
   exercice d'aérobic ► aerobic exercise
   exercice de traction ► push up
   faire de l'exercice ► exercise
exhiber ► display, exhibit, parade, produce
exhibition ► exhibition
exhorter ► urge
exigence ► demand, requirement
exiger ► demand, expect, require
   exiger des frais ► assess
exil ► banishment [banish], exile
exilé (-ée) ► exile
exiler ► banish, exile
existence ► being, fate, life
   d'existence ► living
exister ► exist
exorbitant (-ante) ► extravagant
exotique ► exotic
expansion ► growth
expatrié (-ée) ► exile
expatrier ► exile
expédier ► route, ship
   expédier (par bateau) ► ship

expéditeur (-trice) ▶ sender [send]
expédition ▶ expedition, shipping, trek
expérience ▶ experience, experiment, incident
   d'expérience ▶ veteran
   qui a l'expérience du monde ▶ worldly
expérimentalement ▶ experimentally [experiment], tentatively [tentative]
expérimenté (-ée) ▶ veteran
expérimenter ▶ experiment
expert (-erte) ▶ adept, expert
   de façon experte ▶ adeptly [adept]
explication ▶ account, explanation, instruction
explicite ▶ express
explicitement ▶ specifically [specific]
expliquer ▶ account, explain, interpret
   expliquer clairement ▶ spell out
exploit ▶ achievement, feat
exploitation agricole ▶ farm
exploiter ▶ exploit, harness, operate, tap[2]
explorer ▶ explore
exploser ▶ blow up, burst, erupt, explode
explosion ▶ blast, burst, explosion
exportation ▶ export
exporter ▶ export
exposé ▶ presentation
exposé (-ée) ▶ liable
   exposé (-ée) au vent ▶ bleak
exposer ▶ display, endanger, exhibit, expose, show
   exposer les grandes lignes ▶ outline
   s'exposer à ▶ court
exposition ▶ display, exhibition, show
   simple exposition ▶ bald
exprès ▶ deliberately [deliberate], express, purposely [purpose]
express ▶ express
expressément ▶ expressly [express]
expressif (-ive) ▶ mobile
expression ▶ expression, idiom, phrase, saying, utterance [utter[1]]
   sans expression ▶ blank, vacant, wooden
exprimer ▶ air, couch, express, phrase, put, register, utter[1], voice
expulsé (-ée) ▶ exile
expulser ▶ deport, eject, expel
exquis (-ise) ▶ exquisite
exquisément ▶ exquisitely [exquisite]
extase ▶ ecstasy
s'extasier ▶ rave
extension ▶ extension
exténuer ▶ exhaust
extérieur ▶ exterior, external, outside
   à l'extérieur ▶ foreign, outside
extérieur ▶ exterior, outside, outward

en extérieur ▶ on location
extérieur (-ieure) ▶ external, foreign, outer,
extérieurement ▶ externally [external], outwardly [outward]
extermination ▶ massacre
exterminer ▶ destroy, massacre
externe ▶ external
être en voie d'extinction ▶ endanger
extirpation ▶ pluck
extirper ▶ fish, pull, yank
extraire ▶ core, excerpt, extract, mine[2], quarry[1]
   extraire par fusion ▶ smelt[2]
extrait ▶ excerpt
   extrait de vanille ▶ vanilla
extraordinaire ▶ extraordinary, outstanding, unbelievable, unique, unusual, wonderful
extraordinairement ▶ fantastically [fantastic], unusually [unusual]
extraterrestre ▶ alien, creature
extravagant (-ante) ▶ extravagant
   de façon extravagante ▶ wildly [wild]
extrême ▶ extreme, intense
   extrême pauvreté ▶ wretchedness [wretched]
   extrême tristesse ▶ wretchedness [wretched]
   pousser les choses à l'extrême ▶ go to extremes
extrêmement ▶ enormously [enormous], exceedingly [exceed], extremely [extreme], highly, immensely [immense], mighty, remarkably [remarkable], too, vastly [vast]
extrémiste ▶ extreme
extrémité ▶ end, extreme, peak, tip[1]
   relever une extrémité ▶ tip[2]
exutoire ▶ outlet, vent

F

fable ▶ fable, tale
fabricant (-ante) ▶ maker, manufacturer [manufacture]
fabrication ▶ manufacture
fabrique ▶ factory, mill
fabriquer ▶ fashion, make, make up, manufacture, produce
fabuleusement ▶ fantastically [fantastic]
fabuleux (-euse) ▶ fabulous, fantastic
façade ▶ front
face ▶ face, head
   coup (de pile ou face) ▶ toss
   en face (de) ▶ across
   en face de ▶ opposite
   faire face ▶ cope, face, front, meet
   faire face à ▶ meet with
fâché (-ée) ▶ angry, cross, sore, upset

fâcher ▶ angrily [anger], cross, vex

facial (-ale, -ale, -aux) ▶ facial

facile ▶ easy, effortless [effort], light[2]

facilement ▶ easily, effortlessly [effort], readily

facilité ▶ ease, facility

faciliter ▶ lighten[2]

façon ▶ fashion, manner, way

   de la même façon ▶ similarly [similar]

   de cette façon ▶ thus

   de plusieurs façons différentes ▶ variously [various]

   de toute façon ▶ anyhow, anyway, in any event

   sans façon ▶ informal

façonner ▶ fashion, groom, mould[1], shape

facteur ▶ factor

factoriser ▶ factor

facture ▶ bill[1]

facturer ▶ bill[1]

facultatif (-ive) ▶ optional [option]

faculté ▶ faculty, power

fade ▶ bland, drab, tasteless

faible ▶ dim, faint, feeble, helpless, limp[2], quiet, remote, slack, slim, soft, thin, weak, weakness

   très faible ▶ outside

   par une faible marge ▶ by a nose

faiblement ▶ faintly [faint], helplessly, limply [limp[2]], softly [soft], weakly [weak]

faiblesse ▶ helplessness, weakness

faiblir ▶ fail, falter, weaken

faille ▶ fault, flaw

faillite ▶ crash

   en faillite ▶ bankrupt

   mettre en faillite ▶ bankrupt

faim ▶ hunger

   avoir faim de ▶ hunger

   mourir de faim ▶ starve

fainéant (-ante) ▶ bum, drone, idle, lazy

fainéanter ▶ bum

fainéantise ▶ laziness [lazy]

faire ▶ blow[1], commit, dial, do, give, go, make, pay, run

   se faire ▶ get, go

   pas fait (faite) ▶ undone[1]

   bien fait ▶ well-done

   fait (faite) à la hâte ▶ hurried

   fait (faite) à la maison ▶ homemade

   faire à la hâte ▶ rush[1]

   faire à toute vitesse ▶ race[1], rush[1]

   faire en sorte que ▶ let

   essayer de faire ▶ fling, stab

   venir de faire ▶ just

fair-play ▶ fair[1]

faisan (-ane) ▶ pheasant

faisceau ▶ beam

fait ▶ fact

   de fait ▶ virtual [virtually]

   en fait ▶ actually [actual], really

   fait nouveau ▶ development

faîte ▶ height, ridge

falaise ▶ bluff[2], cliff

falloir ▶ get

falsifier ▶ fake

familial (-ale, -aux) ▶ family

   voiture familiale ▶ station wagon

(se) familiariser ▶ orient

familier (-ière) ▶ chummy [chum], familiar, household, informal

   animal familier ▶ pet

famille ▶ family, folk, house, household, kin

   famille royale ▶ royalty

   membre de la famille royale ▶ royalty

   nom de famille ▶ surname

famine ▶ famine

fanatique ▶ fanatic

fanchon ▶ kerchief

se faner ▶ wither

fantaisie ▶ fancy, fantasy, whim

   articles de fantaisie ▶ novelty

fantaisiste ▶ fancy, whimsical

fantasme ▶ fantasy

fantasque ▶ erratic, temperamental, wise

fantastique ▶ fantastic

fantastiquement ▶ fantastically [fantastic]

fantomatique ▶ ghostly [ghost]

fantôme ▶ ghost, phantom

faon ▶ fawn

farce ▶ dressing, gag, hoax, joke, lark[2], prank, stuffing

farceur (-euse) ▶ clown, mischievous

farcir ▶ stuff

fard à joues ▶ rouge

fardeau (-eaux) ▶ burden, load

farfadet ▶ brown, elf

farfouiller ▶ rummage

farine ▶ flour, meal[2]

farouche ▶ shy

   pas farouche ▶ tame

farouchement ▶ bitterly [bitter]

fascinant (-ante) ▶ glamourous [glamour]

fascination ▶ fascination [fascinate], glamour

fasciner ▶ fascinate

fastidieusement ▶ tediously [tedious]

fastidieux (-euse) ▶ tedious

fatal (-ale, -als) ▶ deadly, fatal, inevitable, mortal

fatalement ▶ inevitably [inevitable]

fatalité ▶ fate

fatidique ▶ fatal

fatigant (-ante) ▶ laborious [labour], pill, strenuous, tire[1]

fatigue ► fatigue, strain[1], tiredness [tired], weariness [weary]
fatigué (-ée) ► run-down, tired, weary, worn
fatiguer ► fatigue, tire[1], weary
faucher ► mow, reap
faucheur (-euse) ► mower [mow]
faucon ► falcon, hawk[1]
se faufiler ► edge, steal, thread, weave, wriggle
    se faufiler furtivement ► sneak
faune ► fauna, wildlife
faussement ► deceptively [deceptive], falsely [false]
fausser ► warp
faute ► blame, error, fault, foul, mistake
    en faute ► at fault
    commettre une faute ► foul
    avoir besoin faute de ► want
fauteuil d'orchestre ► orchestra
fauteuil roulant ► wheelchair
fautif (-ive) ► at fault, guilty
fauve ► tan
faux (fausse) ► fake, false, flat[1], hollow, improper, in (out) of tune, incorrect, mistaken, mock, off-key, sham
    faux bourdon ► drone
    faux nom ► alias
    faux pas ► slip[1]
    faux pli ► crease
chercher des **faux-fuyants** ► hedge
faveur ► favour
    en faveur de ► pro
    faire une faveur ► oblige
    prévenir (contre, en faveur de) ► prejudice
favorable ► fair[1], favourable
favorablement ► favourably [favourable]
favori (-ite) ► favourite, pet
favoris ► sideburns
favoriser ► encourage, favour, forward, further, lean[1], promote, slant
fécond (-onde) ► fertile, productive
féconder ► fertilize
fécule ► starch
féculent ► starchy [starch]
fédéral ► dominion, Dominion
fédéral (-ale, -aux) ► federal
fédéralisme ► dominion, Dominion
fédération ► confederation, dominion, Dominion
fée ► fairy, magician
feindre ► pretend
feinte ► balk
fêler ► crack
félicitations ► compliment
félicité ► bliss
féliciter ► compliment, congratulate, pat on the back

félin (-ine) ► cat, feline
femelle ► cow, female, hen, mate, she
féminin (-ine) ► female, feminine
femme ► female, lady, mate, wife, woman
    de femme ► feminine
    femme (homme) politique ► politician
    femme (homme) d'affaires ► businessman, businesswoman, businessperson [business]
fendre ► chop, knife, slit, split
    se fendre en éclats ► splinter
fenêtre ► window
    fenêtre en baie ► bay[5]
fente ► crack, crevice, slit, slot, split
fer ► iron
    paille de fer ► steel wool
    chemin de fer ► rail, railroad, railway
    fer à cheval ► horseshoe
    donner un coup de fer ► iron
    mettre les fers à ► shackle
fer-blanc ► tin
ferme[1] ► fast[1], firm[1], hard, secure, steady, tight
ferme[2] ► farm, ranch
    ferme laitière ► dairy
fermé (-ée) ► close[2], exclusive, off
    fermé (-ée) à l'aide d'une fermeture éclair ► zipped [zipper]
fermement ► firmly [firm[1]]
fermer ► close[1], fold, shut
    fermer à clé ► lock[1]
    fermer à l'aide d'une fermeture éclair ► zip
    fermer les volets ► shutter
    fermer les yeux ► overlook
    fermer solidement ► fasten
    se fermer d'un coup ► spring
fermeté ► firmness [firm[1]]
    avec fermeté ► firmly [firm[1]]
fermeture ► close[1]
    fermeture à glissière ► zipper
    fermeture éclair ► zipper
    fermer à l'aide d'une fermeture éclair ► zip
fermoir ► catch, clasp
féroce ► ferocious, fierce, savage, vicious
férocement ► ferociously [ferocious], fiercely [fierce]
avec férocité ► ferociously [ferocious]
ferraille ► junk[1], scrap
ferrer ► shoe
système ferroviaire ► railway
fers ► shackle
fertile ► fertile, productive
fertiliser ► fertilize
fervent (-ente) ► passionate [passion]

fesser ► whack
    donner une fessée ► spank
festin ► feast
festival (-als) ► carnival, festival
festivités ► carnival
festonné (-ée) ► scallop
festonner ► scallop
festoyer ► feast
fête ► carnival, feast, festival, party, shower, spree
    les Fêtes ► Yule
    fête de la Confédération ► Dominion Day
    fête des Mères ► Mother's Day
    fête du Canada ► Canada Day, Dominion Day
    Fête du travail ► Labour day
    fête foraine ► carnival, midway
fêter ► celebrate, observe
fétiche ► charm
fétide ► rank[2]
feu (feux) ► fire, light[1]
    feu (de joie) ► bonfire
    feu de camp ► campfire
    feu avant ► headlight
    feu d'artifice ► fireworks
    feu de l'action ► heat
    feu follet ► jack-o'-lantern
    feu de forêt ► wildfire
    coup de feu ► shot[1]
    être mis à feu ► blast off
    mettre le feu à ► fire, ignite
    prendre feu ► flame, ignite
feu (feue) ► late
feuille ► form, leaf, sheet
    à feuilles persistantes ► evergreen
    à feuilles caduques ► deciduous
    feuille de métal ► foil[2]
    feuille de papier ► paper
    feuille odoriférante d'arbre ► bay[4]
feuiller ► leaf
feuilleter ► flip, leaf, scan, skim, thumb
feuilleton ► serial, series
feuillu (-ue) ► leafy [leaf]
feutre ► felt[2]
fève ► bean
février ► February
fiable ► dependable, reliable, responsible
    peu fiable ► unreliable
    de manière fiable ► reliably [reliable]
fiacre ► carriage
fiançailles ► engagement
se fiancer ► engage
fiasco ► flop
    faire fiasco ► flop
fibre ► fibre, strand[2]
fibreux (-euse) ► stringy

ficelle ► string, twine
fiche ► card[1], form, plug, slip[2]
fichier ► document, file[1]
fichu ► kerchief
fictif (-ive) ► fictional [fiction], imaginary, make-believe
fiction ► fiction, make-believe
fidéicommissaire ► trustee
fidèle ► faithful, loyal, regular
    fidèle à ► true
fidèlement ► faithfully [faithful], loyally
fidélité ► allegiance, faithfulness [faithful]
fiduciaire ► trustee
fiducie ► trust
fier (fière) ► proud, proud [pride]
fièrement ► proudly [proud]
fierté ► pride
    qui suscite de la fierté ► proud
se fier ► rely, trust
fièvre ► excitement, fever, temperature
    fièvre jaune ► yellow fever
    fièvre typhoïde ► typhoid fever
figer ► anchor, choke, freeze
figue ► fig
figurant (-ante) ► extra[1]
figure ► face, figure
    figure de proue ► figurehead
    figure de rhétorique ► figure of speech
faire figurer ► feature
fil ► edge, line[1], string, thread, train, wire, yarn
    fil (conducteur) ► thread
    fil électrique ► cord, wire
    coup de fil ► ring[2]
filage ► guy[1]
filandreux (-euse) ► stringy
prendre en filature ► shadow
file ► file[1], row[1]
    file d'attente ► queue
    marcher en file ► file[1]
filer ► dash, fly[1], sail, spin, tail
    filer à toute allure ► race[1], whisk, whiz
filet ► basket, dribble, fillet, net[1], trickle
    ramasser dans ses filets ► net[1]
    prendre au filet ► net[1]
filetage ► thread
fileur (-euse) ► spinner [spin]
filiale ► affiliate
fille ► child, daughter, female, girl, lass
    jeune fille ► girl, lass, maid, maiden, miss[2]
    petite-fille ► girl, granddaughter
film ► film, motion picture, movie
    grand film ► feature
    film à suspense ► thriller
    musique de film ► theme
filmer ► film
filou ► crook
fils ► child, junior, son

petit-fils ▶ grandson
Fils de Dieu ▶ Christ
filtre ▶ filter
filtrer ▶ filter, screen, seep, strain[1]
fin ▶ completion, conclusion, end, fine[1], finish, last[1], tail
    fin de semaine ▶ weekend
    en fin de compte ▶ eventually [eventual]
    sans fin ▶ endless, perpetual
    vers la fin de ▶ late
    mettre fin ▶ terminate
    tirer à sa fin ▶ wind[2]
    prendre fin ▶ break up
fin (fine) ▶ acute, delicate, fine[1], keen, sheer, wispy [wisp]
final (-ale, -aux) ▶ final, terminal, ultimate
    résultat final ▶ grand
finalement ▶ after all, at last, eventually [eventual], finally
finance ▶ finance
    finances ▶ finance
    le ministère des finances ▶ Treasury
financer ▶ finance, fund
financier (-ière) ▶ financial [finance]
    marché financier ▶ stock market
financièrement ▶ financially [finance]
finement ▶ cunningly [cunning], fine[1]
finesse ▶ cunning, thinness [thin]
    avec finesse ▶ exquisitely [exquisite]
fini (-ie) ▶ over, through
    qui manque de fini ▶ crude
finir ▶ cease, close[1], complete, conclude, do, end, finish, terminate, wind[2]
    finir en vitesse ▶ dash off
finition ▶ finish
    finitions ▶ trim
fiole ▶ flask
fiord ▶ fiord, fjord
fioriture ▶ flourish
firme ▶ company, firm[2]
fissure ▶ crack, crevice, split
fixatif à cheveux ▶ spray
fixe ▶ flat[1]
    regard fixe ▶ stare
fixer ▶ appoint, assign, fix, gaze, mount, name, peg, pin, time
    fixer avec une punaise ▶ tack
    regarder fixement ▶ stare
fjord ▶ fiord
flageller ▶ lash[1]
fragrance ▶ perfume
flagrant (-ante) ▶ decided, gross, rank[2]
flair ▶ flair, nose
flairer ▶ nose, scent, sniff
flamant ▶ flamingo
flambeau ▶ torch
flamber ▶ blaze[1], flame

flamboiement ▶ blaze[1], flare
flamboyer ▶ blaze[1], glow
flamme ▶ flame, flare
    flammes ▶ blaze[1]
flanc (de montagne) ▶ hillside
flanelle ▶ flannel
flâner ▶ drift, lounge, moon, stroll, wander
flanquer un coup ▶ sock[2]
    flanquer une claque ▶ box[2]
flaque ▶ pool[1], puddle
flasque ▶ flask, limp[2]
flatter ▶ court, flatter, pat
flatteur (-euse) ▶ complimentary
fléau (-aux) ▶ catastrophe, curse, nuisance, plague
flèche ▶ arrow, spire, steeple
    monter en flèche ▶ jump, rocket, skyrocket, soar
    passer comme une flèche ▶ zip
fléchette ▶ dart
    jeu de fléchettes ▶ dart
fléchir ▶ flex
flegme ▶ coolness [cool]
flet ▶ flounder[2]
flétan ▶ halibut
flétrir ▶ shrivel
    se flétrir ▶ wilt, wither
fleur ▶ bloom, blossom, flower
    fleur de l'âge ▶ prime
    fleurs séchées ▶ potpourri
fleurir ▶ bloom, blossom, flourish, flower
fleuve ▶ river
flexible ▶ flexible, limber
flibustier ▶ pirate
flocon ▶ flake
    flocons d'avoine ▶ oatmeal
    flocon de neige ▶ snowflake
    bouillie de flocons d'avoine ▶ porridge
faune ▶ bloom, blossom
flore ▶ wildlife
florissant (-ante) ▶ thrive
flot continu ▶ stream
    à flot ▶ afloat
    sortir à flots ▶ stream
flottable ▶ buoyant
flotte ▶ armada, fleet[1]
flotter ▶ float, flow, flutter, wave
flotteur ▶ float
flou (floue) ▶ cloudy, fuzzy, hazy, misty [mist], vague
fluet (-ette) ▶ thin
fluide ▶ fluid
fluorescent (-ente) ▶ fluorescent, luminous
fluorure ▶ fluoride
flûte ▶ flute
    flûte à bec ▶ recorder
flux ▶ flow

foi ► belief, faith

foie ► liver

foin ► hay

foire ► carnival, fair[2]

fois ► time
   à la fois ► at once, both
   une fois ► once
   une fois que ► once
   deux fois ► double, twice
   chaque fois que ► whenever
   toutes les fois que ► whenever
   pour la première fois ► first
   (juste) pour une fois ► once

folie ► folly, madness [mad]

folklore ► folklore

follement ► madly [mad]

foncé (-ée) ► dark

foncer ► barrel, bear down, dart, pelt[1], tear[1]

fonction ► duty, function, office
   faire fonction de ► function

fonctionnaire ► official

fonctionnel (-elle) ► convenient

fonctionnement ► operation

fonctionner ► function, operate, work
   qui fonctionne à ► power
   faire fonctionner ► power, run, work

fond ► background, bottom, depth, floor, fund, nucleus, seat
   à fond ► thoroughly [thorough]
   à fond de train ► full tilt [tilt]
   au fond ► back, basically
   de fond ► feature
   sans fond ► bottomless

fondamental (-ale, -aux) ► essential, fundamental, primary, prime

fondamentalement ► essentially, fundamentally [fundamental], radically [radical]

fondant ► fudge

fondateur ► father

fondation ► foundation

fondement ► base[1], foundation

fonder ► base[1], establish, found[2], institute

fondre ► fuse, melt, smelt[2], swoop, thaw
   se fondre ► merge
   faire fondre ► dissolve

fonds ► fund, money

fondu (-ue) ► molten

fondue ► dip

fontaine ► font[1], fountain
   fontaine (à café, à thé) ► urn

fonte ► thaw

fonts baptismaux ► font[1]

football ► football, soccer
   football américain ► football
   ballon de football ► football
   match de football ► bowl[1]

force ► drift, force, loudness [loud], might[2], muscle, strength
   forces ► force
   forces armées ► armed forces
   Forces armées canadiennes ► Canadian Forces
   avoir la force de ses convictions ► backbone
   lancer violemment ► dash, hurl
   reprendre des forces ► rally
   ouvrir en employant la force ► pry[1]

forcé (-ée) ► far-fetched, wry

forcément ► necessarily

forcer ► compel, force, make, obligate, oblige, pry[1]
   forcer à ► pressure
   forcer quelqu'un à faire quelque chose ► railroad

forer ► bore[2], drill

foret ► bit[2]

forêt ► forest, wood
   forêt tropicale (humide) ► rain forest

foreuse ► bore[2], drill

forfait ► package

forger ► invent

formaliste ► formal

formalité ► formality [formal]

format ► format

formation ► background, development, education, formation, training
   recevoir une formation ► train

forme ► figure, form, shape, trim
   en forme ► shape, trim
   en pleine forme ► fit[1]
   en bonne et due forme ► formal
   forme à chaussure ► last[3]
   prendre forme ► brew, form

formel (-elle) ► express, formal, positive

formellement ► positive

former ► form, train, educate, develop, make, mould[1]
   se former ► form
   former des mots avec les lèvres ► mouth

formidable ► fabulous, grand, marvellous, terrific, wonderful

formidablement ► terrifically [terrific]

formulaire ► blank, form
   formulaire de candidature ► application

formulation ► wording

formule ► device, form, formula
   formule magique ► spell[2]

formuler ► couch, express, lodge, utter[1], voice, word

fort[1] ► château, fort

fort[2] ► greatly [great], loudly [loud]

travailler fort ▸ buckle down
parler fort ▸ bluster
fort (forte) ▸ hard, heavy, hot, husky[1], loud, pronounced, stiff, strong, tight
    chambre forte ▸ vault[1]
fortement ▸ hard, heavily, highly, strongly [strong]
forteresse ▸ fortress [fort]
fortifiant ▸ tonic
fortifier ▸ confirm
fortuit (-uite) ▸ casual
fortuitement ▸ by chance [chance], casually [casual]
fortune ▸ estate, fortune, mint[2], wealth
fortuné (-ée) ▸ wealthy
forum ▸ forum
fosse ▸ pit[1], trench
    fosse d'orchestre ▸ orchestra
fossé ▸ ditch, moat
fossette ▸ dimple
fossile ▸ fossil
fou ▸ fool
fou (folle) ▸ crazy, fool, frantic, furious, insane, lunatic, mad, runaway, wild
    fou de joie ▸ beside oneself
    comme un fou (une folle) ▸ frantically [frantic], insanely [insane]
    faire le fou (la folle) ▸ clown
foudre ▸ lightning
    coup de foudre ▸ thunderbolt
fouet ▸ lash[1], switch, whip
    coup de fouet ▸ lash[1], whiplash
fouetter ▸ churn, lash[1], whip
fougère ▸ fern
    crosse de fougère ▸ fiddlehead
fougue ▸ fire, pep
fougueux (-euse) ▸ fiery, spirited
fouiller ▸ burrow, dig, fumble, nose, root[2], rummage, scour[2], search
    fouiller à fond ▸ ransack
    fouiller avec le groin ▸ root[2]
    fouiller avec soin ▸ rake
    fouiller en mettant tout sens dessus dessous ▸ ransack
fouilleur (-euse) d'ordures ▸ scavenger
fouillis ▸ mat, mess, shambles
fouine ▸ snoop
fouiner ▸ nose, pry[2]
fouineur (-euse) ▸ snoop
fouir (la terre) ▸ burrow
foulard ▸ bandana, kerchief, scarf
foule ▸ crowd, crush, drove[3], flock, horde, jam[1], mob, multitude, score, throng
    faire foule autour de ▸ mob
se fouler ▸ sprain, twist
four ▸ kiln, oven
    four à micro-ondes ▸ microwave oven

    (faire) cuir au four ▸ bake
fourche ▸ crotch, fork
fourchette ▸ fork
    manger à coups de fourchette ▸ fork
fourgon ▸ van
    fourgon de queue ▸ caboose
fourgonnette ▸ van
fourmi ▸ ant
fourmilier ▸ aardvark, anteater
fourmilière ▸ hive
fourmillant (-ante) de ▸ alive
fourmillement ▸ tingle
fourmiller ▸ swarm, tingle
fournaise ▸ furnace
fourneau (-eaux) de cuisine ▸ range
fournée ▸ batch
fourni (-ie) ▸ thick
fournir ▸ afford, furnish, provide, supply
    fournir de grands efforts ▸ agonize
    fournir les repas ▸ cater
    fournir une caution ▸ bail[1]
fournisseur (-euse) ▸ dealer
fourniture ▸ provision, supply
fourrage ▸ feed
fourré ▸ brush[2], thicket
fourrer ▸ cram, drum, pop[1], thrust
    fourrer en forçant ▸ jam[1]
fourrière ▸ pound[2]
fourrure ▸ coat, fur, pelt[2]
foyer ▸ fireplace, focus, hearth, home, shelter
fracas ▸ clash, clatter, crash
fracassant (-ante) ▸ thunderous [thunder]
fracassement ▸ smash
fracasser ▸ crash, shatter
    se fracasser contre ▸ slam
fraction ▸ fraction
fragile ▸ breakable, brittle, fragile, rocky [rock[2]], tender[1], unsound
fragilité ▸ weakness
fragment ▸ crumb, debris, fragment, snatch
fragrance ▸ fragrance, perfume
fraîchement ▸ freshly [fresh]
fraîcheur ▸ cool, freshness [fresh]
frais ▸ charge, cool, cost, expense, fee
    frais de douane ▸ duty
    frais de port ▸ postage
    frais de scolarité ▸ tuition
    frais généraux ▸ overhead
    exiger des frais ▸ assess
frais (fraîche) ▸ cool, fresh, sweet, wet
    qui n'est plus frais ▸ stale
fraise[1] ▸ strawberry
fraise[2] ▸ ruffle
fraiser ▸ drill
framboise ▸ raspberry
franc (franche) ▸ candid, clean, direct, frank, genuine, plain, straight, straightforward, truthful

franc jeu ► fair[1]
français ► French-Canadian
    canadien (-ienne) français (-aise) ►
    French Canadian, French-Canadian
    français canadien ► Canadian French
franchement ► frankly [frank], freely [free],
genuinely [genuine], honestly [honest],
outright, truly, truthfully [truthful]
    parler franchement ► level
franchir ► clear, hurdle, negotiate, span
franchise ► concession, frankness [frank],
openness [open]
francophone ► Francophone
frange ► bangs, fringe
franger ► fringe
frappant (-ante) ► impressive, striking
    de façon frappante ► vividly [vivid]
frappé (-ée) ► stricken
frapper ► bang, bump, hammer, hit, impress,
knock, slug[2], strike
    frapper bruyamment ► rap[1]
    frapper fort ► belt
    frapper légèrement ► tap[1]
    frapper à coup de marteau ► hammer
    frapper à grands coups ► pound[2]
    frapper de la monnaie ► coin
    frapper de mildiou ► mildew
    frapper du pied ► stomp
    frapper la balle avec le bâton ► bat[1]
    frapper ou heurter violemment ► pelt[1]
    frapper un simple ► single out [single]
    frapper un roulant ► ground[1]
    frapper une monnaie ► mint[2]
    essayer de frapper ► swing
frappeur (-euse) ► batter[1], slugger [slug[2]]
fraternellement ► brotherly [brother]
fraude ► fraud, racket
fraudeur (-euse) ► fraud
frauduleux (-euse) ► false
frayer ► blaze[2], spawn
    se frayer un chemin ► press, push
    se frayer un chemin des coudes ►
    elbow
    se frayer un chemin à coup d'épaules
    ► shoulder
frayeur ► alarm, dread
fredonner ► hum, sing
frein ► brake
    mettre un frein à ► curb
freiner ► brake
    freiner à fond ► slam
    freiner brutalement ► jam[1]
frêle ► delicate, feeble, puny
frelon ► hornet
frémir ► quiver, tremble, shudder
frémissement ► shudder
frêne ► ash[2]

avec frénésie ► frantically [frantic]
frénétique ► frantic
frénétiquement ► frantically [frantic], wildly
[wild]
fréquemment ► frequently
fréquence ► frequency
fréquent (-ente) ► frequent
fréquentation ► association, company
fréquenter ► associate, frequent, haunt
    se fréquenter ► see
frère ► brother
frétillement ► wag
frétiller ► wag
fretin ► minnow
freux ► rook[1]
friand (-ande) de ► partial
friandise ► candy, tidbit
    friandises ► sweet
friction ► friction
frictionner ► rub
fringant (-ante) ► frisky
fringillidé ► finch
fripon (-onne) ► rascal
fripper ► crease
frire ► fry
    poêle (à frire) ► skillet
frisé (-ée) ► curly [curl]
friser ► curl
frisquet (-ette) ► chilly, cool
frisson ► shiver, shudder, thrill
frissonner ► quiver, shiver, shudder, tremble
    qui fait frissonner ► creepy [creep]
frit (frite) ► fried
frite ► french fry
    pomme de terre frite ► french fry
friture ► fry
frivole ► frivolous, light[2], trivial
froid ► chill, cold
    coup de froid ► snap
    prendre froid ► chill
froid[1] (froide) ► bleak, chilly, cold, cool,
frosty [frost]
froid[2] (froide) ► cold, distant, impersonal,
indifferent
froidement ► coldly [cold], cool
froideur ► chill, coldness [cold], coolness
[cool], distance, indifference [indifferent]
froissement ► rustle
froisser ► crease, ruffle, rumple, rustle, strain[1]
    se froisser ► pull
frôlement ► close shave [shave]
frôler ► graze
fromage ► cheese
froment ► wheat
froncement ► frown
froncer ► gather

froncer les sourcils ▸ frown, scowl
fronde ▸ sling, slingshot
front ▸ brow, forehead, front
    front de mer ▸ waterfront
frontal (-ale, -aux) ▸ front
frontière ▸ border, boundary, frontier, limit
frottement ▸ friction
frotter ▸ rub, scrape
    frotter (à la brosse) ▸ scrub[1]
fructueux (-euse) ▸ productive, profitable
frugal (-ale) ▸ spare
fruit ▸ berry, citrus, fruit, product
    fruit à écale ▸ nut
    fruits de mer ▸ shellfish
    porter fruit ▸ bear[1]
frustration ▸ frustration
frustrer ▸ frustrate
fudge ▸ fudge
fugitif (-ive) ▸ runaway
fugueur (-euse) ▸ runaway
fuir ▸ escape, flee, leak, run
fuite ▸ escape, flight[1], leak
    fuite soudaine ▸ bolt
    avoir une fuite ▸ leak
fulgurant (-ante) ▸ meteoric [meteor]
fulminer ▸ bluster, steam
fumé (-ée) ▸ smoky
fumée ▸ smoke
fumer ▸ smoke, steam
fumeur (-euse) ▸ smoker
fumier ▸ manure
funérailles ▸ funeral
funeste ▸ evil
furet ▸ ferret
fureter ▸ nose, pry[2]
fureteur (-euse) ▸ nosy
fureur ▸ fury, rage
furie ▸ fury, rage
    avec furie ▸ with a vengeance
    [vengeance]
    être en furie ▸ rage
furieusement ▸ furiously [furious]
furieux (-euse) ▸ fierce, furious, mad
    regard furieux ▸ glare
furoncle ▸ boil[2]
furtif (-ive) ▸ quick, stealthy [stealth]
    regard furtif ▸ peek
furtivement ▸ stealthily [stealth]
    suivre furtivement ▸ stalk[2]
    se faufiler furtivement ▸ sneak
fusain ▸ charcoal
fuseau horaire ▸ standard time, time
fusée ▸ rocket, skyrocket
    fusée éclairante ▸ flare
fuseler ▸ taper
fuser ▸ spew
fusible ▸ fuse

fusil ▸ gun, rifle
    fusil de chasse ▸ shotgun
fusionner ▸ fuse, incorporate
futaie ▸ timber
futile ▸ futile, idle, pointless
futilement ▸ futilely [futile]
futilité ▸ futility [futile]
    futilités ▸ trivial
futur ▸ future, tomorrow
futur (-ure) ▸ future
    futur marié ▸ bridegroom
    future mariée ▸ bride
    future vedette ▸ talent
fuyant (-ante) ▸ leaky [leak]
fuyard (-arde) ▸ runaway

G

gâcher ▸ mar, mess, ruin
gâchette ▸ trigger
gâchis ▸ mess, waste
gadget ▸ gadget
gaffe ▸ blunder, slip[1]
    faire une gaffe ▸ blunder, slip[1]
gaffer ▸ blunder
gage ▸ pledge, token
gagnant (-ante) ▸ winner, winning
gagne pain ▸ livelihood
gagner ▸ defeat, earn, gain, make, win,
winning
    gagner (contre toute attente) ▸ upset
gaiement ▸ cheerfully [cheerful]
gain ▸ gain, winning
    gains ▸ earnings
galaxie ▸ galaxy
gale ▸ scab
galère ▸ galley
galerie ▸ tunnel
    galerie (marchande) ▸ arcade
    galerie d'art ▸ gallery
    percer une galerie ▸ tunnel
galet ▸ pebble
galette ▸ bannock, cake
gallon ▸ gallon
galoche ▸ clog
galop ▸ gallop
galoper ▸ gallop
gambade ▸ caper
gambader ▸ caper, scamper
gamin (-ine) ▸ child, kid
gaminet ▸ T-shirt
gamme ▸ scale[3], spectrum
    bas de gamme ▸ cheap
    gamme de produits ▸ line[1]
gang ▸ gang
gangster ▸ gangster
gant ▸ glove

gant de baseball ► mitt
garage ► depot, garage
être le **garant de** ► sponsor
garantie ► coverage, guarantee, insurance, reassurance [reassure], security, warranty
garantir ► certify, ensure, guarantee, insure, sew up
garçon ► boy, fellow, guy[2], lad
  jeune garçon ► youngster
garde ► care, custody, guard
  sur ses gardes ► wary
  garde du corps ► bodyguard
  garde forestier ► ranger
  chien de garde ► watchdog
  mettre en garde ► caution, warn
  monter la garde ► watch
  prendre garde (à) ► beware, heed
garde-à-vous ► attention
  se mettre au garde-à-vous ► snap, stand
garde-fou ► rail
garder ► baby-sit, guard, keep, maintain, mind, reserve, retain, shepherd, tend[2]
  garder (perdre) contact ► keep (lose) track of
  garder (perdre) la notion du temps ► keep (lose) track of
  garder pour soi ► to keep under one's hat
  garder précieusement ► treasure
  garder rancune ► bear[1], harbour
  garder un œil sur ► keep an eye on
garderie ► nursery school
garde-robe ► wardrobe
gardien (-ienne) ► caretaker, guardian, keeper, warden, watchdog
  gardien (-ienne) de parc national ► ranger
  gardien (-ienne) de troupeau (-eaux) ► herd
  gardien de la paix ► cop
gare ► station
gargarisme ► mouthwash
se gargariser ► gargle
gargouille ► gargoyle
gargouillement ► rumble
gargouiller ► rumble
garnir ► coat, garnish, line[2], rig
  garnir de rideaux ► curtain
garniture ► garnish, trim, trimming
garrot ► tourniquet
gars ► chap[1], guy[2]
gaspillage ► waste
gaspillé (-ée) ► lost
gaspiller ► idle, waste
gaspilleur (-euse) ► extravagant
gastronome ► gourmet

gastronomie ► cuisine
gastronomique ► gourmet
gâteau (-eaux) ► cake
  gâteau (-eaux) au chocolat et aux noix ► brownie
gâter ► mar, pamper, spoil
  se gâter ► decay
gâterie ► treat
gauche ► clumsy, inept, left[1], port, ungainly
  à gauche ► left[1]
gauchir ► warp
gaufre ► waffle[1]
gaulthérie ► wintergreen
gaz ► gas
  arrivée de gaz ► throttle
  papillon des gaz ► throttle
gazon ► grass, green
  motte de gazon ► sod
  tondeuse à gazon ► lawnmower
gazouillement ► chirp
gazouiller ► babble, chirp
gazouillis ► chirp, song
geai ► jay
  geai bleu ► bluejay
  geai du Canada ► Canada jay
géant ► Sasquatch
géant (-ante) ► giant, gigantic, mammoth
geindre ► groan, moan, whine
gel ► freeze, frost
gelée ► frost, jelly
geler ► freeze, frost, ice
gémir ► groan, moan, wail, whimper, whine
gémissement ► groan, moan, wail, whine
gemme ► gem
gênant (-ante) ► troublesome
gencive ► gum[2]
gendarme ► cop
gène ► gene
gêne ► discomfort, need
gêné (-ée) ► ill at ease
  être **gêné (-ée)** ► handicap
gêner ► bother, cramp, embarrass, handicap, hinder
général (-ale, -aux) ► background, common, general, master
général (-aux) ► general
  quartier général ► headquarters
  Procureur Général ► Attorney General
  en général ► at large, generally, in general
généralement ► generally
généraliser ► generalize
génération ► generation
  se transmettre entre générations ► run
génératrice ► generator
générer ► generate
généreusement ► generously [generous], handsomely [handsome], liberally [liberal]

généreux (-euse) ► charitable, generous, good, liberal

générosité ► bounty, generousity [generous], goodness, humanity

genèse ► birth

genêt ► broom

génie ► brain, genius, prodigy, wizard

genou (-oux) ► knee
   genoux ► lap[1]
   se mettre à genoux ► kneel

genre ► description, form, genre, kind[2], manner, type
   de ce genre ► such

gens ► folk, people

gentil (-ille) ► gentle, kind[1], kindly, nice, sweet, thoughtful

gentilhomme ► gentleman

gentillesse ► sweetness [sweet]
   avec gentillesse ► kindly

gentiment ► gently [gentle], harmlessly [harmless], helpfully, nicely [nice], thoughtfully [thoughtful]

géographie ► geography

géographique ► geographic [geography]

géologie ► geology

géologique ► geologic [geology]

géomètre ► surveyor

géométrie ► geometry

géométrique ► geometric [geometry]

gerbe ► shock[2], wreath

gerbille ► gerbil

gercer ► chap[2]

gérer ► administer, direct, engineer, govern, manage, operate, run

germe ► germ, seed
   germe de blé ► wheat germ

germer ► sprout

geste ► act, actions, gesture, motion, wave
   gestes ► doings
   geste vif ► grab
   faire un geste ► gesture

gesticuler ► gesture

gestion ► administration, government, management

geyser ► geyser

gibier ► game
   gibier à plumes ► fowl

giclée ► jet, spurt, squirt

gicler ► jet, spout, spurt
   faire gicler ► squirt

gicleur ► nozzle, sprinkler [sprinkle]

gifle ► cuff[2], slap

gifler ► box[2], cuff[2], slap

gigantesque ► gigantic, huge, mountainous

gigoter ► fidget, flop, wriggle

gigue ► jig

gilet ► vest

gingembre ► ginger

girafe ► giraffe

clou de girofle ► clove

giron ► tread

girouette ► vane, weather vane

gisement ► deposit

gîte[1] ► quarter

gîte[2] ► list[2]

givre ► frost

glaçage ► icing

glace ► ice, ice cream, icing, mirror

glacé (-ée) ► chilly, glazed [glaze], icy
   coupe glacée ► sundae

glacer ► frost, glaze

glaciaire ► glacier
   période glaciaire ► Ice Age

glacial (-ale, -als) ► bleak, frosty [frost], glacial [glacier], icy, raw

glacier ► glacier

glacière ► icehouse

glaçon ► icicle

gland ► acorn, tassel

glande ► gland

glapir ► yelp

glissade ► slide

glissant (-ante) ► slick, slippery
   endroit glissant ► slick

glissement ► glide, landslide, shift, slip[1]

glisser ► glide, sail, skim, slide, slip[1], slither
   se glisser ► edge

glissoire ► slide

global (-ale, -aux) ► global [globe], total
   somme globale ► grand

globalement ► globally [globe]

globalité ► package

globe ► globe, world
   globe terrestre ► globe

gloire ► fame, glory, honour

glorieusement ► gloriously [glorious]

glorieux (-euse) ► glorious

glorifier ► praise

glossaire ► glossary

glouglou ► gobble[2]

glouglouter ► gobble[2]

gloussement ► chuckle, giggle

glousser ► cackle, chuckle

glouton ► wolverine

glouton (-onne) ► greedy

gloutonnement ► greedily [greedy]

gloutonnerie ► greed

glu ► glue

gluant (-ante) ► sticky

gnome ► gnome

gnou ► gnu

gobelet ► beaker, mug, tumbler

goéland ► gull

goélette ► schooner

golf ► golf
  jouer au golf ► golf
golfe ► gulf
golfeur (-euse) ► golfer [golf]
gomme ► gum[1]
gommé (-ée) ► adhesive
gomme-laque ► shellac
  traiter à la gomme-laque ► shellac
gommer ► erase
gond ► hinge
gonflé (-ée) ► swollen
gonflement ► inflation
gonfler ► balloon, belly, blow up, inflate, puff, pump, swell
  se gonfler ► billow
gorge ► gorge, throat
  petite gorgée ► sip
  gorge (de serrure) ► tumbler
  rire à gorge déployée ► roar
se gorger ► gorge
gorgée ► swallow[1]
  boire à petites gorgées ► sip
gorille ► gorilla
gosse ► kid
goudron ► tar
goudronner ► tar
gouffre ► black hole, gulf
goulot ► mouth, neck, spout
goulu (-ue) ► greedy
gourde ► canteen
gourdin ► club
gourmet ► gourmet
gousse ► clove, hull
goût ► desire, fancy, flavour, taste, weakness
  goûts ► likes
  sans goût ► tastelessly [tasteless]
  de bon goût ► tasteful
  avec goût ► tastefully [tasteful]
  de mauvais goût ► tacky, tasteless
  avec mauvais goût ► tastelessly [tasteless]
  avoir un goût de ► taste
goûter ► enjoy, tea
goutte ► dole, dribble, drip, drop
  une goutte de ► taste
  tomber goutte à goutte ► dribble
gouttelettes ► spray
gouvernail (-ails) ► rudder
gouvernante ► housekeeper
gouvernement ► government
  chef du gouvernement ► premier
gouverner ► govern, handle, rule
gouverneur (-eure) ► governor, warden
  gouverneur (-eure) général ► Governor General
grâce ► favour, grace
  avec grâce ► gracefully [grace]

Action de grâce(s) ► Thanksgiving
  action de grâces ► grace
  entrer/sortir avec grâce ► glide
  faire grâce ► forgive
  rendre grâces (fait de) ► thanksgiving
gracier ► pardon
gracieusement ► gracefully [grace], graciously [gracious]
gracieux ► complimentary
  à titre gracieux ► complimentary
gracieux (-euse) ► graceful [grace], gracious
grade ► rank[1]
  collation des grades ► graduation
gradin ► tier
graduation ► scale[3]
graduel (-elle) ► gradual
graduellement ► gradually [gradual]
  passer graduellement ► graduate
graduer ► graduate
graffiti ► graffiti
grain[1] ► bean, grain, granola, kernel, speck
  grain de beauté ► mole[1]
  grains de café ► ground[1]
grain[2] ► texture
graine ► bean, seed
  graine de soja ► soybean
graisse ► fat, grease
  graisse (de rognon) ► suet
graisser ► grease, oil
graisseux (-euse) ► greasy [grease], oily [oil]
graminée ► grass
grammaire ► grammar
catégorie grammaticale ► part of speech
gramme ► gram, ounce
grand (grande) ► big, bumper, good, grand, great, healthy, high, large, mass, noble, tall, wide
  très grand (grande) ► vast
Grand bancs ► Grand Banks
Grande Ourse ► dipper
grandement ► highly
grandeur ► height, size
  grandeur nature ► as large as life
grandir ► grow
grand-mère ► grandmother
grand-père ► grandfather
grand-parent ► grandparent
grange ► barn
granit ► granite
granule ► granola
graphique ► chart, graph
grappe ► cluster
  grappe (raisins) ► bunch
gras ► fat
gras (grasse) ► fat, greasy [grease], oily [oil]
grassouillet (-ette) ► chubby, plump
gratis ► free

gratitude ► appreciation, thankfulness [thankful]
    avec gratitude ► gratefully [grateful], thankfully [thankful]
gratte-ciel ► skyscraper
grattement ► scrape, scratch
gratter ► scrape, scratch, strum
gratuit (-uite) ► free, wanton
gratuitement ► free
grave ► critical, deep, grave[2], low, severe, sober, solemn, weighty
gravement ► gravely [grave[2]], terribly
    gravement endommagé ► cripple
graver ► engrave, score
    graver des lettres ► letter
gravier ► gravel
gravillon ► gravel
gravir ► climb
gravité ► gravity
graviter ► orbit
gravure ► print
de bon **gré** ► readily
gréement ► rig
gréer ► rig
greffe ► transplant
greffer ► transplant
greffier (-ière) ► recorder
grêle ► hail[1], thin
grêler ► hail[1]
grenade ► pomegranate
grenaille de plomb ► shot[1]
grenier ► attic, loft
grenouille ► frog
grésillement ► sizzle
grésiller ► crackle, sizzle, sputter
grève ► strike
    en grève ► striking
    faire grève ► strike
    faire le piquet de grève ► picket
gréviste ► picket
gribouillage ► scrawl, scribble
gribouiller ► scribble
gribouillis ► scribble
griffe ► claw, talon
griffer ► claw
griffonnage ► scribble
griffonner ► doodle, scrawl, scribble
grignoter ► nibble
gril ► grill
grillage ► screen
grille ► screen
grille-pain ► toaster
griller ► grill, roast, toast[1]
    griller sur le barbecue ► barbecue
grillon ► cricket
grimacer ► wince
grimper ► climb, creep, shin

grimper à quatre pattes ► scramble
    faire grimper ► train
grinçant (-ante) ► squeaky [squeak]
grincement ► creak, squeak
grincer ► creak, grate, grind, jar, squeak, squeal
grincheux (-euse) ► crab, crabby [crab], crank, cranky
grippe ► flu, influenza
gris ► grey
    gris argenté ► silver
gris (grise) ► grey
grive ► thrush
grizzli ► grizzly bear
grognement ► growl, grunt, snarl[1]
grogner ► growl, grunt, snarl[1], snort
grognon (-onne) ► crabby [crab], whiny [whine]
groin ► snout
    fouiller avec le groin ► root[2]
grondement ► boom[1], growl, roar, rumble, snarl[1]
gronder ► boom[1], growl, roar, rumble, scold, snarl[1]
    gronder (en montrant les dents) ► snarl[1]
gros (grosse) ► fat, foul, heavy, large, stout
    de gros ► wholesale
    en gros ► bulk, wholesale
    vente en gros ► wholesale
grosse ► gross
grosseur ► size
grossier (-ière) ► coarse, crude, foul, gross, impolite, rude, uncouth
grossièrement ► coarsely [coarse], impolitely [impolite], rudely [rude]
grossièreté ► coarseness [coarse], rudeness [rude]
grossir ► magnify, swell, thicken
grossiste ► wholesaler [wholesale]
grotesque ► preposterous
grotesquement ► preposterously [preposterous]
grotte ► cave
grouillant (-ante) de ► alive
grouiller ► crawl, teem
    grouiller autour de ► mill
groupe ► battalion, bracket, bunch, chorus, cluster, clutch[2], den, group, party, squad, troop
    petit groupe ► knot
    groupe de pression ► lobby
    groupe électrogène ► generator
    aller en groupe ► troop
grouper ► bunch, concentrate, gather, group, incorporate
    se grouper ► cluster

gruau ► oatmeal

grue ► crane, hoist

    grue blanche, d'Amérique ► whooping crane

grumeau (-eaux) ► lump

grumeleux (-euse) ► lumpy [lump]

guenilles ► rag

guépard ► cheetah

guêpe ► hornet, wasp, yellow jacket

guérillero ► guerrilla

guérir ► cure, heal, rebound

guérison ► cure

guerre ► war, warfare

    hache de guerre ► tomahawk

    navire de guerre ► warship

    vaisseau (-eaux) de guerre ► warship

    faire la guerre ► wage, war

    se livrer à une guerre d'escarmouches ► skirmish

guerrier (-ière) ► warlike, warrior

faire le **guet** ► watch

    poste de guet ► lookout

guetter ► watch

guetteur (-euse) ► lookout

gueule ► mouth

gueule de loup ► snapdragon

gueuler ► bawl

gui ► mistletoe

guichetier (-ière) ► teller

guidance ► counsel

guide ► counsellor, guide

    guide aînée ► Ranger

guider ► guide, lead[1], shepherd

    être guidé (-ée) ► steer[1]

guignol ► clown

guillemets ► quotation mark

guimauve ► marshmallow

guindé (-ée) ► formal, stiff

agir à sa **guise** ► please

guitare ► guitar

gymnase ► gym, gymnasium

cours de **gymnastique** ► gym

H

habile ► adept, apt, deft, handy, neat, skillful [skill], smart

    habile à ► skilled

habilement ► deftly [deft], skillfully [skill]

habileté ► aptitude, capacity, hang, neatness [neat]

habilité ► skill

habiliter ► enable

habillement ► clothing, costume, dress, dressing, wear

(s')**habiller** ► dress

    bien s'habiller ► dress up

    personne qui s'habille bien ► dresser[2]

habilleur (-euse) ► dresser[2]

habit ► habit

    habits ► clothes

habitants (du coin) ► locals [local]

habitat ► habitat, home

habitation ► dwelling

habiter ► dwell, inhabit, live[1], lodge, occupy, populate, reside

habitude ► custom, habit, practice

    avoir ses habitudes ► set

    avoir l'habitude de ► used to

habitué (-ée) ► familiar, regular, used to

    non habitué (-ée) ► unused

habituel (-elle) ► accustomed, customary, familiar, regular, usual

habituellement ► customarily [customary], generally, ordinarily, usually

(s')**habituer à** ► accustomed to [accustomed]

hache ► axe

    hache de guerre ► tomahawk

hacher ► chop, hack, mince

hachette ► hatchet

hachis de fruits secs ► mincemeat

halda ► haida

haie ► hedge, hurdle

    course de haies ► hurdle

    mettre une haie autour de ► hedge

haïku ► haiku

haillons ► rag

haine ► hate, hatred

haineux (-euse) ► vicious

haïr ► hate

hâle ► tan

hâler ► tan

haleter ► gasp, pant, puff

hall ► hall, lobby

Halloween ► Halloween

halte ► halt, stop

    faire halte ► halt

haltère ► weight

haltérophilie ► weightlifting

hamac ► hammock

hamburger ► hamburger

hambourgeois ► hamburger

hameçon ► hook

hampe ► shaft, staff

hamster ► hamster

hanche ► hip

handicap ► handicap, liability

handicaper ► cripple, handicap

    personne handicapée) ► handicap

    être handicapé (-ée) ► handicap

hangar ► hangar, shed[1]

Hanoukka ► Hanukkah

hanter ► haunt

harceler ► badger, bait, buzz, harass, plague

harde ► herd
hardi (-ie) ► daring, undaunted
hardiesse ► daring
hargneux (-euse) ► crab
haricot ► bean
   haricot vert ► string bean
   haricot/fève de lima ► lima bean
harmonie ► chemistry, harmony
harmonieusement ► agreeably [agreeable]
harmonieux (-euse) ► musical
harnacher ► harness
harnais ► harness
harpe ► harp
   jouer de la harpe ► harp
harpon ► harpoon
harponner ► harpoon
hasard ► accident, chance, fortune, luck
   par hasard ► accidentally [accidental], by chance [chance], casually [casual]
   à tout hasard ► wild
   soumis (-ise) au hasard ► random
   se promener au hasard ► ramble
   se produire par hasard ► chance
   trouver par hasard ► happen
   tomber sur par hasard ► stumble
hasarder ► hazard, venture
hasardeux (-euse) ► adventurous
hase ► doe
hâte ► haste, hastiness [hasty], hurry, rush[1]
   à la hâte ► hastily [hasty], hurriedly [hurried]
   faire à la hâte ► rush[1]
   fait (faite) à la hâte ► hurried
hâter ► hasten, precipitate
   se hâter ► get a move on, hurry, race[1]
hâtif (-ive) ► hasty
hausse ► increase, rise
   forte hausse ► boom[1]
haussement ► lift
   haussement d'épaules ► shrug
hausser ► elevate, increase, inflate, raise, rise
   hausser les épaules ► shrug
haut ► head, high, loud, loudly [loud], top[1]
   du haut ► top[1]
   de haut en bas ► down[1], downward
   en haut ► above, high, up, upstairs
   plus haut ► above, up
   tout haut ► aloud
   vers le haut ► up, uphill, upward
haut (haute) ► high, tall
   haut lieu ► seat
avoir un **haut-le-cœur** ► gag
hautain (-aine) ► haughty, lordly [lord], proud, superior
hautbois ► oboe
hauteur ► elevation, height, level, pitch[1]

hauteurs ► height
   en hauteur ► high
   être à la hauteur ► equal, match[2]
haut-fond ► shoal
haut-parleur ► loudspeaker
havre ► harbour, oasis
havresac ► knapsack
hebdomadaire ► weekly
hebdomadairement ► weekly
héberger ► harbour, house, lodge, put up
hébéter ► daze
hectare ► acre
héler ► flag, hail[2]
hélice ► propeller
   hélice (d'un ventilateur) ► vane
hélicoptère ► helicopter
hélium ► helium
hémisphère ► hemisphere
hennir ► whinny
hennissement ► whinny
héraut ► herald
herbage ► pasture
herbe ► grass
   herbe (aromatique médicinale) ► herb
   herbe à la puce ► poison ivy
   herbe à poux ► ragweed
   fines herbes ► herb
   mauvaise herbe ► weed
herbeux (-euse) ► grassy [grass]
héréditaire ► hereditary
hérédité ► heredity, legacy
hérissé (-ée) ► prickly [prick]
hérisser ► bristle
hérisson ► hedgehog
héritage ► heritage, legacy
hérité (-ée) ► hereditary
hériter ► inherit, succeed
héritier (-ière) ► heir
hermétique ► airtight
héroïque ► epic, heroic
héron ► heron
héros (héroïne) ► hero
hésitant (-ante) ► balky [balk], indecisive, uncertain, unsure
hésitation ► balk, hesitation, uncertainty [uncertain]
   avec hésitation ► uncertainly [uncertain]
hésiter ► balk, falter, grope, hesitate, stumble, waver
   sans hésiter ► decisively [decisive]
hêtre ► beech
heure ► hour
   heure(s) ► hours [hour], o'clock
   des heures ► ages [age]
   à l'heure pile ► punctually [punctual]
   à l'heure ► prompt, punctual, schedule
   heure d'affluence ► rush hour

heure de pointe ▶ rush hour
heure limite ▶ deadline
heure normale ▶ standard time
heures supplémentaires ▶ overtime
heureusement ▶ blissfully [bliss], fortunately [fortunate], happily [happy], luckily
heureux (-euse) ▶ fortunate, glad, happy
de façon heureuse ▶ blissfully [bliss]
heurt ▶ knock
heurter ▶ hit
se heurter ▶ clash
heurter violemment ▶ ram
hexagone ▶ hexagon
hiberner ▶ hibernate
hibiscus ▶ hibiscus
hibou (-oux) ▶ owl
qui a l'air d'un hibou ▶ owlish [owl]
comme un hibou ▶ owlish [owl]
hideux (-euse) ▶ hideous, ugly
hier ▶ yesterday
hiéroglyphe ▶ hieroglyphic
Highlands ▶ Highland [highland]
hilarant (-ante) ▶ hilarious, hysterical
hindou ▶ Hindu
hippocampe ▶ sea horse
hippopotame ▶ hippopotamus
hirondelle ▶ swallow[2]
hirsute ▶ shaggy
hisser ▶ hoist
histoire ▶ history, tale
histoire ancienne ▶ Ancient history [ancient]
longue histoire ▶ yarn
faire un tas d'histoire ▶ fuss
historique ▶ historical
récit historique ▶ historical fiction
hiver ▶ winter
d'hiver ▶ wintry
hivernal (-ale, -aux) ▶ wintry
hocher ▶ nod
hochet ▶ rattle
hockey ▶ hockey
hold-up ▶ holdup
holocauste ▶ holocaust
Holocauste ▶ the Holocaust [holocaust]
homard ▶ lobster
homérique ▶ epic
homicide ▶ murder
hommage ▶ tribute
hommages ▶ compliment, respects [respect]
homme ▶ fellow, man
hommes ▶ man, men
jeune homme ▶ lad, youth
homme (femme) politique ▶ politician
homme (femme) d'affaires ▶ businessman, businesswoman, businessperson [business]

homme de paille ▶ figurehead
hommes de troupe ▶ rank[1]
homographe ▶ homograph
homonyme ▶ homonym
homophone ▶ homophone
honnête ▶ candid, clean, fair[1], genuine, honest, righteous, square, upright
honnêtement ▶ fair[1], fairly, honestly [honest]
honnêteté ▶ fairness [fair[1]], integrity
honneur ▶ credit, honour
honneurs ▶ Honour [honour]
faire honneur ▶ do justice to
honorable ▶ clean, glorious, honourable
honorablement ▶ honourably [honourable], respectably [respectable]
honoraires ▶ fee
honorer ▶ court, grace, honour, worship
honte ▶ disgrace, shame, stigma
avoir honte de ▶ ashamed
couvrir de honte ▶ disgrace
faire honte à ▶ shame
honteusement ▶ disgracefully [disgrace]
honteux (-euse) ▶ ashamed, sinful [sin]
hôpital (-aux) ▶ hospital
hoquet ▶ hiccup
avoir le hoquet ▶ hiccup
hoqueter ▶ hiccup
horaire ▶ schedule, timetable
horde ▶ horde
horizon ▶ horizon
ligne d'horizon ▶ skyline
horizontal (-ale, aux) ▶ horizontal
dans une position horizontale ▶ flat[1]
horizontalement ▶ horizontally [horizontal]
horloge ▶ clock
hormis ▶ except
hormone ▶ hormone
horoscope ▶ horoscope
horreur ▶ fright, horror
horrible ▶ ghastly, horrible, horrid, terrible, ugly, unspeakable
horriblement ▶ dreadfully [dreadful], horribly [horrible]
horrifier ▶ horrify
hors ▶ out
hors de soi ▶ frantic
hors pair ▶ peerless [peer[2]]
hostile ▶ hostile, unfriendly
hôte (hôtesse) ▶ host, steward
hôtel ▶ hotel, inn
hôtel de la Monnaie ▶ mint[2]
hôtel de ville ▶ hall
hôtel particulier ▶ mansion
hotte ▶ hood
houblon ▶ hop[2]
houe ▶ hoe

houle ▸ swell
houppe ▸ puff
houppette ▸ puff
housse ▸ cover
houx ▸ holly
huard ▸ loon
hublot ▸ porthole
huée ▸ hoot
huer ▸ hoot
huile ▸ oil
huiler ▸ oil
huileux (-euse) ▸ greasy [grease], oily [oil]
huit ▸ eight
huitième ▸ eighth [eight]
huître ▸ oyster
hululement ▸ hoot
humain ▸ human, humane
   le genre humain ▸ mankind
   être humain ▸ human
humanité ▸ humanity, mankind
   les humanités ▸ classical
humble ▸ humble, lowly [low], meek, modest
humblement ▸ humbly [humble], meekly [meek]
humecter ▸ dampen, moisten [moist]
humeur ▸ frame of mind, humour, mood, spirit
   bonne humeur ▸ cheer
   d'humeur ▸ spirited
   d'humeur instable ▸ temperamental
   de mauvaise humeur ▸ cantankerous, cross, scowl, temper
humide ▸ damp, humid, moist, muggy, steamy [steam]
   zone humide ▸ wetland
humidité ▸ damp, dampness [damp], humidity, moisture, wetness [wet]
   taux d'humidité ▸ humidex
humilier ▸ humble, humiliate
humilité ▸ humility
humour ▸ humour
   sens de l'humour ▸ sense of humour
humus ▸ humus
huppé (-ée) ▸ exclusive
hurlement ▸ bay[2], howl, roar, yell
hurler ▸ bawl, bay[2], clamour, howl, roar, scream, shriek, wail, yell
huron (-onne) ▸ Huron
husky (huskies) ▸ husky[2]
hutte ▸ hut, lodge, shack
hybride ▸ hybrid, mongrel, mutt
hydravion ▸ seaplane
hydro-électricité ▸ hydro
hydrogène ▸ hydrogen
hyène ▸ hyena
hygiène ▸ hygiene
   hygiène publique ▸ sanitation

hymne ▸ anthem, hymn
hyperbole ▸ hyperbole
hypermétrope ▸ far-sighted
hypnotiser ▸ hypnotize
hypocrite ▸ hypocrite, hypocritical [hypocrite], sneak, underhand
hypothèque ▸ mortgage
hypothéquer ▸ mortgage
hypothèse ▸ assumption, guess, hypothesis, theory
   émettre une hypothèse ▸ theorize
hystérique ▸ hysterical

I

iceberg ▸ iceberg
ici ▸ by, here
   d'ici ▸ here
idéal (-als, -aux) ▸ ideal
idéal (-ale, -als, -aux) ▸ ideal, perfect
idéalement ▸ ideally [ideal]
idéaliste ▸ starry-eyed
idée ▸ concept, drift, idea, image, impulse, intention, mind, notion, thought
   idée préconçue ▸ prejudice
   qui a des idées ▸ smart
   caresser l'idée ▸ toy
identification ▸ challenge, identification, recognition
identifier ▸ diagnose, identify, identify with
identique ▸ identical, same, unchanged
identiquement ▸ identically [identical]
identité ▸ identity
   pièce d'identité ▸ identification
   plaque d'identité ▸ tag[1]
idiomatique ▸ idiomatic
idiome ▸ idiom
idiot (idiote) ▸ ass, crazy, dumb, fool, foolish, silly
   faire l'idiot (idiote) ▸ fool
idiotie ▸ crazy, rubbish, silliness [silly]
   idioties ▸ nonsense
idole ▸ cult, god, idol
idylle ▸ romance
bois d'if ▸ yew
igloo ▸ icehouse, igloo
igname ▸ yam
igné (-ée) ▸ igneous
ignition ▸ ignition
ignoble ▸ base[2], villainous [villain]
ignorance ▸ ignorance
   par ignorance ▸ ignorantly [ignorant]
ignorant (-ante) ▸ ignorant
   ignorant (-ante) de ▸ unaware, unconscious
ignorer ▸ discount
iguane ▸ iguana

il ► he, it

ils ► they

île ► island, isle

illégal (-ale, -aux) ► illegal, unlawful

illégalement ► illegally [illegal]

illettré (-ée) ► ignorant, illiterate

illimité (-ée) ► infinite, unlimited

illisible ► illegible

illogique ► incoherent

illumination ► illumination [illuminate]

illuminer ► illuminate, light[1]

illusion ► illusion, mirage

illusionniste ► magician

illusoire ► deceptive

illustration ► illustration

illustre ► great, noted

illustrer ► illustrate

îlot ► island

image ► illustration, image, metaphor, picture

image de marque ► image

image floue ► blur

imager ► illustrate

poème imagé ► concrete poem

imaginaire ► imaginary, make-believe, unreal

imagination ► fancy, fantasy, imagination, invention

création de l'imagination ► fiction

imaginer ► conceive, devise, imagine, picture, suppose

imbécile ► ass, dumb, fool

faire l'imbécile ► fool, monkey

imbibé (-ée) d'eau ► waterlogged

imitateur (-trice) ► mimic

imitation ► imitation, impression, sham, takeoff

imité (-ée) ► imitation

imiter ► copy, imitate, mimic

immaculé (-ée) ► spotless

immanquable ► certain, inevitable

immanquablement ► consistently [consistent], inevitably [inevitable]

immature ► immature

immédiat (-ate) ► immediate, instant

immédiatement ► at once, directly, immediately [immediate]

immense ► enormous, huge, immense, vast, wide

immensément ► immensely [immense], infinitely [infinite]

immensité ► immensity [immense], vastness [vast]

immerger ► submerge

immigrant (-ante) ► immigrant

immigré (-ée) ► immigrant

immigrer ► immigrate

imminent (-ente) ► upcoming

s'immiscer ► interfere

immobile ► calm, motionless [motion], stationary, still

biens immobiliers ► property, real estate

immobilisation ► standstill

immobiliser ► corner, pin

immonde ► foul

immoral (-ale, -aux) ► obscene

immortel (-elle) ► immortal

immunisé (-ée) ► immune

impact ► impact

impair (-aire) ► odd

impala ► impala

impartial (-ale, -aux) ► disinterested, impartial, objective

impartialement ► fairly

impartialité ► fairness [fair[1]]

impasse ► dead end

impassibilité ► coolness [cool]

impassible ► wooden

impatiemment ► eagerly [eager], impatiently [impatient]

impatience ► impatience [impatient]

avec impatience ► anxiously [anxious]

donner des signes d'impatience ► fidget

impatient (-ente) ► anxious, eager, impatient

impayé (-ée) ► outstanding, unpaid

impeccable ► spotlessly [spotless]

impensable ► unthinkable

imperfection ► defect, flaw, shortcoming

impérial (-ale, -aux) ► imperial

impérissable ► immortal

imperméabiliser ► waterproof

imperméable ► raincoat, waterproof

impersonnel (-elle) ► impersonal

impertinence ► impoliteness [impolite]

impertinent (-ente) ► fresh, gross

impitoyable ► grim, merciless [mercy], ruthless

impitoyablement ► ruthlessly [ruthless]

implacable ► grim

implanter ► locate

impliquer ► involve

implorer ► plead

impoli (-ie) ► gross, impolite, improper, rude, uncouth, unseemly

impoliment ► coarsely [coarse], impolitely [impolite], rudely [rude]

impolitesse ► impoliteness [impolite], rudeness [rude]

importance ► consequence, extent, import, magnitude, significance

sans importance ► insignificant

important (-ante) ► big, considerable, extensive, grand, grave[2], high, important, prominent, substantial, weighty

très important (-ante) ► valuable
importations ► import
importer ► import, matter, value
  peu importe comment ► no matter
  peu importe ► no matter
n'importe lequel (laquelle) ► either
n'importe où ► anyplace, anywhere
n'importe quand ► anytime
importun (-une) ► meddlesome [meddle], unwelcome
importuner ► annoy, badger, cramp, pest
imposant (-ante) ► impressive, massive, noble, towering
  se dresser de manière imposante ► tower
imposer ► command, dictate, impose, intrude, saddle, tax
  imposer une discipline trop stricte ► regiment
imposition ► taxation
impossible ► hopeless, impossible, unlikely
imposteur (-eure) ► fake, fraud, impostor
imposture ► fraud, sham
impôt ► duty
  impôts ► tax
imprécis (-ise) ► indefinite, obscure, vague
imprégné (-ée) d'eau ► waterlogged
impression[1] ► feeling, impression
  avoir l'impression ► feel, guess
impression[2] ► print
impressionnabilité ► impressiveness [impressive]
impressionnant (-ante) ► awesome, awful, grand, impressive, spectacular
  de façon impressionnante ► impressively [impressive]
impressionner ► impress, strike
imprévisible ► unexpected, unpredictable
imprévu (-ue) ► casual, unexpected
imprimante ► printer
  sortie sur imprimante ► print out
imprimé ► print
imprimer ► impress, print
imprimerie ► printer
imprimeur (-euse) ► printer
improbable ► unlikely
improviser ► ad-lib
à l'improviste ► off the cuff
imprudemment ► recklessly [reckless]
imprudence ► recklessness [reckless]
imprudent (-ente) ► rash[2], reckless, unwise
impuissance ► helplessness, inability, weakness
impuissant (-ante) ► helpless, powerless
impulsif (-ive) ► off-hand
impulsion ► impulse
impur (-ure) ► impure

inacceptable ► unacceptable
inaccoutumé (-ée) ► unused
inachevé (-ée) ► incomplete, rough, undone[1], unfinished
inactif (-ive) ► idle
inaction ► idleness [idle]
inactivité ► idleness [idle]
inadapté (-ée) ► inadequate, misfit
inadéquat (-ate) ► inadequate, wrong
inadmissible ► unacceptable
inamical (-ale, -aux) ► unfriendly
inanimé (-ée) ► dead
inanition ► starvation
inappliqué (-ée) ► careless
inapproprié (-ée) ► inadequate, off-key, unfit
inapte ► inept, unable
inattendu (-ue) ► casual, unexpected
  de façon inattendue ► unexpectedly [unexpected]
inattention ► oversight
inaugural (-ale, -aux) ► maiden
incalculable ► untold
incantation ► spell[2]
incapable ► unable
incapacité ► helplessness, inability
incarcérer ► jail
incarnation ► personification
incendie ► fire
  incendie criminel ► arson
  borne d'incendie ► hydrant
incendier ► fire
incertain (-aine) ► uncertain, undecided, up in the air [air]
  d'une manière incertaine ► uncertainly [uncertain]
incertitude ► doubt, question, uncertainty [uncertain]
incessant (-ante) ► endless, relentless
inchangé (-ée) ► unchanged
incidemment ► incidentally
incident ► happening, incident
inciser ► lance, tap[2]
incisif (-ive) ► cutting
incitation ► defiance [defiant]
inciter ► egg[2], encourage, motivate, prod, prompt, provoke, urge
inclinaison ► incline, lean[1], tilt
incliner ► incline, lean[1], slant, tilt
  s'incliner ► bow[2], decline, recline
  incliner la tête ► bow[2], nod
inclure ► contain, count[1], embrace, enclose, include, incorporate, integrate
incognito ► incognito
incohérent (-ente) ► incoherent
incolore ► colourless
incommodant (-ante) ► troublesome
incommode ► inconvenient

incommoder ► wilt
incompatible ► clash, conflict
incomplet (-ète) ► incomplete, unfinished
incompréhensible ► unintelligible
inconcevable ► unbelievable, unthinkable
inconditionnel (-elle) ► unconditional
inconfort ► discomfort
inconfortable ► uncomfortable
inconfortablement ► uncomfortably [uncomfortable]
inconnu (-ue) ► unfamiliar, unknown
inconsciemment ► unconsciously [unconscious]
inconscient (-ente) ► unaware, unconscious
inconsidéré (-ée) ► thoughtless, unwise
inconstant (-ante) ► unstable
inconstitutionnel (-elle) ► unconstitutional
incontestablement ► decidedly [decided]
incontrôlé (-ée) ► unruly
inconvenant (-ante) ► unseemly, unworthy
inconvénient ► bother, disadvantage, discomfort
incorporer ► incorporate, insert, integrate
incorrect (-ecte) ► improper, incorrect, wrong
incorrectement ► incorrectly [incorrect], wrong
incroyable ► incredible, unbelievable
incroyablement ► terrifically [terrific]
incruster ► score
incubateur ► incubator
incuber ► hatch[1]
inculpation ► charge
inculpé (-ée) ► defendant
inculper ► charge
incurable ► terminal
incursion ► raid
indécent (-ente) ► obscene
indécis (-ise) ► indecisive, undecided
indéfini (-ie) ► indefinite
indéfiniment ► indefinitely [indefinite]
indemne ► intact
indemniser ► compensate
indemnité ► benefit, dole
   indemnité de chômage ► dole
indéniable ► certain, gross
indépendamment ► regardless
indépendance ► freedom, liberty
indépendant (-ante) ► independent, rock[1]
indescriptible ► unspeakable
indésirable ► undesirable
indéterminé (-ée) ► indefinite
index ► index
indicateur ► gauge
   indicateur de vitesse ► speedometer

   indicateur de tirage ► draft
indicatif ► theme
indication ► check, clue, cue, guide, indicator [indicate]
indice ► clue, hint, index, indicator [indicate]
   indice d'écoute ► rating
indicible ► unspeakable
indien (-ienne) ► Indian
indifférence ► apathy, distance, indifference [indifferent]
indifférent (-ente) ► disinterested, indifferent, regardless, unmoved
indigence ► need
indigène ► Aborigine, native
indigent (-ente) ► needy [need]
indigestion ► indigestion
indignation ► indignation [indignant], outrage
   avec indignation ► indignantly [indignant]
indigne ► base[2]
indigne ► unreliable, unworthy
indigné (-ée) ► indignant
indigner ► horrify
indiqué (-ée) ► proper
indiquer ► chart, designate, indicate, mark, read, register, tell
indirect (-ecte) ► indirect, roundabout
indirectement ► indirectly [indirect]
indiscipliné (-ée) ► unruly
indiscret (-ète) ► inquisitive
   écouter de façon indiscrète ► eavesdrop
indiscutable ► decided
indispensable ► essential
indisposé (-ée) ► ill
indistinct (-incte) ► dim, obscure
individu ► chap[1], fellow, individual, person
   individus ► selves
individualité ► individual
individuel (-elle) ► individual
individuellement ► individually [individual]
indolence ► laziness [lazy]
indolent (-ente) ► lazy
indubitablement ► undoubtedly, unmistakably [unmistakable]
induire en erreur ► trip up
indulgence ► mercy
   avoir de l'indulgence ► make allowance(s) for [allowance]
   avec indulgence ► tolerantly [tolerant]
indulgent (-ente) ► charitable, tolerant
industrie ► industry
industriel (-ielle) ► industrial
industrieusement ► industriously [industrious]
inébranlable ► steadfast
inébranlablement ► steadfastly [steadfast]
inédit (-ite) ► untold

inégal (-ale, -aux) ► ragged, uneven
inéluctable ► inevitable
inemployé (-ée) ► unused
inepties ► nonsense, tripe
inépuisable ► endless
inéquitable ► unfair, unjust
    d'une façon inéquitable ► unfairly [unfair], unjustly [unjust]
inévitable ► inevitable, necessary
inévitablement ► inevitably [inevitable]
inexact (-acte) ► improper, incorrect, wrong
inexactement ► incorrectly [incorrect]
inexorablement ► grimly [grim]
inexpérimenté (-ée) ► green, raw, unskilled
inexplicable ► uncanny
inexpressif (-ive) ► wooden
inexprimable ► unspeakable
infâme ► infamous, villainous [villain]
infatigable ► tireless
infatigablement ► tirelessly [tireless]
infect (-ecte) ► foul
infecter ► foul, infect
infection ► infection
inférer ► conclude, deduce, infer
inférieur (-eure) ► inferior, lower, lowly [low]
    passage inférieur ► underpass
infester ► invade
infiltration ► leak
infime ► minute[2]
infini (-ie) ► countless, endless, infinite
infiniment ► exceedingly [exceed], infinitely [infinite]
rendre **infirme** ► disable
infirmier (-ière) ► nurse
inflammation ► inflammation
inflation ► inflation
s'infléchir ► curve
inflexible ► grim
inflexiblement ► grimly [grim]
infliger ► impose
influence ► impulse, influence, power, pull
    avoir de l'influence ► weight
influencer ► influence, sway
influenza ► influenza
influer ► affect[1]
information ► communication, information, intelligence
    informations ► data, news, newscast
matériel d'**informatique** ► hardware
mordu (-ue) d'**informatique** ► hacker
de façon **informelle** ► informally [informal]
informer ► advise, brief, communicate, inform, instruct
    informer contre quelqu'un ► inform
infraction ► crime, offence, violation
infructueux (-euse) ► unsuccessful
infuser ► brew

infusion ► tea
s'ingérer ► interfere, meddle
ingénieur ► engineer
ingénieusement ► cleverly [clever]
ingénieux (-euse) ► clever, neat
ingéniosité ► cleverness [clever]
ingénu (-ue) ► starry-eyed
ingrat (-ate) ► ungrateful
ingrédient ► ingredient
inhabité (-ée) ► uninhabited, unsettled
inhabituel (-elle) ► uncommon, unorthodox, unusual
inhaler ► inhale
inimaginable ► unthinkable
inintelligible ► unintelligible
inintéressé (-ée) ► uninterested
ininterrompu (-ue) ► unbroken
initial (-ale, -aux) ► initial
initiale ► initial
initialement ► initially [initial]
initiation ► initiate
initiative ► initiative
initier ► initiate
injecter ► inject
injure ► insult
injurier ► insult
injuste ► partial, unfair, unjust
injustement ► unfairly [unfair], unjustly [unjust]
    traiter injustement ► wrong
injustice ► injustice, wrong
injustifié (-iée) ► wanton
inlassable ► tireless
inlassablement ► tirelessly [tireless]
inné (-ée) ► natural
innocemment ► harmlessly [harmless], innocently [innocent]
innocent (-ente) ► harmless, innocent
innocenter ► clear
innombrable ► countless, untold
innovant (-ante) ► innovative [innovation]
innovateur (-trice) ► original
innovation ► innovation
innu (-ue) ► Innu
inoccupé (-ée) ► idle, vacant
inoffensif (-ive) ► harmless
    serpent inoffensif ► adder
inondation ► flood
inonder ► flood, shower, swamp
inopportun (-une) ► inconvenient
inoubliable ► unforgettable
inouï (-ïe) ► fantastic
inquiet (-iète) ► anxious, concerned, nervous, uneasy
inquiétant (-ante) ► eerie, grave[2], ugly
inquiéter ► disturb
    s'inquiéter ► care, concern, worry

inquiétude ▶ anxiety, care, concern, uneasiness [uneasy], worry

    avec inquiétude ▶ anxiously [anxious], uneasily [uneasy], worriedly [worry]

insalubre ▶ unhealthy

inscription ▶ entry, registration

inscrire ▶ enroll, enter, log, note, put down, register

    s'inscrire ▶ check in, enter, join

    inscrire sur une liste ▶ list[1]

insecte ▶ bug, insect

    insecte nuisible ▶ pest

insensé (-ée) ▶ foolish, insane, lunatic, mad, senseless

insensibilité ▶ indifference [indifferent]

insensible ▶ deaf, indifferent, unmoved

insérer ▶ incorporate, insert

insertion ▶ insert

insigne ▶ badge

insignifiant (-ante) ▶ dull, insignificant, trivial

insinuer ▶ hint, imply, suggest, worm

insipide ▶ dry, flat[1], tame, tasteless

insister ▶ dwell on, insist, underline, underscore

insociable ▶ antisocial

insolation ▶ sunstroke

insolence ▶ impoliteness [impolite]

insolent (-ente) ▶ impolite

    de manière insolente ▶ forward

insomnie ▶ sleeplessness [sleepless]

insonorisé (-ée) ▶ soundproof

insonoriser ▶ soundproof

insouciance ▶ carelessness [careless], recklessness [reckless]

    avec insouciance ▶ carelessly [careless]

insouciant (-ante) ▶ careless, light[2], reckless, regardless

insoutenable ▶ unbearable

inspecter ▶ check, examine, inspect, review, survey

inspection ▶ check, examination, review

inspiration ▶ inspiration, invention

inspirer ▶ draw, inject, inspire, uplift

    inspirer de la répulsion ▶ repel

instable ▶ changeable, rocky [rock[2]], unsettled, unsound, unstable, unsteady

installation ▶ facility, installation [install]

    installation électrique ▶ wiring

    faire l'installation électrique de ▶ wire

installer ▶ equip, install, locate, mount, settle

instant ▶ bit[1], instant, minute[1], moment, spell[3]

    un instant ▶ while

instantané ▶ snapshot

instantané (-ée) ▶ immediate, instant

instantanément ▶ immediately [immediate], instantly [instant]

instinct ▶ instinct

instinctif (-ive) ▶ instinctive [instinct]

instituer ▶ institute

Institut ▶ institute

instituteur (-trice) ▶ teacher

institution ▶ institution

instructif (-ive) ▶ educational

instruction ▶ depth, education, instruction

    instruction civique ▶ civic

instruire ▶ educate, instruct

instruit (-uite) ▶ scholarly [scholar]

instrument ▶ implement, instrument, tool

    instrument à anche ▶ reed

    instrument à vent ▶ wind[1], wind instrument, woodwind

    instruments d'orchestre ▶ orchestra

    joueur (-euse) d'un instrument à clavier ▶ keyboardist

insuccès ▶ breakdown, defeat

insuffisamment ▶ inadequately [inadequate]

insuffisance ▶ deficiency

insuffisant (-ante) ▶ deficient [deficiency], inadequate, scant, scanty [scant]

insuffler ▶ inject

insulte ▶ insult, slur[2]

insulter ▶ insult, outrage, slur[2]

insupportable ▶ unbearable

intact (-acte) ▶ intact, unbroken

intarissable ▶ endless

intègre ▶ upright

intégrer ▶ integrate

intégrité ▶ integrity

intellectuel (-elle) ▶ intellectual

intellectuellement ▶ intellectually [intellectual]

intelligemment ▶ intelligently [intelligence]

intelligence ▶ intelligence, mind, wit

    intelligence artificielle ▶ artificial intelligence

intelligent (-ente) ▶ apt, clever, smart

    très intelligent (-ente) ▶ brilliant

intemporel (-elle) ▶ timeless

intenable ▶ unbearable

intendant (-ante) ▶ steward

intense ▶ acute, extreme, intense, wild

intensément ▶ intensely [intense]

intensif (-ive) ▶ crash

intensité ▶ drift, intensity [intense]

intention ▶ design, drift, idea, intent[2], intention

    avoir l'intention ▶ intend, mean[1]

    à l'intention de ▶ for

intentionnel (-elle) ▶ conscious, deliberate, intentional [intention]

intentionnellement ▶ consciously [conscious]

bien intentionné (-ée) ▶ well-meaning

inter ▶ shortstop

775

intercepter ▸ collar
interdiction ▸ ban
interdire ▸ ban, bar, forbid, prohibit, veto
   interdire de voler ▸ ground[1]
interdit ▸ taboo
intéressant (-ante) ▸ interesting
   de façon intéressante ▸ interestingly
[interesting]
intéresser ▸ concern, interest
   s'intéresser ▸ care
intérêt ▸ good, interest, sake
   intérêts ▸ interest, stake
intérieur ▸ indoor, inside, interior, within
   à l'intérieur de ▸ inside, within
   à l'intérieur ▸ in, indoor, inland, inside,
inwardly [inward]
   vers l'intérieur ▸ inward
intérieur (-eure) ▸ domestic, inland, inner,
inside, interior, internal
   revêtement intérieur ▸ lining
intérieurement ▸ internally [internal],
inwardly [inward]
interjection ▸ interjection
interlocuteur ▸ speaker
interloqué (-ée) ▸ speechless
intermédiaire ▸ intermediate, link
   par l'intermédiaire de ▸ through
interminable ▸ endless, lengthy [length]
interminablement ▸ endlessly [endless]
international (-ale, -aux) ▸ international
internationalement ▸ internationally
[international]
interne ▸ inner, inside, internal
faire **interner** ▸ commit
Internet ▸ Internet
   toile Internet ▸ World Wide Web
interpeller ▸ hail[2]
interprétation ▸ interpretation [interpret]
interpréter ▸ interpret, read
   mal interpréter ▸ misunderstand
   interpréter dans une perspective ▸
slant
interrogation ▸ test
   point d'interrogation ▸ question mark
faire subir un **interrogatoire** ▸ grill
interroger ▸ examine, question, quiz
   s'interroger ▸ speculate
interrompre ▸ break in, cease, disrupt,
disturb, interrupt, punctuate
   s'interrompre ▸ pause
interrupteur ▸ button, switch
interruption ▸ disruption [disrupt], halt,
holdup
   sans interruption ▸ continuously
[continuous]
intervalle ▸ interval, space
intervenir ▸ meddle

interview ▸ interview
interviewer ▸ interview, interviewer
[interview]
intestin ▸ intestine
intime ▸ chummy [chum], close[2], inner,
intimate, near
intimider ▸ bully
intimité ▸ intimacy [intimate], nearness [near]
intituler ▸ title
intolérable ▸ unbearable
intolérant (-ante) ▸ intolerant
intoxiqué (-ée) ▸ addict
intoxiquer ▸ poison
intransigeant (-ante) ▸ intolerant
intrépide ▸ fearless, stout, undaunted
intrigant (-ante) ▸ intriguing, schemer
[scheme]
intrigue ▸ design, manoeuvre, plot
intriguer ▸ intrigue
introduction ▸ introduction, lead[1]
   manuel d'introduction ▸ primer
introduire ▸ enter, introduce
   s'introduire ▸ squeeze
   s'introduire sans permission ▸
trespass
intuition ▸ hunch
   connaître par intuition ▸ sense
inuit (-e) ▸ Inuit
inutile ▸ idle, needless, pointless,
unnecessary, useless, vain
inutilement ▸ needlessly [needless],
unnecessarily [unnecessary]
inutilisé (-ée) ▸ unused
inutilité ▸ idleness [idle]
invariable ▸ constant
invasion ▸ plague
inventaire ▸ inventory
inventer ▸ coin, conceive, devise, invent,
make up, manufacture
inventeur ▸ father
invention ▸ invention
   invention révolutionnaire ▸
breakthrough
inverse ▸ reverse
inverser ▸ reverse
investigateur (-trice) ▸ investigator
[investigate]
investigation ▸ probe
investir ▸ invest
   investir du temps ▸ put in
investissement ▸ investment, security
invincible ▸ invincible
invisible ▸ invisible
invitant (-ante) ▸ invite
invité (-ée) ▸ company, guest
inviter ▸ ask, invite, motion
invraisemblable ▸ fantastic, unbelievable,
unlikely

iode ► iodine
    teinture d'iode ► iodine
iota ► jot
irascible ► cantankerous
iris ► eye, iris
ironie ► irony
    avec une ironie désabusé (-ée) ► wryly
    [wry]
    empreint (-einte) d'une ironie
    désabusé (-ée) ► wry
ironiquement ► ironically [irony]
iroquoien (-ienne) ► Iroquois, Iroquoian
[Iroquois]
iroquois (-oise) ► Iroquois, Iroquoian
[Iroquois]
irradiation ► radiation
irréalisable ► impossible
irréaliste ► unrealistic [unreal]
irréel (-elle) ► imaginary, unreal
irréfléchi (-ie) ► hasty, rash[2], thoughtless,
unwise
irrégularité ► jog[2]
irrégulier (-ière) ► choppy, erratic, irregular,
jagged, ragged, uneven
    de façon irrégulière ► irregularly
    [irregular]
irrégulièrement ► erratically [erratic],
irregularly [irregular]
irresponsable ► reckless
irriguer ► irrigate
irritable ► cantankerous
irritant (-ante) ► vex
irritation ► irritation
irrité (-ée) ► angry, sore
irriter ► inflame, irritate, jar, ruffle, smart
irruption ► descent
    faire brutalement irruption ► barge
Islam ► Islam
islamique ► Islamic [Islam]
isolant ► insulate
isolation ► insulation [insulate]
isolé (-ée) ► lonely, remote
isolement ► loneliness [lonely], remoteness
[remote]
isoler ► insulate, isolate, seclude, single out
[single]
isoloir ► booth
issue ► end, outcome
itinéraire ► itinerary, route
itinérant (-ante) ► migrant, tramp
ivoire ► ivory
ivre ► drunk

J

jabot ► crop, ruffle
jacassement ► chatter

jacasser ► chatter
jacinthe ► hyacinth
jacquet ► backgammon
jade ► jade
jadis ► formerly [former], once
jaguar ► jaguar
jaillir ► jet, leap, spew, spout, spurt
jaillissement ► spurt
jalonner ► stake
jalousement ► jealously [jealous]
jalousie ► envy, jealousy [jealous]
jaloux (-ouse) ► jealous, possessive
jamais ► ever, never
jambe ► leg
    dans les jambes ► underfoot
jambière ► chaps
jambon ► ham
jante ► rim
janvier ► January
jappement ► yelp
japper ► yelp
jardin ► garden
    jardin d'enfants ► kindergarten
jardiner ► garden
jardinière ► planter
jargon ► jargon, vocabulary
jarre ► jar
jars ► gander
jauge ► gauge
jauger ► gauge, size up [size]
jaune ► yellow
    (jaune) citron ► lemon
    jaune d'œuf ► yolk
jaunir ► yellow
javelot ► javelin
jazz ► jazz
je ► I
jean ► denim, jeans
jersey ► jersey
Jésus-Christ ► Christ
    après Jésus-Christ ► A.D.
jet ► jet, leap, spurt, squirt
    jet d'eau ► font[1], fountain
    arroser au jet ► hose
    laver au jet ► hose
    raconter d'un seul jet ► pour out [pour]
jeté (-ée) ► castaway
jetée ► jetty, pier
jeter ► cast, discard, dump, fling, pitch[1], sling,
throw, throw away, throw out, toss
    se jeter ► descend, lunge, plunge, throw
    jeter violemment ► dash
    jeter par derrière l'épaule ► sling
    jeter au rancart ► scrap
    jeter au rebut ► reject
    jeter de la lumière ► shed[2]

jeter un coup d'œil ▸ glance
jeter un coup d'œil discret ▸ peep[1]
jeter un coup d'œil furtif ▸ peek
jeton ▸ chip, token
jeu (jeux) ▸ game
  en jeu ▸ stake
  franc jeu ▸ fair[1]
  jeu de balle ▸ catch
  jeu de cartes ▸ deck
  jeu du chat ▸ tag[2]
  jeu de dames ▸ checkers
  jeu de fléchettes ▸ dart
  jeu de mots ▸ pun
  jeu de quilles ▸ bowling
  jeu d'enfant ▸ snap
  jeu-questionnaire ▸ quiz, trivial
  jeu vidéo ▸ video game
  Jeux olympiques ▸ Olympic Games
  jeu sacrifice ▸ sacrifice
  mise en jeu ▸ face-off
  piste de jeu ▸ lane
  remise en jeu ▸ face-off
  retirer du jeu ▸ bench
  terrain de jeu ▸ playground
jeudi ▸ Thursday
jeune ▸ cub, green, juvenile, kid, young, youth, youthful
  jeunes ▸ the young [young], the youth [youth]
  jeune animal ▸ pup
  jeune enfant ▸ youngster
  jeune fille ▸ girl, lass, maid, maiden, miss[2]
  jeune garçon ▸ youngster
  jeune homme ▸ lad, youth
jeûne ▸ fast[2]
jeûner ▸ fast[2]
jeunesse ▸ the youth [youth]
jeu-questionnaire ▸ quiz, trivial
jockey ▸ jockey
jogging ▸ jog[1]
joie ▸ cheer, delight, gladness [glad], happiness [happy], joy, joyousness [joyous]
  avec joie ▸ gladly [glad]
  fou de joie ▸ beside oneself
joindre ▸ combine, connect, contact, couple, enclose, join, piece, reach
  se joindre ▸ affiliate, merge
joint ▸ joint, seam, washer
jointure ▸ joint
  jointure du doigt ▸ knuckle
joli (-ie) ▸ pretty
jonc ▸ rush[2]
jonction ▸ conjunction
jongler ▸ juggle

jonque ▸ junk[2]
jonquille ▸ dafodil
joue ▸ cheek
  rouge à joues ▸ rouge
  fard à joues ▸ rouge
jouer ▸ act, enact, gamble, perform, pipe, play
  jouer (le rôle de) ▸ portray
  se jouer de ▸ trifle
  jouer avec ▸ toy, worry
  jouer bruyamment ▸ romp
  jouer nerveusement ▸ fiddle
  faire jouer ▸ flex
  jouer cartes sur table ▸ put (one's) cards on the table
jouet ▸ toy
joueur (-euse) ▸ player
  beau joueur (belle joueuse) ▸ sport
  joueur (-euse) d'un instrument à clavier ▸ keyboardist
joufflu (-ue) ▸ full
jouir ▸ enjoy
jouissance ▸ run
jour ▸ day
  un jour ▸ someday
  à jour ▸ up-to-date
  grand jour ▸ board, daylight
  plein jour ▸ board
  jour férié ▸ holiday
  du jour au lendemain ▸ overnight
  de nos jours ▸ nowadays, today
  un jour sur deux ▸ alternate
  un jour ou l'autre ▸ sometime
  faire jour ▸ dawn
  se faire jour ▸ emerge
  jour de congé ▸ holiday
  jour de la semaine ▸ weekday
  jour de l'an ▸ New Year's Day
  jour de naissance ▸ birthday
  lever du jour ▸ daylight
  lumière du jour ▸ daylight
  mis (mise) à jour ▸ up to the minute
  ordre du jour ▸ agenda
  mettre à jour ▸ revise, update
  mettre au jour ▸ uncover
journal (-aux) ▸ diary, journal, log, newspaper
  journal de bord ▸ log
  journal intime ▸ diary
  papier journal ▸ newsprint
journalisme ▸ journalism
journaliste ▸ reporter
journée ▸ day
jovial (-ale, -aux) ▸ jolly
joyau (-aux) ▸ jewel
  joyaux ▸ jewellery

joyeusement ► cheerfully [cheerful], gleefully [glee], joyfully [joyful], joyously [joyous], merrily [merry]

joyeux (-euse) ► cheerful, glad, glee, happy, joyful, joyous, merry, perky [perk], sunny

jubilant (-ante) ► glee

jubilation ► glee

jucher ► perch[1]

   se jucher ► roost

juchoir ► roost

judicieusement ► soundly [sound[2]], wisely [wise]

judicieux (-euse) ► sound[2]

juge ► court, judge, justice

jugement ► conviction, criticism [criticize], decision, estimation [estimate], judgement, trial, verdict

   rendre un jugement ► judge

juger ► criticize, decide, estimate, judge, size up [size], try

juillet ► July

juin ► June

jumeau (-elle, -eaux) ► twin

jumelles ► binoculars

jument ► mare

jungle ► jungle, wilderness

junior ► junior

jupe ► skirt

Jupiter ► Jupiter

jupon ► slip[1]

jurer ► curse, swear, vow

juron ► curse, oath

jury ► jury, panel

jus ► juice

juteux (-euse) ► juicy

jusqu'à ► even, till[1], to

   jusqu'à (ce que) ► until

   jusqu'à présent ► yet

   s'élever jusqu'à ► attain

juste ► accurate, correct, exact, fair[1], fine[1], impartial, in (out) of tune, just, right, tight

   juste à temps ► in the nick of time

   tout juste ► hardly

   tomber juste ► hit the nail on the head

justement ► just

justesse ► accuracy [accurate], correctness [correct]

   de justesse ► barely, just, narrowly [narrow]

   réussi (-ie) de justesse ► narrow

justice ► fairness [fair[1]], justice

   palais de justice ► court

   rendre justice à ► do justice to

justification ► explanation, justification [justify]

justifié (-ée) ► legitimate

justifier ► account, defend, explain, justify, warrant

juvénile ► juvenile, youthful

K

kaki ► khaki

kaléidoscope ► kaleidoscope

kangourou ► kangaroo

karaté ► karate

kascher ► kosher

kayak ► kayak

kérabau ► water buffalo

kérosène ► kerosene

ketchup ► ketchup

kidnapper ► abduct, kidnap

kidnappeur (-euse) ► abductor [abduct]

kidnapping ► abduction [abduct]

kilogramme ► kilogram

kilomètre ► kilometre

   compteur (kilométrique) ► odometer

   des kilomètres et des kilomètres de ► acres

   consommation de carburant au mille (= au kilomètre) ► mileage

kilt ► kilt

kimono ► kimono

kiosque ► stall

kit ► kit

klaxon ► horn

   coup de klaxon ► honk, toot

   donner un coup de klaxon ► toot

klaxonner ► honk, toot

koala ► koala (koala bear)

kootenay ► Kootenay (Kutenai)

Krisna ► Krishna

kung fu ► kung fu

kwanza ► Kwanza

kyste ► cyst

L

la[1] ► her, it

la[2] ► the

là ► here, there

   de là ► hence

   aller çà et là ► ramble

   là où ► where

   là-bas ► yonder

   là-haut ► upstairs, yonder

label ► label

labeur ► labour, toil

laboratoire ► laboratory

laborieux (-euse) ► laborious [labour]

labourer ► tilt[2]

laboureur ► tiller [tilt[2]]

labyrinthe ► labyrinth, maze

lac ► lake
lacer ► lace, tie
lacet ► lace, zigzag
lâche ► coward, cowardly
    de manière lâche ► loosely [loose]
lâcher ► blurt, drop
lacté (-ée) ► milky [milk]
lacune ► gap, hole
Lady ► Lady [lady]
lagon ► lagoon
lagune ► lagoon
laid (laide) ► hideous, ugly
laideur ► ugliness [ugly]
en lainage ► woolen
laine ► wool
    de laine ► wool, woolen
    laine d'acier ► steel wool
laineux (-euse) ► woolly
laïque ► secular
laisser ► drop off, leave[1], let, quit
    laisser aller ► run
    laisser libre cours ► vent
    laisser un acompte ► deposit
    laisser voir ► reveal
laissez-passer ► pass, permit
lait ► milk, whitewash
    au lait ► milky [milk]
    lait écrémé ► skim milk
    lait fouetté ► shake
    lait maternisé ► formula
laiterie ► dairy
laiteux (-euse) ► milky [milk]
laiton ► brass
laitue ► lettuce
lama ► llama
lambeau (-eaux) ► rag, shred
    en lambeaux ► ragged, tattered
lambrisser ► panel
lame ► billow, blade, runner, slat
lamelle ► slat
se lamenter ► lament, whine
lamentable ► miserable, pitiful, sorry
lamentation ► groan, lament, whine
lampe ► lamp
    lampe de poche ► flashlight, torch
    lampe électrique ► flashlight
lance ► harpoon, lance, spear
lance-fusées ► rocket
lancement ► launch[1], promotion
lancer[1] ► cast, fling, initiate, launch[1], pelt[1], pitch[1], throw, toss
    se lancer ► embark, launch[1], plunge, throw
    lancer avec esprit ► quip
    lancer violemment ► dash, hurl
lancer[2] ► throw
    lancer du poids ► shot put

lancer-frappé ► slapshot
lanceur (-euse) ► pitcher[2], shotputter [shot put]
landau ► carriage
lande ► barren, moor[2]
langage ► diction, language, speech
    langage signé ► sign language
langue ► language, tongue
    langue de terre ► spit[2]
    coup de langue ► lick
    claquer la langue ► smack
languette ► tab, tongue
se languir ► pine[2]
lanière ► lash[1], strap
lanterne ► lantern
laper ► lap[3]
lapin (-ine) ► rabbit
    lapin ► bunny
    lapine ► doe
lapsus ► slip[1]
laque ► lacquer, spray
laquer ► lacquer
large ► broad, comprehensive, deep, full, liberal, sweeping, wide
    large sourire ► grin
    de large ► across, wide
    au large ► offshore
largement ► extensively [extensive], liberally [liberal], vastly [vast]
    largement assez ► ample
    sourire largement ► beam
largeur ► breadth, width
larguer ► dump
larme[2] ► tear[2]
    (en) larmes ► tears [tear[2]]
    rire aux larmes ► in stitches
    verser des larmes ► weep
larmoyer ► water
larve ► larva
larynx ► larynx
las (lasse) ► tired, weary, worn
laser ► laser
lasser ► fatigue, weary
lassitude ► tiredness [tired]
    avec lassitude ► wearily [weary]
lasso ► lariat, lasso
    capturer au lasso ► rope
    prendre au lasso ► lasso, rope
latéral (-ale, -aux) ► lateral
latéralement ► laterally [lateral], sideways
latin ► Latin
    latin (-ine) ► Latino [Latin]
    latino-américain (-aine) ► Latino [Latin]
latitude ► latitude
laurier ► bay[4], laurel
    lauriers ► laurel

dormir sur ses lauriers ► rest on
lavabo ► basin
lavage ► wash
    faire un lavage de cerveau ► brainwash
lavande ► lavender
lave ► lava
lave-linge ► washer, washing machine
laver ► wash
    machine à laver ► washer, washing machine
    laver à la batée ► pan
    laver au jet ► hose
laveur (-euse) ► washer
le[1] ► him, it
le[2] ► the
leader ► leader
lécher ► lick
leçon ► homework, lesson, teaching
lecteur ► player
    lecteur de disques ► disk drive
lecteur (-trice) ► reader
    avis au lecteur (-trice) ► foreword
lecture ► reading
    lecture au scanneur ► scan
    livre de lecture ► reader
légal (-ale, -aux) ► lawful, legal
légalement ► lawfully [lawful]
légendaire ► legendary
légende ► caption, fable, legend
léger (-ère) ► buoyant, delicate, faint, fluffy [fluff], frivolous, gentle, light[2], mild, quiet, slight
    à la légère ► thoughtlessly [thoughtless]
    traiter à la légère ► trifle
légèrement ► faintly [faint], light[2], lightly [light[2]], mildly [mild], nimbly [nimble], shade
    légèrement différent (-ente) ► variant
    pleuvoir légèrement ► sprinkle
    secouer légèrement ► jiggle
légèreté ► thinness [thin], thoughtlessness [thoughtless]
légiférer ► legislate
légion ► legion
législateur (-trice) ► legislator
législatif (-ive) ► legislative
    corps législatif ► legislature
législation ► law
légitime ► lawful, legitimate
légitimement ► lawfully [lawful], legitimately [legitimate]
légitimer ► justify, warrant
legs ► legacy
léguer ► bequeath, will[2]
légume ► vegetable
    légumes ► green
    à légumes ► vegetable
    de légumes ► vegetable

légumier (-ière) ► vegetable
lent (lente) ► dull, slow, sluggish, tardy
lentement ► slowly [slow]
lenteur ► slowness [slow], tardiness [tardy]
lentille ► lens
léopard ► leopard
léotard ► leotard
lequel (laquelle, lesquels, lesquelles) ► what, which
    par lequel (laquelle, lesquels, lesquelles) ► whereby
    dans lequel (laquelle, lesquels, lesquelles) ► wherein
les[1] ► them
les[2] ► the
léser ► harm
lésion ► injury
lessive ► laundry, wash
faire du lettrage ► letter
lettre ► letter
    bloc de papier à lettres ► tablet
    graver des lettres ► letter
    marquer avec des lettres ► letter
leur[1] ► them
leur[2] ► their
    le leur ► theirs
    les leurs ► theirs
    leurs ► their
leurre ► lure
leurrer ► decoy
levage ► hoist
    appareil de levage ► tackle
levant ► east
levé (-ée) ► up
levée ► levee
lever ► hoist, lift, raise, rise, uplift
    se lever ► arise, dawn, lift, stand
    lever du jour ► daylight
    lever du soleil ► sunrise
    lever et abaisser régulièrement ► pump
levier ► crowbar, lever, shift
lèvre ► lip
    former des mots avec les lèvres ► mouth
    pincer (les lèvres) ► purse
levure ► yeast
lexique ► dictionary, glossary, vocabulary
lézard ► lizard
    faire le lézard ► sun
liaison ► communication, connection, link
liasse ► wad
libellule ► dragonfly
libéral (-ale, -aux) ► liberal
    Parti Libéral ► Liberal Party
    Libéral (-aux) ► Liberal [liberal]
libéralement ► liberally [liberal]

libérateur (-trice) ► liberator [liberate]
libération ► discharge, release
libéré (-ée) ► freedom
libérer ► clear, discharge, free, liberate, release
    libérer contre une rançon ► ransom
liberté ► freedom, latitude, liberty
    en liberté ► at large, wild
    Charte des droits et libertés ► Charter of Rights and Freedoms
libertinage ► licence
libre ► at large, free, loose, vacant
librement ► freely [free], loose
licence ► licence
    donner une licence ► licence
licencier ► dismiss, fire, lay off
licorne ► unicorn
lié (liée) ► bound[1], relative, relevant
liège ► cork
lien ► attachment, bearing, bond, link, relationship, tie
    établir un lien ► relate
lier ► bind, bond, fasten
    se lier d'amitié ► befriend
    se lier facilement ► relate
lierre ► ivy
lieu (lieux) ► place, spot, whereabouts
    lieux ► premise
    avoir lieu ► be
    au lieu de ► instead, instead of
    haut lieu ► seat
    lieu (lieux) fréquenté(s) ► haunt
    lieu de rencontre ► rendezvous
    lieu de retraite ► retreat
    lieu de séjour ► resort
    lieu de vacances ► resort
    lieu saint ► shrine
    mettre en lieu sûr ► keep
lieue ► league[2]
lieutenant (-ante) ► lieutenant
    lieutenant-colonel ► commander
lièvre ► hare
ligament ► ligament
ligne ► figure, line[1]
    en ligne ► on-line
    hors ligne ► off-line
    grandes lignes ► outline
    ligne aérienne ► airline
    ligne de division ► divide
    ligne de partage ► divide
    ligne de partage des eaux ► watershed
    ligne d'horizon ► skyline
    ligne droite ► rule
liguer ► in league
    se liguer ► align, band[2]
lignée ► descent, strain[2]
ligner ► line[1]

ligneux (-euse) ► woody
ligue ► league[1]
lilas ► lilac
limace ► slug[1]
lime ► file[2], lime[1]
    vert lime ► lime[1]
limer ► file[2]
limerick ► limerick
limitation ► restraint, restriction
limite ► bound[3], boundary, ceiling, confine, end, limit
    limites ► scope
    heure limite ► deadline
limité (-ée) ► narrow
limiter ► confine, limit, narrow, restrict, tie
limousine ► limousine
limpide ► clear
lin ► linen
linceul ► shroud
linge ► linen
    corde à linge ► clothes-lines
lion ► lion
    lionne ► lioness
liquide ► fluid, liquid, thin
    trop liquide ► watery
lire ► read
lisible ► legible
lisière ► edge, fringe
lisse ► sleek, slick, smooth
lisser ► polish, slick, smooth
liste ► list[1], register, roll
    inscrire sur une liste ► list[1]
lister ► list[1]
lit ► bed, channel
    lit d'enfant ► crib
    lit-placard ► bunk
    lit d'eau ► waterbed
    mettre au lit ► bed
litige ► dispute
litre ► litre
littéral (-ale, -aux) ► literal
littéralement ► literally
littérature ► literature
littoral ► coast
littoral (-ale, -aux) ► coastal [coast]
liturgie ► worship
livraison ► delivery
livre[1] ► book, pound[1]
    grand livre ► ledger
    premier livre ► primer
    livre de lecture ► reader
    livre d'orthographe ► speller
    livre élémentaire ► primer
    livre scolaire ► textbook
livre[2] ► sterling
    livre sterling ► pound[1]
livrer ► deliver, fill

livret ► booklet
   livret de chèques ► cheque
lobby ► lobby
local (-ale, -aux) ► local
   locaux ► premise
localement ► locally [local]
localisation ► location
localiser ► locate
   chercher à localiser ► probe
locataire ► tenant
location ► hire, rental
   prix de location ► rent
locomotive ► engine, locomotive
   locomotive à la vapeur ► steam engine
locution ► expression, idiom, phrase
loge ► box[1]
logement ► accomodation [accommodate],
apartment, housing, lodging, quarter
loger ► accommodate, house, lodge, put up
logiciel ► software
logique ► consistent, logic, logical, rational
logiquement ► logically [logical]
loi ► act, law, statute
   sans loi ► lawless
   projet de loi ► bill[1]
   promulguer une loi ► legislate
loin ► away, far
   au loin ► distance
   de loin ► easily
   très loin ► way
   plus loin ► beyond, down[1], farther,
further, past, up,
   loin de la cible ► wide
   être loin ► way
lointain (-aine) ► distant, far, remote
   le (la) plus lointain (-aine) ► farthest
loisir ► leisure
   de loisir ► leisure, recreational
[recreation]
   pour les loisirs ► recreational
[recreation]
long ► long[1]
   le long de ► along
long (longue) ► long[1]
   long métrage ► feature, motion picture
   trop long (longue) ► lengthy [length]
longe ► tether
longer ► follow, hug
longitude ► longitude
longtemps ► long[1], stretch
longueur ► length
   longueur d'ondes ► wavelength
loque ► rag
   en loques ► ragged, tattered
loquet ► catch, latch
Lord ► Lord
lorsque ► when

losange ► diamond
lot ► concession, fate, lot, prize
loterie ► lottery
lotion ► lotion
lotissement ► project, tract
louable ► worthy
louange ► compliment, praise, rave
louanger ► rave
louangeur (-euse) ► complimentary
louche ► dipper, ladle, shady
   servir à la louche ► ladle
loucherie ► squint
louer ► charter, hire, lease, praise, rent
   se louer ► rent
loup (louve) ► wolf
loup-garou ► werewolf
lourd (lourde) ► coarse, heavy, weighty
   pas lourd (lourde) ► tramp
lourdement ► heavily
lourdeur ► heaviness [heavy]
loutre ► otter
louvoyer ► tack
loyal (-ale, -aux) ► fair[1], loyal, staunch
loyalement ► fair[1], fairly, faithfully [faithful],
loyally, staunchly [staunch]
loyaliste ► loyalist
loyauté ► faithfulness [faithful]
loyer ► rent
lubrifiant ► grease
lubrifier ► grease, oil
lucarne ► skylight
luciole ► firefly
lucratif (-ive) ► profitable
lueur ► gleam, glow, ray[1]
luge ► bobsled, coaster, sled, sleigh,
toboggan
   faire de la luge ► bobsled, toboggan
lugubre ► bleak, dingy, dismal
lugubrement ► dismally [dismal]
lui ► her, him
lui-même ► himself
   lui-même (elle-même) ► itself
luire ► gleam, glow
luisant (-ante) ► gleaming [gleam], glossy,
sleek
lumière ► light[1]
   lumière du jour ► daylight
   lumière du soleil ► sun, sunlight,
sunshine
   lumière éblouissante ► glare
   faire la lumière sur ► illuminate
   jeter de la lumière ► shed[2]
lumineux (-euse) ► luminous
   spectre lumineux ► spectrum
lunaire ► lunar
lunch ► lunch
lundi ► Monday

lune ► moon
    croissant de lune ► crescent
    clair de lune ► moonlight
    au clair de lune ► moonlight
    lune de miel ► honeymoon
    partir en lune de miel ► honeymoon
lunettes ► glasses [glass], spectacles [spectacle]
    lunettes de soleil ► sunglasses
lustre ► brightness [bright], brilliance [brilliant], glaze
lustré (-ée) ► glazed [glaze], glossy
lustrer ► glaze
lutin ► brownie, elf, gnome
lutte ► battle, fight, struggle, war, warfare, wrestling
    pratiquer la lutte ► wrestle
lutter ► battle, contend, contest, fight, wrestle
lutteur (-euse) ► fighter
luxe ► luxury
    de luxe ► fancy
luxuriant (-ante) ► lush
luzerne ► alfalfa
lynx ► bobcat, lynx
lys ► lily

M

M.F. (modulation de fréquences) ► FM
macareux ► puffin
macaroni ► macaroni
mâcher ► chew
    mâcher (ses mots) ► mince
    gomme à mâcher ► gum[1]
machin ► gadget, thing
machination ► design
machine ► machine
    machine à coudre ► sewing machine
    machine à écrire ► typewriter
    machine à laver ► washer, washing machine
    machine à vapeur ► steam engine
machinerie ► machinery
mâchoire ► jaw
maculer ► smudge
madame ► ma'am, madam, Mrs., Ms.
mademoiselle ► miss[2]
madrier ► board, plank, timber
magasin ► magazine, shop, store, warehouse
magasiner ► shop
magazine ► magazine
magicien (-ienne) ► magician, wizard
magie ► magic
magique ► magic
magiquement ► magically [magic]
magnat ► baron, tycoon

magnétique ► magnetic
magnétophone ► recorder, tape recorder
magnétoscope ► recorder
magnificence ► magnificence [magnificent]
magnifique ► beautiful, bumper, glorious, golden, gorgeous, grand, great, magnificent, marvellous, splendid, superb, wonderful
mai ► May
maigre ► lean[2], spare, thin
    (très) maigre ► scrawny, skinny
maigreur ► thinness [thin]
maigrir ► slim
mail ► mall
maille ► link, run, stitch
    mailles ► mail[2]
maillon ► link
maillot ► leotard
    maillot de bain ► trunk
main ► hand
    signe de la main ► wave
    tour de main ► knack
    poignée de main ► handshake
    à portée de la main ► ready
    battre des mains ► clap
    donner un coup de main ► lend a hand
    mettre la main sur ► grab
    mettre la dernière main ► finish
    faire passer de main en main ► relay
main courante ► rail
main-d'œuvre ► hand, labour
prêter main-forte ► lend a hand
maintenant ► now
maintenir ► continue, maintain, retain
    se maintenir ► last[2]
    maintenir en équilibre ► balance
    maintenir l'ordre dans ► police
    maintenir ouvert (-te) ► prop
maintien ► bearing, carriage, conservation, upkeep
maire (mairesse) ► mayor
mais ► but, except, however, only, otherwise,
    mais où donc ► wherever
maïs ► corn[1], maize
    maïs éclaté ► popcorn
maison ► dwelling, harbour, home, house
    à la maison ► home, indoor
    vers la maison ► homeward
    maison de campagne ► villa
    maison de santé ► clinic
    maison d'hébergement ► home
    la maison voisine ► next door
    pâté de maisons ► block
    employé (-ée) de maison ► help
    fait à la maison ► homemade
maisonnée ► house, household
maître ► debater [debate], head, instructor, lord

maître (-esse) ► master
    maître de soi ► collect
maîtresse ► mistress
maîtrise ► control, degree, grip
maîtriser ► bridle, control, in check, master, restrain
majesté ► majesty
    Sa (Votre) Majesté ► Majesty
majestueusement ► majestically [majestic]
majestueux (-euse) ► majestic, noble, stately
majeur (-eure) ► major
    majeure partie de ► chunk
majeure ► major
major ► major
majorette ► twirler [twirl]
majoritairement ► largely
majorité ► majority
    la majorité ► most
majuscule ► capital, uppercase [upper]
    écrire en majuscules ► print
mal[1] ► bad, wrong
mal[2] ► badly [bad], messily [mess]
mal[3] ► disease, harm, ill, sin
    faire du mal ► hurt, injure
    faire du mal à ► harm, hurt
    faire mal ► ache, hurt
    faire mal à ► hurt
    sans faire de mal ► harmlessly [harmless]
    se sentir mal ► down[1]
mal (maux) ► evil, hurt, ill, illness
    être mal à l'aise ► squirm
    mal (maux) de tête ► headache
    mal à l'aise ► ill at ease, uncomfortable
    mal du pays ► homesickness [homesick], nostalgia
    mal de ventre ► cramp
    qui a mal au cœur ► sick
    qui a le mal de mer ► seasick
malade ► ill, sick
maladie ► ailment, disease, ill, illness, sickness [sick], trouble
maladresse ► clumsiness [clumsy]
    répondre avec maladresse ► fumble
maladroit (-oite) ► awkward, clumsy, ungainly
maladroitement ► clumsily [clumsy]
    se déplacer maladroitement ► barge
    s'avancer maladroitement ► blunder
malaise ► discomfort, ill, illness
malaria ► malaria
malavisé (-ée) ► misguided, unwise
malaxer ► mix
malchance ► misfortune
malchanceux (-euse) ► unfortunate, unlucky
malcommode ► inconvenient

mâle ► bull, he, male, mate
malédiction ► curse
malentendu ► misunderstanding
malfaisant (-ante) ► evil, wicked
malfaiteur (-euse) ► gangster
malgré ► despite
    malgré (que) ► though
    malgré tout ► nevertheless
malhabile ► inept
malheur ► curse, misfortune, tragedy, woe
malheureusement ► unfortunately [unfortunate], unhappily [unhappy], woefully [woe]
malheureux (-euse) ► miserable, poor, unhappy, woeful [woe], wretch
malhonnête ► crooked
malice ► mischief
    sans malice ► innocent
malicieusement ► wickedly [wicked]
malicieux (-euse) ► arch[2], mischievous
malin (-igne) ► cunning
malin (-ine) ► sly
malingre ► puny
malle ► trunk
malléable ► plastic
malmener ► abuse, bully, punish, rough
malpropre ► dirty, impure
malsain (-aine) ► unhealthy
maltraiter ► abuse, batter[3]
malveillant (-ante) ► evil
malvenu (-ue) ► unwanted
maman ► mom, mother
mammifère ► mammal
mammouth ► mammoth
manche[1] ► crop, handle, shaft, sleeve
manche[2] ► inning
manchette[1] ► cuff[1], ruffle
manchette[2] ► headline
manchon ► muff
manchot ► penguin
mandarine ► tangerine
mandat ► tenure, warrant
mandataire ► attorney, delegate
mandater ► commission, delegate
mandoline ► mandolin
manège ► carousel, manœuvre, merry-go-round
    tour de manège ► ride
manette ► lever, tap[2]
mangeoire ► crib
manger ► eat, feed
    manger à coups de fourchette ► fork
    donner à manger ► feed
maniaque ► maniac
manie ► habit, mania
manier ► finger, wield
    manier gauchement ► fumble

785

manier maladroitement ▶ fumble
manière ▶ fashion, manner, mode, way
  de toute manière ▶ anyhow
  de quelque manière que ▶ however
maniéré (-ée) ▶ affected [affect[2]]
manifestation ▶ demonstration
manifeste ▶ evident
manifestement ▶ evidently [evident],
tangibly [tangible], visibly [visible]
manifester ▶ demonstrate, express
manigancer ▶ hatch[1]
manipuler ▶ handle
manivelle ▶ crank
mannequin ▶ dummy, model
manœuvre ▶ drill, manoeuvre
manœuvrer ▶ handle, manoeuvre
manoir ▶ chateau, mansion
manquant (-ante) ▶ absent, deficient
[deficiency], missing
manque ▶ deficiency, lack, miss[1], shortage
  manque de bon sens ▶ senselessness
[senseless]
  manque de ponctualité ▶ tardiness
[tardy]
  manque de prévenance ou d'égards ▶
thoughtlessness [thoughtless]
  manque de profondeur ▶ shallowness
[shallow]
  manque de soins ▶ neglect
  manque de tranchant ▶ bluntness
[blunt]
  manque de vie ▶ dead
  manque d'empressement ▶ tardiness
[tardy]
  avoir besoin par manque ▶ want
manquer ▶ fail, miss[1]
  manquer à ▶ neglect
  manquer de ▶ lack, shy
mante ▶ mantle
manteau (-eaux) ▶ blanket, cloak, coat,
mantle, wrap
  manteau (-eaux) de pluie ▶ raincoat
  manteau de cheminée ▶ mantel
manuel ▶ guide, manual
  manuel d'introduction ▶ primer
  manuel scolaire ▶ textbook
manuel (-elle) ▶ manual
manuscrit ▶ handwriting, manuscript
maquette ▶ dummy, model
maquillage ▶ make-up
marais ▶ bog, marsh, swamp, wetland
marasme ▶ depression
marathon ▶ marathon
marbre ▶ home, marble
marc ▶ ground[1]
marchand (-ande) ▶ dealer, merchant,
seller, trader, vendor

marchant en gros ▶ wholesaler
[wholesale]
marchander ▶ bargain
marchandise ▶ commodity, goods,
merchandise, ware
marche[1] ▶ march
  de marche ▶ walk
  marche pénible ▶ trudge
marche[2] ▶ stair, step, tide
  en marche ▶ on
  marche arrière ▶ reverse
  mettre en marche ▶ activate, boot, start,
turn on (off) [turn]
marché[1] ▶ bargain, deal
  bon marché ▶ cheap, inexpensive
  à bon marché ▶ cheaply [cheap]
marché[2] ▶ market, marketplace
  marché financier ▶ stock market
  place du marché ▶ marketplace
  faire le marché ▶ market
  mettre en marché ▶ market,
merchandise
marcher ▶ function, march, step, walk
  marcher sur ▶ step, tread
  qui marche à ▶ power
  marcher à grands pas ▶ stride
  marcher à pas feutré ▶ pad
  marcher allègrement ▶ prance
  marcher au pas ▶ march
  marcher avec difficulté ▶ wade
  marcher d'un air digne ▶ stalk[2]
  marcher avec raideur ▶ stalk[2]
  **marcher dans la rue en contrevenant
à la sécurité routière** ▶ jaywalk
  marcher d'un pas léger ▶ trip
  marcher d'un pas lourd ▶ tramp
  marcher d'un pas pressé ▶ trot
  marcher en cadence ▶ pump
  marcher en file ▶ file[1]
  marcher lourdement ▶ clump
  marcher péniblement ▶ trudge
  marcher pesamment ▶ lumber[2]
  marcher sans ordre ▶ straggle
  marcher sur la pointe des pieds ▶
tiptoe
  marcher sur les traces de ▶ in the wake
of [wake[3]]
  marcher voûté ▶ stoop[1]
  (faire) marcher ▶ power, run
  faire marcher quelqu'un ▶ kid
marcheur (-euse) ▶ walker
mardi ▶ Tuesday
mare ▶ pond, pool[1]
marécage ▶ bog, marsh, swamp
marécageux (-euse) ▶ marshy [marsh],
swampy [swamp]
marée ▶ tide

marelle ► hopscotch
margarine ► margarine
marge ► margin
   par une faible marge ► by a nose
marguerite ► daisy
mari ► husband, mate
mariage ► marriage, wedding
   demande en mariage ► proposal
   offre de mariage ► proposal
   demander en mariage ► propose
marié ► bridegroom, groom
   futur marié ► bridegroom
mariée ► bride
   future mariée ► bride
marier ► marry, wed
   se marier ► marry
marin ► sailor
   chanson de marin ► shanty
marin (-ine) ► marine
   bleu marine ► navy
marine ► marine, navy
mariné (-ée) ► pickled
mariner ► pickle
maringouin ► mosquito
marionnette ► puppet
maritime ► maritime
   route maritime ► seaway
marmite ► kettle, pot
marmonner ► mutter
marmotte ► groundhog, woodchuck
marmotter ► mumble, mutter
marque[1] ► blaze[2], brand, check, label, make, mark
   de marque ► premium
   image de marque ► image
   marque de commerce ► trademark
   marque déposée ► trademark
   marque distinctive ► trademark
marque[2] ► score, tag[1], token
marqué (-ée) ► pronounced
marquer ► blaze[2], bowl[2], brand, chalk up, characterize, mark, punctuate, register, score, tag[1], usher in (out) [usher]
   marquer au pochoir ► stencil
   marquer avec des lettres ► letter
   marquer d'un astérisque ► star
   marquer d'une cicatrice ► scar
marqueur ► shadow
marraine ► godmother, sponsor
marron ► brown, chest-nut
   marron clair ► tan
mars ► March
   Mars ► Mars
marsouin ► porpoise
marteau (-eaux) ► hammer
   marteau (-eaux) à panne fendue ► claw
   marteau (-eaux) de forgeron ► sledgehammer

frapper à coup de marteau ► hammer
martèlement ► pound[2]
marteler ► hammer, pound[2], thump
martinet ► swift[2]
martre ► sable
mascotte ► mascot
masculin (-ine) ► male, masculine
masque ► mask
masqué (-ée) ► blind
masquer ► blot out, cloak, conceal, mask, seclude
massacre ► massacre, slaughter
massacrer ► butcher, massacre, slaughter
masse[1] ► crowd, heap, jam[1], mass, score
   la masse ► bulk
   masses ► mass
   de masse ► mass
   en masse ► wholesale
   aller en masse ► swarm
masse[2] ► hammer
masser ► knead, mass
massif ► clump, grove
massif (-ive) ► mass, massive, solid
massue ► club
mastic ► putty
mât ► boom[2], mast, pole[1], staff
   mât de charge ► derrick
match ► game, match[2]
   match de football ► bowl[1]
   match nul ► draw, tie
matelas ► mattress
matelasser ► quilt
mater ► tame
se matérialiser ► materialize
matériau (-aux) ► material
matériel ► equipment, gear, kit, tackle
   matériel d'informatique ► hardware
matériel (-elle) ► material
matériellement ► materially [material]
maternel (-elle) ► motherly [mother]
maternelle ► kindergarten
   école maternelle ► nursery school
materner ► mother
maths ► math
mathématique ► mathematics
matière ► matter, stuff, subject
   matière grasse ► shortening
   matière première ► raw material
   matière scolaire ► discipline
matin ► morning
   du matin ► a.m., morning
matinal (-ale, -aux) ► morning
matinée ► morning
   concert en matinée ► matinée
   spectacle en matinée ► matinée
matraque ► club

matrice ▸ die[3], womb
maturité ▸ maturity [mature]
maudire ▸ curse
maudit (-ite) ▸ wretched
maugréer ▸ moan
maussade ▸ miserable, sullen
mauvais (-aise) ▸ bad, evil, ill, lean[2], poor, wicked, wrong
    plus mauvais (-aise) ▸ worse
    le (la) plus mauvais (-aise) ▸ worst
    mauvais pas ▸ mess
    mauvais perdant (mauvaise perdante) ▸ sport
    mauvais tour ▸ mischief
    mauvais traitement ▸ punishment
    mauvaise herbe ▸ weed
maximal (-ale, -aux) ▸ maximum
maximum ▸ maximum, mileage
    au maximum ▸ fully [full], most
    le maximum ▸ most
mayonnaise ▸ mayonnaise
me ▸ me, myself
mécanicien (-ienne) ▸ engineer, mechanic
mécanique ▸ mechanical, mechanics
mécaniquement ▸ mechanically [mechanical]
mécanisme ▸ device, machinery, mechanics, mechanism, work
méchamment ▸ unkindly [unkind], viciously [vicious]
méchanceté ▸ malice, nastiness [nasty], unkindness [unkind], viciousness [vicious], wickedness [wicked]
    avec méchanceté ▸ maliciously [malice]
méchant (-ante) ▸ bad, cruel, dirty, horrid, ill, malicious [malice], mean[2], nasty, unkind, vicious, villain, wicked
mèche ▸ bit[2], lock[2], strand[2], wick
    fine mèche ▸ wisp
mécontent (-ente) ▸ dissatisfied
médaille ▸ decoration, medal
médaillon ▸ locket
médecin ▸ doctor, physician
médecine ▸ medicine
média ▸ media
médiamat ▸ rating
médiator ▸ pick[1]
médical (-ale, -aux) ▸ medical
médicament ▸ drug, medicine
médiéval (-ale, -aux) ▸ medieval
médiocre ▸ poor
médiocrement ▸ poorly [poor]
médisance ▸ slander
méditer ▸ entertain, muse, ponder
méduse ▸ jellyfish
avec méfiance ▸ suspiciously [suspicious]
méfiant (-ante) ▸ suspicious

méga-octet ▸ megabyte
par mégarde ▸ mistakenly [mistaken]
meilleur (-eure) ▸ best, better
    le meilleur (la meilleure) ▸ best, better, the best
    meilleurs souhaits ▸ best
    meilleurs souvenirs ▸ regard
    meilleurs vœux ▸ regard
mélancolie ▸ gloom, melancholy, wistfulness [wistful]
    avec mélancolie ▸ wistfully [wistful]
mélancolique ▸ gloomy [gloom], melancholy, mournful [mourn], wistful
mélancoliquement ▸ mournfully [mourn], sadly [sad]
mélange ▸ blend, cross, mix
mélangé (-ée) ▸ impure, mixed
mélanger ▸ blend, incorporate, mingle, mix, scramble, shuffle
mêlé (-ée) ▸ mixed
mêlée ▸ scrimmage
mêler ▸ involve, mingle, mix, shuffle
    se mêler ▸ blend, meddle, mingle, mix
    qui se mêle de tout ▸ meddlesome [meddle]
mélodie ▸ harmony, melody
mélodique ▸ melodic [melody]
mélodramatique ▸ melodramatic
    d'un air ou d'une façon mélodramatique ▸ melodramatically [melodramatic]
melon ▸ cantaloupe, melon
    melon d'eau ▸ watermelon
membrane ▸ membrane
membre ▸ limb, member
    devenir membre de ▸ join
    être membre de ▸ serve
    membre de la direction ▸ officer
    membre de la famille royale ▸ royalty
    membre de la Gendarmerie royale du Canada ▸ Mountie
membrure ▸ rib
même ▸ even, proper, same, very
    de même ▸ alike, likewise, same, so
    tout de même ▸ surely [sure]
mémoire ▸ memory
    à la mémoire de ▸ in memory of, memorial
    mémoire morte ▸ ROM
    mise en mémoire ▸ storage
    puce de mémoire ▸ memory chip
    mettre en mémoire ▸ store
    se rafraîchir la mémoire ▸ refresh (one's) memory [refresh]
    rafraîchir la mémoire de quelqu'un ▸ jog someone's memory, refresh (one's) memory [refresh]

mémorable ► unforgettable
mémoriser ► memorize
menaçant (-ante) ► grim, ominous, ugly
   d'un air ou d'un ton menaçant ► menacingly [menace]
menace ► menace, threat
   proférer des menaces ► threaten
menacer ► menace, threaten
ménage ► house, household, housework
ménager ► spare
ménager (-ère) ► household
   travaux ménagers ► housework
mendiant (-ante) ► beggar
mendier ► beg
mener ► boss, carry on, conduct, go, head, hold[1], lead[1]
   se faire mener (de) ► trail
meneur (-euse) ► leader
mensonge ► deceit, lie[2]
mensonger (-ère) ► false
mensuel (-elle) ► monthly
mensuellement ► monthly
mensurations ► measurement
mental (-ale, -aux) ► mental
mentalement ► mentally [mental]
   se préparer mentalement ► brace
menteur (-euse) ► deceptive, impostor, liar
menthe ► mint[1]
   menthe verte ► spearmint
   bonbon à la menthe ► mint[1]
mention ► distinction, Honour [honour], mention
   faire mention de ► mention
mentionner ► bring up, cite, mention, speak
mentir ► lie[2]
menton ► chin
menu ► menu
menu (-ue) ► dainty, fine[1]
menuiserie ► carpentry [carpenter], woodwork
menuisier (-ière) ► carpenter
mépris ► contempt, scorn
   avec mépris ► scornful [scorn]
   rejeter avec mépris ► spurn
   repousser avec mépris ► spurn
   sourire de mépris ► sneer
méprisable ► mean[2]
méprisant (-ante) ► scornfully [scorn]
méprise ► misunderstanding
mépriser ► despise, scorn
mer ► sea
   de mer ► saltwater
   en mer ► offshore
   anémone de mer ► sea anemone
   bras de mer ► sound[4]
   étoile de mer ► starfish
   front de mer ► waterfront

   fruits de mer ► shellfish
   niveau de la mer ► sea level
   tortue de mer ► turtle
   qui a le mal de mer ► seasick
articles de mercerie ► notion
merci ► thanks
mercredi ► Wednesday
mercure ► mercury
   Mercure ► Mercury
mère ► mother, parent
   fête des Mères ► Mother's Day
   servir de mère ► mother
méridional (-ale, -aux) ► south, southern, southerner
mérite ► credit, merit, virtue, worth, worthy
   qui mérite de ► worthwhile
mérité (-ée) ► just
mériter ► deserve, earn, merit
merle ► blackbird
   merle américain ► robin
merveille ► gem, marvel, wonder
   à merveille ► beautifully [beautiful]
merveilleusement ► marvellously [marvellous], wonderfully [wonderful]
merveilleux (-euse) ► great, marvellous, miraculous, wonderful
mésaventure ► mishap
mesdemoiselles ► miss[2]
mesquin (-ine) ► mean[2], small
mesquinement ► shabbily [shabby]
mess ► mess
message ► communication, message
   message télégraphique ► cable
messager (-ère) ► courier, herald, messenger
messe ► Mass
Messie ► Christ
mesurage ► measurement
mesure ► bar, beat, cubic, measure, measurement, metre[2], proportion, step, yardstick
   sur mesure ► custom
   mesures de répressions contre ► crack down
   faire sur mesure ► tailor
mesuré (-ée) ► deliberate, temperate
mesurer ► calculate, gauge, measure, tall, yardstick
   se mesurer ► pit[1]
   mesurer au pas ► pace
métal (-aux) ► metal
   feuille de métal ► foil[2]
métallique ► metallic [metal]
   tampon métallique ► steel wool
métalliser ► plate
métaphore ► metaphor

métaphorique ► metaphorically [metaphor]
métaphoriquement ► metaphorical [metaphor]
météore ► meteor
météorite ► meteorite
méthode ► method, system, tack, way
méticuleux (-euse) ► particular
métier ► business, craft, line[1], occupation, profession, trade
    corps de métier ► profession
    métier à tisser ► loom[1]
Métis (-isse) ► Métis
long **métrage** ► feature, motion picture
mètre ► metre[1], metre[2]
métrique ► metric
    système métrique ► metric system
métro ► subway, tube
métropolitain (-aine) ► metropolitan
mets ► dish
metteur (-eure) en scène ► director
mettre ► apply, change, deposit, lay[1], pack, place, put, put on, set
    mettre à jour ► revise, update
    mis (mise) à jour ► up to the minute
    se mettre ► go
    s'y mettre ► pitch in
    (se) mettre en place ► position
meubles ► furniture
    meuble de rangement ► cabinet
meubler ► furnish
meule ► stack
meurtre ► murder
meurtrier (-ière) ► deadly, killer, murderous [murder]
    d'une façon meurtrière ► murderously [murder]
meurtrir ► bruise
meurtrissure ► bruise
meute ► den
    chien de meute ► hound
mi- ► mid
à **mi-chemin** ► halfway, midway
miche de pain ► loaf[1]
micmac ► Micmac
micro ► mike
microbe ► bug
microfilm ► microfilm
micro-onde ► microwave
    four à micro-ondes ► microwave oven
micro-ordinateur ► microcomputer
    micro-ordinateur portable ► laptop
micro-organisme ► microorganism
microphone ► microphone
    microphone clandestin ► bug
microprocesseur ► microprocessor
microscope ► microscope
microscopique ► microscopic [microscope]

midi ► noon
    avant midi ► a.m.
miel ► honey
    lune de miel ► honeymoon
le mien (la mienne, les miens) ► mine[1]
    (les) miens ► folk
miette ► crumb
mieux ► better, sooner [soon]
    au mieux ► at best
    le mieux ► best
    faire mieux ► top[1]
    faire de son mieux ► best
mignon (-onne) ► cute
migraine ► headache
migrateur (-trice) ► migrant
migrer ► migrate
mijoter ► simmer, stew
milan ► kite
mildiou ► mildew
milieu ► centre, circle, environment, mean[3], medium, middle, midst
    au milieu ► depth
    au milieu de ► mid
militaire ► military, warrior
    militaires ► the military [military]
militant (-ante) ► campaigner [campaign]
militer ► crusade
millage ► mileage
mille[1] ► mile
    mille nautique ► mile
    consommation de carburant au mille (= au kilomètre) ► mileage
mille[2] ► thousand
    dans le mille ► on the nose
mille-pattes ► centipede
millésimé (-ée) ► vintage
milliard ► billion
millième ► thousandth [thousand]
million ► million
millionième ► millionth [million]
minable ► rotten, shoddy
mince ► flimsy, remote, slender, slim, thin, wispy [wisp]
minceur ► thinness [thin]
mine ► face, mine[2], show
    mine de plomb ► lead[2]
    mine de renseignements ► storehouse
    semer des mines ► mine[2]
miner ► conflict, gnaw, mine[2], prey, undermine
minerai ► mineral, ore
minéral (-aux) ► mineral
mineur (-eure) ► minor
miniature ► miniature, toy
miniaturiser ► miniaturize [miniature]
minimal (-ale, -aux) ► minimum
minimum ► minimum

ministère ▸ government, ministry
    ministère des finances ▸ Treasury
ministre ▸ cabinet minister, minister
    Premier ministre ▸ P.M., p.m., premier, prime minister
minorité ▸ minority
minoterie ▸ mill
minuit ▸ midnight
minuscule ▸ lower case, minute[2], scanty [scant], small letter, tiny
minute ▸ minute[1]
minuter ▸ time
minuterie ▸ timer
minutie ▸ precision
minutieusement ▸ elaborately [elaborate], minutely [minute[2]], thoroughly [thorough]
minutieux (-euse) ▸ elaborate, minute[2], thorough
miracle ▸ miracle, wonder
miraculeusement ▸ miraculously [miraculous]
miraculeux (-euse) ▸ miraculous
mirage ▸ illusion, mirage
mire ▸ sight
miroir ▸ mirror
miroiter ▸ glisten, shimmer
mise ▸ setting
    mise à mort ▸ kill
    mise à sac ▸ sack[2]
    mise au point ▸ adjustment
    mise en application ▸ enforcement [enforce]
    mise en jeu ▸ face-off
    mise en scène ▸ production
    mise en travers ▸ jack-knife
    mise en vente ▸ release
    mise en vigueur ▸ enforcement [enforce]
miser ▸ gamble, stake
misérable ▸ bum, mean[2], miserable, wretch, wretched
misérablement ▸ miserably [miserable], wretchedly [wretched]
misère ▸ distress, wretchedness [wretched]
miséricordieux (-euse) ▸ merciful [mercy]
missile ▸ missile, rocket
mission ▸ mission
    durée (d'une mission) ▸ tour
mitaine ▸ mitt, mitten
mite ▸ moth
miteux (-euse) ▸ shabby
mixte ▸ mixed
mobile ▸ incentive, mobile, motive, moving
mobilier ▸ furniture
mobilisation ▸ draft
se mobiliser contre ▸ gang
mocassin ▸ moccasin
moche ▸ tacky

mode ▸ fashion
    à la mode ▸ hot, stylish [style], trendy
mode ▸ mode, pattern, rage, style
    terme à la mode ▸ buzzword
modèle ▸ design, example, model, pattern
    modèle (réduit) ▸ model
    modèle standard ▸ standard
    dessiner d'après le modèle de ▸ model
    présenter les modèles de ▸ model
modeler ▸ model, mould[1], pattern
modem ▸ modem
avec modération ▸ soberly [sober]
modéré (-ée) ▸ easy, moderate, temperate
modérément ▸ moderately [moderate]
modérer ▸ relax, moderate
moderne ▸ contemporary, modern
moderniste ▸ modern
modeste ▸ conservative, humble, lowly [low], modest
modestement ▸ humbly [humble], modestly [modest]
modestie ▸ humility, modesty [modest]
modification ▸ alteration [alter], amendment [amend], change
modifier ▸ alter, change, modify, revise
module ▸ module
moelle épinière ▸ spinal cord
moelleux (-euse) ▸ mellow, puffy [puff]
mœurs ▸ morality
mohawk ▸ Mohawk
moi[1] ▸ I, me, myself
    moi-même ▸ myself
moi[2] ▸ ego
moignon ▸ stump
moindre ▸ inferior, lesser
    moindre preuve ▸ shred
moine ▸ monk
moineau (-eaux) ▸ sparrow
moins ▸ below, least, less, minus
    à moins que ▸ except, unless
    au moins ▸ at least, good
    de moins de ▸ under
    du moins ▸ at least
    en moins ▸ minus, off
    le (la) moins ▸ least
    moins évolué ▸ backward
    moins que rien ▸ nobody
mois ▸ month
moisi (-ie) ▸ mouldy
moisir ▸ mildew, mould[2]
moisissure ▸ mildew, mould[2]
moisson ▸ crop, harvest
moissonner ▸ harvest, reap
moissonneuse-batteuse ▸ combine
moite ▸ moist, sticky
moiteur ▸ damp, dampness [damp]
moitié ▸ half

à moitié ▸ half, halfway
à moitié chemin ▸ halfway
moléculaire ▸ molecular [molecule]
molécule ▸ molecule
mollement ▸ limply [limp[2]], sluggishly [sluggish], weakly [weak]
mollesse ▸ sluggishness [sluggish], weakness
mollet ▸ calf[2]
mollusque ▸ mollusc
moment ▸ instant, minute[1], moment, spell[3], time
   un moment ▸ awhile
   à ce moment-là ▸ then
   en ce moment ▸ currently, now, presently
   moment critique ▸ watershed
   moment décisif (-ive) ▸ watershed
   court moment ▸ wink
momentané (-ée) ▸ momentary [moment]
momentanément ▸ momentarily [moment]
mon (ma, mes) ▸ my
monarchie ▸ crown, monarchy
monarque ▸ monarch
monastère ▸ monastery
mondanité ▸ worldliness [worldly]
monde ▸ earth, world
   de ce monde ▸ worldly
   dans l'autre monde ▸ hereafter
   tout le monde ▸ everybody, everyone
   qui a l'expérience du monde ▸ worldly
   mettre au monde ▸ deliver
mondial (-ale) ▸ worldwide
moniteur ▸ monitor
moniteur (-trice) ▸ coach, counsellor, instructor
monnaie ▸ change, currency, money, pound[1], quarter
   monnaie (10 cents) ▸ dime
   monnaie d'argent ▸ silver
   hôtel de la Monnaie ▸ mint[2]
   faire la monnaie ▸ change
   frapper de la monnaie ▸ coin
   frapper une monnaie ▸ mint[2]
monocycle ▸ unicycle
monogramme ▸ monogram
monologue ▸ monologue
monopole ▸ monopoly
monotone ▸ dreary, flat[1], monotonous, tame
   de façon monotone ▸ flatly [flat[1]]
   parler d'une voix monotone ▸ drone
monotonie ▸ flatness [flat[1]]
monsieur ▸ gentleman, Master, mister, Mr., sir
   messieurs ▸ gentlemen
monstre ▸ monster
monstrueusement ▸ monstrously [monstrous]

monstrueux (-euse) ▸ hideous, horrible, monstrous, outrageous
mont ▸ mount
montage ▸ assembly
Montagnais (-aise) ▸ Montagnais
montagnard (-arde) ▸ mountain
montagne ▸ mound, mountain
   des montagnes ▸ mountain
   montagnes russes ▸ roller coaster
   tour de montagnes russes ▸ ride
   (se) faire une montagne d'un rien ▸ make a mountain out of a molehill
montagneux (-euse) ▸ mountainous
   région montagneuse ▸ highland
montant ▸ amount, size
   montant brut ▸ gross
monte-charge ▸ elevator, lift
montée ▸ ascent, climb, upgrade
monter ▸ arise, ascend, assemble, climb, edit, erect, increase, mount, pitch[1], ride, stage, well[2]
   monter à bord ▸ board
   monter en flèche ▸ jump, rocket, skyrocket, soar
   monter la garde ▸ watch
   monter une accusation ▸ frame
   faire monter ▸ bring, inflate
monticule ▸ knoll, mound
montre ▸ watch
   montre-bracelet ▸ watch, wristwatch
montrer ▸ display, indicate, show, teach
   montrer du doigt ▸ point
   montrer la juste valeur de ▸ do justice to
   montrer ses dents ▸ bare
   se montrer de façon à ▸ forth
monture ▸ mount, setting
monument ▸ memorial, monument
monumental (-ale, -aux) ▸ gigantic
se moquer ▸ mock, sneer, taunt
   se moquer de quelqu'un ▸ make fun of
moquerie ▸ irony, mockery [mock], ridicule, taunt
moquette ▸ carpet
moral ▸ morale, spirit
moral (-ale, -aux) ▸ ethical [ethics], moral, virtuous
morale ▸ ethics, moral, morality
moralement ▸ morally [moral]
moralité ▸ moral, morality, virtue
morceau (-eaux) ▸ excerpt, fragment, hunk, lump, piece, scrap, shred, stick
   (petit) morceau ▸ bit[1]
   bon morceau ▸ tidbit
   gros morceau ▸ chunk
mordant (-ante) ▸ acid
mordiller ▸ nibble

mordre ▸ bite
   mordu (-ue) d'informatique ▸ hacker
se **morfondre** ▸ mope
morne ▸ bleak, colourless, dismal, dreary
   d'un air morne ▸ bleakly [bleak]
transformer par **morphing** ▸ morph
mors ▸ bit[2]
morse ▸ Morse code, walrus
morsure ▸ bite
mort ▸ death
   mise à mort ▸ kill
   sonnerie aux morts ▸ taps
mort (morte) ▸ dead, deceased, the dead
[dead], the deceased [deceased], fallen
   (angle) mort ▸ blind
   au point mort ▸ neutral
mortel (-elle) ▸ deadly, fatal, mortal
mortellement ▸ deathly, fatally [fatal],
mortally [mortal]
veillée **mortuaire** ▸ wake[2]
morue ▸ cod
mosaïque ▸ mosaic
mosquée ▸ mosque
mot[1] ▸ note
mot[2] ▸ word
   jeu de mots ▸ pun
   mot composé ▸ blend, compound word
   mot de passe ▸ password
   mots croisés ▸ puzzle
moteur ▸ engine, motor
   arbre (de moteur) ▸ shaft
   à moteur ▸ motor
   faire ronfler le moteur ▸ gun
moteur (-trice) ▸ motor
motif ▸ cause, design, ground[1], incentive,
motive, occasion, pattern
motion ▸ motion
motivation ▸ incentive, motivation [motivate]
motiver ▸ motivate
motocycliste ▸ rider [ride]
motoneige ▸ snowmobile
motorisé (-ée) ▸ motor
motte de gazon ▸ sod
mou (molle) ▸ limp[2], slack, sluggish, weak
mouchard (-arde) ▸ tattler [tattle]
moucharder ▸ tattle
mouche ▸ fly[2]
   mouche noire ▸ blackfly
moucheron ▸ gnat
moucheté (-ée) ▸ speckled [speck]
mouchoir ▸ handkerchief
   mouchoir en papier ▸ tissue
moudre ▸ grind, mill
moue ▸ pout
   faire la moue ▸ pout, purse
mouette ▸ gull
mouffette ▸ skunk

moufle ▸ mitt, mitten
mouillé (-ée) ▸ sloppy, wet
mouiller ▸ drench, squirt, wet
   (se) mouiller légèrement ▸ moisten
   [moist]
moulage ▸ cast
moule ▸ mussel
mouler ▸ cake, cast, mould[1]
moulin ▸ mill
   moulin à vent ▸ windmill
   aile (d'un moulin à vent) ▸ vane
   roue d'un moulin ▸ mill
moulinet ▸ flourish, reel[1]
mourir ▸ die[1], dying
   mourir de faim ▸ starve
   mourir d'envie ▸ ache, die[1]
mousse ▸ foam, lather, moss
mousser ▸ foam, lather
   faire mousser ▸ hype
mousseux (-euse) ▸ fluffy [fluff], mossy
[moss]
mousson ▸ monsoon
moustache ▸ moustache, whisker
moustiquaire ▸ screen
moustique ▸ mosquito
moutarde ▸ mustard
mouton ▸ sheep
   grand mouton sauvage ▸ bighorn
moutonné (-ée) ▸ fuzzy
mouvement ▸ circulation, fit[2], motion, move,
movement, surge, swing
   mouvement brusque ▸ lunge
   mouvement clandestin ▸ underground
   mouvement rapide ▸ grab
   avoir un mouvement convulsif ▸ twitch
mouvementée (-ée) ▸ hectic
moyen ▸ device, mean[3], way
   avoir les moyens ▸ afford
   au moyen de ▸ via
   moyen (d'expression) ▸ medium
moyen (-enne) ▸ average, mean[3], medium
Moyen Âge ▸ Middle Ages
moyenne ▸ average
   atteindre en moyenne ▸ average
   faire la moyenne ▸ average
moyennement ▸ fairly
mettre en **moyettes** ▸ stook
moyeu (-eux) ▸ hub
muer ▸ crack
muesli ▸ granola
muet (muette) ▸ dumb, speechless
muffin ▸ muffin
mugir ▸ bellow
mugissement ▸ bellow
mukluk ▸ mukluk
mule ▸ mule

mulet ► mule
multiculturel (-elle) ► multicultural
multiple ► multiple
multiplication ► multiplication
multiplier ► multiply
   se multiplier ► mushroom
multitude ► legion, mass, multitude
municipal (-ale, -aux) ► municipal
municipalité ► borough, town
munir ► furnish, rig
   se munir ► arm[2]
munitions ► ammunition, armament
mur ► wall
mûr (mûre) ► mature, ripe
   pas mûr (mûre) ► green, immature
mûre ► blackberry
murer ► brick
mûri (-e) ► mellow
mûrir ► mature, mellow, ripen
murmure ► babble, ripple, whisper
murmurer ► babble, chirp, mumble, murmur, mutter, whisper
musaraigne ► shrew
muscade ► nutmeg
muscadier ► nutmeg
muscle ► muscle
musclé (-ée) ► muscular
musculaire ► muscular
muse ► Muse
museau (-eaux) ► snout
musée ► gallery, museum
museler ► gag
musical (-ale, -aux) ► musical
musique ► music
   musique de film ► theme
muskeg ► muskeg
musulman (-ane) ► Moslem, Muslim
mutation ► transfer
muter ► transfer
mutiler ► wound[1]
mutuel (-elle) ► mutual
myope ► nearsighted
mystère ► mystery, puzzle, riddle[1]
mystérieusement ► mysteriously
mystérieux (-euse) ► mysterious, uncanny
mystifier ► fox
mythe ► myth
mythique ► mythical
   de façon mythique ► mythically [mythical]

N

nabot (nabote) ► dwarf
nage ► swim
nageoire ► fin
nager ► swim

nageur (-euse) ► swimmer
naïf (naïve) ► innocent, naive, naïve, simple
nain (naine) ► dwarf
naissance ► birth, dawn
   jour de naissance ► birthday
   donner naissance à ► bear[1], originate
   prendre naissance ► originate
naître ► dawn, sprout
   faire naître ► provoke, spawn
naïvement ► naively [naïve]
se nantir ► arm[2]
nappe ► cloth
napper ► top[1]
napperon ► mat
narcisse ► narcissus
narine ► nostril
narrateur (-trice) ► narrator
natal (-ale, -als) ► native
natif (-ive) ► Aborigine, native
nation ► dominion, Dominion, nation, people
   Nations Unies ► United Nations
national (-ale, -aux) ► domestic, national, public
nationalisme ► nationalism
nationalité ► nationality
natte ► braid
natter ► braid
nature[1] ► character, complexion
   de nature ► naturally
   par nature ► temperamentally [temperamental]
nature[2] ► nature, plain
naturel ► nature, temperament
   avec naturel ► naturally
   d'un naturel ► temperamental
naturel (-elle) ► candid, native, natural
   ressources naturelles ► natural resources
naturellement ► naturally, of course
naufrage ► shipwreck
naufragé (-ée) ► castaway
nauséabond (-onde) ► foul, mouldy, rank[2]
nautique ► aquatic
   ski nautique ► water-ski
naval (-ale, -als) ► naval
navet ► turnip
navette ► shuttle
   navette spatiale ► space shuttle
   faire la navette ► commute
navigation ► navigation
naviguer ► navigate, sail
navire ► boat, ship
   navires ► shipping
   navire de guerre ► warship
   navire marchand ► trader
né (née) ► born
ne ... pas ► not

néanmoins ► nonetheless, otherwise
néant ► vacuum, zero
nébuleux (-euse) ► cloudy, hazy, misty [mist]
nécessaire ► compulsory, necessary
nécessairement ► necessarily
nécessité ► necessity, requirement
nécessiter ► take
nécessiteux (-euse) ► needy [need]
nectar ► nectar
néfaste ► evil, fatal
négatif ► negative
négatif (-ive) ► minus, negative
négation ► negative
négligé (-ée) ► sloppy, underdog, unkempt
négligeable ► insignificant
négligemment ► carelessly [careless], thoughtlessly [thoughtless]
négligence ► carelessness [careless], neglect
négligent (-ente) ► careless, sloppy
négliger ► fail, neglect, overlook
négociant (-ante) ► trader
négociation ► negotiation [negotiate]
négocier ► negotiate
neige ► snow
  neige fondue ► slush
  boule de neige ► snowball
  bonhomme de neige ► snowman
  banc de neige ► snowbank
  faire boule de neige ► snowball
  flocon de neige ► snowflake
  planche à neige ► snowboard
  tempête de neige ► blizzard
  (blanc) comme neige ► snowy
  couvert (-erte) de neige fondue ► slushy [slush]
neiger ► snow, storm
neigeux (-euse) ► snowy
nénuphar ► lily
néo-écossais (-aise) ► Bluenose
néologisme ► buzzword
néon ► neon
Neptune ► Neptune
nerf ► nerve
nerveusement ► nervously [nervous], restlessly [restless], uneasily [uneasy]
nerveux (-euse) ► nervous, uneasy, wiry
  système nerveux ► nervous system
nervosité ► nerve, nervousness [nervous], restlessness [restless], tension, uneasiness [uneasy]
nervure ► vein
net (nette) ► clean, legible, neat, net[2], sharp, short, trim, vivid
nettement ► flatly [flat[1]], plainly [plain], vastly [vast], vividly [vivid]
netteté ► crispness [crisp], neatness [neat], sharpness [sharp], vividness [vivid]

nettoyant ► cleaner
nettoyer ► clean
nettoyeur (-euse) ► cleaner
neuf ► nine
neuf (neuve) ► mint condition, new
  remettre à neuf ► renovate
neutre ► casual, impersonal, indifferent, neutral
neutron ► neutron
neuvième ► ninth [nine]
neveu (-eux) ► nephew
nez ► nose
  mettre son nez dans ► snoop
  piquer du nez ► dive
  tirer les vers du nez ► pump
ni ► nor
  ni ... ni ► neither
  ni l'un ni l'autre ► neither
niais (-aise) ► simple
niche ► kennel, niche
nichée ► brood
nicher ► nest
nickel ► nickel
nicotine ► nicotine
nid ► nest
nièce ► niece
nier ► deny
niveau (-eaux) ► ladder, level, standard
  bas niveau ► low
  au niveau national ► nationally [national]
  niveau de la mer ► sea level
  niveau de vie ► standard of living
niveler ► even, grade, level
noble ► lordly [lord], noble, peer[2], worthy
noblement ► nobly [noble]
noce ► wedding
  voyage de noces ► honeymoon
  aller en voyage de noces ► honeymoon
  être en voyage de noces ► honeymoon
nocif (-ive) ► harmful
nocturne ► night, nightly, nocturnal
Noël ► Christmas
  Noël (fête de) ► X-mas
  chant de Noël ► carol
  période de Noël ► Yule
nœud ► hitch, kink, knob, knot
  faire un nœud ► knot
noir ► darkness [dark]
  noir absolu ► pitch[2]
  noir complet ► pitch[2]
  dans le noir ► in the dark
  broyer du noir ► mope
  travailler au noir ► moonlight
noir (noire) ► black, dark
  noir (noire) comme l'ébène ► raven
  noir (noire) comme un corbeau ► raven

noir (noire) de suie ▶ sooty [soot]
tableau noir ▶ blackboard
trou noir ▶ black hole
noirceur ▶ gloom, obscurity [obscure]
noisetier ▶ hazel
noisette ▶ hazel
noix ▶ nut, pat, walnut
noix de cajou ▶ cashew
noix de coco ▶ coconut
nom ▶ name, noun
au nom de ▶ behalf, on behalf of
faux nom ▶ alias
nom de famille ▶ surname
nom d'emprunt ▶ alias
nom propre ▶ proper noun
nomade ▶ migrant, nomad
nombre ▶ number, quantity, size
un grand nombre ▶ many, number
petit nombre ▶ handful
nombre cardinal ▶ cardinal number
nombre de victimes ▶ toll[1]
nombre entier ▶ whole number
nombre ordinal ▶ ordinal number
nombre positif ▶ positive
nombre premier ▶ prime number
nombreux (-euse) ▶ frequent, numerous
nombril ▶ navel
nomination ▶ appointment, nomination
nommer ▶ appoint, call, label, name, nominate, term
non ▶ no
non plus ▶ either
nonchalamment ▶ lazily [lazy]
nonchalance ▶ laziness [lazy]
nonchalant (-ante) ▶ lazy
nootka ▶ Nootka
nord ▶ north, North, the North [north], northern
du nord ▶ north, northern
au nord ▶ north
nord-est ▶ northeast
nord-ouest ▶ nortwest
nordique ▶ north, northern, northward
normal (-ale, -aux) ▶ natural, normal, regular, standard
normalement ▶ normally [normal], ordinarily, usually
norme ▶ standard
nostalgie ▶ nostalgia, wistfulness [wistful]
avec nostalgie ▶ wistfully [wistful]
nostalgique ▶ homesick, nostalgic [nostalgia], wistful
notable[1] ▶ conspicuous, notable, visible, worthy
notable[2] ▶ notable
notablement ▶ notably [notable]
notamment ▶ notably [notable]

note[1] ▶ grade, mark,
note[2] ▶ memo, note, tab, toot
note de restaurant ▶ check
note de service ▶ memo
prendre note de ▶ jot, make a note of
régler la note ▶ check out
noter ▶ enter, grade, jot, log, mark, note, notice, put down, record
notification ▶ notification [notify]
notifier ▶ call, notify
notifier une assignation ▶ serve
notion ▶ notion
notoire ▶ notorious
notoirement ▶ notoriously [notorious]
de notoriété publique ▶ popular
notre (nos) ▶ our
le nôtre (la nôtre, les nôtres) ▶ ours
nouer ▶ knot
nouille ▶ noodle
nourricier (-ière) ▶ foster
nourrir ▶ entertain, feed, harbour, nourish, nurse
nourriture ▶ fare, feed, food, nourishment [nourish]
nous ▶ ourselves, us, we
nous-mêmes ▶ ourselves
nouveau (-elle, -eaux) ▶ fresh, further, new, novel[2]
nouveau venu (nouvelle venue) ▶ arrival
nouveauté ▶ novelty, release
nouvelle ▶ short story
nouvelles ▶ news, newscast, tidings, word
nouvelle croustillante ▶ tidbit
nouvellement ▶ newly
nova ▶ nova
novateur (-trice) ▶ creative
novembre ▶ November
novice ▶ novice, rookie
noyau (-aux) ▶ centre, core, kernel, nucleus, pit[2], stone
noyer[1] ▶ drown, flood
noyer[2] ▶ walnut
noyer d'Amérique ▶ hickory
nu (nue) ▶ bare, naked, nude
mettre à nu ▶ bare
nuage ▶ cloud
nuages ▶ billow
(nuage de) gouttelettes ▶ spray
tête de comulonimbus ▶ thunderhead
nuageux (-euse) ▶ cloudy
nuance ▶ hue, shade, tint, undertone
nuancer ▶ qualify, tinge
nucléaire ▶ atomic, nuclear
nucléus ▶ nucleus
nuée ▶ cloud
nuire ▶ harm

nuisible ► harmful
    animal, insecte ou plante nuisible ►
    pest
nuit ► dark, night
    cette nuit ► tonight
    de nuit ► night, nightly
    pendant la nuit ► overnight
    chemise de nuit ► nightgown
    papillon de nuit ► moth
nul[1] (nulle) ► nobody
nul[2] (nulle) ► void, zero
    partie nulle ► draw
nulle part ► nowhere
nullité ► nobody
numérateur ► numerator
numérique ► digital
numéro ► act, character, issue, number,
routine
    numéro comique ► skit
    numéro de série ► serial number
    numéro un ► arch[2]
numéroter ► number
nuptial (-iaux) ► bridal [bride]
nutka ► Nootka
nutriment ► nutrient
nutrition ► nutrition
nylon ► nylon
nymphe ► nymph

O

oasis ► oasis, wash
obéir ► abide
    obéir à ► comply, obey
obéissance ► obedience [obedient]
obéissant (-ante) ► obedient
objecter ► object, protest
objectif ► aim, goal, object, objective
objectif (-ive) ► disinterested, impartial,
objective
objection ► beef, objection, resistance
objectivement ► objectively [objective]
objet ► article, item, object, purpose, thing
    sans objet ► aimless, aimlessly [aimless]
    objet d'aspect cotonneux ► puff
    objet de prédilection ► thing
    objet d'orgueil ► boast
    objet en céramique ► ceramic
    objet exposé ► exhibit
    objet pointu ► sticker
    objets de valeur ► valuable
    complément d'objet ► object
    vente d'objets usagés ► rummage sale
obligation ► bond, commitment, duty,
obligation
obligatoire ► compulsory

obligé (-ée) ► bound[1]
avec obligeance ► kindly
obligeant (-ante) ► neighbourly [neighbour]
obliger ► accommodate, bind, compel, force,
impose, make, obligate, oblige, push, require
obliquer ► angle
oblitération ► postmark
oblitérer ► cancel, postmark
oblong (-ongue) ► oblong
obscène ► obscene
obscur (-ure) ► dark, gloomy [gloom],
obscure, unclear
obscurcir ► complicate, darken, obscure
obscurité ► darkness [dark], gloom,
obscurity [obscure]
obséder ► haunt, possess
obsèques ► funeral
observation ► comment, observation
observer ► eye, obey, observe, regard,
remark, watch
obstacle ► bar, clog, difficulty, hurdle, jump,
obstacle, snag
    faire obstacle ► dam
obstination ► persistence [persist]
obstiné (-ée) ► obstinate, stubborn,
tenacious, willful
s'obstiner ► persist
obstinément ► stubbornly [stubborn],
tenaciously [tenacious], willfully [willful]
obstruer ► block, clog
obtempérer ► obey
obtenir ► gain, get, obtain
    obtenir des votes ► poll
    obtenir un diplôme ► graduate,
    graduation
obtention ► attainment [attain]
obturateur ► shutter
obturer ► plug
obtus (-use) ► dull
obus ► shell
occasion ► break, chance, occasion,
opportunity
    à l'occasion ► occasionally [occasional]
    d'occasion ► secondhand, used
occasionnel (-elle) ► occasional, odd
occasionnellement ► occasionally
[occasional]
occasionner ► determine, give
l'Occident ► west
occidental (-ale, -aux) ► western
occupant (-ante) ► occupant
occupation ► business, occupation, pursuit
occupé (-ée) ► busy
    de façon occupée ► busily [busy]
occuper ► occupy
    s'occuper ► busy, cope, do, handle,
    mind, occupy, see, tend[2]

s'occuper de ses affaires ► stick to (one's) last
occuper un terrain illégalement ► squat
océan ► ocean
océanique ► oceanic [ocean]
océanographie ► oceanography
ocelot ► ocelot
ocre ► tan
octet ► byte
octobre ► October
octogonal (-ale, -aux) ► octagonal [octagon]
octogone ► octagon
octroi ► grant
octroyer ► grant
témoin **oculaire** ► eyewitness
ode ► ode
odeur ► aroma, odour, scent, smell, whiff
odieux (-euse) ► obnoxious
odomètre ► odometer
odorant (-ante) ► fragrant [fragrance]
odorat ► nose, scent, smell
œil (yeux) ► eye
   à l'œil nu ► naked eye
   clin d'œil ► flash
   coup d'œil ► glance, look, peek, peep[1], squint
   d'un œil critique ► critically [critical]
   bander les yeux ► blindfold
   cligner de l'œil ► wink
   cligner des yeux ► blink
   donner un coup d'œil ► squint
   faire un clin d'œil ► wink
   fermer les yeux ► overlook
   garder un œil sur ► keep an eye on
   jeter un coup d'œil ► glance
   jeter un coup d'œil discret ► peep[1]
   jeter un coup d'œil furtif ► peek
   plisser les yeux ► squint
   tourner de l'œil ► keel
œillet ► pink
œuf ► egg[1], spawn
   jaune d'œuf ► yolk
œuvre ► work, writing
   à l'œuvre ► in action [action]
   œuvre de bienfaisance ► charity
   œuvre de charité ► charity
offensant (-ante) ► offensive
offense ► offence, trespass
offenser ► hurt, offend
offensif (-ive) ► offensive
offensive ► offensive
office ► service
officiel[1] **(-elle)** ► official
officiel[2] **(-elle)** ► formal, official
   de façon non officielle ► unofficially [unofficial]

non officiel (-elle) ► unofficial
officiellement ► formally [formal], officially [official]
officier ► officer
   élève officier ► cadet
officieusement ► informally [informal], unofficially [unofficial]
officieux (-euse) ► off the record, unofficial
offrande ► charity, offering
offrant ► bidder [bid]
offre ► proposition
   offre de mariage ► proposal
   faire une offre ► bid
offrir ► afford, extend, give, offer, present[2], put up, treat
offusquer ► horrify, offend
ogive ► warhead
ogre ► ogre
oie ► goose
   oies ► geese
   plume d'oie ► quill
oignon ► corn[2], onion
oiseau (-eaux) ► bird, fowl
   oiseau bleu ► bluebird
   oiseau chanteur ► songbird
   oiseau mâle ► cock
oiseau-mouche ► hummingbird
oiseux (-euse) ► idle
oisif (-ive) ► idle
oison ► gosling
ojibway ► Ojibwa
okanagan ► Okanagan
olive ► olive
   vert olive ► olive
Jeux **olympiques** ► Olympic Games
ombrage ► shadow
ombragé (-ée) ► shady
ombrager ► shade, shadow
ombre ► shade, shadow, trace
   dans l'ombre ► background
ombrer ► shade
omelette ► omelette
omettre ► drop, fail, omit, overlook
omission ► omission [omit], oversight
on ► one, they
once ► ounce
oncle ► uncle
onde ► ripple, wave
   en ondes ► on (off) the air [air]
   longueur d'ondes ► wavelength
   onde porteuse ► carrier
ondoyant (-ante) ► scallop
ondoyer ► billow, flow, scallop
ondulation ► ripple, wave
ondulatoire ► scallop
ondulé (-ée) ► scallop, wavy
onduler ► ripple, roll, scallop

oneida ▶ Oneida
onéreux (-euse) ▶ burdensome [burden]
ongle ▶ fingernail
onguent ▶ ointment, salve
onomatopée ▶ onomatopoeia
onondaga ▶ Onondaga
onze ▶ eleven
onzième ▶ eleventh [eleven]
opaque ▶ opaque
opéra ▶ opera
opérateur (-trice) ▶ operator
  opérateur (-trice) pupitre ▶ keyboarder [keyboard]
opération ▶ operation
opérer ▶ bring about, effect, operate
opinion ▶ climate, concept, estimation [estimate], feeling, idea, judgement, opinion, position, verdict, view, voice
opossum ▶ opossum
opportunément ▶ conveniently [convenient]
à l'**opposé** ▶ counter[2]
opposé (-ée) ▶ contrary, opposite
opposer ▶ pit[1]
  s'opposer ▶ counter[2], mind, object, oppose
  opposer son veto ▶ veto
opposition ▶ conflict, contrast, objection, opposition, opposition, the Opposition [opposition], resistance
  en opposition ▶ contrary
  être en opposition ▶ conflict
  faire opposition à ▶ oppose
opprimé (-ée) ▶ underdog
opter ▶ elect
avec **optimisme** ▶ confidently [confident]
optimiste ▶ optimistic, rosy
option ▶ option
  en option ▶ optional [option]
optionnel (-elle) ▶ optional [option]
optique ▶ optical
optométriste ▶ optometrist
opuscule ▶ pamphlet
or ▶ gold
  d'or ▶ golden
  de l'âge d'or ▶ senior, senior citizen
  en or ▶ golden
orage ▶ storm, thunderstorm
orageux (-euse) ▶ stormy
oral (-ale, -aux) ▶ oral
oralement ▶ orally [oral]
orange ▶ orange
  orange soutenu ▶ tangerine
orang-outang ▶ orangutan
orateur (-trice) ▶ speaker
orbite ▶ orbit
orchestre ▶ orchestra
  chef d'orchestre ▶ conductor

  fosse d'orchestre ▶ orchestra
  instruments d'orchestre ▶ orchestra
  orchestre symphonique ▶ symphony
orchestrer ▶ orchestrate [orchestra]
ordinaire ▶ common, customary, everyday, normal, ordinary, usual
ordinairement ▶ customarily [customary], generally, ordinarily, usually
ordinateur ▶ computer
  ordinateur central ▶ main-frame
  ordinateur personnel ▶ personal computer (pc)
ordonné (-ée) ▶ orderly, tidy
ordonner ▶ bid, command, dictate, direct, enact, order, tell
ordre[1] ▶ bidding, command, direction, order
  ordre(s) ▶ dictate
ordre[2] ▶ order, tidiness [tidy]
  en ordre ▶ in order
  ordre du jour ▶ agenda
  premier ordre ▶ class
  classer par ordre alphabétique ▶ alphabetize
  maintenir l'ordre dans ▶ police
  marcher sans ordre ▶ straggle
ordure ▶ garbage, litter, rat, waste
  ordures ▶ refuse[2], rubbish, trash
  fouilleur (-euse) d'ordures ▶ scavenger
ordurier (-ière) ▶ foul
oreille ▶ ear[1], ear[2]
  casser les oreilles ▶ deafen
  boucle d'oreille ▶ earring
  casser les oreilles ▶ deafen
oreiller ▶ pillow
oreillons ▶ mumps
organe ▶ organ
organique ▶ organic
organisation ▶ organization
organiser ▶ combine, organize, plan, put on, stage
organisme ▶ organism, organization
orge ▶ barley
orgue(s) ▶ organ
orgueil ▶ pride
  objet d'orgueil ▶ boast
orgueilleux (-euse) ▶ proud
orient ▶ east, the East [east]
oriental (-ale, -aux) ▶ east, eastern, easterner
orientation ▶ heading
orienter ▶ channel, direct, orient
orifice ▶ vent
originaire ▶ native
  être originaire de ▶ hail from
original (-ale, -aux) ▶ eccentric, master, original, peculiar, unconventional
original (-aux) ▶ original

originalement ► originally
origine ► cause, origin, root[1]
   à l'origine ► originally
   d'origine ► original
orignal ► elk, moose
orme ► elm
ornement ► adornment [adorn], decoration, flourish, ornament
ornemental (-ale, -aux) ► ornamental [ornement]
ornementation ► decoration
orner ► adorn, deck, decorate, garnish, grace, ornament, trim
   orner de perles ► bead
ornière ► rut
ornithorynque ► platypus
orphelin ► orphan
orteil ► digit, toe
orthodoxe ► orthodox
orthographe ► spelling
   livre d'orthographe ► speller
orthographier ► spell[1]
   mal orthographier ► misspell
os ► bone
   en chair et en os ► as large as life
oscillation ► sway, swing
osciller ► roll, wobble
oseille ► sorrel[1]
oser ► dare
osier ► wicker
osmose ► osmosis
ossature ► frame
osselets ► jack
osseux (-euse) ► bony
otage ► hostage
otarie ► sea lion
ôter ► core, remove
ou ► either, or
où ► where, whereabouts, wherein, whither
   d'où ► hence, whence
   là où ► where
   où où donc ► whereabouts
   où que ► wherever
ouailles ► flock
ouater ► quilt
ouatiner ► quilt
oubli ► oblivion, omission [omit], oversight
oublier ► forget, neglect, omit, overlook, slip[1]
   faire oublier ► smooth
mettre aux **oubliettes** ► scrap
ouest ► west
   à l'ouest ► west, westward
   d'ouest ► west, western
   vers l'ouest ► west
   vers le sud-ouest ► southwest
   vers le nord-ouest ► nortwest
oui ► aye, yea, yes

vieux oui ► yea
   hocher oui ► nod
ouïe ► ear[2], hearing
   ouïes ► gill
ouragan ► hurricane
ourler ► rim
ourlet ► hem
ours ► bear[2]
   ours (ourse) polaire ► polar bear
   ours brun ► grizzly bear
   Grande Ourse ► dipper
outil ► implement, instrument, tool, utensil
outiller ► equip
outrage ► contempt, insult
   outrage au tribunal ► outrage
outrager ► insult, outrage
outrageusement ► outrageously [outrageous]
en **outre** ► additionally [additional], besides, furthermore, moreover
outré (-ée) ► extravagant
outre-mer ► overseas
outrepasser ► exceed
ouvert (-erte) ► frank, open
ouvertement ► openly [open]
ouverture ► gap, intake, mouth, opening, openness [open]
ouvrage ► work
   ouvrage de référence ► reference
ouvrier (-ière) ► hand, labour, worker
ouvrir ► open, pioneer, unlock
   ouvrir d'une chiquenaude ► flip
   ouvrir en employant la force ► pry[1]
   ouvrir une brèche ► breach
   essayer d'ouvrir ► tamper
   s'ouvrir d'un coup ► spring
ovale ► oval
ovation ► cheer
ovule ► egg[2]
oxygène ► oxygen
   bonbonne d'oxygène ► scuba

P

pacifique ► peaceful
pacte ► pact
pagaie ► paddle
pagayer ► paddle
page ► leaf, page[1], page[2]
paie ► pay, wage
paiement ► payment
   paiement illicite ► bribe
paille ► straw
   paille de fer ► steel wool
pain ► bread, cake, loaf[1]
   petit pain ► bun, roll
   pain au levain ► sourdough

pain de sel ▸ lick
pain grillé ▸ toast[1]
pain plat et rond ▸ bannock
miche de pain ▸ loaf[1]
pair ▸ fellow, peer[2]
pairs ▸ peer group
hors pair ▸ peerless [peer[2]]
pair (paire) ▸ even
paire ▸ brace, couple, pair
faire la paire ▸ pair
pairer ▸ couple
paisible ▸ calm, peaceful, quiet, tranquil
paisiblement ▸ calmly [calm], peacefully
[peaceful], quietly [quiet], tranquilly [tranquil]
paître ▸ graze
paix ▸ peace
gardien de la paix ▸ cop
palace ▸ palace
palais ▸ palace
palais de justice ▸ court
pale ▸ blade
pale (d'une hélice) ▸ vane
pâle ▸ dim, pale
palefrenier (-ière) ▸ groom
palet ▸ puck
paletot ▸ overcoat
palette ▸ palette, skid
palier ▸ ladder, landing
pâlir ▸ pale
palissade ▸ fence
palme ▸ fin
palmier ▸ palm[2]
palmure ▸ web
palourde ▸ clam, steamer
palpable ▸ concrete, tangible
palper ▸ feel, finger
palpitant (-ante) ▸ breathtaking, thrill
palpitation ▸ flutter
palpiter ▸ throb
paludisme ▸ malaria
pamplemousse ▸ grapefruit
pan ▸ patch, tail
panache ▸ flourish
panda ▸ panda
paner ▸ bread
panier ▸ basket, hoop
panique ▸ panic, stampede
sujet (-ette) à la panique ▸ panicky
[panic]
semer la panique ▸ stampede
paniquer ▸ panic
panne[1] ▸ failure
en panne ▸ down[1]
panne de courant ▸ blackout
panne d'électricité ▸ blackout
tomber en panne ▸ break down, crash,
fail

panne[2] ▸ claw
panneau (-eaux) ▸ panel, sign
panneau (-eaux) d'affichage ▸ billboard
recouvrir de panneaux ▸ panel
panoplie ▸ battery
panorama ▸ view
pansement ▸ bandage, dressing
mettre un pansement ▸ bandage, dress
panser ▸ dress, groom
pantalon ▸ drawer, pants, slacks, trousers
panthère ▸ panther
pantin ▸ puppet
pantoufle ▸ slipper
papa ▸ dad, pop[1]
pape (papesse) ▸ pope
papeterie ▸ stationery
papier ▸ paper
bloc de papier à lettres ▸ tablet
corbeille à papier ▸ wastebasket
papier ▸ wrapping
mouchoir en papier ▸ tissue
feuille de papier ▸ paper
papier d'aluminium ▸ foil[2], tinfoil
papier de verre ▸ sandpaper
papier d'emballage ▸ wrapper, wrapping
papier journal ▸ newsprint
papier peint ▸ wallpaper
sortie papier ▸ readout
papillon ▸ butterfly
papillon de nuit ▸ moth
papillon des gaz ▸ throttle
papillonner ▸ flutter
paquebot ▸ steamer, steamship
pâquerette ▸ daisy
la Pâque ▸ Passover
Pâques ▸ Easter
paquet ▸ bundle, pack, package, parcel, pile[1]
paqueter ▸ bale
par ▸ a, an, by, in, into, per, via
parachute ▸ parachute
parachutisme en chute libre ▸ skydiving
parade ▸ parade
faire parade ▸ affect[2]
parader ▸ parade
paradis ▸ heaven, paradise, Xanadu
paragraphe ▸ paragraph
paraître[1] ▸ appear, imitate, look, seem
paraître[2] ▸ release
faire paraître ▸ publish
parallèle ▸ parallel
parallèlement ▸ parallel
paralyser ▸ choke, paralyse, petrify
parapher ▸ initial
parapluie ▸ umbrella
parasite ▸ parasite, static
parasol ▸ umbrella
paratonnerre ▸ lightning rod

paravent ▸ screen
parc ▸ park, pen[2], playground
    parc à bestiaux ▸ stockyard
    gardien (-ienne) de parc national ▸ ranger
    aménager en parc ▸ landscape
parce que ▸ because
parcelle ▸ parcel, piece
parchemin ▸ scroll
parcourir ▸ cover, rake, range, roam, run, scan, travel
parcours ▸ circuit, course, haul, journey, route
par-delà ▸ past
pardessus ▸ overcoat
par-dessus ▸ over
    par-dessus bord ▸ overboard
    par-dessus le marché ▸ to boot
pardon ▸ pardon, pardon me or I beg your pardon
    demander pardon ▸ pardon me or I beg your pardon
pardonner ▸ excuse, forgive, pardon
pare-brise ▸ windshield
pare-chocs ▸ bumper
pareil (-eille) ▸ alike, identical, like[2], same, such, unchanged
    sans pareil ▸ peerless [peer[2]]
pareillement ▸ alike, likewise
parent ▸ parent
    grand-parent ▸ grandparent
parent (-ente) ▸ relate, relation, relative
    le (la) plus proche parent (-ente) ▸ next of kin
parents ▸ folk, kin, parent
parenté ▸ family, kinship [kin]
parenthèse ▸ bracket, parenthesis
parer ▸ deck, decorate, ward
pare-soleil ▸ shade, visor
paresse ▸ laziness [lazy]
paresser ▸ idle, loaf[2]
paresseusement ▸ idly [idle], lazily [lazy]
paresseux (-euse) ▸ idle, lazy, sloth
parfaire ▸ complement, complete, perfect
parfait (-aite) ▸ excellent, ideal, perfect, rank[2], utter[2]
parfaitement ▸ excellently [excellent], perfectly
parfois ▸ sometime
parfum ▸ flavour, fragrance, perfume, scent
    être au parfum ▸ in the know
parfumé (-ée) ▸ fragrant [fragrance]
parfumer ▸ flavour, perfume, scent
pari ▸ bet
parier ▸ bet
parka ▸ parka
parlement ▸ parliament

Parlement ▸ parliament
parlementaire ▸ constitutional
parler ▸ speak, talk
    parler avec ▸ meet with
    parler de ▸ deal, mention, speak, talk
    sans parler de ▸ let alone [alone]
    parler avec ambiguïté ▸ waffle[2]
    parler avec enthousiasme ▸ rave
    parler dans le langage des signes ▸ sign
    parler du bout des lèvres ▸ mince
    parler d'une voie flûtée ▸ pipe
    parler d'une voix monotone ▸ drone
    parler fort ▸ bluster
    parler franchement ▸ level
    parler pour ne rien dire ▸ ramble, waffle[2]
    capacité de parler ▸ tongue
    façon de parler ▸ figure of speech
    parlé ▸ spoken
parmi ▸ amid, among
parodie ▸ imitation, parody
paroi ▸ wall
parole ▸ speech, word
    paroles ▸ lyric
    prendre la parole ▸ speak
    retirer ses paroles ▸ back down
    se répandre en flots de paroles ▸ pour out [pour]
parrain ▸ sponsor
parsemer ▸ dot, pepper, stud
part ▸ hand, proportion, quota, share, stake, wedge
    autre part ▸ elsewhere
    de la part ▸ behalf
    de part en part ▸ through
    pour ma part ▸ personally
    prendre part ▸ carry on, take part
    prendre plus que sa part ▸ hog
partage ▸ pool[2]
    ligne de partage ▸ divide
    ligne de partage des eaux ▸ watershed
partager ▸ deal, distribute, divide, parcel, share, split
    partager un appartement ▸ room
    partager une chambre ▸ room
en partance ▸ outgoing
partenaire ▸ companion, partner
parterre ▸ bed
parti ▸ party
    parti pris ▸ bias
    Nouveau parti démocratique ▸ New Democratic Party
    Parti Libéral ▸ Liberal Party
    Parti progressiste-conservateur (du Canada) ▸ Progressive Conservative Party

prendre parti ► side with
prendre le parti de ► defend
partial (-ale, -aux) ► partial
partialement ► partially [partial]
avec **partialité** ► partially [partial]
participation ► contribution
participe ► participle
participer ► collaborate, participate, run, take part
participer à une émeute ► riot
particularité ► characteristic, feature
particule ► particle
particulier (-ière) ► characteristic, individual, particular, peculiar, special, specific
particulièrement ► especially, extra[1], particularly [particular], specifically [specific]
partie[1] ► clan, fraction, part, portion, proportion, section, side
la majeure partie ► better
en partie ► part, partially [partial], partly
partie principale ► body
une grande partie ► much
partie[2] ► game, match[2], round,
partie nulle ► draw
partie[3] ► party
partie de plaisir ► riot
partiel (-ielle) ► partial
élection partielle ► by-election
partiellement ► part, partially [partial], partly
émerger partiellement ► peep[1]
partir ► depart, leave[1], start
à partir de ► onwards
partir à l'eau ► wash
partir de zéro ► from scratch
partir du tee ► tee
partir en catimini ► slink
partir en vitesse ► dash off
partir précipitamment ► dash off
partisan (-ane) de ► pro, supporter [support]
partition ► music, score
partout ► everywhere
partout dans ► throughout
parution ► publication, release
parvenir ► attain, manage, reach
pas[1] ► doorstep, footstep, pace, step, thread, tread
au pas ► crawl
d'un pas lourd ► pound[2]
grands pas ► stride
faux pas ► slip[1]
mauvais pas ► mess
pas (de la porte) ► threshold
pas chancelant ► stagger, wobble
bruit de pas ► tramp, tread
faire les cent pas ► pace, prowl
marcher d'un pas pressé ► trot
marcher d'un pas lourd ► tramp

marcher d'un pas léger ► trip
marcher au pas ► march
marcher à pas feutré ► pad
marcher à grands pas ► stride
mesurer au pas ► pace
pas[2] ► no
pas tellement ► none
sûrement pas ► hardly, scarcely
passable ► fair[1], tolerable
passablement ► tolerably [tolerable]
passage ► excerpt, lane, pass, passage, passing
de passage ► passing
passage étroit ► narrow
passage inférieur ► underpass
passage souterrain ► subway
passager (-ère) ► fare, passenger, passing, voyage
passager (-ère) clandestin (-ine) ► stowaway
en **passant** ► in passing
passe ► assist, pass
mot de passe ► password
passé ► beyond, past, past tense
par le passé ► previously [previous]
passé (-ée) ► past
passe-montagne ► balaclava
passeport ► passport
passer ► by, drop, elapse, fade, hand, pass, put on, run, spend, strain[1], tick[1], while
faire passer ► ferry, manoeuvre
passer (chez quelqu'un) ► call
passer à coté ► wide
passer à travers ► wade
passer en revue ► review
passer en trombe ► rocket
passer graduellement ► graduate
passer inaperçu (-ue) ► escape
passer rapidement ► zip
passer sur ► overlook
qui passe ► passing
se faire passer ► pose
se passer ► happen, run
se passer de ► spare
passe-temps ► hobby, pursuit
passif (-ive) ► passive
passion ► passion
de passion ► smoulder
passionnant (-ante) ► interesting, thrill
passionné (-ée) ► buff, fan[2], hacker, passionate [passion]
passionnément ► eagerly [eager]
passionner ► excite
passivement ► passively [passive]
passoire ► strainer
pastel ► pastel
pastenague ► stingray

pastèque ► watermelon
pasteur ► minister
pastiche ► takeoff
pastille ► drop, tablet
patate ► potato
patate douce ► sweet potato, yam
patauger ► flounder[1], paddle, wade
pâte ► batter[2], dough, paste, pastry, pulp
   pâte alimentaire ► pasta
   pâte feuilletée ► puff
pâté de maisons ► block
pâtée ► mash
   donner de la pâtée ► slop
paternel (-elle) ► fatherly [father]
patiemment ► patiently [patient]
patience ► patience, solitaire
patient (-iente) ► patient
patienter ► wait
patin ► skate[1]
   patin à roulettes ► roller skate
   patin(s) à roues alignées ► in-line
   skates, skate[1]
patiner ► hedge, skate[1]
patinoire ► ice, rink
patio ► patio
pâtisserie ► pastry, roll
pâtissier (-ière) ► baker
patrie ► home, homeland
   vers la patrie ► homeward
patrimoine ► heritage
patriote ► patriot, patriotic [patriot]
patriotique ► patriotic [patriot]
patriotisme ► nationalism
patron ► pattern
patron (-onne) ► boss
patrouille ► patrol
patrouiller ► patrol
patte ► foot, leg, paw, tab
   donner un (des) coup(s) de patte à ► paw
   grimper à quatre pattes ► scramble
pâturage ► pasture, range
pâture ► feed, pasture
paume ► palm[1]
paupière ► eyelid
pause ► break, halt, pause, recess
   faire une pause ► pause
pauvre ► broke, flimsy, poor
   quartier pauvre ► slum
pauvrement ► poorly [poor], shabbily [shabby]
pauvreté ► poverty
   extrême pauvreté ► wretchedness [wretched]
se pavaner ► prance
pavé ► pavement

paver ► pave
pavillon ► bell, lodge, pavilion, ward
payant (-ante) ► profitable
payer ► compensate, give, pay, treat
   faire payer ► charge
   pouvoir se payer ► afford
pays ► country, land, the nation [nation]
   mal du pays ► homesickness [homesick], nostalgia
paysage ► landscape, scenery
paysan (-anne) ► peasant
péage ► toll[1]
peau (peaux) ► hide[2], pelt[2], rind, skin
   peau (du cou) ► scruff
   peau de buffle ► buff
péché ► crime, sin, trespass
pêche[1] ► peach
pêche[2] (à la baleine) ► whaling
pêcher ► fish, sin
   pêcher à la cuiller ► troll[1]
   pêcher au chalut ► trawl
pêcheur (-euse) ► fisher
   pêcheur des Grands Bancs ► banker
pédagogie ► education
pédagogique ► educational
pédale ► pedal
pédaler ► pedal
peigne ► comb
   (se) passer un coup de peigne ► fix
   passer au peigne fin ► comb
peigner ► comb
peignoir ► robe
peindre ► decorate, paint
peine ► grief, pain, penalty, trouble
   à peine ► barely, hardly, only, scarcely
   avoir de la peine ► grieve
   faire de la peine ► hurt
   se donner la peine ► bother
peiné (-ée) ► heartbroken
peiner ► distress, labour, pain, toil
peintre ► painter
peinture ► colour, paint, painting, picture
   peinture murale ► mural
pelage ► coat, fur
peler ► flake, peel
pèlerin (-ine) ► pilgrim
   Père pèlerin ► pilgrim
pelle ► scoop, shovel, spade[1]
pelleter ► scoop, shovel
pellicule ► film
se pelotonner ► curl, nestle
pelouse ► grass, green, lawn
peluche ► fluff
peluché (-ée) ► hairy
pelure ► jacket, peel, rind, skin
pénaliste ► criminal
pénalité ► penalty

banc de pénalité ► penalty box
penchant ► fondness [fond], lean[1], weakness
    avoir un penchant ► lean[1]
pencher ► bend, droop, incline, lean[1], slant, slope, tilt
    se pencher ► stoop[1]
pendant ► during, for, long[1], over, through
    pendant que ► as, while
pendant (-ante) ► sag
penderie ► closet, wardrobe
pendre ► hang, sag
pénétrant (-ante) ► keen
pénétrer ► penetrate
pénible ► hard, laborious [labour], painful, troublesome, uphill
péniblement ► wearily [weary]
péniche ► barge
pénicilline ► penicillin
péninsule ► peninsula
penne ► feather, quill
pensée ► concept, impulse, thought
penser ► design, expect, fancy, figure, guess, imagine, reckon, think
penseur (-euse) ► thinker [think]
pension ► allowance, board, lodging, pension
    pension alimentaire ► alimony
    prendre en pension ► board
pentagone ► pentagon
pente ► descent, incline, rise, slant, slope
    pente raide ► dip
    être en pente ► slope
pénurie ► dearth, shortage
pépiement ► peep[2]
pépier ► peep[2]
pépinière ► nursery
perçant (-ante) ► keen, sharp
    pousser des cris perçants ► screech, squeal
percé (-ée) ► leaky [leak]
percée ► breakthrough
perce-oreille ► earwig
perception ► apprehension
percer ► bore[2], drill, lance, pierce, prick, tap[2]
perceuse ► bore[2], drill
percevoir ► collect, distinguish, levy, perceive
perchaude ► perch[2]
perche ► bass[2], boom[2], perch[2], pole[1], prop, rod
percher ► perch[1]
    se percher ► roost
perchoir ► perch[1], roost
percuter ► crash, ram
perdre ► lose, shed[2]
    se perdre ► lose
    ne pas perdre de vue ► keep an eye on
    se perdre ► lose

perdu (-ue) ► lost, missing, stray, waste
père ► dad, elder, father, parent, senior
    Père Noël ► Santa Claus
    Dieu le Père ► Father
    Père pèlerin ► pilgrim
perfection ► perfection
perfectionnement ► perfection, refinement [refine]
perfectionner ► improve, perfect, upgrade
perfide ► treacherous
perforateur ► punch[2]
perforer ► punch[2]
performance ► performance
péril ► distress, hazard, peril
périlleusement ► perilously [peril]
périlleux (-euse) ► perilous [peril]
    saut périlleux ► flip, somersault
période ► chapter, interval, period, stretch, term
    courte période de temps froid ► snap
    période (de service) ► tour
    période de Noël ► Yule
    période d'essor ► boom[1]
    période glaciaire ► Ice Age
périodique ► periodic
périodiquement ► periodically [periodic]
périphérie ► outskirts
périr ► perish
perle ► bead, gem, jewel, pearl
perlé (-ée) ► pearly [pearl]
permanent (-ente) ► constant, continuous, permanent, standing
    de façon permanente ► permanently [permanent]
permanente ► permanent
permettre ► afford, allow, bring, enable, let, may, permit
    se permettre ► afford, presume
permis ► licence, permit
permis (-ise) ► legal
permission ► approval, leave[2], permission
    permissions ► leaves
    avoir la permission ► may
    s'introduire sans permission ► trespass
pernicieux (-euse) ► fatal
perpendiculaire ► perpendicular
perpétration ► commission
perpétuel (-elle) ► eternal, perpetual
perpétuellement ► eternally [eternal]
perpétuer ► continue
laisser perplexe ► puzzle
    rendre perplexe ► puzzle
perroquet ► parrot
perruche ► parakeet
perruque ► wig
persévérer ► plug

persistance ► persistence [persist]
persistant (-ante) ► constant, persistent [persist]
    à feuilles persistantes ► evergreen
persister ► persist
personnage ► character, figure
personnalité ► celebrity, personality
    personnalité célèbre ► personality
personne[1] ► anybody, creature, individual, people, person, soul
    la personne ► self
    grande personne ► grown-up
    en personne ► as large as life, in person, personal
    pour une personne ► single
    personne à charge ► dependant, dependent
    personne âgée ► senior, senior citizen
    personne austère ► puritan
    personne en deuxième position ► runner-up
    personne ennuyeuse ► bore[1]
    personne handicapée ► handicap
personne[2] ► no one, nobody
personnel ► personnel, staff
    pourvoir en personnel ► man, staff
personnel (-elle) ► close[2], personal, private
personnellement ► personally, personally [personal]
personnification ► personification
perspective ► perspective, prospect, thought, vista
    perspectives ► horizon, outlook
    interpréter dans une perspective ► slant
persuadé (-ée) ► confident
persuader ► coax, convince, determine, persuade, talk, tempt, urge
perte ► drain, loss, undoing [undo], waste
pertinent (-ente) ► apt, relative, relevant
perturbateur (-trice) ► unsettling [unsettled]
perturbation ► disruption [disrupt]
perturbé (-ée) ► unsettled
perturber ► disrupt
pervertir ► corrupt, poison, warp
pesant (-ante) ► heavy, weighty
pesanteur ► heaviness [heavy], weight
peser ► consider, ponder, weigh, weight
peste ► nuisance, pest, plague
pétale ► petal
pétiller ► bubble, sparkle
petit ► young
    petit de ► cub
    petit (de gros animaux) ► calf[1]
petit (-ite) ► kid, light[2], little, short, slight, small, young
    plus petit (-ite) ► least, less

petit-lait ► whey
petit-enfant ► grandchild, great
petite-fille ► granddaughter
petit-fils ► grandson
Petite Ourse ► dipper
pétition ► petition
pétitionner ► petition
pétoncle ► scallop
pétrifier ► petrify, transfix
pétrin ► fix, jam[1], mess, scrape
pétrir ► knead
pétrole ► kerosene, oil, petroleum
pétrolier ► tanker
pétun ► Petun
peu ► few, lick, little, sparsely [sparse]
    à peu près ► about, approximately [approximate], around, halfway, nearly, roughly [rough], somewhere
    tant soit peu ► remotely [remote]
    très peu ► scarcely, tinge
    un peu ► dash, slightly [slight], some, sort of [sort], taste
peu importe ► no matter
peu importe comment ► no matter
peuple ► nation, people
peupler ► people, populate
peuplier ► poplar
peur ► dread, fear, fright, scare
    chose qui fait peur ► creep
    sans peur ► fearless
    avoir peur ► fear
    faire peur ► frighten, scare
phacochère ► warthog
phalène ► moth
pharaon ► pharaoh
phare ► beacon, headlight, lighthouse
phase ► phase, stage
    en phase terminale ► terminal
phénoménal (-ale, -aux) ► phenomenal [phenomenon]
phénomène ► phenomenon
philosophe ► philosopher, philosophical [philosophy]
philosophie ► philosophy
philosophique ► philosophical [philosophy]
philtre ► potion
phonétique ► phonetic, phonetics
phonique ► phonics
phoque ► seal[1]
phosphore ► phosphorus
photo ► photo, photograph, shot[1]
    appareil photographique ► camera
    prendre en photo ► photograph, snap
photocopie ► photocopy, Xerox
photocopier ► duplicate, photocopy, Xerox
photocopieur ► photocopier [photocopy]

photocopieuse ► photocopier [photocopy]
photographie ► photo, photograph
photographier ► photograph, snap
photographique ► photographic [photograph]
    appareil photographique ► camera
photosynthèse ► photosynthesis
phrase ► sentence
    phrase complexe ► compound sentence
physionomie ► face
physique[1] ► physics
physique[2] ► bodily, physical
physiquement ► physically [physical]
piano ► piano
pianoter ► drum
piaulement ► peep[2]
piauler ► peep[2]
pic ► peak, pick[2]
    tomber à pic ► plummet
pic-bois ► woodpecker
pichenette ► flip
pichet ► jug, pitcher[1]
picorer ► peck
picotement ► tingle
picoter ► peck, pick[1], tingle
pièce[1] ► coin
    fausse pièce ► slug[1]
    pièce de un cent ► penny
    pièce de cinq cents ► nickel
    pièce de dix cents ► dime
    pièce de vingt-cinq cents ► quarter
pièce[2] ► component, part, patch, piece
    pièce à conviction ► exhibit
    pièce d'identité ► identification
    pièce insérée ► insert
pièce[3] ► room
pièce[4] ► thriller
    pièce de théâtre ► drama
    pièce satirique ► skit
pied ► foot, leg, stem[1]
    à pied de ► walk
    au pied léger ► fleet[2]
    au pied levé ► off the cuff
    sous les pieds ► underfoot
    coup de pied ► kick
    empreinte de pied ► footprint
    traînement de pieds ► shuffle
    battre des pieds ► kick
    donner un coup de pied ► boot, kick
    faire à pied ► walk
    frapper du pied ► stomp
    lancer un coup de pied ► kick
    marcher sur la pointe des pieds ► tiptoe
    pousser du pied ► prod
    se déplacer à pied ► tramp
    taper du pied ► stamp

pied-de-biche ► claw, crowbar
piège ► catch, snare, trap
    prendre au piège ► snare, trap
piéger ► trap
pierre ► rock[1], stone
    l'âge de (la) pierre ► Stone Age
    pierre à briquet ► flint
    pierre précieuse ► gem
    pierres précieuses ► jewel
piétiner ► trample
piéton (-onne) ► pedestrian, walker
    rue piétonnière ► mall
piètre ► flimsy, lame
pieu (-eux) ► pile[2], stake
    soutenir à l'aide de pieux ► stake
pieuvre ► octopus
pieux (-euse) ► holy
pigeon ► pigeon
pile[1] ► flat[1], on the nose, pile[1]
    coup (de pile ou face) ► toss
pile[2] ► sharp, stack, tail
    élément (de pile) ► cell
    pile sèche ► dry cell
piler ► pound[2]
pilier ► column, pier, pillar
piller ► sack[2]
pilon ► drumstick
pilori ► stocks
pilotage ► navigation
pilote ► pilot
    pilote de brousse ► bush pilot
piloter ► drive, guide, navigate, pilot, sail, shepherd
pilotis ► pile[2]
pilule ► pill
piment rouge ► chili
pimenter ► pepper
pin ► pine[1]
pince ► claw, clip[2], pliers, tongs
pincée ► pinch
    une pincée de ► taste
pincement ► pinch
pincer ► claw, clip[2], pick[1], pinch
    pincer (les lèvres) ► purse
pingouin ► auk
ping-pong ► table tennis
pingre ► miserly [miser]
pinson ► finch
pinte ► pint, quart
pioche ► pick[2]
piocher ► plug
pionnier (-ière) ► pioneer
pipe ► pipe
    Pipe de Bruyère ► briar
pipeau (-eaux) ► pipe
piquant ► quill, sting, thorn
    armé (-ée) de piquants ► prickly [prick]

piquant (-ante) ▸ crisp, hot, pungent, spicy [spice]

pique ▸ spade[2]

pique-nique ▸ picnic

pique-niquer ▸ picnic

descente en **piqué** ▸ swoop

piquer ▸ bite, needle, pit[1], poke, prick, quilt, spear, stick, sting, stitch, tingle

   piquer sur ▸ swoop

   piquer du nez ▸ dive

piquet ▸ peg, picket

piqûre ▸ bite, prick, puncture, shot[1], sting

pirate ▸ pirate

piraté (-ée) ▸ pirate

pirater ▸ pirate

pire ▸ worse, worst

pirogue ▸ dugout

pis ▸ udder

piscine ▸ pool[1]

pissenlit ▸ dandelion

piste ▸ clue, lead[1], ring[1], track, trail, turf

   piste d'atterrissage ▸ runway

   piste de course hippique ▸ turf

   piste de jeu ▸ lane

   piste d'envol ▸ runway

   suivre la piste de ▸ trace, track

   tour (de piste) ▸ lap[2]

pistil ▸ pistil

pistolet ▸ gun, pistol

piston ▸ piston

piteux (-euse) ▸ sorry

pitié ▸ compassion, mercy, pity

   sans pitié ▸ cold-blooded, merciless [mercy], ruthless, ruthlessly [ruthless]

   avoir pitié de ▸ pity

   sans pitié ▸ cold-blooded, merciless [mercy], ruthless, ruthlessly [ruthless]

pitoyable ▸ pitiful, rotten

pitre ▸ clown

pivot ▸ backbone, swivel

pivoter ▸ rotate

   faire pivoter ▸ swivel

pizza ▸ pizza

placage ▸ veneer

placard ▸ bill[1], closet, cup-board

place ▸ accomodation [accommodate], drop, green, place, plaza, position, room, space, square

   à la place ▸ for

   sur place ▸ on location

   place du marché ▸ marketplace

   place forte ▸ fortress [fort]

   clouer sur place ▸ root[1]

   (se) mettre en place ▸ position

   remettre à sa place ▸ replace

   tourner sur place ▸ mill

placement ▸ investment

placer ▸ deposit, invest, lay[1], place, position

placeur (-euse) ▸ usher

plafond ▸ ceiling

plage ▸ beach

plagier ▸ plagiarize

plaid ▸ plaid

plaider ▸ argue, plead

plaie ▸ nuisance, plague, sore

plaindre ▸ pity

   se plaindre ▸ complain, groan, lament, moan

plaine ▸ plain, prairie

plainte ▸ beef, complaint, groan, moan, wail

   porter plainte ▸ lodge

plaire ▸ charm, please

   plaire à ▸ appeal, please

   se plaire ▸ bask

   s'il-vous-plaît ▸ please

plaisanter ▸ fool, joke

plaisanterie ▸ gag, joke, lark[2], quip

plaisir ▸ amusement, enjoyment [enjoy], fun, pleasure, treat

   avec plaisir ▸ gladly [glad]

   grand plaisir ▸ delight

   partie de plaisir ▸ riot

   faire plaisir ▸ bless, please, tickle

   prendre plaisir ▸ delight, enjoy

plan ▸ agenda, blueprint, plan, plane[1], project, proposal, schedule, scheme, tactic

   sur le plan technique ▸ technically [technical]

   faire le plan de ▸ design

   laisser en plan ▸ strand[1]

planche ▸ board, plank

   planche à neige ▸ snowboard

   planche à roulettes ▸ skateboard

   planche de surf ▸ surfboard

   clouer des planches en travers de ▸ board

plancher ▸ floor

plancton ▸ plankton

planer ▸ float, fly[1], glide, hang, plane[2], ride, shave

   vol plané ▸ glide

planète ▸ planet

planifier ▸ plan, schedule

plante ▸ plant

   plante annuelle ▸ annual

   plante grimpante ▸ vine

   plante nuisible ▸ pest

planter ▸ plant

planteur (-euse) ▸ planter

plaquage du quart arrière ▸ sack[2]

plaque ▸ plaque, plate, sheet, slab, tablet

   plaque d'identité ▸ tag[1]

plaquer ▸ plaster, plate

   plaquer (au sol) ▸ tackle

plaqueur (-euse) ▸ tackler [tackle]
plasma ▸ plasma
plastique ▸ plastic
plat ▸ course, dish, platter
   plat en cocotte ▸ casserole
plat (plate) ▸ dead, dry, even, flat[1], level
   à plat ▸ flat[1], perpendicular, run-down
   mettre à plat ▸ knock out [knock]
plateau (-eaux) ▸ plateau, table, tray
plate-forme ▸ platform, rig, shelf
platine ▸ platinum
plâtre ▸ cast, plaster
plâtrer ▸ plaster
plectre ▸ pick[1]
plein (pleine) ▸ full
   à plein ▸ fully [full]
   à son plein ▸ in full swing
   en plein ▸ smack
   se donner à plein dans ▸ kick
pleurs ▸ tears [tear[2]]
pleurer ▸ cry, lament, mourn, wail, water, weep, whine
pleurnicher ▸ sniffle
pleurnicheries ▸ whine
pleurnicheur (-euse) ▸ whiny [whine]
pleuvoir ▸ rain, shower, storm
   pleuvoir légèrement ▸ sprinkle
   pleuvoir à torrents ▸ pour
   pleuvoir à verse ▸ pour
pli ▸ crease, fold, pleat, wrinkle
   faux pli ▸ crease
plié (-ée) ▸ bent
plier ▸ bend, crook, fold
   plier en deux ▸ double
   se plier ▸ humour
plissé (-ée) ▸ pleated
plissement ▸ fold
plisser ▸ crease, gather, pucker
   plisser les yeux ▸ squint
plomb ▸ fuse, lead[2], shot[1]
plomber ▸ fill
plomberie ▸ plumbing
plombier (-ière) ▸ plumber
plongé (-ée) ▸ deep
   plongée sous-marine ▸ skin diving
   faire de la plongée sous-marine ▸ skin-dive
plongeon ▸ dive, plunge
plonger ▸ dip, dive, plummet, plunge, submerge, thrust
   plonger la tête dans l'eau ▸ duck[2]
plongeur (-euse) ▸ diver
ployer ▸ flex, weigh down [weigh]
pluie ▸ hail[1], rain, shower
   manteau (-eaux) de pluie ▸ raincoat
   pluies acides ▸ acid rain
plume ▸ feather

   plume d'oie ▸ quill
plumer ▸ pluck
la plupart ▸ most
pluriel ▸ plural
pluriel (-ielle) ▸ plural
plus ▸ and, any, anymore, further, more, plus
   au plus ▸ most
   de plus ▸ additional, also, else, extra[1], furthermore, moreover, to boot
   de plus en plus ▸ increasingly [increase]
   en plus ▸ additionally [additional], besides, in addition [addition], to boot
   le plus ▸ most
   non plus ▸ either
   plus de ▸ better, in excess of, more, over
plusieurs ▸ several, various
Pluton ▸ Pluto
plutôt ▸ before, instead, pretty, quite, rather, sooner [soon], sort of [sort]
   plutôt que ▸ instead of
pluvieux (-euse) ▸ rainy, wet
pluviosité ▸ rainfall
pneu ▸ tire[2]
   pneu de rechange ▸ spare
   pneu de secours ▸ spare
pneumonie ▸ pneumonia
poche ▸ pocket, pouch
   de poche ▸ pocket
   couteau (-eaux) de poche ▸ jack-knife
   lampe de poche ▸ flashlight, torch
   faire des poches ▸ bag
   mettre dans sa poche ▸ pocket
pochoir ▸ stencil
poêle ▸ pan, stove
   poêle (à frire) ▸ skillet
poème ▸ poem
   poème burlesque et grivois ▸ limerick
   poème imagé ▸ concrete poem
   poème lyrique ▸ lyric
poésie ▸ poetry, romance, verse
poids ▸ burdon, shot[1], weight
   lancer du poids ▸ shot put
   avoir du poids ▸ weight
poignard ▸ dagger
poignarder ▸ stab
poigne ▸ grasp, grip
poignée ▸ doorknob, grip, handful, handle
   poignée de main ▸ handshake
poignet ▸ cuff[1], wrist
poil ▸ fur, hair, pile[3], whisker
   à poil ▸ furry [fur]
   poil raide ▸ bristle
poilu (-ue) ▸ furry [fur], hairy
poinçon ▸ punch[2]
poinçonner ▸ punch[2]
poinçonneuse ▸ punch[2]
poindre ▸ dawn

poing ► fist
  coup de poing ► punch[1]
  donner un coup de poing ► punch[1]
point[1] ► dot, mark, period, point
  deux-points ► colon
  point d'exclamation ► exclamation mark
  point d'interrogation ► question mark
point[2] ► issue, run, way
  au point ► focus
  mettre au point ► debug, focus, tune
  mise au point ► adjustment
  point de vue ► angle, outlook, point of view, side, standpoint, viewpoint
  point déterminant ► head
  point culminant ► apex, climax
  point sensible ► apex, climax
  sur le point de ► about, ready, threshold, verge
  au point mort ► neutral
point[3] ► stitch
pointe ► peak, point, prong, spear, spike[1], tip[1], wedge
  heure de pointe ► rush hour
  pointe de terre ► spit[2]
  tailler en pointe ► taper
pointer ► check, check off, point, pointer, tally
pointeur ► pointer
pointilleux (-euse) ► particular
points ► basket
  égalité (de points) ► tie
pointu (-ue) ► sharp
pointure ► size
point-virgule ► semicolon
poire ► pear
poireau (-eaux) ► leek
pois ► pea, spot
  pois de senteur ► sweet pea
  petit pois ► pea
poison ► poison
poisson ► fish
  banc de poissons ► school[2]
  poisson arctique de la famille des truites ► Arctic char
  poisson rouge ► goldfish
  poisson-chat ► catfish
  soupe au poisson ► chowder
poitrine ► breast, chest
poivre ► pepper
poivrer ► pepper
poivron ► pepper
poker ► poker[2]
polaire ► polar
pôle ► pole[2]
  pôle Nord ► North Pole
poli ► polish
poli (-ie) ► civil, courteous, mannerly [manner], polite

police ► insurance, police, policy[2]
  agent de police ► cop
  agent (-ente) de la police d'état ► troop
  chef de la police ► sheriff
  membre de la Gendarmerie royale du Canada ► Mountie
police de caractères ► font[2]
policier (-ière) ► cop, detective
  drame policier ► mystery
poliment ► courteously [courteous], politely [polite]
polio ► polio
poliomyélite ► polio
polir ► buff, polish, shine
polisson (-onne) ► rascal
politesse ► courteousness [courteous], courtesy, politeness [polite]
politicien (-ienne) ► politician
politique ► policy[1], political, politics
politiquement ► politically [political]
pollen ► pollen
pollué (-ée) ► polluted [pollute]
polluer ► foul, pollute
pollution ► pollution
polo ► polo
  water-polo ► polo
poltron (-onne) ► coward
polyester ► polyester
polygone ► polygon
  polygone de tir ► range
polyvalent (-ente) ► versatile
pommade ► ointment
pomme ► apple, cone
  pomme d'Adam ► Adam's apple
  pomme de terre ► potato
  pomme de terre frite ► french fry
  pomme sauvage ► crab apple
pompe ► pump
  entrepreneur de pompes funèbres ► undertaker
pomper ► pump
pompier (-ière) ► firefighter
  pompier (-ière) bénévole ► volunteer
pompon ► tassel
poncho ► poncho
ponction ► puncture
ponctualité ► promptness [prompt]
  manque de ponctualité ► tardiness [tardy]
ponctuation ► punctuation
ponctuel (-elle) ► prompt, punctual
ponctuellement ► promptly [prompt]
ponctuer ► punctuate
pondre ► lay[1], spawn
poney ► pony
pont ► bridge, deck

pont suspendu ► suspension bridge
pontage ► bypass
populaire ► pop[2], popular
populairement ► popularly [popular]
popularité ► glory, popularity
population ► people, population, public
porc ► hog, pig, pork
porcelaine ► china, porcelain
porc-épic ► porcupine
porche ► porch, stoop[2]
pore ► pore[1]
porridge ► porridge
port[1] ► bearing, carriage, port, wear
    frais de port ► postage
port[2] ► harbour
portable ► portable
portage ► portage
portail (-ails) ► entrance[1]
portatif (-ive) ► portable
porte ► door, doorway, gate
    bouton de porte ► doorknob
    pas (de la porte) ► threshold
    porte de service ► back
    faire du porte à porte ► hawk[2]
porte-avions ► aircraft carrier
portée ► litter, range, reach, span, staff
porte-bonheur ► charm
porte-documents ► portfolio
portefeuille ► wallet
    banquette des députés sans
    portefeuille ► backbench
porte-monnaie ► purse
porte-parole ► representative
porter ► bear[1], bring, carry, deliver, tote, wear
    porter (sur soi) ► carry
    porter atteinte à (la réputation) ►
    smear
    porter fruit ► bear[1]
    porter plainte ► lodge
    porter un toast ► toast[2]
    se porter caution pour ► sponsor
porteur ► carrier
porteur (-euse) ► carrier, porter
portfolio ► portfolio
portière ► door
portillon ► gate
portion ► portion, serving
    petite portion ► dole
portrait ► description, image, portrait, portray
pose ► pose
posé (-ée) ► deliberate, poised [poise], sober
poser ► install, lay[1], pose, posture, rest[1], set
    poser de la tourbe ► sod
    poser sa candidature ► apply
    poser une question ► ask, query
    se poser ► light[3]
poseur (-euse) ► layer

poseur (-euse) de bombes ► bomber
positif ► positive
positif (-ive) ► plus, positive
    de façon positive ► positive
position ► condition, position, stand, standing, station
    avoir une position ► stand
    position affalée ► sprawl
    personne en deuxième position ►
    runner-up
positivement ► positively [positive]
posséder ► have, hold[1], master, own, possess
possesseur (-euse) ► holder
possessif ► possessive
possessif (-ive) ► possessive
possession ► dominion, possession
    fait d'entrer en possession ►
    possession
    être en possession ► possess
possibilité ► chance, possible, possible, possibilities
possible ► eventual, likely, possible, prospective, workable
    pas possible ► dear
possiblement ► possibly
postal (-ale, aux) ► post[2]
    tarif(s) postal (-aux) ► postage
poste[1] ► mail[1], post[2]
    bureau de poste ► post office
    cachet de la poste ► postmark
    poste aérienne ► airmail
    Société canadienne des postes ► post
    office
    timbre-poste ► stamp
    envoyer par la poste ► mail[1], post[2]
poste[2] ► extension, job, post[3], shift, station
    poste d'amarrage ► berth
    poste de guet ► lookout
    poste de télévision ► television
    poste vacant ► opening
poster[1] ► mail[1], post[2]
poster[2] ► position, station
postérieur ► hind
postérieur (-ieure) ► tail
postérité ► generation, posterity
postiche ► toupee, wig
postuler ► apply
posture ► attitude, posture
pot ► jar, planter, pot
pot(s)-pourri(s) ► potpourri
potage ► soup
potager ► garden
pot-de-vin ► bribe
poteau (-eaux) ► column, pole[1], post[1]
    poteau montant ► stud
potelé (-ée) ► chubby

potentiel ► potential
potentiel (-elle) ► eventual, potential
poterie ► pottery
potin ► gossip
potiner ► gossip
potion ► potion
potiron ► gourd
potlatch ► potlatch
poubelle ► can[2]
pouce ► inch, thumb
   faire du pouce ► hitch, hitchhike
pouding ► pudding
poudre ► powder
   comme une traînée de poudre ► like
   wildfire [wildfire]
poudrer ► powder
poudrerie ► blizzard, whiteout
poudrier ► compact
pouffer ► giggle
poulailler ► coop, gallery
poulain ► colt
poule ► hen
   poule naine ► bantam
   donner la chair de poule ► creep
poulet ► chicken
poulie ► pulley
poulpe ► octopus
pouls ► pulse
poumon ► lung
poupe ► stern[2]
poupée ► doll
pouponnière ► nursery
pour ► behalf, by, for, in order to, like[2], pro,
regarding, to, toward
pourboire ► tip[3]
   personne qui donne le pourboire ►
   tipper [tip[3]]
   donner un pourboire ► tip[3]
pourceau (-eaux) ► swine
pourcentage ► percentage, proportion
pourchasser ► hound, hunt, pursue
pourpre ► cardinal, purple
pourquoi ► wherefore, why
pourri (-ie) ► bad, rotten
pourrir ► decay, decompose, perish, rot
pourrissement ► decay
pourriture ► rot
poursuite ► chase, pursuit
poursuivre ► chase, continue, hound,
pursue
   poursuivre en justice ► sue
pourtant ► nevertheless, though
pourvoir ► furnish, provide
   pourvoir en personnel ► man, staff
   se pourvoir en appel ► appeal
pourvu que ► provide
pousse ► shoot, sprout

poussé (-ée) ► extreme
poussée ► boost, drift, hoist, impulse, poke,
push, shove, thrust
pousser ► bear down, egg[2], give, grow, jog[1],
motivate, prompt, provoke, push, shove,
sprout, urge, wheel
   pousser à ► prod, push
   pousser légèrement ► nudge
   pousser à agir ► spur
   pousser du coude ► nudge
   pousser du doigt ► prod
   pousser du pied ► prod
   pousser le long de ► trail
poussette ► carriage, stroller
poussière ► dust, grain, powder, speck
poussif (-ive) asthmatique ► wheeze
poussin ► chick
poutre ► beam, timber
pouvoir ► afford, can[1], clutch[1], could, may,
power
d'une manière pragmatique ► practically
prairie ► meadow, prairie, range
   les Prairies ► prairie, Prairie Provinces
   alouette des prairies ► bobolink
pratique ► down to earth, experience, handy,
practical, useful
   peu pratique ► inconvenient
   en pratique ► practically
   qui a le sens pratique ► practical
   (mise en) pratique ► practice
   mettre en pratique ► apply, implement
pratiquement ► practically, virtually
pratiquer ► practise
   pratiquer à répétition ► drill
   pratiquer la lutte ► wrestle
pré ► meadow
préalable ► previous, prior
   au préalable ► first
préau (-aux) ► yard[1]
préavis ► notice
précaire ► precarious, unsound
précairement ► precariously [precarious]
précaution ► precaution
   avec précaution ► warily
précédemment ► previously [previous]
précédent ► precedent
   sans précédent ► unheard-of
précédent (-ente) ► above, former,
previous, prior
précéder ► precede
précepteur (-trice) ► tutor
prêcher ► preach
précieux (-euse) ► precious, valuable
précipice ► precipice
précipitamment ► hastily [hasty], hurriedly
[hurried]
   partir précipitamment ► dash off

précipitation ► hastiness [hasty], hurry, precipitation, rush[1]

   taux de précipitations ► rainfall

précipité (-ée) ► hasty, hurried

précipiter ► dive, precipitate, send

   se précipiter ► dart, dash, leap, race[1], rush[1], scurry, stampede

précis (-ise) ► accurate, crisp, exact, precise, specific, technical, very

précisément ► exactly [exact], flat[1], just, precisely [precise], specifically [specific]

   pas précisément ► hardly

préciser ► define, determine, specify

précision ► accuracy [accurate], precision, specification

   avec précision ► accurately [accurate]

précoce ► early, precocious

précurseur (-eure) ► pioneer

prédateur (-trice) ► predator, predatory [predator]

prédécesseur (-eure) ► predecessor

prédicat ► predicate

prédilection ► fondness [fond]

   objet de prédilection ► thing

prédire ► predict

prédisposé (-ée) ► prone

préface ► introduction, preface

préférable ► preferable [prefer]

préférablement ► preferably [prefer]

préféré (-ée) ► best, favourite

préférence ► preference

   préférences ► likes

   de préférence ► desirably [desire], preferably [prefer]

préférer ► choose, favour, lean[1], prefer

préfixe ► prefix

préhistorique ► prehistoric

   tigre préhistorique ► sabre-toothed tiger

préjugé ► bias, prejudice

se prélasser ► lounge

prélèvement ► specimen

prélever ► levy

prématernelle ► kindergarten

prématuré (-ée) ► early, premature

prématurément ► prematurely [premature]

premier (-ière) ► early, first, former, initial, maiden, original, premier, primary

   Premier ministre ► premier, prime minister

   première classe ► class

   premier ordre ► class

   premier rôle ► lead[1], principal

   pour la première fois ► first

première ► opening, premiere

   voir en avant-première ► preview

premièrement ► first

prémisses ► premise

prendre ► catch, contract, eat, gain, grab, grasp, handle, hook, invade, ride, take

   s'en prendre à ► pick on

   se prendre ► catch

préoccupation ► care, consideration

préoccuper ► trouble

   se préoccuper ► care

préparatif ► preparation

   préparatifs ► arrangement

préparation ► mix, preparation, training

   préparation rapide ► instant

préparer ► cook, draw, fix, gear, groom, prepare, prime, ready

   préparer le terrain ► pave the way

   préparer un examen ► cram

   se préparer ► train

   se préparer mentalement ► brace

   non préparé (-ée) ► unprepared

préposé (-ée) ► teller, tender[3]

   préposé (-ée) aux soins ► orderly

préposition ► preposition

prérogative ► privilege

près ► near, nearby

   à peu près ► about, approximately [approximate], around, halfway, nearly, somewhere

   près de ► by, close[2], closely [close[2]], near, on

   suivre de près ► dog, tail

   surveiller de près ► watch

présage ► foreshadowing [foreshadow], omen

présager ► foreshadow

presbyte ► far-sighted

prescrire ► prescribe

présence ► attendance, presence

présent[1] ► gift, present[1]

présent[2] ► present tense

présent (-ente) ► contemporary, present[1]

présentateur (-trice) ► announcer

présentation ► exhibition, format, introduction, presentation

présenter ► exhibit, express, extend, give, introduce, lodge, nominate, pay, picture, pose, present[2], report

   se présenter ► report, run

   présenter des excuses ► apologize

   présenter les modèles ► model

préservation ► conservation, preservation

préserver ► conserve, preserve

président (-ente) ► chief, president, speaker

   vice-président (-ente) ► vice-president

présidentiel (-elle) ► presidential [president]

présider ► chair, preside

presque ► almost, hardly, nearly, practically

presqu'île ► peninsula

pressant (-ante) ► urgent

presse ► press
   coupure de presse ► clipping
   presse typographique ► printing press
pressé (-ée) ► eager, hasty, hurried
pressentiment ► hunch
presse-papier ► weight
presser ► crush, hasten, hurry, press, squeeze, urge
   se presser ► hustle
   sans se presser ► leisurely [leisure]
pression ► press, pressure
   à la pression ► draft
   pression de l'air ► air pressure
pressoir ► press
prestance ► presence
preste ► deft, nimble
prestement ► alertly [alert], deftly [deft], nimbly [nimble]
prestige ► glamour, glitter, glory, influence, prestige
prestigieux (-euse) ► glamorous [glamour]
présumer ► presume
prêt ► loan
prêt (prête) ► game, ready, set
   prêt à être tiré ► draft
prétendre ► allege, claim, contend, pretend
prétendu (-ue) ► so-called
prétendument ► allegedly [allege]
prétentieux (-euse) ► conceited
prêter ► lend, loan
   se prêter ► humour
   faire prêter serment (à) ► administer
   prêter assistance ► assist, lend a hand
   prêter attention ► mind
   prêter main-forte ► lend a hand
prêteur (-euse) ► lender [lend]
prétexte ► incentive
prétexter ► object
prêtre ► priest
preuve ► evidence, proof, testimony
   moindre preuve ► shred
prévenance ► thoughtfulness [thoughtful]
   avec prévenance ► considerately [considerate], thoughtfully [thoughtful]
   manque de prévenance ou d'égards ► thoughtlessness [thoughtless]
prévenant (-ante) ► considerate, thoughtful
prévenir ► prevent, tip off [tip[3]], warn
   prévenir (contre, en faveur de) ► prejudice
prévention ► prevention
prévenu (-ue) ► defendant
prévisible ► in the cards, predictable [predict]
prévision ► forecast
prévisionner ► preview
prévoir ► allow for [allow], anticipate, arrange, expect, forecast, provide

prévoir (par extrapolation) ► project
prévoir à son programme ► program
prévoyant (-ante) ► far-sighted
prévu (-ue) ► due
prier ► beg, pray, request
prière ► devotion, prayer
primate ► primate
donner la **primauté à** ► put (place) a premium on
prime ► bonus, bounty, insurance, premium
primitif ► savage
primitif (-ive) ► barbaric, early, primitive
primordial (-ale, -aux) ► capital, primary, prime
prince ► prince
princesse ► princess
principal (-ale, -aux) ► arch[2], capital, cardinal, central, chief, head, main, major, master, primary, prime, principal
   partie principale ► body
principalement ► basically, chiefly [chief], essentially, mainly, mostly [most]
principe ► law, premise, principle
printemps ► spring
prise[1] ► catch, clasp, grasp, grip, haul, hold[1], intake, plug
   avoir une prise de bec avec ► tangle with [tangle]
prise[2] ► strike
   prise à fiche ► jack
   prise de bec ► spat[1]
   prise de contrôle ► takeover
   prise de courant ► outlet, socket
   prise de vue ► shot[1]
   prise de vue(s) ► take
   prise d'eau ► hydrant
   brancher à la prise de terre ► ground[1]
priser ► prize
prisme ► prism
prison ► jail, prison
prisonnier (-ière) ► captive, convict, prisoner
privé (-ée) ► private
priver ► deny, deprive
privilège ► privilege
prix ► award, charge, cost, distinction, fee, price, prize, purse
   à bas prix ► cheap
   prix de location ► rent
   prix d'entrée ► admission
   prix du billet ► fare
   prix Nobel ► Nobel Prize
   attacher beaucoup de prix ► prize
   comparer les prix ► shop around [shop]
   établir un prix ► quote
   s'informer du prix de ► price

probabilité ► probability
   probabilités ► odds
probable ► likely, probable
probablement ► likely, possibly, probably
[probable]
probation ► probation
problème ► difficulty, hassle, issue, matter,
problem, question, trouble
   petit problème ► kink
   problème (informatique) ► bug
procédure ► direction, procedure
procès ► lawsuit, suit, trial
processeur ► processor
procession ► procession
processus ► mechanics, process
procès-verbal ► minute[1]
   hors procès-verbal ► off the record
prochain (-aine) ► next, upcoming
prochainement ► shortly
proche ► close[2], handy, immediate, intimate,
near, nearby
proclamer ► declare, herald, proclaim
procréer ► father
se procurer ► obtain
procureur (-eure) ► attorney
   Procureur Général ► Attorney General
prodige ► prodigy, wonder
prodigieusement ► tremendously
[tremendous]
prodigieux (-euse) ► miraculous,
phenomenal [phenomenon], tremendous
prodigue ► extravagant, generous
producteur (-trice) ► producer
productif (-ive) ► productive
production ► generation, output, production,
yield
produire ► breed, compose, generate, net[2],
produce, shock[1], yield
   produire des étincelles ► sparkle
   produire un bruit retentissant ►
thunder
   produire une étincelle ► spark
   se produire ► happen, occur
   se produire par hasard ► chance
produit ► commodity, crop, proceed, product,
ware
   produit de remplacement ►
replacement
   produits agricoles ► produce
   produits alimentaires ► produce
proéminent (-ente) ► prominent
profane ► secular
proférer (des menaces) ► threaten
professeur (-eure) ► instructor, lecturer
[lecture], professor, teacher
profession ► career, occupation, profession,
vocation

professionnel (-elle) ► pro, professional,
vocational [vocation]
   en professionnel (-elle) ► professionally
[professional]
   de manière professionnelle ►
professionally [professional]
professionnellement ► professionally
[professional]
profil ► outline, profile
profit ► earnings, gain, interest, profit, return
   à profit ► profitably [profitable]
   avec profit ► profitably [profitable]
   représentation au profit ► benefit
   tirer profit ► benefit, profit
profiter ► benefit
   profiter de ► take advantage of
[advantage]
   profiter de quelqu'un ► use
profond (-onde) ► deep, inner, profound
   au plus profond ► depth
   peu profond ► shallow
profondément ► deeply [deep], keenly
[keen], profoundly [profound], sound[2]
profondeur ► depth
   en profondeur ► in depth
   manque de profondeur ► shallowness
[shallow]
profusion ► riot
   à profusion ► wealth
progéniture ► offspring
programmation ► program
programme ► agenda, curriculum, platform,
program
   programme télévisé ► television
programmer ► program
progrès ► advance, improvement, progress
   grands progrès ► stride
progresser ► progress
progressif (-ive) ► gradual, progressive
progression ► advance, progress
progressiste ► progressive
   **Parti progressiste-conservateur (du
Canada)** ► Progressive Conservative
Party
progressivement ► gradually [gradual]
proie ► prey, quarry[2]
   de proie ► predatory [predator]
   animal de proie ► predator
   faire sa proie de ► prey
projecteur ► projector, searchlight, spotlight
projection ► projection
projet ► blueprint, plan, project, proposal,
scheme, venture
   projet de loi ► bill[1]
projeter ► cast, flash, intend, plan, project,
throw

se projeter ▶ shoot
    projeter en silhouette ▶ silhouette
prolifique ▶ productive
prologue ▶ prologue
prolongation ▶ extension, overtime
prolonger ▶ lengthen, prolong
promenade ▶ drive, ride, stroll, walk
    faire une promenade à pied ▶ hike
    faire une petite promenade ▶
    constitutional
promener ▶ walk
    se promener ▶ saunter, stroll
    se promener au hasard ▶ ramble
    se promener en bateau ▶ boat
promeneur (-euse) ▶ walker
promesse ▶ assurance, oath, pledge,
promise, word
    retirer sa promesse ▶ back out
promettre ▶ pledge, promise
promotion ▶ advancement, class, promotion
promouvoir ▶ hype, promote
prompt (prompte) ▶ prompt, quick
promptement ▶ promptly [prompt], quick,
quickly [quick]
promptitude ▶ alertness [alert], promptness
[prompt], quickness [quick]
promulguer ▶ enact
    promulguer une loi ▶ legislate
pronom ▶ pronoun
prononcé (-ée) ▶ pronounced
prononcer ▶ deliver, pronounce, sound[1],
utter[1]
prononciation ▶ diction, pronunciation,
speech
pronostic ▶ forecast
propagande ▶ propaganda
prophétie ▶ prophecy
propice ▶ fair[1], favourable, likely
proportion ▶ percentage, proportion
proportionné (-ée) ▶ proportion
propos ▶ point
    à propos de ▶ about, over
    hors de propos ▶ beside
proposer ▶ counsel, move, nominate, offer,
propose
    se proposer ▶ intend, propose
    se proposer pour faire quelque chose
    ▶ volunteer
proposition ▶ clause, motion, proposal,
proposition
    proposition (de prix) ▶ quote
propre[1] ▶ clean, neat
propre[2] ▶ own
    propre à ▶ peculiar
proprement dit (dite) ▶ proper
propreté ▶ neatness [neat], tidiness [tidy]
    d'une propreté impeccable ▶ spotlessly

[spotless]
propriétaire ▶ landlord
propriété ▶ domain, estate, property
    violer la propriété ▶ trespass
propulser ▶ power, propel
prose ▶ prose
prospecter ▶ prospect
prospectus ▶ circular, flyer, leaflet, literature
prospère ▶ prosperous
prospérer ▶ flourish, prosper, thrive
prospérité ▶ prosperity
prostré (-ée) ▶ prone
protecteur rembourré ▶ pad
protecteur (-trice) ▶ defence, guardian,
protective
protection ▶ conservation, covering,
defence, guard, insurance, preservation,
protection
    de protection ▶ protective
protégé (-ée) ▶ immune
protéger ▶ cover, preserve, protect, secure,
shield
protéine ▶ protein
protestant (-ante) ▶ Protestant
protestation ▶ complaint, protest
protester ▶ complain, protest
prothèse ▶ brace
protocole ▶ etiquette
proton ▶ proton
protozoaire ▶ protozoan
protubérance ▶ knob
proue ▶ bow[3], prow
    figure de proue ▶ figurehead
prouesse ▶ feat
prouver ▶ demonstrate, establish, prove
provenir ▶ derive, originate, stem[2]
proverbe ▶ proverb, saying
province ▶ province
    Provinces maritimes ▶ Maritime
    Provinces
provincial (-ale, iaux) ▶ provincial
[province]
provision ▶ provision
    provisions ▶ store, supply
provisoire ▶ provisional [provision],
temporary, tentative
provisoirement ▶ temporarily [temporary],
tentatively [tentative]
provocant (-ante) ▶ defiant
provocation ▶ defiance [defiant]
    avec provocation ▶ defiantly [defiant]
provoquer ▶ challenge, generate, provoke,
spark, trigger
proximité ▶ closeness [close[2]], nearness
[near]
    à proximité ▶ near, nearby

prudemment ► carefully [careful], cautiously [cautious], wisely [wise]
prudence ► caution
   avec prudence ► warily
prudent (-ente) ► careful, cautious, prudent, wary
prune ► plum
pruneau (-eaux) ► prune[1]
psychiatre ► psychiatrist
psychique ► psychological
psychologie ► psychology
psychologique ► psychological
puanteur ► stink
puberté ► puberty
public ► audience, public
   en public ► in public
public (-ique) ► common, public
   service public ► utility
publication ► publication
   diriger la publication ► edit
ritournelle **publicitaire** ► jingle
publicité ► advertisement, commercial, promotion, publicity
   faire de la publicité à outrance ► hype
publier ► print, publish
publiquement ► publicly [public]
puce ► chip, flea
   puce de mémoire ► memory chip
puceron ► aphid
pudeur ► modesty [modest]
pudique ► modest
puer ► stink
puéril (-ile) ► childish, juvenile
pugiliste ► fighter
puis ► then
puiser ► dip, draw
puisque ► as, since
puissamment ► mightily [mighty]
puissance ► might[2], power
   en puissance ► potential
   puissance en chevaux-vapeur ► horsepower
puissant (-ante) ► mighty, potent, powerful [power]
   tout-puissant ► almighty
puits ► shaft, well[2]
pull-over ► sweater
pulpe ► flesh, pulp
pulsation ► throb
pulvérisateur ► sprayer [spray]
pulvériser ► pound[2], spray
puma ► cougar, puma
punaise ► bug, tack, thumbtack
punch ► punch[3]
punir ► punish
punition ► punishment
pupe ► pupa

pupille ► pupil[2], ward
pupitre ► desk
pur (pure) ► mere, naked, pure, rank[2], sheer, stark
purée ► mash
purement ► merely, purely [pure]
purifier ► filter, purify
puritain (-aine) ► puritan
pur-sang ► thoroughbred
puzzle ► jigsaw puzzle
pyjama ► pyjamas
pyramide ► pyramid
python ► python

Q

quadrilatère ► quadrilateral
quadriller ► check
quadrupède ► quadruped
quadruplet ► quadruplet
quai ► platform, quay, waterfront, wharf
   quai de chargement ► bay[5]
   mettre à quai ► dock[1]
qualification ► qualification
qualifié (-ée) ► capable, competent
qualifier ► qualify, term
qualité ► attribute, grade, point, quality, virtue
   en qualité ► capacity
   de qualité supérieure ► premium
   de première qualité ► prime
   de mauvaise qualité ► cheap
quand ► anytime, once, when, whenever
quand même ► anyway, regardless
quant à ► regarding
quantité ► amount, quantity
   en quantité ► bulk
   petite quantité ► dash
quarantaine ► quarantine
quarante ► forty
quarantième ► fortieth [forty]
quart ► quarter, quarterback
   quart arrière ► quarterback
   quart d'heure ► quarter
   être de quart ► watch
quartier ► area, barracks, block, district, neighbourhood, quarter
   du quartier ► neighbourhood
   quartier général ► headquarters
quartz ► quartz
quasar ► quasar
quasiment ► virtually
quatorze ► fourteen
quatorzième ► fourteenth [fourteen]
quatre ► four
   diviser en quatre ► quarter
quatre-vingt-dix ► ninety

quatre-vingt-dixième ▸ ninetieth [ninety]
quatre-vingtième ▸ eightieth [eighty]
quatre-vingts ▸ eighty
quatrième ▸ fourth [four]
quatuor ▸ quartet
que ▸ than, that, what
quel (quelle) ▸ what, which
  à quel (quelle) ▸ when
  quel (quelle) que soit ▸ no matter,
  whatever, whatsoever
quelconque ▸ plain, some
quelque ▸ any
  quelque chose ▸ something
  quelque part ▸ somewhere
  quelque peu ▸ rather, slightly [slight],
  something, somewhat
  quelque temps ▸ while
quelques ▸ few, several, some
quelqu'un ▸ anybody, anyone, somebody,
someone
se **quereller** ▸ bicker, feud, quarrel
  chercher la querelle ▸ pick a fight
question[1] ▸ issue, matter
  hors de question ▸ out, question
question[2] ▸ query, question
  poser une question ▸ ask, query
questionnaire ▸ questionnaire
  jeu-questionnaire ▸ quiz, trivial
questionner ▸ question
quête ▸ lookout, quest
  être en quête ▸ quest
  faire la quête ▸ to pass the hat
queue ▸ queue, tail
  queue de billard ▸ cue[2]
  fourgon de queue ▸ caboose
  faire la queue ▸ queue
queue de pie ▸ tail
qui ▸ who, whom
  à qui ▸ whose
  qui que ce soit ▸ whoever
quiconque ▸ whoever
quille ▸ keel, pin
  jeu de quilles ▸ bowling
  jouer aux quilles ▸ bowl[2]
quincaillerie ▸ hardware
quinte ▸ fit[2]
quintette ▸ quintet
quintuplé ▸ quintuplet
quinze ▸ fifteen
quinzième ▸ fifteenth [fifteen]
qui plus est ▸ furthermore
quitter ▸ leave[1], quit, vacate
  quitter brusquement ▸ whisk
quoi ▸ what
  après quoi ▸ whereupon
  dans quoi ▸ wherein
  en quoi ▸ wherein

  par quoi ▸ whereby
quoi que ▸ although, whatever, while
  quoi que ce soit ▸ whatever
  sur quoi ▸ whereupon
quoique ▸ though
quolibet ▸ quirk
quota ▸ quota
quote-part ▸ due
quotidien (-ienne) ▸ daily, everyday
quotidiennement ▸ daily
quotient ▸ quotient
  quotient intellectuel (QI) ▸ IQ

R

rabais ▸ discount, rebate
  accorder un rabais ▸ rebate
  consentir un rabais ▸ rebate
  faire un rabais ▸ rebate
rabaisser ▸ humiliate
rabat ▸ flap
rabattre ▸ discount
rabbin ▸ rabbi
rabot ▸ plane[2]
raboter ▸ plane[2], shave
raboteux (-euse) ▸ uneven
rabougrir ▸ stunt[2]
se **raccommoder** ▸ patch up
se **raccorder** ▸ hook up
voie de **raccordement** ▸ switch
raccourci ▸ short cut
raccourcir ▸ abbreviate, shorten
se **raccrocher** ▸ clutch[1]
race ▸ breed, race[2], strain[2]
  de pure race ▸ thoroughbred
  animal de race ▸ thoroughbred
rachat ▸ takeover
racheter ▸ compensate, redeem
racial (-ale, -aux) ▸ racial [race[2]]
racine ▸ base[1], root[1]
  racine carrée ▸ square root
  racine cubique ▸ cube
  prendre racine ▸ root[1]
racinette ▸ root beer
racket ▸ racket
  donner une raclée ▸ belt, lick
racler ▸ scrape, strum
raconter ▸ narrate, relate, tell
  raconter des blagues ▸ kid
  raconter d'un seul jet ▸ pour out [pour]
  jamais raconté (-ée) ▸ untold
radar ▸ radar
radeau (-eaux) ▸ boom[2], catamaran, raft
radiant (-iante) ▸ radiant
radiateur ▸ radiator
radiation ▸ radiation
radical (-ale, -aux) ▸ radical, sweeping

radicalement ► radically [radical]
radieux (-euse) ► radiant, sunny
radio ► radio
    faire une radio ► X-ray
    communiquer par radio ► radio
radioactif (-ive) ► radioactive [radioactivity]
radioactivité ► radioactivity
radioamateur ► ham
radiodiffuser ► broadcast
radiographie ► X-ray
radiographier ► X-ray
radis ► radish
radoter ► ramble
rafale ► gale
    en rafales ► blustery [bluster]
    souffler en rafales ► bluster
raffermir ► harden, steady
raffinage ► refinement [refine]
raffiné (-ée) ► delicate, exquisite, fine[1], sophisticated
    non raffiné (-ée) ► crude
raffiner ► refine
raffinerie ► refinery
rafistoler ► patch up
rafle ► raid, roundup
rafler ► raid, snap
rafraîchir ► cool, ice, refresh
    rafraîchir la mémoire ► jog someone's memory, refresh (one's) memory [refresh]
    se rafraîchir ► chill
rafraîchissement ► refreshment
ragaillardir ► pep
    se ragaillardir ► perk
rage ► rabies, rage
    avec rage ► with a vengeance [vengeance]
    éclater de rage ► blow up
    faire rage ► bluster, rage
rager ► rage
ragoût ► stew
    ragoût en cocotte ► casserole
raid ► raid
raide ► crisp, rigid, steep[1], stiff, straight
    pente raide ► dip
    poil raide ► bristle
raideur ► stiffness [stiff]
    avec raideur ► rigidly [rigid], stiffly [stiff]
    marcher avec raideur ► stalk[2]
raidir ► contract, stiffen
raie[1] ► part, skate[2]
raie[2] ► flounder, ray[2]
rail ► rail, railroad
    rails ► track
railler ► taunt
raillerie ► irony, ridicule, taunt
raisin ► grape
    raisin sec ► raisin

raison ► cause, ground[1], intelligence, mind, motive, occasion, reason, sake, sense
    avec raison ► rightly [right]
    en raison de ► for, owing to
raisonnable ► rational, reasonable
raisonnablement ► reasonably [reasonable], sensibly [sensible]
raisonnement ► reasoning
raisonner ► reason
rajouter ► tack on
tourner au ralenti ► idle
    mettre au ralenti ► throttle
ralentir ► slaken, slow, stunt[2]
râler ► squawk
ralliement ► rally
rallier ► rally
rallonge ► extension, leaf
rallonger ► lengthen
ram ► ram
Rama ► Rama
ramadan ► Ramadan
ramage ► song
ramassage ► collection, pickup
ramasser ► gather, scoop
    ramasser dans ses filets ► net[1]
rame ► oar
    canot à rames ► rowboat
rameau (-eaux) ► bough
ramener ► reel[1]
ramer ► row[2]
ramollir ► soften
rampe ► grade, ramp
ramper ► crawl, creep, slither, worm
ramure ► rack
rance ► rank[2]
ranch ► ranch
rancœur ► grudge
rançon ► ransom
rançonnement ► ransom
rançonner ► ransom
rancune ► grudge, spite
    par rancune ► spitefully [spite]
    garder rancune ► bear[1], harbour
rancunier (-ière) ► spiteful [spite]
randonnée ► hike, trek, walk
    faire de la randonnée ► trek
    faire une randonnée ► tramp
    faire une randonnée pédestre ► hike
rang ► line[1], rank[1], row[1], standing, string
rangée ► bank[3], line[1], rank[1], row[1]
ranger ► file[1], keep, stow, tidy, tuck
    se ranger ► belong, go
    bien rangé (-ée) ► tidy
ranimer ► revive
    se ranimer ► wake up [wake[1]]
rap ► rap[2]
rapace ► greedy

râpé (-ée) ► threadbare
râper ► grate
rapetisser ► dwarf
rapide[1] ► express, fast[1], fleet[2], prompt, quick, rapid, smart, speedy
    préparation rapide ► instant
    restauration rapide ► fast food
rapide[2] ► swift[1], rapids
rapidement ► fast[1], fleet[2], quick, quickly [quick], rapidly [rapid], smartly [smart], soon, speedily [speedy], swiftly [swift[1]]
    très rapidement ► like wildfire [wildfire]
    passer rapidement ► zip
rapidité ► haste, quickness [quick], rapidity [rapid], speed, swiftness [swift[1]]
rapiécer ► patch
rappel ► recall
rappeler ► recall, remind
    se rappeler ► place, recall, remember
rapport[1] ► bearing, ratio, record, report
    rapports ► terms [term]
rapport[2] ► contact, relation, relationship,
    entretenir des bons rapports ► relate
    rapport sexuel ► sex
rapporter ► fetch, give, net[2], report, retrieve, yield
rapporteur (-euse) ► sneak, tattler [tattle]
rapprocher ► compare, relate
raquette ► paddle, racquet, snowshoe
rare ► lean[2], rare[1], scarce, uncommon, unique
rarement ► rarely [rare[1]], seldom
rareté ► curiosity, dearth, scarcity [scarce]
ras (rase) ► level
rasage ► shave
raser ► brush[1], graze, level, shave
rasoir ► razor
se rassasier ► gorge
    état d'être rassasié (-ée) ► fill
rassemblement ► assembly, gathering, rally, roundup
rassembler ► assemble, clump, congregate, gather, herd, piece, raise, rally, scrape
    se rassembler ► cluster, collect, turn out
    rassembler en troupeau ► herd
rassis (-ise) ► stale
rassurer ► reassure
rat (rate) ► rat
    rat musqué ► muskrat
rate ► spleen
raté (-ée) ► failure
râteau (-eaux) ► rake
râteler ► rake
rater ► flop, miss[1]
ratification ► ratification [ratify]
ratifier ► confirm, ratify
ration ► ration

rationaliser ► streamline
rationnel (-elle) ► rational
rationner ► ration
ratisser ► rake
raton laveur ► raccoon
rattacher ► connect
de rattrapage ► remedial
rattraper ► gain on
    se rattraper ► recover
rauque ► hoarse, husky[1]
    pousser des cris rauques ► squawk
ravager ► destroy, devastate
ravaler ► swallow[1]
ravi (-ie) ► overjoyed
ravin ► ravine
ravir ► enchant, entrance[2]
ravissant (-ante) ► darling, lovely
ravitailler ► feed
raviver ► revive
rayer ► blot out, cross, scuff, stripe
rayon[1] ► department, stack
    mettre sur les rayons ► shelve
rayon[2] ► beam, gleam, ray[1], spoke
    rayon x ► X-ray
rayon[3] ► radius
    rayon d'action ► range
rayonnant (-ante) ► radiant, sunny
rayonne ► rayon
rayonnement ► glow, radiation
rayonner ► beam, glow, radiate
rayure ► bar, stripe
raz-de-marée ► tidal wave
réabonnement ► renewal [renew]
réaction ► feedback, reaction, response
    avion à réaction ► jet
    réaction secondaire ► side effect
réagir ► react, respond
réalisable ► workable
réalisateur (-trice) ► director, editor
réalisation ► attainment [attain], execution, production
réaliser ► accomplish, achieve, comprehend, effect, execute, produce
    se réaliser ► come true, materialize
réalisme ► realism
    avec réalisme ► realistically [realistic]
réaliste ► down to earth, lifelike, realistic, true to life
    de façon réaliste ► realistically [realistic]
en réalité ► really
réanimer ► revive
réapparaître ► recur
rebattre (les oreilles) ► harp on
rebelle ► rebel, rebellious [rebellion], stubborn
    se rebeller ► rebel, revolt
rébellion ► rebellion

820

rebond ► bound, rebound
rebondir ► bounce, bound[2], rebound
rebondissement ► development
rebord ► brim, ledge, lip, sill
rébus ► puzzle
rebut ► garbage, reject
   mise au rebut ► disposal
   mettre au rebut ► reject, scrap
   jeter au rebut ► reject
récemment ► lately, newly, recently [recent]
recensement ► census
récent (-ente) ► last[1], late, newly, recent, up to the minute
réceptacle ► receptacle
récepteur ► receiver
réceptif (-ive) ► receptive
réception ► function, party, receipt, reception, shower
   accuser réception (de) ► acknowledge
récession ► depression, recession
recette ► recipe
   recettes ► receipt
receveur ► catcher, conductor
recevoir ► accommodate, entertain, get, host, receive
   recevoir une décharge ► shock[1]
   recevoir une formation ► train
   qui reçoit ► home
rechange ► spare
   pièce de rechange ► replacement
   pneu de rechange ► spare
réchapper ► weather
réchauffer ► heat, warm
   se réchauffer ► thaw, warm
rêche ► rough
recherche ► hunt, lookout, pursuit, quest, research, search
   faire une recherche ► research
   faire des recherches ► probe
rechercher ► check, quest, search, seek
   recherché (-ée) par la police ► hot
rechute ► relapse
rechuter ► relapse
récidive ► relapse
récidiver ► relapse
récif ► reef
récipiendaire ► receiver
récipient ► container, dish, receptacle, vessel
récit ► recitation [recite], relation, tale
   récit historique ► historical fiction
   faire le récit ► recite
récital (-als) ► recital
récitation ► recitation [recite]
réciter ► recite
réclamation ► claim, complaint
réclame ► ad, advertisement
   faire la réclame ► push

réclamer ► claim, complain, demand, insist
reclus (-use) ► recluse
recoin ► corner, recess
récolte ► crop, harvest
récolter ► harvest, reap
recommandation ► caution, counsel
recommander ► advise, advocate, counsel, recommend
recommencer ► renew, resume
récompense ► award, purse, reward
récompenser ► reward
réconcilier ► reconcile
   se réconcilier ► make up
réconfort ► comfort, reassurance [reassure]
réconforter ► comfort
reconnaissable ► unmistakable
reconnaissance ► acknowledgment [acknowledge], appreciation, honour, mercy, recognition, thankfulness [thankful]
   avec reconnaissance ► gratefully [grateful], thankfully [thankful]
   aller en reconnaissance ► scout
reconnaissant (-ante) ► grateful, thankful
reconnaître ► acknowledge, concede, confess, identify with, recognize, tell
   reconnaître coupable ► convict
reconnu (-ue) ► known
record ► record
recoudre ► patch
recourber ► crook
recourir ► refer, resort
recours ► resort
   avoir recours ► apply, resort
recouvrer ► collect
recouvrir ► blanket, cap, coat, cover, cover up, drape, lap[2], line[2], mantle, top[1]
   recouvrir de panneaux ► panel
   recouvrir d'un tapis ► carpet
récréation ► recess, recreation
   cour de récréation ► playground
récrimination ► complaint
récrire ► rewrite
se recroqueviller ► cower
recrue ► recruit
recrutement ► draft
recruter ► draft, recruit
rectangle ► oblong, rectangle
rectangulaire ► oblong, rectangular [rectangle]
rectification ► amendment [amend]
rectifier ► correct, right
reçu ► receipt
recueil ► anthology
recueillir ► gather
reculer ► back, back up, budge, cringe, flinch, recoil, retreat, reverse
   reculer devant ► shrink

à reculons ▸ backward
récupération ▸ retrieval [retrieve]
récupérer ▸ recover, regain, retrieve
récurage ▸ scrub[1]
récurer ▸ clean, scour[1], scrub[1]
recycler ▸ recycle
rédacteur (-trice) en chef ▸ editor
rédaction ▸ composition, essay
rédactionnel (-elle) ▸ editorial
redevance ▸ royalty
reddition ▸ surrender
rédiger ▸ draft, word
redondant (-ante) ▸ redundant
redouter ▸ dread, fear
redresser ▸ straighten
réduction ▸ cut, depletion [deplete], reduction [reduce]
réduire ▸ deplete, discount, drive, lessen, reduce, slash
réduit ▸ curb
reel ▸ reel[3]
réel (-elle) ▸ actual, concrete, genuine, real, tangible
réellement ▸ actually [actual], literally, really, truly, very
réfectoire ▸ hall
référence ▸ reference, standard
se référer ▸ refer
réfléchir ▸ consider, mirror, ponder, reflect, reflect on, think
   réfléchir sur ▸ deliberate
reflet ▸ gleam, image, mirror, reflection
refléter ▸ mirror, reflect; register
réflexe ▸ reflex
réflexion ▸ concentration, consideration, reflection
   ne pas laisser le temps de la réflexion ▸ stampede
refluer ▸ ebb
reflux ▸ ebb
réforme ▸ reform
réformer ▸ reform
refouler ▸ choke, compress, suppress
refrain ▸ chorus, refrain[2]
refréner ▸ bridle
réfrigérateur ▸ refrigerator
réfrigérer ▸ refrigerate
refroidir ▸ cool, ice
   se refroidir ▸ chill
refroidissement ▸ chill
   refroidissement dû au vent ▸ wind chill
refuge ▸ harbour, island, refuge, sanctuary, shelter
réfugié (-ée) ▸ refugee
refus ▸ refusal, rejection [reject]
refuser ▸ decline, deny, refuse[1]
   refuser d'admettre ▸ deny

regard ▸ eye, glance, look, regard
   regard fixe ▸ stare
   regard furieux ▸ glare
   regard furtif ▸ peek
regarder ▸ eye, gaze, look, view, watch
   regarder fixement ▸ stare
régime[1] ▸ regime
régime[2] ▸ diet
   régime (bananes) ▸ bunch
   se mettre au régime ▸ diet
   suivre un régime ▸ diet
régiment ▸ regiment
régimentaire ▸ regimented [regiment]
région ▸ area, belt, country, district, province, region
   région montagneuse ▸ highland
   région reculée ▸ wild
   région sauvage ▸ wild, wilderness
régional (-ale, -aux) ▸ regional [region]
régir ▸ administer, govern, regulate
registre ▸ log, pitch[1], register
réglage ▸ adjustment
règle ▸ regulation, rule, ruler
   dans les règles ▸ formal
   sans règle ▸ no-holds-barred
réglé (-ée) ▸ focus
   non réglé (-ée) ▸ undecided, unsettled
régler ▸ adjust, balance, control, decide, focus, reconcile, regulate, resolve, settle, time, tune
   des comptes à régler ▸ score
   régler la note ▸ check out
règne ▸ crown, kingdom, regime, reign
   prince régnant ▸ prince
régner ▸ reign
regorger ▸ burst
regret ▸ regret, wistfulness [wistful]
regrettable ▸ unfortunate
regretter ▸ lament, miss[1], regret
le (la) regretté (-ée) ▸ late
regroupement ▸ concentration
regrouper ▸ bracket, herd, rally
régularité ▸ steadiness [steadily]
régulier (-ière) ▸ even, regular, steady
régulièrement ▸ consistently [consistent], evenly [even], regularly [regular], steadily [steady]
rein ▸ kidney
reine ▸ queen
rejaillir ▸ spout
rejet ▸ reject, rejection [reject]
rejeter ▸ exclude, reject, throw
   rejeter avec mépris ▸ spurn
   rejeter en arrière ▸ toss
rejoindre ▸ join, reach
réjouir ▸ delight, lighten[2], thrill
   se réjouir ▸ cheer, rejoice

réjouissance ► glee
réjouissant (-ante) ► cheerful, delightful, glee
relâchement ► looseness [loose], release
relâcher ► loosen, relax, release, slaken
relais ► leg, relay, wind up [wind²]
relancer ► boost, revive
relater ► narrate, relate
relatif (-ive) ► comparative, relative
relation ► contact, relation, relationship
relativement ► reasonably [reasonable], relatively [relative]
relaxation ► relaxation [relax]
se **relaxer** ► relax, unwind
relayer ► relay, relieve
relève ► relief¹
   prendre la relève ► relieve
relevé ► statement, survey
relever¹ ► bank²
   ne pas relever ► ignore
   relever de ► depend
   relever une extrémité ► tip²
relever² ► flavour
relié (-ée) ► relative, relevant
relief ► relief²
   carte en relief ► relief map [relief²]
   manque de relief ► flatness [flat¹]
relier ► bind, bridge, connect, join, link, relate, tie, wire
religieuse ► nun
religieux (-euse) ► religious
religion ► faith, religion
reliquaire ► shrine
relique ► relic
relish ► relish
reluire ► gleam
reluquer ► eye
remarquable ► considerable, conspicuous, extraordinary, noble, notable, outstanding, remarkable
remarquablement ► outstandingly [outstanding], remarkably [remarkable], strikingly [striking]
remarque ► comment, observation, remark
   faire une remarque ► comment, remark
remarquer ► note, notice, observe, remark
   remarquer l'absence ► miss¹
remblai ► fill
remblayer ► bank²
rembourrage ► stuffing
rembourré (-ée) ► upholster
   protecteur rembourré ► pad
rembourrer ► cushion, pad, upholster
remboursement ► refund
rembourser ► refund, reimburse, repay
remède ► cure, drug, remedy
remédier ► cure, remedy

remémoration ► recall
remerciement ► acknowledgment [acknowledge]
   remerciements ► thanks
remercier ► thank
remettre ► defer¹, deliver, hand, place, postpone, repay
   remettre à plus tard ► procrastinate
   remettre à neuf ► renovate
   remettre à sa place ► replace
   se remettre ► better
remise¹ ► shack, shed¹
remise² ► discount
   remise des diplômes ► graduation
   remise en jeu ► face-off
   faire une remise ► discount
remontant ► boost
remonte-pente ► lift
remonter ► ascend, boost, crank, hitch, reel¹, wind²
remontoir ► key¹
remords ► remorse
remorquage ► tow
remorque ► trailer
remorquer ► draw, haul, tow
remorqueur ► tug, tugboat
remous ► unrest
remplaçant (-ante) ► alternate, deputy, replacement, substitute
remplacement ► replacement, spare, substitution [substituto]
   produit de remplacement ► replacement
remplacer ► replace, substitute
rempli (-ie) ► full, tuck
   rempli (-ie) de ressentiment ► resentful [resent]
remplir ► brim, fill, invade, load, pack, pump
remporter ► chalk up, win
remue-ménage ► bustle
remue-méninges ► brainstorm
remuement ► wag
remuer ► fidget, flop, stir, wag, wiggle
   se remuer ► bustle
renâcler ► snort
faire **renaître** ► revive
renard ► fox
rencontre ► encounter, meeting
   lieu de rencontre ► rendezvous
rencontrer ► come across, contact, encounter, find, meet, meet with, run
   se rencontrer ► merge, occur, rendezvous
rendement ► output, yield
rendez-vous ► appointment, date¹, engagement, rendezvous
   donner rendez-vous ► meet

rendre ► do, drive, give, make, repay, yield
    se rendre ► get, go, surrender, walk, yield
    se rendre compte ► discover, realize
rendu ► return
rêne ► rein
renfermé (-ée) ► withdrawn
renfermer ► contain, hold[1]
renfoncement ► indent
renfoncer ► indent
renforcement ► reinforcement [reinforce]
renforcer ► reinforce, strengthen, toughen
renfort ► reinforcement [reinforce]
renfrogné (-ée) ► sullen
    d'un air renfrogné ► sullenly [sullen]
se renfrogner ► frown
reniflement ► sniff, sniffle
renifler ► nose, sniff, sniffle
renne ► reindeer
renom ► name
renommé (-ée) ► famous
renommée ► fame
renoncer ► drop, drop out, relinquish,
surrender, waive
renonciation ► waive
renouer ► renew
renouveler ► renew
renouvellement ► renewal [renew]
rénover ► renovate
renseignement ► communication, detail,
information, intelligence, tip[3]
    mine de renseignements ► storehouse
renseigner ► brief, inform, instruct
    se renseigner ► check on, enquire
rentable ► profitable
    de façon peu rentable ► wasteful
[waste]
rente ► income, pension
rentrer ► barge, tuck
renversant (-ante) ► incredible
renverser ► bowl over, reverse, spill, tip[2],
topple, upset
    se renverser ► capsize, reverse
renvoi ► discharge, reference
renvoyer ► discharge, dismiss, echo,
echoed, echoing, expel, fire
    renvoyer d'un coup de tête ► head
repaire ► den
se repaître ► feast
répandre ► broadcast, diffuse, shed[2], spill
    se répandre en flots de paroles ► pour
out [pour]
très répandu (-ue) ► widespread
réparable ► repairable [repair]
réparation ► repair
réparer ► compensate, fix, heal, mend,
patch, repair, right
répartir ► class, classify, deal, distribute,
divide, parcel, portion

répartition ► allotment [allot], assignment
repas ► course, meal[1]
    repas (du midi) ► luncheon
    fournir les repas ► cater
repasser ► iron, press, review
repérage ► location
répercussion ► repercussion
répercuter ► echo, echoed, echoing
    se répercuter ► reflect on
repère ► haunt, lair, landmark
repérer ► locate, spot
répertoire ► directory, index
répéter ► duplicate, echo, echoed, echoing,
practise, rehearse, repeat
    répéter comme un perroquet ► parrot
    se répéter ► recur, repeat
répétiteur (-trice) ► coach
répétition ► rehearsal [rehearse], repeat,
repetition
    pratiquer à répétition ► drill
    s'exercer à répétition ► drill
répétitivité ► sameness [same]
répit ► grace
replacer ► replace
replier ► double, fold, hang
réplique[1] ► replica
    exacte réplique ► twin
réplique[2] ► retort
    souffler (une réplique) ► prompt
répliquer ► retort
répondre ► answer, reply, respond
    répondre avec maladresse ► fumble
    répondre de ► sponsor
réponse ► answer, reply, response
reportage ► article, broadcast, coverage,
report
reporter ► correspondent, defer[1], reporter
repos ► rest[1]
    au repos ► dormant
reposer ► rest[1]
    se reposer ► relax, rest[1], unwind
repousser ► put off, repel
    repousser avec mépris ► spurn
reprendre ► continue, make over, resume
    reprendre des forces ► rally
représailles ► retaliation [retaliate]
    user de représailles ► retaliate
représentant (-ante) ► agent,
correspondent, delegate, representative
représentatif (-ive) ► representative
représentation ► performance, portray,
presentation, representation [represent]
    représentation au profit ► benefit
    série de représentations ► run
représenter ► enact, perform, portray,
represent, spell[1]

représenter un défi ▸ challenge
se représenter ▸ picture, recur, visualize
répression ▸ supression [supress]
   mesures de répressions ▸ crack down
réprimande ▸ lecture
réprimander ▸ scold
réprimer ▸ choke, stifle, suppress
reprise ▸ mend
à plusieurs reprises ▸ repeatedly [repeat]
repriser ▸ mend
reproche ▸ blame, complaint
reprocher ▸ blame, carp[2], scold
reproduction ▸ breeding, copy, reproduction [reproduce]
reproduire ▸ duplicate, reproduce
   reproduire à l'échelle ▸ scale[3]
   se reproduire ▸ recur, reproduce
reptile ▸ reptile
république ▸ republic
répugnance ▸ disgust, horror
répugnant (-ante) ▸ filthy
répugner ▸ repel
réputation ▸ name, reputation
   porter atteinte à (la réputation) ▸ smear
réputé (-ée) ▸ noted
requérir ▸ require
requête ▸ claim, clamour, petition, query, request
requin ▸ shark
requis (-ise) ▸ compulsory
réseau ▸ network
   établir un réseau ▸ network
réservation ▸ reservation
réserve[1] ▸ reservation, qualification
   sous réserve de ▸ subject to [subject]
   sous réserve que ▸ provide
réserve[2] ▸ reserve
   mettre en réserve ▸ keep
réserve[3] ▸ preserve, refuge, sanctuary
réservé (-ée) ▸ aloof, modest, retiring, special
réserver ▸ book, dedicate, intend, reserve
réservoir ▸ reservoir, tank
résidant (-ante) ▸ resident
résidence ▸ dwelling, home, residence
résident (-ente) ▸ citizen
résidentiel (-ielle) ▸ residential
résider ▸ dwell, inhabit, lie[1], reside
résignation ▸ resignation
résigner ▸ reconcile
   se résigner ▸ resign oneself [resign]
résiliation ▸ termination [terminate]
résilier ▸ terminate
résine ▸ resin
résistance ▸ resistance, underground
résistant (-ante) ▸ durable, hardy, resilient

résister ▸ buck, resist, withstand
   résister à l'usure ▸ wear
résolu (-ue) ▸ bent, intent[1]
   non résolu (-ue) ▸ undecided, unsettled
résolument ▸ decidedly [decided]
résolution ▸ decision, détermination, firmness [firm[1]], resolution
résonner ▸ chime, clash, resound, sound[1]
résoudre ▸ crack, decipher, dispose, figure out, resolve, unlock
   se résoudre ▸ resolve
   tenter de résoudre ▸ puzzle
respect ▸ honour, respect
respectable ▸ decent, respectable
respecter ▸ consider, keep, regard, respect
   faire respecter ▸ enforce
respectif (-ive) ▸ respective
respectivement ▸ respectively [respective]
respectueusement ▸ respectfully [respectful]
respectueux (-euse) ▸ respectful
respiration ▸ respiration
   respiration artificielle ▸ artificial respiration
   respiration bruyante ▸ wheeze
   respiration sifflante ▸ wheeze
   chercher sa respiration ▸ gasp
respiratoire ▸ respiratory
respirer ▸ breathe, inhale
   respirer bruyamment ▸ wheeze
responsabilité ▸ blame, care, concern, duty, hand, liability, responsibility
responsable ▸ at fault, charge, guilty, responsible
   de façon responsable ▸ responsibly [responsible]
ressemblant (-ante) ▸ lifelike
ressembler ▸ imitate, resemble
ressemeler ▸ sole[1]
ressentiment ▸ resentment [resent]
   qui éprouve du ressentiment ▸ resentful [resent]
   rempli (-ie) de ressentiment ▸ resentful [resent]
ressentir ▸ feel
   ressentir un élancement (de douleur) ▸ twinge
resserrer ▸ condense, constrict, contract, tighten
ressort ▸ spring
   qui a du ressort ▸ resilient
ressortir ▸ contrast
   faire ressortir ▸ underline, underscore
ressortissant (-ante) ▸ national
ressource ▸ resource
   sans ressource ▸ helplessly
restaurant ▸ restaurant

note de restaurant ► check
petit restaurant ► diner
restauration rapide ► fast food
wagon-restaurant ► diner
restaurer ► renovate, restore
reste ► remainder, rest[2]
restes ► leftover, odds and ends, remain, scrap
rester ► continue, endure, lodge, remain, stay, stick
  rester en arrière ► hang back
  rester fidèle à ► keep
restreindre ► bridle, confine, curb, limit, narrow, restrict
restreint (-einte) ► narrow
restriction ► qualification, restriction
  sans restriction ► no-holds-barred
résumé ► digest, summary
résumer ► condense, sum, summarize
rétabli (-ie) ► up
rétablir ► restore
  se rétablir ► better, rebound, recover, regain
rétameur (-euse) ► tinker
retard ► delay, setback
  en retard ► behind, late, overdue, slow, tardy
  avoir du retard ► behind
  être en retard ► behind
  prendre du retard ► behind
retardé (-ée) ► late
retarder ► delay, put off, stall, stunt[2]
à retardement ► lingeringly [linger]
retenir ► dam, dock[2], hold[1], keep, restrain, retain, swallow[1], withhold
  retenir au sol ► ground[1]
  se retenir ► contain, refrain[1]
retentir ► blare, boom[1], resound, ring[2]
retenue ► detention, restraint
réticent (-ente) ► reluctant
  avec réticence ► reluctantly [reluctant]
rétine ► retina
retiré (-ée) ► out, remote
retirer ► core, draw, scratch, seclude, strike out, withdraw
  se retirer ► retire, retreat, withdraw
  retirer de la vente ► recall
  retirer du jeu ► bench
  retirer sa promesse ► back out
  retirer ses paroles ► back down
rétorquer ► retort
retors (-orse) ► slippery
retoucher ► touch
retour ► return
  de retour ► back, return
  aller-retour ► back and forth, return
  aller et retour ► round trip

retourner ► back, flip, hand, return
retrait ► indent, withdrawal
retraite ► retirement, retreat
  lieu de retraite ► retreat
  prendre sa retraite ► retire
retrancher ► deduct
rétrécir ► narrow
  faire rétrécir ► shrink
retriever ► retriever
rétroaction ► feedback
retrousser ► roll
retrouver ► find, join, trace, track
  se retrouver ► rendezvous
réuni (-ie) ► joint
réunion ► function, gathering, meeting, reunion, social
réunir ► assemble, compile, concentrate, congregate, corral, gather, group, incorporate, mass, raise
  se réunir ► rendezvous
réussi (-ie) ► successful
  réussi (-ie) de justesse ► narrow
réussir ► attain, fare, manage, pass, succeed
  réussir à quelqu'un ► agree with
réussite ► accomplishment [accomplish], achievement, feat, solitaire
revanche ► revenge
rêvasser ► dream
rêvasserie ► dream
rêve ► dream, illusion
revêche ► crabby [crab], crank, cranky, sour
rêvée (-ée) ► golden
réveillé (-ée) ► awake
réveiller ► arouse, awaken, wake[1]
  se réveiller ► awake, wake up [wake[1]]
réveil ► awakening
réveil-matin ► alarm, alarm clock
révéler ► disclose, divulge, expose, indicate, reveal, uncover, unfold, unveil
  se révéler ► prove, turn out
revenant ► ghost
revendication ► claim, demand
revenir sur ► harp on
revenu ► income, revenue
rêver ► dream
révérence ► awe, reverence
  avec révérence ► reverently [reverence]
révérencieux (-euse) ► reverent [reverence]
rêverie ► dream
revers ► cuff[1], reverse
revêtement (intérieur) ► lining
rêveur (-euse) ► dreamer [dream], wistful
revigorer ► pep
  se revigorer ► brace
faire revivre ► revive
réviser ► review, revise

révision ► review, service
au revoir ► aloha, au revoir, goodbye
révolte ► rebellion, revolt, uprising
révolter ► revolt
    se révolter ► rebel, revolt
révolution ► revolution
révolutionnaire ► revolutionary
revolver ► gun, revolver
    étui de revolver ► holster
révoquer ► revoke
revue ► journal, magazine, review
    passer en revue ► review
rez-de-chaussée ► downstairs
rhétorique ► rhetoric
    figure de rhétorique ► figure of speech
rhinocéros ► rhinoceros
rhododendron ► rhododendron
rhumatisme ► rheumatism
rhume ► cold
    petit rhume ► sniffle
ricanement ► sneer, snicker
ricaner ► sneer, snicker
riche ► affluent, mellow, rich, wealthy
richement ► richly [rich]
richesse ► goods, magnificence
[magnificent], riches, wealth
ricocher ► glance, ricochet
    faire ricocher ► skip
ricochet ► rebound, ricochet
ride ► line[1], ripple, wrinkle
rideau (-eaux) ► curtain, drape
    cacher derrière un rideau ► curtain
    garnir de rideaux ► curtain
rider ► wrinkle
ridicule ► insane, laughable [laugh],
preposterous, ridiculous
ridiculement ► preposterously
[preposterous], ridiculously [ridiculous]
ridiculiser ► mock, ridicule
rien ► anything, breeze, nothing, zero
    bon à rien ► worthless
    de rien ► from scratch, you're welcome
[welcome]
    moins que rien ► nobody
    rien que ► only
rigide ► hard, rigid, stiff
rigidement ► rigidly [rigid]
rigole ► ditch, gully
rigoler ► laugh
rigoriste ► puritan
rigoureusement ► rigidly [rigid]
rigoureux (-euse) ► extreme, harsh
rigueur ► strictness [strict], tightness [tight]
rime ► rhyme
rimer ► rhyme
rinçage ► rinse
rince-bouche ► mouthwash
rincer ► rinse

ring ► ring[1]
riposte ► retort
riposter ► retaliate, retort
rire ► break up, laugh
    pas de quoi rire ► no laughing matter
    rire aux larmes ► in stitches
    rire à gorge déployée ► roar
    rire de quelqu'un ► make fun of
    rire étouffé ► giggle
    se tordre de rire ► in stitches
risée ► ridicule
risible ► laughable [laugh]
risque ► chance, hazard, risk
    sans risque ► safely [safe]
risqué (-ée) ► risky
risquer ► chance, compromise, gamble,
hazard, risk, threaten, venture
ristourne ► dividend
rite ► ritual
ritournelle (publicitaire) ► jingle
rituel ► ritual
rivage ► coast, shore
rival (-ale, -aux) ► opponent, rival
rivaliser ► compete, match[2], rival
rivalité ► competition
rive ► bank[2], coast, edge
river ► bridge
rivière ► river
riz ► rice
robe ► coat, dress, gown, robe
    robe chasuble ► jumper[2]
    robe de chambre ► robe
robinet ► faucet, tap[2]
robot ► robot
    robot culinaire ► processor
robuste ► hardy, hearty, resilient, stout,
sturdy, tough, vigorous
robustesse ► sturdiness [sturdy], toughness
[tough]
    avec robustesse ► sturdily [sturdy]
rocailleux (-euse) ► rocky [rock[1]]
Roch ha-Shana ► Rosh Hashanah
roche ► rock[1]
rocher ► boulder, rock[1]
rocheux (-euse) ► rocky [rock[1]]
rock ► rock[2]
rodéo ► rodeo, round-up, stampede
rôder ► prowl
rognon ► kidney
roi ► king
    de roi ► kingly [king]
roitelet ► wren
rôle ► character, hand, part, role
    rôle principal (-aux) ► lead[1]
    premier rôle ► lead[1], principal
    donner le rôle de ► cast
roman ► fiction, novel[1], romance, thriller

romance ► ballad
romanichel (-elle) ► tinker
romantique ► romantic
    de façon romantique ► romantically
    [romantic]
rompre ► breach, break
ronce ► briar
    ronce remarquable ► salmonberry
ronchonnement ► growl
ronchonner ► growl
roncier ► bramble
roncière ► bramble
rond ► ring[1]
    en rond ► around
    tourner en rond ► mill
rond (ronde) ► full, round
    table ronde ► panel
ronde ► beat
rondelle[1] ► puck
rondelle[2] ► washer
    rondelles ► slice
rondin ► log
ronflement ► snore
ronfler ► snore
    faire ronfler le moteur ► gun
ronger ► corrode, eat, erode, gnaw, prey
rongeur ► rodent
ronron ► purr
ronronnement ► drone, purr, whir
ronronner ► drone, hum, purr, whir
rose[1] ► pink, rosy, ruddy
rose[2] ► rose[1]
    à l'eau de rose ► corny
    couronne de roses ou d'épines ►
    crown
rosé (-ée) ► rosy
roseau (-eaux) ► reed
rosée ► dew
Rosh ha-Shana ► Rosh Hashanah
rosier ► rose[1]
    rosier sauvage ► briar
rosser ► thrash
rossignol ► nightingale
rotatif (-ive) ► rotary
    tambour rotatif ► tumbler
rotation ► rotation
    faire en rotation ► rotate
rôtie ► toast[1]
rôtir ► roast
roucouler ► purr
roue ► cartwheel, wheel
    roue d'un moulin ► mill
    roue hydraulique ► waterwheel
    aube (d'une roue hydraulique) ► vane
    aller en roue libre ► coast
rouer (de coups) ► batter[3], thrash
rouet ► spinning wheel

rouge ► red
    rouge à joues ► rouge
    rouge cerise ► cherry
    rouge vif ► cardinal
rouge-gorge ► robin
rougeoiement ► glow
rougeole ► measles
rougeoyant (-ante) ► fiery
rougeoyer ► glow
rougeur ► blush, rash[1]
rougir ► blush, colour
rouille ► mildew, rust
rouillé (-ée) ► rusty [rust]
rouiller ► mildew, rust
rouli-roulant ► skateboard
rouleau (-eaux) ► bolt, coil, reel[1], roll, roller,
scroll
    rouleau compresseur ► steamroller
roulement ► roll
    bande de roulement ► tread
rouler[1] ► cheat
rouler[2] ► roll, wheel
    rouler au sol ► taxi
roulette ► roller
    patin à roulettes ► roller skate
    patins à roues alignées ► in-line skates
    planche à roulettes ► skateboard
rouspéter ► squawk
tache de **rousseur** ► freckle
route ► course, path, road, route, way
    petite route ► lane
    route d'évitement ► bypass
    route rurale ► concession
    route maritime ► seaway
    en route vers ► bound[4]
    sur la route de ► way
    se mettre en route ► activate, set
routier (-ière) ► teamster
routine ► habit, pattern, routine, rut
routinier (-ière) ► routine
    de façon routinière ► routinely [routine]
roux (rousse) ► copper, red
    blond roux ► sandy
    roux ► sorrel[2]
royal (-ale, -aux) ► kingly [king], regal, royal
royalement ► royally [royal]
royaume ► kingdom, realm
royauté ► royalty
ruban ► decoration, ribbon, tape
    ruban adhésif ► tape
    attacher avec du ruban ► tape
rubéole ► measles
rubis ► ruby
ruche ► hive
rucher ► apiary
rude ► barbaric, coarse, rough, rude
rudement ► mighty, rough, rudely [rude]

rudesse ► coarseness [coarse], harshness [harsh], roughness [rough]
    traiter avec rudesse ► rough
rudimentaire ► crude
rue ► place, street
    rues ► block
    rue piétonnière ► mall
ruée ► dash, rush[1], scramble, stampede
ruelle ► alley, lane
se ruer ► stampede
rugby ► rugby
rugir ► roar
rugissement ► roar
rugueux (-euse) ► rough, scratchy [scratch]
ruine ► doom, ruin
ruiner ► bankrupt, ruin
ruisseau (-eaux) ► brook, creek, stream
rumeur ► rumour
    faire courir des rumeurs ► rumour
ruminer ► chew
    nourriture qui a été ruminée ► cud
rupture ► breach, break
rural (-ale, -aux) ► rural
    route rurale ► concession
ruse ► craft, cunning, trick
    avec ruse ► cunningly [cunning], slyly [sly]
rusé (-ée) ► slick, tricky
rutiler ► glitter
rythme ► beat, rate, rhythm, tempo

S

S.O.S. ► mayday
sabbat ► Sabbath
sable ► sand
    sables mouvants ► quicksand
    banc de sable ► shoal
    barre de sable ► sandbar
sabler ► sand
sablonneux (-euse) ► sandy
sabot ► clog, hoof
    à sabots ► hoofed [hoof]
sabotage ► sabotage
saboter ► sabotage
sabre ► sabre
sac ► bag, pack, sac, sack[1]
    mise à sac ► sack[2]
    mettre en sac ► bag
    mettre dans un sac ► sack[1]
    mettre dans le même sac ► lump
    petit sac ► pouch
    sac à dos ► backpack, knapsack
    sac à main ► purse
    sac de couchage ► sleeping bag
saccade ► jerk, twitch, yank
saccadé (-ée) ► choppy

saccager ► sack[2]
sacré (-ée) ► holy, sacred
sacrer ► curse, swear
sacrifice ► sacrifice
sacrifier ► sacrifice
sadique ► cruel
safari ► safari
saga ► saga
sage ► sage[1], wise
sagement ► sagely [sage[1]], wisely [wise]
sagesse ► wisdom
    dent de sagesse ► wisdom tooth
saignant (-ante) ► rare[2]
saigner ► bleed, tap[2]
saillie ► projection
saillir ► project
sain (saine) ► healthy, sound[2], wholesome
    sain (saine) d'esprit ► sane
saindoux ► lard
saint (sainte) ► holy, saint
    digne d'un saint (d'une sainte) ► saintly [saint]
    Écriture sainte ► Scripture
saint-bernard ► Saint Bernard
Saint-Nicolas ► Santa Claus
saint-pierre ► dory[2]
saisie ► capture, haul, seizure
    faire la saisie de ► key in, keyboard
saisir ► capture, catch, clasp, clutch[1], get, grab, grasp, grip, see, seize, snap, snatch, understand
saisissant (-ante) ► impressive, vivid
saison ► season
saisonnier (-ière) ► seasonal
salade ► salad
salaire ► earnings, income, pay, salary, wage
salamandre ► salamander
salaud ► hog, rat
sale ► dirty, filthy, foul, impure, messy [mess]
salé (-ée) ► salty [salt]
salement ► messily [mess]
saler ► salt
saleté ► dirt
salin (-ine) ► saline [salt]
salir ► smear, smudge, soil
salish ► Salish
salissure ► smear
salive ► saliva, spit[1]
salle ► auditorium, hall, house, room, ward
    salle de bain ► bath, bathroom
    salle de cinéma ► theatre
    salle de classe temporaire ► portable
    salle des coffres ► vault[1]
salon ► lounge, parlour, saloon
salopette ► overalls
salubre ► healthy
saluer ► dip, greet, hail[2], salute, wave

salut ▸ hello, hi, salute, salvation
salutaire ▸ healthy
salutation ▸ greeting, salutation
salve ▸ round, salute
samedi ▸ Saturday
sanction ▸ punishment, sanction
sanctionner ▸ approve, sanction
sanctuaire ▸ sanctuary
sandale ▸ sandal
sandwich ▸ sandwich
sang ▸ blood
    à sang chaud ▸ warm-blooded
    à sang froid ▸ cold-blooded
    de sang froid ▸ in cold blood
    par le sang ▸ blood
    pur-sang ▸ thoroughbred
    taché (-ée) de sang ▸ bloody
sang-froid ▸ coolness [cool]
sanglant (-ante) ▸ bloody
sangle ▸ harness, strap
sangler ▸ strap
sanglier ▸ boar
sanglot ▸ sob
sangloter ▸ sob
sangsue ▸ leech
sanitaire ▸ sanitary
    système sanitaire ▸ sanitation
sans ▸ but, free, minus, without
sans abri ▸ homeless
santé ▸ health
    état de santé ▸ condition
    maison de santé ▸ clinic
    en santé ▸ well[1]
    en mauvaise santé ▸ unhealthy
    en bonne santé ▸ all right, fit[1]
    bon pour la santé ▸ healthy
    bonne santé ▸ health
saper ▸ eat, sap[2], undermine
saphir ▸ sapphire
sapin ▸ fir
sarcasme ▸ irony, sarcasm [sarcastic], taunt
    accabler de sarcasmes ▸ taunt
    lancer des sarcasmes ▸ sneer
sarcastique ▸ sarcastic
sarcastiquement ▸ sarcastically [sarcastic]
sarcler ▸ hoe, weed
sardine ▸ sardine
sari ▸ sari
sarracénie ▸ pitcher plant
sarrau ▸ smock
sasquatch ▸ Bigfoot
satellite ▸ satellite
satin ▸ satin
satire ▸ satire
satisfaction ▸ satisfaction
satisfaire ▸ cater, content[2], quench, satisfy
satisfaisant (-ante) ▸ all right, satisfactory

    de manière satisfaisante ▸ satisfactorily [satisfactory]
satisfait (-aite) ▸ content[2]
    satisfait (-aite) de soi-même ▸ smug
saturation ▸ saturate
saturer ▸ saturate
Saturne ▸ Saturn
sauce ▸ dressing, gravy, sauce
    sauce au jus de viande ▸ gravy
saucisse ▸ sausage
saucisson (de Bologne) ▸ bologna
sauf ▸ but, except, save
sauf (sauve) ▸ safe
sauge ▸ sage[2]
saule ▸ willow
    saule blanc ▸ pussy willow
saumon ▸ salmon
saumurer ▸ pickle
saupoudrer ▸ dust, powder, sprinkle
saut ▸ bound[2], bucket, hop[1], jump, leap, vault[2]
    faire des sauts ▸ flop
    saut périlleux ▸ flip, somersault
sauter ▸ bail[2], bound[2], buck, clear, explode, hurdle, jump, leap, skip, spring
    sauter en parachute ▸ parachute
    sauter quelque chose d'un bond ▸ vault[2]
sauterelle ▸ grasshopper, locust
sauteur (-euse) ▸ jumper[1]
sautillement ▸ hop[1]
sautiller ▸ hop[1], skip
sauvage ▸ rugged, savage, savagely [savage], shy, unsettled, wild, wildcat
    pomme sauvage ▸ crab apple
    région sauvage ▸ wild, wilderness
    rosier sauvage ▸ briar
sauvagerie ▸ savagery [savage]
sauvegarde ▸ conservation, preservation
sauvegarder ▸ salvage
sauver ▸ deliver, rescue, salvage, save
    se sauver ▸ flee
sauvetage ▸ rescue, salvage
    canot de sauvetage ▸ lifeboat
sauveteur (-eure) ▸ lifeguard, rescuer [rescue]
sauveur ▸ saviour
savant (-ante) ▸ learned [learn], scholar, scholarly [scholar]
saveur ▸ flavour
savoir ▸ can[1], hear of, know, knowledge
    un (une) je-sais-tout ▸ know-it-all
    à savoir ▸ namely
    savoir gré ▸ oblige
    savoir-faire ▸ know-how
savon ▸ soap
savonner ▸ lather, soap

savonneux (-euse) ► soapy [soap]
savourer ► relish, savour
savoureux (-euse) ► savoury [savour], tasty
saxophone ► saxophone
saynète ► sketch
scalène ► scalene
scandale ► scandal
scandaleusement ► disgracefully [disgrace]
scandaleux (-euse) ► outrageous
scandaliser ► horrify
scander ► chant
scaphandrier ► diver
sceau (-eaux) ► seal²
sceller ► cement, seal²
scénario ► script
scène ► arena, scene, stage
   centre de la scène ► spotlight
   mise en scène ► production
   mettre en scène ► produce, stage
   entrée en scène ► appearance
   entrer en scène ► appear
   porter à la scène ► stage
sceptique ► skeptical
scheik ► sheik
schéma ► diagram
schème ► pattern
schiste (argileux) ► shale
scie ► saw
   brin de scie ► sawdust
   scie à chantourner ► jigsaw puzzle
sciemment ► consciously [conscious]
science ► depth, knowledge, science
   sciences humaines ► social science
scientifique ► scientific, scientist
scientifiquement ► scientifically [scientific]
scier ► saw
scierie ► sawmill
scintillant (-ante) ► glittery, glittering [glitter]
scintillement ► glitter, sparkle, twinkle
scintiller ► glisten, glitter, twinkle
sciure ► sawdust
scolaire ► academic, scholastic
   manuel scolaire ► textbook
scorbut ► scurvy
score ► score
scorpion ► scorpion
scout ► scout
scribe ► scribe
sans scrupules ► unscrupulous
scrupuleusement ► scrupulously [scrupulous]
scuba ► scuba
sculpture ► sculpture
se ► herself, himself, themselves
séance ► hearing, session
   séance d'entraînement ► workout

seau (seaux) ► pail
sec (sèche) ► dry
   pile sèche ► dry cell
sécession ► secession [secede]
   faire sécession ► secede
sécher ► dry
sécheresse ► drought
second ► second¹
second (-onde) ► mate, second¹
   un (une) second (-onde) ► another
secondaire ► minor, secondary, side
   école secondaire ► secondary school
   réaction secondaire ► side effect
seconde ► second²
seconder ► help
secouer ► arouse, buffet², jerk, rock², shake, toss, tremble, worry
secourir ► rescue
secours ► aid, assistance, help, relief¹, rescue
   de secours ► auxiliary, emergency
   pneu de secours ► spare
secousse ► bump, jar, jerk, jolt, shake, shock¹, tremor
   donner une secousse ► jerk
secret ► recipe, secrecy, secret
   dans le secret ► secretly [secret]
   en secret ► secretly [secret]
secret (-ète) ► covert, cryptic, hidden, inner, secret, undercover, underground
secrétaire ► bureau, secretary
secrètement ► secretly [secret], underground
sécréter ► secrete
sécrétion ► secretion [secrete]
sectaire ► bigot, bigoted [bigot]
sectarisme ► bigotry [bigot]
secte ► sect
secteur ► area, sector, zone
   diviser en secteurs ► zoning
section ► chapter, department, division, lodge, section, unit
   section électorale ► ward
sectionner ► divide, section
sécurisant (-ante) ► secure
sécuriser ► secure
sécurité ► safety, security
   en sécurité ► secure
   ceinture de sécurité ► seatbelt
   marcher dans la rue en contrevenant à la sécurité routière ► jaywalk
sédiment ► sediment
séduction ► glamour
séduire ► court, lure
séduisant (-ante) ► attractive, glamourous [glamour]

segment ► segment
ségrégation ► segregation [segregate]
seigle ► rye
seigneur ► lord
sein ► breast
séisme ► earthquake
seize ► sixteen
seizième ► sixteenth [sixteen]
séjour ► stay, visit
    lieu de séjour ► resort
sel ► salt
sélect (-ecte) ► select
sélectif (-ive) ► select
sélection ► draft, pick[1], selection
sélectionné (-ée) ► select
sélectionner ► choose, draft, pick[1], select
selle ► saddle
seller ► saddle
selon ► according to, per
semaine ► week
    de la semaine ► weekly
    chaque semaine ► weekly
    jour de la semaine ► weekday
    fin de semaine ► weekend
semblable ► alike, fellow, like[2], similar, such
semblant ► show
    faire semblant ► fake, make believe, pretend, sham
sembler ► appear, look, seem, sound[1]
semelle ► sole[1], tread
semer ► seed, sow[1]
    semer des mines ► mine[2]
    semer la panique ► stampede
semestre ► semester
semi-conducteur ► semiconductor
sémillant (-ante) ► frisky
séminaire ► seminar, seminary
semoir ► drill
sempiternel (-elle) ► eternal
sempiternellement ► eternally [eternal]
sénat ► senate
sénateur (-trice) ► senator
sénatorial (-ale, -aux) ► senatorial [senator]
sénèque ► Seneca
sens ► heading, meaning, sense
    bon sens ► sense
    plein (pleine) de bon sens ► practical
    dénué (-ée) de sens ► meaningless [meaning]
    (sens du) toucher ► touch
    (sens du) goût ► taste
    sens de l'humour ► sense of humour
    avoir le sens des contacts ► relate
sensation ► feel, feeling, sensation, splash
    à sensation ► sensational
    sensation cuisante ► tingle

sensationnel (-elle) ► fabulous, gorgeous, grand, great, sensational, terrific, wonderful
sensé (-ée) ► sane, sensible
sensibilité ► feeling, sensitivity [sensitive], tenderness [tender[1]]
    avec sensibilité ► sensitively [sensitive]
sensible ► sensitive, sore, susceptible, tender[1]
    point sensible ► quick
sensoriel (-elle) ► sensory [sense]
sentence ► conviction, decision, sentence
senteur ► fragrance, odour, scent
sentier ► path, trail, walk
sentiment ► emotion, feeling, sense, sentiment
sentimental (-ale, -aux) ► emotional, sentimental
sentimentalement ► emotionally, sentimentally [sentimental]
sentinelle ► sentry
sentir ► feel, scent, sense, smell
    se sentir ► feel
    se sentir à l'aise ► at home
    se sentir mal ► down[1]
sépale ► sepal
séparation ► division, secession [secede], separation
séparé (-ée) ► separate
séparément ► separately [separate]
séparer ► detach, divide, divorce, part, segregate, separate
    se séparer ► part, secede, separate
sept ► seven
septembre ► September
septentrional (-ale, -aux) ► northern
septième ► seventh [seven]
sépulture ► grave[1]
séquelle ► sequel
séquence ► sequence
séquestrer ► guard
séquoia ► redwood, sequoia
serein (-eine) ► calm, serene
sereinement ► calmly [calm], serenely [serene]
sérénité ► calm
serf ► serf
sergent (-ente) ► sergeant
série ► chain, round, serial, series, streak
    de série ► serial
    en série ► serial, wholesale
    numéro de série ► serial number
    série de représentations ► run
sérieusement ► earnestly [earnest], gravely [grave[2]], hard, seriously [serious]
    très sérieusement ► deadly
sérieux ► gravity, seriousness [serious]
    avec sérieux ► responsibly [responsible]

sérieux (-euse) ► earnest, grave[2], important, serious, straight, strong
serment ► oath, promise
  sous serment ► under oath
  faire prêter serment (à) ► administer
sermon ► lecture, sermon, speech
serpent ► serpent, snake
  serpent à sonnette ► rattlesnake
  serpent inoffensif ► adder
serpenter ► ramble, snake, twine, twist, wind[2]
serre ► greenhouse, talon
serré (-ée) ► close[2], compact, snug, tight
serrer ► clamp, clasp, clench, clip[2], constrict, cramp, crowd, grip, hug, jam[1], pinch, wring
  serrer amoureusement ► cuddle
  sans serrer ► loosely [loose]
  se serrer ► clench
  se serrer les uns contre les autres ► huddle
sertisseur (-euse) ► setter
sérum ► serum
servant (-ante) ► servant
serviabilité ► helpfulness
serviable ► helpful
service ► department, favour, serve, service
  hors service ► out of commission
  service de table ► service
  service militaire ► service
  service public ► utility
  cuiller de service ► tablespoon
  note de service ► memo
  porte de service ► back
  assurer le service ► run
  être au service de ► attend
  rendre service ► oblige
serviette ► towel
  serviette de table ► napkin, serviette
servir ► dish, further, pour, serve, wait
  se servir ► help oneself
  servir de ► function
  se servir de ► use, utilize
  servir à la louche ► ladle
serviteur ► servant
session ► session
set ► set
setter ► setter
seuil ► doorstep, sill, threshold
  au seuil de ► verge
seul (seule) ► alone, lone, lonely, lonesome, mere, only, single, sole[2]
  tout seul ► alone, single-handed [single]
  tout seuls ► themselves
  toutes seules ► themselves
  un seul coup ► one fell swoop [swoop]
seulement ► but, merely, only, solely [sole[2]]
sève ► sap[1]

sévère ► critical, drastic, hard, harsh, severe, stern[1], strict
  très sévère ► extreme
sévèrement ► harshly [harsh], severely [severe], sternly [stern[1]], strictly [strict]
sévérité ► harshness [harsh], tightness [tight]
sevrage ► withdrawal
sexe ► sex
sexisme ► sexism
sexiste ► sexist [sexism]
sexuel (-elle) ► sexual [sex]
  rapport sexuel ► sex
shampooing ► shampoo
shérif ► sheriff
shilling ► shilling
short ► short, trunk
si ► if, such, that, this, whether
  comme si ► though
sida ► AIDS
sidéré (-ée) ► dumb
siècle ► century
siège ► bench, seat, siege
  siège social ► headquarters
siéger ► sit
le sien (la sienne) ► hers, his, its
sieste ► catnap
  faire une sieste ► nap
sifflement ► hiss, whistle, whiz
siffler ► hiss, hoot, whistle
  faire siffler ► swish
sifflet ► whistle
  coup de sifflet ► toot
  donner un coup de sifflet ► toot
sigle ► acronym
signal ► cue[1], signal
  (signal d') alarme ► alarm
signalement ► description
signaler ► mark, notify, signal, usher in (out) [usher]
signataire ► sign
signature ► signature
signe ► badge, character, characteristic, evidence, gesture, index, indicator [indicate], mark
  consentir d'un signe de tête ► nod
  donner des signes d'impatience ► fidget
signe ► sign, threat, token
  signe d'assentiment ► nod
  signe de la main ► wave
  signe de tête affirmatif ► nod
  langage des signes ► sign language
  faire signe ► motion
  faire signe de s'arrêter ► flag
signer ► autograph, initial, sign
signet ► mark
significatif (-ive) ► meaningful [meaning], significant

d'une manière significative ▶ significantly [significant]

signification ▶ meaning

sans signification ▶ meaningless [meaning]

silence ▶ silence

passer sous silence ▶ ignore

réduire au silence ▶ floor, silence

silencieux ▶ muffler [muffle]

silencieux (-euse) ▶ noiseless [noise], quiet, silent

silex ▶ flint

silhouette ▶ figure, outline, silhouette, skyline

silhouetter ▶ silhouette

silicone ▶ silicon

sillage ▶ wake³

dans le sillage de ▶ in the wake of [wake³]

sillonner ▶ rut, streak

silo ▶ bay⁵, silo

simili- ▶ mock

similitude ▶ like², similarity

simple ▶ easy, informal, mere, natural, plain, simple, single

simple exposition ▶ bald

simple soldat ▶ private

simples soldats ▶ rank¹

frapper un simple ▶ single out [single]

simplement ▶ merely, naturally, plainly [plain], simply

tout simplement ▶ simply

avec **simplicité ▶** simply

simplifier ▶ lighten², simplify

simulation ▶ simulation [simulate]

simuler ▶ affect², simulate

simultané (-ée) ▶ simultaneous

simultanément ▶ simultaneously [simultaneous]

sincère ▶ candid, earnest, genuine, hearty, honest, sincere, truthful

sincèrement ▶ earnestly [earnest], frankly [frank], genuinely [genuine], heartily [hearty], honestly [honest], outright, sincerely [sincere], truthfully [truthful]

sincérité ▶ heartiness [hearty], sincerity [sincere]

singe ▶ monkey

(grand) singe (sans queue) ▶ ape

singulier (-ière) ▶ curious, quaint, singular, weird

singulièrement ▶ curiously [curious]

sinistre ▶ disaster, eerie, grim, sinister

sinistrement ▶ eerily [eerie]

sinon ▶ but, or, otherwise

sinuer ▶ ramble

sinueux (-euse) ▶ winding

sinus ▶ sinus

sioux ▶ siouan [Sioux]

siphon ▶ siphon

siphonner ▶ siphon

sir ▶ sir

sirène ▶ siren

sirop ▶ syrup

faire du sirop d'érable ▶ sugar

sismographe ▶ seismograph

situation ▶ circumstance, condition, context, position, situation

situation difficile ▶ predicament

situation fâcheuse ▶ predicament

connaître la situation ▶ know the score

situé (-ée) ▶ situated

situer ▶ locate

six ▶ six

sixième ▶ sixth [six]

sketch ▶ sketch

ski ▶ ski

ski nautique ▶ water-ski

skier ▶ ski

skieur (-euse) ▶ skier

slalom ▶ slalom

slogan ▶ slogan

sloop ▶ sloop

smog ▶ smog

smoking ▶ tuxedo

snob ▶ snob, stuffy

snober ▶ lord

sobre ▶ sober

sobriquet ▶ nickname

soccer ▶ football, soccer

sociable ▶ outgoing, sociable

pas sociable ▶ antisocial

social (-ale, -aux) ▶ public, social

aide sociale ▶ welfare

siège social ▶ headquarters

socialement ▶ socially [social]

socialiser ▶ chum

socialisme ▶ socialism

socialiste ▶ socialist

société ▶ association, company, corporation, league¹, society

en société ▶ socially [social]

Société canadienne des postes ▶ post office

Société d'état ▶ Crown corporation

socque ▶ clog

soda ▶ pop¹, soda

sodium ▶ sodium

sœur ▶ nun, sister

sofa ▶ couch, sofa

soi-disant ▶ so-called

soie ▶ silk

de soie ▶ silk

en soie ▸ silk
ver à soie ▸ silkworm
soif ▸ thirst
avoir une soif de ▸ appetite
soigné (-ée) ▸ formal, neat, tidy, trim
peu soigné (-ée) ▸ unkempt
soigner ▸ groom, nurse, refine, treat
soigneusement ▸ carefully [careful], elaborately [elaborate], neatly [neat], tidily [tidy]
soigneux (-euse) ▸ careful
soi-même ▸ self
satisfait (-aite) de soi-même ▸ smug
porter (sur soi) ▸ carry
soin ▸ care, treatment
soins ▸ upkeep
avec soin ▸ tidily [tidy]
préposé (-ée) aux soins ▸ orderly
soin du visage ▸ facial
donner des soins à ▸ minister
manque de soins ▸ neglect
prendre soin ▸ mind
prendre soin de ▸ favour
soir ▸ evening
ce soir ▸ tonight
de soir ▸ nightly
du soir ▸ evening
soirée ▸ evening, party, social
de soirée ▸ formal
soirée dansante ▸ dance
soit ▸ either
soixante ▸ sixty
soixante-dix ▸ seventy
soixante-dixième ▸ seventieth [seventy]
soixantième ▸ sixtieth [sixty]
graine de **soja** ▸ soybean
sol ▸ earth, floor, ground[1], land, soil
clouer au sol ▸ transfix
faire le sol ▸ floor
plaquer (au sol) ▸ tackle
retenir au sol ▸ ground[1]
rouler au sol ▸ taxi
clé de **sol** ▸ clef
solaire ▸ solar
système solaire ▸ solar system
tache solaire ▸ sunspot
soldat ▸ soldier, warrior
soldat (de cavalerie) ▸ troop
soldat de deuxième classe ▸ private
simple soldat ▸ private
solde ▸ balance, sale
sans solde ▸ unpaid
soleil ▸ sun
coucher de soleil ▸ sunset
coup de soleil ▸ sunburn
lever du soleil ▸ sunrise
lumière du soleil ▸ sun, sunlight, sunshine

lunettes de soleil ▸ sunglasses
prendre un bain de soleil ▸ sun
solennel (-elle) ▸ grave[2], solemn
solennellement ▸ gravely [grave[2]], solemnly [solemn]
solide ▸ durable, fast[1], firm[1], hearty, rugged, secure, solid, sound[2], stout, strong, substantial, tight, tough
solidement ▸ fast[1], solidly [solid], tightly [tight]
solidité ▸ firmness [firm[1]], soundness [sound[2]], sturdiness [sturdy], toughness [tough]
solitaire ▸ lone, lonely, lonesome, recluse, solitaire, solitary
en solitaire ▸ solo
solitude ▸ loneliness [lonely]
solliciter ▸ court
solo ▸ solo
solstice ▸ solstice
soluble ▸ soluble
solution ▸ solution
sombre ▸ black, cloudy, dark, dingy, dismal, gloomy [gloom], murky, shadowy [shadow], sombre
sombrer ▸ sink
somme ▸ total
somme (d'argent) ▸ sum
somme globale ▸ grand
somme totale ▸ sum
sommeil ▸ sleep, slumber
en sommeil ▸ dormant
sans sommeil ▸ sleepless
sortir du sommeil ▸ wake[1]
tirer du sommeil ▸ wake[1]
sommeiller ▸ doze, nap, slumber, snooze
sommet ▸ apex, crest, crown, height, high, peak, summit, top[1]
somme toute ▸ altogether
somnolent (-ente) ▸ drowsy, sleepy
somptueux (-euse) ▸ gorgeous
son[1] ▸ beat, bran
tache de son ▸ freckle
taché (-ée) de son ▸ freckly, freckled [freckle]
son[2] ▸ noise, sound[1]
son de cloche ▸ toll[2]
son mat ▸ thud
rendre un son discordant ▸ jar
son (sa, ses) ▸ her, his, its
sonar ▸ sonar
sonate ▸ sonata
sondage ▸ poll, survey
sonde ▸ probe
sonder ▸ explore, poll, probe, sound[3]
songer ▸ brood, contemplate, muse

sonique ► sonic
sonner ► chime, ring[2], sound[1], strike, toll[2]
    faire sonner ► jingle
sonnerie ► peal, ring[2]
    sonnerie aux morts ► taps
sonnet ► sonnet
sonnette ► bell, doorbell
    serpent à sonnette ► rattlesnake
sonorité ► loudness [loud], tone
sophistiqué (-ée) ► sophisticated
soprano ► soprano
sorbet ► ice, sherbet
sorcellerie ► magic, witchcraft
sorcier ► medicine man
sorcier (-ière) ► magician, sorcerer, wizard
sorcière ► medicine woman, witch
sort ► doom, fate, spell[2]
    tirage au sort ► draw, lot
sortant (-ante) ► outgoing
sorte ► class, description, kind[2], manner, nature, sort, type
    faire en sorte que ► let
sortie ► exit
    données de sortie ► output
    sortie papier ► readout
sortilège ► spell[2]
sortir ► emerge, erupt, exit, fish, out, poke, release, smuggle
    sortir avec ► date[1]
    sortir (sans être vu) ► slip[1]
    sortir à flots ► stream
    sortir du sommeil ► wake[1]
    faire sortir ► bring out, manoeuvre, produce
    faire sortir discrètement ► spirit
    entrer/sortir avec grâce ► glide
    entrer/sortir avec douceur ► glide
sosie ► double
sot (sotte) ► fool
sottise ► folly, mischief, rubbish
    sottises ► nonsense
souche ► stump
    de souche ► native
souci[1] ► care, heed, trial, worry
souci[2] ► marigold
se soucier ► care
soucieux (-euse) ► anxious, concerned, mindful [mind]
soucoupe ► saucer
soudain (-aine) ► abrupt, flash, sudden
soudainement ► abruptly [abrupt], suddenly [sudden]
soudaineté ► suddenness [sudden]
souder ► solder, weld
    se souder ► knit
soudoyer ► bribe

soudure ► solder
souffle ► breath, puff, wind[1]
soufflé (-ée) ► blown
souffler ► blow out, blow up, blow[1], breathe, puff, storm
    souffler (une réplique) ► prompt
    souffler en rafales ► bluster
souffrance ► hardship, suffering
souffrant (-ante) ► ill
souffrir ► agonize, ail, suffer
    faire souffrir ► hurt, pain, trouble
soufre ► sulphur
souhait ► greeting, wish
    meilleurs souhaits ► best
souhaiter ► bid, desire, may, wish
    souhaiter la bienvenue ► welcome
souiller ► spot, stain, tarnish
soûl (soûle) ► drunk
se soûler ► drink
soulagement ► relief[1]
soulager ► ease, relieve
soulèvement ► upheaval, uprising
soulever ► arouse, boost, lift, offer, raise
    soulever avec un cric ► jack
    soulever un bord ► tip[2]
soulier ► shoe
souligner ► punctuate, underline, underscore
soumettre ► subdue, subject, submit
    se soumettre ► bow[2], comply, obey, submit
    soumettre à un chantage ► blackmail
    soumis (-ise) au hasard ► random
soumission ► bid
soumissionner ► tender[2]
soupçon ► doubt, hint, suggestion, suspicion
    un soupçon (de) ► dash, tinge, touch
soupçonner ► suspect
soupe ► soup
    cuillerée à soupe ► tablespoon
    cuiller à soupe ► tablespoon
    soupe au poisson ► chowder
    soupe aux fruits de mer ► chowder
souper ► dinner, supper
soupir ► rest[1], sigh
soupirer ► sigh
souple ► flexible, limber, resilient, springy [spring], supple
    disque souple ► floppy disk
source ► font[1], fountain, mine[2], origin, source, spring
sourcil ► brow, eyebrow
    froncer les sourcils ► frown, scowl
    arcade sourcilière ► brow
sourciller ► flinch
sourd (sourde) ► deaf, hollow
    émettre un bruit sourd ► thud

rendre sourd ► deafen
sourire ► smile
  sourire de mépris ► sneer
  sourire largement ► beam
souris ► mice, mouse
sournois (-oise) ► sly, sneaky [sneak], tricky, underhand
sournoisement ► slyly [sly]
sous[1] ► below, beneath, under, underneath
sous[2] ► penny
sous-bois ► underbrush
souscrire ► subscribe
sous-développé (-ée) ► underdeveloped
sous-entendu ► undertone
sous-estimer ► misjudge
sous-marin ► submarine
sous-marin (-ine) ► underwater
  plongée sous-marine ► skin diving
sous-produit ► by-product
sous-sol ► basement
sous-titre ► caption, heading
soustraction ► deduction, subtraction
soustraire ► deduct, exclude, subtract
  se soustraire ► escape
sous-vêtement ► underwear
soute ► hold[2]
soutenir ► back, bear[1], brace, cheer, contend, maintain, support, sustain, uphold
soutenu (-ue) ► constant
souterrain ► underground
souterrain (-aine) ► underground
  passage souterrain ► subway
soutien ► crutch, support
  de soutien ► remedial
essayer de **soutirer** ► pump
souvenir ► memento, memory, souvenir
  meilleurs souvenirs ► regard
  se souvenir ► recall, remember
souvent ► frequently, often, oftentimes [often]
souverain (-aine) ► sovereign
soyeux (-euse) ► silken [silk], soft
spacieux (-euse) ► roomy, spacious
spaghetti ► spaghetti
spasme ► spasm
spatule ► spatula
spécial (-ale, -aux) ► special
spécialement ► especially, specially [special]
se **spécialiser** ► specialize
spécialiste ► consultant, expert, specialist
spécialité ► special, specialty
spécification ► specification
spécimen ► specimen
spectacle ► entertainment, show, spectacle
  spectacle en matinée ► matinée
spectaculaire ► spectacular
spectateur (-trice) ► spectator, viewer

spectateurs ► audience
spectral (-ale, -aux) ► ghostly [ghost]
spectre ► ghost, phantom
  spectre lumineux ► spectrum
spéculateur (-trice) ► speculator [speculate]
spéculation ► speculation [speculate]
spéculer ► gamble, speculate
sperme ► sperm
spermophile ► gopher
sphère ► field, globe, sphere
sphérique ► spherical [sphere]
sphinx ► sphinx
spirale ► spiral
  tourner en spirale ► spiral
spirituel (-elle) ► spiritual, witty
spirituellement ► spiritually [spiritual]
spiritueux ► liquor, spirits [spirit]
splendeur ► glory, magnificence [magnificent]
splendide ► glorious, golden, gorgeous, grand, magnificent, marvellous, splendid
splendidement ► splendidly [splendid]
spongieux (-euse) ► spongy [sponge]
spontané (-ée) ► off-hand, spontaneous
spontanément ► spontaneously [spontaneous]
spore ► spore
sport ► casual, sport
  voiture de sport ► sports car
sportif (-ive) ► athletic
sprint ► dash, sprint
sprinter ► sprint
squatter ► squat
squamish ► Squamish
squash ► squash[1]
squelette ► skeleton
stabilité ► steadiness [steady]
stable ► stable[2], steady
stade ► bowl[1], stadium, stage
stagnant (-ante) ► slack, stagnant
stalactite ► stalactite
stalagmite ► stalagmite
stalle ► stall
stand ► booth, stall
  stand de tir ► range
standard ► standard
standardiste ► operator
standing ► status
stationnaire ► stationary
stationnement ► parking [park]
stationner ► park
station-service ► service station
statique ► static
statistique ► statistic [statistics]
  statistiques ► statistics
statue ► statue
statuer ► dispose, resolve

stature ► stature
statut ► status
stégosaure ► stegosaurus
stencil ► stencil
sténo ► shorthand
sténographie ► shorthand
steppe ► steppe
chaîne **stéréo** ► stereo
stéréotype ► stereotype
stéréotyper ► stereotype
stérile ► barren, sterile
stériliser ► sterilize
livre **sterling** ► sterling
stéthoscope ► stethoscope
steward ► steward
stigmate ► stigma
stimulant ► lift
stimulation ► stimulation [stimulate]
stimuler ► cheer, inspire, motivate, stimulate, whet
stimulus ► stimulus
stock ► stock
  en stock ► stock
  avoir en stock ► stock
stocker ► stock
stolon ► runner
store ► blind, shade
strangulation ► strangulation [strangle]
stratégie ► strategy, tactic
stratégique ► strategic [strategy]
stress ► stress
strict (-icte) ► rigid, strict
strictement ► strictly [strict]
strident (-ente) ► harsh
strophe ► cinquain, stanza, verse
structure ► constitution, framework, structure
structurer ► organize, structure
studieux (-euse) ► industrious, studious [study]
studio ► studio
stupéfaction ► amazement [amaze], daze
stupéfiant ► drug
stupéfier ► amaze, astound, daze, stagger
stupide ► ass, dumb, silly, stupid
stupidement ► senselessly [senseless], stupidly [stupid]
stupidité ► stupidity [stupid]
style ► diction, style, vein
stylo ► pen[1]
subalterne ► junior
subir ► experience, suffer, sustain, undergo
subit (-ite) ► flash, immediate, snap
subjuguer ► conquer, subdue
submerger ► flood, overwhelm, submerge
subordonné (-ée) ► subordinate
subordonner ► subordinate
subsistance ► sustenance [sustain]

subsister ► exist
substance ► meat, stuff, substance
  de substance ► substantial
  substance nutritive ► nutrient
substantiel (-elle) ► meaty [meat]
substituer ► substitute
substitution ► substitution [substitute]
subtil (-ile) ► subtle
subtilement ► subtly [subtle]
subtiliser ► palm[1]
subvenir (aux besoins de) ► provide, support
subvention ► grant
suc ► juice
succéder ► succeed
succès ► hit, success
  avec succès ► successfully [successful]
  couronné (-ée) de succès ► successful
  sans succès ► unsuccessful, unsuccessfully [unsuccessful]
successif (-ive) ► successive [succession]
succession ► estate, sequence
successivement ► successively [succession]
succinct (-incte) ► capsule
succion ► suction
succulent (-ente) ► savoury [savour], tasty
succursale ► branch
sucer ► suck
sucre ► sugar
  canne à sucre ► sugarcane
sucré (-ée) ► sweet
sucrer ► sugar, sweeten
sucrerie ► candy
  sucreries ► sweet
sud ► south, southern
  du sud ► south
  vers le sud ► southward
  sud-Est ► southeast
  du sud-est ► southeast, southeastern [southeast]
  sud-Ouest ► southwest
  du sud-ouest ► southwestern [southwest]
  vers le sud-ouest ► southwest
suède ► suede
suer ► sweat
sueur ► sweat
  de sueur ► sweaty [sweat]
  en sueur ► sweaty [sweat]
suffisamment ► adequately [adequate], ample, enough, sufficiently [sufficient]
suffisant (-ante) ► adequate, enough, smug, sufficient
  d'un air suffisant ► smugly [smug]
suffixe ► suffix
suffocation ► choke

suffoquer ► choke, gag, gasp, smother, suffocate

suffrage ► poll

suggérer ► bring up, counsel, imply, propose, suggest

suggestion ► counsel, cue, proposal, suggestion

suicide ► suicide

suicidé (-ée) ► suicide

se suicider ► commit suicide [suicide]

suie ► soot
    couvert (-erte) de suie ► sooty [soot]
    noir (noire) de suie ► sooty [soot]

suinter ► seep

suite ► consequence, escort, round, row[1], sequel, streak, succession, , string, suite
    par la suite ► afterward, subsequently [subsequent]
    tout de suite ► at once

suivant (-ante) ► next, subsequent

suivre ► abide, follow, tag[1], trail
    suivre de près ► dog, tail
    suivre furtivement ► stalk[2]
    suivre la piste de ► trace, track
    suivre les traces de quelqu'un ► follow in someone's footstep

sujet ► issue, matter, subject, theme, topic
    au sujet de ► about

sujet (-ette) à ► liable, prone, subject to [subject]

sulfurique ► sulphuric [sulphur]

sultan ► sultan

sumac ► sumac
    sumac vénéneux ► poison ivy

s'unir contre ► in league

super ► super

superbe ► magnificent, superb, stunning [stun]

superbement ► superbly [superb]

supercherie ► deceit, trick

superficialité ► superficially [superficial]

superficie ► area, extent

superficiel (-ielle) ► frivolous, shallow, superficial

superflu (-ue) ► unnecessary, useless, waste

supérieur (-ieure) ► head, executive, plus, senior, superior, top[1], upper

supériorité ► superiority

superlatif ► superlative

superlatif (-ive) ► superlative

supermarché ► grocery, supermarket

superstitieux (-euse) ► superstitious [superstition]

superstition ► superstition

superviseur (-euse) ► supervisor

suppléant (-ante) ► alternate, deputy, substitute

supplément ► extra[1], supplement
    en supplément ► additionally [additional]
    ajouter un supplément ► supplement

supplémentaire ► additional, extra[1], further, supplementary [supplement]
    heures supplémentaires ► overtime

supplice ► ordeal, torment, torture
    être au supplice ► agonize
    mettre au supplice ► torture

supplier ► beg, plead

support ► bracket, crutch, hanger, mount, prop, rack, rest[1], stand, support

supportable ► tolerable

supporter ► abide, bear[1], endure, put up with, root[3], stand, stomach, sustain, tolerate
    ne pas supporter ► allergic

supporteur (-trice) ► rooter [root[3]]

supposément ► supposedly [suppose]

supposer ► assume, expect, guess, imagine, presume, reckon, suppose
    laisser supposer ► imply

supposition ► assumption, guess, speculation [speculate]

suppression ► cancellation

supprimer ► cancel, delete, dock[2], eliminate, remove

suprême ► supreme, ultimate
    Court suprême ► Supreme Court

suprêmement ► supremely [supreme]

sur ► about, for, on, onto, upon
    sur quoi ► whereupon

sûr[1] (sûre) ► sour, tart[1]

sûr[2] (sûre) ► certain, confident, definite, dependable, fast[1], good, safe, secure, staunch, sure
    bien sûr ► naturally, of course
    peu sûr (sûre) ► unsound, unsure

surcharge ► overload

surcharger ► overload

surdoué (-ée) ► prodigy

sûrement ► certainly, doubtless, surely [sure], unmistakably [unmistakable]
    sûrement pas ► hardly, scarcely

suret (-ette) ► sour

sûreté ► security
    épingle de sûreté ► safety pin

surexciter ► keyed up

surf ► surfing
    planche de surf ► surfboard
    faire du surf ► surf, surfing

surface ► surface

surgir ► arise, emerge, spring, sprout

surhausser ► bank[2]

surir ► sour

sur-le-champ ► at once

surmonter ► bridge, conquer, master, overcome, weather

surnaturel (-elle) ▸ supernatural, the supernatural [supernatural]
surnom ▸ nickname
surnommer ▸ nickname
surpasser ▸ eclipse, surpass
surplomber ▸ project
surplus ▸ leftover, surplus
surprenant (-ante) ▸ incredible, quaint, unheard-of
surprendre ▸ astonish, catch, overtake, surprise
surprise ▸ astonishment [astonish], surprise
   faire une surprise ▸ spring
   prendre par surprise ▸ spring
sursaut ▸ jump, start
sursauter ▸ jump, start
   faire sursauter ▸ startle
sursis ▸ probation
surtout ▸ chiefly [chief], mostly [most]
surveillance ▸ care, observation
   de surveillance ▸ supervisory [supervisor]
surveillant (-ante) ▸ keeper
   surveillant (-ante) de baignade ▸ lifeguard
surveiller ▸ guard, mind, monitor, observe, supervise, watch
   surveiller avec vigilance ▸ watch
   surveiller de près ▸ watch
survenir ▸ arise
survie ▸ survival
survivant (-ante) ▸ survivor [survive]
survivre ▸ survive
   survivre à ▸ weather
en **sus** ▸ extra[1]
susceptible ▸ liable, susceptible, touchy
   susceptible de ▸ apt
susciter ▸ cause, provoke
   qui suscite de la fierté ▸ proud
suspect (-ecte) ▸ suspect, suspicious
   d'une manière suspecte ▸ suspiciously [suspicious]
suspendre ▸ call, dangle, hang, recess, suspend
   pont suspendu ▸ suspension bridge
suspense ▸ suspense
   en suspens ▸ in the balance, unsettled
   film à suspense ▸ thriller
suspension ▸ suspension [suspend]
   en suspension dans l'air ▸ airborne
suturer ▸ stitch
svelte ▸ slender, slim
sycomore ▸ sycamore
syllabe ▸ syllable
symbole ▸ symbol
symbolique ▸ symbolic [symbol], token
symboliquement ▸ symbolically [symbol]

symboliser ▸ symbolize
symétrie ▸ symmetry
symétrique ▸ symmetrical [symmetric]
sympathie ▸ sympathy
   en sympathie ▸ sympathetic
sympathique ▸ likable
sympathiquement ▸ sympathetically [sympathetic]
sympathiser ▸ sympathize
symphonie ▸ symphony
symptôme ▸ symptom
synagogue ▸ synagogue
syncope ▸ blackout
syndic ▸ trustee
syndicat ▸ union
syndrome cervical traumatique ▸ whiplash
synonyme ▸ synonym
   synonyme (de) ▸ synonymous
syntagme ▸ phrase
syntaxe ▸ syntax
synthétique ▸ synthetic
syntonisateur ▸ tuner
syntoniseur ▸ tuner
systématique ▸ routine, systematic [system]
systématiquement ▸ routinely [routine], systematically [system]
système ▸ system, tract
   système d'exploitation DOS ▸ DOS
   système ferroviaire ▸ railway
   système métrique ▸ metric system
   système nerveux ▸ nervous system
   système sanitaire ▸ sanitation
   système solaire ▸ solar system

T

tabac ▸ tobacco
tabasser ▸ hammer
table ▸ table
   table alphabétique ▸ index
   table ronde ▸ panel
   service de table ▸ service
   tennis de table ▸ table tennis
tableau (-eaux) ▸ blackboard, chart, painting, picture, scene, table
   tableau (-eaux) de bord ▸ panel
   tableau (-eaux) d'affichage ▸ bulletin board
   tableau (-eaux) de distribution ▸ switchboard
   tableau (-eaux) noir (s) ▸ blackboard
tablée ▸ table
tablette ▸ bar, tablet
   tablettes ▸ shelves
tablier ▸ apron

tabou ► taboo
tabouret ► stool
tache ► blot, patch, smudge, spot, stain
   petite tache ► speck
   tache de rousseur ► freckle
   tache de son ► freckle
   tache rouge ► rash[1]
   tache solaire ► sunspot
   plein de taches de rousseur ► freckly,
   freckled [freckle]
   couvert (-erte) de taches de rousseur
   ► freckle
tâche ► assignment, chore, concern, job, task
tacher ► blot, spot, stain
   taché (-ée) de sang ► bloody
   taché (-ée) de son ► freckly, freckled
   [freckle]
tâcher ► seek, try
tacheté (-ée) ► speckled [speck]
tacite ► unwritten
tacle ► tackle
tact ► tact
   avec tact ► tactfully [tact]
   plein (pleine) de tact ► diplomatic
   sans tact ► clumsy
tahltan ► Tahltan
taïga ► taiga
taillader ► chop, hack, slash
taille[1] ► fit[1], height, size
   être d'une taille ► size
taille[2] ► waist
tailler ► cut, hack, prune[2], trim
   tailler au couteau ► whittle
   tailler en pointe ► taper
tailleur ► suit, tailor
faire **taire** ► hush, silence
talent ► genius, gift, talent
   aux talents variés ► versatile
   dénicheur (-euse) de talents ► scout
   avoir le talent ► knack
talentueux (-euse) ► gifted, talented [talent]
taloche ► slap
talon ► heel
   coller aux talons ► tag[1]
   être sur les talons de ► heel
talonner ► heel
talure ► bruise
tamanoir ► aardvark, anteater
tambour ► drum
   tambour de basque ► tambourine
   tambour rotatif ► tumbler
   battre le tambour ► drum
tambourin ► drum, tambourine
tambouriner ► drum
tamia ► chipmunk
tamis ► sieve
tamiser ► sift

tampon ► buffer, stamp, wad
   accumulateur en tampon ► buffer
   état tampon ► buffer
   tampon métallique ► steel wool
   faire un tampon de ► wad
tamponner ► dab, postmark
tandis que ► whereas, while
tangible ► tangible
tangiblement ► tangibly [tangible]
tanguer ► pitch[1]
tanière ► den, hole, lair
tank ► tank
tanné (-ée) ► chocolate, leathery [leather]
tanner ► tan
en **tant que** ► as
tant soit peu ► remotely [remote]
tante ► aunt
tapage ► din, fuss, racket
tapageur (-euse) ► jazzy [jazz]
tape ► clap, rap[1], slap
   petite tape ► pat
   donner une tape ► clap
taper ► pound[2]
   taper sur ► punch[1]
   taper des mains ► clap
   taper du pied ► stamp
se **tapir** ► couch, crouch
tapis ► carpet, couch, mat, rug
   mettre sur le tapis ► bring up
   recouvrir d'un tapis ► carpet
coup de **tapette** ► swat
tapisser ► line[2], paper, wallpaper
tapisserie ► tapestry, wallpaper
tapoter ► pat, tap[1]
taquet ► stop
taquin (-ine) ► tease
taquiner ► pick on, tease
tard ► late
   plus tard ► beyond, subsequently
   [subsequent]
   remettre à plus tard ► postpone,
   procrastinate
tardif (-ive) ► tardy
tarentule ► tarantula
tarif douanier ► tariff
tarif(s) d'affranchissement ► postage
tarif(s) postal (-aux) ► postage
tartan ► plaid, tartan
tarte ► pie, tart[2]
   tarte au beurre ► butter tart
tartelette ► tart[2]
tartinade ► spread
tartre ► tartar
tas ► drift, heap, load, mound, mountain,
pile[1], stack
   mettre en tas ► lump
tasse ► cup

tassé (-ée) ▸ compact
tasser ▸ crush, jam[1], ram
tâter ▸ feel, handle
tâtonner ▸ fumble, grope
tatou ▸ armadillo
tatouage ▸ tattoo
tatouer ▸ tattoo
taupe ▸ mole[2]
taudis ▸ slum
taureau (-eaux) ▸ bull
taux ▸ rate
    taux de précipitations ▸ rainfall
    taux d'humidité ▸ humidex
taverne ▸ tavern
taxe ▸ duty, tax
    taxe sur les ventes ▸ sales tax
taxer ▸ tax
taxi ▸ cab, taxi
tchador ▸ chador
technicien (-ienne) ▸ engineer, technician
technique ▸ technical, technique, vocational [vocation]
    sur le plan technique ▸ technically [technical]
techniquement ▸ technically [technical]
technologie ▸ technology
technologique ▸ technological [technology]
teck ▸ teak
tee ▸ tee
tee-shirt ▸ T-shirt
teindre ▸ dye, stain, tint
teint ▸ complexion
teinte ▸ hue, tint
teinter ▸ tinge
teinture ▸ colour, dye
    teinture d'iode ▸ iodine
tel ▸ such
tel (telle) ▸ like[2], such
    tel (telle) que ▸ as, like[2], such as [such]
télécommande ▸ remote control
télécommunications ▸ telecommunications
télégramme ▸ telegram, wire
télégraphe ▸ telegraph
télégraphier ▸ telegraph, wire
téléphone ▸ phone, telephone
    coup de téléphone ▸ ring[2]
    téléphone arabe ▸ grapevine
téléphoner ▸ call, phone, ring[2], telephone
téléphoniste ▸ operator
télescope ▸ telescope
téléspectateur (-trice) ▸ viewer
téléviser ▸ televise
téléviseur ▸ monitor, set, television
télévision ▸ television
    émission de télévision ▸ telecast
    télévision par câble ▸ cable television
    poste de télévision ▸ television

    programme télévisé ▸ television
tellement ▸ so, such, vitally [vital]
    pas tellement ▸ none
témoignage ▸ monument, testimony
témoigner ▸ testify
témoin ▸ model, witness
    témoin oculaire ▸ eyewitness
    être témoin ▸ witness
tempe ▸ temple[2]
tempérament ▸ character, disposition, nature, temper, temperament
    d'un tempérament ▸ temperamental
température ▸ climate, temperature, weather
tempéré (-ée) ▸ mild, moderate, temperate
tempérer ▸ temper
tempête ▸ storm, tempest, thunder
    tempête de neige ▸ blizzard
tempêter ▸ bluster
temple ▸ church, temple[1]
tempo ▸ tempo
temporaire ▸ temporary
    salle de classe temporaire ▸ portable
temporairement ▸ temporarily [temporary]
temporiser ▸ procrastinate
temps ▸ beat, day, season, tense[2], time, weather
    à temps ▸ schedule
    de temps à autre ▸ off and on, once in a while
    de temps en temps ▸ occasional, once in a while
    en ce temps-là ▸ then
    en même temps ▸ at once
    juste à temps ▸ in the nick of time
    pendant ce temps ▸ meantime, meanwhile
    quelque temps ▸ while
    temps légal ▸ standard time
    temps libre ▸ room
    emploi du temps ▸ timetable
    courte période de temps froid ▸ snap
    consacrer du temps ▸ put in
    garder (perdre) la notion du temps ▸ keep (lose) track of
    investir du temps ▸ put in
    passer du temps ▸ put in
    passer le temps ▸ occupy
    perdre son temps ▸ mess about or mess around
    prendre du bon temps ▸ enjoy oneself
tenace ▸ persistent [persist], resilient, tenacious
ténacité ▸ persistence [persist]
    avec ténacité ▸ tenaciously [tenacious]
tenailler ▸ rack
tendance ▸ current, tendency, trend

tendance à ▸ streak
    avoir tendance ▸ apt, incline, tend[1]
tendon ▸ tendon
tendre[1] ▸ fond, soft
tendre[2] ▸ contract, extend, keyed up, strain[1], string, tender[1], tighten
    (se) tendre ▸ tense[1]
    tendre le bras ▸ reach
    tendre le bras pour prendre ▸ reach
    tendre une embuscade ▸ ambush
tendrement ▸ dearly [dear], fondly [fond], tenderly [tender[1]]
tendresse ▸ fondness [fond], tenderness [tender[1]]
tendreté ▸ tenderness [tender[1]]
tendu (-ue) ▸ nervous, taut, tense[1]
    (bien) tendu (-ue) ▸ taut
    d'une manière tendue ▸ tensely [tense[1]]
ténèbres ▸ gloom
ténébreux (-euse) ▸ gloomy [gloom]
tenir ▸ handle, hold[1], keep
    tenir à ▸ treasure
    tenir pour ▸ consider
    tenir au courant ▸ post[2]
    tenir compte de ▸ allow for [allow], heed
    tenir en équilibre ▸ poise
    tenir en grande estime ▸ regard
    tenir le compte ▸ tally
tennis ▸ tennis
    tennis de table ▸ table tennis
ténor ▸ tenor
tension ▸ stress, tension, voltage
    tension artérielle ▸ blood pressure
    sous tension ▸ live[2]
tentacule ▸ tentacle
tentant (-ante) ▸ invite
tentation ▸ temptation
tentative ▸ attempt, bid, try, venture
tente ▸ tent
tenter ▸ attempt, endeavour, stab, try
    tenter de comprendre ▸ puzzle
    tenter de résoudre ▸ puzzle
tenture ▸ drape
tenu (-ue) ▸ liable
tenue ▸ dress, habit, outfit, wear
tercet ▸ triplet
térébenthine ▸ turpentine
tergiverser ▸ procrastinate
terme[1] ▸ conclusion
    avant terme ▸ premature
    arriver à terme ▸ terminate
terme[2] ▸ term, wording
    termes ▸ terms [term]
    terme à la mode ▸ buzzword
terminaison ▸ termination [terminate]
terminal (-ale, -aux) ▸ terminal
terminé (-ée) ▸ complete, through

terminer ▸ close[1], complement, complete, conclude, do, end, finish, wind[2]
    se terminer ▸ break up
terminus ▸ terminal
termite ▸ termite
terne ▸ colourless, dingy, drab, dull, flat[1], tame
ternir ▸ stain, tarnish
ternissure ▸ tarnish
terrain ▸ course, court, field, ground[1], land, lot, plot, terrain
    terrain communal ▸ common
    terrain de jeu ▸ playground
    terrain vague ▸ wasteland
    occuper un terrain illégalement ▸ squat
    préparer le terrain ▸ pave the way
terrarium ▸ terrarium
terrasse ▸ deck, stoop[2], terrace
    en terrasses ▸ terraced [terrace]
terrasser ▸ floor
terre ▸ dirt, earth, estate, globe, ground[1], land, property, shore, soil, topsoil
    Terre ▸ earth, world
    à terre ▸ ashore
    sous (la) terre ▸ underground
    terre boisée ▸ timber
    Terre de la couronne ▸ Crown land
    terre natale ▸ home, homeland
    pointe de terre ▸ spit[2]
    pomme de terre ▸ potato
    pomme de terre frite ▸ french fry
    tremblement de terre ▸ earthquake
    ver de terre ▸ earthworm
    amener à terre ▸ land
terreau (-eaux) ▸ humus
terrestre ▸ worldly
    globe terrestre ▸ globe
terreur ▸ dread, horror, terror
    rendre fou de terreur ▸ terrify
se terrer ▸ burrow
terrible ▸ awful, dread, dreaded, foul, mean[2], terrible
terriblement ▸ awfully, dreadfully [dreadful], terribly, terrifically [terrific]
terrier ▸ burrow, hole, lodge, terrier
terrifiant (-ante) ▸ creepy [creep], scary, terrific
terrifier ▸ terrify
territoire ▸ dominion, territory
territorial (-ale, -aux) ▸ territorial
terroriser ▸ terrorize
terrorisme ▸ terrorism
terroriste ▸ bomber
tertre ▸ knoll
test ▸ test
    petit test ▸ quiz
testament ▸ will[2]
tétanos ▸ tetanus

têtard ▸ tadpole
tête ▸ face, head, lead[1]
   (en) tête ▸ top[1]
   au-dessus de la tête ▸ overhead
   mal (maux) de tête ▸ headache
   consentir d'un signe de tête ▸ nod
   être à la tête ▸ head
   faire une tête ▸ head
   hocher la tête ▸ nod
   incliner la tête ▸ bow[2], nod
   plonger la tête dans l'eau ▸ duck[2]
   renvoyer d'un coup de tête ▸ head
   se creuser la tête ▸ rack one's brain
téter ▸ suck
têtu (-ue) ▸ mulish [mule], stubborn, willful
texte ▸ line[1], script, text
   traitement de texte ▸ word processing
textile ▸ textile
texture ▸ texture
thé ▸ tea
   cuiller à thé ▸ teaspoon
   cuillerée à thé ▸ teaspoon
théâtral (-ale, aux) ▸ theatrical
théâtre ▸ drama, stage, theatre
   coup de théâtre ▸ twist
   pièce de théâtre ▸ drama
théière ▸ pot, teapot
thème ▸ theme, topic
théologie ▸ theology
théologique ▸ theological [theology]
théorie ▸ theory
   élaborer une théorie ▸ theorize
théorique ▸ theoretical
théoriquement ▸ theoretically [theoretical]
thérapie ▸ therapy
thermique ▸ thermal
thermomètre ▸ thermometer
thermos ▸ thermos
thermostat ▸ thermostat
thésaurus ▸ thesaurus
thèse ▸ thesis
thon ▸ tuna
Thora ▸ Torah
thorax ▸ thorax
thym ▸ thyme
thyroïde ▸ thyroid
devant du **tibia** ▸ shin
tic ▸ twitch
tic-tac ▸ tick[1]
tictaquer ▸ tick[1]
tiède ▸ lukewarm
le **tien (la tienne, les tiens, les tiennes)** ▸ yours
tiers ▸ third
tige ▸ rod, stalk[1], stem[1]
tignasse ▸ shock[2]
tigre (tigresse) ▸ tiger

tigre préhistorique ▸ sabre-toothed tiger
timbre[1] ▸ bell, timbre, tone
timbre[2] ▸ stamp
timbrer ▸ stamp
timide ▸ bashful, shy, timid
   qui fait le ou la timide ▸ coy
timidement ▸ bashfully [bashful], shyly [shy], timidly [timid]
timidité ▸ shyness [shy], timidity [timid]
timoré (-ée) ▸ timid
tintement ▸ jingle, tinkle
tinter ▸ tinkle
   faire tinter ▸ jingle
tintinnabuler ▸ tinkle
tipi ▸ teepee
tique ▸ tick[2]
tir ▸ shot[1]
   champ de tir ▸ range
   tir de barrage ▸ barrage
   polygone de tir ▸ range
   stand de tir ▸ range
tirage ▸ circulation, drawing, edition
   tirage au sort ▸ draw, lot
tirailler ▸ tear[1]
tire d'érable ▸ taffy
tiré (-ée) par les cheveux ▸ far-fetched
tirebouchonner ▸ twist
tirer ▸ drag, draw, extract, fire, fish, haul, lug, pinch, pluck, pull, shoot
   tirer de ▸ derive
   tirer (sur) ▸ tug
   tirer à sa fin ▸ wind[2]
   tirer brusquement ▸ jerk
   tirer violemment ▸ wrench
   s'en tirer ▸ cope
tiret ▸ dash
tireur (-euse) ▸ shot[1]
   tireur (-euse) embusqué (-ée) ▸ sniper
tiroir ▸ drawer
   tiroir-caisse ▸ till[3]
tisane ▸ tea
tisonnier ▸ poker[1]
tissage ▸ weave
tisser ▸ spin, weave
   métier à tisser ▸ loom[1]
tissu ▹ cloth, fabric, material, tissue, web
   tissu écossais ▸ plaid
titre ▸ dignity, stock, title
   (gros) titre ▸ headline
   (grand) titre ▸ headline
   à titre de ▸ capacity
   à titre gracieux ▸ complimentary
   à titre d'exemple ▸ illustration
   à titre d'essai ▸ tentatively [tentative]
   à juste titre ▸ rightly [right]
tituber ▸ reel[2], stagger, totter
titulaire ▸ holder

toast ▸ toast[1], toast[2]
toboggan ▸ slide, toboggan
   faire du toboggan ▸ toboggan
toge ▸ gown, robe
toi ▸ you
toile ▸ canvas, cloth, web
   toile d'araignée ▸ cobweb
   toile d'emballage ▸ burlap
   toile goudronnée ▸ tarpaulin
   toile Internet ▸ World Wide Web
toilette ▸ wear
   faire la toilette ▸ groom
toilettes ▸ toilet
toi-même ▸ yourself
toiser ▸ eye
toison ▸ coat
toit ▸ roof
tôle ▸ sheet
tolérable ▸ tolerable
tolérance ▸ tolerance
tolérant (-ante) ▸ liberal, tolerant, understanding
   d'une manière tolérante ▸ tolerantly [tolerant]
tolérer ▸ endure, put up with, tolerate
tomahawk ▸ tomahawk
tomate ▸ tomato
tombe ▸ grave[1], tomb
tombé (-ée) ▸ fallen
tombeau (-eaux) ▸ tomb
tomber ▸ cave, droop, fall, run, sift, spill, topple, tumble
   tomber à pic ▸ plummet
   tomber en panne ▸ break down, crash, fail
   tomber goutte à goutte ▸ dribble
   tomber juste ▸ hit the nail on the head
   tomber sur ▸ chance upon [chance], descend, meet
   tomber sur par hasard ▸ stumble
   laisser tomber ▸ drop, drop out, forget, scrap, sell out
   tomber doucement ▸ sift
tombola ▸ raffle
ton ▸ key[1], pitch[1], shade, tone
   en-dessous du ton ▸ flat[1]
   ton catégorique ▸ decisively [decisive], decisiveness [decisive]
   ton décidé ▸ decisively [decisive]
   d'un air ou d'un ton menaçant ▸ menacingly [menace]
   d'un ton acerbe ▸ crisply [crisp]
   d'un ton tranchant ▸ crisply [crisp]
   donner le ton ▸ pitch[1]
ton (ta, tes) ▸ your
tonalité ▸ tone
   sans tonalité ▸ dead

tondeuse ▸ clipper, mower [mow]
   tondeuse à gazon ▸ lawnmower
tondre ▸ clip[1], mow, shear
tonique ▸ tonic
tonitruant (-ante) ▸ thunderous [thunder]
tonne ▸ ton, tonne
tonneau (-eaux) ▸ barrel
tonnelet ▸ drum
tonner ▸ boom[1], thunder
tonnerre ▸ thunder
   coup de tonnerre ▸ thunderbolt
topaze ▸ topaz
topographie ▸ topography
topographique ▸ topographical [topography]
Tora ▸ Torah
torche ▸ torch
torchon ▸ towel
tordant (-ante) ▸ hilarious, hysterical
tordre ▸ bend, twist, wring
   se tordre ▸ squirm, writhe
tordu (-ue) ▸ crooked
tornade ▸ tornado, whirlwind
toron ▸ strand[2]
torpille ▸ torpedo
torpiller ▸ torpedo
torrent ▸ flood, storm, torrent
   pleuvoir à torrents ▸ pour
torrentiel (-ielle) ▸ torrential [torrent]
torsade ▸ rope
torse ▸ torso
torsion ▸ twist
tort ▸ blame, harm, mischief, wrong
   à tort ▸ falsely [false]
   en tort ▸ at fault
   avouer ses torts ▸ back down
   faire tort à ▸ wrong
   faire du tort à ▸ harm
tortiller ▸ twirl
   se tortiller ▸ squirm, wriggle
tortillon ▸ twist
tortue ▸ tortoise
   tortue de mer ▸ turtle
tortueux (-euse) ▸ crooked, winding
torture ▸ torture
torturer ▸ rack, torment, torture
tôt ▸ early, soon
total (-aux) ▸ total
total (-ale, -aux) ▸ global [globe], outright, total, utter[2]
   somme totale ▸ sum
totalement ▸ totally, utterly [utter[2]]
totaliser ▸ total
totalitaire ▸ totalitarian
totem ▸ totem
toucan ▸ toucan
touche ▸ key[1], note

mettre la touche finale ▸ finish
touché ▸ touchdown
touche-à-tout ▸ meddler [meddle]
toucher ▸ affect[1], border, concern, contact, draw, feel, finger, handle, hit, tag[2], tamper, touch
touffe ▸ clump, tuft
touffu (-ue) ▸ bushy, thick
toujours ▸ always, ever, forever
toundra ▸ tundra
toupet ▸ nerve
toupie ▸ top[2]
tour[1] ▸ castle, rook[2], tower
tour[2] ▸ hoax, joke, prank, trick
  mauvais tour ▸ mischief
tour[3] ▸ lathe
tour[4] ▸ drive, move, ride, rotation, run, spin, turn, twist
  chacun son tour ▸ alternate
  faire un tour ▸ ride
  faire le tour ▸ border, travel
  faire tour à tour ▸ rotate
  tour (de piste) ▸ lap[2]
  tour à tour ▸ alternately
  tour de forage ▸ derrick
  tour de main ▸ knack
  tour de manège ▸ ride
  tour de montagnes russes ▸ ride
tourbe ▸ sod, turf
tourbière ▸ muskeg
tourbillon ▸ hustle, swirl, whirl, whirlpool
tourbillonner ▸ reel[2], whirl
  faire tourbillonner ▸ swirl
tourelle ▸ turret
touriste ▸ tourist
attraction **touristique** ▸ sight
tourment ▸ torment, torture
tourmenter ▸ badger, bait, harass, pest, plague, rack, tantalize, torment, torture
tournant ▸ bend, corner, curve, turn, twist
  grand tournant ▸ watershed
tournée ▸ round, run
  être en tournée ▸ tour
tourner ▸ reel[2], revolve, rotate, round, shoot, spin, stir, swim, turn, veer, wheel
  (se) tourner ▸ turn
  tourner au ralenti ▸ idle
  tourner autour ▸ circle
  tourner de l'œil ▸ keel
  tourner d'une pichenette ▸ flip
  tourner en rond ▸ mill
  tourner en spirale ▸ spiral
  tourner sur place ▸ mill
tournesol ▸ sunflower
tourniquet ▸ tourniquet, turnstile
tournoi ▸ tournament
tournoiement ▸ spin

tournoyer ▸ reel[2], twirl, whirl
tournure ▸ idiom, twist
tourte ▸ pie
tousser ▸ cough, hack
tout[1] ▸ all, everything, whole
  après tout ▸ after all
  du tout ▸ any, at all
  dans tout ▸ throughout
  tout ce que ▸ whatever
  tout de même ▸ surely [sure]
  tout de suite ▸ at once
  tout d'un coup ▸ flash
  tout le monde ▸ everybody, everyone
tout[2] ▸ all
  tout au long de ▸ long[1]
  tout droit ▸ due
  tout haut ▸ aloud
  tout juste ▸ hardly
  tout le long (de) ▸ through
  tout simplement ▸ simply
tout (toute, tous, toutes) ▸ all, entire, every
  à tous (toutes) les ▸ every other
  tout entier ▸ whole
  tout seul ▸ alone, single-handed [single]
  tout seuls ▸ themselves
  toutes seules ▸ themselves
  toutes les fois que ▸ whenever
  tout le monde ▸ everybody, everyone
tout à fait ▸ quite
toutefois ▸ however
tout-puissant (toute-puissante) ▸ almighty
toux ▸ cough
  toux aspirante ▸ whooping cough
  toux coquelucheuse ▸ whooping cough
toxicomane ▸ addict
toxine ▸ toxin
toxique ▸ poisonous [poison], toxic
tracas ▸ care, worry
tracasser ▸ ail, harass
  se tracasser ▸ fret
trace ▸ impression, print, suggestion, trace, track, wake[3]
  traces ▸ trail
  laisser des traces ▸ track
  marcher sur les traces de ▸ in the wake of [wake[3]]
  suivre les traces de quelqu'un ▸ follow in someone's footstep
tracer ▸ draw, map out, plot
  tracer des ornières ▸ rut
tracer un arc ▸ arc
trachée ▸ trachea, windpipe
tract ▸ leaflet
tracteur ▸ tractor
  tracteur à chenilles ▸ caterpillar
traction ▸ traction, tug
  exercice de traction ▸ push up

faire des tractions à la barre fixe ▸ chin

tradition ▸ tradition

traditionnel (-elle) ▸ conservative, old-fashioned, orthodox, traditional

traditionnellement ▸ traditionally [traditional]

traduction ▸ translation, version

traduire ▸ decode, interpret, translate

trafic ▸ racket, traffic

trafiquer ▸ traffic

tragédie ▸ tragedy

tragique ▸ tragic

tragiquement ▸ tragically [tragic]

trahir ▸ betray, sell out

trahison ▸ treason

train ▸ gear, train, wagon
à fond de train ▸ full tilt [tilt]
aller bon train ▸ roll
chef de train ▸ conductor

traînard (-arde) ▸ straggler [straggle]

traîne ▸ train
traîne sauvage ▸ toboggan

traîneau (-eaux) ▸ coaster, sled, sleigh
chien de traîneau ▸ husky[2]
traîneau à chiens ▸ dogsled
aller en traîneau ▸ sled

traînée ▸ smudge, streak, trail

traînement (de pieds) ▸ shuffle

traîner ▸ drag, draw, haul, linger, loaf[2], lug, pull
traîner derrière ▸ lag
traîner en arrière ▸ straggle
se traîner ▸ crawl, trudge

traire ▸ milk

trait ▸ characteristic, feature, trait
de trait ▸ draft
trait d'esprit ▸ quip

trait d'union ▸ hyphen

traité ▸ treaty

traitement ▸ salary, treatment
mauvais traitement ▸ punishment
traitement de texte ▸ word processing

traiter ▸ cover, cure, process, treat
traiter de ▸ deal
traiter à la légère ▸ trifle
traiter avec rudesse ▸ rough
traiter injustement ▸ wrong
traiter sans considération ▸ slight

traiteur (-euse) ▸ processor, treacherous

traître (-esse) ▸ traitor

traîtreusement ▸ treacherously [treacherous]

trajet ▸ circuit, drive, haul, journey, route
trajet dans la voiture de quelqu'un ▸ lift

tramer ▸ devise, hatch[1]

trampoline ▸ trampoline

tramway ▸ streetcar, trolley
voiture (de tramway) ▸ car

tranchant ▸ edge
manque de tranchant ▸ bluntness [blunt]

tranchant (-ante) ▸ crisp, cutting, keen
d'un ton tranchant ▸ crisply [crisp]

tranche ▸ bracket, chapter, slice, steak
petite tranche ▸ sliver
en tranches épaisses ▸ thick
en fines tranches ▸ thin
couper en tranches ▸ slice

tranchée ▸ trench

trancher ▸ contrast, decide, section, sever

tranquille ▸ calm, easy, leisurely [leisure], peaceful, quiet, still, tranquil

tranquillement ▸ calmly [calm], easily, peacefully [peaceful], quietly [quiet], tranquilly [tranquil]

tranquillisant ▸ tranquillizer

tranquilliser ▸ calm, ease, quiet, soothe, still

tranquillité ▸ calm, ease, quiet, still, stillness [still], tranquillity [tranquil]

transaction ▸ compromise
faire des transactions bancaires ▸ bank[1]

transcontinental (-ale, -aux) ▸ transcontinental

transcrire ▸ transcribe

transe ▸ trance
état de transe ▸ trance

transférer ▸ transfer

transfert ▸ transfer

transformer ▸ alter, change, convert, morph, transform
transformer par morphing ▸ morph

transfusion ▸ transfusion

transgresser ▸ invade, violate

transiger ▸ compromise

transistor ▸ transistor

transit ▸ transit

transition ▸ transition

translucide ▸ translucent

transmetteur ▸ transmitter

transmettre ▸ along, bequeath, convey, infect, relay, transmit
se transmettre entre générations ▸ run

transmissible ▸ contagious

transmission ▸ transmission

transparent (-ente) ▸ clear, sheer, transparent
de manière transparente ▸ transparently [transparent]

transpercer ▸ pierce, spear

transpiration ▸ sweat

transpirer ▸ sweat

transplantation ▸ transplant

transplanter ► transplant
transport ► freight, transit, transport, transportation
transportable ► mobile
transporter ► carry, convey, entrance[2], ferry, haul, thrill, transport
   (faire) transporter par camion ► truck
   transporter par tuyau ► pipe
transporteur ► carrier
trapèze ► trapeze, trapezoid
trappe ► hatch[2], trap door
trappeur (-euse) ► trapper
trapu (-ue) ► squat, stocky
traquer ► hound, stalk[2]
traumatique ► trauma
   syndrome cervical traumatique ► whiplash
traumatisant (-ante) ► trauma
traumatisme ► trauma
travail ► chore, job, labour, pursuit, work
   aire de travail ► galley
   cabinet de travail ► den
   dur travail ► toil
   Fête du travail ► Labour day
   faire du travail au noir ► moonlight
   s'appliquer (au travail) ► buckle
   s'atteler au travail ► pitch in
   se vider au travail ► agonize
   travail social ► social work
   travaux ménagers ► housework
travailler ► knead, labour, prey, tool, work
   travailler au noir ► moonlight
   travailler dur ► toil
   travailler fort ► buckle down
   travailler laborieusement ► wade
travailleur (-euse) ► industrious, labour, worker
travée ► bay[5], span
traverse ► rail
à travers ► through
   passer à travers ► wade
   de travers ► amiss, lopsided
   mise en travers ► jack-knife
traverse ► tie
traversée ► crossing, passage, voyage
traverser ► cross, cut, negotiate, span, traverse, voyage
   traverser en trombe ► zoom
   traverser à la nage ► swim
traversier ► ferry
trébucher ► stumble, trip
trèfle ► clover, club, shamrock
treillis ► trellis
treize ► thirteen
treizième ► thirteenth [thirteen]
tremblant (-ante) ► shaky, wobbly [wobble]
   en tremblant ► shakily [shaky]

tremble ► aspen
tremblement ► quake, tremor
   tremblement de terre ► earthquake
trembler ► jar, quake, shake, tremble, wobble
trembloter ► quaver
trempe ► temper
trempé (-ée) ► soggy, wet
tremper ► dip, drench, soak, temper
   faire tremper ► soak, steep[2]
trempette ► dip
tremplin ► springboard
trépidant (-ante) ► hectic
trépied ► tripod
très ► dead, highly, real, terribly, very
trésor ► jewel, treasure
   le Trésor ► Treasury
trésorerie ► treasury
trésorier (-ière) ► treasurer
tressaillir ► flinch, wince
tressauter ► jolt, jump
tresse ► braid
tresser ► braid
tréteau (-eaux) ► horse, trestle
treuil ► hoist, winch
trêve ► truce
triangle ► triangle
triangulaire ► triangular
tribal (-ale, aux) ► tribal
tribord ► starboard
tribu ► clan, tribe
tribunal (-aux) ► court
tribune ► forum, stand
tribut ► tribute
tributaire ► dependent
tricher ► cheat, trick
tricherie ► deceit
tricheur (-euse) ► cheater
tricot ► sweater
tricoter ► knit
   aiguille à tricoter ► needle
tricycle ► tricycle
trier ► sort, weed
trigonométrie ► trigonometry
trilogie ► trilogy
trimballer ► tote
trimer ► slave
trimestre ► quarter
trimestriel (-ielle) ► quarterly
tringle ► rod
trio ► trio
triomphal (-ale, -aux) ► triumphant
triomphalement ► triumphantly [triumphant]
triomphant (-ante) ► triumphant
triomphe ► feat, triumph
   cri de triomphe ► crow[2]
triompher ► overcome, triumph

tripes ▸ tripe
triple ▸ triple
tripler ▸ triple
triplés (-ées) ▸ triplet
tripoter ▸ fiddle, paw, toy
triste ▸ bleak, dark, gloomy [gloom], melancholy, miserable, mournful [mourn], sad, sorry, unhappy
    très triste ▸ woeful [woe]
tristement ▸ bleakly [bleak], mournfully [mourn], sadly [sad], sorrowfully [sorrow], woefully [woe]
    tristement célèbre ▸ notorious
tristesse ▸ gloom, sadness [sad], sorrow, unhappiness [unhappy]
    avec tristesse ▸ wistfully [wistful]
    extrême tristesse ▸ wretchedness [wretched]
triton ▸ newt
troc ▸ barter, swap
trognon ▸ core
trois ▸ three
troisième ▸ third
troll ▸ troll[2]
trolley ▸ trolley
passer en **trombe** ▸ rocket
    traverser en trombe ▸ zoom
trombone ▸ clip[2], trombone
trompe ▸ trunk
tromper ▸ cheat, deceive, dupe, fool, fox, trick
    se tromper ▸ mistake
tromperie ▸ deceit, fraud
trompeter ▸ trumpet
trompette ▸ trumpet
trompeur (-euse) ▸ deceptive, hollow
trompeusement ▸ deceptively [deceptive]
tronc ▸ trunk
tronçonner ▸ log
trône ▸ throne
trop ▸ too
    en trop ▸ spare
trophée ▸ trophy
tropical (-ale, aux) ▸ tropical
tropiques ▸ tropics
troquer ▸ barter
trot ▸ trot
trotter ▸ trot
trotteuse ▸ walker
trottiner ▸ scamper
trottoir ▸ sidewalk
    du trottoir ▸ curb
trou ▸ blowhole, bore[2], cavity, eye, gap, hole, pit[1], room
    trou noir ▸ black hole
trouble ▸ cloudy, commotion, confusion, disorder, flutter, murky, turmoil
troubler ▸ agitate, ail, blur, disturb, fluster, haunt, trouble

trouée ▸ gap
trouer ▸ pit[1]
troupe ▸ chorus, company, gang, horde, swarm, troupe
    hommes de troupe ▸ rank[1]
troupeau (-eaux) ▸ drove[2], flock, herd
    gardien (-ienne) de troupeau (-eaux) ▸ herd
    rassembler en troupeau ▸ herd
troupes ▸ troop
trousse ▸ kit
    aux trousses ▸ hot
trousseau (-eaux) ▸ bunch
trouvaille ▸ find, gimmick
trouver ▸ come across, derive, discover, find, hit, strike
    se trouver ▸ lie[1], occur, stand
    trouver accès à ▸ admission
    trouver par hasard ▸ happen
truc ▸ device, dodge, gadget, gimmick, thing
    trucs ▸ stuff
truie ▸ sow[1]
truite ▸ trout
    poisson arctique de la famille des truites ▸ Arctic char
truquer ▸ fake
trust ▸ trust
tsigane ▸ Gypsy
tslmshlan ▸ Tslmshlan
tu ▸ you
tuba ▸ snorkel, tuba
tube ▸ tube
tuberculose ▸ tuberculosis
tuer ▸ gun, kill, slay
tuerie ▸ massacre
tueur (-euse) ▸ killer
tuile ▸ tile
tulipe ▸ tulip
tumeur ▸ tumour
tumulte ▸ clamour, commotion, tumult, uproar
tumultueux (-euse) ▸ tumultuous [tumult]
tunique ▸ robe, tunic
tunnel ▸ tunnel, underground
tuque ▸ tuque
turban ▸ turban
turbine ▸ turbine
turbulent (-ente) ▸ turbulent
turf ▸ turf
turquoise ▸ turquoise
tuscarora ▸ Tuscarora
tuteur (-trice) ▸ guardian
tuyau (-aux) ▸ hose, pipe, pointer, tube, vent
    tuyau (-aux) d'échappement ▸ exhaust pipe(s)
    tuyau (-aux) d'écoulement ▸ drain(s)
    transporter par tuyau ▸ pipe

tuyauterie ▸ plumbing
tweed ▸ tweed
type ▸ chap[1], type, variety
fièvre typhoïde ▸ typhoid fever
typhon ▸ typhoon
typique ▸ characteristic, typical
typiquement ▸ characteristically [characteristic], typically [typical]
presse typographique ▸ printing press
tyran ▸ tyrant
tyrannie ▸ tyranny
tyrannique ▸ tyrannical [tyranny]
tyrannosaure ▸ tyrannosaurus

U

ukulélé ▸ ukulele
ulcère ▸ ulcer
ultérieur (-ieure) ▸ subsequent
ultime ▸ ultimate
ultimement ▸ ultimately [ultimate]
ultraviolet (-ette) ▸ ultraviolet
ulu ▸ ulu
umiak ▸ umiak
un ▸ one
un (une) ▸ a, an, one, your
à l'unanimité ▸ unanimously [unanimous]
unanime ▸ unanimous
unanimement ▸ solidly [solid], together, unanimously [unanimous]
uni (unie) ▸ even, uniform, united [unite]
unicité ▸ uniqueness [unique]
unifier ▸ fuse, incorporate
uniforme ▸ monotonous, uniform
    en uniforme ▸ uniformed
uniformément ▸ uniformly [uniform]
union ▸ conjunction, union
unique ▸ one of a kind, only, single, sole[2], unique
uniquement ▸ uniquely [unique]
unir ▸ join, unite
unisson ▸ unison
unité ▸ unit
univers ▸ universe
universel (-elle) ▸ universal, worldwide
universellement ▸ universally [universal]
universitaire ▸ academic
université ▸ college, university
uranium ▸ uranium
Uranus ▸ Uranus
urbain (-aine) ▸ urban
urgence ▸ emergency
    d'urgence ▸ emergency, urgently [urgent]
urgent (-ente) ▸ urgent
urine ▸ urine
urne ▸ urn
urticaire ▸ rash[1]

usage ▸ convention, custom, usage, use
    à usages multiples ▸ versatile
    d'usage ▸ correct
usagé (-ée) ▸ secondhand, used
    vente d'objets usagés ▸ rummage sale
usager ▸ user
usé (-ée) ▸ shabby, threadbare, waste, worn
    complètement usé (-ée) ▸ worn-out
    eaux usées ▸ sewage
user ▸ consume, use, utilize, wear, weather
    user de représailles ▸ retaliate
usine ▸ factory, mill, plant
ustensile ▸ utensil
usure ▸ wear
utérus ▸ womb
utile ▸ handy, helpful, useful, worthwhile
    très utile ▸ valuable
utilement ▸ helpfully, profitably [profitable]
utilisateur (-trice) ▸ user
utilisation ▸ usage, use
utiliser ▸ employ, tap[2], use, utilize
utilité ▸ helpfulness, purpose, use, usefulness [useful], utility
utopie ▸ utopia
utopique ▸ utopian [utopia]

V

vacances ▸ holidays [holiday], vacation
    lieu de vacances ▸ resort
    voyage de vacances ▸ vacation
    prendre des vacances ▸ vacation
vacant (-ante) ▸ empty, vacant
    poste vacant ▸ opening
vacarme ▸ clatter, din, racket, tumult, uproar
vaccin ▸ vaccine
vaccination ▸ vaccination [vaccinate]
vacciner ▸ vaccinate
vache ▸ cow
vaciller ▸ blink, falter, quake, reel[2], teeter, totter, waver
vacuum ▸ vacuum
vadrouille ▸ mop
vagabond (-onde) ▸ tramp, truant, vagrant
vagabonder ▸ roam, run
vague[1] ▸ dim, hazy, indefinite, loose, remote, vague
vague[2] ▸ landslide, wave
    vague brisante ▸ breaker
    vague déferlante ▸ breaker, surf
vaguement ▸ faintly [faint], vaguely [vague]
vaillant (-ante) ▸ heroic, valiant
vain (vaine) ▸ futile, idle, pointless, unsuccessful, use
    en vain ▸ helplessly, unsuccessfully [unsuccessful], vainly [vain]

vaincre ► conquer, defeat, overcome, rout, vanquish

vainement ► unsuccessfully [unsuccessful], vainly [vain]

vainqueur (-euse) ► winner

vairon ► minnow

vaisseau (-eaux) ► ship, vessel
    vaisseau (-eaux) de guerre ► warship
    vaisseau (-eaux) spatial (-aux) ► rocket

vaisselle ► china, dishes [dish]

valable ► valid

valentin (-ine) ► valentine

valet ► jack

valeur ► merit, preciousness [precious], value, worth
    de (grande) valeur ► valuable
    sans valeur ► worthless
    aliments sans valeur nutritive ► junk food
    courtier (en valeurs mobilières) ► stockbroker
    objets de valeur ► valuable
    attacher une grande valeur à ► treasure
    montrer la juste valeur de ► do justice to
    prendre de la valeur ► appreciate

valide ► good, valid
    non valide ► void

valise ► suitcase

vallée ► valley

valoir ► cost, worth
    faire valoir que ► object
    qui vaut la peine ► worthwhile

valse ► waltz

valser ► waltz

valve ► valve

valvule ► valve

vampire ► vampire

vandalisme ► vandalism

vanille ► vanilla

vanité ► vanity
    avec vanité ► vainly [vain]

vaniteusement ► vainly [vain]

vaniteux (-euse) ► conceited, proud, vain

vannerie ► wicker

se vanter ► boast, brag

vantard (-arde) ► boastful [boast], conceited

vapeur ► steam, vapour
    plein (pleine) de vapeur ► steamy [steam]
    bateau (-eaux) à vapeur ► steamboat, steamer, steamship
    locomotive à la vapeur ► steam engine
    machine à vapeur ► steam engine
    avancer (à la vapeur) ► steam
    cuire à la vapeur ► steam

vaporisateur ► sprayer [spray]

vaporiser ► spray

varech ► kelp

variable ► changeable, variable

variante ► variant

variation ► variation

varié (-ée) ► assorted, varied

varier ► range, vary

variété ► diversity, variety

variole ► smallpox

vase¹ ► silt, slime

vase² ► china, vase
    vase à bec ► beaker

vaste ► board, comprehensive, extensive, great, immense, sweeping, vast, wide

vautour ► vulture

se vautrer ► wallow

veau (veaux) ► calf¹, veal

vedette ► spotlight, star
    future vedette ► talent
    être la vedette ► star

végétal (-aux) ► plant

végétal (-ale, -aux) ► vegetable

végétarien (-ienne) ► vegetarian

végétation ► vegetation

véhémence ► vehemence [vehement]
    avec véhémence ► vehemently [vehement]

véhément (-ente) ► vehement

véhicule ► medium, vehicle
    petit véhicule ► buggy
    véhicule pour bébés ► buggy
    véhicule amphibie ► amphibian

véhiculer ► shuttle

veille ► eve, vigil
    à la veille ► brink, verge

veillée ► vigil
    veillée mortuaire ► wake²

veiller ► stay

veilleur (-euse) ► lookout
    en veilleuse ► dormant

veine ► seam, vein

veinure ► vein

vélo ► bike

vélocité ► velocity

velours ► velvet

velouté (-ée) ► velvet

velouteux (-euse) ► velvet

velu (-ue) ► hairy

venaison ► venison

vénal (-ale, -aux) ► corrupt

vendetta ► feud

vendeur (-euse) ► clerk, salesperson, seller, vendor

vendre ► carry, handle, market, sell
    se vendre ► price
    vendre aux enchères ► auction

vendredi ▸ Friday
vénéneux (-euse) ▸ poisonous [poison]
vénération ▸ worship
vénérer ▸ worship
vengeance ▸ retaliation [retaliate], revenge, vengeance
se venger ▸ retaliate
venimeux (-euse) ▸ poisonous [poison], venomous [venom]
venin ▸ venom
venir ▸ come
  à venir ▸ upcoming
  aller ou venir en masse ▸ flock
  aller et venir dans une grande agitation ▸ flutter
  venir (à l'esprit) ▸ strike
  venir à l'esprit ▸ occur, suggest
  venir de faire ▸ just
vent ▸ breeze, wind[1]
  grand vent ▸ gale
  coup de vent ▸ gale
  moulin à vent ▸ windmill
  instruments à vent ▸ wind[1]
  instrument à vent ▸ wind instrument, woodwind
  refroidissement dû au vent ▸ wind chill
  flotter au vent ▸ stream
  se laisser porter par le vent ▸ ride
vente ▸ sale
  mise en vente ▸ release
  mettre en vente ▸ release
  (vente aux) enchères ▸ auction
  vente au détail ▸ retail
  vente de bric-à-brac ▸ rummage sale
  vente d'objets usagés ▸ rummage sale
  vente en gros ▸ wholesale
  taxe sur les ventes ▸ sales tax
  retirer de la vente ▸ recall
venteux (-euse) ▸ breezy [breeze], blustery [bluster], windy
ventilateur ▸ fan[1]
ventilation ▸ ventilation
ventre ▸ belly, stomach
  couché (-ée) sur le ventre ▸ prone
  maux de ventre ▸ cramp
ventriloque ▸ ventriloquist
venue ▸ approach
Vénus ▸ Venus
ver ▸ worm
  ver à soie ▸ silkworm
  ver de terre ▸ earthworm
véracité ▸ truthfulness [truthful]
véranda ▸ porch, stoop[2], veranda
verbal (-ale, -aux) ▸ oral, unwritten, verbal
verbalement ▸ orally [oral]
verbe ▸ verb
verbeux (-euse) ▸ windy, wordy

verbosité ▸ wordiness [wordy]
verdict ▸ verdict
verdoyant (-ante) ▸ green
verdure ▸ green
verger ▸ orchard, yard[2]
verglacé (-ée) ▸ icy
verglas ▸ sleet
vergue ▸ yard[2]
véridique ▸ true, truthful
vérification ▸ check, verification [verify]
vérifier ▸ check, edit, verify
véritable ▸ actual, genuine, honest, real, sheer, true, true to life
véritablement ▸ genuinely [genuine], true
vérité ▸ truth
verni (-ie) ▸ glazed [glaze]
vernir ▸ enamel, glaze, varnish
vernis ▸ enamel, glaze, polish, varnish, veneer
verrat ▸ boar
verre ▸ glass, lens
  dessous de verre ▸ coaster
  papier de verre ▸ sandpaper
  verre (droit) ▸ tumbler
verrou ▸ bolt
  mettre sous les verrous ▸ lock[1]
verrouiller ▸ bolt, latch, lock[1]
verrue ▸ wart
vers[1] ▸ rhyme, verse
  tirer les vers du nez ▸ pump
vers[2] ▸ to, toward
versement ▸ payment
verser ▸ pour, shed[2], shower
  verser à la cuiller ▸ spoon
  verser dans un plat ▸ dish
  verser des larmes ▸ weep
  pleuvoir à verse ▸ pour
verset ▸ verse
version ▸ version
verso ▸ reverse
versus ▸ versus
vert ▸ green
vert (verte) ▸ green, immature
  vert lime ▸ lime[1]
  vert olive ▸ olive
vertèbre ▸ vertebra
vertébré ▸ vertebrate
vertébré (-ée) ▸ vertebrate
vertical (-ale, -aux) ▸ vertical
verticalement ▸ upright
pris (prise) de vertige ▸ dizzy
vertu ▸ property, righteousness [righteous], virtue
vertueusement ▸ righteously [righteous]
vertueux (-euse) ▸ virtuous
plein (pleine) de verve ▸ spirited
vésicule ▸ bladder

vésicule biliaire ▶ gall bladder
vessie ▶ bladder, sac
veste ▶ coat, jacket
laisser au **vestiaire** ▶ check
vestibule ▶ entrance[1], hall, lobby
vestige ▶ relic
veston ▶ coat, jacket
vêtement ▶ apparel, garment, wear
   vêtements ▶ clothes, clothing
   vêtements de deuil ▶ mourning
vétéran ▶ veteran
   vétéran (des placers d'Alaska) ▶ sourdough
vétérinaire ▶ veterinarian
vétille ▶ nothing
vêtir ▶ dress
veto ▶ veto
veuf ▶ widower
veuve ▶ widow
vexant (-ante) ▶ offensive, vex
vexé (-ée) ▶ sore
vexer ▶ spite, vex
via ▶ via
viable ▶ viable
viande ▶ meat
   de viande ▶ meaty [meat]
vibrant (-ante) ▶ vibrant
vibration ▶ throb, vibration
vibrer ▶ jar, throb, vibrate
vice ▶ vice[1]
vice versa ▶ vice versa
vice-président (-ente) ▶ vice-president
vicié (-ée) ▶ stale
vicieux (-euse) ▶ vicious
victime ▶ prey, target, victim
   nombre de victimes ▶ toll[1]
   faire sa victime de ▶ prey
victoire ▶ triumph, victory, win
   chanter victoire ▶ crow[2]
victorieux (-euse) ▶ victorious, triumphant
vidanger ▶ empty
vide[1] ▶ bare, blank, empty, vacant, void
vide[2] ▶ gap, hole, vacuum,
vidéo ▶ video
   bande vidéo ▶ video, videotape
   cassette vidéo ▶ tape, video, videocassette
   clip vidéo ▶ video
   jeu vidéo ▶ video game
vidéocassette ▶ video, videocassette
vidéodisque ▶ videodisc
vider ▶ bail[2], down[1], drain, empty, vacate
   se vider au travail ▶ agonize
vie ▶ life, lifetime, living
   de vie ▶ living
   manque de vie ▶ dead
   niveau de vie ▶ standard of living

vieilleries ▶ junk[1]
vieillir ▶ age
vierge ▶ blank, virgin
vieux (vieille) ▶ aged, old
   très vieux ▶ ancient
vif (vive) ▶ alert, brisk, crisp, frisky, keen, nimble, perky [perk], quick, smart, spry, vibrant, vivid
   à vif ▶ raw
   chair à vif ▶ quick
   rouge vif ▶ cardinal
vigie ▶ lookout
vigilance ▶ alertness [alert], care
   surveiller avec vigilance ▶ watch
vigilant (-ante) ▶ alert, jealous, watchful
vigne ▶ grapevine
vignoble ▶ vineyard
vigoureusement ▶ mightily [mighty], strenuously [strenuous], sturdily [sturdy], vigorously [vigorous]
vigoureux (-euse) ▶ hardy, hearty, sturdy, vigorous
vigueur ▶ energy, heartiness [hearty], vigour
   mise en vigueur ▶ enforcement [enforce]
   entrer en vigueur ▶ effective, in effect [effect]
viking ▶ Viking
vil (vile) ▶ base[2]
vilain (-aine) ▶ nasty, naughty, wicked
vilainement ▶ wickedly [wicked]
vilebrequin ▶ drill
villa ▶ cottage, villa
village ▶ village
ville ▶ city, town
   en ville ▶ downtown
   grande ville ▶ city
   (petite) ville ▶ town
   hôtel de ville ▶ hall
lieu de **villégiature** ▶ resort
vin ▶ wine
vinaigre ▶ vinegar
vinaigrette ▶ dressing
vingt ▶ twenty
vingtaine ▶ score
vingtième ▶ twentieth [twenty]
vinyle ▶ vinyl
violateur (-trice) ▶ violator [violate]
violation ▶ violation
   violation de propriété ▶ trespass
violemment ▶ fiercely [fierce], vehemently [vehement], viciously [vicious], violently [violent]
   tirer violemment ▶ wrench
violence ▶ force, fury, intensity [intense], violence
   avec violence ▶ violently [violent]
violent (-ente) ▶ fierce, intense, savage, sharp, stormy, violent

violenter ► assault
violer ► invade, violate
    violer la propriété ► trespass
violet ► purple, violet
violet (-ette) ► violet
violette ► violet
violon ► fiddle, violin
violoncelle ► cello
vipère ► adder
virage ► bend, corner, curve
virer ► veer
virevolter ► flutter
virgule ► comma
virtuel (-elle) ► virtual
virulent (-ente) ► fierce
virus ► virus
vis ► screw
visa ► visa
visage ► face
    soin du visage ► facial
viser ► aim, aspire, calculate, sight, target
viseur ► viewer
visibilité ► visibility
    visibilité nulle à cause de la poudrerie ► whiteout
    sans visibilité ► blind
visible ► distinct, visible
visiblement ► visibly [visible]
visière ► visor
vision ► sight, vision
    champ de vision ► vision
visite ► tour, visit
    de la visite ► company
    courte visite ► call
visiter ► tour, visit
    rendre visite ► call over, visit
visiteur (-euse) ► visitor
vison ► mink
visqueux (-euse) ► slimy [slime]
visser ► screw
visualiser ► visualize
visuel (-elle) ► visual
vital (-ale, -aux) ► vital
vitalité ► life, vigour, zip
vitamine ► vitamin
vite ► fast[1], quick
    trop vite ► hastily [hasty]
vitesse ► pace, quickness [quick], rate, speed, velocity
    à toute vitesse ► full tilt [tilt]
    boîte de vitesses ► transmission
    compteur de vitesse ► speedometer
    indicateur de vitesse ► speedometer
    vitesse acquise ► momentum
    vitesse de croisière ► cruise
    aller à toute vitesse ► career, pelt[1], speed

    avancer à toute vitesse ► hurtle
    changer de vitesse ► shift
    excéder la vitesse limite ► speed
    faire à toute vitesse ► race[1], rush[1]
    partir en vitesse ► dash off
vitre ► glass, windowpane
vitré (-ée) ► glazed [glaze]
vitrer ► glaze
vitreux (-euse) ► glaze
vivacité ► animation, spryness [spry], vividness [vivid]
vivant ► living
vivant (-ante) ► alive, animated cartoon, lifelike, live[2], lively, living, vibrant, vivid
    de façon vivante ► vividly [vivid]
vivement ► briskly [brisk], keenly [keen], spryly [spry], vibrantly [vibrant]
    se baisser vivement ► duck[2]
vivifiant (-ante) ► brisk
vivre ► exist, inhabit, live[1]
    de quoi vivre ► keep
    vivre aux crochets ► bum
    vivre en appartement ► room
    vivre en chambre ► room
vivres ► supply
    s'approvisionner en vivres ► stock
vocabulaire ► vocabulary
vocal (-ale, -aux) ► vocal
vocation ► vocation
vociférer ► clamour
vœu (vœux) ► greeting, vow, wish
    vœux ► compliment
    meilleurs vœux ► regard
vogue ► fashion, rage
voguer ► ride
voie ► avenue, lane, niche
    voie d'accès ► approach, ramp
    voie de fait ► battery
    voie de raccordement ► switch
    voie ferrée ► rail, railroad, railway, track
    Voie lactée ► Milky Way
    voie navigable ► waterway
    voie maritime ► seaway
voilà ► there
voile[1] ► cloak, curtain, mist, veil
    couvrir d'un voile ► veil
voile[2] ► sail, shroud
    mettre les voiles ► ship out [ship]
    voyage en bateau à voile ► sail
voilé (-ée) ► covert
voiler ► buckle, conceal, veil, warp
    se voiler ► cloud
voilier ► sailboat, yacht
voir ► see, tell, view
    voir en avant-première ► preview
    voir un instant ► glimpse
    se voir ► see, show

voisin (-ine) ► adjoining, near, neighbour, neighbourhood
voisinage ► neighbourhood
voiture ► car, coach, wagon
    voiture de sport ► sports car
    voiture familiale ► station wagon
    trajet dans la voiture de quelqu'un ► lift
voix ► voice
    à la voix ► spoken
    à la voie active ► active
    à voix haute (haute voix) ► aloud
    d'une voix rauque/enrouée ► hoarsely [hoarse]
    voix basse ► undertone
    parler d'une voie flûtée ► pipe
    parler d'une voix monotone ► drone
vol[1] ► flight[1]
    en vol ► airborne
    vol plané ► glide
vol[2] ► robbery, theft
    vol à main armée ► holdup
volaille ► fowl, poultry
volant ► wheel
volatile ► fowl
volatiliser ► evaporate
volcan ► volcano
volcanique ► volcanic [volcano]
volée ► flock
voler ► fly[1], pirate, rob, steal, wing
    se dit de ce qui peut voler ► flyer
    empêcher de voler ► ground[1]
    interdire de voler ► ground[1]
    voler du bétail ► rustle
volet ► shutter
voleter ► flutter
voleur (-euse) ► gangster, pirate, thief
    voleur (-euse) à l'étalage ► shoplifter
volley-ball ► volleyball
    ballon de volley-ball ► volleyball
volontaire[1] ► intentional [intention]
volontaire[2] ► voluntary, volunteer
    s'engager comme volontaire ► volunteer
volontairement ► deliberately [deliberate], willingly [willing]
volonté ► way, will[2]
    bonne volonté ► willingness [willing]
volontiers ► gladly [glad], readily, willingly [willing]
volt ► volt
voltage ► voltage
voltiger ► flutter
volume ► body, cubic, volume
vomir ► vomit
vorace ► greedy
voracement ► greedily [greedy], hungrily [hungry]

voracité ► greed
vote ► poll, vote
    bulletin de vote ► ballot
    bureau de vote ► poll
    droit de vote ► suffrage
    obtenir des votes ► poll
voter ► cast, pass, vote
    voter au scrutin ► ballot
le vôtre (la vôtre, les vôtres) ► yours
vouer (un culte) ► worship
vouloir ► care, desire, intend, like[1], mean[1], want, will[2], wish
    vouloir dire ► mean[1]
voulu (-ue) ► deliberate, intentional [intention]
vous ► ye, you
vous-mêmes ► yourself
voûte ► arch[1], roof, vault[1]
vouter ► arch[1]
voyage ► journey, passage, trip
    voyage (par mer) ► voyage
    voyage de noces ► honeymoon
    voyage de vacances ► vacation
    voyage en bateau à voile ► sail
    voyage organisé ► tour
    aller en voyage de noces ► honeymoon
voyager ► journey, tour, travel
    voyager (par mer) ► voyage
    voyager en avion ► fly[1]
voyageur (-euse) ► fare, traveller [travel], voyage
voyant ► show
voyant (-ante) ► conspicuous, loud
voyelle ► vowel
vrai (vraie) ► certain, real, true
vraiment ► dearly [dear], genuinely [genuine], indeed, real, really, sure, true, truly, very
vraisemblable ► likely
vraisemblablement ► likely, presumably [presume]
vrille ► spin
vrombir ► buzz, drone, whir
vrombissement ► buzz, drone, whir
vue ► outlook, prospect, sight, view, vision, vista
    en vue de ► toward
    en vue ► prominent
    bien en vue ► prominent
    point de vue ► angle, outlook, point of view, side, standpoint, viewpoint
    prise de vue ► shot[1], take
    avoir vue sur ► overlook
    confronter des vues ► compare notes
vulgaire ► coarse, vulgar
vulnérable ► vulnerable

W

wagon ► car, coach
    employé (-ée) des wagons-lits ► porter
wagon-restaurant ► diner
wakashan ► Wakashan
wampum ► wampum
water-polo ► polo
watt ► watt
week-end ► weekend
wellingtonia ► redwood
western ► western
whip ► whip
wigwam ► teepee, wigwam
wok ► wok
World Wide Web ► World Wide Web

X

xylophone ► xylophone

Y

yacht ► cruiser, yacht
yack ► yak
Yankee ► Yankee
yaourt ► yogurt
yellowknife ► Yellowknife
yen ► yen[1]
yiddish ► Yiddish
yogourt ► yogurt
Yom Kippour ► Yom Kippur
yo-yo ► yo-yo

Z

zèbre ► zebra
zèle ► industry, zeal
    avec zèle ► zealously [zeal]
zélé (-ée) ► zealous [zeal]
zénith ► zenith
zéro ► nothing, zero
    sous zéro ► below
    partir de zéro ► from scratch
zibeline ► sable
zigzag ► zigzag
    faire des zigzags ► zigzag
zigzaguer ► twist, zigzag
zinc ► zinc
zinnia ► zinnia
zodiaque ► zodiac
zone ► area, belt, zone
    diviser en zones ► zoning
    zone climatique ► zone
    zone humide ► wetland
zoo ► zoo
zoologie ► zoology

GRAMMAR
TOOLKIT

Table of Contents – Grammar Toolkit

GRAMMAR

Grammar is the set of rules that determines how words are put together to make sentences. Understanding the rules of grammar can help you write more effectively. This grammar section explains the basic grammar terminology and various subjects useful in writing and reading. The different parts all work together, so sometimes you may need to read two or three parts to get all the information you need. Look in the Index section at the end of the Grammar Toolkit to find keywords that will help you.

BASIC GRAMMAR TERMINOLOGY

■ PARTS OF SPEECH

Adjectives

Adjectives are words that describe, limit or identify a noun or pronoun. They tell what quality, quantity or order a noun has. The word used to describe what adjectives do is **modify.**

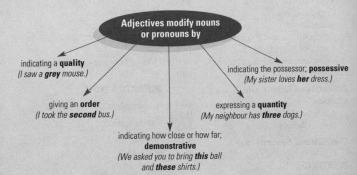

Adjectives modify nouns or pronouns by

indicating a **quality**
(I saw a grey mouse.)

giving an **order**
(I took the second bus.)

indicating how close or how far;
demonstrative
*(We asked you to bring this ball
and these shirts.)*

indicating the possessor; **possessive**
(My sister loves her dress.)

expressing a **quantity**
(My neighbour has three dogs.)

Some things to remember about adjectives

- Adjectives indicating **quality, order** and **quantity** are neither singular nor plural. They do not have a plural form.
  ▷ *Patrick is going to buy a **red** truck.*
  ▷ *Patrick and Todd are going to buy **red** trucks.*
- Adjectives come **immediately before a noun** or **right after the verb *to be*** when the adjective completes the idea of the verb.
  ▷ *He was holding a **cute little** dog.*
  ▷ *Babies are **cute**.*

Basic Grammar Terminology

Adverbs

Adverbs are words that describe or give more details about a verb, adjective or adverb. The word used to describe what adverbs do is **modify.**

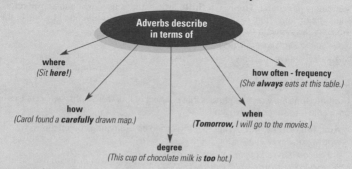

USING ADVERBS

Adverbs that modify verbs can be put in different places in the sentence to emphasize different parts of the sentence.

▷ *Quickly, I rushed home to finish my homework.*
▷ *I rushed home to **quickly** finish my homework.*
▷ *I rushed home to finish my homework **quickly**.*

FORMING ADVERBS WITH ADJECTIVES

Many adverbs are made by adding **-ly** to the adjective form of words. For adjectives that end in **-y,** usually change the **y** to **i** and add **-ly.**

	Adjective + -ly	Adjective (ends in y) + -ily	Same as the adjective
adjective	clear careful poor soft	happy easy busy noisy	far fast first next
adverb	clear**ly** careful**ly** poor**ly** soft**ly**	happ**ily** eas**ily** bus**ily** nois**ily**	far fast first next

Articles

The articles **a, an** and **the** are placed in front of a noun in specific circumstances. **A** and **an** are **indefinite** articles and are used when the noun refers to someone or something in general. **The** is a **definite** article and is used when the noun refers to someone or something in particular. Sometimes a noun is preceded by one of these three articles; sometimes it does not need an article.

▷ *We saw **a** sunflower in **the** garden.*

▷ ***An** elephant eats peanuts.*

Conjunctions

Conjunctions are words or phrases that connect or link words, phrases or clauses into one sentence. There are two kinds:

- **And, but, for, or, not, so** and **yet** are called co-ordinating conjunctions. They link words, phrases or clauses together.

    ▷ *You can have an apple, an orange, **or** a banana.*

    ▷ *I read a book, **but** Sunni watched television.*

- **After, although, as, because, before, even though, if, however, in order to, rather than** and **since** are called subordinating conjunctions. They are used to add a clause that develops what is being said in the main clause of the sentence.

    ▷ ***Now that** the babysitter is here, I can leave.*

    ▷ *I stayed **until** the game was over.*

Interjections

Interjections are short words, phrases or sentences that break the flow of a thought. Some interjections express a feeling or emotion; others are sound words. They are often followed by an exclamation mark (**!**) if the emotion is strong.

- **Feeling or emotion**
    ▷ ***Wow!***
    ▷ ***No way!***
    ▷ ***Get out!***

- **Sound words**
    ▷ ***Psst.***
    ▷ ***Hmmm.***

Nouns

A **noun** is a word used to name a person, animal, place, thing, state or quality.

▷ *boy* (person)
▷ *dog* (animal)
▷ *Chicoutimi* (place)
▷ *table* (thing)
▷ *confusion* (state)
▷ *beauty* (quality)

There are several kinds of nouns:

Kinds of Nouns	Examples
Common nouns Common nouns are the general names of persons, places, things or ideas.	*nurse* *tree* *houses* *hope* *kingdom* *painter*
Proper nouns Proper nouns are the names of specific persons, places, things or ideas. They always begin with a capital letter.	*Aunt Eva* *Niagara Falls* *Nobel Prize* *Buddhism* *Daniel*
Collective nouns Collective nouns are words that name a group of persons, animals or things.	*family* *team* *herd* *flock*
Compound nouns Compound nouns are made up of two or more nouns to express one idea. Some compound nouns are **joined together;** some are **joined by a hyphen;** and some are **separate words.**	*doghouse* *mountaintop* *brother-in-law* *city-state* *tennis match* *television show*
Concrete nouns Concrete nouns are the names of persons, places or things that can be perceived by one or more of the senses (sight, touch, hearing, taste, smell).	*telephone* *river* *chocolate* *snow*
Abstract nouns Abstract nouns are the names of ideas, qualities, feelings or characteristics. Many have one of these endings: **-ance, -ism, -ist, -ity, -ment, -ness, -ship, -tion.**	*health* *agreement* *patriotism* *friendship*

Basic Grammar Terminology

Prepositions

A **preposition** is used to show the relationship of a noun or a pronoun to other words in a sentence. The preposition, its object (noun or pronoun) and the modifiers of the object are called a **prepositional phrase.**

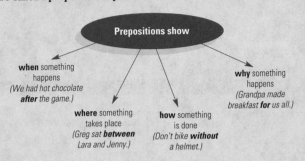

Prepositions show

when something happens
*(We had hot chocolate **after** the game.)*

where something takes place
*(Greg sat **between** Lara and Jenny.)*

how something is done
*(Don't bike **without** a helmet.)*

why something happens
*(Grandpa made breakfast **for** us all.)*

List of common prepositions					
about	at	between	in	out of	until
above	because of	beyond	into	over	up
across	before	by	like	since	upon
after	behind	despite	near	through	with
against	below	down	next to	throughout	within
along	beneath	during	of	to	without
among	beside	for	off	toward(s)	
around		from	on	under	

List of common prepositions of place			
across	beyond	inside	over
above	far from	into	through
around	from	near	to
at	in	on	under
below	in back of	out of	
beside	in front of	outside	

List of preposition combinations with adjectives and verb forms

A
- be absent **from**
- be accused **of**
- be accustomed **to**
- be acquainted **with**
- be addicted **to**
- be afraid **of**
- agree **with**
- be angry **at, with**
- be annoyed **with, by**
- apologize **for**
- apply **to, for**
- approve **of**
- argue **with, about**
- arrive **in, at**
- be associated **with**
- be aware **of**

B
- believe **in**
- blame **for**
- be blessed **with**
- be bored **with, by**

C
- be capable **of**
- be care **about, for**
- be cluttered **with**
- be committed **to**
- compare **to, with**
- complain **about, of**
- be composed **of**
- be concerned **about**
- be connected **to**
- consist **of**
- be content **with**
- contribute **to**
- be convinced **of**
- be coordinated **with**
- count (**upon**) **on**
- be covered **with**
- be crowded **with**

D
- decide (**upon**) **on**
- be dedicated **to**
- depend (**upon**) **on**
- be devoted **to**
- be disappointed **in, with**
- be discriminated **against**
- distinguish **from**
- be divorced **from**
- be done **with**
- dream **of, about**
- be dressed **in**

E
- be engaged **in, to**
- be envious **of**
- be equipped **with**
- escape **from**
- excel **in, at**
- be excited **about**
- be exhausted **from**
- excuse **for**
- be exposed **to**

F
- be faithful **to**
- be familiar **with**
- feel **like**
- fight **for**
- be filled **with**
- be finished **with**
- be fond **of**
- forget **about**
- forgive **for**
- be friendly **to, with**
- be frightened **of, by**
- be furnished **with**

G
- be gone **to**
- be grateful **to, for**
- be guilty **of**

H
- hide **from**
- hope **for**

I
- be innocent **of**
- insist (**upon**) **on**
- be interested **in**
- introduce **to**
- be involved **in**

J
- be jealous **of**

K
- keep **from**
- be known **for**

L
- be limited **to**
- be located **in, on**
- look forward **to**

M
- be made **of, from**
- be married **to**

O
- object **to**
- be opposed **to**

P
- participate **in**
- be patient **with**
- be pleased **with, by**
- be polite **to**
- pray **for, to**
- be prepared **for**
- prevent **from**
- prohibit **from**
- be protected **from**
- be proud **of**
- provide **with**

Q
- be qualified **for**

R
- recover **from**
- be related **to, by**
- be relevant **to**
- rely (**upon**) **on**
- be remembered **for**
- rescue **from**
- respond **to**
- be responsible **for**

S
- be satisfied **with**
- save **from, for**
- be scared **by**
- stare **at**
- stop **from, for**
- subscribe **to**
- substitute **for**
- succeed **in**

T
- take advantage **of**
- take care **of**
- talk **about, of**
- be terrified **of, by**
- thank **for**
- think **about, of**
- be tired **of, from**

U
- be upset **with**
- be used **to**

V
- vote **for, against**

W
- be worried **about**

Basic Grammar Terminology

Pronouns

Pronouns take the place of nouns and are used like nouns.

There are several kinds of pronouns:

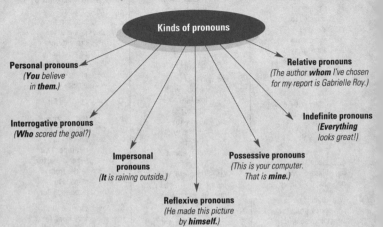

Kinds of pronouns

Personal pronouns
(*You* believe
in *them*.)

Interrogative pronouns
(*Who* scored the goal?)

**Impersonal
pronouns**
(*It* is raining outside.)

Reflexive pronouns
(He made this picture
by *himself*.)

Possessive pronouns
(This is your computer.
That is *mine*.)

Indefinite pronouns
(*Everything*
looks great!)

Relative pronouns
(The author *whom* I've chosen
for my report is Gabrielle Roy.)

Verbs and Verb Tenses

Verbs are words that indicate action or state of being. They also indicate what the subject does or has done to it.

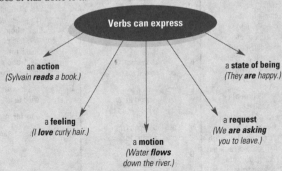

Verbs can express

an **action**
(*Sylvain reads* a book.)

a **feeling**
(I *love* curly hair.)

a **motion**
(Water *flows*
down the river.)

a **request**
(We *are asking*
you to leave.)

a **state of being**
(They *are* happy.)

The subject is the person, place, thing or idea being discussed in the sentence (what the sentence is about). The subject is usually a noun or a pronoun. In the sentence *Duane **ran** down the street*, **ran** is the verb, *Duane* is the subject.

Basic Grammar Terminology

866

SINGULAR AND PLURAL SUBJECTS

In English, verbs usually appear in a different form to indicate how many people are performing the action. If only one person or thing performs the action, the verb is in the **singular.** If more than one person or thing does the action, the verb is in the **plural.**

Singular	Plural
I am thirteen years old.	*We are fourteen years old.*
You watch videos on weekends.	*They watch videos on weekends.*
The clock runs fast.	*They run to English class.*

VERB FORMS

English verbs have four forms that are used in various contexts and in creating the different tenses.

1. the **simple** form   ▷ *They **play** hockey together.*
   *They **sing** a song.*

2. the **simple past** form   ▷ *They **played** hockey yesterday.*
   *They **sang** in a concert last night.*

3. the **past participle** form   ▷ *They have **played** all evening long.*
   *They have **sung** for one hour.*

4. the **present participle** form   ▷ *They are **playing** cards.*
   *They are **singing** a new song.*

■ PARTS OF A SENTENCE

A sentence expresses a complete thought. It has a **subject** and a **predicate,** and it begins with a capital letter and ends with a period, question mark or exclamation mark.

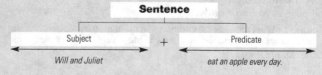

There are four ways in which sentences can express information:

- **statement**
  ▷ *This is my pen.*

- **command**
  ▷ *Hold my pen.*

- **question**
  ▷ *Where's my pen?*

- **exclamation**
  ▷ *That's my pen!*

Basic Grammar Terminology

867

Kinds of Sentences

There are four kinds of sentences:

- A **simple sentence** has one main clause.
  ▷ *Elizabeth likes fishing.*

- A **compound sentence** has two or more main clauses.
  ▷ *Dave likes fishing but doesn't like camping.*

- A **complex sentence** has one or more dependent clauses.
  ▷ *Because Lenny likes fishing, he learned to make lures.*

- A **compound-complex sentence** has two or more main clauses and at least one dependent clause.
  ▷ *Because Luc likes fishing, he learned to make lures and he reads books and magazines about fishing.*

Subject

The **subject** is the person, place, thing or idea being discussed in the sentence (what the sentence is about). The subject is usually a noun or a pronoun. In the following sentences, the subject is in bold.

▷ ***Kyoko*** *danced.*   ▷ ***The big red car*** *stopped.*

Predicate

The **predicate** is the part of the sentence that explains what the subject is doing or what is said about the subject. The predicate can be one word or many words, but it always has a verb. In the following sentences, the predicate is in bold.

▷ *Tony* ***laughed.***   ▷ *The big red car* ***sped off into the night.***

Object

Sometimes the predicate contains an **object.** The object receives the action of the verb.

- A **direct object** answers the question *what* or *who*? In the following sentence, **Hanif's bike** is the direct object.
  ▷ *Tonya borrowed* ***Hanif's bike.***

- An **indirect object** answers the question *to whom, for whom, to what* or *for what* something is done. In the following sentence, **me** is the indirect object.
  ▷ *Nicola lent* ***me*** *her bike.*

Irregular Verbs

Irregular verbs are those that have their own pattern of conjugation for the simple past and past participle forms (adding a suffix that is not -*ed* or using a spelling that is not always the same for both forms).

drink → [handwritten: drank]
drive →

LIST OF IRREGULAR VERBS

Simple	Simple Past	Past Participle	Translation
arise	arose	arisen	► lever
awake	awoke	awaken	► réveiller
be	was	been	► être
bear	bore	borne	► porter
beat	beat	beaten	► battre
become	became	become	► devenir
begin	began	begun	► commencer
bend	bent	bent	► plier
bet	bet	bet	► parier
bid	bid	bid	► souhaiter
bind	bound	bound	► lier
bite	bit	bit/bitten	► mordre
bleed	bled	bled	► saigner
blow	blew	blown	► souffler
break	broke	broken	► casser
breed	bred	bred	► élever
bring	brought	brought	► apporter
broadcast	broadcast	broadcast	► diffuser
build	built	built	► bâtir
burn	burned/burnt	burned/burnt	► brûler
burst	burst	burst	► éclater
buy	bought	bought	► acheter
cast	cast	cast	► jeter
catch	caught	caught	► attraper
choose	chose	chosen	► choisir
cling	clung	clung	► s'accrocher
come	came	come	► venir
cost	cost	cost	► coûter
creep	crept	crept	► ramper
cut	cut	cut	► couper
dig	dug	dug	► creuser
do	did	done	► faire
draw	drew	drawn	► dessiner

Verbs and Verb Tenses

LIST OF IRREGULAR VERBS *(cont'd)*

Simple	Simple Past	Past Participle	Translation
eat	ate	eaten	► manger
fall	fell	fallen	► tomber
feed	fed	fed	► nourrir
feel	felt	felt	► sentir
fight	fought	fought	► se battre
find	found	found	► trouver
fit	fit	fit	► ajuster
flee	fled	fled	► fuir
fling	flung	flung	► lancer
fly	flew	flown	► voler
forbid	forbade	forbidden	► interdire
forecast	forecast	forecast	► prévoir
forget	forgot	forgotten	► oublier
forsake	forsook	forsaken	► abandonner
freeze	froze	frozen	► geler
get	got	gotten	► obtenir
give	gave	given	► donner
go	went	gone	► aller
grind	ground	ground	► moudre
grow	grew	grown	► grandir
hang	hung	hung	► suspendre
have	had	had	► avoir
hear	heard	heard	► entendre
hide	hid	hidden	► cacher
hit	hit	hit	► frapper
hold	held	held	► tenir
hurt	hurt	hurt	► blesser
keep	kept	kept	► garder
know	knew	known	► savoir
lay	laid	laid	► poser
lead	led	led	► mener
leave	left	left	► quitter
lend	lent	lent	► prêter
let	let	let	► laisser
lie	lay	lain	► s'allonger
light	lit/lighted	lit/lighted	► allumer

Verbs and Verb Tenses

LIST OF IRREGULAR VERBS *(cont'd)*

Simple	Simple Past	Past Participle	Translation
lose	lost	lost	► perdre
make	made	made	► faire
mean	meant	meant	► vouloir dire
meet	met	met	► rencontrer
mislay	mislaid	mislaid	► égarer
mistake	mistook	mistaken	► se tromper
pay	paid	paid	► payer
put	put	put	► mettre
quit	quit	quit	► abandonner
read	read	read	► lire
rid	rid	rid	► se débarrasser de
ride	rode	ridden	► monter *(cheval, bicyclette, etc.)*
ring	rang	rung	► sonner
rise	rose	risen	► se lever
run	ran	run	► courir
say	said	said	► dire
see	saw	seen	► voir
seek	sought	sought	► chercher
sell	sold	sold	► vendre
send	sent	sent	► envoyer
set	set	set	► poser
shake	shook	shaken	► secouer
shed	shed	shed	► perdre
shine	shone/shined	shone/shined	► briller
shoot	shot	shot	► tirer
show	showed	shown/showed	► montrer
shrink	shrank/shrunk	shrunk	► faire rétrécir
shut	shut	shut	► fermer
sing	sang	sung	► chanter
sit	sat	sat	► s'asseoir
sleep	slept	slept	► dormir
slide	slid	slid	► glisser
slit	slit	slit	► fendre
speak	spoke	spoken	► parler
speed	sped/speeded	sped/speeded	► aller à toute vitesse
spend	spent	spent	► dépenser

Verbs and Verb Tenses

LIST OF IRREGULAR VERBS *(cont'd)*

Simple	Simple Past	Past Participle	Translation
spin	spun	spun	► tourner
spit	spit/spat	spit/spat	► cracher
split	split	split	► diviser
spread	spread	spread	► étendre
spring	sprang/sprung	sprung	► bondir
stand	stood	stood	► supporter
steal	stole	stolen	► voler
stick	stuck	stuck	► coller
sting	stung	stung	► piquer
stink	stank/stunk	stunk	► puer
strike	struck	struck/stricken	► frapper
string	strung	strung	► enfiler
strive	strove	striven	► s'efforcer de
swear	swore	sworn	► jurer
sweep	swept	swept	► balayer
swim	swam	swum	► nager
swing	swung	swung	► se balancer
take	took	taken	► prendre
teach	taught	taught	► enseigner
tear	tore	torn	► déchirer
tell	told	told	► dire
think	thought	thought	► penser
throw	threw	thrown	► lancer
thrust	thrust	thrust	► enfoncer
understand	understood	understood	► comprendre
undertake	undertook	undertaken	► entreprendre
upset	upset	upset	► déranger
wake	woke/waked	woken/waked	► se réveiller
wear	wore	worn	► porter
weave	wove	woven	► tisser
weep	wept	wept	► pleurer
win	won	won	► gagner
wind	wound	wound	► enrouler
withdraw	withdrew	withdrawn	► retirer
wring	wrung	wrung	► tordre
write	wrote	written	► écrire

Verbs and Verb Tenses

erbs in American English and British English (for
nglish, and **colour** in British English), there are
lar verbs. The following are the most common
n American English and British English for irregular

			British English		
		Past Participle	Simple	Simple Past	Past Participle
			bet	bet/betted	bet/betted
fit	fit	fit	fit	fit/fitted	fit/fitted
get	got	gotten	get	got	got
quit	quit	quit	quit	quitted	quitted

In American English, the following verbs are usually conjugated as regular verbs.
However, in British English, the simple past and past participle forms of these verbs
can be regular but more often end with a *t* and/or have particular spelling
transformations.

American English			British English		
Simple	Simple Past	Past Participle	Simple	Simple Past	Past Participle
burn	burned	burned	burn	burned/burnt	burned/burnt
dream	dreamed	dreamed	dream	dreamed/dreamt	dreamed/dreamt
kneel	kneeled	kneeled	kneel	kneeled/knelt	kneeled/knelt
lean	leaned	leaned	lean	leaned/leant	leaned/leant
leap	leaped	leaped	leap	leaped/leapt	leaped/leapt
learn	learned	learned	learn	learned/learnt	learned/learnt
smell	smelled	smelled	smell	smelled/smelt	smelled/smelt
spill	spilled	spilled	spill	spilled/spilt	spilled/spilt
spoil	spoiled	spoiled	spoil	spoiled/spoilt	spoiled/spoilt

Verbs and Verb Tenses

Basic Auxiliaries or Helping Verbs: *to be, to have* and *to do*

Basic auxiliaries or **helping verbs** are words that accompany verbs to form the progressive and perfect tenses. For example, the verbs **to be, to have** and **to do** are often used as auxiliaries in the progressive and perfect tenses as well as when asking questions.

▷ Tony **has played** baseball all his life.

The following tables show how the three verbs, **to be, to have** and **to do,** are conjugated when used as auxiliaries.

To be (present tense)			
Affirmative Form		**Negative Form**	
long form	contraction	long form	contraction
I am *I am* driving you to school.	**I'm** *I'm* talking with my brother.	**I am not** *I am not* singing tonight.	**I'm not** *I'm not* paying for this.
you are *You are* taking the bus.	**you're** *You're* eating a sandwich.	**you are not** *You are not* coming with me.	**you're not/you aren't** *You're not* thinking straight. *You aren't* walking alone.
he/she/it is *He is* running to the store.	**he's/she's/it's** *She's* listening to the radio.	**he/she/it is not** *It is not* raining yet.	**he's/she's/it's not** **he/she/it isn't** *It's not* snowing very much. *He's not* watching television.
we are *We are* drinking juice.	**we're** *We're* finishing some work.	**we are not** *We are not* sitting down.	**we're not/we aren't** *We're not* fighting anymore. *We aren't* sleeping here.
you are *You are* teaching us well.	**you're** *You're* visiting your aunt.	**you are not** *You are not* reading quietly.	**you're not/you aren't** *You're not* keeping this cat. *You aren't* paying for this.
they are *They are* catching fish.	**they're** *They're* washing the dishes.	**they are not** *They are not* going to the store.	**they're not/they aren't** *They're not* smiling at me. *They aren't* kicking you.

To be (past tense)		
Affirmative Form	**Negative Form**	
long form (only)	long form	contraction
I was *I was* sleeping.	I was not *I was not* reading that book.	I wasn't *I wasn't* trying very hard.
you were *You were* writing.	you were not *You were not* looking.	you weren't *You weren't* eating.
he/she/it was *He was* sitting down.	he/she/it was not *She was not* laughing.	he/she/it wasn't *He wasn't* crying.
we were *We were* driving.	we were not *We were not* drinking.	we weren't *We weren't* helping.
you were *You were* slouching.	you were not *You were not* listening.	you weren't *You weren't* moving.
they were *They were* fighting.	they were not *They were* not sighing.	they weren't *They weren't* clapping.

To have (present tense)		
Affirmative Form	**Negative Form**	
long form (only)	long form	contraction
I have *I have* worked...	I have not *I have not* visited...	I haven't *I haven't* seen...
you have *You have* written...	you have not *You have not* sung...	you haven't *You haven't* built...
he/she/it has *He has* said...	he/she/it has not *She has not* given...	he/she/it hasn't *It hasn't* rained...
we have *We have* sent...	we have not *We have not* been...	we haven't *We haven't* thought...
you have *You have* kept...	you have not *You have not* spoken...	you haven't *You haven't* needed...
they have *They have* wanted...	they have not *They have not* held...	they haven't *They haven't* swum...

Verbs and Verb Tenses

To have (past tense)		
Affirmative Form	**Negative Form**	
long form (only)	**long form**	**contraction**
I had *I had* bought…	I had not *I had not* won…	I hadn't *I hadn't* touched…
you had *You had* started…	you had not *You had not* wanted…	you hadn't *You hadn't* tried…
he/she/it had *He had* told…	he/she/it had not *She had not* spent…	he/she/it hadn't *It hadn't* snowed…
we had *We had* broken…	we had not *We had not* played…	we hadn't *We hadn't* danced…
you had *You had* slept…	you had not *You had not* sent…	you hadn't *You hadn't* forgiven…
they had *They had* seen…	they had not *They had not* given…	they hadn't *They hadn't* told…

To do (present tense)		
Affirmative Form	**Negative Form**	
long form (only)	**long form**	**contraction**
I do *I do* want to eat.	I do not *I do not* like soup.	I don't *I don't* drink.
you do *You do* work well.	you do not *You do not* laugh.	you don't *You don't* draw.
he/she/it does *He does* listen.	he/she/it does not *She does not* speak.	he/she/it doesn't *It doesn't* seem difficult.
we do *We do* believe you.	we do not *We do not* wonder.	we don't *We don't* agree.
you do *You do* ski.	you do not *You do not* skate.	you don't *You don't* argue.
they do *They do* practise..	they do not *They do not* listen.	they don't *They don't* pretend.

To do (past tense)		
Affirmative Form	**Negative Form**	
long form (only)	**long form**	**contraction**
I did *I **did** remember him.*	I did not *I **did not** fight back.*	I didn't *I **didn't** see her.*
you did *You **did** smile at me.*	you did not *You **did not** know them.*	you didn't *You **didn't** go to London.*
he/she/it did *He **did** hear you.*	he/she/it did not *She **did not** like that.*	he/she/it didn't *It **didn't** matter.*
we did *We **did** have lunch.*	we did not *We **did not** drive there.*	we didn't *We **didn't** watch television.*
you did *You **did** skate well.*	you did not *You **did not** mow the lawn.*	you didn't *You **didn't** travel last year.*
they did *They **did** keep the dog.*	they did not *They **did not** feed the cat.*	they didn't *They **didn't** want the bird.*

Contractions of other auxiliary verbs with *not*			
long form	**contraction**		
could not	couldn't	cannot	can't
must not	mustn't	should not	shouldn't
will not	won't	would not	wouldn't

Using *not* and Other Negative Words

Not expresses a negative idea. It immediately follows an auxiliary verb or the verb **to be.**

▷ *An orange is **not** a vegetable.*

If there is more than one auxiliary, **not** comes after the first auxiliary.

▷ *I will **not** be studying that tonight.*

In the simple present, verbs other than **to be** form the negative with **do** or **does + not.**

▷ *I do **not** like this cake.*

In the simple past, verbs other than **to be** form the negative with **did + not.**

▷ *I did **not** like this cake.*

Verbs and Verb Tenses

Non-progressive Verbs

Some verbs are not used in progressive tenses (present progressive, past progressive, future progressive, etc.): **be, believe, belong, exist, forget, hate, have**[1]**, hear, know, like, love, need, own, possess, prefer, remember, see, think**[1]**, understand, want.**

▷ ~~I am wanting this pencil.~~[2]
  I want this pencil.

Adverbs of Frequency

Adverbs of frequency are used with verbs to verbs to specify the frequency of the action (from 100% of the time to 0% of the time).

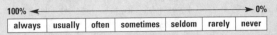

100% ◀						▶ 0%
always	usually	often	sometimes	seldom	rarely	never

NOTE: With the verb **to be,** the adverb of frequency is always put **after** the verb. With any other verb, the adverb of frequency is put **before** the verb.

▷ You are **always** hungry. (verb **to be**)
▷ Nadia **rarely** eats meat.
  Nicolas **often** plays with Samuel.

Phrasal Verbs

A **phrasal verb** is composed of a verb and a particle (a preposition) that have a special meaning together. For example, **work out** means to exercise.

Many phrasal verbs are **separable.** This means that a **noun** can either follow or come between (separate) the verb and the particle.

▷ Jeremy **turns on** the television.
  Jeremy **turns** the television **on.**

If a phrasal verb is separable, a **pronoun** replacing the object of the sentence (*television*) always comes **between** the verb and the particle. This means that the object **cannot** follow the particle without changing the meaning of the verb.

▷ Jeremy turned **it** on.
  Jeremy turned on **it.** (different meaning)

If a phrasal verb is **non-separable,** a noun or a pronoun **always follows** the particle.

▷ They ran **into** their teacher at the shopping mall.
  ~~They ran their teacher into at the shopping mall.~~[3]

---

1. **To have** and **to think** can sometimes be used in progressive tenses. *I think that my English class is easy.* In this case, *think* means believe and is therefore non-progressive. However, when *think* expresses thoughts that are going through one's mind, it can be progressive: *I am thinking about my English class right now.* When the verb **to have** expresses a possession, it is NOT used in the present progressive: *She has a dog.* It would be incorrect to say *She is having a dog right now.* However, in certain idiomatic expressions such as *have a good time,* the verb **to have** can be used in the present progressive: *She is having a good time.*
2. Incorrect form.
3. Incorrect form.

COMMON PHRASAL VERBS

A

| ask out | invite someone to go on a date | ► inviter quelqu'un pour un rendez-vous amoureux |
| ask over | invite someone for a visit | ► inviter quelqu'un pour une visite |

B

break down	1) divide something into parts	► diviser une chose en partie
	2) demolish	► démolir
* break down	1) stop working	► 1) ne plus fonctionner
	2) have a mental collapse	► 2) fondre en larmes
* break up	end a relationship	► mettre fin à une relation
bring about, bring on	cause	► causer
bring up	1) raise children	► élever des enfants
	2) mention/introduce a topic	► mentionner/amener un sujet

C

call back	return a phone call	► rappeler quelqu'un au téléphone
call in	send for someone	► envoyer chercher quelqu'un
call off	cancel	► annuler
* call on	1) ask someone to speak	► 1) demander à quelqu'un de parler
	2) visit	► 2) visiter
call up	telephone somebody	► téléphoner à quelqu'un
* catch up (with)	reach the same position or level	► atteindre la même position ou le même niveau
* check in, check into	register at a hotel or motel	► s'inscrire à la réception d'un hôtel, d'un motel
* check into	investigate something	► vérifier quelque chose
check out	1) take a book from the library	► 1) prendre un livre à la bibliothèque
	2) investigate something	► 2) vérifier quelque chose
* check out (of)	leave a hotel or motel	► quitter un hôtel ou un motel
cheer up	make (someone) feel happier	► divertir quelqu'un
clean up	make clean and orderly	► nettoyer et ranger
* come across	1) meet by chance	► 1) rencontrer par hasard
	2) create a certain impression	► 2) créer une certaine impression
cross out	draw a line through something (usually a word or words)	► tracer une ligne sur quelque chose (habituellement un ou plusieurs mots)
* cut down on	decrease	► réduire
* cut in (on)	interrupt	► interrompre
cut out	stop an annoying activity	► arrêter une activité agaçante

D

do over	do again	► faire une autre fois
* drop by, drop in (on)	visit informally	► faire une visite informelle
drop off	leave something/someone at a place	► laisser quelque chose ou quelqu'un quelque part

Verbs and Verb Tenses

* drop out (of)	stop going to school, to a class, to a club or association	► arrêter d'aller à l'école, à un cours, à une association

F

figure out	understand	► comprendre
fill in/out	complete a form or questionnaire in writing	► remplir le formulaire ou un questionnaire par écrit
find out	discover information	► découvrir de l'information

G

* get along (with)	co-exist satisfactorily	► coexister de façon satisfaisante
* get back (from)	return from a place	► revenir d'un endroit
get back	obtain again	► obtenir de nouveau
* get in, get into	1) enter a car or taxi	► 1) monter dans une voiture ou un taxi
	2) arrive	► 2) arriver
* get off	leave an airplane, a bus, a subway, a train, a boat	► descendre d'un avion, d'un autobus, d'un métro, d'un train, d'un bateau
* get on	enter an airplane, a bus, a subway, a train, a boat	► monter dans un avion, un autobus, un métro, un train, un bateau
* get out of	1) leave a car or taxi	► 1) descendre d'une voiture ou d'un taxi
	2) avoid work or an unpleasant actvity	► 2) éviter une activité ou un travail déplaisants
* get over	recover from an illness or from unpleasant news	► se remettre d'une maladie ou d'une mauvaise nouvelle
* get through	finish	► terminer
* get up	arise from a bed or chair	► se lever d'un lit ou d'un fauteuil
give back	return an item to somebody	► remettre un article, un objet, à quelqu'un
* give in	surrender, admit you cannot do something	► capituler, admettre qu'on ne peut pas faire quelque chose
give out	distribute	► distribuer
give up	stop trying	► arrêter d'essayer
* go over	review or check carefully	► examiner ou vérifier attentivement
* grow up	become an adult	► devenir adulte

H

hand in	submit an assignment, a report	► soumettre un devoir, un rapport
hang up	1) conclude a telephone conversation	► 1) mettre fin à une conversation téléphonique
	2) put clothes on a hanger or a hook	► 2) mettre des vêtements sur un cintre ou un crochet
have on	wear	► porter
heat up	make something hotter	► faire chauffer quelque chose
hold back	1) delay or hesitate	► 1) remettre à plus tard ou hésiter
	2) prevent someone/something from doing something	► 2) empêcher une personne/ une chose de faire quelque chose

K

keep out (of)	not enter	▶ ne pas entrer
* keep up (with)	stay at the same position or level	▶ demeurer dans la même position ou au même niveau
kick out (of)	force (someone) to leave	▶ forcer quelqu'un à partir
knock out	make someone unconscious	▶ faire perdre conscience à quelqu'un

L

leave out	exclude, omit	▶ exclure, omettre
* look after	take care of	▶ prendre soin de
* look forward to	await with excitement	▶ atteindre avec impatience
* look out (for)	be careful	▶ faire attention
look over	review or check carefully	▶ revoir ou vérifier attentivement
look up	look for information about something in a reference book	▶ rechercher de l'information dans un livre de référence

M

make up	invent a story or explanation	▶ inventer une histoire ou une information
* make up	become friends again after a disagreement	▶ redevenir amis après une dispute
mix up	confuse things	▶ confondre les choses

N

name after, name for	give a person the name of another person	▶ donner à une personne le nom d'un autre

P

* pass away	die	▶ mourir
* pass out	lose consciousness	▶ prendre conscience
pass out	distribute	▶ distribuer
pick out	select	▶ sélectionner
pick up	1) take in one's hand 2) go to get someone (e.g., in a car)	▶ 1) prendre avec la main ▶ 2) aller chercher quelqu'un (en voiture par exemple)
point out	call attention to	▶ attirer l'attention
put away	put something in a proper place	▶ mettre quelque chose à sa place
put back	return to original place	▶ remettre à la place originale
put off	postpone	▶ remettre à plus tard
put on	put an article of clothing on one's body	▶ mettre un vêtement sur soi
put out	extinguish a cigarette or fire	▶ éteindre une cigarette ou un incendie
* put up with	tolerate	▶ tolérer

Verbs and Verb Tenses

883

R

* run across, run into	meet by chance	▶ rencontrer par hasard
* run out (of)	finish a supply of something	▶ terminer une provision de quelque chose

S

show off	display with pride	▶ afficher avec fierté
* show up	appear, come	▶ apparaître, arriver
shut off	stop a machine, light, faucet	▶ fermer une machine, une lumière, un robinet

T

* take after	resemble	▶ ressembler
take off	remove clothing, a cover, a lid	▶ retirer des vêtements, un couvercle
* take off	leave on a trip, a plane leaving the ground	▶ partir en voyage, avion qui quitte le sol
take out	1) take someone on a date	▶ 1) inviter quelqu'un pour une sortie en amoureux
	2) remove	▶ 2) retirer
take up	begin a new activity or topic	▶ entreprendre une nouvelle activité
tear down	demolish; reduce to nothing	▶ démolir, réduire à néant
tear up	rip into many little pieces	▶ déchirer en plusieurs morceaux
think over	consider carefully	▶ réfléchir soigneusement
throw away, throw out	discard; get rid of	▶ jeter, se débarrasser de quelques chose
throw up	vomit; regurgitate food	▶ vomir, régurgiter la nourriture
try on	put on clothing to see if it fits	▶ essayer des vêtements
turn down	1) decrease volume or intensity	▶ 1) réduire le volume ou l'intensité
	2) refuse or reject	▶ 2) refuser ou rejeter
turn in	submit an assignment, report, etc.	▶ soumettre un devoir, un rapport, etc.
* turn in	go to bed	▶ se mettre au lit
turn off	stop a machine, light, faucet	▶ fermer une machine, une lumière, un robinet
turn on	start a machine, light, faucet	▶ ouvrir une machine, une lumière, un robinet
turn out	extinguish a light	▶ éteindre une lumière
* turn out	how something develops or results	▶ manière dont une chose évolue
turn up	increase volume or intensity	▶ hausser le volume ou l'intensité
* turn up	appear at or come to a place	▶ apparaître ou se montrer quelque part

---

* These phrasal verbs are non-separable.

	Simple	Progressive	Perfect	Perfect Progressive
Present	**Simple Present**	**Present Progressive**	**Present Perfect**	**Present Perfect Progressive**
	*I **eat** breakfast everyday.*	*I **am eating** breakfast right now.*	*I **have** already **eaten** breakfast.*	*I **have been eating** breakfast for one hour.*
Past	**Simple Past**	**Past Progressive**	**Past Perfect**	**Past Perfect Progressive**
	*I **ate** breakfast yesterday.*	*I **was eating** breakfast when you arrived.*	*I **had** already **eaten** breakfast when you arrived.*	*I **had been eating** breakfast for one hour when you arrived.*
Future	**Simple Future**	**Future Progressive**	**Future Perfect**	**Future Perfect Progressive**
	*I **will eat** breakfast tomorrow.*	*I **will be eating** breakfast when you arrive.*	*I **will** already **have eaten** breakfast by the time you arrive.*	*I **will have been eating** breakfast for two hours when you arrive.*

Present Tense

SIMPLE PRESENT

The **simple present** is used when referring to **daily habits** or **usual activities,** when making **general statements of fact,** when describing a **process** or when speaking of a **job** or **career.** In English, the simple present is not used to speak of right now.

- **Daily habits**
  - ▷ *I **run** every morning.*
- **Usual activities**
  - ▷ *Julia **swims** once a week.*
- **General statements of fact**
  - ▷ *Rabbits **eat** carrots.*
- **Process**
  - ▷ *First you **pour** the milk, then you **add** the flour.*
- **Job/career**
  - ▷ *Martin **is** an author. He **writes** books.*

The Simple Present and the Third Person Singular

In general, with the **simple present,** when using a third person singular proper noun (for example, **Brian** or **Lucinda**) or pronoun **he, she** or **it,** the verb has an -*s* or -*es* ending.

▷ *He **runs** to school every day.*
 *She **watches** television every Saturday night.*

However, after an auxiliary or a modal auxiliary, the verb does not take the **-s** or **-es** ending.

▷ *She **will** go to school tomorrow.*

Verbs and Verb Tenses

885

-s or -es ending		
Rule	**Examples** (simple)	**Examples** (simple present- 3rd person singular)
For most verbs, a final **-s** is added.	walk run listen	*Alicia walks to school.* *Antonio runs every day.* *Amanda always listens to the same music.*
For verbs with **-ch, -sh, -s, -x** or **-z** endings, a final **-es** is added.	watch blush wax cross	*Hadi watches television all day long.* *Samira blushes easily.* *Juliana waxes her car.* *Michael always crosses the street here.*
With the verbs **to do** and **to go**, a final **-es** is added.	do go	*This family does its laundry on Tuesdays.* *That boy goes to school in the city.*
The verbs **to be** and **to have** have a form of their own that ends in **-s.**	be have	*He is happy to be here.* *She has many animals to feed.*
For verbs ending in a consonant and a **-y**, the **-y** changes to an **-i** and **-es** is added.	worry study	*Ben often worries about his parents.* *Josée studies music at the conservatory.*
For verbs ending in a vowel and a **-y**, only a final **-s** is added.	play say	*Matthew plays baseball every summer.* *Zoe says that she likes yogurt.*

PRESENT PROGRESSIVE[1]

The **present progressive** is used to express an action that is currently in progress, taking place right now, at this moment. The present progressive is formed with the auxiliary **to be** (present tense) + present participle form, an **-ing** ending.

▷ *Look! This boy **is smiling** at me!*

▷ *Right now, I **am washing** the dishes.*

▷ *What **are** you **doing**? I **am washing** my bicycle.*

Past Tense

SIMPLE PAST

The **simple past** is used to express an action that began and ended at a specific time in the past. Often, the following words or expressions such as the following are found in the sentence: *yesterday, last night, two days ago*. Regular verbs used in the simple past end with **-ed**; irregular verbs[2] use different endings.

▷ *Yesterday **I walked** to the store.*

▷ *Last night, **I ran** home in the rain.*

Verbs and Verb Tenses

---

1. Also called **present continuous**.
2. See **List of Irregular Verbs** on page 871.

PAST PROGRESSIVE

The **past progressive** is used to express an action that was in progress at a specific time in the past or was in progress when another action occurred. The past progressive is formed with the auxiliary **to be** (past tense) + present participle form, an **-ing** ending.

▷ Last night, I **was sleeping** when you arrived.

▷ Peter **was watching** television when you called.

Future Tense

SIMPLE FUTURE: *WILL* AND *BE GOING TO*

There are two commonly used expressions for actions that will take place in the **simple future,** that is, at a time after the present: **will** and **be going to.** When making predictions about the future, **will** and **be going to** have the same meaning.

▷ Melissa **will jog** tomorrow morning.

▷ Next week, Harry **is going to visit** his mother.

- When expressing a preconceived plan, **be going to** is used.

  ▷ Gilbert is buying some vegetables because he **is going to cook** supper tonight.

- When volunteering or expressing willingness, only **will** may be used.

  ▷ I **will help** you with your homework, if you like.

FUTURE PROGRESSIVE

The **future progressive** is used to express an action that will be in progress at a particular time in the future. The future progressive is formed with the auxiliary **will** + **be** + the present participle form, an **-ing** ending.

▷ She **will be sleeping** when we leave the house.
   (The action **to sleep** will be in progress at a time in the future before the action **to leave** takes place.)

FUTURE PERFECT

The **future perfect** is used to express an action that will be completely finished before a particular time in the future. The future perfect is formed with the auxiliary **will** + the auxiliary **to have** (present tense) + the past participle form.

▷ Kristian **will have eaten** lunch before you arrive.
   (The action **to eat** will be finished at some point in the future before the action **to arrive** takes place.)

Verbs and Verb Tenses

FUTURE PERFECT PROGRESSIVE

The **future perfect progressive** is used to express an action that will be in progress before another event in the future. The future perfect progressive is formed with the auxiliary **will** + the auxiliary **to have** (present tense) + **been** + the present participle form, an **-ing** ending.

▷ Hugh **will have been sleeping** for two hours by the time Janet comes home.
(The action **to sleep** will have been in progress for two hours before the action **to come** takes place.)

Expressing Future Time: Using the Simple Present

In sentences about events that are on a **definite schedule or timetable,** the **simple present** can be used to express future time. These sentences usually contain future time words (**tomorrow, next week, next Saturday,** etc.). Not all verbs are used in this way. The verbs that can be used in this way include **arrive, begin, end, finish, leave** and **start.**

▷ The dance class **starts** next Wednesday.
We **finish** the lesson early tomorrow.

- **Will** and **be going to** are not used in **future time clauses.** When expressing the future in a time clause, the **simple present** is used. Words to look for are **before, after, when, as soon as.**

  ▷ I **will help** you with your homework as soon as you **arrive.**

- **Will** and **be going to** are not used in **if-clauses.** When the meaning of an **if-clause** is future, the **simple present** is used.

  ▷ If we **go** to the party, we **will be** quite tired.

Expressing Future Time: Using the Present Progressive

In a sentence dealing with a planned event or a definite intention, the **future time** may be expressed using the **present progressive.**

▷ Jane **is giving** a conference next Monday.

NOTE: Some verbs, for example, **to rain** or **to snow,** cannot be expressed in future time using the present progressive as they cannot be planned or definitely intended.

Immediate Future Using *be about to*

The idiom **be about to do something** expresses an activity that will happen in the immediate future, usually within a few minutes.

▷ The show **is about to begin.**
Michael **is about to leave.** He is waiting outside for a taxi.

Present Plans for Future Activities

The verbs *to intend, to plan* and *to hope* are often used in present tenses to express present ideas about future activities.

▷ Paul *intends to go* to Paris this summer.
~~Paul~~ *~~will intend to go~~* ~~to Paris this summer.~~[1]

▷ I *plan to take* a Spanish course next month.
~~I~~ *~~will plan to take~~* ~~a Spanish course next month.~~[1]

▷ I *hope to graduate* next month.
~~I~~ *~~will hope to graduate~~* ~~next month.~~[1]

Perfect Tense

PRESENT PERFECT

The **present perfect** is used:

- When expressing an action that occurred before now, at an unspecified time in the past;

  ▷ I *have* already *eaten.*

- for an action that was repeated several times in the past but for which the number of times is unspecified;

  ▷ Sammie *has seen* that movie so many times!

- for an action that began in the past but still holds true in the present.

  ▷ You *have lived* in the same house for eight years now.

The **present perfect** is formed with the auxiliary **to have** (present time) + the past participle form. Important clues for recognizing the present perfect are words like *since, for* and *already.*

Using *since* and *for*

Since is followed by a specific point in time (an hour, a day, a month, a year, etc.).
▷ I have known you *since* Grade 4.
▷ Theresa has worked there *since* last July.

For is followed by a length of time (two minutes, three days, four weeks, etc.).
▷ Mike has lived in the same house *for* seven years.
▷ Donald has worked in this store *for* two months.

---

1. Incorrect form.

PRESENT PERFECT PROGRESSIVE

The **present perfect progressive** is specifically used to express the duration of an action that began in the past and is still in progress. In some contexts, the present perfect progressive and the present perfect are often used interchangeably. However, the present perfect progressive puts more emphasis on the process, whereas the present perfect puts more emphasis on the event or the fact. The present perfect progressive is formed with the auxiliary **to have** (present tense) + been + the present participle form, an **-ing** ending.

▷ You **have been writing** that letter for weeks.

▷ Peter **has been waiting** for more than ten minutes.

PAST PERFECT

The **past perfect** is specifically used to express an action

- that occurred before a particular time in the past;
  ▷ By 2:30 P.M., I **had spoken** to my mother three times.

- that was completed before a particular time in the past.
  ▷ Fiona **had finished** her work when David came over.

The past perfect is formed with the auxiliary **to have** (past tense) + the past participle form.

PAST PERFECT PROGRESSIVE

The **past perfect progressive** is specifically used to express an action that was in progress before another event in the past. The past perfect progressive is formed with the auxiliary **to have** (past tense) + been + the present participle form, an **-ing** ending.

▷ You **had been sleeping** for two hours before I called you.

SUMMARY CHART OF VERB TENSES

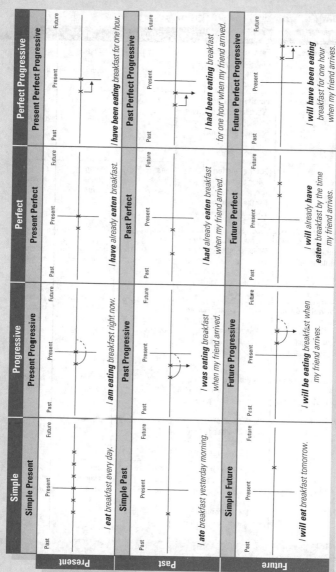

	Simple	Progressive	Perfect	Perfect Progressive
Present	**Simple Present** I **eat** breakfast every day.	**Present Progressive** I **am eating** breakfast right now.	**Present Perfect** I **have** already **eaten** breakfast.	**Present Perfect Progressive** I **have been eating** breakfast for one hour.
Past	**Simple Past** I **ate** breakfast yesterday morning.	**Past Progressive** I **was eating** breakfast when my friend arrived.	**Past Perfect** I **had** already **eaten** breakfast when my friend arrived.	**Past Perfect Progressive** I **had been eating** breakfast for one hour when my friend arrived.
Future	**Simple Future** I **will eat** breakfast tomorrow.	**Future Progressive** I **will be eating** breakfast when my friend arrives.	**Future Perfect** I **will** already **have eaten** breakfast by the time my friend arrives.	**Future Perfect Progressive** I **will have been eating** breakfast for one hour when my friend arrives.

Verbs and Verb Tenses

Spelling of *-ing* and *-ed* Verb Forms

Verb Ending	Rule	Simple	-ing	-ed
For most verbs	**For the *-ing* form:** Add **-ing.** **For the *-ed* form:** Add **-ed.**	*help* *learn* *lift*	*help**ing*** *learn**ing*** *lift**ing***	*help**ed*** *learn**ed*** *lift**ed***
Consonant and *-e*	**For the *-ing* form:** When the verb ends **with -e,** drop the e and add **-ing.** **For the *-ed* form:** When the verb ends with **-e,** just add **-d.**	*love* *skate* *date*	*lov**ing*** *skat**ing*** *dat**ing***	*lov**ed*** *skat**ed*** *dat**ed***
-ee	**For the *-ing* form:** When the verb ends with **-ee,** just add **-ing.** **For the *-ed* form:** When the verb ends with **-ee,** just add **-d.**	*see* *agree* *free*	*see**ing*** *agree**ing*** *free**ing***	*seen*[1] *agree**d*** *free**d***
One vowel and one consonant (one-syllable verbs)	**For the *-ing* and *-ed* form:** When a one-syllable verb ends with one vowel and one consonant, just double the consonant and add **-ing** or **-ed.**	*stop* *plan* *hug*	*stop**ping*** *plan**ning*** *hug**ging***	*stop**ped*** *plan**ned*** *hug**ged***
One vowel and one consonant (two-syllable verbs where the second syllable is stressed)	**For the *-ing* and *-ed* form:** When a two-syllable verb ends with one vowel and one consonant, just double the consonant and add **-ing** or **-ed.**	*begin* *prefer* *control*	*begin**ning*** *prefer**ring*** *control**ling***	*began*[1] *prefer**red*** *control**led***
One consonant and *-y*	**For the *-ing* form:** When a verb ends with a consonant and **-y,** just add **-ing.** **For the *-ed* form:** When a verb ends with a consonant and **-y,** change the **-y** to an **-i** and add **-ed.**	*study* *cry*	*study**ing*** *cry**ing***	*stud**ied*** *cr**ied***
-ie	**For the *-ing* form:** When a verb ends with **-ie,** change the **-ie** to a **-y** and add **-ing.** **For the *-ed* form:** When a verb ends with **-ie,** just add **-d.**	*die* *lie* *tie*	*d**ying*** *l**ying*** *t**ying***	*di**ed*** *li**ed*** *ti**ed***

Verbs and Verb Tenses

---

1. Irregular verb.

NOUNS AND EXPRESSIONS OF QUANTITY

Subject Nouns and Object Nouns

A **subject noun** is the subject of a verb and usually precedes the verb.

An **object noun** is the object of a verb and usually follows the verb.

subject noun	verb	object noun
The **girls**	*love*	**hockey.**

Using Nouns as Adjectives

Sometimes, nouns are used as adjectives. When a noun is used as an adjective, it is in singular form.

▷ *I found **cat** hair all over my sweater.*

▷ *Rachel ate a **chicken** sandwich.*

Plural Forms of Nouns

Singular Ending	Plural Ending	Examples	Exceptions
For most nouns	**s** (general rule)	*cup/cups* *tape/tapes* *table/tables*	
sh **ch** **ss** **x**	**es** **es** **es** **es**	*dish/dishes* *batch/batches* *glass/glasses* *fox/foxes*	
y (consonant)	**ies**	*body/bodies* *city/cities*	
y (vowel)	**s**	*toy/toys* *day/days*	
f **fe**	**es**	*wife/wives* *life/lives* *half/halves* *shelf/shelves*	*belief/beliefs* *chief/chiefs* *cuff/cuffs* *roof/roofs*
o	**s** **es**	*zoo/zoos* *studio/studios* *radio/radios* *potato/potatoes* *tomato/tomatoes* *hero/heroes* *zero/zero(e)s* *volcano/volcano(e)s*	

Singular Ending	Plural Ending	Examples	Exceptions
For some nouns, **the plural form is the same** as the singular form	The same	*sheep/sheep* *species/species* *offspring/offspring* *deer/deer*	
Some **nouns borrowed from a foreign language** keep their foreign plural		*phenomenon/phenomena* *crisis/crises* *cactus/cacti* *bacterium/bacteria*	
Irregular nouns			*person/people* *child/children* *woman/women* *man/men* *mouse/mice* *foot/feet* *tooth/teeth* *goose/geese*

Count and Non-count Nouns

Count nouns are nouns that can come after the article **a/an** and that have a plural form. *For example,* The word **girl** is a **count noun** because you can say **a girl** and because the plural **girls** exists.

Non-count nouns are nouns that usually head a category or group several parts together. They are nouns that cannot immediately follow the article **a/an** and do not have a plural form. For example, The word **rice** is a **non-count noun** because you cannot say **a rice** and because the plural **rices**[1] does not exist. **NOTE:** In a bowl of rice you will find several grains of rice.

NOTE: The ways for discriminating between **count nouns** and **non-count nouns** are not always logical. For example, while the word **pea** is a count noun (*one pea, two peas*), the word **corn** is not (*one corn, two corns*[2]). Also, while the word **fruit** is a non-count noun (*one fruit, two fruits*[3]); the word **vegetable** is a count noun (*one vegetable, two vegetables*).

---

1. Incorrect form.
2. Incorrect form.
3. Incorrect form.

NON-COUNT NOUNS VERSUS COUNT NOUNS

Usually, a **non-count noun** is an umbrella sheltering many other nouns that can be counted and therefore are **count nouns.**

Non-count Nouns	Related Count Nouns
furniture	chairs, tables, desks, beds
mail	letters, bills, postcards
money	coins, bills, pennies, nickels, dimes, quarters, dollars
fruit	apples, bananas, oranges, kiwis, pears
jewellery	earrings, rings, bracelets, necklaces

SOME COMMON NON-COUNT NOUNS

Some Common Non-count Nouns		
clothing	cash	homework
equipment	change	housework
food	postage	work
garbage	scenery	
hardware	stuff	
machinery	traffic	
makeup		
advice		history
information		literature
news		music
		poetry
All languages:		literature
English, Spanish, Japanese, etc.		slang
		vocabulary
corn	pepper	
dirt	rice	
dust	salt	
flour	sand	
grass	sugar	
hair	wheat	

Expressions of Quantity

Expressions of quantity are used to describe the number or amount of a noun. Usually, expressions of quantity are used in front of a noun.

▷ I need **some** time to finish.

▷ I have **three** cookies in my bag.

These expressions of quantity can be:

- Exact numbers such as **one, two, three, four, five…**
- Other adjectives such as **some, any, many, much, a lot (of), a few, a little, several…**

NOTE: At times, expressions of quantity are used alone, without a noun, when the meaning is clear to both the speaker and the listener. When that occurs, those expressions of quantity act as pronouns.

▷ Have you seen **many** movies this year? (adjective)

▷ Yes, I have seen at least **ten.** (ten movies) (pronoun)

▷ Have you had **any** juice? (adjective)

▷ Not yet, but I would like **some,** please. (some juice) (pronoun)

EXPRESSIONS OF QUANTITY USED WITH COUNT AND NON-COUNT NOUNS

Some expressions of quantity are used only with count nouns or with non-count nouns. Also, there are expressions of quantity that are used with either count or non-count nouns.

	Expressions of Quantity	With Count Nouns	With Non-count Nouns
singular	one each every	**one** table **each** table **every** table	
plural	both a couple of a few several many a number of two, three, four… (exact numbers)	**both** tables **a couple of** tables **a few** tables **several** tables **many** tables **a number of** tables **seven** tables	
	a little much a great deal of		**a little** furniture **much** furniture **a great deal of** furniture
	not any/no some a lot of lots of plenty of most all	**not any/no** tables **some** tables **a lot of** tables **lots of** tables **plenty of** tables **most** tables **all** tables	**not any/no** furniture **some** furniture **a lot of** furniture **lots of** furniture **plenty of** furniture **most** furniture **all** furniture

Nouns and Expressions of Quantity

ONE, EACH, EVERY

One, each and *every* are singular expressions of quantity. This means that the noun that each precedes, although it is a count noun, is always presented in its singular form even if it sometimes represents more than one. *One of, each of* and *every one of* are similar expressions. However, they are always used with specific plural count nouns that are, therefore, always presented in their plural form.

Expressions of Quantity: *one, each, every*	
used with a singular count noun	**used with a specific plural count noun**
One *One* bag was lost.	**One of** *One of* the bags was lost.
Each *Each* child brought a lunch. Note: **Each** is used when the speaker is referring to one at a time (in this case, one child at a time).	**Each of** *Each of* the children brought a lunch.
Every *Every* car was damaged. Note: **Every** is used when the speaker is referring to the whole group, as if using the word **all** (in this case, all of the cars).	**Every one of** *Every one of* the cars was damaged. Note: **Every one,** spelled as two words, is an expression of quantity. It should not be confused with **everyone,** spelled as one word, which is a pronoun and has the same meaning as **everybody.**

FEW, A FEW, LITTLE, A LITTLE

The expressions of quantity *few* and *a few* are both used with plural count nouns, whereas *little* and *a little* are both used with non count nouns. However, *a few* and *a little* are used to give a positive view, whereas *few* and *little* are used to give a negative view.

Expressions of Quantity: *few, a few, little, a little*		
	Example	**Explanation**
a few	*Karolyn has **a few** friends.*	Positive view: Karolyn does have more than one friend.
a little	*Lewis has **a little** time left.*	Positive view: Lewis still has some time.
few	*Karolyn has **few** friends.*	Negative view: Karolyn does not have many friends.
little	*Lewis has **little** time left*	Negative view: Lewis does not have much time.

SOME, ANY

Some and **any** are frequently used as adjectives.

- Usually, **some** is used in affirmative sentences.
  ▷ I have **some** time left to eat my lunch.

- In general, **any** is used in negative sentences.
  ▷ I don't have **any** ink left in my printer.

EXPRESSIONS OF QUANTITY FOLLOWED BY "OF + A SPECIFIC NOUN"

Some expressions of quantity must be followed by the word **of**. This occurs when they are placed in front of a **specific noun**. Some expressions of quantity are used with **of** in front of a specific plural count noun, others in front of a specific non-count noun, and still others are used in front of either a specific plural count noun or a specific non-count noun.

A noun is **specific** when it is preceded by:

- **this, that, these** or **those**;
- any **possessive** such as **my, your, Tom's, my mother's**;
- the article **the**.

Expressions of Quantity Used with Specific Nouns: (adjective + of)		
with a plural count noun	**with a non-count noun**	**with either a plural count noun or a non-count noun**
many **(a) few** **several** **both** **two** **one**	**much** **(a) little**	**all** **most** **some** **any** **a lot**
Many of Tom's students did their homework. ~~Many Tom's students did their homework.~~[1]	**Much of** her time is spent skiing. ~~Much her time is spent skiing.~~[2]	**Most of** the snow has melted. **Most of** the children are active. ~~Most the snow has melted.~~[3] ~~Most the children are active.~~[4]

NOTE: When **all** or **both** is placed before a **specific noun**, it can be followed by **of** (but does not have to be). When **all** or **both** is placed before a **non-specific noun**, it is never followed by **of**.

▷ **All of** my friends are coming to the party.
  All my friends are coming to the party.

▷ **Both of** Peter's dogs are brown.
  Both Peter's dogs are brown.

▷ **All** cats meow.
  ~~All of cats meow.~~[5]

▷ **Both** girls wore dresses.
  ~~Both of girls wore dresses.~~[6]

1, 2, 3, 4, 5, 6. Incorrect form.

DEMONSTRATIVES, ARTICLES, POSSESSIVE NOUNS AND POSSESSIVE ADJECTIVES

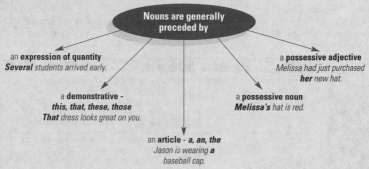

Nouns are generally preceded by

an **expression of quantity**
Several students arrived early.

a **demonstrative** -
this, that, these, those
That dress looks great on you.

an **article** - *a, an, the*
Jason is wearing *a* baseball cap.

a **possessive noun**
Melissa's hat is red.

a **possessive adjective**
Melissa had just purchased *her* new hat.

Demonstratives

The demonstrative adjectives *this, that, these* and *those* precede nouns to indicate how near or far something is in distance or in time.

	Near in Distance or Time	Far in Distance or Time
singular	**This** *This* year I am working twice a week. (referring to the current year) *This* pencil belongs to me. (referring to a pencil that is nearby)	**That** *That* year was memorable. (referring to a specific year in the past) Someone broke *that* window. (referring to a window that is farther away, not nearby)
plural	**These** I have seen many movies *these* days. (lately, recently) I am putting *these* papers in the recycling bin. (referring to papers that are nearby)	**Those** *Those* days were different. (referring to another period of time, sometime in the past) *Those* boys over there aren't friendly. (referring to boys who are farther away, not nearby)

Articles

USING A OR AN

A and *an* are used under the same circumstances, but the choice depends on the noun they precede. *A* is used when the noun begins with a **consonant sound**[1] (for example, *a bird*). *An* is used with a noun beginning with a **vowel sound**[1] (for example, *an oyster*).

	Example	Explanation
With singular count noun	We saw **a** sunflower in the garden. **An** elephant eats peanuts.	The articles **a/an** are used with singular count nouns when making a generalization. In the example, we are not referring to an elephant or a sunflower in particular but to any or all elephants and sunflowers, or to elephants and sunflowers in general.
With plural count nouns or non-count nouns	Elephants eat peanuts. Snow is cold.	**No article** precedes a plural count noun or a non-count noun when making a generalization. In this example, we are referring to any elephant, to all elephants or to elephants in general.

USING THE

The article ***the*** is used with singular count nouns, plural count nouns and non-count nouns when both the speaker/writer and the listener/reader are thinking about the same specific thing(s) or person (people).

Example	Explanation
The teacher asked us to do homework tonight. We saw a sunflower in ***the*** garden.	***The*** is referring to a specific teacher or garden, and it is assumed that the speaker/writer and the listener/reader know which teacher or garden is referred to (there is only one possibility).

Demonstratives, Articles, Possessive Nouns and Possessive Adjectives

---

1. In English, **Y** is sometimes considered a vowel, therefore words beginning with **Y** or **U**, with an initial Y sound, are considered to begin with a consonant sound (for example, *a yogurt* or *a university*, but *an umbrella*).

POSSESSIVE NOUNS AND POSSESSIVE ADJECTIVES

Possessive Nouns

Possessive nouns precede nouns to indicate who is the possessor. Often, the possessor is a person, an animal, a country or a city. Possessive nouns are formed by adding **'s** to nouns. With words that end in an **s** sound, they are formed by adding **'s** or just **'**.

▷ **Greta's** hair is beautiful.
▷ The **children's** toys were stolen.
▷ The **dog's** leash is on the table.
▷ **Lucas's** dog is very big.
▷ The **Marques'** animals are well-fed.
▷ The **cats'** collars were bought at the pet shop.

Possessive Adjectives[1]

The **possessive adjectives** *my, your, his/her/its, our, your* and *their* precede nouns to indicate who is the possessor.

	Possessor	Possessive Adjective	Example
singular	I	my	I left **my** glasses on the table.
	you	your	You wore **your** shoes yesterday.
	he/she/it or Jason, Sylvia, the cat...	his/her/its	Paul forgot **his** mittens. Jackie spoke to **her** father. The dog chased after **its** tail.
plural	we	our	We left **our** car in the parking lot.
	you	your	You bought **your** tickets at the counter.
	they or Valeria and Hector, the dogs	their	Zena and Imad left **their** home in January.

NOTE: In English, **possessive adjectives** always agree with the possessor (the owner). For example, *Alice has a new hat.* We can also say *Alice loves* **her** *new hat.* Because *Alice* is feminine and singular, the possessive adjective used to indicate every single thing Alice owns will be **her**, as in *Alice likes* **her** *dog, Alice went back to* **her** *house* and *Alice wears* **her** *jeans.*

---

1. In some grammar books, possessive adjectives are referred to as "possessive pronouns with a determiner function."

PRONOUNS

Personal Pronouns

A **personal pronoun** can be either a subject pronoun or an object pronoun. A **subject pronoun** is responsible for the action or verb in the sentence and generally comes before the action or verb. An **object pronoun** usually comes after the action or verb in a sentence. It is on the receiving end of the action or verb, or it is the object of a preposition such as **to** or **for**.

		Personal Pronouns	
		Subject	**Object**
singular	1ˢᵗ person	**I** *I threw the ball.*	**me** *You threw the ball to **me**.*
	2ⁿᵈ person	**you** *You wrote a letter.*	**you** *I wrote a letter to **you**.*
	3ʳᵈ person	**he** **she** **it** *She gave Tony a present.*	**him** **her** **it** *She gave **him** a present.*
plural	1ˢᵗ person	**we** *We like Sana.*	**us** *Sana likes **us**.*
	2ⁿᵈ person	**you** *You are talking to Tina.*	**you** *Tina is talking to **you**.*
	3ʳᵈ person	**they** *They read books.*	**them** *Jan and Supinder read **them**.*

Non-specific Object Pronouns

A **non-specific object pronoun** is a pronoun that does not give specific information about the noun it replaces and, just like a personal object pronoun, it is not responsible for the action in the sentence. It is usually placed after the action in the sentence. Non-specific object pronouns are *some*, *any* and *one*.

	Non-specific Object Pronouns		
	replacing singular count nouns	**replacing plural count nouns**	**replacing non-count nouns**
Non-specific object pronoun	**one** *I need a math book.* *Do you have **one**?*	**some/any** *Sean is looking for some skates.* *Do you see **any**?*	**some/any** *Kathy wants some juice.* *Do you have **any**?*
Comparing with personal pronoun (object)	**it/her/him** *I need my math book.* *Do you have **it**?*	**them** *Sean is looking for the hockey skates.* *Do you see **them**?*	**it** *Kathy is looking for the grape juice.* *Do you have **it**?*

Impersonal Pronouns

An **impersonal pronoun** is a pronoun that does not replace a noun but is used when making a general statement. Impersonal pronouns are **one, you, it** and **they.** Impersonal pronouns are considered third person singular pronouns.

- **One** is used in formal contexts.
  ▷ **One** should always wash **one's** hands before eating.

- **You** is used in less formal contexts.
  ▷ **You** should always look both ways before **you** cross the street.

- **It** is used in both formal and informal contexts.
  ▷ **It** appears that this teacher is very popular with her students.

- **They** is used in spoken, informal contexts.
  ▷ **They** say that you should never eat raw meat.

Reflexive Pronouns

A **reflexive pronoun** generally refers to the subject of a sentence. A reflexive pronoun can also be used for emphasis. The expression **by** + reflexive pronoun usually means **alone.**

<table>
<tr><th></th><th></th><th>Reflexive Pronouns</th><th>Examples</th></tr>
<tr><td rowspan="4">singular</td><td>1st person</td><td>myself</td><td>I walked to the store by myself.</td></tr>
<tr><td>2nd person</td><td>yourself</td><td>You wrote the letter yourself.</td></tr>
<tr><td>3rd person</td><td>himself
herself
itself</td><td>She trusts herself to do it right.</td></tr>
<tr><td rowspan="3">plural</td><td>1st person</td><td>ourselves</td><td>We stayed in the room by ourselves.</td></tr>
<tr><td>2nd person</td><td>yourselves</td><td>You stared at yourselves in the mirror.</td></tr>
<tr><td>3rd person</td><td>themselves</td><td>They made breakfast themselves.</td></tr>
</table>

Possessive Pronouns

A **possessive pronoun** replaces the combination of a noun and the possessive noun or adjective preceding that noun. Sometimes the possessive adjective and noun that are replaced by the possessive pronoun are not directly stated but simply implied.

		Possessive Pronouns	Examples
singular	1st person	**mine**	*This is my baseball cap. It is **mine.***
	2nd person	**yours**	*I can't find my coat. Do you have **yours**?*
	3rd person	**his** **hers**	*That is Jeannie's dress. It is **hers**.*
plural	1st person	**ours**	*You put your books on your desk, but we left **ours** on the table.*
	2nd person	**yours**	*This is your computer. It is **yours**.*
	3rd person	**theirs**	*This is where Erik and Peter live. This house is **theirs**.*

Indefinite Pronouns

An **indefinite pronoun** is a pronoun that leaves the identity of the noun it replaces unspecified. An indefinite pronoun can be the subject or object. When it is the subject, it is always followed by a third person singular verb.

Indefinite Pronouns	Examples
everyone	***Everyone*** *is quite content with the election results.*
everybody	***Everybody*** *likes the new teacher.*
everything	***Everything*** *looks great!*
someone	***Someone*** *was here to see you.*
somebody	***Somebody*** *rang the doorbell, but I didn't answer.*
something	*I think **something** is burning in your oven.*
anyone	*I don't think **anyone** is coming to the party.*
anybody	*Does **anybody** have the time?*
anything	*I can't see **anything** without my glasses.*
no one	***No one*** *was here when I arrived.*
nobody	***Nobody*** *lives across the street from me.*
nothing	***Nothing*** *is prettier than the first snowfall of the year.*

ASKING QUESTIONS

There are three kinds of questions that can be asked:

1. Yes/No question
  ▷ *Do you have a bicycle?*

2. Information question
  ▷ *When will you come to Montreal?*

3. Tag question
  ▷ *Today is a beautiful day, isn't it?*

Yes/No Questions

A yes/no question is a question that may be answered with **yes** or **no**. Often, in spoken English, people answer with a simple **yes** or **no**, but this is an improper way to answer grammatically. There are only two ways to answer a yes/no question:

- a **short answer**
  ▷ *Do you have a bicycle?* **Yes, I do.**

- a **long answer**
  ▷ *Do you have a bicycle?* **Yes, I do have a bicycle.**

Yes/No Question	Short Answer	Long Answer
Do you like fish?	Yes, I do. No, I don't.	Yes, I do like fish. No, I don't like fish.
Did you go to the movies last night?	Yes, I did. No, I didn't.	Yes, I did go to the movies last night. No, I didn't go to the movies last night.
Are you going to school today?	Yes, I am. No, I'm not.	Yes, I am going to school today. No, I'm not going to school today.
Were you at the game last night?	Yes, I was. No, I wasn't.	Yes, I was at the game last night. No, I wasn't at the game last night.
Will we go on vacation this summer?	Yes, we will.[1] No, we won't.	Yes, we will go on vacation this summer. No, we won't go on vacation this summer.
Can she swim?	Yes, she can. No, she can't.	Yes, she can swim. No, she can't swim.

NOTE: Often, in spoken English, people will drop the subject **you** and the auxiliary. However, this form is not proper in written English.

▷ *Are you going to school tomorrow?*
▷ *Going to school tomorrow?*

NOTE: In a **negative form** of a yes/no question, usually a contraction **can + not – can't** – is used.

▷ *Can't she talk?* (everyday English)
▷ *Can she not talk?* (formal English or literature)

---

1. It is important to note that with an affirmative answer (**yes**), will or any other auxiliary or helping verb is not contracted with the subject. It would not have been correct to write or say we'll.

Information Questions and Question Words

Information questions are questions that ask for specific information using one of the following question words: *where, when, why, who, whom, what, which, whose* and *how*.

FORMING AN INFORMATION QUESTION

An **information question** is usually formed with a **question word** + an auxiliary (or helping verb) + a subject + a main verb.

	Question Word	Auxiliary (Helping Verb)	Subject	Main Verb
Present	Where	does	she	play?
	Where	do	they	eat?
	Where	are*	Tom and Jerry?	* The main verb is **to be** and, therefore, it has the same position as an auxiliary.
	Who	is*	your friend?	* The main verb is **to be** and, therefore, it has the same position as an auxiliary.
Past	Where	did	she	Play?
	Where	did	they	Eat?
	Where	were*	Tom and Jerry?	* The main verb is **to be** and, therefore, it has the same position as an auxiliary.
	Who	was*	your friend?	* The main verb is **to be** and, therefore, it has the same position as an auxiliary.

If there is one **auxiliary (or helping verb)** in the information question, it is placed before the subject. If there are two auxiliaries in the information question, only one is placed before the subject; the other auxiliary precedes the main verb.

	Question Word	Auxiliary (Helping Verb)	Subject	Main Verb
One auxiliary	Where	is	he	going?
	Where	have	they	been?
	Where	could	she	be?
Two auxiliaries	Where	will	he	be going?
	Where	has	she	been living?
	Where	could	they	have been?

Question Word Table

Question Word	Information Questions	Answer Examples
When **When** is usually used to ask questions about time.	**When** will you come to Vancouver? **When** did you arrive?	Next week. Last night.
Where **Where** is usually used to ask questions about place.	**Where** will the graduation be held? **Where** were you last year?	In the school gymnasium. In Vancouver.
Why **Why** is usually used to ask questions about reason.	**Why** aren't you playing with Tom? **Why** did you get a bad mark?	Because I'm tired. Because I didn't study.
How **How** is usually used to ask questions about manner.	**How** did you come here? **How** does she play basketball?	By train. Very well.
How much and **how many**.	**How much** money do you have? **How many** students are in your class?	Five dollars. Thirty.
How + adjective	**How old** are you? **How nice** are they?	Thirteen. Very nice.
How + adverb	**How soon** can you start practicing? **How fast** can she run?	In twenty minutes. Twenty miles per hour.
How long asks about a length of time.	**How long** have you been a member?	Ten years.
How often asks about frequency.	**How often** do you go skiing in the winter?	Every weekend.
How far asks about distance.	**How far** is your school?	One kilometre.
Who[1] **Who** is usually used to ask questions about a person or people. It can be used as the subject of a question.	**Who** won? **Who** saw the show yesterday? **Who** is coming to the movies?	Nancy. Lucy and I.[2] Samuel and Nicolas.
Whom[1] **Whom** is used as the object of a verb or preposition.	To **whom** did you speak? **Whom** are you meeting? * With **whom** are you spending your summer? **Whom** are you spending your summer with?	Huguette. My friends. My family. My family.
Whose **Whose** is usually used to ask questions about possession.	**Whose** book is it? **Whose** skates did you borrow?	Nicole's. Sophie's.
What[3] **What** can be used as the subject of a question. It refers to things or objects.	**What** scared you? **What** made you cry?	The loud noise. I lost my shoes.

1. **Who** and **whom** can both be used as question words. They are both used to ask questions about a person. However, **whom** can only be used as the object of a verb or preposition. It is also important to note that in spoken English, **whom** is rarely used; **who** is used instead.
2. **Who** is usually followed by a singular verb, even if the answer could be more than one person.
3. Sometimes, **which** or **what** can be used interchangeably, particularly when they accompany a noun.
   ▶ **Which** cities did you visit? Seattle, Vancouver and Victoria.
   ▶ **What** cities did you visit? Seattle, Vancouver and Victoria.

Asking Questions

Question Word	Information Questions	Answer Examples
What can also be used as an object.	**What** are you eating? **What** did she see? **What** did they do?	An apple. A bear. They played.
What + kind of is used to ask about the particular variety or type of something.	**What kind of** dog is that? **What kind of** soap do you use?	Shepherd. Lavender.
What + do/doing can be used as questions about activities.	**What** did you **do** last summer? **What** will you **do** next year? **What** is she **doing**?	I travelled. Go to college. Sleeping.
What + noun can be used to ask a question.	**What** cities did you visit? **What** colour is her hair?	Paris, Berlin and Zurich. Blue.
What + like can be used to ask a question for a general description of qualities.	**What** is your English teacher **like**? **What** is the weather **like**?	Very nice and patient. Cold and windy.
What + look like can be used to ask a question about a physical description.	**What** does your boyfriend **look like**? **What** does her new car **look like**?	He is very tall and has brown hair. It is bright red and has tinted windows.
Which[1] **Which** can be used instead of what to ask a question about the selection from a definite, known quantity or group.	**Which** book do you want? **Which** one do you prefer? **Which** do you want to borrow? **Which** other book should I purchase?	That one. That one. The one about myths and legends. The one about myths and legends.

Tag Questions

A **tag question** is a question usually added at the end of a sentence. Tag questions, usually said with a rising intonation, are intended to confirm that information is correct or to seek agreement. **Affirmative sentences** need negative tags. **Negative sentences** need affirmative tags.

- **Affirmative sentence**

Tag Question	Expected Answer
She likes fish, **doesn't she?**	**Yes, she does.**
Mom is sleeping, **isn't she?**	**Yes, she is.**
They are coming, **aren't they?**	**Yes, they are.**

- **Negative sentence**

Tag Question	Expected Answer
She isn't sad, **is she?**	**No, she isn't.**
Mom isn't sleeping, **is she?**	**No, she isn't.**
They aren't coming, **are they?**	**No, they aren't.**

Asking Questions

---

1. Sometimes, **which** or **what** can be used interchangeably, particularly when they accompany a noun.
  ▶ **Which** cities did you visit? Seattle, Vancouver and Victoria.
  ▶ **What** cities did you visit? Seattle, Vancouver and Victoria.

MODAL AUXILIARIES

Modal auxiliaries generally express a person's attitude or "frame of mind." For example, modal auxiliaries (or modals) can indicate that a person feels something is essential, desirable, permissible, feasible or probable. Modal auxiliaries can also communicate the intensity of a person's attitude. The basic modal auxiliaries are *can, could, had better, may, might, must, ought to, shall, should, will* and *would.*

The phrasal modal auxiliaries are *be able to, be going to, be supposed to, have to, have got to* and *used to.* The meanings of phrasal modals are similar to those of some modal auxiliaries. For example, *be able to* is similar to *can, be going to* is similar to *will, have to* is similar to *must,* etc.

Using Modal Auxiliaries

- **Modal auxiliaries** are followed immediately by the simple form of a verb.
  - ▷ *He can do it.*
  - ▷ *He can to do it.*[1]
  - ▷ *He can does it.*[1]
  - ▷ *He can did it.*[1]

- A **modal auxiliary** cannot be immediately followed by another modal auxiliary. However, it can be followed by the phrasal modals *be able to* and *have to.*
  - ▷ *They **will be able to** help you with your homework.*
  - ▷ *They **will can** help you with your homework.*[1]

- In some cases, it is possible for one phrasal modal to follow another phrasal modal.
  - ▷ *They are not **going to be able to** help you with your homework.*

LIST OF MODAL AUXILIARIES AND SIMILAR EXPRESSIONS

Modal Auxiliary and Use	Present or Future Tenses	Past Tense
BE ABLE TO To express ability	I **am able to** skate. I will go skating with my friends tomorrow.	I **was able to** skate with my friends.
BE TO To express a strong expectation	You **are to** return this book Monday.	You **were to** return that book Monday.

---

1. Incorrect form.

Modal Auxiliary and Use	Present or Future Tenses	Past Tense
BE GOING TO To express certainty	*(future only)* They **are going to** pick you up at 8:00.	
To express a definite plan	I **am going to** build a birdhouse.	I **was going to** build a birdhouse, but I didn't. I didn't have enough time.
BE SUPPOSED TO To express expectation	The game **is supposed to** start at 9:00.	The game **was supposed to** start at 9:00.
CAN To express ability or possibility	I **can** swim.	I **could** swim when I was young, but now I can't.
To express informal permission	You **can** borrow my bicycle tomorrow.	
To express an informal polite request	**Can** I borrow your bicycle?	
To express impossibility or disbelief (negative only)	He **can't** say that.	He **can't** have said that.
COULD To express past ability		I **could** swim when I was young.
To express a polite request	**Could** I please borrow your bicycle?	
To express a suggestion	You need help with your English homework. You **could** ask your teacher.	You **could** have asked your teacher.
To express less than 50% certainty	Where are your parents? They **could** be at the shopping mall.	They **could** have been at the shopping mall.
To express impossibility (negative only)	He **couldn't** say that.	He **couldn't** have said that.
HAD BETTER To express advisability with a threat of bad consequences	You **had better** be home early, or we will eat without you.	
HAVE GOT TO To express necessity	I **have got to** buy milk today.	
HAVE TO To express necessity	I **have to** buy milk today.	I **had to** buy milk yesterday.
To express a lack of necessity (negative)	I **don't have to** buy milk today.	I **didn't have to** buy milk yesterday.
MAY To express a polite request	**May** I go to the bathroom?	
To express formal permission	You **may** go.	
To express less than 50% certainty	Where are your parents? They **may** be at the shopping mall.	They **may** have been at the shopping mall.

Modal Auxiliaries

Modal Auxiliary and Use	Present or Future Tenses	Past Tense
MIGHT To express less than 50% certainty	*Where are your parents? They **might** be at the shopping mall.*	*They **might** have been at the shopping mall.*
MUST To express strong necessity	*I **must** go to school today.*	
To express prohibition (negative)	*You **mustn't** eat fish. You are allergic.*	
To express 95% certainty	*(present only)* *Your parents aren't home. They **must** be at the shopping mall today.*	*They **must** have been at the shopping mall yesterday.*
OUGHT TO To express advisability	*I **ought to** study for my English test.*	*I **ought to** have studied for my English test.*
To express 90% certainty	*(future only)* *They **ought to** do well in the competition.*	*They **ought to** have done well in the competition.*
SHALL To ask a polite question To make a suggestion	***Shall** I turn off the lights?*	
To express future with *I* or *we* as subject	*We **shall** see you tomorrow. (will is more common)*	
SHOULD To express advisability	*I **should** practise today.*	*I **should** have practised yesterday.*
To express 90% certainty	*(future only)* *They **should** do well in the competition.*	*They **should** have done well in the competition.*
USED TO To express a repeated action in the past		*I **used to** walk my dog every day.*
WILL To express 100% certainty	*(future only)* *They **will** be back Saturday.*	
To express willingness	*I **will** help you with your work.*	
To express a polite request	***Will** you please tell her to call me?*	
WOULD To express a polite request	***Would** you mind turning down the music?*	
To express a preference	*I **would** rather have milk than juice.*	*I **would** rather have had milk than juice.*
To express a repeated action in the past		*When I was young, I **would** walk my dog every day.*

Modal Auxiliaries

GERUNDS AND INFINITIVES

Gerunds and infinitives are used as subject nouns or object nouns. A **gerund** is the *-ing* form of a verb used as a noun; an **infinitive** is the preposition **to** + the **simple form** of a verb.

Gerunds	**Infinitives**
▷ *I like **walking**.*	▷ ***To run** is good for your heart.*
▷ ***Listening** to music is my favourite pastime.*	▷ *I like **to ski**.*

Using Gerunds and Infinitives as Subjects

Both gerunds and infinitives can be used as subjects. However, gerunds are more often used as subjects than infinitives.

▷ ***Eating** is important.*

▷ ***To run** is good for your heart.[1]*

Using Gerunds and Infinitives as Objects

Both gerunds and infinitives can be used as objects.

▷ *Many people like **losing** weight in the summer.*

▷ *Many people want **to lose** weight in the summer.*

Using Gerunds as Objects of Prepositions

Only gerunds are used as objects of prepositions.

▷ *These students can complete their assignment **by working** together.*
  ~~These students can complete their assignment by **to work** together.~~[2]

▷ *Valérie **is used to walking** to school.*

▷ *Tess is **accustomed to presenting** in front of the class.*

Using a Verb + Gerunds or Infinitives

Some verbs can be followed by either a gerund or an infinitive: ***begin, can't stand, continue, hate, intend, like, love, plan, prefer*** and ***start.*** In this case, both structures have the same meaning.

▷ *When the bell rang, the students **began leaving**.*

▷ *When the bell rang, the students **began to leave**.*

Nevertheless, the meaning of the sentence might change with the use of some verbs, such as ***forget, go, remember, stop*** and ***try,*** depending on whether the verb is followed by an infinitive or a gerund.

▷ *Audric **stopped to talk** to Daniel.*

▷ *Audric **stopped talking** to Daniel.*

NOTE: In *Audric **stopped to talk** to Daniel,* Audric stopped his movement or action for the purpose of talking to Daniel, or in order to talk to Daniel. In *Audric **stopped talking** to Daniel,* Audric was talking to Daniel and he stopped, possibly to do something else or to speak to someone else.

1. With infinitives, ***it*** is commonly used, as in: *It is good for your heart **to run**.*
2. Incorrect form.

Gerunds and Infinitives

912

Using Gerunds or Infinitives with Verbs of Perception

Verbs of perception such as *feel, hear, listen to, notice, see, smell* and *watch* can be followed by either a gerund or the simple form of the verb.

▷ *I watched Julia play all day.*

▷ *I watched Julia playing all day.*

Using Verbs that Can Only Be Followed by a Gerund

Some verbs can only be followed by a gerund: *admit, appreciate, avoid, consider, delay, deny, discuss, dislike, enjoy, finish, imagine, involve, keep, mention, mind, miss, postpone, practise, quit, recommend, suggest* and *understand.*

▷ *Jessica and Jérémie enjoyed going camping when they were young.*

▷ *Roger dislikes washing the dishes.*

Using Verbs that Can Only Be Followed by an Infinitive

Some verbs can only be followed by an infinitive: *afford, agree, appear, arrange, ask, attempt, choose, consent, decide, demand, deserve, expect, fail, hope, intend, learn, mean, need, plan, prepare, pretend, seem, threaten, wait, want* and *wish.*

▷ *Francis seems to want an ice cream cone.*

▷ *Louise appears to be upset.*

Using Verbs Followed by a Noun/Pronoun and an Infinitive

Some verbs can only be followed by a noun or pronoun and an infinitive: *advise, allow, ask, encourage, expect, force, invite, order, permit, remind, tell, want* and *warn.*

▷ *Huguette asked Ludovic to start working.*

▷ *Josy also encouraged him to work hard.*

Using Gerunds and Infinitives to Express Purpose

In order to or *to* are used to express purpose. They generally answer the question "Why?"

▷ *Some people take the bus in order to avoid traffic.*

▷ *Some people take the bus to avoid traffic.*

The use of a gerund after *for* is common for talking about general use or purpose.

▷ *A laundromat is a place for washing clothes.*

Using an Infinitive after an Adjective

Some adjectives describing feelings or attitudes are usually followed by an infinitive.

▷ *These students were sorry to hear the bad news.*

▷ *We were surprised to see them at the graduation.*

Gerunds and Infinitives

Common Adjectives Usually Followed by Infinitives	
afraid	likely
amazed	lucky
anxious	motivated
ashamed	pleased
astonished	prepared
careful	proud
certain	ready
content	relieved
delighted	reluctant
determined	sad
disappointed	shocked
eager	sorry
fortunate	stunned
glad	surprised
happy	upset
hesitant	willing

Using *enough* and an Infinitive

In spoken or informal English, *enough* follows an adjective and precedes a noun. In formal or written English, *enough* may follow a noun. It is also possible to use a **noun + *enough* + an infinitive.

- **adjective + *enough* + infinitive**
  ▷ *Jacob is **old enough to walk** to school.*

- ***enough* + noun + infinitive**
  ▷ *Jacob has **enough practice to pass** his math test.*

- **noun + *enough* + infinitive**
  ▷ *I have **money enough to purchase** a house. (formal English only)*

COMPARISONS

Comparisons are used to show that people or things are similar or different in some way. Many words or structures can be used to express comparisons.

Types of Comparisons

AS...AS

As...as can be use to say that the two parts of a comparison are equal or the same in some way. Both **adjectives** and **adverbs** can be used in this type of comparison.

▷ *Nathalie is 14 years old. Manuel is also 14. Nathalie is **as** old **as** Manuel.*

▷ *These students are running **as** quickly **as** they can.*

In the negative form, the expressions **not as...as** or **not so...as** are used. **Quite** and **nearly** are also often used with the negative form.

▷ *Nathalie is 14 years old. Mohamed is 15. Nathalie is **not as** old **as** Mohamed.*

▷ *Nathalie isn't **quite as** old **as** Mohamed.*

▷ *Samuel is 4. He isn't **nearly as** old **as** Nathalie.*

Just (meaning "exactly"), **nearly** and **almost** are common modifiers of the **as...as** comparison structure.

▷ *Manuel is **just as** old **as** Nathalie.*

▷ *Nathalie is **almost as** old **as** Mohamed.*

▷ *Nathalie is **nearly as** old **as** Mohamed.*

NOTE: When a pronoun is used in a comparison showing that the two parts are equal in some way, in formal English the nominative form is used after the final **as.** However, it is the objective form that is more commonly used in conversation.

▷ *Manuel is **as** tall **as** I.* (nominative form)

▷ *Manuel is **as** tall **as** me.* (objective form)

THE SAME, SIMILAR AND DIFFERENT

The same, similar and **different** are used as adjectives when making comparisons. **Same** is always preceded by **the.**

▷ *Nathalie and Manuel have **the same/similar/different** schoolbags.*

▷ *Their schoolbags are **the same/similar/different.***

In some structures, **the same** is followed by **as, similar** is followed by **to,** and **different** is followed by **from** (though in informal or spoken English people may use **than** instead of **from** after **different**). It is also possible to place a noun between **the same** and **as.**

▷ *These books are **the same as** those ones.*

▷ *These books are by **the same** author **as** those.*

▷ *These books are **similar to** those ones.*

▷ *These books are **different from** those ones.*

Comparisons

BE LIKE AND ALIKE

Be like and **alike** are also used to make comparisons. The structure for **be like** is: **noun + be like + noun**. The structure for **alike** is: **noun and noun + be alike**.

▷ My dress **is like** your dress.

▷ My dress and your dress **are alike**.

In addition to following **be, like** also follows certain verbs that refer to senses (**look, sound, feel, taste, act, seem,** etc.).

▷ They **look like** their parents.

▷ He **sounds like** his father.

▷ This scarf **feels like** silk.

▷ This water **tastes like** soap.

▷ She is **acting like** a clown.

▷ Giovanni **seems like** a good person.

Alike may also follow some verbs other than **be** (**look, think, act, talk, dress,** etc.).

▷ They **look alike**.

▷ Great minds **think alike**.

▷ Casey and Rebecca **act alike**.

▷ Sebastian and Nadia **talk alike**.

▷ Pierre and Jacob **dress alike**.

Comparatives

FORMING THE COMPARATIVE

The **comparative** generally compares **this/these** to **that/those** using the word **than**. The comparative is usually formed with **verb + more + adjective + than** or **verb + (adjective + the suffix –er) + than**.

▷ Nathalie **is more meticulous than** Manuel.

▷ Manuel is **older than** Nathalie.

▷ Manuel and Nathalie **are older than** Samuel and Nicolas.

USING COMPARATIVES

- In formal and written English, a **subject pronoun** (I, you, he, she, it, we, they) follows **than**. In informal or spoken English, an **object pronoun** (me, you, him, her, it, you, us, them) often follows **than**.

  ▷ I **am taller than** my mother.

  ▷ I **am taller than she is**. (formal English)

  ▷ I **am taller than her**. (informal or spoken English)

- An **auxiliary verb** often follows the subject after **than**.

  ▷ They work **harder than we do**.

  ▷ They finished **earlier than we did**.

- The words **much, a lot, far, a little** and **a little bit** are used to modify the comparative form of adjectives and adverbs.
  - ▷ My parents are **much/a lot/far** more exhausted than we are.
  - ▷ David runs **much/a lot/far** faster than he used to.
  - ▷ Manuel is **a little/a little bit** older than Nathalie.

NOTE: The **adverb "very"** is often used to modify adjectives and adverbs. However, **very** cannot be used to modify comparative adjectives and adverbs.
  - ▷ My parents are ~~very~~ older than we are.[1]
    My parents are **much/a lot/far** older than we are.

NOTE: It is important to avoid repeating the comparison by using both **-er** and **more**.
  - ▷ I was **much more happier** than my brother after going to the movies.[2]
  - ▷ I was **much happier than** my brother after going to the movies.

NOTE: The opposite of **-er/more** is **less** or **not as... as.** They usually have the same meaning. The word **less** is *only* used with adverbs of more than one syllable, whereas **not as...as** can be used with both one-syllable or multi-syllable adjectives or adverbs.
  - ▷ Running is **less** interesting than skating.
    Running is **not as** interesting **as** skating.
  - ▷ My swimming pool is ~~less large than your.~~[3]
    Our swimming pool is **not as** large **as** yours.

- Repeating a comparative with the structure **comparative + and + comparative** suggests that something becomes regularly better, stronger or greater.
  - ▷ Jessica was so nervous that she spoke **faster and faster.**
  - ▷ Cars are becoming **more and more** expensive.

USING DOUBLE COMPARATIVES

A **double comparative** has two parts that both begin with **the.** In general, the second part of the comparative expresses the result of the first part.
- ▷ **The taller** he grew, **the thinner** he became.
- ▷ **The faster** Thierry runs, **the faster** his heart will beat.
- ▷ **The more** nervous she was, **the faster** she spoke.
- ▷ **The colder** the milk (is), **the better** I like it.

NOTE: When using double comparatives, there are common expressions: **The more, the merrier** (the more people somewhere, the better it will be) and **The sooner, the better** (it is better to do it as soon as possible).

---

1. Incorrect form.
2. Incorrect form.
3. Incorrect form.

Superlatives

FORMING THE SUPERLATIVE

The **superlative** compares one part of a whole group (or whole) to all the rest of the group (or whole). The superlative is usually formed with **the** + (adjective + the suffix **–est**) or with **the most** + **adjective.**

▷ *Manuel, Nicolas and Samuel are brothers. Manuel is **the oldest** of all three brothers.*

▷ *A woman in California claims she is **the fastest** woman in the world.*

▷ *Mexico City is one of **the most populated** cities in the world.*

USING SUPERLATIVES

The structures **in** + (a place), *I have ever met/known/etc.*, and **of all** are often used with a superlative.

▷ *Mexico is one of the most populated cities **in the world.***

▷ *Tamika is one of the nicest people **I have ever met/known.***

▷ *Our principal is the best (principal) **of all.***

NOTE: It is important to avoid repeating the comparison by using both **-est** and **the most.**

▷ *He was **the most fastest** sprinter of all.*[1]

▷ *He was **the fastest** sprinter of all.*

NOTE: The opposite of **the most** is **the least.**

▷ *This movie was **the most interesting** one I saw this month.*

▷ *I don't agree. I think it was **the least interesting** of all.*

Comparative and Superlative Forms of Adverbs

	Adverbs	Comparative	Superlative	Explanation
Adverbs ending in -ly	carefully seriously slowly quietly	more carefully more seriously more slowly more quietly	most carefully most seriously most slowly most quietly	With adverbs ending with **-ly more** and **the most** are used to create comparative or superlative forms. **Early** is the only exception, as it is both an adjective and an adverb. It takes the form **earlier/earliest.**
One-syllable adverbs	fast hard	faster harder	fastest hardest	For one-syllable adverbs, **-er** and **-est** are used to create comparative or superlative forms.
Irregular adverbs	badly far well	worse farther/further[2]	the worst	**Badly, far** and **well** have irregular comparative and superlative forms.

1. Incorrect form.
2. Both **farther** and **further** can be used to compare physical distance: *We went **further/farther** than our friends did.* However, only **further** can also mean "additional" or "more": *We will give them **further** information about this homework.*

Comparisons

Comparative and Superlative Forms of Adjectives

	Adjectives	Comparative	Superlative	Explanation
One-syllable adjectives	**small** **wise**	smaller wiser	the smallest the wisest	For most one-syllable adjectives, **-er** and **-est** are used to create comparative or superlative forms.
Two-syllable adjectives	**famous** **crowded**	more famous more crowded	the most famous the most crowded	For most two-syllable adjectives, **more** and **the most** are used to create comparative or superlative forms.
Other two-syllable adjectives	**angry** **clever** **common** **friendly** **gentle** **handsome** **narrow** **pleasant** **polite** **quiet** **simple** **sour**	more angry/angrier more clever/cleverer[1] more common/commoner[1] more friendly/friendlier more gentle/gentler[1] more handsome/handsomer[1] more narrow/narrower more pleasant/pleasanter[1] more polite/politer[1] more quiet/quieter more simple/simpler more sour/sourer[1]	most angry/angriest most clever/cleverest[1] most common/commonest[1] most friendly/friendliest most gentle/gentlest[1] most handsome/handsomest[1] most narrow/narrowest most pleasant/pleasantest[1] most polite/politest[1] most quiet/quietest most simple/simplest most sour/sourest[1]	For some two-syllable adjectives, either **more/the most** or **-er/-est** is used to create comparative or superlative forms.
Two-syllable adjectives that end in **-y**	**easy** **funny**	easier funnier	the easiest the funniest	For most two-syllable adjectives that end in **-y** (exceptions are angry and friendly, see above), the **-y** is changed to **i**, and **-er** and **-est** are used to create comparative or superlative forms.
Adjectives with three or more syllables	**fascinating** **intelligent**	more fascinating more intelligent	most fascinating most intelligent	With adjectives of three or more syllables, **more** and **the most** are used to create comparative or superlative forms.
Irregular adjectives	**bad** **good**	worse better	worst best	**Good** and **bad** have irregular comparative and superlative forms.

1. In Canada and North America, these forms are rarely used in spoken English.

Comparisons

ADJECTIVE CLAUSES AND NOUN CLAUSES

Adjective Clauses

An **adjective clause** is used to modify a noun or a pronoun; it describes, identifies or gives additional information about a noun. It can also be called a **relative clause.** Words used to connect adjective clauses are subject pronouns, such as **who, which,** and **that,** as well as object pronouns, such as **who[1], whom[1], whose, where** and **when.**

USING SUBJECT PRONOUNS *WHO, WHICH* AND *THAT*

- **Who** is used for people.
  - ▷ *I helped the student* **who had problems.**
  - ▷ *I would like to thank everyone* **who volunteered for the tournament.**

- **Which** is used for things. **Which** is always set off by commas.
  - ▷ *The homework,* **which was about chemistry,** *was not completed.*

- **That** is used both for people and things.
  - ▷ *I helped the student* **that had problems.**
  - ▷ *The homework* **that was about chemistry** *was not completed.*
  - ▷ *Those are the ones* **that want to volunteer.**

USING OBJECT PRONOUNS *WHO, WHOM, WHICH* AND *THAT*

- **Who** and **whom** are used for people.
  - ▷ *The person* **who(m) I saw** *was the principal.*

- **Which** is used for things and is always set off by commas.
  - ▷ *The tournament,* **which our school won,** *was held last Saturday.*

- **That** is used both for people and things.
  - ▷ *The person* **that I saw** *was the principal.*
  - ▷ *The tournament* **that our school won** *was held last Saturday.*

NOTE: An **object pronoun** is often omitted from an adjective clause. In general, when an adjective clause modifies a pronoun, the object pronoun is omitted from the adjective clause.

▷ *The person* **who(m) I saw** *was the principal.*
▷ *The person* **I saw** *was the principal.*

NOTE: An **object pronoun** can be used as the object of a preposition. In general and especially in spoken English, the preposition comes at the end of the adjective clause. However, in formal and written English, the preposition is placed at the beginning of the adjective clause.

▷ *Gretzky is a hockey player* **that** *most people know about. (informal or spoken English)*
▷ *Gretzky is a hockey player most people know about. (informal or spoken English)*
▷ *Gretzky is a hockey player* **about whom** *most people know. (formal or written English)*

---

1. **Who** is usually used instead of whom, especially in speaking. **Whom** is generally used as an object pronoun in formal or written English.

USING OBJECT PRONOUN *WHOSE*

- ***Whose*** + **noun** is used to show possession. In general, ***whose*** is used for people, but it can also be used for animals or things.
  - ▷ *The players **whose names were called** left for the game.*
  - ▷ *There is a cat **whose owners feed it fruit.***
  - ▷ *There is a great team **whose name I can't remember.***

USING *WHERE* AND *WHEN*

An **adjective clause** may be introduced by a ***relative adverb*** such as ***where*** or ***when.***

- ***Where*** is used to modify a place noun.
  - ▷ *California is the state **where many electronics companies have their headquarters.***

- ***When*** is used to modify a time noun.
  - *The time period **when** dinosaurs roamed the earth lasted millions of years.*

Place nouns and time nouns can also be modified by a preposition and a clause beginning with ***which.*** The prepositions ***on, in*** or ***at*** are generally used with the pronoun ***which.***

- ▷ *California is the state **in which** many electronics companies have their headquarters.*
- ▷ *My mother will never forget the day **on which** she met my father.*
- ▷ *This is the exact spot **at which** the accident occurred.*

REDUCTION OF ADJECTIVE CLAUSES

Adjective clauses may be reduced (or shortened) **by omitting the pronoun.** When the pronoun appears before the verb *be* (used in the clause as the verb or as an auxiliary verb), the **verb *be* can also be omitted.** By omitting the pronoun and the verb *be,* we change the adjective clause to another grammatical construction.

- ▷ *The car **that we rented Monday** was fast.* (adjective clause)
- ▷ *The car **we rented Monday** was fast.* (adjective clause with ***that*** understood)
- ▷ *The shoes **that are in the locker** are Saima's.* (adjective clause with pronoun and verb ***be***)
- ▷ *The shoes **in the locker** are Saima's.* (adjective phrase)
- ▷ *The teacher who **was working with the Japanese students** was being very attentive.* (adjective clause with pronoun and verb ***be*** as an auxiliary verb)
- ▷ *The teacher **working with the Japanese students** was being very attentive.* (participial phrase)
- ▷ *Marc Garneau, **who was the first Canadian sent into space,** works for the Canadian Space Agency.* (adjective clause with pronoun and verb ***be***)
- ▷ *Marc Garneau, **the first Canadian sent into space,** works for the Canadian Space Agency.* (noun phrase complementing, or in apposition to, the subject "Marc Garneau")

Adjective clauses that contain **subject pronouns + verbs other than** *be* can often be reduced by leaving out the subject pronoun and changing the verb to the *-ing* form (present participle).

▷ *Jamie and David,* **who want to win an Olympic medal next year,** *are training intensively.* (adjective clause with pronoun and verb other than *be*)

▷ *Jamie and David,* **wanting to win an Olympic medal next year,** *are training intensively.* (participial phrase)

Noun Clauses

A noun clause is a dependent or subordinate clause used as a noun.

- It can be used as a **subject.**
  ▷ **The Suzanne is a talented actress** *is obvious.*

- It can also be used as an object of a verb or a preposition.
  ▷ *Barbara and I discussed* **what we should do for our assignment.**
  ▷ *We listened to* **what he told us.**

USING *QUESTION WORDS* TO BEGIN A NOUN CLAUSE

The noun clause uses **question word + subject + predicate** order, without any auxiliary or helping verb like a question word normally introduces.

▷ **Who will be at the game** *is very important for the players.*
▷ *The teacher doesn't know* **why Jordana and Jacob didn't study.**
▷ **What went on** *surprised me.*
▷ **How good your mark will be** *depends on the amount of work you put in.*
  How good will your mark be *depends on the amount of work you put in.*[1]

USING *WHETHER* AND *IF* WITH A NOUN CLAUSE

- **Whether** or **if** can be used to introduce a noun clause. **Whether** is more common in formal or written English, whereas **if** is used in informal or spoken English.
  ▷ *I don't know* **whether they will play at the park.**
  ▷ *I don't know* **if they will play at the park.**
  ▷ *I wonder* **whether they need to be accompanied.**
  ▷ *I wonder* **if they need to be accompanied.**

- The use of **whether** or **if** suggests that there are two implied possibilities: one affirmative ("Yes, they will play at the park") and one negative ("No, they won't play at the park"). The structure or pattern **or not** is often used with noun clauses starting with either **whether** or **if.**
  ▷ *I don't know* **whether or not they will play at the park.**
    I don't know **whether they will play at the park or not.**
  ▷ *I don't know* **if they will play at the park or not.**
    Whether they play at the park or not *is fine by me.*

---

1. Incorrect form.

USING *THAT* WITH A NOUN CLAUSE

- ***That*** can be placed at the beginning of a **noun clause used as a subject.** It is more often used in formal or written English. In informal or spoken English, it is more common to use ***it*** as the subject and place the noun clause at the end of the sentence.

  ▷ ***That this student works hard*** *is very obvious.*
    It is very obvious ***that this student works hard.***

  ▷ ***That we spend a lot of money*** *is a fact.*
    It is a fact ***that we spend a lot of money.***

- ***That*** can be placed at the beginning of a noun clause used as an object. Usually, ***that*** (which may be omitted) follows a verb referring to a mental activity (***believe, complain, decide, dream, expect, forget, hope, regret, remember, understand, etc.***) or a verb used for reporting (***indicate, inform, question, remark, report, think, etc***).

  ▷ *She believes* ***that Justin is a good friend.***
    She believes ***Justin is a good friend.***

  ▷ *We think* ***that she is a good teacher.***
    We think ***she is a good teacher.***

- Noun clauses beginning with ***that*** also follow certain adjectives such as ***amused, amusing, happy, ironic, surprised, surprising,*** and ***unhappy.***

  ▷ *Jorgen and Kim are surprised* ***that there is no class today.***

- Some verbs and adjectives require a subjunctive form of the verb in the noun clause beginning with ***that.*** Verbs such as ***advise, ask, demand, insist, recommend, request*** and ***suggest,*** as well as adjectives such as ***essential, imperative, important, necessary*** and ***vital*** are often followed by the subjunctive.

  ▷ *Our teacher demands* ***that Mike and Jan-Ove see her immediately.***

  ▷ *It is imperative* ***that these students be there right away.***

CONDITIONAL SENTENCES

A conditional sentence usually contains an **if clause**. An **if clause** is a subordinate clause (a clause that gives extra information about the main clause that poses a condition) and a result clause (an independent clause that suggests a result or a consequence). Conditional sentences are generally used to express possible or imagined situations and their results.

if clause (subordinate clause)	+ result clause (independent clause)
▷ **If we invite you to our house,**	*you must stay for supper.*

LIST OF CONDITIONAL SENTENCES

Meaning of the *if clause*	Verb form in the if clause 1 verb form in the result clause	Examples
True in the present/future	simple present + simple present	*If I have a good mark, I go out tonight.*
	simple present + (**will** + simple form)	*If I have a good mark, I will go out tomorrow.*
	simple present + (**can** + simple form)	*If I have a good mark, I can go out tonight.*
Untrue in the present/future	simple past + (**would** + simple form)	*If I had good marks, I would go out every weekend.*
	simple past + (**could** + simple form)	*If I had good marks, I could go out every weekend.*
Untrue in the past	past perfect + (**would have** + past participle)	*If I had had good marks, I would have gone out last weekend.*
	past perfect + (**could have** + past participle)	*If I had had good marks, I could have gone out last weekend.*

WRITING

WRITING FORMATS

Narrative Text

NARRATIVE OUTLINE

It's not much fun to read a story if you know how it's going to end! If you want to surprise your readers, plan what you're going to tell them using the simple outline provided below. An interesting story generally has five main parts: an initial situation, a triggering event, action, a denouement and a closing situation.

Initial Situation

- I position the story in terms of place (where?) and time (when?) and develop the atmosphere.
- I introduce and describe my characters – at least my main character (who?).
- I explain my characters' course of action (what?) at the beginning of the story.

Triggering Event

- I describe the event that upsets, interrupts or interferes with the completion of my characters' course of action.

Action

- I recount or illustrate the episodes in my story in which my characters will try to find a way to continue their adventure or find a solution to their problem so they can complete their course of action.

Denouement

- I explain how my characters succeed or fail with respect to their course of action and how they feel after the events that take place during the story.

Final Situation

- I explain what has happened to my main character.
- I tell my reader whether the main character has learned anything from the experience.
- I use the final situation to balance out the initial situation, after the events of my story have occurred.

NARRATIVE TEXT EXAMPLE

Raspy and Mary Anne

Eager to visit her cousin, Karim, Mary Anne walked along quickly, accompanied by her faithful friend, Raspy. The big dog had earned his nickname from his attempts to imitate his mistress when she suffered from her dreadful coughing fits. Mary Anne was nine years old and had a fiery temperament, despite her frail, delicate appearance. She wore a pretty, polka-dotted dress and, on her right wrist, a lovely little bracelet.

As she hurried along, she tried to walk around a large rock, slipped, struck her head on a tree trunk and lost consciousness. When he saw that Mary Anne failed to respond to his barking, Raspy grabbed her and dragged her under a tree. He stretched out over her, hoping to warm her, but she did not awaken. The dog then dove into a nearby stream, performed a few acrobatic jumps and turns, approached Mary Anne once again and shook himself over her. The cool water brought the young girl back to consciousness. She sat up, realized what had happened and planted a loud, smacking kiss on her friend's muzzle.

When she arrived at Karim's house, safe and sound, Mary Anne introduced him to Raspy, who was in the midst of a coughing fit. She explained what had happened and promised her cousin that she would be more careful on her way home.

OUTLINE OF THE EXAMPLE

Initial Situation

- Introduce character or characters
- Specify atmosphere, setting, time and course of action

Example: Mary Anne is walking along with Raspy and going to visit her cousin.

Note: Setting and atmosphere are not specified in this initial situation.

↓

Triggering Event

- An event that disrupts the initial situation and triggers the story

Example: Mary Anne falls and loses consciousness.

↓

Action	Results
1. Raspy tries to warm his mistress. →	**1.** Mary Anne doesn't move.
2. Raspy finds a way to help his young mistress. He wets his coat and shakes himself over her to wake her up. →	**2.** Mary Anne wakes up.

↓

Denouement

1. The cool water returns the girl to consciousness.
2. She sits up, realizes what has happened and kisses Raspy.

↓

Final Situation

- Return to a stable situation.

Example: Mary Anne and Raspy arrive at Karim's house.
Raspy now has a cold.
Mary Anne promises to be more careful.

Descriptive Text

DESCRIPTIVE OUTLINE

Who and what should you describe? Frequently you can describe characters, events, objects, animals or places. The simple outline below will help you prepare to write a descriptive text. You will discover that this type of writing most often involves the following three stages: introduction, development and conclusion.

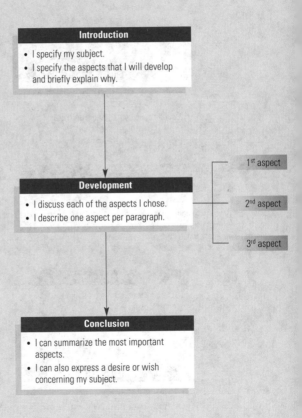

Introduction
- I specify my subject.
- I specify the aspects that I will develop and briefly explain why.

Development
- I discuss each of the aspects I chose.
- I describe one aspect per paragraph.

1st aspect

2nd aspect

3rd aspect

Conclusion
- I can summarize the most important aspects.
- I can also express a desire or wish concerning my subject.

DESCRIPTIVE TEXT EXAMPLE

My Village

I live in a magnificent village located along the shore of the St. Lawrence River. My village resembles many others in my region, but its inhabitants, main street and annual summer festival make it unique.

First, approximately five thousand people live in my village. Most of them are descended from families that have lived here for several generations, but over the last three years, our new arrivals have included two families from Belgium and one from Algeria.

Second, my village's main street is the most beautiful in the entire region. It is narrow and winding, and bordered by houses on both sides. Passersby will often see elderly inhabitants on the balconies, sitting in their rocking chairs or playing cards and dominoes. Our two-hundred-year-old church is located at the village entry point and flanked by two beautiful houses that have been turned into a restaurant and tourist hotel. The old general store, located in the village centre, has retained all of its charm, even though the owners expanded it last year.

Last, every June, all the people in region flock to my village to attend the Raspberry Festival. During this event, the banners and multicoloured decorations all over the main street make the whole village look bright and cheerful.

In conclusion, my village is a unique place and, to those who love raspberries as much as I do, a true heaven on earth.

OUTLINE OF THE EXAMPLE

Introduction

- The subject is "my village."
- Its inhabitants, main street and annual festival make it unique.

Development

- 1st aspect: the inhabitants
- 2nd aspect: the main street
  - 1st sub-aspect: the buildings
  - 2nd sub-aspect: history
- 3rd aspect: the Raspberry Festival

Conclusion

- This village is heaven on earth to everyone who loves raspberries.

THE WRITING PROCESS

When you write, you want your reader to understand and enjoy what you are writing. To make your writing the best it can be, you have to work at it and take it through the **writing process,** from idea to finished form.

The stages of the writing process are not totally separate from each other. For example, when you are concentrating on the content of a story, you would correct the spelling mistakes you see. Or if you noticed an error in logic when you were proofreading, you would make the necessary changes. Here are some suggestions of what to do at each stage of the writing process.

Important things before writing

- Purpose – Why are you writing (to reflect, report, entertain)?
- Audience – Who are you writing for (friends, family, your teacher, the general public or yourself)?
- Format – What format is the best way to present what you have to say?
- Length and style of writing
- Layout, illustrations, diagrams or photographs

Developing ideas

- Brainstorm ideas and discuss them with others.
- Make an idea web.
- Do some research and make notes.
- Organize your information into an outline.

Writing formats

- **Messages:** letters, postcards, invitations, thank-you notes
- **Narrative:** mystery stories, scripts, heroic tales, realistic stories, fables
- **Poetry:** haiku, couplets, free verse, narrative, shape, limericks
- **Informational:** reports, articles, timelines, directions, guides, recipes
- **Word play:** comics, jokes, crosswords, puzzles, tongue twisters
- **Persuasive:** posters, editorials, print ads, jingles, TV ads

Writing

↓

First draft

- Concentrate on getting your ideas down on paper.
- For non-fiction, you need to concentrate on:
  - getting your main ideas down;
  - answering your own questions;
  - finding and adding information to support your ideas;
  - drawing a conclusion.
- For fiction, this is the time to concentrate on:
  - developing your plot;
  - defining the setting;
  - describing the characters;
  - setting the style of writing (humorous, mysterious);
  - writing techniques you can add.

↓

Writing techniques

Writers make their writing more interesting by expressing ideas in original, unusual or descriptive ways or by adding details and information in a subtle way. The following list includes some of the **writing techniques** you can use:

- Alliteration
- Antonyms
- Atmosphere
- Dialogue
- Exaggeration
- Figurative language
- Figures of speech
- Foreshadowing
- Idiom
- Irony
- Metaphors
- Mood
- Personification
- Similes

↓

Revising

Revising focuses on the content. You may need to revise your writing several times before it's ready. Make sure that:

- all the information you need is included;
- the facts are correct;
- nothing needs to be rewritten or explained;
- the information is in a logical order;
- your words and phrases are descriptive and the verbs are in the proper form and tense. Is there a better word you could use? (You can use a dictionary and thesaurus.);
- a variety of sentences and writing techniques are used;
- your sentences and paragraphs are complete.

↓

↓

Editing

Editing focuses on grammar, punctuation and spelling.
This is the time to make sure that:
- you have used words correctly;
- your sentences are complete;
- the writing flows. (You can read the writing aloud to listen to how it flows.);
- the punctuation is correct;
- the words are spelled correctly.

↓

Proofreading

Proofreading is a final check to make sure your spelling and punctuation are correct. You can:
- use a spelling program on a computer to help, but you still need to read each word in context to make sure that you are using it correctly;
- ask someone (a classmate or family member) to help edit and proofread;
- keep a dictionary with you when you edit and proofread to look up the meanings and spellings of words.

↓

Publishing

Publishing your writing allows you to share it with others.
- Think about layout, design, headlines, captions, illustrations or photographs, and a cover.
- Make a clean copy of the work.

CONNECTING IDEAS

Connectors and **transition words** help to organize the information in a text. They also help the reader to understand the logic in the text.

My Village

I live **in** a magnificent village located **along** the shore **of** the St. Lawrence River. My village resembles many others **in** my region, **but** its inhabitants, main street **and** annual summer festival make it unique.

First, approximately five thousand people live **in** my village. Most **of** them are descended **from** families that have lived here **for** several generations, **but** over the last three years, our new arrivals have included two families **from** Belgium **and** one **from** Algeria.

Second, my village's main street is the most beautiful **in** the entire region. It is narrow **and** winding, **and** bordered **by** houses **on** both sides. Passersby will often see elderly inhabitants **on** the balconies, sitting **in** their rocking chairs **or** playing cards **and** dominoes. Our two-hundred-year-old church is located **at** the village entry point **and** flanked **by** two beautiful houses that have been turned **into** a restaurant **and** tourist hotel. The old general store, located **in** the village centre, has retained all **of** its charm, **even though** the owners expanded it last year.

Last, every June, all the people **in** region flock **to** my village **to** attend the Raspberry Festival. During this event, the banners **and** multicoloured decorations all over the main street make the whole village look bright **and** cheerful.

In conclusion, my village is a unique place **and, to** those who love raspberries as much as I do, a true heaven **on** earth.

Writing

934

WORDS THAT HELP CONNECT IDEAS

	coordination	transition	adverb clause	preposition
addition	and not only...but also both...and	in addition, besides, that, furthermore, moreover		in addition to besides
cause and effect	so for	consequently hence therefore thus accordingly as a result	because for since as inasmuch as now that so (that)	because of due to
summary emphasis		in conclusion in short to summarize to conclude indeed in fact in other words		
contrast	but yet	yet however nevertheless on the contrary on the other hand	although though even though while whereas	despite in spite of
time		first second next later finally then	when while as before after since until as soon as whenever	
condition	or nor either...or neither...nor or else	otherwise	if even if whether (or not) unless in case only if in the event that	in case of in the event of

TYPES OF GRAPHS

A **graph** shows the relationship between two changing things. It shows how the one quantity of something depends on or changes with another. On bar and line graphs, the two things being compared are written on the bottom and to the left of the graph. For example, on a line graph comparing how many students use the library at different times of the day, the number of students would be written on the left side of the graph, while the time would be written on the bottom of the graph.

Pictograph

How students get to school	
Transportation	**Number of students**
Walk	🧍 🧍 🧍 🧍 🧍 🧍 🧍 🧍 🧍
Car	🧍 🧍 🧍 🧍 🧍 🧍 🧍
Bike	🧍 🧍 🧍 🧍 🧍 🧍 🧍 🧍
Bus	🧍 🧍 🧍 🧍

Key: 🧍 = 1 student

Bar Graph

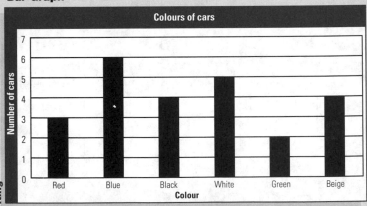

Line Graph

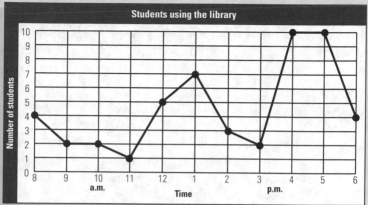

Pie Graph

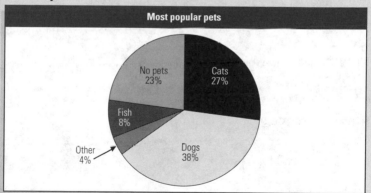

SPELLING

Spelling words in English can be difficult because many words are not spelled the way they sound, and most sounds can be spelled in different ways. However, there are some spelling rules. Learning and understanding these can help you spell more words correctly.

ALTERNATE SPELLINGS

Canadian spelling is often a mix of British and American spellings.
In different parts of Canada, one spelling is more common than the other.
However, the most common Canadian spellings follow this style:

- Use ***our*** (not ***or***) in words such as *honour, colour* and *neighbour*.
- Use ***re*** (not ***er***) at the end of words such as *centre, metre* and *fibre*.
- Double the ***l*** before adding a suffix in words such as *traveller, labelling, signalled* and *jewellery*.
- Use a ***c*** in nouns such as *licence* and *practice*. Use an ***s*** in verbs such as *license* and *practise*.
- Use an ***s*** in words such as *analyse* (analyze), *paralyse* (paralyze) and *cosy* (cozy).
- Other words with alternate spellings are *storey* (story) and *grey* (gray).
- You may also see alternate spellings in advertising: *donut* (doughnut) or *lite* (light). These spellings are not usually considered standard.

IE OR *EI*?

- In most words, ***i*** comes before ***e***: *believe, relief, thief,*
  except after ***c***: *receive, deceive,*
  and in words that rhyme with ***ay***: *eight, weight, freight.*
  Exceptions: *weird, height, species, seize, foreign*

HARD OR SOFT *C* OR *G*?

- An ***e, i*** or ***y*** after a ***c*** or ***g*** usually makes it a soft ***c*** or ***g***.
  pace/pact, ginger/gate
  Exceptions: *get, tiger, gift, giggle*

ADDING PLURALS

Nouns can be **singular** (only one) or **plural** (two or more). The plural form of a noun is listed in the dictionary entry.

- To make most nouns plural, add an ***s*** to the singular word (dogs, cars).
- For most nouns that end in ***s, ch, sh*** or ***x***, add ***es*** to the singular word (bosses, lunches, crashes, boxes).
- For nouns that end in ***y***, change the ***y*** to ***i*** and then add ***es*** (candy/candies, sky/skies). If the noun ends with a vowel followed by a ***y***, only add ***s*** (days, monkeys, toys, guys).

Spelling

938

- For many of the words that end in **f** or **fe,** change the **f** or **fe** to **v** and add **es** (leaf/leaves, knife/knives).

- For words that end in **o** after a single consonant, add **es** (tomatoes, heroes). If the word ends in **o** after two consonants, only add **s** (pros, typos, pueblos). (There are some exceptions where you have a choice: mosquitos, mosquitoes.)

- Some nouns have irregular plurals (child/children, man/men).

- To make most hyphenated words plural, add an **s** (or **es**) to the most important word (mothers-in-law).

ADDING SUFFIXES

A **suffix** is a part of a word that is added to the end of a word to modify its meaning. There are several rules to follow when adding suffixes. When you add a suffix:

- To words ending in a consonant:
  - Just add the suffix. help/helpful sleep/sleeping
  - For words that stress the last syllable or end in **l,** double the last consonant before adding a suffix beginning with a vowel.
  refer/referral travel/traveller occur/occurring

- To one-syllable words:
  - Double the last consonant before adding a suffix beginning with a vowel.
  sad/sadder wet/wettest
  - Except words ending in **x** and some words that end in two or more consonants.
  box/boxes start/started search/searching

- To most words ending in **e**:
  - Drop the **e** before adding a suffix starting with a vowel.
  hope/hoping combine/combination
  - Most words keep the **e** when the suffix starts with a consonant.
  hope/hopeful there/therefore

- To words that end in **y**:
  - Change the **y** to **i** and then add the suffix.
  candy/candies fly/flies happy/happier
  - If the word ends in a **vowel + y,** just add the suffix.
  monkey/monkeys stay/staying

- To words ending in **c**:
  - Add **k** before adding a suffix beginning with **i** or **e** to keep the **c** hard.
  panic/panicking traffic/trafficking

PREFIXES

Prefixes are words or parts of words that can be added to the beginning of words to change the meaning.

- When you add a prefix, you don't add or take away any letters from the original word.
- In some words, a hyphen is added between the prefix and the word.

Prefix	Meaning	Example	Prefix	Meaning	Example
ab	away from	absent, abstract	mid	half	midway
anti	against	antifreeze	mini	very small	miniskirt
auto	self	autobiography	mis	wrong; ill	mistake, misspell
bene	good	beneficial, benefit	mono	one; single	monotonous
bi	two	biweekly, bicycle	multi	many	multifaceted
bio	life	biochemistry, biosphere	non	not	nonviolent
centi	hundred	centimetre	over	too much	overrun
circum	around	circumnavigate	pan	all	pan-Canadian
co	with	co-worker, cooperate	para	beside; near	paramedic
com/con	with	compassion, conjunction		guard against	parachute
			per	throughout; by	perchance
contra	against	contradistinguish	post	after	postgame
counter	against	counter-revolutionary	pre	before	prehistoric
de	negation	debrief, degrade	pro	forward; in favour of	procreate
deci	tenth	decimetre			
dia	through	diameter	re	again	redo, re-read
dis	apart; away	dislike, disagree		back	regain, reaction
eco	earth	ecosystem	semi	half	semisweet
equi	equal	equivalent	sub	below	submarine, subtitle
ex	former; out of	ex-wife, ex-president	super	above; greater	superman, supertanker
extra	out of	extraterrestrial	tele	far	telephone, television
hyper	above	hyperactive	trans	across	transport
il/im/in/ir	not	illegal, impartial	tri	three	tricycle
im/in	in; into	import, include	ultra	beyond	ultrasound
inter	between	interschool	un	not; uncertain	unnecessary
mega	great	megaphone	under	below	underused
micro	small	microscope	uni	one	uniform, unicycle

ROOT WORDS

The **root** of a word is the part of the word that has the meaning. The root is also known as the **base** or **stem**. Prefixes and suffixes are added to roots to make words.

Root	Meaning	Example	Root	Meaning	Example
act	do	*action, activity*	**mot**	move	*motive, motor*
aqua	water	*aquarium*	**nat**	born	*natural, native*
audi	hear	*auditorium*	**nov**	new	*novelty, novice*
bio	life	*biography*	**ology**	the study of	*biology*
cap	head	*capital, captain*	**opt**	eye	*optician, optical*
cent	hundred	*percent*	**ped**	foot	*pedal, expedition*
cred	believe	*credit, credible*	**phono**	sound	*phonograph*
cycl	circle	*bicycle, recycle*	**photo**	light	*photograph*
dict	speak	*dictate, diction*	**poli**	city	*police*
duct	lead	*conduct, induct*	**port**	carry	*transport, portage*
fac	make; do	*factory, faction*	**rupt**	break	*erupt, disrupt*
form	shape	*formation*	**sci**	know	*science, conscious*
geo	earth	*geology*	**scribe**	write	*describe*
gram	write	*program*	**script**	write	*prescription*
graph	write	*graphics*	**sens**	feel	*sensor, sensitive*
ject	throw	*object, reject*	**sign**	mark	*signal, design*
jud/jus	law	*judge, justice*	**spec**	look	*spectator*
loc	place	*location, locate*	**sta**	stand	*stadium, statue*
man	hand	*manufacture*	**struct**	build	*construction*
mand	order	*command*	**temp**	time	*temporary*
min	small	*miniature*	**vid/vis**	see	*video, visual*

SUFFIXES

Suffixes are parts of words that are added on to the end of words.

Suffix	Meaning	Example	Suffix	Meaning	Example
able	likely	*breakable*	**ile**	marked by	*juvenile*
ant/ent	agent; showing	*servant, pleasant*	**ion**	action; result	*union, companion*
ate	having	*affectionate*	**ise**	make; cause	*advertise*
	make; cause	*pollinate*	**ish**	like	*childish*
ation/tion	action	*separation*	**ism**	act; belief	*socialism*
	condition	*rejection*	**ist**	doer; believer	*pianist*
ence	act; condition	*difference*	**ize**	make; cause	*energize*
er	doer; native of	*player, Easterner*	**less**	without	*helpless*
ese	of a place	*Japanese*	**like**	similar to	*childlike*
ful	full of	*beautiful, hopeful*	**ment**	state	*amazement*
fy	make	*magnify*	**ness**	quality	*happiness*
hood	condition	*childhood*	**or**	doer; action	*doctor, error*
ian	belonging to	*Canadian*	**ous**	given to	*dangerous*
ible	likely	*edible, possible*	**y/fly**	like; manner	*friendly*

ABBREVIATIONS

Abbreviations are the shortened forms of words or phrases. Abbreviations are formed by dropping letters from a word. Some abbreviations have a period at the end.

- Sentences should not begin with an abbreviation. Either reword the sentence or write the word out in full.

- The first time you write an abbreviation in a piece of writing, use the long form with the abbreviation following in brackets: *United Nations (UN)*. Then you can use the abbreviation throughout the rest of the piece.

- Try not to use too many abbreviations at once. It makes the sentence harder to read.

- Here are some common abbreviations:

AB/Alta.	Alberta	Feb.	February
A.D.	(Latin, *anno Domini*) in the year of our Lord	Fri.	Friday
		f/x or fx	special effects
a.m.	(Latin, *ante meridiem*) before noon	FYI	for your information
		govt.	government
Apr.	April	GST	Goods and Services Tax
apt.	apartment	Hon.	Honourable
ASAP	as soon as possible	HQ	headquarters
Aug.	August	i.e.	(Latin, *id est*) that is
Ave.	Avenue	incl.	including
BC/B.C.	British Columbia	IOU	I owe you
B.C.	Before Christ	IQ	intelligence quotient
Blvd.	Boulevard	Jan.	January
C	Celsius, centigrade	Jr.	Junior
c. or ca	(Latin, *circa*) around, about	Ltd.	Limited
CAN or Can.	Canada	Mar.	March
CD	compact disk	max.	maximum
c/o	in care of	MB/Man.	Manitoba
C.O.D./c.o.d.	cash on delivery	M.C.	master of ceremonies
Cres.	Crescent	M.D.	medical doctor
DAT	digital audio tape	min.	minimum
Dec.	December	misc.	miscellaneous
dept.	department	MLA	Member of the Legislative Assembly
Dr.	Doctor or Drive		
E	east	M.O.	(Latin, *modus operandi*) mode of operation
ea.	each		
ed.	edited, editor, edition	Mon.	Monday
e.g.	(Latin, *exempli gratia*) for example	MP	Member of Parliament
		MPP	Member of Provincial Parliament
encl.	enclosed, enclosure	Mr.	Mister
esp.	especially	Mt.	Mount
est.	estimated	N	north
et al.	(Latin, *et alii*) and others	N/A	not available or not applicable
etc.	(Latin, *et cetera*) and so forth	NATO	North Atlantic Treaty Organization
F	Fahrenheit		

NB/N.B.	New Brunswick	Rx	prescription
N.B.	(Latin, *nota bene*) note well	SASE	self-addressed stamped envelope
NE	northeast	Sat.	Saturday
NF/Nfld.	Newfoundland	Sept.	September
no.	number	SK/Sask.	Saskatchewan
Nov.	November	S	south
NS/N.S.	Nova Scotia	sq.	square
NT/N.W.T.	North West Territories	Sr.	Senior
NW	Northwest	St.	Saint or Street
Oct.	October	Sun.	Sunday
ON/Ont.	Ontario	TBA/t.b.a.	to be announced
p./pg.	page	temp.	temperature or temporary
PC	personal computer	Thurs.	Thursday
PE/P.E.I.	Prince Edward Island	tr.	translation
PIN	personal identification number	Tues.	Tuesday
p.m.	(Latin, *post meridiem*) after noon	TV/t.v.	television
P.M.	Prime Minister	UFO	unidentified flying object
pop.	population	UN	United Nations
PQ/Que.	Quebec	UNESCO	United Nations Educational, Scientific, and Cultural Organization
P.S.	postscript		
PTA	Parent-Teacher Association		
RCMP	Royal Canadian Mounted Police	UNICEF	United Nations Children's Fund
Rd.	Road	vet.	veterinarian or veteran
ref.	reference	VIP	very important person
RIP	(Latin, *requiescat in pace*) rest in peace	vol.	volume
		V.P.	vice-president
RN	registered nurse	W	west
RR/R.R.	rural route; railroad	Wed.	Wednesday
RSVP	(French, *répondez s'il vous plaît*) please answer	YT/Y.T.	Yukon Territory

CONTRACTIONS

Contractions are two words combined into one word. An apostrophe takes the place of part of one word; for example, the contraction of "do not" is *don't* and the contraction of "they had" is *they'd*. When you write contractions, think about which two words make up the word you want. The following are common contractions listed under the word that has been shortened:

Not	Will	Have	Would/Had	Is/Has
aren't	I'll	I've	I'd	he's
can't	we'll	you've	you'd	she's
couldn't	you'll	they've	he'd	it's
didn't	he'll	could've	she'd	that's
don't	she'll	should've	we'd	there's
hadn't	it'll	might've	they'd	who's
hasn't	one'll	who've	it'd	here's
haven't	they'll	there've	there'd	one's
isn't	these'll	would've	what'd	that's
mustn't	those'll	what've	who'd	what's
shouldn't	that'll		that'd	
wasn't	this'll	**Are**		**Other**
weren't	what'll	you're	**Am**	**Contractions**
won't	who'll	we're	I'm	o'clock
wouldn't		they're		jack-o'-lantern
		who're	**Us**	'twas (it was)
			let's	

SYLLABLES

Syllables are the different sounds in a word. Each syllable makes a beat when you say a word out loud. Every syllable has at least one vowel in it. "Toy" has one beat (one syllable); "happy" has two beats (two syllables); and "Saturday" has three beats (three syllables). Syllables can be used to count beats in poetry or lyrics.

When you write or type, you can use syllables to divide words at the end of a line. Some rules for dividing words are:

- Divide words between double consonants (dim-mer, win-ner).
- Divide words between the prefix or suffix and the root word (pre-judge, talk-ing).
- One- and two-letter syllables should not be divided from the rest of the word; for example, dividing "truly" would leave *ly* on its own.
- Divide hyphenated words at the hyphen (twenty-five).

NOTE: Try not to divide the proper names of people or things.

HOMOPHONES AND HOMOGRAPHS

People are sometimes confused about the difference between **homographs** and **homophones.**

- **Homophones** are words that sound the same but have different spellings and meanings. (*Hint: Phone* means "sound.")

  ▷ *dear* a term of affection   *deer* an animal with antlers

- **Homographs** are words that are spelled the same but have different meanings and sometimes different pronunciations. (*Hint: Graph* means "writing.")

  ▷ *bow* a **bow** and arrow   *bow* the **bow** of a ship

NOTE: When you are revising and editing your writing, check for homophones. Computer spell-checking programs are not able to distinguish between homophones (e.g., their/there) since both words are spelled correctly. Careful rereading is necessary to identify and correct errors using homophones.

Common homophones to watch for:

ate/eight	one/won	sell/cell
bear/bare	pain/pane	side/sighed
beat/beet	pair/pear/pare	sight/site/cite
blue/blew	pale/pail	size/sighs
cent/sent/scent	plane/plain	some/sum
cheap/cheep	pour/pore	son/sun
dear/deer	principal/principle	Sunday/sundae
fair/fare	rain/reign/rein	they're/their/there
for/four/fore	raise/rays	tied/tide
grown/groan	read/reed	to/too/two
hair/hare	ring/wring	warn/worn
here/hear	road/rode/rowed	way/weigh
its/it's	roll/role	we'd/weed
main/mane	sale/sail	week/weak
new/knew	seam/seem	whose/who's
night/knight	seas/sees/seize	write/right
no/know	see/sea	you're/your

PUNCTUATION

Punctuation helps the reader read a group of words as if they were spoken. For example, periods and commas show when there is a pause between words. Following the rules of punctuation makes it easier for a reader to read and understand what you have written.

APOSTROPHES

An **apostrophe** has two uses in written English:

- in contractions, to indicate that some letters or numbers are missing.
  she's (she is); won't (will not); o'clock (of the clock); '02 (2002)

- to indicate possession or ownership.
  Lekh's idea; Sunjay's dinner; the boy's clothes

  - For single nouns that end in **s,** you can use **'** or **'s.**
    my boss' desk or *my boss's desk*   *Luis' dog* or *Luis's dog*

  - For plural nouns that end in **s,** you add only the apostrophe.
    the girls' clubhouse   *the babies' jackets*

CAPITALIZATION

Capital letters are used in the following places:

- The first word in any sentence.
  Where are we going now?

- People's names and other proper nouns.

  - **people**: Sir John A. Macdonald; Dennis Lee

  - **place names**: Nova Scotia; Canadian Rockies; Winnipeg

  - **events**: World Series; the Calgary Stampede

  - **days and months**: Sunday; Monday; January; February

  - **holidays**: Thanksgiving; New Year's Day; Canada Day

  - **organizations**: National Hockey League; the United Nations

  - **trade names**: Roller Blades; Jell-O

  - **nationalities, races, tribes and cultural groups**:
    Chinese; African-American; Cree; First Nations; Europeans

  - **titles of books, magazines, films, songs, plays and poems**:
    Underground to Canada; The Wreck of the Edmund Fitzgerald

  - **titles when they are included with the person's name**:
    Councillor Quon; the Councillor

- The pronoun "I."
  I can't believe what I just did.

- The first word of a direct quotation.
  Sylvie asked, "Where did you leave the keys?"

- Lists when the elements are on separate lines.
  The activities planned are:

  1. *Swimming*   **2.** *Bike riding*   **3.** *Volleyball*

COLONS :

A **colon** tells the reader to "note what follows." A colon is used:

- to introduce a list of items. Often, a word or phrase such as *these, for example* or *the following* comes before the colon.
  *You'll need to bring **the following** items: a bathing suit, a towel and sunscreen.*

- at the beginning of an explanation for what has just been said.
  My vacation was horrible: my luggage was lost and it rained all the time.

- after the greeting in a formal letter.
  Dear Ms. Manley: *Dear Dr. Lopez:*

- when writing the time in numbers.
  4:15   *6:30*   *12:00*

- to introduce a quotation that is four or more lines long.

COMMAS ,

A **comma** makes writing easier to read and understand. Commas generally show where a natural pause occurs in a sentence. They never go between the subject and verb. Commas are placed:

- before a conjunction (and, but, or) joining main clauses.
  The sun was shining brightly, and I went for a walk along the lake.
  However, a comma is not needed to separate **short** main clauses.
  The sun was bright and the clouds were white and fluffy.

- before or after a dependent clause in a sentence.
  Although my door was shut, I could still hear the radio.
  Jennifer overcame her agoraphobia, which is the fear of being in open or public spaces.

- before and after clauses that could be in parentheses.
  When my dog barked, which he doesn't usually do, I checked the door.
  We went to the museum and, of course, the parliament buildings.

- between two or more adjectives that are modifying a noun.
  the hot, bright sun   *the old, green, woolen mittens*

- between words, phrases or clauses in a list or series.
  I need to buy shampoo, toothpaste, and tissues.
  We search in the house, on the lawn, and around the garage.

- to separate spoken words from the rest of the sentence.
  Janice asked, "When are you coming over?"
  "I'll be there early," he replied.

- after the greeting and closing in a friendly letter.
  Dear Elena,   *Sincerely,*

- after introductory phrases or clauses.
  Underneath the floorboards, we found an old box containing a treasure map.
  Using all of her strength, she pulled on the door handle.

- however, a comma is not needed for **short** phrases that refer to time or place.
  At home we take turns washing the dishes.

Punctuation

947

- between a person's name and title when the title follows the name.
  Pierre Trudeau, the former prime minister, gave a speech.
  (No comma is needed when the title goes before the name.)

- in dates.
  July 1, 1967   *Tuesday, May 22nd*

- after exclamations that do not express a strong emotion.
  Well, here we are.   *Oh dear, where did I put my book?*

- before and after words such as *however, indeed* and *obviously.*
  I think, however, that we should go home.

  NOTE: When you revise your writing, read your work out loud. Listen for the natural pauses, and then insert commas there.

DASHES ▬

A **dash** separates one part of a sentence from the rest of the sentence. Dashes let the reader know there will be a break in the flow of the sentence.

- Dashes show a sudden break in a sentence, as if a thought has been interrupted. Commas can be used this way as well, but dashes are stronger.
  Jason — he's my older brother — refused to go camping with me.

- Dashes show a sudden break in speech.
  "Where are —" Deanna began and then stopped suddenly.

- Dashes are used to introduce an explanation or list. The dash takes the place of phrases such as *namely, that is* and *in other words.*
  Stefan has three favourite pastimes — watching television, playing hockey and surfing the Net.

  NOTE: Dashes are a powerful punctuation mark, so use them carefully. You may want to use commas or rewrite the sentence to avoid using dashes, especially in formal writing.

ELLIPSIS ▪▪▪

Ellipsis, or ellipses points, is a series of dots that shows that something has been left out.

- One or more words have been left out of a quotation.
  The story The Hockey Sweater *by Rock Carrier starts "The winters of my childhood were long, long seasons. We lived in three places — the school, the church, and the skating rink — but our real life was on the skating rink."*
  A shorter version could be *"The winters of my childhood were long, long seasons. We lived in three places...but our real life was on the skating rink."*

- A sentence or thought has been left unfinished.
  I stopped to think...but no thoughts would come.

- When a speaker is hesitating.
  Ravi left...well, Ravi and Dave left... I think they went to the store.

  NOTE: If ellipses are used at the end of a sentence, include the period so that there will be four dots.
  One of Shakespeare's most famous lines is "To be or not to be...."

Punctuation

EXCLAMATION MARKS !

An **exclamation mark** is used at the end of a sentence to show surprise, enthusiasm, disbelief, urgency or strong emotion. Exclamation marks are also called exclamation points. Exclamation marks:

- punctuate a sentence, a phrase or a word that expresses surprise or a strong emotion.
  We've finally finished!   *Well done!*   *Stop!*

- replace a question mark when the tone of the question is very strong.
  What are you doing now!

  NOTE: Don't overuse exclamation marks or they won't mean anything special to your reader.

HYPHENS ▬

A **hyphen** is used to break words at the end of a line and to indicate compound words.

- When a word cannot fit on a line, use a hyphen to show that it continues onto the next line. Only divide a word between syllables (car-pet, pen-cil).
  If you are not sure about where to break a word, check the word in the dictionary. Do not divide one-syllable words.

- Some words have hyphens to show that they form one idea, such as:
  – compound words: *mother-in-law*   *a well-written story*
  – words with prefixes: *semi-sweet*   *co-ordinate*   *re-invent*
  – compound numbers from
    twenty-one to ninety-nine: *thirty-two cats*
  – fractions used as adjectives: *two-thirds of an apple*

PARENTHESES () AND BRACKETS []

- **Parentheses** are used to add information that is not closely related to the sentence without changing the structure of the sentence.
  After the game (our last of the season) we are going to Keeghan's house.

- **Square brackets** are used to add information that was not included by the author.
  She grew up in Paris [Ontario] but moved to Montreal.

- Parentheses and brackets are not introduced by any punctuation.

  NOTE: Parentheses and dashes are used the same way. You can choose which one you prefer. Some people think the dash is more noticeable, so they use it when they want the information inside to stand out.

PERIODS .

A **period** shows something is finished.

- Periods end sentences and sentence fragments (incomplete sentences).
  I left my lunch here and now it's gone. Totally gone.

Punctuation

949

- Some abbreviations end with a period. If the abbreviation uses the first letter of each word, the period goes after each letter.

Can.   *Dr.*   *B.A.*   *B.C.*

However, many abbreviations are now being spelled without any periods. Often you can find both spellings.   *U.N.* or *UN*

- Periods go after the initials in someone's name. Usually no space is left between the initials.   *P.E. Trudeau*   *W.C. Fields*

NOTE: Periods go inside quotation marks:
She said, "That's my house."

QUESTION MARKS

A **question mark** lets readers know that the sentence they have just read is a question.

- A question mark ends a sentence that asks a direct question.
What time is it?   *Where is my hat?*

- Question marks are placed inside quotation marks, parentheses and dashes.
After a few minutes, he asked, "What's your name?"

NOTE: A request (an indirect question) ends with a period.
Would you go to the gym, please.

QUOTATION MARKS " "

Quotation marks are punctuation marks that show that someone is speaking or that the information inside is the title of a story, article or poem.

- Quotation marks show direct speech (a quotation that shows what words are said).
"What's that?" he asked.
"I think," Shaunna replied, "it's only a dog."

- All quotations end in punctuation (a comma, period, question mark and so on) and are introduced by a comma when they come after phrases such as *he said* and *she replied.*

- For a direct quotation inside a direct quotation, use single quotation marks.
"And then he told me, 'I've flown a plane,'" Asad said.

- The titles of songs, poems, short stories, magazine articles and essays are surrounded by quotation marks.
"In the Next War" by Robert Priest is my favourite poem.

- Quotation marks always come in pairs. In the Canadian style of writing, the periods, commas, question marks and exclamation marks are put inside quotation marks.

NOTE: Quotation marks are not used for indirect quotations — quotations that do not reproduce exactly what was said. Indirect quotations are often introduced by the word "that."
*Hari said **that** he was coming tonight.*

SEMICOLONS ▪

A **semicolon** is similar to a period and a comma. Some people think of semicolons as weak periods or strong commas. (A semicolon can't end a sentence like a period, but it can identify major sections of a sentence.)

- Semicolons go between main clauses that don't have a conjunction (a connecting word such as *and, or* or *but*)
  The giant panda is endangered; its habitats are disappearing.

- Semicolons separate items in a list, if the items are long phrases or clauses. Generally the last item will follow a conjunction such as *and, or* or *but*.
  On my vacation I went to a baseball game in Montreal; camping with my uncle in Temagami; and whitewater rafting on the Ottawa River.

- Semicolons are put before words and phrases that introduce examples or lists, such as *for example, namely, for instance, i.e., e.g., as* and *that is;* and before clauses that start with words such as *moreover, however, also, therefore* and *consequently*.

- Often it is clearer to use a semicolon rather than a comma to separate a long subordinate clause from the rest of the sentence.
  We worked hard designing, building and painting the model; although we didn't know who would use it.

SLASHES ▪

- The **slash** shows that there is choice.
  We can choose a book and/or a magazine to read.

- A slash is also used in abbreviations and ratios.
  km/h *(kilometres per hour)*   c/o *(in care of)*
  We have a 50/50 chance of winning.   3/4

THESAURUS

Table of Contents

Table of Contents

Table of Contents

Index – Thesaurus

S

T

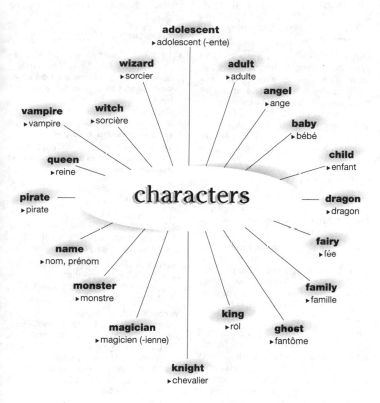

adolescent
▸adolescent (-ente)

wizard
▸sorcier

adult
▸adulte

angel
▸ange

vampire
▸vampire

witch
▸sorcière

baby
▸bébé

child
▸enfant

queen
▸reine

characters

dragon
▸dragon

pirate
▸pirate

fairy
▸fée

name
▸nom, prénom

family
▸famille

monster
▸monstre

king
▸roi

ghost
▸fantôme

magician
▸magicien (-ienne)

knight
▸chevalier

965

adolescent ▸ adolescent (-ente)

nouns adolescence, juvenile, puberty, student, teen, teenager, young adult, young lady, young man, young person, youngster, young woman, youth.

adjectives aggressive, ambitious, athletic, energetic, friendly, funny, happy, immature, mad, mature, mean, nice, outgoing, proud, quiet, rebellious, sad, shy, silly, smart, teenage.

verbs SUBJECT: an adolescent develops, flirts, grows, learns, matures, plays sports, rebels, studies, works. OTHERS: to be an adolescent, to become an adolescent, to befriend an adolescent, to encourage an adolescent, to know an adolescent, to listen to an adolescent, to love an adolescent, to raise an adolescent, to talk to an adolescent.

adult ▸ adulte

nouns adulthood, father, grandparent, grown-up, instructor, man, mother, parent, person, role model, senior citizen, teacher, woman.

adjectives active, angry, brave, calm, caring, charming, confident, educated, famous, fat, fully grown, happy, kind, lonely, loving, lucky, married, mature, old, poor, responsible, rich, sad, short, single, skinny, smart, strong, stupid, tall, weak.

verbs SUBJECT: an adult cooks, disciplines, drives, eats, laughs, loves, parents, reads, relaxes, sleeps, studies, talks, teaches, travels, works. OTHERS: to admire an adult, to become an adult, to love an adult, to please an adult, to respect an adult, to teach an adult.

angel ▸ ange

nouns choir, church, God, guardian angel, harp, heaven, messenger, prayer, religion, song, soul, sky, spirit, virtue, wings.

adjectives blessed, caring, fallen, good, happy, helpful, holy, immortal, kind, loyal, supernatural, sweet, virtuous, winged.

verbs SUBJECT: an angel blesses, brings messages, delivers hope, encourages, helps, inspires, flies, sings, watches over. OTHERS: to believe in angels, to pray to angels.

expressions

- *An angel of mercy:* a person who appears when he/she is particularly needed ▸ **une personne qui apparaît au moment où l'on a particulièrement besoin.**
- *Guardian angel:* a spirit that watches over a person or place ▸ **quelqu'un qui veille sur nous ; un ange gardien.**
- *You're an angel:* you are helpful and kind ▸ **tu es une personne serviable et gentille ; tu es un amour !**

baby ▸ bébé

nouns birth, bottle, buggy, carriage, child, cradle, crib, diaper, doll, grandchild, grandparent, infant, lullaby, milk, new-born, offspring, parent, stroller, toy.

adjectives adorable, big, chubby, cranky, cute, good, happy, healthy, hungry, innocent, newborn, premature, quiet, sick, small, sleepy, sweet, tired.

verbs SUBJECT: a baby crawls, cries, drinks, eats, grows, learns, listens, sleeps, smiles, teethes, wakes, watches. OTHERS: to baby-sit a baby, to be a baby, to change a baby, to cherish a baby, to cradle a baby, to cuddle a baby, to diaper a baby, to have a baby, to hold a baby, to love a baby, to nurse a baby, to protect a baby, to rock a baby, to sing to a baby, to soothe a baby, to walk a baby, to want a baby.

expressions

- *Baby boomer:* a person born during the population increase that followed World War II ▸ **un enfant du baby-boom,** période ayant suivi la Seconde Guerre mondiale au cours de laquelle il y a eu une forte augmentation de la natalité.

- *Baby grand:* a small grand piano ▶ **un petit piano à queue (demi-queue).**

- *Baby kisser:* a person campaigning for votes in his/her quest for elected political office; such people often kiss little children in public ▶ **une personne qui, en campagne électorale, embrasse souvent des enfants en public pour bien paraître et se faire élire.**

- *To act like or to be a big baby:* to be an adult whose behaviour is immature ▶ **agir de façon immature.**

- *To baby someone or something:* to treat with care and attention ▶ **traiter quelqu'un avec soin, prendre soin de quelque chose.**

child ▶ enfant

nouns angel, baby, boy, brat, childhood, childproof, girl, infant, kid, kindergarten, school, youngster, toddler, toy.

adjectives active, adopted, adorable, creative, curious, cute, disobedient, happy, impatient, innocent, intelligent, nice, noisy, only, polite, quiet, sad, sick, small, spoiled, talented, turbulent, young.

verbs SUBJECT: a child argues, cries, draws, fights, grows, grows up, jumps, laughs, learns, likes, listens, loves, plays, reads, runs, screams, skips, speaks, walks, writes. OTHERS: to baby-sit a child, to bear a child, to cherish a child, to congratulate a child, to discipline a child, to feed a child, to have a child, to hug a child, to love a child, to play with a child, to punish a child, to read to a child, to respect a child, to sing to a child, to spoil a child, to take care of a child, to teach a child, to want a child.

expressions

- *To be with child:* to be pregnant ▶ **être enceinte.**

- *A child of the:* a follower of someone ▶ **un disciple, un fidèle ou un initié.**

- *Child's play:* a simple task ▶ **une tâche simple; un jeu d'enfant.**

dragon ▶ dragon

nouns animal, beast, claws, creature, demon, dragonfly, fire, monster, myth, reptile, smoke, tail, teeth, treasure, wings.

adjectives big, cruel, dangerous, evil, fierce, fire-breathing, furious, good, huge, imaginary, legendary, mean, monstrous, mysterious, mythical, powerful, sad, scaly, scary, terrible, vicious.

verbs SUBJECT: a dragon fights, guards treasure, scares people, starts fires, terrorizes. OTHERS: to conquer a dragon, to fight a dragon, to hunt a dragon, to kill a dragon, to save a dragon, to search for a dragon, to slay a dragon, to spare a dragon, to tame a dragon.

expressions

- *Somebody is a dragon:* a fierce person, especially a woman ▶ **une personne redoutable.**

fairy ▶ fée

nouns carriage, king, kingdom, legend, magic, nymph, prince, princess, queen, story, tale, wand, wishes.

adjectives bad, beautiful, brilliant, delicate, enchanted, evil, flying, good, gracious, imaginary, magical, make-believe, marvellous, mean, powerful, small, tiny.

verbs SUBJECT: a fairy appears, charms, conjures, flies, grants wishes, performs magic, transforms. OTHERS: to befriend a fairy, to believe in fairies, to capture a fairy, to catch a fairy, to cherish a fairy, to follow a fairy, to release a fairy, to tease a fairy.

expressions

- *Fairy godmother:* a magical being who watches over a person and helps them ▶ **un être imaginaire qui nous protège et nous aide; une bonne fée.**

- *Fairy tale:* story full of magical and fantastic events ► **une histoire remplie d'événements fantastiques et imaginaires ; un conte de fées.**

family ► famille

nouns ancestor, aunt, blood, brother, clan, cousin, dynasty, father, folks, gathering, generations, grandfather, grandmother, heredity, history, home, household, kin, mother, relative, reunion, roots, sister, uncle.

adjectives adoptive, big, caring, close, distant, extended, famous, happy, loving, noble, nosy, notorious, poor, powerful, respected, rich, royal, small, united.

verbs SUBJECT: a family cares, celebrates, feuds, fights, forgives, gathers, loves, mourns, reunites. OTHERS: to abandon one's family, to belong to a family, to feed a family, to have a family, to miss one's family, to plan a family, to visit a family.

expressions

- *Family man:* a man with a wife and children who enjoys family life ► **un homme avec une femme et des enfants, qui aime la vie de famille.**
- *Family tree:* a chart showing the relationship between family members ► **une représentation graphique qui montre les relations entre les membres d'une même famille ; un arbre généalogique.**
- *In the family way:* pregnant ► **enceinte.**
- *To run in the family:* a feature found in many members of a family ► **un trait ou une caractéristique que l'on retrouve chez plusieurs membres d'une même famille.**

ghost ► fantôme

nouns apparition, creature, graveyard, haunted house, Halloween, illusion, mirage, murder, nightmare, phantom, shadow, soul, spirit, spook, tomb, visitor.

adjectives creepy, dead, frightening, friendly, ghastly, horrible, invisible, mysterious, restless, scary, spooky, supernatural, terrible, terrifying, transparent.

verbs SUBJECT: a ghost flies, haunts houses, rights wrongs, scares people, visits loved ones. OTHERS: to believe in ghosts, to catch a ghost, to see a ghost.

expressions

- *Ghost town:* a town which has been abandoned ► **une ville qui a été abandonnée ; une ville fantôme.**
- *Ghost-writer:* a person who writes a book for someone else without taking credit as the author ► **une personne qui écrit anonymement un livre signé par quelqu'un d'autre.**
- *Give up the ghost:* to die ► **mourir.**
- *Holy Ghost:* the third member of the Christian trinity ► **la troisième entité de la Trinité chrétienne ; le Saint-Esprit.**

king ► roi

nouns baron, castle, chief, conqueror, country, court, crown, duke, dynasty, emperor, kingdom, lord, majesty, master, moat, monarch, nobleman, palace, prince, ruler, sovereign, throne, title, tyrant, warrior.

adjectives arrogant, cruel, determined, fake, handsome, honest, kind, majestic, mean, noble, old, rich, regal, royal, ruthless, stingy, wise, young.

verbs SUBJECT: a king makes decisions, implements laws, reigns over his land, rules his subjects. OTHERS: to admire a king, to approach a king, to betray a king, to defend a king, to protect a king, to kidnap a king, to kill a king, to respect a king, to serve a king.

expressions

- *Kingpin:* an essential person or thing ► **une personne ou un objet essentiel.**
- *King-size:* very large ► **très grand format.**

- *King's ransom:* an excessively large sum of money extorted by kidnappers to let someone go free ► **une rançon très importante exigée par des ravisseurs pour libérer leur otage.**
- *The king of beasts:* the lion ► **le lion; le roi des animaux.**
- *To live like a king:* to live well ► **bien vivre; vivre comme un roi.**

knight ► chevalier

nouns armour, battle, castle, champion, combat, damsel, defender, gentleman, hero, honour, horse, kingdom, military, protector, soldier, sword, valour, vengeance, war, warrior.

adjectives adventurous, brave, charming, courageous, daring, fearless, generous, honourable, invincible, loyal, medieval, noble, powerful, strong, triumphant, valiant, violent.

verbs SUBJECT: a knight defends, fights battles, goes to war, rescues damsels in distress, rides horses, slays dragons. OTHERS: to become a knight, to challenge a knight, to decorate a knight, to fight a knight, to love a knight.

expressions

- *Knight in shining armour:* a rescuer, especially of a woman ► **un sauveur.**

magician ► magicien (-ienne)

nouns costume, crystal ball, entertainer, fantasy, hat, illusion, juggler, magic, mirage, performer, potion, rabbit, showman, sorcerer, spell, surprise, trick, wand.

adjectives amazing, amusing, astounding, clever, entertaining, fabulous, fantastic, glamorous, hypnotic, incredible, mysterious, quick, sly, talented, tricky, vanishing.

verbs SUBJECT: a magician amuses, captivates, entertains, hypnotises, makes things disappear, manipulates, performs, pulls rabbits out of hats, rehearses, retires, surprises, tricks. OTHERS: to admire a magician, to applaud a magician, to apprentice a magician, to become a magician, to watch a magician.

monster ► monstre

nouns animal, Bigfoot, centaur, creature, demon, devil, dragon, freak, giant, legend, mermaid, mutant, nightmare, ogre, Sasquatch, terror, troll, unicorn, werewolf.

adjectives abnormal, cruel, deformed, disgusting, extraordinary, evil, ferocious, fierce, frightening, furious, gigantic, hairy, hideous, horrible, imaginary, incredible, large, menacing, mysterious, savage, scary, sinister, slimy, strange, terrible, ugly, vicious, wicked.

verbs SUBJECT: a monster chases, destroys, escapes, feeds, kills, scares, terrifies, terrorises. OTHERS: to catch a monster, to chase a monster, to destroy a monster, to expose a monster, to kill a monster, to reform a monster, to sabotage a monster.

expressions

- *The green-eyed monster:* jealousy ► **la jalousie.**
- *To be a monster:* a person who is very cruel or evil; a large or ugly animal or thing ► **une personne qui est très cruelle; un animal ou une chose horrible; un monstre.**

name ► nom, prénom

nouns Aaron, Abigail, Adam, Adrian, Adrienne, Agatha, Agnes, Alan, Alana, Albert, Alexander, Alexandra, Alexis, Alfred, Alice, Allison, Alvin, Amanda, Amy, Anastasia, Andrea, Angela, Anita, Anne, Anthony, Antoinette, Archie, Arlene, Arnold, Arthur, Ashley, Astrid, Audrey, Austin, Barbara, Barbie, Beatrice, Benjamin, Bernadette, Bernard, Betty, Beverly, Bianca, Bill, Blanche, Bob, Bonnie, Brad, Brenda, Brendan, Bridget,

Brittany, Bruce, Bruno, Caitlin, Calvin, Cameron, Camille, Candice, Candy, Carl, Carmen, Carol, Caroline, Catherine, Cecilia, Chad, Chantal, Charles, Charlotte, Cheryl, Christine, Christina, Christopher, Cindy, Claire, Claudia, Cliff, Colette, Colin, Connie, Conrad, Constance, Coral, Cordelia, Craig, Curtis, Cynthia, Daisy, Damian, Daniel, Danielle, Daphne, Darlene, Daryl, David, Dawn, Dean, Deborah, Deirdre, Denise, Dennis, Derek, Desmond, Diana, Dolores, Dominique, Donald, Donna, Dorothy, Douglas, Drew, Duncan, Dylan, Earl, Edgar, Edith, Edna, Edward, Eileen, Elisabeth, Ellen, Elvis, Emily, Emma, Eric, Erica, Erin, Ernest, Esther, Eve, Evelyn, Ezra, Faith, Felix, Fern, Fiona, Florence, Floyd, Frances, Frank, Fred, Gabriel, Gabrielle, Gary, Gavin, Genevieve, George, Gerald, Gerard, Gillian, Gina, Glen, Gloria, Gordon, Grace, Graham, Gregory, Gwyneth, Hannah, Harold, Harriet, Harry, Heidi, Helen, Helena, Henry, Herman, Hillary, Holly, Homer, Howard, Hugh, Hugo, Ian, Ingrid, Irene, Irving, Jack, Jacob, Jake, Jacqueline, James, Jane, Janet, Janice, Jarvis, Jason, Jean, Jeff, Jennifer, Jeremy, Jerome, Jessica, Joan, Jocelyne, Joe, Joel, John, Jonathan, Jordan, Joseph, Joshua, Joy, Judy, Julia, Julian, Julie, Karen, Karl, Katherine, Keith, Kelly, Ken, Kevin, Kim, Kirk, Krista, Kurt, Lance, Lara, Larry, Laura, Lawrence, Leonard, Leroy, Lewis, Lilith, Lily, Linda, Lindsey, Lorraine, Lucille, Lucy, Luke, Malcolm, Marcia, Margaret, Marie, Marilyn, Marion, Mark, Martha, Martin, Mary, Matthew, Maurice, Meagan, Melanie, Melinda, Melvin, Meredith, Michael, Michelle, Miles, Molly, Mona, Monica, Murray, Nadine, Nancy, Naomi, Natalie, Natasha, Nathan, Nathaniel, Neil, Nicholas, Nicole, Nigel, Norma, Norman, Olive, Oliver, Opal, Ophelia, Oscar, Owen, Pamela, Patricia, Patrick, Paul, Paula, Penelope, Peter, Philip, Phoebe, Polly, Priscilla, Quentin, Rachel, Ralph, Ramona, Raquel, Rebecca, Rhonda, Richard, Rita, Robert, Roberta, Rod, Rosalie, Rose, Russell, Ruth, Sabrina, Sally, Samantha, Samuel, Sandra, Sarah, Scott, Sean, Sebastian, Shane, Sharon, Sheila, Shelley, Shirley, Simon, Stanley, Stephen, Sylvia, Simone, Stacy, Stanley, Stephanie, Stewart, Susan, Sylvia, Tanya, Tess, Thelma, Theresa, Thomas, Tiffany, Timothy, Toby, Tracey, Trevor, Tyler, Uma, Ursula, Valerie, Vanessa, Veronica, Victor, Victoria, Vincent, Violet, Virginia, Wallace, Walter, Warren, Wayne, William, Winifred, Winona, Yasmin, Yolande, Yvette, Yvonne, Xavier, Yves, Zachary, Zoe.

adjectives common, famous, feminine, first, given, last, long, maiden, married, masculine, middle.

verbs SUBJECT: a name defines, evokes, identifies, impresses. OTHERS: to adopt a name, to change one's name, to choose a name, to give a name, to hate a name, to like a name, to prefer a name.

expressions

- *Call names:* to use ugly or unkind words when speaking to someone or talking about someone ▸ **parler à quelqu'un ou de quelqu'un en le traitant de tous les noms.**

- *In the name of someone:* by the authority of someone ▸ **en vertu de l'autorité de quelqu'un ; au nom de quelqu'un.**

- *Named after:* Given the same name as someone ▸ **porter le même nom que quelqu'un ; nommé en hommage à ou en l'honneur de.**

- *Namedropper:* a person who is always mentioning well-known names ▸ **quelqu'un qui cite toujours le nom de personnes connues ou célèbres dans une conversation.**

- *Name of the game:* What's at the heart of the matter ▸ **ce qui est au cœur du problème, du litige.**

- *Nickname:* a familiar or humorous name given to someone in addition to their real name ▸ **un nom familier ou comique donné à quelqu'un en plus de son nom réel ; un surnom.**

- *Someone's name is mud:* someone is in trouble or no longer liked ▸ **quelqu'un qui est tombé en disgrâce ou qui n'est plus aimé.**

- *To give someone or something a bad name:* to cause harm to the reputation of someone or something ▶ **porter atteinte à la réputation de quelqu'un.**

- *You name it:* everything you can think of ▶ **tout ce à quoi tu peux penser.**

pirate ▶ pirate

nouns adventurer, battle, captain, crime, dagger, danger, eye patch, flag, island, map, mast, mates, ocean, plank, prisoner, sailor, sea, shark, ship, sword, treasure, war.

adjectives adventurous, brave, cold-blooded, corrupt, criminal, cruel, dangerous, disgusting, fat, greedy, grim, mean, old, retired, rowdy, seasick, violent, young.

verbs SUBJECT: a pirate captures, fights, kidnaps, has adventures, robs, sails, steals. OTHERS: to fight a pirate, to follow a pirate, to hate a pirate, to kill a pirate, to know a pirate.

expressions

- *Pirate radio station:* a radio station that broadcasts illegally ▶ **une station de radio qui diffuse illégalement ; une radio pirate.**

- *Pirate ship:* A large boat navigated by pirates ▶ **un grand bateau piloté par des pirates ; un bateau pirate.**

queen ▶ reine

nouns baroness, castle, country, court, crown, duchess, dungeon, dynasty, empress, kingdom, lady, leader, majesty, mistress, moat, monarch, noblewoman, palace, princess, ruler, title, throne, sovereign.

adjectives arrogant, beautiful, caring, charitable, charming, conceited, cruel, deceptive, destructive, evil, fair, feminine, good, happy, icy, impatient, jealous, kind, lonely, loyal, majestic, powerful, rich, royal, secluded, selfish, thoughtful, ugly, wealthy, wicked, young.

verbs SUBJECT: a queen banishes, bans, commands, condemns, governs, rules. OTHERS: to abduct a queen, to assassinate a queen, to crown a queen, to love a queen, to protect a queen, to respect a queen, to serve a queen, to stalk a queen, to wait on a queen.

expressions

- *Queen bee:* the large, fertile female in a beehive; a dominant woman ▶ **la reine des abeilles, seule abeille fertile dans une ruche ; une femme dominante.**

- *Queen's English:* the English language as it is correctly spoken or written in England ▶ **la langue anglaise telle qu'elle est écrite et parlée en Angleterre.**

- *Queen-size:* very large, usually smaller than king-size ▶ **grand format.**

- *Queen mother:* the mother of a queen ▶ **la mère d'une reine.**

vampire ▶ vampire

nouns assassin, bat, blood, cape, cemetery, coffin, creature, death, fangs, garlic, grave, killer, monster, murderer, night, skeleton, superstition, tomb, victim, stake, zombie.

adjectives dead, evil, ghastly, horrible, nocturnal, ruthless, selfish, terrifying, thirsty.

verbs SUBJECT: a vampire feeds, flies, kills people, lives forever, sleeps, sucks blood. OTHERS: to believe in vampires, to chase a vampire, to destroy a vampire, to fear vampires, to kill a vampire, to wake a vampire.

witch ▶ sorcière

nouns alchemist, broomstick, cat, cauldron, curse, fortune, hat, illusion, luck, magic, medium, omen, potion, power, sorcerer, spell, spirit, trick, witchcraft.

adjectives bad, beautiful, capable, enchanted, evil, frightening, good, magical, mysterious, nasty, old, powerful, scary, talented, wicked, white.

verbs SUBJECT: a witch charms, conspires, curses, heals, saves, scares, terrifies, tricks. OTHERS: to apprentice a witch, to believe a witch, catch a witch, drown a witch, to follow a witch, to hunt a witch, to identify a witch, to know a witch, to marry a witch, to save a witch.

expressions

• *Witch-hunt:* a hysterical movement during which people are persecuted for having views considered different or unpopular ▸ **un mouvement hystérique où des personnes sont persécutées parce qu'elles ont des points de vue différents ou impopulaires ; chasse aux sorcières.**

wizard ▸ sorcier

nouns beard, conjurer, crystal ball, genius, hat, magic, magician, medicine man, Merlin, oracle, potion, sorcerer, spell, wand, warlock.

adjectives ancient, knowledgeable, magical, mysterious, old, powerful, smart, wise.

verbs SUBJECT: a wizard casts spells, causes trouble, goes on adventures, makes potions, performs magic, saves people, solves problems. OTHERS: to befriend a wizard, to curse a wizard, to follow a wizard, to kill a wizard, to mourn a wizard, to respect a wizard, to save a wizard.

expressions

• *He's a wiz(ard):* he's very talented ▸ **il est très talentueux, brillant.**

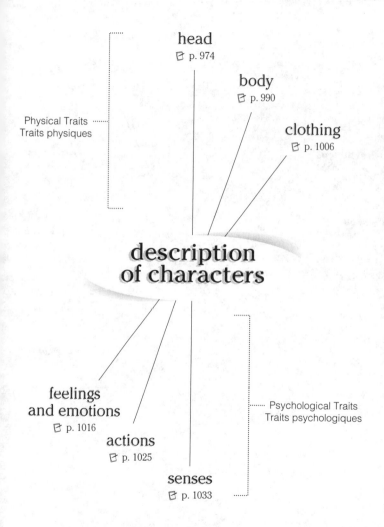

Physical Traits
Traits physiques

head
📖 p. 974

body
📖 p. 990

clothing
📖 p. 1006

description
of characters

feelings
and emotions
📖 p. 1016

actions
📖 p. 1025

senses
📖 p. 1033

Psychological Traits
Traits psychologiques

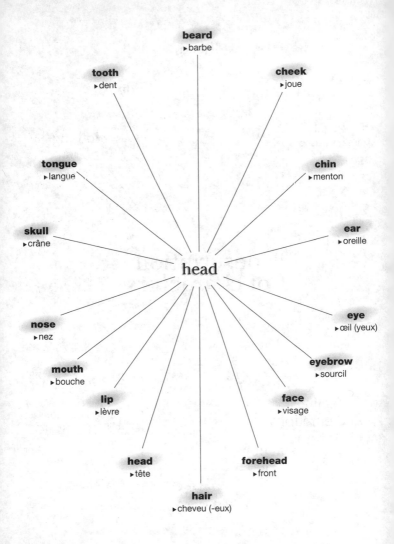

beard
▸barbe

tooth
▸dent

cheek
▸joue

tongue
▸langue

chin
▸menton

skull
▸crâne

ear
▸oreille

head

nose
▸nez

eye
▸œil (yeux)

mouth
▸bouche

eyebrow
▸sourcil

lip
▸lèvre

face
▸visage

head
▸tête

forehead
▸front

hair
▸cheveu (-eux)

beard ► barbe

nouns aftershave (lotion), barber, cheek, facial hair, goatee, hair, jaw, lather, lip, moustache, shaving, shaving brush, shaving cream, shaving foam, sideburns, stubble, razor, whiskers.

adjectives abrasive, badly-groomed, black, brown, bushy, coarse, curly, dark, dishevelled, fair, fake, false, full, fuzzy, grey, greying, groomed, long, neat, patchy, prickly, rough, scraggy, scratchy, shaven, silver, soft, tangled, teased, thick, thin, trimmed, unkempt, unmanageable, well-groomed, white, wild.

verbs SUBJECT: a beard covers, goes grey, greys, grows, hides, itches, masks, stings, thins, tickles. OTHER: to comb a beard, to groom a beard, to grow a beard, to keep a beard, to shave (off) a beard, to trim a beard.

expressions

- *To beard the lion:* to take a risk ► **prendre un risque.**
- *To beard someone in his den:* to confront or face someone ► **affronter quelqu'un ou le braver.**

cheek ► joue

nouns acne, beard, beauty mark, blotch, blush, bone, cheekbone, colour, dimple, face, flush, form, glow, hair, kiss, makeup, mouth, muscle, red, rouge, skin, slap, stroke, shape, stubble, tear, tone.

adjectives aged, big, blemished, blotched, blushing, bright, burning, chubby, coloured, dirty, droopy, feverish, fine, firm, flabby, flawless, fleshy, flushed, fresh, full, gaunt, glowing, hairy, hollow, made-up, pale, pallid, plump, prickly, puffy, reddened, rosy, rouged, rough, round, ruby, scarlet, smooth, soft, streaky, sunken, swollen, taut, unblemished, wrinkled, young, youthful, wan, wet.

verbs SUBJECT: a cheek blushes, clenches, curves, drops, droops, flushes, glows, jiggles, reddens, rounds, shakes, sinks, swells. OTHERS: to caress a cheek, to kiss a cheek, to make up a cheek, to pinch a cheek, to rouge a cheek, to slap a cheek, to stroke a cheek, to tense a cheek.

expressions

- *Cheek by jowl:* side by side, close together ► **côte à côte ; tout près l'un de l'autre.**
- *To be cheek to cheek:* to be affectionately close to somebody ► **être en rapport étroit avec quelqu'un ; être joue à joue.**
- *To turn the other cheek:* to respond to something hurtful without retaliation ► **réagir de façon passive à un outrage ; tendre l'autre joue.**
- *With tongue in cheek:* ironically or as a joke ► **avec ironie ou en plaisantant.**

chin ► menton

nouns beard, dimple, face, form, goatee, hair, jaw, jawbone, protrusion, shape, stubble, whisker, wrinkle.

adjectives angular, clean-shaven, cleft, cute, determined, double, firm, hairless, hairy, long, plump, pointed, protruding, receding, rounded, royal, shapely, shaven, slack, small, square.

verbs SUBJECT: a chin clenches, curves, drops, points, protrudes, quivers, recedes, trembles. OTHERS: to drop a chin.

expressions

- *To keep one's chin up:* to be brave and strong in a difficult situation ► **se montrer brave et fort dans une situation difficile ; tenir le coup.**
- *To lead with one's chin:* to do something risky ► **prendre un risque.**
- *To take it on the chin:* to accept defeat ► **accepter la défaite.**

ear ► oreille

nouns bone, curve, deafness, eardrum, earlobe, ear piece, earplug, earshot, earwax, form, head, hearing, humming, infection, listening, lobe, noise, perception, ringing, secretion, sense, shape, size, sound, vibration, voice, wax, whisper, whistling.

adjectives attentive, big, blocked, clean, cold, cute, deaf, delicate, delicately-shaped, detached, dirty, discrete, distracted, fine, floppy, frozen, hairy, inner, keen, left, listening, little, middle, modest, musical, outer, perked, pointed, prudish, red, right, ringing, sensitive, sharp, small, welcoming.

verbs SUBJECT: an ear blocks up, buzzes, clogs, hangs, hears, listens, perceives, reddens, rings. OTHERS: to block an ear, to bother an ear, to clean an ear, to cover an ear, to grate on an ear, to hurt an ear, to pierce an ear, to plug an ear, to strain an ear, to strike an ear, to whisper into an ear, to yell into an ear.

expressions

- *Coming out of one's ears:* overwhelmed ► **être submergé ou submergée; en avoir par-dessus la tête.**
- *In one ear and out the other:* quickly forgotten ► **vite oublié.**
- *Music to one's ear:* very good news ► **excellente nouvelle; doux à l'oreille.**
- *Out on one's ear:* to be thrown out in disgrace ► **se faire expulser.**
- *To be all ears:* to listen attentively ► **écouter attentivement; être tout ouïe.**
- *To believe one's ears:* to trust what one has heard ► **croire ce que l'on entend.**
- *To fall on deaf ears:* to be ignored or not listened to ► **ne pas se faire écouter; parler aux murs.**
- *To have an ear for music:* to have musical talents ► **avoir du talent pour la musique; avoir l'oreille musicale.**
- *To have one's ear to the ground:* to be well-informed and aware of new trends ► **être bien informé ou informée et au courant des nouvelles tendances.**

- *To have someone's ear:* to have someone listening ► **avoir l'attention de quelqu'un.**
- *To lend one's ear:* to pay attention to and listen ► **écouter attentivement; tendre l'oreille.**
- *To pin someone's ears back:* to defeat or punish ► **vaincre ou punir.**
- *To play by ear:* to play an instrument without the aide of written music ► **jouer d'un instrument sans l'aide de feuilles de musique.**
- *To prick up one's ears:* to pay close attention and listen ► **écouter attentivement; tendre l'oreille.**
- *To turn a deaf ear:* to refuse to listen ► **refuser d'écouter; faire la sourde oreille.**
- *To be wet behind the ears:* to be immature and inexperienced ► **manquer de maturité et d'expérience.**
- *Up to one's ears in something:* to be deeply involved or overworked ► **être très occupé ou occupée; être débordé ou débordée.**
- *Walls have ears:* people can easily hear or listen in on a conversation ► **les gens peuvent facilement entendre une conversation; les murs ont des oreilles.**

eye ► œil (yeux)

nouns bag, ball, blindfold, blindness, blink, blood vessel, blur, circle, clarity, clearness, cloud, colour, colour blindness, contacts, corner, eyebrow, eyeglasses, eyelash, eyelid, eyewitness, expression, flutter, focus, form, glance, glare, glasses, head, infection, lens, longsightedness, look, makeup, mirage, mobility, movement, pair, perception, pupil, retina, sag, sense, short-sightedness, sight, shadow, shape, sparkle, squint, stare, sty, tear, twinkle, vision, view, veil, watch, wink, wrinkle.

adjectives alarmed, angelic, angry, anxious, attentive, attractive, beautiful, big, black, blind, blindfolded, blinking, blue, blue-green, bright, brown, calculating, calm, candid, captivating, cautious, charming, circled, clairvoyant, clear, closed, cold, covered, crafty, crazed, crazy, creased, crossed, cunning, curious, dark, dazzling, deep-set, desirous, dilated, disappointed, dreamy, dry, enraged, evil, expert, expressionless, expressive, far-away, fascinated, fascinating, fixed, fluttering, focused, framed, frantic, fresh, frightened, furious, glassy, glazed, gleeful, gloomy, glowing, glum, good, green, grey, half-closed, half-shut, happy, hazel, heavy, hungry, impassive, indifferent, innocent, inquisitive, intelligent, jealous, lazy, left, light blue, lively, lowered, mischievous, mocking, moving, myopic, naive, nice, open, passionate, penetrating, perceptive, piercing, pleased, probing, proud, puffy, red, right, round, sad, saggy, seductive, set, shifty, shining, shrewd, shut, shy, sickly, slanting, sleepy, small, sneaky, sparkling, squinty, steady, sulky, surprised, sweet, swollen, tender, tinted, tired, troubled, trusting, trustworthy, twinkling, upset, warm, wide-set, wild, winking, wise, wounded, unfocused, yearning.

verbs SUBJECT: an eye blinks, closes, cries, darts, discovers, examines, expresses, finds, follows, glances, glares, hides, observes, perceives, probes, reads, reveals, sees, shifts, shines, shows, shuts, sparkles, squints, stares, stings, tears, tires, twinkles, twitches, watches, winks. OTHERS: to avert an eye, to blind an eye, to bat an eye, to blink an eye, to catch an eye, to close an eye, to cover an eye, to cross an eye, to direct an eye, to flutter an eye, to focus an eye, to follow an eye, to lose an eye, to make up an eye, to move an eye, to open an eye, to protect an eye, to rub an eye, to screw up an eye, to shut an eye, to squint an eye, to turn an eye, to wink an eye.

expressions

- *All eyes:* watching attentively ▸ **surveiller attentivement; avoir l'œil ouvert.**
- *Bird's-eye view:* an overview ▸ **vue d'ensemble; aperçu; survol.**
- *Black eye:* a sign of failure ▸ **signe d'échec.**

- *Bright-eyed and bushy-tailed:* keen and ready ▸ **enthousiaste et prêt à l'action; avoir bon pied bon œil.**
- *Eagle eye:* keen sight and intelligent ▸ **vision claire et intelligente; œil de lynx.**
- *Easy on the eyes:* attractive to look at ▸ **agréable à voir.**
- *Evil eye:* ability to cause harm or misfortune ▸ **capacité de causer du mal ou de porter malchance; mauvais œil; oiseau de malheur.**
- *Eye for an eye:* equal punishment for an offence ▸ **punition égale à l'outrage; œil pour œil, dent pour dent.**
- *Eye opener:* a revelation ▸ **révélation.**
- *Eyeball to eyeball:* face to face in confrontation ▸ **confrontation nez à nez.**
- *Green-eyed monster:* jealousy ▸ **jalousie.**
- *In one's mind's eye:* in imagination or memory ▸ **par imagination ou de mémoire.**
- *In the eye of:* in the focus or centre of something ▸ **au centre de; au cœur de.**
- *In the public eye:* in the view of the public ▸ **en public.**
- *In the twinkling of an eye:* instantly ▸ **instantanément; en un clin d'œil.**
- *More than meets the eye:* something beyond what is seen ▸ **les apparences sont trompeuses; il y a anguille sous roche.**
- *My eye:* nonsense ▸ **balivernes; mon œil.**
- *Naked eye:* sight unaided by a visual instrument or tool ▸ **sans l'aide d'aucun appareil; à l'œil nu.**
- *One eye on:* paying some attention to ▸ **faire attention à; garder l'œil ouvert.**
- *Out of the corner of one's eye:* sideways glance ▸ **discrètement; du coin de l'œil.**
- *Private eye:* a detective who works outside of the police or another authority ▸ **détective privé.**
- *Sight for sore eyes:* someone or something that is a relief or joy to see ▸ **personne ou objet dont la vue est réjouissante.**
- *Stars in one's eyes:* to be in love, naive, idealistic, or optimistic ▸ **être amoureux, naïf, idéaliste ou optimiste; voir la vie en rose.**

- *To be the apple of someone's eye:* to be cherished ► **être aimé.**
- *To be with eyes open:* to be aware and alert ► **être à l'affût; avoir l'œil ouvert.**
- *To believe one's eyes:* to trust what one has seen ► **croire ce que l'on a vu.**
- *To catch someone's eye:* to get someone's attention ► **attirer l'attention de quelqu'un; accrocher le regard de quelqu'un.**
- *To cry one's eyes out:* to weep or sob ► **pleurer ou sangloter; pleurer à chaudes larmes.**
- *To give someone the eye (once-over):* to look at someone attentively ► **observer une personne attentivement; l'avoir à l'œil.**
- *To have an eye for:* to be perceptive about something ► **être perspicace; avoir du nez.**
- *To have eyes bigger than one's stomach:* to want more than one can handle ► **avoir des désirs plus grands que ses capacités; avoir les yeux plus grands que le ventre.**
- *To have eyes in the back of one's head:* to be aware and alert ► **être à l'affût; garder l'œil ouvert.**
- *To have one's eye on:* to watch something or someone carefully, or to have as a goal ► **surveiller quelque chose ou quelqu'un attentivement ou l'avoir dans sa mire; avoir l'œil sur.**
- *To hit between the eyes:* to make someone suddenly aware ► **rendre soudainement conscient; ouvrir les yeux.**
- *To hit the bull's-eye:* to be right ► **avoir raison; frapper dans le mille.**
- *To keep an eye on:* to watch carefully ► **surveiller attentivement; garder l'œil sur.**
- *To keep an eye out for:* to watch for something or someone ► **surveiller l'arrivée de quelque chose ou quelqu'un.**
- *To keep one's eye on the ball:* to stay alert and attentive ► **être attentif et concentré.**
- *To keep one's eyes open:* to be watching for and observant ► **surveiller et observer attentivement.**

- *To lay eyes on:* to look at or see ► **poser les yeux sur.**
- *To look someone in the eye (face):* to face someone directly and honestly ► **regarder quelqu'un droit dans les yeux, de façon honnête.**
- *To open one's eyes:* to become aware of a truth ► **prendre conscience d'une réalité; s'ouvrir les yeux.**
- *To pull the wool over someone's eye:* to deceive or fool someone ► **décevoir ou tromper quelqu'un.**
- *To run one's eye over:* to look over or review ► **consulter rapidement; jeter un coup d'œil.**
- *To make eyes at:* to flirt with or look at with desire ► **flirter ou regarder avec concupiscence; faire de l'œil.**
- *To see eye to eye:* to agree on something ► **s'entendre sur quelque chose; voir les choses du même œil.**
- *To see with half an eye:* to see the obvious quickly and easily ► **comprendre les choses évidentes rapidement; saisir d'un coup d'œil.**
- *To throw dust in someone's eyes:* to mislead someone ► **induire en erreur; jeter la poudre aux yeux.**
- *To turn a blind eye to:* to deliberately overlook or ignore ► **faire semblant de ne pas voir; fermer les yeux sur.**
- *With an eye to:* to have as a goal ► **dans le but de.**
- *With one's eyes open:* with attention ► **avec attention; les yeux grand ouverts.**
- *Without batting an eye:* to react emotionlessly or as though nothing were unusual ► **réagir sans émotion comme si de rien n'était; sans broncher.**

eyebrow ► **sourcil**

nouns arc, arch, brow, colour, eye, eye pencil, face, frown, hair, orbit, tweezers.

adjectives arched, big, black, blonde, brown, bushy, close, even, fair, fine, high, made-up, narrow, natural, perfect, plucked, prominent, pronounced, protruding, raised, screwed up, spaced, sparse, thick, thin, wide, wispy.

verbs SUBJECT: an eyebrow arches, contracts, falls, frames, frowns, moves, rises, twitches. OTHERS: to arch an eyebrow, to make up an eyebrow, to mop an eyebrow, to move an eyebrow, to pencil in an eyebrow, to pluck an eyebrow, to raise an eyebrow, to wiggle an eyebrow.

expressions

• *To raise eyebrows:* to surprise or bring on disapproval ▸ **surprendre ou provoquer la désapprobation.**

face ▸ visage

nouns appearance, beauty, beauty mark, blemish, cheek, chin, colour, complexion, delicacy, dimple, emotion, expression, eye, eyebrow, face-lift, facial, feature, feeling, forehead, form, grimace, happiness, harmonious, head, line, lip, look, makeup, mask, mouth, mystery, nose, oval, prettiness, roundness, scar, serenity, shape, skull, slap, sweetness, tenderness, tone, trait, ugliness, vividness, warmth, wrinkle.

adjectives adorable, aged, ageing, alarmed, alive, amazed, amazing, angelic, angular, attentive, attractive, authoritarian, balanced, beaming, beautiful, bewitched, bewitching, black, blemished, blushing, bored, bothered, brooding, brown, calm, captivated, captivating, caring, changing, charming, clean-shaven, clear, cold, confused, covered, creased, crooked, cruel, crumpled, depressed, determined, dimpled, dreamy, eager, embarrassed, enchanting, energetic, evil, exceptional, exhausted, expressive, expressionless, faceless, familiar, fatty, fine, fixed, fresh, frightening, frightful, frowning, funny, gloomy, glowing, good-looking, grimacing, hairy, handsome, happy, heavenly, heavy, hideous, honest, joyful, known, laughing, lively, long, loving, made-up, marked, maternal, mature, mean, menacing, memorable, mischievous, moving, mysterious, nasty, narrow, nervous, new, normal, oval, pale, paternal, pleasant,

pleasing, plump, pointed, pretty, puffy, puzzled, radiant, red, reddened, relaxed, rosy, round, sad, scarred, scary, scowling, sculpted, serene, serious, sickly, silly, slack, sleek, smeared, smiling, smooth, spotted, stern, strained, strange, strong, stunned, stunning, sullen, sunburned, sunburnt, surprised, sweet, swollen, symmetrical, tanned, taut, tense, tight, tired, thin, thoughtful, threatening, troubled, ugly, ungrateful, unhappy, unknown, unpleasant, unveiled, upset, veiled, vibrant, warm, waxy, welcoming, white, wide, wise, withered, worried, wrinkled, youthful.

verbs SUBJECT: a face ages, beams, blushes, brightens up, expresses, freezes, frowns, grimaces, hardens, lights up, looks away, pales, recoils, reddens, relaxes, scolds, scowls, shines, slackens, smiles, softens, subdues, tans, tenses, tilts, tires, worries, wrinkles. OTHERS: to clean a face, to press a face against, to compose a face, to make up a face, to show a face, to slap a face, to spit in a face, to stroke a face, to wash a face, to uncover a face, to unveil a face.

expressions

• *Blue in the face:* to be exhausted from anger or strain ▸ **être exténué ou exténuée à cause de la colère ou de l'effort.**

• *Face down:* upside placed down ▸ **à l'envers.**

• *Face it:* to look at or accept something unpleasant or difficult ▸ **regarder ou accepter une situation difficile ou désagréable ; regarder les choses en face.**

• *Face to face:* in direct communication opposite each other ▸ **en communication directe l'un avec l'autre ; face à face.**

• *Face up:* up side placed up ▸ **à l'endroit.**

• *Face value:* outward appearance ▸ **apparence extérieure.**

• *Face with:* confront ▸ **confronter ; face à face.**

• *Fly in the face of:* to defy ▸ **défier.**

- *In someone's face:* directly in front of or against someone ► **devant ou contre une personne.**
- *In the face of:* confronted with or despite opposition ► **compte tenu ou malgré l'opposition.**
- *In your face:* daring confrontation or exclamation of contempt ► **confrontation insolente ou mépris évident.**
- *On the face of it:* seemingly ► **apparemment.**
- *Plain as the nose on your face:* obvious and clear ► **clair et évident; comme le nez au milieu de la figure.**
- *Poker face:* expressionless ► **sans expression.**
- *To be red in the face:* to strain oneself or to feel shame ► **faire un effort ou avoir honte; avoir le sang qui monte à la figure.**
- *To do an about-face:* to change one's mind or reverse one's course of action ► **changer d'idée ou de comportement.**
- *To face down:* to overcome someone in a confrontation ► **avoir le dernier mot lors d'une confrontation.**
- *To face the music:* to confront something unpleasant, especially an error made ► **faire face à une situation désagréable, particulièrement à cause d'une erreur que l'on a faite.**
- *To face up to:* to look at or accept something unpleasant or difficult ► **regarder ou accepter une situation difficile ou désagréable; regarder les choses en face.**
- *To feed one's face:* to overeat greedily ► **s'empiffrer; s'en mettre plein la panse.**
- *To get in someone's face:* to annoy or nag someone ► **embêter ou harceler quelqu'un.**
- *To have egg on one's face:* to be embarrassed or to look like a fool ► **avoir l'air stupide ou embarrassé.**
- *To hide one's face:* to feel shame or embarrassment ► **avoir honte ou être embarrassé ou embarrassée.**
- *To keep a straight face:* to avoid laughing or to not show one's feelings

- ► **se retenir de rire ou éviter de montrer ses sentiments.**
- *To look someone in the face:* to look at someone directly and honestly ► **regarder quelqu'un bien en face, honnêtement.**
- *To lose face:* to be publicly embarrassed or humiliated ► **être humilié en public; perdre la face.**
- *To make a face:* to grimace ► **grimacer.**
- *To put on a brave face:* to confront a difficult situation positively or to try to seem brave despite being afraid ► **adopter une attitude positive devant une situation difficile ou se montrer brave malgré la peur.**
- *To put one's face on:* to apply makeup ► **se maquiller; se refaire une beauté.**
- *To save face:* to preserve dignity ► **sauvegarder sa dignité; sauver la face.**
- *To set one's face against:* to disapprove strongly ► **désapprouver fortement.**
- *To show one's face:* to appear ► **apparaître.**
- *To slap in the face:* a verbal blow or insult ► **proférer une parole blessante ou une insulte.**
- *To stare in the face:* to be obvious though originally overlooked ► **évidence qui a été ignorée.**
- *To stuff one's face:* to overeat greedily ► **s'empiffrer; s'en mettre plein la panse.**
- *To take at face value:* to accept from outward appearance ► **accepter d'après les apparences; se fier aux apparences.**
- *To talk until blue in the face:* to fail to convince or be listened to ► **ne pas réussir à convaincre ou à se faire entendre; parler en vain.**
- *To throw in someone's face:* to confront someone with something ► **confronter quelqu'un avec un fait; jeter (la vérité) à la face de quelqu'un.**

forehead ► **front**

nouns brow, bump, colour, edge, expression, eyebrow, face, form, fringe, front, hair, head, profile, scar, shape, skin, sweat, swelling, temperature, temple, wrinkle.

adjectives angular, arched, arrogant, bare, big, beautiful, bulging, concerned, creased, crowned, curved, dark, defined, expressive, fair, feverish, fixed, flat, hairless, handsome, hard, high, hot, large, long, low, lowered, narrow, pale, perfect, prominent, protruding, radiant, receding, rounded, serene, set, severe, shiny, short, sleek, small, smooth, square, straight, sunburned, sunburnt, superb, sweaty, tanned, tormented, troubled, warm, wet, wide, worried, wrinkled.

verbs SUBJECT: a forehead burns, creases, curves, hurts, lightens, pales, reddens, sunburns, sweats, swells, wrinkles. OTHERS: to bump a forehead, to cover a forehead, to crease a forehead, to kiss a forehead, to lower a forehead, to raise a forehead, to wipe a forehead, to wrinkle a forehead.

---

hair ▸ cheveu (-eux)

nouns baldness, bangs, barber, barrette, beard, beauty salon, blade, braid, bristle, brush, bun, clasp, clip, clipper, coat, colour, comb, conditioner, crown, curl, cut, down, dye, forehead, fluff, fringe, fur, head of hair, gel, goatee, growth, hair net, hairball, hairbrush, haircut, hairdo, hairdresser, hairdressing, hairdryer, hairiness, hairline, hairpin, hairstyle, hairstylist, head, helmet, highlights, knot, lacquer, length, lock, mane, mat, mop, mousse, moustache, peach fuzz, perm, permanent, pigtail, ponytail, razor, ribbon, ringlet, rug, scissors, shaft, shag, shampoo, shampooing, sheen, sideburns, streaks, stubble, tangle, toupee, tress, trim, tuft, whiskers, whites, wig, wisp.

adjectives black, bleached, blonde, braided, brown, bunched, bushy, clean, coloured, cropped, cut, dark, dirty, dry, dull, dyed, facial, fake, false, feathery, flat, fleecy, flowing, fluffy, frizzy, full, furry, fuzzy, gorgeous, grey, greying, hairless, hairy, heavy, light, long, matted, messy, mousy, puffy, scraggly, set, shaggy, shaved, shiny, shocking, short, silky, silver, silvery, soft, streaked, styled, thick, thin, tossed, tousled, trimmed, unclean, uncut, untrimmed, unwashed, washed, wavy, wet, white, wild, wispy, woolly.

verbs SUBJECT: hair covers, curls, falls, frames, frizzes, greys, grows, knots, lengthens, shines, sprouts, tangles, tickles, waves, whitens. OTHERS: to braid hair, to brush hair, to clip hair, to comb hair, to colour hair, to crop hair, to cut hair, to dry hair, to dye hair, to lose hair, to mess hair, to pin hair, to perm hair, to pluck hair, to pull hair, to shampoo hair, to shape hair, to shear hair, to streak hair, to style hair, to tease hair, to tie hair, to tint hair, to trim hair, to wash hair, to wet hair.

expressions

- *Bad hair day:* a day when one is not attractive ▸ **journée où l'on n'est pas séduisant.**
- *To have by the short hairs:* to have someone under one's complete control ▸ **avoir le pouvoir sur quelqu'un.**
- *Hair of the dog that bit one:* a remedy from whatever made one ill, especially alcohol ▸ **remède provenant de la cause du malaise, par exemple prendre de l'alcool pour soulager une gueule de bois.**
- *Hair-raising:* terrifying ▸ **terrifiant; à faire dresser les cheveux sur la tête.**
- *Hair shirt:* self-imposed punishment ▸ **punition que l'on s'impose.**
- *Neither hide nor hair:* no sign of something lost or missing ▸ **aucune trace d'une personne ou d'un objet perdu ou disparu.**
- *To be in someone's hair:* to annoy or irritate someone ▸ **ennuyer ou irriter quelqu'un.**
- *To get grey hair from:* to find something worrisome or upsetting ▸ **s'inquiéter ou s'en faire pour quelque chose; se faire du mauvais sang.**
- *To hang by a hair (thread):* to be in a risky situation ▸ **être dans une situation précaire; ne tenir qu'à un fil.**

- *To let one's hair down:* to relax and get casual or informal ▸ **se laisser aller; relaxer.**

- *To lose by a hair (hair's-breadth):* to lose by a very narrow margin ▸ **perdre de très peu.**

- *To make one's hair curl:* to frighten terribly ▸ **faire terriblement peur; faire dresser les cheveux sur la tête.**

- *To make one's hair stand on end:* to frighten terribly ▸ **faire terriblement peur; faire dresser les cheveux sur la tête.**

- *To split hairs:* to quibble and argue over insignificant details or distinctions ▸ **se disputer pour des peccadilles; couper les cheveux en quatre.**

- *To tear (out) one's hair:* to be very upset or distressed about something ▸ **être dans tous ses états; s'arracher les cheveux.**

- *To not turn a hair:* to remain calm and not become frightened ▸ **rester calme et ne pas avoir peur; garder son sang-froid.**

head ▸ **tête**

nouns bobbing, bonnet, brain, bump, cap, character, cheek, chin, crown, ear, eye, eyebrow, face, forehead, form, hair, hat, headache, intelligence, judgement, lip, memory, mind, mouth, nod, nose, portrait, reason, reflection, scalp, shaking, shake, shape, size, skull, spinning, strong, thinking, thought, top.

adjectives bald, bare, beautiful, big, blonde, chopped, cold, comical, confused, covered, cracked, crowned, covered, dirty, enormous, flat, funny, fuzzy, good, grey, hanging, hard, headless, heavy, hideous, inflated, injured, intelligent, interesting, large, light, little, long, monstrous, muddled, nodding, old, pained, plain, pointed, romantic, round, scalped, shaking, shaped, sharp, shaved, short, small, square, swollen, tiny, thick, ugly, wagging, washed, worried, wounded, young.

verbs SUBJECT: a head aches, bleeds, bobs, hangs, hurts, moves, nods, shakes, spins, swells, thinks, tilts, worries. OTHERS: to break a head, to bow a head, to chop off a head, to cover a head, to crack a head, to crown a head, to flatten a head, to go to a head, to hurt a head, to injure a head, to kick a head, to nod a head, to scalp a head, to shake a head, to shave a head, to wag a head, to wash a head, to wound a head.

expressions

- *Can't make head(s) or tail(s) of:* to not understand or be confused ▸ **ne pas comprendre ou être déconcerté par quelque chose; (cela) n'a ni queue ni tête.**

- *From head to toe (heals, foot):* over the whole body ▸ **tout le corps; de la tête aux pieds.**

- *Head and shoulders above:* greatly superior to ▸ **très supérieur à.**

- *Head on:* face first or in direct conflict with ▸ **tête première ou en conflit direct avec.**

- *Heads I win, tails you lose:* I win no matter what ▸ **je gagne de toute façon; face je gagne, pile tu perds.**

- *Heads or tails:* two choices to determine the outcome of a toss of a coin ▸ **pile ou face.**

- *Head over heals:* completely ▸ **complètement, follement.**

- *Head screwed on right:* to be sensible ▸ **être raisonnable; avoir la tête sur les épaules.**

- *Head start:* an advantageous early start ▸ **une longueur d'avance.**

- *Heads up:* a warning of potential danger ▸ **avertissement d'un danger possible.**

- *Heads will roll:* someone will be punished ▸ **quelqu'un sera puni.**

- *Like a chicken with its head cut off:* frenzied, distracted or crazy ▸ **frénétique; éparpillé; fou.**

- *Off one's head:* crazy ▸ **fou; qui a perdu la tête.**

- *Off the top of one's head:* spontaneously, without much thought ► **spontanément; sans trop réfléchir; sur un coup de tête.**

- *On one's (own) head:* one's responsibility or fault ► **sa (propre) responsabilité ou faute.**

- *Over one's head:* in a higher position than another, or beyond one's understanding or ability ► **dans une position supérieure, ou au-delà de sa compréhension ou de ses capacités.**

- *Price on one's head:* a reward for capturing or killing someone usually guilty of a crime ► **récompense offerte pour la capture d'une personne, morte ou vive, habituellement coupable d'un crime; tête mise à prix.**

- *Put one's head on the block:* to take a great risk and make oneself vulnerable ► **prendre un grand risque et se mettre dans une position vulnérable.**

- *Rocks in one's head:* to act with poor judgement or stupidly ► **agir de façon stupide; manquer de jugement; agir comme une tête de linotte.**

- *Roof over one's head:* a shelter or home ► **abri ou maison.**

- *Soft in the head:* silly or foolish ► **stupide; idiot ou idiote; tête de linotte; tête d'oiseau.**

- *Swelled head:* conceited ► **prétentieux; grosse tête.**

- *To be not right in the head:* mentally unsound ► **déséquilibré mentalement; ne pas avoir toute sa tête.**

- *To beat (knock, drum) into one's head:* force someone to learn something ► **forcer une personne à apprendre; lui enfoncer dans la tête.**

- *To beat one's brains out:* to try hard to understand, solve or remember something ► **faire un effort pour comprendre, résoudre un problème ou se souvenir de quelque chose; se casser la tête.**

- *To beat (bang) one's head against the wall:* to waste time on something hopeless ► **perdre son temps avec une situation sans issue; se taper la tête contre les murs.**

- *To bite (snap) someone's head off:* to scold someone ► **réprimander, gronder.**

- *To bring to a head:* to reach a turning point or crisis ► **atteindre un état de crise.**

- *To buck heads:* to run into confrontation ► **entrer en conflit.**

- *To bury one's head in the sand:* to avoid or refuse to face or see something ► **refuser de regarder les choses en face; adopter la politique de l'autruche.**

- *To come to a head:* to reach a crisis point ► **atteindre un état de crise.**

- *To count heads:* to determine the number of people present ► **déterminer le nombre de personnes présentes.**

- *To do standing on one's head:* to do something easily ► **faire quelque chose très facilement, les doigts dans le nez.**

- *To enter one's head:* to occur to one ► **venir à l'esprit.**

- *To get into one's head:* to form an idea ► **avoir une idée.**

- *To get (have) one's head examined:* to be wrong or crazy ► **avoir tort; être détraqué ou détraquée; être tombé ou tombée sur la tête.**

- *To get through one's head:* to understand or be convinced ► **comprendre ou être convaincu ou convaincue.**

- *To give someone his or her head:* to give someone freedom ► **libérer quelqu'un.**

- *To go to one's head:* to make one drunk, or make one proud or vain ► **s'enivrer, s'enorgueillir; monter à la tête.**

- *To hang over one's head:* to threaten or be inevitable ► **menacer ou être inévitable.**

- *To have a big head:* to be conceited ► **être prétentieux; avoir la grosse tête.**

- *To have a good head on one's shoulders:* to be sensible or intelligent ► **être raisonnable ou intelligent; avoir la tête sur les épaules.**

- *To have a (good, strong) head for:* to have a tolerance for something, or to have mental talents for ► **tolérer ou avoir du talent pour.**

- *To have eyes in the back of one's head:* to be more aware of something than is realized ► **être plus conscient ou conciente qu'on en a l'air.**

- *To have one's head in the clouds:* to be forgetful or impractical ► **être distrait ou distraite ou avoir peu de sens pratique; être tête en l'air.**

- *To head off:* to intercept ► **intercepter.**

- *To head out:* to depart on a journey ► **partir.**

- *To head up:* to lead or be in charge of ► **diriger ou être responsable de; être à la tête de.**

- *To hide one's head (in the sand):* to avoid or refuse to face or see something ► **éviter ou refuser de regarder les choses en face; adopter la politique de l'autruche.**

- *To hit the nail on the head:* to be right ► **avoir raison; frapper dans le mille.**

- *To hold a gun to one's head:* to put pressure on someone ► **exercer une pression sur quelqu'un.**

- *To hold one's head high (up):* to be proud or dignified ► **être fier ou fière ou digne; se tenir la tête haute.**

- *To be in over one's head:* to be very involved in something, or to be in trouble ► **être submergé ou submergée par quelque chose ou être en difficulté; en avoir par-dessus la tête.**

- *To keep one's head:* remain calm and in control ► **demeurer calme et conserver son sang-froid; garder la tête froide.**

- *To keep one's head above water:* to stay out of trouble, or keep up with work or demands ► **ne pas être en difficulté; être à jour dans son travail ou répondre à la demande.**

- *To laugh one's head off:* to be very amused ► **être très amusé ou amusée; rire à gorge déployée.**

- *To lose one's head:* to become confused or agitated ► **devenir confus(e) ou agité(e); perdre la tête.**

- *To make headway:* to make progress ► **avancer, progresser.**

- *To make one's head spin:* to make one confused or dazed ► **étourdir ou déconcerter; faire tourner la tête.**

- *To need like a hole in the head:* to not require or desire something ► **n'avoir aucun besoin ou désir pour quelque chose.**

- *To put ideas into someone's head:* to make a suggestion to someone ► **suggérer quelque chose à quelqu'un; lui mettre quelque chose dans la tête.**

- *To put our (their) heads together:* to talk about or plan something ► **planifier ou discuter.**

- *To rear its ugly head:* something unwanted to appear ► **apparition d'un élément indésirable.**

- *To run one's head against:* to waste time on something hopeless ► **perdre son temps sur une situation sans issue.**

- *To scratch one's head:* to think hard, or express confusion ► **réfléchir longuement ou exprimer sa perplexité.**

- *To shake one's head:* to disapprove ► **désapprouver.**

- *To talk someone's head off:* to exhaust the listener by talking so much ► **parler jusqu'à épuiser son interlocuteur.**

- *To trouble one's head with:* to bother or worry ► **déranger ou inquiéter.**

- *To turn one's head:* to draw attention to oneself, or to become vain ► **attirer l'attention sur soi ou devenir prétentieux.**

- *To use one's head:* to be sensible and use common sense ► **être raisonnable et faire preuve de bon sens; se servir de sa tête.**

- *Touched in the head:* somewhat crazy or deranged ► **un peu fou ou dérangé; tête fêlée.**

- *Upside the head:* against the side of a head ► **sur le côté de la tête.**

lip ► **lèvre**

noun contour, corner, edge, flesh, frown, grin, kiss, kissing, laugh, lipstick, makeup, moustache, mouth, murmur, opening, pout, smile, speech, word, whisper.

adjectives arched, big, bleeding, blue, chapped, closed, coloured, cracked, drooping, dry, frowning, full, grimacing, grinning, half-open, hot, hungry, large, loose, lower, lovely, lush, made up, mumbling, murmuring, narrow, open, parting, perfect, pouting, protruding, puckered, pursed, quivering, red, sexy, skinny, smiling, soft, talkative, talking, tender, thick, thin, tight, trembling, upper, uttering, wet, wide, wide-open, whispering.

verbs SUBJECT: a lip chaps, closes, cracks, dries, frowns, grimaces, grins, joins, kisses, mumbles, mutters, opens, parts, pouts, protrudes, puckers, purses, quivers, smiles, touches, trembles, utters, wets, whispers, widens, wrinkles. OTHERS: to bite a lip, to kiss a lip, to lick a lip, to make up a lip, to move a lip, to part a lip, to pucker a lip, to purse a lip, to smack a lip, to touch a lip, to wet a lip.

expressions

- *One's lips are sealed:* keeping a secret and revealing nothing ▶ **garder un secret, ne rien révéler ; motus et bouche cousue.**

- *To button one's lip:* to keep quiet ▶ **ne rien dire, garder le silence ; motus et bouche cousue.**

- *To give lip service:* insincere expression of agreement or support ▶ **faire croire à son accord ou à son appui.**

- *To keep a stiff upper lip:* to show courage in a trying time ▶ **faire preuve de courage dans une situation difficile ; redresser la tête.**

- *To lick one's lips:* to anticipate eagerly ▶ **savourer à l'avance ; s'en lécher les babines.**

- *To pass one's lips:* to speak ▶ **laisser échapper des paroles ; parler.**

- *To pay lip service:* insincere expression of agreement or support ▶ **faire croire à son accord ou à son appui.**

mouth ▶ **bouche**

noun breathe, breathing, cheek, chuckles, cough, diner, eater, food, form, gargling, grimace, gum, kiss, jaw, laugh, lip, moustache, mouthful, mouthing, mouthwash, nutrition, opening, saliva, shape, smile, speech, sucking, talker, taste, thirst, throat, tongue, tonsil, tooth, voice, word, yawn.

adjectives bad, beautiful, big, charming, chewing, clenched, closed, coloured, delicate, dirty, dry, eating, enormous, fiery, foaming, fresh, full, gaping, greedy, grimacing, half-open, huge, hungry, hurtful, hurting, large, loud, loose, mouth-to-mouth, mouthwatering, narrow, open, perfect, round, seductive, sensual, shut, silent, slack, small, smiling, starved, starving, talking, tense, thirsty, tight, tiny, toothless, trap, twisted, wet, wide, wide-open, yawning.

verbs SUBJECT: a mouth bleeds, closes, dribbles, dries, drinks, eats, foams, gapes, grimaces, hurts, laughs, opens, salivates, slackens, spits, shuts, sucks, swallows, yawns, wets. OTHERS: to bleed from a mouth, to breathe through a mouth, to close a mouth, to open a mouth, to rinse out a mouth, to shut a mouth, to wipe a mouth.

expressions

- *By word of mouth:* communicated orally ▶ **communiqué verbalement ; de bouche à oreille.**

- *Down in the mouth:* in low spirits ▶ **d'humeur triste, mélancolique.**

- *From hand to mouth:* existing with difficulty with only the bare necessities ▶ **vivre avec le strict nécessaire ; vivoter.**

- *From the horse's mouth:* from a trustworthy source ▶ **de source sûre.**

- *Out of the mouths of babes:* saying something wise despite one's inexperience ▶ **tenir un discours sensé malgré son inexpérience ; la vérité sort de la bouche des enfants.**

- *To bad mouth:* to speak badly or critically about someone or something

► **parler en mal de quelqu'un ou de quelque chose.**

- *To foam at the mouth:* to be very angry ► **être furieux; écumer de rage.**
- *To have a big mouth:* to talk a lot and be known for revealing secrets ► **être reconnu pour être incapable de garder un secret; avoir une grande gueule.**
- *To have one's heart in one's mouth:* to be very scared or anxious ► **avoir très peur ou être très angoissé; avoir le cœur qui bat la chamade.**
- *To keep one's mouth shut:* to remain quiet and not reveal anything ► **ne rien dire ou révéler; ne souffler mot à personne.**
- *To leave a bad taste in one's mouth:* to make a lasting bad impression ► **laisser une mauvaise impression.**
- *To look a gift horse in the mouth:* to be ungrateful or suspicious of something offered for free ► **ne pas exprimer sa reconnaissance lorsqu'on reçoit un cadeau ou s'en méfier.**
- *To make one's mouth water:* to eagerly await something ► **attendre quelque chose avec impatience; en avoir l'eau à la bouche.**
- *To melt in one's mouth:* to be very tasty ► **être délicieux; fondre dans la bouche.**
- *To mouth off:* to complain loudly or talk back to ► **manifester son mécontentement ou rétorquer avec insolence.**
- *To not open one's mouth:* to remain silent and not reveal one's point of view ► **garder le silence et ne pas révéler son opinion; ne piper mot.**
- *To put one's foot in one's mouth:* to say something one regrets having said ► **prononcer des paroles qu'on regrettera plus tard; se mettre les pieds dans le plat.**
- *To put one's money where one's mouth is:* to act on one's opinion ► **agir selon son opinion.**
- *To put words in someone's mouth:* say something for someone else ► **parler à la place de quelqu'un d'autre.**
- *To run off at the mouth:* to babble on and on ► **parler sans arrêt; jacasser.**

- *To say a mouthful:* to say something important ► **faire une déclaration importante.**
- *To shoot off one's mouth:* to brag, or to say something without thinking ► **se vanter ou parler sans réfléchir.**
- *To shut one's mouth:* to remain silent and not reveal one's point of view ► **se taire et ne pas révéler son opinion; se la fermer.**
- *To take the bit in one's mouth:* to take control ► **prendre les commandes.**
- *To take the bread out of someone's mouth:* to take someone's livelihood away ► **retirer le gagne-pain à quelqu'un; lui retirer le pain de la bouche.**
- *To take the words out of someone's mouth:* to guess what someone is going to say ► **deviner ce que l'autre s'apprête à dire; lui enlever les mots de la bouche.**

nose ► nez

noun aroma, beak, bone, breath, breathing, cartilage, cold, exhalation, face, flu, form, fragrance, glasses, hair, handkerchief, inhalation, muscle, nosebleed, nose ring, nostril, odour, perfume, piercing, protrusion, ridge, scent, secretion, sense of smell, shape, smelling, sneeze, sniff, snore, snort, snout, stink, tip, tissue, trail, whiff.

adjectives angular, beautiful, bent, big, bleeding, blemished, blocked, broken, brown, button, crooked, congested, cute, delicate, dirty, eagle, enormous, fine, flared, flat, hairy, handsome, hooked, huge, long, lovely, normal, odd, perfect, pierced, pinched, pointy, proud, protruding, prying, quivering, red, regal, regular, Roman, round, runny, sculpted, sensitive, short, small, sniffing, straight, strange, strong, stuffed up, tiny, thick, wide, wrinkled.

verbs SUBJECT: a nose bleeds, breaks, breathes, flares, moves, perceives, pokes, quivers, runs, senses, smells, sneezes, sniffs, snores, wrinkles. OTHERS: to blow a nose, to break a nose, to breathe through a nose, to flare a nose, to pick a nose, to pinch a nose, to rub a nose, to stuff a nose, to tickle a nose, to wipe a nose, to wrinkle a nose.

expressions

- *By a nose:* a very small difference ▸ **une infime différence.**

- *Can't see beyond (farther than) the end of one's nose:* unable to see beyond the immediate ▸ **incapable de voir au-delà de la situation immédiate; incapable de voir plus loin que le bout de son nez.**

- *No skin off one's nose:* not a bother or harmful to anyone ▸ **ne dérange ou ne nuit à personne.**

- *Plain as the nose on your face:* obvious and clear ▸ **clair et évident; (cela) se voit comme le nez au milieu de la figure.**

- *On the nose:* exactly or precisely ▸ **exactement ou précisément.**

- *To brown nose:* to try for favour or support ▸ **essayer d'obtenir une faveur ou un soutien.**

- *To count noses:* determine the number of people present ▸ **déterminer le nombre de personnes présentes.**

- *To cut off one's nose to spite one's face:* to cause injury to oneself because of wounded pride ▸ **se faire du tort par fierté ou par dépit.**

- *To follow one's nose:* to go straight ahead ▸ **aller droit devant soi.**

- *To have one's nose in a book:* to often be reading ▸ **s'adonner à la lecture.**

- *To have one's nose in the air:* to be arrogant or defiant ▸ **être arrogant(e) ou hautain(e).**

- *To have one's nose out of joint:* to feel annoyed, upset or wounded ▸ **être ennuyé(e), vexé(e) ou blessé(e).**

- *To keep one's nose clean:* to stay out of trouble ▸ **se tenir tranquille; se tenir à carreau.**

- *To keep one's nose to the grindstone:* to continue to work hard ▸ **travailler sans relâche; avoir le nez dans son travail.**

- *To lead by the nose:* to control someone ▸ **avoir du pouvoir sur quelqu'un; le mener par le bout du nez.**

- *To look down one's nose:* to feel superior to someone else ▸ **se sentir supérieur à autrui; lever le nez sur.**

- *To nose about (around):* to look for something hidden or secret ▸ **fouiner; chercher à découvrir ce qui est caché ou secret; fourrer son nez partout.**

- *To nose in (into):* to snoop, or carefully advance facing forward ▸ **s'avancer avec prudence; mettre son nez dans.**

- *To nose out:* to discover a secret, or to win narrowly ▸ **découvrir un secret ou gagner de peu.**

- *To pay through the nose:* to pay too much for something ▸ **payer trop cher; payer les yeux de la tête.**

- *To poke one's nose into:* to pry into someone else's affairs ▸ **mettre son nez dans les affaires d'autrui.**

- *To rub someone's nose in it:* to forcefully remind someone of a fault or error they have made ▸ **rappeler à une personne une faute ou une erreur qu'elle a commise.**

- *To thumb one's nose:* to show scorn ▸ **faire montre de mépris; rire au nez de quelqu'un.**

- *To turn up one's nose:* to show scorn or arrogance ▸ **montrer du mépris ou de l'arrogance; rire au nez de quelqu'un.**

- *Under one's nose:* in plain view ▸ **sans se cacher; au nez de quelqu'un.**

skull ▸ crâne

noun backbone, bone, brain, bump, crack, danger, death, face, forehead, fracture, form, head, injury, jaw, scalp, shape, size, skeleton, skin, temple, wound.

adjectives big, cracked, crushed, dense, egg-shaped, empty, flat, hard, injured, long, open, oval, pointed, round, shaped, small, soft, tiny, wounded.

verbs SUBJECT: a skull develops, forms, grows, protects. OTHERS: to break a skull, to crack a skull, to crush a skull, to flatten a skull, to injure a skull, to measure a skull, to wound a skull.

tongue ▸ langue

noun click, flavour, kiss, lick, moisture, mouth, muscle, pronunciation, saliva, sense of taste, speech, stammer, stutter, talking, taste, taste bud, tip, tongue-twister, tooth, vocal cords, wag.

adjectives big, clicking, coated, dangerous, dry, flapping, flattering, flickering, furred, gossiping, hanging, licking, mean, moist, nimble, pointed, poisonous, red, slanderous, stammering, stuttering, swollen, wagging, wet.

verbs SUBJECT: a tongue clicks, flaps, licks, points, swells, tastes, wags. OTHERS: to bite a tongue, to burn a tongue, to click a tongue, to moisten a tongue, to stick out a tongue, to tie a tongue.

expressions

- *Cat got one's tongue:* a comment directed to someone who has remained quiet ▸ **se dit d'une personne qui garde le silence ; qui a avalé sa langue.**
- *On the tip of one's tongue:* unable to remember what one was about to say ▸ **incapable de se rappeler ce que l'on voulait dire ; avoir un mot sur le bout de la langue.**
- *One's tongue hangs out:* eager anticipation ▸ **attendre avec impatience ; tirer la langue.**
- *Slip of the tongue:* a mistake in speaking ▸ **erreur d'élocution ; la langue lui a fourché.**
- *To bite one's tongue:* to restrain from speaking ▸ **se retenir de parler ; tenir sa langue.**
- *To find one's tongue:* to find the words to say something ▸ **trouver les mots pour le dire.**

- *To hold one's tongue:* to keep quiet ▸ **se taire ; tenir sa langue.**
- *To keep a civil tongue in one's head:* to speak politely ▸ **parler poliment.**
- *Tongue-tied:* speechless ▸ **bouche bée, incapable de parler.**
- *Tongues wag:* gossip ▸ **commérages ; langue de vipère.**
- *With tongue in cheek:* said ironically or as a joke ▸ **en plaisantant ou avec ironie.**

tooth ▸ dent

noun baby tooth, bite, bone, braces, canine, care, cavity, chew, crown, cutter, dentist, dentures, drill, eating, enamel, erosion, extraction, fang, filling, floss, fluoride, gap, grinder, gum, hygiene, ivories, jaw, molar, mouth, nerve, protection, rage, receding gums, root, sugar, tartar, tooth decay, toothache, toothbrush, toothpaste, toothpick, tusk, wear, whitening, wisdom tooth, tooth fairy.

adjectives adult, artificial, bad, biting, black, brushed, bucked, chattering, chewing, clean, cleaned, clenched, crooked, crunching, crushed, cutting, dazzling, decaying, exposed, fake, false, fallen, fine, gnawing, grinding, growing, hard, healthy, hollow, hollowed out, long, loose, missing, natural, permanent, pointed, pulled, rotten, short, small, soft, spaced, sparkling, spoiled, stained, straight, strong, temporary, tight, toothed, toothless, toothy, ugly, weak, white, wiggling, wisdom, yellow, yellowing.

verbs SUBJECT: a tooth bites, breaks, chatters, chews, chips, clatters, clenches, cracks, crunches, crushes, decays, falls out, gnashes, gnaws, grinds, grows in, hurts, loosens, pierces, rots, tears, sinks into, sparkles, whitens, wiggles, yellows. OTHERS: to break a tooth, to brush a tooth, to chip a tooth, to clench a tooth, to crack a tooth, to crush a tooth, to drill a tooth, to fill a tooth, to floss a tooth, to extract a tooth, to grind a tooth, to grow in a tooth, to loosen a tooth, to lose a tooth, to pull a tooth, to show a tooth, to sink a tooth into, to wiggle a tooth.

expressions

- *Armed to the teeth:* well equipped ▶ **bien équipé ou équipée.**

- *By the skin of one's teeth:* barely or narrowly ▶ **de justesse.**

- *Fine-tooth comb:* to search or investigate by looking at small details ▶ **rechercher jusque dans les moindres détails; passer au peigne fin.**

- *In the teeth of:* straight into, or in opposition to ▶ **directement contre.**

- *Kick in the teeth:* a humiliating setback ▶ **échec humiliant.**

- *Like pulling teeth:* difficulty, especially in getting someone to talk ▶ **difficulté à faire parler quelqu'un.**

- *Long in the tooth:* old ▶ **âgé ou âgée.**

- *Scarce as hen's teeth:* very rare ▶ **très rare.**

- *Sweet tooth:* enjoying sweets ▶ **qui apprécie les sucreries.**

- *To bare (show) one's teeth:* to show one's anger ▶ **montrer sa colère.**

- *To cut one's teeth on:* to learn early in life, or to do in order to get experience ▶ **apprendre à un très jeune âge; faire quelque chose afin d'acquérir de l'expérience.**

- *To fight tooth and nail:* to fight, or to make a great effort ▶ **combattre avec acharnement; faire un grand effort.**

- *To give one's eye-teeth:* to do anything to obtain something ▶ **être prêt ou prête à tous les sacrifices pour obtenir quelque chose.**

- *To gnash one's teeth:* to show rage ▶ **démontrer sa rage.**

- *To grit one's teeth:* to prepare to face something unpleasant or difficult ▶ **se préparer à faire face à une situation désagréable ou difficile; serrer des dents.**

- *To lie through one's teeth:* to say outrageous things ▶ **mentir sans vergogne.**

- *To set one's teeth on edge:* to irritate extremely ▶ **irriter outre mesure; faire grincer des dents.**

- *To sink (get) one's teeth into:* to become wholly involved in ▶ **se lancer totalement dans; mordre à belles dents.**

- *To the teeth:* completely ▶ **jusqu'aux dents; complètement.**

- *Tooth fairy:* a mythical character who offers gifts ▶ **fée qui offre des cadeaux en échange de dents d'enfants.**

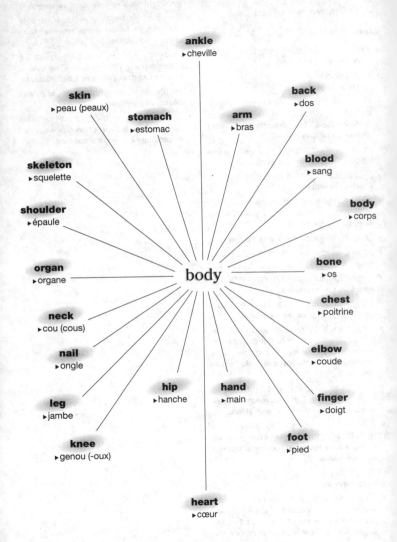

ankle
▸cheville

skin
▸peau (peaux)

stomach
▸estomac

arm
▸bras

back
▸dos

blood
▸sang

skeleton
▸squelette

body
▸corps

shoulder
▸épaule

organ
▸organe

body

bone
▸os

chest
▸poitrine

neck
▸cou (cous)

nail
▸ongle

elbow
▸coude

hip
▸hanche

hand
▸main

finger
▸doigt

leg
▸jambe

foot
▸pied

knee
▸genou (-oux)

heart
▸cœur

ankle ▶ cheville

noun bone, foot, inflammation, joint, leg, limb, limp, sprain, swelling, twist.

adjectives ankle-deep, ankle-length, broken, extended, fat, flexed, hurt, injured, narrow, shattered, sprained, strong, swollen, thin, twisted, weak, wide, wounded.

verbs SUBJECT: an ankle bends, breaks, cracks, extends, flexes, moves, sprains, twists. OTHERS: to bend an ankle, to hurt an ankle, to injure an ankle, to jar an ankle, to shatter an ankle, to sprain an ankle, to twist an ankle, to wound an ankle.

arm ▶ bras

noun armband, armful, armpit, bend, biceps, bone, elbow, embrace, forearm, gesticulation, gesture, hand, hug, length, limb, load, long, movement, muscle, nerve, position, reach, signal, short, shoulder, sleeve, strength, stump, triceps, wrist.

adjectives amputated, bandaged, bare, bending, bent, broken, built, clasping, covered, crossed, dangling, dragging, embracing, extended, fat, flexed, flexible, gesticulating, hanging, hairy, hurt, injured, left, linked, long, lower, lowered, muscular, naked, one-armed, raised, reaching, right, short, shoulder, spread, stiff, straight, swinging, thin, tired, upper, weak, wounded.

verbs an arm balances, bends, breaks, carries, clasps, dangles, drags, embraces, extends, gestures, hangs, holds, hugs, lifts, lowers, moves, raises, reaches, rises, signals, slackens. OTHERS: to amputate an arm, to brush an arm, to cross an arm, to dangle an arm, to drag an arm, to fall into an arm, to grab an arm, to raise an arm, to slacken an arm, to spread an arm, to throw into an arm.

expressions

- *Arm and a leg:* a lot of money ▶ **beaucoup d'argent; (coûter) les yeux de la tête.**
- *Arm in arm:* together, or having one's arms linked ▶ **ensemble; bras dessus bras dessous.**
- *At arm's length:* at a distance avoiding intimacy ▶ **à distance, pour éviter l'intimité; à bout de bras.**
- *Long arm of the law:* the extent of the authorities' powers ▶ **étendue du pouvoir des autorités; le bras de la justice.**
- *One-armed bandit:* a slot machine ▶ **machine à sous.**
- *Open-arms:* inviting ▶ **de manière accueillante; à bras ouverts.**
- *Shot in the arm:* something invigorating ▶ **quelque chose de revigorant; un coup de fouet.**
- *To give one's right arm:* to make a sacrifice ▶ **faire un sacrifice.**
- *To lend an arm:* to offer help ▶ **offrir son aide; prêter main-forte.**
- *To put the arm on:* to ask for money ▶ **réclamer de l'argent.**
- *To talk someone's arm off:* to exhaust a listener by talking so much ▶ **épuiser un interlocuteur à force de parler.**
- *To twist someone's arm:* to persuade someone ▶ **persuader; forcer la main.**
- *Up in arms:* to be angry or rebellious ▶ **être en colère ou révolté(e).**
- *With one arm tied behind one's back:* very easily ▶ **très facilement; les doigts dans le nez.**
- *With open arms:* warmly and enthusiastically ▶ **avec chaleur et enthousiasme; à bras ouverts.**

back ▶ dos

noun back rest, backstroke, bone, broad, buttock, dislocation, hump, kidney, lower, middle, neck, rear, paralysis, posture, shoulder, spinal column, spine, upper, vertebra, vertebrate.

adjectives aching, arched, backache, backbreaking, bare, bent, built, crooked, curved, developed, flexible, humped, hunchbacked, hunched, inflexible, muscular, narrow, plump, rounded, sloping, sore, slumped, stiff, stooped, stooping, straight, strong, twisted, twisting, wide.

verbs SUBJECT: a back aches, bears, bends, carries, curves, moves, narrows, rounds, slopes, slumps, stiffens, stoops, straightens, turns, twists, widens. OBJECTS: to arch a back, to carry on a back, to bend a back, to fall on a back, to lean on a back, to lie on a back, to rub a back, to scratch a back, to slap a back, to sleep on a back, to stretch a back, to swim on a back, to twist a back, to watch a back.

expressions..

- *Back-to-back:* facing opposite directions ► **dos à dos.**
- *Back to (against) the wall:* in a difficult situation with no way out ► **dans une situation difficile et sans issue; acculé ou acculée au pied du mur.**
- *Backslapping:* jovial ► **jovial ou joviale.**
- *Behind someone's back:* without someone knowing ► **à l'insu de quelqu'un; dans le dos de quelqu'un.**
- *Flat on one's back:* sick in bed, or helpless ► **malade au lit; sans défense.**
- *Like water off a duck's back:* easily ► **facilement.**
- *Monkey on one's back:* drug addiction, or a burden ► **dépendance à la drogue ou fardeau.**
- *Off someone's back:* no longer bothering someone ► **cesser de déranger quelqu'un; cesser d'être sur le dos de quelqu'un.**
- *Pat on the back:* support, approval or praise ► **soutien, approbation ou louange.**
- *Slap on the back:* a gesture of congratulations ► **geste de félicitations.**
- *To break one's back:* to work very hard ► **travailler très fort.**
- *To break the back of:* to overpower ► **vaincre.**

- *To give the shirt off someone's back:* to give everything one has ► **être généreux ou généreuse à l'extrême.**
- *To put one's back into it:* to make great effort ► **faire un grand effort.**
- *To put one's back out:* to hurt one's back ► **se faire mal au dos.**
- *To scratch someone's back:* to do something for someone in hopes that the favour will be returned ► **rendre un service dans l'espoir de recevoir la pareille.**
- *To stab in the back:* to betray ► **trahir.**
- *To turn one's back on:* to abandon, deny or reject ► **abandonner, refuser ou rejeter; tourner le dos.**
- *When one's back is turned:* when one is unaware or not looking ► **pendant qu'on n'est pas conscient ou qu'on ne regarde pas; pendant qu'on a le dos tourné.**
- *With one arm tied behind one's back:* very easily ► **très facilement.**
- *You scratch my back and I'll scratch yours:* if you help me, I will help you ► **si tu m'aides, je te rendrai la pareille.**

blood ► sang

noun aorta, artery, blood group, blood taking, blood type, bloodstain, bloodstream, circulation, clot, colour, crust, diabetes, donor, drop, flow, fluid, heart, life, lifeblood, life force, needle, plasma, pressure, pulse, red, scab, serum, transfusion, vein, vessel.

adjectives bleeding, bloodstained, bloody, blue, boiling, burning, clear, dry, fiery, fresh, hot, old, poisoned, poor, pure, red, rich, royal, shed, spilled, splashed, sticky, streaming, thick, thin, young.

verbs SUBJECT: blood boils, circulates, dries, drops, runs, spills, splashes, spurts, stains, streams, trickles. OTHERS: to cover in blood, to drain blood, to lose blood, to shed blood, to spill blood, to replace blood, to transfuse blood.

expressions

- *Bad blood:* hostility between people ▸ **animosité entre personnes.**

- *Blood is thicker than water:* family ties are stronger than other relationships ▸ **les liens familiaux sont plus forts que tous les autres.**

- *Blood relatives:* direct family ▸ **famille directe.**

- *Flesh and blood:* human beings and their faults, or one's kin ▸ **l'être humain et ses défauts, ou sa famille; êtres de chair et de sang.**

- *In cold blood:* ruthless and unfeeling ▸ **sans scrupule ni sentiment; de sang-froid.**

- *In one's blood:* in one's nature ▸ **dans la nature de quelqu'un; dans le sang.**

- *In the blood:* in one's nature ▸ **dans la nature de quelqu'un; dans le sang.**

- *My heart bleeds for you:* I feel no sympathy for you ▸ **je n'ai aucune compassion pour vous.**

- *New blood:* new members to a group with fresh ideas or invigorating energy ▸ **nouveaux membres d'un groupe qui apportent des idées ou une énergie nouvelles; du sang neuf.**

- *Out for blood:* looking for revenge ▸ **chercher à se venger.**

- *Sporting blood:* willing to take risks ▸ **prêt ou prête à prendre des risques.**

- *Sweat blood:* to work very hard ▸ **travailler très fort; suer sang et eau.**

- *To bleed someone white (dry):* to take someone's money ▸ **prendre l'argent de quelqu'un; le saigner à blanc.**

- *To draw blood:* to injure someone emotionally or physically ▸ **infliger une blessure physique ou psychologique.**

- *To make one's blood boil:* to make one very angry ▸ **mettre quelqu'un en colère.**

- *To make one's blood run cold:* to cause to shiver with fear ▸ **faire frissonner de peur; glacer le sang.**

- *To run in the blood (family):* passed on from one generation to the next, or be a family characteristic ▸ **transmis d'une** génération à l'autre; caractéristique familiale.

- *To scream bloody murder:* to angrily protest ▸ **protester avec colère.**

- *To shed (spill) blood:* to violently kill or wound someone ▸ **tuer ou blesser violemment; verser le sang.**

body ▸ corps

noun anatomy, appearance, arm, aspect, attitude, back, bearing, beauty, body bag, bone, build, chest, corpse, exercise, face, feature, fitness, flesh, foot, frame, gesture, gymnastics, hand, head, health, height, hygiene, image, language, leg, limb, look, manner, movement, neck, organ, shape, size, skeleton, skin, stance, stature, stomach, strength, structure, temperature, torso, trunk, waist, weight.

adjectives aged, ageing, agile, attractive, awkward, bare, bent, big, black, bleeding, bony, brittle, broken, built, chubby, clean, clothed, covered, crippled, dancing, defeated, delicate, dirty, dressed, elegant, exhausted, feverish, fat, firm, flexible, giant, graceful, hard, healthy, heavy, inactive, injured, large, lazy, light, limber, lively, moving, naked, old, paralysed, plump, rickety, rigid, scented, scrawny, shaking, shivering, shrivelled, shrunken, shuddering, sickly, skinny, slender, slumped, slim, small, soft, sore, stiff, still, stinky, stocky, stooping, stretched, strong, suffering, sunburnt, tanned, tender, thin, tiny, tired, tired out, trembling, twisted, ugly, undressed, ungraceful, unwashed, vigorous, warm, washed, weak, white, young, youthful.

verbs SUBJECT: a body aches, ages, bends, creaks, dances, dies, leans, lies down, floats, moves, rises, shakes, shrinks, shudders, slumps, smells, stiffens, stinks, stretches, sweats, tans, thins, tires, trembles, weakens. OTHERS: to bathe a body, to bend a body, to bury a body, to cover a body, to dress a body, to dry a body, to feed a body, to head a body, to wash a body.

expressions

- *Body blow:* Some action that causes damage ▶ **action causant des dommages.**
- *Body language:* Body movements that express one's feelings ▶ **mouvements du corps qui expriment des sentiments ; langage non verbal.**
- *Over my dead body:* under no circumstances ▶ **en aucun cas.**
- *To keep body and soul together:* to stay alive or make stay alive ▶ **rester ou garder en vie.**

bone ▶ os

nouns anatomy, body, break, build, cartilage, fracture, frame, framework, limb, skeleton, structure.

adjectives big, bony, broken, cracked, fine, fractured, fragile, skinny, slender, sprained, stiff, strong, twisted, weak.

verbs SUBJECT: a bone aches, breaks, cracks, fractures, pops, sprains, twists. OTHERS: to break a bone, to crack a bone, to fracture a bone, to sprain a bone, to twist a bone.

expressions

- *Bare bones:* basic necessities, or plain ▶ **l'essentiel, ou dans sa plus simple expression.**
- *Bone of contention:* the reason for or matter in a quarrel ▶ **la raison ou l'objet d'une querelle.**
- *Chilled to the bone (marrow):* bitterly cold ▶ **qui a extrêmement froid ; transi(e) jusqu'aux os (jusqu'à la mœlle).**
- *Cut to the bone:* extremely reduced ▶ **réduit ou réduite au minimum.**
- *Funny bone:* a sense of humour, or the elbow ▶ **sens de l'humour ; coude.**
- *Skin and bones:* very thin ▶ **très mince ; n'avoir que la peau et les os.**
- *To bone up:* to study intensely ▶ **étudier de façon intense.**
- *To feel in one's bones:* to have a hunch about something ▶ **avoir un pressentiment.**

- *To have a bone to pick:* have a need to discuss something unpleasant or a grievance ▶ **devoir discuter d'un sujet désagréable ou d'une doléance.**
- *To make no bones about:* to speak freely without hesitation ▶ **parler librement, sans hésitation.**
- *To pull a boner:* to make a silly mistake ▶ **faire une erreur idiote.**
- *To roll the bones:* to throw dice ▶ **lancer les dés.**
- *To work one's fingers to the bone:* to labour or exert oneself very hard ▶ **travailler ou se dépenser intensément.**

chest ▶ poitrine

nouns abdomen, body, breast, breathing, build, bust, cold, heart, lung, pain, pneumonia, respiration, rib, shoulder, skin, thorax, torso, trunk, width.

adjectives attractive, bare, beautiful, big, bony, broad, built, chubby, curved, enormous, fat, firm, flat, fragile, hairless, hairy, handsome, hard, large, muscular, naked, narrow, old, plump, prominent, protruding, rounded, scrawny, sinking, skinny, soft, stocky, strong, sunken, thin, tight, weak, wide, young.

verbs SUBJECTS: a chest contracts, narrows, rises, swells, tightens, widens. OTHERS: to cover a chest, to hold against a chest, to listen to a chest, to pound on a chest, to weigh down on a chest.

expressions

- *To get off one's chest:* to be relieved by saying something one has been meaning to say ▶ **se sentir soulagé d'avoir dit ce que l'on avait sur le cœur.**
- *To play one's cards close to one's chest:* to be secretive ▶ **secret.**

elbow ▶ coude

nouns angle, arm, armrest, bend, biceps, bone, extension, flexion, forearm, elbow rest, funny bone, joint, limb, muscle, triceps.

adjectives bending, bent, big, broken, extended, flexed, fractured, injured, limber, pointed, raised, rounded, wounded.

verbs SUBJECT: an elbow bends, breaks, extends, flexes, fractures, injures, raises, rounds. OTHERS: to bend an elbow, to break an elbow, to extend an elbow, to flex an elbow, to fracture an elbow, to hurt an elbow, to injure an elbow, to rest on an elbow, to raise an elbow, to wound an elbow.

expressions

* *At someone's elbow:* within easy reach ▶ **à portée de la main.**
* *Elbow grease:* tiring physical effort ▶ **effort physique fatigant.**
* *Elbowroom:* sufficient space to move comfortably ▶ **suffisament d'espace pour être à l'aise; avoir les coudées franches.**
* *Out at the elbows (heels, knees):* to wear worn clothes, or be poor ▶ **porter des vêtements usés; être pauvre.**
* *To crook (bend) one's elbow:* to drink alcohol excessively ▶ **boire de l'alcool avec excès.**
* *To elbow one's way through:* to aggressively push one's way through ▶ **jouer des coudes pour se frayer un passage.**
* *To rub elbows (shoulders) with:* to socialise with ▶ **côtoyer.**

finger ▶ **doigt**

nouns agility, bend, bone, digit, dressing, feeling, fingernail, fingerprint, flexibility, hand, index finger, joint, little finger, pinch, plucks, pointer, ring, ring finger, splint, thimble, thumb, tip, touch.

adjectives agile, big, bulging, bumpy, chubby, clean, cold, crooked, crossed, curled, dirty, fat, fine, flexible, fractured, frozen, grabbing, grasping, hairless, hairy, hooked, injured, limber, long, missing, moving, nimble, numb, plump, probing, red, rigid, rough, short, small, stocky,

swollen, tapered, tapping, wounded, wrinkled.

verbs SUBJECT: a finger breaks, bulges, curls, grabs, grasps, hooks, moves, points, pokes, shakes, snaps, tapers, taps, touches. OTHERS: to injure a finger, to fracture a finger, to injure a finger, to miss a finger, to move a finger, to snap a finger, to wound a finger.

expressions

* *At one's fingertips:* readily available ▶ **à portée de la main.**
* *Sticky fingers:* someone with a tendency to steal ▶ **personne qui a tendance à voler.**
* *To burn one's fingers:* to be harmed ▶ **se faire blesser.**
* *To cross one's fingers:* to wish for luck, or to tell a small lie ▶ **souhaiter la chance ou dire un mensonge pieux; croiser les doigts.**
* *To have a finger in the pie:* to be interested in something or meddle in it ▶ **s'intéresser à quelque chose ou s'en mêler.**
* *To keep one's fingers crossed:* to wish for luck ▶ **souhaiter la chance; croiser les doigts.**
* *To lay (put) a finger on:* to barely touch what is prohibited ▶ **à peine toucher ce qui est interdit.**
* *To let slip through the fingers:* to miss an opportunity when one could have had it ▶ **laisser passer la chance; laisser filer la chance.**
* *Not lift a finger:* to refuse to help or exert oneself ▶ **refuser d'aider ou de faire un effort; ne pas lever le petit doigt.**
* *To point the finger at:* to blame or accuse ▶ **blâmer ou accuser; pointer du doigt.**
* *To put (lay) one's finger on:* to identify ▶ **identifier; mettre le doigt sur.**
* *To put the finger on:* to inform on ▶ **dénoncer.**
* *To snap one's fingers at:* to treat disrespectfully or with scorn ▶ **manquer de respect ou traiter avec mépris.**
* *To wrap (turn, twist, wind) somebody*

around one's finger: to have control over someone ► **avoir le pouvoir sur une personne; la mener par le bout du nez.**

- *To work one's fingers to the bone:* to labour or exert oneself very hard ► **trimer dur ou se dépenser avec excès.**

foot ► **pied**

nouns ankle, arch, ball, blister, bone, corn, fallen arch, foot brake, foot mark, football, footprint, footstep, heel, hop, jump, leap, leg, limb, movement, muscle, pace, pedal, pedestrian, run, shoe, size, skeleton, slip, slipper, sole, sprain, stamp, stomp, stand, step, toe, tracks, walk, walker.

adjectives amputated, arched, bare, bent, big, clean, club, cold, crossed, curved, cute, delicate, dirty, dry, extended, fine, flat, flexed, footloose, fractured, frozen, hurt, injured, lame, large, left, limber, long, narrow, numb, pointed, raised, right, rigid, shape, short, small, smelly, sprained, squashed, standing, stinky, sunken, swollen, thin, twisted, ugly, unwashed, walking, warm, washed, wet, wide, wounded.

verbs SUBJECT: a foot kicks, jumps, leaps, moves, runs, slides, stamps, steps, slips, stomps, taps, walks, OTHERS: to balance on a foot, to fall on a foot, to raise a foot, to skip on a foot, to stand on a foot, to twist a foot, to warm a foot, to wipe feet.

expressions

- *Bound hand and foot:* obligated and unable to free oneself ► **être impuissant ou impuissante, incapable de se libérer; avoir les mains liées.**
- *Caught flat-footed:* taken by surprise ► **pris ou prise au dépourvu.**
- *Dead on one's feet:* very tired ► **épuisé ou épuisée; ne plus tenir debout.**
- *Don't let the grass grow under one's feet:* to act without delay ► **agir sans délai.**

- *Feet of clay:* a fault in someone's character ► **défaut de caractère.**
- *Not touch with a ten-foot pole:* to avoid completely ► **éviter à tout prix.**
- *On foot:* walking ► **à pied.**
- *On one's feet:* standing, or healthy ► **être sur pied ou en bonne santé.**
- *Six feet under:* dead and buried ► **mort(e) et enterré(e).**
- *The shoe is on the other foot:* the situation has reversed ► **les rôles sont inversés.**
- *To be at someone's feet:* to be fascinated by someone ► **être fasciné ou fascinée par quelqu'un.**
- *To drag one's feet (heels):* to deliberately delay or work slowly ► **ralentir délibérément le rythme de travail; traîner les pieds.**
- *To fall (land) on one's feet:* to return to a stable situation after a period of difficulty ► **revenir à la normale après une période difficile; retomber sur ses pieds.**
- *To get cold feet:* to stop from doing something because of fear ► **cesser une activité à cause de la peur.**
- *To get off (start off) on the right foot:* to begin well, or establish good relations ► **débuter correctement ou établir de bonnes relations dès le départ; partir du bon pied.**
- *To get off on the wrong foot:* to begin badly, or fail to establish good relations ► **mal débuter ou ne pas réussir à établir de bonnes relations; partir du mauvais pied.**
- *To get one's feet wet:* to start something new ► **essayer quelque chose de nouveau.**
- *To get the lead out of one's feet:* to hurry or move faster ► **se presser ou avancer plus vite.**
- *To get to (on) one's feet:* to stand up ► **se lever.**
- *To have one foot in the grave:* to be near death or be in a very serious condition ► **être mourant(e) ou très gravement malade; avoir un pied dans la tombe.**

- *To have two left feet:* to be clumsy ▸ **être maladroit ou maladroite.**

- *To hold (keep) someone's feet to the fire:* pressure someone into doing something ▸ **pousser quelqu'un à faire quelque chose.**

- *To knock (sweep, carry) off someone's feet:* to make a positive impression on someone ▸ **faire bonne impression.**

- *To land (fall) on one's feet:* to overcome difficulties ▸ **surmonter les difficultés.**

- *To put one's best foot forward:* to try one's best and make a good impression ▸ **faire de son mieux pour faire bonne impression.**

- *To put one's feet up:* to relax sitting down or reclining ▸ **se détendre en s'asseyant ou en s'allongeant.**

- *To put one's foot down:* to take a stand ▸ **prendre position de façon catégorique.**

- *To run (rush) someone off his or her feet:* to hurry someone, or work someone to exhaustion ▸ **bousculer ou faire travailler quelqu'un jusqu'à épuisement.**

- *To set foot in:* to enter ▸ **entrer.**

- *To set foot on:* to step on ▸ **marcher sur.**

- *To set one back on one's feet:* to help someone return to their position or situation ▸ **aider une personne à s'en sortir; aider quelqu'un à se remettre sur pied.**

- *To shake the dust from one's feet:* to leave in a hurry ▸ **partir en vitesse.**

- *To shoot oneself in the foot:* to harm oneself or one's cause ▸ **se nuire ou nuire à sa propre cause.**

- *To stand on one's own feet:* to be or act independent ▸ **être indépendant ou se comporter de façon indépendante.**

- *To take the load off one's feet:* to sit down and relax ▸ **s'asseoir et relaxer.**

- *To think on one's feet:* to mentally react quickly ▸ **penser rapidement.**

- *To vote with one's feet:* to walk away or emigrate as a sign of disapproval ▸ **s'éloigner ou partir en signe de désapprobation.**

- *To wait on hand and foot:* to do everything for someone ▸ **faire tout pour quelqu'un; être à ses pieds.**

- *Under one's feet:* in one's way or path ▸ **déranger.**

- *With both feet on the ground:* to be sensible and practical ▸ **être raisonnable et faire preuve de sens pratique.**

---

hand ▸ **main**

nouns agility, applause, arm, backhand, blister, bone, carrying, clap, corn, feeling, finger, fist, gesture, glove, grasp, grip, handbag, handful, handling, handshake, limb, manual, mitten, palm, palm reader, position, slap, smack, splint, thumb, touch, wrist.

adjectives agile, armed, back, bare, beautiful, big, blistered, bony, bumpy, busy, chapped, chubby, clasped, clasping, clean, clenched, clenching, closed, clumsy, cold, cute, damp, delicate, dry, empty, expert, extended, fat, feeling, fine, folding, free, full, gloved, grabbing, grasping, gripping, hardened, heavy, injured, joined, left, light, limber, limp, long, moist, moving, naked, open, plump, quick, right, rough, shaky, short, skinny, slow, small, soft, stained, stocky, sure, sweaty, swollen, raised, rubbing, tender, touching, trained, trembling, unwashed, warm, washed, waving, wet, wounded, wrinkled.

verbs SUBJECT: a hand brushes, carries, chaps, claps, clasps, clenches, closes, feels, folds, gathers, gestures, grabs, grips, handles, holds, lets go, moves, opens, releases, rubs, slaps, smacks, shakes, squeezes, strokes, touches, trembles. OTHERS: to clap a hand, to extend a hand, to fracture a hand, to give a hand, to hold a hand, to injure a hand, to raise a hand, to rub a hand, to shake a hand, to squeeze a hand, to wash a hand, to wave a hand, to wound a hand.

expressions

- *At first hand:* directly from the origin ▸ **directement de la source; de première main.**
- *At hand:* within easy reach ▸ **tout près; sous la main.**
- *At second hand:* through an intermediary ▸ **par le biais d'un intermédiaire; de seconde main.**
- *At the hand(s) of:* done by ▸ **fait par.**
- *Back of one's hand:* rejection ▸ **rejet du revers de la main.**
- *Bound hand and foot:* unable to be freed from an obligation ▸ **être impuissant, incapable de se libérer; avoir les mains liées.**
- *By hand:* manually ▸ **à la main, manuellement.**
- *Clean hands:* innocent ▸ **innocent.**
- *Cold hands, warm heart:* having feelings without necessarily showing them ▸ **éprouver des sentiments sans pour autant les montrer; mains froides, cœur chaud.**
- *Free hand:* freedom to do as one wants ▸ **avoir toute latitude; ne pas avoir les mains liées.**
- *From hand to hand:* from one person to another ▸ **d'une personne à une autre; de mains en mains.**
- *Glad hand:* an insincere welcome ▸ **accueil faussement chaleureux.**
- *Hand in glove:* on close terms ▸ **en relation très étroite; comme les deux doigts de la main.**
- *Hand in hand:* together ▸ **ensemble; main dans la main.**
- *Hand to hand:* in close combat or nearby ▸ **corps à corps; à côté.**
- *Hat in hand:* humbly ▸ **humblement.**
- *Helping hand:* be of assistance ▸ **aider; donner un coup de main.**
- *Heavy hand:* clumsy ▸ **maladroit.**
- *In good hands:* in safe or able care ▸ **bien traité ou protégé; entre bonnes mains.**
- *In hand:* under one's control, or being settled, or accessible ▸ **maîtrisé, en cours de résolution ou accessible; en mains.**
- *In one's hands:* under one's charge or care ▸ **sous la responsabilité ou les soins de quelqu'un; entre les mains de quelqu'un.**
- *Iron hand:* strong control ▸ **surveillance étroite; main de fer.**
- *Left hand doesn't know what the right hand is doing:* uncoordinated actions ▸ **actions non coordonnées.**
- *Left-handed compliment:* an insult disguised as praise ▸ **une insulte déguisée en louange.**
- *Many hands make light work:* many helpers make a job easier ▸ **plus les participants sont nombreux, plus la tâche est facile.**
- *Off one's hands:* no longer one's responsibility ▸ **se dégager d'une responsabilité; s'en laver les mains.**
- *On hand:* readily available ▸ **facilement accessible; sous la main.**
- *On one's hands:* under one's care ▸ **sous les soins de quelqu'un; entre ses mains.**
- *On the one hand:* one view ▸ **selon un point de vue; d'une part.**
- *On the other hand:* another view ▸ **selon un autre point de vue; d'autre part.**
- *Out of hand:* immediately, or out of control ▸ **d'emblée ou impossible.**
- *Right-hand man:* a trusted helper ▸ **personne de confiance; bras droit.**
- *Show of hands:* an informal vote ▸ **vote non officiel; vote à main levée.**
- *Time on one's hands:* free time ▸ **temps libre.**
- *To bite the hand that feeds you:* to be ungrateful ▸ **être ingrat.**
- *To catch somebody red-handed:* to witness someone committing a crime or wrongdoing ▸ **être témoin d'un crime ou d'un méfait; attraper quelqu'un la main dans le sac.**
- *To change hands:* from one owner to another ▸ **passer d'un propriétaire à un autre; passer de mains en mains.**

- *To dirty one's hands:* to do something illegal ▸ **commettre un acte illégal ; se salir les mains.**
- *To eat out of someone's hand:* to be dominated or manipulated ▸ **être dominé ou manipulé.**
- *To force someone's hand:* to make someone reveal something ▸ **obliger quelqu'un à révéler quelque chose.**
- *To give a hand:* to assist ▸ **aider ; donner un coup de main.**
- *To grease someone's hand:* to bribe someone ▸ **offrir un pot-de-vin.**
- *To have a hand in:* to be involved in ▸ **participer à.**
- *To keep a hand in:* to remain involved in ▸ **continuer de participer.**
- *To know like the back of one's hand:* to understand perfectly or be very familiar with ▸ **connaître ou comprendre parfaitement ; connaître comme sa poche.**
- *To lay hands on:* to get within grasp ▸ **attraper ; mettre la main sur.**
- *To lend a hand:* to be of assistance ▸ **aider ; prêter main-forte.**
- *To lift one's hand against:* to threaten to strike someone ▸ **menacer de frapper quelqu'un ; lever la main sur.**
- *To play into the hands of:* to act as though giving another the advantage ▸ **faire comme si on laissait l'avantage à l'autre.**
- *To put one's hands on:* to find or obtain ▸ **trouver ou obtenir ; mettre la main sur.**
- *To rub one's hands:* to be pleased ▸ **être content ; se frotter les mains de contentement.**
- *To raise a hand against:* to threaten to strike someone ▸ **menacer de frapper quelqu'un ; lever la main sur.**
- *To sit on one's hand:* to not act, or to not applaud ▸ **se croiser les bras ou ne pas applaudir.**
- *To take in hand:* to deal with ▸ **composer avec.**
- *To take into one's hands:* to take control ▸ **prendre la direction ; prendre les choses en mains.**
- *To take the law into one's hands:* to take under one's own control ▸ **se faire justice soi-même.**
- *To tie one's hands:* to prevent one from acting ▸ **empêcher quelqu'un d'agir ; lui lier les mains.**
- *To tip one's hand:* to accidentally reveal one's intentions ▸ **révéler accidentellement ses intentions.**
- *To try one's hand:* to try something for the first time ▸ **essayer quelque chose pour la première fois.**
- *To turn one's hand to:* to attract, or to become vain ▸ **attirer ; devenir prétentieux.**
- *To wash one's hands of:* to refuse responsibility for something ▸ **refuser la responsabilité de quelque chose ; s'en laver les mains.**
- *Upper hand:* in control or having an advantage ▸ **diriger ou avoir l'avantage.**
- *With one hand tied behind one's back:* very easily ▸ **très facilement.**
- *With one's bare hands:* without tools or weapons ▸ **sans outil ou sans arme ; à mains nues.**
- *With one's hand in the till:* stealing from one's boss ▸ **voler l'argent de son employeur.**

heart ▸ **cœur**

nouns aorta, artery, beat, beating, blood, centre, chest, circulation, core, courage, dear, emotion, feelings, flutter, generosity, heart attack, heart beat, heart failure, heartache, heartbreak, life, love, lung, murmur, muscle, nobility, organ, passion, pulse, pump, pumping, sensitivity, spirit, throb, transplant, valve, vein, weakness.

adjectives beating, big, bitter, bleeding, blocked, brave, broken, bursting, closed, compassionate, contracting, courageous, cruel, dedicated, delicate, devoted, disloyal, emotional, faint, faithful, feeling, fluttering, fragile, full, generous, giving, good, happy, hard, heart-shaped, heartbroken, heartless, hungry, keen, kind, joyful, joyous, jumping, leaping, light, lively, lonely, loving, loyal, noble, pained, painful, passionate, pumping, pure, racing, red, ruthless, sensitive, shuddering, sick, sinking, still, stopped, strong, swelling, tender, throbbing, torn, tortured, troubled, wandering, weak, weeping, withered, wounded, young.

verbs SUBJECT: a heart aches, beats, bleeds, breaks, bursts, chills, closes, contracts, feels, flutters, gives, leaps, loves, opens, pulses, pumps, races, sinks, shudders, sickens, starts, stops, swells, throbs, tightens, weeps. OTHERS: to break a heart, to calm a heart, to conquer a heart, to give a heart, to lift a heart, to listen to a heart, to move a heart, to stab a heart, to stir a heart, to strain a heart, to touch a heart, to transplant a heart.

expressions

- *Absence makes the heart grow fonder:* separation strengthens love ► **la séparation renforce l'amour.**
- *After one's own heart:* to one's liking ► **au goût de quelqu'un.**
- *At heart:* basically, or one's deepest feelings ► **au fond ou les sentiments les plus profonds.**
- *By heart:* memorized ► **mémorisé; par cœur.**
- *Change of heart:* changed feelings or opinions ► **changement de sentiment ou d'opinion.**
- *Cold hands, warm heart:* having feelings without necessarily showing them ► **éprouver des sentiments sans pour autant les montrer; mains froides, cœur chaud.**
- *Cross my heart and hope to die:* to promise or speak truthfully ► **promettre de dire la vérité; croix de bois, croix de fer (si je mens, je vais en enfer).**
- *From the bottom of one's heart:* sincerely ► **sincèrement; du fond du cœur.**
- *Heart and soul:* all of one's energies ► **avec toute son énergie; corps et âme.**
- *Heart of gold:* extremely kind and good

- ► **très bon ou bonne et généreux ou généreuse; cœur d'or.**
- *Heart of stone:* a cold and unfriendly personality ► **personne froide et peu sympathique; cœur de pierre.**
- *Heart of the matter:* the basic or most important aspect of an issue ► **l'essentiel ou l'aspect le plus important d'un sujet; le cœur de la question.**
- *Heart to heart:* sincerely ► **sincèrement; à cœur ouvert.**
- *In one's heart of hearts:* according to one's deepest feelings ► **selon les sentiments les plus profonds; du plus profond du cœur.**
- *Near (close) to one's heart:* loved by one ► **aimé.**
- *One's heart goes out to:* to have sympathy for someone ► **éprouver de la sympathie pour quelqu'un.**
- *One's heart misses (skips) a beat:* one is surprised, scared or excited ► **être surpris(e), effrayé(e) ou excité(e).**
- *One's heart sinks:* to be disappointed, or lose courage ► **être déçu(e), ou perdre courage.**
- *One's heart stands still:* one is surprised, scared or excited ► **être surpris(e), effrayé(e) ou excité(e).**
- *Sick at heart:* very sad or disappointed ► **être triste ou déçu(e); avoir le cœur gros.**
- *To break someone's heart:* to cause great emotional pain ► **causer un grand chagrin; briser le cœur de quelqu'un.**
- *To cry one's heart out:* to sob ► **pleurer à chaudes larmes.**
- *To do one's heart good:* to please or satisfy ► **plaire ou satisfaire.**
- *To eat one's heart out:* to feel a strong negative emotion such as grief or worry ► **ressentir une forte émotion négative telle que l'inquiétude ou le chagrin.**
- *To find it in one's heart:* to convince oneself to do something ► **se convaincre de faire quelque chose.**
- *To get to the heart of:* to determine the most important facts or meanings ►

déterminer les significations ou les faits les plus importants; aller au cœur de la question.

- *To give someone heart failure:* to frighten or surprise someone ▸ **surprendre ou faire peur à quelqu'un.**

- *To harden one's heart:* to feel no sympathy for ▸ **ne ressentir aucune sympathie.**

- *To have a heart:* to show pity for ▸ **faire preuve de compassion; avoir du cœur.**

- *To have no heart for:* to lack enthusiasm ▸ **manquer d'enthousiasme; ne pas avoir le cœur à.**

- *To have one's heart in it:* to be enthusiastically involved, or to be emotionally attached to ▸ **s'intéresser à quelque chose avec enthousiasme, ou y être attaché affectivement; prendre quelque chose à cœur.**

- *To have one's heart in one's mouth:* to be frightened or nervous ▸ **avoir peur ou être nerveux; avoir le cœur qui bat la chamade.**

- *To have one's heart in the right place:* to mean well ▸ **avoir de bonnes intentions; avoir bon cœur.**

- *To have one's heart set on:* to strongly want something ▸ **désirer fortement quelque chose; le vouloir de tout son cœur.**

- *To lose one's heart to:* to fall in love ▸ **tomber amoureux ou amoureuse.**

- *To not have the heart for:* to lack enthusiasm ▸ **manquer d'enthousiasme; ne pas avoir le cœur à.**

- *To not have the heart to:* to not feel like saying or doing something ▸ **ne pas avoir envie de faire ou de dire quelque chose; ne pas avoir le cœur de dire ou de faire quelque chose.**

- *To one's heart's content:* to one's full satisfaction ▸ **à son entière satisfaction.**

- *To open one's heart to:* to share one's feelings or thoughts ▸ **partager ses sentiments ou ses pensées; ouvrir son cœur.**

- *To pour out one's heart:* to tell someone one's deepest feelings or thoughts ▸ **révéler ses pensées ou ses senti-**ments les plus profonds; ouvrir son cœur.**

- *To put one's heart in it:* to be enthusiastically involved, or to be emotionally attached to ▸ **s'intéresser à quelque chose avec enthousiasme ou y être attaché ou attachée affectivement; prendre quelque chose à cœur.**

- *To set one's heart on:* to strongly want something ▸ **désirer fortement quelque chose; le vouloir de tout son cœur.**

- *To steal someone's heart:* to win someone's love ▸ **se mériter l'amour de quelqu'un.**

- *To steel one's heart against:* to suppress one's feelings for ▸ **refouler ses sentiments.**

- *To take heart:* to be brave and confident ▸ **être brave et confiant; avoir du cœur au ventre.**

- *To tear out a heart:* to show one's deepest feelings ▸ **révéler ses sentiments les plus profonds; ouvrir son cœur.**

- *To wear one's heart on one's sleeve:* to openly show one's feelings ▸ **montrer ses sentiments; ouvrir son cœur.**

- *With all one's heart:* with deep feeling or enthusiasm ▸ **avec beaucoup d'enthousiasme ou de sentiment; de tout son cœur.**

- *With half a heart:* not fully enthusiastic ▸ **sans enthousiasme; à contrecœur.**

- *Young at heart:* acting young despite one's age ▸ **au comportement plus jeune que son âge; jeune de cœur.**

hip ▸ **hanche**

nouns balance, belt, bone, bump, curve, dance, joint, movement, protrusion, size, sway, thigh, torso, trunk, twist, waist, width, wriggle.

adjectives chubby, fat, flexible, large, moving, narrow, plump, protruding, rigid, shaking, squirming, stocky, strong, swaying, turning, twisting, wide, wriggling.

verbs SUBJECT: a hip bumps, curves, grinds, moves, protrudes, shakes, squirms, sways, wriggles. OTHERS: to fracture a hip, to injure a hip, to wound a hip.

expressions..

• *To shoot from the hip:* to act or speak without thinking ► **agir ou parler sans réfléchir.**

knee ► **genou (-oux)**

nouns bend, bone, calf, joint, knee guard, kneecap, kneel, kneeling, leg, ligament, sprain, tendon, thigh.

adjectives bent, big, chubby, crooked, extended, flexed, flexible, hairy, knock, large, limber, narrow, pointed, rigid, round, scraped, shaky, skinny, sprained, stiff, strong, thin, unsteady, wobbly, wrenched.

verbs SUBJECT: a knee bends, extends, flexes, knocks, shakes, wobbles, wrenches. OTHERS: to extend a knee, to flex a knee, to sprain a knee, to wrench a knee.

expressions..

• *Knee-jerk reaction:* an uncontrollable and strong reaction ► **un réflexe, une réaction forte et incontrôlable.**
• *On bended knee:* humbly ► **humblement.**
• *To be knee-high to a grasshopper:* to be very young or small ► **être très jeune ou de très petite taille.**
• *To bring to one's knees:* to make one submit ► **forcer quelqu'un à se soumettre.**

leg ► **jambe**

nouns ankle, bone, calf, dance, knee, joint, length, limb, movement, muscle, pants, runner, shin, shorts, step, stump, tendon, thigh, walker, walking.

adjectives agile, amputated, artificial, bow, broken, built, chubby, covered, crooked, crossed, dancing, dangling, ele-

gant, extended, fat, firm, flexed, flexible, hairy, kicking, lame, limber, long, nice, one-legged, muscular, paralysed, plump, short, skinny, slender, slim, steady, stocky, straight, strong, swimming, swollen, thick, thin, tired, twisted, unsteady, wobbly.

verbs SUBJECT: a leg extends, flexes, kicks, shakes, straightens, tires, twists. OTHERS: to amputate a leg, to bend a leg, to break a leg, to cross a leg, to fracture a leg, to injure a leg, to shake a leg, to wound a leg.

expressions..

• *A leg up:* an advantage, or the act of helping someone ► **un avantage; un coup de pouce.**
• *Arm and a leg:* a lot of money ► **beaucoup d'argent; (coûter) les yeux de la tête.**
• *On one's last legs:* to be exhausted ► **être épuisé ou épuisée; ne plus tenir debout.**
• *To break a leg:* to injure a leg, or an exclamation of encouragement to a performer for good luck ► **se blesser une jambe ou expression utilisée pour souhaiter bonne chance à un artiste de la scène.**
• *To pull someone's leg:* to tease or play a joke on ► **taquiner quelqu'un ou le faire marcher.**
• *To shake a leg:* to hurry, or to dance ► **se dépêcher ou danser.**
• *To stretch one's legs:* to take a walk after a long time of sitting ► **faire une promenade après avoir passé beaucoup de temps assis; se dégourdir les jambes.**
• *With one's tail between one's legs:* ashamed ► **honteux; la queue entre les jambes.**
• *Without a leg to stand on:* having no chance of success ► **sans aucune chance de succès.**

nail ► **ongle**

nouns biting, clipper, clippings, file, finger, foot, gloss, hand, hygiene, polish, scratch, shape, skin, tip, toe, varnish.

adjectives bitten, broken, chipped, clean, curved, cut, dirty, filed, jagged, long, polished, rounded, short, shiny, smooth, trimmed, varnished.

verbs SUBJECT: a nail breaks, scratches. OTHERS: to bite a nail, to break a nail, to chip a nail, to cut a nail, to do one's nails, to file a nail, to polish a nail, to trim a nail, to varnish a nail.

expressions

- *To bite one's nails:* to show signs of anxiety ► **montrer des signes d'angoisse ; se ronger les sangs.**

- *To fight tooth and nail:* to try hard, or to fight vigorously ► **faire de grands efforts ou se battre avec énergie.**

neck ► **cou (cous)**

nouns Adam's apple, artery, bone, chain, choke, collar, fold, gland, head, jewellery, larynx, ligament, neckline, necklace, scarf, scruff, size, skin, strangling, throat, tie, vein, vertebra, width

adjectives attractive, bare, beautiful, bent, charming, chubby, clean, covered, craned, dirty, fat, flexible, fragile, graceful, long, open-neck, perfumed, plump, scented, short, skinny, slim, square, stiff, stocky, straight, stretched, strong, thick, thin, twisted, unwashed, washed, weak, wide.

verbs SUBJECT: a neck bends, cranes, leans, stiffens, stretches, tilts, turns, twists. OTHERS: to choke a neck, to crane a neck, to hang a neck, to strangle a neck, to twist a neck.

expressions

- *Albatross around one's neck:* a burden of guilt that prevents success ► **sentiment de culpabilité qui constitue une entrave au succès.**

- *Dead from the neck up:* very stupid ► **très stupide.**

- *Neck and neck:* in very close competition ► **presque à égalité ; nez à nez.**

- *Pain in the neck:* a nuisance ► **ennui ou casse-pieds.**

- *To break one's neck:* to work very hard ► **travailler très fort.**

- *To breathe down one's neck:* to follow or watch someone very closely ► **suivre ou surveiller quelqu'un de très près.**

- *To risk one's neck:* to take dangerous risks ► **prendre de grands risques ; risquer sa peau.**

- *To save someone's neck:* to rescue someone from harm or danger ► **sortir quelqu'un d'une situation dangereuse ; lui sauver la peau.**

- *To stick one's neck out:* to take a risk ► **prendre un risque.**

- *Up to one's neck:* deeply involved in ► **très impliqué dans.**

organ ► **organe**

nouns abdomen, appendix, bladder, blood, body, body function, brain, cell, chest, digestive organ, donor, ear, eye, gall bladder, gland, heart, intestine, kidney, liver, lung, small intestine, large intestine, pancreas, reproductive organ, spleen, surgeon, stomach, tissue, transplantation.

adjectives bleeding, damaged, functioning, healthy, unhealthy.

verbs SUBJECT: an organ bleeds, does, functions. OTHERS: to damage an organ, to donate an organ, to operate on an organ, to repair an organ, to transplant an organ.

shoulder ► **épaule**

nouns arm, armpit, back, form, cartilage, curve, joint, junction, movement, muscle, paralysis, shape, shoulder pad, shrug, sling, strap, width.

adjectives achy, bare, bearing, beautiful, broad, broken, chubby, curved, dropped, fractured, hurt, injured, large, knotted, muscular, plump, raised, rounded, shrugging, skinny, slack, slender, square, stocky, strong, sunken, wide, wounded.

verbs SUBJECT: a shoulder aches, bears, drops, hurts, moves, shrugs, sinks. OTHERS: to fracture a shoulder, to injure a shoulder, to wound a shoulder.

expressions

- *Chip on one's shoulder:* to have a bad attitude or resentment ► **avoir une mauvaise attitude ou faire preuve de mauvaise foi.**
- *Cold shoulder:* to deliberately ignore someone ► **ignorer quelqu'un de façon délibérée.**
- *Head and shoulders above:* far superior to ► **bien supérieur à.**
- *On one's shoulders:* one's responsibility ► **sa responsabilité; (responsabilité qui) repose sur les épaules de quelqu'un.**
- *Shoulder to shoulder:* together or nearby ► **ensemble ou côte à côte.**
- *Straight from the shoulder:* in a direct manner ► **de manière directe.**
- *To cry on someone's shoulder:* to tell someone one's problems ► **raconter ses problèmes à quelqu'un; s'épancher.**
- *To have broad shoulders:* to take on a big responsibility ► **accepter de grandes responsabilités; avoir le dos large.**
- *To have a good head on one's shoulders:* to be smart ► **être intelligent; avoir la tête sur les épaules.**
- *To put one's shoulders to the wheel:* to work hard or make a great effort ► **travailler fort ou faire un grand effort.**
- *To rub shoulder's with:* to socialize with ► **côtoyer.**
- *To shrug one's shoulders:* to show indifference ► **se montrer indifférent; hausser les épaules.**

- *To square one's shoulders:* prepare to face confrontation ► **se préparer à une confrontation.**
- *Weight of the world on one's shoulders:* to carry a heavy burden ► **porter un lourd fardeau; porter le poids d'une responsabilité sur ses épaules.**

skeleton ► **squelette**

nouns anatomy, body, bone, broken, cartilage, fractured, frame, framework, limb, muscle, sprain.

adjectives big, bony, fine-boned, fragile, small, strong, thin, weak,

verbs SUBJECT: a skeleton holds together, moves, protects.

expressions

- *Skeleton in the closet:* a shameful secret ► **secret honteux.**

skin ► **peau (peaux)**

nouns blemish, blister, burn, colour, complexion, corn, cream, crust, cut, dryness, feeling, flake, flesh, fold, freckle, graze, hair, hygiene, itch, lotion, makeup, mark, nail, odour, powder, rash, roughness, scar, scratch, scuff, sensitivity, sickness, skincare, smell, softness, sore, stretch mark, sweat, sunburn, tan, texture, tickle, touch, wart, wound, wrinkle.

adjectives bare, beautiful, black, blemished, blistered, branded, breathing, brown, burned, chapped, clean, clear, coarse, cracked, crusty, dark, dead, delicate, dry, dull, faded, fair, fine, flaked, flaky, folded, folding, freckled, fresh, glowing, grazed, hairy, hanging, hard, healed, healthy, itchy, loose, made up, marked, oily, naked, pale, peeling, powdered, puffy, sunburnt, red, reddened, rosy, rough, scarred, scented, scratchy, scuffed, sensitive, shaved, shiny, shivering, shrivelled, silky, soft, smooth, stained, sticky, stretched, sunburned, sunburnt, sweaty, swollen, tanned, tender, thick, tickling, tight, tough, transparent, trembling, ugly, washed, waxy, weak, white, wrinkled, yellow.

verbs SUBJECT: skin blisters, breaths, burns, chaps, clears, darkens, dries, fades, feels, flakes, folds, glows, hangs, heals, itches, pales, peels, reddens, roughens, scars, shivers, shrivels, softens, smoothens, stretches, sweats, swells, tans, tickles, tightens, toughens, trembles, whitens, wrinkles, yellows. OTHERS: to brand skin, to clean skin, to cut skin, to make skin crawl, to mark skin, to scent skin, to scrape skin, to scratch skin, to tear skin, to wash skin.

expressions

- *Beauty is only skin deep:* external appearances do not reveal what is inside someone ▸ **l'apparence d'une personne ne dit rien de sa beauté intérieure.**
- *By the skin of one's teeth:* barely or narrowly ▸ **de justesse.**
- *More than one way to skin a cat:* more than one way of doing things ▸ **il existe plus d'une façon de faire les choses.**
- *No skin off one's nose:* not harmful or annoying to anyone ▸ **qui ne dérange ou ne nuit à personne.**
- *Skin and bones:* extremely thin ▸ **très maigre; n'avoir que la peau et les os.**
- *Soaked to the skin:* very wet ▸ **très mouillé; trempé jusqu'à l'os.**
- *Thick skin:* resistant to criticism or insult ▸ **résiste bien aux critiques ou aux insultes.**
- *To get under someone's skin:* to irritate someone, or to affect someone's deep feelings ▸ **irriter une personne ou toucher ses sentiments profonds.**
- *To jump out of one's skin:* to be extremely startled or scared ▸ **être très effrayé ou surpris; être à fleur de peau.**
- *To make one's skin crawl:* to make one shudder in disgust or fear ▸ **faire frissonner de dégoût ou de peur; donner la chair de poule.**

- *To save one's skin:* to rescue from danger or harm ▸ **se sortir du danger; sauver sa peau.**
- *To skin alive:* to punish severely ▸ **punir sévèrement.**

stomach ▸ **estomac**

nouns abdomen, appetite, belly, belly button, diet, digestion, food, hunger, intestine, organ, pain, pot, punch, stomach-ache, torso, trunk, waist.

adjectives big, bottomless, chubby, cramped, digesting, empty, enormous, fat, flat, full, hard, hungry, muscular, painful, plump, protruding, round, rounded, sleek, small, starving, stocky, swollen, tender, tight.

verbs SUBJECT: a stomach cramps, digests, protrudes, starves, swells, tightens. OTHERS: to fill a stomach, to lie on a stomach, to punch a stomach.

expressions

- *Butterflies in one's stomach:* to feel nervous ▸ **avoir le trac; être nerveux.**
- *Can't stomach the sight of:* to dislike extremely ▸ **détester, ne pas pouvoir blairer quelqu'un ou quelque chose.**
- *Sick to one's stomach:* to become sick or throw up ▸ **avoir mal au cœur ou vomir.**
- *To have eyes bigger than one's stomach:* to want more than one can handle ▸ **avoir des désirs plus grands que ses capacités; avoir les yeux plus grands que le ventre.**
- *To have no stomach for:* to dislike ▸ **détester.**
- *To turn one's stomach:* to disgust one ▸ **dégoûter, écœurer.**

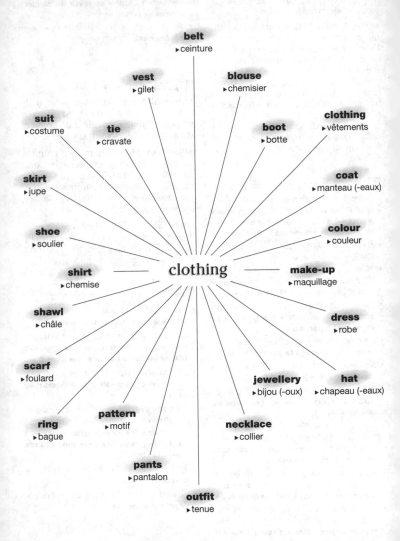

belt
▸ceinture

vest
▸gilet

blouse
▸chemisier

suit
▸costume

tie
▸cravate

boot
▸botte

clothing
▸vêtements

skirt
▸jupe

coat
▸manteau (-eaux)

shoe
▸soulier

colour
▸couleur

clothing

shirt
▸chemise

make-up
▸maquillage

shawl
▸châle

dress
▸robe

scarf
▸foulard

jewellery
▸bijou (-oux)

hat
▸chapeau (-eaux)

ring
▸bague

pattern
▸motif

necklace
▸collier

pants
▸pantalon

outfit
▸tenue

belt ▶ **ceinture**

nouns belt loop, buckle, clasp, cloth, clothing, eye, fabric, fastener, harness, hole, hook, material, leather, loop, looseness, pants, sash, shoulder belt, shorts, size, skirt, strap, tightness, waistband, wearer.

adjectives adorned, buckled, clasped, cloth, coloured, colourful, fabric, fastened, hooked, leather, looped, loose, narrow, plain, stiff, tight, unfastened, wide, worn, woven.

verbs SUBJECT: a belt fastens, holds up, hooks, loops, ties, wears down. OTHERS: to clasp a belt, to put on a belt, to fasten a belt, to loosen a belt, to take off a belt, to tie a belt, to unclasp a belt, to unfasten a belt, to wear a belt.

expressions

- *To hit below the belt:* to break the rules and play unfairly ▶ **tricher; frapper sous la ceinture.**
- *To tighten one's belt:* to spend less and save money ▶ **économiser; se serrer la ceinture.**
- *Under one's belt:* experienced or achieved ▶ **expérimenté(e) ou accompli(e); avoir une nouvelle corde à son arc.**

blouse ▶ **chemisier**

nouns button, buttonhole, buttoning, closet, cloth, clothing, collar, cuff, fabric, fastener, fit, flare, fringe, girl, hanger, ironing, material, neck, neckline, pin, pocket, pressing, ruffle, shirt, size, sleeve, smock, snag, stitch, tail, wardrobe, wearer, woman, wrist, zipper.

adjectives adorned, buttoned, clean, creased, dirty, elegant, embroidered, fastened, fitted, flared, flattering, fringed, gathered, hanging, hung, ironed, large, light, long, long-sleeved, loose, low-cut, open, pressed, puffy, ruffled, see-through, short, short-sleeved, silk, silky, sleeveless, small, snagged, soiled, spotted, stained, stripped, threadbare, tight, torn, tucked, unbuttoned, used, zippered, washed, worn, worn out, wrinkled.

verbs SUBJECT: a blouse bunches, creases, flares, fringes, gathers, wrinkles. OTHERS: to adjust a blouse, to alter a blouse, to button a blouse, to clasp a blouse, to change a blouse, to design a blouse, to fold a blouse, to hang a blouse, to iron a blouse, to make a blouse, to mend a blouse, to press a blouse, to pull on a blouse, to put on a blouse, to sew a blouse, to swim in a blouse, to tear a blouse, to take off a blouse, to tuck in a blouse, to unbutton a blouse, to wash a blouse, to wear a blouse, to wear out a blouse.

boot ▶ **botte**

nouns ankle, ankle boot, bootlace, brush, buckle, clothing, foot, heel, hole, lace, lining, lower leg, leather, pair, polish, rubber, scuff, shoe, shoehorn, shoelace, shoemaker, size, sole, spur, strap, tie, toe, tongue, underfoot, wax, wearer.

adjectives army, brushed, buckled, dirty, dry, fastened, heavy, high, laced, leather, lined, long, low, new, old, polished, resoled, rubber, scuffed, strong, tied, tough, unlaced, used, waxed, wet, worn, worn out.

verbs SUBJECT: a boot wears out. OTHERS: to fasten a boot, to lace a boot, to line a boot, to polish a boot, to pull on a boot, to put on a boot, to resole a boot, to scuff a boot, to take off a boot, to unlace a boot, to wear a boot, to wear out a boot.

expressions

- *To boot:* in addition ▶ **de plus.**
- *To boot out:* to kick out ▶ **expulser.**
- *To die with one's boots on:* to work to the end, or to die working ▶ **travailler jusqu'à la fin de ses jours ou mourir au travail.**
- *To get the boot (axe):* to be fired from a job ▶ **être congédié.**

- *To lick someone's boots:* to serve someone to an extreme degree ► **adopter une attitude servile; lécher les bottes de quelqu'un.**

- *To pull oneself up by the bootstraps:* to succeed on one's own ► **réussir sans l'aide de personne.**

- *To quake (shake) in one's boots:* to tremble with fear ► **trembler de peur.**

- *Too big for one's boots (breeches):* vain ► **prétentieux.**

- *You can bet your boots:* you can be sure ► **vous pouvez en être certain.**

clothing ► vêtements

nouns accessory, adjustment, alterations, apparel, apron, armour, bathrobe, bathing suit, belt loop, bonnet, button, buttonhole, buttoning, cap, cape, clasp, cloth, cotton, covering, cuff, cut, belt, blouse, boot, casual wear, cloak, closet, clothes, coat, collar, colour, costume, crown, drawer, dress, dresser, dressing, evening wear, fabric, fashion, fashion designer, fashion show, fitting, flare, fold, formal wear, fringe, fur, garment, glove, gown, habit, hanger, loop, hat, helmet, hem, hole, hood, hose, hosiery, innerwear, jacket, jumper, kerchief, kilt, kimono, knit, lace, leather, leisure wear, leotard, linen, look, mantle, material, mitten, model, muffler, needle, overcoat, outfit, outerwear, overalls, pants, parka, pattern, pin, pocket, poncho, pyjamas, rags, raincoat, ribbon, robe, ruffle, sash, scarf, sewer, sewing machine, shawl, shirt, shelf, shoe, shorts, shoulder pad, size, skin, skirt, slacks, slippers, smock, snag, sock, stitch, style, suit, suspenders, sweater, swimsuit, tailor, tartan, tear, textile, thimble, tie, tights, thread, tongue, train, trousers, trunks, tunic, tuxedo, underclothes, undress, uniform, veil, vest, wearer, weave, windbreaker, wool, wrinkle.

adjectives adjusted, altered, baby, beautiful, big, bordered, buttoned, clashing, clean, clinging, coloured, colourful, comfortable, cotton, creased, cut-off, dirty, dyed, elegant, expensive, fashionable, fastened, fitted, fitting, flared, flashy, flattering, folded, formal, fringed, furred, gathered, graceful, hanging, hemmed, hung, inside-out, ironed, knit, laced, lacy, large, lined, linen, long-sleeved, loosely-fitting, low-cut clothing, mended, military, modern, new, old, out-of-fashion, oversized, patterned, plain, presentable, pressed, puffy, pulled, quilted, ragged, rolled-up, ruffled, ruined, second-hand, see-through, sewn, short-sleeved, shrunken, silky, simple, skin-tight, small, soiled, sleeved, sleeveless, small, spotted, stained, stretched, striped, stylish, suiting, tailored, tattered, thick, thin, threadbare, tight, torn, unbuttoned, uncomfortable, used, warm, washed, wool, work, worn, woven, wrinkled.

verbs SUBJECT: clothing bunches, clashes, cling, covers, creases, dresses, fits, flares, flatters, gathers, hides, protects, tears, warms, wears out, wraps, wrinkles. OTHERS: to adjust clothing, to button clothing, to change clothing, to clean clothing, to design clothing, to dress in clothing, to dye clothing, to fold clothing, to hang clothing, to hem clothing, to iron clothing, to knit clothing, to lace clothing, to lengthen clothing, to line clothing, to mend clothing, to pack clothing, to pin clothing, to press clothing, to pull on clothing, to put on clothing, to quilt clothing, to remove clothing, to roll up clothing, to ruin clothing, to sew clothing, to shrink clothing, to shorten clothing, to stretch clothing, to tailor clothing, to take off clothing, to tear clothing, to trim clothing, to try on clothing, to unbutton clothing, to undo clothing, to unlace clothing, to wash clothing, to wear clothing, to wear out clothing, to weave clothing.

expressions

- *Wolf in sheep's clothing:* an enemy appearing to be a friend ► **ennemi qui se fait passer pour un ami.**

coat ▸ manteau (-eaux)

nouns belt, belt loop, button, button-hole, buttoning, cape, cloth, clothing, collar, fabric, flare, fringe, fur, hanger, hem, hood, jacket, length, lining, material, overcoat, parka, pocket, poncho, raincoat, shoulder pad, sleeve, smoking, snag, stitch, train, wearer, windbreaker, zipper.

adjectives big, buttoned, clean, dirty, elegant, fancy, fashionable, fastened, fitted, fitting, flared, fringed, full-length, fur, hanging, hung, heavy, hooded, large, lined, loose, long, mended, old, overlapping, light, new, open, plaid, plain, puffy, quilted, ragged, sheepskin, short, small, snagged, soiled, stained, tailored, threadbare, tight, torn, unbuttoned, ugly, used, warm, waterproof, wool, worn, worn out.

verbs SUBJECT: a coat covers, protects, tears, wears out. OTHERS: to button a coat, to clean a coat, to hang a coat, to line a coat, to put on a coat, to sew a coat, to snag a coat, to take off a coat, to tear a coat, to unbutton a coat, to wash a coat, to wear a coat.

expressions

• *On someone's coattails.* to benefit from another's popularity or merits ▸ **profiter de la popularité ou des mérites d'un autre.**

colour ▸ couleur

nouns albino, ash, beet-red, beige, berry, black, blonde, blot, blue, blush, brown, carbon, carrot-orange, charcoal, cherry, cinnamon, clay, coal, copper, cream, crimson, dab, dismal, drab, dye, ebony, eggshell, gold, green, grey, hazel, hue, ink, ivory, ivy-green, khaki, lavender, lemon, lilac, lily-white, mahogany, maroon, ochre, olive-green, orange, peach, pearl, pigment, pink, purple, red, rose, ruby-red, rust, salmon, sapphire, shade, silver, sky-blue, speck, spot, stain, tan, tint, violet, white, yellow.

adjectives artificial, beige, black, bleached, bleeding, blemished, blue, bold, bright, brown, burnt, clear, cold, colourful, dark, deep, defined, diluted, dirty, dull, faded, fiery, flaming, flat, fresh, glowing, grey, happy, heavy, hot, light, lively, loud, main, matching, mixed, murky, natural, neutral, orange, pale, pastel, pink, plain, primary, pure, purple, red, rose, rich, runny, rusty, sad, shaded, shadowy, shiny, shocking, smoky, smudged, soft, sombre, splashy, stained, streaked, strong, subtle, tinted, undefined, uniform, vibrant, violet, warm, washed, waxy, weak, white, yellow.

verbs SUBJECT: a colour accents, adorns, beautifies, bleaches, bleeds, brightens, brings out, clears, covers, dampens, darkens, deepens, defines, dirties, dulls, dyes, fades, flames, flattens, freshens, glows, highlights, hints, lightens, livens up, pales, runs, shines, shocks, smudges, softens, sparkles, splashes, spruces up, stains, streaks, tints, tones, tones down, warms. OTHERS: to apply a colour, to choose a colour, to combine a colour with, to darken a colour, to dilute a colour, to layer a colour, to lighten a colour, to like a colour, to match a colour, to mix a colour, to paint a colour, to pick a colour, to smear a colour, to spread a colour.

expressions

• *Horse of a different (another) colour:* something else entirely ▸ **une toute autre chose; une toute autre histoire.**

• *To come through with flying colours:* to win or succeed ▸ **gagner ou réussir.**

• *To lend colour to:* to expand on to give the appearance of truth ▸ **ajouter des détails pour faire plus vrai.**

• *To look (see) through rose-coloured glasses:* to look at things optimistically ▸ **voir les choses avec optimisme; voir la vie en rose.**

• *To pass with flying colours:* to win or succeed ▸ **gagner ou réussir.**

- *To see the colour of someone's money:* to prove one can pay ► **faire la preuve qu'on peut payer.**
- *(Under) false colours:* pretence or hypocrisy ► **sous un faux prétexte ; hypocritement.**

dress ► robe

nouns belt, belt loop, button, buttonhole, buttoning, clasp, cloth, clothing, crease, cut, fabric, flare, fringe, hanger, hanger loop, hem, gown, kimono, lining, material, model, pattern, pocket, ruffle, shoulder pad, size, sleeve, smock, snag, stitch, train, tunic, wearer, wrinkle.

adjectives adjusted, adorned, altered, belted, bordered, bunched, buttoned, casual, clasped, clinging, colourful, creased, elegant, embroidered, flared, folded, formal, fringed, gathered, hanging, heavy, hemmed, hung, large, lengthened, light, lined, long, long-sleeved, loose, neckline, new, night, old, quilted, plaid, puffy, ragged, ruffled, see-through, sewn, short, shortened, short-sleeved, skin-tight, sleeveless, slip-on, small, snagged, striped, threadbare, tight, torn, unbuttoned, unclasped, used, wool, worn, worn out, wrinkled.

verbs SUBJECT: a dress bunches, creases, flares, fringes, gathers, wrinkles. OTHERS: to adjust a dress, to alter a dress, to button a dress, to clasp a dress, to change a dress, to design a dress, to fold a dress, to hang a dress, to hem a dress, to iron a dress, to knit a dress, to lengthen a dress, to make a dress, to mend a dress, to press a dress, to pull on a dress, to put on a dress, to sew a dress, to shorten a dress, to swim in a dress, to tear a dress, to take off a dress, to unbutton a dress, to wash a dress, to wear a dress, to wear out a dress.

expressions

- *Dress up:* invent ► **inventer.**
- *Dressed to kill:* to be wearing attractive clothes ► **bien habillé ou habillée.**

hat ► chapeau (-eaux)

nouns beret, bonnet, braid, brim, cap, cloth, clothing, edge, fabric, feather, hair, hairdo, hatter, hat maker, hat shop, helmet, hood, hook, leather, material, muffler, peg, rack, ribbon, rim, sunbonnet, tuque, turban, visor, wearer.

adjectives adorned, bowler, brimmed, broad, broad-brimmed, cocked, cowboy, dented, elegant, felt, flattened, hard, heavy, large, leather, light, new, old, pointed, ragged, sailor, small, soft, stiff, straw, stylish, sun, sunken, top, used, wool, worn.

verbs SUBJECT: a hat covers, protects, warms. OTHERS: to crush a hat, to flatten a hat, to take off a hat, to tip a hat, to wear a hat, to wear out a hat.

expressions

- *At the drop of a hat:* immediately ► **instantanément.**
- *Brass hat:* an official of high rank ► **fonctionnaire haut placé.**
- *Hang on to (hold) your hat:* warning of a big surprise ► **avertissement d'une grande surprise.**
- *Hard hat:* a conservative working-class person ► **personne conservatrice de la classe ouvrière.**
- *Hat (cap) in hand:* humbly ► **humblement.**
- *Hat trick:* a clever move or trick ► **mouvement ou tour ingénieux.**
- *Hats off to:* congratulations ► **félicitations ; chapeau bas.**
- *To eat one's hat:* to express that one does not believe something will happen or is true ► **indiquer qu'on ne croit pas que quelque chose arrivera ou est vrai.**
- *To hang up one's hat:* to settle down somewhere ► **s'installer quelque part.**
- *To keep under one's hat:* to keep a secret ► **garder un secret.**
- *To knock into a cocked hat:* to reveal something as false or useless ► **démontrer que quelque chose est faux ou inutile.**

- *To pass the hat:* to ask or beg for money ▸ **faire la quête ; demander de l'argent.**
- *To pull out of a hat:* to produce as if by magic ▸ **faire apparaître comme par magie.**
- *To take off one's hat to:* to show admiration ▸ **témoigner son admiration ; tirer son chapeau.**
- *To talk through one's hat:* to talk about something one knows little about ▸ **parler d'un sujet qu'on ne connaît pas vraiment ; parler à travers son chapeau.**
- *To throw (toss) one's hat in the ring:* to enter a contest ▸ **être en lice ; participer à un concours.**
- *To wear another (different) hat:* to take on another role ▸ **adopter un rôle différent.**
- *To wear more than one hat:* to take on more than one role ▸ **jouer plusieurs rôles.**
- *To wear two hats:* to take on two roles ▸ **jouer deux rôles.**

jewellery ▸ bijou (-oux)

nouns accessory, adornment, alloy, anklet, art, bead, bracelet, brilliance, broach, cameo, chain, chain bracelet, chain necklace, charm, charm bracelet, choker, clasp, collar, copper, coral, cross, crown, diamond, dress up, ear, earring, emerald, fake, fastening, finger, gem, glass, gold, goldsmith, hand, imitation, insurance, jade, jewel, jeweller, jewellery box, jewellery store, junk, karat, leg, masterpiece, medal, medallion, mother-of-pearl, neck, necklace, ornament, pearl, pendant, pin, pirate, ring, ruby, safe, sapphire, shiny, silver, snap, sparkle, stealing, stone, topaz, watch, wealth, wearer, will, wrist.

adjectives antique, beautiful, brilliant, costume, delicate, discreet, dull, engraved, expensive, fake, fine, flashy, gold, gold-plated, hanging, imitation, junk, loud, out-of-fashion, plated, polished, precious, real, shiny, silver, silver-plated,

splashy, sparkling, stolen, subtle, tarnished, valuable, worked.

verbs SUBJECT: jewellery accessorizes, adorns, beautifies, flashes, hangs, shines, sparkles, tarnishes. OTHERS: to cover in jewellery, to insure jewellery, to leave jewellery to, to make jewellery, to plate jewellery, to polish jewellery, to steal jewellery, to wear jewellery.

make-up ▸ maquillage

nouns adornment, appearance, base, beauty, beauty parlour, beauty products, beauty salon, beauty shop, beauty-care products, blush, cold cream, complexion, cream, dye, eye makeup, eye pencil, eye shadow, eyeliner, face, face cream, face makeup, foundation, gloss, hair, hairdresser, hand, hand cream, hand lotion, liner, lip gloss, lip rouge, lipstick, look, lotion, makeup, mascara, mask, mud-pack, nail, nail polish, paint, pancake makeup, powder, puff, rouge, skin.

adjectives beautifying, cake, cream, glossy, powder.

verbs SUBJECT: cosmetics beautify, bring out, enhance, highlight. OTHERS: to apply cosmetics, to cake on cosmetics, to put on cosmetics, to remove cosmetics, to take off cosmetics, to wash off cosmetics, to wear cosmetics.

necklace ▸ collier

nouns adornment, bead, chain, charm, choker, circle, clasp, collar, cross, fastener, gem, gift, gold, jewel, jeweller, jewellery, medallion, metal, neck, ornament, safe, shine, silver, sparkle, stone, thread, wearer.

adjectives beaded, beautiful, brilliant, clasped, delicate, discreet, dull, engraved, expensive, fake, fastened, fine, flashy, gold, gold-plated, hanging, imitation, jewelled, long, loud, original, out-of-fashion, plated, polished, precious, real, shiny, short, silver, silver-plated, splashy, sparkling, stolen, subtle, tarnished, thin, valuable, worked.

verbs SUBJECT: a necklace accessorizes, adorns, beautifies, flashes, hangs, shines, sparkles, tarnishes. OTHERS: to clasp a necklace, to fasten a necklace, to polish a necklace, to steal a necklace, to wear a necklace.

outfit ▶ tenue

nouns accessory, activity, belt, blouse, boot, button, buttonhole, buttoning, coat, cloth, clothing, dress, fabric, hat, jewellery, material, pants, shoe, skirt, suit, tie, vest, wearer, work.

adjectives colour, complete, creased, matching, mended, pattern, wrinkled.

verbs SUBJECT: an outfit creases, matches, wrinkles. OTHERS: to iron an outfit, to mend an outfit, to press an outfit, to put together an outfit, to wear an outfit.

pants ▶ pantalon

nouns button, buttonhole, buttoning, belt, belt loop, cloth, clothing, crease, crotch, elastic, fabric, foot-strap, hem, jeans, leg, lining, material, overalls, pocket, shorts, slacks, suit, suspenders, trousers, wearer, wrinkle, zipper.

adjectives adjusted, altered, Bermuda, buttoned, clasped, clinging, creased, dirty, flared, folded, fringed, hanging, heavy, hemmed, hung, inside-out, large, light, lined, long, loose, low-cut, mended, new, old, ragged, sewn, short, skin-tight, small, snagged, soiled, split, stained, stiff, stripped, tapered, threadbare, tight, torn, unbuttoned, unclasped, unwashed, used, washed, work, worn, worn out, wrinkled.

verbs SUBJECT: pants bunch, crease, flare, fringe, gather, wrinkle. OTHERS: to button pants, to clasp pants, to hem pants, to iron pants, to line pants, to lower pants, to mend pants, to press pants, to pull up pants, to put on pants, to slip into pants, to snag pants, to soil pants, to stain pants, to tear pants, to unbutton pants, to unclasp pants, to wear pants, to wear out pants, to wash pants.

expressions

- *By the seat of the pants:* using feeling rather than experience ▶ **par instinct plutôt que par expérience.**
- *Caught with one's pants down:* surprised or embarrassed ▶ **surpris(e) ou gêné(e).**
- *Kick in the pants (teeth):* something enjoyable, or something humiliating ▶ **situation agréable ou humiliante.**
- *The pants off:* a phrase that intensifies the meaning of the verb used ▶ **expression servant à intensifier la signification du verbe qu'elle accompagne.**
- *To beat the pants off:* to win by a large margin ▶ **gagner avec une avance confortable.**
- *To get the lead out of one's pants (feet):* to hurry up ▶ **se dépêcher.**
- *To have ants in one's pants:* to be keen, uneasy or impatient ▶ **être anxieux ou anxieuse, mal à l'aise ou impatient(e); avoir des fourmis dans les jambes.**
- *To talk someone's pants (arm) off:* talk to the point of exhausting the listener ▶ **épuiser son interlocuteur ou son interlocutrice à force de parler.**
- *To wear the pants:* have control in a household ▶ **mener le ménage; porter la culotte.**

pattern ▶ motif

nouns adornment, arrangement, checkers, checkerboard, colour, design, image, line, model, ornament, plaid, print, repetition, spot, stripe, tweed.

adjectives adorned, decorative, drawn, floral, imaged, lined, ornamental, plaid, printed, repeated, repeating, spotted, striped, textured.

verbs SUBJECT: a pattern clashes, matches, jumps out, stands out. OTHERS: to design a pattern, to choose a pattern, to follow a pattern, to match a pattern, to select a pattern.

ring ▸ bague

nouns adornment, circle, diamond, engagement, finger, gem, gift, gold, hand, jewel, jeweller, jewellery, love, marriage, metal, ornament, safe, setting, shine, silver, sparkle, stone, wearer.

adjectives beautiful, brilliant, delicate, diamond, discreet, dull, engagement, engraved, expensive, fake, fastened, fine, flashy, gold, gold-plated, graduation, imitation, jewelled, loud, out-of-fashion, plated, polished, precious, real, shiny, silver, silver-plated, splashy, sparkling, stolen, subtle, tarnished, tight, valuable, wedding, worked.

verbs SUBJECT: a ring accessorizes, adorns, beautifies, flashes, shines, sparkles, tarnishes. OTHERS: to lose a ring, to polish a ring, to steal a ring, to wear a ring.

expressions

• *Brass ring:* a prize or reward ▸ **prix ou récompense.**

scarf ▸ foulard

nouns band, cloth, clothing, comforter, fabric, fringe, head, head-scarf, kerchief, knit, lining, material, muffler, neck, shawl, shoulder, silk, stitch, wearer, weave, wool.

adjectives clasped, flung, fringed, knitted, knotted, large, lined, long, loose, plaid, pulled, short, silk, soft, striped, threadbare, tied, untied, warm, wool, worn, worn out, woven.

verbs SUBJECT: a scarf adorns, covers, hides, protects, warms, wraps. OTHERS: to fling a scarf, to knit a scarf, to tie a scarf, to untie a scarf, to wash a scarf, to wear a scarf.

shawl ▸ châle

nouns cloth, clothing, fabric, fringe, head, kerchief, knit, material, lining, neck, scarf, shoulder, silk, stitch, throw, wearer, weave, wool.

adjectives clasped, draping, flung, fringed, knitted, lined, pulled, rectangular, square, threadbare, tied, triangular, untied, worn, worn out, woven.

verbs SUBJECT: a shawl adorns, covers, hides, drapes, protects, warms, wraps. OTHERS: to fling a shawl, to knit a shawl, to tie a shawl, to untie a shawl, to wash a shawl, to wear a shawl.

shirt ▸ chemise

nouns blouse, button, buttonhole, buttoning, closet, cloth, clothing, collar, cuff, fastener, fit, flare, fringe, hanger, ironing, material, neck, neckline, pin, pocket, pressing, ruffle, shirt, shirttail, size, sleeve, smock, snag, starch, stitch, tail, wardrobe, wearer, wrist, zipper.

adjectives adorned, buttoned, clean, creased, dirty, dress, elegant, embroidered, fastened, fitted, flared, flattering, fringed, gathered, hanging, hung, ironed, large, light, long, long-sleeved, loose, low-cut, open, pressed, puffy, ruffled, see-through, short, short-sleeved, silk, silky, sleeveless, small, snagged, soiled, spotted, stained, starched, stripped, threadbare, tight, torn, tucked, unbuttoned, used, zippered, washed, work, worn, worn out, wrinkled.

verbs SUBJECT: a shirt bunches, creases, flares, fringes, gathers, wrinkles. OTHERS: to adjust a shirt, to alter a shirt, to button a shirt, to clasp a shirt, to change a shirt, to design a shirt, to fold a shirt, to hang a shirt, to iron a shirt, to make a shirt, to mend a shirt, to press a shirt, to pull on a shirt, to put on a shirt, to sew a shirt, to starch a shirt, to swim in a shirt, to tear a shirt, to take off a shirt, to unbutton a shirt, to wash a shirt, to wear a shirt, to wear out a shirt.

expressions

- *Hair shirt:* punishment of oneself ► **punition que l'on s'inflige.**
- *Stuffed shirt:* an overly formal or vain person ► **personne guindée ou prétentieuse.**
- *To give the shirt off one's back:* to give away everything one has ► **donner tout ce que l'on a.**
- *To keep one's shirt on:* to remain patient or calm ► **faire preuve de patience ou de calme.**
- *To lose one's shirt:* to lose one's money ► **se ruiner ; y laisser sa chemise.**

- *In someone else's shoes (place, stead):* in another person's position or situation ► **se mettre à la place d'autrui.**
- *The shoe is on the other foot:* a situation is reversed ► **situation où les rôles sont renversés.**
- *To fill someone's shoes:* to successfully take over for someone ► **succéder à quelqu'un.**
- *To step into someone's shoes:* to take someone's place ► **prendre la place de quelqu'un.**
- *To wait for the other shoe to drop:* to wait for something that seems inevitable ► **attendre la suite inévitable des événements.**

shoe ► **soulier**

nouns ankle, clothing, brush, buckle, foot, heel, hole, lace, leather, material, overshoe, pair, polish, scuff, shoehorn, shoelace, shoemaker, size, sole, spur, strap, tie, toe, tongue, underfoot, wax, wearer.

adjectives brushed, buckled, dirty, dry, fastened, heavy, laced, leather, long, new, old, polished, resoled, scuffed, strong, tied, tough, unlaced, used, waxed, wet, worn, worn out.

verbs SUBJECT: a shoe wears out. OTHERS: to polish a shoe, to fasten a shoe, to lace a shoe, to pull on a shoe, to put on a shoe, to resole a shoe, to scuff a shoe, to take off a shoe, to unlace a shoe, to wear a shoe, to wear out a shoe.

expressions

- *As comfortable as an old shoe:* familiar and relaxed ► **familier et décontracté.**
- *Goody-two-shoes:* an overly good or nice person ► **personne trop bonne ou trop gentille.**
- *If the shoe (cap) fits, wear it:* If it suits you, accept it ► **si la situation vous convient, acceptez-la.**
- *In someone's shoes (place, stead):* in another person's position or situation ► **se mettre à la place d'autrui.**

skirt ► **jupe**

nouns belt, belt loop, button, buttonhole, buttoning, clasp, cloth, clothing, crease, cut, fabric, flare, fringe, hanger, hanger loop, hem, kilt, leg, lining, material, model, pattern, pocket, ruffle, size, snag, stitch, train, tunic, wearer, wrinkle.

adjectives adjusted, adorned, altered, belted, bordered, bunched, buttoned, casual, clasped, clinging, colourful, creased, elegant, embroidered, flared, folded, formal, fringed, gathered, hanging, heavy, hemmed, hung, large, lengthened, light, lined, long, loose, mini, maxi, neckline, new, old, plaid, puffy, ragged, ruffled, see-through, sewn, short, shortened, skin-tight, small, snagged, striped, threadbare, tight, torn, unbuttoned, unclasped, used, wool, worn, worn out, wrap, wrap-around, wrinkled.

verbs SUBJECT: a skirt bunches, creases, flares, fringes, gathers, wrinkles. OTHERS: to adjust a skirt, to alter a skirt, to button a skirt, to clasp a skirt, to change a skirt, to design a skirt, to fold a skirt, to hang a skirt, to hem a skirt, to iron a skirt, to knit a skirt, to lengthen a skirt, to make a skirt, to mend a skirt, to press a skirt, to pull on a skirt, to put on a skirt, to sew a skirt, to shorten a skirt, to swim in a skirt, to tear a skirt, to take off a skirt, to unbutton a skirt, to wash a skirt, to wear a skirt, to wear out a skirt.

suit ▸ costume

nouns accessory, button, buttonhole, buttoning, cloth, clothing, dress, fabric, fancy dress, jacket, lining, kerchief, material, outfit, pants, skirt, tailor, tie, tuxedo, uniform, vest, wearer.

adjectives adjusted, altered, business, buttoned, casual, clean, colourful, creased, dirty, elegant, fancy, formal, lined, mended, new, old, out-of-fashion, penguin, rented, shabby, smoking, soiled, stained, stylish, threadbare, torn, unbuttoned, used, worn, worn out, wrinkled.

verbs SUBJECT: a suit bunches, creases, gathers, wrinkles. OTHERS: to adjust a suit, to alter a suit, to button a suit, to clasp a suit, to change a suit, to design a suit, to hang a suit, to iron a suit, to make a suit, to mend a suit, to press a suit, to put on a suit, to rent a suit, to sew a suit, to swim in a suit, to tear a suit, to take off a suit, to unbutton a suit, to wash a suit, to wear a suit, to wear out a suit.

expressions

• *To suit up:* to put on clothes for a certain activity ▸ **s'habiller pour une activité en particulier.**

tie ▸ cravate

nouns butterfly, collar, clasp, cloth, clothing, fabric, flap, hang, knot, material, neck, pattern, print, shirt, silk, stain, suit, vest, wearer.

adjectives bow, classic, colourful, flapping, hanging, knotted, long, loose, narrow, plaid, short, slack, soiled, stained, striped, tied, undone, untied, wide, wrinkled.

verbs SUBJECT: a tie comes undone, creases, flaps, hangs, slackens, wrinkles. OTHERS: to crease a tie, to knot a tie, to loosen a tie, to put on a tie, to slacken a tie, to soil a tie, to stain a tie, to swing a tie, to take off a tie, to tie a tie, to undo a tie, to untie a tie, to wear a tie, to wrinkle a tie.

vest ▸ gilet

nouns blouse, button, buttonhole, buttoning, coat, clasp, cloth, clothing, collar, fabric, jacket, lining, material, neckline, pocket, shirt, wearer.

adjectives adjusted, altered, buttoned, clasped, clean, colourful, elegant, fashionable, hanging, hung, knitted, light, lined, long, loose, mended, new, old, open, short, sleeveless, soiled, stained, stylish, threadbare, tight, torn, unbuttoned, used, warm, worn, worn out.

verbs SUBJECT: a vest bunches, creases, gathers, wrinkles. OTHERS: to adjust a vest, to alter a vest, to button a vest, to clasp a vest, to change a vest, to design a vest, to hang a vest, to iron a vest, to knit a vest, to make a vest, to mend a vest, to press a vest, to put on a vest, to sew a vest, to swim in a vest, to tear a vest, to take off a vest, to unbutton a vest, to wash a vest, to wear a vest, to wear out a vest.

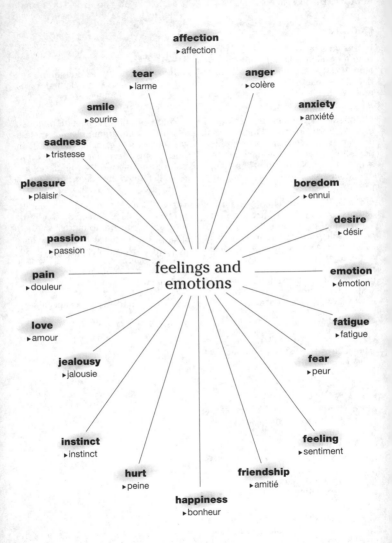

affection
▸affection

tear
▸larme

anger
▸colère

smile
▸sourire

anxiety
▸anxiété

sadness
▸tristesse

pleasure
▸plaisir

boredom
▸ennui

passion
▸passion

desire
▸désir

pain
▸douleur

feelings and emotions

emotion
▸émotion

love
▸amour

fatigue
▸fatigue

jealousy
▸jalousie

fear
▸peur

instinct
▸instinct

feeling
▸sentiment

hurt
▸peine

friendship
▸amitié

happiness
▸bonheur

affection ▸ affection

nouns attachment, bond, caress, emotion, family, feeling, friend, friendship, hug, intimacy, kiss, kissing, love, lover, peck, sentiment, tenderness, touch, union.

adjectives brotherly, constant, growing, intense, loyal, marital, maternal, paternal, returned, tender, touching, undying.

verbs SUBJECT: affection binds, develops, forms, grows, lingers, persists, stops. OTHERS: to feed affection, to feel affection, to form an affection, to get affection, to have affection, to maintain affection, to test affection.

expressions

• *To starve for affection:* to strongly want affection ▸ **éprouver un grand besoin d'affection.**

anger ▸ colère

nouns annoyance, argument, bad humour, burst, disagreement, eruption, explosion, fight, fit, fury, grunt, ill-humour, ill-temper, indignation, irritability, irritation, quarrel, offence, rebellion, rage, scene, short fuse, state, storm, surge, temper, tension, vexation, violence, wrath.

adjectives blinding, devastating, escalating, fierce, fiery, fuming, frequent, frightening, furious, growing, intense, intolerable, justified, liberating, quick, out-of-control, passing, snappy, sour, staggering, stunning, sudden, terrible, terrifying, tremendous, ugly, unstoppable, vengeful, vexing.

verbs SUBJECT: anger boils, comes out, escalates, explodes, grows, injures, lessens, lingers, peaks, persists, rises, stops, wounds. OTHERS: to arouse anger, to awaken anger, to cause anger, to control anger, to fear anger, to free anger, to provoke anger, to restrain anger, to tremble in anger.

expressions

• *More in sorrow than in anger:* saddened instead of made angry by someone's behaviour ▸ **attristé(e) plutôt que fâché(e) à cause du comportement de quelqu'un.**

anxiety ▸ anxiété

nouns anguish, annoyance, apprehension, bother, bravery, courage, distress, dread, emotion, fear, feeling, fit, haunting, heart, impatience, obsession, state, tension, torment, trouble, vexation, waiting, wish, worry.

adjectives atrocious, chronic, constant, deep, dreadful, frightening, growing, intense, intolerable, occasional, permanent, vivid.

verbs SUBJECT: anxiety diminishes, escalates, grows, lessens, lingers, persists, shows, stops. OTHERS: to arouse anxiety, to awaken anxiety, to cause anxiety, to provoke anxiety.

expressions

• *To be anxious to:* to be eager to do something ▸ **avoir hâte de faire quelque chose.**

boredom ▸ ennui

nouns apathy, detachment, discontent, disinterest, displeasure, dissatisfaction, drowsiness, dullness, emptiness, fatigue, flatness, frustration, heaviness, idleness, indifference, irritation, lack of attention, lack of involvement, laziness, lifelessness, passivity, sadness, setback, sleepiness, slowness, tediousness, tedium, tiredness, unease, void, weariness, withdrawal, woe, yawn.

adjectives deep, disagreeable, dragging, frustrating, heavy, intolerable, lingering.

verbs SUBJECT: boredom goes on, lingers, persists, stops, tires, weighs. OTHERS: to cause boredom, to die of boredom.

expressions

- *To bore someone to tears (death):* to tire someone through dull talk or action ▸ **ennuyer quelqu'un par une conversation ou des actions monotones.**

- *To bore someone stiff:* to tire someone through dull talk or action ▸ **ennuyer quelqu'un par une conversation ou des actions monotones.**

desire ▸ désir

nouns ambition, attraction, craving, dream, emotion, fancy, feeling, fire, flame, fondness, frenzy, hope, longing, love, need, passion, want, wish, yearning.

adjectives big, blind, budding, burning, deep, deep-seated, extreme, firm, frantic, frenzied, intense, keen, natural, overwhelming, pressing, profound, secret, sexual, sincere, sole, spontaneous, strong, uncontrollable, unstoppable, urgent.

verbs SUBJECT: desire burns, diminishes, disappears, escalates, goes away, grows, lessens, lingers, persists, rises, stops, vanishes. OTHERS: to awaken desire, to control a desire, to express a desire, to feed a desire, to fuel a desire, to get a desire, to quench a desire, to reveal a desire, to restrain, to satisfy a desire.

expressions

- *To leave a lot to be desired:* to be imperfect or unsatisfying ▸ **être imparfait ou insatisfaisant ; laisser à désirer.**

emotion ▸ émotion

nouns affection, agitation, anger, annoyance, anxiety, attachment, boredom, bother, compassion, confusion, desire, despair, disgust, displeasure, eagerness, ease, emotionality, enthusiasm, exhaustion, experience, fatigue, fear, feeling, friendship, fright, happiness, hurt, increasing, instinct, irritation, jealousy, joy, liveliness, love, melancholy, pain, panic, passion, pleasure, relief, sadness, satisfaction, sensation, shame, shock, smile, sorrow, spirit, state, sympathy, tear, unease, upset, urge, want, wish.

adjectives aroused, bound, burning, calmed, complicated, contained, controlled, deep, denied, dizzying, fake, felt, free, endless, escalating, existing, expressed, extreme, growing, indescribable, intoxicating, keen, lessening, momentary, overwhelming, painful, persisting, pleasant, profound, pure, quenched, provoked, repressed, restrained, revealed, satisfied, secret, sexual, sharp, shown, simple, sincere, slight, strange, strong, subtle, sweet, tender, unbound, unpleasant, violent, vivid.

verbs SUBJECT: emotion disappears, goes away, grows, increases, intensifies, lessens, lingers, moves, overwhelms, pleases, rises, stops, upsets, vanishes. OTHERS: to arouse an emotion, to awaken an emotion, to calm an emotion, to cause an emotion, to control an emotion, to deny an emotion, to experience an emotion, to express an emotion, to fake an emotion, to feed an emotion, to feel an emotion, to free an emotion, to handle emotion, to quench an emotion, to quiver with emotion, to provoke an emotion, to repress an emotion, to restrain an emotion, to reveal an emotion, to satisfy an emotion, to shake with emotion, to show an emotion, to stop an emotion, to tremble with emotion.

fatigue ▸ fatigue

nouns burden, burnout, depression, distress, dullness, exhaustion, faintness, feebleness, mental strain, overstrain, pains, sloth, sleepiness, sluggishness, sorrow, strain, tediousness, tiredness, troubles, weakness, weight.

adjectives chronic, excessive, extreme, intellectual, mental, mortal, nervous, overwhelming, persistent, physical, psychological, relative, terrible, visible.

verbs SUBJECT: fatigue increases, intensifies, goes away, lingers, persist, stops OTHERS: to bring on fatigue, to cause fatigue, to give rise to fatigue, to produce fatigue, to resist fatigue.

fear ▸ peur

nouns alarm, alertness, anxiety, apprehension, coward, dread, emotion, fear, feeling, fright, haunting, horror, intimidation, lack of safety, menace, nervousness, panic, scare, sentiment, shake, shyness, terror, threat, tiring, tremble, unrest, warning, worry.

adjectives alarming, extreme, fleeting, horrible, increasing, indefinable, intense, intolerable, irrational, mortal, overwhelming, petrifying, powerful, rising, terrifying, tremendous, uncontrollable, vague.

verbs SUBJECT: fear alarms, freezes, increases, intensifies, paralyses, recedes, rises, terrifies. OTHERS: to cause fear, to control fear, to lose fear, to feel fear, to produce fear, to resist fear.

expressions

- *Fools rush in where angels fear to tread:* ignorant or inexperienced people are not wise enough to avoid getting involved in bad situations ▸ **les gens ignorants ou sans expérience n'ont pas la sagesse d'éviter les mauvaises situations.**

- *For fear of (that):* in case of ▸ **au cas où; de crainte que.**

- *Never fear:* don't worry if something happens or not ▸ **n'ayez crainte, ne vous inquiétez pas.**

- *To put the fear of God into:* to terrify someone ▸ **terrifier quelqu'un.**

- *To turn white with fear:* to be extremely frightened ▸ **avoir très peur; avoir une peur bleue.**

feeling ▸ sentiment

nouns affection, calm, clearness, cold, disgust, distaste, emotion, emotional charge, exhaustion, fatigue, freedom, happiness, heaviness, hostility, hunger, impression, loneliness, melancholy, pain, perception, relaxation, relief, response, rest, sadness, sensation, sense, shame, spirit, state, state-of-mind, strength, suffering, surprise, triumph, trouble, well-being, warmth, yearning.

adjectives aggressive, annoying, anxious, bad, bitter, brutal, burdensome, comforting, confused, deep, desirable, disagreeable, dizzying, expressed, fleeting, good, hard, hidden, hostile, inexplicable, insensitive, internal, intolerable, heavy, hurt, jealous, maternal, mixed, moving, new, old, oppressive, painful, passing, passionate, paternal, perceptive, pleasant, profound, pure, secret, sensitive, sharp, stimulating, strange, subtle, surprising, tender, terrible, troubling, uncertain, unpleasant, vague, violent, vivid, warm.

verbs SUBJECT: a feeling arises, awakens, burdens, changes, dies, diminishes, disappears, displeases, grows, hurts, increases, intensifies, overwhelms, passes, pleases, returns, rises, startles, terrifies, troubles, vanishes, varies, weighs. OTHERS: to bring on a feeling, to cause a feeling, to express a feeling, to have a feeling, to hide a feeling, to repress a feeling, to share a feeling, to show a feeling, to sustain a feeling.

expressions

- *A sinking feeling:* a sense of apprehension ▸ **sentiment d'appréhension.**

- *Feelings are running high:* emotions are intense ▸ **les émotions sont intenses.**

- *Mixed feelings:* a negative and positive reaction to something ▸ **sentiments ambigus face à une situation.**

- *No hard feelings:* no anger or resentment ▸ **sans rancœur; sans rancune.**

- *The feeling is mutual:* shared feeling ▸ **sentiment partagé.**

friendship ▸ amitié

nouns affection, attachment, buddy, connection, emotion, feeling, friend, kindness, pal, understanding.

adjectives affectionate, boring, broken, brotherly, budding, complicated, constant, deep, fragile, heartfelt, honest, involved, long, longstanding, loyal, mutual, new, old, open, real, reliable, respectful, sad, shaky, short, sincere, sisterly, solid, strange, strong, sweet, tender, touching, tough, troubled, warm.

verbs SUBJECT: friendship buds, develops, dies, grows, survives. OTHERS: to be in a friendship, to betray a friendship, to break a friendship, to end a friendship, to enjoy a friendship, to form a friendship, to harm a friendship, to have a friendship, to lose a friendship, to maintain a friendship, to nurture a friendship, to resume a friendship, to strengthen a friendship, to threaten a friendship, to win a friendship.

expressions.................

- *Fair-weather friend:* someone who is only a friend at good times and not bad ▸ **quelqu'un qui prétend être ami uniquement quand tout va bien.**

- *Friend in court:* people who can help because of their position ▸ **gens qui peuvent être utiles de par leur position.**

- *Friends in high places:* people who can help because of their position ▸ **gens qui peuvent être utiles de par leur position.**

- *To make friends:* to form an acquaintance ▸ **établir des relations avec quelqu'un.**

happiness ▸ bonheur

nouns amusement, celebration, contentment, desire, distraction, dizziness, emotion, enjoyment, enthusiasm, expression, favour, feeling, game, happiness, high spirits, humour, joke, joy, laugh, leisure, pastime, play, pleasure, recreation, relaxation, rest, satisfaction, sense, sensation, smile, state, sweetness, treat, triumph, well-being.

adjectives calm, childlike, contagious, bitter, bubbling, enormous, extraordinary, extreme, false, hidden, immense, indescribable, inexplicable, infectious, infinite, inner, innocent, intense, outer, overwhelming, persistent, pouring, profound, pure, quiet, serene, shamed, sincere, slight, sweet, vivid.

verbs SUBJECT: happiness bursts, dies, disappears, grows, lingers, lives on. OTHERS: to bring happiness, to enjoy happiness, to experience happiness, to express happiness, to fill with happiness, to grab happiness, to have happiness, to hold onto happiness, to share happiness, to strive for happiness, to swim in happiness.

expressions.................

- *Happy as the day is long:* extremely cheerful or glad ▸ **très joyeux(-euse) ou heureux(-euse).**

- *Happy camper:* a satisfied person ▸ **personne satisfaite.**

- *Happy hour:* a bar's promotion of inexpensive drinks in the late afternoon or early evening ▸ **période pendant laquelle un bar offre des boissons à prix réduit; cinq à sept.**

- *Happy hunting ground:* a place where one can do whatever one wants ▸ **endroit où l'on peut faire tout ce que l'on veut.**

- *Happy medium:* the middle point between two extremes ▸ **à mi-chemin entre deux extrêmes.**

- *Many happy returns:* happy birthday and many more ▸ **souhait d'heureux anniversaire et de longue vie.**

- *To live happily ever after:* to spend the rest of one's life happy ▸ **vivre heureux jusqu'à la fin de ses jours.**

- *Trigger-happy:* easily provoked to act violently ▸ **être porté sur la violence; avoir la gâchette facile.**

hurt ► mal (maux)

nouns ache, affliction, anger, anguish, anxiety, betrayal, bitterness, cry, deception, depression, despair, disappointment, discomfort, discouragement, distaste, distress, emotion, feeling, frustration, grief, grimace, heartbreak, ill-being, infliction, injury, irritation, melancholy, misery, mourning, nerve, nostalgia, pain, sadness, sensation, sensitivity, sentiment, setback, sorrow, state, suffering, trouble.

adjectives bad, deep, existing, growing, intense, lingering, overwhelming, painful, profound, strong, tremendous, worsening.

verbs SUBJECT: a hurt diminishes, disappears, goes away, grows, intensifies, lingers, overwhelms. OTHERS: to cause hurt, to feel hurt, to handle hurt, to result in hurt.

expressions

- *To hurt someone's feelings:* to cause someone distress or unhappiness ► **faire de la peine à quelqu'un.**
- *To not hurt a fly:* to be gentle and mild ► **être doux (douce) et gentil (gentille); ne pas faire mal à une mouche.**

instinct ► instinct

nouns ability, feeling, flair, gift, impulse, inkling, inspiration, intuition, perception, reaction, reflex, sense, talent, tendency.

adjectives animal, bad, bruised, correct, maternal, natural, noble, obscure, overwhelming, paternal, raw, right, sexual, slight, strong, violent, wrong.

verbs SUBJECT: instinct awakens, feels, guesses, suspects, tells, warns. OTHERS: to count on instinct, to listen to instinct, to rely on instinct.

expressions

- *To follow one's instincts:* to act on one's feelings ► **agir par instinct.**

- *To trust one's instincts:* to listen to one's feelings ► **se fier à son instinct.**

jealousy ► jalousie

nouns disloyalty, distrust, emotion, family, fear, feeling, friendship, hostility, lie, love, mistrust, notion, sentiment, suspicion, unreliability, want, worry.

adjectives bitter, consuming, crazy, expressed, extreme, fraternal, hidden, hostile, maternal, mean, mutual, petty, sad, slight, strong, terrible, unhealthy, upsetting.

verbs SUBJECT: jealousy arises, bothers, consumes, ends, grows, inspires, intensifies, harms, kills, makes crazy, overwhelms. OTHERS: to cause jealousy, to make jealous.

love ► amour

nouns affair, affection, attachment, bond, crush, emotion, engagement, feeling, flame, flirt, heart, husband, joy, marriage, mistress, lover, obsession, passion, preference, sentiment, spouse, tenderness, wedding, wife.

adjectives attentive, blind, boundless, brotherly, budding, burning, consuming, contradictory, controlled, crazy, deep, demanding, discreet, emotional, excessive, feverish, fiery, fleeting, fragile, frantic, free, generous, healthy, hot, intangible, lasting, lingering, maternal, modest, mutual, needy, overwhelming, painful, passing, passionate, paternal, physical, powerful, profound, puppy, real, restrained, returning, rocky, sensual, shared, sick, sincere, sisterly, strong, tangible, tender, troubled, uncontrollable, undying, unhealthy, youthful.

verbs SUBJECT: love binds, buds, burns, conquers, deepens, destroys, dies, grows, disappears, hurts, lasts, lingers, overwhelms, passes, remains, returns, troubles. OTHERS: to cherish love, to deserve love, to desire love, to feel love, to fight for love, to hold onto love, to need love, to test love, to want love, to yearn for love.

expressions

- *All's fair in love and war:* in some situations any form of behaviour is permissible ▸ **tout est permis dans certaines situations.**
- *For love:* for pleasure ▸ **par amour.**
- *For the love of:* in consideration of ▸ **pour l'amour de.**
- *For the love of God (Mike, Pete):* an exclamation of surprise ▸ **exclamation de surprise ; pour l'amour de Dieu, du ciel, etc.**
- *Misery loves company:* It is easier to cope with difficulty by sharing it with others who understand ▸ **il est plus facile de faire face à une difficulté lorsqu'on peut en parler avec quelqu'un qui la comprend.**
- *Labour of love:* work done for personal enjoyment rather than money ▸ **travail effectué par plaisir et non pour l'argent.**
- *Love affair:* a sexual relationship, or a strong enthusiasm ▸ **aventure amoureuse ; grande passion.**
- *Love at first sight:* an instant attraction to someone or something ▸ **attirance instantanée pour quelqu'un ou quelque chose; coup de foudre ; coup de cœur.**
- *Lovers' lane:* a place of privacy for lovers ▸ **coin tranquille pour les amoureux.**
- *No love lost:* dislike or hate ▸ **animosité ou haine.**
- *Not for love of money:* never ▸ **jamais; pour rien au monde.**
- *Puppy love:* young love or infatuation ▸ **amour de jeunesse ou engouement.**
- *Somebody up there loves me:* I have good luck ▸ **j'ai de la chance ; je suis né sous une bonne étoile.**
- *Tender loving care:* compassionate care ▸ **soins attentionnés.**
- *The course of true love never runs smoothly:* true love has its hardships ▸ **l'amour n'est pas toujours facile.**

- *To be in love with:* to have strong feelings for someone or something ▸ **être amoureux.**
- *To fall in love:* to have strong feelings for someone or something ▸ **tomber amoureux.**
- *To make love:* to have sex ▸ **avoir des relations sexuelles ; faire l'amour.**

pain ▸ **douleur**

nouns ache, anguish, anxiety, arthritis, attack, bitterness, blood, burn, cry, cut, despair, disillusion, distress, drug, emotion, feeling, frustration, grimace, groan, headache, heartbreak, hell, howl, hurt, infliction, injury, irritation, melancholy, moan, mourning, needle, nerve, painkiller, prick, pull, punishment, regret, remedy, sadness, scream, sensation, sensitivity, sentiment, sorrow, state, suffering, swelling, tear, torture, tug, wound, yell.

adjectives burning, clinging, controlled, cutting, deep, destroying, devastating, diffuse, existing, extreme, horrible, intense, internal, intolerable, lingering, localized, mental, overwhelming, penetrating, physical, piercing, profound, punishing, sharp, shooting, short, silent, slight, spreading, swelling, terrible, throbbing, troubling, unpleasant, worsening, vivid.

verbs SUBJECT: pain aggravates, burns, cuts, destroys, devastates, diffuses, diminishes, disappears, goes away, hurts, increases, intensifies, lingers, overwhelms, penetrates, pierces, shoots, spreads, throbs, worsens. OTHERS: to aggravate pain, to cause pain, to control pain, to complain of pain, to cry in pain, to deal with pain, to feel pain, to grimace in pain, to handle pain, to inflict pain, to lessen pain, to share pain, to suffer pain, to take care of pain, to tolerate pain.

expressions

- *For one's pains:* in return for what one has done ▸ **en retour.**
- *Growing pains:* problems encountered when building up a business ▸ **problèmes liés à la croissance d'une entreprise.**

- *No pain, no gain:* without effort there is no reward ► **sans effort, il n'y a pas de récompense.**
- *On (under) pain of:* subject to an assigned penalty ► **assujetti à une pénalité; sous peine de.**
- *Pain in the neck:* a source of bother ► **source d'ennuis; casse-pieds.**
- *To be at pains:* to make a special effort to do something ► **faire un effort tout spécial; prendre la peine de.**
- *To feel no pain:* to be drunk ► **être ivre.**
- *To take pains:* to make a special effort to do something ► **faire un effort tout spécial; prendre la peine de.**

passion ► passion

nouns adoration, affair, affection, anger, burst, craziness, crush, desire, emotion, feeling, fever, fire, flame, heart, hunger, kiss, love, lover, mistress, need, obsession, rage, sensation, sentiment, spirit, suffering, thirst, trance, want, yearning.

adjectives blind, budding, burning, consuming, crazy, dangerous, demanding, destructive, dominating, extreme, fiery, flaming, frightening, guilt, intense, loving, passing, pure, ruling, spirited, strong, sustained, uncontrollable, undying, violent.

verbs SUBJECT: passion dies, diminishes, disappears, explodes, goes out, grows, lessens, thrives, weakens. OTHERS: to awaken a passion, to be ruled by a passion, to control a passion, to follow a passion, to ignite a passion, to lose a passion, to reveal a passion, to share a passion.

expressions

- *Passion fruit:* an exotic fruit ► **fruit exotique; fruit de la passion.**
- *With passion:* passionately ► **avec passion.**

pleasure ► plaisir

nouns amusement, contentment, desire, distraction, dizziness, emotion, enjoyment, favour, feeling, game, happiness, joy, leisure, pastime, recreation, relaxation, rest, satisfaction, sense, sensation, state, treat, well-being.

adjectives bounding, controlled, costly, dangerous, deceptive, deep, diminishing, expressed, growing, intense, mental, physical, profound, pure, sensual, sexual, slight, spousal, sustained, sweet, total, unbounded, uncontrollable.

verbs SUBJECT: pleasure diminishes, ends, grows, increases, satisfies. OTHERS: to die of pleasure, to experience pleasure, to feel pleasure, to ruin pleasure, to seek pleasure, to spoil pleasure, to sustain pleasure, to taste pleasure.

expressions

- *As you please:* whatever you want, ► **comme vous voulez.**
- *Pleased as punch:* delighted ► **ravi.**

sadness ► tristesse

nouns anguish, annoyance, anxiety, bitterness, blue state, boredom, complaint, cry, despair, depression, devastation, disaster, disappointment, discouragement, emotion, expression, feeling, grief, hard time, heartbreak, low-spirits, melancholy, misery, mourning, negativity, pain, sensation, sentiment, setback, sniffle, sob, state, suffering, tear, vexation, void.

adjectives chronic, dark, deep, deep-seated, devastating, distressing, escalating, existing, extreme, heavy, hidden, increasing, inner, intolerable, lingering, mild, ongoing, overwhelming, profound, rising, severe, slight, strong, uncontrollable, worrying.

verbs SUBJECT: sadness deepens, disappears, escalates, exists, hurts, increases, lingers, overwhelms, penetrates, rises. OTHERS: to console sadness, to express sadness, to feel sadness, to live with sadness, to suffer from sadness, to survive sadness.

smile ► sourire

nouns affection, amusement, chuckle, compassion, courtesy, expression, eye, face, friendship, grin, happiness, joy, laugh, lips, manners, mouth, movement, nicety, pity, politeness, resignation, sympathy, tenderness, tooth, understanding.

adjectives affectionate, amused, anxious, astonishing, attractive, awful, beaming, bewildering, big, bitter, blissful, captivating, charming, cold, confident, confiding, confused, confusing, contained, cunning, cute, delicate, discreet, distinguished, distracted, distressed, embarrassed, enchanting, evil, faded, fleeting, fond, friendly, good-looking, gracious, happy, humble, indescribable, infectious, innocent, ironic, irresistible, joyful, likeable, little, lively, melancholic, misleading, mocking, mysterious, narrow, nice, noticeable, persistent, pitying, playful, pleasant, radiant, sad, satisfied, scornful, shamed, showy, shy, sincere, smug, sparkling, strange, subtle, sweet, teasing, tender, tense, threatening, toothy, uncertain, uncomfortable, unpleasant, upset, veiled, welcoming, wicked, wide, winning.

verbs SUBJECT: a smile attracts, beams, charms, drops, fades, forms, grows, misleads, mocks, teases, widens. OTHERS: to contain a smile, to crack a smile, to flash a smile, to force a smile, to get lost in a smile, to greet a smile, to hold a smile, to keep a smile, to notice a smile, to return a smile, to show a smile.

expressions

- *To smile on:* to look on with approval ► **sourire en guise d'approbation.**

tear ► larme

nouns compassion, crier, cry, drop, emotion, eye, feeling, fluid, joy, kerchief, pain, regret, sadness, sob, suffering, sympathy, teardrop, tissue.

adjectives big, bitter, burning, clear, falling, heavy, hot, running, salty.

verbs SUBJECT: a tear clings, drops, falls, flows, hangs, rolls down, runs, shines, slip, wells up. OTHERS: to contain a tear, to drown in tears, to shed a tear, to suppress a tear, to wipe a tear.

expressions

- *Crocodile tears:* insincere grief ► **faux chagrin ; larmes de crocodiles.**
- *Teary-eyed:* to have tears because of joy or sadness ► **avoir les larmes aux yeux (de joie ou de tristesse).**
- *To bore to tears (death):* to tire someone through dull talk or action ► **ennuyer quelqu'un par une conversation ou des actions monotones.**
- *To burst into tears:* to begin crying suddenly ► **éclater en sanglots.**
- *To swallow a tear:* to keep from crying ► **se retenir de pleurer; ravaler ses larmes.**

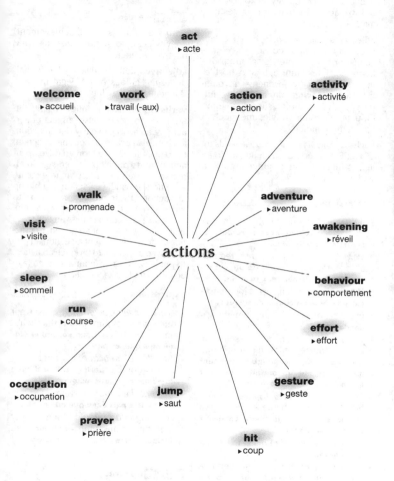

act
▸acte

welcome
▸accueil

work
▸travail (-aux)

action
▸action

activity
▸activité

walk
▸promenade

adventure
▸aventure

visit
▸visite

awakening
▸réveil

actions

sleep
▸sommeil

behaviour
▸comportement

run
▸course

effort
▸effort

occupation
▸occupation

gesture
▸geste

jump
▸saut

prayer
▸prière

hit
▸coup

1025

act ▸ acte

nouns act of bravery, act of chance, act of courage, act of cruelty, act of folly, act of love, action, activity, deed, gesture, manoeuvre, result.

adjectives abusive, brave, brutal, calculated, complicated, conscious, courageous, criminal, cruel, disgusting, dishonest, evil, first, future, heroic, hostile, impulsive, indecent, instinctive, involuntary, latest, moving, planned, powerful, risky, selfish, shameful, simple, solemn, thought out, tough, tragic, unexpected, upcoming, voluntary.

verbs SUBJECT: an act causes, leads to. OTHERS: to accomplish an act, to do an act, to finish an act, to judge an act, to perform an act.

expressions..

- *An act of God:* uncontrollable circumstances ▸ **circonstances hors de tout contrôle ; acte de Dieu.**
- *Hard (tough) act to follow:* a remarkable performance or person ▸ **personne ou prestation remarquable.**
- *High-wire act:* a dangerous job or activity ▸ **activité ou emploi dangereux.**
- *In the act of:* while doing something ▸ **pendant.**
- *To catch in the act:* to capture someone in the course of doing something wrong ▸ **attraper quelqu'un pendant qu'il accomplit un méfait ; attraper quelqu'un la main dans le sac.**
- *To clean up one's act:* to change one's behaviour for the better ▸ **changer son comportement pour le mieux ; améliorer son comportement.**
- *To do a disappearing act:* to vanish ▸ **disparaître.**
- *To get in (into) the act:* to become involved in something ▸ **participer à quelque chose.**
- *To get one's act together:* to get organized, or to behave more appropriately ▸ **s'organiser, ou se comporter de façon plus appropriée.**

- *To put on an act:* to pretend ▸ **jouer un rôle.**

action ▸ action

nouns accomplishment, achievement, activity, call to action, dealing, manoeuvre, operation.

adjectives authoritative, civil, criminal, disgusting, furious, heroic, legal, military, shameful, tragic, voluntary.

verbs SUBJECT: an action results in. OTHERS: to accomplish an action, to achieve an action, to carry out an action, to change an action, to commit an action, to co-operate on an action, to develop an action, to do an action, to engage in an action, to exercise an action, to execute an action, to handle an action, to hold up an action, to improve an action, to influence an action, to interrupt an action, to manage an action, to miss an action, to plan an action, to plot an action, to practice an action, to prevent an action, to proceed with an action, to produce an action, to put in action, to run an action, to take action, to undertake an action.

expressions..

- *Actions speak louder than words:* what one says is less important than what one does ▸ **les actions sont plus éloquentes que les paroles.**
- *All talk and no action:* a lot of talking but no doing ▸ **parler au lieu d'agir ; grand parleur, petit faiseur.**
- *Piece of the action:* a share in something ▸ **une part dans quelque chose.**
- *To swing into action:* to energetically start doing something ▸ **entreprendre quelque chose avec enthousiasme.**

activity ▸ activité

nouns action, calendar, competition, dance, energy, hobby, interest, leisure, liveliness, motion, occupation, painting, pastime, pottery, recreation, schedule, sculpture, sport, theatre, work, vitality.

adjectives after-school, big, calm, cultural, exciting, fall, fantastic, free, important, inside, intellectual, intense, interesting, large, lively, long, mental, motor, musical, mysterious, nervous, nuclear, outside, paid, passing, physical, recreational, restful, scheduled, seasonal, secret, short, social, sporting, spring, summer, voluntary, winter.

verbs SUBJECT: an activity begins, ends, extends, finishes, starts, unfolds. OTHERS: to control an activity, to direct an activity, to do an activity, to get interested in an activity, to participate in an activity, to practice an activity, to present an activity, to register in an activity, to schedule an activity, to sign up for an activity, to start an activity, to stop an activity.

awakening ▸ réveil

nouns alarm, alarm clock, alertness, bed, beginning, birth, dawn, day, dream, drowsiness, excitement, morning, nature, nightmare, rising, sleep, sleep in, sleepiness, spring, start, stretch, wakefulness, yawn.

adjectives abrupt, awful, brutal, exhausted, happy, hurried, joyful, lazy, mean, morning, natural, nocturnal, slow, terrible, tired.

verbs OTHERS: to avoid an awakening, to dread an awakening, to get up at an awakening, to put off an awakening, to rise at an awakening, to stall an awakening, to stretch at an awakening, to yawn at an awakening.

adventure ▸ aventure

nouns accident, adventurer, chance, danger, destiny, discovery, ease, event, exploration, explorer, fate, fear, fire, freedom, hazard, hero, heroine, history, instinct, life, misadventure, passion, peril, racer, risk, spirit, surprise, trip, voyage, whim.

adjectives accidental, bad, chance, crazy, damaging, dangerous, early, emotional, enriching, exciting, exotic, extraordinary, fantastic, fast, funny, future, good, hazardous, human, hurried, imaginary, legendary, love, maddening, marvellous, new, occasional, perilous, pleasant, quick, risky, roaming, romantic, running, sentimental, spontaneous, sudden, surprise, undertaking, unexpected, unplanned, unpleasant, whimsical.

verbs SUBJECT: an adventure begins, ends, finishes, starts. OTHERS: to avoid an adventure, to be in an adventure, to describe an adventure, to discover an adventure, to have an adventure, to imagine an adventure, to invent an adventure, to seek adventure, to run into an adventure.

behaviour ▸ comportement

nouns act, action, appearance, attitude, gesture, impression, look, manner, reaction, seeming, way, way of acting.

adjectives adolescent, adult, aggressive, childish, commendable, dangerous, deviant, funny, good, healthy, honest, human, incomprehensible, linguistic, mysterious, open, passive, praiseworthy, problem, proper, sexual, social, stupid, surprising, troubled, troubling, unhealthy, upsetting, usual, violent.

verbs SUBJECT: behaviour develops, forms. OTHERS: to approve of behaviour, to change behaviour, to criticize behaviour, to deny behaviour, to enjoy behaviour, to explain behaviour, to figure out behaviour, to have behaviour, to improve behaviour, to identify behaviour, to praise behaviour, to predict behaviour, to stop behaviour, to study behaviour.

expressions

- *To be on one's best behaviour:* to be very polite ▸ **être très poli ou polie.**

1027

effort ▶ effort

nouns aim, achievement, act, attempt, concentration, deed, discipline, elbow grease, energy, exercise, feat, impulse, industry, labour, muscle, pains, patience, perseverance, push, strain, stress, struggle, test, toil, trial, training, trouble, try, venture, work.

adjectives accomplished, admirable, apparent, colossal, common, constant, continuous, desperate, determined, difficult, dramatic, energetic, exceptional, generous, grand, heroic, intellectual, intense, long, magnificent, muscular, natural, physical, psychological, powerful, serious, superhuman, supreme, tiring, useless, vain, vigorous, violent.

verbs OTHERS: to appreciate effort, to exert effort, to perceive effort, to reward effort.

expressions..

- *Put some effort into it:* try harder ▶ **faire un plus grand effort.**

gesture ▶ geste

nouns act, action, body, communication, display, flourish, hand, head, hint, indicate, limb, manner, mimic, motion, movement, nod, nudge, show, shrug, sign, signal, wave.

adjectives agitated, automatic, bold, brief, characteristic, circular, elegant, energetic, enthusiastic, expressive, friendly, gracious, impulsive, involuntary, loving, meaningless, menacing, obscene, powerful, precise, rapid, repeated, rude, subtle, threatening, violent.

verbs SUBJECT: a gesture announces, communicates, distracts, expresses, indicates, gives away, manifests, reprimands, reveals, shows, signals, tells. OTHERS: to ignore a gesture, to make a gesture, to notice a gesture, to perceive a gesture, to repeat a gesture.

hit ▶ coup

nouns abuse, accident, ambush, assault, attack, beat, bat, batter, battery, blow, body, boxer, break, chop, claw, clash, club, collision, crack, crash, damage, dodge, drive, drum, fist, harm, hurt, impact, injury, knock, pound, punch, rage, slam, slap, slug, smack, smash, spank, strike, tap, thump, violence, whack, whip, wound.

adjectives accidental, accurate, bodily, brutal, cruel, deliberate, delicate, energetic, fair, first, good, hard, harmful, intentional, light, multiple, painful, senseless, soft, stunning, successful, sudden, traumatic, troublesome, unnecessary, unpleasant, unfriendly, vigorous, violent.

verbs SUBJECT: a hit damages, destroys, frightens, hurts, injures, subdues, wounds. OTHERS: to administer a hit, to fend off a hit, to order a hit, to suffer a hit, to survive a hit, to take a hit.

expressions..

- *A sure-fire hit:* a definite success ▶ **un succès assuré.**
- *Hit and run:* to leave the scene of an accident before being discovered ▶ **quitter les lieux d'un accident sans avoir été vu; délit de fuite.**
- *Hit man:* a hired killer ▶ **tueur à gages.**
- *Something hits the spot:* food or drink that refreshes or satisfies ▶ **aliment ou boisson qui rafraîchit ou satisfait pleinement.**
- *To hit below the belt:* to behave or treat unfairly ▶ **se comporter ou traiter quelqu'un injustement; frapper sous la ceinture.**
- *To hit it off:* to get along well ▶ **bien s'entendre avec quelqu'un.**
- *To hit the books:* to study ▶ **étudier.**
- *To hit the hay:* to go to bed ▶ **aller au lit.**
- *To hit the jackpot:* to be very lucky or successful ▶ **avoir beaucoup de chance ou de succès; tirer le gros lot.**
- *To hit the nail on the head:* to identify precisely, to get something exactly

right ▸ **déterminer de façon précise ; avoir parfaitement raison ; frapper dans le mille.**

- *To hit the road:* to leave, especially in a car ▸ **prendre la route, surtout en voiture.**
- *To hit the sack:* to go to bed ▸ **aller au lit.**

jump ▸ saut

nouns acrobat, air, animal, athlete, bounce, bound, child, dancer, dive, exercise, game, gravity, hop, hopscotch, hurdle, leap, movement, parachute, pounce, skip, sport, spring, vault.

adjectives dangerous, daring, unexpected, high, impressive, incredible, light, little, long, magnificent, playful, quick, silly, sudden, surprising, twisting, winning.

verbs SUBJECT: a jump distances, elevates, separates, surprises, terminates, wins. OTHERS: to jump around, to jump away, to jump back, to jump in, to jump in front of, to jump off, to jump on, to jump out, to jump towards.

expressions

- *Go jump in the lake:* go away and quit being a bother ▸ **va-t'en et cesse de nous déranger ; va voir ailleurs si j'y suis.**
- *Jumpy:* nervous ▸ **nerveux.**
- *To jump on the bandwagon:* to join a popular cause or movement ▸ **épouser une cause ou un mouvement populaire ; prendre le train en marche.**
- *To jump out of one's skin:* to be badly frightened or very surprised ▸ **avoir très peur ou être très surpris ou surprise ; sursauter.**
- *To jump the gun:* to start early ▸ **agir prématurément.**
- *To jump to a conclusion:* to decide quickly without knowing all the facts ▸ **tirer des conclusions sans connaître tous les faits.**

occupation ▸ occupation

nouns action, activity, affair, agriculture, art, artist, attention, boss, business, calling, care, career, charge, chore, commission, company, concern, contract, corporation, craft, day, department, devotion, duty, effort, employee, employer, employment, errand, experience, factory, faculty, function, job, labour, life, manager, mission, occupancy, occupant, office, part, pay, place, possession, post, presence, process, product, production, productivity, profession, province, pursuit, rate, routine, salary, security, service, situation, specialization, specialist, staff, state, student, study, studio, syndicate, task, time, trade, training, undertaking, union, vocation, volunteer, wages, welfare, work, worker.

adjectives academic, active, agricultural, artistic, authorized, automatic, businesslike, cerebral, collective, constant, continuous, creative, dangerous, difficult, domestic, easy, engaged, exhausted, experienced, hard, industrial, intellectual, irregular, functional, lazy, mechanical, military, occupational, occupied, official, permanent, principal, professional, qualified, regular, repetitive, scholarly, specialized, temporary, tiring.

verbs SUBJECT: the occupation tires. OTHERS: to carry on an occupation, to find an occupation, to fill an occupation, to have an occupation, to occupy, to plan an occupation.

prayer ▸ prière

nouns angel, baptism, Bible, cathedral, church, confession, devotion, dream, faith, funeral, grace, hope, mat, miracle, nun, petition, plea, priest, religion, request, shawl, service, Thanksgiving, urge, wish.

adjectives desperate, faithful, healing, holy, humble, important, peaceful, quiet, sacred, short, solemn, tranquil, useless, vain, worthy.

verbs SUBJECT: a prayer blesses, calms, comforts, heals, soothes. OTHERS: to hear a prayer, to mumble a prayer, to say a prayer, to speak a prayer, to whisper a prayer.

expressions

- *To not have a prayer:* to not have a chance ► **ne pas avoir la moindre chance.**

run ► **course**

nouns activity, athlete, competition, course, dash, energy, exercise, foot, gallop, health, hurry, injury, jog, journey, marathon, motion, pad, path, race, runner, shoe, speed, sport, sprint, sweat, trainer, walk.

adjectives annual, boring, competitive, difficult, easy, fast, first, fun, hard, intense, last, Olympic, monotonous, painful, quick, rapid, slow, swift, vigorous.

verbs SUBJECT: a run distances, fatigues, separates, tires. OTHERS: to run around, to run away, to run back, to run from, to run to.

expressions

- *A (good) run for one's money:* a good show or performance – something worthwhile ► **une bonne prestation ou performance; un résultat valable.**

- *Dry run:* Attempt at carrying out a procedure beforehand in order to practise ► **mise à l'essai d'une procédure en guise de pratique; répétition.**

- *In or out of the running:* having a chance or no chance of success ► **avoir ou non une chance de réussir.**

- *In the long run:* in the end – considering something over a period of time ► **au bout du compte; après un certain temps; à long terme.**

- *It runs in the family:* a common family characteristic ► **trait de famille.**

- *Run-down:* in poor condition ► **en mauvaise condition.**

- *Run dry:* to dry up ► **se tarir.**

- *Run-of-the-mill:* ordinary ► **ordinaire.**

- *Runner-up:* the person who finishes second in a race or contest ► **personne qui arrive deuxième dans une course ou un concours.**

- *To be on the run:* to be escaping or running away from something or someone – to be in a rush ► **fuir quelque chose ou quelqu'un; être pressé; être en cavale.**

- *To run a tight ship:* to run an organization with firm rules and regulations ► **mener une entreprise selon des règles strictes et sévères.**

- *To run for it:* to try and escape ► **tenter de s'échapper.**

- *To run into someone:* to encounter someone ► **rencontrer quelqu'un; tomber sur quelqu'un.**

- *To run off at the mouth:* to talk too much ► **parler sans arrêt.**

- *To run out:* to come to the end of a supply ► **épuiser ses réserves.**

- *To run out of steam:* to lose energy and become tired ► **manquer d'énergie et être fatigué ou fatiguée.**

- *To run out on someone:* to leave ► **partir, abandonner quelqu'un.**

sleep ► **sommeil**

nouns bed, bedroom, catnap, coma, death, dream, hammock, morning, nap, night, night-gown, nightmare, pillow, pyjamas, relaxation, rest, slumber.

adjectives brief, deep, drowsy, eternal, long, necessary, nightly, peaceful, poor, quiet, restless, shallow, short, snug, sweet, uncomfortable, uneasy.

verbs SUBJECT: sleep cures, refreshes, remedies. OTHERS: to sleep beside, to sleep off, to sleep near, to sleep on, to sleep with.

expressions

- *Sleeping bag:* a lined or padded bag to sleep in, especially while camping ► **sac de couchage.**

- *Sleeping pill:* a pill to induce sleep ► **somnifère.**
- *Sleepyhead:* a sleepy or inattentive person ► **personne endormie ou inattentive.**
- *Sleepover:* an occasion of spending the night away from home ► **occasion de passer la nuit ailleurs que chez soi.**
- *To sleepwalk:* to walk or perform other actions while asleep ► **marcher ou parler dans son sommeil; être somnambule.**

visit ► **visite**

nouns apartment, city, country, custom, dentist, doctor, friend, holiday, hospital, hotel, house, invitation, luggage, map, monument, museum, parent, passport, place, postcard, region, relative, reunion, suitcase, tour, tourist, town, traveller, vacation, visitor, voyage.

adjectives brief, cautious, dangerous, distant, educational, expensive, extensive, forbidden, foreign, frightening, fun, future, lonely, long, necessary, painful, past, serious, short, sombre, token, unprepared, unwanted.

verbs SUBJECT. a visit accomplishes, educates, refreshes, relaxes. OTHERS: to anticipate a visit, go on visit, to plan a visit, to remember a visit.

expressions

- *Visiting hours:* a designated time when visitors may call, as in a hospital ► **période pendant laquelle on peut visiter les gens (à l'hôpital, par exemple); heures de visite.**

walk ► **promenade**

nouns circuit, energy, exercise, foot, gait, hike, limp, march, motion, move, nature, pace, parade, path, plank, race, run, shoe, stagger, step, stride, stroll, trudge, transport, waddle.

adjectives brisk, long, peaceful, quiet, quick, rambling, rapid, solitary, solo, soothing.

verbs SUBJECT: a walk avoids, begins, ends, follows, winds. OTHERS: to walk along, to walk around, to walk away, to walk behind, to walk beside, to walk down, to walk over, to walk to, to walk under, to walk up.

expressions

- *Walk of life:* way of living ► **mode de vie.**
- *To be walking on air:* to feel happy and excited ► **être heureux ou heureuse et animé(e); marcher sur des nuages.**
- *To walk on eggshells:* to be careful around a sensitive or easily upset person ► **faire très attention à une personne sensible ou susceptible; marcher sur des œufs.**
- *To walk all over someone:* to be disrespectful or inconsiderate of someone's rights or feelings ► **manquer de respect ou de considération à l'égard des droits ou des sentiments de quelqu'un; lui marcher sur les pieds.**
- *To walk away / off with something:* to win something easily ► **gagner facilement.**
- *To walk on air:* to feel extremely happy ► **être extrêmement heureux ou heureuse; marcher sur des nuages.**
- *To walk out:* to go on strike ► **faire la grève.**
- *To walk the plank:* to walk off the board extended off the side of a pirate ship and drown ► **marcher sur une planche tendue hors d'un bateau pirate, sauter et se noyer.**

welcome ► **accueil**

nouns acceptance, embrace, friend, greeting, guest, hold, home, host, house, hug, invitation, kiss, mat, stranger, traveller, visitor.

adjectives comforting, cordial, friendly, gentle, giving, gracious, hearty, hostile, kind, nice, open, polite, rude, trusting, typical, unexpected, unfriendly, unpleasant, warm.

verbs SUBJECT: a welcome comforts, eases, pleases, relieves. OTHERS: to welcome aboard, to welcome back, to welcome home, to welcome in.

expressions

- *To be welcome to do or have something:* to be cheerfully given permission to do or have something ► **obtenir la permission de faire ou de prendre quelque chose.**
- *To make someone welcome:* to be hospitable ► **faire preuve d'hospitalité ; être accueillant.**
- *To outstay one's welcome:* to stay too long as a visitor ► **abuser de l'hospitalité d'autrui.**
- *To put out the welcome mat:* to prepare to welcome a guest ► **se préparer à accueillir un invité.**

expressions

- *To get worked up:* to feel very angry and excited ► **être très en colère et énervé.**
- *To work one's fingers to the bone:* to work very hard ► **travailler très fort.**
- *To work someone over:* to beat someone up ► **battre quelqu'un ; le passer à tabac.**
- *Workout:* a session of physical exercise ► **séance d'exercice physique.**

work ► **travail (-aux)**

nouns achievement, activity, boss, brainstorm, career, colleague, corporation, desk, development, employee, employer, enterprise, factory, job, labour, machine, occupation, office, operation, payment, product, profession, professional, service, slave, slavery, task, toil, vocation, vacation, weekend, worker, workshop.

adjectives administrative, boring, brilliant, creative, daily, dangerous, delicate, easy, equal, everyday, familiar, filthy, fun, good, hard, intellectual, interesting, legal, legislative, new, progressive, risky, simple, steady, strenuous, tiring.

verbs SUBJECT: work begins, starts, terminates. OTHERS: to find work, to hate work, to leave work, to like work, to quit work, to seek work, to stop work.

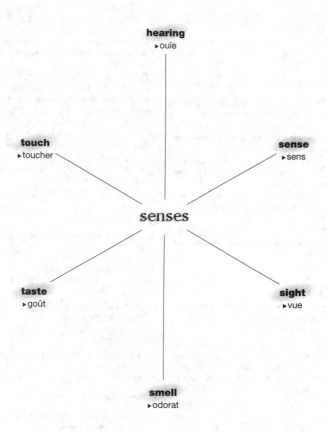

hearing
►ouïe

touch
►toucher

sense
►sens

senses

taste
►goût

sight
►vue

smell
►odorat

hearing ▸ ouïe

nouns ear, ear canal, ear plugs, chatter, communication, eavesdrop, hearing aid, listener, music, musical instruments, noise, radio, silence, sound, stereo, vibrations.

adjectives attuned, excellent, fair, good, impaired, poor, sensitive.

verbs SUBJECT: hearing can be blocked, damaged, impaired, improved, lost, prevented.

expressions

• *Hard of hearing:* to be hearing impaired ▸ **souffrir de déficience auditive.**

• *Hear! Hear!:* to express one's approval ▸ **expression servant à manifester son approbation.**

• *To hear a person out:* to listen to all that a person says ▸ **écouter tout ce qu'une personne a à dire.**

• *To hear one's calling:* to discover one's vocation ▸ **découvrir sa vocation, sa voie.**

• *Will not hear of:* will not allow or agree to ▸ **ne permet ou n'accepte pas; ne veut rien entendre.**

sense ▸ sens

nouns awareness, feeling, hearing, idea, knowledge, meaning, sensation, sight, smell, taste, thought, touch.

adjectives alert, basic, clear, creative, decent, deep, different, dull, effective, familiar, good, hazy, keen, little, magnificent, necessary, poor, profound, sharp, strong , weak.

verbs SUBJECT: a sense aids, assists, develops, distinguishes, identifies, informs, warns. OTHERS: to develop a sense, to have a sense, to ignore a sense, to lose a sense.

expressions

• *Horse sense:* plain good sense ▸ **le bon sens.**

• *In a sense:* in a way, to a certain extent ▸ **dans une certaine mesure.**

• *Out of one's senses:* crazy ▸ **fou; insensé.**

• *Sixth sense:* intuition ▸ **intuition; sixième sens.**

• *To bring someone to their senses:* to make someone understand that they should be more reasonable ▸ **faire comprendre à une personne qu'elle devrait être plus raisonnable; ramener quelqu'un à la raison.**

• *To come to one's senses:* to become sensible after acting foolishly ▸ **retrouver ses sens après avoir posé des gestes stupides.**

• *To make sense:* to be something you can understand or explain ▸ **ce que l'on peut comprendre ou expliquer.**

• *To take leave of one's senses:* to become crazy, slightly mad ▸ **devenir un peu fou; perdre la boule.**

sight ▸ vue

nouns appearance, book, colour, eyes, gaze, glance, glare, glasses, glimpse, light, look, microscope, mirage, observation, perception, reading, recognition, stare, telescope, television, view, viewer, visibility, vision, witness.

adjectives accurate, bad, blind, clear, fading, failing, feeble, good, keen, opaque, poor, powerful, profound, magnificent, terrible.

verbs SUBJECT: sight can be damaged, impaired, lost, prevented. OTHERS: to gain sight, to lose sight.

expressions

• *A sight for sore eyes:* a most welcome sight ▸ **agréable apparition.**

• *Hind sight:* looking to the past ▸ **regard sur le passé.**

• *Hind sight is 20/20:* it is easy to see what should have been done in the past to make things perfect ▸ **il est facile de voir maintenant ce qui aurait** dû être fait dans le passé pour que les choses soient parfaites.

- *Not to be able to stand the sight of someone:* to dislike someone very much ▸ **détester quelqu'un ; ne pas pouvoir le blairer.**
- *Out of sight!:* Fantastic! ▸ **Fantastique !**
- *Out of sight, out of mind:* one stops thinking of someone when that person is absent ▸ **la distance fait oublier les absents ; loin des yeux, loin du cœur.**
- *To catch sight of (something or someone):* to get a brief view – to begin to see ▸ **apercevoir, entrevoir.**
- *To get out of sight:* to hide or disappear ▸ **se cacher ou disparaître.**
- *To have something or someone in one's sight:* to want to get something or someone ▸ **désirer quelqu'un ou quelque chose.**
- *To keep sight of:* to be able to see – to stay focused ▸ **être capable de voir, de se concentrer.**
- *To know someone by sight:* to be able to recognize someone physically without having been introduced ▸ **pouvoir reconnaître une personne sans jamais lui avoir été présenté ou présentée ; connaître quelqu'un de vue.**
- *To lose sight:* to no longer be able to see someone – to lose focus ▸ **perdre quelqu'un de vue ; perdre sa concentration.**
- *To set one's sights on:* to want to get something or someone ▸ **désirer quelqu'un ou quelque chose.**
- *Second sight:* the power of seeing into the future ▸ **pouvoir de connaître l'avenir ; clairvoyance.**

smell ▸ odorat

nouns aroma, bouquet, exhaust, flower, food, fragrance, nose, nostril, odour, paint, perfume, scent, skunk, smoke, sneeze, sniff, snort, stink, whiff.

adjectives aromatic, delicate, delicious, disgusting, excellent, exotic, faint, fine, fragrant, fresh, gross, intense, pleasant, powerful, smoky, soft, sour, spicy, strong, sweet, terrible.

verbs SUBJECT: a smell attracts, draws, drifts, excites, floats, stimulates. OTHERS: to create a smell, to detect a smell, to disguise a smell, to dismiss a smell, to hate a smell, to like a smell, to make a smell, to smell a smell.

expressions

- *To smell a rat:* to suspect that something is wrong ▸ **soupçonner que quelque chose ne tourne pas rond ; anguille sous roche.**
- *To smell of the lamp:* to show signs that a writer has done a lot of research for his work ▸ **indiquer qu'un auteur a effectué beaucoup de recherches pour réaliser son œuvre.**
- *To smell out:* to detect by smell ▸ **reconnaître à l'odeur.**

taste ▸ goût

nouns appetite, bite, breakfast, craving, crumb, diet, dinner, dribble, drop, enjoyment, flavour, food, hunger, lips, lunch, meal, mouth, mouthful, nibble, sample, sip, snack, spoonful, supper, teeth, thirst, tongue.

adjectives acid, bad, bitter, delicate, delicious, disgusting, dry, good, gross, juicy, light, moist, mouldy, particular, pleasant, preferred, rich, rotten, salty, sour, spicy, subtle, sweet, tart, terrible.

verbs SUBJECT: taste cultivates, develops, matures, refines. OTHERS: to crave a taste, to have a taste, to have taste, to lack taste, to like a taste, to request a taste, to want a taste.

expressions

- *To leave a bad taste in one's mouth:* to leave a bad impression or feeling ▸ **laisser une impression ou un sentiment désagréable.**

- *To taste:* (in recipes) to whatever quantity is desired. (For example, "Add salt to taste.") ▸ **autant qu'on le désire ; au goût (dans une recette par exemple).**
- *To one's taste:* to one's liking ▸ **à son goût.**

touch ▸ toucher

nouns affection, aggression, body, bruise, bump, comfort, communication, embrace, feel, finger, hand, hug, kiss, lead, love, manoeuvre, influence, nerves, push, scrape, scratch, skin, slap, support, tap, texture, tickle.

adjectives assuring, careful, cautious, cold, confident, deliberate, electric, first, friendly, gentle, intimate, last, loving, manual, momentary, pleasant, polite, protective, rough, rude, sexual, soft, soothing, violent, warm.

verbs SUBJECT: a touch calms, comforts, communicates, relaxes, reveals, soothes. OTHERS: to crave a touch, to feel a touch, to give a touch, to miss a touch, to want a touch.

expressions..

- *In touch with:* in contact with ▸ **en contact avec.**
- *Touch-and-go:* insecure or uncertain ▸ **précaire, ou incertain.**
- *Touch-type:* to type without looking at the keyboard or one's hands ▸ **taper sans regarder le clavier ou ses mains.**
- *To touch up:* to fix up or paint over ▸ **réparer ou retoucher.**

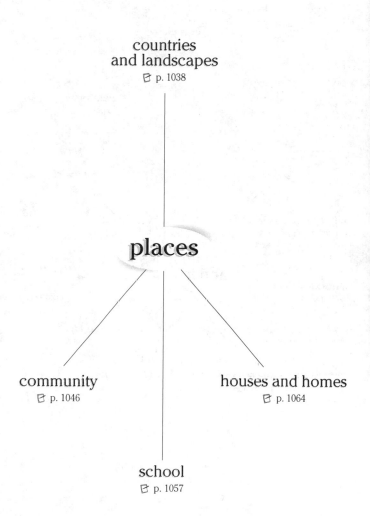

countries
and landscapes
☞ p. 1038

places

community
☞ p. 1046

houses and homes
☞ p. 1064

school
☞ p. 1057

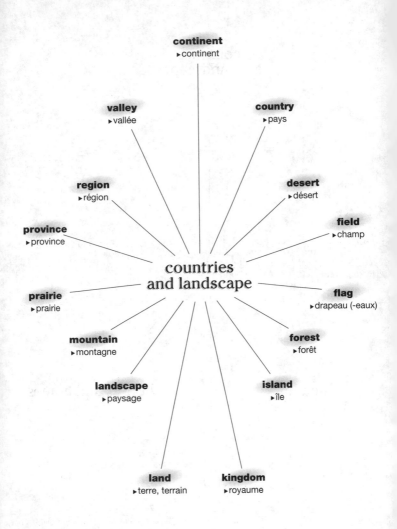

continent
▸continent

valley
▸vallée

country
▸pays

region
▸région

desert
▸désert

province
▸province

field
▸champ

countries
and landscape

flag
▸drapeau (-eaux)

prairie
▸prairie

mountain
▸montagne

forest
▸forêt

landscape
▸paysage

island
▸île

land
▸terre, terrain

kingdom
▸royaume

continent ▸ continent

nouns border, capital, civilization, climate, colony, countries, custom, development, dialect, diversity, earth, empire, environment, expanse, export, folklore, geography, globe, government, import, immigration, immigrants, land, language, latitude, law, longitude, natives, mainland, map, nation, nationality, nature, Occident, ocean, orient, people, place, planet, population, province, refugees, region, soil, state, territory, world, war, zone.

adjectives African, American, ancient, arctic, arid, Asian, Australian, boreal, cold, continental, divided, diversified, dry, eastern, European, hot, humid, indigenous, isolated, large, moderate, native, natural, north American, northern, occidental, oriental, prosperous, rich, small, south American, southern, temperate, western, warm.

verbs SUBJECT: the continent borders, divides, is surrounded, separates, spans across. OTHERS: to cross a continent, to fly to a continent, to invade a continent, to map out a continent, to travel to a continent, to visit a continent.

country ▸ pays

nouns administration, adoption, adventure, agriculture, ancestor, ancestry, area, army, birth, border, capital, city, civilization, coin, colonization, commune, communism, community, country side, county, currency, custom, dialect, democracy, density, development, dictator, district, division, earth, east, empire, explorer, exploration, folklore, foreigner, government, governor, home, identity, immigrant, immigration, inhabitants, institution, island, king, kingdom, lake, land, language, law, leader, lodging, money, name, nation, natives, neighbourhood, north, Occident, ocean, organization, orient, origin, people, politicians, population, port, pride, progress, province, queen, town, track, region, republic, refugee, refuge, republic, road, roots, rule, ruler, sea, senate, soil, south, space, state, suburb, territory, trade, tradition, traveller, trip, tyrant, village, voyage, war, west, world, zone.

adjectives ancient, agricultural, arid, boreal, cold, colonial, communist, cultural, democratic, dense, deserted, developed, diverse, dry, eastern, familiar, foreign, geographical, governmental, historical, hostile, hot, humid, independent, industrial, inhabited, invaded, national, native, new, northern, occidental, occupied, old, oriental, peopled, political, poor, populated, provincial, protected, rich, rural, small, social, socialist, southern, sovereign, temperate, third world, traditional, unfamiliar, united, warm, western, wild.

verbs SUBJECT: the country defends, develops, divides, exports, imports, invests, invites, joins, participates, produces, receives, spans across, sends, trades, welcomes. OTHERS: to be from a country, to border a country, to conquer a country, to defend a country, to die for a country, to discover a country, to escape from a country, to explore a country, to fight for a country, to flee a country, to fly from a country, to live in a country, to move to a country, to return to a country, to stay in a country, to travel to a country, to visit a country.

expressions

- *A country life:* life in a rural community ▸ **vie rurale; vie à la campagne.**
- *A country mile:* any long distance ▸ **toute longue distance.**
- *A country club:* a club devoted mainly to athletic activities ▸ **club d'activités sportives.**
- *To throw one's self upon the country:* to stand for trial ▸ **subir un procès.**
- *To go to the country:* to find out the opinion of the people on a political question by holding an election ▸ **organiser une élection pour connaître l'opinion publique sur une question politique.**

desert ▸ désert

nouns barrens, camel, caravan, climate, desolation, direction, dromedary, dune, earth, east, emptiness, expanse, life, heat, heat stroke, hunger, insects, land, loneliness, mirage, nomad, north, nowhere, oasis, place, plain, prospector, sand, salt, scorpion, silence, snake, solitude, south, thirst, void, wasteland, water, west, wind, zone.

adjectives alive, arid, arctic, barren, cold, dangerous, desolate, dry, empty, expanding, far, flat, harsh, large, long, lost, off-course, polar, rocky, solitary, travelling, tropical, unbearable, uninhabitable, uninhabited, warm, wide.

verbs SUBJECT: the desert covers, expands, reaches, spans across, stretches across. OTHERS: to camp out in the desert, to cross the desert, to die in the desert, to get lost in the desert, to go to the desert, to live in the desert, to scream in the desert, to sleep in the desert, to travel in the desert.

expressions

- *A desert rat:* a person who has lived in the desert for a long time ▸ **personne qui vit dans le désert depuis longtemps.**

field ▸ champ

nouns air, area, agriculture, baseball, battle, city, corn, country, cricket, crops, earth, farm, farmer, fibre, flowers, football, grain, grass, harvest, hay, herbs, hoe, ice, insects, land, moor, pasture, plants, planter, plough, rows, shed, space, stable, sun, tiller, vegetables, weeds, wheat, work.

adjectives abandoned, agricultural, big, biological, closed, cultivated, dry, empty, flat, green, growing, large, long, lush, magnetic, narrow, open, organic, small, tilled, wide.

verbs OTHERS: to burn down the field, to camp out in the field, to cultivate the field, to fight in the field, to harvest the field, to lie in the field, to plant the field, to play in the field, to plough the field, to run in the field, to sit in the field, to sleep in the field, to think in the field, to till the field, to walk in the field, to work in the field.

expressions

- *A field of consciousness:* the totality of what is being observed or considered ▸ **l'ensemble de ce qui est observé ou envisagé.**
- *A field of vision:* what a person is capable of seeing ▸ **ce qu'une personne peut apercevoir; champ de vision.**
- *A field goal:* a drop kick goal in football ▸ **botté de placement au football américain.**
- *A field trip:* a school outing ▸ **excursion scolaire.**
- *The master of the field:* the winner ▸ **le gagnant ou la gagnante.**
- *To have a field day:* to go all out ▸ **se donner à plein; s'en donner à cœur joie.**

flag ▸ drapeau (-eaux)

nouns army, association, banner, celebration, ceremony, city, club, colour, country, culture, crosses, emblem, enemy, honour, identity, nation, nationality, peace, pirate, pole, pride, province, race, regiment, sign, signal, staff, stars, state, symbol, troops, unity, war.

adjectives attached, lowered, mended, military, national, new, oblong, official, old, political, proud, provincial, racing, raised, ripped, sown, stitched, white.

verbs SUBJECT: the flag bends down, hangs, moves, turns, twirls. OTHERS: to burn the flag, to flag someone down, to fold the flag, to hoist the flag, to honour the flag, to lower the flag, to mend the flag, to present the flag, to show raise the flag, to salute the flag, to show the flag, to take the flag, to wave the flag, to wear the flag.

expressions

- *A black flag:* the anarchist or pirate flag ► **pavillon des pirates.**
- *A green flag:* signals the permission to go ► **signe permettant d'avancer, de passer; feu vert.**
- *The flag is down:* signal of distress ► **signal de détresse.**
- *The flag ship:* the ship which carries the flag officer (admiral) ► **navire où se trouve l'amiral; vaisseau amiral.**
- *Something that flags:* something that is drooping or that hangs loose ► **quelque chose qui pend.**
- *To wave a white flag:* to give up ► **abandonner; baisser pavillon.**

forest ► forêt

nouns area, air, animal, bed, biosphere, bush, clearing, clear cutting, climate, conservation, earth, ecology, environment, fauna, fire, flora, flower, forestry, fruit, green, grass, herb, insects, island, life, land, landscape, lake, leaves, life, life forms, log, lumber, maintenance, moor, mountain, mushroom, outdoors, path, plain, plant, plantation, protection, reserve, resources, shrub, site, space, tree, vegetable, vegetation, wetland, wildlife, wood, woods.

adjectives alive, arctic, boreal, clean, deep, dense, ecological, enchanted, endangered, environmental, fresh, growing, immense, inhabited, interconnected, lush, magical, natural, organic, peaceful, private, protected, quiet, splendid, tropical, wild, wonderful.

verbs SUBJECT: the forest borders, dies, stretches across. OTHERS: to camp in the forest, to clear-cut the forest, to cut the forest, to get lost in the forest, to go to the forest, to grow in the forest, to hike in the forest, to live in the forest, to love the forest, to make a fire in the forest, to sleep in the forest, to study the forest, to trek in the forest, to walk in the forest.

expressions

- *Forest city:* nickname for Cleveland, Ohio ► **surnom de la ville de Cleveland, en Ohio.**
- *The forest floor:* the deposit of organic matter on the ground ► **dépôt de matières organiques couvrant le sol en forêt; tapis forestier.**

island ► île

nouns archipelago, bank, bay, beach, city, clay, continent, coral, cove, earth, gulf, ice, inlet, isle, islet, islander, lagoon, land, lake, mainland, map, moor, mount, mountain, ocean, position, reef, rock, sea, shore, soil, sound, strand, stream, swimmer, tourist, tourism, tree, volcano, water.

adjectives alone, arctic, big, continental, deserted, dry, earthy, eastern, elevated, emerging, exotic, floating, forbidden, inhabited, isolated, large, marooned, mountainous, Nordic, northern, oceanic, oriental, peopled, private, rocky, sacred, seaside, small, southern, uninhabited, western, wild.

verbs SUBJECT: the island emerges, floats, separates, sinks. OTHERS: to discover an island, to dream of an island, to live on an island, to swim to an island, to visit an island.

expressions

- *The island city:* nickname for Montreal (Quebec, Canada) ► **surnom de la ville de Montréal (Québec, Canada).**
- *The island of Reil:* the central lobe of the brain ► **lobe central du cerveau; insula de Reil.**
- *The island of the seven cities:* imaginary island filled with gold ► **île imaginaire remplie d'or; île au trésor.**

kingdom ► royaume

nouns animal, area, aristocrat, army, authority, baron, baroness, biology, capital, Christ, classification, colony, colonist, control, count, countess, country, county, crown, death, domain, domination, dominion, divisions, duchess, duke, earth, emperor, empress, empire, extent, God, Goddess, groups, head, heir, hell, idol, inheritance, insect, king, kingship, lady, land, master, monarch, monarchy, nature, noble, place, paradise, prince, princess, quality, queen, rampart, rank, realm, region, reign, republic, science, sovereign, sphere, spirit, state, territory, throne, world.

adjectives animal, aristocratic, authoritarian, divided, ideal, mineral, natural, primary, regal, royal, spiritual, utopian, vegetable.

verbs SUBJECT: the kingdom conquers, imposes, opposes, orders. OTHERS: to divide the kingdom, to expand the kingdom, to inherit the kingdom, to map the kingdom, to reach the kingdom, to study the kingdom.

expressions................................

- *In the kingdom of the blind, the one-eyed man is king:* it is easier to look bright (or good) among people who are not ▶ **il est plus facile de paraître brillant ou brillante (ou bien) parmi ceux et celles qui ne le sont pas ; au royaume des aveugles, les borgnes sont rois.**

- *Kingdom come:* the next world ▶ **l'autre monde ; un monde meilleur.**

- *To go (to be sent) to kingdom come:* to die ▶ **mourir ; partir pour un monde meilleur.**

- *Until kingdom come:* for a very long time ▶ **pour une durée indéterminée ; jusqu'à la fin des temps.**

land ▶ **terre, terrain**

nouns abundance, acre, acreage, agent, agriculture, area, beach, building, cliff, continent, country, crops, desert, draught, earth, estate, farm, farmer, father, fence, fertility, fertilizer, field, floor, forest, frost, ground, home, horizon, house, humidity, indigenous, irrigation, island, kingdom, labour, landlady, landlord, landmark, landscape, latitude, longitude, map, min-

eral, moor, mother, mountain, mud, nation, nationality, nature, ocean, owner, pasture, path, people, plant, plantation, plough, production, property, rain, real estate, river, rock, salt, sand, sea, shore, soil, stone, surface, swamp, tax, tenant, territory, timber, tree, vegetable, vegetation, water, woods, work, yard.

adjectives agricultural, arctic, arid, bad, biological, clean, coarse, cultivated, dry, earthy, eastern, faraway, flat, flooded, frozen, good, hard, harsh, harvested, home, humid, inhabited, mountainous, muddy, native, northern, organic, planted, ploughed, polar, poor, rich, rocky, rough, sandy, smooth, soft, solid, southern, tilled, toxic, uncharted, underground, uninhabited, unploughed, virgin, western, wet.

verbs SUBJECT: the land belongs to, dries, encompasses, grows, needs. OTHERS: to acquire land, to burn the land, to chart land, to clear the land, to cultivate the land, to discover land, to divide land, to inherit land, to land, to live off the land, to own land, to pay taxes on land, to plough the land, to retire on one's land, to run on land, to sell land, to travel on land, to work the land.

expressions................................

- *Land hunger:* desire to acquire land ▶ **désir d'acquérir du terrain.**

- *The land down under:* Australia ▶ **l'Australie.**

- *The land of the living:* the present life ▶ **la vie actuelle ; de ce monde.**

- *The land of the midnight sun:* Norway ▶ **la Norvège.**

- *The land of the rising sun:* Japan ▶ **le Japon.**

- *The lay of the land:* the state of affairs ▶ **l'état des choses.**

- *To go to the land of Nod:* to go to sleep ▶ **s'endormir ; s'en aller au pays des rêves.**

- *To win by a landslide:* to win by a majority ▶ **remporter la victoire par une majorité écrasante.**

landscape ▸ paysage

nouns area, art, artist, brush, camera, canvas, canyon, cliff, colour, country, depth, description, drawing, earth, fog, forest, greenery, hill, horizon, lake, land, lens, light, moor, mount, mountain, nature, object, ocean, paint, painter, painting, photograph, photographer, photography, picture, plan, portion, prospect, river, scene, scenery, sea, shade, shore, sight, site, sketch, territory, tree, view, water, waterfall, woods.

adjectives abstract, actual, alive, amazing, beautiful, breath-taking, bright, charming, dreary, exotic, fancied, far, flat, foggy, frozen, historical, imagined, immense, impressive, incredible, large, lit, long, magnificent, majestic, mountainous, mystical, native, natural, painted, pictorial, sad, strange, urban, visual.

verbs OTHERS: to depict a landscape, to draw a landscape, to imagine a landscape, to paint a landscape, to photograph a landscape, to see a landscape, to view a landscape.

expressions

- *A landscape artist:* someone who paints landscapes ▸ **artiste qui peint des paysages ; paysagiste.**

- *A landscape gardener:* someone who lays out grounds to imitate natural settings ▸ **personne qui crée des jardins rappelant des paysages naturels ; jardinier ou jardinière ; architecte paysagiste.**

mountain ▸ montagne

nouns altitude, animal, ascension, avalanche, base, boots, bottom, boulder, chain, canyon, cave, cavern, cliff, climate, climber, crust, descent, direction, dirt, earth, elevation, equipment, erosion, excursion, fauna, flora, forest, gear, glacier, goat, gorge, group, guide, height, hill, hike, ice, land, lava, level, map, mass, mineral, moor, mound, mount, mountaineer, mud, path, place, range, road, rock, rope, route, sand, sheep, shoes, ski, slope, snow, soil, stone, summit, surface, top, trail, tree, tree line, trek, valley, volcano, wildlife, wind.

adjectives active, alpine, cold, dormant, eroded, gigantic, great, high, huge, humungous, icy, impressive, irregular, isolated, little, low, massive, mountainous, muddy, natural, rocky, round, sacred, sandy, slanted, sloped, small, snowy, steep, tall, volcanic, windy.

verbs SUBJECT: the mountain appears, hides, rises, surrounds. OTHERS: to ascend a mountain, to camp on a mountain, to climb a mountain, to come down a mountain, to fall down a mountain, to hike up a mountain, to live on a mountain, to name a mountain, to paint a mountain, to roll down a mountain, to ski on a mountain, to trek on a mountain.

expressions

- *A mountain of work:* a lot of work ▸ **beaucoup de travail ; un travail fou, un travail monstre.**

- *Mountain dew:* scotch whisky ▸ **whisky écossais.**

- *To make a mountain out of a molehill:* to exaggerate the difficulty of something ▸ **exagérer une difficulté ; se faire une montagne de quelque chose.**

prairie ▸ prairie

nouns agriculture, animal, cattle, chicken, community, corn, country, crops, cultivation, dog, draught, herd, hill, earth, farm, farmer, field, fire, flower, grass, ground, growth, harvest, irrigation, land, landscape, meadow, moor, mount, mountain, nature, pasture, patch, plain, plant, plateau, property, ranch, region, root, shed, soil, tribe, valley, vegetation, village, weed, wheat.

adjectives agricultural, arid, artificial, beautiful, coarse, covered, cultivated, deep, dry, fertile, flat, green, harvested, huge, large, long, natural, planted, rich, rustic, sandy, spacious, treeless, tropical, unlimited, vast, wide.

verbs SUBJECT: the prairie borders, produces, stretches. OTHERS: to cultivate the prairie, to graze in the prairie, to live on the prairie, to love the prairie, to raise animals on the prairie, to work on the prairie.

expressions................................

- *A prairie schooner:* a covered wagon ▸ **grand chariot.**
- *A prairie wolf:* a coyote ▸ **coyote.**
- *Prairie itch:* a skin condition ▸ **irritation cutanée.**

province ▸ province

nouns administration, area, authority, border, candidate, capital, city, coast, community, council, counsellor, country, county, culture, custom, department, dialect, district, division, dominion, dwelling, election, empire, folklore, government, governor, home, house, immigrant, immigration, indigenous, kingdom, language, law, limit, map, nation, nationality, parliament, part, people, place, population, portion, region, representation, representative, republic, residence, riding, senate, sovereignty, state, territory, trade, tradition, unit, village, zone.

adjectives administered, administrative, central, coastal, colonial, conquered, cultural, divided, eastern, federal, geographical, governmental, independent, isolated, local, maritime, national, native, northern, occidental, oriental, outside, poor, prosperous, provincial, purchased, remote, rich, rural, southern, sovereign, territorial, united, urban, wealthy, western.

verbs SUBJECT: a province borders, exports, imports, invites, joins, separates, welcomes. OTHERS: to administer a province, to come from a province, to conquer a province, to divide a province, to immigrate to a province, to join provinces, to live in a province, to map

out a province, to move to a province, to purchase a province, to reside in a province, to rule a province, to travel to a province, to visit a province.

expressions................................

- *It is not within my province:* within my branch of learning ▸ **ce n'est pas mon domaine; cela ne fait pas partie de mes connaissances.**

region ▸ région

nouns area, border, boundary, capital, city, climate, colony, commerce, community, compass, continent, counsel, country, county, department, district, division, domain, east, electorate, empire, expanse, export, fauna, flora, geography, group, guide, height, import, kingdom, land, language, latitude, law, length, limit, longitude, map, natives, navigation, north, Occident, ocean, orient, people, part, place, population, prairie, province, realm, republic, reserve, riding, sea, section, sector, sky, south, space, sphere, spot, state, territory, town, trade, village, way, west, world, zone.

adjectives administrative, agricultural, arctic, boreal, capital, cleared, cold, commercial, cultivated, dangerous, dense, desolate, divided, eastern, economical, expansive, extensive, federal, high, historical, indigenous, inhabited, geographical, large, limited, local, long, low, open, maritime, native, natural, Nordic, northern, occidental, occupied, oriental, productive, protected, quarantined, regional, rural, sectional, sectioned, small, southern, spacious, temperate, tropical, uninhabited, unlimited, urban, vast, void, warm, western, wild.

verbs SUBJECT: the region borders, exports, imports, manufactures, produces, separates, spans across, stretches. OTHERS: to cross a region, to divide a region, to live in a region, to section a region.

valley ► **vallée**

nouns area, bottom, bridge, canyon, cave, cavern, deposit, depression, drainage, erosion, fog, gorge, gravel, hill, hole, inlet, land, mineral, mount, mountain, outlet, plain, pit, ravine, region, river, sand, slope, stream, water, zone.

adjectives covered, cultivated, deep, down, dry, elevated, enclosed, flat, glacial, high, large, long, low, narrow, river, rocky, small, structural, wide, wild.

verbs SUBJECT: the valley crosses, meets, stretches. OTHERS: to cross a valley, to descend into a valley, to dig in a valley, to hike in a valley, to live in a valley, to plant in a valley, to sit in a valley, to walk in a valley, to work in a valley.

expressions...

• *The valley of the shadow of death:* a period of great troubles ► **période très difficile ; période trouble.**

airport ▸ aéroport

nouns abroad, aerodrome, agency, agent, air, air pocket, aisle, aircraft, airline, arrival, aviation, aviator, boarding pass, border, border officer, building, business, cabin, captain, carrier, charter, client, command, company, control tower, co-pilot, counter, courier, crew, customs, departure, emergency, engine, factory, field, fleet, flight, ground, hangar, helicopter, industry, instruments, jet, jet lag, landing, landing strip, lay over, luggage, maintenance, merchandise, navigation, office, overseas, passenger, passport, pilot, place, plane, platform, propeller, restaurant, seat belt, shuttle, steward, stewardess, take-off, ticket, time zone, tourism, tourist, traffic, transit, transport, trip, turbulence, vacation, voyage, waiting room, wind, wing.

adjectives accessible, aeronautical, busy, commercial, designed, efficient, empty, heavy, international, large, local, modern, new, popular, private, public, regional, renovated, reserved.

verbs OTHERS: to board at the airport, to buy a ticket at the airport, to change planes at the airport, to disembark at the airport, to embark at the airport, to evacuate the airport, to fly from the airport, to go to the airport, to land at the airport, to rent a car at the airport, to take off from the airport, to wait at the airport.

bank ▸ banque

nouns account, amount, balance, banker, bank book, bank machine, bankruptcy, bill, branch, business, note, capital, capitalism, capitalist, card, cash, cashier, change, cheque, coin, commercial, commission, corporation, credit, customer, debt, deficit, deposit, debtor, development, director, discount, employee, employer, enterprise, establishment, exchange, finance, firm, fund, government, industry, institution, interest, investment, legal-tender, loan, manager, market, money, mortgage, officer, pay, payment, safe, saving, security, staff, stock, stock exchange, stockholder, exchange, rate, representative, sum, teller, trade, transaction, transfer, transit, value, wages, withdrawal.

adjectives bankrupt, closed, commercial, cooperative, financial, head, important, industrial, modern, national, new, open, payable, private, public, small.

verbs SUBJECT: the bank administers, controls, closes, finances, lends, places, opens, owns, transfers. OTHERS: to borrow from a bank, to deposit at a bank, to enter a bank, to go to a bank, to invest in a bank, to keep a bank, to leave a bank, to overdraw from a bank, to pay at a bank, to save at a bank, to speculate at a bank, to withdraw at a bank.

expressions

- *To bank on:* to place your hopes on ▸ **fonder ses espoirs sur; compter sur, tabler sur.**
- *To break the bank:* to leave oneself or someone else without any money ▸ **se ruiner ou ruiner quelqu'un d'autre.**

bridge ▸ pont

nouns arch, beam, board, boat, canyon, channel, cliff, construction, crossroad, depression, drawbridge, earth, escape, gate, gateway, gorge, ground, guard, head, inlet, iron, lane, mason, masonry, manner, method, moor, obstacle, passage, passenger, path, pier, platform, railroad, railway, ravine, river, road, route, roadway, ship, steel, stream, street, structure, track, train, tunnel, valley, way, wood.

adjectives artificial, covered, crooked, crossing, direct, elevated, erected, fixed, modern, movable, new, old, raised, rusted, stable, straight, supported, suspended, tubular, unstable, wobbling.

verbs SUBJECT: the bridge collapses, crosses, separates. OTHERS: to build a bridge, to cross a bridge, to draw a bridge, to fall from a bridge, to jump off a bridge, to run across a bridge, to traverse under a bridge, to repair a bridge.

expressions

- *Don't burn your bridges before you cross them:* don't ruin your opportunities before you try ► **ne gâchez pas vos chances avant d'essayer.**
- *To make a bridge of gold for someone:* to let someone retreat without losing dignity ► **laisser quelqu'un se retirer avec dignité.**
- *To cross a bridge when one comes to it:* not to bother about a problem about to arise in the future until it actually affects one ► **ne pas s'en faire avec un problème éventuel avant d'y être confronté.**
- *Water under the bridge:* something that is past and is not worth worrying about ► **situation passée qui ne mérite pas qu'on s'en préoccupe.**

building ► bâtiment

nouns apartment, architect, architecture, builder, brick, church, college, construction, contractor, creation, demolition, development, dwelling, factory, fence, frame, government, height, hospital, hotel, house, investment, land, loan, maintenance, mason, masonry, mortgage, museum, office, ownership, place, prison, real estate, renovation, rent, roof, school, shelter, stairs, stone, store, structure, tower, university, value, wall, window.

adjectives architectural, artificial, commercial, constructed, designed, elegant, expensive, framed, governmental, important, large, located, permanent, private, public, religious, residential, run-down, situated, small, tall.

verbs SUBJECT: the building blocks, obstructs, stands. OTHERS: to build a building, to construct a building, to

demolish a building, to erect a building, to fix a building, to purchase a building, to renovate a building, to rent a building, to visit a building.

cemetery ► cimetière

nouns ancestor, ancestry, ashes, autopsy, bell, body, bones, burial, casket, cave, ceremony, chamber, church, clay, coffin, corpse, cremation, cremator, cross, crucifix, crypt, death, earth, end, existence, family, flowers, funeral, funeral home, garden, ghost, grave, grave digger, graveyard, ground, inheritance, knell, land, lot, monument, morgue, mourning, mummy, name, pit, pain, place, rest, row, service, shrine, skeleton, sorrow, tear, tomb, tombstone, urn, vault, void, wake, will, worms.

adjectives buried, calm, Catholic, dead, desolate, difficult, famous, historical, immortal, Jewish, quiet, large, military, mortal, nostalgic, resting, sad, serene.

verbs SUBJECT: a cemetery reminds, saddens. OTHERS: to bury someone in the cemetery, to cry in a cemetery, to dig in the cemetery, to go to the cemetery, to hide in a cemetery, to lay someone in the cemetery, to plant in a cemetery, to remember someone in a cemetery, to visit a cemetery.

expressions

- *A car cemetery:* a junkyard ► **un parc à ferrailles.**

city ► ville

nouns activity, administration, apartment, area, avenue, board, border, boulevard, boundary, building, bus, business, capital, cathedral, charter, church, citizen, citizenship, civilian, clan, commonwealth, confederation, control, council, counsellor, country, county, court, decline, deputy, development, downtown, dump, dwelling, earth, editor, election, environment, family, fusion, garbage, garden, hall, heart, high-rise, highway, history, home, hospital, house, industry, inhabitant, key, kingdom, land, law, library, majority, market, map, mayor, members, metropolis, municipality, neighbour, neighbourhood, noise, occupant, office, organization, park, place, plaza, police, pollution, population, port, province, rent, representation, representative, residence, riding, sewer, shopping centre, space, state, street, square, suburb, subway, taxes, town, tradition, traffic, train, transportation, trip, union, village, water, zone.

adjectives administrative, alive, ancient, big, central, centralized, ceremonial, civil, clean, commercial, conquered, cosmopolitan, dead, dense, dirty, diverse, enormous, federal, ghost, grey, historical, honorary, important, independent, industrial, inhabited, international, legal, major, maritime, metropolitan, minor, municipal, native, political, polluted, populated, provincial, public, quiet, regional, residential, rural, small, sovereign, traditional, uninhabited, university, urban.

verbs SUBJECT: the city changes, develops, expands, grows, runs, sleeps, stretches, welcomes. OTHERS: to build a city, to clean up a city, to conquer a city, to drive through a city, to go to a city, to invade a city, to pollute a city, to shop in a city, to travel in a city, to visit a city, to walk in a city.

expressions

- *City of the dead:* a cemetery ▸ **cimetière.**
- *The big city:* a metropolis ▸ **métropole.**
- *The city of bells:* Strasbourg, Germany ▸ **Strasbourg, en Allemagne.**
- *The city of God:* the Christian church and all the believers ▸ **l'Église chrétienne et l'ensemble de ses fidèles.**
- *The city of a hundred towers:* Pavia, Italy ▸ **Pavie, en Italie.**

drugstore ▸ **pharmacie**

nouns ailment, aspirin, business, candy, cashier, chemist, cold, cosmetics, cough, cough drops, counter, cream, cure, disease, doctor, dose, drug, flu, health, hygiene, infection, injury, insurance, itch, medication, medicine, pain, penicillin, pharmacist, pharmacy, physician, prescription, receipt, remedy, shampoo.

adjectives busy, chemical, clean, closed, convenient, covered, expensive, healthy, inexpensive, itchy, modern, natural, open, organic, pharmaceutical.

verbs SUBJECT: the drugstore closes, opens, OTHERS: to build a drugstore, to find a drugstore, to go to the drugstore, to open a drugstore, to own a drugstore, to pick something up at a drugstore, to prescribe at a drugstore, to recommend a drugstore, to sell a drugstore, to shop at a drugstore.

expressions

- *A drugstore cowboy:* a man who tries to impress women by showing off ▸ **homme qui en met plein la vue afin de faire bonne impression auprès des femmes.**

fire station ▸ **caserne de pompier**

nouns alarm, bell, blaze, bonfire, building, car, chief, city, combustion, community, danger, death, drill, electricity, emergency, employee, engine, escape, extinguisher, fire, fire fighter, flame, flash, fuel, glow, heat, help, home, house, hose, ignition, ladder, light, limits, pole, property, protection, risk, screams, siren, smoke, smoke detector, summer, test, town, traffic, trampoline, truck, volunteer, warmth, water, wind, work.

adjectives active, afraid, alarmed, busy, devoted, far, fast, fireproof, local, loud, near, protected, ready, regional, safe.

verbs SUBJECT: the fire station extinguishes, receives calls, sends help. OTHERS: to call the fire station, to drive to the fire station, to live next to the fire station, to work at the fire station.

garden ▸ jardin

nouns agriculture, area, art, earth, bed, botanist, botany, bush, compost, crop, cultivation, cutter, Eden, farm, farmer, fertilizer, flower, fountain, fruit, gardener, gardening, grass, greenhouse, green thumb, ground, growth, harvest, herb, house, insect, labour, land, lawn, lawn-mower, leaf, market, mineral, occupation, paradise, park, petal, piece, plant, plantation, pot, rake, region, rock, sand, season, seed, seedling, shade, shovel, soil, space, spices, stone, summer, sun, tool, tree, vegetable, weed, warmth, water, wheelbarrow, work, worm, yard, zoology.

adjectives agricultural, botanical, chemical, communal, community, cultivated, fertile, fresh, green, growing, incredible, indoor, inorganic, miniature, natural, organic, ornamental, outdoor, poor, private, public, rich, rocky, seasonal, shady, simple, surrounded, wild, zoological.

verbs SUBJECT: the garden covers, encompasses, dies, grows, lives, stretches. OTHERS: to admire a garden, to cultivate a garden, to dig a garden, to enter a garden, to garden, to grow a garden, to harvest a garden, to lay out a garden, to plant a garden, to share a garden, to spray a garden, to stroll through a garden, to tend a garden, to till a garden, to transplant a garden, to visit gardens, to walk in a garden, to water a garden, to weed a garden.

expressions

* *The Garden:* the philosophy of Epicurus ▸ **philosophie d'Épicure.**
* *To lead up the garden:* to trick ▸ **tromper; monter un bateau, mener en bateau, faire marcher.**

highway ▸ autoroute

nouns asphalt, boulevard, boundary, bus, byway, car, city, cement, collision, concrete, construction, course, curb, detour, development, direction, drive, driver, east, exit, fork, hitchhiking, intersection, lane, load, maintenance, movement, north, number, overpass, path, place, ramp, road, route, radar, rest area, restaurant, rig, robber, shoulder, sign, signal, south, speed, stop, street, tar, town, traffic, transportation, trip, truck, truck stop, way, west.

adjectives blocked, busy, closed, destructive, double, eastern, fast, jammed, interstate, loud, metropolitan, northern, open, paved, principal, private, public, rapid, repaired, right, single, slow, speeding, southern, unnatural, urban, western, wrong.

verbs SUBJECT: the highway divides, finishes, forks, splits. OTHERS: to get lost on a highway, to hitchhike on a highway, to live by a highway, to pass someone on a highway, to repair a highway, to slow down on a highway, to speed on a highway, to stop on a highway, to take a highway, to travel on a highway.

expressions

* *A highwayman:* someone who robs people on the highway ▸ **personne qui vole les gens sur la route; voleur de grand chemin.**

library ▸ bibliothèque

nouns archive, best-seller, book, bookcase, bookseller, building, card, category, circulation, city, clerk, classification, collection, college, congress, consultation, copy, fee, desk, edition, editor, encyclopaedia, fine, furniture, historian, index, institution, librarian, magazine, manual, manuscript, member, membership, microfilm, music, newspaper, novel, paper, people, periodical, place, poem, print, publication, reading, reference, research, researcher, rooms, school, section, shelf, slides, study, university, video, writing.

adjectives calm, classified, filed, historical, indexed, late, legal, local, municipal, national, popular, private, public, quiet, scientific, silent, specialized, universal.

verbs SUBJECT: the library lends out, opens, closes. OTHERS: to borrow a book at the library, to check out a book at a library, to find at a library, to go to a library, to leave a library, to read at a library, to research at a library, to return to a library, to subscribe to a library, to visit a library.

expressions

- *A library rat:* someone who is often at the library ▸ **personne qui fréquente souvent la bibliothèque; rat de bibliothèque.**

---

museum ▸ musée

nouns accumulation, antique, archaeology, architecture, arrangement, art, artist, building, city, collection, conservation, curiosity, display, exhibition, film, gallery, imitation, muse, music, object, original, painting, photographer, photography, piece, place, portrait, relic, reproduction, sculptor, sculpture, shop, souvenir, specimen, tour, town, university, value, visit, wealth, works.

adjectives antique, archaeological, artistic, beautiful, empty, fun, historical, impressive, instructive, interesting, literary, natural, new, old, scientific, small, technological, visual.

verbs SUBJECT: the museum acquires, closes, displays, exhibits, opens, owns, sells. OTHERS: to buy at a museum, to go to a museum, to observe at a museum, to take a tour of a museum, to visit a museum.

expressions

- *A museum piece:* something of historic value or an old person ▸ **objet de grande valeur, ou personne âgée; pièce de musée.**

---

neighbourhood ▸ quartier

nouns address, administration, area, asphalt, association, avenue, bar, bicycle, block, border, boulevard, building, business, bylaw, church, city hall, class, centre, citizen, city, commune, community, country, county, court house, crescent, district, drugstore, dweller, dwelling, environment, farm, fellow, fire station, gang, garden, ghetto, group, home, hospital, hotel, house, inhabitants, intersection, junction, land, mall, map, mayor, members, municipality, nation, neighbour, neighbourhood watch, park, part, path, pavement, pedestrian, people, place, police station, population, poverty, region, residence, resident, restaurant, road, route, school, section, sector, shopping centre, sidewalk, sign, store, street, suburb, surroundings, tavern, tax, traffic, tree, vicinity, village, visit, way, zone.

adjectives abandoned, adjacent, bad, clean, communal, crowded, dangerous, dirty, elegant, empty, expensive, far, friendly, good, green, industrial, inhabited, isolated, kind, large, near, neighbourly, overpopulated, paved, poor, popular, populated, quarantined, quiet, residential, rich, safe, situated, small, suburban, uninhabited, unknown.

verbs SUBJECT: the neighbourhood borders on, finishes at, recycles, starts at. OTHERS: to clean up a neighbourhood, to disturb a neighbourhood, to leave a neighbourhood, to live in a neighbourhood, to map out a neighbourhood, to move to a neighbourhood.

expressions

- *In the neighbourhood of:* approximately ▸ **environ.**

---

office ▸ bureau

nouns accountant, accounting, administration, appointment, archive, assignment, assistant, authority, book, branch, building, business, charge, chief, clerk, company, computer, consultation, corporation, department, desk, director, doctor, document, drawer, duty, employment, fax machine, file, file cabinet, finance, function, hours, lawyer, library, minister, occupation, officer, paper, pen, pencil, people, place, position, post, power, president, prime minister, printer, ministry, requirement, register, research, room, secretary, service, situation, screen, shelf, stapler, study, telephone, trade, transaction, trust, window.

adjectives administrative, big, bright, ceremonial, closed, collective, dark, executive, federal, foreign, friendly, governmental, head, home, huge, important, judicial, legal, medical, official, open, oval, private, provincial, public, small, tiny.

verbs SUBJECT: the office calls, closes, greets, interviews, makes appointments, opens, receives, sends. OTHERS: to appoint to office, to build an office, to consult an office, to drive to an office, to go to an office, to put into office, to research in an office, to read in an office, to sit in an office, to stand in an office, to stay at an office, to study in an office, to wait in an office.

expressions...

- *To do ill office:* to do harm, injury ▸ **blesser; porter atteinte.**

police station ▸ poste de police

nouns abuse, accusation, accused, accuser, administration, alarm, arrest, assembly, brutality, building, car, chief, constable, cop, court, crime, criminal, declaration, defendant, defence, delinquent, detective, emergency, enforcement, felony, fingerprint, force, government, gun, handcuffs, harassment, headquarters, helicopter, holding cell, inspector, judge, judgement, jury, justice, law, lawyer, legislation, magistrate, military, misdemeanour, mugger, murder, murderer, neighbourhood, offence, order, organization, partner, photograph, place,

police officer, power, prison, protection, punishment, regulation, riot, robber, robbery, safety, sergeant, shoplifting, service, sheriff, siren, squadron, stick, surveillance, team, trial, truck, uniform, violation, violence, wagon, weapon, witness.

adjectives federal, legal, legislative, modern, organized, powerful, protected, provincial, regulated, safe.

verbs SUBJECT: the police station dispatches, holds, receives, sends out. OTHERS: to call a police station, to drive to a police station, to find a police station, to handcuff someone at a police station, to leave a police station, to look for a police station, to notify a police station, to release someone at a police station, to take a ride to a police station, to visit a police station, to wait at a police station.

post office ▸ bureau de poste

nouns address, bag, building, city, collection, courier, currency, delivery, department, distance, duty, employee, envelope, government, horse, letter, mail drop, mail, mailbox, mail person, master, message, messenger, money order, neighbourhood, package, paper, parcel, person, pack, people, place, pony, post, postage, postal code, post card, postmark, postmaster-general, rate, road, route, runner, service, size, stamp, station, street, tariff, town, truck, vehicle, village, weight, writing.

adjectives busy, closed, convenient, governmental, international, local, located, national, open, postal, private, public, slow, sorted.

verbs SUBJECT: the post office charges, closes, collects, delivers, opens, posts, receives, returns, rejects, sends, sorts. OTHERS: to buy at a post office, to direct to a post office, to drive to a post office, to go to a post office, to meet at a post office, to pay at a post office, to receive at a post office, to send from a post office, to stop by a post office, to wait in line at a post office, to walk to a post office.

restaurant ▸ restaurant

nouns assistant, bankruptcy, bar, barmaid, barman, bartender, bartending, bill, boss, bowl, breakfast, buffet, building, bus boy, business, cafeteria, cash, catering, chain, chair, change, chef, check, city, client, coin, consumption, cook, counter, course, delivery, dinner, dishes, dishwasher, doggy bag, drink, drive-through, food, employee, employer, entrance, establishment, fast-food, food, hospital, hotel, house, inn, investment, kitchen, leftover, liquor, licence, lunch, meal, manager, menu, napkin, neighbourhood, occupation, order, owner, parking, payment, place, plate, portion, price, receipt, refreshment, reservation, room, service, snack-bar, soup, staff, supper, table, tax, tip, town, truck stop, utensils, valet, village, waiter, waitress, washroom.

adjectives bad, big, busy, cheap, Chinese, classy, clean, comfortable, cosy, crowded, decorated, dirty, elegant, empty, excellent, exotic, expensive, fancy, fast-food, favourite, fine, French, good, greasy, inexpensive, Italian, large, local, located, long, luxurious, Mexican, narrow, normal, ordinary, packed, popular, public, quick, reserved, slow, small, speedy, tiny, take-out, vegetarian.

verbs SUBJECT: the restaurant caters, closes, delivers, empties, fills up, offers, opens, prepares, serves. OTHERS: to buy a restaurant, to call a restaurant, to chat in a restaurant, to drink in a restaurant, to eat at a restaurant, to eat out, to enter a restaurant, to go to a restaurant, to invest in a restaurant, to leave a restaurant, to make reservations at a restaurant, to open a restaurant, to order from a restaurant, to sell a restaurant, to sit in a restaurant, to talk in a restaurant, to wait at a restaurant.

road ▸ chemin

nouns access, accident, alley, automobile, avenue, block, boulevard, bridge, bus, car, circuit, circulation, city, concrete, construction, corner, danger, dead end, detour, direction, distance, ditch, drive, driver, east, flow, fork, highway, hill, hitchhiker, house, intersection, itinerary, journey, junction, land, lane, lights, line, maintenance, map, movement, neighbourhood, north, ocean, outing, overpass, park, passage, passenger, path, pavement, pedestrian, place, repair, ride, river, route, rule, side, sidewalk, sign, signal, south, stop, street, ticket, track, traffic, traffic jam, transportation, trip, turn, U-turn, vacation, vehicle, water, way, west.

adjectives beautiful, black, blocked, bumpy, busy, clean, closed, country, dangerous, dark, different, dirty, far, empty, fast, frozen, green, hot, icy, large, long, loud, muddy, narrow, near, new, old, open, paved, polluted, private, public, quiet, rapid, right, rocky, rural, scenic, short, slow, snowy, stopped, urban, wide, winding, wrong.

verbs SUBJECT: the road divides, finishes, forks, splits, starts, stops, turns, winds, zigzags, OTHERS: to build a road, to clean a road, to close a road, to cross a road, to damage a road, to destroy a road, to drive down the road, to find a road, to follow a road, to pave a road, to rain on a road, to repair a road, to snow on a road, to stop at a road, to stroll down a road, to lose a road, to take a road, to turn at a road, to walk down a road.

expressions

- *All roads lead to Rome:* it all comes to the same thing ▸ **quelle que soit la méthode utilisée, le résultat sera le même; tous les chemins mènent à Rome.**

- *A road monkey:* someone who inspects and repairs the road ▸ **personne chargée d'inspecter et de réparer les routes.**

- *A road runner:* the chaparral bird ▸ **coucou terrestre.**

- *One for the road:* a last drink ▸ **un dernier verre.**

- *On the road to recovery:* to be on the way to better health ▸ **en voie de guérison.**

shopping centre ▸ centre commercial

nouns area, bargain, booth, books, building, business, cart, cinema, city, client, clothes, department, director, discount, display, downtown, drugstore, employee, escalator, establishment, expense, food court, goods, groceries, location, mall, manager, mannequin, neighbourhood, neon, occupation, owner, parking, perfume, place, price, purchase, rendezvous, rent, restaurant, room, sale, Santa Claus, security, shop, shoppers, shopping bag, store, supplies, tag, town, trade, window.

adjectives big, busy, cheap, clean, closed, dark, developing, dirty, empty, expanding, expensive, far, flourishing, growing, huge, large, near, new, open, popular, populated, prosperous, small, successful, underground, sunny, thriving, well lit.

verbs SUBJECT: the shopping centre closes, expands, offers, opens. OTHERS: to buy at a shopping centre, to clean a shopping centre, to eat in a shopping centre, to find in a shopping centre, to go to a shopping centre, to invest in a shopping centre, to meet at a shopping centre, to rendezvous at a shopping centre, to sell in a shopping centre, to shop at a shopping centre, to stroll in a shopping centre, to walk in a shopping centre.

skyscraper ▸ gratte-ciel

nouns administration, apartment, architect, architecture, balcony, boulevard, building, business, city, cement, complex, construction, downtown, dwelling, elevation, elevator, enterprise, floor, height, high-rise, housing, metropolis, office, place, project, rent, restaurant, road, security, security guard, skeleton, steel, storey, structure, sky, tower, window.

adjectives commercial, elegant, elevated, excessive, exclusive, full, high, historical, huge, impressive, incredible, inhabited, large, luxurious, modern, renovated, residential, tall.

verbs SUBJECT: the skyscraper touches, reaches, scrapes. OTHERS: to build a skyscraper, to clean a skyscraper, to live in a skyscraper, to renovate a skyscraper, to work in a skyscraper, to visit a skyscraper.

store ▸ magasin

nouns administration, advertisement, back room, bankruptcy, bargain, boss, bulk, business, buyer, cart, cash, cashier, change, client, clothes, company, convenience store, corner store, credit, demand, department, discount, employee, employer, enterprise, exchange, food, gift, goods, grocer, groceries, hardware, import, inventory, investment, item, lease, liquidation, license, manager, market, merchandise, offer, order, owner, payment, place, price, promotion, provision, publicity, purchase, quality, quantity, receipt, refund, rent, sale, sales person, shelf, shoes, shopping, shopping centre, stock, supplies, tax, warehouse, window.

adjectives affordable, antique, bad, bankrupt, bright, busy, cheap, clean, closed, convenient, crowded, dark, dirty, expensive, far, general, good, huge, inconvenient, inexpensive, international, little, local, long, new, old, old-fashioned, open, organized, packed, popular, quiet, renowned, small, sold, special, stocked, strange, winding.

verbs SUBJECT: the store advertises, charges, closes, delivers, exports, guarantees, imports, labels, offers, opens, refunds, ships. OTHERS: to build a store, to buy at a store, to close a store, to go to a store, to like a store, to manage a store, to open a store, to own a store, to prefer a store, to renovate a store, to return to a store, to run a store, to save at a store, to sell at a store, to shop at a store, to spend in a store, to store.

expressions

- *To store is no sore:* it is good to store for the future ▸ **il est bon de faire des provisions pour l'avenir.**

---

street ▸ rue

nouns address, alley, artery, avenue, boulevard, bus, car, car crash, circulation, city, concrete, construction, corner, dead end, detour, direction, distance, district, ditch, east, highway, hole, house, intersection, junction, lane, name, neighbour, neighbourhood, north, parade, park, path, pavement, pedestrian, people, place, plough truck, repair, road, route, sector, shortcut, side, sidewalk, sign, south, streetcar, street cleaner, strip, traffic, tree, truck, walk, way, west, zone.

adjectives beautiful, blocked, busy, charming, clean, closed, curved, dark, desolate, dirty, dry, empty, famous, far, green, historical, hot, icy, large, lit, little, main, major, narrow, near, new, paved, polluted, popular, principal, private, public, rural, snowy, straight, urban, wet, wide.

verbs SUBJECT: the street connects to, crosses, curves, finishes, follows, forks, divides, meets, splits, turns. OTHERS: to avoid a street, to clean a street, to cross a street, to drive down a street, to find a street, to fix a street, to get to a street, to name a street, to pave a street, to repair a street, to run down a street, to stroll down a street, to take a street, to turn on a street, to walk down a street.

expressions

- *Not to be in the same street as someone or something:* completely different ▸ **complètement différent.**
- *Right up my street:* familiar ▸ **familier.**
- *The man in the street:* the ordinary, typical, average man ▸ **personne ordinaire, typique de la population en général; monsieur ou madame Tout-le-monde; le commun des mortels, l'homme de la rue.**

- *To be on easy street:* to be in a comfortable financial situation ▸ **être fortuné ou fortunée; être à l'aise financièrement.**
- *To be on the street:* to be homeless ▸ **être sans domicile; être à la rue.**
- *To be streets ahead:* to be in advance ▸ **être en avance.**
- *To go on the streets:* to become a prostitute ▸ **se prostituer.**

---

supermarket ▸ supermarché

nouns aisle, bag, bread, business, can, cash, cashier, chain, change, coffee, company, counter, coupon, credit, deli, delivery, discount, eggs, employee, employer, errand, export, flyer, food, fruit, goods, grocer, groceries, hygiene products, import, inventory, line, milk, offer, paper, payment, place, plastic, produce, product, purchase, receipt, savings, section, service, staff, stock, store, supplier, supply, transaction, vegetables, wait.

adjectives big, busy, cheap, cold, crowded, expensive, friendly, hot, inexpensive, large, local, organic, natural, narrow, popular, small, stocked, vegetarian.

verbs SUBJECT: the supermarket closes, delivers, hires, opens. OTHERS: to buy a supermarket, to clean a supermarket, to enter a supermarket, to leave a supermarket, to manage a supermarket, to own a supermarket, to pick something up at a supermarket, to prefer a supermarket, to return to a supermarket, to shop at a supermarket, to wait in line at a supermarket, to walk through a supermarket.

---

train station ▸ gare

nouns agency, agent, arrival, beam, bell, boarding, booth, bridge, building, caboose, cargo, conductor, construction, crossing, delay, departure, destination, dock, engine, engineer, freight, goodbyes, goods, highjack, junction, light, line, load, luggage, merchandise, nail, pass, passenger, rail, railroad, restaurant, return, robber, robbery, schedule, shipment, shoeshine, signal, staff, steam engine, steel, stop, subway, support, ticket, time, track, train, transportation, trip, vacation, wagon, wait, whistle, window, wood, work.

adjectives big, busy, central, convenient, deserted, desolate, empty, famous, historical, located, modern, new, small, warm.

verbs OTHERS: to arrive at a train station, to board at a train station, to buy at a train station, to change trains at a train station, to clean a train station, to disembark at a train station, to embark at a train station, to get off at a train station, to go to a train station, to hurry to a train station, to leave from a train station, to meet at a train station, to pick someone up at a train station, to read in a train station, to sit at a train station, to sleep in a train station, to stop at a train station, to wait at a train station.

university ▶ **université**

nouns administration, admission, advisor, art, artist, article, assistant, association, attendance, average, award, board, books, building, bursary, campus, card, ceremony, chancellor, city, class, club, corporation, course, deadline, dean, degree, department, diploma, director, discipline, discussion, doctor, doctorate, education, employee, evaluation, exam, faculty, failure, geography, grade, graduate, history, homework, institution, instruction, knowledge, language, law, learning, lecture, librarian, library, literature, loan, mathematics, medicine, music, newspaper, office, organization, paper, pass, philosophy, professor, program, radio, reading, rector, registration, residence, resident, school, science, seminar, staff, student, studio, subject, theology, teacher, test, theatre, tuition, tutor, tutoring.

adjectives classical, clean, closed, confusing, crowded, dirty, friendly, educated, educational, expensive, free, funded, large, open, organized, popular, private, provincial, public, renowned, small.

verbs SUBJECT: the university awards, closes, elects, gives, honours, offers, opens, publishes, receives, teaches. OTHERS: to buy at a university, to choose a university, to go to university, to graduate from a university, to leave a university, to live at a university, to pay at a university, to read at a university, to register to a university, to study at a university, to transfer to a university, to visit a university.

expressions

- *A university town:* a town with many universities or a town that only has a university and industry or other business ▶ **ville comptant plusieurs universités.**

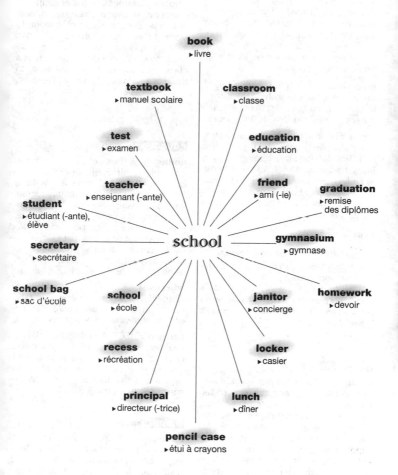

book
▸livre

textbook
▸manuel scolaire

classroom
▸classe

test
▸examen

education
▸éducation

teacher
▸enseignant (-ante)

friend
▸ami (-ie)

graduation
▸remise des diplômes

student
▸étudiant (-ante), élève

school

gymnasium
▸gymnase

secretary
▸secrétaire

school bag
▸sac d'école

school
▸école

janitor
▸concierge

homework
▸devoir

recess
▸récréation

locker
▸casier

principal
▸directeur (-trice)

lunch
▸dîner

pencil case
▸étui à crayons

book ▸ livre

nouns agenda, album, best seller, Bible, bibliography, bookstand, chapter, classic, conclusion, copyright, dedication, diary, edition, introduction, library, literature, log, manual, notebook, novel, pad, preface, production, publication, publisher, reader, reference, shelf, textbook, thriller, title, work.

adjectives big, colouring, English, French, geography, historical, history, interesting, mathematics, new, old, science, science-fiction, small, thick, worn.

verbs SUBJECT: a book captivates, entertains, fascinates, interests, thrills. OTHERS: to borrow a book, to buy a book, to choose a book, to edit a book, to find a book, to lose a book, to publish a book, to read a book, to reserve a book, to return a book, to translate a book, to write a book.

expressions

- *To hit the books:* to study ▸ **étudier.**
- *You can't judge (tell) a book by its cover:* you cannot judge someone or something by the way it looks ▸ **il ne faut pas juger les gens sur l'apparence; l'habit ne fait pas le moine; l'air ne fait pas la chanson.**

classroom ▸ classe

nouns art, auditorium, blackboard, broom, bulletin board, cafeteria, chalk, college, computer, conference, desk, garbage can, gymnasium, kindergarten, laboratory, language, music, open-area, paper, pencil, pencil case, portfolio, projector, radio, recycling bin, room, ruler, school, science, student, substitute, tape recorder, teacher, television, university, white board, workshop.

adjectives attractive, bare, big, dark, decorated, empty, full, large, modern, multicultural, old-fashioned, small, sunny, traditional, unique, welcoming.

verbs OTHERS to clean a classroom, to decorate a classroom, to discuss in a classroom, to dislike a classroom, to empty a classroom, to experiment in a classroom, to have a classroom, to learn in a classroom, to like a classroom, to listen in classroom, to paint a classroom, to play in a classroom, to reserve a classroom, to sit in a classroom, to study in a classroom, to talk in a classroom, to teach in a classroom, to visit a classroom, to want a classroom, to work in a classroom.

education ▸ éducation

nouns book, class, classroom, course, curriculum, direction, discipline, discourse, drill, exercise, exercise, explanation, friend, graduation, grammar, guidance, gymnasium, homework, initiation, instruction, instructor, language, lecture, lesson, monitor, pencil, persuasion, practice, preparation, principal, professor, qualification, school, schooling, secretary, student, study, task, teacher, teaching, test, textbook, training, tuition.

adjectives classical, college, collegiate, elementary, higher, liberal, military, moral, physical, primary, religious, secondary, technical, university, vocational.

verbs SUBJECT: An education allows, enables, helps, opens, structures. OTHERS: to get an education, to give an education, to provide an education, to question one's education, to receive an education, to want an education.

friend ▸ ami (-ie)

nouns acquaintance, affection, ally, associate, buddy, chamber, chum, classmate, companion, fellow, friendship, maid, mate, neighbour, pal, partner, playmate, roommate.

adjectives bosom, childhood, close, conscientious, constant, dependable, devoted, faithful, good, new, old, reliable, stable, trustworthy.

verbs SUBJECT: A friend assists, comforts, cooperates, helps, listens, respects, smiles, trusts, values. OTHERS: to be a friend, to be friends, to become friends, to cherish a friend, to find a friend, to have a friend, to help a friend, to hurt a friend, to like a friend, to lose a friend, to love a friend, to make friends, to smile to a friend, to steal a friend, to treasure a friend.

expressions..

- *Tell me who your friends are and I'll tell you what you are:* you behave or act like the people around you ▸ **on se comporte ou on agit comme les gens de son entourage ; qui s'assemble se ressemble.**

graduation ▸ remise des diplômes

nouns alumni, celebration, certification, commencement, degree, diploma, elementary school, grade, graduate, high school, honour, mark, school, university.

adjectives extraordinary, famous, great, important, memorable, spectacular, terrible.

verbs SUBJECT: A graduation excites, marks, pleases, reunites. OTHERS: to be a part of a graduation, to enjoy a graduation, to graduate, to have a graduation, to organize a graduation, to participate in a graduation, to take part in a graduation.

gymnasium ▸ gymnase

nouns athlete, athletics, ball, contest, education, exercise, fitness, game, gymnastics, play, recreation, school, sports, team.

adjectives big, huge, large, modern, small.

verbs OTHERS: to clean a gymnasium, to learn in a gymnasium, to jump in a gymnasium, to play in a gymnasium, to practice in a gymnasium, to reserve a gymnasium, to run in a gymnasium, to sit a gymnasium, to watch in a gymnasium.

homework ▸ devoir

nouns activity, afternoon, agenda, assignment, chore, desk, due date, evening, exercise, home, obligation, paper, pen, pencil, ruler, school, task.

adjectives complex, compulsory, difficult, easy, enjoyable, fun, interesting, optional, strenuous.

verbs SUBJECT: Homework annoys, enlightens, enriches, helps, provides. OTHERS: to accumulate homework, to assign homework, to complete homework, to copy homework, to correct homework, to do homework, to fail homework, to finish homework, to forget homework, to give homework, to hand in homework, to mail homework, to memorize homework, to pass homework, to post homework, to read homework, to remember homework, to review homework, to understand homework, to verify homework, to work on homework, to write homework.

janitor ▸ concierge

nouns caretaker, cleaner, guard, keeper, occupation, porter, superintendent, watchman.

adjectives careful, dependable, faithful, fast, good, meticulous, neat, nice, organized, quick, reliable, systematic, trusty.

verbs SUBJECT: A janitor brushes, brushes up, cleans, clears, clears off, dusts, polishes, rubs, scrapes, shines, sweeps, takes care of, tidies up, uses, washes, watches, wipes. OTHERS: to argue with a janitor, to ask the janitor, to call the janitor, to depend on a janitor, to dislike a janitor, to help a janitor, to hire a janitor, to like a janitor, to listen to a janitor, to talk to a janitor, to watch a janitor, to work with a janitor.

locker ▸ casier

nouns belonging, box, cabinet, closet, compartment, division, school, section.

adjectives big, functional, handy, huge, new, old, practical, secure, small, useful.

verbs SUBJECT: A locker contains, helps, holds. OTHERS: to acquire a locker, to ask for a locker, to clean a locker, to empty a locker, to get a locker, to give a locker, to have a locker, to keep a locker, to look for a locker, to obtain a locker, to open a locker, to organize a locker, to put in a locker, to remove from a locker, to take from a locker.

lunch ▸ dîner

nouns brunch, chicken, dessert, dinner, drink, egg, fish, fries, fruit, hamburger, hot dog, meal, meat, muffin, noodles, pasta, pizza, poultry, rice, salad, sandwich, snack, soup, spaghetti, supper, toast, vegetables.

adjectives appetising, delightful, extraordinary, good, healthy, nourishing, nutritious, tasty.

verbs SUBJECT: A lunch delights, pleases, satisfies, tastes. OTHERS: to ask for a lunch, to buy a lunch, to devour a lunch, to dislike a lunch, to eat a lunch, to enjoy a lunch, to get a lunch, to have lunch, to like a lunch, to make a lunch, to prepare a lunch, to savour a lunch, to spill a lunch, to swallow a lunch, to taste a lunch, to waste a lunch.

pencil case ▸ étui à crayons

nouns box, calculator, case, eraser, glue, marker, pen, pencil, pencil sharpener, protractor, ruler, scissors, stapler.

adjectives beautiful, big, colourful, handy, hard, huge, large, narrow, new, nice, old, small, ugly, useful, wide.

verbs SUBJECT: A pencil case contains, holds. OTHERS: to acquire a pencil case, to borrow a pencil case, to buy a pencil case, to carry a pencil case, to empty a pencil case, to get a pencil case, to give a pencil case, to have a pencil case, to lend a pencil case, to lose a pencil case,

to need a pencil case, to put in a pencil case, to remove from a pencil case, to take from a pencil case.

principal ▸ directeur (-trice)

nouns administrator, book, chair, chief, class, classroom, college, committee, council, curriculum, direction, discipline, discourse, education, graduation, guidance, head, institution, instructor, kindergarten, professor, pupil, school, school board, secretary, student, teacher, teaching, test, textbook, tuition, union, university.

adjectives demanding, fair, gentle, harsh, just, nice, organized, rigid, severe, stern, strict, unjust.

verbs SUBJECT: A principal administrates, applauds, compliments, conducts, congratulates, controls, disciplines, directs, governs, helps, leads, listens, manages, oversees, pilots, praises, prepares, punishes, rewards, rules, runs, speaks, studies, suspends, teaches, warns, watches, works. OTHERS: to agree with the principal, to answer to a principal, to become a principal, to disagree with the principal, to dislike the principal, to fear the principal, to hate the principal, to help the principal, to like the principal, to listen to the principal, to look for the principal, to love the principal, to obey a principal, to talk to a principal, to work with (for) a principal.

recess ▸ récréation

nouns activity, break, fun, freedom, friend, game, pause, recreation, sport, time.

adjectives amusing, brief, distracting, exciting, exhausting, fun, good, indoor, interesting, lengthy, long, noisy, outdoor, short, thrilling.

verbs SUBJECT: A recess amuses, distracts, relaxes, takes place. OTHERS: to cancel recess, to delay recess, to enjoy recess, to hate recess, to like recess, to play at recess, to postpone recess, to prolong a recess, to run at recess.

school ▶ école

nouns academy, art, board, book, boy, chair, class, classroom, college, committee, convent, council, course, curriculum, desk, dictionary, direction, discipline, discourse, drill, education, encyclopaedia, exercise, explanation, fellowship, friend, girl, government, grade, graduation, grammar, guidance, gymnasium, homework, initiation, institution, instructor, kid, kindergarten, language, lecture, lesson, pencil, principal, professor, pupil, qualification, reading, room, scholarship, schooling, secretary, seminar, student, studies, task, teacher, teaching, test, text, textbook, tuition, university.

adjectives big, boarding, classical, college, collegiate, elementary, foreign, high, higher, liberal, middle, military, moral, national, naval, nursery, physical, primary, private, religious, secondary, small, technical, university, vocational.

verbs SUBJECT: A school changes, educates, instructs, opens, recruits, teaches, trains. OTHERS: to attend (a) school, to be in a school, to build a school, to choose a school, to dislike (a) school, to drop out of school, to enjoy school, to enrol in a school, to go to school, to hate (a) school, to learn at school, to like (a) school, to love (a) school, to pick a school, to run at school, to run the school, to run to school, to select a school, to teach at school, to work at (in) a school.

expressions

* *School's out:* It is the beginning of the summer holidays ▶ **fin des classes ; début des vacances d'été.**

school bag ▶ sac d'école

nouns agenda, backpack, book, box, calculator, case, clothes, diary, eraser, glue, key, knapsack, lunch, manual, marker, newspaper, notebook, novel, pad,

paper, pen, pencil, pencil case, pencil sharpener, protractor, ruler, scissors, shoes, shorts, stapler, textbook, tissue, T-shirt.

adjectives big, colourful, handy, hard, heavy, huge, large, narrow, new, nice, old, small, strong, tough, useful, wide.

verbs SUBJECT: A school bag contains, holds. OTHERS: to acquire a school bag, to borrow a school bag, to buy a school bag, to carry a school bag, to empty a school bag, to get a school bag, to give a school bag, to have a school bag, to hold a school bag, to lend a school bag, to need a school bag, to put in a school bag, to remove from a school bag, to take from a school bag.

secretary ▶ secrétaire

nouns assistant, clerk, desk, employee, office, school, typist, worker.

adjectives careful, dependable, faithful, fast, good, meticulous, meticulous, neat, nice, organized, quick, reliable, systematic, trusty.

verbs SUBJECT: A secretary accompanies, analyses, assists, compares, copies, dislikes, enjoys, gives, helps, likes, listens, notes, prepares, prints, reads, reviews, signs, speaks, supports, takes, takes care of, talks, types, uses, watches, writes. OTHERS: to argue with a secretary, to ask the secretary, to call the secretary, to communicate with a secretary, to depend on a secretary, to dislike a secretary, to gossip with a secretary, to help a secretary, to hire a secretary, to like a secretary, to listen to a secretary, to talk to a secretary, to watch a secretary, to work with a secretary.

student ▶ étudiant (-ante), élève

nouns academy, apprentice, art, board, book, chair, class, classroom, college, committee, convent, council, course, curriculum, desk, dictionary, direction, discipline, discourse, drill, education, encyclopaedia, exercise, explanation, fellowship, friend, government, grade, graduation, grammar, guidance, gymnasium, homework, initiation, institution, instructor, kindergarten, language, lecture, lesson, pencil, principal, professor, pupil, qualification, reading, room, scholarship, school, schooling, secretary, seminar, studies, task, teacher, teaching, test, text, textbook, tuition, university.

adjectives careful, dependable, difficult, disruptive, excellent, faithful, fast, friendly, gentle, good, meticulous, neat, nice, organized, poor, quick, reliable, systematic.

verbs SUBJECT: A student accompanies, acts, analyses, argues, assists, compares, copies, dislikes, displays, enjoys, enrols, gives, helps, likes, listens, notes, performs, plays, pleases, prepares, presents, prints, reads, review, runs, shows, signs, signs up for, skims, speaks, studies, supports, takes, takes care of, talks, types, understands, uses, watches, writes. OTHERS: to argue with a student, to ask the student, to be a student, to call the student, to communicate with a student, to depend on a student, to dislike a student, to fight with a student, to gossip with a student, to help a student, to hire a student, to like a student, to listen to a student, to play with a student, to talk to a student, to teach a student, to watch a student, to work with a student.

---

teacher ▸ enseignant (-ante)

nouns academy, apprentice, art, board, book, boy, chair, class, classroom, coach, college, committee, convent, council, course, curriculum, desk, dictionary, direction, discipline, discourse, drill, education, educator, exercise, explanation, fellowship, friend, girl, government, grade, graduation, grammar, guidance, gymnasium, homework, initiation, institution, instructor, kindergarten, language, lecture, lesson, mentor, pencil, principal, professor, pupil, qualification, reading, room, scholarship, school,

schooling, secretary, seminar, student, studies, task, teaching, test, text, textbook, tuition, tutor, university.

adjectives careful, demanding, dependable, difficult, disruptive, excellent, fair, faithful, fast, gentle, good, harsh, just, meticulous, neat, nice, organized, poor, quick, reliable, rigid, severe, stern, strict, systematic, trusty, unjust.

verbs SUBJECT: A teacher administrates, applauds, compliments, conducts, congratulates, controls, directs, disciplines, dislikes, educates, enlightens, governs, guides, hates, helps, informs, instructs, leads, likes, listens, loves, manages, oversees, pilots, praises, prepares, punishes, rewards, rules, runs, studies, suspends, teaches, trains, tutors, warns, watches, works. OTHERS: to agree with the teacher, to answer to a teacher, to become a teacher, to cooperate with a teacher, to disagree with the teacher, to dislike the teacher, to fear the teacher, to hate the teacher, to help the teacher, to learn from a teacher, to like the teacher, to listen to the teacher, to look for the teacher, to love the teacher, to obey a teacher, to talk to a teacher, to teach with a teacher, to work with (for) a teacher.

---

test ▸ examen

nouns anxiety, essay, exam, examination, grade, homework, mark, paper, query, quiz, report, review, school, stress, teacher, university.

adjectives boring, brief, difficult, easy, elementary, final, good, hard, instructive, interesting, lengthy, long, short, simple, stressful, tedious.

verbs SUBJECT: A test evaluates, grades, measures, prepares, qualifies, ranks, selects, stresses. OTHERS: to avoid a test, to blow a test, to cheat in a test, to copy a test, to correct a test, to dislike a test, to distribute a test, to enjoy a test, to fail a test, to flop a test, to flunk a test, to give a test, to hate a test, to like a test, to make a test, to mark a test, to miss a test, to obtain a test, to pass a test, to photocopy a test, to prepare for a test, to skip a test, to study for a test, to take a test, to write a test.

textbook ▸ **manuel scolaire**

nouns bibliography, book, chapter, classic, conclusion, copyright, edition, introduction, library, literature, manual, notebook, novel, preface, publication, publisher, reader, reference, shelf, text, title, work.

adjectives big, clear, complete, difficult, easy, English, French, geography, helpful, history, interesting, mathematics, new, old, science, small, thick, worn.

verbs SUBJECT: a textbook captivates, entertains, fascinates, helps, interests, teaches, thrills. OTHERS: to borrow a textbook, to buy a textbook, to choose a textbook, to edit a textbook, to find a textbook, to lose a textbook, to publish atextbook, to read a textbook, to reserve a textbook, to return a textbook, to study with a textbook, to translate a textbook, to write a textbook.

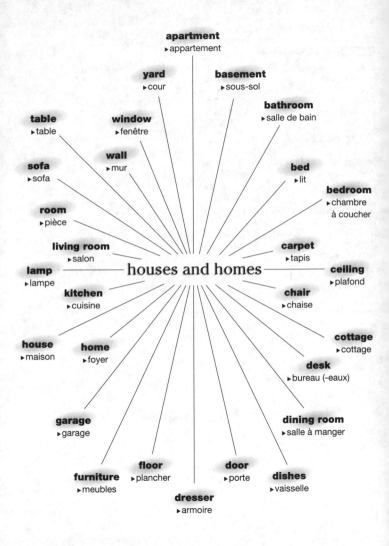

apartment
▸appartement

yard
▸cour

basement
▸sous-sol

bathroom
▸salle de bain

table
▸table

window
▸fenêtre

wall
▸mur

bed
▸lit

bedroom
▸chambre
à coucher

sofa
▸sofa

room
▸pièce

living room
▸salon

carpet
▸tapis

houses and homes

ceiling
▸plafond

lamp
▸lampe

chair
▸chaise

kitchen
▸cuisine

cottage
▸cottage

house
▸maison

home
▸foyer

desk
▸bureau (-eaux)

garage
▸garage

dining room
▸salle à manger

furniture
▸meubles

floor
▸plancher

door
▸porte

dishes
▸vaisselle

dresser
▸armoire

apartment ▸ appartement

nouns antenna, attic, balcony, basement, bathroom, building, bungalow, carpet, ceiling, chimney, closet, condominium, cottage, curtains, door, doorbell, driveway, fence, fireplace, flat, floor, garage, gate, habitat, home, house, household, kitchen, laundry room, living room, mailbox, mansion, nursery, parking, porch, quarters, residence, roof, room, shades, shutters, sidewalk, staircase, stairs, steps, street, wall, window.

adjectives beautiful, big, bright, cold, cosy, dark, expensive, huge, luxurious, nice, noisy, quiet, small, superb, tremendous.

verbs SUBJECT: An apartment contains, holds. OTHERS: to buy an apartment, to clean an apartment, to clear an apartment, to decorate an apartment, to dislike an apartment, to dust an apartment, to find an apartment, to get an apartment, to hate an apartment, to have an apartment, to inherit an apartment, to lend an apartment, to like an apartment, to look for an apartment, to love an apartment, to move into an apartment, to move out of an apartment, to paint an apartment, to possess an apartment, to purchase an apartment, to renovate an apartment, to rent an apartment, to sell an apartment, to watch an apartment.

basement ▸ sous-sol

nouns bathroom, boiler, carpet, ceiling, chimney, closet, colourful, curtains, door, driveway, dryer, electric panel, fireplace, floor, fuel tank, furnace, garage, heater (hot water), home, house, iron, ironing board, laundry room, living room, mop, oil tank, outlet, parking, plug, room, shades, shutters, sidewalk, staircase, stairs, steps, tidy, untidy, vacuum cleaner, wall, washer, washing machine, window.

adjectives beautiful, big, bright, clean, cold, cosy, dark, dirty, dusty, huge, luxurious, modern, nice, quiet, small, superb, tremendous.

verbs OTHERS: to clean a basement, to decorate a basement, to design a basement, to dislike a basement, to dust a basement, to finish a basement, to get a basement, to hate a basement, to have a basement, to insulate a basement, to like a basement, to live in a basement, to love the basement, to paint a basement, to play in a basement, to renovate a basement, to rent a basement, to sleep in the basement, to work in (on) a basement.

bathroom ▸ salle de bain

nouns bath mat, bathtub, cabinet (medicine cabinet), ceiling, curtain, drain, fan, faucet, floor, glass, light, mirror, rack, scale, shower, sink, soap, soap dish, sponge, stopper, tile, toilet, toilet paper (tissue), toothbrush, toothpaste, towel, wall, wallpaper, washcloth.

adjectives beautiful, big, bright, clean, cold, colourful, cosy, dark, dirty, huge, luxurious, modern, nice, quiet, small, superb, tidy, tremendous, untidy.

verbs OTHERS: to clean a bathroom, to decorate a bathroom, to design a bathroom, to dislike a bathroom, to dust a bathroom, to finish a bathroom, to get a bathroom, to hate a bathroom, to have a bathroom, to insulate a bathroom, to like a bathroom, to live in a bathroom, to love a bathroom, to paint a bathroom, to renovate a bathroom, to work on a bathroom.

bed ▸ lit

nouns blanket, box spring, bunk, chesterfield, couch, lamp, mattress, night, pyjamas, pillow, pillowcase, quilt, sheet, sleep, snore, sofa, table.

adjectives beautiful, big, clean, colourful, comfortable, cosy, dirty, huge, large, narrow, new, nice, old, small, tidy, ugly, uncomfortable, untidy, useful, wide.

verbs OTHERS: to borrow a bed, to break a bed, to buy a bed, to choose a bed, to clean a bed, to dislike a bed, to doze in a bed, to dust a bed, to find a bed, to get a bed, to get in a bed, to hate a bed, to have a bed, to jump on a bed, to lie down in (on) a bed, to lift a bed, to like a bed, to look for a bed, to love a bed, to make one's bed, to move a bed, to nap in a bed, to place a bed, to play in a bed, to possess a bed, to purchase a bed, to relax in a bed, to remove a bed, to rest in a bed, to sell a bed, to sit on a bed, to sleep in a bed, to snooze in a bed, to snore in a bed, to stay in bed, to talk in a bed.

expressions...

- *Someone's made his/her bed – now let her/him lie in it:* after creating problems, one must deal them ▸ **il faut composer avec les problèmes dont on est à l'origine ; comme on fait son lit, on se couche ; quand le vin est tiré, il faut le boire.**

- *To be bed-ridden:* to be very ill or incapacitated ▸ **être très malade, frappé ou frappée d'incapacité ; être cloué ou clouée au lit.**

bedroom ▸ **chambre à coucher**

nouns alarm clock, bed, blanket, book, box spring, bunk, carpet, ceiling, chesterfield, closet, comb, couch, curtain, desk, door, drawer, dresser, floor, frame, hairbrush, lamp, light switch, mattress, pyjamas, picture, pillow, pillowcase, quilt, sheet, shelf, sofa, table, wall, window.

adjectives beautiful, big, bright, clean, cold, colourful, cosy, dark, dirty, huge, luxurious, modern, nice, quiet, small, superb, tidy, tremendous, untidy.

verbs OTHERS: to choose a bedroom, to clean a bedroom, to decorate a bedroom, to dislike a bedroom, to doze in a bedroom, to dust a bedroom, to find a bedroom, to finish a bedroom, to get a bedroom, to hate a bedroom, to have a bedroom, to insulate a bedroom, to lie down in a bedroom, to lift a bedroom, to

like a bedroom, to love a bedroom, to nap in a bedroom, to paint a bedroom, to play in a bedroom, to relax in a bedroom, to renovate a bedroom, to rest in a bedroom, to sleep in a bedroom, to study in one's bedroom, to talk in a bedroom, to work in a bedroom.

carpet ▸ **tapis**

nouns door, dust, dust, entrance, floor, living room, mat, plastic, rug, vacuum cleaner, wool.

adjectives beautiful, big, colourful, comfortable, cosy, huge, indoor, large, narrow, new, nice, old, outdoor, shaggy, small, thick, ugly, uncomfortable, useful, wide.

verbs SUBJECT: a carpet absorbs, brightens, decorates. OTHERS to borrow a carpet, to buy a carpet, to choose a carpet, to clean a carpet, to dislike a carpet, to dust a carpet, to find a carpet, to fly on a carpet, to get a carpet, to give a carpet, to hate a carpet, to have a carpet, to lie down on a carpet, to lift a carpet, to like a carpet, to look for a carpet, to love a carpet, to move a carpet, to place a carpet, to purchase a carpet, to remove a carpet, to sell a carpet, to sit on a carpet, to sleep on a carpet, to stain a carpet, to vacuum a carpet.

ceiling ▸ **plafond**

nouns dome, lid, light, mirror, roof, sky, wall.

adjectives colourful, frightening, high, low, scary.

verbs SUBJECT: A ceiling covers, preserves, protects, saves. OTHERS: to build a ceiling, to decorate a ceiling, to dislike a ceiling, to hate a ceiling, to have a ceiling, to like a ceiling, to love a ceiling, to paint a ceiling, to reinforce a ceiling, to renovate a ceiling, to strengthen a ceiling.

chair ▸ chaise

nouns arm, armchair, bench, chester-field, couch, cushion, fabric, furniture, leg, living room, seat, sofa, stool.

adjectives beautiful, big, colourful, comfortable, cosy, huge, large, narrow, new, nice, old, small, ugly, uncomfortable, useful, wide.

verbs SUBJECT: A chair brightens, decorates, sits. OTHERS to borrow a chair, to break a chair, to buy a chair, to choose a chair, to clean a chair, to design a chair, to dislike a chair, to dust a chair, to find a chair, to get a chair, to give a chair, to hate a chair, to have a chair, to lift a chair, to like a chair, to look for a chair, to love a chair, to make a chair, to move a chair, to place a chair, to possess a chair, to purchase a chair, to remove a chair, to see a chair, to sell a chair, to sit on a chair.

cottage ▸ cottage

nouns cabin, country home, decoration, dwelling, escape, habitat, hideaway, hut, inn, isolation, lake, lodging, maintenance, mountain, nature, outdoors, residence, retreat, shed, simplicity, summer house, villa.

adjectives abandoned, calm, cosy, decorated, extravagant, humble, isolated, magnificent, natural, painted, renovated, quiet, run-down, rustic, shady, simple, sunny, tranquil, well-located.

verbs SUBJECT: The cottage looks great, needs repairs, smells great. OTHERS: to abandon a cottage, to build a cottage, to buy a cottage, to design a cottage, to go to the cottage, to live at the cottage, to paint the cottage, to renovate the cottage, to repair the cottage, to rest at the cottage, to relax at the cottage.

expressions

* *Cottage economy:* a slow economy ▸ **économie qui fonctionne au ralenti.**

desk ▸ bureau (-eaux)

nouns binder, book, case, calendar, chair, compartments, desktop computer, diskette, document, drawers, eraser, fax machine, file, frame, furniture, lamp, lectern, marker, office, pencil, photocopy machine, printer, reader, reading desk, scanner, school, screen, secretary, shelves, student, supplies, stapler, table, telephone, work, writer.

adjectives antique, big, broken, computer, executive, hand-made, folding, office, school, small, sturdy, wooden, wobbling.

verbs OBJECTS: to draw at a desk, to lie on a desk, to make a desk, to move a desk, to pull a desk, to read at a desk, to sit at a desk, to stand on a desk, to work at a desk, to write at a desk.

expressions

* *To be glued to one's desk:* to be at one's desk for a long period of time ▸ **être à son bureau pendant une longue période.**

dining room ▸ salle à manger

nouns ambience, banquet, buffet, candles, chairs, cups, cutlery, dessert, dishes, dinner, feast, fruit, meals, place mat, plates, seats, setting, silverware, supper, sweets, table, tablecloth.

adjectives clean, communal, crowded, decorated, dirty, empty, fancy, large, luxurious, narrow, nice, round, small, spacious.

verbs SUBJECT: the dining room looks lovely, the dining room table sits eight, OTHERS: to clean the dining room, to dine in the dining room, to eat in the dining room, to sit at the dining room table, to stand in the dining room, to talk in the dining room, to wait in the dining room.

dishes ► vaisselle

nouns basket, bowl, bottle, bottle-opener, burner, bread basket, breakfast, can-opener, chopping board, coffee pot, container, cup, cutlery, dessert, dinner, dishwasher, dish rack, food, fork, frying pan, glass, grinder, kettle, knife, meal, meat cleaver, metal, mason jars, mug, pan, pepper shaker, plastic containers, platter, plate, porcelain, pot, salt shaker, saucer, serving spoon, silverware, sink, skillet, skewer, snack, spatula, spices, spice rack, spoon, steamer, strainer, sugar bowl, supper, table, tea pot, tongs, vessel, wine glass.

adjectives aluminium, antique, breakable, broken, clean, concave, dirty, disposable, dry, handmade, metal, new, plastic, spotless, stained, unbreakable, wet.

verbs SUBJECT: the dishes break, cost money, don't clean themselves, were made. OTHERS: to break the dishes, to buy dishes, to clean the dishes, to do the dishes, to dry the dishes, to put away the dishes, to rinse the dishes, to scrub the dishes, to sell dishes, to stack the dishes, to throw the dishes, to wash the dishes.

expressions

- *It is his dish:* it is something he really likes ► **activité qu'il ou elle aime vraiment.**
- *To be a dish:* to be an attractive person ► **personne attirante.**

door ► porte

nouns admission, admittance, aluminium, barrier, bolt, chain, door step, doorway, entrance, exit, frame, greetings, handle, hinges, key, keyhole, knob, lock, mat, opening, peephole, plate, portal, screen, security, way, window.

adjectives open, back, bolted, closed, crooked, front, hinged, locked, metal, revolving, secure, sliding, sturdy, swinging, wooden.

verbs SUBJECT: the door is locked. OTHERS: to beat on the door, to break down the door, to close the door, to install a door, to keep the door shut, to knock at the door, to lock the door, to open the door, to push the door, to pull the door, to put in a door, to slam the door, to swing the door.

expressions

- *As dead as a doornail:* really dead ► **vraiment mort ou morte ; raide mort ou morte.**
- *To be "at death's door":* to be near death ► **être mourant ou mourante.**
- *To lay misfortune at one's door:* to blame for ► **blâmer.**
- *He lives next door:* at the next house ► **dans la maison d'à côté ; à côté.**
- *It's no use locking the stable door after the horse has bolted:* what you are doing is useless because it is too late ► **il est inutile de faire ce geste car il est trop tard.**
- *To show someone the door:* to tell that person to leave ► **dire à quelqu'un de partir ; lui montrer la porte.**

dresser ► armoire

nouns antique, bedroom, bench, carpenter, carpentry, chair, chest, clothes, compartment, cupboard, dining room, dishes, door, drawer, furniture, glasses, kitchen, living room, mirror, order, room, set, shelves, space, storage, table, tools, utensils, wood, woodwork, woodworking.

adjectives antique, clean, deep, empty, full, practical, impractical, locked, orderly, packed, ruined, simple, small, spacious, stained, stored, tidy, tiny, unlocked, useful, varnished, wooden.

verbs SUBJECT: the dresser blocks, displays, fills, holds, wobbles. OTHERS: to assemble a dresser, to buy a dresser, to clean a dresser, to damage a dresser, to move a dresser, to obtain a dresser, to purchase a dresser, to sand down a dresser, to sell a dresser, to varnish a dresser, to work on a dresser.

floor ▶ plancher

nouns apartment, area, basement, board, bridge, building, carpenter, carpentry, carpet, cement, ceramic, cleaning, dance, department, division, door, elevation, elevator, escalator, exit, factory, flooring, forest, frame, ground floor, hall, hammer, home, house, level, nail, office, partition, plank, platform, room, saw, sea, skyscraper, space, stairs, story, structure, surface, tools, wall, wax, wood.

adjectives bottom, carpeted, cold, crooked, dirty, dry, even, flat, levelled, main, nailed, oak, open, pine, slippery, smooth, top, wet, waxed.

verbs OTHERS: to clean a floor, to dance on a floor, to dirty a floor, to nail a floor, to put in a floor, to repair a floor, to sand a floor, to sit on a floor, to sleep on a floor, to slip on a floor, to stand on a floor, to sweep a floor, to wax a floor.

expressions

- *To clean (wipe) the floor with someone:* to defeat someone by many points ▶ **vaincre de façon indéniable.**

- *To floor someone:* to defeat someone ▶ **vaincre ; envoyer quelqu'un au tapis.**

- *To hold the floor:* to be the dominant person at a meeting or party because one talks a great deal ▶ **prendre toute la place au cours d'une réunion ou d'une réception en parlant beaucoup ; tenir le crachoir.**

- *To take the floor:* to start talking ▶ **commencer à parler ; prendre la parole.**

furniture ▶ meubles

nouns antique, apartment, armchair, article, bed, bedroom, bench, buffet, building, business, cabinet, carpenter, carpentry, case, cedar, chair, chest, closet, cloth, coffee table, coat, colour, condition, content, couch, cupboards, dishes, door, decoration, desk, drawer, dresser, dust, equipment, era, fabric, factory, file cabinet, finish, floor, garden,

glass, hardware, history, home, house, industry, kitchen, lacquer, leather, leg, library, lock, machine, mahogany, maintenance, metal, oak, object, office, ornament, outfit, oven, parlour, piece, pine, place, plastic, polish, refrigerator, repair, rocking chair, room, sale, sandpaper, scratch, seat, shelf, sofa, space, stain, stand, stool, storage, storing, stove, study, stuffing, supplies, table, trimming, trunk, utensils, varnish, warehouse, window, wood, woodworking, work.

adjectives antique, cedar, cheap, classic, clean, decorated, dusted, dusty, empty, expensive, full, furnished, handmade, historical, inexpensive, lacquered, lawn, luxurious, mahogany, metal, movable, new, oak, old, ornamental, ornamented, period, pine, plastic, polished, rough, second-hand, shining, smooth, stained, stuffed, used, useful, varnished.

verbs OTHERS: to build furniture, to buy furniture, to change furniture, to clean the furniture, to dust the furniture, to furnish, to give away furniture, to keep things in the furniture, to lacquer furniture, to move furniture, to need furniture, to polish furniture, to sell furniture, to shine furniture, to sleep on the furniture, to throw out furniture.

garage ▶ garage

nouns accident, automobile, bicycle, building, business, car, car park, city, damage, dock, door, entrance, garbage, gas, home, house, housing, lot, maintenance, mechanic, motorcycle, oil, parking, place, protection, rent, repair, safety, sale, shed, shelter, storage, storing, tire, truck, tune-up, van, vehicle, way, work.

adjectives affordable, big, closed, dirty, double, dusty, equipped, expensive, general, greasy, loud, mechanical, modern, open, popular, private, rusted, shared, single, small, stinking, trusted, underground.

verbs SUBJECT: the garage, charges, closes, opens, repairs. OTHERS: to close a garage, to drive in a garage, to drop off at a garage, to leave one's car in a garage, to lock a garage, to open a garage, to park in a garage, to put in a garage, to store in a garage.

expressions

- *A garage band:* an amateur music group ► **groupe musical amateur.**
- *A garage sale:* a street sale ► **vente de débarras.**

home ► **foyer**

nouns affairs, ancestor, animal, asylum, birthplace, cabin, core, cottage, country, decoration, dining room, door, dwelling, estate, family, farm, floor, furniture, heart, home base, homeland, home plate, homer, home run, house, household, interior, land, life, living room, lodge, management, nation, nationality, neighbour, neighbourhood, office, origin, people, pet, place, refuge, residence, resident, rest, shelter, studio, suburb, team, village.

adjectives abroad, ancestral, domestic, empty, historical, homeless, home-made, homesick, indigenous, native, private, public, safe, vacant.

verbs OTHERS: to carry home, to come home, to feel at home, to get home, to go home, to invite someone home, to leave home, to make oneself at home, to put in a home, to return home, to run home, to sell a home, to send to a home, to sleep at home, to stay home, to take a bus home.

expressions

- *A home away from home:* a place where one feels as relaxed as when one is at home ► **lieu où l'on se sent comme chez soi.**
- *A home truth:* a plain statement, usually unpleasant but true ► **déclaration simple, habituellement désagréable mais vraie ; pure vérité.**
- *Home and dry:* having succeeded in what one wanted to do ► **avoir réussi ce que l'on voulait faire.**

- *Home is where the heart is:* home is where the love is ► **l'amour se trouve chez soi, parmi les siens.**
- *Home, Jeeves, and don't spare the horses:* go home quickly. This expression is now commonly used as a joke ► **rentrer rapidement à la maison (cette expression est couramment utilisée pour plaisanter).**
- *Nothing to write home about:* not very exciting ► **pas très intéressant.**
- *To bring something home to someone:* to prove something to someone in a way which makes it impossible not to believe it ► **faire la preuve irréfutable d'un fait.**
- *To do one's homework:* to prepare for a meeting by making sure one knows all the facts ► **se préparer à une réunion en s'assurant de bien connaître tous les faits.**
- *To drive something home:* to try to make something completely understood or accepted ► **tenter de faire comprendre ou de faire accepter quelque chose.**
- *To eat one out of house and home:* to eat to the extent of losing all of one's money ► **manger jusqu'à se ruiner ou ruiner quelqu'un d'autre.**
- *To feel at home:* to feel relaxed, as one does in one's own home ► **se sentir à l'aise, comme chez soi.**
- *To make oneself at home:* to make oneself as comfortable as one would at home ► **se mettre à l'aise, prendre ses aises ; faire comme chez soi.**

house ► **maison**

nouns acre, address, apartment, architect, architecture, area, asylum, attic, backyard, basement, beam, bedroom, builder, building, bungalow, castle, ceiling, commons, construction, corridor, cottage, den, dining room, door, dweller, dwelling, entrance, estate, exit, floor, foundation, frame, front, furniture, garage, garden, ground floor, hall, hallway, high-rise, home, housekeeping, household, hut, igloo, kitchen, land, lawn, level, library, living room, lodge, long house, mansion, mason, masonry, mortgage, neighbour, neighbourhood, owner, payment, people, pool, porch, project, renovation, rent, residence, resident, roof, room, shed, shelter, skyscraper, stairs, story, street, structure, study, teepee, temple, tent, tower, trailer, tree, way, wigwam, yard, zone.

adjectives abandoned, architectural, built, clean, cold, comfortable, cosy, crowded, cute, dark, deserted, dirty, domestic, empty, fancy, freezing, full, haunted, hidden, huge, isolated, little, located, long, luxurious, mobile, narrow, renovated, rental, residential, small, split, warm, wide.

verbs SUBJECT: the house burns, cools down, warms up. OTHERS: to abandon a house, to acquire a house, to build a house, to buy a house, to choose a house, to decorate a house, to design a house, to draw a house, to inherit a house, to insulate a house, to keep house, to leave a house, to like a house, to live in a house, to lose a house, to love a house, to make plans for a house, to manage a house, to move from a house, to organize a house, to own a house, to pay for a house, to purchase a house, to renovate a house, to rent a house, to sell a house.

expressions

- *Like a house on fire:* rapidly ► **très rapidement.**
- *The house of God:* a church ► **une église.**
- *The White House:* The US president's residence ► **la résidence du président des États-Unis; la Maison-Blanche.**
- *To be as big as a house:* to be very big ► **être très gros ou grosse.**
- *To be up on the house roof:* to be excited ► **être agité ou agitée; être excité ou excitée comme une puce.**

kitchen ► **cuisine**

nouns appliance, area, board, bowl, breakfast, cabinet, can, chair, cheese, chef, clock, coffee machine, cook, cooker, cooking, counter, cover, cup, cupboards, cutlery, dessert, dinner, dishes, dishwasher, drawer, floor, food, fork, freezer, fruit, frying pan, fryer, furniture, glass, jar, kettle, knife, lunch, meal, meat, oven, pan, pasta, pastry, place, plate, pot, recipe, recipe book, refrigerator, restaurant, sauce, saucer, shelf, silverware, sink, skillet, soap, soup, spatula, spices, spoon, steamer, stove, supper, sweets, table, toaster, tray, work, utensils, vegetables.

adjectives big, clean, closed, communal, decorated, dirty, hot, large, long, narrow, orderly, organized, renovated, shining, simple, small, spacious, spotless, stored, traditional, warm, wide, wooden.

verbs SUBJECT: the kitchen closes, opens, smells OTHERS: to bake in a kitchen, to boil in a kitchen, to burn in a kitchen, to clean a kitchen, to cook in a kitchen, to decorate a kitchen, to extend a kitchen, to fry in a kitchen, to make in a kitchen, to renovate a kitchen, to steam in a kitchen, to taste in a kitchen, to wash in a kitchen, to whip in a kitchen.

expressions

- *To take everything but the kitchen sink:* to take a lot of luggage ► **emporter beaucoup de bagages.**

lamp ► **lampe**

nouns bulb, camping, circuit, combustion, desk, electricity, flame, glass, glow, grow lamp, hall, heat, house, illumination, kitchen, lampshade, lantern, light, night, oil, plug, post, reading, room, safety, street, study, sun, torch, wick.

adjectives antique, artificial, bright, dim, electrical, hazardous, inflammable, lit, off, oil, on, plugged, portable, safe, wired.

verbs SUBJECT: glows, illuminates, lights, shines. OTHERS: to adjust a lamp, to buy a lamp, to change a lamp, to dim a lamp, to light a lamp, to lower a lamp, to raise a lamp, to replace a lamp, to throw out a lamp, to turn off a lamp, to turn on a lamp.

living room ▸ salon

nouns armchair, buffet, chair, chesterfield, coffee table, corridor, couch, dining room, door, family, hall, hallway, home, house, kitchen, lamp, library, nap, party, people, pool, reception, recliner, rest, reunion, room, seat, shelves, sofa, table, tea.

adjectives big, clean, closed off, cold, cosy, crowded, decorated, dirty, divided, heated, hot, huge, joined, modern, shared, small, snug, spacious, warm.

verbs OTHERS: to chat in a living room, to discuss in a living room, to eat in a living room, to host in a living room, to invite in a living room, to meet in a living room, to play cards in a living room, to talk in a living room, to sit in a living room, to sleep in a living room, to walk into a living room.

room ▸ pièce

nouns apartment, attic, bathroom, backroom, ballroom, basement, bedroom, boards, chair, classroom, closet, conference room, corridor, dark room, den, desk, dining room, dresser, emergency room, floor, furniture, hall, hallway, house, kitchen, library, living room, office, operating room, parlour, partition, place, plank, rest room, shelf, sofa, space, storage room, studio, study, table, waiting room, washroom, window, work.

adjectives aired, big, bright, communal, crowded, decorated, deep, elegant, empty, great, huge, little, luxurious, quiet, small, smoky, snug, tiny.

verbs SUBJECT: the room divides, opens, separates. OTHERS: to dance around in a room, to decorate a room, to enliven a room, to lie in a room, to paint a room, to read in a room, to renovate a room, to run in a room, to sit in a room, to sleep in a room, to talk in a room, to vacuum a room, to work in a room.

expressions

- *Your room is better than your company:* people prefer it when you are not there ▸ **les gens préfèrent que vous n'y soyez pas.**
- *Not enough room to swing a cat:* very little room ▸ **très peu d'espace.**

sofa ▸ sofa

nouns arm, back, bed, bench, chair, comfort, couch, cushion, fabric, furniture, house, leather, living room, pillow, recliner, rest, seat, sleep, stuffing, wood.

adjectives antique, comfortable, dusty, heavy, humid, long, mobile, modern, new, old, rigid, ripped, second-hand, soft, stuffed, wet, worn out.

verbs OTHERS: to buy a sofa, to fall asleep on a sofa, to lie on a sofa, to move a sofa, to read on a sofa, to relax on a sofa, to replace a sofa, to rest on a sofa, to sleep on a sofa, to stretch out on a sofa, to throw out a sofa.

table ▸ table

nouns basket, bench, bowl, bread, breakfast, buffet, cards, chair, cook, cooking, courses, cup, desk, dessert, dining room, dinner, dishes, drawer, drink, food, fork, furniture, glasses, kitchen, knife, living room, lunch, meal, place, plate, restaurant, room, service, setting, spoon, supper, surface, table cloth, table mat, cutlery, utensils, waiter, waitress.

adjectives bedside, cedar, cheap, clean, flat, folding, full, heavy, indoor, mahogany, metal, oak, outdoor, oval, pine, plastic, polished, round, square, smooth, thick, thin, wooden.

verbs OTHERS: to buy a table, to clean a table, to come to a table, to discuss around a table, to draw at a table, to lay out on a table, to leave a table, to make a table, to move a table, to place under a table, to polish a table, to put on a table, to serve on a table, to sit at a table, to stand on a table, to work at a table.

expressions

- *Table d'hôte:* regular meal served at a restaurant ▸ **repas à prix fixe au restaurant; table d'hôte.**
- *Table of Pythagoras:* the multiplication table ▸ **table de multiplication.**
- *Table mountain:* flat topped mountain ▸ **montagne au sommet plat.**
- *Table talk:* small talk ▸ **propos légers; papotage.**
- *To be paid under the table:* to be paid illegally ▸ **être rémunéré ou rémunérée illégalement; travailler au noir.**
- *To reverse the tables:* to turn things around ▸ **renverser les rôles.**
- *The knights of the round table:* King Arthur's knights ▸ **les chevaliers du roi Arthur; les chevaliers de la Table ronde.**

wall ▸ mur

nouns brick, building, carpenter, carpentry, cave, defence, door, dry wall, fence, fort, fortress, foundation, frame, height, house, labyrinth, mason, masonry, material, maze, mountain, mural, plaster, prison, protection, room, security, stone, structure, support, vertical, window.

adjectives covered, crooked, decorated, hidden, high, insulated, painted, plastered, short, slanted, small, soundproof, straight, strong, thick, thin.

verbs SUBJECT: the wall blocks, crumbles, obstructs, protects, rises, separates. OTHERS: to build a wall, to climb a wall, to construct a wall, to decorate a wall, to demolish a wall, to destroy a wall, to draw on a wall, to erect a wall, to insulate a wall, to jump over a wall, to lean on a wall, to paint a wall, to take down a wall.

expressions

- *I would like to be a fly on the wall.* I would like to be present without being seen ▸ **j'aimerais pouvoir être présent ou présente sans être vu ou vue; j'aimerais être une petite souris.**
- *The writing on the wall:* something that shows that a disaster is about to happen ▸ **fait indiquant qu'un malheur va bientôt frapper; signe avant-coureur.**
- *To drive (send) someone up the wall:* to annoy someone ▸ **ennuyer quelqu'un; le rendre fou ou folle.**
- *To go to the wall:* to be put out of the way, aside ▸ **être mis ou mise de côté, être tenu ou tenue à l'écart.**
- *To have one's back to the wall:* to be in a difficult situation ▸ **se retrouver dans une situation difficile; être acculé ou acculée au mur.**
- *Wall Street:* the financial centre of the United States of America ▸ **le centre financier des États-Unis d'Amérique.**
- *Walls have ears:* it is important to be discrete as what one says could be overheard even if it seems impossible ▸ **il faut être discret ou discrète, car même si cela semble impossible, on peut être entendu ou entendue; les murs ont des oreilles.**

window ▸ fenêtre

nouns access, air, bar, bay, building, blinds, cover, curtains, entry, envelope, frame, glass, hinges, hole, house, installation, lock, moulding, opening, room, sash, screen, shop, shutter, sill, store, wall, washer, washing, windowpane, wood.

adjectives barred, big, blocked, boarded up, broken, clean, closed, covered, cracked, dirty, fitted, fragile, hinged, large, long, open, round, shut, sliding, small, spotless, transparent, washed.

verbs SUBJECT: the window closes, looks unto, opens, slides. OTHERS: to board a window, to clean a window, to close a window, to lock a window, to enter by a window, to exit by a window, to open a window, to put in a window, to shut a window, to slide open a window, to wash a window, to wipe a window.

expressions..

- *To display all of one's goods in the window:* to show everything one owns ► **montrer tout ce qui nous appartient.**
- *Window-dressing:* the giving to something of an appearance which makes it seem better ► **donner meilleure apparence à quelque chose; maquiller quelque chose.**
- *Window-shopping:* to look at articles without buying ► **examiner des articles sans les acheter; faire du lèche-vitrine.**

yard ► **cour**

nouns activities, amusement, animal, area, backyard, barnyard, business, cattle, courtyard, distance, door, farm-yard, fence, flower, fruit, garden, grass, ground, house, junkyard, lawn, lawn furniture, litter, location, maintenance, measure, park, piece, place, pool, railway-yard, recreation, schoolyard, space, stock-yard, surface, tree, vegetables, vine-yard, yardstick.

adjectives big, busy, commercial, crowded, enclosed, fenced-in, green, large, long, narrow, polluted, private, public, quiet, recreational, small, spacious, wide.

verbs OTHERS: to buy in a yard, to chat in a yard, to find in a yard, to garden in a yard, to look for in a yard, to lose in a yard, to plant in a yard, to pick up in a yard, to play in a yard, to relax in a yard, to run in a yard, to sit in a yard, to stroll in a yard, to sunbathe in a yard, to walk in a yard.

expressions..

- *A yard sale:* a street sale ► **vente de débarras.**
- *Scotland Yard:* British intelligence agency ► **service de renseignements britannique.**
- *The whole nine yards:* all the way, everything ► **en entier, tout; tout le bataclan; tout le bazar.**

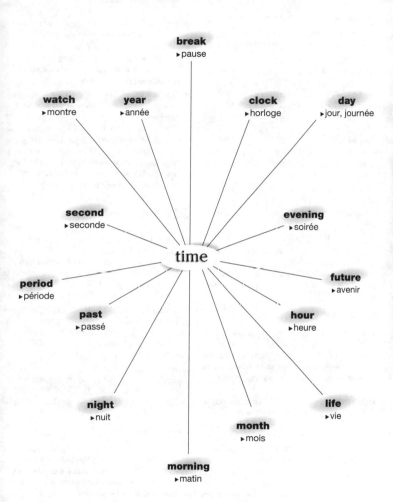

break
▸pause

watch
▸montre

year
▸année

clock
▸horloge

day
▸jour, journée

second
▸seconde

evening
▸soirée

period
▸période

future
▸avenir

past
▸passé

hour
▸heure

time

night
▸nuit

month
▸mois

life
▸vie

morning
▸matin

break ▶ pause

nouns coffee, dinner, division, escape, holiday, interruption, lunch, meal, nap, rest, snack, study, supper, vacation.

adjectives annual, daily, essential, long, monthly, necessary, quick, short, spring, summer, weekly, welcome, winter.

verbs SUBJECT: a break interrupts, refreshes, relaxes. OTHERS: to need a break, to request a break, to skip a break, to take a break, to want a break.

clock ▶ horloge

nouns alarm, cuckoo, face, grandfather, hands, mechanism, motor, tick, time, watch.

adjectives accurate, ancient, antique, biological, broken, digital, early, electrical, faulty, foreign, heirloom, internal, late, old, ticking, windup.

verbs SUBJECT: a clock breaks, keeps time, stops, strikes, ticks, works. OTHERS: to buy a clock, to break a clock, to own a clock, to repair a clock, to see a clock, to stop a clock, to watch a clock, to wind a clock.

expressions

- *Against the clock:* trying to get something accomplished when there does not seem to be enough time ▶ **tenter d'accomplir quelque chose dans un très court laps de temps; course contre la montre.**
- *Around the clock:* for 24 hours a day ▶ **24 heures par jour; jour et nuit.**
- *Clockwise:* to the right, in the same direction as that taken by the hands of a clock ▶ **vers la droite, dans le sens des aiguilles d'une montre.**
- *Counter clockwise:* to the left, in the opposite direction of that taken by the hands of a clock ▶ **vers la gauche, dans le sens contraire des aiguilles d'une montre; rotation rétrograde.**
- *Five o'clock shadow:* a short growth of beard visible on a man's face by the late afternoon ▶ **barbe qu'on peut apercevoir sur le visage d'un homme vers la fin de l'après-midi.**
- *Like clockwork:* very smoothly, without any problems ▶ **très facilement; sans accroc; comme sur des roulettes.**
- *Put back the clock:* to return to the conditions or ways of a past time in history ▶ **revenir à d'anciennes méthodes ou conditions; revenir en arrière.**
- *Regular as clockwork:* very regular ▶ **très régulier; réglé comme du papier à musique.**
- *Time clock:* a clock used by employees which records the time of their arrival at and their departure from work ▶ **horloge qui sert à enregistrer l'heure à laquelle les employés arrivent au travail et le quittent; horloge de pointage.**

day ▶ jour, journée

nouns afternoon, break, breakfast, dawn, dinner, dusk, evening, Friday, hour, lunch, midnight, minute, Monday, month, morning, nap, night, Saturday, second, snack, Sunday, sunrise, sunset, supper, tomorrow, Tuesday, Thursday, Wednesday, week, yesterday.

adjectives beautiful, calm, chilly, cold, difficult, good, hot, humid, important, long, overcast, rainy, sad, short, snowy, special, spring, summer, sunny, stormy, warm, winter.

verbs SUBJECT: a day closes, dawns, drags by, flies by, goes by, passes, speeds by. OTHERS: to count the days, to dread a day, to pick a day, to remember a day, to wait a day, to waste a day.

expressions

- *All in a / the day's work:* not causing any extra or out-of-the-ordinary effort or trouble ▶ **qui ne cause pas d'effort ou de problème supplémentaire ou extraordinaire; routinier.**
- *As happy as the day is long:* very happy in spending one's time in a particular way ▶ **très heureux de passer le temps d'une façon particulière.**

- *At the end of the day:* in the end, with all things considered ▸ **tout compte fait; au bout du compte.**

- *Day by day:* gradually ▸ **graduellement.**

- *Day in, day out:* regularly, consistently ▸ **régulièrement.**

- *Day to day:* daily ▸ **quotidiennement.**

- *Daylight robbery:* excessively high prices ▸ **prix excessifs; c'est du vol.**

- *Every dog has its day:* everybody is entitled or can expect to enjoy a period of success in life ▸ **chacun ou chacune peut espérer ou mérite de réussir dans la vie.**

- *In this day and age:* In the present, modern times ▸ **actuellement; de nos jours.**

- *Not to be someone's day:* a bad or unsuccessful day for someone ▸ **mauvaise journée ou journée marquée par la malchance.**

- *Not to give someone the time of day:* to ignore someone ▸ **faire semblant de ne pas voir une personne.**

- *One of these days:* some time in the near future ▸ **dans un avenir rapproché; un de ces jours.**

- *One of those days:* a day during which everything goes wrong ▸ **une journée où tout va de travers.**

- *Rome was not built in a day:* things that are worthwhile take time to achieve ▸ **pour accomplir quelque chose qui en vaut la peine, il faut y mettre le temps; Paris ne s'est pas fait en un jour.**

- *Some day:* at some time in the near future ▸ **dans un avenir rapproché; un jour.**

- *Someone's days are numbered:* someone is about to be fired from a job; someone is about to die ▸ **personne mourante ou sur le point d'être congédiée; ses jours sont comptés.**

- *That will be the day:* that is very unlikely ▸ **c'est très peu probable.**

- *The order of the day:* something necessary, usual, frequent or particularly fashionable at a certain time ▸ **chose**

nécessaire, habituelle, fréquente ou particulièrement à la mode à un moment donné; au goût du jour.

- *The other day:* not very long ago ▸ **il n'y a pas très longtemps; l'autre jour.**

- *Those were the days:* some time in the past which was very good ▸ **période heureuse appartenant au passé; c'était le bon temps.**

- *To call it a day:* to stop working for the day ▸ **cesser de travailler pour la journée.**

- *To carry the day:* to achieve victory ▸ **triompher.**

- *To have a field day:* to have a great or very successful time ▸ **avoir beaucoup de plaisir ou de succès.**

- *To have had one's day:* to be past one's best or most successful time in life ▸ **dont le succès ou les meilleurs moments sont choses du passé.**

- *To have seen better days:* to be in a worse condition or situation than in the past ▸ **être dans une situation plus difficile que dans le passé.**

- *To live from day to day:* to think only of the present without making any plans for the future ▸ **ne penser qu'au moment présent sans planifier pour l'avenir; vivre au jour le jour.**

- *To make someone's day:* to make someone very happy ▸ **rendre une personne très heureuse.**

- *To name the day:* to announce the date for an important event ▸ **annoncer la date d'un événement important.**

- *To save the day:* to prevent something from going wrong or from failing ▸ **empêcher un malheur ou un échec.**

- *To see daylight:* to near the end of a long task; to understand suddenly ▸ **arriver à la fin d'une tâche difficile ou comprendre soudainement; voir la lumière au bout du tunnel ou commencer à voir clair.**

- *To this day:* even now, until the present moment ▸ **jusqu'à maintenant.**

- *To win the day:* to be successful ▸ **réussir, triompher.**

evening ▸ **soirée**

nouns bed, date, dream, moon, night, nightmare, shade, shadow, sleep, slumber, sunset.

adjectives amusing, busy, chilly, cold, dark, first, fun, humid, last, lonely, magical, pleasant, quiet, rainy, romantic, slow, special, stormy, warm.

verbs SUBJECT: an evening begins, ends, passes. OTHERS: to pass an evening, to remember an evening, to spend an evening.

expressions..

- *Evening dress:* a formal dress to be worn in the evening ▸ **robe du soir.**

future ▸ **avenir**

nouns destiny, hereafter, opportunity, outlook, potential, prospect, time, tomorrow.

adjectives bleak, boring, bright, close, depressing, distant, exciting, grand, grave, great, happy, hopeful, hopeless, lonely, long, positive, possible, potential, scary, uncertain.

verbs SUBJECT: the future approaches, arrives. OTHERS: to anticipate the future, to fear the future, to guess the future, to know the future, to predict the future, to see the future.

expressions..

- *Future shock:* the inability to cope with rapid progress ▸ **incapacité de s'adapter au progrès rapide.**

hour ▸ **heure**

nouns alarm clock, breakfast, clock, day, dinner, hand (of a clock), lunch, midnight, minute, moment, night, noon, period, schedule, second, sunrise, sunset, supper, time, watch.

adjectives busy, determined, crucial, early, evening, given, golden, idle, late,

lonely, long, morning, normal, ordinary, precious, quiet, sad, silent, solitary, tragic, wasted.

verbs SUBJECT: hours drag, fly by, pass. OTHERS: to await an hour, to dread an hour, to gain an hour, to lose an hour, to wait an hour, to watch the hour.

expressions..

- *After hours:* after closing time ▸ **après la fermeture.**
- *At all hours:* any time but often unusual times, particularly late at night ▸ **à n'importe quelle heure, mais souvent à des heures inhabituelles, particulièrement tard dans la nuit; à toute heure du jour et de la nuit.**
- *At the eleventh hour:* at the last possible moment; just in time ▸ **au dernier moment; de justesse.**
- *Hourglass:* a reversible device containing sand which takes one hour to pass from one end to the other ▸ **instrument qui mesure le temps par l'écoulement du sable entre deux vases; sablier.**
- *In someone's hour of need:* at a time of crisis, when someone needs help ▸ **en temps de crise, lorsqu'une personne a besoin d'aide.**
- *Rush hour:* the time of day where there is a lot of traffic because people are going to or coming back from work ▸ **moment de la journée où il y a beaucoup de circulation parce que les gens se rendent au travail ou rentrent à la maison; heure de pointe.**
- *The small hours:* the hours just after midnight ▸ **juste après minuit.**
- *Until all hours:* until very late ▸ **jusqu'à une heure tardive.**

life ▸ **vie**

nouns animal, being, birth, character, day, death, heredity, human, lifetime, mankind, minute, month, murder, period, phase, plant, spirit, second, survival, time, week, year.

adjectives amusing, average, bleak, corrupt, criminal, cruel, difficult, foolish, fortunate, full, fulfilling, happy, honest, honourable, imaginary, isolated, jolly, joyful, lazy, lonely, long, lucky, miraculous, new, noble, past, rewarding, righteous, sensible, short, stubborn, successful, tenacious, tragic, vital.

verbs SUBJECT: a life begins, ends, flies by, goes by, passes, terminates. OTHERS: to cherish life, to destroy life, to give life, to respect life, to spare life, to take life, to waste life.

expressions

• *A matter of life or death:* a matter of great importance ▸ **une question très importante.**

• *As large as life:* in person; actually ▸ **en personne ; en chair et en os.**

• *Come back to life:* to become alert or attentive, to wake up ▸ **retrouver son énergie ou son attention ; se réveiller ; revenir à la vie.**

• *For dear life:* intensely ▸ **intensément.**

• *For the life of me:* even if it was essential in order to save my life ▸ **même si cela me sauvait la vie.**

• *Larger than life:* exaggerated ▸ **exagéré.**

• *Not on your life:* definitely not ▸ **absolument pas ; jamais de la vie.**

• *The life of the party:* an animated or entertaining person ▸ **personne enjouée ou divertissante ; boute-en-train.**

• *The life of Riley:* an easy, carefree life ▸ **vie facile, sans souci ; la belle vie.**

• *To have the time of one's life:* to have a very enjoyable, wonderful time ▸ **avoir beaucoup de plaisir.**

• *To see life:* to find out how other people live ▸ **découvrir comment les autres vivent.**

• *To take one's life in one's hands:* to take the risk of being killed or severely injured ▸ **prendre le risque d'être gravement blessé ou blessée, tué ou tuée ; risquer sa peau.**

• *To the life:* exactly like ▸ **parfaitement semblable ; identique.**

• *While there's life, there's hope:* in a bad situation, one should not despair so long as there is the slightest possibility of improvement ▸ **en situation difficile, on ne doit pas se laisser décourager s'il existe la moindre possibilité d'amélioration ; tant qu'il y a de la vie, il y a de l'espoir.**

month ▸ **mois**

nouns April, August, autumn, birthday, calendar, December, fall, February, January, July, June, March, May, November, October, season, semester, September, spring, summer, trimester, winter, year, zodiac.

adjectives cold, first, hot, last, long, next, rainy, temperate, warm, wintry.

verbs SUBJECT: a month drags, flies by, goes by, passes. OTHERS: to wait a month.

expressions

• *A month of Sundays:* a very long time; never ▸ **délai très long ; jamais ; dans la semaine des quatre jeudis.**

morning ▸ **matin**

nouns bed, breakfast, dawn, daylight, rooster, sun, sunshine, sunrise, today, tomorrow, yesterday.

adjectives blustery, brilliant, busy, calm, cloudy, early, late, noisy, peaceful, previous, quiet, rainy, sad, snowy, special, stormy, sunny, tranquil, typical, wet.

verbs SUBJECT: a morning arrives, drags, ends, passes. OTHER: to waste a morning.

expressions

• *Morning sickness:* nausea felt in the morning during early pregnancy ▸ **nausée matinale caractéristique des premiers mois de grossesse.**

night ▸ nuit

nouns bed, bedroom, blanket, box, bunk, chesterfield, couch, death, dream, evening, lamp, mattress, midnight, moon, moonlight, nightmare, pillow, pillowcase, pyjamas, quilt, rest, shadow, sheet, sleep, snore, sofa, spring, star, sunset, table, time.

adjectives active, bad, black, busy, cold, dark, fun, important, last, lonely, long, quiet, romantic, scary, short, silent, starry, stormy, terrible, tragic, thrilling, unforgettable, windy, wild, wonderful.

verbs SUBJECT: a night begins, drags, ends, passes. OTHERS: to spend a night.

expressions

* *Fly-by-night:* a company that sells many cheap things for a big profit and then disappears ▸ **entreprise qui vend des articles de qualité médiocre pour réaliser des gains importants, puis qui disparaît.**

* *Night-cap:* a drink of an alcoholic nature taken before bedtime ▸ **verre d'alcool consommé avant le coucher.**

* *Night-owl:* a person who tends to stay up late at night ▸ **personne qui a l'habitude de se coucher tard; oiseau de nuit.**

* *To make a night of it:* to spend the night enjoying oneself in a particular way ▸ **passer la nuit à s'amuser à une activité en particulier.**

past ▸ passé

nouns ancestor, heirloom, history, memorial, memory, nostalgia, period, precedent, predecessor, relic, time, tradition, yesterday.

adjectives ancient, criminal, distant, dull, earlier, historical, painful, perfect, prehistoric, previous, recent, remarkable, romantic, secret, stormy, tragic, traumatic, unhappy, violent.

verbs SUBJECT: the past disappears, fades. OTHERS: to cling to the past, to dwell in the past, to forget the past, to live in the past, to question the past, to remember the past, to reject the past.

expressions

* *A past master:* one who is extremely good or skilful at something ▸ **personne qui excelle dans un domaine; expert ou experte.**

* *Someone would not put it past someone else to do something:* to think someone is capable of or immoral enough to do anything bad. ("I would not put it past you to be absent on the day of the test.") ▸ **penser qu'une personne est immorale au point de faire quelque chose de mal. («Cela ne m'étonnerait pas que tu t'absentes le jour de l'examen.»)**

* *To be past one's best (past it):* to be less efficient or good at something than before because one is older ▸ **être moins efficace ou habile que dans le passé à cause de l'âge.**

period ▸ période

nouns age, century, day, decade, episode, era, history, hour, instant, interval, Middle Ages, moment, phase, season, spell, stage, stretch, time, year.

adjectives actual, ancient, annual, controversial, dangerous, distant, glorious, happy, interesting, long, mysterious, painful, primitive, revolutionary, short, sombre, troublesome, violent.

verbs SUBJECT: a period commences, ends, fades, passes. OTHERS: to analyse a period, to remember a period, to study a period.

expressions

* *A period piece:* something very typical of the time in which it was created ▸ **objet typique de l'époque où il a été créé.**

* *Grace period:* the extra time allowed to do something ▸ **délai supplémentaire.**

second ▸ seconde

nouns blink, fraction, instant, last, minute, moment, time.

adjectives critical, disastrous, passing, precious, quick, unforgettable, wonderful.

verbs SUBJECT: a second disappears, passes. OTHERS: to count seconds, to stop a second, to take a second, to time seconds, to wait a second, to watch seconds, to waste seconds.

expressions

• *A split second:* a fraction of a second ▸ **fraction de seconde.**

watch ▸ montre

nouns alarm, battery, face, gears, hands, heirloom, mechanism, jewellery, strap, time.

adjectives antique, beautiful, broken, cheap, digital, elegant, expensive, fake, fancy, modern, new, old, portable, precious, stolen, tacky, ugly.

verbs SUBJECT: a watch breaks, stops, ticks, works. OTHERS: to buy a watch, to give a watch, to steal a watch, to wear a watch, to wind a watch.

year ▸ année

nouns age, April, August, autumn, calendar, century, day, December, fall, February, January, July, June, March, May, month, November, October, season, semester, September, spring, summer, week, winter.

adjectives cold, difficult, disastrous, first, good, hard, important, last, long, lucky, next, present, profitable, rainy, short, unforgettable.

verbs SUBJECT: a year begins, changes, ends, passes, terminates. OTHER: to live a year, to remember a year, to skip a year, to wait a year.

expressions

• *A leap year:* a year in which the month of February has twenty-nine days ▸ **année où le mois de février compte vingt-neuf jours; année bissextile.**

• *Year in, year out:* all the time, every year without exception ▸ **toujours; chaque année sans exception.**

• *Year-round:* all year long ▸ **toute l'année; à longueur d'année.**

animals
p. 1083

living world

plants
p. 1096

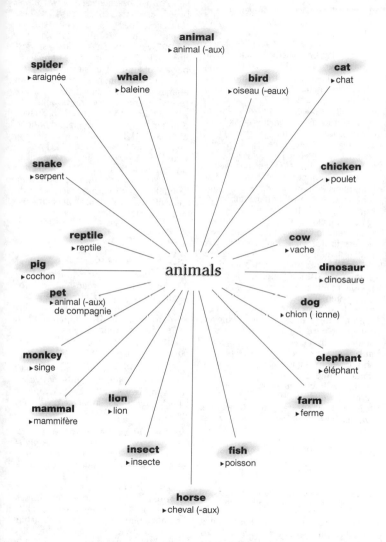

animal
▸animal (-aux)

spider
▸araignée

whale
▸baleine

bird
▸oiseau (-eaux)

cat
▸chat

snake
▸serpent

chicken
▸poulet

reptile
▸reptile

cow
▸vache

pig
▸cochon

animals

dinosaur
▸dinosaure

pet
▸animal (-aux)
de compagnie

dog
▸chion (icnne)

monkey
▸singe

elephant
▸éléphant

mammal
▸mammifère

lion
▸lion

farm
▸ferme

insect
▸insecte

fish
▸poisson

horse
▸cheval (-aux)

animal ▶ animal (-aux)

nouns alligator, alpaca, angelfish, ant, anteater, antelope, anthill, armadillo, baboon, barracuda, bass, bat, beak, bear, beaver, bee, beetle, bill, bird, bison, blackbird, blue jay, bluebird, boar, buffalo, bull, bumblebee, butterfly, buzzard, calf, camel, cardinal, caterpillar, catfish, cattle, centipede, chick, chicken, chimp, chimpanzee, chipmunk, cockroach, cocoon, cod, colt, condor, cow, coyote, crane, cricket, crocodile, crow, crustacean, cub, cuckoo, deer, dolphin, donkey, dove, dragonfly, duck, eagle, eel, egg, elephant, falcon, fawn, feather, fin, firefly, flamingo, flea, fox, frog, gill, giraffe, gnu, goat, goose, gorilla, grasshopper, grizzly bear, gull, halibut, hamster, hare, hawk, hen, herring, hippopotamus, hive, honeycomb, horn, hornet, horse, hummingbird, hyena, iguana, impala, jaguar, jellyfish, kangaroo, koala bear, ladybug, lamb, leopard, lion, lioness, lizard, llama, lobster, loon, lynx, mallard, mink, mole, monkey, moose, mosquito, moth, muskrat, nest, octopus, orangutan, ostrich, otter, owl, oyster, panda, panther, peacock, pelican, penguin, perch, pig, pigeon, pike, polar bear, polar bear, porcupine, praying mantis, puffin, python, racoon, raven, retriever, rhinoceros, roadrunner, robin, rooster, sailfish, salmon, scallop, scorpion, sea gull, sea horse, seal, shark, sheep, shell, shrimp, skunk, snail, snake, sole, sparrow, spider, squid, starfish, stinger, stingray, stork, swallow, swan, swordfish, tentacle, termite, thoroughbred, tiger, tortoise, trout, turkey, turtle, unicorn, vulture, walrus, wasp, web, whale, wolf, woodpecker, zebra.

adjectives annoying, beautiful, big, colourful, deadly, fast, flying, friendly, gentle, gorgeous, huge, hungry, large, lethal, malicious, nice, noisy, poisonous, pretty, quick, slow, small, strong, terrifying, tiny, venomous, weak.

verbs SUBJECT: An animal barks, bites, breathes, builds, carries, catches, chases, chirps, climbs, covers, drinks, eats, escapes, flies, gallops, gives birth, glides, helps, hides, hunts, hurries, jumps, lays, lays down, looks, neighs, observes, plays, protects, races, roars, runs, rushes, scratches, sees, sings, sleeps, speaks, speeds, sprints, swallows, talks, understands, walks, watches, whinnies, whistles. OTHERS: to adopt an animal, to beware of animals, to buy an animal, to care about an animal, to dislike an animal, to eat an animal, to fear animals, to feed an animal, to follow an animal, to get an animal, to give an animal, to hate animals, to have an animal, to hunt an animal, to kill an animal, to like an animal, to look for an animal, to love animals, to observe animals, to own an animal, to pet an animal, to protect an animal, to save an animal, to show an animal, to take care of an animal, to tame an animal, to train an animal, to use an animal, to wash an animal.

bird ▶ oiseau (-eaux)

nouns beak, bill, blackbird, blue jay, bluebird, buzzard, cardinal, condor, crane, crow, cuckoo, dove, egg, falcon, feather, flamingo, goose, gull, hummingbird, loon, mallard, nest, pelican, penguin, pigeon, puffin, raven, roadrunner, robin, sea gull, sparrow, stork, swallow, swan, vulture, wing, woodpecker.

adjectives beautiful, big, colourful, fast, ferocious, friendly, gentle, gorgeous, huge, hungry, large, nice, noisy, pretty, quick, slow, small, strong, terrifying, tiny, weak.

verbs SUBJECT: A bird builds, carries, chirps, covers, eats, escapes, flies, glides, hunts, lays, looks, protects, sees, sings, speaks, swallows, talks, understands, walks, whistles. OTHERS: to buy a bird, to care about a bird, to dislike a bird, to eat a bird, to follow a bird, to get a bird, to give a bird, to hate birds, to have a bird, to hunt a bird, to kill a bird, to like a bird, to love birds, to observe birds, to protect a bird, to save a bird, to sell birds, to show a bird, to tame a bird, to use a bird.

expressions

- *A bird in the hand is worth two in the bush:* what you can have is better than what you could have ► **ce qu'il est possible d'avoir est mieux que ce qu'il serait possible d'avoir; un tien vaut mieux que deux tu l'auras.**

- *A little bird told me:* I cannot reveal my source ► **je ne peux divulguer ma source de renseignements; mon petit doigt me l'a dit.**

- *Birds in their little nest agree:* people who live together should get along ► **les gens qui vivent ensemble devraient s'entendre.**

- *Birds of a feather flock together:* people who are alike stick together ► **les gens qui se ressemblent restent ensemble; qui se ressemble s'assemble.**

- *Bird's-eye view:* the view of an area from high above, as in an airplane ► **vue d'en haut, comme d'un avion; vue d'ensemble.**

- *Fine feathers make fine birds:* attention to detail leads to success ► **l'attention prêtée aux détails entraîne la réussite.**

- *Flip the bird:* to show the middle finger to someone as an insult ► **montrer le majeur en signe d'insulte.**

- *For the birds:* uninteresting, boring ► **inintéressant; ennuyeux.**

- *Free as a bird:* completely free ► **complètement libre; être libre comme un oiseau.**

- *Get the bird:* to be fired or booed ► **être congédié ou congédiée, hué ou huée.**

- *Like a bird:* without arguing or fighting back ► **sans rouspéter ou sans se défendre; comme un mouton.**

- *Sitting in a cat bird seat:* to be in an advantageous position ► **être dans une position avantageuse.**

- *That's not my pigeon:* that is not my business ► **ce ne sont pas mes affaires.**

- *The bird has flown:* someone has fled or escaped ► **quelqu'un qui s'est enfui ou qui a disparu; l'oiseau s'est envolé.**

- *The early bird catches the worm:* we shouldn't postpone until tomorrow what we can do today ► **il ne faut pas remettre au lendemain ce qu'on peut faire aujourd'hui.**

- *The world belongs to the early bird:* there are better chances of success for early-risers, people who wake up early in the morning ► **les chances de réussite sont meilleures pour ceux et celles qui se lèvent tôt; l'avenir appartient à ceux et celles qui se lèvent tôt.**

- *To get up with the lark:* to get up very early ► **se lever vraiment de bonne heure; se lever avec les poules.**

- *To give (someone) the bird:* to tell someone in an abrupt manner to leave or to get out of the way ► **dire avec brusquerie à quelqu'un de partir ou de circuler.**

- *To kill two birds with one stone:* to attain two goals with one action ► **atteindre deux objectifs à la fois; tirer d'une pierre deux coups.**

- *To set the cat among the pigeons:* to introduce some dangerous or disturbing new element ► **entrée en scène de nouveaux éléments dangereux ou dérangeants; c'est le pavé dans la mare.**

cat ► **chat**

nouns bird, claws, cougar, eye, feline, fur, house cat, kitten, kitty, leg, leopard, lion, lynx, milk, mouse, panther, paw, pussycat, saucer, tail, tiger, tomcat, whisker, wildcat.

adjectives affectionate, aggressive, domestic, friendly, gentle, hungry, independent, malicious, mean, nice, scary, soft, terrifying.

verbs SUBJECT: a cat bites catches, chases, climbs, drinks, eats, hides, hunts, jumps, meows, plays, purrs, scratches, sleeps, swallows, runs, walk, washes, watches. OTHERS: to adopt a cat, to beware of cats, to fear cats, to feed a cat, to own a cat, to pet a cat, to tame a cat, to wash a cat.

Expressions

- *A bag of cats:* a bad-tempered person: she's a real bag of cats this morning ► **personne ayant mauvais caractère; personne mal lunée.**

- *A cat can look at a king:* Everyone can be curious about important people ► **n'importe qui peut se montrer curieux à l'égard des gens importants; un chien regarde bien un évêque.**

- *A cat has nine lives:* Cats can survive things that are severe enough to kill them ► **les chats peuvent survivre à des attaques suffisamment graves pour les tuer.**

- *A cat in gloves catches no mice:* Sometimes you cannot get what you want by being careful and polite ► **il est parfois impossible d'arriver à ses fins en étant prudent ou prudente et poli ou polie; trop de précaution nuit.**

- *Alley cat:* Any homeless or stray cat. By extension – a prostitute ► **chat de gouttière et, au figuré, personne qui se prostitue.**

- *As much chance as a wax cat in hell:* no chance at all ► **pas la moindre chance.**

- *Cat got your tongue:* unable to speak ► **incapable de parler; avoir perdu sa langue.**

- *Cat's meow:* the best, the top of the line ► **le mieux, haut-de-gamme.**

- *Copycat:* Someone who mimics someone else ► **quelqu'un qui imite quelqu'un d'autre; copieur ou copieuse.**

- *Do it in a cat's paw:* Do something in a way that no one knows it is you doing it ► **faire quelque chose de manière à ce que personne ne sache qui en est l'auteur ou l'auteure, sans laisser de trace.**

- *Fat cat:* A person with a lot of money ► **personne très riche.**

- *Fight like Kilkenny cats:* to fight until both parties are destroyed ► **se battre jusqu'à épuisement.**

- *High as the hair on a cat's back:* very expensive ► **très cher, qui coûte les yeux de la tête.**

- *It's raining cats and dogs:* it's raining a lot ► **il pleut beaucoup; il pleut à verse; il tombe des cordes.**

- *Like herding cats:* futile, ineffective ► **futile, inefficace.**

- *Not a cat in hell's chance:* no chance at all ► **pas la moindre chance.**

- *Not enough room to swing a cat:* very little room ► **très peu d'espace.**

- *Play cat and mouse:* to play with a person or animal in a cruel or teasing way ► **tourmenter ou se montrer cruel ou cruelle avec une personne ou un animal; jouer au chat et à la souris.**

- *She's a cool cat:* she is calm ► **elle est calme.**

- *Sitting in a cat bird seat:* to be in an advantageous position ► **se trouver dans une position avantageuse.**

- *To be like cat and dog:* disagreeing fiercely ► **ne pas du tout s'entendre; s'entendre ou vivre comme chien et chat.**

- *To let the cat out of the bag:* to reveal a secret ► **divulguer un secret; vendre la mèche.**

- *To look like the cat who swallowed the canary:* to look proud of oneself ► **avoir l'air content ou contente de soi.**

- *To put (set) the cat among the pigeons:* to introduce some dangerous or disturbing new element ► **entrée en scène de nouveaux éléments dangereux ou dérangeants; c'est le pavé dans la mare.**

- *Weak as a kitten:* very weak ► **très faible.**

- *While the cat's away, the mice will play:* more freedom to those unsupervised ► **ceux et celles qui ne sont pas supervisés ou supervisées ont plus de liberté; quand le chat n'est pas là, les souris dansent.**

chicken ► **poulet**

nouns bird, breast, chick, chicken coop, drumstick, egg, farm, farmer, feather, hen house, hen, leg, poultry, roost, rooster, seed, soup, turkey, wing.

adjectives big, breaded, broiled, cooked, delicious, diced, fast, fried, hot, huge, hungry, roasted, slow, small, strong, tiny, white.

verbs SUBJECT: a chicken cackles, eats, pecks, picks, runs, sleeps. OTHERS: to breed chickens, to broil a chicken, to eat a chicken, to feed a chicken, to fry a chicken, to keep chickens.

expressions

- *Chicken:* coward ▸ **lâche.**
- *Chicken feed:* insignificant sum of money ▸ **somme d'argent négligeable.**
- *Chicken livered:* timid ▸ **timide.**
- *Chicken pox:* a mild contagious eruptive disease commonly of children ▸ **éruption cutanée contagieuse courante chez les enfants; varicelle.**
- *Don't count your chickens before they're hatched:* Don't count on things that are not yet yours, done or completed ▸ **il vaut mieux ne pas compter sur les choses que l'on n'a pas encore obtenues ou qui ne sont pas encore terminées; il ne faut pas vendre la peau de l'ours avant de l'avoir tué.**
- *To chicken out, to chicken:* to refrain from doing something because of fear ▸ **s'empêcher de faire quelque chose par peur.**
- *To walk on egg shells:* a dangerous or risky situation ▸ **(être dans une) situation dangereuse ou risquée; marcher sur des œufs.**
- *You can't make an omelette without breaking eggs:* when doing or learning something, it is possible to make mistakes ▸ **il arrive qu'on fasse des erreurs lorsqu'on apprend quelque chose.**

COW ▸ **vache**

nouns barn, beef, bovine, bucket, bull, butter, calf, cattle, cheese, dairy, farm, meat, milk, pitchfork, stable.

adjectives bad, big, docile, gentle, giant, good, huge, hungry, slow, strong, weak.

verbs SUBJECT: A cow bears (a calf), breathes, carries, drinks, eats, escapes, gives birth, helps, helps, looks, moos, observes, protects, sees, swallows, understands, walks. OTHERS: to breed cows, to buy a cow, to feed cows, to get a cow, to have a cow, to herd cows, to kill a cow, to milk a cow, to sell a cow, to watch cows.

expressions

- *A bull in a china shop:* clumsy ▸ **gauche, maladroit ou maladroite; un éléphant dans un magasin de porcelaine.**
- *A sacred cow:* personal possession cherished by its owner ▸ **possessions chères à son propriétaire.**
- *Big enough to choke a cow:* very big ▸ **très gros ou grosse.**
- *Cash cow:* Someone or something that has a lot of cash and supports someone else with it ▸ **quelqu'un ou quelque chose qui fournit beaucoup d'argent et qui sert à soutenir financièrement; vache à lait.**
- *Cow juice:* milk ▸ **lait.**
- *How now, Brown Cow?:* What's next? – or – What's going on? ▸ **Et ensuite? ou Que se passe-t-il?**
- *Steep as a cow's face:* extremely steep ▸ **très escarpé.**
- *The tune the old cow died of:* any tune which has been played a lot (too much) ▸ **chanson qu'on a beaucoup (trop) entendu jouer.**
- *Till the cows come home:* late hours ▸ **tard.**
- *Why buy a cow when you can get the milk for free:* why pay for something that you can get for free otherwise ▸ **pourquoi payer pour quelque chose que l'on peut obtenir gratuitement.**

dinosaur ▸ **dinosaure**

nouns albertosaurus, animal, bones, brontosaurus, digging, excavation, lizard, monster, reptile, skeleton, stegosaurus, tyrannosaurus.

adjectives big, brutal, carnivorous, cruel, enormous, extinct, ferocious, fierce, gentle, giant, gigantic, great, huge, hungry, immense, massive, nice, prehistoric, savage, scary, small, terrifying.

verbs SUBJECT: A dinosaur bites, catches, chases, climbs, drinks, eats, devours, hides, jumps, scratches, sleeps, watches. OTHERS: to beware of dinosaurs, to chase a dinosaur, to fear dinosaurs, to feed a dinosaur, to hunt a dinosaur, to kill a dinosaur, to study dinosaurs, to search for dinosaurs.

dog ▸ chien (-ienne)

nouns bark, bitch, bite, boxer, canine, cat, coat, ear, friend, hair, hound, husky, jaw, kennel, leg, mammal, master, mouth, muzzle, paw, pet, poodle, puppy, retriever, shed, shepherd, smell, tail, terrier, tongue, tooth, veterinary.

adjectives affectionate, aggressive, beautiful, big, domestic, fast, ferocious, friendly, gentle, gorgeous, happy, huge, hungry, independent, large, malicious, mean, nice, noisy, pretty, quick, scary, slow, small, strong, terrifying, tiny, weak.

verbs SUBJECT: A dog barks, bites, carries, catches, chases, climbs, covers, drinks, eats, escapes, fetches, hides, hunts, jumps, lays down, looks, plays, protects, runs, scratches, sees, sleeps, swallows, understands, walks, watches. OTHERS: to adopt a dog, to beware of dogs, to buy a dog, to care about a dog, to dislike a dog, to fear dogs, to feed a dog, to follow a dog, to get a dog, to give a dog, to hate dogs, to have a dog, to like a dog, to look for a dog, to love dogs, to own a dog, to pet a dog, to protect a dog, to save a dog, to show a dog, to take care of a dog, to tame a dog, to train a dog, to wash a dog.

expressions

- *A dog's breakfast:* something bad ▸ **quelque chose de mauvais.**
- *A dog's chance:* no chance at all ▸ **pas la moindre chance.**

- *A dog's life:* a miserable existence ▸ **existence misérable; vie de chien.**
- *Big dog:* important person ▸ **personne importante; ponte.**
- *Call off the dogs:* stop what you are doing ▸ **arrêter ce que l'on est en train de faire.**
- *Crooked as a dog's hind leg:* dishonest ▸ **malhonnête.**
- *Dog does not eat dog:* one bad person will not harm another bad person ▸ **une personne méchante ne fera aucun mal à une autre personne méchante.**
- *Dog tired:* very tired ▸ **très fatigué ou fatiguée; claqué ou claquée.**
- *Gone to the dogs:* to take a turn for the worse ▸ **mal tourner, aller à vau-l'eau.**
- *Happy as a flea in a doghouse:* extremely happy ▸ **très heureux.**
- *If you lie down with dogs, you will get up with fleas:* if you associate with bad people, you will acquire their faults ▸ **à force de fréquenter des gens peu recommandables, on acquiert leurs défauts.**
- *In the doghouse:* in trouble ▸ **en difficulté.**
- *It's a dog eat dog world:* vicious world ▸ **monde sans scrupule.**
- *It's raining cats and dogs:* it's raining a lot ▸ **il pleut beaucoup; il pleut à verse; il tombe des cordes.**
- *Let sleeping dog's lie:* it is better not to say something true that could disturb, hurt or embarrass ▸ **il vaut mieux ne pas dire une vérité qui pourrait être dérangeante, blessante ou gênante; toute vérité n'est pas bonne à dire.**
- *Love me, love my dog:* if you love someone, you should accept everything and everyone that person loves ▸ **si on aime quelqu'un, on accepte tout ce que cette personne aime; qui m'aime me suive.**
- *My dogs are barking:* my feet are hurting or my feet smell ▸ **j'ai mal aux pieds ou j'ai les pieds qui sentent mauvais.**
- *Sick as a dog:* very sick ▸ **très malade; malade comme un chien, comme une bête, à crever.**

- *The tail wagging the dog:* when one does not control something or someone ▸ **situation où l'on n'a aucun pouvoir sur quelqu'un ou quelque chose.**

- *To be like cat and dog:* disagreeing fiercely ▸ **ne pas du tout s'entendre ; s'entendre ou vivre comme chien et chat.**

- *To do the dog and pony show:* to put on a good performance to impress someone ▸ **faire une bonne prestation pour impressionner quelqu'un ; en mettre plein la vue.**

- *To work like a dog:* to work very hard ▸ **travailler très fort, travailler avec acharnement.**

- *Why keep a dog and bark yourself:* why do something you hired someone else to do ▸ **pourquoi faire une chose pour laquelle vous avez engagé quelqu'un.**

- *You cannot teach an old dog new tricks:* someone who is used to doing things a certain way can rarely change ▸ **quelqu'un habitué à faire quelque chose d'une certaine façon peut rarement changer ; on n'apprend pas à un vieux singe à faire la grimace.**

elephant ▸ **éléphant**

nouns animal, ear, eye, ivory, jungle, leg, lip, mammal, mouth, nose, tail, trunk, tusk.

adjectives bad, big, docile, enormous, faithful, fierce, gentle, giant, gigantic, good, great, huge, hungry, immense, mad, massive, nice, obedient, quiet, savage, scary, slow, small, strong, weak.

verbs SUBJECT: An elephant bears (a baby elephant), breathes, carries, drinks, eats, escapes, gives birth, helps, looks, observes, protects, runs, sees, swallows, transports, trumpets, understands, walks. OTHERS: to adopt an elephant, to breed elephants, to buy an elephant, to get an elephant, to have an elephant, to help an elephant, to herd elephants, to kill an elephant, to observe an elephant, to play with an elephant, to protect elephants, to ride an elephant, to save an elephant, to

sell an elephant, to study elephants, to tame an elephant, to wash an elephant.

expressions

- *A white elephant:* a gift you don't want with which you don't know what to do ▸ **cadeau dont on ne veut pas et dont on ne sait pas quoi faire ; objet superflu.**

- *An elephant:* something or someone very big ▸ **quelqu'un ou quelque chose de très gros.**

- *An elephant never forgets:* elephants never forget ▸ **les éléphants n'oublient jamais rien.**

- *A memory like an elephant:* someone with a tremendous memory ▸ **quelqu'un doté d'une excellente mémoire.**

- *Big enough to shade an elephant:* very big ▸ **très gros ou grosse.**

farm ▸ **ferme**

nouns barn, beef, bovine, bucket, bull, butter, calf, cat, cattle, cheese, chick, chicken, chicken coop, colt, cow, dairy, dog, donkey, duck, egg, goat, hay, hen, horse, lamb, meat, milk, pig, pig sty, pitchfork, rooster, shed, sheep, skunk, stable, tractor, turkey, yolk.

adjectives beautiful, big, bright, cosy, enormous, expensive, giant, gigantic, good, great, huge, immense, luxurious, nice, small, superb, tremendous.

verbs SUBJECT: A farm creates, generates, makes, produces. OTHERS: to be in a farm, to build a farm, to buy a farm, to buy at the farm, to choose a farm, to dislike a farm, to give a farm, to hate a farm, to inherit a farm, to like a farm, to love a farm, to pick a farm, to renovate a farm, to rent a farm, to run a farm, to select a farm, to sell a farm, to visit a farm, to work on a farm.

expressions

- *Freckled as a turkey egg:* covered with freckles ▸ **couvert de taches de rousseur.**

- *Nest egg:* savings ▸ **économies ; pécule.**

- *Skunk egg:* an onion ▸ **oignon.**

fish ▶ poisson

nouns angelfish, barracuda, bass, carp, catfish, cod, eel, fin, gill, halibut, herring, mackerel, musky, perch, pike, pickerel, sailfish, salmon, scale, sea horse, shark, smelt, sole, starfish, stingray, sturgeon, swordfish, tail, tomcod, trout, tuna, walleye.

adjectives bad, big, carnivorous, enormous, extinct, ferocious, fierce, gentle, giant, gigantic, good, great, hairy, huge, hungry, immense, mad, massive, mysterious, nice, odd, poisonous, prehistoric, scary, slow, small, sticky, strange, strong, terrifying, unusual, weak, weird.

verbs SUBJECT: A fish attacks bites, breathes, carries, dives, drinks, eats, escapes, flies, floats, glides, jumps, observes, sees, swallows, swims. OTHERS: to breed fish, to buy a fish, to catch a fish, to cook a fish, to cut a fish, to eat a fish, to fish fish, to get a fish, to have a fish, to kill a fish, to observe fish, to play with a fish, to protect fish, to sell fish, to study fish, to wash a fish

expressions

- *As slippery as an eel:* very slippery ▶ **très glissant.**
- *Sleeping with the fishes:* drowned ▶ **noyé ou noyée.**
- *Neither fish, flesh, nor fowl:* neither this nor that ▶ **ni l'un ni l'autre.**
- *A woman needs a man like a fish needs a bicycle:* a woman does not necessarily need a man ▶ **une femme n'a pas nécessairement besoin d'un homme.**
- *Fishing for a compliment:* looking forward to hearing a compliment for one's own self ▶ **rechercher les compliments.**
- *A fine kettle of fish:* a terrible mess ▶ **désordre terrible; une vache n'y trouverait pas son veau.**
- *To be like a fish out of water:* to be out of one's element ▶ **être dans son élément; être comme un poisson dans l'eau.**

- *Busy as a fish peddler in Lent:* very busy ▶ **très occupé ou occupée.**
- *Crooked as a barrel of fish hooks:* extremely dishonest ▶ **absolument malhonnête.**
- *To drink like a fish:* to be a big drinker ▶ **boire beaucoup.**
- *To have better (or other) fish to fry:* to have more important things to worry about ▶ **avoir autre chose à faire; avoir d'autres chats à fouetter.**
- *There's more than one fish in the sea:* there are always other options ▶ **il y a toujours d'autres options.**
- *Like a big fish in a small pond:* someone who has no competition because he or she is either more rich, more beautiful or more talented ▶ **personne qui élimine la concurrence parce qu'elle est la plus riche, la plus belle ou la plus talentueuse.**

horse ▶ cheval (-aux)

nouns armour, barn, bucket, colt, contest, farm, hay, hoof, horseshoe, jockey, knight, leather, leg, mane, neigh, pitchfork, polo, pony, race, race track, rider, rodeo, saddle, sea horse, sleigh, stirrup, tail, thoroughbred, unicorn, whinny.

adjectives bad, big, docile, fast, friendly, gentle, giant, good, hasty, huge, hungry, quick, rapid, slow, strong, weak.

verbs SUBJECT: A horse bears (a colt), breathes, carries, chases, drinks, eats, escapes, gallops, gives birth, helps, hurries, jumps, looks, neighs, observes, protects, pulls, races, runs, rushes, sees, speeds, sprints, swallows, understands, walks, whinnies. OTHERS: to breed a horse, to brush a horse, to buy a horse, to get a horse, to groom a horse, to have a horse, to observe a horse, to ride a horse, to saddle a horse, to sell a horse, to study horses, to train a horse, to watch a horse.

expressions

- *As strong as a horse:* very strong ▶ **très fort ou forte.**

- *Charley horse:* leg cramp ► **crampe dans une jambe.**

- *Don't change horses in mid-stream:* don't change idea in the middle of something important ► **ne changez pas d'avis en cours de route.**

- *Hold your horses:* just wait a second ► **attends un instant.**

- *Horse of another (different) colour:* entirely different situation ► **situation totalement différente; (c'est une) autre paire de manches.**

- *Horse-sense:* common sense ► **le bon sens.**

- *Horsing around:* joking around ► **faire des plaisanteries.**

- *If two ride on a horse, one must ride behind:* when two people do something together, one of them will be the leader and the other will be the subordinate ► **lorsque deux personnes font quelque chose ensemble, il faut nécessairement que l'une dirige et que l'autre suive.**

- *If wishes were horses then beggars would ride:* it's no good just wishing. You have to act ► **il ne suffit pas de désirer, il faut aussi agir.**

- *It is too late to shut the stable door when the horse is stolen:* don't procrastinate ► **il ne faut pas remettre les choses au lendemain.**

- *One horse town:* small town ► **petite ville.**

- *So hungry I could eat a horse:* very hungry ► **être affamé ou affamée.**

- *Straight from the horse's mouth:* from the highest authority ► **provenant des plus hautes autorités.**

- *To beat or flog a dead horse:* to try to make people interested in a subject which everyone has fully discussed ► **tenter d'intéresser les gens à un sujet qui a été épuisé.**

- *To look a gift horse in the mouth:* to have bad manners when accepting a gift ► **mal se comporter lorsqu'on accepte un cadeau.**

- *To put the cart before the horse:* doing something in reversed order ► **faire quelque chose dans le mauvais ordre; mettre la charrue devant les bœufs.**

- *To ride the high horse:* to act pompously ► **agir pompeusement.**

- *Wild horse couldn't drag me away:* even the most disastrous events won't keep me from coming ► **même le pire désastre ne pourrait m'empêcher de venir.**

- *You can lead a horse to water, but you can't make it drink:* you can offer someone something but you cannot insist that they take it ► **on peut offrir quelque chose à quelqu'un, mais on ne peut le forcer à le prendre.**

insect ► **insecte**

nouns ant, anthill, bee, beetle, bumblebee, butterfly, caterpillar, centipede, cockroach, cocoon, cricket, dragonfly, firefly, flea, grasshopper, hive, honeycomb, hornet, ladybug, mosquito, moth, praying mantis, scorpion, spider, stinger, termite, wasp, web, wing.

adjectives annoying, beautiful, big, colourful, deadly, fast, flying, frustrating, gentle, gorgeous, huge, hungry, irritating, large, lethal, malicious, nice, noisy, poisonous, pretty, quick, slow, small, strong, terrifying, tiny, venomous, weak.

verbs SUBJECT: An insect bites, builds, carries, chases, crawls, eats, escapes, flies, glides, hunts, hurts, lays, looks, protects, sees, stings, swallows, walks, whistles. OTHERS: to buy an insect, to dislike an insect, to eat an insect, to hate insects, to have an insect, to kill an insect, to love insects, to observe an insect, to protect an insect, to save an insect, to study insects, to watch an insect.

lion ► **lion**

nouns animal, cat, circus, lynx, park, zoo, claw, cub, den, ear, eye, jungle, leg, mammal, mane, mouth, nose, paw, tail, tamer, tiger, tooth.

adjectives aggressive, beautiful, big, brutal, carnivorous, cruel, enormous, fast, ferocious, fierce, gentle, giant, gigantic, gorgeous, great, happy, huge, hungry, large, malicious, massive, mean, nice, noisy, pretty, quick, savage, scary, slow, small, strong, terrifying, tiny, weak.

verbs SUBJECT: A lion bites, catches, chases, climbs, drinks, eats, devours, hides, jumps, roars, scratches, sleeps, watches. OTHERS: to beware of lions, to chase a lion, to fear lions, to feed a lion, to hunt a lion, to kill a lion, to observe lions, to study lions, to tame a lion, to watch a lion.

expressions

- *To put your head in the lion's den:* to put oneself in trouble or danger ► **se mettre en difficulté ou en danger.**

- *As strong as a lion:* very strong ► **très fort ou forte.**

- *Lionhearted:* very brave; courageous ► **très brave, courageux ou courageuse.**

- *A lion's share:* the greater portion ► **la plus grosse part ; (se tailler) la part du lion.**

- *Better be the head of a dog than the tail of a lion:* it is better to be a decider than a follower ► **il vaut mieux diriger que suivre ; mieux vaut être le premier dans son village que le second à Rome.**

- *In like a lion, out like a lamb:* It comes in rough and goes out gentle – usually the month of March ► **commence durement et se termine doucement, habituellement en partant du mois de mars.**

mammal ► **mammifère**

nouns alpaca, anteater, antelope, armadillo, baboon, bat, beak, bear, beaver, bison, boar, buffalo, bull, calf, camel, cattle, chimp, chimpanzee, chipmunk, colt, cow, coyote, cub, deer, dolphin, donkey, elephant, fawn, fox, giraffe, gnu, goat, goose, gorilla, grizzly bear, hamster, hare, hippopotamus, horn, horse, hump, hyena, impala, jaguar, kangaroo, koala bear, lamb, leopard, lion, lioness, llama, lynx, mink, mole, monkey, moose, muskrat, nest, orangutan, otter, panda, panther, pig, polar bear, porcupine, racoon, retriever, rhinoceros, seal, sheep, skunk, stripe, tail, thoroughbred, tiger, walrus, whale, wolf, zebra.

adjectives annoying, beautiful, big, colourful, deadly, fast, flying, friendly, frustrating, gentle, gorgeous, huge, hungry, irritating, large, lethal, malicious, nice, noisy, poisonous, pretty, quick, slow, small, strong, terrifying, tiny, venomous, weak.

verbs SUBJECT: A mammal barks, bites, breathes, builds, carries, catches, chases, chirps, climbs, covers, drinks, eats, escapes, flies, gallops, gives birth, glides, helps, hides, hunts, hurries, jumps, lays, lays down, looks, neighs, observes, plays, protects, races, runs, rushes, scratches, sees, sings, sleeps, speaks, speeds, sprints, swallows, talks, understands, walks, watches, whinnies, whistles. OTHERS: to adopt a mammal, to beware of mammals, to buy a mammal, to care about a mammal, to dislike a mammal, to eat a mammal, to fear mammals, to feed a mammal, to follow a mammal, to get a mammal, to give a mammal, to hate mammals, to have a mammal, to hunt a mammal, to kill a mammal, to like a mammal, to look for a mammal, to love mammals, to own a mammal, to pet a mammal, to observe a mammal, to protect a mammal, to save a mammal, to show a mammal, to study mammals, to take care of a mammal, to tame a mammal, to train a mammal, to use a mammal, to wash a mammal, to watch mammals.

monkey ► **singe**

nouns agility, baboon, banana, chimp, chimpanzee, face, female, forest, gorilla, head, male, orangutan, primate, quickness, skull, speed, tail, tree.

adjectives aggressive, agile, beautiful, big, domestic, fast, ferocious, flexible, gentle, gorgeous, happy, huge, hungry, large, malicious, mean, nice, noisy, pretty, quick, scary, slow, small, strong, terrifying, tiny, weak.

verbs SUBJECT: A monkey barks, bites, carries, catches, chases, climbs, covers, drinks, eats, escapes, hides, hunts, jumps, lays down, looks, plays, protects, runs, scratches, sees, sleeps, swallows, understands, walks, watches. OTHERS: to adopt a monkey, to beware of monkeys, to buy a monkey, to care about a monkey, to dislike a monkey, to fear monkeys, to feed a monkey, to follow a monkey, to get a monkey, to give a monkey, to hate monkeys, to have a monkey, to like a monkey, to live with monkeys, to look for a monkey, to love monkeys, to observe a monkey, to own a monkey, to pet a monkey, to protect a monkey, to save a monkey, to show a monkey, to study monkeys, to take care of a monkey, to tame a monkey, to train a monkey, to wash a monkey, to watch monkeys.

expressions

- *Monkey see, monkey do:* that which is seen is copied ▶ **ce qui est vu est copié.**
- *Monkey:* naughty person ▶ **personne méchante; peau de vache.**
- *To have a monkey on one's back:* to have an addict's dependence on a drug ▶ **être esclave de la drogue.**
- *To make a monkey of:* to make someone look like a fool ▶ **tourner quelqu'un en ridicule.**
- *Monkey suit:* a man's evening dress (tuxedo, formal suit, etc.) ▶ **habit de soirée (smoking, par exemple).**
- *As fun as a barrel of monkeys:* very funny ▶ **très drôle.**
- *I'll be a monkey's uncle:* I am surprised ▶ **je suis surpris ou surprise.**
- *Monkey business:* bad or illegal happenings ▶ **quelque chose de louche ou d'illégal; combine.**
- *To monkey around:* to do something bad or illegal ▶ **faire quelque chose de louche ou d'illégal.**

- *A monkey in silk is a monkey no less:* no matter how you dress up something, it is still the same underneath ▶ **peu importe comment on déguise une chose, elle reste toujours la même.**

pet ▶ animal (-aux) de compagnie

nouns bark, bitch, bite, boxer, bunny, canary, canine, cat, coat, dog, ear, fish, friend, goldfish, guinea pig, hair, hamster, hound, husky, jaw, kennel, kitten, leg, mammal, master, mice, mouth, muzzle, parakeet, parrot, paw, pet, poodle, puppy, rabbit, retriever, shed, shepherd, smell, tail, terrier, tongue, tooth, turtle, veterinary.

adjectives affectionate, aggressive, beautiful, big, domestic, fast, ferocious, friendly, gentle, gorgeous, happy, huge, hungry, independent, large, malicious, mean, nice, noisy, pretty, quick, scary, slow, small, strong, terrifying, tiny, weak.

verbs SUBJECT: A pet barks, bites, carries, catches, chases, climbs, covers, drinks, eats, escapes, hides, hunts, jumps, lays down, looks, plays, protects, runs, scratches, sees, sleeps, swallows, understands, walks, watches. OTHERS: to adopt a pet, to beware of pets, to buy a pet, to care about a pet, to dislike a pet, to fear pets, to feed a pet, to follow a pet, to get a pet, to give a pet, to hate pets, to have a pet, to like a pet, to look for a pet, to love pets, to own a pet, to pet a pet, to protect a pet, to save a pet, to show a pet, to take care of a pet, to tame a pet, to train a pet, to wash a pet, to watch a pet.

pig ▶ cochon

nouns animal, boar, bucket, farm, farmer, ham, hog, meat, pig sty, piglet, pitchfork, pork, swine.

adjectives bad, big, docile, friendly, gentle, giant, good, huge, hungry, slow, strong, weak.

verbs SUBJECT: A pig attacks, bears (a piglet), breathes, carries, drinks, eats, escapes, gives birth, grunts, helps, looks, observes, protects, sees, swallows, understands, walks. OTHERS: to breed pigs, to buy a pig, to get a pig, to have a pig, to herd pigs, to kill a pig, to milk a pig, to sell a pig, to watch pigs.

expressions

- *Blind pig:* place to buy illicit liquor ▸ **endroit où il est possible d'acheter de l'alcool frelaté.**
- *Buy a pig in a poke:* buy something without seeing it first ▸ **acheter quelque chose sans l'avoir vu; acheter chat en poche.**
- *Even a blind pig finds an acorn once in awhile:* everybody gets lucky sometimes ▸ **un jour ou l'autre, on est chanceux ou chanceuse.**
- *Fat as a pig:* very fat ▸ **très gras ou grasse.**
- *Happy as a pig in mud:* very happy and content ▸ **très heureux ou heureuse.**
- *If that doesn't beat a pig a-pecking:* that's amazing ▸ **c'est renversant.**
- *In a pig's eye:* nonsense ▸ **sottises.**
- *Not fitting to roll with a pig:* uncivilized, bad-mannered and disgusting ▸ **qui a de mauvaises manières et qui est dégoûtant ou dégoûtante; un vrai cochon; un vrai porc.**
- *To be on the pig's back:* to be successful; establishment ▸ **réussir, être établi ou établie.**
- *To bleed like a stuck pig:* to bleed a lot ▸ **saigner beaucoup; pisser le sang.**
- *To eat like a pig:* to eat a lot ▸ **manger beaucoup; se goinfrer; s'empiffrer; s'en mettre plein la panse.**
- *To make a pig of yourself:* to eat too much; all you want ▸ **manger beaucoup trop; se goinfrer; s'empiffrer; s'en mettre plein la panse.**
- *To pig it:* to live in nastiness ▸ **vivre comme des cochons.**
- *To pig out:* to devour food hungrily ▸ **dévorer; s'en mettre plein la panse.**
- *To snore like a pig:* to snore very loudly ▸ **ronfler très fort.**

- *To sweat like a pig:* to sweat a lot ▸ **suer beaucoup.**
- *When pigs fly:* never ▸ **jamais; quand les poules auront des dents.**

reptile ▸ reptile

nouns alligator, amphibians, bite, crocodile, eye, fossils, iguana, jaw, lake, land, lizard, mouth, poison, salamander, scale, skin, snake, swamp, tooth, tortoise, turtle, vertebrates, wildlife.

adjectives beautiful, big, colourful, deadly, fast, flying, frustrating, gentle, gorgeous, huge, hungry, large, lethal, malicious, nice, noisy, poisonous, pretty, quick, slow, small, strong, terrifying, tiny, venomous, weak.

verbs SUBJECT: A reptile bites, builds, carries, chases, crawls, eats, escapes, flies, glides, hunts, hurts, lays, looks, protects, sees, stings, swallows, walks. OTHERS: to buy a reptile, to dislike a reptile, to eat a reptile, to hate reptiles, to have a reptile, to kill a reptile, to love reptiles, to protect a reptile.

snake ▸ serpent

nouns bite, desert, eye, fossils, iguana, jaw, lake, land, lizard, mouth, poison, python, sand, scale, skin, swamp, tooth.

adjectives annoying, beautiful, big, colourful, deadly, fast, huge, hungry, large, lethal, long, malicious, nice, poisonous, pretty, quick, slow, small, strong, terrifying, tiny, venomous.

verbs SUBJECT: A snake bites, chases, crawls, eats, escapes, glides, hides, hunts, hurts, lays, looks, sees, slithers, strangles, swallows, watches. OTHERS: to buy a snake, to charm a snake, to dislike a snake, to eat a snake, to fear snakes, to hate snakes, to have a snake, to kill a snake, to love snakes, to observe a snake, to protect a snake, to watch a snake.

expressions

- *If it was a snake it would have bit you:* very close ▸ **très près ; il s'en fallait de peu.**
- *Mad as a struck snake:* very cruel and angry ▸ **très fâché ou fâchée.**
- *Once a snake, always a snake:* people do not change ▸ **les gens ne changent pas.**
- *Slippery as a snake:* unable to trust ▸ **à qui l'on ne peut faire confiance.**
- *Snake in the grass:* there is trouble ▸ **quelque chose ne tourne pas rond ; il y a anguille sous roche.**

spider ▸ araignée

nouns animal, bite, blood, body, fly, insect, leg, mosquito, poison, reptile, sand, tarantula, web.

adjectives beautiful, big, deadly, fast, hairy, huge, large, lethal, malicious, poisonous, quick, slow, small, terrifying, tiny, venomous.

verbs SUBJECT: A spider bites, chases, crawls, eats, escapes, glides, hurts, lays, sees, spins, stings, swallows, weaves. OTHERS: to be afraid of spiders, to buy a spider, to dislike a spider, to fear spiders, to hate spiders, to have a spider, to kill a spider, to love spiders, to observe, to study spiders.

whale ▸ baleine

noun animal, Antarctic, Arctic, bay, beluga, boat, creature, dolphin, fin, fish, flipper, head, mammal, ocean, sea, tail, water.

adjectives bad, big, enormous, friendly, gentle, giant, gigantic, good, great, huge, hungry, immense, mad, majestic, massive, nice, quiet, scary, slow, small, strong, weak.

verbs SUBJECT: A whale bears (a baby whale), breaches, breathes, drinks, eats, escapes, gives birth, observes, protects, swallows, swims. OTHERS: to help a whale, to kill a whale, to observe whales, to play with a whale, to protect whales, to ride a whale, to save a whale, to study whales, to swim with a whale.

expressions

- *To have a whale of a time:* a lot of fun ▸ **avoir beaucoup de plaisir.**
- *Whale:* something extraordinarily big or great ▸ **quelque chose de très gros ou de très grand.**

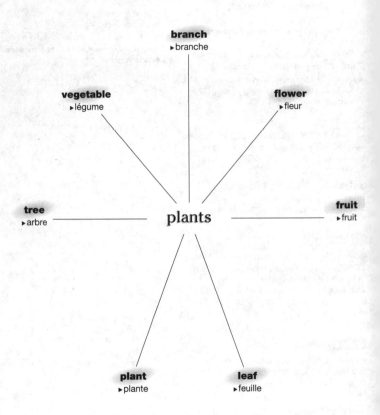

branch
▸branche

vegetable
▸légume

flower
▸fleur

tree
▸arbre

plants

fruit
▸fruit

plant
▸plante

leaf
▸feuille

branch ▸ branche

nouns aspen, bark, birch, bird, bud, bush, cedar, cone, egg, fir, fire, flower, forest, leaf, leafstalk, lumber, needle, nest, oak, pine, plant, poplar, redwood, root, rose tree, saw, sequoia, soil, stem, sun, tree, trunk, water, wood.

adjectives beautiful, big, giant, great, high, large, long, majestic, short, small, strong, superb, tall, thin.

verbs SUBJECT: a branch hides, holds, supports, touches. OTHERS: to attach a branch, to axe a branch, to break a branch, to chop a branch, to cut a branch, to pick up branches, to remove a branch, to slash a branch, to slice a branch, to tie a branch.

expressions

- *Root and branch:* completely and absolutely ▸ **complètement et absolument.**

flower ▸ fleur

nouns bouquet, bud, bulb, chrysanthemum, daffodil, daisy, fragrance, greenhouse, hyacinth, iris, lily, marigold, nose, nursery, orchid, perfume, petal, rose, scent, smell, stem, sunflower, thorn, tulip, violet, wreath, zinnia.

adjectives beautiful, big, blue, bright, charming, colourful, dark, expensive, giant, great, green, high, large, long, lovely, magnificent, majestic, multi-coloured, orange, perfumed, purple, red, short, small, strong, superb, tall, thin, yellow.

verbs SUBJECT: a flower blooms, decorates, grows, smells, wilts. OTHERS: to arrange flowers, to buy flowers, to cut flowers, to deliver flowers, to give a flower, to grow flowers, to hate flowers, to have flowers, to like flowers, to love flowers, to observe flowers, to receive a flower, to sell flowers, to send flowers, to smell flowers, to study flowers, to water flowers.

expressions

- *To push up daisies:* to be dead and buried ▸ **être mort et enterré ou morte et enterrée ; manger les pissenlits par la racine.**
- *The flower of:* the best of ▸ **le meilleur ou la meilleure de ; la crème de.**

fruit ▸ fruit

nouns acorn, apple, apricot, avocado, banana, berry, blueberry, cantaloupe, cherry, chestnut, citrus, coconut, cranberry, fig, gourd, grapefruit, grapes, kiwi, lemon, lime, mango, nectarine, nut, orange, papaya, peach, pear, pineapple, plum, prune, raisin, raspberry, strawberry, sun, tangerine, tree, water, watermelon.

adjectives acid, appetising, big, bitter, delicious, green, hard, juicy, ready, ripe, small, soft, sour, sticky, sweet, tasty.

verbs SUBJECT: a fruit, grows, ripens, tastes. OTHERS: to buy fruit, to cook fruit, to cut fruit, to eat a fruit, to grow fruit, to hate fruit, to like fruit, to love fruit, to pack fruit, to peel a fruit, to pick fruit, to pick up fruit, to rinse a fruit, to sell fruit, to taste a fruit, to wash a fruit.

expressions

- *To bear fruit:* to produce results ▸ **produire des résultats ; porter des fruits.**

leaf ▸ feuille

nouns aspen, bark, birch, bird, branch, bud, bush, cedar, cone, egg, fir, flower, forest, leafstalk, lumber, needle, nest, oak, pine, plant, poplar, redwood, root, rose tree, saw, sequoia, soil, stem, sun, tree, trunk, water, wood.

adjectives beautiful, big, brown, colourful, green, large, long, majestic, nice, old, orange, red, rotten, small, superb, tall, thick, thin, yellow.

verbs SUBJECT: a leaf changes, colours, flies, floats, grows, heals, hides, touches. OTHERS: to burn leaves, to collect leaves, to gather leaves, to pick up leaves, to rake leaves, to remove leaves, to study leaves.

plant ▸ plante

nouns acorn, apple, apricot, artichoke, asparagus, aspen, avocado, banana, bark, bean, beet, birch, bird, blueberry, bouquet, branch, broccoli, Brussels sprout, bud, bulb, bush, cabbage, cantaloupe, carrot, cauliflower, cedar, celery, cherry, chrysanthemum, coconut, cone, corn, cranberry, cucumber, daffodil, daisy, egg, eggplant, fig, fir, flower, forest, fragrance, grapefruit, grapes, green pepper, greenhouse, hyacinth, iris, kiwi, leaf, leafstalk, lemon, lettuce, lily, lime, mango, marigold, mushroom, nectarine, needle, nest, nose, nursery, nut, oak, onion, orange, orchid, papaya, parsnip, pea, peach, pear, perfume, petal, pine, pineapple, plum, poplar, potato, prune, radish, raisin, raspberry, redwood, root, rose, rose tree, scallion, scent, sequoia, smell, soil, spinach, squash, stem, strawberry, sun, sunflower, sweet potato, tangerine, thorn, tomato, tree, trunk, tulip, turnip, violet, water, watermelon, wood, wreath, yam, zinnia, zucchini.

adjectives beautiful, big, blue, bright, brown, carnivorous, charming, colourful, dark, expensive, giant, great, green, high, large, long, lovely, magnificent, majestic, multi-coloured, nice, old, orange, perfumed, purple, red, rotten, short, small, strong, superb, tall, thin, yellow.

verbs SUBJECT: a plant blooms, decorates, grows, hides, holds, smells, supports, touches, wilts. OTHERS: to arrange plants, to attach a plant, to buy plants, to cut a plant, to deliver plants, to give a plant, to grow plants, to hate plants, to have plants, to like plants, to love plants, to observe plants, to pick up plants, to receive a plant, to remove a plant, to sell plants, to send plants, to smell plants, to study plants, to water plants.

tree ▸ arbre

nouns aspen, bark, birch, bird, branch, bud, bush, cedar, cone, deciduous tree, egg, fir, fire, flower, forest, leaf, leafstalk, lumber, needle, nest, oak, pine, plant, poplar, redwood, root, rose tree, saw, sequoia, soil, spruce, stem, sun, trunk, water, wood.

adjectives beautiful, big, giant, great, high, large, long, majestic, short, small, strong, superb, tall, thin.

verbs SUBJECT: A tree grows, hides, touches. OTHERS: to axe a tree, to break a tree, to chop a tree, to cut a tree, to like trees, to plant trees, to protect trees, to push a tree, to remove a tree, to slash a tree, to slice a tree, to study a tree, to tie a tree, to transplant a tree, to water a tree.

expressions

• *To be out of the woods:* out of trouble; difficulties are behind ▸ **ne plus être en difficulté.**

• *A family tree:* a plan showing one's ancestors ▸ **plan montrant les ancêtres de quelqu'un ; arbre généalogique.**

• *Not to be able to see the wood for the trees:* not to understand exactly the nature and purpose of a situation because of too much concern with the details of it ▸ **ne pas comprendre exactement la nature et la raison d'être d'une situation parce qu'on s'empêtre dans les détails.**

vegetable ▸ légume

nouns artichoke, asparagus, beet, broccoli, Brussels sprout, cabbage, carrot, cauliflower, celery, corn, cucumber, eggplant, green pepper, lettuce, bean, mushroom, onion, parsnip, pea, potato, radish, scallion, spinach, squash, sweet potato, tomato, turnip, yam, zucchini.

adjectives appetising, big, bitter, delicious, green, hard, ready, rotten, small, soft, sour, sticky, sweet, tasty.

verbs SUBJECT: a vegetable grows, ripens, tastes. OTHERS: to boil vegetables, to buy vegetables, to cook vegetables, to cut vegetables, to eat a vegetable, to grow vegetables, to hate vegetables, to like vegetables, to love vegetables, to pack vegetables, to peel a vegetable, to pick vegetables, to pick up vegetables, to rinse a vegetable, to sell vegetables, to taste a vegetable, to wash a vegetable.

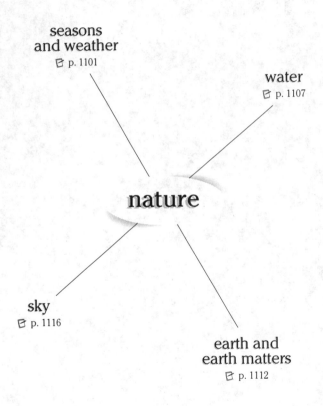

air
▸air

winter
▸hiver

calendar
▸calendrier

weather
▸temps

wind
▸vent

climate
▸climat

dew
▸rosée

tornado
▸tornade

fall
▸automne

temperature
▸température

seasons
and weather

fog
▸brouillard

summer
▸été

heat
▸chaleur

hurricane
▸ouragan

storm
▸tempête

spring
▸printemps

snow
▸neige

rain
▸pluie

season
▸saison

air ► air

nouns aerospace, atmosphere, breath, breeze, climate, cloud, draft, gas, heaven, oxygen, pocket, pollution, sky, smog, smoke, space, wind, ventilation.

adjectives clean, cold, compressed, cool, desert, fresh, hot, humid, light, marine, mountain, poisonous, polluted, pure, smoky, stale, sweet, turbulent, warm.

verbs SUBJECT: air blows, circulates, cools, escapes, flows, stifles, stirs. OTHERS: to breathe air, to compress air, to gasp for air, to inhale air, to need air, to perfume air, to require air, to smell air.

expressions

- *Out of thin air:* out of nothing or from nowhere ► **de nulle part; comme par magie.**
- *To air one's dirty laundry in public:* to discuss private affairs where others can hear ► **discuter d'affaires privées dans un endroit où l'on peut être entendu ou entendue.**
- *To build castles in the air:* to make impossible or imaginary plans ► **échafauder des projets impossibles ou imaginaires; bâtir des châteaux en Espagne.**
- *To walk on air: to be very happy* ► **être très heureux ou heureuse; être sur son petit nuage; être aux anges.**
- *Up in the air:* uncertain ► **incertain.**

calendar ► calendrier

nouns appointment, day, event, holiday, month, occasion, page, paper, schedule, season, time, timetable, wall, year, zodiac.

adjectives annual, current, digital, lunar, personal, solar, yearly.

verbs SUBJECT: a calendar begins, ends, expires, show, tracks. OTHERS: to buy a calendar, to change a calendar, to check a calendar, to mark a calendar, to sell a calendar.

climate ► climat

nouns air, catastrophe, cloud, cyclone, disaster, drizzle, drop, forest, gale, hail, hurricane, lightning, mist, monsoon, nature, precipitation, rain, rainbow, raincoat, rainfall, season, shower, squall, storm, temperature, tempest, thunder, thunderbolt, thunderhead, thunderstorm, tornado, tropics, twister, typhoon, umbrella, water, weather, whirlwind, wind.

adjectives arid, cold, cool, desert, dry, glacial, hot, humid, maritime, mild, pleasant, rainy, regional, seasonal, stormy, temperate, tropical, unpredictable, unstable, warm, wet.

verbs SUBJECT: a climate cools, changes, stabilizes, warms. OTHERS: to enjoy a climate, to hate a climate, to like a climate, to live in a climate.

dew ► rosée

nouns dawn, drops, mist, moisture, morning, night, rain, vapour, water.

adjectives delicate, faint, fine, fresh, heavy, light, morning, summer, wet.

verbs SUBJECT: dew evaporates, falls, refreshes, settles, wets. OTHERS: to see dew, to touch dew.

expressions

- *Dewey-eyed:* having eyes damp with tears ► **avoir les yeux pleins de larmes, avoir les larmes aux yeux.**

fall ► automne

nouns autumn, decline, frost, Halloween, harvest, leaves, November, October, preserves, rain, rake, season, September, time.

adjectives beautiful, brilliant, chilly, colourful, cold, cool, foggy, grey, long, melancholy, rainy, stormy, warm.

verbs SUBJECT: fall begins, ends, passes, terminates. OTHERS: to dread fall, to enjoy fall, to like fall, to love fall, to hate fall, to welcome fall.

fog ▶ brouillard

nouns drops, clouds, drizzle, haze, horn, humidity, lighthouse, mist, moisture, water.

adjectives damp, dense, grey, humid, light, misty, opaque, thick.

verbs SUBJECT: fog clears, cloaks, clings, dampens, drifts, hides, lifts, obscures, rises. OTHERS: to cut the fog, to disappear in the fog, to get lost in the fog, to go into the fog, to penetrate the fog.

expressions

• *In a fog:* mentally confused ▶ **embrouillé ; dans le brouillard.**

heat ▶ chaleur

nouns beach, campfire, climate, degrees, desert, fever, fire, furnace, humidity, insulation, oven, radiator, spark, stove, summer, sun, sunburn, sunshine, thermometer, thermostat.

adjectives arid, desert, dry, excessive, fierce, hot, humid, intense, pleasant, sultry, summer, terrible, tropical, unnatural.

verbs SUBJECT: heat bakes, burns, cooks, decreases, dries, fries, increases, melts, stimulates, suffocates, warms, wilts. OTHERS: to bear the heat, to enjoy the heat.

expressions

• *Heat-stroke:* a feverish condition caused by excessive exposure to high temperature ▶ **fièvre causée par une exposition excessive à la chaleur ; coup de chaleur.**

• *Heatwave:* a prolonged period of unusually hot weather ▶ **période de chaleur inhabituelle ; vague de chaleur.**

• *In the heat of the moment:* during or resulting from intense activity ▶ **pendant ou conséquemment à une activité intense ; dans le feu de l'action.**

hurricane ▶ ouragan

nouns air, catastrophe, climate, cloud, cyclone, disaster, drizzle, drop, forest, gale, hail, lightning, mist, monsoon, nature, precipitation, rain, rainbow, raincoat, rainfall, season, shower, squall, storm, temperature, tempest, thunder, thunderbolt, thunderhead, thunderstorm, tornado, tropics, twister, typhoon, umbrella, water, weather, whirlwind, wind.

adjectives destructive, furious, powerful, scary, strong, terrible, tropical, unbelievable, windy.

verbs SUBJECT: a hurricane blows, destroys, devastates, kills, ruins, scares, strikes, wrecks. OTHERS: to avoid a hurricane, to chase a hurricane, to fear a hurricane, to miss a hurricane, to survive a hurricane.

rain ▶ pluie

nouns acid rain, air, catastrophe, cloud, cyclone, disaster, drizzle, drop, forest, gale, hail, hurricane, lightning, mist, monsoon, nature, precipitation, rainbow, raincoat, rainfall, season, shower, squall, storm, temperature, tempest, thunder, thunderbolt, thunderhead, thunderstorm, tornado, tropics, twister, typhoon, umbrella, water, weather, whirlwind, wind.

adjectives cold, constant, hard, icy, light, mild, misty, monotonous, seasonal, soft, spring, sudden, summer, torrential, warm, welcome, wet.

verbs SUBJECT: rain falls, pelts, pierces, pours, stops, whips. OTHERS: to enjoy rain, to hate rain, to like rain, to want rain.

expressions

• *Rained out:* an event cancelled due to rain ▶ **événement annulé en raison de la pluie.**

• *Rain or shine:* whether the weather is stormy or fair ▶ **quelle que soit la température ; beau temps mauvais temps.**

1103

- *Rainproof:* resistant to rain ► **imperméable.**
- *To rain cats and dogs:* to rain very hard ► **pleuvoir très fort; tomber des cordes.**

season ► saison

nouns autumn, change, equinox, fall, holiday, interval, month, period, quarter, semester, span, spell, sports, spring, summer, term, time, winter, year.

adjectives busy, cold, dry, festive, happy, high, hot, long, low, profitable, rainy, short, warm, wet.

verbs SUBJECT: seasons begin, change, end, fade. OTHERS: to celebrate a season, to dread a season, to enjoy a season, to follow a season, to wait a season.

expressions

- *In season:* available in plenty and good condition ► **abondant et en bon état.**
- *Out of season:* unavailable ► **pas disponible.**

snow ► neige

nouns avalanche, blizzard, crystal, drift, fort, hail, ice, igloo, shovel, skis, sled, snowball, snowbank, snowboard, snowfall, snowflake, snowman, snowmobile, snowplough, snowshoe, storm, toboggan, whiteout, winter.

adjectives cold, fresh, frozen, heavy, icy, new, quiet, wet, white.

verbs SUBJECT: snow accumulates, blankets, covers, drifts, falls, melts, thaws. OTHERS: to melt snow, to shovel snow.

expressions

- *As pure as the driven snow:* completely pure ► **pur; pur comme l'enfant qui vient de naître; blanc comme neige**
- *Snow job:* insincere or exaggerated talk designed to gain the favours of someone ► **propos exagérés ou mensongers exprimés dans le but d'obtenir les faveurs de quelqu'un; baratin.**

- *To be snowed under:* overwhelmed with (for example, a great deal of work) ► **submergé ou submergée (de travail, par exemple).**

spring ► printemps

nouns April, flower, grass, March, May, month, pussy willow, rain, season, shower, sunflower, time, tulip.

adjectives brief, cheerful, cool, early, fresh, glorious, happy, late, long, marvellous, rainy, short, stormy, sudden, sunny, unpleasant, warm, wet, wonderful.

verbs SUBJECT: spring begins, commences, ends, passes, renews. OTHERS: to await spring, to enjoy spring, to celebrate spring, to like spring, to love spring.

expressions

- *Spring chicken:* a young person ► **jeune personne; une jeunesse.**

storm ► tempête

nouns atmosphere, blizzard, cyclone, gale, hail, hurricane, lightning, rain, shower, sleet, snow, squall, tempest, thunder, thunderbolt, thunderhead, thunderstorm, tornado, typhoon, umbrella, wind.

adjectives angry, awesome, brief, dangerous, destructive, electric, fierce, horrible, incredible, intense, passing, relentless, tropical, violent, wet, wild.

verbs SUBJECT: a storm attacks, beats, batters, blows, blusters, breaks, cripples, damages, rages, tapers off, whips. OTHERS: to await a storm, to fear a storm, to predict a storm, to track a storm, to watch a storm.

expressions

- *To take by storm:* to capture by a sudden or very bold attack ► **prendre d'assaut.**
- *A storm in a teacup:* a fuss made over an unimportant matter ► **(faire des) his-**

toires à propos de choses peu importantes ; tempête dans un verre d'eau.

- *To accept any port in a storm:* when one has difficulties, any solution is accepted ▸ **lorsqu'on a des problèmes, toutes les solutions sont acceptables ; nécessité fait loi.**

summer ▸ été

nouns August, barbecue, beach, bicycle, break, bugs, fun, garden, golf, heat, holiday, June, July, picnic, rainbow, roller skate, season, solstice, sun, sunburn, sunglasses, sunstroke, tennis, vacation.

adjectives cloudy, cold, cool, dry, hot, hazy, humid, lazy, muggy, rainy, stormy, sunny, tropical, unforgettable, violent.

verbs SUBJECT: a summer begins, disappears, ends, fades, passes, simmers. OTHERS: to enjoy a summer, to like a summer, to love a summer, to pass a summer, to spend a summer.

expressions

- *Indian summer:* a time of warm weather in the fall ▸ **période de temps chaud pendant l'automne ; été indien.**
- *One swallow doesn't make a summer:* one single or small success does not necessarily indicate an important or global success ▸ **un seul ou un modeste succès n'est pas nécessairement signe de réussite importante ou générale ; une hirondelle ne fait le printemps.**

temperature ▸ température

nouns climate, degrees, season, thermometer, thermostat, weather.

adjectives arid, cold, cool, desert, dry, extreme, hot, humid, local, moderate, mountain, ocean, pleasant, seasonal, tropical, uncomfortable, unpleasant, unpredictable, warm.

verbs SUBJECT: temperature drops, falls, rises, skyrockets, stabilizes. OTHERS: to

have a temperature, to run a temperature, to take a temperature.

expressions

- *To run a temperature:* to have a body temperature that is above normal ▸ **avoir une température corporelle supérieure à la normale ; avoir de la température.**

tornado ▸ tornade

nouns catastrophe, cyclone, disaster, gale, hurricane, nature, rain, squall, storm, tempest, tropics, twister, typhoon, whirlwind, wind.

adjectives destructive, furious, powerful, scary, strong, terrible, tropical, unbelievable, windy.

verbs SUBJECT: a tornado blows, destroys, devastates, kills, ruins, scares, strikes, wrecks. OTHERS: to avoid a tornado, to chase a tornado, to fear a tornado, to miss a tornado, to survive a tornado.

weather ▸ temps

nouns atmosphere, barometer, climate, forecast, front, heat, instrument, precipitation, rain, report, satellite, season, storm, sun, system, temperature, thermometer, wind.

adjectives clear, cloudy, cold, dry, extreme, good, hot, humid, maritime, nice, rainy, snowy, sunny, terrible, tropical, ugly, unfortunate, unpleasant, unusual, variable, violent, wet, windy.

verbs SUBJECT: weather allows, cheers, depresses, discourages, encourages, permits. OTHERS: to curse the weather, to enjoy the weather, to predict weather, to watch weather.

expressions

- *Weatherman:* a person who broadcasts a weather forecast ▸ **personne qui présente les prévisions météorologiques à la télévision.**

- *Keep a weather eye open:* to remain alert or watchful ► **être à l'affût; avoir ou garder l'œil ouvert.**
- *To make heavy weather of something:* to find great difficulty in doing something usually simple and easy to do ► **avoir beaucoup de difficulté à faire quelque chose qui est facile à faire en temps normal.**
- *Under the weather:* in poor health ► **en mauvaise santé.**

wind ► vent

nouns air, blast, blizzard, breath, breeze, Chinook, cyclone, draft, flag, gale, gust, hurricane, kite, sail, squall, storm, tempest, tornado, twister, typhoon, whirlwind, wind chill, wind mill.

adjectives arctic, cold, cool, desert, Eastern, gentle, harsh, hot, light, Northern, ocean, powerful, refreshing, Southern, strong, summer, turbulent, warm, Western, winter.

verbs SUBJECT: wind blows, blasts, carries, cools, dries, roars, scatters, sighs, stimulates, stings, topples, whips, whistles. OTHERS: to feel wind, to smell wind.

expressions

- *To catch wind of:* to hear of ► **entendre dire.**
- *To take the wind out of someone's sails:* to discourage someone ► **décourager quelqu'un.**
- *To throw caution to the wind:* to behave recklessly ► **se comporter avec insouciance.**
- *Windbag:* a person who talks too much ► **personne qui parle trop; moulin à paroles.**
- *Windfall:* an unexpected gift or gain of sizeable proportion ► **cadeau ou gain considérable inattendu; manne tombée du ciel.**

winter ► hiver

nouns snow ball, Christmas, cold, December, February, glacier, hibernation, hockey, holiday, ice, iceberg, icicle, flake, January, New Year's Day, parka, season, shivers, skate, ski, sled, sleigh, snow, snowshoe, solstice, toboggan, tuque.

adjectives cold, cruel, dry, early, enjoyable, frozen, good, harsh, late, long, mild, pleasant, quiet, short, snowy, terrible, typical, unusual, warm, wet.

verbs SUBJECT: winter arrives, blasts, ends, freezes, interrupts. OTHERS: to detest winter, to enjoy winter, to hate winter, to like winter, to pass the winter.

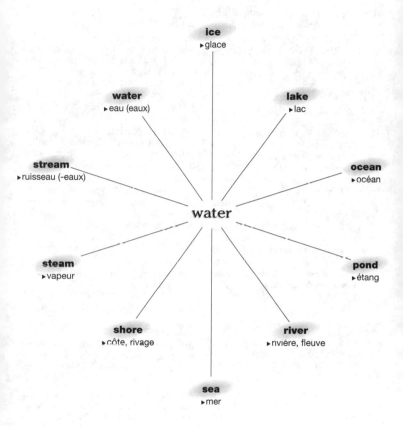

ice
▸glace

water
▸eau (eaux)

lake
▸lac

stream
▸ruisseau (-eaux)

ocean
▸océan

water

steam
▸vapeur

pond
▸étang

shore
▸côte, rivage

river
▸rivière, fleuve

sea
▸mer

ice ► glace

nouns block, cold, crystal, cube, freeze, freezer, glacier, Ice Age, iceberg, ice breaker, ice cream, ice cube, ice house, icicle, skate, sled, sleigh, snow, toboggan, water, winter.

adjectives clear, cold, crushed, dry, fragile, frozen, melting, natural, slippery, solid, thick, thin.

verbs SUBJECT: ice breaks, cracks, forms, melts. OTHERS: to carve ice, to crush ice, to make ice, to slip on ice.

expressions

• *Just (only) the tip of the iceberg:* only a small, visible, part of a very much larger hidden problem ► **aspect à peine visible d'un problème beaucoup plus important; pointe de l'iceberg.**

• *To break the ice:* to start a conversation ► **entamer la conversation; briser ou rompre la glace.**

• *To cut no ice:* to have no effect ► **n'avoir aucun effet.**

• *To put on ice:* to put aside for use or attention at a later date ► **mettre de côté pour y revenir plus tard.**

• *To skate on thin ice:* to do something risky ► **faire quelque chose de risqué; s'aventurer en terrain glissant.**

lake ► lac

nouns bank, boat, cabin, camp, canoe, dive, duck, fish, fog, insect, loon, nature, resort, sailboat, shoal, shore, swim, water, water skis, wave.

adjectives big, calm, clean, clear, deep, fresh, frozen, great, pleasant, polluted, popular, private, quiet, remote, shallow, small, smooth, tiny.

verbs SUBJECT: a lake freezes, melts, mirrors, reflects, sparkles. OTHERS: to bathe in a lake, to drink from a lake, to drown in a lake, to submerge in a lake, to swim in a lake, to visit a lake, to wash in a lake.

expressions

• *Go jump in the lake:* go away and quit being a bother ► **partir et cesser d'ennuyer autrui.**

ocean ► océan

noun bay, beach, boat, coral, cruise, dolphin, fish, gulf, island, journey, mainland, marines, octopus, pirate, reef, sailor, sand, scuba, sea, seal, sea lion, seaweed, shark, ship, shipwreck, shoal, shore, sponge, squid, starfish, submarine, swordfish, tide, tuna, voyage, waterfront, wave, whale.

adjectives Atlantic, Arctic, big, blue, clean, deep, huge, immense, Indian, Pacific, mysterious, polluted, salty, stormy, turbulent, vast, wide.

verbs SUBJECT: an ocean consumes, falls, rises, rocks. OTHERS: to cruise the ocean, to fear the ocean, to love the ocean, to sail the ocean, to see the ocean, to visit the ocean.

expressions

• *A drop in the ocean:* a tiny part of what was needed ► **infime partie de ce qui était nécessaire.**

pond ► étang

nouns bank, beaver, bog, dam, duck, fish, frog, lagoon, lake, marsh, minnow, reed, scum, slime, snail, shore, swamp, tadpole, water.

adjectives calm, clear, country, fresh, frozen, large, murky, natural, peaceful, polluted, secluded, shallow, small, splendid, tranquil.

verbs SUBJECT: a pond dries up, freezes, grows, shrinks. OTHERS: to bathe in a pond, to create a pond, to dig a pond, to drink from a pond, to fish in a pond, to swim in a pond.

expressions

- *A big fish in a small pond:* an important person in a small place or position ▸ **personne importante se trouvant dans une position ou un espace restreint.**

river ▸ rivière, fleuve

nouns barge, bank, boat, bridge, brook, canal, canoe, channel, current, fish, frog, isle, island, lagoon, lake, ocean, pebble, portage, rock, salmon, shoal, source, stream, torrent, trout, waterway.

adjectives clean, clear, cold, dangerous, deep, distant, fresh, frozen, long, mountain, narrow, rapid, raging, rocky, sacred, shallow, swift, wide, winding.

verbs SUBJECT: a river bends, dries up, murmurs, floods, flows, freezes, overflows, rages, rises, runs, rushes, trickles, turns. OTHERS: to bathe in a river, to canoe a river, to cross a river, to drown in a river, to navigate a river, to paddle a river, to swim in a river.

expressions

- *To sell down the river:* to betray or let down ▸ **trahir ou laisser tomber.**

sea ▸ mer

nouns bay, beach, boat, cruise, dolphin, fish, gulf, island, isle, journey, mainland, marines, monster, octopus, pirate, reef, sailor, salt, sand, scuba, sea anemone, seagull, sea horse, seal, sea level, sea lion, seaplane, sea tortoise, seaway, seaweed, shark, ship, shipwreck, shore, sponge, squid, starfish, swordfish, tide, tuna, voyage, waterfront, whale, wave.

adjectives beautiful, big, blue, calm, clean, dead, deep, distant, huge, immense, mysterious, polluted, rough, salty, stormy, turbulent, vast, wide.

verbs SUBJECT: a sea consumes, falls, rises, rocks. OTHERS: to cruise the sea, to drown in the sea, to love the sea, to fear the sea, to pollute the sea, to sail the sea.

expressions

- *At sea:* puzzled or confused ▸ **déconcerté ou déconcertée, confus ou confuse.**
- *Not the only fish in the sea:* not the only one available ▸ **pas le seul disponible; un de perdu, dix de retrouvés.**
- *Sea legs:* adjustment to being in a boat that is rocking on the sea ▸ **adaptation à un bateau qui tangue sur la mer; (avoir, retrouver) le pied marin.**

shore ▸ côte, rivage

nouns bank, beach, border, coast, edge, driftwood, frog, jungle, lake, land, moss, mud, ocean, river, sand, turtle, waterfront, woods.

adjectives distant, mossy, muddy, nearest, rocky, sandy, steep.

verbs SUBJECT: a shore attracts, draws, limits. OTHERS: to stand on shore, to swim to shore, to walk on shore.

expressions

- *Shore leave:* permission given to a person in the Navy to leave the ship for a certain length of time ▸ **dans la marine, permission de quitter le navire pendant une période déterminée; permission à terre.**

steam ▸ vapeur

nouns air, bath, boiler, breath, cloud, condensation, engine, evaporation, fog, gas, geyser, haze, heat, humidity, iron, mist pressure, rain, steamer, steamroller, steamship, temperature, vapour, water.

adjectives aromatic, hot, light, opaque, thick, warm.

verbs SUBJECT: steam disappears, escapes, evaporates, rises. OTHERS: to blow steam, to breathe steam, to inhale steam, to release steam, to see steam.

expressions

- *Full steam ahead:* at the greatest speed possible ▸ **le plus rapidement possible ; à toute vapeur.**
- *Get up steam:* to collect energy to do something ▸ **rassembler ses forces en prévision d'une action.**
- *Let off steam:* to get rid of physical energy or strong feeling through activity ▸ **s'activer pour dépenser de l'énergie ou faire passer de fortes émotions ; se défouler.**
- *Run out of steam:* to become exhausted ▸ **s'épuiser, s'essouffler.**
- *Steamed up:* excited or angry ▸ **agité ou agitée ; en colère.**
- *Under one's own steam:* by one's own efforts ▸ **grâce à ses propres efforts.**

stream ▸ **ruisseau (-eaux)**

nouns bank, bridge, brook, canal, channel, creek, current, fiord, fish, frog, inlet, island, isle, lagoon, lake, pebble, river, rock, source, torrent, waterway.

adjectives clean, clear, cold, distant, fresh, frozen, icy, little, long, mountain, narrow, peaceful, pure, quiet, rapid, rocky, shallow, small, swift, winding.

verbs SUBJECT: a stream flows, freezes, murmurs, runs, trickles. OTHERS: to bathe in a stream, to drink from a stream, to fall in a stream, to jump a stream, to follow a stream.

expressions

- *Stream of consciousness:* a person's thoughts and conscious reactions to events perceived as a continuous flow ▸ **pensées et réactions conscientes d'une personne à l'égard d'événements perçus comme un flux continu.**
- *To change horses midstream:* to make new plans or choose a new leader in the middle of an important activity ▸ **faire de nouveaux plans ou choisir un nouveau ou une nouvelle chef au beau milieu d'un projet important ; changer de cheval au milieu du gué.**

water ▸ **eau (eaux)**

nouns baptism, drip, drop, flood, geyser, hose, ice, irrigation, lake, liquid, ocean, pond, pool, rain, river, sediment, sink, shore, shower, sprinkler, steam, stream, swamp, tear, tidal wave, water, colour, waterfall, waterfront, watershed, waterwheel, wave.

adjectives boiling, clean, clear, cloudy, cold, cool, dirty, frozen, hot, icy, murky, polluted, refreshing, warm, wet.

verbs SUBJECT: water cleans, cleanses, drips, drowns, evaporates, falls, flows, freezes, sprinkles, washes. OTHERS: to carry water, to drink water, to float in water, to sink in water, to submerge in water.

expressions

- *Blood is thicker than water:* a family member is more important than any other person ▸ **les membres de la famille sont les personnes les plus importantes ; rien n'est plus fort que les liens du sang ; c'est la voix du sang.**
- *Milk and water:* something very weak ▸ **quelque chose de très faible.**
- *Of the first water:* of the best quality ▸ **de qualité supérieure.**
- *Through hell and high water:* through troubles or difficulties of any kind ▸ **en ayant des difficultés de toutes sortes.**
- *To be in deep water:* in trouble ▸ **en difficulté ; dans de beaux draps.**
- *To be like a fish out of water:* uncomfortable ▸ **mal à l'aise.**
- *To be like water off a duck's back:* to have no effect at all ▸ **n'avoir aucun effet.**
- *To hold water:* to be correct ▸ **être correct ou correcte ; bien se tenir.**
- *To make one's mouth water:* to make you want to eat or drink something you see or smell ▸ **faire en sorte que l'on désire manger ou boire ce que l'on voit ou ce que l'on sent ; faire venir ou mettre l'eau à la bouche.**

- *To pour oil on troubled waters:* to try to calm things or someone ▶ **tenter de calmer les choses ou les personnes.**

- *To spend money like water:* to spend money very freely ▶ **dépenser sans compter; jeter l'argent par les fenêtres.**

- *To throw cold water on (over) someone:* to discourage someone ▶ **décourager quelqu'un.**

- *To tread water:* to keep oneself afloat in an upright position by moving the legs ▶ **garder la tête hors de l'eau en bougeant les jambes; surnager.**

- *To water something down:* to make something less strong ▶ **rendre moins fort, adoucir, atténuer; mettre de l'eau dans son vin.**

- *Water under the bridge:* something that is past and is not worth worrying about ▶ **chose qui appartient au passé et qui ne vaut plus la peine qu'on s'en préoccupe.**

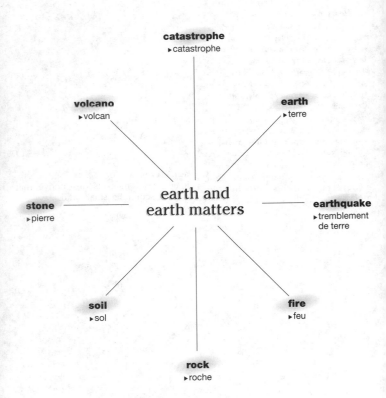

catastrophe
▸catastrophe

volcano
▸volcan

earth
▸terre

earth and earth matters

stone
▸pierre

earthquake
▸tremblement de terre

soil
▸sol

fire
▸feu

rock
▸roche

catastrophe ▸ catastrophe

nouns avalanche, calamity, death, destruction, disaster, earthquake, emergency, epidemic, fire, hurricane, nature, plague, ruin, sickness, tidal wave, tornado, tragedy, twister, war, wrath.

adjectives natural, frightening, great, horrible, huge, massive, nuclear, scary, terrible, tragic, traumatic, unexpected.

verbs SUBJECT: a catastrophe damages, destroys, devastates, kills, ruins, wrecks. OTHERS: to experience a catastrophe, to live through a catastrophe, to predict a catastrophe, to suffer a catastrophe, to survive a catastrophe, to witness a catastrophe.

earth ▸ terre

nouns agriculture, atmosphere, beach, canyon, city, continent, desert, earthquake, ecosystem, equator, estate, farm, geology, gravity, hemisphere, horizon, jungle, land, meadow, mountains, mud, ocean, planet, pole, prairie, rain, region, sand, sea, soil, solar system, territory, topography, topsoil, tundra, universe, vegetation, wasteland.

adjectives arctic, big, cold, dry, fertile, hot, humid, muddy, rainy, rich, rocky, round, wet, windy, vast.

verbs SUBJECT: the earth rotates, spins, turns. OTHERS: to care for the earth, to cultivate the earth, to damage the earth, to heal the earth, to irrigate the earth, to populate the earth, to touch the earth, to walk the earth.

expressions

- *Down to earth:* a quality of someone friendly and approachable ▸ **qualité de quelqu'un d'amical et d'accessible.**
- *To move heaven and earth:* to do everything possible ▸ **faire tout en son pouvoir.**
- *To come back to earth:* to get back to reality ▸ **revenir à la réalité; revenir sur terre.**

earthquake ▸ tremblement de terre

nouns catastrophe, disaster, fault, record, Richter scale, shock, tremor, upheaval.

adjectives big, destructive, natural, small, violent.

verbs SUBJECT: an earthquake alarms, destroys, disrupts, frightens, injures, jolts, kills, rumbles, scares, shakes, surprises, topples. OTHERS: to detect an earthquake, to feel an earthquake, to predict an earthquake, to report an earthquake, to survive an earthquake.

fire ▸ feu

nouns blaze, bonfire, campfire, fire engine, fire hall, fire-fighter, firefly, fireplace, fireworks, flame, forest fire, fuel, gas, gasoline, heat, ignition, log, match, paper, spark, wood.

adjectives big, bright, brilliant, chemical, cosy, dangerous, destructive, hot, roaring, scorching, small, wild.

verbs SUBJECT: fire bakes, blazes, blisters, burns, consumes, cooks, crackles, destroys, dies, glows, illuminates, kills, scorches, sizzles, spreads. OTHERS: to catch fire, to extinguish a fire, to feed a fire, to ignite a fire, to light a fire, to start a fire.

expressions

- *A firebrand:* someone who causes political trouble ▸ **qui cause la dissension politique; brandon de discorde.**
- *Firebug:* an arsonist ▸ **pyromane.**
- *Like a house on fire:* very well or very quickly ▸ **très bien ou très rapidement.**
- *The fat is in the fire:* trouble has been started and something extraordinary can be expected to happen ▸ **les difficultés ont commencé et on peut s'attendre à ce que quelque chose d'extraordinaire se produise; il y a de l'eau dans le gaz.**
- *There is no smoke without fire:* there is always a basis for any rumour ▸ **les rumeurs sont toujours basées sur une quelconque vérité; il n'y a pas de fumée sans feu.**

- *To add fuel to the fire:* to make an argument more heated ▸ **rendre une dispute encore plus aiguë ; jeter de l'huile sur le feu.**
- To be under fire: criticized ▸ **critiqué ou critiquée.**
- *To fight fire with fire:* to fight back in the same way one was attacked ▸ **se défendre de la même façon qu'on a été attaqué ou attaquée ; rendre la pareille ; combattre le feu par le feu.**
- *To fire away:* to go ahead ▸ **aller de l'avant.**
- *To fire on all cylinders:* to work at full strength ▸ **travailler de toutes ses forces ; carburer à plein régime.**
- *To hang fire:* to delay ▸ **reporter.**
- *To have several irons in the fire:* to be involved or to be doing several things at the same time ▸ **mener plusieurs projets de front.**
- *To keep the home fires burning:* to keep things going as usual while someone is away ▸ **faire en sorte que les choses continuent comme d'habitude pendant l'absence de quelqu'un.**
- *To open fire:* to start shooting ▸ **commencer à tirer ; faire feu.**
- *To play with fire:* to do something dangerous ▸ **faire quelque chose de dangereux ; jouer avec le feu.**

rock ▸ roche

nouns boulder, concrete, diamond, flint, fossil, gem, gravel, marble, mineral, pebble, quartz, reef, sandstone, shale, slate, stone.

adjectives ancient, big, broken, crumbling, flat, hard, heavy, huge, irregular, old, rare, round, small, solid, tiny, volcanic.

verbs SUBJECT: rocks fall, roll, sink, slide, tumble. OTHERS: to analyse a rock, to bury a rock, to collect rocks, to kick a rock, to place a rock, to polish a rock, to push a rock, to roll a rock, to skip a rock, to study a rock, to throw a rock, to toss a rock.

expressions

- *As steady as a rock:* very steady ▸ **très stable.**
- *As strong as a rock:* very strong ▸ **très fort ou forte.**
- *Between a rock and a hard place:* to have a tough decision to make ▸ **avoir une décision difficile à prendre.**
- *Something is on the rocks:* something is in danger of breaking up ▸ **quelque chose risque de se briser.**
- *To have a drink on the rocks:* to have ice in one's drink ▸ **mettre de la glace dans une boisson.**

soil ▸ sol

nouns compost, country, dirt, dust, earth, fertilizer, garden, grass, gravel, ground, land, mud, terrain, topsoil, worm.

adjectives damp, dark, dry, dusty, fertile, moist, muddy, organic, rich, rocky, sandy, soft, soggy, wet.

verbs SUBJECT: soil nourishes, supports. OTHERS: to analyse soil, to dig soil, to irrigate soil, to turn over soil, to water soil.

expressions

- *To soil one's hands:* to lower or hurt one's character or name, to do a bad or shameful thing ▸ **s'abaisser ou faire quelque chose de méchant ou de honteux ; se salir les mains.**

stone ▸ pierre

nouns boulder, diamond, gem, pebble, rock, sandstone.

adjectives ancient, big, broken, expensive, flat, hard, huge, irregular, large, old, precious, rare, round, small, solid, tiny.

verbs SUBJECT: stones crack, fall, roll, tumble. OTHERS: to buy a stone, to collect stones, to gather stones, to polish stones, to study stones, to throw stones, to toss stones.

expressions

- *A rolling stone gathers no moss:* a person who moves often will not foster meaningful relationships or receive the other benefits of staying in one place ▸ **une personne qui déménage souvent ne favorise guère la création de liens durables ou ne profite pas des avantages découlant de la stabilité ; pierre qui roule n'amasse pas mousse.**

- *A stone's throw away:* very close ▸ **très près ; à un jet de pierre.**

- *Stone-cold sober:* completely sober ▸ **complètement sobre ; sobre comme un chameau.**

- *To have a heart of stone:* to be cold and uncaring ▸ **être froid ou froide et insensible ; avoir un cœur de pierre, de marbre ; avoir une pierre à la place du cœur.**

- *To kill two birds with one stone:* to succeed in doing two things with only one action ▸ **réussir à accomplir deux choses par une seule action ; faire d'une pierre deux coups.**

- *To leave no stone unturned:* to try every possible means ▸ **essayer par tous les moyens.**

- *To stonewall someone:* to obstruct intentionally ▸ **créer des obstacles intentionnellement.**

volcano ▸ volcan

nouns ash, cloud, crater, explosion, gas, lava, mountain, steam.

adjectives dormant, explosive, inactive, unstable, violent.

verbs SUBJECT: a volcano blankets, burns, covers, destroys, erupts, explodes, kills, lies dormant, rages, rumbles, sleeps. OTHERS: to watch a volcano.

expressions

- *To sit on a volcano:* to be in a place where trouble may start or danger may come suddenly ▸ **se trouver dans un endroit où le danger ou les difficultés peuvent survenir soudainement.**

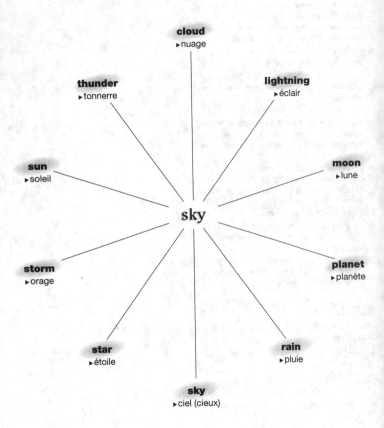

cloud
▸nuage

thunder
▸tonnerre

lightning
▸éclair

sun
▸soleil

moon
▸lune

sky

storm
▸orage

planet
▸planète

star
▸étoile

rain
▸pluie

sky
▸ciel (cieux)

cloud ▸ nuage

nouns climate, cloudburst, cotton, gloom, group, fog, hail, ice, lightning, mass, mist, rain, sadness, shelter, sky, sleet, snow, storm, sun, thermometer, thunder, umbrella, weather, wind, water.

adjectives big, black, clear, dark, dismal, fine, gloomy, grey, high, fast, fluffy, ominous, sad, slow, small, thin, threatening, white.

verbs SUBJECT: clouds, billow, break, change, float, hang, move, threaten. OTHERS: to chase the clouds, to fly in the clouds, to look at a cloud, to study a cloud, to watch a cloud.

expressions

• *A cloud on the horizon:* a problem in the future ▸ **problème éventuel; nuages noirs à l'horizon.**

• *To be under a cloud:* to be unpopular because of something one has said or done ▸ **ne pas être apprécié ou appréciée à cause de ce qu'on a dit ou fait.**

• *Every cloud has a silver lining:* there is something good in every situation ▸ **il y a quelque chose de bon dans toute situation; à quelque chose malheur est bon.**

• *To have one's head in the clouds:* to daydream, to be lost in one's thoughts ▸ **rêver éveillé ou éveillée; être perdu ou perdue dans ses pensées; avoir la tête dans les nuages.**

• *To be on cloud nine:* to be very happy ▸ **être très heureux ou heureuse; être aux anges; être sur son petit nuage.**

lightning ▸ éclair

nouns cloud, charge, electricity, flash, light, rain, rod, storm, thunder.

adjectives blinding, bright, dramatic, instant, scary, sudden, zigzag.

verbs SUBJECT: lightning, breaks, flashes, lights, up, scares, surprises. OTHERS: to be hit by lightning, to be lit by lightning, to protect from lightning, to see lightning, to watch lightning.

expressions

• *Faster than lightning:* extremely fast ▸ **très rapidement; à la vitesse de l'éclair.**

• *Lightening doesn't strike twice:* bad things won't happen twice to the same person ▸ **la malchance ne frappe jamais deux fois la même personne; la foudre ne tombe jamais deux fois au même endroit.**

• *(Someone is) a lightening rod:* one who takes the blame even though others share the responsibility ▸ **personne qui assume l'entière responsabilité même si les autres la partagent.**

moon ▸ lune

nouns astrology, astronomy, atmosphere, body, calendar, cheese, crater, crescent, earth, eclipse, harvest, heaven, light, mountain, night, orbit, planets, rocket, science, sky, space, sun, surface, stars, telescope, water.

adjectives bright, cold, rocky, full, half, new, round, visible.

verbs SUBJECT: the moon appears, glows, revolves, rises, sets, waxes, wanes. OTHERS: to go to the moon, to land on the moon, to see the moon, to study the moon, to walk on the moon.

expressions

• *To moonlight:* to work a second job ▸ **avoir un second emploi.**

• *To ask for the moon:* to ask for more than is reasonable ▸ **faire des demandes déraisonnables; demander la lune.**

• *Once in a blue moon:* rarely, infrequently ▸ **rarement, peu souvent.**

• *To promise the moon:* to promise more than one can give ▸ **promettre quelque chose d'impossible; promettre la lune.**

planet ▸ planète

nouns asteroid, body, Earth, explore, extraterrestrial, galaxy, gasses, gravity, Jupiter, Mars, Mercury, moon, orbit, planetarium, Pluto, Neptune, rings, satellite, Saturn, space, surface, system, telescope, temperature, universe, Uranus, Venus.

adjectives celestial, close, distant, far, huge, massive.

verbs SUBJECT: planets change, correspond, emit, evolve, gravitate, move, revolve. OTHERS: to live on a planet, to observe a planet, to study a planet, to visit a planet.

expressions

• *(Someone is) living on another planet:* someone doesn't notice what's happening around them ▸ **qui ne remarque pas ce qui se passe autour de lui ou d'elle.**

rain ▸ pluie

nouns cloud, earth, humidity, monsoon, plants, precipitation, rainbow, raincoat, season, shower, sky, spring, sprinkling, summer, storm, umbrella, water, weather, worms.

adjectives beating, cold, driving, freezing, heavy, light, refreshing, sudden, warm.

verbs SUBJECT: rain beats, becomes, falls, helps, soaks, sprinkles, starts, stops, wets. OTHERS: to protect from rain, to be thankful for rain, to measure the rain, to need rain, to pray for rain, to seek shelter from rain, to welcome the rain.

expressions

• *To rain on someone's parade:* to spoil someone's enjoyment or success with negative comments or behaviour ▸ **gâcher le plaisir ou le succès de quelqu'un par un comportement ou des commentaires désagréables.**

• *To do something come rain or come shine:* to be determined to do something, no matter what happens ▸ **être déterminé ou déterminée à faire quelque chose, peu importe les conditions.**

• *To be right as rain:* to feel well ▸ **se sentir bien.**

• *To take a rain check:* to agree to do something at a later date ▸ **reporter une activité.**

sky ▸ ciel (cieux)

nouns air, airplane, angel, astrology, astronomy, atmosphere, bird, ceiling, celestial, climate, cloud, galaxy, God, gravity, heaven, horizon, light, lightning, rain, rainbow, rocket, skylight, space, snow, star, sun, moon, storm, weather.

adjectives blue, big, clear, cloudy, changing, dark, foggy, gloomy, heavenly, open, overcast, menacing, sunrise, sunset, stormy, vast.

verbs SUBJECT: the sky becomes, clears, clouds over, covers, darkens, expands, indicates, lightens, stretches. OTHERS: to fall from the sky, to fly in the sky, to look at the sky, to look to the sky, to reach for the sky, to stare at the sky.

expressions

• *Sky high:* extremely high ▸ **très haut.**

• *To skyrocket:* to rise rapidly or suddenly to success, fame and/or fortune ▸ **réussir rapidement ou soudainement.**

• *The sky's the limit:* there is no limit to what you can achieve ▸ **il n'y a aucune limite à ce qui peut être accompli.**

• *Out of a clear blue sky:* an unexpected event ▸ **événement inattendu.**

star ▸ étoile

nouns asterisk, astrology, astronaut, celestial, constellation, explosion, heavens, night, point, sky, space, sparkle, Star of David, telescope.

adjectives bright, celestial, glowing, shining, twinkling, visible.

verbs SUBJECT: stars appear, explode, fade, glow, light, shine, shoot. OTHERS: to count the stars, to draw a star, to see in the stars, to watch the stars.

expressions

• *A star is born:* The moment a person becomes a celebrity ▸ **moment où une personne devient célèbre.**

- *To shoot for the stars:* To aim for the highest goal ► **viser l'objectif le plus élevé.**
- *To be/become a star:* To be/become a celerity ► **être ou devenir une vedette.**
- *To be star struck:* To be in awe of a celebrity ► **être en admiration devant une vedette.**
- *To see stars:* to be temporarily disoriented ► **être désorienté ou désorientée pendant un moment; voir trente-six chandelles.**

storm ► orage

nouns cloud, damage, darkness, destruction, fear, hail, hurricane, ice, lightning, precipitation, rain, rod, shelter, sky, snow, thunder, tornado, weather, wind, warning.

adjectives brewing, brief, close, dangerous, dark, destructive, distant, heavy, rough, sudden, summer, unexpected, wild, winter.

verbs SUBJECT: storms attack, brew, calm, die down, pass, rage, threaten. OTHERS: to fear a storm, to foresee a storm, to escape a storm, to expect a storm, to monitor a storm, to warn about a storm.

expressions

- *A storm is brewing:* A storm is developing ► **une tempête s'annonce.**
- *To talk up a storm:* to talk with a lot of energy ► **parler avec beaucoup d'énergie.**
- *To be in the eye of the storm:* to be in the middle of an argument involving many people ► **être l'objet d'une dispute à laquelle participent plusieurs personnes.**
- *To take by storm:* to have sudden success in a particular place ► **avoir brusquement du succès dans une position particulière.**
- *The calm before the storm:* the peace and quiet before trouble starts ► **temps de paix précédant les difficultés.**

sun ► soleil

nouns asteroid, atmosphere, beach, burn, cancer, chlorophyll, damage, eclipse, fall, freckle, goodness, greenhouse, growth, joy, light, life, happiness, heat, photosynthesis, plants, rainbow, sickness, spring, sky, south, summer, sunflower, sunset, sunrise, sunshine, star, tan, vacation, vitamin, warmth, winter.

adjectives beautiful, hot, necessary, pleasant, tiring, useful, warm.

verbs SUBJECT: the sun beats, bleaches, burns, heats, lights, rises, sets, shines. OTHERS: to avoid the sun, to enjoy the sun, to look at the sun, to need the sun, to seek the sun, to sunbathe.

expressions

- *To make hay while the sun shines:* to do something while conditions are right ► **faire quelque chose pendant que les conditions le permettent.**
- *A place in the sun:* a job or situation that gives you everything you want ► **situation ou emploi très satisfaisant.**
- *Everything under the sun:* everything that exists ► **tout ce qui existe.**
- *To catch the sun:* to become sunburnt ► **avoir un coup de soleil.**
- *Under the sun:* in the whole world ► **dans le monde entier.**

thunder ► tonnerre

nouns air, clap, clouds, crack, explosion, fear, heat, lightning, noise, precipitation, rain, scare, shelter, storm, temperature.

adjectives close, distant, dramatic, loud, noisy, rolling, scary, sudden, violent.

verbs SUBJECT: thunder breaks, claps, crashes, explodes, rumbles. OTHERS: to be afraid of thunder, to hear thunder, to listen for thunder.

expressions

- *To steal someone's thunder:* to do something that detracts from someone else's success ► **faire quelque chose qui porte atteinte au succès de quelqu'un d'autre.**

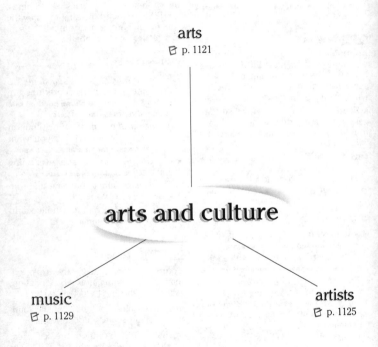

arts
☞ p. 1121

arts and culture

music
☞ p. 1129

artists
☞ p. 1125

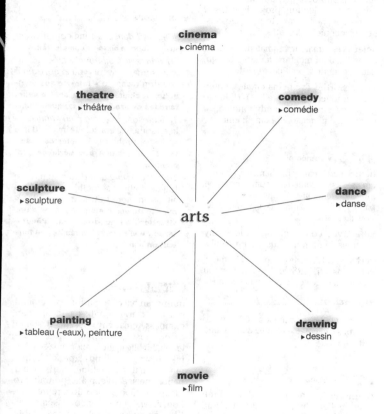

cinema
▸ cinéma

theatre
▸ théâtre

comedy
▸ comédie

sculpture
▸ sculpture

arts

dance
▸ danse

painting
▸ tableau (-eaux), peinture

drawing
▸ dessin

movie
▸ film

cinema ▸ cinéma

nouns actor, actress, art, comedian, critic, comedy, director, documentary, drama, effects, entertainment, experimental, film, horror, lighting, motion, picture, music, musical, performance, persuasion, photography, popular, poster, producer, projection, projectionist, set, sound, spectacle, star, story, studio, suspense, technician, theatre, ticket.

adjectives amateur, animated, classical, comedic, documentary, fantasy, foreign, national, period, political, realistic.

verbs SUBJECT: cinema creates, entertains, produces, shows, tells. OTHERS: to go to the cinema, to study cinema, to work at a cinema, to work in cinema.

comedy ▸ comédie

nouns actor, cartoon, character, cinema, circus, clown, comedian, comic, costume, humour, laughter, make-up, movie, parody, ridicule, satire, stage, stunt, television, theatre, wit.

adjectives comedic, enjoyable, funny, hilarious, humorous, musical, physical.

verbs SUBJECT: clever, comical, comedy, entertains. OTHERS: to do a comedy routine, to practice comedy, to write comedy.

expressions

- *Stand-up comedy:* live comedic monologues ▸ **spectacle d'un ou d'une humoriste.**

dance ▸ danse

nouns action, attitude, audition, audience, ballet, club, creativity, costume, dancer, feet, folk, jazz, hands, imagination, lessons, lighting, movement, muscle, music, night, performance, performer, play, strength, social, sound, stage, technique, theatre, training.

adjectives acrobatic, athletic, classical, childish, contemporary, exotic, expressive, fast, folk, modern, national, popular, rhythmic, sensual, slow, social.

verbs SUBJECT: dance begins, challenges, expresses, inspires moves, touches. OTHERS: to attend a dance, to dance a (particular) dance, to go dancing, to watch dance.

expressions

- *Song and dance:* a long complicated story ▸ **longue histoire compliquée.**
- *To dance to someone's tune:* to do what someone wants you to do, even if you don't want to ▸ **faire ce que quelqu'un souhaite, même à contrecœur; faire les quatre volontés de quelqu'un.**
- *To lead someone to a merry dance:* to keep someone constantly involved in a series of problems ▸ **mêler constamment quelqu'un à une série de problèmes.**
- *To make a song and dance:* to make a big deal about something; to make a situation more important than it is ▸ **faire toute une histoire à propos d'une situation; lui accorder plus d'importance qu'elle n'en a en réalité; en faire tout un plat.**

drawing ▸ dessin

nouns architect, art, artist, background, brushes, canvas, chalk, charcoal, chart, compass, creativity, design, designer, easel, eraser, exhibition, face, figure, graph, highlight, illustration, imagination, ink, instructor, landscape, life, line, model, nature, outline, pad, paper, pencil, perspective, plans, portrait, profile, projection, proportion, representation, ruler, school, shadow, sketch, still-life, study, subject, surface, table, teacher, tracing, training.

adjectives abstract, amateur, careful, colour, computer-generated, figurative, graphic, immature, industrial, old, masterful, quick, rare, studied, talented, weak.

verbs SUBJECT: a drawing expresses, illustrates, represents, reveals, shows. OTHERS: to display a drawing, to enlarge a drawing, to learn to draw, to take a drawing class, to reproduce a drawing, to study a drawing, to teach drawing, to trace a drawing.

expressions

* *To go back to the drawing board:* to start planning again because the first plan failed ▸ **revenir à l'étape de la planification puisque le projet a échoué; recommencer à zéro.**

movie ▸ film

nouns action, actor, actress, art, camera, cinema, comedian, comedy, costumes, critic, director, documentary, drama, effects, entertainment, festival, film, horror, lighting, makeup, motion picture, music, musical, performance, persuasion, photography, popcorn, poster, producer, projection, projectionist, prop, propaganda, review, script, set, sound, spectacle, star, story, studio, suspense, technician, theatre, ticket.

adjectives amateur, animated, classical, comedic, documentary, experimental, fantasy, foreign, funny, gangster, imagination, national, political, popular, realistic, scary, romantic.

verbs SUBJECT: movies challenge, create, delight, demonstrate, disappoint, innovate, entertain, examine, explore, show, tell, thrill. OTHERS: to criticize a movie, to discover a movie, to go to the movies, to rent a movie, to review a movie, to see a movie, to watch a movie.

painting ▸ tableau (-eaux), peinture

nouns abstraction, acrylic, action, artist, brush, canvas, cave, colours, figure, finger, gallery, hobby, horizon, image, imagination, landscape, oil, metal, model, mural, museum, painter, palette, paper, pigment, portrait, profession, realism, representation, restoration,

scene, school, shadow, style, surface, texture, tube, wall, watercolour.

adjectives figurative, abstract, scenic, folk, classical, Western, Eastern, primitive, modern, mural, romantic, contemporary, old, cracked.

verbs SUBJECT: paintings fascinate, intrigue, record, reveal, show. OTHERS: to begin a painting, to compose a painting, to learn to paint, to purchase a painting, to restore a painting, to reproduce a painting, to select a painting, to study a painting, to unveil a painting.

expressions

* *No oil painting:* not very attractive to look at ▸ **pas très agréable à regarder.**
* *To paint the town red:* to go out and enjoy oneself in a noisy, expensive and often eccentric manner ▸ **sortir et s'amuser en faisant du tapage, à grands frais et souvent de manière excentrique.**

sculpture ▸ sculpture

nouns bronze, clay, dimension, figure, form, gesture, marble, model, monument, potter, pottery, reproduction, shape, space, statue, stone, surface, tools, wood, weight.

adjectives abstract, classical, contemporary, figurative, life-sized, miniature, smooth, religious, representational, rough.

verbs SUBJECT: sculptures honour, represent. OTHERS: to admire a sculpture, to carve a sculpture, to cast a sculpture, to fashion a sculpture, to study a sculpture.

theatre ▸ théâtre

nouns accessory, actors, adaptation, amateur, amphitheatre, audience, audition, character, comedy, competition, costumes, critic, crowd, curtain, dance, director, experiment, ghosts, history, illusion, imagination, lights, literature machines, magic, make-up, mask, music, opening, orchestra, performance, play, player, profession, prop, rehearsal, review, role, rows, school, season, seats, set, speakers, story, studio, ticket, time, tour, voice, wings.

adjectives ancient, classical, dramatic, imaginative, innovative, local, musical, national, popular, professional, religious, repertoire, romantic, small.

verbs SUBJECT: theatre creates, entertains, hides, illustrates, reveals, shows, tells. OTHERS: to audition for theatre, to do theatre, to go to the theatre, to study theatre, to work in/at the theatre.

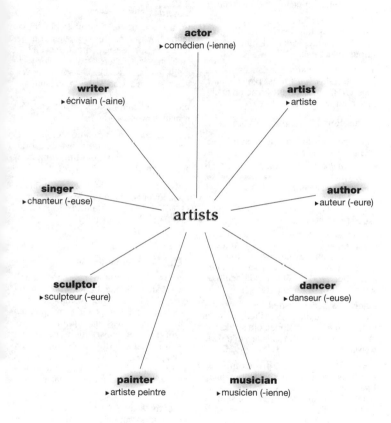

actor
▸comédien (-ienne)

writer
▸écrivain (-aine)

artist
▸artiste

singer
▸chanteur (-euse)

artists

author
▸auteur (-eure)

sculptor
▸sculpteur (-eure)

dancer
▸danseur (-euse)

painter
▸artiste peintre

musician
▸musicien (-ienne)

actor ▶ **comédien (-ienne)**

nouns agent, audience, actress, clown, comedian, comic, costume, dialogue, director, film, impersonator, leading lady, leading man, make-up artist, mime, mimic, motion picture, performer, play-actor, role, puppet, scene, script, theatre, television.

adjectives accomplished, captivating, charismatic, charming, comedic, dramatic, endearing, excellent, funny, good, serious, theatrical.

verbs SUBJECT: an actor dances, dresses up, entertains, performs, plays a part, sings. OTHERS: to admire an actor, to like an actor, to follow an actor.

expressions

- *Bad actor:* a dishonest person ▶ **personne malhonnête.**
- *Good actor:* a dishonest person who is convincing ▶ **personne malhonnête, mais convaincante.**

artist ▶ **artiste**

nouns actor, actress, artisan, author, commercial, composer, critic, dancer, designer, draughtsman, expert, fine arts, genius, masterpiece, musician, painter, performer, prodigy, singer, skill, sculptor, star, virtuoso, writer.

adjectives accomplished, big, clever, creative, comical, dramatic, gifted, imaginative, popular, professional, old-fashioned, ordinary, out-dated, realistic, unknown, well-known.

verbs SUBJECT: an artist composes, conducts, creates, dances, exhibits, imagines, imitates, improvises, innovates, inspires, invents, paints, sings, sculpts, writes. OTHERS: to admire an artist, to discover an artist.

expressions

- *Con artist:* to be a deceiver ▶ **imposteur.**
- *Make-out artist:* to have success with the opposite sex ▶ **avoir du succès auprès du sexe opposé.**

- *Put-on artist:* a fake person ▶ **personne fausse.**
- *Rip-off artist:* someone who steals ▶ **voleur ou voleuse.**

author ▶ **auteur (-eure)**

nouns art, article, autobiography, biography, book, composer, computer, contributor, creator, design, dramatist, editor, fable, fairy tale, fiction, essay, inventor, journalist, letters, magazine, newspaper, novel, novelist, originator, paper, pen, penman, plagiarizer, play, playwright, pulp, poem, prose, publication, satire, style, reporter, romance, work, words.

adjectives bad, brilliant, celebrated, creative, great, ingenious, inventive, original, popular, resourceful, romantic, serious, unknown, well-known.

verbs SUBJECT: an author creates, imagines, invents, inspires, publishes, signs. OTHERS: to cite an author, to read an author, to study an author.

dancer ▶ **danseur (-euse)**

nouns action, attitude, audience, audition, ball, ballerina, ballet, body, choreography, chorus, club, costume, couple, creativity, feet, floor, hands, imagination, jazz, leotard, lessons, lighting, movement, muscle, music, night, orchestra, partner, party, performance, performer, play, professional, prom, public, rhythm, shoes, skill, slipper, social, sound, stage, strength, tap, technique, theatre, time, trainer, training.

adjectives average, bad, classical, deft, energetic, famous, flexible, elegant, excellent, gracious, nude, old-fashioned, second-rate, sensual, social, stylish, supple.

verbs SUBJECT: a dancer accompanies, dances, invites, falls, follows, leads, sways, swirls, turns. OTHERS: to train a dancer, to watch a dancer.

expressions

- *Song and dance:* a long complicated story ► **longue histoire compliquée.**

- *To dance to someone's tune:* to do what someone wants you to do, even if you don't want to ► **faire ce que quelqu'un souhaite, même à contrecœur; faire les quatre volontés de quelqu'un.**

- *To lead someone to a merry dance:* to keep someone constantly involved in a series of problems ► **mêler constamment quelqu'un à une série de problèmes.**

- *To make a song and dance:* to make a big deal out of something; to make a situation more important than it is is ► **faire toute une histoire à propos d'une situation, lui accorder plus d'importance qu'elle n'en a en réalité; en faire tout un plat.**

musician ► musicien (-ienne)

nouns acoustics, amplifier, art, audio, ballad, band, blues, cassette, chant, children, choir, church, compact disk composition, concert, country, dance, duet, ear, film, folk, harmony, hit, hymn, instrument, jazz, key, language, lullaby, music, noise, note, orchestra, perform, performance, piece, player, popular, quartet, rap, recital, record, recording, rhythm, rock, score, sheet, show, singer, skill, solo, soloist, song, sound, stage, style, symphony, talent, teacher, theatre, trio, tune, voice.

adjectives amazing, classical, creative, entertaining, experienced, gifted, inspired, loud, modern, musical, noisy, poetic, popular, rhythmic, talented.

verbs SUBJECT: a musician accompanies, arranges, composes, creates, listens, performs, plays, practices, tunes up, writes. OTHERS: to admire a musician, to conduct musicians, to hear a musician, to hire a musician, to listen to a musician.

expressions

- *Elevator music:* pleasant but boring music played in public places ► **mu-**

sique plaisante mais ennuyeuse qui joue dans les endroits publics.

- *Music to one's ears:* good news ► **bonnes nouvelles; doux à l'oreille.**

- *To face the music:* to face the facts or the consequences ► **regarder les choses en face ou être prêt ou prête à subir les conséquences.**

painter ► artiste peintre

nouns brush, canvas, colour, drawing, easel, figure, frame, gallery, image, inspiration, instrument, landscape, light, masterpiece, material, oil, paint, painting, pastel, pencil, picture, portrait, shape, sketch, style, wall, water colour.

adjectives abstract, amateur, artistic, bold, colourful, creative, famous, inspired, messy, modern, unknown.

verbs SUBJECT: a painter blends, cleans up, creates, draws, mixes, paints, shows, sketches. OTHERS: to admire a painter, to study a painter.

expressions

- *No oil painting:* not very attractive to look at ► **pas très agréable à regarder.**

- *To paint the town red:* to go out and enjoy oneself in a noisy, expensive and often eccentric manner ► **sortir et s'amuser en faisant du tapage, à grands frais et souvent de manière excentrique.**

sculptor ► sculpteur (-euro)

nouns artist, bronze, clay, engraving, form, hand, masterpiece, metal, model, mould, ornament, plaster, pottery, sculpture, shape, spatula, statue, stone, studio, tool, wood, work.

adjectives creative, famous, poor, talented.

verbs SUBJECT: a sculptor carves, chisels, engraves, sculpts, shapes, studies, watches. OTHERS: to observe a sculptor, to watch a sculptor.

singer ▸ chanteur (-euse)

nouns audition, baritone, chord, chorus, concert, fan, hall, interpretation, lyric, microphone, opera, performance, performer, pitch, recital, recording, refrain, rock, show, solo, song, soprano, stage, tenor, tour, voice, word.

adjectives amateur, classical, famous, ordinary, trained, vocal.

verbs SUBJECT: a singer auditions, interprets, performs, practices, records, sings, studies, writes. OTHERS: to discover a singer, to imitate a singer, to listen to a singer, to record a singer.

expressions

- *A song and dance:* a long complicated story ▸ **longue histoire compliquée.**
- *For a song:* for very little money ▸ **pour très peu d'argent; pour une bouchée de pain.**
- *Someone's swan song:* the last work or performance of someone ▸ **dernière œuvre ou prestation de quelqu'un; son chant du cygne.**
- *To make a song and dance:* to make a big deal about something ▸ **faire toute une histoire à propos de quelque chose; en faire tout un plat.**

writer ▸ écrivain (-aine)

nouns article, author, biography, book, comedy, computer, edition, editor, editorial, idea, inspiration, journalism, journalist, letter, literature, lyric, magazine, manual, manuscript, newspaper, notebook, novel, novelist, paper, pen, pencil, poetry, publication, quotation, reporter, spelling, story, verse, word, word processing.

adjectives brilliant, comical, corrected, critical, dramatic, edited, famous, funny, inspired, literary, poetic, poor, published, romantic, sad.

verbs SUBJECT: a writer imagines, invents, publishes, signs, writes. OTHERS: to edit a writer, to hire a writer, to quote a writer, to read a writer, to study a writer.

expressions

- *Writer's block:* Lack of inspiration ▸ **manque d'inspiration; angoisse de la page blanche.**
- *Writer's cramp:* Muscular cramp that develops after excessive writing ▸ **crampe musculaire causée par un excès d'écriture.**
- *Writer-in-residence:* A writer holding a temporary job in a university ▸ **écrivain occupant un poste temporaire dans une université.**

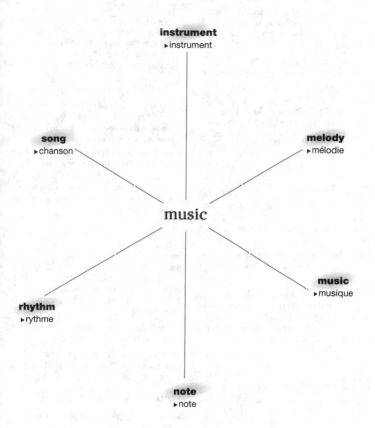

instrument ► instrument

nouns accompaniment, accordion, band, beat, beginner, body, brass, button, composition, drum, flute, gift, guitar, group, harmony, keyboard, keys, lessons, master, melody, music, musician, note, pedal, percussion, piano, orchestra, recording, reed, solo, soul, sound, string, trio, trumpet, tuba, vibration, violin, wind.

adjectives acoustic, brass, electric, expensive, hand-made, heavy, portable, wooden.

verbs SUBJECT: an instrument plays, sounds. OTHERS: to buy an instrument, to learn an instrument, to play an instrument, to master an instrument, to tune an instrument.

melody ► mélodie

nouns composition, ear, jazz, lead, lyric, harmony, note, number, part, piece, phrase, refrain, rhythm, solo, song, tune, voice.

adjectives beautiful, complex, energetic, joyful, lonesome, popular, sad, simple, soft.

verbs SUBJECT: a melody delights, puts to sleep, seduces. OTHERS: to compose a melody, to hum a melody, to learn a melody, to listen to a melody, to sing a melody, to whistle a melody.

music ► musique

nouns art, acoustics, audio, ballad, blues, cassette, chamber, chant, children, choir, church, compact disc (CD), concert, country, dance, ear, film, folk, harmony, hit, hymn, instrument, language, lullaby, jazz, musician, noise, perform, player, popular, rap, recital, record, recording, rock, rhythm, sheet, show, singer, score, sound, style, symphony, teacher, theatre, voice.

adjectives aggressive, alternative, classical, chanted, commercial, contemporary, dramatic, enjoyable, exotic, experimental, harmonious, instrumental, live, local, loud, monotone, obscene, pleasant, recorded, sacred, soft, spiritual, spoken, successful, vocal.

verbs SUBJECT: music calms, creates, expresses, moves, plays. OTHERS: to compose music, to dance to music, to enjoy music, to hear music, to like music, to make music, to read music.

expressions

- *Elevator music:* pleasant but boring music played in public places ► **musique plaisante mais ennuyeuse qui joue dans les endroits publics.**
- *Music to one's ears:* good news ► **bonnes nouvelles; doux à l'oreille.**
- *To face the music:* to face the facts or the consequences ► **regarder les choses en face ou être prêt ou prête à subir les conséquences.**

note ► note

nouns alto, beat, clef, eighth, half, harmony, length, octave, melody, pitch, quarter, range, rest, scale, sign, sixteenth, sound, staff, symbol, time, tenor, tone, tune, whole.

adjectives alto, bass, high, low, pleasant, right, tenor, wrong.

verbs SUBJECT: a note falls, rings, rises, sounds. OTHERS: to hold a note, to miss a note, to play a note, to sing a note.

expressions

- *C-note:* a $100 bill ► **billet de 100 $.**
- *To hit the right note:* to do or say something that has a good effect ► **faire ou dire quelque chose d'efficace.**
- *To make a mental note:* to make an effort to remember something ► **faire un effort pour se souvenir de quelque chose.**

rhythm ▸ rythme

nouns accent, accompanying, beat, dance, measure, music, rhyme, style, stress, swing, tempo.

adjectives continuous, difficult, fast, festive, irregular, merry, slow, steady.

verbs SUBJECT: a rhythm accelerates, intensifies, slows, speeds (up). OTHERS: to alter the rhythm, to change the rhythm, to follow a rhythm, to move/dance to a rhythm, to slow the rhythm (down).

song ▸ chanson

nouns advertisement, choir, chorus, hymn, jingle, lullaby, lyric, melody, music, opera, poem, poetry, pop, radio, rap, refrain, rhythm, serenade, singer, sound, television, video, words.

adjectives folk, long, memorable, new, old, popular, short, special, traditional.

verbs SUBJECT: a song excites, lulls, sells, soothes, tells. OTHERS: to listen to a song, to learn a song, to make up a song, to remember a song, to sing a song, to teach a song, to write a song.

expressions

- *A song and dance:* a long complicated story ▸ **longue histoire compliquée.**
- *For a song:* for very little money ▸ **pour très peu d'argent; pour une bouchée de pain.**
- *Someone's swan song:* the last work or performance of someone ▸ **dernière œuvre ou prestation de quelqu'un; son chant du cygne.**
- *To make a song and dance:* to make a big deal about something; to make a situation more important than it is ▸ **faire toute une histoire à propos d'une situation, lui accorder plus d'importance qu'elle n'en a en réalité; en faire tout un plat.**

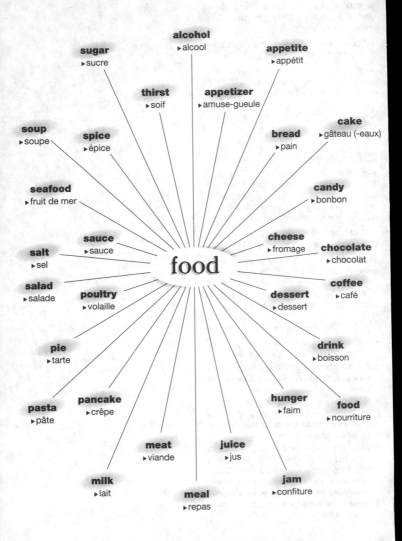

alcohol
▸alcool

sugar
▸sucre

appetite
▸appétit

thirst
▸soif

appetizer
▸amuse-gueule

soup
▸soupe

spice
▸épice

cake
▸gâteau (-eaux)

bread
▸pain

seafood
▸fruit de mer

candy
▸bonbon

sauce
▸sauce

cheese
▸fromage

salt
▸sel

chocolate
▸chocolat

salad
▸salade

coffee
▸café

poultry
▸volaille

dessert
▸dessert

food

pie
▸tarte

drink
▸boisson

pasta
▸pâte

pancake
▸crêpe

hunger
▸faim

food
▸nourriture

meat
▸viande

juice
▸jus

milk
▸lait

jam
▸confiture

meal
▸repas

alcohol ▶ alcool

nouns alcoholism, ale, appetizer, bar, bartender, beer, bottle, bourbon, brandy, celebration, champagne, cognac, control, corkscrew, drink, fruit, fuel, gin, glass, grain, ice, lager, liquid, liquor, medicine, mix, pint, port, punch, refreshment, rum, rye, scotch, serving, sherry, spirits, tequila, toast, vermouth, vintage, vodka, whiskey, wine, yeast.

adjectives aged, alcoholic, bubbly, cheap, colourless, delicious, drunk, expensive, hard, odorous, sober, strong.

verbs SUBJECT: alcohol burns, evaporates, tastes, smells. OTHER: to abuse alcohol, to buy alcohol, to consume alcohol, to drink alcohol, to dilute alcohol, to mix alcohol, to pour alcohol, to smell alcohol, to spill alcohol, to serve alcohol, to splash alcohol, to taste alcohol.

appetizer ▶ amuse-gueule

nouns appetite, bite, cheese, chips, cracker, dip, finger food, flavour, food, good, hunger, napkin, nuts, olive, shrimp, snack, spread, tray, vegetables.

adjectives bite-sized, crunchy, delicious, delightful, flavoursome, mouth-watering, salty, savoury, small, spicy, tasty.

verbs SUBJECT: appetizers crunch, look, smell, taste. OTHER: to bite an appetizer, to eat an appetizer, to enjoy an appetizer, to nibble an appetizer, to prepare an appetizer, to serve an appetizer, to taste an appetizer.

appetite ▶ appétit

nouns course, craving, desire, enjoyment, flavour, fondness, food, greed, hunger, longing, meal, mouth, snack, stomach, taste, thirst, tongue, urge, weakness.

adjectives big, feeble, great, hearty, healthy, large, small, strong, tremendous, weak.

verbs SUBJECT: appetites develop, grow, disappear. OTHER: to have an appetite, to get an appetite (back), to lose one's appetite, to satisfy one's appetite, to stimulate one's appetite.

expressions

- *To have an appetite for something:* to be attracted to something ▶ **être attiré ou attirée par quelque chose; avoir le goût de.**

- *To lose one's appetite:* to become disinterested in something ▶ **se désintéresser de quelque chose; ne plus avoir le goût de.**

- *(Something) whets one's appetite:* makes one want more ▶ **(quelque chose) fait que l'on en veut davantage; aiguise l'appétit.**

- *To whet someone's appetite for something:* to make someone eager to have more of something ▶ **faire que l'on en veut davantage; aiguiser l'appétit.**

bread ▶ pain

nouns aroma, bag, baker, bakery, basket, biscuit, board, box, bun, butter, crumb, crust, dough, flour, food, grain, heel, knife, loaf, oven, pan, recipe, roll, sandwich, slice, staple, toast, water, yeast.

adjectives burnt, brown, crusty, daily, dry, flat, fresh, home-made, mouldy, round, rye, sliced, soft, stale, warm, white, whole-wheat.

verbs SUBJECT: bread dries out, fills, goes mouldy, goes stale, hardens, nourishes, smells, sustains, rises. OTHER: to bake bread, to buy bread, to chew bread, to dip bread, to eat bread, to make bread, to slice bread, to smell bread, to taste bread, to toast bread.

expressions

- *A breadwinner:* a person who earns money to keep a family ▶ **personne qui fait vivre une famille; soutien de famille.**

- *Daily bread:* food needed to live ▸ **nourriture dont on a besoin pour vivre ; pain quotidien.**

- *One cannot live by bread alone:* People need things other than food (like art, music, friends) to be happy ▸ **les gens ont besoin d'autre chose que la nourriture pour être heureux (l'art, la musique, les amis, par exemple).**

- *Something is one's bread and butter:* one's main source of income ▸ **principale source de revenu ; gagne-pain.**

- *The bread basket:* the principle region that produces grain ▸ **principale région productrice de céréales.**

- *The greatest thing since sliced bread:* extremely good ▸ **extrêmement bon.**

- *To be living on the breadline:* with barely enough money to live on ▸ **avec à peine suffisamment d'argent pour vivre.**

- *To bread something:* to coat in batter or crumbs before frying ▸ **enduire de pâte ou de chapelure avant de frire ; paner.**

- *To know which side your bread is buttered on:* to be careful to show respect to people who can help you ▸ **prendre soin de respecter les gens qui peuvent être utiles.**

- *To like one's bread buttered on both sides:* to want to live in great comfort or luxury ▸ **désirer vivre dans le luxe et le confort.**

- *White bread:* ordinary, boring (refers to white, middle-class America) ▸ **ordinaire, ennuyeux (fait allusion aux Nord-américains blancs de classe moyenne).**

cake ▸ **gâteau (-eaux)**

nouns bake, batter, birthday, candle, celebration, chocolate, crumb, dessert, eggs, filling, flour, food, frosting, ice cream, icing, layer, oven, pan, pancake, party, pastry, slice, sugar, vanilla.

adjectives baked, decorated, delicious, fancy, moist, plain, rich, sweet, wedding.

verbs SUBJECT: a cake bakes, burns, costs, rises, tastes, smells. OTHER: to bake a cake, to buy a cake, to decorate a cake, to mix a cake, to serve a cake, to slice a cake, to taste a cake.

expressions

- *A slice of the cake:* a share or part of something ▸ **partie de quelque chose.**

- *Something is a piece of cake:* something is very easy to accomplish ▸ **c'est très facile à accomplir ; c'est du gâteau.**

- *That takes the cake:* that is very bad, even worse than before ▸ **c'est très mauvais, et même pire qu'avant ; c'est le bouquet, le comble.**

- *The icing on the cake:* something that makes a good situation even better ▸ **quelque chose qui améliore une situation déjà intéressante ; la cerise sur le gâteau.**

- *To have one's cake and eat it (too):* to have two things that are usually impossible to have at the same time ▸ **avoir deux choses qu'il est habituellement impossible de posséder en même temps ; on en peut pas tout avoir ; avoir le beurre et l'argent du beurre.**

- *To sell something like hot cakes:* very quickly (when selling something) ▸ **très rapidement (au cours d'une vente).**

candy ▸ **bonbon**

nouns aroma, bag, bar, cavity, child, chocolate, colour, cotton, dentist, drop, flavour, fruit, food, gift, honey, mint, nuts, pleasure, reward, sugar, surprise, sweetener, syrup, temptation, tooth, treat, wrapper.

adjectives delicious, flavoured, flavourful, harmful, rich, small, tempting, tiny, wrapped.

verbs SUBJECT: candies crunch, dissolve, melt, taste. OTHERS: to buy a candy, to crave a candy, to give a candy, to make candies, to offer candies, to swallow a candy, to taste a candy.

expressions

- *Eye candy:* something that is beautiful to look at but not essential ► **quelque chose d'agréable à regarder mais de superflu.**
- *Like taking candy from a baby:* very easy to do, effortless ► **très facile à faire ; sans effort.**
- *To be like a kid in a candy store:* to have a lot of good things to chose from ► **avoir beaucoup de bonnes choses parmi lesquelles choisir.**

cheese ► fromage

nouns appetizer, block, bread, butter, cheddar, cottage, cow, cream, farmer, fat, filling, food, goat, grater, knife, macaroni, milk, mould, mouse, package, piece, pizza, slice, toast, tray, wine, yogurt.

adjectives aged, blue, creamy, grated, fresh, hard, imported, local, melted, mild, mouldy, old, orange, salty, strong, soft, solid, sweet, white, yellow.

verbs SUBJECT: cheese ages, bubbles, burns, dries, hardens, melts, ripens, smells, tastes. OTHERS: to buy cheese, to eat cheese, to grate cheese, to make cheese, to slice cheese, to smell cheese, to sprinkle cheese.

expressions

- *As different/similar as cheese and chalk:* very different ► **très différent.**
- *The big cheese:* the top boss ► **le grand patron ou la grande patronne.**
- *To be cheesed off:* to be bored or depressed ► **être ennuyé ou ennuyée, déprimé ou déprimée.**

chocolate ► chocolat

nouns bakery, baking, bar, beans, bunny, cake, candy, cherry, chip, cocoa, cookie, dessert, Easter, energy, fat, flavour, figure, gift, luxury, milk, nuts, raisins, romance, snack, square, sugar, tooth, Valentine, variety, wrapper.

adjectives bitter, brown, dark, delicious, hard, hollow, hot, light, melted, milk, rich, smooth, soft, solid, square, sweet.

verbs SUBJECT: chocolate hardens, melts, tastes. OTHERS: to buy chocolate, to drink chocolate, to eat chocolate, to find chocolate, to give chocolate, to make chocolate, to melt chocolate, to pour chocolate, to taste chocolate, to serve chocolate, to sprinkle chocolate, to use chocolate.

coffee ► café

nouns aroma, bean, beverage, breakfast, café, cafeteria, caffeine, cream, culture, cup, dinner, drink, energy, filter, flavour, grinder, grounds, liquid, machine, maker, meal, milk, morning, mug, nerves, office, sleep, stain, sugar, sweetener, talk, water.

adjectives alert, awake, black, bitter, bottomless, brewed, brown, hot, instant, rich, smooth, social, strong, warm, weak.

verbs SUBJECT: coffee brews, burns, comforts, drips, excites, irritates, smells, stimulates, wakens. OTHERS: to avoid coffee, to brew coffee, to buy a coffee, to make coffee, to pour coffee, to sell coffee, to re-heat coffee, to serve coffee, to smell coffee, to spill coffee, to take (something) in one's coffee.

expressions

- *Coffee table book:* a large book containing mostly pictures ► **livre de grandes dimensions contenant surtout des photographies.**

dessert ► dessert

nouns bakery, cake, calorie, celebration, chocolate, diet, dinner, dish, fat, flavour, food, fork, fruit, garnish, honey, ice cream, meal, menu, pie, piece, plate, pudding, sauce, serving, slice, spoon, square, vanilla.

adjectives beautiful, expensive, flaming, flavourful, heavy, light, mouth-watering, rich, sweet.

verbs SUBJECT: desserts delight, fill, please, nourish, OTHERS: to bake dessert, to crave dessert, to decorate a dessert, to eat dessert, to garnish dessert, to have dessert, to make dessert, to offer dessert, to savour dessert, to serve dessert.

---

drink ▸ boisson

nouns alcohol, alcoholic, alcoholism, appetizer, apple, bar, bartender, beer, bitters, bottle, breast, bubble, celebration, coffee, control, corkscrew, cream, cup, drunk, food, fruit, glass, grape, grapefruit, herb, ice, juice, pear, lemon, lemonade, lime, litre, liquid, liquor, medicine, milk, mix, mouth, mug, orange, pitcher, pineapple, pint, punch, refreshment, rye, serving, shake, spirits, soda, soft drink, tea, temperature, thermometer, thirst, toast, tomato, tongue, vintage, water, wedge, wine.

adjectives alcoholic, artificial, bitter, brewed, bubbly, cold, cool, distilled, frozen, fruity, hard, herbal, hot, icy, medicinal, mild, natural, non-alcoholic, popular, refreshing, rich, soft, sweet, warm, spicy.

verbs SUBJECT: a drink cools, quenches, refreshes, satisfies, warms, whets. OTHERS: to advertise a drink, to buy a drink, to chill a drink, to colour a drink, to crave a drink, to enjoy a drink, to flavour a drink, to garnish a drink, to heat a drink, to market a drink, to offer a drink, to mix a drink, to need a drink.

expressions

- *To be meat and drink to someone:* to be very important in someone's life ▸ **être très important dans la vie de quelqu'un ; être tout pour lui ou elle.**
- *To drink like a fish:* to drink a lot of alcohol regularly ▸ **boire régulièrement beaucoup d'alcool ; boire comme un trou.**

- *To drink something in:* to take something rapidly or eagerly ▸ **prendre quelque chose rapidement ou avec empressement.**
- *To drink to someone's health:* to drink a toast to someone, wishing him or her good health ▸ **porter un toast à quelqu'un en lui souhaitant la santé ; boire à la santé de quelqu'un.**
- *To drive someone to drink:* to frustrate or aggravate someone by behaving in a difficult way ▸ **exaspérer quelqu'un en se comportant mal.**
- *You can lead a horse to water, but you cannot make it drink:* you cannot force someone to do something, even if you think it is best ▸ **il est impossible de forcer quelqu'un à faire quelque chose, même si c'est pour son bien.**

---

food ▸ nourriture

nouns agriculture, appetizer, appetite, baker, bite, beef, bowl, bread, breakfast, café, cafeteria, carnivore, cheese, cereals, chef, cook, delivery, dessert, diner, energy, farm, farmer, fish, fork, fruit, garden, grain, grocery, growth, hunger, jam, kitchen, knife, ladle, market, meat, milk, mouth, mouthful, pancake, pans, party, pasta, pepper, picnic, pie, plate, pots, poultry, preparation, produce, provision, refrigerator, restaurant, rice, salt, sauce, seafood, snack, soup, spice, spoon, starch, stove, substance, sugar, thirst, tray, vegetable, vegetarian, waiter.

adjectives appetizing, baked, bland, cold, cooked, delicious, exotic, fast, flavourful, fried, grilled, healthy, homemade, hot, light, local, national, nutritious, raw, rich, solid, spicy, substantial, tasteless, tasty, vegetarian, warm.

verbs SUBJECT: food nourishes, sustains. OTHERS: to boil food, to buy food, to chew food, to conserve food, to eat food, to fry food, to offer food, to prepare food, to serve food, to spill food, to stock food.

expressions

- *Food for thought:* something to think about ▸ **sujet de réflexion.**

hunger ▸ faim

nouns appetite, anorexia, craving, diet, desire, emptiness, fast, food, growl, lack, nourishment, poverty, starvation, stomach, taste, thirst, wish.

adjectives big, hungry, famished, ferocious, full, missing, needing, starving, thirsty, weak.

verbs SUBJECT: hunger distracts, tires, weakens. OTHERS: to die of hunger, to feed one's hunger, to feel hunger, to hunger for something, to satisfy one's hunger.

expressions

* *To hunger after/for something:* to want something very much ▸ **désirer ardemment quelque chose.**

jam ▸ confiture

nouns blueberry, bread, breakfast, fall, flavour, food, fruit, jar, knife, marmalade, orange, peanut butter, raspberry, sandwich, spread, strawberry, sugar, summer, toast.

adjectives delicious, homemade, rich, sweet, thick.

verbs SUBJECT: jam nourishes, spreads, sweetens. OTHERS: to boil jam, to eat jam, to lick jam, to make jam, to serve jam, to spread jam, to taste jam.

expressions

* *A jam session:* an informal gathering to play music ▸ **concert improvisé.**
* *To be in a jam:* to be in a difficult situation ▸ **se trouver dans une situation difficile ; être embourbé ou embourbée, coincé ou coincée.**
* *To jam something:* to push, squeeze or force an object into a tight spot ▸ **forcer quelque chose à entrer dans un espace réduit en le poussant ou en l'écrasant.**

juice ▸ jus

nouns appetite, appetizer, apple, bottle, box, breakfast, carrot, citrus, concentrate, crystal, digestion, drink, energy, flesh, fruit, glass, grape, grapefruit, herb, ice, juicer, lime, liquid, litre, lemon, thirst, tomato, meat, mix, orange, peach, pear, pressed, prune, sauce, serving, snack, stomach, syrup, vegetable, vitamin, water, wine.

adjectives acid, bitter, clear, concentrated, energizing, fresh, frozen, healthy, nutritious, orange, pressed, red, refreshing, squeezed, sweet, thick, yellow.

verbs SUBJECT: juice energizes, freezes, melts, moistens, nourishes. OTHERS: to drain juice, to drink juice, to extract juice, to mix juice, to pour juice to sell juice, to serve juice, to squeeze juice, to thaw juice.

expressions

* *To juice up a story:* to add details that are non-essential to a story to make it livelier ▸ **ajouter des détails superflus à une histoire pour la rendre plus vivante ; en rajouter ; en remettre.**
* *To stew in one's own juice:* to suffer as a result of one's own stupidity ▸ **subir les conséquences de sa propre stupidité.**

meal ▸ repas

nouns appetite, bread, breakfast, cafeteria, celebration, cook, course, diner, dining room, dinner, dish, dishes, family, food, grain, guest, hunger, kitchen, lunch, meat, menu, napkin, nutrition, plan, preparation, restaurant, service, snack, supper, table, vegetable, waiter.

adjectives bland, complete, cold, cooked, delicious, delivered, exotic, fancy, fast, flavourful, home-cooked, hot, large, nutritious, popular, simple, small, substantial, take-out, vegetarian.

verbs SUBJECT: a meal comforts, fills, nourishes, satisfies. OTHERS: to digest a meal, to eat a meal, to invite for a meal, to linger over a meal, to miss a meal, to plan a meal, to prepare a meal, to serve a meal, to skip a meal.

expressions

- *A meal ticket:* a job or situation that will provide enough money to live for a long time ▸ **emploi ou situation qui procurera de l'argent pour subsister pendant une longue période.**
- *A square meal:* a hearty, nutritious meal ▸ **repas copieux, nutritif.**
- *Mealy mouthed:* not honest or sincere ▸ **malhonnête ou pas sincère.**
- *To make a meal of something:* to take more time than needed for something ▸ **prendre plus de temps que nécessaire pour faire quelque chose.**

meat ▸ viande

nouns animal, barbecue, batter, beef, bones, butcher, breast, chicken, chop, claws, dish, duck, energy, fat, filet, fire, fish, flavour, flesh, food, goat, gravy, ham, hamburger, heart, juice, kidney, knife, lamb, leg, liver, lobster, lunch, meal, meatloaf, organs, oven, poultry, pork, potato, protein, rack, roast, sandwich, sauce, sausage, seasoning, skin, salt, slice, smoke, spice, spring, steak, stew, stove, substitute, thigh, veal, walnut, wing.

adjectives baked, cooked, chewy, cold, fatty, fresh, fried, frozen, grilled, lean, pink, preserved, raw, red, rotten, salted, stringy, smoked, tender, tough, white, wild.

verbs SUBJECT: meat cooks, freezes, rots, softens, spoils, toughens. OTHERS: to batter meat, to broil meat, to butcher meat, to buy meat, to cut meat, to eat meat, to grill meat, to fry meat, to prepare meat, to preserve meat, to season meat, to salt meat, to slice meat, to smoke meat.

expressions

- *One man's meat is another man's poison:* something liked by one person may be disliked by another ▸ **une chose appréciée par quelqu'un ne l'est pas**

nécessairement par quelqu'un d'autre ; le malheur des uns fait le bonheur des autres.
- *One person's meat is another's poison:* what is important and/or essential to one person may not be so to another ▸ **ce qui est important ou essentiel pour quelqu'un ne l'est pas nécessairement pour quelqu'un d'autre.**
- *The meat and potatoes:* the basic, important parts ▸ **les éléments de base ; l'essentiel.**
- *To be meat and to drink to someone:* to be very important to someone ▸ **être très important pour quelqu'un ; être tout pour lui ou elle.**

milk ▸ lait

nouns baby, bottle, breast, butter, calcium, calf, carton, cheese, chocolate, coffee, cow, cream, drink, energy, fat, food, goat, ice cream, lactose, lamb, life, liquid, mammal, mother, new-born, nipple, nourishment, pasteurization, refrigeration, sheep, sugar, tea, vitamin, yogurt.

adjectives boiled, cold, chocolate, concentrated, creamy, fresh, mother's, powdered, refreshing, separated, skim, sterilized, sour, sweetened, warm.

verbs SUBJECT: milk calms, nourishes, soothes, sours, thickens. OTHERS: to buy milk, to digest milk, to drink milk, to milk an animal, to mix milk, to serve milk, to sterilize milk.

expressions

- *The land of milk and honey:* a country that is perceived by foreigners as a place where everything is good and possible ▸ **pays perçu par les étrangers comme un endroit où tout est agréable et possible.**
- *The milk of human kindness:* being good to others ▸ **être bon pour les autres.**
- *There's no use crying over spilt milk:* it is useless dwell on something that is

lost or a situation that has gone wrong ► **il est inutile de s'attarder à quelque chose qui est perdu ou qui s'est mal passé.**

pancake ► crêpe

nouns aroma, batter, bite, blueberry, bread, breakfast, butter, camp, corn, eggs, flour, fire, food, fruit, hunger, maple, morning, oil, pan, sausages, stack, syrup, water, waffles.

adjectives appetizing, favourite, filling, flavourful, fluffy, hot, light, thick, thin, warm.

verbs SUBJECT: pancakes burn, fry, rise. OTHERS: to eat pancakes, to order pancakes, to make pancakes, to pour syrup onto pancakes, to serve pancakes, to stack pancakes.

pasta ► pâte

nouns bowl, butter, cheese, cream, course, dinner, egg, flavour, flour, food, fork, grain, lunch, macaroni, meal, noodle, pot, salad, sauce, spaghetti, spinach, spoon, starch, supper, tomato, water.

adjectives boiled, cold, cooked, dried, egg, fresh, hot, Italian, packaged, stuffed.

verbs OTHERS: to bake pasta, to boil pasta, to cook pasta, to drain pasta, to eat pasta, to rinse pasta, to serve pasta.

pie ► tarte

nouns aroma, apple, baker, bakery, blueberry, butter, crust, fruit, cherry, dessert, dough, eggs, filling, flour, food, ice, cream, lard, lemon, meal, meat, oven, pecan, piece, plate, raisin, rolling pin, serving, shortening, slice, strawberry, syrup, tart.

adjectives burned, cold, flaky, hot, savoury, sweet, baked, delicious, filling, homemade, sliced.

verbs OTHERS: to bake a pie, to eat a pie, to fill a pie, to heat a pie, to let a pie cool, to roll a piecrust, to serve a pie.

expressions..

- *As easy as pie:* very easy ► **très facile; du gâteau.**
- *Pie in the sky:* good but unlikely ► **bon, mais peu probable.**
- *To eat humble pie:* to face a situation in which you acted wrongly ► **regarder en face une situation où l'on a mal agi.**
- *To have a finger in every pie:* to have many different business dealings ► **avoir plusieurs affaires en cours.**

poultry ► volaille

nouns barbecue, batter, bird, bone, breast, chicken, duck, eggs, farm, feather, food, grain, grill, hen, half, leg, liver, mayonnaise, meal, protein, serving, skin, thigh, quarter, sauce, wing.

adjectives baked, barbecued, battered, crispy, grain-fed, grilled, fried, juicy, lean, raw, roasted, rotten, tender.

verbs SUBJECT: poultry cooks, freezes, rots. OTHERS: to cook poultry, to eat poultry, to prepare poultry, to raise poultry, to serve poultry.

salad ► salade

nouns bar, bean, bowl, carrot, cheese, chicken, crouton, crunch, cucumber, dinner, dressing, fibre, fruit, food, fork, garnish, health, leaf, lettuce, lunch, meal, oil, pasta, potato, serving, sorrel, soup, spinach, tomato, tuna, vinegar, yogurt, vegetarian, vegetable, vitamin.

adjectives bean, green, fresh, mixed, savoury, side, simple, tossed, pasta, warm.

verbs SUBJECT: salad accompanies, nourishes. OTHERS: to eat a salad, to dress a salad, to make a salad, to serve a salad, to toss a salad.

expressions..

- *Salad days:* the time when one' is young and lacking life experience ► **période de jeunesse et d'inexpérience.**

salt ▸ sel

nouns chemical, cooking, grain, iodine, mineral, pepper, pinch, savoury, sea, seasoning, shaker, sodium, table, teaspoon.

adjectives coarse, fine, iodized, salty, sea, table.

verbs SUBJECT: salt corrodes, dries, flavours, preserves, seasons. OTHERS: to avoid salt, to buy salt, to gather salt, to limit salt intake, to mine salt, to ration salt, to salt food.

expressions

• *The salt of the earth:* very good and giving person or persons ▸ **personne(s) bonne(s) et généreuse(s).**

• *To be worth one's salt:* to be deserving of one's pay ▸ **mériter son salaire.**

• *To go through something like a dose of salt:* to finish or accomplish something very quickly ▸ **terminer ou exécuter quelque chose très rapidement.**

• *To rub salt in a wound:* to say or do something that makes someone's difficult situation worse or hurts his or her feelings about a sensitive topic ▸ **dire quelque chose sur un sujet délicat et, ce faisant, empirer une situation déjà difficile ou être blessant ou blessante ; retourner le couteau dans la plaie.**

• *To salt something away:* to store up for future use ▸ **faire des réserves pour l'avenir.**

• *To take it with a grain (pinch) of salt:* not to accept someone's words or actions uncritically or naively ▸ **se montrer sceptique à propos des paroles ou des actions de quelqu'un ; ne pas prendre quelque chose au pied de la lettre.**

sauce ▸ sauce

nouns apple, barbecue, basil, butter, caramel, cheese, chocolate, cranberry, cream, dessert, egg, flavouring, fruit, gravy, herb, juice, lemon, liquid, pasta, peanut, pepper, pink, mayonnaise, meat, mint, mushroom, mustard, onion, relish, seasoning, sorrel, Soya, spinach, syrup, tartar, tomato, vanilla, vegetable, wine.

adjectives bland, brown, chunky, creamy, delicate, fragrant, meaty, pink, savoury, spicy, smooth, stewed, sweet, sweet and sour, thick, thin, white.

verbs SUBJECT: sauces add flavour, coat, cover, enhance, liven. OTHERS: to blend a sauce, to brush (on) a sauce, to cook a sauce, to mix a sauce, to pour a sauce, to prepare a sauce, to serve a sauce, to simmer a sauce, to spread a sauce.

expressions

• *What's sauce for the goose is sauce for the gander:* a rule or treatment that applies to one person must apply to others ▸ **un règlement ou un traitement doit s'appliquer à tous et à toutes sans exception.**

seafood ▸ fruit de mer

nouns anchovy, batter, boat, bones, chowder, clams, crab eel, filet, fish, fisher, flake, flounder, fry, halibut, health, ice, lemon, lobster, mussels, ocean, oysters, parsley, pastry, pickle, piece, protein, salmon, sardine, sauce, scallops, sea, shell, shellfish, shrimp, sole, shark, smoke, squid, steak, trap, trout, tuna.

adjectives baked, canned, cooked, delicate, dried, flaky, frozen, pickled, poached, preserved, raw, salted, smelly, soft, smoked, steamed, white, whole.

verbs SUBJECT: seafood cooks, smells, nourishes, whitens, toughens. OTHERS: to bake seafood, to broil seafood, to buy seafood, to catch seafood, to cook seafood, to eat seafood, to fry seafood, to grill seafood, to prepare seafood, to sell seafood, to serve seafood, to taste seafood.

soup ▸ soupe

nouns base, beans, bowl, bread, broth, can, carrot, chowder, corn, cracker, cup, fish, ladle, liquid, meat, milk, noodle, nutrition, onion, pot, potato, salad, sick, spoon, starter, stock, summer, tomato, vegetable, water, winter.

adjectives canned, chilled, delicate, healthy, hearty, homemade, hot, light, liquid, prepared, smooth, soothing, spicy, warm, warming.

verbs SUBJECT: soup boils, cooks, nourishes, soothes. OTHERS: to boil soup, to cook soup, to garnish soup, to salt the soup, to season the soup, to serve soup, to share the soup, to simmer soup.

expressions

• *From soup to nuts:* from start to finish ▸ **du début à la fin.**

• *(Something is) duck soup:* very easy to do ▸ **très facile à faire ; du gâteau.**

• *To be in the soup:* to be in trouble ▸ **être en difficulté ; être dans de beaux draps.**

• *To be souped-up:* to be made more powerful, faster (usually of a car) ▸ **(voiture) à laquelle on a ajouté un dispositif la rendant plus puissante, plus rapide.**

spice ▸ **épice**

nouns cinnamon, cooking, curry, flavour, food, ginger, grater, herb, jar, market, meats, medicine, mixture, mustard, nutmeg, pepper, powder, sage, seasoning, thyme, trade, vanilla.

adjectives foreign, ground, hot, main, mild, powdered, spicy, strong, whole.

verbs SUBJECT: spices accent, enhance, flavour. OTHERS: to add spice, to avoid spice, to buy spices, to cook with spice, to mix spices, to select spices, to sprinkle spice.

expressions

• *Variety is the spice of life:* variety keeps life interesting and exciting ▸ **la variété donne du piquant à la vie.**

sugar ▸ **sucre**

nouns baking, beets, calorie, cane, coffee, crystal, cube, dessert, diet, energy, grain, honey, lump, maple, measure, powder, sweetener, syrup, weight.

adjectives brown, crystallized, melted, powdered, refined, sweet.

verbs SUBJECT: sugar crystallizes, hardens, melts, sweetens. OTHERS: to add sugar, to avoid sugar, to sugar a recipe.

expressions

• *To sugar coat the pill:* to make something bad seem less unpleasant ▸ **faire en sorte que quelque chose de déplaisant passe mieux ; dorer la pilule.**

• *Sugar daddy:* an elderly man who has a younger friend or girlfriend to whom he gives generous presents ▸ **homme âgé qui offre de généreux cadeaux à sa petite amie plus jeune que lui.**

thirst ▸ **soif**

nouns alcohol, craving, desert, drink, dryness, exercise, feeling, heat, mouth, need, salt, summer, sun, throat, tongue.

adjectives essential, strong, terrible.

verbs SUBJECT: thirst dries out, tires. OTHERS: to relieve one's thirst, to satisfy a thirst, to suffer from thirst, to quench a thirst.

expressions

• *To thirst after/for something:* to want something very much ▸ **désirer ardemment quelque chose.**

accident
▸accident

war
▸guerre

wedding
▸mariage

birth
▸naissance

birthday
▸anniversaire

trip
▸voyage

celebration
▸célébration

show
▸spectacle

ceremony
▸cérémonie

religion
▸religion

events and celebrations

competition
▸compétition

party
▸fête

crime
▸crime

holidays
▸vacances

danger
▸danger

fair
▸foire

death
▸mort

exhibition
▸exposition

demonstration
▸manifestation

event
▸événement

accident ▸ accident

nouns airline, ambulance, car, casualty, catastrophe, chance, collision, crash, damage, derailment, disaster, help, hurt, injury, luck, misadventure, mishap, mistake, police, tow truck, urgent, victim, wound, wreck.

adjectives awful, common, deadly, depressing, devastating, dreadful, fatal, heartbreaking, light, miserable, moving, sad, serious, spectacular, sudden, terrible, unexpected, unfortunate.

verbs SUBJECT: an accident blocks, breaks, cripples, demolishes, destroys, disables, harms, happens, injures, kills, mutilates, takes place. OTHERS: to avoid an accident, to be a witness in an accident, to cause an accident, to have an accident, to see an accident, to suffer from an accident.

expressions

- *By accident:* something that happens by chance ▸ **par hasard.**
- *To be accident prone:* someone who experiences a lot of accidents in their life ▸ **être sujet ou sujette aux accidents.**

birth ▸ naissance

nouns anniversary, ancestry, background, baby, beginning, birthday, blood, breeding, celebration, childbirth, conception, date, delivery, doctor, family, father, hatching, hospital, infant, midwife, mother, new-born, origin, physician, source.

adjectives critical, disastrous, easy, happy, important, moving, multiple, natural, normal, planned, premature, special, spectacular, sudden, twin, unexpected, unfortunate.

verbs SUBJECT: the birth approaches, excites, reunites, thrills. OTHERS: to expect a birth, to give birth, to control births, to induce a birth, to plan a birth.

expressions

- *Of good birth:* from a good family ▸ **de bonne famille.**
- *Of humble birth:* from a poor family ▸ **d'une famille modeste; d'origine modeste.**
- *Birthright:* privilege from birth ▸ **droit acquis de naissance.**

birthday ▸ anniversaire

nouns age, anniversary, beginning, birth, day, date, cake, calendar, candles, card, celebration, feast, festivity, founding, gift, guests, honour, invitation, origin, party, present, treat, wish, year.

adjectives annual, awful, big, boring, depressing, disastrous, entertaining, exciting, famous, fun, happy, important, joyous, moving, sad, special, spectacular, terrible, unhappy.

verbs SUBJECT: a birthday happens, takes place. OTHERS: to acknowledge a birthday, to celebrate a birthday, to honour a birthday, to give a birthday party, to go to a birthday party.

expressions

- *Birthday suit:* to be naked ▸ **être nu ou nue; être nu ou nue comme l'enfant qui vient de naître; être nu ou nue comme un ver.**

celebration ▸ célébration

nouns anniversary, activity, ball, birthday, ceremony, commemoration, dance, event, festival, fireworks, gala, graduation, harvest, holiday, honour, inauguration, jubilee, music, party, performance, praise, reception, speech, wedding.

adjectives annual, artistic, awful, big, boring, civil, common, critical, cultural, daily, deadly, depressing, diplomatic, disastrous, dramatic, entertaining, famous, formal, happy, heartbreaking, historical, important, international, lucky, monthly, moving, municipal, national, planned, political, popular, provincial, regional, religious, sad, scientific, serious, significant, special, spectacular, sudden, terrible, unexpected, unfortunate, unhappy, weekly.

verbs SUBJECT: a celebration amuses, begins, continues, entertains, finishes, lasts, starts. OTHERS: to commemorate a celebration, to go to a celebration, to have a celebration, to join the celebration, to organize a celebration, to participate in a celebration, to plan a celebration.

expressions

• *We must have a celebration:* to have a party ▶ **célébrer; faire la fête.**

• *To join in the celebrations:* to join in the party ▶ **se joindre à la fête.**

ceremony ▶ **cérémonie**

nouns activity, anniversary, ball, birthday, celebration, ceremony, convention, dance, demonstration, dress, event, festival, fireworks, formality, function, gala, graduation, harvest, holiday, honour, inauguration, jubilee, marriage, music, occasion, opening, parade, party, performance, praise, reception, rite, ritual, service, show, speech, tradition, wedding.

adjectives annual, artistic, awful, big, boring, brief, civil, common, critical, cultural, daily, diplomatic, disastrous, dramatic, entertaining, famous, formal, happy, heartbreaking, historical, honorary, important, international, long, monthly, moving, municipal, niceties, official, orthodox, planned, polite, political, popular, pretentious, provincial, regional, religious, sad, serious, short, significant, solemn, special, spectacular, sudden, terrible, weekly.

verbs SUBJECT: a ceremony begins, closes, commences, concludes, finishes, opens, starts, terminates. OTHERS: To animate, a ceremony, to attend a ceremony, to cancel a ceremony, to observe a ceremony, organize a ceremony, to present in a ceremony, to take part in a ceremony.

expressions

• *Master of ceremonies:* The person who conducts the ceremony ▶ **personne qui dirige un événement; maître de cérémonie; chef du protocole.**

• *To leave the room without ceremony:* To leave informally ▶ **partir simplement; partir sans façon, sans cérémonie, sans autre forme de procès.**

• *To stand on ceremony:* To insist on formalities ▶ **tenir aux formalités; faire des cérémonies, faire des façons.**

• *Without ceremony:* To be informal ▶ **simplement; sans façon, sans cérémonie, sans autre forme de procès.**

competition ▶ **compétition**

nouns award, battle, championship, coach, competitor, conflict, contest, elimination, game, honour, judge, loser, match, medal, meeting, opponent, opposition, player, race, referee, rival, sport, struggle, team, trophy, tournament, winner.

adjectives adventurous, athletic, awful, big, celebrated, critical, difficult, extraordinary, heartbreaking, important, impressive, international, local, national, outstanding, provincial, regional, remarkable, significant, spectacular, superb, unfair.

verbs SUBJECT: a competition begins, finishes, starts, takes place. OTHERS: to arbitrate a competition, to enter into a competition, to lose a competition, to offer a competition, to watch a competition, to win a competition, to fail in a competition, to participate in a competition, to succeed in a competition.

crime ▶ **crime**

nouns accused, con, criminal, crook, death, delinquency, imprisonment, felony, fraud, illegal, jail, judge, law, lawyer, misdeed, misconduct, murder, offence, prison, police, punishment, rapist, robber, sentence, sin, thief, treason, trespass, victim, violation, wrongdoing.

adjectives awful, bad, common, cruel, deadly, depressing, devastating, dreadful, fatal, guilty, heartbreaking, horrible, inexcusable, mean, miserable, moving, nasty, outraged, passionate, perfect, sad, serious, spectacular, sudden, terrible, unexpected, unexplainable, unfortunate, wicked.

verbs SUBJECT: crime damages, destroys, dishonours, distresses, hurts, kills. OTHERS: to be accused of a crime, to be charged with a crime, to commit a crime, to investigate a crime.

expressions

- *Copycat crime:* an imitator or mimic ▸ **plagiat.**
- *Crime does not pay:* someone who breaks the law does not benefit from their actions ▸ **ceux et celles qui enfreignent la loi ne profitent pas de leurs crimes; le crime ne paie pas.**

danger ▸ danger

nouns accident, alarm, adventure, chance, caution, complication, conflict, death, difficult, distress, emergency, exposure, fright, harm, hazard, help, helplessness, injury, insecurity, instability, jeopardy, liability, loss, pain, peril, pitfall, scare, risk, trap, threat, vulnerability.

adjectives awful, bad, big, common, critical, cruel, deadly, depressing, devastating, dreadful, eventual, fatal, guilty, harmful, horrible, imminent, inevitable, mean, minor, mortal, nasty, personal, possible, potential, sad, serious, spectacular, sudden, terrible, unexpected, unexplainable, unfortunate, unsafe, wicked.

verbs SUBJECT: danger frightens, scares. OTHERS: to avoid danger, to be attracted to danger, to be exposed to danger, to be in danger, to be put into danger, to confront danger, to encounter danger, to escape danger, to fear danger, to inflict danger, to keep away from danger, to run into danger.

death ▸ mort

nouns accident, agony, bloodshed, body, bury, crime, danger, decease, demise, departure, destruction, downfall, dying, end, exit, expiration, extinction, finish, grave, ruin, funeral, ill, mortality, murder, passing, people, plague, sick, silence, sleep, suicide, rigor mortis, ruin, warrant, watch.

adjectives accidental, awful, common, crib, deadly, depressing, devastating, dreadful, early, fatal, gentle, gradual, heartbreaking, hideous, horrible, light, miserable, moving, mysterious, natural, sad, serene, serious, shocking, slow, spectacular, sudden, terrible, tragic, unexpected, unexplainable, unforeseen, unfortunate, violent.

verbs SUBJECT: death approaches, arrives, claims, occurs, strikes. OTHERS: to accept death, to certify death, to confront death, to contemplate death, to fear death, to fight death, to meet death, to risk death, to surrender to death, to triumph over death.

expressions

- *At death's door:* to be close to death ▸ **près de la mort; mourant ou mourante; à l'article de la mort.**
- *Be the death of:* to cause the death of something or someone ▸ **causer la mort de quelqu'un ou de quelque chose; tuer; faire mourir quelqu'un ou quelque chose.**
- *Bore to death:* someone or something that is very dull ▸ **quelqu'un ou quelque chose de très ennuyeux; ennuyeux à mourir; mortel.**
- *Death row:* area in prison occupied by prisoners sentenced to death ▸ **quartier où se trouvent les prisonniers et les prisonnières condamnés à mort.**
- *Death warmed over:* feeling and looking very ill ▸ **se sentir et avoir l'air très malade.**
- *Fate worse than death:* bad luck ▸ **malchance.**

1145

- *Kiss of death:* an action or a relationship that destroys ▸ **action ou relation destructrice.**
- *Matter of life and death:* urgent situation ▸ **situation urgente; question de vie ou de mort.**
- *Scare to death:* to frighten someone ▸ **effrayer quelqu'un; lui faire une peur bleue.**
- *Sign one's own death warrant:* bring harm to oneself ▸ **se nuire; se saborder.**
- *Tickled or thrilled to death:* overly excited or delighted ▸ **être très agité ou agitée, ravi ou ravie.**

demonstration ▸ manifestation

nouns argument, assembly, banner, clash, convention, crowd, display, exhibition, dispute, flag, gathering, manifestation, march, meet, meeting, parade, presentation, proof, protest, public, reunion, rally, riot, show, spectacle, support, test, trail.

adjectives awful, bloody, calm, collective, common, conclusive, convincing, crucial, cultural, deadly, decisive, depressing, devastating, disorderly, dreadful, enthusiastic, fatal, heartbreaking, hostile, moving, orderly, pacifist, public, sad, serious, spectacular, spontaneous, sudden, terrible, unexpected, unfortunate, violent.

verbs SUBJECT: the demonstration begins, continues, disturbs, finishes, starts, terminates, takes place, unites. OTHERS: to follow a demonstration, to join a demonstration, to march in a demonstration, to organize a demonstration, to participate in a demonstration, to prohibit a demonstration, to settle a demonstration.

event ▸ événement

nouns accident, account, achievement, action, adventure, affair, celebration, commentator, chance, circumstance, contest, consequence, date, day, deed, disaster, episode, experience, fact, fortune, happening, history, holiday, incident, issue, match, milestone, misfortune, occasion, occurrence, outcome, period, program, result, time.

adjectives annual, artistic, awful, big, business, celebrated, common, critical, cultural, current, daily, deadly, depressing, devastating, diplomatic, disastrous, dramatic, dreadful, fatal, happy, heartbreaking, historical, important, literary, lucky, miserable, monthly, moving, planned, political, sad, scientific, serious, significant, spectacular, sporadic, sporting, sudden, terrible, unexpected, unforeseen, unfortunate, unhappy, weekly.

verbs SUBJECT: an event arrives, begins, closes, fails, finishes, happens, occurs, opens, starts, takes place, unfolds. OTHERS: to attend an event, to celebrate an event, to commemorate an event, to look at an event, to miss an event, to organize an event, to participate in an event, to remember an event, to watch an event.

expressions

- *In the unlikely event:* if something improbable should happen ▸ **si quelque chose de peu probable arrivait.**
- *In any event:* no matter what happens or certainly ▸ **peu importe ce qui se produit; à n'importe quelle condition ou certainement.**
- *Blessed event:* the birth of a child ▸ **la naissance d'un enfant; un événement heureux.**

exhibition ▸ exposition

nouns art, artist, author, canvas, cinema, competition, critic, dance, display, drawing, exhibition, gallery, jury, movie, music, opening, painter, painting, presentation, room, sculptor, sculpture, show, theatre, writer.

adjectives agricultural, annual, artistic, awful, big, boring, civil, commercial, common, critical, cultural, cultural, daily, entertaining, famous, historical, important, international, local, monthly, moving, municipal, national, political, popular, provincial, public, regional, religious, scientific, serious, significant, special, spectacular, sudden, temporary, universal, weekly.

verbs SUBJECT: an exhibit arrives, attracts, closes, comes, finishes, happens, interests, opens, takes place. OTHERS: to go to an exhibit, to organize an exhibit, to participate in an exhibit.

---

fair ▶ foire

nouns amusement, animal, art, artist, author, bazaar, buyer, canvas, carnival, charity, competition, country, dance, display, drawing, entertainment, exhibit, exhibition, farm, gallery, goods, hall, jury, market, music, opening, painter, painting, park, pass, presentation, products, public, room, show, theatre, ticket, travelling, visitors, world.

adjectives agricultural, annual, church, commercial, entertaining, international, inexpensive, popular, regional, scientific.

verbs SUBJECT: a fair amuses, attracts, closes, entertains finishes, opens, starts, takes place. OTHERS: to buy at a fair, to gather at a fair, to sell at a fair, to go to a fair, to raise money at a fair.

expression ....

- *A fair shake:* an opportunity or a chance ▶ **occasion ou chance.**
- *Fair and square:* something that is honest ▶ **quelque chose d'honnête.**
- *Fair enough:* something that is reasonable ▶ **quelque chose de raisonnable.**
- *Fair game:* a legitimate target for attack or ridicule ▶ **cible idéale pour les attaques ou les critiques.**
- *Fair play:* conformity to rules ▶ **conformité aux règlements.**
- *Fair to middling:* something that is mediocre ▶ **quelque chose de médiocre.**
- *Fair weather friend:* a dependable friend ▶ **ami ou amie fiable.**
- *Fair-haired:* favourite ▶ **favori.**

---

holidays ▶ vacances

nouns adventure, adventurer, agent, airplane, amusement, autumn, backpack, baggage, bicycle, bike, biker, boat, break, bus, business, car, Christmas, circuit, course, crossing, cruise, cyclist, day, departure, destination, driver, driving, Easter, excursion, expedition, family, fare, festivity, foreign, freedom, guide, hike, hiker, hiking, hotel, itinerary, journey, knapsack, leave, leisure, luggage, map, off, outing, passage, passenger, passport, path, period, plane, pleasure, recess, recreation, reservation, rest, road, route, runner, season, ship, souvenir, spring, suitcase, summer, time, tour, touring, tourism, tourist, train, transport, travel, travelling, trip, vacation, vacationer, voyage, walk, weekend, winter, world.

adjectives amusing, annual, appealing, awful, boring, cheap, costly, cultural, dangerous, dull, educational, enjoyable, entertaining, excellent, exciting, expensive, failure, fascinating, fun, good, great, happy, hazardous, important, interesting, long, nice, organized, pleasant, popular, refreshing, relaxing, restful, rewarding, round, sad, short, special, spectacular, terrible, tiring.

verbs SUBJECT: A holiday begins, continues, finishes, relaxes, starts. OTHERS: to cancel a holiday, to enjoy a holiday, to leave for a holiday, to organize a holiday, to plan a holiday, to reschedule a holiday, to return from a holiday, to ruin a holiday, to take a holiday, to visit during a holiday.

expressions ....

- *Busman's holiday:* To spend free time doing the same thing one does at their job ▶ **passer son temps libre à travailler.**

---

party ▶ fête

nouns activity, anniversary, ball, band, birthday, cake, candles, celebration, ceremony, cocktail, commemoration, dance, dinner, entertainment, event, festival, festivity, fireworks, function, gala, gathering, graduation, group, harvest, holiday, honour, inauguration, invitation, jubilee, music, party, performance, pleasure, praise, reception, speech, tea, wedding.

adjectives amusing, annual, artistic, awful, boring, cheap, cultural, delightful, dull, early, enjoyable, entertaining, exciting, expensive, formal, fun, great, happy, important, municipal, national, pleasant, popular, refreshing, relaxing, rewarding, sad, special, spectacular, terrible, tiring.

verbs SUBJECT: a party begins, finishes, lasts, starts, takes place. OTHERS: to attend a party, to be invited to a party, to enjoy a party, to have a party, to give a party, to go to a party, to plan a party, to prepare for a party.

expressions..

- *Party line:* the official policy of an organization or government ▶ **politique officielle d'un organisme ou d'un gouvernement ; ligne du parti.**
- *Party's over:* It is time now to be serious ▶ **il est maintenant temps d'être sérieux.**
- *Life of the party:* an entertaining and exciting person ▶ **personne animée et amusante ; boute-en-train.**
- *Party animal:* an enthusiastic partygoer ▶ **personne qui aime et fréquente les fêtes.**

religion ▶ **religion**

nouns alter, belief, believer, Bible, cathedral, creed, chapel, church, communion, confession, denomination, divinity, cult, faith, father, god, ministry, monk, mother, nun, parson, prayer, priest, rabbi, reverend, scripture, sect, service, shrine, sister, synagogue, system, temple theology, truth, values, worship.

adjectives Christian, dutiful, faithful, genuine, God-fearing, Hindu, Islamic, Jewish, Moslem, sectarian, strict.

verbs SUBJECT: A religion directs, instructs, teachers, OTHERS: to attend religious services, to be a member of a religious group, to believe in a religion, to follow a certain religion.

expressions..

- *Get religion:* to convert to religion or decide to behave in an honourable way ▶ **se convertir à une religion ou décider de se comporter honorablement.**

show ▶ **spectacle**

nouns act, actor, actress, applause, artist, audience, auditorium, ballet, broadcast, call, cast, cheer, chorus, comedy, concert, costume, critic, curtain, dancer, demonstrate, display, drama, dressing room, event, exhibit, hall, lighting, make-up, mask, master of ceremony, monologue, music, music hall, magic, musician, opera, orchestra, picture, promoter, reservation, review, role, scenery, script, series, set, singer, sound, spectator, stage, talk, tape, television, theatre, ticket, usher.

adjectives annual, artistic, awful, bad, big, boring, brilliant, business, comic, cultural, cultural, daily, disastrous, disturbing, dramatic, funny, good, great, happy, heartbreaking, historical, important, lucky, magical, miserable, moving, musical, sad, spectacular, stupid, superb, terrible, unexpected, variety, weekly.

verbs OTHERS: to appear in a show, to applaud a show, to attend a show, to close a show, to criticize a show, to direct a show, to dislike a show, to enter into a show, to exhibit in a show, to like a show, to open a show, to perform in a show, to present in a show, to produce a show, to repeat a show, to televise a show, to watch a show.

expressions..

- *A show of hands:* an informal vote, which indicates choice ▶ **vote non officiel ; vote à main levée.**

- *The show must go on:* everything must continue as usual ▸ **tout doit continuer comme d'habitude ; la vie continue.**
- To show off: seek attention ▸ **chercher à attirer l'attention.**
- To *show one's heels:* run away or flee ▸ **s'enfuir.**
- To *show one's advantage:* to display in a flattering way ▸ **afficher avantageusement ; se montrer, paraître à son avantage.**
- To *show one's colours:* to reveal oneself ▸ **se révéler.**
- To *show one's face:* to appear on the scene ▸ **apparaître, faire acte de présence ; se montrer le nez.**
- To *show one's hand:* to reveal one's plans ▸ **révéler ses intentions ; annoncer la couleur ; abattre son jeu.**
- To *show one's teeth:* to demonstrate anger ▸ **faire preuve de colère ; montrer les dents.**
- To *show signs of:* exhibit hints of something ▸ **montrer des signes de.**
- To *show someone a good time:* entertain someone ▸ **divertir quelqu'un.**
- To *show someone the door:* order someone to leave ▸ **ordonner à quelqu'un de sortir ; lui montrer la porte.**
- To *show someone the ropes:* familiarize someone with details ▸ **enseigner.**
- To *show someone up:* to surpass someone in ability ▸ **dépasser quelqu'un par ses compétences ; lui en imposer.**
- To *show the way:* guide someone ▸ **guider quelqu'un.**
- To *show the white feather:* display cowardice ▸ **faire preuve de lâcheté.**
- To *show up:* put in an appearance ▸ **apparaître ; se pointer ; se montrer le nez.**

trip ▸ **voyage**

nouns adventure, adventurer, agent, airplane, amusement, autumn, backpack, baggage, bicycle, bike, biker, boat, break, bus, business, car, circuit, course, crossing, cruise, cyclist, day, departure, destination, driver, driving, excursion, excursion, expedition, family, fare, festivity, foreign, freedom, guide, hike, hiker, hiking, holiday, home, hotel, itinerary, journey, knapsack, leave, leisure, luggage, map, off, outing, passage, passenger, passport, path, period, plane, pleasure, recess, recreation, reservation, rest, road, route, runner, season, ship, souvenir, spring, suitcase, summer, time, tour, touring, tourism, tourist, train, transport, travel, travelling, vacation, vacationer, voyage, walk, weekend, winter, world.

adjectives amusing, annual, appealing, attracting, awful, boring, cheap, costly, cultural, dangerous, dull, educational, enjoyable, entertaining, excellent, exciting, expensive, failed, fascinating, fun, good, great, happy, hazardous, important, interesting, long, nice, organized, pleasant, popular, refreshing, relaxing, restful, rewarding, round, sad, short, special, spectacular, terrible, tiring.

verbs SUBJECT: a trip begins, continues, ends, finishes, relaxes, starts. OTHERS: To arrive from a trip, to be on a trip, to go on a trip, to leave for a trip, to postpone a trip, to prepare for a trip, to take a trip.

expressions

- *Bad trip:* to have an unpleasant experience ▸ **expérience désagréable, qui tourne mal.**
- *Ego trip:* behaviour that is conceited ▸ **comportement vaniteux.**
- *Lay a trip:* to inflict one's obsession on another ▸ **imposer ses obsessions.**
- *Round trip:* a journey to a given place and back to the point of departure usually using the same route ▸ **aller-retour, habituellement par le même trajet.**

war ▸ **guerre**

nouns act, action, aggression, air, air force, airplane, alert, alliance, ammunition, arms, armistice, army, assault, attack, base, battle, boat, bomb, bombardment, bomber, bombing, bullet, camp, campaign, cease-fire, clash, combat, command, conflict, confrontation, conquest, conqueror, country, crime, criminal, crisis, crusade, death, debate, declaration, defeat, defence, desertion, destruction, discord, discussion, draft, enemy, engagement, enlistment, evacuation, exercise, extermination, fight, formation, front, game, genocide, ground, gun, hate, hostility, injury, invasion, jeep, line, marine, massacre, mercenary, military, militia, missile, nation, offensive, operation, opposition, order, outbreak, pain, patrol, peace, position, power, prisoner, projectile, raid, rebellion, resistance, retaliation, revolt, revolution, riffle, ruin, shell, soldier, state, strategy, struggle, submarine, tank, tactics, tension, treaty, trench, troops, victory, weapon, wounds, zone.

adjectives aerial, atomic, awful, bacterial, biological, bloody, brutal, chemical, civil, colonial, continuous, deadly, depressing, devastating, dirty, dreadful, economic, fatal, heartbreaking, holy, internal, international, lost, miserable, moving, nuclear, psychological, religious, sad, serious, spectacular, strategic, sudden, terrible, unexpected, unfortunate, victorious.

verbs SUBJECT: A war destroys, hurts, injures, kills, wounds. OTHERS: to be at war, to carry on a war, to declare war, to enlist in a war, to go to war, to make war, to prevent a war, to return from war, to start a war, to stop a war, to wage war.

expressions...

- *War horse:* someone or something who is dependable ▸ **quelqu'un ou quelque chose de fiable.**

- *All is fair in love and war:* in certain conditions any type of conduct is permissible ▸ **dans certaines conditions, tous les comportements sont permis; en amour comme à la guerre, tous les moyens sont bons.**

- *Been to the wars:* someone who shows signs of having received rough treatment or injury ▸ **qui montre des signes de blessure ou de mauvais traitement; amoché ou amochée.**

- *Declare war on (declare war against):* to announce one's intent to wage war against someone or something ▸ **annoncer son intention de faire la guerre à quelqu'un ou quelque chose; déclarer la guerre.**

- *Tug of war:* a power struggle between individuals ▸ **guerre de pouvoir.**

---

wedding ▸ **mariage**

nouns anniversary, bride, day, cake, celebration, ceremony, church, engagement, family, festivities, flower, groom, march, marriage, night, party, guest, ring, shower, stag, union, vows.

adjectives awful, beautiful, big, brilliant, civic, colourful, costly, disastrous, elegant, exciting, expensive, extravagant, formal, good, great, happy, important, lovely, moving, sad, short, spectacular, terrible, unexpected.

verb SUBJECT: a wedding begins, ends, finishes, starts, takes place. OTHERS: to attend a wedding, to go to a wedding, to watch a wedding, to participate in a wedding, to prepare for a wedding.

expressions...

- *Shotgun wedding:* A marriage arranged quickly ▸ **mariage organisé rapidement.**

airplane
▸avion

wagon
▸wagon

airport
▸aéroport

vacation
▸vacances

automobile
▸automobile

truck
▸camion

bicycle
▸bicyclette

travel and transportation

travel
▸voyage

boat
▸bateau (-eaux)

transportation
▸moyen
de transport

bus
▸autobus

train
▸train

car
▸voiture

skate
▸patin

motocycle
▸motocyclette

rocket
▸fusée

airplane ▸ avion

nouns aeronautics, aerodynamics, air, airline, airliner, airport, airspace, airways, aviation, aviator, boarding, bomber, cabin, cargo, class, cockpit, co-pilot, company, connection, controller, departure, factory, fleet, flight, freight, fuselage, glider, hanger, helicopter, hijacker, hijacking, instruments, jet, landing, loading, mail, motor, navigation, passenger, plane, pilot, propeller, runway, squadron, steward, stewardess, takeoff, ticket, traffic, transport, trip, auto-pilot, vacation, voyage, wings.

adjectives automatic, beautiful, big, commercial, computerized, express, fast, international, jumbo, large, light, military, overbooked, quick, rapid, speedy, supersonic.

verbs SUBJECT: a plane crashes, descends, flies, glides, lands, taxies, takes off. OTHERS: to build a plane, to buy a plane, to fly a plane, to get off a plane, to get on a plane, to pilot a plane, to rent a plane, to take a plane, to unload a plane, to wait for a plane.

airport ▸ aéroport

nouns area, airfield, airplane, arrival, aviation, aviator, baggage, board, building, business, cargo, class, cockpit, company, controller, co-pilot, crew, customs, destination, employee, fleet, flight, gear, hanger, helicopter, industry, landing, luggage, mail, maintenance, navigation, office, officer, overseas, passenger, pilot, public, restaurant, runway, staff, stand-by, takeoff, ticket, toilet, tourism, tourist, traffic, transit, transport, traveller, washroom.

adjectives big, busy, huge, international, large, local, massive, military, new, old, private, regional, small.

verbs OTHERS: to arrive at the airport, to be at the airport, to drive to the airport, to have a stopover at the airport, to land at the airport, to leave from the airport, to take off from the airport, to wait at the airport.

automobile ▸ automobile

nouns accelerator, accident, ambulance, battery, belt, blinker, body, brake, breakdown, bumper, car, chauffeur, clutch, collision, compartment, convertible, controls, cylinder, dealership, differential, door, driver, duel, electric, engine, fender, frame, fuel, gas, garage, gears, glove, grease, handle, headlight, hood, horn, hubcap, ignition, industry, interior, jeep, license, lights, limousine, mechanic, mirror, motor, motorist, motor-racing, oil, paint, pedal, race, racing, radiator, reserve, seat, speed, speedometer, starter, steering, suspension, tank, tire, traffic, transmission, trunk, wheel, windshield.

adjectives antique, big, black, blue, broken, brown, clean, comfortable, compact, dirty, electric, expensive, fast, flashy, foreign, gold, green, large, luxury, new, nice, noisy, ordinary, powerful, red, slow, sluggish, small, sports, uncomfortable, white, wrecked, yellow.

verbs SUBJECT: an automobile accelerates, breaks down, crashes, slows down, stalls, starts. OTHERS: to admire an automobile, to buy an automobile, to drive an automobile, to dream of an automobile, to look at an automobile, to sell an automobile, to take place in an automobile, to travel in an automobile.

bicycle ▸ bicyclette

nouns axle, bike, biking, brake, cable, chain, champion, child, city, cycling, cyclist, derailleur, exercise, fork, frame, gears, handlebars, helmet, light, mechanic, messenger, motor, motorcycle, mountain, path, pedal, pump, race, reflector, ride, rim, saddle, stand, seat, speed, spoke, sport, tandem, team, tire, toe-clip, tour, trainer, transport, tricycle, unicycle, valve, wheels.

adjectives big, broken, cheap, equipped, expensive, fast, heavy, light, motorized, new, old, standard, stationary, stolen.

verbs SUBJECT: a bike crashes, glides, skids, works. OTHERS: to adjust a bicycle, to arrive by bicycle, to buy a bicycle, to fix a bicycle, to get on a bicycle, to grease a bicycle, to like bicycling, to mount a bicycle, to repair a bicycle, to sell a bicycle, to travel on a bicycle.

---

boat ▶ bateau (-eaux)

nouns aircraft carrier, anchor, barge, battleship, boarding, boating, bow, cadet, canoe, captain, cargo, coast guard, craft, cruise, cruiser, deck, destroyer, dock, ferryboat, fleet, freight, harbour, headway, kayak, lifeboat, liner, marina, motorboat, navigation, navigator, navy, ocean, passenger, port, pier, pirate, raft, ride, river, row, rowboat, rower, rudder, sail, sailboat, sailor, sea, seaman, seaway, ship, skipper, speedboat, squadron, starboard, steamer, steamship, stern, sternway, submarine, tanker, torpedo, vessel, water, wave, weather, yacht.

adjectives antique, big, damaged, drifting, expensive, fast, large, light, long, luxurious, new, old, old-fashioned, safe, sinking, small.

verbs SUBJECT: a boat arrives, leaves, sails, sinks. OTHERS: to anchor a boat, to board a boat, to build a boat, to get off a boat, to go by boat, to go in a boat, to leave by boat, to live on a boat, to load a boat, to navigate a boat, to ship by boat, to torpedo a boat, to travel by boat, to unload a boat, to watch a boat.

expressions

- *Boat people:* political refugees who escape in a small boat ▶ **réfugiés et réfugiées politiques fuyant leur pays sur des bateaux.**

- *In the same boat:* everyone is in the same situation ▶ **ils et elles sont tous dans la même situation; ils et elles sont tous dans la même galère; ils et elles logent tous à la même enseigne.**

- *To burn one's boats:* to do something which makes it impossible for one to return to one's former position or way of life ▶ **faire quelque chose qui rend tout retour en arrière impossible; brûler ses ponts, ses vaisseaux.**

- *To miss the boat:* to fail to take advantage of an opportunity ▶ **rater une occasion; rater le coche.**

- *To rock the boat:* to cause trouble within a stable situation ▶ **semer le trouble dans une situation stable; jouer les trouble-fêtes.**

---

bus ▶ autobus

nouns back, coach, driver, lane, motorbus, number, pass, passenger, road, route, stop, street, ticket, transport, traveller, trip, trolley, vehicle.

adjective beautiful, big, clean, crowded, dirty, empty, express, large, long, luxurious, modern, municipal, new, nice, old, packed, public, small.

verbs SUBJECT: a bus arrives, continues, leaves, starts, stops. OTHERS: to get on a bus, to get off a bus, to miss a bus, to travel by bus, to wait for the bus.

expressions

- *A busman's holiday:* a holiday spent doing something similar to what one does in one's job ▶ **vacances passées à travailler.**

- *Like the back end of a bus:* very unattractive ▶ **absolument pas attirant.**

- *To miss the bus:* to miss an opportunity or to be left behind ▶ **rater une occasion ou être oublié ou oubliée; rater le coche ou être laissé ou laissée pour compte.**

---

car ▶ voiture

nouns accident, automobile, battery, breakdown, day, dealership, engine, expenses, family, fare, ferry, freight, garage, journey, license, parking, model, motor, movement, passenger, patrol, pool, port, radio, railway, road, seat, street, streetcar, thief, ticket, tracks, tramway, transport, trip, wheels, vacation, vehicle, volume.

adjectives antique, beautiful, big, clean, comfortable, compact, crowded, dirty, economical, empty, expensive, express, fast, foreign, large, long, luxurious, modern, new, nice, old, packed, polished, powerful, public, slow, small.

verbs SUBJECT: a car accelerates, breaks down, crashes, slides, stalls. OTHERS: to buy a car, to clean a car, to drive a car, to go in a car, to look at a car, to park a car, to polish a car, to repair a car, to sell a car, to start a car, to travel by car, to wash a car.

motorcycle ▸ **motocyclette**

nouns accident, association, battery, boots, brake, braking, breakdown, circuit, competition, compression, club, clutch, cylinder, dealership, dirt, driving, exhaust, equipment, gloves, helmet, indicator, jacket, machine, model, motor, motorbike, motocross, muffler, power, racing, rider, road, saddle, scooter, seat, silencer, speed, stand, starter, starting, sunglasses, suspension, tank, transmission, transport, trip, vehicle, volume.

adjectives antique, beautiful, big, clean, comfortable, crowded, dangerous, dirty, economical, empty, expensive, express, fast, foreign, large, long, luxurious, modern, motorized, new, nice, noisy, old, packed, polished, powerful, public, slow, small, sturdy, uncomfortable.

verbs SUBJECT: the motorcycle accelerates, backfires, breaks down, crashes, breaks, stalls, starts, stops. OTHERS: to admire a motorcycle, to buy a motorcycle, to clean a motorcycle, to drive a motorcycle, to polish a motorcycle, to repair a motorcycle, to ride a motorcycle, to sell a motorcycle, to wash a motorcycle.

rocket ▸ **fusée**

nouns air, airplane, astronaut, atmosphere, bomb, capsule, engine, fireworks, frontier, galaxy, gas, instruments, landing, milky way, missile, outer space, orbit, projectile, route, ship, sky, space, spacecraft, stars, station, takeoff, transport, vessel.

adjectives beautiful, big, dangerous, dirty, expensive, explosive, fast, foreign, hazardous, large, long, modern, motorized, new, nice, noisy, old, powerful, slow, small.

verbs SUBJECT: a rocket attacks, explodes, lands, transports, takes off. OTHERS: to attack a rocket, to build a rocket, to design a rocket, to destroy with a rocket, to launch a rocket, to observe a rocket, to put a rocket (into orbit), to transport by rocket, to travel on a rocket.

expressions

• *You don't have to be a rocket scientist:* It does not take super intelligence to understand ▸ **il ne faut pas être très intelligent ou intelligente pour comprendre ; pas besoin d'être une lumière pour comprendre.**

skate ▸ **patin**

nouns activity, arena, athlete, blade, board, boot, clothing, cold, derby, equipment, exercise, floor, frame, freezing, hockey, ice, laces, legs, lane, path, park, roller, road, shoe, skater, skating, socks, sole, sport, stick, straps, surface, team, transport, wheel.

adjectives big, brushed, buckled, cheap, competitive, dirty, dry, expensive, fancy, fastened, fun, heavy, laced, leather, long, new, old, polished, resoled, scuffed, small, strong, tied, tough, unlaced, used, waxed, wet, worn, worn down.

verbs SUBJECT: a skate glides, wears down. OTHERS: to buy skates, to fasten a skate, to get skates, to lace a skate, to polish a skate, to pull on a skate, to put on skates, to race with skates, to resole a skate, to scuff a skate, to sharpen skates, to skate with skates, to take off a skate, to unlace a skate, to wear a skate, to wear down a skate.

expressions..

- *To skate on thin ice:* To be or to put oneself in a dangerous situation ► **être ou se mettre dans une situation dangereuse ; s'aventurer en terrain glissant.**

train ► train

nouns agent, arrival, baggage, brake, check, coach, conductor, corridor, departure, derailment, destination, diesel, door, electric, employee, freight, front, halt, intercom, late, line-up, locomotive, loading, luggage, one-way, pass, passenger, railway, rear, return, round, route, schedule, service, signal, smokestack, speed, station, stop, subway, track, ticket, track, transport, trolley, unloading, window, wreck.

adjectives antique, beautiful, big, clean, comfortable, crowded, dangerous, direct, dirty, economical, empty, expensive, express, fast, foreign, international, large, local, long, luxurious, modern, motorized, national, new, nice, noisy, old, packed, polished, powerful, public, regional, slow, small, sturdy, uncomfortable.

verbs SUBJECT: the train accelerates, arrives, backs up, breaks down, derails, leaves, operates, slows down, starts, stops, transports. OTHERS: to catch a train, to get on a train, to get off a train, to leave on a train, to miss a train, to operate a train, to travel by train, to wait for a train.

expressions..

- *Train of thought:* Ideas that are connected in successive order and have reasoning ► **suite d'idées logiques ; fil de la pensée.**
- *To ride the gravy train:* To experience ease and/or profit that is undeserving ► **avoir une vie facile ou profiter de ce qui n'est pas mérité ; avoir une bonne planque.**

- *Train wreck:* A person with serious medical problems ► **personne qui a de graves problèmes de santé.**

transportation ► moyen de transport

nouns airplane, automobile, baggage, bicycle, boat, bus, cab, car, cargo, carriage, cart, coach, convey, fare, ferry, freight, goods, haul, horses, luggage, messenger, motorcycle, move, movement, passage, passengers, people, plane, post, postage, public, service, ship, shipment, shipping, subway, system, removal, taxi, ticket, traffic, train, transfer, transport, transit, truck, van, wagon.

adjectives clean, comfortable, crowded, dangerous, direct, dirty, economical, expensive, express, fast, foreign, international, large, local, luxurious, modern, motorized, national, new, nice, noisy, old, packed, public, regional, slow, uncomfortable.

verbs OTHERS: to dislike (public) transportation, to like (public) transportation, to need (public) transportation, to praise (public) transportation, to take (public) transportation, to use (public) transportation, to wait for (public) transportation, to work for (public) transportation.

travel ► voyage

nouns adventure, agent, airplane, amusement, annual, autumn, backpack, baggage, bicycle, bike, biker, boat, break, bus, business, car, circuit, course, crossing, cruise, cyclist, day, departure, destination, driver, driving, excursion, expedition, family, fare, festivity, foreign, freedom, guide, hike, hiker, hiking, holiday, home, hotel, itinerary, journey, knapsack, leave, leisure, luggage, map, outing, passage, passenger, passport, path, period, plane, pleasure, recess, recreation, reservation, rest, road, route, runner, season, ship, souvenir, spring, suitcase, summer, time, tour, touring, tourism, tourist, train, transport, travelling, trip, vacation, vacationer, voyage, walk, weekend, winter, world.

adjectives amusing, annual, appealing, attracting, awful, boring, cheap, costly, cultural, dangerous, dull, educational, enjoyable, entertaining, excellent, exciting, expensive, fascinating, fun, good, great, happy, hazardous, important, interesting, long, nice, organized, pleasant, popular, refreshing, relaxing, restful, rewarding, round, sad, short, special, spectacular, terrible, tiring.

verbs SUBJECT: Travel interests, pleases, relaxes. OTHERS: to enjoy one's travel, to like to travel, to love to travel, to remember one's travel.

expressions..

• *To travel light:* to take little baggage on a trip or to have few responsibilities in one's life ▶ **voyager avec peu de bagages ou avoir peu de responsabilités dans la vie.**

---

truck ▶ camion

nouns accident, bulk, cab, cabin, cargo, cart, company, contractor, driver, dump, farm, frame, freight, goods, heavy, jeep, journey, load, map, material, motor, oil, panel, pick-up, road, route, stop, supplies, tanker, teamster, tractor, traffic, trailer, transport, troops trucker, van, vehicle, wagon, weight, wheel.

adjectives beautiful, big, clean, comfortable, crowded, dangerous, direct, dirty, economical, empty, expensive, express, fast, foreign, large, long, luxurious, modern, motorized, new, nice, noisy, old, packed, polished, powerful, slow, small, sturdy, uncomfortable.

verbs SUBJECT: a truck accelerates, breaks down, carries, slows down, starts, stops, transports. OTHERS: to drive a truck, to carry on a truck, to load a truck, to put on a truck, to transport by truck, to unload a truck.

expressions..

• *Have no truck with:* To have no dealings or contact with someone ▶ **n'avoir**

rien à faire avec quelqu'un, ne pas avoir affaire à quelqu'un.

---

vacation ▶ vacances

nouns adventure, agent, airplane, amusement, annual, autumn, backpack, baggage, bicycle, bike, biker, boat, break, bus, business, car, circuit, course, crossing, cruise, cyclist, day, departure, destination, driver, driving, excursion, expedition, family, fare, festivity, foreign, freedom, guide, hike, hiker, hiking, holiday, home, hotel, itinerary, journey, knapsack, leave, leisure, luggage, map, outing, passage, passenger, passport, path, period, plane, pleasure, recess, recreation, reservation, rest, road, route, runner, season, ship, souvenir, spring, suitcase, summer, time, tour, tourism, tourist, train, transport, travel, travelling, trip, vacationer, voyage, walk, weekend, winter, world.

adjectives amusing, annual, appealing, attracting, awful, boring, cheap, costly, cultural, dangerous, dull, educational, enjoyable, entertaining, excellent, exciting, expensive, fascinating, fun, good, great, happy, hazardous, important, interesting, long, nice, organized, pleasant, popular, refreshing, relaxing, restful, rewarding, round, sad, short, special, spectacular, terrible, tiring.

verbs OTHERS: to be on vacation, to cancel a vacation, to enjoy a vacation, to go on vacation, to have a vacation, to leave on vacation, to take a vacation, to return from vacation.

expressions..

• *Vacation:* to serve a prison sentence ▶ **purger une peine en prison.**

---

wagon ▶ wagon

nouns car, cart, chariot, children, delivery, drive, driver, donkey, farm, freight, horse, load, merchandise, motor, mule, police, railway, station, toy, truck, van, vehicle, water, wheel, work, workers.

adjectives antique, attached, beautiful, big, clean, closed, comfortable, covered, crowded, dangerous, direct, dirty, economical, empty, expensive, express, fast, flat, foreign, full, heavy, international, large, loaded, local, long, low, luxurious, modern, motorized, national, new, nice, noisy, old, open, packed, polished, powerful, public, refrigerated, regional, slow, small, sturdy, uncomfortable.

verbs SUBJECT: a wagon moves, rolls, slides, transports. OTHERS: to attach a wagon, to load a wagon, to pull a wagon, to ride in (on) a wagon, to unload a wagon.

expressions

- *To be on the wagon:* to refuse to drink alcoholic beverages ► **refuser de boire de l'alcool; se mettre au régime sec.**

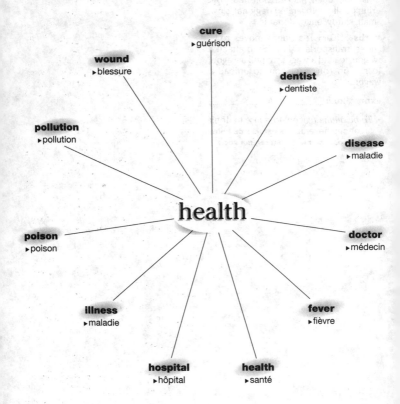

cure
▸guérison

wound
▸blessure

dentist
▸dentiste

pollution
▸pollution

disease
▸maladie

health

poison
▸poison

doctor
▸médecin

illness
▸maladie

fever
▸fièvre

hospital
▸hôpital

health
▸santé

cure ▸ guérison

nouns allergy, antibiotic, antibody, antidote, bacteria, bandage, cancer, capsule, death, diet, disease, doctor, drug, drugstore, health, hope, hospital, illness, infection, injury, life, medicine, needle, ointment, penicillin, pill, prescription, prevention, rash, remedy, research, resistance, serum, sickness, tablet, treatment, vaccine, vitamin, wound.

adjectives calming, helpful, medical, powerful, prescribed, preventive, quick, restoring.

verbs SUBJECT: a cure acts, calms, heals, relieves, restores, saves. OTHERS: to discover a cure, to follow a cure, to hope for a cure, to need a cure, to prescribe a cure, to research a cure.

expressions

- *Cure-all:* A cure for all illnesses ▸ **remède agissant sur toutes les maladies ; panacée.**

dentist ▸ dentiste

nouns assistant, braces, cavity, chair, cleaning, dentistry, disease, doctor, drill, enamel, filling, fluoride, gum, hygiene, infection, instrument, jaw, mirror, mouth, nerve, office, pain, root, smock, surgeon, surgery, tartar, tooth, toothbrush, toothpaste, X-ray.

adjectives busy, caring, clean, dental, precise, professional, skilled, trained, wealthy.

verbs SUBJECT: a dentist cleans, extracts, fills, fixes, makes appointments, operates, studies. OTHERS: to call a dentist, to pay a dentist, to require a dentist.

disease ▸ maladie

nouns ambulance, anesthetic, antibiotic, blood, blood pressure, cancer, clinic, coma, condition, cough, cramp, cure, death, diagnosis, disorder, dizziness, drug, emergency, epidemic, fever,

germ, headache, hospital, illness, immunity, infection, insurance, medicine, nurse, ointment, operation, pain, parasite, patient, rash, recovery, serum, sickness, sneeze, stomach, surgery, symptom, syrup, vaccine, virus, vomiting.

adjectives alarming, bloody, contagious, dangerous, deadly, disabling, diseased, fatal, frightening, harmful, immune, infected, infectious, painful, serious, sudden, transmitted, traumatic, treated.

verbs SUBJECT: a disease affects, develops, disappears, infects, kills, spreads, weakens. OTHERS: to contract a disease, to cure a disease, to fear disease, to recover from disease, to treat a disease.

doctor ▸ médecin

nouns blood, blood pressure, bone, cancer, care, clinic, dentist, diagnosis, disease, drug, heart, hospital, illness, liver, lung, medicine, nurse, office, operation, optometrist, patient, physician, prescription, psychiatrist, school, skin, specialist, stethoscope, surgeon, surgery, therapy, veterinarian, X-ray.

adjectives busy, caring, good, intelligent, medical, popular, professional, specialized, terrible, wealthy.

verbs SUBJECT: a doctor advises, examines, fixes, heals, listens, operates, practices, prescribes, warns. OTHERS: to consult a doctor, to ignore a doctor, to listen to a doctor, to need a doctor.

expressions

- *To doctor something:* To improve something ▸ **améliorer quelque chose.**
- *It's just what the doctor ordered:* That's exactly what I needed ▸ **c'est exactement ce dont j'ai besoin.**

fever ▸ fièvre

nouns bath, bed, body, chill, clinic, disease, dizziness, doctor, face, flu, forehead, headache, heat, hospital, illness, infection, nurse, rest, shivers, sweat, temperature, thermometer, thirst, virus, water.

adjectives alarming, burning, cold, fatal, high, hot, infectious, persistent, raging, red, rising, serious, slight, sweaty, treated, warm.

verbs SUBJECT: a fever disables, hits, lowers, rises, weakens. OTHERS: to have a fever, to feel a fever, to treat a fever.

expressions...

- *Fever blister:* cold sore ► **bouton de fièvre.**
- *Fever pitch:* high excitement ► **grande agitation.**
- *Hay fever:* seasonal allergies ► **allergies saisonnières; rhume des foins.**
- *Spring fever:* restless feeling associated with spring ► **agitation associée à l'arrivée du printemps.**

health ► **santé**

nouns activity, body, care, clinic, club, condition, cure, death, diet, disease, drug, energy, epidemic, exercise, fatigue, food, growth, hazard, healing, hospital, illness, insurance, life, mind, nurse, nutrition, prevention, problem, relaxation, remedy, rest, risk, sleep, sport, strength, supplement, vigour, vitality, vitamin, weakness, weight, well-being.

adjectives ailing, altered, bad, declining, fragile, good, ideal, ill, mental, perfect, physical, poor, restored, strong, weak.

verbs OTHERS: to be in good health, to have one's health, to regain one's health.

expressions...

- *To your health!:* Cheers! ► **À votre santé! À la vôtre!**

hospital ► **hôpital**

nouns accident, admission, ambulance, bed, care, clinic, department, disease, doctor, drug, emergency, examination, gown, illness, injury, institution, medicine, nurse, operation, orderly, patient, reputation, room, sickness, stretcher, surgeon, surgery, treatment, waiting, wheelchair, wound, X-ray.

adjectives busy, clean, closed, crowded, famous, medical, open, teaching.

verbs OTHERS: to avoid the hospital, to drive to the hospital, to send someone to the hospital, to visit the hospital, to walk into a hospital, to work in a hospital.

expressions...

- *Hospital corners:* A specific method of tucking in bed sheets ► **façon particulière de plier les coins de draps.**

illness ► **maladie**

nouns abdomen, ache, acupuncture, AIDS, ailment, alcoholism, allergy, amnesia, anatomy, anemia, anorexia, antibiotic, appendicitis, artery, arthritis, aspirin, asthma, bacteria, blood, body, bone, bronchitis, bruise, burn, cancer, case, chest, chill, clinic, colon, coma, cough, cure, cyst, death, depression, diabetes, diagnosis, disease, disorder, dizziness, doctor, examination, fatigue, fever, handicap, headache, heart, hospital, infection, influenza, intestine, isolation, liver, lung, malaria, mania, measles, medicine, muscle, nerve, nurse, pain, paralysis, patient, penicillin, plague, pneumonia, polio, prescription, pulse, rabies, rash, remedy, rest, serum, sickness, sinus, skin, smallpox, sore, spinal cord, surgery, symptom, tension, tetanus, throat, tonsillitis, trauma, tuberculosis, tumour, vein, virus, vomiting.

adjectives chronic, congenital, contagious, cured, dangerous, deadly, epidemic, fatal, hereditary, imaginary, incurable, long, mental, painful, psychiatric, recurring, serious, treated.

verbs SUBJECT: an illness affects, declares itself, develops, kills, saddens, weakens. OTHERS: to cure an illness, to develop an illness, to fight an illness, to treat an illness.

poison ▸ poison

nouns ambulance, antidote, arsenic, bite, burn, cure, death, disease, dizziness, dose, drug, emergency, fertilizer, gas, headache, insect, ivy, liquid, mushroom, paralysis, plant, powder, rat, snake, spider, sting, toxin, venom, virus, vomiting.

adjectives dangerous, deadly, fatal, frightening, toxic, venomous.

verbs SUBJECT: poison burns, kills, paralyses, stings. OTHERS: to drink poison, to inject poison, to spray poison, to swallow poison.

expressions

• *One man's meat is another man's poison:* not all things are liked or equally liked by all people ▸ **une chose appréciée par une personne ne l'est pas nécessairement par une autre ; le malheur des uns fait le bonheur des autres.**

• *Poison-pen letter:* A nasty, anonymous letter ▸ **lettre anonyme.**

• *Sweet poison:* Something that is both good and bad ▸ **chose à la fois bonne et mauvaise.**

• *To poison one's mind:* To corrupt someone ▸ **corrompre quelqu'un.**

• *What's your poison?:* What's your favourite drink? ▸ **Quelle est votre boisson (alcoolique) préférée ?**

pollution ▸ pollution

nouns acid rain, air, animal, atmosphere, biodegradable, biologist, biology, burning, cancer, car, catastrophe, chimney, cigarette, city, death, disaster, dump, earth, ecology, environment, exhaust, fauna, fog, forest, fuel, garbage, gas, ground, habitat, lake, life, nature, noise, ocean, oil, pipe, plant, poison, prevention, protection, radioactivity, recycling, river, smoke, trash, tree, waste, water, wilderness.

adjectives aggressive, atmospheric, chemical, dangerous, deadly, destructive, dirty, ecological, harmful, natural, organic, poisonous, radioactive, terrible, toxic, tragic.

verbs SUBJECT: pollution dirties, kills, ruins, soils. OTHERS: to create pollution, to fight pollution.

wound ▸ blessure

nouns accident, amputation, antibiotic, bandage, blood, blow, body, break, bruise, bullet, burn, cast, chest, cripple, crutch, cut, emergency, explosion, fall, flesh, gun, handicap, harm, head, heart, hospital, infection, injury, knife, ointment, pain, piercing, scar, skin, sore, stabbing, stretcher, surgery, tissue, trauma, war, wheelchair.

adjectives aching, fresh, healing, infected, old, open, painful, swollen.

verbs SUBJECT: a wound bleeds, heals, hurts, infects. OTHERS: to clean a wound, to cover a wound, to hide a wound, to treat a wound.

expressions

• *To lick one's wounds:* To recover from defeat or disappointment ▸ **récupérer (après un échec ou une déception) ; panser ses plaies.**

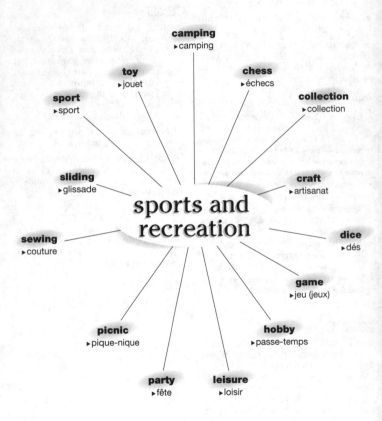

camping
▸camping

toy
▸jouet

chess
▸échecs

collection
▸collection

sport
▸sport

craft
▸artisanat

sliding
▸glissade

sports and recreation

dice
▸dés

sewing
▸couture

game
▸jeu (jeux)

picnic
▸pique-nique

hobby
▸passe-temps

party
▸fête

leisure
▸loisir

camping ▸ camping

nouns ant, backpack, barbecue, beach, blanket, bonfire, bug, cabin, camp, camper, campfire, car, chair, flashlight, food, forest, game, hiking, holiday, lake, log, mountain, night, outdoors, park, party, picnic, pool, provisions, river, sleeping bag, sport, stove, summer, swimming, tent, trailer, wilderness, wildlife, wood, woods.

adjectives chilly, dangerous, fun, recreational, relaxing, warm.

verbs OTHERS: to dislike camping, to enjoy camping, to go camping, to like camping, to pack for camping, to prepare for camping.

chess ▸ échecs

nouns adversary, amateur, attack, bishop, black, champion, chessboard, competition, defence, game, intelligence, king, knight, losing, move, opponent, patience, piece, player, prize, queen, rule, skill, strategy, white, winning.

adjectives boring, challenging, competitive, difficult, fun, long, strategic.

verbs OTHERS: to excel at chess, to love chess, to play chess.

expressions

• *Checkmate:* you have lost (when playing chess) ▸ **expression signifiant que l'on a perdu aux échecs ; échec et mat.**

collection ▸ collection

nouns album, antique, art, assortment, autograph, book, bottle, bug, butterfly, button, car, card, coin, collector, display, doll, exchange, exhibit, expert, gallery, game, group, hat, hobby, jewellery, marble, medal, mug, museum, object, painting, passion, pen, pencil, photograph, pin, plate, postcard, poster, price, pride, purchase, rarity, record, rock, set, shells, souvenir, specimen, spoon, stamp, sticker, toy, trade, trinket, trophy, value.

adjectives amateur, destroyed, expensive, impressive, lost, lovely, new, priceless, private, public, small, unique, unusual, valuable.

verbs OTHERS: to buy a collection, to display a collection, to possess a collection, to sell a collection, to start a collection.

craft ▸ artisanat

nouns activity, art, artist, cardboard, colour, creation, crochet, decoration, display, drawing, fabric, fair, folk, glue, hand, knitting, material, needle, paint, painting, paper, picture, pottery, sculpture, sewing, shop, show, skill, supplies, tool, trade, weaving, wood, wool, yarn.

adjectives beautiful, difficult, easy, expensive, fun, inexpensive, practical.

verbs OTHERS: to learn a craft, to practice a craft, to teach a craft.

expressions

• *Craft guild:* Union of craftspeople ▸ **association d'artisans et d'artisanes.**

dice ▸ dés

nouns adversary, bet, board, card, casino, chance, cheating, cube, dot, five, fortune, four, gambling, game, hand, lottery, luck, magic, number, one, player, rule, six, strategy, table, three, two, winnings.

adjectives large, marked, plastic, small, square, tricked, wooden.

verbs OTHERS: to cheat with dice, to play with dice, to throw dice.

expressions

• *No dice:* No luck ▸ **pas de chance.**
• *To dice with something:* To take risks with something ▸ **prendre un risque à l'égard de quelque chose.**
• *To dice with death:* to do something very risky ▸ **faire quelque chose de très risqué ; jouer avec le feu.**

• *To load the dice against someone:* to take away any chance someone has of succeeding at something ► **éliminer toute chance de réussite.**

game ► jeu (jeux)

nouns ace, action, activity, adventure, adversary, amusement, arcade, backgammon, ball, bet, board, bowling, bridge, card, casino, champion, championship, chance, cheating, checkers, chess, child, chip, club, competition, computer, contest, cricket, croquet, curling, dart, deck, diamond, dice, entertainment, goal, heart, hopscotch, jack, jacks, king, lacrosse, losing, lottery, marble, medal, memory, opponent, outdoors, partner, player, pleasure, poker, puzzle, queen, radio, score, show, skill, sport, strategy, table, tactic, team, television, turn, video, winning.

adjectives animated, bad, challenging, competitive, educational, electronic, entertaining, good, favourite, fun, loud, passionate, strategic, violent.

verbs SUBJECT: a game amuses, entertains. OTHERS: to cheat at a game, to enjoy a game, to organize a game, to participate in a game, to play a game, to win a game.

expressions

• *A mug's game:* something only fools would do ► **chose que seuls les imbéciles feraient; jeu de con.**

• *Fair game:* something which is quite permissible to laugh at ► **chose dont il est permis de se moquer.**

• *Game face:* To be focused and determined during a competition ► **être concentré ou concentrée et déterminé ou déterminée lors d'un concours.**

• *Game over:* There is no more hope ► **il n'y a plus d'espoir.**

• *Game plan:* A strategy ► **stratégie.**

• *The game is not worth the candle:* the project is too difficult for the advan-

tages it would bring ► **le projet est trop difficile compte tenu de ses avantages; le jeu n'en vaut pas la chandelle.**

• *The game is up:* The scheme has been revealed ► **le complot est mis à jour; la partie est perdue.**

• *The name of the game:* the thing that is important, central ► **ce qui est important, crucial.**

• *To give the game away:* To reveal something that should have been hidden ► **révéler quelque chose qui aurait dû rester caché.**

• *To make game of:* To mock ► **se moquer.**

• *To play a losing game:* to attempt to do something in which it is obvious that one is not going to succeed ► **tenter de faire quelque chose sans espoir de réussite.**

• *To play the game:* to act fairly ► **agir honnêtement; jouer franc jeu.**

hobby ► passe-temps

nouns activity, airplane, amateur, baking, baseball, boating, canoeing, casino, chess, collection, comic book, computer, cooking, craft, crochet, curling, cycling, dancing, dart, diving, drawing, entertainment, fishing, football, fun, game, gardening, gliding, golf, hiking, hockey, horseback riding, Internet, inventing, jogging, karate, kayak, kite, leisure, model, motorcycle, movie, museum, music, opera, painting, parachute, passion, photography, pottery, puzzle, reading, relaxation, rest, retirement, sailing, sculpture, skating, ski, sport, stamp, summer, swimming, television, tennis, theatre, trampoline, vacation, volleyball, volunteering, walking, weekend, winter, wrestling, writing.

adjectives artistic, boring, educational, exhausting, expensive, fun, intellectual, musical, relaxing, solitary.

verbs SUBJECT: a hobby bores, entertains, relaxes. OTHERS: to abandon a hobby, to dedicate oneself to a hobby, to discover a hobby, to share a hobby.

expressions

- *He's off on his hobby-horse:* There he goes again ▸ **le voilà qui recommence ; c'est reparti.**

leisure ▸ loisir

nouns activity, baking, baseball, boating, canoeing, casino, chess, comfort, comic book, computer, cooking, craft, crochet, curling, cycling, dancing, darts, diving, drawing, fishing, football, fun, game, gardening, gliding, golf, hiking, hockey, horseback riding, Internet, jogging, karate, kayak, kite, laziness, lounging, model, motorcycle, movie, museum, music, opera, outdoors, painting, parachute, photography, playing, pottery, puzzle, reading, relaxation, rest, retirement, sailing, sculpture, skating, ski, sleep, sport, swimming, television, tennis, theatre, time, vacation, volleyball, walking, weekend.

adjectives fun, relaxing, solitary.

verbs OTHERS: to enjoy leisure, to take time for leisure.

expressions

- *At leisure:* In an unhurried manner ▸ **en prenant son temps ; à tête reposée ; à loisir.**
- *At one's leisure:* When one has time ▸ **lorsqu'on en a le temps, le loisir.**
- *Leisure class:* Rich social class with little need to work ▸ **classe sociale riche qui n'a guère besoin de travailler.**
- *Leisure suit:* Man's casual outfit ▸ **vêtements de sport, décontractés (pour hommes).**

party ▸ fête

nouns affair, amusement, anniversary, announcement, ball, balloon, beverage, birthday, cake, candy, card, celebration, ceremony, Christmas, clown, costume, dance, dinner, dress, entertainment, evening, event, family, food, friend, fun, function, gathering, gift, guest, Halloween, happening, holiday, invitation, music, occasion, popcorn, reception, snack, soft drink, surprise, treat.

adjectives animated, crowded, formal, fun, informal, lively, private, social, unexpected, unforgettable.

verbs SUBJECT: a party amuses, continues, ends, entertains. OTHERS: to attend a party, to expect a party, to leave a party, to organize a party, to throw a party.

expressions

- *Party animal:* Someone who attends many parties ▸ **personne qui fréquente régulièrement les fêtes ; habitué ou habitué des réceptions.**
- *Party manners:* The way someone acts during a public event ▸ **manière dont quelqu'un se comporte en public.**
- *Party pooper:* A person who ruins a party ▸ **personne qui gâche une fête ; rabat-joie ; trouble-fête.**
- *The party is over:* a particularly happy time has come to an end ▸ **fin d'une période particulièrement heureuse.**

picnic ▸ pique-nique

nouns ant, area, barbecue, basket, beach, bee, blanket, bonfire, bug, company, family, flower, food, fruit, game, grill, ham, lake, meal, outdoors, park, rain, river, sandwich, shelter, snack, summer, sun, sunbathing, table, vegetable, woods.

adjectives annual, cloudy, delightful, fun, sunny, warm.

verbs OTHERS: to cancel a picnic, to go on a picnic, to plan a picnic, to prepare a picnic.

expressions

- *It's no picnic:* It's not pleasant ▸ **ce n'est pas agréable ; ce n'est pas une partie de plaisir ; ce n'est pas de la tarte.**
- *Picnic shoulder:* Cut of meat (pork) ▸ **coupe de viande (de porc).**

sewing ▶ couture

nouns badge, blouse, button, chore, collar, cotton, decoration, dress, fabric, garment, hobby, hole, jeans, machine, material, needle, pants, patch, repair, ribbon, rip, seam, shirt, skirt, sleeve, sock, stitch, tear, thread, trim, work, zipper.

adjectives beautiful, creative, difficult, easy, fun, manual, practical.

verbs SUBJECT: sewing relaxes. OTHERS: to enjoy sewing, to learn sewing, to teach sewing.

expressions

• *Sewing up something:* To complete in a satisfactory manner ▶ **terminer d'une manière satisfaisante.**

sliding ▶ glissade

nouns amusement, bump, child, family, hill, ice, mountain, park, playground, pool, sled, slide, slope, snow, summer, surface, toboggan, water, winter, yard.

adjectives amusing, dangerous, fast, fun, inexpensive, slippery, slow, smooth.

verbs OTHERS: to go sliding.

sport ▶ sport

nouns activity, amateur, arena, association, athlete, attack, aviation, badminton, ball, baseball, basketball, bobsled, boomerang, bowling, boxing, canoeing, captain, cheating, climbing, club, coach, competition, court, cricket, croquet, curling, cycling, defence, discipline, diving, effort, elimination, exercise, finals, fishing, football, game, goal, golf, gymnasium, handicap, hockey, hunting, jockey, jogging, judge, karate, knock out, kung fu, lacrosse, league, losing, match, medal, motorcycle, muscle, offence, Olympic Games, opponent, parachute, partner, penalty, performance, player, playing, polo, prize, race, racquet, record, recreation, ring, rink, rugby, runner, sailing, scrimmage, skating, skiing, soccer, squash, stadium, surfing, swimming, target, team, tennis, trainer, training, umpire, volleyball, walking, weight, winning, wrestling.

adjectives aerobic, amateur, athletic, challenging, competitive, dangerous, daring, difficult, educational, expensive, extreme, fun, harsh, horrible, individual, indoor, intense, international, new, old, outdoor, precise, professional, risky, solitary, violent.

verbs OTHERS: to bet on a sport, to excel at a sport, to fail at a sport, to injure oneself in a sport, to lose at a sport, to play a sport, to practice a sport, to train for a sport, to watch a sport, to win at a sport.

expressions

• *He's a sport:* He's great ▶ **il est formidable.**

• *A sporting chance:* a reasonably good chance ▶ **chance raisonnable.**

• *To make sport of someone or something:* to make fun of a person or something ▶ **se moquer de quelqu'un ou de quelque chose.**

toy ▶ jouet

nouns airplane, baby, ball, balloon, bicycle, birthday, box, boy, car, chest, child, Christmas, collection, doll, drum, fair, fireworks, gift, girl, gun, hoops, horse, house, kite, mobile, model, puppet, rattle, robot, rocket, skate, skipping rope, soldier, top, train, tricycle, truck, trunk.

adjectives beautiful, broken, educational, electric, electronic, favourite, fun, miniature, new, old, repaired.

verbs OTHERS: to build a toy, to buy a toy, to give a toy, to lose a toy, to love a toy, to play with a toy.

expressions

• *Don't toy with me:* Don't try to manipulate me ▶ **n'essaie pas de me manipuler ; n'essaie pas de te jouer de moi.**

• *To toy with an idea:* To consider ▶ **envisager ; caresser l'idée.**

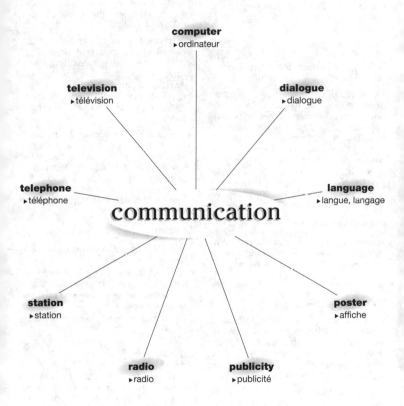

computer
▸ordinateur

television
▸télévision

dialogue
▸dialogue

telephone
▸téléphone

communication

language
▸langue, langage

station
▸station

poster
▸affiche

radio
▸radio

publicity
▸publicité

computer ▸ ordinateur

nouns application, CD-ROM, character, chip, command, connection, data, disk, document, e-mail, file, format, function, game, graphic, hardware, icon, information, Internet, keyboard, machine, memory, modem, monitor, mouse, printer, processor, program, programmer, screen, software, technician, technology, virus, window.

adjectives automated, compatible, complicated, digital, electronic, fun, helpful, interactive, logical, personal, portable, technological, useful.

verbs SUBJECT: a computer analyses, breaks down, calculates, crashes, compiles, corrects, creates, draws, edits, malfunctions, processes. OTHERS: to clean a computer, to communicate with a computer, to e-mail on a computer, to play with a computer, to reboot a computer, to repair a computer, to turn off a computer, to turn on a computer, to type on a computer, to work on a computer, to write with a computer.

expressions

• *To be a computer freak:* to love computers ▸ **aimer les ordinateurs ; être un ou une fanatique des ordinateurs.**

dialogue ▸ dialogue

nouns answer, chat, communication, conversation, disagreement, discussion, ear, expression, hearing, interview, joke, listening, message, mouth, question, screaming, sound, speaker, story, subject, voice, writer, word.

adjectives audio, boring, clear, communicative, dumb, eloquent, engaging, funny, heard, informative, interesting, long, loud, noisy, philosophical, scientific, serious, short, spoken, unpleasant.

verbs OBJECT: to begin a dialogue, to continue a dialogue, to encourage dialogue, to establish dialogue, to end a dialogue, to pursue dialogue, to write

a dialogue, to understand a dialogue. OTHERS: converse, gossip, speak, talk.

language ▸ langage

nouns code, computer, course, dictionary, expression, gesture, grammar, letter, linguist, mistake, music, school, sentence, sign, spelling, syntax, voice, word, world, writing.

adjectives academic, archaic, bad, beautiful, coded, coherent, dead, difficult, everyday, explicit, familiar, fascinating, foreign, impolite, incoherent, international, invented, linguistic, literary, modern, new, old, poetic, popular, proper, regional, spoken, strange, written.

verbs OTHERS: to decode a language, to forget a language, to hear a language, to improve one's language, to interpret a language, to learn a language, to practice a language, to speak a language, to translate a language, to understand a language, to use sign language, to watch one's language.

expressions

• *Strong language:* swearing or abuse ▸ **juron ou grossièreté.**

• *To speak the same language as someone:* to have a mutual understanding ▸ **se comprendre mutuellement ; parler le même langage.**

• *To use bad language:* to curse or swear ▸ **jurer.**

poster ▸ affiche

nouns advertisement, announcement, billboard, frame, graphic, illustration, image, movie, nail, notice, photograph, picture, play, publicity, show, sign, tape, theatre, wall, word.

adjectives colourful, decorative, dramatic, folded, funny, informative, pasted, political, ripped, theatrical, torn.

verbs SUBJECT: a poster advertises, announces, covers up, decorates, displays, informs, promotes. OTHERS: to create a poster, to design a poster, to display a poster, to draw a poster, to frame a poster, to print a poster, to put up a poster, to rip a poster, to tear down a poster.

expressions

- *Poster child:* A person who represents something ► personne qui représente quelque chose.
- *Poster girl or boy:* A female or male model ► **mannequin.**
- *Poster paint:* Paint that is used on posters ► **peinture utilisée sur les affiches.**

publicity ► **publicité**

nouns advertisement, agency, brochure, campaign, consumer, consumption, flyer, media, newspaper, notice, poster, presentation, propaganda, radio, sale, sample, sign, slogan, store, survey, television.

adjectives catchy, commercial, convincing, daring, explicit, false, honest, humorous, intelligent, negative, positive, promotional, subliminal, unusual.

verbs SUBJECT: publicity advertises, amuses, angers, disturbs, informs, promotes, sells, shocks. OBJECT: to avoid publicity, to create publicity, to shun publicity.

expressions

- *Free publicity:* To get publicity without asking or working for it ► **obtenir de la publicité sans effort ou sans l'avoir demandé.**
- *Publicity stunt:* To do something only for the purpose of creating publicity ► **faire quelque chose dans le seul but d'obtenir de la publicité.**

radio ► **radio**

nouns advertisement, affiliate, air, alarm clock, announcer, antenna, audience, broadcast, car, cassette, channel, communication, community, compact disk, dial, director, electricity, engineer, frequency, information, listener, media, message, microphone, music, network, newscast, noise, performer, producer, program, publicity, receiver, reception, record, satellite, set, signal, song, sound, station, stereo, transistor, transmission, volume, wave.

adjectives audio, electric, electronic, good, informative, loud, popular, portable, private, public.

verbs SUBJECT: radio advertises, announces, entertains, informs. OTHERS: to be on the radio, to listen to the radio, to play the radio, to turn off the radio, to turn on the radio.

expressions

- *Radio play:* Broadcast time on the radio ► **temps d'antenne à la radio.**

station ► **station**

nouns affiliate, announcer, antenna, booth, broadcast, building, camera, channel, company, director, engineer, frequency, location, microphone, music, network, producer, radio, reception, satellite, technician, television, wave.

adjectives community, new, old, private, public.

verbs SUBJECT: a station broadcasts. OTHERS: to call a station, to choose a station, to work at a station.

telephone ► **téléphone**

nouns air, answer, apparatus, booth, cable, call, card, coin, communication, company, conference, connection, conversation, dialling, directory, discussion, distance, exchange, extension, information, instrument, key, listener, message, network, number, operator, outlet, receiver, reception, ring, satellite, signal, speaker, speech, subscriber, talk, wire.

adjectives broken, electronic, modern, new, old, portable, public, standard, tapped.

verbs SUBJECT: a telephone annoys, bothers, breaks down, rings, works. OTHERS: to buy a telephone, to hear the telephone, to order on the telephone, to sell by telephone, to speak on the telephone, to use the telephone, to yell on the telephone.

expressions

- *A game of broken telephone:* To unintentionally pass on false information ▶ **transmettre une fausse information sans le vouloir.**
- *She's on the telephone:* She's using the telephone ▶ **elle utilise le téléphone ; elle est au téléphone.**
- *Telephone tag:* A situation where two people call each other repeatedly but fail to establish contact ▶ **situation où deux personnes tentent en vain de se joindre par téléphone.**

television ▶ télévision

nouns actor, advertisement, affiliate, air, announcer, antenna, audience, broadcast, bulletin, cable, channel, circuit, colour, comedy, coverage, dial, director, drama, entertainment, host, image, information, media, movie, network, newscast, picture, producer, production, program, reception, remote control, reporter, screen, set, show, signal, sound, sport, transmission, wire, video.

adjectives broken, dull, educational, electronic, exciting, funny, interesting, repaired, visual.

verbs SUBJECT: television communicates, distracts, informs, instructs. OTHERS: to buy a television, to prefer television, to repair a television, to watch television.

▚ Iconographic References

ILLUSTRATIONS

Maple Syrup Production
François Girard (illustrations of maple syrup products); Bertrand Lachance (thermometer); Jacques Dorion/Sogides Ltée (photos).

Aeronautics
Bertrand Lachance

Aerospace
Canadian Space Agency (Teleoperator System, Radarsat); NASA (International Space Station).

Gymnastics Equipment
Bertrand Lachance

Telephone Equipment
Bertrand Lachance

Hardwood Trees
Monique Chaussé (illustrations); Montreal Botanical Gardens (photo).

Automobile
Bertrand Lachance

Boats
L. Soldano/Archives Bombard (pneumatic boat); CROC « EAU » D'ÎLES (catamaran); Fisheries and Oceans Canada / (trawler); Marc Piché maritime photographer (container freighter, cruise ship, ferry, hydrofoil, sailboat, tugboat, yacht).

Bicycle
Bertrand Lachance

Grains
Monique Chaussé

Food Chain
François Girard

Mushrooms
© Mathieu Sicard (photos); Claire Tremblay (cross section of a gilled mushroom).

Coniferous Trees and Fruit Trees
Monique Chaussé (illustrations); Montreal Botanical Gardens (photos).

Human Body
Anto Dokouzian (respiratory system organs); Christiane Beauregard (digestive system organs and glands, female reproductive system); Bertrand Lachance (human reproduction, male reproductive system); François Escalmel (circulatory system); Antonio Silva (muscular system).

Water Cycle
François Girard

Dinosaurs
Claire Tremblay

Manufacturing Aluminum
Antonio Silva (illustrations); Alcan (photos).

Making Paper
Antonio Silva (illustrations); Smurfit-Stone Inc. (chips); Courtesy of Domtar Inc. (bleaching); Kruger (fourdrinier machine).

Farm
Claire Tremblay (illustrations); Coopérative fédérée de Québec (plough); New Holland Canada (combine reaper-thresher, round baler, spreader).

Ants
Brigitte Fortin

Cheese
Dairy Farmers of Canada (Cheddar, Emmenthal, Oka, Parmesan); Conseil de l'industrie laitière du Québec (blue, brie, Camembert, cheese with herbs, goat cheese, feta, pictograms).

Plant Germination and Growth
Claire Tremblay

Gymnasium
Bertrand Lachance

Hydroelectricity
Antonio Silva (illustrations); Hydro-Québec (photos).

Insects and Spiders
Yves Boudreau

Musical Instruments
Bertrand Lachance

Inventions
François Girard (steam engine); François Girard (steam locomotive); François Girard (photography); François Girard (velocipede); Courtesy Bell Canada Historical Collection (telephone); Monique Chaussé (phonograph); François Girard (light bulb); Daimler-Benz Archives (gas-powered automobile); Monique Chaussé (cinematography); Monique Chaussé (wireless telegraph); Monique Chaussé (airplane); Yves Boudreau (television); Yves Boudreau (atomic bomb); Collection Kharbine-Tapabor (computer); J.-A. Bombardier Museum (snowmobile); Yves Boudreau (inhabited space capsule); François Girard (skateboard); Burton (snowboard); Ralph H. Baer (video game); Baret/Mégapress (microcomputer); Courtesy of Sony (discman, walkman); Monique Chaussé (in-line skates); Canadian Space Agency (Sputnik 1 artificial satellite, Canadarm, Columbia space shuttle, Mir space shuttle, vitual reality game).

Canada's Food Guide to Healthy Eating for People Four Years and Over
Adapted from Canada's Food Guide to Healty Eating with the permission of the Minister of Public Works and Government Services Canada, 2001.

The Seven Wonders of the Ancient World
Monique Chaussé

Mammals of Canada
Yves Boudreau

Microcomputers
Bertrand Lachance

Minerals
© Bruno Beauregard (amethyst, gypsum flower, synthetic bismuth crystal); Minister of Natural Resources (copper, garnet, gold, gypsum, pyrite, salt rock, quartz); National Film Board of Canada (agglomerate, asbestos).

Knots
Bertrand Lachance

Quebec Works of Art
Alfred Pellan–Montreal Museum of Contemporary Art / photo: Denis Farley / © Estate of Alfred Pellan / SODRAC (Montreal) 2001 · Paul-Émile Borduas – Montreal Museum of Fine Arts, gift of the Mr. and Mrs. Maurice Charté Foundation / photo: MBAM · Anne Kahane - © Anne Kahane · Jean Dallaire – Montreal Museum of Contemporary Art / photo: Denis Farley / gift of the Max and Iris Stern Foundation / © Estate of Jean Dallaire / SODRAC (Montreal) 2001 · Jean-Paul Mousseau – Montreal Museum of Contempory Art / photo: Richard-Max Tremblay / © Estate of Jean-Paul Mousseau / SODRAC(Montreal) 2001 · Ulysse Comtois– Montreal Museum of Contemporary Art / photo Denis Farley · Marcel Barbeau – Montreal Museum of Contemporary Art/ photo: MAC / © Marcel Barbeau / SODRAC (Montreal) 2001 · Pierre Ayot – Montreal Museum of Fine Arts, gift of Les Presses de L'université du Québec à Montreal / photo: MBAM / © Estate of Pierre Ayot / SADART · Irene F. Whittome – Montreal Museum of Contemporary Art / Richard-Max Tremblay / © SODART · Betty Goodwin – Montreal Museum of Contemporary Art / photo: Denis Farley / © Galerie René Bluoin · Serge Lemoyne – Montreal Museum of Contemporary Art / photo: Richard-Max Tremblay / © Estate of Serge Lemoyne / SODARC (Montreal) 2001· Armand Vaillancourt – City of Saint-Léonard · René Derouin – © SODART · Michel Goulet – Montreal Museum of Contemporary Art / photo: Ron Diamond · Catherine Widgery – Montreal Museum of Contemporary Art, anonymous gift / photo: Richard-Max Tremblay.

Birds of Canada
Claire Tremblay

Butterflies
Montreal Insectarium

Wildflowers of Quebec
Claire Tremblay

Fish of Canada
François Girard

Pollination
Monique Chaussé

Pollution
Monique Chaussé

Bridges
Boily photo (Confederation Bridge); Terry Charland (Laviolette Bridge, Trois-Rivières); Quebec Transport Ministry (cable-stayed bridge–Papineau Bridge, Montreal), cable-supported bridge (Pierre-Laporte Bridge, Quebec City) cantilever bridge (Quebec City Bridge), single-leaf bascule bridge (lock located at Sainte-Catherine).

Recycling
Monique Chaussé (illustrations); City of Laval (photos) Publiphoto/Alain Dex (sorting center).

Summer Sports
Jacqueline Côté

Winter Sports
Jacqueline Côté

Human Skeleton
Bertrand Lachance

Structure of a Tree
Claire Tremblay

Symbols
Ministère des Transports du Québec

Solar System
Antonio Silva

Vegetation Zone
Publiphoto

ILLUSTRATIONS
Diane Bienvenue, Jocelyne Bouchard, Yves Boudreau, Brigitte Fortin, Pierre Gosselin, Bertrand Lachance, Anne Michaud.